WILEY
CPA
EXAM
REVIEW

WILEY CPA EXAM REVIEW

2012-2013

39th Edition

Volume 1
Outlines and Study Guides

O. Ray Whittington, CPA, PhD

Patrick R. Delaney, CPA, PhD

WILEY

JOHN WILEY & SONS, INC.

CONTENTS

INTRODUCTION

AUDITING AND ATTESTATION

FINANCIAL ACCOUNTING AND REPORTING

REGULATION

BUSINESS ENVIRONMENT AND CONCEPTS

PREFACE

Passing the CPA exam upon your first attempt is possible! The *Wiley CPA Examination Review* preparation materials provide you with the necessary materials (visit our website at www.wiley.com/cpa for more information). It's up to you to add the hard work and commitment. Together we can beat the first-time pass rate of less than 50%. All Wiley CPA products are continuously updated to provide you with the most comprehensive and complete knowledge base. Choose your products from the Wiley preparation materials and you can proceed confidently. You can select support materials that are exam-based and user-friendly. You can select products that will help you pass!

The objective of this work is to provide, in an easily readable format, study outlines of all areas tested on the Uniform Certified Public Accounting (CPA) Examination. The clear, concise phraseology supplemented by brief examples and illustrations is designed to help candidates quickly understand and retain the material. To make the task of preparing for the examination more manageable, we have structured both review volumes into 47 modules (manageable study units). Also, the multiple-choice questions in Volume 2 have been grouped into topical categories within each module. These categories correspond to the sequencing of material as it appears within each of the corresponding modules in this volume. The content of this volume and Volume 2 is based upon current AIPCA Content and Skill Specification Outlines for the Uniform Certified Public Accountant Examination. Actual American Institute of Certified Public Accountants (AICPA) unofficial questions and answers are presented to test your knowledge. With the introduction of the new computerized exam, many author-constructed questions have been added to Volume 2.

Remaining current is one of the keys to examination success. Here is a list of what's new in *Wiley CPA Examination Review*, 39th Edition, 2012-2013.

- The AICPA Content and Skill Specification Outlines for the Computerized CPA Examination
- Coverage of new content beginning January 1, 2011
- Coverage of new accounting and auditing standards, especially

  - The newest FASB and GASB accounting standards
  - International accounting standards
  - SEC reporting requirements

- Coverage of the Tax law changes for 2011 tested in 2012

We are indebted to the American Institute of Certified Public Accountants, the Financial Accounting Standards Board, and the Governmental Accounting Standards Board for permission to reproduce and adapt their publications.

The CPA exam is one of the toughest exams you will ever take. It will not be easy. But if you follow our guidelines and focus on your goal, you will be thrilled with what you can accomplish.

Ray Whittington
June 2012

DON'T FORGET TO VISIT OUR WEB SITE AT WWW.WILEY.COM/CPA FOR SUPPLEMENTS AND UPDATES.

Ray Whittington, PhD, CPA, CMA, CIA, is the dean of the College of Commerce at DePaul University. Prior to joining the faculty at DePaul, Professor Whittington was the Director of Accountancy at San Diego State University. From 1989 through 1991, he was the Director of Auditing Research for the American Institute of Certified Public Accountants (AICPA), and he previously was on the audit staff of KPMG. He previously served as a member of the Auditing Standards Board of the AICPA and as a member of the Accounting and Review Services Committee and the Board of Regents of the Institute of Internal Auditors. Professor Whittington has published numerous textbooks, articles, monographs, and continuing education courses.

Patrick R. Delaney, deceased, was the dedicated author and editor of the *Wiley CPA Exam Review* books for twenty years. He was the Arthur Andersen LLP Alumni Professor of Accountancy and Department Chair at Northern Illinois University. He received his PhD in Accountancy from the University of Illinois. He had public accounting experience with Arthur Andersen LLP and was coauthor of *GAAP: Interpretation and Application*, also published by John Wiley & Sons, Inc. He served as Vice President and a member of the Illinois CPA Society's Board of Directors, and was Chairman of its Accounting Principles Committee; was a past president of the Rockford Chapter, Institute of Management Accountants; and had served on numerous other professional committees. He was a member of the American Accounting Association, American Institute of Certified Public Accountants, and Institute of Management Accountants. Professor Delaney was published in *The Accounting Review* and was a recipient of the Illinois CPA Society's Outstanding Educator Award, NIU's Excellence in Teaching Award, and Lewis University's Distinguished Alumnus Award. He was involved in NIU's CPA Review Course as director and instructor.

ABOUT THE CONTRIBUTORS

Natalie T. Churyk, PhD, CPA is the Caterpillar Professor of Accountancy at Northern Illinois University. She teaches in the undergraduate and M.A.S. programs as well as developing and delivering continuing professional education in Northern Illinois University's CPA and CIA Review programs. Professor Churyk has published in professional and academic journals. She serves on state and national committees relating to education and student initiatives and is a member of several editorial review boards. Professor Churyk is a coauthor on two textbooks: *Accounting and Auditing Research: Tools and Strategies* and *Mastering the FASB Codification and eIFRS: A Case Approach*.

Edward C. Foth, PhD, CPA, Administrator of the Master of Science in Taxation Program at DePaul University. Professor Foth is the author of CCH Incorporated's *Study Guide for Federal Tax Course, Study Guide for CCH Federal Taxation: Comprehensive Topics*, and coauthor of their *S Corporation Guide*. Professor Foth prepared the answer explanations to the multiple-choice and other objective questions in Income Taxes, wrote new questions, selected the mix of questions, and updated items to reflect revisions in the tax law.

Brad McDonald, JD, is an instructor of Business Law and Statistics at Northern Illinois University. He has taught business law since 1987 and has taught the Business Law section of the Northern Illinois CPA review course since 1998. He wrote and revised most of the Business Law modules. He prepared and revised answer explanations for the multiple-choice and simulation questions.

Kurt Pany, PhD, CPA, is a Professor of Accounting at Arizona State University. Prior to entering academe, he worked as a staff auditor for Deloitte and Touche. He is a former member of the AICPA's Auditing Standards Board and has taught in the Arizona CPA Review Course.

INTRODUCTION

To maximize the efficiency of your review program, begin by studying (not merely reading) this chapter and the next three chapters of this volume. They have been carefully organized and written to provide you with important information to assist you in successfully completing the CPA exam. Beyond providing a comprehensive outline to help you organize the material tested, Chapter 1 will assist you in organizing a study program to prepare for the exam. Self-discipline is essential.

Chapter 1: Beginning Your CPA Review Program

GENERAL COMMENTS ON THE EXAMINATION

The Uniform CPA Examination is delivered using computer-based testing (CBT). Computer-based testing has several advantages. You may take the exam one section at a time. As a result, your studies can be focused on that one section, improving your chances for success. In addition, the exam is no longer offered twice a year. During eight months of every year, you may take the exam on your schedule, six days a week and in the morning or in the afternoon.

Successful completion of the Uniform CPA Examination is an attainable goal. Keep this point foremost in your mind as you study the first four chapters in this volume and develop your study plan.

Purpose of the Examination[1]

The Uniform CPA Examination is designed to test the entry-level knowledge and skills necessary to protect the public interest. An entry-level CPA is defined as one who has fulfilled the applicable jurisdiction's educational requirements and has the knowledge and skills typically possessed by a person with up to two years of experience. These knowledge and skills were identified through a Practice Analysis performed in 2008, which served as a basis for the development of the content specifications for the exam beginning in 2011.

The CPA examination is one of many screening devices to assure the competence of those licensed to perform the attest function and to render professional accounting services. Other screening devices include educational requirements, ethics examinations, and work experience.

The examination appears to test the material covered in accounting programs of the better business schools. It also appears to be based upon the body of knowledge essential for the practice of public accounting and the audit of a medium-sized client. Since the examination is primarily a textbook or academic examination, you should plan on taking it as soon as possible after completing your accounting education.

Examination Content

Guidance concerning topical content of the CPA exam can be found in a document prepared by the Board of Examiners of the AICPA entitled *Content and Skill Specifications for the Uniform CPA Exam.* We have included the content outlines in this volume by placing the corresponding outline for each section of the exam in the chapter containing related topical areas. These outlines should be used as an indication of the topics' relative emphasis on the exam.

The Board's objective in preparing this detailed listing of topics tested on the exam is to help "in assuring the continuing validity and reliability of the Uniform CPA Examination." These outlines are an excellent source of guidance concerning the areas and the emphasis to be given each area on future exams.

The Content and Skill Specification Outlines for the CPA examination, including the testing of International Financial Reporting Standards (IFRS™), went into effect January 1, 2011. In addition, the AICPA adopted CBT-e, which is a new computer platform. The major change from your standpoint is that simulations are smaller in size and a larger number of these "task-based simulations" are included on the Auditing and Attestation, Financial Accounting and Reporting, and Regulation exams. In addition, all questions that test writing skills are in the Business Environment and Concepts section. Note that a new set of Content and Skill Specifications will be effective after January 1, 2013. However, the changes from the current Content and Skill Specifications are relatively minor.

A summary of the structure of the four sections of the CPA exam and time allocations is shown below.

Auditing and Attestation

- 3 Multiple-Choice Testlets containing a total of 90 questions
- 1 testlet containing 7 short Task-Based Simulations, including one research simulation   4 hours

Business Environment and Concepts (BEC)

- 3 Multiple-choice Testlets containing a total of 72 questions
- 3 Written Communication Tasks on BEC topics   3 hours

Financial Accounting and Reporting

- 3 Multiple-Choice Testlets containing a total of 90 questions
- 1 Testlet containing 7 short Task-Based Simulations, including one research simulation   4 hours

---

[1] More information may be obtained from the AICPA's *Uniform CPA Examination Candidate Bulletin.* You can find the publication on the AICPA's website at www.cpa-exam.org.

Regulation

• 3 Multiple-Choice Testlets containing a total of 72 questions	
• 1 Testlet containing 6 short Task-Based Simulations, including one research simulation	3 hours

New accounting and auditing pronouncements, including those in the governmental and not-for-profit areas, are tested in the testing window starting six months after the pronouncement's *effective* date. If early application is permitted, a pronouncement is tested six months after the *issuance* date; candidates are responsible for the old pronouncement until it is superseded. The exam covers the Internal Revenue Code and federal tax regulations in effect six months before the beginning of the testing window. For the Business Law and Professional Responsibilities section, federal laws are tested six months following their *effective* date, and for uniform acts, one year after their adoption by a simple majority of jurisdictions. The AICPA posts content changes regularly on its Internet site. The address is www.cpa-exam.org.

Nondisclosure and Computerization of Examination

Beginning May 1996, the Uniform CPA Examination became nondisclosed. For each exam section, candidates are required to agree to a *Statement of Confidentiality*, which states that they will not divulge the nature and content of any exam question. In April of 2004, the CPA exam became computer-based. Candidates take the exam at Prometric sites in the 54 jurisdictions in which the CPA exam is offered. The CPA exam is offered continually during the testing windows shown below.

Testing Window (Exam Available)	January through February	April through May	July through August	October through November
AICPA Review & Update (Exam Unavailable)	March	June	September	December

One or more exam sections may be taken during any exam window, and the sections may be taken in any desired order. **However, no candidate will be allowed to sit for the same section more than once during any given testing window.** In addition, a candidate must pass all four sections of the CPA exam within a "rolling" eighteen-month period, which begins on the date he or she passes a section. In other words, you must pass the other three sections of the exam within eighteen months of when you pass the first section. If you do not pass all sections within the eighteen-month period, credit for any section(s) passed outside the eighteen-month period will expire and the section(s) must be retaken.

Types of Questions

The computer-based Uniform CPA Examination consists of three basic question formats.

1. Multiple-Choice—questions requiring the selection of one of four responses to a short scenario.
2. Simulations—case studies that are used to assess knowledge and skills in a context approximating that found on the job through the use of realistic scenarios and tasks, and access to normally available and familiar resources.
3. Written Communication tasks—questions that require you to write a short communication on Business Environment and Concepts topics.

The multiple-choice questions are much like the ones that have constituted a majority of the CPA examination for years. **And the good news is that these types of questions constitute about 65% of the total examination.** The simulations and written communication tasks are new. However, we have attempted in this manual to use the latest available information to design study materials that will make you successful in answering task-based simulations and written communication questions. You should refer to the AICPA Web site (www.cpa-exam.org) for the latest information about the format and content of this new type of question.

Process for Sitting for the Examination

While there are some variations in the process from state to state, the basic process for sitting for the CPA examination may be described as follows:

1. Apply to take the examination (request, complete, and submit an application).
2. Payment of examination fees
3. Candidates are required to review the tutorial and sample tests.
4. Receive your Notice to Schedule.
5. Schedule your examination.
6. Take your examination(s).
7. Receive your Score Report(s).

Applying to Take the Examination

The right to practice public accounting as a CPA is governed by individual state statutes. While some rules regarding the practice of public accounting vary from state to state, all State Boards of Accountancy use the Uniform CPA

Examination and AICPA advisory grading service as one of the requirements to practice public accounting. To obtain the latest information on requirements to apply and sit for the examination in the various states, every candidate should refer to the website of the National Association of State Boards of Accountancy (NASBA) at www.nasba.org. This website has information or links to sources of information about all of the jurisdictions.

A frequent problem candidates encounter is failure to apply by the deadline. **Apply to sit for the examination early. Also, you should use extreme care in filling out the application and mailing required materials to your State Board of Accountancy.** If possible, have a friend review your completed application before mailing with check and other documentation. The name on your application must appear exactly the same as it appears on the identification you plan to use at the testing center. Candidates miss a particular CPA examination window simply because of minor technical details that were overlooked (checks not signed, items not enclosed, question not answered on application, etc.). **Because of the very high volume of applications received in the more populous states, the administrative staff does not have time to call or write to correct minor details and will simply reject your application.**

Exam Scheduling

Once you have been cleared to take the exam by the applicable state board, you will receive by mail a Notice to Schedule (NTS) and may then schedule to sit for one or more sections of the exam.

You have the following three options for scheduling your examination:

1. **Visit www.prometric.com/cpa on the Internet**

   This is the easiest and quickest way to schedule an examination appointment (or cancel and reschedule an appointment, if necessary). Simply go to the website, select SCHEDULE APPOINTMENT, and follow the directions. It is advised that you print and keep for your records the confirmation number for your appointment.

2. **Call 800-580-9648 (Candidate Services Call Center)**

   Before you call, you must have your NTS in front of you, and have in mind several times, dates, and locations that would work for you. You will not receive written confirmation of your appointment. Be sure to write down the date, time, and location, and confirmation number for each of your appointments.

3. **Call your local test center**

   While this method is not recommended, you may call your local test center and schedule appointments. Again, be sure to have your NTS in front of you and write down the date, time, location, and confirmation number for each of your appointments.

   You should also be aware that if you have to cancel or reschedule your appointment, you may be subject to a cancellation/rescheduling fee. The AICPA's *Uniform CPA Examination Candidate Bulletin* lists the rescheduling and cancellation fees.

To assure that you get your desired location and time period, it is imperative that you schedule early. To get your first choice of dates, you are advised to schedule at least 45 days in advance. You will not be scheduled for an exam fewer than 5 days before testing.

ATTRIBUTES OF EXAMINATION SUCCESS

Your primary objective in preparing for the CPA examination is to pass. Other objectives such as learning new and reviewing old material should be considered secondary. The six attributes of examination success discussed below are **essential**. You should study the attributes and work toward achieving/developing each of them **before** taking the examination.

1. Knowledge of Material

Two points are relevant to "knowledge of material" as an attribute of examination success. **First,** there is a distinct difference between being familiar with material and knowing the material. Frequently candidates confuse familiarity with knowledge. Can you remember when you just could not answer an examination question or did poorly on an examination, but maintained to yourself or your instructor that you knew the material? You probably were only familiar with the material. On the CPA examination, familiarity is insufficient; you must know the material. For example, you may be familiar with the concepts in accounting for leases, but can you compute the present value of an annuity due under a lease agreement and record entries for the lessee and lessor? Once again, a very major concern must be to know the material rather than just being familiar with it. Knowledgeable discussion of the material is required on the CPA examination. **Second,** the Uniform Certified Public Accountant Examination tests a literally overwhelming amount of material at a rigorous level. The CPA examination includes material from the following courses:

Accounting

      Auditing (including Auditing with Technology and Audit Sampling)
      International Auditing Standards
      Intermediate Financial
      Advanced Financial
      International Financial Reporting Standards
      Cost/Managerial
      Governmental and Not-for-Profit
      Tax

Business Law
Accounting Information Systems
Management Information Systems
Finance
Economics
Corporate Governance
Enterprise Risk Management
Project Management
Budgeting and Measurement
Production Operations
Management

Furthermore, as noted earlier, the CPA exam will test new material, sometimes as early as six months after issuance. In other words, you are not only responsible for material in the above courses, but also for all new developments in each of these areas.

This text contains outlines of accounting topics from FASB pronouncements, financial accounting courses, cost accounting courses, finance courses, etc. Return to the original material (e.g., professional standards, your accounting and business textbooks, etc.) only if the outlines do not reinforce topical areas you already know.

2. Commitment to Exam Preparation

Your preparation for the CPA exam should begin at least two months prior to the date you plan to schedule your seating for an exam section. If you plan to take more than one section, you should start earlier. Over the course of your preparation, you will experience many peaks and valleys. There will be days when you feel completely prepared and there will also be days when you feel totally overwhelmed. This is not unusual and, in fact, should be expected.

The CPA exam is a very difficult and challenging exam. How many times in your college career did you study months for an exam? Probably not too many. Therefore, candidates need to remain focused on the objective—succeeding on the CPA exam.

Develop a personal study plan so that you are reviewing material daily. Of course, you should schedule an occasional study break to help you relax, but don't schedule too many breaks. Candidates who dedicate themselves to studying have a much greater chance of going through this process one time. On the other hand, a lack of focus and piecemeal preparation will only extend the process over a number of exam sittings.

3. Solutions Approach

The solutions approach is a systematic approach to solving the questions and simulations found on the CPA examination. Many candidates know the material fairly well when they sit for the CPA exam, but they do not know how to take the examination. Candidates generally neither work nor answer questions efficiently in terms of time or grades. The solutions approach permits you to avoid drawing "blanks" on CPA exam questions; using the solutions approach coupled with grading insights (see below) allows you to pick up a sizable number of points on test material with which you are not familiar. Chapter 3 outlines the solutions approach for multiple-choice questions, simulations, and written communication questions.

4. Grading Insights

Your score on each section of the exam is determined by the sum of points assigned to individual multiple-choice questions, simulations, and written communication questions. Thus, you must attempt to maximize your points on each individual item.

The number of points assigned to a multiple-choice question varies depending upon its difficulty level—easy, medium, or hard. **In other words, you will receive more points for correctly answering a hard question than correctly answering an easy question.** Multiple-choice questions are organized in 24- to 30-question testlets, and each testlet includes questions from all of the content areas of the particular section.

With respect to the multiple-choice testlets, the CPA exam uses a form of adaptive testing known as multistage testing. Using this technique, the average difficulty of subsequent testlet(s) is determined by how the candidate has performed on the previous testlet(s). Therefore, if you get a testlet with a preponderance of very difficult questions, do not become discouraged. It may mean that you performed very well on the previous testlet(s). In addition, since the number of points assigned to hard or medium questions will be greater than the number of points assigned to easy questions, you have an opportunity to accumulate a large number of total points on that testlet.

Each multiple-choice testlet contains "operational" and "pretest" questions. The operational questions are the only ones that are used to determine your score. Pretest questions are not scored; they are being tested for future use as operational questions. However, you have no way of knowing which questions are operational and which questions are pretest questions. Therefore, you must approach each question as if it will be used to determine your grade.

Task-based simulations include more extensive scenarios and requirements. For example, the requirements may involve calculations, spreadsheet completion, journal entries, or research. The points assigned to the requirements will vary according to their difficulty. The task-based simulations make use of a number of commonly used tools such as spreadsheets and electronic research databases. Therefore, you need to become proficient in the use of these tools to maximize your score on the simulations. Task-based simulations will also include "pretest" items that are not counted in your score.

Finally, written communication questions, on the Business Environment and Concepts section, are worth about 5% each, or a total of approximately 15% of that section's score.

CPA Exam scores are reported on a scale from 0 to 99. The total score is not a percent correct score. It is a combination of scores from the multiple-choice and simulation portions of the exam considering the relative difficulty of the items. A total score of 75 is required to pass each section.

The AICPA included a tutorial and sample examinations on its Web site that allow you to get experience with the use of the actual computer tools used on the CPA exam. Also, more experience with computer testing can be obtained by using *Wiley CPA Exam Review Practice Software*.

5. Examination Strategy

Prior to sitting for the examination, it is important to develop an examination strategy (i.e., an approach to working efficiently throughout the exam). Your ability to cope successfully with the examination can be improved by

a. Recognizing the importance and usefulness of an examination strategy
b. Using Chapter 4, Taking the Examination, and previous examination experience to develop a "personal strategy" for the exam
c. Testing your "personal strategy" on example examinations under conditions similar to those at the test centers (using similar tools and databases and with a time limit)

6. Examination Confidence

You need confidence to endure the physical and mental demands of 3 to 4 hours of test-taking under tremendous pressure. Examination confidence results from proper preparation for the exam, which includes mastering the first four attributes of examination success. Examination confidence is necessary to enable you to overcome the initial frustration with problems for which you may not be specifically prepared.

This study manual (in conjunction with Volume 2), when properly used, contributes to your examination confidence. The systematic outlines herein will provide you with a sense of organization such that as you sit for the examination, you will feel reasonably prepared (it is impossible to be completely prepared).

Common Candidate Mistakes

The CPA Exam is a formidable hurdle in your accounting career. With a first-time pass rate of only about 45% on each section, the level of difficulty is obvious. The authors believe that the first-time pass rate could be higher if candidates would be more careful. Eight common mistakes that many candidates make are

1. Failure to understand the exam question requirements
2. Misunderstanding the supporting text of the problem
3. Lack of knowledge of material tested, especially recently issued pronouncements
4. Failure to develop proficiency with practice tools such as electronic research databases and spreadsheets
5. Inability to apply the solutions approach
6. Lack of an exam strategy (e.g., allocation of time)
7. Sloppiness and computational errors
8. Failure to proofread and edit

These mistakes are not mutually exclusive. Candidates may commit one or more of the above items. Remind yourself that when you decrease the number of common mistakes, you increase your chances of successfully becoming a CPA. Take the time to read carefully the exam question requirements. Do not jump into a quick start, only to later find out that you did not understand what information the examiners were asking for. Read slowly and carefully. Take time to recall your knowledge. Respond to the question asked. Apply an exam strategy such as allocating your time among all question formats. Do not spend too much time on the multiple-choice testlets, leaving no time to spend on preparing your simulation responses. Upon completion of any written communications requirements, proofread and edit your answer. Answer questions quickly but precisely, avoid common mistakes, cpa increase your score.

PURPOSE AND ORGANIZATION OF THIS REVIEW TEXTBOOK

Volume 1 and Volume 2 of *CPA Examination Review* are designed to help you prepare adequately for the examination. There is no easy approach to prepare for the successful completion of the CPA Examination; however, through the use of Volumes 1 and 2, your approach will be systematic and logical.

The objective of Volume 1 is to provide study materials supportive to CPA candidates. While no guarantees are made concerning the success of those using this text, this book promotes efficient preparation by

1. Explaining how to **maximize your score** through analysis of examination grading and illustration of the solutions approach.
2. **Defining areas tested** through the use of the content specification outlines. Note that predictions of future exams are not made. You should prepare yourself for all possible topics rather than gambling on the appearance of certain questions.
3. **Organizing your study program** by comprehensively outlining all of the subject matter tested on the examination in 48 easy-to-use study modules. Each study module is a manageable task which facilitates your exam preparation. Turn to the table of contents and peruse it to get a feel for the organization of this volume.

As you read the next few paragraphs that describe the contents of this book (Volume 1), flip through the chapters to gain a general familiarity with the book's organization and contents. Chapters 2, 3, and 4 will help you maximize your score.

Chapter 2   Examination Grading
Chapter 3   The Solutions Approach
Chapter 4   Taking the Examination

Chapters 2, 3, and 4 contain material that should be kept in mind throughout your study program. Refer back to them frequently. Reread them for a final time just before you sit for the exam.

Chapter 5 (Auditing and Attestation) and Chapter 6 (Financial Accounting and Reporting) each contain

1. AICPA Content Specification Outlines
2. Outlines of material tested on that section of the examination

Chapters 7 through 9 outline the Regulation section of the CPA examination. Chapter 7 discusses the coverage of that section of the examination. This chapter also contains the AICPA Content Specification Outlines for all of the Regulation section. The content specification outlines of the topics tested in the Business Environment and Concepts section of the exam are located in Chapter 10.

The first objective of Volume 2 is to provide CPA candidates with previous examination questions and author-developed questions and simulations organized by topic (e.g., audit reports, secured transactions, consolidations, etc.). Volume 2 includes over 2,400 multiple-choice questions, many from previous exams. Multiple-choice questions are an effective means of studying the material tested on the exam. It is also necessary, however, to work with problems and simulations to develop the solutions approach (the ability to solve CPA simulations efficiently).

The second objective of Volume 2 is to provide CPA candidates with an explanation for the answers to the multiple-choice questions and simulations.

Other Textbooks

This text is a comprehensive compilation of study guides and outlines; it should not be necessary to supplement them with textbooks and other materials for most topics. You probably already have accounting, business law, economics, finance, accounting information systems, and tax textbooks. In such a case, you must make the decision whether to replace them and trade familiarity (including notes therein, etc.), with the cost and inconvenience of obtaining the newer texts containing a more updated presentation.

Before spending time and money acquiring new texts, begin your study program with this book to determine your need for a supplemental text.

Ordering Other Materials

Professional materials for study may be ordered from the AICPA at

AICPA (CPA2Biz)
   Telephone: 888-777-7077
   Web site: www.CPA2Biz.com

The AICPA offers candidates a free six-month online subscription to the professional literature to help them prepare for the exam. The package costs includes the Web electronic versions of

- AICPA professional standards
- FASB Original Pronouncements
- FASB Accounting Standards Codification

Candidates may subscribe at www.cpa-exam.org. Only candidates who have applied to take the exam may take advantage of this offer.

The PCAOB website at www.pcaobus.org has the AICPA auditing standards that the PCAOB adopted as its interim standards. It also has the standards it has adopted subsequently.

A variety of supplemental CPA products are available from John Wiley & Sons, Inc. By using a variety of learning techniques, such as software and audio CDs, the candidate is more likely to remain focused during the study process and to retain information for a longer period of time. Visit our website at **www.wiley.com/cpa** for other products, supplements, and updates.

Working CPA Problems

The AICPA Content Outlines, study outlines, etc., in Volume 1 will be used to acquire and assimilate the knowledge tested on the examination. This, however, should be only **one-half** of your preparation program. The other half should be spent practicing how to work problems using Volume 2, "Problems and Solutions."

Most candidates probably spend over 90% of their time reviewing material tested on the CPA exam. Much more time should be allocated to working questions and simulations **under exam conditions**. Working potential examination questions serves two functions. First, it helps you develop a solutions approach as well as solutions that will maximize your score. Second, it provides the best test of your knowledge of the material.

The multiple-choice questions and answer explanations can be used in many ways. First, they may be used as a diagnostic evaluation of your knowledge. For example, before beginning to review commercial paper you may wish to answer 10 to 15 multiple-choice questions to determine your ability to answer CPA examination questions on commercial paper. The apparent difficulty of the questions and the correctness of your answers will allow you to determine the necessary breadth and depth of your review. Additionally, exposure to examination questions prior to review and study of the material should provide motivation. You will develop a feel for your level of proficiency and an understanding of the scope and difficulty of past examination questions. Moreover, your review materials will explain concepts encountered in the diagnostic multiple-choice questions.

Second, the multiple-choice questions can be used as a poststudy or postreview evaluation. You should attempt to understand all concepts mentioned (even in incorrect answers) as you answer the questions. Refer to the explanation of the answer for discussion of the alternatives even though you selected the correct response. Thus, you should read the explanation of the answer unless you completely understand the question and all of the alternative answers.

Third, you may wish to use the multiple-choice questions as a primary study vehicle. This is probably the quickest but least thorough approach to preparing for the exam. Make a sincere effort to understand the question and to select the correct response before referring to the unofficial answer and explanation. In many cases, the explanations will appear inadequate because of your unfamiliarity with the topic. Always refer back to an appropriate study source, such as the outlines and text in this volume, your textbooks, professional standards, etc.

The multiple-choice questions significantly outnumber the task-based simulations in this book. This is similar to the content of the new computer-based examination. One problem with so many multiple-choice questions is that you may overemphasize them. Candidates generally prefer to work multiple-choice questions because they are

1. Shorter and less time-consuming
2. Solvable with less effort
3. Less frustrating than simulations

Another problem with the large number of multiple-choice questions is that you may tend to become overly familiar with the questions. The result may be that you begin reading the facts and assumptions of previously studied questions into the questions on your examination. Guard against this potential problem by reading each multiple-choice question with **extra** care.

Beginning with the April 2004 computer-based examination, the AICPA began testing with simulations, and in 2011 the AICPA moved to shorter task-based simulations and written communication tasks. Simulations released by the AICPA or prepared by the authors, many adopted from prior CPA exam questions and problems, are in Volume 2, "Problems and Solutions." You should also spend significant amount of your study time working these types of questions.

The questions and solutions in Volume 2 provide you with an opportunity to diagnose and correct any exam-taking weaknesses prior to sitting for the examination. Continually analyze your incorrect solutions to determine the cause of the error(s) during your preparation for the exam. Treat each incorrect solution as a mistake that will not be repeated (especially on the examination). Also attempt to generalize your weaknesses so that you may change, reinforce, or develop new approaches to exam preparation and exam taking.

SELF-STUDY PROGRAM

CPA candidates generally find it difficult to organize and to complete their own self-study programs. A major problem is determining **what** and **how** to study. Another major problem is developing the self-discipline to stick to a study program. Relatedly, it is often difficult for CPA candidates to determine how much to study (i.e., determining when they are sufficiently prepared).

The following suggestions will assist you in developing a **systematic, comprehensive,** and **successful** self-study program to help you complete the exam.

Remember that these are only suggestions. You should modify them to suit your personality, available study time, and other constraints. Some of the suggestions may appear trivial, but CPA candidates generally need all the assistance they can get to systemize their study programs.

Study Facilities and Available Time

Locate study facilities that will be conducive to concentrated study. Factors that you should consider include

1. Noise distraction
2. Interruptions
3. Lighting
4. Availability (e.g., a local library is not available at 5:00 A.M.)
5. Accessibility (e.g., your kitchen table vs. your local library)
6. Desk or table space
7. Availability of research resources

You will probably find different study facilities optimal for different times (e.g., your kitchen table during early morning hours and local libraries during early evening hours).

Next review your personal and professional commitments from now until the exam to determine regularly available study time. Formalize a schedule to which you can reasonably commit yourself. At the end of this chapter, you will find a detailed approach to managing your time available for the exam preparation program.

Self-Evaluation

The *CPA Examination Review* self-study program is partitioned into 48 topics or modules. Since each module is clearly defined and should be studied separately, you have the task of preparing for the CPA exam partitioned into 48 manageable tasks. Partitioning the overall project into 48 modules makes preparation psychologically easier, since you sense yourself completing one small step at a time rather than seemingly never completing one or a few large steps.

By completing the following "Preliminary Estimate of Your Knowledge of Subject" inventory, organized by the 48 modules in this program, you will have a tabulation of your strong and weak areas at the beginning of your study program. This will help you budget your limited study time. Note that you should begin studying the material in each module by answering up to 1/4 of the total multiple-choice questions in Volume 2 covering that module's topics. This "mini-exam" should constitute a diagnostic evaluation as to the amount of review and study you need.

PRELIMINARY ESTIMATE OF YOUR PRESENT KNOWLEDGE OF SUBJECT

No.	Module	Proficient	Fairly proficient	Generally familiar	Not familiar
	AUDITING AND ATTESTATION				
1	Professional Responsibilities				
2	Engagement Planning and Understanding				
3	Understanding Internal Control				
4	Responding to Risk Assessment				
5	Reporting				
6	Accounting & Review Services				
7	Audit Sampling				
8	Auditing with Technology				
	FINANCIAL ACCOUNTING AND REPORTING				
9	Basic Theory and Financial Reporting				
10	Inventory				
11	Fixed Assets				
12	Monetary Current Assets and Current Liabilities				
13	Present Value				
14	Deferred Taxes				
15	Stockholders' Equity				
16	Investments				
17	Statement of Cash Flows				
18	Business Combinations and Consolidations				
19	Derivative Instruments and Hedging Activities				

20	Miscellaneous				
21	Governmental Accounting				
22	Not-for-Profit Accounting				
	REGULATION				
23	Professional and Legal Responsibilities				
24	Federal Securities Acts				
25	Business Structure				
26	Contracts				
27	Sales				
28	Commercial Paper				
29	Secured Transactions				
30	Bankruptcy				
31	Debtor-Creditor Relationships				
32	Agency				
33	Regulation of Business				
34	Property				
35	Taxes: Individual				
36	Taxes: Transactions in Property				
37	Taxes: Partnership				
38	Taxes: Corporate				
39	Taxes: Gift and Estate				
	BUSINESS ENVIRONMENT AND CONCEPTS				
40	Corporate Governance, Internal Control, and Enterprise Risk Management				
41	Information Technology				
42	Economics, Strategy, and Globalization				
43	Financial Risk Management and Capital Budgeting				
44	Financial Management				
45	Performance Measures				
46	Cost Measurement				
47	Planning, Control, and Analysis				

Using Note Cards

Key definitions, formulas, lists, etc., can be summarized on note cards to illustrate important concepts. Candidates can organize the note cards into four sections: AUDITING AND ATTESTATION, FINANCIAL ACCOUNTING AND REPORTING, REGULATION, AND BUSINESS ENVIRONMENT AND CONCEPTS. During your study program, you can frequently review your note cards to refresh your memory on certain topics and evaluate your progress. The following examples illustrate one candidate's note cards on various exam topics.

Financial Accounting and Reporting

Investments < 20%
Held-to-Maturity: Amortized Cost
Trading: Fair Market Value
Δs recognized in I/S
Available-for-sale: FMV
Δs during a period recognized in other
comprehensive income

Accounting Changes

	Cum. effect	Pro forma	Restate FS
Δ in estimate	N	N	N
Δ in principle	Y	Y	N
Δ in reporting entity	N	N	Y

Prepared by Greg Graber, CPA, former student, Northern Illinois University

Business Environment and Concepts

Cost-Volume-Profit Sales -Var Exp - Fixed Exp = Profit Breakeven Point In units = $\dfrac{\text{Fixed Exp}}{\text{Cont Mar/Unit}}$ In Sales $ = $\dfrac{\text{Fixed Exp}}{\text{Cont Mar \%}}$	Cash Management

Cash Management detail:

Lock box	Recpt.	Receipts directly to bank
Concentration banking	Recpt.	Branches use local banks
Zero-balance accounts	Disb.	Transferring funds to cover checks
Electronic funds transfer	Disb. or Rec.	Transfer of funds electronically

Prepared by Greg Graber, CPA, former student, Northern Illinois University

Auditing and Attestation

Tolerable Misstatement
Max $ Misstatement for a bal.
Audit Risk: Risk of the existence of a monetary misstatement greater than the tolerable misstatement
Nonsampling Risk:
• Wrong audit procedure
• Audit error
(cont'd)
	Sampling Risk - May cause result diff. than pop. as a whole.
	• Substantive Tests
	  1) Incorrect accep. B
	  2) Incorrect rejec. α
	• Tests of Controls
	  1) Risk of assessing control risk too low (overreliance)
	  2) Risk of assessing control risk too high (underreliance)

Prepared by Rebecca A. Hoger, CPA, former student, Northern Illinois University

Regulation

Negotiable Instrument
1) In writing (semipermeable moveable form)
2) Signed by appropriate person
3) Unconditional promise to pay sum certain in money
4) Words of negotiability
5) No second promise (collateral-ok)
6) Payable on demand or at definite date
	Elements of a binding agreement
	1) Manifestation of mutual assent
	  a. Offer
	  b. Acceptance
	2) Reality of consent
	3) Consideration
	4) Capacity of parties
	5) Legality of object
	6) Compliance with Statute of Frauds

Prepared by Cindy Johnson, CPA, former student, Northern Illinois University

Level of Proficiency Required

What level of proficiency must you develop with respect to each of the topics to pass the exam? You should work toward a minimum correct rate on the multiple-choice questions of 75 to 80%.

Warning: Disproportional study time devoted to multiple-choice (relative to simulation questions/ problems) can be disastrous on the exam. You should work a substantial number of problems and simulations under exam conditions, even though multiple-choice questions are easier to work and are used to gauge your proficiency. The authors believe that practicing simulations and problems will also improve your proficiency on the multiple-choice questions.

Multiple-Choice Feedback

One of the benefits of working through previous exam questions is that it helps you to identify your weak areas. Once you have graded your answers, your strong areas and weak areas should be clearly evident. Yet, the important point here is that you should not stop at a simple percentage evaluation. The percentage only provides general feedback about your knowledge of the material contained within that particular module. The percentage **does not** give you any specific feedback regarding the concepts which were tested. In order to get this feedback, you should look at the questions missed on an individual basis because this will help you gain a better understanding of **why** you missed the question.

This feedback process has been facilitated by the fact that within each module where the multiple-choice answer key appears, two blank lines have been inserted next to the multiple-choice answers. As you grade the multiple-choice questions, mark those questions which you have missed. However, instead of just marking the questions right and wrong, you should now focus on marking the questions in a manner which identifies **why** you missed the question. As an example, a candidate could mark the questions in the following manner: ✓ for math mistakes, X for conceptual mistakes, and ? for areas which the candidate was unfamiliar with. The candidate should then correct these mistakes by reworking through the marked questions.

The objective of this marking technique is to help you identify your weak areas and thus, the concepts which you should be focusing on. While it is still important for you to get between 75% and 80% correct when working multiple-choice questions, it is more important for you to understand the concepts. This understanding applies to both the questions answered correctly and those answered incorrectly. Remember, questions on the CPA exam will be different from the questions in the book; however, the concepts will be the same. Therefore, your preparation should focus on understanding concepts, not just getting the correct answer.

Conditional Candidates

If you have received conditional status on the examination, you must concentrate on the remaining section(s). Unfortunately, many candidates do not study after conditioning the exam, relying on luck to get them through the remaining section(s). Conditional candidates will find that material contained in Chapters 1-4 and the information contained in the appropriate modules will benefit them in preparing for the remaining section(s) of the examination.

PLANNING FOR THE EXAMINATION

Overall Strategy

An overriding concern should be an orderly, systematic approach toward both your preparation program and your examination strategy. A major objective should be to avoid any surprises or anything else that would rattle you during the examination. In other words, you want to be in complete control as much as possible. Control is of paramount importance from both positive and negative viewpoints. The presence of control on your part will add to your confidence and your ability to prepare for and take the exam. Moreover, the presence of control will make your preparation program more enjoyable (or at least less distasteful). On the other hand, a lack of organization will result in inefficiency in preparing and taking the examination, with a highly predictable outcome. Likewise, distractions during the examination (e.g., inadequate lodging, lack of sleep) are generally disastrous.

In summary, establishing a systematic, orderly approach to taking the examination is of paramount importance. Follow these six steps:

1. Develop an overall strategy at the beginning of your preparation program (see below).
2. Supplement your overall strategy with outlines of material tested on the exam.
3. Supplement your overall strategy with an explicitly stated set of problem-solving procedures—the solutions approach.
4. Supplement your overall strategy with an explicitly stated approach to each examination session (see Chapter 4).
5. Evaluate your preparation progress on a regular basis and prepare lists of things "to do" (see Weekly Review of Preparation Program Progress on the following page).
6. **Relax:** You can pass the exam. About 20,000 candidates successfully complete the exam each year. You will be one of them if you complete an efficient preparation program and execute well (i.e., use your solutions approach and exam strategy) while writing the exam.

The following outline is designed to provide you with a general framework of the tasks before you. You should tailor the outline to your needs by adding specific items and comments.

A. Preparation Program (refer to Self-Study Program discussed previously)

1. Obtain and organize study materials.
2. Locate facilities conducive for studying and block out study time.
3. Concentrate your study on one or two sections per exam window. Do not attempt to take more than two sections per window.
4. Develop your solutions approach (including solving simulations and problems as well as multiple-choice questions).
5. Prepare an examination strategy.
6. Study the material tested recently and prepare answers to actual exam questions on these topics under examination conditions.
7. Periodically evaluate your progress.

B. Physical Arrangements

   1. Apply to and obtain acceptance from your state board.
   2. Reserve lodging for examination nights.

C. Taking the Examination (covered in detail in Chapter 4)

   1. Become familiar with exam facilities and procedures.
   2. Implement examination strategies and the solutions approach.

Weekly Review of Preparation Program Progress

The following pages contain a hypothetical weekly review of program progress for the Financial Accounting and Reporting section. You should prepare a similar progress chart. This procedure, which takes only about 5 minutes per week, will help you proceed through a more efficient, complete preparation program.

Make notes of materials and topics

   1. That you have studied
   2. That you have completed
   3. That need additional study

Weeks to go		Comments on progress, "to do" items, etc.
12	1)	Read Basic Theory and Financial Reporting Module
	2)	Made notecards
	3)	Worked the MC Questions and Task-based simulations, on a sample basis
	4)	Need to work Task-Based Simulations using the solutions approach
11	1)	Read Fixed Assets and Stockholders' Equity Modules
	2)	Made notecards
	3)	Read the SFAS and APB outlines that correspond to these topics
	4)	Briefly looked over the MC for both modules
10	1)	Read Monetary Current Assets and Current Liabilities Module
	2)	Made notecards
	3)	Read the corresponding SFAS/APB outlines
	4)	Worked the MC Questions and Task-Based Simulations for Fixed Assets, Stockholders' Equity, and Monetary CA/CL
9	1)	Read the Inventory and Statement of Cash Flows Modules
	2)	Made notecards
	3)	Skimmed the SFAS and APB outlines, taking notes of important areas
	4)	Worked the MC Questions and Task-Based Simulations
8	1)	Read the Present Value Module
	2)	Made notecards
	3)	Studied the SFASs and APBs on leases and pensions
	4)	Completed the MC Questions and Task-Based Simulations
7	1)	Read Deferred Taxes Module
	2)	Made notecards
	3)	Read the corresponding SFAS and APB outlines
	4)	Worked the MC Questions and Task-Based Simulations
6	1)	Read the Derivative Instruments and Hedging Activities and Miscellaneous Modules
	2)	Made notecards
	3)	Read the corresponding SFAS and APB outlines
	4)	Worked the MC Questions and Task-Based Simulations for these modules
	5)	Confident with these mods; only need a quick review

5	1) 2) 3) 4)	*Read Investments Module* *Made notecards* *Read the corresponding SFAS and APB outlines* *Worked the MC Questions and Task-Based Simulations*
4	1) 2) 3) 4)	*Read the Business Combinations and Consolidations Module* *Reviewed consolidations in an advanced accounting textbook* *Made notecards* *Worked the MC Questions and Task-Based Simulations*
3	1)	*Took Financial Accounting and Reporting Sample Exam*
2	1) 2)	*Reviewed all prior topics, picking out a few MC for each topic and working them out* *Did a statement of cash flows*
1	1) 2)	*Reviewed notecards and SFAS and APB outlines* *Worked MC from Deferred Taxes and Stockholders' Equity Modules*
0	1)	*Tried to relax and review topics*

Time Management of Your Preparation

As you begin your CPA exam preparation, you obviously realize that there is a large amount of material to cover over the course of the next two to three months. Therefore, it is very important for you to organize your calendar, and maybe even your daily routine, so that you can allocate sufficient time to studying. An organized approach to your preparation is much more effective than a last week cram session. An organized approach also builds up the confidence necessary to succeed on the CPA exam.

An approach which we have already suggested is to develop weekly "to do" lists. This technique helps you to establish intermediate objectives and goals as you progress through your study plan. You can then focus your efforts on small tasks and not feel overwhelmed by the entire process. And as you accomplish these tasks you will see yourself moving one step closer to realizing the overall goal, succeeding on the CPA exam.

Note, however, that the underlying assumption of this approach is that you have found the time during the week to study and thus accomplish the different tasks. Although this is an obvious step, it is still a very important step. Your exam preparation should be of a continuous nature and not one that jumps around the calendar. Therefore, you should strive to find available study time within your daily schedule, which can be utilized on a consistent basis. For example, everyone has certain hours of the day which are already committed for activities such as jobs, classes, and, of course, sleep. There is also going to be the time you spend relaxing because CPA candidates should try to maintain some balance in their lives. Sometimes too much studying can be counterproductive. But there will be some time available to you for studying and working through the questions. Block off this available time and use it only for exam prep. Use the time to accomplish your weekly tasks and to keep yourself committed to the process. After awhile your preparation will develop into a habit and the preparation will not seem as overwhelming as it once did.

NOW IS THE TIME TO MAKE YOUR COMMITMENT

Chapter 2: Examination Grading

All State Boards of Accountancy use the AICPA advisory grading service. As your grade is to be determined by this process, it is very important that you understand the AICPA grading process and its **implications for your preparation program and for the solution techniques you will use during the examination**. The AICPA has a full-time staff of CPA examination personnel under the supervision of the AICPA Board of Examiners, which has responsibility for the CPA examination.

This chapter contains a description of the AICPA grading process including a determination of the passing standard.

Setting the Passing Standard of the Uniform CPA Examination

As a part of the development of any licensing process, the passing score on the licensing examination must be established. This passing score must be set to distinguish candidates who are qualified to practice from those who are not. After conducting a number of studies of methods to determine passing scores, the Board of Examiners decided to use candidate-centered methods to set passing scores for the computer-based Uniform CPA Examination. In candidate-centered methods, the focus is on looking at actual candidate answers and making judgments about which sets of answers represent the answers of qualified entry-level CPAs. To make these determinations, the AICPA convened panels of CPAs during 2003 to examine candidate responses and set the passing scores for multiple-choice questions and simulations. The data from these panels provide the basis for the development of question and problem points (relative weightings). **A passing score on the computer-based examination is 75 points.**

Grading the Examination

Most of the responses on the computer-based CPA examination are objective in nature. Obviously, this includes the responses to the multiple-choice questions. However, it also includes the responses to the requirements of task-based simulations. Requirements of simulations include responses involving check boxes, entries into spreadsheets, form completion, graphical responses, and drag and drop. All of these responses are computer graded. Therefore, no consideration is given to any comments or explanations outside of the structured responses.

Written communication questions are the only questions that are not computer graded. Graders are used to score the responses involving written communication, (e.g., a written memorandum). These responses are graded for quality of the written communication. While the responses are not graded for technical accuracy, they must be on point. That is, they must be responsive to the requirement.

A **second review** will be performed for all candidates that earn initial grades that are just below the 75-point cutoff.

Multiple-Choice Grading

All of the parts of the CPA examination contain three multiple-choice testlets. **A few of these questions will pretest questions that will not be considered in the candidate's score, but there is no way of determining which are the pretest questions.** Also, the possible score on a question and on a testlet will vary based on the difficulty of the questions. The makeup of the second testlet provided to a candidate will be determined based upon the candidate's performance on the first testlet, and the makeup of the third testlet will be determined by the candidate's performance on the first two testlets. Therefore, you should not be discouraged if you a get a difficult set of questions; it may merely mean that you performed very well on the previous testlet(s). Also, you will receive more raw points for hard and medium questions than for easy questions.

Your grade on the multiple-choice questions is based on the total number of correct answers weighted by their difficulty, (and with no penalty for incorrect answers). As mentioned earlier, several of the multiple-choice questions are pretest items that are not included in the candidate's grade.

Task-Based Simulation and Written Communication Grading

As indicated previously, all of the responses to the task-based simulations will be computer graded. They will typically involve checking a box, selecting a response from a list, or dragging and dropping an answer. As with the multiple-choice questions, a small percentage of the simulation requirements will be pretest items that will not be included in the candidate's grade.

The Business Environment and Concepts examination contains three task-based simulations that involve written communications. The responses to these simulations will be graded for writing skills but not for technical accuracy. These responses are scored based on the following criteria:

1. Coherent organization
2. Development
3. Conciseness
4. Clarity
5. Use of standard English
6. Appropriateness for the reader

Chapter 3 will provide detailed suggestions on ways that you may use the information about grading to maximize your score.

Requesting a Score Review

For an additional fee, you may request a score review. A score review is a verification of your score making certain that the approved answer key was used. Because the AICPA grades your exam at least twice as a part of its normal process, it is unlikely that you will get an adjustment to your score. You should contact the applicable board of accountancy to request a score review.

NOW IS THE TIME TO MAKE YOUR COMMITMENT

Chapter 3: The Solutions Approach

The solutions approach is a systematic problem-solving methodology. The purpose is to assure efficient, complete solutions to CPA exam questions, some of which are complex and confusing relative to most undergraduate accounting questions. This is especially true with regard to the new Simulation type problems. Unfortunately, there appears to be a widespread lack of emphasis on problem-solving techniques in accounting courses. Most accounting books and courses merely provide solutions to specific types of problems. Memorization of these solutions for examinations and preparation of homework problems from examples is "cookbooking." "Cookbooking" is perhaps a necessary step in the learning process, but it is certainly not sufficient training for the complexities of the business world. Professional accountants need to be adaptive to a rapidly changing, complex environment. For example, CPAs have been called on to interpret and issue reports on new concepts such as price controls, energy allocations, and new taxes. These CPAs rely on their problem-solving expertise to understand these problems and to formulate solutions to them.

The steps outlined below are only one of many possible series of solution steps. Admittedly, the procedures suggested are **very** structured; thus, you should adapt the suggestions to your needs. You may find that some steps are occasionally unnecessary, or that certain additional procedures increase your problem-solving efficiency. Whatever the case, substantial time should be allocated to developing an efficient solutions approach before taking the examination. You should develop your solutions approach by working previous CPA questions and problems.

Note that the steps below relate to any specific question or problem; overall examination strategies are discussed in Chapter 4.

Multiple-Choice Questions Screen Layout

The following is a computer screenshot that illustrates the manner in which multiple-choice questions will be presented:

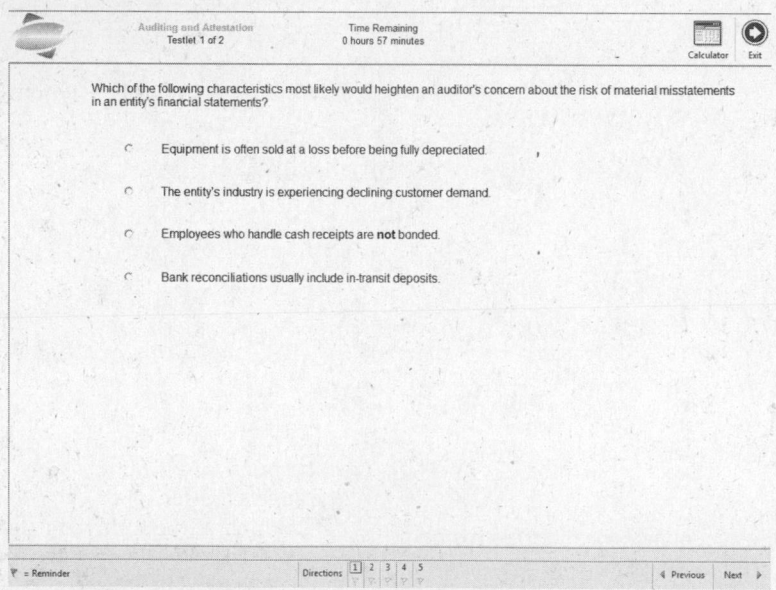

As indicated previously, multiple-choice questions will be presented in three individual testlets of 24 to 30 questions each. Characteristics of the computerized testlets of multiple-choice questions include the following:

1. You may move freely within a particular testlet from one question to the next or back to previous questions until you click the "Exit" button. Once you have indicated that you have finished the testlet by clicking on the "Exit" button, and reconfirmed, you can never return to that set of questions.
2. A button on the screen will allow you to "flag" a question for review if you wish to come back to it later.
3. A four-function computer calculator with an electronic tape is available as a tool.
4. The time remaining for the entire exam section is shown on the screen.
5. The question numbers will be shown at the bottom of the screen. You may navigate between questions by simply clicking on the question number.
6. The "Help" button will provide you with help in navigating and completing the testlet.

The screenshot above was obtained from the AICPA's sample exam at www.cpa-exam.org. Candidates are urged to complete the tutorial and other example questions on the AICPA's Web site to obtain additional experience with the computer-based testing.

Multiple-Choice Questions Solutions Approach

1. **Work individual questions in order.**

   a. If a question appears lengthy or difficult, skip it until you can determine that extra time is available. Mark it for review to remind you to return to it later.

2. **Read the stem of the question without looking at the answers.**

   a. The answers are sometimes misleading and may cause you to misread or misinterpret the question.

3. **Read each question *carefully* to determine the topical area.**

   a. Study the requirements **first** so you know which data are important.
   b. Note keywords and important data.
   c. Identify pertinent information.
   d. Be especially careful to note when the requirement is an **exception** (e.g., "Which of the following is **not** an effective disclaimer of the implied warranty of merchantability?").
   e. If a set of data is the basis for two or more questions, read the requirements of each of the questions before beginning to work the first question (sometimes it is more efficient to work the questions out of order).
   f. Be alert to read questions as they are, not as you would like them to be. You may encounter a familiar looking item; don't jump to the conclusion that you know what the answer is without reading the question completely.

4. **Anticipate the answer before looking at the alternative answers.**

   a. Recall the applicable principle (e.g., offer and acceptance, requisites of negotiability, etc.) and the respective applications thereof.
   b. If a question deals with a complex area, it may be very useful to set up a timeline or diagram using abbreviations.

5. **Read all answers and select the *best* alternative.**
6. **Click on the correct answer (or your educated guess).**
7. **After completing all of the questions including the ones marked for review, click on the "Done" button to close out the testlet. Remember once you have closed out the testlet you can never return to it.**

Multiple-Choice Questions Solutions Approach Example

A good example of the multiple-choice solutions approach follows:

Step 3:

Topical area? Contracts—Revocation and Attempted Acceptance

Step 4:

Principle? An offer may be revoked at any time prior to acceptance and is effective when received by offeree

Step 5:

a. Incorrect - Mason's acceptance was ineffective because the offer had been revoked prior to Mason's acceptance.
b. Incorrect - Same as a.
c. **Correct** - Peters offer was effectively revoked when Mason learned that the lawn mower had been sold to Bronson.
d. Incorrect - Peters was not obligated to keep the offer open because no consideration had been paid by Mason. Note that if consideration had been given, an option contract would have been formed and the offer would have been irrevocable before June 20.

13. On June 15, Peters orally offered to sell a used lawn mower to Mason for $125. Peters specified that Mason had until June 20 to accept the offer. On June 16, Peters received an offer to purchase the lawn mower for $150 from Bronson, Mason's neighbor. Peters accepted Bronson's offer. On June 17, Mason saw Bronson using the lawn mower and was told the mower had been sold to Bronson. Mason immediately wrote to Peters to accept the June 15 offer.

Which of the following statements is correct?

a. Mason's acceptance would be effective when received by Peters.
b. Mason's acceptance would be effective when mailed.
c. Peters' offer had been revoked and Mason's acceptance was ineffective.
d. Peters was obligated to keep the June 15 offer open until June 20.

Currently, all multiple-choice questions are scored based on the number correct, weighted by a difficulty rating (i.e., there is no penalty for guessing). The rationale is that a "good guess" indicates knowledge. Thus, you should answer all multiple-choice questions.

Task-Based Simulations Screen Layouts

Simulations are case-based problems designed to

- Test integrated knowledge
- More closely replicate real-world problems
- Assess research and other skills

Any of the following types of responses might be required on task-based simulations:

- Drop-down selection
- Numeric and monetary inputs
- Formula answers
- Check box response
- Enter spreadsheet formulas
- Research results

The screenshot below illustrates a simulation that requires the candidate to select an answer from a drop-down list.

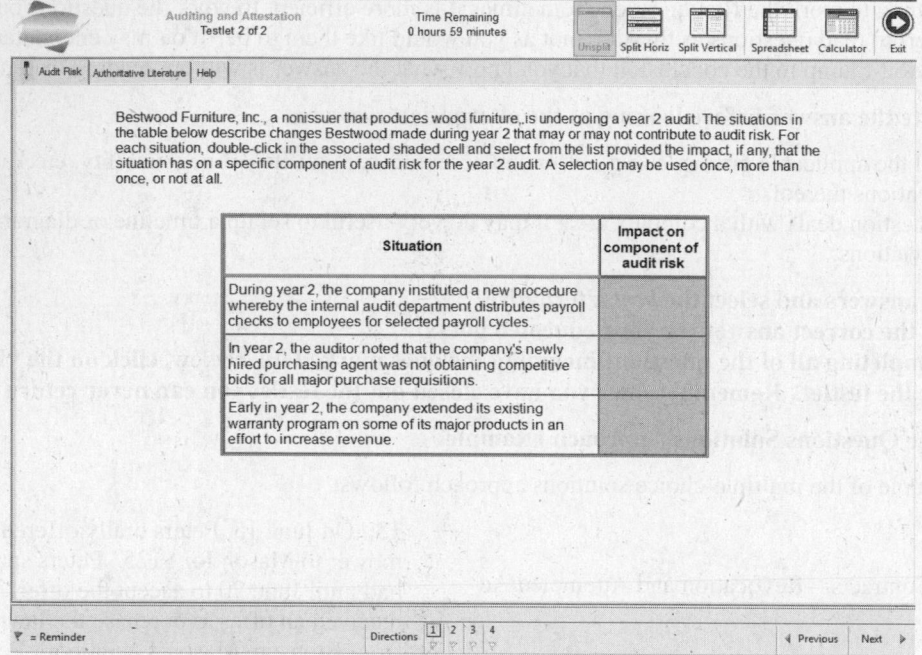

The screenshot below illustrates a simulation that requires the candidate to complete a journal entry by selecting from a list of accounts and inputting amounts.

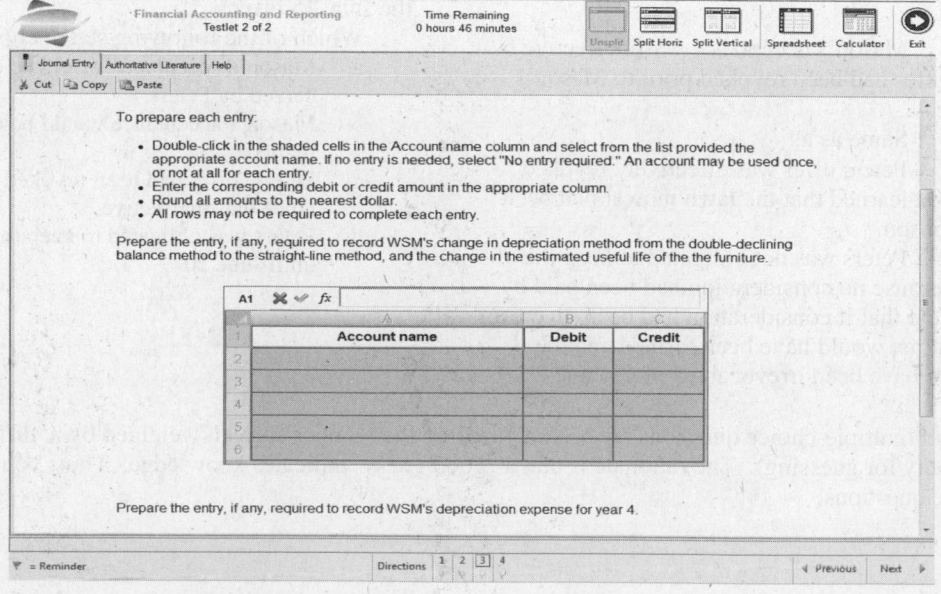

The screenshot below illustrates a simulation that requires the candidate to complete a tax form which might be required in the Regulation section of the exam.

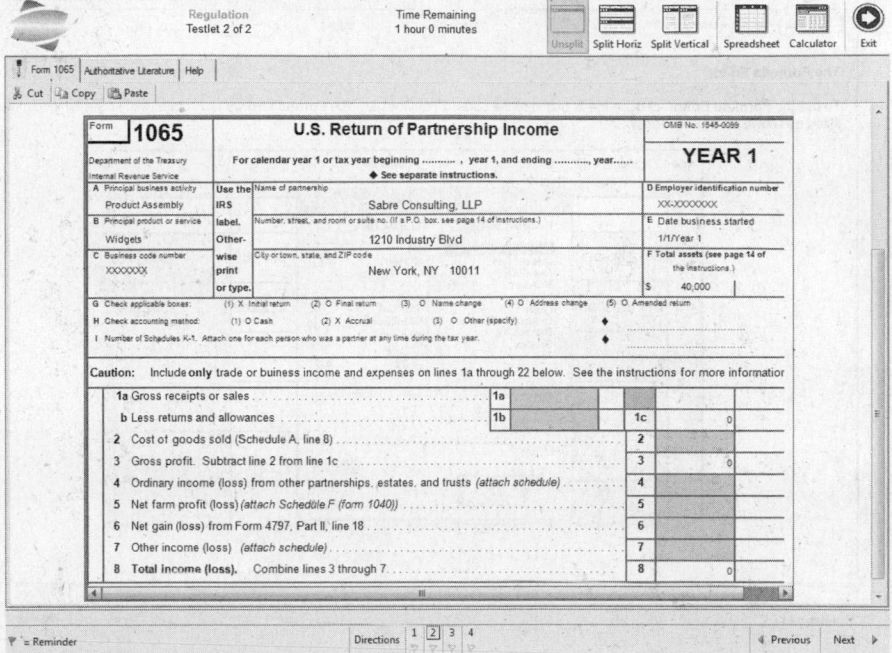

To complete the simulations, candidates are provided with a number of tools, including

- A four-function computer calculator with an electronic tape
- Scratch spreadsheet
- The ability to split windows horizontally or vertically to show two tabs on the screen (e.g., you can examine the situation tab in one window and a requirement tab in a second window)
- Access to professional literature databases to answer research requirements
- Copy and paste functions

In addition, the resource tab provides other resources that may be needed to complete the problem. For example, a resource tab might contain a present value table for use in answering a lease problem.

A window on the screen shows the time remaining for the entire exam and the "Help" button provides instructions for navigating the simulation and completing the requirements.

The screenshots below explain how the spreadsheet operates.

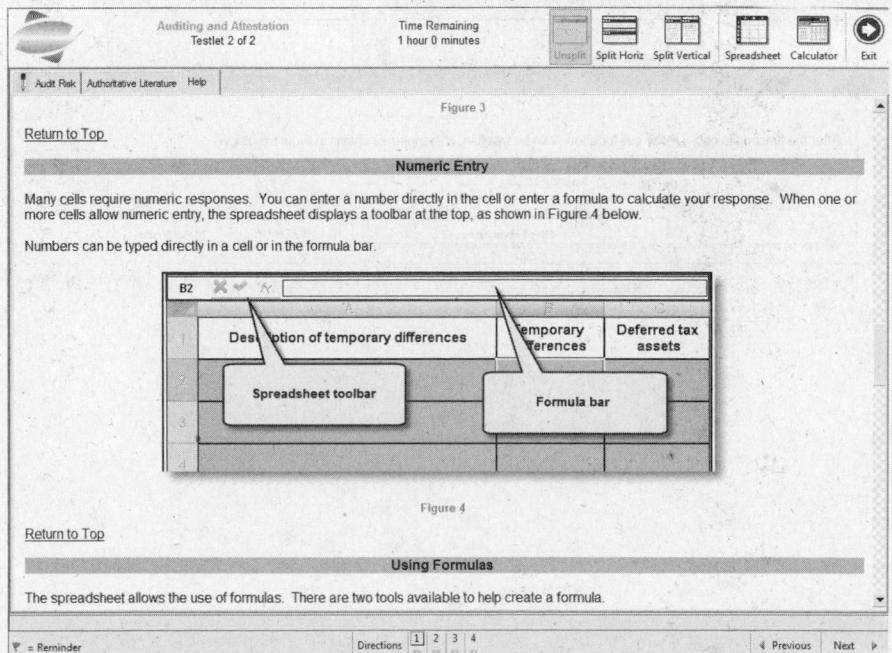

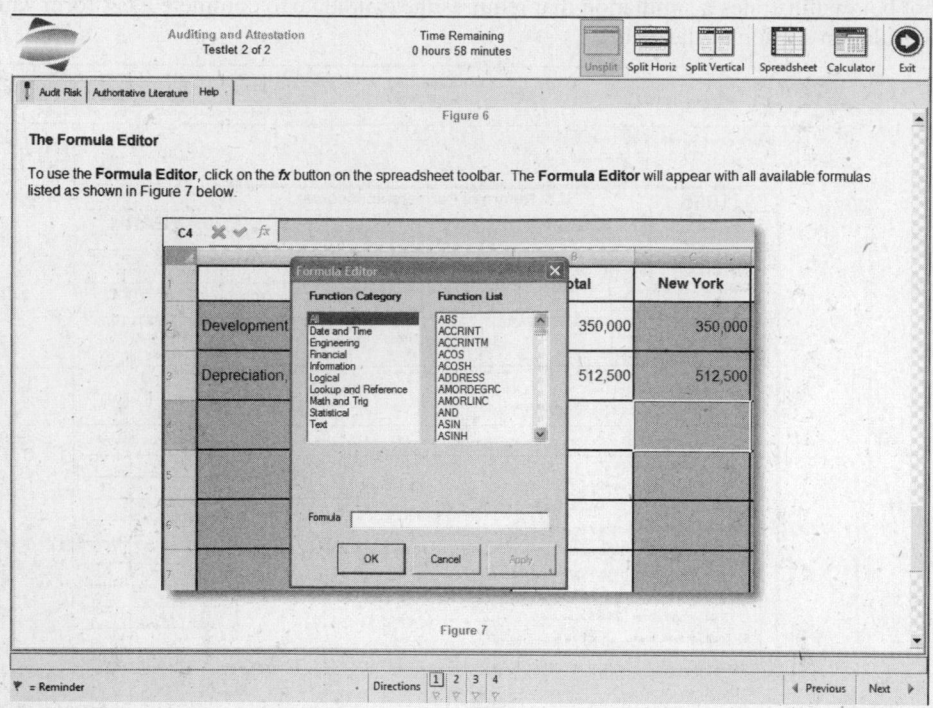

The Formula Editor

To use the **Formula Editor**, click on the *fx* button on the spreadsheet toolbar. The **Formula Editor** will appear with all available formulas listed as shown in Figure 7 below.

Figure 7

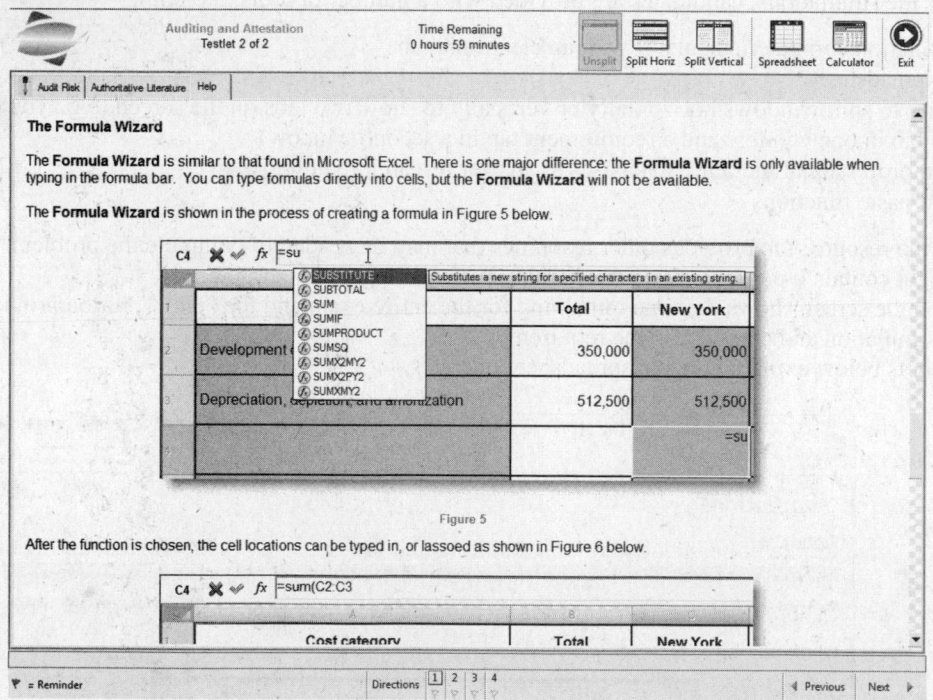

The Formula Wizard

The **Formula Wizard** is similar to that found in Microsoft Excel. There is one major difference: the **Formula Wizard** is only available when typing in the formula bar. You can type formulas directly into cells, but the **Formula Wizard** will not be available.

The **Formula Wizard** is shown in the process of creating a formula in Figure 5 below.

Figure 5

After the function is chosen, the cell locations can be typed in, or lassoed as shown in Figure 6 below.

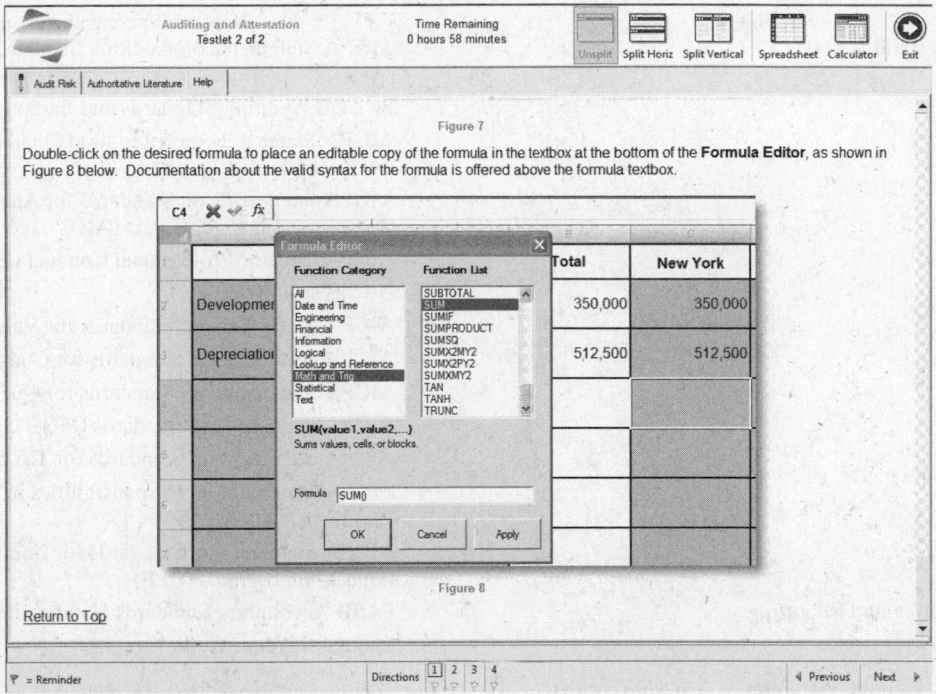

The AICPA has introduced a new simulation interface which is illustrated in this manual. You are urged to complete the tutorial and other sample tests that are on the AICPA's Web site (www.cpa-exam.org) to obtain additional experience with the interface and computer-based testing.

Task-Based Simulations Solutions Approach

The following solutions approach is suggested for answering simulations:

1. **Review the entire background and problem.** Get a feel for the topical area and related concepts that are being tested. Even though the format of the question may vary, the exam continues to test your understanding of applicable principles or concepts. Relax, take a deep breath, and determine your strategy for conquering the simulation.
2. **Identify the requirements of the simulation.** This step will help you focus in more quickly on the solution(s) without wasting time reading irrelevant material.
3. **Study the items to be answered.** As you do this and become familiar with the topical area being tested, you should review the concepts of that area. This will help you organize your thoughts so that you can relate logically the requirements of the simulation with the applicable concepts.
4. **Use the scratch paper (which will be provided) and the spreadsheet and calculator tools to assist you in answering the simulation.**

Task-Based Research Simulations

One research simulation will be included on the Auditing and Attestation, Financial Accounting and Reporting, and Regulation sections of the exam. Research simulations require candidates to search the professional literature and income tax code in electronic format and interpret the results. The table below describes the research material that will be available for each section of the exam that includes research simulations.

Section	**Potential research resources**
Auditing and Attestation	• AICPA Statements on Auditing Standards and Interpretations (AU)
	• PCAOB Auditing Standards and Interpretations (PCAOB)
	• AICPA Statements on Attestation Standards and Interpretations (AT)
	• AICPA Statements on Standards for Accounting and Review Services and Interpretations (AR)
	• AICPA Code of Professional Conduct (ET)
	• AICPA Bylaws (BL)
	• AICPA Statements on Standards for Valuation Services (VS)
	• AICPA Statement on Standards for Consulting Services (CS)
	• AICPA Statements on Standards for Quality Control (QC)
	• AICPA Peer Review Standards (PR)
	• AICPA Statement on Standards for Tax Services (TS)
	• AICPA Statement on Responsibilities in Personal Financial Planning Practice (PFP)
	• AICPA Statement on Standards for Continuing Professional Education Programs (CPE)
Financial Accounting and Reporting	• FASB Accounting Standards Codification
Regulation	• Internal Revenue Code

The research material may be searched using the table of contents or a keyword search. Therefore, knowing important code sections, FASB Codification sections, auditing standards section numbers, etc. may speed up your search.

If possible, it is important to get experience using the electronic version of the research databases to sharpen your skills. If that is not available, you should use the printed copy of the professional standards and the IRS code and regulations to answer the simulations in the manual. Remember, the AICPA offers an electronic version of professional standards to registered candidates. Refer to the AICPA Web site at www.cpa-exam.org.

Written Communication Tasks

The Business Environment and Concepts section of the exam will require the completion of three written communication questions. Communication questions will involve some real-world writing assignment that a CPA might have to perform, such as a memorandum to a client explaining a management technique. The subject of the communication will be a Business Environment and Concepts topic.

It is essential for the communication to be in your own words. In addition, the communication will not be graded for technical accuracy. If it is on point, it will only be graded for usefulness to the intended user and writing skills. The following screenshot illustrates a task requiring the composition of a memorandum to a company president.

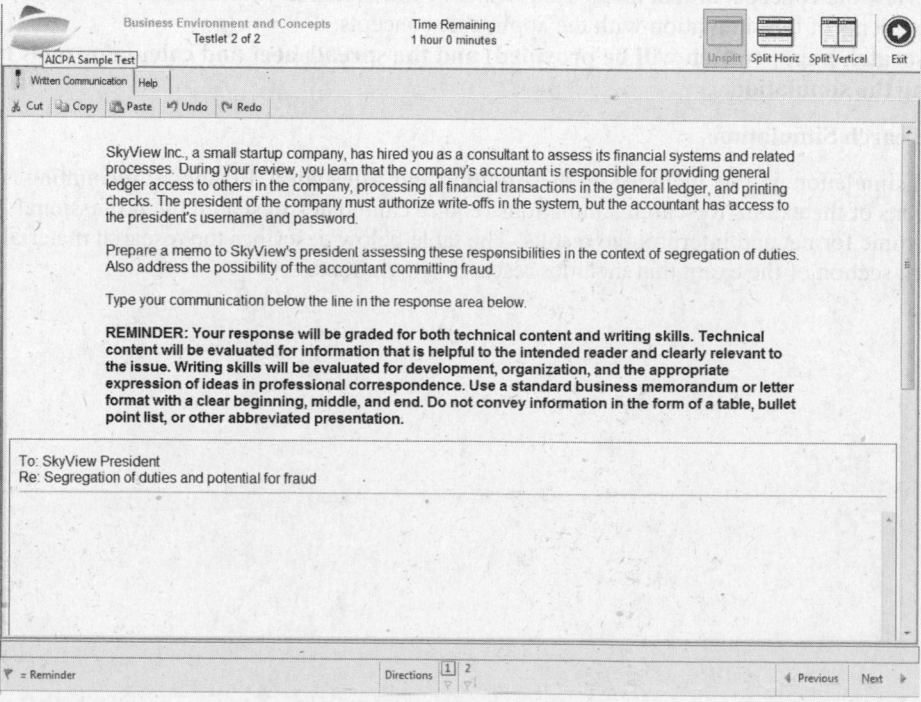

Candidates' writing skills will be graded according to the following characteristics:

1. **Idea formation**

    Candidates should develop coherent ideas from the material provided. Before beginning the communication, the candidate should understand the purpose and the major information to be communicated. Thoughts should be organized in a logical fashion. Prepare an outline to organize your ideas.

2. **Coherent organization**

    Candidates should organize their responses in a manner that is logical and easy to follow. Jumbled paragraphs and disorderly sentences will only confuse the grader and make his/her job more difficult. The following techniques will help improve written coherence.[1]

    • Use short paragraphs composed of short sentences
    • Indent paragraphs to set off lists, equations, key ideas, etc. when appropriate
    • Maintain coherence **within** paragraphs

        - Use a topic sentence at the beginning of each paragraph
        - Develop and support this topic throughout the rest of the paragraph
        - Present old or given information before discussing new information
        - Discuss ideas in chronological order
        - Use parallel grammatical structure
        - Be consistent in person, verb tense, and number
        - Substitute pronouns or synonyms for previously used keywords
        - Use transitions (e.g., therefore, finally)

    • Maintain coherence **between** paragraphs

        - Repeat keywords from previous paragraph
        - Use transitions

    As indicated above, candidates are strongly advised to keyword outline their responses **before** writing their communications. This technique helps the candidate to focus on the flow of ideas s/he wants to convey before starting the actual writing task.

3. **Conciseness**

    Candidates should express themselves in as few words as possible. Complex, wordy sentences are hard to understand. Conciseness can be improved using the following guidelines.

    • Write in short sentences
    • Use a simple word instead of a long word if it serves the same purpose
    • Avoid passive constructions (e.g., **was** evalua**ted**)
    • Use words instead of phrases
    • Combine sentences, if possible
    • Avoid empty fillers (e.g., **it is** apparent; **there seems to be**)
    • Avoid multiple negatives (e.g., **no** reason for **not** using)

4. **Clarity**

    Written responses should leave no doubt in the reader's mind as to the meaning intended. Clarity can be improved as follows:

    • Do **not** use abbreviations
    • Use correct terminology
    • Use examples
    • Use words with specific and precise meanings
    • Write in short, well-constructed sentences
    • Make sure subjects and verbs agree
    • Make sure pronouns and their antecedents agree in number (e.g., the partnership must decide how **it** (not **they**) wants to split profits.)
    • Avoid unclear reference to a pronoun's antecedent (e.g., A should inform B that **he** must perform on the contract by January 1—Who does "he" refer to?)

---

[1] *Adapted from* **Writing for Accountants** *by Aletha S. Hendrickson (Cincinnati, OH: Southwestern Publishing Co., 1993) pp. 128-209.*

5. **Use of standard English**
    Spelling, punctuation, and word usage should follow the norm used in most books, newspapers, and magazines. Note the following common mistakes:

    •   Confusion of its/it's

        The firm issued its stock.
        It's *(it is) the stock of that firm.*

    •   Confusion of there/their/they're

        There *will be a dividend declaration.*
        Their *dividend was declared last week.*
        They're *(they are) declaring a dividend.*

    •   Spelling errors

        *Separate **not** seperate*
        *Receivable **not** recievable*

    The word processing software that you will use to write the communication on the exam will likely have a spell check function. Use it.

6. **Appropriateness for the reader**
    Candidates will be asked to prepare a communication for a certain reader (e.g., a memorandum for a client). Writing that is appropriate for the reader will take into account the reader's background, knowledge of the subject, interests, and concerns. (When the intended reader is not specified, the candidate should write for a knowledgeable CPA.)
    Intended readers may include those who are unfamiliar with most terms and concepts, and who seek financial information because of self-interest (i.e., clients, stockholders). Try the following techniques for these readers:

    •   Avoid jargon, if possible (i.e., GAAS, etc.)
    •   Use parenthetical definitions

        -   *limited partner (liable only to the extent of contributed capital)*
        -   *marketable equity securities (short-term investments in stock)*

    •   Set off definitions as appositives

        A note, a two-party negotiable instrument, may become uncollectible..

    •   Incorporate a "you" attitude

    The requirement of a question may also specify that the response should be directed to professionals who are knowledgeable of most terms and concepts. Employ the following techniques with these readers:

    •   Use jargon
    •   Refer to authoritative sources (i.e., Code section 543 or FASB 13)
    •   Incorporate a "we" attitude

    Again, preparing a keyword outline will assist you in meeting many of these requirements. You should also reread each written communication in its entirety. Writing errors are common during the exam, so take your time to proofread and edit your answers. Again, make use of the spell check function of the word processing software if it is available.

Methods for Improving Your Writing Skills

1. **Organization**
    Logical organization is very important Again, this is where the keyword outline helps.

2. **Syntax, grammar, and style**
    By the time you sit for the CPA exam, you have at your disposal various grammatical constructs from which you may form sentences. Believe it or not, you know quite a bit of English grammar; if you did not, you would never have made it this far in your studies. So in terms of your grammar, relax! You already know it.
    A frequent problem with writing occurs with the syntactic structure of sentences. Although the Board of Examiners does not expect the rhetoric of Cicero, it does expect to read and understand your answer. The way in which the graders will assess writing skills further indicates that they are looking more for writing skills at the micro level (sentence level) than at the macro level (organizational level).

a. Basic syntactic structure (transitive and intransitive action verbs)

    Most English sentences are based on this simple dynamic: that someone or something (the subject) does some action (the predicate). These sentences involve action verbs and are grouped in the following categories:

(1) Subject-Verb

The TAXPAYER WAITED for 3 weeks to get a refund.

(2) Subject-Verb-Direct Object (The object receives the action of the verb.)

The TAXPAYER SIGNED the CONTRACT.

(3) Subject-Verb-Indirect Object-Direct Object (The direct object receives the action of the verb, but the indirect object is also affected by this action, though not in the same way as the direct object.)

The IRS GAVE US a DEFINITE DECISION well beyond our expectations.

b. Syntactic structure (linking verbs)

    Linking verbs are verbs which, rather than expressing action, say something about the subject's state of being. In sentences with linking verbs, the subject is linked to a word which describes it or renames it.

(1) Subject-Linking Verb-Nominative (The nominative renames the subject.)

In the field of Accounting, the FASB IS the standard-setting BOARD.

(2) Subject-Linking Verb-Adjective (The adjective describes the subject.)

Evidence of SCIENTER IS always HELPFUL in proving fraud.

c. Subordinate clauses

(1) Adverbial clauses (subordinating connector + sentence). These clauses modify the action of the main clause.

When amounts are not substantiated, a nondeductible expense is incurred.

(2) Noun clauses (nominal connectors + sentence). These clauses function as nouns in the main sentence.

When a tax return is not signed, we know that the return is not filed.

(3) Adjective clauses [relative pronoun + verb + (object/nominative/adjective)]. These clauses function as noun modifiers.

The court with the highest authority is the one that sets the precedent.

d. The above are patterns which form basic clauses (both dependent and independent). In addition, numerous phrases may function as modifiers of the basic sentence elements.

(1) Prepositional (a preposition + an object)

of the FASB
on the data
about a new type of depreciation

(2) Verbal

(a) Verb + ing + a modifier (noun, verb, adverb, prepositional phrase)

i] Used as an adjective

the expense requiring substantiation
the alternative minimizing taxes

ii] Used as a noun (gerund)

Performing all of the duties required by a contract is necessary to avoid breach.

(b) Verb + ed + modifier (noun, adverb, prepositional phrase)

i] Used as an adjective

The basis used when historical costs cannot be determined is estimated value.

          (c) Infinitive (to + verb + object)

              i] Used as a noun

              The company needs to respond by filing an amended tax return.

3. **Sentence clarity**

    a. When constructing your sentences, do not separate basic sentence elements with too many phrases.

       The liability for partnership losses exceeding capital contributions is another characteristic of a general partnership.

       Better: *One characteristic of a general partnership is the liability for partnership losses which exceed capital contributions.*

    b. Refrain from lumping prepositional and infinitive phrases together.

       The delegation of authority by a corporate director of day-to-day or routine matters to officers and agents of that corporation is a power and a duty of the director.

       Better: *Delegating authority for routine matters to officers and agents is a power and a duty of corporation's directors.*

    c. Make sure that your pronouns have a clear and obvious referent.

       When an accountant contracts with a client for the primary benefit of a third party, they are in privity of contract.

       Better: *When known to be a primary beneficiary of an accountant-client contract, a third party is in privity of contract with the accountant.*

    d. Make sure that any adjectival verbal phrase clearly modifies a noun stated in the sentence.

       To avoid incurring a penalty, each return was prepared exactly as required.

       Better: *To avoid incurring a penalty, we prepared each return exactly as required.*

Time Requirements for the Solutions Approach

Many candidates bypass the solutions approach, because they feel it is too time-consuming. Actually, the solutions approach is a time-saver and, more importantly, it helps you prepare better solutions to all questions and simulations.

Without committing yourself to using the solutions approach, try it step-by-step on several questions and simulations. After you conscientiously go through the step-by-step routine a few times, you will begin to adopt and modify aspects of the technique which will benefit you. Subsequent usage will become subconscious and painless. The important point is that you must try the solutions approach several times to accrue any benefits.

In summary, the solutions approach may appear foreign and somewhat cumbersome. At the same time, if you have worked through the material in this chapter, you should have some appreciation for it. Develop the solutions approach by writing down the steps in the solutions approach algorithm at the beginning of this chapter, and keep them before you as you work CPA exam questions and problems. Remember that even though the suggested procedures appear **very structured** and **time-consuming,** integration of these procedures into your own style of problem solving will help improve **your** solutions approach. The next chapter discusses strategies for the overall examination.

NOW IS THE TIME TO MAKE YOUR COMMITMENT

Chapter 4: Taking the Examination

This chapter is concerned with developing an examination strategy (e.g., how to cope with the environment at the test center, time management, etc.).

EXAMINATION STRATEGIES

Your performance during the examination is final and not subject to revision. While you may sit for a section of the examination again if you are unsuccessful, the majority of your preparation will have to be repeated, requiring substantial, additional amounts of time. Thus, examination strategies (discussed in this chapter) that maximize your exam-taking efficiency are very important.

Getting "Psyched Up"

The CPA exam is quite challenging and worthy of your best effort. Explicitly develop your own psychological strategy to get yourself "up" for the exam. Pace your study program such that you will be able to operate at peak performance when you are actually taking the exam. A significant advantage of the new computerized exam is that if you have scheduled early in a testing window and do not feel well, you can reschedule your sitting. However, once you start the exam, you cannot retake it in the same testing window, so do not leave the exam early. Do the best you can.

Lodging, Meals, Exercise

If you must travel to the test center, make advance reservations for comfortable lodging convenient to the test center. Do not stay with friends, relatives, etc. Both uninterrupted sleep and total concentration on the exam are a must. Consider the following in making your lodging plans:

1. Proximity to the test center
2. Availability of meals and snacks
3. Recreational facilities

Plan your meal schedule to provide maximum energy and alertness during the day and maximum rest at night. Do not experiment with new foods, drinks, etc., around your scheduled date. Within reasonable limits, observe your normal eating and drinking habits. Recognize that overconsumption of coffee during the exam could lead to a hyperactive state and disaster. Likewise, overindulgence in alcohol to overcome nervousness and to induce sleep the night before might contribute to other difficulties the following morning.

Tenseness should be expected before and during the examination. Rely on a regular exercise program to reduce stress. As you select your lodging for the examination, try to accommodate your exercise pleasure (e.g., running, swimming, etc.).

To relieve tension or stress while studying, try breathing or stretching exercises. Use these exercises before and during the examination to start and to keep your adrenaline flowing. Remain determined not to have to sit for the section another time.

In summary, the examination is likely to be both rigorous and fatiguing. Expect it and prepare for it by getting in shape, planning methods of relaxation during the exam and in the evening before, and finally, building the confidence and competence to successfully complete the exam.

Test Center and Procedures

If possible, visit the test center before the examination to assure knowledge of the location. Remember: no surprises. Having a general familiarity with the facilities will lessen anxiety prior to the examination. Talking to a recent veteran of the examination will give you background for the general examination procedures, such as

1. Procedure for taking the examination
2. Accessibility of restrooms
3. Availability of beverages and snacks at the test center
4. Peculiar problems of test center, for example, noise, lighting, temperature, etc. (Prometric has asserted that this will not be a problem)
5. Experience in taking the exam
6. Other important information

Keep in mind the following procedures for taking the exam as set forth in the AICPA *Uniform CPA Examination Candidate Bulletin.*

1. **You must arrive at the test center at least thirty minutes before the scheduled appointment time for your examination.** Your examination should begin within thirty minutes of the scheduled start time. If circumstances

(unrelated to your actions) occur that delay your start time by more than thirty minutes, you will be given the option of taking the exam or rescheduling.

2. You must bring your Notice to Schedule.
3. You are required to present two forms of identification, one of which must contain a recent photograph. **Each form must bear your signature and must not be expired. The names on these documents must exactly match the name on your Notice to Schedule.**

     a. Acceptable primary forms of identification include

         (1) A valid state- or territory-issued driver's license with photograph and signature
         (2) A valid driver's license issued by a foreign government (printed in English)
         (3) A valid state- or territory-issued identification card with a recent photograph and signature
         (4) A valid government-issued passport with photograph and signature
         (5) A United States military identification card with a recent photograph and signature

     b. Acceptable secondary forms of identification include

         (1) An additional government issued identification card (see primary list)
         (2) An identification card issued by your Board of Accountancy
         (3) A valid credit card
         (4) A bank ATM card
         (5) A debit card

4. You must place all personal belongings in a small locker before beginning the exam. Do not bring large items with you.
5. Test center personnel will take a digital photograph of your face.
6. You will be required to sign the test center log book each time you exit or reenter the testing room. You must have your identification with you to be readmitted to the testing room.
7. You will be escorted to a workstation by test center staff, and you will be videotaped while taking the examination.
8. Scratch paper and pencils will be provided to you. You will be directed to enter your examination password on your scratch paper and must return the scratch paper when you complete the exam. If you need additional scratch paper, you may request it but must first turn in the original sheets to get a new supply.
9. Do not pause for an extended period of time between being logged in and starting the first testlet. You will be timed out in about 10 minutes.
10. You should notify the test center staff if you have any problems (e.g., computer problems).
11. When you finish the examination, you will turn in your scratch paper and sign the test center log book.

As you can see, it is important to talk with someone who recently sat for the examination. The objective is to reduce your anxiety just prior to the examination and to minimize any possible distractions. Finally, if you have any remaining questions regarding examination procedure, refer to the AICPA Web site (www.cpa-exam.org), or go to Prometric's Web site (www.prometric.com).

Allocation of Time

Budget your time. Time should be carefully allocated in an attempt to maximize points per minute. While you must develop your own strategy with respect to time allocation, some suggestions may be useful. Allocate 5 minutes to reading the instructions. When you begin the exam you will be given an inventory of the total number of testlets and simulations, including the suggested times. Budget your time based on this inventory.

Plan on spending 1 to 1 1/2 minutes working each of the individual multiple-choice questions. This should leave you sufficient time to complete the simulations.

Techniques for Time Management

Each exam section will have three testlets of multiple-choice questions with from 24 to 30 questions each. As you complete each testlet keep track of how you performed in relation to the AICPA suggested times. After you finish the multiple-choice testlets, budget your time for the simulations based on your remaining time and the AICPA suggested times. Remember that you alone control watching your progress towards successfully completing this exam.

Examination Rules

The following are the significant rules for taking the Uniform CPA Examination:

1. Papers, books, food, or purses are not allowed in the testing room.
2. Eating, drinking, or use of tobacco is not allowed in the testing room.
3. Talking or communicating with other candidates is not allowed in the testing room.
4. Calculators, personal digital assistants, or other computer devices are not allowed in the testing room.
5. Communication devices (e.g., cell phones, pagers, beepers, etc.) are not allowed in the testing room.

6. Recording devices are not allowed in the testing room.
7. You must not leave the testing room without the permission of the test center staff.
8. You must show your identification to the staff to reenter the room after any breaks.

Refer to the brochure *Uniform CPA Examination Candidate Bulletin* for other rules.

Misconduct, cheating, or copyright infringement may result in a candidate's dismissal, or the candidate's scores being canceled by the AICPA.

Breaks

After completing each testlet in an exam section, you will be presented with the option to take a break. You will not be allowed to take a break at any other time during the examination. If you choose to take a break, you will be asked to leave the testing room quietly and sign the test center log book. You do not have to take a break. **The clock will keep running during the break, leaving you less time to complete the section.**

CPA EXAM CHECKLIST

One week before you are scheduled to sit

__ 1. Review notecards and other notes for important terms, lists, and key phrases.
__ 2. If time permits, work through a few questions in your weakest areas so that the applicable principles and concepts are fresh in your mind.
__ 3. Assemble materials listed under 1. above into a "last review" notebook to be taken with you to the exam.

What to bring

__ 1. *Identification*—You should bring your two forms of identification, your Notice to Schedule, and any other required registration material.
__ 2. *Hotel confirmation.* (If you must travel.)
__ 3. *Cash*—Payment for anything by personal check is rarely accepted.
__ 4. *Major credit card*—American Express, Master Card, Visa, etc.
__ 5. *Alarm clock*—This is too important an event to trust to a hotel wake-up call that might be overlooked.
__ 6. *Clothing*—Should be comfortable and layered to suit the possible temperature range in the testing room.
__ 7. *Earplugs*—Even though examinations are being given, there may be constant activity in the testing room (e.g., people walking around, rustling of paper, clicking of keyboards, people coughing, etc.). The use of earplugs may block out some of this distraction and help you concentrate better.
__ 8. *Other*—Any "last review" materials.

Evenings before exams

1. Reviewing the evening before the exam could earn you the extra points needed to pass a section. Just keep this last-minute effort in perspective and do **not** panic yourself into staying up all night trying to cover every possible point. This could lead to disaster by sapping your body of the endurance needed to attack questions creatively during the next day.
2. Reread key outlines or notecards the evening before, reviewing important terms, key phrases, and lists, etc.

3. Go over mnemonics and acronyms you have developed as study aids. Test yourself by writing out the letters on paper while verbally giving a brief explanation of what the letters stand for.
4. **Set your alarm and get a good night's rest!** Being well rested will permit you to meet the day's challenge with a fresh burst of creative energy.

Exam-taking strategy

1. Review the AICPA suggested times for the testlets and simulations to plan your time allocation during the exam.
2. If you are struggling with multiple-choice questions, use the strategy of dividing the questions into two categories.

   a. Questions for which you **know** you lack knowledge to answer: Drawing from any resources you have, narrow answers down to as few as possible; then make an **educated guess**.
   b. Questions for which you feel you should be getting the correct answer: Mark the question for review. Your mental block may clear, or you may spot a simple error in logic that now can be corrected.

3. Remember: **never** change a first impulse answer later unless you are **absolutely certain** you are right. It is a proven fact that your subconscious often guides you to the correct answer.
4. Begin the simulations, carefully monitoring your time. The crucial technique to use for simulations is to read through each fact situation **carefully,** noting keywords. Then **read each requirement** carefully before you start answering it. Save adequate time to complete any communication requirement.
5. Constantly compare your progress with the time remaining. **Never** spend excessive amounts of time on one multiple-choice testlet or simulation.
6. The cardinal rule is **never,** but **never,** leave an answer blank.

AUDITING AND ATTESTATION

As indicated previously, this section consists of 8 modules designed to facilitate your study for the Auditing and Attestation section of the Uniform CPA examination. The table of contents at the right describes the content of each module.

Exam Content Overview

The Auditing & Attestation section of the CPA exam tests the candidate's knowledge primarily of AICPA auditing standards and procedures as they relate to the CPA's functions in the examination of financial statements. However, the section also covers international auditing standards, accounting and review services, other attestation services, ethical standards issued by the AICPA, SEC, PCAOB, Department of Labor, and the GAO, and quality control standards. It also covers auditing standards for issuer (public) companies issued by the PCAOB and the Sarbanes-Oxley Act of 2002. You will increase your chances for success if you have a recent copy of the codification of the Statements on Auditing Standards, Statements on Standards for Accounting and Review Services, Statements on Standards for Attestation Engagements, Statements on Quality Control Standards, and the AICPA Code of Professional Conduct. The codified version, as opposed to the original pronouncements as issued, eliminates all superseded portions. The AICPA publishes the codification as the *AICPA Professional Standards*. Many university bookstores carry this source, as it is often required in undergraduate auditing courses. PCAOB standards are available on its Web site at www.pcaobus.org. An auditing textbook is also helpful.

This chapter reviews topics tested on the Auditing section of the exam. Begin by performing a self-evaluation as suggested in the "self-study program" which appears in Chapter 1 of this volume. After studying each module in this volume, work all of the multiple-choice questions and task-based simulations.

Recognize that most candidates have difficulty with audit sampling and auditing with technology due to limited exposure in their undergraduate programs and in practice. Thus, you should work through the outlines presented in each study module and work the related questions. Unfortunately, this entire volume would be required to provide comprehensive textbook coverage of topics tested on the exam.

AICPA CONTENT AND SKILLS SPECIFICATIONS

The AICPA Content and Skills Specifications for the Uniform CPA Exam set forth the coverage of topics on the Auditing and Attestation exam. This outline was issued by the AICPA and is effective for exams beginning in 2011. The first part of the outline describes the topical coverage of the Auditing and Attestation exam, and the second part provides some insights into the skills tested on all sections of the Uniform CPA exam.

Content Specification Outlines (CSOs)

The Auditing and Attestation section tests knowledge and understanding of the following professional standards: Auditing standards promulgated in the United States of America (related to audits of an "Issuer" (a public company), a "Nonissuer" (an entity that is not a public company), governmental entities, not-for-profit entities, and employee benefit plans, standards related to attestation and assurance engagements, and standards for performing accounting and review services. Candidates are expected to demonstrate an awareness of (1) the International Auditing and Assurance Standards Board (IAASB) and its role in establishing International Standards on Auditing (ISAs), (2) the differences between ISAs and US auditing standards, and (3) the audit requirements under US auditing standards that apply when they perform audit procedures on a US company that supports an audit report based upon the auditing standards of another country, or the ISAs. This section also tests knowledge of professional responsibilities of certified public accountants, including ethics and independence. Candidates are also expected to demonstrate an awareness of (1) the International Ethics Standards Board for Accountants (IESBA) and its role in establishing requirements of the International Federation of Accountants (IFAC) Code of Ethics for Professional Accountants, and (2) the independence requirements that apply when they perform audit procedures on a US company that supports an audit report based upon the auditing standards of another country, or the ISAs. In addition to demonstrating knowledge and understanding of the professional standards, candidates are required to demonstrate the skills required to apply that knowledge in performing auditing and attestation tasks as certified public accountants. The outline below specifies the tasks and related knowledge in which candidates are required to demonstrate proficiency. Candidates are also expected to perform the following tasks:

- Demonstrate an awareness and understanding of the process by which standards and professional requirements are established for audit, attestation, and other services performed by CPAs, including the role of standard-setting bodies within the US and those bodies with the authority to promulgate international standards.
- Differentiate between audits, attestation and assurance services, compilations, and reviews.
- Differentiate between the professional standards for issuers and nonissuers.

- Identify situations that might be unethical or a violation of professional standards, perform research and consultations as appropriate, and determine the appropriate action.
- Recognize potentially unethical behavior of clients and determine the impact on the services being performed.
- Demonstrate the importance of identifying and adhering to requirements, rules, and standards that are established by licensing boards within their states, and which may place additional professional requirements specific to their state of practice.

- Appropriately apply professional requirements in practice, and differentiate between unconditional requirements and presumptively mandatory requirements.
- Exercise due care in the performance of work.
- Demonstrate an appropriate level of professional skepticism in the performance of work.
- Maintain independence in mental attitude in all matters relating to the audit.
- Research relevant professional literature.

The outline below specifies the knowledge in which candidates are required to demonstrate proficiency.

I. Auditing and Attestation: Engagement Acceptance and Understanding the Assignment (12%–16%)

A. Determine Nature and Scope of Engagement

B. Consider the Firm's System of Quality Control for Policies and Procedures Pertaining to Client Acceptance and Continuance, including

1. The CPA firm's ability to perform the engagement within reporting deadlines
2. Experience and availability of firm personnel to meet staffing and supervision requirements
3. Whether independence can be maintained
4. Integrity of client management
5. Appropriateness of the engagement's scope to meet the client's needs

C. Communicate with the Predecessor Auditor

D. Establish an Understanding with the Client and Document the Understanding through an Engagement Letter or Other Written Communication with the Client

E. Consider Other Planning Matters

1. Consider using the work of other independent auditors
2. Determine the extent of the involvement of professionals possessing specialized skills
3. Consider the independence, objectivity, and competency of the internal audit function

F. Identify Matters and Prepare Documentation for Communications with Those Charged with Governance

II. Auditing and Attestation: Understanding the Entity and Its Environment (Including Internal Control) (16%–20%)

A. Determine and Document Materiality Levels for Financial Statements Taken as a Whole

B. Conduct and Document Risk Assessment Discussions among Audit Team, Concurrently with Discussion on Susceptibility of the Entity's Financial Statement to Material Misstatement Due to Fraud

C. Consideration of Fraud

1. Identify characteristics of fraud
2. Document required discussions regarding risk of fraud
3. Document inquiries of management about fraud
4. Identify and assess risks that may result in material misstatements due to fraud

D. Perform and Document Risk Assessment Procedures

1. Identify, conduct, and document appropriate inquiries of management and others within the entity
2. Perform appropriate analytical procedures to understand the entity and identify areas of risk
3. Obtain information to support inquiries through observation and inspection (including reading corporate minutes, etc.)

E. Consider Additional Aspects of the Entity and Its Environment, Including Industry, Regulatory, and Other External Factors; Strategies and Business Risks; Financial Performance

F. Consider Internal Control

1. Perform procedures to assess the control environment, including consideration of the COSO framework and identifying entity-level controls
2. Obtain and document an understanding of business processes and information flows
3. Perform and document walkthroughs of transactions from inception through recording in the general ledger and presentation in financial statements
4. Determine the effect of information technology on the effectiveness of an entity's internal control
5. Perform risk assessment procedures to evaluate the design and implementation of internal controls relevant to an audit of financial statements
6. Identify key risks associated with general controls in a financial IT environment, including change management, backup/recovery, and network access (e.g., administrative rights)
7. Identify key risks associated with application functionality that supports financial transaction cycles, including application access control (e.g., administrative access rights); controls over interfaces, integrations, and e-commerce; significant algorithms, reports, validation, edit checks, error handling, etc.
8. Assess whether the entity has designed controls to mitigate key risks associated with general controls or application functionality
9. Identify controls relevant to reliable financial reporting and the period-end financial reporting process
10. Consider limitations of internal control
11. Consider the effects of service organizations on internal control
12. Consider the risk of management override of internal controls

G. Document an Understanding of the Entity and Its Environment, Including Each Component of the Entity's Internal Control, in Order to Assess Risks

H. Assess and Document the Risk of Material Misstatements

1. Identify and document financial statement assertions and formulate audit objectives including significant financial statement balances, classes of transactions, disclosures, and accounting estimates
2. Relate the identified risks to relevant assertions and consider whether the risks could result in a material misstatement to the financial statements
3. Assess and document the risk of material misstatement that relates to both financial statement level and specific assertions
4. Identify and document conditions and events that may indicate risks of material misstatement

I. Identify and Document Significant Risks That Require Special Audit Consideration

1. Risk of fraud
2. Significant recent economic, accounting, or other developments
3. Related parties and related-party transactions
4. Improper revenue recognition
5. Nonroutine or complex transactions
6. Significant management estimates
7. Illegal acts

III. Auditing and Attestation: Performing Audit Procedures and Evaluating Evidence (16%–20%)

A. Develop Overall Responses to Risks

1. Develop overall responses to risks identified and use the risks of material misstatement to drive the nature, timing, and extent of further audit procedures
2. Document significant risks identified, related controls evaluated, and overall responses to address assessed risks
3. Determine and document level(s) of tolerable misstatement

B. Perform Audit Procedures Responsive to Risks of Material Misstatement; Obtain and Document Evidence to Form a Basis for Conclusions

1. Design and perform audit procedures whose nature, timing, and extent are responsive to the assessed risk of material misstatement
2. Integrating audits: in an integrated audit of internal control over financial reporting and the financial statements, design and perform testing of controls to accomplish the objectives of both audits simultaneously
3. Design, perform, and document tests of controls to evaluate design effectiveness
4. Design, perform, and document tests of controls to evaluate operating effectiveness

5. Perform substantive procedures
6. Perform audit sampling
7. Perform analytical procedures
8. Confirm balances and/or transactions with third parties
9. Examine inventories and other assets
10. Perform other tests of details, balances, and journal entries
11. Perform computer-assisted audit techniques (CAATs), including data query, extraction, and analysis
12. Perform audit procedures on significant management estimates
13. Audit fair value measurements and disclosures, including the use of specialists in evaluating estimates
14. Perform tests on unusual year-end transactions
15. Audits performed in accordance with International Standards on Auditing (ISAs) or auditing standards of another country: determine if differences exist and whether additional audit procedures are required
16. Evaluate contingencies
17. Obtain and evaluate lawyers' letters
18. Review subsequent events
19. Obtain and place reliance on representations from management
20. Identify material weaknesses, significant deficiencies, and other control deficiencies
21. Identify matters for communication with those charged with governance

IV. Auditing and Attestation: Evaluating Audit Findings, Communications, and Reporting (16%–20%)

A. Perform Analytical Procedures

B. Evaluate the Sufficiency and Appropriateness of Audit Evidence and Document Engagement Conclusions

C. Evaluate Whether Audit Documentation Is in Accordance with Professional Standards

D. Review the Work Performed by Others to Provide Reasonable Assurance That Objectives Are Achieved

E. Document the Summary of Uncorrected Misstatements and Related Conclusions

F. Evaluate Whether Financial Statements Are Free of Material Misstatements

G. Consider the Entity's Ability to Continue as a Going Concern

H. Consider Other Information in Documents Containing Audited Financial Statements (e.g., Supplemental Information and Management's Discussion and Analysis)

I. Retain Audit Documentation as Required by Standards and Regulations

J. Prepare Communications

1. Reports on audited financial statements
2. Reports required by government auditing standards

3. Reports on compliance with laws and regulations
4. Reports on internal control
5. Reports on the processing of transactions by service organizations
6. Reports on agreed-upon procedures
7. Reports on financial forecasts and projections
8. Reports on pro forma financial information
9. Special reports
10. Reissue reports
11. Communicate internal control related matters identified in the audit
12. Communications with those charged with governance
13. Subsequent discovery of facts existing at the date of the auditor's report
14. Consideration after the report date of omitted procedures

V. Accounting and Review Services Engagements (12%–16%)

A. Plan the Engagement

1. Determine nature and scope of engagement
2. Decide whether to accept or continue the client and engagement including determining the appropriateness of the engagement to meet the client's needs and consideration of independence standards
3. Establish an understanding with the client and document the understanding through an engagement letter or other written communication with the client
4. Consider change in engagement
5. Determine if reports are to be used by third parties

B. Obtain and Document Evidence to Form a Basis for Conclusions

1. Obtain an understanding of the client's operations, business, and industry
2. Obtain knowledge of accounting principles and practices in the industry and the client
3. Obtain knowledge of stated qualifications of accounting personnel

4. Perform analytical procedures for review services
5. Obtain representations from management for review services
6. Perform other engagement procedures
7. Consider departures from generally accepted accounting principles (GAAP) or other comprehensive basis of accounting (OCBOA)
8. Prepare documentation from evidence gathered
9. Retain documentation as required by standards
10. Review the work performed to provide reasonable assurance that objectives are achieved

C. Prepare Communications

1. Reports on compiled financial statements
2. Reports on reviewed financial statements
3. Restricted use of reports
4. Communicating to management and others
5. Subsequent discovery of facts existing at the date of the report
6. Consider degree of responsibility for supplementary information

VI. Professional Responsibilities (16%–20%)

A. Ethics and Independence

1. Code of Professional Conduct (AICPA)
2. Public Company Accounting Oversight Board (PCAOB)
3. US Securities and Exchange Commission (SEC)
4. Government Accountability Office (GAO)
5. Department of Labor (DOL)
6. Sarbanes-Oxley Act of 2002, Title II
7. Sarbanes-Oxley Act of 2002, Title III, Section 303
8. Code of Ethics for Professional Accountants (IFAC)

B. Other Professional Responsibilities

1. Sarbanes-Oxley Act of 2002, Title IV
2. Sarbanes-Oxley Act of 2002, Title I

References—Auditing and Attestation

- AICPA Statements on Auditing Standards and Interpretations
- AICPA Codification of Statements on Auditing Standards, AU Appendix B, *Analysis of International Standards on Auditing*
- Public Company Accounting Oversight Board (PCAOB) Standards (SEC-Approved) and Related Rules, PCAOB Staff Questions and Answers, and PCAOB Staff Audit Practice Alerts
- US Government Accountability Office Government Auditing Standards
- Single Audit Act, as amended
- Office of Management and Budget (OMB) Circular A-133
- AICPA Statements on Quality Control Standards
- AICPA Statements on Standards for Accounting and Review Services and Interpretations
- AICPA Statements on Standards for Attestation Engagements and Interpretations
- AICPA Audit and Accounting Guides
- AICPA Auditing Practice Releases
- AICPA Code of Professional Conduct

- IFAC Code of Ethics for Professional Accountants
- Sarbanes-Oxley Act of 2002
- Department of Labor Guidelines and Interpretive Bulletins re: Auditor Independence
- SEC Independence Rules
- Employee Retirement Income Security Act of 1974
- The Committee of Sponsoring Organizations of the Treadway Commission (COSO): Internal Control—Integrated Framework
- Current textbooks on auditing, attestation services, ethics, and independence

Skill Specification Outlines (SSOs)

The Skill Specification Outlines (SSOs) identify the skills to be tested on the Uniform CPA Examination. There are three categories of skills, and the weightings will be implemented through the use of different question formats in the exam. For each of the question formats, a different set of tools will be available as resources to the candidates, who will need to use those tools to demonstrate proficiency in the applicable skills categories.

Weights

The percentage range assigned to each skill category will be used to determine the quantity of each type of question, as described below. The percentage range assigned to each skill category represents the approximate percentage to which that category of skills will be used in the different sections of the CPA Examination to assess proficiency. The ranges are designed to provide flexibility in building the examination, and the midpoints of the ranges for each section total 100%. No percentages are given for the bulleted descriptions included in these definitions. The presence of several groups within an area or several topics within a group does not imply equal importance or weight will be given to these bullets on an examination.

Skills Category	Weights (FAR, REG, AUD)	Weights (BEC)
Knowledge and Understanding	50%–60%	80%–90%
Application of the Body of Knowledge	40%–50%	–
Written Communication	–	10%–20%

Knowledge and Understanding. Multiple-choice questions will be used as the proxy for assessing knowledge and understanding, and will be based upon the content topics as outlined in the CSOs. Candidates will not have access to the authoritative literature, spreadsheets, or database tools while answering these questions. A calculator will be accessible for the candidates to use in performing calculations to demonstrate their understanding of the principles or subject matter.

Application of the Body of Knowledge. Task-based simulations will be used as the proxy for assessing application of the body of knowledge and will be based upon the content topics as outlined in the CSOs. Candidates will have access to the authoritative literature, a calculator, spreadsheets, and other resources and tools which they will use to demonstrate proficiency in applying the body of knowledge.

Written Communication will be assessed through the use of responses to essay questions, which will be based upon the content topics as outlined in the CSOs. Candidates will have access to a word processor, which includes a spell-check feature.

Outlines

The outlines below provide additional descriptions of the skills that are represented in each category.

Knowledge and Understanding. Expertise and skills developed through learning processes, recall, and reading comprehension. Knowledge is acquired through experience or education and is the theoretical or practical understanding of a subject; knowledge is also represented through awareness or familiarity with information gained by experience of a fact or situation. Understanding represents a higher level than simple knowledge and is the process of using concepts to deal adequately with given situations, facts, or circumstances. Understanding is the ability to recognize and comprehend the meaning of a particular concept.

Application of the Body of Knowledge, Including Analysis, Judgment, Synthesis, Evaluation, and Research. Higher-level cognitive skills that require individuals to act or transform knowledge in some fashion. These skills are inextricably intertwined and thus are grouped into this single skill area.

- Assess the Business Environment

  - Business Process Evaluation: Assessing and integrating information regarding a business's operational structure, functions, processes, and procedures to develop a broad operational perspective; identify the need for new systems or changes to existing systems and/or processes.
  - Contextual Evaluation: Assessing and integrating information regarding client's type of business or industry.
  - Strategic Analysis—Understanding the Business: Obtaining, assessing, and integrating information on the entity's strategic objectives, strategic management process, business environment, the nature of and value to customers, its products and services, extent of competition within its market space, etc.

- Business Risk Assessment: Obtaining, assessing, and integrating information on conditions and events that could impede the entity's ability to achieve strategic objectives.
- Visualize Abstract Descriptions: Organize and process symbols, pictures, graphs, objects, and other information.

- Research

  - Identify the appropriate research question.
  - Identify key search terms for use in performing electronic searches through large volumes of data.
  - Search through large volumes of electronic data to find required information.
  - Organize information or data from multiple sources.
  - Integrate diverse sources of information to reach conclusions or make decisions.
  - Identify the appropriate authoritative guidance in applicable financial reporting frameworks and auditing standards for the accounting issue being evaluated.

- Application of Technology

  - Using electronic spreadsheets to perform calculations, financial analysis, or other functions to analyze data.
  - Integration of technological applications and resources into work processes.
  - Using a variety of computer software and hardware systems to structure, utilize, and manage data.

- Analysis

  - Review information to determine compliance with specified standards or criteria.
  - Use expectations, empirical data, and analytical methods to determine trends and variances.
  - Perform appropriate calculations on financial and nonfinancial data.
  - Recognize patterns of activity when reviewing large amounts of data or recognize breaks in patterns.
  - Interpretation of financial statement data for a given evaluation purpose.
  - Forecasting future financial statement data from historical financial statement data and other information.
  - Integrating primary financial statements: using data from all primary financial statements to uncover financial transactions, inconsistencies, or other information.

- Complex Problem Solving and Judgment

  - Develop and understand goals, objectives, and strategies for dealing with potential issues, obstacles, or opportunities.
  - Analyze patterns of information and contextual factors to identify potential problems and their implications.
  - Devise and implement a plan of action appropriate for a given problem.
  - Apply professional skepticism, which is an attitude that includes a questioning mind and a critical assessment of information or evidence obtained.
  - Adapt strategies or planned actions in response to changing circumstances.
  - Identify and solve unstructured problems.
  - Develop reasonable hypotheses to answer a question or resolve a problem.
  - Formulate and examine alternative solutions in terms of their relative strengths and weaknesses, level of risk, and appropriateness for a given situation.
  - Develop creative ways of thinking about situations, problems, and opportunities to create insightful and sound solutions.
  - Develop logical conclusions through the use of inductive and deductive reasoning.
  - Apply knowledge of professional standards and laws, as well as legal, ethical, and regulatory issues.
  - Assess the need for consultations with other professionals when gray areas, or areas requiring specialized knowledge, are encountered.

- Decision Making

  - Specify goals and constraints.
  - Generate alternatives.
  - Consider risks.
  - Evaluate and select the best alternative.

- Organization, Efficiency, and Effectiveness

  - Use time effectively and efficiently.
  - Develop detailed work plans, schedule tasks and meetings, and delegate assignments and tasks.
  - Set priorities by determining the relevant urgency or importance of tasks and deciding the order in which they should be performed.
  - File and store information so that it can be found easily and used effectively.

RESEARCHING AICPA PROFESSIONAL STANDARDS

Research components of simulations in the Auditing and Attestation section will involve a research database that includes

- AICPA Statements on Auditing Standards and Interpretations (AU)
- PCAOB Auditing Standards and Interpretations (PCAOB)
- Statements on Attestation Standards and Interpretations (AT)
- Statements on Standards for Accounting and Review Services and Interpretations (AR)
- AICPA Code of Professional Conduct (ET)
- AICPA Bylaws (BL)
- Statements on Standards for Valuation Services (VS)
- Statement on Standards for Consulting Services (CS)
- Statements on Standards for Quality Control (QC)
- Peer Review Standards (PR)
- Statement on Standards for Tax Services (TS)
- Statement on Responsibilities in Personal Financial Planning Practice (PFP)
- Statement on Standards for Continuing Professional Education Programs (CPE)

Database Searching

Searching a database consists of the following five steps:

1. Define the issue. What is the research question to be answered?
2. Select the database to search [e.g., (AU) the Statement on Auditing Standards and Interpretations].
3. Choose a keyword or table of contents search.
4. Execute the search. Enter the keyword(s) or click on the appropriate table of contents item and complete the search.
5. Evaluate the results. Evaluate the research to see if an answer has been found. If not, try a new search.

Advanced Searches

The advanced search screen allows you to use Boolean concepts to perform more precise searches. Examples of searches that can be performed in the advanced search mode include

1. Containing all these words—Allows you to retrieve sections that contain two or more specified words.
2. Not containing any of these words—Allows you to retrieve sections that do not contain specific words.
3. Containing one or more of these words—Allows you to retrieve sections that contain any one or more of the specified words.
4. Containing these words near each other—Allows you to retrieve sections that contain words near to each other.

The advanced search also allows you to select options for the search. One alternative allows you to retrieve alternative word terms. For example, using this approach with a search on the word "cost" would also retrieve sections containing the word "costing." A synonyms option allows you to retrieve sections that contain words that mean the same as the specified word. You also have the option to only search on the selected sections of the literature.

OVERVIEW OF THE ATTEST FUNCTION

In this overview section the general nature of the attest function is first discussed. Second, the general nature of the attest function as it relates to financial statement information is discussed. Third, a diagram is provided for understanding the nature of audits of financial statements. A section on generally accepted auditing standards (GAAS) and Statements on Auditing Standards (SAS) follows.

Attest Function—General Nature

In an attest engagement a CPA is engaged to issue or does issue an examination, a review, or an agreed-upon procedures report on *subject matter*, or an *assertion* about subject matter, that is the responsibility of another party. The attest function adds value to information by having a third party (the CPA) provide assurance over subject matter prepared by a party responsible for that information. For example, in the United States, an attest engagement may be performed under generally accepted auditing standards or PCAOB standards (for historical financial statements and related information) or the attestation standards (for other information). An attestation engagement may be performed under either generally accepted accounting principles (for historical financial statements and related information) **or** the attestation standards (for other information).

As a starting point to thinking about the attest function, consider both the preparation of financial statements and the performance of an audit of those financial statements. The preparation of financial statements may be viewed as consisting of inputs (source documents) being processed (through use of journals, ledgers, etc.) to arrive at an output (the financial information itself). Or shown diagrammatically

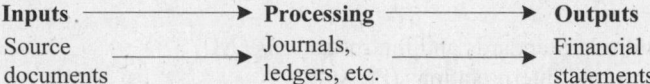

While CPAs often assist in the preparation of the financial statements, the attestation function conceptually begins with financial statements having been prepared by management. The purpose of a CPA financial statement audit is to provide assurance that financial statements which have been prepared by management follow a financial reporting framework—usually generally accepted accounting principles, but sometimes a special-purpose framework such as the cash or tax bases of accounting.

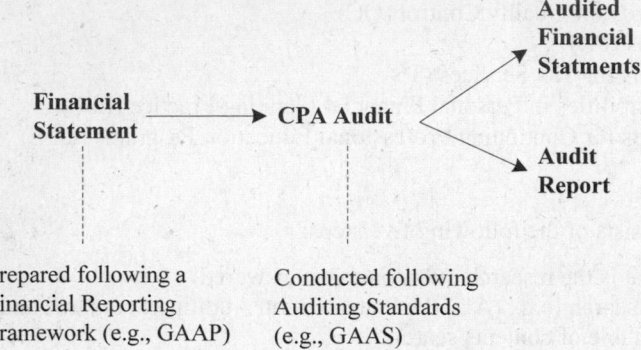

In performing an audit engagement, a CPA gathers various types of evidence relating to the propriety of the recording of economic events and transactions. For financial statements, this evidence will address the assertions that the assets listed in the balance sheet actually exist, that the company has title to these assets, and that the valuations assigned to these assets have been established in conformity with generally accepted accounting principles. The evidence gathered will also address whether the balance sheet contains all the liabilities of the company and that the notes to the financial statements include the needed disclosures. Similarly, a CPA will gather evidence about the income statement and the statement of cash flows. In short, the attest function provides assurance for the overall assertion that the financial statements follow generally accepted accounting principles.

It is helpful to generalize the discussion to information other than financial statements covered by the attestation standards as follows:

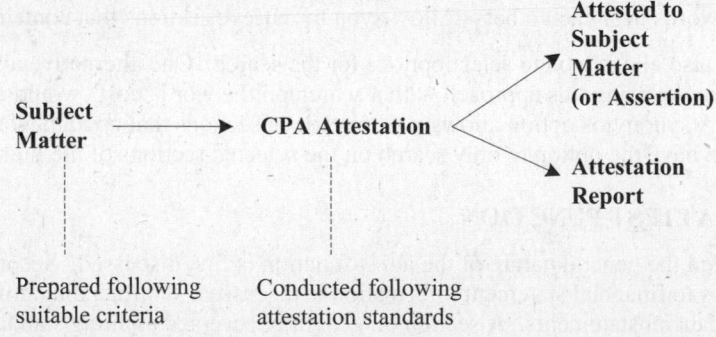

The attestation standards establish three forms of CPA attestation engagements—examinations, reviews, and the performance of agreed-upon procedures. An **examination,** referred to as an **audit** when it involves historical financial statements, normally results in a positive opinion that provides reasonable assurances, the highest form of assurance provided. When performing an examination, the CPAs select from all available evidence a combination that limits to a low level of risk the chance of material misstatement. A **review** is substantially less in scope than an audit and consists primarily of (1) application of analytical procedures, (2) making inquires of management, and (3) obtaining representations from management relating to the financial statements. It results in a report with limited assurance (also referred to as negative assurance since the CPA ordinarily concludes that he or she is not aware of any needed material modifications to the financial statements). For the third form of attestation engagement, a CPA and a specified party that wishes to use the information may mutually decide on specific **agreed-upon procedures** that the CPA will perform. Agreed-upon procedures engagements result in a report that describes the procedures performed and related findings.

CPAs may also provide services to clients in the form of **compilation** and unaudited statement services. The objective of a compilation of financial statements is to present information that is the representation of management without expressing any assurance on the statements. (The Responding to Risk Assessment and Reporting Modules discuss these forms of association in further detail.) For compilations note that the CPA's primary role is to prepare the financial statements. Accordingly, the CPA's report disclaims any opinion and gives no assurances with respect to whether the statements comply with the appropriate criteria. (The Responding to Risk Assessment and Reporting Modules discuss these forms of association in further detail.)

Expansions of the Attest Function

The overall need of individuals and organizations for credible information, combined with changes currently taking place in information technology, is leading to rapid changes in the role of the public accounting profession. CPA firms are already embracing a broader concept of the attest function that is being referred to as the **assurance function,** which includes providing assurance on a broad variety of types of financial or nonfinancial information. The AICPA *Code of Professional Conduct* defines an attest engagement broadly

> An attest engagement is an engagement that requires independence as defined in AICPA Professional Standards.

Assurance services may be structured using the attest standards framework (i.e., examinations, reviews, or agreed-upon procedures engagements), or outside of that framework as the situation merits.

The AICPA Assurance Services Executive Committee has a mission of (1) identifying and prioritizing emerging trends and market needs for assurance, and (2) developing related assurance methodology guidance and tools as needed. Current services developed under this committee's oversight include

- **Trust Services (SysTrust and WebTrust).** These are a set of professional attestation and advisory services based on a core set of principles and criteria that address the risks and opportunities of IT-enabled systems and privacy programs. *SysTrust* is a service designed primarily to build trust and confidence among business depending on IT systems by addressing areas such as security, availability, confidentiality and processing integrity. WebTrust is a service designed to build trust and confidence among customers and businesses doing business on the Internet—it addresses area such as Web site security, privacy, availability, confidentiality and processing integrity.
- **PrimePlus/Elder Care Services.** These services focus on the specific needs and goals of older adults. In providing these services CPAs address a variety of areas, including accounting, cash flow planning and budgeting, pre- and post-retirement plannings, insurance reviews, estate planning, and tax planning.
- **XBRL Services.** E**X**tensible **B**usiness **R**eporting **L**anguage is an international information format designed for business information. The SEC requires companies to provide financial statements in XBRL format, as well as posting such documents to company websites. AICPA develops guidance to assist CPAs in public practice who are requested to provide assurance on XBRL-related documents.

Diagram of an Audit

In the audit process an auditor gathers audit evidence to support a professional opinion. Sufficient appropriate audit evidence must be gathered to adequately restrict **audit risk,** the risk of unknowingly failing to appropriately modify the audit report on materially misstated financial statements.[1] The following diagram outlines the steps in the evidence gathering and evaluation process in which an auditor forms an opinion:

Diagram of an Audit

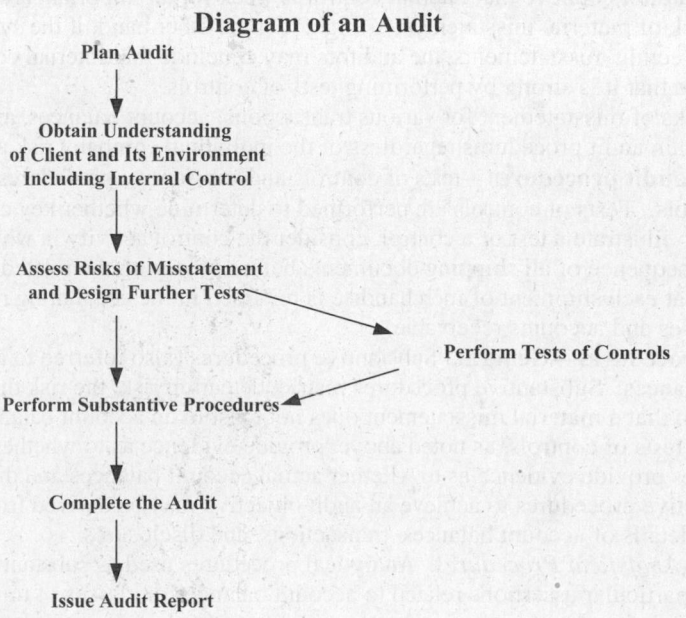

---

[1] The concept of audit risk is presented briefly in this section and is discussed in detail in Section A.2. of Module 1.

Plan Audit. Audit planning involves developing an overall strategy for performing the audit. During planning auditors establish an understanding with their client as to the nature of services to be provided and the responsibilities of each party—this is ordinarily accomplished through use of an engagement letter. In addition, they develop an overall audit strategy, an audit plan, and an audit program.

Although the diagram suggests planning as an initial step, which indeed it is, planning continues throughout the entire audit as the auditor accumulates sufficient appropriate audit evidence to support the audit opinion. This is even more the case in a first year audit of a client in which an understanding of the client must be obtained to even be able to complete initial planning of the audit (e.g., to prepare the audit plan and audit program).

Obtain an Understanding of the Client and Its Environment, Including Internal Control. Auditors must attain a sufficient background to assess the risk of material misstatement of the financial statements and to design the nature, timing, and extent of further audit procedures. **Risk assessment procedures** are used here and include inquiries of management and others within the entity, analytical procedures, observation and inspection, and other procedures. At this stage it is an overall understanding of the client and its environment that is obtained, including its objectives and strategies and related business risks, the manner in which it measures and reviews its financial performance, and its internal control. This understanding helps the auditors to identify relevant assertions related to transaction classes, account balances, and disclosures with a high risk of material misstatement.

Obtaining an understanding of the nature of internal control is an essential part of this understanding as it allows the auditor to identify areas that may be misstated and to design other procedures based on characteristics of the existing system. Information on internal control comes from interviews with client personnel, observing the application of specific control, inspecting documents and reports, and tracing transactions through the information system, as well as reviewing audit working papers.

Assess Risks of Misstatement and Design Further Audit Procedures. Auditors use the information collected while obtaining their understanding of the client and its environment to identify classes of transactions (transaction classes), account balances, and disclosures that might be materially misstated. Assessing the risks of misstatement (the risk assessment) is performed both at the overall financial statement level and at the relevant assertion level and includes considering

- What could go wrong?
- How likely it is that it will go wrong?
- What are the likely amounts involved?

Risk assessment procedures provide the auditors with evidence on potential risks of material misstatement. The risks of material misstatement are composed of inherent and control risks for relevant assertions. Inherent risk is the susceptibility of a relevant assertion to material misstatement, assuming that there are no related controls. Inherent risk arises for a variety of reasons including the business risk faced by management, the possibility of material misstatement due to fraud, and significant measurement uncertainty in accounting estimates and in nonroutine transactions.

Control risk is the risk that a material misstatement could occur in a relevant assertion and not be prevented or detected on a timely basis by the entity's internal control. After analyzing the design and implementation of internal control, the auditors must decide whether the system appears adequate to prevent or detect and correct material misstatements. For example, if the auditors believe that internal control is weak for an important area (that is, control risk is high), they will assess the risk of material misstatement as high. On the other hand, if the system seems capable of preventing or detecting and correcting misstatements, the auditors may conclude that internal control *may* be strong. But in this case they must determine that it is strong by performing tests of controls.

Based on the assessed risks of misstatement for various transactions, account balances, and disclosures, and on various requirements to perform certain audit procedures regardless of the individual company risk assessment, the auditors will design and perform **further audit procedures**—tests of controls and substantive procedures.

Perform Tests of Controls. Tests of controls are performed to determine whether key controls are properly designed and *operating effectively*. To illustrate a test of a control, consider the control activity in which the accounting department accounts for the serial sequence of all shipping documents before preparing the related journal entries. The purpose of this control is to ensure that each shipment of merchandise is recorded in the accounting records (i.e., to ensure the completeness of recorded sales and accounts receivable).

Perform Substantive Procedures—General. Substantive procedures (also referred to as substantive tests) are used to "substantiate" account balances. Substantive procedures restrict detection risk, the risk that audit procedures will incorrectly lead to a conclusion that a material misstatement does not exist in an account balance when in fact such a misstatement does exist. While tests of controls, as noted above, provide evidence as to whether controls are operating effectively, substantive procedures provide evidence as to whether actual account balances and disclosures are proper. The auditor's reliance on substantive procedures to achieve an audit objective may be derived from (1) substantive analytical procedures, and (2) tests of details of account balances, transactions, and disclosures.

Substantive procedures—Analytical Procedures. Analytical procedures used as substantive procedures are used to obtain audit evidence about particular assertions related to account balances or classes of transactions. In these tests auditors gather evidence about relationships among various accounting and nonaccounting data such as industry and economic information. When unexpected changes occur (or expected changes do **not** occur) in these relationships, an auditor obtains an explanation and investigates. Ratio analysis is a frequently used analytical procedure. The auditor would, for example, calculate a ratio and compare it to expectations such as budgets, prior year data, and industry data.

Substantive procedures—Tests of Details of account balances, transactions and disclosures. The objective of these tests is to detect misstatements in the financial statements—more specifically, misstatements of relevant assertions relating to transactions, account balances, and disclosures. The details supporting financial statement accounts are tested to obtain assurance that material misstatements do not exist. Sending confirmations for year-end receivable accounts is an example of a substantive test of details.

Complete the Audit. Auditors perform a number of procedures near the end of the audit. For example, evidence is aggregated and evaluated for sufficiency. Analytical procedures are performed (again) to assist the auditor in assessing conclusions reached and for evaluating overall financial statement presentation. Final decisions are made as to required financial statement disclosures and as to the appropriate audit report.

Audit Report. A standard unqualified audit report is issued by CPAs when their examination and the results thereof are satisfactory. It is also known as a "clean opinion" and is reproduced below. This standard unqualified report is modified as the audit examination deviates from normal, or as the financial statements fail to comply with generally accepted accounting principles (GAAP).

Variations of the audit report include

1. Standard unqualified
2. Unqualified with additional explanatory language
3. Qualified
4. Disclaimer
5. Adverse

The purposes and examples of each are outlined and illustrated in the Reporting Module of this chapter.

Read the standard unqualified report carefully, and note the key points made in it. Remember, the audit report is the primary product of the audit.

Independent Auditor's Report

TO: Board of Directors and Stockholders
        ABC Company

We have audited the accompanying balance sheets of ABC Company as of December 31, 20X1 and 20X0, and the related statements of income, retained earnings, and cash flows for the years then ended. These financial statements are the responsibility of the Company's management. Our responsibility is to express an opinion on these financial statements based on our audits.

We conducted our audits in accordance with US generally accepted auditing standards. Those standards require that we plan and perform the audit to obtain reasonable assurance about whether the financial statements are free of material misstatement. An audit includes examining, on a test basis, evidence supporting the amounts and disclosures in the financial statements. An audit also includes assessing the accounting principles used and significant estimates made by management, as well as evaluating the overall financial statement presentation. We believe that our audits provide a reasonable basis for our opinion.

In our opinion, the financial statements referred to above present fairly, in all material respects, the financial position of ABC Company as of December 31, 20X1 and 20X0, and the results of its operations and its cash flows for the years then ended in conformity with US generally accepted accounting principles.

Joe Smith, CPA
February 23, 20X2

Some key points in the above report include

Required Title ("Independent" must be in title)
Addressee (company, board of directors and/or stockholders—**not** management)
Introductory paragraph

1. We have audited
2. Client's financial statements (statements listed)
3. Financial statements are the responsibility of management.
4. The auditor's responsibility is to express an opinion.

Scope paragraph

1. Audit conducted in accordance with GAAS of the United States of America
2. Those standards require that we plan and perform audit to provide reasonable assurance statements free of material misstatement.
3. Audit involves

    a. Examining on a test basis evidence supporting amounts and disclosures
    b. Assessment of accounting principles

       c. Assessment of significant estimates
       d. Evaluation of overall presentation

    4. Audit provides reasonable basis for opinion

Opinion paragraph

    1. In our opinion
    2. Statements fairly present per US GAAP

Manual or printed signature (firm name)
Date (the date on which sufficient appropriate audit evidence has been obtained)

Generally Accepted Auditing Standards

    Traditionally, CPAs were required to perform their audits of financial statements following generally accepted auditing standards. The figure on the following page summarizes the ten generally accepted auditing standards; for comparative purposes, the eleven attestation standards are also presented.

    The attestation standards relate to all attestation services performed by CPAs. The generally accepted auditing standards may be considered to be the appropriate interpretations as they relate to audits of financial statements. After you have memorized the generally accepted auditing standards, you will find that studying the attestation standards is easy since most are similar. Be familiar with the attestations standards since a question on them is likely.

GENERALLY ACCEPTED AUDITING STANDARDS AND ATTESTATION STANDARDS

Generally Accepted Auditing Standards	Attestation Standards
General Standards	
1. The auditor must have adequate technical **training** and proficiency to perform the audit.	1. The engagement shall be performed by a practitioner or practitioners having adequate technical **training** and proficiency in the attest function.
	2. The engagement shall be performed by a practitioner or practitioners having adequate **knowledge** in the subject matter of the assertion.
	3. The practitioner shall perform an engagement only if he or she has reason to believe that the subject matter is capable of reasonably consistent evaluation against criteria that are suitable and available to users.
2. The auditor must maintain **independence** in mental attitude in all matters relating to the audit.	4. In all matters relating to the engagement, an **independence** in mental attitude shall be maintained by the practitioner or practitioners.
3. The auditor must exercise due **professional care** in the performance of the audit and the preparation of the report.	5. Due **professional care** shall be exercised in the performance of the engagement.
Standards of Fieldwork	
1. The auditor must adequately **plan** the work and must properly supervise any assistants.	1. The work shall be adequately **planned** and assistants, if any, shall be properly supervised.
2. The auditor must obtain a sufficient **understanding** of the entity and its environment, including its internal control, to assess the risk of material misstatement of the financial statements whether due to error or fraud, to design the nature, timing and extent of further audit procedures.	
3. The auditor must obtain sufficient appropriate audit **evidence** by performing audit procedures to afford a reasonable basis for an opinion regarding the financial statements under audit.	2. Sufficient **evidence** shall be obtained to provide a reasonable basis for the conclusion that is expressed in the report.
Standards of Reporting	
1. The auditor must state in the auditor's report whether the financial statements are presented in accordance with **generally accepted accounting principles** (GAAP.	1. The report shall identify the subject matter or the assertion being reported on and state the character of the engagement.
2. The auditor must identify in the auditor's report those circumstances in which such principles have not been **consistently observed** in the current period in relation to the preceding period.	2. The report shall state the practitioner's conclusion about the subject matter or the assertion in relation to the criteria against which the subject matter was evaluated.
3. When the auditor determines that informative **disclosures** are not adequate, the auditor must so state in the auditor's report.	3. The report shall state all of the practitioner's significant reservations about the engagement, the subject matter, and if applicable, the assertion related thereto.

4. The auditor must either express an **opinion** regarding the financial statements, taken as a whole, or state that an opinion cannot be expressed, in the auditor's report. When the auditor cannot express an overall opinion the auditor should state the reasons there for in the auditor's report. In all cases where an auditor's name is associated with financial statements, the auditor should clearly indicate the character of the auditor's work, if any, and the degree of responsibility the auditor is taking, in the auditor's report.

4. The report shall state that the use of the report is restricted to specified parties under the following circumstances:

- When the criteria used to evaluate the subject matter are determined by the practitioner to be suitable only for a limited number or parties who either participated in their establishment or can be presumed to have an adequate understanding of the criteria.
- When the criteria used to evaluate the subject matter are available only to specified parties.
- When reporting on subject matter and a written assertion has not been provided by the responsible party.
- When the report is on an attest engagement to apply agreed-upon procedures to the subject matter.

PROFESSIONAL STANDARDS

The Professional Standards most directly related to the Auditing and Attestation section of the CPA exam (hereafter AUDIT) are

- Statements on Auditing Standards
- Public Company Accounting Oversight Board Pronouncements
- Statements on Standards for Attestation Engagements
- Statements on Standards for Accounting and Review Services
- Statements on Quality Control Standards
- AICPA Code of Professional Conduct

Statements on Auditing Standards

The Auditing Standards Board issues Statements on Auditing Standards that are considered interpretations of GAAS. Outlines of the SAS (except superseded sections) are presented after Module 8 in their codified order with an AU prefix. The manner in which you use these outlines depends upon your educational and practical auditing background. If you have previously read the SAS, you may be able to use the outlines directly without rereading the material. If you are unfamiliar with the SAS, you will probably need to read them, and either simultaneously study the outline, or use the outline to review the major points. In some circumstances you may find that although you haven't read the detailed SAS, your educational and/or practical experience makes studying the outline adequate. At the beginning of each module in this chapter, a study program will refer you to the appropriate SAS. At this point you may read the SAS either before beginning the module or when finished. Many AUDIT exam questions can be directly answered by the SAS outlines. One week before, you can use the outlines as a good review for the AUDIT section. The module presentation provides a summary of the most important information, generally that which has received extremely heavy coverage on past exams.

The SASs (and attestation standards) use two categories of requirements to describe auditor responsibility for following a particular requirement.

- **Unconditional requirement**—The auditor must comply with the requirement in all cases in which the circumstances exist. SASs use the words *must* or *is required* to indicate an unconditional requirement.
- **Presumptively mandatory requirement**—Similarly, the auditor must comply with the requirement, but, in rare circumstances, the auditor may depart from such a requirement. In such circumstances, the auditor documents the departure, the justification for the departure, and how the alternative procedures performed in the circumstances were sufficient. SASs use the word *should* to indicate a presumptively mandatory requirement.*

As discussed earlier in this book, the CPA exam requires the candidates to be able to conduct electronic research of the professional standards. While in most circumstances candidates should expect to use the index or a keyword search to find the relevant topic, knowledge of the overall codified layout of the standards may be helpful. The following table presents the SAS sections in their codified order:

AU 100	**SASs—Introduction**		
	110 Responsibilities and Functions	161	Relationship between GAAS and Quality Control Standards
	120 Defining Professional Requirements		
	150 GAAS		
AU 200	**General Standards**		
	201 Nature	220	Second Gen. Standard—Independence
	210 First General Standard—Training and Proficiency	230	Third Gen. Standard—Due Professional Care

---

* PCAOB standards supplement these two categories with a third category: **Responsibility to Consider**. For these responsibilities, whether the auditor implements these matters will depend on the exercise of professional judgment in the circumstances. PCAOB standards use words such as may, might or could to indicate a responsibility to consider

AU 300   **Standards of Fieldwork**
                  310   Appointment of the Independent Auditor
                  311   Planning and Supervision
                  312   Audit Risk and Materiality
                  313   Substantive Tests Prior to the Balance Sheet
                         Date
                  314   Understanding the Entity and Its Environment
                         and Assessing the Risks of Material Misstate-
                         ment
                  315   Predecessor/Successor Auditors
                  316   Fraud
                  317   Illegal Acts
                  318   Performing Audit Procedures in Response to
                         Assessed Risks and Evaluating the Audit Evi-
                         dence Obtained
                  322   Internal Auditors
                  324   Service Organization

                  325   Commun. of Control-Related Matters
                  326   Audit Evidence
                  328   Fair Value Measurements and Disclosures
                  329   Analytical Procedures
                  330   Confirmation
                  331   Inventories
                  333   Representation Letters
                  334   Related-Party Transactions
                  337   Inquiries of Lawyer
                  339   Audit Documentation
                  341   Going Concern
                  342   Accounting Estimates
                  350   Audit Sampling
                  380   Communication with Audit Committees
                  390   Omitted Procedures

AU 400   **Reporting Standards 1, 2, and 3**
                  410   Adherence to GAAP
                  420   Consistency

                  431   Adequacy of Disclosure

AU 500   **Reporting Standard 4 (Opinion)**
                  504   Association with Financial Statements
                  508   Reports on Audited Financial Statements
                  530   Dating the Audit Report
                  532   Restricting Use of Audit Report
                  534   Reporting on Financial Statements for Use in
                         Other Countries
                  543   Other Auditors
                  544   Lack of Conformity with GAAP

                  550   Other Information in Documents Containing Audited
                         Statements
                  551   Auditor-Submitted Documents
                  552   Condensed Financial Statements
                  558   Required Supplementary Information
                  560   Subsequent Events
                  561   Subsequent Discovery of Facts Existing at Date of
                         Audit Report

AU 600   **Other Types of Reports**
                  622   Agreed-Upon Procedures
                  623   Special Reports

                  625   Reports on Application of Accounting Principles
                  634   Letters for Underwriters

AU 700   **Special Topics**
                  711   Filings under Federal Securities Statutes

                  722   Interim Financial Information

AU 800   **Compliance Auditing**
                  801   Compliance Auditing

AU 900   **Special Reports of the Committee on Auditing**
                  Procedure
                  901   Public Warehouses

The following sections may be particularly important for typical exams:

- AU 312 Audit risk and materiality
- AU 314 Understanding the entity and its environment and assessing the risks of material misstatement
- AU 316 Auditor responsibilities with respect to fraud
- AU 318 Performing audit procedures in response to assessed risks and evaluating the audit evidence obtained
- Various sections are helpful for audit reports, including

  AU 508—Most comprehensive section on types of reports (includes most sample reports, including consistency)
  AU 341—Going concern considerations and reporting (going concern sample paragraph modification)
  AU 420—Consistency
  ALL AU 500 and AU 600 sections, but somewhat less frequently

- Communicating on internal control with audit committees

  AU 325—Significant deficiencies and material weaknesses
  AU 380—Other accounting and auditing matters

- AU 701 Compliance auditing

The Appendix to this chapter presents the individual Statements on Auditing Standards in the order issued.

Public Company Accounting Oversight Board Pronouncements

In the summer of 2002, in reaction to a number of corporate frauds, Congress passed the Sarbanes-Oxley Act authorizing the creation of the Public Company Accounting Oversight Board (PCAOB) to oversee the accounting profession. Establishment of the PCAOB eliminated a significant portion of the accounting profession's system of self-regulation. The Public Company Accounting Oversight Board was established in 2002. The five-member Board's duties include

- Registration of public accounting firms that prepare audit reports for financial statement issuers
- Establishment or adoption of auditing, quality control, ethics, independence and other standards relating to audit reports for issuers
- Conducting inspections of registered public accounting firms
- Performing other duties or functions to promote high professional standards for audits, enforcing compliance with the Sarbanes-Oxley Act, setting the budget, and managing operations

All accounting firms that audit SEC registrants must register with the Board. As part of that registration process, each firm pledges to cooperate with any inquiry made by the Board. The Board may impose monetary damages and may suspend firms and accountants from working on engagements for publicly traded companies. It may also make referrals to the Justice Department to consider criminal cases.

The Board creates auditing standards for the above areas of its listed duties, including audits and reviews of public company financial statements. Information relating to the PCAOB is presented in Modules 1 through 5. Public companies are also referred to as **issuers** indicating that they issue securities under the Securities Acts.

Statements on Standards for Attestation Engagements (SSAEs)

The Statements on Standards for Attestation Engagements relate to attestation engagements on subject matter other than financial statements. Outlines of the SSAEs, which have an AT prefix, are presented following Module 8 and are discussed in the various modules, particularly Module 5. Their codified form may be summarized as

AT 20	Defining Professional Requirements in Statements on Standards for Attestation Engagements (SSAE)
AT 50	SSAE Hierarchy
AT 101	Attest engagements
AT 201	Agreed-upon procedures engagements
AT 301	Financial forecasts and projections
AT 401	Reporting on pro forma financial information
AT 501	An examination of an entity's internal control over financial reporting that is integrated with an audit of its financial statements
AT 601	Compliance attestation
AT 701	Management's discussion and analysis

Statements on Standards for Accounting and Review Services (SSARSs)

The Statements on Standards for Accounting and Review Services provide the authoritative guidance on procedures and reporting of compilation and review engagements of nonissuer (nonpublic) entity financial statements. The outlines of the Codification of the SSARSs is presented in Module 6.

Statements on Quality Control Standards (SQCS)

The Statements on Quality Control Standards apply to the accounting and auditing practices (including all attest services) of all firms. They serve as the standards a firm should be measured against when being evaluated through a peer review—an engagement in which other CPAs evaluate the quality of the firm's auditing and attestation work. In addition to peer reviews conducted under the SCQSs, quality reviews are performed under the Public Company Accounting Oversight Board.

APPENDIX

The following represents a chronological listing of the various Statements on Auditing Standards (SASs), the module in which they are primarily covered in this book, and either their codified section or, in the case of superseded SASs, the SAS that replaced them.

SAS 1 section		Module in this book	New codified SAS section no.
100*	Introduction	Overview	
200*	General GAAS	Overview	
310	Relationship between Appointment and Planning	EVID	
320	Internal Control	IC	Superseded by SAS 55
331	Receivables and Inventories	EVID	
332	Long-Term Investments	EVID	
400*	First 3 Reporting GAAS	REPT	
500*	Fourth Reporting GAAS	REPT	
901	Public Warehouses	EVID	
SAS 2	Audit Reports	REPT	Superseded by SAS 58
SAS 3	EDP and Internal Control	ATEC	Superseded by SAS 48
SAS 4	Firm Quality Controls	ENPL	Superseded by SAS 25
SAS 5	Meaning of Present Fairly	REPT	Superseded by SAS 69
SAS 6	Related-Party Transactions	EVID	Superseded by SAS 45
SAS 7	Predecessor-Successor Communications	EVID	Superseded by SAS 84
SAS 8	Other Information	REPT	Superseded by 118 and 119
SAS 9	Effect of an Internal Audit Function	IC	Superseded by SAS 65
SAS 10	Limited Review	REPT	Superseded by SAS 24
SAS 11	Using Specialists	EVID	Superseded by SAS 73
SAS 12	Inquiry of Client's Lawyer	EVID	337
SAS 13	Limited Review Reports	REPT	Superseded by SAS 24
SAS 14	Special Reports	REPT	Superseded by SAS 62
SAS 15	Comparative Financial Statements	REPT	Superseded by SAS 58
SAS 16	Detection of Errors and Irregularities	ENPL	Superseded by SAS 53
SAS 17	Illegal Acts by Clients	ENPL	Superseded by SAS 54
SAS 18	Replacement Costs	EVID	Deleted by Auditing Standards Board
SAS 19	Client Representations	EVID	Superseded by SAS 85
SAS 20	Required Communications of Material Weaknesses in Internal Accounting Control	IC	Superseded by SAS 60
SAS 21	Segment Reporting	REPT	435
SAS 22	Planning and Supervision	EVID	311
SAS 23	Analytical Review Procedures	EVID	Superseded by SAS 56
SAS 24	Review of Interim Financial Information	EVID	Superseded by SAS 36
SAS 25	The Relationship of Generally Accepted Auditing Standards to Quality Control Standards	ENPL	161
SAS 26	Association with Financial Statements	REPT	504
SAS 27	Supplementary Information Required by the Financial Accounting Standards Board	REPT	Superseded by SAS 52
SAS 28	Supplementary Information on the Effects of Changing Prices	REPT	Withdrawn by SAS 52
SAS 29	Reporting on Information Accompanying the Basic Financial Statements in Auditor-Submitted Documents	REPT	Superseded by SAS 118
SAS 30	Reporting on Internal Accounting Control	REPT	Superseded by SSAE 2
SAS 31	Evidential Matter	EVID	Superseded by SAS 106
SAS 32	Adequacy of Disclosure in Financial Statements	REPT	431
SAS 33	Supplementary Oil and Gas Reserve Information	REPT	Superseded by SAS 45
SAS 34	The Auditor's Considerations When a Question Arises about an Entity's Continued Existence	REPT	Superseded by SAS 59
SAS 35	Special Reports—Applying Agreed-Upon Procedures to Specified Elements, Accounts, or Items of a Financial Statement	REPT	Superseded by SAS 75
SAS 36	Review of and Performing Procedures on Interim Financial Information	EVID	Superseded by SAS 71
SAS 37	Filings under Federal Securities Statutes	REPT	711
SAS 38	Letters for Underwriters	REPT	Superseded by SAS 49
SAS 39	Audit Sampling	AUDS	350
SAS 40	Supplementary Mineral Reserve Information	EVID	Superseded by SAS 52
SAS 41	Working Papers	EVID	339
SAS 42	Reporting on Condensed Financial Statements and Selected Financial Data	REPT	552

* Contains multiple subsections

		Module in this book	New codified SAS section no.
SAS 43	Omnibus Statement on Auditing Standards	VARIOUS	**
SAS 44	Special-Purpose Reports on Internal Accounting Control at Service Organizations	IC	Superseded by SAS 70
SAS 45	Omnibus Statement on Auditing Standards—1983	VARIOUS	**
SAS 46	Consideration of Omitted Procedures after the Report Date	EVID	390
SAS 47	Audit Risk and Materiality in Conducting an Audit	ENPL VARIOUS	Superseded by SAS 107
SAS 48	The Effects of Computer Processing on the Examination of Financial Statements	VARIOUS	**
SAS 49	Letters for Underwriters	REPT	Superseded by SAS 72
SAS 50	Reports on the Application of Accounting Principles	REPT	625
SAS 51	Reporting on Financial Statements Prepared for Use in Other Countries	REPT	534
SAS 52	Omnibus Statement on Auditing Standards	VARIOUS	**
SAS 53	The Auditor's Responsibility to Detect and Report Errors and Irregularities	ENPL	Superseded by SAS 82
SAS 54	Illegal Acts by Clients	ENPL	317
SAS 55	Consideration of the Internal Control Structure in a Financial Statement Audit	IC	Superseded by SAS 109
SAS 56	Analytical Procedures	EVID	329
SAS 57	Auditing Accounting Estimates	EVID	342
SAS 58	Reports on Audited Financial Statements	REPT	508
SAS 59	The Auditor's Consideration of an Entity's Ability to Continue as a Going Concern	EVID REPT	341
SAS 60	The Communication of Internal Control Structure Related Matters Noted in an Audit	IC	Superseded by SAS 112
SAS 61	Communication with Audit Committees	IC	Superseded by SAS 114
SAS 62	Special Reports	REPT	623
SAS 63	Compliance Auditing Applicable to Governmental Entities and Other Specified Recipients of Governmental Financial Assistance	EVID	Superseded by SAS 68
SAS 64	Omnibus Statement on Auditing Standards—1990	VARIOUS	**
SAS 65	The Auditor's Consideration of the Internal Audit Function in an Audit of Financial Statements	IC	322
SAS 66	Communication of Matters about Interim Financial Information Filed or to Be Filed with Specified Regulatory Agencies—an Amendment to SAS 36	IC	Superseded by SAS 71
SAS 67	The Confirmation Process	EVID	330
SAS 68	Compliance Auditing Applicable to Governmental Entities and Other Recipients of Governmental Financial Assistance	EVID	Superseded by SAS 74
SAS 69	The Meaning of *Present Fairly in Conformity with Generally Accepted Accounting Principles* in the Auditor's Report	REPT	Rescinded
SAS 70	Reports on the Processing of Transactions by Service Organizations	ATEC	324
SAS 71	Interim Financial Information	REPT	Superseded by SAS 100
SAS 72	Letters for Underwriters and Certain Other Requesting Parties	REPT	634
SAS 73	Using the Work of a Specialist	EVID	336
SAS 74	Compliance Auditing Considerations in Audits of Governmental Entities and Recipients of Governmental Financial Assistance	REPT	Superseded by SAS 118
SAS 75	Engagements to Apply Agreed-Upon Procedures to Specified Elements, Accounts, or Items of a Financial Statement	REPT	Superseded by SAS 93
SAS 76	Amendments to Statement on Auditing Standards No. 72, *Letters for Underwriters and Certain Other Requesting Parties*	REPT	634
SAS 77	Amendments to Statements on Auditing Standards No. 22, *Planning and Supervision*, No. 59, *The Auditor's Consideration of an Entity's Ability to Continue as a Going Concern*, and No. 62, *Special Reports*	VARIOUS	**
SAS 78	Amendments to Statements on Auditing Standards to Recognize the *Internal Control—Integrated Framework Report*	IC	319
SAS 79	Amendment to Statement on Auditing Standards No. 58, *Reports on Audited Financial Statements*	REPT	508
SAS 80	An Amendment to Statement on Auditing Standards No. 31, *Evidential Matter*	EVID	326
SAS 81	Accounting for Certain Investments in Debt and Equity Securities	EVID	Superseded by SAS 92
SAS 82	Consideration of Fraud in a Financial Statement Audit	ENPL	Superseded by SAS 99

** Outlines of the paragraphs of this statement have been inserted in the outlines of the sections that it superseded.

		Module in this book	New codified SAS section no.
SAS 83	Establishing an Understanding with the Client	ENPL	310
SAS 84	Communications between Predecessor and Successor Auditors	ENPL	315
SAS 85	Management Representations	EVID	333
SAS 86	Amendment to Statement on Auditing Standards No. 72, *Letters for Underwriters and Certain Other Requesting Parties*	REPT	634
SAS 87	Restricting the Use of an Auditor's Report	REPT	532
SAS 88	Service Organizations and Reporting on Consistency	VARIOUS	**
SAS 89	Audit Adjustments	VARIOUS	**
SAS 90	Audit Committee Communications	IC	325
SAS 91	Federal GAAP Hierarchy	REPT	411
SAS 92	Auditing Derivative Instruments, Hedging Activities, and Investments in Securities	EVID	332
SAS 93	Omnibus Statement on Auditing Standards	VARIOUS	
SAS 94	The Effect of Information Technology on the Auditor's Consideration of Internal Control in a Financial Statement Audit	IC	319
SAS 95	Generally Accepted Auditing Standards	ENPL	150
SAS 96	Audit Documentation	EVID	Superseded by SAS 103
SAS 97	Amendment to Statement on Auditing Standards No. 50, *Reports on the Application of Accounting Principles*	REPT	625
SAS 98	Omnibus Statement on Auditing Standards—2002	VARIOUS	**
SAS 99	Consideration of Fraud in a Financial Statement Audit	ENPL	316
SAS 100	Interim Financial Information	EVID	
		REPT	Superseded by SAS 117
SAS 101	Auditing Fair Value Measurements and Disclosures	EVID	328
SAS 102	Defining Professional Requirements	Ch. 5	120
SAS 103	Audit Documentation	EVID	Superseded by SAS 116
SAS 104	Amendment to Statement on Auditing Standards No. 1	PLAN	230
SAS 105	Amendment to Statement on Auditing Standards No. 95, *Generally Accepted Auditing Standards*	PLAN	150
SAS 106	Audit Evidence	EVID	326
SAS 107	Audit Risk and Materiality in Conducting an Audit	PLAN	312
SAS 108	Planning and Supervision	PLAN	311
SAS 109	Understanding the Entity and Its Environment and Assessing the Risks of Material Misstatement	EVID, IC	314
SAS 110	Performing Audit Procedures in Response to Assessed Risks and Evaluating the Audit Evidence Obtained	EVID	318
SAS 111	Amendment to Statement on Auditing Standards No. 39, *Audit Sampling*	AUDS	350
SAS 112	Communicating Internal Control Matters Identified in an Audit	IC	Superseded by SAS 115
SAS 113	Omnibus—2006	VARIOUS	**
SAS 114	The Auditor's Communication with Those Charged with Governance	IC	380
SAS 115	Communicating Internal Control Related Matters Identified in an Audit	IC	325
SAS 116	Interim Financial Information	IC	722
SAS 117	Compliance Audits	REPT	801
SAS 118	Other Information in Documents Containing Audited Financial Statements	REPT	550
SAS 119	Supplementary Information in Relation to the Financial Statements as a Whole	REPT	551
SAS 120	Required Supplementary Information	REPT	558
SAS 121	Revised Applicability of SAS 100, Interim Financial Information	REPT	722

Standards not included on exam (currently expected to be examined in mid-2013; therefore not included in modules or outlines)

SAS 122	Statements on Auditing Standards: Clarification and Recodification
SAS 123	Omnibus Statement on Auditing Standards—2011
SAS 124	Financial Statements Prepared in Accordance with a Financial Reporting Framework Generally Accepted in Another Country
SAS 125	Alert That Restricts the Use of the Auditor's Written Communication

** Outlines of the paragraphs of this statement have been inserted in the outlines of the sections that it superseded.

NOTE: The Auditing Standards Board is currently in the midst of a "clarity" project which will result in the redrafting of all Statements on Auditing Standards. The effort addresses concerns over the clarity, length, and complexity of the existing standards. Redrafted statements will be structured as

- Objectives of the statement
- Definitions (where relevant)
- Requirements
- Application and other explanatory material

In addition, the ASB is converging its standards with those of the International Auditing and Assurance Standards Board (IAASB). We will include redrafted standards as they become eligible for testing on the CPA exam.

The Public Company Accounting Oversight Board has issued a number of standards, the guidance from which is incorporated in the various modules and in outlines following the AICPA codification outlines.

Module 1: Professional Responsibilities

Overview

This module presents requirements relating to a CPA's professional responsibilities related to ethics, including independence, as well as certain other responsibilities. The module begins with the AICPA *Code of Professional Conduct,* which consists of two sections: (1) Principles (the framework) and (2) Rules (govern performance of professional services). Integrated with these two sections are many related interpretations and rules that are also examined. The remainder of the module includes coverage of a number of other areas related to a CPA's professional responsibilities with which you should be familiar.

You should expect a significant number of questions from the AICPA *Code of Professional Conduct,* and somewhat fewer from each of the other areas. Also expect a simulation question in which you must show your research skills relating to finding particular information in the AICPA *Code of Professional Conduct* (codified using ET prefixes).

The primary reference here is the AICPA Code of Professional Conduct. This module incorporates an outline of its key provisions. Yet, access it electronically to gain a familiarity to allow you to efficiently respond to a simulation research question.

A. AICPA Requirements

1. Code of Professional Conduct—General

   a. The Code is applicable to all AICPA members, not merely those in public practice
   b. Compliance with the Code depends primarily on members' understanding and voluntary actions, and only secondarily on

      (1) Reinforcement by peers,
      (2) Public opinion, and
      (3) Disciplinary proceedings.

         (a) Possible disciplinary proceedings include from joint trial board panel **admonishment, suspension** (for up to two years), or **expulsion** from AICPA, or acquittal

   c. The Code provides **minimum** levels of acceptable conduct relating to all services performed by CPAs, unless wording of a standard specifically excludes some members

      (1) For example, some standards do not apply to CPAs not in public practice

   d. Overall structure of the Code goes from very generally worded standards to more specific and operational rules

      (1) Interpretations and rulings remaining from the prior Code are even more specific

   e. The Principles section consists of six Articles

      I. Responsibilities
      II. The Public Interest
      III. Integrity
      IV. Objectivity and Independence
      V. Due Care
      VI. Scope and Nature of Services

2. Code of Professional Conduct—Principles

   a. Outline of six Articles in Section 1 of the Code

   Article I—Responsibilities. In carrying out their responsibilities as professionals, members should exercise sensitive professional and moral judgments in all their activities.
   Article II—The Public Interest. Members should accept the obligation to act in a way that will serve the public interest, honor the public trust, and demonstrate commitment to professionalism.

(1) A distinguishing mark of a professional is acceptance of responsibility to public.

    (a) The accounting profession's public consists of clients, credit grantors, governments, employers, investors, business and financial community, and others.

    (b) In resolving conflicting pressures among groups an accountant should consider the public interest (the collective well-being of the community).

Article III—Integrity. To maintain and broaden public confidence, members should perform all professional responsibilities with the highest sense of integrity.

(1) Integrity can accommodate the inadvertent error and honest difference of opinion, but it cannot accommodate deceit or subordination of principle.

(2) Integrity

    (a) Is measured in terms of what is right and just

    (b) Requires a member to observe **principles of objectivity, independence, and due care**

Article IV—Objectivity and Independence. A member should maintain objectivity and be free of conflicts of interest in discharging professional responsibilities. A member in public practice should be independent in fact and appearance when providing auditing and other attestation services.

(1) Overall

    (a) Objectivity a state of mind

        1] Objectivity imposes obligation to be impartial, intellectually honest, and free of conflicts of interest.

        2] Independence precludes relationships that may appear to impair objectivity in rendering attestation services.

    (b) Regardless of the service performed, members should protect integrity of their work, maintain objectivity, and avoid any subordination of their judgment.

(2) Members in public practice require maintenance of objectivity and independence (includes avoiding conflict of interest).

    (a) Attest services—require independence in fact and in appearance

(3) Members not in public practice

    (a) Are unable to maintain appearance of independence, but must maintain objectivity

    (b) When employed by others to prepare financial statements, or to perform auditing, tax, or consulting services, must remain objective and candid in dealings with members in public practice

Article V—Due Care. A member should observe the profession's technical and ethical standards, strive continually to improve competence and the quality of services, and discharge professional responsibility to the best of the member's ability.

(1) Competence is derived from both education and experience.

(2) Each member is responsible for assessing his or her own competence and for evaluating whether education, experience, and judgment are adequate for the responsibility taken.

Article VI—Scope and Nature of Services. A member in public practice should observe the Principles of the Code of Professional Conduct in determining the scope and nature of services to be provided.

(1) Members should

    (a) Have in place appropriate internal quality control procedures for services rendered

    (b) Determine whether scope and nature of other services provided to an audit client would create a conflict of interest in performance of audit

    (c) Assess whether activities are consistent with role as professionals

3. Code of Professional Conduct—Rules, Interpretations, and Rulings

  a. Combined outline of Section 2 of the code (rules) integrated with interpretation and rulings

ET Section 100.01—Conceptual Framework for AICPA Independence Standards. The conceptual framework describes the risk-based approach to analyzing independence that is used by the AICPA Professional Ethics Executive Committee (PEEC). A member is not independent if there is an unacceptable risk to the member's independence. Risk is unacceptable if the relationship would compromise (or would be perceived as compromising by an informed third party) the member's professional judgment.

(1) In using this framework, the member should identify and evaluate threats (both individually and in the aggregate) to independence. Types of threats include

    (a) *Self-review threat*—Reviewing evidence that results from the member's own work (e.g., preparing source documents for an audit client).

    (b) *Advocacy threat*—Actions promoting the client's interests or position (e.g., promoting a client's securities).

    (c) *Adverse interest threat*—Actions or interests between the member and the client that are in opposition (e.g., litigation between the client and the member).

    (d) *Familiarity threat*—Members having a close or longstanding relationship with client or knowing individuals or entities who performed nonattest services for the client, (e.g., a member of the attest engagement team whose spouse is in a key position at the client).

    (e) *Undue influence threat*—Attempts by a client's management (or others) to coerce the member or exercise excessive influence over the member (e.g., threat to replace the member over a disagreement regarding an accounting principle).

    (f) *Financial self-interest threat*—Potential benefit to a member from a financial interest in, or some financial relationship with, an attest client (e.g., having a direct financial interest in the client).

    (g) *Management participation threat*—Assuming the role of management or performing management functions for the attest client (e.g., serving as an officer of the client).

(2) After considering the threats to independence, the member should consider the safeguards that mitigate or eliminate threats to independence. The three types of safeguards include

    (a) Safeguards created by the profession, legislation, or regulation (e.g., required continuing education on independence and ethics).

    (b) Safeguards implemented by the client (e.g., an effective governance structure, including an active audit committee).

    (c) Safeguards implemented by the firm (e.g., quality controls for attest engagements).

Rule 101 Independence. A member in public practice shall be independent in the performance of professional services as required by standards promulgated by designated bodies.

Interpretation 101-1. Independence is impaired if

(1) During the period of the professional engagement a covered member

    (a) Had or was committed to acquire any direct or material indirect financial interest in the client.

    (b) Was a trustee of any trust or executor or administrator of any estate if such trust or estate had or was committed to acquire any direct or material indirect financial interest in the client.

    (c) Had a joint closely held investment that was material to the covered member.

    (d) Except as specifically permitted in interpretation 101-5, had any loan to or from the client, any officer or director of the client, or any individual owning 10% or more of the client's outstanding equity securities or other ownership interests.

(2) During the period of the professional engagement, a partner or professional employee of the firm, his or her immediate family, or any group of such persons acting together owned more than 5% of a client's outstanding equity securities or other ownership interests.

(3) During the period covered by the financial statements or during the period of the professional engagement, a partner or professional employee of the firm was simultaneously associated with the client as a

    (a) Director, officer, or employee, or in any capacity equivalent to that of a member of management;

    (b) Promoter, underwriter, or voting trustee; or

    (c) Trustee for any pension or profit-sharing trust of the client.

Application of the Independence Rules to a Covered Member's Immediate Family

(1) Except as stated in the following paragraph, a covered member's immediate family is subject to Rule 101 [ET Section 101.01], and its interpretations and rulings.

(2) The exceptions are that independence would not be considered to be impaired solely as a result of the following:

    (a) An individual in a covered member's immediate family was employed by the client in a position other than a key position.

    (b) In connection with his or her employment, an individual in the immediate family of one of the following covered members participated in a retirement, savings, compensation, or similar plan that is sponsored by a client or that invests in a client (provided such plan is normally offered to all employees in similar positions):

1] A partner or manager who provides ten or more hours of nonattest services to the client; or
2] Any partner in the office in which the lead attest engagement partner primarily practices in connection with the attest engagement.

(3) For purposes of determining materiality under Rule 101 [ET Section 101.01], the financial interests of the covered member and his or her immediate family should be aggregated.

Application of the Independence Rules to Close Relatives

(1) Independence would be considered to be impaired if

  (a) An individual participating on the attest engagement team has a close relative who had

    1] A key position with the client; or
    2] A financial interest in the client that

      a] The individual or partner knows or has reason to believe was material to the close relative; or
      b] Enabled the close relative to exercise significant influence over the client.

  (b) An individual in a position to influence the attest engagement or any partner in the office in which the lead attest engagement partner primarily practices in connection with the attest engagement has a close relative who had

    1] A key position with the client; or
    2] A financial interest in the client that

      a] The individual or partner knows or has reason to believe was material to the close relative; and
      b] Enabled the close relative to exercise significant influence over the client.

Application of the Independence Rules to Other Relatives and Friends

(1) Independence is only impaired when a reasonable person aware of all relevant facts relating to a situation would conclude that there is an unacceptable threat to independence (based on the AICPA Conceptual Framework for Independence Standards discussed earlier in this section).

Important Definitions

(1) **Covered member.** A covered member is

  (a) An individual on the attest engagement team;
  (b) An individual in a position to influence the attest engagement;
  (c) A partner or manager who provides nonattest services to the attest client beginning once he or she provides ten hours of nonattest services to the client within any fiscal year and ending on the later of the date:

    1] The firm signs the report on the financial statements for the fiscal year during which those services were provided; or
    2] He or she no longer expects to provide ten or more hours of nonattest services to the attest client on a recurring basis;

  (d) A partner in the office in which the lead attest engagement partner primarily practices in connection with the attest engagement;
  (e) The firm, including the firm's employee benefit plans; or
  (f) An entity whose operating, financial, or accounting policies can be controlled (as defined by generally accepted accounting principles [GAAP] for consolidation purposes) by any of the individuals or entities described in (a) through (e) or by two or more such individuals or entities if they act together.

(2) **Individual in a position to influence the attest engagement.** An individual in a position to influence the attest engagement is one who

  (a) Evaluates the performance or recommends the compensation of the attest engagement partner;
  (b) Directly supervises or manages the attest engagement partner, including all successively senior levels above that individual through the firm's chief executive;
  (c) Consults with the attest engagement team regarding technical or industry-related issues specific to the attest engagement; or
  (d) Participates in or oversees, at all successively senior levels, quality control activities, including internal monitoring, with respect to the specific attest engagement.

(3) **Period of the professional engagement.** The period of the professional engagement begins when a member either signs an initial engagement letter or other agreement to perform attest services or begins to perform an attest engagement for a client, whichever is earlier. The period lasts for the entire duration of the professional relationship (which could cover many periods) and ends with the formal or informal notification, either by the member or the client, of the termination of the professional relationship or by the issuance of a report, whichever is later. Accordingly, the period does not end with the issuance of a report and recommence with the beginning of the following year's attest engagement.

(4) **Key position.** A key position is a position in which an individual

    (a) Has primary responsibility for significant accounting functions that support material components of the financial statements;

    (b) Has primary responsibility for the preparation of the financial statements; or

    (c) Has the ability to exercise influence over the contents of the financial statements, including when the individual is a member of the board of directors or similar governing body, chief executive officer, president, chief financial officer, chief operating officer, general counsel, chief accounting officer, controller, director of internal audit, director of financial reporting, treasurer, or any equivalent position.

(5) **Close relative.** A close relative is a parent, sibling, or nondependent child.

(6) **Immediate family.** Immediate family is a spouse, spousal equivalent, or dependent (whether or not related).

Interpretation 101-2. A firm's independence is considered to be impaired if a partner or professional employee leaves the firm and is subsequently employed by or associated with a client in a key position, unless all of the following conditions are met:

(1) Amounts due to the former partner or professional employee for his or her previous interest in the firm and unfunded benefits are not material to the firm, and the amounts of payments are fixed,

(2) The former partner or professional employee is not in a position to influence the accounting firm's operations or financial policies,

(3) The former partner or professional employee is not associated with the firm (e.g., provides consulting services to the firm, the individual's name is included in the firm directory, etc.),

(4) The ongoing attest engagement team considers the risk of reduced audit effectiveness resulting from the fact that the partner or professional employee has prior knowledge of the audit plan,

(5) The firm assesses whether the existing attest engagement team members have appropriate experience and stature to effectively deal with the former partner or employee if significant interaction will occur, and

(6) The subsequent attest engagement is reviewed to determine whether the team members maintained the appropriate level of skepticism when evaluating the representations of the former partner or employee.

Interpretation 101-3. When a CPA performs nonattest services for an attest client it **may or may not** impair independence.

(1) This interpretation requires compliance with regulatory independence rules by regulators such as the SEC, the General Accounting Office (GAO), and the Department of Labor (DOL).

(2) Must not perform management functions or make management decisions for attest clients.

(3) Client must

    (a) Make management decisions and perform management functions

    (b) Designate a competent employee, preferably in senior management, to oversee services

    (c) Evaluate adequacy and results

    (d) Accept responsibility for results

    (e) Establish and maintain internal controls

(4) Must establish in writing understanding with client (board of directors, audit committee, or management) regarding

    (a) Engagement objectives

    (b) Services to be performed

    (c) Client's acceptance of its responsibilities

    (d) CPA's responsibilities

    (e) Any limitation of the engagement

(5) General activities that impair independence

    (a) Authorizing, executing, or consummating transactions

    (b) Preparing source documents

    (c) Having custody of assets

    (d) Supervising employees

    (e) Determining recommendations to be implemented

    (f) Reporting to the board of directors on behalf of management

    (g) Serving as stock transfer agent, registrar, or general counsel

(6) Independence is impaired by the performance of appraisal, valuation, and actuarial services if the results are material to the financial statements and the service involves a significant degree of subjectivity.

(7) Performing internal audit services for a client impairs independence unless the client understands its responsibility for internal control and designates an officer to manage the internal audit function.

(8) The Sarbanes-Oxley Act of 2002 places additional restrictions on nonattest services for public company audit clients (see Section F).

Interpretation 101-4. CPA who is a director of a nonprofit organization where board is large and representative of community leadership is **not** lacking independence if

(1) Position purely honorary

(2) Position identified as honorary on external materials

(3) CPA participation restricted to use of name

(4) CPA does not vote or participate in management affairs

Interpretation 101-5. Loans from financial institution clients and related terminology

(1) Independence is not impaired by certain "grandfathered" and other loans from financial institution clients

    (a) Grandfathered loans that are permitted (home mortgages, other secured loans, loans immaterial to CPA) that were obtained

        1] Prior to January 1, 1992, under standards then in effect

        2] From a financial institution for which independence was not required, and the financial institution subsequently became an attest client

        3] Obtained from a financial institution for which independence was not required, and the loan was sold to an attest client **or**

        4] Obtained by a CPA prior to becoming a member of CPA firm of which the financial institution is an attest client

> **NOTE:** All of the above must be kept current and not renegotiated after the above dates. Also, the collateral on other secured loans must equal or exceed the remaining loan balance.

    (b) Other permitted loans from a financial institution attest client

        1] Automobile loans and leases collateralized by automobile

        2] Loans of surrender value under an insurance policy

        3] Borrowings fully collateralized by cash deposits at same financial institution (e.g., "passbook loans")

        4] Aggregate outstanding balances from credit card and overdraft accounts that are reduced to $10,000 on a current basis.

(2) Terminology

    (a) Loan—Financial transactions that generally provide for repayment terms and a rate of interest

    (b) Financial institution—An entity that makes loans to the general public as part of its normal business operations

    (c) Normal lending procedures, terms, and requirements—Comparable to those received by other borrowers during period, when considering

        1] Amount of loan and collateral

        2] Repayment terms

        3] Interest rate, including "points"

        4] Closing costs

        5] General availability of such loans to public

Interpretation 101-6. Effect of threatened litigation

(1) Client-CPA actual or threatened litigation

    (a) Commenced by present management alleging audit deficiencies, impairs

    (b) Commenced by auditor against present management for fraud, deceit impairs

    (c) Expressed intention by present management alleging deficiencies in audit work impairs if auditor believes **strong possibility** of claim

    (d) Immaterial not related to audit **usually** does **not** impair (i.e., billing disputes)

(2) Litigation by client security holders or other third parties generally does not impair unless material client-CPA cross-claims develop.

(3) If independence is impaired, CPA should disassociate and/or disclaim an opinion for lack of independence.

Interpretation 101-7. (Deleted)

Interpretation 101-8. (Deleted)

Interpretation 101-9. (Deleted)

Interpretation 101-10. Describes members' duties for independence when auditing entities included in governmental financial statements

(1) Generally, auditor of a material fund type, fund account group, or component unit of entity that should be disclosed in notes of general-purpose financial statements, but is not auditing primary government, should be independent with respect to those financial statements and primary government

(2) Also should be independent if, although funds and accounts are separately immaterial, they are material in the aggregate

Interpretation 101-11. Modified application of Rule 101 for engagements under the Statements on Standards for Attestation Engagements (SSAE)

The Rule 101 independence requirements apply to all attest engagements; exceptions in how they are applied for SSAE engagements:

(1) Those requiring independence other than agreed-upon procedures engagements:

    (a) Covered members must be independent of responsible party

    (b) When someone other than a responsible party engages the CPA, covered members need not be independent of that individual or entity

    (c) Nonattest services otherwise prohibited may be provided when such services do not relate to the specific subject matter of the SSAE engagement.

(2) Agreed-upon procedures (AUP) engagements. Only the following covered members and their immediate families are required to be independent with respect to the responsible party:

    (a) Individuals on AUP Team

    (b) Individuals who directly supervise or manage AUP engagement partner.

    (c) Individuals who consult with attest team on matters specific to AUP engagement.

    Also, independence is impaired if firm had financial relationship covered by outline item (1) of Interpretation 101-1 that was material to the firm (i.e., the section on direct or material indirect financial interests, etc.)

Interpretation 101-12. Independence is impaired if during professional engagement or while expressing an opinion, member's firm had any material cooperative arrangement with client.

(1) Cooperative arrangement exists when member's firm and client participate jointly in business activity such as

    (a) Joint ventures to develop or market a product or service

    (b) Arrangements to provide services or products to a third party

    (c) Arrangements to combine services or products of the member's firm with those of client to market them with references to both parties

    (d) Arrangements under which member firm or client act as distributor of other's products or services

(2) Joint participation with client is not a cooperative arrangement and is thus allowed if all of the following three conditions are present.

    (a) Participation of the firm and client are governed by separate agreements

    (b) Neither firm nor client assumes any responsibility for the other

    (c) Neither party is an agent of the other

Interpretation 101-13. (Deleted)

Interpretation 101-14. If a firm is organized in an alternative practice structure, in which the attest function is part of a larger organization that leases the staff to the attest function, the independence provisions of the AICPA Code of Professional Conduct must be adhered to by all staff and management on attest engagement and every individual that is a direct superior of attest partners or managers. Indirect superiors of attest partners and managers cannot have any relationships prohibited by Interpretation 101-1A.

Interpretation 101-15. This interpretation provides definitions of direct and indirect financial interests that may impair independence.

(1) A **financial interest** is an ownership interest in an equity or a debt security issued by an entity, including derivatives directly related to the interest.
(2) A **direct financial interest** is

    (a) One owned directly by an individual or entity, under control of the individual or entity, or beneficially owned through an investment vehicle,
    (b) Under the control of an individual or entity, or
    (c) Beneficially owned through an investment vehicle, estate, trust or other intermediary when the beneficiary

        1] Controls the intermediary, or
        2] Has the authority to supervise or participate in the intermediary's investment decisions.

Interpretation 101-16 (Reserved)

Interpretation 101-17. A firm member of a network of firms is required to be independent of financial statement audit and review clients of the other members of the network for such clients for which the use of an audit report is not restricted; characteristics of a network include having a brand name, common control, profits/ costs, common business strategy, significant professional resources, common quality controls.

Interpretation 101-18. Financial interests in, or other relationships with, affiliates of a financial statement attest client may impair independence with respect to that client. Examples of affiliates include entities (subsidiaries, partnerships, etc.) the attest client can control, material sister entities of the attest client, entities with a material direct financial interest in the attest client, an entity that controls the attest client, and the sponsor of the attest client's single-employer employee benefit plan. With respect to these entities, the CPA should apply the independence provisions of Rule 101 except in the following situations:

(1) A loan of a covered member from an officer, director, or 10-percent-or-more owner of an affiliate does not automatically impair independence. The member should evaluate the relationship by applying the Conceptual Framework for AICPA Independence Standards.
(2) A member or his or her firm may provide prohibited nonattest services to an affiliate providing it does not present a self-review threat to independence with respect to the attest client.
(3) Former employees of the affiliate may not affect independence if the position did not put them in a key position with respect to the attest client.
(4) Immediate family members and close relatives of a covered member may be employed at an affiliate in a key position provided that position does not put them in a key position with respect to the attest client.

Interpretation 101-19. Employment of a partner or professional staff member of a CPA firm with an educational institution does not impair the firm's independence with respect to the institution, providing that the partner or professional staff member:

(1) Does not hold a key position at the educational institution.
(2) Does not participate on the attest engagement team.
(3) Is not an individual in a position to influence the attest engagement.
(4) Is employed on a part-time and nontenure basis.
(5) Does not participate in the employee benefit plans sponsored by the educational institution.
(6) Does not assume any management responsibilities or set policies for the educational institution.

Rule 102 Integrity and Objectivity. In performance of **any** professional service, a member shall (a) maintain objectivity and integrity, (b) avoid conflicts of interest, and (c) not knowingly misrepresent facts or subordinate judgment.

(1) In tax matters, resolving doubt in favor of client does not, by itself, impair integrity or objectivity.

Interpretation 102-1. Knowingly making or permitting false and misleading entries in an entity's financial statements or records is a violation.

Interpretation 102-2. A conflict of interest may occur if a member performing a professional service has a **significant relationship** with another person, entity, product, or service that **could be viewed** as impairing the member's objectivity.

(1) If the member believes that the professional service can be performed with objectivity, and if the relationship is disclosed to and consent is obtained from the client, employer, or other appropriate parties, the rule does not prohibit performance of the professional service.
(2) Nothing in this interpretation overrides Rule 101 (on independence), its interpretations, and rulings.

Interpretation 102-3. When a member deals with his/her employer's external accountant, the member must be candid and not knowingly misrepresent facts or knowingly fail to disclose material facts.

Interpretation 102-4. If a member and his/her supervisor have a disagreement concerning the preparation of financial statements or the recording of transactions, the member should

(1) Allow the supervisor's position if that position is an acceptable alternative with authoritative support and/or does not result in a material misstatement.
(2) Report the problem to higher levels in firm if supervisor's position could cause material misstatements in records.
(3) Consider quitting firm if after reporting the problem to upper management, action is not taken. Consider reporting this to regulatory authorities and external accountant.

Interpretation 102-5. Those involved in educational services such as teaching full- or part-time at a university, teaching professional education courses, or engaged in research and scholarship are subject to Rule 102.

Interpretation 102-6. Sometimes members are asked by clients to act as advocates in support of clients' position on tax services, consulting services, accounting issues, or financial reporting issues. Member is still subject to Rule 102. Member is also still subject to Rules 201, 202, and 203. Member is also subject to Rule 101 for professional services requiring independence.

> **NOTE:** While CPA candidates should read the rulings to better understand the ethics rules and interpretations, it is **not** necessary to memorize them; consider them to be illustrations. Gaps in sequence are due to deleted sections.

Rule 101, 102 Ethics Rulings

Independence and Integrity Ethics Rulings

2. A member may join a trade association that is a client, without impairing independence, but may not serve in a capacity of management.
8. Extensive accounting and consulting services, including interpretation of statements, forecasts, etc., do not impair independence.
11. Mere designation as executor or trustee, without actual services in either capacity, does not impair independence, but actual service does.
14. Independence of a member serving as director or officer of a local United Way or similar organization is not impaired with respect to a charity receiving funds from that organization unless the organization exercises managerial control over that charity.
17. The acquisition of equity or debt securities as a condition for membership in a country club does not normally impair independence; serving on the club's governing board or taking part in its management does impair independence.
20. Membership on governmental advisory committees does not impair independence with respect to that governmental unit.
31. A member's ownership of an apartment in a co-op apartment building would impair the member's and the firm's independence.

41. Independence is not impaired when a member's retirement plan is invested and managed by an insurance company in a separate account, not a part of the general assets of the insurance company.
52. Independence is impaired when prior year fees for professional services, whether billed or unbilled, remain unpaid for more than one year prior to the date of the report.
64. Independence with respect to a fund-raising foundation is impaired if a member serves on the board of directors of the entity for whose benefit the foundation exists (unless position is purely honorary).
65. Member who is **not** in public practice may use CPA designation in connection with financial statements and correspondence of member's employer. May also use CPA designation on business cards if along with employment title. Member may **not** imply independence from employer. Member cannot state that transmittal is in conformity with GAAP.
67. If a client financial institution merely services a member's loan, independence is not impaired.
70. Maintaining state or federally insured deposits (e.g., checking accounts, savings accounts, certificates of deposit) in a financial institution does not impair independence; uninsured deposits do not impair independence if the uninsured amounts are immaterial.

71. CPA Firm A is not independent of an entity audited by Firm B. CPA Firm B may only use Firm A personnel in a manner similar to internal auditors without impairing Firm B's independence.

72. A member (and the member's firm) are not independent if the member serves on the advisory board of a client unless the advisory board (1) is truly advisory, (2) has no authority to make or appear to make management decisions, and (3) membership is distinct with minimal, if any, common membership with management and the board of directors.

74. A member must be independent to issue an audit opinion or a review report, but need not be independent to issue a compilation report (such lack of independence is disclosed).

75. Membership in a credit union does not impair audit independence if (1) the member qualifies as a credit union member on grounds other than by providing professional services, (2) the member does not exert significant influence over the credit union, (3) the member's loans (if any) from credit union are normal (see Interpretation 101-1), and (4) the conditions of Ruling 70 have been met.

82. When a member is the campaign treasurer for a mayoral candidate, independence is impaired with respect to the candidate's campaign organization, but independence is not impaired with respect to the candidate's political party or the municipality.

85. A member may serve as a bank director, but this is generally not desirable when s/he has clients that are bank customers; performing both services is allowed, however, if the relationship is disclosed and acceptable to all appropriate parties. Revealing confidential client information without client permission is a violation of the Code, even when the failure to disclose such information may breach the member's fiduciary responsibility as a director.

91. Independence is not impaired when a member has an "operating lease" from a client made under normal terms; independence is impaired by a "capital lease" from a client unless the "loan" related to the lease qualifies as "grandfathered."

92. A material joint investment in a vacation home with an officer, director, or principal stockholder of an attest client will impair independence.

93. When a member serves as a director or officer for the United Way or a similar organization and that organization provides funds to local charities that are the member's clients, a conflict of interest will not be considered to exist if the relationship is disclosed and consent is obtained from the appropriate parties.

94. Independence is not impaired if client in the engagement letter agrees to release, indemnify, defend, and hold harmless the member from any liability and costs from misrepresentations of management.

95. An agreement by the member and a client to use alternative dispute resolution techniques in lieu of litigation before a dispute arises does not impair independence.

96. A commencement of an alternative dispute resolution does not impair independence unless the member's and client's positions are materially adverse so that the proceedings are similar to litigation, such as binding arbitration.

99. If a member is asked by a company to provide personal financial planning or tax services for its executives and the member may give the executives recommendations adverse to the company, before accepting and while doing this work, the member should consider Rule 102 on Integrity and Objectivity and Rule 301 on Confidential Client Information. The member can perform the work if s/he believes it can be done with objectivity.

100. A member who was independent when his/her report was issued, may resign the report or consent to its use at a later date when his/her independence is impaired, if no postaudit work is performed while impaired.

102. If a member indemnifies client for damages, losses or costs arising from lawsuits, claims, or settlements relating directly or indirectly to clients acts, this impairs independence.

107. A covered member's participation in a health and welfare plan sponsored by a client would impair independence with respect to the client sponsor and the plan. However, if the covered member's participation results from permitted employment of the covered member's immediate family independence would not be considered impaired.

110. A covered member is associated with an entity in a position that allows him/her to exercise significant influence over the entity. The entity has a loan to or from a client. Independence would be impaired unless the loan is specifically permitted under Interpretation 101-5.

112. Rule 102, *Integrity and Objectivity,* requires the member to disclose to the client that the member uses a third-party service provider to perform certain of the services for the client.

113. Objectivity is impaired if a member receives a gift or entertainment from a client, unless the gift or entertainment is reasonable in the circumstances.

114. Objectivity is impaired if a covered member offers gifts or entertainment to an attest client, unless the gift or entertainment is clearly insignificant to the recipient.

Public Company Accounting Oversight Board (PCAOB) Independence Standards. The PCAOB adopted the *AICPA Code of Professional Conduct* as its interim ethical standards on April 16, 2003. Since then the PCAOB has adopted several additional independence standards. These standards apply to public accounting firms registered with the PCAOB when they are auditing an issuer (a public company).

(1) A registered public accounting firm must comply with all rules and standards of the PCAOB and also those set forth in the rules and regulations of the SEC under the federal securities laws.
(2) A registered public accounting firm is not independent of its audit client if the firm provides any service or product to the client for a contingent fee or a commission, or receives from the audit client a contingent fee or commission.
(3) A registered public accounting firm is not independent of its audit client if the firm provides any nonaudit service to the audit client related to marketing, planning, or opining in favor of

    (a) A *confidential transaction* (a tax transaction that is offered to a client under conditions of confidentiality and for which the client pays the public accounting firm a fee), or
    (b) *Aggressive tax position transaction* initially recommended by the public accounting firm.

(4) A registered public accounting firm is not independent of its audit client if the firm provides any tax service to a person in a financial reporting oversight role at the audit client, or an immediate family member of such person, unless

    (a) The person is in a financial reporting oversight role only because he or she serves as a member of the board of directors or similar body;
    (b) The person is in a financial reporting oversight role at the audit client only because of the person's relationship to an affiliate of the entity being audited, and

        1] The affiliate's financial statements are not material to the consolidated financial statements, or
        2] The affiliate is audited by another public accounting firm; or

    (c) The person was not in a financial reporting oversight role at the audit client before a hiring or some other change in employment and the tax services were

        1] Provided pursuant to an engagement in process prior to the change in employment, and
        2] Completed on or before 180 days after the change in employment.

(5) A registered public accounting firm must get preapproval from the audit committee to perform for an audit client any permissible tax service.
(6) A registered public accounting firm must communicate with the audit committee all relationships between the firm and the audit client that may reasonably be thought to bear on independence.

Rule 201 General Standards. Member must comply with the following standards for all professional engagements:

(1) Only undertake professional services that one can reasonably expect to complete with professional competence
(2) Exercise due professional care

    (a) Member may need to consult with experts to exercise due care

(3) Adequately plan and supervise engagements
(4) Obtain sufficient relevant data to afford a reasonable basis for conclusions and recommendations

Interpretation 201-1. Competence to complete an engagement includes

(1) Technical qualifications of CPA and staff
(2) Financial Accounting Standards Advisory Board for accounting principles for federal governmental entities
(3) Ability to supervise and evaluate work
(4) Knowledge of technical subject matter
(5) Capability to exercise judgment in its application
(6) Ability to research subject matter and consult with others

Interpretations 201-2, 3, 4. (Deleted)

Rule 202 Compliance with Standards. A member who performs auditing, review, compilation, consulting services, tax or other services shall comply with standards promulgated by bodies designated by Council.

> **NOTE:** The designated bodies are
>
> (1) Financial Accounting Standards Board for accounting principles for businesses
> (2) Financial Accounting Standards Advisory Board for accounting principles for federal governmental entities.
> (3) Governmental Accounting Standards Board for accounting principles for state and local governmental entities

(4) Public Company Accounting Oversight Board for auditing, attestation, quality control, ethics and independence standards for companies covered by the Sarbanes-Oxley Act
(5) International Accounting Standards Board for international accounting standards
(6) AICPA designated bodies

(a) Accounting and Review Services Committee
(b) Auditing Standards Board
(c) Management Consulting Services Executive Committee
(d) Tax Executive Committee
(e) Forensic and Valuation Executive Committee

Rule 203 Accounting Principles. Member cannot provide positive or negative assurance that financial statements are in conformity with GAAP if statements contain departures from GAAP having a material effect on
statements taken as a whole except when unusual circumstances would make financial statements following
GAAP misleading.

(1) Sources of GAAP: Financial Accounting Standards Board, financial Accounting Standards Advisory
Board, Governmental Accounting Standards Board, International Accounting Standards Board.
(2) When unusual circumstances require a departure from GAAP, CPA must disclose in report the departure,
its effects (if practicable), and reasons why compliance would result in a misleading statement.

Interpretation 203-1. CPAs are to allow departure from GAAP (without giving qualified or adverse opinion)
only when results of applying will be misleading.

Examples of possible circumstances justifying departure are

(a) New legislation
(b) New form of business transaction

Interpretation 203-2. FASB, GASB and FASAB Interpretations are covered by Rule 203

Interpretation 203-3. (Deleted)

Interpretation 203-4. Rule 203 also applies to communications by employees such as reports to regulatory authorities, creditors, and auditors.

Interpretation 203-5. CPA may report on financial statements prepared using financial frameworks other than
GAAP (e.g., principles of a particular country, principles used in a contract, statutory reporting provisions required by law). The financial statements or reports should not purport that GAAP were followed and should
make clear the financial reporting framework used.

Rule 201, 202, 203 Ethics Rulings

8. A member selecting subcontractors for consulting
services engagements is obligated to select subcontractors on the basis of professional qualifications,
technical skills, etc.
9. A member should be in a position to supervise and
evaluate work of a specialist in his employ.
10. If a member prepares financial statements as a
stockholder, partner, director, or employee of an entity, any transmittal should indicate the member's

relationship and should not imply independence. If
transmittal indicates financial statements are in accordance with GAAP, Rule 203 must be met. If financial statements are on member's letterhead,
member should disclose lack of independence.
12. The CPA firm must provide adequate oversight of
all services performed by a third-party provider for
the firm's clients to ensure that the provider complies with professional standards.

Rule 301 Confidential Client Information. Member in public practice shall not disclose confidential client information without client consent except for

(1) Compliance with Rule 202 and 203 obligations
(2) Compliance with enforceable subpoena or summons
(3) AICPA review of professional practice
(4) Initiating complaint or responding to inquiry made by a recognized investigative or disciplinary body

Interpretation 301-1. (Deleted)

Interpretation 301-2. (Deleted)

Interpretation 301-3. A member who is considering selling his/her practice, or merging with another CPA,
may allow that CPA to review confidential client information without the specific consent of the client.

(1) The member should take appropriate precautions (e.g., obtain a written confidentiality agreement) so that the prospective purchaser does not disclose such information.

> **NOTE:** This exception only relates to a review in conjunction with a purchase or merger. It **does not** apply to the review of working papers **after** a CPA has purchased another's practice. AU 315, discussed in detail later in this module, requires that the successor who wishes to review predecessor auditor working papers should request the client to authorize the predecessor to make such working papers available.

Rule 302 Contingent Fees.

(1) A member in public practice shall not

    (a) Perform for a contingent fee any professional services when the member or member's firm also performs any of the following services for that client:

        1] Audits or reviews of financial statements
        2] Compilations when the member is independent and expects that a third party may use the financial statements
        3] Examinations of prospective financial information

    (b) Prepare an original or amended tax return or claims for a tax refund for a contingent fee for any client

(2) Solely for purposes of this rule, (a) fees fixed by courts or other public authorities, or (b) in tax matters, fees determined based on the results of a judicial proceeding or findings of governmental agency, are not regarded as contingent and are therefore permitted.

Interpretation 302-1. Contingent fees in tax matters

(1) A contingent fee **would be permitted** in various circumstances in which the amounts due are not clear; examples are

    (a) Representing a client in an examination by a revenue agent
    (b) Filing amended tax returns based on a tax issue that is the subject of a test case **involving a different taxpayer** or where the tax authority is developing a position.
    (c) Representing a taxpayer in getting a private ruling

(2) A contingent fee **would not be permitted** for preparing an amended tax return for a client claiming a refund that is clearly due to the client because of an inadvertent omission.

Rule 301, 302 Ethics Rulings

1. A member may utilize outside computer services to process tax returns as long as there is no release of confidential information.
2. With client permission, a member may provide P&L percentages to a trade association.
3. A CPA withdrawing from a tax engagement due to irregularities on the client's return should urge successor CPA to have client grant permission to reveal reasons for withdrawal.
6. A member may be engaged by a municipality to verify taxpayer's books and records for the purpose of assessing property tax. The member must maintain confidentiality.
7. Members may reveal the names of clients without client consent unless such disclosure releases confidential information.
14. A member has a responsibility to honor confidential relationships with nonclients. Accordingly, members may have to withdraw from consulting services engagements where the client will not permit the member to make recommendations without disclosing confidential information about other clients or nonclients.
15. If the member has conducted a similar consulting services study with a negative outcome, the member should advise potential clients of the previous problems providing that earlier confidential relationships are not disclosed. If the earlier confidential relationship may be disclosed (through client knowledge of other clients), the member should seek approval from the first client.
16. In divorce proceedings a member who has prepared joint tax returns for the couple should consider both individuals to be clients for purposes of requests for confidential information relating to prior tax returns. Under such circumstances the CPA should consider reviewing the legal implications of disclosure with an attorney.
17. A contingent fee or a commission is considered to be "received" when the performance of the related services is complete and the fee or commission is determined.
18. Identical to Ruling 85 under Rule 101.
19. A member's spouse may provide services to a member's attest client for a contingent fee and may refer products or services for a commission.
20. When a member learns of a potential claim against him/her, the member may release confidential client information to member's liability carrier used solely to defend against claim.
21. Identical to Ruling 99 under Rule 102.

23. A member may disclose confidential client information to the member's attorney or a court in connection with actual or threatened litigation.

24. A member's fee for investment advisory services for an attest client that is based on a percentage of the portfolio would be considered contingent and a violation of Rule 302, unless

   a. The fee is determined as a specified percentage of the portfolio,
   b. The dollar amount of the portfolio is determined at the beginning of each quarterly period (or longer) and is adjusted only for additions or withdrawals by the client, and
   c. The fee arrangement is not renewed with the client more frequently than on a quarterly basis.

25. A member who provides for a contingent fee investment advisory service, or refers for a commission products or services to the owners, officers, or employees of an attest client would not violate Rule 302 with respect to the client.

ET 400: Responsibilities to colleagues. No current rules or interpretations (section reserved).

Rule 501 Acts Discreditable. A member shall not commit an act discreditable to the profession.

Interpretation 501-1. A CPA's response to a client's request for records depends upon the nature of the records and certain circumstances:

(1) *Records provided by the client*—should be returned to client at the client's request.

(2) *CPA-prepared records that the CPA was not specifically engaged to prepare and are not in the client's books and records, with the result that the client's financial information is incomplete* (e.g., adjusting entries, closing entries and supporting schedules prepared as part of an engagement)—should be provided except that they may be withheld if there are fees due the CPA for the specific work product.

(3) *CPA work products (e.g., "deliverables" such as audit report, tax returns)*—should be provided to the client except that they may be withheld if

   (a) There are fees due on that work product
   (b) Work product is incomplete
   (c) Needed to comply with a professional standard (e.g., withholding an audit report due to outstanding audit issues)
   (d) There is threatened or outstanding litigation concerning the engagement or CPA's work.

(4) *CPA working papers*—prepared solely for the engagement either by the auditor (e.g., audit programs, analytical review procedures schedules) or by the client (at the request of CPA) are CPA's property and need not be provided.

NOTE: In all cases (1 through 4 above), if an authoritative regulatory body such as the CPA's state board of accountancy has a stricter rule, the CPA must follow it.

Interpretation 501-2. Discrimination on basis of race, color, religion, sex, age, or national origin is discreditable.

Interpretation 501-3. In audits of governmental grants, units, or other recipients of governmental monies, failure to follow appropriate governmental standards, procedures, etc. is discreditable.

Interpretation 501-4. Negligently making (or permitting or directing another to make) false or misleading journal entries is discreditable.

Interpretation 501-5. When a governmental body, commission, or other regulatory agency has requirements beyond those required by GAAS, members are required to follow them.

(1) Failure to follow these requirements is considered an act discreditable to the profession, unless the member discloses in the report that such requirements were not followed and the reasons therefor.

Interpretation 501-6. Member who solicits or discloses May 1996 or later Uniform CPA Examination question(s) and/or answer(s) without AICPA written authorization has committed an act discreditable to profession in violation of Rule 501.

Interpretation 501-7. A member who fails to comply with applicable federal, state, or local laws and regulations regarding the timely filing of his or her personal tax returns, or the timely remittance of all payroll and other taxes collected on behalf of others has committed an act discreditable to the profession.

Interpretation 501-8. In some engagements, government regulators prohibit indemnification or limitation of liability agreements. If the CPA engages in such agreements when they are prohibited, he or she has committed an act discreditable to the profession.

Interpretation 501-9. A CPA should maintain confidentiality of his or her employer's confidential information and any information obtained about an organization for which the CPA provides services on a voluntary basis. Disclosure of such information would be considered an act discreditable to the profession. Examples of situations in which the CPA may disclose confidential information include

(1) Disclosure is permitted by law and authorized by the employer.
(2) Disclosure is required by law.
(3) There is a professional responsibility to disclose the information.
(4) Disclosure is permitted on behalf of the employer.

Interpretation 501-10. A CPA is prohibited from promoting or marketing his or her abilities to provide professional services, or making claims about his or her experience or qualifications in a manner that is false, misleading, or deceptive.

Rule 502 Advertising and Other Forms of Solicitation. In public practice, shall not seek to obtain clients by false, misleading, deceptive advertising or other forms of solicitation.

Interpretation 502-1. (Deleted)

Interpretation 502-2. Advertising that is false, misleading or deceptive is prohibited, including advertising that

(1) Creates false or unjustified expectations
(2) Implies ability to influence a court, tribunal, regulatory agency or similar body or official
(3) Contains unrealistic estimates of future fees
(4) Would lead a reasonable person to misunderstand or be deceived

Interpretations 502-3, 4. (Deleted)

Interpretation 502-5. CPA may render services to clients of third parties as long as all promotion efforts are within Code.

Rule 503 Commissions and Referral Fees.

(1) A member in public practice may not accept a commission for recommending a product or service to a client when the member or member's firm also performs any of the following services for that client:

 (a) Audits or reviews of financial statements
 (b) Compilations when the member is independent and expects that a third party may use the financial statements
 (c) Examinations of prospective financial information

(2) A member who receives a commission [not prohibited in (1) above] shall disclose that fact to the client.
(3) A member who accepts a referral fee for recommending or referring any service of a CPA to any person or entity, or who pays a referral fee to obtain a client, must disclose such acceptance or payment to the client.

Rule 504. (Deleted)

Rule 505 Form of Practice and Name. Member may practice public accounting in form of proprietorship, partnership, professional corporation, etc. and may not practice under a misleading name.

(1) May include past partners.
(2) An individual may practice in name of a former partnership for up to two years (applies when all other partners have died or withdrawn).
(3) A firm name may include a fictitious name or indicate specialization if name is not misleading.
(4) Firm may not designate itself as member of AICPA unless all partners or shareholders are members.
(5) Appendix B to Code of Professional Conduct allows non-CPA ownership of CPA firms under certain conditions.

 (a) 66 2/3% (super majority) of ownership (both voting rights and financial interest) must belong to CPAs. Non-CPA owners must be involved in own principal occupation, not practice accounting, and not hold selves out as CPAs.
 (b) CPAs must have ultimate responsibility in firm, not non-CPAs.
 (c) Non-CPA owners must abide by AICPA Code of Professional Conduct, CPE requirements and hold a baccalaureate degree.
 (d) Non-CPAs not eligible to be members of AICPA.

Interpretation 505-1. (Deleted)

Interpretation 505-2. Applicability of rules to members who operate a separate business that provides accounting services.

(1) A member in public practice who participates in the operation of a separate business that performs accounting, tax, etc. services must observe all of the Rules of Conduct.

(2) A member not otherwise in the practice of public accounting must observe the Rules of Conduct if the member holds out as a CPA and performs for a client any professional services included in public accounting.

Interpretation 505-3. CPAs with attest practices that are organized as alternative practice structures must remain financially and otherwise responsible for the attest work.

Rule 591 Ethics Rulings and Other Responsibilities
Ethics Rulings

Due to rescinding the advertising and solicitation prohibition, the majority of the ethics rulings have been suspended.

3. A CPA employed by a firm with non-CPA practitioners must comply with the rules of conduct. If a partner of such a firm is a CPA, the CPA is responsible for all persons associated with the firm to comply with the rules of conduct.

38. A member who is controller of a bank may place his CPA title on bank stationery and in paid advertisements listing the officers and directors of the bank.

78. CPAs who are also attorneys may so indicate on their letterhead.

134. Members who share offices, employees, etc., may not indicate a partnership exists unless a partnership agreement is in effect.

135. CPA firms that are members of an association cannot use letterhead that indicates a partnership rather than an association.

136. Where a firm consisting of a CPA and a non-CPA is dissolved, and an audit is continued to be serviced by both, the audit opinion should be signed by both individuals, such that a partnership is not indicated.

137. The designation "nonproprietary partner" should not be used to describe personnel as it may be misleading.

138. A member may be a partner of a firm of public accountants when all other personnel are not certified, and at the same time practice separately as a CPA.

141. A CPA in partnership with a non-CPA is ethically responsible for all acts of the partnership and those of the non-CPA partner.

145. Newly merged CPA firms may practice under a title that includes the name of a previously retired partner from one of the firms.

183. A CPA firm may designate itself "Accredited Personal Financial Specialists" on its letterhead and in marketing materials if all partners or shareholders of the firm currently have the AICPA-awarded designation.

184. Identical to Ruling 18 under Rule 302.

185. A member may purchase a product from a supplier and resell it to a client at a profit without disclosing the profit to the client.

186. A member may contract for support services from a computer-hardware maintenance servicer and bill them to a client at a profit without disclosing the profit to the client.

187. Identical to Ruling 19 under Rule 302.

188. When a member refers products to clients through distributors and agents, the member may not perform for those clients the services described in Rule 503 [part (1) of the outline of Rule 503].

189. When individuals associated with a client entity have an internal dispute, and have separately asked a member for client records, the member need only supply them once, and to the individual who previously has been designated or held out as the client's representative.

190. A member who is in a partnership with non-CPAs may sign reports with the firm name and below it affix his own signature with the designation "Certified Public Accountant" providing it is clear that the partnership is not being held out as composed entirely of CPAs.

191. If a member (not an owner) of a firm is terminated, he/she may not take copies of the firm's client files without the firm's permission.

192. A member who provides for a contingent fee investment advisory services, or refers for a commission products or services to the owners, officers, or employees of an attest client would not violate Rule 302 or Rule 503 with respect to the client.

4. Responsibilities in Consulting Services

a. In January of 1991 a new series of pronouncements on consulting services, *Statements on Standards for Consulting Services* (SSCS), became effective. This series of pronouncements replaces the three *Statements on Standards for Management Advisory Services*. These standards apply to CPAs in public practice who provide consulting services.

b. Outline of SSCS 1 Definitions and Standards

(1) Comparison of consulting and attest services

    (a) **Attest services**—Practitioner expresses a conclusion about the reliability of a written assertion that is the responsibility of another party (the asserter)

    (b) **Consulting services**—Practitioner develops the findings, conclusions and recommendations presented, generally only for the use and benefit of the client; the nature of the work is determined solely by agreement between the practitioner and the client

    (c) Performance of consulting services **for an attest client** requires that the practitioner maintain independence and does not in and of itself impair independence

> **NOTE:** While one must remain objective in performing consulting services, independence is not required unless the practitioner also performs attest (e.g., audit) services for that client.

(2) Definitions

    (a) **Consulting services practitioner**—A CPA holding out as a CPA (i.e., a CPA in public practice) while engaged in the performance of a consulting service for a client

    (b) **Consulting process**—Analytical approach and process applied in a consulting service

        1] This definition **excludes** services subject to other AICPA technical standards on auditing (SAS), other attest services (SSAE), compilations and reviews (SSARS), most tax engagements, and recommendations made during one of these engagements as a direct result of having performed these excluded services

    (c) **Consulting services**—Professional services that employ the practitioner's technical skills, education, observations, experiences, and knowledge of the consulting process

(3) Types of consulting services

    (a) **Consultations**—Provide counsel in a short time frame, based mostly, if not entirely, on existing personal knowledge about the client

        1] Examples: reviewing and commenting on a client business plan, suggesting software for further client investigation

    (b) **Advisory services**—Develop findings, conclusions and recommendations for client consideration and decision making

        1] Examples: Operational review and improvement study, analysis of accounting system, strategic planning assistance, information system advice

    (c) **Implementation services**—Place an action plan into effect

        1] Examples: Installing and supporting computer system, executing steps to improve productivity, assisting with mergers

    (d) **Transaction services**—Provide services related to a specific client transaction, generally with a third party

        1] Examples: Insolvency services, valuation services, information related to financing, analysis of a possible merger or acquisition, litigation services

    (e) **Staff and other support services**—Provide appropriate staff and possibly other support to perform tasks specified by client

        1] Examples: Data processing facilities management, computer programming, bankruptcy trusteeship, controllership activities

    (f) **Product services**—Provide client with a product and associated support services

        1] Examples: Sale, delivery, installation, and implementation of training programs, computer software, and systems development

(4) Standards for Consulting Services

    (a) General Standards of Rule 201 of Code of Professional Conduct

        1] Professional competence
        2] Due professional care
        3] Planning and supervision
        4] Sufficient relevant data

    (b) Additional standards established for this area (under Rule 202 of Code of Professional Conduct)

        1] Client interest—Must serve client interest while maintaining integrity and objectivity

        2] Understanding with client—Establish either in writing or orally

        3] Communication with client—Inform client of any conflicts of interest, significant reservations about engagement, significant engagement findings

    (c) Professional judgment must be used in applying SSCS

        1] Example: Practitioner not required to decline or withdraw from a consulting engagement when there are mutually agreed upon limitations with respect to gathering relevant data

5. Responsibilities in Personal Financial Planning

    a. Definition, scope and standards of personal financial planning

      (1) Personal financial planning engagements are only those that involve developing strategies and making recommendations to assist a client in defining and achieving personal financial goals

      (2) Personal financial planning engagements involve all of following

        (a) Defining engagement objectives

        (b) Planning specific procedures appropriate to engagement

        (c) Developing basis for recommendations

        (d) Communicating recommendations to client

        (e) Identifying tasks for taking action on planning decisions

      (3) Other engagements may also include

        (a) Assisting client to take action on planning decisions

        (b) Monitoring client's progress in achieving goals

        (c) Updating recommendations and helping client revise planning decisions

      (4) Personal financial planning does not include services that are limited to, for example

        (a) Compiling personal financial statements

        (b) Projecting future taxes

        (c) Tax compliance, including, but not limited to, preparation of tax returns

        (d) Tax advice or consultations

      (5) CPA should act in conformity with AICPA Code of Professional Conduct

        (a) Rule 102, Integrity and Objectivity

            1] A member shall maintain objectivity and integrity, be free of conflicts of interest, and not knowingly misrepresent facts or subordinate his/her judgment to others

        (b) Rule 201

            1] A member shall undertake only those professional services that member can reasonably expect to be completed with professional competence, shall exercise due professional care in the performance of professional services, shall adequately plan and supervise performance of professional services, and shall obtain sufficient relevant data to afford a reasonable basis for conclusions or recommendations

        (c) Rule 301, Confidential Client Information

            1] Member in public practice shall not disclose any confidential client information without specific consent of client

        (d) Rule 302, Contingent Fees

            1] Rules must be followed

      (6) When a personal financial planning engagement includes providing assistance in preparation of personal financial statements or financial projections, the CPA should consider applicable provisions of AICPA pronouncements, including

        (a) Statements on Standards for Accounting and Review Services

        (b) Statement on Standards for Attestation Engagements Financial Forecasts and Projections

        (c) Audit and Accounting Guide for Prospective Financial Information

        (d) Personal Financial Statements Guide

(7) The CPA should document his/her understanding of scope and nature of services to be provided

    (a) Consider engagement letter

(8) Personal financial planning engagement should be adequately planned
(9) Engagement's objectives form basis for planning engagement

    (a) Procedures should reflect materiality and cost-benefit considerations

(10) Relevant information includes understanding of client's goals, financial position, and available resources for achieving goals

    (a) External factors (such as inflation, taxes, and investment markets) and nonfinancial factors (such as client attitudes, risk tolerance, spending habits, and investment preferences) are also relevant information
    (b) Relevant information also includes reasonable estimates furnished by client's advisors, or developed by CPA

(11) Recommendations should ordinarily be in writing and include summary of client's goals and significant assumptions and description of any limitations on work performed
(12) Unless otherwise agreed, CPA is not responsible for additional services, for example,

    (a) Assisting client to take action on planning decisions
    (b) Monitoring progress in achieving goals
    (c) Updating recommendations and revising planning decisions

b. Working with other advisers

(1) If CPA does not provide a service needed to complete an engagement, s/he should restrict scope of engagement and recommend that client engage another adviser
(2) If client declines to engage another adviser, CPA and client may still agree to proceed with engagement

c. Implementation engagement functions and responsibilities

(1) Implementation engagements involve assisting client to take action on planning decisions developed during personal financial planning engagement
(2) Implementation includes activities such as selecting investment advisers, restructuring debt, creating estate documents, establishing cash reserves, preparing budgets, and selecting and acquiring specific investments and insurance products
(3) When undertaking implementation engagement, CPA should apply existing professional standards and published guidance

> **NOW REVIEW MULTIPLE-CHOICE QUESTIONS 1 THROUGH 26 IN VOLUME 2**

B. The Sarbanes-Oxley Act of 2002

1. Title 1—Authorizes establishment of Public Company Accounting Oversight Board

  a. Consists of five members

    (1) Two members must be or have been CPAs
    (2) Three members cannot be or cannot have been CPAs
    (3) None of Board members may receive pay or profits from CPA firms

  b. Board regulates CPA firms ("registrants") that audit SEC registrants ("issuers")

    (1) Main functions are to

      (a) Register and conduct inspections of public accounting firms (this replaces peer reviews)
      (b) Set or adopt standards on auditing, quality control, independence, or preparation of audit reports (as per below, PCAOB adopted AICPA standards on an interim basis as of April 16, 2003)

    (2) Details—PCAOB

      (a) Enforces compliance with professional standards, securities laws relating to accountants and audits.
      (b) May regulate nonaudit services CPA firms perform for clients.
      (c) Performs investigations and disciplinary proceedings on registered public accounting firms.
      (d) May perform any other duties needed to promote high professional standards and to improve auditing quality.

  c. Accounting firms must have second partner review and approve each audit report.

  d. Accounting firms must report on an audit of internal control in addition to the audit of the financial statements for issuers.

  e. Most CPA working papers must be saved for seven years.

  f. Material additional services of auditors must receive preapproval by audit committee, and fees for those services must be disclosed to investors.

 2. Title II—Auditor Independence

  a. The act lists several specific service categories that the issuer's public accounting firm cannot legally perform

   (1) Bookkeeping or other services relating to financial statements or accounting records

   (2) Financial information systems design and/or implementation

   (3) Appraisal services

   (4) Internal audit outsourcing services

   (5) Management functions

   (6) Actuarial services

   (7) Investment or broker-dealer services

   (8) Certain tax services, such as tax planning for potentially abusive tax shelters

    Note that the Act does not restrict auditors from performing these services to nonaudit clients or to private companies. Also, the Act permits the auditor to perform nonaudit services not specifically prohibited (e.g., tax services) when approved by issuer's audit committee.

  b. The audit partner for the job and the audit partner who reviews the audit can do the audit services for only five consecutive years.

   (1) If public company has hired employee of an audit firm to be its CEO, CFO, or CAO within previous year, that audit firm cannot audit the company.

  c. The audit firm should report critical accounting policies, alternative treatments of transactions, etc. and other material written communications between the accounting firm and management to the audit committee.

 3. Title III—Section 303

  a. It is unlawful for any officer or director to take any action to fraudulently influence, coerce, manipulate, or mislead any public accountant engaged in the performance of the audit.

 4. Title IV

  a. Section 404 is particularly important to the overall process of CPA reporting on internal control.

   (1) It in essence led to CPA reporting on client internal control by establishing the following:

    (a) It is management's responsibility to establish adequate internal control

    (b) Management must assess its IC

    (c) The CPA firm attests to management's assessment of IC

  b. Section 406 requires every issuer shall report whether it has adopted a code of ethics for senior financial officers.

  c. CEOs and CFOs of most large companies are now required to certify financial statements filed with SEC

   (1) They certify that the information "fairly presents in all material respects the financial statements and result of operations" of the company.

C. Public Company Accounting Oversight Board

 1. On April 16, 2003, the PCAOB adopted the following AICPA standards as its interim standards to be used on an initial transitional basis:

  a. Auditing Standards Board Standards (through SAS 95).

  b. Attestation Standards

  c. Quality Control Standards

  d. Ethics Standards 101 (Independence) and 102 (Integrity and objectivity) and several standards issued by the Independence Standards Board

 2. The PCAOB has broad authority to oversee the public accounting profession by establishing rules in the above areas; in addition it

    a. Registers public accounting firms that audit issuers companies
    b. Performs inspections of the practices of registered firms
    c. Conducts investigations and disciplinary proceedings of registered firms
    d. Sanctions registered firms.

3. Inspections performed by the PCAOB

    a. The Sarbanes-Oxley Act requires that the PCAOB perform inspections of CPA firms that include at least the following three general components:

        (1) An inspection and review of selected audit and review engagements
        (2) An evaluation of the sufficiency of the quality control system of the CPA firm and the manner of documentation and communication of the system
        (3) Performance of such other testing of the audit, supervisory, and quality control procedures as are considered necessary

    b. Although inspections performed by the PCAOB staff meet the AICPA's practice review requirement for the public auditing practices of CPA firms, they differ from peer reviews conducted by CPA firms. Inspections generally focus on selected quality control issues and may also consider other aspects of practice management, such as how partner compensation is determined. Most of the inspection process is focused on evaluating a CPA firm's performance on a sample of individual audit and review engagements. In selecting the engagements for inspection, the PCAOB staff uses a risk assessment process to identify those engagements that have a higher risk of lack of compliance with professional standards. When an audit is selected, the inspection focuses on the high-risk aspects of that engagement, such as revenue recognition and accounting estimates. When a lack of compliance with professional standards is identified, the PCAOB staff attempts to determine the cause, which may lead to identification of a defect in the firm's quality control system.
    c. Each inspection results in a written report that is transmitted to the SEC and appropriate regulatory authorities. Also included is a letter of comments by the PCAOB inspectors, and any responses by the CPA firm. While the content of most of the reports are made available to the public, discussion of criticisms of a firm's quality control system are not made public unless the firm does not address the criticism within twelve months.

4. Several issues relating to PCAOB implementation of Sarbanes-Oxley independence requirements through rules passed include

    • Prior to accepting an initial engagement (e.g., audit), the CPA firm must

        • Describe in writing to the audit committee all relationships between the CPA firm and the potential audit client (or persons in financial reporting oversight roles with the potential audit client) that may reasonably be thought to bear on independence.
        • Discuss any possible effects on independence of above relationships.
        • Document the substance of the discussion.

    At least annually the above is updated.

    • Recall that the Sarbanes-Oxley Act requires audit committee preapproval of permissible nonaudit services. The PCAOB has issued rules that require that when obtaining preapproval of *permissible tax services* or *permissible nonaudit services related to internal control over financial reporting,* the CPA firm must

        • Describe those services in writing to the audit committee.
        • Discuss any possible effects on independence with the audit committee.
        • Document the substance of the discussion.

    • A CPA firm is not independent if it provides a client nonaudit services related to marketing, planning, or opinion in favor of the tax treatment of confidential transactions or aggressive tax position transactions (unless the proposed tax treatment is at least more likely than not to be allowable).
    • A CPA firm is not independent if it provides any tax services to a person or a financial reporting oversight role to the audit client, or an immediate family member of such person. There are several exceptions if the person the services are provided for only serves as a member of the board of directors.

5. PCAOB Auditing Standards are discussed in subsequent modules; outlines and summary information follow the outline of AU 901.

D. International Standards—Ethical

    The International Ethics Standards Board for Accountants (IESBA) is a standard-setting body within the International Federation of Accountants (IFAC) that issues ethical standards for accountants throughout the world. This group has issued the *Code of Ethics for Professional Accountants,* which is similar to the *Code of Professional Conduct* issued by the AICPA for accountants in the US. The IESBA code has three parts:

- Part A—Framework applies to all professional accountants
- Part B—Applies to professional accountants in public practice
- Part C—Applies to professional accountants in business

Part A—Framework

Section 110—Integrity. Professional accountants should be straightforward and honest in all professional and business relationships. Integrity implies fair dealing and truthfulness. The accountant should not be associated with reports or other communications where the accountant believes the information contains a materially false or misleading statement, contains statements or information furnished recklessly, or omits or obscures information required to be included where such omission or obscurity would be misleading.

Section 120—Objectivity. Professional accountants should not compromise their professional or business judgment.

Section 130—Professional Competence and Due Care. Professional accountants should maintain professional knowledge and skill at the level required to ensure that clients or employers receive competent professional service, and to act diligently in accordance with applicable technical and professional standards.

Section 140—Confidentiality. Professional accountants should refrain from disclosing confidential information unless there is a legal or professional obligation to do so, and using confidential information for personal advantage.

Section 150—Professional Behavior. Professional accountants should comply with laws and regulations and avoid actions that would discredit the profession. In marketing services the professional accountant shall be honest and truthful.

Part B—Accountants in Public Practice

Section 200—Professional Accountants in Public Practice. This section of the code begins with a framework that presents threats to ethical behavior and safeguards to help mitigate these threats.

Section 210—Professional Appointment. Before accepting a new client, a professional accountant should determine whether acceptance would create any threats to compliance with fundamental principles.

Section 220—Conflicts of Interest. A professional accountant should take reasonable steps to identify circumstances that could pose a conflict of interest.

Section 230—Second Opinions. When asked to provide a second opinion on applicable accounting, auditing, reporting or other standards to specific circumstances or transactions, a professional accountant should evaluate the significance of threats and apply necessary safeguards.

Section 240—Fees and Other Types of Remuneration. Commissions, referral fees, fees that are not adequate, and contingent fees may create threats to compliance with professional standards. Therefore, the professional accountant should make sure that necessary safeguards are in effect around fee determination.

Section 250—Marketing Professional Services. Solicitation of new work through advertising or other forms of marketing may create a threat to compliance with fundamental principles. The accountant in public practice should not bring the profession in disrepute when marketing professional services. Assertions in marketing should be honest and truthful.

Section 260—Gifts and Hospitality. Gifts and hospitality from a client may create a threat to independence. The accountant must evaluate the significance of the threat and apply necessary safeguards.

Section 270—Custody of Client Assets. A professional accountant in public practice shall not assume custody of client monies or other assets unless permitted by law.

Section 280—Objectivity—All Services. A professional accountant shall determine when providing professional services whether there are threats to objectivity. If so, the accountant should apply necessary safeguards.

Section 290—Independence—Audit and Review Engagements. The international ethics rules regarding independence in audit and review engagements are similar to the AICPA rules. Both require the concepts of independence in mind and in appearance. However, the international ethics rules have fewer definitive prohibitions. Like the AICPA Code, when there is no definitive prohibition, the following approach is used:

1. Identify threats to independence;
2. Evaluate the significance of the threats identified; and
3. Apply safeguards, when necessary, to eliminate the threats or reduce them to an acceptable level. If safeguards do not reduce the risk to an acceptable level, the firm should not accept or continue the engagement, or assign the particular individual to the engagement team. The firm should document these considerations and the conclusion. Threats to independence arise from self interest, self review, advocacy, familiarity, or intimidation.

a. Like the AICPA *Code of Professional Conduct,* the international ethics rules indicate these types of threats can arise from

- Financial interests in the client;
- Having certain business relationships with the client;
- Serving as a director, officer, or employee of the client; and
- Performing certain non-assurance services to the client.

b. Safeguards are of two categories: (1) those created by the profession, legislation, regulation, and (2) those implemented by the firm in the work environment. For example, legislation may prohibit the performance of certain nonassurance services for audit clients. The audit firm may decide not to assign a particular individual to an audit engagement to mitigate a threat to independence.

Section 291—Independence for Other Assurance Services. These requirements are similar to those established by the AICPA in the US. They relate to maintaining independence from the parties making the assertion on which the accountant is providing assurance.

Part C—Professional Accountants in Business

The rules that apply to professional accountants in business related to the following areas;

- Potential conflicts
- Preparation and reporting on information
- Acting with sufficient expertise
- Financial interests
- Inducements

E. International Standards—Auditing/Assurance

International auditing standards are developed by the **International Auditing and Assurance Standards Board (IAASB)** of the **International Federation of Accountants (IFAC),** a worldwide organization of approximately 160 national accounting bodies (e.g., the AICPA). IFAC was established to help foster a coordinated worldwide accounting profession with harmonized standards. Its boards also establish ethical and quality control standards for accounting professionals and accounting firms. International auditing standards are issued as a series of statements referred to as *International Standards on Auditing*.

The pronouncements of the IAASB do not override the auditing standards of its members. Rather they are meant to help develop consistent worldwide professional standards. Members from countries that do not have their own standards may adopt IAASB standards as their own; members from countries that already have standards are encouraged to compare them to IAASB standards and to seek to eliminate any material inconsistencies. A report commissioned by the European Commission (the executive organization of the European Union) outlines a number of areas in which it suggests there are substantive differences between international and US PCAOB auditing standards. Remaining substantive differences from its list of areas at this point are

1. International standards do not require an audit of internal control, while PCAOB standards do so require.
2. International standards do not allow reference to another audit firm involved in a portion of the audit while PCAOB standards allow the principal auditor to so report (i.e., percentages or dollars audited by the other auditor are reported and the opinion is based in part upon the report of the other auditor).
3. International standards for documentation are less detailed than PCAOB standards, leaving more to professional judgment.
4. International standards in the area of going concern include time horizon of at least, but not limited to, twelve months, while PCAOB standards limit the foreseeable future for a going concern consideration of up to twelve months.

Additional differences not included in the above report as substantive differences include

Topic	International	US Standards (both AIPCA and PCAOB)
Compliance with GAAS	Auditors comply with requirements except in "exceptional circumstances" in which case alternate procedures are performed.	PCAOB standards establish three responsibility levels for compliance: (1) unconditional, (2) presumptively mandatory, and (3) responsibility to consider. Auditing Standards Board standards only include the first two categories (see Chapter 5 under **Statements on Auditing Standards**)

Topic	International	US Standards (both AIPCA and PCAOB)
Confirmation of accounts receivable	Not required. In making a determination on whether to confirm, the auditor should consider the assessed risk of material misstatement at the assertion level and how the audit evidence from other planned audit procedures will reduce the risk of material misstatement at the assertion level to an acceptably low level.	Confirmation is presumptively required unless accounts receivable are immaterial, the use of confirmations would be ineffective or the combined assessed level of inherent and control risk is low.
Fraud definition	An intentional act by one or more individuals among management, those charged with governance, employees, or third parties, involving the use of deception to obtain an unjust or illegal advantage.	An intentional act that results in a material misstatement in financial statements that are the subject of an audit. NOTE: While the international definition is broader, it may have limited significance in that both an audit following International Standards and one following US Standards aim at obtaining reasonable assurance that the financial statements are free from material misstatement, whether due to fraud or error.
Fraud	Auditors should obtain a written representation from management that it has disclosed to the auditor the results of its assessment of the risk of fraud.	Not required. However, various representations on fraud are obtained (management's knowledge of its responsibility, management's knowledge of fraud, allegations of fraud).
Illegal acts	The auditor's concern is with whether laws and regulations may materially affect the financial statements. No explicit distinction is made between direct and indirect effect illegal acts.	The audit obtains reasonable assurance of detection of illegal acts that have a direct and material effect on financial statement amounts; if evidence about possible illegal acts with an indirect effect comes to the auditor's attention it is considered.
Sending letter of audit inquiry to lawyers	Only required when an auditor "assesses a risk of material misstatement."	Presumptively required.
Reviewing predecessor auditor's working papers for evidence on beginning balances	The standard states that this may provide sufficient appropriate audit evidence on opening balances.	This statement is not included in standards.
Terms of audit engagement change, and auditor is unable to agree on new terms	The auditor should withdraw and consider whether there is an obligation to contact other parties.	There is no explicit obligation to consider contacting other parties.
Opinion on financial statements.	Audit opinion may be on either (1) the fair presentation of the financial statements or (2) that the financial statements "give a true and fair view."	Audit opinion may only be on fair presentation of financial statements
Audit report modification for consistency related to changes in accounting principles	Not required.	Audit reports are modified for changes in accounting principles with a material effect on the financial statements.
Inclusion of an emphasis of a matter paragraph in an audit report	Preferably after the opinion paragraph.	No such statement (may be before or after opinion paragraph).
Providing location the auditor practices in an audit report	Required.	Not required.
Dating the audit report for a subsequent event	When management amends financial statements for a subsequent event the auditor should perform necessary procedures and change the date of the audit report to no earlier than the date the financial statements were accepted as amended.	Auditors may "dual date" report (see Section A.2. of Reporting Module).

Topic	International	US Standards (both AIPCA and PCAOB)
Communications to those charged with governance (internal control deficiencies and other matters related to the audit)	While report explicitly addressed to those charged with governance and/or management, the report does not include a restriction on use to these parties (nor does it prohibit such a limitation). Significant deficiencies identified, no category used to identify material weaknesses.	Report explicitly indicates that it is not intended to be, and should not be, used by anyone other than the specified parties (those charged with governance and/or management). Internal control deficiencies divided into two categories: (1) significant deficiencies and (2) material weaknesses.

Switching from auditing standards to accounting standards, you should know that the International Financial Reporting Standards (IFRS) are developed by the International Accounting Standards Board (IASB). These standards represent an alternative financial reporting framework to United States GAAP. When a client follows IFRS it has an effect on the audit process because of the differences between IFRS and US GAAP. Apart from some specific differences in rules, IFRS are considered to be more principle based than US GAAP. Therefore, IFRS generally require the application of more judgment.

F. Other

1. Securities and Exchange Commission (SEC)

   a. The mission of the SEC is to protect investors, maintain fair, orderly, and efficient markets, and facilitate capital formation.
   b. The SEC has the authority to establish standards relating to financial accounting, auditing and CPA professional conduct when involved with public-company financial statements

      (1) Some of those standards differ from AICPA requirements.
      (2) Currently, the SEC works with the PCAOB in this area.

   c. PCAOB pronouncements require SEC approval.
   d. Historically, SEC independence rules have been more restrictive than those than the AICPA in areas such as

      (1) The SEC requirements make clear that performing bookkeeping services impair audit independence; this is allowed under AICPA rules (thereby, only for nonpublic clients).
      (2) The SEC (and PCAOB) have required companies to disclose audit and nonaudit fees earned by CPA firms.

   e. Financial Reporting Releases (FRRs) are designed to communicate the SEC's positions on accounting principles and auditing practices.

2. Government Accountability Office (GAO)

   a. The GAO's mission is to support Congress in meeting its constitutional responsibilities and to help improvement the performance and ensure the accountability of the federal government.
   b. Work includes

      (1) Auditing agency operations to determine whether federal funds are being spent efficiently and effectively
      (2) Investigating allegations of illegal and improper activities
      (3) Reporting on how well government programs meet their objectives
      (4) Performing policy analyses and outlining various options for Congress
      (5) Issuing legal decision and opinions

   c. The GAO develops additional requirements for audits of organizations that receive federal financial assistance.

      (1) These are included in *Government Auditing Standards,* referred to as the "Yellow Book." (the *Government Auditing Standards* outline follow the PCAOB outlines)

   d. GAO independence requirements

      (1) In all matters relating to audit work, the audit organization and the individual auditor must be free of personal, external, and organizational impairments to independence, and must avoid the appearance of such impairments of independence. Many are similar to AICPA restrictions.
      (2) Some are more restrictive in some areas than those of the AICPA; examples are

         (a) CPA firm cannot allow personnel working on nonattest engagements to also work on the audit.
         (b) *Government Auditing Standards* places restrictions on the nature of nonattest services to be performed for an audit client

            1] Nonattest services must be deemed not significant or material to the subject matter of the audit.

3. Department of Labor (DOL)

    a. The DOL's mission involves fostering and promoting the welfare of job seekers, wage earners, and retirees of the United States.

    b. The DOL conducts financial and performance audits following *Government Auditing Standards* relating to its mission, including audits of

        (1) Compliance with applicable laws and regulations

        (2) Evaluation of economy and efficiency of operations

        (3) Evaluation of effectiveness in achieving program results

    c. Employee benefit plans must be audited in accordance with the Employee Retirement Security Act of 1974 (ERISA), as enforced by DOL. Independence requirements are in general similar to those of the AICPA, except that

        (1) Accountant or firm may be engaged on a professional basis by the plan sponsor and the accountant may serve as an actuary.

    d. In some circumstances (e.g., definition of "member" for purposes of those who must maintain independence within a CPA firm) DOL requirements differ from AICPA requirements—in such cases they are generally more restrictive.

NOW REVIEW MULTIPLE-CHOICE QUESTIONS 27 THROUGH 47 IN VOLUME 2

KEY TERMS

Close relative. A parent, sibling, or nondependent child.

Covered member. A covered member is

(a) An individual on the attest engagement team;

(b) An individual in a position to influence the attest engagement;

(c) A partner or manager who provides nonattest services to the attest client, beginning once he or she provides ten hours of nonattest services to the client within any fiscal year and ending on the later of the date.

    1] The firm signs the report on the financial statements for the fiscal year during which those services were provided; or

    2] He or she no longer expects to provide ten or more hours of nonattest services to the attest client on a recurring basis;

(d) A partner in the office in which the lead attest engagement partner primarily practices in connection with the attest engagement;

(e) The firm, including the firm's employee benefit plans; or

(f) An entity whose operating, financial, or accounting policies can be controlled (as defined by generally accepted accounting principles [GAAP] for consolidation purposes) by any of the individuals or entities described in (a) through (e) or by two or more such individuals or entities if they act together.

Direct financial interest. A personal investment under the direct control of the investor. For example, an investment in the stock of a company.

Fraud. An intentional act by one or more individuals among management, those charged with governance, employees, or third parties, involving the use of deception that results in a misstatement in financial statements that are subject of an audit. For financial statement audits, fraud includes two types of intentional misstatements—misstatements arising from fraudulent financial reporting and misstatements arising from misappropriation of assets.

Independence. Defined in the Code of Professional Conduct as

1. *Independence of mind*—The state of mind that permits the performance of an attest service without being affected by influences that compromise professional judgment, thereby allowing an individual to act with integrity and exercise objectivity and professional skepticism.

2. *Independence in appearance*—The avoidance of circumstances that would cause a reasonable and informed third party, having knowledge of all relevant information, including safeguards applied, to reasonably conclude that the integrity, objectivity, or professional skepticism of a firm or a member of the attest engagement team had been compromised.

Immediate family. A spouse, spousal equivalent, or dependent (whether or not related).

Indirect financial interest. An investment in which the specific investment decisions are not under the control of the investor. For example, an investment in a professionally managed mutual fund.

Individual in a position to influence the attest engagement. An individual in a position to influence the attest engagement is one who

1. Evaluates the performance or recommends the compensation of the attest engagement partner;
2. Directly supervises or manages the attest engagement partner, including all successively senior levels above that individual through the firm's chief executive;
3. Consults with the attest engagement team regarding technical or industry-related issues specific to the attest engagement; or
4. Participates in or oversees, at all successively senior levels, quality control activities, including internal monitoring, with respect to the specific attest engagement.

Inspection (conducted by the PCAOB). A process that leads to an assessment of the degree of compliance of each registered public accounting firm and associated persons of that firm with the Sarbanes-Oxley Act of 2002, and the board's requirements in connection with its performance of audits, issuance of audit reports, and related matters.

International Accounting Standards Board. An independent, privately funded accounting standard-setter that is committed to developing a single set of high-quality, understandable, and enforceable global accounting standards.

International Auditing and Assurance Standards Board. A committee of the International Federation of Accountants, established to issue standards on auditing and reporting practices to improve the degree of uniformity of auditing practices and related services throughout the world.

International Federation of Accountants. A worldwide organization of national accounting bodies established to help foster a coordinated worldwide accounting profession with harmonized standards.

Interpretive publications. Auditing interpretations of GAAS, exhibits to GAAS, auditing guidance included in AICPA Audit and Accounting Guides, and AICPA Auditing Statements of Position.

Key position. A key position is a position in which an individual

1. Has primary responsibility for significant accounting functions that support material components of the financial statements;
2. Has primary responsibility for the preparation of the financial statements; or
3. Has the ability to exercise influence over the contents of the financial statements, including when the individual is a member of the board of directors or similar governing body, chief executive officer, president, chief financial officer, chief operating officer, general counsel, chief accounting officer, controller, director of internal audit, director of financial reporting, treasurer, or any equivalent position.

Peer review. A study and appraisal by an independent evaluator of a CPA firm's work.

Period of the professional engagement. The period of the professional engagement begins when a member either signs an initial engagement letter or other agreement to perform attest services or begins to perform an attest engagement for a client, whichever is earlier. The period lasts for the entire duration of the professional relationship (which could cover many periods) and ends with the formal or informal notification, either by the member or the client, of the termination of the professional relationship or by the issuance of a report, whichever is later. Accordingly, the period does not end with the issuance of a report and recommence with the beginning of the following year's attest engagement.

Professional judgment. The application of relevant training, knowledge, and experience, within the context provided by auditing, accounting, and ethical standards, in making informed decisions about the courses of action that are appropriate in the circumstances of the audit engagement.

Professional skepticism. An attitude that includes a questioning mind, being alert to conditions that may indicate possible misstatement due to fraud or error, and a critical assessment of audit evidence.

Public Company Accounting Oversight Board (PCAOB). The five-member board established in 2002 to oversee the audit of public (issuer) companies that are subject to the securities laws. The board has authority to establish or adopt, or both, rules for auditing, quality control, ethics, independence, and other standards relating to the preparation of an audit report.

Quality control standards. AICPA standards designed to provide reasonable assurance that all of a CPA firm's engagements are conducted in accordance with applicable professional responsibilities.

Reporting accountant. An accountant, other than a continuing accountant, in the practice of public accounting, as described in ET section 92.25 of the AICPA Code of Professional Conduct, who prepares a written report or provides oral advice on the application of the requirements of an applicable financial reporting framework to a specific transaction, or on the type of report that may be issued on a specific entity's financial statements. (A reporting accountant who is also engaged to provide accounting and reporting advice to a specific entity on a recurring basis is commonly referred to as an advisory accountant.)

Risk of material misstatement. The risk that the financial statements are materially misstated prior to the audit. This consists of two components, inherent risk and control risk.

Sarbanes-Oxley Act of 2002 (SOX). A set of reforms that strengthened penalties for corporate fraud, restricted the types of consulting CPAs can perform for audit clients, and created the Public Company Accounting Oversight Board to oversee CPAs and public accounting firms.

Module 2: Engagement Planning, Obtaining an Understanding of the Client and Assessing Risks

Overview

The first two standards of fieldwork state

The auditor must adequately plan the work and must properly supervise any assistants.

The auditor must obtain a sufficient understanding of the entity and its environment, including its internal control, to assess the risk of material misstatement of the financial statements whether due to error or fraud, and to design the nature, timing, and extent of further audit procedures.

This module presents requirements relating to both of these standards of fieldwork. Generally, multiple-choice questions are used to test the candidate's knowledge of areas such as

- Audit planning
- Obtaining an understanding of the client
- Auditor responsibility for the detection of misstatements (errors, fraud, and illegal acts)
- Assessing risks, including the components of audit risk

A simulation may require you to examine a situation, evaluate areas of risk related to a company, and to design appropriate audit procedures in response to that situation. The following SAS sections pertain to this module:

AU section

110	Responsibilities and Functions of the Independent Auditor
150	Generally Accepted Auditing Standards
161	Relationship of Generally Accepted Auditing Standards to Quality Control Standards
201	Nature of the General Standards
210	Training and Proficiency of the Independent Auditor
220	Independence
230	Due Care in the Performance of Work
310	Relationship between the Auditor's Appointment and Planning
311	Planning and Supervision
313	Substantive Tests prior to the Balance Sheet Date
314	Understanding the Entity and Its Environment and Assessing the Risks of Material Misstatement
315	Communications between Predecessor and Successor Auditors
316	Consideration of Fraud in a Financial Statement Audit
317	Illegal Acts by Clients
329	Analytical Procedures
AT 101	Attestation Standards

A. Basic Concepts

1. **Financial statement assertions.** Management is responsible for the fair presentation of financial statements. In representing that the financial statements are fairly presented in conformity with generally accepted accounting principles, management implicitly or explicitly makes assertions relating to account balances at year-end (account balances), classes of transactions and events (transactions classes), and presentations and disclosures (disclosures). Those assertions (included in AU 326) are here presented at the transaction class, account balance, and disclosure levels.

Transactions Classes	Account Balances	Disclosures
Occurrence—Transactions and events that have been recorded have occurred and pertain to the entity.	*Existence*—Assets, liabilities, and equity interests exist.	*Occurrence*—Disclosed events and transactions have occurred.
	Rights and obligations—The entity holds or controls the rights to assets, and liabilities are the obligations of the entity.	*Rights and obligations*—Disclosed events pertain to the entity.

Transactions Classes	Account Balances	Disclosures
Completeness—All transactions and events have been recorded.	*Completeness*—All assets, liabilities, and equity interests have been recorded.	*Completeness*—All disclosures that should have been included have been included.
Accuracy—Amounts and other data relating to recorded transactions have been recorded appropriately.	*Valuation and* allocation—Assets, liabilities, and equity interests are included at appropriate amounts.	*Accuracy and valuation*— Information is disclosed fairly and at appropriate amounts.
Cutoff—Transactions and events have been recorded in the correct accounting period.		
Classification—Transactions and events have been recorded in the proper accounts.		*Classification and understandability*—Information is presented and described clearly.

Not all of these assertions are relevant in all circumstances. **Relevant assertions** are those that have a meaningful bearing on whether an account balance, transaction, or disclosure is fairly stated. For example, valuation may not be relevant to the cash account unless currency translation is involved; however, existence and completeness are always relevant.

In planning and performing an audit, the auditor considers these assertions for the various transaction classes, financial statement accounts, and disclosures. When, for example, all of these assertions have been met for an account, the account is in conformity with generally accepted accounting principles. Thus, errors and fraud may be viewed as having the effect of misstating one or more of the assertions. The Responding to Risk Assessment Module presents further illustration of these assertions.

> **NOW REVIEW MULTIPLE-CHOICE QUESTIONS 1 THROUGH 7 IN VOLUME 2**

2. **Audit risk (AU 312).** An audit must be designed to limit audit risk to an appropriately low level. Audit risk, which may be assessed in quantitative or nonquantitative terms, consists of (1) the risk that an account and its related assertions contains material misstatements (composed of two components, referred to as inherent risk and control risk) and (2) the risk that the auditor will not detect such misstatements (referred to as detection risk). Mathematically, we may view this as follows:

Audit Risk = Risk of Material Misstatement *   Risk Auditor Fails to Detect Misstatements

Audit Risk = Inherent Risk * Control Risk   *   Detection Risk

Inherent risk refers to the likelihood of material misstatement of an assertion, assuming no related internal control. This risk differs by account and assertion. For example, cash is more susceptible to theft than an inventory of coal. This risk is assessed using various analytical techniques, available information on the company and its industry, as well as by using overall auditing knowledge.

Control risk is the likelihood that a material misstatement will not be prevented or detected on a timely basis by internal control. This risk is assessed using the results of tests of controls.

Detection risk is the likelihood that an auditor's procedures lead to an improper conclusion that no material misstatement exists in an assertion when in fact such a misstatement does exist. The auditor's substantive procedures are primarily relied upon to restrict detection risk.

Relationship among inherent risk, control risk, and detection risk. Inherent risk and control risk differ from detection risk in that they exist independently of the audit, whereas detection risk relates to the effectiveness of the auditor's procedures. A number of questions are asked concerning the relationship among the three risks. Although the auditor may make either separate or combined assessments of inherent risk and control risk, you may find the audit risk formula that separates the risks helpful for such questions. First, assume that a given audit risk is to be accepted, say .05. Then, the product of inherent risk, control risk and detection risk must be .05 as follows:

Audit Risk	=	Inherent Risk	*	Control Risk	*	Detection Risk
.05	=	Inherent Risk	*	Control Risk	*	Detection Risk

Accordingly, if any risk increases another must decrease to hold audit risk at .05. Therefore, when a question asks for the relationship between control risk and detection risk, for example, you would reply that it is inverse. Stated otherwise, if control risk (or inherent risk) increases, detection risk must decrease.

3. **Materiality (AU 312).** Materiality is "the magnitude of an omission or misstatement of accounting information that, in the light of surrounding circumstances, makes it probable that the judgment of a *reasonable person* relying on the information would have been changed or influenced by the omission or misstatement." This section operationalizes the concept of a reasonable person relying on the financial statements as **users.** Thus the evaluation of

whether a misstatement could influence the economic decision of users involves consideration of the characteristics of those users. Users are assumed to have appropriate knowledge of business and accounting, be willing to study the information, understand that materiality judgments and uncertainty are involved. An auditor's consideration of user needs is as a group, not on specific individual users, whose needs may vary widely. Determining a materiality level helps auditors to (1) assess risks of material misstatements and plan the nature, timing, and extent of further audit procedures and (2) evaluate audit results.

Operationally, the measure of materiality may be either quantitative or nonquantitative. The auditor plans the audit to obtain reasonable assurance of detecting misstatements that could be large enough, individually or when combined, to be quantitatively material to the financial statements. Section 312 suggests that auditors may develop a level of materiality for each financial statement. For example, the auditor may believe that misstatements aggregating approximately $100,000 would have a material effect on income, but that such misstatement would have to aggregate approximately $200,000 to materially affect financial position. In such cases the lower measure would be used for any transactions affecting income.

After determining a materiality level for the various financial statements, the auditor then apportions the amount among the various accounts. This apportionment may be based on factors such as the relative size of various accounts and on professional judgment. The apportioned amount for each account is the "tolerable misstatement" discussed in the Audit Sampling Module (Section C).

The measures of materiality used for evaluation purposes will ordinarily differ from measures of materiality used for planning. This is the result of information encountered during the audit. For evaluation purposes, the auditor is aware of qualitative aspects of actual misstatements that s/he is not aware of during the planning stage. For example, an auditor will consider any fraud in which management is involved to be material, regardless of the amount involved.

> **NOW REVIEW MULTIPLE-CHOICE QUESTIONS 8 THROUGH 23 IN VOLUME 2**

4. **Errors and fraud (AU 316).** An audit should be planned and performed to obtain reasonable assurance about whether the financial statements are free of material misstatements, whether caused by error or fraud. While both errors and fraud may result in misstatements or omissions in the financial statements, they differ in that fraud is intentional. The two types of fraud considered in an audit are (1) **fraudulent financial reporting** that makes the financial statements misleading and (2) **misappropriation of assets** (i.e., theft, defalcation). The Summary of Auditor Responsibility for Errors, Fraud, and Illegal Acts table presents overall auditor responsibilities.

SUMMARY OF AUDITOR RESPONSIBILITY FOR ERRORS, FRAUD, AND ILLEGAL ACTS

	Errors	Fraud	Illegal acts	
			Direct effect	Indirect effect
Definition	Unintentional misstatements or omissions	Intentional misstatements or omissions	Violations of laws or governmental regulations having a material and direct effect on financial statement **amounts**	Violations of laws or governmental regulations **not** having a material and direct effect on financial statement **amounts**
Examples	Mistakes in processing accounting data, incorrect accounting estimates due to oversight, mistakes in application of accounting principles	Two types— **fraudulent financial reporting** (falsification of accounting records) and **misappropriation of assets** (embezzlement)	Tax laws, accrued revenue based on government contracts	Securities trading, occupational safety and health, food and drug administration, environmental protection, equal employment, price fixing

| | Errors | Fraud | Illegal acts | |
			Direct effect	Indirect effect
Detection responsibility	1. Assess risk of misstatement. 2. Based on assessment, design audit to provide reasonable assurance of detection of material misstatements. 3. Exercise due care in planning, performing, and evaluating results of audit procedures, and proper degree of professional skepticism to achieve reasonable assurance of detection.	(Same as for errors)	(Same as for errors)	1. Be aware of possibility that they may have occurred. 2. If specific information comes to attention on an illegal act with a possible material indirect financial statement effect, apply audit procedures necessary to determine whether illegal act has occurred.
Reporting responsibility	1. Modify audit report for remaining departures from GAAP or scope limitations. 2. Report to audit committee (unless clearly inconsequential). 3. In audits in accordance with government auditing standards, consider notification of other parties (e.g., regulatory agencies). 4. Report in various other circumstances (e.g., Form 8-K, successor auditor, subpoena response).	(Same as for errors)	(Same as for errors)	(Similar to errors)
Primary standards	AU 314	AU 316	AU 316, 317	AU 317

You should be very familiar with the information presented in the rather lengthy outline of AU 316, as well as the outline of AU 317 on illegal acts (discussed in detail in the following section). While we summarize some of the most important concepts from them, reading this section of the module alone is insufficient. Although AU 316 does not refer to "steps" involved related to fraud, and indeed in practice the "steps" don't follow one another nicely, we summarize the layout of its guidance in the table below.

Consideration of Fraud

	Step	Approach
Step 1.	Staff discussion of the risk of material misstatement	• Brainstorm • Consider incentives/pressures, opportunities • Exercise professional skepticism
Step 2.	Obtain information needed to identify risks of material misstatement due to fraud	• Make inquiries of management and others • Consider results of analytical procedures • Consider fraud risk factors • Consider other information
Step 3.	Identify risks that may result in a material misstatement due to fraud	For risks identified, consider • Type of risk that may exist • Significance of risk (magnitude) • Likelihood of risk • Pervasiveness of risk
Step 4.	Assess the identified risks after considering programs and controls	• Consider understanding of internal control • Evaluate whether programs and controls address the identified risks • Assess risks taking into account this evaluation

Step	**Approach**
Step 5.	Respond to the results of the assessment	As risk increases

<table>
<tr><td>Step 5.</td><td>Respond to the results of the assessment</td><td>As risk increases</td></tr>
</table>

- Overall response: More experienced staff, more attention to accounting policies, less predictable procedures
- For specifically identified risks: Consider need to increase nature, timing, and extent of audit procedures

On all audits consider the possibility of management override of controls (adjusting journal entries, accounting estimates, unusual transactions)

Step 6.	Evaluate audit evidence

- Assess risk of fraud throughout the audit
- Evaluate analytical procedures performed as substantive procedures and at overall review stage
- Evaluate risk of fraud near completion of fieldwork
- Respond to misstatements that may be due to fraud

Step 7.	Communicate about fraud

- Communicate all fraud to an appropriate level of management
- Communicate all management fraud to audit committee
- Communicate all material fraud to management and audit committee
- Determine if significant deficiencies have been identified

Step 8.	Document consideration of fraud

- Document steps 1-7
- If improper revenue recognition not considered a risk, describe why

AU 316 is the source of many questions. Here are some particularly important points included in the outline.

1. Because an audit is planned and performed to obtain reasonable, not absolute, assurance, even a properly performed audit may miss material misstatements.
2. The auditor must exercise professional skepticism—an attitude that includes a questioning mind and a critical assessment of audit evidence.
3. Make certain you can distinguish between **fraudulent financial reporting** in which the financial statements are intentionally misstated (cooked books) and **misappropriation of assets** when its assets are stolen.
4. Three conditions that are generally present when individuals commit fraud are incentive/pressure, opportunity, and attitude/rationalization.
5. A staff discussion of the risk of material misstatement is required either prior to or in conjunction with obtaining information to identify risks of fraud.
6. In planning the audit, the auditor should perform analytical procedures relating to revenue to identify unusual or unexpected relationships involving revenue accounts.
7. The responses to the results of the assessment as risk are an overall response, a response that specifically addresses identified risks, and a response for the possibility of management override. The response for management override (performed on all audits to some extent) includes

   - Testing the appropriateness of journal entries and adjustments
   - Reviewing accounting estimates for biases
   - Evaluating the rationale for significant unusual transactions

8. Fraud communication responsibility

   - All fraud involving management must be communicated to the audit committee
   - All material fraud should be communicated to the audit committee
   - The auditor should reach an understanding with the audit committee regarding other communications

At this point study the outline of AU 316 in detail.

5. **Illegal acts (AU 317).** Illegal acts are also heavily examined. AU 317 differentiates between illegal acts having a **direct and material effect** in the determination of financial statement amounts (i.e., result in adjusting entries) and those with an **indirect effect** on the financial statements (i.e., result in note disclosures). Examples of illegal acts with a direct effect on the financial statements are (1) violation of tax laws that affect accruals and expenses (e.g., violations of income tax laws) and (2) violations of laws related to the amount of revenue accrued under government contracts. Examples of indirect effect illegal acts include securities purchased or sold based on inside information, price-fixing, and antitrust violations; their indirect effect is normally the result of a need to disclose a contingent liability because of the allegation or determination of illegality. As indicated in the earlier summary, the auditor's responsibility differs for the two types as follows:

Direct—Responsibility same as for errors and fraud (provide reasonable assurance of detection of material misstatements).

Indirect—An audit in accordance with GAAS does not include audit procedures specially designed to detect illegal acts with an indirect effect. However, when procedures applied for other purposes identify possible illegal acts, the auditor should apply audit procedures to determine whether an illegal act has occurred.

When an auditor discovers an act that **might** be illegal, s/he should inquire of management at a level above those involved, if possible. If management does not provide satisfactory information that there has been no illegal act, the auditor should

- Consult with the client's legal counsel or other specialists.
- Apply additional procedures such as

  - Examine supporting documents such as invoices, canceled checks, and agreements and compare them with accounting records.
  - Confirm significant information with the other involved party or with intermediaries, such as banks or lawyers.
  - Determine whether the transaction has been properly authorized.
  - Consider whether other similar transactions may have occurred and apply appropriate procedures.

When, based on procedures such as the above, the auditor believes that an illegal act has or is likely to have occurred, the auditor should

- Consider its financial statement effect.
- Consider its implications to other aspects of the audit, particularly the reliability of representations by management.
- Communicate it to the audit committee.
- Consider the need to modify the audit report as follows:

  - Lack of disclosure is a departure from GAAP and either a qualified or an adverse opinion may be appropriate.
  - Client-imposed scope restrictions will generally lead to a disclaimer of opinion.
  - Circumstance-imposed scope restrictions may lead to either a qualified opinion or a disclaimer of opinion.

Unless the act is clearly inconsequential, the audit committee should be provided with a description of the act, circumstances concerning its occurrence, and its effect on the financial statements. When senior management is involved, the auditor should communicate directly with the audit committee. When a client refuses to give appropriate consideration to handling the illegal act (even an immaterial one), the auditor should consider whether the refusal affects his or her ability to rely on management's representations and whether resignation is desirable.

> **NOW REVIEW MULTIPLE-CHOICE QUESTIONS 24 THROUGH 65 IN VOLUME 2**

B. Audit Planning

CPAs must establish policies for deciding whether to accept (or continue serving) a client in order to minimize the likelihood of being associated with an organization whose management lacks integrity. The auditor must also adequately plan the audit. Much of the information on audit planning is included in AU 311.

Prior to acquiring a client, an auditor should attempt communication with the predecessor auditor and obtain a general understanding of the nature of the organization and its industry. The overall goal is to determine whether to attempt to acquire the client, and to gather adequate information so as to allow the auditor to develop a proposal to be presented to the prospective client.

1. **Communicate with predecessor auditors (AU 315).** Make certain that you are very familiar with the information presented in the outline of AU 315. That standard requires a communication with the predecessor prior to acceptance of the engagement, and strongly recommends one after acceptance of the engagement (see section C.1 of this module). Particularly heavily examined concepts relating to the communication prior to client acceptance are

   a. Initiating the communication is the responsibility of the successor.
   b. If the prospective client refuses to permit the predecessor to respond, or limits the predecessor's response, the successor should inquire as to the reasons and consider the implications in deciding whether to accept the engagement.
   c. The successor's inquiries of the predecessor should include

(1) Information bearing on **integrity** of management
(2) **Disagreements** with management as to accounting principles, auditing procedures or other similarly significant matters
(3) **Communications** to audit committee regarding fraud, illegal acts, and internal control related matters
(4) Predecessor's understanding of the **reasons for the change** in auditors

2. **Establishing an understanding with the client (engagement letters).** Auditors should establish an understanding with the client regarding the services to be performed—see AU 311 (part A of outline). The auditor should document this understanding through a written communication with the client, ordinarily an engagement letter. The engagement letter is sent to the client, who normally indicates approval through returning a signed copy to the CPA.

The understanding must include four general topics: (1) objectives of the engagement, (2) management's responsibilities, (3) auditor's responsibilities, and (4) limitations of the audit. If an auditor believes that an understanding has not been established, he or she should decline to accept or perform the audit.

The following summary presents details of the required understanding with the client.

SUMMARY OF DETAILS OF AN UNDERSTANDING WITH THE CLIENT

General	Details
1. Objectives of the engagement	Expression of an opinion on the financial statements
2. Management's responsibilities	• Establishing and maintaining effective internal control over financial reporting • Identifying and ensuring that the entity complies with laws and regulations • Making financial records and related information available to the auditor • Providing a representation letter (see Responding to Risk Assessment Module) • Adjusting financial statements to correct material misstatements • Affirming in representation letter that effect of uncorrected misstatements aggregated by auditor is immaterial
3. Auditor's responsibilities	• Conducting audit in accordance with US GAAS • Ensuring that audit committee is aware of any significant deficiencies which come to auditor's attention
4. Limitations of the audit	• Obtains reasonable, rather than absolute, assurance • Material misstatement may remain undetected • If auditor is unable to form or has not formed an opinion, auditor may decline to express an opinion or decline to issue a report

Other (not required)	• Arrangements regarding:
	  – Conduct of engagement (timing, client assistance, etc.)
	  – Involvement of specialists or internal auditors
	  – Predecessor auditor
	  – Fees and billing
	  – Additional services to be provided relating to regulatory requirements
	  – Other additional services
	• Any limitation or other arrangement regarding the liability of the auditor or the client
	• Conditions under which access to the auditor's working papers may be granted to others

3. **Preliminary engagement activities.** The auditor performs procedures to determine whether continuance of the client relationship is appropriate and to evaluate the auditor's compliance with ethical considerations (e.g., independence).

4. **Developing an overall strategy.** The nature, timing, and extent of planning will vary with the size and complexity of the audit client, experience with the client, and knowledge of the client's business. The overall audit strategy involves

• Determining the characteristics of the engagement that define its scope (e.g., basis of reporting, industry-specific reporting requirements)
• Determining reporting objectives of the engagement (e.g., deadlines for reporting, key dates)
• Considering important factors that will determine the focus of the audit team's efforts (e.g., materiality levels, high-risk areas)

The above items help the auditor to determine the appropriate resources necessary for the engagement. Once the audit strategy has been established, the auditor is able to start the development of a more detailed audit plan to address the various matters identified in the audit strategy.

5. **The audit plan.** The auditor must develop and document an audit plan in which the auditor determines the audit procedures to be used that, when performed, are expected to reduce audit risk to an acceptably low level. The audit plan should include a description of the nature, timing and extent of planned

   - Risk assessment procedures
   - Further audit procedures (tests of controls and substantive tests) at the relevant assertion level for account balances, transactions classes, and disclosures
   - Other audit procedures (e.g., seeking direct communication with the entity's lawyer)

6. **Audit program.** A written audit program must be developed and used to implement the audit plan. Audit programs are discussed in the Responding to Risk Assessment Module.

7. **Timing of audit procedures (AU 313).** Tests of controls and substantive tests can be conducted at various times. The timing of tests of controls is very flexible; they are often performed at an interim period, and subsequently updated through year-end.

   Auditors also have a certain amount of flexibility in planning the timing of substantive tests. These aspects should be considered.

   a. Factors to be considered before applying tests at an **interim date** before year-end
   b. Auditing procedures to be followed for the **remaining period** (the period after the interim date through year-end)
   c. **Coordination of the timing** of audit procedures

   Before applying procedures at an **interim date,** an auditor should consider the incremental audit risk involved as well as whether performance of such interim procedures is likely to be cost-effective. As an illustration of a substantive test applied at an interim date, consider the confirmation of receivables as of November 30, one month prior to the client's year-end.

   Appropriate auditing procedures must be applied to provide a reasonable basis for extending November 30 interim date results to the **remaining period** (December 1-31). When control risk is assessed at a level below the maximum, the auditor might be able to perform only limited substantive tests during the remaining period to obtain the assurance needed as of the balance sheet date.

   The auditor who intends to apply audit tests at an interim date should consider whether the accounting system will provide information on remaining period transactions that is sufficient to investigate (1) significant unusual transactions, (2) other causes of significant fluctuation (or expected fluctuations that did not occur), and (3) changes in the composition of the account balances.

   A properly performed audit involves **coordination of the timing** of procedures. This especially applies to (1) related-party transactions, (2) interrelated accounts and cutoffs, and (3) negotiable assets. For interrelated accounts and negotiable assets, the auditor is concerned that one might be substituted for another to allow the double counting of a given resource (e.g., sale of securities after they have been counted at year-end and inclusion of proceeds in year-end cash).

NOW REVIEW MULTIPLE CHOICE QUESTIONS 66 THROUGH 87 IN VOLUME 2

C. **Obtain an Understanding of the Entity and Its Environment (AU 314).**
   The procedures followed to obtain an understanding of the entity are referred to as risk assessment procedures. Risk assessment procedures include

   - Inquiries of management and others within the entity
   - Analytical procedures
   - Observation and inspection
   - Other procedures, such as inquiries of others outside the entity (e.g., legal counsel, valuation experts) and reviewing information from external sources such as analysts, banks, etc.

   The following is information on certain specific risk assessment procedures ordinarily performed.

1. **Communicate with predecessor auditors.** Earlier, we discussed the AU 315 requirement that potential successor auditors attempt communication with the predecessor **before** accepting a new client. We also emphasized that you should be very familiar with the outline of AU 315.

   Although strongly recommended, no second communication with the predecessor auditor is required **after** accepting a new client. This second communication would normally involve review of working papers related to opening balances and the consistency of application of accounting principles. With regard to working papers

    a. Documentation examined generally includes

        (1) Planning
        (2) Internal control
        (3) Audit results
        (4) Other matters of continuing accounting **and** auditing significance such as analyses of balance sheet accounts

    b. If in reviewing the working papers the successor identifies financial statement misstatements, the successor should request that the client inform the predecessor and arrange a meeting of the three parties.

    In addition, AU 315 includes a section on "reaudits" of previously audited financial statements. Reaudits may be necessary, for example, when a change in auditors has occurred and the predecessor refuses to reissue his or her audit report on previous year financial statements that are to be reissued (e.g., prior year statements in an SEC filing). In such cases the successor should request the working papers for the period of the reaudit; the extent to which the predecessor permits such access is considered a matter of judgment. Additional procedures beyond those performed by the predecessor are always necessary in such circumstances.

2. **Analytical procedures.** AU 329 requires that analytical procedures be performed in planning the audit (as well as an overall review near completion of the audit). The objective of planning analytical procedures is to assist in planning the nature, timing, and extent of audit procedures that will be used to obtain evidence for specific accounts. Analytical procedures are discussed in further detail in the Responding to Risk Assessment Module.

3. **Consideration of internal control.** In all audits, the CPA must obtain an understanding of internal control sufficient to assess the risk of material misstatement of the financial statements, and to design the nature, timing, and extent of further audit procedures. Internal control is discussed further in the Internal Control Module.

4. **Supervision requirements.** Supervision includes instructing assistants, being informed on significant problems, reviewing audit work, and dealing with differences of opinion among audit personnel. The complexity of the audit and qualifications of audit assistants affect the degree of supervision needed. The work of each assistant should be reviewed (1) to determine whether it was adequately performed and (2) to evaluate whether the results are consistent with the conclusions to be presented in the audit report. Procedures should be established for documenting any disagreements of opinions among staff personnel; the basis for resolution of such disagreements should also be documented.

D. Assess the Risks of Material Misstatement and Design Further Audit Procedures

    The auditor should perform the risk assessment to identify and assess the risks of material misstatement at the financial statement level and at the relevant assertion level for classes of transactions, account balances, and disclosures; the approach is one of

- Identifying risks
- Relating the risks to what can go wrong at the relevant assertion level
- Considering whether the risks are of a magnitude that could result in a material misstatement
- Considering the likelihood that risks could result in material misstatements

    As a part of the risk assessment the auditor is required to identify significant risks that require special audit attention. Although determining the significant risks is a matter of professional judgment, the standards provide some guidance. Routine, noncomplex transactions that are subject to systematic processing are less likely to give rise to significant risks because they have lower inherent risks. Alternatively, significant risks are often derived from business risks that may result in a material misstatement. When evaluating risks, the auditor should consider

- Whether the risk is a risk of fraud
- Whether the risk is related to recent significant economic, accounting or other developments
- The complexity of transactions
- Whether the risk involves significant transactions with related parties
- The degree of subjectivity in the measurement of financial information
- Whether the risk involves significant nonroutine transactions and judgmental matters, or otherwise appear to be unusual

    The "further audit procedures" that are designed are of two types—substantive procedures and tests of controls. When the risk assessment is based on an expectation that controls are operating effectively, the auditor should perform tests of controls to provide evidence on whether those controls are operating effectively—this is discussed further in the Internal Control Module.

    Details on types of substantive tests are presented in the Responding to Risk Assessment Module.

E. Quality Control

1. The Statements on Quality Control Standards (SQCS) apply to the auditing and accounting (compilation and review) practice of CPA firms. While the generally accepted auditing standards and the *Code of Professional Con-*

duct are primarily directed at the **individual practitioner** level, the quality control standards apply to the CPA **firm** itself.

Members of the AICPA who are in public practice and have financial reporting responsibilities must have a sample of their accounting (compilations and reviews) and auditing work reviewed by an independent party. To meet this requirement CPA firms undergo a **peer review** performed directly by a CPA, a CPA firm, or a team of CPAs. There are two types of peer reviews: *system review* and *engagement review*. A *system review* involves peer reviewers' study and appraisal of a CPA firm's system of quality control to perform accounting and auditing work; in essence, the quality control standards serve as the criteria for a system review. The approach of the peer reviewers in a system review is to obtain an understanding of the CPA firm through inquiry of CPA firm personnel, review of documentation about the quality control system (e.g., firm manuals), and selection of a sample of the CPA firm's engagements for review. Subsequently a report is issued by the peer reviewers. A pass rating provides reasonable assurance in that it includes the peer reviewers' opinion that the system is appropriately designed and is being complied with by the CPA firm in all material respects. A pass with deficiencies rating differs in that it indicates that in certain situations (outlined in the report) the system is not appropriately designed or complied with. A fail rating indicates that the peer reviewer has determined that the CPA firm's system is not suitably designed or being complied with.

An *engagement review* is the second type of peer review. The peer reviewers select a sample of a CPA firm's actual accounting work, including accounting reports issued and CPA firm documentation to evaluate whether the reports and procedures are appropriate. This form of peer review is only available for CPA firms that do not perform audits, but do perform accounting work, including reviews and/or compilations. While, as is the case with a systems review, the report issued may be pass, pass with deficiencies, or fail as is the case with a systems review, the restricted nature of an engagement review results in a report in which the pass and pass with deficiencies reports include only limited (negative) assurance.

2. **Overall on a System of Quality Control**

   a. A firm must establish a system of quality control designed to provide it with reasonable assurance that it and its personnel comply with *professional standards and applicable regulatory and legal requirements* (hereafter, simply, "appropriate standards"), and that the firm or engagement partners issue *reports that are appropriate in the circumstances* (hereafter, "appropriate reports").

   b. Statements on Quality Control Standards (SQCSs)

      (1) Contain regulatory requirements and related explanatory material

         (a) *Regulatory requirements* are divided into two categories

            1] Unconditional requirements—the firm is required to comply (words such as *must* or *is required* are used).

            2] Presumptively mandatory requirements—the firm is required to comply, except for rare circumstances, in which it may depart, provided it documents justification for the departure and how alternative procedures were sufficient to achieve the objectives of the requirement (words such as "should" are used).

> **NOTE:** In addition, when the term "should consider" is used, consideration of the procedure is required, whereas carrying out the procedure is not.

         (b) *Explanatory material* in an SQCS provides further explanation or guidance or identifies and describes other procedures or actions relating to the activities of the firm; explanatory material is not intended to impose a professional requirement.

   c. The appropriate nature and extent of a CPA firm's quality control policies and procedures depends on factors such as the firm's size, the nature of its practice and cost/benefit considerations.

   d. Documentation

      (1) The firm should document its quality control policies and procedures.

         (a) The size, *structure*, and nature of the practice of the firm are important considerations in determining the extent of documentation necessary.

      (2) The firm should communicate its quality control policies and procedures to its personnel—although enhanced if it is in writing, it is **not** required to be in writing.

   e. Following are the elements of a firm's system of quality control:

      (1) Leadership responsibilities for quality with the firm ("tone at the top")
      (2) Relevant ethical requirements

    (3) Acceptance and continuance of client relationships and specific engagements
    (4) Human resources
    (5) Engagement performance
    (6) Monitoring

> **NOTE:** The following sections (3 through 8) describe each of the above elements.

3. **Quality Control Element 1: Leadership responsibilities for quality within the firm ("Tone at the top").**

   a. The firm's leadership (e.g., managing partner, chief executive officer, or equivalent) must assume ultimate responsibility for the firm's quality control.
   b. Policies should communicate that the firm's work must comply with appropriate standards and that appropriate reports are issued.

4. **Quality Control Element 2: Relevant ethical requirements.** The firm should establish policies and procedures to provide reasonable assurance that the firm and its personnel comply with relevant ethical requirements.

   a. The SQCS pay particular attention to the importance of providing reasonable assurance of maintaining independence.
   b. At least annually, the firm should obtain written confirmation of compliance with independence policies and procedures from firm personnel.

5. **Quality Control Element 3: Acceptance and continuance of client relationships and specific engagements.** Policies and procedures should provide reasonable assurance of accepting and continuing client relationships where the firm

   a. Has considered client integrity
   b. Is competent to perform the engagement
   c. Can comply with legal and ethical requirements

6. **Quality Control Element 4: Human resources.** The firm should establish policies and procedures to provide reasonable assurance that it has sufficient personnel with necessary capabilities, competence and commitment to ethical principles to (a) perform its engagements in accordance with appropriate standards and (b) enable it to issue appropriate reports. Such policies should address

   a. Recruiting
   b. Determining capabilities and competencies
   c. Assigning personnel to engagements
   d. Professional development
   e. Performance evaluation, compensation, and advancement

7. **Quality Control Element 5: Engagement performance.** The firm should establish policies and procedures to provide reasonable assurance that engagements are performed in accordance with appropriate standards and that appropriate reports are issued.

   a. Policies and procedures should address

       (1) Engagement performance
       (2) Supervision responsibilities
       (3) Review responsibilities

   b. The firm should establish policies and procedures designed to maintain confidentiality, safe custody, integrity, accessibility, and retrievability of engagement documentation.
   c. Controls should include

       (1) Clearly determining when and by whom documentation was prepared or reviewed
       (2) Protection of integrity of information
       (3) Prevention of unauthorized changes
       (4) Allowing access only to those authorized

   d. Consultation—Policies should exist as to consultation with individuals within and outside the firm who have relevant specialized expertise.
   e. Differences of opinion—Differences of opinion may arise within the engagement team, with those consulted, and between the engagement partner and the quality control reviewer.

       (1) Conclusions reached should be documented and implemented and the report should not be released until the matter is resolved.

    f. The firm should establish criteria against which all engagements covered by this statements are to be evaluated to *determine whether an engagement quality control review should be performed;* an engagement quality control review should include

        (1) Objective evaluation of significant judgments made by the engagement team and conclusions reached.

        (2) Reading the financial statements or other subject matter information.

        (3) Review of selected engagement documentation and a discussion with the engagement partner regarding significant findings and issues.

        (4) As necessary, addressing of additional issues such as independence, consultation, etc.

        (5) The quality control review should be properly documented.

8. **Quality Control Element 6: Monitoring.** A firm should establish policies and procedures designed to provide it with reasonable assurance that the policies and procedures relating to the system of quality control are relevant, adequate, operating effectively, and complied with in practice.

    a. Deficiencies identified during monitoring do not necessarily indicate that the system of quality control is insufficient to provide it with reasonable assurance that it complies with appropriate standards and are not necessarily systemic, requiring prompt corrective action.

        (1) Firm must consider the seriousness of such deficiencies.

    b. At least annually, the firm should communicate monitoring results to relevant engagement partners and other appropriate individuals within the firm. This should allow those individuals to take prompt and appropriate corrective action.

    c. A peer review conducted under AICPA standards may substitute for the inspection of engagement working papers, reports and clients' financial statements for some or all engagements for the period covered by the peer review.

9. **Documentation**. The firm should establish policies and procedures requiring appropriate documentation to provide evidence of the operation of each elements of its system of quality control.

NOW REVIEW MULTIPLE-CHOICE QUESTIONS 88 THROUGH 113 IN VOLUME 2

KEY TERMS

    Accounting estimate. An approximation of a monetary amount in the absence of a precise means of measurement. This term is used for an amount measured at fair value where there is estimation uncertainty, as well as for other amounts that require estimation.

    Analytical procedures. Evaluations of financial information through analysis of plausible relationships among both financial and nonfinancial data. Analytical procedures also encompass such investigation, as is necessary, of identified fluctuations or relationships that are inconsistent with other relevant information or that differ from expected values by a significant amount.

    Assertions. Representations by management, explicit or otherwise, that are embodied in the financial statements, as used by the auditor to consider the different types of potential misstatements that may occur.

    Audit evidence. Information used by the auditor in arriving at the conclusions on which the auditor's opinion is based. Audit evidence includes both information contained in the accounting records underlying the financial statements and other information:

    a. Sufficiency of audit evidence is the measure of the quantity of audit evidence. The quantity of the audit evidence needed is affected by the auditor's assessment of the risks of material misstatement and also by the quality of such audit evidence.

    b. Appropriateness of audit evidence is the measure of the quality of audit evidence; that is, its relevance and its reliability in providing support for the conclusions on which the auditor's opinion is based.

    Audit plan. A description of the nature, timing, and extent of the audit procedures to be performed. It is often documented with an audit program.

    Audit program. A detailed listing of the specific audit procedures to be performed in the course of an audit engagement. Audit programs are tailored to the risks and internal control of each engagement.

    Audit risk. The risk that the auditor expresses an inappropriate audit opinion when the financial statements are materially misstated. Audit risk is a function of the risks of material misstatement and detection risk.

    Audit strategy. The approach which involves determining overall characteristics of an audit that define its scope, its reporting objectives, timing of procedures and various important factors relating to the audit. When the overall audit strategy has been established, the auditors start the development of a more detailed audit plan to address the various matters identified in the audit strategy.

Control risk. The risk that a misstatement that could occur in an assertion about a class of transaction, account balance, or disclosure and that could be material, either individually or when aggregated with other misstatements, will not be prevented, or detected and corrected, on a timely basis by the entity's internal control.

Detection risk. The risk that the procedures performed by the auditor to reduce audit risk to an acceptably low level will not detect a misstatement that exists and that could be material, either individually or when aggregated with other misstatements.

Engagement letter. A formal letter sent by the auditors to the client at the beginning of an engagement summarizing such matters as the nature of the engagement, any limitations on the scope of the audit work, work to be performed by the client's staff, and the basis for the audit fee. The purpose of engagement letters is to avoid misunderstandings.

Fraud. An intentional act by one or more individuals among management, those charged with governance, employees, or third parties, involving the use of deception that results in a misstatement in financial statements that are subject of an audit. For financial statement audits, fraud includes two types of intentional misstatements—misstatements arising from fraudulent financial reporting and misstatements arising from misappropriation of assets.

Fraud risk factors. Events or conditions that indicate an incentive or pressure to perpetrate fraud, provide an opportunity to commit fraud, or indicate attitudes or rationalizations to justify a fraudulent action.

Fraudulent financial reporting (management fraud, cooking the books). Material misstatement of financial statements by management with the intent to mislead financial statement users.

Further audit procedures. The additional procedures that are performed based on the results of the auditors' risk assessment procedures. Such procedures include (1) tests of controls (if needed), (2) Detailed tests of transactions, balances, and disclosures and (3) substantive analytical procedures.

Historical financial information. Information expressed in financial terms in relation to a particular entity, derived primarily from that entity's accounting system, about economic events occurring in past time periods or about economic conditions or circumstances at points in time in the past.

Inherent risk. The susceptibility of an assertion about a class of transaction, account balance, or disclosure to a misstatement that could be material, either individually or when aggregated with other misstatements, before consideration of any related controls.

Materiality. The magnitude of an omission or misstatement of accounting information that, in the light of surrounding circumstances, makes it probably that the judgment of a reasonable person relying on the information would have been changed or influenced by the omission or misstatements.

Misappropriation of assets (defalcations). Theft of client assets by an employee or officer of the organization.

Misstatement. A difference between the amount, classification, presentation, or disclosure of a reported financial statement item and the amount, classification, presentation, or disclosure that is required for the item to be in accordance with the applicable financial reporting framework. Misstatements can arise from error or fraud. Misstatements also include those adjustments of amounts, classifications, presentations, or disclosures that, in the auditor's judgment, are necessary for the financial statements to be presented fairly, in all material respects.

  a. **Factual misstatements**—Misstatements about which there is no doubt.
  b. **Judgmental misstatements.** Differences arising from the judgments of management concerning accounting estimates that the auditor considers unreasonable or the selection or application of accounting policies that the auditor considers inappropriate.
  c. **Projected misstatements.** The auditor's best estimate of misstatements in populations, involving the projection of misstatements identified in audit samples to the entire population from which the samples were drawn. For example, if statistical sampling was used with receivables, the difference between auditor estimated total audited value and the book value of receivables is the projected misstatement.

Noncompliance. Acts of omission or commission by the entity, either intentional or unintentional, which are contrary to the prevailing laws or regulations. Such acts involve transactions entered into by, or in the name of the entity, or on its behalf, by those charged with governance, management, or employees. Noncompliance does not include personal misconduct (unrelated to the business activities of the entity) by those charged with governance, management, or employees of the entity.

Predecessor auditor. A CPA firm that formerly served as auditor but has resigned from the engagement or has been notified that its services have been terminated.

Professional judgment. The application of relevant training, knowledge, and experience, within the context provided by auditing, accounting, and ethical standards, in making informed decisions about the courses of action that are appropriate in the circumstances of the audit engagement.

Professional skepticism. An attitude that includes a questioning mind, being alert to conditions that may indicate possible misstatement due to fraud or error, and a critical assessment of audit evidence.

Quality control standards. AICPA standards designed to provide reasonable assurance that all of a CPA firm's engagements are conducted in accordance with applicable professional responsibilities.

Reasonable assurance. In the context of an audit of financial statements, a high, but not absolute, level of assurance.

Relevant assertion. A financial statement assertion that has a reasonable possibility of containing a misstatement or misstatements that would cause the financial statements to be materially misstated. The determination of whether an assertion is a relevant assertion is made without regard to the effect of controls.

Risk assessment procedures. The audit procedures performed to obtain an understanding of the entity and its environment, including the entity's internal control, to identify and assess the risks of material misstatement, whether due to fraud or error, at the financial statement and assertion levels.

Risk of material misstatement. The risk that the financial statements are materially misstated prior to the audit. This consists of two components, inherent risk and control risk.

Significant risk. An identified and assessed risk of material misstatement that, in the auditor's judgment, requires special audit consideration.

Substantive procedure. An audit procedure designed to detect material misstatements at the assertion level. Substantive procedures comprise tests of details (classes of transactions, account balances, and disclosures) and substantive analytical procedures.

Successor auditor. The auditors who have accepted an engagement to replace the CPA firm that formally served as auditor (the predecessor auditor).

Tests of controls. An audit procedure designed to evaluate the operating effectiveness of controls in preventing, or detecting/correcting material misstatements at the assertion level.

Module 3: Understanding Internal Control and Assessing Control Risk

Overview

The second fieldwork standard states

> A sufficient understanding of the entity and its environment, including **internal control,** to assess the risk of material misstatement of the financial statements whether due to error fraud, to design the nature, timing and extent of further audit procedures

AU 314 and AU 318 provide auditors with information in which a client's internal control affects financial statement audits. The guidance first is about obtaining an understanding of the entity including its internal control to help auditors to assess the risk of material misstatement and to design the nature, timing and extent of further audit procedures—this material is in Sections C through E of the outline of AU 314.

Next, AU 318 (see Sections B and C of outline) provides auditors with guidance on the nature of further audit procedures as they relate to internal control (i.e., tests of controls).

The following "Diagram of an Audit," originally presented in the auditing overview section, shows the relationship of internal control to an audit:

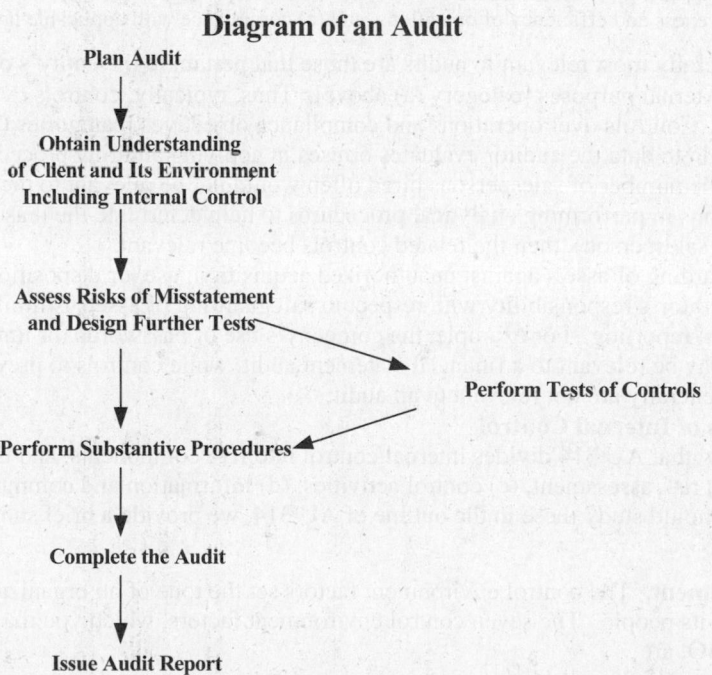

Diagram of an Audit

This module covers obtaining an understanding of internal control and tests of controls. It also develops the relationships among internal control and further audit tests—tests of controls, and substantive tests. Every CPA examination includes numerous questions on internal control and its relationship to various portions of the audit. Multiple-choice questions frequently require specification of a control that would, if present and operating properly, detect a stated weakness or error. Objective questions also have appeared regarding organization responsibility (e.g., who should distribute payroll checks?). A simulation may include a requirement to complete a flowchart of a transaction cycle, evaluate strengths and weaknesses of a system, and/or determine appropriate tests of controls and substantive tests.

Although it is extremely important that you understand the entire outlines of both AU 314 and AU 318, for purposes of this module the sections indicated earlier (C for AU 314 and B for AU 318) are most directly related to this module.

In Section A of this module we begin with the key concepts related to an entity's internal control. In Section B we review the approach suggested by the professional standards for considering internal control in a financial statement audit. Information on audits of internal control is presented in Section C. The Section D discussion is meant to provide you with information that will help you to respond to "applied type" questions that involve actual accounting cycles. Section E involves communications with audit committees, the effects of an internal audit function on an audit, and reports on the processing of transactions by service organizations.

The following SAS sections pertain to internal control and are discussed in this module.

AU Section

AU 314	Understanding the Entity and Its Environment and Assessing the Risks of Material Misstatement
322	The Auditor's Consideration of the Internal Audit Function in an Audit of Financial Statements
324	Reports on the Processing of Transactions by Service Organizations
325	Communication of Internal Control Related Matters Noted in an Audit
318	Performing Audit Procedures in Response to Assessed Risks and Evaluating the Audit Evidence Obtained
380	The Auditor's Communication with Those Charged with Governance
AT 501	An Examination of an Entity's Internal Control over Financial Reporting That Is Integrated with an Audit of Its Financial Statements

A. The Nature of Internal Control

AU 314 and AU 318 present information on (1) the nature of internal control and (2) the auditor's consideration of internal control. In this section we begin by discussing material related to the first area—the nature of internal control. Finally, we present several important, related topics.

1. Definition of Internal Control

AU 314 uses the definition of internal control included in *Internal Control—Integrated Framework*, published by the Committee of Sponsoring Organizations of the Treadway Commission (the COSO Commission). It defines internal control as

> a process—effected by an entity's board of directors, management, and other personnel—designed to provide reasonable assurance regarding the achievement of objectives in the following categories: (a) reliability of financial reporting, (b) effectiveness and efficiency of operations, and (c) compliance with applicable laws and regulations.

The controls generally most relevant to audits are those that pertain to the entity's objective of preparing financial statements for external purposes [category (a) above]. Thus, typically, controls over **financial reporting** are relevant to the audit. Controls over operations and compliance objectives [categories (b) and (c) above] may be relevant if they pertain to data the auditor evaluates or uses in applying auditing procedures. For example, while controls relating to the number of salespersons hired often would not be relevant to the audit, if the auditor uses the number of salespersons in performing analytical procedures to help determine the reasonableness of sales (e.g., by calculating sales per salesperson), then the related controls become relevant.

While the safeguarding of assets against unauthorized acquisition, use, or disposition is an essential part of internal control, the auditor's responsibility with respect to safeguarding of assets is limited to those relevant to the reliability of financial reporting. For example, the company's use of passwords for limiting access to accounts receivable data files may be relevant to a financial statement audit, while controls to prevent the excess use of materials in production generally are not relevant to an audit.

2. Major Components of Internal Control

You need to know that AU 314 divides internal control into five components, and the nature of each—(a) control environment, (b) risk assessment, (c) control activities, (d) information and communication, and (e) monitoring. Although you should study these in the outline of AU 314, we provide a brief summary of each of them at this point.

   a. **Control environment.** The control environment factors set the tone of an organization, influencing the control consciousness of its people. The seven control environment factors, which you may remember using the mnemonic IC HAMBO, are

I	-	Integrity and ethical values
C	-	Commitment to competence
H	-	Human resource policies and practices
A	-	Assignment of authority and responsibility
M	-	Management's philosophy and operating style
B	-	Board of directors or audit committee participation
O	-	Organizational structure

b. **Risk assessment.** For financial reporting purposes an entity's risk assessment is its identification, analysis, and management of risks relevant to the preparation of financial statements following GAAP (or some other comprehensive basis). The following are considered risks that may affect an entity's ability to properly record, process, summarize, and report financial data:

(1) Changes in the operating environment (e.g., increased competition)
(2) New personnel
(3) New information systems
(4) Rapid growth
(5) New technology
(6) New lines, products, or activities
(7) Corporate restructuring
(8) Foreign operations
(9) Accounting pronouncements

c. **Control activities.** The third component of internal control is composed of the various policies and procedures that help ensure that necessary actions are taken to address risks to achieving the entity's objectives. Those policies and procedures include

P - Performance reviews (reviews of actual performance against budgets, forecasts, one another, etc.)
I - Information processing (controls that check accuracy, completeness, and authorization of transactions)
P - Physical controls (activities that assure the physical security of assets and records)
S - Segregation of duties (separate authorization, recordkeeping, and custody)

d. **Information and communication.** The fourth component includes the accounting system, consisting of the methods and records established to **record, process, summarize, and report** entity transactions and to maintain accountability of the related assets and liabilities. To be effective, the information and communication system must accomplish the following goals for transactions:

(1) Identify and record all valid transactions
(2) Describe on a timely basis
(3) Measure the value properly
(4) Record in the proper time period
(5) Properly present and disclose
(6) Communicate responsibilities to employees

e. **Monitoring.** Monitoring assesses the quality of internal control performance over time. Monitoring activities may be **ongoing, separate evaluations**, or a **combination** thereof. Ongoing monitoring activities are often designed into recurring activities such as sales and purchases. **Separate evaluations** are often performed by internal auditors or other personnel and often include communication of information about strengths and weaknesses and recommendations for improving internal control. Monitoring activities may also be performed by external parties (e.g., customers implicitly corroborate billing data by paying invoices).

3. **Related Topics**

a. **Financial statement assertions.** As presented in the Engagement Planning Module, and discussed in further detail in the Responding to Risk Assessment Module, assertions are management representations that are embodied in the transaction class, account balance, and disclosure components of financial statements. For example, for account balances, the assertions include existence, rights/obligations, completeness, and valuation/allocation. The approach embodied in the auditing standards is one of suggesting that for each transaction class, account, or disclosure the auditor determines relevant assertions and then considers the related controls. A control seldom relates to all important assertions. A control over processing sales orders might, for example, be effective at determining the **existence of receivables** (e.g., there was a sale), but would not directly address receivables **valuation** (because collection may be questionable), or **completeness** (whether all receivables have been recorded).

b. **Limitations of internal control.** As we have suggested earlier, internal control provides reasonable, but not absolute, assurance that specific entity objectives will be achieved. Even the best internal control may break down due to

(1) Human judgment in decision making can be faulty
(2) Breakdowns can occur because of human failures such as simple errors or mistakes
(3) Controls, whether manual or automated, can be circumvented by collusion
(4) Management has the ability to override internal control
(5) Cost constraints (the cost of internal control should not exceed the expected benefits expected to be derived)

(6) Custom, culture, and the corporate governance system may inhibit fraud, but they are not absolute deterrents

> **NOTE:** Be familiar with these limitations.

c. **Accounting vs. administrative control.** Previously, the AICPA Professional Standards distinguished between administrative and accounting controls, stating that auditors generally emphasize the latter. While the distinction no longer remains for purposes of the professional standards, it does remain in certain laws, such as the Foreign Corrupt Practices Act.

d. **Foreign Corrupt Practices Act.** A law passed by Congress in 1977 with provisions

   (1) Requiring every corporation registered under the Securities Exchange Act of 1934 to maintain a system of strong internal accounting control (as defined above),
   (2) Requiring corporations [defined in (1)] to maintain accurate books and records, and
   (3) Making it illegal for individuals or business entities to make payments to foreign officials to secure business.

   Violations of the Act can result in fines (up to $1 million for SEC registrants and $10,000 for individuals) and imprisonment (up to five years) of the responsible individuals. Thus, strong internal accounting control is required under federal law.

e. **Committee of Sponsoring Organizations (COSO).** This committee is composed of representatives from various professional organizations, including the AICPA, the Institute of Management Accountants, the Financial Executives Institute, the Institute of Internal Auditors, and the American Accounting Association. COSO commissioned a study for the purpose of integrating various internal control concepts and definitions being used in the business community. The purposes of the study are to establish a common definition of internal control and to provide a standard against which business and other entities can assess internal control. The definition that COSO developed is included in AU 314.

f. **Sarbanes-Oxley Act of 2002 (SOX).** As indicated in Chapter 5, the SOX created a variety of new regulations and eliminated a significant portion of the accounting profession's system of self-regulation. Three particularly relevant sections are

   (1) **Section 302:** Makes officers responsible for maintaining effective internal control and requires the principal executive and financial officers to disclose all significant internal control deficiencies to the company's auditors and audit committee.
   (2) **Section 404:** Requires that management acknowledge its responsibility for establishing adequate internal control over financial reporting and provide an assessment in the annual report of the effectiveness of internal control. Also requires that CPAs attest to management's report on internal control as part of the audit of the financial statements—discussed further in Section D.2 of this module.
   (3) **Section 906:** Requires that management certify reports filed with the SEC (primarily annual 10-K and quarterly 10-Qs) that the reports comply with relevant securities laws and also fairly present, in all material respects, the financial condition and results of operations of the company.

> **NOW REVIEW MULTIPLE-CHOICE QUESTIONS 1 THROUGH 9 IN VOLUME 2**

B. The Auditor's Consideration of Internal Control

AU 314 presents the auditor's consideration of internal control (this begins at Section B in the AU 314 outline). Recall that after planning the audit, auditors

- Obtain an understanding of the entity and its environment, including its internal control
- Assess the risks of material misstatement and design further audit procedures
- Perform further audit procedures, including tests of controls and substantive tests

Internal control is a part of each of these stages. Auditors obtain an understanding of internal control to aid them in their assessment of the risks of material misstatement and to design further audit procedures. Tests of controls, performed to determine whether controls operate effectively, are further audit procedures. While the auditor's consideration of internal control may become quite involved, we will summarize the auditor's approach using the above steps.

If the auditor is performing an audit of a public company, the approach to internal control will be somewhat different. Section C covers the auditor's approach to the audit of a public company.

The relationships among these steps are presented in the flowchart below. We now discuss them in detail.

**SUMMARY FLOWCHART OF INTERNAL CONTROL CONSIDERATION
DURING A FINANCIAL STATEMENT AUDIT**

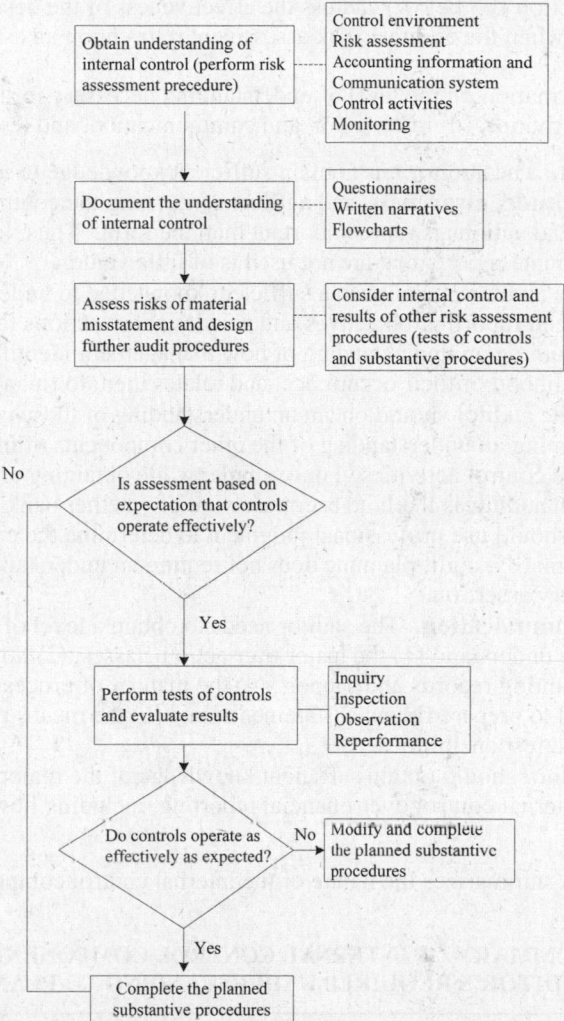

1. **Obtain an understanding of internal control.** As discussed in Module 2, this understanding is obtained as a part of the overall understanding of the entity and its environment. Here we emphasize the internal control portion and its interaction with other audit procedures.

   The auditor performs risk assessment procedures to obtain an understanding of the five components of internal control sufficient to assess the risk of material misstatement of the financial statements, and to design the nature, timing and extent of further audit procedures. Risk assessment procedures for internal control include

   - Inquiries of management and others within the entity
   - Observing the application of specific controls
   - Inspecting documents and records
   - Tracing transactions through the information system

   The knowledge obtained through risk assessment procedures is used to

   - Identify types of potential misstatements
   - Consider factors that affect the risk of material misstatement
   - Design tests of controls and substantive procedures

   Auditor experience in previous years with the entity may also help auditors to assess the risk of material misstatement.

   At this point in the audit, the above procedures are performed primarily to help the auditor to understand the design and whether the controls have been *implemented* (previously referred to as placed in operation). AU 314 distinguishes between determining that controls have been implemented vs. evaluating their operating effectiveness. In determining whether controls have been implemented, the auditor determines that the entity is using them. This is all that is necessary for obtaining an understanding of internal control.

In evaluating operating effectiveness, the auditor goes further and considers (1) how the control was applied; (2) the consistency with which it was applied; and (3) by whom (or what means) it is applied. Tests of controls (described in detail in Section B.3 below) address the effectiveness of the design and operation of a control. Tests of controls are necessary when the auditor's risk assessment relies upon an assumption that controls operate effectively.

AU 314 provides information on the level of understanding necessary for the (a) control environment, (b) risk assessment, (c) control activities, (d) information and communication, and (e) monitoring.

a. **Control environment.** The auditor must obtain sufficient knowledge to understand management's and the board of director's **attitude, awareness,** and **actions** concerning the control environment. The substance of the policies, procedures, and actions is more important than the form. Thus, for example, a budget reporting system that provides adequate reports that are not used is of little value.

b. **Risk assessment.** The auditor must obtain a sufficient knowledge to understand how management considers risks relevant to financial reporting objectives and decides about actions to address those risks. This knowledge generally includes obtaining an understanding of how management identifies risks, estimates the significance of risks, assesses the likelihood of their occurrence, and relates them to financial reporting.

c. **Control activities.** The auditor should obtain an understanding of those control activities relevant to planning the audit. While obtaining an understanding of the other components of internal control, the auditor obtains knowledge about some control activities. For example, while obtaining an understanding of accounting for cash disbursements, an auditor is likely to become aware of whether bank accounts are reconciled (a control activity). An auditor should use professional judgment to determine the extent of additional knowledge needed to plan the audit. Ordinarily, audit planning does not require an understanding of control activities related to each account or to every assertion.

d. **Information and communication.** The auditor needs to obtain a level of knowledge of the information system and communication to understand (1) the major transaction classes, (2) how those transactions are initiated, (3) the available accounting records and support, (4) the manner of processing of transactions, (5) the financial reporting process used to prepare financial statements, and (6) the means the entity uses to communicate financial reporting roles and responsibilities.

e. **Monitoring.** The auditor should obtain sufficient knowledge of the major types of monitoring activities the entity uses to monitor internal control over financial reporting, including how those activities are used to initiate corrective action.

The following illustration summarizes the nature of the internal control components and the auditor's planning responsibility.

SUMMARY OF INTERNAL CONTROL COMPONENTS AND
THE AUDITOR'S REQUIRED UNDERSTANDING TO PLAN THE AUDIT

	Summary of Components	Auditor's Required Understanding to Plan Audit
Overall Internal Control for Financial Reporting	Objective is to prepare financial statements for external purposes that are fairly presented in conformity with GAAP (or another comprehensive basis)	Obtain knowledge about design and whether controls have been implemented; the understanding should be adequate to allow the auditor to (1) Identify types of potential misstatements (2) Consider factors affecting risk of material misstatements (3) Design effective substantive tests
Control Environment	Factors • Integrity and ethical values • Commitment to competence • Human resource policies and practices • Assignment of authority and responsibility • Management's philosophy and operating style • Board of directors or audit committee participation • Organizational structure	Obtain sufficient knowledge to understand management and board of directors (1) Attitudes (2) Awareness (3) Actions
Risk Assessment	The identification, analysis, and management of risks relevant to the preparation of financial statements following GAAP	Obtain understanding of how management (1) Identifies risks (2) Estimates the significance of the risks (3) Assesses the likelihood of occurrence

	Summary of Components	Auditor's Required Understanding to Plan Audit
Control Activities	Policies and procedures that pertain to • Performance reviews • Information processing • Physical controls • Segregation of duties	Obtain additional understanding as necessary to plan the audit. Ordinarily, an understanding of control activities related to each account or to every assertion is not necessary.
Information and Communication	Methods to record, process, summarize, and report transactions, which include • Identify and record all valid transactions • Describe on a timely basis • Measure the value properly • Record in the proper time period • Properly present and disclose • Communicate responsibilities to employees	Obtain understanding of (1) Major transaction classes (2) How transactions are initiated (3) Available accounting records and support (4) Manner of processing of transactions (5) Financial reporting process used to prepare financial statements (6) Means the entity uses to communicate financial reporting roles and responsibilities
Monitoring	Methods to consider whether controls are operating as intended	Obtain sufficient understanding of major types of monitoring activities

Procedures for obtaining an understanding. The auditor relies primarily upon a combination of (1) previous experience with the entity, (2) inquiries, (3) inspection of documents and records, and (4) observation of entity activities to obtain the needed understanding of the internal control. At this point in the audit, these procedures are performed primarily to help the auditor to understand the design and whether the controls have been **implemented**.

AU 314 points out that while obtaining an understanding of the design of a control, including whether it has been implemented, an auditor may either by plan or by chance obtain some information on operating effectiveness. For example, while making inquiries about the design of the client's budgeting system and whether it has been implemented, an auditor may have obtained evidence on the effectiveness of the control in preventing or detecting expense misclassifications. Thus, its operating effectiveness has been tested. In this manner, in essence, some **tests of controls** may have been concurrently performed with obtaining an understanding of internal control.

Documentation of understanding of internal control. The auditor's documentation of his/her understanding of internal control for purposes of planning the audit is influenced by the size and complexity of the entity, as well as the nature of the entity's internal control. For a small client a memorandum may be sufficient. For a larger client, flowcharts, questionnaires, and decision tables may be needed. The more complex the internal control and the more extensive the procedures performed by the auditor, the more extensive should be the documentation. The advantages and disadvantages of using questionnaires, memoranda, and/or flowchart methods are as follows:

Method	Advantages	Disadvantages
Questionnaire	1. Easy to complete 2. Comprehensive list of questions make it unlikely that important portions of internal control will be overlooked 3. Weaknesses become obvious (generally those questions answered with a "no")	1. May be answered without adequate thought being given to questions 2. Questions may not "fit" client adequately
Memoranda	1. Tailor-made for engagement 2. Requires a detailed analysis and thus forces auditor to understand functioning of structure	1. May become very long and time-consuming 2. Weaknesses in structure not always obvious 3. Auditor may overlook important portions of internal control
Flowchart	1. Graphic representation of structure 2. Usually makes it unlikely that important portions of internal control will be overlooked 3. Good for electronic systems 4. No long wording (as in case of memoranda)	1. Preparation is time-consuming 2. Weaknesses in structure not always obvious (especially to inexperienced auditor)

NOTE: Flowcharts, including symbols, are discussed in the Auditing with Technology Module.

In addition to questionnaires, memoranda, and flowcharts, auditors may prepare "decision tables" to document their understanding of internal control. Decision tables are graphic methods of describing the logic of decisions.

Various combinations of **conditions** are matched to one of several **actions**. In an internal control setting, the various important controls are reviewed and, based on the combination of answers received, an action is taken, perhaps a decision on whether to perform tests of controls. The following extremely simplified table will provide you with the information you need for the CPA exam (note, for example, in the case of segregation of functions, a series of detailed segregation conditions—not one summary—would be used).

Conditions		Rules						
		1	2	3	4	5	6	7
(1)	Segregation of function adequate	y	y	y	y	n	n	n
(2)	Adequate documents	y	y	n	n	y	y	n
(3)	Independent checks on performance	y	n	y	n	y	n	-

Actions		Rules						
		1	2	3	4	5	6	7
(1)	Perform all relevant tests of controls	x						
(2)	Perform limited tests of controls		x	x		x		
(3)	Perform no tests of controls				x		x	x

Note that for decision rule 7, after the first two conditions have received "nos" it doesn't matter what the third condition is—tests of controls will not be used. Also, while a decision table is an efficient means of describing the logic of an internal control process, it does not provide an analysis of document flow as does a flowchart.

2. **Assess risks of material misstatement and design further audit procedures.** In Section D of Module 2 we discussed in general terms the process of assessing the risks of material misstatement and designing further audit procedures (tests of controls and substantive procedures). On an overall basis the auditors should perform the risk assessment to identify and assess the risks of material misstatement at the financial statement level and at the relevant assertion level for classes of transactions, account balances, and disclosures; the approach is one of

- Identifying risks
- Relating the risks to what can go wrong at the relevant assertion level
- Considering whether the risks are of a magnitude that could result in a material misstatement
- Considering the likelihood that risks could result in material misstatements

The effectiveness of internal control is important in many situations since particular controls may lessen the likelihood that risks could result in material misstatements (the final bullet). As an example, consider an auditor who identifies a risk of overstated sales. Further, assume that the client has implemented a control with the objective of only allowing proper sales to be recorded. Here the likelihood of material misstatements is affected by the operating effectiveness of the control. In this type of situation the auditors will consider the appropriate combination of tests of controls and substantive procedures to perform.

The decision sequence for considering internal control for the assertions related to classes of transactions, account balances and disclosures depends upon whether controls such as that described in the preceding paragraph appear effective. If the control appears effective, tests of controls will be performed

- When the auditor's risk assessment *includes an expectation of operating effectiveness* of controls because the likelihood of material misstatement is lower if the control operates effectively, *or*
- When substantive procedures alone do not provide sufficient audit evidence.

In the first situation, an auditor's risk assessment will include an expectation of operating effectiveness when the auditor believes that such operating effectiveness decreases the likelihood of material misstatement and that testing such controls is likely to be cost effective. But, since tests of controls alone are not normally sufficient, the further audit procedures will be composed of a combination of tests of controls and substantive procedures. Thus, the decision to perform tests of controls will be made when the auditor believes that a combination of tests of controls and a decreased scope of substantive procedures is likely to be more cost effective than performing more extensive substantive procedures or when this is the only viable approach. The overall approach here, as it relates to controls is to (1) identify controls that are relevant to specific assertions that are likely to prevent or detect material misstatements, and (2) perform tests of controls to evaluate the effectiveness of those controls.

Alternatively, the risk assessment may **not** include an expectation that controls operate effectively. This will be the case when (1) controls appear weak, or (2) the auditor believes that performing extensive substantive procedures is likely to be more cost effective than performing a combination of tests of controls and a decreased scope of substantive procedures. When the risk assessment does not include an expectation that controls operate effectively, further audit procedures will consist entirely of substantive procedures. No evidence on the operating effectiveness of the controls need then be gathered; that is, no tests of controls will be performed. If a separate assessment of control risk is made, control risk is at the maximum level and the auditor will design substantive tests placing no reliance upon the controls operating effectively.

When designing further audit procedures the auditor may design a test of controls to be performed concurrently with a substantive procedure test of details on the same transaction. The objective of tests of controls is to evaluate whether a control operated effectively. The objective of tests of details is to support relevant assertions or detect material misstatements at the assertion level. Although these objectives differ, both may be accomplished concurrently through performance of a test of controls and a test of details on the same transaction; this is known as a **dual purpose test.** For example, an auditor may examine an invoice to determine whether it has been properly approved (a test of a control) and to provide substantive evidence of a transaction (a test of details).

At this point in the audit, the auditor has obtained the needed understanding of internal control. During this process the effectiveness of some controls may have been tested (i.e., some tests of controls may have been performed). If this is the case, the auditors in essence are already using a combination approach involving both tests of controls and substantive tests.

3. **Perform tests of controls.** Tests of controls are used to test either the effectiveness of the design or operation of a control. Approaches include

   a. **Inquiries** of appropriate personnel
   b. **Inspection** of documents and reports
   c. **Observation** of the application of controls
   d. **Reperformance** of the control by the auditor (when evaluating operation)

To illustrate the nature of tests of controls, assume that the client has implemented the control of requiring a second person to review the quantities, prices, extensions, and footing of each sales invoice. The purpose of this control is to prevent material misstatements in the billing of customers and the recording of sales transactions. By using the first approach, inquiry, the auditor would discuss with appropriate client personnel the manner in which the control functions. Generally, because of the indirect nature of the information obtained, inquiry alone is not considered to provide credible enough evidence to conclude on operating effectiveness of controls.

The remaining approaches, inspection, observation, and reperformance, may be illustrated by assuming that a sample of sixty sales invoices has been selected from throughout the year. The auditor might inspect the invoices and determine whether evidence exists that the procedures have been performed (e.g., invoices bearing initials of the individual who reviewed them). Another option is to observe applications of the procedures being applied to the invoices. Note that for controls that leave no documentary trail (e.g., segregation of functions in certain circumstances) inquiry and observation may become the only feasible approaches. Finally, the auditors may reperform the procedure by comparing quantities shown on each invoice to the quantities listed on the related shipping documents, by comparing unit prices to the client's price lists, and by verifying the extensions and footings.

Timeliness of evidence. For reasons of efficiency and practicality, auditors often perform tests of controls at an interim date prior to year-end and then update them to the extent considered necessary at year-end. Also, pertaining to observation approach, note that for many situations only a limited number of observations of individuals performing controls are practical. The auditor must realize that generalizing tests of controls results beyond the periods sampled is risky. It is for this reason that auditors must consider whether additional tests should be performed over untested periods to provide assurance that controls functioned over the entire period.

Audit evidence on operating effectiveness from a prior period. Is an auditor allowed to use the results of prior years' tests of controls in the current audit? PCAOB auditing standards do not allow this. Auditing Standards Board standards allow this in limited circumstances. If the auditor of a nonpublic company plans to use audit evidence about the operating effectiveness of controls obtained in prior audits, the auditor should obtain audit evidence about whether changes in those specific controls have occurred subsequent to the prior audit. When controls have changed since they were last tested, the auditor should test the operating effectiveness of such controls in the current audit. In circumstances in which controls have not changed since they were last tested, the auditor should test the operating effectiveness of such controls at least once in every three years. That is, the auditor should test a control at least once in every third year in an annual audit.

IT controls. Ordinarily an auditor tests a control multiple times to arrive at a conclusion concerning operating effectiveness (e.g., 60 sales invoices). When a control is performed by the computer, must an auditor test the automated control numerous times to conclude on operating effectiveness? No. Generally IT processing is inherently consistent; therefore, the auditor may be able to limit the testing to one or a few instances of the control operation. Note here, however, that an auditor must have confidence that the control operated in the same manner throughout the period (e.g., a computer program didn't inappropriately disable it during part of the period). Also, the timing of tests of controls (and substantive procedures) may be affected by irretrievability of certain client data after a certain period of time.

Evaluating the results of tests of controls. Based on the results of the tests of controls the auditor will determine whether it is necessary to modify substantive procedures. If tests of control reveal that the system operates as expected, there will generally be no need to change the scope of planned substantive procedures. Conversely, if the system does not operate as effectively as expected (control risk is higher than expected), the scope of substantive procedures for the relevant assertion(s) involved will increase (thereby decreasing detection risk).

The entire approach for the consideration of internal control (understand, assess the risks and design further audit procedures, perform tests of controls) may be illustrated through use of an example. Assume that you have been told by the controller that two secretaries are present and open all mail together each morning. These secretaries are supposed to prepare a list of all cash receipts, which is then to be forwarded to the accounts receivable clerk. The cash, according to the controller, is then given to the cashier who deposits it each day. Because you work in the area where the secretaries work, you have observed them following these procedures and conclude that the process seems to have been implemented. To keep the example simple, assume that base on this and other audit evidence you gathered while obtaining an understanding of internal control over receivables, controls seem strong. Assume that to this point you have performed no tests of controls. Thus, you must document your understanding of the structure and make a decision as to whether controls should be tested. Because no tests of controls have been performed, you initial assessment is that you have no evidence on operating effectiveness (control risk is at the maximum level).

Subsequently, you decide to perform tests of controls with the objective of determining whether the structure is actually in operation and may be relied upon. Also, assume you have decided that, if the results of your tests of controls indicate that the controls are operating as described, one substantive procedure will be performed. You intend to confirm 30 of the firm's 250 accounts receivable to verify their existence. That is, despite strong internal control, substantive procedures must generally still be performed.

However, now assume that when you performed your tests of controls by observing the opening of the mail, you discovered that the secretaries, in circumstances in which one is "busy," had decided to minimize their work by having the other individually perform the task periodically. Also, you discovered that the secretaries, when only a "limited" amount of cash is received, decided to omit the step of preparing a list of cash receipts and simply forwarded the receipts to the accounts receivable clerk who then forwarded them to the cashier who deposited them periodically.

You have discovered that the controls over cash receipts are **not** as strong as was indicated when you were gaining an understanding of internal control. In this situation, you might decide that a higher than acceptable likelihood exists that an embezzlement of cash receipts could occur; that is, control risk is high. You might then decide to increase the scope of your substantive procedures; you could, for example, confirm more accounts than originally had been planned. You might also decide to expand your investigation of bad debt write-offs to determine that accounts have not been collected and subsequently have been fraudulently written off. Note that if you had originally obtained a more accurate description of the actual functioning of the internal control over cash receipts, you might have decided to omit the tests of controls and have relied entirely upon substantive procedures, thus resulting in complete reliance upon substantive procedures.

4. **Summary.** The approach presented above may be summarized as follows:

Step 1. Obtain and document understanding of internal control

    (1) Study the control environment, risk assessment, control activities, information and communication, and monitoring
    (2) Document understanding of system—use flowcharts, memoranda, questionnaires, decision tables, etc.

Step 2. Assess risk of material misstatement and design further audit procedures

    (1) Risk assessment procedures are performed to assess the risk of material misstatement
    (2) Risk assessment procedures include inquiries of management and others within the entity, analytical procedures, observation and inspection, and other inquiries
    (3) Appropriate further procedures are designed—tests of controls and substantive procedures

Step 3. Perform tests of controls and evaluate results

    (1) Tests whether controls are operating effectively (through inquiry, inspection, observation, and reperformance)
    (2) Test of control results

    As expected—the planned substantive procedures will be performed

    Not as expected—the scope of planned substantive procedures will be modified and those procedures will be performed

NOW REVIEW MULTIPLE-CHOICE QUESTIONS 10 THROUGH 42 IN VOLUME 2

C. Audits (Examinations) of Internal Control

The Sarbanes-Oxley Act of 2002 created a requirement for an integrated audit of SEC registrants that provides assurance about the fairness of financial statements *and* about the effectiveness of internal control over financial reporting. The financial statement audit portion of the integrated audit is similar to any other financial statement audit, but its integrated nature means that auditors rely much more on internal control and less on substantive procedures.

Section 404 of the Sarbanes-Oxley act of 2002 requires internal control reporting by management and the auditor.

- Section 404a: Requires management to include its assessment of internal control in the annual report filed with the SEC.
- Section 404b: Requires the CPA firm to audit internal control and express an opinion on the effectiveness of internal control. As implemented, the Act applies to companies with a market capitalization of $75,000,000 or more.

Guidance to meet the auditor's responsibilities for reporting upon internal control of a public audit client ("an issuer") as a part of an integrated audit is provided by PCAOB Standard 5; guidance for a nonpublic company ("a nonissuer") is provided by AICPA Statement on Standards for Attestation Engagements (SSAE) 15. While integrated audits are required for public companies, they are not required for nonpublic companies unless required by some other regulatory body. Both PCAOB Standard 5 and SSAE 15 require when performing an audit of internal control that the auditor examine the design and operating effectiveness of internal control over financial reporting (hereafter IC or internal control) to provide a sufficient basis to issue an opinion on the effectiveness of IC in preventing or detecting material misstatements of the financial statements. Also, the report issued may be either a separate report on IC or combined with the audit report on the financial statements.

PCAOB Standard 5 and SSAE 15 are very similar to one another. Our approach here is to first present an outline of PCAOB Standard 5 (which essentially includes a summary of most of the key information in SSAE 15), and then provide a brief section presenting some of the differences between the two standards. The following serves as an overall outline of Standard 5 and a summary of the most important points of that standard and of SSAE 15.

1. General

   a. Objective of audit of IC—express an opinion on the effectiveness of the company's IC

      (1) To form a basis for such an opinion, the auditor must plan and perform the audit to obtain reasonable assurance about whether material weaknesses exist as of the date of management's assessment.
      (2) The existence of one or more material weaknesses leads to a conclusion that IC is not effective.

   b. The general group of GAAS are applicable (adequate training, independence, due professional care); the fieldwork and reporting standards for an audit of IC are established in Standard 5.

   c. Important terms

      (1) Deficiencies in IC

         (a) **Deficiency**—The design or operation of a control does not allow management or employees, in the normal course of performing their assigned functions, to prevent or detect misstatements on a timely basis. A deficiency is also referred to as a control deficiency in Standard 5.
         (b) **Significant deficiency**—A deficiency, or combination of deficiencies, in IC that is less severe than a material weakness, yet important enough to merit attention by those responsible for oversight of the company's financial reporting.
         (c) **Material weakness**— A deficiency, or combination of deficiencies, in IC such that there is *a reasonable possibility* that a material misstatement of the company's annual or interim financial statements will not be prevented or detected on a timely basis.

            1] A reasonable possibility is either "reasonably possible" or "probable" as those terms are used in SFAS 5, *Accounting for Contingencies.*
            2] Note that this definition of material weakness is slightly different from the AICPA definition.

      (2) **Control objective**—A specific target against which to evaluate the effectiveness of controls. A control objective for IC generally relates to a relevant assertion and states a criterion for evaluating whether the company's control procedures in a specific area provide reasonable assurance that a misstatement in that relevant assertion is prevented or detected on a timely basis.
      (3) **Management's assessment**—The assessment required under provisions of the Sarbanes-Oxley Act (Item 308(a)3 of Regulations S-B and S-K) that is included in management's annual report on internal control over financial reporting.
      (4) **Relevant assertion**—A financial statement assertion that has a reasonable possibility of containing misstatements that could cause the financial statements to be materially misstated (determination made without regard to the effect of controls).
      (5) **Significant accounts and disclosures**—An account or disclosure for which there is a reasonable possibility of material misstatement. The determination is based on inherent risk, without regard to the effect of controls.

   d. In summary, the standard may be viewed as having the following structure:

      - Plan the audit
      - Use a top-down approach to identify controls to test

- Test design and operating effectiveness of controls
- Evaluate identified deficiencies
- Wrap-up
- Report on internal control

> **NOTE:** Sections 2. through 7. of this outline describe the above bulleted points.

2. Plan the audit

   a. The opinion on internal control is as to whether internal control is effective at a point in time—the "as of date"—as contrasted to a period of time (e.g., the entire year). The as of date is the last day of the company's fiscal period.

   b. Similar to a typical audit of financial statements, the auditor should obtain an understanding of the company's industry, regulations affecting the company, the company's business, and recent changes in operations and internal control.

   c. Risk assessment underlies the entire audit process

      (1) As risk of material misstatement increases, so should the auditor's attention to that area.
      (2) The risk that a company's IC will fail to prevent or detect misstatement caused by *fraud* usually is higher than the risk of failure to prevent or detect *errors*.

   d. Scaling the audit (for smaller and/or less complex companies)—size and complexity affect how companies achieve control objectives. Scaling is a natural extension of the risk-based approach to audits.

   e. Addressing the risk of fraud

      (1) The auditor should take into account the AU 316 fraud risk assessment results.
      (2) Controls that might address risk of fraud and management override include controls over

         (a) Significant, unusual transactions
         (b) Journal entries and adjustments made in the period-end financial reporting process
         (c) Related-party transactions
         (d) Significant management estimates
         (e) Incentives or pressures of management to falsify or inappropriately manage financial results

> **NOTE:** Be familiar with the above, as a lack of controls in these areas may result in fraud and/or management override.

   f. In an IC audit, to use the work of others (e.g., internal auditors and other client personnel), the auditor should

      (1) Assess their competence and objectivity; do not use the work of those with low competence and/or low objectivity
      (2) In general, use the work in lower risk areas

   g. Entity-level controls vary in nature and precision.

      (1) Some entity-level controls have an important but indirect effect on the likelihood of misstatement (e.g., certain control environment controls such as tone at the top). These controls might affect the other controls the auditor decides to test, and the nature, timing and extent of procedures performed on other controls.
      (2) Some entity-level controls monitor the effectiveness of other controls, but not at a level of precision that would address the assessed risk that misstatements will be prevented or detected (e.g., controls that monitor the operation of other controls). These entity-level controls, when operating effectively, might allow the auditor to reduce testing of the other controls.
      (3) Some entity-level controls by themselves adequately prevent or detect misstatements. If an entity-level control sufficiently addresses the risk of misstatement, the auditor need not test additional controls related to that risk.

   h. The auditor should use the same materiality considerations as s/he would use in planning the annual financial statement audit.

3. Use a top-down approach to identify controls to test.

   a. A top-down approach, beginning at the financial statement level, should be used to select controls to test.

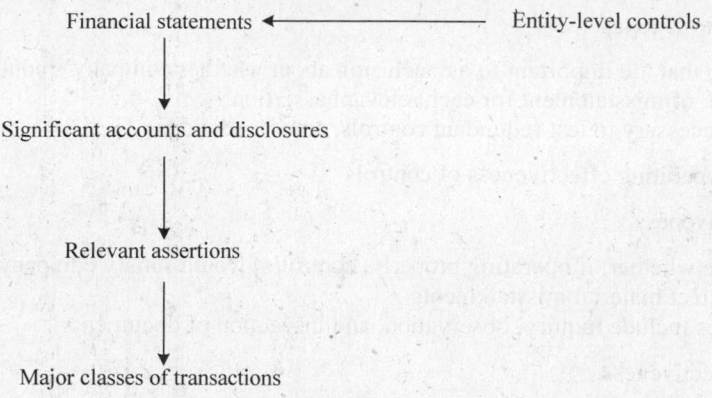

b. Entity-level controls

    (1) Controls related to the control environment; particularly whether

        (a) Management's philosophy and operating style promotes effective IC

        (b) Sound integrity and ethical values are developed and understood

        (c) The board of directors or audit committee understands and exercises oversight responsibility over financial reporting and IC

    (2) Controls over management override

    (3) The company's risk assessment process

    (4) Centralized processing and controls

    (5) Controls to monitor results of operations

    (6) Controls to monitor other controls (e.g., internal auditing, the audit committee, self-assessment programs)

    (7) Controls over the period-end financial reporting process

    (8) Policies that address significant business control and risk management practices

c. The auditor must evaluate the period-end financial reporting process (e.g., entering transaction totals to the general ledger, selection of accounting policies, adjustments, preparing financial statements).

d. Identifying significant accounts and disclosures

    (1) Consider

        (a) Size and composition of account

        (b) Susceptibility to misstatement

        (c) Volume of activity, complexity, homogeneity of transactions

        (d) Nature of account

        (e) Accounting and reporting complexities

        (f) Exposure to losses in account

        (g) Possibility of significant contingent liabilities

        (h) Related-party transactions

        (i) Changes from the prior period in accounts or disclosures

    (2) The auditor should identify significant accounts and disclosures and their relevant assertions; relevant assertions include

        (a) Existence or occurrence

        (b) Completeness

        (c) Valuation or allocation

        (d) Rights and obligations

        (e) Presentation and disclosure

e. To obtain a further understanding of the likely sources of misstatement, and as a part of selecting the controls to test, the auditor should achieve the following objectives:

    (1) Understand the flow of transactions

    (2) Verify that he or she has identified points at which a material misstatement could arise

    (3) Identify controls implemented by management to address potential misstatements

    (4) Identify controls to prevent or detect unauthorized acquisition, use or disposition of assets that could result in a material misstatement

    f. Selecting controls to test

        (1) Test those that are important to a conclusion about whether company's controls sufficiently address the assessed risk of misstatement for each relevant assertion.

        (2) It is not necessary to test redundant controls, unless redundancy is itself a control objective.

4. Test design and operating effectiveness of controls

    a. Design effectiveness

        (1) Determine whether, if operating properly, control(s) would satisfy company's control objectives and prevent or detect material misstatements

        (2) Procedures include inquiry, observation, and inspection of documents

    b. Operating effectiveness.

        (1) Determine whether control is operating as designed and whether person performing the control possesses the necessary authority and competence.

        (2) Procedures include inquiry, observation, inspection, and reperformance.

        (3) Walk-throughs may be used to test operating effectiveness; walk-throughs

            (a) Involve following a transaction from origination through the company processes until it is reflected in the financial statements

            (b) Usually consist of a combination of inquiry of appropriate personnel, observation of the company's operations, inspection of relevant documentation, and reperformance of the control

                1] Included in inquires are questions of company personnel about their understanding of what is required by the company's procedures and controls

            (c) Might provide sufficient evidence on operating effectiveness, depending on the risk associated with the control being tested, the specific procedures performed as a part of the walk-through and the results of those procedures

    c. Auditors are not responsible for obtaining sufficient evidence to support an opinion about the effectiveness of each individual control; rather, their objective is to express an overall opinion on IC.

    d. When the auditor identifies deviations from established controls, s/he should determine the effect of the deviations on his/her assessment of the risk associated with the control and on operating effectiveness.

        (1) Any individual control does not necessarily have to operate without deviation to be considered effective.

    e. Timing of testing controls

        (1) Testing controls over a greater period of time provides more evidence of the effectiveness of control.

        (2) Testing performed closer to the date of management's assessment provides more evidence than testing performed earlier.

    f. The more extensively a control is tested, the greater the evidence obtained from that test.

    g. When the auditor obtains evidence about operating effectiveness at an interim date (e.g., October 31 for a December 31 year-end client), s/he should determine what additional evidence is needed for the remaining period (referred to as "roll-forward procedures"); the needed additional evidence depends upon

        (1) Details of the control itself and results of tests performed

        (2) Sufficiency of evidence of effectiveness obtained at interim date

        (3) Length of remaining period

        (4) Possibility of significant changes in IC since interim date

    h. In subsequent years' audits, the auditor should incorporate knowledge obtained during past audits of IC.

        (1) Risk associated with the control must be considered.

        (2) The amount of work performed in previous audits, results, and whether there have been changes must also considered.

5. Evaluate identified deficiencies.

    a. Although the audit is designed to identify material weaknesses, any deficiencies the auditor has identified must be considered; the severity of a deficiency depends on

        (1) Whether there is reasonable possibility that the control will fail to prevent or detect a misstatement

        (2) The magnitude of the potential misstatement

    b. Details on evaluating deficiencies

(1) Factors affecting the magnitude include

    (a) Financial statement amounts or total transactions exposed to the deficiency
    (b) Volume of activity exposed to the deficiency in the current period

(2) The maximum amount that an account balance can be overstated is generally the recorded amount, while understatements can be larger.
(3) The auditor should consider the effect of compensating controls which might detect such a misstatement; if an adequate compensating control exists, the deficiency is not a material weakness.
(4) The auditor need **not** identify a material, misstatement for a deficiency to be considered a material weakness—rather, there must be a reasonable possibility of a material misstatement.

c. Indicators of material weaknesses

(1) Identification of fraud, whether or not material, on the part of senior management
(2) Restatement of previously issued financial statements to reflect a correction of a misstatement
(3) Identification by the auditor of a material misstatement that would not have been detected by the company's IC
(4) Ineffective oversight of external reporting and IC by the audit committee

> **NOTE:** Make certain that you know the above 4 indicators.

6. Wrap-up

  a. The auditor should form an opinion.
  b. Written representations from the client should be obtained.
  c. Communicating certain matters

(1) Material weaknesses—Communicate, in writing, to management and the audit committee prior to issuing the auditor's report on IC.

    (a) If oversight by the audit committee of external financial reporting and IC is ineffective, the auditor should communicate in writing to the board of directors.

(2) Significant deficiencies—Communicate in writing to management and the audit committee.
(3) Significant deficiencies and deficiencies (those that are not material weaknesses)—Communicate in writing to management and inform the audit committee when such a communication has been made.

    (a) Significant deficiencies and deficiencies previously communicated to management in writing by the auditor, internal auditors, or others in the organization, need not be repeated to *management*.
    (b) Significant deficiencies that are not corrected and were previously communicated to the audit committee should be recommunicated. The auditor may recommunicate them by referring to the prior communication.

(4) The auditor should not issue a report stating that no significant deficiencies or deficiencies were noted during the audit.

> **NOTE:** Make certain that you know all of the above communication requirements.

7. Report on internal control

  a. Report should include

(1) Title with word independent
(2) Statement that management is responsible for IC
(3) Identification of management's report on IC
(4) Statement that the auditor's responsibility is to express an opinion on IC
(5) Definition of IC
(6) Audit conducted in accordance with standards of PCAOB
(7) Standards of PCAOB require auditor to plan and perform audit to obtain reasonable assurance
(8) Audit includes obtaining an understanding of IC, assessing risk that a material weakness exists, testing and evaluating the design and operating effectiveness of IC, and performing other necessary procedures
(9) The auditor believes the audit provides a reasonable basis for his/her opinion.
(10) Paragraph on inherent limitation of IC
(11) Auditor's opinion on whether company maintained effective IC
(12) Manual or printed signature of firm

        (13) City and state of firm

        (14) Date of report

  b. Separate reports on the financial statements and IC or a combined report are acceptable.

  c. Report date—no earlier than date on which auditor has obtained sufficient competent evidence to support opinion.

  d. Material weaknesses result in an adverse opinion.

  e. The auditor should inquire of management as to any subsequent events affecting IC and should obtain written representation.

  f. Other reporting situations

      (1) Management's report on IC is incomplete or improperly represented—auditor should include an explanatory paragraph describing

      (2) Scope limitation—withdraw from engagement or disclaim an opinion

        (a) If the auditor concludes that a material weakness exists and a disclaimer is being issued, the report should include the definition of material weakness and a description of any material weakness identified.

      (3) Opinion based, in part, on report of another auditor—follow advice from AU 543

      (4) If management's report on IC includes information beyond that normally presented, the auditor ordinarily should disclaim an opinion on that information.

        (a) If that information includes a material misstatement of fact, the auditor should notify management and the audit committee.

8. The following is an example of a combined unqualified audit report on the financial statements and IC:

Report of Independent Registered Public Accounting Firm

To the Audit Committee and Stockholders of Carver Company

[Introductory paragraph]

    We have audited the accompanying balance sheets of Carver Company as of December 31, 20X8 and 20X7, and the related statements of income, stockholders' equity and comprehensive income, and cash flows for each of the years in the three-year period ended December 31, 20X8. We also have audited Carver Company's internal control over financial reporting as of December 31, 20X8, based on [*Identify control criteria, for example, "criteria established in Internal Control—Integrated Framework issued by the Committee of Sponsoring Organizations of the Treadway Commission (COSO)."*]. Carver Company's management is responsible for these financial statements, for maintaining effective internal control over financial reporting, and for its assessment of the effectiveness of internal control over financial reporting, included in the accompanying [*title of management's report*]. Our responsibility is to express an opinion on these financial statements and an opinion on the company's internal control over financial reporting based on our audits.

[Scope paragraph]

    We conducted our audits in accordance with the standards of the Public Company Accounting Oversight Board (United States). Those standards require that we plan and perform the audits to obtain reasonable assurance about whether the financial statements are free of material misstatement and whether effective internal control over financial reporting was maintained in all material respects. Our audits of the financial statements include examining, on a test basis, evidence supporting the amounts and disclosures in the financial statements, assessing the accounting principles used and significant estimates made by management, and evaluating the overall financial statement presentation. Our audit of internal control over financial reporting included obtaining an understanding of internal control over financial reporting, assessing the risk that a material weakness exists, and testing and evaluating the design and operating effectiveness of internal control based on the assessed risk. Our audits also included performing such other procedures as we considered necessary in the circumstances. We believe that our audits provide a reasonable basis for our opinions.

[Definition paragraph]

    A company's internal control over financial reporting is a process designed to provide reasonable assurance regarding the reliability of financial reporting and the preparation of financial statements for external purposes in accordance with generally accepted accounting principles. A company's internal control over financial reporting includes those policies and procedures that (1) pertain to the maintenance of records that, in reasonable detail, accurately and fairly reflect the transactions and dispositions of the assets of the company; (2) provide reasonable assurance that transactions are recorded as necessary to permit preparation of financial statements in accordance with generally accepted accounting principles, and that receipts and expenditures of the company are being made only in accordance with authorizations of management and directors of the company; and (3) provide reasonable assurance regarding prevention or timely detection of unauthorized acquisition, use, or disposition of the company's assets that could have a material effect on the financial statements.

[Inherent limitations paragraph]

Because of its inherent limitations, internal control over financial reporting may not prevent or detect misstatements. Also, projections of any evaluation of effectiveness to future periods are subject to the risk that controls may become inadequate because of changes in conditions, or that the degree of compliance with the policies or procedures may deteriorate.

[Opinion paragraph]

In our opinion, the financial statements referred to above present fairly, in all material respects, the financial position of Carver Company as of December 31, 20X8 and 20X7, and the results of its operations and its cash flows for each of the years in the three-year period ended December 31, 20X8, in conformity with accounting principles generally accepted in the United States of America. Also in our opinion, Carver Company maintained, in all material respects, effective internal control over financial reporting as of December 31, 20X8, based on [*Identify control criteria, for example, "criteria established in Internal Control—Integrated Framework issued by the Committee of Sponsoring Organizations of the Treadway Commission (COSO)*.]

Willington & Co., CPAs
Bisbee, Arizona, United States of America
February 20X9.

9. **Differences between PCAOB** Standard **5 and SSAE 15.** The following are differences between PCAOB 5 and SSAE 15 that you should be aware of:

- PCAOB 5 refers to this as an "audit," while SSAE 15 refers to it as an "examination."
- Both standards are structured about reporting on internal control at a point in time (the "as of" date), but SSAE 15 also allows an auditor to examine effectiveness of internal control for a period of time (e.g., for the year 20X7).
- Both standards provide for reporting on the subject matter (internal control), but SSAE 15 also allows for reporting on management's assertion. However, when a material weakness exists in an SSAE 15 engagement, the auditor must report on the subject matter.
- Both standards require that the auditor not issue a report stating that no significant deficiencies exist, but only SSAE 15 explicitly requires that no such report be issued stating that no material weaknesses were identified during the examination.
- The stage referred to as "wrapping-up" by PCAOB 5 (step 6 in the preceding outline) is referred to as "concluding procedures" by SSAE 15.
- The reports issued on IC are very similar, but differ in that PCAOB 5 states that the audit was conducted in accordance with standards of the PCAOB while SSAE 15 states that the examination was conducted in accordance with attestation standards established by the AICPA.

10. **Reporting on Whether a Previously Reported Material Weakness Continues to Exist (PCAOB Standard 4).** After the existence of a material weakness has lead to an adverse opinion in an internal control audit report, the company is ordinarily motivated to eliminate the weakness as quickly as is reasonably possible. When management believes that the material weakness continues to exist.

The overall approach under PCAOB Standard 4 is one in which management gathers evidence, including documentation that the material weakness no longer exists, and then prepares a written report so indicating. The auditors then plan and perform an engagement emphasizing the controls over the material weakness. The report issued indicates the auditor's opinion that the material weakness "no longer exists" or "exists" as of the date of management's assertion. At this point you should study the outline of PCAOB Standard 4.

> **NOW REVIEW MULTIPLE-CHOICE QUESTIONS 43 THROUGH 78 IN VOLUME 2**

D. Accounting Cycles

We now consider CPA exam questions that require an understanding of a transaction cycle.[1] These questions may, for example, require a candidate to perform one or more of the following:

- Identify an audit test that will meet some specified objective (or financial statement assertion).
- Identify internal control strengths/weaknesses.
- Complete a flowchart which includes a number of symbols without descriptors.
- Evaluate an internal control questionnaire.

---

[1] What is the relationship between an accounting cycle and a class of transactions? This is a largely definitional issue with no firm agreement. Many consider an accounting cycle to be broad—for example, we discuss later in this module the "purchase, payables, and cash disbursements cycle." Within that cycle are both purchase and cash disbursement transactions. While some would consider this one transaction cycle, most would consider the purchases and the cash disbursement as classes of transactions.

These questions may be difficult because a candidate (1) may not have an understanding of the various source documents and accounting records and how they relate to one another in an accounting system, and (2) does not know what types of detailed controls should exist. To help you prepare for these questions we are presenting information on both directional testing (which is also helpful for evidence questions) and a summary of transaction cycles.

Directional Testing. As a starting point, you should understand the notion of directional testing. Directional testing has a **from** and **to.** The basic idea is that testing **from** source documents forward **to** recorded entries accomplishes a different objective than testing **from** recorded entries back **to** source documents.

Diagrammatically, directional testing suggests

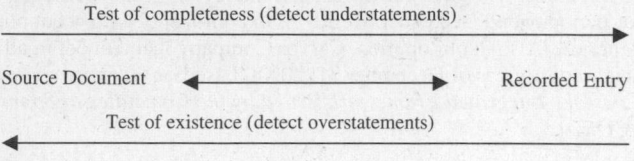

In sentence form, the rules are

1. Tracing forward (source document to recorded entry) primarily tests completeness of recording, and has a primary objective of detecting understatements.
2. Vouching (tracing backwards—recorded entry to source document) primarily tests existence and has a primary objective of detecting overstatements.

To understand the basic concept here, think about sales invoices (a source document) and the sales journal (the recorded entry).

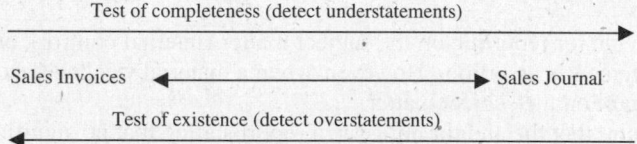

An auditor may select a group of sales invoices and compare them to the sales journal. On the other hand, the auditor may also vouch sales journal entries back to the sales invoices (and other support such as shipping documents, customer purchase orders). If an auditor is testing for **understated** sales, it would be best to start with possible sales, not those that were already recorded in the sales journal. Thus, for finding understatements of sales, a CPA would sample from the sales invoices (which are prepared when a sale occurs) in an effort to determine whether individual sales are being recorded. On the other hand, when testing for overstated sales, the CPA would test from the sales recorded in the sales journal back to sales invoices (as well as other source documents such as shipping documents, customer purchase orders). This is because for each recorded sale there should be support. We will apply the concept of directional testing in our discussion of the detailed transaction cycles.

Financial Accounting Reporting Cycle. In the overview section we suggested that an accounting system may be viewed as follows:

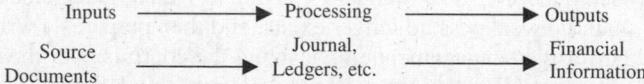

At this point review "The Financial Reporting Cycle" on the following page and simply look it over and note the various **source documents** (inputs), and **accounting records** such as journals and ledgers which are used to process the inputs (processing), and financial statements (outputs). Recall that our objectives are to (1) learn an approach for addressing questions pertaining to internal control weaknesses and for preparing internal control questionnaires, and (2) learn how to answer other questions pertaining to the effectiveness of audit tests.

When you consider a simulation question pertaining to internal control weaknesses an organized approach is to

1. Read the simulation to identify the type of transaction cycle
2. Obtain an understanding of how the accounting system works by carefully reading the simulation in detail (and possibly informally flowcharting it if the description is very detailed)
3. Consider the control activities (PIPS—**P**erformance reviews, **I**nformation processing, **P**hysical controls, and **S**egregation of duties), but particularly segregation of duties
4. Recall typical weaknesses (presented subsequently) for the transaction cycle involved to find additional internal control weaknesses

Steps 1 and 2 are clearly necessary since you need to understand the simulation and its requirements. When performing the second step, realize that on an overall basis, controls are aimed at safeguarding both assets and

THE FINANCIAL REPORTING CYCLE

Inputs (Source Documents)	Processing (Accounting Records)	Outputs (Financial Statements)

Inputs (Source Documents)

- Sales Order
- Shipping Document
- Sales Invoice
- Check — To Bank
- Remittance Advice
- Purchase Requisition
- Purchase Order
- Receiving Report
- Vendor's Invoice
- Check and Remittance Advice — To Vendor
- Job Time Tickets
- Employee Clock Cards
- Salaried Employee Time Summaries
- Miscellaneous Support

Processing (Accounting Records)

- Sales Journal[1]
- Cash Receipts Journal[2]
- Purchases Journal[3]
- Cash Disbursements Journal[4]
- Paychecks to Employees
- Payroll Journal[5]
- General Journal[6]

GENERAL LEDGER

Working* Trial Balance

Outputs (Financial Statements)

- Balance Sheet
- Income Statement
- Statement of Cash Flows

Journal Entries

1.	Accounts Receivable		4.	Accounts Payable
	Sales			Cash
	Cost of Goods Sold		5.	Work In Process
	Inventory			Salary Expense
2.	Cash			Cash
	Accounts Receivable		6.	Miscellaneous Entries
3.	Inventory (Purchases)			
	Accounts Payable			

*As a result of the audit, the auditor's adjustments and reclassifications will be used to modify the working trial balance accounts and balances.

financial records. Also, be aware of each department's operational objective (e.g., the shipping department ships goods). Also, know that one way to consider controls is to classify them by function.

Functions of controls. Although the word "controls" has different meanings in different contexts, from an internal control perspective controls within a business organization serve to ensure that information is processed correctly. Controls can in general be viewed as having a function of either (1) preventing misstatements, (2) detecting and correcting misstatements that have occurred, although a particular control may have elements of each. Preventive controls are typically most effective since they are designed to prevent a misstatement from occurring (e.g., two persons opening the mail which includes cash receipts may prevent embezzlement). Detective and corrective controls most frequently occur together. They detect and correct a misstatement that has already occurred (e.g., bank account reconciliation by an individual not otherwise involved with cash receipts or cash disbursements). While these controls are typically less expensive to implement than preventive controls, they may detect misstatements too late. They may detect that an employee embezzled $1,000,000, but may only be corrective in the sense that an embezzlement loss journal entry is made in cases where the employee has disappeared. For purposes of the CPA exam, ask yourself how effective each of the detective and corrective controls is—their effectiveness depends on the details of the system being examined.

Segregation of duties. When using the control activities to find internal control weaknesses (step 3), segregation of duties is especially important since many of the weaknesses relate to inadequate segregation. Recall that inadequate segregation exists whenever one individual is performing two or more of the following:

- Authorization
- Recordkeeping
- Custodianship

For example, when a cashier (custodian) authorizes the write-off of bad debts (authorization), a weakness exists. Also, know that for good internal control reconciliation of an account with some other information should be performed by an individual otherwise independent of the function. To illustrate, the individual preparing checks should not perform the reconciliation of the bank account.

We now analyze in detail each of the following accounting cycles:

1. Sales, Receivables, and Cash Receipts
2. Purchases, Payables, and Cash Disbursements
3. Inventories and Production
4. Personnel and Payroll
5. Financing
6. Investing

1. **Sales, Receivables, and Cash Receipts.** The following is a possible flow of documents:

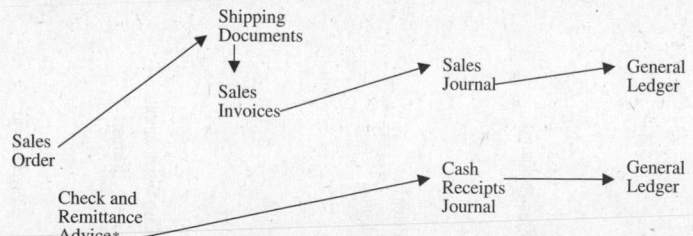

* *Checks are sent to banks and remittance advices (or a list of remittance advices) are used to prepare journal entries.*

   Assume that the firm's sales personnel prepare sales orders for potential sales (many other possibilities, such as the customer filling out the sales order, are found in practice). The sale is approved by the credit department, the goods are shipped, and the billing department (a part of accounting) prepares a sales invoice (a copy of which becomes the customer's "bill"). After the sales invoice is prepared, the sales journal, the general ledger, and the accounts receivable subsidiary ledger are posted. The customer pays the account with a check, and a remittance advice is enclosed to describe which invoice the check is paying. As a preventive control, two individuals open the mail that includes these customer remittances. The checks are listed and sent to the cashier who daily deposits them in the bank (recall that the checks should not go to the accounting department, as that would give the accounting department custody of assets [checks in this case] as well as recordkeeping responsibility). Another copy of the list of checks and the remittance advices is sent to accounting to be used to post the cash receipts journal, which is subsequently posted to the general and accounts receivable subsidiary ledgers.

Major Controls

Sales

(1) Credit granted by a credit department
(2) Sales orders and invoices prenumbered and controlled
(3) Sales returns are presented to receiving clerk who prepares a receiving report which supports prenumbered sales return credit memoranda

Accounts Receivable

(1) Subsidiary ledger reconciled to control ledger regularly
(2) Individual independent of receivable posting reviews statements before sending to customers
(3) Monthly statements sent to all customers
(4) Write-offs approved by management official independent of recordkeeping responsibility (e.g., the treasurer is appropriate)

Cash Receipts

(1) Cash receipts received in mail listed by individuals with no recordkeeping responsibility

   (a) Cash goes to cashier
   (b) Remittance advices go to accounting

(2) Over-the-counter cash receipts controlled (cash register tapes)
(3) Cash deposited daily
(4) Employees handling cash are bonded
(5) **Lockbox,** a post office box controlled by the company's bank at which cash remittances from customers are received. The bank collects customer remittances, immediately credits the cash to the company's bank account, and forwards the remittance advices to the company. A lockbox system is considered an extremely effective control because company employees have no access to cash and bank employees have no access to the company's accounting records.
(6) Bank reconciliation prepared by individuals independent of cash receipts recordkeeping

Sales, Receivables, and Cash Receipts CPA Exam Questions

1. Which assertion is being most directly addressed when an auditor selects a sample of sales invoices and compares them to the subsequent journal entries recorded in the sales journal?
   a. Occurrence.
   b. Classification.
   c. Accuracy.
   d. Completeness.

(d) This question is about directional testing. The step will help the auditor to determine that **all** sales invoices have been properly recorded. Accordingly answer (d) is correct since completeness relates most directly to whether **all** items are recorded. Answer (a), occurrence, would be a good reply for the opposite direction of testing—from sales journal entries to sales invoices. Answer (b), classification, would be to a limited extent also tested by tracing from the sales journal to the sales invoices. But, one would also wish to examine other documents such as contracts relating to classification. Little evidence is obtained here on accuracy, answer (c), in that recorded transactions are not being selected for testing.

2. When a client's physical count of inventories is lower than the inventory quantities shown on its perpetual records, the situation would most likely be caused by unrecorded
   a. Sales.
   b. Sales returns.
   c. Purchases.
   d. Purchase discounts.

(a) The question is asking what situation could cause the actual inventory to be lower than the amount recorded in the perpetual records. If sales had not been recorded, the perpetual records would not reflect the shipment of inventory; this would result in an overstatement of inventory in the accounting records. Answers (b) and (c) would address cases for which the physical count is higher than the perpetual records since physical goods would be in inventory with no recordkeeping having been performed. Purchase discounts, answer (d), relates to the cost of items as contrasted to the quantity.

3. How would you test credit sales for understatement?

ANSWER: Compare a sample of approved sales orders to the subsequent posting in the sales journal (and through to the general ledger). You are interested in finding out whether the approved sales order made it all the way to the general ledger. Note that you may find overstatements by this audit procedure (e.g., a $10 sale recorded for a higher amount) but that the primary emphasis is in finding understatements.

4. How would you test credit sales for overstatements?

ANSWER: Opposite of 3. above.

5. Are you mainly testing for over or understatements of cash when you agree remittance advices to the cash receipts journal?

ANSWER: Understatements. That is, did the cash that the firm received get recorded?

6. What could cause a remittance advice with no subsequent cash receipt entry?

ANSWER: An embezzlement.

7. Should there be a sales invoice for each sales order?

ANSWER: No. Sales in process and sales not approved will not be invoiced.

Illustrative Task-Based Simulation

Illustrative Simulation A, which follows, involves internal control strengths and deficiencies over the revenue cycle. Consider the following:

Illustrative Simulation A

Items 1 through 11 present various internal control strengths or internal control deficiencies. For each item, select from the list below the appropriate response.

   A. Internal control strength for the revenue cycle (including cash receipts).
   B. Internal control deficiency for the revenue cycle (including cash receipts).
   C. Internal control strength unrelated to the revenue cycle.

Items to be answered

1. Credit is granted by a credit department.

2. Sales returns are presented to a sales department clerk who prepares a written, prenumbered shipping report.

3. Statements sent monthly to customers.

4. Write-offs of accounts receivable are approved by the controller.

5. Cash disbursements over $10,000 require two signatures on the check.

6. Cash receipts received in the mail are received by a secretary with no recordkeeping responsibility.

7. Cash receipts received in the mail are forwarded unopened with remittance advices to accounting.

8. The cash receipts journal is prepared by the treasurer's department.

9. Cash is deposited weekly.

10. Support for disbursement checks is canceled after payment by the treasurer.

11. Bank reconciliation is prepared by individuals independent of cash receipts recordkeeping.

Solution to Illustrative Simulation A

1. **(A)** The function of a credit department is to follow the company's credit policies to make decisions on the granting of credit.

2. **(B)** Sales returns should be presented to the receiving clerk (not a sales department clerk) who should prepare a receiving report (not a shipping report).

3. **(A)** Sending monthly statements to customers represents a control strength as errors and fraud may be discovered.

4. **(B)** Write-offs of accounts receivable should be approved by a management official independent of recordkeeping responsibility, not by the controller who is responsible for recordkeeping. Frequently, the treasurer approves write-offs.

5. **(C)** While requiring two signatures on large checks is a good control over expenditures, it relates much more directly to the purchases/disbursements cycle than to the revenue cycle.

6.   **(A)** Mailed cash receipts should be received by an individual with no recordkeeping responsibility—a secretary with no recordkeeping responsibility is appropriate. That individual should open the mail and prepare a list of the receipts. The cash should be forwarded with a copy of the listed receipts to a cashier (or the individual who makes deposits) and the remittance advices should be forwarded with another copy of the listed receipts to accounting.

7.   **(B)** As indicated in the answer explanation to item 6, the cash receipts should be opened by an individual with no recordkeeping responsibility. The cash should be forwarded with a copy of the listed receipts to a cashier (or the individual who makes deposits) and the remittance advices should be forwarded with another copy of the listed receipts to accounting.

8.   **(B)** The cash receipts journal should be prepared by the department responsible for recordkeeping—accounting—under the leadership of the controller.

9.   **(B)** Cash should ordinarily be deposited **daily**.

10.   **(C)** This control relates to the purchases/disbursements cycle.

11.   **(A)** Bank reconciliations should be prepared by individuals independent of cash receipts (and cash disbursements) recordkeeping.

NOW REVIEW MULTIPLE-CHOICE QUESTIONS 79 THROUGH 94

---

2. **Purchases, Payables, and Cash Disbursements.** The following is a possible flow of documents:

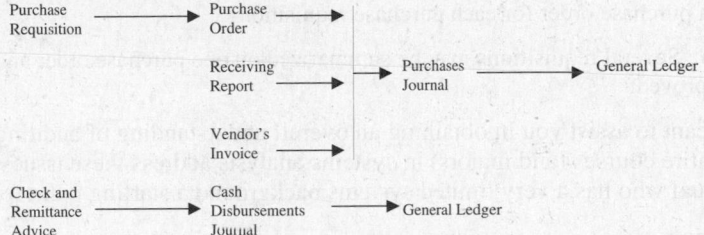

Assume that the purchase requisition is an internal document sent by the department in need of the supplies to the purchasing department. The purchasing department determines the proper quantity and vendor for the purchase and prepares a purchase order. One copy of the purchase order is sent to the vendor. Another copy is sent to the receiving department to allow receiving personnel to know that items received have been ordered; however, the copy of the purchase order sent to receiving will not have a quantity of items on it so as to encourage personnel to count the goods when they are received. When the goods are received, a receiving report is prepared by the receiving department and forwarded to the accounting department. A vendor's invoice or "bill" is received by the accounting department from the vendor. When the accounting department has the purchase order, receiving report, and vendor's invoice, the payment is approved and then recorded in the purchases journal since evidence exists that the item was ordered, received, and billed. A check and remittance advice is subsequently sent to the vendor in accordance with the terms of the sale. The purchase order, receiving report, and vendor's invoice are stamped paid to prevent duplicate payments.

Major Controls

Purchases

    (1) Prenumbered purchase orders used
    (2) Separate purchasing department makes purchases
    (3) Purchasing personnel independent of receiving and recordkeeping
    (4) Suppliers' monthly statements compared with recorded payables

Accounts Payable

    (1) Accounts payable personnel independent of purchasing, receiving, and disbursements
    (2) Clerical accuracy of vendors' invoices tested
    (3) Purchase order, receiving report, and vendor's invoice matched

Cash Disbursements

    (1) Prenumbered checks with a mechanical check protector used
    (2) Two signatures on large check amounts
    (3) Checks signed only with appropriate support (purchase order, receiving report, vendor's invoice). Treasurer signs checks and mails them

(4) Support for checks canceled after payment

(5) Voided checks mutilated, retained, and accounted for

(6) Bank reconciliations prepared by individual independent of cash disbursements recordkeeping

(7) Physical control of unused checks

Purchases, Payables, and Cash Disbursement Questions

1. Which documents need to be present before payment is approved?

    ANSWER: Purchase order, receiving report, vendor's invoice. (This shows that the firm ordered the goods, received the goods, and has been billed for the goods.)

2. How can a firm control disbursements so that if a duplicate invoice is sent by the supplier the payment will not be made a second time?

    ANSWER: Cancel the required supporting documents in 1. after the invoice is paid the first time.

3. What audit test could be used to determine whether recorded purchases represent valid business expenses?

    ANSWER: Compare a sample of recorded disbursements with properly approved purchase orders, purchase requisitions, vendor's invoices, and receiving reports.

4. What audit procedure would test whether actual purchases are recorded?

    ANSWER: Select a sample of purchase requisitions and agree them to the purchase orders and to the purchases journal (as well as to subsequent general ledger posting).

5. Should there be a purchase order for each purchase requisition?

    ANSWER: No. Several requisitions may be summarized on one purchase order and some requisitions may not be approved.

The above are meant to assist you in obtaining an overall understanding of auditing procedures and internal control. Note that entire courses (and majors) in systems analysis address these issues. The purpose of the above is to give the individual who has a very limited systems background a starting point for analysis.

Task-Based Simulation

Illustrative Simulation B, a purchase/disbursements simulation, is typical of a number of questions which have presented a flowchart with certain information on operations omitted—the candidate is to determine what description belongs in the blocks, circles, etc. which simply contain a number or letter. This type of question does **not** require a knowledge of internal control weaknesses. What is necessary is an understanding of how accounting systems generally work.

First, you must know the common flowchart symbols (presented in the Auditing with Technology Module under "Flowcharting"). This information will be helpful to you because when you see, for example, a trapezoid, you will know that a manual operation has been performed. Additionally, for such simulations, you should consider the department the missing information is in and that department's purpose (e.g., the purchasing department purchases appropriate goods from vendors at acceptable prices). Finally, consider both the step preceding and succeeding the missing information to provide you with a clue as to what is being represented.

Starting with A in the purchasing department, we note that an approved requisition has been received from stores. Step A represents some form of manual operation (due to the existence of a trapezoid) out of which a 5-copied purchase order as well as the requisition come. The only possible manual operation here is the preparation of a 5-part purchase order. At this point, the various copies are either filed or sent elsewhere (the circles represent connectors to other portions of the flowchart or possibly represent a document leaving the system). In this case, we see the various copies being filed and sent to receiving and vouchers payable. Step B represents a copy being sent elsewhere. When we consider the fact that the purpose of the purchasing department is to purchase the items, it becomes obvious that this copy must be sent to the vendor—otherwise no order would occur.

Because a receiving report appears for the first time under step C, it obviously represents the preparation of a receiving report. Next are connectors D and E. We know that the use of the circle indicates that something— probably a document or form of some sort—has been received. For D, a clue is given in that requisition 1 has also been received. We know that this is from purchasing by recalling that requisition 1 and purchase order 5 were sent to vouchers payable—this is shown on the flowchart under purchasing. Similarly, we know that receiving sent a copy of the receiving report to vouchers payable and that E and G relate to it. Thus, through understanding the nature of the various symbols and by considering preceding and succeeding information, we are able to determine the nature of the omitted information. The following is the complete solution to this simulation:

Illustrative Simulation B

The following illustrates a manual system for executing purchases and cash disbursements transactions.

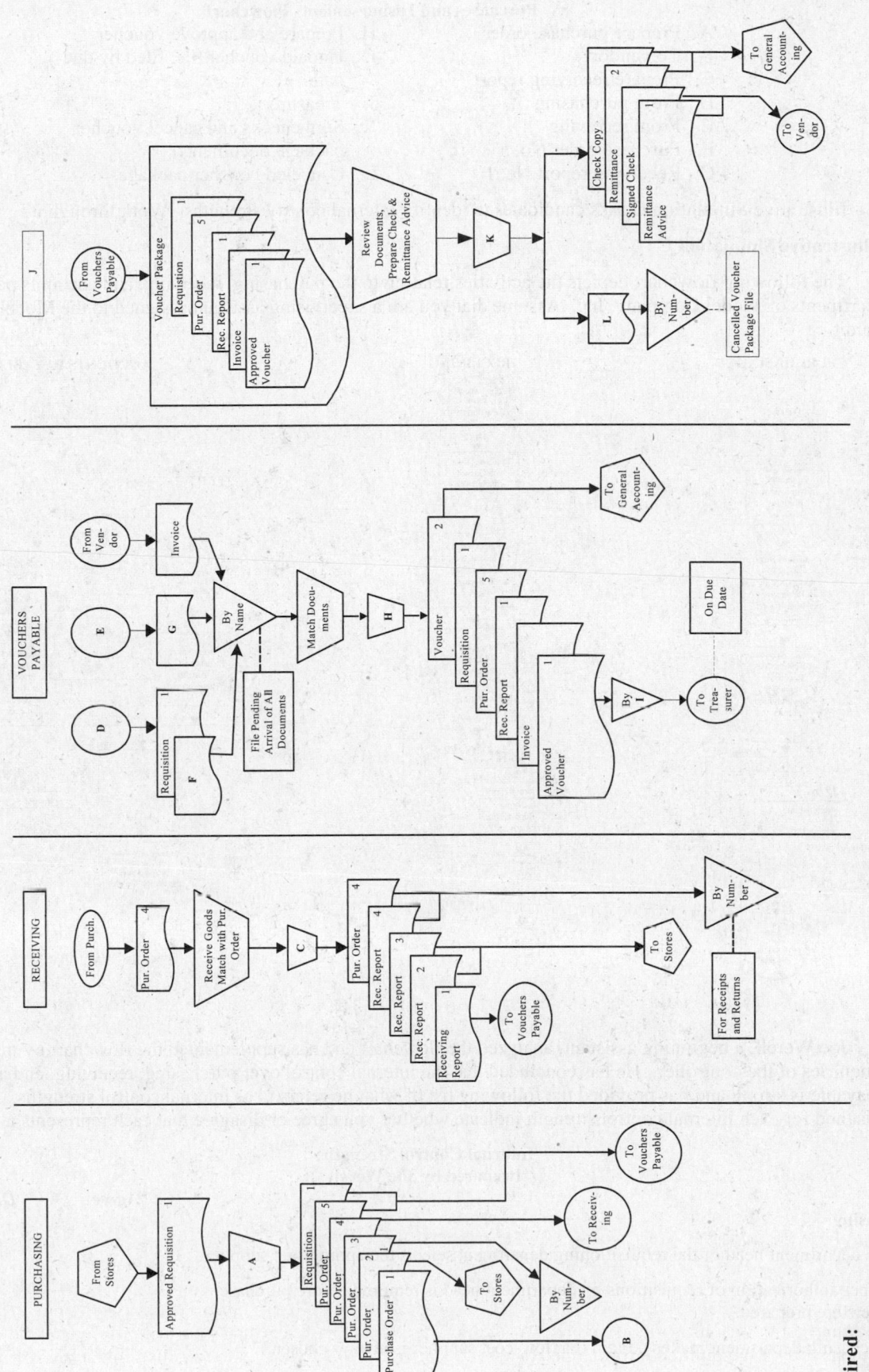

Required:

Indicate what each of the letters (A) through (L) represent. Do not discuss adequacies or inadequacies in the system of internal control.

Purchases and Disbursements Flowchart

A. Prepare purchase order
B. To vendor
C. Prepare receiving report
D. From purchasing
E. From receiving
F. Purchase order No. 5
G. Receiving report No. 1

H. Prepare and approve voucher
I. Unpaid voucher file, filed by due date
J. Treasurer
K. Sign checks and cancel voucher package documents
L. Canceled voucher package

Illustrative Simulation C asks candidates to identify internal control strengths. Work through it.

Illustrative Simulation C

The following flowchart depicts the activities relating to the purchasing, receiving, and accounts payable departments of Model Company, Inc. Assume that you are a supervising assistant assigned to the Model Company audit.

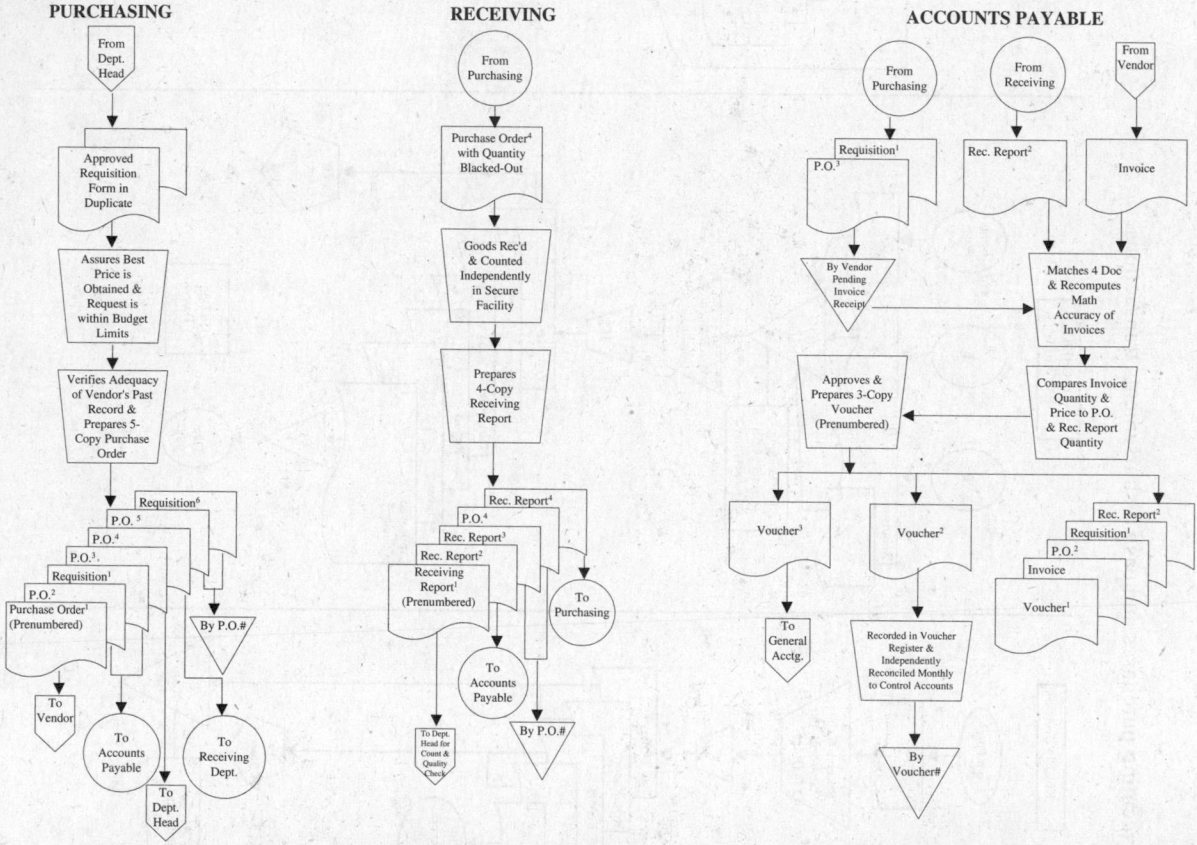

Joe Werell, a beginning assistant, analyzed the flowchart and has supplemented the flowchart by making certain inquiries of the controller. He has concluded that the internal control over purchasing, receiving, and accounts payable is strong and has provided the following list of what he refers to as internal control strengths. Review his list and for each internal control strength indicate whether you agree or disagree that each represents a strength.

Internal Control Strengths
Prepared by Joe Werell

	Agree	Disagree
Purchasing		
1. The department head of the requisitioning department selects the appropriate supplier.	○	○
2. Proper authorization of requisitions by department head is required before purchase orders are prepared.	○	○
3. Purchasing department makes certain that low-cost supplier is always chosen.	○	○
4. Purchasing department assures that requisitions are within budget limits before purchase orders are prepared.	○	○
5. The adequacy of each vendor's past record as a supplier is verified.	○	○

		Agree	*Disagree*

Receiving

6. Secure facilities limit access to the goods during the receiving activity.   ○   ○

7. Receiving department compares its count of the quantity of goods received with that listed on its copy of the purchase order.   ○   ○

8. A receiving report is required for all purchases, including purchases of services.   ○   ○

9. The requisitioning department head independently verifies the quantity and quality of the goods received.   ○   ○

10. Requisitions, purchase orders, and receiving reports are matched with vendor invoices as to quantity and price.   ○   ○

Accounts Payable

11. Accounts payable department recomputes the mathematical accuracy of each invoice.   ○   ○

12. The voucher register is independently reconciled to the control accounts monthly by the originators of the related vouchers.   ○   ○

13. All supporting documentation is marked "paid" by accounts payable immediately prior to making it available to the treasurer.   ○   ○

14. All supporting documentation is required for payment and is made available to the treasurer.   ○   ○

15. The purchasing, receiving, and accounts payable functions are segregated.   ○   ○

Solution to Illustrative Simulation C

1. Disagree. Someone independent of requisitioning should select the supplier.

2. Agree.

3. Disagree. Often, factors in addition to cost are considered (e.g., quality, dependability).

4. Agree.

5. Agree.

6. Agree.

7. Disagree. A comparison of quantities is not possible because quantity is blacked out on the purchase order provided to receiving.

8. No receiving report is ordinarily necessary for purchases of services.

9. Agree.

10. Agree.

11. Agree.

12. Disagree. The reconciliation should be performed by an independent party.

13. Disagree. Documentation should be marked "paid" by the individual making the payment.

14. Agree.

15. Agree.

3. **Inventories and Production.** Inventories and production fit under the first two cycles. However, due to the unique nature of inventories, separate coverage is warranted. Two cases will be considered here: a nonmanufacturing firm and a manufacturing firm.

   Assume you are auditing a retailer who purchases products from a wholesaler and then sells the goods to the public. As in the acquisitions and payments cycle, purchase requisitions and purchase orders are used and controlled to purchase the inventory items that are of a "finished goods" nature. Likewise, when ordered goods are received, a receiving report is filled out by personnel in the receiving department. Perpetual inventory records are maintained for large dollar items. The firm has calculated economic reorder points and quantities. When quantities on hand reach the reorder point, a purchase requisition is prepared and sent to the purchasing department that places the order.

   At the end of the year, a physical inventory is taken during which items on hand are counted. In the case of items for which perpetual records exist, the perpetuals are corrected for any errors—large errors must be explained. For items without perpetual records, the total on hand is used to adjust the cost of goods sold at year-end (Beginning inventory + Purchases – Ending inventory = Cost of goods sold).

   The case of the manufacturing firm is somewhat more involved. Recall that basically three types of inventory accounts are involved. First, supplies and raw materials are purchased from suppliers in much the same manner as described above for the nonmanufacturing firm. Second, work in process is the combination of raw materials, direct labor, and factory overhead. Third, when the items in process have been completed, they are transferred at their cost (typically standard cost) to finished goods. Finally, when the goods are sold, the entry is to credit finished goods and to debit cost of goods sold.

Work in process is controlled through use of a standard cost system as described in elementary cost accounting courses. Recall that raw materials are those that typically can be directly identified with the product (e.g., transistors in a radio). Direct labor is also identified with the product (e.g., assembly line labor). Overhead includes materials not specifically identified with the product (amount of glue used) and supervisory, nonadministrative labor. Variances may be calculated for all three components—raw materials, direct labor, and overhead. Variances will be allocated between cost of goods sold and ending inventory (finished goods and work in process) based on the proportion of items sold and those remaining in inventory, although any "abnormal" waste will be directly expensed. This allocation is necessary because generally accepted accounting principles require that the firm report inventory based on the lower of actual cost or market—not standard cost.

Major Inventory and Production Controls

(1) Perpetual inventory records for large dollar items
(2) Prenumbered receiving reports prepared when inventory received; receiving reports accounted for
(3) Adequate standard cost system to cost inventory items
(4) Physical controls against theft
(5) Written inventory requisitions used
(6) Proper authorization of purchases and use of prenumbered purchase orders

Inventories and Production CPA Exam Multiple-Choice Questions

1. To verify debits to the perpetual inventory records an auditor would sample from the recorded debits to a sample of
  a. Purchase approvals.
  b. Purchase requisitions.
  c. Purchase invoices.
  d. Purchase orders.

1.   **(c)**   The question is asking what an auditor would sample **to** when testing debits in the perpetual inventory records. The invoice from the vendor (purchase invoice) will include both the quantity and cost of items sent to the client company. Note that none of the other replies will include the quantities actually shipped. Answer (a) would address a question relating to internal control over purchases. Answer (b) would address: "When verifying that recorded purchases of inventory were requisitioned by stores, an auditor would be most interested in examining a sample of. . .?" Answer (d) would address: "When verifying that recorded purchases of inventory have been properly ordered, an auditor would be most interest in examining a sample of. . .?"

2. The best procedure to allow an auditor to determine that a client has completely included merchandise it owns in its ending inventory is to review and test the
  a. Terms of the open purchase orders.
  b. Purchase cutoff.
  c. Commitments.
  d. Purchase invoices received around year-end.

2.   **(b)**   The question is asking how best to address the completeness of inventory. Purchase cutoff procedures include the other choices and are thus more complete. Answers (a) and (c) would be good answers for a question such as "To determine the amount of future purchase commitments a client has, an auditor should test the. . .?" Answer (d) would address: "An effective procedure for determining that a proper year-end cutoff of purchases has occurred is to test the. . .?"

4. **Personnel and Payroll.** The following is a possible flow of documents:

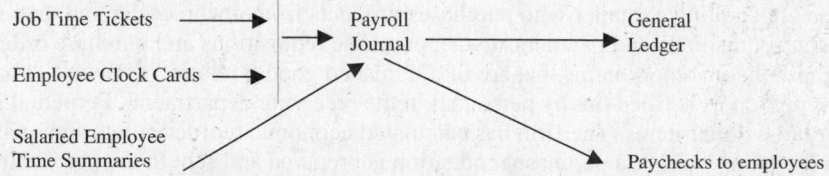

Assume that a separate personnel department maintains complete, up-to-date records for each employee. Included in such records is information on level of education, basic payroll information, experience, and authorization for any changes in pay rates. Assume that the firm's factory direct labor personnel use a time clock to punch in each morning and out each evening. Their employee clock card thus shows the total hours worked each day. These direct labor personnel also fill out job time tickets for each job they work on each day. At the end of each week their supervisor compares job time tickets with employee clock cards that have already been signed by the employees. Assume also that salaried and other employees fill out weekly time summaries indicating hours worked. All of the above information is sent to the payroll accounting department whose responsibility is to prepare the payroll journal and to prepare the unsigned payroll checks. The checks are then signed by the treasurer and distributed by an independent paymaster who has no other payroll functions. The summary payroll entry is then posted to the general ledger in the accounting department.

The internal auditing department periodically compares the payroll department's file on each employee with that in the personnel department's file to determine that no unauthorized changes in payroll records have been made. Employees with cash handling and recordkeeping responsibilities should be covered by fidelity bonds, a form of insurance which protects an employer against losses caused by dishonest employees (fidelity bonds also serve as a control when new employees are hired since the insurer will typically perform a background check on prospective employees).

Major Personnel and Payroll Controls

    (1) Segregate: Timekeeping
                       Payroll Preparation
                       Personnel
                       Paycheck Distribution
    (2) Time clocks used where possible
    (3) Job time tickets reconciled to time clock cards
    (4) Time clock cards approved by supervisors (overtime and regular hours)
    (5) Treasurer signs paychecks
    (6) Unclaimed paychecks controlled by someone otherwise independent of the payroll function (locked up and eventually destroyed if not claimed). In cases in which employees are paid cash (as opposed to checks) unclaimed pay should be deposited into a special bank account.
    (7) Personnel department promptly sends termination notices to the payroll department.

Personnel and Payroll CPA Exam Multiple-Choice Questions

1. From the perspective of good internal control, which of the following is the most appropriate individual to distribute payroll checks?
    a.   The payroll clerk.
    b.   A personnel employee.
    c.   Accounts receivable clerk.
    d.   Employee supervisors.

1. **(c)** When considering internal control, a person not otherwise involved in personnel or payroll procedures, an "independent paymaster," should distribute paychecks. Of the choices provided, the accounts receivable clerk [answer (c)] is best. Answers (a) and (b) are improper because the payroll clerk prepares the payroll and the personnel department is involved in hiring and terminating employees. Employee supervisors are inappropriate due to the potential problem of employees who have quit, but for which paychecks are still, improperly, being prepared. Note that the key for this question is **not** that the accounts receivable clerk should distribute checks, but that an individual otherwise independent of the process should perform the function. Previous CPA questions, for example, have included the receptionist as an appropriate individual to distribute checks.

2. If an auditor is concerned about whether all individuals being paid are bona fide employees, would s/he sample from source documents to the payroll journal, or from the payroll journal to source documents?

2. The direction of testing will be **from** the payroll journal that represents the population of employees who are being paid **to** support. This support will include personnel records, employees' Form W-4, and clock cards or time tickets. In addition, the auditor might observe the distribution of the paychecks, or observe employees listed in the payroll journal at work. Note here that the auditor must sample from the population representing the firm's paid employees, here the payroll journal, to determine whether they are all bona fide.

Illustrative Simulation

Illustrative Simulation Problem D, which follows, provides an illustration of the relationship between controls and tests of controls in the payroll area.

Illustrative Simulation D

You are working in the payroll area of the Remlo Company Audit. For each of the listed controls, select the **best** test of a control to determine whether the control is operating effectively. Each test of a control may be used only once (or not at all).

Controls

1. The Human Resources Department authorizes all hires.

2. The Human Resources Department authorizes all pay rate changes.

3. Authorized **decreases** in pay rate have been reflected in subsequent remuneration.

4. Factory workers on the payroll exist as working employees of the company.

5. The individual signing the payroll checks (the maker) is properly authorized.

6. Individual payroll checks are signed by the authorized check maker.

7. The payroll bank account is reconciled by an individual who is not involved in preparation of payroll checks.

8. Employee overtime is approved by the employee's supervisor.

9. Sales commissions are properly calculated.

Tests of Controls

A. Agree pay rate change authorizations to subsequent pay rates in the payroll journal.

B. Compare current employee time cards to the subsequent payroll journal.

C. Compare payroll budgets to the preceding period budget.

D. Compare the total payroll costs per the payroll journal to the amounts as posted to ledger accounts.

E. Confirm the payroll account using the Standard Form to Confirm Account Balance Information with Financial Institutions.

F. Confirm with the bank that all checks have been issued bearing the signature of the proper check maker.

G. Confirm with the bank the individual responsible for account reconciliation.

H. Examine employee time cards for proper authorization.

I. Observe and make inquiries about the performance of the reconciliation and payroll check preparation function.

J. Obtain a list of authorized check signers (makers) from the bank.

K. Recalculate employee gross pay using supporting information.

L. Select a sample of cancelled payroll checks and determine that the maker's signature is proper.

M. Select a sample of employees on the payroll and determine that each has a properly approved hiring authorization form in his or her personnel file.

N. Select a sample of employee names from the payroll register and briefly interview each on a surprise basis.

O. Select a sample of hiring authorization forms and agree each to an employee in the payroll journal.

P. Vouch changes in pay rates as per two periods to pay rate change authorizations.

Solution to Illustrative Simulation Problem D

1. (**M**) To test whether all hires are authorized, selecting a sample of employees on the payroll to determine whether they have the proper documentation is the best approach. Notice that reply (o), selecting a sample of hiring authorization forms and agreeing each to employees in the payroll journal tests in the wrong direction. If one starts with a hiring authorization form one is not going to identify an employee without such a form. Reply (o) would more directly address whether those with hiring authorization forms are being paid—not typically a problem given individuals' tendency to complain if they are not paid.

2. (**P**) To test whether pay rate changes have been authorized, one must identify situations in which there is an actual change in pay and determine whether it was authorized. Reply (p) provides a good test since it identifies such a change and tests whether there is a pay rate change authorization.

3. (**A**) To determine whether authorized pay **decreases** have been properly processed, one must begin with the authorized decreases and test whether they have been recorded. In this case, the only documents likely to serve as the source documents are the pay rate change authorization forms.

4. (**N**) To determine whether factory workers being paid are actually at work, one would expect to test from source documents relating to paychecks (or the payroll journal) to some evidence that the person is on the job, whether it be evi-

dence of work performed or the employee him or herself. Reply (n) is in the proper direction in that those on the payroll register are being paid, and should be on the job.

5. (J) The list of authorized check signers is maintained by the bank. Also, the board of directors may authorize signers. Since none of the replies deal with the Board of Directors the confirmation obtaining a list of authorized check signers from the bank is the best option.

6. (L) To determine whether the authorized check maker is signing the checks, one must examine individual checks. Notice that this control would ordinarily be tested following testing of the preceding control.

7. (I) Observation and inquiry about reconciliation and the payroll check preparation functions will serve to test this segregation.

8. (H) To determine whether overtime is approved by the employee's supervisor, one must understand the approval process. But in a question such as this, one must find a reply that implies authorization, as does reply (h).

9. (K) The proper calculation of sales commission requires a comparison of sales with pay. The general reply (k) on recalculating gross pay accomplishes this task.

5. **Financing.** This cycle includes issuance and repurchase of debt (bank loans, mortgages, bonds payable) and capital stock, and payment of interest and dividends. Debt and capital stock transactions should be authorized by the board of directors. Often an independent trustee issues bonds, monitors company compliance with the provisions of the debt agreement, and pays interest.

For capital stock transactions, corporations may either employ an independent stock registrar and a stock transfer agent, or handle their own transactions. Normally, internal control is stronger when a stock registrar and a stock transfer agent are utilized. A stock registrar's primary responsibility is to verify that stock is issued in accordance with the authorization of the board of directors and the articles of incorporation; the stock transfer agent's primary responsibility is maintaining detailed stockholder records and carrying out transfers of stock ownership.

Major Financing Controls Frequently Missing in CPA Exam Questions

(1) Debt and equity transactions are properly approved by the company's board of directors.
(2) An independent trustee handles bond transactions.
(3) A stock registrar and a stock transfer agent handle capital stock transactions.
(4) Canceled stock certificates are defaced to prevent their reissuance.

6. **Investing.** This cycle includes investments in the debt and equity of other organizations, and purchases of property, plant, and equipment. Investments may be categorized as marketable securities and long-term investments. Purchases are recorded at cost, and reported at the lower of cost or market, as guided by SFAS 12.

Major Investment Controls Frequently Missing in CPA Exam Questions

(1) Segregation of duties among the individuals authorizing purchases and sales of securities, maintaining custody of the securities, and maintaining the records of securities
(2) Use of an independent agent such as a stockbroker, bank or trust company to maintain custody of securities
(3) Securities **not** in the custody of an independent agent maintained in a bank safe-deposit box under the joint control of the treasurer and one other company official; both individuals must be present to gain access
(4) Registration of securities in the name of the company
(5) Detailed records of all securities and related revenue from interest and dividends
(6) Periodical physical inspection of securities by individuals with no responsibility for the authorization, custody, or recordkeeping for investments

Property, plant, and equipment acquisitions require board of directors' approval for purchases over a certain amount. Otherwise, the purchase is handled similarly to a merchandise purchase. As in the case of merchandise purchases, the item is recorded as an addition when some form of purchase authorization is present with a vendor's invoice and a receiving report. The company then selects an appropriate life and depreciation method (e.g., straight-line, sum-of-the-years' digits, double-declining balance). Depreciation entries are made in the general journal with a debit to depreciation expense (manufacturing overhead for manufacturing equipment) and a credit to accumulated depreciation. The company must also have controls to determine that repair and maintenance expenses have not been capitalized.

Asset retirements are recorded by removing the asset and accumulated depreciation from the general ledger—a gain (loss) may occur on the transaction. In the case of an exchange of assets, the firm has policies to determine that GAAP is properly followed in recording the transaction.

Major Property, Plant, and Equipment Controls Frequently Missing in CPA Exam Questions

(1) Major asset acquisitions are properly approved by the firm's board of directors and properly controlled through capital budgeting techniques.
(2) Detailed records are available for property assets and accumulated depreciation.
(3) Written policies exist for capitalization vs. expensing decisions.
(4) Depreciation properly calculated.
(5) Retirements approved by an appropriate level of management.
(6) Physical control over assets to prevent theft.
(7) Periodic physical inspection of plant and equipment by individuals who are otherwise independent of property, plant, and equipment (e.g., internal auditors).

7. **Overall Internal Control Questionnaires (checklists).** The following internal control questionnaires (in checklist form) outline the controls that are typically necessary in various transaction cycles and accounts. While the lists are clearly too lengthy to memorize, review them and obtain a general familiarity. **Candidates with little actual business experience will probably find them especially helpful for questions that require analysis of internal control deficiencies.** Study in detail the questionnaire checklists on cash receipts (#3), cash disbursements (#4), and on payroll (#14)—as indicated above, a large percentage of the internal control weakness type questions relate to these three areas.

The checklists are organized into subtopics—generally by category of balance sheet account (e.g., cash, receivables, fixed assets, liabilities, shareholders' equity, etc.). The related nominal accounts should be considered with the real accounts (e.g., depreciation and fixed assets, sales and accounts receivable).

1. General

   Chart of accounts
   Accounting procedures manual
   Organizational chart to define responsibilities
   Absence of entries direct to ledgers
   Posting references in ledgers
   Review of journal entries
   Use of standard journal entries
   Use of prenumbered forms
   Support for all journal entries
   Access to records limited to authorized persons
   Rotation of accounting personnel
   Required vacations
   Review of system at every level
   Appropriate revision of chart of accounts
   Appropriate revision of procedures
   Separation of recordkeeping from operations
   Separation of recordkeeping from custodianship
   Record retention policy
   Bonding of employees
   A conflict of interest policy

2. Cash funds

   Imprest system
   Reasonable amount
   Completeness of vouchers
   Custodian responsible for fund
   Reimbursement checks to order of custodian
   Surprise audits
   No employee check cashing
   Physically secure
   Custodian has no access to cash receipts
   Custodian has no access to accounting records

3. Cash receipts

   Detail listing of mail receipts
   Restrictive endorsement of checks
   Special handling of postdated checks
   Daily deposit
   Cash custodians bonded
   Cash custodians apart from negotiable instruments
   Bank accounts properly authorized
   Handling of returned NSF items
   Comparison of duplicate deposit slips with cash book
   Comparison of duplicate deposit slips with detail AR
   Banks instructed not to cash checks to company
   Control over cash from other sources
   Separation of cashier personnel from accounting duties
   Separation of cashier personnel from credit duties
   Use of cash registers
   Cash register tapes
   Numbered cash receipt tickets
   Outside salesmen cash control
   Daily reconciliation of cash collections

4. Cash disbursements

   Numbered checks
   Sufficient support for check
   Limited authorization to sign checks
   No signing of blank checks
   All checks accounted for
   Detail listing of checks
   Mutilation of voided checks
   Specific approval for unusually large checks
   Proper authorization of persons signing checks
   Control over signature machines
   Check listing compared with cash book
   Control over interbank transfers
   Prompt accounting for interbank transfers
   Checks not payable to cash
   Physical control of unused checks

Cancellation of supporting documents
Control over long outstanding checks
Reconciliation of bank account
Independence of person reconciling bank
  statement
Bank statement direct to person reconciling
No access to cash records or receipts by check
  signers

5. Investments

Proper authorization of transactions
Under control of a custodian
Custodian bonded
Custodian separate from cash receipts
Custodian separate from investment records
Safety-deposit box
Record of all safety-deposit visits
Access limited
Presence of two required for access
Periodic reconciliation of detail with control
Record of all aspects of all securities
Availability of brokerage advices, etc.
Periodic internal audit
Securities in name of company
Proper segregation of collateral
Physical control of collateral
Periodic appraisal of collateral
Periodic appraisal of investments
Adequate records of investments for applica-
  tion of equity method

6. Accounts receivable and sales

Sales orders prenumbered
Credit approval
Credit and sales departments independent
Control of back orders
Sales order and sales invoice comparison
Shipping invoices prenumbered
Names and addresses on shipping invoice
Review of sales invoices
Control over returned merchandise
Credit memoranda prenumbered
Matching of credit memoranda and receiving
  reports
Control over credit memoranda
Control over scrap sales
Control over sales to employees
Control over COD sales
Sales reconciled with cash receipts and AR
Sales reconciled with inventory change
AR statement to all customers
Periodic preparation of aging schedule
Control over collections of written-off receiv-
  ables
Control over AR write-offs (e.g., proper au-
  thorization)
Control over AR written off (i.e., review for
  possible collection)
Independence of sales, AR, receipts, billing,
  and shipping personnel

7. Notes receivable

Proper authorization of notes
Detailed records of notes
Periodic detail to control comparison
Periodic confirmation with makers
Control over notes discounted
Control over delinquent notes
Physical safety of notes
Periodic count of notes
Control over collateral
Control over revenue from notes
Custodian of notes independent from cash and
  recordkeeping

8. Inventory and cost of sales

Periodic inventory counts
Written inventory instructions
Counts by noncustodians
Control over count tags
Control over inventory adjustments
Use of perpetual records
Periodic comparison of G/L and perpetual rec-
  ords
Investigation of discrepancies
Control over consignment inventory
Control over inventory stored at warehouses
Control over returnable containers left with
  customers
Preparation of receiving reports
Prenumbered receiving reports
Receiving reports in numerical order
Independence of custodian from recordkeeping
Adequacy of insurance
Physical safeguards against theft
Physical safeguards against fire
Adequacy of cost system
Cost system tied into general ledger
Periodic review of overhead rates
Use of standard costs
Use of inventory requisitions
Periodic summaries of inventory usage
Control over intracompany inventory transfers
Purchase orders prenumbered
Proper authorization for purchases
Review of open purchase orders

9. Prepaid expenses and deferred charges

Proper authorization to incur
Authorization and support of amortization
Detailed records
Periodic review of amortization policies
Control over insurance policies
Periodic review of insurance needs
Control over premium refunds
Beneficiaries of company policies
Physical control of policies

10. Intangibles

Authorization to incur
Detailed records

Authorization to amortize
Periodic review of amortization

11. Fixed assets

Detailed property records
Periodic comparison with control accounts
Proper authorization for acquisition
Written policies for acquisition
Control over expenditures for self-construction
Use of work orders
Individual asset identification plates
Written authorization for sale
Written authorization for retirement
Physical safeguard from theft
Control over fully depreciated assets
Written capitalization—expense policies
Responsibilities charged for asset and depreciation records
Written, detailed depreciation records
Depreciation adjustments for sales and retirements
Control over intracompany transfers
Adequacy of insurance
Control over returnable containers

12. Accounts payable

Designation of responsibility
Independence of AP personnel from purchasing, cashier, receiving functions
Periodic comparison of detail and control
Control over purchase returns
Clerical accuracy of vendors' invoices
Matching of purchase order, receiving report, and vendor invoice
Reconciliation of vendor statements with AP detail
Control over debit memos
Control over advance payments
Review of unmatched receiving reports
Mutilation of supporting documents at payment
Review of debit balances
Investigation of discounts not taken

13. Accrued liabilities and other expenses

Proper authorization for expenditure and incurrence
Control over partial deliveries
Postage meter
Purchasing department
Bids from vendors
Verification of invoices
Imprest cash account

Detailed records
Responsibility charged
Independence from G/L and cashier functions
Periodic comparison with budget

14. Payroll

Authorization to employ
Personnel data records
Tax records
Time clock
Supervisor review of time cards
Review of payroll calculations
Comparison of time cards to job sheets
Imprest payroll account
Responsibility for payroll records
Compliance with labor statutes
Distribution of payroll checks
Control over unclaimed wages
Profit-sharing authorization
Responsibility for profit-sharing computations

15. Long-term liabilities

Authorization to incur
Executed in company name
Detailed records of long-term debt
Reports of independent transfer agent
Reports of independent registrar
Otherwise adequate records of creditors
Control over unissued instruments
Signers independent of each other
Adequacy of records of collateral
Periodic review of debt agreement compliance
Recordkeeping of detachable warrants
Recordkeeping of conversion features

16. Shareholders' equity

Use of registrar
Use of transfer agent
Adequacy of detailed records
Comparison of transfer agent's report with records
Physical control over blank certificates
Physical control over treasury certificates
Authorization for transactions
Tax stamp compliance for canceled certificates
Independent dividend agent
Imprest dividend account
Periodic reconciliation of dividend account
Adequacy of stockholders' ledger
Review of stock restrictions and provisions
Valuation procedures for stock issuances
Other paid-in capital entries
Other retained earnings entries

NOW REVIEW MULTIPLE-CHOICE QUESTIONS 95 THROUGH 137 IN VOLUME 2

E. Other Considerations

1. **Additional Financial Statement Audit Communications**

   a. **Communication of internal control related matters.** AU 325 requires auditors to communicate significant deficiencies and material weaknesses to management and to those charged with governance.[2] At this point study the outline of AU 325. Make certain that you know the following points related to the AU 325 communication:

      • Summary of likelihood and potential amount involved

Deficiency	Severity	Required Communication to Management and Those Charged with Governance?
Control Deficiency	Design or operation of control does not allow management or employees, in the normal course of performing their assigned functions, to prevent or detect and correct misstatements on a timely basis.	No
Significant Deficiency	Less severe than a material weakness, yet important enough to merit attention by those charged with governance.	Yes
Material Weakness	A reasonable possibility that a material misstatement will not be prevented, or detected and corrected on a timely basis.	Yes

      • The report issued should be **written** and include

        • Purpose of consideration of IC was to express an opinion on the financial statements, **not** to express an opinion on IC.
        • Auditor is not expressing an opinion on IC effectiveness.
        • Consideration of IC not designed to identify all significant deficiencies or material weaknesses.
        • Definition of material weakness and significant deficiency.
        • Separately describe significant deficiencies and material weaknesses identified.
        • Indication that the communication is for management, those charged with governance and others within the organization; it **should not be used by others.**

      • While a written report indicating that no significant deficiencies were identified should **not** be issued, a report indicating that no material weaknesses were identified **may** be issued. Notice that this differs from an SSAE 15 internal control engagement (discussed in Section C of this module) in which a report directly stating that no material weaknesses were identified **cannot** be issued.
      • Communications are best if issued by the audit report release date (the date the auditor grants client permission to use report), but should be issued not later than 60 days following the audit report release date.
      • A previously communicated significant deficiency or material weakness that has not been corrected should be recommunicated; it may be communicated by simply referring to the prior communication and its date.

   b. **The auditor's communication with those charged with governance.** AU 380 requires that a communication (orally or in writing) of certain information occur between the auditor and those charged with governance of the company being audited (e.g., the board of directors, audit committee). Recall that the audit committee is a group of outside (non management) directors whose functions typically include

      • Nominating, terminating, and negotiating CPA firm audit fees
      • Discussing broad, general matters concerning the type, scope, and timing of the audit with the public accounting firm
      • Discussing internal control weaknesses with the public accounting firm
      • Reviewing the financial statements and the public accounting firm's audit report
      • Working with the company's internal auditors

---

[2] Those charged with governance are the person(s) with responsibility for overseeing the strategic direction of the entity and obligations related to the accountability of the entity.

The following summarizes the required matters communicated:

Audit responsibilities under GAAS

1. Responsibility to form and express an opinion
2. An audit does not relieve management for those charged with governance of their responsibilities.

Planned scope and timing of the audit

Planned scope and timing of the audit—An overview of the planned scope and timing of the audit; this may assist those charged with governance in understanding the consequences of the auditor's work for their oversight activities and the auditor to understand better the entity and its environment.

Significant findings from the audit

1. Qualitative aspects of the entity's significant accounting practices
2. Significant difficulties encountered during the audit
3. Uncorrected misstatements
4. Disagreements with management
5. Management's consultations with other accountants
6. Significant issues discussed, or subject to correspondence with management
7. Auditor independence issues
8. If those charged with governance are not involved in managing the entity, the following should also be communicated

   - Material corrected misstatements resulting from audit
   - Representations requested from management
   - Other significant issues

A simulation question might make the Professional Standards available and ask the candidate to prepare a report on internal control deficiencies or on matters to be communicated to those charged with governance. While you might use either the index or keyword approach to identify the appropriate standards, bear in mind that the two primary sections here are AU 325 and AU 380. At this point you should study the outline of AU 380.

NOW REVIEW MULTIPLE-CHOICE QUESTIONS 138 THROUGH 152 IN VOLUME 2

---

2. **Effects of an Internal Audit Function.** AU 322 discusses the effect of an internal audit function on the CPA's audit.

   Internal auditors have two primary effects on the audit: (1) their existence and work may **affect the nature, timing, and extent of audit procedures**, and (2) CPAs may use internal auditors to **provide direct assistance** in performing procedures. The CPA should assess both the **competence** and **objectivity** of internal auditors. Competence is evaluated by considering education, experience, professional certification, audit policies, and various work policies. Objectivity is assessed by considering organizational status within the company, and policies for assuring that internal auditors are objective with respect to the areas being audited. Section B of the outline of Section AU 322 presents more detailed information on the heavily tested area of internal auditor competence and objectivity.

   Internal auditors may affect the CPA's understanding of internal control, control risk assessment, and substantive procedures. You should know that for assertions with high audit risk, the internal auditor's work alone cannot eliminate the need for CPA's tests. A number of questions may be expected on this topic. At this point, you should study the section outline.

3. **Reports on Processing of Transactions by Service Organizations (AT 801 and AU 324)**

   A service organization provides services to user entities. Those services are likely to be relevant to the user entities' internal control over financial reporting. For example, a payroll processing service organization's controls related to the timely remittance of payroll deductions to government authorities may be relevant to a user entity because late remittances could incur interest and penalties. Auditors of user entities are concerned with service organization controls. Accordingly, service organizations often obtain from their CPAs a report on those elements of internal control that are relevant to the users and their auditors—related guidance is in AT 801. Guidance on how the users' auditor should consider those reports is presented in AU 324.

   Two types of service auditor reports are described in detail in this section. The first addresses whether service organization controls have been implemented. The following is an example of such a report:

   To the XYZ Loan Servicer:

   We have examined the accompanying description of the loan servicing application of XYZ Loan Servicer. Our examination included procedures to obtain reasonable assurance about whether (1) the accompanying description presents fairly, in all material respects, the aspects of XYZ Loan Servicer's policies and procedures that may be relevant to a user organization's internal control, (2) the control structure policies and procedures included in the description were suitably designed to achieve the control objectives specified in the description, if those policies and procedures were complied with satisfactorily, and (3) such policies and procedures had been implemented as of December 31, 20X2. The control objectives were specified by the State of Arizona Loan Servicing Authority. Our examination was performed in accordance with standards established by the American Institute of Certified Public Accountants and included those procedures we considered necessary in the circumstances to obtain a reasonable basis for rendering an opinion.

We did not perform procedures to determine the operating effectiveness of policies and procedures for any period. Accordingly, we express no opinion on the operating effectiveness of any aspects of XYZ Loan Servicer's policies and procedures, individually or in the aggregate.

In our opinion, the accompanying description of the aforementioned application presents fairly, in all material respects, the relevant aspects of XYZ Loan Servicer's policies and procedures that had been implemented as of December 31, 20X2. Also, in our opinion, the policies and procedures, as described, are suitably designed to provide reasonable assurance that the specified control objectives would be achieved if the described policies and procedures were complied with satisfactorily.

The description of policies and procedures at XYZ Loan Servicer is as of December 31, 20X2, and any projection of such information to the future is subject to the risk that, because of change, the description may no longer portray the system in existence. The potential effectiveness of specific policies and procedures at the service organization is subject to inherent limitations and, accordingly, misstatements or fraud may occur and not be detected. Furthermore, the projection of any conclusions, based on our findings, to future periods is subject to the risk that changes may alter the validity of such conclusions.

This report is intended solely for use by the management of XYZ Loan Servicer, its customers, and the independent auditors of its customers.

The second, issued when the effectiveness of controls has been tested, includes the information presented in the first type of report plus an opinion on the operating effectiveness of those controls. Of the two reports, only the second type provides the user auditor a basis for reducing the assessment of control risk. At this point, you may wish to study the outlines of AT 801 and AU 324.

Section C.3.g of the Reporting Module discusses the reports discussed in this section and two other types of service organization control (SOC) reports. Those discussed here are referred to as SOC 1 reports in that section.

> **NOW REVIEW MULTIPLE-CHOICE QUESTIONS 153 THROUGH 166 IN VOLUME 2**

KEY TERMS

Assertions. Representations by management, explicit or otherwise, that are embodied in the financial statements, as used by the auditor to consider the different types of potential misstatements that may occur.

Control risk. The risk that a misstatement that could occur in an assertion about a class of transaction, account balance, or disclosure and that could be material, either individually or when aggregated with other misstatements, will not be prevented, or detected and corrected, on a timely basis by the entity's internal control.

Deficiency in internal control. A deficiency in internal control exists when the design or operation of a control does not allow management or employees, in the normal course of performing their assigned functions, to prevent, or detect and correct, misstatements on a timely basis. A *deficiency in design* exists when (a) a control necessary to meet the control objective is missing or (b) an existing control is not properly designed so that, even if the control operates as designed, the control objective would not be met. A *deficiency in operation* exists when a properly designed control does not operate as designed, or when the person performing the control does not possess the necessary authority or competence to perform the control effectively.

Foreign Corrupt Practices Act of 1977. Federal legislation prohibiting payments to foreign officials for the purpose of securing business. The act also requires all companies under SEC jurisdiction to maintain a system of internal control to provide reasonable assurance that transactions are executed only with the knowledge and authorization of management.

Internal control. A process—effected by those charged with governance, management, and other personnel—designed to provide reasonable assurance about the achievement of the entity's objectives with regard to the reliability of financial reporting, effectiveness and efficiency of operations, and compliance with applicable laws and regulations. Internal control over safeguarding of assets against unauthorized acquisition, use, or disposition may include controls relating to financial reporting and operations objectives.

Internal control checklist. One of several methods of describing internal control in audit working papers. Checklists are usually designed so that "no" answers prominently identify weaknesses in internal control.

Internal control flowchart. One of several methods of describing internal control in audit working papers. A symbolic representation of a system or series of procedures with each procedure shown in sequence.

Internal control questionnaire. One of several methods of describing internal control in audit working papers. Questionnaires may either ask (1) ask open-ended questions or (2) "yes/no questions in which case it in essence becomes the same as an internal control checklist).

Internal control written narrative. One of several methods of describing internal control in audit working papers. A written summary of internal control for inclusion in audit working paper—generally a memo.

Material weakness. A deficiency, or a combination of deficiencies, in internal control, such that there is a reasonable possibility that a material misstatement of the entity's financial statements will not be prevented, or detected and corrected, on a timely basis.

Report on management's description of a service organization's system and the suitability of the design of controls. A report that comprises

1. Management's description of the service organization's system.
2. A written assertion by management of the service organization about whether, in all material respects, and based on suitable criteria

   a. Management's description of the service organization's system fairly presents the service organization's system that was designed and implemented as of a specified date.
   b. The controls related to the control objectives stated in management's description of the service organization's system were suitably designed to achieve those control objectives as of the specified date.

3. A service auditor's report that expresses an opinion on the matters in 2.a. – 2.b.

Report on management's description of a service organization's system and the suitability of the design and operating effectiveness of controls (referred to in this section as a *type 2 report*). A report that comprises

1. Management's description of the service organization's system.
2. A written assertion by management of the service organization, about whether in all material respects and, based on suitable criteria,

   a. The description of the service organization's system fairly presents the service organization's system that was designed and implemented throughout the specified period.
   b. The controls related to the control objectives stated in the description of the service organization's system were suitably designed throughout the specified period to achieve those control objectives.
   c. The controls related to the control objectives stated in the description of the service organization's system operated effectively throughout the specified period to achieve those control objectives.

3. A service auditor's report that

   a. Expresses an opinion about the matters in 2.a. - 2.c.
   b. Includes a description of the service auditor's tests of controls and the results thereof.

> **NOTE:** The two primary differences between a type 1 and type 2 report are that (1) a type 2 report deals with controls over a time period (often a year) while a type 1 deals with controls at a point in time and (2) only a type 2 report addresses operating effectiveness.

Sarbanes-Oxley Act of 2002 (SOX). A set of reforms that strengthened penalties for corporate fraud, restricted the types of consulting CPAs can perform for audit clients, and created the Public Company Accounting Oversight Board to oversee CPAs and public accounting firms.

Service auditor. A practitioner who reports on controls at a service organization.

Service organization. An organization or segment of an organization that provides services to user entities that are likely to be relevant to user entities' internal control as it relates to financial reporting.

Service organization's system. The policies and procedures designed, implemented and documented by management of the service organization to provide user entities with the services covered by the service auditor's report. Management's description of the service organization's system identifies the services covered, the period to which the description relates (or I the case of a type 1 report, the date to which the description relates), the control objectives specified by management or an outside party, the party specifying the control objectives (if not specified by management), and the related controls.

Significant deficiency. A deficiency, or a combination of deficiencies, in internal control that is less severe than a material weakness, yet important enough to merit attention by those charged with governance.

Substantive procedure. An audit procedure designed to detect material misstatements at the assertion level. Substantive procedures comprise tests of details (classes of transactions, account balances, and disclosures) and substantive analytical procedures.

Those charged with governance. The person(s) or organization(s) (for example, a corporate trustee) with responsibility for overseeing the strategic direction of the entity and the obligations related to the accountability of the entity. This includes overseeing the financial reporting process. Those charged with governance may include management personnel; for example, executive members of a governance board or an owner-manager.

Tests of controls. An audit procedure designed to evaluate the operating effectiveness of controls in preventing, or detecting/correcting material misstatements at the assertion level.

User auditor. An auditor who audits and reports on the financial statements of a user entity.

User entity. An entity that uses a service organization and whose financial statements are being audited.

Walk-through. A procedure in which an auditor follows a transaction from origination through the company's processes, including information systems, until it is reflected in the company's financial records, using the same documents and information technology that company personnel use. Walkthrough procedures usually include a combination of inquiry, observation, inspection of relevant documentation, and reperformance of controls.

Module 4: Responding to Risk Assessment: Evidence Accumulation and Evaluation

Overview

The entire financial statement audit may be described as a process of evidence accumulation and evaluation. This process enables the auditor to formulate an informed opinion as to whether the financial statements are presented fairly in accordance with US generally accepted accounting principles. The following "Diagram of an Audit" was first presented and explained in the auditing overview section.

Diagram of an Audit

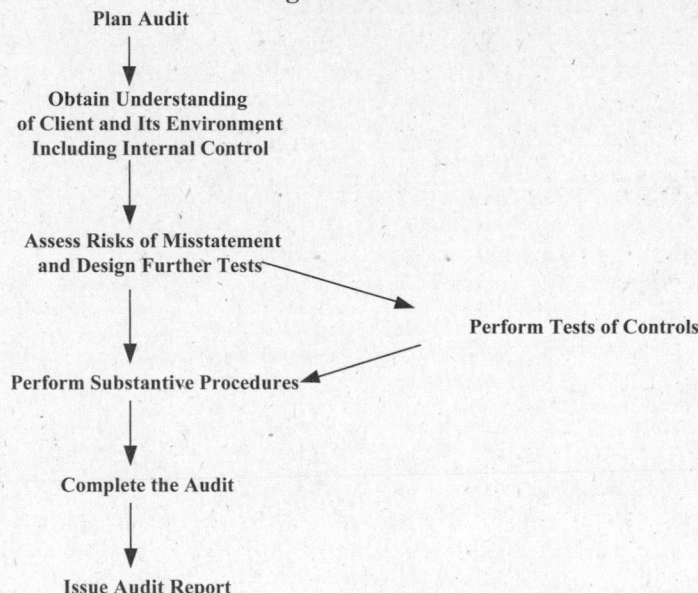

After assessing the risks of material misstatement, the auditors design and perform further audit procedures—tests of controls and substantive tests. The internal control module discussed tests of controls. This module emphasizes substantive procedures. It first covers audit evidence as a concept and discusses types of audit evidence generated through performance of substantive procedures, both (1) substantive analytical procedures and (2) tests of details of transactions, account balances, and disclosures. It concludes with audit procedures involved in completing the audit.

Numerous questions on audit evidence appear on each CPA exam. Multiple-choice questions frequently ask the candidate to select the audit procedure most likely to detect misstatements that have occurred in given situations, and to distinguish among various concepts such as

1. Appropriate vs. sufficient evidence
2. Analytical procedures vs. tests of details of transactions, account balances, and disclosures
3. Audit objectives vs. audit procedures

A simulation question may require the candidate to select appropriate audit procedures for a particular account and to research the professional standards on some aspect of that account (e.g., when are negative confirmation requests appropriate). Alternatively, the candidate may be required to calculate various ratios using a spreadsheet and to then interpret those ratios.

This module covers information included in the Evidence and Procedures Section of the AICPA Content Specification Outline with the following exceptions: (1) Use of the Computer in Performing the Audit is covered in the Auditing with Technology Module; and (2) Use of Statistical Sampling in Performing the Audit is covered in the Audit Sampling Module.

The following SAS sections pertain to audit evidence:

AU Section

326	Audit Evidence
328	Auditing Fair Value Measurements and Disclosures
329	Analytical Procedures
330	The Confirmation Process
331	Inventories
332	Auditing Derivative Instruments, Hedging Activities, and Investments in Securities
333	Client Representations
334	Related-Party Transactions
336	Using the Work of a Specialist
337	Inquiry of a Client's Lawyer Concerning Litigation, Claims, and Assessments
342	Auditing Accounting Estimates
390	Consideration of Omitted Procedures After the Report Date
558	Supplementary Information Required by the FASB
560	Subsequent Events
561	Subsequent Discovery of Facts Existing at the Date of the Auditor's Report
722	Review of Interim Financial Information
801	Compliance Auditing Applicable to Governmental Entities and Other Recipients of Governmental Financial Assistance

Read the various sections and study the outlines for each of the above SAS separately. After studying each outline, attempt to summarize in your own words the "sum and substance" of the pronouncement. If you cannot explain the pronouncement in your own words, you do not understand it. Go back and study it again.

A. Evidence—General

The second attestation standard and the third audit fieldwork standard both require the collection of sufficient appropriate evidence to provide a reasonable basis for the conclusion to be issued in the report. Audit evidence is all the information used by the auditor in arriving at the conclusions on which the audit opinion is based. It includes information contained in the accounting records underlying the financial statements and other information.

As background pertaining to financial statements, bear in mind that when management prepares financial statements that are supposed to be in conformity with generally accepted accounting principles, certain assertions (implicit or explicit) are made. AU 326 identifies and classifies these assertions which we originally presented in Module 2 as

Account Balances	Transaction Classes	Disclosures
Existence—Assets, liabilities, and equity interests exist.	*Occurrence*—Transactions and events that have been recorded have occurred and pertain to the entity.	*Occurrence*—Disclosed events and transactions have occurred.
Rights and obligations—The entity holds or controls the rights to assets, and liabilities are the obligations of the entity.		*Rights and obligations*—Disclosed events pertain to the entity.
Completeness—All assets, liabilities, and equity interests have been recorded.	*Completeness*—All transactions and events have been recorded.	*Completeness*—All disclosures that should have been included have been included.
Valuation and allocation—Assets, liabilities, and equity interests are included at appropriate amounts.	*Accuracy*—Amounts and other data relating to recorded transactions have been recorded appropriately.	*Accuracy and valuation*—Information is disclosed fairly and at appropriate amounts.
	Cutoff—Transactions and events have been recorded in the correct accounting period.	
	Classification—Transactions and events have been recorded in the proper accounts.	*Classification and understandability*—Information is presented and described clearly.

Later in this module we will discuss audit programs in detail. In those audit programs, which emphasize account balances, we will summarize the assertions into one list (based primarily upon account balances) as follows:

Presentation and disclosure—accounts are described and classified in accordance with generally accepted accounting principles, and financial statement disclosures are complete, appropriate, and clearly expressed.

Existence and occurrence—assets, liabilities, and equity interests exist, and recorded transactions and events have occurred.

Rights and obligations—the company holds rights to the assets, and liabilities are the obligations of the company.

Completeness and cutoff—all assets, liabilities, equity interests, and transactions that should have been recorded have been recorded, and all transactions and events are recorded in the appropriate accounting period.

Valuation, allocation, and accuracy—all transactions, assets, liabilities, and equity interests are included in the financial statements at proper amounts.

(PERCV—as in, "I perceive the need to pass the CPA exam.")

Note the relationship between existence and completeness. The existence assertion relates to whether the recorded amount is bona fide (e.g., recorded receivables are legitimate). Completeness, on the other hand, addresses the issue of whether all transactions have been recorded (e.g., are all receivables recorded?). An auditor must test for both existence and completeness. This concept of "directional testing" is discussed in Section D of the Internal Control Module.

The Statement on Attestation Standards suggests two basic types of evidence collection procedures: (1) search and verification, and (2) internal inquiries and comparisons. Search and verification procedures include procedures such as inspecting assets, confirming receivables, and observing the counting of inventory. Internal inquiry and comparison procedures include discussions with firm representatives and analytical procedures such as ratio analysis.

As described in greater detail in the Reporting Module, accountants perform (1) examinations, (2) reviews, (3) agreed-upon procedures, and (4) compilation accounting engagements. Of these forms of association, an examination offers the highest level of assurance. (An "audit" is considered to be an examination of financial statements.) In examinations, accountants select from among all available audit procedures to determine whether the appropriate assertions (generally PERCV in the case of financial statements) have been met.

A review offers limited assurance (also referred to as negative assurance) with respect to information. It is composed primarily of internal inquiries and comparisons. However, when evidence with respect to an assertion seems incomplete or inaccurate, search and verification procedures may be performed.

Agreed-upon procedures result in a report in which a summary of findings is provided. The extent of the procedures is specified by the user, but must exceed the attester's mere reading of the assertions.

Compilations, which are considered accounting and attest services, result in a report that provides no explicit assurance on the information. While the accountant who performs a compilation should understand the nature of the client's business and its accounting records, s/he is not required to make any inquiries or perform any other verification procedures beyond reading the information. As is the case with all other forms of association, material known misstatements or omissions must be disclosed in the accountant's report that is expanded to disclose the situation.

Three presumptions (asked directly and indirectly on several previous exams) relate to the validity of evidence: (1) evidence from independent sources provides more assurance than evidence secured solely from within the entity, (2) information from direct personal knowledge is more persuasive than information obtained indirectly, and (3) assertions developed under effective internal control are more reliable than those developed in the absence of internal control.

1. **Sufficient Appropriate Audit Evidence.** The third fieldwork standard requires that the auditor obtain sufficient appropriate audit evidence. Sufficient appropriate evidence has been obtained when audit risk is reduced to an acceptable level. What do the terms sufficient and appropriate mean? Section AU 326 points out that *sufficiency* is the measure of the quantity of audit evidence that must be obtained. *Appropriateness* is the measure of the quality of that audit evidence—both its *relevance* and *reliability* in providing support for, or detecting misstatements. *Relevance* relates to the assertion being addressed. For example, analyzing the confirmation with a client's customers of accounts receivable may provide evidence on the existence of receivables at year-end, yet only limited information relating to whether the client has completely recorded all receivable accounts. The *reliability* of evidence is dependent on the circumstances in which it is obtained. While generalizations are difficult and subject to exceptions, audit evidence is *ordinarily* more reliable when it is

   • Obtained from knowledgeable independent sources *outside the client company* rather than nonindependent sources
   • Generated internally through a system of *effective controls* rather than ineffective controls
   • Obtained *directly* by the auditor rather than indirectly or by inference (e.g., observation of application of a control is more reliable than an inquiry to the client concerning the control)
   • *Documentary* in form (paper, electronic, or other) rather than an oral representation
   • Provided by *original documents* rather than copies or facsimiles

   AU 326 suggests that in the great majority of cases the auditor finds it necessary to rely on evidence that is persuasive rather than conclusive. An acceptable level of audit risk does not indicate that **all** uncertainty be eliminated for sufficient evidence to have been gathered. The auditor must be able to form an opinion within a reasonable length of time, at a reasonable cost. However, the difficulty or expense involved in testing a particular item is not in itself a valid reason for omitting a test. Auditors use professional judgment to determine the extent of tests necessary to obtain sufficient evidence. In exercising this professional judgment, auditors consider both the materiality of the item in question (e.g., dollar size) as well as the inherent risk of the item (e.g., cash, due to its liquidity, may have a higher inherent risk than do certain property, plant, and equipment items).

The following example distinguishes between appropriate vs. sufficient evidence. Assume that an auditor has highly credible evidence on one account receivable for $400 out of a total receivable balance of $1,000,000. While this evidence is appropriate, most auditors would suggest that it is not sufficient evidence for the $1,000,000 balance; to be sufficient, more evidence verifying the account's **total** value must be collected.

Obtaining sufficient appropriate evidence is particularly difficult when auditing client accounting estimates (e.g., allowance for doubtful accounts, loss reserves, pension expenses). AU 342 suggests that the auditor's objectives relating to estimates are to determine that all estimates (1) have been developed, (2) are reasonable, and (3) follow GAAP. Typically these estimates are needed because the valuation of some accounts is based on future events or because certain evidence cannot be accumulated on a timely, cost-effective basis. Know that the three basic approaches for evaluating the reasonableness of these estimates are (1) to review and test management's process of deriving the estimate (consider the reasonableness and accuracy of management's approach), (2) develop one's own expectation of the accounting estimate and compare it to management's, and (3) review subsequent events or transactions occurring prior to the completion of fieldwork which bear on the estimate.

2. **Types of Audit Evidence.** Recall from Module 2 that at the account level audit risk is composed of the risk of material misstatement (inherent risk and control risk) and the risk that the auditor's procedures do not detect a material misstatement). The auditor should obtain audit evidence to draw reasonable conclusions on which to base the audit opinion by performing audit procedures. The following are the basic procedures used in an audit:

- **Risk assessment procedures**—Used to obtain an understanding of the entity and its environment, including its internal control. Risk assessment procedures are discussed in detail in Module 2.
- **Tests of controls**—When necessary, or when the auditor has decided to do so, used to test the operating effectiveness of controls at the relevant assertion level. Tests of controls are discussed in detail in Module 3.
- **Substantive procedures**—Used to detect material misstatements in transactions, account balances, and disclosures. Substantive procedures include substantive analytical procedures and test of details of account balances, transactions, and disclosures.

Tests of controls and substantive procedures are referred to as "further procedures" in that they are designed based on the risk assessment and follow that stage. Substantive procedures are used to restrict detection risk. As the acceptable level of detection risk decreases, the assurance provided by substantive procedures must increase. This increased assurance may be obtained by modifying the nature, timing, and/or extent of substantive procedures as follows:

- **Nature**—Use more effective procedures, such as tests directed toward independent parties rather than toward parties within the entity.
- **Timing**—Perform tests at year-end rather than at an interim date.
- **Extent**—Use a larger sample size.

Audit evidence includes the information contained in the *accounting records* underlying the financial statements and *other information*. *Accounting records* generally include the records of initial entries and supporting records, such as

- Documents, including checks and records of electronic fund transfers, invoices, contracts
- General and subsidiary ledgers, journal entries, and other adjustments to the financial statements that are not reflected in formal journal entries
- Records such as worksheets and spreadsheets supporting cost allocations, computations, reconciliations, and disclosures

Other information that the auditor may use as audit evidence includes

- Minutes of meetings
- Confirmations from third parties
- Industry analysts' reports
- Comparable data about competitors (benchmarking)
- Controls manuals
- Information obtained by the auditor from such audit procedures as inquiry, observation, and inspection
- Other information developed by or available to the auditor that permits the auditor to reach conclusions through valid reasoning

Since the quality of audit evidence depends upon the financial statement assertion under consideration, the auditor must use professional judgment when deciding which type of evidence is most appropriate in a specific situation. Conceptually, the auditor should attempt to gather a sufficient quantity of appropriate evidence at a minimum cost.

Audit procedures (acts to be performed) are used as risk assessment procedures, tests of controls, and substantive procedures. The following is a list of types of procedures:

- *Inspection of records or documents* (e.g., invoice for an equipment purchase transaction)
- *Inspection of tangible assets* (e.g., inventory items)
- *Observation* (e.g. observation of inventory count, observation of control activities)
- *Inquiry* (e.g., written inquiries and oral inquiries)
- *Confirmation* (e.g., accounts receivable)
- *Recalculation* (e.g., checking the mathematical accuracy of documents or records.)
- *Reperformance* (e.g., reperforming the aging of accounts receivable)
- *Analytical procedures* (e.g., scanning numbers for reasonableness, calculating ratios)

Numerous other terms have been used in both the professional standards and in auditing texts. Some of the more frequent terms that you will find in written audit programs include the following:

Agree (schedule balances to general ledger)
Analyze (account transactions)
Compare (beginning balances with last year's audited figures)
Count (cash, inventory, etc.)
Examine (authoritative documents)
Foot (totals)
Prove (totals)
Read (minutes of directors' meetings)
Reconcile (cash balance)
Review (disclosure, legal documents)
Scan (for unusual items)
Trace (from support to recorded entry)
Vouch (from recorded entry to support)

The auditor may obtain the assistance of client personnel to perform certain tasks (e.g., prepare schedules) providing the auditor adequately tests the work performed by these individuals.

NOW REVIEW MULTIPLE-CHOICE QUESTIONS 1 THROUGH 14 IN VOLUME 2

B. Evidence—Specific (Substantive Procedures)

As noted earlier, the objective of an audit is to express an opinion on whether the company's financial statements are fairly presented in conformity with generally accepted accounting principles. Substantive procedures are designed to assist the auditor in reaching this goal by determining whether the specific balances of financial statement accounts, transactions, and disclosures are in conformity with generally accepted accounting principles. While tests of controls are used to test the "means" of processing (internal control), substantive procedures are used to directly test the "ends" of processing—the financial statements.

When evaluating evidence, auditors estimate the amount of misstatements within the financial statements, and determine whether it exceeds a material amount. The auditor estimates the likely misstatement in the financial statements and attempts to determine whether an unacceptably high audit risk exists. Note that in the evaluation of audit evidence, because of the information obtained during the audit, the auditor may revise his/her preliminary estimate of materiality (see discussion in Module 2).

1. **Types of Substantive Procedures.** Substantive procedures are of two types: (1) Substantive analytical procedures, (2) Tests of details of transactions, account balances, and disclosures.

   a. **Analytical procedures.** Analytical procedures consist of evaluations of financial information made by a study of plausible relationships among financial and nonfinancial data. Analytical procedures are used for the following purposes:

      Planning—Determine the nature, timing, and extent of tests (Required)

      Substantive procedures—Substantiate accounts for which overall comparisons are helpful

      Overall review—Assess conclusions reached and evaluate overall financial statement presentation (Required)

      > **NOTE:** GAAS requires the use of analytical procedures during the planning stage and the final review stage. Analytical procedures are **not** a required substantive procedure.

      The following table summarizes some important characteristics of analytical procedures performed at the three stages of an audit. Make certain that you know all of the information presented on it.

Stage of audit	Required?	Purpose	Comment
Planning	Yes	To assist in planning the nature, timing and extent of other auditing procedures	Generally use data aggregated at a high level
Substantive Procedures	No	To obtain evidence about particular assertions related to account balances or classes of transactions	Effectiveness depends upon (a) Nature of assertion (b) Plausibility and predictability of relations (c) Reliability of data (d) Precision of expectation
Overall Review	Yes	To assist in assessing the conclusions reached and in the evaluation of the overall financial statement presentation	Includes reading financial statements to consider (a) Adequacy of evidence gathered for unusual or unexpected balances identified during planning or during course of audit (b) Unusual or unexpected balances or relationships not previously identified

Perhaps the most familiar example of analytical procedures used in auditing is the calculation of ratios. However, analytical procedures range from simple comparisons of information through the use of complex models such as regression and time series analysis. The typical approach is

(1) Develop an expectation for the account balance
(2) Determine the amount of difference from the expectation that can be accepted without investigation
(3) Compare the company's account balance (or ratio) with the expected account balance
(4) Investigate significant differences from the expected account balance

When developing an expectation, the auditor must attempt to identify plausible relationships. These expectations may be derived from

(1) The information itself in prior periods
(2) Anticipated results such as budgets and forecasts
(3) Relationships among elements of financial information within the period
(4) Industry information
(5) Relevant **nonfinancial** information

Relationships differ in their predictability. Be familiar with the following principles:

(1) Relationships in a dynamic or unstable environment are less predictable than those in a stable environment.
(2) Relationships involving balance sheet accounts are less predictable than income statement accounts (because balance sheet accounts represent balances at one arbitrary point in time).
(3) Relationships involving management discretion are sometimes less predictable (e.g., decision to incur maintenance expense rather than replace plant).

Recall from earlier in this module (section A) that the reliability of evidence varies based on whether it is obtained from (1) independent sources, (2) personal knowledge, or (3) developed under strong internal control. In addition, in the case of analytical procedures be aware that use of data that has been subjected to audit testing and data available from a variety of sources increases the reliability of the data used in the analysis.

Principal limitations concerning analytical procedures include

(1) The guidelines for evaluation may be inadequate (e.g., Why is an industry average good? Why should the ratio be the same as last year?).
(2) It is difficult to determine whether a change is due to a misstatement or is the result of random change in the account.
(3) Cost-based accounting records hinder comparisons between firms of different ages and/or asset compositions.
(4) Accounting differences hinder comparisons between firms (e.g., if one firm uses LIFO and another uses FIFO the information is not comparable).
(5) Analytical procedures present only "circumstantial" evidence in that a "significant" difference will lead to additional audit procedures as opposed to direct detection of a misstatement.

b. **Tests of details of transactions, balances, and disclosures.** These tests are used to examine the actual details making up the various account balances and disclosures. For example, if receivables total $1,000,000 at year-end, tests of details may be made of the individual components of the total account. Assume the $1,000,000 is the accumulation of 250 individual accounts. As a test of details, an auditor might decide to confirm a sample of these 250 accounts. Based on the results of the auditor's consideration of internal control and tests of controls, the auditor might determine that 60 accounts should be confirmed. Thus, when responses are received and when the balances have been reconciled, the auditor has actually tested the detail supporting the account; the **existence** of the accounts has been confirmed. As an additional test (and also as an alternative procedure when confirmation replies have not been received from debtors), the auditor may examine cash receipts received subsequent to year-end on individual accounts. This substantive procedure provides evidence pertaining to both the **existence** and the **valuation** of the account.

> **NOTE:** In gathering sufficient appropriate audit evidence, auditors seek an efficient and effective combination of (1) tests of controls, (2) analytical procedures, and (3) tests of details to afford a reasonable basis for an opinion.

2. **Substantive Procedure Audit Programs.** An audit program is a detailed list of the audit procedures to be performed in the course of an audit. It is helpful to understand the nature of audit programs for various accounts to help reply to a variety of multiple choice questions and, possibly, to a simulation. The professional standards require a written audit program for each audit.

As noted earlier under "Evidence—Specific (Substantive Procedures)," financial statements that purport to be in conformity with generally accepted accounting principles contain certain assertions: presentation and disclosure, existence or occurrence, rights and obligations, completeness and cutoff, and valuation, allocation, or accuracy (PERCV). Auditors gather evidence to form an opinion with respect to these assertions. The experienced auditor should be able to prepare an audit program for an audit area (e.g., inventory) to test whether these assertions are supportable. The process is one in which specific audit objectives are developed (also either explicitly or implicitly) based on the assertions being made in the financial statements. Finally, audit procedures to meet these audit objectives are formulated and listed in an audit program. These relationships may be illustrated as

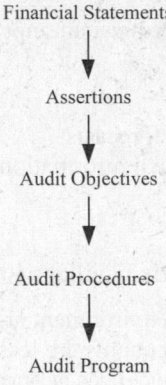

Financial Statements

↓

Assertions

↓

Audit Objectives

↓

Audit Procedures

↓

Audit Program

For purposes of the CPA exam, consider two possible approaches for auditing an account

(1) Direct tests of ending balance ("tests of balances")
(2) Tests of inputs and outputs during the year ("tests of details of transactions")

An auditor may emphasize the first approach to directly test ending balances for high turnover accounts such as cash, accounts receivable, accounts payable, etc. (e.g., confirm year-end balances). The second approach, tests of transactions (inputs and outputs during the year), is used most extensively for lower turnover accounts (e.g., fixed assets, long-term debt, etc.). For example, for fixed assets, a low turnover account, the emphasis will be on vouching additions or retirements—not on auditing the entire account for a continuing audit engagement. Bear in mind, however, that during an audit it is **not** an either/or proposition—a **combination of approaches** with an emphasis of one approach over the other will generally be used.

The tables that appear at the end of this section present summarized substantive audit programs for the major balance sheet accounts. Although the programs are constructed to present the pertinent procedures under only one assertion, be aware that many audit procedures provide support for multiple assertions. The purpose is to use the PERCV assertions to organize your thoughts about audit programs. When you think about a program you need not worry about which assertion an audit procedure "best fits under." However, recall from Section A of this module and Section C of the Internal Control Module on directional testing, that some objective questions may ask which assertion a procedure applies most directly to (e.g., analysis of inventory turnover rates most directly applies to valuation). You must use your understanding of the assertions for the specific procedure presented in that type of question. Section C of this module should help you understand the nature of various audit procedures.

In reviewing the summary audit procedures, you will find a number of similarities between areas. We have provided the following "overall framework" to help you identify the similarities.

Overall: The following are typical procedures included in a substantive audit program.

Presentation and Disclosure:

Review disclosure. Always include a general disclosure requirement related to overall compliance with GAAP.

Inquire about disclosures. Consider specific disclosure requirements for the account, as well as for related accounts. Example: for receivables, you would recall from your accounting courses such possibilities as factoring, pledging, or discounting.

Existence or Occurrence:

Confirmation. Often an account will lend itself to confirmation (e.g., bank for cash, debtor for receivables, stock registrar and transfer agent for stock authorized and outstanding).

Observation. Always consider whether you can observe the item itself and/or a legal document representing the item. Examples: cash on hand, inventory, loan agreements.

Trace/Vouch transactions. This step relates directly to "directional testing" as presented in Section C of the Internal Control Module. Example: for receivables the auditor may examine shipping documents, invoices, and credit memos.

Rights and Obligations:

Authorization. Consider whether there are transactions that require specific authorization. Authorization of transactions relates to whether proper rights and obligations have been established. This step is not always included, but programs for accounts such as receivables, debt, and owners' equity accounts are affected.

Completeness and Cutoff:

Analytical procedures. Always include a step on analytical procedures. Also, mention specific procedures for the account being audited. Section C of this module provides examples for the various accounts.

Omissions. Consider how transactions (adjustment) could improperly have been omitted from the account. Examples here include inventory count sheets not included, accruals not made, debt not recorded.

Cutoff. Auditors must consider whether transactions have been reported in the proper period. Think about the transactions affecting the account to determine the proper cutoff. For example, cash cutoffs will relate to receipts and disbursements of cash, while receivables will relate to credit sales and cash receipts.

> **NOTE:** Be careful here. Cutoffs also apply directly to the existence/occurrence and completeness assertions. If a multiple-choice question is asked, the specific details of the question determine the most directly related assertion.

Valuation, Allocation, and Accuracy:

Foot schedules. Consider the actual schedules involved with the account and include a step to foot and cross-foot them.

Agree schedules balances to general ledger balances.

Agree financial statement balances to schedules. Because financial statements are derived from accounting information, the general and subsidiary ledgers as well as other accounting records must be summarized. Examples: accounts receivable, inventory count sheets.

Consider valuation method of account. You should consider the accounting method used, and whether it has been properly applied. Most accounts have a number of steps here. Examples: Receivables must be valued net of an appropriate allowance, inventory costing methods (e.g., LIFO, FIFO), and application of the lower of cost or market rule. Always integrate your accounting knowledge with auditing procedures here.

Consider related accounts. When you are considering an audit program for a balance sheet account, know that it ordinarily will include procedures used to audit the related income statement accounts. Examples: analytical procedures for bad debt expense may provide evidence as to the valuation of receivables; recalculating interest expense may provide evidence as to the existence of long-term debt; and recalculating depreciation and applying analytical procedures to repairs and maintenance expense may provide evidence as to the completeness and/or valuation of property, plant, and equipment.

Audit objectives. The CPA exam may ask for the auditor's "objectives" in the audit of an account. In general there will be one or more "objectives" relating to each of the financial statement assertions. For example, in the case of long-term debt, the following could serve as objectives:

1. Determine whether internal control over long-term debt is adequate
2. Determine whether long-term debt disclosures comply with GAAP (presentation and disclosure)
3. Determine whether recorded long-term debt exists at year-end (existence or occurrence)
4. Determine whether long-term debt represents an obligation to the firm at year-end (rights and obligations)
5. Determine whether all long-term debt has been completely recorded at year-end (completeness)
6. Determine whether all long-term debt has been properly valued at year-end (valuation)

Areas in which a SAS prescribes procedures. The Professional Standards include a number of areas in which specific procedures are either required or suggested. A simulation question may require you to find them. Although you need not memorize the AU section, know that such procedures have been presented in areas such as the following:

Specific types of transactions	
Illegal Acts	AU 317
Related Parties	AU 334
Litigation (Loss Contingencies)	AU 337
Information with which "limited" procedures are required	
Other Information in Documents Containing Audited Statements	AU 550
Interim Reviews	AU 722
Compilations	AR 100
Reviews	AR 100
Supplemental information required by the FASB	
General Procedures	AU 558
Areas in which "audit" procedures are required	
Receivables	AU 330
Inventories	AU 331
Investment Securities	AU 332
Subsequent Events	AU 560
Other	
Other Auditors Involved	AU 543
Public Warehouses	AU 901, AU 331

While we discuss these areas throughout the various modules, the Summary of Prescribed Audit Procedures: Other Areas (see the following pages) presents lists of the primary procedures for several of the areas for which you may expect an exam question. Do not try to memorize the procedures for each of the areas. Instead, review them well before the exam and then again shortly before the exam. A simulation question might ask you to find certain of these procedures and paste them to your answer.

NOW REVIEW MULTIPLE-CHOICE QUESTIONS 15-33 IN VOLUME 2

SUMMARY AUDIT PROCEDURES[1]: CASH, RECEIVABLES, INVENTORY

	Cash	Receivables	Inventory
Presentation and Disclosure	1. Review disclosures for compliance with GAAP 2. Inquire about compensating balance requirements and restrictions	1. Review disclosures for compliance with GAAP 2. Inquire about pledging, discounting 3. Review loan agreements for pledging, factoring	1. Review disclosures for compliance with GAAP 2. Inquire about pledging 3. Review purchase commitments
Existence or Occurrence	3. Confirmation 4. Count cash on hand 5. Prepare bank transfer schedule	4. Confirmation 5. Inspect notes 6. Vouch (examine shipping documents, invoices, credit memos)	4. Confirmation of consigned inventory and inventory in warehouses 5. Observe inventory count
Rights and Obligations	6. Review bank statements	7. Inquire about factoring of receivables	6. Inquire about inventory from vendors on consignment

---
[1] Audit procedures are described in detail in Section C.

	Cash		Receivables		Inventory
Completeness and Cutoff	7. Review cutoffs (receipts and disbursements) 8. Perform analytical procedures 9. Review bank reconciliation 10. Obtain bank cutoff statement to verify reconciling items on bank reconciliation		8. Review cutoffs (sales, cash receipts, sales returns) 9. Perform analytical procedures		7. Review cutoffs (sales, sales returns, purchases, purchase returns) 8. Perform test counts and compare with client's counts/summary 9. Inquire about consigned inventory 10. Perform analytical procedures 11. Account for all inventory tags and count sheets
Valuation, Allocation and Accuracy	11. Foot summary schedules 12. Reconcile summary schedules to general ledger 13. Test translation of any foreign currencies		10. Foot subsidiary ledger 11. Reconcile subsidiary ledger to general ledger 12. Examine subsequent cash receipts 13. Age receivables to test adequacy of allowance for doubtful accounts 14. Discuss adequacy of allowance for doubtful accounts with management and compare to historical experience		12. Foot and extend summary schedules 13. Reconcile summary schedules to general ledger 14. Test inventory costing method 15. Determine that inventory is valued at lower of cost or market 16. Examine inventory quality (salable condition) 17. Test inventory obsolescence

SUMMARY AUDIT PROCEDURES:
MARKETABLE SECURITIES, PROPERTY, PLANT, AND EQUIPMENT, PREPAIDS

	Marketable securities		Property, plant, equipment		Prepaids
Presentation and Disclosure	1. Review disclosures for compliance with GAAP 2. Inquire about pledging 3. Review loan agreements for pledging 4. Review management's classification of securities		1. Review disclosures for compliance with GAAP 2. Inquire about liens and restrictions 3. Review loan agreements for liens and restrictions		1. Review disclosures for compliance with GAAP 2. Review adequacy of insurance coverage
Existence or Occurrence	5. Confirmation of securities held by third parties 6. Inspect and count 7. Vouch (to available documentation)		4. Inspect additions 5. Vouch additions 6. Review any leases for proper accounting 7. Perform search for unrecorded retirements		3. Confirmation of deposits and insurance 4. Vouch (examine) insurance polices (miscellaneous support for deposit)
Rights and Obligations	(See Existence or Occurrence)		8. Review minutes for approval of additions		(See Existence or Occurrence)
Completeness and Cutoff	8. Review cutoffs (examine transactions near year-end) 9. Perform analytical procedures 10. Reconcile dividends received to publish records		9. Perform analytical procedures 10. Vouch major entries to repairs and maintenance expense		5. Review cutoffs 6. Perform analytical procedures
Valuation, Allocation and Accuracy	11. Foot summary schedules 12. Reconcile summary schedules to general ledger 13. Test amortization of premiums and discounts 14. Determine the market value for trading and available-for-sale securities 15. Review audited financial statements of major investees		11. Foot summary schedules 12. Reconcile summary schedules to general ledger 13. Recalculate depreciation		7. Foot summary schedules 8. Reconcile summary schedules to general ledger 9. Recalculate prepaid portions

SUMMARY AUDIT PROCEDURES:
PAYABLES (CURRENT), LONG-TERM DEBT, OWNERS' EQUITY

	Payables (current)	Long-term debt	Owners' equity
Presentation and Disclosure	1. Review disclosures for compliance with GAAP 2. Review purchase commitments	1. Review disclosures for compliance with GAAP 2. Inquire about pledging of assets 3. Review debt agreements for pledging and events causing default	1. Review disclosures for compliance with GAAP 2. Review information on stock options, dividend restrictions
Existence or Occurrence	3 Confirmation 4. Inspect copies of notes and note agreements 5. Vouch payables (examine purchase order, receiving reports, invoices)	4. Confirmation 5. Inspect copies of notes and note agreements 6. Trace receipt of funds (and payment) to bank account and cash receipts journal	3. Confirmation with registrar and transfer agent (if applicable) 4. Inspect stock certificate book (when no registrar or transfer agent) 5. Vouch capital stock entries
Rights and Obligations	(See Existence or Occurrence)	7. Review minutes for proper authorization	6. Review minutes for proper authorization 7. Inquire of legal counsel on legal issues 8. Review Articles of Incorporation and bylaws for propriety of equity securities
Completeness and Cutoff	6. Review cutoffs (purchases, purchase returns, disbursements) 7. Perform analytical procedures 8. Perform search for unrecorded payables (examine unrecorded invoices, receiving reports, purchase orders) 9. Inquire of management as to completeness	8. Review cutoffs (examine transactions near year-end) 9. Perform analytical procedures 10. Inquire of management as to completeness 11. Review bank confirmations for unrecorded debt	9. Perform analytical procedures 10. Inspect treasury stock certificates
Valuation, Allocation and Accuracy	10. Foot subsidiary ledger 11. Reconcile subsidiary ledger to general ledger 12. Recalculate interest expense (if any) 13. For payroll, review year-end accrual 14. Recalculate other accrued liabilities	12. Foot summary schedules 13. Reconcile summary schedules to general ledger 14. Vouch entries to account 15. Recalculate interest expense and accrued interest payable	11. Agree amounts to general ledger 12. Vouch dividend payments 13. Vouch all entries to retained earnings 14. Recalculate treasury stock transactions

SUMMARY OF PRESCRIBED AUDIT PROCEDURES: OTHER AREAS

Professional Standard Section	Illegal acts AU 317	Related parties—identifying transactions AU 334	Related parties—determining existence AU 334	Litigation, claims, and assessments AU 337	Required supplemental information AU 558	Subsequent events AU 560
1. Discuss with Management	a. Policies for prevention b. Policies for identifying, evaluating, and accounting c. Inquire as to existence NOTE: Audits do not include procedures designed specifically to detect illegal acts. However, normal audit procedures may bring illegal acts to the auditor's attention.	a. Inquire as to existence	a. Policies for identifying and accounting b. Obtain list of related parties c. Inquire as to existence	a. Policies for identifying, evaluating, and accounting for b. Obtain description	a. Measurement methods, significant assumptions, consistency with prior periods	a. Contingent liabilities b. Significant changes in capital stock, debt, working capital c. Current status of estimated items d. Unusual items after balance sheet date
2. Examine	a. Consider laws and regulations b. Normal tests of controls (compliance tests) and substantive test examination procedures	a. SEC filings b. Minutes of Board of Directors and others c. Conflict of interest statements	a. SEC filings b. Pensions, other trusts, and identify officers thereof c. Stockholder listings (for closely held firms) d. Prior year audit workpapers	a. Correspondence and invoices from lawyers b. Minutes—stockholders, directors, others c. Read contracts, agreements, etc. d. Other documents.	a. Compare with financial statements and other information	a. Latest interim statements b. Minutes of stockholders, directors, etc.
3. Other Procedures	a. Coordinate with loss contingency procedures b. Consideration of internal control c. Read minutes d. Overall substantive tests e. Include in representation letter	a. Review business with major customers, suppliers, etc. b. Consider services being provided (received) at unreasonable prices c. Review accounting records for large, unusual transactions d. Review confirmations e. Review invoices from lawyers f. Consideration of internal control g. Provide audit personnel with names of known related parties	a. Contact predecessor and other auditors b. Review material investment transactions c. Know that such transactions are more likely for firms in financial difficulty	a. Letters of audit inquiry to clients's lawyers	a. Add to representation letter b. Perform further inquiries if information seems incorrect c. Apply any other required procedures for specific area being considered	a. Include in representation letter b. Coordinate with loss contingency procedures c. Cutoff procedures (sales, purchases)

3. **Documentation (AU 339 and PCAOB 3).** Make certain that you are familiar with the information in the outline of AU 339. You should know that

   a. Audit documentation should be prepared so as to enable an experienced auditor, with no previous connection to the audit, to understand procedures performed, audit evidence obtained, and conclusions reached.

   b. While it is not necessary to document every matter considered during an audit, oral explanations alone (absent working paper documentation) are not sufficient to support the work of the auditor.

   c. Audit documentation should include a written audit program (or set of audit programs) for every audit.

   d. Documentation relating to documents inspected by the auditor should allow an experienced auditor to determine which ones were tested.

   e. The auditor should identify any information that contradicts or is inconsistent with auditor's final conclusion regarding significant matter and how the matter was addressed in forming a conclusion, but need not retain documentation that is incorrect or superseded. Documentation of the contradiction or inconsistency may include procedures performed, records documenting consultations, differences in professional judgment among team members or between team members and others consulted.

   f. If information is added to the working papers after the issuance of the audit report, documentation should include (1) when and by whom changes were made and reviewed, (2) specific reasons for changes, and (3) the effect, if any, of the changes on the auditor's conclusion.

   g. The documentation completion period is 60 days following the report release date. That means that changes resulting from the process of assembling and completing the audit file may be made within 60 days following the date the audit report was released to the client. The fact that these changes have been made need not be documented. Examples of such changes include routine file-assembling procedures, deleting discarded documentation, sorting, and signing off file completion checklists. However, the auditor may not add new information to the working papers unless it is documented per f. above.

   h. After the documentation completion date, the auditor should not delete or discard audit documentation. Additions are treated as per f. above.

   i. The retention period (how long audit documentation must be kept) should not be less than five years from the report release date (longer if legal and regulatory requirements so require).

   j. Audit documentation is the property of the auditor and is confidential.

PCAOB Standard 3 contains documentation requirements for audits and reviews of issuer (public) companies—you should review the outline of Standard 3, which follows the AU Outlines. The requirements differ from AICPA standards in these significant ways.

   1. The documentation must demonstrate that the engagement complied with PCAOB standards.

   2. The documentation completion period is 45 days (not 60 days) following the report release date.

   3. The retention period is seven years (rather than five years).

Additionally, candidates should be aware of the following terms:

Working Trial Balance—A listing of ledger accounts with current year-end balances (as well as last year's ending balances), with columns for adjusting and reclassifying entries as well as for final balances for the current year. Typically both balance sheet and income statement accounts are included.

Lead Schedules—Schedules that summarize like accounts, the total of which is typically transferred to the working trial balance. For example, a client's various cash accounts may be summarized on a lead schedule with only the total cash being transferred to the working trial balance.

Index—The combination of numbers and/or letters given to a workpaper page for identification and organization purposes. For example, cash workpaper may be indexed A-1.

Cross-Reference—When the same information is included on two workpapers, auditors indicate on each workpaper the index of the other workpaper containing the identical information. For example, if Schedule A-1 includes a bank reconciliation with total outstanding checks listed, while Schedule A-2 has a detailed list of these outstanding checks plus the total figure, the totals on the two workpapers will be cross-referenced to one another.

Current Workpaper Files—Files that contain corroborating information pertaining to the current year's audit program (e.g., cash confirmation)

Permanent Workpaper Files—Files that contain information that is expected to be used by the auditor on many future audits of a client (e.g., copies of articles of incorporation and bylaws, schedules of ratios by year, analyses of capital stock accounts, debt agreements, and internal control)

> **NOW REVIEW MULTIPLE-CHOICE QUESTIONS 34 THROUGH 47 IN VOLUME 2**

C. Other Specific Audit Evidence Topics

1. Cash

a. **Special audit considerations for cash**

(1) **Kiting.** Kiting is a form of fraud that overstates cash by causing it to be simultaneously included in two or more bank accounts. Kiting is possible because a check takes several days to clear the bank on which it is drawn (the "float period"). Following is an example of how kiting can be used to conceal a prior embezzlement in a company that has two bank accounts (one in Valley State Bank and one in First City Bank).

Date	Situation
12/15	Bookkeeper writes himself a $10,000 check on the Valley account, and cashes it—no journal entry is made
12/16	Bookkeeper loses the money gambling in Bullhead City
12/31	Bookkeeper, fearing the auditors will detect the fraud, conceals the shortage by

1. Writing a $10,000 unrecorded check on First City account and depositing it in the Valley account. This will cover up the shortage because Valley will credit the account for the $10,000, and the check will not clear the First City account until January—no journal entry is made until after year-end.
2. When the First City bank reconciliation is prepared at 12/31, the check is not listed as outstanding.

Kiting may be detected by preparing a bank transfer schedule, by preparing a four-column bank reconciliation for the Valley account, or by obtaining a cutoff statement for the First City account.

(2) **Bank transfer schedule.** A bank transfer schedule shows the dates of all transfers of cash among the client's various bank accounts. Know that its primary purpose is to help auditors to **detect kiting**. The schedule is prepared by using bank statements for the periods before and after year-end **and** by using the firm's cash receipts and disbursements journals. The following is an example of a bank transfer schedule that will help an auditor to detect the kiting described in (1) above:

		Date			Date	
Amount	Bank drawn on	Books	Bank	Bank deposited in	Books	Bank
$10,000	First City	1/2	1/2	Valley	1/2	12/31

Note that analysis of the schedule reveals that at December 31, the cash is double counted: it is included in both the Valley account (the bank gave credit for the deposit on 12/31) and in the First City account. Another misstatement that may arise is caused when the date per books for deposit and withdrawal are in different periods (e.g., 12/31 and 1/1).

(3) **Bank reconciliations.** Auditors generally prepare either a two- or a four-column bank reconciliation for the difference between the cash per bank and per books. The four column approach (also called a proof of cash) **will** allow the auditor to reconcile

(a) All cash receipts and disbursements recorded on the books to those on the bank statement and
(b) All deposits and disbursements recorded on the bank statement to the books.

A four-column reconciliation **will not** allow the auditor to verify whether

(a) Checks written have been for the wrong amounts and so recorded on both the books and the bank statement and
(b) Unrecorded checks or deposits exist that have not cleared the bank.

In the earlier kiting example, note that the Valley four-column reconciliation will detect the kiting because the 12/15 credit for the check used in the embezzlement will have been included in the Valley bank statement disbursements, but not on the books as of 12/31. This is because the embezzlement will result in a $10,000 unreconciled difference between the book and bank totals in the disbursements column of the reconciliation. The First City reconciliation, by itself, will not assist in detection of the kiting because both book and bank entries occur after year-end.

(4) **Bank cutoff statements.** A cutoff statement is a bank statement for the first 8-10 business days after year-end. Know that its primary purpose is to help auditors to **verify reconciling items** on the year-end bank reconciliation. Tests performed using a cutoff statement include verifying that outstanding checks have been completely and accurately recorded as of year-end, and that deposits in transit have cleared within a reasonable period. The statement is sent directly by the bank to the auditor. In the above kiting example, the cutoff statement for the First City account will allow the auditor to detect the fraud since it will include the December 31 unrecorded check.

(5) **Standard confirmation form.** Auditors use a standard form to obtain information from financial institutions (Standard Form to Confirm Account Balance Information with Financial Institutions). The form requests information on two types of balances—**deposits** and **loans**. The form requests financial institutions to indicate any exceptions to the information noted, and to confirm any additional account or loan balance information that comes to their attention while completing the form. Know that the form is designed to substantiate evidence primarily on the **existence** assertion, and not to discover or provide assurance about accounts not listed on the form (evidence on the completeness assertion is not elicited).

b. **Typical substantive audit procedures for cash**

(1) Review disclosures for compliance with generally accepted accounting principles.

(2) Inquire of management concerning compensating balance requirements and restrictions on cash. A compensating balance is an account with a bank in which a company has agreed to maintain a specified minimum amount; compensating balances are typically required under the terms of bank loan agreements. Such restrictions on cash, when material, should be disclosed in the financial statements.

(3) Send confirmation letters to financial institutions to verify existence of the amounts on deposit. See Section a.(5) above.

(4) Count cash on hand at year-end to verify its existence.

(5) Prepare a bank transfer schedule for the last week of the audit year and the first week of the following year to disclose misstatements of cash balances resulting from kiting. See Section a. above.

(6) Review the cutoff of cash receipts and cash disbursements around year-end to verify that transactions affecting cash are recorded accurately and in the proper period.

(7) Review bank statements to verify that book balances represent amounts to which the client has rights.

(8) Perform analytical procedures to test the reasonableness of cash balances. Tests here may include comparisons to prior year cash balances. These procedures help verify the existence and completeness as well as the accuracy of cash transactions.

(9) Review year-end bank reconciliations to verify that cash has been properly stated as of year-end. See Section a. above.

(10) Obtain a bank cutoff statement to verify whether the reconciling items on the year-end bank reconciliation have been properly reflected. See Section a. above.

(11) Foot summary schedules of cash and agree their total to the amount which will appear on the financial statements.

(12) Reconcile summary schedules of cash to the general ledger.

(13) Test translation of any foreign currencies.

2. **Receivables (AU 330)**

a. **Special audit considerations for receivables**

(1) **Lapping.** Lapping is an embezzlement scheme in which cash collections from customers are stolen and the shortage is concealed by delaying the recording of subsequent cash receipts. A simplified lapping scheme is shown below.

Date	Situation	Bookkeeping entry		
1/7	Jones pays $500 on account	No entry, bookkeeper cashes check and keeps proceeds		
1/8	Smith pays $200 on account	Cash	500	
	Adam pays $300 on account	Accounts Receivable—Jones		500
1/9	Brock pays $500 on account	Cash	500	
		Accounts Receivable—Smith		200
		Accounts Receivable—Adam		300
1/10	Bookkeeper determines Brock is unlikely to purchase from company in the future	Allowance for Doubtful Accts.	500	
		Accounts Receivable—Brock		500

Lapping most frequently occurs when one individual has responsibility for both recordkeeping and custody of cash. Although the best way to control lapping is to segregate duties and thereby make its occurrence difficult, it may be detected by using the following procedures:

(a) Analytical procedures—calculate age of receivables and turnover of receivables (lapping increases the age and decreases turnover).

(b) Confirm receivables—investigate all exceptions noted, emphasize accounts that have been written off and old accounts. For all accounts watch for postings of cash receipts which have taken an unusually long time. For example, when a reply to a confirmation suggests that the account was paid on December 29, investigate when the posting occurred.

(c) Deposit slips

        1] Obtain authenticated deposit slips from bank and compare names, dates, and amounts on remittance advices to information on deposit slips (where possible).

        2] Perform surprise inspection of deposits, and compare deposit slip with remittances.

   (d) Bookkeeping system

        1] Compare remittance advices with information recorded.

        2] Verify propriety of noncash credits to accounts receivable.

        3] Foot cash receipts journal, customers' ledger accounts, and accounts receivable control account.

        4] Reconcile individual customer accounts to accounts receivable control account.

        5] Compare copies of monthly statements with customer accounts.

(2) **Confirmations.** Confirmation of accounts receivable is a generally accepted auditing procedure. Auditors are to confirm receivables unless (1) accounts receivable are immaterial, (2) confirmations would be ineffective as an audit procedure, or (3) the combined assessment of inherent and control risk is low, and that assessment, with other substantive evidence, is sufficient to reduce audit risk to an acceptably low level.

    Receivable confirmations primarily test the **existence** assertion, and only to a limited extent the completeness and valuation assertions. Know the difference between the **positive** and **negative** forms of confirmation request.

    The positive form requests a reply from debtors. Some positive forms request the recipient to indicate either agreement or disagreement with the information stated on the request. Other positive forms, "blank forms," do not state the amount (or other information), but request the respondent to fill in the balance or furnish other information, and when used, often result in lower response rates.

    The negative form requests the recipient to respond only if he or she disagrees with the information stated on the request. Negative confirmation requests may be used when

   (a) The combined assessed level of inherent risk and control risk is low,

   (b) A large number of small balances is involved, and

   (c) The auditor has no reason to believe that recipients are unlikely to give them adequate consideration.

Note that when no reply is received to the negative form, the assumption is made that the debtor agrees with the amount and that evidence as to the existence assertion has been collected. When no reply is received to a positive confirmation, a second request is normally mailed to the debtor; if no reply to the second request is received, the auditor normally performs **alternative procedures** (e.g., examination of shipping documents, subsequent cash receipts, sales agreements). However, the auditor may consider **not performing alternative procedures** when (1) no unusual qualitative factors or systematic characteristics related to responses have been identified, and (2) the nonresponses in total, when projected as 100% misstatements to the population, are immaterial.

b. **Typical substantive audit procedures for receivables**

(1) Review disclosures for compliance with generally accepted accounting principles.

(2) Inquire of management about pledging, or discounting of receivables to verify that appropriate disclosure is provided.

(3) Review loan agreements for pledging and factoring of receivables to verify that appropriate disclosure is provided.

(4) Confirm accounts and notes receivable by direct communication with debtors to verify the existence and gross valuation of the accounts. See Section C.2.a. above.

(5) Inspect notes on hand and confirm those not on hand by direct communication with holders. For notes receivable, the auditor will generally be able to inspect the actual note. This procedure is particularly important in situations in which the note is negotiable (i.e., salable) to third parties.

(6) Vouch receivables to supporting customer orders, sales orders, invoices, shipping documents, and credit memos to verify the existence of accounts, and occurrence and accuracy of sales transactions.

(7) Review the cutoff of sales and cash receipts around year-end to verify that transactions affecting accounts receivable are recorded in the proper period. A sale is properly recorded when title passes on the items being sold. Title passes for items sold FOB shipping point when the item is shipped from inventory; title passes for items sold FOB destination when the item is received by the purchaser. You should realize that a proper credit sales cutoff generally affects at least four components of the financial statements: accounts receivable, sales, cost of goods sold, and inventory. Cash receipts should be recorded when the check (or cash) is received from a customer.

(8) Inquire about factoring of receivables to verify that the client maintains rights to the accounts.

(9) Perform analytical procedures for accounts receivable, sales, notes receivable, and interest revenue. Typical ratios include: (a) the gross profit rate, (b) accounts receivable turnover, (c) the ratio of accounts receivable to credit sales, (d) the ratio of accounts written off to the ending accounts receivable, and (e) the

ratio of interest revenue to notes receivable. These procedures typically provide evidence to support the existence, completeness, accuracy, and valuation assertions.

(10) Foot the accounts and notes receivable subsidiary ledgers to verify clerical accuracy.

(11) Reconcile subsidiary ledgers to the general ledger control accounts to verify clerical accuracy.

(12) Examine cash receipts subsequent to year-end to test the adequacy of the allowance for doubtful accounts to determine appropriate valuation.

(13) Age accounts receivable to test the adequacy of the allowance for doubtful accounts. An aging schedule is used to address the receivable valuation assertion. Such a schedule summarizes receivables by their age (e.g., 0-30 days since sale, 31-60 days since sale...). Estimates of the likely amount of bad debts in each age group are then made (typically based on historical experience) to estimate whether the amount in the allowance for doubtful accounts is adequate at year-end.

(14) Discuss the adequacy of the allowance for doubtful accounts with management and the credit department and compare it to historical experience to verify valuation.

(15) Consider changes in the economy or the company's customers that might affect the valuation of accounts receivable.

> **NOW REVIEW MULTIPLE-CHOICE QUESTIONS 48 THROUGH 74 IN VOLUME 2**

3. **Inventory (AU 331)**

   a. **Special audit consideration for inventory**

      (1) **Observation.** Observation by the auditor of the client's counting of inventory is a generally accepted auditing procedure and departure from it must be justified. During the inventory observation the auditor seeks to determine that recorded inventory items do not exist (addressing the existence assertion), that all items are recorded (completeness), and that the client has properly considered the condition of the items (valuation). You should be familiar with various situations that may affect the auditor's observation.

         (a) When a client uses statistical methods in determining inventory quantities, the auditor must be satisfied that the sampling plan has statistical validity.

         (b) The existence of good internal control, including an accurate perpetual inventory system, may allow an effective count to be made prior to year-end. In such circumstances, the auditor will rely upon internal control and tests of updating of inventory through year-end to determine that year-end inventory exists and is properly valued. The auditor may verify the accuracy of the perpetual inventory records by examining receiving reports and vendor invoices.

         (c) For a first-year client the auditor will probably not have been present for the count of the beginning inventory, a necessary input to determining cost of goods sold. If adequate evidence is available (e.g., acceptable predecessor workpapers), no report modification may be necessary. When adequate evidence is not available, the auditor may be required to qualify his/her audit report due to the scope limitation. Any resulting misstatement affects both current and prior year income and is therefore likely to result in qualification of the opinion on the income statement. The balance sheet at year-end will be unaffected due to the self-correcting nature of such an error.

         (d) Related to (c), a first-year client may have engaged the auditor subsequent to year-end and the auditor may also have missed the year-end inventory count. In addition, other events may make it impossible for the auditor to be present for the client's count of inventory. In such circumstances, alternate procedures may sometimes be used to establish the accuracy of the count (e.g., good internal control); however, these alternate procedures **must include some physical counts of inventory items** and must include appropriate tests of intervening transactions.

   b. **Typical substantive audit procedures for inventory**

      (1) Review disclosures for compliance with generally accepted accounting principles.

      (2) Inquire of management about pledging of inventory and verify the adequacy of disclosure.

      (3) Review purchase and sales commitments to verify whether there may be a need to either accrue a loss and/or provide disclosure. Generally, commitments are not disclosed in the financial statements unless uneconomic commitments result in a need to accrue significant losses (due to current price changes).

      (4) Confirm consigned inventory and inventory in warehouses. Some companies store inventory items in public warehouses. In such a situation, the auditor should confirm in writing with the custodian that the goods are being held. Additionally, if such holdings are significant, the auditor should apply one or more of the following procedures:

         (a) Review the client's control procedures relating to the warehouseman.

         (b) Obtain a CPA's report on the warehouseman's internal control.

(c) Observe physical counts of the goods.

(d) If warehouse receipts have been pledged as collateral, confirm with lenders details of the pledged receipts.

(5) Observe the taking of the physical inventory and make test counts to verify the existence (and to a limited extent the ownership and valuation) of inventory. See Section C.3.a. above.

(6) Review cutoffs of sales, sales returns, purchases, and purchase returns around year-end to verify that transactions affecting inventory are recorded in the proper period. Know here that the objective is to include in inventory those items for which the client has legal title.

(7) Perform test counts during the observation of the taking of the inventory and compare them to the client's counts and subsequently to the accumulated inventory to verify the accuracy of the count and its accumulation. See Section C.3.a. above.

(8) Inquire of management as to the existence of consigned inventory to verify the adequacy of its disclosure. Know that inventory consigned out remains the property of the client until it is sold. Inventory consigned to the client must not be included in the physical count since it belongs to the consignor.

(9) Perform analytical procedures to test the reasonableness of inventory. Analytical procedures include calculation of gross profit margins by product, and inventory turnover rates. Analytical procedures are particularly effective at identifying obsolete inventory and, therefore, are useful in determining its proper valuation.

(10) Account for all inventory tags and count sheets to verify that inventory has been completely recorded.

(11) Foot and extend summary inventory schedules to verify clerical accuracy.

(12) Reconcile inventory summary schedules to the general ledger to verify clerical accuracy.

(13) Test the inventory cost method to verify that it is in conformity with generally accepted accounting principles. Here the auditor will determine the method of pricing used and whether it is acceptable and consistent with the prior years (e.g., LIFO, FIFO).

(14) Test the pricing of inventory to verify that it is valued at the lower of cost or market and that inventory and cost of goods sold transactions are accurately recorded. As a general rule, inventories should not be carried in excess of their net realizable value. The accuracy of pricing is determined by reference to vendor invoices (for wholesalers and retailers) and to vendor invoices, requisitions, and labor reports (for manufacturers). In certain circumstances a specialist may be needed to assist in valuation of inventory (see Section 13, Using the Work of a Specialist, below).

(15) Examine inventory quality and condition to assess whether there may be evidence suggesting that it is in unsatisfactory condition.

(16) Perform any necessary additional tests of inventory obsolescence to verify the valuation of inventory.

4. **Investment Securities (AU 332)**
(Review outline of AU 332 at this point)

a. **Special audit considerations for investment securities**

(1) **GAAP requirements.** Recall the criteria for deciding whether the cost adjusted for fair value, equity, or consolidated basis should be used for the investments (see outlines of APB 18 and SFAS 94). Also recall the distinction in accounting treatment under SFAS 115 for debt securities and equity securities where significant influence does not exist. Accounting for derivative instruments is presented in SFAS 133.

(2) **Audit approach.** Evidence related to the **existence** assertion is obtained by inspecting any securities that are held by a client (often in a safe deposit box) and by confirming securities held by custodians (e.g., a bank or trust company). A client employee should be present during the inspection to avoid confusion over any missing securities. In examining the security certificates, the auditor determines whether securities held are identical to the recorded securities (certificate numbers, number of shares, face value, etc.).

Evidence pertaining to **valuation** (carrying amount) for long-term investments for an investee may be obtained by examining investee (a) audited financial statements, (b) unaudited financial statements (insufficient evidence in and of itself), (c) market quotations, and (d) other evidence.

(3) **Simultaneous verification.** Because of the liquid nature of securities, the auditor's inspection is generally performed at year-end simultaneously with the audit of cash, bank loans (e.g., a revolving credit agreement), and other related items.

(4) **Client controls.** The liquid nature of marketable securities makes certain controls, such as the following, desirable:

(a) The treasurer should authorize purchases and sales up to a certain value. After that value has been reached, transactions should be authorized by the board of directors.

(b) Two individuals should be present when access to the securities is necessary.

(c) Recorded balances for investments should periodically be compared with the actual securities held by individuals independent of the function.

b. **Typical substantive audit procedures for investment securities**

(1) Review disclosures for compliance with generally accepted accounting principles.
(2) Inquire of management about pledging of investment securities and verify that appropriate disclosure is provided.
(3) Review loan agreements for pledging of investment securities and verify that appropriate disclosure is provided.
(4) Review management's classification of securities held for investment.
(5) Obtain confirmation of securities in the custody of others to verify their existence.
(6) Inspect and count securities on hand and compare serial numbers with those shown on the records and, if appropriate, with prior year audit working papers. This procedure addresses the existence of the securities and provides evidence that no fraud involving "substitution" (e.g., unauthorized sale and subsequent repurchase) of securities has occurred during the year. When an auditor is unable to inspect and count securities held in a safe-deposit box at a bank until after the balance sheet date, a bank representative should be asked to confirm that there has been no access between the balance sheet date and the security count date.
(7) Vouch purchases and sales of securities during the year. This audit procedure will provide evidence relating to all financial statement assertions. Included here will be recomputation of gains and losses on security sales.
(8) Review the cutoff of cash receipts and disbursements around year-end to verify that transactions affecting investment securities transactions are recorded accurately and in the proper period.
(9) Perform analytical procedures to test the reasonableness of investment securities. A typical analytical procedure is to verify the relationship between interest and dividend income to the related securities. The auditor will also be able to recompute the interest and dividend income if so desired.
(10) Reconcile amounts of dividends received to published dividend records generally available from databases maintained on the Internet to verify the completeness and accuracy of dividend revenue.
(11) Foot and extend summary investment security schedules to verify clerical accuracy.
(12) Reconcile summary inventory schedules to the general ledger to verify clerical accuracy.
(13) Test amortization of premiums and discounts to verify that investments are properly valued.
(14) Determine the market value of securities classified as trading or available-for-sale at the date of the balance sheet.
(15) Review audited financial statements of major investments to test whether they are properly valued at year-end.

5. **Property, Plant, and Equipment (PP&E)**

a. **Special audit considerations for PP&E**

(1) **Accounting considerations.** Many PP&E acquisitions involve trades of used assets. Module 11, Section C, points out that under SFAS 153 most nonmonetary exchanges of these assets are recorded using the fair value of the asset exchanged.
      Assets constructed by a company for its own use should be recorded at the cost of direct material, direct labor, and applicable overhead. Recall that interest may be capitalized.
      PP&E must be tested for impairment when facts and circumstances indicate that the asset's value may be impaired.
(2) **Overall approach.** The reasonableness of the entire account balance must be audited in detail for a client that has not previously been audited. When a predecessor auditor exists, the successor will normally review that auditor's workpapers.
      For a continuing audit client, the audit of PP&E consists largely of an analysis of the year's acquisitions and disposals (an input and output approach). Subsequent to the first year, the account's slow rate of turnover generally permits effective auditing of the account in less time than accounts of comparable size.
(3) **Relationship with repairs and maintenance.** A number of CPA questions address this area. A PP&E acquisition may improperly be recorded in the repair and maintenance expense account. Therefore, an analysis of repairs and maintenance may detect **understatements** of PP&E. Alternatively, an analysis of PP&E may disclose repairs and maintenance that have improperly been capitalized, thereby resulting in **overstatements** of PP&E. Expenditures that make the asset more productive or extend its useful life should be capitalized in the asset account (betterment) or as a debit to accumulated depreciation (life extension).
(4) **Unrecorded retirements.** Disposals may occur due to retirements or thefts of PP&E items. Simple retirements of equipment are often difficult to detect since no journal entry may have been recorded to reflect the event. Unrecorded or improperly recorded retirements (and thefts) may be discovered through examination of changes in insurance policies, consideration of the purpose of recorded acquisition, examination of property tax files, discussions, observation, or through an examination of debits to accumulated depreciation and of credits to miscellaneous revenue accounts. Inquiry of the plant manager may disclose unrecorded retirements and/or obsolete equipment.

b. **Typical substantive audit procedures for PP&E**

(1) Review disclosures for compliance with generally accepted accounting principles.

(2) Inquire of management concerning any liens and restrictions on PP&E. PP&E may be pledged as security on a loan agreement. Such restrictions are disclosed in the notes to the financial statements.

(3) Review loan agreements for liens and restrictions on PP&E and verify that appropriate disclosure is provided.

(4) Inspect major acquisitions of PP&E to verify their existence.

(5) Vouch additions and retirements to PP&E to verify their existence, accuracy, and the client's rights to them. Typically large PP&E transactions support will include original documents such as contracts, deeds, construction work orders, invoices, and authorization by the directors. This procedure will also help to identify transactions that should be expensed rather than capitalized.

(6) Review any leases for proper accounting to determine whether the related PP&E assets should be capitalized.

(7) Perform search for unrecorded retirements and for obsolete equipment. See Section C.5.a. above.

(8) Review minutes of the board of directors (and shareholders) to verify that additions have been properly approved.

(9) Perform analytical procedures to test the reasonableness (existence, completeness, and valuation) of PP&E. Typical analytical procedures involve a (a) comparison of total cost of PP&E divided by cost of goods sold, (b) comparison of repairs and maintenance on a monthly and annual basis, and (c) comparison of acquisitions and retirements for the current year with prior years.

(10) Obtain or prepare an analysis of repairs and maintenance expense and vouch transactions to discover items that should have been capitalized. See Section C.5.a. above.

(11) Foot PP&E summary schedules to verify clerical accuracy.

(12) Reconcile summary PP&E schedules to the general ledger to verify clerical accuracy.

(13) Recalculate depreciation to establish proper valuation of PP&E. In addition, the existence of recurring losses on retired assets may indicate that depreciation charges are generally insufficient.

(14) Consider any conditions that indicate that assets may be impaired to determine that the assets are properly valued. Indications of possible impairment include discontinuance of a business segment or type of product, excessive capacity, loss of major customers, etc.

c. **Intangible assets** are audited similar to PP&E. They are generally valued at cost and amortized over their useful lives. However, goodwill is not amortized; instead it is tested for impairment at least annually. Research and development expenditures are not capitalized. They are expensed as incurred.

6. **Prepaid Assets**

a. **Special audit considerations for prepaid assets**

(1) **Overall.** Prepaid assets typically consist of items such as insurance and deposits. Insurance policies may be examined and the prepaid portion of any expenditure may be recalculated. Additionally, policies may be confirmed with the company's insurance agent and/or payments may be vouched. Deposits and other prepaid amounts are typically immaterial. When they are considered material, an auditor may confirm their existence, recalculate prepaid portions, and examine any available support.

(2) **Self-insurance.** The lack of insurance on an asset (or inadequate insurance) will not typically result in report modification, although this may be disclosed in the notes to the financial statements. Also, an auditor may serve an advisory role by pointing out assets that, unknown to management, may have inadequate insurance.

b. **Typical substantive audit procedures for prepaid assets**

(1) Review disclosures for compliance with generally accepted accounting principles.

(2) Review the adequacy of insurance coverage.

(3) Confirm deposits and insurance with third party to verify their existence and valuation.

(4) Vouch additions to accounts (examine insurance policies and miscellaneous other support for deposit) to verify existence and accuracy.

(5) Perform analytical procedures to test the reasonableness of prepaid assets. A primary procedure here is comparison with prior year balances and obtaining explanations for any significant changes.

(6) Foot prepaid summary schedules to verify accuracy.

(7) Reconcile summary schedules to the general ledger to verify proper accuracy and valuation.

(8) Recalculate prepaid portions of prepaid assets to verify proper valuation.

NOW REVIEW MULTIPLE-CHOICE QUESTIONS 75 THROUGH 98 IN VOLUME 2

7. **Payables (Current)**

   a. **Special audit considerations for payables**

      (1) **Confirmation.** Confirmations may be sent to vendors. However, such confirmation procedures are sometimes omitted due to the availability of externally generated evidence (e.g., both purchase agreements and vendors' invoices) and due to the inability of confirmations to adequately address the completeness assertion. (Auditors are primarily concerned about the possibility of understated payables; a major payable will not in general be confirmed if the client completely omits it from the trial balance of payables.)

          Accounts payable confirmations are most frequently used in circumstances involving (1) bad internal control, (2) bad financial position, and (3) situations when vendors do not send month-end statements. However, when an auditor has chosen to confirm payables despite the existence of vendor statements, the confirmation will generally request the vendor to send the month-end statement to the auditor. For this reason, the balance per the client's books is not included on such a confirmation.

          Confirmations are sent to (1) major suppliers, (2) disputed accounts, and (3) a sample of other suppliers: Major suppliers are selected because they represent a possible source of large understatement: the client will normally have established large credit lines. The size of the **recorded** payable at year-end is of less importance than for receivables. While as a practical matter large year-end recorded balances will normally be confirmed, the emphasis on detecting understated payables may lead the auditor to also confirm accounts with relatively low recorded year-end balances. Also, if the payables to be confirmed are selected from a list of vendors instead of from the recorded year-end payables, the completeness assertion as well as the existence assertion may be addressed.

      (2) **The search for unrecorded liabilities.** The search for unrecorded liabilities is an effort to discover any liabilities that may have been omitted from recorded year-end payables (completeness). Typical procedures include the following:

        (a) Examination of vendors' invoices and statements both immediately prior to and following year-end
        (b) Examination, **after year-end,** of the following to test whether proper cutoffs have occurred:

            1] Cash disbursements
            2] Purchases
            3] Unrecorded vouchers (receiving reports, vendors' invoices, purchase orders)

        (c) Analytical procedures
        (d) Internal control is analyzed to evaluate its likely effectiveness in preventing and detecting the occurrence of such misstatements.

   b. **Typical substantive audit procedures for payables**

      (1) Review disclosures for compliance with generally accepted accounting principles.
      (2) Review purchase commitments to determine whether there may be a need to either accrue a loss and/or provide disclosure (see also step 3 of inventory program).
      (3) Confirm accounts payable by direct correspondence with vendors. Confirmation of payables provides evidence relating to the occurrence, obligation, completeness, accuracy, and valuation assertions. See Section C.7.a. above.
      (4) Inspect copies of notes and note agreements.
      (5) Vouch balances payable to selected creditors by inspecting purchase orders, receiving reports, and invoices to verify existence, accuracy, valuation, and to a lesser extent, completeness.
      (6) Review the cutoff of purchases, purchase returns, and disbursements around year-end to verify that transactions are recorded in the proper period.
      (7) Perform analytical procedures to test the reasonableness of payables. Examples here are ratios such as accounts payable divided by purchases, and accounts payable divided by total current liabilities.
      (8) Perform search for unrecorded payables to determine whether liabilities have been completely recorded. See Section C.7.a. above.
      (9) Inquire of management as to the completeness of payables.
    (10) Foot the subsidiary accounts payable ledger to test clerical accuracy.
    (11) Reconcile the subsidiary ledger to the general ledger control account to verify clerical accuracy.
    (12) Recalculate interest expense on interest-bearing debt.
    (13) Recalculate year-end accrual for payroll. A typical procedure here is to allocate the total days in the payroll subsequent to year-end between the old and new years and to determine whether the accrual is reasonable.
    (14) Recalculate other accrued liabilities. The approach for accruals is largely one of (1) testing computations made by the client in setting up the accrual, and (2) determining that the accruals have been treated consistently with the past. Note that the audit approach here is somewhat different than for accounts payable that, because one or more transactions usually directly indicate the year-end liability, do not require such a computation. Examples of accounts requiring accrual include property taxes, pension plans, vacation pay, service guarantees, commissions, and income taxes payable.

8. **Long-Term Debt**

   a. **Special audit considerations for long-term debt**

      (1) **Overall approach.** Despite the fact that this account's turnover rate is low, considerable analysis is performed on its ending balance. Confirmations are frequently used; recall that when the debt is owed to banks, confirmation is obtained with the standard bank confirmation. In addition, minutes of director and/or stockholder meetings will be reviewed to determine whether new borrowings have been properly authorized.

      The proceeds of any new borrowings are traced to the cash receipts journal, deposit slips, and bank statements. Repayments are traced to the cash disbursements journal, canceled checks, and canceled notes. If a debt trustee is used, it will be possible to obtain information through use of a confirmation whether the repayments have been made.

   b. **Typical substantive audit procedures for long-term debt**

      (1) Review disclosures for compliance with generally accepted accounting principles.
      (2) Inquire of management concerning pledging of assets related to debt.
      (3) Review debt agreements for details on pledged assets and for events that may result in default on the loan.
      (4) Confirm long-term debt with payees or appropriate third parties (including any applicable sinking fund transactions).
      (5) Obtain and inspect copies of debt agreements to verify whether provisions have been met and disclosed.
      (6) Trace receipt of funds (and payments) to the bank account and to the cash receipts journal to verify that the funds were properly received (or disbursed) by the company.
      (7) Review the cutoff of cash receipts and disbursements around year-end to verify that transactions affecting debt are recorded in the proper period.
      (8) Review minutes of board of directors' and/or shareholders' meetings to verify that transactions have been properly authorized and, if necessary, that an opinion of an attorney has been obtained regarding the legality of the debt.
      (9) Perform analytical procedures to verify the overall reasonableness of long-term debt and interest expense.
      (10) Inquire of management as to the completeness of debt.
      (11) Review bank confirmations for any indication of unrecorded debt.
      (12) Foot summary schedules of long-term debt to test clerical accuracy.
      (13) Reconcile summary schedules of long-term debt to the general ledger to verify clerical accuracy.
      (14) Vouch entries in long-term debt accounts to test existence, obligation, and accuracy of debt.
      (15) Recalculate interest expense and accrued interest payable to determine accuracy of the amounts.

9. **Owners' Equity**

   a. **Special audit considerations for owners' equity**

      (1) **Control of capital stock transactions.** Clients use one of two approaches for capital stock transactions. First, a stock certificate book may be used which summarizes shares issued through use of "stubs" which remain after a certificate has been removed. The certificates for outstanding shares are held by the stockholders; canceled certificates (for repurchased stock or received when a change in stock ownership occurs) are held by the client. When a stock certificate book is used auditors reconcile outstanding shares, par value, etc., with the "stubs" in the book. Confirmations are sometimes sent to stockholders. Since capital stock transactions are generally few in number, the audit of this area takes relatively less audit time.

      The second approach, typically used by large clients, is to engage a registrar and a stock transfer agent to manage the company's stock transactions. The primary responsibility of the registrar is to verify that stock which is issued is properly authorized. Stock transfer agents maintain detailed stockholder records and carry out transfers of stock ownership. The number of shares authorized, issued, and outstanding will usually be confirmed to the auditor directly by the registrar and stock transfer agent.

      (2) **Retained earnings.** Little effort will be exerted in auditing the retained earnings of a continued client. The audit procedures for dividends will allow the auditor to verify the propriety of that debit to retained earnings. The entry to record the year's net income (loss) is readily available. Finally, the nature of any prior period adjustments is examined to determine whether they meet the criteria for an adjustment to retained earnings. Recall that the type of adjustment typically encountered is a correction of prior years' income.

   b. **Typical substantive audit procedures for stockholders' equity**

      (1) Review disclosures for compliance with generally accepted accounting principles.
      (2) Review Articles of Incorporation, bylaws, and minutes for provisions relating to stock options, and dividends restriction.

(3) Confirm stocks authorized, issued, and outstanding with the independent registrar and stock transfer agent (if applicable).

(4) For a corporation that acts as its own stock registrar and transfer agent, reconcile the stock certificate book to transactions recorded in the general ledger.

(5) Vouch transactions and trace receipt of funds (and payment) to the bank account and to the cash receipts journal to verify that the funds were properly received (or disbursed) by the company.

(6) Review minutes of the board of directors' and/or shareholders' meetings to verify that stock transactions and dividends have been properly authorized.

(7) Inquire of the client's legal counsel to obtain information concerning any unresolved legal issues.

(8) Review the Articles of Incorporation and bylaws for the propriety of equity transactions.

(9) Perform analytical procedures to test the reasonableness of dividends.

(10) Inspect treasury stock certificates to verify that transactions have been completely recorded and that client has control of certificates.

(11) Agree amounts that will appear on the financial statements to the general ledger.

(12) Vouch dividend payments to verify that amounts have been paid.

(13) Vouch all entries affecting retained earnings.

(14) Recalculate treasury stock transactions.

10. **Revenue**

   a. **Special audit considerations for revenue**

      (1) **Overall approach.** Most revenue accounts are verified in conjunction with the audit of a related asset or liability account. For example

Balance Sheet Account	Revenue Account
Accounts receivable	Sales
Notes receivable	Interest
Investments	Interest, dividends, gains on sales
Property, plant, and equipment	Rent, gains on sales

      (2) Module 9 discusses revenue recognition. Most frequently sales are recorded during the period in which title has passed, or services have been rendered to customers who have made firm, enforceable commitments to purchase such goods or services. SEC Staff Accounting Bulletin 101 provides a more specific, helpful overall set of criteria for revenue recognition.

         (a) Persuasive evidence of an arrangement exists.
         (b) Delivery has occurred or services have been rendered.
         (c) The seller's price to the buyer is fixed or determinable.
         (d) Collectibility is reasonably assured.

      (3) **Potential problem areas for revenues**

         (a) **Bill and hold transactions.** Transactions in which a customer agrees to purchase goods but the seller retains physical possession until the customer requests shipment to designated locations. Because delivery has not yet occurred, such transactions do not ordinarily qualify. The primary requirements to qualify for revenue recognition are that the buyer make an absolute commitment to purchase, has assumed the risks and rewards of the product, and is unable to accept delivery because of some compelling reason.

         (b) **Side agreements.** Agreements used to alter the terms and conditions of recorded sales transactions, often to convince customers to accept delivery of goods and services. Side agreements are frequently hidden from the board of directors and may create obligations that relieve the customer of the risks and rewards of ownership. Accordingly, side agreement terms *may* preclude revenue recognition.

         (c) **Channel stuffing (trade loading).** A marketing practice that suppliers sometimes use to boost sales by inducing distributors to buy substantially more inventory than they can promptly resell. Inducements may range from deep discounts on the inventory to threats of losing the distributorship if inventory is not purchased. Channel stuffing may result in the need to increase the level of anticipated sales returns.

         (d) **Related-party transactions.** A variety of potential misstatements may occur due to transactions with related parties. For example, sales of the same inventory back and forth among affiliated companies may "freshen" receivables.

   b. **Substantive test approach for revenues not verified in the audit of balance sheet accounts**

      (1) Perform analytical procedures related to revenue accounts.
      (2) Obtain or prepare analyses of selected revenue accounts.
      (3) Vouch selected transactions and determine that they represent proper revenue for the period.

11. **Expenses**

    a. **Special audit considerations for expenses**

       (1) **Overall approach.** Most expense accounts are verified in conjunction with the audit of a related asset or liability account. For example

Balance Sheet Account	Expense Account
Accounts receivable	Uncollectible accounts
Inventories	Purchases, cost of goods sold, payroll
Property, plant, and equipment	Depreciation, repairs, and maintenance
Accrued liabilities	Commissions, fees, product warranty expenses

    b. **Substantive test approach for expenses not verified in the audit of balance sheet accounts**

       (1) Perform analytical procedures related to the expense accounts.
       (2) Obtain or prepare analyses of selected expense accounts.
       (3) Vouch selected transactions.

> **NOW REVIEW MULTIPLE-CHOICE QUESTIONS 99 THROUGH 120 IN VOLUME 2**

12. **Client Representation Letters (AU 333).** Review the outline and note that representation letters are required for audits. In reviewing the outline be generally familiar with the various representations obtained by auditors. Expect multiple-choice questions on matters such as the following:

    a. The representation letter should be addressed to the auditor, in a letter dated no earlier than the date of the auditor's report.
    b. The representation letter should be signed by the chief executive officer and the chief financial officer.
    c. Representations from management are not a substitute for the application of other necessary auditing procedures.
    d. Representations should be obtained for all periods being reported upon, even if management was not present during all of those periods.
    e. Management refusal to furnish written representations **precludes** an unqualified opinion, and ordinarily results in a disclaimer, although a qualified opinion may be appropriate in some circumstances.

13. **Using the Work of a Specialist (AU 336).** Read the outline of this standard. Auditors increasingly are finding it necessary to use the work of specialists in areas such as postemployment and postretirement benefits, environmental cleanup obligations, fair value disclosures and derivatives, as well as in more traditional areas such as the valuation of inventory (e.g., diamonds). This standard provides guidance both in situations in which an auditor (1) uses the work of specialists that have already performed services for a client (including client employees and specialists hired by the client such as the consulting services personnel of the CPA firm) and (2) engages specialists to perform various procedures. In all cases, the auditors should evaluate the specialist's professional qualifications, understand the objectives and scope of the specialist's work, the appropriateness of using the specialist's work, and the form and content of the specialist's findings. Several other key points from AU 336 include

    a. AU 336 applies whenever auditors use a specialist's work as evidence in performing substantive tests to evaluate financial statement assertions. For purposes of this standard, internal auditors are **not** considered specialists.
    b. To assess the qualifications of the specialist, the CPA should consider specialist professional certification, reputation, and experience in the type of work under consideration.
    c. While the work of a specialist who is a client employee may be used, the standard requires the CPA to evaluate the relationship and consider whether it might impair the specialist's objectivity. If objectivity may be impaired, additional procedures should be performed, possibly including using another specialist.
    d. The specialist is not referred to in the auditor's report unless such a reference would help report users to understand the need for an explanatory paragraph or a departure from an unmodified opinion. (If the work of the specialist is consistent with the client's financial statements, no reference is permitted.)

> **NOW REVIEW MULTIPLE-CHOICE QUESTIONS 121 THROUGH 137 IN VOLUME 2**

14. **Loss Contingencies and Inquiry of a Client's Lawyer (AU 337).** Accounting standard (e.g., FAS 5) require disclosures relating to loss contingencies, as well as adjusting journal entries for those which are probable and estimable. Loss contingencies arise due to occurrences such as

- Litigation
- Income tax disputes
- Various guarantees made by the client
- Accounts receivable sold or assigned with recourse
- Environmental issues

While auditors obtain information on many of these issues through inquiry of management, reading related correspondence, and various analyses of transactions, the client's lawyer is the primary source for corroboration of information obtained from the client concerning loss contingencies. At this point, read the outline of AU 337.

The process relating to the attorney is one in which the client prepares a list and describes claims, litigation, assessments, and unasserted claims pending against the firm. This information is sent by the auditor to the attorney who is to review it and provide additional input, if possible.

Refusal of the lawyer to reply is a scope limitation that may affect the audit report. If the lawyer is unable to estimate the effect of litigation, claims, and assessments on the financial statements, it may result in an uncertainty that would also have an effect on the audit report. In the case of unasserted claims that the client has not disclosed, the lawyer is **not** required to note them in his/her reply to the auditor. However, the lawyer is generally required to inform the client of the omission and to consider withdrawing if the client fails to inform the auditor. The following is a sample lawyer's letter:

> In connection with an examination of our financial statements at (balance sheet date) and for the (period) then ended, management of the Company has prepared, and furnished to our auditors (name and address of auditors), a description and evaluation of certain contingencies, including those set forth below involving matters with respect to which you have been engaged and to which you have devoted substantive attention on behalf of the Company in the form of legal consultation or representation. These contingencies are regarded by management of the Company as material for this purpose (management may indicate a materiality limit if an understanding has been reached with the auditor). Your response should include matters that existed at (balance sheet date) and during the period from that date to the date of your response.

> #### Pending or Threatened Litigation (excluding unasserted claims)

> [Ordinarily the information would include the following: (1) the nature of the litigation, (2) the progress of the case to date, (3) how management is responding or intends to respond to the litigation (for example, to contest the case vigorously or to seek an out-of-court settlement), and (4) an evaluation of the likelihood of an unfavorable outcome and an estimate, if one can be made, of the amount or range of potential loss.] Please furnish to our auditors such explanation, if any, that you consider necessary to supplement the foregoing information, including an explanation of those matters as to which your views may differ from those stated and an identification of the omission of any pending or threatened litigation, claims, and assessments or a statement that the list of such matters is complete.

> #### Unasserted Claims and Assessments (considered by management to be probable of assertion, and that, if asserted, would have at least a reasonable possibility of an unfavorable outcome)

> [Ordinarily management's information would include the following: (1) the nature of the matter, (2) how management intends to respond if the claim is asserted, and (3) an evaluation of the likelihood of an unfavorable outcome and an estimate, if one can be made, of the amount or range of potential loss.] Please furnish to our auditors such explanation, if any, that you consider necessary to supplement the foregoing information, including an explanation of those matters as to which your views may differ from those stated.

> We understand that, in the course of performing legal services for us with respect to a matter recognized to involve an unasserted possible claim or assessment that may call for financial statement disclosure, if you have formed a professional conclusion that we should disclose or consider disclosure concerning such possible claim or assessment, as a matter of professional responsibility to us, you will so advise us and will consult with us concerning the question of such disclosure and the applicable requirements of Statement of Financial Accounting Standards No. 5. Please specifically confirm to our auditors that our understanding is correct.

> Please specifically identify the nature of and reasons for any limitation on your response.

> [The auditor may request the client to inquire about additional matters, for example, unpaid or unbilled charges or specified information on certain contractually assumed obligations of the company, such as guarantees of indebtedness of others.]

(Section 337, Appendix)

15. **Fair Values (AU 328).** Generally accepted accounting principles require companies to use "fair value" for measuring, presenting, and disclosing various accounts (e.g., investments, intangible assets, impaired assets, derivatives). Fair value is generally considered to be the amount at which an asset (or liability) could be bought or sold in a current transaction between willing parties.

The determination of fair value is easiest when there are published price quotations in an active market (e.g., a stock exchange). Determining fair value is more difficult when an active market does not exist for items such as various investment properties or complex derivative financial instruments. In such circumstances fair value may be calculated through the use of a valuation model (e.g., a model based on forecasts and discounting of future cash flows). Auditing fair values is similar to that of other estimates (see topic A.1 of this module) in that a combination of three approaches is often used—(1) review and test management's process, (2) independently develop as estimate, or (3) review subsequent events.

When reviewing management's process (approach 1), the auditors consider whether the assumptions used by management are reasonable, whether the valuation model seems appropriate, and whether management has used relevant information that is reasonably available. Developing one's own estimate (approach 2) offers the advantage of allowing the auditors to compare that estimate with that developed by management. Reviewing subsequent events (approach 3) allows the auditors to use information obtained subsequent to year-end to help evaluate the reasonableness of management's estimate. Often auditors will use a combination of the approaches. Regardless of the approach(es) followed, the auditors should evaluate whether the disclosures of fair values required by GAAP have been properly presented.

16. **Related-Party Transactions (AU 334).** Review the outline of AU 334. The main issue with related-party transactions concerns the price at which a transaction occurs. This price may not be the one that would have resulted from an "arm's-length bargaining." Note the procedures suggested in Section 334 for discovering related-party transactions. Further note that it is generally not possible for the auditor to determine whether such a transaction would have occurred if no related party had existed, and, if so, the price thereof.

17. **Subsequent Events and Subsequent Discovery of Facts Existing at the Date of the Audit Report (AU 560, 561).** These two sections deal with accounting issues (e.g., how to measure and disclose certain events) as well as audit responsibility with respect to subsequent events. Section 560 classifies subsequent events into two types.

    a. Those events that provide additional evidence with respect to conditions that existed at the date of the balance sheet (for which the financial statements are to be adjusted for any changes in estimates)

    b. Those events that provide evidence with respect to conditions that did **not** exist at the date of the balance sheet but arose subsequent to that date (for which there is to be footnote disclosure)

    The following diagram depicts the two types of subsequent events.

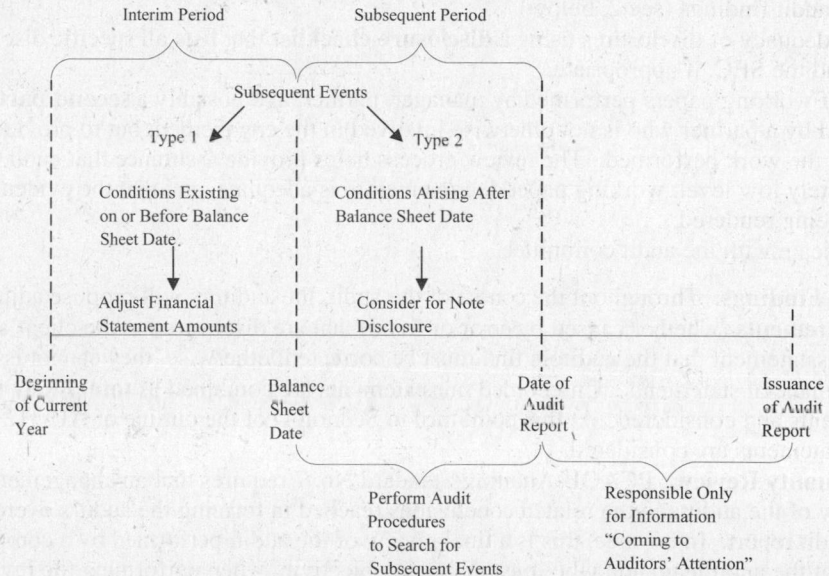

Section 560 also deals with the auditing issues involved when these types of events are noted prior to release of the audit report. Be familiar with the audit procedures that may reveal the existence of subsequent events—see Section C. In the Reports Module we discuss dating of the audit report when a subsequent event has occurred.

Section 561 deals with the auditing of events existing at the report date that are not discovered until after the release of the financial statements. Read carefully the outline of the auditor's responsibilities with respect to these events—a number of questions have been asked concerning subsequent events.

18. **Omitted Procedures Discovered after the Report Date (AU 390).** Subsequent to issuance of an audit report, an auditor may realize that one or more necessary procedures were omitted from the audit. When this occurs, the auditor should first assess its importance. If omission is considered important (i.e., it affects present ability to support the previously expressed opinion) and if the auditor believes individuals are relying or are likely to rely on the financial statements, the procedures or alternate procedures should be promptly applied. If the procedure is then applied and misstatements are detected, the auditor should review his/her responsibilities under AU 561 on subsequent discovery of facts existing at the date of the auditor's report. If the client does not allow the auditor to apply the necessary procedure(s), the auditor should consult his/her attorney as to appropriate action.

19. **Audit of the Statement of Cash Flows.** The statement of cash flows is prepared from the other financial statements and from analyses of increases and decreases in selected account balances. Since the amounts included in

the statement of cash flows are audited in conjunction with the audit of balance sheet and income statement accounts, only limited substantive procedures are necessary.

The statement of cash flows divides cash receipts and cash disbursements into three categories: operating, investing, and financing. In addition to comparing this information to the balance sheet and income statement, the auditors must determine whether it has been properly classified among the three categories. For example, cash flow from operations should not be overstated through inclusion of funds from either investing or financing. The auditors must also determine that the concept of cash or cash equivalents analyzed in the statement agrees with an amount shown on the balance sheet. Finally, the auditors should determine that a statement of cash flows is presented for each year for which an income statement is presented.

> **NOW REVIEW MULTIPLE-CHOICE QUESTIONS 138 THROUGH 163 IN VOLUME 2**

D. Completing the Audit

1. **Procedures Completed near the End of the Audit.** A number of audit procedures (most discussed in sections B and C) are involved in completing the audit. These procedures, completed on or near the last day of fieldwork, include

   - Search for unrecorded liabilities.
   - Review minutes of meetings of shareholders, board of directors, and the audit committee.
   - Perform final review stage analytical procedures.
   - Perform procedures, including the inquiry of client's lawyers, to identify loss contingencies.
   - Perform review for subsequent events.
   - Obtain representation letter.
   - Evaluate audit findings (see 2. below).
   - Review adequacy of disclosures using a **disclosure checklist** that lists all specific disclosures required by GAAP and the SEC, if appropriate.
   - Review of working papers performed by manager, partner, and possibly a **second partner review** performed by a partner who is not otherwise involved in the engagement but to provide an independent review of the work performed. The review process helps provide assurance that audit risk is an appropriately low level, working paper documentation is adequate, and that the evidence supports the opinion being rendered.
   - Communicate with the audit committee.

2. **Evaluate Audit Findings.** Throughout the course of the audit, the auditors will propose adjusting entries for all **material misstatements** (whether caused by error or fraud) that are discovered in the client's financial records. Any material misstatement that the auditors find must be corrected; otherwise, they cannot issue an unqualified opinion on the financial statements. Unrecorded misstatements are combined as **total likely misstatement** in the financial statements and considered. At this point turn to Section D of the outline of AU 312 to review details on how these misstatements are considered.

3. **Engagement Quality Review.** PCAOB Auditing Standard No. 7 requires that an engagement quality reviewer perform a review of the audit and the related conclusions reached in forming the audit's overall conclusions and in preparing the audit report. In essence, this is a final review of the audit, performed by a competent reviewer who isn't a member of the audit team and who must maintain objectivity when performing the review. The audit report may only be issued after the engagement quality reviewer provides concurring approval of issuance.

   The quality review process is one in which the quality reviewer evaluates the significant judgments made by the engagement team throughout the audit. This includes considering significant ricks identified by the engagement team, reviewing the engagements team's evaluation of firm independence in relation to the engagement, reviewing the financial statements, and considering other areas of the audit. The engagement quality reviewer may provide concurring approval to issue the audit report only if he or she is not aware of a significant engagement deficiency. Documentation of an engagement quality review should contain sufficient information to enable an experienced auditor having no previous connection with the engagement to understand the procedures performed by the quality reviewer.

   The AICPA *Quality Control Standards* for nonpublic company engagements require that a CPA firm establish criteria to determine which of its engagements should undergo a quality control review. Thus, the audit of a nonpublic client that meets the firm's criteria will have a quality review prior to audit report issuance. In addition, and related, various laws require certain nonpublic companies to have quality control reviews. A result of this overall situation is that many, but not all, audits of nonpublic companies also undergo a quality control review.

E. Other Related Topics

Operational Auditing. Operational audits, generally performed by internal auditors, typically evaluate the effectiveness and efficiency of various operational processes. As such they are similar to "performance audits" as presented in the outline of *Government Auditing Standards*. In fact, the topic "operational auditing" was dropped from the AICPA Content Specification Outline when compliance auditing was added.

As an example of an operational audit, consider an auditor's examination of the sales, receivables, and cash receipts cycle to consider whether policies and procedures concerning the effectiveness and efficiency of related management decision-making processes. A financial statement audit, on the other hand, would deal more directly with controls relating to the entity's ability to record, process, summarize, and report financial data consistent with the assertions in the financial statements.

NOW REVIEW MULTIPLE-CHOICE QUESTIONS 164 THROUGH 169 IN VOLUME 2

KEY TERMS

Accounting estimate. An approximation of a monetary amount in the absence of a precise means of measurement. This term is used for an amount measured at fair value where there is estimation uncertainty, as well as for other amounts that require estimation. Where this section addresses only accounting estimates involving measurement at fair value, the term fair value accounting estimates is used.

Analytical procedures. Evaluations of financial information through analysis of plausible relationships among both financial and nonfinancial data. Analytical procedures also encompass such investigation, as is necessary, of identified fluctuations or relationships that are inconsistent with other relevant information or that differ from expected values by a significant amount.

Appropriateness (of audit evidence). The measure of the quality of audit evidence; that is, its relevance and its reliability in providing support for the conclusions on which the auditor's opinion is based.

Arm's length transaction. A transaction conducted on such terms and conditions between a willing buyer and a willing seller who are unrelated and are acting independently of each other and pursuing their own best interests.

Assertions. Representations by management, explicit or otherwise, that are embodied in the financial statements, as used by the auditor to consider the different types of potential misstatements that may occur.

Audit evidence. Information used by the auditor in arriving at the conclusions on which the auditor's opinion is based. Audit evidence includes both information contained in the accounting records underlying the financial statements and other information:

1. Sufficiency of audit evidence is the measure of the quantity of audit evidence. The quantity of the audit evidence needed is affected by the auditor's assessment of the risks of material misstatement and also by the quality of such audit evidence.
2. Appropriateness of audit evidence is the measure of the quality of audit evidence; that is, its relevance and its reliability in providing support for the conclusions on which the auditor's opinion is based.

Control risk. The risk that a misstatement that could occur in an assertion about a class of transaction, account balance, or disclosure and that could be material, either individually or when aggregated with other misstatements, will not be prevented, or detected and corrected, on a timely basis by the entity's internal control.

Detection risk. The risk that the procedures performed by the auditor to reduce audit risk to an acceptably low level will not detect a misstatement that exists and that could be material, either individually or when aggregated with other misstatements.

Exception (to external confirmation request). A response that indicates a difference between information requested to be confirmed, or contained in the entity's records, and information provided by the confirming party.

External confirmation. Audit evidence obtained as a direct written response to the auditor from a third party (the confirming party), either in paper form or by electronic or other medium (for example, through the auditor's direct access to information held by a third party).

1. The auditor's direct access to information held by the confirming party may meet the definition of an external confirmation when for example, the auditor is provided by the confirming party with the electronic access codes or information necessary to access a secure website where data that addresses the subject matter of the confirmation is held.
2. The auditor's access to information held by the confirming party may also be facilitated by a third party provider. Where access codes or information necessary to access data held by a third party is provided to the auditor by management (i.e., not by the confirming party), evidence obtained by the auditor from access to such information does not meet the definition of an external confirmation.

Fraud. An intentional act by one or more individuals among management, those charged with governance, employees, or third parties, involving the use of deception that results in a misstatement in financial statements that are the subject of an audit. For financial statement audits, fraud includes two types of intentional misstatements—misstatements arising from fraudulent financial reporting and misstatements arising from misappropriation of assets.

Fraud risk factors. Events or conditions that indicate an incentive or pressure to perpetrate fraud, provide an opportunity to commit fraud, or indicate attitudes or rationalizations to justify a fraudulent action.

Fraudulent financial reporting (management fraud, cooking the books). Material misstatement of financial statements by management with the intent to mislead financial statement users.

Further audit procedures. The additional procedures that are performed based on the results of the auditors' risk assessment procedures. Such procedures include (1) tests of controls (if needed), (2) Detailed tests of transactions, balances, and disclosures, and (3) substantive analytical procedures.

Internal auditing. An independent, objective assurance and consulting activity designed to add value and improve an organization's operations. It helps an organization accomplish its objective by bring a systematic, disciplined approach to evaluate and improve the effectiveness of risk management, control, and governance processes.

Negative confirmation request. A request that the confirming party respond directly to the auditor only if the confirming party disagrees with the information provided in the request.

Nonresponse. A failure of the confirming party to respond, or fully respond, to a positive confirmation request, or a confirmation request returned undelivered.

Omitted procedure. An auditing procedure that the auditor considered necessary in the circumstances existing at the date of the audit of financial statements, but which was not performed.

Positive confirmation request. A request that the confirming party respond directly to the auditor providing the requested information or indicating whether the confirming party agrees or disagrees with the information in the request.

Related party transaction. A transaction in which one party has the ability to influence significantly the management or operating policies of the other party, to the extent that one of the transacting parties might be prevented from pursuing fully its own separate interests.

Risk assessment procedures. The audit procedures performed to obtain an understanding of the entity and its environment, including the entity's internal control, to identify and assess the risks of material misstatement, whether due to fraud or error, at the financial statement and assertion levels.

Relevant assertion. A financial statement assertion that has a reasonable possibility of containing a misstatement or misstatements that would cause the financial statements to be materially misstated. The determination of whether an assertion is a relevant assertion is made without regard to the effect of controls.

Risk of material misstatement. The risk that the financial statements are materially misstated prior to the audit. This consists of two components, inherent risk and control risk.

Scanning. A type of analytical procedure involving the auditor's use of professional judgment to review accounting data to identify significant or unusual items.

Specialist. An individual or organization possessing expertise in a field other than accounting or auditing, whose work in that field is used by the auditor to assist the auditor in obtaining sufficient appropriate audit evidence.

Subsequent events. Events occurring between the date of the financial statements and the date of the auditor's report that require adjustment of, or disclosure in, the financial statements.

Subsequently discovered facts. Facts that become known to the auditor after the date of the auditor's report that, had they been known to the auditor at that date, may have caused the auditor to amend the auditor's report.

Substantive procedure. An audit procedure designed to detect material misstatements at the assertion level. Substantive procedures comprise tests of details (classes of transactions, account balances, and disclosures) and substantive analytical procedures.

Sufficiency (of audit evidence). The measure of the quantity of audit evidence. The quantity of the audit evidence needed is affected by the auditor's assessment of the risks of material misstatement and also by the quality of such audit evidence.

Written representation. A written statement by management provided to the auditor to confirm certain matters or to support other audit evidence. Written reorientations, for purposes of his section, do not include financial statements, the assertions therein, or supporting books and records.

Module 5: Reporting

Overview

The report represents the end product of the auditor's association with the client's financial statements. The following "Diagram of an Audit," originally presented in the auditing overview section, shows the relationship of the audit report to the entire financial statement audit.

Diagram of an Audit

Plan Audit

↓

Obtain Understanding
of Client and Its Environment
Including Internal Control

↓

Assess Risks of Misstatement
and Design Further Tests

→ Perform Tests of Controls

↓

Perform Substantive Procedures

↓

Complete the Audit

↓

Issue Audit Report

This module covers the topics listed in the Reporting area of the AICPA Content Specification Outline and subsequent events (which the AICPA includes in the Audit Evidence and Procedures area of the Outline). The emphasis in this module is upon audit reports, but it also includes information on other reports (e.g., compilation reports, review reports, attestation reports).

Candidate knowledge of reports is tested on every examination. While most of the report questions refer to audit reports, a significant number refer to the other types of reports that CPAs issue. Multiple-choice questions present a circumstance that calls for a departure from the standard short form report and ask specifically what type of report is to be issued. A simulation question may require preparation of a report using electronic access to the appropriate professional standards.

All of the following sections of Statements on Auditing Standards apply to reports.

AU Section

341	The Auditor's Consideration of an Entity's Ability to Continue as a Going Concern
410	Adherence to GAAP
420	Consistency of Application of GAAP
431	Adequacy of Informative Disclosure
435	Segment Information
504	Association with Financial Statements
508	Reports on Audited Financial Statements
530	Dating the Independent Auditor's Report
534	Reporting on Financial Statements Prepared for Use in Other Countries
543	Part of Examination Made by Other Independent Auditors
550	Other Information in Documents Containing Audited Financial Statements
551	Information in Auditor-Submitted Documents
552	Reporting on Condensed Financial Statements and Selected Financial Data
558	Required Supplementary Information
560	Subsequent Events

AU Section

561	Subsequent Discovery of Facts Existing at the Report Date
623	Special Reports
625	Reports on the Application of Accounting Principles
634	Letters for Underwriters
722	Interim Financial Information
801	Compliance Auditing Considerations in Audits of Governmental Entities and Recipients of Governmental Financial Assistance

The following attestation standards outlines (all have AT prefixes) apply to this module:

Statements on Standards for Attestation Engagements (SSAE)

AT 101	Attestation Standards
AT 201	Agreed-Upon Procedures Engagements
AT 301	Financial Forecast and Projections
AT 401	Reporting on Pro Forma Financial Statements
AT 601	Compliance Attestation
AT 701	Management's Discussion and Analysis

AT 501, *Reporting on an Entity's Internal Control over Financial Reporting*, is included in the Internal Control Module.

The AU and AT sections listed earlier are very detailed. In this module, we present an overview of this information contained in those sections. In order to simplify the discussion, the topics are covered in a sequence that is different than the order in which they are presented in the codified professional standards. The best way to cover this material is to first read the background material presented in Section A of this module. Then, read each subsequent section together with the AU section outline presented later in this volume. The purpose of this module is to give you an overview of the information that will make it easier for you to understand the actual professional standards. But you should also carefully study the various outlines.

This module covers the topics listed in the Reporting area of the AICPA Content Specification Outline plus subsequent events that the AICPA includes in the Audit Evidence and Procedures area of the Outline.

A. Financial Statement Audit Reports—General

1. **Overall issues**

    a. **Forms of association.** It is useful to think about four primary forms of accountant association with information; examinations, reviews, agreed-upon procedures, and compilations.

    Examinations (referred to as audits in the case of financial statements) provide a positive opinion with reasonable assurance on whether assertions follow the appropriate criteria. The unqualified report for financial statement audits includes three paragraphs: introductory, scope, and opinion.

    Reviews provide a report that includes limited assurance. Limited assurance is also referred to as "negative assurance" because a phrase such as "I am not aware of any material modifications that should be made" is included in the report. The first paragraph of the report states that a review in accordance with AICPA standards was performed. The second paragraph indicates the limited scope of the review and the third paragraph provides the limited assurance. The procedures of a review are largely limited to internal inquiries and analytical procedures and are thus significantly more limited than an examination. In this module we discuss reviews of interim information, while in the following module we discuss reviews of financial statements of nonpublic companies that do not have audits.

    Agreed-upon procedures result in a report that provides a summary of findings. Because agreed-upon procedures will ordinarily be less in scope than examination, the report disclaims a positive opinion on the financial statements.

    Compilations provide no assurance in the report. The first paragraph states that a compilation in conformity with AICPA standards has been performed, the second paragraph states that no opinion or assurance is provided. Compilations are discussed in the following module.

    b. **Restricted-use reports vs. general-use reports (AU 532).** Reports issued by auditors differ in that some are available for only "restricted use" while others are available for "general use."

    Restricted-use auditors' reports are intended only for specified parties. Ordinarily "specified parties" are those parties to the agreement (e.g., management, the board of directors, the audit committee, others within the organization, and sometimes, regulatory agencies). The following three circumstances result in a restricted-use auditors' report and should be issued:

    (1) The subject is based on criteria in contractual agreements or regulatory provisions that are not in accordance with GAAP or another comprehensive basis of accounting
    (2) Agreed-upon procedures engagements

(3) "By-products" of an audit (for example, internal control significant deficiencies letters [AU 325], and communications with audit committees [AU 380])

An auditor's report that is restricted should contain a separate paragraph at the end of the report that includes

(1) A statement that the report is intended solely for the information and use of the specified parties
(2) An identification of the specified parties to whom use is restricted
(3) A statement that the report is not intended to be and should not be used by anyone other than the specified parties

General-use auditors' reports are not restricted to specified parties. These reports are on information that is ordinarily understandable by a broader set of individuals than is the information reported upon in restricted-use reports. For example, audit reports on financial statements prepared in accordance with GAAP provide an illustration of what is ordinarily a general-use report.

2. **Financial Statement Audit Reports—Nonissuer (Nonpublic) Companies.** Most CPA exam questions pertain to audits of financial statements. The following standard short-form report for a nonpublic company was originally presented in the overview section:

Independent Auditor's Report

To: Board of Directors and Stockholders
ABC Company

We have audited the accompanying balance sheets of ABC Company as of December 31, 20X2 and 20X1, and the related statements of income, retained earnings, and cash flows for the years then ended. These financial statements are the responsibility of the Company's management. Our responsibility is to express an opinion on these financial statements based on our audits.

We conducted our audits in accordance with US generally accepted auditing standards. Those standards require that we plan and perform the audit to obtain reasonable assurance about whether the financial statements are free of material misstatement. An audit includes examining, on a test basis, evidence supporting the amounts and disclosures in the financial statements. An audit also includes assessing the accounting principles used and significant estimates made by management, as well as evaluating the overall financial statement presentation. We believe that our audits provide a reasonable basis for our opinion.

In our opinion, the financial statements referred to above present fairly, in all material respects, the financial position of ABC Company as of December 31, 20X2 and 20X1, and the results of its operations and its cash flows for the years then ended in conformity with US generally accepted accounting principles.

Joe Smith, CPA
February 23, 20X3

Some key details relating to the above report include

Title ("Independent" must be in title)
Addressee (company, board of directors, and/or stockholders—**not** management)
Introductory paragraph

1. We have audited
2. Client's financial statements (statements listed)

> **NOTE:** SFAS 130 establishes standards for the reporting and display of comprehensive income and its components when a full set of financial statements is being issued. While it does not require a specific format, the statement provides illustrations that display comprehensive income and its components in three manners.
>
> 1. A separate statement
> 2. As an add-on to the statement of income
> 3. Integrated with the statement of changes in equity
>
> When a separate statement of comprehensive income is presented (method 1. above), the introductory paragraph of the auditor's report should refer to that statement.

3. Financial statements are the responsibility of management.
4. The auditor's responsibility is to express an opinion.

Scope paragraph

1. Audit conducted in accordance with US generally accepted auditing standards
2. Those standards require that we plan and perform audit to provide reasonable assurance statements free of material misstatement
3. Audit involves

      a. Examining on a test basis evidence supporting amounts and disclosures
      b. Assessment of accounting principles
      c. Assessment of significant estimates
      d. Evaluation of overall presentation

   4. Audit provides reasonable basis for opinion

Opinion paragraph

   1. In our opinion
   2. Statements present fairly per US generally accepted accounting principles

Manual or printed signature (Firm name)
Date (The date on which the auditors have obtained sufficient appropriate evidence to support their opinion, ordinarily the last day of fieldwork)

     Remember that the generally accepted auditing standards include four reporting standards (GAAP, Opinion, Disclosure, Consistency—the GODC mnemonic presented in the Overview Section). Read Sections 410 and 431. Note especially in Section 411 that the term "present fairly" in the opinion paragraph is normally to be interpreted within the framework of GAAP. That is, if financial statements are in conformity with GAAP, they normally are presented fairly. Nevertheless, there may be unusual circumstances in which a generally accepted accounting principle may cause the financial statements to be misleading (e.g., new legislation); in such a case, the principle is not to be followed.

     Section 431 addresses the adequacy of financial statement disclosures. Disclosures are to be regarded as reasonably adequate unless otherwise stated in the audit report. When the auditor issues a qualified or an adverse opinion, the report should provide, **if practicable,** the information causing the departure from an unqualified report. Thus, if the client omits information in the notes concerning a loan agreement's restriction of future dividends, the auditor would provide the additional information. However, if the client has omitted a statement of cash flows, the auditor would not be required to prepare it, since it is not practicable to easily and directly obtain this information from the client's records.

     As indicated earlier in this module, the date of the report is not earlier than the date on which the auditors have obtained sufficient appropriate audit evidence to support the audit opinion, normally the last day of fieldwork. AU 530 discusses an often-tested exception to this rule. When a subsequent event requiring note disclosure has occurred after the date of the audit report but prior to its issuance, the auditor may either dual date the report or change its date to that of the subsequent event. For example, assume that March 2 was the date sufficient appropriate audit evidence had been accumulated (other than that related to the subsequent event). A dual-dated report would be dated as "March 2, 20X2, except for note X for which the date is March 6, 20X2." Alternatively, the auditor may change the report date to March 6. This latter option is generally less desirable since the auditor's responsibility with respect to other possible subsequent events is extended to the date of the report—here March 6.

     AU 530 also addresses the proper date of an audit report when a CPA is asked to either furnish additional copies of a previously issued report or to reissue a previously issued report (e.g., for inclusion in a report filed with the SEC). In both circumstances, the date is not normally changed from that originally used. However, if the CPA has become aware of an event requiring note disclosure (as contrasted to requiring an adjusting entry), the financial statements should disclose the event in a separate unaudited note to the financial statements. The note should be captioned in a manner such as "Event (Unaudited) Subsequent to the Date of the Independent Auditor's Report." When the event is such that the financial statements require adjustment, the auditor should reissue the report as dual dated (as discussed above).

3. **Financial Statement Audit Reports—Public (Issuer) Companies.** The Sarbanes-Oxley Act of 2002 created a requirement for an integrated audit that provides assurance about the fairness of financial statements and about the effectiveness of internal control over financial reporting—the internal control module discusses audit reports on internal control. The audit report on financial statements is different from that of a nonpublic (nonissuer) company in the following ways:

   1. The report includes the title "Report of Independent Registered Public Accounting Firm."
   2. The report refers to the standards of the PCAOB rather than generally accepted auditing standards.
   3. The report includes a paragraph referring to the auditor's report on internal control. (This reference is obviously only required when the reports on the financial statements and internal control are separate.)
   4. The report should contain the city and state or country of the office that issued the report.

The following is a sample audit report on the financial statements of a public company.

Report of Independent Registered Public Accounting Firm

     We have audited the accompanying balance sheets of X Company as of December 31, 20X3 and 20X2, and the related statements of operations, stockholders' equity, and cash flows for each of the three years in the period ended

December 31, 20X3. These financial statements are the responsibility of the Company's management. Our responsibility is to express an opinion on these financial statements based on our audits.

We conducted our audits in accordance with the standards of the Public Company Accounting Oversight Board (United States). Those standards require that we plan and perform the audit to obtain reasonable assurance about whether the financial statements are free of material misstatement. An audit includes examining, on a test basis, evidence supporting the amounts and disclosures in the financial statements. An audit also includes assessing the accounting principles used and significant estimates made by management, as well as evaluating the overall financial statement presentation. We believe that our audits provide a reasonable basis for our opinion.

In our opinion, the financial statements referred to above present fairly, in all material respects, the financial position of the Company as of [at] December 31, 20X3 and 20X2, and the results of its operations and its cash flows for each of the three years in the period ended December 31, 20X3, in conformity with US generally accepted accounting principles.

We also have audited, in accordance with the standards of the Public Company Accounting Oversight Board (United States), the effectiveness of X Company's internal control over financial reporting as of December 31, 20X3, based on criteria established in Internal Control—Integrated Framework issued by the Committee of Sponsoring Organizations of the Treadway Commission and our report dated February 24, 20X4, expressed an unqualified opinion thereon.

[*Signature*]
[*City and State or Country*]
[*Date*]

The examples in the following portions of this module follow the format for nonissuer (nonpublic) company audit reports. At this point, the rules for modifying reports of issuer (public) companies are the same as those for nonissuer companies—one simply begins with a slightly different standard report. Accordingly, this material applies to both issuer and nonissuer company audit reports.

> **NOW REVIEW MULTIPLE-CHOICE QUESTIONS 1 THROUGH 18 IN VOLUME 2**

B. Financial Statement Audit Reports—Detailed

1. **Circumstances Resulting in Departure from the Auditor's Standard Report**.

    The AICPA does not present a list of necessary conditions for an auditor to render a standard, unqualified report. The approach is one of presenting circumstances that may require departure from the standard report. These situations may be divided into circumstances requiring additional explanatory language be added to an unqualified report, and those which result in other than an unqualified report as follows:

    Circumstances requiring unqualified report with additional explanatory language

    a. Opinion based, in part, on report of another auditor
    b. Unusual circumstances requiring a departure from promulgated GAAP
    c. Substantial doubt about ability to remain a going concern (may also lead to a disclaimer)
    d. Inconsistency in application of GAAP
    e. Certain circumstances affecting comparative statements
    f. Required quarterly data for SEC reporting companies
    g. Required supplementary information
    h. Other information included with the audited financial statements
    i. Emphasis of a matter

    Circumstances requiring **other** than an unqualified report

    j. Departure from GAAP
    k. Scope limitation
    l. Lack of independence

    You should be familiar with the effect that each of the above circumstances has on an audit report. The following pages contain a summary of some of the most important "must know" material. While the outlines of the various audit report AU sections present the information in more detail, we provide you with a more structured, organized approach to these topics than is possible with the outlines alone.

    a. **Opinion based, in part, on report of another auditor (AU 543, 508).** Opinions based, in part, on the report of another auditor may differ from the standard report. This situation arises when two or more auditors are involved in the audit of a single entity. An example of this is the case in which one CPA firm audits the entire firm except for a subsidiary in a distant location. The auditor who audited the single subsidiary will generally issue a report on the subsidiary. The auditor who audited the remainder of the firm could give a report on that portion of the entity examined. However, there will generally be a preference (and indeed often a legal requirement) for an audit report on the overall entity.

The overall audit report must be signed by the principal auditor. The principal auditor is designated based on the materiality of the portion of financial statements examined, knowledge of the overall financial statements, and the importance of the components audited. The principal auditor is required to

(1) Make inquiries regarding the other auditor's reputation (e.g., contact AICPA, state society of CPAs, other practitioners, bankers, etc.)
(2) Obtain representation from the other auditor concerning independence
(3) Ascertain that the other auditor knows US auditing standards, SEC standards (if appropriate), and knows that the financial statements he or she audited are a component of, and to be included with, the financial statements on which the principal auditor will report

If the results of any of the above inquiries are unsatisfactory, the principal auditor must either modify the overall audit report (qualify or disclaim), or audit the component. If the results of the inquiries are satisfactory, the following summarizes the principal auditor's required decisions and responsibilities:

PRINCIPAL OTHER AUDITOR RELATIONSHIP

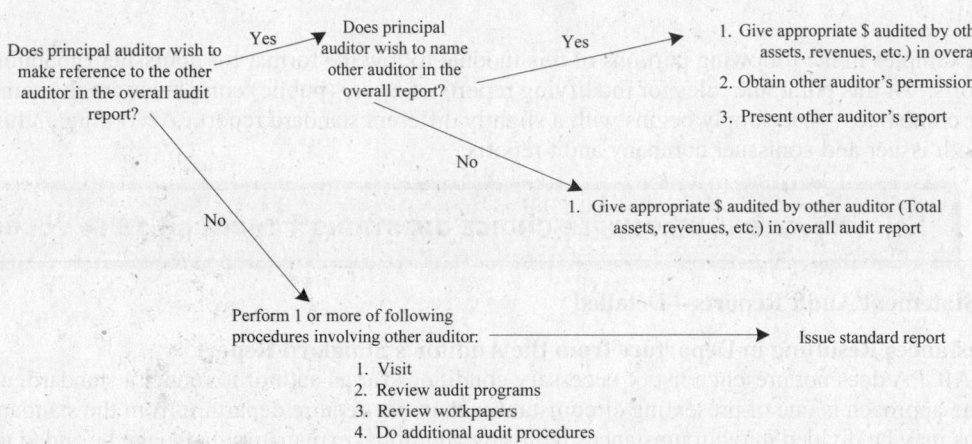

The decision to make reference to the other auditor indicates **divided** (or **shared**) **responsibility** between the auditors and is **not** considered an audit report qualification. The decision **not** to make reference to the other report indicates that the principal auditor assumes responsibility for the work of the other auditor. Reasons for assuming responsibility include

1.   The other auditor is an affiliate of the principal auditor.
2.   The principal auditor hired the other auditor.
3.   The portion audited by the other auditor is not material.
4.   Other miscellaneous reasons as the principal auditor (or client) desires.

Finally, note that in situations in which the other auditor's report is other than unqualified, the materiality of the matter (causing a departure from the standard report of the other auditor) to the overall financial statements determines whether the principal auditor's report must be modified.

b.   **Unusual circumstances requiring a departure from promulgated GAAP (AU 508).** This section only applies to entities that follow standards promulgated by either the Government Accounting Standards Board or the Federal Accounting Standards Advisory Board. Entities that follow Financial Accounting Standards Board pronouncements are excluded since there are no longer any justified departures from FASB (and predecessor group) pronouncements. This circumstance occurs when the auditor of the a company that follows GASB or FASAB standards agrees with a client that a departure from GAAP is justified due to unusual circumstances (e.g., new legislation or a new type of transaction). The situation considered here is one in which following those standards would result in misleading financial statements. When such unusual circumstances do exist, the GASB or FASAB standard should be departed from and the auditor should issue a report with an unqualified opinion and an explanatory paragraph describing the departure.

c.   **Substantial doubt about ability to remain a going concern (AU 341).** Auditors must make a judgment as to whether there is substantial doubt about the ability of a client to continue as a going concern for a reasonable period of time—a period not to exceed **one year** from the **date** of the **financial statements**.

The use of accruals by generally accepted accounting principles relies on an assumption that an entity will continue indefinitely as a going concern. For example, capitalizing assets and depreciating them over future periods is justified on the basis that the costs will be "matched" against future revenues. While audits do not contain specific procedures to test the appropriateness of this going concern assumption, procedures performed for other objectives (i.e., the PERCV objectives) may identify conditions and events indicating substantial doubt as to whether an entity will remain a going concern. AU 341 suggests that such procedures include (1) analytical procedures, (2) the review of subsequent events, (3) review for (non)compliance with debt agreements, (4) reading of minutes, (5) inquiry of legal counsel, and (6) confirmation of arrangements with various organizations to maintain financial support. When such procedures indicate that substantial doubt may exist as to whether an entity will remain a going concern, the auditor must obtain management's plans (including significant prospective financial information) for dealing with the situation and assess the likelihood that these plans can be implemented. If after evaluating management's plans substantial doubt still exists, the auditor should either add an explanatory paragraph to an unqualified report (following the opinion paragraph) or disclaim an opinion. In either case the report must explicitly include the phrases "substantial doubt" and "going concern." If analysis of management's plans convinces the auditor that substantial doubt does not exist, he or she still must consider the adequacy of financial statement note disclosures related to the matter. The following diagram summarizes the entire decision process.

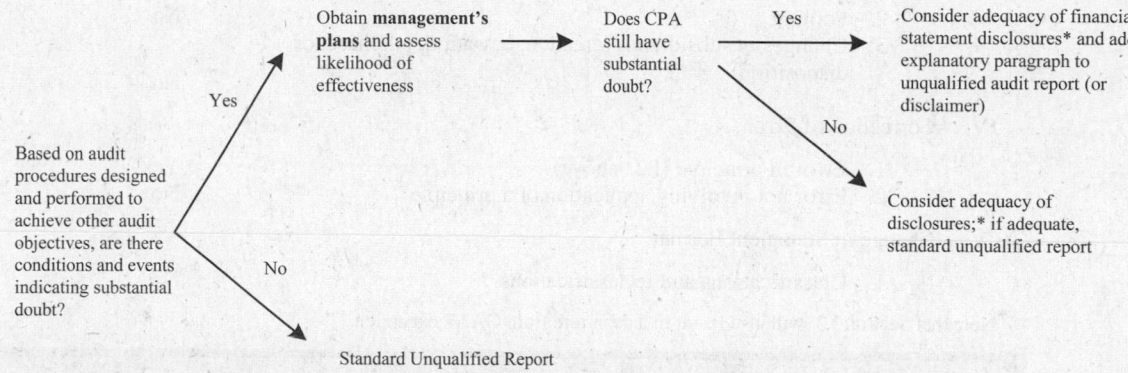

If disclosures are not adequate a departure from GAAP exists which may lead to a qualified or adverse opinion.

At this point review in detail the outline of AU 341.

d. **Inconsistency in application of GAAP (AU 420, 508).** A change in accounting principle that has a material effect on the comparability of a company's financial statements ordinarily results in a report with an unqualified opinion followed by an explanatory paragraph. Review FASB 154 on accounting changes when studying this section.

The general rule is that changes in accounting principles result in the addition of explanatory language, while changes in accounting estimates, corrections of clerical errors, and minor reclassifications of accounts from one year to the next do not. Changes in business entities and changes among carrying bases (cost, equity, consolidated) for continuing subsidiaries result in explanatory language; creation, cessation, purchase, or disposition of subsidiaries do not result in explanatory language.

Bear in mind that consistency pertains to the accounting treatment for items **between periods**. Also, in comparative reports for changes that are not accounted for by retroactive restatement, the explanatory paragraph is retained as long as the year of change is presented. Retroactive changes require the explanatory paragraph only in the year of the change.

Here are several other important points relating to consistency.

(1) Differing accounting principles may be used for different portions of an account. For example, a client may choose to use FIFO for valuation of a portion of its inventory and LIFO for the remainder. Similarly, for fixed assets, differing depreciation methods may be used for differing classes (types) of assets.

(2) A change that is immaterial this year, but is expected to become material in the future, **does not** result in explanatory language if the client has properly disclosed it in the notes to the financial statements.

(3) If the auditor does not concur with a change in principle, or if the change has not been properly accounted for, a qualified or adverse opinion is required because this represents a departure from GAAP.

(4) The audit report does not mention consistency when there has been no change in principle.

The most frequent changes in principle relating to consistency are summarized below.

Type of change	Consistency explanatory paragraph
I. Change in Accounting Principle	
1. GAAP to GAAP	Yes
2. Non-GAAP to GAAP	Yes
3. GAAP to non-GAAP	Yes*
4. For newly acquired assets in an existing class of assets (whether 1, 2, or 3 above)	Yes
5. For a new class of asset (whether 1, 2, or 3 above)	No
II. Change in Accounting Estimate	
1. Judgmental adjustments	No
2. Inseparable estimate and principle change	Yes
III. Change in Entity	
1. Changes between carrying basis (cost, equity, consolidated)	Yes
2. Pooling	No
3. Changes in subsidiaries (creation, cessation, purchase, or disposition)	No
IV. Correction of Error	
1. Error in principle (I.2., above)	Yes
2. Error not involving application of a principle	No
V. Change in Statement Format	
1. Classifications and reclassifications	No

*Note that Section I.3. will also result in a departure from GAAP exception.

> **NOW REVIEW MULTIPLE-CHOICE QUESTIONS 19 THROUGH 45 IN VOLUME 2**

e. **Certain circumstances affecting comparative financial statements (AU 508).** When comparative statements are issued (i.e., financial statements for two or more periods are presented), the auditor must report on the statements for all years presented. One overall report, dated as of the date on which the auditor has obtained sufficient appropriate audit evidence for the most recent audit, addressing the years presented, is issued. Two major situations may result in an unqualified report with explanatory language.

(1) An opinion on the prior period financial statements may differ from the opinion previously issued. For example, an auditor previously may have qualified the opinion on the prior period statements because of a departure from GAAP, and the prior period statements may be restated in the current period to follow GAAP. In such a circumstance the auditor's updated report on the prior period statements should indicate that the statements have been restated and should express an unqualified opinion with respect to the restated statements. Whenever an updated report has an opinion different from that previously expressed, the auditor should disclose all substantive reasons for the different opinion in a separate explanatory paragraph preceding the opinion paragraph. The explanatory paragraph should disclose

   (a) The date of the previous report
   (b) The type of opinion previously expressed
   (c) The circumstances causing the auditor to express a different opinion
   (d) That the updated opinion is different from the previous opinion

(2) When a predecessor auditor has examined the prior period statements, a decision needs to be made as to whether the predecessor's report is to be reissued. If the report is **not** to be reissued, the successor auditor's report should indicate in the introductory paragraph

   (a) That the financial statements of the prior period were examined by other auditors
   (b) The date of the predecessor's report
   (c) The type of report issued by the predecessor
   (d) The substantive reasons therefor, if it was other than a standard unqualified report

If the predecessor's report is to be reissued, the predecessor should read the current statements, compare the prior period statements to the current statements, and obtain from the successor a letter of representation as to whether any material matters concerning the prior period statements have arisen.

Regardless of whether the predecessor's report is being reissued, the opinion paragraph of the successor auditor's report refers only to the second year.

f. **Required quarterly data for SEC reporting companies (AU 722).** Certain SEC reporting companies are required to include unaudited quarterly information in their annual reports or other documents filed with the SEC that contain audited financial statements. Auditors are engaged to perform review procedures either at the conclusion of each quarter, or at the end of the year when the information is included with the annual information. When dealing with the annual financial statements, omission, misstatement, or auditor inability to review the quarterly information all lead to inclusion of an explanatory paragraph in the annual audit report. Be aware that the information is to be reviewed, not audited. Therefore, its misstatement will **not** lead to a qualified or an adverse opinion.

g. **Required supplementary information**. AU 558 provides the related guidance. Required supplementary information is required by a designated accounting standards setter (FASB, GASB, IASB, or FASAB) to accompany a company's basic financial statements. As an example, GASB 50 requires certain disclosures for defined benefit pension plans. Procedures that auditors must perform include

(1) *Inquire* of management about methods of preparing information—including whether it was prepared following prescribed guidelines, whether methods of measurement or presentation have changed from prior period, and whether there were any significant assumptions or interpretations underlying the measurement or presentation of information.

(2) *Compare information* for consistency with

(a) Management's responses to the inquiries.
(b) The basic financial statements.
(c) Other knowledge obtained during the audit.

(3) *Obtain written representations* from management acknowledging its responsibility that the information is measured within guidelines, methods have not changed, and significant assumptions.

For a public company, the professional standards state that if no deviations from accounting standards are identified, no report modification is necessary. For a nonpublic company in such a situation, an emphasis of matter paragraph such as the following is added to the audit report:

> Accounting principles generally accepted in the United States of America require that the [identify the supplementary information] on page xx be presented to supplement the basic financial statements. Such information, although not a part of the basic financial statements, is required by the [indicate designated accounting standards setter] who considers it to be an essential part of the financial reporting and for placing the basic financial statements and related notes in an appropriate operational, economic, or historical context. We have applied limited procedures to the required supplementary information in accordance with auditing standards generally accepted in the USA, which consisted of inquiries of management about the methods of preparing the information and comparing the information for consistency with management's responses to our inquiries, the basic financial statements, and other knowledge we obtained during our audit of the basic financial statements. We do not express an opinion or provide any assurance on the information because the limited procedures do not provide us with sufficient evidence to express an opinion or provide any assurance.

When the supplementary information is omitted or improperly stated that information is added to the emphasis of matter paragraph (for either a public or nonpublic company). The opinion paragraph of the report is not modified since the supplementary information is not considered a part of the audited information. Realize that when such information is presented the audit report refers to it, regardless of whether it is properly stated or improperly stated.

h. **Other information included with the audited financial statements.** AU 550 and AU 551 address this area. AU 550 addresses financial and nonfinancial information (other than required supplementary information) that is included in a document that contains audited financial statements. The document is often an annual report, which includes information such as a report by management, financial summaries, employment data, planned capital expenditures, financial ratios, names officers and directors, and selected quarter information. Auditors are required to *read* this information for inconsistencies, if any, with the audited financial statements.

If the auditor identifies no inconsistencies, *no additional paragraph is added to the audit report*. Thus, the report contains no indication that the auditors have read the other information when no inconsistencies or material misstatement are identified. If inconsistencies or material misstatements are identified, the auditor will first request the client to revise any incorrect information. If the client refuses to revise the incorrect information, one or both of the following must be true:

(1) Financial statements are incorrect—This will lead to a qualified opinion or an adverse opinion since it is a departure from GAAP (see Section B.1.j. below).

(2) Other information is incorrect—This will lead to a report with an unqualified opinion and an explanatory paragraph, withholding the auditor's report or withdrawing from the engagement.

The auditor may note no inconsistency, but may believe that the other information **seems** incorrect. In such cases the auditor discusses the matter with the client, consults with other parties such as legal counsel, and uses judgment as to the resolution of the matter.

AU 551 addresses certain other information which the client desires an auditor to provide an opinion on whether it is fairly presented in relation to the financial statements as a whole. What makes this section of the standards different than AU 558 and 550 requirements is that it presents a service that is not required as a part of performing an audit; the service is ordinarily selected by management or those charged with corporate governance. With this service auditors perform procedures to allow them to provide assurance on whether supplementary information is fairly stated, in all material respects, in relation to the financial statements as a whole. The information may be presented in a document containing audited financial statements or separate from the financial statements. The information must be derived from and relate directly to the underlying accounting and other records used to prepare the financial statements to allow this service to be performed. Examples of such information are consolidating information, historical summaries of accounts, and statistical data. As presented in the outline of AU 551, the auditor's procedure for this service goes well beyond those of the preceding two sections, including

- Inquiring of management about the purpose of the information and criteria used to prepare it.
- Determining the propriety of the form and content of the information.
- Obtaining an understanding of how the information was prepared.
- Comparing and reconciling information to underlying accounting and other records.
- Inquiring of management concerning significant assumptions.
- Evaluating the appropriateness and completeness of the information.
- Obtaining written reorientations.

When the information is found to be fairly stated in relation to the financial statements an emphasis of matter paragraph such as the following is added:

> Our audit was conducted for the purpose of forming an opinion on the financial statements as a whole. The [identify the supplementary information] is presented for purposes of additional analysis and is not a required part of the financial statements. Such information is the responsibility of management and was derived from and relates directly to the underlying and other records used to prepare the financial statements. The information has been subjected to the auditing procedures applied in the audit of the financial statements and certain additional procedures, including comparing and reconciling such information directly to the underlying accounting and other records used to prepare the financial statements and other additional procedures prescribed by auditing standards generally accepted in the United States of America. In our opinion, the information is fairly stated in all material respects in relation to the financial statements as a whole.

If the auditors conclude that the information is not fairly stated in all material respects, the paragraph so states. The opinion paragraph of the audit report is not modified since the supplementary information is not considered a part of the audited information.

NOW REVIEW MULTIPLE-CHOICE QUESTIONS 46 THROUGH 57 IN VOLUME 2

---

i. **Emphasis of a matter (AU 508).** The auditor may wish to emphasize a matter (through adding an explanatory paragraph) regarding the financial statements, but nevertheless, may intend to render an unqualified opinion. Examples include cases in which the entity is a component of a larger entity, or in which significant related-party transactions exist, or the auditor wishes to draw attention to an important subsequent event. Such information is included in an explanatory paragraph.

Until 1996, significant uncertainties affecting the financial statements (e.g., a significant lawsuit, which nevertheless did not raise a question concerning going concern status) were considered a distinct circumstance that might result in the addition of an explanatory paragraph to an audit report. Standards relating to uncertainty modifications were eliminated, and now an auditor may wish to emphasize an uncertainty through inclusion under the emphasis of a matter paragraph.

> **NOTE:** The following sections require other than an unqualified report.

j. **Departures from generally accepted accounting principles (AU 508).** Departures from GAAP result in either a qualified opinion or an adverse opinion; both types of reports include an explanatory paragraph preceding the opinion paragraph. Examples of departures from GAAP include the use of an unacceptable inventory valuation method (e.g., current sales value) or incorrectly treating a capital lease as an operating lease.

The type of report depends on the materiality of the departure. **Know** that materiality depends on

(1) Dollar magnitude of effects

(2) Significance of item to enterprise
(3) Pervasiveness of misstatement
(4) Impact of misstatement on financial statements taken as a whole

As the effects of such departures become more material, the likelihood of an adverse opinion increases. If the departure from GAAP consists of inadequate disclosure of required information, the correct information, if available, should be included in an explanatory paragraph that **precedes** the qualified or adverse opinion paragraph. When the information is not available, the explanatory paragraph of the report should so state.

When an adverse opinion is being issued, an auditor may be asked to add a comment in the audit report indicating that certain identified accounts or disclosures in the financial statements are fairly presented. The auditor should not comply with this type of request since such "piecemeal opinions" are considered inappropriate because they might overshadow or contradict the overall adverse opinion.

Be familiar with two specific circumstances relating to departures from GAAP: omission of the statement of cash flows and incorrect segment disclosures. When a company presents financial statements that purport to present financial position **and** results of operations (e.g., balance sheet **and** an income statement) a statement of cash flows must also be presented. The omission of a statement of cash flows in such a circumstance is a departure from GAAP that requires issuance of a qualified opinion (an adverse opinion is not recommended). Additionally, the auditor need not present the missing statement of cash flows in an explanatory paragraph of the audit report.

The second circumstance involves incorrect (or omitted) segment disclosures required under SFAS 131 issued by the Financial Accounting Standards Board. Inaccurate (or omitted) segment disclosures constitute a departure from GAAP and lead to a qualified opinion or an adverse opinion. When a client changes operating segments from one year to the next for acceptable reasons, no consistency modification or other report modification is necessary.

An auditor considers segment disclosures (as other disclosures) in relation to the financial statements taken as a whole. Accordingly, the auditor is not required to apply procedures as extensive as would be necessary to express an opinion on the segment information itself. The procedures performed include

Procedures to evaluate identification of segments:	Procedures to evaluate adequacy of segment disclosures:
• Inquire about methods of identifying segments. • Review corroborating evidence. • Assess whether SFAS 131 procedures were appropriately followed to determine segments. • Obtain management's written representation that segments are appropriately identified.	• Perform analytical procedures. • Evaluate adequacy with regard to general information, information about segments, reconciliations of revenues, losses, etc. • Review reconciliations of totals of segment revenues, etc. • If an entity has had a reorganization of its structure, assess whether segment disclosures for prior periods have been restated.

k. **Scope limitations (AU 508).** Scope limitations result in either a qualified opinion or a disclaimer. In both cases, the opinion paragraph indicates that the opinion modification is based on the possible effects on the financial statements, and not due to the scope limitation itself, and the explanatory paragraph is added preceding the opinion paragraph. The type of report issued depends on the importance of the omitted procedures. This assessment is affected by the nature and magnitude of the potential effects of the matters in question and by their significance to the financial statements (e.g., number of accounts involved). An auditor may issue a disclaimer whenever he or she is unable to form an opinion or has not formed an opinion as to the fairness of presentation of the financial statements.

Two types of scope limitations must be considered: client-imposed and circumstance-imposed. Client-imposed limitations result when a client will not allow the auditor to perform an audit procedure (e.g., confirm receivables). Circumstance-imposed limitations occur in situations **other** than the client saying, "No, I will not allow you to perform that procedure." For example, weak internal control may make it impossible for the auditor to perform the audit. This is considered a circumstance-imposed limitation. The following diagram summarizes the effect of scope limitations on the report.

SCOPE LIMITATION DECISIONS

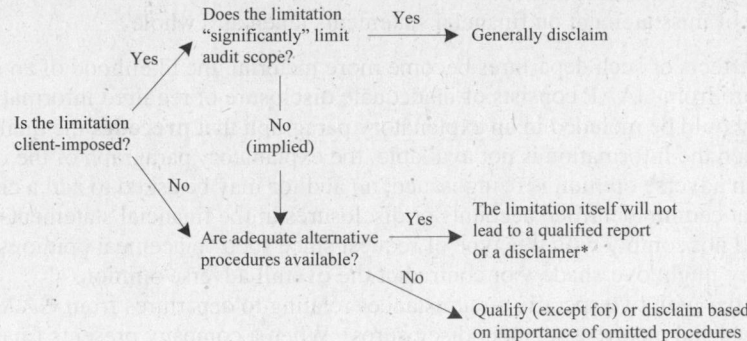

* *The alternative procedures used should not be mentioned in the report.*

Know that scope limitations may result in different opinions on individual financial statements. For example, if the auditor of a first-year client has been unable to verify the accuracy of the beginning inventory, the scope limitation will affect the current year's income statement (through cost of goods sold) but not the year-end balance sheet. In such a situation, the auditor might issue an unqualified opinion on the balance sheet and a disclaimer on the income statement.

Note the distinction between scope limitations and limited reporting objectives. Consider two circumstances. First, the auditor may, when requested, report on only one statement (e.g., the balance sheet). If access to information underlying the financial statements is not limited, such a situation does not involve a scope limitation. The auditor may report on the financial statement.

Second, as is the case with issuance of an adverse opinion, when issuing a disclaimer the auditor may not include a "piecemeal opinion" that identifies certain accounts that are properly stated.

Several multiple-choice questions have required knowledge of the "circumstance for which it is **not** appropriate to refer a reader of an auditor's report to a financial statement note for details." The proper answer is generally a scope limitation since details of audit scope are not presented in the financial statement notes.

l. **Lack of independence (AU 504).** When an auditor is not independent, a disclaimer must be issued stating that the auditor is not independent. No mention of the reason for the lack of independence nor any audit procedures followed is to be given in the report. These circumstances might occur when the CPA firm has neglected to sell an equity (e.g., common stock) interest in the client being audited.

Summary. Know that circumstances a. through i. may result in unqualified reports with additional explanatory language. Circumstance c., doubt about ability to remain a going concern, may also result in a disclaimer of opinion. The circumstances requiring other than an unqualified opinion may be summarized as

Circumstances	Type of opinion
j. Departure from GAAP	Qualified or adverse
k. Scope limitation	
1. Client-imposed	"Generally disclaim," otherwise qualified
2. Circumstance-imposed	Qualified or disclaimer
l. Lack of independence	Disclaimer

SUMMARY OF DEPARTURES FROM STANDARD REPORT

Circumstance	Introductory paragraph modified	Scope paragraph modified	Opinion paragraph modified	Explanatory paragraph modified
UNQUALIFIED WITH EXPLANATORY LANGUAGE				
a. Other Auditor—Make reference	Yes	Yes	Yes	No
b. Justified GAAP departure*				
c. Going concern				
d. Inconsistency				
e. Report reissued				
f. Required SEC quarterly data	No	No	No	Yes
g. Supplementary information				
h. Other information				
i. Emphasis of a matter				
e. Predecessor report not reissued	Yes	No	No	No
QUALIFIED OPINIONS				
j. Departure from GAAP	No	No	Yes	Yes
k. Scope limitation	No	Yes	Yes	Yes
DISCLAIMER				
c. Going concern**	Yes	Yes	Yes	Yes
k. Scope limitation	Yes	Omit	Yes	Yes
l. Lack of independence	(A one-paragraph disclaimer is issued)			
ADVERSE				
j. Departure from GAAP	No	No	Yes	Yes

* Only applies to companies that follow Government Accounting Standards Board or Federal Accounting Standards Advisory Board Standards.
** No sample report presented in Professional Standards.

> **NOW REVIEW MULTIPLE-CHOICE QUESTIONS 58 THROUGH 79 IN VOLUME 2**

C. Accountant Association other than Audits

As indicated in the overview section, accountants become involved with financial information on engagements less than "full" audits. These forms may be categorized as: (1) other forms of accountant association with historical financial statements, and (2) other reports.

1. **Other Forms of Accountant Association with Historical Financial Statements.** Here we discuss four primary "other" forms of accountant association. The candidate should be very familiar with each of these forms of association.

   a. **Unaudited statements (AU 504).** For those relatively few issuer (public) firms that are not required to have an annual audit, the option of unaudited statements exists. In this case, a simple disclaimer of opinion is generally issued; also, each page of the financial statements should be marked "unaudited." As a minimum, the auditor must read the financial statements for obvious material misstatements. If the auditor is aware of any significant departures from GAAP, s/he should suggest that the statements be revised and, failing that, should include such information in the disclaimer.

   b. **Compiled or reviewed statements (AR 100-600).** Compilations and reviews require far fewer procedures than do audits. Guidance for compilations of interim information of public companies is included in the *Statements on Auditing Standards* (AU 722)—we cover the material in the next section. Compilations and reviews of nonpublic company financial statements performed under the *Statements on Standards for Accounting and Review Services* (SSARS) are discussed in the following module. Compilations and reviews (whether performed under SAS or SSARS standards) represent a heavily tested area.

   c. **Reviewed interim (quarterly) statements (AU 722).** The standards discussed above in section b. are most frequently for reviews of annual financial statements. Reviews are also performed on interim (ordinarily, quarterly) financial information. Public companies ("issuers") are required to have interim reviews, while nonpublic companies ("nonissuers") may choose to have reviews.

   AU 722, as originally promulgated by the Auditing Standards Board, was written primarily for issuer companies. When the Public Company Accounting Oversight Board adopted the AICPA standards as its "interim standards," it adopted AU 722. Subsequently, the Auditing Standards Board revised AU 722 to apply to nonpublic companies. Today, two versions of AU 722 currently exist—the PCAOB version for issuer companies and the Auditing Standards Board version for nonissuer companies.

Both versions of AU 722 outline a service very similar to reviews investments Statement on Standards for Accounting and Review Services (SSARs, codified as AR sections—discussed in detail in the next module). Rather than provide a detailed outline of AU 722, which in many ways duplicates the SSARs outlines, the outline summarizes significant differences between SSARs reviews and AU 722. At this point you should study that outline.

The objective of a review of interim information is to provide the accountant with a basis for communicating whether he or she is aware of any material modifications that should be made to the interim financial information for it to conform with the applicable financial reporting framework (e.g., GAAP). Particularly important to this area are

- Overall, the procedures should be sufficient to provide a reasonable basis for obtaining the limited (negative) assurance that there are no material modifications needed.
- The accountant must obtain an understanding of the industry and knowledge of the client (the business itself and accounting principles followed).
- While the Accounting and Review Services module includes much more information on the nature of reviews, know that AU 722 interim reviews involve performing analytical procedures, making inquiries of management (and others within the organization), and the obtaining an understanding of internal control. The understanding of internal control must be sufficient to identify types of procedures. As discussed investments the Accounting and Review Services module, this understanding of internal control is not required under reviews performed under SSARS.

The following is the standard review report for a public company:

Report of Independent Registered Public Accounting Firm

We have reviewed the accompanying [*describe the interim financial information*] of ABC Company and consolidated subsidiaries as of September 30, 20X1, and for the three-month and nine-month periods then ended. This interim financial information is the responsibility of the company's management.

We conducted our review in accordance with standards of the Public Company Accounting Oversight Board. A review of interim financial information consists principally of applying analytical procedures and making inquiries of persons responsible for financial and accounting matters. It is substantially less in scope than an audit conducted in accordance with generally accepted auditing standards, the objective of which is the expression of an opinion regarding the financial statements taken as a whole. Accordingly, we do not express such an opinion.

Based on our review, we are not aware of any material modifications that should be made to the accompanying interim financial information for it to be in conformity with US generally accepted accounting principles.

d. **Condensed financial statements (AU 552).** A client who must file a set of audited financial statements at least annually with a regulatory agency may choose to prepare condensed financial statements for other purposes. In such cases the auditor's report on condensed statements should disclose

(1) That the auditor has expressed an opinion on the complete audited financial statements
(2) The date of the audit report on the complete statements
(3) The type of opinion expressed on the complete statements
(4) Whether the condensed statements are fairly stated in relation to the complete financial statements

e. **Financial statements prepared for use in other countries (AU 534).** An auditor may be asked to report on the financial statements of a United States client that follow the accounting principles of a foreign country. The general rule is that in such circumstances the auditor must follow US general and fieldwork standards to the extent that they are appropriate. Certain procedures, however, may **not** be appropriate (e.g., procedures related to the tax deferral account in a country which does not allow tax deferral). Also, the auditor may be requested to apply the other country's auditing standards. This may be done if US standards have been followed and if the auditor is familiar with the standards of the other country.

The report issued depends on whether it is for use primarily outside the US (the most frequent case) or within the US. If it is intended primarily for outside the US, a modified US report may be issued which (1) describes the basis followed, (2) states that US standards (and other national standards if appropriate) were followed, and (3) states whether the statements present fairly and consistently the basis followed. If, however, the auditor has made certain that s/he understands the responsibilities relating to the standard report of the other country, then such report may be issued. Financial statements for use primarily outside of the US may be distributed to limited US individuals and organizations (such as banks) if differences between the US and the foreign country standards are understood.

If distribution within the US is **more than limited,** the auditor should use the US standard report and modify it as necessary for any departures from GAAP. Additionally, for distribution outside the US, a report may be prepared as indicated in the prior paragraph.

NOW REVIEW MULTIPLE-CHOICE QUESTIONS 80 THROUGH 92 IN VOLUME 2

2. **Other Reports—Statements on Auditing Standards Based.** In addition to guidance on financial statement audits, the Statements on Auditing Standards (those with AU prefix in the outlines that follow Module 8) also present guidance on a number of engagements not discussed earlier in this module, including

   a. Special reports
   b. Letters for underwriters
   c. Application of accounting principles

a. **Special reports (AU 623).** AU 623 presents guidance on five basic types of reports. You should have a general familiarity with each. Your approach here should be to study the information in this section in combination with the outline of AU 623. Here we present only summary information and sample reports; details are presented in the outline of AU 623.

   The first type of special report deals with reporting on financial statements that follow a comprehensive basis other than GAAP (e.g., cash basis, tax basis, or a basis prescribed by a regulatory agency). In general, the report issued parallels the standard audit report, with a fourth paragraph added indicating the basis being followed, and that it is a comprehensive basis of accounting other than GAAP. When the basis is prescribed by a regulatory agency, an additional paragraph limiting distribution to the company and to the regulatory agency is added at the end of the report. Terms such as "balance sheet" and "income statement" are **not** used for statements that follow a comprehensive basis other than GAAP. Instead, an other comprehensive basis of accounting may use, for example, "statement of assets and liabilities arising from cash transactions." (The use of such terms will require the auditor to qualify the opinion.)

   The following is the suggested standard form for cash-basis statements:

Financial Statements Prepared on the Cash Basis

Independent Auditor's Report

We have audited the accompanying statements of assets and liabilities arising from cash transactions of XYZ Company as of December 31, 20X2 and 20X1, and the related statements of revenue collected and expenses paid for the years then ended. These financial statements are the responsibility of the Company's management. Our responsibility is to express an opinion on these financial statements based on our audits.

We conducted our audits in accordance with US generally accepted auditing standards. Those standards require that we plan and perform the audit to obtain reasonable assurance about whether the financial statements are free of material misstatement. An audit includes examining, on a test basis, evidence supporting the amounts and disclosures in the financial statements. An audit also includes assessing the accounting principles used and significant estimates made by management, as well as evaluating the overall financial statement presentation. We believe that our audits provide a reasonable basis for our opinion.

As described in Note X, these financial statements were prepared on the basis of cash receipts and disbursements, which is a comprehensive basis of accounting other than US generally accepted accounting principles.

In our opinion, the financial statements referred to above present fairly, in all material respects, the assets and liabilities arising from cash transactions of XYZ Company as of December 31, 20X2 and 20X1, and its revenue collected and expenses paid during the years then ended, on the basis of accounting described in Note X.

A comprehensive-basis report prepared solely for filing with a regulatory agency, following a basis prescribed by that agency, would be similar to the above report, but would also add the following as a final paragraph:

This report is intended solely for the information and use of the board of directors and management of XYZ Insurance Company and for filing with the [name of regulatory agency] and should not be used for any other purpose.

The second type of special report is that on special elements, accounts, or items. An auditor may, if allowed to perform the procedures s/he believes necessary, issue an opinion on one or more accounts (e.g., receivables or rentals). However, if a specified element is, or is based upon, an entity's net income or stockholders' equity, the CPA should have audited the complete financial statements in order to express an opinion. On the other hand, if the auditor is hired to perform only agreed-upon procedures, a summary of findings is provided.

The overall area of agreed-upon procedure engagements is discussed below in section C.3.b, and in the outline of AT 201. At this point simply read the reports.

Special Elements Report Examples

Report Relating to Accounts Receivable

Independent Auditor's Report

We have audited the accompanying schedule of accounts receivable of ABC Company as of December 31, 20X2. This schedule is the responsibility of the Company's management. Our responsibility is to express an opinion on this schedule based on our audit.

We conducted our audit in accordance with US generally accepted auditing standards. Those standards require that we plan and perform the audit to obtain reasonable assurance about whether the schedule of accounts receivable is free of material misstatement. An audit includes examining, on a test basis, evidence supporting the amounts and disclosures in the schedule of accounts receivable. An audit also includes assessing the accounting principles used and significant estimates made by management, as well as evaluating the overall schedule presentation. We believe that our audit provides a reasonable basis for our opinion.

In our opinion, the schedule of accounts receivable referred to above presents fairly, in all material respects, the accounts receivable of ABC Company as of December 31, 20X2, in conformity with US generally accepted accounting principles.

> **NOTE:** As is the case with all special reports, an additional paragraph is added limiting distribution when a basis which is not GAAP or another comprehensive basis is used.

Independent Accountant's Report on Applying Agreed-Upon Procedures

To the Board of Directors and Management of X Company:

We have performed the procedures enumerated below, which were agreed to by the Board of Directors and Management of X Company, solely to assist you in connection with the proposed acquisition of Y Company as of December 31, 20XX. This agreed-upon procedures engagement was conducted in accordance with attestation standards established by the American Institute of Certified Public Accountants. The sufficiency of these procedures is solely the responsibility of the parties specified in this report. Consequently, we make no representation regarding the sufficiency of the procedures described below either for the purpose for which this report has been requested or for any other purpose.

The procedures and the associated findings are as follows:

Accounts Receivable

1. We added the individual customer account balances shown in an aged trial balance of accounts receivable (identified as exhibit A) and compared the resultant total with the balance in the general ledger account.

[*Present Findings*]

2. We mailed confirmations directly to the customers representing the 150 largest customer account balances selected from the accounts receivable trial balance, and we received responses as indicated below. We also traced the items constituting the outstanding customer account balance to invoices and supporting shipping documents for customers from which there was no reply. As agreed, any individual differences in a customer account balance of less than $300 were to be considered minor, and no further procedures were performed.

[*Present Findings*]

We were not engaged to, and did not, perform an examination, the objective of which would be the expression of an opinion on cash and accounts receivable. Accordingly, we do not express such an opinion. Had we performed additional procedures, other matters might have come to our attention that would have been reported to you.

This report is intended solely for the information and use of the board of directors and management of X Company and is not intended to be and should not be used by anyone other than these specified parties.

[*Signature*]
[*Date*]

The third type of special report is one that results from an engagement in which the auditor is hired to test whether a client is in compliance with some form of agreement. For example, an auditor may provide negative assurance to a bank on whether a client is in conformity with restrictions contained in a debt agreement. This type of report may only be issued when the CPA has performed an audit of the financial statements. Section D of this Module discusses other compliance reports; those reports relate to audits performed under *Government Auditing Standards* and reports providing positive assurance on compliance with contractual agreements or regulatory provisions when no financial statement audit has been performed.

Compliance Report Examples

Contractual Compliance Independent Auditor's Report

Compliance Report as a Separate Report	**Compliance Report Included in Unqualified Report**
We have audited, in accordance with US generally accepted auditing standards, the balance sheet of XYZ Company as of December 31, 20X1, and the related statement of income, retained earnings, and cash flows for the year then ended, and have issued our report thereon dated February 16, 20X2.	Standard Unqualified Report
In connection with our audit, nothing came to our attention that caused us to believe that the Company failed to comply with the terms, covenants, provisions, or conditions of sections, XX to XX, inclusive, of the Indenture dated July 21, 19X8, with ABC Bank insofar as they relate to accounting matters. However, our audit was not directed primarily toward obtaining knowledge of such noncompliance.	Then add these two paragraphs
This report is intended solely for the information and use of the boards of directors and managements of XYZ Company and ABC Bank and should not be used for any other purpose.	

The fourth type of special report is for client special-purpose financial presentations that have been prepared by the client to comply with an agreement (e.g., a loan agreement). The information presented is more substantial than specified elements, but is different in some ways, and generally less complete than required by a comprehensive basis of accounting. Unless the report is to be filed with a regulatory agency such as the SEC and to be included in a publicly available document (e.g., a prospectus), a paragraph limiting distribution is added to the report.

Special-Purpose Financial Presentation Examples

Loan Agreement
(GAAP not followed)

[Introductory paragraph refers to specific report]

[Standard scope paragraph]

The accompanying special-purpose financial statements were prepared for the purpose of complying with Section 4 of a loan agreement between DEF Bank and the Company as discussed in Note X, and are not intended to be a presentation in conformity with US generally accepted accounting principles.

In our opinion, the special-purpose financial statements referred to above present fairly, in all material respects, the assets and liabilities of ABC Company at December 31, 20X1 and 20X0, and the revenues, expenses and cash flows for the years then ended, on the basis of accounting described in Note X.

This report is intended solely for the information and use of the boards of directors and managements of ABC Company and DEF Bank and should not be used for any other purpose.

Schedule of Apartment Revenues and Expenses Included in a Document
to Be Distributed to the General Public

[Introductory paragraph refers to specific report]

[Standard scope paragraph]

The accompanying Historical Summaries were prepared for the purpose of complying with the rules and regulations of the Securities and Exchange Commission (for inclusion in the registration statement on Form S-11 of DEF Corporation) as described in Note X and are not intended to be a complete presentation of the Apartments' revenues and expenses.

In our opinion, the Historical Summaries referred to above present fairly, in all material respects, the gross income and direct operating expenses described in Note X of ABC Apartments for each of the three years in the period ended December 31, 20XX, in conformity with US generally accepted accounting principles.

The fifth special report is that for which a client is required to present information on prescribed forms or schedules. For example, a state corporate commission may require all corporations within its jurisdiction to report assets, liabilities, and equities per a standard form. If that form calls for the auditor to make an assertion that s/he believes to be unjustified, s/he is to either reword the form or attach a separate report to the form.

The "Special Reports Summary" presents the essential elements of each type of special report. In the past, the most frequently examined report formats have been the comprehensive basis and agreed-upon procedures applied to specified elements.

SPECIAL REPORTS SUMMARY*

	Comprehensive basis	Specified Elements — a. Opinion	Specified Elements — b. Agreed-upon procedures	Compliance Reports — a. Within standard report	Compliance Reports — b. Separate report	Special purpose presentation
Introductory Paragraph	1. Standard report except for, in first sentence (a) names of statements (b) name reporting basis used	1. Standard report except for, in first sentence (a) names of accounts (b) name reporting basis used	1. We have performed agreed-upon procedures 2. Report solely to assist (specified parties) 3. AICPA attestation standards followed 4. Sufficiency of procedures responsibility of users 5. No representation made as to sufficiency of procedures	1. Standard report	1. Standard report except for, add "and have issued our report thereon dated ___" (to end of first sentence)	1. Standard report except for, in first sentence (a) names of statements
Scope Paragraph	1. Standard report	1. Standard report except for naming of accounts	1. Enumerate procedures and findings	1. Standard report		1. Standard report except for names of accounts
Explanatory Paragraph	1. Mention basis and refer to note which describes	1. Description of reporting basis if not given in scope paragraph		1. No explanatory paragraph	1. No explanatory paragraph	1. Mention basis and refer to note which describes
Opinion (Assurance) Paragraph	**Opinion** 1. Standard report except for (a) Names of statements (b) Refer to reporting basis used	**Opinion** 1. Standard report except for (a) Names of accounts (b) Name reporting basis used	**Assurance** 1. We did not perform an audit and do not express an opinion 2. If additional procedures had been performed other matters might have come to our attention — An additional paragraph follows indicating report intended solely for specified parties	**Opinion and negative assurance** 2 paragraphs: A. Standard opinion para B. Negative assurance on compliance para 1. Nothing came to our attention to lead us to believe not in compliance 2. Exam was not directed primarily toward obtaining knowledge of such noncompliance	**Negative assurance** 1. Nothing came to our attention to lead us to believe not in compliance 2. Exam was not directed primarily toward obtaining knowledge of such noncompliance	**Opinion** 1. Standard report except for (a) Names of statements (b) Refer to reporting basis used
How to Report Departures from Reporting Criteria**	1. Same as standard report	1. Add comment to opinion para and add explanatory para describing 2. If significant client interpretations of criteria have been made, add explanatory para describing	1. Prepare schedules summarizing accounts 2. Add comment to negative assurance para and add explanatory para describing	1. Add comment to negative assurance para and add explanatory para describing	1. Add comment to negative assurance para and add explanatory para describing	1. Same as standard report

* Note that no report form has been proposed for the Special Report based on Prescribed Forms or Schedules. Prospective financial statements are summarized in the outline section (following the SAS [AU] outlines).

** All special reports include an additional paragraph when distribution is limited (see outline of AU 623).

b. **Letters for underwriters (AU 634).** When an issuer (public) company wishes to issue new securities to the public, the underwriters of the securities will generally ask the company's auditor to provide "comfort" on the financial and accounting data in the prospectus that is not covered by an accountant's report of some form (e.g., an audit report on the financial statements). In comfort letters, the CPAs will provide positive assurance that they are independent and that their audit followed SEC standards. They will provide negative assurance or a summary of findings on various types of accounting related matters such as the following: unaudited condensed and summarized interim information, pro forma financial information, change subsequent to the balance sheet date, and on various tables of data. At this point quickly review the outline of AU 634.

c. **Application of accounting principles (AU 625).** CPAs may be asked by specified users (e.g., management, the board of directors, and others) to report on the application of accounting principles to new transactions and products, or to increase the specified users' knowledge of certain financial reporting issues. This section applies to public accountants when they get a request from a prospective client for a **written or oral** report on the accounting treatment of a prospective or completed transaction.

Before providing a report on accounting principles, AU 625 requires the accountants to take steps to make sure they have a complete understanding of the form and substance of the transaction, including consulting with the company's current auditors. They should also review existing accounting principles and consult appropriate references and experts to provide an adequate basis for their conclusions. Also, such reports should not be issued on a hypothetical transaction that does not involve facts or circumstances relating to the specific company. Use of such reports is restricted to the specified parties involved.

> **NOW REVIEW MULTIPLE-CHOICE QUESTIONS 93 THROUGH 112 IN VOLUME 2**

3. **Other Reports—Attestation Standards Based.** CPAs[1] also become involved with a variety of other types of information which result in the following reports:

   a. Attestation engagements—general (AT 101)
   b. Agreed-upon procedures engagements (AT 201)
   c. Financial forecasts and projections (AT 301)
   d. Pro forma financial information (AT 401)
   e. Management discussion and analysis (AT 701)
   f. Trust services
   g. Service organization control (SOC) reports

Points a. and b. provide overall general guidance for attestation engagements of all types. For example, the overall eleven attestation standards are presented in AT 101, and the overall standards for agreed-upon procedures engagements in AT 201.

The remaining points (c. through g.) relate to specific guidance for attestation engagements related to a particular topic (e.g., AT 301 [topic c. above] relates to providing assurance on forecasts). Thus, the individual performing an attestation engagement for a financial forecast has two sources of guidance—the general and the specific. In situations in which an attestation engagement is being performed on a type of information for which a detailed standard has not been provided, the CPA uses that information provided in AT 101 and AT 201. In addition to the above detailed types of engagements, recall that auditors may issue reports on internal control over financial reporting (AT 501); this topic is summarized in the Internal Control Module. Also, information on compliance attestation (AT 601) is presented later in this module.

a. **Attestation engagements—general (AT 101).** AT 101 provides the framework for all attest engagements. Attestation standards apply to engagements in which CPAs are engaged to issue or do issue an examination, a review, or an agreed-upon procedures report on subject matter, or an assertion about subject matter, that is the responsibility of another party. It is important to distinguish between the subject matter and the assertion about the subject matter.

The **subject matter** of an attestation engagement may take many forms, including

- Historical or prospective performance or condition (e.g., historical prospective financial information, performance measurements, and backlog data)
- Physical characteristics (e.g., narrative descriptions, square footage of facilities)
- Historical events (e.g., price of a market basket of goods on a certain date)
- Analyses (e.g., breakeven analyses)
- Systems or processes (e.g., internal control)
- Behavior (e.g., corporate governance, compliance with laws and regulations, and human resource practices)

---

[1] The attestation standards use the term "practitioner" throughout.

An **assertion** is a declaration about whether the subject matter is presented in accordance with certain criteria. For example, management might assert that the price of a market basket of goods at its store was the lowest in the city as of a certain date. While such an assertion is generally obtained, in those circumstances in which it is not, the attest report must be restricted in those few circumstances in which a written assertion is not obtained.

CPAs may ordinarily report on either the assertion about the subject matter, **or** on the subject matter itself either as of a point in time or for a period of time. Continuing with our market basket engagement example, if reporting on the assertion, the CPAs' opinion would include assurance about management's assertion concerning the prices. Alternatively, when reporting on the subject matter, the CPAs' opinion would include assurance directly on the price of that market basket. An exception to allowing reporting on either the subject matter or on the assertion is when the examination reveals material departures from the suitable criteria. In such circumstance the CPA should report directly upon the subject matter, and not on the assertion.

If the CPAs are reporting on an assertion about the subject matter, the assertion is presented with the subject matter or in the CPAs' report. If the CPAs are reporting **directly** on the subject matter, the assertion normally is included only in a representation letter that the CPAs obtain from the responsible party.

Recall the eleven attestation standards presented in Chapter 5. Those standards provide a general framework for all such engagements. You should consider several important concepts related to those standards, including criteria and types of engagements.

Criteria. Criteria are standards or benchmarks that are used to evaluate the subject matter of the engagements. Criteria are important in reporting the CPAs' conclusion to the users because they convey the basis on which the conclusion was formed. For example, generally accepted accounting principles are ordinarily used as the frame of reference—criteria—to evaluate the financial statements.

A CPA must evaluate the criteria being followed. As indicated in the third general standard, the criteria used in an attestation engagement must be **suitable** and **available** to the users. **Suitable criteria** must have an appropriate combination of the following characteristics: objective, measurable, complete, and relevant. The following are general rules relating to criteria suitability:

- Criteria are ordinarily suitable if they are developed by regulatory agencies or other bodies composed of experts that use due process, including exposing the proposed criteria for public comment.
- Criteria developed by management or industry groups without due process may be suitable, but the CPA should carefully evaluate them in relation to the characteristics described in the previous paragraph.
- Criteria that are overly subjective should not be used in an attestation engagement. For example, an assertion that a particular software product is the *best on the market* is too subjective for an attestation engagement. There are no generally accepted criteria for what constitutes the *best* software product. Some criteria may be suitable in evaluating subject matter for only those specified parties who established them (e.g., management and the CPA) and are not suitable for general use.

In addition to meeting the requirement that they be *suitable*, the criteria must also be available to users. This requirement of availability actually has two parts in that not only must the criteria be available, they must be understandable to users. Criteria should be available in one or more of the following ways:

- Publicly
- Inclusions—with the subject matter or in the assertion
- Inclusion in CPA's report
- Well understood by most users (e.g., the distance between A and B is 20 feet)
- Available only to specified parties (in this case the CPA's report is restricted to those parties)

Forms of engagements. As indicated in Chapter 5, the forms of attestation engagements are **examinations, reviews,** or the performance of **agreed-upon procedures**.

An examination is designed to provide the highest level of assurance that CPAs provide—the same level of assurance about other types of subject matter as an audit provides for financial statements. When performing an examination, CPAs select from all available procedures to gather sufficient evidence to allow the issuance of a report with a positive opinion about whether the subject matter being examined follows some established or stated criteria. Sufficient evidence exists when it is enough to drive attestation risk to an appropriate **low level**.

At the completion of the examination, the CPAs issue an appropriate report. The following is an example of a standard unqualified examination report **directly on the subject matter:**

Independent Accountant's Report

We have examined the accompanying schedule of investment performance statistics of Yorn Investment Fund for the year ended December 31, 20X2. This schedule is the responsibility of Yorn Investment Fund's management. Our responsibility is to express an opinion on this schedule based on our examination.

Our examination was conducted in accordance with attestation standards established by the American Institute of Certified Public Accountants and, accordingly, included examining, on a test basis, evidence supporting the schedule and performing such other procedures as we considered necessary in the circumstances. We believe our examination provides a reasonable basis for our opinion.

In our opinion, the schedule of investment performance statistics referred to above presents, in all material respects, the performance of Yorn Investment Fund for the year ended December 31, 20X2, in conformity with the measurement and disclosure criteria set forth by the Association of Investment Management Research, Inc., as described in Note 1.

Jane Zhang, CPA, LLP
January 22, 20X3

This standard report, however, is not appropriate in all cases. The following illustrates circumstances that result in modification of the standard unqualified report.

Situation	Report modification
1. Criteria are agreed upon or only available to specified users	A statement of limitations on the use of the report
2. Departure of subject matter from criteria	Qualified or adverse opinion depending on materiality of the departure
3. Limitation on scope of engagement	Qualified opinion or disclaimer
4. When reporting on subject matter and a written assertion is not obtained from the responsible party	A statement of limitations on the use of the report

Reviews. A review engagement involves performing limited procedures, such as inquiries and analytical procedures. In performing a review, the CPAs endeavor to gather sufficient evidence to drive attestation risk to a **moderate level**. Accordingly, the resulting report provides only limited assurance that the information is fairly presented. **Limited assurance** is also referred to as **negative assurance** because the CPAs' report disclaims an opinion on the reviewed information, but includes a statement such as "We are not aware of any material modifications that should be made in order for the information to be in conformity with the criteria." Of course, when uncorrected material departures from the criteria are noted, the report must be modified to so indicate. The following is an example of an unmodified review report **directly on the subject matter:**

Independent Accountant's Report

We have examined the accompanying schedule of investment performance statistics of King Investment Fund for the year ended December 31, 20X2. This schedule is the responsibility of King Investment Fund's management.

Our examination was conducted in accordance with attestation standards established by the American Institute of Certified Public Accountants. A review is substantially less in scope than an examination, the objective of which is the expression of an opinion on the schedule. Accordingly, we do not express such an opinion.

Based on our review, nothing came to our attention that caused us to believe that the accompanying schedule of investment performance statistics of King Investment Fund for the year ended December 31, 20X2, is not presented, in all material respects, in accordance with the measurement and disclosure criteria set forth by the Association of Investment Management Research, Inc., as described in Note 1.

George Williams & Associates, LLP
January 15, 20X3

The following lists circumstances that result in modification of the CPAs' review report.

Situation	Report modification
1. Criteria are agreed upon or only available to specified users	A statement of limitations on the use of the report
2. Departure of subject matter from criteria	Modified report describing the departure
3. Limitation on scope of the engagement	Report cannot be issued
4. When reporting on subject matter and a written assertion is not obtained from the responsible party	A statement of limitations on the use of the report

At this point you should carefully study the outline of AT 101.

b. **Agreed-upon procedures engagements.** AT 201 provides guidance for agreed-upon procedures engagements. The section applied to both engagements relating to historical financial information (e.g., specified elements of a financial statement—section 2.a. of this module) and engagements related to information other than historical financial statements. Agreed-upon procedures reports include a list of procedures performed (or reference thereto) and the related findings. Because specified parties have agreed upon the nature of the procedures, the reports for such engagements are intended only for those parties. Consequently, reports on agreed-upon procedures are referred to as **restricted use** reports, as contrasted to **general use** reports, such as those on examinations and reviews. As previously indicated, examination and review reports ordinarily may be used by all third parties. Only when the criteria have been agreed upon by the parties involved and such criteria are not generally understandable to those not involved with the information must an examination or review report be restricted. Examples of the later type of engagement include the application of agreed-upon procedures to an entity's internal control over financial reporting, compliance with various laws and regulations, or on a schedule of statistical production data. At this point you should carefully study the outline of AT 201.

c. **Financial forecasts and projections (AT 301).** AT 301 presents three forms of accountant association with forecasts or projections—compilation, examination, and application of agreed-upon procedures.

The following are the standard report forms suggested for compilation and examination of forecasts or projections:

Compilation Report

We have compiled the accompanying forecasted balance sheet, statements of income, retained earnings, and cash flows of XYZ Company as of December 31, 20XX, and for the year then ending, in accordance with standards established by the American Institute of Certified Public Accountants.

A compilation is limited to presenting in the form of a forecast information that is the representation of management and does not include evaluation of the support for the assumptions underlying the forecast. We have not examined the forecast and, accordingly, do not express an opinion or any other form of assurance on the accompanying statements or assumptions. Furthermore, there will usually be differences between the forecasted and actual results, because events and circumstances frequently do not occur as expected, and those differences may be material. We have no responsibility to update this report for events and circumstances occurring after the date of this report.

Examination Report

We have examined the accompanying forecasted balance sheet, statements of income, retained earnings, and cash flows for XYZ Company as of December 31, 20XX, and for the year then ended. XYZ Company's management is responsible for the forecast. Our responsibility is to express an opinion on the forecast based on our examination.

Our examination was conducted in accordance with attestation standards established by the American Institute of Certified Public Accountants and, accordingly, included such procedures as we considered necessary to evaluate both the assumptions used by management and the preparation and presentation of the forecast. We believe that our examination provides a reasonable basis for our opinion.

In our opinion, the accompanying forecast is presented in conformity with guidelines for presentation of a forecast established by the American Institute of Certified Public Accountants, and the underlying assumptions provide a reasonable basis for management's forecast. However, there will usually be differences between the forecasted and actual results, because events and circumstances frequently do not occur as expected, and those differences may be material. We have no responsibility to update this report for events and circumstances occurring after the date of this report.

Departures from the standard report for forecasts/projections are very similar to those for historical financial statement audit reports. While it is not necessary that you read the entire Statement (on forecasts/projections), you should at this point turn to the outline of AT 301. Several **extremely** important points relative to that outline are

(1) An accountant should not be associated with forecasts/projections that do not disclose assumptions.
(2) Forecasts may be for general or limited use, while projections are for limited use only (see Section A.1. of outline for AT 301 for discussion).
(3) Independence is **not** required for compilations (recall this is also the case for financial statement compilations).
(4) Concerning assurance provided: Know that a compilation report provides no assurance (again, this is also the case with financial statement compilations); an examination report provides positive assurance with respect to the reasonableness of assumptions; and an agreed-upon procedures report provides a summary of findings.

d. **Reporting on pro forma financial information (AT 401).** High levels of business combinations and various types of changes in capitalization created a significant demand for auditor association with "pro forma financial information" which adjusts earlier historical financial information prospectively for the effects of an actual or proposed transaction (or event). Accountants may either review or examine the information. The following is an example of an examination report:

Pro Forma Financial Information

Independent Auditor's Report

We have examined the pro forma adjustments reflecting the transaction described in Note 1 and the application of those adjustments to the historical amounts in the accompanying pro forma condensed balance sheet of X Company as of December 31, 20X0, and the pro forma condensed statement of income for the year then ended. The historical condensed financial statements are derived from the historical financial statements of X Company, which were audited by us, and of Y Company, which were audited by other accountants, appearing elsewhere herein. Such pro forma adjustments are based upon management's assumptions described in Note 2. X Company's management is responsible for the pro forma financial information. Our responsibility is to express an opinion on the pro forma financial information based on our examination.

Our examination was conducted in accordance with attestation standards established by the American Institute of Certified Public Accountants and, accordingly, included such procedures as were considered necessary in the circumstances. We believe that our examination provides a reasonable basis for our opinion.

The objective of this pro forma financial information is to show what the significant effects on the historical financial information might have been had the transaction [or event] occurred at an earlier date. However, the pro forma condensed financial statements are not necessarily indicative of the results of operations or related effects on financial position that would have been attained had the above-mentioned transaction [or event] actually occurred earlier.

[Additional paragraph(s) may be added to emphasize certain matters relating to the attest engagement of the subject matter.]

In our opinion, management's assumptions provide a reasonable basis for presenting the significant effects directly attributable to the above-mentioned transaction described in Note 1, the related pro forma adjustments give appropriate effect to those assumptions, and the pro forma column reflects the proper application of those adjustments to the historical financial statement amounts in the pro forma condensed balance sheet as of December 31, 20X0, and the pro forma condensed statement of income for the year then ended.

Review reports, as is the case with reviews of historical financial information, indicate that they are less in scope than examinations, and provide negative assurance (e.g., "I am not aware of any material modifications that should be made. . .").

Scope restrictions, departures from AICPA standards, etc., are treated in a manner similar to that for reviews and audits of historical financial statements. At this point, review the outline of the section that precedes the AU outline.

e. **Management discussion and analysis.** AT 701 provides guidance for performing review and examination of management's discussion and analysis (MD&A). MD&A is included in reports filed with the SEC (e.g., Form 10K and 10Q) and in annual reports sent directly to shareholders. In addition, a number of companies that do not report to the SEC prepare such information. This service allows a CPA to provide assurance ("negative assurance" for a review, and "reasonable assurance" for an examination) on a client's MD&A. At this point you should review carefully the outline of AT 701, including the summary tables that follow that outline.

f. **Trust Services.** Trust Services—jointly developed with the Canadian Institute of Chartered Accountants (CICA)—are designed to provide information system business assurance and advisory services that instill confidence in an organization, system, or other entity by improving the quality or context of information for decision makers. They were developed by the AICPA's Assurance Services Executive Committee (discussed in Overview).

Trust Services view a system as consisting of five key components organized to achieve a specified objective—infrastructure, software, people, procedures, and data. It may be as simple as a personal-computer-based payroll application with only one user, or as complex as a multi-application, multicomputer banking system accessed by many users both within and outside the banks involved.

In a Trust Services engagement, management prepares and communicates a system description that can be included on the company's Web site, attached to the practitioners' report, or communicated to users in some other manner. It must clearly articulate the boundaries of the system so as to allow individuals to understand both the scope of management's assertions related to it and the CPA's report.

In performing a Trust Services engagement the CPA (practitioner) performs procedures to determine that management's description of the system is fairly stated, and obtains evidence that the controls over the system are designed and operating effectively to meet the Trust Services **Principles** and **Criteria**—the suitable criteria required for an attest engagement. The CPA reports on whether the system meets one or more of the following **principles** over a particular reporting period:

1. **Security.** The system (infrastructure, software, people, procedures, and data) is protected against unauthorized access (both physical and logical).
2. **Availability.** The system is available for operation and use as committed or agreed.
3. **Processing Integrity.** System processing is complete, accurate, timely, and authorized.
4. **Online Privacy.** Private information obtained as a result of electronic commerce is collected, used, disclosed, and retained as committed or agreed.
5. **Confidentiality.** Information designated as confidential is protected as committed or agreed.

For each principle reported upon by the auditor, the auditor considers each of the following four criteria:

1. **Policies.** The entity has defined and documented its policies relevant to the particular principle. These policies are written statements that communicate management's intent, objectives, requirements, responsibilities, and/or standards for a particular subject.
2. **Communications.** The entity has communicated its defined policies to authorized users.
3. **Procedures.** The entity utilizes procedures to achieve the objectives in accordance with its defined policies.
4. **Monitoring.** The entity monitors the system and takes action to maintain compliance with its defined policies.

Key points related to a Trust Services engagement

1. Management ordinarily provides the CPA with a written assertion on the system and the CPA may report either on management's assertion or the subject matter of the engagement (one or more of the principles). When the CPA reports on the assertion, the assertion should accompany the CPA's report or the first paragraph of the report should contain a statement of the assertion. The CPA's report and management's assertion should specify the period covered—that may be for a period of time (ordinarily one year or less) or at a point in time.

2. If one or more criteria relating to a principle have not been achieved, the CPA issues a qualified or adverse report. If management refuses to provide a written assertion, a disclaimer of opinion is ordinarily appropriate.

3. When reporting on more than one principle, the CPA may issue either a combined report on all principles, or individual reports.

4. Either an examination or an agreed-upon procedures engagement may be performed for a Trust Services engagement.

5. At present CPAs offer two types of trust services—WebTrust and SysTrust.

    a. **WebTrust** provides assurance on electronic commerce (including Web sites). The CPA is engaged to examine *both* that a client *complied* with the Trust Services criteria (e.g., the company uses procedures in accordance with its defined policies) and that it *maintained effective controls* over the system based on Trust Services criteria (e.g., the company's procedures are effective).

    b. **SysTrust** provides assurance on any defined electronic system. In a SysTrust engagement the CPA is engaged to examine only that a client *maintained effective controls* over the system based on the Trust Services criteria.

6. Both WebTrust and SysTrust are designed to incorporate a seal management process by which a seal (logo) may be included on a client's Web site as an electronic representation of the practitioner's unqualified WebTrust report. If the client wishes to use the seal (logo), the engagement must be updated at least annually. Also, the initial reporting period must include at least two months. Following are sample reports for WebTrust and SysTrust.

Independent Practitioner's WebTrust Report on Consumer Protection

To the Management of ABC Company:

We have examined ABC Company's compliance with the AICPA/CICA Trust Services Criteria for consumer protection, and based on these criteria, the effectiveness of controls over the Online Privacy and Processing Integrity of the Customer Order Placement System during the period January 1, 20X2, through June 30, 20X2. The compliance with these criteria and maintaining the effectiveness of these controls is the responsibility of ABC Company's management. Our responsibility is to express an opinion based on our examination.

Within the context of AICPA/CICA Trust Services, consumer protection addresses the controls over personally identifiable information and the processing of electronic commerce transactions. The AICPA/CICA Trust Services On-line Privacy and Processing Integrity Criteria are used to evaluate whether ABC Company's controls over consumer protection of its Customer Order Placement System are effective. Consumer protection does not address the quality of ABC Company's goods, nor their suitability for any customer's intended purpose.

Our examination was conducted in accordance with attestation standards established by the American Institute of Certified Public Accountants and, accordingly, included (1) obtaining an understanding of ABC Company's relevant on-line privacy and processing integrity controls; (2) testing and evaluating the operating effectiveness of the controls; (3) testing compliance with the Online Privacy and Processing Integrity Criteria; and (4) performing such other procedures as we considered necessary in the circumstances. We believe that our examination provides a reasonable basis for our opinion.

In our opinion, ABC Company complied, in all material respects, with the criteria for consumer protection and maintained, in all material respects, effective controls over the Customer Order Placement System to provide reasonable assurance that

- Personal information obtained as a result of electronic commerce was collected, used, disclosed, and retained as committed or agreed, and
- System processing was complete, accurate, timely and authorized during the period of January 1, 20X2, through June 30, 20X2, based on the AICPA/CICA Trust Services Criteria for consumer protection.

Because of inherent limitations in controls, error or fraud may occur and not be detected. Furthermore, the projection of any conclusions, based on our findings, to future periods is subject to the risk that the validity of such conclusions may be altered because of changes made to the system or controls, the failure to make needed changes to the system or controls, or a deterioration in the degree of effectiveness of the controls.

The WebTrust Seal of Assurance on ABC Company's Web site constitutes a symbolic representation of the contents of this report and it is not intended, nor should it be construed, to update this report or provide any additional assurance.

This report does not include any representation as to the quality of ABC Company's goods nor their suitability for any customer's intended purpose.

[*Name of CPA* Firm*, City, State, Date*]

Independent Practitioner's SysTrust Report

To the Management of ABC Company:

We have examined the effectiveness of ABC Company's control described in Schedule X, over the security of its Cash Disbursements System during the period January 1, 20X2, to June 30, 20X2, based on the AICPA/CICA Trust Services Security Criteria. Maintaining the effectiveness of these controls is the responsibility of ABC Company's management. Our responsibility is to express an opinion based on our examination.

Our examination was conducted in accordance with attestation standards established by the American Institute of Certified Public Accountants and, accordingly, included (1) obtaining an understanding of ABC Company's relevant on-line privacy and processing integrity controls; (2) testing and evaluating the operating effectiveness of the controls; (3) testing compliance with the Online Privacy and Processing Integrity Criteria; and (4) performing such other procedures as we considered necessary in the circumstances. We believe that our examination provides a reasonable basis for our opinion.

In our opinion, ABC Company maintained, in all material respects, effective controls described in Schedule X, over the security of the Cash Disbursements System to provide reasonable assurance that the Cash Disbursements System was protected against unauthorized access (both physical and logical) during the period January 1, 20X2 to June 30, 20X2, based on the AICPA/CICA Trust Services Security Criteria.

Because of inherent limitations in controls, error or fraud may occur and not be detected. Furthermore, the projection of any conclusions, based on our findings, to future periods is subject to the risk that the validity of such conclusions may be altered because of changes made to the system or controls, the failure to make needed changes to the system or controls, or a deterioration in the degree of effectiveness of the controls.

The SysTrust Seal on ABC Company's Web site constitutes a symbolic representation of the contents of this report and it is not intended, nor should it be construed, to update this report or provide any additional assurance.

[*Name of CPA Firm, City, State, Date*]

g. **Service Organization Control (SOC) Reports.** Service organization provide processing services to customers who decide to outsource their processing of particular data. Examples of service organizations include data centers, flexible spending account servicers, and medical claims processers. The AICPA has established three types of examination services that result in the following three types of CPA reports on service organization controls (SOC):

- SOC 1: Restricted use reports on controls at a service organization relevant to a user entity's internal control over financial reporting.
- SOC 2: Restricted use reports on controls at a service organization related to security, availability, processing integrity, confidentiality, and/or privacy.
- SOC 3: General use SysTrust reports related to security, availability, processing integrity, confidentiality, and/or privacy.

SOC 1 Reports. Section E3 of the Understanding Internal Control and Assessing Control Risk module discusses SOC 1 reports. These reports are intended primarily for the use of user auditors and the company that uses the services of the service organization. AT 801 provides guidance to CPAs providing SOC 1 reports and AU 324 addresses the use of such reports.

SOC 2 Reports. SOC 2 reports are performed under AT Section 101, Attest Engagements and address one or more of the Trust Services principles of security, availability, processing integrity, confidentiality, and/or privacy. SOC 2 reports are designed to provide

- Organizations that outsource tasks and functions a mechanism for improving governance and oversight of service providers.
- Service organizations the ability to communicate the suitability of the design and operating effectiveness of their controls.

In a SOC 2 engagement, management prepares a detailed description of the service organization's system, including controls designed to achieve the criteria for one or more of the Trust Services Principles. In essence, the CPA reports on the fairness of the description. Service organizations can distribute the report to their customers and other intended recipients, such as regulators and business partners.

SOC 3 Reports. SOC 3 reports are in essence Trust Services reports for service organizations. These reports provide users with an assertion by management that it maintained effective controls to meet the Trust Services criteria, a short description of its system, and a CPA's report on either management's assertion or on the effectiveness of controls that meet the Trust Services criteria as described earlier in this chapter. The following figure compares the various types of service organization reports.

	SOC 1	**SOC 2**	**SOC 3**
Professional Standards	• AT 801 (SSAE No. 16) • AICPA Guide *Applying SSAE No. 16 Reporting on Controls at a Service Organization* • AU 324 (on use of such reports)	• AT 101 • AICPA Guide, *Reporting on Controls at a Service Organization Relevant to Security, Availability, Processing Integrity, Confidentiality, or Privacy*	• AT 101 • AICPA Technical Practice Aid, *Trust Services Principles, Criteria and Illustrations*
Primary Purpose	Report on service organization controls over financial reporting, particularly on those controls likely to be relevant to user entities' financial statements. These reports are primarily for auditors of companies that outsource processing to a service organization.	Report on service organization controls related to compliance with the Trust Services Principles and Criteria (controls over security, availability, processing integrity, confidentiality, and/or privacy).	
Assertion provided by service organization management	A specific, detailed assertion on the part of the system the CPA is reporting upon.		A more general assertion on the organization having met one or more of the AICPA Trust Services Criteria.
Report	Detailed Type 1 or Type 2 report on controls tested.*	Detailed Type 1 or Type 2 report on service organization's compliance with one or more Trust Service Principles. *	A less detailed report on whether service organization maintained effective controls based on the Trust Services Criteria.
Use of Report	Restricted use report primarily for user auditors (auditors auditing the financial statements of companies that use the service auditor).	Restricted use report primarily for service organization and user stakeholders such as customers, regulators, business partners, suppliers, and directors.	General use report (for use by anyone).

*Type 1 reports address whether the description of the controls is fairly presented and whether the controls described are suitably designed. A Type 2 report includes the information in a Type 1 report and an opinion on whether the controls were operating effectively.

NOW REVIEW MULTIPLE-CHOICE QUESTIONS 113 THROUGH 144 IN VOLUME 2

D. Reporting on Compliance

Compliance auditing involves testing and reporting on whether an organization has complied with the requirements of various laws, regulations, contracts, and grants. Congress and various regulatory agencies have adopted compliance auditing requirements for a variety of governmental and other organizations. While not a new type of auditing, it has become more significant in the last decade. A primary purpose of compliance auditing is to provide assurance that requirements of various federal programs have been met. Currently, the major engagements are (1) compliance attestation engagements, or (2) compliance auditing of federal financial assistance programs.

1. **Compliance Attestation Engagements.** AT 601 provides guidance to CPAs on providing assurance—either through agreed-upon procedures or through examination engagements—concerning an organization's compliance with requirements of certain laws, regulations, rules, contracts, or grants (referred to as compliance with **specified requirements**). The following are examples of agreed-upon procedures engagements (which occur much more frequently than examinations):

EXAMPLE 1

The Federal Depository Insurance Corporation (FDIC) Improvement Act of 1991 requires that CPAs be engaged by certain financial institutions to perform agreed-upon procedures engagements to test financial institution compliance with certain "safety and soundness" laws designated by the FDIC.

> **EXAMPLE 2**
>
> The Environmental Protection Agency (EPA) requires that CPAs (or internal auditors) be engaged to perform agreed-upon procedures engagements to test certain entities' compliance with an EPA regulation that gasoline contains at least 2.0% oxygen.

As an alternative to performing agreed-upon procedures in engagements such as the above, a CPA may perform agreed-upon procedures on the portion of the internal control that is designed to provide reasonable assurance of compliance with such specified requirements. Using the second illustration, a control over compliance engagement would analyze controls related to providing management with reasonable assurance that gasoline contains at least 2.0% oxygen.

Basic to compliance attestation engagements **is a written management assertion** concerning compliance. In this assertion, management ordinarily states that it believes that the company is in compliance with the specified requirements or acknowledges certain instances of noncompliance. This written assertion is included in a representation letter addressed by management to the auditor, and may also be included in a separate management report. For example, in the second earlier example, the written management assertion relates to its compliance with the EPA regulation; alternatively, structured on internal control, the assertion relates to internal control over compliance with the EPA regulation. The CPA performs procedures to test whether the written assertion is correct. AT 601 establishes standards for agreed-upon procedures engagements on compliance and internal control, and for examination engagements on compliance. The statement does not permit review engagements.

a. **Agreed-upon procedures engagements**

   (1) **Applicability**—These engagements may be related either to management's assertion about compliance with specified requirements or to management's assertion about the effectiveness of its internal control over compliance.

   (2) **Engagement scope**—The scope of these engagements is often fixed by the regulatory agency involved (e.g., the EPA in the second example presented earlier). The CPA is required to obtain an understanding of the compliance requirements addressed in management's assertion and must obtain a representation letter from management.

   (3) **Reporting**—As with other agreed-upon procedures engagements, the report is a limited distribution report, in this case restricted to the audit committee, management, and the parties for whom the procedures were performed (e.g., the EPA). The accountant provides a summary of findings in the report. The report must include any material noncompliance noted, regardless of whether the CPA became aware of it as a direct result of the procedures performed or in some other manner (e.g., through a discussion with an internal auditor). The following is an example of an agreed-upon procedures report:

Independent Practitioner's Report

To XYZ Company:

   We have performed the procedures enumerated below, which were agreed to by the Minnesota Department of Education, solely to assist the specified parties in evaluating XYZ Company's compliance with Section F.2. of Minnesota Department of Education Regulation 76A of *Employment Health Requirements* during the period ended December 31, 20XX. Management is responsible for XYZ Company's compliance with those requirements. This agreed-upon procedures engagement was conducted in accordance with attestation standards established by the American Institute of Certified Public Accountants. The sufficiency of these procedures is solely the responsibility of those parties specified in this report. Consequently, we make no representation regarding the sufficiency of the procedures described below either for the purpose for which this report has been requested or for any other purpose.

[Include paragraphs to enumerate procedures and findings.]

   We were not engaged to, and did not, perform an examination, the objective of which would be the expression of an opinion on compliance. Accordingly, we do not express such an opinion. Had we performed additional procedures, other matters might have come to our attention that would have been reported to you.

   This report is intended solely for the information of the audit committee, management, and the parties listed in the first paragraph, and is not intended to be and should not be used by anyone other than those specified parties.

b. **Examination engagements**

   (1) **Applicability**—These engagements relate to management's written assertion about the entity's compliance with specified requirements. (AT 601 does not provide guidance for examinations of the internal control over compliance. General guidance for such engagements is provided in AT 101.)

   (2) **Engagement scope**—The procedures and scope of an examination of compliance are similar to those of an audit of financial statements. Following are the major stages:

   (a) Obtain an understanding of specified compliance requirements.

    (b) Plan the engagement.

    (c) Consider relevant portions of internal control over compliance (when control risk is to be assessed below maximum, tests of controls must be performed).

    (d) Obtain sufficient evidence through substantive tests of compliance with specified requirements.

    (e) Consider whether any subsequent events affect compliance.

    (f) Form an opinion about whether management's assertion about the entity's compliance with specified requirements is fairly stated in all material respects based on established or agreed-upon criteria.

(3) **Reporting**—The CPA's report may either be (1) directly upon compliance, or (2) on management's assertion. The following is an unqualified report directly upon compliance:

Independent Practitioner's Report

To XYZ Company:

We have examined XYZ Company's compliance with Section F.2. of Minnesota Department of Education Regulation 76A of *Employment Health Requirements* during the period ended December 31, 20XX. Management is responsible for XYZ Company's compliance with those requirements. Our responsibility is to express an opinion on XYZ Company's compliance based on our examination.

Our examination was conducted in accordance with attestation standards established by the American Institute of Certified Public Accountants, and, accordingly, included examining, on a test basis, evidence about XYZ Company's compliance with those requirements and performing such other procedures as we considered necessary in the circumstances. We believe that our examination provides a reasonable basis for our opinion. Our examination does not provide a legal determination on XYZ Company's compliance with specified requirements.

In our opinion, XYZ Company complied, in all material respects, with the aforementioned requirements for the year ended December 31, 20XX.

This report is intended solely for the information and use of XYZ Company and the State of Minnesota and is not intended to be and should not be used by anyone other than these specified parties.

As is the case with other attestation reports, if an opinion other than unqualified is being issued the CPA should follow the first reporting option, reporting directly upon compliance. The following table presents the primary circumstances:

Circumstance	Examination Report Effect
1. Entity did not comply	Qualified or adverse opinion with an explanatory paragraph added before the opinion paragraph
2. Material uncertainty relating to future events makes determination of compliance insusceptible to reasonable estimation	Qualified opinion or disclaimer of opinion with an explanatory paragraph added before the opinion paragraph
3. Scope restriction	When client-imposed, generally disclaim an opinion; when circumstance-imposed, consider qualified opinion or disclaimer of opinion
4. Involvement of another CPA firm	When the principal CPA does not wish to take responsibility for the other CPA's work, the other CPA's report is referred to.

2. **Compliance Auditing, Government Auditing Standards, and the Single Audit Act.** Governments frequently establish requirements that entities undergo a "compliance audit" to address their compliance with applicable requirements relating to various laws, regulations, contracts, and grants. The scope of compliance audits differs from one another, ordinarily due to differing requirements of the particular situation involved. Yet, the overall goal is for the auditor to provide assurance about whether the law, regulation, contract or grant has been administered in accordance with applicable laws and regulations. Further guidance for compliance auditing is provided by AU 801 and *Government Auditing Standards (GAS),* Also referred to as the "yellow book," published by the Comptroller General of the United States (the top executive within the Government Accountability Office).

AU 801 applies when an auditor is engaged, or required by law or regulation, to perform a compliance audit in accordance with any of the following:

- GAAS
- Standards for financial statements under Government Auditing Standards.
- A governmental audit requirement that requires an auditor to express an opinion on compliance (e.g., a requirement of organizations governed by the US Department of Housing and Urban Development).

Read the outline of AU 801. *Government Auditing Standards* provides what it refers to a as "generally accepted government auditing standards (GAGAS)—read the summary information relating to Government Auditing Standards presented following the outline of AU 901.

To provide a perspective on this area, we discuss compliance auditing in three contexts—GAAS audits, Government Auditing Standard audits, and audits performed under the Single Audit Act.

a. **Audits conducted in accordance with GAAS**

(1) **Applicability**—This form of audit is generally performed for governmental entities for which no law requires either a *GAS* or Single Audit. It is also performed for certain nongovernmental entities that have received federal financial assistance.

(2) **Audit scope**—Recall from Section A of the Engagement Planning Module that auditors have a responsibility to design all audits to provide reasonable assurance of detecting misstatements resulting from violations of laws and regulations that have a direct and material effect on line item amounts (hereafter "direct effect") in the financial statements; this responsibility remains the same for these audits. Because entities that receive financial aid must comply with a number of laws that, if violated, result in illegal acts with a direct effect on the financial statements, an audit must provide reasonable assurance of their detection.

To identify laws having a direct effect on an organization's financial statements, auditors (1) discuss laws with management, other administrators, and government auditors, (2) review relevant grant and loan agreements, (3) review minutes of the legislative body of the governmental organization, and (4) obtain written representations from management about the completeness of laws identified. They then assess the risk that financial statement amounts might be materially misstated by violations of laws and design and perform appropriate substantive tests of compliance with the laws.

The objectives, scope, methodology, and results of the audit should be summarized in audit working papers in a legible manner and should contain evidence of supervisory reviews of the work conducted. These working papers should "stand alone" without the need for any supplementary explanations to describe the nature of the audit and should include a written audit program, with proper cross-referencing to the working papers.

(3) **Reporting**—The standard audit report is normally issued. If material noncompliance is detected, it must be disclosed in the financial statements or treated as a departure from GAAP in the audit report, thus requiring a qualified or an adverse opinion. **No** compliance report (see next section) is issued, and a report on internal control is only issued when significant deficiencies have been identified.

b. **Audits conducted in accordance with generally accepted government auditing standards (GAGAS)**

(1) **Applicability**—These audits are required for certain organizations that receive federal financial assistance. Whether a governmental organization is so required depends upon requirements of the federal financial assistance programs in which it participates and whether it is required to have a Single Audit (see c. below).

(2) **Audit scope**—In addition to GAAS requirements, depending upon the nature of the entity being audited, additional auditor responsibilities may exist. (See outline of *Government Auditing Standards* following AU 901 outline.)

(3) **Reporting**—While GAGAS require reporting on the **financial statements** (i.e., the "audit report"), **internal control**, and on **compliance with laws and regulations**, other government audits may not require a report on internal control. The AU 801 reporting requirements outline reports for reporting on compliance alone, combining a report on compliance and internal control, and reporting on internal control over compliance.

c. **Audits conducted in accordance with the Single Audit Act.** Audits in accordance with the Single Audit Act of 1984 (as amended in 1996) are more extensive than GAAS or GAS audits. This act, passed by Congress, is implemented by the Office of Management and Budget (OMB) through its Circular A-133 and its related Compliance Supplement. Circular A-133 is the OMB's key policy document that implements the Single Audit Act. The Compliance Supplement is the document that provides guidance to auditors who are engaged to test for compliance with program requirements.

Audits in accordance with the Single Audit Act include requirements that supplement the GAS audit procedures. The auditors' report(s) may be presented in the form of either combined or separate reports, but should include the following:

(1) Opinion (or disclaimer) on whether financial statements conform to GAAP.

(2) Opinion on schedule of expenditures of federal awards. The schedule summarized program expenditures for all programs. The auditors' report includes an opinion as to whether the information is presented fairly, in all material respects, in relation to the financial statements taken as a whole.

(3) Report on internal control related to the financial statements and major programs. Under the single audit requirements, auditors are responsible for understanding internal control over major programs and reporting the results of their tests; significant deficiencies and material weaknesses must be disclosed. Auditors are required to obtain an understanding of the recipient's internal control over financial reporting and over federal programs sufficient to plan the audit to support a low assessed level of control risk for major programs.

While this provision does not require that auditors achieve a low assessed level of risk, it does require auditors to test the controls over federal programs to determine whether they are effective.

The internal control report (or internal control portion of a combined report) includes the following:

First paragraph

- Management is responsible for establishing and maintaining effective internal control over compliance with requirements of laws.
- We considered internal control over compliance that could have a direct and material effect on a major federal program.

Second paragraph

- Our consideration would not necessarily disclose all material weaknesses.
- Definition of material weakness
- Material weaknesses noted (or statement that none were noted)

Third paragraph

- Other matters (less than material weaknesses) noted

Fourth paragraph

- Report is for information of audit committee, management, and federal awarding agencies.
- Report is a matter of public record and its distribution is not limited.

Opinion paragraph

- Entity complied, in all material respects, with types of requirements described above for each of its major programs.
- Auditing procedures disclosed immaterial instances of noncompliance described in the accompanying Schedule of Findings and Questioned Costs.

(4) **Report on major financial assistance program compliance.** A major program is one that is determined by using a risk-based approach that considers both the amount of the program's expenditures and the risk of material noncompliance. In general, the major programs must constitute at least 50% of the total federal expenditures by the organization.

Under the Single Audit Act, compliance procedures are performed for the specific requirements of all major programs. The specific requirements that must be audited are those that, if not complied with, could have a material effect on a major program. These requirements relate to such matters as activities allowed, allowable costs, cash management, and eligibility. In testing compliance under the Single Audit Act, a lower level of planning materiality is used because auditors must consider compliance from the perspective of a material effect on each major federal assistance program. When evaluating whether an instance of noncompliance with law is material, auditors should consider the frequency of noncompliance and whether it results in a material amount of questioned costs. Questioned costs are those costs not allowed by the program, not adequately supported with documentation, unnecessary, or unreasonable.

The compliance report (or compliance portion of a combined report) in general follows the format of the standard unqualified report, with modifications including the following:

Introductory paragraph

- We have audited in compliance with requirements of Circular A-133.
- Compliance is the responsibility of management.
- Our responsibility is to express an opinion on compliance.

Scope paragraph

- Conducted audit in compliance with US GAAS; *Government Auditing Standards*, and OMB Circular A-133

Opinion paragraph

- Entity complied, in all material respects, with types of requirements described above for each of its major programs.
- Auditing procedures disclosed immaterial instances of noncompliance described in the accompanying Schedule of Findings and Questioned Costs.

(5) **A summary report on audit results relating to financial statements, internal control, and compliance.** This report includes a summary of the auditors' findings relating to the financial statements, internal control, compliance matters, questioned costs, or suspected fraud.

NOW REVIEW MULTIPLE-CHOICE QUESTIONS 145 THROUGH 166 IN VOLUME 2

KEY TERMS

Adverse opinion. The opinion expressed when the auditor concludes that the financial statements are materially and pervasively misstated and accordingly are **not** prepared in accordance with the applicable financial reporting framework (ordinarily GAAP).

Agreed-upon procedures. An attest engagement in which the CPAs agree to perform procedures for a specified party and to issue a report that is restricted to use by that party (and management).

Audit report on financial statements. A document designed to communicate the nature of the audit, including responsibilities taken, limitations, and a conclusion as to the fairness of presentation of the financial statements.

Comparative financial statements. A complete set of financial statements for one or more prior periods included with current year financial statements of the current period.

Compliance audit. An audit that emphasizes performing audit procedures to test an organization's compliance with laws and regulations.

Condensed (summary) financial statements. Historical financial information that is derived from the financial statements but contains less detail, while still providing a structured representation consistent with the financial statements.

Consistency. The concept of using the same accounting principles from year to year so that the successive financial statements issued by a business entity will be comparable.

Continuing accountant. An accountant who has been engaged to report on the financial statements of a specific entity.

Date of the auditor's report. A date no earlier than the date on which the auditor has obtained sufficient appropriate audit evidence, including evidence that the audit documentation has been reviewed.

Date of the financial statements. The date of the end of the latest period covered by the financial statements.

Disclaimer of opinion. An auditor's conclusion in an audit report that he or she is unable to form an opinion on whether the financial statements are prepared in accordance with the applicable financial reporting framework (ordinarily GAAP). This conclusion most frequently occurs due to a lack of sufficient appropriate audit evidence. It may also occur due to uncertainties, including going concern uncertainties.

Examination. An attest engagement designed to provide the highest level of assurance that CPAs provide on an assertion. An examination of financial statements is referred to as an audit.

Explanatory paragraph. A paragraph inserted in an audit report in which the auditors describe the reasons for giving a report other than a standard report.

Fraud. An intentional act by one or more individuals among management, those charged with governance, employees, or third parties, involving the use of deception that results in a misstatement in financial statements that are subject of an audit. For financial statement audits, fraud includes two types of intentional misstatements—misstatements arising from fraudulent financial reporting and misstatements arising from misappropriation of assets.

Hypothetical transaction. A transaction or financial reporting issue that does not involve facts or circumstances of a specific entity.

Integrated audit. As required by the Sarbanes-Oxley Act and the Public Company Accounting Oversight Board, an audit that includes providing assurance on both the financial statements and internal control over financial reporting. Integrated audits are required of large publicly traded companies in the United States.

Issuer. A company whose stock is traded on a public market or a company in the process of registering its stock for public sale.

Letter for underwriter. A letter issued by the independent auditors to the underwriters of securities registered with the SEC under the Securities Act of 1933. Letters for underwriters deal with matters such as the auditor's independence and the compliance of unaudited data with requirements of the SEC. These letters are also referred to as "comfort letters."

Modified opinion. A qualified opinion, an adverse opinion, or a disclaimer of opinion.

Negative assurance. A conclusion by CPAs that, after applying limited investigative techniques to certain information, they are not aware of the need to modify the presentation of the information. Negative assurance is equivalent to limited assurance.

Nonissuer. A company whose securities are *not* registered under requirements of the Securities and Exchange Commission; ordinarily, a "nonissuer" is a nonpublic company. This is in contrast to an issuer, a company whose securities are registered under the requirements of the Securities and Exchange Commission.

Nonpublic company A company other than one whose securities are traded on a public market or one that makes a filing with a regulatory agency in preparation for the sale of securities on a public market.

Other auditor. Within the context of a situation in which more than one auditing firm is involved with an audit, the auditor that has performed some of the audit work, but is not the principal auditor.

Other comprehensive basis of accounting. A basis for financial reporting other than GAAP, including (1) any basis required by a governmental regulatory agency, (2) income tax basis, (3) cash basis, and (4) a definite set of criteria having substantial support.

Pervasive. The effects on financial statements of misstatements or possible effects of misstatements that are undetected due to an inability to obtain sufficient appropriate audit evidence. Pervasive effects on the financial statements are those that, in the auditor's judgment are not confined to specific elements, accounts or items of the financial statements or if so confined, represent or could represent a substantial proportion of the financial statements or in relation to disclosures, are fundamental to users' understanding of the financial statements.

Predecessor auditor. A CPA firm that formerly served as auditor but has resigned from the engagement or has been notified that its services have been terminated.

Principal auditor. Auditors who use the work and reports of other auditors who have audited the financial statements of one or more subsidiaries, branches, or other segments of the principal auditor's client.

Qualified opinion. The opinion expressed when the auditor concludes that the financial statements are prepared in all material respects, in accordance with the applicable financial reporting framework (ordinarily GAAP) except for the effects of some limitation in the scope of the audit or some departure from GAAP.

Reasonable assurance. In the context of an audit of financial statements, a high, but not absolute, level of assurance.

Shared responsibility opinion. An audit report in which the principal auditors decide to refer to an other auditor involved with the audit of some component of the company.

Single Audit Act. Legislation passed by the US Congress that establishes uniform requirements for audits of federal financial assistance provided to state and local government.

Special report. An auditors' report issued on any of the following: (1) financial statements prepared on a comprehensive basis of accounting other than GAAP, (2) elements of financial statements, (3) compliance with regulatory or contractual requirements, (4) financial presentations to comply with contractual agreements or regulatory provisions, or (5) audited information presented in prescribed forms.

Standard audit report. The wording of an unqualified audit report that includes no modifications for matters such as substantial doubt about going concern status, a change in accounting principle, emphasis of a matter described in the financial statements, or a shared responsibility opinion.

Successor auditor. The auditors who have accepted an engagement to replace the CPA firm that formerly served as auditor (the predecessor auditor).

Unqualified opinion. The opinion expressed when the auditor concludes that the financial statements are prepared in all material respects, in accordance with the applicable financial reporting framework.

Module 6: Accounting and Review Services

Overview

This module presents guidance on engagements performed under the AICPA *Statements on Standards for Accounting and Review Services (SSARS—codified with an AR prefix)*. The *SSARS* outline two forms of accountant association with financial statements—compilations and reviews. A compilation is a service in which the accountant assists in the preparation of financial statements; compilation reports provide no assurance. A review is an attest service in which the accountants (1) perform analytical procedures, (2) make inquiries of management and others, and (3) obtain representations from management relating to the financial statements. Review reports include limited (negative) assurance.

Determining the appropriate standards for reviews may be confusing. Make certain that you understand the appropriate standards for reviews performed under the SAS and SSARS, as follows:

- SAS Reviews: These are for interim (ordinarily quarterly) financial statements of either public or nonpublic companies. Public company ("issuer") interim reviews are required by the SEC. Nonpublic company ("nonissuer") interim reviews are ordinarily not required, but are performed for companies that select the service. The two very similar versions of AU 722 (PCAOB and the Auditing Standards Board) apply to interim reviews of companies that have an annual audit. The Reporting module presents guidance on AU reviews.
- SSARS Reviews: These reviews are only for nonpublic companies. Most frequently they are performed on annual financial statements of companies that choose not to have an audit, although they may also be performed on interim financial statements. This module presents guidance on SSARS (AR) reviews.

The professional standards underlying compilations and reviews have far less quantity than those for audits. Yet, this topic is heavily tested on every exam. The limited quantity of guidance makes this a particularly "manageable" area for candidates, although the need for the exam to include enough questions on this topic to meet the percentages included on the content specification outline requires that it be examined in depth. You might expect a number of multiple-choice questions related to this area, but also, frequently, a research oriented simulation question which requires you to perform research finding an appropriate compilation or review report, or appropriate procedures in a particular situation.

The following SSARS sections pertain to this module:

Section	Title
AR 60	Framework for Performing and Reporting on Compilation and Review Engagements
AR 80	Compilation of Financial Statements
AR 90	Review of Financial Statements
AR 110	Compilation of Specified Elements, Accounts or Items of a Financial Statement
AR 120	Compilation of Pro Forma Financial Information
AR 200	Reporting on Comparative Financial Statements
AR 300	Compilation Reports on Financial Statements Included in Certain Prescribed Forms
AR 400	Communications between Predecessor and Successor Accountants
AR 500	Reporting on Compiled Financial Statements
AR 600	Reporting on Personal Financial Statements Included in Written Personal Financial Plans

Virtually all of the information in the ***Overall Objectives and Approach*** section at the beginning of each AR outline is essential. In addition, while material from all of the outlines is examined heavily, make absolutely certain you know virtually all the information presented in the outlines of AR 60, 80, and 90. The remaining sections (110 +) are also important, but ordinarily slightly less thoroughly examined.

The next section of this outline provides you with an introductory summary of some of the very most important points followed by the AR outlines. It can serve to provide you with both introductory and final study information. But you must be very familiar with the guidance in the AR outlines.

FINANCIAL STATEMENT COMPILATIONS

A. Nature of Compilations

1. A compilation involves assisting management in presenting financial information in the form of financial statements. To perform a compilation *Statements on Standards for Accounting and Review Services* require the accountants to have knowledge of the accounting principles and practices used within the client's industry and a general understanding of the client's business transactions and accounting records.

   a. At a minimum, the accountants must *read* the compiled statements for appropriate format and obvious material misstatement. CPAs performing a compilation must not accept patently unreasonable information.

      (1) If the client's information appears to be incorrect, incomplete, or otherwise unsatisfactory, the CPAs should insist upon revised information. If the client refuses to provide revised information, the CPAs should withdraw from the engagement.

      (2) Beyond these basic requirements, CPAs have no responsibility to perform any investigative procedures to substantiate the client's representations.

   b. Proper CPA reporting on compiled statements is dependent upon whether the financial statements are expected to be used by a third party other than management

      (1) When no such third-party use is expected, an accountant may either (1) issue a compilation report or (2) not issue a compilation report, but document the understanding with the client through use of an engagement letter.

         (a) When not issuing a compilation report, the engagement letter, signed by management, must make clear the services performed and the limitations on the use of the financial statements. A phrase such as "Restricted for Management's Use Only" should be included on each page of the financial statements.

      (2) When the financial statements are to be used by a third party (or reasonably might be expected to be used by a third party) a compilation report must be issued by the CPA. This report disclaims an opinion or any other form of assurance on the financial statements.

2. AR 60 states that a compilation is an attest service, but not an assurance service.

B. Planning Compilations

1. The accountant should establish an understanding with management re the compilation and should document the understanding through a written communication with management.

2. The CPAs may, with the permission of management or those charged with governance, decide to make inquiries of the predecessor accountants before accepting a compilation (or review) engagement. These inquiries include questions regarding the integrity of management, disagreements over accounting principles, the willingness of management to provide or to revise information, and the reasons for the change in accountants. The decision of whether to contact the predecessor accountants is left to the judgment of the successor CPAs. Ordinarily the predecessor is expected to respond fully to inquiries. (AR 400 provides guidance on communicating with the predecessor.)

3. A CPA may accept a compilation (or review) engagement in an industry s/he is unfamiliar with if s/he is able to obtain the required level of knowledge before compiling (reviewing) the financial statements.

C. Compilation Procedures

1. Sections A and B of the outline of AR 80 provide guidance on requirements to establish an understanding with the client (note that a written engagement letter should be obtained) and the compilation performance requirements.

2. The accountant is not required to perform other procedures such as making inquiries or performing procedures to verify information supplied by the entity. However, whenever an accountant becomes aware of information that is incorrect, incomplete, or otherwise unsatisfactory, the accountant should obtain additional or revised information. If the entity refuses to provide (or correct) such information, the accountant should withdraw from the compilation. Finally, independence is not required when performing a compilation.

D. Overall Compilation Reporting Issues

1. Standard Report

   We have compiled the accompanying balance sheet of XYZ Company as of December 31, 20XX, and the related statements of income, retained earnings, and cash flows for the year then ended. We have not audited or reviewed the accompanying financial statements and, accordingly, do not express an opinion or any assurance about whether the financial statements are in accordance with accounting principles generally accepted in the United States of America.

Management is responsible for the preparation and fair presentation of the financial statements in accordance with accounting principles generally accepted in the United States of America and for designing, implementing, and maintaining internal control relevant to the preparation and fair presentation of the financial statements.

Our responsibility is to conduct the compilation in accordance with Statements on Standards for Accounting and Review Services issued by the American Institute of Certified Public Accountants. The objective of a compilation is to assist management in presenting financial information in the form of financial statements without undertaking to obtain any assurance that there are no material modifications that should be made to the financial statements.

2. Related issues

    a. Each page of the unaudited financial statements should be marked "See Accountants' Compilation Report."
    b. The compilation report should be dated as of the completion of the compilation.
    c. A compilation report may be issued on one or more individual financial statements, without compiling a complete set of statements.
    d. Financial statements may be compiled on a special purpose framework (i.e., comprehensive basis of accounting) *other than* generally accepted accounting principles. In this case, the basis of accounting used must be disclosed either in the statements or in the accountants' report.

3. Other compilation reporting circumstances

Circumstance	Resolution
Departures from GAAP	A departure from generally accepted accounting principles requires the accountants to discuss the departure in a separate paragraph in the compilation report.
Lack of consistent application of GAAP, substantial doubt about ability to remain a going concern properly disclosed in financial statements	Compilation report not required to be altered.
Lack of consistent application of GAAP, substantial doubt about ability to remain a going concern **not** properly disclosed in financial statements	Modify the compilation report for a departure from generally accepted accounting principles.
Compilations of information that omits substantially all disclosures (e.g., note disclosures omitted)	This is permissible. In such situations the accountants should add the following last paragraph to their report: • Management has elected to omit substantially all of the disclosures (and the statement of cash flows) required by generally accepted accounting principles. If the omitted disclosures were included in the financial statements, they might influence the user's conclusions about the company's financial position, results of operations, and cash flows. Accordingly, these financial statements are not designed for those who are not informed about such matters. The financial statements should also indicate "Selected Information—Substantially All Disclosures Required by Generally Accepted Accounting Principles Are Not Included."
Compilations when the CPAs are not independent	Independence is not required. The following may be added to the compilation report: • We are not independent with respect to XYZ Company. In addition the CPAs may also provide reason(s) for the lack of independence (e.g., a member of the audit team had a direct financial interest in XYZ Company).

FINANCIAL STATEMENT REVIEWS

A. Nature of Reviews

1. A review is a service, the objective of which is to obtain limited assurance (also referred to as negative assurance) that there are no material modifications that should be made to the financial statements in order for the statements to be in conformity with the applicable financial reporting framework.

    a. In a review engagement, the accountant should accumulate review evidence to obtain a limited level of assurance.

2. A review engagement is an assurance engagement as well as an attest engagement.

B. Planning Reviews

1. The CPAs may decide to make inquiries of the predecessor accountants before accepting a compilation or review engagement. These inquiries include questions regarding the integrity of management, disagreements over accounting principles, the willingness of management to provide or to revise information, and the reasons for the change in accountants. The decision of whether to contact the predecessor accountants is left to the judgment of the successor CPAs. However, if inquiries are made with the client's consent, the predecessor accountants are generally required to respond.
2. CPAs must prepare an *engagement letter* clearly specifying the objectives of the review engagement, management's responsibilities, the accountant's responsibilities, and limitations of the engagement.

C. Review Procedures

1. Sections A and B of the outline of AR 90 provide guidance on requirements to establish an understanding with the client (as is the case with compilations, a written engagement letter should be obtained) and the review performance requirements. Particularly important points include

   a. Overall, the procedures should be sufficient to provide a reasonable basis for obtaining limited assurance that there are no material modifications needed.
   b. As is the case with compilations, the accountant must obtain an understanding of the industry and knowledge of the client (the business itself and accounting principles followed).
   c. Know that the procedures involve primarily analytical procedures, inquiries, and obtaining written representations from management. The inquiries are primarily of management and others within the company and ordinarily do not include inquiries of third parties (e.g., lawyers, confirmations of receivables). The accountant investigates differences from expectations developed when performing analytical procedures.

2. Unexpected results obtained through the use of analytical procedures are followed up by inquiries to management and certain other procedures.

   a. While a review ordinarily does not require accountants to corroborate management's responses with other evidence, they should consider the consistency of management responses in light of the results of other review procedures and their knowledge of the client's business and internal control.
   b. Additional procedures should be performed if the accountants become aware that information may be incorrect, incomplete, or otherwise unsatisfactory. The accountants should perform these procedures to the extent considered necessary to provide limited assurance that there are no material modifications that should be made to the statements.

      (1) For example, if review procedures lead an accountant to question whether a significant sales transaction is recorded in conformity with generally accepted accounting principles, it may become necessary to discuss the terms of the transaction with both senior marketing and accounting personnel and to read the sales contract.

3. Summary of review procedures

Analytical Procedures	Inquiries of Management Members with Responsibility for Financial and Accounting Matters about
• Develop *expectations* by identifying and using plausible relationships that are reasonably expected to exist.	• Whether financial statements are prepared in conformity with GAAP.
• Compare recorded amounts or ratios developed from recorded amounts to expectations.	• Whether accounting principles, practices, and methods are applied.
• Compare the consistency of management's responses in light of results of other review procedures and knowledge of business and industry.	• Any unusual or complex situations that might affect the financial statements.
	• Significant transactions taking place near the end of the period.
Obtain written representations from management and perform other procedure such as	• Status of uncorrected misstatements identified in a previous engagement.
• Inquire as to actions taken at shareholder, board of director, and other committees of board of directors.	• Questions that have arisen in applying review procedures.
• Read financial statements.	• Subsequent events.
• Obtain reports from other accountants, if any, that have reviewed significant components.	• Knowledge of potentially material fraud or suspected fraud.
	• Significant journal entries and other adjustments.
	• Communications from regulatory agencies.

4. Other procedures performed in a review include reading available minutes of stockholder and director meetings, reading the interim financial information, and obtaining reports from other accountants who have reviewed significant components of the company. Evidence must also be obtained showing that the interim financial information agrees or reconciles with the accounting records.

5. A review does *not* contemplate (a) obtaining an understanding of the entity's internal control, (b) assessing fraud risk, (c) tests of accounting records by obtaining sufficient appropriate audit evidence through inspection, observation, confirmation, (d) the examination of source documents (for example, cancelled checks or bank images); or (e) other procedures ordinarily performed in an audit.

6. A representation letter signed by management should be dated the date of the review report and should include management's acknowledgement of its

   - Responsibility for the financial statements' conformity with generally accepted accounting principles and its belief that it has met this responsibility.
   - Responsibility to prevent and detect fraud, as well as to divulge any knowledge that it has of any actual or suspected fraud that is material.
   - Responsibility to respond fully and truthfully to all inquiries and to provide complete information, including that on subsequent events.

D. Overall Review Reporting Issues

1. Standard review report

   We have reviewed the accompanying balance sheet of XYZ Company as of December 31, 20XX, and the related statements of income, retained earnings, and cash flows for the year then ended. A review includes primarily applying analytical procedures to management's financial data and making inquiries of company management. A review is substantially less in scope than an audit, the objective of which is the expression of an opinion regarding the financial statements as a whole. Accordingly, we do not express such an opinion.

   Management is responsible for the preparation and fair presentation of the financial statements in accordance with accounting principles generally accepted in the United States of America and for designing, implementing, and maintaining internal control relevant to the preparation and fair presentation of the financial statements.

   Our responsibility is to conduct the review in accordance with Statements on Standards for Accounting and Review Services issued by the American Institute of Certified Public Accountants. Those standards require us to perform procedures to obtain limited assurance that there are no material modifications that should be made to the financial statements. We believe that the results of our procedures provide a reasonable basis for our report.

   Based on our review, we are not aware of any material modifications that should be made to the accompanying financial statements in order for them to be in conformity with accounting principles generally accepted in the United States of America.

2. Departures from GAAP. Departures from GAAP, when the accountant concludes that modification of the standard report is appropriate, result in modification of the fourth paragraph and inclusion of an explanatory paragraph; for example

   With the exception of the matter described in the following paragraph, we are not aware of any material modifications....

   As disclosed in Note 6 to the financial statements, generally accepted accounting principles require that land be stated at cost. Management has informed us that the Company has stated its land at appraised value and that, if generally accepted accounting principles had been followed, the land account and stockholders' equity would have been decreased by $500,000.

   Notice that the report is neither "qualified" nor "adverse" in form as would be the case with an audit report in which a departure from GAAP exists. Audit reports, not review reports, result in an opinion, be it unmodified, qualified or adverse. Also, if the accountant believes that modification of the report is not adequate to indicate the deficiencies in the financial statements, the accountant should withdraw from the review engagement and provide no further services with respect to those financial statements.

3. As is the case for compilation reports, review reports are not required to be altered in situations involving a lack of consistent application of generally accepted accounting principles or the existence of major uncertainties (including going-concern uncertainties) that have been properly reported in the financial statements. However, when that information is not properly presented or disclosed in the financial statements, the financial statements contain a departure from generally accepted accounting principles, and the review report should be appropriately modified.

4. Other issues

   a. Because reviews are attest services, an accountant must be independent to perform a review.
   b. Each page of the financial statements should include a reference such as "See Accountant's Review Report."
   c. If the client restricts the scope of review procedures or refuses to provide an accountant with a representation letter, the review is incomplete and no review report may be issued.
   d. When current year financial statements have been reviewed and prior year financial statements were audited, an accountant may either reissue the audit report and issue a review report, *or* may refer to the audit in the review report. In referring to the audit in the review report, an accountant should indicate that the statements were audited, the date of the previous opinion, reasons for any departures from an unqualified form, and that no auditing procedures were performed after the date of the previous report. (When the current year financial statements have been compiled, the same procedures are followed.)

    e. When the current year financial statements have been audited and prior year financial statements were reviewed the audit report should include a statement indicating the type of service performed, the date of the report, a description of any material modifications noted in the report, and a statement that the service was less in scope than an audit and does not provide a basis for the expression of an opinion on the financial statements. (When prior year financial statements have been compiled, the same procedures are followed.)

    f. An audit engagement may be changed to a review engagement (or a review to a compilation) if the reason for the client's request is considered reasonable. In such a situation, this change is not referred to in the report issued.

5. Other communications.

    a. As with annual financial statement audits, the CPAs should communicate to the audit committee the information about significant adjustments found during the review and the acceptability and quality of significant accounting policies and estimates. The audit committee should also be informed about any disagreements with management over accounting principles or review procedures, or any other difficulties encountered in performing the review. These communication responsibilities with respect to an audit were described in detail in the internal control module.

    b. The CPAs should make sure that the audit committee is informed about any instances of fraud or illegal acts that come to their attention, as well as any significant deficiencies and material weaknesses related to the preparation of interim financial statements.

The outlines of the SSARS follow.

STATEMENTS ON STANDARDS FOR ACCOUNTING AND REVIEW SERVICES

The following outlines emphasize the standards as represented by the *Statements on Standards for Accounting and Review Services* (SSARS) Numerous questions related to the SSARS appear on a typical exam. The SSARS have been codified as follows:

Section	Title
AR 60	Framework for Performing and Reporting on Compilation and Review Engagements
AR 80	Compilation of Financial Statements
AR 90	Review of Financial Statements
AR 110	Compilation of Specified Elements, Accounts or Items of a Financial Statement
AR 120	Compilation of Pro Forma Financial Information
AR 200	Reporting on Comparative Financial Statements
AR 300	Compilation Reports on Financial Statements Included in Certain Prescribed Forms
AR 400	Communications between Predecessor and Successor Accountants
AR 500	Reporting on Compiled Financial Statements
AR 600	Reporting on Personal Financial Statements Included in Written Personal Financial Plans

AR 60, 80 and 90 Compilation and Review Engagements).

Overall Objectives and Approach—These sections present guidance on appropriate procedures and reporting for **compilation** and **review** engagements of *nonissuer* financial statements. In general terms, a *nonissuer* is one whose securities are *not* registered with the Securities and Exchange Commission—that is, a nonpublic company. AICPA pronouncements apply to *nonissuers* while PCAOB pronouncements apply to *issuers*.

For nonissuers, in addition to this section (and other AR sections), AU 722 provides guidance for reviews. In each circumstance either AU 722 *or* the ARs apply. AU 722 applies for interim financial information of nonissuers if the following conditions are met:

- Entity's latest annual financial statements have been audited by the accountant or a predecessor;
- Accountant has been engaged to audit the entity's current year financial statements; and
- Client prepares interim financial information in accordance with the same financial reporting framework as that used for annual financial statements.
- In addition, if the interim information involved is condensed

    - It must comply with appropriate accounting standards
    - It must include a note that condensed information should be read in conjunction with latest audited annual financial statements
    - The audited annual financial statements should accompany it, or be readily available

If the above requirements are not met, AR 100 (and other AR sections) apply.

Important to the section is the concept of "**submitting financial statements,**" defined as presenting to a client or third parties financial statements that the accountant has prepared either manually or through the use of computer software. A CPA should not submit unaudited financial statements of a nonissuer unless he or she, at a minimum, performs a compilation. While performing a compilation is the minimum service, issuance of a compilation report is only required when third-party reliance upon the compiled financial statements is reasonably expected.

Although performance of a compilation is the minimum requirement for submitting financial statements, services such as the following do **not** result in submission and accordingly may be performed without meeting the requirements included in this section.

- Simply reading or typing client-prepared financial statements
- Preparing a working trial balance
- Proposing adjusting or correcting entries
- Providing a client with financial statement format that does not include amounts

A CPA should not consent to the use of his/her name in a document containing unaudited financial statements unless he or she has compiled or reviewed the financial statements, or the financial statements are accompanied by an indication that the accountant has not compiled or reviewed the financial statements and assumes no responsibility for them (e.g., "The accompanying [list the financial statements] were not audited, reviewed, or compiled by us and, accordingly, we do not express an opinion or any other form of assurance on them.") The outline is organized as follows:

- Framework for Performing and Reporting on Compilation and Review Engagements (AR 60)
- Compilation of Financial Statements (AR 80)
- Review of Financial Statements (AR 90)

AR 60 Framework for Performing and Reporting on Compilation and Review Engagements

A. Selected relevant definitions

1. **Assurance engagement.** An engagement in which an accountant expresses a conclusion designed to enhance the degree of confidence of third parties and management about the outcome of an evaluation or measurement of the financial statements (subject matter) against the applicable financial reporting framework (criteria).

   > **NOTE:** There must always be subject matter and an applicable financial reporting framework in an assurance or attest engagement.

2. **Attest engagement.** An engagement that requires independence—as independence is defined by the AICPA *Professional Standards.*

   > **NOTE:** Independence is defined in ET 100.06 as requiring both independence of mind and independence in appearance.

3. **Financial reporting framework.** A set of criteria used to determine measurement, recognition, presentation, and disclosure of all material items appearing in the financial statements.

   a. **Applicable financial reporting framework**. The financial reporting framework adopted by management and, where appropriate, those charged with governance. (Most frequently this is either GAAP or IFRS—International Financial Reporting Standards.)

   b. **Other comprehensive basis of accounting (OCBOA).** A definite set of criteria, other than GAAP or IFRS, having substantial support underlying the preparation of financial statements prepared pursuant to that basis. Examples include tax and cash basis accounting.

4. **Nonissuer**. In general, nonpublic companies. That is, companies not required to register securities or file reports with the SEC.

5. **Review evidence.** The information used by the accountant to provide a reasonable basis for the obtaining of limited assurance.

6. **Submission of financial statements.** Presenting to management financial statements that the accountant has prepared.

B. Objectives and overall guidance on compilation and review engagements

1. Compilations

   a. Objective—To assist management in presenting financial information in the form of financial statements, information that is the representation of management (owners) without undertaking to obtain any assurance that there are no material modifications that should be made to the financial statements in order for the statements to be in conformity with the applicable financial reporting framework

      (1) The standard states that, although a compilation is not an assurance engagement, it is an attest engagement.

   b. A compilation differs from a review or an audit as follows:

(1) Review—It does not contemplate performing inquiry, analytical procedures, or other procedures performed in a review.
(2) Audit—It does not contemplate obtaining an understanding of internal control, assessing fraud risk, tests of accounting records by obtaining sufficient appropriate audit evidence, or other procedure ordinarily performed in an audit.

2. Reviews

a. Objective of a review—Obtain limited assurance that there are no material modifications that should be made to the financial statements in order for the statements to be in conformity with the applicable financial reporting framework

(1) In a review the accountant should accumulate review evidence to obtain a limited level of assurance.
(2) A review engagement is an assurance engagement as well as an attest engagement.

b. A review differs from an audit in that it does not contemplate obtaining an understanding of internal control, assessing fraud risk, tests of accounting records by obtaining sufficient appropriate audit evidence, or other procedure ordinarily performed in an audit.

(1) Accordingly, a review only provides limited assurance that there are no material modifications needed.

c. Materiality considerations for a review engagement are similar to those of an audit.

3. Much like the auditing standards, the SSARS use two categories of professional requirements identified by specific terms to describe the degree of responsibility they impose on accountants:

a. **Unconditional requirements.** The accountant is required to comply with an unconditional requirement in all cases in which the circumstances exist to which the unconditional requirement applies. SSARS use the words *must* or *is required* to indicate an unconditional requirement.
b. **Presumptively mandatory requirements.** The accountant is also required to comply with a presumptively mandatory requirement in all cases in which the circumstances exist to which the presumptively mandatory requirement applies; however, in rare circumstances, the accountant may depart from a presumptively mandatory requirement provided that the accountant documents his or her justification for the departure and how the alternative procedures performed in the circumstances were sufficient to achieve the objectives of the presumptively mandatory requirement. SSARS use the word *should* to indicate a presumptively mandatory requirement.
c. In addition to (a) and (b) above, if a SSARS states that an accountant "should consider" a procedure, the consideration of the procedure is presumptively required, whereas carrying out the procedure is not.

4. Application guidance is defined as the text within a SSARS (excluding appendices and interpretations) that may provide *further explanation and guidance* on professional requirements *or* identify and describe *other procedures* or actions relating to the accountant's activities.

a. *Further explanation and guidance.* It is descriptive, not imperative (required)—such guidance explains the objective of the requirements, explains why the accountant might consider procedure and additional information to consider in exercising professional judgment.
b. *Other procedures.* Not intended to impose a professional requirement. Procedures or actions require the accountant's attention and understanding; how and whether accountant carries out such procedures depends upon exercise of professional judgment. The words *may, might,* and *could* are used to describe.

5. If an accountant is not in the practice of public accounting, the issuance of a written communication or report under SSARS would be inappropriate.

C. Hierarchy of compilation and review standards and guidance

1. Levels (In the event of a conflict between levels, the lower numbered level prevails)

a. Level 1: Compilation and Review Standards (SSARS).
b. Level 2: Interpretative publications (compilation and review interpretations of the SSARS, appendixes to the SSARS, compilation and review guidance included in AICPA Audit and Accounting Guides, and AICPA Statements of Positions).
c. Level 3: Other compilation and review publications (e.g., other AICPA accounting and review publications, AICPA annual compilation and review alert, other articles and related programs).

2. AICPA members performing compilations and reviews are governed by the AICPA Code of Professional Conduct and Statements of Quality Control Standards.

D. Elements of a compilation or review engagement

1. A three-party relationship involving the (1) responsible party (management), (2) an accountant, and (3) intended users

    a. Responsible party—Management is responsible for the financial statements.
    b. Accountant—Should possess a level of knowledge of the accounting principles and practices of the industry in which the entity operates that will enable him/her to compile or review financial statements that are appropriate in form for an entity operating in that industry

       (1) In some cases this requirement can be satisfied by the accountant using the work of experts or specialists.

    c. Intended users—Persons who understand the limitations of the compilation or review and of financial statements; the accountant has no responsibility to identify the intended users

       (1) In some cases intended users may impose additional procedures or requirements for a specific purpose—an accountant may comply as long as s/he adheres to the professional standards.
       (2) In some cases, management and the intended users may be the same.

2. An applicable financial reporting framework (e.g., GAAP or International Financial Reporting Standards)
3. Financial statement or financial information

    a. An accountant may compile or review a complete set of financial statements, an individual financial statement (e.g., a balance sheet only) for an annual period or for a shorter or longer period, depending on management's needs.

4. Evidence

    a. Compilations—No responsibility to obtain evidence about accuracy or completeness of financial statement (this is why no assurance is provided)
    b. Reviews—Procedures (analytical procedures and inquiries) designed to accumulate review evidence that will provide a reasonable basis for obtaining limited assurance that there are no material modifications needed

5. Reports

    a. Compilation

       (1) Third-party reliance expected—A report or written communication is required unless the accountant withdraws. If the accountant is not independent, s/he may issue a compilation report provided s/he complies with compilation standards.
       (2) No third-party reliance expected—A report is not required, although one may be issued.

    b. Review

       (1) A written report is required unless the accountant withdraws from the engagement.

E. Materiality—these requirements are essentially the same as materiality considerations on audits.

AR 80 Compilation of Financial Statements

A. Establishing an understanding for a compilation

1. An accountant should establish an understanding with management regarding services to be performed and should document it through a written communication (in an engagement letter); an understanding should include

    a. Objective of compilation is to assist management in presenting financial information in the form of financial statements
    b. Accountant uses information that is the representation of management without undertaking to obtain any assurance on its accuracy
    c. Management is responsible for

       (1) Preparation and fair presentation of financial statements
       (2) Designing, implementing and maintaining IC
       (3) Preventing and detecting fraud
       (4) Entity compliance with laws and regulations
       (5) Making all financial records and related information available to the accountant

    d. The accountant is responsible for conducting engagement as per Statements on Standards on Accounting and Review Services (SSARS) issued by AICPA
    e. Differences between a compilation and a review or an audit
    f. Compilation cannot be relied upon to disclose errors, fraud, or illegal acts

   g. Accountant will inform management of material misstatements and illegal acts
   h. The effect of any independence impairments on the expected compilation report

2. Other matters can be added to the engagement letter (e.g., fees, additional services).
3. If the compilation is not expected to be used by a third party, the accountant should so indicate in the engagement letter.

B. Compilation Performance Requirements

1. *Understanding of industry*—The accountant should possess such an understanding

   a. Yet, an accountant may accept a compilation engagement of an entity in an industry with which the accountant has no previous experience—s/he must obtain the required level of knowledge (e.g., through AICPA guides, industry publications, textbooks, CPE, etc.) so as to be able to perform the engagement competently.

2. *Knowledge of the client*—this includes the client's business and the accounting principles followed by the client.
3. *Reading the financial statements*—Read and consider whether they appear to be appropriate in form and free from material errors.
4. *Other compilation procedures*—The accountant is *not* required to make inquiries or perform other procedures to verify, corroborate, or review information supplied by the entity.

   a. However, the accountant may have made inquiries or performed other procedures which revealed misstatements, illegal acts, etc.; in such cases

      (1) The accountant should request that management consider the matters.
      (2) When accountant believes financial statements are materially misstated, obtain additional, or revised information; if the entity refuses to provide such information the accountant should withdraw from the engagement.

C. Documentation in a compilation engagement should include

1. Signed engagement letter (by management and the accountant)
2. Any findings or issues that, in the accountant's judgment are significant, such as

   a. Results of compilation procedures that indicate financial statements could be misstated, including actions taken to address such findings
   b. To the extent the accountant had questions or concerns as a result of compilation procedures, how they were resolved

3. Communication (oral or written) to the appropriate level of management regarding fraud or illegal acts that came to the accountant's attention

D. Reporting on compiled financial statements—general

1. When the accountant is engaged to report on compiled statements or submits financial statements that are *reasonably expected to be used by a third-party* the financial statements should be accompanied by a compilation report.
2. Basic elements of a compilation report

   a. *Title*, such as "Accountant's Compilation Report"
   b. *Addressee*, as appropriate in the circumstances
   c. *Introductory paragraph:*

      (1) Identify the financial statements and indicate they have been compiled
      (2) Date of each financial statement
      (3) A statement that the financial statements have not been audited or reviewed and, accordingly, no opinion, or any assurance is expressed

   d. Management's responsibility for the financial statements and for IC over financial reporting
   e. Accountant's responsibility

      (1) Conduct compilation in accordance with SSARS issued by AICPA
      (2) Objective of a compilation is to assist management in presenting financial information in the form of financial statements without undertaking to obtain any assurance that there are no material modifications that should be made to the financial statements.

   f. *Signature of the accountant*—manual or printed
   g. *Date of the accountant's report*—Date of completion of the compilation

3. Other

    a. Any procedures that the accountant might have performed before or during the compilation should *not* be described in the report.

    b. Each page of the compiled statements should include a reference, such as "See Accountant's Compilation Report."

    c. Other comprehensive basis of accounting (OCBOA) statements should include a description of the OCBOA and informative disclosures similar to those required by GAAP.

E. Reporting on financial statements—Circumstances resulting in modification of the compilation report

1. Financial statements that omit substantially all disclosures (e.g., the notes)

    a. An accountant may compile and report on such statements if the intent, to the accountant's knowledge, is not to mislead users.

    b. Report modifications—in the report indicate that

        (1) Management has elected to omit substantially all disclosures (and the statement of cash flows, if applicable) required by the applicable financial reporting framework.

        (2) The omitted disclosures might influence the user's conclusions about the company's financial position, results of operations and cash flows.

        (3) The financial statements are not designed for those who are not informed about such matters.

    c. When the entity wishes to include disclosures about only a few matters in the form of notes to the financial statements, such disclosures should be labeled "Selected Information—Substantially All Disclosures Required by [identify applicable financial reporting framework, e.g., GAAP] are not included."

2. Accountant is not independent

    a. The accountant need not provide the reason for a lack of independence, but should add "I am (we are) not independent with respect to XYZ Company" in a final paragraph to the report.

    b. However, an accountant may choose to provide the reason for a lack of independence; examples: "I am (we are) not independent with respect to XYZ Company during the year ended December 31, 20XX because

        (1) A member of the engagement team had a direct financial interest in XYZ company."

        (2) An individual of my immediate family was employed by XYZ company."

        (3) We performed certain accounting services [describe] that impaired our independence."

    c. If an accountant elects to disclose reasons for a lack of independence, s/he must disclosure all of them.

3. When the financial statements are **not** expected to be used by a third party

    a. Accountant is not required to issue a compilation report.

    b. This must be so indicated in the engagement letter (returned, signed by management).

    c. Add a reference on each page of the financial statements restricting their use, such as "Restricted for Management's Use Only."

    d. If accountant finds such financial statements have been distributed to third parties, discuss with client and request that the client have the statements returned.

        (1) If the client refuses, notify the known third parties that the financial statements are not intended for third-party use, preferably in consultation with accountant's attorney.

4. Emphasis of a matter

    a. Accountant may, in a separate paragraph, emphasize a matter concerning the financial statements; such paragraphs are never required.

    b. Examples of matters: uncertainties, entity a component of a larger enterprise, significant transactions with related parties, unusually important subsequent events, accounting matters.

5. Departures from applicable financial reporting framework

    a. If accountant believes modification of standard report is appropriate, disclose departure in a separate paragraph of the report, including the effects of such departure if known.

        (1) The accountant is not required to determine the effects of a departure if management has not done so, provided the accountant states in the report that such determination has not been made.

    b. If the accountant believes modification is not adequate to indicate the deficiencies, withdraw from the engagement and provide no further services with respect to those financial statements.

NOTE: Departures from an applicable financial reporting framework do not result in a "qualified" or "adverse" opinion when one is conducting a compilation or review—opinions only result from audits.

6. Restricting the use of an accountant's compilation report

   a. Overall, general use vs. restricted use reports

     (1) General use—An accountant's report not restricted to specified parties. Accountants' reports on financial statements prepared in conformity with an applicable financial reporting framework ordinarily are not restricted regarding use.

       (a) However, nothing in this section precludes the accountant from restricting the use of any report.

     (2) Restricted use—An accountant's report intended only for one or more specified third parties. Use is restricted in a number of circumstances, including

       (a) Report may be misunderstood when taken out of context in which it was intended to be used.
       (b) Subject matter of the accountant's report or the presentation being reported on is based on measurement or disclosure criteria contained in contractual agreements or regulatory provision that are not in conformity with an applicable financial reporting framework.
       (c) As per (1) above, nothing in this section precludes the accountant from restricting the use of any report.

   b. Other situations

     (1) When one accountant's report covers both the restricted subject matter and the not restricted subject matter—the accountant's report should indicate that the restricted portion is for the specified parties.
     (2) When required by law, a separate restricted use report may be included in a document that *also contains a general use report.* In this circumstance inclusions of the restricted use report in the document that contains a general use report is acceptable—the restricted use report remains restricted, and the general use report continues for general use.
     (3) Subsequent to completion of the engagement resulting in a restricted use report, the accountant may be asked to consider adding other parties as specified parties—the accountant may agree to this if it seems reasonable. If so, the accountant should

       (a) Obtain affirmative acknowledge, preferably in writing, from the other parties of their understanding of the nature of the engagement, measurement criteria, and related report.
       (b) The accountant may either reissue the report with the new specified party added, or provide written acknowledgement of the fact.

         • If reissued, the report date should not be changed.
         • If written acknowledgement, such acknowledgment should state no procedures have been performed subsequent to the date of the report.

   c. The report modification to restrict use should

     (1) State that the report is intended solely for information and use of specified parties
     (2) Identify those specified parties
     (3) Say that report is not intended for and should not be used by anyone other than the specified parties

7. Uncertainty about an entity's ability to continue as a going concern

   a. Request management to consider possible effects on the financial statements, including need for related disclosure.
   b. If accountant determines management's conclusions are unreasonable or the disclosure of uncertainty on going concern is not adequate, it should be treated as a departure from the applicable financial reporting framework.
   c. Accountant may wish to emphasize an uncertainty (emphasis of a matter) concerning going concern; but this emphasis is not required.

8. Subsequent events and subsequent discovery of facts existing at date of report—treated similarly to audits, see AU 561.

9. Supplementary information presented

   a. Accountant should clearly indicate degree of responsibility, if any, being taken with respect to such information.

F. Communicating to management and others when performing a compilation

1. When fraud or an illegal act come to the accountant's attention—communicate to an appropriate level of management.

    a. Accountant need not report matters regarding illegal acts that are clearly inconsequential.

    b. Matters involving senior management should be reported to an individual or group higher in the organization (e.g., manager [owner] or those charged with governance).

       (1) Communication may be oral or written; if oral document it.

    c. If owner is involved, consider resigning.

    d. Accountant should consider consulting legal counsel whenever evidence that fraud or an illegal act has occurred comes to his/her attention, unless it is clearly inconsequential.

  2. Contacting a party outside the organization is not ordinarily part of the accountant's responsibility and the accountant should not do so. Exceptions are as follows:

    a. To comply with certain legal and regulatory requirements

    b. Response to a successor auditor inquiry

    c. Response to a subpoena

G. Change in engagement from audit or review to a compilation

  1. Before agreeing to a change consider

    a. Reasonableness of reason for client's request

       (1) Examples of acceptable reasons:

          (a) Change in circumstances

          (b) Misunderstanding of nature of audit, review, or compilation

    b. Additional audit or review effort needed to complete the engagement—generally, the closer to complete, the less reasonable

    c. Estimated additional cost to complete the audit or review

  2. Other

    a. Situations in which an accountant ordinarily cannot change to a compilation

       (1) In an audit, the accountant has been prohibited from corresponding with entity's legal counsel.

       (2) In an audit or review the client does not provide a signed representation letter.

    b. If accountant concludes the change is reasonable, the compilation report should not include reference to the original engagement, procedures performed, scope limitations.

NOW REVIEW MULTIPLE-CHOICE QUESTIONS 1 THROUGH 26 IN VOLUME 2

AR 90 Review of Financial Statements

A. Applicability—This section establishes review standards on reviews of financial statements

  1. It does not apply when AU 722 applies (accountant also audits annual financial statements).

  2. An accountant may not perform a review if the accountant's independence is impaired for any reason other than the performance of an internal control service.

B. Establishing an understanding for a review

  1. An accountant should establish an understanding with management, and if applicable, those charged with governance regarding services to be performed and should document it in an engagement letter signed by management and the accountant; an understanding should include

    a. Objective of review is to obtain limited assurance that there are no material modifications that should be made to the financial statements in order for the statements to be in conformity with the applicable financial reporting framework.

NOTE: Make certain that you know the above objective.

    b. Management is responsible for

       (1) Preparation and fair presentation of financial statements

       (2) Designing, implementing, and maintaining IC

       (3) Preventing and detecting fraud

        (4) Complying with laws and regulations

        (5) Making all financial records and related information available to the accountant

        (6) Providing the accountant, at the conclusion of the engagement, a representation letter

    c. The accountant is responsible for conducting engagement as per Statements on Standards for Accounting and Review Services (SSARS) issued by AICPA.

    d. A review

        (1) Consists primarily of inquiries of company personnel and analytical procedures applied to financial data

        (2) Is substantially less in scope than an audit (and then describe how it is different)

        (3) Cannot be relied upon to disclose errors, fraud, or illegal acts

    e. The accountant will inform management of material misstatements and illegal acts that are identified.

  2. The understanding should be communicated in the form of an engagement letter, signed by the accountant and management (or, if applicable, those charged with governance).

  3. Other matters can be added to the letter (e.g., fees, additional services).

C. Review performance requirements—general

  1. Procedures must be sufficient to accumulate review evidence that will provide a reasonable basis for obtaining limited assurance that there are no material modifications needed.

  2. Understanding of industry—The accountant should possess such an understanding.

    a. Yet, an accountant may accept a review engagement of an entity in an industry with which the accountant has no previous experience—s/he must obtain the required level of knowledge (e.g., through AICPA guides, industry publications, textbooks, CPE, etc.) so as to be able to perform the engagement competently.

  3. Knowledge of the client—this includes the client's business and the accounting principles followed by the client

D. Designing and performing review procedures

  1. Based on the accountant's understanding of the industry and client, the accountant designs and performs analytical procedures and makes inquires and performs other procedures as appropriate to obtain limited assurance that there are no needed material modifications.

  2. Analytical procedures

    a. Involve comparisons of recorded amounts, or ratios developed from recorded amounts to expectations developed by the accountant. Expectations are developed by identifying and using plausible relationships. Examples of sources of information for developing expectations

        (1) Financial information for comparable prior periods

        (2) Anticipated results (e.g., budgets)

        (3) Relationships among elements of financial information within the period

        (4) Information regarding the industry (e.g., gross margin information)

        (5) Relationships of financial information with relevant nonfinancial information (e.g., payroll costs to number of employees)

    b. When analytical procedures identify unexpected fluctuations or relationships, the accountant should investigate these differences by inquiring of management and performing other procedures as necessary in the circumstances.

        (1) Although the accountant is not required to corroborate management's responses with other evidence, the accountant may need to perform other procedures when, for example, management is unable to provide an explanation, or its explanation is not considered adequate.

  3. Inquiries and other review procedures

    a. Inquiries to management concerning

        (1) Whether statements prepared in conformity with applicable financial reporting framework

        (2) Entity's accounting principles followed

        (3) Unusual or complex situations that may have an effect on financial statements

        (4) Significant transactions near end of reporting period

        (5) Status of uncorrected misstatements identified during previous engagement

        (6) Questions that have arisen in the course of applying review procedures

        (7) Events subsequent to date of financial statements

        (8) Knowledge of fraud or suspected fraud affecting entity involving management or others that could have a material effect on financial statements

      (9) Significant journal entries and other adjustments
     (10) Communications with regulatory agencies

  b. Inquiries concerning actions taken at meetings of stockholders, board of directors, etc.
  c. Reading the financial statements to consider whether they appear to conform with the applicable financial reporting framework
  d. Obtaining reports from other accountants, if any, which are involved with significant components

4. The accountant ordinarily is not required to corroborate management's responses with other evidence; however, the accountant should consider the reasonableness and consistency of management's responses in light of the results of other review procedures and the accountant's knowledge of the client's business and the industry in which it operates.

5. Incorrect, incomplete or otherwise unsatisfactory information

  a. Request management to consider the effects of these matters on the financial statements and communicate results to the accountant.
  b. If the accountant believes financial statements may be materially misstated, perform additional procedures to obtain limited assurance there are no material modifications needed. If the accountant concludes the financial statements are materially misstated, follow guidance on reporting departures from the applicable financial reporting framework.

6. Management's representations

  a. Written representations are required from management for all financial statements and periods covered by the review report.

    (1) If current management was not present during all periods covered, the accountant should nevertheless obtain written representations from current management for all such periods.

  b. The accountant should obtain written representations from management on

    (1) Its responsibility for fair presentation of financial statements
    (2) Its belief the financial statements are fairly presented
    (3) Its acknowledgement of its responsibility to design, implement, and maintain IC
    (4) Its knowledge of any fraud or suspected fraud that could have a material effect on the financial statements.
    (5) Its knowledge of any fraud or suspected fraud affecting the entity involving management or others where the fraud could have a material effect on the financial statements
    (6) Its full and truthful response to all inquiries
    (7) Completeness of information
    (8) Information concerning subsequent events
    (9) Other matters specific to the entity's business or industry

  c. Representations should be made as of the date of the accountant's review report.

    (1) Normally the CEO and CFO or others with equivalent positions sign the representation letter.

E. Documentation in a review engagement

  1. Documentation provides

    a. Principal support that the review was performed in accordance with SSARS
    b. Principal support for conclusion that accountant is not aware of any material modifications needed to financial statements

  2. Documentation should include

    a. Engagement letter
    b. Analytical procedures performed, including

      (1) Expectations
      (2) Results of comparison of expectations to recorded amounts/ratios
      (3) Management's responses to accountant's inquires regarding fluctuations

    c. Any additional review procedure performed in response to significant unexpected differences
    d. Significant matters covered in inquiry procedures and responses thereto
    e. Findings that in the accountant's judgment are significant
    f. Significant unusual matters
    g. Evidence from performance of internal control services, if applicable

    h. Communications, whether oral or written, to management concerning fraud or illegal acts

    i. Representation letter

F. Reporting on the Financial Statements—General

1. Objective in reporting: Prevent misinterpretation of the degree of responsibility the accountant is assuming when his/her name is associated with the financial statements

2. Basic elements of a review report

    a. *Title*, such as "Independent Accountant's Review Report"

    b. *Addressee*, as appropriate in the circumstances

    c. *Introductory paragraph*

      (1) Identify the financial statements and indicate that have been reviewed.

      (2) Date of each financial statement.

      (3) A review consists primarily of applying analytical procedures to management's financial data and making inquiries of company management.

      (4) A statement that a review is substantially less in scope than an audit, the objective of which is the expression of an opinion; the accountant does not express such an opinion.

    d. Management's responsibility for the financial statements and for IC over financial reporting

    e. Accountant's responsibility

      (1) Conduct review in accordance with SSARS issued by AICPA.

      (2) Review standards require the accountant to perform the procedures to obtain limited assurance that there are no material modifications needed.

      (3) Accountant believes the results of his/her procedures provide a reasonable basis for the report.

    f. *Results of the engagement*—Accountant is not aware of any material modifications that should be made to the financial statement, other than those modifications (if any) indicated in the report

    g. *Signature of the accountant*—manual or printed

    h. *Date of accountant's report*—Not earlier than the date on which the accountant has accumulated review evidence sufficient to provide a reasonable basis for expressing limited assurance

3. Other

    a. Each page of the financial statements should include a reference such as "See Accountant's Review Report."

    b. When the accountant is unable to perform inquiry and analytical procedures considered necessary, or the client does not provide a representation letter, the review is incomplete—no review report should be issued. The accountant should consider whether it is appropriate to issue a compilation report on the financial statements.

    c. An accountant may review one financial statement (e.g., balance sheet) as long as inquiry and analytical procedures are not restricted.

    d. OCBOA financial statements should include a description of the OCBOA and informative disclosures similar to those required by GAAP.

G. Reporting on financial statements—Circumstances resulting in modification of the review report

1. Emphasis of a matter

    a. Accountant may, in a separate paragraph, emphasize a matter concerning the financial statements.

    b. Such paragraphs are never required.

    c. Examples of matters: uncertainties, entity a component of a larger enterprise, significant transactions with related parties, unusually important subsequent events, accounting matters.

2. Departures from applicable financial reporting framework

    a. If accountant believes modification of standard report is appropriate, disclose departure in a separate paragraph of the report, including the effects of such departure if known.

      (1) The accountant is not required to determine the effects of a departure if management has not done so, provided the accountant states in the report that such determination has not been made.

    b. If the accountant believes modification is not adequate to indicate the deficiencies, withdraw from the engagement and provide no further services with respect to those financial statements.

3. Restricting the use of an accountant's review report—The restrictions are very similar to those for a compilation (see E.6. of this outline).

4. Uncertainty about an entity's ability to continue as a going concern

   a. Request management to consider possible effects on the financial statements, including need for related disclosure.

   b. If accountant determines management's conclusions are unreasonable or the disclosure of uncertainty on going concern is not adequate, it should be treated as a departure from the applicable financial reporting framework.

   c. Accountant may wish to emphasize an uncertainty (emphasis of a matter) concerning going concern; this emphasis is not required.

5. Subsequent events and subsequent discovery of acts existing at date of report—treated similarly to audits, see AU 561
6. Supplementary information presented

   a. Accountant should clearly indicate degree of responsibility, if any, being taken with respect to such information

H. Communicating to management and others—The requirements are very similar to that of a compilation— The communications are very similar to those for a compilation (see F. of AR 80 outline) and include

1. When fraud or an illegal act come to the accountant's attention—communicate to an appropriate level of management.

   a. Account need not report matters regarding illegal acts that are clearly inconsequential.

   b. Matters involving senior management should be reported to an individual or group higher in the organization (e.g., manager [owner] or those charged with governance).

      (1) Communication may be oral or written; if oral document it.

   c. If owner is involved, consider resigning.

   d. Accountant should consider consulting legal counsel whenever evidence that fraud or an illegal act has occurred comes to his/her attention, unless it is clearly inconsequential.

2. Contacting a party outside the organization is not ordinarily part of the accountant's responsibility and the accountant should not do so. Exceptions are as follows:

   a. To comply with certain legal and regulatory requirements

   b. Response to a successor auditor inquiry

   c. Response to a subpoena

I. Change in engagement from audit to review

1. Before agreeing to a change consider

   a. Reasonableness of reason for client's request

      (1) Examples of acceptable reasons:

         (a) Change in circumstances
         (b) Misunderstanding of nature of audit or review

   b. Additional audit effort needed to complete the audit—generally, the closer to complete, the less reasonable.

   c. Estimated additional cost to complete the audit

2. Other

   a. In considering the implications of an audit scope restriction, the accountant should evaluate the possibility that information affected by the scope restriction may be incorrect. When in an audit the accountant has been prohibited by the client from corresponding with the entity's legal counsel, the accountant ordinarily would be precluded from issuing a review report.

   b. If accountant concludes the change is reasonable, the review report should not include reference to original engagement, procedures performed, or scope limitations.

AR 110 Compilation of Specified Elements, Accounts, or Items of a Financial Statement

Overall Objectives and Approach—This section expands SSARS to apply to compilations of one or more specified elements, accounts or items of a financial statement (hereafter, specified elements). Examples of specified elements include schedules of rentals, royalties, profit participation, or provision for income taxes. The section outlines the required understanding with the entity that must be obtained, performance requirements, and reporting requirements.

A. The accountant should obtain overall understanding with the entity that includes

1. The engagement cannot be relied upon to disclose errors, fraud or illegal acts
2. The accountant will inform an appropriate level of management of any material errors, fraud or illegal acts that are discovered

B. Performance requirements include adherence to SSARS and, prior to issuance of a compilation report, reading the specified elements and consideration of whether the information appears appropriate in form and free of obvious material misstatements

C. Reporting requirements

1. The report should include

    a. A statement that the specified elements were compiled. If the compilation was performed in conjunction with a compilation of the company's financial statements, indicate this and the date of that compilation report. Any departure from the standard report on the financial statements should be disclosed if it is relevant to the specified element

    b. Compilation performed in accordance with SSARS issued by AICPA

    c. Description of the reporting basis followed if basis is not GAAP (e.g., tax basis)

    d. Financial information that is the representation of management (owners)

    e. Specified elements not audited or reviewed, and no opinion or assurance is provided

    f. Signature of accounting firm or accountant, as appropriate

    g. Date of report (completion of compilation)

2. Each page of compiled specified elements should include a reference such as "See Accountant's Compilation Report"

AR 120 Compilation of Pro Forma Financial Information

Overall Objectives and Approach—This section is very similar to AR 110, but applies to pro forma financial information. The objective of pro forma financial information is to show what the significant effects on historical financial information might have been had a consummated or proposed transaction (or event) occurred at an earlier date. Pro forma information is commonly used to show the effect of transactions such as business combinations, changes in capitalization, disposal of a significant portion of the business, changes in the form of the business, and the proposed sale of securities.

The overall understanding of the entity and the performance requirements for a compilation of pro forma financial information correspond to those in AR 110 for specified elements, accounts, or items of a financial statement and are not repeated here. The reporting requirements include those as per AR 110, plus

- A reference to the financial statements from which the historical information is derived and a statement as to whether that information was compiled, reviewed or audited
- A separate paragraph explaining the objective of the pro forma financial information and its limitations

AR 200 Reporting on Comparative Financial Statements

Overall Objectives and Approach—This section presents guidance for reporting on comparative statements of a non-issuer, at least a portion of which are not audited (i.e., one or more years is compiled or reviewed). The existence of compiled, reviewed, and audited financial statements, as well as financial statements with which the auditor has had no association, presents a situation in which there are numerous implementation issues related to compiled statements. For example, perhaps the first year's statements have been reviewed, and the second year's compiled.

This section presents and resolves an overwhelming number of situations which may occur in practice. In the outline we attempt to provide information on the most frequent cases which one would expect to see on the CPA exam. You should be aware that several questions on the exam have required candidates either to prepare or to critique comparative reports of this nature.

The outline provides (a) overall guidance as well as (b) enumerating important situations.

A. Overall guidance

1. The accountant's report should cover each period presented as a comparative statement

    a. An entity may include financial information with which the accountant is not associated (e.g., last year's statements) in a report that also includes information with which the accountant is associated (e.g., this year's compiled or reviewed statements)

        (1) When the information is presented on separate pages, the information should clearly indicate that the accountant is not associated

        (2) The accountant should not allow his/her name to be associated with such financial statements (i.e., the year which s/he is not associated) that are presented in columnar form with financial statements on which s/he has reported

            (a) If the entity still intends to use the accountant's name, the accountant should consult with his/her attorney

2. When compiled statements of one year omit most of the disclosures required per GAAP (e.g., do not include foot-notes) they should not be presented with another year's which do have such disclosures, and the accountant should **not** issue a report on such comparative statements

3. Each page of comparative financial statements compiled or reviewed by an accountant should include a reference such as "See Accountant's Report"

4. The following is general guidance on the overall form of comparative reports

   a. When both years have been compiled or reviewed, the report uses the standard form, modified to include both years

   b. A continuing accountant who performs the same or a **higher level of service** with respect to financial statements of the current period (e.g., review this year, compilation last year) should update his/her report on the financial statements of a prior period presented with those of the current period

---

EXAMPLE

Issue a standard review report supplemented with the following paragraph:

The accompanying 20X1 financial statements of XYZ were compiled by me. A compilation is limited to representing in the form of financial statements information that is the representation of management. I have not audited or reviewed the 20X1 financial statements and accordingly, do not express an opinion or any other form of assurance on them.

---

   c. A continuing accountant who performs a **lower level of service** with respect to the financial statements of the current period (e.g., compilation this year, review last year) should either

   (1) Include a separate paragraph in his/her report with a description of the responsibility assumed for the prior period statements or

   (2) Reissue his/her report on the financial statements of the prior period

---

EXAMPLE

Approaches (1) and (2)

(1) Issue a compilation report on 20X4 which includes a paragraph summarizing the responsibility assumed for the 20X3 financial statements. The description should include the original date of the review report and should state that no procedures have been performed on the review after that date.

(2) Combine the compilation report on 20X4 with the reissued report on the financial statements of the prior period or print them separately. The combined report should state that the accountant has not performed any procedures in connection with that review engagement after the date of the review report.

B. Other situations

1. **Existence of a predecessor auditor**—as is the case with audited financial statements, a decision must be made as to whether the predecessor will reissue his/her compilation or review report

> **NOTE:** The situation here is one in which a choice is made as to whether two reports will be associated with the comparative information (20X3 the predecessor's, 20X4 the successor's) **or** one report in which the successor summarizes the predecessor's findings.

   a. Reissuance of the predecessor's report

   (1) The predecessor must determine whether his/her report is appropriate based on

      (a) Current vs. prior period statement format
      (b) Newly discovered subsequent events
      (c) Changes in the financial statements affecting the report

   (2) The predecessor should also perform the following procedures:

      (a) Read the current statements and the successor's report
      (b) Compare prior and current statements
      (c) Obtain representation letter from successor suggesting that s/he is not aware of any matters having a material effect on the prior statements

   (3) If anything comes to the predecessor's attention that affects the report, the predecessor should

        (a) Make any necessary inquiries and perform any necessary procedures

        (b) If necessary insist that the client revise the statements and revise the report as appropriate (normally add an explanatory paragraph)

           1] The report will be "dual dated"—see outline of AU 530 on dual dating

    b. No reissuance of predecessor's report (i.e., it is not presented)

      (1) The successor auditor should add a paragraph stating that the

        (a) Prior (comparative) statements were compiled (or reviewed) by another accountant

        (b) Date of the predecessor's report

        (c) Assurance, if any, provided in the predecessor's report

        (d) Reasons for any modification of the predecessor's report

2. **20X3 reviewed (or compiled) and 20X4 audited**—The situation here is similar to above with a predecessor auditor in that the prior years report may be reissued, or a summary of it included in the 20X4 report

3. When an accountant is reporting on financial statements that now omit substantially all disclosures (i.e., notes), which when originally issued did not omit such disclosures, a paragraph is added to the report indicating that the disclosures have been omitted; also, the final paragraph indicates the accountant's prior form of association with the information.

EXAMPLE

20X4 has been reviewed, and now, in 20X5, 20X4 statements have been compiled from the previously reviewed statements. A compilation report is issued on 20X5, with a paragraph on the omitted disclosures (see Section A.4.e. above) and with a paragraph on the 20X4 statements such as the following:

> The accompanying 20X4 financial statements were compiled by me from financial statements that did not omit substantially all of the disclosures required by generally accepted accounting principles and that I previously reviewed as indicated in my report dated March 1, 20X5.

---

4. When a company changes its status (i.e., nonpublic to public, or vice versa) the proper reporting responsibility is determined by the status at the time of reporting

AR 300 Compilation Reports on Financial Statements Included in Certain Prescribed Forms

Overall Objectives and Approach—This section presents guidance on issuing compilation reports related to information presented on prescribed forms, designed by the bodies with which they filed (e.g., governmental bodies, trade associations, banks). For example, assume that a state governmental body has a balance sheet form which all companies incorporated in that state are required to fill out with appropriate financial information. Also, assume that the state requires that a compilation report be filed with the report. This section deals with the manner in which the auditor should report on such forms. This section also relates directly to the material presented in AU 623, special reports, on prescribed forms (in that section some form of association other than compilation for a nonissuer [nonpublic] entity is assumed). The following outline provides general guidance on the report issued.

A. General guidance on compilation reports for prescribed forms

1. An overall presumption is made that the form is sufficient to meet the needs of the body which has designed or adopted it

2. Departures from GAAP

    a. **Required to appropriately complete the form**—There is **no need** to advise such bodies of this type of departure

---

EXAMPLE

If, because of the requirements of the form, inventory is included on the form at cost, rather than the lower of cost and market, no indication would be provided that this departure from GAAP existed.

---

    b. **Other departures**—Indicate in second paragraph and add a final paragraph

3. Departures from the requirements of the prescribed form—treat in the same manner as 2.b. above

4. When a prescribed form does not conform to the guidance provided in either AR 100 or AR 300, the accountant should not sign it, but should append an appropriate report to the prescribed form

AR 400 Communications between Predecessor and Successor Accountants

Overall Objectives and Approach—This section presents guidance for situations in which a successor accountant **decides to communicate** with a predecessor accountant concerning acceptance of a compilation or a review engagement of a nonissuer (nonpublic) entity; such communication is **not** required.

The guidance provided is similar to that in AU 315, which requires such communication prior to accepting an **audit**. As is the case with that section, inquiries of a predecessor may occur: (a) in conjunction with acceptance of the engagement, and (b) other inquiries, subsequent to acceptance of the engagement. The section also provides guidance for situations in which the successor becomes aware of information indicating the need for revision of the statements with which the predecessor is associated.

A. Inquiries in conjunction with accepting an engagement

1. Circumstances in which a successor might choose to communicate

    a. Information concerning client, principals, and management is limited or appears to be in need of special attention

    b. Change in accountants occurs substantially after end of period for which financial statements are to be compiled or reviewed

    c. There have been frequent changes in accountants

2. An accountant may not disclose confidential information without consent of client

    a. Except as permitted by AICPA Code of Conduct

    b. Successor accountant should request client to

        (1) Permit him/her to make inquiries

        (2) Authorize predecessor to respond completely

    c. If client refuses to comply with request for inquiry, accountant should consider reasons for, and implications of, such denial as they relate to accepting the engagement

3. May be oral or written and typically would include requests for information on

    a. Matters which might affect the integrity of management (owners)

    b. Disagreement about accounting principles or necessity of certain procedures

    c. If necessary, cooperation of management (owners) in providing additional or revised information

    d. Predecessor's understanding of reason for change in accountants

4. The predecessor should respond promptly and completely to requests made in connection with engagements

    a. If, due to unusual circumstances, response must be limited, accountant should so indicate

        (1) For example, unusual circumstances include pending litigation but do not include unpaid fees

B. Other inquiries

1. May be made before/after acceptance of engagement to facilitate a compilation or review

2. Might include questions about prior periods' circumstances such as

    a. Deficiencies in underlying financial data

    b. Necessity of performing other accounting services

    c. Areas requiring inordinate amounts of time

3. May include request for access to predecessor's working papers

    a. Successor should request client authorization

    b. Customary for predecessor to be available for consultation and provide certain of his/her workpapers

    c. Predecessor and successor should agree on which workpapers

        (1) Will be available

        (2) May be copied

    d. Generally, predecessor should provide access to workpapers relating to

        (1) Matters of continuing accounting significance

        (2) Contingencies

    e. Predecessor may refuse for valid business reasons, including but not limited to, unpaid fees

    f. If client is considering several successors

        (1) Predecessor and working papers need not be made available until client names an accountant as successor

      g. Successor should not reference report on work of predecessor in his/her report except when comparative statements are being issued—see outline of AR 200.

C. Predecessor accountant's financial statements

    1. If successor becomes aware of information indicating the need for revision of financial statements reported on by predecessor, the successor should

      a. Request that the client inform the predecessor accountant

    2. If the client refuses to inform the predecessor or the successor is not satisfied with the predecessor's actions, the successor should consult his/her attorney

AR 500 Reporting on Compiled Financial Statements
(Deleted)

AR 600 Reporting on Personal Financial Statements Included in Written Personal Financial Plans

    Overall Objectives and Approach—This section provides an exception to the AR 100 requirement that accountants either compile, review, or audit financial statements with which they are associated. The section allows accountant association with unaudited statements included in written personal financial plans prepared by the accountant. The outline presents related details.

A. Requirements relating to "unaudited" association with personal financial plans

    1. Financial statements in personal financial plans need not be compiled, reviewed, or audited if

      a. The accountant establishes an understanding (preferably in writing) with the client that statements will be used solely to assist the client and the client's advisors to develop and achieve personal financial goals and objectives

      b. Nothing came to accountant's attention to cause him/her to believe that the financial statements will be used for other purposes

    2. The accountant's report should state that the financial statements

      a. Are for the financial plan

      b. May be incomplete or contain GAAP departures and should not be used for other purposes

      c. Have not been audited, reviewed, or compiled

NOW REVIEW MULTIPLE-CHOICE QUESTIONS 27 THROUGH 49 IN VOLUME 2

KEY TERMS

    Assurance engagement. An engagement in which an accountant issues a report designed to enhance the degree of confidence of third parties and management about the outcome of an evaluation or measurement of financial statements (subject matter) against an applicable financial reporting framework.

    Attest engagement. Defined somewhat differently in the Code of Professional Conduct and the attestation standards: The Code of Professional Conduct defines an attest engagement as an engagement performed by public accountants that requires independence. The attest standards define it as one in which the public accountants issue an examination, a review, or an agreed–upon procedures report on subject matter or on an assertion about subject matter that is the responsibility of another party (ordinarily management).

    Compilation of financial statements. An accounting service that involves the preparation of financial statements from client records. No assurance is provided in a compilation. The current professional standards consider compilations to be attest engagements.

    Financial reporting framework. A set of criteria used to determine measurement, recognition, presentation and disclosure of all material items appearing in the financial statements; for example, accounting principles generally accepted in the United States of America, International Financial Reporting Standards (IFRS) issued by the International Accounting Standards Board (IASB). An "applicable financial reporting framework" is the framework adopted by management of the company being audited in a particular situation.

    Issuer. A company whose stock is traded on a public market or a company in the process of registering its stock for public sale.

    Limited (negative) assurance. A conclusion by CPAs that, after applying limited investigative techniques to certain information, they are not aware of the need to modify the presentation of the information.

    Nonissuer. A company whose securities are *not* registered under requirements of the Securities and Exchange Commission; ordinarily, a "nonissuer" is a nonpublic company. This is in contrast to an issuer, a company whose securities are registered under the requirements of the Securities and Exchange Commission. The *Statements on Accounting and Review Services* apply to nonissuers.

Review of financial statement. A form of attestation based on inquiry and analytical procedures applied for the purpose of expressing limited assurance that the historical financial statements are presented in accordance with GAAP or some other appropriate basis.

Module 7: Audit Sampling

Overview

Sampling is essential throughout audits as auditors attempt to gather sufficient competent evidence in a cost efficient manner. The following "Diagram of an Audit" was originally presented in the auditing overview section.

Diagram of an Audit

Plan Audit

↓

Obtain Understanding
of Client and Its Environment
Including Internal Control

↓

Assess Risks of Misstatement
and Design Further Tests

→ Perform Tests of Controls

Perform Substantive Procedures ←

↓

Complete the Audit

↓

Issue Audit Report

Audit sampling is used for both tests of controls (attributes sampling) and for tests of details of transactions and balances (usually, variables sampling). In both attributes sampling and variables sampling, the plans may be either nonstatistical or statistical. The chart at the bottom of this page summarizes methods of audit sampling.

Audit sampling has been tested on most recent auditing examinations, usually in the form of multiple-choice questions. One might anticipate additional questions dealing with concepts such as sampling risk, nonsampling risk, tolerable misstatement, and the projection of sample results to an overall population. Also, as in the past, one might expect exam questions dealing with the relationships between statistical concepts and basic audit concepts such as assessing control risk, materiality, and audit decision making. One might expect a portion of a simulation to require candidates to calculate or interpret statistical results.

Detailed Audit Sampling Techniques

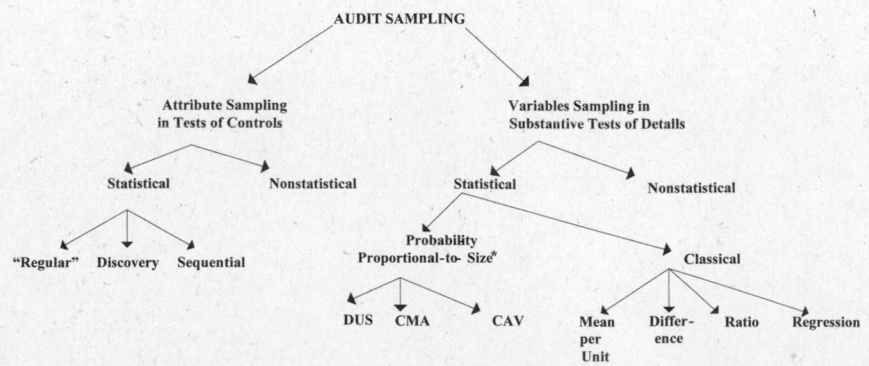

* Probability-proportional-to-size sampling may also be used for attributes sampling. A number of variations of probability-proportional-to-size sampling exist, including dollar-unit sampling and monetary-unit sampling.

The material in this module is primarily structured around both AU 350 and the *Audit Sampling* guide. It is presented in outline form to allow an efficient review of the material. Additionally, AU 312 on audit risk and materiality relates to this area.

A. Basic Audit Sampling Concepts

1. **Definition of Sampling**

   a. **Audit sampling** is the application of an audit procedure to less than 100% of the items within an account balance or class of transactions for the purpose of evaluating some characteristic of the balance or class (AU 350).

   b. The AICPA Audit and Accounting Guide, *Audit Sampling*, lists procedures that **do not** involve sampling as follows:

      (1) Inquiry and observation

         (a) Interview management and employees
         (b) Obtain an understanding of internal control
         (c) Obtain written representations from management
         (d) Scan accounting records for unusual items
         (e) Observe behavior of personnel and functioning of business operations
         (f) Observe cash-handling procedures
         (g) Inspect land and buildings

      (2) Analytical procedures
      (3) Procedures applied to every item in a population

         (a) For example, some audit plans include the audit of all "large" accounts and a portion of the small accounts. In such situations only the "small" accounts would be subject to sampling.

      (4) Tests of controls where application is not documented

         (a) Procedures that depend on segregation of duties or that otherwise provide no documentary evidence

      (5) Procedures from which the auditor does not intend to extend a conclusion to the remaining items in the account

         (a) For example, tracing several transactions through accounting system to obtain understanding

      (6) Untested balances

2. **General Approaches to Audit Sampling—Nonstatistical and Statistical**

   a. Both involve judgment in planning, executing the sampling plan, and evaluating the results of the sample
   b. Both can provide sufficient competent evidential matter
   c. Statistical sampling helps the auditor to

      (1) Design an efficient sample
      (2) Measure the sufficiency of the evidential matter obtained
      (3) Evaluate the sample results

         (a) The auditor can objectively **quantify sampling risk** to limit it to a level considered acceptable. (This has been the proper reply to numerous multiple-choice questions on the advantages of sampling.)

   d. Costs of statistical sampling

      (1) Training auditors
      (2) Designing samples
      (3) Selecting items to be tested

3. **Uncertainty and Audit Sampling**—Eliminating all uncertainty, even if possible, would delay release of audited information and greatly increase audit cost

   a. **Audit risk** is a combination of the risk that a material misstatement will occur and the risk that it will not be detected by the auditor. It consists of (1) the risk (inherent risk and control risk) that the balance or class and related assertions contain misstatements that could be material when aggregated with other misstatements, and (2) the risk (detection risk) that the auditor will not detect such misstatement. Recall our discussion of audit risk in the Engagement Planning Module (Section A.1.a.).

      (1) **Audit risk** may be expressed using the following model:

$$AR = IR \times CR \times DR$$

$$AR = IR \times CR \times AP \times TD$$

where: AR   =   Audit risk
             IR   =   Inherent risk
             CR   =   Control risk
             DR   =   Detection risk
             AP   =   Analytical procedures risk and other relevant substantive tests
             TD   =   Test of details allowable risk of incorrect acceptance for this substantive test

> **NOTE:** The second equation is presented in the Appendix to AU 350. This model separates detection risk into the two components of AP and TD.

(2) **Nonsampling risk** includes all aspects of audit risk that are not due to sampling. It is controlled by adequate planning and supervision of audit work and proper adherence to quality control standards. The following are examples of nonsampling risk:

(a) The failure to select appropriate audit procedures
(b) The failure to recognize misstatements in documents examined
(c) Misinterpreting the results of audit tests

(3) **Sampling risk** is the risk that the auditor's conclusion, based on a sample, might be different from the conclusion that would be reached if the test were applied in the same way to the entire population (AU 350).

(a) Tests of controls sampling risks include the risk of assessing control risk too high and the risk of assessing control risk too low. These risks are discussed in section B.1. of this outline.
(b) Substantive test sampling risks include the risk of incorrect rejection and the risk of incorrect acceptance. These risks are discussed in section C.1. of this outline.

> **NOTE:** A number of exam multiple-choice questions have required candidates to identify the response that is an example of nonsampling risk. For example, illustrations of three of the above sampling risks may be presented with one of nonsampling risk. To identify nonsampling risk, think of it as the risk of "human" type errors (e.g., failure to detect a misstatement).

4. **Types of Audit Tests in Which Sampling May Be Used**

a. **Tests of controls** are directed toward the design or operation of a control to assess its effectiveness in preventing or detecting material misstatements in a financial statement assertion.
b. **Substantive tests** are used to obtain evidence about the validity and propriety of the accounting treatment of transactions and balances.
c. **Dual-purpose tests** are those in which a single sample is used to test a control **and** to serve as a substantive test of a recorded balance or class of transactions. When a dual-purpose test is used, auditors select the sample size as the higher of that required for the two purposes. For example, if the test of control test required thirty-five items, and the substantive test required forty, both tests would be performed using the forty items.

5. **Types of Statistical Sampling Plans**

a. **Attributes sampling** (used in tests of controls) reaches a conclusion in terms of a rate of occurrence—discussed in section B. below.
b. **Variables sampling** (used in substantive testing) reaches a conclusion in dollar amounts (or possibly in units).

(1) **Probability-proportional-to-size (PPS) sampling**—discussion in section C.2
(2) **Classical variables sampling techniques**—discussed in section C.3

Below is an outline organized around the audit guide's steps involved in attributes and variables sampling.

AUDIT AND ACCOUNTING GUIDE SAMPLING STEPS

Attributes Sampling (used in Tests of Controls)	Variables Sampling (used in Substantive Testing)
1. **Determine** the objectives of the test	**Determine** the objectives of the test

2. **Define** the deviation conditions	**Define** the population
	  a. Define the sampling unit
	  b. Consider the completeness of the population
	  c. Identify individually significant items

3. **Define** the population
  a. Define the period covered by the test
  b. Define the sampling unit
  c. Consider the completeness of the population
	Select an audit sampling technique

4. **Determine** the method of selecting the sample
  a. Random-number sampling
  b. Systematic sampling
  c. Other sampling
	Determine the sample size
	  a. Consider the variation within the population
	  b. Consider the acceptable level of risk
	  c. Consider the tolerable misstatement
	  d. Consider the expected amount of misstatement
	  e. Consider the population size

5. **Determine** the sample size
  a. Consider the acceptable risk of assessing control risk too low
  b. Consider the tolerable rate
  c. Consider the expected population deviation rate
  d. Consider the effect of population size
  e. Consider a sequential or a fixed sample-size approach
	Determine the method of selecting the sample

6. **Perform** the sampling plan	**Perform** the sampling plan

7. **Evaluate** the sample results
  a. Calculate the deviation rate
  b. Consider sampling risk
  c. Consider the qualitative aspects of the deviations
  d. Reach an overall conclusion
	Evaluate the sample results
	  a. Project the misstatement to the population and consider sampling risk
	  b. Consider the qualitative aspects of the misstatements and reach an overall conclusion

8. **Document** the sampling procedure	**Document** the sampling procedure

> **NOTE:** Be familiar with the preceding steps as the CPA exam questions have required candidates to list and explain them.

NOW REVIEW MULTIPLE-CHOICE QUESTIONS 1 THROUGH 19 IN VOLUME 2

B. Sampling in Tests of Controls

1. Sampling Risk

  a. **Risk of assessing control risk too high (alpha risk, type I error)** is the risk that the assessed level of control risk based on the sample is **greater** than the true operating effectiveness of the control structure policy or procedure. Know that this risk relates to **audit efficiency**. If the auditor assesses control risk too high, substantive tests will consequently be expanded beyond the necessary level, leading to audit inefficiency.

  b. **Risk of assessing control risk too low (beta risk, type II error)** is the risk that the assessed level of control risk based on the sample is **less** than the true operating effectiveness of the control structure policy or procedure. Know that this risk relates to **audit effectiveness**. If the auditor assesses control risk too low, substantive tests will not be expanded to the necessary level to ensure an effective audit. Because materially misstated financial statements may result from this situation, controlling this risk is generally considered of greater audit concern than controlling the risk of assessing control risk too high. The table below illustrates the two aspects of sampling risk for tests of controls.

TRUE OPERATING EFFECTIVENESS OF THE CONTROLS IS

The test of controls sample indicates:	Adequate for planned assessed level of control risk	Inadequate for planned assessed level of control risk
Extent of operating effectiveness is adequate	Correct Decision	Incorrect Decision (risk of assessing control risk too low)
Extent of operating effectiveness is inadequate	Incorrect Decision (risk of assessing control risk too high)	Correct Decision

2. **Statistical (Attributes) Sampling for Tests of Controls**

   a. **Steps involved in attributes sampling**

   (1) **Determine the objectives of the test**—Remember that tests of controls are designed to provide reasonable assurance that internal control is operating effectively. For example, attributes sampling might test controls for voucher processing, billing systems, payroll systems, inventory pricing, fixed-asset additions, and depreciation computations.

   (a) Attributes sampling is generally used when there is a trail of documentary evidence.

   (2) **Define the deviation conditions**—An auditor should identify characteristics (attributes) that would indicate operation of the internal control procedures. The auditor next defines the possible deviation conditions. A deviation is a departure from the prescribed internal control policy or procedure.

   EXAMPLE

   If the prescribed procedure to be tested requires the cancellation of each paid voucher, a paid but uncanceled voucher would constitute a deviation.

   ---

   (3) **Define the population**—For tests of controls, the population is the class of transactions being tested. Conclusions based on sample results can be projected only to the population from which the sample was selected. Three steps are involved in defining the population.

   (a) **Define the period covered by the test**—Ideally, tests of controls should be applied to transactions executed during the entire period under audit. In some cases it is more efficient to test transactions at an interim date and use supplemental procedures to obtain reasonable assurance regarding the remaining period.

   (b) **Define the sampling unit**—The sampling unit is one of the individual elements constituting the population. In our earlier example, the sampling unit is the voucher.

   (c) **Consider the completeness of the population**—The auditor actually selects sampling units from a physical representation of the population (in our example, the recorded paid vouchers). Because subsequent statistical conclusions relate to the physical representation, the auditor should consider whether it includes the entire population.

   (4) **Determine the method of selecting the sample**—The sample should be representative of the population. All items in the population should have an opportunity to be selected. Methods include

   (a) **Random-number sampling**—Every sampling unit has the same probability of being selected, and every combination of sampling units of equal size has the same probability of being selected. Random numbers can be generated using a random number table or a computer program.

   (b) **Systematic sampling**—Every nth (population size/sample size) item is selected after a random start. When a random starting point is used, this method provides every sampling unit in the population an equal chance of being selected. If the population is arranged randomly, systematic selection is essentially the same as random number selection.

   1] One problem with systematic sampling is that the population may be systematically ordered; for example, the identification number of all large items ends with a nine. A biased sample may result since nine's may be selected either too frequently **or** never. This limitation may be overcome by using multiple random starts or by using an interval that does not coincide with the pattern in the population.

2] An advantage of systematic sampling, as compared to random-number sampling, is that the population items do not have to be consecutively numbered for the auditor to use this method.

(c) **Haphazard sampling**—A sample consisting of units selected without any conscious bias, that is, without any special reason for including or omitting items from the sample. It does not consist of sampling units selected in a "careless" manner, but in a manner that the auditor hopes to be representative of the population. Haphazard sampling is not used for statistical sampling because it does not allow the auditor to measure the probability of selecting a given combination of sampling units.

(d) **Block sampling**—A sample consisting of contiguous units.

EXAMPLE

An auditor selects three blocks of ten vouchers for examination.

The advantage of block sampling is the ease of sample unit selection. The disadvantage is that the sample selected may not be representative of the overall population. Because of this disadvantage, use of this method is **generally the least desirable** method.

(5) **Determine the sample size**—A series of decisions must be made.

(a) **Allowable risk of assessing control risk too low.** Since the auditor uses the results of tests of controls as the source of evidence for assessing control risk at levels below the maximum, a low allowable risk is normally selected.

   1] Risk levels between 1% and 10% are normally used.
   2] There is an inverse relationship (e.g., as one increases the other decreases) between the risk of assessing control risk too low and sample size.

(b) **Tolerable rate (tolerable deviation rate)**—The maximum rate of deviation from a prescribed control structure policy or procedure that an auditor is willing to accept without modifying the planned assessed level of control risk.

   1] The auditor's determination of the tolerable deviation rate is a function of

      a] The planned assessed level of control risk.
      b] The degree of assurance desired by the sample.

   2] When the auditor's planned assessed level of control risk is low, and the degree of assurance desired from the sample is high, the tolerable rate should be low.

      a] This will be the case, for example, when the auditor does not perform other tests of controls for an assertion.

(c) **Expected population deviation rate (expected rate of occurrence)**—An estimate of the deviation rate in the entire population

   1] If the expected population deviation rate exceeds the tolerable rate, tests (tests of controls/attributes sampling) will not be performed.
   2] Although the risk of assessing control risk too high is often not explicitly controlled when determining attributes sample size, it can be controlled to some extent by specifying a conservative (larger) expected deviation rate.
   3] There is a direct relationship (e.g., as one increases, the other also increases) between the expected deviation rate and sample size.
   4] The expected population deviation rate is

      a] Typically determined by using last year's deviation rate adjusted judgmentally for current year changes in the control procedure, or by determining the deviation rate in a small preliminary sample.
      b] Used only to determine sample size and not to evaluate sample results, so the estimate need not be exact.

   5] Because a deviation from a control procedure does not necessarily result in a misstatement (e.g., an unapproved invoice may still represent a valid business expenditure), the rate of misstatements is generally lower than the deviation rate.

(d) **Population effect**—Increases in the size of the population normally increase the sample size. However, it is generally appropriate to treat any population of more than 5,000 sample units as if it were infinite.

(e) When (a) through (d) above have been quantified, the sample size can be easily determined through the use of sample size tables. For the CPA exam **remember the following relationships**:

ATTRIBUTES SAMPLING
SUMMARY OF RELATIONSHIPS TO SAMPLE SIZE

Increases in	Effect on Sample Size
Risk of assessing control risk too low	Decrease
Tolerable rate	Decrease
Expected population deviation rate	Increase
Population	Increase (slightly for large samples)

(f) **Fixed vs. sequential sample size approach**—Audit samples may be designed using either a fixed or a sequential sample size approach. Supplementing traditional attributes (fixed size) sampling approaches are

1] **Sequential (stop-or-go) sampling**—a sampling plan for which the sample is selected in several steps, with the need to perform each step conditional on the results of the previous steps. That is, the results may either be so poor as to indicate that the control may not be relied upon, or so good as to justify reliance at each step.

2] **Discovery sampling**—a procedure for determining the sample size required to have a stipulated probability of observing at least one occurrence when the expected population deviation rate is at a designated level. It is most appropriate when the expected deviation rate is zero or near zero. If a deviation is detected, the auditor must either (1) use an alternate approach, or (2) if the deviation is of sufficient importance, audit all transactions.

(6) **Perform the sampling plan**—The auditor should apply the appropriate audit procedures to all items in the sample to determine if there are any deviations from the prescribed control procedures. Each deviation should be analyzed to determine whether it is an isolated or recurring type of occurrence.

(a) The auditor should select extra sample items (more than the needed sample size) so that voided, unused, or inapplicable documents can be excluded from the sample and be replaced.

(b) If the auditor is unable to examine a selected item (e.g., a document has been misplaced), it should be considered a deviation for evaluation purposes. Furthermore, the auditor should consider the reasons for this limitation and its implications for the audit.

(c) In some cases the auditor may find enough deviations early in the sampling process to indicate that a control cannot be relied upon. The auditor need not continue the tests in such circumstances.

(7) **Evaluate the sample results**—Once audit procedures have been performed on all sample items, the sample results must be evaluated and projected to the entire population from which the sample was selected.

(a) Calculate the sample deviation rate.

1] $\text{Deviation rate} = \dfrac{\text{Number of observed deviations}}{\text{Sample size}}$

2] The deviation rate is the auditor's best estimate of the true (but unknown) deviation rate in the population.

(b) For the risk of assessing control risk too low that is being used, determine the **upper deviation limit** (upper occurrence limit, achieved upper precision limit).

1] The auditor uses the number of deviations noted, and the appropriate sampling table (not presented here) to calculate the upper deviation limit.

a] This upper deviation limit represents the sample deviation rate plus an **allowance for sampling risk**.

(c) Compare the upper deviation limit to the tolerable rate specified in designing the sample.

1] If the upper deviation limit is less than or equal to the tolerable rate, the sample results support reliance on the control procedure tested.

> **EXAMPLE:**
>
> Assume that the auditor established the following criteria for an attributes sampling plan:
>
> > Population size: over 5,000 units
> >
> > Allowable risk of assessing control risk too low: 5%
> >
> > Tolerable deviation rate: 6%
> >
> > Estimated population deviation rate: 2.5%

By referencing the appropriate sample size table (not included here) the auditor determined that the required sample size was 150 units.

The auditor applied appropriate audit procedures to the 150 sample units and found eight deviations.

a] The sample deviation rate = 8/150 = 5.3%

b] The upper deviation limit found from the table (not presented) for a 5% risk of assessing control risk too low and eight deviations = 9.5%

c] The allowance for sampling risk = 9.5 – 5.3 = 4.2%

d] The conclusions that can be drawn include

   i] There is a 5% chance of the true population deviation rate being greater than or equal to 9.5%.

   ii] Since the upper deviation limit (9.5%) exceeds the tolerable deviation rate (6%), the sample results indicate that control risk for the control procedure being tested is higher than planned, and, therefore, the scope of resulting substantive tests must be increased.

(d) In addition to the frequency of deviations found, the auditor should consider the qualitative aspects of each deviation.

1] The nature and cause of each deviation should be analyzed. For example, are the deviations due to a misunderstanding of instructions or to carelessness?

2] The possible relationship of the deviations to other phases of the audit should be considered. For example, the discovery of fraud ordinarily requires broader consideration than does the discovery of an error.

(e) Reach an overall conclusion by applying audit judgment

1] If all evidence obtained, including sample results, supports the auditor's planned assessed level of control risk, the auditor generally does not need to modify planned substantive tests.

2] If the planned level is not supported, the auditor will

   a] Test other related controls

   b] Modify the related substantive tests to reflect increased control risk assessment

(8) **Document the sampling procedure.** Each of the prior seven steps, as well as the basis for overall conclusions, should be documented in the workpapers.

3. **Nonstatistical Sampling for Tests of Controls**—The steps involved in the design and implementation of a nonstatistical sampling plan are similar to statistical plans. Differences in determining sample size, sample selection, and evaluating sample results are discussed below.

   a. **Determine sample size**—As in statistical sampling, the major factors are the risk of assessing control risk too low, the tolerable rate, and the expected population deviation rate.

      (1) In nonstatistical sampling it is not necessary to quantify these factors.

      (2) The auditor should still consider the effects on sample size as described in section B.2.a.(5).

   b. **Sample selection**—Any of the sample selection methods discussed under statistical sampling (B.2.) may be used (i.e., random-number, systematic, haphazard, or, less desirably, block).

   c. **Evaluate sample results**—In nonstatistical sampling it is impossible to determine an upper deviation limit or to quantify sampling risk.

      (1) The auditor should relate the deviation rate in the sample to the tolerable rate established in the design stage to determine whether an adequate allowance for sampling risk has been provided to draw the conclusion that the sample provides an acceptably low level of risk.

(a) **Rule of thumb**—If the deviation rate in a properly designed sample does not exceed the expected population deviation rate used in determining sample size, the auditor can generally "accept" the population and conclude that the control is operating effectively.

(2) As in statistical sampling, the qualitative aspects of deviations should be considered in addition to the frequency of deviations.

(3) Again the auditor must use his/her professional judgment to reach an overall conclusion as to the assessed level of control risk for the assertion(s) related to the internal control procedure tested.

NOW REVIEW MULTIPLE-CHOICE QUESTIONS 20 THROUGH 38 IN VOLUME 2

C. Sampling in Substantive Tests of Details

1. Sampling Risk

a. **Risk of incorrect rejection (alpha risk, type I error)** is the risk that the sample supports the conclusion that the recorded account balance is materially misstated when it is not materially misstated. Know that like the risk of assessing control risk too high, this risk relates to **audit efficiency**. If the sample results incorrectly indicate that an account balance is materially misstated, the performance of additional audit procedures will generally lead to the correct conclusion.

b. **Risk of incorrect acceptance (beta risk, type II error)** is the risk that the sample supports the conclusion that the recorded account balance is not materially misstated when it is materially misstated. Know that like the risk of assessing control risk too low, this risk relates to **audit effectiveness**. If the sample results indicate that an account balance is not misstated, when it is misstated, the auditor will not perform additional procedures and the financial statements may include such misstatements.

c. Although the two risks are mutually exclusive (the auditor cannot incorrectly decide to reject an account balance at the same time s/he incorrectly decides to accept an account balance), both risks may be considered in the sample design stage. The following table illustrates both aspects of sampling risk for substantive tests.

	THE POPULATION ACTUALLY IS	
The Substantive Test Sample Indicates	**Not Materially Misstated**	**Materially Misstated**
The population is not materially misstated	Correct Decision	Incorrect Decision (risk of incorrect acceptance)
The population is materially misstated	Incorrect Decision (risk of incorrect rejection)	Correct Decision

NOTE: The following portions of this outline summarize the steps involved in substantive testing (section C.1.d.), probability- proportional-to-size sampling (section C.2.), and classical variables sampling (section C.3.). Finally, PPS and classical variables sampling are compared (section C.4.).

d. Steps involved in variables sampling

(1) **Determine the objectives of the test**—Remember that variables sampling is used primarily for substantive testing and that its conclusion is generally stated in dollar terms (although conclusions in terms of units [e.g., inventory] are possible). Variables sampling might test, for example, the recorded amount of accounts receivable, inventory quantities and amounts, payroll expense, and fixed asset additions.

(2) **Define the population**—The population consists of the items constituting the account balance or class of transactions of interest. Three areas need to be considered.

(a) **Sampling unit**—The sampling unit is any of the individual elements that constitute the population.

EXAMPLE

If the population to be tested is defined as total accounts receivable, the sampling unit used to confirm the balance of accounts receivable could be each individual account receivable.

(b) **Consider the completeness of the population**—Since sampling units are selected from a physical representation (e.g., a trial balance of receivables), the auditor should consider whether the physical representation includes the entire population.

(c) **Identify individually significant items**—Items that are individually significant for which sampling risk is not justified should be tested separately and not be subjected to sampling. These are items in which potential misstatements could individually equal or exceed tolerable misstatement.

(3) **Select an audit sampling technique**—Either nonstatistical or statistical sampling may be used. If statistical sampling is used, either probability-proportional-to-size sampling (PPS) or classical variables techniques are appropriate.

(4) **Determine the sample size**—Five items need to be considered.

(a) **Variation within the population**—Increases in variation (standard deviation in classical sampling) result in increases in sample size.

(b) **Acceptable level of risk**—The risk of incorrect acceptance is related to audit risk (see AU 312 outline and Engagement Planning Module Section A.2.). The auditor may also control the risk of incorrect rejection so as to allow an efficiently performed audit. Increases in these risks result in decreases in sample size.

> **NOTE:** The risk of incorrect rejection **is not** typically controlled when using PPS sampling, but **is** controlled when using classical methods.

(c) **Tolerable misstatement (error)**—An estimate of the maximum monetary misstatement that may exist in an account balance or class of transactions, when combined with misstatements in other accounts, without causing the financial statements to be materially misstated. As tolerable misstatement increases, sample size decreases.

(d) **Expected amount of misstatement (error)**—Expected misstatement is estimated using an understanding of the business, prior year information, a pilot sample, and/or the results of the review and evaluation of internal control. As expected misstatement increases, a larger sample size is required.

(e) **Population size**—Sample size increases as population size increases. The effect is more significant in classical variables sampling than PPS sampling.

VARIABLES SAMPLING
SUMMARY OF RELATIONSHIPS TO SAMPLE SIZE

Increases in	Effect on sampling size
Risk—Incorrect Acceptance	Decrease
Risk—Incorrect Rejection	Decrease
Tolerable Misstatement (Error)	Decrease
Expected Misstatement (Error)	Increase
Population	Increase
Variation (standard deviation)	Increase

> **NOTE:** Memorize the above relationships. As an aid remember that, in both variables sampling and attributes sampling, increases in risk and in the "tolerables" (tolerable misstatement and tolerable rate) lead to decreases in sample size. For the risks especially, this result is intuitively appealing in that one expects more risk in many contexts when one does less work. Increases in the other factors increase sample size.

(5) **Determine the method of selecting the sample**—Generally random number or systematic sampling

(6) **Perform the sampling plan**—Perform appropriate audit procedures to determine an audit value for each sample item.

(7) **Evaluate the sample results**—The auditor should project the results of the sample to the population. The total projected misstatement, after any adjustments made by the entity, should be compared with the tolerable misstatement and the auditor should consider whether the risk of misstatement in excess of the tolerable amount is at an acceptably low level. Also, qualitative factors (such as the nature of the misstatements and their relationship to other phases of the audit) should be considered. For example, when fraud has been discovered, a simple projection of them will not in general be sufficient as the auditor will need to obtain a thorough understanding of them and of their likely effects.

(8) **Document the sampling procedure**—Each of the prior seven steps, as well as the basis for overall conclusions, should be documented.

e. **Comments on nonstatistical sampling**—Both statistical and nonstatistical sampling require judgment. The major differences between statistical and nonstatistical sampling in substantive testing are in the steps for determining sample size and evaluating sample results.

(1) **Determination of sample size**—Be aware of the relationships summarized in section C.1.d.(4)(e). Also, know that the statistical tables **may** be used to assist in the determination of sample size.

(2) **Evaluation of sample results**—The auditor should project misstatements found in the sample to the population and consider sampling risk.

(a) Projecting misstatements can be accomplished by

1] Dividing the total dollar amount of misstatement in the sample by the fraction of total dollars from the population included in the sample, or

2] Multiplying the average difference between audit and book values for sample items times the number of units in the population.

(b) If tolerable misstatement exceeds projected misstatement by a large amount, the auditor may be reasonably sure that an acceptably low level of sampling risk exists. Sampling risk increases as projected misstatement approaches tolerable error.

(c) When sampling results do not support the book value, the auditor can

1] Examine additional sampling units,

2] Apply alternative auditing procedures, or

3] Ask the client to investigate and, if appropriate, make necessary adjustments.

(d) Qualitative aspects of misstatements need to be considered as well as frequency and amounts of misstatements.

2. **Probability-Proportional-to-Size (PPS) Sampling [dollar-unit, cumulative monetary amount (CMA) sampling]**

a. Uses attributes sampling theory to express a conclusion in dollar amounts. PPS sampling has gained popularity in practice because it is easier to apply than classical variables sampling.

b. Steps in PPS sampling

(1) **Determine the objectives of the test**—PPS tests the reasonableness of a recorded account balance or class of transactions. PPS is primarily applicable in testing account balances and transactions for **overstatements**.

(2) **Define the population**—The population is the account balance or class of transactions being tested.

(a) **Define the sampling unit**—The sampling units in PPS are the individual dollars in the population. The auditor ordinarily examines each individual account or transaction (called a **logical unit**) that includes a sampled dollar.

(b) **Consider the completeness of the population**—As with other sampling plans, the auditor must assure him/herself that the physical representation of the population being tested includes the entire population.

(c) **Identify individually significant items**—PPS automatically includes in the sample any unit that is individually significant.

(3) **Select an audit sampling technique**—Here we have selected PPS.

(4) **Determine the sample size**—A PPS sample divides the population into sampling intervals and selects a logical unit from each sampling interval.

(a) Sample size $= \dfrac{\text{Book value of population} \times \text{Reliability factor}}{\text{Tolerable error} - (\text{Expected error} \times \text{Expansion factor})}$

Sampling interval $= \dfrac{\text{Book value of population}}{\text{Sample size}}$

Expansion Factors (from the *Audit Sampling* guide) for expected misstatements

	Risk of Incorrect Acceptance								
	1%	5%	10%	15%	20%	25%	30%	37%	50%
Factor	1.9	1.6	1.5	1.4	1.3	1.25	1.2	1.15	1.0

Reliability Factors (from the *Audit Sampling* guide) for misstatements of overstatement. (Use 0 errors for determining Reliability Factor.)

Number of	Risk of Incorrect Acceptance								
Overstatements	1%	5%	10%	15%	20%	25%	30%	37%	50%
0	4.61	3.00	2.31	1.90	1.61	1.39	1.21	1.00	.70
1	6.64	4.75	3.89	3.38	3.00	2.70	2.44	2.14	1.68
2	8.41	6.30	5.33	4.72	4.28	3.93	3.62	3.25	2.68
3	10.05	7.76	6.69	6.02	5.52	5.11	4.77	4.34	3.68

(b) Observations

1] The size of the **sampling interval** is related to the risk of incorrect acceptance and tolerable misstatement. The auditor controls the risk of incorrect rejection by making an allowance for expected misstatements. The auditor specifies a planned allowance for sampling risk so that the estimate of projected misstatement plus the allowance for sampling risk will be less than or equal to tolerable misstatement.

2] If no misstatements are expected, the sampling interval is determined by dividing tolerable misstatement by a factor that corresponds to the risk of incorrect acceptance (i.e., the reliability factor).

3] A reliability factor table such as the one above has been included with CPA exam questions.

(5) **Determine the method of selecting the sample**—PPS samples are generally selected using **systematic sampling** with a random start. All logical units (e.g., accounts) with dollar amounts greater than or equal to the sampling interval are certain to be selected.

(6) **Perform the sampling plan**—The auditor must apply appropriate audit procedures to determine an audit value for each logical unit included in the sample.

(7) **Evaluate the sample results**—Misstatements found should be projected to the population and an allowance for sampling risk should be calculated. When the sample contains misstatements, the **upper limit on misstatements** is the total of projected misstatement and the allowance for sampling risk (with its two subcomponents).

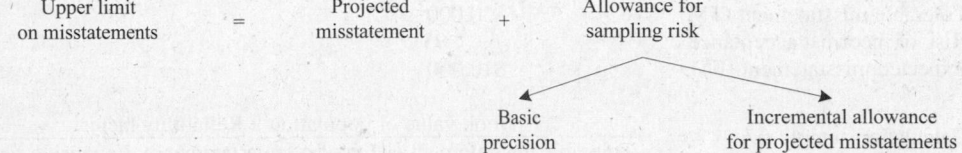

Projected misstatement is calculated for each logical unit containing misstatements and totaled. The approach differs based on whether the book value of the specific logical unit is less than or greater than the size of the sampling interval.

Logical unit less than sampling interval—Multiply the percentage the account is misstated (misstatement/book value, referred to as the "taint") times the sampling interval. For example, an account with a book value of $100 has an audited value of $95, and a sampling interval of $3,000. The tainting percentage of 5% ($5 misstatement/$100) is multiplied times the $3,000 sampling interval, or

$$\$5/\$100 \times \$3,000 = \$150 \text{ projected misstatement}$$

Logical unit greater than sampling interval—The actual amount of misstatement is considered to be the projected misstatement. For example, consider an account with a book value of $4,000, an audited value of $40, and a sampling interval of $3,000; the projected misstatement is $3,960 ($4,000 – $40). Similarly, if the audited value is $3,300, the projected misstatement is $700 ($4,000 – $3,300).

> **NOTE:** Questions have required candidates to calculate a projected misstatement for one or more accounts. If more than one account is involved, the various projected misstatements are simply totaled.
>
> For completeness' sake we also present computations of basic precision and the incremental allowance for projected misstatements. That information has not been heavily examined to this point.

Basic precision is found by multiplying the reliability factor [see section C.2.b.(4)] times the sampling interval.

Incremental allowance for projected misstatements is determined by ranking the misstatements for logical units that are less than the sampling interval from highest to lowest and considering the incremental changes in reliability factors for the actual number of misstatements found. The table of Reliability Factors presented earlier [section C.2.b.(4)] presents values for zero through three misstatements. The *Audit Sampling* guide presents additional values for situations in which more misstatements are detected. One must subtract 1.00 from each incremental change to isolate the incremental allowance for projected misstatements.

(a) **Decision rule:** Compare the upper limit on misstatements to tolerable misstatement.

1] If the upper limit on misstatements is less than or equal to tolerable misstatement, the sample results support the conclusion that the population is not misstated by more than tolerable misstatement at the specified risk of incorrect acceptance.

2] If the upper limit on misstatements is greater than the tolerable misstatement, the sample results do not support the conclusion that the population is not misstated by more than the tolerable misstatement. This may be due to the fact that (a) the population is misstated, (b) the auditor's expectation of misstatement was low and resulted in too small of a sample, or (c) the sample is not representative of the population.

3] The auditor should consider qualitative aspects of errors found as well as quantitative factors.

(b) **Observation:** If no misstatements are found, projected misstatement and the incremental allowance for projected misstatements will equal zero, leaving the basic precision as the only nonzero component of the upper limit on misstatements. No further calculations are needed since the tolerable misstatement will be greater than this amount.

(8) **Document the sampling procedure**—Each of the prior seven steps, as well as the basis for overall conclusions, should be documented.

The following example illustrates the probability-proportional-to-size method:

Probability-Proportional-to-Size Sampling Example

Step 1.   Objective of test—determine reasonableness of accounts receivable
Step 2.   Define population—individual dollars in account
Step 3.   Select sampling technique—probability-proportional-to-size
Step 4.   Determine sample size

Given:

Tolerable misstatement (TM)	$50,000
Risk of incorrect acceptance	.05
Expected misstatement (EM)	$10,000

$$\text{Calculation sample size} = \frac{\text{Book value of population} \times \text{Reliability factor}}{\text{Tolerable misstatement} - (\text{Expected misstatement} \times \text{Expansion factor})}$$

$$= \frac{\$1,000,000 \times 3}{\$50,000 (10,000 \times 1.6)} \approx 88$$

$$\text{Sampling interval} = \frac{\text{Book value of population}}{\text{Sample size}}$$

$$= \frac{\$1,000,000}{88} \approx \$11,333.33$$

Step 5.   Determine method of selecting sample—systematic
Step 6.   Perform sampling plan
Step 7.   Evaluate and project results

Projected misstatement—Assume 3 misstatements

Book value	Audited value	Misstatement	Taint %	Sampling interval	Projected misstatement
$ 100	$ 95.00	$ 5.00	5%	$11,333	$ 567
11,700	212.00	11,488.00	--*	NA	11,488
65	58.50	6.50	10%	11,333	1,133
Projected misstatement					$13,188

* Not applicable; book value larger than sampling interval.

NOTE: Make certain that you understand details of the projected misstatement computation as it has been required on various CPA examination questions.

Basic precision	=	Reliability factor	×	Sampling interval
	=	3.0	×	$11,333.33
	=	$34,000.00		

Incremental allowance for projected misstatements

Reliability factor	Increment	(Increm – 1)	Projected misstatements	Incremental allowance
3.00	--	--	--	--
4.75	1.75	.75	$1,133	$ 850
6.30	1.55	.55	567	312
Incremental allowance for projected misstatements				$1,162

Upper limit on misstatements	=	Projected misstatement	+	Basic precision	+	Incremental allowance for projected misstatements

$$= \quad \$13,188 \quad + \quad \$34,000 \quad + \quad \$1,162$$
$$= \quad \$48,350 \quad \text{(Accept, this is less than tolerable misstatement)}$$

3. **Classical Variables Sampling**

   a. **Classical variables sampling models** use normal distribution theory to evaluate selected characteristics of a population on the basis of a sample of the items constituting the population.

   (1) For any normal distribution, the following fixed relationships exist concerning the area under the curve and the distance from the mean in standard deviations. This table assumes a two-tailed approach that is appropriate since classical variables sampling models generally test for both overstatement and understatement.

Distance in Stan. Dev. (Reliability coefficient)	Area under the Curve (Reliability level)	
± 1.0	68%	
1.64	90%	*
1.96	95%	
2.0	95.5%	
2.7	99%	

   * Most frequently tested on CPA exam

   Example where the mean = 250 and the standard deviation = 10:

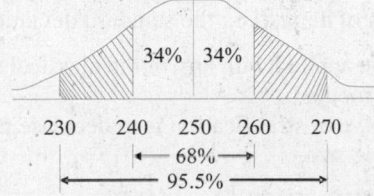

   (2) For large samples (greater than or equal to thirty) the distribution of sample means tends to be normally distributed about its own mean which is equal to the true population mean, even if the population is not normally distributed (Central Limit Theorem). Since many populations sampled in auditing are not normally distributed, this is important.

   (3) **The standard deviation** in the above model measures the dispersion among the respective amounts of a particular characteristic, for all items in the population for which a sample estimate is developed.

   b. **Variations of classical variables sampling**

   (1) **Mean-per-unit estimation** is a classical variables sampling technique that projects the sample average to the total population by multiplying the sample average by the number of items in the population.

   (a) Determine audit values for each sample item.
   (b) Calculate the average audit amount.
   (c) Multiply this average audit amount times the number of units in the population to obtain the estimated population value.

   (2) **Difference estimation** is a classical variables sampling technique that uses the average difference between audited amounts and individual recorded amounts to estimate the total audited amount of a population and an allowance for sampling risk.

   (a) Determine audit values for each sample item.
   (b) Calculate the difference between the audit value and book value for each sample item.
   (c) Calculate the average difference.
   (d) Determine the estimated population value by multiplying the average difference by the total population units and adding or subtracting this value from the recorded book value.

   (3) **Ratio estimation** is a classical variables sampling technique that uses the ratio of audited amounts to recorded amounts in the sample to estimate the total dollar amount of the population and an allowance for sampling risk.

   (a) Determine audit values for each sample item.
   (b) Calculate the ratio between the sum of sample audit values and sample book values.

(c) Determine the estimated population value by multiplying the total population book value times this ratio.

(4) **The regression approach** is similar to the difference and ratio approaches. This approach has the effect of using both the average ratio and the average difference in calculating an estimate of the total amount for the population.

(5) **Difference and ratio estimation** are used as alternatives to mean-per-unit estimation. The auditor should use these approaches when applicable because they require a smaller sample size (i.e., they are more efficient than mean-per-unit estimation).

    (a) One factor in the calculation of sample size for classical variables sampling models is the estimated standard deviation. If the standard deviation of differences or ratios is smaller than the standard deviation of audit values, these two methods will produce a smaller sample size.

        1] Difference estimation will be used if the differences between sample audit values and book values are a relatively constant dollar amount, regardless of account size.
        2] Ratio estimation will be used if the differences are a constant percentage of book values.

    (b) In order to use either difference or ratio estimation, the following constraints must be met:

        1] The individual book values must be known and must sum to the total book value.
        2] There must be more than a few differences (twenty is often suggested as a minimum) between audit and book values.

    (c) These two methods will usually be more efficient than mean-per-unit estimation when stratification of the population is not possible.

(6) **Stratification** separates a population into relatively homogeneous groups to reduce the sample size by minimizing the effect of variation of items (i.e., the standard deviation) in the population.

    (a) Although stratification may be applied with any of the classical methods, it is most frequently used with the mean-per-unit estimation method.
    (b) Know that the primary objective of stratification is to decrease the effect of variance in the total population and thereby reduce sample size.

c. Variables sampling steps applied to classical variables sampling

(1) **Determine the objectives of the test**—Recall that variables sampling models are designed to draw conclusions in dollar amounts.

(2) **Define the population**—The population consists of the items constituting the account balance or class of transactions.

    (a) **Sampling unit**—As with PPS sampling, the sampling unit is any of the individual elements that constitute the population. For example, the sampling unit in receivables is often an individual customer's account.
    (b) **Consider the completeness of the population**—As discussed in PPS, the auditor must consider whether the physical representation includes the entire population.
    (c) **Identify individually significant items**—Items which are individually significant for which sampling risk is not justified, should be tested separately and not be subject to sampling. These are items for which potential error could individually equal or exceed tolerable misstatement. Note that in PPS these items were automatically selected.

(3) **Select an audit sampling technique**—Here we would select among mean-per-unit, difference, ratio, and regression estimation.

(4) **Determine the sample size**—The following factors are included in the sample size calculation:

    (a) **The population size** is directly related to sample size.
    (b) **Estimated standard deviation**—An estimate must be made of the dispersion of audit values for the units constituting the population. This value can be estimated by

        1] Calculating the standard deviation of recorded amounts,
        2] Auditing a small pilot sample, or
        3] Using the standard deviation found in the previous audit.

    (c) **Tolerable misstatement**—An estimate of the maximum monetary misstatement that may exist in an account balance or class of transactions, when combined with error in other accounts, without causing the financial statements to be materially misstated.

(d) **Risk of incorrect rejection (alpha risk)**—Since the risk of incorrect rejection is inversely related to sample size, the auditor must weigh the costs of a larger sample size against the potential additional costs associated with expanded audit procedures following the initial rejection resulting from a sample size that was too small.

(e) **Risk of incorrect acceptance (beta risk)**—In specifying an acceptable level of risk of incorrect acceptance, the auditor considers the level of audit risk that s/he is willing to accept. Recall this discussion in section A.1.a. of the Engagement Planning Module.

(f) **Planned allowance for sampling risk (desired precision)**—The allowance is a function of the auditor's estimates of tolerable misstatement, risk of incorrect rejection, and risk of incorrect acceptance. The risk of incorrect acceptance is not explicitly included in the sample size equation, but the allowance for sampling risk controls the level of risk the auditor is assuming.

Various approaches are used to calculate the planned allowance for sampling risk. Since these approaches are not frequently examined, we will not present them. Depending upon the risk assumed (incorrect acceptance and rejection) the planned allowance for sampling risk is either equal to or less than the tolerable misstatement. For example, when a 5% and 10% risk of incorrect acceptance and rejection respectively are established, the planned allowance for sampling risk is established at 1/2 the amount of the tolerable misstatement.

(g) **Sample size equation**

$$ n = \left(\frac{N \times SD \times U_R}{A} \right)^2 $$

n = Sample size
N' = Population size
SD = Estimated population standard deviation
U_R = The standard normal deviate for the acceptable risk of incorrect rejection
A = Planned allowance for sampling risk

(h) The above formula assumes sampling with replacement and may be adjusted by a finite correction factor (thereby reducing sample size) when sampling without replacement.

$$ n' = \frac{n}{1 + n/N} \qquad n' = \text{Sample size adjusted for finite correction factor} $$

(5) **Determine the method of selecting the sample**—Classical samples are generally selected using random sampling or stratified random sampling.

(6) **Perform the sampling plan**—Perform appropriate audit procedures to determine an audit value for each item.

(a) If the auditor is unable to examine selected items (i.e., accounts receivable confirmations are not returned), s/he should perform alternative procedures that provide sufficient evidence to form a conclusion.

(7) **Evaluate and project the sample results**—As was the case with sample selection, the actual evaluation and projection of sample results is affected by the method used. Additionally, the various auditing textbooks do not agree on the approach for evaluating sample results. We provide a summarized approach. Assume a population of 10,000 accounts with a book value of $1,000,000; this represents an average book value of $100 ($1,000,000/10,000 accounts). Further, assume that a sample has been selected and the following results obtained:

Average book value of items in sample $101
Average audited value of items in sample $ 98

Projected misstatement and estimated total audited value (ETAV). As was the case with PPS sampling a projected misstatement may be calculated.

Mean-Per-Unit Method

ETAV = Population size × Average audited value

= 10,000 × $98 = $980,000

Projected misstatement = $1,000,000 – $980,000 = $20,000 overstatement

Difference Estimation Method

Average difference (in sample): Average BV – Average AV.

$101 – $98 = $3

Projected misstatement: 10,000 accounts × $3 = $30,000 overstatement

ETAV = $1,000,000 – $30,000 = $970,000

Ratio Estimation Method

ETAV = (Sample Avg. AV/Sample Avg. BV) × Population BV

= ($98 / $101) × $1,000,000 = $970,297

Projected Misstatement = $1,000,000 – $970,297 = $29,703 overstatement

> **NOTE:** The difference and ratio estimation methods use the book value of the sample items in the analysis, while the mean-per-unit method **does not**.

Considering sampling risk. When statistical sampling is used, the auditors utilize statistical formulas to determine whether the account balance should be accepted. In essence, these formulas help the auditor to determine whether the projected misstatement may reveal a materially misstated account. One approach is to construct an adjusted allowance for sampling risk (plus or minus) around the estimated audited population value. (The CPA exam does not generally require such a computation.)

If the book value falls within this interval, the auditors will accept that the population is materially correct. If not, the auditors will conclude that there is an unacceptably high risk that the inventory account is materially misstated. When a conclusion is reached that an account is materially misstated, the auditors may decide to (1) increase the sample size of the test, (2) perform other audit tests of the account, or (3) work with the client's personnel to locate other misstated items in the account.

4. **Comparison of PPS Sampling to Classical Variables Sampling**

   a. Advantages of PPS sampling

      (1) Generally easier to use
      (2) Size of sample not based on variation of audited amounts
      (3) Automatically results in a stratified sample
      (4) Individually significant items are automatically identified.
      (5) Usually results in a smaller sample size if no misstatements are expected
      (6) Can be easily designed and sample selection can begin before the complete population is available

   b. Advantages of classical variables sampling

      (1) May result in a smaller sample size if there are many differences between audited and book values
      (2) Easier to expand sample size if that becomes necessary
      (3) Selection of zero balances does not require special sample design considerations.
      (4) Inclusion of negative balances does not require special sample design considerations.

> **NOW REVIEW MULTIPLE-CHOICE QUESTIONS 39 THROUGH 58 IN VOLUME 2**

KEY TERMS

Attributes sampling. A sampling plan enabling the auditors to estimate the deviation rate in a population.

Audit sampling (sampling). The selection of less than 100% of a population of audit relevance, and the evaluation of that sample, such that the auditor expects the items selected (the sample) to be representative of the population, and thus likely to provide a reasonable basis for conclusions about the population. In this context, *representative* means that the sample will result in conclusions that, subject to the limitations of sampling risk, are similar to those that would be drawn if the same procedures were applied to the entire population.

Deviation rate. A defined rate of departure from prescribed controls. Also referred to as occurrence rate or exception rate.

Difference estimation. A classical variables sampling plan that uses the difference between the audited (correct) values and the book values of items in a sample to calculate the estimated total audited value of the population.

Discovery sampling. A procedure for determining the sample size required to have a stipulated probability of observing at least one occurrence when the expected population deviation rate is at a designated level. It is most appropriate when the expected deviation rate is zero or near zero. If a deviation is detected, the auditor must either (1) use an alternate approach, or (2) if the deviation is of sufficient importance, audit all transactions.

Mean-per-unit estimation. A classical variables sampling plan enabling auditors to estimate the average dollar value of items in a population by determining the average value of items in a sample.

Misstatement. A difference between the amount, classification, presentation, or disclosure of a reported financial statement item and the amount, classification, presentation, or disclosure that is required for the item to be in accordance with the applicable financial reporting framework. Misstatements can arise from error or fraud.   Misstatements also include those adjustments of amounts, classifications, presentations, or disclosures that, in the auditor's judgment, are necessary for the financial statements to be presented fairly, in all material respects.

a. **Factual misstatements**—Misstatements about which there is no doubt.
b. **Judgmental misstatements.** Differences arising from the judgments of management concerning accounting estimates that the auditor considers unreasonable or the selection or application of accounting policies that the auditor considers inappropriate.
c. **Projected misstatements.** The auditor's best estimate of misstatements in populations, involving the projection of misstatements identified in audit samples to the entire population from which the samples were drawn. For example, if statistical sampling was used with receivables, the difference between auditor estimated total audited value and the book value of receivables is the projected misstatement.

Nonsampling risk. The risk that the auditor reaches an erroneous conclusion for any reason not related to sampling risk. Examples of nonsampling risk include use of inappropriate audit procedures or misinterpretation of audit evidence and failure to recognize misstatement or deviation.

Population. The entire set of data from which a sample is selected and about which the auditor wishes to draw conclusions.

Probability-proportional-to-size (PPS) sampling. A variables sampling procedure that uses attributes theory to express a conclusion in monetary (dollar) amounts.

Ratio estimation. A classical variables sampling plan enabling auditors to use the ratio of audited (correct) values to book values of items in a sample to calculate the estimated total audited value of the population.

Risk of assessing control risk too high. The risk that the assessed level of control risk based on the sample is greater than the true operating effectiveness of the control. That is, the auditor concludes that the system operates less effectively than it actually does.

Risk of assessing control risk too low. This risk is the possibility that the assessed level of control risk based on the sample is less than the true operating effectiveness of the controls. That is, the auditor concludes that the system operates more effectively than it actually does.

Risk of incorrect acceptance. The risk that sample results indicate that a population is not materially misstated when, in fact, it is materially misstated.

Risk of incorrect rejection. The risk that sample results indicate that a population is materially misstated when, in fact, it is not.

Sampling risk. The risk that the auditor's conclusion based on a sample may be different from the conclusion if the entire population was subjected to the same audit procedure.

Sampling unit. The individual items constituting a population.

Statistical sampling. Audit sampling that uses the laws of probability for selecting and evaluating a sample from a population for the purpose of reaching a conclusion about the population.

Stratification. Division of the population into groups.

Tolerable misstatement. A monetary amount set by the auditor in respect of which the auditor seeks to obtain an appropriate level of assurance that the monetary amount set by the auditor is not exceeded by the actual misstatement in the population.

a. The professional standards require that the auditor determine performance materiality to reduce to an appropriately low level the probability that the aggregate of uncorrected and undetected misstatements in the fanatical statements exceeds materiality for the financial statements as a whole.
b. Tolerable misstatement is the application of performance materiality to a particular sampling procedure. Tolerable misstatement may be the same amount or an amount smaller than performance materiality (for example, when the population from which the population is selected is smaller than the account balance).

Tolerable rate of deviation. A rate of deviation from prescribed internal control procedures set by the auditor in respect of which the auditor seeks to obtain an appropriate level of assurance that that rate of deviation set by the auditor is not exceeded by the actual rate of deviation in the population.

Uncorrected misstatements. Misstatements that the auditor has accumulated during the audit and that have not been corrected.

Variables sampling. Sampling plans designed to estimate a numerical measurement of a population, such as dollar value.

Module 8: Auditing with Technology

Overview

Computers have become the primary means used to process financial accounting information and have resulted in a situation in which auditors must be able to use and understand current information technology (IT) to audit a client's financial statements. Accordingly, knowledge of computer terminology, computer systems, and related audit procedures is tested both on the Business Environment and Concepts section and on the Auditing and Attestation section of the CPA exam.

The following "Diagram of an Audit" was first presented and explained in the auditing overview section:

Diagram of an Audit

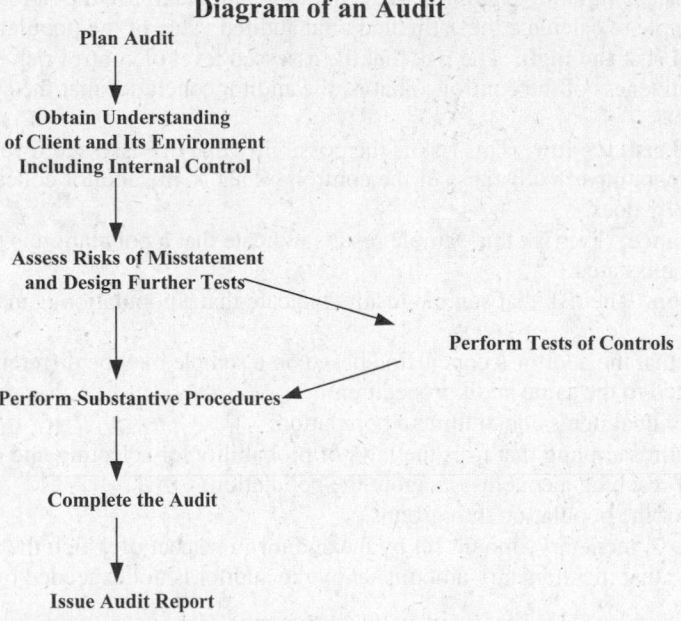

Computer processing (historically referred to as electronic data processing or EDP) does not necessitate modification of the diagram. However, the auditor's consideration of internal control includes an assessment of computerized as well as manual controls. Also, audit procedures may include computerized and manual procedures for considering internal control and for performing substantive tests. AU 318 addresses computer processing.

Because much of the IT information you need to know for auditing relates to IT systems, you should refer to the material that appears in Module 41 of this volume. The coverage here is limited to audit considerations.

A. The Auditor's Consideration of Internal Control When a Computer Is Present

1. General

The auditor's responsibilities with respect to internal control over computer systems remain the same as with manual systems, that is, to obtain an understanding adequate (1) to aid in planning the remainder of the audit and (2) to assess control risk. Yet the auditor's consideration of internal control may be affected in that computer systems may

a. Result in transaction trails that exist for a short period of time or only in computer-readable form
b. Include program errors that cause uniform mishandling of transactions—clerical errors become much less frequent
c. Include computer controls that need to be tested in addition to the segregation of functions
d. Involve increased difficulty in detecting unauthorized access
e. Allow increased management supervisory potential resulting from more timely reports
f. Include less documentation of initiation and execution of transactions

g. Include computer controls that affect the effectiveness of related manual control activities that use computer output

As is the case for all controls, the auditor needs to test operating effectiveness only when control risk is to be assessed below the maximum. General application controls may be tested through inquiry, observation, and inspection techniques. In addition, application controls may be tested using reperformance techniques outlined in the following section. Because general controls affect all computer applications, the auditor's initial focus should be on them since the effectiveness of specific application controls depends upon the effectiveness of the general controls.

2. **Computerized Audit Tools (CAAT) for Tests of Controls**

Tests of controls may be divided into the following categories of techniques: (a) program analysis, (b) program testing, (c) continuous testing, and (d) review of operating systems and other systems software.

a. **Techniques for program analysis.** These techniques allow the auditor to gain an understanding of the client's program. Because these techniques ordinarily are relatively time-consuming and require a high level of computer expertise, they are infrequently used in financial statement audits.

 (1) **Code review**—This technique involves actual analysis of the logic of the program's processing routines. The primary advantage is that the auditor obtains a detailed understanding of the program. Difficulties with the approach include the fact that it is extremely time-consuming, it requires a very high level of computer expertise, and difficulties involved with making certain that the program being verified is in fact the program in use throughout the accounting period.

 (2) **Comparison programs**—These programs allow the auditor to compare computerized files. For example, they can be used in a program analysis to determine that the auditor has the same version of the program that the client is using.

 (3) **Flowcharting software**—Flowcharting software is used to produce a flowchart of a program's logic and may be used both in mainframe and microcomputer environments. A difficulty involved is that the flowcharts of large programs become extremely involved.

 (4) **Program tracing and mapping**—Program tracing is a technique in which each instruction executed is listed along with control information affecting that instruction. Program mapping identifies sections of code that can be "entered" and thus are executable. These techniques allow an auditor to recognize logic sequences or dormant section of code that may be a potential source of abuse. The techniques are infrequently used because they are extremely time-consuming.

 (5) **Snapshot**—This technique in essence "takes a picture" of the status of program execution, intermediate results, or transaction data at specified processing points in the program processing. This technique helps an auditor to analyze the processing logic of specific programs.

b. **Techniques for program testing.** Program testing involves the use of auditor-controlled actual or simulated data. The approach provides direct evidence about the operation of programs and programmed controls. Historically, knowledge of these techniques has been tested relatively frequently on the CPA exam.

 (1) **Test data**—A set of dummy transactions is developed by the auditor and processed by the client's computer programs to determine whether the controls which the auditor intends to test (not necessarily all controls) to restrict control risk are operating effectively. Some of these dummy transactions may include errors to test effectiveness of programmed controls and to determine how transactions are handled (e.g., time tickets with invalid job numbers). When using test data, each control generally need only be tested once. Several possible problems include

   (a) Making certain the test data is not included in the client's accounting records
   (b) Determining that the program tested is actually used by the client to process data
   (c) Adequately developing test data for every possible control
   (d) Developing adequate data to test key controls may be extremely time-consuming

 (2) **Integrated test facility (ITF)**—This method introduces dummy transactions into a system in the midst of live transactions and is usually built into the system during the original design. One way to accomplish this is to incorporate a simulated or subsidiary into the accounting system with the sole purpose of running test data through it. The test data approach is similar and therefore its limitations are also similar, although the test data approach does not run simultaneously through the live system. The running of dummy transactions in the midst of live transactions makes the task of keeping the two transaction types separate more difficult.

 (3) **Parallel simulation**—Parallel simulation processes actual client data through an **auditor's generalized audit software program** and frequently, although not necessarily, the auditor's computer (generalized audit software is discussed in Section G. of this module). After processing the data the auditor compares the output obtained with output obtained from the client. The method verifies processing of **actual** transactions

(as opposed to test data and ITF that use dummy transactions) and allows the auditor to verify actual client results. This method allows an auditor to simply test portions of the system to reduce the overall time and concentrate on key controls. The limitations of this method include

(a) The time it takes to build an exact duplicate of the client's system
(b) Incompatibility between auditor and client software
(c) Tracing differences between the two sets of outputs to differences in the programs may be difficult
(d) The time involved in processing large quantities of data

(4) **Controlled reprocessing**—Controlled reprocessing, a variation of parallel simulation, processes actual client data through a copy of the **client's application program**. As with parallel simulation, this method uses actual transactions and the auditor compares the output obtained with output obtained from the client. Limitations of this method include

(a) Determining that the copy of the program is identical to that currently being used by the client
(b) Keeping current with changes in the program
(c) The time involved in reprocessing large quantities of data

c. **Techniques for continuous (or concurrent) testing.** Advanced computer systems, particularly those utilizing EDI, sometimes do not retain permanent audit trails, thus requiring capture of audit data as transactions are processed. Such systems may require audit procedures that are able to identify and capture audit data as transactions occur.

(1) **Embedded audit modules and audit hooks**—Embedded audit modules are programmed routines incorporated into an application program that are designed to perform an audit function such as a calculation, or logging activity. Because embedded audit modules require that the auditor be involved in system design of the application to be monitored, this approach is often not practical. An audit hook is an exit point in an application program that allows an auditor to subsequently add an audit module (or particular instructions) by activating the hook to transfer control to an audit module.

(2) **Systems control audit review files (SCARF)**—A SCARF is a log, usually created by an embedded audit module, used to collect information for subsequent review and analysis. The auditor determines the appropriate criteria for review and the SCARF selects that type of transaction, dollar limit, or other characteristic.

(3) **Extended records**—This technique attaches additional data that would not otherwise be saved to regular historic records and thereby helps to provide a more complicated audit trail. The extended record information may subsequently be analyzed.

(4) **Transaction tagging**—Tagging is a technique in which an identifier providing a transaction with a special designation is added to the transaction record. The tag is often used to allow logging of transactions or snapshot of activities.

d. **Techniques for review of operating systems and other systems software.** Systems software may perform controls for computer systems. Related audit techniques range from user-written programs to the use of purchasing operating systems monitoring software.

(1) **Job accounting data/operating systems logs**—These logs, created by either the operating system itself or additional software packages that track particular functions, include reports of the resources used by the computer system. Because these logs provide a record of the activity of the computer system, the auditor may be able to use them to review the work processed, to determine whether unauthorized applications were processed, and to determine that authorized applications were processed properly.

(2) **Library management software**—This software logs changes in programs, program modules, job control language, and other processing activities. Auditors may review these logs.

(3) **Access control and security software**—This software supplements the physical and control measures relating to the computer and is particularly helpful in online environments or in systems with data communications because of difficulties of physically securing computers. Access control and security software restricts access to computers to authorized personnel through techniques such as only allowing certain users with "read-only" access or through use of encryption. An auditor may perform tests of the effectiveness of the use of such software.

3. Information technology (IT) provides potential benefits of effectiveness and efficiency because it enables an entity to

a. Consistently apply predefined business rules and perform complex calculations on large volumes of transactions
b. Enhance timeliness, availability, and accuracy of information
c. Facilitate the additional analysis of information
d. Enhance the ability to monitor the performance of the entity's activities and its policies and procedures

   e. Reduce risk that controls will be circumvented
   f. Enhance ability to achieve effective segregation of duties by implementing security controls in applications, databases, and operating systems

4. IT poses specific risks to internal control including

   a. Systems or programs may inaccurately process information
   b. Unauthorized access to data may lead to destruction of data or inappropriate changes to data
   c. Unauthorized changes to data in master files
   d. Unauthorized changes to systems or programs
   e. Failure to make necessary changes to systems or programs
   f. Inappropriate manual intervention
   g. Potential loss of data

5. Use of an IT specialist

   a. In determining whether specialized IT skills are needed to design and perform the audit, the auditor considers factors such as

      (1) Complexity of entity's systems and IT controls
      (2) Significance of changes made to existing systems, or implementation of new systems
      (3) Extent to which data is shared among systems
      (4) Extent of entity's participation in electronic commerce
      (5) Entity's use of emerging technologies
      (6) Significance of audit evidence available only in electronic form

   b. Procedures an auditor may assign to a professional possessing IT skills

      (1) Inquiring of entity's IT personnel on how data and transaction are initiated, recorded, processed, and reported, and how IT controls are designed
      (2) Inspecting systems documentation
      (3) Observing operation of IT controls
      (4) Planning and performing of tests of IT controls

6. Documenting the understanding of internal control

   a. For an information system with a large volume of transactions that are electronically initiated, recorded, processed, or reported, may include flowcharts, questionnaires, or decision tables
   b. For an information system with limited or no use of IT, or for which few transactions are processed (e.g., long-term debt) a memorandum may be sufficient
   c. When an auditor is performing only substantive tests to restrict detection risk to an acceptable level, the auditor should obtain evidence about the accuracy and completeness of the information

7. Effects of IT on assessment of control risk

   a. In determining whether to assess control risk at the maximum level or at a lower level, the auditor should consider

      (1) Nature of the assertion
      (2) Volume of transactions
      (3) Nature and complexity of systems, including use of IT
      (4) Nature of available evidential matter, including evidence in electronic form

   b. In designing tests of automated controls

      (1) The inherent consistency of IT processing may allow the auditor to reduce the extent of testing (e.g., use a smaller sample)
      (2) Computer-assisted audit techniques may be needed for automated controls

8. Effects of IT on restriction of detection risk

   a. An auditor may assess control risk at the maximum and perform substantive tests to restrict detection risk when he or she believes that the substantive tests by themselves would be more efficient than performing tests of controls; for example

      (1) Client has only a limited number of transactions related to fixed assets and long-term debt and the auditor can readily obtain corroborating evidence in the form of documents and confirmations.

b. When evidence is entirely or almost entirely electronic, the auditor in some circumstances may need to perform tests of controls. This is because it may be impossible to design effective substantive tests that by themselves provide sufficient evidence in circumstances such as when the client

   (1) Uses IT to initiate order using predetermined decisions rules and to pay related payables based on system-generating information, and no other documentation is produced
   (2) Provides electronic service to customers (e.g., Internet service provider or telephone company) and uses IT to log service provided, initiate bills, process billing, and automatically record amounts in accounting records

---

NOW REVIEW MULTIPLE-CHOICE QUESTIONS 1 THROUGH 18 IN VOLUME 2

B. Computerized Audit Tools

A variety of computerized audit tools (which may also be viewed as computer assisted audit techniques) are available for administering, planning, performing, and reporting of an audit. We present a summary of major types.

1. **Generalized Audit Software (GAS)**

   The auditor may use various types of software on PCs (or other computers) and may include customized programs, utility software, and generalized audit software for performing tests of controls and substantive tests. Customized programs are written specifically for a client. Commercially produced utility software is used for sorting, merging, and other file maintenance tasks. Generalized audit software also performs such file maintenance tasks but generally requires a more limited understanding of the client's hardware and software features. The following is a list of functions performed by GAS (it is based on the AICPA Auditing Procedure Study *Auditing with Computers*):

   a. Record extraction—Extract (copy) records that meet certain criteria, such as

      (1) Accounts receivable balances over the credit limit
      (2) Inventory items with negative quantities or unreasonably large quantities
      (3) Uncosted inventory items
      (4) Transactions with related parties

   b. Sorting (e.g., ascending or descending order)
   c. Summarization, such as

      (1) By customer account number
      (2) Inventory turnover statistics
      (3) Duplicate sales invoices

   d. Field statistics, such as

      (1) Net value
      (2) Total of all debt (credit values)
      (3) Number of records
      (4) Average value
      (5) Maximum (minimum) value
      (6) Standard deviation

   e. File comparison, such as

      (1) Compare payroll details with personnel records
      (2) Compare current and prior period inventory files

   f. Gap detection/duplicate detection—Find missing or duplicate records
   g. Sampling
   h. Calculation
   i. Exportation—Select an application that has been performed using GAS and export to another file format (for additional analysis)

2. **Electronic Spreadsheets**

   Electronic spreadsheets, often included in generalized audit software, may be used for applications such as analytical procedures and performing mathematical procedures. Also, auditors often use microcomputer electronic spreadsheets to prepare working trial balances, lead, and other schedules. Such spreadsheets may significantly simplify the computational aspects of tasks such as incorporating adjustments and reclassifications on a worksheet and are relatively easy to use, inexpensive, and can be saved and easily modified in the future. Disadvantages include the need for auditor training, and the fact that original spreadsheet development takes a significant amount of time.

3. **Automated Workpaper Software**

Automated workpaper software, generally microcomputer based, is increasingly being used by auditors. Originally used to generate trial balances, lead schedules, and other workpapers, advances in computer technology (e.g., improvements in scanning) make possible an electronic workpaper environment. Ordinarily, this type of software is easy to use and inexpensive. The primary disadvantage is the time required to enter the data for the first year being audited.

4. **Database Management Systems**

We have discussed database management systems in Section C. of this module. Database management software may be used to perform analytical procedures, mathematical calculations, generation of confirmation requests, and to prepare customized automated workpapers. An auditor may, for example, download relevant client files into his or her database and analyze the data as desired. Advantages of this approach include a great opportunity for the auditor to rearrange, edit, analyze, and evaluate a data file in a manner well beyond that possible to be performed manually and the ability to download client data without time-consuming data entry. Disadvantages include auditor training (more than with spreadsheets) and the need for adequate client documentation of applications.

5. **Text Retrieval Software**

Text retrieval software (also referred to as text database software) enables access to such databases as the AICPA Professional Standards and various FASB and SEC pronouncements. This software allows an auditor to research technical issues quickly and requires minimal training. Disadvantages include the fact that some training is required and that some professional literature is not currently available in software form.

6. **Public Databases**

Public databases may be used to obtain accounting information related to particular companies and industries as well as other publicly available information on, for example, electronic bulletin boards, that an auditor may use. Current developments for companies and their industries may be obtained from the Internet. The Internet provides online access to newspaper and journal articles. In addition, many companies and industry associations have World Wide Web home pages that describe current developments and statistics.

7. **Word Processing Software**

Auditors use word processing software in a variety of communication-related manners including the consideration of internal control, developing audit programs, and reporting.

> **NOW REVIEW MULTIPLE-CHOICE QUESTIONS 19 THROUGH 32 IN VOLUME 2**

KEY TERMS

Computer assisted auditing techniques. The practice of using computers to automate or simplify the audit process In the broadest sense of the term, they can refer to any use of a computer during the audit.

Controlled reprocessing. A variation of parallel simulation, processes actual client data through a copy of the client's application program. As with parallel simulation, this method uses actual transactions and the auditor compares the output obtained with output obtained from the client.

Generalized audit software. Software designed to read, process, and write data with the help of functions performing specific audit routines and with self-made macros. It is a tool in applying computer assisted auditing techniques. Functions of generalized audit software include importing computerized data; thereafter other functions can be applied (e.g., the data can be browsed, sorted, summarized, stratified, analyzed, taken samples from, and made calculations, conversions, and other operations with).

Integrated test facility (ITF). This method introduces dummy transactions into a system in the midst of live transactions and is usually built into the system during the original design. One way to accomplish this is to incorporate a simulated or subsidiary into the accounting system with the sole purpose of running test data through it. The test data approach is similar and therefore its limitations are also similar, although the test data approach does not run simultaneously through the live system. The running of dummy transactions in the midst of live transactions makes the task of keeping the two transaction types separate more difficult.

Parallel simulation. Parallel simulation processes actual client data through an auditor's generalized audit software program and frequently, although not necessarily, the auditor's computer (generalized audit software is discussed in Section G. of this module). After processing the data the auditor compares the output obtained with output obtained from the client. The method verifies processing of actual transactions (as opposed to test data and ITF that use dummy transactions) and allows the auditor to verify actual client results. This method allows an auditor to simply test portions of the system to reduce the overall time and concentrate on key controls.

Test data. A set of dummy transactions is developed by the auditor and processed by the client's computer programs to determine whether the controls which the auditor intends to test (not necessarily all controls) to restrict control risk are operating effectively. Some of these dummy transactions may include errors to test effectiveness of programmed controls and to determine how transactions are handled (e.g., time tickets with invalid job numbers). When using test data, each control generally need only be tested once.

Outlines of Professional Standards

This section presents outlines of (1) the Statements on Standards for Attestation Engagements, (2) the Statements on Auditing Standards, and (3) the Statements on Standards for Accounting and Review Services. When codified sequence differs from chronological sequence, we have presented the outlines in codified sequence. Study these outlines in conjunction with the related topical material (e.g., ethics, reports, etc.).

STATEMENTS ON STANDARDS FOR ATTESTATION ENGAGEMENTS

Overview. The Statements on Standards for Attestation Engagements are issued by three organizations: (1) the Auditing Standards Board, (2) the Accounting and Review Services Committee, and (3) the Management Advisory Services Executive Committee.

AT 20 Defining Professional Requirements in Statements on Standards for Attestation Engagements (SSAE 13)—This section sets forth the meaning of terms in SSAEs. Similar to Statements on Auditing Standards, SSAEs includes the following type of requirements:

A. **Unconditional requirements**—The accountant is required to comply in all cases in which the circumstances exist. SSAEs use the words *must* or *is required* to indicate an unconditional requirement.

B. **Presumptively mandatory requirements**—The accountant is required to comply in all cases in which the circumstances exist. However, in rare cases the accountant may depart provided that the accountant documents the justification and how alternative procedures performed were adequate. SSAEs use the word *should* to indicate a presumptively mandatory requirement.

AT 50 SSAE Hierarchy (SSAE 14)—This section sets forth the authoritative level of various attestation guidance.

A. **Generally Accepted Attestation Standards and Statements on Standards for Attestation Engagements**

   1. An accountant must identify those applicable to the engagement and exercise professional judgment in applying SSAEs.
   2. An accountant must document justification for departures and explain how alternative procedures were sufficient.

B. **Attestation Interpretations** consist of Interpretations of SSAEs, appendixes to SSAEs, attestation guidance in AICPA Audit and Accounting Guides, and AICPA Statements of Position.

   1. Accountant must be aware of this guidance.
   2. Accountant who does not apply should be prepared to explain how s/he complied with the applicable SSAE.

C. **Other attestation publications,** such as articles, textbooks, etc.

   1. Have no authoritative status, but may help the accountant apply SSAEs.

AT 101 Attestation Standards

Overall Objectives and Approach—This section is composed of (1) definitions and underlying concepts and (2) the eleven attestation standards with related explanations. This information is the general framework for attest services. Subsequent AT sections take the information included in AT 101 as a starting point and provide additional guidance, generally a particular type of service (e.g., reporting on internal control, or compliance with laws and regulations).

The scope of the section includes engagements in which a CPA is engaged to issue or does issue an examination, a review, or an agreed-upon procedures report on subject matter—or an assertion about the subject matter—that is the responsibility of another party. However, only limited guidance is provided relating to agreed-upon procedures engagements, which are discussed in detail in AT 201. Be aware that services explicitly **excluded** from this section's coverage include services and engagements performed

- Under Statements on Auditing Standards (see the AU outlines)
- Under Statements on Standards for Accounting and Review Services (see the AR outlines)
- Under Statements on Standards for Consulting Services
- Advocating a client's position (e.g., matters being reviewed by the Internal Revenue Service)
- Preparing tax returns or providing tax advice.

The following outline has four sections. Section A defines and provides underlying concepts relating to attest engagements. Sections B, C, and D present the general, fieldwork, and reporting standards, respectively. Note that the attest standards are included in *italics* as numbered subheadings under Sections B, C, and D. Finally, while the standards use the term "practitioner" in most places, we will use the term "CPA."

A. Definitions and underlying concepts

1. **Subject matter**—May take many forms, including

   a. Historical or prospective performance or condition (e.g., prospective financial statements)
   b. Physical characteristics (e.g., narrative descriptions, square footage of facilities)
   c. Historical events (e.g., price of goods at a certain date)
   d. Analyses (e.g., breakeven analyses)
   e. Systems and processes (e.g., internal control)
   f. Behavior (e.g., corporate governance, compliance with laws and regulations, human resource practices)

2. **Assertion**—Any declaration or set of declarations about whether the subject matter is based on or in conformity with the criteria selected

   a. A CPA may report on a written assertion or on the subject matter
   b. When a written assertion is not obtained the use of the report should be restricted

3. **Responsible party**—The party responsible for the subject matter

   a. A CPA should obtain written acknowledgement or other evidence of responsible party's responsibility
   b. Most frequently, the responsible party is top management

B. General standards

1. First general standard—The engagement shall be performed by a practitioner having adequate technical training and proficiency in the attest function
2. Second general standard—The engagement shall be performed by a practitioner having adequate knowledge of the subject matter
3. Third general standard—The practitioner shall perform the engagement only if he or she has reason to believe that the subject matter is capable of reasonably consistent evaluation against criteria that are suitable and available to users

   a. Suitable criteria

      (1) Are the standards or benchmarks used to measure and present the subject matter and against which the CPA evaluates the subject matter

      > **NOTE:** To illustrate the suitable criteria concept, think of financial statements—the suitable criteria are frequently generally accepted accounting principles. We use this illustration because most are familiar with generally accepted accounting principles. Recognize that historical financial statements are not included under the attestation standards.

      (2) Although trade-offs exist, suitable criteria must be

         (a) Objective
         (b) Measurable
         (c) Complete
         (d) Relevant

   b. Guidelines on suitable criteria

      (1) Criteria established or developed by groups composed of experts that follow due process (e.g., FASB) are ordinarily considered suitable
      (2) Criteria established or developed by management, industry associations, or other groups that do not follow due process may or may not be suitable
      (3) Some criteria are suitable only to a limited number of parties who participated in their establishment or have an understanding of them

         (a) In such circumstance use of the report should be restricted to those parties

   c. Criteria should be available in one or more of the following ways

      (1) Publicly
      (2) Inclusion with the subject matter or in the assertion
      (3) Inclusion in CPA's report
      (4) Well understood by most users (e.g., The distance between A and B is twenty feet)
      (5) Available only to specified parties

         (a) In this circumstance the CPA's report should be restricted to those parties

4. Fourth general standard—In all matters relating to the engagement, an independence in mental attitude shall be maintained by the practitioner

C. Standards of fieldwork

1. First fieldwork standard—The work shall be adequately planned and assistants, if any, shall be properly supervised
2. Second fieldwork standard—Sufficient evidence shall be obtained to provide a reasonable basis for the conclusion that is expressed in the report

   a. Presumptions

      (1) Evidence from independent sources provides greater assurance than evidence secured solely from within the entity
      (2) Information obtained from direct personal knowledge is more persuasive than information obtained indirectly
      (3) The more effective the controls over subject matter, the more assurance they provide about the subject matter or assertion

      NOTE: Recall that the above presumptions are also presented in AU 326.

3. Types of attest engagements

   a. **Examination**—CPA selects from all available procedures and provides a high level of assurance to limit attestation risk to an appropriately low level
   b. **Review**—CPA generally limits procedures to inquiries and analytical procedures and provides a moderate level of assurance to limit attestation risk to moderate level
   c. **Agreed-upon procedures**—Presented in AT 201

D. Standards of reporting

1. First reporting standard—The report shall identify the subject matter or the assertion being reported on and state the character of the engagement
2. Second reporting standard—The report shall state the practitioner's conclusion about the subject matter or the assertion in relation to the criteria against which the subject matter was evaluated
3. Third reporting standard—The report shall state all of the practitioner's significant reservations about the engagement, the subject matter, and if applicable, the assertion related thereto
4. Fourth reporting standard—The report shall state that the use of the report is restricted to specified parties under the following circumstances [abridged]:

   a. Criteria are suitable only for a limited number of parties
   b. Subject matter is available only to specified parties
   c. Written assertion has not been provided by the responsible party
   d. Agreed-upon procedures engagements

5. An examination report on subject matter [assertion] should include

   a. Title with word "independent"
   b. Identification of subject matter [assertion]
   c. Subject matter [assertion] is the responsibility of the responsible party
   d. CPA's responsibility is to express opinion on subject matter [assertion]
   e. Examination conducted in accordance with attestation standard established by AICPA
   f. Examination provides reasonable basis for opinion
   g. Opinion on whether subject matter [assertion] follows criteria
   h. Statement restricting use of report as per fourth reporting standard (D.4. above)
   i. Manual or printed signature of firm
   j. Date of report

6. A review report on subject matter [assertion] should include

   a. Title with word "independent"
   b. Identification of subject matter [assertion]
   c. Subject matter [assertion] is the responsibility of the responsible party
   d. Review conducted in accordance with attestation standards established by AICPA
   e. Review substantially less in scope than an examination, the objective of which is expression of an opinion, and accordingly, no such opinion is expressed
   f. Statement about whether CPA is aware of any material modifications needed for subject matter [assertion] to comply with criteria

g. Statement restricting use of report as per fourth reporting standard (D.4. above)
h. Manual or printed signature of firm
i. Date of report

E. Attest documentation

1. Purposes

   a. Principal support for practitioner's report
   b. Aid in conduct and supervision of engagement

2. Should be sufficient to

   a. Enable members of engagement team with supervision and review responsibilities to understand nature, timing, extent, and results of attest procedures performed and information obtained
   b. Indicate who performed and reviewed the work

AT 201 Agreed-Upon Procedures Engagements

Overall Objectives and Approach—This section sets forth attestation requirements and provides guidance for a CPA's performance of agreed-upon procedures (AUP) engagements. Recall that auditors currently perform three types of attestation engagements—examinations and reviews (emphasized in AT 101) and agreed-upon procedures. Because many of the concepts in AT 201 carry over from AT 101, make certain that you are familiar with that information.

A. An agreed-upon procedures engagement is one in which a CPA is engaged by a client to issue a report of findings based on specific procedures performed on subject matter

1. The client engages the CPA to assist specified parties in evaluating subject matter or an assertion

   a. Specified parties and the CPA agree upon the procedures that the specified parties believe appropriate
   b. Specified parties assume responsibility for the sufficiency of the procedures
   c. CPA's report should indicate that its use is restricted to those specified parties

> **EXAMPLE**
>
> Assume that representatives of a bank ask that specified procedures be performed on balance sheet accounts that are to serve as collateral for a loan to a CPA's client. Those representatives would ordinarily be considered specified parties.

2. A CPA may perform an AUP engagement provided that

   a. CPA is independent
   b. Party that wishes to engage CPA is

      (1) Responsible for subject matter, or has a reasonable basis for providing a written assertion about the subject matter **or**
      (2) **Not** responsible for the subject matter but is able to provide CPA, or have a third party who is responsible for the subject matter provide evidence of third party's responsibility for the subject matter

   c. CPA and specified parties agree on procedures to be performed
   d. Specified parties take responsibility for sufficiency of procedures
   e. Subject matter involved is subject to reasonably consistent measurement
   f. Criteria used to determine findings are agreed upon between CPA and specified parties
   g. Procedures applied are expected to result in reasonably consistent findings using the criteria
   h. Evidential matter is expected to provide reasonable basis for expressing findings
   i. Where applicable, CPA and specified parties agree on materiality limits
   j. Use of report restricted to specified parties
   k. For AUP engagements on prospective financial information, the statements include a summary of significant findings

3. A written assertion is generally **not** required
4. CPA should establish an understanding with client about a variety of matters including—nature of engagement, identification of subject matter, specified parties, use restrictions, etc.

B. Procedures, findings, and working papers

1. Responsibility

   a. Specified parties—sufficiency of agreed-upon procedures

b. CPA—perform procedures and report findings in accordance with attest standards and have adequate knowledge of subject matter

2. Procedures performed may be limited or extensive

a. But mere reading of an assertion or specified information about subject matter does not constitute a sufficient procedure to report on AUP

b. CPA should not agree to perform procedures so overly subjective and possibly open to varying interpretations; examples are

(1) Reading work performed by others solely to describe their findings
(2) Evaluating competency or objectivity of another party
(3) Obtaining understanding about a particular subject
(4) Interpreting documents outside scope of CPA's expertise

c. In certain circumstances a specialist may be called to assist the CPA in performing one or more procedures

3. Report should be in form of findings, and should **not** include negative assurance
4. The concept of materiality limits does not in general apply, unless agreed to by the specified parties
5. Working papers should indicate that work was adequately planned and supervised and that adequate evidential matter was obtained

C. Reporting

1. Required elements

a. Title with word "independent"
b. Identification of specified parties
c. Identification of subject matter (or written assertion related thereto) and character of engagement
d. Subject matter responsibility of responsible party
e. Procedures performed agreed to by specified parties
f. AUP engagements conducted in accordance with attestation standards established by AICPA
g. Sufficiency of procedures responsibility of specified parties
h. List of procedures performed and related findings
i. Description of agreed-upon materiality limits (if any)
j. CPA not engaged to perform examination, disclaimer on subject matter, statement that if additional procedures had been performed other matters might come to CPA's attention
k. Statement restricting use of report to specified parties
l. For AUP on prospective financial information, items required under AT 301
m. Where applicable, description of nature of assistance provided by specialist
n Manual or printed signature of CPA's firm
o. Date of report

2. Explanatory language may be included, such as

a. Stipulated facts, assumptions, interpretations
b. Condition of records, controls, etc.
c. Explanation that CPA has no responsibility to update report
d. Explanation of sampling risk

3. Report should be dated as of date of completion of agreed-upon procedures
4. If CPA's procedures restricted, CPA should describe restrictions in report or withdraw
5. Additional specified parties may be added if they agree to take responsibility for sufficiency of procedures

D. Other

1. CPA may wish to, but is not required to, obtain representation letter from responsible party
2. A CPA who has performed another form of attest or nonattest engagement may be requested to change engagement to AUP engagement

a. Before changing to AUP, the CPA should consider

(1) Possibility that procedures performed for other engagement not appropriate for AUP
(2) Reason for request
(3) Additional effort required
(4) If applicable, reasons for changing from general-use report to restricted-use report

    b. In all circumstances, if original engagement substantially complete, CPA should consider propriety of accepting a change in the engagement

  3. AUP reports may be combined with reports on other services (e.g., audit of financial statements) providing types of services clearly distinguished and report remains restricted

AT 301 Financial Forecasts and Projections

Overall Objectives and Approach—This section sets forth standards and provides guidance for CPAs who are engaged to issue examination, compilation, or agreed-upon procedures reports on prospective financial information. As a starting point, it is important that you understand the basic information presented in Section A of the outline. That information is used throughout the remainder of the outline. Sections B, C, and D of the outline provide information on the three basic forms of CPA association with prospective financial information—compilations, examinations, and agreed-upon procedures. (CPAs do **not** perform reviews on prospective information.) Recognize that standards for the compilation form of association is not included in AT sections other than AT 301.

A. Definition and basic concepts

  1. Prospective financial statements—Partial presentations, financial forecasts, and financial projections

    a. Types

      (1) **Prospective forecasts**—Either financial forecasts or financial projections, including summaries of significant assumptions and accounting policies

      (2) **Partial presentations**—A presentation of prospective financial information that excludes one or more of the items required for prospective financial statements (see b. below)

      (3) **Financial forecasts**—Prospective financial statements that present the responsible party's beliefs about the entity's expected financial position, results of operations, and cash flows

      (4) **Financial projection**—Prospective financial statements that present expected results, to the best of the responsible party's knowledge and belief **given one or more hypothetical assumptions**. A projection is a "what would happen if. . .?" statement.

    b. Minimum disclosures

      (1) **Financial statement information:** sales, gross profit (or cost of goods sold), unusual or infrequently occurring items, provision for income taxes, discontinued operations, extraordinary items, income from continuing operations, net income, earnings per share, and significant cash flows

      (2) **Background information:** purpose of prospective statements, assumptions, and significant accounting policies

      (3) **Assumptions**

> **NOTE:** Omission of group 1 items creates a "partial presentation" not considered in the Statement. Omission of group 2 items in the presence of group 1 items results in a presentation subject to the provisions of this Statement. The accountant should not compile or examine statements lacking disclosure of assumptions (group 3).

    c. **Pro forma statements** (those which show how a hypothetical transaction might have affected historical statements) and accountant financial analysis of a particular project are not included under provisions of this statement

    d. Financial forecasts and projections may both be in the form of single point estimates or ranges (in which case a paragraph discussing the estimates or ranges is added to report)

    e. Uses of prospective financial statements

      (1) **General**—May be used by persons with whom the responsible party is not negotiating directly (e.g., in an offering statement for debt or equity interests). Only a forecast is appropriate for general use

      (2) **Limited**—May only be used by responsible party or by responsible party and third parties with whom responsible party is negotiating directly. A forecast or a projection is appropriate for limited use

  2. Accountant independence—an accountant need **not** be independent to perform a compilation, but must be independent to perform an examination or agreed-upon procedures

    a. When the accountant is not independent when performing a compilation, this is indicated in a separate paragraph added to the report. If the accountant elects to disclose a description about the reasons for a lack of independence, he or she should ensure that all reasons are included.

  3. The accountant's report should not indicate that engagement included "preparation" of prospective financial statements

B. Compilations of prospective financial statements

  1. Compilation procedures

    a. Assemble, to extent necessary, based on responsible party's assumptions

    b. **Perform required compilation procedures**

      (1) Establish understanding with client (preferably in writing) about services to be performed

      (2) Inquire about accounting principles used

      (3) Ask how responsible party identifies key factors and assumptions

      (4) List (or obtain a list of) significant assumptions and consider its completeness

      (5) Consider whether there are obvious inconsistencies in assumptions

      (6) Test mathematical accuracy

      (7) Read statements for conformity with AICPA guidelines and determine that assumptions are not obviously inappropriate

      (8) If a significant portion of prospective period has expired, inquire about actual results

      (9) Obtain written client representation letter (signed by responsible party at highest level of authority)

     (10) Attempt to obtain additional or revised information when above procedures make errors seem likely

  2. Compilation reports (see the standard report in the Reporting Module)

    a. A compilation report on prospective financial information should include

      (1) Identification of prospective financial statements

      (2) Statements compiled in accordance with attestation standards established by AICPA

      (3) Compilation limited in scope and does not enable accountant to express opinion or any other form of assurance on prospective financial statements

      (4) Prospective results may not be achieved

      (5) Accountant assumes no responsibility to update the report after its issuance

    b. Circumstances resulting in departure from standard compilation report

      (1) Presentation deficiencies or disclosure omissions, other than a significant assumption (clearly indicate deficiency in report)

      (2) Comprehensive basis statements which do not disclose the basis used (disclose the basis in the report)

      (3) Summary of significant accounting policies omitted (a paragraph is needed which discloses that the policies have been omitted)

C. Examinations of prospective financial statements

  1. Examination procedures

    a. Evaluate preparation

    b. Perform examination procedures

      (1) Reach an **understanding with client** (ordinarily confirmed in an engagement letter)

      (2) **Evaluate the support for underlying assumptions** (consider available support, consistency, reliability of underlying historical information, logical arguments or theory)

      (3) **Obtain written representation letter** (signed by responsible party at highest level of authority)

    c. Evaluate presentation for conformity with AICPA presentation guidelines (especially, that presentations reflect assumptions)

  2. The examination report on prospective financial statements should include

    a. Title with the word independent

    b. Identification of prospective financial statements

    c. Identification of responsible party

    d. CPA's responsibility is to express opinion on the prospective financial information

    e. Examination conducted in accordance with attestation standards established by AICPA

    f. Examination provides reasonable basis for opinion

    g. Opinion on whether subject matter (assertion) follows criteria

    h. Caveat that prospective results may not be obtained

    i. CPA assumes no responsibility to update report

    j. Manual or printed signature of firm

    k. Date of report

  3. Circumstances resulting in departure from standard examination report

a. Departure from AICPA presentation guidelines (result in a qualified or adverse opinion)
b. Unreasonable assumptions (adverse opinion)
c. Scope limitation (disclaimer)
d. Emphasis of a matter (unqualified)
e. Evaluation based in part on report of another auditor (unqualified—divided responsibility)

D. Application of agreed-upon procedures to prospective financial statements

1. An accountant engaged to perform agreed-upon procedures on prospective financial statements should follow SSAE 4 guidance (included in outline of AU 622)
2. An agreed-upon procedures engagement may be performed if

    a. The accountant is independent
    b. The accountant and specified users agree on procedures
    c. The specified users take responsibility for sufficiency of the agreed-upon procedures
    d. The prospective financial statements include a summary of significant assumptions
    e. The prospective financial statements to which the procedures are applied are subject to reasonably consistent estimation or measurement
    f. Criteria to be used (accounting principles, policies and assumptions) are agreed upon between the accountant and the specified users
    g. Procedures are expected to result in reasonably consistent findings using the criteria
    h. Evidential matter to which the procedures are applied is expected to exist to provide a reasonable basis for expressing the findings in the accountant's report
    i. Where applicable, there is agreement on any materiality limits
    j. Use of the report is restricted to the specified users (although an accountant may perform an engagement pursuant to which his or her report will be matter of public record)

3. The procedures may be as limited or as extensive as specified users desire, but must exceed mere reading of the prospective financial statements
4. The report on agreed-upon procedures should be in the form of procedures and findings and include

    a. Title with word "independent"
    b. Identification of specified parties
    c. Reference to the prospective financial statements and the character of the engagement
    d. Statement that procedures were agreed to by specified parties
    e. Identification of responsible party
    f. Reference to attestation standards established by AICPA
    g. Sufficiency of procedures responsibility of specified parties and a disclaimer of responsibility for sufficiency of those procedures
    h. List of procedures performed (or reference thereto) and related findings
    i. Where applicable, a description of any agreed-upon materiality limits
    j. Statement that CPA did not perform an examination of prospective financial statements; a disclaimer of opinion; if the CPA had performed additional procedures, other matters might have come to his or her attention that would have been reported
    k. A statement of restriction on the use of report because it is intended to be used solely by the specified parties
    l. Various other restrictions
    m. A caveat that prospective results may not be achieved
    n. A statement that accountant assumes no responsibility to update report
    o. Description of nature of assistance provided by a specialist (if applicable)
    p. Manual or printed signature of practitioner's firm
    q. The report should be dated as of the completion of the agreed-upon procedures

AT 401 Reporting on Pro Forma Financial Information

Overall Objective and Approach—This section presents guidance on appropriate procedures and for reporting on certain pro forma financial information. As a starting point, this section **does not** apply to circumstances in which (1) pro forma information is presented within the same document, but not with financial statements (see the outline of AU 550) or (2) financial statements footnote information includes pro forma information (e.g., to show a revision of debt maturities, or a revision of earnings per share for a stock split).

This section **does** apply to pro forma financial information, presented with the basic financial statements, used to show the effects of an underlying transaction or event (hereafter, simply transaction). Such transactions include possible (1) business combinations, (2) changes in capitalization, (3) disposition of a significant portion of a business, and (4) proposed sale of securities and the application of proceeds. For example, a company which is considering issuing debt might prepare pro forma financial information to indicate what the effect of granting a loan in the prior period would have been. The pro forma financial information must be included with the historical financial statements. Thus, financial statements would generally have a column for historical information, and one for pro forma information.

This section divides much of the procedural and reporting advice into three areas—(1) determining that the assumptions are reasonable, (2) determining that the assumptions lead to the adjustments, and (3) determining that the adjustments have been properly reflected in the "pro forma column." The outline is divided into (a) procedural requirements and (b) reporting requirements.

A. Procedural requirements

1. The overall approach is to apply pro forma adjustments to historical financial information
2. An accountant may agree to report on an **examination** or a **review** of pro forma financial information if the following conditions are met

    a. The document with the pro forma financial information includes (or incorporates by reference) complete financial statements for the most recent period
    b. The historical financial statements on which the pro forma financial information is based have been audited or reviewed

    (1) The level of assurance for the pro forma financial information should be limited to the level of assurance provided on the historical financial statements

    > **EXAMPLE**
    >
    > When the historical financial statements have been audited, the pro forma financial information may be examined or reviewed. When the historical financial statements have been reviewed, the pro forma financial information may only be reviewed.

    c. The accountant must have an appropriate level of knowledge of the accounting and financial reporting practices of each significant part of the combined entity

    > **EXAMPLE**
    >
    > In a business combination between Company A and Company B, the accountant reporting on the pro forma financial information must obtain the knowledge relating to both companies, even if s/he has only audited one of them.

3. The objective of an accountant's examination or review procedures relates to whether

    a. Management's assumptions are reasonable
    b. The pro forma adjustments appropriately follow from the assumptions
    c. The pro forma financial information column of numbers reflects proper application of the adjustments

    > **NOTE:** When performing an examination, or review, reasonable assurance and negative assurance, respectively, are provided.

4. The following procedures should be applied to assumptions and pro forma adjustments for either an examination or a review

    a. Obtain knowledge of each part of the combined entity in a business combination
    b. Obtain an understanding of the underlying transaction (e.g., read contracts, minutes of meetings, make inquiries)
    c. Procedures applied to the assumptions

    (1) Discuss with management
    (2) Evaluate whether they are presented in a clear and comprehensive manner and are consistent with one another

    d. Procedures applied to the adjustments and their accumulation

    (1) Obtain sufficient evidence in support of adjustments
    (2) Evaluate whether pro forma adjustments are included for all significant effects of the transaction
    (3) Evaluate whether adjustments are consistent with one another and with the data used to develop them
    (4) Determine that computation of pro forma adjustments are mathematically correct and properly accumulated

    e. Obtain written representations from management concerning their

  (1) Responsibility for the assumptions
  (2) Belief that the assumptions are reasonable, that adjustments give effect to the assumptions, and that pro forma column reflects application of those adjustments
  (3) Belief that significant effects attributable to the transactions are properly disclosed

f. Read the pro forma financial information and determine that the following disclosures are presented

  (1) Underlying transaction, pro forma adjustments, significant assumptions, and significant uncertainties
  (2) The source of the historical financial information on which the pro forma financial information is based has been appropriately identified

B. Reporting on pro forma financial information

  1. Overall issues

    a. The report on the pro forma financial information may be added to the accountant's report on the historical financial information, or it may appear separately
    b. The report on pro forma financial information should be dated as of the completion of the appropriate procedures

      (1) When the reports on the historical and the pro forma financial information are combined, and when the completion of the pro forma procedures is after the completion of fieldwork for the audit or review of the historical financial information, the report should be dual dated

        (a) For example, "March 1, 20X8, except for the paragraphs referring to the pro forma financial information, for which the date is March 20, 20X8"

  2. The CPA's report on pro forma financial information should include

    a. Title with word "independent"
    b. Identification of pro forma financial information
    c. Reference to financial statements from which historical information derived
    d. Identification of responsible party
    e. CPA's responsibility is to express opinion on the pro forma financial
    f. Examination conducted in accordance with attestation standards established by AICPA
    g. Examination provides reasonable basis for opinion
    h. Objective of pro forma financial information and limitations
    i. Opinion on whether subject matter (assertion) follows criteria
    j. Manual or printed signature of CPA's firm
    k. Date of the examination report

> **NOTE:** A review report is similar to the above, but presents negative assurance instead of an opinion.

  3. The accountant may qualify the opinion, render an adverse opinion, disclaim or withdraw due to circumstances such as scope limitation, uncertainties about the assumptions, conformity with presentation with assumptions or other reservations

AT 501 An Examination of an Entity's Internal Control over Financial Reporting That Is Integrated with an Audit of Its Financial Statements

Overall Objectives and Approach—This section provides guidance for examining and reporting on an entity's internal control over financial reporting. In essence this section is the nonpublic company companion to PCAOB Standard 5's public company requirements for performing the internal control portion integrated audit. Because the procedures and requirements are very similar in the two documents, our approach is to discuss them together in Section C of the Internal Control Module rather than provide separate outlines. Section C provides an outline of PCAOB Standard 5 and a summary of a number of areas where the two documents differ.

AT 601 Compliance Attestation

Overall Objectives and Approach—This section provides guidance on the CPA's (referred to as the "practitioner's") responsibilities with respect to attestation engagements to test compliance with specified requirements which arise through laws, regulations, contracts, rules, or grants. As indicated in part A.2. of the outline, not included in this section are engagements in accordance with *Government Auditing Standards* and various related acts (see AU 801) and several other areas.

The emphasis in this section is upon agreed-upon procedures engagements, although procedures and reporting responsibilities for examination engagements are also presented. Guidance for three types of engagements is provided:
(1) agreed-upon procedures engagements on compliance with **specified requirements,** (2) agreed-upon procedures en-

gagements on the effectiveness of an entity's **internal control over compliance,** and (3) examination engagements on compliance with **specified requirements**. (Reviews are not permitted for any of these engagements; general guidance for examinations of the internal control over compliance is in AT 101.)

Section A of the outline presents general information. Sections B and C provide information on agreed-upon procedures and examination engagements respectively. Section D provides guidance on the required management representation letter that must be obtained on all of these engagements.

A. Introduction and general requirements

1. This section provides guidance for engagements related to **management's written assertion** about either

   a. An entity's compliance with requirements of specified laws, regulations, rules, contracts, or grants (hereafter, compliance with specified requirements) or
   b. Effectiveness of internal control over compliance with specified requirements

      (1) Management's assertions may be either financial or nonfinancial in nature
      (2) Engagements should comply with SSAE 1, *Attestation Standards,* which provides the overall attestation "umbrella" under which this more specific guidance exists

2. Section does **not** apply to

   a. GAAS audit responsibility
   b. Auditor reports on compliance based solely on an audit (see AU 623 outline)
   c. *Government Auditing Standards* and other governmental type engagements such as Single Audit Act engagements (see AU 801 outline)
   d. Letters for Underwriter (see AU 634 outline)
   e. Internal control engagements for a broker or dealer required by SEC Act of 1934

3. Allowed scope of services

   a. Three types of engagements are permitted

      (1) Agreed-upon procedures related to management's assertion about compliance with specified requirements
      (2) Agreed-upon procedures related to management's assertion about the effectiveness of an entity's internal control over compliance

      NOTE: This type of engagement differs from an AT 501 engagement on internal control in that AT 501 is about management's internal control over financial reporting and this section is on management's internal control over compliance with specified requirements.

      (3) Examination of management's assertion about compliance with specified requirements

   b. Review engagements are **not** permitted

4. Conditions for engagement performance

   a. Overall, management must

      (1) Accept responsibility for compliance with requirements **and** effectiveness of internal control over compliance
      (2) Evaluate compliance with specified requirements (or effectiveness of internal control over compliance)
      (3) Provide to the practitioner its written assertion about compliance with specified requirements (or effectiveness of internal control over compliance)

         (a) The written assertion must be in a separate management report if a general distribution **examination** report is to be issued (**all agreed-upon procedures** engagements and examinations with only a representation letter written assertion result in limited distribution reports)

      (4) For examinations

         (a) Assertion must be capable of evaluation against reasonable criteria that are expected to result in findings that are capable of reasonably consistent estimation
         (b) Sufficient evidential matter must support management's evaluation

   b. Management must identify applicable compliance requirements, establish policies to provide reasonable assurance of compliance, evaluate compliance, and produce specific reports that satisfy requirements.

B. Agreed-upon procedures engagements

    1. The **objective** of an agreed-upon procedures engagement is to present specific findings to assist users in evaluating management's assertion about an entity's compliance with specified requirements or about the effectiveness of an entity's internal control over compliance based on procedures agreed upon by the users of the report

        a. The practitioner may be engaged to perform agreed-upon procedures about compliance with specified requirements **or** about effectiveness of internal control over compliance

    2. Ordinarily the accountant will communicate directly to obtain acknowledgment as to procedures from specified users; when this is not possible accountant may

        a. Compare procedures to written requirements of specified users
        b. Discuss procedures to be applied with representatives of the specified users, and/or
        c. Review relevant contracts or communication from specified users

    3. The report on agreed-upon procedures should include

        a. Title with word "independent"
        b. Identification of specified parties
        c. Identification of subject matter (internal control over financial reporting)
        d. Identification of responsible party
        e. Subject matter is responsibility of responsible party
        f. Procedures agreed to by the specified parties
        g. Examination conducted in accordance with attestation standards established by AICPA
        h. Sufficiency of procedures responsibility of specified parties
        i. List of procedures performed and related findings
        j. Where applicable, description of materiality limits
        k. CPA not engaged to perform an examination (and other limitations)
        l. Restriction of use of report to specified parties
        m. Where applicable, reservations or restrictions concerning procedures or findings
        n. Where applicable, description of nature of assistance provided by specialist
        o. Manual or printed signature of CPA's firm
        p. Date of the examination report

C. Examination engagements

    1. The audit risk model (AU 312) is adapted to compliance as follows:

        a. Attestation risk—Risk practitioner unknowingly fails to modify opinion on management's assertion, composed of

            (1) Inherent risk—Risk of material noncompliance assuming no internal control
            (2) Control risk—Risk material noncompliance could occur and not be prevented or detected on a timely basis by internal control
            (3) Detection risk—Practitioner's procedures lead to conclusion that material noncompliance does not exist when it does

    2. Materiality differs from GAAS audit in that it is affected more by

        a. Nature of assertion and compliance requirements, which may or may not be quantifiable in monetary terms
        b. Nature and frequency of noncompliance identified with appropriate consideration of sampling risk
        c. Qualitative considerations, including needs and expectations of report's users

            (1) In some cases practitioner may provide a supplemental report of all or certain noncompliance discovered

    3. Procedures to be followed

        a. Obtain understanding of specified compliance requirements
        b. Plan the engagement

            (1) Testing compliance at every location may be unnecessary
            (2) Practitioner may decide to use work of a specialist and to consider and use work of internal auditors

        c. Consider relevant portions of internal control over compliance

            (1) When control risk to be assessed below maximum, perform tests of controls

        d. Obtain sufficient evidence including testing compliance with specified requirements
        e. Consider subsequent events

(1) Responsibility similar to that of audits (see outline of AU 560)

 f. Form opinion about whether entity compiled, in all material respects, with specified requirements (or management's assertion abort such compliance is fairly stated in all material respects)

4. Report should include

 a. Title with word "independent"
 b. Identification of compliance requirements
 c. Compliance is the responsibility of management
 d. Practitioner's responsibility is to express an opinion on compliance
 e. Examination was made in accordance with the attestation standards of AICPA, and included examining evidence about compliance
 f. Examination provides reasonable basis for opinion
 g. Examination does not provide a legal determination of compliance
 h. Opinion on whether entity complied, in all material respects, with specified requirements (or whether management's assertion about compliance is fairly stated) based on established or agreed-upon criteria
 i. Limitation on use when prepared in conformity with criteria specified by regulatory agency
 j. Manual or printed signature of firm
 k. Date of examination report

5. Report modifications

 a. Material noncompliance

  (1) Practitioner should state an opinion on compliance with specified requirements, not on management's assertion
  (2) If management discloses noncompliance and appropriately modifies its assertion, practitioner should modify opinion paragraph by including a reference to the noncompliance and add an explanatory paragraph (before the opinion paragraph) that describes the noncompliance
  (3) Depending upon significance either a qualified or an adverse opinion is appropriate

 b. Material uncertainty—may lead to a qualified opinion or a disclaimer of opinion

D. Management's representations

1. On all engagements a representation letter must be obtained from management
2. Management's refusal to furnish a representation letter is a scope limitation sufficient to require withdrawal in an agreed-upon procedures engagement and a qualified opinion or disclaimer in an examination engagement
3. When management's assertion is included in a report with other information the practitioner's only responsibility is to read that other information and consider whether it is materially inconsistent with the information appearing in management's report or whether it contains a material misstatement of fact

AT 701 Management's Discussion and Analysis

Overall Objectives and Approach—This section presents guidance on management's discussion and analysis (MD&A) presented pursuant to the Securities and Exchange Commission's (SEC) rules and regulations (also, nonregistrants may voluntarily choose to present such information). It presents guidance for performing either a review or an examination on such information. The SEC does **not** require registrants to have MD&A information either reviewed or examined—the only current requirement is that an auditor meet the AU 550 requirement by reading all information accompanying the audited financial statements for consistency with those statements. While the section is extremely lengthy, in this outline we present only its most major points. You should be familiar with all of the information in the outline and the accompanying summary tables.

A. Review

1. Overall considerations

 a. Objective is to report whether any information came to practitioner's attention leading him/her to believe

  (1) MD&A presentation does **not** include, in all material respects, the SEC **required elements,** including a discussion of the entity's

   (a) Financial condition
   (b) Changes in financial condition and results of operations
   (c) Liquidity and capital resources

    (2) Historical amounts included in MD&A **not** accurately derived from financial statements

    (3) Underlying information, determinations, estimates and assumptions do **not** provide a reasonable basis for MD&A disclosures

  b. Consists principally of applying analytical procedures and making inquiries of persons responsible for financial accounting and operational matters; does **not** contemplate

    (1) Tests of accounting records through inspection, observation, or confirmation

    (2) Obtaining corroborative evidential matter

    (3) Applications of other examination type procedures

  c. A review of annual MD&A may be performed when practitioner has audited the historical financial statements of latest period to which MD&A relates, and other periods have been audited

  d. A review of interim information may be performed if a quarterly review (or audit) of interim information has been performed

2. The review approach is similar to that for financial statements (analytical procedures and inquiry emphasis)
3. The review report of an issuer (public) company (or a nonissuer [nonpublic] company that is making a public offering) should be restricted to the use of specified parties
4. See MD&A General and Reporting Summaries at the end of this outline for guidance on planning, internal control, procedures, and reports

B. Examination

  1. Overall considerations

    a. Objectives are to express an opinion on whether

      (1) Presentation includes SEC **required elements,** including a discussion of the entity's

        (a) Financial condition

        (b) Changes in financial condition and results of operations

        (c) Liquidity and capital resources

      (2) Historical amounts accurately derived from financial statements

      (3) Underlying information, determinations, estimates, and assumptions provide a reasonable basis for MD&A disclosures

    b. Engagement may be performed when practitioner has audited the historical financial statements of the latest period to which MD&A relates, and other periods have been audited

  2. Practitioner should obtain reasonable assurance of detecting both intentional and unintentional misstatements, and adequately restrict attestation risk and its components—inherent risk, control risk, detection risk
  3. The assertions embodied in MD&A include

    a. Occurrence

    b. Consistency with financial statements

    c. Completeness

    d. Presentation and disclosure

> **NOTE:** Points 1. and 2. above are the MD&A adaptations of "audit risk" and point 3. is the MD&A adaptation of the financial statement assertions—see AU 312.

  4. See MD&A General and Reporting Summaries below for guidance on planning, internal control, procedures, and reports

MD&A SUMMARY—GENERAL SUMMARY

	Review	Examination
Planning	1. Obtain understanding of SEC MD&A rules and regulations	1. Same as for reviews
	2. Develop an overall strategy for the analytical procedures and inquiries to be performed to provide negative assurance	2. Develop an overall strategy for the expected scope and performance of the engagement to obtain reasonable assurance to express an opinion
Internal Control	Consider relevant portions to identify types of potential misstatement and to select the inquires and analytical procedures—no tests of controls performed	Obtain understanding to plan the engagement and assess control risk (tests of controls may be performed)

	Review	Examination
Procedures (test assertions)	1. Read MD&A, compare to financial statements, recompute increases, decreases, and percentages 2. Compare nonfinancial amounts to financial statements or other records 3. Consider consistency of MD&A explanations with information obtained during financial statement review or audit; make any necessary further inquiries 4. Compare MD&A to SEC requirements 5. Obtain and read available prospective financial information, inquire concerning this information 6. Obtain public communications and minutes of meetings and compare to MD&A 7. Make inquiries of officers with responsibility for operating areas and financial accounting matters as to their plans and expectations for the future 8. Inquire as to prior SEC experience 9. Consider whether there are additional matters that should be disclosed in MD&A based on results of preceding procedures	1. Same as review 2. Same as review, but also perform tests on other records 3. Same as review, but investigate further explanations that cannot be substantiated by information in audit working papers 4. Same as review 5. Same as review, plus evaluate whether the underlying information, determinations, estimates, and assumptions provide a reasonable basis for MD&A disclosures 6. Same as review, plus consider obtaining other types of publicly available information for comparison to MD&A 7. Same as review 8. Same as review 9. Test completeness of results 10. Examine documents in support of existence, occurrence, or expected occurrence of events, transactions, etc.
Report	Includes negative assurance	Includes an opinion (reasonable assurance)
Other	1. Must consider events subsequent to balance sheet 2. Must obtain management written representations	1. Same as review 2. Same as review

MD&A SUMMARY—REPORTING SUMMARY

	Review	Examination
Report should include	1. Title with word independent 2. Identification of MD&A and period covered 3. Management responsible for MD&A 4. Reference to audit report on financial statements and, if nonstandard, reasons therefor 5. Review conducted in accordance with attestation standards and description of scope of examination established by AICPA; a description of review procedures 6. Review substantially less in scope than an examination 7. Paragraph stating that preparation of MD&A requires interpretations, and actual future results may vary 8. If nonissuer (nonpublic) entity, MD&A intended to follow SEC rules 9. Statement about whether any information came to practitioner's attention concerning misstatements relating to (1) required elements, (2) historical amounts accurately derived, (3) underlying information provides reasonable basis (negative assurance provided) 10. Restriction on distribution if issuer (public) company 11. Manual or printed signature 12. Date of a review	1. Same as review 2. Same as review 3. Same as review 4. Same as review 5. Examination conducted in accordance with attestation standards established by AICPA and description of scope of examination 6. Practitioner believes examination provides reasonable basis for opinion 7. Same as review 8. Same as review 9. Practitioner's opinion on (1) presentation includes required elements, (2) historical amounts accurately derived, (3) underlying information provides reasonable basis 10. (No such requirement) 11. Same as review 12. Same as review
Report modified for	1. Exclusion of a material required element 2. Historical financial amounts not accurately derived from financial statements 3. Underlying information has no reasonable basis 4. Practitioner decides to refer to report of another practitioner 5. Practitioner reviews MD&A after it has already been filed with SEC	1. through 5., same as review, but also when there is a restriction on the scope of the engagement
Other	1. Must consider events subsequent to balance sheet 2. Must obtain management written representations	1. Same as review 2. Same as review

AT 801 Reporting on Controls at a Service Organization

A. Introduction and objectives

1. This section addresses examination engagements undertaken by a service auditor to report on controls at organizations that provide services to user entities when those controls are likely to be part of the user entities' information and communication systems relevant to financial reporting. (Study it in conjunction with your study of AU 324— that section deals with a user auditor using the report of a service auditor).
2. The objectives of the service auditor are to obtain reasonable assurance and report about whether, in all material respects, based on suitable criteria

   a. Management's description of the service organization's system is fairly represented.
   b. The controls are suitably designed to achieve the control objectives stated in management's description of the service organization's system.
   c. When included in the scope of the engagement, the controls operated effectively throughout the specified period to achieve the control objectives.

   > **NOTE:** Make certain that you know that in general, the service auditor is engaged to issue one of two types of reports. Type 1 deals with points a. and b. above; this report addresses whether controls have been properly designed and implemented. Type 2 deals with points a., b. and c.; that is, they also address control operating effectiveness. Type 1 reports are as of a specific date, while Type 2 are for a time period.

B. Selected definitions

1. **Complementary user entity controls.** Controls that management of the service organization assumes, in the design of its service, will be implemented by user entities, and which, if necessary to achieve the control objectives stated in management's description of the service organization's system, are identified as such in that description.
2. **Report on management's description of a service organization's system and the suitability of the design of controls** (referred to in this section as a *type 1 report*). A report that comprises

   a. Management's description of the service organization's system, prepared by management of the service organization.
   b. A written assertion by the service organization's management about whether, in all material respects, and based on suitable criteria

      (1) Management's description of the service organization's system fairly presents the service organization's system that was designed and implemented as of a specified date.
      (2) The controls related to the control objectives stated in the description were suitably designed to achieve those control objectives as of the specified date.

   c. A service auditor's report that expresses an opinion on the matters in b(1)-b(2).

3. **Report on management's description of a service organization's system and the suitability of the design and operating effectiveness of controls** (referred to in this section as a *type 2 report*). (Ref: par. A1) A report that comprises

   a. A description of the service organization's system prepared by management of the service organization.
   b. A written assertion by the service organization's management, about whether in all material respects and, based on suitable criteria,

      (1) Management's description of the service organization's system fairly presents the service organization's system that was designed and implemented throughout the specified period.
      (2) The controls related to the control objectives stated in the description of the service organization's system were suitably designed throughout the specified period to achieve those control objectives.
      (3) The controls related to the control objectives stated in the description of the service organization's system operated effectively throughout the specified period to achieve those control objectives.

   c. A service auditor's report that

      (1) Expresses an opinion about the matters in b(1)-b(3).
      (2) Includes a description of the service auditor's tests of controls and the results thereof.

   > **NOTE:** The difference between a type 1 and type 2 report is that only a type 2 report addresses operating effectiveness. They both address how controls have been designed and implemented.

4. **Service auditor.** A practitioner who reports on controls at a service organization.

5. **Service organization.** An organization or segment of an organization that provides services to user entities that are likely to be relevant to those user entities' internal control over financial reporting.

6. **Subservice organization.** A service organization used by another service organization to perform some of the services provided to user entities that are part of the user entities' information and communication systems relevant to financial reporting.

7. **User auditor.** An auditor who audits and reports on the financial statements of a user entity.

8. **User entity.** An entity that uses a service organization and whose financial statements are being audited.

C. Requirements—General

1. Acceptance and continuance

   a. A service auditor should accept or continue an engagement to report on controls at a service organization only if

      (1) The service auditor has the capabilities and competence to perform the engagement.

      (2) The service auditor's preliminary knowledge of the engagement circumstance indicates that the criteria to be used will be suitable, sufficient appropriate evidence will be available, and the scope of the engagement will not be restricted.

      (3) Management agrees to the terms of the engagement by accepting responsibility for

         (a) Preparing its description of the service organization's system and the accompanying assertion.

         (b) Having a reasonable basis for the assertion.

         (c) Selecting criteria used and stating them in the assertion.

         (d) Specifying control objectives.

         (e) Identifying risks

         (f) Providing a written assertion that will be included in, or attached to management's description of the service organization's system and provided to user entities.

2. The service auditor must assess the suitability of the criteria being followed by the service organization

3. When the service organization has an internal audit function, the service auditor should obtain an understanding of that function and may use the work of that function. In such circumstances, the service auditor should make no reference to the internal audit function's work *in the service auditor's opinion.*

   a. But when a Type 2 report is issued and the internal audit function has been used in performing tests of controls, the service auditor's *description of controls* should include description of the internal auditor's work and the service auditor's procedures with respect to that work.

4. If the service auditor intends to use the work of a specialist, the service auditor should follow procedures similar to those required of a financial statement auditor in such a situation—see AU 336.

D. Requirements—Performance of examination

1. To issue a Type 1 report, the service auditor should

   a. Obtain an understanding of the service organization's system

      (1) When obtaining this understanding, the service auditor should obtain information for use in identifying risks that the service organization's system is not fairly presented (in management's description and assertion) or that the control objectives stated were not achieved.

   b. Obtain evidence regarding the description of the service organization's system.

      (1) The service auditor should obtain and read the description and evaluate accuracy

      (2) The service auditor should determine whether the service organization's system described in management's description has been implemented.

   c. Obtain evidence regarding the design of controls.

      (1) The service auditor should determine which of the controls are necessary to achieve the control objective stated in the description and should assess whether they were suitably designed to achieve those control objectives.

2. To issue a Type 2 report, the service auditor should

   a. Perform the procedures listed above for a Type 1 report.

   b. Obtain evidence regarding the operating effectiveness of controls

(1) Here the requirements are similar to when a financial statement auditor performs tests of controls performed for a financial statement audit. In essence, the auditor tests controls to determine whether they operate effectively to meet the control objectives in the management's description.

3. A service auditor should ask management to provide written representations

 a. Reaffirming the assertion.
 b. All records were made available.
 c. The following were disclosed to the service auditor

 (1) Any noncompliance with laws or uncorrected errors that affect a user entity.
 (2) Knowledge of overrides of controls or misappropriation of assets.
 (3) Design deficiencies.
 (4) Instances where controls have not operated as described.
 (5) Subsequent events.

4. The service auditor should prepare documentation that would enable an experienced service auditor having no previous connection with the engagement to understand the

 a. Procedures performed.
 b. Results obtained.
 c. Significant matters arising during the engagement, the conclusions reached thereon, and significant professional judgments made in reaching those conclusions.

5. Report issued

 a. The opinion

 (1) Type 1

 (a) The description of the service organization's system fairly presents it.
 (b) The controls related to the control objective stated in the description of the service organization's system were suitably designed to provide reasonable assurance that those control objectives would be achieved if the controls operated effectively.

 (2) Type 2

 (a) Points (1) and (2) above
 (b) The controls the service auditor tested, which were those necessary to provide reasonable assurance that the control objectives stated in the description were achieved, operated effectively throughout the specified period.

 b. Use of service auditor reports is restricted to customers of the service organization.
 c. Modified opinions (generally qualified) result from

 (1) A management description of the system which is not fairly presented in all material respects.
 (2) Controls that are not suitably designed to provide reasonable assurance that the control objectives stated in the description would be achieved if the controls operated as described.
 (3) The service auditor is unable to obtain sufficient, appropriate evidence.
 (4) For a Type 2 report—controls did not operate effectively.

STATEMENTS ON AUDITING STANDARDS

Overview. The Statements on Auditing Standards (SAS) are issued by the Auditing Standards Board. The SAS which have been issued are codified into the following **overall** categories:

Section	Title
AU 100	Introduction
AU 200	The General Standards
AU 300	The Standards of Fieldwork
AU 400	The First, Second, and Third Standards of Reporting
AU 500	The Fourth Standard of Reporting
AU 600	Other Types of Reports
AU 700	Special Topics
AU 800	Compliance Auditing
AU 900	Special Reports of the Committee on Auditing Procedure

Included following AU 901 is the outline of *Government Auditing Standards*, published by the Comptroller General of the United States. *Government Auditing Standards*, which is listed in *Information for Uniform CPA Examination Candidates* as a publication which candidates should study, provides background material upon which much of AU 801 is based.

110 Responsibilities and Functions of the Independent Auditor (SAS 1)

Overall Objectives and Approach—This section presents the objective of audits, compares the responsibilities of the auditor with those of management, and discusses the professional requirements necessary for an auditor.

A. Objective of a financial statement audit—the expression of an opinion on the fairness with which the financial statements present financial position, results of operations, and cash flows in conformity with GAAP

B. Responsibilities

1. Management—adopting sound accounting policies and internal control that will record, process, summarize, and report financial data that is consistent with management's assertions in the financial statements
2. Auditor—expression of an opinion on the financial statements

> **NOTE:** A number of exam questions have addressed the idea that management's role includes the preparation of the statements while that of the auditor is expressing an opinion.

C. An independent auditor must have adequate levels of education and experience

120 Defining Professional Requirements (SAS 102)

Overall Objectives and Approach—This brief section defines certain terms used in the standards.

A. General

1. SASs contain both professional requirements and related guidance
2. Auditors must consider the entire text of the SAS (AU), but not every paragraph must be followed

B. Categories of requirements

1. Unconditional requirements—Auditors must comply in all cases in which the circumstances exist to which the requirement applies. The words *must* or *required to* are used to indicate an unconditional requirement
2. Presumptively mandatory requirements—Auditors must comply in all circumstances in which the requirement applies, except in rare circumstances the auditor may depart from the requirement provided that the auditor documents his or her justification for the departure and how the alternative procedures were sufficient to meet the audit objectives. The word *should* is used to indicate a presumptively mandatory requirement
3. If a SAS states that the auditor *should consider* a procedure or action, such a consideration is required, but carrying out the procedure or action is not required

C. Explanatory material

1. This type of material provides further explanation and guidance on the professional requirements and is descriptive rather than imperative (i.e., it is not required). The words *may, might*, or *could* are used to describe these actions and procedures.

150 Generally Accepted Auditing Standards (SAS 1, 43, 95, 105)

Overall Objectives and Approach—This section (a) distinguishes between auditing standards and auditing procedures, (b) presents the 10 generally accepted auditing standards (GAAS), and (c) discusses the status of Statements on Auditing Standards (SAS), interpretative publications, and other auditing publications.

A. A CPA plans, conducts, and reports the results of an audit in accordance with GAAS

1. Auditing standards—provide a measure of audit quality and objectives to be achieved in an audit
2. Auditing procedures—acts the auditor performs during an audit to comply with GAAS

B. General standards

1. **T**raining—the audit must be performed by a person or persons having adequate technical **training** and proficiency as an auditor
2. **I**ndependence—in all matters relating to the assignment, an **independence** in mental attitude is to be maintained by the auditor or auditors
3. **P**rofessional Care—due **professional care** is to be exercised in the performance of the examination and the preparation of the report

C. Standards of fieldwork

1. **Plan**—the auditor must adequately **plan** the work and must properly supervise any assistants
2. **Understanding**—The auditor must obtain a sufficient **understanding** of the entity and its environment, including its internal control to assess the risk of misstatement of the financial statements
3. **Evidence**—The auditor must obtain sufficient appropriate audit **evidence** by performing audit procedures to afford a reasonable basis for an opinion

D. Standards of reporting

1. **Generally accepted accounting principles**—the report shall state whether the financial statements are presented in accordance with **generally accepted accounting principles**
2. **Consistency**—the report shall identify those circumstances in which such principles have not been **consistently** observed in the current period in relation to the preceding period
3. **Disclosures**—informative **disclosures** in the financial statements are to be regarded as reasonably adequate unless otherwise stated in the report
4. **Opinion**—the report shall either contain an expression of **opinion** regarding the financial statements, taken as a whole, or an assertion to the effect that an opinion cannot be expressed. When an overall opinion cannot be expressed, the reasons therefore should be stated. In all cases where an auditor's name is associated with financial statements, the report should contain a clear-cut indication of the character of the auditor's examination, if any, and the degree of responsibility s/he is taking

> **NOTE:** You need not memorize the exact wording, but know the 10 standards. Recall TIP, PUE, and GODC (reordered standards of reporting—1, 4, 3, 2).

E. GAAS and Statements on Auditing Standards (SAS)

1. An auditor must identify those applicable to his/her audit and exercise professional judgment in applying SAS
2. An auditor must document his or her justification for departures from a presumptively mandatory requirement and how alternative procedures performed in the circumstances were sufficient to achieve the objectives of the requirement
3. Materiality and audit risk underlie application of GAAS and SAS
4. An auditor must be prepared to justify departures from SAS
5. **Interpretative publications** consist of Auditing Interpretations, AICPA Audit and Accounting Guides and AICPA Auditing Statements of Position

   a. Are recommendations, not auditing standards
   b. An auditor who does not apply should be prepared to explain how he or she complied with the SAS provisions addressed by such guidance

6. **Other auditing publications** include other AICPA auditing publications, *Journal of Accountancy* and *CPA Letter* articles, continuing education programs, texts, etc.

   a. Have no authoritative status, but may help auditor to apply SAS

161 The Relationship of Generally Accepted Auditing Standards to Quality Control Standards (SAS 25)

Overall Objectives and Approach—This section states that a CPA firm has a responsibility to adopt a system of quality control that will provide it with reasonable assurance that its personnel comply with generally accepted auditing standards in its audit standards. For details on the actual quality control standards that have been promulgated, see the Engagement Planning Module.

A. Rule 202 of the Code of Professional Conduct requires that individual CPAs comply with GAAS

1. GAAS relate to the conduct of individual audits; quality control standards relate to the conduct of a firm's audit practice as a whole
2. Deficiencies or instances of noncomplicance with quality control policies and procedures do not, in and of themselves, indicate that an audit was not performed in accordance with GAAS

B. CPA firms should comply with GAAS and establish quality control policies and procedures

1. The nature and extent of quality control policies and procedures depends on the firm's

   a. Size
   b. Autonomy of personnel and practice offices
   c. Nature of the firm's practice

    d. Firm's organizational structure

    e. Appropriate cost-benefit considerations

C. GAAS and quality control standards are related

  1. GAAS related to the conduct of **individual audits**

  2. Quality control standards relate to **overall audit practice**

  3. GAAS and quality control standards may affect both the conduct of individual audits and the conduct of a firm's entire audit practice

201 through 230 The General Standards (SAS 1)

Overall Objectives and Approach—These brief sections present information on the general group (training; independence, professional care) of GAAS. We combine discussion of these sections.

A. The general standards are personal in nature and are concerned with the qualifications of the auditor and the quality of the auditor's work

B. Training—the examination is to be performed by a person or persons having adequate technical training and proficiency as an auditor

  1. Both proper education and professional experience are necessary

  2. A CPA must exercise objectivity and professional judgment when performing an audit

C. Independence—in all matters relating to the assignment, an **independence** in mental attitude is to be maintained by the auditor or auditors

  1. The CPA should not only be **independent in fact,** but should also **appear independent** (i.e., avoid situations that may lead outsiders to doubt his/her independence)

  2. To stress the CPA's independence, many companies follow the practice of having the independent auditor appointed by the board of directors or the stockholders

D. Professional Care—due **professional care** is to be exercised in the planning and performance of the audit and the preparation of the report

  1. At a minimum, the auditor with final responsibility for the engagement should know the relevant accounting and auditing standards and should be knowledgeable about the client

  2. Due professional care requires the auditor to exercise professional skepticism

    a. Professional skepticism is an attitude that includes a questioning mind and a critical assessment of audit evidence

    b. The auditor neither assumes that management is dishonest nor assumes unqualified honesty

  3. The auditor must plan and perform the audit to obtain sufficient appropriate audit evidence so that audit risk will be limited to a low level that is appropriate for expressing an opinion on the financial statements

    a. A low level of audit risk means that there is a remote likelihood that an auditor may unknowingly fail to appropriately modify the opinion on financial statements that are materially misstated

    b. This is referred to as providing "reasonable assurance" (rather than "absolute assurance")

    c. Because of the characteristics of fraud, a properly planned and performed audit may not detect a material misstatement; characteristics include

      (1) Collusion among management, employees, or third parties

      (2) Withheld, misrepresented, or falsified documentation

      (3) Ability of management to override or instruct others to override what otherwise appear to be effective controls

311 Planning and Supervision (SAS 108)

Overall Objectives and Approach—This section presents information on planning and supervising the audit. Audit planning involves developing an overall audit strategy for the expected conduct, organization, and staffing of the audit. The auditor must plan the audit so that it is responsive to the assessment of the risk of material misstatement based on the auditor's understanding of the entity and its environment, including its internal control. Planning is an iterative process that begins with engagement acceptance and continues throughout the audit. Notice that points 1. through 7. under topic A. provide a good overview of procedures considered to be planning procedures. Supervision involves directing the efforts of assistants who are involved in accomplishing the objective of the audit and determining whether those objectives were accomplished.

A. Planning

  1. Appointment of the independent auditor

    a. Early appointment of the auditor is preferable, although an auditor may accept an engagement near or after the close of the fiscal year

  2. Establishing an understanding with the client

    a. The auditor should establish an understanding with the client through a written communication (i.e., an engagement letter)

    b. The understanding should include the objectives of the engagement, management's responsibilities, the auditor's responsibilities, and limitations of the engagement, including

      (1) Objective of audit is expression of an opinion on the financial statements

      (2) Management is responsible for

        (a) Financial statements

        (b) Establishing and maintaining effective internal control over financial reporting

        (c) Designing and implementing programs and controls to prevent and detect fraud

        (d) Identifying and ensuring that the entity complies with laws and regulations

        (e) Making financial records and related information available to auditor

        (f) Providing a representation letter

        (g) Adjusting financial statements to correct material misstatements and for affirming to auditor that effects of uncorrected misstatements aggregated by auditor are immaterial

      (3) The auditor is responsible for conducting audit in accordance with GAAS; limitations

        (a) An auditor obtains reasonable and not absolute assurance that financial statements are free of material misstatement, whether due to error or fraud

        (b) Material misstatement may remain undetected

        (c) If for any reason auditor is unable to complete the audit or to form an opinion, the auditor may decline to express an opinion or issue a report

      (4) An audit includes obtaining an understanding of internal control sufficient to plan the audit and to determine the nature, timing, and extent of audit procedures

        (a) An audit is **not** designed to provide assurance on internal control or to identify significant deficiencies

        (b) However, if significant deficiencies are identified, the auditor must ensure that the audit committee is aware of them

    c. An understanding might also include other matters such as

      (1) The arrangements regarding the conduct of the audit (e.g., timing, client assistance, availability of documents)

      (2) Involvement of specialists

      (3) Involvement of a predecessor auditor

      (4) Fees and billing

      (5) Any limitation of or other arrangements regarding auditor liability

      (6) Conditions under which access to audit documentation may be granted to others

      (7) Additional services to be provided relating to regulatory requirements

      (8) Other services to be provided in connection with the engagement (e.g., reviews of interim financial information)

  3. Preliminary engagement activities

    a. The auditor should

      (1) Perform procedures regarding the continuance of the client relationship and the specific audit

      (2) Evaluate own compliance with ethical requirements, including independence

    b. The purpose of the above procedures are to ensure that

      (1) Auditor maintains independence and ability to perform engagement

      (2) There are no issues with management integrity

      (3) There is no misunderstanding with the client as to the terms of the engagement

  4. Overall audit strategy

    a. Overall audit strategy involves

    (1) Determining characteristics of the engagement that define its scope (e.g., basis of reporting, industry reporting requirements, location of entity)

    (2) Ascertaining reporting objectives to plan timing of audit, such as meeting deadlines for interim and financial reporting and other key dates

    (3) Considering important factors that will determine the focus of audit team's efforts, including

        (a) Materiality

        (b) Areas of higher risk of material misstatement

        (c) Material locations and accounts

        (d) Evaluation of whether auditor may plan to obtain evidence on effectiveness of internal control

        (e) Identification of significant entity-specific, industry, financial reporting or other relevant developments

  b. Developing the audit strategy helps the auditor to determine the resources necessary to perform the engagement

  c. When the audit strategy has been established, the auditor is able to start the development of a more detailed audit plan to address the various matters identified in the audit strategy

    (1) The two planning activities, *developing an overall audit strategy* and *developing an audit plan*, are closely interrelated since changes in one may result in changes to the other

    (2) In audits of a small company, audit team coordination and communication is ordinarily easier and establishing an overall audit strategy need not be complex or time consuming (e.g., it may involve preparation of a brief memorandum based on a review of prior year audit)

5. The audit plan

  a. The auditor must develop an audit plan for the audit in order to reduce audit risk to an acceptably low level

  b. The audit plan is more detailed than the audit strategy and includes the nature, timing, and extent of audit procedures to be performed by audit team members

  c. Documentation of the audit plan also serves as a record of the proper planning and performance of the audit procedures that can be reviewed and approved prior to the performance of further audit procedures

  d. The audit plan should include a description of

    (1) Nature, timing, and extent of planned risk assessment procedures

    (2) Nature, timing, and extent of planned further audit procedures at the relevant assertion level for each material class of transactions, account balance, and disclosure

    (3) Other audit procedures to be carried out for the engagement to comply with GAAS

  e. Should include information on the extent of the involvement of professionals possessing specialized skills (e.g., tax, IT)

6. Communications with those charged with governance and management

  a. Ordinarily includes information on the overall audit strategy and timing of the audit, including any limitations thereon, or additional requirements

  b. The overall audit strategy and the audit plan remain the auditor's responsibility, and when discussing them with the client, the auditor should be careful to not compromise the effectiveness of the audit

7. Additional considerations in initial audit engagements

  a. Prior to starting an initial audit

    (1) Perform procedures regarding the acceptance of the client relationship and the specific audit engagement (as per Quality Control Standards)

    (2) Communicate with the previous auditor, when there has been a change of auditors

  b. Additional matters auditor should consider in developing overall strategy and audit plan

    (1) Arrangements to review previous auditor's audit documentation

    (2) Any major issues discussed with management in connection with initial selection

    (3) Planned audit procedures regarding opening balances

    (4) Assignment of firm personnel with appropriate levels of capabilities and competence to respond to anticipated significant risks

    (5) Other procedures required by the firm's system of quality control for initial audits

B. Supervision

1. The auditor with final responsibility for the audit should communicate with members of the audit team regarding the susceptibility of the entity's financial statements to material misstatement due to error or fraud, with special emphasis on fraud

a. The conversation should emphasize the need to maintain a questioning mind and to exercise professional skepticism in gathering and evaluating audit evidence

2. Assistants should be informed of their responsibilities and the objectives of the audit procedures they are to perform

   a. The auditor with final responsibility for the audit should direct assistants to bring to his/her attention accounting and auditing issues that the assistant believes are significant
   b. Assistants should also be directed to bring to the attention of appropriate individuals in the firm difficulties encountered in performing the audit, such as missing documents or resistance from client personnel in providing access to information or in responding to inquiries
   c. The work of each assistant, including the audit documentation, should be reviewed to determine whether it was adequately performed and documented and to evaluate the results
   d. Each assistant has a professional responsibility to bring to the attention of appropriate individuals in the firm disagreements or concerns with respect to accounting and auditing issues that the assistant believes are of significance to the financial statements or auditor's report

      (1) The auditor with final responsibility for the audit and assistants should be aware of the procedures to be followed when differences of opinion concerning accounting and auditing issues exist among firm personnel
      (2) Procedures should enable an assistant to document his/her disagreement with the conclusions reached if, after appropriate consultation, he or she believes it necessary to disassociate himself or herself from the resolution of the matter; in this situation, the basis for the final resolution should also be documented

312 Audit Risk and Materiality in Conducting an Audit (SAS 107)

Overall Objectives and Approach—This section presents guidance on the auditor's consideration of audit risk and materiality when performing an audit. The existence of audit risk is recognized in the professional standards in that auditors provide reasonable, but not absolute, assurance that material misstatements are detected.

The concept of materiality recognizes that some matters are important for fair presentation of financial statements in conformity with GAAP, while other matters are not important. In performing the audit, the auditor is concerned with matters that could be material to the financial statements. The auditor's responsibility is to plan and perform the audit to obtain reasonable assurance that material misstatements, whether caused by errors or fraud, are detected.

A. Overall

1. The perceived needs of **users of financial statements** are recognized in the discussion of materiality in SFA Concepts 2, which defines materiality as "the magnitude of an omission or misstatement of accounting information that in the light of surrounding circumstances, makes it probable that the judgment of a reasonable person relying on the information would have been changed or influenced by the omission or misstatement."
2. The auditor's judgment as to matters that are material to **users of financial statements** is based on a consideration of the needs of the users as a group; the auditor does **not** consider the possible effect of misstatements on a specific individual user. Users are assumed to

   a. Have appropriate knowledge of business and economic activities and accounting and a willingness to study the information in the financial statements with an appropriate diligence
   b. Understand that financial statements are prepared and audited to levels of materiality
   c. Recognize the uncertainties inherent in financial statements
   d. Make appropriate economic decisions on the basis of the information in the financial statements

3. Misstatements

   a. Errors vs. fraud

      (1) Errors—**unintentional** misstatements of amounts or disclosures
      (2) Fraud—an **intentional** act by one or more individuals involving the use of deception to obtain an unjust or illegal advantage. Two types of misstatements resulting from fraud are relevant to the audit.

         (a) Fraudulent financial reporting
         (b) Misappropriation of assets

   b. An auditor does not have a responsibility to plan and perform the audit to detect immaterial misstatements
   c. When an auditor encounters evidence of potential fraud, regardless of its materiality, the auditor should consider the implications for the integrity of management or employees and the possible effect on other aspects of the audit

B. Audit risk and materiality considerations

1. At the financial statement level

a. The auditor must consider audit risk and must determine a materiality level for the financial statements as a whole for the purpose of

    (1) Determining the extent and nature of risk assessment procedures
    (2) Identifying and assessing the risks of material misstatement
    (3) Determining the nature, timing, and extent of further audit procedures
    (4) Evaluating whether the financial statements as a whole are presented fairly, in conformity with GAAP

b. The auditor should consider audit risk in relation to the individual account balances, classes of transactions, and disclosures and relevant assertions and at the overall financial statement level

c. The audit should be performed to reduce audit risk to a low level

    (1) Audit risk may be assessed in quantitative or nonquantitative terms

2. At the individual account balance, class of transactions, or disclosure level

a. There is an inverse relationship between audit risk and materiality

    (1) Either a decrease in the acceptable level of audit risk or a decrease in the material amount for the account (tolerable misstatement) will result in one or more of the following:

        (a) Perform more effective audit procedures
        (b) Perform audit procedures closer to year-end
        (c) Increase the extent of particular audit procedures

b. At the account balance, class of transactions, or disclosure level, audit risk (AR) consists of

    (1) Risk of material misstatement—the risk that the balance, class, or disclosure and relevant assertions contain misstatements that could be material; composed of

        (a) Inherent risk—susceptibility to misstatement, assuming there are no related controls; examples

            1] Cash is more susceptible to theft than an inventory of coal
            2] Accounts consisting of estimates (e.g., allowance for doubtful accounts) pose greater risks of measurement errors than accounts composed of routine transactions
            3] Inventory for a high-tech company may have more inherent risk of obsolescence than an inventory of a company that sells salt

        (b) Control risk—risk that a misstatement could occur that could be material and not be prevented or detected on a timely basis by the entity's internal control

    (2) Detection risk—the risk that the auditor will not detect a misstatement that exists that could be material

        (a) Detection risk may be disaggregated into

            1] Tests of details risk
            2] Substantive analytical procedures risk

> **NOTE:** Notice that inherent risk and control risk are directly related to the company itself and exist regardless of whether there is an audit. Detection risk is a function of the effectiveness of audit procedures and the effectiveness of the application of those audit procedures by the auditor.

    (3) Various relationships exist between the components of audit risk. Consider the following:

$$\text{Audit Risk} = \text{Risk of Material Misstatement} \times \text{Detection Risk}$$
$$\text{AR} = \text{RMM} \times \text{DR}$$

$$\text{RMM} = \text{Risk of Material Misstatement} = \text{IR} \times \text{CR}$$
Where IR = Inherent Risk
$$\text{CR} = \text{Control Risk}$$

$$\text{DR} = \text{Detection Risk} = \text{TD} \times \text{AP}$$
Where TD = Test of Details Risk
$$\text{AP} = \text{Substantive Analytical Procedures Risk}$$

    (4) Using the above relationships, one may derive the following equivalent forms of the "audit risk model":

$$\text{AR} = \text{RMM} \times \text{DR}$$
$$\text{AR} = \text{RMM} \times \text{TD} \times \text{AP}$$
$$\text{AR} = \text{IR} \times \text{CR} \times \text{TD} \times \text{AP}$$

> **NOTE:** The model is not meant to be a mathematical formula including all factors in an audit; however, some auditors find such a model useful in planning appropriate risk levels for audit procedures to reduce the desired audit risk to an appropriate level. The model should also be helpful for multiple-choice questions which ask questions such as, "When the risk of material misstatement increases, the required detection risk increases, decreases, etc." Here the answer would be decreases because an increase in the one risk must be accompanied by a decrease in the other to keep the audit risk at its desired level.

C. Materiality when planning the audit

1. Determining materiality for the financial statements as a whole

   a. The auditor should determine a materiality level for the financial statements as a whole when establishing the overall audit strategy

      (1) However, some misstatements below this materiality level may still be considered material due to their nature

      (2) In determining what is material, the auditor often applies a percentage to a chosen **benchmark,** while considering

         (a) Elements of financial statements (e.g., assets, liabilities, equity, income, and expenses)
         (b) Whether there are financial statement items on which, for the particular entity, users' attention seems to be focused (e.g., for purpose of evaluating financial forecast)
         (c) Nature of the entity and its industry
         (d) Size of the entity, nature of ownership and the way it is financed

      (3) **Benchmarks** for materiality that auditors often use include total revenues, gross profit, other categories of reported income, such as profit before tax from continuing operations

         (a) For example, an auditor may use 5% of profit before tax from continuing operations
         (b) Appropriate benchmarks may differ based on the nature of the company, for example

            1] For an owner-managed business where the owner takes much of pretax income out of business in the form of remuneration, profit before tax from continuing operations may not be an appropriate benchmark
            2] For an asset-based entity (e.g., an investment fund) an appropriate benchmark might be net assets

      (4) When determining materiality, the auditor should consider the prior period's financial results and financial position, the period-to-date financial results and financial position, and budgets or forecasts for the current period, taking into account changes in the entity's circumstances and relevant changes in conditions in the economy as a whole or the industry

         (a) An exceptional increase or decrease in profit may lead the auditor to conclude that materiality is better determined using a normalized profit figure based on past results (e.g., an average of the benchmark for the past three years)

2. A lower level of materiality for particular items than the materiality level determined for the financial statements taken as a whole is sometimes appropriate

   a. Considering factors such as the following may result in a lower level for materiality:

      (1) Accounting standards, laws, or regulations that particularly affect users' expectations regarding certain items (e.g., related-party transactions, remuneration of management)
      (2) Key disclosures in relation to the industry and environment (e.g., research and development in a pharmaceutical company)
      (3) Whether attention is focused on financial performance of a particular segment that is separately disclosed (e.g., a newly acquired business)

3. Tolerable misstatement

   a. Tolerable misstatement is the maximum misstatement in a population (for example, a class of transactions or account balance) that the auditor is willing to accept

      (1) The auditor should determine one or more levels of tolerable misstatement for classes of transactions, account balances, and disclosures

   b. This is a disaggregation of the materiality measure for use with the various classes of transactions and balances; for example, if $1,000,000 is considered material, a lesser amount might represent the tolerable misstatement for auditing various accounts

4. Consideration of materiality as the audit progresses

   a. Because it is not feasible to anticipate all circumstances that may ultimately influence materiality judgments, the auditor's judgment for planning purposes may differ from the judgment about materiality used in evaluating audit findings

   b. As the aggregate misstatement (**known** and **likely**) that the auditor has identified approaches the materiality level, the auditor should consider whether there is a greater than acceptably low level of risk that material misstatements in total do exist

      (1) **Known misstatements**—Specific misstatements identified during audit arising from incorrect selection or application of accounting principles or misstatements of facts

      (2) **Likely misstatements** are from two sources

         (a) Differences between the client's and the auditor's judgments about accounting estimates

         (b) Amounts the auditor considers likely to exist based on an extrapolation from audit evidence obtained (e.g., projecting known misstatements identified in an audit sample of accounts receivable to the entire population)

5. Communication of misstatements to management

   a. Accumulate all known and likely misstatements identified, other than those that the auditor believes are trivial

   b. Communicate misstatements to management on a timely basis, distinguishing between known and likely misstatements

   c. Other requirements

      (1) The auditor should request management to correct all **known misstatements,** including the effect of prior period misstatements, other than those that are trivial

      (2) Where the amount of **likely misstatement** from a sample is projected as material, the auditor should request management to examine the class of transactions, account, or disclosure in order to identify and correct misstatements (e.g., while testing the cost of prices of raw material inventory, the auditor extrapolates this misstatement to the raw materials account balance and the amount is material)

      (3) When the auditor evaluates the amount of likely misstatement, the auditor should request management to review assumptions and method used to develop its estimate

      (4) If management decides not to correct some or all misstatements communicated by the auditor, the auditor should obtain an understanding of management's reason for not making the corrections and should take that into account when considering the qualitative aspects of the entity's accounting practices and the implications for the audit report

D. Evaluating audit findings

1. The auditor must consider the effects, both individually and in the aggregate, of misstatements (known and likely) that are not corrected by the entity

   a. The consideration and aggregation of misstatements should include likely misstatements (the auditor's best estimate of the total misstatements in the account balances or class of transactions that he or she has examined), not just known misstatements (the amount of misstatements specifically identified)

   > **NOTE:** The standards provide the following illustration on the relationship between known and likely misstatements: "If the auditor were to examine all of the items in a balance or a class, the likely misstatement applicable to recorded transactions in the balance or class would be the amount of known misstatements specifically identified." It follows that the likely misstatement is the best estimate of total misstatements in the account and that this amount includes the known misstatements. Some textbooks establish likely misstatement as this amount minus known misstatement.

   b. Before considering the aggregate effect of identified uncorrected misstatements, the auditor should consider each misstatement separately to evaluate

      (1) Its effect to the relevant classes of transactions, account balances, or disclosures

      (2) Whether it is appropriate to offset misstatements (e.g., it may be inappropriate to offset misstatements of items that are disclosed separately in the financial statements)

      (3) Effect of misstatements related to prior period that also affect this year

         (a) In aggregating misstatements, the auditor should include the effect on the current period's financial statements of those prior period misstatements

   c. In aggregating misstatements, the auditor should include the effect on the current financial statements of those prior period misstatements; in doing this, the auditor should consider both

(1) Adjustments necessary to correct misstatements in the ending balance sheet, even if they arose in whole or part in prior years, including the effect of the adjustments of the most recent income statement and

(2) Adjustments necessary to correct misstatements affecting the most recent income statement

2. When substantive analytical procedures are used, the auditor ordinarily would not specifically identify misstatements, but would obtain an indication of whether misstatement might exist

   a. If the substantive analytical procedure indicates that a misstatement might exist, but not its approximate amount, the auditor should request management to investigate and, if necessary, expand his or her work on it

3. When an auditor uses audit sampling to test a relevant assertion for an account balance or class of transactions, he or she should project the amount of known misstatement in the sample to the overall balance or class

4. Estimates such as those for inventory obsolescence, uncollectible receivables and warranty obligations are subject not only to the unpredictability of future events, but also to misstatements that may arise from using inadequate or inappropriate data or misapplication of appropriate data

   a. Because no one accounting estimate can be considered accurate with certainty, the auditor recognizes that a difference between an estimated amount best supported by the audit evidence and the financial statement estimated amount may not be significant, and such difference would not be considered to be a likely misstatement

      (1) But if the auditor believes the financial statement amount is unreasonable, he or she should treat the difference between the estimate and the closest reasonable estimate as a likely misstatement

          (a) The closest reasonable estimate may be a range of acceptable amounts or a specific amount

      (2) Example of range: Assume the auditor concludes that the allowance for doubtful accounts should be between $130,000 and $160,000

          (a) If management's estimate is in that range, the auditor ordinarily would conclude that the recorded amount is reasonable and no difference would be aggregated. There is no likely misstatement

          (b) If management's estimate is outside the auditor's range, the difference between the recorded amount and the amount at the closest end of the auditor's range would be aggregated as a likely misstatement

          (c) Illustrations

              1] Management's estimate is $132,000. The likely misstatement would be zero

              2] Management's estimate is $124,000. The likely misstatement would be $6,000.

   b. The auditor should watch for situations in which all such estimates seem biased in one direction—in such a case an adjustment may be necessary

5. Qualitative factors may also cause an auditor to consider a misstatement to be material, including

   a. Potential effect on trends, particularly profitability trends
   b. Misstatement that changes loss into income or vice versa
   c. Potential effect on entity's compliance with loan covenants, contracts, etc.
   d. Existence of statutory or regulatory reporting requirements
   e. Masks a change in earnings or other trends
   f. Increases management's compensation
   g. Sensitivity of the circumstances surrounding the misstatements (e.g., when a possible illegal act is involved)
   h. Significance of the financial statement element affected by the misstatement
   i. Effect of misclassifications (e.g., between operating and nonoperating income or recurring and nonrecurring income)
   j. Significance relative to reasonable user needs (earnings to investors, equity to creditors)
   k. Definitive character of misstatements, for example, the precision of an error that is objectively determinable versus an estimate
   l. Motivation of management with respect to the misstatement
   m. Existence of offsetting effects of individually significant but different misstatements
   n. Likelihood it will become material in the future
   o. Cost of correction
   p. Risk that possible additional undetected misstatements could exist

E. Evaluating whether the financial statements as a whole are free of material misstatements

1. The auditor should consider both the uncorrected misstatements (known and likely) and the qualitative factors

   a. As the aggregate misstatements approach materiality, the risk that the financial statements may be materially misstated increases

2. If the auditor concludes that, or is unable to conclude whether, the financial statements are materially misstated, the auditor must determine the implications for the auditor's report

    a. If financial statements depart materially from GAAP, a qualified opinion or adverse opinion is appropriate

    b. If a scope limitation is involved which makes it impossible for the auditor to determine whether the financial statements depart materially from GAAP, a qualified opinion or a disclaimer of opinion is appropriate

3. AU 380 provides guidance on communication responsibilities

F. Documentation

1. The auditor should document

    a. Levels of materiality, and tolerable misstatement, including any changes hereto, and the basis on which those levels were determined

    b. A summary of uncorrected misstatements, other than those that are trivial, related to known and likely misstatements

    c. Conclusion as to whether uncorrected misstatements, individually or in aggregate, do or do not cause the financial statements to be materially misstated, and the basis for that conclusion

    d. All known and likely misstatements, other than those that are clearly trivial, that have been corrected by management

2. Uncorrected misstatements should be documented in a manner that allows the auditor to

    a. Separately consider the effects of known and likely misstatements, including uncorrected misstatements identified in prior periods

    b. Consider the aggregate effect of misstatements on the financial statements and

    c. Consider the qualitative factors that are relevant to the auditor's consideration whether misstatements are material.

313 Substantive Tests prior to the Balance Sheet Date (SAS 45)

Overall Objectives and Approach—This section presents guidance related to performing substantive tests at a date prior to the balance sheet date ("interim testing"). For example, in certain circumstances an auditor might wish to audit an account as of November 30, and then apply certain procedures for the period through December 31, the balance sheet date. In addition to discussing the effect of interim procedures on audit risk, the section provides guidance on (1) factors to be considered prior to applying such procedures at an interim date, (2) extending interim date audit conclusions to the balance sheet date, and (3) coordinating the timing of auditing procedures.

A. Overall relationship of interim substantive testing to audit risk

1. Potentially increases audit risk (the risk that the auditor may **unknowingly fail to modify his/her opinion** on financial statements that are materially misstated—see outline of AU 312)

2. Potential for increased audit risk increases as interim period is lengthened

3. Effective substantive tests to cover the remaining period should be designed to control for the potentially increased audit risk

B. Performing substantive tests at an interim date

1. Factors to be considered before performing tests at an interim date

    a. Difficulty in controlling the incremental audit risk due to performing test early

    b. Cost of subsequent tests necessary in remaining period (period after principal substantive tests through year-end)

    c. Effectiveness of remaining period substantive tests, especially when control risk is assessed at the maximum

        (1) In some circumstances a reasonable basis for extending audit conclusions from an interim date to the balance sheet date when control risk is assessed at the maximum level

    d. Existence of rapidly changing business conditions which might cause management to misstate financial statements

    e. Predictability of year-end balances

2. Extending interim date audit conclusions to balance sheet date

    a. **Compare interim balances with year-end balances for unusual changes** and perform other analytical procedures and/or substantive tests of detail

    b. Consider implications of interim period errors in determining scope of remaining period tests

3. Coordinate timing of audit procedures such as

     a. Related-party transactions
     b. Interrelated accounts and accounting cutoffs (e.g., cash with marketable securities)
     c. Negotiable assets (e.g., cash) and liabilities (e.g., loans)

314 Understanding the Entity and Its Environment and Assessing the Risks of Material Misstatement (SAS 109)

Overall Objectives and Approach—This section establishes standards and provides guidance for implementing the second standard of fieldwork.

> *The auditor must obtain a sufficient understanding of the entity and its environment, including its internal control, to assess the risk of material misstatement of the financial statements whether due to error or fraud, and to design the nature, timing, and extent of further audit procedures.*

The understanding of the entity and its environment helps the auditor in a variety of ways throughout the audit, including

- Establishing materiality
- Considering appropriateness of accounting policies
- Identifying areas where special audit consideration is necessary
- Developing expectations for analytical procedures
- Designing audit procedures
- Evaluating sufficiency of evidence

The following is an overview of the outline:

A. Risk assessment procedures and sources of information about the entity and its environment, including its internal control
B. Understanding the entity and its environment, including its internal control
C. Internal control (logically fits under B., but due to its comprehensiveness was provided a separate section)
D. Assessing the risks of material misstatement
E. Documentation
F. Appendices

A. Risk assessment procedures and sources of information about the entity and its environment, including its internal control

     1. Risk assessment procedures

         a. Relationship between (1) risk assessment procedures, and (2) obtaining an understanding of the entity and its environment, including its internal control

             (1) Risk assessment procedures are the audit procedures used to obtain this understanding
             (2) The term "risk assessment procedures" is used because such procedures are used by the auditor as audit evidence to support assessment of the risks of material misstatement

                 (a) Such procedures may also provide audit evidence about the relevant assertions—that is, they may sometimes serve as substantive tests or tests of controls

         b. Procedures include

             (1) Inquiries of management and others within the entity

                 (a) Others within the entity include those charged with governance, internal audit personnel, employees involved in initiating processing, or recording complex or unusual transactions, in-house legal counsel, marketing, sales, etc.

             (2) Analytical procedures

                 (a) AU 329 provides guidance on analytical procedures

             (3) Observation and inquiry

                 (a) Examples

                     1] Observation of entity activities and operations
                     2] Inspection of documents, records, and internal control manuals
                     3] Reading reports prepared by management and by those charged with governance (e.g., board of directors' meeting minutes) and internal audit
                     4] Visits to the entity's premises

5] Tracing transactions through the information system relevant to financial reporting, which may be performed as part of a walk-through

> **NOTE:** The above procedures integrate well with AU 316's requirement that the auditor consider fraud risk factors and assess the risk of material misstatement due to fraud. Thus identifying fraud risk factors helps auditors obtain their understanding of the client and in assessing the risks of material misstatement.

2. Discussion among the audit team

a. Objective: For members of audit team to gain a better understanding of the potential for material misstatements of the financial statements resulting from fraud or error in the specific areas assigned to them, and to understand how the results of the audit procedures affect other aspects of the audit

b. Key members of the audit team are ordinarily involved in the discussion; it is not necessary for all team members to have a comprehensive knowledge of all aspects of the audit

c. The discussion should emphasize the need to exercise professional skepticism throughout the engagement, and to be alert for possible fraud or errors

> **NOTE:** One would expect this discussion to often be held concurrently with the discussion required by AU 316 on the susceptibility of the financial statements to fraud.

B. Understanding the entity and its environment, including its internal control; the understanding should include information on

1. Industry, regulatory, and other external factors

a. Examples—industry conditions, regulatory environment, relevant accounting pronouncements, legal and political environment, environmental requirements, other external factors such as general economic donations

2. Nature of the entity

a. Refers to: entity's operations, its ownership, governance, types of investments it makes, its structure, and how it is financed

3. Objectives and strategies and related business risks

a. The entity's objectives and strategies and related business risks that may result in material misstatement of the financial statements

b. While business risk is broader than the risk of misstatements, it includes that risk; examples

(1) A new competitor's product makes obsolete a portion of inventory
(2) New products may fail
(3) New types of contracts (e.g., percentage completion for a new product)

4. Measurement and review of the entity's financial performance

a. Performance measures create pressures that may motivate management to take action to misstate the financial statements

b. Misstatements may occur in performance measurement

5. Internal control—although internal control is a part of obtaining an understanding of the client, because of the depth covered in this section, we provide it with its own major section, following

C. Internal control

1. Overall

a. The auditor should obtain an understanding of the five components of internal control (IC) sufficient to assess the risk of material misstatement of the financial statements, whether due to error or fraud, and to design the nature, timing, and extent of further audit procedures

b. Auditor's approach

(1) Identify types of potential misstatements
(2) Consider factors that affect the risks of material misstatement
(3) Design test of controls, when applicable, and substantive procedures

c. Internal control is a process effected by an entity's board of directors, management, and other personnel, designed to provide reasonable assurance regarding the achievement of objectives in the following categories: (a) reliability of financial reporting, (b) effectiveness and efficiency of operations, and (c) compliance with applicable laws and regulations; IC consists of five interrelated components

    (1) Control environment
    (2) Entity's risk assessment
    (3) Information and communication
    (4) Control activities
    (5) Monitoring

  d. Auditors may use different terminology or IC frameworks to describe the various aspects of IC, provided all the components described in this section are addressed

2. Controls relevant to the audit

  a. Ordinarily, controls that are relevant to an audit pertain to preparing proper financial statements

  b. Controls over operations and compliance may be relevant to an audit if they pertain to information or data the auditor evaluates or uses in applying audit procedures; examples

    (1) Analytical procedures often rely on such information
    (2) Controls pertaining to detecting noncompliance with laws may have a direct and material effect on the financial statements

  c. Other controls are ordinarily not relevant to an audit (e.g., sophisticated system of automated controls in a commercial airline's system to maintain flight schedules)

  d. An auditor's consideration of asset safeguarding controls is generally limited to those relevant to reliable financial reporting

    (1) Passwords to control access to assets may be relevant; controls to prevent excessive use of materials in production generally are not relevant

3. Depth of understanding of internal control

  a. Obtaining an understanding of IC involves evaluating the design of a control and determining whether it has been implemented

    (1) Implemented means that the control exists and that the entity is using it
    (2) An improperly designed control may be a material weakness
    (3) Procedures to obtain audit evidence about the design and implementation of relevant controls include

      (a) *Inquiring* of entity personnel
      (b) *Observing* the application of specific controls
      (c) *Inspecting* documents and reports
      (d) *Tracing* transactions through the information system relevant to financial reporting

> **NOTE:** Inquiry alone is not sufficient to evaluate the design of a control and to determine whether it has been implemented.

  b. Obtaining an understanding of an entity's controls is not sufficient to serve as testing of operating effectiveness, unless there is some automation that provides for the consistent application of the operation of the control

    (1) The inherent consistency of IT processing may make this possible

4. Characteristics of manual and automated elements of internal control relevant to the auditor's risk assessment

  a. Benefits of IT

    (1) Consistent application of business rules and performance of complex calculations
    (2) Enhance timeliness, availability, and accuracy of information
    (3) Facilitate additional analysis of information
    (4) Enhance ability to monitor performance of entity's activities and its policies and procedures
    (5) Reduce risk that controls will be circumvented
    (6) Enhance ability to achieve effective segregation of duties

  b. Risks of IT

    (1) Reliance on systems and programs
    (2) Unauthorized access to data
    (3) Unauthorized changes to data in master files
    (4) Unauthorized changes to systems or programs
    (5) Failure to make necessary changes to systems
    (6) Inappropriate manual intervention
    (7) Potential loss of data or inability to access data as required

   c. Manual controls may be more suitable where judgment and discretion are required, such as

     (1) Large, unusual, or nonrecurring transactions
     (2) Circumstances where misstatements are difficult to define, anticipate, or predict
     (3) Changing circumstances that require a control response outside the scope of an existing automated control
     (4) Monitoring effectiveness of automated controls

   d. Manual controls may be less suitable when

     (1) High volume or recurring transactions, or when errors can be anticipated if done manually
     (2) A control activity is involved for which there are specific ways to effectively automate the control

   e. Limitations of internal control

     (1) Can only provide reasonable, not absolute, assurance about achieving an entity's objectives
     (2) Specific limitations

       (a) Human judgment in decision making can be faulty
       (b) Breakdowns in IC due to human failures such as simple mistakes
       (c) Collusion of two or more people may circumvent controls
       (d) Inappropriate management override of IC
       (e) Segregation of duties may be difficult in very small entities

5. Components of internal control

   a. Control environment

     (1) Elements

       (a) Communication and enforcement of integrity and ethical values
       (b) Commitment to competence
       (c) Participation by those charged with governance
       (d) Management's philosophy and operating style
       (e) Organizational structure
       (f) Assignment of authority and responsibility
       (g) Human resource policies and practices

     (2) **Understanding needed by auditor**

       (a) Understand attitudes, awareness, and actions of those charged with governance; concentrate on implementation of controls
       (b) Consider the collective effect of control environment strengths and weaknesses

     (3) The control environment itself does not prevent or detect and correct a material misstatement; therefore, auditor should consider the effect of other components of IC in conjunction with the control environment

       (a) Example: An auditor might consider an entity's monitoring of controls in conjunction with the control environment

   b. The entity's risk assessment process

     (1) Definition—Identification, analysis, and management of risks relevant to the preparation of financial statements that are fairly presented in conformity with GAAP
     (2) Risks

       (a) Change in operating environment
       (b) New personnel
       (c) New or revamped information systems
       (d) Rapid growth
       (e) New technology
       (f) New business models, products, or activities
       (g) Corporate restructurings
       (h) Expanded foreign operations
       (i) New accounting pronouncement

     (3) **Understanding needed by auditor**

       (a) Understand how management considers risks relevant to financial reporting and how it decides about actions to address those risks

(b) Inquire about business risks that management has identified and consider whether they may result in material misstatements

c. Information systems, including related business processes relevant to financial reporting, and communication

(1) Includes the accounting system and consists of the procedures and records established to initiate, record, process, and report entity transactions, and to maintain accountability for the related assets, liabilities, and equity

(2) **Understanding needed by auditor**

(a) Significant classes of transactions
(b) Procedures by which transactions are initiated, recorded, processed, and reported
(c) Related accounting records
(d) How information system captures events and conditions, other than classes of transactions, that are significant to the financial statements
(e) Financial reporting process used to prepare financial statements, including estimates and disclosures
(f) The auditor should also obtain an understanding of how incorrect processing of transactions is resolved (e.g., suspense items, overrides, bypasses of controls)

(3) Detailed procedures that auditor must understand include those to

(a) Enter transaction totals into the general ledger
(b) Initiate, record, and process journal entries in the general ledger
(c) Initiate and record recurring and nonrecurring adjustments to the financial statements
(d) Prepare financial statements and disclosures

d. Control activities

(1) The policies and procedures that help ensure that management directives are carried out; for example, policies that ensure that necessary actions are taken to address risks that threaten the achievement of entity objectives

(2) Types of control activities

(a) Authorization
(b) Segregation of duties
(c) Safeguarding
(d) Asset accountability

(3) **Understanding needed by the auditor**

(a) Consider knowledge about control activities obtained from understanding other components in determining whether it is necessary to devote additional attention to control activities
(b) Ordinarily those relevant are those relating to authorization, segregation of duties, safeguarding of assets, and asset accountability
(c) The main concern is whether control activity individually or in combination with others prevents or detects and corrects material misstatements

(4) IT application controls may be performed by IT or individuals (e.g., edit checks, numerical sequence checks, manual follow-up of exceptions)

(a) Application controls performed by individuals interacting with IT may be referred to as *user controls*

(5) General controls are policies and procedures that relate to many applications and support the effective functioning of application controls

(a) Include controls over data center and network operations; system software acquisition, change, and maintenance; access security; application system acquisition, development and maintenance
(b) General controls should be assessed in relation to their effect on applications and data that become part of the financial statements

e. Monitoring of controls

(1) A process to assess the quality of IC performance over time

(a) Involves assessing design and operation of controls on a timely basis and taking necessary corrective actions
(b) Much of the information may be produced by the entity's information system

(2) **Understanding needed by the auditor**

    (a) Major types of activities the entity uses to monitor IC, including the sources of the information related to those activities and how those activities are used to initiate corrective actions

D. Assessing the risks of material misstatement

1. Overall

  a. The auditor should identify and assess the risks of material misstatement at the financial statement level and at the relevant assertion level for classes of transactions, account balances, and disclosures; approach

    (1) Identify risks throughout the process of obtaining an understanding
    (2) Relate the identified risks to what can go wrong at the relevant assertion level
    (3) Consider whether the risks are of a magnitude that could result in a material misstatement
    (4) Consider likelihood that risks could result in a material misstatement

> **NOTE:** This is referred to as "the risk assessment."

  b. When the risk assessment is based on an expectation that controls are operating effectively to prevent or detect material misstatement, the auditor should perform test of controls to provide evidence as to whether controls are operating effectively
  c. The auditor should determine whether identified risks of material misstatement relate to specific classes of transactions, account balances, and disclosures at the relevant assertion level, **or** whether they relate more pervasively to the financial statements as a whole and potentially affect many relevant assertions

    (1) Those risks affecting many assertions may result from a weak control environment

  d. In making risk assessments, the auditor should identify controls that are likely to prevent or detect and correct material misstatements in specific relevant assertions

    (1) Often only multiple control activities, together with other elements of internal control will address a risk
    (2) Other control activities may have specific effect on an individual relevant assertion (e.g., control activities established to ensure that its personnel are properly counting and recording the annual physical inventory)

  e. Controls may be directly or indirectly related to an assertion

    (1) The more indirect, the less effect (e.g., sales manager's review of a summary of sales addresses completeness less directly than a process of matching shipping documents with billing documents)

2. Significant risks that require special audit consideration

  a. Determining significant risks is a matter for the auditor's professional judgment

    (1) In determining significant risks, the auditor should exclude the effect of identified controls and determine whether the nature of the risk, its likely magnitude of misstatement, and its likelihood of occurring are such that they require specific audit consideration
    (2) Routine, noncomplex transactions that are subject to systematic processing are less likely to give rise to significant risks because they have lower inherent risks
    (3) Significant risks are often derived from **business risks,** and the auditor should consider

      (a) Whether the risk is a risk of fraud
      (b) Whether the risk is related to recent significant economic, accounting, or other developments
      (c) The complexity of transactions
      (d) Whether the risk involves significant transactions with related parties
      (e) The degree of subjectivity in the measurement of financial information
      (f) Whether the risk involves significant nonroutine transactions that are outside the normal course of business for the entity, or that appear to be unusual

    (4) Significant risks are also often related to **significant nonroutine transactions and judgmental matters** arising from matters such as

      (a) Greater management intervention to specify accounting treatment
      (b) Grater manual intervention for data collection and processing
      (c) Complex calculations or accounting principles
      (d) Nonroutine transactions that are difficult to control
      (e) Significant related-party transactions

    (5) Risks of material misstatement may be greater for risks relating to significant judgmental matters that require **accounting estimates** such as

        (a) Accounting principles for accounting estimates or revenue recognition that are subject to differing interpretation

        (b) Those requiring judgment because of their subjectivity or complexity

        (c) Those requiring assumptions about the effects of future events (e.g., judgments about fair value)

  b. For significant risks, to extent not already done, the auditor should evaluate the design of the entity's related controls and determine whether they have been implemented

    (1) If management has not appropriately responded by implementing controls over significant risks, the auditor may judge that there is a material weakness that must be communicated to those charged with governance (e.g., the audit committee)

3. For routine transactions, substantive procedures alone (i.e., no tests of controls) may be sufficient, depending upon the risk of misstatement involved

4. Examples of situations in which it may be impossible to design effective substantive procedures that by themselves provide sufficient appropriate audit evidence (i.e., test of controls may also be required)

  a. IT is used to initiate orders for purchases and delivery of goods based on predetermined rules and to pay related accounts payable based on system-generated decisions

  b. An entity that provides services to customers via electronic media (e.g., internet service provider or a telecommunications company) and uses IT to create a log of the service provided to its customers, etc.

5. Revision of risk assessment

  a. Risk is revised throughout the audit—for example, as test of control and substantive procedures audit evidence is collected

E. Documentation; the auditor should document

1. Discussion among audit team, including how and when the discussion occurred, subject matter discussed, audit team members who participated, and significant decisions reached concerning planned responses at the financial statement and relevant assertion level

2. Key elements of the understanding obtained, including each of the components of IC, sources of information, and risk assessment procedures

3. Assessment of the risks of material misstatement both at the financial statement level and at the relevant assertion level

4. Risks identified and related controls

F. Appendices

1. Appendix A—Provides details on matters the auditor may consider when obtaining an understanding of the industry, regulatory, and other external factors that affect the entity; the nature of the entity; objectives and strategies and related business risks; and measurement and review of the entity's financial statements

2. Appendix B—Provides details on the five internal control components—control environment; risk assessment; information and communications systems; control activities; and monitoring

3. Appendix C—Composed of the following examples that may indicate the existence of risks of material misstatement:

- Operations in regions that are economically unstable
- Operations exposed to volatile market (e.g., futures trading)
- High degree of complex regulation
- Going concern and liquidity issues
- Marginally achieving explicitly-stated strategic objectives
- Constraints on the availability of capital and credit
- Changes in the industry in which the entity operates
- Changes in the supply chain
- Developing or offering new products or services
- Expanding into new locations
- Changes in the entity, such as through acquisitions, etc.
- Entities or business segments likely to be sold
- Complex alliances and joint ventures
- Use of off-balance-sheet finance, special-purpose entities, and other complex financing arrangements
- Significant transactions with related parties

- Lack of personnel with appropriate accounting and financial reporting skills
- Change in key personnel
- Weaknesses in internal control
- Inconsistencies between entity's IT strategy and its business strategies
- Changes in the IT environment and systems
- Inquiries into entity's operations or financial results by regulators
- Past misstatements, history of errors, or a significant amount of adjustments at period end
- Significant amount of nonroutine or nonsystematic transactions
- Transactions recorded based on management's intent (e.g., debt refinancing, assets to be sold, classification of marketable securities)
- Application of new accounting pronouncements
- Complex processes related to accounting measurements
- Events or transactions that result in significant measurement uncertainty, including accounting estimates
- Pending litigation and contingent liabilities

315 Communications between Predecessor and Successor Auditors (SAS 84)

Overall Objectives and Approach—This section presents guidance on communications between predecessor and successor auditors when a change of auditors has taken place or is in process. The section presents information on (a) several definitions and key concepts, (b) a **required** communication by the potential successor **before** accepting the engagement, (c) **other** advisable communications **after** the successor auditor has accepted the engagement, and (d) audits of financial statements that have been previously audited (**reaudits**).

A. Definitions and key concepts

1. **Predecessor auditor**—Auditor who has reported on the most recent audited financial statements or was engaged to perform but did not complete an audit of any subsequent financial statements and has resigned, declined to stand for reappointment, or been notified that his/her services have been, or may be terminated
2. **Successor auditor**—Auditor who is considering accepting an engagement to audit financial statements or an auditor who has accepted such an engagement
3. The responsibility for beginning the communication process is with the successor
4. The communication may be written or oral

B. Required communications **before** successor accepts engagement

1. The successor should obtain prospective client's permission to contact the predecessor

   a. If the prospective client refuses permission, the successor should inquire as to the reasons and consider the implications of such refusal in deciding whether to accept the engagement

2. Successor's inquiries of the predecessor should include

   a. Information bearing on **integrity** of management
   b. **Disagreements** with management as to accounting principles, auditing procedures, or other similarly significant matters
   c. **Communications** to audit committee regarding fraud, illegal acts, and internal control related matters
   d. Predecessor's understanding of the **reasons for change** in auditors

3. Predecessor should respond promptly and fully to reasonable inquiries; however, unusual circumstances (e.g., litigation, disciplinary proceedings) may lead to a limited response

C. Other advisable communications **after acceptance** of the engagement

1. Successor should request client to authorize predecessor to allow a review of the predecessor auditor's working papers

   a. Although the review of working papers affects nature, timing, and extent of procedures with respect to **opening balances** and **consistency** of accounting principles, all conclusions reached are solely the responsibility of the successor
   b. The predecessor may wish to request the successor to sign a consent and acknowledgment letter from the client to document this authorization and reduce misunderstandings about the scope of the communication being authorized

      (1) **Consent letter**—From predecessor auditor to client (then signed by client) acknowledging client's permission to allow communication with the successor
      (2) **Acknowledgment letter**—From predecessor to successor (then signed by successor), indicating that successor **will not**

    (a) Comment as to whether predecessor's engagement was performed in accordance with GAAS
    (b) Provide expert testimony on predecessor's audit
    (c) Use audit procedures in predecessor auditor's working papers as evidential matter

2. Predecessor should determine working papers to be made available, and should ordinarily include

    a. Documentation of planning
    b. Internal control
    c. Audit results
    d. Other matters of continuing accounting and auditing significance, such as analysis of balance sheet accounts

3. Extent to which predecessor permits access to working papers is a matter of judgment
4. Audit evidence includes

    a. Most recent financial statements
    b. Predecessor auditor's report
    c. Results of successor's review of predecessor auditor's working papers

5. If the successor auditor discovers financial misstatements, the successor should request client to inform predecessor auditor and arrange meeting of the three parties

    a. AU 561 provides further information
    b. If client refuses to inform predecessor, the successor should

        (1) Evaluate implications on current audit
        (2) Decide whether to resign
        (3) Consider need to consult with legal counsel concerning future action

D. Audits of financial statements that have been previously audited (**reaudits**)

1. If an auditor is asked to audit financial statements that have been previously audited (a reaudit), the auditor as a successor should follow procedures presented above in this outline; additional audit procedures are necessary in the reaudit
2. The successor should request working papers for period under reaudit, and the period prior to the reaudit period; the extent to which the predecessor permits access to working papers is a matter of judgment
3. If material, the successor performing the reaudit should perform some physical counts of inventory at a date subsequent to the period of reaudit; additional procedures may include

    a. Tests of prior transactions
    b. Review of records of prior counts
    c. Application of analytical procedures such as gross profit tests

316 Consideration of Fraud in a Financial Statement Audit (SAS 99)

Overall Objectives and Approach—It is an auditor's responsibility to plan and perform the audit to obtain reasonable assurance about whether the financial statements are free of material misstatement, whether caused by error or fraud. Concerning fraud, the emphasis in the Professional Standards is on situations in which it causes material misstatements, **not** on making determinations of whether legally fraud has occurred in any particular situation.

This section deals with the auditor's responsibility as it relates to the risk of material misstatement due to fraud. Its major sections describe

A. Characteristics of fraud
B. Professional skepticism
C. Staff discussion of the risk of material misstatement
D. Obtaining the information needed to identify risks of material misstatement due to fraud
E. Identifying risks that may result in a material misstatement due to fraud
F. Assessing the identified risks after considering the client's programs and controls
G. Responding to the results of the assessment
H. Evaluating audit evidence
I. Communicating about fraud to management, the audit committee, and others
J. Documenting the auditor's consideration of fraud

In considering the outline, you might think of point A. as including background information, with point B. discussing the concept of professional skepticism. Although a simplification, the remaining sections may be viewed as "steps" to be performed relating to fraud.

Following point J. of the outline is a summary of AU 316's fraud risk factors and information on antifraud programs and controls. Those items are included as appendices to AU 316.

A. Characteristics of fraud

    1. Fraud is intentional, errors are unintentional

        a. Although fraud is considered an intentional act, when a misstatement exists, intent is often difficult to determine

    2. **Types of intentional misstatements**

        a. **Fraudulent financial reporting**—intentional misstatements, omissions of amounts or disclosures
        b. **Misappropriation of assets**—theft of an entity's assets, also referred to as defalcation

    3. Three conditions are generally present when fraud occurs

        a. **Incentive/pressure**—a reason to commit fraud
        b. **Opportunity**—for example, ineffective controls, override of controls
        c. **Attitude/rationalization**—ability to justify the fraud to oneself

    4. Management has a unique ability to perpetrate fraud because it can directly or indirectly manipulate accounting records and present fraudulent financial information; it may

        a. Override controls
        b. Direct or solicit employees to carry out fraud

    5. Although fraud is ordinarily concealed, certain conditions (e.g., missing documents) may suggest the possibility of fraud
    6. An auditor is unable to provide absolute assurance of detecting fraud

B. Professional Skepticism

    1. Professional skepticism is an attitude that includes a questioning mind and a critical assessment of audit evidence
    2. An audit should be conducted with a mindset that recognizes the possibility of material misstatement due to fraud, even if

        a. Past experience with the client has not revealed fraud, and
        b. Regardless of the auditor's belief about management's honesty and integrity

    3. An auditor should not be satisfied with less than persuasive evidence because of a belief that management is honest

C. Staff discussion of the risk of material misstatement

    1. Prior to or in conjunction with obtaining information to identify risks of fraud (part D of this outline), the audit team should discuss the potential for a material misstatement due to fraud, including

        a. "Brainstorming" among team members about how and where the financial statements might be susceptible to fraud, how management could perpetrate and conceal fraudulent financial reporting, and how assets could be misappropriated
        b. Emphasizing the importance of maintaining the proper state of mind regarding the potential for material misstatement due to fraud

    2. The discussion should

        a. Include consideration of known factors affecting **incentives/pressures** for fraud, **opportunities,** and culture or environment that enables management to **rationalize** committing fraud
        b. Emphasize the need to maintain a questioning mind and to exercise professional skepticism
        c. Include key members of the audit team

            (1) If multiple locations are involved there could be multiple discussions in different locations
            (2) It may be useful to include any specialists assigned to the audit team in the discussion

D. Obtaining the information needed to identify risks of material misstatement due to fraud; procedures should include

    1. Inquiries of management and others

        a. Examples of inquiries of management

            (1) Does it have knowledge of fraud or suspected fraud
            (2) Have there been allegations of fraud or suspected fraud
            (3) Its understanding of fraud risks
            (4) Programs and controls established to mitigate fraud risks
            (5) Control over multiple locations

(6) Communications to employees about business practices and ethical behavior

(7) Whether management has reported to the audit committee the nature of the company's internal control

    b. Inquiries of the audit committee, internal audit function, and others should include their views about risks of fraud and their knowledge of any fraud or suspected fraud

2. Considering the results of analytical procedures performed in planning the audit

    a. When unexpected results occur, consider the risk of material misstatement due to fraud

    b. Perform analytical procedures on revenue to identify unusual or unexpected relationships

> **NOTE:** Make certain that you know that analytical procedures relating to revenue must be performed during planning of the audit.

    c. Because analytical procedures performed during planning often use data aggregated at a high level, results obtained often only provide a broad initial indication about whether a material misstatement exists

3. Considering fraud risk factors

    a. **Fraud risk factors** are events or conditions that indicate **incentives/pressures** to perpetrate fraud, **opportunities** to carry out fraud, or **attitude/rationalizations** to justify a fraudulent action

> **NOTE:** Recall that **incentives/pressures, opportunities,** and **attitudes/rationalizations** are the conditions generally present in individuals who commit fraud presented in A.3 of the outline.

    b. The auditor should use professional judgment in determining whether a risk factor is present and in identifying and assessing the risk of material misstatement due to fraud

    c. While fraud risk factors do **not** necessarily indicate the existence of fraud, they often are present when fraud exists

    d. Fraud risk factors are presented following point I. of this outline

4. Consider other information: the discussion among audit team members, reviews of interim financial statements, consideration of identified inherent risks

E. Identifying risks that may result in a material misstatement due to fraud

1. It is helpful at this stage to consider the three conditions present when a material misstatement due to fraud ordinarily occurs—incentives/pressures, opportunities, and attitudes/rationalizations

    a. But fraud may exist even if all three haven't been identified

2. The auditor should evaluate whether identified risks of material misstatement due to fraud can be related to specific accounts, assertions, or whether they relate more pervasively to the financial statements as a whole

3. The identification of a risk of material misstatement due to fraud includes consideration of

    a. Type of risk that may exist (fraudulent financial reporting or misappropriation of assets)

    b. Significance of risk (magnitude)

    c. Likelihood of risk

    d. Pervasiveness of risk (overall financial statements, or a particular assertion or account)

4. A presumption of improper revenue recognition is a fraud risk

5. The auditor should always address the risk of management override of controls

> **NOTE:** Make certain that you know points 4. and 5. above are required for all audits. That is, the auditor should ordinarily presume that there is a risk of material misstatement due to fraud relating to revenue recognition and of management override.

F. Assessing the identified risks after considering programs and controls

1. AU 319 requires the auditor to obtain an understanding of internal control sufficient to plan the audit; this understanding allows the auditor to

    a. Identify types of potential misstatements

    b. Consider factors that affect the risk of material misstatement

    c. Design tests of controls when applicable

    d. Design substantive tests

2. As a part of obtaining an understanding of internal control sufficient to plan the audit, the auditor should evaluate whether the client's programs and controls that address the identified risks of material misstatement due to fraud have been suitably designed and placed in operation

3. After the auditor has evaluated the client's programs and controls in this area, the auditor's assessment of the risk of material misstatement due to fraud should consider these results

4. Appendix 2 to this section provides programs and controls

G. Responding to the results of the assessment—as risk increases

1. **Overall responses**

   a. Assign personnel with more experience and have more supervision
   b. More carefully consider significant accounting policies
   c. Make auditing procedures less predictable

2. **Responses that address specifically identified risks**

   a. General types of responses

      (1) Nature—more reliable evidence or additional corroborative information
      (2) Timing—perform at or near end of reporting period, but apply substantive procedures to transactions occurring throughout the year
      (3) Extent—increase sample sizes, perform more detailed analytical procedures

   b. Examples of modification of the nature, timing, and extent of procedures

      (1) Perform procedures on a surprise or unannounced basis (e.g., inventory observations, counting of cash)
      (2) Request inventory counts at end of reporting period
      (3) Make oral inquiries of major customers and suppliers in addition to written confirmations
      (4) Perform substantive analytical procedures using disaggregated data
      (5) Interview personnel in areas where risk of material misstatement due to fraud has been identified
      (6) Discuss the situation with any other auditors involved with audit (e.g., an "other auditor" who audits subsidiary)

   c. Additional examples of responses for a high risk of **fraudulent financial reporting** may result in increased

      (1) Analysis of revenue recognition
      (2) Consideration of inventory quantities
      (3) Consideration of management estimates (e.g., allowance for doubtful accounts)

   d. Additional responses for a high risk of **misappropriation of assets**

      (1) If a particular asset is susceptible to misappropriation, obtain understanding of controls and/or physical inspection may be appropriate
      (2) More precise analytical procedures may be used

3. **Responses to further address the risk of management override of controls**

   a. **Examine journal entries and other adjustments** for evidence of possible material misstatement due to fraud
   b. **Review accounting estimates** for biases, including a retrospective review of previous year estimates so as to provide guidance on management's past performance in this area
   c. **Evaluate the business rationale** for significant unusual transactions

   > **NOTE:** 1. through 3. above are distinct types of responses—(1) overall responses, (2) responses that address specifically identified risks, and (3) responses for management override of controls. Although differing combinations of each might be expected on an audit, those for management override are ordinarily required on an audit.

H. Evaluating audit evidence

1. The assessment of risks of material misstatement should be ongoing throughout the audit
2. Conditions identified during fieldwork may change or support a judgment concerning the assessment

   a. Discrepancies in accounting records; examples

      (1) Transactions not recorded in a complete or timely manner, or improperly recorded
      (2) Unsupported or unauthorized balances or transactions
      (3) Significant last-minute adjustments
      (4) Evidence of employee inappropriate access to systems

   b. Conflicting or missing audit evidence; examples

     (1) Missing, unavailable, or altered documents
     (2) Unexplained items on reconciliations
     (3) Inconsistent, vague, or implausible responses to inquiries
     (4) Unusual discrepancies between records and confirmation replies
     (5) Missing inventory or physical assets
     (6) Unavailable or missing electronic evidence, inconsistent retention policies

   c. Problematic or unusual relationships between auditor and management; examples

     (1) Denial of access to records, facilities, employees, customers, vendors, and others
     (2) Undue time pressures
     (3) Management complaints, intimidation
     (4) Unusual delays in providing information
     (5) Tips or complaints about alleged fraud
     (6) Unwillingness to facilitate auditor access to electronic files
     (7) Denial of access to IT operations staff and facilities
     (8) Unwillingness to add or revise disclosures in financial statements

3. The auditor should evaluate whether analytical procedures performed as substantive tests or in the overall review stage indicate a previously unrecognized risk of material misstatement due to fraud

   a. If not already performed, the auditor should perform analytical procedures at the overall review stage of the audit; unusual situations include

     (1) Large amounts of income recorded in the last week or two of the year
     (2) Income inconsistent with trends in cash flows from operations

   b. Examples of unusual or unexpected analytical relationships

Change	Possible cause
Net income to cash flows may appear unusual	Fictitious revenue and receivables
Changes in inventory, payables, sales, or cost of goods sold as compared to preceding period	Theft of inventory, but inability to manipulate all related accounts
Company profitability inconsistent with industry trends	Numerous possible misstatements
Bad debt write-offs high	Theft of cash receipts
Sales volume per accounting records differs from production statistics	Misstatement of sales

4. The auditor should evaluate risks of material misstatement due to fraud at or near completion of fieldwork

   a. This is primarily a qualitative consideration based on the auditor's judgment

5. When audit procedures identify misstatements, the auditor should consider whether such misstatements may indicate fraud

6. When misstatements are or may be the result of fraud, but the effects are not material to the financial statements, the auditor should evaluate the implications

   a. A misappropriation of cash from a small petty cash fund normally would have little significance
   b. A misappropriation involving management may be indicative of a more pervasive problem and may require the auditor to consider the impact on the nature, timing, and extent of tests of balances or transactions, and the assessment of the effectiveness of controls

7. If the auditor believes the misstatements may be the result of fraud and has determined it could be material to the financial statements, but has been unable to evaluate whether the effect is material, the auditor should

   a. Attempt to obtain audit evidence to determine whether fraud has occurred and its effect
   b. Consider implications for other aspects of the audit
   c. Discuss the matter and an approach for further investigation with an appropriate level of management at least one level above those involved, and with senior management and the audit committee
   d. If appropriate, suggest the client consult with legal counsel

8. The risk of fraud may be so high as to cause the auditor to consider withdrawing from engagement; factors affecting decision

   a. Implications about integrity of management
   b. Diligence and cooperation of management or the board of directors

I. Communicating about fraud to management, the audit committee, and others

1. Whenever there is evidence that fraud may exist, the matter should be brought to an appropriate level of management, even if the matter might be considered inconsequential

    a. All fraud involving senior management, and any fraud (by anyone) that causes a material misstatement should be reported directly to the audit committee
    b. The auditor should reach an understanding with the audit committee regarding communications about misappropriations perpetrated by lower-level employees

2. If risks have continued control implications, the auditor should determine whether they represent significant deficiencies and need to be communicated to the audit committee—see outline of AU 325
3. The auditor may choose to communicate other risks of fraud
4. Disclosure of fraud beyond senior management and its audit committee is not ordinarily a part of the auditor's responsibility, unless

    a. Required by specific legal and regulatory requirements
    b. To a successor auditor—see outline of AU 315
    c. In response to a subpoena
    d. To a funding agency or other specified agency in accordance with requirements of audits of entities that receive governmental financial assistance

J. Documenting the auditor's consideration of fraud; document the following:

1. Discussion among audit team of risk of material misstatement due to fraud, including how and when discussion occurred, participants, and subject matter
2. Procedures performed to obtain information to identify and assess risks of material misstatement due to fraud
3. Specific risks of material misstatement due to fraud that were identified and auditor's response to those risks
4. If auditor has **not** identified improper revenue recognition as a risk of material misstatement due to fraud, the reasons for that conclusion
5. Results of procedures performed to further assess risk of management override of controls
6. Other conditions and analytical relationships or other responses required and any further responses the auditor concluded were appropriate to address such risks or conditions
7. Nature of communications about fraud made to management, the audit committee, and others

APPENDIX 1: EXAMPLES OF FRAUD RISK FACTORS

Misstatements Arising from Fraudulent Financial Reporting

Incentives/Pressures	Opportunities	Attitudes/Rationalizations

Incentives/Pressures

1. Threatened financial stability or profitability
   - High degree of competition or sales saturation
   - High vulnerability to rapid changes (e.g., technology, interest rates)
   - Declines in customer demand, business failures in industry
   - Operating losses
     Negative cash flows from operations
   - Rapid growth or unusual profitability
   - New accounting, statutory, or regulatory requirements

2. Excessive pressure on management to meet requirements or third-party expectations due to
   - Profitability or trend level expectations
   - Need for additional debt or equity financing
   - Marginal ability to meet exchange listing requirements
   - Likely poor financial results on pending transactions

3. Management or directors' financial situation threatened by
   - Significant financial interests in company
   - Significant portions of compensation contingent on results of company
   - Personal guarantees of debts of company

4. Excessive pressure to meet financial target set up by directors or management

Opportunities

1. Industry provides opportunities for
   - Related-party transactions beyond ordinary
   - Company can dictate terms or conditions to suppliers or customers (may result in inappropriate transactions)
   - Accounts based on significant estimates
   - Significant, unusual, or highly complex transactions
   - Significant operations across international borders with differing business environments and cultures
   - Significant bank accounts in tax haven jurisdictions

2. Ineffective monitoring of management allows
   - Domination of management by a single person or small group without controls
   - Ineffective board of director or audit committee oversight

3. Complex or unstable organizational structure
   - Difficulty in determining organization or individuals with control of company
   - Overly complex structure
   - High turnover of senior management, counsel, or board members

Internal control deficient
   - Inadequate monitoring of controls
   - High turnover rate or ineffective accounting, internal audit, or information technology staff
   - Ineffective accounting and information systems

Attitudes/Rationalizations

Relating to board members, management, or employees
   - Ineffective communications, implementation, support, or enforcement of ethics
   - Nonfinancial management excessive participation in selecting accounting principles or determining estimates
   - Known history of violations of securities or other laws
   - Excessive interest in maintaining or increasing stock price
   - Aggressive or unrealistic forecasts
   - Failure to correct significant deficiencies on a timely basis
   - Interest by management of employing inappropriate means to minimize earnings for tax reasons
   - Recurring management attempts to justify marginal or inappropriate accounting based on materiality
   - Strained relationship with current or predecessor auditor

Misstatements Arising from Misappropriation of Assets

Incentives/Pressures	Opportunities	Attitudes/Rationalizations

1. Personal financial obligations
 	
2. Adverse relationship between company and employees
 	
  • Known or anticipated layoffs
  • Changes in compensation
  • Promotions, compensation, or other rewards inconsistent with expectations
	1. Characteristics of assets
	
	  • Large amounts of cash on hand or processed
	  • Small, high-value, or high-demand inventory items
	  • Easily convertible assets (bearer bonds, diamonds, computer chips)
	  • Small marketable fixed assets
	
	2. Inadequate internal control, including inadequate
	
	  • Segregation of duties
	  • Job application screening of employees with access to assets
	  • Recordkeeping for assets
	  • Authorization or approval of transactions
	  • Reconciliation of assets
	  • Documentation of transactions (e.g., credits for merchandise returns)
	  • No requirements for mandatory vacations
	  • Management understanding of information technology
	  • Access controls over automated records
		Attitudes or behavior of those with access to assets susceptible to misappropriation
		
		  • Disregard for need for monitoring or reducing risks
		  • Disregard for internal control
		  • Behavior indicating displeasure or dissatisfaction with company or its treatment of employees
		  • Changes in behavior or lifestyle that indicate assets may have been misappropriated

APPENDIX 2: PROGRAMS AND CONTROLS RELATED TO FRAUD

This appendix includes a discussion of examples of programs and controls that management can implement to help deter, prevent, and detect fraud, which may be briefly summarized as

A. Creating a culture of honesty and high ethics

1. Setting tone at the top
2. Creating a positive workplace environment
3. Hiring and promoting appropriate employees
4. Proper training
5. Proper discipline for those committing fraud

B. Management's evaluation of processes and controls to mitigate risk of and reduce opportunities for fraud include policies and procedures to

1. Identify and measure fraud risks
2. Mitigate fraud risks
3. Implement and monitor appropriate controls and other measures

C. Develop an appropriate oversight process

1. Effective audit committee or board of directors
2. Effective internal auditors
3. Assistance from independent auditors

317 Illegal Acts by Clients (SAS 54)

Overall Objectives and Approach—This section presents guidance on the nature and extent of consideration given to client illegal acts during audits. The guidance relates both to considering the possibility of illegal acts, and to the responsibility when such illegal acts are detected.

A. Overall definition of illegal acts and summary of auditor responsibility

1. Illegal acts—violations of laws or governmental regulations

   a. Illegal acts by clients are acts attributable to entity under audit acts of management, or employees acting on behalf of entity
   b. Illegal acts by clients **do not include personal misconduct** by entity's personnel that is unrelated to business

2. Determination of legality of act is normally beyond auditor's professional competence and depends on legal judgment
3. The further removed illegal act is from the events and transactions ordinarily reflected in financial statements the less likely it is that the auditor will become aware

   a. Examples of illegal acts more likely to be detected (those with a direct and material effect on determination of financial statement amounts)

      (1) Tax laws affecting accruals
      (2) Revenue accrued on governmental contracts

   b. Examples of illegal acts less likely to be detected (those with an indirect effect on financial statements—often a contingent liability)

      (1) Laws related to securities trading
      (2) Occupational safety and health
      (3) Price fixing

      > **NOTE:** a. items typically relate to financial and accounting aspects; b. items typically relate more to an entity's operating aspects. The auditor's responsibility for illegal acts having a direct and material effect on determination of financial statement amounts (a.) is the same as for errors and fraud—to design the audit to provide reasonable assurance of their detection when they are material; see AU 316. An auditor does not ordinarily have a sufficient basis for recognizing possible violations of those illegal acts having only indirect effects (b.).

   c. **The remainder of this section is only on illegal acts having material but indirect effect on the financial statements (b. above).**

B. Auditor's consideration of possibility of illegal acts **on all audits**

   1. Summary of the auditor's responsibility

      a. Be aware of possibility of such illegal acts
      b. If specific information comes to the auditor's attention concerning the existence of illegal acts, apply audit procedures specifically directed to ascertaining whether such an illegal act has occurred
      c. An audit provides no assurance that illegal acts will be detected or that any contingent liabilities that may result will be disclosed

   2. **Audit procedures when there is no evidence** concerning the existence of possible illegal acts

      a. Audits normally do not include procedures designed to detect illegal acts, but other procedures may identify such acts (e.g., reading minutes, inquiries to management and legal counsel, substantive tests)
      b. The auditor should make inquiries of management concerning the client's compliance with laws and regulations. Where applicable, the auditor should inquire of management concerning

         (1) Client's policies related to prevention of illegal acts
         (2) Directives issued by client and representations obtained by client from management on compliance with laws

      c. The auditor should ordinarily also obtain written representations from management concerning the absence of violations of laws whose effects should be considered for disclosure in the financial statements or as a basis for recording a loss contingency

      > **NOTE:** The section states that audits **do not** include procedures designed to detect illegal acts (a. above) and then suggests several inquiry-type procedures (b. and c. above).

   3. **Information** that **may suggest** the possibility of **illegal acts**

      a. Unauthorized, improperly recorded, or unrecorded transactions
      b. Investigation by a governmental agency
      c. Reports of regulatory agencies citing law violations
      d. Large payments for unspecified services to consultants, affiliates, or employees
      e. Excessive sales commissions
      f. Unusually large payment to cash, bearer, transfers to numbered bank accounts
      g. Unexplained payments to government officials or employees
      h. Failure to file tax returns or pay other fees

   4. Audit procedures required **when the auditor becomes aware** of information concerning a **possible illegal act**

      a. Obtain an understanding of the act and its implications

         (1) Inquire of management at a level above those involved

      b. If management **does not** provide satisfactory information that there has been no illegal act

         (1) Consult client's legal counsel or other specialists (client arranges this consultation)
         (2) Apply additional necessary procedures such as

            (a) Examine supporting documents
            (b) Confirm significant information
            (c) Determine whether transaction authorized
            (d) Consider whether other similar transactions have occurred and apply procedures to identify

C. Auditor's response to detected illegal acts

   > **NOTE:** This section only relates to audits in which the procedures followed in B. above have revealed that an illegal act is likely to have occurred.

   1. If necessary contact legal counsel
   2. Consider financial statement effect

      a. Quantitative and qualitative aspects
      b. Determine that act adequately disclosed in financial statements

          (1) Consider possible loss contingency (e.g., threat of expropriation of assets, enforced discontinuance of operations in another country, and litigation)

    3. Consider implications of illegal act on other aspects of audit (e.g., reliability of management representations)

D. Communication with audit committee

    1. **Determine that audit committee is informed,** unless clearly inconsequential
    2. Communication should include

        a. **Description of act**
        b. **Circumstances of occurrence**
        c. **Effects on financial statements**

    3. If senior management is involved, auditor should communicate directly with audit committee
    4. **Communication may be written or oral (if oral, document)**

E. Effect on auditor's report

    1. Improper accounting, a qualified or adverse opinion due to the departure from GAAP
    2. If auditor precluded from obtaining sufficient information (i.e., a scope limitation exists), generally disclaim
    3. If client refuses to accept report, withdraw and indicate reasons in writing to audit committee or board of directors
    4. When circumstances (not the client) make it impossible to determine legality, the auditor should consider the effect on the report

> **NOTE:** In this circumstance either a "circumstance imposed" scope limitation or an "uncertainty" may be involved. See the outline of AU 508.

F. Other considerations

    1. Withdrawal may be necessary, even when client does not take remedial actions for illegal acts having an immaterial effect on the financial statements (auditor may wish to contact legal counsel)
    2. Situations in which there may be a duty to notify parties outside the client

        a. Form 8-K disclosures (change of auditors)
        b. Disclosure to successor auditor (AU 315)
        c. Disclosure in response to subpoena
        d. Disclosure to funding agency for entities receiving governmental financial assistance

    3. Additional responsibilities may exist for audits of governmental units under the Single Audit Act of 1984

318 Performing Audit Procedures in Response to Assessed Risks and Evaluating the Audit Evidence Obtained (SAS 110)

Overall Objectives and Approach—This section establishes standards and provides guidance on determining overall responses and designing and performing "further audit procedures" (tests of controls and substantive procedures) to respond to the assessed risks of material misstatement at the financial statement and relevant assertion levels in a financial statement audit and on evaluating the sufficiency and appropriateness of the audit evidence obtained. You might wish to study this standard after you have studied SAS 109, *Understanding the Entity and Its Environment and Assessing the Risks of Material Misstatement.*
This section includes guidance on

A. Overall responses to assessed risks
B. Audit procedures responsive to risks of material misstatement at the relevant assertion level
C. Evaluating the sufficiency and appropriateness of audit evidence obtained
D. Documentation

A. Overall responses

    1. Possible overall responses to address the assessed risks of material misstatement at the financial statement level

        a. Emphasize to the audit team the need to maintain professional skepticism in gathering and evaluating audit evidence
        b. Assign more experienced staff, or staff with specialized skills
        c. Provide more supervision
        d. Incorporate additional elements of unpredictability in the selection of audit procedures
        e. Make general changes to the nature, timing, or extent of audit procedures (e.g., performing substantive procedures at period end instead of at an interim date)

2. Effects of the control environment ordinarily include the following:

   a. If the control environment is effective it may allow the auditor to have more confidence in internal control and the reliability of audit evidence generated internally, thus allowing the auditor to perform some audit procedures at an interim date rather than at period end

   b. If there are weaknesses in the control environment the auditor ordinarily should

      (1) Conduct more audit procedures at the period end rather than at an interim date,

      (2) Seek more extensive audit evidence from substantive procedures,

      (3) Modify the nature of audit procedures to obtain more persuasive evidence, or

      (4) Increase the number of locations included in audit scope

B. Audit procedures responsive to risks of material misstatement at the relevant assertion level

1. This section discusses in detail **further audit procedures**—audit procedures beyond those involved with obtaining an understanding of the entity that include

   a. Test of controls

      (1) Situations in which tests of controls will not be performed

         (a) Auditors have not identified any (potentially) effective controls relevant to the assertion, or

         (b) When testing operating effectiveness of the controls would be inefficient and substantive procedures are sufficient to reduce the risk of material misstatement to an acceptable level

      (2) Tests of controls reduce, but do not eliminate, the need for substantive procedures

   b. Substantive procedures

      (1) Types

         (a) Detailed tests of classes of transactions, account balances and disclosures (frequently referred to as tests of details of transactions, accounts and disclosures)

         (b) Substantive analytical procedures

      (2) Substantive procedures must be performed for all relevant assertions

   c. Often, a combined approach of using tests of controls and substantive procedures is appropriate for reducing the risk of material misstatement

2. The auditor should provide a clear linkage between the nature, timing, and extent of the auditor's further audit procedures and the risk assessments; the auditor should consider matters such as

   a. Significance of risk

   b. Likelihood that a material misstatement will occur

   c. Characteristics of the class of transactions, account balance or disclosure involved

   d. Nature of specific controls used by the entity

   e. Whether the auditor expects to obtain audit evidence to determine if the controls are effective in preventing or detecting material misstatements (i.e., whether auditor plans to perform tests of controls)

3. Considering the nature, timing, and extent of further audit procedures

   a. **Nature**

      (1) Types—inspection, observation, inquiry, confirmation, recalculation, reperformance, and analytical procedures

      (2) The higher the assessment of risk, the more reliable and relevant is the audit evidence sought from substantive procedures

         (a) Example: If the auditor believes the risk of misstatement is high related to receivables that arose due to a credit sale, the auditor may (1) confirm the completeness of the terms of a contract with a third party, (2) inspect sales-related documents and (3) obtain management representations concerning the sale

      (3) If there is a lower risk that a material misstatement may occur, the auditor may determine that substantive analytical procedures alone may provide sufficient appropriate audit evidence

   b. **Timing**

      (1) The higher the risk of material misstatement, the more likely it is that the auditor may decide it is more effective to

(a) Perform substantive procedures nearer to, or at, the period end rather than at an earlier date, or
(b) Perform audit procedures unannounced or at unpredictable times

(2) If the auditor performs tests of operating effectiveness of controls or substantive procedures before period end, the auditor should consider the additional evidence that is needed for the remaining period
(3) Other timing considerations

(a) Control environment strength
(b) When relevant information is available (e.g., electronic files may subsequently be overwritten; as a result, the auditor may have to perform tests at several times during the year rather than at year-end)
(c) Nature of risk (e.g., risk of inflated revenues to meet earnings expectations)
(d) Period or date to which audit evidence relates

c. **Extent**

(1) Determined by judgment of auditor after considering materiality, assessed risk of material misstatement, and the degree of assurance the auditor plans to obtain; extent increases as risk of material misstatement increases

4. Tests of controls

a. Tests of controls must be performed

(1) When the risk assessment includes an expectation of operating effectiveness of controls, *or*
(2) When substantive procedures alone do not provide sufficient appropriate audit evidence at the relevant assertion level

b. Tests of operating effectiveness of controls are performed only on controls that the auditor has determined are suitably designed to prevent or detect a material misstatement in a relevant assertion
c. Control implementation vs. tests of operating effectiveness

(1) **Control implementation**—audit evidence based on performing risk assessment procedures to determine that the entity is using the controls
(2) **Tests of operating effectiveness** of controls ("tests of controls")—audit evidence that control operates effectively and includes

(a) **How** control was applied during period
(b) **Consistency** with which they were applied
(c) **By whom** (or by what means) they were applied

(3) When an auditor determines that a control has been implemented, the auditor may sometimes have obtained audit evidence about operating effectiveness; in such circumstances the evidence on implementation also serves as a test of controls (e.g., in determining that an automated control has been implemented the auditor may have substantial evidence on the control's operating effectiveness)

d. **Nature** of tests of controls

(1) Ordinarily include

(a) **Inquiries** of appropriate entity personnel
(b) **Inspection** of documents, reports, or electronic files, indicating performance of the control
(c) **Observation** of the application of the control
(d) **Reperformance** of the application of the control

> **NOTE:** Ordinarily, inquiries alone are insufficient.

(2) Objectives of tests of controls vs. substantive procedure tests of details

(a) Tests of controls—to determine whether a control operated effectively
(b) Tests of details—to support relevant assertions or to detect material misstatements at the assertion level

> **NOTE:** A test that accomplishes both (a) and (b) is referred to as a **dual purpose test** (e.g., a control is found ineffective and leads to discovery of a misstatement).

e. **Timing** of tests of controls

(1) If the auditor tests controls at a particular point in time, the auditor only obtains audit evidence that the control operated effectively at that time

(a) This may be sufficient when testing certain controls such as the entity's physical inventory counting at period end

(2) If a control operates throughout a period, the auditor should obtain audit evidence of the effectiveness of the operation of controls during the period

(a) When an auditor obtains evidence about operating effectiveness during an interim period (for example, the first nine months of the year), the auditor should determine what additional audit evidence should be obtained for the remaining period

(3) The auditor may under certain circumstances rely on evidence on operating effectiveness of controls obtained in prior periods; in such situations the auditor should obtain evidence about whether changes have occurred

(a) If changes have occurred, tests of operating effectiveness are necessary

(b) If no changes have occurred, tests of operating effectiveness may not be necessary. However, auditor should test operating effectiveness at least once in every three audits

(c) In general, the higher the risk of material misstatement, or the greater the reliance on controls, the shorter should be the time that has elapsed in testing controls; additional factors that decrease the time period include

1] Weak control environment
2] Weak monitoring controls
3] A significant manual element to controls
4] Personnel changes
5] Changing circumstances
6] Weak IT general controls

f. **Extent** of tests of controls

(1) Factors affecting extent

(a) Frequency of performance of control

(b) Length of time during audit period auditor is relying on operating effectiveness of control (e.g., a control that operates daily vs. a control that occurs only at year-end)

(c) Relevance and reliability of audit evidence obtained in supporting effectiveness of control

(d) Extent to which audit evidence exists from tests of other controls that are related to the relevant assertion

(e) Extent to which auditor plans to rely on operating effectiveness of control in assessment of risk (to reduce substantive procedures)

(f) Expected deviation from the control

(2) With IT processing, the auditor may be able to limit testing to one or a few instances of the control operation

5. Substantive procedures

a. Overall

(1) Substantive procedures are performed to detect material misstatements at the relevant assertion level, and include

(a) Tests of details of

1] Classes of transactions
2] Account balances
3] Disclosures

(b) Substantive analytical procedures

(2) Regardless of the assessed risk of material misstatement, the auditor *should design and perform substantive procedures for all relevant assertions* related to each material class of transactions, account balance, and disclosure

(a) This is because

1] The auditor's assessment of risk is judgmental and may not be sufficiently precise to identify all risks of material misstatement, and

2] There are inherent limitations of internal control, including management override, and even effective internal controls generally reduce, but do not eliminate the risk of material misstatement

(b) Even if the auditor determines that the risk of material misstatement may not be reduced to an acceptably low level by performing only tests of controls for a particular assertion related to a class of transactions, account balance, or disclosure, the auditor should also perform substantive procedures

(3) Substantive procedures should include the following audit procedures related to the financial statement reporting process:

(a) Agreeing financial statements, including notes, to the underlying accounting records
(b) Examining material journal entries and other adjustments made during the course of preparing the financial statements

(4) When an auditor has determined that the assessed risk of material misstatement for a relevant assertion is a significant risk, the auditor should perform substantive procedures that are specifically in response to that risk

(a) Example: If management is under pressure to meet earning expectations, there may be a risk of inflating sales by improperly recognizing revenue. In such circumstance the auditor may design confirmation requests to not only confirm outstanding amounts, but also details of sales agreements. In addition, the auditor may perform inquiries of nonfinancial personnel in the entity regarding any changes in sales agreements or delivery terms.

(5) When the approach to significant risks consists only of substantive procedures, the audit procedures appropriate consist of tests of details only, or a combination of tests of details and substantive analytical procedures

b. **Nature** of substantive procedures

(1) Nature of substantive procedures—tests of details (of transactions, balances, and disclosures) and substantive analytical procedures
(2) Tests of details are ordinarily more appropriate to obtain audit evidence regarding certain relevant assertions about account balances, including existence and valuation
(3) Substantive analytical procedures are generally more applicable to large volumes of transactions that tend to be predictable over time

(a) These alone may be appropriate when tests of operating effectiveness of controls have been performed and the risk of material misstatement is assessed at a relatively low level

(4) Financial statement assertions and substantive tests of details illustrations

(a) Existence/occurrence assertion—select from items contained in a financial statement amount and obtain relevant audit evidence
(b) Completeness assertion—select from audit evidence and investigate whether item is included in financial statement amount

NOTE: (a) and (b) above are examples of "directional testing" where one may test from the recorded item to the source document, or vice versa.

(5) In designing substantive analytical procedures consider

(a) Suitability, given the assertions
(b) Reliability of the data
(c) Whether expectation is sufficiently precise to identify the possibility of a material misstatement at the desired level of assurance
(d) Amount of any difference from expected that is acceptable

(6) The auditor should consider testing controls over the entity's preparation of information used in substantive analytical procedures

c. **Timing** of substantive procedures

(1) When performed at an interim date (e.g., September 30, for a December 31 year-end audit), the auditor should perform further substantive procedures or substantive procedures combined with tests of controls to cover the remaining period
(2) The following should be considered when performing substantive procedures at an interim date:

(a) Control environment

      (b) Availability of information at a later date
      (c) Objective of substantive procedure
      (d) Assessed risk of material misstatement
      (e) Nature of class of transactions, or account balance and relevant assertions
      (f) Ability to reduce risk of misstatements at year-end

    (3) When a risk of material misstatement due to fraud has been identified, the auditor might conclude that substantive procedures should be performed at or near the end of the reporting period

    (4) In most cases, audit evidence from the performance of substantive procedures in a prior audit provides little or no audit evidence for the current period

> **NOTE:** This is different than for tests of controls which under certain circumstances need be performed only once every three years.

  d. Extent of the performance of substantive procedures

    (1) The greater the need to restrict detection risk, the greater the extent of substantive procedures

    (2) In addition to considering increasing sample size, the auditor should also consider matters such as using other selective means of testing, such as selecting large or unusual items rather than performing sampling or stratifying the population

6. Adequacy of presentation and disclosure

  a. This relates to the form, arrangement, and content of the financial statements and their related notes, including, for example, terminology used, level of detail given, classification of items in the financial statements, and the bases of amounts set forth

C. Evaluating the sufficiency and appropriateness of the audit evidence obtained

1. An audit is a cumulative and iterative process. Identification of misstatements, control deviations, and other information lead the auditor to revise considerations of assessed risks and to reevaluate the adequacy of planned audit procedures

  a. When control deviations are identified, the auditor should make specific inquiries to understand them and their potential consequences

  b. When misstatements are detected while performing substantive procedures, the auditor should consider the effectiveness of related controls

2. The auditor should conclude whether sufficient appropriate audit evidence has been obtained to reduce to an appropriately low level the risk of material misstatement; this is influenced by

  a. Significance of the potential misstatement
  b. Effectiveness of management's responses and controls to address the risks
  c. Experience gained during previous audits with respect to similar potential misstatements
  d. Results of audit procedures performed
  e. Source and reliability of available information
  f. Persuasiveness of audit evidence
  g. Understanding of the entity and its environment, including its internal control

D. Documentation

1. The auditor should document

  a. Overall response to address the assessed risks of misstatement at the financial statement level
  b. Nature, timing, and extent of further audit procedures
  c. Linkage of those procedures with the assessed risks at the relevant assertion level
  d. Results of audit procedures
  e. Conclusions reached on use of current audit of evidence about operating effectiveness of controls that was obtained in a prior audit

E. Appendix—Illustrates the use of assertions in designing substantive procedures for inventories

322 The Auditor's Consideration of the Internal Audit Function in an Audit of Financial Statements (SAS 65)

Overall Objectives and Approach—This section presents guidance on how CPAs (1) **consider the effect of work** of internal auditors on the nature, timing, and extent of audit procedures and (2) use internal auditors to **provide direct assistance** on the audit. When considering internal auditors' work, the CPA must assess both **competence** and **objectivity**. Internal auditors may affect CPA understanding of internal control, control risk assessment, and substantive tests.

A. Obtaining an understanding of the internal auditing function

1. CPA should obtain an understanding of the internal auditing function sufficient to aid in planning the audit
2. The CPA should make inquiries concerning internal auditors'

   a. Organizational status within the entity
   b. Application of professional standards
   c. Audit plan
   d. Access to records, including any scope limitations placed on internal auditors
   e. Charter, mission statement, etc.

3. Consider relevant activities (those pertaining to entity's ability to record, process, summarize, and report financial data) using knowledge from prior-year audits, reviewing internal audit function allocation of its audit resources, and by reading internal auditors' reports
4. If CPA concludes internal auditors' activities are not relevant to audit, those activities need not be considered further unless CPA wishes to obtain internal auditors' direct assistance on audit (part D of this outline)

> **EXAMPLE**
>
> A CPA is not typically interested in internal auditors' evaluation of management decision-making processes.

B. Assessing **competence** and **objectivity** of internal auditors

1. When assessing **competence** CPA should consider internal auditors'

   a. Education and experience
   b. Professional certification and continuing education
   c. Audit policies, programs, and procedures
   d. Practices regarding assignments
   e. Supervision and review activities
   f. Quality of working paper documentation, reports, and recommendations
   g. Evaluation of performance

2. When assessing **objectivity** CPA should consider internal auditors'

   a. Organizational status, including whether

      (1) Internal auditors report to officer of sufficient status
      (2) Internal auditors have direct access to board of directors, audit committee, or owner-manager
      (3) Board of directors, audit committee, or owner/manager oversees internal auditors' employment decisions

   b. Policies to maintain internal auditors' objectivity about areas audited, such as policies prohibiting internal auditors from auditing areas where

      (1) Relatives are employed in important or audit-sensitive positions
      (2) An internal auditor was recently assigned or is scheduled to be assigned

3. Sources of information for assessing competence and objectivity

   a. Previous experience
   b. Discussions with management
   c. Recent external quality review of internal auditors' activities
   d. Professional internal auditing standards

C. Effect of internal auditors' work on the audit

1. Effect of internal auditors' work on the nature, timing, and extent of audit (effect on 3 stages of audit)

   a. **Understanding of internal control**—Internal auditors may have developed useful information for CPA (e.g., flowcharts, evidence on whether controls have been placed in operation)
   b. **Risk assessment**

      (1) **Financial statement level**—May affect many financial statement assertions (e.g., CPA and internal auditors may coordinate work to reduce number of entity's locations CPA performs auditing procedures)
      (2) **Account-balance or class-or-transaction level**—May affect nature, timing, and extent of tests

   c. **Substantive procedures**—CPA has ultimate responsibility for opinion

    (1) Responsibility for opinion cannot be shared with internal auditors

    (2) In determining extent of effect, CPA should consider materiality, risk of misstatement, and subjectivity of evidence

    (3) For assertions with high risk of material misstatement, internal auditors' work cannot alone eliminate need for CPA testing

        (a) Examples: Assertion on valuation of accounting estimates, related-party transactions, contingencies, uncertainties, subsequent events

    (4) For assertions related to immaterial financial statement amounts where risk of material misstatements is low, CPA in some circumstances may not need to do additional procedures

        (a) Examples: Existence of cash, prepaid assets, fixed asset additions

2. Work of internal auditors and CPA should be coordinated through periodic meetings, scheduling audit work, access of internal auditors' working papers, reviewing audit reports, and discussions

3. When evaluating the effectiveness of internal auditors' **work** the CPA should

    a. Consider whether

        (1) Scope of work appropriate

        (2) Audit programs appropriate

        (3) Adequate documentation in working papers

        (4) Appropriate conclusions in reports

        (5) Reports consistent with results of work

    b. Test internal auditors' work through examining controls, transactions, or balances either examined by internal auditors or similar to those examined by internal auditors

D. Using internal auditors to **provide direct assistance,** CPA should

1. Consider internal auditors' competence and objectivity

2. Supervise, review, evaluate, and test internal auditors' work performed

324 Reports on the Processing of Transactions by Service Organizations (SAS 70)

Overall Objectives and Approach—This section provides guidance on performing audits of entities that use a service organization. As examples of service organizations, consider organizations that (1) process the payroll information of other entities, (2) execute and process transactions for trust departments of banks that invest and hold assets for employee benefit plans for various entities, and (3) service mortgages for mortgage bankers.

As discussed in Section C.3.g of the Reporting Module, the AICPA has developed a *Service Organization Control (SOC)* framework with three reporting options:

- SOC 1: Restricted use reports on controls at a service organization relevant to a user entity's internal control over financial reporting.
- SOC 2: Restricted use reports on controls at a service organization related to security, availability, processing integrity, confidentiality, and/or privacy.
- SOC 3: General use SysTrust Reports related to security, availability, processing integrity, confidentiality, and/or privacy.

SOC 1 engagements, the reports covered by AU 324, are examinations addressing a service organization's internal control over financial reporting. When considering these engagements the following terms are important:

User organization—The entity whose financial statements are being audited (this organization hires the service auditor).

User auditor—The auditor who reports on the financial statements of the user organization.

Service organization—The entity that provides services to the client organization.

Service auditor—The auditor who reports on the processing of transactions by the service organization.

AU 324 presents guidance on how user auditors may use a SOC 1 report, while AT 801 addresses requirements for service auditors when issuing such a report. Know that SOC 1 reports are generally used by the user organization's auditors as part of their consideration of the user organization's internal control.

Section A of this outline presents information on the user auditor's consideration of the service organization's controls on the audit of the user organization. Section B presents summary information on the reports issued under SOC 1 (presented in detail in the outline of AT 801) and user auditor reliance thereon.

A. User auditor considerations of the effect of a service organization on the internal control of a user organization

1. A service organization's services are part of an entity's information system if they affect

    a. Transaction initiation
    b. Accounting records, supporting information and accounts
    c. Accounting processing from transaction initiation to inclusion in financial statements, **or**
    d. Financial reporting process used to prepare financial statements

2. The significance of controls of the service organization for the user organization depends on

    a. Nature and materiality of transactions processed
    b. Degree of interaction of activities with those of user organization

3. In **planning the audit** when a service organization is involved, information about the nature of services provided may be available from

    a. User manuals
    b. Technical manuals
    c. Contract between user and service organization
    d. Reports by service auditors, internal auditors, or regulatory authorities on service organization controls

4. If services are highly standardized, the auditor's experience with the service organization may be helpful in planning the audit

5. If the user auditor is unable to obtain sufficient evidence, a scope limitation exists that may lead to a qualified opinion or a disclaimer

6. **Assessing control risk** of the user organization

    a. The following types of evidential matter may assist the user auditor

        (1) Tests of user organization's controls over activities of service organization
        (2) A service auditor's report on controls tests of operating effectiveness (see Section B of this outline)
        (3) Tests of controls by the user auditor at the service organization

    b. The user auditor is responsible for evaluating the evidence presented by the service auditor and for determining its effect on the assessment of control risk at the user organization

7. When using a service auditor's report, the user auditor should

    a. Make inquiries concerning service auditor's professional reputation
    b. If necessary, supplement the understanding of service auditor's procedures by discussing them with the service auditor
    c. **Not** make reference to the report of the service auditor in his/her audit report

B. The two types of reports described below are

1. **Type 1:** A report on service organization's management description of the service organization's system and the suitability of the design of the controls to achieve the related control objectives included in the description as of a specified date

    a. Because no tests of controls are performed, the report itself is not intended to provide user auditor with basis for reducing assessments of control risk

2. **Type 2:** A report on the service organization's management description of the service organization's system and the suitability of the design *and operating effectiveness* of the controls to achieve the related control objectives included in the description as of a specified date.

    a. The italicized "and operating effectiveness" is the difference between the two types.
    b. This report also includes a description of the service auditor's tests of operating effectiveness and results of those tests.
    c. Only this type of test will provide a basis for reducing the assessment of control risk.

> **NOTE:** When considering this area, bear in mind that **control objectives** are designated by the service organization or by outside parties (e.g., a regulatory agency, or a user group). Controls are then designed to achieve the specified control objectives. Management prepares a description of the control objectives and policies and procedures. The CPA provides assurance on whether the description presents fairly policies and procedures placed in operation and whether the controls were suitably designed to provide reasonable assurance that control objectives will be achieved if the controls are complied with satisfactorily. In addition, in the second type report, assurance is provided on operating effectiveness of the controls in meeting the control objectives.

325 Communicating Internal Control Related Matters Identified in an Audit

Overall Objectives and Approach—This section establishes standards and provides guidance on communicating internal control related matters identified in a financial statement audit. Throughout this outline, when the word "audit" is used, it means an audit of financial statements.

A. Introduction

   1. Internal control (IC) is a process—effected by those charged with governance, management, and other personnel—designed to provide reasonable assurance about the achievement of the entity's objectives with regard to the reliability of financial reporting, effectiveness and efficiency of operations, and compliance with applicable laws and regulations

     a. Generally, controls relevant to an audit are those pertaining to reliable financial reporting

   2. An auditor is not required to perform procedures to identify IC deficiencies, but during various stages of the audit may become aware of such deficiencies

B. Definitions

   1. IC deficiencies

     a. **Deficiency in design.** When a control necessary to meet control objectives is missing or an existing control is not properly designed so that, even if it operates as designed, the control objective is not met

     b. **Deficiency in operation.** A properly designed control does not operate as designed or the person performing the control does not possess the necessary authority or competence to perform the control effectively

   2. **Material weakness**—A deficiency in IC such that there is a reasonable possibility that a material misstatement will not be prevented, or detected and corrected on a timely basis

   3. **Significant deficiency**—A deficiency in IC that is less severe than a material weakness, yet important enough to merit attention by those charged with governance

C. Evaluating deficiencies identified as part of the audit

   1. The severity of a deficiency depends on

     a. The magnitude of the potential misstatement resulting from the deficiency; factors affecting magnitude include

       (1) Financial statement amounts or total transactions exposed to deficiency

       (2) Volume of activity exposed to the deficiency

       (3) The maximum amount of overstatement generally is the recorded amount; the maximum understatement could be larger

     b. Whether there is a reasonable possibility controls will fail to prevent, or detect/correct a misstatement

       (1) Evaluation of a reasonable possibility may be made without quantifying the probability of occurrence

     c. Compensating controls may limit the severity of a deficiency since a compensating control may limit exposure

   2. Indicators that material weaknesses exist

     a. Identification of any fraud (material or immaterial) on the part of senior management

     b. Restatement of previously issued financial statements due to correction of a material misstatement due to error or fraud

     c. Identification of a material misstatement that would not have been detected by IC

     d. Ineffective oversight of financial reporting and IC by those charged with governance

   3. When a deficiency that is less than a material weakness is identified, the auditor should consider whether prudent officials having knowledge of the facts would reach the same conclusion (i.e., that it is not a material weakness)

D. Communication—Form, Content, and Timing

   1. Significant deficiencies and material weaknesses—Communicate in writing to management and those charged with governance

     a. Timing of communication—Best if by report release date, the date the auditor grants the entity permission to use the audit report; but no later than 60 days following the report release date.

       (1) Certain timely matters should be communicated earlier

   b. Significant deficiencies and material weaknesses previously identified and communicated, but not acted upon by management, should be communicated again—this may be done by referring to the previously issued written communication and the date of that communication

   c. Other deficiencies may be communicated either in writing or orally (if orally, document in work papers)

2. Information included in written communication on significant deficiencies and material weaknesses

   a. Purpose of consideration of IC was to express an opinion on financial statements, not on IC
   b. Auditor is not expressing an opinion on effectiveness of IC
   c. Auditor's consideration of IC not designed to identify all significant deficiencies or material weaknesses
   d. Definition of significant deficiencies and material weaknesses
   e. Provide a description of the significant deficiencies and material weaknesses separately identified
   f. Communication is intended solely for management, those charged with governance, and others within the organization. (If an organization is required to furnish such communication to a government authority, this may be added and allowed)

3. Other information in the written communication

   a. Communication may include inherent limitations of IC (e.g., management override of controls).
   b. A letter may be issued indicating that no material weaknesses were identified; a communication should **not** be issued indicating no significant deficiencies were identified
   c. If management is required by a regulator to provide a written response, the auditor should add a comment indicating that s/he disclaims an opinion on management's response

E. Document appendices

1. Illustrative written communications.
2. Examples of circumstances that may be IC deficiencies

326 Audit Evidence (SAS 106)

Overall Objectives and Approach—This section presents information related to the third standard of fieldwork which requires that sufficient audit evidence be obtained. The statement

- Defines audit evidence
- Defines relevant assertions and discusses their use in *assessing risks* and *designing appropriate further audit procedures*
- Discusses qualitative aspects that the auditor considers in determining the sufficient and appropriateness of audit evidence; and
- Describes various audit procedures and discusses their purposes

A. Audit evidence

1. Audit evidence is all the information used by the auditor in arriving at conclusions on which the audit opinion is based and includes (a) the information contained in the *accounting records* underlying the financial statements and (b) other information
2. Audit evidence includes that obtained from audit procedures performed during the course of audit, but may include audit evidence obtained from other sources, such as previous audits and a firm's quality control procedures for client acceptance and continuance
3. Accounting records generally include the records of initial entries and supporting records such as checks, records of electronic fund transfers, invoices, contracts, general and subsidiary ledgers, journal entries, other adjustments, etc.

   a. The auditor should obtain some audit evidence by testing accounting records, (e.g., through analysis and review, reperforming procedures, reconciling related types of information)
   b. Accounting records themselves do not provide sufficient audit evidence on which to base an audit opinion and *other information* (audit evidence) should be examined

4. Other information that may be used as audit evidence includes minutes of meetings, confirmations from third parties, industry analysts' reports, comparable data about competitors (benchmarking), controls manuals, etc.

B. Sufficient appropriate audit evidence

1. The auditor must obtain sufficient appropriate evidence

   a. Sufficient—a measure of quantity
   b. Appropriate—a measure of quality, that is, its *relevance* and *reliability* in providing support for, or detecting misstatements in transactions, account balances, and disclosures

2. The auditor considers the sufficiency and appropriateness of audit evidence to be obtained when assessing risks and designing further audit procedures
3. The higher the risk of misstatement, the greater the need for more evidence and/or higher quality evidence
4. Generalizations about reliability of audit evidence (there are exceptions); audit evidence is more reliable when

   a. Obtained from knowledgeable independent sources outside the entity
   b. Internally generated under effective controls
   c. Obtained directly by the auditor rather than indirectly obtained (e.g., observation of application of control is more reliable than when obtained through inquiry concerning the control)
   d. It exists in documentary form (paper or electronic) rather than oral representation
   e. Provided by original documents rather than photocopies or facsimiles

5. While an auditor should consider the reliability of information to be used as audit evidence, an audit rarely involves the authentication of documentation, nor is the auditor an expert at authentication
6. The auditor ordinarily obtains more assurance from *consistent* audit evidence obtained from different sources than from items of audit evidence considered individually
7. Although the auditor may consider the relationship between the cost and usefulness of possible audit evidence, difficulty or expense involved is not itself a valid basis for omitting an audit procedure for which there is no reliable valid alternative

C. Use of assertions in obtaining audit evidence

   1. Management implicitly or explicitly makes assertions regarding the recognition, measurement, presentation, and disclosure of information in the financial statements and related disclosures
   2. Categories of assertions

      a. Assertions about **classes of transactions and events** for the period under audit

         (1) **Occurrence:** Transactions and events that have been recorded have occurred and pertain to the entity
         (2) **Completeness:** All transitions and events that should have been recorded have been recorded
         (3) **Accuracy:** Amounts and other data relating to recorded transactions and events have been recorded appropriately
         (4) **Cutoff:** Transactions and events have been recorded in the correct accounting period
         (5) **Classification:** Transaction and events have been recorded in the proper accounts

      b. Assertions about **account balances** at the period end

         (1) **Existence:** Assets, liabilities, and equity interests exist
         (2) **Rights and obligations:** The entity holds or controls the rights to assets, and liabilities are the obligations of the entity
         (3) **Completeness:** All assets, liabilities, and equity interests that should have been recorded have been recorded
         (4) **Valuation and allocation:** Assets, liabilities, and equity interests are included in the financial statements at the appropriate amounts and any resulting valuation or allocation adjustments are appropriately recorded

      c. Assertions about presentation and disclosure

         (1) **Occurrence and rights and obligations:** Disclosed events and transactions have occurred and pertain to the entity
         (2) **Completeness:** All disclosures that should have been included in the financial statements have been included
         (3) **Classification and understandability:** Financial information is appropriately presented and described and information in disclosures is clearly expressed
         (4) **Accuracy and valuation:** Financial and other information is disclosed fairly and at appropriate amounts

      d. The above assertions may be used as presented, or combined as appropriate

   3. **Relevant assertions** are assertions that have a meaningful bearing on whether the account is fairly stated (e.g., valuation may not be relevant to the cash account unless currency transaction is involved; but existence and completeness are always relevant to cash)

      a. To identify relevant assertions, the auditor should determine the source of likely misstatements in each significant class of transactions, account balance, and presentation and disclosure; to determine whether a particular assertion is relevant the auditor should evaluate the

         (1) Nature of assertion
         (2) Volume of transactions or data related to assertion

(3) Nature and complexity of systems, including use of information technology (IT)

D. Audit procedures for obtaining audit evidence

1. An auditor should obtain audit evidence to draw reasonable conclusions by performing the following types of audit procedures:

    a. **Risk assessment procedures**—To obtain an understanding of the entity and its environment (including internal control) to assess the risks of material misstatement at the financial statement and relevant assertions levels

        (1) Risk assessment procedures by themselves do not provide sufficient appropriate audit evidence on which to base the audit opinion, and must be supplemented by procedures included in b. and c. below

    b. **Tests of controls**—When necessary, or when the auditor wishes to do so, the auditor should test operating effectiveness of controls at the relevant assertion level

        (1) Tests of controls are necessary in two circumstances

            (a) When the auditor's risk assessment includes an expectation of operating effectiveness of controls
            (b) When planned substantive procedures alone do not provide sufficient appropriate evidence

    c. **Substantive procedures**—To detect material misstatements at the relevant assertion level

        (1) Substantive procedures include

            (a) **Tests of details** of classes of transactions, account balances, and disclosures, and
            (b) **Substantive analytical procedures**

2. The auditor should use one or more types of audit procedures described in section E. of this outline; these procedures may be used as risk assessment procedures, tests of controls, or substantive procedures.

E. Types of audit procedures

1. Inspection of records or documents

    a. Some documents represent direct audit evidence of the existence of an asset (a financial instrument such as a stock or bond), yet may provide little evidence on ownership

2. Inspection of tangible assets

    a. For example, physical examination of assets such as inventory
    b. Inspection may provide audit evidence on existence, but not necessarily on rights/obligations or valuation

3. Observation

    a. Looking at a process or procedure being performed by others (counting inventories, observation of control activities)
    b. Observation provides audit evidence about performance of process or procedure, but is limited to the point of time at which it was performed

4. Inquiry

    a. In inquiry the auditor should

        (1) Consider the knowledge, objectivity, experience, responsibility, and qualification of the individual to be questioned
        (2) Ask clear, concise, and relevant questions
        (3) Use open or closed questions appropriately
        (4) Listen actively and effectively
        (5) Consider reactions and responses and ask follow-up questions
        (6) Evaluate the response

    b. In some cases the auditor should request written replies (e.g., representation letter)
    c. Procedures in addition to inquiry should be performed, as inquiry alone ordinarily does not provide sufficient appropriate audit evidence to detect a material misstatement at the relevant assertion level; inquiry alone is not sufficient to test control operating effectiveness

5. Confirmation

    a. A specific type of inquiry involves obtaining a representation of information or of an existing condition directly from a third party (e.g., receivable confirmations)

6. Recalculation

   a. Checking mathematical accuracy manually or through use of IT

7. Reperformance

   a. Auditor's independent execution of procedures or controls that were originally performed as part of the entity's internal control

328 Auditing Fair Value Measurements and Disclosures

Overall Objectives and Approach—Generally accepted accounting principles require companies to use fair value for measuring, representing, and disclosing a number of the companies' assets, liabilities, and components of equity. Examples include complex derivative financial instruments, marketable securities with quoted market prices, and nonmarketable securities that must be priced using a valuation model. This section provides auditing guidance related to auditing fair value measurements and disclosures.

Fair value measurements may arise both at the initial recording of transactions and later when values change. Fair value measurements may be relatively simple in situations in which active markets exist, but more complex when no such markets exist. When there are no active markets the measurements are often imprecise, as they often involve uncertainty in both the amount and timing of future cash flows. They also may be based on assumptions about future conditions, transactions, or events.

A. The auditor's evaluation of the conformity of fair value measurements and disclosures with GAAP should include a(n)

1. Evaluation of management's intent and ability to carry out certain courses of action by considering matters such as

   a. Management's history of carrying out its stated intentions for assets and liabilities
   b. Written plans and other documentation, including budgets, minutes, and other such items
   c. Management's stated reasons for choosing a particular course of action
   d. Management's ability to carry out a particular course of action

2. Evaluation of whether the entity's fair value measurements are applied consistently
3. Consideration whether to use the work of a specialist to help with the above issues

B. The three general approaches for auditing estimates are appropriate for testing fair value measurements and disclosures

1. Review and test management's process of deriving the estimate by testing management's significant assumptions, the valuation, and the underlying data to evaluate whether

   a. The assumptions are reasonable
   b. Fair value was determined using an appropriate model
   c. Management used relevant information that was reasonably available

2. Develop the auditor's own expectation of the estimate and compare it to management's estimate of fair value
3. Review subsequent events and transactions occurring after period end may help the auditor with respect to fair value measurements

C. Other

1. Measurements become more complex, and uncertainty increases with the

   a. Length of the forecast period
   b. Number of significant and complex assumptions
   c. Degree of subjectivity associated with assumptions
   d. Degree of uncertainty with the future occurrence of events
   e. Lack of objective data when highly subjective factors are used

2. The auditor should evaluate whether disclosures about fair values are in conformity with GAAP
3. The auditor should consider the effects of subsequent events
4. Management representations may be obtained on

   a. Appropriateness of measurement methods
   b. Completeness and adequacy of disclosures
   c. Whether subsequent events require adjustment to the fair value measurements

5. The auditor should determine that the audit committee is informed about the process used by management to form sensitive accounting estimates, including fair value estimates as per AU 380

329 Analytical Procedures (SAS 56)

Overall Objectives and Approach—This section presents information on analytical procedures. It suggests that analytical procedures are normally used at three stages of the audit: (1) planning, (2) substantive testing, and (3) overall review at the conclusion of an audit. They are required during the planning and overall review stages. In addition, the section presents information on the manner in which analytical procedures are applied.

A. Analytical procedures consist of **evaluations of financial information made by a study of plausible relationships among financial and nonfinancial data**

   1. **Basic premise—Plausible relationships** among data may be expected to exist in the absence of known conditions to the contrary

   2. Analytical procedures used for **3 purposes:**

      a. **Planning** nature, timing, and extent of other auditing procedures
      b. **Substantive tests** about particular assertions
      c. **Overall review** in the final stage of audit

      > **NOTE:** The section requires the use of analytical procedures in a. and c. above.

   3. The auditor **compares recorded amounts to expectations** developed from sources such as

      a. **Prior period** financial information
      b. **Anticipated results** such as projections or forecasts
      c. **Relationships among elements** of financial information within the period
      d. **Industry** information
      e. **Relevant nonfinancial information** (e.g., number of employees, volume of goods produced)

B. Analytical procedures for **planning**

   1. The purpose is to assist in planning the nature, timing, and extent of other substantive tests and therefore should

      a. Enhance auditor's understanding of client's business and events since the last audit
      b. Identify high risk areas (e.g., **unusual transactions**)

   2. Generally use data aggregated at a high level

C. Analytical procedures for **substantive tests**

   1. Especially effective for assertions for which detailed evidence does not make misstatement apparent (e.g., comparing aggregate wages paid to number of employees)

   2. Auditors must understand the reasons that relationships are plausible

      a. For higher assurance more predictable relationships are required to develop an expectation
      b. Principles involving **usual** predictability of relationships:

         (1) Relationships in a **dynamic** or unstable environment are **less predictable** than those in a stable environment
         (2) Relationships involving **balance sheet accounts are less predictable** than income statement accounts (because balance sheet accounts represent balances at one arbitrary point in time)
         (3) Relationships involving management discretion are sometimes less predictable (e.g., decision to incur maintenance expense rather than replace plant)

      > **NOTE:** Know the above three principles.

   3. The following factors generally **increase the reliability** of data used to develop an expectation

      a. Data generated from **independent sources outside entity**
      b. **Internal data** developed by **sources independent** of amount being audited
      c. **Internal data** developed under **effective internal control**
      d. **Data subjected to audit testing** in current or prior year
      e. **Expectations developed** using data from a **variety of sources**

   4. Expectations developed at a detailed level generally have a greater chance of detecting misstatement

      a. Monthly amounts will generally be more effective than annual amounts
      b. Comparisons by line of business usually more effective than company-wide comparisons

5. The auditor should use the materiality amount and level of assurance desired from the procedure to determine the amount of difference from expectation that can be accepted without further investigation

6. When an analytical procedure is used as the principal substantive test for a significant assertion, the auditor should document

   a. The expectation and factors considered in its development
   b. Results of comparison of the expectation to the recorded amounts (or ratios)
   c. Any additional procedures performed in response to significant unexpected differences and results of such additional procedures

D. Analytical procedures in **overall review**

   1. Purposes are to assist auditor in

      a. **Assessing the conclusions** reached
      b. **Evaluating the overall financial statement presentation**

   2. Should include reading the financial statements and notes to consider

      a. Adequacy of data gathered in response to unusual or unexpected balances identified during preliminary analysis
      b. Unusual or unexpected balances or relationships not identified during the audit

330 The Confirmation Process (SAS 67)

Overall Objectives and Approach—This section provides guidance on the confirmation process. Confirmation is defined as "the process of obtaining and evaluating direct communication from a third party in response to a request for information about a particular item affecting financial statement assertions."

The first portion of the outline discusses the relationship of the confirmation process to the auditor's assessment of audit risk. This portion of the section builds on AU 312 and AU 326 on audit risk and financial statement assertions, respectively. Recall that audit risk has three components—inherent risk, control risk, and detection risk. The five management assertions relating to financial statements are presentation, existence/occurrence, rights/obligations, completeness, and valuation. If you are not familiar with these sections you may wish to study them prior to studying Section A (both are discussed in the Engagement Planning Module).

Section B of this outline discusses overall issues related to the confirmation process. Sections C and D discuss alternative procedures and the evaluation of confirmation results. Finally, the outline addresses the confirmation of accounts receivable.

A. Relationship of confirmation procedures to the auditor's assessment of audit risk and financial statement assertions.

   1. The greater the combined assessed levels of inherent risk and control risk, the greater the assurance needed from substantive tests

      a. In these situations the auditor might use confirmation procedures
      b. When the client has entered into an unusual or complex transaction the auditor should consider confirming the terms
      c. Procedures **in addition to confirmation** may be necessary to achieve a low level of audit risk (e.g., perform sales cutoff tests in addition to confirming receivables)

   2. Confirmation may not be necessary if inherent and control risks are assessed as low

      a. For example, when inherent and control risks are low for cash, the auditor might inspect client-provided bank statements rather than confirm cash balances

   3. Assertions addressed by confirmations

      a. Confirmation requests sent to a sample selected from recorded accounts are more likely to address existence than completeness; examples are

         (1) Receivables and payables samples selected from a trial balance
         (2) The standard form for cash confirmations is sent to recorded accounts and is not designed to test completeness

      b. To address completeness an appropriate population must be used (e.g., a list of vendors for payables)
      c. Confirmations may provide information on rights/obligations as well as existence (e.g., confirmation of goods held on consignment with the consignee)
      d. Confirmations generally provide only limited evidence relating to the valuation assertion

B. The confirmation process

  1. Steps involved in confirmation

    a. Select items to be confirmed
    b. Design confirmation request
    c. Send confirmation request
    d. Obtain response
    e. Evaluate the information provided

  2. Forms of confirmation requests

    a. **Positive form**

      (1) Two methods are possible

        (a) Request the respondent to indicate whether s/he agrees with the amount (or other information) included on the request
        (b) Do not include the amount (or other information) on the request and ask respondent to fill in the information (referred to as the "blank" positive form)

          1] Use of the blank positive form may result in a lower response rate, although it may decrease the risk that respondents sign and return the confirmation without verifying the information

    b. **Negative form**

      (1) Request recipient to respond only if s/he disagrees with the information stated on the request
      (2) Negatives may be used when

        (a) Combined assessed level of inherent and control risk is low,
        (b) Large number of small balances are involved, and
        (c) The auditor has no reason to believe that recipients are unlikely to give them consideration

      (3) Unreturned negatives rarely provide significant evidence other than for certain aspects of existence

  3. When using confirmations the auditor should consider

    a. **Prior experience**—response rates, misstatements identified, and inaccurate replies
    b. **Nature of information being confirmed**—consider whether respondents may reply effectively and understand the information being confirmed
    c. **Appropriate respondent**—consider who should receive the confirmation request so as to help assure a meaningful response

  4. The auditor should maintain control over the confirmation requests and the responses

    a. Oral replies (e.g., by telephone)—when significant, the auditor should request written confirmation
    b. Fax replies—consider verifying source and contents through a telephone call and by asking that the original request be mailed (in addition to the fax replies) to the auditor
    c. Second, and sometimes third requests should be sent when positive requests used

C. Alternative procedures

  1. Should generally be performed when no reply to a positive confirmation request has been received
  2. Omission of alternative procedures may be acceptable when

    a. No unusual factors related to nonresponses have been noted (e.g., they don't all relate to year-end transactions) and
    b. The total of nonresponses in aggregate, when projected as 100% misstatements, and all other unadjusted differences noted in the audit are still immaterial

D. When evaluating confirmation results the auditor should consider

  1. The reliability of the confirmations and alternative procedures
  2. The nature of any exceptions
  3. Evidence provided by other procedures
  4. Whether additional evidence is needed

E. Accounts receivable should be confirmed unless

  1. They are immaterial,
  2. The use of confirmations would be ineffective, or

3. The combined assessment of inherent and control risk is low and that assessment, with other substantive tests, reduces audit risk to an acceptably low level

> **NOTE:** Accounts receivable should normally be confirmed and the auditor who has not confirmed them should document how s/he overcame that presumption.

331 Inventories (SAS 1)

Overall Objectives and Approach—This section establishes the observation of inventories as a **generally accepted auditing procedure**. An auditor who omits the observation of inventories must be able to justify the decision (in the working papers—not in the report). The section discusses a number of complications that may arise when observing the client's inventory count, and establishes procedures which may be necessary when inventories are held in public warehouses.

A. Inventories—held by clients

1. It is normally necessary for the CPA to be present when inventory quantities are determined by means of a physical count
2. When perpetual records are well maintained and checked by the client periodically by comparisons with physical counts, the auditor may perform observation procedures either during or after the end of the period under audit
3. When a client uses statistical sampling to determine inventory quantities, the auditor must determine that

   a. It is reasonable and has statistical validity
   b. It has been properly applied
   c. The results are reasonable in the circumstances

4. When a CPA has not observed the counting of inventory

   a. It will **always** be necessary to make some physical counts of inventory and apply appropriate tests of intervening transactions subsequent to the client's count

   > **EXAMPLE**
   >
   > Assume the client counted inventory on December 31, and the auditor was not present. At some point, say January 15, the auditor must make some physical counts and reconcile the January 15 quantities back to those of December 31.

5. When a CPA is satisfied as to the current inventory, s/he may satisfy him/herself as to a **prior period's inventory** (e.g., the beginning inventory for the year under audit) by

   a. Tests of prior transactions
   b. Review of prior count records
   c. Gross profit tests

B. Inventories—held in public warehouses

1. Direct confirmation in writing from custodian is ordinarily obtained
2. If such inventories represent a significant portion of current or total assets, auditor should

   a. Review and test owner's control procedures for investigating and evaluating performance of the warehouseman
   b. Obtain report from independent accountant as to the reliability of internal control over custody of goods and, if applicable, pledging of receipts

      (1) Alternatively, test the structure to gain assurance that information received is reliable

   c. Observe physical counts where reasonable and practical
   d. Confirm pertinent details of pledged receipts with lenders, if any

332 Auditing Derivative Instruments, Hedging Activities, and Investments in Securities

Overall Objectives and Approach—This section presents guidance on auditing derivative instruments, hedging activities, and investments in securities. This guidance, which applies to both debt and equity securities.

A. Overall

1. The auditor may need special skill or knowledge to plan and perform auditing procedures for certain assertions about derivatives and securities

2. Auditors must design procedures to obtain reasonable assurance of detecting material misstatements of assertions about derivatives and securities

B. Inherent risk assessment—Examples of factors that affect inherent risk

1. Management's objectives

   a. For example, using hedges subject to the risk of market conditions may increase risk

2. Complexity of the features of the derivative or security
3. Whether the transaction that gave rise to the derivative or security involved the exchange of cash

   a. Those not involving an initial exchange of cash are more risky for valuation and disclosure

4. The entity's experience with the derivative or security
5. Whether a derivative is freestanding or an embedded feature of an agreement

   a. Embedded are more risky because they may be less likely to be identified by management

6. Whether external factors affect the assertion (e.g., credit risk, market risk, basis risk, legal risk)
7. Evolving nature of derivatives and applicable GAAP
8. Significant reliance on outside parties increases risk
9. GAAP may require developing assumptions about future conditions, which increases risk

C. Control risk assessment

1. Examples of controls include

   a. Monitoring by a control staff that is independent of derivative activities
   b. Prior to exceeding limits, senior management approval of transactions
   c. Senior management addresses limit excesses and divergences from approved derivatives strategies
   d. Derivatives positions accurately transmitted to risk measurement systems
   e. Appropriate reconciliations
   f. Constraints defined
   g. Regular review of controls by senior management, an independent group, or a designated individual
   h. Review of limits

2. When a service organization is involved, it may be a part of the entity's information system, and thereby the auditor should consider procedures from a variety of sources, such as

   a. User manuals
   b. System overviews
   c. Technical manuals
   d. Contract between entity and service organization
   e. Reports of auditors, regulatory agencies
   f. Inquiry of personnel at the entity or service organization

> **NOTE:** See AU 324 for more information on service organizations.

3. If the auditor plans to assess control risk below the maximum, he or she should identify specific controls applicable to assertions and gather evidential matter about their operating effectiveness (i.e., perform tests of controls)

D. Designing substantive procedures

1. Existence or occurrence assertion *example* procedures

   a. Confirm (security issuer, security holder, broker-dealer)
   b. Inspect security or derivative contract
   c. Read executed partnership or similar agreements
   d. Inspect supporting documentation for subsequent realization or settlement after end of reporting period
   e. Perform analytical procedures

2. Completeness

   a. Request counterparties or holders to state whether there are any side agreements or agreements to repurchase old securities sold
   b. Request frequently used counterparties or holders with whom accounting records indicate there are no *current* derivatives or securities to state whether any exist
   c. Inspect financial instruments and other agreements to identify embedded derivatives
   d. Perform analytical procedures

      e. Compare previous account detail with current account detail

      f. Read other information (e.g., minutes of board of directors, other committees)

  3. Rights and obligations

      a. Confirm significant terms with counterparty or holder

      b. Inspect underlying agreements

      c. Consider findings of other audit procedures (e.g., reading minutes of meetings)

  4. Valuation

      a. Determine whether GAAP specifies the method to be used to determine the fair value of the derivatives and securities, and, if so, whether they have been properly handled.

      b. The section also identifies sources of fair value information for derivatives and securities, the hierarchy of such sources, procedures to follow when market prices are not available, and the auditor's overall responsibility.

  5. Presentation and disclosure

      a. Since certain derivatives have particular presentation and disclosure requirements, the auditor must be aware of them

E. Hedging activities

  1. A hedge is a defensive strategy to protect an entity against the risk of adverse price or interest-rate movements on certain of its assets, liabilities, or anticipated transactions

  2. In an audit, the auditor should gather evidence to determine whether management

      a. Complied with GAAP hedge accounting requirements

      b. Originally expected that the hedging relationship would be highly effective

      c. Periodically assessed the hedge's ongoing effectiveness

  3. For a cash flow hedge of a forecasted transaction, management must determine the probability of occurrence; probability should be supported by circumstances such as

      a. Frequency of similar past transactions

      b. Financial and operational ability of entity to carry out transaction

      c. Extent of loss that could result if the transaction does not occur

      d. Likelihood transaction with substantially different characteristics might be used to achieve same business purposes

333 Management Representations

Overall Objectives and Approach—This section establishes a requirement that auditors obtain written representations from management (representation letters) as part of any audit and provides related guidance.

A. Reliance upon management's representations

  1. Written representations by management to an auditor (in a representation letter)

      a. **Confirm** representations explicitly or implicitly provided throughout the audit

      b. Indicate and document the continuing appropriateness of such representations, and

      c. Reduce the possibility of misunderstanding

  2. Although written representations are **not** a substitute for other necessary audit procedures, in some cases they provide additional evidential matter

      a. For example, as to management's intent to discontinue a line of business

  3. If a representation is contradicted by other audit evidence, the auditor should investigate the circumstances and consider whether reliance upon other representations during the audit is appropriate and justified

B. Written representation obtained

  1. Representations should be obtained for **all** financial statements and periods covered by the auditor's report

  2. Representations should be tailored by engagement, but should include the following matters:

      a. Financial statements

          (1) Management acknowledges its responsibility for the financial statements being prepared in conformity with GAAP

          (2) Management believes financial statements presented in conformity with GAAP

(3) Management believes effects of uncorrected financial statement misstatements are immaterial, both individually and in the aggregate

b. Completeness of information

(1) Availability of all financial records and related data
(2) Completeness and availability of all minutes of meetings of stockholders, directors, and committees of directors
(3) Communications from regulatory agencies
(4) Absence of unrecorded transactions

c. Recognition, measurement, and disclosure

(1) Management's acknowledgement of its responsibility to design and implement programs and controls to prevent or detect fraud
(2) Information concerning fraud or suspected fraud affecting the company
(3) Information concerning any allegations of fraud or suspected fraud affecting the company, for example, because of communications from employees, former employees, analysts, regulators, short sellers, or other investors
(4) Plans or intentions that may affect carrying value or classification of assets or liabilities
(5) Information about related-party transactions and receivable or payables
(6) Guarantee (written or oral) under which the entity is contingently liable
(7) All significant estimates and material concentrations known to management are disclosed as per FASB ASC 275
(8) Violations or possible violations of laws whose effects should be considered for disclosure or as basis for recording loss contingency
(9) Unasserted claims or assessments that entity's lawyer has advised are probable of assertion and must be disclosed as per FASB ASC 450
(10) Satisfactory title to assets, liens on assets, and assets pledged as collateral
(11) Compliance with aspects of contractual agreements that may affect financial statements

C. Details of Representations

1. Representations may be limited to matters considered either individually or collectively **material** to the financial statements, provided management and the auditor have an agreement on materiality

   a. But no materiality limitations should exist for management's responsibility for the financial statements, the availability of financial records, the completeness of records, or communications from regulatory agencies—all included in B.2. above

2. Written representation should be

   a. **Addressed to the auditor**
   b. **Dated no earlier than** the date of the **auditor's report**
   c. **Signed** by **chief executive officer** and **chief financial officer**

      (1) Representations should be obtained from current management for all periods reported upon, even if current management was not present during all those periods

D. Scope limitations

1. **Management refusal** to furnish written representations constitutes a **scope limitation** that **precludes an unqualified opinion** and ordinarily is sufficient to cause a **disclaimer of opinion**

   a. Based on nature of representations not obtained, a qualified opinion may be appropriate

334 Related Parties (SAS 45)

Overall Objectives and Approach—This section presents guidance on **accounting** and **auditing** considerations for related-party transactions. The subsection on audit procedures, after providing some general advice, provides guidance on (1) identifying **conditions** in which related-party transactions are likely, (2) identifying **parties** that are related to the entity, (3) identifying **transactions** with related parties, and (4) **examining related-party transactions** that have been **identified**. The section closes with information on required disclosures.

A. Accounting (including disclosures) considerations for related-party transactions

1. FASB ASC 850 provides accounting requirements for related-party disclosures

   a. Nature of relationship(s)

b. Description of transaction(s)
c. Dollar amount of transactions
d. Amounts due to/from related parties, including terms

> **NOTE:** See outline of FASB ASC 850 for more details.

2. Transactions should reflect their substance (rather than merely their legal form)
3. Except for routine transactions, it will generally **not be possible** to determine whether a particular transaction would have taken place, or what its terms would have been

   a. If management makes such a representation, **and if it is unsubstantiated,** it may result in either a qualified or an adverse opinion due to a departure from GAAP—see outline of AU 508 and Reporting Module for information on departures from GAAP

> **NOTE:** Points 3. and 3.a. have been asked several times in multiple-choice questions.

4. Example transactions that may be indicative of related-party transactions

   a. Borrowing or lending at interest rates above or below the market rate
   b. Selling real estate at a price significantly different from its appraised value
   c. Exchanging property for similar property in a nonmonetary transaction
   d. Making loans with no scheduled repayment terms

> **NOTE:** Several multiple-choice questions have asked for a situation in which the existence of related parties is likely, and have used one of the above as the correct reply.

B. Auditing considerations for related-party transactions

1. An audit cannot be expected to provide assurance that all related-party transactions will be discovered

   a. Nevertheless, an auditor should be aware of the possible existence of material related-party transactions

      (1) Experience has shown, for example, that business structure and operating style are occasionally deliberately designed to obscure such transactions.

2. **Conditions in which related-party transactions are likely**

   a. Lack of sufficient working capital or credit to continue the business
   b. An urgent desire for favorable EPS trends
   c. Overly optimistic EPS forecast
   d. Dependence on a few products, customers, or transactions
   e. Declining industry profitability
   f. Excess capacity
   g. Significant litigation
   h. Significant obsolescence

3. Procedures to identify **parties** that are related to the entity

   a. Evaluate the client's procedures for related-party transactions
   b. Ask client for names of all related parties and whether there have been any transactions with these parties
   c. Review SEC filings
   d. Determine names of officers of all employee trusts
   e. Review stockholder listings of closely held companies
   f. Review prior workpapers for the names of related parties
   g. Inquire of predecessor and/or principal auditors
   h. Review material investment transactions

4. Procedures to identify **transactions** with related parties

   a. Provide audit personnel with related-party names
   b. Review Board of Directors' minutes (and other committees)
   c. Review SEC filings
   d. Review client "conflict of interest" statements obtained by company from management
   e. Review nature of transactions with major customers, suppliers, etc.
   f. Consider whether unrecorded transactions exist
   g. Review accounting records for large, nonrecurring transactions

    h. Review confirmations of compensating balances for indications that balances are maintained for or by related parties

    i. Review legal invoices

    j. Review confirmations of loans receivable and payable for guarantees

5. Procedures (beyond management inquiry) for **examining** related-party transactions that have been **identified**

    a. Obtain understanding of the purpose of the transaction

    b. Examine supporting documents

    c. Verify existence of required approval

    d. Evaluate reasonableness of amounts to be disclosed

    e. Consider simultaneous or joint audit of intercompany balances

    f. Inspect/confirm transferability and value of collateral

    g. Extend auditing procedures further as necessary to understand transactions

        (1) Confirm transaction details with other party

        (2) Inspect evidence held by other party

        (3) Confirm information with intermediaries (e.g., banks)

        (4) Refer to trade journals, credit agencies, etc.

        (5) Seek assurance on material uncollected balances

336 Using the Work of a Specialist (SAS 73)

Overall Objectives and Approach—This section presents guidance on an auditor's use of the work of a specialist. For example, an auditor may engage an appraiser to help verify a client's valuation of an inventory of diamond rings. Other specialists whose work might be used by auditors include actuaries, engineers, environmental consultants, geologists, and attorneys providing services other than those related to litigation (AU 337 addresses litigation); internal auditors are **not** considered specialists for purposes of this section. The section applies to situations in which either management or the auditor engage a specialist. Note that when management has engaged the specialist the work will often have been performed prior to the audit; for example, prior to the audit a specialist may have appraised assets in support of loans issued by a bank.

Section A of this outline summarizes the types of matters that may result in an auditor using the work of a specialist, and an auditor's consideration of specialist qualifications and work of the specialist; Section B considers the effect of the specialist's findings on the audit report.

A. Types of matters, specialist qualifications, and findings

1. Among the **types of matters** for which an auditor may decide to use the work of a specialist are the determination of

    a. Valuation (e.g., inventories, complex financial instruments, real estate, art)

    b. Physical characteristics (e.g., mineral content, mineral reserves, materials stored in stockpiles)

    c. Amounts derived by using specialized methods (e.g., actuarial determinations for employee benefits, insurance loss reserves)

    d. Technical requirements, regulations or agreements (significance of contracts or other legal documents)

2. The auditor should evaluate the professional **qualifications** of the specialist by considering

    a. Professional certification, licenses, etc.

    b. Reputation

    c. Experience in this type of work

3. The auditor should obtain an understanding of the **work** performed by the specialist including

    a. Objectives

    b. Specialist's relationship to client

        (1) No relationship—work usually provides greater assurance of reliability

        (2) A relationship—although using the work of such a specialist is acceptable under certain circumstances

            (a) When such a relationship exists the auditor should assess the risk that the specialist's objectivity might be impaired

            (b) If objectivity might be impaired, the auditor should perform additional procedures or engage another specialist

    c. Methods or assumptions used

    d. Comparison of methods or assumptions with those used in preceding period

    e. Appropriateness of using specialist's work

f. Form and content of specialist's findings that will enable the auditor to

    (1) Obtain an understanding of the methods and assumptions and their reasonableness
    (2) Make appropriate tests of data provided to the specialist, including the auditor's assessment of control risk
    (3) Evaluate whether the specialist's findings support the related assertions in the financial statements

> **NOTE:** The appropriateness and reasonableness of the methods and assumptions used are the responsibility of the specialist. However, if at any point the auditor believes the specialist's findings are unreasonable, additional procedures should be applied.

B. Effect of specialist's work on the auditor's report

1. If the specialist's findings support the related financial statement assertions, the auditor may conclude that sufficient competent evidential matter has been obtained, and no reference should be made to the specialist's work in the audit report
2. If the specialist's findings do not support the related financial statement assertions,

    a. The auditor should (1) apply additional procedures and (2) if necessary, obtain the opinion of another specialist (unless it appears that the matter cannot be resolved)
    b. If the difference cannot be resolved, the auditor will ordinarily qualify the opinion or disclaim an opinion because the inability to obtain sufficient competent evidential matter is a scope limitation
    c. If the financial statements are incorrect, the auditor should express a qualified or adverse opinion due to a departure from GAAP

> **NOTE:** Only in b. and c. may the specialist be referred to.

337 Inquiry of a Client's Lawyer Concerning Litigation, Claims, and Assessments (LCA) (SAS 12)

Overall Objectives and Approach—This section presents guidance on the manner in which a CPA is to obtain information from a client's lawyer concerning litigation, claims, and assessments (LCA) that affect a client. LCA may result in contingent, as well as direct liabilities. At this point, if you are unable to recall the FASB ASC 450 accounting standard related to contingencies, we suggest that you review that outline.

After a brief reference to FASB ASC 450, the section presents information on the types of evidential matter that should be gathered and the appropriate audit procedures to be followed. Next, details of the inquiry which is to be sent to the client's lawyer are provided. The section concludes by discussing how CPAs should handle various limitations in the lawyer's response to the inquiry.

A. Evidential matter and appropriate audit procedures

1. The auditor should obtain evidential matter relating to LCA relevant to the following factors:

    a. Conditions indicating a possible loss from LCA
    b. The period in which the underlying cause occurred
    c. The degree of probability of an unfavorable outcome
    d. The amount or range of potential loss

2. Because **management** is the primary source of information about such contingencies, the CPA's procedures for LCA should include

    a. Inquiring as to the policies and procedures adopted for identifying, evaluating, and accounting for contingencies
    b. Obtaining a description and evaluation of all pending contingencies at the balance sheet date and any contingencies arising after the balance sheet date
    c. Examining relevant documents including correspondence and invoices from lawyers
    d. Obtaining management's written assurance that all unasserted claims required to be disclosed by SFAS 5 (per client's lawyer) are disclosed

        (1) Obtain client's permission to inform lawyer that client has given this assurance

3. Other audit procedures which may reveal pending or possible contingencies

    a. Reading board of directors' and other appropriate meeting minutes
    b. Reading contracts, leases, correspondence, and other similar documents
    c. Guarantees of indebtedness disclosed on bank confirmations
    d. Inspecting other documents for possible client-made guarantees

B. Inquiry **sent to** the client's lawyer

> **NOTE:** Although not explicitly stated in the section, the auditor mails this inquiry (typed on the client's letterhead) to the lawyer.

1. This inquiry may be sent to the client's **inside general counsel** or legal department (i.e., lawyers that are employees of the client) **and outside counsel**

    a. Information obtained from inside counsel is **not** a substitute for information outside counsel refuses to furnish

2. Information included in the inquiry to the lawyer

    a. Identification of the client and the date of the audit
    b. A list prepared by management (or a request by management that the lawyer prepare a list) describing **pending or threatened LCA** for which the lawyer has been engaged and devoted substantive attention with a request that the **lawyer indicate**

        (1) A description of the **nature** of the matter, **progress** of the case to date, and the **action** the company intends to take (e.g., contest vigorously)
        (2) If possible, an evaluation of the likelihood and amount of potential loss
        (3) Identification of any omissions from list, or a statement that the list is complete with respect to LCA

    c. A list prepared by management that describes and evaluates **unasserted claims and assessments** which management considers **probable of assertion,** and that, **if asserted,** would have a **reasonable possibility** of an unfavorable outcome and a request that the lawyer indicate any disagreements with the description or evaluation

        (1) For unasserted claims, the lawyer **will not** inform the CPA of omissions from management's list

            (a) The lawyer is to advise the client of the omission
            (b) If the client does not then inform the CPA about the omission, the lawyer is generally required to resign

        > **NOTE:** Several exam multiple-choice questions have addressed the idea that resignation of a lawyer is to be investigated by the auditor; such resignation may indicate the existence of undisclosed unasserted claims. The auditor should inquire about reasons for changes in or resignations of lawyers.

            (c) A request that the lawyer specifically identify the nature of and reasons for any limitations in his/her response

3. The client and CPA should agree on materiality limits, and then inquiry need not be made of immaterial items
4. In some circumstances the auditor may obtain a response to the inquiry in a conference with the lawyer

    a. The CPA should appropriately document the conference

C. Limitations on the lawyer's response to the inquiry

1. A lawyer may limit his/her response to material matters to which s/he has devoted substantive attention—such limitations are not considered audit scope limitations
2. **Refusal to furnish either in writing or orally information** requested in the inquiry letter is a **scope limitation sufficient to preclude an unqualified opinion**

    a. Scope limitations lead to either qualified opinions or disclaimers of opinion

3. Inherent uncertainties involving the situation may make it impossible for the lawyer to respond as to the likelihood of loss, or the amount

    a. This is an uncertainty situation which, if material, may lead to an unqualified opinion with an explanatory paragraph, or a disclaimer of opinion

> **NOTE:** For more on scope limitations and uncertainties, see the outline of AU 508 and Section B of the Reporting Module.

339 Audit Documentation (AU 103 [redrafted])

Overall Scope—This section addresses the auditor's responsibility to prepare audit documentation for a financial statement audit. Audit documentation provides (1) evidence of the auditor's basis for a conclusion about the overall objective of the auditor and (2) evidence that the audit was planned and performed in accordance with GAAS and applicable legal and regulatory requirements. Audit documentation also serves additional purposes, including

- Assisting the engagement team to plan and perform the audit
- Assisting team members to direct and supervise the audit, and to review the quality of work performed
- Retaining records of continuing significance for future audits
- Enabling the conduct of quality review and inspections
- Assisting a successor auditor
- Assisting auditors to understand prior year work performed to aid in planning and performing the current engagement

A. Objective

1. The objective of the auditor is to prepare documentation that provides

   a. A sufficient and appropriate record of the basis for the auditor's report
   b. Evidence that the audit was planned and performed in accordance with GAAS and applicable legal and regulatory requirements

B. Definitions

1. **Audit documentation.** The record of audit procedures performed, relevant audit evidence obtained, and conclusions the auditor reached (terms such as working papers or workpapers are also sometimes used)
2. **Audit file.** One or more folders or other storage media, in physical or electronic form, containing the records that comprise the audit documentation for a specific engagement
3. **Experienced auditor.** An individual, whether internal or external to the firm, who has practical audit experience (i.e., an individual with competencies and skills that would have enabled him/her to perform the audit), and a reasonable understanding of

   a. Audit processes;
   b. SASs and applicable legal and regulatory requirements;
   c. The business environment in which the entity operates; and
   d. Auditing and financial reporting issues relevant to the entity's industry

4. **Report release date.** The date the auditor grants the entity permission to use the auditor's report in connection with the financial statements. In many cases, this is the date the auditor delivers the audit report to the entity
5. **Documentation completion date.** The date, no later than 60 days following the report release date, on which the auditor has assembled for retention, a complete and final set of documentation in an audit file

C. Requirements

1. Form and content requirements

   a. The audit documentation should be sufficient to enable an experienced auditor having no previous connection with the audit to understand

      (1) The nature, timing and extent of audit procedures performed
      (2) The results of the audit procedures performed and audit evidence obtained
      (3) Significant findings or issues arising during the audit, conclusions reached, and significant judgments made in reaching those conclusions

   b. Includes abstracts or copies of significant contracts or agreements
   c. In documenting the nature, timing and extent of audit procedures performed, record information identifying

      (1) Characteristics of specific items or matters tested
      (2) Who performed the audit work and the date it was completed
      (3) Who reviewed the audit work and the date and extent of review

   d. Document discussions of significant findings or issues with management, those charged with governance and others, including significant findings, responses, and when and with whom the discussions took place
   e. Document any information inconsistent with final audit conclusions.

2. Document and justify any departures from any relevant presumptively mandatory requirements and how alternative audit procedures were sufficient
3. If additional procedures are performed after the date of the auditor's report, the auditor should document the circumstances, the new or additional procedure(s), and when/by whom changes to audit documentation were made and reviewed

D. Assembly and retention of the final audit file

1. Must be complete no later than 60 days after the report release date
2. The report release date should be documented

3. After the documentation completion date, the auditor should not delete or discard audit documentation of any nature before the end of the specified retention period (not less than 5 years)
4. When documentation changes are necessary after the documentation completion date, the auditor should document the reasons for making them and when and by whom they were made and reviewed.

    a. Example: The auditor becomes aware of facts that existed at that date and if known, might have caused the modification of the financial statements and/or the audit opinion

341 The Auditor's Consideration of an Entity's Ability to Continue as a Going Concern (SAS 59)

Overall Objectives and Approach—This section presents guidance on CPA responsibility for evaluating whether there is **substantial doubt** about a client's ability to continue as a going concern. The section suggests that continuation as a going concern is assumed in the absence of information to the contrary. The section first discusses an auditor's responsibility related to a client. Second, audit procedures which may identify conditions and events which raise a question about going concern status are presented. The third subsection, which is only appropriate after such conditions and/or events have been identified, discusses the manner in which an auditor evaluates management's plans for dealing with such adverse circumstances. The fourth and fifth subsections discuss proper financial statement and audit report reflections of such conditions and events.

A. The auditor's responsibility

1. The auditor must evaluate whether there is substantial doubt about the entity's ability to continue as a going concern for a period not to exceed one year from the date of the financial statements being audited

    a. Ordinarily, information that significantly **contradicts the going concern assumption** relates to inability to meet obligations as they become due without

        (1) Substantial disposition of assets
        (2) Restructuring debt
        (3) Externally forced revisions of operations
        (4) Similar actions

2. The evaluation is based on audit procedures planned and performed to achieve the audit objectives related to the management assertions—for more on the assertions see AU 326 outline and Section A of the Evidence Module
3. The process for evaluating whether there is substantial doubt

    a. Consider whether audit procedures identify conditions and events suggesting substantial doubt
    b. If substantial doubt from a.,

        (1) Obtain management's plans
        (2) Assess likelihood plans can be implemented

    c. If substantial doubt remains, consider

        (1) Adequacy of disclosures on inability to continue and
        (2) Include explanatory paragraph following opinion paragraph in audit report

> **NOTE:** Be familiar with this process.

4. **Auditors are not responsible for predicting future** conditions and events

    a. The fact that an entity ceases to exist after an audit report which does not refer to substantial doubt does not in itself indicate inadequate auditor performance
    b. Absence of reference to substantial doubt in an audit report should not be viewed as providing assurance entity will continue as a going concern

B. Audit procedures and consideration of conditions and events

1. **It is not necessary to design audit procedures for identifying substantial doubt**
2. **Procedures for other objectives are sufficient** to identify conditions and events indicating substantial doubt. Examples of procedures

    a. Analytical procedures
    b. Review of subsequent events
    c. Compliance with terms of debt and loan agreements
    d. Reading minutes of shareholders' and board of directors' meetings
    e. Inquiry of legal counsel on litigation, claims, and assessments
    f. Confirmation of arrangements to maintain financial support

3. **Conditions** and events that **may indicate substantial doubt**

   a. Negative trends—(e.g., losses, working capital deficiencies)
   b. Other indications of financial difficulties—(e.g., defaults)
   c. Internal matters—(e.g., work stoppages, dependence on one project)
   d. External matters—(e.g., legal proceedings, loss of key franchise)

C. Consideration of management's plans

1. Auditor's consideration of management's plans may include the following

   a. **Plans to dispose** of assets—Consider restrictions, marketability, effects of disposal
   b. **Plans to borrow** money or restructure debt—Consider availability of financing, existing arrangements, possible effects of borrowing
   c. **Plans to reduce** or delay **expenditures**—Consider feasibility, possible effects
   d. **Plans to increase ownership equity**—Consider feasibility and existing arrangements to reduce dividend requirements, etc.

2. When prospective financial information is significant to management's plans

   a. Request such information
   b. Consider adequacy of support for assumptions
   c. If important factors are not considered, request revision

D. Financial statement effects

1. **When substantial doubt exists consider** the need for the following **disclosures**

   a. **Conditions** and events giving rise to substantial doubt
   b. **Possible effects** of such conditions and events
   c. **Management's evaluation** of conditions and events
   d. **Possible discontinuance** of operations
   e. **Information on recoverability and classification** of assets and liabilities

2. When, primarily because of auditor's consideration of management's plans, no substantial doubt remains, still consider need for appropriate disclosures

E. Effects on auditor's report

1. When substantial doubt exists, modify report to include an explanatory paragraph following opinion paragraph

   a. The report must include the phrase "substantial doubt about its ability to continue as a going concern"

2. If disclosures are inadequate, a departure from GAAP exists which may result in qualified or adverse opinion
3. When issuing comparative statements, resolution of prior substantial doubt eliminates need for modification and a standard report covering both years is appropriate
4. The auditor may also choose to disclaim an opinion when substantial doubt remains

F. Documentation

1. Conditions that led to belief that substantial doubt exists
2. Elements of management's plans considered important to overcoming significant doubt
3. Auditing procedures performed and evidence obtained to evaluate management's plans
4. Auditor's conclusion as to whether substantial doubt remains or is alleviated

   a. If it remains, document possible effects on the financial statements and adequacy of disclosures
   b. If it is alleviated, document conclusion as to need for disclosure of principal conditions and events that caused substantial doubt

342 Auditing Accounting Estimates (SAS 57)

Overall Objectives and Approach—This section provides guidance on auditing accounting estimates (e.g., allowance for doubtful accounts, revenues recognized on construction contracts accounted for by the percentage-of-completion method). The section discusses (a) the need for and characteristics of accounting estimates, (b) management's role in developing accounting estimates, and (c) the auditor's evaluation of accounting estimates

A. The need for and characteristics of accounting estimates

1. Accounting estimates are needed because

   a. Measurement or valuation of some accounts is based on future events

    b. Evidence on some accounts cannot be accumulated on a timely, cost-effective basis

  2. Examples of accounting estimates: net realizable values of inventory and accounts receivable, loss reserves, percentage-of-completion revenues, pension and warranty expenses

  3. Estimates are based on subjective as well as objective factors

    a. Difficult for management to establish controls over them

  4. **Responsibility of the auditor** with respect to estimates

    a. Evaluate the reasonableness of accounting estimates in the context of the financial statements taken as a whole

    b. Plan and perform procedures with attitude of **professional skepticism**

B. Management's role in developing accounting estimates

  1. Steps involved in making estimates

    a. Identify situations for which estimates are needed
    b. Identify relevant factors affecting estimate
    c. Accumulate data on which to base estimate
    d. Develop assumptions based on most likely circumstance and events
    e. Determine estimated amount
    f. Determine estimate follows GAAP and that disclosure is adequate

  2. The risk of misstatement of accounting estimates is affected by

    a. Complexity and subjectivity involved in process
    b. Availability and reliability of relevant data
    c. The number and significance of assumptions made
    d. Degree of uncertainty associated with assumptions

  3. An entity's internal control may reduce the likelihood of material misstatements of estimates. Relevant aspects of internal control include

    a. Communication to management need for estimate
    b. Accumulation of accurate data on which to base estimate
    c. Preparation of estimate by qualified personnel
    d. Adequate review and approval of estimates
    e. Comparison of prior estimates with subsequent results
    f. Consideration by management of whether estimate is consistent with operational plans of entity

C. Auditor's evaluation of accounting estimates

  1. Auditor's objectives are to provide reasonable assurance that

    a. All estimates have been developed
    b. Estimates are reasonable
    c. Estimates follow GAAP and are properly disclosed

> **NOTE:** Know the above objectives.

  2. Procedures for determining all estimates have been developed (C.1.a. above)

    a. **Consider assertions** in financial statements to determine need for estimates
    b. **Evaluate information from other procedures** such as

      (1) Changes in entity's business or operating strategy
      (2) Change in methods of accumulating information
      (3) Information concerning litigation, claims and assessments
      (4) Minutes of stockholder, directors, and appropriate committees' meetings
      (5) Information in regulatory reports

    c. **Inquiry of management**

  3. Evaluating reasonableness (C.1.b. above)

    a. Three basic approaches (of which a combination may be used)

      (1) **Review and test management's process**

        (a) Identify related controls

    (b) Identify sources of data and factors used and consider whether appropriate

    (c) Consider whether there are additional key factors or alternate assumptions about the factors

    (d) Evaluate consistency of assumptions with one another, supporting data, historical data, and industry data

    (e) Analyze historical data used

    (f) Consider changes in business or industry

    (g) Review documentation of assumptions and inquire about other plans, etc.

    (h) Consider using a specialist (see outline of AU 336)

    (i) Test management calculations

(2) **Develop own expectation of estimate**

    (a) Auditor independently develops an expectation

(3) **Review subsequent events** or transactions prior to completion of fieldwork

> **NOTE:** Know the above three approaches.

350 Audit Sampling (SAS 39, 111)

Overall Objectives and Approach—This section presents guidance on the use of sampling while **planning, performing,** and **evaluating results** of an audit of financial statements. The objective is to provide the conceptual background for audit sampling. In addition to this guidance, the AICPA issued the *Audit Sampling Guide,* which provides more detailed guidance. Both this section and the *Guide* are summarized in the Audit Sampling Module, which includes detailed examples.

The various subsections of our outline are divided as follows:

A. General background information;
B., C., D. Sampling in substantive procedures (tests of details);
E., F., G. Sampling in tests of controls;
H. Dual-purpose testing, and
I. Selecting a sampling approach.

A. General background information

1. Audit sampling is the application of an audit procedure to less than 100% of the items within an account balance or class of transactions (hereafter, "account")

    a. The purpose of audit sampling is to evaluate some characteristics of an account (e.g., its balance)

    b. The use of a few items to obtain an understanding of a system or operation is not covered by the guidance in this section

2. Both nonstatistical and statistical approaches to sampling are addressed in this statement, and both

    a. Are considered **acceptable**

    b. May be used to **provide sufficient appropriate audit evidence**

    c. Require the use of **judgment**

3. The relationship of uncertainty to audit sampling

    a. The third standard of fieldwork ("...sufficient appropriate audit evidence...") implies some degree of uncertainty

    b. Some items do not justify the acceptance of any uncertainty, and must be examined 100% (e.g., individually material items)

    c. This section refers to uncertainty as audit risk. Audit risk includes the risk of material misstatement (consisting of inherent risk and control risk) and the risk that any material misstatements will not be detected by the auditor (detection risk)

        (1) The auditor relies on internal control to reduce the first risk

        (2) The auditor relies on substantive procedures to reduce the second risk. Substantive procedures include

            (a) Detail tests (tests of transactions)

            (b) Analytical procedures

            (c) Tests of ending balances

4. Audit risk includes uncertainties due to sampling, called sampling risk, and uncertainties due to factors other than sampling, called nonsampling risk

    a. Sampling risk arises from the possibility that the conclusions derived from the sample will differ from the conclusions that would be derived from the population (the sample is nonrepresentative of the population). Sampling risk varies inversely with sample size.

    b. Nonsampling risk arises from uncertainties due to factors other than sampling. For example

        (1) Inappropriate audit procedures for a given objective, and
        (2) The failure to recognize errors

    c. Nonsampling risk can be reduced through adequate planning and supervision and adherence to quality control standards.

5. In performing substantive procedures, the auditor is concerned with two aspects of sampling

    a. The risk of incorrect acceptance
    b. The risk of incorrect rejection

6. In performing tests of controls, the auditor is concerned with two aspects of sampling

    a. The risk of assessing control risk too low
    b. The risk of assessing control risk too high

> **NOTE:** Risks 5.a. and 6.a. relate to the effectiveness and are most important of the audit. Risks 5.b. and 6.b. relate to the efficiency of the audit.

B. Sampling in substantive procedures (tests of details)—planning

1. In **planning** a sample the auditor should consider

    a. The relationship of the sample to the relevant audit objective
    b. Preliminary estimates of materiality levels (the maximum error is called **tolerable misstatement** for a particular sample)

        (1) Auditors should normally set tolerable misstatement at less than financial statement materiality.

    c. The auditor's allowable risk of incorrect acceptance
    d. Characteristics of items comprising the account balance or class of transactions to be sampled

2. The auditor must select a **population** from which to sample and which is consistent with the specified audit objective of concern

    a. The **population** consists of items in the account balance or transaction class of interest
    b. For example, understatement due to omission could not be detected by sampling recorded items. Sampling from subsequent activities records would be preferred.

3. The extent of **substantive procedures required will vary inversely with the auditor's assessment of the risk of material misstatement (inherent risk and control risk)**

4. The greater the reliance on analytical procedures and other substantive procedures of a nonsampling nature, the greater the allowable risk of incorrect acceptance and, thus, the smaller the required sample size for substantive procedures

5. The auditor uses his/her judgment in determining which items should be individually tested and which items should be subject to sampling

    a. The efficiency of a sample may be improved by separating items subject to sampling into relatively homogeneous groups

C. Sampling in substantive procedures (tests of details)—in selecting sample items, the auditor should ensure that

1. The sample is representative of the population
2. All the items have a chance of being chosen
3. Acceptable random-based selection techniques include

    a. Random sampling
    b. Stratified random sampling
    c. Probability-proportional-to-size
    d. Systematic sampling

D. Sampling in substantive procedures (tests of details)—in **performing** audit procedures on selected items and when **evaluating** sampling results, the auditor should

1. Apply auditing procedures to each sample item

a. Unexamined items should be evaluated to determine their effect on the sample results
b. In addition, the auditor should consider the reasons for his/her inability to examine the item (e.g., a lack of supporting documentation)

2. Project the misstatement results from the sample to the population from which the sample was selected
3. Compare projected population misstatement results (including misstatements from the 100% examined items) to the tolerable misstatement

   a. This evaluation requires the use of judgment in both statistical and nonstatistical sampling
   b. The auditor should also consider the qualitative aspects of the misstatements

      (1) The nature and cause of the misstatement
      (2) The possible relationship of the misstatement to other phases of the audit

   c. A fraud usually requires more consideration than a misstatement

4. The auditor should consider projected misstatement results in the aggregate from statistical and nonstatistical sources when evaluating whether the financial statements as a whole may be misstated

E. Sampling in tests of controls—planning

1. In planning a sample the auditor should consider

   a. The relationship of the sample to the objective of the test
   b. The maximum rate of deviation from (tolerable rate) prescribed control procedures that would support his/her allowable risk of assessing control risk too low.
   c. The auditor's allowable risk of assessing control risk too low.

      (1) Low levels usually required because tests of controls are the primary source of evidence about whether a control procedure is being applied as prescribed
      (2) Quantitatively the auditor might consider 5% to 10% risk of assessing control risk too low as acceptable

   d. The characteristics of the population of interest

      (1) The auditor should consider the likely rate of deviation
      (2) The auditor should consider whether to test controls singly or in combination

2. The auditor should realize that deviations from important control procedures at a given rate ordinarily result in misstatements at a lower rate
3. Sampling applies when an auditor needs to decide whether the rate of deviation from a control is no greater than a tolerable rate

   a. Risk assessment procedures to obtain an understanding of internal control do not involve sampling
   b. Sampling concepts also do not apply for some tests of controls

      (1) Some automated controls need to be tested only once or a few times if effective IT controls exist.
      (2) Determining whether an appropriate segregation of duties exists
      (3) Operation of the control environment, such as examining the actions of those charged with governance

F. Sampling in tests of controls—sample selection should ensure that

1. The sample is representative of the population
2. The probability of inclusion of every item in the population is **known**

G. Sampling in tests of controls—performance and evaluation

1. The auditor should apply auditing procedures to each sample item

   a. If the auditor cannot apply procedures to all sample items, s/he should consider reasons for the limitations
   b. Items to which procedures cannot be applied should be considered deviations for sample evaluation

2. Whether statistical or nonstatistical sampling is used, if the auditor decides that s/he is not going to rely on internal control, the planned substantive procedures should be adjusted

H. **Dual-purpose samples** have two purposes

1. To test the operating effectiveness of a control
2. **To test whether the recorded dollar amount of a transaction is correct** (substantive procedures)

   a. The auditor usually assumes that there is an acceptably small planned assessed level of control risk which is greater than the tolerable level
   b. The size of the sample should be the larger of the samples otherwise designed for two separate purposes

I. Selecting a sampling approach

1. Statistical or nonstatistical approaches can provide sufficient audit evidence
2. Choice between statistical and nonstatistical approach depends on relative

    a. Cost
    b. Effectiveness

3. Statistical sampling helps

    a. Design efficient sampling plans
    b. Measure sufficiency of audit evidence
    c. To quantitatively evaluate sample results

380 The Auditor's Communication with Those Charged with Governance (SAS 114)

Overall Scope—This section addresses the auditor's responsibility to communicate with those charged with governance in relation to an audit of financial statements. It does **not** establish requirements regarding communications with management or owners, unless they are also charged with a governance role.

A. Objectives in communicating with those charged with governance include

1. Communicate auditor responsibilities and an overview of the audit scope and timing
2. Obtain information from those charged with governance relevant to the audit
3. Provide those charged with governance timely observations arising from the audit
4. Promote effective two-way communication between the auditor and those charged with governance

B. Definitions

1. **Those charged with governance.** Person(s) or organization(s) with responsibility for overseeing the strategic direction of the entity and the obligations relating to the accountability of the entity. This includes overseeing the financial reporting process. Those charged with governance may include management personnel, for example, executive members of a governance board or an owner-manager. (For entities with a board of directors, this term encompasses the board of directors or audit committee.)
2. **Management.** Person(s) with executive responsibility for the conduct of the entity's operations.

C. Requirements

1. Determine who is charged with governance. When the auditor communicates with a subgroup (e.g., the audit committee), the auditor should determine whether s/he also needs to communicate with the governing body (e.g., the entire board of directors). When all those charged with governance are also involved in managing the entity, the auditor must also make certain that they are aware of the matters.

D. Matters to be communicated

1. Auditor responsibility to form and express an opinion, and that an audit does not release management or those charged with governance of their responsibilities
2. Planned scope and timing of the audit
3. Significant findings from the audit, including

    a. Auditor views of qualitative aspects of significant accounting practices
    b. Significant difficulties encountered during the audit
    c. Disagreements with management
    d. Other findings or issues which the auditor believes are significant and relevant to those charged with governance

4. Uncorrected misstatements other than those that are trivial, as well as the effect of uncorrected misstatements related to prior periods
5. When not all of those charged with governance are involved with management, also communicate

    a. Material corrected misstatements
    b. Significant issues discussed with management
    c. Auditor's views about significant matters on which management consulted with other accountants
    d. Written representations the auditor is requesting

NOTE: A number of multiple-choice questions have asked which matter is communicated (or not communicated). You should be familiar with the nature of the above matters.

E. Communication process

1. **Form.** The auditor should communicate in writing with those charged with governance significant findings from the audit when, in the auditor's professional judgment, oral communication would not be adequate. When communicated orally, the communication should be documented in the working papers, including when and to whom they were communicated; when in writing, retain a copy of the communication.

2. **Restricted use.** When the communication is in writing, the auditor should indicate that it is intended solely for the information of those charged with governance (and, if appropriate, management) and is not intended to be used by anyone else.

3. **Timing.** On a sufficiently timely basis to enable those charged with governance to take appropriate action.

4. **Adequacy of process.** If the process has not been considered adequate, the auditor should evaluate the effect, if any, on the assessment of the risks of the material misstatements and the ability to obtain sufficient appropriate audit evidence and should take appropriate action.

390 Consideration of Omitted Procedures after Report Date (SAS 46)

Overall Objectives and Approach—This brief section presents guidance on how to approach a situation in which subsequent to issuance of an audit report, an auditor determines that one or more necessary procedures may have been omitted. While the auditor has no responsibility to retroactively review his/her work, the section does address the situation in which a post issuance review (e.g., an internal inspection of a peer review) may have disclosed such an omitted procedure(s). Also, the guidance only relates to a situation in which there is no indication that the financial statements depart from GAAP—when known departures exist see the outline of AU 561 and Section C of the Evidence Module. Make certain that you are able to distinguish the omitted audit procedure responsibility described in this section from the discovery of facts relating to the financial statements in Section 561.

A. When it is determined that a procedure has been omitted, the auditor should assess its importance, considering other procedures which may have compensated for its omission

1. This section only covers cases in which there is **no** indication that financial statements depart from GAAP. (See AU 561 when errors exist.)

2. Although auditor has no responsibility to retroactively review his/her work, such postissuance review may occur as part of internal inspection, or peer review

3. In all such circumstances, the auditor may be well advised to consult an attorney

B. When it is determined that a procedure has been omitted, auditor must

1. **Assess its importance.** (Consider other procedures which may have compensated for its omission.)

   a. If omission is considered important and if auditor believes individuals are relying on financial statements, procedures (or alternate procedures) should be promptly applied

      (1) The auditor may, however, discover that the results of other procedures that **were** applied compensate for the omitted procedure

   b. If financial statement errors are detected, consult AU 561

   c. If the auditor is unable to apply procedures, consult attorney

410 Adherence to Generally Accepted Accounting Principles (SAS 1)

Overall Objectives and Approach—This very brief section states that (1) GAAP, as used in the reporting standards, includes not only accounting principles, but also the methods of applying them and (2) the auditor's report does not represent a statement of fact by the auditor, but an opinion.

420 Consistency of Application of GAAP (SAS 1)

Overall Objectives and Approach—This section presents guidance on applying the consistency reporting standard, which was revised in 1988 (it now reads, "The report shall identify those circumstances in which such principles have not been consistently observed in the current period in relation to the preceding period"). This section relates very directly to APB 20 which prescribes accounting for three types of accounting changes—change in principles, change in estimate, and change in reporting entity—and for corrections of errors in prior statements.

The general rule is that changes in accounting principles, changes in the reporting entity, and correction of error in principles require explanatory language as to consistency (i.e., an explanatory paragraph added to an unqualified report); changes in estimates do not. Yet, there are several exceptions to the rules (described below) with which you need to be familiar.

A. Changes that require the addition of an explanatory paragraph referring to the inconsistency

1. **Change in accounting principle**

   a. As a typical example, consider changing from straight-line to the sum-of-the-years' digits method
   b. Special cases of changes in accounting principles (which still require an explanatory paragraph)

      (1) **Correction of an error in principle**—For example, assume that in the preceding year a client used an unacceptable method for valuing inventory; changing to a proper method (e.g., LIFO) still requires an explanatory paragraph. There is a tendency to **incorrectly** think that since the client is eliminating an error, no mention of the inconsistency is necessary.
      (2) **Change in principle inseparable from a change in estimate**—For example, changing from deferring a cost to expensing it in the year incurred represents a change in principle from capitalization to expensing; but it also represents a change in estimate in that the life is now assessed at one year or less.

2. **Change in the reporting entity**

   a. The following require an explanatory paragraph

      (1) Presenting consolidated or combined statements in place of individual company statements
      (2) Changing the specific subsidiaries in the group for which consolidated statements are presented
      (3) Changing the companies included in combined statements
      (4) Changing among the cost, equity, and consolidation methods of accounting for subsidiaries

   b. Application of the consistency standard for a pooling of interests

   > **NOTE:** APB 16 requires that comparative financial statements restate prior years' results to give recognition of the pooling of interests. When single-year statements are presented, the financial statement notes should adequately disclose the pooling transaction and state the revenues, extraordinary items, and net income of the constituent companies for the preceding year on a combined basis. For more information see outline of APB 16.

      (1) When prior year financial statements are presented and not restated

         (a) Add an explanatory paragraph on the inconsistency (due to the lack of application to the prior years, not due to a change in application in accounting principle in the current year)
         (b) Also, the failure to restate comparative statements to reflect the pooling is a departure from GAAP—see outline of AU 508 for proper reporting treatment (i.e., qualified or adverse opinion)

      (2) When single-year statements do not properly disclose pooling transaction in notes the auditor should

         (a) Add an explanatory paragraph on the inconsistency between the current and preceding (not presented) year
         (b) Qualify the opinion due to the lack of disclosure

   > **NOTE:** As indicated below, when the accounting treatment of a pooling of interests has been proper, no consistency modification is necessary.

B. Changes that **do not** require the addition of an explanatory paragraph referring to the inconsistency

   1. Change in estimate

      a. For example, changing either the life or salvage value of fixed assets

   2. Correction of an error **not involving a principle**

      a. For example, correction of a mathematical error in previously issued financial statements

   3. Change in classification

      a. For example, adding an additional line item expense to this year's income statement which in the preceding year was included in "miscellaneous expense"

   4. Creation, cessation, purchase, or disposition of a subsidiary or business unit

   > **NOTE:** Be careful here to distinguish the above circumstances from those described in A.2. above. These situations are normal business events. Those described in A.2. above may be viewed as using different accounting methods.

   5. Properly accounted-for pooling of interest combinations
   6. Changes in principles that **do not materially** affect this year's financial statements, even when reasonably certain the change will materially affect them in later years

7. Accounting principles are adopted when events or transactions first become material in their effect

   a. Modification or adoption of a principle at this point does not require a paragraph referring to consistency

C. Miscellaneous

1. Accounting changes may also lead to a departure from GAAP situation

   a. When a material change in principles occurs, with which the auditor does not concur, a departure from GAAP exists and a qualified opinion or an adverse opinion is appropriate—see outline of AU 508

   b. Whenever an accounting change has not been appropriately described in the financial statements, a departure from GAAP exists (in this case, inadequate disclosure) and a qualified opinion or an adverse opinion is appropriate—see outline of AU 508

2. Periods to which the consistency standard relates

   a. When the CPA reports only on the current period, the consistency standard relates to the preceding period, regardless of whether that period is presented

   b. When the CPA reports on two or more years, the consistency standard relates to the years reported upon, and with the year prior thereto **only if** such prior year is presented

3. For a first year audit

   a. Normally the auditor will be able to determine whether accounting principles employed are consistent with the prior year

      (1) When inadequate records make this determination impossible, when such amounts could materially affect current operating results, the auditor may be unable to express an opinion on the income statement and the statement of cash flows

431 Adequacy of Disclosure in Financial Statements (SAS 32)

Overall Objectives and Approach—This brief section interprets the third standard of reporting, which states that informative disclosures are to be regarded as reasonably adequate unless otherwise stated in the report. Omission of required information is a departure from GAAP which requires the auditor to issue either a qualified or an adverse opinion—see outline of AU 508 for details. If practicable, the auditor should provide the omitted information in his/her report; practicable means that the information is reasonably obtainable from the accounts and records and does not require the auditor to assume the position of a preparer of financial information. Thus, the auditor would **not** be expected to prepare a basic financial statement (e.g., a statement of cash flows) or segment information and include it in his/her report.

504 Association with Financial Statements (SAS 26)

Overall Objectives and Approach—This section defines what is meant by a CPA being "associated with financial statements," and discusses "unaudited statements." The issue of being "associated with financial statements" is important because the fourth standard of reporting (which requires an opinion, or a statement that an opinion cannot be expressed) requires that a CPA must make clear the character of his/her examination, and the responsibility taken, when s/he is **associated** with financial statements.

The section related to "unaudited statements" is of limited applicability since there are no "unaudited statements" for nonissuer (nonpublic) companies—statements for such companies are compiled, reviewed, or audited. Thus, "unaudited statements" are only relevant for the occasional public company which for some reason does not require audited financial statements. In this outline we present information on (a) general association with financial information, (b) reporting on unaudited statements, and (c) reporting on comparative statements when one period is unaudited and when one period is audited.

A. General association with financial information

1. The objective of the fourth standard of reporting is **to prevent misinterpretation of the degree of responsibility** assumed by the accountant when his/her name is **associated** with financial statements

2. An accountant is **associated** with financial statements when s/he

   a. Has consented to the use of his/her name in a report, document, or written communication containing the statements or

    b. Submits to a client financial statements that s/he has prepared or assisted in preparing, even though the accountant does not append his/her name to the statements

  3. Before issuing a report, **the accountant has a responsibility to read the statements for obvious material misstatements;** no other procedural requirements exist

    a. When other procedures have been performed, mention of them should **not** be made in the report issued

B. Reporting on unaudited statements

  1. The following disclaimer may accompany or be on the statements:
The accompanying balance sheet of X Company as of December 31, 20X1, and the related statement of income, retained earnings, and cash flows for the year then ended were not audited by us and accordingly, we do not express an opinion on them.

  2. Each page of the statements **should be marked as "unaudited"**

  3. When the client has prepared a document which includes unaudited statements, the auditor should request that

    a. His/her name not be included in the communication **or**

    b. That the financial statement be marked as unaudited and that there be a notation that s/he does not express an opinion on them

  4. If the accountant is **not** independent, the disclaimer issued should indicate such nonindependence, but should **not** indicate any procedures performed or the reason for nonindependence

  5. When the accountant believes that the unaudited statements do not follow GAAP

    a. S/he should request appropriate revision

    b. If unsuccessful, modify the disclaimer to refer to the departure

> **NOTE:** Some CPA exam questions have suggested that a qualified or adverse opinion is appropriate when such statements do not follow GAAP. This is incorrect since an audit has not been performed. A disclaimer with the appropriate information **is** appropriate. If the client refuses to accept such a report, the accountant should disassociate him/herself from the statements.

  6. In no case should a report on unaudited statements include negative assurance (e.g., "nothing came to our attention"—see the outline of AU 623 for more information on negative assurance)

  7. When unaudited financial statements are presented in comparative form with audited financial statements in *SEC documents*, the statements should be marked as "unaudited" but not referred to in the auditor's report

    a. In any other document, the CPA's report on the unaudited prior period financial statements should be reissued or the report on the subsequent year should include a separate paragraph describing the CPA's association with the unaudited statements

508 Reports on Audited Financial Statements (SAS 58 and SAS 79)

Overall Objectives and Approach—This section presents guidance on the nature of audit reports. The information presented constitutes the primary reporting guidance for normal GAAP GAAS audits. It is also summarized in the Reporting Module, which includes sample reports.

You should know that the objective of the fourth reporting standard (i.e., the report is to contain an opinion on the financial statements **taken as a whole** or an assertion that an opinion cannot be expressed) is to **prevent misinterpretation of the degree of responsibility** taken by the auditor. Also, the phrase "taken as a whole" applies equally to the complete set of financial statements and to the individual financial statements.

Section A of this outline summarizes information relating to the auditor's standard report. Section B deals with circumstances in which an auditor issues an unqualified report with explanatory language added. Qualified, adverse, and disclaimers of opinion are considered in Sections C through E. Sections F and G relate to comparative statements.

A. The auditor's standard report

  1. Basic elements

    a. Title that includes word "independent"

    b. Statements were audited

    c. Financial statements are management's responsibility; expressing an opinion is the auditor's responsibility

    d. Audit conducted in accordance with US GAAS

    e. Those standards require planning and performing audit to obtain reasonable assurance financial statements free of material misstatement

    f. Statement that an audit includes

      (1) Examining, on a test basis, evidence

        (2) Assessing accounting principles and estimates

        (3) Evaluating financial statement presentation

    g. Statement that auditor believes audit provides reasonable basis for opinion

    h. Opinion statements present fairly per US GAAP

    i. Manual or printed signature of firm

    j. Date of report

2. **The report is addressed to company, board of directors, or shareholders**

    a. When an auditor is engaged by a client to report on statements of a nonclient, the report is addressed to client (e.g., a client may hire the auditor to audit statements of an acquisition candidate)

B. Explanatory language added to the auditor's standard report

> **NOTE:** The report issued may still be unqualified in the following circumstances. The unqualified report includes an explanatory paragraph (or other explanatory language).

1. Opinion based in part on report of another auditor

    a. **Reference is made to other auditor in all three paragraphs**

2. Departure from a promulgated accounting principle

    a. Pertains to situations in which unusual circumstances result in a situation in which following GAAP would lead to misleading results

    b. **An explanatory paragraph is added** (either preceding or following opinion paragraph)

3. Consistency

    a. The auditor must concur with the change

        (1) **If the auditor does not concur, a departure from GAAP exists** which leads to either a qualified or adverse opinion

    b. **Explanatory paragraph added** (following opinion paragraph)

        (1) Nonrestatement cases—as long as year of change presented and reported on

        (2) Restatements—only in year of change

    c. See AU 420 outline

4. Emphasis of a matter

    a. Pertains to situations in which **auditor wishes to draw attention** to a matter concerning financial statements (e.g., when client is component of larger entity, related-party transactions, subsequent events, matter affecting comparability)

    b. **Explanatory paragraph** added (either preceding or following opinion paragraph)

C. Qualified opinions

1. Scope limitation

    a. Types—**client- and circumstance-imposed**

    b. Type of report (unqualified, qualified, or disclaimer)

        (1) Depends upon importance of omitted procedure (consider nature, magnitude, potential effect, and number of accounts involved)

        (2) **Generally disclaim for client-imposed scope restrictions**

    c. **Limitation described in scope, explanatory, and opinion paragraphs**

        (1) Explanatory paragraph precedes opinion paragraph

    d. Opinion qualification pertains to possible effects on financial statements, not to scope limitation itself

    e. A **report on only one statement** (e.g., balance sheet) **is not a scope restriction** if auditor has access to necessary information

2. Departure from generally accepted accounting principle

    a. Type of report (unqualified, qualified, or adverse)

(1) Depends on dollar magnitude, significance to operations, pervasiveness, and impact on statements as a whole

(2) Inadequate disclosure is a departure from GAAP

b. **Explanatory paragraph added** (preceding opinion paragraph), and **opinion paragraph altered**

c. **Omission of statement of cash flows**

(1) Auditor not required to prepare one

(2) Ordinarily qualify report

d. Accounting principle changes

(1) Auditor evaluates whether

(a) New principle is GAAP

(b) Method of accounting for change is GAAP

(c) Management justification is reasonable

(2) If any of (1) is "no," a departure from GAAP exists

(3) Qualification (or adverse) remains as long as statements provided

D. Adverse opinion

1. Statements taken as a whole are not fairly presented

2. Explanatory paragraph (preceding opinion paragraph), opinion paragraph altered

E. Disclaimer

1. A disclaimer states that the auditor does not express an opinion on the financial statements

2. Disclaimer is appropriate when the auditor is unable to form an opinion or has not formed an opinion as to the fairness of presentation of the financial statements

> **NOTE:** Scope limitations are emphasized in the standards as a circumstance resulting in a disclaimer (or a qualified opinion). Other circumstances in which disclaimers are issued include [1] unaudited statements (AU 504), [2] a lack of auditor independence (AU 504), [3] substantial doubt about a client's ability to continue as a going concern when an auditor does not wish to issue an unqualified opinion with an explanatory paragraph (AU 341), and [4] an auditor believes that a particularly important uncertainty makes it impossible to form an opinion (AU 508).

F. Comparative financial statements

1. Continuing auditors should update report to cover comparative statements

2. Date report not earlier than the date on which the auditor has obtained sufficient appropriate audit evidence to support the opinion (ordinarily the date of completion of fieldwork of most recent audit)

3. **Updating** prior period reports may result in an opinion different from that originally issued

a. Example—departure from GAAP in prior year statements eliminated

b. If opinion different from previous period, explanatory paragraph should disclose

(1) Date of previous report

(2) Type of opinion previously expressed

(3) Circumstances calling for changed report

(4) State that updated opinion differs from previous opinion

G. Comparative statements—When a predecessor auditor has audited the preceding year his/her audit report may be reissued **or** summarized in the successor auditor's report

1. Before reissuing report predecessor should

a. **Read** the current statements

b. **Compare** prior statements with current

c. **Obtain letter of representations from successor** indicating any matters that might have effect on prior statements

d. **If predecessor is aware of events** affecting previous opinion, s/he should **perform necessary audit procedures**

e. Dating report

(1) Not revised—use original report date

(2) Revised—dual date

2. Predecessor's report not presented

    a. Successor's report should indicate

        (1) **Prior statements audited by other auditors**
        (2) **Date of their report**
        (3) **Type of report issued by predecessor**
        (4) **Substantive reasons if other than unqualified**

            (a) Also, if other than standard, give reasons for explanatory paragraph

530 Dating the Independent Auditor's Report (SAS 1, 29)

Overall Objectives and Approach—This section presents guidance on dating of the auditor's report. **The general rule is that the report is dated no earlier than the date on which the auditor has obtained sufficient appropriate audit evidence to support the audit opinion (ordinarily the date of the completion of fieldwork).** The section discusses two exceptions—(a) events have occurred after fieldwork, but before issuance of the report, and (b) certain circumstances in which an audit report is being reissued.

A. Dating the audit report when subsequent events have occurred after fieldwork, but before issuance of the report

> **NOTE:** An understanding of this section requires knowledge of AU 560 on subsequent events. That section distinguishes between the "event" (i.e., the subsequent event) which occurred after the balance sheet date, but prior to the issuance of the financial statements, and the "condition" which caused the event. The basic accounting rule developed in AU 560 is that when a subsequent event occurs the auditor must determine whether the condition which caused the event existed at the date of the balance sheet. When the condition existed at the balance sheet date, adjustment of the financial statements is appropriate. When the condition came into effect after year-end, note disclosure is appropriate. For more information on this, see the outline of AU 560.

1. Dating of the audit report when the **condition came into effect before year-end**

    a. When an adjustment is needed, and no note disclosure is needed, the audit report need not be changed
    b. When an adjustment **and** note disclosure is needed, the auditor must change the report date as indicated in 3. below

2. Dating of the audit report when the condition came into existence after year-end

    a. Note disclosure is needed, and the auditor must change the report date as indicated in 3. below

3. When the report date must be changed (from the date on which the auditor obtained sufficient appropriate audit evidence), two methods are available

    a. **A dual date** in which the overall report is dated as of the report's original date, but a note such as "except for Note X, as to which the date is ____," is added following the date.

> **EXAMPLE**
>
> A report might be dated as follows: February 17, 20X9, except for Note 1, as to which the date is February 27, 20X9.

    b. The report date might be changed to the **date of the subsequent event**

> **EXAMPLE**
>
> Using the above example: February 27, 20X9

        (1) When the report date is changed in this manner, the CPA's responsibility for subsequent events extends to the date of his/her report—see outline of AU 560 for these procedures

B. Dating the audit report when it is being reissued

    The situation here is one in which an auditor has already issued a report, and is being asked to reissue it. This may occur, for example, when the financial statements are included in a report being filed with the SEC, or, more simply, when a client asks the CPA to furnish additional copies of a previously issued report. The overall rule is that the CPA has no responsibility to make any further investigation as to events which may have occurred during the period between the original report date and the date of the release of the additional reports. The original report date is retained for the reissued report. A complicating factor arises when the CPA becomes aware of an event subsequent to the date of the original report that requires adjustment and/or disclosure.

1. When the auditor is asked to reissue his/her report, and s/he

   a. Is **not** aware of the existence of any subsequent event, the original report date should be used
   b. Is aware of the existence of a subsequent event which requires adjustment or disclosure, the report should be dated in accordance with A.3. above
   c. Is aware of an event which requires disclosure only (i.e., no adjustment) which has occurred **between the date of the original report and the date of reissuance,** the event may be disclosed in a separate **unaudited note to the financial statements;** the audit report date is **not** changed from that used for the original report

532 Restricting the Use of an Auditor's Report

Overall Objectives and Approach—This section presents guidance on when and how auditors should restrict audit reports.

A. General-Use and Restricted-Use Reports

1. General-use reports are not restricted to specified parties

   a. Financial statements prepared in accordance with GAAP are ordinarily general use

2. Restricted-use reports are intended only for specified parties; an auditor should restrict the use of a report in the following circumstances:

   a. The subject matter of the auditor's report is based on measurement or disclosure criteria in contractual agreements or regulatory provisions that are not in accordance with GAAP or an other comprehensive basis of accounting

      (1) Use should be restricted to the parties to the agreement or regulatory agencies responsible for the provisions

   b. The accountant's report is based on agreed-upon procedures

      (1) Use should be restricted to the "specified parties" as per AU 622

   c. The auditor's report is issued as a "by-product" of an audit

      (1) Examples

         (a) AU 325 on internal control significant deficiencies
         (b) AU 380 on communication with audit committees
         (c) AU 623 on compliance with aspects of contractual agreements or regulatory requirements

      (2) Use should be restricted to the audit committee, board of directors, management, others with the organization, specified regulatory agencies, and in compliance reports to the parties of the contract

3. An auditor's report that is restricted should contain a separate paragraph at the end of the report that includes

   a. A statement that the report is intended solely for the information and use of the specified parties
   b. An identification of the specified parties to whom use is restricted
   c. A statement that the report is not intended to be and should not be used by anyone other than the specified parties

B. Other issues

1. When an auditor issues a single combined report covering both subject matter that requires a restriction and subject matter that does not ordinarily require restriction, the use of such a single combined report should be restricted to the specified parties
2. Additional users may be added as "specified parties" if those parties specify, ordinarily in writing, that they understand the nature of the engagement, the measurement or disclosure criteria, and the related report
3. While an auditor is not responsible for controlling the distribution of reports by the client, an auditor should consider informing the client that restricted-use reports are not intended for distribution to specified party
4. Nothing this section precludes an auditor from restricting the use of any report

   a. For example, if the auditor and client agreed, an audit report could be made "restricted use"

534 Reporting on Financial Statements Prepared for Use in Other Countries (SAS 51)

Overall Objectives and Approach—This section presents guidance for a CPA practicing **in the US** who is engaged to report on the **financial statements of a US entity** that have been prepared in conformity with the **accounting principles**

of another country. For example, consider a US subsidiary of a multinational corporation with a non-US parent. Often such a subsidiary issues GAAP-based financial statements intended for use in the US, and other financial statements that are prepared in conformity with accounting principles generally accepted in another country. This section addresses the approach the CPA should use for the financial statements prepared following the principles of the other country. The guidance provided in Section A of this outline deals with the applicability of the following standards—(1) US GAAS, (2) other country accounting standards, and (3) other country auditing standards. Section B of this outline provides information on reporting requirements.

A. Applicable standards and procedures other than reporting

   Overall requirements—before reporting on the statements, the auditor should have a clear understanding of, and obtain written representations from, management regarding the purpose and uses of the financial statements

   1. Applicability of **US GAAS**

      a. The general rule is that the CPA must perform US **general** and **fieldwork** standards

         (1) Exceptions to the rule occur when differences in the other country's accounting principles require modification of the procedures that are followed.
         (2) Examples

            (a) When the principles of the other country do not require deferred taxes, procedures for testing deferred tax balances would not be applicable
            (b) When principles of the other country do not require or permit disclosure of related-party transactions, audit procedures related to meeting US disclosure standards would not be appropriate

   2. Other country **accounting** standards

      a. The auditor should understand the accounting principles of the other country; this knowledge may be obtained by considering

         (1) The professional literature of that country
         (2) Information obtained by consulting with individuals with the necessary expertise
         (3) International Accounting Standards (when the other country's principles are not well established)

   3. Other country auditing standards

      a. When the auditor is requested to apply the other country's auditing standards s/he may do so if

         (1) US standards are also applied
         (2) S/he has read pertinent literature, and to the extent necessary, has consulted with persons having the necessary expertise

B. Reporting requirements

   1. Report issued for the financial statements (which are to be used outside the US)—either a modified US report or the standard report of the other country **may** be appropriate

      a. Modified US report should

         (1) Identify the financial statements that have been audited
         (2) Refer to the note in the financial statements that describes the basis of presentation (including the nationality) of the principles
         (3) State that the audit followed US auditing standards (and other country standards if appropriate)
         (4) Include a paragraph on whether the statements present fairly in conformity with the basis being followed

      b. The standard report of the other country may be used if

         (1) Such a report would be used by auditors in the other country in similar circumstances
         (2) The auditor understands the attestations contained in the report

      c. Limited distribution of the reports described above in a. and b. is acceptable (e.g., to banks, institutional investors) if the statements are to be allowed in a manner that permits such parties to discuss differences in US and other country reporting practices

   2. When the distribution in the US is more than limited, the auditor should report using the US standard form of report, modified as appropriate for departures from GAAP

      a. The CPA may choose to include a separate report expressing an opinion on whether the financial statements are in conformity with the other country's standards **or**

b. May issue a US report for distribution in the US, and a report as described in B.1.a. and B.1.b. above in the other country

> **NOTE:** The above section is actually requiring that when the statements following the other country's basis are being used on more than a limited basis in the US, the auditor must indicate departures from GAAP in a US style report. This will **not** normally be necessary because the statements will not in general be used in the US. Recall from our introduction of this section that more typically, when there is a US demand for such statements, dual statements will be issued—one set following US GAAP and the other set following other country's accounting principles. The auditor would then issue a standard US report on the first set of statements, and one of the reports described in "B.1." for the other country's statements.

543 Part of the Examination Made by Other Independent Auditors (SAS 1)

Overall Objectives and Approach—This section presents guidance on reporting requirements when more than one CPA firm is involved with the audit of a particular company. As an example, consider a situation in which a parent company owns four subsidiaries. CPA firm A has audited the parent (a holding company with no operations of its own) and three of the subsidiaries; CPA firm B has audited the fourth subsidiary. This situation may occur, for example, when the parent has recently purchased the subsidiary and as a part of the purchase agreement the acquired subsidiary is allowed to keep its CPA firm for some period of time.

In such a situation a number of audit reports may be issued. First, reports might be issued for each of the four subsidiaries. The reporting for those is quite straightforward—CPA firm A would issue three reports while CPA firm B would issue one.

The situation with respect to the parent is more complicated. After consolidation, the parent will be composed of the three subsidiaries audited by CPA firm A, and one audited by CPA firm B. It is the reporting for this situation that AU 543 addresses. The section requires that a "principal" auditor be determined to report on the consolidated parent's overall financial statements and prescribes certain requirements of the CPA firm—Section A of the outline presents that material. Two basic approaches to presenting the audit report are presented—Section B discusses a decision by the principal auditor **not** to make reference to the other auditor; Section C discusses a decision **to make reference** to the other auditor. Section D of the outline provides miscellaneous related points.

A. Determining the principal auditor and his/her responsibilities

1. The following factors should be considered in determining which firm is to serve as the principal auditor

    a. Materiality of the portion of the financial statements audited by each CPA
    b. Each CPA's relative knowledge of the overall financial statements
    c. The importance of the components audited by each CPA

    > **NOTE:** This will normally be an easy decision since in practice one CPA will normally have much more than one-half of the overall work.

2. The principal auditor is required to make the following types of inquiries about the other auditor

    a. His/her **reputation**[*]—contact

        (1) AICPA, state society, local chapter
        (2) Other CPAs
        (3) Bankers and other credit grantors
        (4) Others

    b. Obtain representation from the other CPA that s/he is independent per AICPA requirements, and if appropriate, per the requirements of the SEC
    c. Ascertain through communication with the other auditor that s/he

        (1) Knows the statements and his/her report will be used by the principal CPA
        (2) Is familiar with GAAP and GAAS[*]
        (3) Is familiar with SEC rules (if applicable)[*]
        (4) Knows a review of matters affecting elimination of intercompany transactions will be made by the principal CPA

[*] These items are ordinarily unnecessary if the principal auditor already knows the professional reputation and standing of the other auditor and if the other auditor's primary place of business is in the US.

> **NOTE:** If the CPA determines that s/he can neither assume responsibility nor rely on the work of the other CPA, s/he should qualify or disclaim an opinion, stating the reasons and the magnitude of the financial statements affected. As a practical matter, in such a situation one would expect that the principal CPA would perform the procedures necessary to eliminate the problem.

3. The principal CPA must determine whether s/he wishes to refer to the other CPA in the audit report

    a. When no reference is made, the principal auditor is assuming responsibility for the work of the other auditor

B. Deciding **not** to make reference to the other CPA

1. No mention of the other CPA or of the procedures indicated in Section A.2. above are made in the report—(e.g., if a standard unqualified report is appropriate, the report would be identical to that issued if no other CPA were involved)

2. Situations in which a principal auditor might choose this course of action (not making reference)

    a. The other CPA is associated with the principal auditor in some manner
    b. The other CPA was retained by the principal auditor (e.g., the principal auditor did not have a branch, and did not wish to travel to the city in which the subsidiary was headquartered)
    c. The principal auditor is satisfied with the other auditor's work
    d. The portion of the statement examined by the other CPA is not material to the overall financial statements

3. When the principal auditor is following this course of action (not making reference), s/he should also consider whether to perform one or more of the following

    a. Visit the other CPA and discuss the audit
    b. Review the other CPA's audit programs
    c. Review the other CPA's working papers
    d. Perform additional auditing procedures

C. Deciding to **make reference** to the other CPA

1. The audit report will indicate the other auditor involvement in the introductory, scope, and opinion paragraphs

    a. The report should indicate the dollar amount of assets, income, and other appropriate criteria included in the other CPA's audit
    b. The other auditor may be named, but only

        (1) With his/her permission
        (2) When his/her report is presented with the principal CPA's report

    c. Absent other circumstances (e.g., a scope limitation or a departure from GAAP), the report issued is unqualified with explanatory language

> **NOTE:** When studying how to actually write audit reports, it is most efficient to study the various modifications of the standard report together. Section B.2. of the Reporting Module presents the necessary information.

D. Miscellaneous

1. Principal auditor treatment of a situation in which the other auditor's report is **not** standard unqualified in form

    a. If the matter is material to the overall financial statements it will require modification of the principal auditor's report
    b. If the matter is **not** material to the overall financial statements, and if the other auditor's report is not presented, the principal auditor need not make reference to the matter

        (1) If the other auditor's report is presented, the principal auditor may wish to make reference to it as to its disposition

2. The advice in this section may also relate to the situation in which an investment is accounted for by use of the equity method; reference to the other auditor who is associated with the investee may be appropriate

3. Following a pooling, a CPA may express an opinion on the restated statements of prior periods; several complications may arise

    a. If the CPA cannot satisfy him/herself with respect to the restated statements

        (1) The CPA should issue the appropriate report on the current year statements (e.g., a standard unqualified one-year report), with an additional paragraph following the opinion paragraph in which the CPA expresses an opinion solely on the proper combination of the pooled companies
        (2) In these circumstances the CPA does not take responsibility for the work of the other CPAs nor for expressing an opinion on the restated statements taken as a whole; procedures should be taken to enable him/her to express an opinion as to the proper combination of the statements

550 Other Information in Documents Containing Audited Financial Statements (SAS 118)

A. Introduction

1. This section addresses the auditor's responsibility in relation to other information in documents containing audited financial statements and the auditor's report thereon. In the absence of any separate requirement in the particular circumstances of the engagement, the auditor's opinion does not cover other information and the auditor has no responsibility for determining whether such information is properly stated. This section establishes the requirement for the auditor to read the other information because the credibility of the audited financial statements may be undermined by material inconsistencies between the audited financial statements and other information.

2. In this section, *documents containing audited financial statements* refers to annual reports (or similar documents) that are issued to owners (or similar stakeholders) and annual reports of governments and organizations for charitable or philanthropic purposes that are available to the public that contain audited financial statements and the auditor's report thereon. This section also may be applied to other documents to which the auditor, at the client's request, devotes attention.

   a. Examples of other information: A report by management on operations, financial summaries or highlights, employment data, financial ratios, names of officer and directors, selected quarterly data

   b. Examples of information not considered "other information:" A press release or cover letter accompanying the document with audited financial statements, information contained in analyst briefings, information contained on the entity's website

B. Objective: The auditor's objective is to respond appropriately when he or she becomes aware that documents containing audited financial statements and the auditor's report thereon include other information that could undermine the credibility of those financial statements and the auditor's report.

C. Definitions

1. **Other information.** Financial and nonfinancial information (other than the financial statements and the auditor's report thereon) that is included in a document containing audited financial statements and the auditor's report thereon, excluding required supplementary information.

2. **Inconsistency.** Other information that conflicts with information contained in the audited financial statements. A material inconsistency may raise doubt about the audit conclusions drawn from audit evidence previously obtained and, possibly, about the basis for the auditor's opinion on the financial statements.

3. **Misstatement of fact.** Other information that is unrelated to matters appearing in the audited financial statements that is incorrectly stated or presented. A material misstatement of fact may undermine the credibility of the document containing audited financial statements.

D. Requirements, application and other explanatory material

1. Reading other information

   a. The auditor should read the other information of which the auditor is aware in order to identify material inconsistencies, if any, with the audited financial statements

   b. The auditor should attempt to obtain the other information prior to the report release date; if this is not possible, the auditor should read other information as soon as possible

      (1) The auditor may delay the report release date until management provides the other information

   c. The auditor should communicate with those charged with governance the auditor responsibility and other procedures performed relating to other information

2. Inconsistencies between the audited information and the other information identified: If the auditor identifies a material inconsistency, the auditor should determine whether the audited financial statements or the other information needs to be revised; when management refuses

   a. If the audited financial statements are incorrect: The auditor should modify the auditor's report for a departure from GAAP (assuming management does not correct the statements).

   b. If the other information is incorrect: the auditor should do one of the following:

      (1) Include an explanatory (emphasis of matter) paragraph in the audit report
      (2) Withhold the auditor's report; or
      (3) Where withdrawal is legally permitted, withdraw.

3. If material inconsistencies are identified subsequent to the report release date the auditor should refer to AU 561.
4. If the other information includes misstatements of fact, the auditor should

   a. Discuss with management

b. If still unresolved, request management to consult with a qualified third party (e.g., legal counsel) and the auditor should consider the advice received

c. If still unresolved, the auditor's reaction depends upon the particular circumstances

   (1) Possible reactions include notifying the client in writing about the auditor's view and consulting legal counsel as to further appropriate action

551 Supplementary Information in Relation to the Financial Statements as a Whole (SAS 119)

A. Introduction

1. Scope: This section addresses the auditor's responsibility when engaged to report on whether supplementary information is fairly stated, in all material respects, in relation to the financial statements as a whole. The information covered by this section is presented outside the basic financial statements and is not considered necessary for the financial statements to be fairly presented. This SAS also may be applied when the auditor is engaged to report on whether *required* supplementary information is fairly stated, in all material respects, in relation to the financial statements as a whole.

2. This section applies to *other information* (defined below). An example of other information is a schedule of details of officers' salaries expense that presents detailed information on each top officer's salary—information beyond what is required by GAAP. This section deals with the situation in which the entity wishes to have that other information also audited. Auditors can do that, and in essence use the same materiality measure(s) they use for the financial statements as a whole (not materiality measures based alone on the other information, here officers' salaries). AU 550 addresses the situation in which the other information is presented, but the entity does not engage the auditor to audit that information.

B. Objective: The objective is to evaluate and report on whether the supplementary information is fairly stated, in all material respects, in relation to the financial statements as a whole.

C. Definition

1. **Supplementary information.** Information outside the basic financial statements (excluding required supplementary information) that is not considered necessary for the financial statements to be fairly presented in accordance with the applicable financial reporting framework. Such information may be presented in a document containing the audited financial statements or separate from the financial statements.

   a. Examples of supplementary information: Additional details on items related to the basic financial statements, consolidating information, historical summaries of financial statement items, statistical data, other material, some of which may be from sources outside the accounting system or outside the entity

   b. AU 550 (SAS 118) addresses other information in documents containing audited financial statements. Only the part of that information obtained or derived from the accounting records would be appropriately covered under this section (i.e., if so engaged an accountant could provide an opinion on it in relation to the financial statements as a whole).

D. Requirements, application and other explanatory material

1. To accept an engagement to apply procedures to determine whether supplementary information is fairly stated, in all material respects, in relation to the financial statements as a whole, the auditor should determine that all of the following conditions are met:

   a. Supplementary information was derived from and relates directly to the underlying accounting and other records used to prepare financial statements.

   b. The other information relates to the same period as the financial statements.

   c. The financial statements were audited and the auditor served as the principal (group) auditor.

   d. Neither an adverse opinion nor a disclaimer of opinion was issued on the financial statements.

   e. The supplementary information will accompany the audited financial statements, or such audited financial statements will be made readily available by the entity (e.g., they are posted on a website).

2. The auditor should obtain the agreement of management that it acknowledges and understands its responsibility

   a. For proper preparation of supplementary information

   b. To provide auditor with written representations on information

   c. To include the auditor's report on the supplementary information in any document that includes that information

   d. To present the supplementary information with the audited financial statements or to make the audited financial statements available

3. Perform the following procedures using the same materiality level used in the audit of the financial statements:

     a. Inquire of management about the purpose of the information and whether it has been prepared in accordance with the applicable financial reporting framework (e.g., GAAP)

     b. Determine form and content of supplementary information complies with applicable criteria

     c. Obtain understanding about methods of preparing information

     d. Compare and reconcile information to underlying accounting and other records

     e. Inquire of management as to significant assumptions, interpretations, etc.

     f. Evaluate appropriateness and completeness of information

     g. Obtain written representations from management

     h. While the auditor has no responsibility for considering subsequent events with respect to supplementary information, if such information comes to his/her attention, AU 560 and AU 561 are relevant.

4. Reporting

     a. The auditor should include an explanatory paragraph with the following elements:

         (1) Audit conducted for purposes of forming an opinion on the financial statements as a whole

         (2) Supplementary information is presented for purposes of additional analysis and is not a required part of the financial statements

         (3) Supplementary information is the responsibility of management and was derived from and relates directly to the underlying accounting and other records used to prepare the financial statements

         (4) The other information has been subjected to the auditing procedures applied in the audit of financial statements and certain additional procedures, including reconciling information to the underlying accounting and other records used to prepare the financial statements and additional procedures in accordance with US GAAS

         (5) If the auditor has issued an unqualified opinion on the financial statements, a statement that the supplementary information is fairly stated in all material respects in relation to the financial statements taken as a whole

         (6) If the auditor is issuing a qualified opinion on the financial statements and the qualification has an effect on the supplementary information, a statement that, in the auditor's opinion, except for the effects of the matter referred to, such information is fairly stated in all material respects in relation to the financial statements as a whole

     b. When the entity does not present the other information with the financial statements, the auditor should include the required reporting in a separate report on the other information

     c. When the auditor's report on the financial statements includes an adverse opinion or a disclaimer of opinion, the auditor is precluded from expressing an opinion on the supplementary information

         (1) When permitted by law, the auditor may withdraw from the engagement

         (2) If the auditor does not withdraw, the auditor's report on the supplementary information should state that because of the significance of the matter described in the auditor's report, it is inappropriate to, and the auditor does not, express an opinion on the supplementary information

     d. The date of the auditor's opinion on the other information should not be earlier than the date on which the auditor completed the required procedures

     e. If the auditor concludes the supplementary information is materially misstated, discuss with management and proper revisions; if management does not revise

         (1) Modify opinion on supplementary information and describe the misstatement, or

         (2) If a separate report is being issued on the supplementary information, withhold the auditor's report on the supplementary information

552 Reporting on Condensed Financial Statements and Selected Financial Data (SAS 42)

Overall Objectives and Approach—This section presents guidance for reporting on a client-prepared document which contains **condensed financial statements** or **selected financial data** derived from the complete audited financial statements. This section only applies when the CPA has reported on the overall financial statements from which the information is being abstracted. The section provides for separate reports on condensed financial statements and on selected financial data. Sections A and B of the outline discuss the nature of the CPA's report on condensed financial statements and selected financial data, respectively. Section C discusses miscellaneous related points.

A. Reporting on **condensed financial statements**

1. The report should indicate

     a. That the complete financial statements have been audited and that the auditor has expressed an opinion on them

b. The date of the auditor's report on the complete financial statements
c. The type of opinion expressed on the complete financial statements
d. Whether the information in the condensed financial statements is fairly presented in all material respects in relation to the complete financial statements from which it is derived

2. Example report

We have audited, in accordance with US generally accepted auditing standards, the consolidated balance sheet of X Company and subsidiaries as of December 3, 20X3, and the related consolidated statements of income, retained earnings, and cash flows for the year then ended (not presented herein); and in our report dated February 15, 20X4, we expressed an unqualified opinion on those consolidated financial statements. In our opinion, the information set forth in the accompanying condensed consolidated financial statements is fairly stated in all material respects in relation to the consolidated financial statements from which it has been derived.

B. Reporting on **selected financial data**

1. The report should be limited to data derived from the audited complete financial statements
2. The CPA's report should indicate items a., c., and d. from A.1. above

   a. The reference in d. is changed from condensed financial statements to the selected financial data

3. When comparative selected financial data are presented and some of the data were derived from financial statements audited by another CPA, the report should so state, and the auditor should not express an opinion on that data

C. Miscellaneous

1. When a client prepares a document with condensed financial statements or selected financial data which **names the CPA** but **does not present the complete financial statements,** the CPA should request that the client

   a. Not include the CPA's name in the document or
   b. Engage the CPA to report on the information or
   c. Include the complete financial statements in the document

558 Required Supplementary Information (RSI) (SAS 120)

A. Scope: This section addresses the auditor's responsibility in relation to information supplementary to the basic financial statements that is required by a designated accounting standard setter to accompany such financial statements. In the absence of any separate requirement in the circumstances of the engagement, the auditor's opinion on the basic financial statements does not cover this required supplementary information (RSI).
B. Objective: When a designated accounting standard setter requires information to accompany an entity's basic financial statements, the auditor's objectives are to

1. Describe in the auditor's report whether required supplementary information is presented and
2. Communicate when some or all of the required supplementary information has not been prepared in accordance with guidelines established by a designated accounting standard setter or when the auditor has identified material modifications needed to required supplementary information.

C. Definitions

1. **Required supplementary information (RSI).** Information that a designated accounting standard setter requires to accompany an entity's basic financial statements. RSI is not a part of the basic financial statements; however, a designated accounting standard setter considers the information to be an essential part of financial reporting. In addition, authoritative guidelines for measurement and presentation have been established.
2. **Designated accounting standard setter.** A body designated by the AICPA council to establish accounting standards pursuant to Rule 203, *Accounting Principles* (AICPA, *Professional Standards,* vol. 2, ET sec. 200), of the AICPA *Code of Professional Conduct.* Bodies designated by the AICPA council to establish accounting standards are listed in appendix A of the AICPA *Code of Professional Conduct.*
3. **Basic financial statements.** Financial statements presented in accordance with an applicable financial reporting framework as established by a designated accounting standard setter, excluding RSI.
4. **Applicable financial reporting framework.** The financial reporting framework adopted by management, and when appropriate, those charged with governance in the preparation of financial statements that is acceptable in view of the nature of the entity and the objective of the financial statements, or that is required by law or regulation (for example, accounting principles generally accepted in the United States of America, International Financial Reporting Standards issued by the International Accounting Standards Board, or comprehensive bases of accounting other than generally accepted accounting principles).

5. **Prescribed guidelines.** The authoritative guidelines established by the designated accounting standard setter for the methods of measurement and presentation of the RSI.

D. Requirements, application and other explanatory material

1. Procedures

   a. The auditor should

      (1) *Inquire* of management about methods of preparing information—including whether it was prepared following prescribed guidelines, whether methods of measurement or presentation have changed from prior period, and whether there were any significant assumptions or interpretations underlying the measurement or presentation of information

      (2) *Compare information* for consistency with

         (a) Management's responses to the inquiries
         (b) The basic financial statements
         (c) Other knowledge obtained during the audit

      (3) *Obtain written representations* from management acknowledging its responsibility that the information is measured within guidelines, methods have not changed, and significant assumptions

   b. If the auditor is unable to complete the above procedures, the auditor should consider whether management contributed to the auditor's inability to complete the procedures—if so, inform those charged with governance.

2. Reporting

   a. Overall, add an explanatory paragraph to the auditor's report and, depending upon the circumstances, indicate that

      (1) RSI is included and the auditor has applied the procedures (described earlier)
      (2) RSI is omitted
      (3) Some RSI is missing and some is presented
      (4) The auditor has identified material departures from the applicable financial reporting framework
      (5) The auditor is unable to complete the prescribed procedures
      (6) The auditor has unresolved doubts about whether the RSI conforms to guidelines

   b. If all or some of the RSI is included, the explanatory paragraph in the auditor's report should include the following elements:

      (1) A statement that (identify applicable financial reporting framework, e.g., US GAAP) requires the RSI
      (2) RSI, although not a part of basic financial statements, is required and considered essential.
      (3) If auditor is able to complete prescribed procedures

         (a) Auditor has applied procedures in accordance with GAAS, which consisted of inquires of management and comparing the information for consistency with management's responses, the basic financial statements, and other knowledge the auditor obtained during the audit
         (b) The auditor does not express an opinion or provide any assurance on the information because the limited procedures do not provide sufficient evidence

      (4) If auditor is unable to complete prescribed procedures—indicate and say the auditor does not express an opinion or any other form of assurance on the RSI.
      (5) If some RSI omitted—indicate.
      (6) If RSI departs materially from guidelines, so indicate.
      (7) If auditor has unresolved doubts about whether RSI conforms with guidelines, so indicate.

   c. If all RSI is omitted, the explanatory paragraph should include the following elements:

      (1) Management has elected to omit RSI
      (2) Although not a part of basic financial statements, the RSI is considered essential
      (3) A statements that although the auditor's opinion on the basic financial statements is not affected by the missing information, the entity has not complied with the applicable financial reporting framework

> **NOTE:** Omission or incorrect RSI results in an explanatory paragraph describing the matter—yet it does not result in modification of the auditor's opinion. Also, the auditor does not provide the RSI in the audit report.

560 Subsequent Events (SAS 1)

Overall Objectives and Approach—This section presents guidance on accounting for and auditing "subsequent events." Carefully distinguish between the information presented in this section and that of AU 561. This section relates to proper accounting and auditing procedures related to events occurring subsequent to the balance sheet date, but prior to issuance of the audit report. AU 561 relates to events occurring after the date of the auditor's report, most frequently when the financial statements have been issued.

This outline first defines the relevant terms from throughout the section. Section B summarizes proper accounting for subsequent events. Section C lists normal audit procedures which should be performed to detect subsequent events.

A. Definitions

  1. **Subsequent events**—Events or transactions having a material effect on the financial statements that occur subsequent to the balance sheet date, but prior to issuance of the financial statements

    a. **Type 1 subsequent events**—Those events that provide additional evidence about **conditions that existed** at the date of the balance sheet and affect the estimates used in preparing financial statements

    b. **Type 2 subsequent events**—Those events that provide evidence with respect to **conditions that did not exist** at the date of the balance sheet being reported on, but arose after that date

  2. **Subsequent period**—The period after the balance sheet date, extending to the date of the auditor's report

B. Proper accounting for subsequent events

  1. **Type 1**—Make an adjusting entry to adjust the financial statements

    a. Examples

      (1) Settlement of litigation for an amount different from the liability recorded in the accounts, assuming the event causing the litigation occurred before year-end

      (2) Loss on an uncollectible account receivable as a result of a customer's deteriorating financial condition that led to bankruptcy subsequent to the balance sheet date

> **NOTE:** Think about the above example. Although the customer filed for bankruptcy after year-end, an adjustment is appropriate because filing for bankruptcy was simply the conclusion of the condition—deteriorating financial position—which began prior to year-end.

  2. **Type 2—Disclose in notes** to the financial statements

    a. Examples

      (1) Sale of bond or stock issue
      (2) Purchase of a business
      (3) Litigation settlement, but only when the litigation is based on a post-balance-sheet event

        (a) Because of the time involved with litigation, this would presumably be rare

      (4) Fire or flood loss
      (5) Receivable loss, but only when the loss occurred due to a post-balance-sheet event such as a customer's major casualty arising after the balance sheet date

> **NOTE:** Distinguish between this example and example 1.a.(2) above.

  3. Several related points for Type 2 subsequent events

    a. The disclosures related to subsequent event may include pro forma statements included in the notes
    b. An auditor may wish to add an explanatory paragraph to an unqualified report to emphasize the subsequent event matter—see Emphasis of a Matter in the outline of AU 508 and Section B of the Reporting Module
    c. When statements are reissued (for example, in an SEC filing) the statements should not be adjusted for events occurring after the original issuance date

C. Subsequent period auditing procedures

  1. Certain procedures are applied to transactions after year-end

    a. To assure proper year-end cutoff
    b. To help evaluate asset and liability valuation

  2. In addition, the CPA should perform other procedures near completion of fieldwork to identify subsequent events

a. Read latest interim statements

   (1) Make comparison with other data

b. Discuss with management

   (1) Existence of contingent liabilities
   (2) Significant changes in shareholders' equity items
   (3) Statement items accounted for on tentative data
   (4) Unusual adjustments in the subsequent period

c. Read minutes of Board of Directors and other committees

   (1) Make inquiries when minutes are not available

d. Obtain lawyer's letter on

   (1) Litigation
   (2) Impending litigation, claims
   (3) Contingent liabilities

e. Include in management representation letter representations on subsequent events

561 Subsequent Discovery of Facts Existing at the Date of the Auditor's Report (SAS 1)

Overall Objectives and Approach—This section presents guidance on procedures to be followed by the CPA who, after the date of his/her audit report, becomes aware of facts that may have existed when the audit report was issued and that might have affected that report. You might wish to study and compare this section with AU 560, which deals with events occurring subsequent to the balance sheet date, but prior to issuance of the audit report.

This outline summarizes the section's procedural guidance in a series of four steps. The outline deviates from a strict format to make obvious the sequence of audit procedures.

A. Appropriate procedures for events discovered subsequent to the date of the audit report

> **NOTE:** The auditor has no obligation to perform additional procedures after the audit report date, **unless** s/he becomes aware of facts that may have existed at the report date. As overall advice, when any of these circumstances arise, the CPA should consult with his/her attorney.

Step 1. The CPA should determine if the subsequently discovered information is reliable and existed at the date of the audit report

   a. To accomplish this, the auditor should discuss the matter with the appropriate level(s) of management, the board of directors (if deemed necessary), and should request cooperation in whatever investigation is necessary

Step 2. When the CPA determines that the information is reliable and did exist at the date of the audit report, the following procedures are required

   a. Determine whether the audit report would have been affected if the information had been known at the time of report issuance
   b. Assess whether persons are likely to still be relying upon the report

      (1) The auditor will consider, among other things, the time that has elapsed since the financial statements were issued

Step 3. When the CPA believes that the report would be affected, and that persons are relying upon the information, the CPA should insist that the client undertake appropriate disclosure, which may vary with the circumstances

   a. If the effect on the financial statements and/or the auditor's report can be promptly determined, the statements should be revised and reissued

      (1) The reason for the revision should be described in a note to the financial statements and referred to in the auditor's report
      (2) Generally, only the most recently issued audited statements would need to be revised, even though the revision resulted from events that had happened in prior years

   b. If issuance of statements of a subsequent period is imminent, appropriate revision can be made in those statements; disclosures should be similar to those in a. above

c. If the effect cannot be promptly determined and it appears that the statements will be revised after the investigation, **persons known to be relying or who are likely to rely** on the financial statements should be notified

   (1) If appropriate, the client should disclose the information to the proper regulatory bodies (e.g., SEC)

Step 4. This step is appropriate only if the client **refuses** to cooperate with the CPA

a. Notify each member of the board of directors of the client's refusal to make disclosures and that the CPA will take the steps outlined in b. below

b. Unless the CPA's attorney recommends a different course of action, the CPA should undertake the following steps (to the extent applicable)

   (1) Notify the client that the audit report cannot be associated with the financial statements
   (2) Notify regulatory agencies that the audit report should not be relied upon
   (3) Notify each person known to be relying on the statements that the report should not be relied upon

> **NOTE:** Know that the notification is limited to the client, regulatory agencies (e.g., the SEC), and persons **known** to be relying on the statements. It will not, in general, be practicable to notify all stockholders or investors at large.

c. Appropriate disclosures

   (1) If the CPA makes a satisfactory investigation and believes the information is reliable

      (a) Disclose the nature of the information and effect on the report and statements
      (b) Disclosures should be precise and factual, and should not comment on the motives of any person who is involved

   (2) If the client has not cooperated, and the auditor has been unable to conduct a satisfactory investigation, the auditor should disclose that the

      (a) Information has come to his/her attention and that
      (b) The client has not cooperated in attempting to substantiate it, and if true, the auditor believes his report should no longer be relied upon

623 Special Reports (SAS 63)

Overall Objectives and Approach—This section was passed in 1989 to update the area of "special reports" to reflect the 1988 statements (SAS 52-61). It describes five specific types of special reports issued by auditors which are based on—(a) Financial statements prepared using a **comprehensive basis of accounting other than GAAP** (hereafter, simply **a comprehensive basis**), (b) **Specified elements, accounts or items** of statements (e.g., cash, accounts receivable), (c) **Compliance** with aspects of contractual or regulatory requirements related to audited financial statements, (d) **Financial presentations** to comply with contractual or regulatory requirements, and (e) Financial information presented in **prescribed forms** or schedules that require a prescribed form of auditor's report. Be aware that the above 5 types of reports are the only types of special reports. Thus, for example, reviews of interim statements (AU 722) and forecast examinations (AT 200) are not "special reports." (A number of multiple-choice questions have presented 3 special reports, plus another type of report, and have asked "which is not a special report?")

A confusing portion of this section relates to whether the distribution of the various reports is limited (generally to the preparer, appropriate regulatory agency and/or party to a contract), or is available to the general public. The following are the primary types of reports **not** publicly available:

1. Presentations prepared following a basis **other than GAAP or a comprehensive basis**
2. Comprehensive basis statements **prepared using a basis of accounting used to comply with requirements of a governmental regulatory agency** (A.2.a. below)
3. Incomplete GAAP or comprehensive basis presentations unless the presentation is to be filed with a regulatory agency (e.g., the SEC) **and** to be included in a document that is distributed to the general public [D.1.a.(1) below]
4. Report on compliance with contractual agreements or regulatory requirements related to audited financial statements (C. below)

The sections of the following outline summarize proper reporting and procedural requirements for each of the five types of special reports as well as a discussion of circumstances that require explanatory language in an auditor's special report.

A. Reports prepared following a **comprehensive basis** of accounting

1. GAAS apply when an auditor conducts an audit of and reports on **any financial statement**

2. A comprehensive basis is one of the following

    a. A basis of accounting used to comply with governmental regulatory agency (e.g., rules of state insurance commission)
    b. The basis of accounting used for tax purposes
    c. The cash receipts and disbursements basis of accounting, including a method with widely accepted modifications of the method (e.g., recording depreciation, accruing income taxes)
    d. A definite set of criteria with **substantial authoritative support** applied to all material items (e.g., price level basis of accounting)

    > **NOTE:** The effect of the above section is to limit comprehensive basis statements to regulatory basis, tax basis, cash basis, or another one with **substantial authoritative support**. Thus, a basis developed by a client or another party (e.g., a bank for use in assessing a company's compliance with debt covenants) will not in general qualify.

3. Reports on statements following a comprehensive basis

    a. A title that includes the word independent
    b. A paragraph stating that the financial statements

        (1) Were audited
        (2) Are the responsibility of management and that the auditor is responsible for expressing an opinion on them

    c. A paragraph stating that

        (1) The audit was conducted per GAAS
        (2) GAAS require that the auditor plan and perform the audit to obtain reasonable assurance about whether the financial statements are free of material misstatement
        (3) An audit includes

            (a) Examining on a test basis evidence supporting the amounts and disclosures in the financial statements
            (b) Assessing the accounting principles used and significant estimates and
            (c) Evaluating overall financial statement presentation

        (4) The auditor believes that the audit provides a reasonable basis for the opinion

    d. A paragraph indicating

        (1) The basis of presentation and refers to the note in the financial statement describing the basis
        (2) That the basis is a comprehensive basis of accounting other than GAAP

    e. A paragraph with an opinion on whether the financial statements are presented fairly, in all material respects, in conformity with the basis of accounting described
    f. When statements are prepared in conformity with a regulatory agency's principles, a paragraph that restricts distribution of the report solely to those within the entity and for filing with the regulatory agency—see A.2.a. above
    g. The manual or printed firm signature
    h. The date (generally the last day of fieldwork—see AU 530 outline)

    > **NOTE:** One might expect an occasional simulation that requires preparation of a comprehensive basis report. Notice how closely it parallels the standard audit report on whether financial statements follow GAAP. Also, an example of the report is provided in the Reporting Module, Section C.2.a.

4. Terms such as statement of financial position, statement of income (or operations), and statement of cash flows should not be used for comprehensive basis statements

    a. Examples of appropriate (cash basis) titles: statements of assets and liabilities arising from cash flows, statement of revenue collected and expenses paid

    > **NOTE:** Different titles are used so as to prevent misleading anyone into believing that the statements follow GAAP.

5. While comprehensive basis statement notes should include a summary of significant accounting policies and describe how the basis differs from GAAP, the differences **need not be quantified**
6. When evaluating the adequacy of disclosures, the auditor should consider disclosure of matters such as related-party transactions, restrictions on assets and owners' equity, subsequent events, and uncertainties

B. Reports on **specified elements, accounts, or items** of a financial statement

1. Examples—rentals, royalties, a profit participation, provision for income tax, accounts receivable
2. There are two basic approaches

    a. Express an opinion on one or more elements
    b. Provide "negative assurance" relating to the results of applying agreed-upon procedures to one or more elements

    > **NOTE:** This section only deals with expressing an opinion (2.a.). Section AT 201 presents guidance for expressing negative assurance as a result of applying agreed-upon procedures.

3. In general, GAAS apply
4. The measure of materiality must be related to the individual element, **not** the financial statements taken as a whole
5. A special report may **only** be issued on specific elements in statements upon which an adverse opinion or a disclaimer was issued when

    a. The element(s) are not a major part of the financial statements
    b. The special report does not accompany the financial statements of the entity

6. Reports on specific elements

    a. The report issued is similar to that for comprehensive basis statements (see A.3. above); major exceptions are

        (1) The terms relating to the financial statements are replaced with a term relating to the elements, accounts or items presented
        (2) The "opinion paragraph" (A.3.e. above) should include

            (a) A description of the basis on which the elements are presented, and when applicable, any agreements specifying such basis
            (b) If considered necessary, a description and the source of significant interpretations made by management relating to the agreement

    > **NOTE:** Review both A.3. and this section since periodically an exam will require preparation of such a report. Section C.2.a. of the Reporting Module provides a sample report.

7. If a specified element, account, or item is based on income or stockholders' equity, the auditor should have audited the complete financial statements to express an opinion on it

C. Reports on **compliance with contractual agreements** or with regulatory requirements related to audited financial statements

1. The situation being considered here is one in which an audit has been performed on the financial statements, and some organization (e.g., a bank) wants assurance with respect to compliance with the conditions of an agreement

    a. Examples—loan agreements often require restriction of dividend payments and maintenance of the current ratio at a specific level

2. The auditor provides negative assurance as to compliance with the agreement, either

    a. As a separate report, or
    b. As one or more paragraphs added to the auditor's report accompanying the financial statements

        (1) In either case indication that the negative assurance is given in connection with the audit
        (2) When a separate report is issued, it should indicate that an audit has been performed, the date of the report, and whether GAAS were followed

3. Negative assurance should **not** be provided

    a. For covenants that relate to matters that have not been subjected to the audit procedures applied in the audit of the financial statements
    b. When the auditor has expressed an adverse opinion or disclaimed an opinion on the financial statements to which the covenants relate

4. A separate report on compliance with contractual agreements should include

    a. A title that includes the word independent
    b. A paragraph stating that the financial statements were audited per GAAS, the date of that report, and describing any departures from standard report

c. A paragraph that includes reference to the specific covenants, provides negative assurance relative to compliance, and specifies that the negative assurance is being given in connection with the audit

d. A paragraph that includes a description and the source of any significant interpretations (if needed)

e. A paragraph that restricts distribution of report solely to those within the entity and for filing with the regulatory agency

f. The manual or printed firm signature

g. The date

5. When the report on compliance is included in the audit report, the auditor should include paragraphs similar to 4.c., d., and e. above (following the opinion paragraph)

> **NOTE:** See Section C.2.a. of the Reporting Module for a sample report.

D. Special-purpose financial presentations to comply with contractual agreements or regulatory provisions

1. In this situation the financial statements have been prepared to comply with some agreement (e.g., a loan agreement) or regulatory provision and are intended solely for the use of the parties to the agreement, regulatory bodies, or other specified parties; two types of special-purpose presentations are discussed

   a. Special-purpose financial presentations that do not constitute complete presentation of assets and liabilities, revenues and expenses, but otherwise are **presented per GAAP** or other comprehensive basis

      (1) The procedural and reporting requirements are similar to those for comprehensive basis statements (A. above), although a paragraph restricting distribution of the report is necessary unless the information is filed with a regulatory agency (e.g., the SEC) and is to be included in a publicly available report

   b. Special-purpose financial presentations which may or may not be a complete set of financial statements that do **not follow GAAP or another comprehensive basis** of accounting

      (1) As an example, consider an acquisition agreement that requires the borrower to prepare financial statements per GAAP, except for certain assets such as receivables, inventories, and properties for which a net realizable valuation basis is specified in the agreement

      (2) The report, while similar to that for comprehensive basis statements (A. above) includes an opinion paragraph that explains what the presentation is intended to present and refers to the note describing that basis, and states that the presentation is not per GAAP

      (3) A paragraph limiting distribution is included

> **NOTE:** See Section C.2.a. of the Reporting Module for sample reports.

E. Reports on information in prescribed forms or schedules

1. Printed forms or schedules (hereafter, forms) that are designed by the bodies with which they are filed often suggest a required wording for an auditor's report

> **EXAMPLE**
>
> Assume that a state has a balance sheet form which companies incorporated in that state are to fill out with appropriate financial information. Also, assume that the state requires a standard unqualified report be filed with the report. The difficulty here is that the form may not provide adequate or proper disclosures. This section deals with the manner in which an auditor should report on such forms.

2. When a schedule requires that an auditor make a statement that is incorrect, the auditor should respond in a manner such as the following

   a. Revise the form so that it complies with the required statement to be made by the auditor

   b. Attach a separate report

3. In no case should an auditor make an assertion that is not justified

> **EXAMPLE**
>
> Continuing the above example, if the information can be made to follow GAAP an unqualified report could be issued. Otherwise, the auditor would not be able to meet the legal requirement as his/her report would include departures from the standard form.

F. Circumstances requiring explanatory language in an auditor's special report

> **NOTE:** Throughout the special reports, in general the circumstances which lead auditors to qualified, adverse, and disclaimers of opinions in GAAP audits generally apply. Several special considerations apply to the following circumstances which normally result in the auditor adding additional explanatory language to an unqualified report.

1. Lack of consistency

   a. An explanatory paragraph is added
   b. When financial statements (or specified elements, accounts or items) have been prepared in conformity with GAAP in prior years, and the basis is changed to another comprehensive basis, the auditor is not required to add an explanatory paragraph on consistency (although s/he may choose to do so)

2. Uncertainties (including going concern uncertainties)

   a. An explanatory paragraph is only added when the uncertainties are relevant to the presentation

      (1) For example, an explanatory paragraph may be necessary for cash basis statements, but may **not** be necessary for a report based on compliance with loan covenants

3. Other auditors

   a. When reference is made to other auditors whose report is being relied upon, the AU 508 requirements for other auditors apply (mention them in introductory, scope, and opinion paragraphs)

4. Comparative financial statements when a different opinion than originally issued is being issued

   a. The auditor should disclose that the opinion is different, with all reasons therefore in a separate explanatory paragraph preceding the opinion paragraph

634 Letters for Underwriters and Certain Other Requesting Parties (SAS 72)

Overall Objectives and Approach—This section presents guidance on letters to underwriters (also referred to as "comfort letters") which CPAs may prepare to assist underwriters who are involved with the selling of securities under the Securities Act of 1933, as well as certain other acts. Consider, for example, a company selling stock to the public. The underwriter will assist the company in meeting the various legal requirements, and may purchase and then resell the securities to the public. Under the Securities Act of 1933 the underwriter is required to perform, with "due diligence," a "reasonable investigation" of the financial and accounting data that is not audited (referred to as information "not expertized"). A comfort letter, although not specifically required by the Act, is issued by the CPA to the underwriter on certain of this information.

Because the CPA exam has only asked a few questions pertaining to letters for underwriters, less detail is provided in this outline than has been included in prior outlines. The outline is organized as follows: (a) overall issues, (b) general information, and (c) detailed information.

A. Overall issues

1. A comfort letter is normally for an underwriter, although it may be for a law firm or other party that has a due diligence defense
2. CPAs may only

   a. Comment on matters upon which their professional expertise is substantially relevant
   b. At the most, provide negative assurance on information that is not audited

B. General comfort letter information

1. Dates relevant to filings

   a. Closing date—securities delivered to underwriter (letter normally so dated)
   b. Cutoff date—last date of CPA's procedures related to comfort letter
   c. Effective date—securities registration becomes effective
   d. Filing date—securities first filed (recorded) with SEC

2. While the letter is most frequently addressed to the underwriter and the client, it may also be addressed to involved broker-dealers, financial intermediaries, buyers or sellers
3. In describing work, auditor should not use terms such as "general review," "check," and "test"

C. Detailed information often included in a comfort letter

1. **Pertaining to audit**—CPAs explicitly state that they are independent and that in their opinion their audit of the financial statements complied with SEC requirements

2. **Other information**

   a. The CPAs must have obtained knowledge of internal control as it relates to preparation of annual and interim financial information before providing assurance on other information

      (1) If an audit has been performed, this knowledge will normally have been obtained
      (2) If the CPAs have not audited the company, they should perform procedures to obtain the necessary knowledge

   b. Types of other information

      (1) Unaudited condensed interim financial information—provide negative assurance
      (2) Unaudited summarized interim information (capsule financial information)—provide negative assurance
      (3) Pro forma financial information—provide a summary of tests performed and findings
      (4) Subsequent changes (e.g., changes in capital stock, debt, decreases in certain accounts)—provide negative assurance or a summary of tests performed and findings

         (a) Negative assurance may only be provided within 135 days of most recent audit or review; thereafter, only a summary of tests performed and findings may be provided
         (b) While the report may indicate changes, terms such as "adverse changes" should not be used due to lack of a clearly understood meaning

      (5) Tables, statistics, and other financial information—provide negative assurance, but only on information obtained or derived from accounting records that is subject to the accounting system of internal control

         (a) The term "presents fairly" should not be used

711 Filings under Federal Securities Statutes (SAS 37)

Overall Objectives and Approach—This section presents overall information on a CPA's responsibilities when s/he is associated with information included in a client's filing with the SEC. Section A of the outline presents overall responsibilities. Section B provides information on subsequent events in 1933 Act filings—this supplements the guidance in AU 560. Section C relates to the appropriate response when subsequent events have been discovered—this supplements the guidance in both AU 560 and AU 561.

A. Overall responsibilities under Federal Securities Statutes

1. An accountant has a defense against lawsuits filed under Section 11 of the 1933 Securities Act if s/he can prove that s/he had, after a **reasonable** investigation, **reasonable** grounds to believe and did believe that the statements were true and not misleading at the effective date of the financial statements

   a. The standard of **reasonableness** is that of a prudent person in the management of his/her own property

2. CPA should read the **experts section** of the prospectus under a 1933 Securities Act filing to make certain that his/her name is not used in a misleading manner

3. When a CPA's review report is included with interim financial information in a registration statement, a statement should be included that this is not a **report** under the meaning of Section 7 or 11 of the Securities Act of 1933

   > **NOTE:** The effect of the above statement is to limit CPA responsibility with respect to interim information contained in a registration statement.

4. When an independent audit report is incorporated in a registration statement by reference, the CPA is described as an "expert in auditing and accounting"

B. Procedures for finding subsequent events under a 1933 Securities Act Filing

1. A CPA should extend his/her investigation from that of his/her report to the effective date of the filing, or as close as possible; this investigation should include

   a. Subsequent event procedures in AU 560—see outline of AU 560
   b. Additional procedures

      (1) Reading of the prospectus and relevant portions of the registration statement
      (2) Obtaining written confirmation from managerial and accounting officers as to any subsequent events not mentioned in the registration statement

2. A predecessor accountant who has not examined the most current statements should

a. Read applicable portions of the prospectus and registration statement
b. Obtain a letter of representation from the successor CPA regarding the existence of any subsequent events

C. Appropriate response when subsequent events have been discovered

1. Use any AU 560 or 561 guidance—see outlines of AU 560 and AU 561
2. Overall

   a. Insist upon revision
   b. Comment on the matter in the audit report
   c. Inquire of attorney, and consider withholding opinion if client will not correct financial statements

3. If the unaudited financial statements are not in conformity with GAAP, insist on revision, and failing that

   a. If CPA has issued a review report, refer to AU 561 and AU 722 for guidance
   b. If no review has been performed, modify report on audited financial statements to describe the departure

722 Interim Financial Information (SAS 117)

Overall Objectives and Approach—There are currently two forms of AU 722—one for nonissuers (nonpublic companies) and one for issuers (public companies). The interim information for an issuer is ordinarily that which is included in form 10Q for the first three quarters of the year (after the fourth quarter, an annual form 10K is issued). Reviews of each quarter's interim information are required.

The interim information for a nonissuer includes information for periods shorter than one year or for a 12-month period ending on a date other than the entity's fiscal year-end; financial information may be condensed or in the form of a complete set of financial statements. A review of nonissuer information is not required unless a regulatory agency requires it.

For nonissuers, in addition to AU 722, the various *Statements on Standards for Accounting and Review Services (SSAEs, codified as AR)* provide guidance. In each circumstance *either* AU 722 *or* the SSAEs apply. AU 722 applies for interim financial information of nonissuers if the following conditions are met:

- Entity's latest annual financial statements have been audited by the accountant or a predecessor
- Accountant either

  - Has been engaged to audit the entity's current year financial statements or
  - Audited the latest financial statements and, when it is expected that the current year financial statements will be audited by the appointment of another accountant to audit the current year financial statements is not effective prior to the beginning of the period covered by the review and
  - In addition, if the interim information involved is condensed

    - It must comply with appropriate standards (e.g., APB Opinion 28)
    - It must include a note that condensed information should be read in conjunction with latest audited annual financial statements
    - The audited annual financial statements should accompany it, or be readily available

If the above requirements are not met, the *SSAEs* apply (see AR outlines following the AU outlines)

Reviews performed under either form of AU 722 or the SSAEs are very similar. To simplify things, we only present overall details of review guidance with the SSAEs; we recommend that you carefully study AR 100 (and to a lesser extent the remaining AR sections) at this point. Then study the following table, which emphasizes a number of areas in which interim financial reviews differ from SSAE reviews.

	AU 722	**SSAEs (AR 100)**
Establishing an understanding with the client	Must be through a written communication with the client.	Preferably in writing
Objective	Provide the accountant with a basis for communicating whether he or she is aware of any material modifications that should be made	Express limited assurance that there are no material modifications that should be made to the financial statements
Internal control	The accountant should have sufficient knowledge of IC to • Identify types of potential misstatements • Select inquiries and analytical procedures to provide a basis for communicating whether he or she is aware of any material modifications that should be made to the interim financial information	An AR review does not contemplate obtaining an understanding of the entity's internal control

	AU 722	SSAEs (AR 100)
Written representations by management	Required. AU 722 details more overall procedures, but two primary differences are that management must • Acknowledge its responsibility to establish sufficient controls • Disclose all significant deficiencies and weaknesses	Required, but no representations on internal control
Communicating with management and those charged with governance	Basically the AU 325 (material weaknesses and significant deficiencies) and AU 380 requirements (a variety of disclosures) are required if such information has come to the accountant's attention The communication may be written or oral	Although communication of any matters coming to the accountant's attention is appropriate, no examples relating to internal control are included. The communication may be written or oral
Written review report	Only required if the entity states that the interim financial information has been reviewed by an independent public accountant or makes other reference to the accountant's association	Required
Condensed interim information	The review report should indicate that the interim financial information does not represent the complete financial statements of the entity and should be read in conjunction with the entity's latest annual audited financial statements	Not addressed

801 Compliance Auditing Considerations in Audits of Governmental Entities and Recipient of Governmental Financial Assistance (SAS 74)

Compliance Audits

A. Introduction and objective

1. Governments frequently establish governmental audit requirements for entities to undergo an audit of their compliance with applicable compliance requirements. This section is applicable when an auditor is engaged to perform a compliance audit in accordance with

    a. GAAS
    b. Government Auditing Standards (generally accepted government auditing standards [GAGAS] or the "Yellow Book")
    c. A governmental audit requirement

2. This section addresses the application of GAAS to a compliance audit. Compliance audits usually are performed in conjunction with a financial statement audit.
3. Management is responsible for the entity's compliance, including

    a. Identifying the entity's government programs and compliance requirements
    b. Establishing related controls
    c. Evaluating and monitoring the entity's compliance
    d. Taking corrective action on audit findings of the compliance audit

B. The objectives of a compliance audit are

1. Obtain sufficient appropriate audit evidence to form an opinion and report at the level specified on the governmental audit requirement on whether the entity complied in all material respects with the applicable compliance requirements
2. Meet the supplementary audit requirements of the governmental audit requirement, if any

C. The auditor should

1. Adapt and apply the AU sections to the objectives of a compliance audit
2. Establish materiality levels for the audit based on the governmental audit requirement
3. Identify government programs and applicable compliance requirements

    a. Sources an auditor may consult include

        (1) Compliance Supplement issued by the Office of Management and Budget
        (2) Applicable program-specific audit guide information issued by the grantor agency which requires the various compliance requirements

4. Perform risk assessment procedures

5. Assess the risks of material noncompliance whether due to error or fraud for each applicable compliance requirement; factors include

   a. Complexity of compliance requirements
   b. Susceptibility of compliance requirements to noncompliance
   c. Time entity has been subject to compliance requirements
   d. Auditor's observation about company prior year compliance
   e. Potential effect on the entity of noncompliance
   f. Degree of judgment involved
   g. Auditor's assessment of the risks of material misstatement in the financial statement audit

6. Perform further audit procedures in response to assessed risks

   a. If the auditor identifies a risk of material noncompliance that is pervasive to the entity's compliance, the auditor should develop an overall response to the assessed risks of material noncompliance

      (1) Examples of risks of noncompliance that are pervasive

         (a) An entity experiencing financial difficulty which increases the likelihood of improper diversion of funds
         (b) An entity has poor recordkeeping for government programs

   b. Perform further audit procedures, including test of details, to obtain sufficient appropriate audit evidence about compliance with each applicable requirement in response to the assessed risks of material noncompliance
   c. Adapt and apply requirements from applicable SASs in designing and performing further audit procedures in response to the assessed risks of noncompliance. Test of controls over compliance should be performed if the auditor's risk assessment

      (1) Includes an expectation of operating effectiveness,
      (2) Substantive procedures alone do not provide sufficient appropriate audit evidence, or
      (3) Such test of controls are required by the governmental audit requirements.

7. Identify audit requirements specified in the governmental audit requirement that are supplemental to GAAS and GAGAS and perform procedures to address these requirements
8. Obtain written representations from management related to the entity's compliance with applicable compliance requirements.
9. Consider subsequent events as per AU 561
10. Forming an opinion and reporting

   a. An auditor's report on compliance includes an opinion on the governmental audit requirement.

      (1) If noncompliance is identified, the opinion is modified.

   b. An auditor's report on compliance may be combined with a report on internal control over compliance, and related information on internal control over compliance should be added.
   c. If a report on internal control over compliance is required and the auditor chooses to issue a separate report on internal control, this is acceptable.
   d. Reports on compliance are modified for

      (1) Scope restrictions
      (2) Making reference to the report of another auditor
      (3) Inability to comply with GAAS, GAGAS, or the governmental audit requirement, as well as for noncompliance

   e. The auditor should document

      (1) Risk assessment procedures performed
      (2) Responses to assessed risk of material noncompliance, the procedures performed to test compliance with applicable compliance requirements and the results of those procedures, including any tests of controls over compliance
      (3) Materiality levels and how they were determined
      (4) How s/he complied with specific governmental audit requirements that are supplemental to GAAS and GAGAS

901 Public Warehouses—Controls and Procedures for Goods Held

Overall Objectives and Approach—This section, from which relatively few exam questions have been asked, presents guidance on auditing a public warehouse and its internal control. Concerning the auditing of a public warehouse, a CPA should

1. Obtain an understanding of internal control relating to accountability and custody over goods and perform tests of controls to evaluate their effectiveness
2. Test the warehouseman's records for goods placed in warehouse
3. Test the warehouseman's system of receipts (a receipt is provided to entity that stores goods in the warehouse)
4. Observe physical counts of goods in the warehouse and reconcile them to the records
5. To the extent considered necessary, confirm with holders of warehouse receipts (the entities that store the goods in the warehouse)

See Section C of the internal control module for guidance on internal control over inventories; see part B of the outline of AU 331 for procedures relating to auditing inventories held in public warehouses.

STANDARDS OF THE PUBLIC COMPANY ACCOUNTING OVERSIGHT BOARD

Overview. The Public Company Accounting Oversight Board issues its own series of Standards. At this point they have not been codified.

PCAOB Auditing Standard No. 1 (and related reporting guidance)—References in Auditors' Reports to the Standards of the PCAOB

Overall Objectives and Approach—This very brief statement requires auditors to refer to standards of the Public Company Accounting Oversight Board (rather than to generally accepted auditing standards) in their reports on audits of issuer (public) companies.

A. Auditors' reports for audits of issuer (public) company financial statements

1. The PCAOB adopted as interim standards, the AICPA Statements on Auditing Standards and other auditing guidance
2. The financial statement audit report for an issuer (public) client

   a. Refers to "standards of Public Company Accounting Oversight Board (United States)" rather than to generally accepted auditing standards
   b. Has a title of "Report of Independent Registered Public Accounting Firm"
   c. Includes a paragraph referring to the auditor's report on internal control (this requirement was added subsequent to passage of Standard 1)
   d. Includes the city and state (or country) in which the report was issued

3. For reports on interim financial statements

   a. Refers to "standards of the Public Company Accounting Oversight Board (United States)" rather than standards of the AICPA
   b. Has a title of "Report of Independent Registered Public Accounting Firm"
   c. Includes the city and state (or country in which the report was issued

B. Sample audit report for financial statements

Report of Independent Registered Public Accounting Firm

We have audited the accompanying balance sheets of X Company as of December 31, 20X3 and 20X2, and the related statements of operations, stockholders' equity, and cash flows for each of the three years in the period ended December 31, 20X3. These financial statements are the responsibility of the Company's management. Our responsibility is to express an opinion on these financial statements based on our audits.

We conducted our audits in accordance with the standards of the Public Company Accounting Oversight Board (United States). Those standards require that we plan and perform the audit to obtain reasonable assurance about whether the financial statements are free of material misstatement. An audit includes examining, on a test basis, evidence supporting the amounts and disclosures in the financial statements. An audit also includes assessing the accounting principles used and significant estimates made by management, as well as evaluating the overall financial statement presentation. We believe that our audits provide a reasonable basis for our opinion.

In our opinion, the financial statements referred to above present fairly, in all material respects, the financial position of the Company as of [at] December 31, 20X3, and 20X2, and the results of its operations and its cash flows for each of the three years in the period ended December 31, 20X3, in conformity with US generally accepted accounting principles.

We also have audited, in accordance with the standards of the Public Company Accounting Oversight Board (United States), the effectiveness of X Company's internal control over financial reporting as of December 31, 20X3, based on criteria established in Internal Control–Integrated Framework issued by the Committee of Sponsoring Organizations of the Treadway Commission and our report dated February 24, 20X4, expressed an unqualified opinion thereon.

[Signature]

[City and State or Country]

[Date]

PCAOB Auditing Standard No. 2—An Audit of Internal Control over Financial Reporting Performed in Conjunction with an Audit of Financial Statements—Superseded by PCAOB Auditing Standard No. 5.

PCAOB Auditing Standard No. 3—Audit Documentation

Overall Objectives and Approach—This standard establishes general guidelines for audit documentation (working papers) that the auditor should prepare and retain in connection with engagements under the PCAOB standards—audits of financial statements, audits of internal control over financial reporting, and reviews of interim financial information.

A. General

1. **Audit documentation**—the written record of the basis for the auditor's conclusion that provides the support for the auditor's representations, whether those representations are contained in the auditor's report or otherwise

   a. Audit documentation also facilitates planning, performance and supervision of the engagement.
   b. It is the basis for the review of the quality of the work because it provides the reviewer with written documentation of the evidence supporting the auditor's significant conclusions

2. Audit documentation should

   a. Demonstrate that the engagement complied with PCAOB standards
   b. Support the auditor's conclusions for every relevant financial statement assertion
   c. Demonstrate that the underlying accounting records agree or reconcile with the financial statements

3. Audit documentation must contain sufficient information to enable an *experienced auditor* having no previous connection with the engagement to

   a. Understand the nature, timing, extent, and results of the procedures performed, evidence obtained, and conclusions reached
   b. Determine who performed the work, the date such work was completed, the person who reviewed the work, and the date of such review

B. The Standard also contains the following specific documentation requirements:

1. Documentation must make it possible to identify the items examined by the auditor in areas such as the inspection of documents, confirmation, tests of details, tests of operating effectiveness of controls, and walk-throughs
2. Significant findings or issues must be documented, including

   a. Significant matters involving accounting principles
   b. Results of auditing procedures that indicate (1) the need to modify planned auditing procedures, (2) the existence of material misstatements, (3) omissions in the financial statements, or (4) the existence of significant deficiencies or material weaknesses in internal control over financial reporting
   c. Audit adjustments
   d. Disagreements among members of the engagement team or others consulted about final conclusions reached on significant accounting or auditing matters
   e. Circumstances causing difficulty in applying auditing procedures
   f. Significant changes in the assessed level of audit risk
   g. Any matters that could result in modification of the auditor's report

   The above information should be included in an *engagement completion document*
3. In addition, the auditor must obtain, review, and retain information from other auditors that are involved in the audit

C. Retention of and subsequent changes to audit documentation

1. Important dates

   a. **Report release date**—The date the auditor grants permission to use the auditor's report. On this date the auditor has

      (1) Completed all necessary auditing procedures, including clearing review notes and providing support for all final conclusions
      (2) Obtained sufficient evidence to support the representations in the auditor's report

   b. **Documentation completion date**—Not more than 45 days after the report release date

2. Audit documentation requirements

   a. Should be retained for 7 years from the report release date, unless a longer period of time is required by law

    b. No deletions or discarding after the documentation completion date, but information may be added (indicating date added, name of person who prepared the additional documentation, and the reason for adding it)

    c. Audit documentation related to the work of other auditors should also be retained

    d. If after the documentation completion date the auditor becomes aware that documentation of necessary audit procedures is lacking, the auditor should investigate whether sufficient procedures were performed

        (1) If "yes," the auditor should consider what additional documentation is needed and add that documentation

        (2) If the auditor is unable to determine whether sufficient procedures were performed, the auditor should comply with AU 390 (consideration of omitted procedures)

PCAOB Auditing Standard No. 4—Reporting on Whether a Previously Reported Material Weakness Continues to Exist

Overall Objectives and Approach—This standard applies when an auditor is engaged to report on whether a previously reported material weakness in internal control continues to exist as of a date specified by management. The situation here is one in which the existence of a material weakness previously led to an adverse opinion in an internal control report. In such a circumstance, the company is ordinarily motivated to eliminate the weakness as quickly as reasonably possible, and may voluntarily engage the auditors to report on whether the material weakness continues to exist.

A. Conditions for CPA engagement performance; management must

    1. Accept responsibility for effectiveness of IC

    2. Evaluate the effectiveness of the specific controls that address the material weakness using the same control criteria (e.g., COSO)

    3. Assert that the control(s) identified is effective in achieving the control objective

    4. Support its assertion with sufficient evidence

    5. Present a written report that will accompany auditor's report

B. Overall

    1. Terminology

        a. A control objective relates to a relevant financial statement assertion and states a criterion for evaluating whether the company's control procedures in a specific area provide reasonable assurance that a misstatement in that relevant assertion is prevented or detected by controls on a timely basis.

        b. If a material weakness has previously been reported, a necessary control objective (or objectives) has not been met

        c. Examples of control objectives and related assertions

            (1) Recorded sales of product are real (existence or occurrence)

            (2) The company has legal title to recorded product X inventory (rights and obligations)

    2. The control objective provides management and the auditor with a target against which to evaluate whether the material weakness continues to exist

    3. Management and the auditor must be satisfied that the control objective has been achieved (and therefore the material weakness no longer exists)

        a. If management and the auditor have difficulty in identifying all stated control objectives affected by a material weakness (e.g., a weakness related to the control environment), the material weakness probably is not suitable for this engagement

    4. An engagement includes

        a. Planning

        b. Obtaining an understanding of IC

        c. Testing and evaluating whether material weakness continues to exist

        d. Forming an opinion on whether previously reported material weakness continues to exist

    5. Applying procedures

        a. Consistent with Standard 2, the auditor should evaluate operating effectiveness of a specified control for an adequate period of time

        b. Substantive procedures may be necessary

    6. The auditor should evaluate whether to use work performed by others

    7. Written representations should be obtained from management

C. Reporting

1. Auditor may issue an opinion only when there have been no restrictions on the scope of work
2. Management's report

   a. Management responsibility for maintaining IC
   b. Control criteria followed (e.g., COSO)
   c. Identification of the material weakness
   d. Identification of control objectives
   e. Statement that material weakness no longer exists

3. Auditor's report

   a. Title with word "independent"
   b. Statement about previous audit and a description of the material weakness
   c. Identification of management's report that includes the assertion that the material weakness no longer exists and a statement that management is responsible for its assertion
   d. Identification of specific controls management asserts address the material weakness and an identification of the company's stated control objective that is achieved by these controls
   e. It is the auditor's responsibility to express an opinion on whether the material weakness continues to exist as of the date of management's assertion
   f. Engagement conducted in accordance with PCAOB standards, standards that require the auditor to plan and perform engagement to obtain evidence that will allow auditor to provide reasonable assurance about whether the material weakness continues to exist
   g. Auditor believes auditing procedures provide a reasonable basis for opinion
   h. Opinion on whether identified material weakness exists (or no longer exists) as of date of management's assertion
   i. An audit of IC was not performed and inherent limitations of IC may not prevent or detect misstatements
   j. Signature of firm, city and state, and date

4. The report is modified if any of the following exist:

   a. Other material weaknesses are not addressed in the auditor's report (that is, if other material weaknesses existed that are not being addressed here, the auditor's report must so indicate)
   b. A subsequent event since the date being reported on (e.g., a change in effectiveness of identified controls)
   c. Management's report includes additional information (auditor should indicate that no opinion or other assurance is provided on that information)

5. If auditor believes material weakness continues to exist, this is so indicated in the audit report
6. If a new material weakness is identified, the auditor must communicate it to the audit committee (but not in this report)

PCAOB Auditing Standard No. 5—An Audit of Internal Control over Financial Reporting That Is Integrated with an Audit of Financial Statements

Overall Objectives and Approach—Section 404 of the Sarbanes-Oxley Act of 2002 requires that company management assess and report on the effectiveness of the company's internal control, and that the company's auditor attest to management's disclosures regarding the effectiveness of internal control. PCAOB Standard 5 (which replaced Standard 2) provides guidance for auditing issuer (public) companies' internal control over financial reporting in conjunction with an audit of the financial statements (i.e., an "integrated audit"). Specifically, the standard requires the auditor to examine the design and operating effectiveness of internal control over financial reporting to provide a sufficient basis to provide an opinion on its effectiveness in preventing or detecting material misstatement of the financial statements. We have integrated the outline of Standard 5 into Module 3, Internal Control, as Section C.

PCAOB Auditing Standard No. 6—Evaluating Consistency of Financial Statements

Overall Objectives and Approach—This Standard addresses when audit reports are modified to reflect a lack of consistency in audits performed in accordance with PCAOB Standards. It is in response to FASB Statement No. 154 which establishes a requirement that, unless impracticable, retrospective application is the required method for reporting a change in accounting principles; for public company audits it replaces AU 420.

A. Consistency and the auditor's report on financial statements

1. The periods covered in the auditor's evaluation of consistency depend on the periods covered by the auditor's report

    a. When the auditor reports only on the current period (e.g., as a successor auditor) s/he should evaluate whether the current period financial statements are consistent with those of the preceding period

    b. When the auditor reports on two or more periods, s/he should evaluate consistency between such periods and the consistency of such periods with the period prior thereto *if* such prior period is presented with the financial statements being reported upon

  2. The following situations, when material, result in a consistency modification (i.e., a paragraph following the opinion paragraph indicating a lack of consistency):

    a. A change in accounting principle

    b. An adjustment to correct a misstatement in previously issued financial statements

B. Change in accounting principle

  1. A change in accounting principle that has a material effect on the financial statements should be recognized in the auditor's report

    a. If the change is treated properly in the financial statements (i.e., it and its method of application are generally accepted, disclosures are adequate, the company has justified that it is preferable), an explanatory paragraph indicating the lack of consistency is added following the opinion paragraph of the audit report

    b. If the change is not handled properly, the auditor should treat it as a departure from GAAP (i.e., issue a qualified or adverse opinion)

C. Correction of a material misstatement in previously issued financial statements

  1. A correction of a material misstatement in previously issued financial statements should be recognized in the auditor's report

    a. If the change is treated properly in the financial statements, an explanatory paragraph describing the correction and the lack of consistency is added following the opinion paragraph of the audit report

    b. If the correction is not handled properly, the auditor should treat it as a departure from GAAP (i.e., issue a qualified or adverse opinion)

D. Change in classification

  1. Does not require recognition in the auditor's report unless the change represents the correction of a material misstatement or a change in accounting principle

    a. Examples of a correction of a material misstatement: Reclassification of debt from long-term to short-term or reclassifications of cash flows from operating activities to financing, when those items were incorrectly classified in the previously issued financial statements

      (1) In such situations, the reclassification is also a correction of a misstatement and the audit report is modified for consistency (as per C. above)

PCAOB Standard No. 7—Engagement Quality Review

    Overall Objective and Approach—This standard provides guidance relating to engagement quality review which must be completed prior to issuance of an audit report on a public company. An independent quality reviewer in essence reviews the primary areas of the audit and determines whether he or she concurs with the audit as performed and has not identified one or more significant engagement deficiencies. We have integrated coverage of this material into topic D3 of Module 4, Responding to Risk Assessment: Evidence Accumulation and Evaluation.

PCOAB Standards 8 through 15—The Auditor's Assessment of, and Response to, Risk

    These standards are similar in most areas to the AICPA and international risk assessment standards. In this manual we emphasize the AICPA risk assessment standards, but, throughout the text, we identify areas in which the various standards differ when we consider it appropriate. The following are the PCAOB brief summaries of its risk assessment standards.

Auditing Standard 8—Audit Risk

    This standard discusses the auditor's consideration of audit risk in an audit of financial statements as part of an integrated audit or an audit of financial statements only. It describes the components of audit risk and the auditor's responsibilities for reducing audit risk to an appropriately low level in order to obtain reasonable assurance that the financial statements are free of material misstatement.

Auditing Standard 9—Audit Planning

This standard establishes requirements regarding planning an audit, including assessing matters that are important to the audit, and establishing an appropriate audit strategy and audit plan.

Auditing Standard 10—Supervision of the Audit Engagement

This standard sets forth requirements for supervision of the audit engagement, including, in particular, supervising the work of engagement team members. It applies to the engagement partner and to other engagement team members who assist the engagement partner with supervision.

Auditing Standard 11—Consideration of Materiality in Planning and Performing an Audit

This standard describes the auditor's responsibilities for consideration of materiality in planning and performing an audit.

Auditing Standard 12—Identifying and Assessing Risks of Material Misstatement

This standard establishes requirements regarding the process of identifying and assessing risks of material misstatement of the financial statements. The risk assessment process discussed in the standard includes information-gathering procedures to identify risks and an analysis of the identified risks.

Auditing Standard 13—The Auditor's Responses to the Risks of Material Misstatement

This standard establishes requirements for responding to the risks of material misstatement in financial statements through the general conduct of the audit and performing audit procedures regarding significant accounts and disclosures.

Auditing Standard 14—Evaluating Audit Results

This standard establishes requirements regarding the auditor's evaluation of audit results and determination of whether the auditor has obtained sufficient appropriate audit evidence. The evaluation process set forth in this standard includes, among other things, evaluation of misstatements identified during the audit; the overall presentation of the financial statements, including disclosures; and the potential for management bias in the financial statements.

Auditing Standard 15—Audit Evidence

This standard explains what constitutes audit evidence and establishes requirements for designing and performing audit procedures to obtain sufficient appropriate audit evidence to support the opinion expressed in the auditor's report.

GOVERNMENT AUDITING STANDARDS
(Issued by the Comptroller General of the United States, General Accounting Office)

Background—Government Auditing Standards (GAS), also referred to as the "Yellow Book," is a book of standards issued by the Comptroller General of the United States. The standards (referred to as generally accepted government auditing standards—GAGAS) are for the use of auditors of government entities and entities that receive government awards. When studying this information also review the outline of AU 801 on AICPA audit requirements in this area. In this outline we present a brief outline of the information on three types of government audits: (a) financial audits, (b) attestation engagements, and (c) performance audits.

A. Overall

    1. All *GAS* audits and attestation engagements begin with objectives, and those objectives determine the type of audit to be performed and the applicable standards to be followed
    2. GAGAS requirements apply to the following types of audit and attestation engagements:

        a. Financial audits
        b. Attestation engagements
        c. Performance audits

B. Financial Audits

    1. Provide an independent assessment and reasonable assurance about whether an entity's reported financial condition, results, and use of resources are presented fairly in accordance with recognized criteria
    2. Reporting on financial audits performed in accordance with GAGAS include an audit report on the financial information, but also reports on

    a. Internal control over financial reporting (hereafter IC).

    b. Compliance with laws and regulations, and provisions of contracts and grant agreements as they relate to financial transactions, systems and processes.

3. There are two types of financial audits

    a. Financial statement audits—The primary purpose is to provide reasonable assurance through an opinion (or a disclaimer) about whether an entity's financial statements are presented fairly in all material respects in conformity with GAAP or with a comprehensive basis of accounting other than GAAP.

    b. Other financial audits—Other types of financial audits under GAGAS provide for different levels of assurance and entail various scopes of work, including

        (1) Special reports (e.g., on specified elements)
        (2) Reviews of interim financial information
        (3) Letters for underwriters and certain other requesting parties
        (4) Reports on the controls over processing of transactions by a service organization
        (5) Compliance with regulations relating to federal award expenditures and other governmental financial assistance in connection with a financial statement audit

4. Require following generally accepted auditing standards reporting standards, plus reporting on

    a. Compliance with GAGAS (report should say auditors performed audit in accordance with GAGAS)

    b. IC *and* compliance with laws, regulations, and provisions of contracts or grant agreements

        (1) The auditors should report on the scope of the auditor's testing of compliance and internal control, and state in the reports whether the tests they performed provided sufficient appropriate evidence to support an opinion on IC over financial reporting and on compliance with laws, regulations, and provisions of contracts or grant agreements.

            (a) Although auditors test compliance with laws and regulations, responsibility for compliance is the responsibility of management

        (2) The reports on IC and compliance may be combined or separate.

    c. A variety of additional matters, including various deficiencies related to

        (1) IC—significant deficiencies and material weaknesses are reported
        (2) Fraud, illegal acts, violations, and abuse

            (a) Under GAAS and GAGAS—Auditors have a responsibility to provide reasonable assurance of detecting fraud and illegal acts with a material effect on the financial statements and to determine that those charged with governance are informed

            (b) Auditors should include in their audit report the following that are discovered during the audit:

                1] Fraud and illegal acts that are more than inconsequential
                2] Violations of provisions of contracts or grant agreements with a material effect on financial statements
                3] Abuse that is material, either quantitatively or qualitatively

            (c) Auditors should report known or likely fraud, illegal acts, or abuse directly to parties *outside the audited entity* in two circumstances:

                1] When management does not satisfy legal or regulatory requirements to report
                2] When management fails to take timely and appropriate steps to respond to known or likely fraud, illegal acts, violations of contracts, or abuse

    d. Communicating significant matters in the auditors' report

        (1) The auditors may emphasize in the report significant matters regarding the financial statements.

> **NOTE:** This is like GAAS "emphasis of a matter" reporting.

    e. Reporting on the restatement of previously issued financial statements

        (1) The auditors should update the audit report as appropriate. They should notify those charged with governance if management doesn't timely (a) disclose new information that should be disclosed or (b) restate financial statements when necessary

    f. Reporting views of responsible officials

(1) If the auditors' report discloses deficiencies in IC, fraud, illegal acts, violations of contracts, or abuse, auditors should obtain and report the views of responsible officials concerning the information.

(2) When auditors receive written comments from the responsible officials, they should include in their report a copy of them, or a summary. When only oral comments are provided, the auditor should prepare a summary and include in report as appropriate

g. Reporting confidential or sensitive information

(1) If certain information is prohibited from public disclosure, auditors should disclose in the report that certain information has been omitted and the reason or circumstances that make the omission necessary.

h. Distribution of audit reports

(1) Distribution depends on the relationship of the auditors to the audited organization and the nature of the information contained in the report. If the subject involves material that is classified for security purposes or contains confidential or sensitive information, the auditors may limit the report distribution. The auditors should document any limitation on report distribution.

C. Attestation Engagements

1. Can cover a broad range of financial or nonfinancial objectives and may provide different levels of assurance about the subject matter or assertion depending on the users' needs
2. They are examination, review, or agreed-upon procedures engagements
3. Examples of subject matter are similar to those of attestation standards, for example

a. Prospective financial or performance information
b. Management discussion and analysis
c. Internal control over financial reporting
d. Effectiveness of internal control over compliance

4. Reporting standards for attestation engagements; AICPA attestation reporting standards *plus* reporting on

a. Compliance with GAGAS (report should say auditors performed audit in accordance with GAGAS)
b. Reporting deficiencies in IC, fraud, illegal acts, violations of provisions of contracts or grant agreements, and abuse
c. Reporting views of responsible officials
d. Reporting confidential or sensitive information
e. Distribution of reports

> **NOTE:** Overall reporting standards are similar to those for financial audits described earlier in Section B of this outline.

D. Performance audits

1. Engagements that provide assurance or conclusions based on an evaluation of sufficient, appropriate evidence against stated criteria, such as specific requirements, measures, or defined business practices
2. They provide objective analysis so that management and those charged with governance and oversight can use the information to improve program performance and operations, reduce costs, facilitate decision making by parties with responsibility to oversee or initiate corrective action, and contribute to public accountability
3. Performance audits that comply with GAGAS provide reasonable assurance that the auditors have obtained sufficient appropriate evidence to support the conclusions reached
4. Performance audit objectives may vary widely and include assessments of program effectiveness, economy and efficiency, internal control, compliance, and prospective analyses.
5. Audit objectives that focus on economy and efficiency address the costs and resources used to achieve program objectives; examples

a. Assessing relative ability of alternative approaches to yield better program performance or eliminate factors that inhibit program effectiveness
b. Analyzing the relative cost-effectiveness of a program or activity
c. Determining whether a program produced intended results

6. Examples of audit objectives related to internal control include an assessment of whether the IC provides reasonable assurance about whether

a. Organizational missions, goals, and objectives are achieved effectively and efficiently
b. Resources are used in compliance with laws, regulations, or other requirements
c. The integrity of information from computerized systems is achieved

7. Examples of compliance audit objectives include determining whether

    a. The purpose of the program, the manner in which it is to be conducted, the services delivered, the outcomes or the population it serves is in compliance with laws, regulations, contract provisions, grant agreements, and other requirements.
    b. Government services and benefits are distributed to citizens based on the individual's eligibility to obtain those services and benefits.
    c. Incurred or proposed costs are in compliance with applicable laws, regulations, and contracts or grant agreements.

8. Examples of prospective analysis audit objectives include providing conclusions based on

    a. Current or projected trends and future potential impact on government programs and services
    b. Program or policy alternatives, including forecasting program outcomes under various assumptions
    c. Management's assumptions on which prospective information is based

9. Reporting standards for performance audits; auditors should perform audit reports that contain

    a. The objectives, scope, and methodology of the audit
    b. The audit results, including findings, conclusions, and recommendations, as appropriate
    c. A statement about the auditors' compliance with GAGAS
    d. A summary of the views of responsible officials
    e. If applicable, the nature of any confidential or sensitive information

> **NOTE:** Although the overall requirements are similar to those of financial statement audits, the great variety of performance audits results in less specific requirements.

As indicated previously, this section consists of 14 modules designed to facilitate your study for the Financial Accounting and Reporting section of the Uniform CPA Examination. The table of contents at the right describes the content of each module.

Exam Content Overview

This chapter is written to help you review intermediate and advanced accounting (financial accounting) for the Financial Accounting and Reporting section of the exam. The AICPA Content Specification Outline of financial accounting coverage appears below.

The chapter is organized along the lines of the traditional intermediate and advanced accounting texts. The topics are arranged per the fourteen financial modules (on the previous pages). The objective is to provide you with the basic concepts, journal entries, and formulas for each topic and subtopic. Hopefully you will be able to expand, adapt, and apply the basics to specific problem situations as presented in multiple-choice questions and simulations appearing on the CPA exam. Keep in mind the importance of working questions and simulations under exam conditions as you study the basics set forth in this chapter. Refer to the multiple-choice questions, problems, and simulation problems on each of the financial accounting topics.

As you work through this chapter, remember that there are many possible series of journal entries and account titles that can be used in accounting for a specific type of economic transaction (e.g., long-term construction contracts). Reconcile the approach illustrated in the chapter with the approach you studied as an undergraduate per your intermediate or advanced text.

In this chapter, you will be referred frequently to the authoritative literature. As of July 1, 2009, the FASB Accounting Standards Codification is the single source of all US GAAP, except for the SEC authoritative literature. Task-based research simulations test research using the Accounting Standards Codification beginning in 2011.

AICPA CONTENT AND SKILLS SPECIFICATION

The AICPA Content and Skills Specifications for the Uniform CPA Exam set forth the coverage of topics on the Financial Accounting and Reporting exam. This outline was issued by the AICPA and is effective beginning in 2011. The first part of the outline describes the topical coverage of the Financial Accounting and Reporting exam, and the second part provides some insights into the skills tested on all sections of the Uniform CPA exam.

Content Specification Outlines (CSOs)

The Financial Accounting and Reporting section tests knowledge and understanding of the financial reporting framework used by business enterprises, not for profit organizations, and governmental entities. The financial reporting frameworks that are included in this section are those issued by the standard setters identified in the references to these CSOs, which include standards issued by the Financial Accounting Standards Board, the International Accounting Standards Board, the US Securities and Exchange Commission, and the Governmental Accounting Standards Board. In addition to demonstrating knowledge and understanding of accounting principles, candidates are required to demonstrate the skills required to apply that knowledge in performing financial reporting and other tasks as certified public accountants. To demonstrate such knowledge and skills, candidates will be expected to perform the following tasks:

- Identify and understand the differences between financial statements prepared on the basis of accounting principles generally accepted in the United States of America (US GAAP) and International Financial Reporting Standards (IFRS).
- Prepare and/or review source documents including account classification, and enter data into subsidiary and general ledgers.
- Calculate amounts for financial statement components.
- Reconcile the general ledger to the subsidiary ledgers or underlying account details.
- Prepare account reconciliation and related schedules; analyze accounts for unusual fluctuations and make necessary adjustments.
- Prepare consolidating and eliminating entries for the period.
- Identify financial accounting and reporting methods and select those that are appropriate.
- Prepare consolidated financial statements, including balance sheets, income statements, and statements of retained earnings, equity, comprehensive income, and cash flows.
- Prepare appropriate notes to the financial statements.
- Analyze financial statements including analysis of accounts, variances, trends, and ratios.
- Exercise judgment in the application of accounting principles.
- Apply judgment to evaluate assumptions and methods underlying estimates, including fair value measures of financial statement components.
- Produce required financial statement filings in order to meet regulatory or reporting requirements (e.g. Form 10-Q, 10-K, annual report).
- Determine appropriate accounting treatment for new or unusual transactions and evaluate the economic substance of transactions in making the determinations.
- Research relevant professional literature.

The outline below specifies the knowledge in which candidates are required to demonstrate proficiency:

I. Conceptual Framework, Standards, Standard Setting, and Presentation of Financial Statements (17%–23%)

A. Process by Which Accounting Standards Are Set and Roles of Accounting Standard-Setting Bodies

1. US Securities and Exchange Commission (SEC)
2. Financial Accounting Standards Board (FASB)
3. International Accounting Standards Board (IASB)
4. Governmental Accounting Standards Board (GASB)

B. Conceptual Framework

1. Financial reporting by business entities
2. Financial reporting by not-for-profit (nongovernmental) entities
3. Financial reporting by state and local governmental entities

C. Financial Reporting, Presentation and Disclosures in General-Purpose Financial Statements

1. Balance sheet
2. Income statement
3. Statement of comprehensive income
4. Statement of changes in equity
5. Statement of cash flows
6. Notes to financial statements
7. Consolidated and combined financial statements
8. First-time adoption of IFRS

D. SEC Reporting Requirements (e.g. Form 10-Q, 10-K)

E. Other Financial Statement Presentations, Including Other Comprehensive Bases of Accounting (OCBOA)

1. Cash basis
2. Modified cash basis
3. Income tax basis
4. Personal financial statements
5. Financial statements of employee benefit plans/trusts

II. Financial Statement Accounts: Recognition, Measurement, Valuation, Calculation, Presentation, and Disclosures (27%–33%)

A. Cash and Cash Equivalents
B. Receivables
C. Inventory
D. Property, Plant, and Equipment
E. Investments

1. Financial assets at fair value through profit or loss
2. Available-for-sale financial assets
3. Held-to-maturity investments
4. Joint ventures

5. Equity method investments (investments in associates)
6. Investment property

F. Intangible Assets—Goodwill and Other
G. Payables and Accrued Liabilities
H. Deferred Revenue
I. Long-Term Debt (Financial Liabilities)

1. Notes payable
2. Bonds payable
3. Debt with conversion features and other options
4. Modifications and extinguishments
5. Troubled debt restructurings by debtors
6. Debt covenant compliance

J. Equity
K. Revenue Recognition
L. Costs and Expenses
M. Compensation and Benefits

1. Compensated absences
2. Deferred compensation arrangements
3. Nonretirement postemployment benefits
4. Retirement benefits
5. Stock compensation (share-based payments)

N. Income Taxes

III. Specific Transactions, Events and Disclosures: Recognition, Measurement, Valuation, Calculation, Presentation, and Disclosures (27%–33%)

A. Accounting Changes and Error Corrections
B. Asset Retirement and Environmental Obligations
C. Business Combinations
D. Consolidation (Including Off-Balance-Sheet Transactions, Variable-Interest Entities and Noncontrolling Interests)
E. Contingencies, Commitments, and Guarantees (Provisions)
F. Earnings Per Share
G. Exit or Disposal Activities and Discontinued Operations
H. Extraordinary and Unusual Items
I. Fair Value Measurements, Disclosures, and Reporting
J. Derivatives and Hedge Accounting
K. Foreign Currency Transactions and Translation
L. Impairment
M. Interim Financial Reporting
N. Leases
O. Distinguishing Liabilities from Equity
P. Nonmonetary Transactions (Barter Transactions)
Q. Related Parties and Related-Party Transactions
R. Research and Development Costs
S. Risks and Uncertainties
T. Segment Reporting
U. Software Costs
V. Subsequent Events

W. Transfers and Servicing of Financial Assets and Derecognition

IV. Governmental Accounting and Reporting (8%–12%)

A. Governmental Accounting Concepts

1. Measurement focus and basis of accounting
2. Fund accounting concepts and applications
3. Budgetary accounting

B. Format and Content of Comprehensive Annual Financial Report (CAFR)

1. Government-wide financial statements
2. Governmental funds financial statements
3. Proprietary funds financial statements
4. Fiduciary funds financial statements
5. Notes to financial statements
6. Management's discussion and analysis
7. Required supplementary information (RSI) other than Management's Discussion and Analysis
8. Combining statements and individual fund statements and schedules
9. Deriving government-wide financial statements and reconciliation requirements

C. Financial Reporting Entity, Including Blended and Discrete Component Units

D. Typical Items and Specific Types of Transactions and Events: Recognition, Measurement, Valuation, Calculation, and Presentation in Governmental Entity Financial Statements

1. Net assets and components thereof
2. Fund balances and components thereof
3. Capital assets and infrastructure assets
4. General long-term liabilities
5. Interfund activity, including transfers
6. Nonexchange revenue transactions
7. Expenditures
8. Special items
9. Encumbrances

E. Accounting and Reporting for Governmental Not-for-Profit Organizations

V. Not-for-Profit (Nongovernmental) Accounting and Reporting (8%–12%)

A. Financial Statements

1. Statement of financial position
2. Statement of activities
3. Statement of cash flows
4. Statement of functional expenses

B. Typical Items and Specific Types of Transactions and Events: Recognition, Measurement, Valuation, Calculation, and Presentation in Financial Statements of Not-for-Profit Organizations

1. Support, revenues, and contributions
2. Types of restrictions on resources
3. Types of net assets
4. Expenses, including depreciation and functional expenses
5. Investments

References—Financial Accounting and Reporting

- Financial Accounting Standards Board (FASB) Accounting Standards Codification
- Governmental Accounting Standards Board (GASB) Codification of Governmental Accounting and Financial Reporting Standards
- Standards Issued by the US Securities and Exchange Commission (SEC):

  - Regulation S-X of the Code of Federal Regulations (17 CFR Part 210)
  - Financial Reporting Releases (FRR)/Accounting Series Releases (ASR)
  - Interpretive Releases (IR)
  - SEC Staff Guidance in Staff Accounting Bulletins (SAB)
  - SEC Staff Guidance in EITF Topic D and SEC Staff Observer Comments

- International Accounting Standards Board (IASB) International Financial Reporting Standards (IFRS), International Accounting Standards (IAS), and Interpretations
- AICPA Auditing and Accounting Guides
- Current textbooks on accounting for business enterprises, not-for-profit organizations, and governmental entities

Skill Specification Outlines (SSOs)

The Skill Specification Outlines (SSOs) identify the skills to be tested on the Uniform CPA Examination. There are three categories of skills, and the weightings will be implemented through the use of different question formats in the exam. For each of the question formats, a different set of tools will be available as resources to the candidates, who will need to use those tools to demonstrate proficiency in the applicable skills categories.

Weights

The percentage range assigned to each skill category will be used to determine the quantity of each type of question, as described below. The percentage range assigned to each skill category represents the approximate percentage to which that category of skills will be used in the different sections of the CPA Examination to assess proficiency. The ranges are designed to provide flexibility in building the examination, and the midpoints of the ranges for each section total 100%.

No percentages are given for the bulleted descriptions included in these definitions. The presence of several groups within an area or several topics within a group does not imply equal importance or weight will be given to these bullets on an examination.

Skills Category	Weights (FAR, REG, AUD)	Weights (BEC)
Knowledge and Understanding	50%–60%	80%–90%
Application of the Body of Knowledge	40%–50%	—
Written Communication	—	10%–20%

Knowledge and Understanding. Multiple-choice questions will be used as the proxy for assessing knowledge and understanding and will be based upon the content topics as outlined in the CSOs. Candidates will not have access to the authoritative literature, spreadsheets, or database tools while answering these questions. A calculator will be accessible for the candidates to use in performing calculations to demonstrate their understanding of the principles or subject matter.

Application of the Body of Knowledge. Task-based simulations will be used as the proxy for assessing application of the body of knowledge and will be based upon the content topics as outlined in the CSOs. Candidates will have access to the authoritative literature, a calculator, spreadsheets, and other resources and tools which they will use to demonstrate proficiency in applying the body of knowledge.

Written Communication will be assessed through the use of responses to essay questions, which will be based upon the content topics as outlined in the CSOs. Candidates will have access to a word processor, which includes a spell-check feature.

Outlines

The outlines below provide additional descriptions of the skills that are represented in each category.

Knowledge and Understanding. Expertise and skills developed through learning processes, recall, and reading comprehension. Knowledge is acquired through experience or education and is the theoretical or practical understanding of a subject; knowledge is also represented through awareness or familiarity with information gained by experience of a fact or situation. Understanding represents a higher level than simple knowledge and is the process of using concepts to deal adequately with given situations, facts, or circumstances. Understanding is the ability to recognize and comprehend the meaning of a particular concept.

Application of the Body of Knowledge, Including Analysis, Judgment, Synthesis, Evaluation, and Research. Higher-level cognitive skills that require individuals to act or transform knowledge in some fashion. These skills are inextricably intertwined and thus are grouped into this single skill area.

- Assess the Business Environment

  - Business Process Evaluation: Assessing and integrating information regarding a business's operational structure, functions, processes, and procedures to develop a broad operational perspective; identify the need for new systems or changes to existing systems and/or processes.
  - Contextual Evaluation: Assessing and integrating information regarding client's type of business or industry.
  - Strategic Analysis—Understanding the Business: Obtaining, assessing and integrating information on the entity's strategic objectives, strategic management process, business environment, the nature of and value to customers, its products and services, extent of competition within its market space, etc.).
  - Business Risk Assessment: Obtaining, assessing and integrating information on conditions and events that could impede the entity's ability to achieve strategic objectives.
  - Visualize Abstract Descriptions: Organize and process symbols, pictures, graphs, objects, and other information.

- Research

  - Identify the appropriate research question.
  - Identify key search terms for use in performing electronic searches through large volumes of data.
  - Search through large volumes of electronic data to find required information.
  - Organize information or data from multiple sources.
  - Integrate diverse sources of information to reach conclusions or make decisions.
  - Identify the appropriate authoritative guidance in applicable financial reporting frameworks and auditing standards for the accounting issue being evaluated.

- Application of Technology:

  - Using electronic spreadsheets to perform calculations, financial analysis, or other functions to analyze data.
  - Integration of technological applications and resources into work processes.
  - Using a variety of computer software and hardware systems to structure, utilize, and manage data.

- Analysis

    - Review information to determine compliance with specified standards or criteria.
    - Use expectations, empirical data, and analytical methods to determine trends and variances.
    - Perform appropriate calculations on financial and nonfinancial data.
    - Recognize patterns of activity when reviewing large amounts of data or recognize breaks in patterns.
    - Interpretation of financial statement data for a given evaluation purpose.
    - Forecasting future financial statement data from historical financial statement data and other information.
    - Integrating primary financial statements: using data from all primary financial statements to uncover financial transactions, inconsistencies, or other information.

- Complex Problem Solving and Judgment

    - Develop and understand goals, objectives, and strategies for dealing with potential issues, obstacles, or opportunities.
    - Analyze patterns of information and contextual factors to identify potential problems and their implications.
    - Devise and implement a plan of action appropriate for a given problem.
    - Apply professional skepticism, which is an attitude that includes a questioning mind and a critical assessment of information or evidence obtained.
    - Adapt strategies or planned actions in response to changing circumstances.
    - Identify and solve unstructured problems.
    - Develop reasonable hypotheses to answer a question or resolve a problem.
    - Formulate and examine alternative solutions in terms of their relative strengths and weaknesses, level of risk, and appropriateness for a given situation.
    - Develop creative ways of thinking about situations, problems, and opportunities to create insightful and sound solutions.
    - Develop logical conclusions through the use of inductive and deductive reasoning.
    - Apply knowledge of professional standards and laws, as well as legal, ethical, and regulatory issues.
    - Assess the need for consultations with other professionals when gray areas, or areas requiring specialized knowledge, are encountered.

- Decision Making

    - Specify goals and constraints.
    - Generate alternatives.
    - Consider risks.
    - Evaluate and select the best alternative.

- Organization, Efficiency, and Effectiveness:

    - Use time effectively and efficiently.
    - Develop detailed work plans, schedule tasks and meetings, and delegate assignments and tasks.
    - Set priorities by determining the relevant urgency or importance of tasks and deciding the order in which they should be performed.
    - File and store information so that it can be found easily and used effectively.

Written Communication. The various skills involved in preparing written communication, including

- Basic writing mechanics, such as grammar, spelling, word usage, punctuation, and sentence structure.
- Effective business writing principles, including organization, clarity, and conciseness.
- Exchange technical information and ideas with coworkers and other professionals to meet goals of job assignment.
- Documentation:

    - Prepare documents and presentations that are concise, accurate, and supportive of the subject matter.
    - Document and cross-reference work performed and conclusions reached in a complete and accurate manner.

- Assist client to recognize and understand implications of critical business issues by providing recommendations and informed opinions.
- Persuade others to take recommended courses of action.
- Follow directions.

RESEARCHING FASB ACCOUNTING STANDARDS

Research components of simulations in the Financial Accounting and Reporting section will involve a research database. Beginning in 2011, that database will be the FASB Accounting Standards Codification (ASC)

Database Searching

Searching a database consists of the following five steps:

1. Define the issue. What is the research question to be answered?
2. Choose appropriate search technique. Select keywords that will locate the needed information or use the table of contents.
3. Execute the search. Enter the keyword(s) or click on the table of contents item and complete the search.
4. Evaluate the results. Evaluate the research to see if an answer has been found. If not, try a new search.
5. Select an answer by clicking on one of the citations provided in the answer selections on the right-hand side of the screen.

Advanced Searches

The advanced search screen allows you to use Boolean concepts to perform more precise searches. Examples of searches that can be performed in the advanced search mode include

1. Containing all these words—Allows you to retrieve sections that contain two or more specified words.
2. Not containing any of these words—Allows you to retrieve sections that do not contain specific words.
3. Containing one or more of these words—Allows you to retrieve sections that contain any one or more of the specified words.
4. Containing these words near each other—Allows you to retrieve sections that contain words near to each other.

The advanced search also allows you to select options for the search. One alternative allows you to retrieve alternative word terms. For example, using this approach with a search on the word "cost" would also retrieve sections containing the word "costing." A synonyms option allows you to retrieve sections that contain words that mean the same as the specified word. You also have the option to only search on the selected sections of the literature.

Module 9: Basic Theory and Financial Reporting

Overview

This module covers **basic concepts** such as the conceptual framework and revenue recognition, **error correction** such as counterbalancing and classification errors, **accounting changes** such as changes in principle and changes in estimates, and **financial statements** such as the income statement and balance sheet.

US GAAP is the basis for financial reporting but it does not constitute a cohesive body of accounting theory. Concept Statements were issued to provide a theoretical framework for accounting standard development and a basis for financial reporting.

As of July 1, 2009, the Accounting Standards Codification (ASC) became the single source for US GAAP. **The relevant Accounting Standards Codification topic is indicated in the discussion with a cross-reference to the previous accounting literature (i.e., ARB, APB, SFAS, and SFAC).** Appendix A of this text includes an outline of the pre-Codification standards with a cross reference to the appropriate Codification topics to help candidates transition to the FASB's Accounting Standards Codification. Note these outlines appear in the following sequence: ARB, APB, SFAS, and SFAC. Turn to each outline as directed and study the outline while reviewing the related journal entries, computations, etc.

The AICPA began testing International Financial Reporting Standards (IFRS) on January 1, 2011. Coverage of international standards and outlines of the differences between US GAAP and IFRS are located at the end of each module.

A. Basic Concepts

Basic concepts include theory, income determination, accruals, deferrals, and revenue recognition.

1. **Basic Accounting Theory**

    Effective July 1, 2009, the FASB's Accounting Standards Codification became the single source of US GAAP for nongovernmental entities.

    a. The Accounting Standards Codification (ASC) replaced all previously issued non-SEC accounting literature. The Codification did not change GAAP, but merely restructured the existing accounting standards to provide one cohesive set of accounting standards.

       (1) Included in the Codification is all GAAP, as well as relevant literature issued by the SEC.
       (2) The FASB issues Accounting Standards Updates (ASUs) to update the Codification.

       > **NOTE:** To help the CPA candidate transition to the Accounting Standards Codification, the Codification citation is shown first, and the cross-reference to previous GAAP citations are shown in parentheses.

    b. Theory can be defined as a coherent set of hypothetical, conceptual, and pragmatic principles forming a general frame of reference for a field of inquiry; thus, accounting theory should be the basic principles of accounting rather than its practice (which GAAP describes or dictates).

       (1) Although GAAP is the current basis for financial reporting, it does not constitute a cohesive body of accounting theory. Generally, authoritative pronouncements have been the result of a problem-by-problem approach that have dealt with specific problems as they occur and are not predicated on an underlying body of theory.
       (2) Accounting has a definite need for conceptual theoretical structure if an authoritative body such as the FASB is to promulgate consistent standards.
       (3) A body of accounting theory should be the foundation of the standard-setting process and should provide guidance where no authoritative GAAP exists.
       (4) The FASB issued concept statements to develop a theoretical framework. As of December 2011, the FASB had issued eight concept statements to develop a frame of reference.

(a) The purpose of the concept statements is "to set forth objectives and fundamental concepts that will be the basis for development of financial accounting and reporting guidance" (SFAC 8). In other words, the SFAC attempt to organize a framework that can serve as a reference point in formulating financial accounting standards.

> **NOTE:** The SFAC do not constitute authoritative GAAP and therefore are not part of the Codification.

(b) Three concept statements have been superseded by other concept statements: SFAC 1 and SFAC 2 were superseded by SFAC 8, and SFAC 3 was superseded by SFAC 6. The remaining concept statements are as follows: SFAC 4, *Objectives of Financial Reporting of Nonbusiness Organizations*; SFAC 5, *Recognition and Measurement in Financial Statements*; SFAC 6, *Elements of Financial Statements*; SFAC 7, *Using Cash Flow Information and Present Value in Accounting Measurements*; and SFAC 8, *Conceptual Framework for Financial Reporting*.

(c) SFAC 8 is the most recent attempt to develop accounting theory as a joint project between the FASB and the International Accounting Standards Board (IASB).

   1] SFAC 8 contains two chapters of the revised conceptual framework and replaces SFACs 1 and 2.

      a] Chapter 1, The Objective of General-Purpose Financial Reporting replaces SFAC 1.
      b] Chapter 3, Qualitative Characteristics of Useful Financial Information, replaces SFAC 2.

(d) As additional phases of the joint project between the FASB and the IASB are completed, the revised concept statements will be included as new chapters to SFAC 8.

c. **Financial Reporting.** "The objective of general-purpose financial reporting is to provide financial information about the reporting entity that is useful to existing and potential investors, lenders, and other creditors in making decisions about providing resources to the entity" (SFAC 8).

> **NOTE:** Not all informational needs are met by accounting or financial reporting.

(1) The following diagram from SFAC 5 describes the information spectrum.

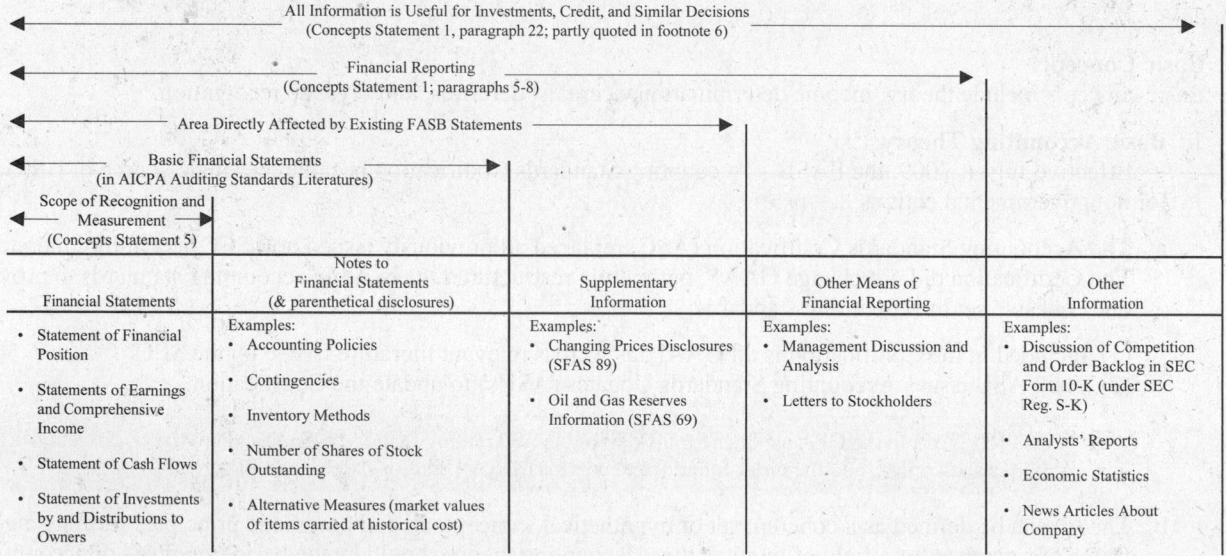

* The SFAC 5 diagram has not been updated to reflect the issuance of SFAC 8.

d. **Components of the Conceptual Framework.** The components of the conceptual framework for financial accounting and reporting include objectives, qualitative characteristics, elements, recognition, measurement, financial statements, earnings, funds flow, and liquidity.

(1) The relationship between these components is illustrated in the following diagram from *Financial Statements and Other Means of Financial Reporting*, a FASB Invitation to Comment.

   (a) In the diagram below, components to the left are more basic and those to the right depend on components to their left. Components are closely related to those above or below them.
   (b) The most basic component of the conceptual framework is the objectives.

    1] The objectives underlie the other phases and are derived from the needs of those for whom financial information is intended.

    2] The objectives provide a focal point for financial reporting by identifying what types of information are relevant.

Conceptual Framework
For Financial Accounting and Reporting

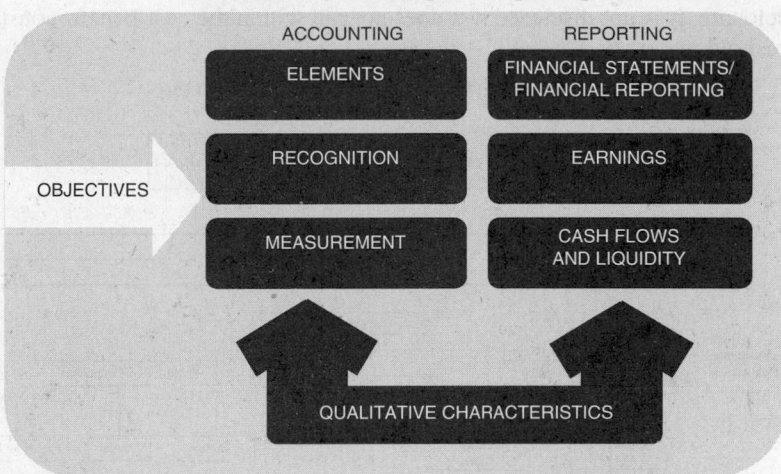

  (c) The qualitative characteristics also underlie most of the other phases.

    1] They are the criteria to be used in choosing and evaluating accounting and reporting policies.

  (d) Elements of financial statements are the components from which financial statements are created. They include assets, liabilities, equity, investments by owners, distributions to owners, comprehensive income, revenues, expenses, gains, and losses.

  (e) In order to be included in financial statements, an element must meet criteria for recognition and possess an attribute which is relevant and can be reliably measured.

  (f) Finally, reporting and display considerations are concerned with what information should be provided, who should provide it, and where it should be displayed.

  (g) How the financial statements (financial position, earnings, and cash flow) are presented is the focal point of this part of the conceptual framework project.

(2) **Objectives of Financial Reporting.** (See outline of SFAC 8, Chapter 1.) The objectives of general-purpose financial reporting focus on users of financial information.

  (a) The primary users of financial reporting are investors, lenders, and other creditors who must rely on reporting entities to provide information to them.

    1] Although management is also interested in financial information, management does not rely on general-purpose reports because information can be obtained internally.

    2] In addition, although other parties such as regulators and members of the public may use financial information, they are not considered primary users according to SFAC 8.

  (b) SFAC 8, Chapter 1, states that the objective of financial reporting is to provide

    1] Information that is useful to potential and existing investors, lenders, and other creditors (primary users)

    2] Information about the reporting entity's economic resources and claims against the reporting entity

    3] Changes in economic resources and claims

    4] Financial performance reflected by accrual accounting

    5] Financial performance reflected by past cash flow

    6] Changes in economic resources and claims not resulting from financial performance

(3) **Qualitative Characteristics.** (See outline of SFAC 8, Chapter 3.) The qualitative characteristics also underlie the conceptual framework, but in a different way. While the objectives provide an overall basis, the qualitative characteristics establish criteria for selecting and evaluating accounting alternatives which will meet the objectives. In other words, information must possess the qualitative characteristics if that information is to fulfill the objectives.

(a) SFAC 8 views these characteristics as a hierarchy of accounting qualities, as represented in the diagram below.

    1] The diagram below reveals many important relationships. At the top is the cost-benefit constraint. If the benefits of information do not exceed the costs of providing that information, it would not be reported. At the bottom of the diagram is the materiality threshold. An item that is not material is not required to be disclosed. Although an item may possess the other qualitative characteristics for disclosure, it is not disclosed if it does not fall within the cost-benefit constraint or the materiality threshold.

A HIERARCHY OF ACCOUNTING QUALITIES

(b) The two fundamental qualitative characteristics of accounting information are relevance and faithful representation.

    1] Relevant information is capable of making a difference in a user's decision. Financial information is relevant if it has predictive value, confirmatory value, or both.

        a] **Predictive value** requires that information be used to predict future outcomes.
        b] **Confirmatory value** requires that information either confirms or changes prior evaluations.
        c] An item is material if omitting it or misstating it could influence a user's decision. Therefore, the materiality threshold relates to the qualitative characteristic of relevance.

    2] Information has the quality of **faithful representation** if the information depicts what it purports to represent. A faithful representation should be complete, neutral, and free from error.

        a] Completeness requires that information is presented or depicted in a way that users can understand the item being depicted.
        b] Neutrality requires that the item is depicted without bias either favorably or unfavorably to users.
        c] Free from error means that there are no errors or omissions in the information reported.

(c) The enhancing qualitative characteristics of accounting information are comparability, verifiability, timeliness, and understandability.

    1] **Comparability** enables users to identify and understand similarities and differences between items.

        a] Consistency refers to the use of the same accounting methods in different periods. Consistency, therefore, helps achieve comparability because it helps the user make comparisons across different time periods.

    2] **Verifiability** occurs when different sources reach consensus or agreement on an amount of representation of an item. Direct verification occurs through direct observation; indirect verification occurs by using techniques such as checking formulas or recalculating amounts. Although forward-looking information cannot be verified, the underlying assumptions, methods, facts, and circumstances can be disclosed to help users determine if the information is useful.

3] **Timelines** requires that information is available to a decision maker when it is useful to make the decision.

4] **Understandability** involves classifying, characterizing, and presenting information clearly and concisely. Understandability assumes that a user has a reasonable knowledge of business and economic activities to comprehend financial reports.

(4) **Basic Elements.** (See outline of SFAC 6.) Elements of financial statements are the ten basic building blocks from which financial statements are constructed. These definitions are based upon the objectives of SFAC 8. They are intended to assure that users will receive decision-useful information about enterprise resources (assets), claims to those resources (liabilities and equity), and changes therein (the other seven elements). In order to be included in the statements, an item must qualify as an element, meet recognition criteria, and be measurable.

(a) The meaning of financial statement elements depends on the conceptual view of earnings which is adopted. Two basic views are the asset-liability view and the revenue-expense view.

1] Under the **asset-liability view**, earnings are measured by the change (other than investments or withdrawals) in the net economic resources of an enterprise during a period. Therefore, definitions of assets and liabilities are the key under this view, and definitions of revenues, expenses, gains, and losses are secondary and are based on assets and liabilities.

2] The **revenue-expense view** holds that earnings are a measure of an enterprise's effectiveness in using its inputs to obtain and sell outputs. Thus, definitions of revenues and expenses are basic to this view, and definitions of assets, liabilities, and other elements are derived from revenues and expenses.

(b) The definitions of all ten elements are contained in the outline of SFAC 6. Let us examine one definition in more detail.

EXAMPLE

"Assets are probable future economic benefits obtained or controlled by a particular entity as a result of past transactions or events." This definition is based on the objectives and qualities of SFAC 8. The overall thrust of the objectives—predicting and evaluating future cash flows—is reflected in the phrase "probable future economic benefits." "Control by a particular entity" is crucial if reporting an item as an asset is to have decision usefulness (or relevance). The quality of reliability is assured by the phrase "as a result of past transactions." Information is more verifiable, valid, and neutral (the components of reliability) if based on past transactions. A similar analysis can be applied to liabilities, equity, investments by owners, distributions to owners, comprehensive income, revenues, expenses, gains and losses.

(c) SFAC 6 also defines some other concepts in addition to the ten elements. Especially important among these eleven additional concepts are accrual accounting, realization, recognition, and matching.

1] Realization and recognition are addressed by the FASB in SFAC 5.

2] The definition of accrual accounting is important because SFAC 8 stated that accrual accounting should be used since it provides a better indication of future cash flows than the cash basis. This is true because accrual accounting records transactions with cash consequences (involving future cash flows) as they occur, not when the cash actually moves.

3] Matching is referred to in most accounting literature as a principle, or fundamental law, of accounting.

(5) **Recognition and Measurement.** (See outline of SFAC 5.) Recognition principles establish criteria concerning when an element should be included in the statements, while measurement principles govern the valuation of those elements.

(a) SFAC 5 established four fundamental recognition criteria: definitions, measurability, relevance, and reliability. If an item meets the definition of an element, can be reliably measured, is capable of making a difference in user decisions, and is verifiable, neutral, and representationally faithful, it should be included in the financial statements.

(b) Five different attributes are used to measure assets and liabilities in present practice. These are discussed below in an excerpt from SFAC 5.

1] **Historical cost (historical proceeds).** Property, plant, and equipment and most inventories are reported at their historical cost, which is the amount of cash, or its equivalent, paid to acquire an asset, commonly adjusted after acquisition for amortization or other allocations. Liabilities that involve obligations to provide goods or services to customers are generally reported at historical proceeds, which is the amount of cash, or its equivalent, received when the obligation was incurred and may be adjusted after acquisition for amortization or other allocations.

2] **Current cost.** Some inventories are reported at their current (replacement) cost, which is the amount of cash, or its equivalent, that would have to be paid if the same or an equivalent asset were acquired currently.

3] **Current market value.** Some investments in marketable securities are reported at their current market value, which is the amount of cash or its equivalent, that could be obtained by selling an asset in orderly liquidation. Current market value is also generally used for assets expected to be sold at prices lower than previous carrying amounts. Some liabilities that involve marketable commodities and securities, for example, the obligations of writers of options or sellers of common shares who do not own the underlying commodities or securities, are reported at current market value. Current market value is now referred to as fair value.

4] **Net realizable (settlement) value.** Short-term receivables and some inventories are reported at their net realizable value, which is the nondiscounted amount of cash, or its equivalent, into which an asset is expected to be converted in due course of business less direct costs, if any, necessary to make that conversion. Liabilities that involve known or estimated amounts of money payable at unknown future dates, for example, trade payables or warranty obligations, generally are reported at their net settlement value, which is the nondiscounted amount of cash, or its equivalent, expected to be paid to liquidate an obligation in the due course of business, including direct costs, if any, necessary to make that payment.

5] **Present (or discounted) value of future cash flows.** Long-term receivables are reported at their present or discounted value (discounted at the implicit or historical rate), which is the present value of future cash inflows into which an asset is expected to be converted in due course of business less present values of cash outflows necessary to obtain those inflows. Long-term payables are similarly reported at their present or discounted value (discounted at the implicit or historical rate), which is the present or discounted value of future cash outflows expected to be required to satisfy the liability in due course of business.

(c) SFAC 5 states that each of these attributes is appropriate in different situations and that all five attributes will continue to be used in the future.

(d) Similarly, SFAC 5 states that nominal units of money will continue to be the measurement unit. However, if inflation increases to a level where the FASB feels that financial statements become too distorted, another unit (such as units of constant purchasing power) could be adopted.

(e) SFAC 5 is based on the concept of financial capital maintenance. Two basic concepts of capital maintenance (financial and physical) can be used to separate return **on** capital (earnings) from return **of** capital (capital recovery). Remember, any capital which is "used up" during a period must be returned before earnings can be recognized. In other words, earnings is the amount an entity can distribute to its owners and be as well-off at the end of the year as at the beginning.

1] One way "well-offness" can be measured is in terms of *financial capital*. This concept of capital maintenance holds that the capital to be maintained is measured by the amount of cash (possibly restated into constant dollars) invested by owners. Earnings may not be recognized until the dollar investment in net assets, measured in units of money or purchasing power, is returned. The financial capital maintenance concept is the traditional view which is reflected in most present financial statements.

2] An alternative definition of "well-offness" is expressed in terms of *physical capital*. This concept holds that the capital to be maintained is the physical productive capacity of the enterprise. Earnings may not be recognized until the current replacement costs of assets with the same productive capabilities of the assets used up are returned. The physical capital maintenance concept supports current cost accounting. Again, the physical productive capacity may be measured in nominal or constant dollars.

EXAMPLE

Suppose an enterprise invests $10 in an inventory item. At year-end, the enterprise sells the item for $15. In order to replace the item at year-end, they would have to pay $12 rather than $10. To further simplify, assume the increase in replacement cost is due to specific price changes, and there is no general inflation.

The **financial capital** concept would maintain that the firm is as well-off once the dollar investment ($10) is returned. At that point, the financial capital is maintained and the remaining $5 is a return **on** capital, or income. The **physical capital** concept maintains that the firm is not as well-off until the physical capacity (a similar inventory item) is returned. Therefore, the firm must reinvest $12 to be as well-off. Then physical capital is maintained, and only the remaining $3 is a return **on** capital or income.

(f) SFAC 5 also gives specific guidance as to recognition of revenues and gains, and expenses and losses, as indicated below.

1] Recognize **revenues** when realized or realizable (when related assets received or held are readily convertible to known amounts of cash or claims to cash) and earned

2] Recognize **gains** when realized or realizable

3] Recognize **expenses** when economic benefits are consumed in revenue-earning activities, or when future economic benefits are reduced or eliminated

   a] When economic benefits are consumed during a period, the expense may be recognized by matching (such as cost of goods sold), immediate recognition (such as selling and administrative salaries), or systematic and rational allocation (such as depreciation).

4] Recognize **losses** when future economic benefits are reduced or eliminated

(g) Revenues, expenses, gains, and losses are used to compute **earnings**.

1] Earnings is the extent to which revenues and gains associated with cash-to-cash cycles substantially completed during the period exceed expenses and losses directly or indirectly associated with those cycles.

2] Earnings adjusted for cumulative accounting adjustments and other nonowner changes in equity (such as foreign currency translation adjustments) is **comprehensive income**.

   a] Per SFAC 5, comprehensive income would reflect all changes in the equity of an entity during a period, except investments by owners and distributions to owners. However, accounting standards only go part way in implementing this concept.

NOW REVIEW MULTIPLE-CHOICE QUESTIONS 1 THROUGH 17 IN VOLUME 2

---

(6) **Cash Flow Information and Present Value.** (See outline of SFAC 7.) As discussed earlier, the attributes most often used to measure assets and liabilities include observable marketplace-determined amounts. These observable marketplace amounts (such as current cost) are generally more reliable and are determined more efficiently than measurements which employ estimates of future cash flows. However, when observable amounts are unavailable, accountants often turn to estimated cash flows to determine the carrying amount of an asset or liability. Since those cash flows often occur in one or more future periods, questions arise regarding whether the accounting measurement should reflect the present value or the undiscounted sum of those cash flows.

(a) In February 2000, the FASB issued SFAC 7, *Using Cash Flow Information and Present Value in Accounting Measurements*.

1] SFAC 7 provides a framework for using future cash flows as the basis of an accounting measurement.

NOTE: SFAC 7 addresses measurement issues, not recognition questions.

EXAMPLE

SFAC 7 does not specify **when** fresh-start measurements are appropriate. Fresh-start measurements are defined by the FASB as measurements in periods following initial recognition that establish a new carrying amount unrelated to previous amounts and accounting conventions.

2] SFAC 7 applies only to measurements at initial recognition, fresh-start measurements, and amortization techniques based on future cash flows.

3] SFAC 7 does not apply to measurements based on the amount of cash or other assets paid or received, or on observation of fair values in the marketplace.

   a] If such observations or transactions are present, the measurement would be based on them, not on future cash flows. The marketplace assessment of present value is already embodied in the transaction price.

(b) The framework provides general principles governing the use of present value, especially when the amount of future cash flows, their timing, or both, are uncertain. The framework provided by SFAC 7 also describes the objective of present value in accounting measurements.

    1] The present value formula is a tool used to incorporate the time value of money in a measurement. Thus, it is useful in financial reporting whenever an item is measured using estimated future cash flows.

    2] The FASB defines present value as the current measure of an estimated future cash inflow or outflow, discounted at an interest rate for the number of periods between today and the date of the estimated cash flow.

    3] The objective of using present value in an accounting measurement is to capture, to the extent possible, the economic difference between sets of future cash flows.

(c) Assets with the same cash flows are distinguished from one another by the timing and uncertainty of those cash flows.

> **NOTE:** Accounting measurement based on undiscounted cash flows would measure assets with the same cash flows at the same amount.

EXAMPLE

An asset with a contractual cash flow of $28,000 due in ten days would be equal to an asset with an *expected* cash flow of $28,000 due in ten years.

    1] Present value helps to distinguish between cash flows that might otherwise appear similar.

    2] A present value measurement that incorporates the uncertainty in estimated cash flows always provides more relevant information than a measurement based on the undiscounted sum of those cash flows, or a discounted measurement that ignores uncertainty.

(d) To provide relevant information for financial reporting, present value must represent some observable measurement attribute of assets or liabilities. This attribute is fair value. Fair value is "the price that would be received to sell an asset or paid to transfer a liability in an orderly transaction between market participants at the measurement date under market conditions."

(e) **The only objective of present value, when used in accounting measurements at initial recognition and fresh-start measurements, is to estimate fair value.**

    1] In the absence of observed transaction prices, accounting measurements at initial recognition and fresh-start measurements should attempt to capture the elements that taken together would comprise a market price if one existed.

        a] Marketplace participants attribute prices to assets and liabilities. In doing so they distinguish the risks and rewards of one asset or liability from those of another. An observed market price encompasses the consensus view of all marketplace participants about an asset's or liability's utility, future cash flows, the uncertainties surrounding those cash flows, and the amount that marketplace participants demand for bearing those uncertainties.

        b] While the expectations of an entity's management are often useful and informative in estimating asset and liability values, the marketplace is the final judge of asset and liability values. An entity is required to pay the market's price when it acquires an asset or settles a liability in a current transaction, regardless of the intentions or expectations of the entity's management. Therefore, for measurements at initial recognition or for fresh-start measurements, fair value provides the most complete and representationally faithful measurement of the economic characteristics of an asset or a liability.

(f) A present value measurement that is able to capture the economic differences between various assets and liabilities would include the following elements according to SFAC 7:

    1] An estimate of the future cash flow, or in more complex cases, series of future cash flows at different times.

    2] Expectations about possible variations in the amount or timing of those cash flows.

    3] The time value of money, represented by the risk-free rate of interest.

    4] The price for bearing the uncertainty inherent in the asset or liability.

    5] Other, sometimes unidentifiable factors, including illiquidity and market imperfections.

(g) SFAC 7 contrasts two approaches to computing present value. Either approach may be used to estimate the fair value of an asset or a liability, depending on the circumstances.

    1] In the expected cash flow approach only the time value of money, represented by the risk-free rate of interest, is included in the discount rate; the other factors cause adjustments in arriving at risk-adjusted expected cash flows.

    2] In a traditional approach to present value, adjustments for factors [2] – [5] are embedded in the discount rate.

(h) While techniques used to estimate future cash flows and interest rates vary due to situational differences, certain general principles govern any application of present value techniques in measuring assets. These are discussed in the outline of SFAC 7.

(i) Traditionally, accounting applications of present value have used a single set of estimated cash flows and a single interest rate, often described as "the rate commensurate with risk."

    1] The *discount rate adjustment approach* assumes that a single interest rate convention can reflect all of the expectations about future cash flows and the appropriate risk premium. While the traditional approach may be adequate for some simple measurements, the FASB found that it does not provide the tools needed to address more complex problems.

    2] The *expected cash flow (present value) approach* was found to be a more effective measurement tool than the discount rate adjustment approach in many situations. **The expected cash flow approach** uses all expectations about possible cash flows instead of the single most-likely cash flow. The expected cash flow approach focuses on direct analysis of the cash flows in question and on explicit assumptions about the range of possible estimated cash flows and their respective probabilities.

EXAMPLE

A cash flow might be $100, $200, or $300 with probabilities of 10%, 60%, and 30%, respectively. The expected cash flow is $220 ($100 × .1) + ($200 × .6) + ($300 × .3) = $220. However, the traditional approach would choose $200 as the best estimate or most-likely amount.

    3] When the timing of cash flows is uncertain, the expected cash flow approach allows present value techniques to be utilized. The following example is from SFAC 7.

EXAMPLE

A cash flow of $1,000 may be received in one year, two years, or three years with probabilities of 10%, 60%, and 30%, respectively. Notice that the expected present value of $892.36 differs from the traditional notion of a best estimate of $902.73 (the 60% probability). The following shows the computation of expected present value:

Present value of $1,000 in one year at 5%	$952.38	
Probability	10.00%	$95.24
Present value of $1,000 in two years at 5.25%	$902.73	
Probability	60.00%	541.64
Present value of $1,000 in three years at 5.50%	$851.61	
Probability	30.00%	255.48
Expected present value		$892.36

---

    a] An interest rate in a traditional present value computation is unable to reflect any uncertainties in the timing of cash flows.

    b] By incorporating a range of possible outcomes (with their respective timing differences), the expected cash flow approach accommodates the use of present value techniques when the timing of cash flows is uncertain.

(j) An estimate of fair value should include an adjustment for risk.

    1] The risk adjustment is the price that marketplace participants are able to receive for bearing the uncertainties in cash flows.

    2] This assumes that the amount is identifiable, measurable, and significant.

    3] Present value measurements occur under conditions of uncertainty. In SFAC 7, the term **uncertainty** refers to the fact that the cash flows used in a present value measurement are estimates, rather than known amounts. Uncertainty has accounting implications because it has economic consequences. Business and individuals routinely enter into transactions based on expectations about uncertain future events. The outcome of those events will place the entity in a financial position that may be better or worse than expected, but until the uncertainties are resolved, the entity is **at risk**.

4] In common usage, the word **risk** refers to any exposure to uncertainty in which that exposure has potential negative consequences. Risk is a relational concept. A particular risk can only be understood in context. In most situations, marketplace participants are said to be **risk adverse**. They prefer situations with less uncertainty relative to an expected outcome. Marketplace participants seek compensation for accepting uncertainty. This is referred to as a **risk premium**. They demand more compensation (a higher premium) to assume a liability with expected cash flows that are uncertain, than to assume a liability with cash flows of the same expected amount but no uncertainty. This phenomenon can be described with the financial axiom, "the greater the risk, the greater the return." The objective of including uncertainty and risk in accounting measurements is to imitate, to the extent possible, the market's behavior toward assets and liabilities with uncertain cash flows.

(k) If prices for an asset or liability or an essentially similar asset or liability can be observed in the marketplace, there is no need to use present value measurements. The marketplace assessment of present value is already embodied in the price. However, if observed prices are unavailable, present value measurements are often the best available technique with which to estimate what a price would be.

(l) The measurement of liabilities sometimes involves problems different from those encountered in the measurement of assets. Thus, measurement of liabilities may require different techniques in arriving at fair value. Liabilities can be held by individuals who sell their rights differently than they would sell other assets. Liabilities are sometimes settled through assumption by a third party. To estimate the liability's fair value, accountants must estimate the price necessary to pay the third party to assume the liability.

1] The most relevant measure of a liability always reflects the credit standing of the entity obligated to pay. An entity's credit standing affects the interest rate at which it borrows in the marketplace. The initial proceeds of a loan, therefore, always reflect the entity's credit standing at that time. Likewise, the price at which others buy and sell the entity's loan includes their assessment of the entity's ability to repay. The failure to include changes in credit standing in the measurement of a liability ignores economic differences between liabilities.

(m) Present value techniques are also used in periodic reporting conventions knows collectively as **interest methods of allocation**. Financial statements usually attempt to represent changes in assets and liabilities from one period to the next. In principle, the purpose of all accounting allocations is to report changes in the value, utility, or substance of assets and liabilities over time.

1] Accounting allocations attempt to relate the change in an asset or liability to some observable real-world phenomenon. An interest method of allocation relates changes in the reported amount with changes in the present value of a set of future cash inflows or outflows. However, allocation methods are only representations. They are not measurements of an asset or liability. The selection of a particular allocation method and the underlying assumptions always involves a degree of arbitrariness. As a result, no allocation method can be demonstrated to be superior to others in all circumstances. The FASB will continue to decide whether to require an interest method of allocation on a project-by-project basis. Refer to the outline of SFAC 7 for further information regarding the interest method of allocation.

> **NOW REVIEW MULTIPLE-CHOICE QUESTIONS 18 THROUGH 25 IN VOLUME 2**

2. **Income Determination** (See outlines of SFAC 5, 6, and 8.)

   a. The primary objective of accounting is to measure income. Income is a measure of management's efficiency in combining the factors of production into desired goods and services.

   (1) Efficient firms with prospects of increased efficiency (higher profits) have greater access to financial capital and at lower costs. Their stock usually sells at a higher price-earnings ratio than the stock of a company with less enthusiastic prospects. The credit rating of the prospectively efficient company is probably higher than the prospectively less efficient company. Thus, the "cost of capital" will be lower for the company with the brighter outlook (i.e., lower stock dividend yield rates and/or lower interest rates).

b. The entire process of acquiring the factors of production, processing them, and selling the resulting goods and services produces revenue. The acquisition of raw materials is part of the revenue-producing process, as is providing warranty protection.

c. Under the accrual basis of accounting, revenue is generally recognized at the point of sale (ASC Topic 605) or as service is performed. The point of sale is when title passes: generally when seller ships (FOB shipping point) or when buyer receives (FOB destination).

   (1) Three exceptions exist to the general revenue recognition rule: during production, at the point where production is complete, and at the point of cash collection. The table below compares the three exceptions with the general revenue recognition rule (point of sale).

Recognition basis/ source of GAAP	Accounting method	Criteria for use of basis	Reason(s) for departing from sale basis
• **Point of sale/ ASC Topic 605**	• Transactions approach (sales basis)	• Exchange has taken place • Earnings process is (virtually) complete	
• **During production basis/ASC Topic 605**	• Percentage-of-completion	• Long-term construction,* property, or service contract • Dependable estimates of extent of progress and cost to complete • Reasonable assurance of collectibility of contract price	• Availability of evidence of ultimate proceeds • Better measure of periodic income • Avoidance of fluctuations in revenues, expenses, and income
• **Completion-of-production basis/ ASC Topic 330**	• Net realizable value	• Immediate marketability at quoted prices • Unit interchangeability • Difficulty of determining costs	• Known or determinable revenues • Inability to determine costs and thereby defer expense recognition until sale
• **Cash collection basis/ASC Topic 605**	• Installment and cost recovery methods	• Absence of a reasonable basis for estimating degree of collectibility	• Level of uncertainty with respect to collection of the receivable precludes recognition of gross profit before cash is received

* Note that the "completed contract" method for construction contracts is not a departure from the sale basis.

SOURCE: Adapted from Henry R. Jaenicke, *Survey of Present Practices in Recognizing Revenues, Expenses, Gains, and Losses,* FASB, 1981.

   (2) Under accrual accounting, expenses are recognized as related revenues are recognized, that is, (product) expenses are matched with revenues. Some (period) expenses, however, cannot be associated with particular revenues. These expenses are recognized as incurred.

   (a) **Product costs** are those which can be associated with particular sales (e.g., cost of sales). Product costs attach to a unit of product and become an expense only when the unit to which they attach is sold. This is known as associating "cause and effect."

   (b) **Period costs** are not particularly or conveniently assignable to a product. They become expenses due to the passage of time by

      1] Immediate recognition if the future benefit cannot be measured (e.g., advertising)
      2] Systematic and rational allocation if benefits are produced in certain future periods (e.g., asset depreciation)

   (c) Thus, income is the net effect of inflows of revenue and outflows of expense during a period of time. The period in which revenues and expenses are taken to the income statement (recognized) is determined by the above criteria.

   (3) **Cash basis accounting**, in contrast to accrual basis accounting, recognizes income when cash is received and expenses when cash is disbursed. Cash basis accounting is subject to manipulation (i.e., cash receipts and expenses can be switched from one year to another by management). Another reason for adopting accrual basis accounting is that economic transactions have become more involved and multiperiod. An expenditure for a fixed asset may produce revenue for years and years.

> **NOW REVIEW MULTIPLE-CHOICE QUESTIONS 26 THROUGH 28 IN VOLUME 2**

3. **Accruals and Deferrals**

   a. **Accrual**—accrual-basis recognition precedes (leads to) cash receipt/expenditure

      (1) Revenue—recognition of revenue earned, but not received

      (2) Expense—recognition of expense incurred, but not paid

  b. **Deferral**—cash receipt/expenditure precedes (leads to) accrual-basis recognition

      (1) Revenue—postponement of recognition of revenue; cash is received, but revenue is not earned

      (2) Expense—postponement of recognition of expense; cash is paid, but expense is not incurred

      (3) A deferral postpones recognition of revenue or expense by placing the amount in liability or asset accounts.

      (4) Two methods are possible for deferring revenues and expenses depending on whether real or nominal accounts are originally used to record the cash transaction.

EXAMPLE

BOOKKEEPING METHODS

Deferrals of Expense

	Expense method			Asset method	
When paid	Insurance expense	xx		Prepaid insurance	xx
	Cash		xx	Cash		xx
Year-end	Prepaid insurance	xx		Insurance expense	xx
	Insurance expense		xx	Prepaid insurance		xx
Reverse	Yes			No	

Deferrals of Revenue

	Revenue method			Liability method	
When received	Cash	xx		Cash	xx
	Rent revenue		xx	Unearned rent		xx
Year-end	Rent revenue	xx		Unearned rent	xx
	Unearned rent		xx	Rent revenue		xx
Reverse	Yes			No	

Accruals

	Expense			Revenue	
Adjustment	Wages expense	xx		Interest receivable	xx
	Wages payable		xx	Interest revenue		xx
Reverse	Yes			Yes	

---

  c. Entries are reversed for bookkeeping expediency. If accruals are reversed, the subsequent cash transaction is reflected in the associated nominal account. If accruals are not reversed, the subsequent cash transaction must be apportioned between a nominal and real account.

      Cash   (amount received)

          Revenue   (earned in current period)

         Revenue receivable   (accrual at last year-end)

      (1) Accruals do not have two methods, but can be complicated by failure to reverse adjusting entries (also true for deferrals initially recorded in nominal accounts).

4. **Cash to Accrual**

  a. Many smaller companies use the **cash basis** of accounting, where revenues are recorded when cash is received and expenses are recorded when cash is paid (except for purchases of fixed assets, which are capitalized and depreciated). Often the accountant is called upon to convert cash basis accounting records to the accrual basis. This type of problem is also found on the CPA examination.

  b. When making journal entries to adjust from the cash basis to the accrual basis, it is important to identify two types of amounts:

      (1) The **current balance** in the given account (cash basis) and

      (2) The **correct balance** in the account (accrual basis).

         (a) The journal entries must adjust the account balances from their current amounts to the correct amounts.

  c. It is also important to understand relationships between balance sheet accounts and income statement accounts.

(1) When adjusting a balance sheet account from the cash basis to the accrual basis, the other half of the entry will generally be to the related income statement account. Thus, when adjusting accounts receivable, the related account is sales; for accounts payable, purchases; for prepaid rent, rent expense; and so on.

EXAMPLE

Assume a company adjusts to the accrual basis every 12/31; during the year, they use the cash basis. The 12/31/10 balance in accounts receivable, after adjustment, is $17,000. During 2011, whenever cash is collected, the company debits cash and credits sales. Therefore, the 12/31/11 balance in accounts receivable **before adjustment** is still $17,000. Suppose the **correct** 12/31/11 balance in accounts receivable is $28,000. The necessary entry is

Accounts receivable	11,000	
Sales		11,000

This entry not only corrects the accounts receivable account, but also increases sales since unrecorded receivables means that there are also unrecorded sales. On the other hand, suppose the **correct** 12/31/11 balance of accounts receivable is $12,500. The necessary entry is

Sales	4,500	
Accounts receivable		4,500

Sales is debited because during 2011, $4,500 more cash was collected on account than should be reported as sales. When cash is received on account the transaction is recorded as a credit to sales, not accounts receivable. This overstates the sales account.

EXAMPLE

Some problems do not require journal entries, but instead a computation of accrual amounts from cash basis amounts, as in the example below.

	12/31/10	12/31/11	2011
Rent payable	$4,000	$6,000	
Prepaid rent	8,000	4,500	
Cash paid for rent			$27,000

The rent expense can be computed using either T-accounts or a formula.

T-accounts are shown below.

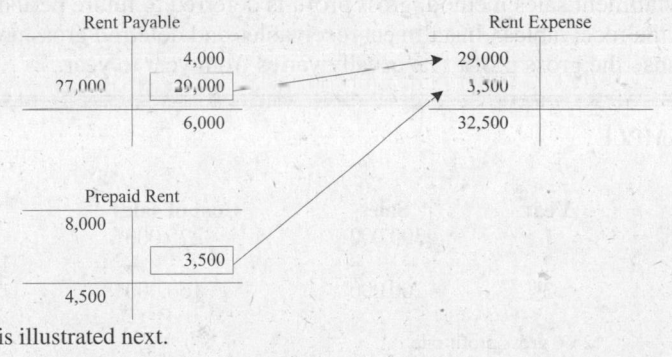

The use of a formula is illustrated next.

Payments		Beginning prepaid		Ending payable		Ending prepaid		Beginning payable		Expense
$27,000	+	8,000	+	6,000	–	4,500	–	4,000	=	$32,500

(2) Formulas for conversion of various income statement amounts from the cash basis to the accrual basis are summarized in the following equations.

 (a) Since the accrual-basis numbers can be derived with T-accounts, you should not have to memorize the formulas.

Cash basis		*Additions*		*Deductions*		*Accrual basis*
Collections from sales	+	Ending AR (a) / AR written off (b)	–	Beginning AR (c)	=	Sales
Collections from other revenues	+	Beginning unearned revenue (d) / Ending revenue receivable (e)	–	Ending unearned revenue (f) / Beginning revenue receivable (g)	=	Other revenues
Payments for purchases	+	Beginning inventory (h) / Ending AP (i)	–	Ending inventory (j) / Beginning AP (k)	=	Cost of goods sold
Payments for expenses	+	Beginning prepaid expenses (l) / Ending accrued expenses payable (m)	–	Ending prepaid expenses (n) / Beginning accrued expenses payable (o)	=	Operating expenses*

*Provision must also be made for depreciation expense and similar write-offs and bad debt expense.

(a) Ending AR and related sales have not yet been recorded
(b) AR written off reduced AR but did not result in cash collected
(c) Beginning AR was collected and recorded as sale during the period but was sale of the prior period
(d) Beginning unearned revenue was collected and recorded as revenue in the prior period but was earned in the current period
(e) Ending revenue receivable was earned during the period but has not yet been recorded because it has not been collected
(f) Ending unearned revenue was recorded upon collection as revenue but has not yet been earned
(g) Beginning revenue receivable was recorded during the current period upon collection as revenue but was earned last period
(h) Beginning inventory was sold during the period
(i) Ending AP and related purchases have not yet been recorded
(j) Ending inventory must be excluded from cost of goods sold
(k) Beginning AP reflects purchases last period which were not paid for or recorded until the current period
(l) Beginning prepaid expenses were recorded as expenses when paid in a prior period but are expenses of the current period
(m) Ending accrued expenses payable have not yet been recorded
(n) Ending prepaid expenses were recorded as expenses when paid this period but are expenses of future periods
(o) Beginning accrued expenses payable were recorded currently as expenses when paid but are expenses of the prior period

---

NOW REVIEW MULTIPLE-CHOICE QUESTIONS 29 THROUGH 53 IN VOLUME 2

---

5. **Installment Sales**

a. Revenue is recognized as cash is collected. Thus, revenue recognition takes place at the point of cash collection rather than the point of sale. Installment sales accounting can only be used where "collection of the sale price is not reasonably assured" (ASC Topic 605) (APB 10).

b. Under the installment sales method, gross profit is deferred to future periods and recognized proportionately to collection of the receivables. Installment receivables and deferred gross profit accounts must be kept separate by year, because the gross profit rate usually varies from year to year.

EXAMPLE

			Collections of	
Year	Sales	Cost of sales	Year 1	Year 3
1	300,000	225,000*	80,000	--
2	--	--	120,000	--
3	200,000	160,000**	100,000	100,000

*25% gross profit rate
**20% gross profit rate

To record sale	Year 1	Year 2	Year 3
Install AR-1	300,000	--	--
Install AR-3	--	--	200,000
Install sales	300,000	--	200,000
To record cash receipt			
Cash	80,000	120,000	200,000
Install AR-1	80,000	120,000	100,000
Install AR-3	--	--	100,000

To record CGS

Install cost of sales	225,000	--	160,000
Inventory (or Purchases)	225,000	--	160,000
To defer gross profit			
Install sales	300,000	--	200,000
Install cost of sales	225,000	--	160,000
Deferred install GP-1	75,000	--	--
Deferred install GP-3	--	--	40,000

	Year 1	**Year 2**	**Year 3**
To recognize gross profit			
Deferred install GP-1	20,000^a	30,000^b	25,000^c
Deferred install GP-3	--	--	20,000^d
GP realized on install method	20,000	30,000	45,000

^{a}(25% × 80,000) ^{c}(25% × 100,000)
^{b}(25% × 120,000) ^{d}(20% × 100,000)

c. Summary of accounts used in installment sales accounting

BALANCE SHEET

Cash			Installment AR—Year 1			Installment AR—Year 3	
(B)			Ending balance from year 1 sales	(B)		(A)	(B)

Inventory (or Purchases)			Deferred Gross Profit—Year 1			Deferred Gross Profit—Year 3	
	(C)		(E)	Ending balance from year 1 installment sales		(E)	(D)

INCOME STATEMENT

Cost of Installment Sales			Installment Sales	
(C)	(D)		(D)	(A)

Realized Gross Profit on Installment Sales			Income Summary	
(F)	(E)			(F)

Explanation of Select Journal Entries

(A) To record installment sales
(B) To record cash collected from year one and year three installment receivables
(C) To record cost of goods sold (perpetual or periodic) for year one and year three
(D) To close installment sales and cost of installment sales accounts
(E) To remove gross profit realized through collections from the deferred gross profit account
      (Gross profit rate for year one × Cash collections from year one receivables)
      (Gross profit rate for year two × Cash collections from year three receivables)
(F) To close realized gross profit at year-end

6. **Cost Recovery Method**

    a. The cost recovery method is similar to the installment sales method in that gross profit on the sale is deferred. The difference is that no profit is recognized until the cumulative receipts exceed the cost of the asset sold.

    > **EXAMPLE**
    >
    > In our installment sales example, the entire profit from year one sales ($75,000) would be recognized in year three. Profit on year three sales will be recognized in year four to the extent that in year four cash collections on year three sales exceed the $60,000 ($160,000 cost – $100,000 cash collected) unrecovered cost on year three sales.

    b. If interest revenue was to be earned by the seller, it would likewise be deferred until the entire cost was recovered.

    c. The cost recovery method is used when the uncertainty of collection is so great that even use of the installment method is precluded.

NOW REVIEW MULTIPLE-CHOICE QUESTIONS 54 THROUGH 66 IN VOLUME 2

7. **Franchise Agreements**

   a. ASC Topic 952 (SFAS 45—see outline) provides that the initial franchise fee be recognized as revenue by the franchiser **only** upon substantial performance of their initial service obligation.
   b. The amount and timing of revenue recognized depends upon whether the contract contains bargain purchase agreements, tangible property, and whether the continuing franchise fees are reasonable in relation to future service obligations.
   c. Direct franchise costs are deferred until the related revenue is recognized.

8. **Real Estate Transactions**

   a. Accounting treatment for real estate sales is provided by ASC Topics 360 and 976 (SFAS 66). Due to the variety of methods of financing real estate transactions, determining when the risks and rewards of ownership have been clearly transferred and when revenue should be recognized becomes very complex.
   b. Profit from real estate sales may be recognized in full, provided the profit is determinable and the earnings process is virtually complete. Additionally, the following four criteria must be met to recognize profit in full at the point of sale:

      (1) A sale is consummated.
      (2) The buyer's initial and continuing investments are adequate to demonstrate a commitment to pay for the property.
      (3) The seller's receivable is not subject to future subordination.
      (4) The seller has transferred to the buyer the usual risks and rewards of ownership in a transaction that is, in substance, a sale and does not have a substantial continuing involvement in the property.

   c. Depending on which combination of criteria is met, the real estate sales will be recorded using one of the following methods:

      (1) Deposit.
      (2) Cost recovery.
      (3) Installment.
      (4) Reduced profit.
      (5) Percentage-of-completion.
      (6) Full accrual.

         (a) The deposit and reduced profit methods require explanation. In accordance with the **deposit method**, payments received are recorded as a liability until the contract is canceled or a sale is achieved.
         (b) Under the **reduced profit method**, the seller recognizes a portion of profit at the time of sale with the remaining portion recognized in future periods. Profit recognized at the time of sale is determined by calculating the present value of the buyer's receivable and applying a formula. The reduced profit recognized at the time of sale is the gross profit less the present value of the receivable as determined above. The remaining profit is recognized in future periods. See the outline of SFAS 66.

9. **Multiple-Deliverable Revenue Arrangements**
   Another exception to the general revenue recognition principles is for multiple-deliverable revenue arrangements.

   a. If an entity has revenue generating activities to provide multiple products or services at different times, the arrangement should be evaluated to determine if there are separate units being delivered. Two conditions must be met for an item to be considered a separate unit of accounting:

      (1) The delivered item has value on a stand-alone basis (i.e., it can be sold separately by the vendor or customer) and
      (2) If the arrangement includes a right of return for the delivered item, the undelivered item must be substantially in control of the vendor.
      (3) If it meets both requirements, the revenue arrangement is divided into separate units based on the relative selling prices. Revenue recognition criteria are then applied to each of the separate units.

10. **Research or Development Accounted for on the Milestone Basis**

    a. The **milestone method** of accounting may be used in accounting for research and development arrangements in which revenue (payments) to the vendor is contingent on achieving one or more substantive milestones related to deliverables or units of accounting.

       (1) A substantive milestone is an uncertain event that can only be achieved based on the vendor's performance and

         (a) It is commensurate with the vendor's performance or enhancement of value resulting from the vendor's performance.
         (b) It relates solely to past performance.
         (c) It is reasonable relative to all of the deliverables and payment terms.

       (2) If all of these circumstances are met, the vendor may recognize the contingent revenue in its entirety in the period in which the milestone is achieved.

    b. The notes to the financial statements should disclose its accounting policy for the recognition of milestone payments. In addition the following should be disclosed:

       (1) A description of the overall arrangement.
       (2) A description of each milestone and related contingent consideration.
       (3) A determination of whether each milestone is considered substantive.
       (4) The factors considered in determining whether the milestones are substantive.
       (5) The amount of consideration recognized during the period for the milestone or milestones.

11. **Software Revenue Recognition**

    a. Software products that require significant production, modification, or customization should be accounted for using ASC Topic 605 (ARB 45, *Long-Term Construction-Type Contracts*).

       (1) Software products that are included with tangible products (i.e., hardware) and are required for the product's functionality are excluded from these software revenue recognition rules.

    b. Software products that do not require significant production, modification, or customization should recognize revenue when all of the following criteria are met:

       (1) Persuasive evidence of an arrangement exists.
       (2) Delivery has occurred.
       (3) Vendor's fee is fixed or determinable.
       (4) Collectibility is probable.

    c. The portion of the fee allocated to an element should be recognized using the same list of criteria.

       (1) Delivery of an element is considered not to have occurred if other elements essential to the functionality of it are undelivered.
       (2) No portion of the fee meets the criterion of collectibility if the portion of the fee allocable to delivered elements is subject to forfeiture, refund, or other concession if undelivered elements are not delivered.

    d. Arrangement that includes multiple elements should allocate the fee to the elements based on vendor-specific objective evidence of fair value, regardless of stated prices in a contract.

    (1) Multiple elements

       (a) Arrangements consisting of multiple software deliverables including

         1] Software products.
         2] Upgrades/enhancements.
         3] Postcontract customer service (PCS).
         4] Services.
         5] Elements deliverable on a when-and-if-available basis.

    (2) Vendor-specific objective evidence of fair value

       (a) Limited to

         1] Price charged when the same element is sold separately.
         2] Price established by management if not sold separately yet. It should be probable that the price will not change before being sold separately.

       (b) Amount allocated to an undelivered element should not be adjusted. If it is probable that the amount allocated will result in a loss, ASC Topic 450, *Contingencies* (SFAS 5), should be followed.

    (3) Insufficient vendor-specific objective evidence of fair value

       (a) Defer revenue until whichever one of the following occurs first:

　　　　　　　　1] Sufficient vendor-specific objective evidence does exist.
　　　　　　　　2] All elements have been delivered.

　　　　　　(b) Exceptions

　　　　　　　　1] The PCS is the only undelivered element—recognize entire fee ratably.
　　　　　　　　2] Only undelivered element is services that don't require significant production, modification, or customization—recognize the entire fee over the period in which the services will be performed.
　　　　　　　　3] Arrangement is a subscription in substance—recognize entire fee ratably.
　　　　　　　　4] Fee based on the number of copies.

　　　e. Separate accounting for service element of an arrangement is required if both of following criteria met

　　　　　(1) Services not essential to functionality of any other element of the transaction.
　　　　　(2) Services are described in the contract such that total price of the arrangement would be expected to vary as result of inclusion or exclusion of the services.

12. **Sales Basis Criteria for Selected Transactions**

　　a. Under GAAP, specific rules have been developed which are stated in the form of conditions which must be met before it is acceptable to recognize profit from "a sale in the ordinary course of business."　Unfortunately, these rules represent a patchwork set of criteria for applying the sales basis of revenue recognition.　This patchwork set of criteria contains many inconsistencies either in the results obtained or in the rationale justifying the criteria.

　　b. The table below summarizes the criteria which have been devised for applying the sales basis to selected transactions involving the sale of assets.

Recognition issue/ source of GAAP	Factors to be considered before recognizing revenue on the sale basis	Conditions that cause recognition to be delayed beyond time of sale
• **Sale with a right of return/ASC Topic 605 (SFAS 48)**	• Whether economic substance of the transaction is a sale or a financing arrangement • Determination of sales price • Probability of collection of sales price • Seller's future obligations • Predictability of returns	• Sales price not fixed or determinable • Payment excused until product is sold • Payment excused if property stolen or damaged • Buyer without separate economic substance • Seller's obligation to bring about resale of the property • Inability to predict future returns
• **Product financing arrangement/ ASC Topic 470 (SFAS 49)**	• Whether risks and rewards of ownership are transferred	• Agreement requires repurchase at specified prices or provides compensation for losses
• **Real estate sale/ ASC Topics 360 and 976 (SFAS 66)**	• Probability of collection • Seller's continued involvement • Whether economic substance of the transaction is a sale of real estate or another type of transaction such as a service contract	• Inadequate buyer investment in the property • Seller's continuing obligations, such as participation in future losses, responsibility to obtain financing, construct buildings, or initiate or support operations
• **Sales-type lease/ ASC Topic 840 (SFAS 13)**	• Transfer of benefits and risks of ownership • Probability of collection • Predictability of future unreimbursable costs	• Inability to meet conditions specified above for real estate sales • Inability to meet specified conditions (four criteria) indicating transfer of benefits and risks of ownership • Collectibility not predictable • Uncertainty about future unreimbursable costs
• **Sale of receivables with recourse/ ASC Topic 860 (SFAS 140)**	• Isolation of transferred assets • Right to pledge or exchange transferred assets • Control of receivables	• Transferred assets can be reached by transferor or its creditors • Transferee's inability to pledge or exchange transferred assets • Control of receivables not surrendered due to repurchase or redemption agreement

Recognition issue/ source of GAAP	Factors to be considered before recognizing revenue on the sale basis	Conditions that cause recognition to be delayed beyond time of sale
• Nonmonetary exchange/ASC Topic 845 (APB 29 and SFAS 153)	• Transaction has commercial substance	• Fair value not determinable • Exchange transaction to facilitate sales to customers • Transaction lacks commercial substance
• Sale-leaseback transaction/ASC Topic 840 (SFAS 13)	• Substance of the transaction • Portion of property leased back • Length of leaseback period	• All sale-leaseback transactions are financing transactions and not sales transactions unless leaseback covers only a small part of the property or is for a short period of time

SOURCE: Adapted from Henry R. Jaenicke, *Survey of Present Practices in Recognizing Revenues, Expenses, Gains, and Losses*, FASB, 1981.

13. **Reporting Start-up Costs**

ASC Topic 720-15 (Statement of Position (SOP) 98-5) provides the guidance for accounting for a company's start-up costs. These costs include those incurred during the course of undertaking one-time activities related to opening a new facility, introducing a new product or service, conducting business in a new territory, conducting business with a new class of customer or beneficiary, initiating a new process in an existing facility, commencing some new operation, or organizing a new entity. ASC Topic 720-15 requires start-up costs to be expensed rather than capitalized.

NOW REVIEW MULTIPLE-CHOICE QUESTIONS 67 THROUGH 73 IN VOLUME 2

14. **Research Component—Accounting Standards Codification**

a. Basic concepts are included in the Financial Accounting Concepts (SFACs). However, the concept statements are not considered authoritative literature, and, therefore, are not included in the Accounting Standards Codification (ASC).

b. The Accounting Standards Codification database uses the following categories on the main menu: Presentation, Assets, Liabilities, Equity, Revenue, Expenses, Broad Transactions, Industry, and Master Glossary. Under each of these main categories are Topics. Topics are further divided into subtopics, sections, and subsections.

c. Citations in this text for information on a certain topic are cited as ASC Topic XXX. Complete citations for a specific rule are referenced by topic-subtopic-section-subsection. An example of a full research citation is ASC 350-10-25-1.

d. The following table lists the topical areas within the Codification.

Presentation

105	Generally Accepted Accounting Principles
205	Presentation of Financial Statements
210	Balance Sheet
215	Statement of Shareholder Equity
220	Comprehensive Income
225	Income Statement
230	Statement of Cash Flows
235	Notes to Financial Statements
250	Accounting Changes and Error Corrections
255	Changing Prices
260	Earnings per Share
270	Interim Reporting
272	Limited Liability Entities
274	Personal Financial Statements
275	Risks and Uncertainties
280	Segment Reporting

Assets

305	Cash and Cash Equivalents
310	Receivables
320	Investments—Debt and Equity Securities
323	Investments—Equity Method and Joint Ventures
325	Investments—Other
330	Inventory
340	Deferred Costs and Other Assets
350	Intangibles—Goodwill and Other
360	Property, Plant, and Equipment

Liabilities

405	Liabilities
410	Asset Retirement and Environmental Obligations
420	Exit or Disposal Cost Obligations
430	Deferred Revenue
440	Commitments
450	Contingencies
460	Guarantees
470	Debt
480	Distinguishing Liabilities from Equity

Equity

505	Equity

Revenue

605	Revenue

Expenses

705	Cost of Sales and Services
710	Compensation—General
712	Compensation—Nonretirement Postemployment Benefits
715	Compensation—Retirement Benefits
718	Compensation—Stock Compensation

720 Other Expenses	835 Interest
730 Research and Development	840 Leases
740 Income Taxes	845 Nonmonetary Transactions
	850 Related-Party Disclosures
Broad Transactions	852 Reorganizations
805 Business Combinations	855 Subsequent Events
810 Consolidation	860 Transfers and Servicing
815 Derivatives and Hedging	
820 Fair Value Measurements and Disclosures	**Industry**
825 Financial Instruments	905 through 995
830 Foreign Currency Matters	

> **NOTE:** The accounting rules for development stage enterprises, franchising, not-for-profit entities, real estate, and software issues are located under "Industry" in the Codification. SEC content is included in each topic as appropriate and labeled "S." The SEC content is provided for convenience and is not the complete SEC literature.

e. Keywords for researching basic concepts are shown below.

Area franchise	Installment accounting	Sales type lease
Bargain purchase	Installment method	Sales value
Capital surplus	Net income	Security interest
Collectibility	Persuasive evidence arrangement	Seller obligation
Collection reasonably assured	Proceeds of sale	Services substantially performed
Consummated sale	Product financing	Significant customization
Consummation sale	Product financing arrangements	Significant production
Continuing franchise fees	Profit and loss	Software products
Continuing involvement	Profit on transactions	Specified prices resale
Culmination of earning process	Reasonable estimate returns	Sponsor purchase
Earned surplus	Recognizing revenue software	Sponsor repurchase
Fair value determinable	Related transaction purchase	Sponsor sells
Financial asset	Repurchase product	Substantial performance
Franchise fee revenue	Retained earnings	Substantially identical product
Franchisee	Return privilege expired	Transaction completed
Franchisor	Revenue recognized	Transfer financial asset
Full accrual method	Right of return	Unrealized profit
Initial franchise fee	Sales leaseback	Vendor specific evidence
Initial services	Sales price	

15. **International Financial Reporting Standards (IFRS)**

a. The International Accounting Standards Committee (IASC) issued International Accounting Standards (IAS) from 1973 to 2001. In addition, the IASC created a Standing Interpretations Committee (SIC) that provided further interpretive guidance on accounting issues not addressed in the standards. In 2001, the International Accounting Standards Board (IASB) replaced the IASC. The IASB adopted the existing International Accounting Standards (IAS) and interpretations issued by the Standing Interpretations Committee (SIC). Since 2001, the IASB is responsible for issuing International Financial Reporting Standards (IFRS), and the IFRS Interpretations Committee (IFRIC) is responsible for issuing interpretations of the standards. Therefore, the current international accounting guidelines are contained in the IAS and IFRS pronouncements, together with SIC and IFRIC interpretations.

b. It is often said that US GAAP employs a "rules"-based approach. In other words, the standards are usually explicit as to precise rules that must be followed for recognition, measurement, and financial statement presentation. IFRS, on the other hand, is considered a "principles"-based approach because it attempts to set general principles for recognition, measurement and reporting, and allows professional judgment in applying these

principles. This principles-based approach should focus on a true and fair view or a fair representation of the financial information.
- c. In 2002, the FASB and the IASB agreed to work toward convergence in the accounting standards. Therefore, you will find some IFRS accounting treatments identical, some similar, and others different from US GAAP. An effective study strategy is to study US GAAP and then learn the significant differences between US GAAP and IFRS. This compare/contrast strategy will help the candidate to remember which method is US GAAP and which method is IFRS. As you study this module, notice the differences in the following areas:

    (1) **Vocabulary or definition differences.** Although the concepts of US GAAP and IFRS may be similar, vocabulary and definitions are often somewhat different.
    (2) **Recognition and measurement differences.** Differences may exist in when and how an item is recognized in the financial statements. Alternative methods may be acceptable in US GAAP whereas only one method may be allowed for IFRS (or vice versa). In some instances, either IFRS or US GAAP may not require an item to be recognized in the financial statements. In addition, the amount recognized (measurement of the item) may be different in the two sets of standards.
    (3) **Presentation and disclosure differences.** Presentation refers to the presentation of items on the financial statements, whereas disclosure refers to the additional information contained in the notes to financial statements. Again, differences exist as to whether an item must be presented in the financial statements or disclosed in the footnotes, as well as the types of information that must be disclosed.
    (4) The table below highlights the major accounting differences between US GAAP and IFRS.

Major Differences— US GAAP versus IFRS

US GAAP	IFRS
Financial Statement Presentation	
No specific requirement regarding comparative information.	Requires comparative information for prior year.
Comprehensive income may be presented as a stand-alone statement or at the bottom of the income statement and changes in equity may be presented in the notes.	Requires a separate statement of comprehensive income and statement of changes in equity.
Presentation of certain items as extraordinary is required.	Extraordinary items are not allowed.
Revenue Recognition	
Construction contracts are accounted for using the percentage-of-completion method if certain criteria are met. Otherwise the completed-contract method is used.	Construction contracts are accounted for using the percentage-of-completion method if certain criteria are met. Otherwise, revenue recognition is limited to the costs incurred. The completed-contract method is not allowed.
Consolidated Financial Statements	
No exemption from consolidating subsidiaries in general-purpose financial statements.	Under certain restrictive situations a subsidiary (normally required to be consolidated) may be exempt from the requirement.
Noncontrolling interest measured at fair value.	Noncontrolling interest may be measured either at fair value or the proportionate share of the value of the identifiable assets and liabilities of the acquiree.
Monetary Current Assets and Current Liabilities	
Short-term obligations expected to be refinanced can be classified as noncurrent if the entity has the intent and ability to refinance.	Short-term obligations expected to be refinanced can be classified as noncurrent only if the entity has entered into an agreement to refinance prior to the balance sheet date.
Contingencies that are probable and can be reasonably estimated are accrued.	Contingencies that are probable and measurable are considered provisions and accrued.
Inventory	
LIFO cost flow assumption is an acceptable method.	The LIFO cost flow assumption is not allowed.
Inventories are valued at lower of cost of market (between a floor and a ceiling).	Inventories are valued at lower of cost or net realizable value.
Any impairment write-downs create a new cost basis; previously recognized impairment losses are not reversed.	Previously recognized impairment losses are reversed.
Fixed Assets	
Revaluation not permitted.	Revaluation of assets is permitted as an election for an entire class of assets but must be done consistently.
No separate accounting for investment property.	Separate accounting is prescribed for investment property versus property, plant, and equipment.

US GAAP	IFRS
Unless the assets are "held for sale" they are valued using the cost model.	Investment property may be measured at fair value.
Biological assets are not a separate category.	Biological assets are a separate category and not included in property, plant, and equipment.
There is no requirement to account for separate components of an asset.	If the major components of an asset have significantly different patterns of consumption or economic benefits, the entity must allocate the costs to the major components and depreciate them separately.
Impairment losses are not reversed.	Impairment losses may be reversed in future periods.

Financial Investments

Compound (hybrid) financial instruments are not split into debt and equity components unless certain requirements are met, but they may be bifurcated into debt and derivative components.	Compound financial interests (e.g., convertible bonds) are split into debt, equity and, if applicable, derivative components.
Declines in fair value below cost may result in impairment loss solely based on a change in interest rate unless entity has the ability and intent to hold the debt till maturity.	Generally, only evidence of a credit default results in impairment loss for an available-for-sale debt instrument.
When impairment is recognized through the income statement, a new cost basis is established and such losses cannot be reversed.	Impairment losses in available-for-sale investments may be reversed in future periods.
Unless the fair value option is elected, loans and receivables are classified as either (1) held for investment, which is measured at amortized cost, or (2) held for sale, which is measured at lower of cost or fair value.	Loans and receivables are measured at amortized cost unless classified into the Fair Value Through Profit or Loss category or the Available-for-Sale category, both of which are carried at fair value.

Leases

Operating leased assets are never recorded on the balance sheet.	Assets held by lessee under operating leases may be capitalized on the balance sheet if they meet certain requirements.
A lease for land and building that transfers ownership to the lessee or contains a bargain purchase option would be classified as a capital lease regardless of the relative value of the land. If the fair value of the land at inception represents 25% or more of the total fair value, the lessee must consider the components separately when evaluating the lease.	When land and buildings are leased, elements of the lease are considered separately when evaluating the lease unless the amount for the land element is immaterial.

Income Taxes

Deferred tax assets are recognized in full but valuation allowances reduce them to the amount that is more likely than not to be realized.	Deferred tax assets are recognized only to the extent it is probable that they will be realized.

d. **Underlying Concepts—The IASB *Framework***

(1) The IASB *Framework for the Preparation and Presentation of Financial Statements* establishes the underlying concepts for preparing financial statements.
(2) This framework addresses the objectives of financial statements, underlying assumptions, qualitative characteristics of financial statement information, definitions, recognition, measurement, and capital maintenance concepts.
(3) Although the IASB *Framework* contains information similar to the Statement of Financial Accounting Concepts by the US Financial Accounting Standards Board (FASB), several important differences exist.

    (a) First, some terms and definitions are different.
    (b) Second, the elements of financial statements are not identical.
    (c) Candidates should become familiar with these subtle differences in the two sets of concepts.

(4) The IASB *Framework* is not considered an accounting standard and therefore does not override any accounting treatment required by the International Accounting Standards (IAS) or International Financial Reporting Standards (IFRS). The *Framework* exists to assist in the development of future international accounting standards and to assist preparers in accounting for topics that do not have guidance in an existing standard.
(5) In September 2010, the IASB completed two chapters on a joint conceptual framework project with the FASB.

    (a) The new conceptual framework contains Chapter 1, The Objective of General-Purpose Financial Reporting, and Chapter 3, Qualitative Characteristics of Useful Financial Information.

(b) Because this is a joint project, the FASB and IASB chapters 1 and 3 are identical. You may refer to the information earlier in this chapter on those topics.

(c) However, until the remaining parts of the joint project are completed, there are subtle differences between the two frameworks. The most significant differences are terms, definitions, and elements of financial statements.

(6) FASB SFAC 6 contains ten elements of financial statements: assets, liabilities, equity, investments by owners, distributions to owners, comprehensive income, revenues, expenses, gains, and losses. The IASB *Framework* contains only five elements: assets, liabilities, equity, income, and expense.

> **NOTE:** There are several significant vocabulary differences regarding the elements of financial statements. With US GAAP, the term "income" is not a financial statement element. In US GAAP, the term income is used to describe a calculation of some type (e.g., income from continuing operations, net income) or to designate a specific type of income such as interest income. However, with IFRS, the term income is a financial statement element, and the items that are considered "income" are revenues and gains. IFRS uses the term "profit" whereas US GAAP uses the term "net income."

(7) The IASB *Framework*'s formal definitions of the five elements are shown below.

IASB *Framework*—Elements of Financial Statements	
Asset	An asset is a resource controlled by the entity as a result of past events and from which future economic benefits are expected to flow to the entity.
Liability	A liability is a present obligation of the entity arising from past events, the settlement of which is expected to result in an outflow from the entity of resources embodying economic benefits.
Equity	Equity is the residual interest in the assets of the entity after deducting all its liabilities.
Income	Income is increases in economic benefits during the accounting period in the form of inflows or enhancements of assets or decreases of liabilities that result in increases in equity, other than those relating to contributions from equity participants.
Expenses	Expenses are decreases in economic benefits during the accounting period in the form of outflows or depletions of assets or incurrence of liabilities that result in decreases in equity, other than those relating to distributions to equity participants.

(a) An important point to understand is that the definition of income includes both revenue and gains. Revenues arise in the normal course of business and are often referred to as sales, fees, interest, dividends, royalties, and rent. Gains are other items that meet the definition of income, which may or may not arise in the normal course of business. The IASB *Framework* indicates that gains are increases in economic benefits and are no different in nature from revenues. Therefore, they are not regarded as a separate element in the *Framework*. The *Framework* treats losses in the same way, as no different in nature from other expenses. However, the *Framework* also indicates that when gains or losses are reported in the income statement, they are usually displayed separately because this knowledge may be useful to the decision maker. Gains may be reported net of their related expenses, and losses may be reported net of their related income.

(8) The IASB *Framework* provides for capital maintenance adjustments. When assets or liabilities are revalued or restated, and there is a corresponding increase or decrease to equity, the definition of income or expense may not be met. Therefore, certain items may be included in equity as revaluation reserves.

(9) The IASB *Framework* defines recognition as the process of incorporating into the balance sheet or income statement an item that meets the definition of an element and satisfies the criteria for recognition.

(a) The two criteria for recognition are (1) it is probable that a future economic benefit will flow to the entity, and (2) the item has a cost or value that can be measured reliably.

(10) The *Framework* also outlines various bases of measurement such as historical cost, current cost, realizable (settlement) value, and present value. Current cost is the amount of cash or cash equivalent that would be paid if the same or equivalent asset were acquired currently. Realizable (settlement) value is the amount of cash that could be currently obtained by settling (e.g., selling) the asset in an orderly disposal. Although the measurement basis is commonly historical cost, certain accounts use different measurement methods.

e. **Revenue Recognition.** As indicated above, revenue is the gross inflow of economic benefits resulting from an entity's ordinary activities. These inflows must increase equity and not increase the contribution of owners or equity participants. Revenue is generated from the sale of goods, the rendering of services, and the use of an entity's assets by others. Various titles are used for revenue including sales, fees, interest, dividends, and royalties. Revenue is measured at the fair value of the consideration received or the receivable, net of trade discounts or rebates.

(1) Revenue is recognized from the sale of goods if all five of the following criteria are met:

  (a) The significant risks and rewards of ownership of the goods are transferred to the buyer,
  (b) The entity does not retain either a continuing managerial involvement or control over the goods,
  (c) The amount of revenue can be measured reliably,
  (d) It is probable that economic benefits will flow to the entity from the transaction, and
  (e) The costs incurred can be measured reliably.

(2) Revenue can be recognized from rendering services when the outcome of rendering services can be estimated reliably. This method is often referred to as the percentage-of-completion method.

> **NOTE:** Progress payments or advances from customers are not used to determine the state of completion. The outcomes can be estimated reliably if all the following criteria are met:
>
> 1. The amount of revenue can be measured reliably,
> 2. It is probable that economic benefits will flow to the entity,
> 3. The stage of completion at the end of the reporting period can be measured reliably, and
> 4. The costs incurred and the costs to complete the transaction can be measured reliably.

  (a) If the outcomes cannot be estimated reliably, then revenue should be recognized using the cost recovery method.

      1] The cost recovery method recognizes revenue only to the extent that the expenses recognized are recoverable.

> **NOTE:** IFRS does not permit use of the completed-contract method, which is allowed for US GAAP.

(3) Barter transactions are not recognized if the exchanged goods are similar in nature and value. If the goods are dissimilar, revenue is recognized at fair value of the goods received. If the fair value of the goods received cannot be measured, revenue is recognized at the fair value of goods or services given up.

(4) Interest income is recognized using the effective interest method. Royalties should be accrued as provided for in the contractual agreement. Dividends should be recognized when the shareholder has a right to receive the dividend payment.

f. **First-Time Adoption of IFRS.** There are a number of options available upon first-time adoption of IFRS, as described below.

(1) Generally the adoption involves restating assets, liabilities, and equity using IFRS principles. The "date of transition to IFRS" is defined as the beginning of the earliest period for which an entity presents full comparative information under IFRSs in its first IFRS financial statements. The "first IFRS reporting period" is defined as the latest reporting period covered by an entity's first IFRS financial statements.

(2) **Business combinations.** With respect to business combinations, the first-time adopter has the option of retrospectively adopting IFRS 3 for all periods presented, or adjusting the assets and liabilities through retained earnings in the period of adoption.

(3) **Plant, property, and equipment.** Unless an entity decides to use a fair value election, it will need to recalculate the life-to-date depreciation or amortization of any PPE or intangible assets under IFRS. This can be quite time-consuming. Alternatively, the entity may use various methods to determine the fair value of the assets and use those amounts as the deemed cost at the time of adoption. IFRS would then be used going forward. The fair value election may be applied on an individual item basis.

> **NOW REVIEW MULTIPLE-CHOICE QUESTIONS 74 THROUGH 83 IN VOLUME 2**

KEY TERMS

Accounting Standards Codification (ASC). The single source for all US GAAP.
Accrual. Recognition precedes cash receipt/expenditure.
Accrual basis. Expenses are recognized as related revenues are recognized.
Cash basis. Recognizes income when cash is received and expenses when cash is disbursed.
Current cost. The amount of cash, or its equivalent, that would be paid if the same asset were to be acquired currently.

Current market value. The amount of cash, or its equivalent, that could be obtained by selling as asset in orderly liquidation.

Deferral. Cash receipt/expenditure precedes accrual-basis recognition.

Fair value. The price that would be received to sell an asset or paid to transfer a liability in an orderly transaction between market participants at the measurement date under current market conditions.

Historical cost. The amount of cash, or its equivalent, paid to acquire an asset.

Installment sales. Revenue is recognized as cash is collected.

Net realizable value. The nondiscounted amount of cash, or its equivalent, into which an asset is expected to be converted during the normal course of business less direct costs to make the conversion.

Period costs. Costs not particularly or conveniently assignable to a product.

Present value. The current measure of an estimated future cash inflow or outflow, discounted at an interest rate for the number of period between today and the date of the estimated cash outflow.

Product costs. Costs which can be associated with particular sales.

Realized (realizable). When related assets received or held are readily convertible into known amounts of cash or claims to cash.

Risk adverse. Market place participants prefer situations with less uncertainty relative to an expected outcome.

Start-up costs. The costs incurred during the course of undertaking on-time activities related to opening a new facility.

B. Error Correction

1. Accountants must be in a position to anticipate, locate, and correct errors in their functions of systems and procedures design, controllership, and attestation.

   a. Errors which are discovered in the same year that they are made are corrected by

      (1) Determining the entry that was made
      (2) Determining the correct entry
      (3) Analyzing increases or decreases needed in affected accounts
      (4) Making the correct entry

   b. Errors in classification (e.g., sales expense instead of R&D expense) affect only one period.
   c. Nonsystematic errors in adjusting entries (e.g., an error in ending inventory of one period) affect two periods and are known as self-correcting (counterbalancing) errors.

> **EXAMPLE**
>
> Overstating ending inventory of 2010 will overstate the income of 2010 and understate the income of 2011.

   d. Other errors will affect the income of several periods, such as misrecording the cost of a long-lived asset (i.e., depreciation will be misstated for all periods).

2. The chart below shows four examples of counterbalancing errors.

Errors Which Will Self-Correct After Two Years
Omitting Accruals

Case #1

	12/31/10	12/31/11	1/1/12
Expense (wages)	Understated	Overstated	Correct
Net income	Overstated	Understated	Correct
Payable (wages)	Understated	Correct	Correct
Retained earnings	Overstated	Correct	Correct

Case #2

Revenue (interest)	Understated	Overstated	Correct
Net income	Understated	Overstated	Correct
Receivable (interest)	Understated	Correct	Correct
Retained earnings	Understated	Correct	Correct

Omitting Deferrals (Prepaids)

Case #3

Expense (insurance)	Overstated	Understated	Correct
Net income	Understated	Overstated	Correct
Prepaid asset	Understated	Correct	Correct
Retained earnings	Understated	Correct	Correct

Case #4

Revenue (unearned)	Overstated	Understated	Correct
Net income	Overstated	Understated	Correct
Liability (un. rev.)	Understated	Correct	Correct
Retained earnings	Overstated	Correct	Correct

NOTE: In all four cases the income statement errors have the opposite effect in 2010 and 2011. Also notice that by the end of 2011 the balance sheet accounts are correct. Therefore, even if the error is not discovered, the financial statements will be correct by the beginning of the third year.

3. When an error is discovered in a period subsequent to the period when the error occurred, an entry must be made to correct the accounts as if the error had not been made.

EXAMPLE

Assume the entry to accrue wage expense in the amount of $10,000 is omitted on 12/31/10. The effects that would be caused by such an omission may be categorized as follows:

	2010	2011	2012
Expense	Understated	Overstated	Correct
Income	Overstated	Understated	Correct
Wages payable	Understated	Correct	Correct
Retained earnings	Overstated	Correct	Correct

If the company follows the policy of reversing adjusting entries for accruals, then correction of the error any time during 2011 will require

Adjustment to correct error	10,000	
Wage expense		10,000

The adjustment account, when closed to retained earnings, will correct for the 1/1/11 overstatement in retained earnings due to the overstatement of 2010 income. The credit to wage expense will reduce the expense account for 2011 to an amount equal to 2011 wages.

If the error was discovered in 2012, no entry would be required since the error self-corrects during 2011. The 2012 balances would be the same with or without the error.

NOTE: The requirements of error analysis questions vary considerably. When asked for the effect of errors, be careful to determine the effect rather than the correction; they are opposite. The effect of revenue overstatement on income is over or plus; therefore, the correction to income is to subtract. Also distinguish between correcting/adjusting entries (which can be made in the accounts to correct the current period) and "worksheet entries" which adjust amounts reported in prior periods (i.e., journal entries are not recorded to correct nominal accounts of prior periods).

4. Accounting errors are errors in recognition, measurement, presentation, or disclosure in the financial statements. An error can occur from mathematical mistakes, mistakes in applying GAAP, or oversight of facts that existed when the financial statements were prepared. A change in accounting principle from non-GAAP to GAAP is also a correction of an error.

   a. An error in the financial statements is treated as a prior period adjustment by restating the prior period financial statements. The cumulative effect of the error is reflected in the carrying value of assets and liabilities at the beginning of the first period presented, with an offsetting adjustment to the opening balance in retained earnings for that period. Financial statements for each period are then adjusted to reflect the correction of the period-specific effects of the error.

   b. Footnote disclosures should disclose that the previously issued financial statements were restated, along with a description of the error. The line item effects of the error and any per share amounts must also be disclosed for each period presented. The gross effects and net effects from applicable income taxes on the net income of the prior period must be disclosed, as well as the effects on retained earnings and net income. Footnote disclosures must also indicate the cumulative effect of the change on retained earnings or other components of equity or net assets at the beginning of the earliest period presented. Once the correction of the error is disclosed, the financial statements of subsequent years do not need to repeat the disclosures.

EXAMPLE

Income Statement Effects

	Year 1	Year 2	Year 3
Wages expense	− $10,000	+ $10,000	-0-
Income tax expense	+ 3,000	− 3,000	-0-
Net income	+ 7,000	− 7,000	-0-

Comparative Income Statement
Issued in Year 3, for Year 2 and Year 3

	Year 2 Restated	Year 3
Wages expense	($ xxxx − 10,000)	$ xxxx
Income tax expense	($ xxx+ 3,000)	$ xxxx
Net income	($ xxx+ 7,000)	$ xxxx

Balance Sheet

	Year 1	Year 2	Year 3
Wages payable	− $10,000	-0-	-0-
Taxes payable	+ 3,000	-0-	-0-
Retained earnings	+ 7,000	-0-	-0-

Comparative Retained Earnings Statement
Issued in Year 3, for Year 2 and Year 3

	Year 2 as restated	Year 3
Beginning balance	$ xxxx	$ xxxx
Prior period adjustment — Understatment of wages expense (net of tax $3,000)	− 7,000	--
Retained earnings as adjusted	$ xxxx	$ xxxx
Net income as corrected	xxxx	xxxx
Dividends	(xxxx)	(xxxx)
Ending retained earnings	$ xxxx	$ xxxx

5. Inventory errors have an impact on both the balance sheet and the income statement.

   a. Inventory errors include a misstatement of the ending inventory balance, which is followed by a misstatement of the beginning balance for the next period, or an inventory error could be a misstatement of purchases for the period.

   b. The analysis of inventory errors in a periodic inventory system is facilitated by setting up a statement of cost of goods sold. The statement of cost of goods sold shows the relationship between the inventory and purchases accounts and the impact of incorrect amounts.

   c. The four examples shown below use the statement of cost of goods sold format to analyze different inventory errors. Items that are correct are identified by an "OK," while items that are incorrect are listed as overstated (over) or understated (under).

EXAMPLE

INVENTORY ERRORS

	Case #1 (Overstated Inventory Count)		Case #2 (Understated Inventory Count)	
	2010	2011	2010	2011
Beginning inventory	OK	Over	OK	Under
+ Purchases	OK	OK	OK	OK
Goods available for sale	OK	Over	OK	Under
− Ending inventory*	Over	OK	Under	OK
Cost of goods sold	Under	Over	Over	Under
Net income	Over	Under	Under	Over
Retained earnings	Over	OK	Under	OK
Accounts payable	OK	OK	OK	OK

* Determined by physical count.

	Case #3 (Overstated Purchases**)		Case #4 (Understated Purchases***)	
	2010	2011	2010	2011
Beginning inventory	OK	OK	OK	Under
+ Purchases	Over	Under	Under	Over
Goods available for sale	Over	Under	Under	OK
− Ending inventory*	OK	OK	Under	OK
Cost of goods sold	Over	Under	OK	OK
Net income	Under	Over	OK	OK
Retained earnings	Under	OK	OK	OK
Accounts payable	Over	OK	Under	OK

* Determined by physical count.
** Vendor shipped goods FOB destination. Goods were not received by 12/31, but recorded as purchases and not included in physical inventory count.
*** Vendor shipped goods FOB shipping point prior to 12/31, but not recorded as purchases or included in physical inventory count.

6. Research Component—Accounting Standards Codification

ASC Topic 250, found in the Presentation area of the Codification, outlines the accounting rules for accounting changes and error corrections. Keywords for researching accounting errors are shown below.

Correction error	Period-specific effects	Prior period adjustments error
Disclosure correction error	Prior period adjustment	Reporting correction error

7. International Financial Reporting Standards (IFRS)

Accounting for error correction is similar to US GAAP. A prior period error includes arithmetic mistakes, mistakes in applying accounting policies, and mistakes in recognition, measurement, presentation or disclosures in the financial statements. IFRS requires the entity to correct the error by restating the comparative amounts for prior periods. If the error occurred before the earliest period presented, then the opening balances of assets, liabilities, and equity should be restated for the earliest period presented. Similar to US GAAP, if it is impracticable to determine the periodic effects of the error, comparative information is restated from the earliest date practicable.

NOW REVIEW MULTIPLE-CHOICE QUESTIONS 1 THROUGH 15 IN VOLUME 2

C. Accounting Changes

Accounting changes include a change in accounting principle, a change in estimate, or a change in the reporting entity. The correction of an error in previous financial statements is not an accounting change. The statement further defines two important terms: restatement and retrospective application. A **restatement** is the process of revising previously issued financial statements to correct an error. A **retrospective application** is the application of a different accounting principle to previously issued financial statements, as if that principle had always been used. Retrospective application is required for changes in accounting principle and changes in reporting entity.

1. Changes in Accounting Principles

a. An entity may change accounting principle only if the change is required by a newly issued accounting pronouncement, or if the entity can justify the use of the alternative accounting principle because it is **preferable**.

b. A change in accounting principle is accounted for through retrospective application of the new accounting principle to all prior periods, unless it is impracticable to do so. Retrospective changes require the following:

(1) The cumulative effects of the change are presented in the carrying amounts of assets and liabilities as of **the beginning of the first period presented**.

(2) An offsetting adjustment is made to the opening balance of retained earnings for that period (the beginning of the first period presented).

(3) Financial statements for each individual prior period presented are adjusted to reflect the **period-specific effects** of applying the new accounting principle.

(a) Only the **direct effects** of the change are recognized in prior periods. An example of a direct effect is an adjustment to an inventory balance due to a change in inventory valuation method. Related changes, such as the effect on deferred taxes or an impairment adjustment, are also considered direct effects and must be recognized in prior periods.

(b) **Indirect effects** are any changes to current or future cash flows that result from making a change in accounting principle. An example of an indirect effect is a change in a profit sharing or royalty payment based on revenue or net income. Any indirect effects of the change are reported in the period in which the accounting change is made.

(c) If the cumulative effect of applying the accounting change can be determined but the period-specific effects on all prior periods cannot be determined, the cumulative effect is applied to the carrying amounts of assets and liabilities at the beginning of the earliest period to which it can be applied or calculated. An offsetting adjustment is then made to the opening balance of retained earnings for that period.

EXAMPLE

Wagner Corporation began operations on January 1, 2009. On January 1, 2011, Wagner changes from the weighted-average method of accounting for inventory to the FIFO method. Wagner provides a profit-sharing plan for its employees. The bonus or profit-sharing plan allows all employees to share in a 5% bonus based on earnings before income taxes and bonus. The income tax rate for all periods is 30%. Assume there are no book/tax differences or deferred taxes. All taxes and bonuses are accrued at the end of each year on December 31 and paid in January of the following year.

Assume that Wagner's accounting records are adequate to determine the effects of the change in accounting principle for each year. Ending inventory for the weighted-average and FIFO methods are shown below.

Ending Inventory

	Weighted-average method	FIFO method
12-31-09	1,000	1,200
12-31-10	2,000	2,500
12-31-11	2,400	3,200

The income statements for 2009 through 2011 calculated using weighted-average method are shown below.

Wagner Corporation
Income Statements

	For the period ending 12-31-11 (before change)	For the period ending 12-31-10 (before change)	For the period ending 12-31-09 (before change)
Sales	$15,000	$12,000	$ 8,000
Less: Cost of good sold	(8,900)	(7,000)	(5,000)
Gross profit	6,100	5,000	3,000
Sales, general & admin. expenses	(3,500)	(3,000)	(2,000)

Earnings before bonus and income taxes	2,600	2,000	1,000
Bonus compensation expense	(130)	(100)	(50)
Earnings before income taxes	2,470	1,900	950
Income tax expense	(741)	(570)	(285)
Net income	$ 1,729	$ 1,330	$ 665

Balance sheets calculated using the weighted-average inventory method before the change to FIFO for 2009-2011 are shown below.

Wagner Corporation
Balance Sheets

	Dec. 31, 2011 (before change)	Dec. 31, 2010 (before change)	Dec. 31, 2009 (before change)
Cash	$ 1,900	$ 1,000	$ 1,000
Inventory	2,400	2,000	1,000
Plant, property, and equipment	11,000	10,000	10,000
Total assets	15,300	13,000	12,000
Accounts payable	1,370	1,000	1,665
Accrued bonus liability	130	100	50
Income tax liability	741	570	285
Total liabilities	2,241	1,670	2,000
Common stock	500	500	500
Additional paid-in capital	8,835	8,835	8,835
Retained earnings	3,724	1,995	665
Total liabilities and owners' equity	$15,300	$13,000	$12,000

To account for the change in accounting for inventory, the new accounting method is applied retrospectively. Retrospective application requires restatement of the financial statements for the period-specific effects. The period-specific effects for Wagner include the direct effects on inventory, cost of goods sold, income tax expense, and income tax liability for each period. The change in bonus compensation expense and accrued bonus liability are indirect effects and are accounted for in the year of the change, which is the current year, 2011.

To calculate the adjustments in inventory and cost of goods sold for each year, use a T-account. First, calculate the purchases for each year using the weighted-average method.

Inventory
(Weighted-average method)

1-1-09	-0-	5,000	CGS
Purchases	6,000		
12-31-09	1,000	7,000	CGS
Purchases	8,000		
12-31-10	2,000	8,900	CGS
Purchases	9,300		
12-31-11	2,400		

Then, using the amount of purchases for each period and the information given in the problem for ending inventory using the FIFO method, calculate the adjusted cost of goods sold for each period using the FIFO method.

Inventory
(FIFO method)

1-1-09	-0-	4,800	CGS
Purchases	6,000		
12-31-09	1,200	6,700	CGS
Purchases	8,000		
12-31-10	2,500	8,600	CGS
Purchases	9,300		
12-31-11	3,200		

After you have calculated the period-specific effects on ending inventory and cost of goods sold, prepare an adjusted income statement for each period.

The adjusted income statement for the period ending December 31, 2009, is shown below.

Wagner Corporation—Income Statement
For the year ending 12-31-09

	For the period ending 12-31-09 as originally reported	For the period ending 12-31-09 as adjusted	Effect of the change
Sales	$ 8,000	$ 8,000	$ --
Less: Cost of good sold	(5,000)	(4,800)	(200)
Gross profit	3,000	3,200	200
Sales, general & admin. expenses	(2,000)	2,000	--
Earnings before bonus and income taxes	1,000	1,200	200
Bonus compensation expense*	(50)	(50)*	--
Earnings before income taxes	950	1,150	200
Income tax expense	(285)	(345)	(60)
Net income	$ 665	$ 805	$ 140

* Bonus expense is an indirect effect of the change; therefore, bonus expense is not adjusted retrospectively. Instead, the indirect effects of the bonus are adjusted in the current year, 2011.

Wagner Corporation—Income Statement
For the year ending 12-31-10

	For the period ending 12-31-10 as originally reported	For the period ending 12-31-10 as adjusted	Effect of the change
Sales	$ 12,000	$ 12,000	$ --
Less: Cost of good sold	(7,000)	(6,700)	(300)
Gross profit	5,000	5,300	300
Sales, general & admin. expenses	(3,000)	3,000	--
Earnings before bonus and income taxes	2,000	2,300	300
Bonus compensation expense*	(100)	(100)*	--
Earnings before income taxes	1,900	2,200	300
Income tax expense	(570)	(660)	(90)
Net income	$ 1,330	$ 1,540	$ 210

* Bonus expense is an indirect effect of the change; therefore, it is adjusted and expensed in the current year, 2011.

Wagner Corporation—Income Statement
For the year ending 12-31-11

	For the period ending 12-31-11 current year before adjustment	For the period ending 12-31-11 as adjusted
Sales	$15,000	$15,000
Less: Cost of good sold	(8,900)	(8,600)
Gross profit	6,100	6,400
Sales, general & admin. expenses	(3,500)	(3,500)
Earnings before bonus and income taxes	2,600	2,900
Bonus compensation expense*	(130)	(170)*
Earnings before income taxes	2,470	2,730
Income tax expense	(741)	819
Net income	$ 1,729	$ 1,911

* Bonus compensation expense for 2011 is calculated as follows:

2011	Earnings before bonus and taxes	$2,900	x	5%	$145
2010	Adjustment to earnings before bonus and taxes	300	x	5%	15
2009	Adjustment to earnings before bonus and taxes	200	x	5%	10
	Total bonus compensation expense for 2011 (adjusted for effects of the accounting change)				$170

The adjusted income statements for years 2009 through 2011, resented on a comparative basis are shown below.

Wagner Corporation
Income Statement

	For the period ending 12-31-11	For the period ending 12-31-10 as adjusted	For the period ending 12-31-09 as adjusted
Sales	$15,000	$12,000	$ 8,000
Less: Cost of good sold	(8,600)	(6,700)	(4,800)
Gross profit	6,400	5,300	3,200
Sales, general & admin. expenses	(3,500)	(3,000)	(2,000)
Earnings before bonus and income taxes	2,900	2,300	1,200
Bonus compensation expense	(170)	(100)	(50)
Earnings before income taxes	2,730	2,200	1,150
Income tax expense	(819)	(660)	(345)
Net income	$ 1,911	$ 1,540	$ 805

The balance sheet is presented on a comparative basis for two years. Therefore, the assets and liabilities must be retrospectively adjusted for the period-specific effects as of December 31, 2010, the first year presented. In addition, any previous years' adjustment are shown as an adjustment to retained earnings for the earliest year presented.

Wagner Corporation—Balance Sheet
December 31, 2010

	Dec. 31, 2010 as originally reported	Dec. 31, 2010 as adjusted
Cash	$ 1,000	$ 1,000
Inventory	2,000	2,500
Plant, property, and equipment	10,000	10,000
Total assets	13,000	13,500
Accounts payable	1,000	1,000
Accrued bonus liability	100	100
Income tax liability	570	720*
Total liabilities	1,670	1,820
Common stock	500	500
Additional paid-in capital	8,835	8,835
Retained earnings	1,995	2,345**
Total liabilities and owners' equity	$13,000	$13,500

*   Tax liability is adjusted for the increase in income tax expense and income tax liability for 2009 and 2010 ($60 in 2009 and $90 in 2010, for a total of $150 increase in income tax liability).
** Retained earnings is adjusted as follows:

Retained earnings (with adjustments)	
665	NI 2009, as originally reported
140	Adjustment to NI for 2009
805	Bal. in R/E, 12-31-09 adjusted
1,330	NI 2010, as originally reported
210	Adjustment to NI for 2010
2,345	Bal. in R/E, 12-31-10 after adjustments
1,911	Net income in 2011 using FIFO method
4,256	Bal. in R/E, 12-31-11

The balance sheet presented on a comparative basis for two years, is as follows:

Wagner Corporation
Comparative Balance Sheets

	Dec. 31, 2011	Dec. 31, 2010 (as adjusted)
Cash	$ 1,900	$ 1,000
Inventory	3,200	2,500
Plant, property, and equipment	11,000	10,000
Total assets	16,100	13,500
Accounts payable	1,370	1,000
Accrued bonus liability	170*	100
Income tax liability	969**	720**
Total liabilities	2,509	1,820

	Dec. 31, 2011	Dec. 31, 2010 (as adjusted)
Common stock	500	500
Additional paid-in capital	8,835	8,835
Retained earnings	4,256	2,345**
Total liabilities and owners' equity	$16,100	$13,500

* Bonus liability calculation

Bonus liability will be accrued in 2011 and paid in 2012. Therefore, the bonus liability at the end of December 31, 2011, is calculated as follows:

2011	Earnings before bonus and taxes	$2,900	x	5%	$145
2010	Adjustment to earnings before bonus and taxes	300	x	5%	15
2009	Adjustment to earnings before bonus and taxes	200	x	5%	10
	Total bonus compensation liability as of 12-31-11 (adjusted for effects of the accounting change)				$170

** Tax liability calculation

Because the change in accounting method occurred in 2011, the tax liability resulting from the change will be accrued in 2011 and paid in January, 2012. The tax liability on the balance sheet is calculated as follows:

2011	Earnings before income taxes	$2,730	x	30%	$819
2010	Adjustment to earnings before income taxes	300	x	30%	90
2009	Adjustment to earnings before income taxes	200	x	30%	60
	Total tax liability for 2011 (adjusted for effects of the accounting change)				$969

c. If it is impracticable to determine the cumulative effect to any of the prior periods, the new accounting principle is applied as if the change was made prospectively at the earliest date practicable. It is considered impracticable only if one of the following three conditions is met:

(1) After making every reasonable effort to apply the new principle to the previous period, the entity is unable to do so.
(2) Retrospective application requires assumptions about management's intentions in a prior period that cannot be independently substantiated.
(3) Retrospective application requires significant estimates, and it is impossible to obtain objective information about the estimates.

d. Notes to the financial statements to describe a change in accounting principle must include

(1) The nature and reason for the change, and explanation as to why the new method is preferable
(2) The method of applying the change
(3) A description of the prior period information that is retrospectively adjusted
(4) The effect of the change on income from continuing operations, net income, and any other affected financial statement line item, and any affected per share amounts for the current period and all periods adjusted retrospectively
(5) The cumulative effect of the change on retained earnings or other components of equity or net assets as of the earliest period presented
(6) If retrospective application is impracticable, the reason, and a description of how the change was reported
(7) A description of the indirect effects of the change, including amounts recognized in the current period, and related per share amounts
(8) Unless impracticable, the amounts of the indirect effects of the change and the per share amounts for each prior period presented

e. Disclosures are also required for interim periods. In the year of the change to the new accounting principle, interim financial statements should disclose the effect of the change on income from continuing operations, net income, and related per share amounts for the postchange interim periods.

f. Once the change in method is disclosed, financial statements in subsequent periods do not need to repeat the disclosures.

NOW REVIEW MULTIPLE-CHOICE QUESTIONS 1 THROUGH 18 IN VOLUME 2

2. **Changes in Accounting Estimates**

    a. Changes in accounting estimates are accounted for on a prospective basis. The financial statements are not restated or retrospectively adjusted. The change is accounted for in the current period and future periods.

    b. If a change in accounting estimate is effected by a change in principle (e.g., a change in depreciation method), it is treated as a change in estimate.

    (1) In cases where an entity effects a change in estimate by changing an accounting principle, the footnote disclosures required by a change in accounting principle apply and must be included in the notes to the financial statements.

EXAMPLE

Gonzalez Corporation acquires equipment on January 1, 2009 for $100,000. Gonzalez depreciates the equipment using the double-declining balance method. The equipment has a ten-year life and a $20,000 salvage value. In January, 2011, Gonzalez changes its depreciation method to straight-line.

This change in depreciation method is considered a change in estimate effected by a change in accounting principle. According to ASC Topic 250, it is accounted for in the current year and future years.

Step 1: Calculate accumulated depreciation and book value at the beginning of the year of the change in depreciation method.

Double declining balance method

The double-declining rate is $\dfrac{1}{10} \times 2 = 20\%$

Year		Book value at beginning of year	Depreciation rate	Depreciation expense
2009	Year 1	$100,000	20%	$20,000
2010	Year 2	$ 80,000	20%	16,000
Accum. Depr. Jan. 1, 2011				$36,000

To calculate book value on January 1, 2011:

Historical cost	$100,000
– Accum. depr.	36,000
Book value 1-1-11	$ 64,000

Step 2: Calculate depreciation expense for current year and future years using the new method.

($64,000 BV – $20,000 salvage value) ÷ 8 years remaining life = $5,500 depreciation expense per year

Journal entry for 2011

In 2011 and in future years, the following depreciation entry is recorded:

Depreciation expense	5,500	
Accumulated depreciation		5,500

---

3. **Changes in Reporting Entities**

    a. Another type of accounting change is a change in reporting entity. A change in reporting entity occurs when a change in the structure of the organization is made which results in financial statements that represent a different or changed entity.

    (1) Some examples of a change in reporting entity include presenting consolidated statements in place of individual statements, a change in subsidiaries, or a change in the use of the equity method for an investment.

    b. When there is a change in reporting entity, the change is retrospectively applied to the financial statements of all prior periods presented. Previously issued interim statements are also presented on a retrospective basis. Footnote disclosures for change in reporting entity include the nature and reason for the change, net income, other comprehensive income, and any related per share amounts for all periods presented.

4. **Correction of an Error**

    a. A correction of an error in previously issued financial statements requires a prior period adjustment by restating the financial statements. Prior period adjustments are covered in the previous section of this module.

TYPES OF ACCOUNTING CHANGES

Type of accounting change	Definition	Financial statement treatment	Financial statement disclosure
1. Change in accounting principle	Change from the use of one generally accepted accounting principle to another generally accepted accounting principle	**Retrospective application:** Report cumulative effect of change in the carrying amounts of assets and liabilities as of the beginning of the first period presented, with an offsetting adjustment to the opening balance of retained earnings for that period. Financial statements for each period are adjusted to reflect period-specific effects of the change for direct effects.	Disclose the nature and reason for the change; method of applying the change; description of prior period information that is retrospectively adjusted; effect of the change on income from continuing operations, net income, and any other financial statement line item; per share amounts for current period and adjusted periods; and a description of the indirect effects of the change and related per share amounts.
2. Change in estimate	Change of estimated FS amount based on new information or experience	**Prospective:** Report in the period of the change and future periods. Do not adjust financial statements of previous periods.	Disclose the effect on income from continuing operations, net income, and related per share amounts if the change affects several future periods.
3. Change in reporting entity	Change that results in the financial statements representing a different entity	**Retrospective application:** Report financial statements of all periods to show financial information for the new reporting entity for those periods.	Disclose the type of change and the reasons for the change, the related effects on income before extraordinary items, net income, other comprehensive income, and related per share effects on EPS for all periods presented.

> **NOW REVIEW MULTIPLE-CHOICE QUESTIONS 19 THROUGH 26 IN VOLUME 2**

5. **International Financial Reporting Standards (IFRS)**

   a. **Change in accounting principle.** The rules for accounting changes are also similar to US GAAP.

      (1) Accounting changes may occur only when a change is required by an IFRS, or there is a voluntary change in accounting methods.

         (a) In the case of a new IFRS pronouncement, the transition rules in the new IFRS statement should be followed.

         (b) A voluntary change in accounting method may only be made if it provides reliable and more relevant information about the transactions, entity's financial position, performance, or cash flows.

            1] A voluntary change in accounting method is given retrospective application by applying the policy as if the new policy had always been applied. Retrospective application provides that the opening balance of equity is adjusted for the earliest period presented, and that other amounts are disclosed for each prior period as if the new accounting policy had always been applied.

            2] If it is impracticable to determine the effects of the change, then the change may be applied on a prospective basis.

      (2) Disclosures include the title of the IFRS requiring the change, the nature of the change, the amount of the adjustments to each financial statement line item, and effects on earnings per share.

   b. **Change in accounting estimate.** A change in accounting estimate occurs due to uncertainties in measuring items on the financial statements. Changes in estimates include changes in estimates for bad debts, inventory obsolescence, the fair value of financial assets or liabilities, the useful life of a depreciable asset, or warranty obligations. A change in estimate is accounted for on a prospective basis in the period of the change (current period) and future periods.

> **NOW REVIEW MULTIPLE-CHOICE QUESTIONS 27 THROUGH 29 IN VOLUME 2**

KEY TERMS

Prospective application. The change is accounted for in the current period and future periods.

Restatement. The process of revising previously issued financial statements to correct an error.

Retrospective application. The application of a different accounting principle to previously issued financial statements, as if that principle had always been used.

D. Financial Statements

1. Income and Retained Earnings Statement Formats

Income statements may be prepared using a multiple-step or single-step form. The income (earnings) and comprehensive income statement illustrated below for Totman Company includes separate categories for continuing operations, discontinued operations, and extraordinary items. The purpose of these separate categories is to enable users to assess future cash flows. Retrospective application is required for all changes in accounting principle. Other comprehensive income is required and may be disclosed in several methods (covered later in this module).

a. The Totman Company statement is a combined statement of income and comprehensive income.

EXAMPLE

Totman Company
STATEMENT OF EARNINGS AND COMPREHENSIVE INCOME
For the year Ended December 31, 2008

	Sales		$2,677
	Cost of goods sold		1,489
See	Gross margin on sales		1,188
Note	Operating expenses		
#5	Selling expenses	$ 220	
below	Administrative expenses	255	475
	Operating income		713
	Other revenues and gains		
	Interest revenue	$ 5	
	Equity in Huskie Co. earnings	15	
	Gain on sale of available-for-sale securities	45	65
	Other expenses and losses		
	Interest expense	(60)	
	Loss from permanent impairment of value of manufacturing facilities	(120)	(180)
	Income from continuing operations before provision for income taxes		598
	Provision for income taxes		
	Current	$ 189	
	Deferred	50	239
	Income from continuing operations		359(a)
	Discontinued operations:		
	Loss from operations of discontinued Division Z, including loss on disposal of $230	(1,265)	
	Income tax benefit	(466)	(799)(b)
	Income (loss) before extraordinary item		(440)
	Extraordinary item: Loss due earthquake (less applicable income taxes of $30)		(45)(b)
	Net earnings (loss)		(485)(a)
	Other comprehensive income:		
	Foreign currency translation adjustments (less applicable income taxes of $6)		26
	Unrealized gains on securities:		
	Unrealized holding gains arising during period (Less applicable income taxes of $43)	179	
	Less: reclassification adjustment (less applicable income taxes of $10) for gain		
	included in net income	(35)	144
	Other comprehensive income		170
	Comprehensive income		$ (315)

Note:

1. Assumes a tax rate of 40% on applicable items
2. (a) indicates where earnings per share (EPS) amounts would be necessary on the face of the IS. (b) EPS may be shown on the face of the income statement or in the notes. On the CPA exam, rather than memorizing these, simply calculate an EPS number for all numbers starting with income from continuing operations through net earnings.
3. Footnote explanations would also be required for many of the above events and transactions.
4. In the multiple-step format above, the Securities and Exchange Commission (SEC) requires that public companies place impairment losses in operating income instead of under "Other expenses and losses."
5. This is the format for a multiple-step income statement. A single-step income statement would differ only for the portion of the statement shown below. Otherwise, the single-step statement format is the same.

Revenues		
Sales	$2,677	
Interest	5	
Gain on sale of available-for-sale securities	45	
Equity in Huskie Co. earnings	15	
Total revenues		$2,742
Expenses		
Cost of goods sold	1,489	
Selling expenses	220	
Administrative expenses	255	
Interest expense	60	
Loss from permanent impairment of value of manufacturing facilities	120	
Total expenses		2,144
Income from continuing operations before provision for income taxes		598

b. The following chart summarizes the various category definitions and their placement on the income statement and retained earnings statement. These categories are all discussed in various parts of this module.

Income Statement and Retained Earnings Statement Categories

	Description	Definition	Placement on income statement or statement of retained earnings
1.	Unusual or Infrequent Items	An unusual or infrequent event considered to be material that does not qualify as extraordinary	Placed as part of income from continuing operations after normal recurring revenues and expenses
2.	Discontinued Operations*	Results from disposal of a business component	Placed as a separate category after income from continuing operations
3.	Extraordinary Items*	An unusual and infrequent nonrecurring event which has material effects	Placed as a separate category after discontinued operations
4.	Change in Accounting Principle:	Change from one generally accepted accounting principle to another	No longer on income statement. **Retrospective application:** Report cumulative effect of change in the carrying amounts of assets and liabilities as of the beginning of the first period presented, with an offsetting adjustment to the opening balance of retained earnings for that period. Financial statements for each period are adjusted to reflect period-specific effects of the change for direct effects.
5.	Correction of an Error	A correction of a material error from a prior period	Report as prior period adjustment by restating the prior-period financial statements. Cumulative effect of the error on prior periods is reflected in the carrying value of assets and liabilities at the beginning of the first period, with an offsetting adjustment made to the opening balance of retained earnings for that period. Financial statements are adjusted to reflect correction of period-specific effects of the error.

* These items are all presented net of applicable income tax effects.

2. **Unusual or Infrequent Items**

a. Items that are unusual or infrequent but not both should not be presented as extraordinary items. However, they are often presented in a separate section in the income statement above income before extraordinary items. A common example of such items is a "restructuring charge."

   (1) A restructuring is a program that is planned and controlled by management and materially changes either the scope of the business undertaken by the company, or the manner in which that business is conducted. Examples include

       (a) Sale or termination of a line of business
       (b) Closure of business activities in a particular location
       (c) Relocation of business activities from one location to another
       (d) Changes in management structure, or
       (e) Fundamental reorganizations that affect the nature and focus of operations

(2) Another unusual or infrequent item is accounting for the costs of exit and disposal activities (which include, among other items, restructurings). A liability for a cost associated with an exit or disposal activity should be recognized and measured initially at fair value in the period in which the liability is incurred. The fair value is usually determined as the present value of the estimated future payments discounted at the credit-adjusted, risk-free rate of interest.

   (a) In the unusual circumstance when fair value cannot be reasonably estimated, the liability shall be initially recognized in the period in which fair value can be reasonably estimated. Examples of such liabilities include

      1] Onetime termination benefits provided to current employees that are involuntarily terminated
      2] Costs to terminate a contract that is not a capital lease
      3] Costs to consolidate facilities or relocate employees

   (b) The recognition of the liability and expense for onetime termination benefits depends on whether the employees are required to provide services beyond the minimum retention period. If so, the expense is recognized over the period that the services are provided. If they are not required to provide future services, the liability is recognized when the plan is communicated to the employees.

   (c) In periods subsequent to initial measurement, changes to the liability shall be measured using the credit-adjusted risk-free rate that was used to measure the liability initially.

   (d) Costs associated with an exit or disposal activity that does not involve discontinued operations shall be included in income from continuing operations before income taxes. The footnotes to the financial statements should provide extensive disclosure of the activities.

3. **Discontinued Operations**

   a. As shown on the Totman Co. income statement, "Discontinued operations" is broken out separately. The "Loss from discontinued operations" includes the loss or income of the component for the period, and the gain or loss on its disposal. Income taxes or tax benefit are deducted from or added to that amount to determine the gain or loss after taxes.

   b. To qualify for treatment as discontinued operations the assets must comprise a component of the entity with operations and cash flows that are clearly distinguished, operationally and for financial reporting purposes, from the rest of the entity. A component may be a reportable or operating segment, a reporting unit, a subsidiary, or an asset group.

   c. To be reported as discontinued operations, two requirements must be met: (1) the operations and cash flows of the component have been (or will be) eliminated from the ongoing operations of the entity as a result of the disposal, and (2) the entity will not have any significant involvement in the operations of the component after disposal.

   d. Many of the assets disposed of as discontinued operations are long-lived assets. Accordingly, the component is classified as discontinued operations in the first period that it meets the criteria as being "held for sale":

      (1) Management commits to a plan of disposal.
      (2) The assets are available for sale.
      (3) An active program to locate a buyer has been initiated.
      (4) The sale is probable.
      (5) The asset is being actively marketed for sale at a fair price.
      (6) It is unlikely that the disposal plan will significantly change.

      (a) Long-lived assets classified as "held for sale" are reported at the lower of their carrying amounts or fair values less costs to sell. Therefore, the gain or loss on disposal of discontinued operations is the actual gain or loss if disposal occurs in the same period that the component meets the criteria to be classified as "held for sale."

      (b) If the criteria to classify the component as "held for sale" is met in a period before it is disposed of, the amount of the loss (if applicable) on disposal is an estimated loss resulting from the write-down of the group of assets to their estimated fair values. Estimated gains cannot be initially recognized.

      (c) However, if the component is held for sale over several reporting periods, estimated gains can be recognized based on new information but are limited to the amount of losses previously recognized.

      (d) Thus, the assets can be written up but not above their carrying amounts when they met the criteria as being held for sale.

   e. When "discontinued operations" are disclosed in a comparative income statement, the income statement presented for each previous year must be adjusted retroactively to enhance comparability with the current year's income statement. Accordingly, the revenues, cost of goods sold, and operating expenses (including income taxes) for the discontinued component are removed from the revenues, cost of goods sold, and operating expenses of continuing operations and are netted into one figure, that is, "Income (loss) from discontinued operations."

(1) The following excerpt from a comparative income statement shows the proper disclosure (2010 figures assumed).

	2011	2010
Discontinued operations:		
Loss from operations of discontinued Division Z, including loss on disposal in 2011 of $230	$699	$990
Income tax benefit	466	300

> **NOW REVIEW MULTIPLE-CHOICE QUESTIONS 1 THROUGH 32 IN VOLUME 2**

4. **Comprehensive Income**

   a. **Reporting.** Comprehensive income is the sum of net earnings (loss) and other comprehensive income. It requires disclosure of **changes during a period** of the following components of other comprehensive income: unrealized gains and losses on available-for-sale investments and foreign currency items, including any reclassification adjustments and any adjustments necessary to recognize the funding status of pension plans or other postemployment benefits.

   b. This standard allows the management of an enterprise two choices for presenting **other comprehensive income**. These are as follows:

      (1) At the bottom of income statement, continue from net income to arrive at a comprehensive income. An entity shall present the following:

         (a) A total amount for net income and its components.
         (b) A total amount for other comprehensive income and its components.
         (c) Total comprehensive income.

      (2) In a separate statement that may start with net income, (illustrated below) and that **directly** follows the statement of income. An entity shall present the following:

         (a) Net income and it's components in the statement of net income.
         (b) Comprehensive and its components along with total comprehensive income.

      The accumulated (total) comprehensive income shall be presented separately from retained earnings and additional paid in capital in the statement of financial position. The changes in the accumulated balances are to be presented in the notes to the financial statements or on the face of the financial statements. (See the balance sheet on the following page and the statement of changes in stockholders' equity at the beginning of Module 15).

   c. **Reclassification adjustments.** As unrealized gains (losses) recorded and reported in other comprehensive income for the current or prior periods are later realized, they are recognized and reported in net income. To avoid double counting it is necessary to reverse the unrealized amounts that have been recognized.

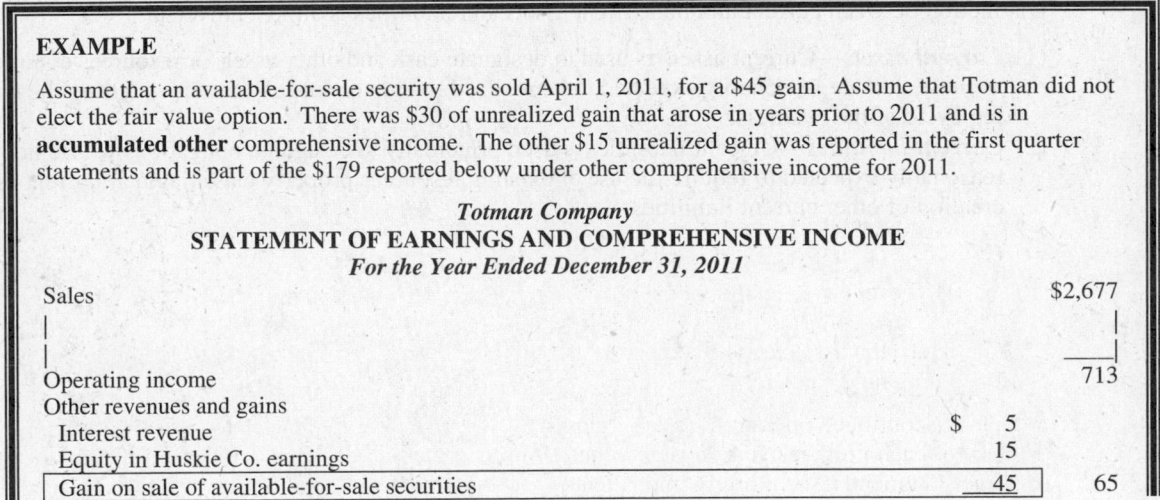

EXAMPLE

Assume that an available-for-sale security was sold April 1, 2011, for a $45 gain. Assume that Totman did not elect the fair value option. There was $30 of unrealized gain that arose in years prior to 2011 and is in **accumulated other** comprehensive income. The other $15 unrealized gain was reported in the first quarter statements and is part of the $179 reported below under other comprehensive income for 2011.

Totman Company
STATEMENT OF EARNINGS AND COMPREHENSIVE INCOME
For the Year Ended December 31, 2011

Sales		$2,677
		713
Operating income		713
Other revenues and gains		
Interest revenue	$ 5	
Equity in Huskie Co. earnings	15	
Gain on sale of available-for-sale securities	45	65

Other expenses and losses		
Interest expense	(60)	
Loss from permanent impairment of value of manufacturing facilities	(120)	(180)
Income from continuing operations before provision for income taxes		598
Provision for income taxes		
Current	$ 189	
Deferred	50	239
Income from continuing operations		359

Net earnings (loss)		(485)
Other comprehensive income:		
Foreign currency translation adjustments (less applicable income taxes of $6)		26
Unrealized gains on securities:		
Unrealized holding gains arising during period (less applicable income taxes of $43)	179	
Less: Reclassification adjustment (less applicable income taxes of $10) for gain in-cluded in net income	(35)	144
Other comprehensive income		170
Comprehensive income		$(315)

The reclassification adjustment to avoid double counting is $45 less a tax effect of $10 or $35 net. Since the $45 was realized in the current period, a realized gain of $45 was reported in the income from continuing operations under other revenues and gains above before provisions for income taxes of $598. The $10 of income tax on the $45 is reported as part of provision for income taxes in the current portion of income tax expense of $189. Recall that all items reported above the provision for income taxes are reported "gross," not net of taxes as in the case of items such as discontinued operations. Also, note the tax effects reported under other comprehensive income are **deferred** since the unrealized components are not recognized for tax purposes until realized.

d. **Balance sheet.** Accumulated other comprehensive income is reported in the stockholders' equity section of the balance sheet. When an entity has components of other comprehensive income, the total of these is closed to the balance sheet account entitled **accumulated other comprehensive income,** not retained earnings. In the case above, the other comprehensive income of $170 for the period would need to be closed to accumulated other comprehensive income, not retained earnings. The net loss is closed to retained earnings.

> **NOW REVIEW MULTIPLE-CHOICE QUESTIONS 33 THROUGH 46 IN VOLUME 2**

5. **Balance Sheets (Statements of Financial Position)**

a. Balance sheets or statements of financial position present assets, liabilities, and stockholders' equity. The balance sheet reports the effect of transactions at a point in time, whereas the statement of earnings (income) and comprehensive income, statement of retained earnings, and statement of cash flows report the effect of transactions over a period of time. An example of balance sheet classification and presentation is illustrated by the comprehensive balance sheet on the previous page.

b. Distinction between current and noncurrent assets and liabilities is almost universal.

  (1) *Current assets*—Current assets is used to designate cash and other assets or resources commonly identified as those that are reasonably expected to be realized in cash or sold or consumed during the normal operating cycle of the business.

  (2) *Current liabilities*—Current liabilities is used principally to designate obligations whose liquidation is reasonably expected to require the use of existing resources properly classifiable as current assets, or the creation of other current liabilities.

EXAMPLE

Totman Company
BALANCE SHEET
December 31, 2011

Assets			*Liabilities and Stockholders' Equity*		
Current assets:			*Current liabilities:*		
Cash and bank deposits:			Commercial paper and other short-term notes	$xxx	
Restricted to current bond maturity	$xxx		Accounts payable	xxx	
Unrestricted	xxx	$xxx	Salaries, wages, and commissions	xxx	
Short-term investments:			Taxes withheld from employees	xxx	
Marketable securities (Trading)		xxx	Income taxes payable	xxx	
Refundable income taxes		xxx	Dividends payable	xxx	
Receivables from affiliates		xxx	Rent revenue collected in advance	xxx	
Accounts receivable	xxx		Other advances from customers	xxx	
Less allowance for doubtful accounts	(xxx)	xxx	Current portion of long-term debt	xxx	
Notes receivable due in 2012		xxx	Current obligations under capital leases	xxx	
Installment notes due in 2012		xxx	Deferred tax liability	xxx	
Interest receivable		xxx	Short-term portion of accrued warranty	xxx	
Creditors' accounts with debit balances		xxx	Other accrued liabilities	xxx	
Advances to employees		xxx	Total current liabilities		$xxx
Inventories (carried at lower of cost or market by FIFO)			*Noncurrent liabilities:*		
Finished goods	xxx		Notes payable due after 2012	xxx	
Work in process	xxx		Plus unamortized note premium	xxx	$xxx
Raw materials	xxx	xxx	Long-term bonds:		
Prepaid expenses:			10% debentures due in 2022	xxx	
Prepaid rent	xxx		9-1/2% collateralized obligations maturing		
Prepaid insurance	xxx	xxx	serially to 2014	xxx	
Total current assets		$xxx	8% convertible subordinated debentures due in 2027	xxx	
			Less unamortized discounts net of premiums	(xxx)	xxx
Long-term investments:			Accrued pension cost		xxx
Investments in marketable securities (available-for-sale)		xxx	Obligations under capital leases		xxx
Investments in bonds (held-to-maturity)		xxx	Deferred tax liability		xxx
Investments in unused land		xxx	Long-term portion of accrued warranty		xxx
Cash surrender value of officers' life insurance policies		xxx	Total noncurrent liabilities		$xxx
Sinking fund for bond retirement		xxx	Total liabilities		$xxx
Plant expansion fund		xxx	*Capital stock:*		
Total long-term investments		$xxx	$12.50 convertible preferred stock, $100 stated value, 200,000 shares authorized, 175,000 outstanding	xxx	
Property, plant, and equipment:			12% cumulative preferred stock, $100 stated value, callable at $115, 100,000 shares authorized and outstanding	xxx	
Land	xxx				
Buildings	xxx				
Machinery and equipment	xxx		Common stock, $10 stated value, 500,000 shares authorized, 450,000 issued, 15,000 held in treasury	xxx	
Furniture and fixtures	xxx				
Leasehold improvements	xxx				
Leased assets	xxx		Common stock subscribed 10,000 shares	xxx	
Less accumulated depreciation and amortization	(xxx)		Less: Subscriptions receivable	(xxx)	xxx
Total property, plant, and equipment		$xxx	*Additional paid-in capital:*		
			From 12% cumulative preferred	xxx	
Intangible assets net of amortization:			From common stock	xxx	
Goodwill		xxx	From treasury stock transactions	xxx	
Patents		xxx	From stock dividends	xxx	
Trademarks		xxx	From expiration of stock options	xxx	
Total intangible assets, net		$xxx	Warrants outstanding	xxx	xxx
Other assets:			*Retained earnings:*		
Installment notes due after 2012		xxx	Appropriated for bond indebtedness	xxx	
Unamortized bond issue costs		xxx	Free and unappropriated	xxx	xxx
Equipment to be disposed of		xxx			
Total other noncurrent assets		$xxx	*Accumulated other comprehensive income:*		xxx*
Total assets		$xxx	Total stockholders' equity		
			Less: Treasury stock at cost		
			Total liabilities and stockholders' equity		

* Assumes components thereof are disclosed either in a statement of changes in stockholders' equity or in the notes to FS.

NOTE: Current assets include those expected to be

1.   Realized in cash
2.   Sold
3.   Consumed

Current liabilities are those expected to

1.   Use current assets
2.   Create other current liabilities

The operating cycle is the average time between acquisition of materials and final cash realization.

> **NOW REVIEW MULTIPLE-CHOICE QUESTIONS 47 THROUGH 53 IN VOLUME 2**

6.   **Other Financial Statement Concepts**

a.   **Disclosures.** Related-party disclosures are covered by ASC Topic 850 (SFAS 57). Additional disclosures required for specific situations were specified at the end of most pronouncements.

b.   **Accounting policies** must be set forth as the initial footnote to the statements. Disclosures are required of

(1) Accounting principles used when alternatives exist
(2) Principles peculiar to a particular industry
(3) Unusual or innovative applications of accounting principles

c.   **Subsequent events.** Subsequent events are those occurring after the balance sheet date but before the financial statements are issued or available to be issued. Financial statements are issued when they are distributed to shareholders and other users. Financial statements are "available to be issued" when they are in a form and format that is complete and complies with GAAP and all necessary approvals for issuance have been obtained.

(1) An entity that is an SEC filer or is a conduit bond obligor for conduit debt securities traded in a public market must evaluate subsequent events through the date the financial statements are issued. All other entities must evaluate subsequent events through the date that the financial statements are available to be issued. There are two types of subsequent events: recognized and nonrecognized.
(2) A recognized subsequent event is one in which the condition existed at the balance sheet date and, therefore, is recognized in the financial statements.

> **EXAMPLE**
>
> Recognized events include an estimate for warranty liability, an estimate of a contingent liability due to a lawsuit, or an estimate of allowance for uncollectible accounts.

(a) If a recognized subsequent event is settled after the balance sheet date but before the financial statements are issued or available to be issued, then the settlement amounts should be used as the liability in the balance sheet.

(3) A nonrecognized subsequent event is one in which the condition did NOT exist at the balance sheet date, but arose AFTER the balance sheet date. In such cases, the event is NOT recognized in the financial statements. However, if the event is such that the financial statements would be misleading, then a footnote disclosure should be made indicating the nature of the event and an estimate of the financial statement effects.
(4) An entity that is an SEC filer is not required to disclose the date through which subsequent events are evaluated. However, a non-SEC filer must also disclose the date through which the subsequent events were evaluated and whether that date is the date the financial statements are issued or available to be issued. The provisions of ASC Topics 855 apply both interim and annual reports for all subsequent events that are not addressed by other areas of the Codification.

> **NOW REVIEW MULTIPLE-CHOICE QUESTIONS 54 THROUGH 64 IN VOLUME 2**

d.   **Fair value measurements.** Fair value measurements are required for certain assets and liabilities (investments, derivatives, asset impairments, asset retirement obligations, goodwill, business combinations, troubled debt restructuring).

(1) Applying the fair value measurement approach involves the following six steps:

    (a) Identify the asset or liability to be measured.
    (b) Determine the principal or most advantageous market.
    (c) Determine the valuation premise.
    (d) Determine the appropriate valuation technique (*market, income, or cost approach*).
    (e) Obtain inputs for valuation (*Level 1, Level 2, or Level 3*).
    (f) Calculate the fair value of the asset.

(2) Fair value is the price that would be received to sell an asset or paid to transfer a liability in an orderly transaction between market participants at the measurement date (at exit price) under current market conditions. An orderderly transaction is a transaction that allows for normal marketing activities that are usual and customary. In other words, it is not a forced transaction or sale.

(3) The fair value measurement assumes that the asset or liability is sold or transferred in the principal market, or if no principal market exists, the most advantageous market. The **principal market** is a market in which the greatest volume and level of activity occurs. The **most advantageous market** maximizes price received for the asset or minimizes the amount paid to transfer the liability. Market participants in the principal or most advantageous market should have the following characteristics:

    (a) Be independent of the reporting entity (not related parties),
    (b) Be knowledgeable,
    (c) Able to transact, and
    (d) Willing to transact (i.e., motivated, but not compelled to transact).

(4) The price in the principal or most advantageous market shall **not** be adjusted for transaction costs, such as costs to sell. However, the cost to sell is used to determine which market is the most advantageous. If location is a characteristic of the asset or liability, the price **is adjusted** for costs necessary to transport the asset or liability to the market.

EXAMPLE 1

(Adapted from ASC 820-10-55-42 through 45A)

Company A is valuing a trading security to fair value at year-end. The stock is traded on two stock exchanges, the NYSE and NASDAQ. The price quoted on December 31, 2011, on the NYSE is $50 per share, and the brokerage fees are $4 per share. The price quoted on the NASDAQ is $48 per share with brokerage fees of $1 per share.

  a. Assume the NYSE is the principal market. The fair value would be $50 because the FV is the price in the principal market for the asset.

  b. Assume that there is no principal market, and the stock is exchanged equally on both markets. The fair value would be the price in the most advantageous market. The NYSE price would allow Company A to receive $46 per share for the stock ($50 – $4). The NASDAQ price would allow company A to receive $47 per share for the stock ($48 – $1 per share). Therefore, the NASDAQ price would maximize the price received for the asset, and the NASDAQ market would be considered the most advantageous market. The fair value of $48 per share would be the fair value of the stock.

NOTE: Although the selling fees may be used to determine the most advantageous market, selling costs or brokerage fees are NOT used in calculating the fair value.

EXAMPLE 2

(Adapted from SFAS 157, Appendix A)

Company B is valuing a commodity at year-end. The commodity is traded on an open-exchange, and the price quoted at December 31, 2011, is $10,000. Transportation costs to deliver the goods to market are $500. The fair value of the commodity is $9,500 ($10,000 less the cost to transfer the goods to market of $500).

---

(5) Fair value measurement also assumes the highest and best use of the nonfinancial asset.

NOTE: For financial assets and financial liabilities, the highest and best use concept is not relevant since they do not have alternative uses and their fair values do not depend upon their use within a group.

    The **highest and best use** will maximize the value of the asset or group of assets. The use of the asset must be physically possible, legally permissible, and financially feasible at the measurement date. The highest and best use of the asset is then used to determine the valuation premise used to measure fair value as follows:

(a) If the asset provides maximum value by using it with other assets as a group. The fair value of the asset is the price that would be received to sell the asset assuming the asset is used with other assets as a group.

(b) If the asset provides maximum value on a stand-alone basis, the fair value of the asset is the price that would be received in a current transaction to sell the asset stand-alone.

(6) Three valuation techniques can be used to measure fair value: the market approach, the income approach, and the cost approach. The **market approach** uses prices and relevant information from market transactions for identical or comparable assets or liabilities. The **income approach** converts future amounts to a single current (discounted) amount. The **cost approach** relies on the current replacement cost to replace the asset with a comparable asset, adjusted for obsolescence.

(a) If a firm changes its valuation technique or approach for measuring fair value, the change is accounted for as a change in accounting estimate and treated on a prospective basis. The disclosure provisions for a change in accounting estimate are not required for revisions or changes to valuation techniques used in fair value measurements.

(b) Applying the market approach, income approach, and the cost approach requires gathering information to value the asset or liability. A fair value hierarchy is used to prioritize the inputs to valuation techniques. The fair value hierarchy is referred to as Level 1, Level 2, and Level 3, with the fair value hierarchy based on the lowest level of input. The lowest level that is practical should be used to value the asset or liability.

1] Level 1 uses quoted prices (unadjusted prices) from active markets for identical assets or liabilities. Quoted prices in active markets provide the most reliable evidence of fair value and should be used without adjustment whenever available. Examples of Level 1 inputs are stock quotations from the New York Stock Exchange, quotations from dealer markets such as NASDAQ or the market from US Treasury securities, brokered markets wherein brokers match buyers and sellers, and principal-to-principal markets. The fair value of a security measured within Level 1 is the quoted price times the quantity held, and it is not adjusted for the quantity of shares (blockage factor) held.

2] Level 2 inputs are directly or indirectly observable inputs other than quoted prices of Level 1. Examples of Level 2 inputs include quoted prices for similar assets or liabilities in active markets, quoted prices for identical or similar assets that are in markets where few transaction occur, the prices are not current, or prices vary substantially over time. Level 2 inputs also include observable inputs such as yield curves, bank prime rates, interest rates, volatilities, prepayment speeds, loss severities, credit risks, and default rates.

3] Level 3 inputs are unobservable inputs. Level 3 inputs may only be used to measure fair value if observable inputs are not available (i.e., there is little market activity for the asset or liability). These unobservable inputs may reflect the reporting entity's own assumptions about the market and are based on the best information available. Example of Level 3 inputs would include pricing a three-year option using the historical volatility on shares, valuing an asset retirement obligation using expected cash flows estimated by the company, or valuing a reporting unit using a firm's financial forecasts for cash flows or earnings.

e. **The fair value option for reporting financial assets and financial liabilities.** An election can be made to value certain financial assets and financial liabilities at fair value. A financial asset is cash, evidence of an ownership interest in an entity, or a contract that conveys a right to receive cash or another financial instrument or to exchange financial instruments on favorable terms. A financial liability is a contract that imposes an obligation to deliver cash or another financial instrument.

(1) The fair value option applies to all financial assets including available-for-sale, held-to-maturity, and equity method investments. The fair value option also applies to certain financial liabilities, firm commitments that involve financial instruments, written loan commitments, nonfinancial insurance contracts that can be settled by paying a third party, warranties that can be settled by paying a third party, and a host financial instrument that is an embedded nonfinancial derivative instrument separated from a nonfinancial hybrid instrument.

(2) The fair value method does **not** apply to consolidations, pensions, share-based payments, stock options, other postemployment benefits (OPEB), exit or disposal activities, leases, or financial instruments that are a component of equity.

(3) The fair value is the price that would be received to sell an asset or paid to transfer a liability in an orderly transaction between market participants at the measurement date under current market conditions.

(4) A company can elect to measure the applicable financial assets or financial liabilities at fair value on the date an eligible item is first recognized, the date the entity enters into a firm commitment, the date financial assets cease to qualify for fair value treatment due to specialized accounting rules.

    (a) For companies using the equity method of accounting, a company can elect to measure the investment at fair value on the date the percentage of ownership changes and the entity is no longer required to consolidate.

    (b) For debt modifications, the fair value option can be elected on the date the debt is modified. **Once the fair value option is elected, it is irrevocable.**

(5) The fair value election can be made on an instrument-by-instrument basis. For example, a company has two available-for-sale securities, Security A and Security B. The company can account for Security A using the cost adjusted fair value method for available-for-sale securities and it can elect the fair value option and account for Security B at fair value. **However, if the fair value option is elected, it must be applied to the entire instrument and not a portion of the instrument**. For example, if there are multiple advances to a borrower for a single contract, it must be applied to the entire balance of the contract. If the fair value option is applied to an investment in an entity that would normally use the equity method, it must be applied to all debt and equity interests in that entity.

    (a) Similarly, if the fair value option is elected for insurance contracts, it must be applied to all claims and obligations for that contract.

    (b) If the fair value option is elected, any unrealized gains and losses are reported in earnings for the period. Therefore, any unrealized gains and losses on an available-for-sale security would be reported on the income statement rather than in other comprehensive income. For a held-to-maturity security, the company would no longer report the investment at amortized cost. Instead, the held-to-maturity security would be marked to fair value at the end of the period, and the resulting unrealized gain or loss would be reported on the income statement. The rules remain in effect for classifying items on the statement of cash flows as operating or investing activities.

(6) If a reporting entity holds a group of financial assets and financial liabilities that are exposed to market and credit risks of counterparties, the reporting entity may apply fair value to the net position if the following conditions are met:

    (a) The group of financial assets and financial liabilities are managed on the basis of net exposure;

    (b) Information about the group is provided on a net basis; and

    (c) The reporting entity has elected or is required to measure the group at fair value.

(7) Additional financial statement disclosures are required if the fair value option is elected. Two methods are permissible for balance sheet disclosure: (1) present the aggregate fair value and non–fair value amounts in the same line with amounts measured at fair value parenthetically disclosed, or (2) present two separate line items for fair value and non–fair value carrying amounts.

f. **Disclosures for fair value measurements.** Additional footnote disclosures are required for fair value measurements. Fair value measurements are reported by class of assets or liabilities. The class is determined on the basis of the nature and risks of the assets or liability.

(1) For assets and liabilities that are measured at fair value on a **recurring** basis, the following disclosures are required for each major class of assets and liabilities:

    (a) The fair value measurement at the end of the reporting date.

    (b) The level within the fair value hierarchy used, segregating the fair value measurements, which use Levels 1, 2, and 3 inputs.

    (c) The amount of any transfers between Level 1 and Level 2 of the fair value hierarchy and the reason for the transfer along with the entity's transfer policy. Transfers into and out of each level are disclosed separately.

    (d) For fair value measures using significant other observable inputs (Level 2) and significant unobservable inputs (Level 3), a description of valuation techniques used, the inputs used to determine fair values of each class of assets or liabilities. If there is a change in valuation techniques, the reason for the change must be disclosed.

    (e) For fair value measurements using unobservable inputs (Level 3) a reconciliation of the beginning and ending balance, showing

        1] Total gains and losses for the period realized and unrealized, presenting gains and losses in earnings and gains and losses in other comprehensive income, and a description of where those gains or losses are included in the income statement, or in other comprehensive income.

        2] Purchases, sales, issues, and settlements shown separately.

   3] Transfers in and out of Level 3 are shown separately with reasons for the transfers, along with the
       entity's transfer policy.

   (f) For fair value measurements using unobservable inputs (Level 3) the amount of total gains or losses for
        the period included in earnings from unrealized gains and losses for those assets and liabilities still held
        at the end of the reporting period and the line item in the statement of income (or activities) where the
        gains and losses are recognized.
   (g) For fair value measurements using unobservable inputs (Level 3) a description of the valuation
        processes (policies, procedures, and analyses of change from period to period), the sensitivity of the
        measurement, and any interrelationships.
   (h) For fair value measurements, a description of nonfinancial assets with a current use differing from the
        highest and best use.

(2) For assets and liabilities that are measured at fair value on a **nonrecurring** basis, the following information
     must be disclosed in interim and annual period financial statements:

   (a) The fair value measurement at the end of the reporting period and the reasons for the measurement.
   (b) The level within the fair value hierarchy, Level 1, 2, and 3.
   (c) For fair value measurements categorized within Level 2 or Level 3 of the fair value hierarchy, the in-
        puts and valuation techniques to measure fair value.
   (d) For fair value measurements using significant unobservable inputs (Level 3), a description of valuation
        processes (policies, procedures, and analyses of change from period to period).
   (e) For fair value measurements a description of nonfinancial assets with a current use differing from the
        highest and best use.

NOW REVIEW MULTIPLE-CHOICE QUESTIONS 65 THROUGH 76 IN VOLUME 2

---

g. **Development stage enterprise accounting** should follow generally accepted accounting principles. The only
    additional disclosure required is that cumulative amounts from inception of losses, revenues, expenses, and
    cash flows should be shown in the income statement and statement of cash flows. Furthermore, the stockhold-
    ers' equity section of the balance sheet should include cumulative net losses termed "deficit accumulated during
    development stage." These statements should be identified as those of a development stage enterprise. (More
    detailed coverage appears in Module 11.)

h. **Constant dollar accounting.** The accounting standards encourage, but do not require, a business enterprise
    that prepares its financial statements in US dollars and in accordance with US generally accepted accounting
    principles to disclose supplementary information on the effects of changing prices. This statement presents re-
    quirements to be followed by enterprises that voluntarily elect to disclose this information.

(1) Constant dollar accounting is a method of reporting financial statement elements in dollars which have the
     same purchasing power. This method is often described as accounting in units of current purchasing power.

   (a) Purchasing power indicates the ability of a dollar to command goods and services.

EXAMPLE

If the inflation rate during a given year for a group of items is 10%, then 110 end-of-year dollars are needed
to purchase the same group of items which cost $100 at the beginning of the year. Similarly, a machine
purchased at the beginning of that year for $1,000 would be presented in a year-end constant dollar balance
sheet at a restated cost of $1,100. This represents the basic thrust of constant dollar accounting: the
adjustment of historical data (nominal dollars) for changes in the general price level.

---

(2) The adjustment of nominal dollar data is facilitated by the use of the Consumer Price Index, which reflects
     the average change in the retail prices of a wide variety of consumer goods. The adjustment is made by
     multiplying historical cost by the TO/FROM ratio.

$$\text{Historical cost (nominal dollars)} \times \frac{\text{Price level adjusting to}}{\text{Price level adjusting from}} = \text{Restated historical cost (constant dollar)}$$

EXAMPLE

An asset was purchased on 12/31/08 for $20,000 and the Consumer Price Index was 100 on 12/31/08, 110 on 12/31/09, and 120 on 12/31/10. Restatement for end-of-year balance sheets would be

12/31/08	$20,000	$\times$	$\dfrac{100}{100}$	$=$	$20,000
12/31/09	$20,000	$\times$	$\dfrac{110}{100}$	$=$	$22,000
12/31/10	$20,000	$\times$	$\dfrac{120}{100}$	$=$	$24,000
		or			
	$22,000	$\times$	$\dfrac{120}{110}$	$=$	$24,000

(3) The preparation of constant dollar financial statements requires the classification of balance sheet items as either monetary or nonmonetary.

  (a) Items are monetary if their amounts are fixed by statute or contract in terms of numbers of dollars. Examples include cash, accounts and notes receivable, accounts and notes payable, and bonds payable.

    1] By contract or statute, these items are already stated in current dollars and require no restatement.

  (b) Nonmonetary items, on the other hand, do require restatement to current dollars. Inventory, property, plant, and equipment, and unearned service revenue are examples of nonmonetary items.

    1] Under some increasingly popular loan arrangements, when the repayment of loan principal is adjusted by an index, the receivable/payable is classified as a nonmonetary item.

NOTE: The holding of a nonmonetary asset such as land during a period of inflation need not result in a loss of purchasing power because the value of that land can "flow" with the price level (hence, the need for restatement). However, if a monetary asset such as cash is held during a period of inflation with no interest, purchasing power is lost because the cash will be able to purchase less goods and services at year-end than at the beginning of the year. This type of loss is simply called a "purchasing power loss." Holding a monetary liability has the opposite effect. Therefore, if a firm's balance sheet included more monetary liabilities than monetary assets throughout a given year, a purchasing power **gain** would result, since the firm could pay its liabilities using cash which is "worth less" than the cash it borrowed.

  (c) A simple example can illustrate both the restatement process and the effect of holding monetary assets. Assume that the Static Company has the following balance sheet at the beginning of period 1:

EXAMPLE

Static Co.
End of Period 1
Consumer Price Index = 110

Cash	$1,000	Common Stock	$2,200[b]
Land	1,000		
	$2,000		$2,000

Further assume
• Index increases to 110 by the end of year 1
• No transactions have taken place, land and common stock would be restated to end-of-year dollars.
• Cash is still stated at $1,000.
• To have the same level of purchasing power that was present at the beginning of the year, Static Co. should also have cash of $1,100 at year-end. The fact that the company held $1,000 cash throughout the year has resulted in a $100 purchasing power loss. The balance sheet at the end of period 1 would therefore be

Static Co.
End of Period 1
Consumer Price Index = 110

Cash	$1,000	Common Stock	$2,200[b]
Land	1,100[a]	Retained Earnings	(100)[c]
	$2,100		$2,100

^{a}$1,000 \times \dfrac{110}{100}$ ^{b}$2,000 \times \dfrac{110}{100}$ ^{c}Purchasing power loss $1,000 - \left($1,000 \times \dfrac{110}{100}\right)$

What if the entity had acquired equipment costing $1,000 at the beginning of the year by issuing a $1,000 note payable? At the end of the year, under constant dollar accounting, the equipment would be carried at $1,100 and the note payable would be still reported at $1,000. What would the net purchasing power gain (loss) be? The answer is zero because the loss of $100 is offset by a $100 gain from holding the note payable.

i. **Current cost accounting** is a method of valuing and reporting assets, liabilities, revenues, and expenses at their current cost at the balance sheet date or at the date of their use or sale.

(1) It is important to distinguish between constant dollar and current cost accounting. Constant dollar accounting is concerned only with changes in the unit of measure—from nominal dollars to units of general purchasing power. Current cost accounting discards historical cost as a reporting model.

(2) Preparation of a current cost income statement requires an understanding of certain basic current cost concepts. **Current cost income from continuing operations** is sales revenue less expenses on a current cost basis. **Realized holding gains** (the difference between current cost and historical cost of assets consumed) are then added to arrive at **realized income,** which will always be equal to historical cost net income. Finally, **unrealized holding gains** (increases in the current cost of assets held throughout the year) are included to result in **current cost net income**.

EXAMPLE

Bell Company went into business on 1/1/10. 2010 sales revenue was $200,000 and purchases totaled $150,000. Inventory with a historical cost of $100,000 was sold when its current cost was $160,000. Ending inventory (historical cost, $50,000) had a year-end current cost of $80,000. No other revenue was realized or expenses incurred during 2010. Historical and current cost income statements for 2010 are presented below.

Bell Company
INCOME STATEMENTS

Historical cost		Current cost	
Sales	$200,000	Sales	$200,000
Less CGS	(100,000)	Less CGS	(160,000)
		Cur. cost income from cont. oper.	40,000
		Realized holding gains (160,000 – 100,000)	60,000
Net income	$100,000	Realized income	100,000
		Unrealized holding gains (80,000 – 50,000)	30,000
		Current cost net income	$130,000

2010 journal entries for Bell Company in current cost system would be as follows:

a)	Inventory	150,000		d)	Cost of goods sold	160,000	
	Cash		150,000		Inventory		160,000
b)	Inventory	90,000		e)	Realizable holding gain	90,000	
	Realizable				Realized holding gain		60,000
	holding gain		90,000		Unrealized holding gain		30,000
c)	Cash	200,000					
	Sales revenue		200,000				

---

(3) In general, sales and some expense amounts (salaries, rent, etc.) will be the same under historical and current cost systems. However, whenever an expense represents the use or consumption of an asset whose current cost has changed since its acquisition (as with the inventory in the Bell Company example), that expense must be expressed at the current cost of the asset when used. Realized holding gains are computed by comparing the current cost of assets when used or consumed with their historical cost. Unrealized holding gains for the period are determined by identifying changes in the current cost of assets held throughout the year (not used or consumed).

NOTE: Holding gains do not reflect changes in the general purchasing power. In other words, holding gains are not reported net of general inflation when the reporting model is current cost/nominal dollar.

(4) **Current cost/constant dollars.** The relationship measured is current cost, but the measuring unit is restated dollars. Changes in both the general and specific price levels are separately recorded.

> **NOW REVIEW MULTIPLE-CHOICE QUESTIONS 77 THROUGH 87 IN VOLUME 2**

j. **Risks and uncertainties.** Disclosure is required in financial statements about the risks and uncertainties existing as of the date of those statements. The four areas of disclosure are

   (1) Nature of operations

      (a) Major products/services and principal markets served.
      (b) Industries operating within and relative importance of each industry, including basis of determination (assets, revenue, or earnings).

   > **NOTE:** Quantification not required and words such as predominantly, equally, major, or other may be used.

   (2) Use of estimates in preparation of financial statements.

      (a) This fact must be disclosed by an explanation that management must use estimates.
      (b) The purpose is to alert users clearly to pervasiveness of estimates.

   (3) Certain significant estimates:

      (a) Potential impact of estimates to value assets, liabilities, gains, or losses when

         1] Reasonably possible the estimate will change in the near term.
         2] Effect of change would be material to financial statements.

   > **NOTE:** Near term is defined as not to exceed one year from date of financial statements.

      (b) Contingencies.
      (c) Disclosure of factors causing the estimate to be sensitive to change is encouraged, but not required.
      (d) Materiality is measured by the effect that using a different estimate would have on the financial statements.

   (4) Current vulnerability due to concentrations.

      (a) Before issuance of financial statements, management knows that concentrations:

         1] Exist at balance sheet date.
         2] Make entity vulnerable to risk of near-term severe impact.
         3] Reasonably possible events could cause severe impact in near future.

   > **NOTE:** Severe impact is defined as higher than materiality and would have a significant financially disruptive effect on the normal functioning of the entity.

      (b) Examples are concentrations in

         1] Volume of business transacted with a particular customer, supplier, lender, grantor, or contributor.
         2] Revenue from particular products, services, or fund-raising events.
         3] Available sources of supply of materials, labor, or services, or of licenses or other rights used in the entity's operations.
         4] Market or geographical area in which an entity conducts its operations.

      (c) Disclose the percentage of labor covered by a collective bargaining agreement and the percentage covered whose agreement expires within one year.
      (d) Describe for operations outside of home country, the carrying value of net assets and location.

7. **Comparative Financial Statements**
   The Totman Company balance sheet and income statement illustrated in this module are presented for a single year. Most companies present comparative financial statements. Comparative financial statements present not only the current year's information, but prior periods also. The purpose of comparative financial statements is to enable users to evaluate trends which may reveal information about the company's future performance. The SEC requires that a two-year comparative balance sheet and a three-year comparative income statement and statement of cash flows be presented.

8. **Other Comprehensive Bases of Accounting (OCBOA)**

a. Financial statements may be prepared in conformity with a comprehensive basis of accounting other than generally accepted accounting principles (GAAP) or international accounting standards. The four types of OCBOA include

(1) **Cash-basis** financial statements—In pure cash-basis financial statements the only asset is cash; revenue is recognized when cash is received; and expenses are recognized when they are paid. The pure basis is rarely used.

(2) **Modified cash-basis** financial statements—Modified cash basis financial statements are cash basis statements with modifications that have substantial support. For example, fixed assets, inventories, and the related liabilities are typically recorded in modified cash-basis financial statements. Modifications that have substantial support involve presenting the items as they would be in GAAP financial statements providing that the presentation is not illogical. As an example, an illogical modification would involve recording inventories but not recording the accounts payable related to the inventories.

(3) **Tax-basis** financial statements—Tax-basis financial statements are statements prepared on the basis of tax laws and regulations. When financial statements are prepared on an income tax basis, the financial statements should not simply repeat items and amounts reported in the tax return. Thus, items such as nontaxable municipal interest and the nondeductible portion of travel and entertainment expense should be **fully** reflected in the tax-basis income statement.

(4) **Regulatory-basis** financial statements—Regulatory financial statements are prepared based on rules established by a regulatory agency.

b. OCBOA financial statements should not include titles such as "balance sheet" and "statement of income" (unmodified) because these terms are reserved for GAAP-basis statements. Titles such as "balance sheet—tax basis," "statement of revenues and expenses—income tax basis," "statement of assets and liabilities—modified cash basis," and "statement of cash receipts and disbursements" are appropriate. In addition, the notes to the financial statements should disclose the differences between the OCBOA- and GAAP-basis financial statements, as well as the other information normally included in GAAP-basis financial statements.

9. **Prospective Financial Information**

a. Definitions

(1) **Prospective financial information**—any financial information about the future.
(2) **Responsible party**—person(s), usually management, who are responsible for assumptions underlying the information.
(3) Users of prospective financial information

(a) General—use of financial statements by parties with whom responsible party is not negotiating directly.
(b) Limited use—use of prospective financial information by the responsible party only or by responsible party and third parties with whom responsible party is negotiating directly.

(4) **Financial forecast**—prospective FS that present the knowledge and belief of responsible party in terms of expected financial position, results of operations, and cash flows

(a) May be prepared for **general** or **limited** use.
(b) Monetary amounts are expressed as a single-point estimate of results or range.

(5) **Financial projection**—prospective FS that present the knowledge and belief of responsible party, based on one or more **hypothetical** assumptions, the enterprise's financial position, results of operations, and cash flows.

(a) Assumptions **not necessarily** expected to occur.
(b) May contain a single-point estimate of results or a range of dollars.
(c) May be prepared only for **limited** use.

b. Reasons for preparation are to

(1) Obtain external financing.
(2) Consider a change in accounting or operations.
(3) Prepare budgets.

c. Process for preparing forecasts and projections may consist of any of the following:

(1) Formal system.
(2) Carrying out a work program that outlines steps followed in preparation.
(3) Documented procedures, methods, and practices used in preparation.

d. Financial forecasts and projections should reflect **a reasonably objective basis** as a result of preparing them

(1) In good faith.
(2) With due care by qualified personnel.
(3) In accordance with GAAP.
(4) With the highest quality information that is reasonably available.
(5) Using information that is in accordance with plans of the entity.
(6) Identifying key factors as basis for assumptions.

(a) Key factors are important matters for which outcomes are expected to depend.

(7) Using appropriate assumptions.

(a) Quality of these is crucial.
(b) **Hypothetical** assumptions used in projections do **not** need to meet a strict reasonableness test; they must, however, be appropriate in light of the purpose of the projection.

(8) Providing ways to determine relative effect of variations in main assumptions (i.e., sensitivity analysis).
(9) Documenting forecast/projection and process used.
(10) Providing for comparison of forecast/projection with attained results.
(11) Providing adequate review of the responsible party at appropriate levels of authority in the organization.
(12) Prospective financial statement disclosures include.

(a) Summary of significant accounting policies.
(b) Summary of significant assumptions.

> **NOW REVIEW MULTIPLE-CHOICE QUESTIONS 88 THROUGH 97 IN VOLUME 2**

10. SEC Reporting Requirements

a. Unless exempt by regulation, companies with assets of more than $10 million and 500 or more shareholders and securities that trade on a national securities exchange or an over-the-counter market must have the securities registered.

b. Companies with registered securities (termed issuers) must file the following reports with the SEC:

(1) **Regulation S-X** describes the form and content of financial statements filed with the SEC.
(2) **Regulation S-K** describes the requirements for information and forms required by Regulation S-X.
(3) **Regulation AB** describes reporting requirements for asset-backed securities.
(4) **Regulation Fair Disclosure (FD)** mandates that publicly traded companies disclose material information to all investors simultaneously.

c. Companies with registered securities (termed issuers) must file the following reports with the SEC:

(1) **Form S-1/F-1**-registration statement for US/ foreign companies.
(2) **Form 8-K/6-K**- information about material events for US/foreign companies.
(3) **Form 10-K/20F**-annual report for US/foreign companies.

(a) A foreign registrant can omit the reconciliation between US GAAP and home-country GAAP (e.g. IFRS) if the foreign-based company follows IFRS as issued by the IASB.

(4) **Form 10-Q**- quarterly reports.
(5) **Schedule 14A**- proxy statement.

d. Information statements (**Form 8-K**) provide information about material events that affect the company, such as mergers and acquisitions, changes in directors or CEO, other major changes in operations or status, changes in auditors, etc. The Form 8-K must be filed within 4 business days of the occurrence of the events.

EXAMPLE

ITEM 7.01. REGULATION FD DISCLOSURE[*]

On May 26, 2011, management of Rand Logistics, Inc. ("Rand") presented to institutional investors a summary of Rand's business, historical financial performance, and future earnings guidance at the CJS Securities 2nd Annual Midwest Investor Conference. The presentation is attached as Exhibit 99.1 and is incorporated by reference herein.

[*]SEC Edgar Filing

---

(1) The 8-K includes the following information (*Italicized items may be omitted*):

    (a) Item 1.01, Entry into a Material Definitive Agreement.

    (b) Item 1.02, Termination of a Material Definitive Agreement.

    (c) Item 1.03, Bankruptcy or Receivership.

    (d) *Item 2.01, Completion of Acquisition or Disposition of Assets.*

    (e) *Item 2.02, Results of Operations And Financial Condition.*

    (f) *Item 2.03, Creation of A Direct Financial Obligation or an Obligation Under an Off-Balance Sheet Arrangement of a Registrant.*

    (g) Item 2.04, Triggering Events That Accelerate or Increase a Direct Financial Obligation or an Obligation Under an Off-Balance Sheet Arrangement.

    (h) *Item 2.05, Costs Associated with Exit or Disposal Activities.*

    (i) *Item 2.06, Material Impairments.*

    (j) *Item 3.01, Notice of Delisting or Failure to Satisfy a Continued Listing Rule or Standard; Transfer of Listing.*

    (k) *Item 3.02, Unregistered Sales of Equity Securities.*

    (l) Item 3.03, Material Modification to Rights of Security Holders.

    (m) *Item 4.01, Changes in Registrant's Certifying Accountant.*

    (n) *Item 4.02, Non-Reliance on Previously Issued Financial Statements or a Related Audit Reports or Completed Interim Review.*

    (o) *Item 5.01, Changes in Control of Registrant.*

    (p) *Item 5.02, Departure of Directors or Principal Officers; Election of Directors; Appointment of Principal Officers.*

    (q) Item 5.03, Amendments to Articles of Incorporation or Bylaws; Change in Fiscal Year.

    (r) *Item 5.04, Temporary Suspension of Trading Under Registrant's Employee Benefit Plans; and*

    (s) *Item 5.05, Amendments to the Registrant's Code of Ethics, or Waiver of a Provision of the Code of Ethics.*

    (t) Section 5.06, Change in Shell Company Status.

    (u) Item 5.07, Submission of Matters to a Vote of Security Holders.

    (v) Item 6.01, ABS Informational and Computational Material.

    (w) Item 6.02, Change of Servicer or Trustee.

    (x) Item 6.03, Change In Credit Enhancement or Other External Support.

    (y) Item 6.04, Failure to Make a Required Distribution.

    (z) Item 6.05, Securities Act Updating Disclosure.

    (aa) Item 7.01, Regulation FD Disclosure.

    (bb) Item 8.01, Other Events.

    (cc) Item 9, Financial Statements and Exhibits.

e. A quarterly report (**Form 10-Q**) provides quarterly information similar to that in the 10-K but is less detail. It includes quarterly financial statements that are reviewed (not audited) by public accountants. The company files three Form 10-Qs every year and the Form 10-K contains the quarterly results for the fourth quarter. Form 10-Qs are due 40 days after the end of the fiscal quarter for accelerated filers and 45 days after the end of the fiscal quarter for all other companies.

f. An annual report (**Form 10-K**) provides a comprehensive picture of a company's performance, including audited financial statements. The 10-K includes the following sections:

Item No.	Reg. S-K No. (unless otherwise noted)	Description
Part I		
1	101	Business
1A	503(c)	Risk factors
2	102	Properties
3	103	Legal proceedings
4	104	Removed
Part II		
5	201, 701, 703	Market for common equity and related matters
6	301	Selected financial data
7	303	Management's discussion and analysis
7A	305	Quantitiative and qualitative disclosures about market risk
8	302	Financial statements and supplementary data
9	304 (b)	Changes in and disagreement with auditors
9A	307, 308	Controls and procedures

Item No.	Reg. S-K No. (unless otherwise noted)	Description
Part III		
10	401, 405,406,407(c)(3), (d)(4), (d)(5)	Directors and executive officers (may be omitted)
11	402	Executive compensation (may be omitted)
12	201(d)	Security ownership of owners and management (may be omitted)
13	404	Relationships and related transactions (may be omitted)
14	9 (e) of Schedule 14A	Principal accountant fees and services
Part IV		
15	302 and 601 of Reg. S-K, Reg. S-X	Exhibits, financial statement schedules
Other		
	Reg. AB1112(b), 1114(b), 1117, 1119, 1122, 1123	Substitute information to be included

* SOURCE: Modified from Natalie T. Churyk, NIU CPA Review

Form 10-Ks are due 60 days after the end of the fiscal year for large accelerated filers (more than $700 million of aggregate worldwide market value of voting and nonvoting common stock), 75 days after the end of the fiscal year for accelerated files (between $70 million of aggregated worldwide market value of voting and nonvoting common stock), and 90 days after the end of the fiscal year for all other companies.

11. **Financial Statements of Trusts**

a. Trusts are entities formed to hold assets for the benefit of the beneficiaries. They are administered by trustees. Trusts generally present the following financial statements:

   (1) A statement of assets and liabilities.
   (2) A statement of operations.
   (3) A statement of changes in net assets.

b. The financial statements of a trust are generally presented on the accrual basis and the assets are generally presented at their fair values.

> **NOW REVIEW MULTIPLE-CHOICE QUESTIONS 98 THROUGH 104 IN VOLUME 2**

12. **Research Component—Accounting Standards Codification**

a. The rules for presentation of financial statements are located in the category labeled "Presentation" in the Accounting Standards Codification. The topics are numbered in the 200 series. Note that discontinued operations are included under the rules of Topic 205. Treatment of extraordinary items is found in Topic 225. Below is a list of topics related to financial statement disclosures:

   Presentation
205	Presentation of Financial Statements
210	Balance Sheet
215	Statement of Shareholder Equity
220	Comprehensive Income
225	Income Statement
230	Statement of Cash Flows
235	Notes to Financial Statements
250	Accounting Changes and Error Corrections
255	Changing Prices
260	Earnings Per Share
270	Interim Reporting
275	Risks and Uncertainties
280	Segment Reporting

b. Other topics covered in the module are located under the category "Broad Transactions" and include the following topics:

   Broad Transactions
820	Fair Value Measurements and Disclosures
825	Financial Instruments
850	Related-Party Disclosures
855	Subsequent Events

c. Keywords for research financial statements and related disclosures are shown below.

Accounting policies	Disposal of segment	Period-specific effects
Balance sheet	Earned surplus	Principal market
Capital stock	External revenue	Prior period adjustments
Capital surplus	Extraordinary items	Pro forma amounts
Cash flow estimation	Fair value hierarchy	Pro forma effects
Change in accounting	Fair value option	Profit and loss
Change in principle	Financial position	Purchasing power gain/loss
Changes in entity	Highest and best use	Reclassification adjustments
Changes in equity	Impairment loss	Reconciliations of totals
Changes in estimates	Inclusive net income	Recurring operations
Classifications net income	Income approach	Reportable segment
Comparative financial statements	Income statement	Results of operations
Comparative purposes	Infrequency of occurrence	Retroactive adjustment
Component held for sale	Interim period information	Retrospective application
Component of an entity	Market approach	Segment item
Comprehensive income	Measure impairment loss	Surplus statement
Correction of error	Monetary asset	Translation adjustment
Cost approach	Monetary liability	Unusual nature
Current assets	Nature products services	Valuation techniques
Current cost purchasing power	Net income period	Working capital
Current liabilities	Obligations operating cycle	
Disclosure accounting policies	Operating cycle	
Discontinued operation	Operating segment	
Disposal activity	Other comprehensive income	

13. **International Financial Reporting Standards (IFRS)**

a. **Financial statements.** IAS 1 provides that a complete set of financial statements must be prepared annually. A complete set of financial statements includes a statement of financial position, a statement of comprehensive income, a statement of changes in equity, a statement of cash flows, and notes containing significant accounting policies and explanations.

(1) The headings on the financial statements should include the name of the entity, the title of the statement, and the date of the statement.

(2) The financial statements should present a "true and fair view" of the company. IFRS must be used unless there is a rare circumstance where the use of IFRS would produce misleading financial statements.

(3) Whenever an entity retrospectively applies an accounting policy, retrospectively restates its financial statements, or reclassifies items, three years of statements of financial position are required for comparative purposes. Presentation and classification of items on the financial statements should be consistent for the periods presented.

(4) The accrual basis of accounting is used to prepare the financial statements, with the assumption that the entity is a going concern.

(a) Assets and liabilities may not be offset against each other unless specifically permitted by an IFRS.

(b) Similarly, income and expenses may not be offset unless specifically permitted.

(c) Offsets may be used for valuation purposes, such as contra accounts (allowance for uncollectible accounts or accumulated depreciation).

(d) Items on the financial statements should be presented separately for each material class of similar items. If an item is not material, it may be aggregated with other items.

b. **Statement of financial position**.

(1) Assets are classified as current and noncurrent.

(a) An asset is current if it is expected to be realized or held for consumption in the normal course of the entity's operating cycle, held primarily for trading purposes, expected to be realized within 12 months of the end of the period, or is cash or a cash equivalent that is not restricted.

(b) Noncurrent assets include tangible, intangible, operating, and financial assets that are long term, such as held-to-maturity investments, investment property, property and equipment, intangible assets, assets held for sale, and miscellaneous assets.

(2) Liabilities are classified as current and noncurrent.

(a) A liability is current if it is expected to be settled in the normal course of business during the operating cycle, due to be settled within 12 months, held primarily for trading purposes, or does not have an unconditional right to defer settlement beyond 12 months.

    1] However, certain payables such as trade payables and accruals for operating costs are classified as current liabilities regardless of the settlement date.

(b) Interest-bearing liabilities are classified based upon whether they are due within 12 months.

    1] However, if an agreement to refinance the liability on a long-term basis is executed prior to the financial statement date, the liability may be classified as noncurrent.

NOTE: This is different from US GAAP, where if there is the intent and ability to refinance before the issuance of the financial statements, reclassification is permitted.

      a] An executed agreement prior to the balance sheet is not required.

    2] For IFRS, if the agreement to refinance is made after the balance sheet date, then the liability must be classified as current at the balance sheet date. Similar to US GAAP, if a long-term debt becomes callable due to violation of a loan covenant, the liability must be classified as a current liability.

(3) For shareholders' equity the financial statements must disclose the number of shares of common stock authorized, issued, and outstanding. If there are preference shares (e.g., preferred stock), they must be reported separately including the number of shares authorized, issued, and outstanding. Preference shares that are redeemable at the option of the holder must be classified as liabilities. Treasury shares repurchased are stated at cost and shown as a reduction to shareholders' equity. Accumulated other comprehensive income is reported in the shareholder's equity section of the balance sheet, and noncontrolling interests are disclosed as a separate item in the equity section of the balance sheet.

(4) Although IAS 1 does not require a specific format for the statement of financial position, the following categories should be displayed:

    (a) Property, plant, and equipment
    (b) Investment property
    (c) Intangible assets
    (d) Financial assets
    (e) Investments accounted for using the equity method
    (f) Biological assets
    (g) Inventories
    (h) Trade and other receivables
    (i) Cash and cash equivalents
    (j) The total assets classified as held for sale and assets included in disposal groups classified as held for sale under IFRS 5
    (k) Trade and other payables
    (l) Provisions
    (m) Financial liabilities
    (n) Liabilities and assets for current tax
    (o) Deferred tax liabilities and deferred tax assets
    (p) Liabilities included in disposal groups classified as held for sale
    (q) Noncontrolling interest
    (r) Issued capital and reserves attributable to owners of the parent

c. **The income statement.** IAS 1 requires that at a minimum, the following items should be included on an income statement:

    (1) Revenue (referred to as income)
    (2) Finance costs (interest expense)
    (3) Share of profits and losses of associates and joint ventures accounted for using equity method
    (4) Tax expense
    (5) Discontinued operations
    (6) Profit or loss
    (7) Noncontrolling interest in profit and loss
    (8) Net profit (loss) attributable to equity holders in the parent

    (a) If an entity acquires less than 100% of a subsidiary, the income statement should indicate the profit or loss attributable to the noncontrolling interest and the owners of the parent.

(b) A significant difference between US GAAP and IFRS is that IFRS does not permit the classification of items as "extraordinary items" on the income statement. Any gains or losses should be reported as income or expense.

     1] In addition, operating expenses may be classified either by nature or by function. Classification by nature is based on the character of the expense, such as salaries and wages, raw materials used, interest expense, tax expense, and depreciation of assets. Classification by function is based on the purpose of the expenditure, such as manufacturing, distribution, or administration. If the entity classifies expenses by function, cost of sales must be stated separately from other expenses. (Note that in US GAAP, expenses are classified by function, e.g., cost of goods sold, operating expenses, etc.).

     2] For IFRS, finance costs (interest expense) must be identified separately regardless of which classification scheme is used.

(c) Operating expenses are normally classified as distribution costs (selling expenses) and general and administrative expenses.

     1] If an item is material in amount and of such a size, nature, or incidence that disclosure is important to understand the performance of the entity, then the item should be disclosed separately.

EXAMPLE

Examples of those disclosures include write-downs of inventories; write-downs of plant, property, and equipment; restructuring costs; costs of litigation settlements; and reversals of provisions.

(d) The treatment of discontinued operations is similar to US GAAP. If an asset is classified as held for sale or is part of a disposal group, it is valued at the lower of carrying value or fair value less costs to sell. The write-down net of tax is included in discontinued operations in the income statement. For discontinued operations, several calculations are required.

     1] First, the revenues, expenses, pretax profit or loss, and the related income tax expense are calculated.

     2] Second, the gain or loss on disposal or remeasurement is calculated with the related income tax expense.

     3] Finally, the total of these two amounts is determined (net of tax) and must be disclosed on the income statement.

     4] The footnote disclosures must include the pretax profit or loss, gain or loss on disposal, and tax effects, as well as the net cash flows from operating, investing, and financing activities.

d. **Statement of comprehensive income.** The statement of comprehensive income may be presented in either one statement or in two statements.

(1) The two-statement approach presents a separate income statement, and then presents a second statement, which begins with profit or loss and displays the components of comprehensive income.

     (a) Items that are included in comprehensive income are changes in revaluation surplus for plant, property, and equipment, actuarial gains and losses on defined benefit plans, gains and losses from foreign currency translations, gains and losses on remeasuring available-for-sale financial assets, and the effective portion of gains and losses on hedging instruments used as cash flow hedges.

     (b) Each component of comprehensive income should be stated separately on the statement of comprehensive income.

e. **Statement of cash flows.** The accounting rules for the Statement of Cash Flows are similar to US GAAP. For IFRS, cash flows include the inflows and outflows of both cash and cash equivalents. Cash equivalents include cash on hand, bank balances for immediate use, other demand deposits, and short-term investments with maturities of three months or less. Both the direct method and indirect method are acceptable methods for preparing the statement of cash flows. However, for the indirect method, operating activities may be presented using a modified approach. This modified indirect method shows revenues and expenses in operating activities, and then reports the changes in working capital accounts.

(1) As in US GAAP, the statement of cash flows is divided into three parts: operating, investing, and financing activities. At the bottom of the statement of cash flows, a reconciliation must be made with the amounts in the statement of cash flows and the cash and cash equivalents reported in the statement of financial position.

(2) The most significant difference between IFRS and US GAAP is where certain items are presented on the statement of cash flows.

> **EXAMPLE**
>
> Interest and dividends received may be reported on the statement of cash flows as operating or investing activities. Interest and dividends paid may be reported either in the operating activities or the financing activities sections.

    (a) Although the entity has discretion on where interest and dividends are reported, it must be reported on a consistent basis.

    (b) Cash from the purchase and sale of trading securities are classified as operating activities.

    (c) Cash advances and loans (bank overdrafts) are also usually classified as operating activities.

    (d) Taxes paid on income must be disclosed separately in operating activities. However, cash flows from certain taxes may be classified elsewhere if they are related to investing or financing activities.

    (e) In addition, the effects of noncash transactions are not reported on the statement of cash flows. Instead, significant noncash activities must be disclosed in the notes to the financial statements.

NOW REVIEW MULTIPLE-CHOICE QUESTIONS 105 THROUGH 115 IN VOLUME 2

KEY TERMS

Active market. A market in which transactions for the asset or liability take place with sufficient frequency and volume to provide pricing information on an ongoing basis.

Cash basis financial statement. The only asset is cash, revenue is recognized when cash is received; and expenses are recognized when they are paid.

Change in accounting principle. Change from one generally accepted accounting principle to another.

Constant dollar accounting. A method of reporting financial statement elements in dollar which have the same purchasing power.

Correction of an error. A correction of a material error from a prior period.

Cost approach. A valuation technique that reflects the amount that would be required currently to replace the service capacity of an asset.

Current assets. Cash and other assets or resources that are reasonably expected to be realized in cash or sold or consumed during the normal operating cycle of the business.

Current cost accounting. A method of valuing and reporting assets, liabilities, revenues, and expenses at their current cost at the balance sheet date or at the date of their use or sale.

Current liabilities. Obligations whose liquidation is reasonably expected to require the use of existing resources properly classifiable as current assets, or the creation of other current liabilities.

Discontinued operation. Results from disposal of a business component.

Discount rate adjustment technique. A present value technique that uses a risk-adjusted discount rate and contractual, promised, or most likely cash flows.

Expected cash flow. The probability-weighted average of possible future cash flows.

Extraordinary items. An unusual and infrequent event which has material effects.

Fair value. The price that would be received to sell an asset or paid to transfer a liability in an orderly transaction between market participants at the measurement date under current market conditions.

Fair value option for reporting financial assets and financial liabilities. An election can be made to value certain financial assets and financial liabilities at fair value.

Financial forecast. Prospective financial statements that present the knowledge and belief of responsible party in terms of expected financial position, results of operations, and cash flows.

Financial projection. Prospective financial statements that present the knowledge and belief of responsible party, based on one or more **hypothetical** assumptions, the enterprise's financial position, results of operations, and cash flows.

Form S-1/F-1. Registration statement for US/foreign companies.

Form 8-K/6-K. Information about material events for US/foreign companies.

Form 10-K/20F. Annual report for US/foreign companies.

Form 10-Q. Quarterly reports.

Highest and best use. The use of a nonfinancial asset by market participants that would maximize the value of the asset or the group of assets and liabilities within which the asset would be used.

Income approach. A valuation technique that converts future amounts to a single current amount. The fair value measurement is determined on the basis of the value indicated by current market expectations about those future amounts.

Level 1 inputs. Quoted prices in active markets for identical assets or liabilities that the reporting entity can access at the measurement date.

Level 2 inputs. Inputs other than quoted prices included in Level 1 that are observable for the asset or liability, either directly or indirectly.

Level 3 inputs. Unobservable inputs for the asset or liability.

Market approach. A valuation technique that uses prices and other relevant information generated by market transactions involving identical or comparable assets, liabilities, or a group of assets and liabilities, such as a business.

Modified cash-basis financial statements. Cash basis financial statements with modifications that have substantial support.

Most advantageous market. The market that maximizes the price that would be received to sell the asset or minimizes the amount to be paid to transfer the liability taking into account transaction costs and transportation cost.

Observable inputs. Inputs that are developed using market data and that refect the assumptions that market participants would use when pricing the asset or liability.

Present value. A tool used to link future amounts to a present amount using a discount rate.

Principle market. A market in which the greatest volume and level of activity occurs.

Prospective financial information. Any financial information about the future.

Realized holding gains. The difference between current cost and historical cost of asset consumed.

Regulation AB. Describes reporting requirements for asset-backed securities.

Regulation Fair Disclosure (FD). Mandates that publicly traded companies disclose material information to all investors simultaneously.

Regulation S-X. Describes the form and content of financial statements filed with the SEC.

Regulation S-K. Describes the requirements for information and forms required by Regulation S-X.

Regulatory-basis financial statements. Based on rules established by a regulatory agency.

Responsible party. Person(s), usually management, who are responsible for assumptions underlying the information.

Restructuring. A program that is planned and controlled by management and materially changes either (1) the scope of the business or (2) the manner in which the business is conducted.

Risk premium. Compensation sought by risk-averse market participants for bearing the uncertainty inherent in the cash flows of an asset or a liability.

Schedule 14A. Proxy statement.

Subsequent events. Events occurring after the balance sheet date but before the financial statements are issued or available to be issued.

Systematic risk. The common risk shared by an asset or a liability with the other items in a diversified portfolio.

Tax-basis financial statements. Prepared on the basis of tax laws and regulations.

Unrealized holding gains. Increases in the current cost of assets held throughout the year.

Unsystematic risk. The risk specific to a particular asset or liability.

Unusual or infrequent items. An unusual or infrequent event considered to be material that does not qualify as extraordinary.

Module 10: Inventory

Overview

Inventory is defined as tangible personal property (1) held for sale in the ordinary course of business, (2) in the process of production for such sale, or (3) to be used currently in the production of items for sale.

Inventory is tested on the Financial Accounting and Reporting section of the exam. The primary topics covered by questions on the exam are

1. **Ownership of goods:** The determination of which items are to be included in inventory taking into account items such as shipping terms and consignments.
2. **Cost:** The determination of which costs are to be assigned to inventory such as freight and overhead.
3. **Cost flow assumptions:** The determination of costs assigned to cost of goods sold and inventory under the various cost flow methods such as LIFO and FIFO.
4. **Valuation:** The determination of how and when inventories should reflect their market values using rules such as LCM.

A. Determining Inventory and Cost of Goods Sold

1. The primary basis of accounting for inventories is cost, which includes the cash or other fair value of consideration given in exchange for it. Inventory cost is a function of two variables

   a. The number of units included in inventory, and
   b. The costs attached to those units.

2. The units to be included in inventory are those which the firm owns; ownership is usually determined by legal title.
3. The costs to be included in inventory include all costs necessary to prepare the goods for sale. Normal costs for freight-in, handling costs, and normal spoilage are included in inventory.

   a. For a manufacturing entity, the cost of inventory includes direct materials, direct labor, and both direct and indirect factory overhead. These costs are then allocated to the work in progress and finished goods inventory account. Variable production overhead is allocated to each unit of production based on the actual use of the production facilities. Fixed overhead is allocated based on the normal capacity of the production facilities. The normal capacity of the production facility is the production expected to be achieved over a number of periods or seasons under normal circumstances, taking into account the loss of capacity resulting from planned maintenance. The range of normal capacity will vary based on business and industry-specific factors. The actual level of production may be used if it approximates normal capacity. Unallocated fixed overhead costs are recognized as an expense in the period in which they are incurred.

      (1) Any abnormal costs for freight-in, handling costs, and spoilage are treated as current period expenses, and are not allocated to inventory.
      (2) Interest on inventories routinely produced, or repetitively produced in large quantities, is not capitalized as part of inventory cost.

   b. For a merchandising concern, the costs to be included in inventory include the purchase price of the goods, freight-in, insurance, warehousing, and any other costs incurred in the preparation of these goods for sale. The amount used as a purchase price for the goods will vary depending upon whether the gross or net method is used in the recording of purchases.

      (1) If the gross method is used to record the purchases, then any subsequent discount taken is shown as purchase discount which is netted against the purchases account in determining cost of goods sold.

(2) If the net method is used to record purchases, then any purchase discounts offered are assumed taken and the purchase account reflects the net price. If subsequent to the recording of the purchases the discount is not taken (i.e., payment is tendered after the discount period has elapsed), a purchase discounts lost account is debited. The balance in the purchase discounts lost account does **not** enter into the determination of cost of goods sold; this amount is treated as a period expense.

> **NOTE:** Regardless of the method used, purchases are always recorded net of any allowable **trade discounts**. These are discounts that are allowed to the entity because of its being a wholesaler, a good customer, or merely the fact that the item is on sale at a reduced price.

> **NOTE:** Interest paid to vendors is not included in the cost of inventory.

4. The determination of cost of goods sold and inventory under each of the cost flow assumptions depends upon the method used to record the inventory: periodic or perpetual.

     a. **Periodic system.** Inventory is counted periodically and then priced. The ending inventory is usually recorded in the cost of goods sold (CGS) entry.

Ending inventory (EI)	xx	
CGS	(plug)	
Beginning inventory (BI)		xx
Purchases		xx

       (1) CGS = Purchases – (the change in inventory). For example, if ending inventory decreases, all of the purchases and some of the beginning inventory have been sold. If ending inventory increases, not all of the purchases have been sold.

     b. **Perpetual system.** A running total is kept of the units on hand (and possibly their value) by recording all increases and decreases as they occur. When inventory is purchased, the inventory account, rather than purchases, is debited. As inventory is sold, the following entry is recorded.

CGS	(cost)	
Inventory		(cost)

> **NOW REVIEW MULTIPLE-CHOICE QUESTIONS 1 THROUGH 13 IN VOLUME 2**

B. Inventory Valuation and Cost-Flow Methods

1. Specific identification
2. Weighted-average
3. Simple average
4. Moving average
5. Lower of cost or market
6. Losses on purchase commitments
7. First-in, first-out (FIFO)
8. Last-in, first-out (LIFO)
9. Dollar-value LIFO
10. Gross profit
11. Standard costs
12. Direct (variable) costing
13. Market
14. Cost apportionment by relative sales value

1. Specific Identification

     a. The seller determines which item is sold.

> **EXAMPLE**
>
> A seller has for sale four identical machines costing $260, $230, $180, and $110. Since the machines are identical, a purchaser will have no preference as to which machine s/he receives when purchased.

> **NOTE:** The seller is able to manipulate income as s/he can sell any machine (and charge the appropriate amount to CGS). Significant dollar value items are frequently accounted for by specific identification.

     b. The use of the specific identification method is appropriate when there is a relatively small number of significant dollar value items in inventory.

2. Weighted-Average

a. The seller averages the cost of all items on hand and purchased during the period. The units in ending inventory and units sold (CGS) are costed at this average cost.

EXAMPLE

	Cost	Units	
Beginning inventory	$200	100	($2.00 unit)
Purchase 1	315	150	($2.10 unit)
Purchase 2	85	50	($1.70 unit)
	$600	300	

Weighted-average cost $600/300 = $2.00 unit

---

3. Simple Average

a. The seller does not weight the average for units purchased or in beginning inventory (e.g., the above $2.00, $2.10, and $1.70 unit costs would be averaged to $1.93).

b. The method is fairly accurate if all purchases, production runs, and beginning inventory quantities are equal.

4. Moving Average

a. The average cost of goods on hand must be recalculated any time additional inventory is purchased at a unit cost different from the previously calculated average cost of goods on hand.

EXAMPLE

	Dollar cost of units on hand	Units on hand	Inventory unit cost
Beginning inventory	$200	100	$2.00
Sale of 50 units @ $2.00 = $100	100	50	2.00
Purchase of 150 units for $320	420	200	2.10
Sale of 50 units @ $2.10 = $105	315	150	2.10
Purchase of 50 units for $109	424	200	2.12

NOTE: Sales do not change the unit price because they are taken out of inventory at the average price.

b. Moving average may only be used with perpetual systems which account for changes in value with each change in inventory (and not with perpetual systems only accounting for changes in the number of units).

NOW REVIEW MULTIPLE-CHOICE QUESTIONS 14 THROUGH 17 IN VOLUME 2

5. Lower of Cost or Market

a. "A departure from the cost basis of pricing the inventory is required when the utility of the goods is no longer as great as its cost." The following steps should be used to apply the lower of cost or market rule:

(1) Determine market

(a) Market is replacement cost limited to

1] **Ceiling**—which is net realizable value (selling price less selling costs and costs to complete).
2] **Floor**—which is net realizable value less normal profit.

NOTE: If replacement cost is greater than net realizable value, market equals net realizable value. Likewise, market equals net realizable value minus normal profit if replacement cost is less than net realizable value minus normal profit.

(2) Determine cost

NOTE: The floor and ceiling have nothing to do with cost

(3) Select the lower of cost or market either for each individual item or for inventory as a whole (compute total market and total cost, and select lower).

EXAMPLE

LOWER OF COST OR MARKET EXAMPLE

Item	Cost	Replacement cost	Selling price	Selling cost	Normal profit
A	$10.50	$10.25	$15.00	$2.50	$2.50
B	5.75	5.25	8.00	1.50	1.00
C	4.25	4.75	5.50	1.00	1.50

Item	Replacement cost	NRV (ceiling)	NRV-Profit (floor)	Designated market value	Cost	LCM
A	$10.25	$12.50	$10.00	$10.25	$10.50	$10.25
B	5.25	6.50	5.50	5.50	5.75	5.50
C	4.75	4.50	3.00	4.50	4.25	4.25

Item A—Market is replacement cost, $10.25, because it is between the floor ($10.00) and the ceiling ($12.50). Lower of cost or market is $10.25.

Item B—Market is limited to the floor, $5.50 ($8.00 – $1.50 – $1.00) because the $5.25 replacement cost is beneath the floor. Lower of cost or market is $5.50.

Item C—Market is limited to the ceiling, $4.50 ($5.50 – $1.00) because the $4.75 replacement cost is above the ceiling. Lower of cost or market is $4.25.

---

b. Observations about the lower of cost or market rule

(1) The floor limitation on market prevents recognition of more than normal profit in future periods (if market is less than cost).

(2) The ceiling limitation on market prevents recognition of a loss in future periods (if market is less than cost).

(3) Cost or market applied to individual items will always be as low as, and usually lower than, cost or market applied to the inventory as a whole. They will be the same when all items at market or all items at cost are lower.

(4) Once inventory has been written down there can be no recovery from the write-down until the units are sold. Recall that this differs from marketable securities where recoveries of prior write-downs are required to be taken into the income stream.

c. Methods of recording the write-down

(1) If market is less than cost at the end of any period, there are two methods available to record the market decline. The entry to establish the ending inventory can be made using the market figure. The difficulty with this procedure is that it forces the loss to be included in the cost of goods sold, thus overstating the cost of goods sold by the amount of the loss.

NOTE: Under this method the loss is not separately disclosed.

(2) An alternative treatment is to debit the inventory account for the actual cost (not market) of goods on hand, and then to make the following entry to give separate recognition to the market decline.

Loss due to market decline	xx	
Inventory		xx

NOW REVIEW MULTIPLE-CHOICE QUESTIONS 18 THROUGH 22 IN VOLUME 2

6. **Losses on Purchase Commitments**

a. **Purchase commitments** (PC) result from legally enforceable contracts to purchase specific quantities of goods at fixed prices in the future. When there is a decline in market value below the contract price at the balance sheet date and the contracts are noncancellable, an unrealized loss has occurred and, if material, should be recorded in the period of decline.

Estimated loss on PC	(excess of PC over mkt.)
Accrued loss on PC	(excess of PC over mkt.)

b. If further declines in market value are estimated to occur before delivery is made, the amount of the loss to be accrued should be increased to include this additional decline in market value. The loss is taken to the income statement; the accrued loss on PC is a liability account and shown on the balance sheet.

When the goods are subsequently received

Purchases	xx	
Accrued loss on PC	xx	
Cash		xx

c. If a partial or full recovery occurs before the inventory is received, the accrued loss account would be reduced by the amount of the recovery. Likewise, an income statement account, "Recovery on Loss of PC," would be credited.

> **NOW REVIEW MULTIPLE-CHOICE QUESTIONS 23 THROUGH 24 IN VOLUME 2**

7. **First-In, First-Out (FIFO)**

   a. The goods from beginning inventory and the earliest purchases are assumed to be the goods sold first.
   b. In a period of rising prices, cost of goods sold is made up of the earlier, lower-priced goods resulting in a larger profit (relative to LIFO). The ending inventory is made up of more recent purchases and thus represents a more current value (relative to LIFO) on the balance sheet.

   > **NOTE:** This cost-flow assumption may be used even when it does not match the physical flow of goods.

   c. Whenever the FIFO method is used, the results of inventory and cost of goods sold are the same at the end of the period under either a perpetual or a periodic system.

8. **Last-In, First-Out (LIFO)**

   a. Under this cost-flow method, the most recent purchases are assumed to be the first goods sold; thus, ending inventory is assumed to be composed of the oldest goods. Therefore, the cost of goods sold contains relatively current costs (resulting in the matching of current costs with sales).

   > **NOTE:** This cost-flow assumption usually does not parallel the physical flow of goods.

   b. LIFO is widely adopted because it is acceptable for tax purposes and because in periods of rising prices it reduces tax liability due to the lower reported income (resulting from the higher cost of goods sold).
   c. LIFO smooths out fluctuations in the income stream relative to FIFO because it matches current costs with current revenues.
   d. A primary disadvantage of LIFO is that it results in large profits if inventory decreases because earlier, lower valued layers are included in the cost of goods sold. This is generally known as a LIFO liquidation.

   (1) Another disadvantage is the cost involved in maintaining separate LIFO records for each item in inventory.

   e. If LIFO is used for tax purposes, it must be used for financial reporting purposes. This is known as the **LIFO conformity rule**.

   (1) Under current tax law, inventory layers may be added using the (1) earliest acquisition costs, (2) weighted-average unit cost for the period, or (3) latest acquisition costs.

   > **NOTE:** In solving questions on the CPA Exam, use the earliest acquisition costs unless you are instructed to use one of the other alternatives.

   f. When a company uses LIFO for external reporting purposes and another inventory method for internal purposes, a **LIFO Reserve** account is used to reduce inventory from the internal valuation to the LIFO valuation. LIFO Reserve is a contra account to inventory, and is adjusted up or down at year-end with a corresponding increase or decrease to **Cost of Goods Sold**.

9. **Dollar-Value LIFO**

   a. Dollar-value LIFO is LIFO applied to **pools** of inventory items rather than to **individual** items. Thus, the cost of keeping inventory records is less under dollar-value LIFO than under unit LIFO.

(1) Because the LIFO conformity rule (if LIFO is used for tax, it must also be used for external financial statements) also applies to dollar-value LIFO, companies using dollar-value LIFO define their LIFO pools so as to conform with IRS regulations.

(2) Under these regulations, a LIFO pool can contain all of the inventory items for a natural business unit, or a multiple pool approach can be elected whereby a business can group similarly used inventory items into several groups or pools.

b. The advantage of using inventory pools is that an involuntary liquidation of LIFO layers is less likely to occur because of the increased number of items in the pool (if the level of one item decreases it can be offset by increases in the levels of other items), and because the pools can be adjusted for changes in product composition or product mix.

c. Like unit LIFO, dollar-value LIFO is a layering method. Unlike unit LIFO, dollar-value LIFO determines increases or decreases in ending inventory in terms of dollars of the same purchasing power rather than in terms of units. Dollar-value LIFO seeks to determine the real dollar change in inventory.

(1) Ending inventory is deflated to base-year cost by dividing ending inventory by the current year's conversion price index and comparing the resulting amount with the beginning inventory, which has also been stated in base-year dollars. The difference represents the layer which, after conversion, must be added or subtracted to arrive at the appropriate value of ending inventory.

> **NOTE:** The individual layers in a dollar-value LIFO inventory are valued as follows:
>
> $ value LIFO = Inventory at base-year prices × Conversion price index

d. In applying dollar-value LIFO, manufacturers develop their own indexes while retailers and wholesalers use published figures. In computing the conversion price index, the **double-extension technique** is used, named so because each year the ending inventory is extended at both base-year prices and current-year prices. The index, computed as follows, measures the change in the inventory prices since the base year.

$$\frac{\text{EI at end-of-year prices}}{\text{EI at base-year prices}} = \text{Conversion price index}$$

EXAMPLE

To illustrate the computation of the index, assume that the base-year price of products A and B is $3 and $5, respectively, and at the end of the year, the price of product A is $3.20 and B, $5.75, with 2,000 and 800 units on hand, respectively. The index for the year is 110%, computed as follows:

	EI at end-of-year prices	÷	EI at base-year prices	=	Conversion price index
Product A	2,000 @ $3.20 = $ 6,400		2,000 @ $3 = $ 6,000		
Product B	800 @ $5.75 = $ 4,600		800 @ $5 = $ 4,000		
	$11,000		$10,000		1.10 (or 110%)

---

e. Steps in dollar-value LIFO

Manufacturers	**Retailers and wholesalers**
1. Compute the conversion price index	1. Determine index from appropriate published source
2. Compare BI at base-year prices to EI at base-year prices to determine the	2. Divide EI by conversion price index to restate to base-year prices
a. New inventory layer added, or b. Old inventory layer removed (LIFO liquidation)	3. Same as 2. for manufacturers
3. If there is an increase at base-year prices, value this new layer by multiplying the layer (stated in base-year dollars) by the conversion price index. If there is a decrease at base-year prices, the remaining layers are valued at the index in effect when the layer was first added.	4. Same as 3. for manufacturers

EXAMPLE

Assume the following:

	EI at end-of-year prices	÷	Conversion price index	=	EI at base-year prices		Change as measured in base-year dollars
Year 1 (base)	$100,000		1.00		$100,000		
Year 2	121,000		1.10		110,000	>	$10,000
Year 3	150,000		1.20		125,000	>	15,000
Year 4	135,000		1.25		108,000	>	(17,000)

In both year 2 and year 3, ending inventory in terms of base-year dollars increased 10,000 and 15,000 base-year dollars, respectively. Since layers are added every year that ending inventory at base-year prices is greater than the previous year's ending inventory at base-year prices, the ending inventory for year 3 would be computed as follows:

Ending inventory, Year 3

	Base-year prices	×	Index	=	EI at dollar-value LIFO cost
Year 1 (base)	$100,000		1.00		$100,000
Year 2 layer	10,000		1.10		11,000
Year 3 layer	15,000		1.20		18,000
Ending inventory	$125,000				$129,000

> **NOTE:** Each layer added is multiplied by the conversion price index in effect when the layer was added. Thus, the year 2 layer is multiplied by the year 2 index of 1.10 and the year 3 layer is multiplied by the year 3 index of 1.20.

In year 4, ending inventory decreased by 17,000 base-year dollars. Therefore, a LIFO liquidation has occurred whereby 17,000 base-year dollars will have to be removed from the previous year's ending inventory. Because LIFO is being used, the liquidation affects the most recently added layer first and then, if necessary, the next most recently added layer(s). Ending inventory in year 4 is composed of

	Base-year prices	×	Index	=	EI at dollar-value LIFO cost
Year 1 (base)	$100,000		1.00		$100,000
Year 2 layer	8,000		1.10		8,800
Ending inventory	$108,000				$108,800

> **NOTE:** The liquidation of 17,000 base-year dollars in year 4 caused the entire year 3 layer of 15,000 base-year dollars to be liquidated as well as 2,000 base-year dollars from year 2. Also note that the remaining 8,000 base-year dollars in the year 2 layer is still multiplied by the year 2 index of 1.10.

f. **Link-chain technique.** The computations for application of the double-extension technique can become very arduous even if only a few items exist in the inventory. Also, consider the problems that arise when there is a constant change in the inventory mix or in situations in which the breadth of the inventory is large.

  (1) The link-chain method was originally developed for (and limited to) those companies that wanted to use LIFO but, because of a substantial change in product lines over time, were unable to recreate or keep the historical records necessary to make accurate use of the double-extension method.

  (2) The link-chain method is the process of developing a single cumulative index. Technological change is allowed for by the method used to calculate each current year index. The index is derived by double extending a representative sample (generally thought to be between 50% and 75% of the dollar value of the pool) at both beginning-of-year prices and end-of-year prices. This annual index is then applied (multiplied) to the previous period's cumulative index to arrive at the new current year cumulative index.

> **EXAMPLE**
>
> How the links and cumulative index are computed.
>
> | End of period | Ratio of end of period prices to beginning prices* | Cumulative index number** |
> |---|---|---|
> | 0 | -- | 1.000 |
> | 1 | 1.10 | 1.100 |
> | 2 | 1.05 | 1.155 |
> | 3 | 1.07 | 1.236 |
>
> * $\dfrac{\text{End of period prices}}{\text{Beginning of period prices}}$ = Index number for **this period only**
>
> ** Multiply the cumulative index number at the beginning of the period by the ratio computed with the formula shown above.

(a) The ending inventory is divided by the cumulative index number to derive the ending inventory at base period prices. An increase (layer) in base period dollars for the period is priced using the newly derived index number.

NOW REVIEW MULTIPLE-CHOICE QUESTIONS 25 THROUGH 35 IN VOLUME 2

10. Gross Profit

a. Ending inventory is estimated by using the gross profit (GP) percentage to convert sales to cost of goods presumed sold.

b. Since ending inventory is only estimated, the gross method is not acceptable for either tax or annual financial reporting purposes.

c. Its major uses are to estimate ending inventory for internal use, for use in interim financial statements, and for establishing the amount of loss due to the destruction of inventory by fire, flood, or other catastrophes.

> **EXAMPLE**
>
> Suppose the inventory of the Luckless Company has been destroyed by fire and the following information is available from duplicate records stored at a separate facility: beginning inventory of $30,000, purchases for the period of $40,000, sales of $60,000, and an average GP percentage of 25%. The cost of the inventory destroyed is computed as follows:
>
> | | | |
> |---|---|---|
> | | Beginning inventory | $30,000 |
> | + | Purchases | 40,000 |
> | | Goods available | 70,000 |
> | – | Cost of goods sold | 45,000* |
> | | Inventory destroyed | $25,000 |
>
> * Cost of goods sold is computed as (1) sales of $60,000 – ($60,000 × 25%) or (2) sales of $60,000 × 75%.

d. If you need to convert a GP rate on cost to a markup (MU) rate on the selling price, divide the GP rate on cost by 1 **plus** the GP rate on cost, that is, if the GP rate on cost is 50%, then .50/(1 + .50) = 33 1/3% is the MU rate on the selling price.

e. If you need to convert a MU rate on the selling price to a GP rate on cost, divide the MU rate on the selling price by 1 **minus** the MU rate on the selling price, that is, if the MU rate on the selling price is 20%, then .20/(1 – .20) = 25% GP rate on cost.

f. Always be cautious about gross profit rates (on cost or the selling price).

11. Standard Costs

a. Standard costs are predetermined costs in a cost accounting system, generally used for control purposes.

b. Inventory may be costed at standard only if variances are reasonable (i.e., not large).

(1) Large debit (unfavorable) variances would indicate inventory (and cost of sales) were undervalued, whereas large credit (favorable) variances would indicate inventory is overvalued.

12. **Direct (Variable) Costing**

   a. Direct costing is not an acceptable method for valuing inventory (ARB 43, chap 4).
   b. Direct costing considers only variable costs as product costs and fixed production costs as period costs. In contrast, absorption costing considers both variable and fixed manufacturing costs as product costs.

13. **Market**

   a. Inventory is usually valued at market value when market is lower than cost. However, occasionally, inventory will be valued at market even if it is above cost. This usually occurs with

   (1) Precious metals with a fixed market value
   (2) Industries such as meatpacking where costs cannot be allocated and

       (a) Quoted market prices exist
       (b) Goods are interchangeable (e.g., agricultural commodities)

14. **Cost Apportionment by Relative Sales Value**

   a. Basket purchases and similar situations require cost allocation based on relative value.

   > **EXAMPLE**
   >
   > A developer may spend $400,000 to acquire land, survey, curb and gutter, pave streets, etc. for a subdivision. Due to location and size, the lots may vary in selling price. If the total of all selling prices were $600,000, the developer could cost each lot at 2/3 (400/600; COST/RETAIL ratio) of its selling price.

   NOW REVIEW MULTIPLE-CHOICE QUESTIONS 36 THROUGH 37 IN VOLUME 2

C. Items to Include in Inventory

1. Goods shipped FOB shipping point which are in transit should be included in the inventory of the buyer since title passes to the buyer when the carrier receives the goods.
2. Goods shipped FOB destination should be included in the inventory of the seller until the goods are received by the buyer since title passes to the buyer when the goods are received at their final destination.

   > **NOTE:** The more complicated UCC rules concerning transfer of title should be used for the law portion, not the financial accounting and reporting portion, of the exam.

D. Consignments

1. Consignors consign their goods to consignees who are sales agents of the consignors. Consigned goods remain the property of the consignor until sold. Therefore, any unsold goods (including a proportionate share of freight costs incurred in shipping the goods to the consignee) must be included in the consignor's inventory.
2. Consignment sales revenue should be recognized by the consignor when the consignee sells the consigned goods to the ultimate customer. Therefore, no revenue is recognized at the time the consignor ships the goods to the consignee.

   > **NOTE:** Sales commission made by the consignee would be reported as a selling expense by the consignor and would **not** be netted against the sales revenue recognized by the consignor.

   > **NOTE:** The UCC rules concerning consignments should be used for the law portion, not the financial accounting and reporting portion, of the exam.

E. Ratios
The two ratios below relate to inventory.

1. **Inventory turnover**—Measures the number of times inventory was sold and reflects inventory order and investment policies

$$\frac{\text{Cost of goods sold}}{\text{Average inventory}}$$

2. **Number of days' supply in average inventory**—Number of days inventory is held before sale; reflects on efficiency of inventory policies

$$\frac{365}{\text{Inventory turnover}}$$

NOW REVIEW MULTIPLE-CHOICE QUESTIONS 38 THROUGH 50 IN VOLUME 2

F. Long-Term Construction Contracts

1. Long-term contracts are accounted for by two methods: completed-contract method and percentage-of-completion method.

   a. **Completed-contract method**—Recognition of contract revenue and profit at contract completion. All related costs are deferred until completion and then matched to revenues.

      (1) The completed-contract method is preferable in circumstances in which estimates cannot meet the criteria for reasonable dependability or one of the above conditions does not exist.

      (2) The advantage of the completed-contract method is that it is based on results, not estimates, and the disadvantage is that current performance is not reflected and income recognition may be irregular.

   b. **Percentage-of-completion**—Recognition of contract revenue and profit during construction based on expected total profit and estimated progress towards completion in the current period. All related costs are recognized in the period in which they occur.

      (1) The use of the percentage-of-completion method depends on the ability to make reasonably dependable estimates of contract revenues, contract costs, and the extent of progress toward completion. For entities which customarily operate under contractual arrangements and for whom contracting represents a significant part of their operations, the **presumption** is that they have the ability to make estimates that are sufficiently dependable to justify the use of the percentage-of-completion method of accounting.

      (2) The percentage-of-completion method is **preferable** in circumstances in which reasonably dependable estimates can be made and in which all of the following conditions exist:

         (a) Contracts executed by the parties normally include provisions that clearly specify the enforceable rights regarding goods or services to be provided and received by the parties, the consideration to be exchanged, and the manner and terms of settlement.
         (b) The buyer can be expected to satisfy obligations under the contract.
         (c) The contractor can be expected to perform contractual obligation.

      (3) The advantage of percentage-of-completion is periodic recognition of income, and the disadvantage is dependence on estimates.

      (4) In practice, various procedures are used to measure the extent of progress toward completion under the percentage-of-completion method, but the most widely used one is **cost-to-cost** which is based on the assumed relationship between a unit of input and productivity. Under cost-to-cost, either revenue and/or profit to be recognized in the current period can be determined by the following formula:

$$\text{Revenue (profit)} = \left(\frac{\text{Cost to date}}{\substack{\text{Total expected} \\ \text{cost based on} \\ \text{latest estimate}}} \times \substack{\text{Contract price} \\ \text{(Expected profit)}} \right) - \substack{\text{Revenue (profit)} \\ \text{recognized in} \\ \text{previous periods}}$$

NOTE: Revenue and profit are two different terms. Profit is calculated by subtracting construction expenses from revenue. Revenue is the contract price. Therefore, pay particular attention to what item the CPA exam asks you to calculate.

2. The ledger account titles used in the following discussion are unique to long-term construction contracts. In practice, there are numerous account titles for the same item (e.g., "billings on LT contracts" vs. "partial billings on construction in progress") and various methodologies for journalizing the same transactions (e.g., separate revenue and expense control accounts in lieu of an "income on LT contracts" account). The following example has been simplified to highlight the main concepts.

EXAMPLE

Assume a 3-year contract at a contract price of $500,000 as well as the following data:

	Year 1	Year 2	Year 3
Cost incurred this year	$135,000	$225,000	$ 45,000
Prior years' costs	-0-	135,000	360,000
Estimated costs to complete	$315,000	40,000	-0-
Total costs	$450,000	400,000	$405,000
Progress billings made during the year	$200,000	$200,000	$100,000
Collection of billings each year	$175,000	$200,000	$125,000

From the above information, the following may be determined.

Percent of completion (costs to date/total costs)
Year 1: $135,000/$450,000 = 30%
Year 2: $360,000/$400,000 = 90%
Year 3: $405,000/$405,000 = 100%

	Year 1	Year 2	Year 3
Total revenue	$500,000	$500,000	$500,000
× Percent of completion	× 30%	× 90%	× 100%
Total revenue to be recognized by end of year	$150,000	$450,000	$500,000
− Revenue recognized in prior periods	--	(150,000)	(450,000)
Current year's revenue (to be recognized)	$150,000	$300,000	$ 50,000
Contract price	$500,000	$500,000	$500,000
− Total estimated costs	(450,000)	(400,000)	(405,000)
Estimated profit	$ 50,000	$100,000	$ 95,000
× Percent of completion	× 30%	× 90%	× 100%
Total profit to be recognized by end of year	$ 15,000	$ 90,000	$ 95,000
− Profit recognized in prior periods	--	(15,000)	(90,000)
Current year's profit (to be recognized)	$ 15,000	$ 75,000	$ 5,000

		Percentage-of-completion		Completed-contract	
Year 1 Costs	Construction in progress	135,000		135,000	
	Cash		135,000		135,000
Year 1 Progress billings	Accounts receivable	200,000		200,000	
	Billings on LT contracts		200,000		200,000
Year 1 Cash collected	Cash	175,000		175,000	
	Accounts receivable		175,000		175,000
Year 1 Profit recognition	Construction expenses	135,000		none	
	Construction in progress	15,000			
	Construction revenue		150,000		
Year 2 Costs	Construction in progress	225,000		225,000	
	Cash		225,000		225,000
Year 2 Progress billings	Accounts receivable	200,000		200,000	
	Billings on LT contracts		200,000		200,000
Year 2 Cash collected	Cash	200,000		200,000	
	Accounts receivable		200,000		200,000
Year 2 Profit recognition	Construction expenses	225,000		none	
	Construction in progress	75,000			
	Construction revenue		300,000		
Year 3 Costs	Construction in progress	45,000		45,000	
	Cash		45,000		45,000
Year 3 Progress billings	Accounts receivable	100,000		100,000	
	Billings on LT contracts		100,000		100,000
Year 3 Cash collected	Cash	125,000		125,000	
	Accounts receivable		125,000		125,000

Year 3 Profit recog-
nition and closing
of special ac-
counts
	Construction expenses
	Construction in progress
	   Construction revenue
	Billings on LT contracts
	   Const. in progress
	Construction expenses
	   Const. in progress
	Billings on LT contracts
	   Construction revenue
		45,000
		5,000
		
		500,000
			
			50,000
			
			500,000
			
			405,000
			
			500,000
				
				405,000
				
				500,000

3. The "construction in progress" (CIP) account is a cost accumulation account similar to "work in process" for job-order costing, except that the percentage-of-completion method includes interim profits in the account. The "billings on LT contracts" account is similar to an unearned revenue account. At each financial statement date, the "construction in progress" account should be netted against the "billings on LT contracts" account on a project-by-project basis, resulting in a net current asset and/or a net current liability.

EXAMPLE

Under the percentage of completion method in the above example, a net current asset of $50,000 [($135,000 + $15,000 + $225,000 + $75,000) – ($200,000 + $200,000)] would be reported at the end of year 2. A net current liability of $40,000 would result under the completed-contract method [($200,000 + $200,000) – ($135,000 + $225,000)] for the same year.

SUMMARY OF ACCOUNTS USED IN CONSTRUCTION ACCOUNTING
(NO LOSS EXPECTED OR INCURRED)

Balance sheet

Construction in Progress			A/P, Materials, etc.	
(A)	(E)		(A)	
(F)	(G)			

Accounts Receivable			Billings on LT Contracts	
(B)	(C)		(D)	(B)
			(G)	

Cash	
(C)	

Income statement

Construction Revenue	
	(D)
	(F)

Construction Expenses	
(E)	
(F)	

Explanation of Journal Entries

Both methods	**Completed-contract method**	**Percentage-of-completion method**
(A) To record accumulated costs (B) To record progress billings (C) To record cash collections	(D) To record revenue upon completion and to close billings account (E) To record expenses upon completion and to close construction in progress account	(F) To record recognition of interim revenue and expense (G) To close construction-in-progress and billings accounts at project completion

Balance Sheet Classification*

Current asset	**Current liability**
Projects where CIP at year-end** > Billings	Projects where billings > CIP at year-end** Estimated loss on uncompleted contract***

   * Evaluate and classify on a project-by-project basis.
  ** Construction in progress including income (when percentage-of-completion method is used) or loss recognized.
*** When recognizing and reporting losses, it is necessary to use a current liability account instead of reducing CIP in those cases in which a contract's billings exceed its accumulated costs.

---

4. **Contract losses**

    a. In any year when a **percentage-of-completion** contract has an expected loss on the entire contract, the amount of the loss reported in that year is the total expected loss on the entire contract **plus** all profit previously recognized.

EXAMPLE

If the expected costs yet to be incurred at the end of year two were $147,000, the total expected loss is $7,000 [$500,000 − ($135,000 + $225,000 + $147,000)] and the total loss reported in year two would be $22,000 ($7,000 + $15,000).

---

b. Similarly, under the **completed-contract** method, total expected losses on the entire contract are recognized as soon as they are estimated. The loss recognized is similar to that for percentage-of-completion except the amount is for the expected loss on the entire contract.

EXAMPLE

In the aforementioned example, the loss to be recognized is only $7,000 (the entire loss on the contract expected in year two) because interim profits have not been recorded.

---

c. Journal entries and a schedule for profit or loss recognized on the contract under the percentage-of-completion method follow.

EXAMPLE

Journal entry at end of year 2	Percentage-of-completion	Completed-contract
Construction expenses	227,000*	
Construction in progress (loss)	22,000	
Construction revenue	205,000**	
Loss on uncompleted LT contracts		7,000
Construction in progress (loss)		7,000

* Year 2 costs $225,000

Loss attributable to year 3:		
Year 3 revenue ($500,000 − $150,000 − $205,000)	$145,000	
Year 3 costs (expected)	147,000	2,000
Total		$227,000

** ($360,000/$507,000) (Costs to date/Total estimated costs) = 71% (rounded); (71% × $500,000) − $150,000 = $205,000

PERCENTAGE-OF-COMPLETION METHOD

	Year 1	Year 2	Year 3
Contract price:	$ 500,000	$500,000	$500,000
Estimated total costs:			
Costs incurred this year	$ 135,000	$225,000	$ 144,000***
Prior year's costs	--	135,000	360,000
Estimated cost yet to be incurred	315,000	147,000	--
Estimated total costs for the three-year period, actual for year 3	$ 450,000	$507,000	$504,000
Estimated total income (loss) for three-year period, actual for year 3	$ 15,000	$ (7,000)	$ (4,000)
Income (loss) on entire contract previously recognized	--	15,000	(7,000)
Amount of estimated income (loss) recognized in the current period, actual for year 3	$ 15,000	$(22,000)	$ 3,000

*** Assumed

NOW REVIEW MULTIPLE-CHOICE QUESTIONS 51 THROUGH 61 IN VOLUME 2

G. Research Component—Accounting Standards Codification

1. The authoritative literature for inventory is found primarily in two places in the Codification: Topic 330 and Topic 605.

    a. Topic 330 contains the definition of inventory, the significance of inventories, the basis of accounting, cost flows, and application of lower of cost or market.

b. Topic 605 focuses on long-term construction contracts and the percentage-of-completion and completed-contract methods.

c. Although the weighted-average, moving-average, and gross profit methods of accounting for inventory are acceptable methods, few, if any, references are made to these methods in the accounting literature.

   (1) The only references to methods are first-in first-out, average and last-in first-out.

> **NOTE:** Typing the keywords with correct hyphenation should produce faster and more accurate results.

Accumulated costs billings	Expected losses contract	Mark-up inventory
Basis consistently applied	Finished goods	Net realizable value
Clearly reflects income	Firm purchase commitments	Percentage-of-completion method
Completed-contract method	First-in first-out	Physical deterioration
Contract costs loss	Held for sale	Raw materials
Contracts in process	Inventory obsolescence	Utility of goods
Cost or market	Last-in first-out	Work in process
Cost principle inventories	Lower of cost or market	

H. International Financial Reporting Standards (IFRS)

1. IFRS accounting for inventory differs from US GAAP in three areas: cost flow assumption, valuation of inventory at year-end, and capitalization of interest.

   a. With IFRS, the LIFO cost flow assumption is not permissible. Specific ID is required for inventory of goods that are not interchangeable, or goods that are produced and segregated for specific projects. FIFO and weighted-average methods are acceptable methods under IFRS for other types of inventory. The retail method may only be used for certain industries. In addition, the gross profit method can be used to estimate ending inventory when a physical count is not possible.

   b. Inventories are carried at the lower of cost or net realizable value (LCNRV). An exception to the LCNRV rule applies to agricultural inventories (biological assets) which are carried at fair value less costs to sell at the point of harvest.

      (1) Recall that in US GAAP, lower of cost or market (LCM) is used to value inventories. Market is defined as replacement cost, subject to a ceiling and floor. The ceiling is net realizable value (NRV), and the floor is NRV less a normal profit margin. Once inventory is written down, a loss may not be recovered.

      (2) Although IFRS uses a similar valuation concept, IFRS values inventory at the lower of cost or net realizable value (LCNRV). Note that the calculations are different from US GAAP. NRV is calculated as estimated selling price less estimated costs of completion and sale. Generally, LCNRV is applied on an item-by-item basis. However, under IFRS if there are groups of items that have similar characteristics, they may be grouped for the application of LCNRV.

> **EXAMPLE**
>
> Assume the following facts for an inventory:
>
> | | |
> |---|---|
> | Historical cost | $100 |
> | Estimated selling price | 90 |
> | Estimated costs to complete and sell | 5 |
> | NRV | $ 85 |
>
> To apply LCNRV to this example, you compare the cost of $100 to the estimated selling price less estimated costs to complete and sell ($90 – $5). NRV is $85. Therefore, the LCNRV is $85. The inventory would be written down to $85 with a corresponding expense on the income statement. If the inventory value at the end of Year 2 was $90, a recovery of the loss would be recorded by debiting Inventory and crediting an income account.

> **NOTE:** If LCM were applied under US standards, additional information would be needed. Specifically, US GAAP would require the replacement cost and the normal profit margin in order to arrive at the ceiling and the floor.

   c. Rules for capitalization of interest are also different.

      (1) US GAAP allows no capitalization of interest for inventories that are routinely manufactured or otherwise produced in quantities on a repetitive basis.

(2) Similar to US GAAP, IFRS does not allow interest or financing costs to be capitalized as an inventory cost if it is paid under normal credit terms. However, IFRS allows interest costs to be capitalized if there is a lengthy production period to prepare the goods for sale.

NOW REVIEW MULTIPLE-CHOICE QUESTIONS 62 THROUGH 68 IN VOLUME 2

KEY TERMS

Absorption costing. Considers both variable and fixed manufacturing costs as product costs.

Ceiling. Which is net realizable value (selling price less selling costs and costs to complete).

Completed-contract method. Recognition of contract revenue and profit at contract completion.

Direct (Variable) costing. Considers only variable costs as product costs and fixed production costs as period costs.

Dollar-value LIFO. LIFO applied to pools of inventory items rather than to individual items.

First-In, First-Out (FIFO). The goods from beginning inventory and the earliest purchases are assumed to be the goods sold first.

Floor. Which is net realizable value less normal profit.

FOB destination. Title passes to the buyer when the goods are received at their final destination.

FOB shipping point. Title passes to the buyer when the carrier receives the goods.

Gross method. Any subsequent discount taken is shown as purchase discount which is netted against the purchases account in determining cost of goods sold.

Inventory turnover. Measures the number of times inventory was sold and reflects inventory order and investment policies.

Last-In, First-Out (LIFO). The most recent purchases are assumed to be the first goods sold; thus, ending inventory is assumed to be composed of the oldest goods.

LIFO conformity rule. If LIFO is used for tax purposes, it must be used for financial reporting purposes.

LIFO reserve. The account used to reduce inventory from the internal valuation to the LIFO valuation.

Moving-average. The average cost of goods on hand must be recalculated any time additional inventory is purchased at a unit cost different from the previously calculated average cost of goods on hand.

Net method. Any purchase discounts offered are assumed taken and the purchase account reflects the net price.

Number of days' supply in average inventory. Number of days inventory is held before sale; reflects on efficiency of inventory policies.

Percentage-of-completion. Recognition of contract revenue and profit during construction based on expected total profit and estimated progress towards completion in the current period.

Periodic system. Inventory is counted periodically and then priced.

Perpetual system. A running total is kept of the units on hand (and possibly their value) by recording all increases and decreases as they occur.

Purchase commitments. Result from legally enforceable contracts to purchase specific quantities of goods at fixed prices in the future.

Simple average. The seller does not weight the average for units purchased or in beginning inventory.

Specific identification. The seller determines which item is sold.

Standard costs. Predetermined costs in a cost accounting system, generally used for control purposes.

Trade discounts. These are discounts that are allowed to the entity because of its being a wholesaler, a good customer, or merely the fact that the item is on sale at a reduced price.

Weighted-average. The seller averages the cost of all items on hand and purchased during the period. The units in ending inventory and units sold (CGS) are costed at this average cost.

Module 11: Fixed Assets

Overview

Fixed assets are defined as the capitalized amount of expenditures made to acquire tangible property which will be used for a period of more than one year. Tangible property includes property that physically exists. Intangible assets are nonphysical assets.

Fixed and intangible asset concepts are tested on the Financial Accounting and Reporting section of the exam. The primary topics covered include

1. Fixed and intangible asset acquisitions including the costs to be capitalized.
2. Self-constructed assets including capitalization of interest.
3. Asset exchanges including how to account for exchanges that lack commercial substance or include some monetary amount.
4. Asset cost allocation including depreciation, amortization, and depletion methods and impairment.

A. Acquisition Cost

1. **Fixed assets** represent the capitalized amount of expenditures made to acquire tangible property which will be used for a period of more than one year. Their cost, therefore, is deferred to future periods in compliance with the matching principle.
2. **Tangible property** includes land, buildings, equipment, or any other property that physically exists.

   a. All of the costs necessary to get the asset to the work site and to prepare it for use are capitalized, including the cost of negotiations, sales taxes, finders' fees, razing an old building, shipment, installation, preliminary testing, and so forth.

      (1) When capitalizing such costs it is necessary to associate them with the asset which is being prepared for use. Thus, the cost of razing an old building is added to the cost of acquiring the land on which the building stood.

3. Charges for self-constructed fixed assets include direct materials, direct construction labor, variable overhead, and a fair share of fixed overhead.
4. Assets received through donation should be recorded at fair value with a corresponding credit to revenue; if fair value is not determinable, book value should be used.

   a. If the entity incurs a liability associated with future retirement of the asset, the fair value (present value) of that obligation should be added to the carrying value of the asset.

B. Capitalization of Interest

1. The capitalization of interest is part of the cost of certain assets. Only assets which require a period of time to be prepared for use qualify for interest capitalization.

   a. These include assets constructed for sale produced as discrete projects (e.g., ships) and assets constructed for a firm's own use, whether by the entity itself or by an outsider.

EXAMPLE

A building purchased by an entity **would not** qualify, but one constructed over a period of time **would**.

---

    (1) Other assets that do **not** qualify include those in use or ready for use and ones not being used in the earnings activities of a firm (e.g., idle land).

2. The amount of interest to be capitalized is the amount which could have been avoided if the project had not been undertaken. This amount includes amortization of any discount, premium, or issue costs; but, it shall not exceed the actual interest incurred during the period. The amount of "avoidable" interest is computed as

      Average accumulated expenditures during construction   ×   Interest rate   ×   Construction period

3. The interest rate used is the rate on specific borrowings for the asset, or a weighted-average of other borrowings when a specific rate is not available. Capitalized interest should be compounded.

    a. This is usually accomplished by including the interest capitalized in a previous period in the calculation of average accumulated expenditures of subsequent periods.
    b. Furthermore, noninterest-bearing payables (e.g., trade payables and accruals) are excluded in determining these expenditures.
    c. In practice, both the weighted-average interest rate and the average accumulated expenditures have been computed on the following bases: monthly, quarterly, semiannual, and annual.

4. The interest capitalization period begins when, and continues as long as, all three of the following conditions are met:

    a. Expenditures for the asset have been made
    b. Activities necessary to get the asset ready for its intended use are in progress
    c. Interest cost is being incurred

5. The period ends when the asset is substantially complete. Brief interruptions and delays do not suspend interest capitalization, while suspension of the activities will.

NOTE: In no case should the amount capitalized exceed the interest actually incurred.

EXAMPLE

Interest Capitalization

Assume the company is constructing an asset which qualifies for interest capitalization. By the beginning of July $3,000,000 had been spent on the asset, and an additional $800,000 was spent during July. The following debt was outstanding for the entire month.

1. A loan of $2,000,000, interest of 1% per month, specifically related to the asset.
2. A note payable of $1,500,000, interest of 1.5% per month.
3. Bonds payable of $1,000,000, interest of 1% per month.

The amount of interest to be capitalized is computed below.

Average accumulated expenditures (for the month of July) = ($3,000,000 + $3,800,000) ÷ 2 = $3,400,000

Avoidable interest			Actual interest		
$2,000,000 × 1%	=	$20,000	$2,000,000 × 1%	=	$20,000
1,400,000 × 1.3%*	=	18,200	1,500,000 × 1.5%	=	22,500
			1,000,000 × 1%	=	10,000
$3,400,000		$38,200	$4,500,000		$52,500

$38,200 < $52,500 ∴ $38,200 is capitalized

Amount of interest to be capitalized is $38,200

Asset	38,200	
Interest expense		38,200

* The average rate on other borrowings is ($22,500 + $10,000) ÷ ($1,500,000 + $1,000,000) = 1.3%. Notice that a specific rate is used to the extent possible and the average rate is used only on any excess. Alternatively, the rate on all debt may be used.

---

6. Interest on expenditures made to acquire land on which a building is to be constructed qualifies for interest capitalization. The capitalization period begins when activities necessary to construct the building commence and

ends when the building is substantially complete. Interest so capitalized becomes part of the cost of the building. Thus, it is charged to expense as the building is depreciated.

7. Frequently, the funds borrowed to finance the construction project are temporarily invested until needed. The interest earned on these funds must be recognized as revenue and may not be offset against the interest expense to be capitalized.

8. The diagram below outlines the requirements pertaining to capitalization of interest.

SUMMARY OF ACCOUNTING FOR INTEREST CAPITALIZATION

Capitalization of Interest During Construction

Qualifying Assets:
Capitalize means to include an expenditure in an asset's cost.
Interest costs, when material, incurred in acquiring the following types of assets, shall be capitalized

  1. Assets constructed or produced for a firm's own use

      a. Including construction by outside contractors requiring progress payments

  2. Assets intended for lease or sale that are produced as discrete projects

      a. For example, ships and real estate developments

  3. But **not** on

      a. Routinely produced inventories (e.g., widgets)
      b. Assets ready for their intended use when acquired
      c. Assets not being used nor being readied for use (e.g., idle equipment)
      d. Land, unless it is being developed (e.g., as a plant site, real estate development, etc.).
          Then capitalized interest resulting from land expenditure (cash outlay) is added to building.

When to Capitalize Interest (All three must be met):
  1. Expenditures for asset have been made
  2. Activities intended to get asset ready are in progress
  3. Interest cost is being incurred

Applicable Interest (Net of discounts, premiums, and issue costs):
  1. Interest obligations having explicit rates
  2. Imputed interest on certain payables/receivables
  3. Interest related to capital leases

How Much Interest Cost Is Capitalized?

$$\left(\begin{array}{l} \text{Accumulated expenditures beg. of period (C - I - P ** bal.) +} \\ \text{Accumulated expenditures end of period (C - I - P bal.)} \end{array} \right) \div 2 \times \text{Portion of year} = \text{Weighted-average accumulated expenditures}$$

$$\text{Weighted-average accumulated expenditures} \times \left(\begin{array}{c} \text{Interest*} \\ \text{rate} \end{array} \right) = \text{Amount capitalized (cannot exceed total interest incurred)}$$

  * AICPA questions have given the specific borrowing rate on debt incurred to finance a project and indicated that expenditures were incurred evenly throughout the year. ASC Topic 835 (SFAS 34) requires that the firm's weighted-average borrowing rate be used after the amount of a specific borrowing is exhausted. Alternatively, only the firm's weighted-average borrowing rate may be used on all expenditures.
** C-I-P-Construction-in-Progress

Qualifications:
  1. Amount of interest to be capitalized cannot exceed total interest costs incurred during the entire reporting period
  2. Interest earned on temporarily invested borrowings may not be offset against interest to be capitalized

a. **Rationale** for interest capitalization

 (1) To reflect asset's acquisition cost
 (2) To match asset's cost with revenue of periods that benefit from its use

NOW REVIEW MULTIPLE-CHOICE QUESTIONS 1 THROUGH 5 IN VOLUME 2

C. Nonmonetary Exchanges

1. A nonmonetary exchange is a reciprocal transfer wherein the transferor has no substantial continuing involvement in the asset, and the risks and rewards of ownership are transferred.

2. The guidance on nonmonetary exchanges does not apply to (1) business combinations, (2) transfers of nonmonetary assets between companies under common control, (3) acquisition of nonmonetary assets or services for the issuance of capital stock, (4) stock issued or received in stock dividends or stock splits, (5) transfer of assets in exchange for equity interests, (6) a pooling of assets in joint undertaking for gas or oil, (7) exchanging part of an operating interest owned for a part of another operating interest owned by another party, and (8) certain transfers of financial assets.

3. Nonmonetary exchanges are usually recorded using the fair value of the asset exchanged.

 a. If one of the parties could have elected to receive cash instead of the nonmonetary asset, the amount of cash that could have been received is evidence of the fair value of the assets exchanged.
 b. If the fair value (FV) of the asset given up cannot be determined, assume it is equal to the fair value of the asset received.
 c. Three exceptions exist to the fair value treatment:

  (1) If fair value is not determinable;
  (2) If it is an exchange transaction to facilitate sales to customers; or
  (3) The transaction lacks commercial substance.

   (a) A transaction has **commercial substance** if the configuration of cash flows are significantly different as a result of the exchange. The configuration of cash flows includes the risk, timing, and the amount of future cash flows.
   (b) Cash flows from tax effects are not considered in determining if the transaction has commercial substance.

  (4) In these three exceptions, the transaction is measured using the recorded amount (book value) of the asset exchanged.
  (5) For exception (1) when neither of the fair values is determinable, the exchange is accounted for at book value, and no gain or loss is recognized. For exceptions (2) and (3), the transaction is measured using the recorded amount (book value) of the exchanged asset, and any losses are recognized. When book values are used, a part of the gain may be recognized when boot is received.

4. The exchange of nonmonetary assets (such as inventory, property, and equipment) for other nonmonetary assets requires special consideration of two amounts.

 a. Gain or loss, if any
 b. Fair market value of the nonmonetary assets received

EXAMPLE

Gain or loss on a nonmonetary exchange is computed as follows:

  Fair value of the asset given   –   Book value of the asset given   =   Gain (loss)

  (1) The asset received is generally recorded at the fair value of the asset surrendered (or the FV of the asset received if "more clearly evident"). Some exceptions do exist. Remember, however, that the asset given up will always be removed from the books at book value.

5. The following rules apply in recording nonmonetary exchanges:

 a. Losses are always recognized
 b. Gains are recognized if the exchange is measured at fair value.
 c. If any of the three conditions for exception to fair value treatment are met, use book value (recorded amount) of the asset exchanged. If no boot is involved, no gain is recognized. If boot is given, no gain is recognized, and

the new asset is recorded at the book value of the exchanged asset plus the boot given. If boot is received, a portion of the gain is recognized.

d. The following chart summarizes the process involved in accounting for nonmonetary exchanges. Refer to this chart as you work through the following examples.

ACCOUNTING FOR NONMONETARY EXCHANGES
Concepts Summary

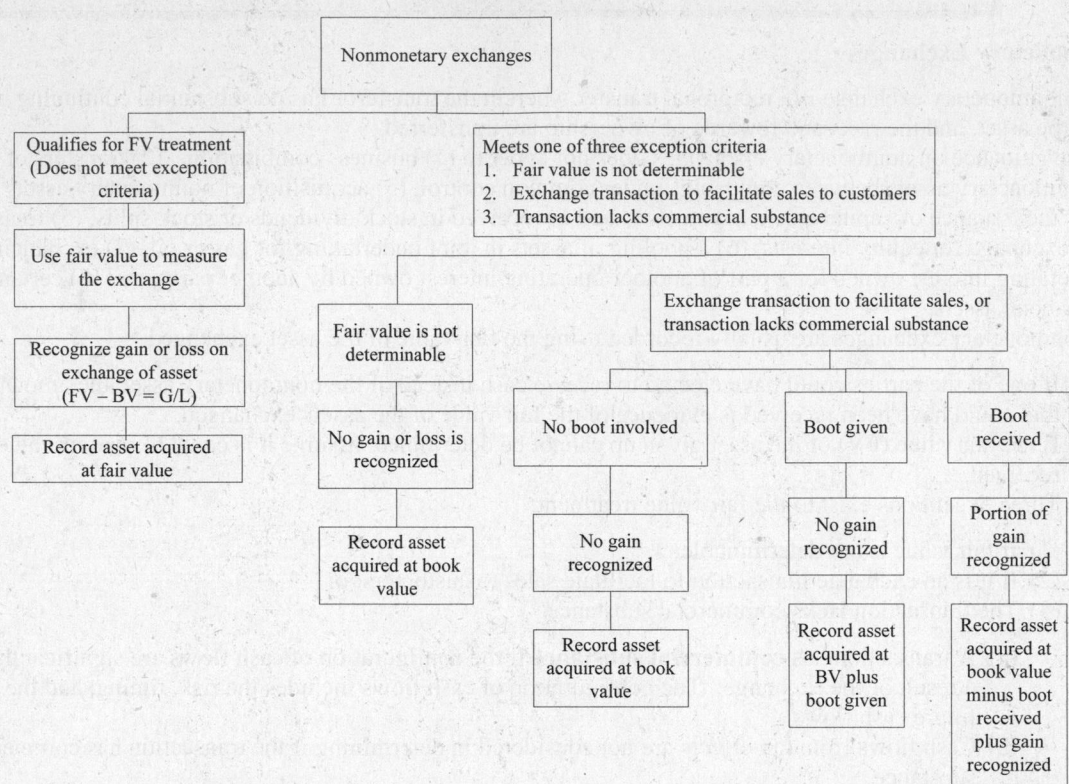

* For tax purposes losses are not recognized on exchanges of similar assets; they are adjustments to the asset's basis as are gains.

1. **FV is not determinable.** When fair value of the asset given up or the asset received is not determinable, book value is used to record the exchanged asset.

EXAMPLE

A company trades a machine (cost, $10,000; accumulated depreciation, $3,000) for land. Neither the FV of the machine or the land is determinable.

Land	7,000	(BV given)
Accumulated depreciation	3,000	
Machine		10,000

Since FV is unknown, no gain can be computed, and the asset received is recorded at the BV of the asset given up ($10,000 – $3,000).

---

2. **Loss situations.** Normally, an exchanged asset is valued at fair value of the asset exchanged, or the fair value of the asset received, whichever is more clearly evident. When the fair value is less than the book value, a loss occurs. Because losses are recognized immediately, the treatment in a loss situation is the same for all nonmonetary exchanges, regardless of whether it meets the exception criteria.

EXAMPLE

Situation 1. Loss, no boot involved.

A company trades a machine with a FV of $5,000 (cost, $10,000; accumulated depreciation, $3,000) for land. It is assumed that the transaction has commercial substance and does not meet the exception criteria to fair value measurement.

	FV	BV	Gain (loss)
Machine given	$5,000	$7,000	$(2,000)
Land received			

The loss (FV – BV) is recognized immediately and the land is recorded at the FV of the machine given up.

Land	5,000	(FV given)
Accumulated depreciation	3,000	
Loss	2,000	
Machine		10,000

NOTE: This transaction would be treated the same way if the transaction lacked commercial substance.

A company trades a machine (cost, $10,000; accumulated depreciation, $3,000) for another machine with a FV of $6,000. It is assumed that the transaction has commercial substance and does not meet the exception criteria to fair value measurement.

	FV	BV	Gain (loss)
Machine given		$7,000	$(1,000)
Machine received	$6,000		

In this case, the FV of the asset given is unknown. You can substitute the FV of the asset received for FV given when computing gain/loss. The fair value of the asset given is implied in this case.

$$\underset{\substack{\text{FV given}\\\text{(assumed or implied)}}}{\$6,000} - \underset{\text{BV given}}{\$7,000} = \underset{\text{Loss}}{\$(1,000)}$$

Machine	6,000	(FV received)
Accumulated depreciation	3,000	
Loss	1,000	
Machine		10,000

NOTE: If the treatment lacked commercial substance, the entries would be the same because of the loss.

Situation 2. Loss, boot given.

A company trades a machine with a FV of $6,000 (cost, $10,000; accumulated depreciation, $3,000) and $500 cash for land. It is assumed that the transaction has commercial substance and does not meet the exception criteria to fair value measurement.

	Boot	FV	BV	Gain (loss)
Machine given	$500	$6,000	$7,000	$(1,000)
Land received				

Gain (loss) still equals FV less BV. Boot given is added to the value of the asset given.

Land	6,500	(FV given + Boot given)
Accumulated depreciation	3,000	
Loss	1,000	
Machine		10,000
Cash		500

Assume the FV of the machine was unknown, but the FV of the land received was known to be $6,000.

	Boot	FV	BV	Gain (loss)
Machine given	$500		$7,000	$(1,500)
Land received		$6,000		

To compute gain (loss), you can assume FV given is equal to FV received less boot given ($6,000 – $500).

$5,500	–	$7,000	=	$(1,500)
FV given		BV given		Loss
(assumed)				

Land	6,000	(FV received)
Accumulated depreciation	3,000	
Loss	1,500	
Machine		10,000
Cash		500

NOTE: If the transaction lacked commercial substance, the entries would be the same because of the loss.

Situation 3. Loss, boot received.

A company trades a machine with a FV of $6,000 (cost, $10,000; accumulated depreciation, $3,000) for land and $500 cash.

	Boot	FV	BV	Gain (loss)
Machine given		$6,000	$7,000	$(1,000)
Land received	$500			

Boot received is deducted from the value of the asset given.

Land	5,500	(FV given – Boot received)
Accumulated depreciation	3,000	
Cash	500	
Loss	1,000	
Machine		10,000

Now assume the FV of the machine is unknown but the FV of the land received is known to be $6,000.

	Boot	FV	BV	Gain (loss)
Machine given			$7,000	$(500)
Land received	$500	$6,000		

In this case, you can assume FV given is equal to FV received **plus** the boot received ($6,000 + $500).

$6,500	–	$7,000	=	$(500)
FV given		BV given		Loss
(assumed)				

Land	6,000	(FV received)
Accumulated depreciation	3,000	
Cash	500	
Loss	500	
Machine		10,000

3. **Gain Situations**

EXAMPLE

Situation 1. Gain, fair value measurement.

A company trades a computer with a FV of $12,000 (cost, $11,000; accumulated depreciation, $4,000) for a building. The transaction has commercial substance and does not meet any of the exception criteria; therefore the transaction should be valued at fair value.

	FV	BV	Gain (loss)
Computer given	$12,000	$7,000	$5,000
Building received			

Since the transaction has commercial substance, the earnings process is considered complete and the entire gain is recognized.

Building	12,000	(FV received)
Accumulated depreciation	4,000	
Computer		11,000
Gain		5,000

> **NOTE:** If boot had been involved, the accounting would be similar to that illustrated in the loss situation.

Situation 2. Gain, transaction lacks commercial substance, no boot involved.

A company trades equipment with a FV of $12,000 (cost, $11,000; accumulated depreciation, $4,000) for another piece of equipment. The configuration of cash flows of the asset exchanged does not significantly differ from the cash flows of the new asset.

	FV	BV	Gain (loss)
Equipment given	$12,000	$7,000	$5,000
Equipment received			

Since this transaction lacks commercial substance, the earnings process is **not** considered complete and no gain is recognized. The asset received is debited at the book value (**not** fair value) of the asset given.

Equipment	7,000	(BV given)
Accumulated depreciation	4,000	
Equipment		11,000

The unrecognized gain of $5,000 will be deferred; it will be recognized as the equipment received is depreciated (lower depreciation results than if FV had been used) and/or sold or disposed of in a subsequent transaction.

Situation 3. Gain, transaction lacks commercial substance, boot given.

A company trades a machine (cost, $10,000; accumulated depreciation, $2,000) and $4,000 in cash for another machine with a FV of $16,000. The configuration of cash flows of the asset exchanged does not significantly differ from the cash flows of the new asset.

	Boot	FV	BV	Gain (loss)
Machine given	$4,000		$8,000	$4,000
Machine received		$16,000		

As in the loss situation, the FV of the asset given can be assumed equal to the FV received less the boot given ($16,000 – $4,000).

$$\underset{\substack{\text{FV given} \\ \text{(assumed)}}}{\$12,000} - \underset{\text{BV given}}{\$8,000} = \underset{\text{Gain}}{\$4,000}$$

Boot given is added to the value of the asset given (in this case, book value). Gain is still unrecognized.

Machine	12,000	(BV given + Boot given)
Accumulated depreciation	2,000	
Machine		10,000
Cash		4,000

Below are alternative ways to calculate the asset received.

FV received	$16,000	BV given	$ 8,000
Gain deferred	(4,000)	Cash paid	4,000
	12,000		12,000

Situation 4. Gain, transaction lacks commercial substance, boot received.

An exception to nonrecognition of gain on exchange for a transaction lacking commercial substance arises when boot is received in the exchange. This type of earnings process is assumed complete for the portion related to the boot received (i.e., "sale" portion), but is **not** assumed complete for the portion related to the asset received (i.e., "exchange" portion). Therefore, a gain is recognized only for that portion related to the boot. Gain recognized is computed as follows:

$$\left(\frac{\text{Boot received}}{\text{Boot received} + \text{FV of asset received}} \right) \times \text{Total gain} = \text{Gain recognized}$$

If the FV of the asset received is not given, it may be determined by subtracting the boot received from the FV of the asset given up.

A company trades a machine with a FV of $12,000 (cost, $9,000; accumulated depreciation, $2,000) for a different machine and $2,000 cash.

	Boot received	Machine		Gain (loss)
		FV	BV	
Given		$12,000	$7,000	$5,000
Received	$2,000	?	?	

Since boot was received, the portion of the gain relating to the boot must be recognized.

$$\left(\frac{\$2,000}{\$2,000 + \$10,000 *}\right) \times (\$5,000) = \$833$$

* The FV of the asset received ($10,000) was derived by deducting boot received from the FV of the machine given.

$12,000		$2,000		$10,000
FV given	−	Boot received	=	FV received
				(assumed)

Thus, only $833 of the gain will be recognized. The machine received would be recorded at its BV given less boot received, plus gain recognized ($7,000 − $2,000 + $833 = $5,833). Alternatively this could be calculated by taking its FV less the gain deferred [$10,000 − ($5,000 gain − $833 gain recognized)].

Cash	2,000	
Machine (received)	5,833	$\left(\begin{array}{c}\text{BV given} - \text{Boot received} \\ + \text{Gain recognized}\end{array}\right)$ or $\left(\begin{array}{c}\text{FV received} - \\ \text{Gain deferred}\end{array}\right)$
Accumulated depreciation	2,000	
Machine (given)		9,000
Gain		833

NOW REVIEW MULTIPLE-CHOICE QUESTIONS 6 THROUGH 19 IN VOLUME 2

D. Purchase of Groups of Fixed Assets (Basket Purchase)

1. Cost should be allocated based on relative market value.

$$\text{Cost of all assets acquired} \times \frac{\text{Market value of A}}{\text{Market value of all assets acquired}}$$

EXAMPLE

Purchase of Asset 1 with a FMV of $60,000, Asset 2 with a FMV of $120,000, and Asset 3 with a FMV of $20,000 all for $150,000 cash.

	FMV	Relative FMV	Total cost	Allocated cost
Asset 1	$ 60,000	60/200	$150,000	$45,000
Asset 2	120,000	120/200	150,000	90,000
Asset 3	20,000	20/200	150,000	15,000
Total FMV	$200,000			

Journalized:

Asset 1	$45,000	
Asset 2	90,000	
Asset 3	15,000	
Cash		$150,000

E. Capital vs. Revenue Expenditures

1. Capital expenditures and revenue expenditures are charges that are incurred after the acquisition cost has been determined and the related fixed asset is in operation.

   a. **Capital expenditures** are not normal, recurring expenses; they benefit the operations of more than one period. The cost of major rearrangements of assets to increase efficiency is an example of a capital expenditure.
   b. **Revenue expenditures** are normal recurring expenditures. However, some expenditures that meet the test for capital expenditures are expensed because they are immaterial (e.g., less than $50).

2. Expenditures to improve the efficiency or extend the asset life should be capitalized and charged to future periods.

   a. A subtle distinction is sometimes made between an improvement in efficiency and an extension of the asset life. Some accountants feel improvements in efficiency should be charged to the asset account, and improvements extending the asset life should be charged to the accumulated depreciation account. The rationale is that improvements extending the asset life will need to be depreciated over an extended period of time, requiring revision of depreciation schedules.

3. The chart on the following page summarizes the appropriate treatment of expenditures related to fixed assets.

NOW REVIEW MULTIPLE-CHOICE QUESTIONS 20 THROUGH 24 IN VOLUME 2

F. Depreciation

1. **Depreciation** is the annual charge to income for asset use during the period. Since depreciation is a noncash expense, it does not provide resources for the replacement of assets. It is simply a means of spreading asset costs to periods in which the assets produce revenue.

   a. Essentially, the "depreciation base" is allocated over the asset's useful life in a rational and systematic manner. The meaning of the key terms is as follows:

   (1) **Systematic**—Formula or plan
   (2) **Rational**—Representational faithfulness (fits with reality)
   (3) **Allocation**—Not a process of valuation

2. The objective is to match asset cost with revenue produced. The depreciation base is cost less salvage value (except for the declining balance method which ignores salvage value). The cost of an asset will include any reasonable cost incurred in bringing an asset to an enterprise and getting it ready for its intended use. The useful life can be limited by

   a. Technological change
   b. Normal deterioration
   c. Physical usage

   (1) The first two indicate depreciation is a function of time whereas the third indicates depreciation is a function of the level of activity. Other depreciation methods include inventory, retirement, replacement, group, composite, etc.

3. Depreciation methods based on time are

   a. Straight-line (SL)
   b. Accelerated

   (1) Declining balance (DB)

      (a) Most common is double-declining balance (DDB)

   (2) Sum-of-the-years' digits (SYD)

4. **Straight-line** and **accelerated** depreciation are illustrated by the following example:

EXAMPLE

$10,000 asset, four-year life, $2,000 salvage value.

Year	Straight line	DDB	SYD
1	$2,000	$5,000	$3,200
2	$2,000	$2,500	$2,400
3	$2,000	$ 500*	$1,600
4	$2,000	--	$ 800

$$\text{Straight-line} \rightarrow \frac{\$10,000 - \$2,000}{4}$$

DDB Twice the straight-line rate ($2 \times 25\%$) times the net book value at beginning of each year, but not below salvage value (salvage value is not deducted for depreciation base).

SYD 4/10**, 3/10, 2/10, 1/10 of ($10,000 − $2,000).

   * $10,000 − ($5,000 + 2,500) = $2,500 Book value at beginning of year three. $2,500 − 2,000 salvage value = $500.

   ** $\dfrac{n(n+1)}{2} = \dfrac{4 \times 5}{2} = 10$

COSTS SUBSEQUENT TO ACQUISITION OF PROPERTY, PLANT, AND EQUIPMENT

Type of expenditure	Characteristics	Expense when incurred	Capitalize — Debit (credit) to asset	Capitalize — Debit (credit) to accum. deprec.	Other
1. Additions	• Extensions, enlargements, or expansions made to an existing asset		x		
2. Repairs and maintenance					
a. Ordinary	• Recurring, relatively small expenditures				
	1. Maintain normal operating condition	x			
	2. **Do not** add materially to use value	x			
	3. **Do not** extend useful life	x			
b. Extraordinary (major)	• Not recurring, relatively large expenditures				
	1. Primarily increase the quality and/or output of services		x		
	2. Primarily extend the useful life			x	
3. Replacements and improvements	• Major component of asset is removed and replaced with the same type of component with comparable performance capabilities (replacement) or a different type of component having superior performance capabilities (betterment)			x	
a. Book value of old component is known	• Old component amounts		(x)	x	• Recognize any proceeds and loss (or gain) on old asset
	• New component outlay		x		
b. Book value of old component is **not** known	• Primarily increases the use value		x		
	• Primarily extends the useful life			x	
4. Reinstallations and rearrangements	• Provide greater efficiency in production or reduce production costs				
	1. Material costs, benefits extend into future accounting periods		x		
	2. No measurable future benefit	x			

a. Straight-line and accelerated depreciation methods are illustrated by the following graphs:

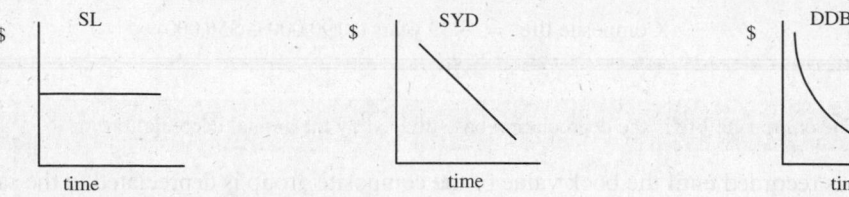

b. Accelerated depreciation is justified by

(1) Increased productivity when asset is new
(2) Increasing maintenance charges with age
(3) Risk of obsolescence

c. Accelerated depreciation methods result in a better matching of costs and revenues when one or more of these factors are present.

5. **Physical usage depreciation** is based on activity (e.g., machine hours) or output (e.g., finished widgets).

$$\text{Annual depreciation} = \frac{\text{Current activity or output}}{\text{Total expected activity or output}} \times \text{Depreciation base}$$

> **EXAMPLE**
>
> A machine costs $60,000. The machine's total output is expected to be 500,000 units. If 100,000 units are produced in the first year, $12,000 of depreciation would be incurred (100/500 × $60,000).

> **NOTE:** Physical usage depreciation results in a varying charge (i.e., not constant). Also physical usage depreciation is based on asset activity rather than expiration of time.

6. **Inventory depreciation** is a method typically used in situations where there are many low-cost tangible assets, such as hand tools for a manufacturer or utensils for a restaurant.

a. Using this method, an inventory of the assets is taken at the beginning and the end of the year. Valuation of these assets is based on appraisal value. Depreciation is calculated as follows:

= Beginning inventory + Cost of acquisitions − Ending inventory

b. The inventory method is advantageous in situations involving such small assets because it is not practical to maintain separate depreciation schedules for them. On the other hand, this method is often criticized because it is not systematic and rational.

7. **Composite (group) depreciation** averages the service life of a number of property units and depreciates the group as if it were a single unit.

a. The term "group" is used when the assets are similar; "composite" when they are dissimilar.
b. The depreciation rate is the following ratio:

$$\frac{\text{Sum of annual SL depreciation of individual assets}}{\text{Total asset cost}}$$

c. Thus, composite depreciation is a weighted-average of a group of assets—usually of a similar nature, expected life, etc.

> **EXAMPLE**
>
> Three types of assets (A, B, and C) are depreciated under the composite method.
>
> | Asset type | Asset cost | Salvage value | Depreciation base | Useful life (yrs.) | SL annual depreciation |
> |---|---|---|---|---|---|
> | A | $ 45,000 | $ 15,000 | $ 30,000 | 5 | $ 6,000 |
> | B | 90,000 | 50,000 | 40,000 | 4 | 10,000 |
> | C | 145,000 | 25,000 | 120,000 | 3 | 40,000 |
> | | $280,000 | $ 90,000 | $190,000 | | $ 56,000 |

$$\text{Depreciation or composite rate} = \frac{\$56,000}{\$280,000} = 20\%$$

$$\text{Composite life} = 3.39 \text{ years } (\$190,000 \div \$56,000)$$

NOTE: The composite life is the depreciation base divided by the annual depreciation.

(1) Depreciation is recorded until the book value of the composite group is depreciated to the salvage value of the then remaining assets. As assets are retired the composite group salvage value is reduced.

NOTE: Gains and losses are not recognized on disposal (i.e., gains and losses are netted into accumulated depreciation). This latter practice also affects the length of time required to reduce the book value (cost less accumulated depreciation) to the group salvage value.

The entry to record a retirement is

Cash, other consideration	(amount received)	
Accumulated depreciation	(plug)	
Asset		(original cost)

8. **Changes in depreciation.** A change in depreciation method is a change in accounting estimate effected by a change in accounting principle. Therefore, a change in depreciation method is treated as a change in accounting estimate.

   a. Changes in depreciation estimates also include changes in the expected useful life or salvage value. Changes in accounting estimates are accounted for on a prospective basis in the current and future periods. Make the change prospectively from the beginning of the year in which the change in estimate occurs. The procedure for straight-line depreciation is

      (1) Divide the periods remaining (from the beginning of the year of change) into
      (2) The remaining depreciation base (i.e., undepreciated cost to date less revised salvage value)

9. **Fractional year depreciation.** Many conventions exist for accounting for depreciation for midyear asset acquisitions. They include

   a. A whole year's depreciation in year of acquisition and none in year of disposal
   b. One-half year's depreciation in year of acquisition and year of disposal
   c. Depreciation to nearest whole month in both year of acquisition and year of disposal

NOTE: CPA exam questions generally specify the convention to be followed.

NOW REVIEW MULTIPLE-CHOICE QUESTIONS 25 THROUGH 37 IN VOLUME 2

G. Disposals and Impairment of Value

1. The entry to record the disposal (sale) of an asset is

Cash	(amount received)		
Accumulated depreciation	(old asset)		
Old asset		(cost)	
Gain or loss	(loss)	(gain)	

   a. Remember to record depreciation for disposed assets up to the point of disposal.

EXAMPLE

Jimco, a manufacturer of sports equipment, purchased a machine for $6,000 on 1/1/05. The machine had an eight-year life, a $600 salvage value, and was depreciated using the straight-line method. Thus, depreciation was charged at a rate of $56.25 per month [($6,000 cost – $600 salvage) ÷ (8 yrs × 12 mos/yr)]. If Jimco sells the asset on 9/1/10 for $3,000, the following entries must be made to record 2010 depreciation and to record the sale:

Depreciation expense	450	
Accumulated depreciation ($56.25 × 8 mos)		450
Cash	3,000	
Accumulated depreciation ($56.25 × 68 mos)	3,825	
Equipment		6,000
Gain on sale of equip. [$3,000 cash − ($6,000 − $3,825)CV]		825

2. In some cases, assets are intended to be **disposed of** in a future reporting period rather than held for use. If management has adopted such a plan for disposal, a loss is recognized if the fair value minus selling costs (NRV) is less than the recorded carrying value.

EXAMPLE

Assume that the asset in the above example has not been sold yet. However, management intends to dispose of it in the next year at NRV of $1,500. The entry to record management's intents would be as follows:

Loss on planned disposition*	675	
Equipment to be disposed of	1,500	
Accumulated depreciation	3,825	
Equipment		6,000

* 1,500 − (6,000 − 3,825)

---

   a. Fixed assets intended for disposal are not subsequently depreciated. The equipment to be disposed of would be classified as other assets on the balance sheet.

   b. **Losses on fixed assets to be disposed of can be recovered** due to changes in the fair value or selling costs associated with the asset. This write-up, however, **cannot** exceed the carrying amount prior to recognition of impairment. If the NRV for this asset increases in the next period, the maximum recovery (gain) that could be recognized is $675.

3. **Assets that are intended to be held and used** should be tested for impairment. Impairment occurs when the carrying amount of a long-lived asset or asset group exceeds its fair value. However, an impairment loss is recognized only if the carrying amount of the asset is not recoverable. The carrying value is considered not recoverable if it exceeds the sum of the expected value of the undiscounted cash flows.

   a. The loss on impairment recognized is the difference between the asset's fair value and its carrying value. In determining the fair value, the principal or most advantageous market for the asset should be used consistent with the asset's highest and best use. The in-use valuation premise assumes the highest value of the asset is achieved by using it in the business with other assets. An in-exchange premise assumes that the highest value of the asset is the amount received to sell the asset stand-alone.

EXAMPLE

Assume that the asset in the previous example is not to be sold. A test for impairment indicates that the net undiscounted cash flows from the machine are $2,000. Since the carrying value is equal to $2,175 ($6,000 − $3,825), the asset is impaired as of 9/1/10. If the machine's fair value at this date is $1,400, its carrying value is reduced, as shown below.

Loss on impairment [($6,000 − $3,825) CV − $1,400 FV]	775	
Accumulated depreciation		775

It will continue to be depreciated at $50.00 per month for its remaining useful life ($1,400 ÷ 28 mos = $50.00). At 12/31/12, when the asset is fully depreciated, Jimco retires it and writes the machine off with the following entry:

Accumulated depreciation	6,000	
Equipment		6,000

NOTE: The entire cost has been depreciated because upon impairment of the asset it was determined that the equipment did not have a salvage value.

   b. When management has alternative courses of action to recover the carrying amount of the assets or a particular course has multiple outcomes in terms of cash flow, ASC 360-10-35-30 (SFAS 144) indicates that probability-weighted cash flow approach should be considered. **Recoveries of previously recognized impairment losses may not be recognized in subsequent periods.**

H. Depletion

1. **Depletion** is "depreciation" of natural resources. The depletion base is the total cost of the property providing the natural resources. This includes all development costs such as exploring, drilling, excavating, and other preparatory costs.

     a. The depletion base is usually allocated by the ratio of extracted units over the total expected recoverable units.

$$\frac{\text{Units extracted}}{\text{Total expected recoverable units}} \times \quad \text{Depletion base}$$

     b. The unit depletion rate is frequently revised due to the uncertainties surrounding the recovery of natural resources. The revised unit rate in any year takes the following form:

$$\frac{\text{Orig. cost + Addl. cost incurred – Resid. value – Depletion taken in prev. yrs.}}{\text{Units withdrawn currently + Estimated units recoverable at year-end}}$$

> **NOTE:** The adjustment is being made prospectively (i.e., the remaining undepleted cost is being expensed over the remaining recoverable units).

     c. Depletion on resources extracted during an accounting period is allocated between inventory and cost of goods sold.

NOW REVIEW MULTIPLE-CHOICE QUESTIONS 38 THROUGH 57 IN VOLUME 2

I. Insurance

1. **Loss account for fixed assets.** When an insured loss occurs, an insurance loss account should be set up and charged for all losses. These losses include decreases in asset value, earned insurance premiums, etc. The account should be credited for any payments from the insurance company. The remainder is closed to revenue and expense summary.
2. **Coinsurance.** This area is tested on the Business Environment and Concepts section of the exam.

J. Goodwill and Other Intangible Assets

1. Intangible assets are nonphysical assets. Intangible assets normally include only noncurrent intangibles (e.g., accounts receivable are not considered intangibles). Examples of intangible assets include copyrights, leaseholds, organizational costs, trademarks, franchises, patents, and goodwill. These intangibles may be categorized according to the following characteristics:

     a. Identifiability. Separately identifiable or lacking specific identification.
     b. Manner of acquisition. Acquired singly, in groups, or in business combinations; or developed internally.
     c. Expected period of benefit. Limited by law or contract, related to human or economic factors, or indefinite or indeterminate duration.
     d. Separability from enterprise. Rights transferable without title, salable, or inseparable from the entire enterprise.

2. **Acquisition of intangibles.** Purchased intangibles should be recorded at cost, which represents the fair value of the intangible at time of acquisition. Internally developed intangibles are written off as research and development expense; an exception is the cost to register a patent.
3. **Acquisition of goodwill and allocation to reporting units.** Goodwill is recorded only when an entire business is purchased. Purchase of goodwill as part of acquiring a business is discussed in the Investment and Business Combinations and Consolidations modules.

     a. In a business acquisition, the recognized goodwill should be assigned to one or more reporting units. In essence, the goodwill assigned to a reporting unit is the difference between the fair value of the unit and the value of its individual assets and liabilities. A reporting unit can be an operating segment or one level below.

EXAMPLE

Allocation of Goodwill to a Reporting Unit

Dunn Corporation acquired all of the assets of Yeager Corporation for $12,000,000 cash. The assets were seen as relating to three different reporting units (operating segments)—Communications, Technology, and Consulting. The fair value of the Communications reporting unit at the date of acquisition was $4,700,000. Goodwill associated with the unit would be assigned based on a comparison of its total fair value to the value of its assets and liabilities as shown below.

Communications Reporting Unit (In 000s)

	Fair value
Cash	$ 200
Accounts receivable	900
Net Equipment	2,700
Patents	1,000
Customer contracts	700
Current liabilities	(1,100)
Fair value of net assets	$4,400

The amount of goodwill assigned to the reporting unit would be $300,000 ($4,700,000 – $4,400,000), the excess of the fair value of the reporting unit over the value of its net assets. Goodwill would be assigned to the other two reporting units in a similar manner.

---

4. **Amortization of intangibles.** Intangible assets that have a definite useful life are amortized by crediting the intangible account directly (ordinarily, contra accounts are not used).

Amortization expense	xx	
Intangible asset		xx

a. The method of amortization of intangibles should mirror the pattern that the asset is consumed. If the pattern cannot be reliably determined, the straight-line basis should be used.

EXAMPLE

Determination of Useful Life of an Intangible Asset

Yeager Communications owns several radio stations and has $5,000,000 recorded as the carrying value of broadcast rights. The rights have a legal life of 7 more years but may be extended upon appropriate application for an indefinite period. Since the company has the right and intent to extend the rights indefinitely, the useful life of the asset should be considered indefinite and the rights should not be amortized.

---

5. **Impairment of intangible assets.** An intangible asset that is amortized should be tested for impairment.

a. An intangible asset that is determined to have an indefinite useful life should not be amortized. However, it should be reevaluated every reporting period to determine if facts and circumstances have changed creating a limited life and requiring it to be amortized. Also, such intangible assets should be tested for impairment annually or more frequently if facts and circumstances indicate that impairment may have occurred.

(1) If the carrying value of the intangible asset exceeds its fair value, an impairment loss should be recorded in the amount of the difference.

EXAMPLE

Impairment of an Intangible Asset with an Indefinite Life

Wilson Company acquired a trademark for a major consumer product several years ago for $50,000. At the time it was expected that the asset had an indefinite life. During its annual impairment test of this asset, the company determined that unexpected competition has entered the market that will significantly reduce the future sales of the product. Based on an analysis of cash flows, the trademark is determined to have a fair market value of $30,000 and is expected to continue to have an indefinite useful life. The $20,000 ($50,000 – $30,000) impairment loss should be recognized as shown below.

Impairment loss	20,000	
Trademark		20,000

---

6. **Impairment of goodwill.** The goodwill assigned to a reporting unit should be examined for impairment on an annual basis and between annual tests in certain circumstances. The annual examination may be performed any time during the company's fiscal year as long as it is done at the same time every year. Different reporting units may be examined at different times during the year. An entity has the option to first qualitatively determine if it is more likely than not (greater than 50%) that the fair value of a reporting unit is less than its carrying value, including goodwill. Circumstances to be examined include, but are not limited to, examination of: macroeconomic conditions, industry and market considerations, cost factors, overall financial performance, entity-specific events, reporting unit events, and share price decreases. If it is found that it is **not** more likely than not that the fair value of the reporting unit is less than its carrying value, the goodwill impairment tests are deemed unnecessary. Then entity can choose to bypass the qualitative assessment and proceed directly to the first step of the goodwill impairment test. The test of impairment is a two-step process as described below.

   a. Compare the fair value of the reporting unit with its carrying amount.

      (1) To determine fair value, a valuation premise should be used that is consistent with the asset's highest and best use. The valuation premise can either be an in-use or an in-exchange premise. An in-use premise is used if the asset is used in a business in combination with other assets, such as a reporting unit.

         (a) If the carrying amount of the unit is greater than zero and exceeds its fair value, the second step is performed.
         (b) If the carrying amount of the unit is zero or negative, step 2 of the goodwill impairment test should be performed if it is more likely than not that a goodwill impairment exists.

   b. Compare the implied fair value of the reporting unit goodwill with the carrying amount of that goodwill.

      (1) The implied fair value of goodwill is determined in the same manner as the amount of goodwill recognized in a business combination. That is, all assets in the segment are valued, and the excess of the fair value of the reporting unit as a whole over the amounts assigned to its assets and liabilities is the implied goodwill.

         (a) If the implied value of goodwill is less than its carrying amount, goodwill is written down to its implied value and an impairment loss is recognized.

EXAMPLE

Test of Impairment of Goodwill

Dunn Corporation is performing the test of impairment of the Communications reporting unit at 9/30/10. In performing the first step in the test of impairment, the Communications reporting unit is valued through a multiple of earnings approach at $4,450,000. The carrying amount of the unit at 9/30/10 is $4,650,000, requiring the second step to be performed. The fair value of the assets and liabilities are valued as shown below.

Communications Reporting Unit
Estimated Fair Values 9/30/10 (In 000s)

	Fair value
Cash	$ 150
Accounts receivable	1,000
Net Equipment	2,600
Patents	950
Customer contracts	800
Current liabilities	(1,100)
Fair value of net assets	$4,400

The implied value of goodwill is $50,000 ($4,450,000 – $4,400,000) and this is less than the carrying amount of $300,000. Therefore, an impairment of goodwill should be recognized as shown below.

Impairment loss	250,000	
Goodwill—Communications		250,000

NOW REVIEW MULTIPLE-CHOICE QUESTIONS 58 THROUGH 68 IN VOLUME 2

K. Reporting on the Costs of Start-Up Activities

Start-up costs, including organization costs, are to be expensed as incurred. Start-up costs are defined as one-time activities related to opening a new facility or new class of customer, initiating a new process in an existing facility, or some new operation. In practice, these are referred to as preopening costs, preoperating costs, and organization costs. Routine ongoing efforts to improve existing quality of products, services, or facilities, are not start-up costs.

L. Research and Development Costs

1. R&D costs are expensed as incurred except for intangibles or fixed assets purchased from others having alternative future uses. These should be capitalized and amortized over their useful life. Thus, the cost of patents and R&D equipment purchased from third parties may be deferred and amortized over the asset's useful life. Internally developed R&D may not be deferred.

2. Finally, R&D done under contract for others is not required to be expensed. The costs incurred would be matched with revenue using the completed-contract or percentage-of-completion method.

M. Computer Software Costs

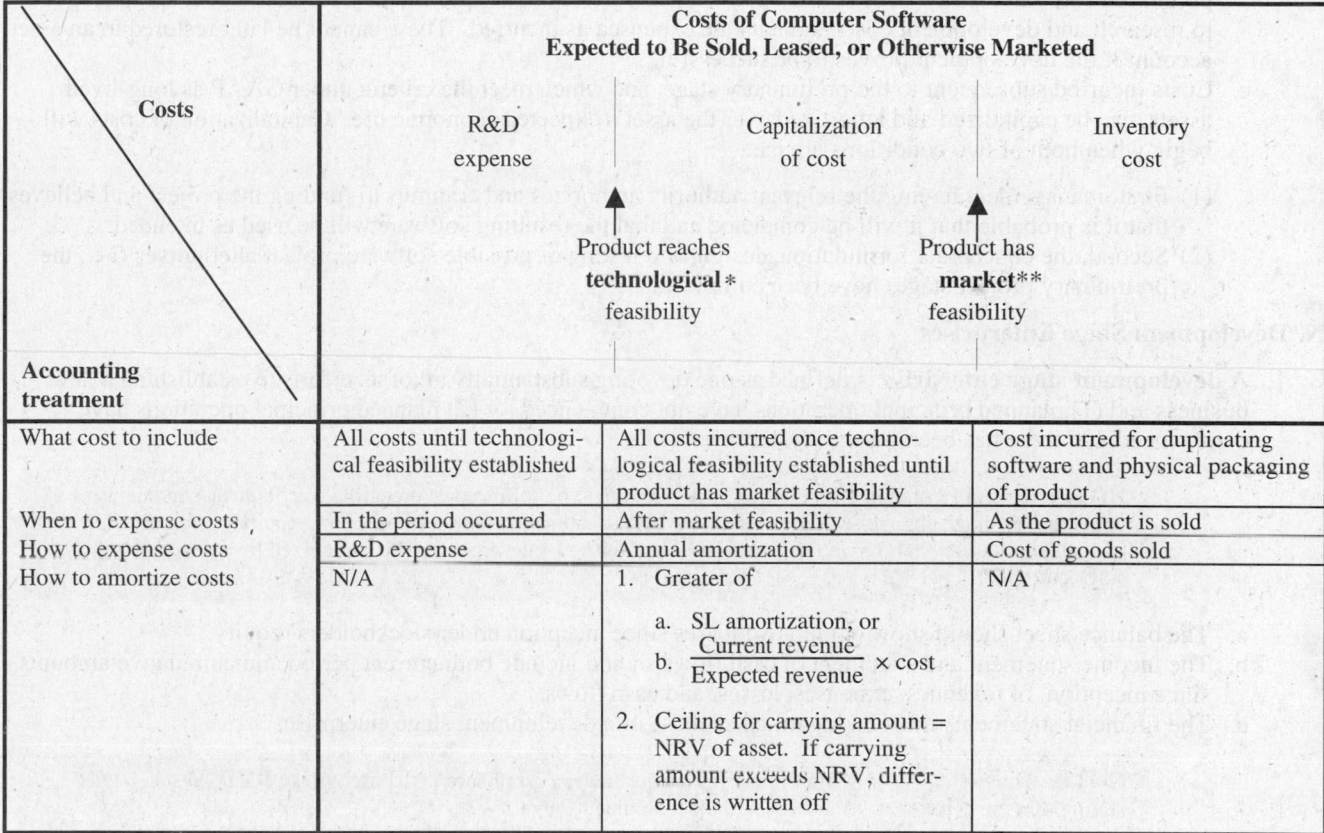

	Costs of Computer Software Expected to Be Sold, Leased, or Otherwise Marketed		
Costs	R&D expense	Capitalization of cost	Inventory cost
	↑ Product reaches **technological** * feasibility	↑ Product has **market** ** feasibility	
Accounting treatment			
What cost to include	All costs until technological feasibility established	All costs incurred once technological feasibility established until product has market feasibility	Cost incurred for duplicating software and physical packaging of product
When to expense costs	In the period occurred	After market feasibility	As the product is sold
How to expense costs	R&D expense	Annual amortization	Cost of goods sold

How to amortize costs	N/A	1. Greater of
		
		  a. SL amortization, or
		
		  b. $\dfrac{\text{Current revenue}}{\text{Expected revenue}} \times \text{cost}$
		
		2. Ceiling for carrying amount = NRV of asset. If carrying amount exceeds NRV, difference is written off
			N/A

* Software creation process includes a detail program design.
** Product ready for release to customers.

1. **Software developed for sale or lease.** If software is developed for sale or lease, the costs incurred to internally create software should be expensed as research and development until technological feasibility is established. Thereafter, all costs should be capitalized and reported at the lower of unamortized cost or net realizable value. Capitalization should cease when the software is available for general release to customers.

   a. The annual amortization of capitalized computer software costs will be the greater of the ratio of current revenues to anticipated total revenues or the straight-line amortization which is based on the estimated economic life.

   b. Once the software is available for general release to customers, the inventory costs should include costs for duplicating software and for physically packaging the product.

   c. The cost of maintenance and customer support should be charged to expense in the period incurred.

2. **Software developed for internal use.** Software must meet two criteria to be accounted for as internally developed software.

   a. First, the software's specifications must be designed or modified to meet the reporting entity's internal needs, including costs to customize purchased software.

   b. Second, during the period in which the software is being developed, there can be no plan or intent to market the software externally, although development of the software can be jointly funded by several entities that each plan to use the software internally.

(1) In order to justify capitalization of related costs, it is necessary for management to conclude that it is probable that the project will be completed and that the software will be used as intended.

    (a) Absent that level of expectation, costs must be expensed currently as research and development costs are required to be.

    (b) Entities which historically were engaged in both research and development of software for internal use and for sale to others would have to carefully identify costs with one or the other activity, since the former would (if all conditions are met) be subject to capitalization, while the latter might be expensed as research and development costs until technological feasibility had been demonstrated.

b. Under terms of the standard, cost capitalization commences when an entity has completed the conceptual formulation, design, and testing of possible project alternatives, including the process of vendor selection for purchased software, if any. These early-phase costs (referred to as "preliminary project stage") are analogous to research and development costs and must be expensed as incurred. These cannot be later restored to an asset account if the development proves to be successful.

c. Costs incurred subsequent to the preliminary stage, and which meet the criteria under GAAP as long-lived assets, can be capitalized and amortized over the asset's expected economic life. Capitalization of costs will begin when both of two conditions are met.

    (1) First, management having the relevant authority authorizes and commits to funding the project and believes that it is probable that it will be completed and that the resulting software will be used as intended.

    (2) Second, the conceptual formulation, design, and testing of possible software project alternatives (i.e., the preliminary project stage) have been completed.

N. Development Stage Enterprises

1. A **development stage enterprise** is defined as one devoting substantially all of its efforts to establishing a new business and (1) planned principal operations have not commenced, or (2) planned principal operations have commenced, but there has been no significant revenue.

> **NOTE:** Generally accepted accounting principles are to be followed in preparing the financial statements of a development stage enterprise. Therefore, no special treatment is allowed concerning capitalization or deferral of costs; only costs that may be deferred for an established enterprise may be capitalized by a development stage enterprise.

a. The balance sheet should show cumulative losses since inception under stockholders' equity.

b. The income statement and statement of cash flows should include both current period and cumulative amounts, since inception, of revenues, expenses, losses, and cash flows.

c. The financial statements must be identified as those of a development stage enterprise.

> **NOTE:** The first fiscal year after the development stage, a disclosure is required in the financial statements stating that the entity was previously in the development stage.

NOW REVIEW MULTIPLE-CHOICE QUESTIONS 69 THROUGH 84 IN VOLUME 2

O. Research Component—Accounting Standards Codification

Research on fixed assets is found in several locations in the accounting standards. The most basic accounting rules for fixed assets are in ASC Topic 360, titled *Property, Plant, and Equipment*. Other accounting standards may apply to fixed assets. The following table lists these standards with the corresponding ASC topic numbers and relevant account issues.

Topic number	Topic	Accounting issue(s)
250	Accounting Changes	Changes in Depreciation
280	Segment Reporting	Defining a Reporting Unit
350	Intangibles—Goodwill and Other	Valuation, Impairment
360	Property, Plant, and Equipment	Cost, Measurement, Impairment, Disclosures
410	Asset Retirement Obligations	Capitalizing Costs of Retirement Obligation
720	Other Expenses (Including Start-Up Costs)	Start-Up Activities/Costs
730	Research and Development	Capitalizing R&D
805	Business Combinations	Valuation in Business Combination
820	Fair Value Measurements and Disclosures	Fair Value Measures
835	Interest (Capitalization of Interest)	Capitalization of Interest
845	Nonmonetary Transactions	Exchanges of Nonmonetary Assets

Topic number	Topic	Accounting issue(s)
915	Development Stage Enterprises	Accounting for Development Stage Enterprises
958	Not-For-Profit Entities	Donated Assets
985	Software	Capitalizing Software Costs

P. International Financial Reporting Standards (IFRS)

1. Some of the most significant differences between US GAAP and IFRS exist in the area of accounting for fixed assets. Items which are classified as noncurrent assets under US GAAP may be classified differently under IFRS. Specifically, noncurrent assets must be identified in categories such as plant, property, and equipment, investment property, intangible assets, and biological assets.

2. Plant, Property, and Equipment

   a. Plant, property, and equipment are tangible items which are expected to be used during more than one period, and used in the production or supply of goods or services, for rental to others, or for administrative purposes. Plant, property, and equipment are recorded at cost.

      (1) Cost includes the purchase price net of discounts and rebates, the expenditures to bring the asset to its required location and condition, delivery and handling, site preparation, installation, assembly costs, professional fees, and the estimate of the cost of obligations required for the asset's disposal (decommissioning or site restoration).
      (2) Similar to US GAAP, costs of self-constructed assets include material, labor, and interest costs.

   b. After an asset is initially recognized at cost, it is subsequently measured using either the cost model or the revaluation model. Long-lived assets are divided into classes, and a decision is made for each class on which valuation method is applied.

      > **NOTE:** A different valuation model can be used for different classes of assets but not individual assets within a class. Examples of classes of assets include land, equipment, motor vehicles, land and buildings, ships, aircraft, and furniture and fixtures.

      (1) The cost model provides that the asset is carried at cost less an accumulated depreciation and less any accumulated impairment loss.

         (a) The depreciation method chosen should reflect the pattern of economic benefits expected to be consumed. The straight-line, declining balance, and units of production methods are acceptable depreciation methods. A change in depreciation method is considered a change in accounting estimate and is accounted for on a prospective basis.

      (2) Under the revaluation model, the carrying amount of the asset is the fair value at the date of revaluation less any subsequent accumulated depreciation and subsequent accumulated impairment loss. The revaluation model should be applied to assets whose value can be reliably measured. There is no rule regarding the frequency or date of revaluation; therefore, annual revaluations are not required. However, when revaluation is performed, it must be performed for the entire class of assets.

         (a) Revaluation to fair value usually involves obtaining appraisals. When a class of assets is revalued, the asset account is written up or down, and the adjustment is recorded to the revaluation surplus account which is reported in other comprehensive income for the period.
         (b) If the revaluation model is used, accumulated depreciation can be adjusted proportionately, or the accumulated depreciation account can be eliminated and the asset shown net.
         (c) When an asset is disposed of, a gain or loss is recognized and reported on the income statement. Any balance in the revaluation surplus account is transferred directly to retained earnings (not to profit or loss).

3. **Investment Property**

   a. Investment property is defined as property held to earn rentals, for capital appreciation, or both. To qualify as investment property, it may not be used in the production or supply of goods or services or for administrative purposes, nor can it be held for sale in the ordinary course of business.

      (1) Investment property includes land or a building and can be held by the owner or by a lessee under a financing lease.
      (2) Examples of investment property also include land held for long-term appreciation, land held for an undetermined future use, buildings owned by the entity, or a vacant building held to be leased under an operating lease.

b. Investment property is recognized when it is probable that the future economic benefits of the property will flow to the entity and the cost of the property can be measured reliably. Investment property is measured at cost. After initial recognition, the investment property is measured under the fair value model or the cost model, with certain exceptions.

(1) Under the fair value model, investment property is initially measured at fair value. Changes in fair value are recognized in profit or loss in the period of the change. Notice that this is different treatment than for plant, property, and equipment, where the revaluation is recorded in other comprehensive income.

(a) If the fair value model is used, no depreciation is recorded.
(b) The fair value is the price at which the property could be exchanged between knowledgeable parties in an arm's-length transaction.

(2) The cost model requires investment property to be carried on the balance sheet at cost less accumulated depreciation and less accumulated impairment losses. If an entity chooses the cost model, it must still disclose fair values in the notes to the financial statements.

c. Another difference between IFRS and US GAAP involves investment property leased under operating leases. Under IFRS, an entity has the option to record investment property leased under an operating lease as an asset on the balance sheet if the lessee can reliably measure the fair value of the lease. Once this option is selected for one leased property, other investment property must also be accounted for using the fair value model.

d. Investment property does not include property used in the business, property being constructed or developed for others, property under construction that will be future investment property, and property held for sale in the normal course of business.

4. **Intangible Assets**

a. Intangible assets either have no physical substance or have a value that is not represented by its physical substance. Intangible assets are categorized as either identifiable or unidentifiable.

(1) An asset is identifiable if meets one of the two criteria: (1) it is based on contractual or legal rights, or (2) it can be separated from the entity and sold, transferred, licensed, rented, or exchanged.

(a) Notice this is similar to US GAAP where an identifiable intangible must meet the legal, contractual, or separability criteria.

(2) Identifiable intangibles include patents, copyrights, brand names, customer lists, trade names, computer software, formulae, licenses, and franchises.

b. Accounting for intangibles under IFRS depends upon whether the intangible assets were acquired or internally developed.

(1) If the intangible assets were acquired, the intangible asset is recorded at cost.
(2) If the intangible assets were acquired in a business combination, newly identified intangibles are recognized at fair value separately from goodwill.
(3) Internally generated intangibles are initially recognized at the cost of development. However, to be recognized, they must meet the definition of identifiable assets (i.e., they must have future economic benefits and can be measured reliably).

(a) Although internally generated goodwill may provide future economic benefits, it cannot be measured reliably. Therefore, internally generated goodwill is not recognized as an asset.
(b) Similarly, expenditures on research may not result in probable future economic benefits; therefore, research expenditures are treated as an expense of the period.
(c) Development is the application of research findings for the production of new products or technology. Development costs may be recognized as an intangible asset if the following six criteria are met: (1) technological feasibility of completing the asset for use or sale has been achieved; (2) the entity intends to complete and use or sell the asset; (3) the entity has the ability to use or sell the asset; (4) the entity understands how the asset will generate probable future economic benefits; (5) technical, financial, and other resources are available to complete development of the asset; (6) the entity has the ability to reliably measure the expenditures. If all six conditions are not met, development costs should be expensed in the current period. Once development costs are expensed, they cannot be capitalized in the future.

c. Intangible assets may use either the cost model or the revaluation model.

(1) Similar to plant, property, and equipment, the cost model requires the asset to be recorded at its cost less any accumulated amortization or accumulated impairment losses.

(2) The revaluation model requires that the fair value must be determined in an active market. Therefore, only intangible assets that are traded with active market prices may be valued using the revaluation model. The revaluation model requires gains and losses on revaluation to be recorded in other comprehensive income.

d. The useful life of an intangible asset is either finite or indefinite. Intangible assets with finite lives are amortized over the useful life; intangible assets with indefinite lives are not amortized, but tested for impairment annually (at the reporting date).

5. **Impairment of Assets**

a. An entity should determine at each reporting date if there are conditions that would cause an asset to be impaired.

   (1) Asset impairment exists if the carrying value of the asset is greater than its recoverable amount.

      (a) The recoverable amount is the greater of the net selling price or its value in use.

   (2) An impairment loss for an asset accounted for at historical cost is recognized as an expense of the current period. The loss may be included with depreciation expense or identified separately on the income statement.

   (3) If the revaluation model was used, an impairment adjustment may be treated as a reversal of an upward revaluation. Once the entire revaluation account is eliminated, the excess charge is recognized in expense of the period. Hence, the revaluation account cannot have a debit balance.

b. Intangible assets with finite lives are tested for impairment when the asset's carrying value is more than its recoverable amount. However, if an intangible asset has an indefinite life, a test for impairment must be made annually.

   (1) If an intangible asset's carrying value is more than its recoverable amount, the asset is considered impaired.

      (a) The recoverable amount is the greater of the net selling price (fair value less costs of disposal) or its value in use.
      (b) The value in use is determined by estimating the future cash flows expected from the continued use of the asset and its disposal.

   (2) Impairments of intangible assets carried at historical cost are recognized as charges against the current period profit or loss.

   (3) If the revaluation method was used for long-lived assets, any increase in value was recorded in a revaluation account in other comprehensive income. Therefore, the impairment adjustment is used to reverse any previous revaluation adjustment. Once the revaluation account is reduced to zero, the impairment is then charged to expense of the period.

c. An important difference between US GAAP and IFRS is that IFRS allows reversals of previously recognized impairments if the historical cost method is used.

   (1) If the cost method is used, a reversal of impairment losses may be recognized in the income statement up to the amount of the impairments previously recognized.

   (2) However, if the revaluation method is used, the recovery of impairments would be recognized in other comprehensive income.

6. **Biological Assets**

a. Biological assets (agricultural assets) are living animals or plants and must be disclosed as a separate item on the balance sheet. Biological assets are recognized when a future economic benefit is probable, the entity controls the asset as a result of past events, and the cost or fair value can be measured reliably. Agricultural produce should be measured as fair value less costs to sell at harvest.

NOW REVIEW MULTIPLE-CHOICE QUESTIONS 85 THROUGH 102 IN VOLUME 2

KEY TERMS

Capital expenditures are not normal, recurring expenses; they benefit the operations of more than one period.

Capitalize. To include an expenditure in an asset's cost.

Commercial substance. A transaction lacks commercial substance if the configuration of cash flows is significantly different as a result of the exchange.

Depletion. "Depreciation" of natural resources.

Depreciation is the annual charge to income for asset use during the period.

Development stage enterprise. One devoting substantially all of its efforts to establishing a new business and (1) planned principal operations have not commenced, or (2) planned principal operations have commenced, but there has been no significant revenue.

Fixed assets. The capitalized amount of expenditures made to acquire tangible property which will be used for a period of more than one year.

Impairment. Occurs when the carrying amount of a long-lived asset or asset group exceeds its fair value.

Intangible assets. Nonphysical assets.

Nonmonetary exchange is a reciprocal transfer wherein the transferor has no substantial continuing involvement in the asset, and the risks and rewards of ownership are transferred.

Revenue expenditures are normal recurring expenditures.

Start-up costs. One-time activities related to opening a new facility or new class of customer, initiating a new process in an existing facility, or some new operation.

Tangible property. Property that physically exists.

Module 12: Monetary Current Assets and Current Liabilities

Overview

This study module reviews accounting for current assets (except inventory which is presented in Module 10) and short-term investments (which are presented in Module 16). The primary topics covered on the Financial Accounting Reporting Section of the exam include

1. Cash and bank reconciliations.
2. Receivables with respect to initial recording, bad debts, borrowing, factoring, transferring, servicing, and securitizing.

This module also reviews current liabilities. The primary topics tested on the exam include accounting for payroll and contingencies (e.g., warranties, lawsuits.) Additionally, this module covers ratio analysis for solvency (e.g. current ratio) and operational efficiency (e.g. inventory turnover).

A. Cash

The definition of **cash** includes both cash (cash on hand and demand deposits) and cash equivalents (short-term, highly liquid investments).

1. **Cash equivalents** have to be readily convertible into cash and so near maturity that they carry little risk of changing in value due to interest rate changes. Generally this will include only those investments with original maturities of three months or less from the **date of purchase** by the enterprise.

   a. Common examples of cash equivalents include Treasury bills, commercial paper, and money market funds. Unrestricted cash and cash equivalents available for general use are presented as the first current asset.

2. Cash set aside for special uses is usually disclosed separately. The entry to set up a special fund is

Special cash fund	xx	
Cash		xx

3. Cash restricted as to use (e.g., not transferable out of a foreign country) should be disclosed separately, but not as a current asset if it cannot be used in the next year (this is true of special funds also).

4. Imprest (petty) cash funds are generally included in the total cash figure, but unreimbursed expense vouchers are excluded.

B. Bank Reconciliations

1. Bank reconciliations are prepared by bank depositors when they receive their monthly bank statements. The reconciliation is made to determine any required adjustments to the cash balance. Two types of reconciling items are possible.

   a. Reconciling items not requiring adjustment on the books (type A)

      (1) There are three type A reconciling items. They do not require adjusting journal entries.

         (a) Outstanding checks
         (b) Deposits in transit
         (c) Bank errors

   b. Reconciling items requiring adjustment on the books (type B)

      (1) All other reconciling items (type B) require adjusting journal entries. Examples of type B reconciling items include

         (a) Unrecorded returned nonsufficient funds (NSF) checks

    (b) Unrecorded bank charges
    (c) Errors in the cash account
    (d) Unrecorded bank collections of notes receivable

2. Two types of formats are used in bank reconciliations.

Format 1	**Format 2**
Balance per bank	Balance per bank
+(–) A adjustments	+(–) A adjustments
Correct cash balance	+(–) B adjustments
	Balance per books
Balance per books	+(–) B adjustments
+(–) B adjustments	Correct cash balance
Correct cash balance	

  a. Type A and B adjustments can be either added or subtracted depending upon the type of format and the nature of the item.

  b. Reconciling items must be analyzed to determine whether they are included in (1) the balance per bank, and/or (2) the balance per books.

    (1) If they are included in one, but not the other, an adjustment is required.

       (a) For instance, the $1,800 deposit in transit in the following example is included in the balance per books but not in the balance per bank. Thus, it must be added to the balance per bank to reconcile to the correct cash balance.

       (b) Deposits in transit do not require an adjusting journal entry. Analyze all reconciling items in this manner, but remember, only journalize type B reconciling items.

SAMPLE BANK RECONCILIATION (FORMAT 1)

Per bank statement	$ 4,702
Deposits in transit	1,800
Outstanding checks	(1,200)
Bank error	50
Correct cash balance	$ 5,352
Per books	$ 5,332
Service charges	(5)
Note collected by bank	150
Customer's NSF check	(170)
Deposit of July 10 recorded as $749 instead of $794	45
Correct cash balance	$ 5,352

NOTE: The balance per bank and balance per books each are reconciled directly to the corrected balance.

  c. **Adjusting journal entries.** All of the items in the per books section of a bank reconciliation (type B) require adjusting entries. The entries for the above example appear below.

Miscellaneous expense	5		AR	170	
Cash		5	Cash		170
Cash	150		Cash	45	
Notes receivable		150	AR (or sales)		45

3. Four-column cash reconciliation

  a. Unlike the bank reconciliation above, which is as of a specific date, a four-column cash reconciliation, also known as a "proof of cash," reconciles bank and book cash balances over a specified time period.

  b. A proof of cash consists of four columns: beginning of the period bank reconciliation, receipts, disbursements, and end-of-the-period bank reconciliation. Thus, the proof of cash cross-foots as well as foots.

SAMPLE PROOF OF CASH (FORMAT 2)

	Bank reconciliation June 30, 2010	Receipts	Disbursements	Bank reconciliation July 31, 2010
Balance per bank statement	$3,402	$25,200	$23,900	$ 4,702
Deposits in transit				
June 30, 2010	1,610	(1,610)		
July 31, 2010		1,800		1,800
Outstanding checks				
June 30, 2010	(450)		(450)	
July 31, 2010			1,200	(1,200)
Service charges			(5)	5
Note collected by bank		(150)		(150)
Customer's NSF check			(170)	170
Deposit of July 10 recorded as $749 instead of $794		(45)		(45)
Bank error			(50)	50
Balance per books	$4,562	$25,195	$24,425	$ 5,332

(1) There are no type B reconciling items in the beginning reconciliation column. This is because the $4,562 has been adjusted when the June bank statement was reconciled.

(2) Figures appearing in the center columns have unlike signs if they are adjacent and like signs if they are not adjacent to amounts in the side columns.

c. The purpose of the proof of cash is to disclose any cash misstatements, such as unrecorded disbursements and receipts within a month, which would not be detected by a bank reconciliation.

> **EXAMPLE**
>
> If the center two columns each required a negative $1,000 to make the top line reconcile with the bottom line, there may be unrecorded receipts and deposits of $1,000.

NOW REVIEW MULTIPLE-CHOICE QUESTIONS 1 THROUGH 6 IN VOLUME 2

C. Receivables

Accounts receivable should be disclosed in the balance sheet at net realizable value (gross amount less estimated uncollectibles) by source (e.g., trade, officer, etc.). Officer, employee, and affiliate company receivables should be separately disclosed. Unearned interest and finance charges should be deducted from gross receivables.

1. Anticipation of Sales Discounts

a. Cash discounts are generally recognized as expense when cash payment is received within the discount period. As long as cash discounts to be taken on year-end receivables remain constant from year to year, there is no problem. If, however, discounts on year-end receivables fluctuate, a year-end allowance can be set up or sales can be recorded net of the discounts.

(1) The entries to record sales at net are shown below in comparison to the sales recorded at **gross**.

		Sales at net		Sales at gross	
a.	Sale	AR (net)		AR (gross)	
		Sales	(net)	Sales	(gross)
b.	Cash receipt within discount period	Cash (net)		Sales disc. (disc.)	
		AR	(net)	Cash (net)	
				AR	(gross)
c.	Cash receipt after discount period	Cash (gross)		Cash (gross)	
		AR	(net)	AR	(gross)
		Disc. not taken	(disc.)		

(a) The rationale for the net method is that sales are recorded at the cash equivalent amount and receivables nearer realizable value.

> **NOTE:** Under both the net and gross methods, sales and accounts receivable are recorded net of trade discounts for the same reason.

(b) If a sales discount allowance method is used, the entry below is made with the gross method entries. The entry should be reversed.

Sales discounts   (expected disc. on year-end AR)
   Allowance for sales disc.   (expected disc. on year-end AR)

(c) Similarly, when using the **"net method,"** an entry should be made to pick up discounts not expected to be taken on year-end receivables. Generally, however, these latter adjustments are not made, because they are assumed to be about the same each period.

2. **Bad Debts Expense**

There are two approaches to bad debts.

- Direct write-off method
- Allowance method

a. Under the **direct write-off method**, bad debts are considered expenses in the period in which they are written off.

> **NOTE:** The direct write-off method is not considered acceptable under GAAP, unless the amounts are immaterial.

(1) The direct write-off method is the method required for tax purposes.

Bad debts expense   (uncollectible AR)
   AR   (uncollectible AR)

b. The **allowance method** seeks to estimate the amount of uncollectible receivables, and establishes a contra valuation account (allowance for bad debts) for the amount estimated to be uncollectible.

(1) The adjusting entry to set up the allowance is

Bad debts expense   (estimated)
   Allowance for bad debts   (estimated)

(2) The entry to write off bad debts is

Allowance for bad debts   (uncollectible AR)
   AR   (uncollectible AR)

(a) There are two methods to determine the annual charge to bad debts expense.

1] **Annual sales**

a] Charging bad debts expense for 1% of annual sales is based on the theory that bad debts are a function of sales; this method emphasizes the income statement.

b] When bad debts expense is estimated as a function of sales, any balance in the allowance account is ignored in making the adjusting entry. Bad debts expense under this method is simply the total amount computed (i.e., Sales × Percentage).

2] **Year-end AR**

a] Charging bad debts on year-end AR is based on the theory that bad debts are a function of AR collections during the period; this method emphasizes the balance sheet.

b] A bad debts percentage can be applied to total AR or subsets of AR. Often an aging schedule is prepared for this purpose. An AR aging schedule classifies AR by their age (e.g., 30, 60, 90, 120, etc., days overdue).

c] When bad debts expense is estimated using outstanding receivables, the expense is the amount needed to adjust the allowance account to the amount computed (i.e., AR × Percentage[s]). Thus, bad debts expense under this method is the amount computed less any credit balance currently in the allowance account (or plus any debit balance).

(3) **Net accounts receivable** is the balance in accounts receivable less the allowance for bad debts.

> **NOTE:** Net receivables **do not change** when a specific account is written off since both accounts receivable and the allowance account are reduced by the same amount.

(4) The policy for charging off uncollectible trade accounts receivable must be disclosed for receivables that have a contractual maturity of one year or less and arise from the sale of goods or services.

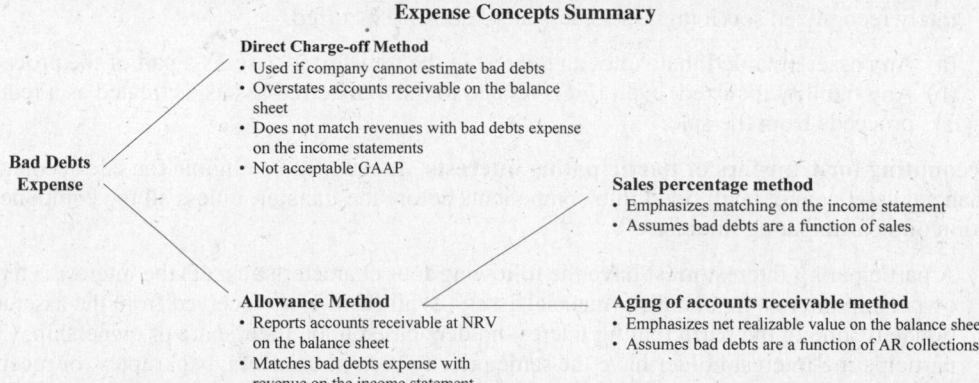

Methods of Recognizing Bad Debts
Expense Concepts Summary

Direct Charge-off Method
- Used if company cannot estimate bad debts
- Overstates accounts receivable on the balance sheet
- Does not match revenues with bad debts expense on the income statements
- Not acceptable GAAP

Bad Debts Expense

Sales percentage method
- Emphasizes matching on the income statement
- Assumes bad debts are a function of sales

Allowance Method
- Reports accounts receivable at NRV on the balance sheet
- Matches bad debts expense with revenue on the income statement

Aging of accounts receivable method
- Emphasizes net realizable value on the balance sheet
- Assumes bad debts are a function of AR collections

> **NOW REVIEW MULTIPLE-CHOICE QUESTIONS 7 THROUGH 23 IN VOLUME 2**

3. **Transfers and servicing of financial assets (ASC Topic 860).** Transfers of financial assets include the transfer of an entire financial asset, a group of financial assets, or a participating interest in an entire financial asset. Specifically, this topic includes servicing arrangements, recourse arrangements, guarantees, agreements to purchase or redeem transferred financial assets, options written or held, derivative financial instruments that are entered into with contemplation of a transfer, arrangements to provide financial support, pledges of collateral, and transferor's beneficial interests in the transferred financial asset.

   a. The major types of transfers include

   (1) **Securitizations**—Purchasing and selling securities that are collateralized by a pool of assets, such as a group of receivables.
   (2) **Factoring**—Selling receivables at a discount to obtain immediate cash.
   (3) **Transfers of receivables with recourse**—Selling receivables at a discount to obtain immediate cash but retaining the risk of loss if the customer does not pay the amount owed.
   (4) **Repurchase agreements**—An agreement to sell an asset to a lender and later repurchase the asset. These agreements are in effect using the asset as collateral for a loan.
   (5) **Loan participations**—A situation where a group of financial institutions (called participating interest holders) purchases a share of a financial instruments (e.g., a loan).
   (6) **Banker's acceptances**—An order from a customer of a bank for the payment of a specified sum of money (like a post-dated check) that may be bought and sold.

   b. The important determination in accounting for transfers of assets is whether the transaction is accounted for as a sale of the asset or a secured loan with the asset as collateral.

   (1) A transfer may be accounted for as a sale only when the transferor surrenders control of the financial asset(s) and all of the following conditions are met:

   (a) The transferred financial asset(s) are isolated and beyond the reach of the transferor and its creditors, even in bankruptcy or receivership.
   (b) The transferee can pledge or exchange the asset(s) without unreasonable constraints or conditions.
   (c) The transferor does not maintain effective control over the transferred financial asset(s) or a third-party beneficial interest in the asset(s).

   > **EXAMPLE**
   >
   > The transferor may not have a repurchase or redemption agreement, an agreement to cause the holder to return the asset (other than a cleanup call), or an agreement that requires the transferor to repurchase the financial asset at a favorable price wherein it is probable that the repurchase will occur.

   (2) Transfers of financial assets are disaggregated into separate components of assets and liabilities. Each entity involved in the transaction

   (a) Recognizes only the assets it controls and liabilities it incurs after the transaction has occurred, and
   (b) Derecognizes assets for which control has been given up or lost, and liabilities for which extinguishment has occurred.

(3) The proceeds received from the sale of financial assets is the cash or other assets obtained, including separately recognized servicing assets, less any liabilities incurred.

    (a) Any asset obtained that is not an interest in the transferred asset is a part of the proceeds of the sale.

    (b) Any liability incurred, even if it is related to the transferred assets, is treated as a reduction of the proceeds from the sale.

c. **Accounting for transfers of participating interests.** In order to be eligible for sale accounting, the entire financial asset cannot be divided into components before the transfer, unless all the components meet the definition of a participating interest.

(1) A participating interest must have the following four characteristics: (1) the interest is a proportionate ownership interest in an entire financial asset; (2) all cash flows received from the asset are divided proportionately among the participating interest holders based upon their share of ownership; (3) the rights of each participating interest holder have the same priority (i.e., in transfers, bankruptcy, or receivership); and (4) no party has the right to pledge or exchange the financial asset unless all participating interest holders agree.

(2) When a transfer of a participating interest(s) qualifies as a sale, the transferor should

    (a) Allocate the carrying amount of the entire financial asset(s) between the participating interest(s) sold and the participating interest that continues to be held by the transferor. Relative fair values at the date of transfer are used to allocate the carrying amount.

    (b) Derecognize the participating interest(s) sold.

    (c) Recognize and measure at fair value servicing assets, servicing liabilities, and any other assets obtained or liabilities incurred in the sale.

    (d) Recognize any gain or loss on the sale in earnings.

    (e) Report any participating interest that continues to be held as the difference between the previous carrying amount and the amount derecognized.

(3) If the transfer of a financial asset does not meet the criteria for a sale, the transferor and transferee account for the transfer as a secured borrowing with the financial asset(s) pledged as collateral.

d. **Factoring of receivables.** This category of financing is the most significant in terms of accounting implications. **Factoring** traditionally involves the outright sale of receivables to a financing institution known as a factor. These arrangements usually involve (1) notification to the customer to forward future payments to the factor and (2) transfer of receivables **without recourse**, which means that the factor assumes the risk of loss from noncollection. Thus, once a factoring arrangement is completed, the entity has no further involvement with the receivables, unless the customer decides to return the merchandise. In its simplistic form, the receivables are sold and the difference between the cash received and the carrying value of the receivables is recognized as a gain or loss.

(1) Factoring **without** recourse provides two financial benefits to the business: it permits the entity to obtain cash earlier, and the risk of bad debts is transferred to the factor.

    (a) The factor is compensated for each of the aspects of the transaction.

    (b) Interest is charged based on the anticipated length of time between the date the factoring is consummated and the expected collection date of the receivables sold, and a fee is charged based upon the anticipated bad debt losses.

EXAMPLE

Thirsty Corp., on July 1, 2011, enters into an agreement with Rich Company (the factor) to sell a group of its receivables **without recourse**. A total face value of $200,000 of accounts receivable are involved. The factor charges 20% interest computed on the weighted-average time to maturity of the receivables of thirty-six days plus a 3% fee.

The entries required by the transferor are as follows:

Cash	190,055	
Interest expense (or prepaid) (200,000 × .20 × 36/365)	3,945	
Factoring fee (200,000 × .03)	6,000	
Accounts receivable		200,000

The interest expense and factor's fee can be combined into a $9,945 loss on the sale of receivables.

    (c) Merchandise returns will normally be the responsibility of the transferor, who must then make the appropriate settlement with the factor.

1] To protect against the possibility of merchandise returns which diminish the total amount of the receivables to be collected, a factor will often holdback a portion of the amount of the receivables factored in addition to taking the interest and fee.

2] The transferor will charge any merchandise returns to a "factor's holdback receivable" account that is created when the receivables are factored. At the end of the return privilege period, any remaining holdback will become due and payable to the borrower.

EXAMPLE

Accounting by the transferor for the transfer of receivables without recourse

1. Thirsty Corp., on July 1, 2011, enters into an agreement with Rich Company to sell a group of its receivables **without recourse**. A total face value of $200,000 accounts receivable are involved. Rich (the factor) charges 20% interest computed on the weighted-average time to maturity of the receivables of thirty-six days plus a 3% fee. A 5% holdback is also retained.
2. Thirsty's customers return for credit $4,800 of merchandise.
3. The customer return privilege period expires and the remaining holdback is paid to the transferor.

The entries required are as follows:

1. Cash	180,055	
Loss on sale of receivables	9,945*	
Factor's holdback receivable (200,000 × .05)	10,000	
Accounts receivable		200,000

  * ($3,945 interest expense + $6,000 factoring fee)

2. Sales returns and allowances	4,800	
Factor's holdback receivable		4,800
3. Cash	5,200	
Factor's holdback receivable		5,200

(d) Factoring transfers title to the receivables. Thus, if there is a **without recourse** provision, the removal of these receivables from the borrower's balance sheet is clearly warranted.

(2) Factoring arrangements may also involve factoring **with** recourse.

  (a) In a with-recourse arrangement, if the customer does not pay the factor, the transferor must pay the factor the amount due on the account.

  (b) The rules for transfer of receivables with recourse vary by jurisdiction; therefore, transfers with recourse may or may not qualify for sale treatment.

  (c) If the factoring with recourse arrangement qualifies as a sale, the recourse liability is treated as reduction of the proceeds received in the transfer.

    1] In computing the gain or loss to be recognized at the date of the transfer of the receivables, the borrower (transferor) must take into account the anticipated chargebacks from the transferee for bad debts expected to be incurred. This action requires an estimate by the transferor, based on past experience.

    2] Adjustments should also be made at the time of sale for the estimated effects of any accelerated payments by customers (where the receivables are interest-bearing or where cash discounts are available).

EXAMPLE

Accounting by the transferor for the transfer of receivables with recourse

1. Thirsty Corp., on July 1, 2011, enters into an agreement with Rich Company to sell a group of its receivables with a face value of $200,000. Rich Company (the factor) charges 20% interest computed on the weighted-average time to maturity of the receivables of thirty-six days and a 3% fee. A 5% holdback is also retained.
2. Assume Thirsty Corp. surrenders control of the receivables, per ASC Topic 860, Thirsty's future obligation for uncollectible accounts is reasonably estimable, and Rich Co. does not have a unilateral ability to require Thirsty to repurchase the receivables.
3. The factor accepts the receivables **subject to recourse** for nonpayment. The recourse obligation has a fair value of $10,000.

Fair Values

Cash proceeds	180,055
Factor's holdback receivable	10,000
Recourse obligation	(10,000)
Net proceeds	180,055
Less: Carrying value of receivables	(200,000)
Loss on sale of receivables	(19,945)

The entries required to record the sale are

Cash	180,055	
Factor's holdback receivable (200,000 × .05)	10,000	
Loss on sale of receivables	19,945	
Accounts receivable		200,000
Recourse obligation		10,000

(d) The accounts receivable are removed from the transferor's books because they have been sold. The loss on sale of receivables is the sum of the interest charged by the factor ($3,945), the factor's fee ($6,000), and the fair value of the recourse obligation ($10,000), which is the estimated amount of uncollectible accounts.

(e) Because the transaction resulted in a "sale" rather than a borrowing, the "interest" and "fee" elements relate directly to the sale transaction. In a sale, these components are in essence part of a negotiated price for the receivables.

(f) If, subsequent to the sale of the receivables, the actual experience relative to the recourse terms differs from the provision made at the time of the sale, a change in an accounting estimate results. It is reflected as an additional gain or loss in the subsequent period. These changes are not corrections of errors or retroactive adjustments.

(g) If the above transfer did not meet the requirements for sale treatment, it would be accounted for as a secured borrowing.

(3) The chart below summarizes the accounting for the transfer of receivables.

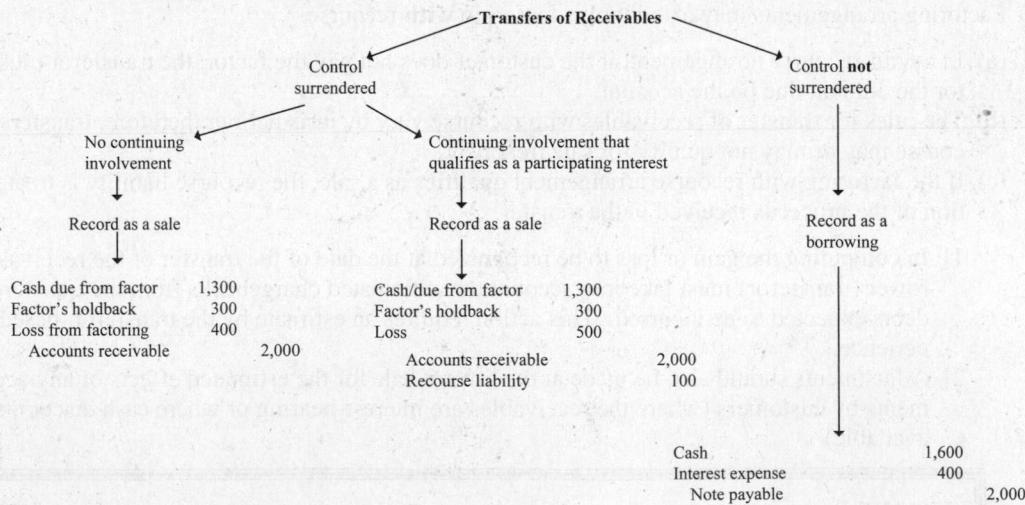

e. **Servicing of financial assets.**

(1) Servicing of financial assets may involve any one or all of the following activities:

    (a) Collecting payments
    (b) Paying taxes and insurance
    (c) Monitoring delinquencies
    (d) Foreclosing
    (e) Investing
    (f) Remitting fees
    (g) Accounting

(2) Although inherent in transfers of most financial assets, **servicing** is a distinct asset or liability only when separated contractually from the underlying financial asset. The servicing asset usually results either from

separate purchase or assumption of the servicing rights, or from securitization with retained servicing. The servicer's obligations are specified in the contract.

(3) Typically, the servicing contract results in an asset because the benefits are more than adequate compensation for the cost of servicing. The benefits include fees, late charges, float, and other income.

(4) If the benefits do not provide fair compensation, the servicing contract is a liability. The fair value of a servicing contract is based on its value in the market and is not based on the internal cost structure of the servicer. Thus, the concept of adequate compensation is judged by requirements that would be imposed by a new or outside servicer. In cases where there is not a reliable market for the contract, present value methods may be used to value the servicing contract.

(5) In summary, the servicer should record the servicing contract based on the following criteria:

   (a) More than adequate—resulting in a recorded asset
   (b) Adequate compensation—resulting in no asset or liability
   (c) Less than adequate—resulting in a recorded liability

(6) Servicing assets or servicing liabilities are to be accounted for separately as follows:

   (a) Assets are reported separately from liabilities. They are not netted.
   (b) Initially measure servicing assets that are retained by the transferor by allocating the carrying amount based on relative fair values at the date of transfer.
   (c) Initially measure at fair value all purchased assets, assumed liabilities, and liabilities undertaken in a sale or securitization.
   (d) Account separately for interest-only strips (future interest income from serviced assets that exceed servicing fees).
   (e) Measure servicing assets and servicing liabilities using one of two methods: amortization method, or fair value method. An election must be made to use the fair value method for each class of servicing assets and servicing liabilities. Once the election is made to value using the fair value method, the election cannot be reversed.
   (f) Report servicing assets and servicing liabilities on the balance sheet in one of two ways:

      1] Display separate line items for amounts valued at fair value and amounts measured by amortization method, **or**
      2] Display aggregate amounts for all servicing assets and servicing liabilities, and disclose parenthetically the amount that is measured at fair value that is included in the aggregate amount.

(7) The **amortization method** requires servicing assets and servicing liabilities to be initially recorded at fair value. Assets are then amortized in proportion to, and over the period of, receipt of estimated net servicing income or net servicing loss. At the end of each period, the assets are assessed for impairment or increased obligation based on fair value. Over time, the asset is tested for impairment which is recognized in a valuation allowance account. Liabilities are amortized in proportion to, and over the period of, the net servicing loss. In cases where changes have increased the fair value above the book value, an increased liability and a loss should be recognized.

(8) Under the **fair value method,** servicing assets and servicing liabilities are initially recorded at fair value. The fair value is measured at each reporting date. Changes in fair value are reported in earnings in the period in which the change in fair value occurs.

(9) Required disclosures for **all** servicing assets and servicing liabilities include management's basis for determining classes, a description of risks, the instruments used to mitigate income statement effect of changes in fair value, the amount of contractually specified servicing fees, late fees, and ancillary fees for each period, and quantitative and qualitative information about assumptions used to estimate fair value.

   (a) For servicing assets and liabilities subsequently measured at fair value, disclosures must also be provided showing the beginning and ending balances, additions, disposals, changes in fair value inputs or assumptions used, and changes in fair value.
   (b) For servicing assets and liabilities that use the amortization method, disclosures must include the beginning and ending balances, additions, disposals, amortization, application of valuation allowance to adjust carrying value, and other changes that affect the balance, as well as a description of the changes. In addition, the fair value at the beginning and end of each period should be disclosed if it is practicable to estimate the value. The activity in the valuation account, including beginning and ending balances, recoveries made, and write-downs charged against the allowance for each period should also be disclosed.

f. **Securitizations.** As described above, securitization is the transformation of financial assets into securities (asset-backed securities). Various assets including mortgages, credit cards, trade receivables, loans, and leases are grouped and securitized. These groupings of relatively homogeneous assets are then pooled and divided into securities with cash flows that can be quite different from those of the original individual assets. With an established market, most of these securities cost less than the alternative use of the assets as collateral for borrowing. Thus, the benefits of most securitizations include lower financing costs, increased liquidity, and lower credit risk.

(1) The transferor (also called issuer or sponsor) forms a securitization mechanism to buy the assets and to issue the securities. Sometimes, another transfer is made to a trust and the trust issues the securities. These different structures are generally referred to as one-tier or two-tier respectively. The securitization mechanism then generates beneficial interests in the assets or resulting cash flows which are sold. The form of the securities chosen depends on such things as the nature of the assets, income tax considerations, and returns to be received.

(2) Various financial components (assets or liabilities) arise from securitizations. Examples include servicing contracts, interest-only strips, retained interests, recourse obligations, options, swaps, and forward contracts. All controlled assets and liabilities must be recognized.

EXAMPLE

Sale of loans with servicing contract and an interest-strip of 1% (transferor retains 1% of the interest paid).

(This problem is adapted from ASC 860-10-65-3)

Facts given:

Cash proceeds	$16,000
Loan's book value	15,000
Fair value of servicing asset	1,200
Fair value of interest strip	800

Net Proceeds

Cash proceeds	$16,000
Servicing asset	1,200
Interest strip	800
Net proceeds	18,000
Less: Carrying amount of loans	(15,000)
Gain on sale of loans	3,000

Journal entry

Cash	16,000	
Servicing asset	1,200	
Interest strip	800	
Loans		15,000
Gain on sale		3,000

---

(3) The transferor generally wants to take the assets off the balance sheet. This result can be accomplished if the transaction results in a sale. The key criterion in this case is to be sure that the assets are beyond control of the transferor even in bankruptcy.

g. **Secured borrowings.** In a **secured borrowing** arrangement, receivables are pledged as collateral for a loan. The customers whose accounts have been pledged are not aware of this event, and their payments are still remitted to the borrower. The pledged accounts merely serve as security to the lender, giving comfort that sufficient assets exist which will generate cash flows adequate in amount and timing to repay the debt. However the debt is paid by the borrower whether or not the pledged receivables are collected and whether or not the pattern of such collections matches the payments due on the debt.

EXAMPLE

Thirsty Corp., on July 1, 2011, enters into an agreement with Rich Company (the factor) to sell a group of its receivables **with recourse**. A total face value of $200,000 of accounts receivable are involved. The factor charges 20% interest computed on the weighted-average time to maturity of the receivables of thirty-six days plus a 3% fee. Assume the transfer does not qualify as a sale.

Since the transfer does not qualify as a sale, it is treated as a secured borrowing. The borrower's entry will be

Cash	190,055	
Interest expense (or prepaid)	3,945	
Factoring fee	6,000	
Factor borrowing payable		200,000

---

(1) The accounts receivable remain on the borrower's books. Both the accounts receivable and the factor borrowing payable should be cross-referenced in the balance sheet.

(2) In a secured borrowing, the assets of the borrowing entity continue to be shown as assets in its financial statements but must be identified as having been pledged. This identification can be accomplished either parenthetically or by footnote disclosures. Similarly, the related debt should be identified as having been secured by the receivables or other asset.

EXAMPLE

Proper disclosure for pledged receivable shown parenthetically on the balance sheet

Current assets:
    Accounts receivable, net of allowance for doubtful accounts of $600,000
        ($3,500,000 of which has been pledged as collateral for bank loans)   8,450,000
Current liabilities:
    Bank loans payable (secured by pledged accounts receivable)   2,700,000

---

h. **Accounting for collateral.** The method of accounting for a collateral agreement depends both on control of the assets and on the liabilities incurred under the agreement.

(1) Ordinarily, the transferor should carry the collateral as an asset and the transferee should not record the pledged asset.

(2) If the transferee, however, has control of the asset, the secured party should record the asset at fair value and also the liability to return it. The transferor should reclassify the asset (probably as a receivable) and report it separately in the balance sheet.

(3) If the transferor defaults and is not entitled to the return of the collateral, it should be derecognized. If not already recognized, the transferee should record collateral as an asset at fair value.

4. **Disclosures.** Additional disclosures required for receivables, off-balance-sheet credit exposure, and foreclosed and repossessed assets include the following:

  a. Accounting policies for loans and trade receivables
  b. Assets serving as collateral
  c. Nonaccrual and past due financing receivables
  d. Accounting policies for off-balance sheet credit exposures
  e. Foreclosed and repossessed assets
  f. Allowance for credit losses
  g. Impaired loans
  h. Loss contingencies
  i. Risks and uncertainties
  j. Fair value disclosures
  k. Credit quality information
  l. Modifications

NOW REVIEW MULTIPLE-CHOICE QUESTIONS 24 THROUGH 46 IN VOLUME 2

D. Current Liabilities

Current liabilities are "obligations whose liquidation is reasonably expected to require the use of existing resources properly classifiable as current assets, or the creation of other current liabilities."

1. **Examples of current liabilities** (as they fall within the above definition)

  a. Trade accounts and notes payable
  b. Loan obligations—Including current portions of long-term debt. This is not true if the current portion of long-term debt will not require the use of current assets (e.g., be paid from a sinking fund which is not classified as current).
  c. Short-term obligations expected to be refinanced cannot be reclassified as noncurrent liabilities unless there is both an intent and an ability to refinance.
  d. Dividends payable—Cash dividends are a liability when declared. They cannot be rescinded.
  e. Accrued liabilities—Adjusting entries to reflect the use of goods or services before paying for them. Will pay in future periods even though the expense is incurred in this period (e.g., interest, payroll, rent expenses).

      Expense account   xx
         Liability (usually current) account   xx

f. Payroll—There are two entries to record payroll. The first records the employee's payment and deductions on behalf of the employee. The second is to record the employer's taxes.

Payroll expense	xx (gross pay)
Payroll payable, cash	xx (net pay)
Income taxes payable	xx
FICA taxes payable	xx
Union dues payable	xx
Medical insurance payable	xx
Payroll tax expense	xx
FICA taxes payable	xx
Federal unemployment tax payable	xx
State unemployment tax payable	xx

g. Property taxes. Generally, there is a monthly accrual for property taxes over the fiscal period of the taxing authority. If taxes are payable at the end of the tax authority's fiscal period, the monthly accrual would be

Property tax expense	xx
Property tax payable	xx

(1) If the taxes were paid at the beginning of the period, the entry to record the prepayment would be followed by monthly entries to expense the prepayment.

Prepaid property taxes	xx	Property tax expense	xx
Cash	xx	Prepaid property taxes	xx

(2) If taxes are due, but not paid at the beginning of the year, the liability should be recorded and the deferred charge expensed over the fiscal year of the taxing body.

Deferred property taxes	xx	Property tax expense	xx
Property tax payable	xx	Deferred property taxes	xx

h. Bonus arrangements

Bonus expense	xx
Bonus payable	xx

(1) Set up equations to describe the terms of the bonus agreement. The general forms of the equations follow:

$$B = P(NI - B - T)$$
$$T = R(NI - B)$$
$$B = \text{Bonus}$$
$$P = \text{Bonus or profit sharing rate (10\%)}$$
$$NI = \text{Net income (\$150,000)}$$
$$T = \text{Taxes}$$
$$R = \text{Tax rate (40\%)}$$

EXAMPLE

Work through the above equations using the data in parentheses.

$$T = .40(150,000 - B)$$
$$T = 60,000 - .4B$$
$$B = .10(150,000 - B - T)$$
$$B = .10(150,000 - B - 60,000 + .4B)$$
$$B = 15,000 - .1B - 6,000 + .04B$$
$$1.06B = 9,000$$
$$B = \$8,491$$

---

i. Advances from customers—Record as deferred revenue and recognize as revenue when earned

Cash	xx	Deferred revenue	xx
Deferred revenue	xx	Revenue	xx

NOW REVIEW MULTIPLE-CHOICE QUESTIONS 47 THROUGH 76 IN VOLUME 2

2. **Contingencies**

   a. **Definitions**—An obligation may be either determinable (fixed) or contingent in accordance with the following definitions.

      (1) **Determinable liabilities**—The amount of cash and time of payment are known and reasonably precise. Such liabilities are usually evidenced by written contracts but may also arise from implied agreements or imposed legal statutes. Examples include notes payable and liabilities for various taxes as shown above.

      (2) **Contingent liabilities**—Such obligations **may** exist but are dependent on uncertain future events. A contingency is defined as an existing condition, situation, or set of circumstances involving uncertainty as to possible gain or loss to an enterprise that will ultimately be resolved when one or more future events occur or fail to occur.

   b. **Recording and disclosing contingencies**—The accounting problems related to contingencies involve the following issues.

      (1) When is it appropriate to record and report the effects of a contingency in the financial statements? Should the financial impact of the contingency be reported in the period when the contingency is still unresolved or in the period in which the contingency is resolved?

      (2) For contingencies not recorded and reported on the financial statements before they are resolved, what disclosures, if any, are needed in the footnotes to the financial statements?

   c. A loss contingency should be accrued if it is **probable** that an asset has been impaired or a liability has been incurred at the balance sheet date **and** the amount of the loss is **reasonably estimable**. When loss contingencies are accrued, a debit should be made to an expense or to a loss account and a credit should be made to either a liability or to a contra asset account.

> **NOTE:** To accrue a loss contingency means that the financial effects are reported in the financial statements **before** the contingency is resolved.

      (1) When making the decision concerning the accrual of a loss contingency, the term **probable** relates to the likelihood of a future event taking place or failing to take place which would resolve the uncertainty. However, the likelihood of a future event taking place or failing to take place may not always be judged to be probable. The likelihood of the future event taking place or failing to take place may instead be judged to be **reasonably possible** or **remote**. In these last two situations, it is **not** appropriate to accrue the loss contingency as of the balance sheet date, although footnote disclosure may be necessary. Footnote disclosure will be discussed later in this section.

      (2) In addition to being probable, the accrual of a loss contingency also requires that the amount of the loss be **reasonably estimable**. In most situations, a single amount can be estimated, and this represents the loss that is accrued. In other situations, the loss may be estimated in terms of a range, for example, the range of loss may be $100,000 to $500,000. In these situations, the amount of loss to accrue is the best estimate within the range. For example, if the best estimate within the range is $200,000, the loss should be accrued in the amount of $200,000. However, if no number in the range is a better estimate of the loss than any other number in the range, the lower number in the range is accrued as the loss. Thus, $100,000 would be accrued if no other number in the range from $100,000 to $500,000 were a better estimate of the loss than any other number in the range.

EXAMPLE

The accounting problems related to contingencies involve the following issues:

- Collectibility of receivables (Bad debts expense/Allowance for uncollectible accounts),
- Obligations related to product warranties and product defects (Warranty expense/Warranty liability), and
- Premiums offered to customers (Premium expense/Premium liability)

      (a) These contingencies are usually accrued because it is **probable** that some receivables will not be collected, that some of the products sold will be defective and may need warranty work, and that some customers will take advantage of premiums offered by the company.

      (b) In addition, the **amounts** in each case can usually be **estimated** because of past experience with each of these situations.

EXAMPLE

Product warranty loss contingency.

Facts related to the illustration for ABC Company.

Year	Sales	Actual warranty expenditures	Estimated warranty costs related to dollar sales
2011	$500,000	$15,000	Year of sale 4%
2012	$700,000	$47,000	Year after sale 6%

In 2011, ABC should accrue a loss contingency related to product warranties for $50,000 [$500,000 × (4% + 6%)]. The entry would appear as follows:

Warranty expense	50,000	
Liability for product warranty		50,000

The **actual** warranty expenditures in 2011 would be recorded in the following manner. (Note that the actual expenditures reduce the liability and have no effect on the expense account.)

Liability for product warranty	15,000	
Cash, parts inventory, etc.		15,000

ABC's income statement for 2011 would report an expense for $50,000 related to its product warranty, and its December 31, 2011 balance sheet would report a current liability for product warranty of $35,000 ($50,000 – $15,000). In 2012, ABC should accrue a loss contingency related to product warranties for $70,000 [$700,000 × (4% + 6%)]. The entry would appear as follows:

Warranty expense	70,000	
Liability for product warranty		70,000

The actual warranty expenditures for 2012 would be recorded in the following manner. (Again, note that the actual expenditures only affect the liability account.)

Liability for product warranty	47,000	
Cash, parts inventory, etc.		47,000

ABC's income statement for 2012 should report an expense related to product warranties of $70,000, and its December 31, 2012 balance sheet should report a current liability for product warranty of $58,000 (the 1/1/12 balance of $35,000 + the 2012 expense of $70,000 less the actual warranty expenditures of $47,000 in 2012).

EXAMPLE

Premium (e.g., towels, knives, and other prizes) **contingency accrual**.

Companies often have premium liability for outstanding coupons when it is probable that some of the coupons will be redeemed and the amount can be estimated. The expense should be accrued in the period of sale based on the estimated redemption rate.

Premium plan expense	xx	
Premium plan liability		xx

As coupons are actually redeemed by customers, the liability is reduced.

Premium plan liability	xx	
Premiums		xx

EXAMPLE

Environmental Liabilities [e.g., Asset Retirement Obligation (ARO)]

Companies often have environmental liabilities related to nuclear facilities, oil and gas properties, mining facilities, or landfills and these liabilities are often estimable. The cost associated with the ARO is initially measured at fair value and is included in the carrying amount of the associated asset. A related liability is also recorded.

Landfill	xx	
Asset retirement obligation		xx

The cost of the ARO is allocated over the asset's life.

Depreciation expense	xx	
Accumulated deprecation		xx

Interest is accrued (accretion expense).

Interest expense	xx	
Asset retirement obligation		xx

An entry is made to record the retirement of the settlement

Asset retirement obligation	xx	
Loss on settlement of ARO	xx	
Cash		xx

(3) Loss contingencies that may be accrued (depending upon whether or not the two conditions of probable and reasonably estimable are satisfied) include the following events.

- Threat of expropriation of assets
- Pending or threatened litigation
- Actual or possible claims and assessments
- Guarantees of indebtedness of others
- Obligations of commercial banks under "Standby letters of credit," and
- Agreements to repurchase receivables (or the related property) that have been sold

(a) **Litigation**—The one event listed above that appears frequently on the exam involves pending litigation. If the loss from litigation is reasonably estimable, and it is probable as of the balance sheet date that the lawsuit will be lost, the loss should be accrued.

EXAMPLE

Litigation

Assume that XYZ Company is presently involved in litigation involving patent infringement that allegedly occurred during 2011. The financial statements for 2011 are being prepared, and XYZ's legal counsel believes it is probable that XYZ will lose the lawsuit and that the damages will be in the range from $500,000 to $800,000 with the most likely amount being $700,000. Based upon XYZ's legal counsel, it should accrue the loss contingency in the following manner at December 31, 2011.

Loss from litigation	700,000	
Liability from litigation		700,000

The $700,000 loss from litigation should be reported on XYZ's 2011 income statement, and the liability should be reported on the December 31, 2011 balance sheet.

If XYZ settles the litigation in 2012 by paying damages of $600,000, the following journal entry should be made.

Liability from litigation	700,000	
Cash		600,000
Recovery of loss from litigation		100,000

The above entry results in a loss recovery for 2012 because the damages were settled for less than their estimated amount. This situation is not unusual because the loss contingency related to the litigation was based upon an estimate. Note that the loss recovery cannot exceed the estimated loss, which in this case was $700,000. It would be incorrect to revise the 2011 financial statements so that the loss contingency reflected the actual damages of $600,000. When the financial statements for 2011 were issued, the best estimate of loss was $700,000. This estimate is not revised subsequent to the issuance of the 2011 financial statements.

Since loss contingencies involving litigation are only accrued if the conditions of probable and reasonably estimable are present, you should be aware of what is reported if either or both of these conditions are not present. For XYZ's case, suppose that its legal counsel believed it was only **reasonably possible** (not probable) as of the balance sheet date, December 31, 2011, that XYZ would lose its lawsuit. In this situation, it would **not** be appropriate for XYZ to accrue a loss at December 31, 2011. However, because XYZ's legal counsel believes it is reasonably possible to lose the lawsuit, XYZ should disclose this litigation in its footnotes for its 2011 financial statements. The range of loss, noted before as being from $500,000 to $800,000, would also be disclosed in the footnote. In 2012, when the actual damages of $600,000 are known, XYZ would record a loss of this amount and report it on its 2012 income statement.

If XYZ's legal counsel believed that it was **remote** as of December 31, 2011, that the lawsuit would be lost, no accrual or disclosure of the litigation would be necessary.

(4) Loss contingencies that are not accrued or even disclosed in the footnotes include the following events.

- Risk of loss or damage of enterprise property by fire, explosion, or other hazards
- General or unspecified business risks
- Risk of loss from catastrophes assumed by property and casualty insurance companies including reinsurance companies

(a) Losses that result from the above events are recorded and reported in the period when the event occurs that causes the loss.

> **EXAMPLE**
>
> If XYZ's factory is destroyed by fire in 2011, the loss from this event should be recorded and reported in 2011. If the damages from the fire amount to $1,000,000, and XYZ's insurance company reimburses XYZ $800,000, XYZ's loss is $200,000. If XYZ does not insure for fire with an insurance company, XYZ's loss for 2011 would be $1,000,000.

d. **Compensated absences**—Knowledge of the conditions that must be present in order to accrue a loss contingency is helpful in the accounting for compensated absences (vacation, sick leave pay, etc.).

(1) An employer shall accrue a liability for employees' compensation for future absences if all of the following conditions are met:

(a) The employer's obligation relating to employees' rights to receive compensation for future absences is attributable to employees' **services already rendered**
(b) The obligation relates to rights that **vest or accumulate**
(c) Payment of the compensation is **probable**
(d) The amount can be reasonably **estimated**

> **NOTE:** The last two criteria are the general criteria for recognizing a loss contingency.

> **EXAMPLE**
>
> Assume MNO Company employees earn two weeks of paid vacation for each year of employment. Unused vacation time can be accumulated and carried forward to succeeding years, and will be paid at the salary level in effect when the vacation is taken. As of December 31, 2011 when John Baker's salary was $600 per week, John Baker had earned eighteen weeks vacation time and had used twelve weeks of accumulated vacation time. At December 31, 2011, MNO should report a liability for John Baker's accumulated vacation time of $3,600 (six weeks of accumulated vacation time times $600 per week). The journal entry at December 31, 2011, would appear as follows (assume previous year's entry was reversed).
>
> | | | |
> |---|---|---|
> | Salary and wages expense | 3,600 | |
> | Accrued liability for compensated absences | | 3,600 |

e. **Gain contingencies**—The discussion relating to contingencies has focused on the accounting for loss contingencies. On the other hand, contingencies exist that may also result in possible **gains**.

(1) Contingencies that might result in gains usually are not reflected in the accounts since to do so might be to recognize revenue prior to its realization. This means that any gains that result from gain contingencies should be recorded and reported in the period during which the contingency is resolved.

(a) For example, the plaintiff in a lawsuit should not record or report the expected damages to be received until the lawsuit has been decided.

E. Fair Value Option

As discussed in Module 9D, a company can elect the fair value option for reporting financial assets and financial liabilities. The fair value option also applies to firm commitments that would otherwise not be recognized at inception that only involve financial instruments. Nonfinancial insurance contracts and warranties may only be reported at fair value if the obligation can be settled by paying a third party to provide the goods and services.

NOW REVIEW MULTIPLE-CHOICE QUESTIONS 77 THROUGH 103 IN VOLUME 2

F. Ratios

1. **Solvency**—Measures short-term viability

   a. **Acid-test (quick) ratio**—Measures ability to pay current liabilities from cash and near-cash items

   $$\frac{\text{Cash, Net receivables, Marketable securities}}{\text{Current liabilities}}$$

   b. **Current ratio**—Measures ability to pay current liabilities from cash, near-cash, and cash flow items

   $$\frac{\text{Current assets}}{\text{Current liabilities}}$$

2. **Operational efficiency**—Measures utilization of assets

   a. **Receivable turnover**—Measures how rapidly cash is collected from credit sales

   $$\frac{\text{Net credit sales}}{\text{Average net receivables}}$$

   b. **Number of days' sales in average receivables**—Average length of time receivables are outstanding, which reflects credit and collection policies

   $$\frac{365}{\text{Receivable turnover}}$$

   c. **Inventory turnover**—Indicates how rapidly inventory is sold

   $$\frac{\text{Cost of goods sold}}{\text{Average inventory}}$$

   d. **Number of days' supply in average inventory**—Measures the number of days inventory is held before sale and therefore reflects the efficiency of the entity's inventory policies

   $$\frac{365}{\text{Inventory turnover}}$$

   e. **Length of operating cycle**—Measures length of time from purchase of inventory to collection of cash

   $$\begin{matrix} \text{Number of days'} \\ \text{supply in average} \\ \text{inventory} \end{matrix} + \begin{matrix} \text{Number of days'} \\ \text{sales in average} \\ \text{receivables} \end{matrix}$$

> **NOW REVIEW MULTIPLE-CHOICE QUESTIONS 104 THROUGH 111 IN VOLUME 2**

G. Research Component—Accounting Standards Codification

1. Basic concepts regarding balance sheet classification of current assets and current liabilities are found in ASC Section 210-10-45, which is contained under the heading "Presentation" in the Codification. Specific rules for monetary current assets and current liabilities are located throughout the Codification as shown in the following table.

Topic number	Topic	Accounting issues
305	Cash and cash equivalents	Classification and disclosures
310	Receivables	A/R, bad debts
405	Liabilities	Cross referencing to specific issues
440	Commitments	Unconditional purchase obligations
450	Contingencies	Contingent liabilities
470	Debt	Liability issues
720	Compensation—general	Compensated absences
820	Fair value measurements	Measuring FV
825	Financial instruments	FV option
835	Interest	Interest rates, imputed interest, interest calculations and disclosures
860	Transfers and servicing	Factoring, pledging, assigning A/R

2. Keywords for research are listed below.

Agreement to refinance	Estimated or accrued amounts	Refinance obligation
Appropriated retained earnings	Examples loss contingencies	Remote
Beneficial interests	Extinguished debt	Retained interests
Benefits of servicing	Extinguished liability	Rights that vest
Classification current liabilities	Fair value retained interests	Sale of financial assets
Collateral	Financial assets	Sale of receivables
Collateral pledged	Financial assets exchange	Securitization
Compensation future absences	Financial liability	Securitized financial assets
Contingency	Loss contingency	Servicing fees
Control transferred assets	Operating cycle	SPE
Current assets	Ordinary operations	Transferor surrendered control
Current liabilities	Primary obligor	Transfers financial assets
Debtor security interest	Probable	Undivided interests
Deduction from receivables	Probable future events	Unilateral ability
Derecognize assets	Proceeds	With recourse
Derecognize liability	Reasonably possible	Without recourse
Estimated loss	Recourse	Working capital

H. International Financial Reporting Standards (IFRS)

1. Normally, assets are reported as current and noncurrent, and liabilities are reported as current and noncurrent on the balance sheet. If a liquidity presentation provides more relevant and reliable information, then balance sheet items may be reported based on their liquidity without segregation.

   a. In a balance sheet segregated between current and noncurrent items, an asset is classified as current (1) when the entity expects to realize the asset or to consume or sell it within 12 months or the normal operating cycle, or (2) it holds the asset primarily for the purpose of trading. A liability is classified as current when it expects to settle the liability within the normal operating cycle, the liability will be settled within 12 months after the reporting period, or it holds the liability for the purpose of trading.

2. IFRS defines the terms financial assets and financial liabilities.

   a. A financial asset is any asset that is cash, an equity instrument of another entity, a contractual right to receive cash or another financial asset, a contractual right to exchange a financial instrument, or a contract that will be settled in the reporting entity's own equity instruments.

   (1) IFRS 9 requires that financial assets be measured at amortized cost or fair value based on the entity's business model for managing the financial asset and the contractual cash flow characteristics of the financial asset.

   (a) A financial asset should be measured at amortized cost if the business model's objective is to hold the asset in order to collect contractual cash flows, and the terms of the contract indicate specific dates for the payment of principal and interest on the principle amount outstanding.
   (b) An entity may also elect at initial recognition to value a financial asset at fair value through profit or loss (FVTPL).

   b. A financial liability is any liability that is a contractual obligation to deliver cash or another financial asset, a contractual obligation to exchange financial instruments under potentially unfavorable conditions, or a contract that may be settled in the entity's own equity instruments.

   (1) Financial liabilities are measured at either amortized cost using the effective interest method, or an election may be made to value the financial liability at fair value through profit or loss (FVTPL).

3. There are two important areas where IFRS differ from US GAAP.

   a. The first relates to short-term obligations expected to be refinanced. Under US GAAP, short-term obligations expected to be refinanced may be reported in the noncurrent liability section of the balance sheet if the company has the intent and ability to refinance. However, IFRS requires obligations expected to be refinanced to be reported as current liabilities unless there is an agreement to refinance in place prior to the balance sheet date.

b. The second area in which the terminology and rules are different is "provisions" and "contingencies." Under IFRS, a "provision" is a liability that is uncertain in timing or amount. Provisions are made for items such as taxes payable, compensated absences, bad debts, warranties, and other estimated liabilities. A "contingency," however, depends upon some future uncertainty or event.

(1) A contingent asset is a possible asset that arises from past events that will be confirmed only by occurrence or nonoccurrence of uncertain future events that are not within the control of the reporting entity. As with US GAAP, a contingent asset is not recognized, but it is disclosed if the economic benefits are probable.

(2) Under IFRS, a contingent liability does not have the same definition as in the US standards. Recall that under US GAAP, the accounting for a contingency depends on whether the outcome is probable, reasonably possible, or remote, and whether the contingency is measureable. In contrast, under IFRS if the outcome is probable and measureable, it is not considered a contingency. Instead, it is classified as a "provision."

(3) Under IFRS, the term contingency is used to describe an event which is not recognized because it is not probable that an outflow will be required or the amount cannot be measured reliably.

(4) If an item qualifies as a contingency, the notes to the financial statements should include an estimate of the financial effect, and indication of the uncertainties, and the possibility of reimbursement. If the possibility of the event occurring is remote, no disclosure is required in the notes to the financial statements.

(5) It should be noted that the "probable" threshold test for determining whether a provision should be made is "more likely than not" which is defined as a probability over 50%.

NOW REVIEW MULTIPLE-CHOICE QUESTIONS 112 THROUGH 116 IN VOLUME 2

KEY TERMS

Acid-test (quick) ratio. Measures ability to pay current liabilities from cash and near-cash items.

Allowance method. Seeks to estimate the amount of uncollectible receivables, and establishes a contra valuation account (allowance for bad debts) for the amount estimated to be uncollectible.

Amortization method. Requires servicing assets and servicing liabilities to be initially recorded at fair value. Assets are then amortized in proportion to, and over the period of, receipt of estimated net servicing income or net servicing loss.

Banker's acceptance. An order from a customer of a bank for the payment of specified sum of money (like a post-dated check) that may be bought and sold.

Cash. Includes both cash (cash on hand and demand deposits) and cash equivalents (short-term, highly liquid investments).

Cash equivalents. Readily convertible into cash and so near maturity that they carry little risk of changing in value due to interest rate changes.

Contingent liabilities. Obligations may exist but are dependent on uncertain future events.

Current liabilities. Obligations whose liquidation is reasonably expected to require the use of existing resources properly classifiable as current assets, or the creation of other current liabilities.

Current ratio. Measures ability to pay current liabilities form cash, near-cash, and cash flow items.

Determinable liabilities. The amount of cash and time of payment are known and reasonably precise.

Direct write-off method. Bad debts are considered expenses in the period in which they are written off.

Factoring. Selling receivables at a discount to obtain immediate cash. Traditionally involves the outright sale of receivables to a financing institution know as a factor.

Fair value method. Servicing assets and servicing liabilities are initially recorded at fair value. The fair value is measured at each reporting date.

Inventory turnover. Indicated how rapidly inventory is sold.

Length of operating cycle. Measures length of time from purchase of inventory to collection of cash.

Loan participations. A situation where a group of financial institutions (called participating interest holders) purchases a share of a financial instruments (e.g., a loan).

Net realizable value. Gross amount of receivables less estimated uncollectibles.

Number of days' sales in average receivables. Average length of time receivables are outstanding, which reflects credit and collection policies.

Number of days' supply in average inventory. Measures the number of days inventory is held before sale and therefore reflects the efficiency of the entity's inventory policies.

Operation efficiency. Measures utilization of assets.

Probable. The likelihood of a future event taking place or failing to take place which would resolve the uncertainty.

Receivable turnover. Measures how rapidly cash is collected from credit sales.

Repurchase agreements. An agreement to sell an asset to a lender and later repurchase the asset. These agreements are in effect using the asset as collateral for a loan.

Secured borrowing. Receivables are pledged as collateral for a loan.

Securitizations. Purchasing and selling securities that are collateralized by a pool of assets, such as a group of receivables.

Servicing. A distinct asset or liability only when separated contractually from the underlying.

Solvency. Measures short-term viability.

Transfers of receivables with recourse. Selling receivables at a discount to obtain immediate cash but retaining the risk of loss if the customer does not pay the amount owned.

Transfer of receivables without recourse. The factor assumes the risk of loss from noncollection.

Module 13: Present Value

Overview

This module begins by reviewing the basic concepts related to time value of money such as present and future value. The module then covers four major topics in which time value of money applications are used extensively:

1. **Bonds** payable and bond investments including initial accounting, sales, conversions, warrants, and extinguishments.
2. **Debt** restructure including settlement, modification of terms, and impairment.
3. **Pensions** including defined contribution plans, defined benefit plans, and other post employment benefits.
4. **Leases** including operating leases and capital leases for both lessees and lessor.

All of these topics are tested on the Financial Accounting and Reporting section of the exam to varying degrees.

A. Fundamentals

The concepts of time value of money are essential for successful completion of the CPA exam. Time value of money concepts are central to capital budgeting, leases, pensions, bonds, and other topics. You must understand the mechanics as well as the concepts. After studying the next few pages, work the multiple-choice questions entitled "Fundamentals." Note that the following abbreviations are used in the text that follows.

$$i = \text{interest rate}$$

$$n = \text{number of periods or rents}$$

On the CPA exam, you do not have to know the complex formulas that are used to compute time value of money factors (TVMF). The factors will be given to you or enough information will be given to you so that you can easily compute them (see section A.8. TVMF Applications). Your main focus of attention should be centered on understanding which TVMF should be used in a given situation.

1. **Future Value (FV) of an Amount** (future value of $1)

   a. The future value of an amount is the amount that will be available at some point in the future if an amount is deposited today and earns compound interest for "n" periods.

      (1) The most common application is savings deposits.

> **EXAMPLE**
>
> If you deposited $100 today at 10%, you would have $110 [$100 + ($100 × 10%)] at the end of the first year, $121[$100 + ($110 × 10%)] at the end of the second year, etc. The compounding feature allows you to earn interest on interest. In the second year of the example you earn $11 interest: $10 on the original $100 and $1 on the first year's interest of $10.

2. **Present Value (PV) of a Future Amount** (present value of $1)

   a. The present value of a future amount is the amount you would pay now for an amount to be received "n" periods in the future given an interest rate of "i."

      (1) A common application would be the money you would lend today for a noninterest-bearing note receivable in the future.

> **EXAMPLE**
>
> If you were lending money at 10%, you would lend $100 for a $110 note due in one year or for a $121 note due in two years.

b. The present value of $1 is the inverse of the future value of $1. Thus, given a future value of $1 table, you have a present value of $1 by dividing each value into 1.00.

> **EXAMPLE**
>
> Look at the present value of $1 and future value of $1 tables on the next page. The future value of $1 at 10% in five years is 1.611. Thus, the present value of $1 in five years would be $1.00 \div 1.611$ which is .621 (check the table). Conversely, the future value of $1 is found by dividing the present value of $1 into 1.00, that is, $1.00 \div .621 = 1.611$.

3. **Compounding**

   a. When interest is compounded more than once a year, two extra steps are needed.

      (1) First, **multiply** "n" by the number of times interest is compounded annually. This will give you the total number of interest periods.
      (2) Second, **divide** "i" by the number of times interest is compounded annually. This will give you the appropriate interest rate for each interest period.

> **EXAMPLE**
>
> If the 10% was compounded semiannually, the amount of $100 at the end of one year would be $110.25 $[(1.05)^2]$ instead of $110.00. The extra $.25 is 5% of the $5.00 interest earned in the first half of the year.

4. **Future Value of an Ordinary Annuity**

   a. The **future value of an ordinary annuity** is the amount available "n" periods in the future as a result of the deposit of an amount (A) at the end of every period "1" through "n."
   b. Compound interest is earned at the rate of "i" on the deposits.

      (1) A common application is a bond sinking fund. A deposit is made at the end of the first period and earns compound interest for n-1 periods (not during the first period, because the deposit is made at the end of the first period). The next to the last payment earns one period's interest, that is, $n - (n-1) = 1$. The last payment earns no interest, because it is deposited at the end of the last (nth) period.

> **NOTE:** In the FUTURE AMOUNT OF AN ORDINARY ANNUITY TABLE, all of the factors for any "n" row are based on one less interest period than the number of payments.

TIME VALUE OF MONEY FACTOR (TVMF) TABLES

Future Value (Amount) of $1

n	6%	8%	10%	12%	15%
1	1.060	1.080	1.100	1.120	1.150
2	1.124	1.166	1.210	1.254	1.323
3	1.191	1.260	1.331	1.405	1.521
4	1.262	1.360	1.464	1.574	1.749
5	1.338	1.469	1.611	1.762	2.011

Present Value of $1

n	6%	8%	10%	12%	15%
1	.943	.926	.909	.893	.870
2	.890	.857	.826	.797	.756
3	.840	.794	.751	.712	.658
4	.792	.735	.683	.636	.572
5	.747	.681	.621	.567	.497

Future Value (Amount) of an Ordinary Annuity of $1

n	6%	8%	10%	12%	15%
1	1.000	1.000	1.000	1.000	1.000
2	2.060	2.080	2.100	2.120	2.150
3	3.184	3.246	3.310	3.374	3.473
4	4.375	4.506	4.506	4.641	4.993
5	5.637	5.867	6.105	6.353	6.742

Present Value of an Ordinary Annuity of $1

n	6%	8%	10%	12%	15%
1	.943	.926	.909	.893	.870
2	1.833	1.783	1.736	1.690	1.626
3	2.673	2.577	2.487	2.402	2.283
4	3.465	3.312	3.170	3.037	2.855
5	4.212	3.993	3.791	3.605	3.352

5. **Present Value of an Ordinary Annuity**

   a. The present value of an ordinary annuity is the value today, given a discount rate, of a series of future payments.

      (1) A common application is the capitalization of lease payments by either lessors or lessees. Payments "1" through "n" are assumed to be made at the end of years "1" through "n," and are discounted back to the present.

EXAMPLE

Assume a five-year lease of equipment requiring payments of $1,000 at the end of each of the five years, which is to be capitalized. If the discount rate is 10%, the present value is $3,791 ($1,000 × 3.791).

The behavior of the present value of the lease payment stream over the five-year period is shown below. Note that the liability (principal amount) grows by interest in the amount of 10% during each period and decreases by $1,000 at the end of each period.

```
            1                2               3               4               5
$3,791 + 380 Int. =  $4,171
                   -  1,000  Payment
                     $3,171 + 320 Int. = $3,491
                                       - 1,000  Payment
                                         $2,491 +  250 Int. = $2,741
                                                            -  1,000  Payment
                                                              $1,741 + 170 Int. =  $1,911
                                                                                 - 1,000  Payment
                                                                                 $  911 + 91 Int. =  $1,002  Payment
                                                                                                      1,000
                                                                                                         2*
```

* Due to rounding

---

6. **Distinguishing a Future Value of an Annuity from a Present Value of an Annuity**

   a. Sometimes confusion arises in distinguishing between the future value (amount) of an annuity and the present value of an annuity. These two may be distinguished by determining whether the total dollar amount in the problem comes at the beginning (e.g., cost of equipment acquired for leasing) or at the end (e.g., the amount needed to retire bonds) of the series of payments as illustrated as follows.

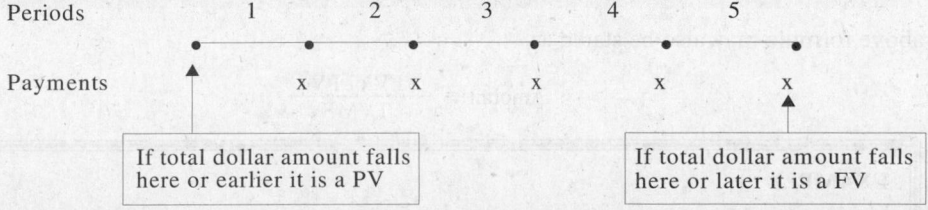

NOTE: If the total amount comes at the end of the series of payments, it is a **future value** of annuity situation. If the total amount comes at the beginning of the series of payments, it is a **present value** of annuity situation. The total dollar amount may be given in the problem or you may have to compute it; either way, it makes no difference in determining whether a problem involves a present value or future value situation.

> **NOTE:** Some students feel the need to "convert" all time value of money problems into either present value or future value problems, depending on which they're most comfortable with. This process involves more work and more chance for errors, because an additional TVMF equation must be solved in the conversion. This is inefficient, and unnecessary if you are able to correctly identify between the two initially. Become proficient at determining present value and future value situations, so that you may efficiently select the correct TVMF from the corresponding table. Drawing a timeline for the facts in each problem will help you determine if you need to solve for a present value or a future value.

7. **Annuities Due**

   a. In some cases, the payments or annuities may not conform to the assumptions inherent in the annuity tables. For example, the payments might be made at the beginning of each of the five years instead of at the end of each year. This is an annuity due (annuity in advance) in contrast to an ordinary annuity (annuity in arrears). Both annuity due and ordinary annuity payments are represented by the "x's" in the illustration below.

Periods	1	2	3	4	5
Annuity	x	x	x	x	x
Annuity Due	x	x	x	x	x

> **EXAMPLE**
>
> If the payments in the 5-period lease example presented previously were made at the beginning of the period, the present value of the first payment which is made today is $1,000 (i.e., the TVMF is 1.00). The remaining 4 payments comprise an ordinary annuity for 4 periods as you can see on the above diagram. Always use time diagrams to analyze application of annuities.

   b. To convert either a future value of an ordinary annuity or the present value of an ordinary annuity factor to an annuity due factor, multiply the ordinary annuity factor times $(1 + i)$.

> **EXAMPLE**
>
> For the above lease example, you would find the present value of an ordinary annuity factor for n = 5 which is 3.993. Then multiply 3.993 by 1.08 to arrive at the annuity due factor, 4.312. The present value of the payments would be $4,312 (4.312 × $1,000).

> **NOTE:** The present value of the annuity due in the above example is $319 greater than the present value of the ordinary annuity because the payments are moved closer to the present.

8. **TVMF Applications**

   a. The basic formula to use is

$$\text{FV or PV} = \text{TVMF} \times \text{Amount}$$

   b. If an annuity is involved, the amount is the periodic payment or deposit; if not, it is a single sum.

> **NOTE:** FV or PV is determined by three variables: time, interest rate, and payment. TVMF represents two variables: time and interest rate. The tables usually have the interest rate on the horizontal axis and time on the vertical axis.

   c. The above formula may also be stated as

$$\text{Amount} = \frac{\text{FV or PV}}{\text{TVMF}}$$

> **EXAMPLE**
>
> If we need to accumulate $12,210 in five years to repay a loan, we could determine the required annual deposit with the above formula. If the savings rate were 10%, we would divide the FV ($12,210) by the TVMF of the future value of annuity, n=5, i=.10 (6.105) and get $2,000. Thus, $2,000 deposited at the end of each of five years earning 10% will result in $12,210. This formula may also be used to find future values of an amount, present values of amounts, and annuities in the same manner.

Another variation of the formula is

$$TVMF = \frac{FV \text{ or } PV}{\text{Amount}}$$

EXAMPLE

We may be offered a choice between paying $3,312 in cash or $1,000 a year at the end of each of the next four years. We determine the interest rate by dividing the annual payment into the present value of the annuity to obtain the TVMF (3.312) for n=4. We then find the interest rate which has the same or similar TVMF (in this case 8%). Alternatively, using the above formula, we may know the interest rate but not know the number of payments. Given the TVMF, we can determine "n" by looking in the TVMF table under the known interest rate. Remember the TVMF reflects two variables: time and interest rate.

> **NOW REVIEW MULTIPLE-CHOICE QUESTIONS 1 THROUGH 5 IN VOLUME 2**

9. **Notes Receivable and Payable**

   a. This section assumes that the entity does not elect the fair value option for accounting for receivables or payables (see section A.12 "Fair Value Option"). Short-term notes receivable and notes payable that arise from transactions with customers and suppliers in the normal course of business and are due in one year are classified as current liabilities. These short-term notes are recorded at their maturity value.

   b. Notes receivable and notes payable due in more than one year (long-term notes) should be recorded at their present values. Upon receipt or issuance of a long-term note, record the net value of the note receivable or payable (i.e., note plus or minus premium or discount) at

      (1) Cash received or paid

         (a) Assumes no other rights or privileges

      (2) Established exchange price (fair market value) or property or services received or provided

         (a) If not determinable, determine present value with imputed interest rate

   c. Record interest revenue (on notes receivable) or interest expense (on notes payable) as the effective rate of interest times the net receivable or payable during the period.

   d. **Note exchanged for cash only**

      (1) When a note is exchanged for cash and no other rights or privileges are exchanged, the present value of the note is equivalent to the cash exchanged.

         (a) The cash exchanged, however, may not be equal to the face amount of the note (the amount paid at maturity).

      (2) When the face amount of a note does not equal its present value, the difference is either a discount or a premium.

         (a) A discount results when the face of the note exceeds its present value, and a premium results when the present value of the note exceeds its face (see section B.1. in this module for a more detailed discussion of discounts and premiums).

   e. **Note exchanged for cash and unstated rights and privileges**

      (1) In the preceding discussion, notes were issued solely for cash, and no other rights or privileges were exchanged. The accounting treatment differs, however, when a note is issued for cash and unstated rights and/or privileges are also exchanged. The cash exchanged for such a note consists of two elements:

         (a) The present value of the note, and
         (b) The present value of the unstated right or privilege.

      (2) Proper accounting for this situation requires that one of the two present values above be determined. Once this is done, the remaining present value is simply the difference between the face amount of the note and the present value that was determined.

EXAMPLE

On January 1, 2010, Zilch Company borrowed $200,000 from its major customer, Martha Corporation. The borrowing is evidenced by a note payable due in three years. The note is noninterest-bearing. In consideration for the borrowing, Zilch Company agrees to supply Martha Corporation's inventory needs for the loan period at favorable prices. This last feature of the transaction is the unstated right or privilege; that is, the ability of Martha to purchase inventory at less than regular prices.

The present value of the note (assuming it is easier to determine) should be based upon the interest rate Zilch would have to pay in a normal borrowing of $200,000 (i.e., in a transaction that did not include unstated rights or privileges). Assume that Zilch would have to pay interest at 12% in a normal borrowing. The present value of $200,000 discounted for three years at 12% is $142,400 ($200,000 × .712). The difference between the face amount of the note, $200,000, and its present value of $142,400 represents the present value of the unstated right or privilege. The amount of this present value is $57,600.

The entries below show how both Zilch and Martha should account for this transaction during 2010.

Zilch			Martha		
1/1/10			**1/1/10**		
Cash	142,400		Note receivable	200,000	
Discount on note payable	57,600		Discount on note receivable		57,600
Note payable		200,000	Cash		142,400
Cash	57,600		Advance payments on inventory	57,600	
Deferred revenue		57,600	Cash		57,600
12/31/10			**12/31/10**		
Interest expense	17,088*		Discount on note receivable	17,088	
Discount on note payable		17,088	Interest income		17,088
* $142,400 × .12 = $17,088					
Deferred revenue	xx		Inventory (purchases)	xx	
Sales		xx	Advance payments on inventory		xx

The amounts represented by "xx" in the entries above depend upon the amount of goods acquired by Martha during 2010.

On the December 31, 2010 balance sheets of both Zilch and Martha, the above notes should be disclosed in the noncurrent liability (Zilch) and asset (Martha) sections net of the unamortized discount applicable to each note.

f. **Note exchanged in a noncash transaction**

(1) In addition to notes issued for cash, a note may also be received or issued in a noncash transaction; that is, for goods, property, or services. The problem created in this situation is how to determine the note's present value in the absence of cash.

(a) One way to solve this problem is to assume that the stated rate or contractual rate stated on the note represents a fair rate of return to the supplier for the use of the related funds. If the interest rate is presumed to be fair, then the face amount of the note is presumed to equal its present value. Interest revenue (expense) is computed by multiplying the interest rate stated on the face of the note by the face of the note. There is no discount or premium to consider because the face of the note is assumed to be equal to its present value.

(b) The assumption that the interest rate on the face of the note is fair is not always valid. The assumption is not valid if

1] The interest rate is not stated (usually, this means the note is noninterest-bearing), or

2] The stated rate is unreasonable (this refers to both unreasonably low and high rates), or

3] The stated face amount of the note is materially different from the current cash sales price for the same or similar items, or from the market value of the note at the date of the transaction.

(c) When the interest rate is not fair, the face amount of the note does not equal its present value. In the absence of cash, the present value of a note is determined according to the following priorities:

1] First, determine if the goods, property, or services exchanged have a reliable fair market value. If they do, the fair market value is presumed to be the present value of the note.

2] If a reliable fair market value does not exist for the goods, property, or services exchanged, then determine if the note has a market value. If it does, the note's market value is equal to the present value of the note.

3] Finally, if market values do not exist for either the goods, property, or services or for the note, then an interest rate must be **imputed**. This imputed interest rate is then used to determine the present value of the note. The imputed interest rate represents the **debtor's** incremental borrowing rate.

EXAMPLE

The situation where the interest rate on a note is not fair, yet the fair market value of the property exchanged is known.

Doink Co. sold a building on January 1, 2011, which originally cost $7,000,000 and which had a book value of $4,000,000 for a $14,000,000 (face amount) noninterest-bearing note due in three years. Since zero interest is not considered to be a fair rate of return, the face amount of Doink's note does not equal its present value. In Doink's case, the face of its note is $14,000,000. The present value of the note is the unknown and must be calculated.

To determine the present value of Doink's $14,000,000 noninterest-bearing note, you should first see if the building sold had a reliable fair market value at the date it was sold. Assume that Doink's building could have been sold on January 1, 2011, for $10,000,000 in a straight cash transaction. Given the information about the building, its fair market value of $10,000,000 on January 1, 2011 represents the note's present value. Since the face of the note is $14,000,000 and its present value is $10,000,000, the $4,000,000 difference represents the discount. Doink should record this transaction in the following manner:

Note receivable	14,000,000	
Accumulated depreciation	3,000,000	
Building		7,000,000
Gain on sale of building		6,000,000
Discount on note receivable		4,000,000

NOTE: It is important that you note how the gain is calculated in the entry above. The gain is the difference between the present value of the note ($10,000,000) and the book value of the property sold ($4,000,000). The difference between the face amount of the note ($14,000,000) and its present value ($10,000,000) represents the discount of $4,000,000. This discount should be amortized to interest income using the effective interest method. However, before this discount can be amortized, the interest rate must be determined. In situations like this, the interest rate can be determined by reference to present value tables. In Doink's situation, the present value of the note, $10,000,000, divided by its face amount, $14,000,000, results in the number .714. This number represents a factor from the present value of $1 table. Since Doink's note is for 3 periods, the factor .712 in the present value of $1 table is under the 12% interest rate. Thus, Doink's interest rate is approximately 12%.

If the building sold by Doink did not have a reliable fair market value on January 1, 2011, the next step would be to determine if the note had a market value on that date.

Finally, if the building sold by Doink did not possess a reliable fair market value on January 1, 2011, and the note did not have a market value on that date, the present value of Doink's note would have to be determined by **imputation**. This means that Doink would determine the present value of its note by reference to the incremental borrowing rate of the company which acquired its building.

(2) The following diagram represents the forementioned relationships and procedures for determining the present value of a note receivable or payable (monetary assets and liabilities) and the amount of a discount/premium.

ACCOUNTING FOR MONETARY ASSETS AND LIABILITIES WHICH HAVE
MATURITIES GREATER THAN ONE YEAR FROM THE BALANCE SHEET DATE

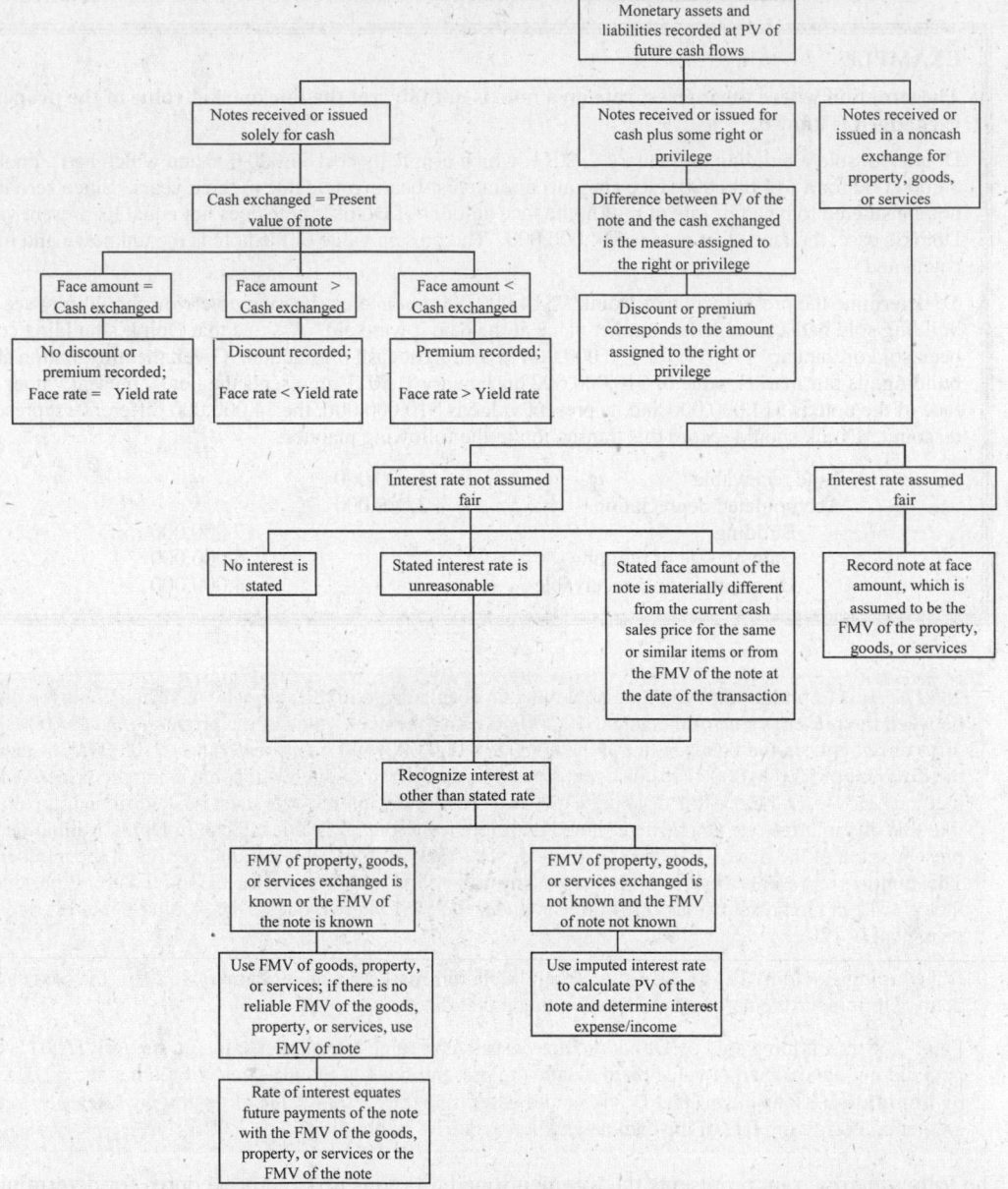

NOW REVIEW MULTIPLE-CHOICE QUESTIONS 6 THROUGH 18 IN VOLUME 2

10. **Loan Origination Costs and Fees**

   a. Sometimes the lender incurs various loan origination costs when originating or acquiring a loan. The lender shall defer and recognize these costs over the life of the loan only when the costs relate directly to the loan, and would not have been incurred but for the loan. Otherwise, the costs are considered indirect and are charged to expense as incurred.

   b. Sometimes the lender charges the borrower a nonrefundable loan origination fee. Both lender and borrower shall defer and recognize the nonrefundable fee over the life of the loan. The fee is frequently assessed in the form of points, where a point is 1% of the face amount of the loan.

EXAMPLE

Assume that Bannon Bank grants a ten-year loan to VerSteiner, Inc. in the amount of $100,000 with a stated interest rate of 8%. Payments are due monthly, and are computed to be $1,213. In addition, Bannon Bank incurs $3,000 of direct loan origination costs (attorney's fees, title insurance, wages of employees' direct work on loan origination), and also charges VerSteiner a 5-point nonrefundable loan origination fee.

Bannon Bank, the lender, has a carrying amount of $98,000. This reflects the $100,000 face amount of the loan less the $5,000 nonrefundable fee, plus the $3,000 additional investment Bannon Bank incurs to generate the $145,560 total payments from the borrower, VerSteiner. The effective interest rate is approximately 8.5%.

VerSteiner, the borrower, receives 5% less than the face amount of $100,000, or $95,000, but is still required to pay $1,213 per month under the terms of the loan. VerSteiner's carrying amount is then $100,000 – $5,000 = $95,000, with an effective interest rate of approximately 9.2%.

NOTE: Both the rates can be derived with a financial calculator. It is not likely that you would be asked to compute these on the CPA exam because the computerized exam provides a simple four-function calculator, and the formula to calculate interest is not included in the spreadsheet formulas. What you are expected to know is the concept of effective interest. You also need to know that the loan origination costs are to be added to the principal, by the lender, and any fee charged to the client is deducted from the principal by both parties in calculating the carrying amount.

11. **Disclosures**

    a. The basic loan situation involves a borrower receiving the face amount of a loan from a lender, with no related discount or premium. The liability is the face amount, and the effective interest rate is the stated interest rate on the interest-bearing note.

        (1) When a note is issued for an amount other than the face of the loan or when a noninterest-bearing note is used, and the fair value option is not elected, a premium or discount must be recorded for the note. The discount amount is additional interest over the life of the note; the premium amount is a reduction in interest expense over the life of the loan. The amount in the discount or premium account is amortized to interest expense over the life of the note using the effective interest rate.

    b. Notes are reported on the financial statement at their net carrying value.

        (1) Discount on notes payable is a liability valuation account (contra account). It should be reported as a direct reduction from the face amount of the note on the balance sheet.
        (2) A premium on the note is reported as an addition to the face amount of the note (adjunct account) on the balance sheet.

    c. In the footnotes to the financial statements, a disclosure must be made for the aggregate amounts of maturities and the sinking fund requirements for all long-term borrowings for each of the five years following the balance sheet date.

12. **Fair Value Option**

    a. A company may elect the fair value option for reporting financial assets and financial liabilities. The financial liability is reported at fair value at the end of each reporting period, and the resulting gain or loss is reported in earnings of the period. A company may calculate interest expense in various ways, but must disclose in the notes to the financial statements the method used to determine interest expense.

> **NOW REVIEW MULTIPLE-CHOICE QUESTIONS 19 THROUGH 25 IN VOLUME 2**

13. **Research Component—Accounting Standards Codification**

    a. The authoritative literature on payables and receivables is found in several locations in the Codification: Topics 310, 825, and 835. ASC Topic 835 addresses the valuation of the note, determining appropriate interest rates, amortization of discounts and premiums, and financial statement presentation of the discount and premium account.

    b. A list of keywords that may be helpful in your research is shown below.

Determining present value	Indirect costs loan	Note issued
Direct costs loan	Loan origination fees	Note received
Disclosure long-term borrowings	Maturities long-term	Points fees
Effective interest note	Noncash transaction note	Present value note
Exchange price note	Nonrefundable fees loan	

14. **International Financial Reporting Standards (IFRS)**

   a. IAS 23 requires borrowing costs to be capitalized if they meet certain criteria. Borrowing costs must be capitalized if they are related to the acquisition, construction, or production of a qualifying asset.

   (1) A qualifying asset is one that takes a substantial period of time to get ready for its intended use. Qualifying assets include inventory, plant, property, and equipment, intangible assets, or investment property.

   (2) Borrowing costs that do not meet the rules for capitalization are expensed in the current period. Note that finance costs (interest expense) must be disclosed separately in the income statement.

KEY TERMS

Future value. The amount that will be available at some point in the future if an amount is deposited today and earns compound interest for "n" periods.

Future value of an ordinary annuity. The amount available "n" periods in the future as a result of the deposit of an amount (A) at the end of every period "l" through "n."

Present value. The amount you would pay now for an amount to be received "n" periods in the future given an interest rate of "i."

Present value of an ordinary annuity. The value today, given a discount rate, of a series of future payments.

B. Bonds

1. **Bonds Payable and Bond Investments**

   a. Investment in bonds and bonds payable are discussed together to contrast their treatment.[1] Bonds generally provide for periodic fixed interest payments at a contract rate of interest. At issuance, or thereafter, the market rate of interest for the particular type of bond may be above, the same, or below the contract rate.

      (1) If the market rate exceeds the contract rate, the book value will be less than the maturity value. The difference (discount) will make up for the contract rate being below the market rate.
      (2) Conversely, when the contract rate exceeds the market rate, the bond will sell for more than maturity value to bring the effective rate to the market rate. This difference (premium) will make up for the contract rate being above the market rate.
      (3) When the contract rate equals the market rate, the bond will sell for the maturity value.

   b. The market value of a bond is equal to the maturity value and interest payments discounted to the present.

   > **NOTE:** You may have to refer to the discussion of time value of money concepts in the previous section before working with the subsequent material. Finally, when solving bond problems, candidates must be careful when determining the number of months to use in the calculation of interest and discount/premium amortization. For example, candidates frequently look at a bond issue with an interest date of September 1 and count three months to December 31. This error is easy to make because candidates focus only on the fact that September is the ninth month instead of also noting whether the date is at the beginning or end of the month. Candidates should also be aware that bond issues that mature on a single date are called term bonds, and bond issues that mature in installments are called serial bonds.

2. **Accounting for Bonds**

   a. A company may elect the fair value option for reporting financial assets and financial liabilities. If the fair value option is elected for a bond, the measurement of the financial liability should include adjustments for nonperformance risk, credit risk, or instrument-specific credit risk.

      (1) The election to value a financial liability at fair value should be made on the date the entity initially recognizes the item.
      (2) Although the fair value option may be made on an instrument-by-instrument basis, it must be applied to the entire instrument.

   b. If the fair value option is elected for a financial liability, the bond is not reported with a discount or premium. In addition, if the fair value option is elected for a bond, the effective interest method is not required for measuring interest expense.

      (1) Interest expense may be calculated using various methods, but the company must disclose in the notes to the financial statements the manner in which interest expense was measured.
      (2) Any gain or loss in revaluing the bond to fair value should be included on the income statement for the current period.
      (3) Two methods are allowed for disclosing financial liabilities on the balance sheet.

         (a) The first method is to disclose the total fair value and non–fair value amounts in the aggregate, with a parenthetical disclosure of the amounts measured at fair value.
         (b) The second method of disclosure is to present two separate line items to display the fair value and non–fair value carrying amounts separately.

      (4) In addition, the standards require footnote disclosure of the difference between the aggregate fair value and the aggregate unpaid principal balance.
      (5) If the fair value of a liability is significantly affected by instrument-specific credit risk, disclosures must also indicate the estimated amount of gains and losses from fair value changes that are attributable to changes in the credit risk.

   c. If an entity does not elect the fair value option, the bond is recorded at its issue price, and the effective interest method is used to amortize any premium or discount on the bond. The remainder of this module will focus on the pricing of the bond using the effective interest method of amortizing a bond.

---

[1] Coverage in this module focuses on a bond's book or carrying value. Issues concerning FV, holding gains and losses, and financial statement presentation of bond investments are covered with other marketable debt securities in Module 16, Investments.

> **EXAMPLE**
>
> **Bond Valuation Example**
>
> $10,000 in bonds, interest at 6% contract rate, paid semiannually, maturing in six years, and market rate of 5%.
>
> - Find present value of maturity value. Use present value of $1 factor. Discount $10,000 back 12 periods at 2 1/2% interest (Factor = .7436). (Semiannual compounding is going to be required to discount the semiannual payments so it is also assumed here.)
>
> $$\$10,000 \quad \times \quad .7436 \quad = \quad \$7,436$$
>
> - Find the present value of the annuity of twelve $300 interest payments. Use present value of an ordinary annuity of $1 factor for twelve periods at 2 1/2% interest (Factor = 10.26).
>
> $$\$300 \quad \times \quad 10.26 \quad = \quad \$3,078$$
>
> - Today's value is $10,514 (7,436 + 3,078)
>
> The $514 premium is to be recognized over the life of the bond issue. It is a reduction of interest expense on the books of the issuer and a reduction of interest revenue on the books of the investor. Amortization is to be on the present value basis.

d. The following summarizes when bonds are issued/acquired at a premium or discount:

ISSUE/ACQUISITION PRICE OF BONDS—PRESENT VALUE OF INTEREST ANNUITY PLUS THE PRESENT VALUE OF THE MATURITY AMOUNT USING THE YIELD OR MARKET RATE

Face amount	Premium	Discount
Yield rate = Face rate	Yield rate < Face rate	Yield rate > Face rate

3. **Journal Entries**

> **EXAMPLE**
>
> **Bond Journal Entries**
> The issuer's books will be illustrated at gross (including a premium or discount account) and the investor's books will be illustrated at net (no discount or premium account).
>
> The investor may record the bonds either net or gross, but the issuer records at gross.
> In the past, CPA examination problems and solutions have followed the net method on the books of the investor.
>
> | | | | Issuer | | | Investor | |
> |---|---|---|---|---|---|---|---|
> | a. | Issue and | Cash | 10,514 | | Bond invest. | 10,514 | |
> | | Acquisition | Bonds pay. | | 10,000 | Cash | | 10,514 |
> | | | Bonds prem. | | 514 | | | |
> | b. | First int. | Interest exp. | 300 | | Cash | 300 | |
> | | payment | Cash | | 300 | Interest rev. | | 300 |
> | c. | Premium— | Bond prem. | 37.15* | | Interest rev. | 37.15 | |
> | | Amortization | Interest exp. | | 37.15 | Bond invest. | | 37.15* |
>
> * Interest receipt (payment) minus effective interest = 300 – 262.85 = 37.15
>
> Effective interest = net book value times effective rate = 10,514 × .025 = 262.85

a. Entry a. assumes that the bonds are issued on the interest payment date. If bonds are purchased between interest payment dates, the purchaser will also include accrued interest through the purchase date in the total cash paid for the bonds.

b. The payment of this accrued interest on the purchase date will serve to reduce the subsequent receipt of interest income (which covers a time period longer than the time the purchaser held the bond). Subsequent interest payments are recorded the same as entry b. shown above. The amount of subsequent amortization (entry c. above) changes. Interest to be recorded under the interest method is always computed by

$$\text{Effective interest rate} \times \text{Net book value}$$

c. This formula is true of all applications of the interest method. The effective rate of interest times net book value is the actual interest revenue or expense for the period. The difference between the actual interest and the amount received or paid is the amortization. The amortization table below shows the effective interest amounts and premium amortizations for the first 4 periods.

EXAMPLE

Effective Interest Table and Journal Entries

Period	3% cash interest	2 1/2% effective interest	Decrease in book value	Book value of bonds
0				$10,514.00
1	$300[a]	$262.85[b]	$37.15[c]	10,476.85[d]
2	300	261.92	38.08	10,438.77
3	300	260.97	39.03	10,399.74
4	300	259.99	40.01	10,359.73

(a) 3% × $10,000   (c) $300 – $262.85

(b) 2 1/2% × $10,514.00   (d) $10,514.00 – $37.15

Since the interest is paid semiannually, interest (including premium amortization) is recorded every six months. The journal entries for periods 2, 3, and 4 are

	Issuer				Investor		
Period 2	Interest expense	261.92		Cash	300.00		
	Bond premium	38.08			Interest rev.		261.92
	Cash		300.00		Bond invest.		38.08
Period 3	Interest expense	260.97		Cash	300.00		
	Bond premium	39.03			Interest rev		260.97
	Cash		300.00		Bond invest.		39.03
Period 4	Interest expense	259.99		Cash	300.00		
	Bond premium	40.01			Interest rev.		259.99
	Cash		300.00		Bond invest		40.01

NOTE: The interest (revenue and expense) decreases over time. This is because the net book value (which is also the present value) is decreasing from the maturity value plus premium to the maturity value. Thus, the effective rate is being multiplied by a smaller amount each six months.

NOTE: The change in interest each period is the prior period's premium amortization times the effective rate.

EXAMPLE

Change in Interest

The interest in period 3 is $.95 less than in period 2, and $38.08 of premium was amortized in period 2. The effective rate of 2½% (every six months) times $38.08 is $.95. Thus, if the interest changes due to the changing level of net book value, the change in interest will be equal to the change in the net book value times the effective rate of interest.

---

d. Another complication may arise if the year-end does not coincide with the interest dates. In such a case, an adjusting entry must be made. The proportional share of interest payable or receivable should be recognized along with the amortization of discount or premium. The amortization of discount or premium should be straight-line within the amortization period.

EXAMPLE

Assume that in the above example, both issuer and investor have reporting periods ending three months after the issuance of the bonds.

	Issuer			Investor		
Entries on the	Interest expense	150		Interest receivable	150	
closing date	Interest payable		150	Interest revenue		150
	Bond premium	18.57		Interest revenue	18.57	
	Interest expense		18.57	Bond investment		18.57

Reverse at beginning of new period and make regular entry at next interest payment date.

e. If bonds are sold (bought) between interest dates, premium/discount amortization must be computed for the period between sale (purchase) date and last (next) interest date. This is accomplished by straight-lining the six-month amount which was calculated using the effective interest method.

EXAMPLE

Sale of bonds between interest dates

The investor sold $5,000 of bonds in the above example, two months after issuance, for $5,250 plus interest.

1. The bond premium which must be amortized to the point of sale ($5,000 for two months) is $1/2 \times 1/3 \times$ $37.15 or $6.19.

Interest revenue	6.19	
Investment		6.19

2. The sale is recorded. The investment account was $5,257 before amortization of $6.19. The cash received would be $5,250 plus $50 interest ($1/2 \times 1/3 \times \$300$). The loss is a forced figure.

Cash	5,300.00	
Loss	.81	
Interest revenue		50.00
Investment		5,250.81 [($10,514.00/2) − $6.19]

3. Check the interest revenue recorded ($50.00 − $6.19) to the interest earned: $5,257 \times 2\ 1/2\% \times 1/3$ (which equals $43.81).

---

f. Bonds issue costs are treated as deferred charges and amortized on a straight-line basis over the life of the bond.

4. Comparison of Effective Interest and Straight-Line Amortization Methods

Method of Amortization	Interest Revenue/Expense	Interest Rate**
Effective interest method	Changes each period*	Constant each period
Straight-line method	Constant each period	Changes each period

* Carrying amount of the bond investment or bonds payable at the beginning of the interest period multiplied times the yield rate
** Interest revenue/expense for a period divided by the carrying amount of the bond investment or bond liability at the beginning of the interest period

a. The following table summarizes the various behavior patterns related to the use of the effective interest method:

	Amortization of	
Description	Discount	Premium
Interest revenue/expense	↑Increases each period	↓Decreases each period
Amount of amortization	↑Increases each period	↑Increases each period
Carrying amount of bonds payable/investment in bonds	↑Increases each period	↓Decreases each period

---

NOW REVIEW MULTIPLE-CHOICE QUESTIONS 1 THROUGH 30 IN VOLUME 2

---

5. Convertible Bonds

a. Bonds are frequently issued with the right to convert the bonds into common stock. When issued, no value is apportioned to the conversion feature. Two approaches are possible to account for bond conversions:

(1) Valuing the transaction at cost (book value of the bonds)

  (a) Conversion under the cost method would result in debits to bonds payable and bond premium (or a credit to bond discount) equal to the book value of the bonds, and credits to common stock and paid-in excess of par equal to the book value.

  (b) In practice, conversations are usually recorded at book value.

NOTE: Under the cost conversion method no gain (loss) is recorded, as no gain (loss) should result from an equity transaction.

(2) Valuing at market (of the stocks or bonds), whichever is more reliable.

  (a) At market, assuming market value exceeds book value, the entries would be

Issuer		Investor	
Loss on redemption	(plug)	Stock invest	(mkt)
Bonds payable	(book value)	Invest in bonds	(carrying value)
Bond premium	(book value)	Gain on conversion	(plug)
Common stock	(par)		
Paid-in excess of par	(mkt-par)		

(b) On the issuer's books, the debit (credit) to the loss (gain) account (ordinary) would be for the difference between the market value of the stock (bonds) and the book value of the bonds.

(c) The conversion is treated as the culmination of an earnings process; thus the loss (gain) should be recognized.

(d) The bonds and the related accounts must be written off, and paid-in excess of par is credited for the excess of the market value of the stock (bonds) over the stock's par value.

(e) On the investor's books, the gain (loss) would also be the difference between the market value the stock (bonds) and the book value of the bonds.

NOTE: In both cases that the accrued interest and discount or premium amortization must be recorded prior to the conversion

b. To induce conversion, firms sometimes change the original conversion privilege or give additional considerations to the bondholders.

(1) The fair value of these "sweeteners" should be recognized as an expense (ordinary in nature) upon conversion, determined as the excess of the FV of all securities and consideration transferred over the FV of the securities issuable per the original conversion terms.

NOW REVIEW MULTIPLE-CHOICE QUESTIONS 31 THROUGH 34 IN VOLUME 2

6. **Debt Issued with Detachable Purchase Warrants**

a. The proceeds of debt issued with detachable stock purchase warrants are allocated between the debt and stock warrants based on relative market values.

EXAMPLE

Units of one bond and one warrant (to buy 10 shares of stock at $50/share) are issued for $1,030. Thereafter, warrants trade at $40 and the bonds at $960. The relative market value of the warrants is 4% (40/1,000) and the relative market value of the bonds is 96% (960/1,000). Thus, $41.20 (.04 × $1,030) of the issue price is assigned to the warrants.

Cash	1,030.00	
Bond discount	11.20	
Bonds payable		1,000.00
Paid-in capital—stock warrants		41.20

If one warrant was subsequently exercised

Cash	500.00	
Paid-in capital—stock warrants	41.20	
Common stock		(par of 10 shs)
Paid-in excess		(plug)

Alternatively, the example above could have indicated the market value of the stock (e.g., $54) rather than the market values of the bonds and warrants. In such a case, one would value the warrants based on the difference between option price and market price, for example, [$54 (market) − $50 (option)] × 10 shares = $40 value for the warrants.

NOTE: The effect of requiring allocation of the cash received to the stock warrants. The final effect is to increase interest costs on the bond issue by reducing the premium or increasing the discount.

> **NOTE:** The allocation to equity shown above is only applicable where the purchase warrants are **detachable**. In contrast, no allocation is made to equity if the bonds are issued with **nondetachable** stock purchase warrants. Detachable warrants are often traded separately from the debt and therefore have a readily determinable market value of their own. The inseparability of nondetachable warrants prevents the determination of a separate market value; therefore, no allocation to equity is permitted.

7. **Extinguishment of Debt**

   a. Debt is considered extinguished whenever the debtor pays the creditor and is relieved of all obligations relating to the debt.

      (1) Typical examples of this are the calling of a bond by the debtor, requiring the bondholder to sell the bond to the issuing corporation at a certain date and stated price, and the open market repurchase of a debt issue.
      (2) Refunding of debt (replacement of debt with other debt) is also considered an extinguishment.
      (3) However, troubled debt restructures (situations where creditors agree to grant relief to debtors) and debt conversions initiated by the debt holders are not.
      (4) Additionally, when the debtor is legally released from being the primary obligor of the debt either judicially or by the creditor, and it is probable the debtor will make no further payments on it, the debt is considered extinguished.

   b. All gains (losses) resulting from the extinguishment of debt should be recognized in the period of extinguishment.

      (1) The gain (loss) is the difference between the bond's reacquisition price and its net book value (face value plus [minus] any unamortized premium [discount] and issue costs).

         (a) The rule is not affected by the reissuance of debt before or after the refunding.
         (b) Furthermore, this rule applies to convertible bonds when reacquired with cash. The gain or loss is considered an ordinary gain or loss, and is a separate item in net income before extraordinary items.

   c. Because most companies use debt refinancing as a normal risk management tool, early extinguishment of debt is no longer considered an extraordinary item. If, however, the company can meet the criteria for extraordinary (infrequent in occurrence and unusual in nature), the early extinguishment of debt may be considered for extraordinary treatment.

Loss or gain	xx	xx
Bonds payable	xx	
Bond premium	xx	
Unamortized issue costs		xx
Bond discount		xx
Cash		xx

NOW REVIEW MULTIPLE-CHOICE QUESTIONS 35 THROUGH 39 IN VOLUME 2

8. **Research Component—Accounting Standards Codification**

   The Codification lists Liabilities as Topic 405. This topic lists the various issues related to liabilities and provides for cross-references for topics related to debt. Topic 470, entitled *Debt*, contains subtopics that outline the rules for debt with conversion and other options, product financing, modifications and extinguishments, and troubled debt restructuring by debtors. ASC Topic 835 outlines the rules relating to interest on debt.

NOW REVIEW MULTIPLE-CHOICE QUESTIONS 40 THROUGH 42 IN VOLUME 2

9. **International Financial Reporting Standards (IFRS)**

   a. Similar to US accounting standards, IAS 39 provides that financial liabilities are initially measured at fair value, and subsequently measured at amortized cost using the effective interest method.

      (1) An option can be made to value financial liabilities at fair value.

   b. Financial instruments with characteristics of both debt and equity are referred to as "compound instruments."

      (1) Accounting for compounds instruments is another area where IFRS differs from US GAAP. Convertible bonds, bonds with detachable warrants, and other compound instruments must be separated into their components of debt and equity.

(a) The liability component is initially recorded at fair value, and the residual value is assigned to the equity component.
(b) Each component is presented in the appropriate section of the balance sheet. IFRS refers to the fair value option as "Fair Value through Profit or Loss" (FVTPL).
(c) If the fair value option is elected for a financial liability, then the liability is revalued at the end of the reporting period and the resulting gain or loss is recognized in profit or loss for the period.

NOW REVIEW MULTIPLE-CHOICE QUESTIONS 43 THROUGH 45 IN VOLUME 2

KEY TERMS

Discount. The difference between the net proceeds, after expense, received upon issuance of debt and the amount repayable at its maturity.

Premium. The excess of the net proceeds, after expense, received upon issuance of debt over the amount repayable at its maturity.

Serial bands. Bond issues that mature in installments.

Term bonds. Bond issues that mature on a single date.

Warrant. A security that gives the holder the right to purchase shares of common stock in accordance with the terms of the instrument, usually upon payment of a specified amount.

C. Debt Restructure

1. Creditors may grant relief to debtors. Two types of restructure are described. The first is a settlement of the debt at less than the carrying amount and the second is a continuation of the debt with a modification of terms.

   a. ASC 310 addresses the accounting by creditors for impairment of certain loans. Impaired loans include all loans that are restructured in a troubled debt restructuring involving a modification of terms. Two requirements must be met for a creditor to classify a restructuring as a trouble debt restructuring

      (1) The restructuring constitutes a concession
      (2) The debtor is experiencing financial difficulties

   b. An election can also be made to value certain financial assets or financial liabilities at fair value. Included in the list of eligible items is modification of debt. If the fair value option is elected, the debt is revalued at fair value and any resulting gain or loss is recognized in earnings for the period. If the fair value option is not elected, then the rules of ASC Topic 470 (SFAS 15) apply for the debtor, and the rules of ASC Topic 310 (SFAS 114) apply to the creditor. The remainder of this chapter will focus on the rules when the fair value option is **not** elected and when the restructuring qualifies as a troubled debt restructuring.

2. **Settlement of Debt**

   a. **Debtors.** If the debt is settled by the exchange of assets, a gain is recognized for the difference between the carrying amount of the debt and the consideration given to extinguish the debt. Such gains are no longer extraordinary.

      (1) If a noncash asset is given, a separate gain or loss is recorded to revalue the noncash asset to fair value (FV) as the basis of the noncash asset given. Thus, a two-step process is used: (1) revalue the noncash asset to FV and (2) determine the restructuring gain. If stock is issued to settle the liability, record the stock at FV.

   b. **Creditors**

      (1) Assets received in full settlement are recorded at FV

         (a) The excess of receivable over asset FV is an ordinary loss
         (b) Subsequently account for the assets as if purchased for cash

---

EXAMPLE

Settlement of Debt. Debtor company transfers land in full settlement of its loan payable.

Loan payable (5 years remaining)		$90,000
Accrued interest payable on loan		10,000
Land:		
Book value		70,000
Fair value		80,000

Debtor				**Creditor**		
1. Land	10,000		1.	Land	80,000	
Gain on transfer of				Loss on settlement	20,000	
assets		10,000		Loan receivable		90,000
2. Loan payable	90,000			Interest receivable		10,000*
Interest payable	10,000					
Land		80,000				
Gain on settlement						
of debt		20,000				

* If the creditor was a bank or other finance company, this amount would be included as part of Loan receivable.

---

3. **Modification of Terms**

   a. **Debtors.** If the debt is continued with a modification of terms, it is necessary to compare the total future cash flows of the restructured debt (both principal and stated interest) with the prerestructured carrying value.

      (1) If the total amount of future cash flows is greater than the carrying value, no adjustment is made to the carrying value of the debt; however, a new effective interest rate must be computed.

         (a) This rate makes the present value of the total future cash flows equal to the present carrying value of debt (principal and accrued interest).

(2) If the total future cash flows of the restructured debt are less than the present carrying value, the current debt should be reduced to the amount of the future cash flows and a gain should be recognized.

    (a) No interest expense would be recognized in subsequent periods because the loan was written down below its carrying value.

    (b) All payments including those designated as interest would be applied to the principal amount.

(3) If the restructuring consists of part settlement and part modification of payments, first account for the part settlement per the above, and then account for the modification of payments per the above.

b. **Creditors**

(1) Under ASC 310 (SFAS 114), a creditor measures impairment based on the present value of expected future cash flows discounted at the loan's effective interest rate.

    (a) The effective interest rate for a loan restructured in a troubled debt restructuring is based on the original contractual rate, not the rate specified in the restructuring agreement.

    (b) As a practical expedient, a creditor may measure impairment based on a loan's observable market price, or the fair value of the collateral if the loan is collateral dependent.

        1] A loan is collateral dependent if the repayment of the loan is expected to be provided solely by the underlying collateral.

(2) If the measure of the impaired loan is less than the recorded investment in the loan (including accrued interest, net deferred loan fees or costs, and unamortized premium or discount), a creditor shall recognize an impairment by creating a valuation allowance with a corresponding charge to bad debt expense or by adjusting an existing valuation allowance for the impaired loan with a corresponding charge or credit to bad debt expense.

(3) The present value of an impaired loan's expected future cash flows will change from one reporting period to the next because of the passage of time and also may change because of revised estimates in the amount or timing of those cash flows. No guidance is provided on how the creditor should recognize the change in the present value.

(4) The following example of the treatment of modification of terms for creditors demonstrates the accounting for the **debtor** under ASC Topic 470 (SFAS 15) and for the **creditor** under ASC Topic 310 (SFAS 114).

EXAMPLE

Modification of Terms—Gain/Loss Recognized—Using the previous example with a loan payable of $90,000 and accrued interest payable on the loan of $10,000, assume the interest rate on above loan is 5% and the following modification of terms is made:

1. Interest rate is reduced to 4%.
2. The accrued interest is forgiven.
3. The principal at date of restructure is reduced to $80,000.

        Debtor

Future cash flows (after restructuring):	
Principal	$80,000
Interest (5 years × $80,000 × 4%; $3,200 per year)	+16,000
Total cash to be repaid	$96,000
Amount prior to restructure ($90,000 principal + $10,000 accrued interest)	– 100,000
Gain to be recognized	$ 4,000

Analysis of Debtor's Loan Payable Account

		90,000	Loan payable before modification of terms
Gain	4,000	10,000	Additional amount payable from accrued interest
4% modified interest payments in years 1-5	3,200* 3,200 3,200 3,200 3,200	96,000	Balance after restructure

* Note that the $3,200 is recorded as a reduction of principal, not as an interest expense.

Creditor

    Present value of future cash flows (after restructuring) discounted at
        the original effective interest rate of 5% for the 5 years remaining:

Principal ($80,000 × .78353)**	$ 62,682
Interest ($80,000 × 4% × 4.32948)***	13,854
Present value of future cash flows	$ 76,536
Recorded investment in loan by creditor	$100,000
Present value of future cash flows after restructuring	76,536
Impairment loan loss to be recognized by creditor	$ 23,464

  **   PV of 1 for 5 periods at 5%.
*** PV of ordinary annuity for 5 periods at 5%.

Debtor (ASC Topic 470 [SFAS 15])			**Creditor (ASC Topic 310 [SFAS 114])**		
Beginning of Year 1			**Beginning of Year 1**		
Interest payable	10,000		Bad debt expense	23,464	
Loan payable	4,000		Loan receivable		10,000
Loan payable		10,000	Accrued interest receivable		10,000
Gain on restructure of debt		4,000	Valuation allowance for impaired		
			loans		3,464

(The accrued interest is added to the loan payable to arrive at the prerestructure carrying value. The gain reduces the loan payable to the total future cash flows of the restructured debt.)	(This entry reduces the principal to $80,000 forgives the accrued interest, and recognizes a loss on impairment.)

Debtor			**Creditor**		
End of Year 1			**End of Year 1**		
Loan payable	3,200		Cash	3,200	
Cash		3,200	Valuation allowance for impaired loans	627	
			Interest revenue/bad debts expense		3,827*

        * [($80,000 – $3,464) × 5% = $3,827

End of Year 2			**End of Year 2**		
Loan payable	3,200		Cash	3,200	
Cash		3,200	Valuation allowance for impaired loans	658	
			Interest revenue/bad debts expense		3,858*

        * [$80,000 – ($3,464 – $627)] × 5% = $3,858

End of Year 3			**End of Year 3**		
Loan payable	3,200		Cash	3,200	
Cash		3,200	Valuation allowance for impaired loans	691	
			Interest revenue/bad debts expense		3,891*

        * [$80,000 – ($3,464 – $627 – $658)] × 5% = $3,891

End of Year 4			**End of Year 4**		
Loan payable	3,200		Cash	3,200	
Cash		3,200	Valuation allowance for impaired loans	726	
			Interest revenue/bad debts expense		3,926*

        * [$80,000 – ($3,464 – $627 – $658 – $691)] × 5% = $3,926

End of Year 5			**End of Year 5**		
Loan payable	3,200		Cash	3,200	
Cash		3,200	Valuation allowance for impaired loans	762	
			Interest revenue/bad debts expense		3,962*

        * [$80,000 – ($3,464 – $627 – $658 – $691 – $726)] × 5% = $3,962

Loan payable	80,000		Cash	80,000	
Cash		80,000	Loan receivable		80,000

NOTE: This example does not include any future changes in the amount and timing of future cash flows, due to the complexity of the accounting.

EXAMPLE

Modification of Terms—No Gain Recognized by Debtor

Assume the $90,000 principal is reduced to $85,000. The interest rate of 5% is reduced to 4%.

Future cash flows (after restructuring):	
Principal	$ 85,000
Interest (5 years × $85,000 × 4%)	17,000
Total cash to be repaid	$102,000
Amount prior to restructure:	
($90,000 principal + $10,000 accrued interest)	– 100,000
Interest expense/revenue to be recognized over 5 years	$ 2,000

NOTE: A new effective interest rate must be computed so that the PV of future payments = $100,000. A trial and error approach would be used. For the exam, you need to be prepared to describe this process and the related entries, but you will not have to make such a computation.

End of Year 1-5

	Debtor	
Loan payable	xxxx	
Interest expense	xxx	
Cash		3,400

End of Year 5

Loan payable	85,000	
Cash		85,000

NOTE: x's equal different amounts each year based on effective interest rate computed.

By Creditor—The creditor would account for the modification in the same way as in the previous example that shows the ASC Topic 310 (SFAS 114) approach. That is, the original effective rate would be used to measure the loss.

c. To summarize the two basic situations

(1) **Settlement of debt:** The debtor transfers assets or grants an equity interest to the creditor in full satisfaction of the claim. Both debtor and creditor account for the fair values of assets transferred and equity interest granted. A gain or loss is recognized on the asset transferred. The debtor recognizes a gain and the creditor recognizes a loss for the difference between the recorded value of the debt and the fair values accounted for.

(2) **Restructuring of the debt:** Under ASC Topic 470 (SFAS 15), the terms of the debt are modified in order to reduce or defer cash payments that the debtor is obligated to make to the creditor, but the debt itself is continued. The debtor accounts for the modification of terms as a reduction in interest expense from the date of restructuring until maturity. Gains and losses will generally not be recognized unless the total future cash payments specified by the new terms are less than the recorded amount of the debt. Then the debtor would recognize a gain for the difference. Under ASC Topic 310 (SFAS 114), the creditor accounts for a restructuring using the original effective rate to measure losses.

d. Refer to the outlines of ASC Topic 470 (SFAS 15) and ASC Topic 310 (SFAS 114) for the disclosure requirements.

3. **Impairment**

a. **Debtors.** The debtor still has a legal obligation to repay the debt, so no entry is made for impairment on the debtor's accounting records.

b. **Creditors.** If the creditor determines that, based on current information and events, it is probable that they will be unable to collect all amounts due on an outstanding note receivable, then the note is considered to be impaired. The criteria for determining uncollectibility of a note should be based on the creditor's normal review procedures.

(1) When a note receivable is considered to be impaired, a loss should be recorded at the time the impairment is discovered. The loss will be based upon the difference between the current carrying value of the note and

the present value of the expected future cash flows from the impaired note, discounted at the loan's contractual rate.

EXAMPLE

On January 1, 2011, Spot Corporation issued a $100,000, three-year noninterest-bearing note to yield 10%, to Grover Corporation. The amortization schedule using the effective interest method for the note is calculated as follows:

Date	10% interest	Carrying value	
1/1/11	--	$ 75,132	(present value of 100,000 at 10% for 3 periods, 100,000 × .75132)
12/31/11	7,513	82,645	(75,132 + 7,513)
12/31/12	8,265	90,910	(82,645 + 8,265)
12/31/13	9,090	100,000	(90,910 + 9,090)

On December 31, 2011, Spot Co. management determines that it is probable that Grover Co. will be unable to repay the entire note. It appears as though only $75,000 will be repaid. Using the effective interest method, the impairment is calculated as follows:

Carrying value at 12/31/11	$82,645
Present value of future receipts	
($75,000, 10%, 2 periods = $75,000 × .82645)	61,984
Impairment at 12/31/11	$20,661

The loss due to the impairment of the Grover Co. note will be recorded on Spot Corporation's (the creditor's) books as follows:

Bad debt expense	20,661	
Allowance for doubtful accounts		20,661

The debtor, Grover Co., should not record anything, as it still has a legal obligation to repay the entire $100,000. The future interest revenue recorded by Spot Co. will be based upon the new carrying value of $61,984. If there is a significant change in the expected future cash flows, then the impairment should be recalculated and the allowance adjusted accordingly.

---

4. **Research Component—Accounting Standards Codification**

    a. The Accounting Standards Codification addresses debt restructure in ASC Subtopics 470-50, 470-60, and 310-40.
    b. When researching impaired loans, it is important that you first distinguish whether you are taking the perspective of the debtor or the creditor. Using the word debtor or creditor in your search string may help to find the appropriate sites more quickly.
    c. ASC Topic 825 applies only if the entity elects the fair value option for accounting for a debt modification.
    d. Keywords for researching in this area are shown below.

Carrying amount payable	Impairment loan	Restructuring
Fair value collateral	Measure impaired loan	Restructuring payables
Future cash flows impairment	Modification terms	Troubled debt restructurings
Impaired loan	Original contract rate	

5. **International Financial Reporting Standards (IFRS)**

    IFRS 9 provides that a modification of debt, or an exchange of an original liability with a new financial liability with substantially different terms, are accounted for as an extinguishment of the original liability and the recognition of a new financial liability.

> **NOW REVIEW MULTIPLE-CHOICE QUESTIONS 1 THROUGH 8 IN VOLUME 2**

KEY TERMS

Debt. A receivable or payable (collectively referred to as debt) represents a contractual right to receive money or a contractual obligation to pay money on demand or on fixed or determinable dates that is already included as an asset or liability in the creditor's or debtor's balance sheet at the time of the restructuring.

Effective interest rate. The rate of return implicit in the loan, that is, the contractual interest rate adjusted for any net deferred loan fees or costs, premium, or discount existing at the origination or acquisition of the loan.

Fair value. The price that would be received to sell an asset or paid to transfer a liability in an orderly transaction between market participants at the measurement date.

Probable. The future event or events are likely to occur.

Recorded investment. The amount of the investment in a loan, which is not net of a valuation allowance, but which does reflect any direct write-down of the investment.

Troubled debt restructuring. A restructuring of a debt constitutes a troubled debt restructuring if the creditor for economic or legal reasons related to the debtor's financial difficulties grants a concession to the debtor that it would not otherwise consider.

D. Pensions

Accounting for pensions involves the use of special terminology. Mastery of this terminology is essential both to an understanding of problem requirements and to the ability to respond correctly to theory questions.

a. In this section the key points covered are as follows:

    (1) The differences between a defined contribution pension plan and a defined benefit pension plan and the resulting accounting and reporting differences between these two types of plans.

    (2) The bookkeeping entries made to record an employer's pension expense and the funding of pension cost.

    (3) The benefits-years-of-service approach.

    (4) The calculation and reporting of the net pension asset/liability for employers who sponsor defined benefit pension plans.

    (5) The five elements which, if they all exist, an employer sponsoring a defined benefit pension plan must evaluate for inclusion in its pension expense each year. These factors are

        (a) Service cost

        (b) Interest cost

        (c) Actual return on plan assets

        (d) Amortization of unrecognized prior service cost

        (e) Gain or loss.

    (6) The required disclosures in the financial statements of employers who sponsor pension plans.

1. **Employer Sponsor's vs. Plan's Accounting and Reporting**

    a. In order to understand the accounting and reporting requirements for pension plans, you must keep in mind that there are two accounting entities involved: the employer sponsor of the plan, and the pension plan which is usually under the control of a pension trustee.

        (1) The employer sponsor reports Pension Cost (Pension Expense) in its income statement. In its balance sheet it usually reports a net Pension Asset/Liability representing the difference between the Projected Benefit Obligation and the Plan Assets; both of the latter accounts, are under the control of the pension trustee. As discussed later, another entry may be required to accumulated other comprehensive income to report the funding status of the plan.

    b. A separate accounting entity, the pension plan, maintains the following accounts: Projected Benefit Obligation, Accumulated Benefit Obligation (for reporting purposes only), Vested Benefits (for reporting purposes only), and Plan Assets. The pension plan pays benefits to the retired employees.

    c. The diagram below shows the relationship of the entities involved in a pension plan, the accounts usually used by each, and the flow of cash.

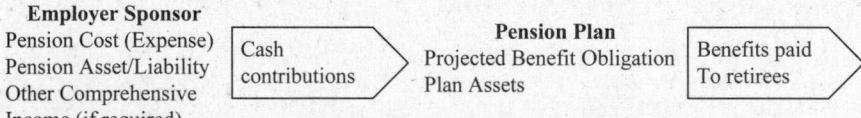

        (1) The employer sponsor must maintain, accounts for Unrecognized Prior Service Cost and Unrecognized Gains and Losses within Other Comprehensive Income (OCI).

> **NOTE:** The projected benefit obligations of the pension plan, the interest on these obligations, the pension plan assets available to meet these obligations, and returns (income) on these plan assets are all economic variables which impact the employer sponsor's yearly calculations of pension expense and its year-end pension asset/liability. (Key concepts are **boldfaced** to call attention to those terms and phrases that must be clearly understood.)

        (2) Plan information must be made available to the participants and beneficiaries. Furthermore, after filing under ERISA (the Employee Retirement Income Security Act of 1974), the DOL (Department of Labor) must make the annual report available to the public. Certain funding information must be filed with the PBGC (Pension Benefit Guarantee Corporation).

2. **An Overview of Employer's Accounting for Pension Plans**

    a. Under a **defined contribution plan** the employer agrees to make a defined contribution to a pension plan as determined by the provisions of the plan. Consequently, plan participants will receive at retirement whatever benefits (i.e., payments) the contributions can provide.

(1) Accounting for a defined contribution plan is relatively straightforward. Each year the employer records an expense and a related liability for the agreed-upon contribution.

(2) Payments are charged against the liability with an offsetting reduction in cash.

(3) Additional disclosure requirements include a description of the plan including employee groups covered, the basis for determining contributions, and the nature and effects of events affecting comparability.

b. Under a **defined benefit plan** the employer agrees to provide a benefit at retirement that is defined or fixed by a formula. Because the benefits are defined, the employer accepts the risk associated with changes in the variables that determine the amounts needed to meet the obligation to plan participants. These amounts require the use of estimates that may become very complex. However, these estimates are made by actuaries hired by the management of the employer sponsor. They are not made by the sponsoring company's accountants. The remainder of our pension coverage is devoted to a discussion of the issues that arise under this type of plan.

(1) The **accrual accounting objective** for pension costs recognizes the compensation cost of an employee's pension benefits including prior service costs over that employee's service period. Under accrual accounting, pension expense should not be determined on the basis of the employer's cash payout (funding) practices.

(2) The **funding of the pension obligation** refers to the amount that the employer contributes to an independent trustee for the pension plan (plans where the fund is under the control of the employer are considered unfunded). Many factors including tax considerations, working capital management, and contractual agreements influence funding decisions.

(a) Thus, the amount selected for funding should not govern the determination of the amount to be reported as pension expense under accrual accounting; these events should be distinguished. Although both events can be recorded with one entry, we use two entries in this section to better illustrate this distinction.

Pension expense	xxxx	
Pension asset/liability		xxxx

1] This adjusting entry is to record the accrued expense. The use of the Pension asset/liability account simplifies the accounting. If the account has a net debit balance, it is an asset. If the account has a net credit balance, it is a liability.

Pension asset/liability	xxxx	
Cash		xxxx

2] This entry is to record the funding of the pension obligation at the time cash is transferred to the plan's trustee.

(b) The determination of the amounts to be used in the above entries requires the professional expertise of actuaries who assess the benefits to be provided under the pension formula and the characteristics of the employees covered under the plan (e.g., average age). With these factors as given, the actuaries must estimate the values of the variables that will influence the actual amounts to be paid at retirement by making actuarial assumptions about factors such as longevity, early retirements, turnover rate, and the rates of return to be earned on invested funds.

(3) The actuarial present value of the obligation determined under the benefits-years-of-service method is referred to as the **projected benefit obligation**. The **accumulated benefit obligation** is the amount computed using the current salary amounts instead of the estimated future salary amounts. Therefore, if the defined benefit formula is not dependent on the amount of a future salary (say a retiree receives a fixed amount for each month worked), there would be no difference between the two approaches. If the defined benefit formula is pay-related and salaries are assumed to increase over time, the projected benefit obligation will be a greater amount than the accumulated benefit obligation.

(4) The Codification requires reporting the funded status of a pension plan. Overfunded and underfunded plans must be reported on the balance sheet as either assets or liabilities.

3. **Funded Status of Pension Plan**

a. The funded status of the plan must be reported in the balance sheet. The funded status is the difference between the projected benefit obligation and the fair value of the plan assets at the measurement date.

(1) If the plan is overfunded, a noncurrent asset is recorded on the balance sheet.

(2) If the plan is underfunded, either a current liability, a noncurrent liability, or both are reported on the balance sheet.

(3) Any additional asset or liability not already recognized as pension expense is recognized in other comprehensive income (net of tax).

(4) If a plan is amended and either increases or decreases the projected benefit obligation, this amount should be recognized as either a prior service cost or credit. Prior service costs or credits should be amortized over the future periods of service of the employees expected to receive benefits.

b. For an employer with multiple plans, all overfunded plans are aggregated and disclosed as a noncurrent asset. All underfunded plans are aggregated and disclosed as a current liability, noncurrent liability, or both. **In other words, the funding status of plans may NOT be netted (overfunded plans may not be netted with underfunded plans).** The measurement date for plans is the fiscal year-end (i.e., balance sheet date) of the entity.

4. **Determination of Pension Expense**

a. The general term **Pension Cost** is preferred over pension expense because pension cost is included in overhead in the determination of product costs and therefore may be part of inventory in the balance sheet.

(1) When permissible the term "Pension Expense" is used instead because it is simpler and clearer.
(2) The disclosure of the elements included in pension expense is one of the most significant disclosures required. A comprehensive illustration is presented in Section 7 below.

(a) This illustration integrates the concepts and calculations that have been introduced in the preceding discussions.

b. Pension Expense is a net amount calculated by adding together five factors. These factors are (1) service cost, (2) interest on the projected benefit obligation, (3) return on plan assets, (4) amortization of unrecognized prior service cost or credit, and (5) the effect of gains and losses. Each of these components is discussed below.

(1) **Service cost—Increases pension expense**

(a) **Service cost** is defined as the actuarial present value of benefits attributed by the pension benefit formula to employee service during the current period.
(b) ASC Topic 715 (SFAS 87) requires that future salary levels be taken into consideration in this calculation (i.e., the benefits-years-of-service approach).

(2) **Interest on projected benefit obligation—Increases pension expense**

(a) The **interest on the projected benefit obligation** is defined as the increase in the amount of the projected benefit obligation due to the passage of time. Since the pension plan's obligation at the beginning of the year is stated in terms of present value, a provision for interest is required. By the end of the period, the plan's obligation will increase by the amount of interest that would accrue based on the discount (settlement) rate selected.

1] The discount rate selected should be determined by reference to market conditions using such rates as the return on high quality investments or the implicit rate of return in retirement annuities as a basis for comparison.
2] Also, the rate selected must be **explicit** and an unreasonable rate cannot be justified by an argument that the unreasonable rate is **implicitly** valid because of other offsetting actuarial assumptions. The selected discount rate is referred to as the **settlement rate** because it is the rate at which the plan's obligation could be settled.

EXAMPLE

Compute the "interest" component of net pension expense for 2010, if the projected benefit obligation was $4,800,000 on January 1, 2010, and the settlement rate is 9%. Answer: Net pension expense for 2010 is increased by $432,000 (9% × $4,800,000) to provide for interest on the projected benefit obligation.

---

(3) **Actual return on plan assets—Decreases or possibly increases pension expense**

(a) The **actual return on plan assets** is defined as the difference in the fair value of plan assets at the beginning and the end of the period adjusted for contributions made to the plan and benefit payments made by the plan during the period. The formula for determining the actual return is as follows:

Actual return = (End. Bal. of plan assets at fair value – Beg. bal. of plan assets at fair value) + Benefits – Contributions

(b) The **fair value or market value** of plan assets is defined as the price expected in a sales transaction between a willing buyer and seller.

1] **Plan assets** typically include marketable securities and other investments such as real estate that are held in trust for the plan participants.

2] Assets that are under the control of the employer are not considered to be plan assets.

3] In calculating the return on plan assets, considerable leeway has been allowed in measuring the fair value of plan assets.

EXAMPLE

Compute the "actual return on plan assets" component of net pension expense, if the fair value of plan assets was $3,100,000 at the beginning of the year and $3,820,000 at year-end. The employer sponsor contributed $450,000 to the plan and the plan paid benefits of $200,000 during the year. Answer: Net pension expense is decreased by $470,000 [($3,820,000 – $3,100,000) + $200,000 – $450,000] due to the actual return earned on the fair value of plan assets.

(c) Although the **actual** return on plan assets is measured and disclosed as one of the components of net pension expense, net pension expense will include only an amount equal to the **expected** return on plan assets.

1] This methodology is followed because the difference between the actual return on plan assets and the expected return on plan assets is a canceling adjustment that is included in the gain or loss calculation to be discussed below.

(4) **Prior service cost or credit—Increases or possibly decreases pension expense**

(a) **Prior service costs** are retroactive adjustments that are granted to recognize services rendered in previous periods.

1] These costs are caused by either an amendment to an existing plan or the initiation of a new plan where a **retroactive allowance** is made for past services rendered.

2] If, as a result of an amendment to an existing plan, the benefits are increased, then the amount of the plan's projected benefit obligation will increase.

a] The amount of the prior service costs is measured by the increase in the projected benefit obligation caused by the amendment or the initiation of the plan.

(b) While the prior service costs are related to the past, it is assumed that the initiation or amendment of the plan was made with the intent of benefiting the employer's future operations rather than its past operations. Because of this assumption, prior service costs should be amortized over the present and future periods affected. The unamortized portion is located in OCI. Two methods approved for use in determining the assignment of prior service costs are (1) the expected future years of service method, and (2) the straight-line basis over the average remaining service period of active employees method.

1] Under the **expected future years of service** method, the total number of employee service years is calculated by grouping employees according to the time remaining to their retirement, based on actuarial assumptions, and multiplying the number in each group by the number of periods remaining to retirement.

EXAMPLE

Eight employees expected to work ten years until retirement would contribute eighty expected future years of service to the total.

---

a] To calculate the amortization of prior service costs for a given year, the number of employee service years applicable to that period is used as the numerator of the fraction and the denominator is the total employee service years based on all the identified groups. This method produces a declining pattern similar to the amortization applicable to premiums or discounts on serial bonds and the sum-of-the-years' digits method of depreciation.

2] The **straight-line basis over the average remaining service period** of active employees is a simpler method. The projected average remaining service period for the affected participants is estimated by the use of a weighted-average method.

EXAMPLE

Ten employees with ten years remaining to retirement, and fifteen employees with twenty years remaining to retirement would have a weighted-average service life of sixteen years computed as follows: $(10 \times 10 + 15 \times 20)/25$. In this example, the prior service costs would be amortized and included in pension expense over sixteen years.

---

a] Although the costs are gradually recognized in Pension Expense over the sixteen years, the costs are fully recognized on the balance sheet in OCI immediately resulting in an adjustment to the Pension Asset/Liability account.

EXAMPLE

Compute the "amortization of prior service cost" component of net pension expense for the first three years after an amendment, based on the following facts. The prior service cost associated with the amendment is determined by the actuaries to be \$650,000 (the difference between the projected benefit obligation before and after the amendment). The employer has 200 employees at the time of the amendment. It is expected that workers will retire or terminate at the rate of 4% per year, and the employer will use the "expected future years of service" method of amortization.

Answer: Since the workers will leave at the rate of 8 per year $(4\% \times 200$ employees), the denominator of the amortization fraction is computed by summing $200 + 192 + 184 + ... + 8$. This series can be written as $8(25 + 24 + 23 + ... + 1)$ or $8n(n+1)/2 = 8(25)(26)/2 = 2,600$. The calculations for the first three years and the unamortized balance at year-end are presented in the table below.

Year	Amortization fraction	Annual amortization	Unamortized balances
0			\$650,000
1	200/2,600	\$50,000	600,000
2	192/2,600	48,000	552,000
3	184/2,600	46,000	506,000

---

(5) **Gain or loss—Increases or decreases pension expense**

(a) Net gain or loss is defined as the change in the amount of the projected benefit obligation as well as the change in the value of plan assets (realized and unrealized), resulting from experience being different from that assumed, or from a change in an actuarial assumption. For this calculation, plan assets are valued at the market-related value, discussed under (3) above.

(b) The gain or loss component included in net pension expense consists of two items:

1] The current period difference between the actual and expected return on plan assets.

a] (Expected rate of return on plan assets) × (Market-related value of plan assets at the beginning of the period)

2] Amortization of the unrecognized net gain or loss from **previous** periods.

a] The current period difference is reported as a component of the current period net pension expense and the unrecognized net gain or loss is located in OCI until it is subject to amortization.

b] In the unusual case when a gain or loss arises from an event such as the discontinuation of a business component, the gain or loss should be recognized immediately and associated with the event that was the cause (e.g., discontinued operations) rather than the pension plan.

(c) When the amortization of the cumulative unrecognized net gain or loss from previous periods is required, the procedure is comparable to the amortization of prior service cost and, in general, it requires the use of a systematic method applied on a consistent basis that is dependent on the average remaining service period for active employees.

1] Unlike past service cost, however, the amount to be amortized is not necessarily the calculated amount of the cumulative unrecognized net gain or loss.

2] Instead, the minimum amount subject to amortization is determined by the use of a method sometimes referred to as the "**corridor**" approach and is determined by computing, at the beginning of the fiscal year, the excess of the cumulative unrecognized gain or loss over 10% of the greater of the projected benefit obligation or the market-related asset value.

a] If the cumulative unrecognized gain or loss is equal to or less than the 10% calculated value, no amount need be amortized.

EXAMPLE

Compute the "gain or loss" component of net pension expense and the other elements of pension expense based on the following facts:

At the beginning of the year the cumulative unrecognized net loss was $500,000, the fair value and market-related value of plan assets was $3,100,000, and the projected benefit obligation was $4,800,000. The expected return on assets for the year was 9% and the settlement rate was 11%. The fair value of plan assets at the end of the year was $3,400,000. There were no contributions to the plan during the year. The plan made no benefit payments during the year. Service costs for the year were $400,000. At the beginning of the year the average remaining service period of active employees was ten years. There are no other factors to be considered in computing pension expense for the year.

Answer: The elements of net pension expense are calculated as follows:

Service cost	$400,000	
Interest (.11 × $4,800,000)	528,000	
Actual return on plan assets	(300,000)	(1)
Amortization of unrecognized net loss	2,000	(2)
Asset gain deferred	21,000	(3)
Net pension expense	$651,000	

> **NOTE:** The above components of pension expense are required to be disclosed in the employer sponsor's financial statements. This would be done in the footnotes to those statements.

(1) $3,400,000 less $3,100,000 less contributions to the plan of $0 plus benefit payments of the plan of $0.
(2) Amortization of unrecognized net loss is calculated as follows:

"Corridor" 10% × $4,800,000	$480,000
Cumulative unrecognized net loss at the beginning of the year	500,000
Excess to be amortized	$ 20,000

Amortization of unrecognized loss is: $20,000/10 years = $2,000.

(3) The asset gain deferred of $21,000 is calculated as follows: Actual return on plan assets of $300,000 less expected return on plan assets of $279,000. The expected return on plan assets is determined by multiplying the expected return on plan assets of 9% times the market-related value of plan assets at the beginning of the year of $3,100,000. Note that in the above computation of pension expense actual return on assets of $300,000 is deducted. However, the expected return on plan assets of $279,000 ($300,000 – $21,000) is the amount that is actually included in pension expense for the year.

---

5. **Reconciling the Projected Benefit Obligation**

a. The projected benefit obligation (PBO) is the actuarial present value of all benefits attributed to employee service rendered prior to that date. The PBO is measured by using actuarial assumptions and estimates regarding discount rates, retirement dates, and life expectancies. Any changes in these actuarial assumptions may increase or decrease the PBO.

  (1) Changes to the PBO due to changes in actuarial assumptions are referred to as actuarial gains or losses in calculating the PBO.
  (2) The PBO is also affected by any changes or amendments to the plan made during the current period.
  (3) The total change to the PBO caused by a plan amendment is referred to as the prior service cost or credit.

> **NOTE:** The entire amount of the prior service cost or credit will affect the PBO in the year of the change. However, only the amortized amount of the prior service cost or credit is included in pension cost (expense) for the period.

b. The following formula is used to reconcile the projected benefit obligation:

Change in projected benefit obligation:

	Beginning of year PBO
+	Service cost
+	Interest cost
±	Prior service cost or credit (from changes to plan in current year)
±	Actuarial gain or loss (from changes in actuarial or underlying assumptions)
−	Benefits paid
	End of year PBO

6. **Disclosures for Pensions**

   a. The required disclosures for pensions and other postretirement benefits are as follows:

      (1) A reconciliation schedule of the benefit obligation showing the components separately
      (2) A reconciliation schedule of the fair value of plan assets with the components shown separately
      (3) The funded status of the plans, and the amounts recognized in the balance sheet showing separately the noncurrent assets, current liabilities, and noncurrent liabilities recognized
      (4) Information about plan assets including equity securities and debt securities, a narrative description of investment policies and strategies, a narrative description of the basis used to determine overall expected rate-of-return on assets, disclosure of classes of plan assets, and information about assets if information is expected to be useful
      (5) For defined benefit pension plans, the accumulated benefit obligation
      (6) The benefits expected to be paid in each of the next five fiscal years and in the aggregate for the five fiscal years thereafter
      (7) The employer's best estimate of contributions expected to be paid to the plan during the rest of the fiscal year
      (8) The net periodic benefit cost recognized with the components shown separately
      (9) The net gain or loss and net prior service cost or credit recognized in other comprehensive income (OCI) for the period, and any reclassification adjustments of OCI (amortization of items) that are recognized in pension cost
      (10) The amounts in accumulated OCI that have not yet been recognized as pension costs, showing separately the net gain or loss, the net prior service cost or credit, and net transition asset or obligation
      (11) On a weighted-average basis, the rates used for the assumed discount rate, rate of compensation increase, and expected long-term rate of return on plan assets, and the assumptions used to determine benefit obligations and net benefit cost
      (12) The assumed health care cost trend rate, a description of the pattern of change
      (13) The effect a 1-percentage-point increase or decrease would have on the aggregated service and interest cost components and the accumulated postretirement benefit obligation for health-care benefits
      (14) The amounts and types of securities of the employer and related parties included in plan assets, the approximate amount of future annual benefits of plan participants covered by insurance contracts issued by employer or related parties, and any significant transactions between the employer or related parties and the plan during the year
      (15) Any alternative method used to amortize prior service amounts or unrecognized net gains and losses
      (16) Any substantive commitments, such as past practice or history of regular benefit increases used to account for benefit obligation
      (17) The cost of providing special or contractual termination benefits recognized during the period and a description of the nature of the event
      (18) An explanation of any significant changes in the plan assets or the benefit obligation
      (19) The amounts in accumulated OCI expected to be recognized as components of pension cost over the fiscal year-end that follows the most recent balance sheet presented, showing separately net gain or loss, net prior service cost or credit, and net transition asset or obligation
      (20) The amount and timing of any plan assets expected to be returned to the employer during the next 12-month period (or operating cycle, if longer) after the most recent balance sheet

   b. The required disclosures for multiemployer plans are as follows:

      (1) The significant multiemployer plans in which an employer participates.
      (2) The level of an employer's participation (the contribution to the plan and whether that contribution represents more than 5% of the total contributions).
      (3) The financial health of the plan such as funded status, improvement plans, and surcharges.
      (4) The nature of the employer commitments to the plans such as collective bargaining agreements and minimum contribution requirements.
      (5) For plans in which users are unable to obtain additional information from outside sources:

         (a) A description of the nature of the plan benefits.
         (b) A qualitative description of the employer responsibility for plan obligations.
         (c) Other quantitative information available such as total plan assets, actuarial present value of accumulated vested benefits, and total contributions received by the plan.

7. Comprehensive Illustration

EXAMPLE

Schaefer Company has sponsored a noncontributory (i.e., employees make no contributions) defined benefit plan for its 100 employees for several years. Within this group of 100 employees, it is expected that workers will retire or terminate at the rate of 5 per year for the next twenty years starting January 1, 2011. Prior to 2011, cumulative pension expense recognized in compliance with ASC Topic 715 exceeded cumulative contributions by $150,000, resulting in a $150,000 balance sheet liability. As of January 1, 2011, the company has agreed to an amendment to its plan that includes a retroactive provision to recognize prior service. To illustrate how the provisions of ASC Topic 715 should be applied, assumptions about the facts relevant to the pension plan for the years 2010 and 2011 are presented in the tables that follow:

	1/1/2010	1/1/2011	12/31/2011
Plan assets (at fair value = market-related value)	$400,000	$ 455,000	$ 760,500
Accumulated benefit obligation (ABO; 60% vested)	460,000	640,000*	710,000*
Projected benefit obligation	550,000	821,500*	1,033,650*
Unrecognized cumulative gain (loss)—due to unexpected decrease in asset value	--	(106,000)	?
Prior service cost amendment	--	105,000	?
Pension asset/(liability)	(150,000)	?	?

* Includes effects of amendment

	12/31/2010	12/31/2011
Service cost	$117,000	$130,000
Employer's funding contribution	125,000	260,000
Plan assets (at fair value = market-related value)	455,000	760,500
Accumulated benefit obligation (60% vested)	620,000	710,000
Benefits paid by the plan	--	--
Unrecognized cumulative gain (loss)—due to unexpected decrease in asset value	(106,000)	(103,729)
Rate of return on assets	9%	10%
Settlement rate	9%	10%

Schedule of Changes in Plan Assets

	2010	2011
Plan assets at 12/31	$455,000	$760,500
Plan assets at 1/1	400,000	455,000
Increase in plan assets	55,000	305,500
Add: Benefits paid	--	--
Less: Funding contributions for the year	(125,000)	(260,000)
Actual return or (loss) on plan assets	(70,000)	45,500
Expected return on plan assets		
2010: 9% × $400,000	36,000	
2011: 10% × $455,000		45,500
Unrecognized gain (loss)	$(106,000)	$ --

Required:

A. Prepare a supporting schedule to determine the amounts to be reported as pension expense for 2010 and 2011. The company has decided to use the "expected future years of service" method to amortize the effects of the amendment made in 2011.

B. Prepare the journal entries required for 2010 and 2011 with respect to the pension plan including any entry necessary to comply with the minimum liability requirement.

C. Prepare pension worksheets for 2010 and 2011.

> **NOTE:** These worksheets summarize Schaefer's general journal entries and changes in its pension-related accounts. These worksheets also summarize the changes in the pension plan's accounts, unrecognized prior service cost, and unrecognized gain or loss. Study these worksheets as they are an excellent tool for pulling together the elements of this comprehensive illustration.

D. Indicate the pension-related amounts that should appear in the company's financial statements prepared at the end of 2010 and 2011.

E. Prepare disclosures of the funded status of the plan to the liability shown in the company's balance sheet at 1/1/10, 12/31/10, and 12/31/11.

EXAMPLE

Solution Part A

REQUIRED FOOTNOTE DISCLOSURE
Pension Expense

	12/31/10	12/31/11
Components of net periodic benefit cost		
1. Service cost	$117,000	$130,000
2. Interest cost on projected benefit obligation	49,500	82,150
3. Actual loss or (actual return) on plan assets	70,000	(45,500)
4. Amortization of prior service cost	--	10,000
5. Deferral of "gain" or (loss)	(106,000)	--
6. Loss amortization	--	2,271
7. Recognized actuarial loss	--	--
Net periodic benefit cost	$130,500	$178,921

Calculations

1. **Service cost** is given.
2. **Interest:** 9% × $550,000 (2010), and 10% × $821,500 (2011). The settlement rate times PBO.
3. **Actual return:** ($70,000) for 2010 and $45,500 (same as expected) for 2011. Note that in 2010, the $70,000 actual loss on plan assets less the $106,000 unrecognized loss equals the expected return ($36,000).
4. **Prior service cost amortization:** Compute the denominator of the fraction for amortization by calculating the sum of the estimated remaining service years by adding 100 + 95 + 90 + ... + 10 + 5. This series can be written as 5(20 + 19 + 18 + ... + 2 + 1) or 5n(n+1)/2, where n = 100/5 = 20, or 5(20)(21)/2 = 1,050. For 2011 the amount is (100/1,050) × $105,000 = $10,000.
5. **Loss:** The $106,000 unrecognized loss that arose in 2010 is not amortized until 2011, because no unrecognized net gain or loss existed at the beginning of the year. The amortization of the unrecognized net gain or loss should be included as a component of pension expense only if the unrecognized net gain or loss existed as of the beginning of the year and the unrecognized gain or loss exceeded the corridor. At 1/1/2011 10% of the greater of the projected benefit obligation ($821,500) or the market-related asset value ($455,000) is equal to $82,150. The minimum loss to be amortized is $106,000 − $82,150 or $23,850. The average employee service remaining as of 1/1/2010 assuming a constant work force of 100 and an attrition rate of 5 workers per year is (100 + 95 + 90 + ... + 10 + 5)/110 or 1,050/110 = 10.5 years. The amount of the loss recognized in 2011 is $23,850/11.5 = $2,271. Since actual and expected returns are equal in 2011, no further adjustment is required.

EXAMPLE

Solution Part B

The journal entries will include three entries: (1) record pension expense for the period; (2) report the cash paid to fund the plan; and (3) report any pension asset or liability caused by overfunding or underfunding the plan. Below are the journal entries required for Schaefer for the first two entries. Below are the journal entries required for Schaefer. A compound entry is provided with the worksheet.

Journal Entries

	2010		2011	
Pension expense	130,500		178,921	
Pension asset/liability		130,500		178,921
To record pension expense				
Pension asset/liability	125,000		260,000	
Cash		125,000		260,000
To record funding				

The journal entry to record other comprehensive income for the unexpected gain/loss and prior service cost, shown net of tax, are as follows:

Assuming a 40% tax rate, the entries for 2010 and 2011 would be

2010 entries		
Other comprehensive income G/L	106,000	
Pension asset/liability		106,000
Deferred tax asset	42,400	
Other comprehensive income—deferred tax asset		42,400

2011 entries

Other comprehensive income PSC	105,000	
Other comprehensive income PSC		10,000
Other comprehensive income G/L		2,271
Pension asset/liability		92,729
Deferred tax asset	37,092	
Other comprehensive income—deferred tax asset		37,092

Therefore, in 2010, OCI would decrease by $63,600 net of tax, and in 2011, OCI would decrease $55,637 net of tax.

The total change in the pension asset/liability account resulting from the above journal entries tries to the change in the required pension asset/liability account as calculated by the change in the funded status of the plan. For example, for 2010, the entries to the pension asset/liability account include: $130,500 (CR) + 125,000 (DR) + 106,000 (CR) = $111,500. The funded status (as shown on the next page, at the beginning of the year is $150,000 (CR). The funded status at the end of the year is $261,500 (CR). The change in funded status is $261,600 − 150,000 = $111,500.

The balance sheet reflects the funded status of the plan. The status is determined by comparing the projected benefit obligation to the fair value of the plan assets. The end-of-year projected benefit obligation is calculated as shown below.

	2010	2011
Projected benefit obligation at beginning of year	$550,000	$ 821,500
Service cost	117,000	130,000
Interest cost*	49,500	82,150
Benefits paid	0	0
Projected benefit obligation at end of year	$716,500	$1,033,650

* The interest cost is determined by multiplying the Settlement rate times the beginning projected benefit obligation. ($49,500 = $550,000 × 9%) ($82,150 = $821,500 × 10%)

Then the funded status of the plan for the two years may be calculated as follows:

	12/31/2010	12/31/2011
Projected benefit obligation	$716,500	$1,033,650
Fair value of plan assets	455,000	760,500
Funded status of plan	$(261,500)	$(273,150)

Because the plan is underfunded at the end of both years, a liability must be included on the balance sheet equal to the underfunded amount. However, the entity will often already have an accrued/prepaid pension account. To determine the liability adjustment needed, the balance in the accrued/prepaid pension cost must be considered. The balances at 12/31/10 and 12/31/11 are calculated below.

	2010	2011
Pension asset/liability at beginning of year	$(150,000)	$(155,500)
Funding contributions	125,000	260,000
Pension cost (expense)	(130,500)	(178,921)
Other comprehensive income—G/L	(106,000)	2,271
Other comprehensive income—PSC (net)		(95,000)
Pension asset/liability at end of year	$(261,500)	$ (273,150)

Finally, the adjustment to establish to recognize the funding status of the plan for each year is calculated as follows:

	12/31/2010	12/31/2011
Liability required	$261,500	$273,150
Pension asset/liability at beginning of year	(150,000)	(261,500)
Adjustment to liability*	$111,500	$ (11,650)

* The adjustment must tie to the journal entries provided on previous page.

Similarly, if the pension plan were overfunded, Schaefer would record an adjusting entry to record a noncurrent asset for the amount of the plan that is overfunded.

Often, a compound journal entry will be used to reflect the changes in the pension asset/liability account. The compound journal entry can be derived from the previous information or the worksheet on the following page.

	2010	2011
Pension cost (expense)	130,500	178,921
Other comprehensive income G/L	106,000	--
Other comprehensive income PSC	--	105,000
Cash	125,000	260,000
Other comprehensive income G/L	--	2,271
Other comprehensive income PSC	--	10,000
Pension asset/liability	111,500	11,650

EXAMPLE

Solution Part C

SCHAEFER COMPANY
Pension Worksheet—2010

	Debit (credit)						Debit (credit)	
	General journal entries						Memo entries	
	Pension expense	Cash	Accumulated OCI PSC	Accumulated OCI G/L	Deferred tax asset (liab)	Pension asset (liab)	Projected benefit obligation	Plan assets
Bal. 1/1/2010						(150,000)	(550,000)	400,000
Service cost	117,000						(117,000)	
Interest cost	49,500						(49,500)	
Actual loss	70,000							(70,000)
Deferred gain (loss)	(106,000)			106,000				
Contribution		(125,000)						125,000
Journal entry for 2010	130,500	(125,000)		106,000		(111,500)		
Def. tax adjustment				42,400	42,400			
Bal. 12/31/2010				(63,600)	42,400	(261,500)	(716,500)*	455,000

* Before plan amendment on 1/1/11

SCHAEFER COMPANY
Pension Worksheet—2011

	Debit (credit)						Debit (credit)	
	General journal entries						Memo entries	
	Pension expense	Cash	Accumulated OCI PSC	Accumulated OCI G/L	Deferred tax asset (liab)	Pension asset (liab)	Projected benefit obligation	Plan assets
Bal. 1/1/2011						(261,500)	(716,500)	455,000
Prior service cost amendment			105,000				(105,000)	
Service cost	130,000						(130,000)	
Interest cost	82,150						(82,150)	
Actual return	(45,500)							45,500
Prior service cost amortization	10,000		(10,000)					
Loss amortization	2,271			(2,271)				
Contribution		(260,000)						260,000
Journal entry for 2011	178,921	(260,000)	95,000	(2,271)		(11,650)		
OCI 12/31/10 Bal				63,600	42,400			
Def. tax adjustment			(38,000)	908	37,092			
Bal. 12/31/2011			57,000	62,237	79,492	(273,492)	(1,033,650)	760,500

EXAMPLE

Solutions Part D and E

Required Footnote Disclosure
(Pension expense disclosure shown in Part A)

	12/31/2010	12/31/2011
Change in projected benefit obligation		
Benefit obligation at beginning of year*	$ 550,000	$ 716,500*
Service cost	117,000	130,000
Interest cost	49,500	82,150
Amendment (prior service cost)	--	105,000
Actuarial loss (gain)	--	--
Benefits paid	--	--
Benefit obligation at end of year	$ 716,500	$1,033,650

* Before effect of plan amendment

	12/31/2010	12/31/2011
Change in plan assets		
Fair value of plan assets at beginning of year	$ 400,000	$ 455,000
Actual return (loss) on plan assets	(70,000)	45,500
Employer contribution	125,000	260,000
Benefits paid	--	--
Fair value of plan assets at end of year	$ 455,000	$ 760,500
Funded status	$(261,500)	$ (273,150)
Other changes recognized in other comprehensive income		
Net actuarial loss	$(150,000)	$ --
Amortization of net loss		2,271
Plan amendment for PSC		(105,000)
Amortization of PSC		10,000
Deferred tax	42,400	37,092
Total recognized change in other comprehensive income	$(63,600)	$(55,637)
Amounts recognized in the statement of financial position (balance sheet) consists of		
Pension asset/liability	$(261,500)	$(273,150)
Deferred tax asset	42,400	79,492
Other comprehensive income G/L	(63,600)	(62,237)
Other comprehensive income PSC	--	(57,000)

NOW REVIEW MULTIPLE-CHOICE QUESTIONS 1 THROUGH 35 IN VOLUME 2

8. **Postretirement Benefits other than Pensions (OPEB)**

   a. ASC Subtopic 715-60 (refer to outline) establishes the standard for employers' accounting for other (than pension) postretirement benefits (OPEB). This standard requires a single method for measuring and recognizing an employer's accumulated postretirement benefit obligation (APBO). It applies to all forms of postretirement benefits, although the most material benefit is usually postretirement health care. To the extent that the promised benefits are similar, the accounting provisions are similar. Only when there is a compelling reason is the accounting different. Companies must disclose the status of overfunded and underfunded postretirement plans on their balance sheets.

   b. There are, however, some fundamental differences between defined benefit pension plans and postretirement benefits other than pensions. The following list presents these differences.

Differences between Pensions and Postretirement Health Care Benefits*

Item	Pensions	Health care benefits
Funding	Generally funded.	Generally *NOT* funded.
Benefit	Well-defined and level dollar amount.	Generally uncapped and great variability.
Beneficiary	Retiree (maybe some benefit to surviving spouse).	Retiree, spouse, and other dependents.
Benefit payable	Monthly.	As needed and used.
Predictability	Variables are reasonably predictable.	Utilization difficult to predict. Level of cost varies geographically and fluctuates over time.

    *   D. Gerald Searfoss and Naomi Erickson, "The Big Unfunded Liability: Postretirement Health Care Benefits," **Journal of Accountancy**, November 1988, pp. 28-39.

    c.   OPEB requires accrual accounting and adopts the three primary characteristics of pension accounting: (1) delayed recognition (changes are not recognized immediately, but are subsequently recognized in a gradual and systematic way), (2) reporting net cost (aggregates of various items are reported as one net amount), and (3) offsetting assets and liabilities (assets and liabilities are sometimes shown net).

    d.   The Codification distinguishes between the **substantive** plan and **written** plan. Although generally the same, the substantive plan (the one understood as evidenced by past practice or by communication of intended changes) is the basis for the accounting if it differs from the written plan.

    e.   OPEBs are considered to be deferred compensation earned in an exchange transaction during the time periods that the employee provides services. The expected cost generally should be attributed in equal amounts (unless the plan attributes a disproportionate share of benefits to early years) over the periods from the employee's hiring date (unless credit for the service is only granted from a later date) to the date that the employee attains full eligibility for all benefits expected to be received. This accrual should be followed even if the employee provides service beyond the date of full eligibility.

        (1)   The transition obligation is the unrecognized and unfunded APBO (accumulated postretirement benefit obligation) for all of the participants in the plan. This obligation can either (1) be recognized immediately as the effect of an accounting change, subject to certain limitations, or (2) be recognized on a delayed basis over future service periods with disclosure of the unrecognized amount. The delayed recognition has to result in, at least, as rapid a recognition as would have been recognized on a pay-as-you-go basis.

EXAMPLE

A sample illustration of the basic accounting for OPEB follows: Firstime Accrual Co. plans to adopt accrual accounting for OPEB as of January 1, 2010. All employees were hired at age 30 and are fully eligible for benefits at age 60. There are no plan assets. This first calculation determines the unrecognized transition obligation (UTO).

Firstime Accrual Co.
December 31, 2009

Employee	Age	Years of service	Total years when fully eligible	Expected retirement age	Remaining service to retirement	EPBO	APBO
A	35	5	30	60	25	$ 14,000	$ 2,333
B	40	10	30	60	20	22,000	7,333
C	45	15	30	60	15	30,000	15,000
D	50	20	30	60	10	38,000	25,333
E	55	25	30	65	10	46,000	38,333
F	60	30	30	65	5	54,000	54,000
G	65	RET	--		--	46,000	46,000
H	70	RET	--		--	38,000	38,000
					85	$288,000	$226,332

Calculations

1. EPBO (expected postretirement benefit obligation) is usually determined by an actuary, although it can be calculated if complete data is available.
2. APBO is calculated using the EPBO. Specifically, it is EPBO × (Years of service/total years when fully eligible)
3. The unrecognized transition obligation (UTO) is the APBO at 12/31/09 since there are no plan assets to be deducted. The $226,332 can be amortized over the average remaining service to retirement of 14.17 (85/6) years or an optional period of twenty years, if longer. Firstime Accrual selected the twenty-year period of amortization.
4. Note that Employee F has attained full eligibility for benefits and yet plans to continue working.

5. Note that the above 2009 table is used in the calculation of the 2010 components of OPEB cost that follows.

After the establishment of UTO, the next step is to determine the benefit cost for the year ended December 31, 2010. The discount rate is assumed to be 10%.

Firstime Accrual Co.
OPEB COST
December 31, 2010

1.	Service Cost	$ 5,000
2.	Interest Cost	22,633
3.	Actual Return on Plan Assets	--
4.	Gain or Loss	--
5.	Amortization of Unrecognized Prior Service Cost	--
6.	Amortization of UTO	11,317
	Total OPEB Cost	$38,950

Calculations

1. Service cost calculation uses only employees not yet fully eligible for benefits.

Employee	1/1/10 EPBO	Total years when fully eligible	Service cost
A	$14,000	30	$ 467
B	22,000	30	733
C	30,000	30	1,000
D	38,000	30	1,267
E	46,000	30	1,533
Total service cost			$5,000

2. Interest cost is the 1/1/10 APBO of $226,332 × 10% = $22,633.
3. There are no plan assets so there is no return.
4. There is no gain (loss) since there are no changes yet.
5. There is no unrecognized prior service cost initially.
6. Amortization of UTO is the 1/1/10 UTO of $226,332/20 year optional election = $11,317.

Assume that Firstime Accrual makes a year-end cash benefit payment of $20,000. Firstime Accrual's year-end entry to record other postretirement benefit cost for 2010 would be as follows:

Postretirement benefit cost	38,950	
Cash		20,000
Accrued postretirement benefit cost		18,950

f. Required disclosures for a postretirement benefit plan are stated in ASC Subtopic 715-60. The requirements are the same as the requirements for pensions, which have already been covered in this module.

9. **Nonretirement Postemployment Benefits**

a. Benefits made available to former/inactive employees after employment but before retirement. Examples include continuation of health care and life insurance coverage, severance pay, and disability-related benefits. Criteria for accrual of these benefits are the same as for compensated absences.

(1) Obligation relates to **services already provided** by the employee,
(2) Rights to compensation **vest or accumulate,**
(3) Payment of obligation is **probable,** and
(4) Amount to be paid is **reasonably estimable**.

> **NOTE:** The last two are the general criteria for recognizing a loss contingency per ASC Topic 450. If is not possible to reliably estimate benefits, disclosure of that fact is required in the footnotes to the financial statements.

10. **Deferred Compensation**

Deferred compensation is the payment at a future date for work done in an earlier period(s). Account for these contracts individually on an accrual basis that reflects the terms of the agreement. Accrue amounts to be paid in future over the employment period from date agreement is signed to full eligibility date. The rationale for this treatment is matching.

┌──┐
│   **NOW REVIEW MULTIPLE-CHOICE QUESTIONS 36 THROUGH 41 IN VOLUME 2**   │
└──┘

11. **Research Component—Accounting Standards Codification**

In the Codification, the accounting rules for pensions are found in Expenses under Compensation, which is labeled 71X. Topic 71X includes Topics 710, 712, 715, and 718. Topic 710 is Compensation—General. Topic 712 is Compensation—Nonretirement Postemployment Benefits. Topic 715 is Compensation—Retirement Benefits. Topic 715 is organized by subtopics as shown in the following table:

Subtopic	Title
715-10	Overall
715-20	Defined Benefit Plans—General
715-30	Defined Benefit Plans—Pensions
715-60	Defined Benefit Plans—Other Postretirement Plans
715-70	Defined Contribution Plans
715-80	Multiemployer Plans

12. **International Financial Reporting Standards (IFRS)**

The area of employee benefits, and more specifically pensions, is where there are many similarities between US GAAP and IFRS.

a. In a defined contribution pension plan, the accounting is similar to US GAAP. The employer recognizes an expense for the period equal to the required contribution. If payment is made to the plan, then cash is credited. If the contribution is not made by the end of the accounting period, then the entity would recognize a liability for the accrued contributions.

b. With respect to defined benefit plans, some vocabulary is different.

(1) In US GAAP, the benefits-years-of-service method is used to calculate the projected benefit obligation (PBO). Under IFRS, the Projected Unit Credit Method is used to calculate the present value of the defined benefit obligation (PV-DBO). The concept is the same, but the terms are different.

(2) In addition, rather than the term "accumulated benefit obligation," IFRS uses the term "accrued benefit obligation."

(3) In a defined benefit pension plan, the calculation of pension cost for the period is also similar to US GAAP. Under IFRS, net periodic pension cost is comprised of six components:

(a) Current service cost,

(b) Interest cost for the current period on the accrued benefit obligation,

(c) Expected return on plan assets,

(d) Actuarial gains and losses,

(e) Past service costs, and

(f) Effects of curtailments and settlements.

(4) Under US GAAP, the discount rate used is the "settlement rate" (the rate at which the plan's obligations could be settled). With IFRS the discount rate is determined by the market yields at the end of the reporting period for high-quality corporate bonds having a similar term or maturity.

(5) Another difference in accounting for pensions is that under IFRS, an entity may recognize a portion of the net accumulated actuarial gains or losses, or they may elect to recognize all of the actuarial gains and losses.

(a) If the entity wishes to recognize a portion, then the amount recognized is the excess of a "corridor" amount. The corridor amount is the greater of 10% of the present value of the defined benefit obligation, or 10% of the fair value of any plan assets. This excess gain or loss above the corridor amount is then amortized over the expected remaining working lives of the employees.

(b) Although the corridor rule is similar in US GAAP, the other option for recognizing all actuarial gains and losses is allowed only under IFRS.

(6) Finally, IFRS has specific rules for netting the balances of pension plan assets and pension liabilities. Netting of plan assets and liability balances is only permissible when there is a legally enforceable right to use the assets of one plan to settle the obligations of another plan.

c. **Termination benefits.** When an entity provides voluntary termination benefits, a liability and expense are reported when the entity is demonstrably committed to a detailed formal plan that it cannot withdraw. The plan should include information such as location, function, number of employees, benefits provided, and when the plan will be implemented.

NOW REVIEW MULTIPLE-CHOICE QUESTIONS 42 THROUGH 43 IN VOLUME 2

KEY TERMS

Accumulated benefit obligation. The actuarial present value of benefits (whether vested or nonvested) attributed to employee service rendered before a specified date and based on employee service and compensation before that date.

Actual return on plan assets. The difference between the fair value of plan assets at the end of the period and the fair value at the beginning of the period, adjusted for contribution and payments of benefits during the period.

Benefit-years-of-service approach. An equal portion of the total estimated benefit is attributed to each year of service. The actuarial present value of the benefits is derived after the benefits are attributed to the periods.

Benefits. Payments to which participants may be entitled under pension plan, including pension benefits, death benefits, and benefits due on termination of employment.

Contributory plan. A pension plan under which employees contribute part of the cost.

Cost approach. Assigns net pension costs to periods as level amounts or constant percentages of compensation.

Defined benefit pension plan. A pension plan that defines an amount of pension benefit to be provided, usually as a function of one or more factors such as age, years of service, or compensation.

Defined contribution plan. A plan that provides an individual account for each participant and provides benefits that are based on amounts contributed.

Expected return on plan assets. An amount calculated as a basis for determining the extent of delayed recognition of the effects of changes in the fair value of assets. The expected return on plan assets in determined based on the expected long-term rate of return on plan assets and the market-related value of plan assets.

Gain or loss. A change in the value of either the projected benefit obligation or the plan assets resulting from experience different from that assumed or from a change in an actuarial assumption. Gains and losses that are not recognized in net periodic pension cost when they arise are recognized in other comprehensive income.

Interest cost. The amount recognized in a period determined as the increase in the projected benefit obligation due to the passage of time.

Market-related value of plan assets. A balance used to calculate the expected return on plan assets. The market-related value of plan assets is either fair value or a calculated value that recognizes changes in fair value in a systematic and rational manner over not more than five years.

Multiple-employer plan. A pension plan maintained by more than one employer but not treated as a multiemployer plan.

Net periodic pension cost. The amount recognized in an employer's financial statements as the cost of a pension plan for a period. Components of net periodic pension cost are service cost, interest cost, actual return on plan assets, gain or loss, amortization of prior service cost or credit, and amortization of the transition asset or obligation.

Pension benefits. Periodic (usually monthly) payments made pursuant to the terms of the pension plan to a person who has retired from employment or to that person's beneficiary.

Plan amendment. A change in the terms of an existing plan or the initiation of a new plan. A plan amendment may increase benefits, including those attributed to years of service already rendered.

Plan assets. Assets—usually stocks, bonds, and other investments—that have been segregated and restricted, usually in a trust, to provide for pension benefits. The amount of plan assets includes amounts contributed by the employer, and by employees for a contributory plan, and amounts earned from investing the contributions, less benefits paid.

Prior service cost. The cost of retroactive benefits granted in a plan amendment. Retroactive benefits are benefits granted in a plan amendment (or initiation) that are attributed by the pension benefit formula to employee services rendered in periods before the amendment.

Projected benefit obligation. The actuarial present value as of a date for all benefits attributed by the pension benefit formula to employee service rendered before that date.

Service cost. A component of net periodic pension cost recognized in a period determined as the actuarial present value of benefits attributed by the pension benefit formula to services rendered by employees during that period.

Single-employer plan. A pension plan that is maintained by one employer. The term also may be used to describe a plan that is maintained by related parties such as a parent and its subsidiaries.

Unfunded projected benefit obligation. The excess of the projected benefit obligation over plan assets.

Vested benefit obligation. The actuarial present value of vested benefits.

E. Leases

A lease is a contract between two parties—a lessor and a lessee. A lease contract gives a lessee rights to use the lessor's property for a specified period of time in return for periodic cash payments (rent) to the lessor.

1. A major goal in accounting for leases is to recognize the economic substance of the lease agreement over its mere legal form. For example, many lease agreements are similar to the purchase of an asset financed by the issuance of debt. The economic substance of a lease agreement generally takes one of two forms:

   a. Periodic payments of rent by the lessee for the **use** of the lessor's property
   b. Periodic payments similar to an installment purchase by the lessee for the rights to **acquire** the lessor's property in the future (i.e., acquisition of property by financing)

       (1) In a., the risks and rewards of owning the asset remain with the lessor. Accordingly, the asset is **not** treated as sold by the lessor to the lessee, and remains on the lessor's books. This form of leasing arrangement is called an **operating lease**.
       (2) By contrast, in b., a lease agreement may transfer many of the risks and rewards of ownership to the lessee. This form of lease is treated as a sale by the lessor and as a purchase by the lessee. This concept is clearly stated as follows:

   > The objective of the **lease** classification criteria in the Subtopic derives from the concept that a lease that transfers **substantially all** of the benefits and risks incident to the ownership of property should be accounted for as the acquisition of an asset and the incurrence of an obligation by the lessee and as a **sale or financing** by the lessor. All other leases should be accounted for as **operating leases** (ASC 840).

   c. When the risks and rewards of ownership are deemed to have been passed from the lessor to the lessee, the lessor will account for the lease as either a **direct financing** or as a **sales-type lease,** and the lessee will account for the lease as a **capital lease**.

       (1) To determine whether the risks and rewards of ownership have been transferred to the lessee, **at least one** of the following four criteria must be met:

           (a) The lease **transfers title** to the lessee.
           (b) The lease contains a **bargain purchase** option.
           (c) The lease **term is 75% or more** of useful life and the lease is not first executed within the last 25% of the original useful life.
           (d) The **present value** of minimum lease payments **is 90% or more** of the net of the **fair value** of the asset reduced by the investment tax credit (when in effect) retained by the lessor and the lease is not executed in the last 25% of the original useful life.

       (2) These four criteria apply to both the lessor and to the lessee. The lessor, however, must meet two additional criteria:

           (a) **Collectibility** of minimum lease payments is predictable, and
           (b) There are **no important uncertainties** concerning costs yet to be incurred by the lessor under the lease.
           (c) **Both** of the above must be satisfied by the lessor in order for the lessor to treat the lease in substance as a capital lease.

   d. The classification of leases can be summarized as follows:

	Lessor		*Lessee*
Risks and rewards remain with lessor (no sale and purchase of asset)	Operating	———————————	Operating
Risks and rewards transfer to lessee (sale and purchase of asset)	Direct financing	———————————	Capital
	Sales-type		

2. **Study Program for Leases**

   a. Begin by reviewing the terms peculiar to leases that appear at the beginning of the outline of ASC Topic 840 (SFAS 13) in the pronouncement outlines that begin after Module 22.
   b. Review the material in this module so that you will be familiar with the major concepts and applications in the leasing area.

c. After you have developed a solid base of understanding, you should review the outline of SFAS 13 (ASC Topic 840).

d. The discussion of accounting for leases is structured to follow the lease classification matrix listed above.

(1) Operating Lease—Lessor/Lessee

An operating lease is any lease not meeting the criteria for a direct financing or sales-type lease in the case of a lessor, or for a capital lease in the case of a lessee. Under an operating lease, leased assets continue to be carried on the lessor's balance sheet and are depreciated in the normal manner. These assets, however, are not shown on the lessee's balance sheet since the lessee cannot expect to derive any future economic benefit from the assets beyond the lease term. Several issues are frequently encountered when dealing with operating leases. These issues are discussed in the remainder of this section.

(a) Free rent/uneven payments

Some lease agreements might call for uneven payments or scheduled rent increases over the lease term. Other agreements might include, as an incentive to the lessee, several months of "free rent" during which the lessee may use the asset without owing rent to the lessor. In these cases, rental revenue (expense) is still recognized by the lessor (lessee) on a straight-line basis and is prorated over the full term of the lease during which the lessee has possession of the asset. This is due to the matching principle; if physical usage is relatively the same over the lease term, then an equal amount of benefit is being obtained by both parties to the lease.

> **NOTE:** Another method to allocate rental revenue (expense) may be used if it better represents the actual physical use of the leased asset.

1] When the pattern of actual cash received (paid) as rent is other than straight-line, it will be necessary for both parties to record accruals, or deferrals, depending upon the payment schedule.

		Accruals	**(or)**	**Deferrals**
Lessor	--	Rent receivable		Unearned rent
Lessee	--	Rent payable		Prepaid rent

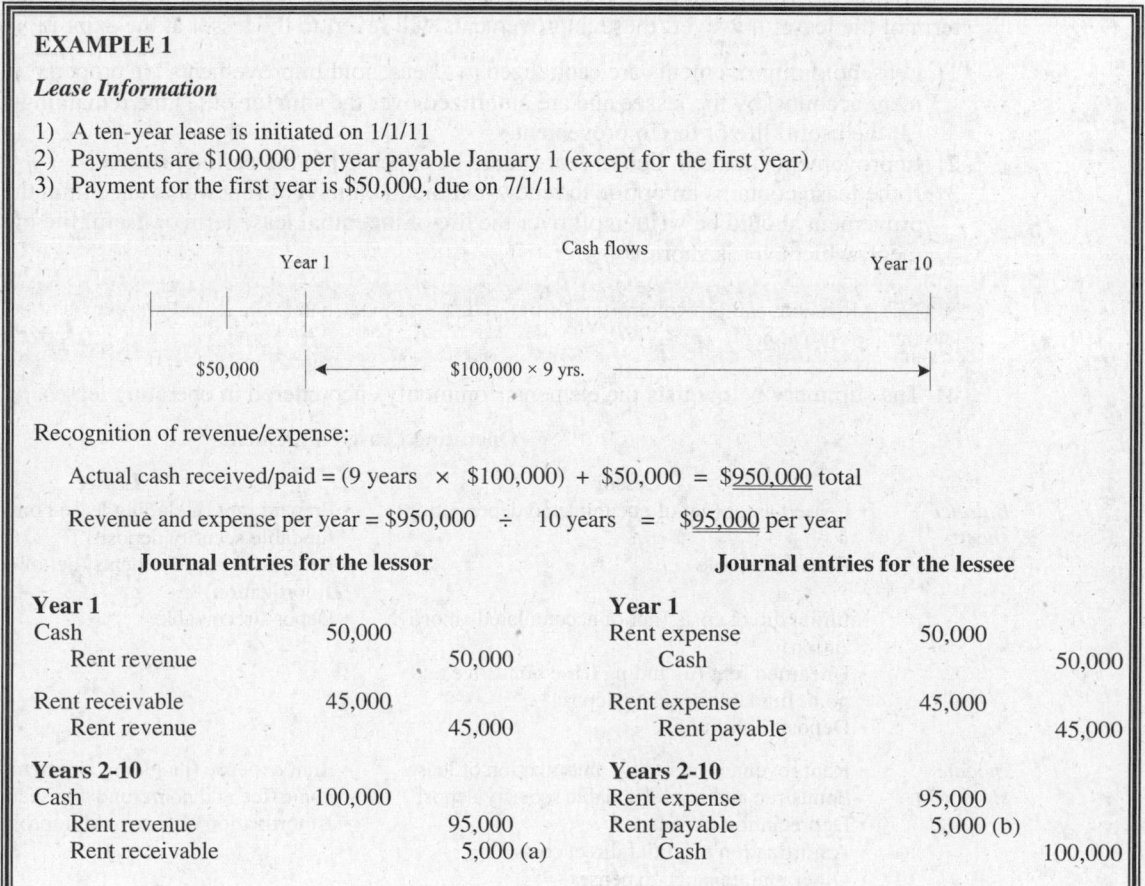

EXAMPLE 1

Lease Information

1) A ten-year lease is initiated on 1/1/11
2) Payments are $100,000 per year payable January 1 (except for the first year)
3) Payment for the first year is $50,000, due on 7/1/11

Cash flows

Year 1   Year 10

$50,000   ← —— $100,000 × 9 yrs. —— →

Recognition of revenue/expense:

Actual cash received/paid = (9 years × $100,000) + $50,000 = $950,000 total

Revenue and expense per year = $950,000 ÷ 10 years = $95,000 per year

Journal entries for the lessor			**Journal entries for the lessee**		
Year 1			**Year 1**		
Cash	50,000		Rent expense	50,000	
Rent revenue		50,000	Cash		50,000
Rent receivable	45,000		Rent expense	45,000	
Rent revenue		45,000	Rent payable		45,000
Years 2-10			**Years 2-10**		
Cash	100,000		Rent expense	95,000	
Rent revenue		95,000	Rent payable	5,000 (b)	
Rent receivable		5,000 (a)	Cash		100,000

Rent Receivable		**(a)**	**(b)**	Rent Payable	
yr. 1 45,000	5,000	yr. 2	yr. 2	5,000	45,000 yr. 1
	•			•	
	•			•	
	•	yr. 10	yr. 10	•	

(b) **Initial direct costs**

The lessor may incur costs in setting up the lease agreement. Such costs might include finder's fees, appraisal fees, document processing fees, negotiation fees, and any costs in closing the transaction. These costs, called initial direct costs, are carried as an asset on the lessor's balance sheet. Initial direct costs are amortized on a straight-line basis to expense over the lease term by the lessor, and are shown net of accumulated amortization on the lessor's balance sheet.

(c) **Lease bonus (fee)**

At the inception of the lease, the lessee may pay a nonrefundable lease bonus (fee) to the lessor in order to obtain more favorable leasing terms (e.g., a lease term of three years instead of five years). The lease bonus (fee) would be treated as unearned rent by the lessor and would be amortized to rental revenue on a straight-line basis over the lease term. The lessee would treat the lease bonus (fee) as prepaid rent and would recognize it as rental expense over the lease term on a straight-line basis.

(d) **Security deposits**

Some lease agreements may require that the lessee pay the lessor a security deposit at the inception of the lease. Security deposits may be either refundable or nonrefundable. A **refundable** security deposit is treated as a liability by the lessor and as a receivable by the lessee until the deposit is returned to the lessee. A **nonrefundable** security deposit is recorded as unearned revenue by the lessor and as prepaid rent by the lessee until the deposit is considered earned by the lessor (usually at the end of the lease term).

(e) **Leasehold improvements**

Frequently, the lessee will make improvements to leased property by constructing new buildings or improving existing structures. The lessee has the right to use these leasehold improvements over the term of the lease; however, these improvements will revert to the lessor at the expiration of the lease.

1] Leasehold improvements are capitalized to "Leasehold Improvements" (a property, plant and equipment account) by the lessee and are amortized over the **shorter** of (1) the remaining lease term, **or** (2) the useful life of the improvement.

2] Improvements made in lieu of rent should be expensed in the period incurred.

3] If the lease contains an option to renew and the likelihood of renewal is uncertain, the leasehold improvement should be written off over the life of the initial lease term or useful life of the improvement, whichever is shorter.

NOTE: Moveable equipment or office furniture that is not attached to the leased property is **not** considered a leasehold improvement.

4] The summary below lists the elements commonly encountered in operating leases.

Operating Lease FS Elements

	Lessor	Lessee
Balance sheet:	• Leased asset (net of accumulated depreciation)	• Prepaid rent (including lease bonus/fee and nonrefundable security deposit)
	• Rent receivable	• Leasehold improvements (net of accumulated amortization)
	• Initial direct costs (net of accumulated amortization)	• Deposit receivable
	• Unearned rent (including lease bonus/fee and nonrefundable security deposit)	
	• Deposit liability	
Income statement:	• Rent revenue (including amortization of lease bonus/fee and nonrefundable security deposit)	• Rent expense (including amortization of lease bonus/fee and nonrefundable security deposit)
	• Depreciation expense	• Amortization of leasehold improvements
	• Amortization of initial direct costs	
	• Other maintenance expenses	

NOTE: Knowledge of these elements is helpful in answering questions that require a determination of lessor's net income or lessee's total expense in connection with an operating lease.

(f) **Modifications and terminations to capital leases**

A company may modify a capital lease in such a way that it changes the lease to an operating lease.

1] If a capital lease is modified as such, it is treated as a sales-leaseback transaction.

2] If a company terminates a capital lease, the accounting for the termination depends on whether the lease was a capital lease for real estate or for an asset other than real estate.

a] If the capital lease was for real estate, then the criteria for recognition of gains must be met in order for the company to recognize a gain on termination of the lease. However, any loss on the transaction is recognized immediately.

b] If the lease was for assets other than real estate, then the asset and obligation of the lease are removed from the accounts and a gain or loss is recognized for the difference.

i] If the original lessee remains secondarily liable, the guarantee obligation is recognized.

(g) **Termination costs**

If a lessee terminates an operating lease before the end of its term, the lessee must recognize any termination costs. Termination costs may include a lump-sum payment or payments that continue during the remaining lease term. Such costs are measured and recognized at fair value on the date the agreement is terminated, the entity no longer receives rights to the assets, or the company ceases to use the assets (cease-use date).

1] If the company remains liable for payments after the cease-use date, the fair value of the termination costs is based on the remaining lease rentals reduced by the estimated sublease rentals that could be obtained for the property, even if the entity does not intend to sublease.

2] Termination costs of an operating lease are included in calculating income from continuing operations.

3] If the termination of an operating lease is associated with the exit or disposal of a discontinued operation, these costs are included in the results of discontinued operations.

NOW REVIEW MULTIPLE-CHOICE QUESTIONS 1 THROUGH 18 IN VOLUME 2

(2) **Direct Financing Lease—Lessor**

NOTE: Although most discussions begin with the lessee's accounting for a capital lease, we have chosen to present the lessor's accounting first because the lessor is the party that determines the fixed cash schedule of lease payments that are to be made by the lessee.

(a) A direct financing lease arises when a consumer needs equipment but does not want to purchase the equipment outright, and/or is unable to obtain conventional financing. In this situation, the consumer will turn to a leasing company (e.g., a bank) which will purchase the desired asset from a manufacturer (or dealer) and lease it to the consumer. Direct financing leases apply to leasing companies, as opposed to manufacturers or dealers, because leasing companies purchase the assets solely for leasing, not for resale. Leasing companies are usually involved in financing activities (e.g., banking and insurance), not in the sale of property of the type being leased. The following situation shows when a direct financing lease would arise:

EXAMPLE

ABC Company needs new equipment to expand its manufacturing operations but does not have enough capital to purchase the equipment at present. ABC Company employs Universal Leasing Company to purchase the equipment. ABC will lease the asset from Universal. Universal records a direct financing lease.

(b) The relationships in a direct financing lease arrangement are illustrated below.

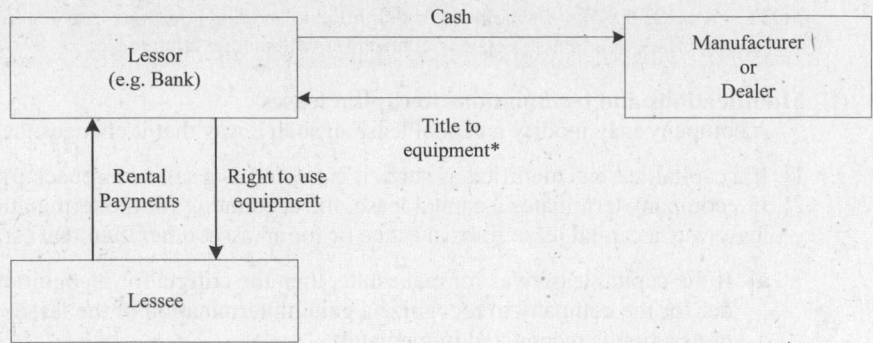

* Title would stay with the lessor unless criterion (1) or (2) previously presented is met, in which case title would pass to the lessee.

(c) As mentioned, a lease is considered to be a direct financing lease by the **lessor** if at least one of the four criteria applicable to both lessors and lessees is met, and **both** of the additional criteria applicable to lessors are met.

(d) Direct financing leases result in only interest revenue for the lessor. In essence, no product has been sold by the lessor, so no gain/loss, sales, or cost of sales is recognized from the lease transaction. Thus the FV (selling price) of the leased asset equals its cost to the lessor.

   1] The lessor's entry to record the acquisition of title to the asset to be leased is as follows:

Asset to be leased	(cost of asset = FV)	
Cash		(cash paid)

   2] At the inception of the lease, the lessor makes the following entry:

Lease receivable	xx	
Asset to be leased		xx
Unearned interest revenue		xx

   3] In effect, the asset is removed from the lessor's books; it will be transferred to the lessee's books if one of the four criteria applicable to lessees is met. It is possible that the lessee's analysis might result in an operating lease.

(e) In order to calculate the amounts in the entry above, you must first become familiar with several important terms.

   1] **Minimum lease payments (MLP)**

   MLP are the payments that the lessor/lessee is or can be required to make in connection with the leased property.

   a] Rent payments (excluding executory costs and contingent rentals)
   b] Bargain purchase option (if any)
   c] Guaranteed residual value (if any)
   d] Penalty for failure to renew (if any)
   e] Executory costs (e.g., property taxes, insurance, etc.) and contingent rentals are treated as revenues in the period earned.

   2] **Bargain purchase option (BPO)**

   This option allows the lessee to purchase leased property for an amount substantially lower than the expected FMV at the exercise date of the option.

   3] **Residual value**

   Residual value can be unguaranteed or guaranteed. Some lease contracts require lessees to guarantee residual value to lessors. The lessee can either buy the leased asset at the end of the lease term for the guaranteed residual value or allow the lessor to sell the leased asset (with the lessee paying any deficiency or receiving any excess over the guaranteed residual value).

   a] **Guaranteed residual value (GRV)** is considered part of the "minimum lease payment" and is reflected in the lessor's lease receivable account and the lessee's lease payable account. At the end of the lease term, the receivable and payable on the respective lessor's and lessee's books should be equal to the guaranteed residual value. Both lessor and lessee consider the guaranteed residual value a final lease payment. The lessee should amortize (depreciate) the asset down to the guaranteed residual value.

b] **Unguaranteed residual value** is the estimated residual value of the leased asset at the end of the lease (if a guaranteed residual value exists, the unguaranteed residual value is the excess of estimated value over the guaranteed residual value). The present value of the unguaranteed residual value should be included in the lessor's net investment in the lease unless the lease transfers title to the leased asset or there is a bargain purchase option.

    i] At the end of the lease, the lessor's receivable account should be equal to the unguaranteed residual value. The lessor must review the estimated residual value annually and recognize any decreases as a loss. No upward adjustments of the residual value are permitted.

(f) Now you are ready to calculate the amounts for the lessor's entry using the following formulas:

EXAMPLE

Lease receivable* (= gross investment)	=	Total MLP**	+	URV (if any)
Asset to be leased (= net investment) (= FV or cost of asset)	=	PV of gross investment		
Unearned interest revenue	=	Gross investment	–	FV (or cost) of asset

  * The title **Gross investment** is used when there is an unguaranteed residual value because the lower probability of collection of the residual value makes the use of the term **Receivable** undesirable.

  ** Include guaranteed residual value.

Alternative methods of recording the lease transaction are shown below.

Lease receivable (gross)	xx			Lease receivable (net)	xx
Asset to be leased		xx	-or-	Asset to be leased	xx
Unearned interest revenue		xx			

NOTE: We will follow the gross method in our examples for the lessor because it is consistent with the questions on the CPA exam.

(g) Below are additional guidelines when accounting for the lessor.

1] The lease receivable should be separated into current and noncurrent components on the lessor's balance sheet.

2] Unearned interest revenue must be amortized to produce a constant periodic rate of return on the net investment using the interest method.

3] No residual value is assumed to accrue to the value of the lessor if the lease transfers ownership or contains a BPO.

4] At the termination of the lease, the balance in the receivable should equal the guaranteed or unguaranteed residual value, assuming title is not transferred and there is no bargain purchase option.

EXAMPLE 2

Lease Information

1) A three-year lease is initiated on 1/1/11 for equipment costing $131,858 with an expected useful life of five years. The FV of the equipment on 1/1/11 is $131,858.

2) Three annual payments are due to the lessor beginning 12/31/11. The property reverts back to the lessor upon termination of the lease.

3) The guaranteed residual value at the end of year 3 is $10,000.

4) The lessor is to receive a 10% return (implicit rate).

5) Collectivity of minimum lease payments is predictable, and there are no important uncertainties concerning costs yet to be incurred by the lessor under the lease.

6) The cost (FV) of the asset incurred by the lessor to acquire the asset for leasing is to be recovered through two components: annual rent payments and guaranteed residual value using a discount (implicit) rate of 10%.

7) The annual rent payment to the lessor is computed as follows:

a) Find PV of guaranteed residual value

$$\underset{\text{GRV}}{\$10,000} \quad \times \quad .7513 \quad = \quad \$7,513$$

b) Find PV of annual rent payments

$$\underset{\text{FV of asset}}{\$131,858} \quad - \quad \$7,513 \quad = \quad \$124,345$$

c) Find annual rent payment

$$\$124,345 \quad \div \quad PVA_{n=3;\ i=10\%}$$

$$\$124,345 \quad \div \quad 2.4869 \quad = \quad \$50,000$$

Lease Classification

This lease is a direct financing lease because criterion 4 (the 90% test) is satisfied.

$$\$124,345 + \$7,513 \geq (.9)(\$131,858)$$

(Since the residual value is guaranteed, the PV of the MLP is 100% of the FV.) The two additional criteria for the lessor are satisfied, and FV equals cost. If the residual value had been unguaranteed, the 90% test would still have been met because $\$124,345 \geq (.9)\,(\$131,858)$.

Accounting for Lease

1) The lease should be recorded at the beginning of year 1 by the lessor.
2) The lease receivable is calculated as follows:

$$\begin{array}{ccccc}
(\text{Annual rent payment} & \times & \text{Lease term}) & + & \text{GRV} \\
\$50,000 & & 3 \text{ yrs.} & & \$10,000 \quad = \$160,000
\end{array}$$

3) Unearned interest revenue is calculated as follows:

$$\begin{array}{ccc}
\text{Lease receivable} & - & \text{FV of asset} \\
\$160,000 & & \$131,858 \quad = \$28,142
\end{array}$$

4) Unearned interest is amortized during the lease term using the following amortization schedule:

AMORTIZATION SCHEDULE

Carrying value at beg. of yr. 1 (= PV of gross investment)		$131,858
Interest revenue (10%)	$ 13,186	
Rent payment	(50,000)	(36,814)
Carrying value at beg. of yr. 2		95,044
Interest revenue	9,504	
Rent payment	(50,000)	(40,496)
Carrying value at beg. of yr. 3		54,548
Interest revenue	5,452	
Rent payment	(50,000)	(44,548)
Carrying value at end of yr. 3 (= residual value)		10,000

Lease receivable on balance sheet:

End of Year 1	–	current portion	= $40,496	principal reduction in year 2
		noncurrent portion	= $54,548	principal reductions after year 2
End of Year 2	–	current portion	= $54,548	principal reduction in the following year
				(includes residual value)

> **NOTE:** As the lease expires, interest revenue decreases and the reduction of principal increases.

5) The journal entries for the lessor are shown below.

JOURNAL ENTRIES FOR THE LESSOR

Initial entries (Beg. of Yr. 1)			End of Year 2		
Equipment for leasing	131,858		Cash	50,000	
Cash		131,858	Lease receivable		50,000
Lease receivable	160,000		Unearned interest	9,504	
Equipment for leasing		131,858	Interest revenue		9,504
Unearned interest		28,142			

Cash	50,000		Cash	50,000	
Lease receivable		50,000	Lease receivable		50,000
Unearned interest	13,186		Unearned interest	5,452	
Interest revenue		13,186	Interest revenue		5,452

6) Assume that when the asset is returned at the end of year 3 the asset has a FV of only $4,000. The lessee will need to make a payment of $6,000 ($10,000 − $4,000) because the residual value was guaranteed. The lessor would make the following entry:

Cash	6,000	
Residual value of equipment	4,000	
Lease receivable		10,000

NOW REVIEW MULTIPLE-CHOICE QUESTIONS 19 THROUGH 20 IN VOLUME 2

---

(3) **Sales-Type Lease—Lessor**

A sales-type lease arises when a manufacturer or dealer leases an asset which otherwise might be sold outright for a profit. These manufacturers (dealers) use leasing as a way to market their own products (e.g., a car dealership). The leasing, or financing arrangement, is a means for the manufacturer to sell its products and realize a profit from sales. (By contrast, direct financing leases serve purely as financing arrangements.) The following situation shows when a sales-type lease would arise:

> ABC Company needs equipment to expand its manufacturing operations. ABC Company enters into a lease agreement with XYZ Manufacturing, Inc. for the equipment. XYZ Manufacturing Inc. records a sales-type lease.

(a) The relationships in a sales-type lease arrangement are illustrated below.

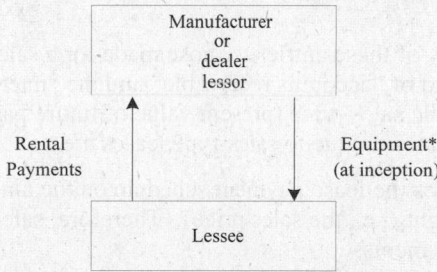

* Title stays with lessor and property will be returned to lessor at the end of the lease term unless criterion (1) or (2) previously presented is met.

(b) Sales-type leases, unlike direct financing leases, result in **both** (1) gross profit (loss) in the period of sales, **and** (2) interest revenue to be earned over the lease term using the effective interest method. The diagram below compares and contrasts direct financing leases with sales-type leases.

Direct Financing Lease (Lessor)

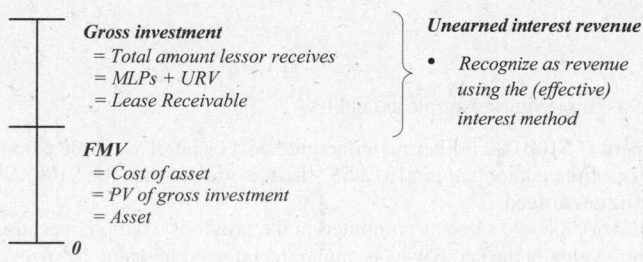

Sales-Type Lease (Lessor)

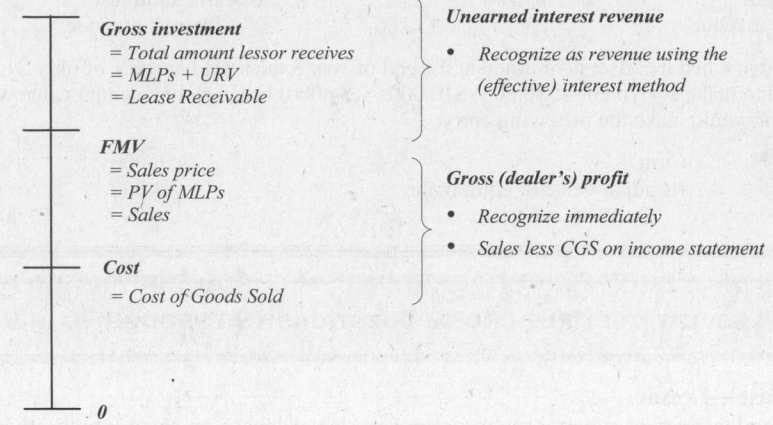

Gross investment
= Total amount lessor receives
= MLPs + URV
= Lease Receivable

Unearned interest revenue
• Recognize as revenue using the
  (effective) interest method

FMV
= Sales price
= PV of MLPs
= Sales

Gross (dealer's) profit
• Recognize immediately
• Sales less CGS on income statement

Cost
= Cost of Goods Sold

0

(c) A lease is considered to be a sales-type lease from the viewpoint of the lessor if the criteria mentioned earlier for direct financing leases are satisfied. However, in the case of a sales-type lease, the FV of the asset, which is the sales price in the ordinary course of the lessor's business is **greater than** the cost or carrying value of the leased asset. Because of this difference, a sales-type lease is more complex than a direct financing lease. The journal entries to record a sales-type lease are

Lease receivable (Gross)	xx	
Sales		xx
Unearned interest		xx
CGS	xx	
Inventory		xx

Note the similarity of these entries to those made for a sale on account. The differences are "lease receivable" instead of "accounts receivable" and the "unearned interest" for the excess of the receivables over the sales price (present value of future payments).

(d) Additional guidelines unique to sales-type leases are

1] The lessor bases the lease payment schedule on the amount the lessee would have paid to purchase the asset outright (i.e., the sales price). Therefore, sales are equal to the present value of the minimum lease payments.

2] The cost of goods sold to be charged against income is equal to the historic cost or carrying value of the leased asset (most likely inventory) **less** the present value of any unguaranteed residual value.

3] The difference between the selling price and cost of goods sold is the gross profit (loss) recognized by the lessor at the inception of the lease.

4] When accounting for sales-type leases, guaranteed residual value is considered part of sales revenue because the lessor knows the entire asset has been sold. Unguaranteed residual value, however, is excluded from both sales and cost of sales at its present value because there is less certainty that unguaranteed residual value will be realized.

EXAMPLE 3

Lease Information

Assume same information as in previous example except

1) The cost of the equipment is $100,000 (either manufactured cost or purchase price paid by dealer).
2) The normal selling price of the equipment is $131,858 which is greater than the $100,000 cost.
3) The residual value is **unguaranteed**.
4) The lease payments are $50,000, the same as computed in the previous example, because the lessor treats an **un**guaranteed residual value in the same way as a guaranteed residual value. However, as mentioned below, the present value of the unguaranteed residual value is not included in the 90% test.

Lease Classification

This is a sales-type lease since the 90% test is satisfied; 90% of the $131,858 FV = $118,672, which is less than $124,345, the present value of the minimum lease payments (see Numerical Example 2); the present value of the residual value is excluded because it is unguaranteed. Additionally, the cost of the asset is less than its fair value (also the present value of the minimum lease payments plus the unguaranteed residual value). Assume the two additional criteria for the lessor have been satisfied.

Accounting for Lease

1) The gross investment is: $160,000 [3 payments of $50,000 (same as Numerical Example 2) plus a $10,000 unguaranteed residual value]

   The PV of gross investment is: $131,858 [($50,000 × 2.4869) + ($10,000 × .7513)]
   The unearned interest revenue is: $28,142 ($160,000 − $131,858)
   Sales are: $124,345 [$131,858 − ($10,000 × .7513)[*]]
   CGS is: $92,487 [$100,000 − ($10,000 × .7513)[*]]

   > [*] There is no effect on gross profit of not including the present value of the unguaranteed residual value in either sales or cost of goods sold. In both cases, the gross profit is $31,858. If the residual value were guaranteed, this adjustment would not be made.

2) The entry to record the lease is

Lease receivable[**]	160,000	
Cost of goods sold	92,487	
Sales		124,345
Inventory[***]		100,000
Unearned interest		28,142

   > [**] On the balance sheet this amount is termed gross investment since it includes an unguaranteed residual value.
   > [***] Either acquisition cost to dealer or manufacturer's cost of production.

   Interest revenue will be recognized at 10% of the outstanding net investment (lease receivable less unearned interest) each period (i.e., interest revenue in year 1 is $131,858 × 10% = $13,186).

   At the end of year 1, the following entry(ies) would be made:

Cash	50,000	
Lease receivable		50,000
Unearned interest revenue	13,186	
Interest revenue		13,186

   At termination, the lease receivable will have a balance of $10,000 which is the unguaranteed residual value. Note that the same amortization schedule that appears in Numerical Example 2 above is applicable to this one. The fact that the residual value is unguaranteed in this example does not affect the amortization schedule because the lessor is projecting that it will get back an asset worth $10,000. If the asset is returned to the lessor and its fair market value is only $4,000, the following entry is made on the lessor's books:

Loss	6,000	
Residual value of equipment	4,000	
Lease receivable		10,000

(e) Now that we have completed our discussion of lessor's direct financing and sales-type leases, it should be helpful to review the financial statement elements for the lessor, and to preview elements that appear on the lessee's financial statements. These elements are shown below.

Lessor

	Direct financing lease	**Sales-type lease**
Balance sheet:	Lease receivable (current and noncurrent)	Lease receivable (current and noncurrent)
	Initial direct costs (added to net investment causing a new implicit rate of interest)	
Income statement:	Unearned interest revenue	Unearned interest revenue
	Interest revenue	Interest revenue
	Amortization of initial direct costs	Initial direct costs (expensed immediately)
		Dealer's profit

Lessee

Capital lease

Balance sheet:	Leased asset (net of accumulated depreciation)
	Lease obligation (current and noncurrent)
Income Statement:	Depreciation expense
	Interest expense
	Other maintenance expense

NOW REVIEW MULTIPLE-CHOICE QUESTIONS 21 THROUGH 24 IN VOLUME 2

---

(4) Capital Leases—Lessee

When a lessor records a direct financing or sales-type lease, the lessee, in turn, must record a capital lease. Capital leases reflect the transfer of risks and benefits associated with the asset to the lessee.

(a) A lease is considered to be a capital lease to the lessee if **any one** of the four criteria is satisfied.

  1] Transfer of title
  2] Bargain purchase
  3] 75% of useful life
  4] 90% of net FV

  a] Lease agreements not meeting at least one of the criteria for capital leases are treated as operating leases on the lessee's books. If the lease is classified as a capital lease, the lessee must record an asset and a liability based on the present value of the minimum lease payments as follows:

Leased asset	(PV of MLP)	
Lease obligation		(PV of MLP)

  b] The above entry reflects recording the transaction "net" (i.e., at present value). If the lease was recorded gross, the lease obligation would be credited for the total amount of the MLP and there would be a debit to "Discount on lease obligation."

Leased asset	(PV of MLP)	
Discount on lease obligation	(plug)	
Lease obligation		(gross MLP)

(b) The gross method is similar to the accounting for deferred payment contracts.

(c) To determine the present value of the MLP, the lessee discounts the future payments using the **lesser** of

  1] The lessee's incremental borrowing rate, **or**
  2] The lessor's implicit rate if known by the lessee

NOTE: Using a lower interest rate increases the present value.

(d) Leased assets, however, should **not** be recorded at an amount greater than the FV of the asset. If the FV is less than the PV of the MLP, the lease should be recorded at the FV and a new implicit interest rate calculated to reflect a constant periodic rate applied to the remaining balance of the obligation.

(e) During the term of the lease, the lessee must use the (effective) interest method to allocate cash paid between interest expense and reduction of the lease obligation. This method is the same as the one used by the lessor as previously described.

(f) Lessees must amortize leased assets recorded on the books under a capital lease. The amortization (depreciation) method used should be consistent with the lessee's normal depreciation policy. The term over which the asset is amortized may differ depending upon which criteria qualified the lease as a capital lease.

  1] If the lease transfers ownership or contains a BPO (criteria 1 or 2), the asset will be amortized over its estimated useful life (since the asset actually becomes the property of the lessee at the end of the lease term and will be used for the remainder of its useful life).

  2] If the 75% of useful life or the 90% test (criteria 3 or 4) is met, the leased asset is amortized over the lease term only (since the property will revert to the lessor at the end of the lease term and will be used for the remainder of its useful life).

(g) The lease term does not extend beyond the date of a bargain purchase option. Lease terms, however, may include the following:

1] Bargain renewal periods
2] Periods when the lessor has the option to renew or extend
3] Periods during which the lessee guarantees the debt of the lessor
4] Periods in which a material penalty exists for failure to renew

(h) When the lease terminates, the balance in the obligation account should equal the bargain purchase option price or the expected residual value (guaranteed residual value, or salvage value if lower).

1] Leased assets and obligations should be disclosed as such in the balance sheet. The lease obligation should be separated into both current and noncurrent components.

EXAMPLE 4

Lease Information

1) A three-year lease is initiated on 1/1/11 for equipment with an expected useful life of five years. The equipment reverts back to the lessor upon expiration of the lease agreement.
2) Three payments are due to the lessor in the amount of $50,000 per year **beginning 12/31/11**. An additional sum of $1,000 is to be paid annually by the lessee for insurance.
3) Lessee guarantees a $10,000 residual value on 12/31/13 to the lessor.
4) The leased asset is expected to have only a $7,000 salvage value on 12/31/13 despite the $10,000 residual value guarantee; therefore, the asset should be depreciated down to the $7,000 expected residual value.
5) The lessee's incremental borrowing rate is 10% (same as lessor's implicit rate).
6) The present value of the lease obligation is

PV of guaranteed residual value	=	$10,000	×	.7513	=	$ 7,513
PV of annual payments	=	$50,000	×	2.4869	=	124,345
						$131,858

Since the lessee's incremental borrowing rate is 10% and the residual value is guaranteed, the present value of $131,858 is the same amount used by the lessor in the direct financing lease example (Numerical Example 2) to determine the payments to be made by the lessee. If an incremental borrowing rate different than the lessor's is used and/or the lease contains an unguaranteed residual value, the present value computed by the lessee will differ from the lessor's present value (FV). These differences account for the fact that many leases are not capitalized by lessees because they don't meet the 90% test.

Lease Classification

The 90% test is met because the present value of the minimum lease payments ($131,858) is 100% of the FV of the leased asset.

Accounting for Lease

1) Note that executory costs (e.g., insurance, property taxes, etc.) are not included in the present value calculations
2) The entry to recognize the lease is

1/1/11	Leased equipment	131,858	
	Lease obligation		131,858

3) The entries to record the payments and depreciation are

	12/31/11	12/31/12	12/31/13
Insurance expense	1,000	1,000	1,000
Lease obligation*	36,814	40,496	44,548
Interest expense*	13,186	9,504	5,452
Cash	51,000	51,000	51,000
Depreciation expense**	41,619	41,619	41,620
Accumulated depreciation	41,619	41,619	41,620***

* Refer to the amortization table in the direct financing lease discussion (Numeric Example 2). Note that classification of the lease obligation into current and noncurrent on the lessee's books would parallel classification of the lease receivable on the lessor's books.

NOTE: Classification of the lease obligation into current and noncurrent on the lessee's books would parallel classification of the lease receivable on the lessor's books.

** [($131,858 − 7,000) ÷ 3 years]
*** Rounding error of $1

4) The 12/31/13 entry to record the guaranteed residual value payment (assuming salvage value = estimated residual value = $7,000) and to clear the lease related accounts from the lessee's books is

Lease obligation	10,000	
Accumulated depreciation	124,858	
Cash		3,000
Leased equipment		131,858

If the actual residual value were only $5,000, the credit to "cash" would be $5,000 and a $2,000 loss would be recognized by the lessee.

(i) Remember that leased assets are amortized over the lease term unless title transfers or a bargain purchase option exists—then over the useful life of the leased asset. At the end of the lease, the balance of the lease obligation should equal the guaranteed residual value or the bargain purchase option price. To illustrate, consider the following example.

EXAMPLE 5

Lease Information

1) A three-year lease is initiated on 1/1/11 for equipment with an expected useful life of five years.
2) Three annual $50,000 payments are due the lessor **beginning 1/1/11**.
3) The lessee can exercise a bargain purchase option on 12/31/13 for $10,000. The expected residual value at 12/31/15 is $1,000.
4) The lessee's incremental borrowing rate is 10% (lessor's implicit rate is unknown).

Lease Classification

Although the lease term is for only 60% of the asset's useful life, the lessee would account for this as a capital lease because it contains a bargain purchase option. Also, the PV of the minimum lease payments is greater than 90% of the FV of the leased asset.

Accounting for Lease

1) The present value of the lease obligation is

PV of bargain purchase option	=	$10,000	×	.7513	=	$ 7,513	
PV of annual payments	=	$50,000	×	2.7355	=	136,775	
						$144,288	

2) The following amortization table summarizes the liability amortization:

AMORTIZATION TABLE

Carrying value at beg. of yr. 1		$144,288
Lease payment	$(50,000)	(50,000)
Carrying value at beg. of yr. 1 after first payment		94,288
Interest expense	9,429	
Lease payment	(50,000)	(40,571)
Carrying value at beg. of year 2 after second payment		53,717
Interest expense	5,372	
Lease payment	(50,000)	(44,628)
Carrying value at beg. of yr. 3 after third payment		9,089
Interest expense	911*	911
Bargain purchase option		10,000
Option payment	(10,000)	(10,000)
		--

*   Rounding error of $2

NOTE: This table reflects the fact that the lease is an annuity due with cash payments on 1/1 and interest expense accruals on 12/31; thus, the first payment does not include any interest expense.

3) The entry to record the lease is

1/1/11	Leased equipment	144,288	
	Lease obligation		144,288

4) The entries to record the payments, interest expense, depreciation (amortization) expense, and the exercise of the bargain purchase are

		2011		2012		2013	
1/1	Lease obligation	50,000		40,571		44,628	
	Accrued interest payable or						
	interest expense*			9,429		5,372	
	Cash		50,000		50,000		50,000
12/31	Interest expense	9,429		5,372		911	
	Accrued int. payable		9,429		5,372		
	Lease obligation						911
12/31	Depreciation expense**	28,658		28,658		28,658	
	Accumulated depreciation		28,658		28,658		28,658
12/31	Lease obligation					10,000	
	Cash						10,000

 * If 12/31 accruals are reversed
 ** (143,288 ÷ 5 years)

3. Other Considerations

To supplement the review of lease accounting presented above, the following topics have been selected for further discussion:

 a. Initial direct costs
 b. Sale-leaseback
 c. Disclosure requirements

a. Initial direct costs

(1) Initial direct costs are the lessor's costs directly associated with negotiation and consummation of leases. These costs include commissions, legal fees, credit investigations, document preparation, etc. In operating leases, initial direct costs are capitalized and subsequently amortized to expense in proportion to the recognition of rental revenue (which is usually straight-line).

(2) Initial direct costs of direct financing and sales-type leases are accounted for differently

 (a) In sales-type leases, charge initial direct costs to operations in the year the sale is recorded;
 (b) In direct financing leases add the initial direct costs to the net investment in the lease.
 (c) Compute a new effective interest rate that equates the minimum lease payments and any unguaranteed residual value with the combined outlay for the leased asset and initial direct costs. Finally, the unearned lease (interest) revenue and the initial direct costs are to be amortized to income over the lease term so that a constant periodic rate is earned on the net investment.

b. Sale-leaseback

(1) Sale-leaseback describes a transaction where the owner of property (seller-lessee) sells the property, and then immediately leases all or part of it back from the new owner (buyer-lessor). The important consideration in this type of transaction is the recognition of two separate and distinct economic transactions. It is important, however, to note that there is not a physical transfer of property. First, there is a sale of property, and second, there is a lease agreement for the same property in which the seller is the lessee and the buyer is the lessor. This is illustrated below.

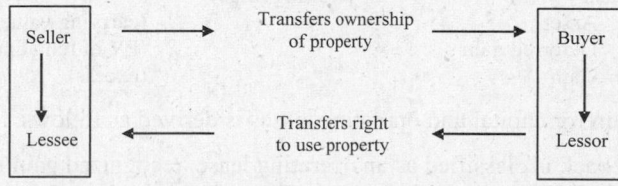

> **NOTE:** Sale-leaseback transactions only affect accounting for the seller-lessee. Buyer-lessor accounting is unaffected.

(2) The accounting treatment from the seller-lessee's point of view will depend upon the degree of rights to use the property retained by the seller-lessee. The degree of rights may be categorized in one of three ways:

 (a) Substantially all
 (b) Minor
 (c) More than minor but less than substantially all

(3) A seller-lessee retains **substantially all** the rights to use the property if the PV of the rental payments is 90% or more of the fair value of the asset sold. This test is based on the criteria used earlier to classify leases. Since the seller-lessee retains use of the asset, this type of sale-leaseback is considered, in substance, a form of financing to the seller-lessee rather than a sale. In this case, any gain on the sale is deferred by the seller-lessee.

Cash	(selling price)	
Asset		(carrying value)
Deferred gain		(excess)

(a) The asset would be reported on the seller-lessee's balance sheet as follows:

Leased asset	xx
Less: Deferred gain	(xx)
	xx

(b) The net value of the leased asset is the same amount the asset would be if it had not been sold.

(c) If the lease is classified as a capital lease, the deferred gain is amortized over the life of the asset at the same rate as the asset is being depreciated. As deferred gain is amortized, it is charged to depreciation expense.

Deferred gain	xx	
Depreciation expense		xx

(d) Alternatively, the gain may be recognized as income over the term of the lease.

(e) Although most leases in the "substantially all" category are capital leases, a sale-leaseback occurring in the last 25% of an asset's economic life would be classified as an operating lease.

(f) If the lease is classified as an operating lease, any deferred gain is amortized over the lease term in proportion to the related gross rental charges to expense over the lease term. Amortization in this case is charged to rent expense by the seller-lessee.

Deferred gain	xx	
Rent expense		xx

(4) The seller-lessee retains only a **minor** portion of rights to use the property when the PV of the rental payments is 10% or less of the fair value of the asset sold. Since the seller-lessee has given up the right to use the asset, the leaseback is considered in substance a sale. Any gain on the sale is recognized in full since the earnings process is considered complete.

Cash	(selling price)	
Asset		(carrying value)
Gain		(excess)

(a) When only a minor portion of use is retained, the seller-lessee accounts for the lease as an operating lease.

(5) The seller-lessee retains **more than a minor portion but less than substantially all** the rights to use the property when the PV of the rental payments is more than 10% but less than 90% of the fair value of the asset sold. In this situation, gain is recognized only to the extent that it exceeds the PV of the rental payments.

Cash	(selling price)	
Asset		(carrying value)
Deferred gain		(PV of rental payments)
Gain		(excess)

(6) Recognized gain for capital and operating leases is derived as follows:

(a) If the leaseback is classified as an operating lease, recognized gain is the portion of gain that exceeds the PV of the MLP over the lease term. The seller-lessee should use its incremental borrowing rate to compute the PV of the MLP. If the implicit rate of interest in the lease is known and lower, it should be used instead.

(b) If the leaseback is classified as a capital lease, recognized gain is the amount of gain that exceeds the recorded amount of the leased asset.

(7) In all cases, the seller-lessee should immediately recognize a loss when the fair value of the property at the time of the leaseback is less than its undepreciated cost (book value). In the example below, the sales price is less than the book value of the property. However, there is no economic loss because the FV which equals the PV is greater than the book value.

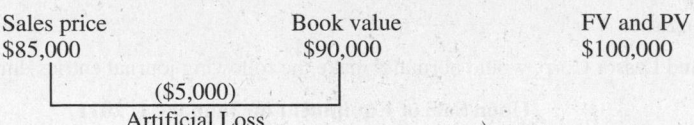

Sales price   Book value   FV and PV
$85,000 $90,000 $100,000

($5,000)
Artificial Loss

(a) The artificial loss must be deferred and amortized as an addition to depreciation.

(8) In the following chart, when the leased asset is land only, any amortization should be on a straight-line basis over the lease term, regardless of whether the lease is classified as a capital or operating lease.

(a) The buyer-lessor should account for the transaction as a purchase and a direct financing lease if the agreement meets the criteria of **either** a direct financing lease **or** a sales-type lease. Otherwise, the agreement should be accounted for as a purchase and an operating lease.

(b) To illustrate a sale-leaseback transaction, consider the example below.

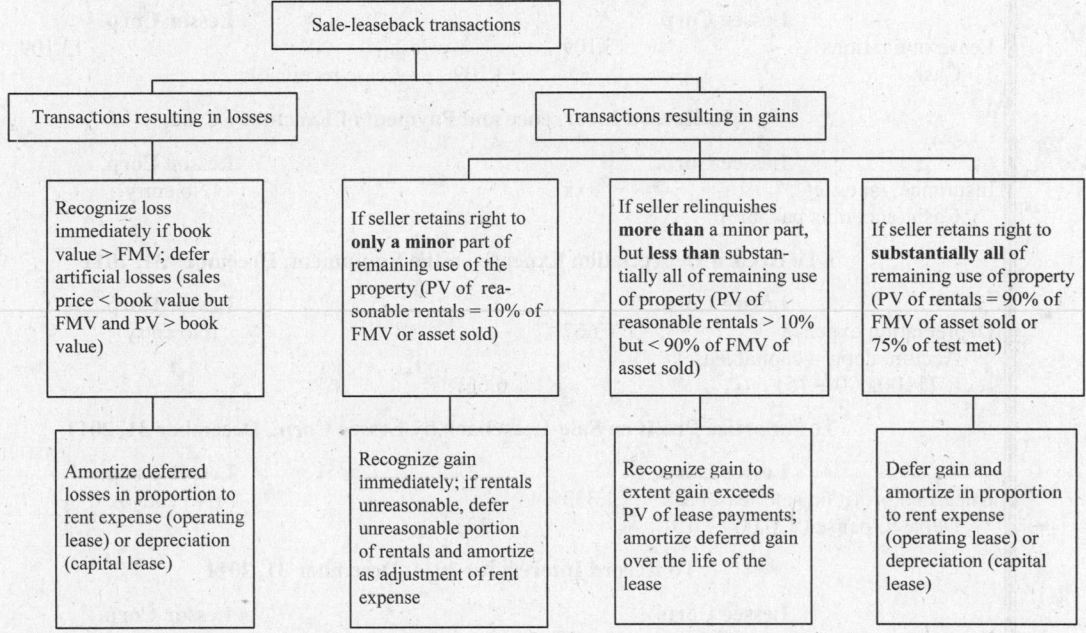

EXAMPLE 6

Lease Information

1) Lessee Corporation sells equipment that has a book value of $80,000 and a fair value of $100,000 to Lessor Corporation, and then immediately leases it back.
2) The sale date is January 1, 2011, and the equipment has a fair value of $100,000 on that date and an estimated useful life of fifteen years.
3) The lease term is fifteen years, noncancelable, and requires equal rental payments of $13,109 at the beginning of each year.
4) Lessee Corp. has the option to renew the lease annually at the same rental payments upon expiration of the original lease.
5) Lessee Corp. has the obligation to pay all executory costs.
6) The annual rental payments provide the lessor with a 12% return on investment.
7) The incremental borrowing rate of Lessee Corp. is 12%.
8) Lessee Corp. depreciates similar equipment on a straight-line basis.

Lease Classification

Lessee Corp. should classify the agreement as a capital lease since the lease term exceeds 75% of the estimated economic life of the equipment, and because the present value of the lease payments is greater than 90% of the fair value of the equipment. Assuming that collectibility of the lease payments is reasonably predictable and that no important uncertainties exist concerning the amount of unreimbursable costs yet to be incurred by the lessor, Lessor Corp. should classify the transaction as a direct financing lease because the present value of the minimum lease payments is equal to the fair market value of $100,000.

Accounting for Lease

Lessee Corp. and Lessor Corp. would normally make the following journal entries during the first year:

Upon Sale of Equipment on January 1, 2011

Lessee Corp.			**Lessor Corp.**		
Cash	100,000		Equipment	100,000	
Equipment		80,000	Cash		100,000
Unearned profit on sale-leaseback		20,000	Lease receivable	196,635*	
			Equipment		100,000
Leased equipment	100,000		Unearned interest		96,635
Lease obligations		100,000			
			* ($13,109 × 15)		

To Record First Payment on January 1, 2011

Lessee Corp.			**Lessor Corp.**		
Lease obligations	13,109		Cash	13,109	
Cash		13,109	Lease receivable		13,109

To Record Incurrence and Payment of Executory Costs

Lessee Corp.		**Lessor Corp.**
Insurance, taxes, etc.	xxx	(No entry)
Cash (accounts payable)	xxx	

To Record Depreciation Expense on the Equipment, December 31, 2011

Lessee Corp.			**Lessor Corp.**
Depreciation expense	6,667		(No entry)
Accum. depr.—capital leases			
($100,000 ÷ 15)		6,667	

To Amortize Profit on Sale-Leaseback by Lessee Corp., December 31, 2011

Lessee Corp.			**Lessor Corp.**
Unearned profit on sale-leaseback	1,333		(No entry)
Depr. Expense ($20,000 ÷ 15)		1,333	

To Record Interest for 2011, December 31, 2011

Lessee Corp.			**Lessor Corp**		
Interest expense	10,427		Unearned interest revenue	10,427	
Accrued interest payable		10,427	Interest revenue		10,427

(Carrying value $86,891 × .12 = $10,427)

c. **Disclosure requirements**

The disclosures required of the lessor and lessee are very comprehensive and detailed. In essence, all terms of the leasing arrangement are required (i.e., contingent rentals, subleases, residual values, unearned interest revenue, etc.). There are, however, some generic disclosure requirements. First, a **general description** of the leasing arrangement is required. Second, the minimum future payments to be received (paid) by the lessor (lessee) for each of the **five succeeding fiscal years** should also be disclosed.

SUMMARY OF KEY PROBLEM SOLUTION POINTS

(1) **Lessor—direct financing and sales-type leases**

    (a) Periodic lease payments (PLP)

$$= \frac{\text{FV of leased property–PV of RV*/BPO}}{\text{PV of an annuity factor** using the lessor's implicit rate}}$$

    * Guaranteed/unguaranteed
  ** Annuity due or ordinary

    (b) Lease payments receivable/Gross investments = (Periodic lease payments × Number of rents) + Residual value/BPO

    (c) Unearned interest revenue = Gross investment – PV of PLP, PV of G/U RV, PV of BPO

    (d) Net investment = Gross investment – Unearned interest revenue

   (e)   Gross profit (only for sales-type leases)   =   Selling price* – Cost of leased asset sold

        * (FV/PV of PLP + G/URV + BPO)

   (f)   Interest revenue   =   Carrying value of lease receivable* × Implicit % × Time

        * (Gross investment – Unearned interest revenue)

Periodic Journal Entries

Unearned interest revenue	xxx	
Interest revenue		xxx
Cash	xxx	
Lease payments receivable		xxx

(2) Lessee—capital lease

   (a)   Determine capital   =   (Periodic lease payment [PLP] × Present value factor *) +
           lease liability   (G/URV or BPO × PV of 1.00 factor)

        * Annuity due or ordinary annuity

- Use lessee's incremental borrowing %, unless lessor's implicit % is lower and lessee knows it
- PLP is exclusive of executory costs

   (b)   Leased asset   =   Capital lease liability at inception of lease as computed above—PV ×
                                MLP [Exception: where FV of leased asset < PV of MLP (PLP +
                                GRV or BPO), then leased asset and capital lease liability are
                                recorded at the FV of leased asset.]

   (c)   Depreciation   •   Over useful life, regardless of lease term, if either criterion (1) or (2) is
           (amortization) of   met: title transfer or bargain purchase option.
           leased asset

- Over lease term if criterion (3) or (4) is met: ≥ 75% test or ≥ 90% test

   (d)   Lease liability   =   (1) Carrying value at inception of lease $xxx
                              (2) Less first payment (usually the first payment is all principal   (xx)
                                   because the lease liability is the PV of an annuity due)
                            (3) Carrying value (CV) $xxx
   (e)   CV × % = Interest   (4) Less principal part of second payment [PLP – (CV × interest %)] (xxx)
           expense   (5) Carrying value $xxx
                                                                                 etc.

NOW REVIEW MULTIPLE-CHOICE QUESTIONS 25 THROUGH 56 IN VOLUME 2

---

4. **Research Component—Accounting Standards Codification**

   a. The accounting rules for leases are found in the area of the Codification labeled "Broad Transactions" under Topic 840 Broad Transactions—Leases is divided into the following subtopics:

Broad Transactions	
840-10	Overall
840-20	Operating Leases
840-30	Capital Leases
840-40	Sales-Leaseback Transactions

   b. Care should be taken when researching this area of the standards, as the rules for lessee and lessor are intertwined throughout each section of the Codification. Candidates should take special care to read the titles of each subtopic and section to ensure the question is answered appropriately for either the lessee or lessor. Typical research questions may include determining whether a lease is an operating lease or a capital lease or determining which items to include in calculating the minimum lease payments.

   c. Keywords are shown below.

Bargain purchase option	Lease modification	Sales-type lease
Capital lease	Leasehold improvement	Substantial rights
Costs to terminate	Minimum lease payments	Termination costs
Direct financing lease	Modified lease	Termination of agreement
Guaranteed residual	New agreement operating lease	Transfer title
Initial direct costs	Operating lease	Unguaranteed residual
Lease bonus	Sale-leaseback	

5. **International Financial Reporting Standards (IFRS)**

  a. Leasing is a topic where the IASB rules focus on substance over form. Unlike US GAAP, which uses certain thresholds to determine whether a lease should be classified as a capital lease, IAS 17 classifies leases based on whether substantially all the risks or benefits of ownership have been transferred. Leasing is also a topic where subtle terminology differences exist, for example, capital lease (US GAAP) versus finance lease (IFRS).

  b. **Criteria for treatment of leases.** Under US GAAP, a lessee classifies a lease as either an operating lease or a capital lease. For the lessor, the lease is classified as an operating lease, a direct-financing lease, or a sales-type lease. However, under IAS 17 the lease is classified as either an operating lease or a finance lease for the lessee and the lessor. Of course, with a finance lease, the lessor is usually financing the item, or, if the lessor is a manufacturer or dealer, the lessor is selling the item through the leasing process.

  c. Lease payments under an operating lease are recognized as expense on a straight-line basis over the lease term. The lessee must disclose in the footnotes the total future minimum payments for the next 12 months, payments due in Years 2-5, and payments due after five years, as well as a general description of the lease terms and restrictions imposed by the lease.

  d. IFRS provides that a lease is a finance lease if substantially all of the risks or benefits of ownership have been transferred to the lessee. If any one of the four criteria is met, the lease is considered a finance lease.

    (1) The lease transfers ownership to the lessee by the end of the lease term or the lease contains a bargain purchase option, and it is reasonably certain that the option will be exercised.

    (2) The lease term is for the major part of the economic life of the asset (title may or may not pass to the lessee).

    (3) The present value of the minimum lease payments at the inception of the lease is at least equal to substantially all of the fair value of the leased asset.

    (4) The leased assets are of a specialized nature such that only the lessee can use them without modifications.

      (a) Although these four criteria are similar to the rules under US GAAP, notice that these rules do not carry specific thresholds such as 75% of the economic life or 90% of the fair value of the leased asset. Therefore, the proper classification is determined based on judgments about the substance of the transaction.

      (b) In addition, the following three other circumstances may indicate that the lease should be treated as a finance lease:

        1] If the lessee can cancel the lease, and the lessor's losses are borne by the lessee.

        2] Gains or losses resulting from the fluctuations in fair value will accrue to the lessee.

        3] The lessee has the ability to continue the lease for a supplemental term at a rent substantially lower than market value.

  e. Under IFRS, a lease is classified as either an operating or a finance lease at the inception of the lease. The inception of the lease is the earlier of the date of the lease agreement or the date of commitment to the lease agreement. The commencement date of the lease term is the date on which the lessee is entitled to use the leased asset. Although the lease must be classified as either an operating or a finance lease on the date of inception, the lease is not recognized in the financial statements until the commencement date when the lessee is entitled to use the asset.

  f. Another significant difference in classifying leases arises when land and buildings are leased together. Because land has an indefinite life, if title does not pass by the end of the lease term, the substantial risks and rewards of ownership do not transfer. Thus, in such cases the land lease cannot be classified as a finance lease. Under IFRS, the land and building would be treated as separate components; the land lease would be classified as an operating lease, and the building lease would be classified as a finance lease (assuming substantially all risks and rewards of ownership transferred). The minimum lease payments would be allocated between the land and the buildings elements in proportion to the relative fair values of the leasehold interests of each element. If both elements of the lease are expected to pass to the lessee at the end of the lease term, then the entire lease is classified as a finance lease.

    (1) **Accounting by lessees.** Under IFRS, the finance lease is recorded as an asset and as a liability by the lessee at the fair value of the leased property at the inception of the lease or the present value of the minimum lease payments. For the lessee, the minimum lease payments include the payments over the lease term that are required to be made, the bargain purchase option, and amounts guaranteed by the lessee. For the lessor, the minimum lease payments also include any residual value guaranteed by a third party not related to the lessor.

      (a) The interest rate used to calculate the present value of the minimum lease payments is the implicit rate. However, if the implicit rate cannot be determined, then the lessee's incremental borrowing rate is used. Any indirect costs incurred by the lessee in connection with negotiating and arranging the lease are added to the cost of the asset.

(b) Each period the minimum lease payments are apportioned between the finance charge and the reduction of the principal outstanding. Any contingent rents are charged to expense as they are incurred. In addition, depreciation expense should be recognized for the leased asset. If ownership transfers at the end of the lease term, then the asset is depreciated over its useful life. If ownership does not transfer, then the finance lease is depreciated over the shorter of the lease term or the asset's useful life.

(c) Disclosures required for leases include the net carrying amount at the end of the reporting period, the future minimum lease payments at the end of the reporting period, and the present value of the lease payments due within one year, due after one year and less than five years, and after five years. Disclosures should also indicate the contingent rents recognized as expense during the period, a description of the lease, and its terms and restrictions.

(2) **Accounting by lessors.** In a finance lease, the asset is removed from the lessor's balance sheet, and the net investment in the lease is recorded as an asset. The net investment in the lease is calculated as gross lease receivables less the unearned finance income (interest income).

(a) Similar to US GAAP, a manufacturer or dealer will recognize the sale, cost of goods sold, lease receivable, and unearned finance income.

(b) **Sales and leaseback.** A sale and leaseback transaction may be classified as either an operating lease or a finance lease. The same criteria (risk and benefits of ownership, substance over form) determine whether the sale and leaseback is an operating or a finance lease. If it is classified as a finance lease, the gain is deferred and amortized over the lease term. If it is classified as an operating lease, the profit or loss is recognized immediately. If it is an operating lease and the fair value at the time of the sale and leaseback transaction is less than the carrying amount of the asset, then a loss is recognized immediately.

> **NOW REVIEW MULTIPLE-CHOICE QUESTIONS 57 THROUGH 60 IN VOLUME 2**

KEY TERMS

Bargain purchase option (BPO). Allows the lessee to purchase leased property for an amount substantially lower than the expected FMV at the exercise date of the option.

Capital lease. A lease that transfers substantially all of the benefits and risks incident to the ownership of property.

Guaranteed residual value (GRV) . A guaranteed residual value of the leased asset at the end of the lease.

Initial direct costs. Costs in setting up the lease agreement.

Lease. A contract between two parties—a lessor and a lessee that gives a lessee rights to use the lessor's property for a specified period of time in return for periodic cash payments (rent) to the lessor.

Minimum lease payments (MLP). The payments that the lessor/lessee is or can be required to make in connection with the leased property.

Operating lease. The risks and rewards of owning the asset remain with the lessor.

Unguaranteed residual value. The estimated residual value of the leased asset at the end of the lease.

Module 14: Deferred Taxes

Overview

Income for financial reporting purposes (book income) and income for tax purposes (taxable income) usually differ. Differences are due to the fact that for financial reporting, firms are required to follow GAAP. However, for tax purposes, firms must follow the Internal Revenue Code. The differences can either (1) permanently differ, in which case there is no deferral, or (2) reverse over time (e.g., straight line depreciation is used for book purposes and MACRS is used for tax purposes) which leads to a temporary difference or deferred tax.

ASC Topic 740, *Income Taxes* (SFAS 109), requires an asset and liability (balance sheet) approach to recognizing and measuring deferred taxes. This means that Income Tax Expense reporting in a firm's GAAP financial statements is a function of the current taxes owed to the Internal Revenue Service (Income Tax Payable) and the deferred taxes. To understand the basic concepts of deferred taxes, study this module and the outlines of SFAS 109 and APB 23 (ASC Topic 740).

A. Overview of Deferred Tax Theory

1. There are numerous differences between the recognition and measurement of pretax financial (book) income and asset/liability valuation under GAAP and the recognition and measurement of taxable income and asset/liability valuation under the Internal Revenue Code. Because of these differences between the two bodies of promulgated rules, pretax financial (book) income usually differs from taxable income. The amount of Income Tax Expense and the amount of Income Taxes Payable are, therefore, often different amounts.

2. Financial income tax expense (the **current and deferred** tax consequences of **all** events that have been recognized in the financial statements) is charged to Income Tax Expense.

   a. Income Tax Expense equals the taxes actually owed (a current tax liability) for the current period plus or minus the change during the current period in amounts payable in the future and in future tax benefits.

      (1) By using this procedure, any possible income statement or balance sheet distortion that may result from differences in the timing of revenue recognition or expense deductibility and asset or liability valuation between GAAP and the Internal Revenue Code is avoided.

      (2) The Income Tax Expense reported in the entity's income statement reflects the amount of taxes related to transactions recognized in the financial statements prepared under GAAP for the specific period.

      (3) The deferred tax asset or liability (the difference between Income Tax Expense and Income Tax Payable) reported in the entity's balance sheet clearly reflects the amount of taxes that the entity has prepaid (an asset) or will have to pay in the future (a liability) because of temporary differences that result from differences in timing of revenue recognition or expense deductibility between GAAP and the Internal Revenue Code.

B. Permanent and Temporary Differences Defined

Differences between pretax financial (book) income and taxable income can be divided into two types: temporary differences or permanent differences. The Codification does **not** use the term permanent differences. However, to ease our explanation and your comprehension, the term "permanent difference" will be used in this module, as it is in several intermediate accounting textbooks.

1. **Temporary Differences**

    A temporary difference is "a difference between the tax basis of an asset or liability and its reported amount in the financial statements that will result in taxable or deductible amounts in future years when the reported amount of the asset or liability is recovered or settled, respectively."

    a. This definition of a temporary difference is based on the assumption that assets and liabilities reported on an entity's balance sheet will eventually be recovered or settled at their net reported (book) value.

        (1) This recovery or settling process will create income statement items (revenues/gains or expenses/losses) as the life of the asset or liability progresses.

        (2) If the reported financial (book) value of the balance sheet item differs from its tax basis, the correct period for recognition of the related income statement item will differ between the entity's financial statements and the entity's tax return. Thus, from an income statement perspective, a temporary difference occurs when a revenue or expense item: (1) is included in both financial accounting income and taxable income, **and,** (2) is recognized in one period for financial accounting purposes and in another period for income tax purposes because of differences between the promulgated rules of GAAP and the Internal Revenue Code.

            (a) If such a temporary difference exists, an amount will be recorded and reported as either a deferred tax liability or a deferred tax asset depending upon the relationship between the reported net financial (book) value and the tax basis of the related asset or liability.

            (b) When the temporary difference reverses, the recorded deferred tax amount is removed from the balance sheet; the amount removed results in an increase or decrease in income tax expense. Some examples of temporary differences are presented below.

                1] **Estimated warranty liability:** Expense recognized in the financial statements when the liability is incurred. Deduction recognized for tax purposes when the work is actually performed.

                2] **Unearned rent (royalty) revenue:** Recognized in the financial statements as a liability when the rent (royalty) is received and as revenue when earned. Recognized as revenue for tax purposes when the cash is received. (Note that the Internal Revenue Code refers to revenue received in advance as "prepaid income," not "unearned revenue.")

                3] **Plant assets and accumulated depreciation:** Changes in these assets and the related contra asset are recognized in the financial statements according to depreciation methods acceptable to GAAP. Changes in these assets and the related contra asset are usually recognized for tax purposes according to accelerated methods acceptable to the IRS such as ACRS and MACRS. Note that recovery of these assets occurs as the asset is used in the entity's operations to generate revenue. In essence, a portion of the investment in the asset is being recovered as the product or service is sold.

                4] **Donated asset:** According to GAAP, initial valuation in the financial statements of a donated asset is based upon fair market value, and revenue is recognized for the same amount. Depreciation on the asset is computed according to the entity's normal policies. Upon sale of the asset, a gain is recognized for the difference between cash received and net book value. According to the Internal Revenue Code, a donated asset has the same basis for the donee as it did in the donor's hands. Thus, no tax deductions for depreciation are allowed for the asset if the tax basis is zero. When the asset is sold, the entire amount received is a taxable gain.

                5] **Involuntary conversion of assets:** According to GAAP, a gain (loss) must be recognized when a nonmonetary asset is involuntarily converted into a monetary asset, even though the entity reinvests the monetary assets in replacement nonmonetary assets. The replacement asset is valued at its cost or fair value on date of acquisition. According to the Internal Revenue Code, no gain is recognized on an involuntary conversion if the amount reinvested in replacement property equals or exceeds the amount realized from the converted property. The tax basis of the replacement asset is valued at its cost less the deferred gain.

                6] **Goodwill:** Under GAAP, goodwill is not amortized. The Internal Revenue Code however, mandates an amortization period of fifteen years.

2. **Permanent Differences**

    A permanent difference occurs when a revenue or expense item is only included in pretax financial (book) income or in taxable income but will never be included in both. For example, interest income on municipal bonds is included in pretax financial (book) income but is never included in taxable income because it is tax exempt by law.

    a. No deferred taxes need to be recognized because no future tax consequences are created.
    b. The tax exempt income (or deduction not allowed for taxes) is simply subtracted from (or added to) book income in the book to tax reconciliation. Thus, a permanent difference affects only the current reconciliation of book income to taxable income, and has no effect on the computation of deferred taxes. Some common permanent differences are

(1) **State and municipal bond interest income:** included in book income but not included in taxable income.

(2) **Life insurance premium expense when the corporation is the beneficiary:** deducted for book income but not for taxable income; proceeds received on such policies result in a book gain but are not taxable.

(3) **Federal income tax expense:** deducted for book income but not for taxable income.

(4) **Payment of penalty or fine:** deducted for book income but not for taxable income.

(5) **Dividend received deduction (DRD):** deducted for taxable income but not for book income.

c. The example below shows how permanent and temporary differences are used in calculating taxable income, given a corporation's pretax financial (book) income.

EXAMPLE 1

A corporation has pretax financial accounting (book) income of $146,000 in 2010. Additional information is as follows:

1. Municipal bond interest income is $35,000.
2. Life insurance premium expense, where the corporation is the beneficiary, per books is $4,000.
3. Accelerated depreciation is used for tax purposes, while straight-line is used for books. Tax depreciation is $10,000; book depreciation is $5,000.
4. Estimated warranty expense of $500 is accrued for book purposes.

Taxable income can be determined as follows:

Financial (book) income before income taxes	$146,000
Permanent differences	
Life insurance premium	4,000
Municipal bond interest	(35,000)
Temporary differences	
Amount added to tax accum. depr. and deducted on the tax return >	
Amount added to book accum. deprec. and deprec. exp.	(5,000)
Amount recognized for book estimated warranty	
liability and warranty exp. not recognized on the tax return	500
Taxable income	$110,500

The above schedule is known as the reconciliation of book income to taxable income. It is similar to the Schedule M-1 of the US Corporate Income Tax Return (Form 1120) except it starts with pretax financial accounting income instead of net income as Schedule M-1 does.

NOTE: The permanent differences only impact the current year (2010 in this case) whereas the temporary differences will have future tax consequences.

NOW REVIEW MULTIPLE-CHOICE QUESTIONS 1 THROUGH 5 IN VOLUME 2

C. Deferred Tax Assets and Liabilities

A **deferred tax asset** is the deferred tax consequences attributable to deductible temporary differences and carryforwards. The deferred tax asset must be reduced by a valuation account if a portion or all of the deferred tax asset will not be realized in the future. A **deferred tax liability** is defined as an amount that is recognized for the deferred tax consequence of temporary differences that will result in taxable amounts in future years. Discounting of these deferred tax assets and liabilities is not permitted.

1. **Identification and Measurement of Deferred Tax Items**

NOTE: The candidate's ability to work an income tax accounting problem depends upon his/her ability to correctly identify permanent and temporary differences. In order to recognize the tax consequences of a temporary difference, it must be the result of event(s) that have already been recognized in the entity's financial statements for the current or previous years. With regard to a fixed asset, this means that the fixed asset has been acquired before the end of the year for which income taxes are being determined. Thus, planned asset acquisitions for future years cannot result in temporary differences and thereby affect the determination of deferred income taxes.

a. A **temporary difference** between pretax financial (book) income and taxable income occurs when the tax basis of an asset (or liability) differs from its reported financial statement amount. As shown in Example 1, a temporary difference resulting from timing of GAAP recognition vs. timing of recognition for tax purposes can create the need for additions to or subtractions from book income in order to arrive at taxable income.

(1) These **additions (taxable amounts) or subtractions (deductible amounts)** can occur in the year an event takes place and a deferred asset or liability is incurred as well to account for future years when the asset is recovered or the liability is settled.

(2) The table below presents the various possible relationships between financial statement (book) and tax recognition of revenue and expense and assets and liabilities as well as the nature of the resulting future tax consequences.

Acctg. Income > or < taxable income*	B/S relationships	Temp. differ.** Cur.	Fut.	Type of BS tax deferral	Current deferred tax expense effect	Future deferred tax expense effect
	Assets					
>	(1) on books > tax return	D	T	Liability	(+)	(−)
<	(2) on books < tax return	T	D	Asset	(−)	(+)
	Liabilities					
<	(3) on books > tax return	T	D	Asset	(−)	(+)
	(4) on books < tax return	D	T	Liability	(+)	(−)

* Relationship in the year the temporary difference originates.
** Deductible (D) /Taxable (T).

 (a) For example, a type 1 temporary difference (such as the difference between the financial statement amount and the **zero** tax basis of an asset obtained by a donation) creates a deferred tax liability.

  1] If the donated asset is sold for more than its tax basis, recognition of the difference between the asset's financial statement amount and its tax return basis results in a gain for taxable income and either a smaller gain or a loss for book income depending on the amount of book depreciation taken on the asset since it was received by the enterprise. The amount of cash that will be needed to pay the taxes due will be increased because the entire amount of cash received for the donated asset will be reported as gain (taxable amount) on the tax return.

  2] A liability is defined in SFAC 6 as "probable future sacrifices of economic benefits arising from present obligations of a particular entity to transfer assets...as a result of past transactions or events." The increase in cash paid out for taxes (a sacrifice of economic benefits) will result when the donated asset (from a past transaction or event) is disposed of; therefore, the future tax impact of the current period difference between financial statement value and tax basis represents a deferred liability. When the liability is recognized, deferred income tax expense is also recognized.

 (b) In contrast, a contingent liability recognized in the current period financial statements represents a type 3 temporary difference because a contingent liability has a zero basis for tax accounting. The amount of expense stemming from this contingent liability must be added back to financial (book) income to arrive at taxable income. Therefore, a deferred tax asset is created.

  1] When the probable and measurable future event does actually occur, the contingent liability will then represent a loss (deductible amount) on the tax return. Because the tax loss recognized will reduce taxable income and income taxes payable, the amount of cash that will be needed to pay the taxes due will be decreased.

  2] Remember, an asset is defined in SFAC 6 as a "probable future economic benefit obtained or controlled by a particular entity as a result of past transactions or events." The reduction of current tax expense and the resulting future decrease in cash paid out for taxes (an economic benefit) will result from the contingent liability (a past transaction or event). Therefore, the future tax impact of the current period difference between the financial statement value and tax basis represents a deferred tax asset in the year the contingency is recognized.

> **NOTE:** The deferred tax expense recorded in this situation is a credit because it represents a current period benefit.

2. **Scheduling and Recording Deferred Tax Amounts**

 a. An entity's total income statement provision for income taxes is the sum of that entity's current and deferred tax amounts.

  (1) The **current tax expense or benefit** is defined by ASC Topic 740 (SFAS 109) as "the amount of income taxes paid or payable (or refundable) for a year as determined by applying the provisions of the tax law to the taxable income or excess of deductions over revenues for that year."

  (2) The **deferred tax expense or benefit** is defined as "the change during the year in an enterprise's deferred tax liabilities or assets."

  (3) Current and deferred tax amounts are computed independently.

b. The deferred tax amount (the future tax consequences of temporary differences) should be recorded in the current financial statements at the amounts that will be paid or recovered based upon tax laws and rates that are already in place and due to be in effect at the date of payment or recovery.

    (1) These are known as **enacted** tax laws and **enacted** tax rates. An entity must, therefore, determine when the identified and measured temporary differences will become taxable or deductible.
    (2) Future **taxable amounts** cause taxable income to be greater than financial (book) income in future periods. They are a result of existing temporary differences and are reported as deferred tax liabilities in the current year.
    (3) Future **deductible amounts** cause taxable income to be less than financial (book) income in future periods. They are a result of existing temporary differences and are reported as a deferred tax asset in the current year.
    (4) For illustrative purposes, the following examples show the scheduling of future temporary differences.

    > **NOTE:** In practice and on the CPA exam, extensive scheduling is generally not necessary unless (1) there is a change in future enacted tax rates or (2) the problem requires the use of a valuation allowance account.

c. Deferred tax liabilities and assets are determined separately for each tax-paying component (an individual entity or group of entities that is consolidated for tax purposes) in each tax jurisdiction. That determination includes the following procedures:

    (1) Identify the types and amounts of existing temporary differences.
    (2) Identify the nature and amount of each type of operating loss and tax credit carryforward and the remaining length of the carryforward period.
    (3) Measure the total deferred tax liability for taxable temporary differences using the applicable tax rate.
    (4) Measure the total deferred tax asset for deductible temporary differences and operating loss carryforwards using the applicable tax rate.
    (5) Measure deferred tax assets for each type of tax credit carryforward.
    (6) Reduce deferred tax assets by a valuation allowance if, based on the weight of available evidence, it is *more likely than not* (a likelihood of more than 50%) that some portion or all of the deferred tax assets will not be realized. The valuation allowance should be sufficient to reduce the deferred tax asset to the amount that is more likely than not to be realized.
    (7) Deferred tax assets and liabilities are **not** discounted to reflect their present value.

EXAMPLE 2

This example shows the **deferred tax accounting in 2010, 2011, and 2012** for the temporary differences included in Example 1 earlier in this module. Additional details are

a. On 1/1/08 the enterprise acquired a depreciable asset for $30,000 that had an estimated life of six years and is depreciated on a straight-line basis for book purposes. For tax purposes, the asset is depreciated using the straight-line election under MACRS and qualifies as a three-year asset.
b. The enterprise deducted warranty expense of $500 for book purposes in 2010 that is expected to be deductible for tax purposes in 2011.
c. Taxable income was $110,500 in 2010, $112,000 in 2011, and $113,500 in 2012.
d. The applicable tax rate is 40% for all years affected.

The deferred component of income tax expense for 2010 is computed as follows. First, a schedule of **the temporary depreciation differences** for all affected years is prepared:

	2008	2009	2010	2011	2012	2013
Book depreciation	$ 5,000	$ 5,000	$ 5,000	$5,000	$5,000	$5,000
Tax depreciation	5,000*	10,000	10,000	5,000*	--	--
Temporary difference:						
No difference	$ 0			$ 0		
Book deprec. < Tax deprec.		$(5,000)	$(5,000)			
Book deprec. > Tax deprec.					$5,000	$5,000

*   Due to MACRS half-year convention

Then, a schedule of **future taxable (deductible) amounts** is prepared.

	2011 Taxable (deductible)	2012 Taxable (deductible)	2013 Taxable (deductible)	Tax rate	Deferred tax liability (asset)
Scheduled taxable (deductible) amounts:					
Depreciation differences:					
taxable amounts		$5,000	$5000	40%	$4,000 Noncurrent
Warranty differences:					
deductible amounts	$(500)			40%	$(200) Current

The above schedule shows that the future tax benefit (deductible amount) in 2011 of the $500 temporary difference resulting from the Warranty Expense Liability must be recognized automatically as a deferred tax asset in 2010. The deferred tax asset of $200 ($500 × 40%) should be reported as a current asset at 12/31/10 because the classification of the temporary difference is based on the related asset or liability, in this case a warranty liability that is expected to be satisfied in the next year. The amount of future taxes payable (deferred tax liability) associated with the total temporary difference of $10,000 resulting from excess depreciation [$5,000 (2010) + $5,000 (2011)] is $4,000 [($5,000 + 5,000) × 40%]. The $4,000 amount is reported as a noncurrent deferred tax liability at 12/31/10, because classification as current or noncurrent is based on the classification of the related asset or liability, in this case a depreciable asset that is noncurrent.

Once the deferred tax asset and deferred tax liability have been measured at year-end, a journal entry is necessary to adjust the deferred tax account balances to the current year-end amount. As stated earlier, income tax expense for the year will consist of the taxes currently payable (based on taxable income) plus or minus any change in the deferred tax accounts.

EQUATION FOR DETERMINING INCOME TAX EXPENSE

$$\begin{array}{ccccc} \text{Income tax} & & \text{Income tax} & & \text{Change in} \\ \text{expense for} & = & \text{payable from} & \pm & \text{deferred} \\ \text{financial reporting} & & \text{the tax return} & & \text{taxes (net)*} \end{array}$$

* Ending balance of deferred tax liability/asset (net) less beginning balance of deferred tax liability/asset (net)

Notes:
1. Income Tax Expense is the sum of the two numbers on the right side of the equation. Each of these two numbers is determined directly using independent calculations. It is not possible to derive Income Tax Expense from pretax financial accounting income adjusted for permanent differences, unless the tax rate is constant for all years affected.
2. The $\pm$ refers to whether the change is a credit or additional liability (+) or a debit or additional asset (–).
3. Income Tax Payable is the amount of taxes calculated on the corporate tax return. It is the amount legally owed the government (after credits).
4. One deferred tax (net) balance sheet account may be used in practice. If separate asset and liability accounts are used, the changes in each account would all be netted to determine the deferred tax component of income tax expense.

EXAMPLE

To illustrate, we will use the deferred tax liability computed in Example 2 above and the taxable income derived in Example 1. Note that at the end of 2010, but prior to adjustment, the deferred tax asset account had a zero balance and the deferred tax liability account had a balance of $2,000 ($5,000 × 40%) that was recognized as a result of the accumulated depreciation temporary difference that originated in 2008. (Refer to the schedule following the additional information given in Example 2 showing depreciation and the pattern of temporary differences and to the T-account under (c) below.) To focus on the two components of income tax expense, two entries rather than the typical combined entry will be used.

Income tax expense—current	44,200	
Income tax payable (a)		44,200

(a) $110,500 taxable income (from Example 1) × 40% = $44,200

Income tax expense—deferred (d)	1,800	
Deferred tax asset—current (b)	200	
Deferred tax liability—noncurrent (c)		2,000

(b) $500 × 40% = $200 needed Ending balance; $200 Ending balance – $0 Beginning balance = $200 increase needed in the account

```
                    Deferred Tax Asset
Beg. bal.                  0
Increase (b)             200
End. bal.                200
```

(c) $10,000 × 40% = $4,000 needed Ending balance; $4,000 Ending balance − $2,000 Beginning balance = $2,000 increase needed in the account

```
          Deferred Tax Liability
                              2,000    Beg. bal.
                              2,000    Increase (c)
                              4,000    End. bal.
```

(d) $2,000 increase in noncurrent deferred tax liability account − $200 increase in current deferred tax asset account = $1,800

The bottom of the income statement for 2010 would appear as follows:

Income before income tax		$146,000
Income tax expense		
Current	$44,200	
Deferred	1,800	46,000
Net income		$100,000

To determine the deferred component of income tax expense for **2010,** a schedule of future taxable (deductible) amounts is prepared.

	2011 Taxable (deductible)	2012 Taxable (deductible)	2013 Taxable (deductible)	Tax rate	Deferred tax liability (asset)
Scheduled taxable (deductible) amounts:					
Depreciation differences:					
taxable amounts	-0-	$5,000	$5,000	40%	$4,000 Noncurrent

The temporary depreciation difference of $10,000 results in future taxes payable (a deferred tax liability) of $4,000 [($5,000 + 5,000) × 40%]. Note that the amount of the deferred tax liability in this example does not change from 2010 to 2011. The $4,000 amount would be reported as a noncurrent deferred tax liability at 12/31/11, based upon the noncurrent classification of the related depreciable asset. The $500 warranty expense deducted in 2010 for book purposes is deducted in 2011 for tax purposes. Therefore, the deferred tax asset related to warranty expense is realized in 2011 and the temporary difference related to warranty expense no longer exists.

Once the deferred tax amounts have been measured at year-end, a journal entry is required to adjust the deferred tax account balances to the current year-end amount. Income tax expense for the year consists of the taxes currently payable plus or minus any change in the deferred tax accounts. The following journal entries are needed to record income tax expense for 2011:

```
Income tax expense—current            44,800
    Income tax payable (a)                        44,800
```

(a) $112,000 taxable income x 40% = $44,800

```
Income tax expense deferred (c)          200
    Deferred tax asset current (b)                  200
```

(b) The credit to the deferred tax asset is the adjustment necessary to reduce the existing balance to the desired ending balance.

```
              Deferred Tax Asset
Beg. bal.          200
                              200    Decrease (b)
End. bal.            0
```

(c) Income tax expense—deferred results from the decrease in the deferred tax asset. There is no adjustment to the deferred tax liability account.

```
              Deferred Tax Liability
                              4,000    Beg. bal.
                                  0
                              4,000    End. bal.
```

To determine the deferred component of income tax expense for **2012** the following journal entries are required:

```
Income tax expense—current            45,400
    Income tax payable (a)                        45,400
```

(a) $113,500 taxable income × 40% = $45,400

Deferred tax liability—noncurrent (b)	2,000
Income tax expense—deferred (c)	2,000

(b) The debit to the deferred tax liability is the adjustment necessary to reduce the existing balance to the desired ending balance.

Deferred Tax Liability

	4,000	Beg. bal.
2,000		Decrease (b)
	2,000	End. bal.

(c) Income tax expense—deferred results from the decrease in the deferred tax liability. The deferred tax asset account was closed in 2011 because all temporary differences have reversed.

The income tax liability per the tax return in 2012 is higher than total tax expense reported on the income statement since depreciation is not deducted for tax purposes anymore. In effect, the income tax liability in 2012 includes a portion of the tax deferred from 2010-2012 that was recorded as a liability; therefore, the deferred tax liability is reduced in 2012. There is a corresponding decrease in income tax expense—deferred that will reconcile the income tax liability per the tax return to income tax expense on the books.

Income tax expense—current	45,400
Income tax expense—deferred	(2,000)
Income tax expense per income statement	43,400

d. **Changing tax rates.** The previous examples assumed a constant enacted tax rate of 40%.

(1) Under the **liability method**, future taxable or deductible amounts (deferred tax assets or liabilities) must be measured using enacted tax rates expected to be in effect in the periods such amounts will impact taxable income.

(2) However, when tax rates change, adjustments to reflect such changes are automatically included in the journal entry amount to increase or decrease the deferred tax accounts to the balances needed to properly reflect balance sheet amounts and to recognize the deferred component of income tax expense.

(a) The rate change effect would be included because the amount of the journal entry is determined by comparing the needed balance in deferred taxes at the end of the period which would be based on the newly enacted rates with the balance at the beginning of the period and taking the difference.

EXAMPLE 3

Assume that in June 2012 a new income tax law is passed which lowers the corporate tax rate to 35% effective January 1, 2013. The entry debiting income tax expense—current and crediting income tax payable for 2012 is identical to that above.

However, the debit to the deferred tax liability account is the adjustment necessary to reduce the existing balance to the desired ending **balance under the new tax rate**.

Deferred tax liability—noncurrent	2,250
Income tax expense—deferred	2,250

Deferred Tax Liability

	4,000	Beg. bal.
2,250		Decrease
	1,750	End. bal.

The $1,750 is the necessary balance for the 2013 reversal of the remaining $5,000 at 35%.

EXAMPLE 4

Dart Corporation has the following temporary differences from its first year of operations:

			Treatment in the book to tax reconciliation
1.	**Long-term contracts:**		
	Year 1 (Current year):	Book contract income > tax contract income	$300 subtraction
	Year 2:		$300 addition
		Book contract income < tax contract income	
2.	**Accumulated depreciation:**		
	Year 1 (Current year):	Book deprec. < tax deprec.	$1,000 subtraction
	Year 2:	Book deprec. < tax deprec.	$500 subtraction
	Year 3:	Book deprec. > tax deprec.	$600 addition
	Year 4:	Book deprec. > tax deprec.	$400 addition
	Year 7:		$500 addition
3.	**Estimated expense liability:**	Book est. exp./loss > tax deduction	$200 addition
	Year 1 (Current year):	Book exp./loss < tax deduction	$200 subtraction
	Year 7:		
4.	**Rent revenue:**		
	Year 1 (Current year):	Book rev. < tax rev.	$500 addition
	Year 4:	Book rev. > tax rev.	$200 subtraction
	Year 7:	Book rev. > tax rev.	$300 subtraction
5.	**Tax rates:**	Current year: 40%	
		Years 2-4: 35%	
		Years 5-7: 30%	

The schedule below combines (1) the pretax accounting income to taxable income reconciliation and (2) the future taxable (deductible) amounts schedule. Remember that **taxable amounts** are added to financial (book) income in the book to tax reconciliation schedule in the future years in which they increase taxable income. **Deductible amounts** are subtracted from financial (book) income in the book to tax reconciliation schedule in the future years in which they decrease taxable income. Taxable income and deferred tax liability (asset) balances for year 1 (the current year) would be determined as follows:

	Current year		Future years			
	Year 1	Year 2 taxable (deductible)	Year 3 taxable (deductible)	Year 4 taxable (deductible)	Year 7 taxable (deductible)	Deferred tax liability (asset)
Tax rate	40%	35%	35%	35%	30%	
Pretax accounting income	$1,600					
Temporary differences:						
LT contracts	(300)	300				$ 105 Current
Accumulated deprec.	(1,000)	(500)*	600	400	500	$ 325 Noncurrent
Estimated expense liability	200			(200)	(200)	$ (60) Noncurrent
Rent revenue	500			(200)	(300)	$(160) Noncurrent
Taxable income	$1,000					
Income tax payable ($1,000 × 40%)	$ 400					

* Note that in year 2 there is excess tax depreciation as there was in year 1.

Income tax expense would be computed as follows:

$$\text{Income tax expense} = \text{Income taxes} \pm \text{Change in deferred taxes (net)}$$

Under ASC Topic 740, deferred tax assets and liabilities are classified as current or long-term based on the related asset or liability, rather than on the expected timing of the future deductible or taxable amounts. However, if a deferred tax asset or liability is not related to an asset or liability for financial reporting purposes, it is classified based upon its expected reversal date. Presented below is a solution for Example 4.

Temporary difference	Deferred tax asset or liability	Related account	Classification*
LT contracts	$300 × 35% = $105 liability	Const-in-Progress	Current
Depreciation	[(500) + 600 + 400] × 35% + $500 × 30% = $325 liability	Accumulated depr.	Noncurrent
Est. expense	$200 × 30% = $60 asset	Estimated liability	Noncurrent
Rent revenue	$200 × 35% + $300 x 30% = $160 asset	Unearned rent	Noncurrent

* Balance sheet disclosure is explained for this example in Section F.3.

The journal entries required are as follows:

Income tax expense current	400	
Income tax payable		400 (a)

(a) $1,000 taxable income × 40% = $400

Income tax expense deferred (e)	210	
Deferred tax asset noncurrent (b)	220	
Deferred tax liability current (c)		105
Deferred tax liability noncurrent (d)		325

(b) $200 × 30% + $200 × 35% + $300 × 30%= $220 needed Ending balance; $220 Ending balance – $0 Beginning balance = $220 increase needed in the account.

Deferred Tax Asset—Noncurrent		
	-0-	Beg. bal.
	220	Increase (b)
	220	End. bal.

(c) $300 × 35% = $105 Ending balance; $105 Ending balance – $0 Beginning balance = $105 increase needed in the account

Deferred Tax Liability—Current		
Beg. bal.	-0-	
Increase (c)	105	
End. bal.	105	

(d) $1,000 × 35% + ($500) × 35% + $500 × 30% = $325 Ending balance; $325 Ending balance –$0 Beginning balance = $325 increase needed in the account.

Deferred Tax Liability—Noncurrent		
Beg. bal.	-0-	
Increase (c)	325	
End. bal.	325	

(e) $105 increase in current deferred tax liability amount + $325 increase in noncurrent deferred tax liability account – $220 increase in noncurrent deferred tax asset account = $210.

> **NOTE:** Since this is the firm's first year of operations, there are no beginning balances in the deferred tax accounts. If there were any permanent differences, such differences would affect only the current year as they did in Example 1. In addition, the need for a valuation allowance to reduce the deferred tax asset to its net realizable value would need to be considered.

e. **Deferred tax asset valuation allowance**. A deferred tax asset is reduced by a valuation allowance if, based on the weight of available evidence, it is more likely than not (a likelihood of more than 50%) that some portion or all of the deferred tax asset will not be realized.

(1) All available evidence, both positive and negative, should be considered to determine whether a valuation allowance is needed. The need for a valuation allowance ultimately depends on the existence of sufficient taxable income (necessary to receive the benefit of a future deductible amount) within the carryback/carryforward period, as described in Section E of this module. If any one of the following sources is sufficient to support a conclusion that a valuation allowance is not necessary, other sources need not be considered.

(2) Possible sources of taxable income

   (a) Future reversals of existing taxable temporary differences
   (b) Future taxable income exclusive of reversing temporary differences and carryforwards
   (c) Taxable income in prior carryback year(s) if carryback is permitted under the tax law
   (d) **Tax-planning strategies** that would, if necessary, be implemented to

      1] Accelerate taxable amounts to utilize expiring carryforwards
      2] Change the character of taxable or deductible amounts from ordinary income or loss to capital gain or loss
      3] Switch from tax-exempt to taxable investments.

(3) Examples of evidence to be considered when evaluating the need for a valuation allowance are summarized as follows:

   (a) Negative evidence—Indicates need for a valuation allowance

1] Cumulative losses in recent years

2] A history of operating loss or tax credit carryforwards expiring unused

3] Losses expected in early future years (by a presently profitable entity)

4] Unsettled circumstances that, if unfavorably resolved, would adversely affect future operations and profit levels on a continuing basis in future years

5] A carryback/carryforward period that is so brief that it would limit realization of tax benefits if (1) a significant deductible temporary difference is expected to reverse in a single year or (2) the enterprise operates in a traditionally cyclical business.

(b) Positive evidence—Can offset the impact of negative evidence

1] Existing contracts or firm sales backlog that will produce more than enough taxable income to realize the deferred tax asset based on existing sales prices and cost structures

2] An excess of appreciated asset value over the tax basis of the entity's net assets in an amount sufficient to realize the deferred tax asset

3] A strong earnings history exclusive of the loss that created the future deductible amount (tax loss carryforward or deductible temporary difference) coupled with evidence indicating that the loss (for example, an unusual, infrequent, or extraordinary item) is an aberration rather than a continuing condition.

EXAMPLE

Valuation allowance

Assume Jeremiah Corporation has determined it has a noncurrent deferred tax asset of $800,000. Note that in the current and prior periods when this asset was recognized, income tax expense was reduced. Based on the weight of available evidence, Jeremiah feels it is more likely than not that $300,000 of this deferred tax asset will not be realized. Jeremiah would prepare the following journal entry:

Income tax expense	300,000	
Allowance to reduce deferred tax asset to expected realizable value		300,000

The balance sheet presentation is

Other Assets (Noncurrent)
Deferred tax asset $800,000
Less Allowance to reduce deferred tax asset
to expected realizable value (300,000)
$500,000

At each year-end, the balance on the allowance account is adjusted upward or downward based on the evidence available at that time, resulting in an increase or decrease of income tax expense. For example, if $600,000 was deemed to be the net realizable value at the end of the next year, the following entry would be made:

Allowance to reduce deferred tax asset to expected realizable value	100,000	
Deferred income tax expense		100,000

D. Deferred Tax Related to Business Investments

One additional issue concerns temporary differences from income on long-term investments that are accounted for using the equity method. For these investments a corporation may assume that the temporary difference (the undistributed income since date of acquisition) will ultimately become taxable in the form of a dividend or in the form of a capital gain. Obviously, the tax expense and deferred tax liability recorded when the difference originates will be a function of whichever of these assumptions is made.

EXAMPLE

Assume Parent Company owns 70% of the outstanding common stock of Subsidiary Company and 30% of the outstanding common stock of Investee Company. Additional data for Subsidiary and Investee Companies for the year 2010 are as follows:

	Investee Co	Subsidiary Co
Net income	$50,000	$100,000
Dividends paid	20,000	60,000

Income Tax Effects from Investee Co.

The pretax accounting income of Parent Company will include equity in Investee income equal to $15,000 ($50,000 × 30%). Parent's taxable income, however, will include dividend income of $6,000 ($20,000 × 30%), and a dividends received deduction of 80% of the $6,000, or $4,800, will also be allowed for the dividends received. This 80% dividends received deduction is a permanent difference between pretax accounting and taxable income and is allowed for dividends received from domestic corporations in which the ownership percentage is less than 80% and equal to or greater than 20%. The originating temporary difference results from Parent's equity ($9,000 = $30,000 × 30%) in Investee's undistributed income of $30,000 ($50,000 – $20,000). The amount by which the deferred tax liability account would increase in 2010 depends upon the expectations of Parent Co. as to the manner in which the $9,000 of undistributed income will be received. If the expectation of receipt is via dividends, then the temporary difference is 20% of $9,000 because 80% of the expected dividend will be excluded from taxable income when received. This temporary difference in 2010 of $1,800, multiplied by the tax rate, will give the amount of the increase in the deferred tax liability. If the expectation of receipt, however, is through future sale of the investment, then the temporary difference is $9,000, and the change in the deferred tax liability is the capital gains rate (currently the same as ordinary rate) times the $9,000.

The entries below illustrate these alternatives. A tax rate of 34% is used for both ordinary income and capital gains. Note that the amounts in the entries below relate only to Investee Company's incremental impact upon Parent Company's tax accounts.

| | Expectations for undistributed income | |
	Dividends	Capital gains
Income tax expense	1,020	3,468
Deferred taxes (net)	612[b]	3,060[c]
Income taxes payable	408[a]	408[a]

[a]Computation of income taxes payable
Dividend income—30% ($20,000)	$6,000
Less: 80% dividends received deduction	(4,800)
Amount included in Parent's taxable income	$1,200
Tax liability—34% ($1,200)	$ 408

[b]Computation of deferred tax liability (dividend assumption)
Temporary difference—Parent's share of undistributed income—30% ($30,000)	$9,000
Less: 80% dividends received deduction	(7,200)
Originating temporary difference	$1,800
Deferred tax liability—34% ($1,800)	$ 612

[c]Computation of deferred tax liability (capital gain assumption)
Temporary difference—Parent's share of undistributed income—30% ($30,000)	$9,000
Deferred tax liability—34% ($9,000)	$3,060

Income Tax Effects from Subsidiary Co.

The pretax accounting income of Parent will also include equity in Subsidiary income of $70,000 (70% of $100,000). Note also that this $70,000 will be included in pretax consolidated income if Parent and Subsidiary consolidate. For tax purposes, Parent and Subsidiary cannot file a consolidated tax return because the minimum level of control (80%) is not present. Consequently, the taxable income of Parent will include dividend income of $42,000 (70% of $60,000) and there will be an 80% dividends received deduction of $33,600. The temporary difference results from Parent's equity ($28,000 = $40,000 × 70%) in Subsidiary's undistributed earnings of $40,000 ($100,000 – $60,000). Remember that the undistributed income of Subsidiary has been recognized for book purposes, but only distributed income (dividends) has been included in taxable income. The amount of the deferred tax liability in 2010 depends upon the expectations of Parent Company as to the manner in which this $28,000 of undistributed income will be received in the future. The same expectations can exist as previously discussed for Parent's equity in Investee's undistributed earnings (i.e., through future dividend distributions or capital gains). Determination of the amounts and the accounts affected for these two assumptions would be similar. The following diagram illustrates the accounting and income tax treatment of the undistributed investee/subsidiary earnings by corporate investors under different levels of ownership.

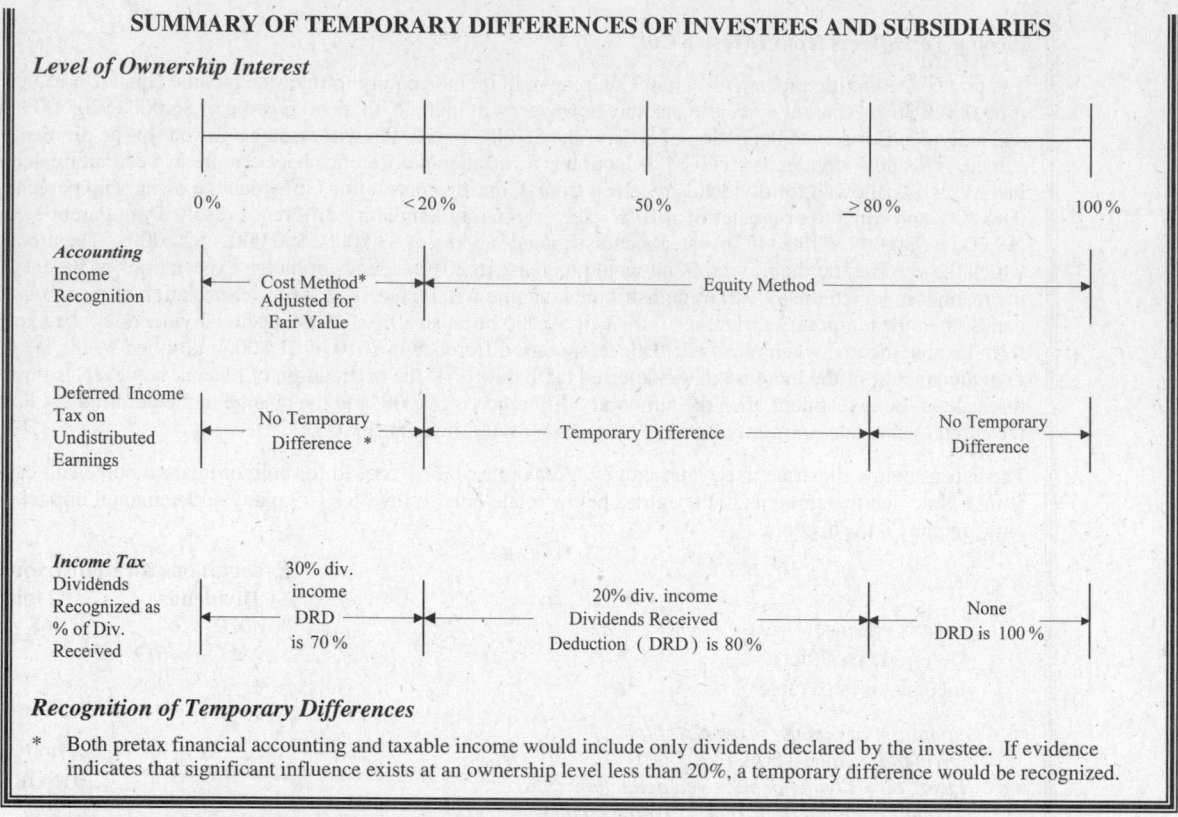

SUMMARY OF TEMPORARY DIFFERENCES OF INVESTEES AND SUBSIDIARIES

Level of Ownership Interest

Recognition of Temporary Differences

*   Both pretax financial accounting and taxable income would include only dividends declared by the investee. If evidence indicates that significant influence exists at an ownership level less than 20%, a temporary difference would be recognized.

> **NOW REVIEW MULTIPLE-CHOICE QUESTIONS 6 THROUGH 29 IN VOLUME 2**

E. Loss Carryforwards and Carrybacks

1. Operating losses of a particular period can be carried back to the two immediate past periods' income resulting in a refund. Losses still remaining after carrybacks may also be carried forward for twenty years to offset income if income arises in any of those twenty years. Companies may at the time of the loss elect to use only the carryforward provision.

    a. **Loss carrybacks** occur when losses in the current period are carried back to periods in which there was income. Loss carrybacks result in tax refunds in the loss period and thus should be recognized in the year of the loss. The entry to record the benefit is

    Tax refund receivable   (based on tax credit due to loss)
        Tax loss benefit (income tax expense)   (same)

    (1) The tax loss benefit account would be closed to revenue and expense summary in the year of the loss.

    b. **Tax loss carryforwards** are recognized in the year the loss occurs. Under ASC Topic 740 (SFAS 109), the benefit of a loss carryforward is **always** recognized as a deferred tax asset which may be reduced by a valuation allowance if necessary.

EXAMPLE

Assume Caleb Corporation has a loss carryforward of $300,000 which could result in future tax savings of $120,000 (40% × $300,000). Caleb feels that based on the weight of available evidence it is more likely than not that $50,000 of these savings will not be realized. Caleb's entries to record the benefit and the valuation allowance are

Deferred tax asset	120,000	
Tax loss benefit (income tax expense)		120,000
Tax loss benefit (income tax expense)	50,000	
Allowance to reduce deferred tax asset to expected realizable value		50,000

c. **Income statement presentation.** The income statement for the year in which both a loss carryback and carryforward are realized would appear as follows:

Loss before income taxes		$ (xx)
Less:		
Benefit from operating loss carryback	xx	
Benefit from operating loss carryforward	xx	xx
Net loss		$ (xx)

> **NOW REVIEW MULTIPLE-CHOICE QUESTIONS 30 THROUGH 33 IN VOLUME 2**

F. Financial Statement Presentation of Income Tax

1. Income Statement

a. **Continuing operations.** For each year presented, the significant components of income tax expense arising from continuing operations shall be disclosed on the face of the income statement or in the notes. These components would include

(1) Current tax expense or benefit
(2) Deferred tax expense or benefit (exclusive of the effects of other components listed below).
(3) The benefits of operating loss carryforwards
(4) Adjustments of a deferred tax liability or asset for enacted changes in tax laws or rates or a change in the tax status of the enterprise
(5) Adjustments of the beginning-of-the-year balance of a valuation allowance because of a change in circumstances that causes a change in judgment about the realizability of the related deferred tax asset in future years.

c. **Other components of net income.** Income tax expense must be allocated within an accounting period between continuing operations and other components of net income (i.e., discontinued operations, extraordinary items, etc.).

(1) The amount of income tax expense allocated to continuing operations is equal to the tax on pretax income or loss from continuing operations.

   (a) However, if net income includes "special items" such as discontinued operations, extraordinary items, and accounting changes, the amount of income tax expense allocated to continuing operations must consider these items.

(2) The amount allocated to an item other than continuing operations (e.g., discontinued operations, extraordinary items, and accounting changes) is equal to the incremental effect on income taxes resulting from that item.

EXAMPLE

Benjamin Corporation's ordinary loss from continuing operations is $1,000. Benjamin also has an extraordinary gain of $1,800 that is a capital gain for tax purposes. The tax rate is 40% on ordinary income and 30% on capital gains. Income taxes currently payable are $240 [($1,800 – $1,000) × 30%]. Since the effect of the $1,000 loss was to offset a capital gain, the benefit allocated to continuing operations is $300 (30% × $1,000) rather than $400 (40% × $1,000). The incremental tax expense allocated to the extraordinary gain is $540 (difference between the $300 tax benefit and the $240 total tax expense).

EXAMPLE

Alco Co. has income from continuing operations of $2,000,000, an extraordinary gain of $450,000, and no permanent or temporary differences. The current tax rate is 34%. Total income tax expense is $833,000 ($2,450,000 × 34%). This amount will first be allocated to income from continuing operations, and the remainder (incremental tax consequences attributable to the remaining components of net income) will be allocated to the extraordinary gain.

Total income tax expense	$ 833,000
Tax consequences associated with income from continuing	
operations ($2,000,000 × 34%)	680,000
Remainder to extraordinary gain	$ 153,000
The bottom of the income statement would appear as follows:	
Income from continuing operations	$2,000,000
Income tax expense	680,000
Income before extraordinary item	$1,320,000
Extraordinary gain (net of $153,000 tax)	297,000
Net income	$1,617,000

    d. **Other comprehensive income.** Components of other comprehensive income may be displayed net of related deferred tax effects or before related deferred tax effects with one amount shown for the aggregate income tax effect (with detail shown in notes). Refer to Module 9D for more information regarding comprehensive income.

 2. **Retained Earnings**

    Any income tax effects associated with adjustments of the opening balance of retained earnings for a **special type** change in accounting principle or correction of an error are to be charged or credited directly to retained earnings. The income tax effects of other stockholders' equity items (e.g., cumulative translation adjustment) are charged or credited to stockholders' equity.

 3. **Balance Sheet**

    a. The classification of deferred tax liabilities and assets is a two-stage process.

      (1) First, all deferred tax liabilities and assets are classified as current or noncurrent.

        (a) Deferred tax liabilities and assets are classified as current or long-term based on the related asset or liability.

          1] A deferred tax liability or asset is related to an asset or liability if reduction of the asset or liability will cause the temporary difference to reverse.

        (b) If the deferred tax liability or asset is **not** related to any asset or liability for financial reporting purposes (such as a deferred tax asset caused by a loss carryforward), it is classified based on the timing of its expected reversal or utilization date.

      (2) Once classification has been determined, all current amounts are netted to get a net current asset or liability and the noncurrent amounts are likewise netted to obtain a net noncurrent amount.

      (3) This process is illustrated in Example 4 that appeared earlier in this module. In Example 4, the only current deferred tax asset/liability is the $105 current liability. Thus the net current amount is a $105 liability. The other amounts are netted to find the net noncurrent amount. In this case the net noncurrent amount is a $105 liability ($325 – $220).

    b. If an allowance account has been recognized for a deferred tax asset, it would be deducted from the related deferred tax asset before the netting process described above is done. If the allowance account balance relates to a deferred tax asset that is classified partially as current and partially as noncurrent, the allowance balance should be allocated between them in the ratio of each asset balance to the total asset balance.

> **NOTE:** If a tax refund receivable results from a loss carryback in the current period, this element would not be included in the netting process; only deferred tax assets and liabilities are netted.

NOW REVIEW MULTIPLE-CHOICE QUESTIONS 34 THROUGH 41 IN VOLUME 2

G. Treatment of Selected Temporary Differences

    The table on the next page summarizes the treatment of selected temporary differences from the period of origination to the period of reversal.

TREATMENT OF SELECTED TEMPORARY DIFFERENCES

	Book value		Tax basis		Previous and current reconciliations of book income to tax income	Future years(s) reconciliation of book income to tax income	Deferred consequence
a. Estimated liability under warranties	56,000	Less	≡	=	56,000 addition(s)	56,000 subtraction(s)	Asset
b. Unearned rent (royalty) revenue received (liability)	40,000	Less	≡	=	40,000 addition(s)	40,000 subtraction(s)	Asset
c. Long-term contracts:							
Construction in process (asset)	1,125,000	Less	1,000,000	=	125,000 subtraction	125,000 addition	Liability
d. Plant assets and accumulated depreciation:							
Equipment (asset)	50,000	Less	50,000				
Accumulated depreciation (contra asset)	10,000		18,500				
End of period basis	40,000		31,500	=	8,500 subtraction(s)	8,500 addition(s)	Liability
e. Donated assets:							
Year of acquisition:							
Machinery (asset)	90,000	Less	≡	=	Not included because donat. recorded in S/E	See deprec. below	Liability
Depreciation:							
Machinery (asset)	90,000	Less					
Accumulated depreciation (contra asset)	18,000						
End of period basis	72,000		80,000	=	18,000 addition(s)	18,000 addition(s)	Reduction of liability
Sale of asset:							
Cash received	80,000	Less	80,000				
Basis of asset	72,000		80,000				
Gain (revenue)	8,000			=		72,000 addition	Reduction of liability
f. Replacement asset for involuntarily converted asset:							
Year of acquisition:							
Building (asset)	280,000		280,000				
Deferred gain from involuntary conversion	—*		(110,000)				
Initial basis of asset	280,000	Less	170,000		110,000 subtraction		Liability
Depreciation:							
Building (asset)	280,000		170,000				
Accumulated depreciation (contra asset)	(14,000)	Less	(28,900)				
End of period basis	266,000		141,100		14,900 subtraction		Liability
Sale of replacement asset:							
Cash received	270,000		270,000				
Basis of asset	(266,000)	Less	(141,100)				
Gain (revenue)	4,000		128,900	=		124,900 addition	Reduction of liability

* The $110,000 gain was recognized in the financial statements in the period the involuntary conversion occurred.

H. Research Component—Accounting Standards Codification

ASC Topic 740 addresses most research questions on deferred taxes. An important concept is that SFAS 109 uses the asset/liability method in recognizing deferred taxes. The most likely research questions are defining temporary differences, identifying the tax rates used to calculate deferred taxes, classifying items as current or noncurrent, and the use of valuation accounts. ASC Topic 740 defines temporary differences and lists examples. An important point is that the statement does not define the term "permanent differences," nor does it use this term in the standard.

Keywords for researching the most important issues in deferred taxes are shown below.

Carrybacks	Deferred tax consequences	Income taxes currently payable
Carryforwards	Deferred tax expense	Negative evidence
Change tax rates	Deferred tax liability	Positive evidence
Current tax expense	Enacted tax rates	Taxable income
Deductible temporary differences	Future deductible amount(s)	Taxable temporary differences
Deferred tax asset	Future taxable amount(s)	Valuation allowance tax
Deferred tax benefit	Income tax expense	

I. International Financial Reporting Standards (IFRS)

1. IFRS requires the use of the "liability method" to account for income taxes. Similar to US GAAP, its primary purpose is to focus on the statement of financial position and report deferred tax assets and deferred tax liabilities.

    a. IAS 12 prohibits deferred tax assets or deferred tax liabilities from being classified as current. Therefore, deferred taxes are classified as noncurrent items in the statement of financial position.

2. Current tax is the amount of income taxes payable or recoverable on the taxable profit or loss for the period.
3. Deferred tax assets and liabilities arise due to temporary differences.

    a. Temporary differences are either taxable temporary differences or deductible temporary differences.

       (1) A taxable temporary difference will result in an increase in taxable amounts in a future period.
       (2) A deductible temporary difference will result in amounts that can be deducted in future periods.

    b. A deferred tax asset arises when there is a deductible temporary difference. A deferred tax asset also arises when an entity has unused tax losses that can be deducted in the future or tax credits which can be used in the future.
    c. An entity can recognize a deferred tax asset if it is probable (more likely than not) that the tax benefit can be used.

4. Deferred tax assets and liabilities are measured using the enacted rate or substantially enacted rate (unlike US GAAP which requires the use of the enacted tax rate).
5. The liability method requires an entity to identify all temporary differences. The differences are then classified as those giving rise to deferred tax liabilities, and those giving rise to deferred tax assets.

    a. This distinction is important because all deferred tax liabilities are reported, whereas deferred tax assets can only be recognized if it is probable (more likely than not) that the asset will be realized.
    b. Similar to US GAAP, tax expense is the sum of current tax expense and the deferred tax expense.

6. One of the significant differences in accounting for income taxes between US GAAP and IFRS is the classification of deferred taxes on the balance sheet.

    a. Recall that for US GAAP, the netting procedures involve netting current deferred tax assets (DTA) with current deferred tax liabilities (DTL) to present one amount, and netting noncurrent DTA with noncurrent DTL to present another amount.
    b. Under IFRS, deferred tax assets and liabilities may not be classified as current.
    c. The netting rules are also different.

       (1) Netting of the components of deferred taxes is only permissible in certain situations.

          (a) The rules for presentation and disclosure require that a current tax payable and a current tax recoverable (receivable) can be offset only if it relates to the same taxing authority.
          (b) Likewise, the netting of deferred tax assets and deferred tax liabilities must relate to the same taxing authority. Therefore, in order to net these amounts, the entity must have a legal right to offset the amounts, and the amounts must relate to the same taxing authority.

NOW REVIEW MULTIPLE-CHOICE QUESTIONS 42 THROUGH 44 IN VOLUME 2

KEY TERMS

Asset. A "probable future economic benefit obtained or controlled by a particular entity as a result of past transactions or events: (SFAC 6).

Current tax expense or benefit. "The amount of income taxes paid or payable (or refundable) for a year as determined by applying the provisions of the tax law to the taxable income or excess of deductions over revenues for that year" (ASC Topic 740).

Deferred tax asset. The deferred tax consequences attributable to deductible temporary differences and carryforwards.

Deferred tax expense or benefit. "The change during the year in an enterprise's deferred tax liabilities or assets" (ASC Topic 740).

Deferred tax liability. An amount that is recognized for the deferred tax consequence of temporary differences that will result in taxable amounts in future years.

Liability. A "probable futures sacrifices of economic benefits arising from present obligations" (SFAC 6).

Loss carrybacks. Occur when losses in the current period are carried back to periods in which there was income.

Tax loss carryforwards. Occurs when losses in the current period are carried forward to future years.

Temporary difference. "A difference between the tax basis of an asset or liability and its reported amount in the financial statements that will result in taxable or deductible amounts in future years when the reported amount of the asset or liability is recovered or settled, respectively."

Module 15: Stockholders' Equity

Overview

Stockholders' equity is the residual of assets minus liabilities (i.e., net assets). Due to the number of fraudulent manipulations involving stocks, many states have legislated accounting for stockholders' equity transactions, and they are controlled to some degree (e.g., conditions under which dividends may be paid).

This module covers accounts located within stockholders' equity (e.g., common stock) and events affecting stockholders' equity (e.g., bankruptcy).

Common stockholders' equity consists of two major categories: contributed capital and retained earnings. Retained earnings are either appropriated or unappropriated. Paid-in capital consists of paid-in excess and legal capital. Legal capital is the par or stated value of stock.

When significant changes occur in stockholders' equity accounts, enterprises are required to disclose them. Most companies satisfy this requirement by issuing a statement of changes in stockholders' equity (illustrated below). These statements show changes in the number of shares (not included due to space limits) as well as dollars between balance sheet dates. The statement of changes in stockholders' equity may also be used to report comprehensive income.

Northern Corporation
STATEMENT OF CHANGES IN STOCKHOLDERS' EQUITY
For the Year Ended December 31, 2010

	Common stock	Comprehensive income	Retained earnings	Accumulated other comprehensive income	Total
Balances, January 1, 2010	$1,500,000		$213,675	$ (3,450)	$1,710,225
Comprehensive income					
Net income		$63,250	63,250		
Other comprehensive income:					
Foreign currency translation adjustments, net of tax		8,000			
Unrealized gains on securities:					
Unrealized holding gains arising during period, net of tax		13,000			
Less: reclassification adjustment, net of tax, for gain included in net income		(4,000)			
Other comprehensive income		17,000		17,000	
Comprehensive income		80,250			80,250
Proceeds from issuance of shares	200,000				200,000
Dividends paid	--		(24,825)		(24,825)
Balances, December 31, 2010	$1,700,000		$252,100	$13,550	$1,965,650

A. Common Stock

1. The entry to record the issuance of common stock is

Cash	(amount received)
Common stock	(par or stated value)
Paid-in capital in excess of par	(forced)

   a. If stock is sold for less than par, a discount account is debited.

   b. Very little stock is issued at a discount because of the resulting potential liability to the original purchaser for the difference between the issue price (when less than par) and par which in many states is legal capital. This liability has been avoided by the use of stated value and no par stock, but is mainly avoided by establishing par values below market.

2. Control accounts are occasionally used to control unissued stock.

   a. At authorization

Unissued common stock	(total par or stated value)
Common stock authorized	(same)

   b. At issuance

Cash	(cash received)
Unissued common stock	(par or stated value)
Paid-in capital in excess of par	(forced)

     (1) The credit balance in the authorized account is the total available for issuance. The debit balance in the unissued account is the amount not issued. Thus, authorized (cr) – unissued (dr) = issued (cr). The unissued account is an offset account to the authorized account.

3. No-par stock is occasionally issued (i.e., no par or stated value exists). All of the proceeds from issuance of no-par stock are credited to "common stock."

4. Costs of registering and issuing common stock are generally netted against the proceeds (i.e., reduce "paid-in capital in excess of par"). An alternative method is to consider stock issue costs an organizational cost.

Legal expenses	(FMV)
Assets	(FMV)
Common stock	(par)
Paid-in capital in excess of par	(forced)

B. Preferred Stock

As implied, preferred stock has preferential rights: most commonly the right to receive dividends prior to common stockholders. Generally the dividend payout is specified (e.g., 7% of par). Additional possible features are

1. **Participating**—share with common stockholders in dividend distributions after both preferred and common stockholders receive a specified level of dividend payment

   a. Participation with common stockholders in dividends is usually specified in terms of a percentage of legal capital. For example, 7% preferred receive 7% of their par value in dividends before common stockholders receive dividends. Fully participating preferred would receive the same percentage dividend as common stockholders if the common stockholders received over a 7% (of par value) dividend.

2. **Cumulative**—dividends not paid in any year (dividends in arrears) must be made up before distributions can be made to common stockholders

   a. However, dividends in arrears are not a liability until declared. They should be disclosed parenthetically or in the footnotes.

3. **Convertible**—preferred stockholders have an option of exchanging their stock for common stock at a specified ratio

   a. Conversion is usually accounted for at book value

Preferred stock	(par converted)
Preferred paid-in accounts	(related balances)
Common stock	(par)
Paid-in capital in excess of par	(forced)

   b. If market value is used, common stock and paid-in excess are credited for the market value, usually resulting in a large debit to retained earnings. (Plug figure in the journal entry.)

4. **Callable**—the corporation has the option to repurchase the preferred stock at a specified price

   a. If called, no gain or loss is recognized on the income statement. Gains are taken to a paid-in capital account; losses are charged to retained earnings.

Preferred stock	(par)
Preferred paid-in accounts	(related balances)
Retained earnings	(if dr. needed)
Cash	(amount paid)
Paid-in capital from preferred retirement	(if cr. needed)

5. Any of the above features present in a preferred stock issuance should be disclosed parenthetically in the balance sheet next to the account title.

6. Any financial instrument that imposes an obligation on the issuer to transfer assets or issue equity shares is classified as a liability.

   a. Therefore, mandatorily **redeemable preferred stock** must be classified as liabilities on the balance sheet.

   b. The SEC requires that preferred securities redeemable for cash or other assets should be classified outside of permanent equity (as temporary equity) if the preferred stock is redeemable at a fixed or determinable price on a fixed or determinable date; at the option of the holder, or upon the occurrence of an event not within the control of the issuer.

C. Stock Subscriptions

Stock (common/preferred) can be subscribed by investors. A receivable is established and "stock subscribed" credited. When the total subscription price is received, the stock (common/preferred) is issued.

1. At subscription

Cash	(any cash received)
Subscription receivable	(balance)
Common stock subscribed	(par)
Paid-in capital in excess of par	(subscription price > par)

2. Cash receipt and issuance

Cash	(balance)
Subscriptions receivable	(balance)
Common stock subscribed	(par)
Common stock*	(par)

   * Unissued common stock, if unissued and authorized accounts are being used.

3. Upon default of subscription agreements, depending on the agreement, the amount paid to date may be

   a. Returned to subscriber
   b. Kept by company
   c. Held to cover any losses on resale and balance returned

4. If returned

Common stock subscribed	(par)
Paid-in capital in excess of par	(subscription price > par)
Cash	(any cash received)
Subscriptions receivable	(balance)

   a. If kept by the company, no cash would be paid and "paid-in from subscription default" credited instead of cash.

   b. If held to cover any losses on resale, a "refundable subscription deposit" liability would be credited instead of cash. If the stock were resold at less than the original subscription price, the difference would be debited to "refundable subscription deposit."

Cash	(payment)
Refundable subscription deposit	(forced)
Stock	(par)
Paid-in capital in excess of par	(amount from original sale)

   (1) The balance in the refundable subscription account would be paid (possibly in an equivalent number of shares) to the original subscriber.

> **NOW REVIEW MULTIPLE-CHOICE QUESTIONS 1 THROUGH 11 IN VOLUME 2**

D. Treasury Stock Transactions

A firm's own stock repurchased on the open market is known as treasury stock. Treasury stock is **not** an asset, as a firm may not own shares of itself. Instead it is treated as a reduction of stockholders' equity. Furthermore, a firm may only recognize a gain or loss on assets, not on transactions with its own stockholders. Therefore the terms "above cost" and "below cost" will be used instead of gain or loss. There are two methods of accounting for treasury stock: cost and par value.

1. Cost Method

a. Under the **cost method,** treasury stock is debited for the cost of treasury stock.
b. Any difference between the cost of the treasury stock and the resale price is recognized at the point of resale. However, such amounts are not included in the determination of periodic income.

  (1) Resale amounts **above cost** are credited to "paid-in capital from treasury stock transactions."
  (2) Resale amounts **below cost** should be charged first to "paid-in capital from treasury stock (TS) transactions" or "paid-in capital from stock retirement" to the extent that either of these exists for that class of stock. The remainder of any amount from sales below cost is to be charged to retained earnings.
  (3) In essence a one-transaction viewpoint is used, as the firm is treated as a middle "person" for the transfer of stock between two shareholders.

2. Par Value Method

Under the **par value** method, all capital balances associated with the treasury shares are removed upon acquisition.

a. Any excess of treasury stock cost over par value is accounted for by charging "paid-in capital from common stock" for the amount in excess of par received when the shares were originally issued.
b. Any excess of the cost of acquiring the treasury stock over the original issue cost is charged to retained earnings.
c. If treasury stock is acquired at a cost equal to or less than the original issue cost, "paid-in capital from common stock" is charged (debited) for the original amount in excess of par and "paid-in capital from treasury stock" is credited for the difference between the original issue price and the cost to acquire the treasury stock.
d. When the treasury stock is resold, it is treated as a typical issuance, with the excess of selling price over par credited to "paid-in capital from common stock."

> **NOTE:** The par value method takes on a two-transaction viewpoint. The purchase is treated as a "retirement" of the shares, while the subsequent sale of the shares is treated as a "new" issue.

EXAMPLE

100 shares ($50 par) are originally sold at $60, reacquired at $70, and subsequently resold at $75.

Cost method			Par value method		
Treasury stock	7,000		Treasury stock	5,000	
Cash		7,000	Paid-in capital—common		
			stock	1,000	
			Retained earnings	1,000	
			Cash		7,000
Cash	7,500		Cash	7,500	
Treasury stock		7,000	Treasury stock		5,000
Paid-in capital—			Paid-in capital—		
treasury stock		500	common stock		2,500

If the shares had been resold at $65:

Cost method			Par value method		
Cash	6,500		Cash	6,500	
Retained earnings*	500		Treasury stock		5,000
Treasury stock		7,000	Paid-in capital—		
			common stock		1,500

* "Paid-in capital—treasury stock" or "paid-in capital—retired stock" of that issue would be debited first to the extent it exists.

> **NOTE:** Total stockholders' equity is not affected by the method selected; only the allocation among the equity accounts is different.

E. Retirement of Stock

    Formal retirement or constructive retirement (purchase with no intent of reissue) of stock is handled very similarly to treasury stock.

  1. When formally retired

Common stock	xx
Paid-in capital in excess of par*	xx
Retained earnings*	xx
Treasury stock*	xx

    * Assuming a loss on the retirement of treasury stock

    a. "Paid-in capital from treasury stock transactions" may be debited to the extent it exists

    b. A pro rata portion of all paid-in capital existing for that issue (e.g., if 2% of an issue is retired, up to 2% of all existing paid-in capital for that issue may be debited)

      (1) Alternatively, the entire or any portion of the loss may be debited to retained earnings. Any gains are credited to a "paid-in capital from retirement" account.

> **NOW REVIEW MULTIPLE-CHOICE QUESTIONS 12 THROUGH 22 IN VOLUME 2**

F. Dividends

  1. At the date of declaration, an entry is made to record the dividend liability.

Retained earnings (dividends)	xx
Dividends payable	xx

  2. No entry is made at the date of record. Those owning stock at the date of record will be paid the previously declared dividends.

    a. The stockholder records consist of

      (1) General ledger account
      (2) Subsidiary ledger

         (a) Contains names and addresses of stockholders

      (3) Stock certificate book

    b. Outside services: (usually banks)

      (1) Transfer agent issues new certificates, canceling old, and maintains stockholder ledger
      (2) Registrar validates new certificates and controls against overissuance
      (3) Functions are now becoming combined

  3. At the payment date, the liability is paid.

Dividends payable	xx
Cash	xx

  4. **Property dividends** are dividends payable in an asset other than cash, but the entries are similar to those of cash dividends.

    a. They are recorded at fair value (FV) of the asset transferred with a gain (loss) recognized on the difference between the asset's book value (BV) and FV at disposition.

  5. **Liquidating dividends** (dividends based on other than earnings) are a return of capital to stockholders and should be so disclosed.

    a. Paid-in capital is usually debited rather than retained earnings. Common stock cannot be debited because it is the legal capital which can only be eliminated upon corporate dissolution.

  6. **Scrip dividends** are issuance of promises to pay dividends in the future (and may bear interest) instead of cash.

Retained earnings	xx
Scrip dividends payable	xx

Scrip dividends are a liability which is extinguished by payment.

Scrip dividends payable	xx
Interest expense (maybe)	xx
Cash	xx

7. Unlike cash and property dividends, stock dividends are not a liability when declared. They can be rescinded, as nothing is actually being distributed to stockholders except more stock certificates. Current assets are not used to "pay" the dividend.

    a. After stock dividends, shareholders continue to own the same proportion of the corporation.

    b. At declaration

Retained earnings	(FV of shares)	
Stock dividend distributable		(par)
Paid-in capital in excess of par		(plug)

    c. At issuance

Stock dividend distributable	xx	
Common stock		xx

    d. Charge retained earnings for FV of stock dividend if less than 20%-25% increase in stock outstanding; charge RE for **par value** of stock dividend if greater than 20-25% increase in stock outstanding.

       (1) Not required if closely held company

NOW REVIEW MULTIPLE-CHOICE QUESTIONS 23 THROUGH 35 IN VOLUME 2

G. Stock Splits
Stock splits change the number of shares outstanding and the par value per share.

1. Par value is reduced in proportion to the increase in the number of shares.
2. The total par value outstanding does not change and no charge is made to retained earnings.
3. If legal requirements preclude changing the par or stated value, charge retained earnings only for the par or stated value issued.

STOCK DIVIDENDS AND SPLITS: SUMMARY OF EFFECTS

	Total S.E.	Par value per share	Total par outstanding	RE	Legal capital	Additional paid-in capital	No. of shares outstanding
Stock dividend < 20-25% of shares outstanding	N/C	N/C	+	Decrease by market value of shares issued	+	+	+
Stock split effected in form of dividend > 20 – 25% of shares outstanding	N/C	N/C	+	Decrease by par value of shares issued	+	N/C	+
Stock split	N/C	Decrease proportion-ately	N/C	N/C	N/C	N/C	+

    N/C = No Change
    + = Increase
    Prepared by Professor John R. Simon, Northern Illinois University

H. Appropriations of Retained Earnings (Reserves)
An entry to appropriate retained earnings restricts the amount of retained earnings that is available for dividends.

RE (or Unappropriated RE)	xx	
Reserve for RE (or Appropriated RE)		xx

NOTE: The restriction of retained earnings does not necessarily provide cash for any intended purpose. The purpose is to show that **assets** in the amount of the appropriation are not available for dividends. When a reserve is no longer needed it must be returned directly to unappropriated retained earnings by reversing the entry that created it.

NOW REVIEW MULTIPLE-CHOICE QUESTIONS 36 THROUGH 41 IN VOLUME 2

I. Share-Based Payments

Share-based payments are transactions wherein an entity acquires goods or services by issuing shares (stock), share options, or other equity instruments. It also includes transactions with an employee or supplier wherein the entity incurs a liability that is based on the price of the entity's shares or that will be settled using equity shares.

1. There are two important distinctions for applying the rules for share-based payments:

   a. Is the share-based payment to employees or nonemployees?
   b. Is the share-based payment considered equity or a liability?

2. **Share-based payments to nonemployees.** Share-based payments to nonemployees for goods and services are measured at the fair value of the equity instruments or the fair value of the goods and services, whichever is more reliable.

3. **Share-based payments to employees.** Share-based payments to employees are measured based on the fair-value-based method. The cost of the services is measured at the grant-date fair value of the equity instruments issued, or the fair value of the liability incurred. Employee service cost is based on fair value net of any amount the employee pays or is obligated to pay for the instrument.

   a. The fair value of an equity share option is measured based on the observable market price of an option with the same or similar terms and conditions, or estimated using an option-pricing model.

      (1) If it is not possible to estimate fair value at the grant date, the compensation cost is measured using the intrinsic value at the end of each reporting period, and final compensation cost is measured at the settlement date.

         (a) The intrinsic value is the difference between the market value of the stock and the price the employee must pay.

   b. Compensation cost for share-based employee compensation classified as equity is amortized on a straight-line basis over the requisite service period.

      (1) The **requisite service period** is the period in which the employee is required to provide services, which is usually the vesting period.
      (2) The **service inception date** is the beginning of the requisite service period.
      (3) Firms must estimate the number of forfeitures that will occur.

         (a) No compensation cost is recognized if an employee forfeits shares because a service or performance condition is not met.
         (b) However, if an employee renders the requisite service and the share option expires or is unexercised, previously recognized compensation cost is not reversed.

   c. Share-based payments may also be classified as liabilities.

      (1) Puttable shares are considered liabilities if the repurchase feature allows the employee to avoid bearing the risks and rewards for a reasonable period (six months or more).
      (2) The measurement date for liability instruments is the settlement date; therefore, share-based payments are remeasured at the end of each reporting period.
      (3) Compensation cost is the change in fair value of the instrument from one period to the next.

Share-Based Payments		
	Classified as Equity	**Classified as Liability**
When to measure	Grant-date fair value of equity instrument	Each reporting period Final measurement on settlement date
How to measure	Observable market price of option with same or similar terms OR Estimate using option pricing model OR Intrinsic value at end of each reporting period if no market price or estimate can be determined (net of amounts that employee must pay)	Fair value of liability incurred
How to allocate compensation expense	Straight-line over requisite service period	Straight-line over requisite service period

   d. If an option-pricing model (such as Black-Scholes model) is used, the option-pricing model should consider the following variables:

(1) Current price of the underlying stock
(2) Exercise price of the option
(3) Expected life of the option
(4) Expected volatility of the underlying stock
(5) Expected dividends on the stock
(6) Risk-free interest rate during the expected option term

   (a) The resulting fair value shall be applied to the number of options expected to vest (based on the grant date estimate) or the total number of options issued.

J. Accounting Entries for the Share-Based Payments to Employees

  1. **Share-based payments classified as equity**

EXAMPLE

To illustrate the recognition and measurement of stock compensation expense, suppose ABC Corporation (a public company) establishes an employee stock option plan on January 1, 2011. The plan allows its employees to acquire 10,000 shares of its $1 par value common stock at $52 per share, when the market price is also $52. The options may not be exercised until five years from the grant date. The grant-date fair value of an option with similar terms and conditions is $8.62.

Accounting for Stock-Based Compensation
Calculation of Compensation Cost

Fair Value of Option at grant-date	$ 8.62
× Number of options	10,000
Deferred comp. expense	$86,200

The journal entry to recognize the deferred compensation expense in Year 1 is shown below.

Deferred comp. expense	86,200	
Stock options outstanding		86,200

During each of the next five years which is the requisite service period, compensation expense is recognizes as follows:

Compensation expense	17,240	
Deferred comp. expense		17,240

When the option is exercised, cash is received and stock is issued as reflected in the following entry (assume exercise after the five-year period):

Cash	52,000	(option price)	
Stock options outstanding	86,200		
Common stock		10,000	(par)
Additional paid-in capital		128,200	(plug)

---

   a. If modifications are made to a shared-based payment plan, the incremental compensation cost is measured by comparing the fair value of the modified plan with the fair value of the plan immediately before the modification.

   b. Deferred compensation is presented in the balance sheet by subtracting the balance in the deferred compensation expense account from stock options outstanding in the paid-in capital section of owners' equity to indicate the net contributed services on any date.

  2. **Share-based payments classified as liabilities**

   a. When a share-based payment is treated as a liability, it is measured at the fair value of the liability incurred. The measurement date is the date of settlement. Therefore, the liability is remeasured at the end of each reporting period until the date of settlement.

     (1) Compensation cost for each period is based on the change in fair value of the instrument for each reporting period.

     (2) If the requisite service period has not been completed, the compensation cost recognized is equal to the percentage of the requisite service that has been rendered as of that date.

   b. An example of share-based payment classified as a liability is a stock appreciation right. **Stock appreciation rights** (SAR) allow employees to receive stock or cash equal in amount to the difference between the market value and some predetermined amount per share for a certain number of shares. SARs allow employees to receive the amount of share appreciation without having to make a cash outlay as is common in stock option plans.

c. For financial reporting purposes, compensation expense is the excess of market value over a predetermined amount.

    (1) Compensation expense is recorded in each period prior to exercise based on the excess of market value at the end of each period over a predetermined amount.

    (2) Compensation expense is adjusted up or down as the market value of the stock changes before the measurement date (which is the exercise date). Therefore, compensation expense could be credited (reduced) if the stock's market value drops from one period to the next.

EXAMPLE

Assume a company grants 100 SAR, payable in cash, to an employee on 1/1/11. The predetermined amount for the SAR plan is $50 per right, and the market value of the stock is $55 on 12/31/11, $53 on 12/31/12, and $61 on 12/31/13. Compensation expense recorded in each year would be

Total expense – Exp. previously accrued = Current expense

2011	100 ($55 – $50)	=	$ 500 – $ 0	=	$ 500
2012	100 ($53 – $50)	=	$ 300 – $500	=	$ (200)
2013	100 ($61 – $50)	=	$1,100 – $300	=	$ 800

The total expense recognized over the three-year period is $1,100 [100($61 – $50)]. Journal entries would be

2011 and 2013		**2012**	
Compensation expense $500/$800		Liability under SAR plan $200	
Liability under SAR plan $500/$800		Compensation expense $200	

[If the SAR were to be redeemed in common stock, Stock Rights Outstanding (a paid-in capital account) would replace the liability account in the above entries.]

The above example assumes no service or vesting period, which is the period of time until the SAR become exercisable. If the above plan had a two-year service period, 50% of the total expense would be recognized at the end of the first year, and 100% at the end of the second year and thereafter until exercised. The compensation would be accrued as follows:

2011	$ (500) (50%)	=	$ 250 – $ 0	=	$250
2012	$ (300) (100%)	=	$ 300 – $250	=	$ 50
2013	$(1,100) (100%)	=	$1,100 – $300	=	$800

---

3. **Disclosures**

    a. Excess tax benefits are recognized as additional paid-in capital.

    b. Cash retained as a result of excess tax benefits are presented in the statement of cash flows as a cash inflow from financing activities (not as a reduction of taxes paid).

    c. Diluted earnings per share is based on the actual number of options or shares granted and not yet forfeited, unless the shares are antidilutive.

       (1) If equity share options are outstanding for only a part of a period, the shares are weighted to reflect the portion of time outstanding.

    d. Disclosures for share-based payments should include the following:

       (1) The nature and terms of arrangements during the period and potential effects on shareholders

       (2) The effect of compensation cost from share-based arrangements on the income statement

       (3) The method of estimating the fair value of goods or services received, or fair value of the equity instruments granted during the period

       (4) The cash flow effects from share-based payments

NOW REVIEW MULTIPLE-CHOICE QUESTIONS 42 THROUGH 54 IN VOLUME 2

K. Basic Earnings Per Share

NOTE: CPA candidates must be able to compute both basic and diluted earnings per share (EPS). In addition to the computations, candidates should also understand the presentation and disclosure requirements.

1. Only public entities (those who trade their stock on the major stock exchanges and over the counter) are required to present earnings per share.

a. Nonpublic companies often choose to present such information, but they are not required to do so.
b. Before continuing, it is recommended that candidates read the outline of SFAS 128, *Earnings Per Share* (ASC Topic 260), in the back of the FAR section.

2. The objective of EPS is to measure the performance of an entity over the reporting period. Required presentation calls for a **basic** EPS in all situations and a **diluted** EPS in those situations where an entity's capital structure includes potential dilutive securities. Basic and dilutive (when applicable) earnings per share amounts must be presented on the face of the income statement for two elements.

    a. Income from continuing operations **and**
    b. Net income

3. In those situations where an entity also reports discontinued operations, and/or extraordinary items, the entity **may report** EPS on the face of the income statement or disclose such information in the footnotes to the financial statements.

> **NOTE:** The only required EPS presentations are for income from continuing operations and net income. All other presentations of EPS are optional.

4. Public corporations begin by computing **basic** earnings per share. In this calculation, only those shares of common stock **outstanding** are included. Any **potential** issuance of securities is **ignored**. The computational formula is as follows:

$$\text{Basic EPS} = \frac{\text{Net income available to common stockholders}}{\text{Weighted-average number of common shares \textbf{outstanding}}}$$

    a. The **numerator** (net income available to common stockholders) for EPS on **net income** is computed by taking the **net income** and **subtracting**

       (1) The dividends **declared** in the period on the **noncumulative preferred stock** (whether paid or not) **and**
       (2) The dividends **accumulated** for the current period only on the **cumulative preferred stock** (whether or not declared).

> **NOTE:** Dividends in arrears are excluded from this calculation.

    b. The **numerator** (net income available to common stockholders) for EPS on **net income from continuing operations** is computed by taking the **net income** and subtracting any net income or adding any net loss from the following:

       (1) Discontinued operations
       (2) Extraordinary items
       (3) The net income from continuing operations is then adjusted by subtracting the preferred stock dividends as described in points number 1. and 2. above.

    c. The following example will illustrate the application of this formula:

EXAMPLE

Numerator information		Denominator information	
a. Net income	$100,000	a. Common shares outstanding 1/1/09	100,000
b. Extraordinary loss (net of tax)	30,000	b. Shares issued for cash 4/1	20,000
c. 6% preferred stock, $100 par, 1,000 shares issued and outstanding ($100,000 × .06)	6,000	c. Shares issued in 10% stock dividend declared in July	12,000
		d. Shares of treasury stock purchased 10/1	10,000

Earnings per common share:

$$\text{On income from continuing operations} = \frac{\$130,000 - 6,000}{\text{Common shares outstanding}}$$

$$\text{Our net income} = \frac{\$100,000 - 6,000}{\text{Common shares outstanding}}$$

---

d. When calculating the amount of the numerator, the claims of senior securities (i.e., preferred stock) should be deducted to arrive at the earnings attributable to common shareholders.

   (1) In the example, the preferred stock is cumulative. Thus, regardless of whether or not the board of directors declares a preferred dividend, holders of the preferred stock have a claim of $6,000 (1,000 shares × $6 per share) against 2009 earnings. Therefore, $6,000 is deducted from the numerator to arrive at the net income attributable to common shareholders. Note that this $6,000 would have been **deducted for noncumulative preferred only if a dividend of this amount had been declared**. Cumulative preferred stock dividends for the current period are always deducted whether or not declared.

e. The numerator of the EPS calculation covers a particular time period such as a month, a quarter, or a year. It is, therefore, consistent to calculate the average number of common shares which were outstanding during this same time period. The calculation below in Table I illustrates the determination of weighted-average common shares outstanding.

> **NOTE:** For stock dividends the number of shares is adjusted retroactively for the shares which were outstanding prior to the stock dividend.

   (1) Since the stock dividend was issued **after** the issuance of additional shares for cash on 4/1, the shareholders of those additional shares and the shareholders of the shares outstanding at the beginning of the year will receive the stock dividend.

   (2) However, if the stock dividend had been issued **before** the issuance of additional shares of stock for cash on 4/1, only the shareholders who own the shares outstanding at the beginning of the period would have received the stock dividend.

   (3) Stock splits are handled in an identical fashion.

TABLE I

Dates	Number common shares outstanding	Months outstanding	Fraction of year	Shares × Fraction of year
1/1 to 4/1	100,000 + 10% (100,000) = 110,000	3	¼	27,500
4/1 to 10/1	110,000 + 20,000 + 10% (20,000) = 132,000	6	½	66,000
10/1 to 12/31	132,000 – 10,000 = 122,000	3	¼	30,500
	Weighted-average of common shares outstanding			124,000

   (a) There is an exception to the general rule that stock dividends and stock splits are treated as if outstanding the entire year. If a stock dividend provides that the shareholders may receive either cash or stock, the dividend is treated as a share issuance, and weighted for the time period outstanding.

   (4) In the weighted-average computation, if common shares are issued in a business combination during the year, the common shares are weighted from the date of issuance.

   (5) Other complications in the weighted-average calculation are posed by actual conversions of debt and preferred stock to common during the year and by exercise of warrants and options. These situations are introduced in the example presented with diluted earnings per share in the next section.

f. To complete the basic EPS example, the weighted-average number of common shares determined in Table I is divided into the income elements previously computed to arrive at the following:

Earnings per common share

On income from continuing operations $\dfrac{\$130,000 - 6,000}{124,000 \text{ common shares}} = \$1,000$

On net income $\dfrac{\$100,000 - 6,000}{124,000 \text{ common shares}} = \$\ .76$

   (1) The above EPS numbers should be presented on the face of the income statement. Reporting a $.24 loss per share due to the extraordinary item is optional.

> **NOW REVIEW MULTIPLE-CHOICE QUESTIONS 55 THROUGH 61 IN VOLUME 2**

L. Diluted Earnings Per Share

1. **Diluted EPS** measures the performance of the entity over the reporting period (same as basic EPS) while also taking into account the effect of all dilutive potential common shares that were outstanding during the period.

  a. One difference between the computation of diluted and basic EPS is that the denominator of the diluted EPS computation is increased to include the number of additional common shares that would have been outstanding if the dilutive potential common shares had been issued.

  b. In addition, the numerator is adjusted to add back any convertible preferred dividends, the after-tax amount of interest recognized in the period associated with any convertible debt, and any other changes in income (loss) that would result from the assumed conversion of the potential common shares.

  c. Diluted EPS should be based on the security holder's most advantageous conversion rate or exercise price.

  d. Similar to basic EPS, all antidilutive securities are disregarded.

2. The following two independent examples will illustrate the procedures necessary to calculate basic and diluted EPS.

EXAMPLE 1

For both examples, assume net income is $50,000, and the weighted-average of common shares outstanding is 10,000.

In the first example, assume the following additional information with respect to the capital structure:

    1. 4% nonconvertible, cumulative preferred stock, par $100, 1,000 shares issued and outstanding the entire year

    2. Options and warrants to purchase 1,000 shares of common stock at $8 per share. The average market price of common stock during the year was $10 and the closing market price was $12 per share. The options and warrants were outstanding all year.

Diluted EPS must be computed because of the presence of the options and warrants. The preferred stock is not convertible; therefore, it is not a potentially dilutive security.

The first step in the solution of this problem is the determination of the basic EPS. This calculation appears as follows:

$$\frac{\text{Net income} - \text{Preferred dividends}}{\text{Weighted-average of common shares}} = \frac{\$50,000 - 4,000}{10,000 \text{ shares}} = \$4.60$$

NOTE: Preferred dividends are deducted to arrive at net income applicable to common stock. When preferred stock is cumulative, this deduction is made whether or not dividends have been declared.

The calculation of diluted EPS is based upon outstanding common stock and all dilutive common shares that were outstanding during the period. In the example, the options and warrants are the only potentially dilutive security. Options and warrants are considered to be common stock equivalents at all times. Consequently, the only question that must be resolved is whether or not the options and warrants are dilutive.

This question is resolved by comparing the average market price per common share of $10 with the exercise price of $8. If the average market price is > the exercise price, the effect of assuming the exercise of options and warrants is dilutive. However, if the average market price is ≤ the exercise price, the effect of assuming the exercise of options and warrants would be antidilutive (i.e., EPS would stay the same or increase). In the example, the options and warrants are dilutive ($10 > $8).

The method used to determine the dilutive effects of options and warrants is called the **treasury stock method**.

This method assumes:

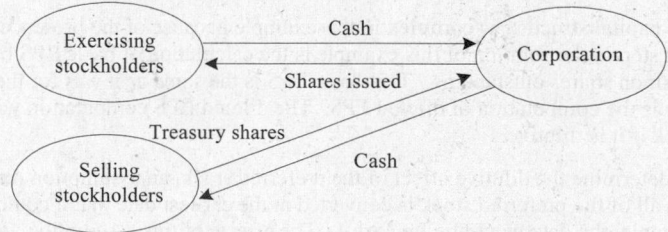

Dilutive effect = Number of shares issued to exercising stockholders − Shares acquired from selling stockholders

In the example above, all of the options and warrants are assumed to be exercised at the beginning of the year (the options and warrants were outstanding the entire year) and the cash received is used to reacquire shares (treasury stock) at the average market price. The computation below illustrates the "treasury stock" method.

Proceeds from assumed exercise of options and warrants (1,000 shares × $8)	$8,000
Number of shares issued	1,000
Number of shares reacquired ($8,000 ÷ $10)	800
Number of shares assumed issued and not reacquired	200

* An alternative approach that can be used to calculate this number for diluted EPS is demonstrated below.

$$\frac{\text{Average market price} - \text{Exercise price}}{\text{Average market price}} \times \text{Number of shares under options/warrants} = \text{Shares not reacquired}$$

$$\frac{\$10 - 8}{\$10} \times 1{,}000 \text{ shares} = 200 \text{ shares}$$

Diluted EPS can now be calculated, as follows, including the effects of applying the "treasury stock" method.

$$\frac{\text{Net income} - \text{Preferred dividends}}{\substack{\text{Weighted-average of common shares} \\ \text{outstanding} + \text{Number of shares not acquired} \\ \text{with proceeds from options and warrants}}} = \frac{\$50{,}000 - 4{,}000}{10{,}000 + 200 \text{ shares}} = \$4.51$$

> **NOTE:** The incremental effects of the treasury stock method; there was no effect on the numerator of the EPS calculation while there were 200 shares added to the denominator. Note also that the options and warrants are dilutive. EPS is reduced from $4.60 to $4.51.

a. Table II summarizes the calculations made for the first example involving diluted EPS.

TABLE II

Items	Basic EPS Numerator	Basic EPS Denominator	Diluted EPS Numerator	Diluted EPS Denominator
Net income	$50,000		$50,000	
Preferred div.	(4,000)		(4,000)	
Common shares outstanding		10,000 shs.		10,000 shs.
Options and warrants				200
Totals	$46,000 ÷	10,000 shs.	$46,000 ÷	10,200 shs.
EPS	$4.60		$4.51	

> **EXAMPLE 2**
>
> Assume net income is $50,000, and the weighted-average of common shares outstanding is 10,000.
>
> Assume the following additional information:
>
> 1. 8% convertible debt, 200 bonds each convertible into 40 common shares. The bonds were outstanding the entire year. The average AA corporate bond yield was 10% at the date the bonds were issued. The income tax rate is 40%. The bonds were issued at par ($1,000 per bond). No bonds were converted during the year.
> 2. 4% convertible, cumulative preferred stock, par $100, 1,000 shares issued and outstanding. Each preferred share is convertible into 2 common shares. The preferred stock was outstanding the entire year, and the average AA corporate bond yield at the date the preferred stock was issued was 10%. The preferred stock was issued at par. No preferred stock was converted during the year.
>
> The capital structure is **complex** in this example because of the presence of the two convertible securities. The first step in the solution of this example is the calculation of basic EPS based upon weighted-average of common shares outstanding. This basic EPS is the same as it was for the first example (i.e., $4.60). The next step is the computation of diluted EPS. The diluted EPS computation will include the convertible preferred stock if it is dilutive.
>
> To determine the dilutive effect of the preferred stock, an assumption (called the **if-converted method**) is made that all of the preferred stock is converted at the earliest date that it could have occurred during the year. In this example, the date would be January 1. The effects of this assumption are twofold. One, if the preferred stock is converted, there will be no preferred dividend of $4,000 for the year; and, two, there will be an additional 2,000 shares of common stock outstanding during the year (the conversion rate is 2 common for 1 preferred). EPS is computed, as follows, reflecting these two assumptions.
>
> $$\frac{\text{Net income}}{\substack{\text{Weighted-average of common shares} \\ \text{outstanding} + \text{Shares issued upon} \\ \text{conversion of preferred stock}}} = \frac{\$50{,}000}{10{,}000 + 2{,}000 \text{ shares}} = \$4.17$$
>
> The convertible preferred stock is **dilutive** because it reduced EPS from $4.60 to $4.17.

In the example, the convertible bonds are assumed to have been converted at the beginning of the year. The effects of this assumption are twofold. One, if the bonds are converted, there will be no interest expense of $16,000 ($8\% \times \$200,000$ face value); and, two, there will be an additional 8,000 shares (200 bonds × 40 shares) of common stock outstanding during the year. One note of caution, however, must be mentioned; namely, the effect of not having $16,000 of interest expense will increase income, but it will also increase tax expense. Consequently, the net effect of not having interest expense is $9,600 [$16,000 – (40\% \times \$16,000)]$. Diluted EPS is computed, as follows, reflecting the dilutive preferred stock and the effects noted above for the convertible bonds:

$$\frac{\text{Net income} + \text{Interest expense (net of tax)}}{\substack{\text{Weighted-average of common shares outstanding} \\ + \text{Shares issued upon conversion of preferred and} \\ \text{conversion of bonds}}} = \frac{\$50,000 + 9,600}{10,000 + 2,000 + 8,000 \text{ shares}} = \$2.98$$

The convertible debt is **dilutive**. Both the convertible bonds and preferred stock reduced EPS from $4.60 to $2.98. Table III summarizes the computations made for the second example.

The income statement **disclosures** for EPS, as a result of the second example, would be as follows:

Earnings per common share (see Note X)	$4.60
Earnings per common share assuming dilution	2.98

Note X would state the assumptions made in determining both basic and diluted EPS numbers.

b. Table III summarizes the computations made for the second example.

TABLE III

	Basic EPS		Diluted EPS	
Items	Numerator	Denominator	Numerator	Denominator
Net income	$50,000		$50,000	
Preferred div.	(4,000)			
Common shares outstanding		10,000 shs.		10,000 shs.
Conversion of preferred				200
Conversion of bonds			9,600	8,000
Totals	$46,000 ÷	10,000 shs.	$59,600 ÷	20,000 shs.
EPS	$4.60		$2.98	

c. In the two examples, all of the potentially dilutive securities were outstanding the entire year and no conversions or exercises were made during the year. If a potentially dilutive security was not outstanding the entire year, then the numerator and denominator effects would have to be "time-weighted."

EXAMPLE

Suppose the convertible bonds in the second example were issued during the current year on July 1. If all other facts remain unchanged, diluted EPS would be computed as follows:

$$\frac{\text{Net income} + \text{Interest expense (net of tax)}}{\substack{\text{Weighted-average of common shares outstanding} + \\ \text{Shares issued upon conversion of preferred and} \\ \text{conversion of bonds}}} = \frac{\$50,000 + 1/2\,(9,600)}{10,000 + 2,000 + \frac{1}{2}(8,000)} = \$3.43$$

The convertible debt is dilutive whether or not it is outstanding the entire year or for part of a year.

d. If actual conversions or exercises take place during a period, the common shares issued will be outstanding from their date of issuance and, therefore, will be in the weighted-average of common shares outstanding. These shares are then weighted from their respective times of issuance.

EXAMPLE

For example, assume that all the bonds in the second example are converted on July 1 into 8,000 common shares. Several important effects should be noted, as follows:

1. The weighted-average of common shares outstanding will be increased by (8,000)(.5) or 4,000. Income will increase by $4,800 net of tax because the bonds are no longer outstanding.
2. The "if converted" method is applied to the period January 1 to July 1 because it was during this period that the bonds were potentially dilutive. The interest expense, net of tax, of $4,800 is added to the income, and 4,000 shares (.5 of 8,000) are added to the denominator.

> 3. Interestingly, the net effect of items 1 and 2 is the same for the period whether these dilutive bonds were outstanding the entire period or converted during the period.

   e. It should also be noted that when convertible debt is issued for a premium or discount, the interest expense net of taxes must be computed after giving effect to premium/discount amortization.
   f. The benchmark used to determine if including individual securities decreases income is income from continuing operations unless an enterprise has no discontinued operations. In that case income before extraordinary items would be the benchmark number.

3. **Redemption of preferred stock.** The SEC requires that if preferred stock is redeemed, the difference between the fair value of the consideration transferred and the carrying amount of the preferred stock should be treated the same as a divided to preferred shareholders in calculating earnings per share.

   a. If the consideration transferred is greater than the carrying amount of the preferred stock, it should be subtracted from net income in the calculation of EPS.
   b. If the consideration transferred is less than the carrying amount, then it should be added to net income in calculating the numerator for EPS.

4. **Contingent issuances of common stock.** Also mentioned are **contingent issuances** of common stock (e.g., stock subscriptions). If shares are to be issued in the future with no restrictions on issuance other than the passage of time, they are to be considered issued and treated as outstanding in the computation of dilutive EPS. Other issuances that are dependent upon certain conditions being met are to be evaluated in a different respect.

   a. If the contingency is to merely maintain the earnings levels currently being attained, then the shares are considered outstanding for the entire period and considered in the computation of dilutive EPS if the effect is dilutive.
   b. If the requirement is to increase earnings over a period of time, the diluted EPS computation shall include those shares that would be issued based on the assumption that current amount of earnings will remain unchanged, if the effect is dilutive.

5. **EPS on comprehensive income and other comprehensive income components.** EPS numbers below net income are not required for comprehensive income components.

> **NOW REVIEW MULTIPLE-CHOICE QUESTIONS 62 THROUGH 70 IN VOLUME 2**

M. Corporate Bankruptcy

1. The **going concern** assumption is one of the basic principles underlying the primary financial statements (balance sheet, income statement and statement of cash flows). However, this assumption of continued existence is threatened in corporations that are in severe financial trouble.

   a. A range of alternative actions is available to a company before it enters bankruptcy, such as seeking extensions on due dates of debt, restructuring its debt, or allowing a court-appointed trustee to manage the corporation.

      (1) These pre-bankruptcy options are presented in the following modules:

         (a) Creditor's agreements—Module 30, Bankruptcy
         (b) Troubled debt restructurings—Module 13, Present Value, Section C

2. Bankruptcy is the final legal act for a company. In bankruptcy, the accounting and financial reporting must present the information necessary for the liquidation of the business.

   a. The **Statement of Affairs** is prepared to present the current market values of the assets and the status of the various categories of the equity interests of the corporation.

      (1) The **Statement of Affairs** classifies assets in the following order of priority (highest to lowest):

         (a) Assets pledged with fully secured creditors—assets having a fair valuation equal to or greater than the debts for which they serve as collateral
         (b) Assets pledged with partially secured creditors—assets having a fair valuation less than their associated debts
         (c) Free assets—uncommitted assets available for remaining equity interests

   b. The accountant must provide a prioritization of the creditors' claims against the net assets of the corporation. The legal rights of each creditor are determined by the terms of the credit agreement it has with the company and by the National Bankruptcy Act.

(1) The equity interests are classified in the following order (highest to lowest):

    (a) Preferred claims—these claims have priority as specified in the Bankruptcy Act

    (b) Fully secured creditors—these are claims which should be fully covered with the realizations from the assets pledged to the claims

    (c) Partially secured creditors—these are claims which may not be fully covered by the realizations of the pledged assets for these claims; the amount of the uncovered claims goes to the unsecured creditors category

    (d) Unsecured creditors—these are claims that have no priority and do not have any collateral claims to any specific assets

    (e) Stockholders' equity—this represents any residual claim

c. The historical cost valuation principles used in a balance sheet assume a going concern assumption.

    (1) As a business enters bankruptcy, the liquidation values of the assets become the most relevant measures. In addition, anticipated costs of liquidation should be recognized.

    (2) The Statement of Affairs begins with the present book values of the company's assets in order to articulate with the balance sheet. After relating the projected proceeds from the liquidation of the assets to the various equity interests, the statement concludes with the estimated dollar amount of unsecured claims that cannot be paid (estimated deficiency).

EXAMPLE

The Vann Corporation's balance sheet for December 31, 2011, is shown below. The corporation is entering bankruptcy and expects to incur $8,000 of costs for the liquidation process. The estimated current values of the assets are determined and the various equity claims are prioritized. The Statement of Affairs for Vann Corporation is presented on the following page.

The Vann Corporation
BALANCE SHEET
December 31, 2011

Assets	
Cash	$ 1,500
Marketable securities	10,000
Accounts receivable (net)	18,000
Merchandise inventory	41,000
Prepaid expenses	2,000
Land	6,000
Building (net of depreciation)	65,000
Machinery (net of depreciation)	21,000
Goodwill	10,000
	$174,500
Equities	
Accounts payable	$ 30,000
Notes payable	37,000
Accrued wages	6,500
Mortgages payable	45,000
Capital stock ($10 par)	100,000
Retained earnings (deficit)	(44,000)
	$174,500

NOW REVIEW MULTIPLE-CHOICE QUESTIONS 71 THROUGH 73 IN VOLUME 2

N. Reorganizations

Chapter 11 of the Bankruptcy Reform Act of 1978 and The Bankruptcy Abuse and Consumer Protection Act of 2005 allow legal protection from creditors to provide time for a bankrupt corporation to return its operations to a profitable level.

1. The balance sheet, income statement, and statement of cash flows must distinguish events and transactions related with the reorganization from those related to ongoing operations.
2. Liabilities should be reported at expected amounts per the plan on the balance sheet. Liabilities should be classified as unsecured or secured liabilities before reorganization and liabilities incurred after the filing date for Chapter 11.

3. Transactions directly related to the reorganization should be reported separately on the income statement in the period incurred, and disclosure should be made of any anticipated changes in common stock or common stock equivalents.

4. Cash flows related to the reorganization should be reported separately from those related to regular operations.

5. At confirmation of the plan of reorganization, an entity may be considered a new entity for reporting purposes if the reorganization value of assets before confirmation is less than liabilities incurred after petition for Chapter 11 and voting shareholders before confirmation receive less than 50% of the voting shares of the emerging entity.

6. If the entity does not qualify as a new entity, the reorganization should be accounted for as troubled debt restructuring which is discussed in Module 13C.

O. Quasi Reorganization

The purpose of a quasi reorganization is to allow companies to avoid formal bankruptcy proceedings through an informal proceeding. The procedure is applicable for a situation where a going concern exists except for overvalued assets and a possible deficit. The overvalued assets result in high depreciation charges and losses or lower net income. The deficit precludes payment of dividends. The procedure is applicable during a period of declining price levels (normally associated with decreased economic activity), such as the 1930s.

1. The procedures involve

   a. Proper authorization including that from stockholders and creditors where required
   b. Revaluation of assets to current values
   c. Elimination of any deficit by charging paid-in capital

      (1) First, capital surplus
      (2) Second, capital stock

2. To write down assets: here the adjustments are taken directly to retained earnings. An alternative is to use an intermediary account such as "adjustment account" which would later be closed to retained earnings.

Retained earnings	(write-down)	
Assets		(write-down)

3. To eliminate the deficit

Paid-in capital	(deficit)	
Retained earnings		(deficit)

4. In many cases, paid-in capital in excess of par value will be insufficient, and the par or stated value of the capital stock must be reduced to eliminate the deficit.

Existing paid-in capital	(amount on the books)	
Capital stock	(total reduction in par)	
Retained earnings		(deficit)
Paid-in capital from		
quasi reorganization		(forced figure)

   a. The paid-in capital arises from reducing the par or stated value from, for example, $100 to $50 rather than to $59.415. The $59.415 would come from dividing the shares outstanding into the retained earnings deficit.
   b. Retained earnings must be dated for ten years (less than ten years justified under exceptional circumstances) after a quasi reorganization takes place. Disclosure similar to "since quasi reorganization of June 30, 2010," would be appropriate.

> **NOW REVIEW MULTIPLE-CHOICE QUESTIONS 74 THROUGH 77 IN VOLUME 2**

P. Stock Rights

1. Generally, before additional stock is offered to the public, stock rights are issued to existing shareholders to prevent involuntary dilution of their voting rights (e.g., the preemptive privilege). The stock rights, evidenced by warrants, indicate the number and price at which the shares may be purchased. At issuance, the issuer makes only a memorandum entry. Upon exercise, the following entry is made:

Cash	(proceeds)	
Common stock		(par)
Paid-in capital		(plug)

The Vann Corporation
STATEMENT OF AFFAIRS
December 31, 2011

ASSETS

Book values		Estimated current values	Amount available to unsecured claims
	(1) Assets Pledged with Fully Secured Creditors:		
$ 6,000	Land	$12,000	
65,000	Building	41,000	
		$53,000	
	Less Mortgages Payable	45,000	
		$ 8,000	$ 8,000
	(2) Assets Pledged with Partially Secured Creditors:		
10,000	Marketable Securities	$12,000	
	Notes Payable	37,000	
	(3) Free Assets		
1,500	Cash	1,500	
18,000	Accounts Receivable (net)	14,000	
41,000	Merchandise Inventory	22,500	
2,000	Prepaid Expenses	0	
21,000	Machinery	13,200	
10,000	Goodwill	0	51,200
	Estimated amount available		59,200
	Less: creditors with priority		(14,500)
	Net Estimated amount available to unsecured creditors		44,700
	(81 cents on the dollar)		
	Estimated deficiency to unsecured creditors		10,300
$174,500			$55,000

EQUITIES

Book values		Amount unsecured
	(1) Creditors with Priority	
$ 0	Estimated Liquidation Expenses (accounting, legal and other costs of liquidation process)	$ 8,000
6,500	Accrued Wages	6,500
		$14,500
	(2) Fully Secured Creditors	
45,000	Mortgages Payable	45,000
	(3) Partially Secured Creditors	
37,000	Notes Payable	37,000
	Less Marketable Securities	12,000
		25,000
	(4) Unsecured Creditors	
30,000	Accounts Payable	30,000
	(5) Stockholders' Equity	
100,000	Capital Stock	
(44,000)	Retained Earnings (deficit)	
$174,500		$55,000

2. Information relating to stock rights outstanding must be disclosed. Detachable stock rights issued with preferred stock are treated like those on bonds (see Module 11, Section B.6.). Treatment of stock rights by recipients is discussed in Module 14, Section F.

Q. Employee Stock Ownership Plan (ESOP)

An employee stock ownership plan (ESOP) is a qualified stock bonus plan designed to invest primarily in qualifying employer securities, including stock and other marketable obligations.

1. In some instances, the ESOP will borrow funds from a bank or other lender in order to acquire shares of the employer's stock.

     a. If such an obligation of the ESOP is guaranteed by the employer (assumption by the employer of the ESOP's debt), it should be recorded as a liability in the employer's financial statements.

     b. The offsetting debit to the liability should be accounted for as a reduction of shareholders' equity.

        (1) Shareholders' equity will increase symmetrically with the reduction of the liability as the ESOP makes payments on the debt.

     c. Assets held by an ESOP should not be included in the employer's financial statements, because such assets are owned by the employees, not the employer.

     d. Additionally, the employer should charge to compensation expense the amount the employer contributed or committed to be contributed to an ESOP with respect to a given year. This is done regardless of whether or not the ESOP has borrowed funds.

NOW REVIEW MULTIPLE-CHOICE QUESTIONS 78 THROUGH 86 IN VOLUME 2

R. Ratios

The following ratios use stockholders' equity components in their calculations:

1. **Dividend payout**—measures percentage of earnings distributed as dividends

$$\frac{\text{Dividends per share}}{\text{Earnings per share}}$$

2. **Book value of common stock** (at a point in time)—not a meaningful measure because assets are carried at historical costs

$$\frac{\text{Common stockholders' equity}}{\text{Common shares outstanding}}$$

3. **Rate of return on common stockholders' equity**—measures the return earned on the stockholders' investment in the firm

$$\frac{\text{Net income available to common stockholders}}{\text{Common stockholders' equity}}$$

4. **Debt to equity**—shows creditors the corporation's ability to sustain losses

$$\frac{\text{Total debt (all liabilities)}}{\text{Stockholders' equity}}$$

NOW REVIEW MULTIPLE-CHOICE QUESTIONS 87 THROUGH 91 IN VOLUME 2

S. Research Component—Accounting Standards Codification

1. Stockholders' equity includes a variety of transactions and accounts that are addressed in several places in the Codification. The Statement of Shareholder Equity is found in ASC Topic 215. Earnings per Share rules are in ASC Topic 260. Accounting rules for specific shareholder equity transactions are found in ASC Topic 505, *Equity*. ASC Topic 505 includes accounting for stock dividends and stock splits, treasury stock, and equity-based payments to nonemployees. Although share-based payments to employees and nonemployees were previously covered by one accounting standard, SFAS 123(R), the rules for share-based payments are now located in two areas of the Codification. Share-based payments to nonemployees are located in ASC Topic 505 and are referred to as equity-based payments. Share-based payments to employees are located in ASC Topic 718, *Compensation— Stock Compensation*. Notice that Topic 718 is further divided into the following subtopics:

718-20	Awards Classified as Equity	
718-30	Awards Classified as Liabilities	
718-40	Employee Stock Ownership Plans	
718-50	Employee Share Purchase Plans	

2. A list of useful keywords for research is shown below.

a. Basic stockholders' equity definitions and issues

Appropriation retained earnings	Earned surplus	Undistributed profits
Capital stock	Retained earnings	
Capital surplus	Retained income	

b. Stock dividends, stock splits, property dividends, treasury stock

Gains on sales treasury stock	Sales of treasury stock	Stock retirement
Nonmonetary asset transfer	Stock dividend	Stock split-up
Nonreciprocal transfer to owners	Stock purchased	Treasury stock
Recipient stock dividend	Stock retired	

c. Earnings per share

Antidilutive effect	Convertible securities	Numerator EPS
Basic EPS	Denominator EPS	Options EPS
Contingent issuable shares	Diluted EPS	Treasury stock method
Contingently issuable shares EPS	Dilutive potential shares	Warrants EPS
Conversion rate EPS	If-converted method	Weighted-average common shares

d. Capital structure disclosures

Dividend liquidation preferences	Per-share amounts	Redeemable stock
Information about securities	Redeemable preferred stock	

e. Stock options, stock warrants, conversion of bonds

Black-Scholes	Grand date option	Restricted stock
Compensation cost option	Intrinsic value method	Service inception date
Compensatory plans	Measurement date option	Service period
Employee stock option	Measuring compensation	Share-based payments
Employee stock purchase plan	Noncompensatory plans	Stock-based compensation
Expected volatility	Nonvested stock options	Vested employee options
Fair value method	Option pricing model	Volatility
Fixed award	Requisite service period	

f. Comprehensive income

Classified items income	Display of income	Reclassification adjustments
Comprehensive income	Other comprehensive income	

T. International Financial Reporting Standards (IFRS)

1. Accounting for shareholders' equity may be influenced by the laws of a particular jurisdiction or country. Therefore, IFRS does not contain a comprehensive set of requirements for reporting shareholders' equity. Instead, IFRS provides some rules as to the minimum required disclosures. **Note that in this area, there may be vocabulary differences when describing certain components of shareholders' equity.**

   a. IFRS requires disclosure of the issued share capital, retained earnings, and other components of equity. The par value and the number of authorized, issued, and outstanding shares must be disclosed.

      (1) If shares were issued but not fully paid (referred to as "subscribed stock" in the US and "calls" in other countries), the amount not collected is shown as a contra account in the equity section.

      (2) A schedule must be presented that reconciles the number of shares of stock at the beginning and end of each period.

b. Additional items that are disclosed in the shareholders' equity section are the capital contributions in excess of par (also called additional paid-in capital, or "share premium"), the revaluation reserve, reserves for other items, and retained earnings.

(1) Mandatorily redeemable shares or puttable shares may not be treated as equity and should be classified as liabilities.
(2) Compound financial instruments that have the features of both debt and equity must be separated into a liability component and an equity component and recognized in the appropriate section of the balance sheet.
(3) Noncontrolling interest is included in the shareholders' equity section of the balance sheet.

2. Preferred shares that are convertible into ordinary shares are recorded in the preferred share account. Later, if the shares are converted, the book value method is used to account for the conversion of preferred stock into common stock.
3. Shares issued for services or property should be recorded at the fair value of the property or services.

a. If the fair value of the property or services is not available, then the shares should be recorded at the fair value of the shares.
b. However, if convertible debt is issued, the instrument is viewed as having a debt feature and an equity feature and should be allocated accordingly.

(1) The amount allocated to liabilities is the fair value of the liability component, and the residual amount is allocated to equity.

4. Notes to the financial statements should describe the rights, preferences, and restrictions with respect to dividends for each class of stock, cumulative dividends in arrears, reacquired shares, and shares reserved for future issuances under options and sales contracts.
5. Cash dividends are recorded in the same way as US GAAP. Although IFRS does not address share (stock) dividends, guidance is based on national accounting rules.

a. If dividends have been proposed but not declared or formally approved, such dividends must be reported in the notes to the financial statements.
b. In addition, information regarding dividends declared after the end of the period but prior to issuance of the financial statements should be disclosed in the notes to the financial statements.

6. If ordinary and preferred shares are issued to investors as a unit (referred to as share units), the proceeds are allocated in proportion to the relative market values of the securities issued.

a. If only one security is publicly traded, that security is valued at market value, and the residual is allocated to the other security.
b. If the market value of neither security is known, then an appraisal value may be used.

7. For share subscriptions, the accounting relies on the laws of the particular jurisdiction. In some instances, the subscription receivable is shown as either a current or noncurrent asset based upon the payment due date. However, in other instances, the subscription receivable is a contra account and reduces shareholders' equity.
8. For US GAAP, donated assets are recognized at fair value and as revenue when the contribution is received. IFRS does not currently address donated assets.
9. Treasury shares are the entity's shares that have been reacquired. There are three methods for accounting for treasury shares: cost method, par value method, and constructive retirement method.

a. The cost method and par method entries are the same as US GAAP.
b. The construction retirement method is similar to the par value method except that the par value of the reacquired shares is charged to the share account instead of the treasury stock account.

(1) The constructive retirement method is used when management does not intend to reissue the shares or the jurisdiction of incorporation requires that reacquired shares be retired.

10. Share-Based Payments. IFRS accounting for share-based payments and US GAAP are similar due to the convergence project. However, some vocabulary differences exist.

a. IFRS has three categories for share-based payments: equity-settled, cash-settled, or a choice to settle in either cash or equity.

(1) Equity-settled share-based payments to **nonemployees** are valued at fair value of goods or services received if it can be measured reliably. If the fair value of goods or services cannot be measured, then the fair value of the equity instrument is used.
(2) Equity-settled payments to **employees** are valued at the fair value of the security. A debit is made to either an expense or an asset, and a credit is made to equity. For cash-settled, share-based payments, such as stock appreciation rights or options, a liability is measured at the fair value at the measurement date. The

liability is then remeasured at every reporting date, and additional income or expense is recognized in profit or loss.

> **NOW REVIEW MULTIPLE-CHOICE QUESTIONS 92 THROUGH 94 IN VOLUME 2**

KEY TERMS

Basic EPS. Measures the performance of the entity over the reporting period.

Book value of common stock (at a point in time). Not a meaningful measure because assets are carried at historical costs.

Callable. The corporation has the option to repurchase the preferred stock at a specified price.

Convertible. Preferred stockholders have an option of exchanging their stock for common stock at a specified ratio.

Cost method. Treasury stock is debited for the cost of treasury stock.

Cumulative. Dividends not paid in any year (dividends in arrears) must be made up before distributions can be made to common stockholders.

Debt to equity. Shows creditors the corporation's ability to sustain losses.

Diluted EPS. Measures the performance of the entity over the reporting period (same as basic EPS) while also taking into account the effect of all dilutive potential common shares that were outstanding during the period.

Dividend payout. Measures percentage of earnings distributed as dividends.

Employee Stock Ownership Plan (ESOP). A qualified stock bonus plan designed to invest primarily in qualifying employer securities, including stock and other marketable obligations.

Intrinsic value. The difference between the market value of the stock and the price the employee must pay.

Liquidating dividends (dividends based on other than earnings). A return of capital to stockholders.

Par value method. All capital balances associated with the treasury shares are removed upon acquisition.

Participating. Share with common stockholders in dividend distributions after both preferred and common stockholders receive a specified level of dividend payment.

Preferred stock. Stock with preferential rights.

Property dividends. Dividends payable in an asset other than cash; the entries are similar to those of cash dividend.

Quasi reorganization. Allows companies to avoid formal bankruptcy proceedings through an informal proceeding.

Rate of return on common stockholders' equity. Measures the return earned on the stockholders' investment in the firm.

Scrip dividends. Issuance of promises to pay dividends in the future (may bear interest) instead of cash.

Share-based payments. Transactions wherein an entity acquires goods or services by issuing shares (stock), share options, or other equity instruments.

Stock appreciation rights (SAR). Allows employees to receive stock or cash equal in amount to the difference between the market value and some predetermined amount per share for a certain number of shares.

Stock splits. Change the number of shares outstanding and the par value per share.

Treasury stock. A firm's own stock repurchased on the open market.

Overview

Investments in debt and equity securities are accounted for using ASC Topics 320, 323, 325, and 825 (SFAS 115, APB 18, or SFAS 159). The accounting treatment for investments is different depending upon the percentage of ownership, the classification of the security, and the election of the fair value option for reporting financial assets. This module will begin by covering the rules for trading, available-for-sale, and held-to-maturity securities. The coverage includes discussions on the initial recording of the securities, subsequent accounting, transfers between categories, and financial statement presentation.

This module also covers the equity method of accounting for investments where significant influence exists. After you understand the reporting rules for investments the fair value option will be discussed.

A. Concepts of Accounting and Investment Percentage

1. **Debt securities** are "any security representing a creditor relationship with an entity."

   a. This includes corporate debt, convertible bonds, US Treasury and municipal securities, redeemable preferred stock, commercial paper, and other secured debt instruments.
   b. Excluded are unsecured trade receivables and consumer loans and notes receivable because they are not normally traded on organized exchanges and because of cost/benefit considerations.
   c. Investments in debt securities are classified into three categories: trading securities, available-for-sale securities, and held-to-maturity securities.

      (1) Debt securities are discussed in Section B of this module and also in Module 13, Section B.

2. **Equity securities** include ownership interests (common, preferred, and other capital stock), rights to acquire ownership interests (rights, warrants, call options), and rights to dispose of ownership interests (put options).

   a. The accounting rules for investments in the common stock of another corporation are generally based on the percentage of the voting stock obtained.

      (1) *Investments of less than 20% of the outstanding stock*
         In most cases, "small" investments in marketable equity securities are classified into two categories: trading securities and available-for-sale securities. Discussion of these smaller investments is presented in Section B of this module.
      (2) *Investments between 20% and 50% of the outstanding stock*
         At 20% or more ownership, the investor is presumed to be able to significantly influence the operating or financial decisions of the investee. Most investments in this range will result in significant influence; however, the 20% level is just a guide.

         (a) An example in which an investor owning between 20% and 50% may not be able to exercise influence over the investee is when the majority ownership is concentrated among a small group of investors who ignore the views of the minority investor.
         (b) The equity method of accounting is used for investments resulting in significant influence.
         (c) Investments where significant influence does exist are discussed in Section C of this module.

      (3) *Investments of more than 50% of the outstanding stock*
         At more than 50% ownership, the investor has control because of its majority ownership of the voting stock.

(a) Most of these investments will require the preparation of consolidated financial statements. Consolidations are discussed in Module 18.

3. Securities are originally recorded at cost, including any broker's fees, taxes, etc.; this amount is the best estimate of fair value at acquisition.

 a. Cost equals the cash paid or, in noncash transactions, the fair value of either the securities received or the resources sacrificed, whichever is more clearly determinable.

  (1) The fair value of debt securities equals the present value of their future cash inflows.

   (a) The present value is calculated using the current market rate of interest for similar instruments with similar risk.
   (b) Any accrued interest is accounted for separately.

  (2) The fair value of equity securities to be marked to market must be readily determinable from quotes obtainable from a securities exchange registered with the SEC or from the over-the-counter market.

   (a) Investments which are considered to be nontradeable or investments which do not have determinable market values should be carried at cost and adjusted only for permanent declines in value.

 b. The exhibit that follows illustrates the major concepts of accounting for investments in equity securities.

PERCENTAGE OF OUTSTANDING VOTING STOCK ACQUIRED

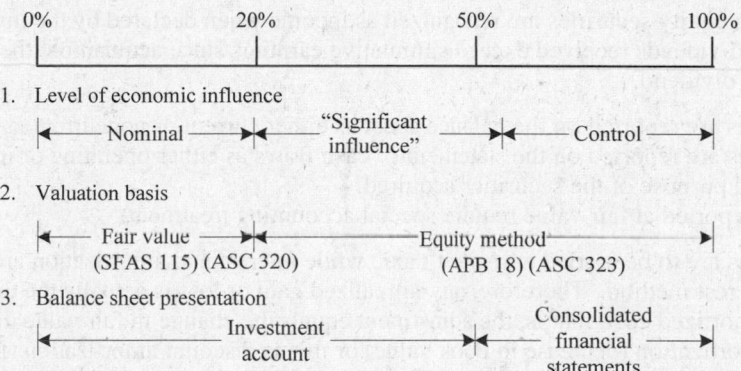

 (1) Several exceptions to these general concepts exist. These exceptions are noted in the following discussions.

B. Investments in Which Significant Influence Does *Not* Exist

Investments which do not confer significant influence over the operating or financial decisions of the investee consist of all debt securities and generally all small (less than 20%) investments in equity securities. Such investments should be segregated into held-to-maturity securities (debt securities only), trading securities, and available-for-sale securities; the appropriateness of the classification should be reviewed at each reporting date.

1. Held-to-Maturity Securities (amortized cost)

 a. This category includes only debt securities and requires the positive intent and ability to hold the securities to maturity (not simply an absence of intent to sell).
 b. Held-to-maturity securities are carried at amortized cost (acquisition cost adjusted for amortization of premium or discount) using effective interest method; thus, unrealized holding gains and losses are not reported.

  (1) However, realized gains and losses are included in earnings, as are interest income and premium and discount amortization.

 c. These securities are classified on the balance sheet as current or noncurrent on an individual basis, and on the statement of cash flows as investing activities.
 d. In rare instances, the investor company's intent to hold a security to maturity may change without casting doubt on its intent to hold other debt securities to maturity.

  (1) The circumstances must be nonrecurring and unforeseeable, such as the continuing deterioration of the issuer's credit.
  (2) Premature sale of held-to-maturity securities may be considered as maturities if either of the following conditions are met:

      (a) The sale occurs so close to the maturity date that interest rate risk is virtually eliminated, or

      (b) The sale occurs after at least 85% of the principal has been collected.

  e. Investments in held-to-maturity securities are accounted for under the cost method (unless the fair value option is elected), which requires that they be carried at amortized cost (acquisition cost adjusted for amortization of premium or discount). Coverage of accounting for these appears under bond investments in Module 13B.

2. **Trading Securities (mark-to-market)**

  a. Debt and equity securities purchased and held principally for the purpose of generating gains on current resale are classified as trading securities.

  b. Trading securities are accounted for according to the cost adjusted for fair value (mark-to-market) method, under which the carrying amount is adjusted at financial statement dates for subsequent changes in fair value (i.e., they are carried at market value). (See Module 9D for a discussion of ASC Topic 820 [SFAS 157] and fair value measurements.)

  c. Trading securities are generally held by brokers, bankers, and other financial institutions which engage in active buying and selling activities.

  d. Both unrealized and realized gains and losses are included in income.

    (1) However, to the extent that realized gains/losses have been previously reported as unrealized, only changes in the current period shall be reported as realized in the period of sale.

  e. Other components of earnings include dividend and interest revenue.

    (1) Dividends on equity securities are recognized as income when declared by the investee.

    (2) However, if dividends received exceed cumulative earnings since acquisition, the excess is accounted for as a liquidating dividend.

  f. Trading securities are reported on the balance sheet as either current or noncurrent as appropriate.

  g. Trading securities are reported on the statement of cash flows as either operating or investing activities based on the nature and purpose of the securities acquired.

  h. Debt securities reported at fair value require special accounting treatment.

    (1) The securities are to be carried at market value while interest and amortization are to be calculated using the effective interest method. Therefore, any unrealized gain or loss is actually the difference between fair value and amortized cost, that is, the adjustment equals the change in fair value during the period, plus premium amortization (decrease in book value) or minus discount amortization (increase in book value).

    (2) Both the interest revenue and the unrealized holding gain/loss are included in current earnings.

    (3) An example of accounting for trading debt securities is presented in the comprehensive example at the end of Section B.

3. **Available-for-Sale Securities (mark-to-market)**

  a. Available-for-sale securities include debt and equity securities not categorized as either held-to-maturity securities or trading securities. For example, a company such as a manufacturing firm may purchase securities to make use of idle cash. These securities are not actively traded, nor will they necessarily be held to maturity.

  b. Included in earnings are realized gains and losses (which include previously unrealized holding gains and losses) and dividend and interest income.

  c. Available-for-sale securities are accounted for according to the cost adjusted for fair value (mark-to-market) method, under which the carrying amount is adjusted at financial statement dates for subsequent changes in fair value (i.e., they are carried at market value).

  d. Unrealized gains and losses on available-for-sale debt and equity securities are calculated in the same manner as those on trading securities.

    (1) These gains and losses, however, are not recognized in income of the period. Instead, the changes in fair value during a period (unrealized gains/losses) are reported as other comprehensive income (see Module 9D), and the accumulated unrealized gain/loss on marketable securities account is presented as accumulated other comprehensive income in stockholders' equity.

  e. The following chart summarizes the three categories of marketable securities and the accounting treatment of each.

ACCOUNTING AND REPORTING OF MARKETABLE DEBT AND EQUITY SECURITIES

Category	Definition	How the security is reported on the balance sheet	How unrealized holding gains and losses are reported on the income statement*	How realized gains and losses are reported on the income statement
Trading (trading securities)	Debt and equity securities bought and held principally for the purpose of selling them in the near term	Reported at fair market value and grouped with current assets on the balance sheet	Unrealized gains and losses are included in earnings in the period they occur	Realized gains and losses not already recognized as unrealized components are recognized
Available-for-sale	Debt and equity securities not classified as trading or held-to-maturity	Reported at fair market value and may be classified as current or noncurrent	Unrealized gains and losses for a period are excluded from earnings and reported as other comprehensive income (If decline is "other than temporary" then recognized in earnings)	Realized gains and losses are recognized (which include unrealized holding gains and losses recognized previously as unrealized)
Held-to-maturity	Debt securities that the organization has the positive intent and ability to hold to the maturity date	Reported at amortized cost and may be classified as current or noncurrent	Unrealized gains and losses are excluded from earnings (unless decline is "other than temporary")	Realized gains and losses are recognized in accordance with amortized cost method

* Or on the statement where items of other comprehensive income are reported.

f. The fair value of a debt security minus its amortized cost represents the correct unrealized gain or loss for this security in the accumulated other comprehensive income account at year-end.

   (1) The adjusting entry for this account at the end of the period will equal the difference between the account's balance before adjustment and the cumulative unrealized gain or loss on the debt and equity securities at the end of the period.

g. Available-for-sale securities are classified on the balance sheet as current or noncurrent on an individual basis based on management's intent concerning the holding period and appear on the statement of cash flows as investing activities.

EXAMPLE

On 1/01/10, when interest rates were 12%, STC Corp. purchased the following securities:

Security description	Acquisition cost
• Shaner Enterprise ten-year, 10%, $1,000 face value bonds (STC Corp. intends to hold the bond until it matures)	$ 887
• Harmony Corporation five-year, 14%, $5,000 face value bond (STC Corp. expects that interest rates will fall and the bond will be sold at a profit)	$5,360
• 100 shares Keswick Corporation common stock (STC anticipates that the price of the stock will rise 10%, at which time the stock will be sold)	$2,200
• 150 shares Rusell Inc. common stock (STC has no immediate plans to sell this stock)	$5,600

The Shaner bond must be classified as held-to-maturity and carried at amortized cost since management has the ability and intent to hold the investment to the maturity date. The Harmony and Keswick securities are classified as trading securities because STC intends to hold these investments for only a short period of time expressly to realize a quick profit. The Rusell Inc. stock is classified as available-for-sale because STC has not expressed an intent to hold the stock for current resale. The Harmony, Keswick, and Rusell investments are all carried at fair market value.

At the end of 2010, the fair values of the Keswick and Rusell stock are $2,700 and $5,190, respectively. Interest rates have fallen to 10%, boosting the value of the Harmony bond to $5,634. Interest income, premium amortization, and unrealized gain on this bond are calculated as

Date	14% Cash interest	12% Effective interest	Premium amortization	Carrying value	Fair value	Unrealized gain (loss)
1/01/10				$5,360	$5,360	
12/31/10	$700	$643	$57	5,303	5,634	$331

NOTE: The unrealized gain ($331) equals the increase in fair value ($274) plus the premium amortization ($57).

Interest income and discount/premium amortization must be recorded for the bonds in any of the three portfolios. Both the Harmony and Shaner bonds were purchased to yield 12%. The adjusting journal entries required at 12/31/10 are

Interest receivable	100	
Investment in Shaner bond—held-to-maturity	6	
Interest income ($887 × 12%)		106

Interest receivable	700	
Investment in Harmony securities—trading		57
Interest income		643

On 12/31/10 after the two adjusting entries above are posted, the carrying values and fair values are

	12/31/10 Carrying amount	**12/31/10 Fair value**
Held-to-maturity:		
Shaner bond	$ 893	NA
Trading:		
Harmony bond	5,303	$5,634
Keswick stock	2,200	2,700
Available-for-sale:		
Rusell stock	5,600	5,190

At this time, the adjusting journal valuation entries are made for the trading and the available-for-sale portfolios of securities, as follows:

Investment in Harmony securities—trading	331	
Unrealized gain on holding debt securities (income statement) ($5,634 FV – $5,303 CV)		331
Investment in Keswick securities—trading	500	
Unrealized gain on holding equity securities (income statement) ($2,700 FV – $2,200 CV)		500
Unrealized loss on Rusell securities—available-for-sale (other comprehensive income account)	410	
Investment in Rusell securities—available-for-sale ($5,600 CV – $5,190 FV)		410

The unrealized holding gain on trading securities is a nominal account which is closed to income at 12/31/10. The unrealized loss on available-for-sale securities is closed out to the "accumulated other comprehensive income" account at year-end, which is presented in the stockholders' equity section of the 12/31/10 balance sheet. It is important to note that the increases and decreases in market value recorded above may alternatively be recorded in a separate fair value adjustment account (contra asset account). If a fair value adjustment account is used to carry the holding gains and losses, then the fair value adjustment account and the investment account would be netted for presentation purposes. The carrying amount of the Shaner bond at 12/31/10 is $893 ($887 + $6).

Now assume that in July 2011, 75 of the 150 shares of Rusell stock were sold for $30 per share. The entry to record the sale is

Cash ($30 × 75)	2,250	
Loss on sale of securities	550	
Investment in Rusell securities—available-for-sale*		2,595
Reclassification adjustment of unrealized loss on Rusell securities—available-for-sale		205

* Carrying value = $5,190 ($5,600 – 410) market value on books ÷ 150 shares = $34.60/share. $2,595 = $34.60 × 75 shares

The loss on sale of securities equals the initial acquisition cost of the securities less the sales price. Because the Rusell securities are classified as available-for-sale, the proportionate amount of unrealized holding gains or losses ($205 = ½ × $410) which had accumulated in the stockholders' equity account would be reclassified and becomes part of the realized loss for inclusion in earnings of the period of the sale.

> **NOTE:** The accumulated other comprehensive income account in stockholders' equity is a "holding account" for the difference between the initial acquisition cost of the available-for-sale security and its current fair market value at the balance sheet date.

No other holding gains or losses beyond the $410 holding loss recognized on December 31, 2010, had accumulated since December 31, 2010. When the available-for-sale security is sold, the amount of the previously recognized unrealized holding gain or loss is reclassified and becomes part of the realized gain or loss on the sale of available-for-sale securities. The realized gain or loss on the sale is then the difference between the selling price and the initial acquisition cost ($550 = $2,250 – $2,800 acquisition cost of 75 shares).

In September 2011, Keswick Corp. declared a 10% stock dividend. Stock dividends should not be reflected in income. The stock's current carrying value of $2,700 should be allocated to the additional shares received from the dividend. Since STC holds 100 shares, the dividend will be 10 shares, resulting in a total of 110 shares. After the dividend, the 110 shares will each have a carrying value of $24.55 ($2,700 ÷ 110) which will be adjusted to market at the end of the reporting period.

STC Corp. periodically reviews its intent to hold or actively trade its securities. At 12/31/11, when interest rates are 8%, STC decides that it will hold the Harmony bond indefinitely. Because this bond was originally classified as trading, it must be transferred to available-for-sale. Market value on this date is $5,773. The entries to record interest income and to transfer the bond are

Interest receivable	700	
Investment in Harmony securities—trading		64
Interest income		636
Investment in Harmony securities—trading	204	
Unrealized gain on holding debt securities		204
Investment in Harmony securities—available-for-sale	5,773	
Investment in Harmony securities—trading		5,773

The holding gain of $204 ($5,773 FV 12/11 – $5,634 FV 12/10 plus premium amortization of $64) is recognized in current earnings, and the value recorded in the available-for-sale portfolio reflects the market value of $5,773 at the transfer date. Note that from this point forward any holding gains or losses should be recognized as other comprehensive income and included in accumulated other comprehensive income in stockholders' equity in accordance with the available-for-sale classification.

Also on 12/31/11, STC sold its held-for-trading Keswick stock for $32 per share. This transaction was recorded as follows:

Cash ($32 × 110 shares)	3,520	
Investment in Keswick securities—trading		2,700
Gain on sale of securities		820

On 12/31/11, STC also recorded the appropriate entries for amortization of the Shaner bond ($7 discount amortization and $107 interest income) and to adjust the Rusell stock to its current fair value of $29 per share.

Finally, on 12/31/11 STC discovered that Shaner Enterprise is experiencing financial difficulty due to mismanagement, and the full amount of the bond will not be collected. This impairment would be considered other than temporary, so the investment in Shaner Enterprise bonds must be reduced to its current fair value of $500. The realized loss of $400 ($900 12/31/11 current carrying value – $500 FV) is reported in earnings, and no write-up will be allowed if a recovery is made at a later date.

To summarize STC Corp.'s marketable securities transactions for 2010 and 2011, T-accounts for each security are shown below, followed by earnings information relating to the investments.

Harmony Bond—Trading			
1/01/10 Acquisition	5,360	57	12/31/10 Amort.
12/31/10 Adj. to FV	331	64	12/31/11 Amort.
12/31/11 Adj. to FV	204	5,773	12/31/11 Transfer
Bal. 12/31/11	0		

Harmony Bond—Available-for-Sale		
12/31/11 Transfer	5,773	
Bal. 12/31/11	5,773	

Shaner Bond—Held-to-Maturity			
1/01/10 Acquisition	887		
12/31/10 Amort.	6		
12/31/11 Amort.	7	400	12/31/11 Write-down
Bal. 12/31/11	500		

Keswick Stock—Trading			
1/01/10 Acquisition			
(100 shares)	2,200		
12/31/10 Adj. to FV	500		
(9/10 Stock div.—10 shares)		2,700	12/31/11 Sale
Bal. 12/31/11	0		

Rusell Stock—Available-for-Sale			
1/01/10 Acquisition			
(150 shares)	5,600	410	12/31/10 Adj. to FV
		2,595	7/11 Sale (75 shares)
		420	12/31/11 Adj. to FV
Bal. 12/31/11	2,175		

Year	Transaction	Income/Gain	Loss	Net earnings	Other comprehensive income
2010	Harmony adj. to FV	$ 331			
	Keswick adj. to FV	500			
	Interest on Shaner bond	106			
	Interest on Harmony bond	643			
	Rusell adj. to FV				$(410)
	2010 total	$1,580		$1,580	(410)
2011	Write-down of Shaner bond		$(400)		
	Sale of one-half of Rusell securities		(550)		$ 205
	Gain on Keswick securities	$ 820			
	Harmony adj. to FV	203			
	Interest on Shaner bond	107			
	Interest on Harmony bond	636			
	Rusell adj. to FV				(420)
	2011 total	$1,766	$(950)	$ 816	$(215)

4. **Transfers between Categories**

a. The classification of securities should be reviewed at each balance sheet date. Although a reclassification should be rare, a company may deem it necessary to transfer a security from one category to another.

(1) Such transfers are accounted for at fair value, taking into consideration any unrealized holding gains or losses.

(a) For example, when a security is transferred **from** trading securities, any recognized unrealized gain or loss as of the date of transfer should not be reversed.

(b) On the other hand, in a transfer **to** trading securities, unrealized holding gains and losses are recognized immediately.

(c) Held-to-maturity securities reclassified **to** available-for-sale securities must be restated to fair value; any unrealized holding gain or loss that results is reported as accumulated other comprehensive income in stockholders' equity.

(d) However, transfers **from** held-to-maturity should be rare.

(e) Unrealized holding gain or loss on securities transferred **to** held-to-maturity from available-for-sale is also reported as accumulated other comprehensive income in stockholders' equity, but this gain or loss is then amortized over the remaining life of the security as an adjustment to yield.

(2) The treatment of securities transfers is summarized in the chart that follows.

Securities transferred to:

		Held-to-maturity	Available-for-sale	Trading
Securities transferred from:	Held-to-maturity		Report unrealized G/L as accumulated other comprehensive income in SE	Recognize unrealized G/L immediately
	Available-for-sale	Report unrealized G/L as accumulated other comprehensive income in SE & amortize the gain or loss over remaining life of security		Recognize unrealized G/L immediately
	Trading	Do not reverse unrealized G/L previously recognized in income	Do not reverse unrealized G/L previously recognized in income	

5. **Income Statement Presentation**

a. Since held-to-maturity and available-for-sale securities are held for some length of time, these securities may become impaired at some point.

(1) If the decline in value is other than temporary, then the impaired security must be written down to fair value and the realized loss included in earnings.

(2) Any subsequent recovery would not be recognized in earnings unless realized through sale of the security.

(3) An other than temporary impairment cannot occur in the context of trading securities because holding gains and losses are recognized in current earnings without limitation.

    b. Cash dividends or interest income should be included in the current period's income.

    c. Stock dividends should not be reflected in income.

        (1) Additional shares received from a stock dividend should be added to the original shares and the per share value should be calculated upon the original shares' carrying value.

        (2) At the end of the period the carrying value of the stock is adjusted to the fair value, and any unrealized holding gain or loss is recorded.

    d. Realized and **unrealized** gains and losses on trading securities are included in the current period's earnings.

        (1) Only realized gains and losses on sales of available-for-sale and held-to-maturity securities should be included in earnings.

        (2) Unrealized gains (losses) on available-for-sale securities are reported as other comprehensive income in one of three ways (see Module 9D).

        (3) Amortization of any unrealized holding gain or loss on securities transferred to held-to-maturity from available-for-sale is included in income.

> **NOW REVIEW MULTIPLE-CHOICE QUESTIONS 1 THROUGH 31 IN VOLUME 2**

C. Investments Where Significant Influence *Does* Exist

    Use of the **equity method** is required for investments which give the investor the ability to exercise significant influence over the operating and financial policies of the investee.

1. Ownership of 20% or more of the outstanding stock will result in that ability.

    a. Exceptions to the use of the equity method (i.e., the cost adjusted for fair value method) are related to an assessment of the investor's level of influence over the investee.

        (1) The cost adjusted for fair value method should be used if an investment of more than 20% is judged to be temporary, if the investment is in a company operating in a foreign country which has severe restrictions on the operations of companies and on the transfer of monies outside the country, and for other investments of more than 20% that do not result in significant influence.

    b. There may be unusual circumstances in which a less than 20% investor may have significant influence over the investee, in which case the equity method must be used to account for the investment.

2. **Cost adjusted for fair value method**—The cost adjusted for fair value and the equity methods differ in the treatment of the investment account and in the recognition of earnings from the investment.

    a. The cost adjusted for fair value method first records the cost of the investment in the investment account.

    b. Income is recognized for dividends distributed from income of the investee earned since the date the investor acquired the stock.

        (1) Any dividends distributed by the investee which exceed earnings since the acquisition date are classified as return of capital and recorded as a reduction of the investment account.

    c. Under the cost adjusted for fair value method, equity securities must be adjusted for subsequent changes in market value, and the unrealized holding gain or loss on equity securities for the period equals the current fair value minus the previous period's fair value on the books.

3. **Equity method**—The equity method also begins with recording the cost of the investment in the investment account but the two methods differ from this point on.

    a. A basic concept of the equity method is the reciprocal relationship formed between the investment account on the investor's books and the book values of the net assets on the investee's books.

    b. As changes in the investee's net assets occur (e.g., earnings, dividends, etc.), the investor will recognize in the investment account the percentage of ownership share of those changes.

    c. Another aspect of the equity method is the computation and accounting for the difference between the cost of the investment and the book value of the acquired asset share at the investment date.

        (1) The abundance of advanced accounting texts currently in print use an assortment of terms to describe the characteristics of this concept. For purposes of uniformity, the following boldfaced terms shall be used throughout this module.

            Differential: The difference between the cost of the investment and the underlying book value of the net assets of the investee. This difference can be either positive or negative, as follows:

Excess of Cost over Book Value, which is generally attributable to

- **Excess of fair value over book value,** when the fair values of the investee's assets are greater than their book values, and
- **Goodwill,** when the investee has high earnings potential for which the investor has paid more than the fair values of the other net assets

Excess of Book Value over Cost, which is generally attributable to

- **Excess of book value over fair value,** when the book values of the net assets of the investee are greater than their fair values, and
- **Excess of fair value over cost,** when the cost of the investment is less than even the fair values of the investee's net assets. Some authors term this "negative goodwill."

If the differential is related to assets with finite useful lives, it will be amortized to the investment account. Goodwill will not be amortized; it will be written down if the investment is determined to be impaired.

EXAMPLE

A Company purchased 20 shares of B Company's 100 shares of common stock outstanding for $25,000. The book value of B's total net worth (i.e., stockholders' equity) at the date of the investment was $120,000. Any excess of cost over book value is due to equipment that has a ten-year remaining useful life.

Investment cost		$ 25,000
Book value of B Company	$120,000	
Percentage owned	20%	
Investor's share		24,000
Excess of cost over book value (due to equipment)		$ 1,000

Amortization over forty years
$1,000 ÷ 10 years = $100

---

d. Under the equity method, the Income from Investment account is a parallel income statement account to the Investment in Stock balance sheet account. These two accounts should include all the income recognition and amortization resulting from the investment.

> **NOTE:** Under the equity method, dividends received from the investee are a reduction in the Investment balance sheet account and are **not** part of the Income from Investment account.

e. Alternative levels of recording the results of intercompany transactions and amortization in both the investment and investment income accounts are used in accounting practice. The alternatives are presented below.

(1) **Cost adjusted for fair value method**—No intercompany transactions or amortization are recognized in either the investment account or investment income account under this method.

(2) **"Partial" equity**—Includes recognition of percentage share of income or loss, dividends, and any changes in the investment percentage. This method is often used for investments that will be consolidated. Thus, amortization and other adjustments are made on the worksheets, not in the investment account.

(3) **"Full" equity**—In addition to the factors above, this level includes any necessary amortization or write-off of the differential between the investment cost and book value of the investment. This level also recognizes the effects of any intercompany transactions (e.g., inventory, fixed assets, and bonds) between the investor and investee corporations. All unconsolidated investments are reported in the financial statements using the "full" equity method.

EXAMPLE

Assume the same facts for A Company and B Company as stated above. In addition, B Company earned $10,000 income for the year and paid $6,000 in dividends. There were no intercompany transactions. If A Company does not have significant influence over B Company, the investment would be accounted for by the cost adjusted for fair value method. If A Company can significantly influence B Company, the equity method is used to account for and report the investment. The appropriate entries are

Cost adjusted for fair value method			Equity method		
1. To record purchase of 20% interest					
Investment in stock of B	25,000		Investment in stock of B	25,000	
Cash		25,000	Cash		25,000

2. To record percentage of share of investee's reported income

No entry	Investment in stock of B	2,000	
	Income from investment		2,000
	(20% × $10,000)		

3. To record percentage share of dividend received as distribution of income

Cash	1,200		Cash	1,200	
Dividend income from invest-		1,200	Investment in stock of B		1,200
ment (20% × $6,000)					

4. To record amortization of equipment in accordance with ASC Topic 323

| No entry (no differential amortization under this method) | Income from investment | 100 | |
| | Investment in stock of B | | 100 |

The differences in the account balances under the equity method vs. the cost adjusted for fair value method reflect the different income recognition processes and underlying asset valuation concepts of the two methods. The investment account balance under the cost adjusted for fair value method remains at the investment cost of $25,000 (although subsequent changes in fair value would require that the investment account be adjusted to market value), while under the equity method, the investment balance increases to $25,700. The $700 difference is the investor's share of the increase in the investee's undistributed earnings less the investor's amortization of the differential (excess of cost over the book value of the investment).

The amount of the investment income to be recognized by the investor also depends upon the length of time during the year the investment is owned.

For example, assume that A Company acquired the 20% interest on July 1, 2010, and B Company earned $10,000 of income ratably over the period from January 1 to December 31, 2010. The entry to record A Company's percentage share of B Company's income for the period of July 1 to December 31, 2010, would be

Cost adjusted for fair value method	**Equity method**		
No entry	Investment in stock of B	1,000	
	Income from investment (20% × $10,000 × 6/12)		1,000

The receipt of the $1,200 dividends after the acquisition date would require additional analysis since the $1,200 dividend received is greater than the investor's share of the investee's income ($1,000) since acquisition. The difference of $200 ($1,200 – $1,000) is a return of capital under the cost adjusted for fair value method, and is recorded as follows:

Cost adjusted for fair value method			**Equity method**		
Cash	1,200		Cash	1,200	
Dividend income from investment		1,000	Investment in stock of B		1,200
Investment in stock of B		200			

The amortization of equipment will also be prorated to the time period the investment was held.

4. **Changes to or from the equity method**—when an investor changes from the cost adjusted for fair value to the equity method, the investment account must be adjusted retroactively and prior years' income and retained earnings must be retroactively restated.

a. A change to the equity method would be made if an investor made additional purchases of stock and, for the first time, is able to exercise significant influence over the operating and financial decisions of the investee.

(1) Remember that ASC Topic 323 (APB 18) states that investments of 20% or more of the investee's outstanding stock carry the "presumption" that the investor has the ability to exercise significant influence. Therefore, in most cases, when an investment of less than 20% increases to more than 20%, the investor will retroactively change from the cost adjusted for fair value method to the equity method.

(a) The retroactive change to the equity method requires a prior period adjustment for the difference in the investment account and retained earnings account between the amounts that were recognized in prior periods under the cost adjusted for fair value method and the amounts that would have been recognized if the equity method had been used.

1] In the full-year investment example on the previous page where A Company had a $25,000 balance in its Investment in B account under the cost adjusted for fair value method and $25,700 under the equity method, if A changed from the cost to the equity method because of its increased influence over B, the change entry would be

Investment in B Company	700	
Retained earnings		700
($700 = $2,000 – $1,200 – $100)		

(b) In addition, any balance in the Unrealized holding gain or loss account must be reversed.

1] Assume that the fair value of the B Company stock had increased from $25,000 to $27,000 as of the end of the year of acquisition. The investment account would have been debited for $2,000 and the Unrealized gain on MES account credited for $2,000 to bring the carrying value of the stock up to its market value. Upon retroactive change to the equity method, the following reversing entry would be made:

Unrealized gain on MES	2,000	
Investment in stock of B		2,000

(2) If the change is made at any time point other than the beginning of the fiscal period, the change entry would also include an adjustment to the period's Income from investment account to record the difference between the cost adjusted for fair value and equity methods handling of the investor's share of the investee's income for the current period.

b. When an investor discontinues using the equity method because of an inability to influence the investee's financial and operating policies, no retroactive restatement is allowed.

(1) An example of this would be a disposal of stock resulting in a decrease in the percentage of stock owned from more than 20% to less than 20%.

(2) The earnings or losses that relate to the shares retained by the investor that were previously recognized by the investor should remain as a part of the carrying amount.

(a) However, if dividends received by the investor in subsequent periods exceed the investor's share of the investee's earnings for such periods, the excess should be accounted for as a return of capital and recorded as a reduction in the investment carrying amount.

c. A T-account is used to exhibit the major changes in the Investment in stock account under the equity method.

Investment in Stock	
Original cost of investment	Percentage share of investee's losses since acquisition
Percentage share of investee's income since acquisition	Percentage share of dividends received
Amortization of excess of book value over cost	Amortization of excess of cost over book value
Increase above "significant influence" ownership— retroactive adjustment for change to equity	Disposal or sales of investment in stock

d. In addition to the above, several adjustments may be added if the "full equity" method is used. This method eliminates the effects of intercompany profits from transactions such as sales of inventory between the investor and investee corporations. This method is rarely required on the exam but candidates should briefly review these additions in association with the discussion of the elimination entries required for consolidated working papers presented later in Module 18.

Investment in Stock (continued)	
Realized portion of intercompany profit from last period confirmed this period	Elimination of unrealized portion of intercompany profit transactions from current period

NOW REVIEW MULTIPLE-CHOICE QUESTIONS 32 THROUGH 48 IN VOLUME 2

D. Equity Method and Deferred Income Taxes

1. Recognition of deferred taxes may be required when the equity method is used.

a. The difference between the income recognized using the equity method and the dividends received from the investee represents a temporary difference for which interperiod allocation is necessary.

> **NOTE:** Companies are allowed to exclude 80% of the dividend income from domestic investees. If an investor owns 80% or more of the investee's stock, the dividend exclusion is increased to 100% (i.e., no taxes are due on investee dividend distributions). The dividend exclusion (dividends received deduction) is a permanent difference.

2. A discussion of deferred income taxes arising from equity method investments and several examples are provided in Module 14, Deferred Taxes.

E. The Fair Value Option

1. An entity may elect to value its securities at fair value.

   a. A firm can elect the fair value option on an instrument-by-instrument basis.
   b. If the firm elects the fair value option for reporting available-for-sale or held-to-maturity securities, the security is revalued to fair value and any gain or loss is recorded in earnings for the period.
   c. Likewise, if the fair value option is elected for instruments that would otherwise be reported using the equity method, the securities are revalued to fair value. Any gain or loss is recorded in earnings for the period.
   d. If the fair value option is elected for instruments that would normally use the equity method, it must be applied to all interests in that entity (i.e., both debt and equity instruments would be valued at fair value).

2. The fair value option can be elected on the date an investment is first recognized, or when the investment no longer qualifies for fair value treatment.

   a. For example, if Company A has a trading security in Company B stock and acquires more than 20% of Company B, the rules of the equity method of reporting would normally be applied. However, if the fair value option is elected, Company A is no longer required to use the equity method, but instead values the security at year-end at fair value. Any unrealized gain or loss is recognized in earnings for the period.

3. The rules for the statement of cash flows continue to apply for determining the classification of a purchase or sale of security on the statement of cash flows. Additional disclosures in the notes to the financial statements are required if the fair value option is elected. Refer to the outline of SFAS 159 (ASC Topic 825) for these disclosures.

F. Stock Dividends and Splits

Stock dividends and stock splits are not recorded as income. The recipient continues to own the same proportion of the investee as before the stock split or stock dividend. The investor should make a memo entry to record the receipt of the additional shares and recompute the per share cost of the stock.

G. Stock Rights

1. Investors in common stock occasionally receive stock rights to purchase additional common stock below the existing market price. The investee company has probably issued the stock rights to satisfy the investor's preemptive right to maintain an existing level of ownership of the investee. It is possible to waive these preemptive rights in some jurisdictions.

2. Rights are issued below the existing market price to encourage the exercise of the rights (i.e., the investor's use thereof resulting in acquisitions of additional shares of stock).

   a. The rights are separable, having their own markets, and should be accounted for separately from the investment in common stock.
   b. The rights represent a possible dilution of investor ownership and should be recorded by allocating the cost of the stock between the market value of the rights and the market value of the stock.

      (1) This is accomplished by multiplying the following ratio by the cost basis of the stock:

$$\frac{\text{Market value of right}}{\text{Market value of right} + \text{Market value of stock}}$$

3. The following entry is made to record the receipt of the rights:

Investment in stock rights	xx	
Investment in common stock		xx

4. The rights can be sold or exercised. The entry for exercise is

Investment in common stock	xx	
Investment in stock rights		xx
Cash		xx

5. If the stock rights lapse

Loss on expiration of stock rights	xx	
Investment in stock rights		xx

EXAMPLE

A Company acquired 1,000 shares of common stock in B Company for $12,000. A Company subsequently received two stock rights for every share owned in B Company. Four rights and $12 are required to purchase one new share of common stock. At the date of issuance the market value of the stock rights and the common stock is $5 and $20, respectively. The entry to record the receipt of the rights is as follows:

Investment in stock rights	4,000	
Investment in common stock		4,000

The $4,000 above was computed as follows:

Total market value of rights	2,000 rights × $ 5 =	$10,000
Total market value of shares	1,000 shares × $20 =	$20,000
Combined market value		$30,000
Cost allocated to stock rights	$\dfrac{\$10,000}{\$30,000}$ × $12,000 = $4,000	
Cost allocated to common stock	$\dfrac{\$20,000}{\$30,000}$ × $12,000 = $8,000	

NOTE: $2 ($4,000 ÷ 2,000 rights) of cost is assigned to each stock right and $8 ($8,000 ÷ 1,000 shares) of cost to each share of stock.

If A uses 800 rights to purchase 200 additional shares of stock, the following entry would be made to record the transaction.

Investment in common stock	4,000	
Investment in stock rights		1,600*
Cash		2,400**

  * (800 rights × $2/right)
 ** (200 shares × $12/share)

If 1,000 stock rights are sold outright for $5 per right, the following entry would be made to record the transaction.

Cash	5,000*	
Investment in stock rights		2,000**
Gain on sale of rights		3,000

  * (1,000 rights × $5/right)
 ** (1,000 rights × $2/right)

If the 200 remaining stock rights are permitted to expire, the following entry would be made:

Loss on expiration of stock rights	400*	
Investment in stock rights		400*

* (200 rights × $2/right)

The journal entries above can be summarized as follows:

Investment in common stock				Investment in stock rights		
Purchase, 1,000 shares @ $12	12,000	4,000	← Cost allocated to stock rights →	4,000	1,600	Exercise of 800 rights
Purchase, 200 shares by exercise of rights	4,000				2,000	Sale of 1,000 rights
					400	Expiration of 200 rights
	12,000				--	

NOW REVIEW MULTIPLE-CHOICE QUESTIONS 49 THROUGH 52 IN VOLUME 2

H. Cash Surrender Value of Life Insurance

1. The cash surrender value of life insurance policies represents a noncurrent investment when the company is the beneficiary (rather than insured employees). The entry to record insurance premiums that increase cash surrender value is

Insurance expense	(plug)	
Cash surrender value	(increase in CSV)	
Cash		(total premium)

   a. Cash surrender value remains a noncurrent asset unless the company plans to cash in the policy within the next period.

2. During the first few years of a policy, no cash surrender value may attach to the policy. During this period, the entire insurance premium would be expense. In addition, any dividends received from the life insurance policy are not recorded as revenue, but instead are offset against insurance expense.

I. Research Component—Accounting Standards Codification

1. Research for investments is found in three topics in the Codification: ASC Topics 320, 323, and 825. ASC Topic 320, *Investments—Debt and Equity Securities*, outlines the rules for trading securities, available-for-sale securities, and held-to-maturity securities. ASC Topic 323, *Investments—Equity Method and Joint Ventures*, covers the accounting rules for securities where significant influence exists and the equity method of accounting is required. ASC Topic 825, *Financial Instruments*, outlines the rules for electing the fair value option for reporting investments in debt and equity.

2. Keywords for research are listed below.

Asset-liability management	Fair value investment	Other comprehensive income loss
Available-for-sale	Fair value option	Readily determinable fair value
Carrying amount investment	Fair value security	Security maturity date
Cash flows securities	50% or less	Shares of investee
Classified securities	Held-to-maturity	Significant influence
Change intent	Increase in ownership investee	Trading
Debt equity securities	Intent indefinite period	Transfer between categories
Decline in fair value	Intercompany profits	Unrealized holding gains
Disclosure securities	Interest income	Unrealized holding losses
Dividend income	Investments equity securities	Voting privileges
Enterprise disclose	Loss temporary decline	
Equity method investment	Other comprehensive income gain	

> **NOW REVIEW MULTIPLE-CHOICE QUESTIONS 53 THROUGH 59 IN VOLUME 2**

J. International Financial Reporting Standards (IFRS)

1. As discussed earlier in fixed assets, the term investment is used in the area of investment property as well as investments in financial instruments of other entities. The accounting rules for investment property were covered under the section on fixed assets.

2. The term "investments" refers to investments that are held for trading (HFT), available for sale (AFS), and held to maturity (HTM), as well as investments accounted for using the equity method, and investments that require consolidated financial statements. The accounting for investments is covered by various IASs, depending upon the type of investment.

3. A financial instrument should be classified as either fair value through profit or loss (FVTPL), held to maturity (HTM), available for sale (AFS), or loans and receivables.

   a. The FVTPL category includes financial assets in the held for trading (HFT) category.
   b. HTM instruments have fixed and determinable payments and fixed maturity dates.
   c. Held for trading (HFT) securities are securities that the entity has the intent to sell in the near term.
   d. Available for sale financial assets are those that are not classified as FVTPL, HTM, or loans and receivables.

4. If an asset is classified as fair value through profit or loss (FVTPL), it is remeasured to fair value at the end of each accounting period, and any profit or loss is recorded in that period.

a. An election can be made to use the FVTPL method for accounting purposes for an asset normally classified as available for sale (AFS) or held to maturity (HTM).

   (1) However, if an equity security has no active market in which to determine fair value, then the equity security may not be classified as FVTPL.

b. Once the item is classified as FVTPL, it may not be subsequently reclassified.

c. Any equity instrument that does not have a quoted market price or a determinable fair value should be accounted for using the cost method.

5. If FVTPL is not elected, different rules apply.

   a. If the investment is classified as held to maturity (HTM), the investment is recorded at cost, and is subsequently measured at amortized cost using the effective interest method.

   b. Similarly, if a financial asset is classified as loans or receivables, it is accounted for by using amortized cost and the effective interest method.

   c. If the investment is classified as available-for-sale (AFS), the asset is measured at fair value, and any income or loss is recognized in other comprehensive income for the period.

      (1) If a debt security is classified as available-for-sale, any premium or discount must be amortized using the effective interest method on the income statement, with the increase or decrease in fair value reported in other comprehensive income.

6. Investments in associates (affiliates) are accounted for using either the equity method or the FVTPL method.

   a. To qualify for the equity method, the entity must have significant influence over the investee.

      (1) Significant influence is presumed when the investor owns between 20% and 50% of the voting power of another entity.

   b. Consistent with US GAAP, the equity method requires the investment to be recorded at cost, with the investor's share of profit or loss recognized at year-end in the investment account, and the investor's share of dividend distributions recognized as a reduction in the investment account.

      (1) If the cost of the investment is greater than the investor's share of the fair value of net assets, it is not recorded as goodwill.

         (a) However, this portion of the cost of the investment over the carrying amount is amortized as the assets are realized.

      (2) If the cost is less than the fair value of net assets (goodwill is negative), this difference is recognized as income in the year of acquisition.

      (3) An impairment of an investment is recognized if the carrying amount of the investment is greater than its recoverable amount.

NOW REVIEW MULTIPLE-CHOICE QUESTIONS 60 THROUGH 64 IN VOLUME 2

KEY TERMS

Amortized cost. Acquisition cost adjusted for amortization of premium or discount.

Available-for-sale securities. Include debt and equity securities not categorized as either held-to-maturity securities or trading securities.

Debt securities. "Any security representing a creditor relationship with an entity."

Differential. The difference between the cost of the investment and the underlying book value of the net assets of the investee.

Equity method. Required for investments which give the investor the ability to exercise significant influence over the operating and financial policies of the investee.

Equity securities. Include ownership interests (common, preferred, and other capital stock), rights to acquire ownership interests (put options).

Fair value option. An entity may elect to value its securities at fair value.

Held-to-maturity securities (amortized cost). This category includes only debt securities and requires the positive intent and ability to hold the securities to maturity (not simply an absence of intent to sell).

Trading securities (mark-to-market). Debt and equity securities purchased and held principally for the purpose of generating gains on current resale are classified as trading securities.

Module 17: Statement of Cash Flows

Overview

The primary purposes of the statement of **cash flows** are to provide information about an entity's cash receipts and cash payments and to disclose information about the financing and investing activities of an entity. As such, the statement divides cash receipts and cash payments into three sections: operating, investing, and financing.

1. **Operating activities** include delivering or producing goods for sale and providing services. Generally, operating activities are related to net income and the current asset and current liability sections of the balance sheet.
2. **Investing activities** include the acquisition or disposition of long-term productive assets or securities. Investing activities are generally related to the noncurrent section of the balance sheet.
3. **Financing activities** include obtaining resources from creditors and repaying amounts borrowed. Generally, financing activities are related to the noncurrent liability and equity sections of the balance sheet.

This module also covers the two methods of presenting cash flows from operating activities: direct or indirect. The FASB prefers the direct method. Cash flow presentations for investing and financing activities do not differ between the two methods.

A. Objectives of the Statement of Cash Flows (See outline of SFAS 95, [ASC Topic 230])

1. The primary purposes of this statement are to provide information about an entity's cash receipts and cash payments and to disclose information about the financing and investing activities of an entity. This statement should help the users of the statement assess:

   a. An entity's ability to generate positive future cash flows;
   b. An entity's ability to meet its obligations and pay dividends;
   c. The reasons for differences between income and associated cash receipts and payments; and
   d. The cash and noncash aspects of an entity's investing and financing transactions.

2. In order to facilitate the users in making those assessments, a statement of cash flows shall report cash receipts and cash payments of an entity's operations, its investing transactions, and its financing transactions. A separate schedule accompanying the statement should also report the effects of investing and financing transactions that **do not affect cash**.

3. The statement of cash flows is required to be prepared based on changes during the period in cash and cash equivalents. Cash equivalents include short-term, highly liquid investments that (1) are readily convertible to known amounts of cash and (2) are so near their maturity (original maturity of three months or less from **date of purchase** by the enterprise) that they present negligible risk of changes in value because of changes in interest rates. Treasury bills, commercial paper, and money market funds are all examples of cash equivalents.

B. Statement of Cash Flows Classification

1. Cash receipts and cash payments are to be classified into operating, financing, and investing activities.

    a. Operating activities include delivering or producing goods for sale and providing services.

        (1) Operating activities include all transactions that are **not** investing and financing activities.
        (2) More specifically, cash flows from operations should not include cash flows from transactions whose effects are included in income but are investing and financing activities.

            (a) For example, a gain (loss) on extinguishment of debt should properly be classified as a financing activity, and a gain (loss) from disposal of property should be classified as an investing activity.

    b. Investing activities include the acquisition and disposition of long-term productive assets or securities that are not considered cash equivalents.

        (1) Investing activities also include the lending of money and collection on loans.

    c. Financing activities include obtaining resources from owners and returning the investment.

        (1) Also included is obtaining resources from creditors and repaying the amount borrowed.

2. The FASB has listed the following as examples of classifications of transactions.

ACTIVITIES REPORTED ON THE STATEMENT OF CASH FLOWS

Description of the activity	Positive cash flow	Negative cash flow
Operating activities (direct method):		
• Cash received from customers	xx	
• Cash received from interest	xx	
• Cash received from dividends	xx	
• Cash received from sales of securities classified as trading	xx	
• Cash paid to suppliers		xx
• Cash paid for operating expenses		xx
• Cash paid for interest		xx
• Cash paid for income taxes		xx
• Cash paid for securities classified as trading (based on nature and purpose acquired)		xx
Investing activities		
• Proceeds from sales of property, plant, and equipment	xx	
• Proceeds from sales of investments in stocks (available for sale) and bonds (available for sale)	xx	
• Cash paid for securities classified as trading (based on nature and purpose acquired)		xx
• Proceeds from the sale or redemption of investments in bonds classified as held to maturity	xx	
• Proceeds from collection of loans (principal only)	xx	
• Proceeds from selling components of the company	xx	
• Acquisition of property, plant, and equipment (capital expenditures)		xx
• Acquisition of investments in stocks and bonds (available for sale or held to maturity)		xx
• Making loans to other entities		xx
• Acquiring other businesses		xx
Financing activities:		
• Proceeds from issuing common and preferred stock	xx	
• Proceeds from reissuing treasury stock	xx	
• Proceeds from issuing short-term debt	xx	
• Proceeds from issuing long-term debt	xx	
• Paying cash dividends		xx
• Repurchasing common stock (treasury stock)		xx
• Repaying short-term loans (principal only)		xx
• Repaying long-term loans, including capital lease obligations (principal only)		xx

Noncash investing and financing activities (reported in a separate schedule)
- Acquiring an asset through a capital lease
- Conversion of debt to equity
- Exchange of noncash assets or liabilities for other noncash assets or liabilities
- Issuance of stock to acquire assets

a. Cash flows from trading securities are classified as operating or investing activities based on the nature and purpose for which the securities were acquired.

> **NOTE:** Noncash investing and financing activities should be excluded from the statement itself. These transactions involve no cash inflows and outflows, but they have a significant effect on the prospective cash flows of a company. Therefore, they must be distinguished from activities that involved cash receipts and payments and must be reported in a separate schedule or in the footnotes to the financial statements.

b. In the statement, the inflows and outflows for each category (operating, investing, and financing) should be shown separately, and the **net** cash flows (the difference between the inflows and outflows) should be reported.

> **NOW REVIEW MULTIPLE-CHOICE QUESTIONS 1 THROUGH 15 IN VOLUME 2**

C. Direct or Indirect Presentation in Reporting Operating Activities

1. The FASB decided that the preferable method of presenting net cash flows from operating activities is by **directly** showing major classes of operating cash receipts and payments.

   a. However, the **indirect (reconciliation) method** is also permitted.
   b. When the direct method is used, it is also necessary to present a separate accompanying schedule showing the indirect method.
   c. The **direct method** is discussed first, followed by a discussion of the **indirect method**.

2. Under the direct approach, cash flow elements of operating activities are derived from the accrual basis components of net income.

   a. In converting to the cash basis, accounts that should be analyzed under operating activities are those which are debited or credited when recording transactions that affect the income statement.

      (1) These transactions include transactions with outsiders and adjusting entries.
      (2) For example, these accounts include sales, cost of sales, operating expenses, and tax expense, as well as assets and liabilities which are related to them, such as accounts receivable, inventory, accounts payable, accrued expenses, and prepaid expenses.

      > **NOTE:** Interest expense and interest revenue are included within operating activities.

      (3) Formulas for conversion of various income statement amounts from the accrual basis to the cash basis are summarized in the following table:

Accrual basis		Additions		Deductions		Cash basis
Net sales	+	Beginning AR	–	Ending AR AR written off	=	Cash received from customers
Cost of goods sold	+	Ending inventory Beginning AP	–	Depreciation and amortization* Beginning inventory Ending AP	=	Cash paid to suppliers
Operating expenses	+	Ending prepaid expenses Beginning accrued expenses payable	–	Depreciation and amortization Beginning prepaid expenses Ending accrued expenses payable	=	Cash paid for operating expenses

      * Applies to a manufacturing entity

   b. A T-account analysis method may be used instead of the above formulas to determine cash received and cash paid. T-account analysis provides a quick, systematic way to accumulate the information needed to prepare the statement.

c. The direct approach would be presented in the statement of cash flows as follows:

Cash flows from operating activities

Cash received from dividends	$ 500	
Cash received from interest	1,000	
Cash received from sale of goods	9,000	
Cash provided by operating activities		$10,500
Cash paid to suppliers	5,000	
Cash paid for operating expenses	500	
Cash paid for interest	500	
Cash paid for taxes	500	
Cash disbursed from operating activities		6,500
Net cash flows from operating activities		$ 4,000

3. The other way of reporting net cash flows from operations is known as the **indirect method**.

a. This is done by starting with income from continuing operations and adjusting for changes in operating related accounts (e.g., inventory and accounts payable) and noncash expenses, revenues, losses, and gains.

(1) Noncash items that were subtracted in determining income must be added back in determining net cash flows from operations. Each of these noncash items is a charge against income but does not decrease cash.

(2) Items to be added back include depreciation, amortization of intangibles, amortization of discount on bonds payable, bad debt expense, and any increase in the deferred tax liability. Note each of these items is charged against income but does not decrease cash.

(3) Noncash items that were added in determining income must be subtracted from net income in determining net cash flows from operations. Each of these noncash items is an increase to income but does not increase cash.

(4) Items to be deducted from income include decreases in the deferred tax liability and amortization of the premium on bonds payable.

(5) Finally, gains (losses) on fixed assets require adjustment, since the cash received is not measured by the gain (loss), that is, a fixed asset with a book value of $10, sold for $15 in cash, provides $15 in cash but is reported as only a $5 gain on the income statement. The $15 is shown as a separate item on the cash flow statement under investing activities and the $5 gain is subtracted from income. Losses on asset disposals are added back to income.

b. When preparing the cash flows from operating activities section of a Statement of Cash Flows under the indirect method, reconstructing journal entries may help in determining if an item should be added or subtracted to net income.

EXAMPLE

If accounts receivable increased by $20,000 over the year, the journal entry that would result in an increase to accounts receivable would be

Accounts receivable	xx	
Sales		xx

This entry results in an increase to net income (through sales), but cash is not affected. Therefore, the amount of the increase is deducted from net income in determining cash flows from operating activities.

If accounts payable decreased by $35,000, the entry for a decrease in accounts payable would be

Accounts payable	xx	
Cash		xx

Since the corresponding credit results in a decrease to cash, the amount of this decrease should be deducted from net income in determining cash flows from operating activities.

---

c. When the **indirect** method is used, separate disclosure of cash flows related to extraordinary items and discontinued operations is permitted, but is not required.

(1) If an entity chooses to disclose this information, disclosure must be consistent for all periods affected.

(2) Extraordinary items, if disclosed, should be added to (or subtracted from) operating activities (adjustment to net income) at the gross amount, not the net-of-tax amount.

(a) Under either method, the extraordinary item should be included in financing or investing activities, whichever is appropriate.

ADJUSTMENTS TO NET INCOME FOR INDIRECT METHOD

Add to net income	Deduct from net income
Decreases in:	**Increases in:**
Accounts receivable (net)	Accounts receivable (net)
Inventories	Inventories
Prepaid expenses	Prepaid expenses
Deferred tax asset	Deferred tax asset
Increases in:	**Decreases in:**
Accounts payable	Accounts payable
Income taxes payable	Income taxes payable
Deferred tax liability	Deferred tax liability
Interest payable	Interest payable
Other accrued payables	Other accrued payables
Unearned revenue	Unearned revenue

Other items:
- Losses from disposals of property, plant, and equipment and available-for-sale investments
- Depreciation expense
- Amortization expense related to intangible assets and bond discounts
- Bad debts expense (if adjustment for accounts receivable is based upon the gross, not the net, change in accounts receivable)
- Losses from early extinguishments of debt

Other items:
- Gains from disposals of property, plant and equipment and available-for-sale investments
- Undistributed income from equity method investments (equity income less the cash dividends received during the period)
- Amortization of a bond premium
- Gains from early extinguishments of debt

5. The direct and indirect approaches will both be illustrated throughout the remainder of this module.

NOW REVIEW MULTIPLE-CHOICE QUESTIONS 16 THROUGH 29 IN VOLUME 2

D. Example of Statement of Cash Flows

The following information pertains to the Haner Company at December 31, 2010. Comparative balance sheets for 2009 and 2010 are as follows:

EXAMPLE

	2010	2009	Net change
Cash	$ 9,000	$ 8,000	$ 1,000
Treasury bills	4,000	3,000	1,000
Accounts receivable	4,000	5,000	(1,000)
Inventory	1,000	2,000	(1,000)
Prepaid insurance	2,000	3,000	(1,000)
Investment in Simba Co. (held-for-trading)	15,000	15,000	--
Market increase adjustment (trading)	3,000	--	3,000
Investment in ABC Co. (available-for-sale)	15,400	22,000	(6,600)
Market decrease adjustment (available-for-sale)	(3,500)	--	(3,500)
Fixed assets	22,000	17,000	5,000
Deferred tax asset	1,400	--	1,400
	$68,300	$71,000	$(2,700)
Accounts payable	$ 4,000	$ 7,000	$(3,000)
Income tax payable	3,000	1,000	2,000
Deferred tax liability	6,360	3,000	3,360
Bonds payable	5,000	10,000	(5,000)
Common stock	20,000	20,000	--
Accumulated other comprehensive income			
Unrealized loss on available-for-sale securities (net of tax)	(2,100)	--	(2,100)
Retained earnings	32,040	30,000	2,040
	$68,300	$71,000	$(2,700)

Income Statement for 2010 is as follows:

Net sales		$50,000
Cost of goods sold		(20,000)
Gross profit		30,000
Operating expenses		(17,000)
Income from operations		13,000
Other revenue and gains	$5,000	
Other expenses and losses	(2,560)	2,440
Income before extraordinary item and income taxes		15,440
Income tax expense:		
Current portion	5,000	
Deferred portion	3,360	8,360
Net income		$7,080

Statement of Comprehensive Income for 2010 is as follows:

Net income		$7,080
Other comprehensive income		
Unrealized loss on available-for-sale securities, (net of tax of $2,000)	($3,000)	
Less:		
Reclassification on sale of available-for-sale securities, (net of tax of $600)	(900)	(2,100)
Comprehensive income		$4,980

Additional information includes

- Treasury bills have a maturity of less than three months from date of purchase
- Fixed assets costing $5,000 with a book value of $2,000 were sold for $4,000
- Three-year insurance policy was purchased in 2008
- At 12/31/10, available-for-sale investments with a book value of $6,600 at 12/31/09 and $5,100 at 12/31/10 sold for $5,100.
- Additional bonds were issued on 12/31/10 for $4,000. There was no premium or discount.
- Bonds with a book value of $9,000 were retired on 12/31/10.
- Other revenue and gains include a $3,000 unrealized gain recognized for trading securities
- Other expenses and losses consist of $1,060 interest paid and $1,500 realized loss on available-for-sale securities
- Changes in investments:

  - No changes in fair value of the investments occurred prior to 2010
  - There were no sales or purchases of trading securities during 2010
  - The tax rate is 40%

1. **Procedural Steps**

   a. The first step is to calculate the change in cash and cash equivalents.

	2010	2009	Change
Cash	$9,000	$8,000	+$1,000
Treasury bills	4,000	3,000	+ 1,000
Net change in cash and cash equivalents			+$2,000

   b. Calculate net cash flows from operating activities

      (1) Indirect approach

Net income	$ 7,080	
Decrease in accounts receivable	1,000	(a)
Decrease in inventory	1,000	(b)
Decrease in prepaid insurance	1,000	(c)
Decrease in accounts payable	(3,000)	(d)
Increase in income tax payable	2,000	(e)
Increase in deferred tax liability	3,360	(f)
Unrealized gain on trading securities	(3,000)	(g)
Realized loss on available-for-sale securities	1,500	(h)
Gain on sale of fixed assets	(2,000)	(i)
Depreciation expense	4,000	(j)
Net cash flows from operating activities		$12,940

   Reconstructing journal entries may serve to explain the effect on net income of an increase or decrease of a particular account.

(a) **Accounts receivable.** For accounts receivable to decrease, the journal entry must have been

Cash	xx	
Accounts receivable		xx

Cash increased as a result of the collection of accounts receivable. The $1,000 decrease in accounts receivable should be added to net income.

(b) **Inventory.** For inventory to decrease, the entry must have been

Cost of goods sold	xx	
Inventory		xx

Expenses (CGS) increased without an additional cash outlay for inventory, so the $1,000 decrease is added back to net income.

(c) **Prepaid insurance.** For prepaid insurance to decrease, the entry must have been

Insurance expense	xx	
Prepaid insurance		xx

Because expenses increased without a corresponding cash outlay, the $1,000 decrease in prepaid insurance should be added to net income.

(d) **Accounts payable.** For accounts payable to decrease, the entry must have been

Accounts payable	xx	
Cash		xx

The entry involves a cash outlay, so the $3,000 decrease in accounts payable is deducted from net income.

(e) **Income tax payable.** For income tax payable to increase, the entry must have been

Income tax expense	xx	
Income tax payable		xx

Expenses increased without an actual cash outlay; therefore the $2,000 increase in the liability is added back to net income.

(f) **Deferred tax liability.** For deferred tax liability to increase, the entry must have been

Income tax expense	xx	
Deferred tax liability		xx

Expenses increased without an actual cash outlay; therefore the $3,360 increase in the liability, which is a noncash expense, is added back to net income.

(g) **Unrealized gain on trading securities.** The entry to record the unrealized gain on trading securities would have been

Investment in Simba Co.—held-for-trading	3,000	
Unrealized holding gain		3,000

Since unrealized gains on trading securities are recognized as income but do not involve a cash inflow, such gains must be subtracted from net income.

(h) **Realized loss on available-for-sale securities.** When $5,100 stock in ABC Co. was sold, the previously unrealized loss of $1,500 ($5,100 FV at 12/31/10 – $6,600 FV at 12/31/09) which arose in 2010 became realized. The entry to record the sale would have been

Cash	5,100	
Realized loss	1,500	
Available for sale		6,600

Because the realized loss does not involve any cash outflow, it must be added back to net income. Note that a $1,500 unrealized loss would have been recognized in financial statements prepared during 2010. The entry to remove this amount from the other comprehensive income account entitled "Unrealized loss on available-for-sale securities account" and the tax effect is

Adjustment to market (available-for-sale securities)	1,500	
Deferred tax benefit—unrealized loss	600	
Unrealized loss on available-for-sale securities		1,500
Deferred tax asset		600

Since an unrealized loss on AFS securities of $3,500 was recognized during 2010 (from 2009 to 2010), a $5,000 decline in FV must have occurred in 2010, as shown below. The deferred tax asset of $1,400 came from recognizing the future benefit of the unrealized loss of $3,500. The entry was

| Deferred tax asset | 1,400 | |
| Deferred tax expense (benefit) | | 1,400 |

Market Adjustment (Available-for-Sale Securities)

	--		2009 Bal.
Sale	1,500	5,000	2010 Unreal. loss
		3,500	2010 Bal.

Available-for-Sale Securities

2009 Bal.	22,000		
		6,600	Sale
2010 Bal.	15,400		

Accumulated Other Comprehensive Income

	--		
		1,400	Closing entry
Closing entry	3,500		
2010 Bal.	2,100		

Unrealized Loss on AFS Securities

2009 Bal.	--	1,500	Realized upon sale
Unreal. Loss recog. During year	5,000		
		3,500	Closing entry
2010 Bal.	--		

Deferred Tax Benefit— Unrealized Loss

Sale	600	--	
Closing entry	1,400	2,000	2010 adj.
2010 Bal.	--		

Deferred Tax Asset

2009 Bal.	--	600	Sale
2010 Adj.	2,000		
2010 Bal.	1,400		

Because unrealized gains/losses on available-for-sale securities do not affect cash flows, no adjustment for this change is necessary on the statement of cash flows.

(i) **Gain on sale of fixed assets.** The entry to record the sale would have been

Cash	4,000	
Accumulated depreciation	3,000	
Gain on sale		2,000
Asset		5,000

The total amount of cash received in payment for the asset, not just the amount of the gain, represents the cash inflow. Since cash inflow from the sale (including the amount of the gain) appears in the investing section, the gain should be subtracted from net income.

(j) **Depreciation expense.** The entry to record depreciation is

| Depreciation expense | 4,000 | |
| Accumulated depreciation | | 4,000 |

Because expenses increased without a corresponding cash outlay, the amount recorded for depreciation expense should be added to net income. In this case, the increase in accumulated depreciation must take into consideration the accumulated depreciation removed with the sale of the asset.

AD

AD of sold asset	3,000*	4,000	Beg. bal.
		4,000	Depreciation (plug)
		5,000	End. bal.

* $5,000 Cost – $2,000 book value

(2) Direct approach

Cash received from customers		$51,000 (a)
Cash provided by operating activities		
Cash paid to suppliers	22,000 (b)	
Cash paid for operating expenses	12,000 (c)	
Cash paid for interest	1,060 (d)	
Cash paid for income taxes	3,000 (e)	
Cash disbursed for operating activities		38,060
Net cash flows from operating activities		$12,940

(a) **Cash received from customers.** Net sales + Beginning AR – Ending AR = Cash received from customers ($50,000 + $5,000 – $4,000 = $51,000). Cash received from customers also may be calculated by analyzing T-accounts.

Accounts Receivable

Beg. bal.	5,000		
Sales	50,000	51,000	Cash collected
End. bal.	4,000		

(b) **Cash paid to suppliers.** Cost of goods sold + Beginning AP – Ending AP + Ending inventory – Beginning inventory = Cash paid to suppliers ($20,000 + $7,000 – $4,000 + $1,000 – $2,000 = $22,000). This is a two-account analysis. The amount for cash paid to suppliers equals the debit to accounts payable, but to solve for that amount, you must first determine purchases. To calculate purchases you must analyze the inventory account.

Step 1. Calculate purchases

	Inventory		
Beg. bal.	2,000	20,000	CGS
Purchases	19,000		
End. bal.	1,000		

Step 2. Calculate cash payments to suppliers

	Accounts Payable		
		7,000	Beg. bal.
Cash paid to suppliers	22,000	19,000	Purchases
		4,000	End. bal.

Note that the $2,000 difference between the $20,000 CGS (accrual-basis amount) and the $22,000 cash payments made to suppliers (cash-basis amount) equals the difference between the $1,000 decrease in inventory and the $3,000 decrease in accounts payable when the indirect method is used. However, under the indirect method the difference is deducted from net income. This is because when the direct method is used, expenses such as CGS are examined as **outflows** of cash, whereas when the indirect method is used, net income (revenue-expenses, including CGS) is treated as a net cash **inflow**.

(c) **Cash paid for operating expenses.** Operating expenses + Ending prepaid expenses – Beginning prepaid expenses – Depreciation expense (and other noncash operating expenses) = Cash paid for operating expenses ($17,000 + $2,000 – $3,000 – $4,000 = $12,000). The two accounts in this problem that relate to operating expenses are accumulated depreciation and prepaid insurance.

	Prepaid Insurance					Accumulated Depreciation	
Beg. bal.	3,000					4,000	Beg. bal.
		1,000	Insurance expense	AD of sold asset	3,000	4,000	Depreciation expense
End. bal.	2,000					5,000	End. bal.

Since neither the expiration of prepaid insurance nor depreciation expense required a cash outlay, cash basis operating expenses are accrual expenses of $17,000 less depreciation ($4,000) and insurance expense ($1,000), or $12,000.

(d) **Cash paid for interest.** No analysis needed; amount was given in problem

(e) **Cash paid for income taxes.** Current portion of income tax expense + Beginning income tax payable – Ending income tax payable = Cash paid for income taxes ($5,000 + $1,000 – $3,000 = $3,000). The journal entry for income tax expense is

Income tax expense—current	5,000	
Income tax expense—deferred	1,360	
Income tax payable (current portion)		5,000
Deferred tax liability		1,360

Therefore, taxes paid are $3,000, as shown in the T-account below.

	Income Tax Payable		
		1,000	Beg. bal.
Income taxes paid	3,000	5,000	Current portion
		3,000	End. bal.

c. Analyze other accounts and determine whether the change is a cash inflow or outflow and whether it is a financing, an investing, or a noncash investing and financing activity.

(1) Investments in ABC Co. decreased by $5,100 when this portion was sold (cash inflow, investing activity). The entry to record the sale was

Cash	5,100	
Investment in ABC Co.— available-for-sale		5,100

(2) Fixed assets increased by $5,000 after $5,000 of assets were sold for $4,000 (cash inflow, investing activity). Thus, $10,000 of fixed assets were purchased (cash outflow, investing activity).

	Fixed Assets		
Beg. bal.	$17,000		
Purchase of new assets	10,000	5,000	Sold asset
End. bal.	22,000		

(3) Bonds payable increased by $4,000 when additional bonds were issued (cash inflow, financing activity).

(4) Bonds payable decreased by $9,000 when they were retired (cash outflow, financing activity). The entry to record the retirement of debt was

Bonds payable	9,000	
Cash		9,000

(5) Common stock had no change.

(6) Retained earnings increased $2,040 after net income of $7,080, indicating a dividend of $5,040 (cash outflow, financing activity).

	Retained Earnings		
		30,000	Beg. bal.
Cash dividend	5,040	7,080	Net income
		32,040	End. bal.

d. Prepare formal statement

Haner Company
STATEMENT OF CASH FLOWS
For the Year Ended December 31, 2010

Cash flows from operating activities:		
Cash received from customers	$51,000	
Cash provided by operating activities		$51,000
Cash paid to suppliers	22,000	
Cash paid for operating expenses	12,000	
Cash paid for income taxes	3,000	
Cash paid for interest expense	1,060	
Cash disbursed for operating activities		38,060
Net cash flows from operating activities		$12,940
Cash flows from investing activities:		
Proceeds from sale of investments	$ 5,100	
Proceeds from sale of fixed assets	4,000	
Acquisition of fixed assets	(10,000)	
Net cash used by investing activities		(900)
Cash flows from financing activities:		
Proceeds from sale of bonds	$ 4,000	
Repayment of long-term debt	(9,000)	
Dividends paid	(5,040)	
Net cash used by financing activities		(10,040)
Net increase in cash and cash equivalents		$ 2,000
Cash and cash equivalents at beginning of year		11,000
Cash and cash equivalents at end of year		$13,000

Reconciliation of net income to cash provided by operating activities:
[This schedule would include the amounts from D.1.b.(1) (near the beginning of this example) starting with "net income" and ending with Net cash flows from operating activities of $13,040.]

Disclosure of accounting policy:
For purposes of the statement of cash flows, the Company considers all highly liquid debt instruments purchased with a maturity of three months or less to be cash equivalents.

NOTE: If the reconciliation approach for operating activities had been shown in the body of the statement instead of the direct approach, an additional schedule showing interest paid and income taxes paid would be necessary.

NOW REVIEW MULTIPLE-CHOICE QUESTIONS 30 THROUGH 37 IN VOLUME 2

E. Capital Leases

In the period an entity enters into a capital lease, a noncash financing and investing activity in the amount of the present value of the minimum lease payments is reported following the cash flow statement. As payments are made by the lessee, the principal reduction component is reported as a cash outflow under financing activities. The interest component is reported in the operating activities section under the direct method. Under the indirect method, interest paid must be disclosed as supplementary information.

F. Research Component—Accounting Standards Codification

1. ASC Topic 230 outlines the accounting rules for the statement of cash flows. Typical research issues may involve determining the cash equivalents of the enterprise; classifying items as either operating, investing, or financing activities; and identifying significant noncash transactions. Note that ASC Topic 230 specifically prohibits reporting cash flow per share information on the statement of cash flows.

2. Below are keywords for researching issues on the statement of cash flows. Note that in some paragraphs in FARS, the word "transaction" or "transactions" (rather than "activity") is used to discuss whether an item is included in the operating, investing, or financing section of the statement of cash flows.

Cash equivalents	Noncash activities
Financing activities	Noncash transactions
Financing transactions	Operating activities
Investing activities	Operating transactions
Investing transactions	Reconciliation of net income

G. International Financial Reporting Standards (IFRS)

1. **Statement of cash flows.** The accounting rules for the statement of cash flows are similar to US GAAP.

   a. For IFRS, cash flows include the inflows and outflows of both cash and cash equivalents.

      (1) Cash equivalents include cash on hand, bank balances for immediate use, other demand deposits, and short-term investments with maturities of three months or less.

   b. Both the direct method and indirect method are acceptable methods for preparing the statement of cash flows.

      (1) However, for the indirect method, operating activities may be presented using a modified approach.
      (2) This modified indirect method shows revenues and expenses in operating activities, and then reports the changes in working capital accounts.

2. As in US GAAP, the statement of cash flows is divided into three parts: operating, investing, and financing activities. At the bottom of the statement of cash flows, a reconciliation must be made with the amounts in the statement of cash flows and the cash and cash equivalents reported in the statement of financial position.

3. The most significant difference between IFRS and US GAAP is where certain items are presented on the statement of cash flows.

   a. For example, interest and dividends received may be reported on the statement of cash flows as operating or investing activities.
   b. Interest and dividends paid may be reported either in the operating activities or the financing activities sections.

      (1) Although the entity has discretion on where interest and dividends are reported, it must be reported on a consistent basis.

   c. Cash from the purchase and sale of trading securities are classified as operating activities.
   d. Cash advances and loans (bank overdrafts) are also usually classified as operating activities.
   e. Taxes paid on income must be disclosed separately in operating activities.

      (1) However, cash flows from certain taxes may be classified elsewhere if they are related to investing or financing activities.

   f. In addition, the effects of noncash transactions are not reported on the statement of cash flows. Instead, significant noncash activities must be disclosed in the notes to the financial statements.

NOW REVIEW MULTIPLE-CHOICE QUESTIONS 38 THROUGH 39 IN VOLUME 2

KEY TERMS

Cash equivalents. Short-term, highly liquid investments that (1) are readily convertible to known amounts of cash and (2) are so near their maturity (original of three months or less from **date of purchase** by the enterprise) that they present negligible risk of changes in value because of changes in interest rates.

Direct approach. Cash flow elements of operating activities are derived from the accrual basis components of net income.

Indirect method. Starts with income from continuing operations and adjusts for changes in operating related accounts (e.g., inventory and accounts payable) and noncash expenses, revenues, losses, and gains.

Statement of Cash Flow. Provides information about an entity's cash receipts and cash payments and discloses information about the financing and investing activities of an entity.

Module 18: Business Combinations and Consolidations

Overview

This module covers business combinations and consolidations. To qualify for treatment as a business combination, the entity must meet the definition of a business. If an entity is not considered a business, the transaction is accounted for as an asset acquisition and goodwill is not recognized.

Acquisition accounting is the method to account for a business combination and it consists of four steps: (1) identifying the acquirer; (2) determining the acquisition date; (3) recognizing and measuring assets acquired, liabilities assumed, and noncontrolling interest in the acquirer; and (4) recognizing goodwill. Each of these steps is discussed in detail. Numerous examples relating to variations in acquisition accounting are presented along with the calculation of goodwill and intercompany eliminating entries.

This module also discusses required disclosures, combined financial statements, and push-down accounting. Push-down accounting is required by the SEC. It requires the subsidiary to revalue its assets and liabilities to fair value.

A. Scope—Acquisition Method

1. ASC Topic 805 (SFAS 141[Revised]) applies to business acquisitions.

   a. It does not apply to the formation of joint ventures, the acquisition of assets or groups of assets that do not constitute a business, or the combination of entities under common control.

2. **Asset acquisition** scope exception

   a. If the assets and liabilities acquired do not constitute a business, then the transaction is accounted for as an asset acquisition.

   b. In an asset acquisition, the assets are recorded at the amount of cash paid, or the cost of the assets.

      (1) If the assets are not acquired with cash, then the assets are recorded at either fair value of the assets given up (transferred) by the acquiring entity, or the fair value of the assets acquired, whichever is more reliable.

   c. If assets are acquired in a group, the cost of each asset is determined by allocating the total cost to the individual assets based on their relative fair values.

   d. **No goodwill is recorded in an asset acquisition.**

3. Common control scope exception

   a. ASC Topic 805 (SFAS 141[R]) also does not apply to entities under common control.

(1) For example, an entity may create a new corporation and transfer some or all of its assets to the new corporation, or a parent may transfer the net assets of a wholly owned subsidiary into the parent and then liquidate the subsidiary.

b. These types of changes are considered a change in legal organization, not a change in the reporting entity.

(1) In situations where entities are under common control, the assets and liabilities transferred are recorded at their carrying amounts at the date of the transfer.

4. Definition of a business

a. To qualify for treatment as a business combination, the entity must meet the definition of a business.

(1) A **business** is defined as "an integrated set of activities and assets that is capable of being conducted and managed for the purpose of providing a return in the form of dividends, lower costs, or other economic benefits directly to investors or other owners, members or participants."

(2) A business normally consists of inputs, processes, and outputs. However, outputs are NOT required for the entity to qualify as a business.

5. Common terminology

a. The **acquiree** is the business that is being acquired.

b. The **acquirer** is the entity that obtains control of the acquiree.

c. The **acquisition date** is the date on which the acquirer obtains control of the acquiree.

d. A **business combination** is a transaction or event in which the acquirer obtains control of one or more businesses.

e. **Control** is defined as a controlling financial interest by ownership of a majority of the voting shares of stock. The general rule is that ownership either directly or indirectly by one company of more than 50% of the outstanding voting shares of another company constitutes control.

B. The Acquisition Method for Business Combinations

1. If an acquisition qualifies as a business combination, then the acquisition method is used. The four steps in applying the acquisition method are as follows:

a. Identify the acquirer.

b. Determine the acquisition date.

c. Recognize and measure identifiable assets acquired, liabilities assumed, and noncontrolling (minority) interest in the acquiree.

d. Recognize and measure goodwill, or recognize a gain from a bargain purchase.

2. Acquirer identification.

a. Acquirer identification is the first step in a business combination.

b. Distinguishing between the acquirer and the acquiree is important because only the acquiree's assets are revalued to fair value at the acquisition date.

c. Normally the acquirer is the entity that obtains control of the acquiree.

(1) The acquirer is usually the entity that transfers cash or incurs the liabilities in order to acquire the other firm.

(2) However, if it is unclear which entity is the acquirer, one of the combining entities must be identified as the acquirer by examining the facts and circumstances.

(a) The entity that retains the largest portion of voting rights is usually the acquirer.

(b) The acquirer may also be determined by identifying the company that retains more individuals on its governing body or in its senior management.

(c) If the business was acquired by exchanging equity interests, the acquirer is usually the entity that pays a premium over the fair value of the equity interests of the other firm.

(d) The acquirer may also be determined by identifying the entity that is significantly larger in size, measured by its assets, revenues, or earnings.

3. Acquisition date identification.

a. Acquisition date identification is the second step in a business combination.

b. The acquisition date is important for two reasons:

(1) The acquisition date is the date when the identifiable assets and the liabilities of the acquiree are measured at fair values, and

(2) The acquirer recognizes net income of the acquiree only after the date of acquisition.

c. Acquisition date determination:

    (1) The date on which the acquirer obtains control over the acquiree. Usually, the date on which the acquirer transfers the consideration, acquires the assets, and assumes the liabilities of the acquiree.

        (a) However, it is possible that the acquirer could obtain control either before or after the closing date when the consideration is transferred. In that case, the facts and circumstances should be examined to determine the date at which control was acquired.

4. Recognition and Measurement.

    a. Recognition and measurement of identifiable assets, liabilities and noncontrolling interest is the third step in a business combination.

    b. On the acquisition date, the identifiable assets acquired, the liabilities assumed, and any noncontrolling interest (previously referred to as minority interest) are measured at fair value. The acquirer also recognizes assets that were not previously recognized on the acquiree's books if the assets are identifiable.

        (1) An asset is an **identifiable asset** if it arises from a contractual or legal right, or if it is separable.

        (2) An asset is separable if it can be separated or divided from the entity and sold, transferred, licensed, rented, or exchanged.

    c. At the acquisition date, the acquirer must classify the assets acquired and liabilities assumed so that GAAP can be applied.

        (1) Examples of items that must be classified include trading, available-for-sale, and held-to-maturity securities, derivatives, and embedded derivative instruments.

        (2) Leases, however, are classified as either an operating or a capital lease based upon their contractual terms at the inception of the contracts.

            (a) Therefore, if the lease was a capital lease for the acquiree, then it is classified as a capital lease on the books of the acquirer.

            (b) Similarly, if the lease was an operating lease on the books of the acquiree, then the lease continues to be an operating lease on the books of the acquirer.

            (c) An exception to this rule occurs when a lease contract is modified. If a lease contract is modified at the date of acquisition, the new terms of the modified contract are used to classify the lease.

    d. On the date of acquisition, the acquirer should recognize any newly identified intangible assets of the acquiree that meet the contractual-legal or separability criteria. Examples of items that meet the contractual-legal or separability criteria include the following items:

        (1) Marketing-related intangibles, such as trademarks, trade names, service marks, certification marks, newspaper mastheads, internet domain names, and noncompetition agreements.

        (2) Customer-related intangibles, such as customer lists, order or production backlog, customer contracts, and noncontractual customer relationships.

        (3) Artistic-related intangible assets, such as plays, operas, ballets, books, magazines, newspapers, literary works, musical works, pictures, photographs, videos, motion pictures, films, music videos, and television programs.

        (4) Contract-based intangibles, such as licensing, royalty, advertising, construction, management, lease, or franchise agreements. Other examples include construction permits, operating and broadcast rights, supply or service contracts, employment contracts, and drilling, water, air, and timber cutting rights.

        (5) Technology-based intangibles, such as patented technology, computer software and mask works, unpatented technology, and databases. Another example is trade secrets, such as secret formulas, processes, and recipes.

        (6) Items that do not meet the contractual-legal or separability criteria may not be recognized as assets.

            (a) Nonqualifying assets include the value of an assembled workforce, intellectual capital, and potential contracts.

5. Recognize goodwill

    a. Goodwill recognition is the fourth step in a business combination.

    b. At the date of acquisition, the assets and liabilities of the acquiree are measured at fair value.

        (1) If the acquirer has previously held equity interests in the acquiree, these shares are revalued to fair value at acquisition date.

        (2) Any noncontrolling interest is also valued at fair value at acquisition date.

        (3) After the assets, liabilities, previously held conterests, and noncontrolling interest are valued at fair value, the goodwill or gain from a bargain purchase is calculated, as illustrated below.

Fair value of consideration transferred (cost to the acquirer)
Plus: Fair value of previously held equity interests in acquiree
Plus: Fair value of noncontrolling interest
<u>Less: Fair value of net identifiable assets</u>
Goodwill or gain from bargain purchase

(4) If the fair value of net identifiable assets is less than the aggregate of the consideration transferred, plus the acquisition date fair value of previously held interests, plus the fair value of noncontrolling interest, goodwill is recognized.

(a) **Goodwill** is defined as "an asset representing the future economic benefits that arises from other assets acquired in a business combination that are not individually identified and separately recognized."

(b) Although an intangible asset is defined as an asset that lacks physical substance for purposes of business combinations, goodwill is not considered an intangible asset. Instead, goodwill is classified separately, and the accounting rules for goodwill apply.

(5) If the fair value of net identifiable assets exceeds the aggregate of the consideration transferred, plus the acquisition date fair value of previously held interests, plus the fair value of the noncontrolling interest, then a bargain purchase occurs. A gain is recognized by the acquirer in the current period for the bargain purchase.

c. The consideration transferred is measured at fair value at the acquisition date.

(1) Consideration may include assets transferred, liabilities incurred, and equity interests issued by the acquirer.

(2) If the fair values of the acquirer's assets or liabilities transferred are different from their carrying values, the acquirer should recognize a gain or loss on the assets transferred in earnings of the current period.

(3) However, if the acquirer retains control of the transferred assets or liabilities, then the assets and liabilities are measured at their carrying amounts immediately before the acquisition date.

(4) If the acquirer transfers contingent consideration, then the fair value of the contingent consideration is included as part of the consideration paid for the acquiree. Measurement of contingent consideration is discussed later in this module.

6. Step acquisition.

a. Sometimes the acquirer obtains control through a step acquisition, wherein the acquirer invests in less than 50% of the voting shares of the acquiree, and at a later date, acquires enough shares to obtain voting control.

b. Depending upon the percentage of ownership previously acquired, the acquirer may have accounted for shares of stock using the cost adjusted for fair value method, the equity method, or the fair value option.

c. In a step acquisition, the acquisition date fair value of the previously held shares is also included in the acquisition cost. If the fair values of the previously held shares at the acquisition date are not equal to their carrying values, a gain or loss is recognized in the current period.

d. If the acquirer had previously recognized any changes in fair value of the securities in other comprehensive income, then the amounts recognized in other comprehensive income should be reclassified and included as a gain or loss on the income statement in the current period.

7. Noncontrolling interest.

a. Noncontrolling interest is measured by using the active market prices on the acquisition date for the equity shares not held by the acquirer.

> **NOTE:** The fair values of the acquirer's investment and the noncontrolling interest may not be the same on a per-share basis.

(1) This difference can be attributed to the acquirer paying a premium to obtain control of the acquiree, or to a noncontrolling interest discount due to lack of control.

(2) This difference should be ignored, and the noncontrolling interest should be valued by multiplying the active market price on the acquisition date times the number of shares held by the noncontrolling parties.

b. Noncontrolling interest should be classified as equity in the statement of financial position of the consolidated financial statements. On the statement of earnings, consolidated net income is adjusted to disclose the net income or loss attributed to the noncontrolling interest. Comprehensive income is also adjusted to include the comprehensive income attributed to the noncontrolling interest.

8. Acquisition-related costs

  a. Acquisition-related costs for a business acquisition are normally treated as an expense in the period in which the costs are incurred or the services are received.
  b. Acquisition-related costs may include finder's, advisory, legal, accounting, valuation, consulting and other professional fees. They also include general administrative costs.
  c. Although the costs of registering and issuing debt and equity securities are considered part of acquisition costs, these costs are not expensed in the period of the acquisition, but are recognized in accordance with other GAAP.

     (1) Costs of registering and issuing common stock are normally netted against the proceeds of the stock and reduce the paid-in capital in excess of par account.
     (2) Bond issue costs are treated as a deferred charge and amortized on a straight-line basis over the life of the bond.

C. Consolidated Financial Statements

1. An acquisition of more than 50% of the outstanding voting stock will normally result in control and require the preparation of consolidated financial statements.

  a. The complete consolidation process is presented in the next section of this module.
  b. The investment account will be eliminated in the consolidation working papers and will be replaced with the specific assets and liabilities of the investee corporation.
  c. Consolidation is generally required for investments of more than 50% of the outstanding voting stock except when the control is not held by the majority owner, Examples of noncontrol include

     (1) The investee is in legal reorganization or bankruptcy.
     (2) The investee operates in a foreign country, which has severe restrictions on the financial transactions of its business firms or is subject to material political or economic uncertainty that casts significant doubt on the parent's ability to control the subsidiary.

        (a) In these limited cases, the investment will be reported as a long-term investment in an unconsolidated subsidiary on the investor's balance sheet.
        (b) The cost method is used unless the acquirer qualifies to use the equity method or elects to use the fair value option for reporting financial assets. As you recall from Module 16 on investments, the equity method is used in cases where the investor has significant influence over the investee.

2. Variable interest entities

  a. In certain instances, control over an entity may be achieved through arrangements that do not involve ownership or voting interests.
  b. Special rules apply to **variable interest entities** (VIEs, also referred to as special-purpose entities) in which control is achieved based on contractual, ownership, or other pecuniary interests that change with changes in the entity's net asset value.
  c. The initial determination of whether a legal entity is a VIE is made on the date the reporting entity becomes involved with the legal entity.

     (1) The status of a VIE is reconsidered if certain events occur such as a change in the legal entity's contractual arrangements or characteristics, a change in the equity investment by investors, or changes in facts and circumstances that change the power from voting rights or similar rights to direct the activities of the VIE.

  d. If an entity has a controlling financial interest in the VIE, the entity is considered **the primary beneficiary** of the VIE. A primary beneficiary is required to consolidate the VIE in its financial statements.

     (1) An entity has a controlling financial interest in a VIE if both of the following conditions exist:

        (a) The entity has the power to direct the activities of a VIE that most significantly impact the VIE's economic performance.
        (b) The entity has the obligation to absorb losses of the VIE that could potentially be significant to the VIE, or has the right to receive benefits from the VIE that could potentially be significant to the VIE.

     (2) A qualitative approach is used to determine if the entity has the power to control the VIE.

        (a) If power is shared among unrelated parties and consent of the other parties is required to direct the activities of the VIE, then no one party has the power to direct the activities of the VIE. In such cases where power is shared, none of the parties is required to consolidate the VIE.

1] If power is shared by unrelated parties and the nature of the activities directed by each party is not the same, then the entities must identify which party has the power to direct the activities that most significantly affect the VIE's economic performance.

2] If the party that has the power to direct the economic performance is also obligated to absorb the losses or receive the benefits, that entity is the primary beneficiary and must consolidate the VIE.

(b) An entity should determine whether it is the primary beneficiary on the date it becomes involved with a VIE. The reporting entity must also reassess whether it is the primary beneficiary throughout its involvement with the VIE.

(c) Kick-out rights are the ability to remove the reporting entity who has the power to direct the activities that most significantly impact the VIE's economic performance.

(d) Participating rights are the ability to block the actions of a reporting entity with power to direct the activities of the VIE.

(e) Kick-out and participating rights will not affect an entity from being considered the primary beneficiary unless those rights are held by a single equity holder who has the ability to exercise those rights.

e. Additional disclosures are required for entities that have interests in VIEs.

(1) The primary beneficiary that is required to consolidate the VIE must present separately on the face of the statement of financial position the assets of the VIE that can be used only to settle obligations of the consolidated VIE and the liabilities of the VIE for which creditors do not have recourse to the general credit of the primary beneficiary. Disclosures in the notes to financial statements by the primary beneficiary that consolidates the VIE are

(a) The carrying amounts and classification of the VIE's assets and liabilities that are consolidated, as well as qualitative information about the assets and restrictions on the assets.

(b) Lack of recourse if creditors have no recourse to the general credit of the primary beneficiary.

(c) Terms of arrangements.

(2) A reporting entity that is not the primary beneficiary is not required to consolidate the VIE, but must disclose the following:

(a) The carrying amounts and classification of the assets and liabilities that relate to the reporting entity's variable interest in the VIE.

(b) The maximum exposure to loss from involvement with the VIE.

(c) A comparison of the carrying amounts of assets and liabilities and the maximum exposure to loss, together with supporting information explaining the differences in amounts.

(d) Information about any liquidity arrangements, guarantees, or other commitments by third parties that may affect the fair value or risk of the interest in the VIE.

(e) If applicable, significant factors considered and judgments in determining that the power to direct the activities of the VIE is shared.

(3) All entities with interests in VIEs (both primary beneficiaries and other holders of variable interests in VIEs that are not required to consolidate) must disclose the following:

(a) The methodology for determining whether the reporting entity is the primary beneficiary of a VIE.

(b) If facts and circumstances regarding consolidation of VIE have changed.

(c) Whether the reporting entity has provided financial or other support to the VIE that was not contractually required during the periods presented.

(d) Qualitative and quantitative information about the reporting entity's involvement with the VIE, including nature, purpose, size, and activities of the VIE, and how the VIE is financed.

3. The concept of consolidated statements is that the resources of two or more companies are under the control of the parent company.

a. Consolidated statements are prepared as if the group of legal entities were one economic entity group.

b. Consolidated statements are presumed to be more meaningful for management, owners, and creditors of the acquirer company and they are required for fair presentation of the financially-related companies.

c. Individual company statements should continue to be prepared for noncontrolling ownership and creditors of the acquiree companies.

4. The accounting principles used to record and report events for a single legal entity are also applicable to a consolidated economic entity of two or more companies.

a. The concept of the reporting entity is expanded to include more than one company, but all other accounting principles are applied in the same way as for an individual company.

b. The consolidation process eliminates reciprocal items that are shown on both the acquirer's and acquiree's books. These eliminations are necessary to avoid double counting the same items, which would misstate the financials of the combined economic entity.

5. Consolidated financial statements are prepared from worksheets, which begin with the trial balances of the acquirer and acquiree companies.

   a. Eliminating worksheet entries are made to reflect the two separate companies' results of operations and financial position as one combined economic entity.

   b. The entire consolidation process takes place **only on a worksheet;** no consolidation elimination entries are ever recorded on either the parent's or subsidiary's books.

6. Consolidated balance sheets are typically prepared at the date of combination to determine the initial financial position of the economic entity.

   a. Any intercompany accounts between the acquirer and acquiree must be eliminated against each other.

   b. The "Investment in acquiree's stock" account from the acquirer's books will be eliminated against the reciprocal accounts of the acquiree's stockholders' equity.

   c. The remaining accounts are then combined to prepare the consolidated balance sheet.

7. The preparation of consolidated statements after the date of combination becomes a little more complex because the acquirer and acquiree income statements may include reciprocal intercompany accounts, which must be eliminated.

8. The next section of the module will present an example of the preparation of a consolidated balance sheet at the date of combination for the acquisition method. You should carefully review the date of combination consolidation process before proceeding to the preparation of consolidation statements subsequent to combination.

NOW REVIEW MULTIPLE-CHOICE QUESTIONS 1 THROUGH 15 IN VOLUME 2

D. Pelican Corp. and Swan Corp.—Acquisition of Swan, 100% Acquisition

A presentation of the date of combination entries for the acquisition method will be made first for a 100% acquisition. This problem will be expanded to present the method for preparing the income statement, statement of retained earnings, and balance sheet at year-end for a 100% acquisition. The example will then be modified to apply the accounting for less than a 100% acquisition with noncontrolling interest.

EXAMPLE

On January 1, 2011, Pelican Corporation acquired Swan Corporation by acquiring all of Swan's outstanding stock by issuing 16,000 shares of Pelican $1 par value common stock, with a fair value of $10 per share. The balance sheets for Pelican and Swan immediately before the acquisition are shown below.

Pelican Company and Swan Company
BALANCE SHEETS 1/1/11
(Immediately before combination)

Assets	Pelican Corp.	Swan Corp.
Cash	$ 30,000	$ 24,000
Accounts receivable	35,000	9,000
Inventories	23,000	16,000
Equipment	240,000	60,000
Accumulated depreciation	(40,000)	(10,000)
Patents	--	12,000
Total assets	$288,000	$111,000
Liabilities and Equity		
Accounts payable	$ 6,000	$ 7,000
Bonds payable	80,000	--
Capital stock ($10 par)	120,000	60,000
Additional paid-in capital	20,000	10,000
Retained earnings	62,000	34,000
Total liabilities and equity	$288,000	$111,000

Additional Information:

1. At the time of the acquisition, it was determined that Swan had a client list with a fair value of $5,000, and a trademark with a fair value of $14,000. The client list has a remaining life of five years, and the trademark has a remaining life of ten years.

2.   The fair values of Swan's assets and liabilities on the date of the acquisition are shown below.
3.   The existing equipment of Swan will be depreciated over its remaining useful life of four years.
4.   The patent on Swan's books will be depreciated over a remaining life of six years.

Swan Corporation
BALANCE SHEETS 1/1/11
(Immediately before combination)

Assets	Book value	Fair value	Difference between BV and FV
Cash	$ 24,000	24,000	$ --
Accounts receivable	9,000	9,000	--
Inventories	16,000	17,000	1,000
Equipment	60,000	72,000	12,000
Less: Accumulated depreciation	(10,000)	(12,000)*	(2,000)
Patents	12,000	15,000	3,000
Client list	--	5,000	5,000
Trademark	--	14,000	14,000
Total assets	$111,000	$144,000	

Liabilities and Equity			
Accounts payable	$ 7,000	$ 7,000	--
Bonds payable	--	--	
Capital stock ($10 par)	60,000		
Additional paid-in capital	10,000		
Retained earnings	34,000		
Total liabilities and equity	$111,000		

*   When the asset is revalued and increased by 20% ($60,000 × 20% = $12,000), there is also a corresponding increase in the accumulated depreciation account ($10,000 × 20% =$2,000).

> **NOTE:** Although there are no previously held interests or noncontrolling interest in this example, these items are shown in the following formulas for completeness.

The entry to record the investment in Swan is

Investment in Swan	160,000	
Common stock (Pelican)		16,000
Additional paid-in capital		144,000

To record the issuance of 16,000 shares of Pelican's $1 par value stock with a fair value of $10 per share to acquire Swan Corp.

Goodwill should be calculated using a three-step process.

Step 1:   Compute the difference between (1) the aggregate of acquisition cost, the fair value of previously held shares, and the fair value of noncontrolling interest and (2) the book value of Swan's net assets:

Acquisition cost	$160,000
Plus: Fair value of previously held shares	--
Plus: Fair value of noncontrolling interest	--
Less: Book value of Swan ($111,000 assets – $7,000 liabilities)	104,000
Differential	$ 56,000

This differential can be attributed to assets written up to fair value, newly identified intangible assets, and goodwill.

Step 2:   Compute the fair value of net identifiable assets.

Book value ($111,000 assets – $7,000 liability)	$104,000
Plus: Asset write-ups ($1,000 + $12,000 – $2,000 + $3,000)	14,000
Plus: Newly identified Intangibles ($5,000 + $14,000)	19,000
Fair value of net identifiable assets	$137,000

Step 3:   Compute goodwill.

Acquisition cost	$160,000
Plus: Fair value of previously held shares	--
Plus: Fair value of noncontrolling interest	--
Less: Fair value of net identifiable assets	(137,000)
Goodwill	$ 23,000

If the cost of acquisition is greater than the fair value of the net identifiable assets acquired, then goodwill is recorded as a noncurrent asset on the balance sheet. In this situation, Pelican would report goodwill of $23,000 on the date of acquisition. After the date of acquisition, goodwill is tested for impairment each year.

Assuming Pelican paid $120,000 for Swan

Acquisition cost	$120,000
Plus: Fair value of previously held shares	--
Plus: Fair value of noncontrolling interest	--
Less: Fair value, net identifiable assets	(137,000)
Bargain Purchase	$ (17,000)

The $17,000 bargain purchase would be recorded as a gain in the current period on Pelican's income statement.

E. Pelican Corp. and Swan Corp.—Date of Combination Consolidated Balance Sheet—Acquisition Method (100% Acquisition)

At the date of acquisition, a consolidated balance sheet is prepared. This section continues our example of Pelican's 100% acquisition of Swan. The entry below is the entry recorded on Pelican's books at the date of acquisition.

EXAMPLE

1. **Investment Entry on Pelican Company's Books**

The entry to record the 100% acquisition on Pelican Company's books was

Investment in stock of Swan Corp.	160,000	
Common stock		16,000
Additional paid-in capital		144,000

To record the issuance of 16,000 shares of Pelican's $1 par value stock with a fair value of $10 per share to acquire 100% of Swan Corp.

Although common stock is used for the consideration in our example, Pelican could have used debentures, cash, or any other form of consideration acceptable to Swan's stockholders to make the business acquisition.

The following is the worksheet to prepare the consolidated balance sheet immediately after Pelican's acquisition of Swan. Notice that the balance sheet of Pelican has changed from the balance sheet issued prior to the acquisition of Swan. The investment account increased Pelican's assets by $160,000, the acquisition cost of the investment. Also the capital stock and additional paid-in capital account of Pelican (the acquirer) have increased for the 16,000 shares of $1 par value Pelican stock issued. Common stock increased $16,000 ($1 par × 16,000 shares), and additional paid-in capital increased by $144,000 ($9 × 16,000 shares).

PELICAN CORP. AND SWAN CORP.—CONSOLIDATED WORKING PAPERS
For Date of Acquisition—1/1/11
Acquisition Method—100% Acquisition

	Pelican	Swan	Adjustments and eliminations Debit		Adjustments and eliminations Credit		Consolidated balances
Balance sheet 1/1/11							
Cash	30,000	24,000					54,000
Accounts receivable	35,000	9,000					44,000
Inventories	23,000	16,000	(b)	1,000			40,000
Equipment	240,000	60,000	(b)	12,000			312,000
Accumulated depreciation	(40,000)	(10,000)			(b)	2,000	(52,000)
Investment in stock of Swan	160,000				(a)	160,000	--
Difference between cost and book value			(a)	56,000	(b)	56,000	--
Goodwill	--		(b)	23,000			23,000
Patents	--	12,000	(b)	3,000			15,000
Client list	--		(b)	5,000			5,000
Trademark	--		(b)	14,000			14,000
Total assets	448,000	111,000					455,000
Accounts payable	6,000	7,000					13,000
Bonds payable	80,000	--					80,000
Capital stock	136,000	60,000	(a)	60,000			136,000
Additional paid-in capital	164,000	10,000	(a)	10,000			164,000
Retained earnings	62,000	34,000	(a)	34,000			62,000
Total liabilities and equity	448,000	111,000		218,000		218,000	455,000

2. **Difference between Acquisition Cost and Book Value of Acquiree**

To prepare the consolidated balance sheet, calculate the difference between (1) the aggregate of the acquisition cost, plus the fair value of previously held shares, plus the fair value of noncontrolling interest, and (2) the acquirer's interest in the net book value of the assets of the acquiree. This difference can be attributed to undervalued assets, newly identified intangible assets, and goodwill as shown below:

Swan Corp.

Undervalued assets	
Inventory	1,000
Equipment	12,000
Accumulated depreciation	(2,000)
Patents	3,000
New identifiable intangible assets	
Client list	5,000
Trademark	14,000
Goodwill	23,000
Total undervalued assets, new intangible assets, and goodwill	56,000

The difference of $56,000 will be accounted for by preparing consolidated working paper entries to eliminate the acquiree's equity accounts, revalue the acquiree's existing assets to fair values, record any newly identified intangible assets, and record goodwill. Note that the book value of the acquiree can also be calculated by adding the equity accounts of the acquiree at date of acquisition. A reconciliation of the cost to acquire Swan and the book value of Swan can also be calculated by using the equity accounts of Swan as shown below.

Acquisition cost		$160,000
Plus: Fair value of previously held shares		
Plus: Fair value of noncontrolling interest		
Less: Book value at date of acquisition		
Swan Corp.'s:		
Capital stock	(60,000)	
Additional paid-in capital	(10,000)	
Retained earnings	(34,000)	
Total		(104,000)
Differential		$56,000

Again, this difference is due to undervalued assets, newly identified intangible assets, and unrecorded goodwill.

3. **Completing the Consolidated Trial Balance Worksheet**

The worksheet on the date of acquisition is completed in two steps.

Step 1: Eliminate the acquiree's equity accounts, the acquirer's investment account, and establish the differential (the difference between acquisition cost and the book value of the acquiree's net assets).

Step 2: Eliminate the differential account and record asset write-ups to fair value, new identifiable intangible assets, and goodwill.

The elimination entries are then posted to the worksheet, and the consolidated worksheet is totaled.

The Step 1 entry is to eliminate the acquiree's equity account, eliminate the investment account on the acquirer's books, and record the differential as shown below.

(a)	Capital stock—B Co.	60,000	
	Additional paid-in capital—Swan Corp.	10,000	
	Retained earnings—Swan Corp.	34,000	
	Differential	56,000	
	Investment in stock of Swan Corp.		160,000

NOTE: Swan's stockholders' equity accounts are eliminated. Also an account called "Differential" is debited in the workpaper entry. The differential account is a temporary account to record the difference between the cost of the investment in Swan on the Pelican's books and the book value of Pelican's 100% interest in Swan.

The next step is to allocate the differential to the specific accounts by making the following workpaper entry:

(b) Inventories	1,000	
Equipment	12,000	
Patents	3,000	
Goodwill	23,000	
Client list	5,000	
Trademark	14,000	
Accumulated depreciation		2,000
Differential		56,000

This entry reflects the allocations prepared in Step 2 and recognizes the Pelican's revaluation of assets to fair value, the newly identified intangible assets, and goodwill.

Our example does not include any other intercompany accounts as of the date of combination. If any existed, they would be eliminated to fairly present the consolidated entity. Examples of other reciprocal accounts will be shown later in this module.

When the consolidated worksheet is finished, check the worksheet for possible errors. First, you should reduce the investment in Swan's account to zero. If the entries for write-up of existing assets to fair value, recording newly identified intangible assets, and recording goodwill are done accurately, the differential account will also be zero. The common stock account and additional paid-in capital account in the consolidated worksheet should reflect only the balances of the acquirer's accounts. At date of acquisition, the retained earnings account will only reflect the balance of the acquirer's account. Finally, check to see that the acquiree's equity accounts are eliminated.

NOW REVIEW MULTIPLE-CHOICE QUESTION 16 THROUGH 25 IN VOLUME 2

F. **Consolidated Financial Statements Subsequent to Acquisition**

1. The concepts used to prepare subsequent consolidated statements are essentially the same as those used to prepare the consolidated balance sheet at the acquisition date.

    a. The income statement and statement of retained earnings are added to reflect the results of operations since the acquisition date.
    b. Furthermore, some additional reciprocal accounts may have to be eliminated because of intercompany transactions between the acquirer and the acquiree.
    c. Please note that the financial statements of a consolidated entity are prepared using the same accounting principles that would be employed by a single, unconsolidated enterprise. The only difference is that some reciprocal accounts appearing on both companies' books must be eliminated against each other before the two corporations may be presented as one consolidated economic entity.
    d. Your review should concentrate on the accounts and amounts appearing on the consolidated statements (amounts in the last column of the worksheet). This "end-result" focus will help provide the understanding of why certain elimination entries are necessary.

2. An expanded version of the consolidated worksheet is necessary if the income statement and retained earnings statement must also be prepared.

    a. A comprehensive format often called "the three statement layout" is an integrated vertical array of the income statement, the retained earnings statement, and the balance sheet.
    b. The net income of the period is carried to the retained earnings statement and the ending retained earnings are carried down to the balance sheet.
    c. If you are required to prepare just the consolidated balance sheet, then eliminating entries involving nominal accounts (income statement accounts and the "Dividends declared" account) would be made directly against the ending balance of retained earnings presented on the balance sheet.

3. The following discussion assumes the acquirer is using the partial equity method to account for the majority investment.

    a. Some firms may use the cost method during the period to account for investment income because it requires fewer book adjustments to the investment account.

       (1) In cases where the cost method is used during the period, one approach is to adjust the investment and investment income accounts to the equity method through an entry on the workpaper and the consolidation process may then be continued.
       (2) Assuming that an income statement and retained earnings statement are being prepared in addition to the balance sheet, the general form of this restatement from cost to equity entry is made on the workpapers.

Dividend income (for income recognized using cost method)	xx
Investment in acquiree (% of undistributed income of sub)	xx
Equity in subsidiary's income (for income recognized using equity method)	xx

(3) Additional workpaper restatement entries would be required to recognize the equity income in prior periods if the investment were owned for more than one period and to recognize the amortizations of any differential for all periods the investment was held. After these entries are made, the investment and equity in the acquiree's income accounts would be stated on the equity basis and the consolidation process may be continued.

> **NOTE:** The formal consolidated statements will be the same regardless of the method used by the acquirer to account for the investment on its books.

b. The concept of measurement used in the preparation of the consolidated statements is equivalent to the full equity method and the elimination process will result in statements presented under that concept. Regardless of which method was used to initially record the investment, when the consolidated worksheet is finished, the investment in acquiree must be zero.

> **NOW REVIEW MULTIPLE-CHOICE QUESTIONS 26 THROUGH 41 IN VOLUME 2**

G. Intercompany Transactions and Profit Confirmations

1. Three general types of intercompany transactions may occur between the acquirer and acquiree companies:

   a. Intercompany sales of merchandise,
   b. Transactions in fixed assets, and
   c. Intercompany debt/equity transactions.

      (1) Intercompany transactions require special handling because the profit or loss from these events must be properly presented on the consolidated financial statements.
      (2) These events may generate "unrealized profit" (also referred to as unconfirmed profit) which is a profit or gain shown in the trial balance from one of the company's books that should not be shown in the consolidated financial statements.
      (3) Intercompany bond transactions may require recognition of a gain or loss on the consolidated financials, which is not in the trial balances of either the acquirer or acquiree companies.

2. **Intercompany Inventory Transactions**

   a. Unrealized profit in ending inventory arises through intercompany sales above cost that are not resold to third parties prior to year-end.

      (1) The profit on the selling corporation's books is overstated, because an arm's-length transaction has not yet taken place.
      (2) The inventory is overstated on the purchaser's books for the amount of the unrealized intercompany profit.
      (3) An exhibit of the relationships is shown below.

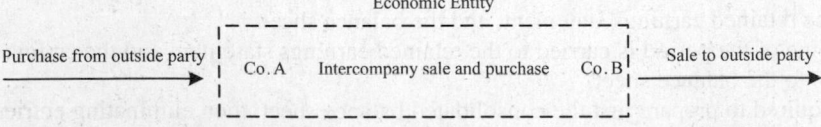

      (a) Companies A and B are two separate legal entities and will each record the sale or purchase of goods. From a consolidated or economic entity viewpoint, however, the intercompany transaction is a transfer of assets which cannot result in revenue recognition until these goods are sold to a third party.
      (b) Assuming a sale from Company A to Company B (a "downstream" intercompany sale), the sale income of Company A cannot be recognized until the goods are sold to third parties by Company B.
      (c) In addition, the ending inventory of Company B is overstated by the amount of profit in the inventory acquired from Company A.
      (d) Once intercompany sales have been sold to third parties, the earning process has been verified by an arm's-length transaction with third parties. Thus, recognition of previously unrecognized profit may occur at that time.

3. **Intercompany Fixed Asset Transactions**

   a. Unrealized profits on fixed assets arise through intercompany sales of fixed assets above undepreciated cost. From a consolidated viewpoint, the transaction represents the internal transfer of assets and no gain (loss) should be recognized. Any gain (loss) must be eliminated and the carrying value of the transferred asset must be returned to its initial book value basis.

      (1) In subsequent periods, in the case of an intercompany gain, depreciation expense is overstated, because an overvalued asset is being depreciated on the books of the company showing the asset. This overstatement of depreciation must also be eliminated in the consolidation process. In essence, the company that acquired the intercompany asset is including the intercompany gain (loss) in its depreciation expense.

4. **Intercompany Bond Transactions**

   a. When one consolidated company buys bonds of another consolidated company, there are several reciprocal items to eliminate: investment in bonds and bonds payable, interest income and interest expense, and interest payable and interest receivable. Intercompany gains and losses **cannot** arise from direct intercompany bond purchases. The book value would be the same on both books and the interest accounts would be reciprocal. The effective interest method for debt transactions between acquirer and acquiree companies is not required. Straight-line amortizations of premiums or discounts are sometimes used in these instances.

   b. Gains and losses on intercompany bond holdings occur when

      (1) Already outstanding bonds of the acquirer (acquiree) are purchased by an acquiree (acquirer),
      (2) From a third party, and
      (3) For an amount different from the carrying value of the issuer.

   c. From a consolidated viewpoint, these bonds are viewed as retired. However, the bonds are still recorded as liabilities on the issuer's separate books and as investment in bonds on the purchasing corporation's books.

      (1) The eliminating entry is to recognize the imputed gain (loss) on the consolidated "retirement of debt" in the year of intercompany bond purchase. Gains on early extinguishment of debt are no longer routinely considered extraordinary.

H. **Pelican Corp. and Swan Corp. — Subsequent Consolidated Financial Statements**

   The following information extends the basic example of Pelican and Swan begun earlier in this module. The example illustrates the major consolidation concepts and procedures most likely to appear on the CPA exam. The following intercompany transactions occurred during 2011.

EXAMPLE

During 2011, Pelican sold merchandise to Swan for $30,000. The merchandise originally cost Pelican $24,000. During 2011, Swan sold 40% of the merchandise purchased from Pelican to third parties for $15,000. On December 31, 2011, Swan's inventory included 60% of the merchandise purchased from Pelican.

During 2011, Swan sold merchandise to Pelican for $16,000. The cost of goods sold to Swan was $11,000. During 2011, Pelican subsequently sold all of these goods to an unrelated third party for $23,000.

Swan reduced its intercompany account payable to Pelican to a balance of $3,000 as of December 31, 2011, by making a payment of $1,000 on December 30. This $1,000 payment was still in transit on December 31, 2011.

On January 2, 2011, Swan acquired equipment from Pelican for $8,000. The equipment was originally purchased by Pelican for $12,000 and had a book value of $5,000 at the date of sale to Swan. Pelican was depreciating the equipment over an estimated ten-year useful life with no salvage value. Swan has determined the equipment's estimated remaining life is four years as of January 2, 2011, when the equipment was purchased. Swan uses straight-line depreciation with no salvage value and a four-year remaining life to depreciate the equipment.

On December 31, 2011, Swan purchased for $39,000, 50% of the $80,000 of outstanding bonds issued by Pelican to third parties. The bonds mature on December 31, 2016, and were originally issued at par. The bonds pay interest annually on December 31 of each year and the interest was paid to the prior investor immediately before Swan's purchase of the bonds.

The consolidated worksheet for the preparation of consolidated financial statements as of December 31, 2011, is presented on the next page.

To begin the problem, the investment account balance at the statement date should be reconciled to ensure the acquirer made the proper entries under the method of accounting used to account for the investment.

NOTE: Pelican is using the partial equity method, without amortizations. The amortizations of the excess of cost over book value will be recognized only on the worksheets. This method is the one typically followed on the CPA exam; however, be sure you determine the method used in the exam problem—do not assume!

The "proof" of the investment account of Pelican is:

	Investment in Stock of Swan Corp.			
Original cost	160,000			
100% of Swan Corp.'s Income	38,000	15,000	100% of Swan Corp.'s dividends declared	
Bal. 12/31/11	183,000			

Any errors will require correcting entries before the consolidation process is continued. Correcting entries will be posted to the books of the appropriate company; eliminating entries are **not** posted to either company's books. Eliminating entries are only recorded on the worksheet in order to prepare consolidated financial statements.

The difference between the investment cost and the book value of the net assets acquired was determined and allocated in the preparation of the date of acquisition consolidated statements presented earlier in this section. For purposes of brevity, that process will not be duplicated here since the same computations are used in preparing financial statements for as long as the investment is owned.

PELICAN CORP. AND SWAN CORP. CONSOLIDATED WORKING PAPERS
Year Ended December 31, 2011

Acquisition Method—100% Acquisition
Subsequent, partial equity

	Pelican	Swan	Adjustments and eliminations Debit		Adjustments and eliminations Credit		Consolidated balances
Income statement for year ended 12/31/11							
Sales	800,000	400,000	(c)	30,000			1,154,000
			(d)	16,000			
Cost of sales	580,000	250,000			26,400	(c)	787,600
					16,000	(d)	
Gross margin	220,000	150,000					366,400
Depreciation and amort. expense	28,000	14,000	(k)	5,400	800	(f)	46,600
Other operating expenses	115,000	98,000					213,000
Net income from operations	77,000	38,000					106,800
Gain on sale of equipment	3,000		(e)	3,000			--
Gain on bonds					1,000	(g)	1,000
Income from acquiree	38,000		(h)	38,000			--
Net income	118,000	38,000		92,400	44,200		107,800
Statement of retained earnings for year ended 12/31/11							
1/1/11 Retained earnings							
Pelican Corp.	62,000						62,000
Swan Corp.		34,000	(i)	34,000			--
Add net income (from above)	118,000	38,000		92,400	44,200		107,800
Total	180,000	72,000					169,800
Deduct dividends	(26,000)	(15,000)			15,000	(h)	(26,000)
Balance December 31, 2011	154,000	57,000		126,400	59,200		143,800
Balance sheet 12/31/11							
Cash	50,000	21,000	(a)	1,000			72,000
Accounts receivable (net)	42,000	8,000			1,000	(a)	46,000
					3,000	(b)	
Inventories	34,000	14,000	(j)	1,000	3,600	(c)	45,400
Equipment	290,000	68,000	(e)	4,000			374,000
			(j)	12,000			
Accumulated depreciation	(50,000)	(17,000)	(f)	800	7,000	(e)	(77,700)
					2,000	(k)	
					2,500	(j)	
Investment in stock of Swan Corp.	183,000				23,000	(i)	--
					160,000	(h)	
Differential			(i)	56,000	56,000	(j)	--
Goodwill			(j)	23,000			23,000
Investment in bonds of Pelican Corp.		39,000			39,000	(g)	--
Patents	--	12,000	(j)	3,000	500	(k)	14,500
Client list			(j)	5,000	1,000	(k)	4,000

Trademarks			(j)	14,000	1,400	(k)	12,600
Total assets	549,000	145,000					513,800
Accounts payable	15,000	18,000	(b)	3,000			30,000
Bonds payable	80,000	--	(g)	40,000			40,000
Capital stock	136,000	60,000	(i)	60,000			136,000
Additional paid-in capital	164,000	10,000	(i)	10,000			164,000
Retained earnings (from above)	154,000	57,000		126,400	59,200		143,800
Total liabilities and equity	549,000	145,000		359,200	359,200		513,800

The following adjusting and eliminating entries will be required to prepare consolidated financials as of December 31, 2011.

> **NOTE:** A consolidated income statement is required and, therefore, the nominal accounts are still "open." The number or letter in parentheses to the left of the entry corresponds to the key used on the worksheet.

Step 1. Complete the transaction for any intercompany items in transit at the end of the year.

(a) Cash   1,000
          Accounts receivable   1,000

This entry eliminates the cash in transit at year-end.

Step 2. Prepare the eliminating entries.

(b) Accounts payable   3,000
          Accounts receivable   3,000

This eliminates the remaining intercompany receivable/payable owed by Swan to Pelican. This eliminating entry is necessary to avoid overstating the consolidated entity's balance sheet. The receivable/payable is not extinguished and Swan must still transfer $3,000 to Pelican in the future.

(c) Sales   30,000
          Cost of goods sold   26,400
          Inventory   3,600

This eliminates the effects of the intercompany sale of merchandise by Pelican to Swan. When Swan purchased the inventory, Swan recorded the items in its inventory account at a cost of $30,000. Swan sold 40% of the goods to third parties for $15,000. Therefore, the revenue recognized for the period should be $15,000. Swan's cost of goods sold related to the sale to third parties was $12,000 (40% × $30,000). The remaining inventory, which is 60% of the amount purchased, is $18,000 (60% × $30,000). Although Swan has $18,000 of goods remaining in its ending inventory, the value of the inventory is overstated. A reconstruction of the entries for the sales, cost of goods sold, and inventory related to the intercompany sale is shown below.

	Pelican Corp.	Swan Corp.
Sales	$30,000	$15,000
Cost of goods sold	(24,000)	(12,000)
Gross profit	6,000	3,000
Inventory purchased	24,000	$30,000
Inventory sold	(24,000)	12,000
Ending inventory	--	18,000

Since 60% of the inventory remains, the original cost to Pelican for the remaining inventory is $14,400 (60% × $24,000). If 40% of the inventory has been sold, then the actual cost of the inventory sold should be $9,600 (40% × $24,000 [Pelican's cost]). Therefore, an adjusting entry must be made to eliminate the overstatement of sales, cost of goods sold, and inventory. Analyzing the calculations above, the sale made to third parties was $15,000. This is the only sale amount that should be reflected in the consolidated financial statements. Therefore, the $30,000 sale recorded by Pelican must be eliminated. The total cost of goods sold without eliminations is $36,000, but this amount must be reduced by $26,400 to $9,600 (40% × $24,000), which is the cost to Pelican. Inventory is currently stated at $18,000, but the actual cost (Pelican's cost) of the remaining inventory is $14,400 (60% × 24,000). Therefore, inventory must be reduced by the difference $3,600 ($18,000 – $14,400).

(d) Sales   16,000
          Cost of goods sold   16,000

This entry eliminates the effects of the sale of merchandise by Swan to Pelican. Since all of the goods were sold to third parties, there is no effect on ending inventory. The effects of the sale are illustrated below.

	Swan Corp.	Pelican Corp.
Sales	$16,000	$23,000
Cost of goods sold	(11,000)	(16,000)

An elimination entry must be made to prevent double counting sales and cost of goods sold by Swan to Pelican. The sale by Pelican to third parties for $23,000 must remain on the books. The cost of goods sold of $11,000, the original cost of purchasing the inventory, is the correct cost of goods sold. Therefore, the sale of $16,000 and the cost of goods sold of $16,000 must be eliminated.

(e) Equipment	4,000	
Gain on sale of equipment	3,000	
Accumulated depreciation		7,000

This entry eliminates the gain on the intercompany sale of the equipment, eliminates the overstatement of equipment, and restores accumulated depreciation to its balance as of the date of acquisition. To understand this entry, reconstruct the accounts for both Pelican and Swan.

Pelican's books		**Swan's books**	
Historical cost	$12,000	Historical cost	$8,000
Less: Accum. depr.	(7,000)		
Book value	$ 5,000		
Fair value received	$ 8,000		
Less: Book value	(5,000)		
Gain on sale of asset	$ 3,000		

If the intercompany sale had not occurred, Pelican would not have recorded a gain of $3,000. The asset would continue to be valued at historical cost of $12,000 (instead of $8,000) with accumulated depreciation of $7,000. Because Swan recorded the asset at $8,000 in its records, the equipment account is not recorded at cost. The entry adjusts the accounts to eliminate the effects of the intercompany transaction.

(f) Accumulated depreciation	800	
Depreciation expense		800

This entry eliminates the excess depreciation taken on the equipment by Swan. The depreciation recorded when Pelican owned the equipment was $12,000 cost divided by ten years, or $1,200 per year. Swan acquired the asset at a cost of $8,000 and depreciates the asset over a four-year useful life. The depreciation recorded by Swan for the asset was $8,000 divided by 4 years, or $2,000 depreciation expense per year. The excess depreciation of $800 ($2,000 – $1,200) must be eliminated.

(g) Bonds payable	40,000	
Investment in bonds of Pelican Corp.		39,000
Gain on extinguishment of debt		1,000

This entry eliminates the book value of Pelican's debt against the bond investment account of Swan. To the consolidated entity, this transaction must be shown as a retirement of debt even though Pelican still has the outstanding intercompany debt to Swan. In future periods, Swan will amortize the discount, thereby bringing the investment account up to par value and a retained earnings account will be used in the eliminating entry instead of the gain account.

(h) Income from Swan	38,000	
Dividends declared—Swan Corp.		15,000
Investment in stock of Swan Corp.		23,000

This elimination entry adjusts the investment account back to its balance at the beginning of the period and also eliminates the income from subsidiary account and the dividends from subsidiary account.

(i) Capital stock—Swan Corp.	60,000	
Additional paid-in capital—Swan Corp.	10,000	
Retained earnings—Swan Corp.	34,000	
Differential	56,000	
Investment in stock of Swan Corp.		160,000

This entry eliminates Swan's stockholders' equity at the beginning of the year, 1/1/11.

NOTE: The changes **during** the year were eliminated in entry (f) above. The differential account reflects the excess of investment cost greater than the book value of the assets acquired on the date of acquisition. Notice that in a three-part worksheet with an income statement, statement of retained earnings, and balance sheet, the eliminating entry for beginning retained earnings is posted to the retained earnings section of the worksheet.

(j) Inventories	1,000	
Equipment	12,000	
Patents	3,000	
Goodwill	23,000	
Client List	5,000	
Trademark	14,000	
Accumulated depreciation		2,000
Differential		56,000

This entry allocates the differential (excess of investment cost over the book values of the assets acquired). Note that this entry is the same as the allocation entry made to prepare consolidated financial statements for January 1, 2011, the date of acquisition.

(k) Depreciation and amortization expense	5,400	
Accumulated depreciation		2,500
Patents		500
Client list		1,000
Trademarks		1,400

This records depreciation on the net write-up on the equipment to fair value of $10,000 (equipment less accumulated depreciation). The entry also amortizes the write-up on the patent to fair value, and amortizes the newly acquired identifiable intangible assets.

As indicated earlier in the problem, the existing equipment has a remaining useful life of four years, and the patent has a remaining useful life of six years. The depreciation and amortization expense entry of $5,400 is calculated by totaling the following amounts:

Depreciation expense on equipment write-up ($10,000/4 years)	$2,500
Patent amortization ($3,000/ 6 years)	500
Client list amortization ($5,000/ 5 years)	1,000
Trademark amortization ($14,000/11 years)	1,400
Total depreciation and amortization	$5,400

After all adjusting and eliminating entries are made and posted to the worksheet, the worksheet is totaled. Notice that the total adjustments to the income statement (debit of $92,400 and credit of $42,200) are posted as adjustments to net income in the retained earnings section of the worksheet. Notice that the total adjustments to retained earnings (debit of $126,400 and credit of $59,200) are carried down and posted as adjustments to retained earnings on the balance sheet. The consolidated balances are then totaled. In the consolidated balance column, notice that net income flows into the retained earnings part of the worksheet, and the ending balance in retained earnings flows to the balance sheet.

NOW REVIEW MULTIPLE-CHOICE QUESTIONS 42 THROUGH 54 IN VOLUME 2

I. Noncontrolling Interest

1. The acquirer often acquires less than 100% (but more than 50%) of the acquiree's outstanding stock. Under the acquisition method, the consolidated financial statements will include all of the assets, liabilities, revenues, and expenses of these less than wholly owned businesses.
2. The percentage of the stock not owned by the acquirer represents the noncontrolling interest's share of the fair values of the acquiree.
3. Noncontrolling interest is disclosed as a separate line item on the balance sheet in owner's equity. In addition, the portion of net income and comprehensive income attributed to the noncontrolling interest must be disclosed on the acquirer's income statement.
4. The following procedures apply to cases of less than 100% business acquisition.

   a. The equity accounts of the acquiree are eliminated in consolidation, and a noncontrolling interest is established for the fair value of the shares of stock held by the noncontrolling interest at the date of acquisition.
   b. The effects of intercompany transactions are eliminated.
   c. A portion of net income and dividends of the acquiree are allocated to the noncontrolling interest.

5. The financial statements are consolidated and combined with the parent including 100% of the acquiree's revenues and expenses after the date of acquisition. The noncontrolling interest's share of the acquiree's income is shown as a deduction on the consolidated income statement.
6. The following problem illustrates the worksheets for a company that acquires less than 100% of the acquiree.

> **EXAMPLE**
>
> On January 1, 2011, Pearl purchases 90% of Sapphire by issuing 15,000 shares of Pearl's $1 par value common stock with a fair value of $10 per share on the date of acquisition. At the date of acquisition Sapphire had 6,000 shares of stock outstanding with a value of $17.50 per share. Assume the book values of Sapphire's assets are equal to their fair values on the acquisition date. The financial statements at the date of acquisition for Pearl and Sapphire were as follows:

Pearl Corp. and Sapphire Corp.
BALANCE SHEETS 1/1/11
(Immediately before combination)

Assets	Pearl Corp.	Sapphire Corp.
Cash	$ 30,000	$ 24,000
Accounts receivable	35,000	9,000
Inventories	23,000	16,000
Equipment	240,000	60,000
Accumulated depreciation	(40,000)	(10,000)
Patents	--	12,000
Total assets	$288,000	$111,000
Liabilities and Equity		
Accounts payable	$ 6,000	$ 6,000
Bonds payable	80,000	--
Capital stock ($10 par)	120,000	60,000
Additional paid-in capital	20,000	10,000
Retained earnings	62,000	35,000
Total liabilities and equity	$288,000	$111,000

The entry to record the investment in Sapphire is

Investment in Sapphire	150,000	
Common stock (Pearl)		15,000
Additional paid-in capital		135,000

To calculate goodwill, we use the three-step process.

Step 1: Compute the difference between (1) the acquisition cost, plus the fair value of previously acquired shares, plus the fair value of the noncontrolling interest, and (2) the book value of Sapphire's net assets. This is referred to as the differential or difference between fair value and book value.

Acquisition cost	$150,000	
Plus: Fair value of previously acquired shares*	--	
Plus: Fair value of noncontrolling interest	10,500	(600 shares × $17.50 fair value)
Less: Book value of Sapphire	105,000	($111,000 total assets – $6,000 liability)
Differential	$ 55,500	

    * In this example, no shares of stock were previously acquired.

Step 2: Compute the fair value of net identifiable assets.

Book value of Sapphire	$105,000
Plus: Asset write-ups*	--
Plus: Newly identified intangibles*	--
Fair value of net identifiable assets	$105,000

    * In this case, the fair value of net identifiable asset is equal to the book value because there are no asset write-ups or newly identified intangibles.

Step 3: Compute goodwill.

Acquisition cost	$150,000	
+ Fair value of previously acquired shares	--	
Plus: FV of noncontrolling interest	10,500	(600 shares × $17.50 per share)
Less: Fair value, net identifiable assets	(105,000)	
Goodwill	$ 55,500	

Goodwill is then allocated between the controlling interest and noncontrolling interest, as shown below.

	Pearl (90%)	Sapphire (10%)
FV of consideration given and noncontrolling interest shares	$150,000	$10,500
Less: FV of net identifiable assets ($105,000)	(94,500)	(10,500)
Goodwill allocation	$ 55,500	$ 0

Goodwill is allocated to the controlling interest and noncontrolling interest, so that it may be tested for impairment at the end of each reporting period. In this case, no goodwill is allocated to the noncontrolling interest because the fair value of the noncontrolling interest is equal to the noncontrolling interest's share of the fair value of net identifiable assets. If the noncontrolling interest's share of net identifiable assets were less than the fair value of the noncontrolling interest's shares, then a portion of the goodwill would be allocated to the noncontrolling interest. If the consideration paid by the acquirer plus the fair value of noncontrolling interest is less than the fair value of the net identifiable assets, then a **bargain purchase** occurs. The entire gain on the bargain purchase is recognized by the acquirer. No gain on the bargain purchase is recognized by the noncontrolling interest.

a. On the date of acquisition, the working paper eliminations for a less-than-100% acquisition are similar to a 100% acquisition. However, entries must be made for the noncontrolling interest. When there is a noncontrolling interest, the entries required at date of acquisition are modified slightly.

(1) Step 1: Eliminate the acquiree's equity accounts and the acquirer's investment account, establish the differential (the difference between acquisition cost and the book value of the acquiree's net assets), and record the fair value of the noncontrolling interest.

(2) Step 2: Eliminate the differential account, and record the asset write-ups to fair value, the new identifiable intangible assets, and goodwill.

EXAMPLE

Using the information from the prior example, the Step 1 entry is illustrated below.

(a)	Capital stock—Sapphire Corp.	60,000	
	Additional paid-in capital—Sapphire Corp.	10,000	
	Retained earnings—Sapphire Corp.	35,000	
	Differential	55,500	
	Investment in stock of Sapphire Corp.		150,000
	Noncontrolling interest in Sapphire		10,500

NOTE: 100% of Sapphire's stockholders' equity accounts are eliminated. Also, an account called "Differential" is debited in the workpaper entry.

Step 2 allocates the differential to the specific accounts. In this case, all of the differential is attributed to goodwill. The following entry is made to record goodwill:

(b)	Goodwill	55,500	
	Differential		55,500

These entries are then posted to the worksheet in order to prepare consolidated financial statements.

PEARL CORP. AND SAPPHIRE CORP.—CONSOLIDATED WORKING PAPERS
For Date of Acquisition—1/1/11

Acquisition Method—90% Acquisition

	Pearl	Sapphire	Adjustments and eliminations Debit		Credit	Noncontrolling interest	Consolidated balances
Balance sheet 1/1/11							
Cash	30,000	24,000					54,000
Accounts receivable	35,000	9,000					44,000
Inventories	23,000	16,000					39,000
Equipment	240,000	60,000					300,000
Accumulated depreciation	(40,000)	(10,000)					(50,000)
Investment in stock of Sapphire Corp.	150,000			(a)	150,000		--
Difference between cost and book value			(a)	55,500	(b) 55,500		--
Goodwill	--		(b)	55,500			55,500
Patents	--	12,000					12,000
Total assets	438,000	111,000					454,500
Accounts payable	6,000	6,000					12,000
Bonds payable	80,000	--					80,000
Capital stock	135,000	60,000	(a)	60,000			135,000
Additional paid-in capital	155,000	10,000	(a)	10,000			155,000
Noncontrolling interest in Sapphire					10,500	10,500	10,500
Retained earnings	62,000	35,000	(a)	35,000			62,000
Total liabilities and equity	438,000	111,000		216,000	216,000		454,500

When consolidated financial statements are prepared in subsequent years, the working paper eliminations are similar to the 100% acquisition method with a few exceptions. The next worksheet is a continuation of our 90% acquisition of Sapphire for the end of the year subsequent to acquisition. Assume the following additional facts for Pearl and Sapphire:

1. During 2011, Sapphire has $38,000 of net income and pays a dividend of $15,000.
2. Pearl sold $30,000 of goods to Sapphire. Pearl's cost of goods sold was $18,000. All of the goods remain in Sapphire's inventory.
3. At December 31, 2011, Sapphire owes Pearl $5,000 for a portion of the inventory purchased in 2.

Step 1. Eliminate the acquiree's equity accounts, write-up assets to fair value, recognize newly acquired intangibles, and record noncontrolling interests.

(a) Capital stock—Sapphire Corp.	60,000	
Additional paid-in capital—Sapphire Corp.	10,000	
Retained earnings—Sapphire Corp.	35,000	
Differential	55,500	
Investment in stock of Sapphire Corp.		150,000
Noncontrolling interest in Sapphire		10,500
(b) Goodwill	55,500	
Differential		55,500

Note that in this problem, the book value of assets equals the fair value, so no asset write-ups and no newly acquired intangible assets are recorded.

Step 2. Prepare the eliminating entries for intercompany transactions.

(c) Accounts payable	5,000	
Accounts receivable		5,000

This entry eliminates the remaining intercompany receivable/payable owed by Sapphire to Pearl.

(d) Sales	30,000	
Cost of goods sold		18,000
Inventory		12,000

This entry eliminates the intercompany sale of merchandise by Pearl to Sapphire for $30,000, eliminates the cost of goods sold, and restores the inventory to its original historical cost. Also, note that this is a "downstream" sale from the parent to the subsidiary; therefore, the entire transaction must be eliminated.

After the intercompany transactions are eliminated, the income and dividend accounts of the subsidiary must be eliminated.

(e) Income from Sapphire	34,200	
Dividend from Sapphire		13,500
Investment in Sapphire		20,700

This entry eliminates the income from Sapphire recorded on Pearl's books under the equity method, and eliminates the dividends from Sapphire. Note that since only 90% of Sapphire's income was recorded by Pearl, only $34,200 (90% × $38,000) is included in the elimination entry. Also, note that since only 90% of Sapphire's $15,000 dividends declared were paid to Pearl, only $13,500 (90% × $15,000) in dividends are eliminated. The portion that is not eliminated will be included in the balance of the noncontrolling interest in acquiree. Notice that in a three-part worksheet with an income statement, statement of retained earnings, and balance sheet, the debit to income from Sapphire is posted in the income statement portion of the worksheet. The credit to dividends from Sapphire is posted in the retained earnings section of the balance sheet.

There are several differences in the worksheet for a less-than-100% acquisition. Notice that in our example for the 90% acquisition, the initial noncontrolling interest is established by crediting noncontrolling interest for the fair value of the shares of the Sapphire stock at date of acquisition. Also, notice in the income statement portion of the worksheet, that the net income attributable to the noncontrolling interest is subtracted to determine the amount of net income attributable to the acquirer. In the retained earnings section, the net income attributable to the noncontrolling interest less the dividends paid to the noncontrolling interest will be the change in the noncontrolling interest account. The change in noncontrolling interest is added to the beginning balance in noncontrolling interest to arrive at end-of-year controlling interest.

To check for accuracy, it is important to reconcile the noncontrolling interest account. In our example, the noncontrolling interest deduction on the income statement is computed as follows:

Sapphire Corp.'s reported income	$ 38,000
Noncontrolling interest share (10%)	(3,800)
Acquirer's interest in acquiree's income	$34,200

The noncontrolling interest's share of the fair value of net identifiable assets at date of acquisition is shown on the consolidated balance sheet in the owners' equity section. The computation for the noncontrolling interest shown in the balance sheet for our example is

Fair value of noncontrolling interest at date of acquisition	$10,500
Plus: % of noncontrolling interest's share of net income	3,800
Less: % of noncontrolling interest's share of dividends	(1,500)
End of year balance, noncontrolling interest	$12,800

PEARL CORP. AND SAPPHIRE CORP. CONSOLIDATED WORKING PAPERS
Year Ended December 31, 2011

Acquisition Method—90% Acquisition
Subsequent, partial equity

Adjustments and eliminations

	Pearl	Sapphire	Debit		Credit		Noncontrolling interest	Consolidated balances
Income statement for year ended 12/31/11								
Sales	800,000	400,000	(d)	30,000				1,170,000
Cost of sales	580,000	250,000			18,000	(d)		(812,000)
Gross margin	220,000	150,000						358,000
Depreciation and amort. expense	25,000	14,000						39,000
Other operating expenses	115,000	98,000						213,000
Income from operations	80,000	38,000		30,000	18,000			106,000
Income from Sapphire	34,200		(e)	34,200				--
Net income	114,200	38,000		64,200	18,000			106,000
Net income attributable to non-controlling interest in acquiree							3,800	(3,800)
Net income attributable to acquirer								102,200
Statement of retained earnings for year ended 12/31/11								
1/1/11 Retained earnings								
Pearl Corp.	62,000							62,000
Sapphire Corp.		35,000	(a)	35,000				--
Add net income (from above)	114,200	38,000		64,200	18,000		3,800	102,200
Total	176,200	73,000		99,200	18,000		3,800	164,200
Deduct dividends	(26,000)	(15,000)			13,500	(e)	(1,500)	(26,000)
Balance December 31, 2011	150,200	58,000		99,200	31,500		2,300	138,200
Balance sheet 12/31/11								
Cash	48,500	21,000						69,500
Accounts receivable (net)	42,000	8,000			5,000	(c)		45,000
Inventories	34,000	14,000			12,000	(d)		36,000
Equipment	290,000	107,000						397,000
Accumulated depreciation	(50,000)	(17,000)						(67,000)
Investment in stock of Sapphire Corp.	170,700				20,700	(e)		--
					150,000	(a)		
Differential			(a)	55,500	55,500	(b)		--
Goodwill	--	--	(b)	55,500				55,500
Patents	--	12,000						12,000
Total assets	535,200	145,000						548,000
Accounts payable	15,000	17,000	(b)	5,000				27,000
Bonds payable	80,000	--						80,000
Capital stock	135,000	60,000	(a)	60,000				135,000
Additional paid-in capital	155,000	10,000	(a)	10,000				155,000
Retained earnings (from above)	150,200	58,000		99,200	31,500		(2,300)	138,200
Noncontrolling interest in Sapphire					10,500	(a)	2,300	12,800
Total liabilities and equity	535,200	145,000		285,200	285,200		2,300	548,000

7. The remainder of the consolidation process is just worksheet techniques, as described below.

   a. Take all income items across horizontally and foot the adjustments, noncontrolling interest, and consolidated columns down to the net income line.

   b. Take the amounts on the net income line (on income statement) in the adjustments, noncontrolling interest, and consolidated balances columns **down to** retained earnings items across the consolidated balances column. Foot and crossfoot the retained earnings statement.

   c. Take the amounts of ending retained earnings in each of the four columns down to the ending retained earnings line in the balance sheet. Foot the noncontrolling interest column and place its total in the consolidated balances column. Take all the balance sheet items across to consolidated balances column.

8. Take a few minutes to study this worksheet so that you understand how to subtotal and total the three areas of the worksheet.

NOTE: The totals flow from the income statement section to the retained earnings section of the worksheet. Notice how the adjustments to retained earnings flow to the balance sheet.

9. Business consolidation problems may require only the completion of a balance sheet. If you encounter only a balance sheet in a simulation exercise, remember that the entries posted to net income and retained earnings can be posted directly to the appropriate accounts in the stockholders' equity and noncontrolling interest accounts on the balance sheet. Intercompany transactions that involve nominal accounts on the income statement, as well as dividends declared, would be posted to the retained earnings account.

10. More complex business combination problems with noncontrolling interests involve the write-up of assets to fair value, the subsequent depreciation of the increase in fair value on depreciable assets, intercompany sales of inventory by the subsidiary to the parent (upstream sales), and gains and losses from the intercompany sale of fixed assets. ASC Topic 805 states the following:

> *The amount of intra-entity income or loss to be eliminated in accordance with paragraph 810-10-45-1 is not affected by the existence of a noncontrolling interest. The complete elimination of the intercompany income or loss is consistent with the underlying assumption that consolidated financial statements represent the financial position and operating results of a single economic entity. The elimination of the intercompany income or loss may be allocated between the parent and non-controlling interests.*

11. Currently, alternative methods for eliminating intercompany transactions may be used when a noncontrolling interest exists.

   a. The entire intercompany transaction may be eliminated (similar to the 100% acquisition problem earlier in this module for Pelican and Swan).
   b. Another alternative for an acquisition of less than 100% is to allocate the income or loss on intercompany transactions between the parent and the noncontrolling interest. This would apply to situations in which the subsidiary sold inventory or fixed assets to the parent (upstream sales).
   c. Another issue that was not addressed by the FASB is whether the depreciation on asset write-ups should be allocated to the acquirer and the noncontrolling interest. Current practice and accounting texts discuss the logic of allocating the additional depreciation between the acquirer and the noncontrolling interest.
   d. Inasmuch as there are alternative approaches for these transactions, either answer would be acceptable.

> **NOW REVIEW MULTIPLE-CHOICE QUESTIONS 55 THROUGH 67 IN VOLUME 2**

J. Additional Issues Regarding Business Combinations

1. **Incomplete Information**—At the date of acquisition, the accounting for a business combination may be incomplete. For example, the acquirer may not have complete information on valuing certain assets or liabilities.

   a. If the information is not yet complete by the end of the reporting period, then provisional amounts are recorded for those items.

   (1) These provisional amounts may be retrospectively adjusted during the **measurement period**.
   (2) The measurement period ends when the acquirer receives information or learns the information is not obtainable.
   (3) The measurement period may not exceed one year from date of acquisition.

   b. Any changes in the provisional amounts are recognized by retrospectively adjusted the provisional amounts recognized at acquisition date and making a corresponding adjustment to goodwill.
   c. Once the measurement period has ended, the acquirer accounts for changes as a correction of an error by making a prior period adjustment and restating the financial statements.

2. **Transfer of assets**—As discussed earlier, consideration transferred may include cash, assets, liabilities incurred by the acquirer, equity interests of the acquirer, and contingent consideration.

   a. Any assets transferred by the acquirer as part of the consideration in a business acquisition should be remeasured to fair value. Any gain or loss on the remeasurement should be included in earnings for the period.
   b. If the assets remain within the combined entity after the business combination or the acquirer retains control of those assets, then the assets are measured at their carrying values.

3. **Contingent Consideration**—Contingent consideration may be transferred in a business acquisition by promising to pay additional cash or to issue additional shares of the equity of the acquirer. The contingent consideration is measured at fair value at acquisition date.

   a. After the date of acquisition, additional information may indicate the initial value has changed.

(1) If the changes in value occur during the measurement period, then it is treated as a change in a provisional amount and accounted for by an adjustment to goodwill.

(2) After the measurement date, a change in the fair value of contingent consideration classified as an asset or liability is reported in earnings of the period.

b. Any contingent consideration classified as equity is not remeasured.

c. Any settlement of contingent consideration classified as equity is accounted for within owner's equity.

4. **Recognition and Measurement Issues**—Normally, assets and liabilities are measured at fair values and classified at date of acquisition so that the appropriate GAAP rules are applied. Other accounting exceptions exist for recognition and measurement of certain items. Below is a discussion of each of these items.

   a. **Lease classification.** As we discussed earlier, an exception exists for leases. A lease should be recorded on the acquirer's book based on its classification at the inception of the lease. However, if the lease terms are modified or changed at date of acquisition, then the lease is classified as required by the modified terms.

   b. **Operating lease.** If the acquiree is a lessee in operating leases, the acquirer determines whether the lease terms are favorable or unfavorable compared to market terms at the acquisition date. If the terms are favorable, an intangible asset can be recognized apart from goodwill. If the terms are unfavorable, then a liability should be recognized.

      (1) If the acquiree is the lessor in an operating lease, the underlying asset is measured at fair value. The acquirer may also recognize a separate asset or liability if the lease terms are favorable or unfavorable with regard to market terms.

   c. **Contingencies.** Contingencies of the acquiree are considered as contractual contingencies or noncontractual contingencies.

      (1) The acquirer should recognize any contractual contingencies at fair value at the acquisition date.

      (2) For noncontractual contingencies, the acquirer must assess whether it is "more likely than not" that the contingency gives rise to either an asset or a liability as defined in SFAC 6.

         (a) If the noncontractual contingency is more likely than not to meet the definition of an asset, then it is measured at fair value at date of acquisition.

         (b) If the noncontractual contingency is not likely to give rise to either an asset or a liability, the rules for contingencies are applied.

      (3) Recall, that the rules for contingencies use the distinction of probable, reasonably possible, or remote to determine the appropriate accounting.

         (a) Subsequent to acquisition date, if new information is obtained about the possible outcome of the contingency, the acquirer would measure the asset at the lower of its acquisition-date fair value, or the best estimate of its future settlement amount.

         (b) A liability is subsequently measured at the higher of its acquisition-date fair value or the amount recognized by applying the rules for accounting for contingencies.

      (4) The acquirer may only derecognize an asset or liability arising from a contingency when the contingency is resolved.

   d. **Income taxes.** Income taxes of the acquiree are measured at the acquisition date.

   e. **Employee benefits.** Employee benefits of the acquiree are recognized at date of acquisition. This includes compensated absences, pensions, other postemployment benefits, and deferred compensation agreements.

   f. **Indemnification contracts.** Occasionally, the seller of a business may contractually indemnify (guarantee against loss) the acquirer for some uncertainty of contingency. If the seller indemnifies the acquirer, then the acquirer has an indemnification asset, which is measured at fair value at acquisition date.

   g. **Reacquired rights**—Occasionally, the seller of the business may reacquire a right that has been transferred previous to the business acquisition. Examples of reacquired right include rights to use a trade name under a franchise agreement or rights to use technology.

      (1) For example, assume that Company A licenses a trade name to Company B. Company A may or may not have recognized this right as an asset on its books. Later, Company A reacquires the right to the license when it acquires Company B in a business acquisition. At the date of acquisition, Company A, the acquirer, would measure the fair value of this reacquired right and recognize it as an intangible asset on the balance sheet. The reacquired right would be amortized over the remaining contract period.

   h. **Valuation allowances.** At the date of acquisition, the assets of the acquiree are measured at fair value. Uncertainties about cash flows should be considered in the fair value measurements. Therefore, the acquirer would not recognize a separate valuation allowance for cash flows that are considered uncollectible or uncertain at the acquisition date.

    i. **Share-based payment awards.** If the acquirer is required to replace the acquiree's share-based payment awards with new share-based payment awards of the acquirer, then the fair value of the replacement awards are included in the consideration transferred in the business acquisition. If the acquirer is not required to replace the awards, but voluntarily chooses to do so, then the fair value of the replacement awards is recognized as compensation cost in the postcombination financial statements.

    j. **Assets held for sale.** If the acquiree has assets held for sale at the acquisition date, the acquirer measures the assets held for sale at fair value less cost to sell.

K. Additional Disclosures

1. The following items should be disclosed in the notes to the financial statements for business combinations that occur during the reporting period.

    a. Name and description of the acquiree.

    b. Acquisition date.

    c. Percentage of voting equity shares acquired.

    d. Primary reasons for the business combination and how acquirer obtained control of acquiree.

    e. Qualitative description of the factors that make up the goodwill recognized.

    f. Acquisition-date fair value of total consideration transferred and the fair value of each major class of consideration including cash, other assets, liabilities assumed, contingent consideration, and equity instruments (including the number of instruments issued and method of determining fair value).

    g. For contingent consideration and indemnification assets, the amount recognized, a description of arrangement, basis for determining amount of payment, and an estimate of the range of outcomes.

    h. The amounts recognized at the acquisition date for each major class of assets acquired and liabilities assumed.

    i. For assets and liabilities arising from contingencies, the amounts recognized and the nature of recognized and unrecognized contingencies, together with a range of outcomes for the contingencies.

    j. The total amount of goodwill expected to be deducted for tax purposes.

    k. If segment information is reported, the amount of goodwill by reportable segment.

    l. For transactions recognized separately from the business combination, description, accounting, amounts and line items where it is recognized.

    m. Amounts of acquisition-related costs recognized as expense and where those expenses are recognized in the income statement. Amounts of acquisition-related costs not recognized in the income statement.

    n. The gain recognized from bargain purchase and the reason for the gain.

    o. The fair value of any noncontrolling interest in the acquiree at acquisition date, and the valuation techniques used to measure fair value of the noncontrolling interest.

    p. If the business was acquired in stages, the acquisition-date fair value of the equity interest in the acquiree held immediately before the acquisition date, as well as the amount of gain or loss recognized as a result of remeasuring those securities to fair value, valuation techniques, and information on valuation inputs.

    q. If the acquirer is a public company, the amount of revenue and earnings of the acquiree since acquisition date that is included in the consolidated income statement. Also, supplemental pro forma information for revenue and earnings as if the combination had occurred at the beginning of the period, and pro forma comparative statements for the prior reporting period as if the combination had occurred in the beginning of the prior period.

    r. If the acquisition occurs after the reporting date but before the financial statements are issued, the acquirer should make the disclosures of the business combination information listed above.

    s. Any information that enables users of financial statements to evaluate the financial effects of adjustments recognized in the current reporting period related to business combinations that occurred in the current or previous period.

    t. If accounting for a business combination is incomplete, the reason why it is incomplete, and the assets, liabilities, equity interests or items that are incomplete, and the nature and amount of any measurement period adjustments recognized during the period.

    u. Any changes in a contingent consideration asset or liability, differences arising from settlement, and changes in the range of outcomes and reasons for changes.

    v. A reconciliation of the carrying amount of goodwill at the beginning and end of the period.

L. Combined Financial Statements

1. **Combined financial statements** is the term used to describe financial statements prepared for companies that are owned by the same parent company or individual. These statements are often prepared when several subsidiaries of a common parent are not consolidated. Combined financial statements are prepared by combining all of the separate companies' financial statement classifications. Intercompany transactions, balances, and profit (loss) should be eliminated in the same way as in consolidated statements.

NOW REVIEW MULTIPLE-CHOICE QUESTIONS 68 THROUGH 77 IN VOLUME 2

M. Push-Down Accounting

1. "Push-down accounting" describes the method used to prepare the separate financial statements for significant, very large subsidiaries that are either wholly owned or substantially owned ($\geq$ 90%). For publicly traded companies, the SEC requires a onetime adjustment under the acquisition method to revalue the subsidiary's assets and liabilities to fair value, and this entry is made directly on the books of the subsidiary.
2. Push-down accounting requires the subsidiary to record an entry revaluing all assets and liabilities with a balancing entry to a revaluation capital account. The revaluation capital account will be eliminated in consolidation against the investment in subsidiary account.
3. Push-down accounting will have no effect on the presentation of the consolidated financial statements or the separate financial statements of the parent company. However, the subsidiary's financial statements would be reported at fair value rather than historical cost.
4. Advocates of push-down accounting believe that a change of ownership through an acquisition-combination justifies the use of a new basis for the acquired entity. Thus, the new basis should be pushed down or directly recorded on the acquired entity's books.

N. Research Component—Accounting Standards Codification

ASC Topic 805 applies to business combinations. ASC topic 810 provides the rules for consolidation. Below is a list of keywords for searching business combination issues.

Acquired research and development	Contingent consideration	Intercompany balances
Acquirer	Contractual rights	Intercompany profit or loss
Acquiree	Contractual-legal criterion	Legal rights
Allocate cost assets	Controlling interest	Noncontrolling interest
Allocating cost asset	Costs registering securities	Obtains control
Asset apart from goodwill	Date of acquisition	Parent-company
Assigning amounts to assets	Derecognized	Purchase method
Bargain purchase	Disclosure financial statement	Reportable segment
Business combinations	Fair value exchanged	Reporting unit
Combined entity notes to financial statements	Financial assets	Rights transferable or separable
	Goodwill	Separability criterion
Combined financial statements	Initial measurement	Stock dividends subsidiary
Commonly controlled companies	Initial recognition	Subsequent accounting acquisition
Consolidated financial statements	Intangible asset class	
Consolidation purposes	Intangible assets acquired	
Contingency	Intangible assets subject to amortization	

O. International Financial Reporting Standards (IFRS)

1. IFRS requires business combinations to be accounted for using the acquisition method. Although the accounting for business combinations is similar for US GAAP and IFRS, it is different in several respects.
2. Under US GAAP noncontrolling interest is recorded at its fair value. IFRS, on the other hand, allows noncontrolling interest to be valued at either fair value or the proportionate share of the value of the identifiable net assets of the acquiree.

   a. If the noncontrolling interest is valued at fair value, the noncontrolling interest is calculated by determining the market price for equity shares not held by the acquirer. If the market value is not available, other valuation techniques may be used to measure the fair value.
   b. The second method for valuing noncontrolling interest is to calculate the fair value of net assets acquired and multiply that amount times the percentage of shares owned by the noncontrolling interest. Note that these two methods may result in different amounts of goodwill being recognized by the acquirer.
   The calculation of goodwill is

Consideration transferred
+ Noncontrolling interest in acquiree (valued at % of FV or % share of net assets)
+ Fair value of previously held interests in acquiree
– Fair value of net assets acquired
Goodwill

c. If goodwill is negative, a gain from bargain purchase should be recognized in the current period on the income statement.

3. Consolidated financial statements are required for all parent and subsidiaries wherein the parent has control. Similar to US GAAP, control is presumed if the entity has more than 50% of the voting shares of another entity. However, under IFRS, a parent may exclude a subsidiary only if three conditions are met: (1) is it wholly or partially owned and its other owners do not object to nonconsolidation; (2) it does not have any debt or equity instruments publicly traded; and (3) its parent prepares consolidated financial statements that comply with IFRS.

4. The SEC requires the use of "push-down" accounting as described in M. above whereas IFRS disallows its use.

> **NOW REVIEW MULTIPLE-CHOICE QUESTIONS 78 THROUGH 79 IN VOLUME 2**

KEY TERMS

Business. "An integrated set of activities and assets that is capable of being conducted and managed for the purpose of providing a return in the form of dividends, lower costs, or other economic benefits directly to.

Acquiree. The business that is being acquired.

Acquirer. The entity that obtains control of the acquire.

Acquisition date. The date on which the acquirer obtains control of the acquiree.

Business combination. A transaction or event in which the acquirer obtains control of one or more businesses.

Control. A controlling financial interest by ownership of a majority of the voting shares of stock. The general rule is that ownership either directly or indirectly by one company or more than 50% of the outstanding voting shares of another company constitutes control.

Identifiable asset. Arise from a contractual or legal right, or if it is separable.

Separable. It can be separated or divided from the entity and sold, transferred, licensed, rented, or exchanged.

Goodwill. "An asset representing the future economic benefits that arises from other assets acquired in a business combination that are not individually identified and separately recognized"

Variable interest entities (VIE). Control is achieved based on contractual, ownership, or other pecuniary interest that change with changes in the entity's net asset value.

Primary beneficiary. An entity that has a controlling financial interest in a VIE.

Combined financial statements. The term used to describe financial statements prepared for companies that are owned by the same parent company or individual.

Contingent consideration. A promise to pay additional cash or to issue additional shares of the equity of the acquirer.

Bargain purchase. If the consideration paid by the acquirer plus the fair value of noncontrolling interest is less than the fair value of the net identifiable assets.

Module 19: Derivative Instruments and Hedging Activities

Overview

This module covers foreign currency **transactions** (foreign currency **translations** are discussed in Module 20), derivative instruments, and hedging activities. A **foreign currency transaction** is a transaction denominated in a currency other than the entity's functional currency. Foreign currency transactions are discussed in this module because exchange rate risk can be hedged.

A **derivative instrument** derives its value as a financial instrument from something else and must meet three specific criteria to qualify as such. These criteria are discussed in this module. The most relevant measure for reporting derivatives is fair value. Some instruments, hybrid instruments, must be bifurcated (separated) between the derivative and the basic contract.

Hedging instruments are derivative instruments that meet two primary criteria: (1) sufficient documentation relating to the objective of the hedge, identification of the hedge, and the assessment of the hedge must be provided and (2) the hedge must be highly effective. Hedges are classified as fair value hedges, cash flow hedges, or foreign currency hedges.

Derivative accounting and reporting can be very complex. It requires the adherence to many specific criteria to distinguish how to account for certain derivatives. The candidate is urged to spend considerable time reading through and understanding the definitions in the key terms before studying this module.

A. Foreign Currency Transactions

1. A foreign currency transaction, according to ASC Topic 830, is a transaction denominated in a currency other than the entity's functional currency. **Denominated** means that the balance is fixed in terms of the number of units of a foreign currency regardless of changes in the exchange rate. When a US company purchases or sells goods or services (or borrows or lends money) to a foreign entity, and the transaction is denominated in foreign currency units, the US company has a foreign currency transaction in which the US dollar is the functional currency.

   a. In these situations, the US company has "crossed currencies" and directly assumes the risk of fluctuating foreign exchange rates of the foreign currency units.
   b. This exposed foreign currency risk may lead to recognition of foreign exchange transaction gains or losses in the income statement of the US company.
   c. If the US company pays or receives US dollars in import and export transactions, the risk resulting from fluctuating foreign exchange rates is borne by the foreign supplier or customer, and there is no need to apply the procedures outlined in ASC Topic 830 to the transaction reported in US dollars on the US company's books.
   d. The following example illustrates the terminology and procedures applicable to the translation of foreign currency transactions.

> **EXAMPLE**
>
> Assume that US Company, an exporter, sells merchandise to a customer in Germany on December 1, 2010, for 10,000 euros (€). Receipt of €10,000 is due on January 31, 2011, and US Company prepares financial statements on December 31, 2010. At the transaction date (December 1, 2010), the spot rate for immediate exchange of foreign currencies indicates that €1 is equivalent to $.90. This quotation is referred to as a direct quotation since the exchange rate is stated in terms of a direct translation of the currency in which the debt is measured. To find the US dollar equivalent of this transaction, simply multiply the foreign currency amount, €10,000, by $.90 to get $9,000. Occasionally, spot rates are quoted indirectly (e.g., $1 is equivalent to €1.1111). In the example used, since $1 is equivalent to €1.1111, the foreign currency amount would be divided by €1.1111 to get the US dollar amount of $9,000 (assuming the calculation is performed using four decimal places and rounded to the nearest dollar).
>
> At December 1, 2010, the foreign currency transaction should be recorded by US Company in the following manner:
>
> | | | |
> |---|---|---|
> | Accounts receivable (€) | 9,000 | |
> | Sales | | 9,000 |

> The accounts receivable and sales are measured in US dollars at the transaction date using the spot rate at the time of the transaction. While the accounts receivable is measured and reported in US dollars, the receivable is also denominated or fixed in euros. This characteristic can result in foreign exchange transaction gains or losses if the spot rate for euros changes between the transaction date and the date the transaction is settled.

2. If financial statements are prepared between the transaction date and the settlement date, the FASB requires that receivables and liabilities denominated in a currency other than the functional currency be restated to reflect the spot rates in existence at the balance sheet date.

EXAMPLE

Assume the same facts as the previous example and that, on December 31, 2010, the spot rate for euros is €1 = $.93. This means that €10,000 are worth $9,300, and that the accounts receivable denominated in euros are increased by $300. The following journal entry should be recorded as of December 31, 2010:

Accounts receivable (€)	300	
Foreign currency transaction gain		300

NOTE: The sales account, which was credited on the transaction date for $9,000, is not affected by changes in the spot rate.

---

a. This treatment exemplifies the "two-transaction" viewpoint adopted by the FASB. In other words, making the sale is the result of an operating decision, while bearing the risk of fluctuating spot rates is the result of an investment decision. Therefore, the amount determined as sales revenue at the transaction date should not be altered because of an investment decision to wait until January 31, 2011, for payment of the account.

    (1) The risk of a foreign exchange transaction loss can be avoided either by demanding immediate payment on December 1 or by entering into a forward exchange contract to hedge the exposed asset (accounts receivable).

    (2) The fact that US Company in the example did not act in either of these two ways is reflected by the required recognition of foreign currency transaction gains or losses on this type of transaction. These gains or losses are reported on US Company's income statement as financial (nonoperating) items in the period during which the exchange rates changed.

NOTE: Reporting transaction gains or losses before the transaction is settled results in reporting unrealized gains or losses. This represents an exception to the conventional realization principle which normally applies. This practice also results in a temporary difference between pretax accounting income and taxable income because foreign exchange transaction gains and losses do not enter into the determination of taxable income until the year they are realized. Thus, the recognition of foreign currency transaction gains and losses on unsettled foreign currency transactions results in deferred tax assets/liabilities (depending on whether the temporary differences result in future taxable or future deductible amounts).

EXAMPLE

To complete the previous illustration, assume that on January 31, 2011, the foreign currency transaction is settled when the spot rate is €1 = $.91. Note that the account receivable is still valued at $9,300 at this point. The receipt of euros and their conversion into dollars should be journalized as follows:

Foreign currency (€)	9,100	
Foreign currency transaction loss	200	
Accounts receivable (€)		9,300
Cash	9,100	
Foreign currency (€)		9,100

The net effect of this foreign currency transaction was the receipt of $9,100 from a sale which was measured originally at $9,000. This realized net foreign currency transaction gain of $100 is reported on the income statements of more than one period—a $300 gain in 2010 and a $200 loss in 2011.

---

3. The financial statement disclosures required by ASC Topic 830 include the following:

    a. Aggregate transaction gain (loss) that is included in the entity's net income

    b. Significant rate changes subsequent to the date of the financial statements including effects on unsettled foreign currency transactions

NOW REVIEW MULTIPLE-CHOICE QUESTIONS 1 THROUGH 9 IN VOLUME 2

B. Derivative Instruments and Hedging Activities

1. Financial instruments include cash, accounts/notes receivable, accounts/notes payable, bonds, common stock, preferred stock, stock options, foreign currency forward contracts, futures contracts, various financial swaps, etc. Other contracts which are also considered financial instruments meet the following two criteria:

   a. The contract imposes a contractual obligation on one party (to the contract) to deliver cash or another financial instrument to the second party, or to exchange financial instruments on potentially unfavorable terms with the second party;

   b. The contract conveys a contractual right to the second party to receive cash or another financial instrument from the first party, or to exchange financial instruments on favorable terms with the first party.

   A glossary of derivative-related terms is presented at the end of this section.

   c. It is from the above universe of financial instruments and other contracts that a subset is identified that qualifies as derivative instruments. **Derivative instruments** are so called because they derive their value as a financial instrument from something outside the instrument itself.

   (1) For example, a call option to purchase an exchange-traded stock would qualify as a derivative instrument. The value of the call option can only be determined by the market price of the related stock.

   EXAMPLE

   A call option allows the holder to purchase 1,000 shares of stock at $50 per share, but no determination can be made as to the value of the call option until the stock price is determined. If the market value of the stock is $58 per share, the value of the call option is easily determined to be $8,000 [1,000 shares × ($58 – $50)].

   (a) The stock price is called the **"underlying,"** the rate or price that exists outside the derivative instrument that is used to determine the value of the derivative instrument.

   (b) The 1,000 shares of stock is known as the **"notional amount,"** that is the number of units related to the derivative instrument.

   (c) Both of these terms are important for two reasons:

   1] Their existence is a necessary condition for determining whether or not a financial instrument or other contract is a derivative instrument;

   2] They are determining factors in calculating the "settlement amount" of a derivative instrument.

   (d) All of these terms are discussed in more detail later in this section, but this basic understanding of derivative instruments may be helpful in working through the remaining definitions, explanations, and examples.

2. **Foundation Principles for Accounting for Derivatives and Hedging**—The basic principles driving the structure of accounting for derivatives and hedging are

   a. **Fair value measurement.** Derivative instruments meet the definition of assets and liabilities (probable future economic benefits or sacrifices of future economic benefits resulting from past transactions or events). As such they should be reported on an entity's financial statements. The most relevant measure for reporting financial instruments is "fair value."

   (1) ASC Topic 820 defines **fair value** as "the price that would be received to sell an asset or paid to transfer a liability in an orderly transaction between market participants at the measurement date."

   (2) As a corollary to this principle, gains and losses that result from the change in the fair value of derivative instruments are **not** assets and liabilities. Therefore, gains and losses should not be reported on the balance sheet but rather should either appear in comprehensive income or be reported in current earnings.

   (3) The details for reporting gains and losses appear in a subsequent section.

   b. **Hedging.** Certain derivative instruments will qualify under the definition of hedging instruments. Those that qualify will be accounted for using hedge accounting, which generally provides for matching the recognition of gains and losses of the hedging instrument and the hedged asset or liability. (More details about hedge accounting are provided in a later section.) Three kinds of hedges have been defined in the standard.

   (1) **Fair value hedge**—A hedge of the exposure to changes in the fair value of (a) a recognized asset or liability, or (b) an unrecognized firm commitment.

(2) **Cash flow hedge**—A hedge of the exposure to variability in the cash flows of (a) a recognized asset or liability, or (b) a forecasted transaction.

(3) **Foreign currency hedge**—A hedge of the foreign currency exposure of (a) an unrecognized firm commitment, (b) an available-for-sale security, (c) a forecasted transaction, or (d) a net investment in a foreign operation.

If a derivative instrument does not qualify as a hedging instrument under one of the three categories shown above, then its gains or losses must be reported and recognized in current earnings.

3. **Definition of a Derivative Instrument**—Three distinguishing characteristics of a derivative instrument, must be present for a financial instrument or other contract to be considered a derivative instrument. All three characteristics must be present.

   a. The financial instrument or other contract must contain (a) one or more **underlyings,** and (b) one or more **notional amounts** (or payment provisions or both).

   (1) An **underlying** is any financial or physical variable that has either observable changes or objectively verifiable changes. Therefore, underlyings would include traditional financial measures such as commodity prices, interest rates, exchange rates, or indexes related to any of these items. More broadly, measures such as an entity's credit rating, rainfall, or temperature changes would also meet the definition of an underlying.

   (2) **Notional** amounts are the "number of currency or other units" specified in the financial instrument or other contract. In the case of options, this could include bushels of wheat, shares of stock, etc.

   (3) The **settlement amount** of a financial instrument or other contract is calculated using the underlying(s) and notional amount(s) in some combination.

      (a) Computation of the settlement amount may be as simple as multiplying the fair value of a stock times a specified number of shares.

      (b) On the other hand, calculation of the settlement amount may require a very complex calculation, involving ratios, stepwise variables, and other leveraging techniques.

> **NOTE:** The term "notional amount" is sometimes used interchangeably with "settlement amount." Watch to determine if the context in which the term is used is calling for a number of units (notional amount), or a dollar value (settlement amount).

   b. The financial instrument or other contract requires no initial net investment or an initial net investment that is smaller than would be required for other types of contracts that would be expected to have a similar response to changes in market factors.

   (1) Many derivative instruments require no net investment or simply a premium as compensation for the time value of money.

      (a) Futures contracts may require the establishment of a margin account with a balance equal to a small percentage (2 – 3%) of the value of the contract.

      (b) A call option on a foreign currency contract would again only cost a small fraction of the value of the contract.

      (c) These are typical contracts that would meet this definition and would be included in the definition of derivative instruments.

   c. The terms of the financial instrument or other contract do one of the following with regard to settlement:

   (1) Require or permit net settlement, either within the contract or by a means outside the contract.

      (a) Net settlement means that a contract can be settled through the payment of cash rather than the exchange of the specific assets referenced in the contract.

      (b) This type of settlement typically occurs with a currency swap or an interest rate swap.

      (c) This definition may have some unanticipated consequences. For example, a contract with a liquidating damages clause for nonperformance, the amount of which is determined by an underlying, would meet this criterion.

   (2) Provide for the delivery of an asset that puts the recipient in a position not substantially different from net settlement.

      (a) This might include a futures contract where one party to the contract delivers an asset, but a "market mechanism" exists (such as an exchange) so that the asset can be readily converted to cash.

         1] Convertibility to cash requires an active market and is a determining factor in whether or not a financial instrument or other contract will be treated as a derivative instrument.

NOW REVIEW MULTIPLE-CHOICE QUESTIONS 10 THROUGH 18 IN VOLUME 2

4. **Inclusions in and Exclusions from Derivative Instruments**

   The following table provides a list of those financial instruments and other contracts that meet the definition of derivative instruments and those that do not meet the definition of derivative instruments or because they are specifically excluded from treatment.

Included	**Excluded**
• Options to purchase (call) or sell (put) exchange-traded securities	• Normal purchases and sales (does not exclude "take or pay" contracts with little or no initial net investment and products that are readily convertible to cash)
• Futures contracts	• Equity securities
• Interest rate swaps	• Debt securities
• Currency swaps	• Regular-way (three-day settlement) security trades (this exclusion applies to "to be announced" and "when issued" trades)
• Swaptions (an option on a swap)	• Leases
• Credit indexed contracts	• Mortgage-backed securities
• Interest rate caps/floors/collars	• Employee stock options
	• Royalty agreements and other contracts tied to sales volumes
	• Variable annuity contracts
	• Adjustable rate loans
	• Guaranteed investment contracts
	• Nonexchanged traded contracts tied to physical variables
	• Derivatives that serve as impediments to sales accounting (e.g., guaranteed residual value in a leasing arrangement)

   a. **Interest rate swaps** are one of the most commonly used derivative instruments in business. The following discussion first describes an interest rate swap and then shows how it meets the definition of a derivative instrument.

      (1) In a common example, two parties may agree to swap interest payments on debt. Usually this occurs when one party (Company F) has issued fixed-rate debt and believes that interest rates are going to drop, while a second party (Company V) has issued variable-rate debt and believes that interest rates are going to rise. In this case, both companies would be interested in exchanging interest payments since both believe that their interest expense would decrease as a result of the swap. Variable-rate interest may be determined by any number of indices (e.g., London Interbank Offered Rate [LIBOR], S&P 500 index, some fixed relationship to T-bill rates, AAA corporate bonds, etc.).

         (a) In this example, the **notional amount** is defined as the principal portion of the debt, which would be the same for both the fixed and variable rate debt. The **underlying** is the index that determines the variable interest rate, for example, six-month LIBOR. There is no initial **net investment** required for this contract since the first payment will not occur until the first interest date arrives, and net settlement can be achieved through the payment of interest and principal at the maturity date. Therefore, all three of the criteria for a derivative instrument are present, and it is accounted for as an interest rate swap. Similar examples could be developed for the other financial instruments listed in the "included" column below.

5. **Embedded Derivative Instruments and Bifurcation**

   Financial instruments and other contracts may contain features which, if they stood alone, would meet the definition of a derivative instrument. These financial instruments and other contracts are known as **"hybrid instruments."** This means that there is a basic contract, known as the **"host contract,"** that has an embedded derivative instrument. In these circumstances, the embedded derivative instrument may have to be separated from the host contract, a process known as **bifurcation,** and treated as if it were a stand-alone instrument. In this case, the host contract (excluding the embedded derivative) would be accounted for in the normal manner (as if it had never contained the embedded derivative), and the now stand-alone derivative instrument would be accounted for using the rules for derivatives.

  a. Three criteria are used to determine if **bifurcation** must occur. **All** criteria must be met.

    (1) The embedded derivative meets the definition of a derivative.

    (2) The hybrid instrument is **not** regularly recorded at fair value, with changes reported in current earnings as they occur under other GAAP. If the hybrid instrument is regularly recorded at fair value, then there is no need to bifurcate the embedded derivative since the same end result is being accomplished already.

    (3) The economic characteristics and risks of the embedded derivative instrument are **not** "clearly and closely related" to the economic characteristics and risks of the host contract.

  b. Below are listed a number of hybrid instruments that would normally require bifurcation:

    (1) A bond payable with an interest rate based on the S&P 500 index.

    (2) An equity instrument (stock) with a call option, allowing the issuing company to buy back the stock.

    (3) An equity instrument with a put option, requiring the issuing company to buy back the stock at the request of the holder.

    (4) A loan agreement that permits the debtor to pay off the loan prior to its maturity with the loan payoff penalty based on the short-term T-bill rates.

    (5) Loans with term-extending options whose values are based on the prime rate at the time of the extension.

    (6) Convertible debt (from the investor's viewpoint)

  c. The holder of a hybrid instrument normally requiring bifurcation can make an election **not** to bifurcate the instrument. Instead, the entire instrument is valued at fair value.

    (1) This election is irrevocable and is made on an instrument-by-instrument basis.

    (2) Changes in fair value of the hybrid instruments are recognized each year in earnings.

    (3) If a company elects to use fair value measurement on selected hybrid instruments, the balance sheet disclosure may be presented in one of two ways:

      (a) As separate line items for the fair value and non–fair value instruments on the balance sheet,

      (b) As an aggregate amount of all hybrid instruments with the amount of the hybrid instruments at fair value shown in parentheses.

  d. The fair value option may be applied to host financial instruments resulting from separation of an embedded nonfinancial derivative instrument from a nonfinancial hybrid instrument. If the fair value option is elected, the disclosure rules for fair value apply.

> **NOW REVIEW MULTIPLE-CHOICE QUESTIONS 19 THROUGH 27 IN VOLUME 2**

6. Hedging Instruments—General Criteria

Two primary criteria must be met in order for a derivative instrument to qualify as a hedging instrument.

  a. Sufficient documentation must be provided at the beginning of the process to identify at a minimum (1) the objective and strategy of the hedge, (2) the hedging instrument and the hedged item, and (3) how the effectiveness (see below) of the hedge will be assessed on an ongoing basis.

  b. The hedge must be **"highly effective"** throughout its life.

    (1) Effectiveness is measured by analyzing the hedging instrument's (the derivative instrument) ability to generate changes in fair value that offset the changes in value of the hedged item.

    (2) At a minimum, its effectiveness will be measured every three months and whenever earnings or financial statements are reported.

    (3) A "highly effective" hedge has been interpreted to mean that "the cumulative change in the value of the hedging instrument should be between 80 and 125% of the inverse cumulative changes in the fair value or cash flows of the hedged item."

    (4) The method used to assess effectiveness must be used throughout the hedge period and must be consistent with the approach used for managing risk.

    (5) Similar hedges should usually be assessed for effectiveness in a similar manner unless a different method can be justified. (Even though a hedging instrument may meet the criterion for being highly effective, it may not eliminate variations in reported earnings, because to the extent that a hedging instrument is not 100% effective, the difference in net loss or gain in each period must be reported in current earnings.)

7. Fair Value Hedges

A fair value hedge is the use of a derivative instrument to hedge the exposure to changes in the fair value of an asset or a liability.

a. **Specific criteria.** The hedged asset/liability must meet certain criteria in order to qualify as a fair value hedge. The hedged item must be either **all** or a **specific portion** (e.g., a percentage, a contractual cash flow) of a recognized asset/liability or an unrecognized firm commitment.

(1) Both of these situations arise frequently in foreign currency transactions.

> **EXAMPLE**
>
> A company may enter into a firm commitment with a foreign supplier to purchase a piece of equipment, the price of which is denominated in a foreign currency and both the delivery date and the payment date are in the future. The company may decide to hedge the commitment to pay for the equipment in a foreign currency in order to protect itself from currency fluctuations between the firm commitment date and the payment date. For the period between the firm commitment date and the delivery date, the company will be hedging against an unrecognized firm commitment. For the period between the delivery date and the payment date, the company is hedging against a recognized liability. (See Section 9 of this module for the accounting associated with this example.)

(2) For an unrecognized firm commitment to qualify it must be (1) binding on both parties, (2) specific with respect to all significant terms, and (3) contain a nonperformance clause that makes performance probable.

b. **Accounting for a fair value hedge.** Gains and losses on the hedged asset/liability and the hedging instrument will be recognized in current earnings.

> **EXAMPLE**
>
> On 10/1/09, Dover Corp. purchases 20 shares of Porter, Inc. stock at $40. The securities are classified as available-for-sale. The market price moves to $45 by the end of the year. Assume Dover does not elect the fair value option to report its shares of Porter stock. In order to protect itself from a possible decline in the stock value of its available-for-sale security, Dover purchases an at-the-money put option for $300 on 12/31/09. The put option gives Dover the right, but not the obligation, to sell 200 shares of Porter stock at $45 per share, and the option expires on 12/31/11. Dover designates the hedge as a fair value hedge because it is hedging changes in the security's fair value. The fair value of an option is made up of two components, the time value and the intrinsic value. At the time of purchase, the time value is the purchase price of the options and the intrinsic value is $0 (because the option was purchased at-the-money).
>
> Over the life of the option, the time value will drop to $0. This is due to the fact that time value relates to the ability to exercise the option over a specified period of time. As the option moves toward the expiration date, the perceived value of the time value portion of the option will decrease as a function of the time value of money (TVM) issues and other market forces. The time value will generally decrease over the life of the option, but not necessarily in a linear fashion. The intrinsic value will vary based on the difference between the current stock price vs. the stock price on the date the option was purchased. As shown in the table below, the intrinsic value of the option increases from $0 to $200 between 12/31/09 and 12/31/10 because the stock price has dropped by $1 (× 200 shares), and the hedge has been effective for that same amount. As can be seen by analyzing the two components of the put option, the market is the primary driver of the value that should be assigned to the option. As is often the case, the intrinsic value of the option is considered to be a "highly effective" hedge against changes in the stock price, while the time value is ineffective and is reflected in current earnings. Additional information is provided below.
>
> | Item | 1/1/09 | 12/31/09 | 12/31/10 | 12/31/11 |
> |---|---|---|---|---|
> | Porter stock price | $40 | $ 45 | $ 44 | $ 42 |
> | Put option | | | | |
> | Time value | | $300 | $160 | $0 |
> | Intrinsic value | | $ 0 | $200 | $600 |
> | | | | (200 × $1) | (200 × $3) |
>
> **1/1/09**
>
> 1. Available-for-sale securities   8,000
>   Cash   8,000
>   *Record the purchase of Porter stock (200 × $40).*
>
> **12/31/09**
>
> 2. Available-for-sale securities   1,000
>   Other comprehensive income   1,000
>   *Record the unrealized gain on Porter stock (accounting prior to the hedge in accordance with ASC Topic 320. (200 × $5 valuation increase from holding gain to market value)*
>
> 3. Put option   300
>   Cash   300
>   *Record the purchase of at-the-money put option.*

12/31/10
4. Put option   200
      Gain on hedge activity   200
Record the increase in the intrinsic value (fair value) of the option.

5. Loss on hedge activity   200
      Available-for-sale securities   200
Record the decrease in the fair value of the securities (accounting after the hedge is established) $200 = 200 shares × $1 holding loss.

> **NOTE:** The $200 gain on hedge activity from the put option is balanced effectively against the $200 loss on hedge activity from the hedged available-for-sale security. The portion of the unrealized holding gain or loss on an available-for-sale security that is designated as a hedged item in a fair value hedge is recognized in earnings during the period of the hedge. This is why the $200 holding loss on the available-for-sale securities is recognized in the period's earnings.

6. Loss on hedge activity   140
      Put option   140
Record the loss related to the time value of the option. $140 = $300 – $160

12/31/11
7. Put option   400
      Gain on hedge activity   400
Record the increase in the intrinsic value of the put option.

8. Loss on hedge activity   400
      Available-for-sale securities   400
To record the decrease in the fair value of the securities (accounting after the hedge is established); $400 = 200 shares × $2 holding loss on available-for-sale securities.

9. Loss on hedge activity   160
      Put option   160
Record the loss related to the time value of the option. $140 = $300 – $160

10. Cash   9,000
      Put option   600
      Available-for-sale securities   8,400
Record the exercise of the put option (sell the 200 shares of stock @ $45) and close out the put option investment.

11. Other comprehensive income   1,000
      Gain on Porter stock   1,000
To reclassify the unrealized holding gain recognized in entry 2., from other comprehensive income to earnings, because the securities were sold.

8. **Cash Flow Hedges**

Cash flow hedges use derivative instruments to hedge the exposure to variability in expected future cash flows.

a. **Specific criteria.** Additional criteria must be met in order to qualify as a **cash flow hedge**.

  (1) The primary criterion is that the hedged asset/liability and the hedging instrument must be **"linked."**

    (a) **Linking** is established if the basis (the specified rate or index) for the change in cash flows is the same for the hedged asset/liability and the hedging instrument.

  (2) Cash flows do not have to be identical, but they must meet the **highly effective** threshold discussed above.

  (3) In addition, if the hedged asset/liability is a **forecasted transaction,** it must be considered **probable,** based on appropriate facts and circumstances (i.e., past history).

  (4) Also, if the forecasted hedged asset/liability is a series of transactions, they must "share the same risk exposure."

    (a) Purchases of a particular product from the same supplier over a period of time would meet this requirement.

b. **Accounting for a cash flow hedge.** For the hedging instrument:

  (1) The effective portion is reported in other comprehensive income, and

  (2) The ineffective portion and/or excluded components are reported on a cumulative basis to reflect the lesser of

    (a) The cumulative gain/loss on the derivative since the creation of the hedge, or

    (b) The cumulative gain/loss from the change in expected cash flows from the hedged instrument since the creation of the hedge.

1] The above amounts need to be adjusted to reflect any reclassification of other comprehensive income to current earnings. This will occur when the hedged asset/liability affects earnings (e.g., when hedged inventory is sold and the cost of inventory passes through to cost of goods sold).

EXAMPLE

A commercial bakery believes that wheat prices may increase over the next few months. To protect itself against this risk, the bakery purchases call options on wheat futures to hedge the price risk of their forecasted inventory purchases. If wheat prices increase, the profit on the purchased call options will offset the higher price the bakery must pay for the wheat. If wheat prices decline, the bakery will lose the premium it paid for the call options, but can then buy the wheat at the lower price. On June 1, 2010, the bakery pays a premium of $350 to purchase a September 30, 2010 call for 1,000 bushels of wheat at the futures price of $16.60 per bushel. The call option is considered a cash flow hedge because the designated risk that is being hedged is the risk of changes in the cash flows relating to changes in the purchase price of the wheat. On September 30, the bakery settles its call options and purchases wheat on the open market. Pertinent wheat prices are shown below.

Spot price (June 1)	$16.50
Futures price (as of June 1 for September 30)	$16.60
Spot price (September 30)	$17.30

June 1

1. Call option	350	
Cash		350

Record the purchase of the call option.

September 30

2. Loss on hedge activity	350	
Call option		350

Record the expiration (change in time value) of the call option.

3. Call option	700	
Other comprehensive income		700

Record the increase in intrinsic value of the call option. $700 = {1,000 bushels × [$17.30 (the spot price per bushel on September 30) − $16.60 (the futures price as of June 1 for September 30)]}

4. Cash	700	
Call option		700

Record the cash settlement of the call option.

5. Inventory	17,300	
Cash		17,300

Record the purchase of the wheat at the spot price. $17,300 = 1,000 bushels × $17.30

---

9. Foreign Currency Hedges

Foreign currency denominated assets/liabilities that arise in the course of normal business are often hedged with offsetting forward exchange contracts. This process, in effect, creates a natural hedge. Normal accounting rules apply, and the FASB did not change this accounting treatment in the implementation of hedge accounting. Hedge accounting is required in four areas related to foreign currency hedges. The four foreign currency hedges are discussed below.

a. **Unrecognized firm commitment.** Either a derivative instrument or a nonderivative financial instrument (such as a receivable in a foreign currency) can be designated as a hedge of an unrecognized firm commitment attributable to changes in foreign currency exchange rates. If the requirements for a fair value hedge are met, then this hedging arrangement can be accounted for as a **fair value hedge,** discussed above.

b. **Available-for-sale securities.** Hedge accounting is not used for trading and held-to-maturity securities. The use of hedge accounting for transactions for securities designated as available-for-sale may be allowed in some instances. Derivative instruments can be used to hedge debt or equity available-for-sale securities. However, equity securities must meet two additional criteria.

(1) They cannot be traded on an exchange denominated in the investor's functional currency.

(2) Dividends must be denominated in the same foreign currency as is expected to be received on the sale of the security.

If the above criteria are met, hedging instruments related to available-for-sale securities can be accounted for as **fair value hedges,** discussed above.

c. **Foreign currency denominated forecasted transactions.** Only derivative instruments can be designated as hedges of foreign currency denominated forecasted transactions. A forecasted export sale with the price denominated in a foreign currency might qualify for this type of hedge treatment.

(1) Forecasted transactions are distinguished from firm commitments (discussed in a. above) because the timing of the cash flows remains uncertain.

(a) This additional complexity results in hedging instruments related to foreign currency denominated forecasted transactions being accounted for as cash flow hedges, discussed above.

(b) Hedge accounting is permissible for transactions between unrelated parties, and under special circumstances (not discussed here) for intercompany transactions.

d. **Net investments in foreign operations.** The accounting for net investments in foreign operations has not changed from the ASC Topic 830 rules, except that the hedging instrument has to meet the new "effective" criterion. The change in the fair value of the hedging derivative is recorded in a manner consistent with a translation adjustment in other comprehensive income which is then closed to the accumulated other comprehensive income account in the equity section of the balance sheet.

Hedge Accounting ASC Topic 815 (SFAS 133)

		Type of Hedge	
Attribute	**Fair Value**	**Cash Flow**	**Foreign Currency (FC)**
Types of hedging instruments permitted	Derivatives	Derivatives	Derivatives or nonderivatives depending on the type of hedge
Balance sheet valuation of hedging instrument	Fair value	Fair value	Fair value
Recognition of gain or loss on changes in value of hedging instrument	Currently in earnings	Effective portion currently as a component of other comprehensive income (OCI) and reclassified to earnings in future period(s) that forecasted transaction affects earnings	**FC denominated firm commitment** Currently in earnings **Available-for-sale security (AFS)** Currently in earnings
		Ineffective portion currently in earnings	**Forecasted FC transaction** Same as cash flow hedge **Net investment in a foreign operation** OCI as part of the cumulative translation adjustment to the extent it is effective as a hedge
Recognition of gain or loss on changes in the fair value of the hedged item	Currently in earnings	Not applicable; these hedges are not associated with recognized assets or liabilities	**FC denominated firm commitment** Currently in earnings **Available-for-sale security (AFS)** Currently in earnings **Forecasted FC transaction** Not applicable; same as cash flow hedge

> **NOW REVIEW MULTIPLE-CHOICE QUESTIONS 28 THROUGH 37 IN VOLUME 2**

10. **Forward Exchange Contracts**

It was stated previously that foreign currency transaction gains and losses on assets and liabilities which are denominated in a currency other than the functional currency can be hedged if a US company enters into a forward exchange contract.

a. The following example shows how a forward exchange contract can be used as a hedge, first against a firm commitment and then, following delivery date, as a hedge against a recognized liability.

b. The general rule for estimating the fair value of forward exchange contracts is to use the forward exchange rate for the remaining term of the contract.

EXAMPLE

Baker Simon, Inc. enters into a firm commitment with Dempsey Ing., Inc. of Germany, on October 1, 2010, to purchase a computerized robotic system for €6,000,000. The system will be delivered on March 1, 2010, with payment due sixty days after delivery (April 30, 2011). Baker Simon, Inc. decides to hedge this foreign currency firm commitment and enters into a forward exchange contract on the firm commitment date to receive €6,000,000 on the payment date. The applicable exchange rates are shown in the table below.

Date	Spot rates	Forward rates for April 30, 2010
October 1, 2010	€1 = $.90	€1 = $ .91
December 31, 2010	€1 = $.92	€1 = $ .94
March 1, 2011	€1 = $.92	€1 = $.935
April 30, 2011	€1 = $.96	

---

c. The following example separately presents both the forward contract receivable and the dollars payable liability in order to show all aspects of the forward contract.

(1) For financial reporting purposes, most companies present just the net fair value of the forward contract, which would be the difference between the current value of the forward contract receivable and the dollars payable accounts.

(2) The transactions which reflect the forward exchange contract, the firm commitment and the acquisition of the asset and retirement of the related liability appear as follows:

Forward contract entries

(1) 10/1/10 (forward rate for 4/30/11
€1 = $.91)

Forward contract receivable (€)	5,460,000	
Dollars payable		5,460,000

This entry recognizes the existence of the forward exchange contract using the gross method. Under the net method, this entry would not appear at all, since the fair value of the forward contract is zero when the contract is initiated. The amount is calculated using the 10/1/10 forward rate for 4/30/11 (€6,000,000 × $.91 = $5,460,000). Note that the **net** fair value of the forward exchange contact on 10/1/10 is zero because there is an exact amount offset of the forward contract receivable with the dollars payable liability.

(2) 12/31/10 (forward rate for 4/30/10
€1 = $.94)

Forward contract receivable (€)	180,000	
Gain on hedge activity		180,000

€6,000,000 × ($ .94 – $ .91) = $180,000. The dollar values for this entry reflect, among other things, the change in the forward rate from 10/1/10 to 12/31/10. However, the actual amount recorded as gain or loss (gain in this case) will be determined by all market factors.

(4) 3/1/11 (forward rate for 4/30/11 €1
= $.935)

Loss on hedge activity	30,000	
Forward contract receivable (€)		30,000

€6,000,000 × ($ .935 – $ .94) = $30,000. These entries again will be driven by market factors, and they are calculated the same way as entries (2) and (3) above. Notice that the decline in the forward rate from 12/31/10 to 3/1/11 resulted in a loss against the forward contract receivable and a gain against the firm commitment.

Hedge against firm commitment entries

(3) 12/31/10

Loss on hedge activity	180,000	
Firm commitment		180,000

The dollar values for this entry are identical to entry (2), reflecting the fact that the hedge is highly effective (100%) and also the fact that the market recognizes the same factors in this transaction as for entry (2). This entry reflects the first use of the firm commitment account, a temporary liability account pending the receipt of the asset against which the firm commitment has been hedged.

(5) 3/1/11

Firm commitment	30,000	
Gain on hedge activity		30,000

(6) 3/1/11 (spot rate €1 = $.92)

Equipment	5,370,000	
Firm commitment	150,000	
Accounts payable (€)		5,520,000

This entry records the receipt of the equipment (recorded at fair value determined on a discounted net present value basis), the elimination of the temporary liability account (firm commitment), and the recognition of the payable, calculated using the spot rate on the date of receipt (€6,000,000 × $.92 = $5,520,000).

(7)   4/30/11 (spot rate €1 = $.96)

Forward contract receivable (€)	150,000	
Gain on forward contract		150,000

The gain or loss (gain in this case) on the forward contract is calculated using the change in the forward to the spot rate from 3/1/11 to 4/30/11 [€6,000,000 × ($..96 – $.935) = $150,000]

(9)   4/30/11

Dollars payable	5,460,000	
Cash		5,460,000
Foreign currency units (€)	5,760,000	
Forward contract receivable (€)		5,760,000

This entry reflects the settlement of the forward contract at the 10/1/10 contracted forward rate (€6,000,000 × $.91 = $5,460,000) and the receipt of foreign currency units valued at the spot rate (€6,000,000 × $.96 = $5,760,000).

(8)   4/30/11

Transaction loss	240,000	
Accounts payable (€)		240,000

The transaction loss related to the accounts payable reflects only the change in the spot rates and ignores the accrual of interest. [€6,000,000 × ($.96 – $.92) = $180,000]

(10)

Accounts payable (€)	5,760,000	
Foreign currency units		5,760,000

This entry reflects the use of the foreign currency units to settle the account payable.

    d.   In the case of using a forward exchange contract to speculate in a specific foreign currency, the general rule to estimate the fair value of the forward contract is to use the forward exchange rate for the remainder of the term of the forward contract.

11. **Disclosures**

    Disclosures related to financial instruments, both derivative and nonderivative, that are used as hedging instruments must include the following information:

    a.   Objectives and the strategies for achieving them,
    b.   Context to understand the instrument,
    c.   Risk management policies, and
    d.   A list of hedged instruments.

      (1)   These disclosures have to be separated by type of hedge and reported every time a complete set of financial statements is issued.
      (2)   In addition, disclosure requirements exist for derivative instruments that are not designated as hedging instruments.

NOW REVIEW MULTIPLE-CHOICE QUESTIONS 38 THROUGH 41 IN VOLUME 2

---

12. **Fair Value and Concentration of Credit Risk Disclosures of Financial Instruments other than Derivatives**

    Disclosure of fair values of financial instruments is required if it is practicable to estimate fair value. This requirement pertains to both asset and liability financial instruments, whether recognized in the balance sheet or not. Disclosure of concentrations of credit risk is required.

    a.   Credit risk is the risk that a loss will occur because parties to the instrument do not perform as expected.

      (1)   Such concentrations exist when a number of an entity's financial instruments are associated with similar activities and economic characteristics that could be affected by changes in similar conditions (e.g., an entity whose principal activity is to supply parts to one type of industry).

Lenaburg, Inc.
Notes to Financial Statements
FAIR VALUE OF FINANCIAL INSTRUMENTS HELD OR ISSUED FOR PURPOSES
OTHER THAN TRADING *(in thousands)*

	December 31, 2011	
	Carrying amount	**Fair value**
Assets		
Cash and cash equivalents	32,656	32,656
Long-term investments	12,719	14,682
Liabilities		
Short-term debt	3,223	3,223
Long-term debt	150,000	182,500

FAIR VALUE OF FINANCIAL INSTRUMENTS HELD FOR TRADING PURPOSES (in thousands)

	December 31, 2011	
	Carrying amount	**Fair value**
Assets		
Short-term investments	4,074	4,074

Cash and cash equivalents—The carrying amount of cash and cash equivalents approximates fair value due to their short-term maturities.

Long-term investments—The fair value is estimated based on quoted market prices for these or similar investments.

Short-term investments—The Company holds US Treasury notes and highly liquid investments for trading purposes. The carrying value of these instruments approximates fair value.

Short- and long-term debt—The fair value of short- and long-term debt is estimated using quoted market prices for the same or similar instruments or on the current rates offered to the Company for debt of equivalent remaining maturities.

Summary of Disclosure Standards for Financial Instruments other than Derivatives

ASC	Pertains to	Required disclosures
825-10-50	Financial Instruments (Assets and Liabilities), Whether on Balance Sheet or Not	• Fair value, when practicable to estimate • Information pertinent to estimating fair value (carrying value, effective interest rate, maturity) if not practicable to estimate, and reasons for impracticability of estimation • Distinguish between instruments held or issued for trading purposes and instruments held or issued for purposes other than trading • Do not net or aggregate fair values of derivative financial instruments with fair values of nonderivative financial instruments or with fair values of other derivative financial instruments
	Financial Instruments with Concentrations of Credit Risk	• Information about similar activity, region, or economic characteristics • Maximum potential accounting loss • Information about collateral or security requirements

> **NOW REVIEW MULTIPLE-CHOICE QUESTIONS 42 THROUGH 50 IN VOLUME 2**

C. Research Component—Accounting Standards Codification

ASC Topic 815, *Derivatives and Hedging*, contains the accounting and disclosure rules for derivatives and hedging. ASC Topic 830, *Foreign Currency Matters*, contains the rules for foreign currency transactions and foreign currency translations. ASC Topic 825, *Financial Instruments*, covers the accounting rules for reporting financial instruments.

A list of research terms is listed below.

At the money	Financial instrument	Insurance contracts
Bifurcation	Firm commitment hedge	Intrinsic value
Call option	Forecasted transaction hedge	LIBOR
Cash flow hedge	Foreign currency derivative	Net settlement
Changes in fair value	Foreign currency hedge	Notional amounts
Derivative instrument	Forward contract	Out of the money
Designation as hedged item	Forward exchange contract	Payment provision hedge
Discount forward contract	Futures contract	Premium forward contract
Embedded derivative	Hedged item	Put option
Embedded derivative instruments	Hybrid instrument	Regular way securities trades
Fair value financial instruments	Impediments to sales accounting	Swaption
Fair value hedge	In the money	Transaction gain or loss
Financial guarantee contracts	Initial net investment	Underlyings

D. International Financial Reporting Standards (IFRS)

1. A derivative is a financial instrument that (1) requires little or no initial investment, (2) changes in value in response to a change in the value of another instrument or index (called an underlying), and (3) is settled in the future.

a. Examples of derivatives include options, futures, forward contracts, and swaps. Derivatives are recognized in the financial statements using the fair value through profit and loss method (FVTPL).

b. Derivatives are remeasured at fair value, with gains and losses recorded in profit or loss for the period.

2. A hedging instrument is a type of derivative that is classified as a fair value hedge, a cash flow hedge, or a hedge of a net investment in operations.

    a. Hedge accounting allows the optional treatment to offset profits and losses on hedged items.

    b. If a company elects to use hedge accounting, the accounting treatment differs depending on the type of hedge.

      (1) A fair value hedge is accounted for by recognizing the gains and losses in profit and loss of the period.

      (2) A cash flow hedge and a hedge of a net investment are accounted for by reporting gains and losses in other comprehensive income for the period.

NOW REVIEW MULTIPLE-CHOICE QUESTION 51 IN VOLUME 2

KEY TERMS

At the money. An at-the-money option is one in which the price of the underlying is equal to the strike or exercise price.

Bifurcation. The process of separating an embedded derivative from its host contract. This process is necessary so that hybrid instruments (a financial instrument or other contract that contains an embedded derivative) can be separated into their component parts, each being accounted for using the appropriate valuation techniques.

Call option. An American call option provides the holder the right to acquire an underlying at an exercise or strike price, anytime during the option term. A premium is paid by the holder for the right to benefit from the appreciation in the underlying.

Derivative instruments. Derivative instruments are defined by their three distinguishing characteristics. Specifically, derivative instruments are financial instruments or other contracts that have

1. One or more underlyings and one or more notional amounts (or payment provisions or both);
2. No initial net investment or a smaller net investment than required for contracts expected to have a similar response to market changes; and
3. Terms that require or permit

    a. Net settlement
    b. Net settlement by means outside the contract
    c. Delivery of an asset that results in a position substantially the same as net settlement

Discount or premium on a forward contract. The foreign currency amount of the contact multiplied by the difference between the contracted forward rate and the spot rate at the date of inception of the contract.

Embedded derivative. A feature on a financial instrument or other contract, which if the feature stood alone, would meet the definition of a derivative.

Fair value. Defined as the amount at which the asset or liability could be bought or settled in an arm's-length transaction; measured by reference to market prices or estimated by net present value of future cash flows, options pricing models, or by other techniques.

Financial instrument. Financial instruments include cash, accounts/notes receivable, accounts/notes payable, bonds, common stock, preferred stock, stock options, foreign currency forward contracts, futures contracts, various financial swaps, etc. Other contracts which are also considered financial instruments meet the following two criteria: (1) the contract imposes a contractual obligation on one party (to the contract) to deliver cash or another financial instrument to the second party or to exchange potentially unfavorable terms with the second party; (2) the contract conveys a contractual right to the second party to receive cash or another financial instrument from the first party or to exchange financial instruments on favorable terms with the first party.

Firm commitment. An agreement with an unrelated party, binding on both, usually legally enforceable, specifying all significant terms and including a disincentive for nonperformance sufficient to make performance likely.

Forecasted transaction. A transaction expected to occur for which there is no firm commitment, and thus, which gives the entity no present rights or obligations. Forecasted transactions can be hedged and special hedge accounting can be applied.

Foreign currency transactions. Transactions whose terms are denominated in a currency other than the entity's functional currency. Foreign currency transactions arise when an enterprise (1) buys or sells on credit goods or services whose prices are denominated in foreign currency, (2) borrows or lends funds and the amounts payable or receivable are denominated in foreign currency, (3) is a party to an unperformed forward exchange contract, or (4) for other reasons, acquires or disposes of assets, or incurs or settles liabilities denominated in foreign currency.

Forward contract. A forward contract is an agreement between two parties to buy and sell a specific quantity of a commodity, foreign currency, or financial instrument at an agreed-upon price, with delivery and/or settlement at a designated future date. Because a forward contract is not formally regulated by an organized exchange, each party to the contract is subject to the default of the other party.

Forward exchange contract. An agreement to exchange at a specified future date currencies of different countries at a specified rate (forward rate).

Futures contract. A futures contract is a forward-based contract to make or take delivery of a designated financial instrument, foreign currency, or commodity during a designated period, at a specified price or yield. The contract frequently has provisions for cash settlement. A futures contract is traded on a regulated exchange and, therefore, involves less credit risk than a forward contract.

In the money. A call option is in the money if the price of the underlying is greater than the strike or exercise price of the underlying.

Initial net investment. A derivative instrument is one where the initial net investment is zero or is less than the notional amount (possibly plus a premium or minus a discount). This characteristic refers to the relative amount of investment. Derivative instruments allow the opportunity to take part in the rate or price change without owning the asset or owing the liability. If an amount approximating the notional amount must be invested or received, it is not a derivative instrument. The two basic forms of derivative instruments are futures contracts and options. The futures contract involves little or no initial net investment. Settlement is usually near the delivery date. Call options, when purchased, require a premium payment that is less than the cost of purchasing the equivalent number of shares. Even though this distinguishing characteristic is the result of only one of the parties, it determines the application for both.

Intrinsic value. With regard to call (put) options, it is the larger of zero or the spread between the stock (exercise) price and the exercise (stock) price.

LIBOR. London Interbank Offer Rate. A widely used measure of average interest rates at a point in time.

Net settlements. To qualify as derivative instruments, one of the following settlement criteria must be met:

1. No delivery of an asset equal to the notional amount is required. For example, an interest rate swap does not involve delivery of the instrument in which the notional amount is expressed.
2. Delivery of an asset equal to the notional amount is required of one of the parties, but an exchange (or other market mechanism, institutional arrangement or side agreement) facilitates net settlement. For example, a call option has this attribute.
3. Delivery by one of the parties of an asset equal to the notional amount is required but the asset is either readily convertible to cash (as with a contract for the delivery of a marketable equity security), or is required but that asset is itself a derivative instrument (as is the case for a swaption [an option on a swap]).

This characteristic means that the derivative instrument can be settled by a net delivery of assets (the medium of exchange does not have to be cash). Contract terms based on changes in the price or rate of the notional amount that implicitly or explicitly require or permit net settlement qualify. Situations where one of the parties can liquidate their net investment or be relieved of the contract rights or obligations without significant transaction costs because of a market arrangement (broadly interpreted) or where the delivered asset can be readily converted to cash also meet the requirements for net settlement. It is assumed that an exchange traded security is readily converted to cash. Thus, commodity-based contracts for gold, oil, wheat, etc. are now included under this standard. The convertible to cash condition requires an active market and consideration of interchangeability and transaction volume. Determining if delivery of a financial asset or liability equal to the notional amount is a derivative instrument may depend upon whether it is readily convertible into cash. Different accounting will result if the notional amount is not readily converted to cash. Using the notional amount as collateral does not necessarily mean it is readily convertible to cash.

Notional amount. The notional amount (or payment provision) is the referenced associated asset or liability. A notional amount is commonly a number of units such as shares of stock, principal amount, face value, stated value, basis points, barrels of oil, etc. It may be that amount plus a premium or minus a discount. The interaction of the price or rate (underlying) with the referenced associated asset or liability (notional amount) determines whether settlement is required and, if so, the amount.

Out of the money. A call option is out of the money if the strike or exercise price is greater than the price of the underlying. A put option is out of the money if the price of the underlying is greater than the strike or exercise price.

Put option. An American put option provides the holder the right to sell the underlying at an exercise or strike price, anytime during the option term. A gain accrues to the holder as the market price of the underlying falls below the strike price.

Swap. A swap is a forward-based contract or agreement generally between two counterparties to exchange streams of cash flows over a specified period in the future.

Swaption. A swaption is an option on a swap that provides the holder with the right to enter into a swap at a specified future date at specified terms (freestanding option on a swap) or to extend or terminate the life of an existing swap (embedded option on a swap). These derivatives have characteristics of an option and an interest rate swap.

Time value. The difference between an option's price and its intrinsic value.

Transaction gain or loss. Transaction gains or losses result from a change in exchange rates between the functional currency and the currency in which a foreign currency transaction is denominated. They represent an increase or decrease in (1) the actual functional currency cash flows realized upon settlement of foreign currency transactions, and (2) the expected functional currency cash flows on unsettled foreign currency transactions.

Underlyings. An underlying is commonly a specified price or rate such as a stock price, interest rate, currency rate, commodity price, or a related index. However, any variable (financial or physical) with (1) observable changes or (2) objectively verifiable changes such as a credit rating, insurance index, climatic or geological condition (temperature, rainfall) qualifies. Unless it is specifically excluded, a contract based on any qualifying variable is accounted for under ASC Topic 815 (SFAS 133) if it has the distinguishing characteristics stated above.

Module 20: Miscellaneous

Overview

This module covers personal financial statements, interim reporting, segment reporting, partnership accounting, and foreign currency translation.

The personal financial statements section covers how to report assets and liabilities and tax estimates. This topic is located in ASC Topic 274.

Interim reporting describes financial reporting for periods less than a year. This topic is located in ASC Topic 270.

Segment reporting presents disclosure standards for the components of an entity's operations, its products and services, its geographic areas, and its major customers. This topic is located in ASC Topic 280.

Partnership accounting describes and events related to formation, income allocation, dissolution, admission of a new partner, withdrawal of an existing partner, and liquidation. The ASC does not provide guidance for partnership accounting and reporting. Guidance is provided within the Uniform Partnership Acts of 1914 and 1997; and the Revised Uniform Partnership Act of 1994.

The foreign currency translation section covers translations and remeasurement. Determining if a subsidiary's transactions are denominated in a foreign currency or US Dollars establishes which method should be applied. This topic is located in ASC Topic 830.

A. Personal Financial Statements[1] (ASC Topic 274)

1. Personal financial statements may be prepared for an individual, husband and wife, or family. Personal financial statements (PFS) consist of

   a. **Statement of financial condition**—presents estimated current values of assets, estimated current amounts of liabilities, estimated income taxes, and net worth at a specified date.
   b. **Statement of changes in net worth**—presents main sources of increases (decreases) in net worth over the time period included by the statement of changes in net worth.

2. Assets and liabilities, including changes therein, should be recognized using the accrual basis of accounting. Assets and liabilities should be listed by order of liquidity and maturity, not a current/noncurrent basis.

3. In PFS, **assets** should be presented at their estimated current value. This is an amount at which the item could be exchanged assuming both parties are well informed, neither party is compelled to buy or sell, and material disposal costs are deducted to arrive at current values. **Liabilities** should be presented at the lesser of the discounted amount of cash to be paid or the current cash settlement amount. Income taxes payable should include unpaid income taxes as of the date of the statement of financial condition. Also, PFS should include the **estimated income tax** on the difference between the current value (amount) of assets (liabilities) and their respective tax bases as if they had been realized or liquidated. The table below summarizes the methods of determining "estimated current values" for assets and "estimated current amounts" for liabilities.

4. Business interests which comprise a large portion of a person's total assets should be shown separately from other investments. An investment in a separate entity which is marketable as a going concern (e.g., closely held corporation) should be presented as one amount for its fair value. If the investment is a limited business activity, not conducted in a separate business entity, separate asset and liability amounts should be shown (e.g., investment in real estate and related mortgage). Of course, only the person's beneficial interest in the investment is included in their PFS.

---

[1] The source of GAAP for personal financial statements is ASC Topic 274, which has been summarized in this module.

Assets and liabilities	Discounted cash flow	Market price	Appraised value	Other
• Receivables	x			
• Marketable securities		x		
• Options		x		
• Investment in life insurance				Cash value less outstanding loans
• Investment in closely held business	x		x	Liquidation value, multiple of earnings, reproduction value, adjustment of book value or cost
• Real estate	x		x	Sales of similar property
• Intangible assets	x			
• Future interests (nonforfeitable rights)	x			
• Payables and other liabilities	x			Discharge amount if lower than discounted amount
• Noncancelable commitments	x			
• Income taxes payable				Unpaid income tax for completed tax years and estimated income tax for elapsed portion of current tax year to date of financial statements
• Estimated income tax on difference between current values of assets and current amounts of liabilities and their respective tax bases				Computed as if current value of assets and liabilities had been respectively realized or liquidated considering applicable tax laws and regulations, recapture provisions and carryovers

NOW REVIEW MULTIPLE-CHOICE QUESTIONS 1 THROUGH 17 IN VOLUME 2

B. Interim Reporting

The term interim reporting is used to describe financial reporting for periods of less than one year, generally quarterly financial statements.

1. The primary purposes of interim reporting are to provide information which is more timely than is available in annual reports, and to highlight business turning points which could be "buried" in annual reports.
2. There are two basic conceptual approaches to interim reporting: the **discrete view** and the **integral view**.

   a. **Discrete view**—Each interim period is a separate accounting period; interim period must stand on its own; same principles and procedures as for annual reports; no special accruals or deferrals.
   b. **Integral view**—Each interim period is an integral part of an annual period; expectations for annual period must be reflected in interim reports; special accruals, deferrals, and allocations utilized.
   c. The **integral view** is used for interim reporting.

3. The table below summarizes the accounting standards.

Income statement item	General rule	Exceptions
Revenues	Same basis as annual reports	None
Cost of goods sold	Same basis as annual reports	1. Gross profit method may be used to estimate CGS and ending inventory for each interim period 2. Liquidation of LIFO base-period inventory, if expected to be replaced by year-end, is changed to CGS at its estimated replacement cost 3. Temporary declines in inventory market value need not be recognized 4. Planned manufacturing variances should be deferred if expected to be absorbed by year-end
All other costs and expenses	Same basis as annual reports	Expenditures which **clearly benefit** more than one interim period may be allocated among periods benefited (e.g., annual repairs, property taxes).
Income taxes	(Year-to-date income × Estimated annual effective tax rate) – (Expense recognized in previous quarters)	None
Discontinued operations	Recognized in interim period as incurred	None
Extraordinary items	Recognized in interim period as incurred. Materiality is evaluated based on expected annual results	None
Change in accounting principle	Retrospective application. Cumulative effect of change reflected in the carrying amounts of assets and liabilities as of the first period presented with offsetting adjustment to retained earnings for that period. Financial statements are adjusted for period-specific effects of the change.	None

   a. A key disclosure item for interim reporting is the seasonal nature of the firm's operations. This disclosure helps prevent misleading inferences and predictions about annual results.
   b. Income tax expense is estimated each period using an estimated annual effective tax rate. The example below illustrates the application of this requirement.

EXAMPLE

Qtr	(a) Quarterly income before income taxes	(b) Year-to-date income before income taxes	(c) Estimated annual effective tax rate	(d) = (b) × (c) Year-to-date income tax expense	(e) Previous quarter's expense	(f) = (d) – (e) Current quarter's expense
1	$100,000	$100,000	30%	$ 30,000	$ 0	$ 30,000
2	150,000	250,000	32%	80,000	30,000	50,000
3	300,000	550,000	36%	198,000	80,000	118,000
4	200,000	750,000	35%	262,500	198,000	64,500

(1) In the prior chart, columns (a) and (c) are assumed to be given. Column (b) is obtained by accumulating column (a) figures. Column (e) is either the preceding quarter's entry in column (d) or the **cumulative** total of previous quarters in column (f).

4. **Research Component—Accounting Standards Codification**

a. The research on interim reporting is found in ASC Topic 270. A general search using the term "interim" should locate the updated rules for specific areas.

b. Keywords for research are shown below.

Costs and expenses interim   Interim reporting
Costs interim periods   Inventory interim
Costs of goods sold interim periods   Seasonal variations
Interim period

5. **International Financial Reporting Standards (IFRS)**
IFRS does not mandate interim reporting. However, when interim reports are required, four financial statements are required: the statement of financial position, the statement of comprehensive income, the statement of changes in equity, and the statement of cash flows. For consistency purposes, the entity must use the same accounting policies as used in year-end financial statements.

> **NOW REVIEW MULTIPLE-CHOICE QUESTIONS 1 THROUGH 19 IN VOLUME 2**

KEY TERMS

Discrete view. Each interim period is a separate accounting period; interim period must stand on its own; same principles and procedures as for annual reports; no special accruals or deferrals.

Integral view. Each interim period is an integral part of an annual period; expectations for annual period must be reflected in interim reports; special accruals, deferrals, and allocations, utilized.

Interim reporting. Describe financial reporting for periods of less than one year.

C. Segment Reporting

1. ASC Topic 280 (SFAS 131—see outline) sets forth financial reporting standards for segment reporting, the disclosure of information about different components of an enterprise's operations as well as information related to the enterprise's products and services, its geographic areas, and its major customers.

    a. The purpose of segment disclosure is to assist investors and lenders in assessing the future potential of an enterprise. Consolidated statements give the user the overall view (results of operations, financial position, cash flows). However, trends, opportunities, risk factors, etc., can get lost when data for a diversified company are merged into consolidated statements. Additionally, most intersegment transactions that are eliminated from consolidated financial information are included in segment information.

    b. The approach used in segment reporting is a "management approach," meaning it is based on the way management organizes segments internally to make operating decisions and assess performance.

        (1) Companies can segment their financial information by products or services, by geography, by legal entity, or by type of customer.
        (2) The management approach facilitates consistent descriptions of an enterprise for both internal and external reporting and, in general, provides that external financial reporting closely conforms to internal reporting.

    c. Segment reporting does not apply to not-for-profit organizations or nonpublic enterprises.

2. **Operating Segments**

    a. An **operating segment** is defined as

        (1) A component of an enterprise engaged in business activity for which it may earn revenues and incur expenses, about which separate financial information is available that is evaluated regularly by the chief operating decision makers in deciding how to allocate resources and in assessing performance.

    b. A segment is significant (reportable) if it satisfies **at least one** of the following three 10% tests:

        (1) **Revenues**—Segment revenue (including intersegment revenue) is 10% or more of combined segment revenue (including intersegment revenue)
        (2) **Operating profit or loss**—The absolute amount of segment profit or loss is 10% or more of the **greater,** in absolute amount, of combined profit of segments reporting profit, or combined loss of segments reporting loss
        (3) **Segment assets**—Segment assets are 10% or more of total segment assets

    c. Operating profit or loss is unaffiliated revenue and intersegment revenue, less **all** operating expenses as defined by the chief operating decision maker to evaluate the performance of the segments.

        (1) Since segment revenue includes **intersegment sales, transfer pricing** becomes an issue.

            (a) FASB requires companies to use the same transfer prices for segment reporting purposes as are used internally.
            (b) Since most segments are **profit centers,** internal transfer prices generally reflect market prices.

    d. Common costs are operating expenses incurred by the enterprise for the benefit of more than one operating segment.

        (1) These costs should only be allocated to a segment for external reporting purposes if they are included in the measure of the segments profit or loss that is used internally by the chief operating decision maker.

    e. Similarly, only those assets that are included internally in the measure of the segment's assets used to make operating decisions shall be reported as assets of the segment in external financial reports.
    f. Interperiod comparability must be considered in conjunction with the results of the 10% tests. If a segment fails to meet the tests, but has satisfied the tests in the past and is expected to in the future, it should be considered reportable in the current year for the sake of comparability. Similarly, if a segment which rarely passes the tests does so in the current year as the result of an unusual event, that segment may be excluded to preserve comparability.
    g. There are some limitations to the number of segments which are to be reported.

        (1) There must be enough segments separately reported so that at least 75% of unaffiliated revenues are shown by reportable segments (75% test).
        (2) If the 75% test is not satisfied, additional segments must be designated as reportable until the test is satisfied.
        (3) Also, the number of reportable segments should not be so large (ten is a rule of thumb) as to make the information less useful.

(a) The following example illustrates the three 10% tests (revenues, operating profit or loss, and identifiable assets) and the 75% test:

EXAMPLE

Segment	Unaffiliated revenue	Intersegment revenue	Total revenue	Operating profit (loss)	Segment assets
A	$ 90	$ 90	$ 180	$ 20	$ 70
B	120		120	10	50
C	110	20	130	(40)	90
D	200		200	0	140
E	330	110	440	(100)	230
F	380		380	60	260
Total	$1,230	$220	$1,450	$ (50)	$840

Revenues test: (10%)($1,450) = $145

   Reportable segments: A, D, E, F

Operating profit or loss test: (10%)($140) = $14

   Reportable segments: A, C, E, F

> **NOTE:** Operating loss ($140) is greater than operating profit, $90

Segment assets test: (10%)($840) = $84

   Reportable segments: C, D, E, F

Reportable segments: Those segments which pass **at least one** of the 10% tests. Segments A, C, D, E, and F are reportable in this example.

75% test: (75%)($1,230) = $922.50

Segments A, C, D, E, and F have total unaffiliated revenue of $1,110, which is greater than $922.50.

The 75% test is satisfied; no additional segments need be reported.

---

(4) Certain other factors must be considered when identifying reportable segments. An enterprise may consider aggregating two or more operating segments if they have similar economic characteristics and if the segments are similar in each of the following areas:

   (a) The nature of the products and services
   (b) The nature of the production processes
   (c) The type of customer for their products and services
   (d) The methods used to distribute their products or provide their services
   (e) The nature of the regulatory environment

(5) Aggregation can occur prior to performing the 10% tests if the enterprise desires.
(6) Additionally, the enterprise may combine information on operating segments that do not meet any of the 10% tests to produce a reportable segment, but only if the segments meet a majority of the aggregation criteria presented above. It should be noted that information about operating segments that do not meet any of the 10% thresholds may still be disclosed separately, rather than as an aggregated total.

3. **Segment Disclosures**
Several disclosures are required regarding the enterprise's reportable segments. They include

a. **General information**—An explanation of how management identified the enterprise's reportable segments, including whether operating segments have been aggregated. Additionally, a description of the types of products and services from which each reportable segment derives its revenues.
b. **Certain information about reported segment profit and loss, segment assets, and the basis of measurement**—The enterprise shall disclose the following about each reportable segment if the specified amounts are reviewed by the chief operating decision maker:

   (1) Revenues from external customers
   (2) Intersegment revenues
   (3) Interest revenue and expense (reported separately unless majority of segment's revenues are from interest and management relies primarily on net interest revenue to assess performance)
   (4) Depreciation, depletion, and amortization expense

(5) Unusual items, extraordinary items
(6) Equity in the net income of investees accounted for by the equity method
(7) Income tax expense or benefit
(8) Significant noncash items

Also, the basis of measurement for these items must be disclosed, including differences in measurement practices between a segment and the complete entity and differences in measurement practices in a segment between periods.

c. **Reconciliations**—The enterprise will need to reconcile the segment amounts disclosed to the corresponding enterprise amounts.

d. **Interim period information**—Although the interim disclosures are not as extensive as in the annual financial report, certain segment disclosures are required in interim financial reports.

4. **Restatement of Previously Reported Segment Information**
Segment reporting is required on a comparative basis. Therefore, the information must be restated to preserve comparability whenever the enterprise has changed the structure of its internal organization in a manner that causes a change to its reportable segments. The enterprise must explicitly disclose that it has restated the segment information of earlier periods.

5. **Enterprise-Wide Disclosures about Products and Services, Geographic Areas, and Major Customers**
The enterprise-wide disclosures are required for all enterprises, even those that have a single reportable segment. Disclosures need to be provided only if not provided as part of the segment information. Disclosures are required regardless of whether the information is used in making operating decisions.

a. **Products and services.** Revenue from external customers for each product and service shall be reported by the enterprise, unless it is impractical to do so.

b. **Geographic areas.** An enterprise shall report revenues from external customers and long-lived assets attributable to its domestic operations and **foreign operations,** unless it is impractical to do so. If revenues or assets of an individual foreign country are material, then these amounts should be separately disclosed. In addition, the enterprise's basis for attributing revenue to individual countries shall be disclosed.

c. **Major customers.** Certain disclosures are made concerning major customers if the following 10% test is met. If 10% or more of **consolidated revenue** comes from a **single** external customer, the enterprise must disclose this fact in addition to the amount of such revenues, and the identity of the segment or segments making the sales. (A group of customers under common control, such as subsidiaries of a parent, is regarded as a single customer. Similarly, the various agencies of a government are considered to be a single customer.)

6. **Research Component—Accounting Standards Codification**
ASC Topic 280 uses a management approach to segment and enterprise reporting. A careful analysis of the vocabulary used in the standards is slightly different than most individuals would use in discussion. For example, we may use the term "total revenue" whereas the standard uses the term "combined revenue." Instead of using the word "tests," the standard refers to them as "quantitative thresholds." Although these differences seem trivial, they will affect your ability to find the material using a keyword search.

a. Below is a list of keywords that are useful in researching ASC Topic 280. If you add the word "segment" or "segments" to your search string, it may significantly reduce the number of irrelevant paragraphs.

Aggregation segments	Enterprise disclosure	Management approach
Combined assets segments	External revenue segments	Operating segment
Combined profit segments	Geographic areas	Products services segment
Combined revenue operating segments	Geographic information	Reportable segment
Enterprise disclose	Major customer	Single reportable segment

Flowchart for Identifying Reportable Operating Segments[*]

Identify operating segments by utilizing management approach

Do some segments meet all aggregation criteria? — Yes → Aggregate segments, if desired

No

Do segments meet the 10% tests for revenue, profit, or assets? — Yes → These are reportable segments to be separately disclosed

No

Is revenue of reportable segments at least 75% of consolidated revenue (75% test)? — Yes

No

Identify additional segments until 75% test is met.

Combine remaining segments/activities into "all other" category.

[*] Adapted from ASC Topic 280.

7. **International Financial Reporting Standards (IFRS)**

   a. IFRS 8 on segment reporting includes guidance very similar to US GAAP. It requires a management approach to identifying operating segments. An operating segment is a reportable segment if it meets one of the following defined quantitative thresholds:

      (1) The segments revenue (including internal and external sales) is 10% or more of combined revenue of all segments,

      (2) The absolute value of the profit or loss is 10% or more than the greater (in absolute value) of the (1) combined reported profit of all segments that did not report a loss or (2) the combined reported loss of all segments that reported a loss, or

      (3) The assets are 10% or more of the combined assets of all segments.

   b. In addition, the total external revenue by reportable segments must be a least 75% of the entity's revenue; otherwise additional segments must be identified and reported. Note that these thresholds are the same as for US GAAP.

NOW REVIEW MULTIPLE-CHOICE QUESTIONS 1 THROUGH 12 IN VOLUME 2

KEY TERMS

Management approach. Segment reporting is based on the way management organizes segments internally to make operating decisions and assess performance.

Operating segment. A component of an enterprise engaged in business activity for which it may earn revenues and incur expenses, about which separate financial information is available that is evaluated regularly by the chief operating decision makers in deciding how to allocate resources and in assessing performance.

Segment assets. Segment assets are 10% or more of total segment assets.

Segment operating profit or loss. The absolute amount of segment profit or loss is 10% or more of the greater, in absolute amount, of combined profit of segments reporting profit, or combined loss of segments reporting loss.

Segment revenues. Segment revenue (including intersegment revenue) is 10% or more of combined segment revenue (including intersegment revenue).

D. Partnership Accounting

There are no authoritative pronouncements concerning the accounting for partnerships; thus, all of the principles described below have evolved through accounting practice.

> **NOTE:** Partnership accounting typically is tested through a few multiple-choice questions on the Financial Accounting and Reporting Exam. Occasionally, the material is tested through a problem.

1. Partnership Formation

a. The partnership is a separate **accounting entity** (not to be confused with a separate legal entity), and therefore its assets and liabilities should remain separate and distinct from the individual partner's personal assets and liabilities.

   (1) Thus, all assets contributed to the partnership are recorded by the partnership at their **fair market values**. All liabilities assumed by the partnership are recorded at their **present values**.

b. Upon formation, the amount credited to each partner's capital account is the difference between the fair market value of the assets contributed and the present value of the liabilities assumed from that partner.

   (1) The capital accounts represent the residual equity of the partnership.
   (2) The capital account of each partner reflects all of the activity of an individual partner: contributions, withdrawals, and the distributive share of net income (loss).
   (3) In some cases, a **drawing** account is used as a clearing account for each partner's transactions with only the net effect of each period's activity shown in the capital account.

EXAMPLE

Partnership Formation

A and B form a partnership. A contributes cash of $50,000, while B contributed land with a fair market value of $50,000 and the partnership assumes a liability on the land of $25,000.

The entry to record the formation of the partnership is

Cash	50,000	
Land	50,000	
Liabilities		25,000
A Capital		50,000
B Capital		25,000

NOW REVIEW MULTIPLE-CHOICE QUESTIONS 1 THROUGH 4 IN VOLUME 2

2. Allocation of Partnership Income (Loss)

a. The partners should have a written agreement (articles of copartnership) specifying the manner in which partnership income (loss) is to be distributed.

> **NOTE:** In the absence of a predetermined agreement, the profit and loss (P&L) is divided equally among the partners.

b. It is important to remember that P&L should **not** be distributed using a ratio based on the partners' capital balances unless this is the ratio specified in the articles of copartnership.

c. A number of issues arise which complicate the allocation of partnership income (loss).

   (1) Partners may receive interest on their capital balances. If so, it must be determined what will constitute the capital balance (e.g., the year-end amount or some type of weighted-average).
   (2) Some of the partners may receive a salary.
   (3) Some of the partners may receive a bonus on distributable net income. If so, you need to determine if the bonus should be computed before or after salary and interest allocations.
   (4) A formula needs to be determined for allocating the remaining income. The formula agreed upon is usually termed the **residual, remainder**, or **profit (loss) sharing ratio**.
   (5) Finally, the partners should decide upon how income is to be allocated if net income is insufficient to cover partners' salaries, bonuses, and interest allocations.

(a) These allocations are usually made even if the effect is to create a negative remainder. This remainder is usually allocated in accordance with the profit (loss) ratio.

(b) However, it is important to note that partners may choose to allocate losses (or a negative remainder) in a different manner than income.

EXAMPLE

Partnership P&L Distribution

Partners receive 5% interest on beginning capital balances
Partner B receives a $6,000 salary
Partner C receives a 10% bonus after interest and salaries
The P&L ratios are A — 50%, B — 30%, C — 20%

Assuming partnership net income of $18,250, the following distribution schedule would be prepared:

	A	B	C	Total
P&L ratio	50%	30%	20%	
Beginning capital balance	30,000	10,000	5,000	45,000
Net income				(18,250)
5% interest	1,500	500	250	2,250
Salary		6,000		6,000
Bonus			1,000*	1,000
Distribution of residual	4,500	2,700	1,800	9,000
Total	6,000	9,200	3,050	0 --
Ending capital balances	36,000	19,200	8,050	

* ($18,250 – $8,250) × .10 = $1,000

Note that if the interest, salary, and bonus allocation had exceeded net income, the excess would have been deducted on the distribution schedule in the P&L ratio.

NOW REVIEW MULTIPLE-CHOICE QUESTIONS 5 THROUGH 9 IN VOLUME 2

---

3. **Partnership Dissolution (Changes in Ownership)**

Partnership dissolution occurs whenever there is a change in ownership (e.g., the addition of a new partner, or the retirement or death of an existing partner). This is not to be confused with partnership liquidation, which is the winding up of partnership affairs and termination of the business. Under dissolution the partnership business continues, but under different ownership.

a. When partnership dissolution occurs a new accounting entity results.

(1) The partnership should first adjust its records so that all accounts are properly stated at the date of dissolution.

(2) After the income (loss) has been properly allocated to the existing partners' capital accounts, all assets and liabilities should be adjusted to their fair market value and their present values, respectively.

(a) The latter step is performed because the dissolution results in a new accounting entity.

(3) After all adjustments have been made, the accounting for dissolution depends on the type of transaction that caused the dissolution. These transactions can be broken down into two types:

(a) Transactions between the partnership and a partner (e.g., a new partner contributes assets, or a retiring partner withdraws assets)

(b) Transactions between partners (e.g., a new partner purchases an interest from one or more existing partners, or a retiring partner sells his/her interest to one or more existing partners).

b. **Transactions between a partner and the partnership**

(1) **Admission of a new partner**

When a new partner is admitted to the partnership essentially three cases can result. The new partner can invest assets into the partnership and receive a capital balance:

(a) Equal to his/her purchase price

1] If the new partner's capital balance is equal to the assets invested, then the entry debits the asset(s) contributed and credits the new partner's capital account for the fair value of the asset(s) contributed.

(b) Greater than his/her purchase price

(c) Less than his/her purchase price

1] If the new partner's capital balance is not equal to the assets invested [as in situation (b) and (c) above], then either the **bonus** or **goodwill** method must be used to account for the difference.

a] **Bonus method**—The old partnership capital plus the new partner's asset contribution is equal to the new partnership capital. The new partner's capital is allocated his purchase share (e.g., 40%) and the old partner's capital accounts are adjusted as if they had been paid (or as if they paid) a bonus. The adjustment to the old partners' capital accounts is made in accordance with their profit (loss) sharing ratio.

i] The bonus method implies that the old partners either received a bonus from the new partner, or they paid a bonus to the new partner. As a result the old partners' capital accounts are either debited to reflect a bonus paid, or credited to reflect a bonus received. The new partner's capital account is **never** equal to the amount of assets contributed in a case where the bonus method is used.

b] **Goodwill method**—The old partnership capital plus the new partner's asset contribution is **not** equal to the new partnership capital. This is because goodwill is recorded on the partnership books for the difference between the total identifiable assets of the partnership (not including goodwill) and the deemed value of the partnership entity (which includes goodwill). Under the goodwill method, valuation of the new partnership is the objective.

i] How the value of the partnership is determined depends on whether the book value acquired is greater or less than the asset(s) invested. If the book value acquired is less than the asset(s) invested, the value is determined based upon the new partner's contribution, and goodwill is allocated to the old partners' accounts. If the book value acquired is greater than the asset(s) contributed, the value is based upon the existing capital accounts, and goodwill is attributed to the new partner.

2] The decision as to whether the bonus or goodwill method should be used rests with the partners involved. In other words, the bonus and goodwill methods are alternative solutions to the same problem.

EXAMPLE

Partnership Dissolution—Bonus Method

Total old capital for ABC Partnership is $60,000.

Partner	A	B	C
Capital	$10,000	$20,000	$30,000
P&L Ratio	40%	40%	20%

Case 1

D is admitted to the partnership and is given a 20% interest in the capital in return for a cash contribution of $30,000.

Cash	30,000	
D Capital		18,000
A Capital		4,800
B Capital		4,800
C Capital		2,400

The total partnership capital to be shown on the books is $90,000 ($60,000 + $30,000) of which D is entitled to a 20% interest, or a capital balance of $18,000. The remaining $12,000 is treated as a bonus to the old partners and is allocated to their capital accounts in accordance with their P&L ratio.

Case 2

D is admitted to the partnership and is given a 20% interest in the capital in return for a cash contribution of $10,000.

Cash	10,000	
A Capital	1,600	
B Capital	1,600	
C Capital	800	
D Capital		14,000

The total partnership capital to be shown on the books is $70,000 ($60,000 + $10,000) of which D is entitled to a 20% interest, or a capital balance of $14,000. The difference of $4,000 ($10,000 – $14,000) is allocated to the old partners' accounts as if they had paid a bonus to the new partner.

EXAMPLE

Partnership Dissolution—Goodwill Method

Use the same original data as given above.

Case 1

D is admitted to the partnership and is given a 20% interest in the capital in return for a cash contribution of $20,000. The partners elect to record goodwill. The book value acquired [($60,000 + $20,000) × 20% = $16,000] is less than the asset contributed.

The value of the partnership is determined based upon the contribution of the new partner. In this case it is assumed that the partnership value is $100,000 ($20,000/20%). The resulting goodwill is $20,000 ($100,000 – $80,000). The $80,000 represents the total current capital, exclusive of goodwill, $60,000 of which is attributable to the old partners and $20,000 of which is attributable to the new partner.

Goodwill	20,000	
A Capital		8,000
B Capital		8,000
C Capital		4,000
Cash	20,000	
D Capital		20,000

Goodwill was allocated to the old partners in their P&L ratio. Also note that the capital balance of D represents 20% of the total capital of the partnership.

Case 2

D is admitted to the partnership and is given a 20% interest in the capital in return for a cash contribution of $10,000. The partners elect to record goodwill. The book value acquired [($60,000 + $10,000) × 20% = $14,000] is greater than the asset contributed.

The partnership value is based upon the capital accounts of the existing partners. Because D is entitled to a 20% interest, the $60,000 capital of the old partners must represent 80% of the capital. This means that the total value of the partnership is $75,000 ($60,000/80%). D's total contribution consists of the $10,000 in cash and $5,000 of goodwill. The goodwill is determined as the difference between the cash contribution and the 20% of the partnership capital.

Cash	10,000	
Goodwill	5,000	
D Capital		15,000

NOTE: In this last case no adjustment is made to the capital accounts of partners A, B, and C.

3] The table below summarizes the bonus and goodwill situations discussed above:

When to Apply Bonus Method			When to Apply Goodwill Method		
New	Old	New Partner's	New	Old	New Partner's
Partnership = Partners' +		Asset	Partnership > Partners' +		Asset
Capital	Capital	Investment	Capital	Capital	Investment

Which Partner(s) Receive Bonus	**Which Partner(s) Goodwill Is Recognized**
• **New Partner**	• **New Partner's Goodwill**
New Partner's New Partner's	New Partner's New Partner's
Capital Credit > Asset Investment	Capital Credit > Asset Investment
(The difference represents the bonus.)	(The difference represents goodwill.)

- **Old Partners**
  New Partner's   New Partner's
  Capital Credit   <   Asset Investment
  (The difference represents the bonus allocated to
  old partners in their P&L Ratio.)

- **Old Partners' Goodwill**
  New Partner's   New Partner's
  Capital Credit   =   Asset Investment
  (Goodwill is allocated to old partners in their
  P & L Ratio.)

NOW REVIEW MULTIPLE-CHOICE QUESTIONS 10 THROUGH 15 IN VOLUME 2

---

(2) Partner death or withdrawal

The death or withdrawal of a partner is treated in much the same manner as the admission of a new partner. However, there is no new capital account to be recorded; we are dealing only with the capital accounts of the original partners. Either the bonus or goodwill method may be used. The key thing to remember in regard to a partner's withdrawal from the partnership is that the withdrawing partner's capital account must be adjusted to the amount that the withdrawing partner is expected to receive.

EXAMPLE

Partner Withdrawal

Assume the same partnership data as given for the ABC partnership earlier.

Case 1

Assume that A withdraws from the partnership after reaching an agreement with partners B & C that would pay him $16,000. The remaining partners elect not to record goodwill.

B Capital	4,000	
C Capital	2,000	
A Capital		6,000
A Capital	16,000	
Cash		16,000

The $6,000 bonus is determined as the difference between the current balance of A's capital account and the amount of his buyout agreement. This "bonus" is then allocated between the remaining partners' capital accounts in proportion to their P&L ratios.

Case 2

Assume again that A withdraws from the partnership pursuant to the same agreement except that this time the partners elect to record goodwill.

The first step is to determine the amount of goodwill to be recorded. In this case we know that A's capital account must have a balance of $16,000, the agreed buyout payment he is to receive. In order to accomplish this, the total partnership assets must be increased by some amount of which $6,000 represents 40%, A's P&L ratio. Therefore, the amount of goodwill to be recorded is $15,000 ($6,000/40%).

Goodwill	15,000	
A Capital		6,000
B Capital		6,000
C Capital		3,000
A Capital	16,000	
Cash		16,000

NOTE: In this case all of the partners' capital accounts are adjusted to record the goodwill in accordance with their P&L ratios.

NOW REVIEW MULTIPLE-CHOICE QUESTIONS 16 THROUGH 20 IN VOLUME 2

---

c. **Transactions between partners**

(1) The sale of a partnership interest is a transaction only between the partners. Thus, the treatment accorded the transaction is determined by the partners involved.

(2) There are two means of dealing with such a transaction.

(a) The first is to simply transfer a portion of the existing partners' capital to a new capital account for the buying partner.

EXAMPLE

Sale of a Partnership Interest—No Goodwill Recorded

Assume the following for the AB partnership:

Partner	A	B
Capital	$50,000	$50,000
P&L Ratio	60%	40%

Case 1

Assume that C wishes to enter the partnership by buying 50% of the partnership interest from both A and B for a total of $80,000. It is important to note that the $80,000 is being paid to the individual partners and not to the partnership. Thus, we are only concerned with the proper adjustment between the capital accounts, not the recording of the cash. This approach ignores the price that C paid for the partnership interest.

A Capital	25,000	
B Capital	25,000	
C Capital		50,000

(b) The other method available for recording a transaction between partners involves the recording of implied goodwill.

EXAMPLE

Sale of Partnership Interest—Recording Goodwill

Assume the same facts presented above for the sale of the partnership interest except that in this case the partners elect to record goodwill.

Case 1

Assuming that C paid $80,000 for a 50% interest in the partnership the implied value of the partnership assets is $160,000 ($80,000/50%). Because total capital prior to the purchase is only $100,000, the amount of goodwill that must be recorded is $60,000. The goodwill is allocated to the prior partners' accounts in proportion to their P&L ratios. Note that this entry is made before an adjustment is made to reflect C's admission to the partnership.

Goodwill	60,000	
A Capital		36,000
B Capital		24,000

Now we can record the sale of the partnership interest to C. The capital balance of A is now $86,000 ($50,000 + $36,000) while the capital balance of B is $74,000 ($50,000 + $24,000). Recall that C is to receive 50% of each balance.

A Capital	43,000	
B Capital	37,000	
C Capital		80,000

NOTE: In this situation the capital balance of C after the purchase is equal to the amount of the purchase price. Again no entry is made to record the receipt of cash because the cash goes directly to the individual partners, A and B.

---

4. **Partnership Liquidation**

a. A liquidation is the winding up of the partnership business. That is, it sells all of its noncash assets, pays its liabilities, and makes a final liquidating distribution to the remaining partners.

There are four basic steps to a partnership liquidation.

(1) Any operating income or loss up to the date of the liquidation should be computed and allocated to the partners' capital accounts on the basis of their P&L ratio.
(2) All noncash assets are sold and converted to cash. The gain (loss) realized on the sale of such assets is allocated to the partners' capital accounts on the basis of their P&L ratio.

(3) Any creditors' claims, including liquidation expenses or anticipated future claims, are satisfied through the payment or reserve of cash.

(4) The remaining unreserved cash is distributed to the remaining partners in accordance with the balance in their capital accounts. Note that this is **not** necessarily the P&L ratio.

b. Two factors that may complicate the liquidation process are the existence of loans or advances between the partnership and one or more of the partners, or the creation of a deficit in a partner's capital account because of the allocation of a loss.

(1) When loans exist between the partnership and a partner, the capital account and the loan(s) are combined to give a net amount. This is often referred to as the **right of offset**.

(2) When a deficit exists, the amount of the deficit is allocated to the remaining solvent partners' capital accounts on the basis of their relative P&L ratio.

> **NOTE:** If the partner with the capital deficit is personally solvent, he has a liability to the remaining partners for the amount of the deficit.

c. There are two topics that appear with regularity on the CPA examination in regard to the liquidation of a partnership. They are the **statement of partnership liquidation** and the determination of a **"safe payment"** in an installment liquidation.

(1) **Statement of partnership liquidation**
   The statement of partnership liquidation shows in detail all of the transactions associated with the liquidation of the partnership.

   (a) The liquidation of a partnership can take one of two forms: **simple** or **installment**.

   1] A **simple liquidation** (illustrated below) is one in which all of the assets are sold in bulk and all of the creditors' claims are satisfied before a single liquidating distribution is made to the partners.

   a] Because the assets are sold in bulk there is a tendency to realize greater losses than if the assets were sold over a period of time. As a result, many partnerships liquidate on an installment basis.

   2] In an **installment liquidation** the assets are sold over a period of time and the cash is distributed to the partners as it becomes available.

EXAMPLE

Statement of Partnership Liquidation—Simple Liquidation

Assume the following:

The capital balances are as given below.

The P&L ratio is 5:3:2 for A, B, and C, respectively.

STATEMENT OF PARTNERSHIP LIQUIDATION

	Cash	Other assets	Liabilities	Capital A (50%)	B (30%)	C (20%)
Balances	5,000	75,000	45,000	12,000	17,000	6,000
Sale of assets ($20,000 loss)	40,000	(60,000)		(10,000)	(6,000)	(4,000)
	45,000	15,000	45,000	2,000	11,000	2,000
Payment of liabilities	(45,000)		(45,000)			
	0	15,000	0	2,000	11,000	2,000
Sale of assets ($5,000 loss)	10,000	(15,000)		(2,500)	(1,500)	(1,000)
	10,000	0	0	(500)	9,500	1,000
Distribution of A's deficit				500	(300)	(200)
	10,000	0	0	0	9,200	800
Final distribution of cash	(10,000)				(9,200)	(800)

> **NOTE:** After the noncash assets have been sold and the creditors satisfied, a $500 deficit remains in A's capital account. The deficit is allocated to the remaining solvent partners on the basis of their relative P&L ratios, in this case, 3:2. A is liable to the partnership for the $500. If A is personally solvent and repays the $500, then $300 will go to B and $200 will go to C.

(b) If in the above example there had been liquidation expenses or loans between the partnership and partners, these would have to be recognized in the statement prior to any distribution to partners. A loan receivable from or payable to a partner is simply offset to (closed against) that partner's capital account.

(2) **Installment method of cash distribution**

(a) There are two keys to preparing a statement of partnership liquidation under the **installment method**:

1] The determination of the available cash balance at any given point in time and
2] The determination of which partner(s) is(are) to receive the payment of that cash.

(b) The reason that the cash is not distributed in accordance with the P&L ratio is twofold:

1] The final cash distribution is based upon the balance in each partner's capital account, **not** the P&L ratio, and
2] There will be situations, as illustrated in the previous example, where one or more partners will have deficit balances in their capital accounts. If this is the case, they should **never** receive a cash distribution, even if the deficit does not arise until late in the liquidation process.

(c) The determination of the available cash balance is generally very straightforward. The beginning cash balance (cash on hand at the start of the liquidation process) is adjusted for the cash receipts from receivables, sale of noncash assets, payment to creditors, and liquidation expenses incurred.

1] A situation may occur where a certain amount of cash is to be reserved for payment of future liabilities that may arise. If this is the case, this cash should be treated as an escrowed, or restricted, asset which makes it unavailable for current distribution to the partners.

(d) The determination of which partner(s) is(are) to receive the available cash is somewhat more difficult. There are a number of ways to make this computation, all of which are equally correct in the eyes of the examiners.

1] This determination can be made at the beginning of the liquidation process or at the time of each payment. In making this determination there are two key assumptions that must be made:

a] The individual partners are assumed to be personally insolvent, and
b] The remaining noncash assets are deemed to be worthless (thus creating a maximum possible amount of loss).

(e) One method of determining the amount of the "**safe payment**" is the use of an **Installment Cash Distribution Schedule**. This schedule is prepared by determining the amount of loss required to eliminate each partner's capital account.

1] As noted above, all of the remaining noncash assets are to be considered worthless at the time a safe payment is determined. Thus, if we determine the amount of loss required to eliminate each partner's capital balance, we can determine the order in which the partners should receive the cash payments.
2] When preparing this schedule it is important to make sure that the proper capital balance is used.

a] The capital balance used **must** be inclusive of any loans or advances between the partnership and partners. Thus, the capital balance at the beginning of the liquidation process is increased by any amount owed to the partner by the partnership, and decreased by any amount owed to the partnership by the partner.

EXAMPLE

SCHEDULE OF POSSIBLE LOSSES

	Total	A (50%)	B (30%)	C (20%)
Net capital balances	$35,000	$12,000	$17,000	$6,000
Loss to eliminate A	24,000	(12,000)	(7,200)	(4,800)
		0	$ 9,800	$1,200
Additional loss to eliminate C	3,000*		(1,800)	(1,200)
			8,000	0
Additional loss to eliminate B	8,000		(8,000)	
	$35,000		0	

* Allocated 60:40

The total capital balance of $35,000 indicates that if the noncash assets are sold for $35,000 less than their book value, then none of the partners will receive a cash distribution. The purpose of this schedule is to determine how much of a loss each partner's capital account can withstand based on that partner's P&L ratio. In this example A's capital would be eliminated if the partnership incurred a $24,000 ($12,000/50%) loss, B's would be eliminated by a $56,667 ($17,000/30%) loss, and C's by a $30,000 ($6,000/20%) loss. A is assumed to be eliminated first because it would take the smallest amount of loss to eliminate his account. Once A is eliminated as a partner, the P&L ratios change to reflect the relative P&L ratio of the remaining partners, in this case B and C. Based on the remaining capital balances and the relative P&L ratio, it would take a $16,333 ($9,800/60%) loss to eliminate B and a $3,000 ($1,200/40%) loss to eliminate C. Now that C is eliminated B will share all of the profits and losses as a sole partner (i.e., 100%). It will now take an $8,000 loss to eliminate B's capital. The resulting installment cash distribution schedule would appear as follows.

Schedule of Possible Losses and Installment Cash Distribution

Assume the same data as used for the previous example.

This schedule assumes that all creditors have already received full payment; thus, the cash amount represents available cash:

INSTALLMENT CASH DISTRIBUTION SCHEDULE

Partner		A	B	C
First	$ 8,000		100%	
Next	3,000		60%	40%
Next	24,000	50%	30%	20%
Any other		50%	30%	20%

While the example shown in section 4.a. was not an installment liquidation, the Installment Cash Distribution Schedule shown above could still be used to determine how the available cash of $10,000 is to be distributed. This is illustrated below.

Partner		A	B	C
First	$ 8,000		$8,000	
Next	2,000		1,200	$800
Total	$10,000	--	$9,200	$800

NOTE: It is important to note that this method is acceptable for most purposes; however, a CPA exam problem may require the "safe payment" approach where the amount of the safe payment is computed at a specific point in time.

NOW REVIEW MULTIPLE-CHOICE QUESTIONS 21 THROUGH 22 IN VOLUME 2

5. **Incorporation of a Partnership**

   a. The incorporation of a partnership results in the formation of a new accounting (and legal) entity. This means that the partnership must adjust its records up to the date of incorporation.

      (1) First, the partnership closes its books and recognizes any income or loss up to the date of incorporation.
      (2) Second, the books of the partnership are adjusted to reflect the fair market value of the partnership assets and the present value of partnership liabilities.
      (3) A corresponding adjustment is made to the capital accounts in accordance with the partners' P&L ratio. Third, common stock is distributed to the partners in accordance with the amounts in their capital accounts.

      NOTE: The entries to record the receipt of stock by the corporation are different depending upon whether the corporation retains the partnership books or establishes new books.

   b. Retention of the partnership books means that the issuance of common stock results in the closing of the partners' capital accounts with credits going to common stock and additional paid-in capital.
   c. Establishing new books means that the assets and liabilities are closed out and the difference between their net value and the value of the corporate stock is debited to an asset "capital stock from corporation." This account is then credited and the partners' capital accounts debited to record the distribution of stock.

NOW REVIEW MULTIPLE-CHOICE QUESTION 23 IN VOLUME 2

6. **Research Component**
    Because there are no authoritative pronouncements in the accounting standards for partnerships, research in the partnership area is limited to the concepts statements that apply for all for-profit entities. You should be prepared to answer conceptual questions on typical accounting concepts such as revenue recognition, matching, valuation, allocation, and other accrual basis accounting concepts that are applicable to all business entities.

KEY TERMS

Bonus method. The old partnership capital plus the new partner's asset contribution is equal to the new partnership capital.

Dissolution. Occurs whenever there is a change in ownership (e.g., the addition of a new partner, or the retirement or death of an existing partner).

Goodwill method. The old partnership capital plus the new partner's asset contribution is not equal to the new partnership capital.

Installment liquidation. The assets are sold over a period of time and the cash is distributed to the partners as it becomes available.

Liquidation. The winding up of partnership affairs and termination of the business.

Right of offset. When loans exist between the partnership and a partner, the capital account and the loan(s) are combined to give a net amount.

Simple liquidation. One in which all the assets are sold in bulk and all of the creditors' claims are satisfied before a single liquidating distribution is made to the partners.

Statement of partnership liquidation. Shows in detail all of the transactions associated with the liquidation of the partnership.

E. Foreign Currency Translation

1. **Objective of Foreign Currency Translation**

   a. The rules for the translation of foreign currency into US dollars apply to two major areas.

      (1) Foreign currency transactions which are denominated in other than a company's functional currency (e.g., exports, imports, loans), and
      (2) Foreign currency financial statements of branches, divisions, subsidiaries, and other investees which are incorporated with the financial statements of a US company by combination, consolidation, or the equity method

   b. The objectives of translation are

      (1) To provide information relative to the expected economic effects of rate changes on an enterprise's cash flows and equity, and
      (2) To provide information in consolidated statements relative to the financial results and relationships of each individual foreign consolidated entity as reflected by the functional currency of each reporting entity

   The first objective influences the rules for the translation of foreign currency transactions, while both objectives influence the rules for the translation of foreign currency financial statements. After working through this module, read through the outline of ASC Topic 830 (SFAS 52).

2. **Translation of Foreign Currency Statements**

EXAMPLE

Assume that a US company has a 100% owned subsidiary in France. The subsidiary's operations consist of leasing space in an office building. Its balance sheet at December 31, 2010, and its income statement for 2010 are presented below.

French Company
BALANCE SHEET
December 31, 2010

Assets	Euros	Liabilities and Owners' Equity	Euros
Cash	60	Accounts payable	100
Accounts receivable (net)	100	Mortgage payable	200
Land	200	Common stock	100
Building	500	Retained earnings	360
Less accumulated depr.	(100)	Total liabilities and	
Total assets	€760	Owners' equity	€760

French Company
INCOME STATEMENT
For Year Ended December 31, 2010

Revenues	€260
Operating Expenses (excluding depreciation expense)	140
Depreciation expense	20
Net Income	€100

In addition to the information above, the following data are also needed for the translation process:

1. Transactions involving land, building, mortgage payable, and common stock all occurred in 2008.
2. No dividends were paid during the period 2008-2010.
3. Exchange rates for various dates follow.

   €1 = $.90 in 2008
   €1 = $1.05 at beginning of 2010
   €1 = $1.12 at end of 2010
   €1 = $1.10 weighted-average for 2010

---

   a. If the US company wants to present consolidated financial statements which include the results of its French subsidiary, the financial statements of the French company must be translated into US dollars. However, before this can be accomplished, the management of the US company must determine the functional currency of its French subsidiary. An entity's functional currency is the currency of the primary economic environment in which the entity operates; normally, that is the currency of the environment in which an entity primarily generates and expends cash. The decision concerning the functional currency is important because, once determined, it should be used consistently, unless it is clear that economic facts and circumstances have changed. The selection of the functional currency depends upon an evaluation of several factors. These factors include the following:

(1) Cash flows—Do the foreign entity's cash flows directly affect the parent's cash flows and are they immediately available for remittance to the parent?
(2) Sales prices—Are the foreign entity's sales prices responsive to exchange rate changes and to international competition?
(3) Sales markets—Is the foreign entity's sales market the parent's country or are sales denominated in the parent's currency?
(4) Expenses—Are the foreign entity's expenses incurred in the parent's country?
(5) Financing—Is the foreign entity's financing primarily from the parent or is it denominated in the parent's currency?
(6) Intercompany transactions—Is there a high volume of intercompany transactions between the parent and foreign entity?

b. If the answers to the questions above are predominantly yes, the functional currency would be the reporting currency of the parent (i.e., the US dollar). On the other hand, if the answers to the questions were predominantly no, the functional currency would be the foreign currency. In the example described previously, the euro would be the functional currency if the answers were no.

> **NOTE:** That the functional currency does not necessarily have to be the local currency of the foreign country when the answers to the questions are negative. In other words, it is possible for a foreign currency other than the euro to be the functional currency of our French company. For example, Swiss francs or British pounds could be the functional currency for the French company if one of these currencies is the currency of the primary economic environment in which the entity operates. However, assume these other possibilities are not alternatives in the example mentioned previously.

c. If the circumstances indicate the euro to be the functional currency, the current rate method is used for translation of the foreign currency financial statements. The rules for applying the current rate method are

(1) All assets and liabilities are translated using the current rate at the balance sheet date.
(2) All revenues and expenses are translated at the rates in effect when these items are recognized during the period. Due to practical considerations, however, weighted-average rates can be used to translate revenues and expenses which were incurred throughout the year.
(3) Owners' equity accounts are translated using historical exchange rates.
(4) Dividends are translated at the historic rate on the date of declaration.
(5) The translation adjustment for the period is reported as other comprehensive income under one of several acceptable reporting alternatives and the parent company's share of the accumulated amount is reported as accumulated other comprehensive income in the stockholders' equity section of the consolidated balance sheet.

d. This current rate method is illustrated below for the French financial statements shown previously.

EXAMPLE

Current Rate Method

French Company
BALANCE SHEET
December 31, 2010
(Euro is Functional Currency)

	Euros	Exchange rates	US dollars
Assets			
Cash	60	1.12	67.20
Accounts receivable (net)	100	1.12	112.00
Land	200	1.12	224.00
Building (net)	400	1.12	448.00
Totals	€760		$851.20
Liabilities and Owners' Equity			
Accounts payable	100	1.12	112.00
Mortgage payable	200	1.12	224.00
Common stock	100	.90	90.00
Retained earnings, 12/31/10	360	see income statement	352.00
Translation adjustment (gain)	___		73.20 (plug)
Totals	€760		$851.20

French Company
COMBINED INCOME AND RETAINED EARNINGS STATEMENT
For the Year Ending December 31, 2010

	Euros	Exchange rates	US dollars
Revenues	260	1.10	$ 286
Operating expenses (excluding €20 of depreciation expense)	(140)	1.10	(154)
Depreciation expense	(20)	1.10	(22)
Net income	100		110
Retained earnings calculation:			
Retained earnings at 1/1/10	260		242*
Net income	100		110
Retained earnings at 12/31/10	€360		$352

* The US dollar amount of retained earnings results from applying weighted-average exchange rates to translate revenues and expenses during the period 2008 through 2010. Retained earnings cannot be translated using a single exchange rate. The beginning retained earnings would be taken from the prior period's translated financial statements.

The translation adjustments result from translating all assets and liabilities at the current rate, while owners' equity is translated using historical rates. Common stock was issued in 2008 when the exchange rate was €1 = $.90. The beginning balance of retained earnings for 2010 was accumulated during the period 2008 through 2010. The new balance in ending retained earnings is placed on the balance sheet, and the translation adjustment is a plug figure to bring the balance sheet back into balance. In this situation, there is a translation gain of $73.20 that is credited to other comprehensive income.

You can use a trial balance technique as shown below. Translate all balance sheet and income statement items as indicated in the rules for the current rate method. The foreign currency translation gain/loss is the amount that will bring the trial balance back into balance.

French Company
TRIAL BALANCE
December 31, 2010

	Euros		Exchange rates	US dollars	
	DR	CR		DR	CR
Cash	60		1.12	67.20	
Accounts rec. (net)	100		1.12	112.00	
Land	200		1.12	224.00	
Building (net)	400		1.12	448.00	
Accounts payable		100	1.12		112.00
Mortgage payable		200	1.12		224.00
Common stock		100	.90		90.00
Retained earnings 1/1/10		260			242.00
Revenues		260	1.10		286.00
Expenses	140		1.10	154.00	
Depreciation exp.	20		1.10	22.00	
Totals	€920	€920		$1,027.20	$954.00
Translation adjustment (gain)					73.20
Totals				$1,027.20	$1,027.20

e. The previous illustration of the current rate technique assumed the euro to be the functional currency. Assume, however, that the circumstances were evaluated by the US company, and the US dollar was chosen as the functional currency. Under this alternative, the foreign currency financial statements are remeasured into US dollars.

(1) The remeasurement process is intended to produce the same result as if the entity's books of record had been maintained in the functional currency.
(2) If the US dollar is the functional currency, the remeasurement of foreign currency financial statements into US dollars results in a remeasurement gain or loss that is included in the subsidiary's income for the period.
(3) The remeasurement process begins by classifying assets and liabilities as either monetary or nonmonetary items and then applying the appropriate exchange rate depending on whether the item is monetary or nonmonetary. The following rules apply to the remeasurement process:

(a) Monetary assets and monetary liabilities are remeasured using the current rate at the balance sheet date.
(b) Nonmonetary assets and liabilities (e.g., land, building) which have historical cost balances are remeasured using historical exchange rates at the date the item entered the subsidiary.

(c) Owners' equity accounts such as common stock and additional paid in capital are translated using historic rates.

(d) Dividends is translated at the historic rate at the date of declaration

(e) Retained earnings is brought forward from the translated statement of the previous year.

(f) Revenues and most expenses that occur during a period are remeasured, for practical purposes, using the weighted-average exchange rate for the period. However, revenues and expenses that represent allocations of historical balances (e.g. depreciation) are remeasured using the same historical exchange rates as used for those items on the balance sheet.

(g) The remeasurement loss is reported on the consolidated income statement. The loss is the result of a remeasurement process which assumes that the US dollar is the functional currency.

(h) The calculation of the remeasurement loss is the result of the rules employed in the remeasurement process. In mechanical terms, the remeasurement loss is the amount needed to make the debits equal the credits in the French company's US dollar trial balance.

(4) The remeasurement process is illustrated below for the French subsidiary.

EXAMPLE

Remeasurement Method

French Company
BALANCE SHEET
December 31, 2010
(US dollar is Functional Currency)

Assets	(Classification)	Euros	Exchange rates	US dollars
Cash	(Monetary)	60 100	1.12	67.20
Accounts receivable (net)	(Monetary)	200	1.12	112.00
Land	(Nonmonetary)	400	.90	180.00
Building (net)	(Nonmonetary)	€760	.90	360.00
Totals				$719.20
Liabilities and Owners' Equity				
Accounts payable	(Monetary)	100	1.12	112.00
Mortgage payable	(Monetary)	200	1.12	224.00
Common stock		100	.90	90.00
Retained earnings, 12/31/10		360		293.20 (plug) (A)
Totals		€760		$719.20

The end retained earnings number is a plug figure to bring the balance sheet back into balance (**A**). This number is then used as end retained earnings in the statement of retained earnings to calculate net income after the remeasurement gain or loss (**B**). The remeasurement gain or loss (**C**) is the plug figure needed on the income statement to arrive at the calculated net income figure (**B**).

French Company
COMBINED INCOME AND RETAINED EARNINGS STATEMENT
For the Year Ending December 31, 2010

	Euros	Exchange rates	US dollars	
Revenues	260	1.10	286.00	
Expenses (exclusive of depreciation)	(140)	1.10	(154.00)	
Depreciation	(20)	.90	(18.00)	
Earnings before remeasurement loss			114.00	
Remeasurement loss	--	--	(40.80)	(plug) (C)
Net income (loss)	100		73.20	(Taken from R/E Stmt)
Calculation of retained earnings, net Income and measurement loss:				
Retained earnings at 1/1/10	260		220.00*	(given in problem)
Net income			73.20	(plug) (B)
Retained earnings at 12/31/10	€360		$293.20	(plug from balance sheet)

* Retained earnings of $220 includes remeasured income from the period 2008 through 2009, which includes remeasurement losses applicable to those years due to the strengthening of the euro compared to the US dollar. Beginning retained earnings were taken from the prior period's financial statements.

An easier way to calculate the foreign currency translation gain or loss is to use the trial balance approach. The remeasurement gain/loss is the amount needed to bring the trial balance back into balance. The trial balance approach is shown below.

French Company
TRIAL BALANCE
December 31, 2010

	Euro DR	Euro CR	Exchange rates	US dollars DR	US dollars CR	
Cash	60		1.12	67.20		
Accounts rec. (net)	100		1.12	112.00		
Land	200		.90	180.00		
Building (net)	400		.90	360.00		
Accounts payable		100	1.12		112.00	
Mortgage payable		200	1.12		224.00	
Common stock		100	.90		90.00	
Retained earnings 1/1/10		260			220.00*	(given in problem)
Revenues		260	1.10		286.00	
Expenses	140		1.10	154.00		
Depreciation exp.	20		.90	18.00		
Totals	€920	€920		$891.20	$932.00	
Remeasurement loss				40.80	--	(plug)
Totals				$932.00	$932.00	

(5) The significant points to remember about the French illustration are summarized below.

(a) Before foreign currency financial statements can be translated into US dollars, a decision must be made regarding the functional currency.

(b) If the functional currency is the foreign currency, the current rate method is used to translate to US dollars.

1] All assets and liabilities are translated using the current rate at the balance sheet date.

2] Owners' equity is translated using historical rates while revenues (and gains) and expenses (and losses) are translated at the rates in existence during the period when the transactions occurred.

3] A weighted-average rate can be used for items occurring numerous times throughout the period.

4] The translation adjustments (debit or credit) which result from the application of these rules are reported as a separate item in owners' equity in the consolidated balance sheet of the US parent.

(c) If the functional currency is not the reporting currency (the US dollar), the foreign currency financial statements are **remeasured** into US dollars.

1] All foreign currency balances are restated to US dollars using either historical or current exchange rates.

2] Foreign currency balances which reflect prices from past transactions (e.g., inventories carried at cost, prepaid insurance, property, plant, and equipment, etc.) are remeasured using historical rates while foreign currency balances which reflect prices from current transactions (e.g., inventories and trading and available-for-sale securities carried at market, etc.) are remeasured using the current rate.

3] Monetary assets and liabilities are remeasured using the current rate. (Deferred taxes are remeasured using the current rate.)

4] Remeasurement gains/losses that result from the remeasurement process are reported on the consolidated income statement under "Other Income (Expense)."

(6) The above summary can be arranged in tabular form as shown below.

Functional currency	Functional currency determinants	Translation method	Reporting
Local currency of foreign company	a. Operations not integrated with parent's operations b. Buying and selling activities primarily in local currency c. Cash flows not immediately available for remittance to parent	Current Rate (All assets/ liabilities translated using current rate; revenues/expenses use weighted-average rate; equity accounts use historical rates)	Translation adjustments are reported as other comprehensive income under one of several acceptable reporting alternatives and as accumulated other comprehensive income in the equity section of consolidated balance sheet. Analysis of changes in accumulated translation adjustments disclosed via footnote
US Dollar	a. Operations integrated with parent's operations b. Buying and selling activities primarily in US and/or US dollars c. Cash flows immediately available for remittance to parent	Remeasurement (Monetary assets/ liabilities use current rate; historical cost balances use historical rates; revenues/ expenses use weighted-average rates and historical rates, the latter for allocations such as depr. exp.).	Remeasurement gain/loss is reported on the consolidated income statement.

3. A few comments concerning the translation of foreign currency financial statements in highly inflationary economies should be made. If the cumulative inflation rate is $\geq$ 100% over a three-year period in a foreign country, the foreign currency statements of a company located in that country are remeasured into the reporting currency (i.e., the US dollar). In other words, it is assumed the US dollar is the functional currency. The following flowchart summarizes the requirements of foreign currency financial statements.

FOREIGN CURRENCY FINANCIAL STATEMENTS

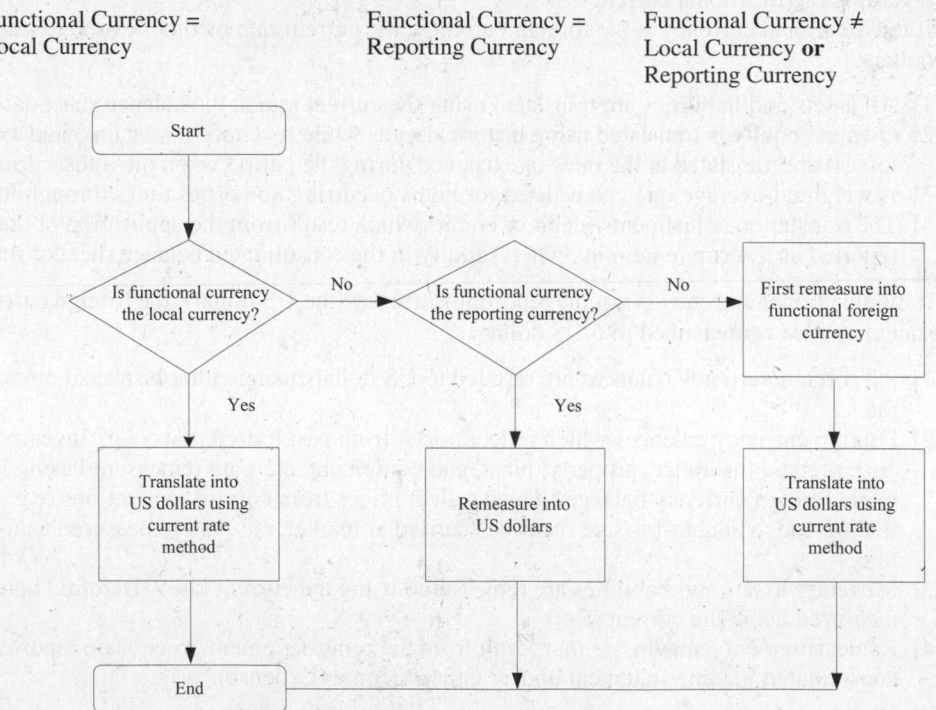

4. **Research Component—Accounting Standards Codification**

ASC Topic 830 addresses the issues related to translation of financial statements. A list of keywords helpful in locating foreign currency translation issues is shown below.

Exchange rate	Foreign operations	Reporting currency
Foreign currency	Functional currency	Translation adjustment(s)
Foreign currency statements	Highly inflationary economy	Translation financial statement
Foreign currency translation	Primary economic environment	
Foreign entity	Remeasurement functional currency	

5. **International Financial Reporting Standards (IFRS)**

   a. Currencies are defined as either foreign, functional currency, or presentation currency. The functional currency is the currency of the primary economic environment in which the entity operates. A foreign currency is a currency other than the functional currency. The presentation currency is the currency in which financial statements are presented. Similar to US GAAP, the three-step process for translating financial statements is as follows:

      (1) Determine the functional currency.
      (2) Translate items into the functional currency.
      (3) Translate items into the presentation currency.

   b. When translating financial statement items, the items are classified into two categories: monetary and nonmonetary items.

      (1) Monetary items are translated at the year-end spot rate.
      (2) Nonmonetary items measured at historical cost are translated at the historical exchange rate.
      (3) Nonmonetary items measured at fair value are translated at the rate in effect when fair value was determined.
      (4) If the functional currency is the same as the presentation currency, any gains and losses on translation are recognized in profit or loss in the period. However, there are several exceptions to this rule.
      (5) Currency gains or losses on nonmonetary items for which gains and losses are recorded in other comprehensive income should also be reported in other comprehensive income.

   c. If the functional currency is not the same as the presentation currency, then any translation gains and losses are recorded in other comprehensive income. In this case, assets and liabilities are recorded at the closing exchange rate, and income and expenses are recorded at the rate when the transaction occurred.

KEY TERMS

Foreign Currency Statements. Financial statements that employ as the unit of measure a functional currency that is not the reporting currency of the enterprise.

Foreign Currency Translation. The process of expressing in the reporting currency of the enterprise those amounts that are denominated or measured in a different currency.

Functional Currency. An entity's functional currency is the currency of the primary economic environment in which the entity operates; normally, that is the currency of the environment in which an entity primarily generates and expends cash.

Local Currency. The currency of a particular country being referred to.

Remeasurement. If an entity's books and records are not kept in its functional currency, remeasurement into the functional currency is required. Monetary balances are translated using the current exchange rate and nonmonetary balances are translated using historical exchange rates. If the US dollar is the functional currency, remeasurement into the reporting currency (the US dollar) makes translation unnecessary.

Reporting Currency. The currency in which an enterprise prepares its financial statements.

Translation Adjustments. Translation adjustments result from the process of translating financial statements from the entity's functional currency into the reporting currency.

Module 21: Governmental (State and Local) Accounting

Overview

Governmental accounting has some similarities to commercial accounting. For example, governmental accounting uses the double-entry system, journals, ledgers, trial balances, financial statements, internal control, etc. However, differences arise due to the objectives and environment of government. The major differences include

1. The absence of a profit motive, except for enterprise activities, such as utilities
2. A legal emphasis that involves restrictions both in the raising and spending of revenues
3. An inability to "match" revenues with expenditures, as revenues are often provided by persons other than those receiving the services
4. An emphasis on accountability or stewardship of resources entrusted to public officials
5. The use of fund accounting and reporting, as well as government-wide reporting
6. The recording of the budget in governmental funds which legally adopt a budget (i.e., General Fund)
7. The use of modified accrual accounting rather than full accrual accounting in some funds (governmental fund types)

Before beginning the reading you should review the key terms at the end of the module.

A. The Governmental Accounting Standards Board

The Governmental Accounting Standards Board (GASB), which has the authority to establish standards of financial reporting for all units of state and local governments, was created in 1984. It should be noted that the Financial Accounting Standards Board (FASB) has the authority to establish standards for nongovernmental not-for-profit organizations. GASB Statement No. 55 established a hierarchy of sources of generally accepted accounting principles (GAAP) for states and local governments as shown below (in descending order of authority):

1. Officially established accounting principles—GASB Statements and Interpretations.
2. GASB Technical Bulletins and AICPA Industry Audit and Accounting Guides and Statements of Position cleared by the GASB.

3. AICPA Practice Bulletins cleared by the GASB and consensus positions of groups of accountants organized by the GASB.
4. Implementation guides published by the GASB staff and practices that are widely recognized and prevalent.

In 2010, the GASB issued Statement No. 62 which incorporated into GASB's authoritative literature certain accounting and financial reporting guidance that is included in the following pronouncements issued on or before November 30, 1989:

1. FASB Statements and Interpretations
2. Accounting Principles Board Opinions
3. Accounting Research Bulletins

Major topics in GASB Statement No. 62 include

1. Capitalization of interest cost
2. Revenue recognition for exchange transactions
3. Revenue recognition when the right of return exists
4. Classification of items in the statement of net position
5. Special and extraordinary items
6. Comparative financial statements
7. Related parties
8. Prior-period adjustments
9. Accounting changes and error corrections
10. Disclosure of accounting policies
11. Contingencies
12. Long-term construction contracts
13. Extinguishment of debts
14. Troubled-debt restructuring
15. Foreign currency transactions
16. Imputation of interest costs
17. Inventory
18. Investments in common stock
19. Leases
20. Nonmonetary transactions
21. Real estate transactions
22. Research and development arrangements
23. Guidance for specialized industries, such as broadcasters and insurance entities

For these areas accounting by state and local government is similar to the accounting by business enterprises.

B. Governmental Accounting Concepts

GASB Concept Statements are much like the FASB Concepts Statements in that they set fourth fundamentals on which governmental accounting and reporting standards will be based.

1. Objectives of Financial Reporting

   a. GASB Concepts Statement No. 1 establishes the objectives of general purpose external financial reporting by state and local governmental entities and applies to both governmental-type and business-type activities.
   b. The nature of the governmental environment affects the financial reporting of governmental-type activities. The governmental environment is characterized by representative forms of government with separation of powers, a prevalence of intergovernmental revenues, and services that are provided to taxpayers. The budget is very significant in accounting for government-type activities because it expresses public policy, funding intent, and provides control over government expenditures. Control over revenues and expenditures is also provided by the use of fund accounting.
   c. Governmental business-type activities are more akin to private business activities. Generally, they involve exchanges that involve charging fees for providing particular services. However, many business-type activities receive subsidies, grants, or taxes from the general government, making them part of the government and publicly accountable.
   d. Concepts Statement No. 1 identified three primary users of the external state and local governmental financial reports:

      (1) The citizenry,
      (2) Legislative and oversight bodies, and
      (3) Investors and creditors.

e. Government financial reports are primarily used to compare actual financial results with budgets, to assess financial condition and results of operations, to assist in determining compliance with finance-related laws and regulations, and to assist in evaluating effectiveness and efficiency.

f. State and local governmental financial reports should possess the basic characteristics of understandability, reliability, relevance, timeliness, consistency, and comparability. See Module 9A for definitions of these characteristics.

2. Service Efforts and Accomplishments Reporting (SEA Reporting)

a. GASB Concepts Statement No. 2 (as amended by Concepts Statement No. 5) describes the objective, elements and characteristics of SEA reporting. The objective of SEA Reporting is to provide more complete information about a governmental entity's performance than can be provided by traditional financial statements and schedules. Such information is necessary for assessing accountability and making informed decisions.

b. Ideally a governmental entity should (1) establish and communicate clear, relevant goals and objectives, set measureable targets for accomplishment, and develop and report indicators that measure its progress. The elements of SEA reporting include measures of service effort, measures of service accomplishments (output and outcome measures), measures that relate service efforts to service accomplishments (efficiency and cost-outcome measures) and narrative or explanatory information.

3. Communication Methods in General-Purpose External Financial Reports

a. GASB Concepts Statement No. 3 provides a conceptual basis for selecting communication methods to present items of information within general-purpose external reports that contain financial statements. The alternative methods of communication include recognition in the basic financial statements, disclosure in notes to the basic financial statements, presentation as required supplementary information, and presentation as supplementary information.

b. GASB Concepts Statement No. 4 establishes definitions for the seven elements of historically based financial statements of state and local governments. The elements of a statement of financial position are defined as

(1) Assets—resources with present service capacity that the government presently controls.
(2) Liabilities—present obligations to sacrifice resources that the government has little or no discretion to avoid.
(3) Deferred outflow of resources—a consumption of net assets by the government that is applicable to a future reporting period. This is similar to an asset (e.g., a prepaid asset).
(4) Deferred inflow of resources—an acquisition of net assets by the government that is applicable to a future reporting period. This is similar to a liability (e.g., unearned revenue).
(5) Net position—the residual of all other elements presented in a statement of financial position.

c. The elements of the resource flows statements are defined as

(1) Outflow of resources—a consumption of net assets by the government that is applicable to the reporting period.
(2) Inflow of resources—an acquisition of net assets by the government that is applicable to the reporting period.

C. The Government Reporting Model

Governmental accounting focuses on two types of accountability: operational accountability and fiscal accountability. Operational accountability is demonstrated by government-wide financial statements which illustrate how effective and efficient the organization has been at using its resources, and the resources available to meet its future obligations. Fiscal accountability is illustrated by fund financial statements which show the organization's compliance with laws and regulations affecting its spending activities. The integrated approach refers to the fact that government financial statements show operational and fiscal accountability and the relationship between the two. The integrated approach requires a reconciliation between the government-wide financial statements and the fund financial statements.

GASB Statement No. 34, as amended by GASB Statement No. 63, provides the minimum requirements for basic financial statements and required supplemental information (RSI) to be in compliance with GAAP. These requirements for **general-purpose** governmental units (i.e., states, cities, counties) are

- Management's Discussion and Analysis (MD&A) (Required Supplementary Information)
- Government-Wide Financial Statements
  Statement of Net Position
  Statement of Activities
- Fund Financial Statements
  Governmental Funds
    Balance Sheet
    Statement of Revenues, Expenditures, and Changes in Fund Balances

        Proprietary Funds
            Statement of Net Position
            Statement of Revenues, Expenses, and Changes in Fund Net Position
            Statement of Cash Flows
        Fiduciary Funds
            Statement of Fiduciary Net Position
            Statement of Changes in Fiduciary Net Position
- Notes to the Financial Statements
- Required Supplementary Information (RSI) other than Management's Discussion and Analysis
            Schedule of Funding Progress (for Entities Reporting Pension Trust Funds)
            Schedule of Employer Contributions (for Entities Reporting Pension Trust Funds)
            Budgetary Comparison Schedules
            Information about Infrastructure Assets (for Entities Reported Using the Modified Approach)
            Claims Development Information When the Government Sponsors a Public Entity Risk Pool

In addition, general-purpose governments may choose to provide certain **other supplementary information,** including combining statements for nonmajor funds. If a government wishes to prepare a complete **Comprehensive Annual Financial Report (CAFR) ,** three major sections would be included. First, an **introductory section** (unaudited) would include a letter of transmittal, organization chart, and list of principal officials. Second, a **financial section** would be prepared, including an auditor's report, the required information, and other supplementary information listed above. Finally, a **statistical section** would include a number of schedules such as net position by component, changes in net position, revenue capacity, debt capacity, and demographic and economic statistics.

Special-purpose governments include park districts, tollway authorities, school districts, and sanitation districts. GASB has categorized special-purpose governments as those that are engaged in governmental activities, business-type activities, fiduciary activities, and both governmental and business-type activities. Special-purpose governments that are engaged in governmental activities and have more than one program and special-purpose governments that are engaged in both governmental and business-type activities must prepare both the government-wide and fund financial statements. Special-purpose governments that are engaged in a single governmental activity (such as a cemetery district) may combine the government-wide and fund financial statements or use other methods allowed by GASB. Special-purpose governments that are engaged in only business-type activities or fiduciary activities are not required to prepare the government-wide statements, but only prepare the proprietary or fiduciary fund statements. All governments must include the MD&A, Notes, and RSI.

> **NOTE:** Public colleges and universities and other governmental not-for-profit organizations may choose to report as special-purpose governments engaged in only business-type activities, engaged in only governmental activities, or engaged in both governmental and business-type activities.

D. The Reporting Entity

The GASB carefully defines the **reporting entity** in an effort to ensure that all boards, commissions, agencies, etc. that are under the control of the reporting entity are included. The reporting entity consists of a primary government and appropriate component units. A **primary government** is either (1) a state government, (2) a general-purpose local government, or (3) a special-purpose local government that has a separately elected governing body, is legally separate, and is fiscally independent of other state or local governments. A **component unit** is a legally separate organization for which the elected officials of a primary government are financially accountable. As clarified by GASB Statement No. 61, financial accountability for a legally separate organization is assumed in the following circumstances:

1. The primary government appoints a voting majority of the organization's governing body and (1) it is able to impose its will on that organization, or (2) there is a potential for the organization to provide specific financial benefits to, or impose specific financial burdens on, the primary government.
2. The organization is fiscally dependent on and there is a potential for the organization to provide specific financial benefits to, or burdens on, the primary government regardless of the primary government's influence on the governing board.

A component unit is also one in which the nature and significance of their relationships with a primary government is such that omission would cause the primary government's financial statements to be misleading. Generally, the financial statements would be misleading if they excluded organizations that are closely related to, or financially integrated with, the primary unit.

Most component units are reported, in the government-wide financial statements, in a separate column or columns to the right of the information related to the primary government (**discretely presented**). However, component units should be **blended** with the primary government figures in the following circumstances:

1. The governing body of the component unit is substantially the same as that of the primary government and (1) there is a financial benefit or burden relationship between the primary government and the component unit, or (2) management of the primary government has operational responsibility for the component unit.

2. The component unit provides services entirely, or almost entirely, for the primary government or for the benefit of the primary government.

3. The component unit's total debt outstanding, including leases, is expected to be repaid entirely or almost entirely by the primary government.

GASB Statement No. 39, *Determining Whether Certain Organizations Are Component Units—An Amendment of GASB Statement No. 14*, requires that a fund-raising foundation and similar organization whose primary purpose is to raise or hold significant resources for the benefit of a specific governmental unit should be reported as a component unit of that government.

E. **Management's Discussion and Analysis**

The **Management's Discussion and Analysis (MD&A)** provides, in plain English terms, an overview of the government's financial activities. This section is to provide a comparison of the current year results with the results of the prior year, with emphasis on the prior year. Included will be

- A brief discussion of the financial statements
- Condensed financial information from the government-wide financial statements and individual fund statements
- An analysis of significant variations between the original budget, final budget, and actual results for the year
- A description of significant capital asset and long-term debt activity for the year
- A discussion by governments that use the modified approach to report infrastructure assets regarding the condition of these capital assets and changes from the prior year
- A description of any known facts, decisions, or conditions that would have a significant effect on the government's financial position or results of operations.

MD&A is considered to be Required Supplementary Information (RSI). The nature of RSI is described in Section G. Only items required by GASB are included.

F. **Government-Wide Financial Statements**

The **government-wide** statements include the Statement of Net Position and the Statement of Activities, both of which are reproduced in this module. The government-wide statements are prepared on the economic resources measurement focus and accrual basis of accounting. All activities of the primary government are included, with the exception of fiduciary activities, as well as discretely presented component units.

The **Statement of Net Position** is similar to a balance sheet, except that the form, "Assets + Deferred Outflows of Resources – Liabilities – Deferred Inflows of Resources = Net Position" is used. Governmental accounting standards provide that (1) deferred outflows should be reported in a separate section following assets, and (2) deferred inflows should be reported in a separate section following liabilities. The statement then arrives at net position which includes the net effects of assets, deferred outflows of resources, liabilities, and deferred inflows of resources. Remember that a deferred outflow of resources is a consumption of net assets that is applicable to a future reporting period. An example would be where a government hedges a future transaction and the fair value becomes negative. A deferred inflow of resources is an acquisition of net assets that is applicable to a future reporting period. An example would be concession arrangement that involves the sale by a government of the future income from a toll road. The payment from the toll operator represents deferred revenue that should be recognized in the applicable future periods. Therefore it is similar to a liability.

If deferred outflows or deferred inflows are disclosed in the aggregate, the notes to the financial statements should describe the different types of deferred amounts. In addition, an explanation in the notes is required if the amount reported for a component of net position is significantly affected by the difference between deferred inflows or outflows and their related assets and liabilities.

GASB Statement No. 65, Items Previously Recognized as Assets and Liabilities, clarifies which financial statement items should continue to be presented as assets and liabilities, which should be reclassified as deferred outflows and deferred inflows, and which items should be treated as current period expenditures (outflows) or current period inflows.

Examples of Deferred Outflows of Resources	**Examples of Deferred Inflows of Resources**
• Grant expenditures paid in advance of meeting timing requirements	• Grant amounts received in advance of meeting timing requirements
• Deferred amounts from refunding of debt (debits)	• Deferred amounts from refunding debt (credits)
• Cost to acquire rights to future revenues	• Proceeds from sale of future revenues
• Deferred loss from sale and leaseback	• Deferred gain from a sale-leaseback transaction
• Negative fair value of government hedge of a future transaction	• Positive fair value of government hedge of a future transaction
	• Advance of revenue from imposed nonexchange transactions

Examples of Items that Continue to be Reported as Assets
- Prepayments
- Net pension plan position in excess of employer's total liability
- Capitalized incurred costs for regulated activities

Examples of Items that Continue to be Reported as Liabilities
- Advances of derived tax revenues
- Grant amounts received in advance of meeting requirements other than timing
- Receipt of prepayment
- Loan commitment fees
- Refunds imposed by a regulator

Examples of Items Reported as Current Outflows
- Debt issuance costs
- Initial direct cost incurred by lessor for operating leases
- Fees related to purchased loans

Examples of Items Reported as Current Inflows
- Loan origination fees related to lending activities
- Commitment fees charged to make a loan
- Loan origination fees for mortgage loans held for investment

Full accrual accounting is to be used on the statement of net position, including the recording and depreciation of fixed assets, including infrastructure. Capital assets generally are presented in the asset section of the statement of net position net of related depreciation. Note that "net position" is broken down into three categories: (1) net investment in capital assets, (2) restricted, and (3) unrestricted. The term "net investment in capital assets" is computed by taking the value of capital (fixed) assets, less accumulated depreciation, less the debt associated with the acquisition or improvement of the capital assets. Deferred outflows of resources and deferred inflows of resources that are related to the acquisition, construction, or improvement of those assets or the related debt should also be included in this component of net position. The term "restricted," as defined by GASB means "(a) externally imposed by creditors (such as through debt covenants), grantors, contributors, or laws or regulations of other governments, and (b) imposed by law through constitutional provisions or enabling legislation." Unrestricted net position is a "plug" figure, computed by taking the total net position and subtracting the net investment in capital assets and the restricted net position.

Note also that the columns are separated into (1) governmental activities, (2) business-type activities, (3) total primary government, and (4) component units. Governmental activities are those that are financed primarily through taxes and other nonexchange transactions. Business-type activities are those normally financed through user charges. The terms "primary government" and "component units" are described above. If a government has more component units than can be displayed effectively in the Statement of Net Position, then the detail of each component unit should be disclosed in the notes to the financial statements.

The **Statement of Activities** reports revenues and expenses on the full accrual basis. This is a consolidated statement except that interfund transactions are not eliminated, when those transactions are between governmental and business-type activities, and between the primary government and discretely presented component units. Expenses are reported by function. Revenues are also reported on the accrual basis and may be exchange revenues or nonexchange revenues. **Exchange revenues** are reported when goods or services are transferred for payment of (approximately) equal value, as is true for business enterprises. **Nonexchange transactions** are reported in accord with Section K. below.

Program revenues, those that are directly associated with the functional expense categories, are deducted to arrive at the net expense or revenue. Note that program revenues include (1) charges for services, (2) operating grants and contributions, and (3) capital grants and contributions, although program revenues are not limited to the three categories. Examples of program revenue would be the fees charged for park operations under "culture and recreation," and fines and forfeits, such as fines for traffic violations. Charges for services are deducted from the function which creates the revenues. Grants and contributions (both operating and capital) are reported in the function to which their use is restricted. The net expense or revenue is broken out between governmental activities, business-type activities, and component units, the same as in the Statement of Net Position. General revenues are deducted from the net expenses to obtain net revenues. General revenues include all taxes levied by the reporting government and other nonexchange revenues not restricted to a particular program. After that, separate additions or deductions are made for special items, extraordinary items, and transfers (between categories). If a government had contributions to term and permanent endowments and contributions to permanent fund principal, these would also be shown after general revenues. Finally, the net position at the beginning and end of the year are reconciled. (This is called an "all-inclusive activity" statement.)

Extraordinary items are those that are both unusual in nature and infrequent in occurrence (the same as for business enterprises). **Special items** are those events within the control of management that are either unusual in nature or infrequent in occurrence. An example of a special item would be the gain on sale of park land.

> Alternatively, the internal balances could be reported on
> separate lines as assets and liabilities. A notation would need
> to be added to inform the reader that the "Total" column is
> adjusted for those amounts.

Sample City
STATEMENT OF NET POSITION
December 31, 2013

	Governmental activities	Primary government Business-type activities	Total	Component units
Assets				
Cash and cash equivalents	$ 13,597,899	$ 10,279,143	$ 23,877,042	$ 303,935
Investments	27,365,221	--	27,365,221	7,428,952
Receivables (net)	12,833,132	3,609,615	16,442,747	4,042,290
Internal balances	175,000	(175,000)	--	--
Inventories	322,149	126,674	448,823	83,697
Capital assets, net (Note 1)	170,022,760	151,388,751	321,411,511	37,744,786
Total assets	224,316,161	165,229,183	389,545,344	49,603,660
Deferred outflow				
Payment to acquire rights to future parking revenue	--	27,520	27,520	--
Liabilities				
Accounts payable	6,783,310	751,430	7,534,740	1,803,332
Accrued and other liabilities	1,435,599	--	1,435,599	38,911
Noncurrent liabilities (Note 2):				
Due within one year	9,236,000	4,426,286	113,662,286	1,426,639
Due in more than one year	83,302,378	74,482,273	157,784,651	27,106,151
Total liabilities	100,757,287	79,659,989	180,417,276	30,375,033
Deferred inflow				
Deferred gain from sale and leaseback of building	16,300	--	16,300	--
Net position				
Net investment in capital assets	103,711,386	73,088,574	176,799,960	15,906,392
Restricted for:				
Capital projects	11,705,864	--	11,705,864	492,445
Debt service	3,020,708	1,451,996	4,472,704	--
Community development projects	4,811,043	--	4,811,043	--
Other purposes	3,214,302	--	3,214,302	--
Unrestricted (deficit)	(2,920,729)	11,056,144	8,135,415	2,829,790
Total net position	$123,542,574	$ 85,596,714	$209,139,288	$19,228,627

> *Assets restricted for capital projects* includes approximately $13 million of capital debt for which the proceeds have not yet been used to construct capital assets.

SOURCE: Revised from GASB 34, page 201.

All governments are required to report those expenses that are directly associated with each function on the appropriate line. If a government chooses to allocate some indirect expenses to functions, separate columns should show the direct, indirect, and total costs charged to each function. Direct expenses include depreciation that can be directly charged. Depreciation expense that serves all functions may be allocated as an indirect expense or charged to general government or as unallocated depreciation expense. Depreciation expense for general **infrastructure assets** (roads, bridges, storm sewers, etc.) should not be allocated but shown as an expense of that function that normally is used for capital outlay (public works, for example) or as a separate line. Interest on long-term debt would be included in direct expenses if the interest is due to a single function. Most interest, however, cannot be identified with a single function and should be shown in a separate line. Interest is capitalized for business-type activities but not for governmental activities.

A government may choose to use a **modified approach for recording eligible infrastructure assets**. Under the modified approach eligible infrastructure assets are **not required to be depreciated** as long as the following two requirements are met: (1) the government manages the eligible infrastructure assets using an asset management system and (2) the government documents that the eligible infrastructure assets are being preserved approximately at (or above) a condition level established and disclosed by the government. Under the modified approach, if a government meets the above criteria and infrastructure, assets are not depreciated and all expenditures (except for additions and improvements) made for eligible infrastructure assets should be expensed in the period incurred. Expenditures for additions and improvements of eligible infrastructure assets should be capitalized.

> **NOW REVIEW MULTIPLE-CHOICE QUESTIONS 1 THROUGH 21 IN VOLUME 2**

G. Fund Financial Statements

In addition to government-wide statements, governmental accounting standards require a number of fund financial statements. Most governments use fund accounting internally and prepare the government-wide statements with worksheet adjustments from this fund accounting base. A fund is defined by the GASB as

> A fiscal and accounting entity with a self-balancing set of accounts recording cash and other financial resources, together with all related liabilities and residual equities and balances, and changes therein, which are segregated for the purpose of carrying on specific activities or attaining certain objectives in accordance with special regulations, restrictions, or limitations.

Under GASB standards there are 11 fund types, which are classified into three general categories.

Governmental funds	Proprietary funds	Fiduciary funds
(1) General	(6) Internal service	(8) Agency
(2) Special revenue	(7) Enterprise	(9) Pension and other employee benefit trust funds
(3) Debt service		(10) Investment trust funds
(4) Capital projects		(11) Private-purpose trust funds
(5) Permanent		

Fund financial statements are presented separately for the governmental, proprietary, and fiduciary fund categories. Each government has only one general fund; each other fund type may have any number of individual funds, although GASB encourages having as few funds as possible. Fixed assets and long-term debt are not reported in the fund financial statements for governmental funds. Fixed assets and long-term debt related to governmental funds only are reported in the government-wide financial statements (statement of net position).

The fund financial statements for the governmental and enterprise fund categories report **major funds,** not all funds. The general fund is always a major fund. Other funds must be considered major when both of the following conditions exist: (1) total assets, liabilities, deferred inflows and outflows, revenues, expenditures/expenses of that individual governmental or enterprise fund constitute 10% of the governmental or enterprise category **and** (2) total assets, liabilities, deferred inflows and outflows, revenues, expenditures/expenses are 5% of the total of the governmental and enterprise category combined. In addition, a government may choose to call any fund major if it feels that reporting that fund would be useful. In governmental and enterprise fund statements, the nonmajor funds are aggregated and reported as a single column. Combining statements for nonmajor funds are shown as "Other supplementary information" later in the financial section of CAFR. Internal service funds are reported in a single column on the proprietary fund statements.

Fiduciary fund financial statements report a separate column for fund type (agency, pension and other employee benefit trust, investment trust, and private purpose). If separate reports are not available for each pension trust fund, then the notes must disclose this information. If separate reports are available, then the notes must disclose how readers can obtain those reports.

A reconciliation between the information presented in the governmental fund financial statements and the governmental activities column of the government-wide financial statements is required either at the bottom of the fund financial statements or in a schedule immediately following the fund financial statements. Explanations should either accompany the reconciliation or be in the notes.

Governmental funds focus on the current financial resources raised and expended to carry out general government purposes. Governmental funds include the general, special revenue, debt service, capital projects, and permanent funds. GASB Statement No. 54 provides definitions of the governmental fund types. The **General fund** accounts for and reports all financial resources except those required to be accounted for and reported in another fund. The general fund includes expenditures for functions such as general government, public safety, culture and recreation, public works and engineering, and other activities not set aside in other funds. **Special revenue funds** are

---

[1] The determination of whether or not a fund is major or nonmajor can be illustrated by the HUD Programs Fund, shown in the governmental funds statements as a major fund. The first step is to determine whether or not the HUD Programs Fund is 10% of the governmental funds assets ($7,504,765/51,705,690 = 14.5%), liabilities ($6,428,389/16,812,584 = 38.3%), revenues ($2,731,473/97,482,467 = 2.80%), or expenditures ($2,954,389/121,332,470 = 2.44%). The first (10%) criterion is met for assets and liabilities but not for revenues and expenditures. As a result, the 5% test will be applied for assets and liabilities only. See the statements for governmental and proprietary funds. The assets do not qualify [$7,504,765/(51,705,690 + 165,404,18) = 3.45%]. However, the liabilities do exceed 5% [$6,428,389/(16,812,584 + 79,834,989) = 6.65%]. Thus, the HUD Programs Fund must be shown as a major fund.

used to account for and report specific revenue sources that are restricted or committed to expenditures for specified current purposes other than debt service and capital projects. An example would include a motor fuel tax limited by law to highway and street construction and repair. **Debt service funds** are used to account for and report financial resources that are restricted, committed, or assigned to expenditures for the payment of general long-term debt principal and interest. **Capital projects funds** are used to account for and report financial resources that are restricted, committed, or assigned to expenditures for capital outlays, including the acquisition or construction of capital facilities and other capital assets. Capital projects funds exclude capital-related outflows financed by proprietary funds or for assets that will be held in trust funds. **Permanent funds** are used to account for and report resources that are restricted to the extent that only earnings, and not principal, may be used to support government programs which benefit the government or its citizens. Permanent funds exclude private purpose trust funds which benefit individuals, private organizations, or other governments.

Financial statements required for governmental fund types include (1) **Balance Sheet** and (2) **Statement of Revenues, Expenditures, and Changes in Fund Balances**. Both of these are illustrated in this module. Governmental fund financial statements are prepared on the current financial resources measurement focus and modified accrual basis of accounting (see Section H., "Measurement Focus and Basis of Accounting"). Like the government-wide statement of net position, the balance sheet of a governmental fund would include deferred outflows of resources and deferred inflow of resources. GASB Statement No. 54 established fund balance classifications that are to be used by governmental funds based on the extent to which the government is obligated to observe constraints imposed upon the use of the resources. Fund balance classifications provided by GASB Statement No. 54 are nonspendable, restricted, committed, assigned and unassigned balances. The classifications are based on the relative strength of the constraints that control how specific amounts can be spent. The **nonspendable** fund balance classification includes amounts that cannot be spent because they are either (1) not in spendable form, or (2) they are legally or contractually required to be maintained intact. "Not in spendable form" includes items that are not expected to be converted to cash, such as inventories and prepaid amounts. It also includes the long-term amount of loans and notes receivable, as well as property acquired for resale. However, if the proceeds from collection of receivables or from the sale of property is restricted, committed, or assigned, the amounts should be included in the appropriate fund balance classification, rather than in the nonspendable fund balance. **Restricted** fund balances include amounts that are restricted to specific purposes and should be reported as restricted when constraints placed upon the resources are either: (1) externally imposed by creditors, contributors, or laws or regulations of other governments or (2) imposed by law through constitutional provisions or enabling legislation. **Committed** fund balances are amounts that can only be used for specific purposes pursuant to constraints imposed by formal action of the government's highest level of decision-making authority. The **assigned** classification of fund balance includes amounts that are constrained by the government's *intent* to be used for specific purposes but are neither restricted nor committed. It also includes any remaining positive amounts that are reported in governmental funds, other than the general fund, that are not classified as nonspendable, restricted, or committed and amounts in the general fund that are intended to be used for a specific purpose. To be classified as assigned "intent" should be expressed by (1) the governing body or (2) a body (i.e., budget or finance committee) or official who has the authority to assign amounts to be used for specific purposes. Finally, the **unassigned** fund balance is the residual classification for the general fund. The unassigned classification represents the fund balance that has not been assigned to other funds and that has not been restricted, committed, or assigned to specific purposes within the general fund. GASB Statement No. 54 indicates that the general fund should be the only fund that reports a positive unassigned fund balance amount. The balance sheet or the notes to the financial statements should disclose the details of the items in each of the five fund balance classifications. GASB Statement No. 54 indicates that *encumbrances* are not a specific purpose and should not be displayed as a separate item on the balance sheet but should be included in the appropriate fund balance classification based on the definition and criteria for fund balance classifications. Significant encumbrances should be disclosed in the notes to the financial statements in conjunction with disclosures of other significant commitments.

Note in the Statement of Revenues, Expenditures, and Changes in Fund Balances that revenues are reported by source, expenditures are reported by character (current, debt service, capital outlay) and then by function (general government, public safety, etc.). The category "other financing sources and uses" includes transfers between funds and proceeds from the issuance of long-term debt and proceeds from the sale of fixed assets. Special and extraordinary items are reported in this statement in the same manner as in the government-wide Statement of Activities, and reconciliation between the beginning and ending fund balance completes the statement. Interest expenditures related to fixed assets are **not** capitalized.

Sample City
STATEMENT OF ACTIVITIES
For the Year Ended December 31, 2013

> The detail presented for government activities represents the *minimum* requirement. Governments are encouraged to provide more details—for example, police, fire, EMS, and inspections—rather than simply "Public safety."

Functions/Programs	Expenses	Program revenues			Net (expense) revenue and changes in net position			
		Charges for services	Operating grants and Contributions	Capital grants and contributions	Primary government			Component units
					Governmental activities	Business-type activities	Total	
Primary government								
Governmental activities								
General government	$ 9,571,410	$ 3,146,915	$ 843,617	$	$ (5,580,878)	$	$ (5,580,878)	$
Public safety	34,844,749	1,198,855	1,307,693	62,300	(32,275,901)		(32,275,901)	
Public works	10,128,538	850,000		2,252,615	(7,025,923)		(7,025,923)	
Engineering services	1,299,645	704,793			(594,852)		(594,852)	
Health and sanitation	6,738,672	5,612,267	575,000		(551,405)		(551,405)	
Cemetery	735,866	212,496			(523,370)		(523,370)	
Culture and recreation	11,532,350	3,995,199	2,450,000		(5,087,151)		(5,087,151)	
Community development	2,994,389			2,580,000	(414,389)		(414,389)	
Education (payment to school district)	21,893,273				(21,893,273)		(21,893,273)	
Interest on long-term debt	6,068,121				(6,068,121)		(6,068,121)	
Total governmental activities	105,807,013	15,720,525	5,176,310	4,894,915	(80,015,263)		(80,015,263)	
Business-type activities								
Water	3,595,733	4,159,350		1,159,909		1,723,526	1,723,526	
Sewer	4,912,853	7,170,533		486,010		2,743,690	2,743,690	
Parking facilities	2,796,283	1,344,087				(1,452,196)	(1,452,196)	
Total business-type activities	11,304,869	12,673,970		1,645,919		3,015,020	3,015,020	
Total primary government	$117,111,882	$28,394,495	$5,176,310	$6,540,834	(80,015,263)	3,015,020	(77,000,243)	
Component units								
Landfill	$ 3,382,157	$ 3,857,858	$	$ 11,397				487,098
Public school system	31,186,498	705,765	3,937,083					(26,543,650)
Total component units	$ 34,568,655	$ 4,563,623	$3,937,083	$ 11,397				(26,056,552)

	Governmental activities	Business-type activities	Total	Component units
General revenues:				
Taxes:				
Property taxes, levied for general purposes	51,693,573		51,693,573	
Property taxes, levied for debt service	4,726,244		4,726,244	
Franchise taxes	4,055,505		4,055,505	
Public service taxes	8,969,887		8,969,887	
Payment from Sample City				21,893,273
Grants and contributions not restricted to specific programs	1,457,820		1,457,820	6,461,708
Investment earnings	1,958,144	601,349	2,559,493	881,763
Miscellaneous	884,907	104,925	989,832	22,464
Special item—gain on sale of park land	2,653,488		2,653,488	
Transfers	501,409	(501,409)		
Total general revenues, special items, and transfers	76,900,977	204,865	77,105,842	29,259,208
Change in net position	(3,114,286)	3,219,885	105,599	3,202,656
Net position—beginning	126,656,860	82,376,829	209,033,689	16,025,971
Net position—ending	$123,542,574	$85,596,714	$209,139,288	$19,228,627

SOURCE: Revised from GASB 34, pp. 208-9.

Proprietary funds focus on total economic resources, income determination, and cash flow presentation. Proprietary funds include internal service funds (which are reported as governmental activities in the government-wide financial statements) and enterprise funds (which are considered business-type activities in the government-wide financial statements). **Internal service funds** report any activity that provides goods or services to other funds of the primary government on a cost-reimbursement basis. Examples might include print shops, motor pools, and self-insurance activities. Internal service funds may incidentally provide services to other governments on a cost-reimbursement basis. **Enterprise funds** may be used to provide goods or services to external users for a fee. Enterprise funds must be used if (1) the activity is financed with debt that is secured solely by a pledge of the net revenues from fees and charges of that activity, (2) laws or regulations require that the activity's cost of providing services be recovered with fees and charges, rather than from taxes or similar revenues, or (3) the pricing policies of the activity establish fees and charges designed to cover its costs including capital costs (e.g., depreciation and debt service). Examples of enterprise funds would include water utilities, airports, and swimming pools.

Statements required for proprietary funds include (1) **Statement of Net Position,** (2) **Statement of Revenues, Expenses, and Changes in Fund Net Position,** and (3) **Statement of Cash Flows**. These statements are all included in this module. Note that the Statement of Net Position is prepared in the same "Assets + Deferred Outflows of Resources – Liabilities – Deferred Inflows of Resources = Net Position" format as the Statement of Net Position in the government-wide financial statements. GASB permits the more traditional balance sheet format, "Assets + Deferred Outflows of Resources = Liabilities + Deferred Inflows of Resources + Net Position" for this proprietary funds statement. The net position category has the same breakdown as the government-wide statement of net positions, "net investment in capital assets," "restricted (distinguishing between major categories of restrictions)," and "unrestricted." Note also that the internal service funds are shown separately to the right as a fund type in the proprietary fund financial statements, with all internal service funds grouped together. A classified format, with current and noncurrent assets and liabilities shown separately, is required by GASB for the proprietary fund statement of net position (or balance sheet).

The Statement of Revenues, Expenses, and Changes in Fund Net Position is an all-inclusive operating statement, with a reconciliation of the beginning and ending fund net position as the last item. Major enterprise funds are shown, along with a total of all enterprise fund activity, and the total of internal service funds is shown separately. GASB standards require an operating income figure, with operating revenues and expenses shown separately from nonoperating revenues and expenses. Capital contributions, transfers, extraordinary items, and special items are to be shown after the nonoperating revenues and expenses. GASB requires that depreciation be shown separately as an operating expense and that interest be shown as a nonoperating expense. Interest expense related to fixed assets is capitalized.

The Statement of Cash Flows is prepared in accord with the requirements of GASB Statement No. 9, as modified by GASB Statement No. 34, and contains several major differences from the familiar business cash flow statement required by FASB. First, only the direct method is acceptable, and reconciliation is required. Second, the reconciliation is from operating income to net cash flow from operating activities, not from net income as required by FASB. Third, GASB has four categories instead of the three required by FASB. The four categories of activities used are operating, noncapital financing, capital and related financing, and investing. Fourth, cash receipts from interest are classified as investing, not operating activities. Fifth, cash payments for interest are classified as financing (either noncapital or capital and related), not as operating activities. Finally, purchases of capital assets (resources provided by financing activities) are considered financing, not investing, activities.

Sample City
BALANCE SHEET
GOVERNMENTAL FUNDS
December 31, 2013

	General	HUD programs	Community redevelopment	Route 7 construction	Other governmental funds	Total governmental funds
Assets						
Cash and cash equivalents	$3,418,485	$1,236,523	$—	$—	$5,606,792	$10,261,800
Investments	—	—	13,262,695	10,467,037	3,485,252	27,214,984
Receivables, net	3,644,561	2,953,438	353,340	11,000	10,221	6,972,560
Due from other funds	1,370,757	—	—	—	—	1,370,757
Receivables from other governments	—	119,059	—	—	1,596,038	1,715,097
Liens receivable	791,926	3,195,745	—	—	—	3,987,671
Inventories	182,821	—	—	—	—	182,821
Total assets	$9,408,550	$7,504,765	$13,616,035	$10,478,037	$10,698,303	$51,705,690
Liabilities and fund balances						
Liabilities						
Accounts payable	$3,408,680	$129,975	$190,548	$1,104,632	$1,074,831	$5,908,666
Due to other funds	—	25,369	—	—	—	25,369
Payable to other governments	94,074	—	—	—	—	94,074
Total liabilities	3,502,754	155,344	190,548	1,104,632	1,074,831	6,028,109
Deferred inflows	4,266,730	6,273,045	250,000	11,000	—	10,800,775
Fund balances						
Nonspendable	958,447					958,447
Restricted			100,000			100,000
Committed	40,292	41,034	19,314	5,792,587	1,814,122	7,707,349
Assigned		1,035,342	13,056,173	3,569,818	7,809,350	25,470,683
Unassigned	640,327					640,327
Total fund balances	$1,639,066	$1,076,376	$13,175,487	$9,362,405	$9,623,472	$34,876,806

Amounts reported for governmental activities in the statement of net position are different because:

Capital assets used in governmental activities are not financial resources and therefore are not reported in the funds.	161,082,708
Other long-term assets are not available to pay for current-period expenditures and therefore are deferred in the funds.	9,348,876
Internal service funds are used by management to charge the costs of certain activities, such as insurance and telecommunications, to individual funds. The assets and liabilities of the internal service funds are included in governmental activities in the statement of net position.	2,994,691
Long-term liabilities, including bonds payable, are not due and payable in the current period and therefore are not reported in the funds.	(84,760,507)
Net position of governmental activities	$123,542,574

SOURCE: Revised from GASB 34, pp. 220-1.

Sample City

STATEMENT OF REVENUES, EXPENDITURES, AND CHANGES IN FUND BALANCES

GOVERNMENTAL FUNDS

For the Year Ended December 31, 2013

	General	HUD programs	Community redevelopment	Route 7 construction	Other governmental funds	Total governmental funds
Revenues						
Property taxes	$51,173,436	$ —	$ —	$ —	$ 4,680,192	$ 55,853,628
Franchise taxes	4,055,505	—	—	—	—	4,055,505
Public service taxes	8,969,887	—	—	—	—	8,969,887
Fees and fines	606,946	—	—	—	—	606,946
Licenses and permits	2,287,794	—	—	—	—	2,287,794
Intergovernmental	6,119,938	2,578,191	—	—	2,830,916	11,529,045
Charges for services	11,374,460	—	—	—	30,708	11,405,168
Investment earnings	552,325	87,106	549,489	270,161	364,330	1,823,411
Miscellaneous	881,874	66,176	—	2,939	94	951,083
Total revenues	86,022,165	2,731,473	549,489	273,100	7,906,240	97,482,467
Expenditures						
Current						
General government	8,630,835	—	417,814	16,700	121,052	9,186,401
Public safety	33,729,623	—	—	—	—	33,729,623
Public works	4,975,775	—	—	—	3,721,542	8,697,317
Engineering services	1,299,645	—	—	—	—	1,299,645
Health and sanitation	6,070,032	—	—	—	—	6,070,032
Cemetery	706,305	—	—	—	—	706,305
Culture and recreation	11,411,685	—	—	—	—	11,411,685
Community development	—	2,954,389	—	—	—	2,954,389
Education—payment to school district	21,893,273	—	—	—	—	21,893,273
Debt service						
Principal	—	—	—	—	3,450,000	3,450,000
Interest and other charges	—	—	—	—	5,215,151	5,215,151
Capital outlay	—	—	2,246,671	11,281,769	3,190,209	16,718,649
Total expenditures	88,717,173	2,954,389	2,664,485	11,298,469	15,697,954	121,332,470
Excess (deficiency) of revenues over expenditures	(2,695,008)	(222,916)	(2,114,996)	(11,025,369)	(7,791,714)	(23,850,003)
Other Financing Sources (Uses)						
Proceeds of refunding bonds	—	—	—	—	38,045,000	38,045,000
Proceeds of long-term capital-related debt	—	—	17,529,560	—	1,300,000	18,829,560
Payment to bond refunding escrow agent	—	—	—	—	(37,284,144)	(37,284,144)
Transfers in	129,323	—	—	—	5,551,187	5,680,510
Transfers out	(2,163,759)	(348,046)	(2,273,187)	—	(219,076)	(5,004,068)
Total other financing sources and uses	(2,034,436)	(348,046)	15,256,373	—	7,392,967	20,266,858
Special Item						
Proceeds from sale of park land	3,476,488	—	—	—	—	3,476,488
Net change in fund balances	(1,252,956)	(570,962)	13,141,377	(11,025,369)	(398,747)	(106,657)
Fund balances—beginning	2,908,322	1,647,338	34,110	20,387,774	10,022,219	34,999,763
Fund balances—ending	$ 1,655,366	$1,076,376	$13,175,487	$ 9,362,405	$ 9,623,472	$ 34,893,106

SOURCE: GASB 34, pp. 222-3

Sample City
STATEMENT OF NET POSITION
PROPRIETARY FUNDS
December 31, 2013

This statement illustrates the "net position" format; the "balance sheet" format also is permitted. Classification of assets and liabilities is required in either case.

	Business-type activities—enterprise funds			Governmental activities—internal Service funds
	Water and sewer	Parking facilities	Totals	
Assets				
Current assets:				
Cash and cash equivalents	$ 8,416,653	$ 369,168	$ 8,785,821	$ 3,336,099
Investments	--	--	--	150,237
Receivables, net	3,564,586	3,535	3,568,121	157,804
Due from other governments	41,494	--	41,494	--
Inventories	126,674	--	126,674	139,328
Total current assets	12,149,407	372,703	12,522,110	3,783,468
Noncurrent assets:				
Restricted cash and cash equivalents	--	1,493,322	1,493,322	--
Capital assets:				
Land	813,513	3,021,637	3,835,150	--
Distribution and collection systems	39,504,183	--	39,504,183	--
Buildings and equipment	106,135,666	23,029,166	129,164,832	14,721,786
Less accumulated depreciation	(15,328,911)	(5,786,503)	(21,115,414)	(5,781,734)
Total noncurrent assets	131,124,451	21,757,622	152,882,073	8,940,052
Total assets	143,273,858	22,130,325	165,404,183	12,723,520
Deferred outflow				
Payment to receive rights to future parking revenue		27,520	27,520	
Liabilities				
Current liabilities:				
Accounts payable	447,427	304,003	751,430	780,570
Due to other funds	175,000	--	175,000	1,170,388
Compensated absences	112,850	8,827	121,677	237,690
Claims and judgments	--	--	--	1,687,975
Bonds, notes, and loans payable	3,944,609	360,000	4,304,609	249,306
Total current liabilities	4,679,886	672,830	5,352,716	4,125,929
Noncurrent liabilities:				
Compensated absences	451,399	35,306	486,705	--
Claims and judgments	--	--	--	5,602,900
Bonds, notes, and loans payable	54,451,549	19,544,019	73,995,568	--
Total noncurrent liabilities	54,902,948	19,579,325	74,482,273	5,602,900
Total liabilities	59,582,834	20,252,155	79,834,989	9,728,829
Net Position				
Net investment in capital assets	72,728,293	360,281	73,088,574	8,690,746
Restricted for debt service	--	1,451,996	1,451,996	--
Unrestricted	10,962,731	93,413	11,056,144	(5,696,055)
Total net position	$ 83,691,024	$ 1,905,690	$ 85,596,714	$ 2,994,691

SOURCE: Revised from GASB 34, page 227.

Fiduciary fund financial statements provide information, based on the economic resources measurement focus and accrual accounting, on resources held and used by governments for the benefit of individuals and entities other than the government. Fiduciary fund statements are the Statement of Fiduciary Net Position and the Statement of Changes in Fiduciary Net Position. Unlike the statements for the governmental and enterprise fund categories, fiduciary fund statements report totals for each of the four fund types. The fiduciary fund types are (1) pension (and other employee benefit) trust funds, (2) investment trust funds, (3) private-purpose trust funds, and (4) agency funds. However, each individual pension or employee benefit trust fund report must be reported in the notes if separate reports have not been issued. If separate reports have been issued, the notes to the financial statement must indicate how the reader might obtain such reports.

Pension (and other employee benefit) trust funds account for funds held in trust for the payment of employee retirement and other benefits. These trust funds exist when the government is the trustee for the pension plan. Accounting for these plans is covered by GASB Statement Nos. 25, 43, 50, and 57. **Investment trust funds** are used to report the external portions of investment pools, when the reporting government is trustee. **Private-purpose trust funds** should be used to report all other trust arrangements where the principal must remain intact and the income generated is used to benefit individuals, private organizations, and other governments. An example would be a fund to report scholarship funds contributed by individuals and businesses, by a public school system. Finally, **agency funds** report resources held by the reporting government in a purely custodial capacity. Agency funds report only assets and liabilities and are not included in the Statement of Changes in Fiduciary Net Position.

Sample City
STATEMENT OF REVENUES, EXPENSES, AND CHANGES IN FUND NET POSITION
PROPRIETARY FUNDS
For the Year Ended December 31, 2013

	Business-type activities—enterprise funds			Governmental activities—internal service funds
	Water and sewer	Parking facilities	Totals	
Operating revenues:				
Charges for service	$11,329,883	$1,340,261	$12,670,144	$15,256,164
Miscellaneous	--	3,826	3,826	1,066,761
Total operating revenues	11,329,883	1,344,087	12,673,970	16,322,925
Operating expenses:				
Personal services	3,400,559	762,348	4,162,907	4,157,156
Contractual services	344,422	96,032	440,454	584,396
Utilities	754,107	100,726	854,833	214,812
Repairs and maintenance	747,315	64,617	811,932	1,960,490
Other supplies and expenses	498,213	17,119	515,332	234,445
Insurance claims and expenses	--	--	--	8,004,286
Depreciation	1,163,140	542,049	1,705,189	1,707,872
Total operating expenses	6,907,756	1,582,891	8,490,647	16,863,457
Operating income (loss)	4,422,127	(238,804)	4,183,323	(540,532)
Nonoperating revenues (expenses):				
Interest and investment revenue	454,793	146,556	601,349	134,733
Miscellaneous revenue	--	104,925	104,925	20,855
Interest expense	(1,600,830)	(1,166,546)	(2,767,376)	(41,616)
Miscellaneous expense	--	(46,846)	(46,846)	(176,003)
Total nonoperating revenues (expenses)	(1,146,037)	(961,911)	(2,107,948)	(62,031)
Income (loss) before contributions and transfers	3,276,090	(1,200,715)	2,075,375	(602,563)
Capital contributions	1,645,919	--	1,645,919	18,788
Transfers out	(290,000)	(211,409)	(501,409)	(175,033)
Change in net position	4,632,009	(1,412,124)	3,219,885	(758,808)
Total net position—beginning	79,059,015	3,377,814	82,376,944	3,753,499
Total net position—ending	$83,691,024	$1,905,690	$85,596,714	$ 2,994,691

SOURCE: Revised from GASB 34, page 229.

The statements required for fiduciary funds are the **Statement of Fiduciary Net Position** and **Statement of Changes in Fiduciary Net Position**. Examples of these statements are reflected in this module. The Statement of Fiduciary Net Position is prepared in the form "Assets + Deferred Outflows of Resources – Liabilities – Deferred Inflows of Resources = Net Position." Columns are included for each fund type. The Statement of Changes in Fiduciary Net Position uses the terms "additions" and "deductions" instead of revenues and expenses, but the additions and deductions are computed on the full accrual basis. This, like all other GASB operating statements, is an "all-inclusive" statement with reconciliation of the beginning and ending net position at the bottom of the statement. Note that agency funds have only assets and liabilities (assets = liabilities) and are not reported in the Statement of Changes in Fiduciary Net Position.

H. Notes to the Financial Statements

Note disclosure requirements are found in the GASB *Codification* Section 2300 and in GASB Statement Nos. 34, 38, and 40. Some of the major disclosures are (1) a summary of accounting policies, (2) a description of the reporting entity, (3) disclosures on cash and investments (including securitization), (4) information relating to fixed assets, long-term debt, pensions, commitments and contingencies, (5) information on exceeding the budget at the legal level of control, (6) disclosures of individual funds with deficit fund balances, and (7) risks related to deposits and investments. Some disclosures brought about by GASB Statement No. 34 include a description of the government-wide financial statements, the policy for capitalizing fixed assets and estimating useful lives, segment information for enterprise funds, and the policy for recording infrastructure, including the use of the modified approach, if applicable.

Sample City
STATEMENT OF CASH FLOWS
PROPRIETARY FUNDS
For the Year Ended December 31, 2013

	Business-type activities—enterprise funds			Governmental activities—internal service funds
	Water and sewer	Parking facilities	Totals	
Cash flows from operating activities				
Receipts from customers	$11,400,200	$ 1,345,292	$12,745,492	$15,326,343
Payments to suppliers	(2,725,349)	(365,137)	(3,090,486)	(2,812,238)
Payments to employees	(3,360,055)	(750,828)	(4,110,883)	(4,209,688)
Internal activity—payments to other funds	(1,296,768)	--	(1,296,768)	--
Claims paid	--	--	--	(8,482,451)
Other receipts (payments)	(2,325,483)	--	(2,325,483)	1,061,118
Net cash provided by operating activities	1,692,545	229,327	1,921,872	883,084
Cash flows from noncapital financing activities				
Operating subsidies and transfers to other funds	(290,000)	(211,409)	(501,409)	(175,033)
Cash flows from capital and related financing activities				
Proceeds from capital debt	4,041,322	8,660,778	12,702,100	--
Capital contributions	1,645,919	--	1,645,919	--
Purchases of capital assets	(4,194,035)	(144,716)	(4,338,751)	(400,086)
Principal paid on capital debt	(2,178,491)	(8,895,000)	(11,073,491)	(954,137)
Interest paid on capital debt	(1,479,708)	(1,166,546)	(2,646,254)	41,616
Other receipts (payments)	--	19,174	19,174	131,416
Net cash (used) by capital and related financing activities	(2,164,993)	(1,526,310)	(3,691,303)	(1,264,423)
Cash flows from investing activities				
Proceeds from sales and maturities of investments	454,793	143,747	598,540	15,684
Interest and dividends	454,793	143,747	598,540	129,550
Net cash provided by investing activities	(307,655)	(1,364,645)	(1,672,300)	145,234
Net (decrease) in cash and cash equivalents	8,724,308	3,227,135	11,951,443	(411,138)
Balances—beginning of the year	$ 8,416,653	$ 1,862,490	$10,279,143	3,747,237
Balances—end of the year				$ 3,336,099
Reconciliation of operating income (loss) to net cash provided (used) by operating activities				
Operating income (loss)	$ 4,422,127	$ (238,804)	$ 4,183,323	$ (540,532)
Adjustments to reconcile operating income to net cash provided (used) by operating activities:				
Depreciation expense	1,163,140	542,049	1,705,189	1,707,872
Change in assets and liabilities:				
Receivables, net	653,264	1,205	654,469	31,941
Inventories	2,829		2,829	39,790
Accounts and other payables	(297,446)	(86,643)	(384,089)	475,212
Accrued expenses	(4,251,369)	(11,520)	(4,239,849)	(831,199)
Net cash provided by operating activities	$ 1,692,545	$ 229,327	$ 1,921,872	$ 883,084

SOURCE: GASB 34, pp. 230–231

I. Required Supplementary Information (RSI) other than MD&A

GASB requires four types of information that should be included immediately after the notes to the financial statements. These four items, along with MD & A (see Section C) are considered Required Supplementary Information (RSI). RSI is information presented outside the basic financial statements. While RSI is not covered in the audit opinion, omission of RSI, incomplete RSI, or misleading RSI requires a comment by the auditor. However, an auditor may not modify the report on the basic financial statements as a result of problems discovered related to RSI.

The four types of RSI other than MD&A are (1) two pension schedules, (2) schedules when the government sponsors a public entity risk pool, (3) budgetary comparison schedules, and (4) certain schedules when using the modified approach for reporting infrastructure. The pension schedules include a **Schedule of Funding Progress** and a **Schedule of Employer Contributions**. These statements are required when a government reports a defined benefit pension plan. The Schedule of Funding Progress provides actuarial information regarding the actuarial value of assets, the actuarial accrued liability, and the unfunded actuarial liability, if any. The Schedule of Employer Contributions reflects the amount contributed compared with the amount required to be contributed.

The second type of schedule required when the government is sponsor of a public entity risk pool provides revenue and claims development information.

Sample City
STATEMENT OF FIDUCIARY NET POSITION
FIDUCIARY FUNDS
December 31, 2013

	Employee retirement plan	Private-purpose trusts	Agency funds
Assets			
Cash and cash equivalents	$ 1,973	$ 1,250	$ 44,889
Receivables:			
Interest and dividends	508,475	760	--
Other receivables	6,826	--	183,161
Total receivables	515,301	760	183,161
Investments, at fair value:			
US government obligations	13,056,037	80,000	--
Municipal bonds	6,528,019	--	--
Corporate bonds	16,320,047	--	--
Corporate stocks	26,112,075	--	--
Other investments	3,264,009	--	--
Total investments	65,280,187	80,000	--
Total assets	65,797,461	82,010	$228,050
Liabilities			
Accounts payable	--	1,234	--
Refunds payable and others	1,358	--	228,050
Total liabilities	1,358	1,234	$228,050
Net Position			
Held in trust for pension benefits and other purposes	$65,796,103	$80,776	

SOURCE: GASB 34, page 235.

Sample City
STATEMENT OF CHANGES IN FIDUCIARY NET POSITION
FIDUCIARY FUNDS
For the Year Ended December 31, 2013

	Employee retirement plan	Private-purpose trusts
Additions		
Contributions:		
Employer	$ 2,721,341	$ --
Plan members	1,421,233	--
Total contributions	4,142,574	--
Investment earnings:		
Net (decrease) in fair value of investments	(272,522)	--
Interest	2,460,871	4,560
Dividends	1,445,273	--
Total investment earnings	3,633,622	4,560
Less investment expense	216,428	--
Net investment earnings	3,417,194	4,560
Total additions	7,559,768	4,560

	Employee retirement plan	Private-purpose trusts
Deductions		
Benefits	2,453,047	3,800
Refunds of contributions	464,691	--
Administrative expenses	87,532	678
Total deductions	3,005,270	4,478
Change in net position	4,554,498	82
Net position—beginning of the year	61,241,605	80,694
Net position—end of the year	$65,796,103	$80,776

SOURCE: GASB 34, pages 235-236.

The third type of information is to provide **budgetary comparison schedules** for the general fund and all major special revenue funds for which an annual budget has been legally adopted by the governmental unit. Governments may elect to report the budgetary comparison information in a budgetary comparison statement as part of the basic financial statements, rather than as RSI. If the government has significant budgetary perspective differences that result in it not being able to present budgetary comparison information for its general fund and major special revenue funds, the government must present a budget comparison schedule based on the structure of its legally adopted budget. Budgetary comparison schedules include the original budget, the final appropriated budget, and the actual revenues and expenditures stated on the budgetary basis. A separate variance column to report the differences between the final budget and actual amounts is encouraged but not required. The format may be that of the original budget document or in the format, terminology, and classifications in the Statement of Revenues, Expenditures, and Changes in Fund Balances. Information must be provided, either in this schedule or in notes to the RSI, that reconciles budgetary information basis to GAAP information. An example of a Budget—Actual Statement is included below.

Sample City
STATEMENT OF REVENUES, EXPENDITURES, AND CHANGES IN FUND BALANCES—
BUDGET AND ACTUAL
GENERAL FUND
For the Year Ended December 31, 2013

	Budgeted amounts		Actual amounts
Revenues	Original	Final	(budgetary basis)
Property taxes	$52,017,833	$51,853,018	$51,173,436
Other taxes—franchise and public service	12,841,209	12,836,024	13,025,392
Fees and fines	718,800	718,800	606,946
Licenses and permits	2,126,600	2,126,600	2,287,794
Intergovernmental	6,905,898	6,571,360	6,119,938
Charges for services	12,392,972	11,202,150	11,374,460
Interest	1,501,945	550,000	552,325
Miscellaneous	3,024,292	1,220,991	881,874
Total revenues	91,043,549	87,078,943	86,022,165
Expenditures			
Current			
General government (including contingencies and miscellaneous)	11,837,534	9,468,155	8,621,500
Public safety	33,050,966	33,983,706	33,799,709
Public works	5,215,630	5,025,848	4,993,187
Engineering services	1,296,275	1,296,990	1,296,990
Health and sanitation	5,756,250	6,174,653	6,174,653
Cemetery	724,500	724,500	706,305
Culture and recreation	11,059,140	11,368,070	11,289,146
Education—payment to school district	22,000,000	22,000,000	21,893,273
Total expenditures	90,940,295	90,041,922	88,774,763
Excess (deficiency) of revenues over expenditures	103,254	(2,962,979)	(2,752,598)
Other Financing Sources (Uses)			
Transfers in	939,525	130,000	129,323
Transfers out	(2,970,256)	(2,163,759)	(2,163,759)
Total other financing sources and uses	(2,030,731)	(2,033,759)	(2,034,436)
Special Item			
Proceeds from sale of park land	1,355,250	3,500,000	3,476,488
Net change in fund balance	(572,227)	(1,496,738)	(1,310,546)
Fund balances—beginning	3,528,750	2,742,799	2,742,799
Fund balances—ending	$ 2,956,523	$ 1,246,061	$ 1,432,253

SOURCE: GASB 34, pages 272-273. Budget to GAAP Reconciliation Omitted.

The fourth type of information is presented only when the government is using the **modified approach for reporting infrastructure**. Governments have the option of not depreciating their infrastructure assets if they adopt the "modified" approach for recording infrastructure. Two requirements must be met to adopt this approach. First, the government must manage the eligible infrastructure assets using an asset management system that has certain characteristics. These characteristics include (1) keeping an up-to-date inventory of infrastructure assets, (2) performing condition assessments of eligible infrastructure assets, summarizing the results using a measurement scale, and (3) estimating the costs each year to preserve the infrastructure assets at the condition level established and disclosed by the government. Second, the government must document that the infrastructure assets have been preserved at the condition level prescribed by the government. Two schedules are required: (1) a schedule reflecting the condition of the government's infrastructure, and (2) a comparison of the needed and actual expenditures to maintain the government's infrastructure. Disclosures that should be included in notes to the RSI are (1) the basis of the condition measurement and the measurement scale used to assess and report the condition of the government's infrastructure assets, (2) the condition level at which the government intends to preserve its eligible infrastructure assets reported using the modified approach, and (3) factors that significantly affect trends in the information reported in the required schedules.

An example is provided to illustrate the difference between the "depreciation approach" and the "modified approach" to record infrastructure. Assume a government had $1,000,000 in ordinary maintenance expenses, $2,000,000 in expenditures to extend the life of existing infrastructure, and $3,000,000 in expenditures to add to or improve existing infrastructure. Depreciation (if recorded) amounted to $2,500,000. If the "depreciation approach" were used, $3,500,000 would be charged to expense ($1,000,000 + $2,500,000). If the modified approach were used, the amount charged to expense would be $3,000,000 ($1,000,000 + $2,000,000). In both cases, the $1,000,000 would be charged to expense, and the $3,000,000 would be capitalized. Under the "modified approach," the $2,000,000 in expenditures to extend the life of infrastructure is substituted for depreciation expense.

J. Measurement Focus and Basis of Accounting (MFBA)

GASB Standards require two types of measurement focus: *economic resources measurement focus and current financial resources measurement focus* and two types of basis of accounting: *accrual and modified accrual*. The measurement focus and basis of accounting varies depending upon the financial statement being reported. **The economic resources measurement focus and accrual basis of accounting** is a method similar to accounting for business enterprises. The objective is to measure all of the economic resources available to the governmental entity, including fixed assets and subtracting long-term debt. Full accrual accounting is used, where revenues are recognized when earned and expenses are recognized when incurred. Fixed assets are recorded and depreciated. The economic resources measurement focus and accrual basis of accounting is used for the government-wide statements, the proprietary fund statements, and the fiduciary fund statements.

The objective of the **current financial resources measurement focus and modified accrual basis of accounting** is to measure only the current financial resources available to the governmental entity. As a result governmental funds (i.e., general fund) do not account for fixed assets or long-term debt within the fund. Modified accrual accounting is used by governmental funds. Under modified accrual accounting, revenues are recognized when measurable and available to finance expenditures of the current period. Property taxes may be considered "available" when collected within sixty days of the end of the fiscal year. The recognition of expenditures (not expenses) is modified in the following way. First, expenditures may be recorded for current items (salaries, supplies), capital outlays (purchase of a police car, construction expenditures), or debt service (matured interest, matured principal). Second, payment of principal and interest on long-term indebtedness, including bonds, notes, capital leases, compensated absences, claims and judgments, pensions, special termination benefits, and landfill closure and postclosure care are recorded when due, rather than accrued. However, a government may accrue an additional amount if it has provided financial resources to a debt service fund for payment of liabilities that will mature early in the following period (not more than a month). As noted previously, the current financial resources measurement focus and modified accrual basis of accounting are used in the governmental fund financial statements and will be illustrated later.

NOW REVIEW MULTIPLE-CHOICE QUESTIONS 22 THROUGH 49 IN VOLUME 2

K. Accounting by Governments for Certain Events and Transactions

1. **Accounting for nonexchange transactions.** The previous section indicated that, under the accrual basis of accounting, revenues are recognized when earned. Revenues and inflows of resources include **exchange transactions**, in which goods or services of equal or approximately equal values are exchanged, and **nonexchange transactions.** GASB indicates that revenues from exchange transactions are to be recognized in accordance with generally accepted accounting principles as those principles have evolved over the years and provides no special guidance. However, GASB Statement No. 33, *Accounting and Financial Reporting for Nonexchange Transactions*, defines nonexchange transactions as transactions "in which a government gives (or receives) value without directly receiving (or giving) equal value in exchange." GASB Statement No. 33 is written under the presumption that an entity is following full accrual accounting. When governmental fund financial statements are issued, modified accrual accounting "modifies" the provisions of GASB Statement No. 33 to require that resources must be measurable and available to finance the expenditures of the current period, as described in Section H. above.

GASB Statement No. 33 classifies nonexchange transactions into four categories, and revenue recognition depends upon the category. The categories are: (1) derived tax revenues, (2) imposed nonexchange revenues, (3) government-mandated nonexchange transactions, and (4) voluntary nonexchange transactions. For the government-wide financial statements, revenue from nonexchange transactions is considered to be an increase in unrestricted net position unless the revenue is restricted by the grantor, donor, or legislation. For example, a hotel-motel tax may have to be used, by legislation, for promotion of tourism. Purpose restrictions do not affect the timing of revenue recognition.

In order for a receivable and revenue to be recognized, four types of **eligibility requirements** must be met. First is the **required characteristics of the recipients**. The recipient of resources must have the characteristics required by the provider. For example, the recipient of certain state funds allocated for road repairs may have to be a county government, a municipality, or a township. Second, **time requirements** must be met, if a provider specifies that resources must be expended in a certain future period. For example, if a state indicates that funds are appropriated for water system improvements for the fiscal year ended June 30, 2012, then neither a receivable nor revenue would be recognized by the local governments receiving the funds until that fiscal year. In the absence of specified time requirements, a receivable and revenue would be recognized when a promise is unconditional. Third, certain grants from one government to another cannot be provided until the receiving government has expended the funds. This is a condition the GASB calls a **reimbursement**. Reimbursement grant revenues are recognized only when expenditures are recognized. Finally, resources pledged that have a **contingency** attached are not to be recognized until that contingency is removed.

Derived tax revenues result from taxes assessed by governments on exchange transactions. Examples include sales taxes, income taxes, and motor fuel taxes. Receivables and revenues are to be recognized when the underlying transaction (the sale, the income, etc.) takes place. For example, under accrual accounting, if a state imposed a sales tax of 6%, the state would record a revenue of $6 when a merchant recorded a sale of $100. If resources are received before the underlying transaction takes place, then the asset would be offset by revenues received in advance, a liability.

Imposed nonexchange transactions are taxes and other assessments by governments that are not derived from underlying transactions. Examples include property taxes, special assessments, and fines and forfeits. Assets from imposed nonexchange transactions should be recognized when an enforceable legal claim exists, or when the resources are received, whichever occurs first. In the case of property taxes, this would normally be specified in the enabling legislation, such as the lien or assessment date. Revenues for property taxes should be recognized, net of estimated refunds and estimated uncollectible taxes, in the period for which the taxes are levied, regardless of when the enforcement date or collection date might be. All other imposed nonexchange transactions should be recognized as revenues at the same time as the assets, or as soon as use is first permitted. On the modified accrual basis, property taxes may not be recognized unless collected within sixty days after the end of a fiscal year.

Government-mandated nonexchange transactions exist when the providing government, such as the federal government or a state government, requires the receiving government to expend funds for a specific purpose. For example, a state may require school districts to "mainstream" certain children by including them in regular classes and also to provide additional assistance in the form of extra aides. Funding for this purpose would be considered to be a government-mandated nonexchange transaction. Receiving governments should recognize assets and revenues when all eligibility requirements have been met.

Voluntary nonexchange transactions include grants and entitlements from one government to another where the providing government does not impose specific requirements upon the receiving government. For example, a state provides a grant for new technology for school districts but does not require those school districts to accept the grant or utilize that technology. Even though the use of the grant is restricted, it is a voluntary nonexchange transaction. It also includes voluntary contributions from individuals and other entities to governments. An example of this type of transaction would be the gift of funds from an individual to a school district or a college. Voluntary nonexchange transactions may or may not have purpose restrictions. The recognition of assets and revenues would be when all eligibility requirements have been met, the same as government-mandated nonexchange transactions.

If after a revenue has been recognized by a governmental entity (in a later fiscal year), and those funds must be returned to the provider, then the recipient government must record an expense and liability (or reduction of cash). If there is a difference in the provider government's and recipient government's fiscal year, then the provider's fiscal year would govern for purposes of determining eligibility requirements. If the providing government, a state, has a biennial fiscal year, then half of the grant would be recognized by the recipient government in each of the providing government's two fiscal years.

2. **Accounting for intangible assets.** GASB Statement No. 51, *Accounting and Financial Reporting for Intangible Assets,* allows only **identifiable** intangible assets to be recognized as capital assets in the statement of net position (at historical cost). Costs related to internally generated intangibles (e.g., proprietary software systems) may begin to be capitalized when

   a. The government's specific **objective** for the project and the proposed **service capacity** has been determined,

   b. The **feasibility** of completing the project has been demonstrated, and

   c. The government's **intention** to complete or to continue the development of the asset has been demonstrated.

Intangible assets should be amortized over their useful lives. An intangible asset that has no legal, contractual, regulatory, technological, or other factors limiting its useful life should be considered to have an indefinite useful life and should not be amortized unless its useful life is later determined to be no longer indefinite.

3. **Sales and pledges of receivables and future revenues.** In some situations a state or local government may decide to sell receivables or future revenues (e.g., future tobacco settlement receipts, or delinquent tax receivables). GASB Statement No. 48, *Sales and Pledges of Receivables and Future Revenues and Intraentity Transfers of Assets and Future Revenues,* provides guidance for accounting for such transactions. Specifically, this statement provides criteria for determining when the assets have been sold and should be removed from the government's financial statements as opposed to treating the transaction as a collateralized loan.

GASB Statement No. 48 establishes that a transaction is a collateralized borrowing unless the government both transfers the receivables or future revenues and has no continued involvement with them. Circumstances that would indicate continued involvement and prevent accounting for the transaction as a sale include

- The government or the buyer can cancel the sale.
- The government can limit the buyer's ability to subsequently sell or pledge the receivables or future revenue.
- The government has access to the receivables, future revenues, or the cash collected from them.
- The government can substitute for or reacquire specific receivables without the buyer's consent.
- The government is actively involved in the future generation of sold revenues (e.g., the revenues are the product of goods or services provided by the government).

Receivables that meet the requirements for sale should be removed from the assets of the selling government's financial statements. The difference between the carrying value of the receivables and the funds received is reported as a gain or loss on accrual-basis financial statements or as revenue in modified-accrual-basis financial statements. In a sale of future revenue, the government reports the proceeds as a deferred inflow and recognizes the revenue over the life of the sales agreement.

If the transaction does not meet the requirements of a sale, it is accounted for as a collateralized loan. The proceeds represent a liability that is repaid as the receivables or revenues are collected.

4. **Accounting for derivative instruments.** GASB Statement No. 53, *Accounting and Financial Reporting for Derivative Instruments*, specifies the appropriate accounting for derivative instruments. State and local governments use derivative instruments to make investments or manage (hedge) specific risks. The rules for accounting for these instruments are similar to those for other entities under SFAS 133. Derivative instruments derive value as a financial instrument from something outside the instrument itself.

Under GASB Statement No. 53, derivative instruments are reported on the statement of net position at their fair value (except for certain Synthetic Guaranteed Investment Contracts). If the derivative is an investment or an ineffective hedge, changes in fair value should be reported as investment revenue in the flow of resources statement. Changes in the values of hedging derivatives are reported as deferred inflows or deferred outflows in the statement of net position. In proprietary or fiduciary fund-based financial statements, the fund that reports or expects to report the hedged item should report the hedging derivative instrument.

A derivative is evaluated for effectiveness as a hedge when it is acquired and reevaluated at the end of each subsequent financial reporting period. Methods used to evaluate the effectiveness include

1. Consistent critical terms method—evaluates the hedge by qualitatively evaluating the terms of the hedgeable item and the potential hedging derivative instrument. If the critical terms between the hedgeable item and the derivative instrument are the same or similar, the instrument is considered to be an effective hedge.

2. Quantitative methods

   a. Synthetic instrument method—combines the cash flow effects of the hedgeable item with the potential hedging derivative instrument to see if they offset.

   b. Dollar-offset method—compares changes in the fair value (or expected cash flows) of the hedgeable item with the potential hedging derivative.

   c. Regression analysis method—evaluates effectiveness by examining the statistical relationship between the hedgeable item and the potential hedging derivative instrument.

If in a subsequent period the derivative is determined to be no longer effective, it is terminated as a hedge and the balance in the deferral account should be reported in the flow of resources statement within the investment revenue classification. GASB No. 64 amends GASB No. 53 to clarify whether an effective hedge of a financial instrument can be maintained after the replacement of the swap counterparty or the swap counterparty's credit support provider. GASB No. 64 indicates that a hedging relationship is maintained and hedge accounting should continue if there are no changes in terms or risk of the instrument other than a replacement of the counterparty or the counterparty's credit support provider.

5. **Accounting for pollution remediation obligations.** GASB Statement No. 49, *Accounting and Financial Reporting for Pollution Remediation Obligations,* establishes rules for accounting for estimated obligations for pollution remediation. A government must estimate its expected outlays for pollution remediation if it knows a site is polluted and any of the following recognition triggers occur:

- Pollution poses an imminent danger to the public or environment and the government has little or no discretion to avoid fixing the problem.
- The government has violated a pollution prevention-related permit or license.
- A regulator (e.g., the EPA) has identified the government as responsible or potentially responsible for cleaning up pollution or paying some of the cost of the cleanup.
- The government is named in a lawsuit to compel it to address the pollution.
- The government begins or legally obligates itself to begin cleanup or post-cleanup activities.

Liabilities and expenses are estimated using an "expected cash flows" measurement technique.

6. **Service concession arrangements.** A service concession arrangement is an agreement between a government unit and an operator in which

a. The government unit conveys to the operator the right and obligation to provide public services through the operation of a facility (capital asset) in exchange for consideration;
b. The operator collects and is compensated by fees from third parties;
c. The government unit has the ability to modify or approve the services to be provided, to whom the operator is required to provide the services, and the price of the services; and
d. The government unit is entitled to significant residual interest in the facility at the end of the arrangement.

Common examples of service concession arrangements include

1. Arrangements in which an operator agrees to design and build or improve a facility and collect fees from third parties (e.g., construct a municipal complex or a tollway).
2. Arrangements in which an operator will pay the government unit for the right to operate a government facility (e.g., a parking structure) and collect fees from third party for its use.

If the facility associated with the arrangement is an existing facility, the government unit should continue to report the facility as a capital asset. If the facility is purchased, constructed or improved by the operator, the government unit should record (a) the new facility (capital asset) at its fair value when it is placed in operation, (b) any related contractual obligations as liabilities, and (c) a corresponding deferred inflow of resources equal to the difference. A contractual obligation is one that is significant and related to the facility (e.g., an obligation by the government unit to provide insurance for the facility). These obligations should be measured at their present values.

EXAMPLE

A state government through its Department of Transportation (DOT) enters into an agreement with the Local Tunnel Authority (LTA), a governmental operator, in which LTA agrees to design, build and operate a tunnel for 40 years. In exchange for building the tunnel, the LTA is entitled to collect and retain tolls generated by the tunnel for the term of the agreement. The cost of the tunnel is $1 billion. The fair value of the tunnel when it is placed in operation is $1.5 billion. When the tunnel is placed in operation, the state government would record the asset at its $1.5 billion fair value, and record $1.5 billion in deferred (revenue) inflow of resources.

In future years, the state government would apply existing capital asset guidance, including depreciation, if applicable, to the tunnel. If the state elects to use the straight-line method of amortization of revenue, it would recognize $37,500,000 ($1.5 billion ÷ 40 years) in revenue for the next 40 years and reduce the deferred inflow by the same amount.

In the Notes to the financial statements, the government should disclose

1. A general description of the arrangement, including the government's objectives for entering into the arrangement.
2. Nature of amounts of assets, liabilities, and deferred outflows and inflows of resources related to the agreement.
3. Nature and extent of rights retained by the government.
4. The details of any related guarantees and commitments.

7. **Related-party transactions.** State and local governments must disclose certain related-party transactions. In addition, if the substance of a particular transaction is significantly different from its form because of the involve-

ment of related parties, financial statements should recognize the substance of the transaction rather than merely its legal form.

8. **Subsequent events.** The requirements regarding the effect of subsequent events on financial statements are similar to those for commercial businesses under GAAP. If the event provides additional evidence about conditions that existed at the date of the statement of net position and affect the estimates in the financial statements, the effect of the event should be recognized in the financial statements. If the event provides evidence about conditions that did not exist at the date of the statement of net position but arose subsequent to that date, the event should be disclosed in the notes to the financial statements.

9. **Going concern considerations.** The guidance regarding going concern for state and local governments is similar to that for commercial business under GAAP. The financial reporting model assumes that the entity will be a going concern for a reasonable period of time (i.e., 12 months from the financial statement date). Indicators that there may be substantial doubt about the entity's ability to continue as a going concern include

   a. Negative trends (e.g., recurring losses).
   b. Other indicators of financial difficulties (e.g., defaults on loan agreements).
   c. Internal matters (e.g., work stoppages).
   d. External matters (e.g., legal proceedings).

   If it is determined that there is substantial doubt about a governmental entity's ability to continue as a going concern for a reasonable period of time, the notes to the financial statements should disclose details of the sources of the concerns and the government official's plan for dealing with those concerns.

   GASB Statement No. 58, *Accounting and Financial Reporting for Chapter 9 Bankruptcies,* provides accounting and financial reporting guidance when a governmental unit has been granted relief under the provisions of Chapter 9 of the US Bankruptcy Code. The standard provides that assets and liabilities should be remeasured in accordance with the court's Plan of Adjustment. In addition, the statement requires disclosure of the details of the bankruptcy and how users can obtain a copy of the Plan of Adjustment.

10. **Financial Instruments Reporting Changes.** In June 2010 the GASB issued Statement No. 59, *Financial Instruments Omnibus,* which updated and improved existing standards regarding reporting and disclosure requirements of certain financial instruments and external investment pools. The specific issues related to financial instruments addressed by GASB Statement No. 59 include

    a. Amended NCGA Statement 4 to be consistent with GASB Statement No. 53 regarding the guarantees of the indebtedness of others.
    b. Amended GASB Statements Nos. 25 and 43 to be consistent with the provisions of GASB Statement No. 31. The amendment removed the fair value exemption for unallocated insurance contracts. The effect is to report investments in unallocated insurance contracts as interest-earning investment contracts.
    c. Clarified GASB Statement No. 31 by indicating the 2a7-like investment pool is an external investment pool that operates in conformity with Security and Exchange (SEC) Rule 2a7 as promulgated under the Investment Company Act of 1940.
    d. Amended GASB Statement No. 40 to indicate that interest-rate risk information should be disclosed only for debt investment pools that do not meet the requirements to be reported as a 2a7-like pool.
    e. Amended GASB Statement No. 53 as follows:

       (1) A penalty payment for nonperformance that is dependent on the failure of the counterparty to comply with the terms of construction or purchase contract does not meet the net settlement characteristic included in the definition of a derivative instrument.
       (2) To be included with the scope of GASB Statement No. 53 a financial guarantee contract must meet the definitions of a derivative instrument and be entered into primarily for the purpose of obtaining income or profit.
       (3) The scope of GASB Statement No. 53 excludes contracts that are not exchange-traded and have reference rates based on specific volumes of sales or service revenue of one of the parties to the contract.
       (4) Provides that a hybrid instrument should be reported according to GASB Statement No. 53 if the investor's initial rate of return on the companion instrument has the potential for at least a doubled yield.

NOW REVIEW MULTIPLE-CHOICE QUESTIONS 50 THROUGH 64 IN VOLUME 2

L. Budgetary Accounting for the General and Special Revenue Funds

The GASB, in one of its basic principles, states

1. An annual budget(s) should be adopted by every governmental unit.
2. The accounting system should provide the basis for appropriate budgetary control.
3. A common terminology and classification should be used consistently throughout the budget, the accounts, and the financial reports of each fund.

In accordance with the principle above, budgets should be prepared for each of the fund types used by governmental units. This directive, by itself, does not differentiate governmental from commercial enterprises. What is different, however, is the inclusion of budgetary accounts in the formal accounting system for the general and major special revenue funds. Inclusion of the budgetary accounts facilitates a budget-actual comparison in Required Supplementary Information (RSI) or as a basic financial statement. The budget-actual comparison is required for the general fund and all major special revenue funds that have a legally adopted annual budget. Budgetary accounts are generally used in those funds for which the budget-actual comparison is made. *As a result, CPA examination questions always assume budgetary accounts for the general fund and sometimes, but not always, assume budgetary accounts for special revenue funds.*

Budgetary accounts (Estimated Revenues, Appropriations, Estimated Other Financing Sources, Estimated Other Financing Uses, and Budgetary Fund Balance) are incorporated into governmental accounting systems to provide legislative control over revenues and other resource inflows and expenditures and other resource outflows. Recording the budget also provides an assessment of management's stewardship by facilitating a comparison of budget vs. actual. The journal entries that follow illustrate the budgetary accounts used by the general and special revenue funds.

Upon adoption of the estimated revenues and appropriations included in the legally adopted budget (at the beginning of the period), the following entry is made and posted to the general ledger:

Estimated Revenues[2] (individual items are posted to subsidiary ledger)	1,000,000 (anticipated resources/revenues)	
Appropriations (individual items are posted to subsidiary ledger)		980,000 (anticipated expenditures/liabilities)
Budgetary Fund Balance		20,000 (a surplus is anticipated since estimated revenues are more the appropriations)

Estimated Revenues, Appropriations, and Budgetary Fund Balance are budgetary accounts. This budgetary entry is reversed at year-end during the closing process.

As actual resource inflows and outflows occur during the year, they are recorded in Revenues and Expenditures accounts, and the detail is posted to the revenues and expenditures subsidiary ledgers to facilitate budget vs. actual comparisons. To prevent the overspending of appropriations (which is the legal authority to spend resources) an additional budgetary account is maintained during the year. This budgetary account is called Encumbrances. When goods or services are ordered, encumbrances are recorded so that appropriations are not overspent. The following entry is used to record encumbrances:

Encumbrances (detail posted to subsidiary ledger)	5,000 (cost estimate)	
Reserved for Encumbrances		5,000 (cost estimate)

The Reserved for Encumbrances is a fund equity account that is used to segregate the amount of encumbrances outstanding. When the debit in the entry is posted, the amount that can still be obligated or expended for an individual budget line item is reduced. Thereafter, when the goods or services ordered are received, the encumbrance entry is reversed and the actual resource outflow (expenditures) is recorded.

Reserved for Encumbrances	5,000	
Encumbrances (detail posted to subsidiary ledger)		5,000
Expenditures (detail posted to subsidiary ledger)	5,200 (actual cost)	
Vouchers Payable		5,200 (actual cost)

The encumbrances account does not represent an expenditure; it is a budgetary account which represents the estimated cost of goods or services which have yet to be received. In effect, the recording of encumbrances represents the recording of executory contracts, which is essential to prevent overspending of an appropriation, which is the legal authority to spend resources). As noted above, the account reserved for encumbrances is a fund equity account, not a liability account. If encumbrances are outstanding at the end of a period, the encumbrances account is closed to the fund balance, and the reserved for encumbrances account is reported in the fund balance section of the balance sheet based on GASB Statement No. 54 fund balance classifications.

At the end of the year, the following closing entries would be recorded, assuming actual revenues for the year totaled $1,005,000, actual expenditures for the year were $950,000, and encumbrances outstanding at year-end were $10,000:

1.	Budgetary Fund Balance	20,000	
	Appropriations	980,000	
	Estimated Revenues		1,000,000

---

[2] Appropriations, estimated revenues, encumbrances, revenues, expenditures, estimated other financing sources, estimated other financing uses, other financing sources, and other financing uses are **"Control"** accounts which require detail be posted to a subsidiary ledger.

2.　Revenues　　　　　　　　　　　　　　　　　　　　　1,005,000
　　　　Expenditures　　　　　　　　　　　　　　　　　　　　　　　　950,000
　　　　Encumbrances　　　　　　　　　　　　　　　　　　　　　　　　10,000
　　　　Fund Balance—Unreserved　　　　　　　　　　　　　　　　　　45,000

> *If Expenditures and Encumbrances had exceeded Revenues, Fund Balance—Unreserved, an equity account, would have been debited in this closing entry.*

It is important to remember that Fund Balance—Unreserved and Reserved for Encumbrances are balance sheet equity accounts.

M. Expenditure Classification for Governmental Funds

Expenditure classification. The GASB *Codification* includes guidelines for the classification of governmental fund expenditure data as set forth in GASB Statement No. 1. Both internal and external management control benefit from multiple classification of expenditures. In addition, multiple classifications prove important from an accountability standpoint. This classification system provides assistance in aggregating data and performing data analysis. Internal evaluations, external reporting, and intergovernmental comparisons can be enhanced by this multiple classification system. The following chart describes each expenditure classification with examples.

Classification	Description	Examples
Function (or program)	• Provides information on the overall purposes or objectives of expenditures • Represents a major service or area of responsibility	Highways and streets Health and welfare Education General government Public safety
Organization unit (department)	• Grouped according to the government's organizational structure • The responsibility for a department is fixed	Police department Fire department Parks and recreational department Personnel department City clerk
Activity	• Specific and distinguishable line of work performed by an organizational unit as part of one of its functions or programs • More meaningful if the performance of each activity is fixed	Police protection function Subactivities: 　Police administration 　Crime control and investigation 　Traffic control 　Police training 　Support services
Character	• Classifies expenditures by the fiscal period benefited	Current expenditures Capital outlays Debt service
Object	• Classified according to the types of items purchased or services obtained	Personal services Supplies Rent Utilities Buildings

The Statement of Revenues, Expenditures, and Changes in Fund Balances (earlier in this module) generally reports expenditures by function within character classifications. Budgets often report expenditures by object class at the departmental level.

N. Accounting for the General Fund

The general fund is the most significant governmental fund. It accounts for all transactions not accounted for in any other fund. Revenues come from many sources (taxes, licenses and permits, fines and forfeits, charges for services, etc.), and the expenditures cover the major functions of government (public safety, health and welfare, highways and streets, education, etc.). The illustration below presents an overview of the general fund account structure.

GENERAL FUND ACCOUNT STRUCTURE

Real Accounts
Current Assets (DR)
Current Liabilities (CR)
Fund Balance (Fund Equity) (CR) (See note 1 below)
　　Reserved (Encumbrances, Inventories, etc.)
　　Unreserved

Nominal Accounts
Revenues (Control Account) (CR) (See note 2 below)
Other Financing Sources (Control Account) (CR)
　　(Transfers In)
　　(Bond Issue Proceeds)
　　(Sale of Capital Assets)

Budgetary Accounts
Estimated Revenues (Control Account) (DR)
Estimated Other Financing
　　Sources (Control Account) (DR)

Expenditures (Control Account) (DR)	Appropriations (Control Account) (CR)	
	Encumbrances (Control Account) (DR)	
Other Financing Uses (Control Account) (DR)	Estimated Other Financing	
(Transfers Out)	Uses (Control Account) (CR)	
	Budgetary Fund Balance (DR) (CR)	

Note 1: For accounting purposes two fund balance classifications (reserved and unreserved) are used. However, for financial reporting under GASB Statement No. 54, five fund balance classifications (nonspendable, restricted, committed, assigned, and unassigned) are used.

Note 2: Remember that whenever a journal entry is made to a "control account" the detail needs to be posted to the subsidiary ledger.

The following represents an accounting cycle problem for the general fund. Some of these entries have been illustrated previously.

a. Adoption of a budget where estimated revenues exceed appropriations and estimated other financing uses (planned transfer out to another fund) by $10,000. (Assume it is the first year of existence for this governmental unit.)

Estimated Revenues (detail posted to subsidiary ledger)	300,000	
Appropriations (detail posted to subsidiary ledger)		240,000
Estimated Other Financing Uses		50,000
Budgetary Fund Balance		10,000

b. Transfers to a debt service fund (for general long-term debt payments) amount to $50,000.

Other Financing Uses—Transfers Out	50,000	
Due to Debt Service Fund		50,000

According to the GASB, transfers should be recognized in the accounting period in which the interfund receivable and payable arises. The account "Other Financing Uses—Transfers Out" is a temporary/nominal account that is compared with the budgetary account "Estimated Other Financing Uses." The account "Due to other funds (or Due to X fund)" is a current liability. Note that the debt service fund would record a receivable as follows:

Debt Service

Due from General Fund	50,000	
Other Financing Sources—Transfers In		50,000

The account "Due from other funds (or Due from X fund)" is a current asset account. The "Transfers" accounts are closed at the end of the year. It is important to note that the account "Transfers Out" is not an expenditure account, but is an Other Financing Use, and that the account "Transfers In" is not a revenue account, but is an Other Financing Source. (See the combined statement of revenues, expenditures, and changes in fund balance shown previously.) There is a complete discussion of interfund transactions and transfers later in this module (Section T).

c. The property tax levy is recorded as revenues, under the modified accrual basis, in the year for which the tax levy is enacted by the governmental unit, if collections will be in time to finance expenditures of the current period. The tax bills amount to $250,000, and $20,000 is estimated to be uncollectible.

Property Taxes Receivable—Current	250,000	
Allowance for Uncollectible Taxes—Current		20,000
Revenues		230,000

Under the modified accrual basis, revenues should be recorded in the period in which they are both measurable and available. The GASB requires that property taxes be recognized as a revenue if the taxes are

1. Available—collected by year-end or soon enough to pay liabilities of the current period (no more than sixty days after the end of the fiscal year)
2. To finance the budget of the current period

To the extent the modified accrual criteria for recognition are not met, the property tax levy would be recorded with a credit to Deferred Inflow of Resources Property Taxes, a liability, instead of Revenues.

If cash is needed to pay for expenditures before the property tax receivables are collected, it is not uncommon for governmental units to borrow on tax anticipation notes. The property taxes receivable serves as security for this loan and, as taxes are collected, the liability is paid (i.e., Tax Anticipation Notes Payable is debited).

The treatment of the allowance for uncollectible accounts should be noted. Expendable funds account for resource inflows (revenues) and resource outflows (expenditures). Expenses are not recorded. The Allowance for Uncollectible Accounts (contra asset account) represents an estimated reduction in a resource inflow and, accordingly, revenues are recorded net of estimated uncollectible taxes.

d. Revenues from fines, licenses, and permits amount to $40,000.

Cash	40,000	
Revenues (detail posted)		40,000

Resource inflows from fines, licenses, permits, etc. are usually not measurable until the cash is collected. Sometimes, it is possible to measure the potential resource inflow; however, because the availability is questionable, revenues are recorded when cash is collected.

e. The state owes the city $25,000 for the city's share of the state sales tax. The amount has not been received at year-end, but it is expected within the first few months of the next fiscal year (in time to pay the liabilities as of the current fiscal year).

State Sales Tax Receivable	25,000	
Revenues (detail posted)		25,000

Sales taxes, income taxes, etc. may be accrued before collection by a governmental unit, if collection is anticipated in time to pay for current year expenditures. Other firm commitments from the state or other governmental units for grants, etc. are also recorded.

f. Incurred liabilities for salaries, repairs, utilities, rent, and other regularly occurring items for $200,000.

Expenditures (detail posted)	200,000	
Vouchers Payable		200,000

Note that all resource outflows which are legally authorized appropriations are debited to Expenditures. It makes no difference whether the outflow is for a fire truck or for rent. Remember, expendable funds do not have a capital maintenance objective. Also, note that the encumbrance accounts were not used in this example. There is usually no need to encumber appropriations for items that occur regularly, and which possess a highly predictable amount (e.g., salaries, rent, etc.). It should be pointed out, however, that there is no hard and fast rule for when to use encumbrances, and encumbrance policies do vary tremendously (i.e., from every expenditure being encumbered to virtually no expenditures being encumbered).

g. Ordered one police car; estimated cost is $17,000. One month later, ordered second police car; estimated cost is $16,500.

Encumbrances	17,000	
Reserved for Encumbrances		17,000
Encumbrances	16,500	
Reserved for Encumbrances		16,500

Recording encumbrances prevents overspending line-item appropriations. In the case of the police cars, assume that appropriations were authorized in the amount of $34,000 for police vehicles. After the first police car was ordered, the unencumbered appropriation for police vehicles was reduced to $17,000. This placed a dollar limit on what could be spent on the second car.

h. Police car ordered first was received; actual cost is $16,800. Note that the encumbrance is reversed in the first journal entry in the amount of $17,000 which is the estimated cost of the police car. In the second entry the expenditures account is debited for the actual cost of the police car.

Reserved for Encumbrances	17,000	
Encumbrances		17,000
Expenditures	16,800	
Vouchers Payable		16,800

i. Property tax collections amounted to $233,000, payments to other funds amounted to $50,000 (see item b.), and payments of vouchers were $190,000.

Cash	233,000	
Property Taxes Receivable—Current		233,000
Due to Debt Service Fund	50,000	
Cash		50,000
Vouchers Payable	190,000	
Cash		190,000
Allowance for Uncollectible Taxes—Current	3,000	
Revenues		3,000

The last entry above is made because the Allowance for Uncollectible Taxes—Current was overstated. Note that the estimate was $20,000 in entry c. above. Tax revenues were estimated to be $230,000. Since property tax collections exceeded $230,000 for the current year, an increase in revenues is recorded.

j. Recorded $5,000 inventory of materials and supplies, reduced the allowance for uncollectible property taxes to $10,000, and reclassified uncollected property taxes to delinquent accounts.

Materials and Supplies Inventory[3]	5,000	
Reserved for Inventory of Materials and Supplies		5,000
Allowance for Uncollectible Taxes—Current	7,000	
Revenues		7,000
Property Taxes Receivable—Delinquent	17,000	
Allowance for Uncollectible Taxes—Current	10,000	
Allowance for Uncollectible Taxes—Delinquent		10,000
Property Taxes Receivable—Current		17,000

One of the reasons for recording the inventory of materials and supplies is to inform the preparers of the budget that items purchased during the year and charged to expenditures (item f.) are still unused. The account "Reserved for Inventory of Materials and Supplies" is a reservation of Fund Balance. In this respect, it is similar to "Reserved for Encumbrances."

The second entry adjusts the estimate of uncollectible property taxes to $10,000. This is the result of collecting more property taxes than anticipated (see entries made in c. and i. above) and of an estimate that $7,000 will now be collected.

The third entry reclassifies property taxes receivable from current to delinquent at the end of the year. Generally, interest and penalty charges accrue on the unpaid taxes from the date they become delinquent. If these items have accrued at the end of a fiscal period, they would be recorded in the following way:

Interest and Penalties Receivable on Delinquent Taxes	xx	
Allowance for Uncollectible Interest and Penalties		xx
Revenues		xx

k. Appropriate closing entries are made.

Budgetary Fund Balance	10,000	
Appropriations	240,000	
Estimated Other Financing Uses	50,000	
Estimated Revenues		300,000

The above entry reverses the entry to record the budget.

Revenues	305,000	
Expenditures		216,800
Encumbrances		16,500
Other Financing Uses—Transfers Out		50,000
Fund Balance—Unreserved		21,700

The above entry indicates that the unreserved fund balance increased by $21,700 since actual revenues exceeded expenditures, encumbrances and other financing uses.

Financial statements. Under the GASB *Codification*, individual fund statements should not be prepared that simply repeat information found in the basic or combining statements but may be prepared to present individual fund budgetary comparisons (not needed for the general or major special revenue funds), to present prior year comparative data, or to present more detailed information than is found in the basic or combining statements.

The balance sheet below would represent the general fund portion of the governmental funds balance sheet. Note the following points from the balance sheet:

1. The total fund balance (equity) is $43,200, but only $21,700 is unreserved. This $21,700 represents the appropriable component of total fund balance (i.e., the amount that can be used next period to help finance a deficit budget). The $21,700 represents unreserved net liquid resources.
2. The reason for crediting "Reserved for Inventory of Materials and Supplies" in item j. previously should now be more meaningful. The inventory of materials and supplies is not a liquid resource that can be used to finance future expenditures. Consequently, if this asset is disclosed, it must be disclosed via a fund restriction.
3. The "Reserved for Encumbrances" which is disclosed on the balance sheet relates to the second police car that was ordered but not delivered at year-end. When the car is received in the next period, the following journal entries could be made, assuming the actual cost is $16,600. It should be noted that the first journal entry reverses the encumbrances which were closed at the end of the prior year. Also note the $100 difference between the estimated cost ($16,500) and the actual cost ($16,600) of the police car is charged to current year expenditures.

Encumbrances—Prior Year	16,500	
Fund Balance—Unreserved		16,500

---

[3] The illustration covers the "purchases method" for materials and supplies. The "consumption method" is not covered in this illustration. Consult an advanced or governmental textbook for coverage of the "consumption method."

Reserved for Encumbrances	16,500	
Encumbrances—Prior Year		16,500
Expenditures—Prior Year	16,500	
Expenditure	100	
Vouchers Payable		16,600

The police car would not be recorded in the general fund as a fixed asset; rather it would be displayed as a fixed asset in the government-wide Statement of Net Position.

City of X
GENERAL FUND
BALANCE SHEET
At June 30, 2013

Assets			*Liabilities and Fund Equity*		
Cash		$33,000	*Liabilities:*		
Property Taxes Receivable—			Accounts Payable		$26,800
Delinquent	$17,000				
Less: Allowance for Uncollectible			*Fund Equity:* (See note below)		
Taxes—Delinquent	10,000	7,000	Reserved for Inventory of Materials		
State Sales Tax Receivable		25,000	and Supplies	$ 5,000	
Inventory of Materials and Supplies		5,000	Reserved for Encumbrances	16,500	
			Unreserved Fund Balance	21,700	
			Total Fund Equity		$43,200
Total Assets		$70,000	Total Liabilities and Fund Equity		$70,000

NOTE: For financial reporting purposes, GASB Statement No. 54 would require the reserve for inventory of material and supplies to be reported as nonspendable fund balance, the reserve for encumbrance would be included in the assigned fund balance classification, unless it was restricted or committed, and the unreserved fund balance would most likely be reported as unassigned fund balance.

The following would be the general fund portion of the Budgetary Comparison Schedule:

City of X
BUDGETARY COMPARISON SCHEDULE
GENERAL FUND
For the Year Ended June 30, 2013

	Budgeted amounts		Actual amounts	Variances with final budget
	Original	Final	(Budgetary basis)	positive (negative)
Budgetary Fund Balance, July 1, 2012	--	--	--	--
Resources (Inflows)	$300,000	$300,000	$305,000	$ 5,000
Amounts Available for Appropriation	300,000	300,000	305,000	5,000
Charges to Appropriations (Outflows)	240,000	240,000	233,300	6,700
Transfers to Other Funds	50,000	50,000	50,000	--
Total Charges to Appropriations	290,000	290,000	283,300	6,700
Budgetary Fund Balance, June 30, 2013	$ 10,000	$ 10,000	$ 21,700	$11,700

The Budgetary Comparison Schedule is included in Required Supplementary Information (RSI), presented after the notes to the basic statements. The format may be in accord with the budget or in accord with the Statement of Revenues, Expenditures, and Changes in Fund Balances (earlier in this module). The Budgetary Fund Balance may or may not be the same as the Unreserved Fund Balance reported in the Balance Sheet for the General Fund. (In this example, it is the same.)

One additional point needs to be covered before going to special revenue funds; that is, how to account for the inventory of materials and supplies in the second or any subsequent year. Accordingly, assume that at the end of the second year, $4,000 of materials and supplies were unused. The adjusting entry would appear as follows:

Reserved for Inventory of Materials and Supplies	1,000	
Materials and Supplies Inventory		1,000

This entry, when posted, will result in a balance of $4,000 in the inventory and reserve accounts. Note the entry at the end of the first year established a $5,000 balance in these accounts. Thereafter, the inventory and reserve accounts are adjusted upward or downward to whatever the balance is at the end of the year.[4]

---

[4] Again, this entry illustrates the "purchases method" of accounting for inventories. Consult a governmental or advanced textbook for illustration of the "consumption method."

O. Accounting for Special Revenue Funds

Special revenue funds account for and report the proceeds of specific revenue sources that are restricted or committed to expenditure for specified purposes other than debt service or capital projects. The specific revenue is then used to finance various authorized expenditures. For example, a city might place its share of the state's gasoline tax revenues into a State Gasoline Tax Fund, which could then be used to maintain streets.

> **NOTE:** A governmental unit has some discretion in terms of how many special revenue funds it creates. Sometimes separate funds are required by law or grant requirements. Many federal and state grants are reported in special revenue funds.

The accounting for special revenue funds parallels that of the general fund. One type of transaction that often takes place in a special revenue fund is a "reimbursement" grant from a federal or state government. **GASB Statement No. 33** lists reimbursement grant requirements as one of the conditions that must be satisfied before a revenue can be recognized, either for accrual or modified accrual accounting. With a reimbursement grant, the granting government will not provide resources unless the receiving government provides evidence that an appropriate expenditure has taken place; **GASB Statement No. 33** requires that the expenditure must be recognized prior to the revenue being recognized.

For example, assume a government with a calendar fiscal year receives a grant award on November 1, 2012, in the amount of $30,000. No entry would be recorded (either a receivable or revenue) until the expenditure takes place. Assume the expenditure takes place on March 1, 2013. The entries would be

Expenditures	30,000	
Cash		30,000
Grants Receivable	30,000	
Revenues—Grants		30,000

Assume cash is received on April 1, 2013; the entry would be

Cash	30,000	
Grants Receivable		30,000

The budgetary comparison schedule in RSI must include "major" special revenue funds for which annual budgets have been legally adopted.

P. Accounting for Capital Projects Funds

Capital projects funds account for and report financial resources that are restricted, committed, or assigned to expenditure for capital outlay, including the acquisition and construction of capital facilities and other capital assets. Capital projects funds exclude capital-related outflows which are financed by proprietary or fiduciary funds. Resources for construction or purchase of capital assets normally come from the issuance of general long-term debt, from government grants (federal, state, and local), and from interfund transfers.

Project budgets for estimated resources and expenditures must be approved before the project can begin. However, unlike the budgets of general and special revenue funds, an annual budget for capital projects funds may not be legally adopted and need not be recorded formally in the accounts.

The following transactions illustrate the entries encountered in a capital projects fund:

a. City Council approved the construction of a new city hall at an estimated cost of $10,000,000. General obligation long-term serial bonds were authorized for issuance in the face amount of $10,000,000. **(No formal entries are required for approval of capital projects.)**

b. $10,000,000 in 8% general obligation serial bonds were issued for $10,100,000. Assume that the premium is transferred to a debt service fund for the eventual payment of the debt. (Premiums and discounts in governmental funds are not amortized in the fund financial statements.)

Cash	10,100,000	
Other Financing Sources—Proceeds of Bonds		10,100,000
Other Financing Uses—Transfers Out	100,000	
Cash		100,000

Note the credit to Proceeds of Bonds. This is an Other Financing Source on the operating statement, whereas the Transfers Out is an Other Financing Use. Both accounts are temporary accounts that are closed to Unreserved Fund Balance at year-end.

The transfer requires an entry in the debt service fund.

Debt Service Fund

Cash	100,000	
Other Financing Sources—Transfer In		100,000

This entry will be explained in more detail later.

c. The bond issue proceeds are temporarily invested in a Certificate of Deposit (CD) and earn $50,000. The earnings are authorized to be sent to the debt service fund for the payment of bonds.

Capital Projects Fund

Investment in CD	10,000,000	
Cash		10,000,000
Cash	50,000	
Revenues—Interest		50,000

Debt Service Fund

Cash	50,000	
Other financing sources—		
Transfers in		50,000

Capital Projects Fund side:

Other financing uses—		
Transfers out	50,000	
Cash		50,000

d. The lowest bid, $9,800,000, is accepted from a general contractor.

Encumbrances	9,800,000	
Reserved for Encumbrances[5]		9,800,000

e. $2,000,000 of the temporary investments are liquidated.

Cash	2,000,000	
Investment in CD		2,000,000

f. Progress billings due to the general contractor for work performed amount to $2,000,000. The contract allows 10% of the billings to be retained until final inspection and approval of the building. The contractor was paid $1,800,000.

Reserved for Encumbrances	2,000,000	
Encumbrances		2,000,000
Expenditures—Construction	2,000,000	
Contracts Payable		2,000,000
Contracts Payable	2,000,000	
Cash		1,800,000
Contracts Payable—Retained Percentage		200,000

The account "Contracts Payable—Retained Percentage" is a liability account. Note, also, that the fixed asset is not recorded in the capital projects fund because the capital projects fund is a governmental fund and governmental funds are expendable and do not have a capital maintenance objective.

g. Interest accrued on a CD at the end of the year amounted to $40,000. This was authorized to be sent to the debt service fund for the payment of debt.

Capital Projects Fund

Interest Receivable	40,000	
Revenues—Interest		40,000

Debt Service Fund

Due from Other Funds	40,000	
Other Financing Sources—		
Transfers In		40,000

Capital Projects Fund side:

Other Financing Uses—		
Transfers Out	40,000	
Due to Other Funds		40,000

The interest is recognized because it is measurable and will soon be available to finance debt service fund expenditures.

h. Closing entries for the capital projects fund would appear as follows:

(1)

Revenues—Interest	90,000	
Other Financing Sources—Proceeds of Bonds	10,100,000	
Fund Balance—Unreserved		10,190,000

(2)

Fund Balance—Unreserved	9,800,000	
Encumbrances		7,800,000
Expenditures—Construction		2,000,000

(3)

Fund Balance—Unreserved	190,000	
Other Financing Uses—Transfers Out		190,000

The GASB requires that the totals for "major" capital projects funds appear in the balance sheet and the Statement of Revenues, Expenditures, and Changes in Fund Balances, for governmental funds. Combining statements are required in the CAFR for nonmajor capital projects funds along with other nonmajor governmental funds.

---

[5] As previously noted reserve for encumbrances is a fund equity account used to segregate the portion of fund balance related to outstanding encumbrances.

A "stand-alone" Statement of Revenues, Expenditures, and Changes in Fund Balances is shown below for the capital projects fund example.

City of X
Capital Projects Fund
STATEMENT OF REVENUES, EXPENDITURES, AND CHANGES
IN FUND BALANCES
Year Ended June 30, 2013

Revenues:		
Interest on Temporary Investments		$ 90,000
Expenditures:		
Construction of City Hall		2,000,000
Excess of Expenditures over Revenues		(1,910,000)
Other Financing Sources and Uses:		
Proceeds of General Obligation Bonds	$10,100,000	
Transfer to Debt Service Fund	(190,000)	9,910,000
Excess of Revenues and Other Financing Sources over Expenditures and		
Other Financing Uses		8,000,000
Fund Balance—Beginning of Year		--
Fund Balance—End of Year		$8,000,000

At the beginning of the second year, the following entry would be made to reestablish the Encumbrances balance:

Encumbrances	7,800,000	
Fund Balance—Unreserved		7,800,000

The purpose of this entry is to permit the recording of expenditures in the normal manner (i.e., reverse the encumbrances before recording the expenditures). It should be noted that capital projects funds differ from other governmental fund types because they have a "project focus" rather than a fiscal year focus. However, closing entries are made in capital projects funds in order to facilitate the preparation of financial statements at the end of the fiscal year.

When the city hall project is finished, the capital projects fund should be closed. Assuming there are no cost overruns, the excess cash left in the fund upon project completion must be transferred to some other fund, normally a debt service fund. This entry is described along with other interfund transactions and transfers in Section S.

Impairment of capital assets. In accordance with GASB Statement No. 42, *Accounting and Financial Reporting for Impairment of Capital Assets and for Insurance Recoveries*, governments must evaluate prominent events or changes in circumstances affecting capital assets to determine whether impairment of the assets has occurred. Such events include evidence of physical damage, enactment or approval of laws or regulations, changes in environmental factors, technological changes or evidence of considered impaired if (a) the decline in service utility of the asset is large in magnitude, and (b) the event or change in circumstance is outside the normal life cycle of the capital asset (e.g., unexpected).

Impaired capital assets that are no longer used by the government should be reported at the lower of carrying value or fair value. Impairment losses on capital assets that will continue to be used by the government should be measured using the method that best reflects the asset's diminished service utility. As an example, if the asset is damaged, the loss should be measured at an estimate of the cost to restore the capital asset (the restoration approach). If the asset is affected by changes in environmental factors or obsolescence, the impairment should be measured using an approach that compares the service units provided by the asset before and after the impairment (the service units approach). If the asset is affected by a change in the manner or duration of use, the loss generally should be measured using the service units approach or the depreciated replacement cost approach which quantifies the cost of the service currently provided by the capital asset and converts that cost to historical cost.

Any insurance recovery associated with events or changes in circumstances resulting in impairment of a capital asset should be netted against the impairment loss.

Q. Debt Service Funds

Debt service funds account for and report financial resources that are restricted, committed, or assigned to expenditure for the payment of general obligation long-term debt principal and related interest. General obligation debt is secured by the full faith and taxing power of the governmental unit. Repayment of debt financed by internal service and enterprise funds (proprietary fund types) is accounted for in those individual funds. Consequently, debt service funds are normally established as the result of issuing general obligation bonds for capital projects. The bond liability to be extinguished is not recorded in the debt service fund until it matures (is legally due). Outstanding general long-term debt is reported only in the government-wide financial statements (statement of net position).

Assume the City of X authorizes a debt service fund for the general obligation serial bonds issued to finance the city hall project. The debt service fund is also authorized to pay the 8% interest on the $10,000,000 of debt on December 31 and June 30. The fiscal year-end is June 30. Note that the debt service fund has received resources from the general and capital projects funds. Transactions showing recognition and receipt of these resources were illustrated in the discussions of the general and capital projects funds. They are repeated below as follows:

(1)	Due from General Fund	50,000		(Transaction b.
	Other Financing Sources—Transfers In		50,000	in Section L.)
(2)	Cash	50,000		(Transaction i.
	Due from General Fund		50,000	in Section L.)
(3)	Cash	100,000		(Transaction b.
	Other Financing Sources—Transfers In		100,000	in Section N.)
(4)	Cash	50,000		(Transaction c.
	Other Financing Sources—Transfers In		50,000	in Section N.)
(5)	Due from Capital Projects Fund	40,000		(Transaction g.
	Other Financing Sources—Transfers In		40,000	in Section N.)

Assume the bonds were issued on July 1. In addition, assume that $250,000 of the bonds mature each six months, starting June 30.

a. The property tax levy contains $870,000 portion allocable to the debt service fund. $20,000 of this amount is estimated to be uncollectible.

Property Taxes Receivable—Current	870,000	
Allowance for Uncollectible Taxes—Current		20,000
Revenues—Property Taxes		850,000

b. $840,000 of property taxes are collected during the year. The remainder of the property taxes is reclassified as delinquent.

Cash	840,000	
Property Taxes Receivable—Current		840,000
Property Taxes Receivable—Delinquent	30,000	
Allowance for Uncollectible Taxes—Current	20,000	
Property Taxes Receivable—Current		30,000
Allowance for Uncollectible Taxes—Delinquent		20,000

c. The semiannual interest is paid on December 31 and June 30. The following entries are made on December 31:

Expenditures—Interest	400,000	
Matured Interest Payable		400,000
Matured Interest Payable	400,000	
Cash		400,000

The following entries are made on June 30:

Expenditures—Interest	400,000	
Matured Interest Payable		400,000
Matured Interest Payable	400,000	
Cash		400,000

Note that if interest were paid on dates other than December 31 and June 30, interest would not be recorded in the debt service fund until it is legally due, but would be accrued at the end of the fiscal year in the government-wide financial statements.

d. On June 30, the first $250,000 principal payment became due, and $200,000 was paid. The following entries would be made in the debt service fund:

Expenditures—Principal	250,000	
Matured Bonds Payable		250,000
Matured Bonds Payable	200,000	
Cash		200,000

If a bank were used as the fiscal agent, cash would first be transferred to a "Cash with Fiscal Agent" account, and payment would then be made from that account.

e. Appropriate closing entries are made based upon all information presented.

Revenues—Property Taxes	850,000	
Other Financing Sources—Transfers In	240,000	
Expenditures—Interest		800,000
Expenditures—Principal		250,000
Fund Balance—Reserved for Debt Service		40,000

The balance sheet for the debt service fund would appear as follows:

City of X
DEBT SERVICE FUND
BALANCE SHEET
June 30, 2013

Assets		*Liabilities and Fund Equity*	
Cash	$40,000	*Liabilities:*	
Due from Capital Projects Fund	40,000	Matured Bonds Payable	$50,000
Property taxes receivable—Delinquent (net of		*Fund Equity:* (See note below)	
$20,000 allowance for uncollectible taxes)	10,000	Fund Balance—Reserved for Debt Service	40,000
Total Assets	$90,000	Total Liabilities and Fund Equity	$90,000

NOTE: For financial reporting purposes, GASB Statement No. 54 would require the fund balance—reserved for debt service to be reported as restricted, committed, or assigned.

Under modified accrual accounting, expenditures for principal and interest are generally not accrued but recorded when legally due. However, GASB Statement No. 36, *Recipient Reporting for Certain Shared Nonexchange Revenues—An Amendment of GASB Statement No. 33*, provides that if resources are available at year-end and payment is to be made within one month after year-end, an accrual may be made, if a debt service fund is used.

R. Permanent Funds

A fifth type of governmental fund, introduced by GASB Statement No. 34, is the **permanent fund** type. Permanent funds account for and report resources that are restricted to the extent that only the earnings and not the principal may be used to support government programs which benefit the government or its citizens. For illustrative purposes all revenue and expenditure transactions below are recorded in the permanent fund. An alternative approach is to record interest from investments as revenue in the permanent fund, then record the transfer of the interest as an other financing use—transfer out to the general (or a special revenue fund). The general fund (or special revenue fund) would record the transfer as an other financing source—transfer in and record the expenditures of the earnings for the specified purpose.

A common example would be a cemetery perpetual care fund. Assume a local citizen was concerned about the deplorable condition of the city cemetery and on January 2, 2012, contributed $500,000 with the stipulation that the funds be invested and held; the income is to be used for the purpose of maintaining the city cemetery. On January 2, the cash was received and invested.

Cash	500,000	
Revenues—Additions to Permanent Endowments		500,000
Investments	500,000	
Cash		500,000

During 2012, $30,000 was earned on the investment, and $25,000 was expended.

Cash (and/or interest receivable)	30,000	
Revenues—Investment Income		30,000
Expenditures	25,000	
Cash (or Vouchers Payable)		25,000

S. Accounting for Special Assessments

GASB Statement No. 52, *Land and Other Real Estate Held as Investments by Endowments,* provides that land and other real estate held by an endowment for investment purposes should be reported at fair value at each reporting date. Changes in fair value during the period should be reported as a part of investment income. GASB Statement No. 6, *Accounting and Reporting for Special Assessments,* outlines the accounting and financial reporting for special assessments. Special assessments are levied for projects to be paid primarily by the property owners who benefit from the improvement project (for example, a street lighting or sidewalk project).

Under GASB Statement No. 6, the accounting and reporting for special assessment capital projects depends on the liability of the governmental unit for the special assessment debt. If the governmental unit is not obligated in any way for the debt and merely acting in a collecting capacity, the special assessment activities will be accounted for in an agency fund. However, if the governmental unit is either **primarily** or **potentially liable** for the debt, the accounting and reporting will take place as if it were any other capital improvement and financing transaction. Construction activities will be recorded in a capital projects fund and debt principal and interest activities would be recorded in a debt service fund.

T. Accounting for Proprietary Funds

GASB standards provide two types of proprietary funds: Internal Service and Enterprise Funds. **Internal service funds** are established to account for the provision of goods and services by one department of the government to other departments within the government, generally on a cost-reimbursement basis. The extent of the use of internal service fund services are managed through the budgets of the user departments. Internal service funds are normally established for the following types of activities: central garages, motor pools, central printing and duplicating, stores departments, self-insurance, etc. **Enterprise funds,** on the other hand, account for activities for which the government provides goods and services that are (1) rendered primarily to the general public, (2) financed substantially or entirely through user charges, and (3) intended to be self-supporting. Enterprise funds are usually established for public utilities, airports, toll roads and bridges, transit systems, golf courses, solid waste landfills, etc.

Proprietary funds use the accrual basis of accounting and are nonexpendable; capital is to be maintained. Revenues and expenses are recorded generally as they would be in commercial enterprises. Fixed assets are recorded in proprietary funds, and depreciation expense is deducted from revenues. Proprietary funds also report their own long-term liabilities. The GASB has provided a special rule regarding the use of FASB pronouncements in accounting for enterprise funds of state and local governments. That rule has two parts.

1. Enterprise funds should follow FASB pronouncements issued prior to November 30, 1989, unless those FASB pronouncements conflict with GASB pronouncements.
2. Enterprise funds may or may not follow FASB pronouncements issued after November 30, 1989, which do not conflict with GASB pronouncements. The decision regarding whether or not to follow such FASB pronouncements must be applied consistently to all FASB pronouncements, and the choice must be disclosed.

When proprietary funds are initially established, a contribution or advance is usually received from the general fund. A contribution is a transfer and would be recorded by the internal service or enterprise fund as follows:

Cash	xx	
Transfer from the General Fund		xx

The transfer from the general fund would be closed to net position—unrestricted at the end of the fiscal year. The transfer would be reported in the Statement of Revenues, Expenses, and Changes in Net Position. On the other hand, an advance from the general fund is a long-term loan and would be recorded by an internal service or enterprise fund as follows:

Cash	xx	
Advance from General Fund		xx

The term "advance from" is used to indicate that the liability is long term and would be reported on the proprietary fund's balance sheet as a long-term liability. The advance would be reported as a long-term asset on the general fund's balance sheet, which requires a reservation of fund balance because it is not available for current operations.

Accounting entries for proprietary funds are similar to those for business enterprises. "Operating Revenues—Charges for Services" is a common operating revenue account for both internal service and enterprise funds. As indicated earlier, revenues and expenses are recognized on the full accrual basis and are classified as operating and non-operating. Some features that distinguish the accounting for proprietary funds are

1. Long-term debt is recorded directly in internal service and enterprise funds. Revenue bonds are those that are backed only by the revenues of the proprietary fund activity. However, revenue bonds with general obligation backing and general obligation bonds that are to be paid with revenues of the proprietary fund activities are also recorded in the proprietary funds.
2. Interest on long-term debt is accrued as an expense, unlike interest on general long-term debt, which is generally not recorded until it is legally due (see debt service funds). Premiums and discounts on debt issuances, as well as debt issue costs, are recorded with the debt and amortized over the life of the bonds.
3. Fixed assets are capitalized and depreciated, using one of the generally accepted methods used by business enterprises. Interest incurred during construction is capitalized.
4. Revenues, expenses, capital contributions, and transfers are closed out to net position at year-end. Three categories of net position exist, as indicated earlier: (a) net investment in capital assets, (b) restricted, and (c) unrestricted. These are the same asset categories as are used in the government-wide Statement of Net Position.
5. Net position—net investment in capital assets, would be the net of fixed assets, less accumulated depreciation, less any long-term debt issued to finance capital assets. Net position—restricted would offset, for example, by any resources held for future debt service in accord with bond indenture requirements.
6. A special problem exists with self-insurance funds, which are often classified as internal service funds.[6] Governments transfer resources from other funds to self-insurance funds, from which claims are paid. To the extent that the transfers do not exceed the actuarially determined liability of the government, they are recorded as expenditures or expenses. Any transfers in addition to the actuarially determined liability are classified as transfers.
7. Another special problem exists with municipal waste landfills, which are often classified as enterprise funds. Many of the solid waste landfills in the US are operated by local governmental units. The problem which arises in accounting for municipal landfills is that most revenue is earned early in the useful life of the landfill, as

---

[6] GASB requires that, if self-insurance is to be recorded in a single fund, that fund must be an internal service or the general fund.

various persons and organizations pay to dispose of waste; conversely, a significant portion of the costs, termed closure and postclosure care costs as defined by US Government regulations, occur up to twenty to thirty years later. The GASB requires that these future costs be estimated and charged against periodic revenues on a "units of production" basis according to the amount of landfill capacity consumed during each period. If a municipal waste landfill is operated as an enterprise fund, expenses and liabilities are accounted for on a full accrual basis and recorded directly in the enterprise fund. If the municipal waste landfill is operated through a governmental fund, the expenditure and fund liability would be limited to the amount that will be paid with currently available resources, and the remaining liability would be reported in the government-wide statements.

CPA exam questions sometimes portray a situation, such as a federal government grant for bus purchases, and ask candidates to provide accounting treatment for when the transaction is recorded in a governmental fund (record a revenue if expended, defer revenue if not), and for when the transaction is recorded in a proprietary fund (record as capital contributions). When uncertain, candidates should generally recall business accounting principles to record the proprietary fund transaction.

U. Accounting for Fiduciary Funds

Fiduciary funds (also referred to as "trust and agency" funds) are used to account for assets held by the governmental unit in a trustee capacity or as an agent for individuals, private organizations, and other governmental units. Fiduciary funds include private-purpose trust funds which account for resources received under a trust agreement in which the investment income of an endowment is intended to benefit an external individual, private organization, or government. (Remember that resources held and invested for the benefit of the reporting government are classified as permanent funds, a governmental fund category.) In addition to private-purpose trust funds, the fiduciary fund category includes pension (and other employee benefit) trust funds, investment trust funds, and agency funds.

Pension (and other employee benefit) trust funds are maintained when the governmental unit is trustee for the pension (or other employee benefit) plan. In addition, many state governments operate statewide Public Employee Retirement Systems (PERS) for local governments, teachers, university employees, judges, etc. These PERS are normally a part of the state government reporting entity. Full accrual accounting is used for pension trust funds, and investments are reported at fair value. Pension trust funds are required to have two financial statements and two schedules (included as required supplementary information). The pension trust funds are included in the (1) Statement of Fiduciary Net Position and the (2) Statement of Changes in Fiduciary Net Position. The two RSI schedules are the (1) Schedule of Funding Progress (which illustrates actuarial status) and the (2) Schedule of Employer Contributions. Accounting for pension plans by government employers is covered by GASBS 27 and 50. Accounting by pension plans is covered by GASBS 25 and 50.

Government pension plans do not include the accrued actuarial liability in the statement of fiduciary net position. Rather, the actuarial liability is reported in the schedule of funding progress and in the notes. Extensive note disclosures are required, both for the PERS and for the government as employer, whether or not it is trustee of the pension plan.

The above requirements relate to **defined benefit** pension plans. Under **defined contribution** plans, the government is liable only for the required contributions not made.

Employer accounting for defined benefit plans is the same, regardless of whether or not the government is the trustee for the pension plan. Expenditures (or expenses) are charged in the appropriate funds (especially the general, special revenue, and enterprise funds) in an amount equal to the amount provided to the pension plan. The pension trust fund (or statewide PERS) would record those contributions as additions. Other additions for the pension trust fund would include employee contributions, investment income, and gains in the market value of investments. Deductions would include retirement benefit payments, disability payments, refunds to terminated (nonvested) employees, and losses in the market value of investments.

Statewide PERS may be **agency** defined benefit, **cost-sharing** defined benefit, or defined contribution. **Agency** plans maintain separate balances for each participating government so that it is possible to determine its unfunded actuarial liability (or assets in excess of accrued actuarial benefits). **Cost-sharing** plans normally compute balances on a statewide basis only; it is not the responsibility of each participating government to fund its own liability.

A final use for pension trust funds is IRS Sec. 457 Deferred Compensation Plans (tax-deferred annuities for government employees). In many cases, these plans will not be recorded. However, when the plan meets the criteria for inclusion in a government financial statement, GASB Statement No. 34 requires that a pension trust fund be used.

The financial reporting framework for **postretirement benefits other than pensions** under GASB Statement No. 45 is similar to the reporting for pensions under GASB Statement No. 27. Employers are required to measure and disclose the amount for annual other post employment benefits (OPEB) cost on the accrual basis. Annual OPEB cost is equal to the employer's annual required contribution to the plan with certain adjustments if the OPEB obligation is under- or overfunded. This is essentially the same as the accounting required by commercial enterprises under SFAS 106 (See Module 13). GASB Statement No. 45 discussed an alternative measurement method for employers with fewer than 100 total plan members. GASB Statement No. 57, *OPEB Measurements by Agent Employers and Agent Multiple-Employer Plans,* addressed issues related to the use of the alternative measurement method and the frequency and timing of measurements by employers that participate in agent multiple-employer OPEB plans. GASB Statement

No. 57 amended GASB Statement No. 45 to permit an agent employer that has an individual-employer OPEB plan with fewer than 100 total plan members to use the alternative measurement method at its option regardless of the number of total plan members in the agent multiple-employer OPEB plan in which it participates. GASB Statement No. 57 also amended the GASB Statement No. 43 requirement that a defined OPEB plan obtain an actuarial valuation. GASB Statement No. 57 indicates that this requirement can be met by reporting aggregated individual-employer OPEB information determined by actuarial valuations or measurements using the alternative measurement method for individual-employer OPEB plans that are eligible. In addition, GASB Statement No. 57 indicated that actuarially de-termined OPEB measures should be determined at a common date and at a minimum frequency to satisfy the agent multiple-employer OPEB plan's financial reporting requirements.

A government may decide to provide **voluntary termination benefits,** such as early-retirement incentives to its employees. They may also provide **involuntary termination benefits,** such as severance pay. In governmental fi-nancial statements prepared on the accrual basis, governments should recognize a liability and expense for voluntary termination benefits when the offer has been accepted by the employees and the amount of liability can be estimated. For involuntary termination benefits, the liability should be recognized when the plan has been approved and commu-nicated to the employees and the amount of the liability can be estimated. GASB Statement No. 47, *Accounting for Termination Benefits,* provides that the liability for termination benefits should be measured at the present value of the expected future benefit payments. In financial statements prepared on the modified accrual basis, the liability and ex-penditures for termination benefits should be recognized to the extent the liabilities are normally expected to be liqui-dated with expendable available financial resources.

Investment trust funds are required when a government sponsors an external investment pool; for example, when a county sponsors an investment pool for all cities, school districts, and other governments within its borders. The **ex-ternal portion** of investment pools are to be reported (by the county) in a manner similar to pension trust funds. The Statements of Net Fiduciary Assets and of Changes in Fiduciary Net Position are required. However, Statements of Cash Flows are not required.

Private-purpose trust funds represent all other trust arrangements under which principal and income benefit ex-ternal individuals, private organizations, or other governments. Private-purpose trust funds may be **nonexpendable** or **expendable**. A nonexpendable trust fund is one in which the principal cannot be expended but which provide that in-come may be expended for some agreed-upon purpose. Sometimes, this is called an endowment.

EXAMPLE

Assume a donor gives $500,000 to a city with instructions that the principal be invested permanently and that the income is to be used to provide scholarships for low-income children to attend a private, not-for-profit day care program. The receipt and investment of the gift would be recorded as

Cash	500,000	
Additions—Nonexpendable Donation		500,000
Investments	500,000	
Cash		500,000

Assume $30,000 is received in investment income and expended.

Cash	30,000	
Additions—Investment Income		30,000
Deductions—Awarding of Scholarships	30,000	
Cash		30,000

Expendable private-purpose trust funds are accounted for in the same manner, except that the principal as well as investment income may be expended. For example, a donor may give $10,000 to a school district with instructions that each year $2,000 plus investment income be awarded to the top student in the senior class, as a scholarship.

Another use of private-purpose trust funds, in some cases, is for **escheat property**. Escheat property is property taken over by a government, usually state government, when the property is abandoned and the legal owners cannot be found. GASB Statement No. 37 concluded that escheat property generally is recorded in the governmental or pro-prietary fund to which the property ultimately escheats (e.g., an educational fund). A liability is recorded for esti-mated amounts to potential claimants. A private-purpose trust fund is used when resources are held for individuals, private organizations, or another government.

Agency funds are used to account for activities where the government is acting as an agent for others. Agency funds have only assets and liabilities; no fund equity, revenue, or expenditure (expense) accounts are used. The GASB requires the use of agency funds for special assessments where the government is not obligated in any manner for the special assessment debt.

Another common use of agency funds is to account for property taxes. Property taxes are usually remitted to a county treasurer who places the monies in a county Tax Agency Fund. The taxes are held until such time as they are remitted to each of the other local governments located within the county. Often, a fee is charged, which decreases the amount that is distributed to the other local governments and increases the amount that is distributed to the County General Fund.

V. Reporting Interfund Activity

Under GASB Statement No. 34, interfund activity is shown between individual funds in fund financial statements and between business-type and governmental-type activities in the government-wide financial statements. GASB provides for two major types of interfund activity, each with two subtypes.

1. Reciprocal interfund activity

   a. Interfund loan and advances
   b. Interfund services provided and used

2. Nonreciprocal interfund activity

   a. Interfund transfers
   b. Interfund reimbursements

Interfund loans and advances are transactions in which one fund provides resources with a requirement for repayment. Short-term loans are recorded with "Due from" and "Due to" accounts.

EXAMPLE

Assume an enterprise fund made a short-term loan to the general fund, the entry would be

Enterprise Fund			*General Fund*		
Due from General Fund	100,000		Cash	100,000	
Cash		100,000	Due to Enterprise Fund		100,000

Long-term interfund receivables and payables use the terms "Advance to" and "Advance from." If a governmental fund makes a long-term loan to another fund, it is necessary to reserve fund balance in the amount of the advance, as the resources are not "available" for expenditure in the current period.

EXAMPLE

Assume the general fund advances $50,000 to an internal service fund. The entries would be

General Fund			*Internal Service Fund*		
Advance to Internal Service					
Fund	50,000		Cash	50,000	
Cash		50,000	Advance from General Fund		50,000
Fund Balance—Unreserved	50,000				
Fund Balance—Reserved					
for Long-Term Advances		50,000			

Loans and advances to and from component units are to be separately identified in the government-wide financial statements.

Interfund services provided and used represent transactions in which sales and purchases of goods and services between funds are made at prices approximating their external exchange price. Examples would include the sale of water from an enterprise fund to the general fund, the provision of services by an internal service fund to a governmental fund, a payment in lieu of taxes from an enterprise fund to the general fund (where payment is approximately equal to services provided), and the payment of a retirement fund contribution from the general fund to a pension trust fund. Revenues (or additions) are recognized by one fund, and an expenditure or expense is recorded by another fund. As a result, the operating statements will include these revenues and expenditures/expenses.

EXAMPLE

Assume an internal services fund charges the general fund for goods or services provided.

Internal Service Fund			*General Fund*		
Due from General Fund	30,000		Expenditures	30,000	
Operating Revenues—			Due to Internal Service		
Charges for Services		30,000	Fund		30,000

Interfund transfers are nonreciprocal transfers between funds, where payment is not expected. Examples would include an annual subsidy from an enterprise fund to the general fund or an annual transfer from the general fund to a debt service fund. To illustrate the latter in the amount of $300,000

General Fund			*Debt Service Fund*		
Other Financing Uses—Transfer					
to Debt Service Fund	300,000		Cash	300,000	
Cash		300,000	Other Financing Sources—		
			Transfer from General Fund		300,000

Transfers are reported as "Other Financing Sources (Uses)" in the governmental funds statement of revenues, expenditures, and changes in fund balance.

Interfund reimbursements are repayments from funds responsible for expenditures or expenses to those funds that initially paid for them.

EXAMPLE

Assume the general fund paid an enterprise fund for a consultant's fee that was initially paid by the enterprise fund and charged to expense.

General Fund			*Enterprise Fund*		
Expenditures	50,000		Cash	50,000	
Cash		50,000	Consultant Fee Expense		50,000

W. Accounting for Investments

GASB's rules for investment accounting are included in GASB Statement No. 31, *Accounting and Financial Reporting for Certain Investments and for External Investment Pools.* GASB Statement No. 31 provides that investments in debt securities and in equity securities with determinable fair values be reported at fair value. Changes in fair value should be reported as a part of operations, using modified accrual or accrual accounting, as appropriate. No distinction is to be made on the face of the financial statements between realized and unrealized gains and losses, although disclosure may be made of realized gains in the notes. Investment income should be reported in the fund for which investments are held, when investments are pooled.

X. Conversion from Fund Financial Statements to Government-Wide Financial Statements

Most state and local governments will keep their books on a fund basis in order to facilitate the preparation of fund financial statements and to prepare the budget-actual schedule as a part of RSI. This will mean that governments will record transactions on the modified accrual basis for governmental funds and on the accrual basis for proprietary and fiduciary funds. Many governments will make changes, on a worksheet basis, in order to prepare the government-wide financial statements (Statement of Net Position and Statement of Activities). The following are the worksheet changes that will be necessary to convert from governmental fund statements to the governmental activities portion of the government-wide statements. It should be emphasized that the journal entries illustrated below are made only for worksheet purposes and will not be posted to the funds ledger.

1. **Capitalization of Capital Outlay Expenditure**

   Costs incurred for capital assets acquired or constructed by governmental funds are recorded as expenditures. Governmental funds do not record capital assets. Therefore it will be necessary to record capital outlay expenditures as capital assets in the governmental activities column of the government-wide Statement of Net Position. A worksheet adjusting entry needs to be made to reduce capital outlay expenditures to zero and capitalize the costs in appropriate capital asset accounts. These capital assets will increase the net position of the governmental activities. Assuming the amount is $10,000,000, the entry would be

Fixed Assets (Land, Buildings, Equipment, etc.)	10,000,000	
Expenditures		10,000,000

   In addition, depreciation expense will be required to be recorded for the buildings and equipment.

2. **Issuance of general long-term debt**

   When general long-term debt is issued, governmental funds credit Proceeds of Debt, which is an Other Financing Source. Also, premiums and discounts are not amortized but simply add to or deduct from the amount of resources available. On a worksheet it will be necessary to eliminate Other Financing Sources—Proceeds of Bonds and record the debt as a liability. Moreover, any premium or discount must be associated with the liability and amortized over the life of the bonds. The worksheet entry to convert the sale of bonds from governmental fund accounting to government-wide statements, assuming a sale of $5,000,000 bonds at par, would be

Other Financing Sources—Proceeds of Bonds	5,000,000	
Bonds Payable		5,000,000

3. **Debt service payments**

    When making principal payments on long-term debt, governmental funds debit Expenditures—bond principal retirement. Those expenditures will need to be eliminated and replaced with a debit to the bond principal when preparing the government-wide statements. Bond principal retirement does not affect the government-wide Statement of Activities but reduces the bonds payable balance in the Statement of Net Position. In addition, governmental funds do not accrue interest payable but record expenditures on the maturity date. Accrual of interest payable will be required for the government-wide statements, including adjustments for amortization of premiums and discounts. Assuming that a payment of $100,000 was made for the retirement of bond principal, then the worksheet entry to convert the $100,000 principal payment from governmental fund accounting to government-wide statements would be

Bonds Payable	100,000	
Expenditures—Bond Principal Retirement		100,000

4. **Adjustment of revenue recognition**

    Governmental funds recognize revenues only when measurable and available to finance expenditures of the current period. In the case of property taxes, revenues cannot be recognized if those revenues will be collected more than sixty days after the end of the fiscal year. When preparing the government-wide financial statements, some adjustments will be required to recognize all revenues, net of uncollectible receivables, in accord with revenue accounting for exchange and nonexchange transactions, as described earlier in this module. Assume a government levied $10,000,000 in property taxes for the year 2012 with 2% uncollectible. The amount to be recognized on the government-wide statements is $9,800,000. Assume that during 2012 and the first sixty days of 2013, $9,600,000 had been and was expected to be collected, limiting the amount reported as revenues in the governmental funds Statement of Revenues, Expenditures, and Changes in Fund Balances to $9,600,000. The $200,000 would have been shown as deferred inflow of resources in the Governmental Funds Balance Sheet. The worksheet entry would be

Deferred Inflow—Property Taxes	200,000	
Revenues—Taxes		200,000

5. **Accrual of expenses**

    Under modified accrual accounting, expenditures are recorded for items that are current, capital outlay, and debt service. As indicated earlier, adjustments must be made to convert expenditures for capital outlay and debt service principal payments to the accrual basis. In addition, adjustments must be made to record the noncurrent portion of certain liabilities (claims and judgments, compensated absences, etc.). These worksheet entries would debit expenses and credit liabilities.

6. **Other**

    Some governments use the purchases method to record governmental fund inventories, and these must be changed to the consumption method when using accrual accounting. Other governments do not record and amortize certain prepaid items, such as prepaid insurance and prepaid rent. Adjustments must also be made for these items.

7. **Reclassifications**

    Fund financial statements are presented separately for governmental, proprietary, and fiduciary fund categories. Government-wide financial statements have columns for governmental activities, business-type activities, and component units. In order to make the transition from fund financial statements, the fiduciary funds will be eliminated. Internal service funds, which are proprietary funds, are to be classified as governmental activities in the government-wide statements. Discretely presented component units, which are not presented at all in the fund financial statements, will be added when preparing the government-wide financial statements.

> **NOW REVIEW MULTIPLE-CHOICE QUESTIONS 65 THROUGH 129 IN VOLUME 2**

Y. Public College and University Accounting (Governmental)—GASB Statement No. 35

GASB Statement No. 35, *Basic Financial Statements—and Management's Discussion and Analysis—for Public Colleges and Universities,* established accounting and financial reporting standards for public colleges and universities within the guidelines of GASB Statement No. 34.

GASB Statement No. 35 requires that public colleges and universities follow the standards for special purpose governments outlined in GASB Statement No. 34. This means that public colleges may choose to use the guidance for special purpose governments engaged in (1) only business-type activities, (2) engaged in only governmental activities, or (3) engaged in both governmental and business-type activities.

Public colleges and universities which elect to report as special purpose governments that are engaged in only governmental activities or in governmental and business-type activities are required to follow the reporting model for state and local governments. This model requires (1) a Management's Discussion and Analysis (MD&A), (2) Government-

Wide Financial Statements, (3) Fund Financial Statements, (4) Notes to the Financial Statements, and (5) Required Supplementary Information (RSI) other than MD&A.

While a number of community colleges may choose to report in the manner described in the previous paragraph, most public colleges and universities will choose to report as special entities engaged only in **business-type** activities. In this case, proprietary fund statements only are required. These institutions will report (1) an MD&A, (2) a Statement of Net Position, (3) a Statement of Revenues, Expenses, and Changes in Net Position, (4) a Statement of Cash Flows, and (5) Required Supplementary Information (RSI) other than MD&A. Public colleges and universities reporting as business-type activities present financial statements using the **economic resources measurement focus and the accrual basis of accounting**.

The **Statement of Net Position** (as illustrated) may be presented in the format: Assets + Deferred Outflows of Resources – Liabilities – Deferred Inflows of Resources = Net Position. Alternatively, a balance sheet format (Assets + Deferred Outflows of Resources = Liabilities + Deferred Inflows of Resources + Net Position) may be presented. In either case, a classified financial statement must be presented, distinguishing between current and long-term assets and between current and long-term liabilities. As is the case for state and local governments, net position must be segregated into three categories: (1) net investment in capital assets, (2) restricted, and (3) unrestricted. Restricted net position should show major categories of restrictions. It is **not** permissible to show designations of unrestricted net position.

The **Statement of Revenues, Expenses, and Changes in Net Position** is reported in an "all-inclusive" format that reconciles to the ending total net position. GASB requires that revenues be reported by major source and that a distinction be made between operating and nonoperating revenues and expenses. The general format is

	Operating Revenues
–	Operating Expenses
=	Operating Income (Loss)
±	Nonoperating Revenues and Expenses
=	Income Before Other Revenues, Expenses Gains, Losses, and Transfers
±	Capital Contributions, Additions to Permanent and Term Endowments, Special and Extraordinary Items, and Transfers
=	Increase (Decrease) in Net Position
+	Net Position, Beginning of Period
=	Net Position, End of Period

Group ASB Statement No. 35 requires that state appropriations for operating purposes be reported as nonoperating revenue. State appropriations for capital outlay are shown separately as capital appropriations. Capital grants and gifts, additions to permanent endowments, extraordinary items, and special items are also displayed separately.

The **Statement of Cash Flows** is prepared using the GASB format described earlier in this module. The direct method must be used, along with a reconciliation between net operating income (loss) and net cash provided (used) by operating activities. Four categories are used: (1) operating activities, (2) noncapital financing activities, (3) capital and related financing activities, and (4) investing activities. Note that interest paid is classified as a (capital or noncapital) financing activity and interest received is classified as cash flows from investing activities.

GASB Statement No. 35 requires that cash flows from state appropriations for operations be reported as cash flows from noncapital financing activities. It also requires that cash flows from state appropriations for construction be reported as cash flows from capital and related financing activities.

ABC University
STATEMENT OF NET POSITION
June 30, 2013

	Primary institution	Component unit hospital
Assets		
Current assets:		
Cash and cash equivalents	$ 4,571,218	$ 977,694
Short-term investments	15,278,981	2,248,884
Accounts receivable, net	6,412,520	9,529,196
Inventories	585,874	1,268,045
Deposit with bond trustee	4,254,341	--
Notes and mortgages receivable, net	359,175	--
Other assets	432,263	426,427
Total current assets	$31,894,372	$14,450,246
Noncurrent assets:		
Restricted cash and cash equivalents	24,200	18,500
Endowment investments	21,548,723	--
Notes and mortgages receivable, net	2,035,323	--
Other long-term investments	--	6,441,710

	Primary institution	Component unit hospital
Investments in real estate	6,426,555	--
Capital assets, net	158,977,329	32,602,940
Total noncurrent assets	189,012,130	39,063,150
Total assets	$220,906,502	$53,513,396
Deferred outflows of assets	$1,294,500	

Liabilities
Current liabilities:

Accounts payable and accrued liabilities	4,897,470	2,911,419
Long-term liabilities—current portion	4,082,486	989,321
Total current liabilities	$8,979,956	$3,900,740

Noncurrent liabilities:

Deposits	1,124,128	--
Long-term liabilities	31,611,427	2,194,236
Total noncurrent liabilities	32,735,555	2,194,236
Total liabilities	$41,715,511	$6,094,976
Deferred inflows of assets	$ 6,737,213	--

Net Position

Net investment in capital assets	$126,861,400	$32,199,938

Restricted for:
Nonexpendable:

Scholarships and fellowships	10,839,473	--
Research	3,767,564	2,286,865

Expendable:

Scholarships and fellowships	2,803,756	--
Research	5,202,732	--
Instructional department uses	938,571	--
Loans	2,417,101	--
Capital projects	4,952,101	913,758
Debt service	4,254,341	152,947
Other	403,632	--
Unrestricted	11,307,607	11,864,912
Total net position	$173,748,278	$47,418,420

SOURCE: Revised GASB 35, page 27.

ABC University
STATEMENT OF REVENUES, EXPENSES, AND CHANGES IN NET POSITION
For the Year Ended June 30, 2013

> Operating expenses may be displayed using either object or functional classification.

	Primary institution	Component unit hospital
Revenues		
Operating revenues:		
Student tuition and fees (net of scholarship allowances of $3,214,454)	$ 36,913,194	$ --
Patient services (net of charity care of $5,114,352)	--	46,296,957
Federal grants and contracts	10,614,660	--
State and local grants and contracts	3,036,953	7,475,987
Nongovernmental grants and contracts	873,740	--
Sales and services of educational departments	19,802	--
Auxiliary enterprises:		
Residential life (net of scholarship allowances of $428,641)	28,079,274	--
Bookstore (net of scholarship allowances of $166,279)	9,092,363	--
Other operating revenues	143,357	421,571
Total operating revenues	88,773,343	54,194,515
Expenses		
Operating expenses:		
Salaries:		
Faculty (physicians for the hospital)	34,829,499	16,703,805
Exempt staff	29,597,676	8,209,882
Nonexempt wages	5,913,762	2,065,267
Benefits	18,486,559	7,752,067
Scholarships and fellowships	3,809,374	--

	Primary institution	Component unit hospital
Utilities	16,463,492	9,121,352
Supplies and other services	12,451,064	7,342,009
Depreciation	6,847,377	2,976,212
Total operating expenses	128,398,803	54,170,594
Operating income (loss)	(39,625,460)	23,921
Nonoperating Revenues (Expenses)		
State appropriations	39,760,508	--
Gifts	1,822,442	--
Investment income (net of investment expense of $87,316 for the primary institution and $19,823 for the hospital)	2,182,921	495,594
Interest on capital asset—related debt	(1,330,126)	(34,538)
Other nonoperating revenues	313,001	321,449
Net operating revenues	42,748,746	782,505
Income before other revenues, expenses, gains, or losses	3,123,286	806,426
Capital appropriations	2,075,750	--
Capital grants and gifts	690,813	711,619
Additions to permanent endowments	85,203	--
Increase in net position	5,975,052	1,518,045
Net Position		
Net position—beginning of year	167,773,226	45,900,375
Net position—end of year	$173,748,278	$47,418,420

SOURCE: GASB 35, page 28.

GASB Statement No. 39, *Determining Whether Certain Organizations Are Component Units—An Amendment of GASB Statement No. 14*, provides guidance relating to whether or not certain legally separate tax-exempt entities are to be reported in the financial statements of governments. These provisions are especially important to public colleges and universities, many of which have legally separate foundations. GASB Statement No. 39 will result in many of these foundations being reported as discretely presented component units in public college and university financial statements. All three of the following criteria must be met before these foundations are included:

1. The economic resources received or held by the separate organization are entirely or almost entirely for the benefit of the primary government, its component units, or its constituents.
2. The primary government or its component units is entitled to, or has the ability to otherwise access a majority of the economic resources received or held by the separate organization.
3. The economic resources received or held by an individual organization that the specific primary government is entitled to, or has the ability to otherwise access are significant to that primary government.

ABC University
STATEMENT OF CASH FLOWS
For the Year Ended June 30, 2013

> The direct method of reporting cash flows is required.

	Primary institution	Component unit hospital
Cash Flows from Operating Activities		
Tuition and fees	$ 33,628,945	$ --
Research grants and contracts	13,884,747	--
Payments from insurance and patients	--	18,582,530
Medicaid and Medicare	--	31,640,524
Payments to suppliers	(28,175,500)	(13,084,643)
Payments to employees	(87,233,881)	(32,988,044)
Loans issued to students and employees	(384,628)	--
Collection of loans to students and employees	291,642	--
Auxiliary enterprise charges:		
Residence halls	26,327,644	--
Bookstore	8,463,939	--
Other receipts (payments)	1,415,502	(997,502)
Net cash provided (used) by operating activities	(31,781,590)	3,152,865
Cash Flows from Noncapital Financing Activities		
State appropriations	39,388,534	--
Gifts and grants received for other than capital purposes:		
Private gifts for endowment purposes	85,203	--
Net cash flows provided by noncapital financing activities	39,473,737	--

	Primary institution	Component unit hospital
Cash Flows from Capital and Related Financing Activities		
Proceeds from capital debt	4,125,000	--
Capital appropriations	1,918,750	--
Capital grants and gifts received	640,813	711,619
Proceeds from sale of capital assets	22,335	5,066
Purchases of capital assets	(8,420,247)	(1,950,410)
Principal paid on capital debt and lease	(3,788,102)	(134,095)
Interest paid on capital debt and lease	(1,330,126)	(34,538)
Net cash used by capital and related financing activities	(6,831,577)	(1,402,358)
Cash Flows from Investing Activities		
Proceeds from sales and maturities of investments	16,741,252	2,843,124
Interest on investments	2,111,597	70,501
Purchase of investments	(17,680,113)	(4,546,278)
Net cash provided (used) by investing activities	1,172,736	(1,632,653)
Net increase in cash	2,033,306	117,854
Cash—beginning of year	2,562,112	878,340
Cash—end of year	$ 4,595,418	$ 996,194

Reconciliation of net operating revenues (expenses) to net cash provided (used) by operating activities:

	Primary institution	Component unit hospital
Operating income (loss)	$(39,625,460)	$ 23,921
Adjustments to reconcile net income (loss) to net cash provided (used) by operating activities:		
Depreciation expense	6,847,377	2,976,212
Change in assets and liabilities:		
Receivables, net	1,295,704	330,414
Inventories	37,284	(160,922)
Deposit with bond trustee	67,115	--
Other assets	(136,229)	75,456
Accounts payable	(323,989)	(75,973)
Deferred inflows of resources	217,630	--
Deposits held for others	(299,428)	--
Compensated absences	138,406	(16,243)
Net cash provided (used) by operating activities	$(31,781,590)	$3,152,865

NOTE: The required information about noncash investing, capital, and financing activities is not illustrated.

SOURCE: Revised from GASB 35, pages 29-30.

NOW REVIEW MULTIPLE-CHOICE QUESTIONS 130 THROUGH 133 IN VOLUME 2

KEY TERMS

Agency fund. Accounts for resources held by the reporting government in a purely custodial capacity.

Capital projects fund. Accounts for financial resources that are restricted, committed, or assigned to expenditures for acquisition or construction of capital assets.

Component unit. A legally separate organization for which the elected officials of a primary government are financially accountable.

Comprehensive Annual Financial Report (CAFR). A complete annual report for a state or local government, consisting of an introductory section, a financial section, and a statistical section.

Debt service fund. Accounts for resources that are restricted, committed, or assigned to expenditures for the payment of general long-term debt principal and interest.

Enterprise fund. Accounts for activities that involve providing goods or services to external users for a fee.

Exchange revenues. Transactions that involve the transfer of goods or services for payment of (approximately) equal value.

Fiduciary funds. Account for resources held and used by governments for the benefit of individuals and entities other than the government. Fiduciary funds include agency funds, pension and other employee benefit trust funds, investment trust funds, and private-purpose trust funds.

General fund. Accounts for all financial resources except those required to be accounted for in another fund.

Governmental funds. Account for the current financial resources raised and expended to carry out general government purposes. Governmental funds include the general fund, special revenue funds, debt service funds, capital projects funds, and permanent funds.

Infrastructure assets. Long-lived capital assets that normally are stationary in nature and can normally be preserved for a significant number of years, (e.g., roads, tunnels, bridges, dams, etc.).

Internal service fund. Reports activities that provide goods or services to other funds of the primary government on a cost-reimbursement basis.

Investment trust fund. Reports the external portions of investment pools, when the reporting government is the trustee.

Nonexchange revenues. Transactions in which a government gives or receives value without providing equal value in return, (e.g., property taxes, income taxes, etc.).

Pension and other employee benefit trust funds. Account for funds held in trust for the payment of employee retirement and other benefits.

Permanent fund. Accounts for resources that are restricted to the extent that only earnings and not principal may be used to support specified government programs.

Primary government. A state government, a general purpose local government, or a special-purpose local government that has a separately elected governing body, is legally separate, and is fiscally independent of other state or local governments.

Private-purpose trust fund. Reports all trust arrangements where the principal must remain intact and the income generated is used to benefit individuals, private organizations, and other governments.

Proprietary funds. Account for a government's business-type activities. Proprietary funds include internal service funds and enterprise funds.

Special revenue fund. Accounts for specific revenues that are restricted or committed to expenditures for specific current purposes other than debt service or capital projects.

Module 22: Not-for-Profit Accounting

Overview

Nonprofit[1] organizations provide socially desirable services without the intention of realizing a profit. Nonprofit organizations are financed by user charges, contributions from donors and/or foundations, investment income, and government grants. The nature and extent of support depends upon the type of nonprofit organization.

Examples of private sector nonprofits would be private colleges (University of Chicago), private sector health care entities operated by religious or other nonprofit organizations, voluntary health and welfare organizations, and various "other" nonprofits, such as performing arts companies. Examples of government nonprofits would be public colleges (Northern Illinois University), government hospitals, and government museums. Private sector nonprofit organizations have GAAP set primarily by the FASB; governmental nonprofit organizations have GAAP set primarily by the GASB.

In June of 1993, the FASB issued SFAS 116, *Accounting for Contributions Received and Contributions Made,* and SFAS 117, *Financial Statements of Not-for-Profit Organizations.* These standards are applicable to private sector not-for-profit organizations of all types. This module presents GAAP for private sector nonprofits under SFAS 116 and 117 (FASB ASC 958). The AICPA has developed two *Audit Guides* that correspond and add to the new FASB principles: (1) Not-for-Profit Organizations, and (2) Health Care Organizations. The *Not-for-Profit Guide* applies only to private sector not-for-profits. The *Health Care Guide* applies to all health care entities, private for-profit, private not-for-profit, and governmental.

Governmental nonprofits are not permitted to follow SFAS 116 and 117 (FASB ASC 958). (The definition of a government is provided in the introductory section of Module 21.) As applied to colleges, health care entities, and other not-for-profit organizations, that guidance has been outlined through different pronouncements.

First, in November 1999, the GASB issued Statement 35, *Basic Financial Statements—and Management's Discussion and Analysis—for Public Colleges and Universities.* GASB 35 permits public colleges to report as special-purpose entities engaged in governmental or business-type activities, or both. Most four-year institutions are expected to report as special-purpose entities engaged only in business-type activities. Some community colleges may choose to report as special-purpose entities engaged in governmental activities due to the extent of state and local government tax support. The provisions of GASB 35 are outlined in Module 21.

Second, GASB 34 indicates that hospitals and other health care providers may be considered special-purpose entities that may be engaged in either governmental or business-type activities, or both. Most health care organizations will choose to report as special-purpose entities that are engaged in business-type activities. As a result, proprietary fund statements will be required for those health care entities. The AICPA Audit and Accounting Guide, *Health Care Organizations*, contains guidance for both private sector and governmental health care organizations; both are presented in this module.

Third, other governmental not-for-profit organizations (essentially governmental voluntary health and welfare and "other" not-for-profit organizations) also may be considered special-purpose entities that may be engaged in either governmental or business-type activities, or both. However, GASB 34 specifically permits these organizations that were using the "AICPA Not-for-Profit Model" upon adoption of GASB 34 to report as special-purpose entities engaged in business-type activities. These entities will present proprietary fund statements. The AICPA Audit and Accounting Guide, *Not-for-Profit Organizations*, applies only to private sector organizations and these principles are contained in this module; governmental not-for-profits are less significant and are not illustrated in this module.

The first section of this module presents the FASB and AICPA standards for all nongovernmental nonprofits, including private sector colleges, universities, and health care entities. The second section presents standards that apply primarily to private colleges and universities. The third and fourth sections present standards for health care entities; first for private sector health care entities; next for governmental health care entities. Module 21 presents standards for public colleges and universities. Before beginning the reading you should review key terms at the end of the module.

A. FASB and AICPA Standards for Private Sector Nonprofits

FASB ASC 958 applies to private sector nonprofits subject to FASB guidance; they do not apply to governmental nonprofits subject to GASB guidance.

---

[1] The terms not-for-profit and nonprofit are used interchangeably here and in practice.

More recently, FASB issued Statement 124, *Accounting for Certain Investments Held by Not-for-Profit Organizations*. This statement requires fair value accounting for most equity and debt investments by not-for-profit organizations and requires reporting of realized and unrealized gains and losses directly in the Statement of Activities.

Most recently, FASB issued Statement 136, *Transfers of Assets to a Not-for-Profit Organization or Charitable Trust That Raises or Holds Contributions for Others*. This statement provides guidance regarding proper reporting by foundations and similar not-for-profits when funds are raised for others, as described in 1.n. and o. below.

The FASB guidance is intended to eliminate the differences in accounting and reporting standards that existed previously between four types of not-for-profit organizations. While some differences exist, for example, in functional categories reported, private sector nonprofit colleges and universities, health care entities, voluntary health and welfare organizations, and "other" organizations follow the basic guidance in the FASB standards; some differences between health care entities and other private sector not-for-profits will be illustrated later. The section lists a number of basic requirements, illustrates financial statements, and presents a few journal entries as required by SFAS 116, 117, 124, and 136 (FASB ASC 958). All illustrations are for a general nongovernmental not-for-profit organization, but remember that the principles apply to all four types (colleges and universities, health care organizations, voluntary health and welfare organizations, and "other" not-for-profit organizations).

1. Important Features of the FASB Guidance

a. The standards apply to **all** nongovernmental nonprofit organizations, except those that operate for the direct economic benefit of members (such as mutual insurance companies). General FASB standards, unless specifically prohibited by those standards or do not apply because of their nature (capital stock, etc.) or unless modified by these standards, are presumed to apply.

b. Net assets are divided into three classes: unrestricted, temporarily restricted, and permanently restricted. Fund classifications are not reported, unless the information can be shown as subdivisions of the three major classes. To be restricted, resources must be restricted by donors or grantors; internally designated resources are unrestricted. Only contributed resources may be restricted.

c. Permanently restricted resources include (1) certain assets, such as artwork, etc. that must be maintained or used in a certain way, (2) endowments, which represent resources that must be invested permanently with income to be used for either restricted or unrestricted purposes, and (3) land, when that land must be held in perpetuity.

d. Temporarily restricted resources include unexpended resources that are to be used for a particular purpose, at a time in the future, or are to be invested for a period of time (a term endowment). Temporarily restricted resources might also be used for the acquisition or receipt of a gift of plant and would represent the undepreciated amount. As the plant is depreciated, the amount depreciated would be reclassified from temporarily restricted net assets to unrestricted net assets and shown as a deduction from unrestricted revenues, gains, and other support on the statement of activities. Alternatively, plant may be initially recorded as unrestricted.

e. Unrestricted resources include all other resources including unrestricted contributions, the net amount from providing services, unrestricted income from investments, etc. Resources are presumed to be unrestricted, unless evidence exists that donor-imposed restrictions exist. As mentioned above, undepreciated plant may be included as unrestricted or temporarily restricted.

f. Statements required are (1) Statement of Financial Position, (2) Statement of Activities, and (3) Statement of Cash Flows. Certain note disclosures are also required and others recommended. In addition, voluntary health and welfare organizations are required to report a Statement of Functional Expenses that show expenses by function and by natural classifications.

g. The Statement of Financial Position reports assets, liabilities, and net assets. Organization-wide totals must be provided for assets, liabilities and net assets, and net assets must be broken down between unrestricted, temporarily restricted, and permanently restricted.

h. The Statement of Activities reports revenues, expenses, gains, losses, and reclassifications (between classes of net assets). Organization-wide totals must be provided. Separate revenues, expenses, gains, losses, and reclassifications for each class may or may not be reported, but the changes in net assets for each class must be reported.

i. Revenues, expenses, gains, and losses are reported on the full accrual basis. A revenue is presumed to be unrestricted unless donor-imposed restrictions apply, either permanent or temporary. A presumption is made, in the absence of contrary information, that a given expense would use restricted resources first, rather than unrestricted resources. Revenues and expenses should be reported at gross amounts; gains and losses are often reported net. Investment gains and losses may be reported net.

j. Unconditional contributions are to be recorded as assets (contributions receivable) and as revenues (contribution revenue). However, a donor-imposed **condition** causes a not-for-profit organization to not recognize either a receivable or a revenue. A donor-imposed condition specifies a future or uncertain event whose occurrence or failure to occur gives the promisor a right of return of the assets transferred or releases the promisor from its obligation to transfer the assets promised.

> **EXAMPLE**
>
> A not-for-profit organization receives a pledge from a donor that she will transfer $1,000,000 if matching funds can be raised within a year. The $1,000,000 would not be recognized as a revenue until the possibility of raising the matching funds is reasonably certain.

k. Multiyear contributions receivable would be recorded at the present value of the future collections. Moneys to be collected in future years would be presumed to be temporarily restricted revenues (based on time restrictions) and then reclassified in the year of receipt. The difference between the previously recorded temporarily restricted revenue at present value amounts and the current value would be recorded as contribution revenue, not interest. **All** contributions are to be recorded at fair market value as of the date of the contribution.

l. Organizations making the contributions, including businesses and other nonprofits, would recognize contribution expense using the same rules as followed by the receiving organization.

m. Contributions are to be distinguished from exchange revenues. The *Not-for-Profit Guide* indicates criteria that indicate when an increase in net assets is a contribution and when it is an exchange revenue; the most important rule is that if nothing is given by the not-for-profit organization in exchange in a transaction, that transaction would be considered a contribution. Contributions are recognized as additions to any of the net asset classifications. Exchange revenues (tuition, membership dues, charges for services, etc.) are increases in unrestricted net assets and are recognized in accordance with GAAP as applied to business enterprises.

n. Accounting standards require that when a not-for-profit organization (such as a foundation) is an **intermediary** or an **agent** for the transfer of assets to another not-for-profit organization, that intermediary or agent would not recognize a contribution. Unless the intermediary or agent not-for-profit organization is granted **variance power** to redirect the resources, or unless it is financially interrelated, the receipt of resources would be offset with the recognition of a liability to the recipient organization. If variance power exists, the recipient organization would recognize contribution revenue.

o. Accounting standards also require that the recipient organization recognize a revenue when the intermediary or agent recognizes a liability. When the intermediary or agent and the beneficiary are **financially interrelated,** the intermediary or agent would recognize contribution revenue; the beneficiary would recognize its interest in the net assets of the intermediary or agent.

p. Expenses are to be reported by function either in the statements or in the notes. The FASB does not prescribe functional classifications but does describe functions as program and supporting. Major program classifications should be shown. Supporting activities include management and general, fund raising, and membership development. Other classifications may be included, such as operating income, but are not required, except for health care entities. All expenses are reported as decreases in unrestricted net assets.

q. Plant is recorded, as mentioned above, either as temporarily restricted or unrestricted, and depreciated. Depreciation is to be charged for exhaustible fixed assets.

r. An entity may or may not capitalize "collections." "Collections" are works of art, historical treasures, and similar assets if those assets meet all of the following conditions:

(1) They are held for public exhibition, education, or research in furtherance of public service rather than financial gain;

(2) They are protected, kept encumbered, cared for, and preserved;

(3) They are subject to an organizational policy that requires the proceeds from sales of collection items to be used to acquire other items for collections.

If collections are not capitalized, revenues (contributions) would not be recognized for donated collections. Extensive note disclosure regarding accessions, disposals, etc. are required.

s. Investments in all debt securities and investments in equity securities that have readily determinable fair values (except equity securities accounted for under the equity method and investments in consolidated subsidiaries) are to be reported at fair value in the Statement of Net Assets. Unlike accounting standards for business enterprises, all unrealized gains and losses are to be reflected in the Statement of Activities along with realized gains and losses, in the appropriate net asset class.

t. Contributed services, when recognized, are recognized as both revenue and expense. However, contributed services should be recognized only when the services: (1) create or enhance nonfinancial assets, or (2) require specialized skills, are provided by individuals possessing those skills, and would typically be purchased if not provided by donation.

> **EXAMPLE**
>
> Jenna Wu, an attorney, provides necessary legal services to a not-for-profit organization gratis. The value of these services may be recognized by the not-for-profit as contributed services because they require

> specialized skills, are provided by an individual possessing those skills, and would typically be purchased in not provided by Jenna.

u. All expenses are reported as unrestricted. Expenses using resources that are temporarily restricted, including depreciation of plant, would be matched by a reclassification of resources from temporarily restricted to unrestricted net assets.

v. The "Reclassification" category of the Statement of Activities is unique. Sometimes "Reclassifications" are called "Net Assets Released from Restrictions." Reclassifications generally include (1) satisfaction of program restrictions (a purpose restriction by a donor), (2) satisfaction of equipment acquisition restrictions (depreciation of assets classified as temporarily restricted), (3) satisfaction of time restrictions (donor actual or implied restrictions as to when funds be used), and (4) expiration of term endowment.

w. Cash Flow statements are required for nonprofit organizations. The three FASB categories (operating, investing, and financing) are to be used. As is true for business organizations, either the direct or indirect method may be used. The indirect method, or reconciliation schedule for the direct method, will reconcile the change in **total** net assets to the net cash used by operating activities. Restricted contributions for long-term purposes (endowments, plant, future program purposes, etc.) are reported as financing activities.

x. Note disclosures are required for all items required for generally accepted accounting principles that are relevant to nonprofit organizations. In addition, specific requirements of SFAS 117 (FASB ASC 958) include (1) policy disclosures related to choices related to restricted contributions received and expended in the same period, and to the recording of plant as temporarily restricted or unrestricted, and (2) more detailed information regarding the nature of temporarily and permanently restricted resources.

y. The FASB specifically encourages note disclosures on (1) detail of the reclassification, (2) detail of investments and (3) breakdown of expenses by function and natural classifications (except for Voluntary Health and Welfare Organizations, which must include this information in a Statement of Functional Expenses).

z. The *Not-for-Profit Guide* provides guidance for **split-interest agreements,** such as charitable lead trusts and charitable remainder trusts. Split-interest agreements represent arrangements whereby both a donor (or beneficiary) and a not-for-profit organization receive benefits, often at different times in a multiyear arrangement. Specific rules exist for each type of split-interest agreement. The general rule is that the not-for-profit will record revenues in an amount equal to the present value of anticipated receipts.

EXAMPLE

Roger Smith established a charitable lead trust for a donation to the Salvation Army. Roger put $1,000,000 in the trust to be invested for 10 years. The Salvation Army receives the trust income for the 10-year period. At the end of the 10-year period, the principal of the trust goes to Roger's children.

---

aa. FASB requires that fund-raising expenses be reported either on the face of the financial statements or in the notes. AICPA Statement of Position 98-2 indicates that when an activity, such as a mailing, might involve fund-raising and either program or management and general activities, it is presumed to be fund-raising unless three criteria exist. Those criteria are

(1) **Purpose.** The activity has more than one purpose, as evidenced by whether compensation or fees for performing the activity are based strictly on the amount raised or on the performance of some program and/or management and general activity.

(2) **Audience.** If the audience is selected on the basis of its likelihood to contribute to the not-for-profit, this criterion is not met.

(3) **Content.** In order for this criterion to be met, the mailing or event must include a call to action other than raising money. For example, a mailing from the American Cancer Society might call for recipients to have regular check-ups, to exercise, to eat the right kinds of food, etc.

2. **Illustrative Financial Statements**

    The FASB requires three financial statements for nongovernmental, not-for-profit organizations, including (1) Statement of Financial Position, (2) Statement of Activities, and (3) Statement of Cash Flows. Voluntary health and welfare organizations (such as the American Red Cross, a mental health association, or a Big Brothers/Big Sisters organization) are required to prepare a fourth statement, a Statement of Functional Expenses. The first three of these statements are described and illustrated below.

    a. **Statement of Financial Position.** A Balance Sheet or Statement of Financial Position must show total assets, total liabilities, and total net assets. Net assets must be broken down between those that are unrestricted, temporarily restricted, and permanently restricted. Assets and liabilities may be classified or reported in order of liquidity and payment date. Assets restricted for long-term purposes must be reported separately from those that are not. The comparative format illustrated is optional; entities may report only balances for one year.

Contributions receivable are to be reported at the present value of future receipts. Investments in securities with determinable fair values are to be reported at fair value. The following reflects one of the permissible formats of FASB ASC 958:

Not-for-Profit Organization
STATEMENTS OF FINANCIAL POSITION
June 30, 20X1 and 20X0
(in thousands)

	20X1	20X0
Assets		
Cash and cash equivalents	$ 75	$ 460
Accounts and interest receivable	2,130	1,670
Inventories and prepaid expenses	610	1,000
Contributions receivable	3,025	2,700
Short-term investments	1,400	1,000
Assets restricted to investment in land, buildings, and equipment	5,210	4,560
Land, buildings, and equipment	61,700	63,590
Long-term investments	218,070	203,500
Total assets	$292,220	$278,480
Liabilities and net assets		
Accounts payable	$ 2,570	$ 1,050
Refundable advance		650
Grants payable	875	1,300
Notes payable		1,140
Annuity obligations	1,685	1,700
Long-term debt	5,500	6,500
Total liabilities	10,630	12,340
Net assets		
Unrestricted	115,228	103,670
Temporarily restricted	24,342	25,470
Permanently restricted	142,020	137,000
Total net assets	281,590	266,140
Total liabilities and net assets	$292,220	$278,480

SOURCE: SFAS 117, page 56

b. **Statement of Activities.** Note the following from the example Statement of Activities:

(1) Contributions, income on long-term investments, and net unrealized and realized gains on long-term investments may increase unrestricted, temporarily restricted, and permanently restricted net assets. All of these revenue sources increase unrestricted net assets unless restricted by donors.

(2) Fees increase unrestricted net assets. All exchange revenues increase unrestricted net assets. Exchange revenues include admissions charges, fees, and membership dues.

(3) Net unrealized gains are shown together with realized gains and investments. FASB prohibits displaying net unrealized and realized gains separately.

(4) All expenses decrease unrestricted net assets. (Losses, such as the actuarial loss, may decrease restricted net assets.)

(5) At some point net assets are released from restrictions (reclassified) from temporarily restricted to unrestricted net assets. This might be for satisfaction of program restrictions, satisfaction of equipment acquisition restrictions, expiration of time restrictions, or expiration of term endowments. Note that when net assets are released from restrictions, temporarily restricted net assets decrease and unrestricted net assets increase.

(6) Expenses are broken down between programs (A, B, C) and supporting (management and general, fundraising). While the FASB does not require these functional breakdowns, the FASB does have two requirements.

    (a) Expenses must be reported by function in the notes if not in this statement, and
    (b) Fund-raising expenses must be disclosed in the notes, if not in this statement.

The FASB permits other formats. For example, some entities prepare two statements.

    (a) Statement of Revenues, Expenses, and Changes in Unrestricted Net Assets, and
    (b) Statement of Changes in Net Assets.

Regardless of the format used, the change in net assets must be reported, by net asset class and in total.

Not-for-Profit Organization
STATEMENT OF ACTIVITIES
Year Ended June 30, 20X1
(in thousands)

	Unrestricted	Temporarily restricted	Permanently restricted	Total
Revenues, gains, and other support:				
Contributions	$ 8,640	$ 8,110	$ 280	$ 17,030
Fees	5,400			5,400
Income on long-term investments	5,600	2,580	120	8,300
Other investment income	850			850
Net unrealized and realized gains on long-term investments	8,228	2,952	4,620	15,800
Other	150			150
Net assets released from restrictions:				
Satisfaction of program restrictions	11,990	(11,990)		
Satisfaction of equipment acquisition restrictions	1,500	(1,500)		
Expiration of time restrictions	1,250	(1,250)		
Total revenues, gains, and other support	43,608	(1,098)	5,020	47,530
Expenses and losses:				
Program A	13,100			13,100
Program B	8,540			8,540
Program C	5,760			5,760
Management and general	2,420			2,420
Fund raising	2,150			2,150
Total expenses	31,970			31,970
Fire loss	80			80
Actuarial loss on annuity obligations		30		30
Total expenses and losses	32,050	30		32,080
Change in net assets	11,558	(1,128)	5,020	15,450
Net assets at beginning of year	103,670	25,470	137,000	266,140
Net assets at end of year	$115,228	$24,342	$142,020	$281,590

SOURCE: SFAS 117, page 59.

c. **Statement of Cash Flows.** In general, the FASB rules for cash flow statements, required for business enterprises, apply to not-for-profit organizations.

> **NOTE**: GASB rules, illustrated in Module 21, do not apply. The only major difference is that cash receipts for contributions restricted for long-term purposes are classified as financing activities.

Not-for-Profit Organization
STATEMENT OF CASH FLOWS
Year Ended June 30, 20X1
(in thousands)

Cash flows from operating activities:	
Cash received from service recipients	$ 5,220
Cash received from contributors	8,030
Cash collected on contributions receivable	2,615
Interest and dividends received	8,570
Miscellaneous receipts	150
Interest paid	(382)
Cash paid to employees and suppliers	(23,808)
Grants paid	(425)
Net cash used by operating activities	(30)

Cash flows from investing activities:

Insurance proceeds from fire loss on building	250
Purchase of equipment	(1,500)
Proceeds from sale of investments	76,100
Purchase of investments	(74,900)
Net cash used by investing activities	(50)

Cash flows from financing activities:

Proceeds from contributions restricted for:

Investment in endowment	200
Investment in term endowment	70
Investment in plant	1,210
Investment subject to annuity agreements	200
	1,680

Other financing activities:

Interest and dividends restricted for reinvestment	300
Payments of annuity obligations	(145)
Payments on notes payable	(1,140)
Payments on long-term debt	(1,000)
	(1,985)
Net cash used by financing activities	(305)
Net decrease in cash and cash equivalents	(385)
Cash and cash equivalents at beginning of year	460
Cash and cash equivalents at end of year	$ 75

Reconciliation of change in net assets to net cash used by operating activities:

Change in net assets	$ 15,450

Adjustments to reconcile change in net assets to net cash used by operating activities:

Depreciation	3,200
Fire loss	80
Actuarial loss on annuity obligations	30
Increase in accounts and interest receivable	(460)
Decrease in inventories and prepaid expenses	390
Increase in contributions receivable	(325)
Increase in accounts payable	1,520
Decrease in refundable advance	(650)
Decrease in grants payable	(425)
Contributions restricted for long-term investment	(2,740)
Interest and dividends restricted for long-term investment	(300)
Net unrealized and realized gains on long-term investments	(15,800)
Net cash used by operating activities	$ (30)

Supplemental data for noncash investing and financing activities:

Gifts of equipment	$140
Gift of paid-up life insurance, cash surrender value	$80

SOURCE: SFAS 117, pages 64-65.

3. Illustrative Transactions

a. Unrestricted revenues and expenses.

Under FASB guidance, full accrual accounting is used. A look at the Statement of Activities indicates that revenues might include contributions, fees, investment income, and realized and unrealized gains on investments. Expenses must be reported as unrestricted and reported by function, either in the statements or in the notes.

Assume the following unrestricted revenues:

Cash	1,000,000	
Contributions Receivable	200,000	
Accounts Receivable	100,000	
Interest Receivable	50,000	
Contributions—Unrestricted		700,000
Fees—Unrestricted		300,000
Income on Long-Term Investments—Unrestricted		350,000

Income earned from investments can be unrestricted, temporarily restricted, or permanently restricted depending on the wishes of the donor. If the donor does not specify, the investment income is unrestricted, even if the investment principal itself is permanently restricted.

Assume the following expenses, reported by function:

Program A Expense	400,000	
Program B Expense	300,000	
Program C Expense	200,000	
Management and General Expense	100,000	
Fund Raising Expense	200,000	
Cash		900,000
Accounts Payable		300,000

b. Purpose restrictions—temporarily restricted resources

Temporarily restricted resources are generally restricted by purpose, by time, and for the acquisition of plant. Assume that in 20X0 a donor gives $100,000 in cash for cancer research and that the funds are expended in 20X1. In 20X0, the following entry would be made:

Cash	100,000	
Contributions—Temporarily Restricted		100,000

At the end of 20X0 the $100,000 would be a part of the net assets of the temporarily restricted net asset class. In 20X1, the following entries would be made, assuming the funds are expended for cancer research.

Program A Expense (Research)	100,000	
Cash		100,000
Reclassifications from Temporarily Restricted Net Assets—		
Satisfaction of Program Restrictions	100,000	
Reclassifications to Unrestricted Net Assets—Satisfaction of		
Program Restrictions		100,000

NOTE: The assets are released from restriction by the expense, by conducting the research. Looking at the example statement of activities, the $100,000 would be included as a part of the $11,990,000 in program reclassifications.

c. Time restrictions—temporarily restricted resources

If a donor makes a contribution and indicates that the contribution should be used in a future period, that contribution would be recorded as a revenue in the temporarily restricted net asset class and then transferred to the unrestricted net asset class in the time period specified by the donor. In the absence of other information, if a pledge is made, the schedule of anticipated receipts would determine when the net assets are reclassified. Assume a $100,000 pledge in late 20X0, intended to be used by the nonprofit organization in 20X1; the entry in 20X0 would be

Pledges receivable	100,000	
Contributions—Temporarily Restricted		100,000

At the end of 20X0, the $100,000 would be reflected in the net assets of the temporarily restricted in class. In 20X1, the following entries would be made:

Cash	100,000	
Pledges receivable		100,000
Reclassifications from Temporarily Restricted Net Assets—		
Satisfaction of Time Restrictions	100,000	
Reclassifications to Unrestricted Net Assets—Satisfaction of		
Time Restrictions		100,000

The $100,000 above would be a part of the $1,250,000 in reclassifications for satisfaction of time restrictions in the statement of activities. Note that time, not an expense, determines when the asset is released from restrictions. In the special case of multiyear pledges, the present value of the future payments should be recorded as a revenue in the year of the pledge. In future years, the increase in the present value, due to the passage of time, is to be recorded as contribution revenue, not interest.

Finally, note that a time restriction might be explicit or implicit. An explicit time restriction would occur when a donor states specifically that the funds are for a certain year (this might be printed on pledge cards). An implicit time restriction reflects the provision that cash must be received from a donor during an accounting period, or the pledge will be assumed to carry a time restriction. The idea is that, if a donor wished a nonprofit to spend the money this year, the donor would have contributed the cash.

d. Plant acquisition restrictions—temporarily restricted resources

Sometimes donors give moneys restricted for the acquisition of plant, often in connection with a fund drive. The resources, whether in the form of pledges, cash, or investments, would be held in the temporarily restricted net asset class until expended. When expended, the nonprofit organization has a choice of two options: (1) reclassify the resources to the unrestricted class and record the entire plant as unrestricted, or (2) record the plant as temporarily restricted and reclassify to unrestricted in accordance with the depreciation schedule. Under the first option, assume that a donor gives $50,000 to a nonprofit organization in 20X0 for the purchase of equipment. The equipment is purchased in 20X1. The following entry would be made in the temporarily restricted class in 20X0:

Cash	50,000	
Contributions		50,000

In 20X1, the following entries would be made:

Equipment	50,000	
Cash		50,000
Reclassifications from Temporarily Restricted Net Assets—		
Satisfaction of Equipment Acquisition Restrictions	50,000	
Reclassification to Unrestricted Net Assets—Satisfaction of		
Equipment Acquisition Restrictions		50,000

The equipment would then be depreciated as a charge to expense in the unrestricted class as would be normal in business accounting. Remember that depreciation may be allocated to functional categories. Assume a ten-year life and that the equipment was purchased at the beginning of the year and that the equipment was used solely for Program A.

Program A Expense	5,000	
Accumulated Depreciation—Equipment		5,000

The above alternative has normally been used in the CPA Examination. When this is the case, the problem often states that, "the Not-for-Profit Organization implies no restriction on the acquisition of fixed assets."

The second alternative is to record the equipment as an increase in temporarily restricted net assets and reclassify it over time. The entries are illustrated below. Assume the contribution was received but unexpended in 20X0.

Cash	50,000	
Contributions—Temporarily Restricted		50,000

Assume the equipment was acquired early in 20X1.

Equipment	50,000	
Cash		50,000

Note that the $50,000 remains in temporarily restricted net assets. At the end of 20X1, the depreciation entry is made, and $5,000 is reclassified.

Program A Expense	5,000	
Accumulated Depreciation—Equipment		5,000
Reclassification from Temporarily Restricted Net Assets—		
Satisfaction of Equipment Acquisition Restrictions	5,000	
Reclassification to Unrestricted Net Assets—Satisfaction of		
Equipment Acquisition Restrictions		5,000

Using the first alternative, at the end of 20X1, the net asset balance of $45,000 would be in the unrestricted net asset class; in the second alternative, the $45,000 net asset balance would be in the temporarily restricted net asset class.

e. Permanently restricted resources

Resources in the permanently restricted class are held permanently. An example would be an endowment, where a donor makes a contribution with the instructions that the amount be permanently invested. The income might be unrestricted or restricted for a particular activity or program. Assume that in 20X1 a donor gave $100,000 for the purpose of creating an endowment. An entry would be made in the permanently restricted class (this would be part of the $280,000 shown in the Statement of Activities).

Cash	100,000	
Contributions—Permanently Restricted		100,000

> **NOTE:** Revenues can be recorded in any of the three net asset classes but expenses are recorded only in the unrestricted class. Note also that the expiration of restrictions is recorded by reclassifications.

B. College and University Accounting—Private Sector Institutions

Private colleges and universities are subject to the same guidance as other not-for-profit organizations that are included under the *Not-for-Profit Guide*. However, a few comments that specifically impact colleges and universities are in order.

1. Student tuition and fees are reported net of those scholarships and fellowships that are provided not in return for compensation.

> **EXAMPLE**
>
> Assume a university provides a scholarship based on grades, entering ACT or SAT, etc. The scholarship would be recorded as follows:
>
> | | | |
> |---|---|---|
> | Cash | 8,000 | |
> | Revenue Deduction—Student Scholarships | 2,000 | |
> | Revenue—Student Tuition and Fees | | 10,000 |

2. Student graduate assistantships and other amounts given as tuition remissions (for example for full-time employees) that are given in return for services provided to the institution are charged as expenses, to the department and function where the services are provided.

> **EXAMPLE**
>
> Assume that an assistantship was given with services provided to the Biology Department. The assistantship would be recorded as follows:
>
> | | | |
> |---|---|---|
> | Cash | 8,000 | |
> | Expense—Instruction (Biology Department) | 2,000 | |
> | Revenue—Student Tuition and Fees | | 10,000 |

3. The AICPA *Not-for-Profit Guide* specifically states that operation and maintenance of physical plant is not to be reported as a functional expense. Those costs, including depreciation, are to be allocated to other functions.
4. The *Not-for-Profit Guide* does not include examples of financial statements for colleges and universities, or other not-for-profit organizations. The illustrative statement of activities for an educational institution is taken from the *Financial Accounting and Reporting Manual for Higher Education* published by the National Association of College and University Business Officers. Many other formats are possible, as long as the changes in net assets are shown separately for unrestricted, temporarily restricted, and permanently restricted net assets.

> **NOTE:** All expenses are reported as decreases in unrestricted net assets; losses may be reported as decreases in any of the net asset classes.

Educational Institution
ILLUSTRATIVE STATEMENT OF ACTIVITIES
Multicolumn Format

	Unrestricted	Temporarily restricted	Permanently restricted	Total
Revenues and gains:				
Tuition and fees	$xxx	--	--	$xxx
Contributions	xxx	$xxx	$xxx	xxx
Contracts and other exchange transactions	xxx	--	--	xxx
Investment income on life income and annuity agreements	--	xxx	--	xxx
Investment income on endowment	xxx	xxx	xxx	xxx
Other investment income	xxx	xxx	xxx	xxx
Net realized gains on endowment	xxx	xxx	xxx	xxx
Net realized gains on other investments	xxx	xxx	xxx	xxx
Sales and services of auxiliary enterprises	xxx	--	--	xxx
Total revenues and gains	xxx	xxx	xxx	xxx
Net assets released from restrictions	xxx	(xxx)	--	--
Total revenues and gains and other support	xxx	xxx	xxx	xxx

	Unrestricted	Temporarily restricted	Permanently restricted	Total
Expenses and losses:				
Educational and general:				
Instruction	xxx	--	--	xxx
Research	xxx	--	--	xxx
Public service	xxx	--	--	xxx
Academic support	xxx	--	--	xxx
Student services	xxx	--	--	xxx
Institutional support	xxx	--	--	xxx
Total educational and general expenses	xxx	--	--	xxx
Auxiliary enterprises	xxx	--	--	xxx
Total expenses	xxx	--	--	xxx
Fire loss	xxx	--	--	xxx
Payments to life income beneficiaries	--	xxx	--	xxx
Actuarial loss on annuity obligations	xxx	--	--	xxx
Total expenses and losses	xxx	--	--	xxx
Increase (decrease) in net assets	xxx	xxx	xxx	xxx
Net assets at beginning of year	xxx	xxx	xxx	xxx
Net assets at end of year	$xxx	$xxx	$xxx	$xxx

SOURCE: National Association of College and University Business Officers, *Financial Accounting and Reporting Manual for Higher Education*, Chapter 500, as modified with the exclusion of Operation and Maintenance of Physical Plant and Scholarships and Fellowships as functional expenses.

NOW REVIEW MULTIPLE-CHOICE QUESTIONS 1 THROUGH 62 IN VOLUME 2

C. Health Care Organization Accounting—Private Sector

The AICPA has issued an AICPA Audit and Accounting Guide, *Health Care Organizations*. This *Guide* applies both to private sector and governmental health care organizations; separate illustrative statements are presented for each. This section of the module presents private sector health care principles, first by indicating the unique features (beyond part A of this module) that apply and second by presenting illustrative statements. A few of the major features are as follows:

1. Requirements of the *Guide* apply to clinics, medical group practices, individual practice associations, individual practitioners, emergency care facilities, laboratories, surgery centers, other ambulatory care organizations, continuing care retirement communities, health maintenance organizations, home health agencies, hospitals, nursing homes, and rehabilitation centers. Sometimes, a fine line is drawn between those organizations that are considered health care entities and those that are considered voluntary health and welfare organizations, which are not covered by this *Guide*. The distinction is made by the source of revenues, not by the services provided. A nonprofit organization providing health care service in return for payment (an exchange transaction) by the recipient of the service, by a third-party payor, or a government program would be considered a health care organization. A nonprofit organization providing health care service funded primarily by voluntary contributions (from persons or organizations not receiving the service) would be considered a voluntary health and welfare organization.

2. Health care organizations may be not-for-profit, investor owned, or governmental. When possible, accounting and reporting for all types should be similar.

3. Financial statements include a balance sheet, a statement of operations, a statement of changes in net assets, a cash flow statement, and notes to the financial statements.

4. The statement of operations should include a performance indicator, such as operating income, revenues over expenses, etc. The *Guide* specifically indicates that the following must be reported separately from (underneath) that performance indicator (this is a partial list):

   a. Equity transfers involving other entities that control the reporting entity, are controlled by the reporting entity, or are under the common control of the reporting entity.
   b. Receipt of restricted contributions.
   c. Contributions of (and assets released from donor restrictions related to) long-lived assets.
   d. Unrealized gains and losses on investments not restricted by donors or by law, except for those investments classified as trading securities.
   e. Investment returns restricted by donors or by law.
   f. Other items that are required by GAAP to be reported separately (such as extraordinary items, the effect of discontinued operations, accounting changes).

5. Note disclosure must indicate the policies adopted by the entity to determine what is and what is not included in the performance indicator.

6. Patient service revenue is to be reported on the accrual basis net of adjustments for contractual and other adjustments in the operating statement. Provisions recognizing contractual adjustments and other adjustments (for example, hospital employee discounts) are deducted from gross patient revenue to determine **net patient** revenue. Significant revenue under capitation agreements (revenues from third party payors based on number of employees to be covered, etc. instead of services performed) is to be reported separately. Note disclosure should indicate the methods of revenue recognition and description of the types and amounts of contractual adjustments.

7. Patient service revenue does not include charity care. Management's policy for providing charity care and the level of charity care provided should be disclosed in the notes.

8. "Other revenues, gains, and losses" (included in operative revenues) include items such as

   a. Investment income
   b. Fees from educational programs
   c. Proceeds from sale of cafeteria meals
   d. Proceeds from gift shop, parking lot revenue, etc.

9. As is true for other not-for-profit organizations, contributions restricted to long-term purposes (plant acquisition, endowment, term endowment, etc.) would not be reported in the Statement of Operations (as unrestricted revenue) but would be reported in the Statement of Changes in Net Assets as a revenue increasing temporarily restricted or permanently restricted net assets, as appropriate.

10. Expenses are decreases in unrestricted net assets. Expenses may be reported by either natural (salaries, supplies, etc.) or functional classification. Not-for-profit health care entities must disclose expenses in the notes by function if functional classification is not presented on the operating statement. Functional classifications should be based on full cost allocations. Unlike organizations subject to the *Not-for-Profit Guide,* health care organizations may report depreciation, interest, and bad debt expense along with functional categories.

11. Health care organizations, except for continuing care retirement communities, are to present a classified balance sheet, with current assets and current liabilities shown separately. Continuing care retirement communities may sequence assets in terms of nearness to cash and liabilities in accordance with the maturity date.

Two statements are presented for a private sector not-for-profit hospital, both taken from the *Guide*. The statement of operations is presented with one line shown for "excess of revenues over expenses." This is the performance indicator. Note the separation of items above and below that line. Also note the presentation separately for depreciation, interest, and provision for bad debts. In addition, note that the net assets released from restrictions includes separate amounts for those net assets released for operations and those released for other items. The statement of changes in net assets presents the other changes required by FASB ASC 958.

Sample Not-for-Profit Hospital
STATEMENTS OF OPERATIONS
Years Ended December 31, 20X7 and 20X6
(in thousands)

	20X7	20X6
Unrestricted revenues, gains and other support:		
Net patient service revenue	$85,156	$78,942
Premium revenue	11,150	10,950
Other revenue	2,601	5,212
Net assets released from restrictions used for operations	300	--
Total revenues, gains and other support	99,207	95,104
Expenses:		
Operating expenses	88,521	80,585
Depreciation and amortization	4,782	4,280
Interest	1,752	1,825
Provision for bad debts	1,000	1,300
Other	2,000	1,300
Total expenses	98,055	89,290
Operating income	1,152	5,814

	20X7	20X6
Other income:		
Investment income	3,900	3,025
Excess of revenues over expenses	5,052	8,839
Change in net unrealized gains and losses on other than trading securities	300	375
Net assets released from restrictions used for purchase of property and equipment	200	
Change in interest in net assets of Sample Hospital Foundation	283	536
Transfers to parent	(688)	(3,051)
Increase in unrestricted net assets, before extraordinary item	5,147	6,699
Extraordinary loss from extinguishment of debt	(500)	--
Increase in unrestricted net assets	$ 4,647	$ 6,699

See accompanying notes to financial statements.

SOURCE: AICPA Audit and Accounting Guide, *Health Care Organizations.*

Sample Not-for-Profit Hospital
STATEMENTS OF CHANGES IN NET ASSETS
Years Ended December 31, 20X7 and 20X6
(in thousands)

	20X7	20X6
Unrestricted net assets:		
Excess of revenues over expenses	$ 5,052	$ 8,839
Net unrealized gains on investments, other than trading securities	300	375
Change in interest in net assets of Sample Hospital Foundation	283	536
Transfers to parent	(688)	(3,051)
Net assets released from restrictions used for purchase of property and equipment	200	--
Increase in unrestricted net assets before extraordinary item	5,147	6,699
Extraordinary loss from extinguishment of debt	(500)	--
Increase in unrestricted net assets	4,647	6,699
Temporarily restricted net assets:		
Contributions for charity care	140	996
Net realized and unrealized gains on investments	5	8
Net assets released from restrictions	(500)	--
Increase (decrease) in temporarily restricted net assets	(355)	1,004
Permanently restricted net assets:		
Contributions for endowment funds	50	411
Net realized and unrealized gains on investments	5	2
Increase in permanently restricted net assets	55	413
Increase in net assets	4,347	8,116
Net assets, beginning of year	72,202	64,086
Net assets, end of year	$76,549	$72,202

See accompanying notes to financial statements.

SOURCE: AICPA Audit and Accounting Guide, *Health Care Organizations.*

D. Health Care Organization Accounting—Governmental

Governmental health care organizations, as mentioned earlier, are not allowed to use the principles established in SFAS 116 and 117 for not-for-profit organizations. The AICPA *Health Care Guide,* however, attempts to present accounting and reporting principles allowed by the GASB in as close a fashion as possible to private sector health care entities. A few major observations should be noted.

1. Governmental health care organizations are permitted by GASB 34 to report as special-purpose entities engaged in governmental or business-type activities, or both. Most will choose to report as special-purpose entities engaged in business-type activities.
2. Governmental health care organizations reporting as special-purpose entities engaged in business-type activities will prepare the statements required for proprietary funds. These are the (a) Balance Sheets, (b) Statement of Revenues, Expenses, and Changes in Net Assets, and (c) Statement of Cash Flows
3. GASB principles must be followed in the separate reports of governmental health care organizations. For example, net assets are to be categorized as (a) invested in capital assets, net of related debt; (b) restricted, and (c) unrestricted. The GASB cash flow format should be used. Refer to the proprietary fund example statements in Module 21.
4. To the extent possible, AICPA *Health Care Guide* principles should also be followed. For example, the items listed above in Section C.4. should be reported below the performance indicator, net patient revenue should be calculated in the same manner as described previously in C.6. and should not include charity care cases.

> **NOW REVIEW MULTIPLE-CHOICE QUESTIONS 63 THROUGH 83 IN VOLUME 2**

KEY TERMS

Contributions (of cash). A voluntary transfer of resources to a charitable organization motivated by generosity.

Contributions (of services). A voluntary providing of personal services to a charitable organization.

Permanently restricted resources. Resources such as (1) certain assets, such as artwork, etc. that must be maintained or used in a certain way, (2) endowments that represent funds that must be invested permanently, and (3) land when it must be held in perpetuity.

Split-interest agreement. An arrangement whereby both a donor (or beneficiary) and a not-for-profit organization receive benefits (e.g., charitable lead trusts and charitable remainder trusts).

Temporarily restricted resources. Resources restricted to be (1) used for a particular purpose, (2) expended at a time in the future, or (3) invested for a period of time.

Unrestricted resources. All resources that do not have restrictions by donors or grantors.

ARB, APB, and FASB Pronouncements

Study Program for the Accounting Pronouncements

As of July 1, 2009, the FASB Accounting Standards Codification is the only source of US GAAP, other than SEC literature. Older pronouncements, such as the Accounting Research Bulletins, Accounting Principles Board Opinions, and FASB Statements, are no longer considered authoritative. Outlines of the pronouncements that were used in the Codification are included in this edition to assist the CPA candidate in his/her transition to the Codification. The outlines of these previous sources of accounting literature are presented by Accounting Standard Codification (ASC) Topic order (e.g., ASC Topic 205, 210, 505), with cross-references to their location in the new ASC. For standards with the same ASC Topic cross-reference (e.g., both APB 6 and SFAS 129 relate to ASC Topic 505), the earlier issued standard is presented first. For standards relating to multiple ASC Topic areas (e.g., SFAS 6 is related to ASC Topic 210 and ASC Topic 470), the entire standard is presented in both locations. A cross references list by standard type precedes the outlines.

Study through the outlines as you are referred to them in the modules throughout the text. Note that on the CPA exam, it is not necessary to know the Codification Topic numbers or pronouncement numbers; however, being familiar with the numbering system will greatly aid the candidate in the research component of the FAR exam. Also, note that it is not necessary to memorize all the required disclosures. A good approach to take is to take the position of a financial analyst: What data would you want to know? Utilizing this approach will help you remember any exceptions (i.e., items you would not normally think an analyst would be interested in.)

References to FASB Materials

In studying the outlines, you might notice that parts of some pronouncements have not been outlined. The reason some sections of the pronouncements are excluded from the outlines is that they have never been tested on the exam. Also, outlines for very specialized pronouncements (e.g., SFAS 50, *Financial Reporting in the Record and Music Industry*) are not included in this manual. Several others are outlined more generally. Only those FASB Interpretations and Technical Bulletins having widespread applicability are included in this chapter. They are set apart with solid lines **only** to distinguish them from the SFAS.

ACCOUNTING RESEARCH BULLETINS

ARB 43—Chapter 1A Rules Adopted by Membership (ASC Topics 310, 505, 605, and 850)
Chapter 1B—Profits or Losses on Treasury Stock (ASC Topic 505)
Chapter 2A—Comparative Financial Statements (ASC Topic 205)
Chapter 3A—Current Assets and Current Liabilities (ASC Topics 210, 310, 340, 470)
Chapter 4—Inventory Pricing (ASC Topic 330)
Chapter 7A—Quasi Reorganization (ASC Topic 852)
Chapter 7B—Stock Dividends and Stock Splits (ASC Topic 505—Equity)
Chapter 10A—Real and Personal Property Taxes (ASC Topic 720—Other Expenses)
ARB 45—Long-Term Construction Contracts (ASC Topic 605—Revenue)
ARB 51—Consolidated Financial Statements (ASC Topic 810—Consolidation)

ACCOUNTING PRINCIPLES BOARD OPINIONS CROSS-REFERENCE

APB 6—Status of Accounting Research Bulletins (ASC Topic 505—Equity)
APB 9—Reporting the Results of Operations (ASC Topics 225, 250, 505)
APB 10—Omnibus Opinion—1966 (ASC Topics 210, 605, 740)
APB 12—Omnibus Opinion—1967 (ASC Topics 310, 360, 505, 710, 835)
APB 14—Convertible Debt and Debt Issued with Stock Warrants (ASC Topic 470—Debt)
APB 18—The Equity Method for Investments (ASC Topics 323, 325, 850)
APB 21—Interest on Receivables and Payables (ASC Topic 835—Interest)
APB 22—Disclosure of Accounting Policies (ASC Topic 235—Notes to Financial Statement)
APB 23—Accounting for Income Taxes—Special Areas (ASC Topic 740—Income Taxes) (Amended by SFAS 109)
APB 26—Early Extinguishment of Debt (ASC Topic 470—Debt) (Amended by SFAS 84 and SFAS 145)
APB 28—Interim Financial Reporting (ASC Topic 270—Interim Reporting)
APB 29—Accounting for Nonmonetary Transactions (ASC Topic 845—Nonmonetary Transactions)
APB 30—Reporting the Results of Operations (ASC Topic 225—Income Statement)

STATEMENTS OF FINANCIAL ACCOUNTING STANDARDS CROSS-REFERENCE

SFAS 2—Accounting for Research and Development Costs (R&D) (ASC Topic 730—Research & Development)

SFAS 6—Classification of Short-Term Obligations Expected to Be Refinanced (ASC Topics 210 and 470)

SFAS 7—Accounting and Reporting by Development Stage Companies (ASC Topic 915—Development Stage Entities)

SFAS 13—Accounting for Leases (ASC Topic 840—Leases)

SFAS 15—Accounting by Debtors and Creditors for Troubled Debt Restructurings (ASC Topics 310 and 470) (Superseded by SFAS 114 with regard to creditors)

SFAS 16—Prior Period Adjustments (ASC Topics 250 and 270)

SFAS 34—Capitalization of Interest Cost (ASC Topic 835—Interest)

SFAS 43—Accounting for Compensated Absences (ASC Topics 710—Compensation—General)

SFAS 45—Accounting for Franchise Fee Revenue (ASC Topic 952—Franchisors)

SFAS 47—Disclosure of Long-Term Obligations (ASC Topics 440 and 470)

SFAS 48—Revenue Recognition When Right of Return Exists (ASC Topic 605—Revenue) (Also ASC Topics 450 and 460)

SFAS 52—Foreign Currency Translation (ASC Topic 830—Foreign Currency Matters)

SFAS 57—Related-Party Disclosures (ASC Topic 850—Related-Party Disclosures)

SFAS 66—Accounting for Sales of Real Estate (ASC Topics 360, 605, and 976)

SFAS 78—Classification of Obligations That Are Callable by the Creditor (ASC Topic 470—Debt)

SFAS 86—Accounting for the Costs of Computer Software to Be Sold, Leased, or Otherwise Marketed (ASC Topic 985—Software)

SFAS 87—Employers' Accounting for Pensions (ASC Topic 715—Compensation—Retirement Benefits)

SFAS 88—Employers' Accounting for Settlements and Curtailments of Defined Benefit Pension Plans and for Termination Benefits (ASC Topic 715—Retirement Benefits)

SFAS 89—Financial Reporting and Changing Prices (ASC Topic 255—Changing Prices)

SFAS 91—Accounting for Nonrefundable Fees and Costs Associated with Originating or Acquiring Loans and Initial Direct Costs of Leases (ASC Topic 310—Receivables)

SFAS 94—Consolidation of All Majority-Owned Subsidiaries (ASC Topic 810—Consolidation)

SFAS 95—Statement of Cash Flows (ASC Topic 230—Statement of Cash Flows)

SFAS 98—Accounting for Leases (ASC Topic 840—Leases)

SFAS 106—Employers' Accounting for Postretirement Benefits other than Pensions (ASC Topic 715—Compensation—Retirement Benefits)

SFAS 107—Disclosures about Fair Value of Financial Instruments (ASC Topic 825—Financial Instruments)

SFAS 109 (I27)—Accounting for Income Taxes (ASC Topic 740—Income Taxes)

SFAS 112—Employers' Accounting for Postemployment Benefits (ASC Topic 712—Compensation—Nonretirement Postemployment Benefits)

SFAS 114—Accounting by Creditors for Impairment of a Loan (ASC Topic 310—Receivables)

SFAS 115—Accounting for Certain Investments in Debt and Equity Securities (ASC Topic 320—Investments—Debt and Equity Securities)

SFAS 116—Accounting for Contributions Received and Contributions Made (ASC Topic 958—Not-for-Profit Entities)

SFAS 117—Financial Statements of Not-for-Profit Organizations (ASC Topic 958—Not-for-Profit Entities)

SFAS 123—Revised (C36) Share-Based Payment (ASC Topic 718—Compensation—Stock Compensation and ASC Topic 505—Equity)

SFAS 124—Accounting for Certain Investments Held by Not-for-Profit Organizations (ASC Topic 958—Not-for-Profit Entities)

SFAS 128—Earnings Per Share (ASC Topic 260—Earnings per Share)

SFAS 129—Disclosure of Information about Capital Structure (ASC Topic 505—Equity)

SFAS 130—Reporting Comprehensive Income (ASC Topic 220—Comprehensive Income)

SFAS 131—Disclosures about Segments of an Enterprise and Related Information (ASC Topic 280—Segment Reporting)

SFAS 132 (Revised)—Employers' Disclosures about Pensions and Other Postretirement Benefits (ASC Topic 715—Compensation—Retirement Benefits)

SFAS 133—Accounting for Derivative Instruments and Hedging Activities (ASC Topic 815—Derivatives and Hedging)

SFAS 138—Accounting Certain Derivative Instruments and Certain Hedging Activities: (ASC Topic 815—Derivatives and Hedging)

SFAS 140—Accounting for Transfers and Servicing of Financial Assets and Extinguishment of Liabilities (ASC Topic 860—Transfers and Servicing)

SFAS 141(R)—Business Combinations (ASC Topic 805—Business Combinations)

SFAS 142—Goodwill and Other Intangible Assets (ASC Topic 350—Intangibles—Goodwill and Other)

SFAS 143—Accounting for Asset Retirement Obligations (ASC Topic 410—Asset Retirement and Environmental Obligations)

SFAS 144—Accounting for the Impairment or Disposal of Long-Lived Assets (ASC Topic 360—Property, Plant, and Equipment; ASC Topic 205—Presentation of Financial Statements; and ASC Topic 225—Income Statement)

SFAS 145—Rescission of FASB Statements No. 4, 44, and 64, Amendment of FASB Statement No. 13, and Technical Corrections (Rescinds SFAS 4, 44, and 64 and amends SFAS 13)

SFAS 146—Liabilities: Exit or Disposal Costs (ASC Topic 420—Exit or Disposal Cost Obligation)

SFAS 147—Acquisitions of Certain Financial Institutions, An Amendment of FASB Statements No. 72 and 144 and FASB Interpretation No. 9 (The authors believe that this topic is too specialized for the CPA exam)

SFAS 149—Amendment of Statement 133 on Derivative Instruments and Hedging Activities (ASC Topic 815)

SFAS 150—Accounting for Certain Financial Instruments with Characteristics of Both Liabilities and Equity (ASC Topic 480—Distinguishing Liabilities from Equity)

SFAS 151—Inventory Costs (ASC Topic 330—Inventory)

SFAS 152—Accounting for Real Estate Time Sharing Transactions—An Amendment of FASB Statements No. 66 and 67 (Amends SFAS 66 and SFAS 67)

SFAS 153—Exchanges of Nonmonetary Assets—An Amendment of APB Opinion No. 29 (ASC Topic 845—Nonmonetary Transactions)

SFAS 154—Accounting Changes and Error Corrections (ASC Topic 250—Accounting Changes and Error Corrections)

SFAS 155—Accounting for Certain Hybrid Financial Instruments (ASC Topic 815—Derivatives and Hedging)

SFAS 156—Accounting for Servicing of Financial Assets (ASC Topic 860—Transfers and Servicing)

SFAS 157—Fair Value Measurements (ASC Topic 820—Fair Value Measurement and Disclosures)

SFAS 158—Employers' Accounting for Defined Benefit Pension and Other Postretirement Plans (An Amendment of FASB Statements 87, 88, 106, and 132[R]) (ASC Topic 715—Compensation—Retirement Benefits and ASC Topic 958—Not-for-Profit Entities)

SFAS 159—The Fair Value Option for Financial Assets and Financial Liabilities—including an amendment of FASB Statement 115 (ASC Topic 825—Financial Instruments)

SFAS 160—Noncontrolling Interests in Consolidated Financial Statements—An Amendment of ARB No. 51 (ASC Topic 810—Consolidation)

SFAS 161—Disclosures about Derivative Instruments and Hedging Activities—An Amendment of FASB Statement No. 133 (ASC Topic 815—Derivatives and Hedging)

SFAS 162—The Hierarchy of Generally Accepted Accounting Principles

SFAS 163—Accounting for Financial Guarantee Insurance Contracts—An Interpretation of FASB Statement No. 60. (The authors believe that this topic is too specialized for the CPA exam.)

SFAS 164—Not-for-Profit Entities: Mergers and Acquisitions—Including an Amendment of FASB Statement No. 142 (ASC Topic 958) (The authors believe that this topic is too specialized for the CPA exam.)

SFAS 165—Subsequent Events (ASC Topic 855)

SFAS 166—Accounting for Transfers of Financial Assets—An Amendment of FASB Statement No. 140 (ASC Topic 860)

SFAS 167—Amendments to FASB Interpretation No. 46(R) (ASC Topic 810)

SFAS 168—The FASB Accounting Standards Codification and the Hierarchy of Generally Accepted Accounting Principles—A Replacement of FASB Statement No. 162 (ASC Topic 105)

GENERAL PRINCIPLES (ASC TOPIC 100)

SFAS 168—The FASB Accounting Standards Codification and the Hierarchy of Generally Accepted Accounting Principles—A Replacement of FASB Statement No. 162 (ASC Topic 105)

A. Establishes the Codification as the single source of US GAAP for nongovernmental entities, except for SEC authoritative literature which applies to SEC registrants

B. Content in SEC Sections of the Codification is provided for convenience and is not the complete SEC literature.

PRESENTATION (ASC TOPIC 200)

ARB 43—Chapter 2A Comparative Financial Statements (ASC Topics 205)

Comparative statements enhance the usefulness of financial statements and should be presented.

SFAS 144 Accounting for the Impairment or Disposal of Long-Lived Assets (ASC Topic 360—Property, Plant, and Equipment; ASC Topic 205—Presentation of Financial Statements; and ASC Topic 225—Income Statement)

A. Establishes financial and reporting requirements for the impairment or disposal of long-lived assets. In addition to property, plant, equipment, and intangible assets being amortized, SFAS 144 applies to capital leases of lessees, long-lived assets of lessors subject to operating leases, proved oil and gas properties that are being accounted for using the successful efforts method of accounting, and long-term prepaid assets.

B. If a long-lived asset (or assets) is part of a group that includes other assets and liabilities not covered by SFAS 144, the statement applies to the group.

C. Assets to be held and used

1. Reviewed for impairment when circumstances indicate that the carrying amount of a long-term asset (or group) is not recoverable and exceeds its fair value. The carrying amount of a long-lived asset (asset group) is not recoverable it if exceeds the sum of the undiscounted cash flows expected to result from its use and eventual disposal.
2. A long-lived asset (asset group) shall be tested for recoverability whenever events or changes in circumstances indicate that its carrying amount may not be recoverable. Examples of such events include

   a. Significant decrease in market value
   b. Change in way asset used or physical change in asset
   c. Legal factors or change in business climate that might affect asset's fair value or adverse action or assessment by regulator
   d. Asset costs incurred greater than planned
   e. Current-period operating or cash flow loss combined with historical or projection of such amounts demonstrates continuing losses from the asset
   f. A current expectation that, more likely than not a long-lived asset will be disposed of significantly before the end of its previously estimated useful life

3. Impaired if the expected total future cash flows are less than the carrying amount of the asset (asset group)

   a. Assets should be grouped at lowest level for which there are identifiable cash flows independent of other groupings
   b. Expected future cash flows are future cash inflows to be generated by the asset (asset group) less the future cash outflows expected to be necessary to obtain those inflows
   c. Expected future cash flows are **not** discounted and do not consider interest charges
   d. If the management has alternative courses of action to recover the carrying amount, or if a range of possible cash flows are associated with a particular course of action, a probability-weighted approach may be useful

4. Written down to fair value and loss recognized upon impairment

   a. Fair value is "the price that would be received to sell an asset or paid to transfer a liability in an orderly transaction between market participants at the measurement date." (SFAS 157)
   b. If quoted market price in active market is not available, the estimate of fair value should be based on best information available

5. An impairment loss for an asset group shall reduce only the carrying amounts of the long-lived assets. Impairment of other assets in the group should be accounted for in accordance with other applicable accounting standards
6. If an impairment loss is recognized, the adjusted carrying amount becomes its new cost basis
7. Fair value increases on assets previously written down for impairment losses may not be recognized
8. Disclosures

   a. Description of impaired asset (asset group) and circumstances which led to impairment
   b. Amount of impairment and manner in which fair value was determined
   c. Caption in income statement in which impairment loss is aggregated, if it is not presented separately thereon
   d. Business segment(s) affected (if applicable)

D. Long-lived assets to be disposed of other than by sale

1. Long-lived assets to be abandoned are disposed of when they cease to be used
2. Long-lived assets to be exchanged for similar assets or to be distributed to owners are disposed of when they are exchanged or distributed

E. Long-lived assets to be disposed of by sale

1. Long-lived assets to be sold shall be classified as "held-for-sale" in the period in which all of the following criteria are met:

   a. Management commits to a plan of disposal
   b. The assets are available for sale
   c. An active program to locate a buyer has been initiated
   d. The sale is probable
   e. The asset is being actively marketed for sale at a fair price
   f. It is unlikely that the disposal plan will significantly change

2. Reported at lesser of the carrying amount or fair value less cost to sell

  a. Cost to sell includes broker commissions, legal and title transfer fees, and closing costs prior to legal title transfer

3. In future periods, adjusted carrying amount of asset shall be revised down or up to extent of changes in estimate of fair value less cost to sell, provided that the adjusted carrying amount does not exceed the carrying amount of the asset prior to the adjustment reflecting the decision to dispose of the asset

  a. Thus, recoveries may be recognized when assets are to be **disposed of** but not on impaired assets that continue to be used

F. Reporting long-lived assets and disposal groups to be disposed of

1. Discontinued operations of a component of an entity

  a. A component of an entity comprises operations and cash flows that can be clearly distinguished, operationally and for financial reporting purposes

  b. The results of a component of an entity that either has been disposed of or is classified as held for sale shall be reported as discontinued operations if both of the following conditions are met:

    (1) The operations and cash flows of the component have been (will be) eliminated from ongoing operations
    (2) The entity will not have any significant continuing involvement in the operations of the component after disposal

  c. In reporting discontinued operations, the income statement should present the results of discontinued operations separately after income from continuing operations and before extraordinary items as shown below

Income from continuing operations before income taxes	$xxxxx	
Income taxes	xxx	
Income from continuing operations		$xxxx
Discontinued operations (Note X)		
Loss from operations of discontinued Component Z (including loss on disposal of $xxx)	xxxx	
Income tax benefit	xxxx	
Loss on discontinued operations	xxxx	
Net income		$xxxx

2. A gain or loss recognized for long-term asset (group) classified for sale that is not a component of an entity shall be included in income from continuing operations before income taxes

3. Disclosures

  a. Description of assets to be disposed of, reasons for disposal, expected disposal date, and carrying amount of those assets
  b. Gain or loss, if any, resulting from changes in carrying amount due to further changes in market value
  c. If applicable, amounts of revenue and pretax profit or loss reported in discontinued operations
  d. If applicable, the segment of the business affected (see outline of SFAS 131)

ARB 43—Chapter 3A Current Assets and Current Liabilities (ASC Topics 210, 310, 340, 470)

Chapter 3A contains the definitions and examples of current assets and liabilities.

A. **Current assets** are "cash and other assets or resources commonly identified as those which are reasonably expected to be (1) realized in cash, (2) sold, or (3) consumed during the ordinary operating cycle of the business."

1. Cash available for current operations
2. Inventories
3. Trade receivables
4. Other receivables collectible in one year
5. Installment, deferred accounts, and notes receivable
6. Prepaid expenses

B. **Current liabilities** are "obligations whose liquidation is reasonably expected to require the use of existing resources properly classifiable as current assets or the creation of other current liabilities during the ordinary operating cycle of the business."

1. Trade payables
2. Collections received in advance of services
3. Accruals of expenses

4. Other liabilities coming due in one year
5. Note that liabilities not using current assets for liquidation are not current liabilities (e.g., bonds being repaid from a sinking fund)

C. Operating cycle is "average time intervening between the acquisition of materials or services entering this process and the final cash realization."

APB 10 Omnibus Opinion—1966 (ASC Topics 210, 605, 740)

A. ARB 43, Chapter 3B Working Capital

1. Offsetting of liabilities and assets in the balance sheet is not acceptable unless a right of offset exists.
2. Most government securities are not designed to be prepayment of taxes and thus may not be offset against tax liabilities. Only where an explicit prepayment exists may an offset be used.

FASB INTERPRETATION NO. 39 OFFSETTING OF AMOUNTS RELATED TO CERTAIN CONTRACTS

A right of setoff exists when all of the following conditions are met: (a) each of the two parties to a contract owes the other determinable amounts, (b) the reporting entity has the right to set off the amount owed with the amount owed by the other entity, (c) the reporting entity intends to set off, and (d) the right of setoff is enforceable at law.

B. Installment method of accounting

Revenues should be recognized at the point of sale unless receivables are in doubt. The installment or cost recovery method may be used.

SFAS 6 Classification of Short-Term Obligations Expected to Be Refinanced (ASC Topics 210 and 470)

A. Short-term obligations shall be classified as a current liability unless

1. Enterprise intends to refinance the obligation on a long-term basis
2. AND the intent is supported by ability to refinance

   a. Post-balance-sheet issuance of long-term debt or equity securities, or
   b. Financing agreement that clearly permits refinancing on a long-term basis

     (1) Does not expire or is not callable for one year
     (2) No violation of the agreement exists at the balance sheet date or has occurred to date

3. The amount of the short-term obligation excluded from current liability status should not exceed the

   a. Net proceeds of debt or securities issued
   b. Net amounts available under refinancing agreements

     (1) The enterprise must intend to exercise the financing agreement when the short-term obligation becomes due.

4. Refinancing of short-term obligations is a FS **classification** issue, **not** a **recognition** and **measurement** issue.

FASB INTERPRETATION NO. 8 CLASSIFICATION OF A SHORT-TERM OBLIGATION REPAID PRIOR TO BEING REPLACED BY A LONG-TERM SECURITY

Short-term obligations that are repaid after the balance sheet date but **before** funds are obtained from long-term financing are to be classified as current liabilities at the balance sheet date.

EXAMPLES

In situation 1 below, the obligation will be classified as a noncurrent liability at the balance sheet date. Why? Proceeds from refinancing were obtained prior to the due date of the obligation.

12/31 Year-end	2/1 Stock/long-term debt issued	2/15 Short-term obligation due	3/15 Financial statements issued

Situation 1: Classify obligation due 2/15 as noncurrent liability at balance sheet date.

In situation 2 below, the short-term obligation will be classified as a current liability. Why? Proceeds from the issuance of stock or long-term debt were not obtained until after the due date of the short-term obligation. Therefore, current assets must have been used to pay the short-term obligation.

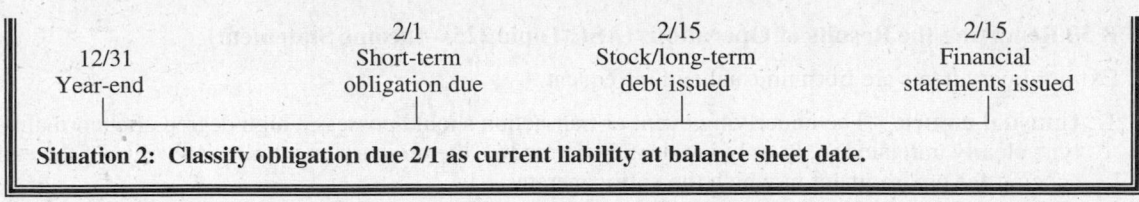

Situation 2: Classify obligation due 2/1 as current liability at balance sheet date.

SFAS 130 Reporting Comprehensive Income (ASC Topic 220—Comprehensive Income)

A. Establishes standards for reporting and display of comprehensive income (net income plus **other comprehensive income**) in a full set of general-purpose FS

B. Items, and changes therein, to be included as part of and separately classified in **other comprehensive income**

    1. Foreign currency items

    2. Unrealized gains (losses) on certain investments in debt and equity securities

    3. The amounts for overfunded or underfunded pension plans

C. Presentation of comprehensive income

    1. Alternative display options

        a. At the bottom of IS, continue from net income to arrive at a **comprehensive income** figure (equals net income plus other comprehensive income), or

        b. In a separate statement that starts with net income.

    2. Components of other comprehensive income may be displayed net of related tax effects or before related tax effects with one amount shown for the aggregate income tax effect (with detail shown in notes)

    3. Reclassification (recycling) adjustments

        a. Made to avoid double counting of items included in other comprehensive income in a prior year or current year that are included in net income (earnings) for the period

        b. Display separately from the balance of each item adjusted (B.1. and B.2. above) (gross display)

            (1) For reclassification adjustments related to the minimum pension liability, a single amount shall be displayed (net display)

D. Separate EPS numbers are not required for other comprehensive income or comprehensive income

APB 9 Reporting the Results of Operations (ASC Topics 225, 250, 505)

A. Designates a new format for income statement in which all normal operating items would be presented at the top of the income statement resulting in "net income before extraordinary items."

    1. "Net income before extraordinary items" is followed by extraordinary items resulting in "net income."

B. "Prior period adjustments" are excluded from the income statement and constitute adjustments of beginning retained earnings disclosed at the top of the retained earnings statement.

    1. Beginning retained earnings are adjusted by "prior period adjustments" resulting in "restated beginning retained earnings."

    2. "Restated retained earnings" is then adjusted for net income and dividends which results in ending retained earnings.

C. Prior period adjustments should be disclosed in the period of adjustment.

    1. The effect on each prior period presented should be disclosed including restated income taxes.

    2. Disclosure in subsequent periods is not normally required.

    3. Historical summary data should also be restated and disclosed in the period of adjustment.

D. The APB also reaffirmed earlier positions that the following should not affect determination of net income:

    1. Transactions in the company's own stock

    2. Transfers to or from retained earnings

    3. Quasi reorganization adjustments

APB 30 Reporting the Results of Operations (ASC Topic 225—Income Statement)

A. Extraordinary items are **both** unusual and infrequent.

1. **Unusual nature.** "The underlying event or transaction should possess a high degree of abnormality and be of a type clearly unrelated to, or only incidentally related to, the ordinary and typical activities of the entity, taking into account the environment in which the entity operates."

   a. Special characteristics of the entity

      (1) Type and scope of operations
      (2) Lines of business
      (3) Operating policies

2. **Infrequency of occurrence.** "The underlying event or transaction should be of a type that would not reasonably be expected to recur in the foreseeable future, taking into account the environment in which the entity operates."

3. Example of extraordinary presentation

Income before extraordinary items	$xxx
Extraordinary items (less applicable income taxes of $__) (Note __)	xxx
Net income	$xxx

4. Examples of gains and losses that are **not** generally extraordinary

   a. Write-downs or write-offs of receivables, inventories, R&D, etc.
   b. Translation of foreign exchange including major devaluations
   c. Disposal of a component of a business
   d. Sale of productive assets
   e. Effects of strikes
   f. Accruals on long-term contracts

5. Extraordinary items should be classified separately if material on an individual basis.

6. Gains or losses that are unusual **or** infrequent but not both should be disclosed separately (but not net of tax) in the income statement or notes.

SFAS 95 Statement of Cash Flows (ASC Topic 230—Statement of Cash Flows)

A. Statement of Cash Flows in General

1. Required for each period results of operation (income statement) are provided
2. Objectives

   a. Provide information about cash receipts and cash payments
   b. Provide information about operating, investing, and financing activities
   c. Helps users to assess

      (1) Ability to generate future net cash flows
      (2) Ability to meet obligations and pay dividends
      (3) Reasons for differences between income and associated cash receipts and payments
      (4) Both cash and noncash aspects of entity's investing and financing activities

3. Shall report

   a. Cash effects during a period from

      (1) Operating activities
      (2) Investing activities
      (3) Financing activities

   b. Noncash financing and investing activities in supplemental schedule

B. Gross and Net Cash Flows

1. Gross amount of cash receipts and payments is relevant.

   a. For example, must show issuance of bonds and retirement of bonds separately

2. Statement should explain change during the period in **cash and cash equivalents**.

   a. Cash equivalents

      (1) Short-term, highly liquid investments that are

(a) Readily convertible into known amounts of cash
(b) Near maturity (original maturity of three months or less from **date of purchase** by the enterprise) and present negligible risk of changes in value

(2) Examples

(a) Treasury bills
(b) Commercial paper
(c) Money market funds

C. Classification

1. Investing activities

a. Include

(1) Lending money and collecting on those loans
(2) Acquiring and selling, or disposing

(a) Securities that are neither cash equivalents nor held in a trading portfolio
(b) Productive assets expected to generate revenue over long periods of time

(3) Cash inflows

(a) Receipts from loans by

1] Principal repayments
2] Sale of loans made by the entity

(b) Receipts from sale of

1] Securities of other entities carried in held-to-maturity (debt only) or available-for-sale portfolios (debt or equity)
2] Property, plant, and equipment

(4) Cash outflows

(a) Loans made or purchased by the entity
(b) Payments to acquire assets

1] Securities of other entities carried in held-to-maturity (debt only) or available-for-sale portfolios (debt or equity)
2] Property, plant, and equipment

2. Financing activities

a. Include

(1) Obtaining resources from owners and providing them with a return on, and a return of, their investment
(2) Obtaining resources from creditors and repaying the amounts borrowed

b. Cash inflows

(1) Proceeds from the issuance of

(a) Equity securities
(b) Bonds
(c) Mortgages
(d) Notes
(e) Other short- or long-term borrowing

c. Cash outflows

(1) Payments of dividends
(2) Outlays to repurchase entity's shares
(3) Repayments of amounts borrowed

3. Operating activities

a. Include

(1) All transactions and other events that are not investing and financing
(2) Delivering or producing goods for sale and providing services
(3) Cash effects of transactions and other events that enter into the determination of income

      b. Cash inflows

         (1) Cash receipts from sale of goods or services
         (2) Interest and dividends received
         (3) Other operating cash receipts
         (4) Sales of "trading portfolio" securities

      c. Cash outflows

         (1) Payments to employees and other suppliers of goods or services
         (2) Income taxes paid
         (3) Interest paid
         (4) Other operating cash payments
         (5) Purchases of "trading portfolio" securities

D. Exchange Rate Effects

   1. Report the reporting currency equivalent of foreign currency cash flows using exchange rates in effect at time of cash flows

      a. Weighted-average exchange rate may be used, if result substantially same.

E. Content and Form

   1. Report net cash provided or used by operating, investing, and financing activities
   2. At end of statement, reconcile beginning and ending cash and cash equivalents by showing net increase or decrease for period as addition to beginning balance to obtain ending balance
   3. Cash flow from operating activities

      a. Direct presentation (encouraged by FASB)

         (1) Report major classes of operating receipts and payments (C.3.b.–c. above)
         (2) Difference between cash receipts and payments—net cash flow from operating activities
         (3) Supplemental schedule using indirect presentation must be presented when direct method used in body of statement

      b. Indirect presentation (acceptable format)

         (1) Shall separately report all major classes of reconciling items

            (a) Deferrals of past operating cash receipts and cash payments such as depreciation and changes during the period in inventory and unearned revenue
            (b) Accruals of expected future operating cash receipts and cash payments such as changes during the period in receivables and payables

         (2) Interest paid (net of amounts capitalized) and income taxes paid must appear in related disclosures

      c. Does not include cash flows from transactions or events whose effects are included in income, but which are not operating activities; for example,

         (1) Gain or loss on extinguishment of debt—financing activities
         (2) Gain or loss on sale of assets or from disposal of discontinued operations—investing activities

   4. Inflows and outflows of cash from investing and financing activities

      a. Noncash aspects should be clearly identified in separate schedule; for example,

         (1) Conversion of debt to equity
         (2) Acquisition of assets by assuming liabilities

            (a) Includes capital lease obligations

         (3) Exchanges of assets or of liabilities

   5. Enterprise shall disclose policy for determining items included in cash equivalent.

      a. Change in policy is change in accounting principle requiring restatement of comparative FS.

F. Cash flow per share shall not be reported.

APB 22 Disclosure of Accounting Policies (ASC Topic 235—Notes to Financial Statement)

A. Accounting policies can affect reported results significantly and the usefulness of the financial statements depends on the user's understanding of the accounting policies adopted by the reporting entity. Disclosure of accounting policies are

1. Essential to users
2. Integral part of financial statements
3. Required for one or more financial statements
4. Required for not-for-profit entities
5. Not required for unaudited interim statements

   a. If no change in accounting policy has occurred

B. Disclosure should include accounting principles and methods of applying them if material to reported amounts.

1. Generally, disclosure pertinent to principles involving recognition of revenue and expense
2. Specifically, disclosure pertinent to

   a. Selection from existing alternatives
   b. Principles peculiar to a particular industry
   c. Unusual or innovative applications

3. Examples

   a. Consolidation method
   b. Depreciation method
   c. Amortization of intangibles
   d. Inventory pricing
   e. R&D references amended by SFAS 2
   f. Translation of foreign currencies
   g. Long-term contract accounting
   h. Franchising and leasing activities

4. Accounting policy disclosure should not duplicate disclosures elsewhere in the statements.

C. Particularly useful is a separate **Summary of Significant Accounting Policies** either preceding or as the initial note.

SFAS 16 Prior Period Adjustments (ASC Topics 250 and 270)

A. All P&L items are included in the determination of net income except the correction of an error in statements of a prior period.

1. Account for and report as a prior period adjustment to beginning retained earnings

B. An exception exists for interim reporting regarding certain adjustments relating to prior interim periods of the current year.

1. These "adjustments" (affecting prior interim periods of the current fiscal year) are settlements or adjustments of

   a. Litigation or similar claims
   b. Income taxes
   c. Renegotiation proceedings
   d. Utility revenue per the rate-making process

2. These "adjustments" must also

   a. Be material to operating income, trends in income, etc.
   b. All or part of the adjustment is specifically identified with specified prior interim periods of the current fiscal year.
   c. Not subject to reasonable estimation prior to the current interim period (e.g., new retroactive tax legislation)

SFAS 154 Accounting Changes and Error Corrections (ASC Topic 250—Accounting Changes and Error Corrections)

A. Defines an accounting change as (1) change in principle; (2) change in an estimate; or (3) change in reporting entity. The correction of an error is not an accounting change.
B. Once an accounting principle is adopted, it must be used consistently for similar events and transactions. An entity may change an accounting principle only if the change is required by a new accounting pronouncement, or if the entity can justify that the alternative method is preferable.

C. Change in accounting principle

1. Is given retrospective application of the new accounting principle to all prior periods, unless it is impracticable to do so. This includes

   a. Cumulative effects of the change are presented in the carrying amounts of assets and liabilities as of the beginning of the first period presented
   b. Offsetting adjustment is made to opening balance of retained earnings for that period
   c. Financial statements of each period are adjusted to reflect period-specific effects of the new accounting principle

   Only direct effects of change are recognized (i.e., changes in inventory balances, deferred taxes, impairment adjustments). Indirect effects are reported in period in which the accounting change is made.
D. If cumulative effect can be determined, but period-specific effects cannot be determined, cumulative effect is applied to the earliest period to which it can be calculated. Offsetting adjustment is made to retained earnings of that period.
E. If it is impracticable to determine the cumulative effect of the change in any prior period, treat prospectively.
F. Notes to the financial statements must include

1. The nature and reason for the change with explanation as to why the new method is preferable
2. The method of applying the change
3. A description of the prior period information retrospectively adjusted
4. Effect of change on income from continuing operations, net income, and other affected line items on financial statements, and any per share amounts for current period and all periods adjusted
5. The cumulative effect of the change on retained earnings and other components of equity or net assets as of the earliest period presented
6. If retrospective application is impracticable, the reason and a description of how the change was reported
7. A description of the indirect effects of the change and amounts recognized in the current period and related per share amounts
8. The amounts of indirect effects of the change and per share amounts

G. Disclosures for interim periods should disclose the effect of change on income from continuing operations, net income, and related per share amounts for postchange interim periods.
H. Once the change in method is disclosed, financial statements in subsequent periods do not need to repeat disclosures.
I. Change in accounting estimate

1. Treat on prospective basis in current and future periods
2. If change is effected by change in principle, treat as change in estimate
3. Change in depreciation method is treated as change in estimate
4. If change in estimate is caused by change in principle, must show footnote disclosures required by change in accounting principle

J. Change in reporting entities

1. Change is retrospectively applied to the financial statements of all periods presented
2. Previously issued interim statements presented on a retrospective basis
3. Footnote disclosures include the nature and reason for change, net income, other comprehensive income, and any related per share amounts for all periods presented

K. Correction of an error

1. Errors are errors in recognition, measurement, presentation, or disclosure (Change from non-GAAP to GAAP is a correction of error)
2. Treat as prior period adjustment by restating financial statements
3. Cumulative effect of error is reflected in carrying value of assets and liabilities at the beginning of the first period presented, with an offsetting adjustment in the opening balance in retained earnings
4. Restate financial statements to reflect period-specific effects of error
5. Footnote disclosures must disclose that previously issued statements were restated, along with description of error.
6. Effects of error and any per share amounts must also be disclosed for each period presented
7. Cumulative effect of the change on retained earnings or other components of equity should be presented for the earliest period presented.
8. Gross effects and net effects from income taxes on net income of prior period must be disclosed. Amount of income tax applicable to each prior period must be disclosed.
9. Once correction of error is disclosed, financial statements of subsequent years do not need to repeat disclosure

SFAS 89 Financial Reporting and Changing Prices (ASC Topic 255—Changing Prices)

This statement **encourages** but does not require a business enterprise that prepares its financial statements in US dollars and in accordance with US generally accepted accounting principles to disclose supplementary information on changing prices.

A. Measurement

  1. Inventory

    a. Current cost is the current cost of purchasing or manufacturing, whichever is applicable

      (1) Or recoverable amount if lower

  2. Property, plant, and equipment

    a. Current cost is current cost of acquiring same service potential (or recoverable amount if lower)

      (1) That is, the same operating costs and output
      (2) Three valuation methods

        (a) Current cost of new asset less depreciation
        (b) Cost of comparable used asset
        (c) Adjusting new asset cost for differences in

          1] Useful life
          2] Output capacity
          3] Nature of service
          4] Operating costs

  3. Recoverable amount

    a. Current worth of net amount of cash expected to be recoverable from the use or sale of an asset

  4. Increase or decrease in current cost amount of inventory and PP&E, net of inflation

    a. Differences between current cost at entry dates and exit dates

      (1) Entry dates are the later of the beginning of the year or date of acquisition
      (2) Exit dates are the earlier of date of use, sale, etc., or year-end

SFAS 128 Earnings Per Share (ASC Topic 260—Earnings per Share)

A. Presentation on Financial Statements

  1. Entities with publicly held common stock and simple capital structures (no potential common shares) need only present basic per share amounts. All other entities must present basic and diluted per share amounts with equal prominence.
  2. Must present EPS on face of income statement for

    a. Income from continuing operations
    b. Net income

  3. May present on face of income statement or in notes

    a. Discontinued operations
    b. Extraordinary items
    c. Cumulative effect of change in accounting principle

B. Basic EPS—Measures entity performance over a period of time

  1. Computed as net income minus preferred dividends divided by the weighted-average number of common shares outstanding. The claims of senior securities (nonconvertible preferred dividends) should be deducted from income prior to computing EPS to properly determine net income available to **common** shareholders. Therefore, dividends on cumulative preferred are deducted whether or not declared, while dividends on noncumulative preferred are deducted only if declared.
  2. EPS figures should be based upon consolidated income figures after consolidating adjustments and eliminations.
  3. To compute the weighted-average of common shares outstanding, treasury shares should be excluded as of date of repurchase.
  4. EPS data for all periods presented should be retroactively adjusted for all splits and dividends, even those subsequent to the period being presented.

5. For stock issued in purchase combinations, use weighted-average from date of combination. For pooling combination, shares assumed outstanding the entire period regardless of when issued.

C. For Diluted EPS, these additional procedures apply

1. The "if-converted" method is used to adjust EPS on outstanding common shares for dilutive convertible securities.

   a. The convertible securities are considered to have been converted at the beginning of the period (or at issuance if later) increasing the denominator of EPS.
   b. For convertible bonds, the interest savings net of tax is added to the numerator of EPS.
   c. For convertible preferred, the preferred dividends deducted in arriving at EPS are not deducted, thereby increasing the numerator. There is no tax effect because dividends are not an expense.

2. The "treasury stock" method is used to adjust EPS on outstanding common shares for dilutive options and warrants (i.e., those for which the exercise price is below the market price).

   a. The options and warrants are assumed to be exercised at the beginning of the period (or the date the options and warrants were issued if later). The shares assumed issued increase the denominator of EPS.
   b. The hypothetical proceeds are used to purchase treasury stock at the average price over the year.
   c. No retroactive adjustment should be made to EPS figures for options and warrants as a result of market price changes.

3. When convertible securities require payment of cash at conversion, they are considered the equivalent of warrants. The "if-converted" method is used for the conversion and the "treasury stock" method is applied to the cash proceeds.

4. Fixed awards and nonvested stock to be issued to an employee under a stock-based compensation arrangement are considered options and are considered to be outstanding as of the grant date even though their exercise may be contingent upon vesting.

5. Contingently issuable shares are shares whose issuance is contingent upon the satisfaction of certain conditions and shall be considered outstanding and included in the diluted EPS computation as follows:

   a. If all necessary conditions have been satisfied by the end of the period, the shares should be included as of the beginning of the period in which the conditions were satisfied (or as of the date of the contingent stock agreement, if later).
   b. If all necessary conditions have not been satisfied, the number of contingently issuable shares shall be based on the number of shares (if any) that would be issuable if the end of the reporting period were the end of the contingency period and if the result would be dilutive. These shares shall be included in the diluted EPS denominator as of the beginning of the period (or as of the date of the contingent stock agreement if later).

6. Antidilutive securities shall not be included in diluted EPS computations.

D. Additional Disclosure Requirements

1. A reconciliation of the numerators and denominators of the basic and diluted per share computations for income from continuing operations, including the individual income and share amount effects of all securities that affect earnings per share.

2. The effect that has been given to preferred dividends in arriving at income available to common shareholders in computing basic EPS.

3. Securities that are antidilutive for the period(s) presented but could potentially dilute basic EPS in the future.

4. A description of any transaction that occurs after the end of the most recent period but before issuance of the financial statements that would materially change the number of shares outstanding at the end of the period if the transaction had occurred before the end of the period.

APB 28 Interim Financial Reporting (ASC Topic 270—Interim Reporting)

PART I Application of GAAP to Interim Periods

A. APB faced basic question about interim periods

1. Are interim periods basic accounting periods?
2. Are interim periods integral parts of the annual period?

B. The APB decided interim periods are an integral part of an annual period.

1. Certain GAAP must be modified for interim reporting to better relate the interim period to the annual period.

C. Revenue should be recognized on the same basis as for the annual period.

D. Costs directly associated with revenue should be reported as in annual periods with the following exceptions:

1. Estimated gross profit rates may be used to estimate inventory. Disclose method used and significant adjustments to reconcile to later physical inventory.
2. When LIFO base period inventories are liquidated during the interim period but are expected to be replaced by the end of the annual period, cost of sales should be priced at replacement costs rather than at base period costs.
3. Declines in inventory market values, unless temporary, should be recognized. Subsequent recovery of market value should be recognized as a cost recovery in the subsequent period.
4. Unanticipated and unplanned standard cost variances should be recognized in the respective interim period.

E. The objective of reporting all other costs is to obtain fair measure of operations for the annual period. These expenses include

1. Direct expenditures—salaries
2. Accruals—vacation pay
3. Amortization of deferrals—insurance

F. These costs should be applied in interim statements as follows:

1. Charge to income as incurred, or based on time expiration, benefit received, etc. Follow procedures used in annual reports.
2. Items not identified with specific period are charged as incurred.
3. No arbitrary assignment.
4. Gains and losses of any interim period that would not be deferred at year-end cannot be deferred in the interim period.
5. Costs frequently subjected to year-end adjustments should be anticipated in the interim periods.

   a. Inventory shrinkage
   b. Allowance for uncollectibles, quantity discounts
   c. Discretionary year-end bonuses

G. Seasonal variations in above items require disclosure and one may add twelve-month reports ending at the interim date for current and preceding years.
H. The best estimate of the annual tax rate should be used to provide taxes on a year-to-date basis.

1. The best estimate should take investment credits, capital gains, etc. into account, but not extraordinary items.
2. Tax effects of losses in early portion of the year should not be recognized unless realization in subsequent interim periods is assured beyond a reasonable doubt (e.g., an established pattern of loss in early periods).

   a. When tax effects of losses in early periods are not recognized, no taxes should be accrued in later periods until loss credit has been used.

I. Extraordinary items should be disclosed separately and recognized in the interim period in which they occur.

1. The materiality of extraordinary items should be determined in relation to expected annual income.
2. Effects of disposals of a component of a business are not extraordinary items, but should be disclosed separately.
3. Extraordinary items should **not** be prorated over remainder of the year.
4. Contingencies should be disclosed in the same manner as required in annual reports.

J. Each interim report should disclose any change in accounting principle from

1. Comparable period of prior year
2. Preceding periods of current year
3. Prior annual report

K. Reporting these changes

1. SFAS 154 should be applied.
2. A change in accounting estimate (including effect on estimated tax rate) should be accounted for in period of change and disclosed in subsequent periods if material.
3. Changes in principle should be given retrospective application. Financial statements are retrospectively adjusted showing the effects of the change on the carrying amounts of assets and liabilities for the earliest period presented, with an adjustment to beginning retained earnings for that period. Period-specific effects of the change should be shown for all direct effects of the change.

PART II Required Interim Disclosures by Publicly Traded Companies

A. Minimum disclosure includes

1. Sales, provision for taxes, extraordinary items, cumulative effect of principle changes, and net income
2. BEPS and DEPS

3. Seasonal revenue, costs, and expenses
4. Significant changes in estimates of taxes
5. Disposal of a business component and extraordinary items
6. Contingent items
7. Changes in accounting principles and estimates
8. Significant changes in financial position
9. Reportable operating segments

   a. External revenues
   b. Intersegment revenues
   c. Segment profit/loss
   d. Total assets (if material change from last annual report)
   e. Description of changes from last annual report in method of determining segments or measurement of segment profit/loss
   f. Reconciliation of total of reportable segments' profit/loss to corresponding enterprise amount

B. When **summarized interim data** are reported regularly, the above should be reported for the

1. Current quarter
2. Current year-to-date or last twelve months with comparable data for the preceding year

C. If fourth quarter data are not separately reported, disclose in annual report

1. Disposal of business component
2. Extraordinary, unusual, and infrequent items
3. Aggregate year-end adjustments

D. The APB encourages interim disclosure of financial position and funds flow data.

1. If not disclosed, significant changes therein should be disclosed.

FASB INTERPRETATION NO. 18 ACCOUNTING FOR INCOME TAXES IN INTERIM PERIODS

Tax on income from continuing operations for an interim period is based on estimated annual effective rate, which reflects anticipated tax planning alternatives. Expense of interim period is (Year-to-date income) × (Estimated rate) less (Expense recognized in prior interim periods). Tax effect of special items (below continuing operations) computed as they occur.

SFAS 131 Disclosures about Segments of an Enterprise and Related Information (ASC Topic 280—Segment Reporting)

A. Requires disclosures about

1. Operating segments of an enterprise, products and services, geographic areas, major customers

   a. Disclosures are required for **public** companies in complete annual FS per GAAP and in condensed FS of interim periods including comparative presentations
   b. Purpose of disclosures is to better assist statement users in appraising past and future performance of the enterprise and assessing prospects for future net cash flows.

B. Definitions

1. **Management approach.** Method chosen by the FASB to determine what information should be reported; it is based on the way that management organizes segments internally for making operating decisions and assessing performance.
2. **Operating segment.** Component of an enterprise that may earn revenues and incur expenses, about which separate financial information is available that is evaluated regularly by the chief operating decision maker in deciding how to allocate resources and in assessing performance.
3. **Chief operating decision maker.** Person whose general function (not specific title) is to allocate resources to, and assess the performance of, the segments of an enterprise.
4. **Segment revenue.** Includes revenue from unaffiliated customers and intersegment sales (use company transfer prices to determine intersegment sales).
5. **Segment operating profit (loss).** Segment revenue less all operating expenses, including any allocated revenues or expenses.
6. **Segment assets.** Tangible and intangible assets directly associable or used by the segment, including any allocated portion of assets used jointly by more than one segment

C. To determine reportable segments

1. Identify operating segments under management approach
2. Determine if aggregation of operating segments is appropriate.
3. Perform quantitative threshold tests (10% tests).

D. Operating segments may be aggregated by management if they have similar economic characteristics and if segments are similar in each of the following areas:

1. Nature of products and services
2. Nature of production processes
3. Type of customer for their products and services
4. Methods used to distribute their products or provide their services
5. Nature of regulatory environment; for example, banking

E. Operating segments that meet any of the three quantitative thresholds (10% tests) are immediately deemed reportable segments.

1. Segment revenue is $\geq$ 10% of combined revenue (revenue includes intersegment revenue).
2. Segment operating profit or loss is $\geq$ 10% of the greater of, in absolute amount

   a. Combined operating profit of all operating segments with profit, or
   b. Combined operating loss of all operating segments with loss

3. Segment assets are $\geq$ 10% of combined assets of all segments.

F. Additional considerations when determining reportable segments

1. Management may combine information about operating segments that do not meet the 10% tests with information on other operating segments that do meet the 10% tests to produce reportable segment only if majority of the aggregation criteria exists.
2. Segment that was reported previously should continue to be reported if judged to be of continuing significance by management even if it does not meet the 10% tests in current period.
3. Combined sales to nonaffiliated customers of segments reporting separately must be at least 75% of total consolidated sales

   a. If not, additional segments must be identified as reportable segments

4. All other operating segments which are not reportable shall be combined with any other business activities (e.g., corporate headquarters) and disclosed in "all other" category.
5. Number of reportable segments probably should not exceed ten.

   a. Combine closely related segments if number of segments becomes impracticable

G. Information is to be presented for each reportable segment and in aggregate for remaining segments not reported separately

1. General information, including

   a. Explanation of factors used to identify the enterprise's reportable segments
   b. Types of products and services from which revenue is derived

2. An enterprise shall report a measure of profit or loss and total assets for each reportable segment. To the extent the following is included in the measure of profit or loss or assets it shall also be disclosed:

   a. Revenues from external customers
   b. Revenues from transactions with other operating segments of the same enterprise
   c. Interest revenue
   d. Interest expense
   e. Depreciation, depletion, and amortization expense
   f. Unusual items not qualifying as extraordinary items
   g. Equity in net income of investees accounted for by equity method
   h. Income tax expense or benefit
   i. Extraordinary items
   j. Significant noncash items other than depreciation, depletion, and amortization expense

   3. For segment assets

     a. Total expenditures for additions to long-lived assets
     b. Amount of investment in equity method investees

   4. Enterprise shall provide an explanation of the measurements of segment profit or loss and assets, including

     a. Basis of accounting
     b. Nature of any differences between measurement of profit and loss or assets for the segment and that of the consolidated enterprise
     c. Nature of any changes from prior periods
     d. Nature and effect of asymmetrical allocations (e.g., allocating depreciation, but not related assets to segment)

   5. Enterprise will need to provide reconciliations for the segment amounts disclosed to the corresponding enterprise amounts.
   6. Although not as extensive as in the annual report, certain disclosures are required in the interim reports.

H. Previously issued segment information must be restated (unless impractical to do so) if any enterprise changes structure of internal organization that causes composition of reportable segments to change
I. Information about products and services

   1. Enterprise-wide disclosure required even if only one and segment disclosures required.
   2. Revenue from external customers for each product and service shall be reported by the enterprise.

J. Information about geographic areas (individual countries)

   1. Enterprise-wide disclosure required even if only one and segment disclosures required.
   2. Enterprise shall report revenues from external customers and long-lived assets attributable to its domestic operations and foreign operations.
   3. If enterprise functions in two or more foreign geographic areas, to the extent revenues or assets of an individual foreign geographic area are material, then these amounts should be separately disclosed.

K. Major customers

   1. Enterprise-wide disclosure required even if segment disclosures are not required
   2. Disclose amount of revenue to each customer accounting for ≥ 10% of revenue
   3. Disclose similarly if ≥ 10% of revenue derived from sales to domestic government agencies or foreign governments
   4. Identify segment making sales

ASSETS (ASC TOPIC 300)

ARB 43—Chapter 1A Rules[1] Adopted by Membership (ASC Topics 310, 505, 605, and 850)

Four rules recommended by the Committee on Cooperation with Stock Exchanges in 1934. The last rule is from another 1934 Institute committee.

   1. Profit is realized at the point of sale unless collection is not reasonably assured.
   2. Capital (paid-in) surplus should not be charged with losses or expenses, except in quasi reorganizations.
   3. Receivables from officers, employees, and affiliates must be separately disclosed.
   4. Par value of stock issued for assets cannot be used to value the assets if some of the stock is subsequently donated back to the corporation.

Chapter 3A Current Assets and Current Liabilities (ASC Topics 210, 310, 340, 470)

Chapter 3A contains the definitions and examples of current assets and liabilities.

A. Current assets are "cash and other assets or resources commonly identified as those which are reasonably expected to be (1) realized in cash, (2) sold, or (3) consumed during the ordinary operating cycle of the business."

   1. Cash available for current operations
   2. Inventories
   3. Trade receivables
   4. Other receivables collectible in one year
   5. Installment, deferred accounts, and notes receivable
   6. Prepaid expenses

---

[1] The references in parentheses are from the FASB Accounting Standards—Current Texts: Volumes 1 and 2, John Wiley & Sons, Inc. These are included only for facilitating the use of the Current Texts for candidates who have access to them.

B. **Current liabilities** are "obligations whose liquidation is reasonably expected to require the use of existing resources properly classifiable as current assets or the creation of other current liabilities during the ordinary operating cycle of the business."

1. Trade payables
2. Collections received in advance of services
3. Accruals of expenses
4. Other liabilities coming due in one year
5. Note that liabilities not using current assets for liquidation are not current liabilities (e.g., bonds being repaid from a sinking fund)

C. **Operating cycle** is "average time intervening between the acquisition of materials or services entering this process and the final cash realization."

APB 12 Omnibus Opinion—1967 (ASC Topics 310, 360, 505, 710, 835)

A. Allowance or contra accounts (allowance for bad debts, accumulated depreciation, etc.) should be deducted from assets or groups of assets with appropriate disclosure.

B. Disclosure of depreciable assets should include

1. Depreciation expense for the period
2. Balances of major classes of depreciable assets by nature or function
3. Accumulated depreciation either by major class or in total
4. Description of method(s) of depreciation by major classes of assets

C. Changes in the separate shareholder equity accounts in addition to retained earnings and changes in number of equity securities must be disclosed in the year of change

1. In separate statements
2. Or the financial statements
3. Or the notes

SFAS 15 Accounting by Debtors and Creditors for Troubled Debt Restructurings (ASC Topics 310 and 470)
(Superseded by SFAS 114 with regard to creditors)

A. Troubled debt restructurings occur when a creditor is compelled to grant relief to a debtor due to the debtor's inability to service the debt. This SFAS prescribes accounting for such debt restructurings if

1. By creditor-debtor agreement
2. Imposed by a court
3. Result of repossessions and foreclosures
4. But not changes in lease agreements

    a. Nor legal actions to collect receivables
    b. Nor quasi reorganizations

B. If a **debtor** transfers assets to settle fully a payable, recognize a gain on restructuring equal to the book value of the payable less FV of assets transferred.

1. Use fair value measurements as outlined by SFAS 157.
2. The difference between set FV and carrying value of the assets transferred is a gain or loss in disposition of assets per APB 30.

C. If a **debtor** issues an equity interest to settle fully a payable, account for equity issued at FV.

1. Excess of carrying value of payable over equity FV is a gain on restructuring.

D. A **debtor** having the terms of troubled debt modified should account for the restructure prospectively (i.e., no adjustment of the payable).

1. Recompute the new effective rate of interest based on the new terms

    a. Total cash payments to be paid, less carrying value of payable is the interest
    b. Amortize the payable by the interest method (APB 21) using the new interest rate

2. Exception is if restructured terms require total cash payments (including interest) which are less than the carrying value of the payable, write down the payable to the total cash to be paid

    a. Include contingent payments in calculation; this precludes recognizing a gain currently and interest expense later

b. Recognize gain on the write-down
c. All future cash payments reduce the payable (i.e., no interest expense is recognized)

E. If restructured by partial settlement (assets and/or equity issuance) and modified terms

1. First account for asset and/or equity issuance per above
2. Then account for modified terms per above

F. Related matters

1. A repossession or foreclosure is accounted for per the above.
2. Contingent payments on restructured debt shall be recognized per SFAS 5 (i.e., its payment is probable and subject to reasonable estimate).
3. Legal fees on debt restructuring involving equity issuance reduce the amounts credited to the equity accounts.

   a. All other direct costs of debt restructuring reduce gain or are expenses of the period if there is no gain.

G. Disclosures by **debtors**

1. Description of major changes in debt of each restructuring
2. Aggregate gain on debt restructuring and related tax effect
3. Aggregate net gain (loss) on asset transfers due to restructuring
4. EPS amount of aggregate gain on restructuring net of tax effect

SFAS 91 Accounting for Nonrefundable Fees and Costs Associated with Originating or Acquiring Loans and Initial Direct Costs of Leases (ASC Topic 310—Receivables)

Establishes the accounting for nonrefundable fees and costs associated with lending, committing to lend, or purchasing a loan or group of loans. Applies to all types of loans.

A. Loan origination fees shall be recognized over life of related loan as adjustment of yield.
B. Certain direct loan origination costs shall be deferred over the life of the related loan as a reduction of the loan's yield.
C. All loan commitment fees shall be deferred except for certain retrospectively determined fees.

1. Those commitment fees meeting specified criteria shall be recognized over the loan commitment period.
2. All other commitment fees shall be recognized as an adjustment of yield over the related loan's life.
3. If commitment expires unexercised, then recognize in income upon expiration of the commitment.

D. Loan fees, certain direct loan origination costs, and purchase premiums and discounts on loans shall be recognized as an adjustment of yield generally by the interest method based on contractual terms of the loan.

1. Prepayments by debtors may be anticipated in certain specified circumstances.

SFAS 114 Accounting by Creditors for Impairment of a Loan (ASC Topic 310—Receivables)

A. Scope of SFAS 114

1. Applies to all creditors and to all loans except for those specified in A.3 (a.-d.)
2. Applies to all loans (including A.3.a.) that are restructured in a troubled debt restructuring involving a modification of terms
3. Exceptions

   a. Large groups of smaller-balance homogeneous loans collectively evaluated for impairment
   b. Loans that are measured at fair value or at the lower of cost or fair value
   c. Leases
   d. Debt securities

4. Does not specify how a creditor should identify loans that are to be evaluated for collectibility

B. Recognition of Impairment

1. A loan is impaired when it is probable that a creditor will be unable to collect all amounts due according to the contractual terms.

   a. Probable—future event or events are likely to occur
   b. All amounts due according to the contractual terms include both interest and principal payments collected as scheduled in loan agreement.

2. If a loan qualifies as exception A.3.a., the creditor may not apply the provisions of SFAS 114 until the debt is restructured.
3. Instances when a loan is not impaired

      a. Insignificant delays or shortfalls

      b. A delay in which creditor expects to collect all amounts due including interest accrued for the period of delay

C. Measurement of Impairment

    1. Creditor measures impairment based on present value of expected future cash flows discounted at the loan's effective interest rate

      a. Effective interest rate—rate implicit in loan at time of origination

      b. If effective interest rate varies (based on an independent index or rate)

        (1) May be calculated based on the index or rate as it changes over life of loan

        (2) Or may be fixed at rate in effect at date the loan meets impairment criterion

      c. Expected future cash flows determined as creditor's best estimate based on reasonable and supportable assumptions and projections (including estimated costs to sell)

    2. Loans with common risk characteristics may be aggregated and impairment measured using historical statistics and a composite effective interest rate.

    3. Alternative measures of impairment

      a. Loan's observable market price

      b. Fair value of collateral if loan is collateral dependent

        (1) Collateral dependent means repayment provided solely by the underlying collateral

        (2) This method must be used when foreclosure is probable (and loan is collateral dependent)

    4. When measure of impaired loan is less than recorded investment in loan

      a. Create valuation allowance with charge to bad debt expense

      b. Or adjust existing valuation allowance with charge to bad debt expense

    5. Significant changes (increases or decreases) subsequent to initial measure of impairment

      a. Recalculate impairment

      b. Adjust valuation allowance

      c. Net carrying amount of loan may never exceed recorded investment in loan

D. Income Recognition

    1. The present value of an impaired loan changes over time and also changes because of revised estimates in the amount or timing of cash flows.

    2. Recognition and measurement methods to reflect changes in present value are not specified in this statement as amended.

E. Disclosures

    1. The recorded investment in impaired loans, total allowance for credit losses related to impaired loans, and amount for which no allowance for credit losses

    2. The creditor's income recognition method, including cash receipts

    3. For each period presented which relates to the impaired loans

      a. Average recorded investment

      b. Interest revenue recognized

      c. If practicable, interest revenue recognized on a cash basis

SFAS 115 Accounting for Certain Investments in Debt and Equity Securities (ASC Topic 320—Investments—Debt and Equity Securities)

A. Establishes financial accounting and reporting requirements for all investments in debt securities and for small investments in equity securities with readily determinable fair values

    1. "Small" investments are those not accounted for by the equity method or involving consolidated subsidiaries

B. Segregates debt and equity securities into three categories

    1. Held-to-maturity securities

      a. Applies only to debt securities

      b. Requires intent and ability to hold to maturity

         (1) Will **not** sell in response to changes in

           (a) Funding terms and sources
           (b) Interest rates and prepayment risk
           (c) Foreign currency risk
           (d) Attractiveness of alternative investments
           (e) Liquidity needs

         (2) In rare cases, intent may change due to nonrecurring and unforeseeable circumstances.

           (a) Continuing deterioration of issuer's credit
           (b) Elimination of tax-exempt status of interest
           (c) Business combination or disposition that increases interest rate risk or credit risk
           (d) Regulatory change in permissible investments
           (e) Downsizing to meet industry capital requirements
           (f) Increased risk weight of debt securities held as regulatory risk-based capital

         (3) Considered maturity if

           (a) Sale occurs so close to maturity that interest rate risk is virtually eliminated
           (b) Sale occurs after at least 85% of the principal has been collected

    c. Balance sheet

      (1) Report at amortized cost
      (2) Classify as current or noncurrent on an individual basis

    d. Income statement

      (1) Do not report unrealized holding gains and losses
      (2) Include realized G(L) in earnings
      (3) Include interest income and premium/discount amortization in earnings

    e. Statement of cash flows

      (1) Classify cash inflows from sales and outflows from purchases gross (not netted) as investing activities

2. Trading securities

    a. Applies to debt and equity securities held for current resale
    b. Balance sheet

      (1) Report at fair value (See SFAS 157 for fair value measurements)
      (2) Classify as current assets, generally

    c. Income statement

      (1) Include unrealized holding G(L) in earnings
      (2) Exclude previously recognized realized G(L) from earnings
      (3) Include dividend and interest revenue

    d. Statement of cash flows

      (1) Classify purchases and sales as operating activity

3. Available-for-sale securities

    a. Applies to debt and equity securities not categorized as held-to-maturity or trading securities
    b. Balance sheet

      (1) Report at fair value (See SFAS 157 for fair value measurements)
      (2) Classify as current or noncurrent on an individual basis
      (3) Report net unrealized holding G(L) in other comprehensive income and accumulated other comprehensive income as separate component of stockholders' equity

    c. Income statement

      (1) Include realized G(L) in earnings
      (2) Include dividend and interest revenue and premium/discount amortization in earnings

    d. Statement of cash flows

      (1) Classify sales and purchases gross (not netted) as investing activity

C. Transfers between categories are accounted for at fair value

1. From trading

   a. Do not reverse recognized unrealized holding G(L) at date of transfer

2. To trading

   a. Recognize unrealized holding G(L) immediately

3. To available-for-sale from held-to-maturity

   a. Report unrealized holding G(L) as other comprehensive income
   b. Transfers from held-to-maturity should be rare

4. To held-to-maturity from available-for-sale

   a. Report unrealized holding G(L) as other comprehensive income
   b. Amortize G(L) over remaining life of security as adjustment to yield

D. Impairment of Securities

1. Applies to held-to-maturity and available-for-sale securities
2. If permanent decline

   a. Write down to fair value
   b. Include realized loss in earnings

3. No write-up for subsequent recoveries

E. Disclosures

1. Only held-to-maturity and available-for-sale securities
2. By major security type

   a. Aggregate fair value
   b. Gross unrealized holding gains and losses
   c. Amortized cost basis

3. By maturity of debt securities

   a. All enterprises disclose contractual information.
   b. Financial institutions disclose fair value and amortized cost for four or more groups of maturities

      (1) Up to one year
      (2) Over one through five years
      (3) Over five through ten years
      (4) Over ten years

   c. Securities maturing at multiple dates

      (1) May disclose separately
      (2) May allocate over groupings

4. Available-for-sale securities

   a. Proceeds from sales
   b. Gross realized G(L)
   c. Cost basis for determining G(L)
   d. Change in net unrealized holding G(L) reported as comprehensive income in stockholders' equity

5. Trading securities

   a. Change in net unrealized holding G(L) reported in earnings

6. Transfers

   a. Gross G(L) on transfer from available-for-sale to trading
   b. Of held-to-maturity securities

      (1) Amortized cost
      (2) Realized or unrealized G(L)
      (3) Reason for sale

APB 18 The Equity Method for Investments (ASC Topics 323, 325, 850)

A. The equity method should be used for corporate joint ventures.

B. The equity method should be applied to investments where less than 50% ownership is held but the investor **can exercise significant influence over operating and financing policies of the investee.**

1. Twenty percent (20%) or more ownership should lead to presumption of substantial influence, unless there is evidence to the contrary.
2. Conversely, less than 20% ownership leads to the presumption of no substantial influence unless there is evidence to the contrary.
3. The 20% test should be based on voting stock outstanding and disregard common stock equivalents.
4. The following procedures should be used in applying the equity method:

   a. Intercompany profits should be eliminated.
   b. Difference between cost and book value of net assets acquired should be accounted for per SFAS 141 and 142.
   c. The investment account and investor's share of investee income should be presented as single amounts in investor statements with the exception of d. below.
   d. Investor's share of discontinued operations, extraordinary items, cumulative effects of accounting changes, and prior period adjustments of investee should be so presented in statements of investor.
   e. Investee capital transactions should be accounted for as are subsidiary capital transactions in consolidated statements.
   f. Gains on sale of investment are the difference between selling price and carrying value of investment.
   g. When investee and investor fiscal periods do not coincide, use most recent investee statement and have consistent time lag.
   h. Losses, not temporary in nature, of investment value should be recognized by investor.
   i. Investor's share of investee loss should not be recorded once investment account is written to zero. Subsequent income should be recognized after losses not recognized are made up.
   j. Investor's share of investee's earnings should be computed after deducting investee's cumulative preferred dividends whether declared or not.
   k. If an investor's holding falls below 20%, discontinue applying the equity method but make no retroactive adjustment.
   l. When an investor's holding increases from a level less than 20% to a level equal to or greater than 20%, the investment account and retained earnings of the investor should be adjusted retroactively to reflect balances as if the equity account had been used. This is accounted for like a prior period adjustment.

5. Statements of investors applying the equity method should disclose

   a. Investees and percentages held

      (1) Accounting policies followed
      (2) Treatment of goodwill, if any

   b. Aggregate market value of investment (not for subsidiaries)
   c. When investments are material to investor, summarized information of assets, liabilities, and results of operations of investee may be necessary
   d. Conversion of securities, exercise of warrants, or issuances of investee's common stock which significantly affects investor's share of investee's income

---

FASB INTERPRETATION NO. 35   CRITERIA FOR APPLYING THE EQUITY METHOD OF ACCOUNTING FOR INVESTMENTS IN COMMON STOCK.   Interprets APB 18.

Investors owning between 20 and 50% of an investee may **not** be able to exercise significant influence over the investee's operating and financial policies. The presumption of significant influence stands until overcome by evidence to the contrary, such as (1) opposition by the investee, (2) agreements under which the investor surrenders shareholder rights, (3) majority ownership by a small group of shareholders, (4) inability to obtain desired information from the investee, (5) inability to obtain representation on investee board of directors, etc. Whether contrary evidence is sufficient to negate the presumption of significant influence is a matter of judgment requiring a careful evaluation of all pertinent facts and circumstances, in some cases over an extended period of time. Application of this interpretation resulting in changes to or from the equity method shall be treated per APB 18, paras 19l and 19m.

FASB INTERPRETATION NO. 1   ACCOUNTING CHANGES RELATED TO THE COST OF INVENTORY

Changes in the cost composition of inventory is an accounting change and must conform to APB 20, including justification for the change. Preferably should be based on financial reporting objectives rather than tax-related benefits.

Chapter 4 Inventory Pricing (ASC Topic 330)

Contains 10 statements outlining inventory valuation

1. Inventory consists of tangible personal property

   a. Held for sale in ordinary course of business
   b. In process of production for such sale
   c. To be currently consumed in the production of such goods

2. Major objective of inventory valuation is proper income determination

   a. Matching of costs and revenues

3. Primary basis is cost. Cost includes all reasonable and necessary costs of preparing inventory for sale. These costs would include expenditures to bring inventory to existing condition and location.

   a. Direct or variable costing is not acceptable (use absorption costing)

4. Cost may be determined under any flow assumption. Use method which most clearly reflects income.
5. Departure from cost to market required when utility of goods, in their disposal in the ordinary course of business, is not as great as cost.

   a. Write-down recognized as a loss of the current period
   b. Use of lower of cost or market method more fairly reflects income of the period than would the cost method
   c. Results in a more realistic estimate of future cash flows to be realized from the assets
   d. Supported by doctrine of conservatism

6. Market means current replacement cost subject to

   a. Market should not exceed net realizable value (sales price less selling and completion costs)
   b. Market should not be less than net realizable value less normal profit

7. Lower of cost or market may be applied to individual items or the inventory as a whole. Use method that most clearly reflects income.
8. Basis for stating inventories and changes therein should be consistent and disclosed.
9. Inventories may be stated above cost in exceptional cases

   a. No basis for cost allocation (e.g., meatpacking)
   b. Disposal assured and price known (e.g., precious metals)

10. Purchase commitment loss should be recognized in the same manner as inventory losses.

SFAS 151 Inventory Costs (ASC Topic 330—Inventory)

A. Requires that abnormal amounts of idle facility expense, freight, handling costs, and wasted material (spoilage) may be treated as current period charges.
B. Requires that fixed overhead allocation be based on normal capacity of production facilities.

1. Normal capacity is a range of production levels.
2. Normal capacity is production expected to be achieved over a number of periods or seasons under normal circumstances, taking into account loss of capacity due to planned maintenance.
3. Normal capacity varies on business and industry-specific factors.

C. Factors that might cause abnormally low production level include significantly reduced demand, labor and material shortages, unplanned facility or equipment downtime.
D. Actual level of production may be used if it approximates normal capacity.
E. In periods of abnormally high production, amount of fixed overhead allocated to each unit is decreased so inventories are not measured above cost.
F. Items treated as period costs include

1. Unallocated overhead costs are recognized as expense in period in which they are incurred.
2. General and administrative expenses (under most circumstances).
3. Selling expense.
4. Abnormal freight, handling costs, amount of wasted materials (spoilage).

SFAS 142 Goodwill and Other Intangible Assets (ASC Topic 350—Intangibles—Goodwill and Other)

This standard provides guidance on accounting for intangible assets including goodwill.

A. Initial Recognition and Measurement of Intangible Assets

1. Intangible assets not acquired in a business combination

   a. An intangible asset that is acquired either individually or with a group of other assets shall be initially recognized at its fair value

   b. The cost of assets acquired as a group should be allocated to the individual assets based on their relative fair values and shall not give rise to goodwill

2. Intangible assets (including goodwill) acquired in a business combination shall be recognized in accordance with SFAS 141

3. Costs of internally developing, maintaining, or restoring intangible assets that are not specifically identifiable, that have indeterminate lives, or that are inherent in a continuing business and related to an entity as a whole, shall be recognized as an expense when incurred

B. Accounting for Intangible Assets

1. The cost of an intangible asset with a finite useful life is amortized over its estimated useful life

   a. The useful life of an intangible asset should be estimated by considering factors such as

      (1) Expected use
      (2) Expected useful life of assets related to the intangible asset
      (3) Legal, regulatory, and contractual provisions that may limit or extend the useful life
      (4) The effects of obsolescence, demand, competition, and other economic factors
      (5) The level of expenditures expected to be required to maintain the asset

   b. The method of amortization shall reflect the pattern in which the economic benefits of the intangible assets are consumed; if the pattern cannot be reliable determined, a straight-line amortization method shall be used

   c. The residual value of the intangible asset will be presumed to be zero unless there is a commitment from a third party to purchase the asset at the end of its useful life, or the residual value can be determined by reference to an exchange transaction in an existing market

   d. The remaining useful life of the intangible asset should be reevaluated each reporting period—if it is no longer appropriate the carrying amount should be amortized prospectively over the revised remaining useful life

   e. Intangible assets with finite useful lives should be reviewed for impairment in accordance with SFAS 144

2. An intangible asset that is determined to have an indefinite useful life should not be amortized until its useful life is determined to be no longer indefinite

   a. An intangible asset that is not subject to amortization should be tested for impairment annually, or more frequently if events or changes in circumstances indicate that the asset might be impaired

   b. The impairment test involves comparison of the carrying amount of the asset to its fair value

3. Goodwill should not be amortized

   a. Goodwill should be examined for impairment at the level of reporting referred to as a reporting unit (an operating segment or one level below). See the outline of SFAS 131

   b. An entity has the option to first qualitatively determine if it is more likely than not (greater than 50%) that the fair value of a reporting unit is less than its carrying value, including goodwill. Circumstances to be examined include, but are not limited to, examinations of macroeconomic conditions, industry and market considerations, cost factors, overall financial performance, entity-specific events, reporting unit events, and share price decreases. If it is found that it is not more likely than not that the fair value of the reporting unit is less than its carrying value, the goodwill impairment tests are deemed unnecessary. The entity can choose to bypass the qualitative assessment and proceed directly to the first step of the goodwill impairment test. The test of impairment is a two-step process as described below.

      (1) The first step involves a comparison of the fair value of the reporting unit with its carrying amount. If the carrying amount of the unit exceeds its fair value, the second step is performed. In estimating the fair value of a reporting unit, a valuation technique based on multiples of earnings or revenue or other performance measure may be used.

      (2) The second step involves a comparison of the implied fair value of goodwill of the reporting unit with the carrying amount of that goodwill

      (3) The implied fair value of goodwill is determined in the same manner as the amount of goodwill recognized in a business combination—see outline of SFAS 141. That is, all assets in the segment are valued in accordance with SFAS 141 and the excess of the fair value of the reporting unit as a whole over the

amounts assigned to its recorded assets and liabilities is the implied goodwill. If the implied value of goodwill is less than the carrying amount, goodwill is written down to its implied value and an impairment loss is recognized.

c. Goodwill should be tested for impairment on an annual basis and between annual dates if one or more of the following events occur:

(1) A significant adverse change in legal factors or in the business climate
(2) An adverse action or assessment by a regulator
(3) Unanticipated competition
(4) A loss of key personnel
(5) A more-likely-than-not expectation that a reporting unit or a significant portion of a reporting unit will be sold or otherwise disposed of
(6) The test for recoverability under SFAS 144 within a reporting unit reveals that a significant group of assets are recorded at amounts above their recoverable values
(7) Recognition of a goodwill impairment loss in the financial statements of a subsidiary that is a component of a reporting unit

d. A reporting unit may be tested at any time during the fiscal year as long as it is tested at the same time each year. Different reporting units may be tested at different times during the year.
e. Initially goodwill is allocated to reporting units. Then the assets and liabilities of the reporting units are valued individually with goodwill being measured as the difference between the cost assigned to the reporting unit and the fair value of the individual assets and liabilities.

C. Disclosures

1. In the period of acquisition

a. For intangible assets subject to amortization

(1) The amount assigned in total and by major intangible asset class
(2) Significant residual value, in total and by major intangible asset class
(3) The weighted-average amortization period, in total and by major intangible asset class

b. For intangible assets not subject to amortization, the amount assigned in total and by major intangible asset class
c. The amount of research and development assets acquired and written off and in which financial statement line items the amounts are included

2. Continuing disclosures

a. For intangible assets subject to amortization

(1) The gross carrying amount and accumulated amortization, in total and by major intangible asset class
(2) The aggregate amortization expense for the period
(3) The estimated aggregate amortization expense for each of the five succeeding fiscal years

b. For intangible assets not subject to amortization, the carrying amount in total and by each major intangible asset class
c. The changes in the carrying amount of goodwill during the period including

(1) The aggregate amount of goodwill acquired
(2) The aggregate amount of impairment losses recognized
(3) The amount of goodwill included in the gain or loss on disposal of all or a portion of a reporting unit

d. For each other-than-goodwill impairment loss recognized (other than for goodwill)

(1) A description of the impaired intangible asset and the facts and circumstances leading to the impairment
(2) The amount of the impairment loss and the method of determining fair value
(3) The caption in the income statement or the statement of activities in which the impairment loss is aggregated
(4) If applicable, the segment in which the impaired intangible asset is reported under SFAS 131

e. For each goodwill impairment loss recognized

(1) A description of the facts and circumstances leading to the impairment
(2) The amount of the impairment loss and the method of determining the fair value of the associated reporting unit

          (3) If a recognized impairment loss is an estimate that has not yet been finalized, the facts and circumstances and the amount of subsequent adjustments

SFAS 66 Accounting for Sales of Real Estate (ASC Topics 360, 605, and 976)

A. Other than retail land sales

    1. Use the full accrual method if the following criteria are satisfied:

        a. Sale is consummated
        b. Buyer's initial and continuing investments demonstrate a commitment to pay for the property
        c. Seller's receivable is not subject to future subordination
        d. Risks and rewards of ownership have been transferred

    2. When the criteria are not met and dependent upon the particular circumstance, use one of the following methods:

        a. Installment method
        b. Cost recovery method
        c. Deposit method
        d. Reduced profit method
        e. Percentage-of-completion

B. Retail land sales (not outlined due to specialized nature)

SFAS 144 Accounting for the Impairment or Disposal of Long-Lived Assets (ASC Topic 360—Property, Plant, and Equipment; ASC Topic 205—Presentation of Financial Statements; and ASC Topic 225—Income Statement)

A. Establishes financial and reporting requirements for the impairment or disposal of long-lived assets. In addition to property, plant, equipment, and intangible assets being amortized, SFAS 144 applies to capital leases of lessees, long-lived assets of lessors subject to operating leases, proved oil and gas properties that are being accounted for using the successful efforts method of accounting, and long-term prepaid assets.

B. If a long-lived asset (or assets) is part of a group that includes other assets and liabilities not covered by SFAS 144, the statement applies to the group.

C. Assets to be held and used

    1. Reviewed for impairment when circumstances indicate that the carrying amount of a long-term asset (or group) is not recoverable and exceeds its fair value. The carrying amount of a long-lived asset (asset group) is not recoverable it if exceeds the sum of the undiscounted cash flows expected to result from its use and eventual disposal.

    2. A long-lived asset (asset group) shall be tested for recoverability whenever events or changes in circumstances indicate that its carrying amount may not be recoverable. Examples of such events include

        a. Significant decrease in market value
        b. Change in way asset used or physical change in asset
        c. Legal factors or change in business climate that might affect asset's fair value or adverse action or assessment by regulator
        d. Asset costs incurred greater than planned
        e. Current-period operating or cash flow loss combined with historical or projection of such amounts demonstrates continuing losses from the asset
        f. A current expectation that, more likely than not a long-lived asset will be disposed of significantly before the end of its previously estimated useful life

    3. Impaired if the expected total future cash flows are less than the carrying amount of the asset (asset group)

        a. Assets should be grouped at lowest level for which there are identifiable cash flows independent of other groupings
        b. Expected future cash flows are future cash inflows to be generated by the asset (asset group) less the future cash outflows expected to be necessary to obtain those inflows
        c. Expected future cash flows are **not** discounted and do not consider interest charges
        d. If the management has alternative courses of action to recover the carrying amount, or if a range of possible cash flows are associated with a particular course of action, a probability-weighted approach may be useful

    4. Written down to fair value and loss recognized upon impairment

        a. Fair value is "the price that would be received to sell an asset or paid to transfer a liability in an orderly transaction between market participants at the measurement date." (SFAS 157)
        b. If quoted market price in active market is not available, the estimate of fair value should be based on best information available

5. An impairment loss for an asset group shall reduce only the carrying amounts of the long-lived assets. Impairment of other assets in the group should be accounted for in accordance with other applicable accounting standards
6. If an impairment loss is recognized, the adjusted carrying amount becomes its new cost basis
7. Fair value increases on assets previously written down for impairment losses may not be recognized
8. Disclosures

   a. Description of impaired asset (asset group) and circumstances which led to impairment
   b. Amount of impairment and manner in which fair value was determined
   c. Caption in income statement in which impairment loss is aggregated, if it is not presented separately thereon
   d. Business segment(s) affected (if applicable)

D. Long-lived assets to be disposed of other than by sale

1. Long-lived assets to be abandoned are disposed of when they cease to be used
2. Long-lived assets to be exchanged for similar assets or to be distributed to owners are disposed of when they are exchanged or distributed

E. Long-lived assets to be disposed of by sale

1. Long-lived assets to be sold shall be classified as "held-for-sale" in the period in which all of the following criteria are met:

   a. Management commits to a plan of disposal
   b. The assets are available for sale
   c. An active program to locate a buyer has been initiated
   d. The sale is probable
   e. The asset is being actively marketed for sale at a fair price
   f. It is unlikely that the disposal plan will significantly change

2. Reported at lesser of the carrying amount or fair value less cost to sell

   a. Cost to sell includes broker commissions, legal and title transfer fees, and closing costs prior to legal title transfer

3. In future periods, adjusted carrying amount of asset shall be revised down or up to extent of changes in estimate of fair value less cost to sell, provided that the adjusted carrying amount does not exceed the carrying amount of the asset prior to the adjustment reflecting the decision to dispose of the asset

   a. Thus, recoveries may be recognized when assets are to be **disposed of** but not on impaired assets that continue to be used

F. Reporting long-lived assets and disposal groups to be disposed of

1. Discontinued operations of a component of an entity

   a. A component of an entity comprises operations and cash flows that can be clearly distinguished, operationally and for financial reporting purposes
   b. The results of a component of an entity that either has been disposed of or is classified as held for sale shall be reported as discontinued operations if both of the following conditions are met:

      (1) The operations and cash flows of the component have been (will be) eliminated from ongoing operations
      (2) The entity will not have any significant continuing involvement in the operations of the component after disposal

   c. In reporting discontinued operations, the income statement should present the results of discontinued operations separately after income from continuing operations and before extraordinary items as shown below

Income from continuing operations before income taxes	$xxxxx	
Income taxes	xxx	
Income from continuing operations		$xxxx
Discontinued operations (Note X)		
Loss from operations of discontinued Component Z (including loss on disposal of $xxx)		xxxx
Income tax benefit		xxxx
Loss on discontinued operations		xxxx
Net income		$xxxx

2. A gain or loss recognized for long-term asset (group) classified for sale that is not a component of an entity shall be included in income from continuing operations before income taxes

3. Disclosures

   a. Description of assets to be disposed of, reasons for disposal, expected disposal date, and carrying amount of those assets
   b. Gain or loss, if any, resulting from changes in carrying amount due to further changes in market value
   c. If applicable, amounts of revenue and pretax profit or loss reported in discontinued operations
   d. If applicable, the segment of the business affected (see outline of SFAS 131)

LIABILITIES (ASC TOPIC 400)

SFAS 143 Accounting for Asset Retirement Obligations (ASC Topic 410—Asset Retirement and Environmental Obligations)

This standard provides guidance on accounting for obligations associated with the retirement of tangible long-lived assets.

A. The guidance applies to legal obligations associated with the retirement of long-lived assets that result from the acquisition, construction, development and/or normal operation of a long-lived asset, except for certain obligations of lessees. Examples include

   1. Costs to decommission a nuclear utility plant at the end of its useful life
   2. Costs to dismantle and remove an offshore oil platform at the end of its useful life

B. Such legal obligation may arise from

   1. Existing or enacted law, statute, ordinance
   2. Written or oral contract
   3. Legal construction of a contract under the doctrine of promissory estoppel (inferred legal obligation)

C. An asset retirement obligation is recognized at its fair value in the period in which it is incurred providing that a reasonable estimate of fair value can be made
D. Upon initial recognition of a liability, the entity shall increase the carrying amount of the related long-lived asset by the same amount as that recognized for the liability
E. The cost shall be subsequently expensed using a systematic and rational method over periods no longer than that for which the related asset is expected to provide benefits
F. Initial measurement of the liability

   1. The best source of fair value of the liability would be provided by market-determined values but they will seldom be available
   2. In the absence of a market, expected present value of future cash flows should be used. In determining the expected present value, the entity should

      a. Use probability-weighted present values in a range of the expected cash flows
      b. The amounts should be discounted to present value using a credit-adjusted risk-free rate

G. Subsequent to the initial measurement of the liability the obligation should be adjusted for

   1. The passage of time, and
   2. Revisions in estimates of timing or amounts of future cash flows

H. Adjustments to the liability for revisions in estimates of timing or amounts of cash flows should also be reflected in the carrying value of the related asset
I. Disclosures related to asset retirement obligations should include

   1. Description of the obligation and related asset
   2. Description of how fair value was determined
   3. The funding policy, if any
   4. A reconciliation of the beginning and ending aggregate carrying value

SFAS 146 Liabilities: Exit or Disposal Costs (ASC Topic 420—Exit or Disposal Cost Obligation)

A. A liability for cost associated with an exit or disposal shall be recognized and measured initially at its fair value in the period in which the liability is incurred

   1. There is an exception for a liability for one-time termination benefits that involves employees providing future services
   2. When fair value cannot be reasonably estimated, the liability shall be recognized initially in the period in which fair value can be reasonably estimated

B. An exit activity includes but is not limited to restructurings which are programs that are planned and controlled by management, and materially changes either

1. The scope of a business undertaken by the company, or
2. The manner in which that business is conducted
3. Examples include

    a. Sale or termination of line of business
    b. Closure of business activities at a particular location
    c. Relocation of business activities from one location to another
    d. Changes in management structure
    e. Fundamental reorganization of the business

C. Exit or disposal activities covered by this statement do not include those that involve an entity acquired in a business combination, nor do they include disposals covered by SFAS 144. It also does not apply to costs associated with the retirement of a long-lived asset covered by SFAS 143. Examples of exit or disposal activities covered by this statement include

1. Termination benefits provided to involuntarily terminated employees (other than ongoing arrangements and deferred compensation agreements)
2. Costs to terminate a contract that is not a capital lease
3. Costs to consolidate facilities or relocate employees

D. A liability for a cost associated with an exit or disposal activity shall be recognized and measured initially at fair value in the period in which the liability is incurred

1. This typically is measured by determining the present value of the liability by discounting it using the entity's credit-adjusted risk-free interest rate

E. In the unusual circumstance in which fair value cannot be reasonably estimated, the liability shall be recognized initially in the period in which fair value can be reasonably estimated
F. Subsequent to initial recognition, the liability is adjusted over time by using the discount rate used to initially determine the liability
G. Measurement of onetime termination benefits

1. A onetime termination agreement exists when the plan of termination meets the following criteria and has been communicated to the employees:

    a. Management commits to the plan
    b. The plan identifies the number of employees to be terminated, their job classifications and locations, and the expected completion date
    c. The plan establishes the terms of the benefit arrangement
    d. It is unlikely that significant changes in the plan will be made

2. The liability is recognized and measured at the communication date if

    a. The employees are not required to perform additional services to receive termination benefits, or
    b. The employees will not be retained to render services beyond the minimum retention period (not to exceed the legal notification period)

3. If the employees are required to render service until they are terminated in order to receive termination benefits and will render service beyond the minimum retention period

    a. The liability for termination benefits shall be initially measured at the communication date based on the fair value of the liability as of the termination date, and
    b. The liability shall be recognized ratably over the future service period

H. Measurement of contract termination costs

1. Costs to terminate the contract before term end

    a. Recognized and measured when the contract is terminated

2. Costs that will be incurred for the remaining term without benefit to the entity

    a. Recognized and measured when the entity ceases to use the rights conveyed by the contract (e.g., when the entity returns the leased assets)

I. Disclosure

   1. A description of the exit or disposal activity
   2. For each major type of cost associated with the activity

      a. The total amount expected to be incurred
      b. A reconciliation of the beginning and ending liability amounts

   3. The line items in the income statements in which the costs are included
   4. For each reportable segment, the total amount of costs expected to be incurred in connection with the activity
   5. If a liability cannot be reasonably estimated, the reasons therefor

SFAS 47 Disclosure of Long-Term Obligations (ASC Topics 440 and 470)

A. This statement requires that firm disclose

   1. Commitments under unconditional purchase obligations that are associated with suppliers (financing arrangements)
   2. Future payments on long-term borrowings

B. **Unconditional purchase obligations** are obligations to transfer funds in the future for fixed or minimum amounts of goods or services at fixed or minimum prices.
C. Unconditional purchase obligations that have all the following characteristics must be disclosed; they are not recorded on the balance sheet.

   1. Is noncancelable or cancelable only

      a. Upon occurrence of a remote contingency, or
      b. With permission of another party, or
      c. If a replacement agreement is signed between same parties, or
      d. Upon penalty payment such that continuation appears reasonably assured

   2. Was negotiated as part of arranging financing for the facilities that will provide the contracted goods
   3. Has a remaining term greater than one year

D. Disclosure of those unconditional purchase obligations not recorded on the balance sheet shall include

   1. Nature and term of obligation
   2. Amount of fixed and determinable portion of obligation as of most recent BS in aggregate and if determinable for each of next five years
   3. Description of any variable elements of the obligation
   4. Amounts purchased under the obligation(s) for each year an income statement is presented
   5. Encourages disclosing imputed interest to reduce the obligation to present value using

      a. Effective interest rate, or if unknown
      b. Purchaser's incremental borrowing rate at date obligation was entered into

E. This statement **does not change** the accounting for obligations that are recorded on the balance sheet, nor does it suggest that disclosure is a substitute for accounting recognition. For recorded obligations, the following information should be disclosed for each of the next five years:

   1. Aggregate amount of payments for unconditional obligations that meet criteria for balance sheet recognition
   2. Combined aggregate amount of maturities and sinking fund requirements for all long-term borrowings

SFAS 5 Accounting for Contingencies (ASC Topic 450—Contingencies)

A. Contingency is "an existing condition, situation, or set of circumstances involving uncertainty as to possible gain (loss) to an enterprise that will ultimately be resolved when one or more future events occur or fail to occur."

   1. Definitions

      a. Probable—future events are likely to occur
      b. Reasonably possible—chance of occurrence is more than remote, but less than likely
      c. Remote—chance of occurrence is slight

   2. Loss contingency examples

      a. Receivable collection
      b. Product warranty obligations
      c. Risk of property losses by fire, explosion, etc.
      d. Asset expropriation threat

    e. Pending, threatened, etc., litigation
    f. Actual or possible claims and assessments
    g. Catastrophe losses faced by insurance companies
    h. Guarantees of indebtedness of others
    i. Banks' obligations under "standby letters of credit"
    j. Agreements to repurchase receivables, related property, etc. that have been sold
    k. Asset retirement obligations

B. Estimated loss from contingencies shall be accrued and charged to income when

  1. It is probable (at balance sheet date) that an asset has been impaired or liability incurred
  2. **And** the amount of loss can be reasonably estimated

    a. Difference between estimate recorded and actual amount determined in subsequent period is a change in accounting estimate

C. Loss contingency disclosures

  1. Nature and amount of material items
  2. Nonaccrued loss contingencies for which a reasonable possibility of loss exists

    a. Disclose nature of contingency
    b. Estimate possible range of loss

      (1) Or state estimate cannot be made

  3. If a loss contingency develops after year-end, but before statements are issued, disclosure of the nature of the contingency and amount may be necessary.

    a. If a year-end contingency results in a loss before issuance of the statements, disclosure (possibly pro forma amounts) may be necessary.

  4. Disclose nature and amount of the following loss contingencies (even if remote)

    a. Guarantees of others' debts
    b. Standby letters of credit by banks
    c. Agreements to repurchase receivables

D. General, unspecified risks are not contingencies.
E. Appropriation of RE for contingencies shown within shareholders' equity is not prohibited.

  1. Cannot be shown outside shareholders' equity
  2. Contingency costs and losses cannot be charged to appropriation.

F. Gain contingency accounting

  1. Normally not reflected in accounts until realized.
  2. Adequate disclosure should be made without misleading implications of likelihood of realization.

G. Rationale for accounting for contingencies per SFAS 5

  1. Reflects **conservatism**—recognize losses immediately (if probable and reasonably estimable), but recognize gains only when realized.
  2. Results in better matching—contingent losses are recognized in time period of origin.

FASB INTERPRETATION NO. 14 REASONABLE ESTIMATION OF THE AMOUNT OF LOSS

A range of the amount of a loss is sufficient to meet the criteria of SFAS 5 that the amount of loss be "subject to reasonable estimate." When one amount in the range is a better estimate, use it; otherwise, use the minimum of the range and disclose range.

STATEMENTS OF POSITION NO. 96-1 ENVIRONMENTAL REMEDIATION LIABILITIES

This SOP includes accounting guidance, preceded by a very detailed description of relevant laws, remediation laws, remediation provisions and other pertinent information, useful to auditors as well as clients. Auditing guidance is limited to recitation of SFAS 5 concerns about reasonable estimation of loss accruals.

Accounting guidance includes the following provisions:

A. Interprets SFAS 5 in the context of environmental obligations (e.g., threshold for accrual of liability, etc.) and sets "benchmarks" for recognition.

B. Benchmarks for accrual and evaluation of estimated liability (stages which are deemed to be important to ascertaining the existence and amount of the liability) are

1. Identification and verification of an entity as a potentially responsible party (PRP), since the proposal stipulated that accrual should be based on premise that expected costs will be borne by only the "participating potentially responsible parties" and that the "recalcitrant, unproven and unidentified" PRP will not contribute to costs of remediation
2. Receipt of unilateral administrative order
3. Participation, as a PRP, in the remedial investigation/feasibility study (RI/FS)
4. Completion of the feasibility study
5. Issuance of the Record of Decision (ROD)
6. Remedial design through operation and maintenance, including postremediation monitoring

C. The amount of liability is affected by

1. The entity's allocable share of liability for a specified site; and
2. Its share of the amounts related to the site that will not be paid by the other PRP or the government

D. Costs to be included in the accrued liability are

1. Incremental direct costs of the remediation effort itself; and

   a. Fees to outside law firms for work related to the remediation effort
   b. Costs relating to completing the RI/FS
   c. Fees to outside consulting and engineering firms for site investigations and development of remedial action plans and remedial actions
   d. Costs of contractors performing remedial actions
   e. Government oversight costs and past costs
   f. Cost of machinery and equipment dedicated to the remedial actions that do not have an alternative use
   g. Assessments by a PRP group covering costs incurred by the group in dealing with a site
   h. Costs of operation and maintenance of the remedial action, including costs of postremediation monitoring required by the remedial action plan

2. Costs of compensation and benefits for employees directly involved in the remediation effort
3. Costs are to be estimated based on existing laws and technologies, and not discounted to present value unless timing of cash payments is fixed or reliably determinable

---

ARB 43— Chapter 3A Current Assets and Current Liabilities (ASC Topics 210, 310, 340, 470)

Chapter 3A contains the definitions and examples of current assets and liabilities.

A. Current assets are "cash and other assets or resources commonly identified as those which are reasonably expected to be (1) realized in cash, (2) sold, or (3) consumed during the ordinary operating cycle of the business."

1. Cash available for current operations
2. Inventories
3. Trade receivables
4. Other receivables collectible in one year
5. Installment, deferred accounts, and notes receivable
6. Prepaid expenses

B. Current liabilities are "obligations whose liquidation is reasonably expected to require the use of existing resources properly classifiable as current assets or the creation of other current liabilities during the ordinary operating cycle of the business."

1. Trade payables
2. Collections received in advance of services
3. Accruals of expenses
4. Other liabilities coming due in one year
5. Note that liabilities not using current assets for liquidation are not current liabilities (e.g., bonds being repaid from a sinking fund)

C. Operating cycle is "average time intervening between the acquisition of materials or services entering this process and the final cash realization."

APB 14 Convertible Debt and Debt Issued with Stock Warrants (ASC Topic 470—Debt)

A. Convertible debt constitutes securities which are convertible into common stock of the user or affiliate. Terms generally include

1. Lower interest rate than on ordinary debt
2. Initial conversion price greater than the common price at time of issuance
3. A conversion price which does not decrease except to protect against dilution

B. While there are arguments to account for the debt and equity characteristics separately, the APB has concluded no proceeds of a convertible issue should be attributed to the conversion factor.

1. Primary **reasons** are

    a. The inseparability of the debt and conversion features
    b. The practical difficulties of valuing the conversion feature

C. When debt is issued with detachable purchase warrants, the debt and warrants generally trade separately and should be treated separately.

1. The allocation of proceeds should be based on relative market value at date of issuance.
2. Any resulting debt discount or premium should be accounted for as such.

D. Separate valuation of debt and warrants is applicable where the debt may be used as consideration when exercising the warrants. Separate valuation is not acceptable where the debt must be tendered to exercise the warrants (i.e., the warrants are, in essence, nondetachable).

APB 26 Early Extinguishment of Debt (ASC Topic 470—Debt)
(Amended by SFAS 84 and SFAS 145)

A. Definitions

1. **Net carrying amount.** "Amount due at maturity, adjusted for unamortized premium, discount, and cost of issuance."
2. **Reacquisition price.** "Amount paid on extinguishment, including a call premium and miscellaneous costs of reacquisition."
3. **Refunding.** Replacement of debt with other debt

B. Retirement is usually achieved by use of liquid assets.

1. Currently in existence
2. From sale of equity securities
3. From sale of debt securities

C. **A difference** between **reacquisition price** and **net carrying amount** of the extinguished debt should be recognized in the year of extinguishment as a separate item.

1. Gains and losses should not be amortized to future years.
2. Gains and losses are ordinary.

SFAS 6 Classification of Short-Term Obligations Expected to Be Refinanced (ASC Topics 210 and 470)

A. Short-term obligations shall be classified as a current liability unless

1. Enterprise intends to refinance the obligation on a long-term basis
2. AND the intent is supported by ability to refinance

    a. Post-balance-sheet issuance of long-term debt or equity securities, or
    b. Financing agreement that clearly permits refinancing on a long-term basis

       (1) Does not expire or is not callable for one year
       (2) No violation of the agreement exists at the balance sheet date or has occurred to date

3. The amount of the short-term obligation excluded from current liability status should not exceed the

    a. Net proceeds of debt or securities issued
    b. Net amounts available under refinancing agreements

       (1) The enterprise must intend to exercise the financing agreement when the short-term obligation becomes due.

4. Refinancing of short-term obligations is a FS **classification** issue, **not** a **recognition** and **measurement** issue.

FASB INTERPRETATION NO. 8 CLASSIFICATION OF A SHORT-TERM OBLIGATION REPAID PRIOR TO BEING REPLACED BY A LONG-TERM SECURITY

Short-term obligations that are repaid after the balance sheet date but **before** funds are obtained from long-term financing are to be classified as current liabilities at the balance sheet date.

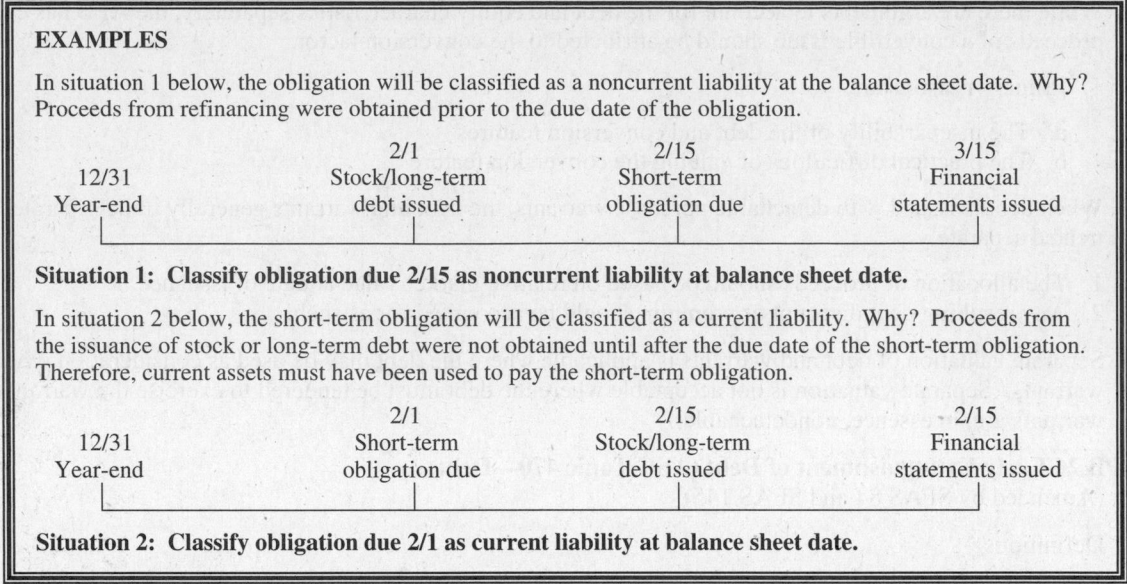

EXAMPLES

In situation 1 below, the obligation will be classified as a noncurrent liability at the balance sheet date. Why? Proceeds from refinancing were obtained prior to the due date of the obligation.

| 12/31
Year-end | 2/1
Stock/long-term
debt issued | 2/15
Short-term
obligation due | 3/15
Financial
statements issued |

Situation 1: Classify obligation due 2/15 as noncurrent liability at balance sheet date.

In situation 2 below, the short-term obligation will be classified as a current liability. Why? Proceeds from the issuance of stock or long-term debt were not obtained until after the due date of the short-term obligation. Therefore, current assets must have been used to pay the short-term obligation.

| 12/31
Year-end | 2/1
Short-term
obligation due | 2/15
Stock/long-term
debt issued | 2/15
Financial
statements issued |

Situation 2: Classify obligation due 2/1 as current liability at balance sheet date.

SFAS 15 Accounting by Debtors and Creditors for Troubled Debt Restructurings (ASC Topics 310 and 470)
(Superseded by SFAS 114 with regard to creditors)

A. Troubled debt restructurings occur when a creditor is compelled to grant relief to a debtor due to the debtor's inability to service the debt. This SFAS prescribes accounting for such debt restructurings if

1. By creditor-debtor agreement
2. Imposed by a court
3. Result of repossessions and foreclosures
4. But not changes in lease agreements

    a. Nor legal actions to collect receivables
    b. Nor quasi reorganizations

B. If a **debtor** transfers assets to settle fully a payable, recognize a gain on restructuring equal to the book value of the payable less FV of assets transferred.

1. Use fair value measurements as outlined by SFAS 157.
2. The difference between set FV and carrying value of the assets transferred is a gain or loss in disposition of assets per APB 30.

C. If a **debtor** issues an equity interest to settle fully a payable, account for equity issued at FV.

1. Excess of carrying value of payable over equity FV is a gain on restructuring.

D. A **debtor** having the terms of troubled debt modified should account for the restructure prospectively (i.e., no adjustment of the payable).

1. Recompute the new effective rate of interest based on the new terms

    a. Total cash payments to be paid, less carrying value of payable is the interest
    b. Amortize the payable by the interest method (APB 21) using the new interest rate

2. Exception is if restructured terms require total cash payments (including interest) which are less than the carrying value of the payable, write down the payable to the total cash to be paid

    a. Include contingent payments in calculation; this precludes recognizing a gain currently and interest expense later
    b. Recognize gain on the write-down
    c. All future cash payments reduce the payable (i.e., no interest expense is recognized)

E. If restructured by partial settlement (assets and/or equity issuance) and modified terms

1. First account for asset and/or equity issuance per above
2. Then account for modified terms per above

F. Related matters

1. A repossession or foreclosure is accounted for per the above.
2. Contingent payments on restructured debt shall be recognized per SFAS 5 (i.e., its payment is probable and subject to reasonable estimate).
3. Legal fees on debt restructuring involving equity issuance reduce the amounts credited to the equity accounts.

   a. All other direct costs of debt restructuring reduce gain or are expenses of the period if there is no gain.

G. Disclosures by **debtors**

1. Description of major changes in debt of each restructuring
2. Aggregate gain on debt restructuring and related tax effect
3. Aggregate net gain (loss) on asset transfers due to restructuring
4. EPS amount of aggregate gain on restructuring net of tax effect

SFAS 78 Classification of Obligations That Are Callable by the Creditor (ASC Topic 470—Debt)

A. Statement specifies that the current liability classification is also intended to include

1. Obligations that, by their terms, are due on demand or will be due on demand within one year (or operating cycle, if longer) from balance sheet date, even though liquidation may not be expected within that period
2. Long-term obligations that are or will be callable by creditor either because

   a. Debtor's violation of debt agreement provision at balance sheet date makes obligation callable **or**
   b. Violation, if not cured within grace period, will make obligation callable

B. Callable obligations in A.2. should be classified current unless one of the following conditions is met:

1. Creditor has waived or subsequently lost the right to demand repayment for more than one year (or operating cycle, if longer) from balance sheet date
2. For long-term obligations containing grace period within which debtor may cure violation, it is probable violation will be cured within that period

   a. If obligation meets this condition, the circumstances shall be disclosed

C. This statement does not modify SFAS 6 or 47

SFAS 84 Induced Conversions of Convertible Debt (ASC Topic 470—Debt)

A. Establishes accounting and reporting standards for conversion of convertible debt to equity securities when debtor induces conversion of the debt

1. Applies only to conversions that both

   a. Occur pursuant to changed conversion privileges exercisable only for limited period of time
   b. Include issuance of all of the equity securities issuable pursuant to the original conversion privileges for each instrument that is converted

2. Examples of changed terms to induce conversion

   a. Reduction of original conversion price
   b. Issuance of warrants or other securities not included in original conversion terms
   c. Payment of cash or other consideration to debt holders who convert during the specified time period

B. Debtor enterprise shall recognize expense equal to excess of fair value of all securities and other consideration transferred in the transaction over fair value of securities issuable pursuant to the original conversion terms.

1. Expense is not an extraordinary item.
2. Fair value of securities/other consideration measured as of inducement date

   a. Typically date converted by debt holder or binding agreement entered into

SFAS 150 Accounting for Certain Financial Instruments with Characteristics of Both Liabilities and Equity (ASC Topic 480—Distinguishing Liabilities from Equity)

A. This statement addresses how an issuer classifies and measures certain financial instruments with characteristics of both liabilities and equity. If the financial instrument embodies an obligation to the issuer, then it should be reported as a liability.

B. Terms: An obligation is a conditional or unconditional duty or responsibility to transfer assets or to issue equity shares. The duty may require a physical settlement (repurchasing its equity shares), a net cash settlement (transferring cash), or a net share settlement (issuing shares to settle).

C. This pronouncement applies to three classes of financial instruments: mandatorily redeemable preferred stock, obligations to repurchase the issuer's equity shares by transferring assets, and certain obligations to issue a variable number of shares.

1. Mandatorily redeemable preferred stock is classified as a liability unless the redemption only occurs upon liquidation or termination of the entity.
2. If a financial instrument embodies an obligation to repurchase the issuer's equity shares and requires settlement by transferring assets, then the instrument is classified as a liability.
3. If the financial instrument has an obligation that the issuer must settle by issuing a variable number of its equity shares, then it is classified as a liability if the value of the obligation is based on a fixed monetary amount or an amount tied to variations or inverse variations in something other than the issuer's securities.

D. These items are presented in the liabilities section of the statement of financial position. For EPS purposes, mandatorily redeemable preferred and forward contracts to repurchase equity shares are excluded in the calculation of earnings per share. Dividends and participation rights are deducted in computing income available to common shareholders in calculating EPS.

E. Disclosure: The following must be disclosed in the notes to financial statements:

1. The amount that would be paid or number of shares that would be issued and their fair value if settlement were to occur at reporting date
2. How changes in fair value of the shares would affect the settlement amounts
3. The maximum number of shares that could be required to be paid for a physical settlement
4. The maximum number of shares that could be required to be issued
5. That a contract does not limit the amount that the issuer could be required to pay or issue shares
6. If the forward contract or option indexed to the issuer's equity shares, the forward price or option strike price, the number of issuer's shares to which the contract is indexed and the settlement date or dates

EQUITY (ASC TOPIC 500)

ARB 43—Chapter 1A Rules[2] Adopted by Membership (ASC Topics 310, 505, 605, and 850)

Four rules recommended by the Committee on Cooperation with Stock Exchanges in 1934. The last rule is from another 1934 Institute committee.

1. Profit is realized at the point of sale unless collection is not reasonably assured.
2. Capital (paid-in) surplus should not be charged with losses or expenses, except in quasi reorganizations.
3. Receivables from officers, employees, and affiliates must be separately disclosed.
4. Par value of stock issued for assets cannot be used to value the assets if some of the stock is subsequently donated back to the corporation.

ARB 43—Chapter 1B Profits or Losses on Treasury Stock (ASC Topic 505)

Profits on treasury stock are not income and should be reflected in capital surplus.

ARB 43— Chapter 7B Stock Dividends and Stock Splits (ASC Topic 505—Equity)

A. Dividend—evidence given to shareholders of their share of accumulated earnings that are going to be retained in the business

B. Split—stock issued to increase number of outstanding shares to reduce market price and/or to obtain a wider distribution of ownership

C. To the recipient, splits and dividends are not income. Dividends and splits take nothing from the property of the corporation and add nothing to the property of the recipient.

1. Upon receipt of stock dividend or split, recipient should reallocate cost of shares previously held to all shares held.

D. Issuer of a stock dividend (issuance is small in relation to shares outstanding and consequently has no apparent effect on market price) should capitalize retained earnings equal to the fair market value of shares issued.

1. Unless retained earnings are capitalized, retained earnings thought to be distributed by the recipient will be available for subsequent distribution.

---

[2] The references in parentheses are from the FASB Accounting Standards—Current Texts: Volumes 1 and 2, John Wiley & Sons, Inc. These are included only for facilitating the use of the Current Texts for candidates who have access to them.

2. Issuances less than 20-25% of previously outstanding shares are dividends. Issuances greater than 20-25% of previously outstanding shares are splits.

3. Where stock dividend is so large it may materially affect price (a split effected in the form of a dividend), no capitalization is necessary other than that required by law.

   a. Some jurisdictions require that the par value of splits be capitalized (i.e., changes in par value are not permitted).

4. For closely held corporations, there is no need to capitalize retained earnings other than to meet legal requirements.

APB 6 Status of Accounting Research Bulletins (ASC Topic 505—Equity)

A. ARB 43, Chapter 1B Treasury Stock

1. An excess of purchase price of treasury stock, purchased for retirement or constructive retirement, over par or stated value may be allocated between paid-in capital and retained earnings.

   a. The charge to paid-in capital is limited to all paid-in capital from treasury stock transactions and retirements of the same issue and a pro rata portion of all other paid-in capital of that issue.
   b. Also, paid-in capital applicable to fully retired issues may be charged.

2. Alternatively, losses may be charged entirely to retained earnings.
3. All gains on retirement of treasury stock go to paid-in capital.
4. When the decision to retire treasury stock has not been made, the cost of such is a contra shareholders' equity item. Losses may only be charged to paid-in capital from treasury transactions and retirements of the same issue.
5. Some state laws prescribe accounting for treasury stock. The laws are to be followed where they are at variance with this APB. Disclose all statutory requirements concerning treasury stock such as dividend restrictions.

B. ARB 43, Chapter 3A Current Assets and Liabilities

   Unearned interest, finance charges, etc. included in receivables should be deducted from the related receivable.

C. ARB 43, Chapter 7B Stock Dividends and Splits

   States "the shareholder has no income solely as a result of the fact that the corporation has income," but does not preclude use of the equity method.

APB 9 Reporting the Results of Operations (ASC Topics 225, 250, 505)

A. Designates a new format for income statement in which all normal operating items would be presented at the top of the income statement resulting in "net income before extraordinary items."

1. "Net income before extraordinary items" is followed by extraordinary items resulting in "net income."

B. "Prior period adjustments" are excluded from the income statement and constitute adjustments of beginning retained earnings disclosed at the top of the retained earnings statement.

1. Beginning retained earnings are adjusted by "prior period adjustments" resulting in "restated beginning retained earnings."
2. "Restated retained earnings" is then adjusted for net income and dividends which results in ending retained earnings.

C. Prior period adjustments should be disclosed in the period of adjustment.

1. The effect on each prior period presented should be disclosed including restated income taxes.
2. Disclosure in subsequent periods is not normally required.
3. Historical summary data should also be restated and disclosed in the period of adjustment.

D. The APB also reaffirmed earlier positions that the following should not affect determination of net income:

1. Transactions in the company's own stock
2. Transfers to or from retained earnings
3. Quasi reorganization adjustments

APB 12 Omnibus Opinion—1967 (ASC Topics 310, 360, 505, 710, and 835)

A. Allowance or contra accounts (allowance for bad debts, accumulated depreciation, etc.) should be deducted from assets or groups of assets with appropriate disclosure.

B. Disclosure of depreciable assets should include

1. Depreciation expense for the period
2. Balances of major classes of depreciable assets by nature or function

3. Accumulated depreciation either by major class or in total
4. Description of method(s) of depreciation by major classes of assets

C. Changes in the separate shareholder equity accounts in addition to retained earnings and changes in number of equity securities must be disclosed in the year of change

1. In separate statements
2. Or the financial statements
3. Or the notes

SFAS 123 (Revised) (C36) Share-Based Payment (ASC Topic 718—Compensation—Stock Compensation and ASC Topic 505—Equity)

A. Provides a fair value based method of accounting for stock-based payment plans

1. Supersedes APB 25, amends SFAS 123
2. Applies to all transactions between an entity and its "suppliers" (whether employees or nonemployees) in which the entity acquires goods or services through issuance of equity instruments or incurrence of liabilities based on fair value of the entity's common stock or other equity instruments
3. Examples include stock purchase plans, stock options, restricted stock, and stock appreciation rights
4. Classifies share-based payment as either equity or liability

B. Transactions with Nonemployees—Accounted for based on fair value of consideration received or fair value of equity instruments given, whichever is more readily determinable.

C. Transactions with Employees—Uses fair value based method

D. Measurement Methods

1. Share-based payments recorded as equity

    a. Measured at fair value at grant date
    b. Stock options are measured at fair value which is based on the observable market price of an option with the same or similar terms and conditions, or via use of an option pricing model which considers, as of grant date, exercise price and expected life of the option, current price of underlying stock and its anticipated volatility, expected dividends on the stock, and risk-free interest rate for expected term of the option.
    c. If fair value cannot be determined as of grant date, final measure shall be based on stock price and any other pertinent factors when it becomes reasonably possible to estimate that value. Current intrinsic value shall be used as a measure until a final determination of fair value can be made.

2. Share-based payments recorded as liabilities
    Requires the recording of liability based on current stock price at end of each period. Changes in stock price during service period are recognized as compensation cost over service period. A change in stock price subsequent to service period is recognized as compensation cost of that period.

E. Recognition of Compensation Cost

1. Total compensation cost is based on the number of instruments that eventually vest

    a. Vesting is defined as moment when employee's right to receive or retain such instruments or cash is no longer contingent on performance of additional services
    b. No compensation cost shall be recognized for employees that forfeit eligibility due to failure either to achieve service requirement or performance condition
    c. Compensation cost shall not be reversed if vested employee's stock option expires unexercised
    d. Company must estimate forfeitures due to service or performance condition not being met
    e. Total compensation cost is amortized straight-line over the requisite service period

2. Acceptable accrual methods

    a. As of grant date, base accruals of compensation cost on best available estimate of the number of options or instruments expected to vest, with estimates for forfeitures
    b. As of grant date, accrue compensation cost as if all options or instruments that are subject only to a service requirement will vest

F. Tax consequences of stock-based compensation transactions shall be accounted for pursuant to SFAS 109

1. Excess tax benefits are recognized as additional paid-in capital
2. Cash retained as a result of excess tax benefits is presented on the statement of cash flows as a cash inflow from financing activities

G. Disclosures

1. The method of estimating the fair value of goods or services received or fair value of the equity instruments granted during the period
2. The cash flow effects from share-based payments
3. Vesting requirements, maximum term of options granted, and number of shares authorized for grants of options or other equity instruments
4. The number and weighted-average exercise prices of each group of options
5. The weighted-average grant-date fair value of options granted during the year, classified according to whether exercise price equals, exceeds, or is less than fair value of stock at date of grant
6. A description of methods used and assumptions made in determining fair values of the options
7. Total compensation cost recognized for the year

SFAS 129 Disclosure of Information about Capital Structure (ASC Topic 505—Equity)

A. Information to Be Disclosed about Securities within the Financial Statements

1. The rights and privileges of the various securities outstanding; for example

   a. Dividend and liquidation preferences
   b. Participation rights
   c. Call prices and dates
   d. Conversion/exercise prices/rates and dates
   e. Sinking fund requirements
   f. Unusual voting rights
   g. Significant terms of contracts to issue additional shares

2. The number of shares issued upon conversion, exercise, or satisfaction of required conditions during at least the most recent annual fiscal period and any subsequent interim period presented.

B. Disclosure of Liquidation Preference of Preferred Stock within the Financial Statements

1. Relationship between the preference in liquidation and the par/stated value of the shares when preferred stock (or other senior stock) has a preference in involuntary liquidation considerably in excess of the par/stated value of the shares. This disclosure should be made in the equity section of the balance sheet in the aggregate, either parenthetically or "in short."
2. Aggregate or per share amounts at which preferred stock may be called or is subject to redemption through sinking fund operations or otherwise.
3. Aggregate and per share amount of arrearages in cumulative preferred dividends.

C. Disclosure of Redeemable Stock within the Financial Statements

1. The amount of redemption requirements, separately by issue or combined, for all issues of capital stock that are redeemable at fixed or determinable prices on fixed or determinable dates in each of the five years following the date of the latest balance sheet presented.

REVENUE (ASC TOPIC 600)

ARB 43—Chapter 1A Rules[3] Adopted by Membership (ASC Topics 310, 505, 605, and 850)

Four rules recommended by the Committee on Cooperation with Stock Exchanges in 1934. The last rule is from another 1934 Institute committee.

1. Profit is realized at the point of sale unless collection is not reasonably assured.
2. Capital (paid-in) surplus should not be charged with losses or expenses, except in quasi reorganizations.
3. Receivables from officers, employees, and affiliates must be separately disclosed.
4. Par value of stock issued for assets cannot be used to value the assets if some of the stock is subsequently donated back to the corporation.

ARB 45 Long-Term Construction Contracts (ASC Topic 605—Revenue)

Discusses accounting for multiple-period projects

A. The percentage-of-completion method recognizes income as work progresses.

1. Recognized income based upon a percentage of estimated total income

---

[3] The references in parentheses are from the FASB Accounting Standards—Current Texts: Volumes 1 and 2, John Wiley & Sons, Inc. These are included only for facilitating the use of the Current Texts for candidates who have access to them.

    a. (Incurred costs to date)/(Total expected costs) known as cost-to-cost measure

    b. Other measure of progress based on work performed (e.g., engineering or architectural estimate)

2. Costs, for percentage-of-completion estimate, might exclude materials and subcontracts, especially in the early stages of a contract.

    a. Avoids overstating the percentage-of-completion

3. If a loss is estimated on the contract, the **entire loss** should be recognized currently.
4. Contracts should be separated into net assets and net liabilities.

    a. Current assets include costs and income (loss) in excess of billings.

    b. Current liabilities include billings in excess of costs and income (loss).

    c. Contracts should not be offset on the balance sheet.

5. Advantages of percentage-of-completion are periodic recognition of income and reflection of the status of the contract.

    a. Results in appropriate matching of costs and revenues

    b. Avoids distortions in income from year to year and thus provides more relevant information to financial statement users

6. The principal disadvantage is the reliance on estimates.
7. The percentage-of-completion method is required when total costs and percent of completion can be reasonably estimated.

B. The completed-contract method recognizes income when the contract is complete.

1. General and administrative expenses can be allocated to contracts.

    a. Not necessary if many projects are in process

    b. No excessive deferring of costs

2. Provision should be made for **entire amount of any expected loss** prior to job completion.

    a. That is, losses are recognized immediately in their entirety—conservative treatment

3. An excess of accumulated costs over related billings is a current asset. An excess of accumulated billings over related costs is a liability (current in most cases).

    a. Balance sheet accounts are determined as in A.4., except no income is included

    b. Recognized losses in B.2. reduce accumulated costs.

4. The advantage of the completed-contract method is that it is based on final results, and its primary disadvantage is that it does not reflect current performance.

    a. Overall, the completed-contract method represents a conservative approach.

APB 10 Omnibus Opinion—1966 (ASC Topics 210, 605, 740)

A. ARB 43, Chapter 3B Working Capital

1. Offsetting of liabilities and assets in the balance sheet is not acceptable unless a right of offset exists.
2. Most government securities are not designed to be prepayment of taxes and thus may not be offset against tax liabilities. Only where an explicit prepayment exists may an offset be used.

FASB INTERPRETATION NO. 39 OFFSETTING OF AMOUNTS RELATED TO CERTAIN CONTRACTS

  A right of setoff exists when all of the following conditions are met: (a) each of the two parties to a contract owes the other determinable amounts, (b) the reporting entity has the right to set off the amount owed with the amount owed by the other entity, (c) the reporting entity intends to set off, and (d) the right of setoff is enforceable at law.

B. Installment method of accounting

  Revenues should be recognized at the point of sale unless receivables are in doubt. The installment or cost recovery method may be used.

SFAS 48 Revenue Recognition When Right of Return Exists (ASC Topic 605—Revenue)
(Also ASC Topics 450 and 460)

A. Specifies accounting for sales in which a product may be returned for refund, credit applied to amounts owed, or in exchange for other products.

   1. Right is specified by contract or is a matter of existing practice.
   2. Right may be exercised by ultimate customer or party who resells product to others.
   3. Not applicable to service revenue, real estate or lease transactions, or return of defective goods

B. Recognize revenue from right of return sales only if all of the following conditions are met:

   1. Price is substantially fixed or determinable at date of sale.
   2. Buyer has paid or is unconditionally obligated to pay.
   3. Obligation is not changed by theft, destruction, or damage of product.
   4. Buyer has "economic substance" apart from seller (i.e., sale is not with a party established mainly for purpose of recognizing sales revenue).
   5. Seller has no significant obligation for performance to directly cause resale of product.
   6. Amount of future returns can be reasonably estimated.

C. If all of the conditions in B. above are met, record sales and cost of sales **and**

   1. Reduce sales revenue and cost of sales to reflect estimated returns
   2. Accrue expected costs or losses in accordance with SFAS 5

D. If any condition in B. above is not met, do not recognize sales and cost of sales until either

   1. All conditions are subsequently met, or
   2. Return privilege has substantially expired

E. Factors which may impair ability to make a reasonable estimate of returns include

   1. Susceptibility of product to significant external factors (e.g., obsolescence or changes in demand)
   2. Long period of return privilege
   3. Absence of experience with similar products or inability to apply such experience due to changing circumstances (e.g., marketing policies or customer relationships)
   4. Absence of large volume of similar transactions

SFAS 66 Accounting for Sales of Real Estate (ASC Topics 360, 605, and 976)

A. Other than retail land sales

   1. Use the full accrual method if the following criteria are satisfied:

     a. Sale is consummated
     b. Buyer's initial and continuing investments demonstrate a commitment to pay for the property
     c. Seller's receivable is not subject to future subordination
     d. Risks and rewards of ownership have been transferred

   2. When the criteria are not met and dependent upon the particular circumstance, use one of the following methods:

     a. Installment method
     b. Cost recovery method
     c. Deposit method
     d. Reduced profit method
     e. Percentage-of-completion

B. Retail land sales (not outlined due to specialized nature)

EXPENSES (ASC TOPIC 700)

APB 12 Omnibus Opinion—1967 (ASC Topics 310, 360, 505, 710, 835)

A. Allowance or contra accounts (allowance for bad debts, accumulated depreciation, etc.) should be deducted from assets or groups of assets with appropriate disclosure.
B. Disclosure of depreciable assets should include

   1. Depreciation expense for the period
   2. Balances of major classes of depreciable assets by nature or function
   3. Accumulated depreciation either by major class or in total
   4. Description of method(s) of depreciation by major classes of assets

C. Changes in the separate shareholder equity accounts in addition to retained earnings and changes in number of equity securities must be disclosed in the year of change

 1. In separate statements
 2. Or the financial statements
 3. Or the notes

SFAS 43 Accounting for Compensated Absences (ASC Topics 710—Compensation—General)

A. This statement addresses the accounting for future sick pay benefits, holidays, vacation benefits, and other like compensated absences.

B. Accrual of a liability for future compensated absences is required if all of the conditions listed below exist.

 1. Obligation of employer to compensate employees arises from services already performed
 2. Obligation arises from vesting or accumulation of rights
 3. Probable payment of compensation
 4. Amount can be reasonably estimated

C. Above criteria require accrual of a liability for vacation benefits; however, other compensated absences typically may not require accrual of a liability.

 1. In spite of the above criteria, accrual of a liability is not required for accumulating nonvesting rights to receive sick pay benefits because amounts are typically not large enough to justify cost.

SFAS 112 Employers' Accounting for Postemployment Benefits (ASC Topic 712—Compensation—Nonretirement Postemployment Benefits)

A. Statement sets forth accounting standards for employers providing **postemployment** benefits to former/ inactive employees, **after employment but before retirement.**

 1. Applies to any postemployment benefits provided to former employers and their beneficiaries and dependents except

    a. Special or contractual termination benefits addressed by SFAS 88 and 106.
    b. Postemployment benefits derived from post**retirement** benefit or pension plans.
    c. Stock compensation plans covered by APB 25.
    d. Deferred compensation plans for individual employees that are covered by APB 12.

 2. Postemployment benefits may

    a. Result from death, disability, layoff, etc.
    b. Be paid in cash or in kind
    c. Be paid upon assumption of inactive status or over a period of time

B. Applicable postemployment benefits must be accounted for according to SFAS 43, which states:

 1. Liability for future compensated absences must be accrued if

    a. Obligation relates to services already provided by the employee,
    b. Rights to compensation vest or accumulate,
    c. Payment of obligation is probable, **and**
    d. Amount to be paid is reasonably estimable.

C. If conditions listed above are not met but the benefits are within scope of SFAS 43, they are accounted for according to SFAS 5, which states

 1. Estimated loss contingency accrued if

    a. It is known before FS are issued that it is probable that asset has been impaired or a liability incurred and that future events will probably confirm the loss, **and**
    b. Amount of loss is reasonably estimable.

D. Disclosure required if liability for postemployment benefits not accrued solely because amount not reasonably estimable.

SFAS 87 Employers' Accounting for Pensions (ASC Topic 715—Compensation—Retirement Benefits)

Applies to any arrangement that is similar in substance to pension plan regardless of form or means of financing. Applies to written plan and to plan whose existence may be implied from well-defined, although perhaps unwritten, practice of paying postretirement benefits. Does not apply to plan that provides only life insurance benefits or health insurance benefits, or both, to retirees. Does not apply to postemployment health care benefits.

The following terms are given specific definitions for the purposes of SFAS 87:

Accumulated benefit obligation—Actuarial present value of benefits (whether vested or nonvested) attributed by the pension benefit formula to employee service rendered before a specified date and based on employee service and compensation (if applicable) prior to that date. The accumulated benefit obligation differs from the projected benefit obligation in that it includes no assumption about future compensation levels. For plans with flat-benefit or non-pay-related pension benefit formulas, the accumulated benefit obligation and the projected benefit obligation are the same.

Actual return on plan assets component (of net periodic pension cost)—Difference between fair value of plan assets at the end of the period and the fair value at the beginning of the period, adjusted for contributions and payments of benefits during the period.

Actuarial present value—Value, as of a specified date, of an amount or series of amounts payable or receivable thereafter, with each amount adjusted to reflect (a) the time value of money (through discounts for interest) and (b) the probability of payment (by means of decrements for events such as death, disability, withdrawal, or retirement) between the specified date and the expected date of payment.

Amortization—Usually refers to the process of reducing a recognized liability systematically by recognizing revenues or reducing a recognized asset systematically by recognizing expenses or costs. In pension accounting, amortization is also used to refer to the systematic recognition in net pension cost over several periods of previously **unrecognized** amounts, including unrecognized prior service cost and unrecognized net gain or loss.

Defined contribution pension plan—Plan that provides pension benefits in return for services rendered, provides an individual account for each participant, and specifies how contributions to the individual's account are to be determined instead of specifying the amount of benefits the individual is to receive. Under a defined contribution pension plan, the benefits a participant will receive depend solely on the amount contributed to the participant's account, the returns earned on investments of those contributions, and forfeitures of other participants' benefits that may be allocated to such participant's account.

Gain or loss—Change in the value of either the projected benefit obligation or the plan assets resulting from experience different from that assumed or from a change in an actuarial assumption. See also **Unrecognized net gain or loss**.

Gain or loss component (of net periodic pension cost)—The gain or loss component is the net effect of delayed recognition of gains and losses (the net change in the unrecognized net gain or loss) except that it does not include changes in the projected benefit obligation occurring during the period and deferred for later recognition.

Interest cost component (of net periodic pension cost)—Increase in the projected benefit obligation due to passage of time.

Market-related value of plan assets—Balance used to calculate the expected return on plan assets. Market-related value can be either fair market value or a calculated value that recognizes changes in fair value in a systematic and rational manner over not more than five years. Different ways of calculating market-related value may be used for different classes of assets, but the manner of determining market-related value shall be applied consistently from year to year for each asset class.

Net periodic pension cost—Amount recognized in an employer's financial statements as the cost of a pension plan for a period. Components of net periodic pension cost are service cost, interest cost, actual return on plan assets, gain or loss, amortization of unrecognized prior service cost, and amortization of the unrecognized net obligation or asset existing at the date of initial application of SFAS 87. SFAS 87 uses the term **net periodic pension cost** instead of **net pension expense** because part of the cost recognized in a period may be capitalized along with other costs as part of an asset such as inventory.

Prior service cost or credit—Cost of retroactive benefits or credit granted in a plan amendment.

Projected benefit obligation—Actuarial present value as of a date of all benefits attributed by the pension benefit formula to employee service rendered prior to that date. The projected benefit obligation is measured using assumptions as to future compensation levels if the pension benefit formula is based on those future compensation levels (pay-related, final-pay, final-average-pay, or career-average-pay plans).

Service cost component (of net periodic pension cost)—Actuarial present value of benefits attributed by the pension benefit formula to services rendered by employees during the period. The service cost component is a portion of the projected benefit obligation and is unaffected by the funded status of the plan.

Unfunded projected benefit obligation—Excess of the projected obligation over plan assets.

Unrecognized net gain or loss—Cumulative net gain (loss) that has not been recognized as a part of net periodic pension cost. See **Gain or loss**.

Unamortized prior service cost or credit—Portion of prior service cost or credit that has not been recognized as a part of net periodic pension cost.

A. Single-Employer Defined Benefit Plans

1. Pension benefits are part of compensation paid to employees for services

    a. Amount of benefits to be paid depends on a number of future events specified in the **plan's benefit formula**.

2. Any method of pension accounting that recognizes cost before payment of benefits to retirees must deal with two problems

    a. Assumptions must be made concerning future events that will determine amount and timing of benefits

    b. Approach to attributing cost of pension benefits to individual years of service must be selected

B. Basic Elements of Pension Accounting

1. Prior service cost

    a. Except as specified otherwise, prior service cost shall be amortized by assigning an equal amount to each future service period of each employee active at the date of a plan amendment who is expected to receive benefits under plan.

    b. If all/almost all of plan's participants are inactive, cost of retroactive plan benefits should be amortized over remaining life expectancy of those participants.

    c. Consistent use of alternative amortization approach that more rapidly reduces unrecognized cost of retroactive amendments is acceptable.

        (1) Alternative method used should be disclosed.

    d. When period during which employer expects to realize economic benefits from amendment granting retroactive benefits is shorter than entire remaining service period of active employees, amortization of prior service cost should be accelerated.

    e. Plan amendment can reduce, rather than increase, the projected benefit obligation.

        (1) Reduction should be used to reduce any existing unrecognized prior service cost.

        (2) Excess should be amortized on same basis as cost of benefit increases.

2. Gains and losses

    a. Gains (losses)

        (1) Result from changes in amount of either projected benefit obligation or plan assets due to experience different than assumed and changes in assumptions

        (2) Include both **realized** and **unrealized** amounts

    b. Asset gains (losses) include both changes reflected in the market-related value of assets and changes not yet reflected in the market-related value.

        (1) Asset gains (losses) not yet reflected in market-related value are not required to be amortized as B.2.c. below.

    c. As a minimum, amortization of unrecognized net gain (loss) should be included as a component of net pension cost for a year if, as of the beginning of the year, that unrecognized net gain (loss) $\geq .10$ of the larger of the projected benefit obligation or the market-related value of plan assets.

        (1) Minimum amortization should be the excess divided by the average remaining service period of active employees expected to receive benefits under the plan.

            (a) Amortization must always reduce beginning-of-the-year balance.

            (b) Amortization of a net unrecognized gain (loss) results in a decrease (increase) in net periodic pension cost.

        (2) If all or almost all of plan's participants are inactive, average remaining life expectancy of inactive participants should be used instead of average remaining service.

    d. Any systematic method of amortization of unrecognized gains (losses) may be used in lieu of the minimum specified above provided that

        (1) Minimum is used in any period in which minimum amortization is greater (reduces the net balance by more)

        (2) Method is applied consistently and disclosed

3. Recognition of liabilities and assets

    a. Liability (asset) is recognized if net periodic pension cost recognized exceeds (is less than) amounts the employer has contributed to the plan and if the projected benefit obligations exceeds (is less than) plan asset.

C. Attribution

 1. Pension benefits should be attributed to periods of employee service based on plan's benefit formula.
 2. When employer has a present commitment to make future amendments, and substance of plan is to provide benefits attributable to prior service that are greater than benefits defined by written terms of the plan.

    a. The substantive commitment should be basis for accounting, and
    b. Existence and nature of the commitment to make future amendments should be disclosed

 3. Assumptions

    a. Assumed discount rates reflect rates at which pension benefits could be effectively settled

       (1) Used in measurements of projected and accumulated benefit obligations and the service and interest cost components of net periodic pension cost

    b. Assumed compensation levels (when measuring service cost and the projected benefit obligation) should reflect an estimate of the actual future compensation levels of employees involved, including future changes attributed to general price levels, productivity, seniority, promotion, and other factors.
    c. Accumulated benefit obligation shall be measured based on employees' history of service and compensation without estimate of future compensation levels.
    d. Automatic benefit increases specified by plan that are expected to occur should be included in measurements of projected and accumulated benefit obligations and the service cost component.
    e. Retroactive plan amendments should be included in computations of projected and accumulated benefit obligations.

       (1) Once they have been contractually agreed to
       (2) Even if some provisions take effect only in future periods

D. Measurement of Plan Assets

 1. For purposes of determining the funded status of the plan and required disclosures, plan investments, whether equity or debt securities, real estate, or other, should be measured at their fair value as of measurement date.
 2. Market-related asset value is used for purposes of determining the expected return on plan assets and accounting for asset gains and losses.

E. Acceptable Measurement Dates

 1. As of date of financial statements, or
 2. If used consistently from year to year, as of a date < 3 months prior to that date
 3. Measurement date is not intended to require that all procedures be performed after that date.
 4. Information for items requiring estimates can be prepared as of an earlier date and projected forward to account for subsequent events (e.g., employee service).
 5. The "assets and liabilities" reported in interim financial statements should be the same "assets and liabilities" recognized in previous year-end balance sheet.

    a. Adjusted for subsequent accruals and contributions unless measures of both the obligation and plan assets are available as of a current date or a significant event occurs, such as plan amendment, that would call for such measurements

 6. Measurements of net periodic pension cost for both interim and annual financial statements should be based on assumptions used for previous year-end measurements.

    a. If more recent measurements are available or a significant event occurs, use these more recent measurements.

 7. For fiscal years ending after December 15, 2008, the measurement date is the fiscal year-end of firm

F. Disclosures (Amended by SFAS 132[R] and SFAS 158)

SFAS 88 Employers' Accounting for Settlements and Curtailments of Defined Benefit Pension Plans and for Termination Benefits (ASC Topic 715—Retirement Benefits)

Statement applies to an employer that sponsors a defined benefit pension plan accounted for under the provisions of SFAS 87 if all or part of the plan's pension benefit obligation is settled or the plan is curtailed. It also applies to an employer that offers benefits to employees in connection with their termination of employment.

The following terms are given specific definitions for the purposes of SFAS 88:

Settlement—Transaction that (a) is an irrevocable action, (b) relieves the employer (or the plan) of primary responsibility for a pension benefit obligation, and (c) eliminates significant risks related to the obligation and the assets used to effect the settlement.

Annuity contract—Irrevocable contract in which an insurance company[4] unconditionally undertakes a legal obligation to provide specified benefits to specific individuals in return for a fixed consideration or premium. It involves the transfer of significant risk from the employer to the insurance company.

Curtailment—Event that significantly reduces the expected years of future service of present employees or eliminates for a significant number of employees the accrual of defined benefits for some or all of their future services.

A. Relationship of Settlements and Curtailments to Other Events

1. Settlement and curtailment may occur separately or together.

B. Accounting for Settlement of Pension Obligation

1. For purposes of this statement, when a pension obligation is settled, the maximum gain or loss subject to recognition is the unrecognized gain or loss defined in SFAS 87 plus any remaining unrecognized net asset existing at the date of initial application of SFAS 87.
2. If the purchase of a participating annuity contract constitutes a settlement, the maximum gain (but not the maximum loss) should be reduced by the cost of the participation right before determining the amount to be recognized in earnings.
3. If the cost of all settlements in a year is less than or equal to the sum of the service cost and interest cost components of net periodic pension cost for the plan for the year, gain or loss recognition is permitted but not required for those settlements.

C. Accounting for Plan Curtailment

1. Unrecognized prior service cost is a loss.
2. The projected benefit obligation may be decreased (a gain) or increased (a loss) by a curtailment.

D. Termination Benefits

1. Employer may provide benefits to employees in connection with their termination of employment.
2. Termination benefits may take many forms consisting of

   a. Lump-sum payments
   b. Periodic future payments

3. The cost of termination benefits recognized as a liability and a loss shall include the amount of any lump-sum payments and present value of any expected future payments.

SFAS 106 Employers' Accounting for Postretirement Benefits other than Pensions (ASC Topic 715—Compensation—Retirement Benefits)

Standard applies to all forms of postretirement benefits, particularly postretirement health care benefits. Applies to written plan and to a plan whose existence may be implied from well-defined, although perhaps unwritten, practice of paying postretirement benefits (called the substantive plan). Does not apply to pensions.

The following terms are given specific definitions for purposes of SFAS 106:

Attribution period—The period of an employee's service to which the expected postretirement benefit obligation for that employee is assigned. The beginning of the attribution period is the employee's date of hire unless the plan's benefit formula grants credit only for service from a later date, in which case the beginning of the attribution period is generally the beginning of that credited service period. The end of the attribution period is the full eligibility date.

Benefit formula—The basis for determining benefits to which participants may be entitled under a postretirement benefit plan. A plan's benefit formula specifies the years of service to be rendered, age to be attained while in service, or a combination of both that must be met for an employee to be eligible to receive benefits under the plan.

Full eligibility date—The date at which an employee has rendered all of the service necessary to have earned the right to receive all of the benefits expected to be received by that employee (including any beneficiaries and dependents expected to receive benefits).

Health care cost trend rates—An assumption about the annual rate(s) of change in the cost of health care benefits currently provided by the postretirement benefit plan, due to factors other than changes in the composition of the plan population by age and dependency status, for each year from the measurement date until the end of the period in which benefits are expected to be paid.

Incurred claims cost (by age)—The cost of providing the postretirement health care benefits covered by the plan to a plan participant, after adjusting for reimbursements from Medicare and other providers of health care benefits and for deductibles, coinsurance provisions, and other specific claims costs borne by the retiree.

---

[4] If the insurance company is controlled by the employer or there is any reasonable doubt that the insurance company will meet its obligation under the contract, the purchase of the contract does not constitute a settlement for purposes of this statement.

Net periodic postretirement benefit cost—The amount recognized in an employer's financial statements as the cost of a postretirement benefit plan for a period. Components of net periodic postretirement benefit cost include service cost, interest cost, actual return on plan assets, gain or loss, amortization of unrecognized prior service cost, and amortization of the unrecognized transition obligation or asset.

Plan amendment—A change in the existing terms of a plan. A plan amendment may increase or decrease benefits, including those attributed to years of service already rendered.

Transition asset—The unrecognized amount, as of the date this statement is initially applied, of (a) the fair value of plan assets plus any recognized accrued postretirement benefit cost or less any recognized prepaid postretirement benefit cost in excess of (b) the accumulated postretirement benefit obligation.

Transition obligation—The unrecognized amount, as of the date this statement is initially applied, of (a) the accumulated postretirement benefit obligation in excess of (b) the fair value of plan assets plus any recognized accrued postretirement benefit cost or less any recognized prepaid postretirement benefit cost.

Unrecognized transition asset—The portion of the transition asset that has not been recognized either immediately as the effect of a change in accounting or on a delayed basis as a part of net periodic postretirement benefit cost, as an offset to certain losses, or as a part of accounting for the effects of a settlement or a curtailment.

Unrecognized transition obligation—The portion of the transition obligation that has not been recognized either immediately as the effect of a change in accounting or on a delayed basis as a part of net periodic postretirement benefit cost, as an offset to certain gains, or as a part of accounting for the effects of a settlement or a curtailment.

A. Single Employer Defined Benefit Plans

1. Postretirement benefits are part of compensation paid to employees for services

    a. Amount of benefits to be paid depends on future events specified in plan's benefit formula

2. Postretirement benefits formerly were accounted for on a pay-as-you-go (cash) basis. SFAS 106 changes this practice by requiring accrual, during the years that the employee renders necessary service, of **expected** cost of providing those benefits to an employee. Any method of postretirement benefits accounting that recognizes cost before payment of benefits to retirees must deal with two problems.

    a. Assumptions must be made concerning future events that will determine amount and timing of benefits.
    b. Approach to attributing cost of postretirement benefits to individual years of service must be selected.

B. Basic Elements of Postretirement Benefits Accounting

1. Prior service cost

    a. Except as specified otherwise, prior service cost shall be amortized by assigning an equal amount to each future service period of each employee active at the date of a plan amendment who was not yet fully eligible for benefits at that date.
    b. If all or almost all of a plan's participants are fully eligible for benefits, prior service cost shall be amortized over remaining life expectancy of those participants.
    c. Consistent use of alternative amortization approach that more rapidly reduces unrecognized cost of retroactive amendments is acceptable.

        (1) Alternative method used should be disclosed.

    d. When period during which employer expects to realize economic benefits from amendment granting increased benefits is shorter than entire remaining service period of active employees, amortization of prior service cost shall be accelerated.
    e. Plan amendment can reduce, rather than increase, accumulated postretirement benefit obligation

        (1) Reduction should be used to reduce any existing unrecognized prior service cost
        (2) Then to reduce any remaining unrecognized transition obligation
        (3) Excess, if any, shall be amortized on same basis as specified for prior service cost

2. Gains and losses

    a. Gains (losses)

        (1) Result from changes in amount of either accumulated postretirement benefit obligation or plan assets due to experience different than assumed and changes in assumptions
        (2) Include both **realized** and **unrealized** amounts

    b. Asset gains (losses) include both (a) changes reflected in market-related value of assets and (b) changes not yet reflected in market-related value.

        (1) Asset gains (losses) not yet reflected in market-related value are not required to be amortized as c. below.

    c. As a minimum, amortization of unrecognized net gain (loss) should be included as a component of net postretirement benefit cost for a year if, as of the beginning of the year, that unrecognized net gain (loss) > .10 of the larger of the accumulated postretirement benefit obligation or the market-related value of plan assets.

      (1) Minimum amortization should be the excess divided by the average remaining service period of active employees expected to receive benefits under the plan

        (a) Amortization must always reduce beginning of the year balance
        (b) Amortization of a net unrecognized gain (loss) results in a decrease (increase) in net periodic pension cost

      (2) If all or almost all of plan's participants are inactive, average remaining life expectancy of inactive participants should be used instead of average remaining service.

    d. Any systematic method of amortization of unrecognized gains (losses) may be used in lieu of the minimum specified above provided that

      (1) Minimum is used in any period in which minimum amortization is greater (reduces the net balance by more)
      (2) Method is applied consistently and disclosed

  3. Recognition of liabilities and assets

    a. SFAS 106 requires an employer's obligation for postretirement benefits expected to be provided to an employee be **fully** accrued by the full eligibility date of employee, even if employee is to render additional service beyond that date
    b. Transition obligations

      (1) SFAS 106 measures the transition obligation as the unfunded and unrecognized accumulated postretirement benefit obligation for all plan participants. Two options are provided for recognizing that transition obligation.

        (a) **Immediate** recognition of the transition obligation as the effect of an accounting change (i.e., include all of the obligation as part of the net periodic postretirement benefit cost)
        (b) Recognize the transition obligation in the balance sheet and income statement on a delayed basis over the plan participants' future service periods, with proper disclosure of the remaining unrecognized amount. Note that delayed recognition **cannot** result in less rapid recognition than accounting for the transition obligation on a pay-as-you-go basis.

C. Attribution

  1. The expected postretirement benefit obligation shall be attributed, in equal amounts, to each year of service in the attribution period.
  2. However, if a benefit plan contains a benefit formula that attributes a disproportionate share of the expected postretirement benefit obligation to employees' early years of service, the postretirement benefits should be attributed based on the plan's benefit formula.
  3. Assumptions

    a. Assumed discount rates shall reflect time value of money in determining present value of future cash outflows currently expected to be required to satisfy postretirement benefit obligation

      (1) Used in measurements of expected and accumulated postretirement benefit obligations and service and interest cost components of net periodic postretirement benefit cost

    b. Assumed compensation levels (when measuring service cost and expected and accumulated postretirement benefit obligations) shall reflect estimate of actual future compensation levels of employees involved, including future changes attributed to general price levels, productivity, seniority, promotion, and other factors.
    c. Accumulated postretirement benefit obligation shall be measured based on employees' history of service and compensation without estimate of future compensation levels.
    d. Automatic benefit changes specified by plan that are expected to occur should be included in measurements of projected and accumulated benefit obligations and the service cost component.
    e. Plan amendments should be included in computations of projected and accumulated benefit obligations.

      (1) Once they have been contractually agreed to
      (2) Even if some provisions take effect only in future periods

D. Measurement of Plan Assets

1. For purposes of required disclosures, plan investments, whether equity or debt securities, real estate, or other, shall be measured at FMV as of measurement date.
2. Market-related asset value is used for purposes of determining the expected return on plan assets and accounting for asset gains and losses.

E. Acceptable Measurement Dates

1. As of date of financial statements, or
2. If used consistently from year to year, as of a date < 3 months prior to that date
3. Measurement date is not intended to require that all procedures be performed after that date
4. Information for items requiring estimates can be prepared as of an earlier date and projected forward to account for subsequent events (e.g., employee service)
5. Measurements of net periodic postretirement benefit cost for both interim and annual financial statements shall be based on assumptions used for previous year-end measurements

    a. If more recent measurements are available or a significant event occurs, use more recent measurements

F. Disclosures (amended by SFAS 132)

SFAS 132 (Revised) Employers' Disclosures about Pensions and Other Postretirement Benefits (ASC Topic 715—Compensation—Retirement Benefits)

A. Disclosures for defined benefit pensions plans and defined benefit postretirement plans

1. A reconciliation of beginning and ending balances of the benefit obligation with the effects of the following shown separately:

    a. Service cost
    b. Interest cost
    c. Contributions by plan participants
    d. Actuarial gains and losses
    e. Foreign currency exchange rate changes
    f. Benefits paid
    g. Plan amendments
    h. Business combinations
    i. Divestitures
    j. Curtailments
    k. Settlements
    l. Special termination benefits

2. A reconciliation of beginning and ending balances of the fair value of plan assets with the effects of the following shown separately:

    a. Actual return on plan assets
    b. Foreign currency exchange rate changes
    c. Contributions by the employer
    d. Contributions by plan participants
    e. Benefits paid
    f. Business combinations
    g. Divestitures
    h. Settlements

3. The funded status of the plans
4. The amounts recognized and the amounts not recognized in the statement of financial position such as

    a. Any unamortized prior service cost or credit
    b. Any unrecognized net gain or loss
    c. Any unamortized net obligation or net asset existing at the initial date of prior SFAS 87 or 106 that are still unrecognized
    d. Prepaid assets or accrued liabilities of the net pension or other postretirement benefits
    e. Any intangible asset
    f. The amount of other comprehensive income recognized

5. Information about plan assets including

a. For each major category of plan assets, including equity securities, debt securities, real estate, and all other assets, the percentage of the fair value of total plan assets held as of the measurement date

b. A description of investment policies and strategies, including target allocation percentages or ranges of percentages for each major category of plan assets, and other factors that are pertinent to understanding the investment policies and strategies, (i.e., investment goals, risk management practices, permitted and prohibited investments)

c. A description of the basis used to determine the overall expected long-term rate-of-return-of-assets assumption, the general approach used, the extent to which ROA assumption was based on historical returns, adjustments made to reflect expectations of future returns, and how adjustments were determined.

d. Disclosure of additional asset categories and additional information about specific assets is encouraged if the information is useful in understanding risks and long-term rate of return.

6. For defined benefit pension plans, the accumulated benefit obligation.

7. The benefits are expected to be paid in each of the next five fiscal years, and in the aggregate for the five fiscal years thereafter.

8. The employer's best estimate of contributions expected to be paid to the plan during the next fiscal year. The estimated contributions may be presented in the aggregate combining contributions required by funding regulations or laws, discretionary contributions, and noncash contributions.

9. The recognized amount of the net periodic benefit cost with the components shown separately

10. The amount caused from a change in the additional minimum pension liability that was included in other comprehensive income

11. On a weighted-average basis, the rates for

    a. Assumed discount rate
    b. Rate of compensation increase
    c. Expected long-term rate of return on plan assets

12. The assumptions used to determine the benefit obligation and the net benefit cost

13. Trend rates assumed for health care cost for the next year and thereafter

14. The measurement date(s) used to determine pension and other postretirement benefit measurements for plans that make up the majority of assets and benefit obligations

15. The effects of a one-percentage-point increase or decrease of the trend rates for health care costs on

    a. The aggregate of the service and interest cost components
    b. The accumulated postretirement benefit obligation

16. If applicable

    a. The amounts and types of securities of the employer or a related party in plan assets
    b. The amount of future benefits covered by insurance contracts issued by the employer or a related party
    c. Any significant transactions between the plan and the employer or a related party
    d. Any substantive commitment used as the basis for accounting for the benefit obligation
    e. The cost of special or contractual termination benefits recognized during the period with a description of the event

17. An explanation of significant changes in the benefit obligation or plan assets that is not apparent in the other disclosures required

B. Disclosures for employers with more than one plan

1. Disclosures required in this statement may be disclosed in aggregate for an employer's defined benefit pension plans and in aggregate for an employer's defined benefit postretirement plans but must still present separately prepaid benefit costs and accrued benefit liabilities recognized in the statement of financial position.

2. An employer may not combine the disclosures of plans outside the US and plans in the US if the benefit obligation of the plans outside the US represent a significant portion of the total benefit obligation and significant differences exist in the assumptions used.

C. Disclosure requirements for nonpublic entities

1. Nonpublic entities may choose to disclose the following instead of the disclosures stated in A.:

    a. Benefit obligation
    b. Fair value of plan assets
    c. Funded status of the plan
    d. Contributions by the employer and the participant
    e. Amounts recognized in the statement of financial position of

(1) Prepaid assets or accrued liabilities
(2) Any intangible asset

f. Amount of accumulated other comprehensive income recognized and the amount resulting from a change in the minimum pension liability recognized
g. Net periodic benefit cost recognized
h. Rates for

(1) Assumed discount rate
(2) Rate of compensation increase
(3) Expected long-term rate of return on plan assets

i. Trend rates assumed for health care cost for the next year and thereafter
j. If applicable

(1) Amounts and types of securities of the employer or a related party
(2) Future annual benefits covered by insurance contracts issued by the employer or a related party
(3) Any significant transactions between the plan and the employer or a related party

k. Nature and effect of significant nonroutine events

D. Disclosures for defined contribution plans

1. Amount of cost recognized for pension or postretirement benefit plans must be separate from the cost recognized for defined benefit plans
2. Nature and effect of any significant changes that affect comparability must be disclosed

E. Disclosures for multiemployer plans

1. Amount of contributions to multiemployer plans
2. Nature and effect of changes which affect comparability
3. If withdrawals made by an employer from a multiemployer plan will result in an obligation for a portion of the unfunded benefit obligation or the unfunded accumulated postretirement benefit obligation, follow the provision of SFAS 5, *Accounting for Contingencies*
4. The significant multiemployer plans in which an employer participates
5. The level of an employer's participation (the contribution to the plan and whether that contribution represents more than 5% of the total contributions).
6. The financial health of the plan, such as funded status, improvement plans, and surcharges.
7. The nature of the employer commitments to the plans, such as collective bargaining agreements and minimum contribution requirements.
8. For plans in which users are unable to obtain additional information from outside sources:

a. A description of the nature of the plan benefits
b. A qualitative description of the employer responsibility for plan obligations
c. Other quantitative information available, such as total plan assets, actuarial present value of accumulated vested benefits, and total contributions received by the plan

SFAS 158 Employers' Accounting for Defined Benefit Pension and Other Postretirement Plans (An Amendment of FASB Statements 87, 88, 106, and 132[R]) (ASC Topic 715—Compensation—Retirement Benefits and ASC Topic 958—Not-for-Profit Entities)

A. Recognize funded status of benefit plans

1. Aggregate status of all overfunded plans and show as noncurrent asset on balance sheet
2. Aggregate status of all underfunded plans, and show as current liability, noncurrent liability, or both on balance sheet.
3. Recognize as other comprehensive income the gain and loss and the prior service costs or credits that arise during the period but are not a part of pension expense.

B. Effective for fiscal years ending after December 15, 2008, the measurement date is the employer's fiscal year-end balance sheet date.

C. Disclosures

1. Funded status of the plans, and the amounts recognized in the balance sheet, showing separately the noncurrent assets, current liabilities, and noncurrent liabilities recognized.
2. Disclose the net gain or loss, net prior service cost or credit recognized in OCI for the period, and any reclassification adjustments of OCI that are recognized in pension cost.

3. The amounts in accumulated OCI that have not yet been recognized as pension costs. Show separately the following items:

    a. Net gain or loss
    b. Net prior service cost or credit
    c. Net transition asset or obligation

4. The amount and timing of any plan assets expected to be returned to the employer during the next 12-month period after the most recent balance sheet date.

SFAS 123 (Revised) (C36) Share-Based Payment (ASC Topic 718—Compensation—Stock Compensation and ASC Topic 505—Equity)

A. Provides a fair value based method of accounting for stock-based payment plans

1. Supersedes APB 25, amends SFAS 123
2. Applies to all transactions between an entity and its "suppliers" (whether employees or nonemployees) in which the entity acquires goods or services through issuance of equity instruments or incurrence of liabilities based on fair value of the entity's common stock or other equity instruments
3. Examples include stock purchase plans, stock options, restricted stock, and stock appreciation rights
4. Classifies share-based payment as either equity or liability

B. Transactions with Nonemployees—Accounted for based on fair value of consideration received or fair value of equity instruments given, whichever is more readily determinable.
C. Transactions with Employees—Uses fair value based method
D. Measurement Methods

1. Share-based payments recorded as equity

    a. Measured at fair value at grant date
    b. Stock options are measured at fair value which is based on the observable market price of an option with the same or similar terms and conditions, or via use of an option pricing model which considers, as of grant date, exercise price and expected life of the option, current price of underlying stock and its anticipated volatility, expected dividends on the stock, and risk-free interest rate for expected term of the option.
    c. If fair value cannot be determined as of grant date, final measure shall be based on stock price and any other pertinent factors when it becomes reasonably possible to estimate that value. Current intrinsic value shall be used as a measure until a final determination of fair value can be made.

2. Share-based payments recorded as liabilities
    Requires the recording of liability based on current stock price at end of each period. Changes in stock price during service period are recognized as compensation cost over service period. A change in stock price subsequent to service period is recognized as compensation cost of that period.

E. Recognition of Compensation Cost

1. Total compensation cost is based on the number of instruments that eventually vest

    a. Vesting is defined as moment when employee's right to receive or retain such instruments or cash is no longer contingent on performance of additional services
    b. No compensation cost shall be recognized for employees that forfeit eligibility due to failure either to achieve service requirement or performance condition
    c. Compensation cost shall not be reversed if vested employee's stock option expires unexercised
    d. Company must estimate forfeitures due to service or performance condition not being met
    e. Total compensation cost is amortized straight-line over the requisite service period

2. Acceptable accrual methods

    a. As of grant date, base accruals of compensation cost on best available estimate of the number of options or instruments expected to vest, with estimates for forfeitures
    b. As of grant date, accrue compensation cost as if all options or instruments that are subject only to a service requirement will vest

F. Tax consequences of stock-based compensation transactions shall be accounted for pursuant to SFAS 109

1. Excess tax benefits are recognized as additional paid-in capital
2. Cash retained as a result of excess tax benefits is presented on the statement of cash flows as a cash inflow from financing activities

G. Disclosures

1. The method of estimating the fair value of goods or services received or fair value of the equity instruments granted during the period
2. The cash flow effects from share-based payments
3. Vesting requirements, maximum term of options granted, and number of shares authorized for grants of options or other equity instruments
4. The number and weighted-average exercise prices of each group of options
5. The weighted-average grant-date fair value of options granted during the year, classified according to whether exercise price equals, exceeds, or is less than fair value of stock at date of grant
6. A description of methods used and assumptions made in determining fair values of the options
7. Total compensation cost recognized for the year

ARB 43— Chapter 10A Real and Personal Property Taxes (ASC Topic 720—Other Expenses)

Accounting for personal and real property taxes which vary in time of determination and collection from state to state

A. In practice, the dates below have been used to apportion taxes between accounting periods.

1. Assessment date
2. Beginning of fiscal period of taxing authority
3. End of fiscal period of taxing authority
4. Lien date
5. Date of tax levy
6. Date tax is payable
7. Date tax is delinquent
8. Period appearing on tax bill

B. The most acceptable basis is a monthly accrual on the taxpayer's books during the fiscal period of the taxing authority.

1. At year-end, the books will show the appropriate prepayment or accrual.
2. An accrued liability, whether known or estimated, should be shown as a current liability.
3. On income statement, property taxes may be charged to operating expense, deducted separately from income, prorated among accounts to which they apply, or combined with other taxes (but not with income taxes).

SFAS 2 Accounting for Research and Development Costs (R&D) (ASC Topic 730—Research & Development)

A. Establishes accounting standards for R&D costs with objective of reducing alternative practices. In summary, all R&D costs are expensed except intangible assets purchased from others and tangible assets that have alternative future uses (which are capitalized and depreciated or amortized as R&D expense).

1. SFAS 2 specifies

    a. R&D activities
    b. Elements of R&D costs
    c. Accounting for R&D costs
    d. Required disclosures for R&D

2. SFAS 2 does not cover

    a. R&D conducted for others under contract
    b. Activities unique to extractive industries

B. R&D activities

1. Research is "planned search or critical investigation aimed at discovery of new knowledge with the hope that such knowledge will be useful in developing a new product or service or a new process or technique in bringing about a significant improvement to an existing product or process."
2. Development is "the translation of research findings or other knowledge into a plan or design for a new product or process or for a significant improvement to an existing product or process whether intended for sale or use."
3. R&D examples

    a. Laboratory research to discover new knowledge

        (1) Seeking applications for new research findings

    b. Formulation and design of product alternatives

        (1) Testing for product alternatives
        (2) Modification of products or processes

   c. Preproduction prototypes and models

     (1) Tools, dies, etc. for new technology
     (2) Pilot plants not capable of commercial production

   d. Engineering activity until product is ready for manufacture

  4. Exclusions from R&D

   a. Engineering during an early phase of commercial production
   b. Quality control for commercial production
   c. Troubleshooting during commercial production breakdowns
   d. Routine, ongoing efforts to improve products
   e. Adaptation of existing capability for a specific customer or other requirements
   f. Seasonal design changes to products
   g. Routine design of tools, dies, etc.
   h. Design, construction, startup, etc. of equipment except that used solely for R&D
   i. Legal work for patents or litigation
   j. Items a.–h. above are normally expensed but not as R&D; i. is capitalized

C. Elements of R&D costs

  1. Materials, equipment, and facilities

   a. If acquired for a specific R&D project and have no alternative use
   b. If there are alternative uses, costs should be capitalized

     (1) Charge to R&D as these materials, etc., are used

  2. Salaries, wages, and related costs
  3. Intangibles purchased from others are treated as materials, etc. in 1. above

   a. If capitalized, amortization is covered by APB 17

  4. R&D services **performed by others**
  5. A reasonable allocation of indirect costs

   a. Exclude general and administrative costs not clearly related to R&D

D. Accounting for R&D

  1. Expense R&D as incurred

E. Disclosure required on face of IS or notes

  1. Total R&D expensed per period

APB 10 Omnibus Opinion—1966 (ASC Topics 210, 605, 740)

A. ARB 43, Chapter 3B Working Capital

  1. Offsetting of liabilities and assets in the balance sheet is not acceptable unless a right of offset exists.
  2. Most government securities are not designed to be prepayment of taxes and thus may not be offset against tax liabilities. Only where an explicit prepayment exists may an offset be used.

FASB INTERPRETATION NO. 39 OFFSETTING OF AMOUNTS RELATED TO CERTAIN CONTRACTS

A right of setoff exists when all of the following conditions are met: (a) each of the two parties to a contract owes the other determinable amounts, (b) the reporting entity has the right to set off the amount owed with the amount owed by the other entity, (c) the reporting entity intends to set off, and (d) the right of setoff is enforceable at law.

B. Installment method of accounting

Revenues should be recognized at the point of sale unless receivables are in doubt. The installment or cost recovery method may be used.

APB 23 Accounting for Income Taxes—Special Areas (ASC Topic 740—Income Taxes)
(Amended by SFAS 109)

A. Undistributed earnings of domestic subsidiaries

1. Inclusion of undistributed earnings in pretax accounting income of parent (either through consolidation or equity method) results in temporary difference.

   a. Tax effect may be based on assumptions such as

      (1) Earnings would be distributed currently as dividends or
      (2) Earnings would be distributed in form of capital gain.

B. Foreign subsidiaries are not required to accrue deferred taxes for undistributed earnings if sufficient evidence exists that subsidiary would reinvest the undistributed earnings indefinitely or remit them tax-free.

SFAS 109 (I27) Accounting for Income Taxes (ASC Topic 740—Income Taxes)

A. Establishes financial accounting and reporting requirements for income taxes resulting from an entity's activities during the current and preceding years.

1. Continues BS-oriented asset and liability approach consistent with SFAC 6.
2. Objectives

   a. Recognize taxes payable or refundable for current year.
   b. Recognize deferred tax liabilities and assets for future tax consequences of events previously recognized in financial statements or tax returns.

B. Basic principles

1. Recognize current tax liability or asset for estimated taxes payable or refundable on tax returns for current year
2. Measure and recognize deferred tax liability or asset using enacted tax rate(s) expected to apply to taxable income in periods in which the deferred tax assets and liabilities are expected to be realized or settled
3. Adjust measurement of deferred tax assets so as to not recognize tax benefits not expected to be realized
4. Deferred tax assets and liabilities are **not** discounted to reflect their present value

C. Measurement of Deferred Taxes

1. Temporary differences

   a. Difference between tax basis of asset or liability and its reported amount for financial accounting which results in taxable or deductible amounts in future years

      (1) Includes all timing differences
      (2) Includes tax-book differences in asset's bases

   b. Future effects

      (1) **Taxable amounts** are from temporary differences that will result in lower amounts of expense or higher amounts of revenue being reported on the tax return than are reported on the books in the future period.
      (2) **Deductible amounts** are from temporary differences that will result in higher amounts of expense or lower amounts of revenue being reported on the tax return than are reported on the books in the future period.

2. Deferred tax liability or asset measured each BS date

   a. Identify types and amounts of existing temporary differences **and** nature of each type of operating loss and tax credit carryforward and the remaining length of the carryforward period
   b. Measure total deferred tax liability for taxable temporary differences using the enacted applicable tax rate
   c. Measure total deferred tax asset for deductible temporary differences and operating loss carryforwards using the enacted applicable tax rate
   d. Measure deferred tax assets for each type of tax credit carryforward
   e. Reduce deferred tax assets by a valuation allowance, **if more likely than not** (a likelihood of more than 50%) that some or all of deferred tax asset will not be realized

      (1) All available evidence (positive and negative) should be considered to determine whether valuation allowance is needed.

D. Changes in Tax Rates

1. Change in rates

   a. Change previously recorded amounts of deferred tax liabilities or assets
   b. Net adjustments shall be reflected in tax expense on continuing operations in period that includes enactment date.

E. Business Combinations

1. Recognize deferred tax asset or liability for differences between assigned values and tax basis of assets and liabilities recognized in a purchase combination

F. Intraperiod Tax Allocation

1. Allocate income tax expense or benefit for the period among continuing operations, extraordinary items, other comprehensive income, and items charged or credited to stockholders' equity

   a. In cases where there is only one item after continuing operations, portion of income tax expense (benefit) remaining after allocation to continuing operations is amount allocated to that item.
   b. In cases where there are two or more items after continuing operations, portion left after allocation to continuing operations is allocated among other items in proportion to their individual effects on income tax expense (benefit).

G. Financial Statement Presentation and Disclosure

1. Balance sheet

   a. Report deferred tax liabilities and assets as current or noncurrent based on classification of related asset or liability
   b. Classify deferred tax liabilities or assets not related to an asset or liability (i.e., one related to a carryforward) according to the expected reversal date of the temporary difference
   c. For a taxpaying component of an enterprise and within a particular tax jurisdiction

      (1) All current deferred tax liabilities and assets should be offset and reported as a single amount
      (2) All noncurrent deferred tax liabilities and assets should be offset and reported as a single amount

2. Must disclose the following components of the net deferred tax liability or asset:

   a. The total of all deferred tax liabilities
   b. The total of all deferred tax assets
   c. The total valuation allowance for deferred tax assets

3. Additional disclosures

   a. Disclose any net change in the total valuation allowance
   b. Disclose the types of temporary differences, carryforwards, and carrybacks

4. Income statement

   a. Components of tax expense attributable to continuing operations shall be disclosed in financial statements or notes. For example

      (1) Current tax expense or benefit
      (2) Deferred tax expense or benefit (exclusive of other components listed below)
      (3) Investment tax credits
      (4) Government grants (to the extent recognized as a reduction of income tax expense)
      (5) Benefits of operating loss carryforwards
      (6) Tax expense resulting from allocation of certain tax benefits either directly to contributed capital or to reduce goodwill or other noncurrent intangible assets of an acquired entity
      (7) Adjustments of a deferred tax liability or asset resulting from enacted changes in tax laws, rates, or status

   b. Variances between statutory and effective tax rates must be disclosed.

      (1) Public entities should disclose reconciliation using percentages or dollar amounts.
      (2) Nonpublic entities must disclose nature of significant reconciling items.

   c. Disclose amounts and expiration dates of operating loss and tax credit carryforwards **and** any portion of the deferred tax asset valuation allowance for which subsequently recognized tax benefits will be allocated to reduce intangible assets or directly reduce accumulated other comprehensive income.

BROAD TRANSACTIONS (ASC TOPIC 800)

SFAS 141(R) Business Combinations (ASC Topic 805—Business Combinations)

A. Scope

1. Applies to transactions or events that meet the definition of a business combination.
2. Does not apply to joint venture, acquisition of group of assets that are not a business, or combination of entities or businesses under common control.
3. The acquisition method is required for all business combinations.

B. Key terms

1. Acquiree—business of which the acquirer obtains control.
2. Acquirer—entity that obtains control of acquiree.
3. Acquisition date—date which acquirer obtains control.
4. Business—integrated set of activities and assets that are capable of being conducted and managed for the purpose of providing a return in the form of dividends, lower costs, or other economic benefits directly to investors or other owners, members, or participants.
5. Business combination—transaction or other event in which acquirer obtains control of one or more businesses.
6. Contingent consideration—obligation to transfer additional assets or equity interests to the former owners as part of the exchange for control of the acquiree if certain events or conditions occur.
7. Control is ownership of more than 50% of the voting stock.
8. Equity interest is an ownership interest.
9. Fair value is the price that would be received to sell an asset or paid to transfer a liability in an orderly transaction between market participants at the measurement date.
10. Goodwill—an asset representing the future economic benefit arising from other assets acquired in a business combination that are not individually identified and separately recognized.
11. Intangible asset lacks physical substance. For purposes of SFAS 141(R), intangible assets exclude goodwill.
12. Noncontrolling interest is the equity in a subsidiary not attributable directly or indirectly to a parent.

C. Application of the acquisition method.

1. Identify the acquirer (the entity that obtains control over the acquiree). Factors to consider

    a. The relative voting rights in the combined entity after the combination.
    b. The existence of a large minority voting interest in the combined entity when no other owner or organized group of owners has a significant voting interest.
    c. The composition of the governing body of the combined entity.
    d. The composition of the senior management of the combined entity.
    e. The terms of the exchange of equity securities.
    f. Examine the facts and circumstances.

2. Determine the acquisition date.

    a. Usually the date the acquirer legally transfers consideration and acquires the assets and liabilities of the acquiree.
    b. Usually the closing date.
    c. Examine facts and circumstances if necessary.

3. Recognize and measure the identifiable assets acquired, the liabilities assumed, and any noncontrolling interest in the acquiree.

    a. Assets, liabilities, and noncontrolling interest are measured at fair value.

4. Recognize and measure goodwill or gain from a bargain purchase.

    a. Consideration transferred includes

       (1) Assets transferred.
       (2) Liabilities incurred.
       (3) Equity interests issued by acquirer.
       (4) Contingent consideration.

    b. Goodwill

       (1) Defined as an asset representing the future economic benefits that arise from other assets acquired in a business combination that are not individually identified and separately recognized.

    (2) Calculated as the aggregate of the fair value of consideration given, plus the fair value of previously held interests, plus the fair value of noncontrolling interests, less the fair value of assets acquired.

    (3) Not considered an intangible asset.

    (4) Test for impairment using rules of SFAS 142.

  c. Bargain purchase

    (1) Excess of the fair value of assets acquired over the aggregate of the fair value of consideration transferred, plus the fair value of previously held interests, plus the fair value of the noncontrolling interests.

    (2) Recognized as a gain in the current period.

5. Acquisition-related costs are expensed in the period incurred (finder's fees, advisory, legal, accounting, valuation, consulting, general administrative costs, and other professional fees).

6. Cost of registering and issuing debt securities are recognized in accordance with GAAP.

  a. For equity securities, net against the proceeds of the stock and reduce additional paid-in capital.

  b. Bond issue costs are treated as deferred charge and amortized on a straight-line over life of bond.

D. Exceptions to Recognition or Measurement Principles.

1. Provisional Amounts.

  a. Record for items that have incomplete information.

  b. Adjust during the measurement period.

  c. Measurement period ends when acquirer receives information or learns information is not available.

  d. Changes in provisional amounts recognized by retrospectively adjusting provisional amounts and making an adjustment to goodwill.

  e. After measurement period ends, changes are made as error corrections in accordance with SFAS 154.

2. Transferred assets

  a. Measured at fair value.

  b. Gain or loss is reported in earnings of the period.

  c. If acquirer retains control, then measure at carrying value.

3. Contingent consideration

  a. Measure at fair value at acquisition date.

  b. Changes in value are treated as changes in provisional amounts.

  c. After measurement date, changes in value are remeasured to fair value at each reporting date until contingency is resolved, with changes reported in earnings of the period.

  d. Contingent consideration classified as equity is not remeasured.

4. Lease classification.

  a. Leases are classified based on classification at inception of lease.

  b. If lease is modified at acquisition date, classify lease by its new terms.

  c. When acquiree is lessee in an operating lease, if terms are favorable, record an intangible asset apart from goodwill. If unfavorable, record a liability.

  d. If acquiree is lessor in operating lease, measure at fair value, and recognize a separate asset or liability if lease terms are favorable or unfavorable with regard to market terms.

5. Contingencies

  a. Categorize as contractual or noncontractual.

  b. Contractual contingencies recorded at fair value at acquisition date.

  c. Noncontractual contingencies are assessed as to whether it is more likely than not that the contingency gives rise to an asset or liability. If more likely than not, record a liability.

  d. May derecognize an asset or liability from the contingency only when the contingency is resolved.

6. Income taxes measured at acquisition date in accordance with SFAS 109.

7. Employee benefits measured at acquisition date.

8. Indemnification contracts (guarantees against loss). If seller indemnifies acquirer, an indemnification asset is recorded.

9. Reacquired rights recorded as intangible asset and amortized over remaining contract period.

10. Valuation allowances of the acquiree are not recorded.

11. Share-based payments

a. If acquirer is required to replace, then the fair value of awards are part of consideration transferred.

b. If acquirer voluntarily replaces, then fair value of awards is recognized in compensation cost in accordance with SFAS 123(R).

12. Assets held for sale are recorded at fair value less cost to sell, as provided by SFAS 144.

E. Disclosures in Notes to Financial Statements

1. Name and description of the acquiree.
2. Acquisition date.
3. Percentage of voting equity shares acquired.
4. Primary reasons for the business combination and how acquirer obtained control of acquiree.
5. Qualitative description of the factors that make up the goodwill recognized.
6. Acquisition-date fair value of total consideration transferred and the fair value of each major class of consideration including cash, other assets, business or subsidiary of the acquirer, liabilities, contingent consideration, and equity instruments (including the number of instruments issued and method of determining fair value).
7. For contingent consideration and indemnification assets, the amount recognized, a description of arrangement, basis for determining amount of payment, and an estimate of the range of outcomes.
8. The amounts recognized at the acquisition date for each major class of assets acquired and liabilities assumed.
9. For assets and liabilities arising from contingencies, the amounts recognized and the nature of recognized and unrecognized contingencies, together with a range of outcomes for the contingencies.
10. The total amount of goodwill expected to be deducted for tax purposes.
11. If segment information is reported, the amount of goodwill by reportable segment.
12. Transaction that are recognized separately from the business combination.
13. The gain recognized from bargain purchase and a reason for the gain.
14. The fair value of any noncontrolling interest in the acquiree at acquisition date, and the valuation techniques used to measure fair value of the noncontrolling interest.
15. If the business was achieved in stages, the acquisition-date fair value of the equity interest in the acquiree held immediately before the acquisition date, as well as the amount of gain or loss recognized as a result of remeasuring those securities to fair value.
16. If the acquirer is a public company, the amount of revenue and earnings of the acquiree since acquisition date that is included in the consolidated income statement. Also, supplemental pro forma information for revenue and earnings as if the combination had occurred at the beginning of the period, and pro forma comparative statements for the prior reporting period as if the combination had occurred in the beginning of the prior period.
17. If the acquisition occurs after the reporting date but before the financial statements are issued, the acquirer should make the disclosures of the business combination information listed above.
18. Any information that enables users of financial statements to evaluate the financial effects of adjustments recognized in the current reporting period related to business combinations that occurred in the current or previous period.
19. If accounting for a business combination is incomplete, the reason why it is incomplete, and the assets, liabilities, equity interests or items that are incomplete, and the nature and amount of any measurement period adjustments recognized during the period.
20. Any changes in a contingent consideration asset or liability, differences arising from settlement, and changes in the range of outcomes and reasons for changes.
21. A reconciliation of the carrying amount of goodwill at the beginning and end of the period as required by SFAS 142.

ARB 51 Consolidated Financial Statements (ASC Topic 810—Consolidation)

A. Consolidated statements present financial statements of a parent and subsidiaries, as if the group were a single company for the benefit of the parent's stockholders and creditors.

1. Substance (effectively a single entity) takes precedence over **legal form** (legally separate entities).
2. Consolidated financial statements result in **more meaningful presentation of financial position and operating results** than if separate statements were presented for the parent and subsidiary.

B. The general condition for consolidation is over 50% ownership of subsidiaries.

1. Theoretical condition is **control** of the subsidiaries.

   a. This is generally implicit in greater than 50% ownership.

2. Subsidiaries that are a temporary investment (in reorganization, in bankruptcy, etc.) should not be consolidated.
3. Large indebtedness to bondholders should not preclude consolidation.

FASB INTERPRETATION NO. 46 CONSOLIDATION OF VARIABLE INTEREST ENTITIES

Variable interest entities are entities that must be consolidated because they do not have sufficient funding to finance their future activities without the infusion of additional subordinated investment. Entities are presumed to be variable interest entities subject to consolidation if their equity is less than ten percent of total assets. To avoid consolidation of such entities, definitive evidence must be provided that they can fund their future activities without additional subordinated investment. Entities with equity of ten percent or more of total assets may also be a variable interest entity if it appears that the entity will not be able to fund its activities without obtaining additional subordinated investment. A variable interest entity is consolidated by the primary beneficiary, which is the enterprise that is obligated to fund the majority of the variable interest entity's expected losses if they occur, or will receive the majority of the residual returns if they occur, or both.

C. A difference in fiscal periods should not preclude consolidation.

  1. Differences of three months are acceptable if one discloses material intervening events.
  2. Differences in excess of three months should be consolidated on the basis of interim statements of the subsidiary.

D. Consolidation policy should be disclosed by headings or footnotes.
E. Intercompany balances and transactions should be eliminated in consolidated statements.

  1. Intercompany gains and losses on assets remaining in the group should be eliminated (eliminate entire gross profit or loss even on transactions with minority interest subsidiaries).

F. Retained earnings of subsidiaries at the acquisition date should not appear in the consolidated statements.
G. When a parent purchases a subsidiary in several blocks of stock, the subsidiary's retained earnings should be determined by the step method (apply equity method to subsidiary retroactively).
H. When a subsidiary is purchased in midyear, subsidiary operations may be included in the consolidated income statement for the year and then the operating results prior to acquisition would be deducted.

  1. As an alternative for a subsidiary purchased in midyear, postacquisition operations can be included in the consolidated income statement.
  2. For midyear disposals, omit operations from the consolidated income statement and include equity in subsidiary's operations up to disposal date as a separate item in the income statement.

> **NOTE:** F. through H. pertain only to acquisitions accounted for as purchases per APB 16.

I. Sometimes combined, as distinguished from consolidated, financial statements are appropriate for commonly owned companies and are prepared when consolidated statements are not appropriate.

SFAS 94 Consolidation of All Majority-Owned Subsidiaries (ASC Topic 810—Consolidation)

A. Precludes use of parent company FS prepared for issuance to stockholders as FS of primary reporting entity
B. Requires consolidation of all majority-owned (ownerships, directly or indirectly, of more than 50% of outstanding voting shares of another company) subsidiaries

  1. Unless control

    a. Temporary
    b. Not held by majority owner (e.g., subsidiary)

      (1) Is in legal reorganization or bankruptcy
      (2) Operates under foreign exchange restrictions, controls, or other governmentally imposed uncertainties

  2. Even if

    a. Subsidiary's operations nonhomogeneous
    b. Large minority interest exists
    c. Subsidiary located in foreign country

SFAS 160 Noncontrolling Interests in Consolidated Financial Statements—An Amendment of ARB No. 51 (ASC Topic 810—Consolidation)

A. Scope—Applies to all entities that prepare consolidated financial statements except for not-for-profit organizations.
B. Classification of noncontrolling interest on the balance sheet.

  1. Noncontrolling interest is classified as equity.
  2. Noncontrolling interest is attributed its share of income or loss.

3. The amount of net income attributable to the parent and the noncontrolling interest must be presented on the face of the consolidated income statement.
4. Noncontrolling interest is attributed losses even if it results in a deficit balance.

C. Income Statement Disclosures

1. Consolidated net income includes net income attributed to the noncontrolling interest.
2. Consolidated comprehensive income includes comprehensive income attributed to the noncontrolling interest.

D. Changes in Ownership Interests

1. Accounted for as equity transaction.
2. No gain or loss recognized in net income or comprehensive income.
3. The carrying amount of the noncontrolling interest is adjusted to reflect change in ownership in subsidiary.
4. Difference between the fair value of consideration received or paid and amount by which controlling interest is adjusted is recognized in additional paid-in capital of the parent.

E. Deconsolidation

1. The parent recognizes a gain or loss in net income when subsidiary is deconsolidated.
2. Deconsolidation occurs as of the date parent ceases to have control.
3. Gain or loss on deconsolidation of the subsidiary is measured using the fair value of the noncontrolling equity investment.
4. Gain or loss is calculated as aggregate of (1) fair value of consideration received PLUS (2) fair value of retained noncontrolling investment, PLUS (3) carrying amount of noncontrolling interest in former subsidiary LESS (4) the carrying amount of the former subsidiary's assets and liabilities.
5. If parent deconsolidates by a nonreciprocal transfer to owners (such as spin-off), then APB Opinion 29 applies for nonmonetary transactions.
6. Disclosures for deconsolidation

   a. Amount of gain or loss.
   b. Portion of gain or loss related to remeasurement of retained investment in the former subsidiary.
   c. The caption in the income statement in which gain or loss is recognized.

F. Disclosures in Consolidated Financial Statements
   A parent with a less than wholly owned subsidiary shall disclose the following:

1. On the face of the financial statements, the amounts of consolidated net income and consolidated comprehensive income attributed to the parent and the noncontrolling interests.
2. In the notes or on the face of the income statement, amounts attributable to the parent for the following:

   a. Income from continuing operations.
   b. Discontinued operations.
   c. Extraordinary items.

3. In either the consolidated statement of changes in equity or the notes to the financial statements, a reconciliation at the beginning and end of the period carrying amount of total equity, equity attributable to the parent, and equity attributable to the noncontrolling interest. The reconciliation must disclose separately

   a. Net income.
   b. Transactions with owners, contributions from and distributions to owners.
   c. Each component of other comprehensive income.
   d. In the notes to financial statements, a schedule showing effects of changes in parent's ownership interest in subsidiary.

SFAS 167—Amendments to FASB Interpretation No. 46(R) (ASC Topic 810)

A. Eliminates the quantitative-based risks and rewards calculation for determining if an enterprise has a controlling financial interest in a variable interest entity
B. Approach focuses on identifying which entity has the power to direct the activities of a variable interest entity that can significantly impact the entity's performance and

1. The obligation to absorb the losses of the entity, or
2. The rights to receive benefits from the entity

C. Amends FASB Interpretation 46(R) to require additional disclosures about an enterprise's involvement in variable interest entities

SFAS 133 Accounting for Derivative Instruments and Hedging Activities (ASC Topic 815—Derivatives and Hedging)

A. Foundation principles for SFAS 133

1. Financial instruments should be measured at fair value (See SFAS 157 for fair value measurements)
2. Changes in fair value, or gains and losses, should be reported in comprehensive income or in current earnings
3. Hedging instrument criteria

   a. Fair value hedge

      (1) Recognized asset or liability
      (2) Unrecognized firm commitment

   b. Cash flow hedge

      (1) Recognized asset or liability
      (2) Forecasted transaction

   c. Foreign currency hedge

      (1) Unrecognized firm commitment
      (2) Available-for-sale security
      (3) Forecasted transaction
      (4) Net investment in foreign operations

B. Definition of derivative instrument

1. Contract must contain one or more underlyings and one or more notional amounts
2. Contract requires no initial net investment, or a smaller initial net investment than required for contracts with an expected similar response to market changes
3. Terms that require or permit net settlement, net settlement by means outside the contract, or delivery of an asset that results in a position no substantially different from net settlement

C. Embedded derivative instruments

1. Financial instruments which contain features which separately meet the definition of a derivative instrument
2. Three criteria used to determine whether the instrument should be separated from the host contract

   a. The embedded derivative instrument meets the definition of a derivative instrument (e.g., strips)
   b. The hybrid instrument is not regularly recorded at fair value
   c. The economic characteristics and risks of the embedded instrument are not clearly and closely related to the economic characteristics of the host contract

3. An election can be made not to bifurcate the instrument. See outline of SFAS 155.

D. Hedging instruments criteria

1. Sufficient documentation must be provided at the beginning of the process

   a. Identify the objective and strategy of the hedge
   b. Identify the hedging instrument and the hedged item
   c. Identify how the effectiveness of the hedge will be assessed on an ongoing basis

2. The hedge must be highly effective throughout its life

   a. Measured every three months and whenever earnings or financial statements are reported

E. Fair value hedges

1. Specific criteria

   a. Hedged item must be a specific portion of a recognized asset/liability or an unrecognized firm commitment
   b. An unrecognized firm commitment must be binding on both parties, specific with respect to all significant terms, and contain a nonperformance clause that makes performance probable.

2. Gains and losses will be recognized in current earnings

F. Cash flow hedges

1. Specific hedges

   a. The change in cash flows must be the same, or linked, for the hedge's asset/liability and the hedging instrument
   b. A forecasted transaction's cash flows must be considered probable
   c. A forecasted series of transactions must share the same risk exposure

2. Accounting for

   a. Effective portion reported in other comprehensive income
   b. Ineffective portion reported in earnings

G. Foreign currency hedge

1. Unrecognized firm commitment

   a. Accounted for as fair value hedge if requirements met

2. Available-for-sale securities

   a. Accounted for as fair value hedge if requirements met and

      (1) Cannot be traded on exchange denominated in investor's functional currency
      (2) Dividends must be denominated in same foreign currency as expected sale proceeds

3. Foreign currency denominated forecasted transactions

   a. Accounted for as cash flow hedges

4. Net investments in foreign operations

   a. Must meet hedge effectiveness criterion
   b. Change in fair value recorded in other comprehensive income

H. Forward exchange contracts

1. Mark to market using the forward exchange rate at each reporting date
2. Recognize changes in fair value in current earnings

I. Disclosures

1. Objectives and strategies for achieving financial instruments
2. Context to understand the instrument
3. Risk management policies
4. A list of hedged instruments
5. Disclosure of fair value of financial instruments required when practicable to estimate fair value

SFAS 138 Accounting Certain Derivative Instruments and Certain Hedging Activities: (ASC Topic 815—Derivatives and Hedging)

A. Amended four specific items in SFAS 133

1. Normal purchases and sales exception extended

   a. Applies to contracts that require delivery of nonfinancial assets to be used in the normal operations of an entity
   b. These contracts need not be accounted for as derivative instruments unless the contracts require net settlements of gains or losses

2. Redefined the interest rate risk

   a. Permits a benchmark interest rate to be designated as the hedged risk in a hedge of interest rate risk
   b. This benchmark presents the risk-free rate and is the interest rate on direct Treasury obligations of the US government, or the London Interbank Offered Rate (LIBOR)
   c. A company's actual interest rate above the benchmark interest rate reflects that company's credit risk which is separate from the risk-free rate of interest

3. Hedging recognized foreign currency denominated assets or liabilities

   a. Permits a recognized foreign currency denominated asset or liability, for which a foreign currency transaction gain or loss is recognized in earnings under the provisions of SFAS 52, to be the hedged item in a fair value or cash flow hedge.

      b. The foreign currency denominated asset or liability continues to be remeasured using the spot exchange rates to compute the transaction gain or loss for the period.

      c. In the case of cash flow hedges, the transaction gain or loss would be offset by an equal amount of reclassified from other comprehensive income. In the case of fair market value hedges, the hedging instrument would be a hedge of both interest rate risk and foreign exchange rate risk. The foreign currency denominated asset or liability would be adjusted for changes in fair value attributable to changes in foreign interest rates before remeasurement at the spot exchange rate. This eliminates the differences on earnings related to the use of different measurement criteria for the hedged item and the hedging instrument

   4. Hedging with intercompany derivatives

      a. Permits derivative instruments entered into with another member of the consolidated group to qualify as hedging instruments in the consolidated financial statements if those internal derivatives are offset by unrelated third-party contracts on a net basis

      b. Previously, the internal derivative had to be offset on an individual derivative contract basis with a third party

SFAS 149 Amendment of Statement 133 on Derivative Instruments and Hedging Activities (ASC Topic 815)

A. This statement clarifies under what circumstances a contract with an initial net investment meets the characteristics of a derivatives. It also clarifies when a derivative contains a financing component, and amends the definition of an underlying to conform to language used in FASB Interpretation 45, and amends other existing pronouncements.

B. This statement amended existing pronouncements to clarify that the use of the term "expected cash flows" does not have the same meaning as the term is defined and used in SFAC 7, *Using Cash Flow Information and Present Value in Accounting Measurements.*

SFAS 155 Accounting for Certain Hybrid Financial Instruments (ASC Topic 815—Derivatives and Hedging)

SFAS 155, issued in February 2006, amends SFAS 133. SFAS 155 changes the accounting for hybrid financial instruments that would normally be required to be bifurcated.

A. An election can be made **not** to bifurcate the instrument

B. The election is irrevocable and is made on an instrument-by-instrument basis

C. Changes in fair value of the hybrid instruments are recognized in earnings each year

D. Balance sheet disclosure may be presented in one of two ways

   1. As a separate line item for the fair value and non–fair value instruments, **or**

   2. As an aggregate amount of all hybrid instruments with the amount of the hybrid instruments at fair value shown in parentheses

E. Initial adoption of SFAS 155 requires the difference between the total carrying amount of the components of the bifurcated hybrid instruments and the fair value of the hybrid instruments to be recognized as a cumulative effect adjustment to the beginning balance of retained earnings

F. Notes to financial statements should indicate the gross gains and losses of the cumulative effect adjustments. Prior periods are not restated

G. SFAS 155 does not apply to hedging instruments

SFAS 161 Disclosures about Derivative Instruments and Hedging Activities—An Amendment of FASB Statement No. 133 (ASC Topic 815—Derivatives and Hedging)

A. Additional disclosures required for derivative instruments

   1. How and why an entity uses derivatives

   2. How derivatives and hedges are accounted for

   3. How derivatives and hedges affect the financial position, financial performance, and cash flows

B. Type of information disclosed

   1. Risk exposure such as interest rate, credit, foreign exchange rate, and price risk

   2. Purpose of instrument, (i.e., risk management or other)

   3. Location and fair value amounts of derivative instruments reported in balance sheet

   4. Location and amounts recognized on the income statement

SFAS 157 Fair Value Measurements (ASC Topic 820—Fair Value Measurement and Disclosures)

A. Fair value is the price that would be received to sell an asset or paid to transfer a liability in an orderly transaction between market participants at the measurement date (an exit price).

B. Applying the fair value measurement approach involves

1. Identify the asset or liability to be measured
2. Determine the principal or most advantageous market *(highest and best use)*
3. Determine the valuation premise *(in-use or in-exchange)*
4. Determine the appropriate valuation technique *(market, income, or cost approach)*
5. Obtain inputs for valuation *(Level 1, Level 2, or Level 3)*
6. Calculate the fair value of the asset

C. Assumes the asset or liability is sold or transferred in either the principal market or most advantageous market

1. Principal market has greatest volume and level of activity
2. Most advantageous market minimizes price received for the asset or minimizes amount paid to transfer liability
3. Market participants have the following characteristics:

   a. Be independent of the reporting entity (not related parties)
   b. Knowledgeable
   c. Able to transact
   d. Willing to transact (motivated, but not compelled to transact)

4. Do not adjust prices for costs to sell
5. If location is attribute of asset or liability, price is adjusted for costs necessary to transport asset or liability to market

D. Assumes the highest and best use of the asset

1. Highest and best use maximizes the value of asset or group of assets
2. Highest and best use must be

   a. Physically possible
   b. Legally permissible
   c. Financially feasible at measurement date

3. Highest and best use determines the valuation premise used

E. Valuation Premise

1. In use:

   a. Asset provides maximum value by using it with other assets as a group
   b. Valuation based on price to sell asset assuming it is used with other assets

2. In-exchange:

   a. Asset provides maximum value on stand-alone basis
   b. Valuation based on price to sell the asset stand-alone

F. Valuation Techniques

1. Market approach

   a. Uses prices and relevant information from market transaction for identical or comparable assets or liabilities

2. Income approach

   a. Uses present value techniques to discount cash flows or earnings to present value amounts

3. Cost approach

   a. Relies on current replacement cost to replace the asset with a comparable asset, adjusted for obsolescence.

G. Levels of Input for Valuation

1. Use fair value hierarchy to prioritize inputs to valuation techniques
2. Fair value hierarchy is Level 1, Level 2, and Level 3
3. Inputs should be based on lowest level of input (i.e., highest priority is lowest level)
4. Level 1 inputs—lowest level, highest priority

   a. Uses quoted prices (unadjusted prices) from active markets
   b. Examples are quotes from NYSE, quotations from dealer markets

   5. Level 2 inputs

      a. Inputs that are directly or indirectly observable other than quoted prices of Level 1.
      b. Examples are quoted prices for similar assets or liabilities, observable inputs such as yield curves, bank prime rates, interest rates, volatilities, loss severities, credit risks, and default rates.

   6. Level 3 inputs

      a. Unobservable inputs
      b. May only be used if observable inputs are not available
      c. May reflect reporting entity's own assumptions about market
      d. Based on best information available

H. Change in Valuation Premise or Technique

   1. Treat as change in estimate on a prospective basis
   2. Requirements of SFAS 154 do not apply

I. Disclosures

   1. For assets measured at fair value on recurring basis

      a. Valuation techniques used
      b. Identify level of hierarchy or measurements used
      c. The amount of significant transfers between Level 1 and Level 2 and reason for the transfer along with the entity's transfer policy.
      d. If Level 2 or Level 3 using significant other observable inputs and unobservable inputs respectively, the valuation techniques and the inputs used.
      e. If Level 3 used, the effect of measurements on earnings for the period, purchases, sales, issuances, and settlements, and any transfers in or out of Level 3 are disclosed

   2. For assets and liabilities measured at fair values on a nonrecurring basis (i.e., impaired assets), identify the following:

      a. The fair value measurements used
      b. The reasons for the measurements
      c. The level within the hierarchy
      d. For Level 2 or Level 3, the inputs and valuation techniques used to measure fair value.
      e. A description of nonfinancial assets with a current use differing from the highest and best use.

SFAS 107 Disclosures about Fair Value of Financial Instruments (ASC Topic 825—Financial Instruments)

A. Statement requires entities to disclose the fair value of financial instruments, both assets and liabilities whether recognized or not recognized in the statement of financial position, for which it is practicable to estimate fair value.

   1. Applies to all entities
   2. Does not change any recognition, measurement, or classification requirements for financial instruments in financial statements
   3. Fair value disclosures of financial instruments previously prescribed by GAAP meet the requirements of this statement.

B. Financial instruments include

   1. Cash
   2. Evidence of ownership interest in an entity, or
   3. A contract that both

      a. Imposes contractual obligation on one entity to deliver cash or another financial instrument to second entity or to exchange financial instruments on potentially unfavorable terms with second entity, and
      b. Conveys contractual right to second entity to receive cash or another financial instrument from first entity or to exchange financial instruments on potentially favorable terms with first entity

C. Fair value of a financial instrument is defined by SFAS 157 as "the price that would be received to sell an asset or paid to transfer a liability in an orderly transaction between market participants at the measurement date."

D. Standard lists a number of areas for which the disclosure requirements are not applicable, including pensions and other deferred compensation arrangements and leases.

E. Disclosure Requirements

1. When practicable (i.e., without incurring excessive costs), an entity must disclose the fair value of financial instruments in either the body of the financial statements or in the accompanying notes.

   a. Disclosure must include the method(s) and significant assumptions used in estimating fair value

   (1) Quoted market price is generally the best estimate of fair value.
   (2) If quoted market price is not available, management must estimate fair value based upon similar financial instruments or valuation techniques.
   (3) No disclosure is required for trade receivables and payables when carrying amount approximates fair value.

   b. Disclosure must distinguish between financial instruments held or issued for

   (1) Trading purposes
   (2) Purposes other than trading

2. If estimation of the fair value of financial instruments is not practicable, entity must disclose

   a. Information pertinent to estimating the fair value (i.e., the carrying amount, effective interest rate, and maturity), and
   b. The reason why estimation of fair value is not practicable.

3. Derivative financial instruments may not be combined, aggregated or netted with nonderivative or other derivative financial instruments.
4. If financial instruments disclosed in more than one area in FS, one note must contain a summary table cross-referencing the location of the other instruments.
5. Disclosure of concentrations of credit risk of all financial instruments

   a. Disclose all significant concentrations of credit risk from **all** financial instruments, whether from an individual counterparty or groups of counterparties.
   b. Group concentrations exist if a number of counterparties are engaged in similar activities and have similar economic characteristics such that they would be similarly affected by changes in conditions.
   c. Disclose for each significant concentration

   (1) Information about the (shared) activity, region, or economic characteristics
   (2) The amount of accounting loss the entity would incur should any party to the financial instrument fail to perform according to the terms of the contract and the collateral or security, if any, is of no value.
   (3) The entity's policy of requiring collateral or security, the entity's access to that collateral or security, and the nature and brief description of the collateral or security.

SFAS 159 The Fair Value Option for Financial Assets and Financial Liabilities—including an amendment of FASB Statement 115 (ASC Topic 825—Financial Instruments)

A. Scope

1. Applies to

   a. Financial assets and financial liabilities (includes available-for-sale, held-to-maturity, and equity method investments, and liabilities)
   b. Firm commitments that involve financial instruments
   c. Written loan commitments
   d. Nonfinancial insurance contracts that can be settled by paying third party
   e. Warranties that can be settled by paying third party
   f. Host financial instruments resulting from separation of embedded nonfinancial derivative instrument from a nonfinancial hybrid instrument

2. Does **not** apply to consolidations, pensions, share-based payments, stock options, OPEB, exit or disposal activities, leases, and financial instruments that are component of equity

B. Definitions

1. **Fair value**—The price that would be received to sell an asset or paid to transfer a liability in an orderly transaction between market participants at the measurement date
2. **Financial asset**—Cash, evidence of an ownership interest in an entity or a contract that conveys a right to receive cash or another financial instrument or to exchange other financial instruments on potentially favorable items
3. **Financial liability**—A contract that imposes an obligation to deliver cash or another financial instrument to exchange other financial instruments on potentially favorable terms

4. **Firm commitment**—An agreement, usually legally enforceable, that specifies all significant terms, including quantity, fixed price, and timing of transaction. The agreement includes a disincentive for nonperformance that makes performance probable

C. Fair Value Option (FVO)

1. Can elect to measure financial asset or financial liability at fair value
2. Must elect to use fair value method on specific items

   a. Can be elected on instrument-by-instrument basis

      (1) If multiple advances to one borrower for single contract, fair value options is applied to larger balance and not each individual advance
      (2) If fair value applied to investment that can use equity method, it must be applied to all interests in same entity (i.e., debt and equity)
      (3) If applied to insurance contracts, must be applied to all claims and obligations for that contract

   b. Is irrevocable
   c. Must apply to entire instrument, not a portion of instrument

3. Report unrealized gains and losses in earnings
4. Classification on statement of cash flows—rules of FAS 95 apply

D. Election Dates

1. The date an eligible item is first recognized
2. The date the entity enters into a firm commitment
3. When financial assets cease to qualify for fair value treatment due to specialized accounting rules, can elect to use fair value (i.e. equity method for investments)
4. Percentage of ownership change and can no longer consolidate
5. Modifications of debt

E. Financial Statement Disclosure Requirements—two methods permissible

1. Present aggregate fair value and non–fair value amounts in same line, with amounts measured at fair value parenthetically disclosed
2. Present two separate line items for fair value and non–fair value carrying amounts

F. Disclosures to Notes to Financial Statements—Balance Sheet

1. Management's reasons for electing fair value option for each item or group of items
2. If fair value option is elected for some but not all items

   a. Description of similar items and reason for partial election
   b. Information to understand how group of similar items relates to individual line items on balance sheet

3. Information to understand how line items relate to major categories of assets and liabilities presented in SFAS 157 fair value disclosure requirements
4. Aggregate carrying amount of items included in each line item in balance sheet that are not eligible for fair value option
5. Difference between aggregate fair value and aggregate unpaid principal balance of

   a. Loans and long-term receivables using FVO
   b. Long-term debt instruments using FVO
   c. Aggregate fair value of loans that are 90 days or more past due
   d. Aggregate fair value of loans in nonaccrual status if interest is recognized separately from changes in fair value
   e. Difference between aggregate fair value and aggregate unpaid principal balance for loans 90 days or more past due

6. For investments that would have used equity method, the information required by APB 18 for equity method

G. Required Disclosures for Income Statement Items

1. Amounts of gains/losses included in earnings for each line item in balance sheet
2. Description of how interest and dividends are measured and reported on the income statement
3. For loans and receivables held as assets

   a. Estimated amount of gains/losses in earnings that is attributed to changes in credit risk
   b. How the gains/losses were determined

4. For liabilities affected by credit risk

    a. Amount of gains/losses attributable to changes in credit risk
    b. Qualitative information about reasons for changes
    c. How gains/losses were determined

5. Methods and significant assumptions to estimate fair value

H. Transition Requirements

1. Report as cumulative effect adjustment to opening balance of retained earnings
2. Remove balance sheet effects such as

    a. Amortized deferred costs, fees, premiums, discounts
    b. Valuation allowances (such as allowance for loan losses)
    c. Accrued interest

SFAS 52 Foreign Currency Translation (ASC Topic 830—Foreign Currency Matters)

A. Primary objectives of foreign currency translation

1. Should provide information disclosing effects of rate changes on enterprise cash flows and equity
2. Should also provide information in consolidated statements as to financial results and relationships of individual consolidated entities measured in their respective functional currencies in accordance with US GAAP

B. Functional currency is the currency of the primary economic environment in which a foreign entity operates (i.e., the environment in which the entity generates and spends cash).

1. A foreign entity's assets, liabilities, revenues, expenses, gains, and losses shall be measured in that entity's functional currency.
2. The functional currency could be the currency of the country in which the entity operates if the entity is a self-contained unit operating in a foreign country.

> **EXAMPLE**
>
> An entity (1) whose operations are not integrated with those of the parent, (2) whose buying and selling activities are primarily local, and (3) whose cash flows are primarily in the foreign currency.

3. There may be several functional currencies if there are many self-contained entities operating in different countries.
4. The functional currency might be the US dollar if the foreign entity's operations are considered to be a direct and integral part of the US parent's operations.

> **EXAMPLE**
>
> An entity (1) whose operations are integrated with those of the parent, (2) whose buying and selling activities are primarily in the parent's country and/or the parent's currency, and (3) whose cash flows are available for remittance to the parent.

5. Functional currency for a foreign entity, once determined, shall be used consistently unless it is clear that economic facts and circumstances have changed.

    a. If a change is made, do not restate previously issued financial statements

6. If a foreign entity's bookkeeping is not done in the functional currency, the process of converting from the currency used for the books and records to the functional currency is called remeasurement.

    a. Remeasurement is intended to produce the same result (e.g., balances for assets, expenses, liabilities, etc.) as if the functional currency had been used for bookkeeping purposes.
    b. In highly inflationary economies (cumulative inflation over a 3-year period is > 100%), the remeasurement of a foreign entity's financial statements shall be done as if the functional currency were the reporting currency (i.e., the US dollar).

7. The functional currency (if not the US dollar) is translated to the reporting currency (assumed to be the US dollar) by using appropriate exchange rates (see item C. below).

    a. If the functional currency is the US dollar, there is no need to translate (if the books and records are maintained in US dollars).

C. The translation of foreign currency FS (those incorporated in the FS of a reporting enterprise by consolidation, combination, or the equity method of accounting) should use a current exchange rate if the foreign currency is the functional currency.

1. Assets and liabilities—exchange rate at the balance sheet date is used to translate the functional currency to the reporting currency
2. Revenues (expenses) and gains (losses)—exchange rates when the transactions were recorded shall be used to translate from the functional currency to the reporting currency

   a. Weighted-averages for exchange rates may be used for items occurring numerous times during the period.

3. Translation adjustments will result from the translation process if the functional currency is a foreign currency.

   a. Translation adjustments are not an element of net income of the reporting entity.
   b. Effects of current translation adjustments are reported in other comprehensive income for the period with the accumulated amount reported as part of the reporting entity's owners' equity and labeled accumulated other comprehensive income.
   c. Accumulated translation adjustments remain part of the owners' equity until the reporting entity disposes of the foreign entity.

      (1) In period of disposal, these adjustments are reported as part of the gain (loss) on sale or liquidation.

D. Foreign currency transactions are those which are denominated (fixed) in other than the entity's functional currency.

1. Receivables and/or payables which are fixed in a currency other than the functional currency may result in transaction gains (losses) due to changes in exchange rates after the transaction date.
2. Transaction gains or losses generally are reported on the income statement in the period during which the exchange rates change.
3. Deferred taxes may have to be provided for transaction gains or losses that are realized for income tax purposes in a time period different than that for financial reporting.

E. A forward exchange contract represents an agreement to exchange different currencies at a specified future rate and at a specified future date. (Accounting and reporting now specified by SFAS 133)

F. FS disclosures required

1. Aggregate transaction gain (loss) that is included in the entity's net income
2. Analysis of changes in accumulated translation adjustments which are reported as part of other comprehensive income
3. Significant rate changes subsequent to the date of the financial statements including effects on unsettled foreign currency transactions

---

FASB INTERPRETATION NO. 37 ACCOUNTING FOR TRANSLATION ADJUSTMENTS UPON SALE OF PART OF AN INVESTMENT IN A FOREIGN ENTITY

If an enterprise sells part of its ownership interest in a foreign entity, a pro rata portion of the accumulated translation adjustment component of equity attributable to that investment shall be recognized in measuring the gain (loss) on the sale.

SFAS 34 Capitalization of Interest Cost (ASC Topic 835—Interest)

A. Interest costs, when material, incurred in acquiring the following types of assets, shall be capitalized:

1. Assets constructed or produced for a firm's own use

   a. Including construction by others requiring progress payments

2. Assets intended for lease or sale that are produced as discrete projects

   a. For example, ships and real estate developments

3. But not on

   a. Routinely produced inventories
   b. Assets ready for their intended use
   c. Assets not being used nor being readied for use
   d. Land, unless it is being developed (e.g., as a plant site, real estate development, etc.)

4. The objective of interest capitalization is to

    a. Reflect the acquisition cost of assets
    b. Match costs to revenues in the period benefited

5. Capitalized interest shall be treated as any other asset cost for depreciation and other purposes.
6. Required interest cost disclosures

    a. Total interest cost incurred
    b. Interest capitalized, if any

B. Amount of interest to be capitalized

1. Conceptually, the interest that would have been avoided if the expenditures had not been made
2. Based on the average accumulated expenditures on the asset for the period

    a. Includes payment of cash, transfer of other assets, and incurring interest-bearing liabilities
    b. Reasonable approximations are permitted

3. Use the interest rates incurred during period

    a. First, the rates on specific new borrowings for the asset
    b. Second, a weighted-average of other borrowings

        (1) Use judgment to identify borrowings

4. Interest cost capitalized in any period cannot exceed interest cost incurred in that period.

    a. On a consolidated basis for consolidated statements
    b. On an individual company basis for individual company statements

5. Capitalized interest should be compounded.

C. Interest capitalization period

1. Begins when all the following three conditions are present:

    a. Asset expenditures have been made
    b. Activities to ready asset for intended use are in progress

        (1) Includes planning stages

    c. Interest cost is being incurred

2. If activities to ready asset for intended use cease, interest capitalization ceases

    a. Not for brief interruptions that are externally imposed

3. Capitalization period ends when asset is substantially complete

    a. For assets completed in parts, interest capitalization on a part of the asset ends when that part is complete
    b. Capitalize all interest on assets required to be completed in entirety until entire project is finished

4. Interest capitalization continues if capitalized interest raises cost above market values

    a. Apply impairment accounting per SFAS 144

APB 12 Omnibus Opinion—1967 (ASC Topics 310, 360, 505, 710, 835)

A. Allowance or contra accounts (allowance for bad debts, accumulated depreciation, etc.) should be deducted from assets or groups of assets with appropriate disclosure.
B. Disclosure of depreciable assets should include

1. Depreciation expense for the period
2. Balances of major classes of depreciable assets by nature or function
3. Accumulated depreciation either by major class or in total
4. Description of method(s) of depreciation by major classes of assets

C. Changes in the separate shareholder equity accounts in addition to retained earnings and changes in number of equity securities must be disclosed in the year of change

1. In separate statements
2. Or the financial statements
3. Or the notes

APB 21 Interest on Receivables and Payables (ASC Topic 835—Interest)

Accounting for receivables and payables whose face value does not approximate their present value

A. Applies to receivables and payables except

1. Normal course of business receivables and payables maturing in less than one year
2. Amounts not requiring repayment in the future (will be applied to future purchases or sales)
3. Security deposits and retainages
4. Customary transactions of those whose primary business is lending money
5. Transactions where interest rates are tax affected or legally prescribed (e.g., municipal bonds and tax settlements)
6. Parent-subsidiary transactions
7. Estimates of contractual obligations such as warranties

B. Notes exchanged for cash are recorded at their present value. Present value equals the cash paid/received. If face value of note ≠ cash paid/received, difference is a discount/premium.

1. If unstated **rights or privileges** are exchanged in issuance of note for cash, adjust cash payment to obtain present value of the note and unstated rights.

C. Notes exchanged for goods or services in arm's-length transaction are recorded at face amount (presumption that face amount = present value).

1. Presumption not valid if note is

   a. Noninterest-bearing
   b. Stated interest rate is unreasonable
   c. Face amount of the note differs materially from sales price of goods or services

2. When presumption not valid, record note at fair value of goods or services

   a. Compute **implicit** rate (rate that discounts the future value [face of note plus cash interest, if any] to fair value of goods and services) for interest expense/revenue recognition

3. When no established market price for goods and services exists, record note at its fair market value.

   a. Compute **implicit** rate (rate that discounts the future value [face of note plus cash interest, if any] to fair [present] value of note) for interest expense/revenue recognition

4. When no fair market value exists for either the goods and services or the note, record note at approximation of market value.

   a. Use **imputed** rate to compute present value of (and discount on) note.
   b. Imputed rate should approximate the rate an independent borrower and lender would negotiate in a similar transaction. Consider

      (1) Credit standing of issuer
      (2) Restrictive covenants
      (3) Collateral
      (4) Payment and other terms
      (5) Tax consequences to buyer and seller
      (6) Market rate for sale or assignment
      (7) Prime rate
      (8) Published rates of similar bonds
      (9) Current rates charged for mortgages on similar property

D. Discount or premium should be amortized by the interest method (constant rate of interest on the amount outstanding).

1. Other methods (e.g., straight-line) may be used if the results are not materially different from those of the interest method.

E. Discount or premium should be netted with the related asset or liability and **not** shown as separate asset or liability.

1. Issue costs should be reported as deferred charges.

SFAS 13 Accounting for Leases (ASC Topic 840—Leases)

Applies to agreements for use of property, plant, and equipment, but not natural resources and not for licensing agreements such as patents and copyrights.

The major issue in accounting for leases is whether the benefits and risks incident to ownership have been transferred from lessor to lessee. If so, the lessor treats the lease as a sale or financing transaction and the lessee treats it as a purchase. Otherwise, the lease is accounted for as a rental agreement. These different treatments recognize the **substance** of a transaction rather than its **form;** that is, what is legally a lease may be effectively the same as or similar to an installment purchase by the lessee and a sale or financing transaction by the lessor.

The following terms are given specific definitions for the purpose of SFAS 13:

Bargain purchase option—A provision allowing the lessee the option of purchasing the leased property for an amount that is sufficiently lower than the expected fair value of the property at the date the option becomes exercisable. Exercise of the option must appear reasonably assured at the inception of the lease.

Contingent rentals—Rentals that represent the increases or decreases in lease payments which result from changes in the factors on which the lease payments are based occurring subsequent to the inception of the lease.

Estimated economic life of lease property—The estimated remaining time which the property is expected to be economically usable by one or more users, with normal maintenance and repairs, for its intended purpose at the inception of the lease. This estimated time period should not be limited by the lease term.

Estimated residual value of leased property—The estimated fair value of the leased property at the end of the lease term.

Executory costs—Those costs such as insurance, maintenance, and taxes incurred for leased property, whether paid by the lessor or lessee. Amounts paid by a lessee in consideration for a guarantee from an unrelated third party of the residual value are also executory costs. If executory costs are paid by the lessor, any lessor's profit on those costs is considered the same as executory costs.

Fair value of leased property—The price that would be received to sell the property in an orderly transaction between market participants at the measurement date.

When the lessor is a manufacturer or dealer, the fair value of the property at the inception of the lease will ordinarily be its normal selling price net of volume or trade discounts.

When the lessor is not a **manufacturer or dealer,** the fair value of the property at the inception of the lease will ordinarily be its costs net of volume or trade discounts.

Implicit interest rate—The discount rate that, when applied to the minimum lease payments, excluding that portion of the payments representing executory costs to be paid by the lessor, together with any profit thereon, and the unguaranteed residual value accruing to the benefit of the lessor, causes the aggregate present value at the beginning of the lease term to be equal to the fair value of the leased property to the lessor at the inception of the lease.

Inception of the lease—The date of the written lease agreement or commitment (if earlier) wherein all principal provisions are fixed and no principal provisions remain to be negotiated.

Incremental borrowing rate—The rate that, at the inception of the lease, the lessee would have incurred to borrow over a similar term (i.e., a loan term equal to the lease term) the funds necessary to purchase the leased asset.

Initial direct costs—(See outline of SFAS 91)

Lease term—The fixed, noncancelable term of the lease plus all renewal terms when renewal is reasonably assured.

> **NOTE:** The lease term should not extend beyond the date of a bargain purchase option.

Minimum lease payments—For the **lessee:** The payments that the lessee is or can be required to make in connection with the leased property. Contingent rental guarantees by the lessee of the lessor's debt, and the lessee's obligation to pay executory costs are excluded from minimum lease payments. If the lease contains a bargain purchase option, only the minimum rental payments over the lease term and the payment called for in the bargain purchase option are included in minimum lease payments. Otherwise, minimum lease payments include the following:

1. The minimum rental payments called for by the lease over the lease term
2. Any guarantee of residual value at the expiration of the lease term made by the lessee (or any party related to the lessee), whether or not the guarantee payment constitutes a purchase of the leased property. When the lessor has the right to require the lessee to purchase the property at termination of the lease for a certain or determinable amount, that amount shall be considered a lessee guarantee. When the lessee agrees to make up any deficiency below a stated amount in the lessor's realization of the residual value, the guarantee to be included in the MLP is the stated amount rather than an estimate of the deficiency to be made up.
3. Any payment that the lessee must or can be required to make upon **failure to renew or extend** the lease at the expiration of the lease term, whether or not the payment would constitute a purchase of the leased property

For the **lessor:** The payments described above plus any guarantee of the residual value or of the rental payments beyond the lease term by a third party unrelated to either the lessee or lessor (provided the third party is financially capable of discharging the guaranteed obligation).

Unguaranteed residual value—the estimated residual value of the leased property exclusive of any portion guaranteed by the lessee, by any party related to the lessee, or any party unrelated to the lessee. If the guarantor is related to the lessor, the residual value shall be considered as unguaranteed.

A. Classification of leases by lessees. Leases that meet one or more of the following criteria are accounted for as capital leases; all other leases are accounted for as operating leases:

1. Lease transfers ownership (title) to lessee during lease term.
2. Lease contains a bargain purchase option.
3. Lease term is 75% or more of economic useful life of property.
4. Present value of minimum lease payments equals 90% or more of FV of the leased property.

     a. Present value is computed with lessee's incremental borrowing rate, unless lessor's implicit rate is known and is less than lessee's incremental rate (then use lessor's implicit rate).
     b. FMV is cash selling price for sales-type lease; lessor's cost for direct financing of lease. (If not recently purchased, estimate FV)

> **NOTE:** 3. and 4. do not apply if lease begins in last 25% of asset's life.

B. Classification of leases by lessors

1. Sales-type leases provide for a manufacturer or dealer profit (i.e., FV of leased property is greater than lessor cost or carrying value).

     a. Sales-type leases must meet one of the four criteria for lessee capital leases (A.1. to A.4. above) and **both** of the following two criteria:

         (1) Collectibility is reasonably predictable, and
         (2) No important uncertainties regarding costs to be incurred by lessor exist, such as unusual guarantees of performance. Note estimation of executory expense such as insurance, maintenance, etc., is not considered.

2. Direct financing leases must meet same criteria as sales-type leases (just above) but do not include a manufacturer's or dealer's profit.
3. Operating leases are all other leases that have not been classified as sales-type, direct financing, or leveraged.

C. Lease classification is determined at the inception of the lease.

1. If changes in the lease are subsequently made which change the classification, the lease generally should be considered a new agreement and reclassified and accounted for as a new lease. Exercise of renewal options, etc., are not changes in the lease. However, if the terms of a capital lease are modified such that it should be reclassified as an operating lease, the lessee should account for it under the sale-leaseback provisions of SFAS 98.
2. Changes in estimates (e.g., economic life or residual value) or other circumstances (e.g., default) do not result in a new agreement but accounts should be adjusted and gains or losses recognized.
3. An important goal of SFAS 13 was to achieve **symmetry** in lease accounting (i.e., an operating lease for the lessee will be an operating lease for the lessor) and likewise for capital leases.

D. Accounting and reporting by lessees

1. Record capital leases as an asset and liability

     a. Leased asset shall not be recorded in excess of FV. If the present value of the lease payments is greater than the FV, the leased asset and related liability are recorded at FV and the effective interest rate is thereby increased.
     b. Recognize interest expense using the effective interest method.
     c. If there is a transfer of ownership or a bargain purchase option, the asset's depreciation/amortization period is its economic life. Otherwise, depreciate/amortize assets to the expected residual value at the end of the lease term.

2. Rent on operating leases should be expensed on a straight-line basis unless another method is better suited to the particular benefits and costs associated with the lease.
3. Contingent rentals are reported as rent expense in the period incurred.
4. Disclosures by lessees include

     a. General description of leasing arrangement including

         (1) Basis of computing contingent payments
         (2) Existence and terms of renewal or purchase options and escalation clauses
         (3) Restrictions imposed by the lease agreement such as limitations on dividends and further leasing arrangements

     b. Capital lease requirements

         (1) Usual current/noncurrent classifications
         (2) Depreciation/amortization should be separately disclosed

      (3) Future minimum lease payments in the aggregate and for each of the five succeeding fiscal years with separate deductions being made to show the amounts representing executory cost and interest

      (4) Total minimum sublease rentals to be received in the future under noncancelable subleases

      (5) Total contingent rental actually incurred for each period for which an income statement is presented

  c. Operating leases which have initial or remaining noncancelable term > 1 year

      (1) Future minimum lease payments in the aggregate and for each of the five succeeding fiscal years

      (2) Total minimum sublease rentals to be received in the future under noncancelable subleases

      (3) All operating leases—rent expense of each IS period

         (a) Present separate amounts for minimum rentals, contingent rentals, and sublease rentals

         (b) Rental payments for leases with a term of a month or less may be excluded

E. Accounting and reporting by lessors

  1. Sales-type leases

    a. Lease receivable is charged for the gross investment in the lease (the total net minimum lease payments plus the unguaranteed residual value). Sales is credited for the present value of the minimum lease payments.

    b. Cost of sales is the carrying value of the leased asset plus any initial direct costs less the present value of the unguaranteed residual value. Note that in a sales-type lease, initial direct costs are deducted in full in the period when the sale is recorded. Unearned interest income is credited for the difference between the gross investment and the sales price.

    c. Recognize interest revenue using the effective interest method

    d. At the end of the lease term, the balance in the receivable account should equal the amount of residual value guaranteed, if any.

    e. Contingent rental payments are reported as income in the period earned.

  2. Direct financing leases

    a. Accounting is similar to sales-type lease except that no manufacturer's or dealer's profit is recognized.

    b. Lease receivable is charged for the gross investment in the lease, the asset account is credited for the net investment in the lease (cost to be acquired for purpose of leasing) and the difference is recorded as unearned income.

    c. Initial direct costs are recorded in a separate account. A new effective interest rate is computed that equates the minimum lease payments and any unguaranteed residual value with the combined outlay for the leased asset and initial direct costs. The initial direct costs and unearned lease revenue are both amortized so as to produce a constant rate of return over the life of the lease.

    d. The remaining requirements are the same as those for the sales-type lease.

  3. Operating leases

    a. Leased property is to be included with or near PP&E on the BS, and lessor's normal depreciation policies should be applied.

    b. Rental revenue should be recognized on a straight-line basis unless another method is better suited to the particular benefits and costs associated with the lease.

    c. Initial direct costs should be deferred and allocated over the lease term in proportion to the recognition of rental revenue.

F. Related-party leases shall be accounted for as unrelated-party leases except when terms have been significantly affected by relationship.

G. Sale-leasebacks

  1. Legally two separate transactions

  2. Lessee (seller) accounts for the gain (loss) as follows:

    a. Loss (when FV < Book value) on the sale should be recognized immediately.

    b. Gain treatment

      (1) Seller relinquishes the right to substantially all of the remaining use of the property sold (PV of reasonable rentals < 10% of fair value of asset sold)—then separate transactions, and entire gain is recognized.

      (2) Seller retains more than a minor part, but less than substantially all of the remaining use (PV of reasonable rentals are > 10% but < 90% of fair value of asset sold)—then gain on sale is recognized to the extent of the excess of gain over the present value of minimum lease payments (operating) or the recorded amount of the leased asset (capital).

      (3) Seller retains right to substantially all of the remaining use—then entire gain on sale is deferred.

    c. If the gain is deferred and lease is accounted for as

       (1) Capital lease—defer and amortize gain over lease term using same method and life used for depreciating/amortizing cost of leased asset

         (a) Deferral and amortization of the gain are required because the sale and leaseback are components of a single transaction and are interdependent.

       (2) Operating lease—recognize gain on straight-line basis

         (a) Treat as a reduction of rent expense.

  3. Lessor records as a purchase of asset to be leased and as a direct financing or operating lease

---

FASB TECHNICAL BULLETIN 85-3 ACCOUNTING FOR OPERATING LEASES WITH SCHEDULED RENT INCREASES

SFAS 13 requires lessees or lessors to recognize rent expense or rental income for an operating lease on a straight-line basis. Certain operating lease agreements specify scheduled rent increases over the lease term. The effects of these scheduled rent increases, which are included in minimum lease payments under SFAS 13, should also be recognized by lessors and lessees on a straight-line basis over the lease term.

SFAS 98 Accounting for Leases (ASC Topic 840—Leases)

> **NOTE:** The outline below includes those changes that relate to all leases. The remainder of SFAS 98 deals with real estate leases that are not outlined since they are not expected to be tested on the exam.

A. Lease term, as redefined, includes

1. All periods covered by bargain renewal options
2. All periods for which failure to renew the lease imposes a penalty
3. All periods during which a loan, directly or indirectly related to the leased property, is outstanding
4. All periods covered by ordinary renewal options preceding the exercisable date of a bargain purchase option
5. All periods representing renewals or extensions of the lease at the lessor's option

APB 29 Accounting for Nonmonetary Transactions (ASC Topic 845—Nonmonetary Transactions)

A. Definitions

1. **Monetary assets and liabilities.** "Assets and liabilities whose amounts are fixed in terms of units of currency by contract or otherwise. Examples are cash, short- or long-term accounts and notes receivable in cash, and short- or long-term accounts and notes payable in cash."
2. **Nonmonetary assets and liabilities.** "Assets and liabilities other than monetary ones. Examples are inventories; investments in common stocks; property, plant, and equipment; and liabilities for rent collected in advance."
3. **Exchange.** "A reciprocal transfer between an enterprise and another entity that results in the enterprise's acquiring assets or services or satisfying liabilities by surrendering other assets or services or incurring other obligations. A reciprocal transfer of a nonmonetary asset shall be deemed an exchange only if the transferor has no substantial continuing involvement in the transferred asset such that the usual risks and rewards of ownership of the asset are transferred."
4. **Nonreciprocal transfer.** "Transfer of assets or services in one direction, either from an enterprise to its owners (whether or not in exchange for their ownership interests) or another entity or from owners or another entity to enterprise. An entity's reacquisition of its outstanding stock is an example of a nonreciprocal transfer."
5. **Productive assets.** "Assets held for or used in the production of goods or services by the enterprise. Productive assets include an investment in another entity if the investment is accounted for by the equity method but exclude an investment not accounted for by that method."

B. APB 29 does **not** apply to

1. Business combinations
2. Transfer of nonmonetary assets between companies under common control
3. Acquisition of nonmonetary assets with capital stock of an enterprise
4. Stock dividends and splits, issued or received
5. A transfer of assets for an equity interest
6. A transfer of a financial asset under SFAS 140

C. APB 29 does apply to

1. Nonreciprocal transfers with owners. Examples are distributions to stockholders

   a. Dividends
   b. To redeem capital stock
   c. In liquidation
   d. To settle rescission of a business combination

2. Nonreciprocal transfer with other than owners. Examples are

   a. Contribution to charitable institutions
   b. Contribution of land by governmental unit to a business

3. Nonmonetary exchange

D. Nonmonetary transactions should generally be accounted for as are monetary transactions.

1. Cost of a nonmonetary asset is the fair value of the asset surrendered to obtain it.

   a. The difference between fair value and book value is a gain or loss.
   b. Fair value of asset received, if clearer than that of asset given, should value transaction.

2. Recorded (book) value shall be used for exchanges in which

   a. Fair value is not determinable
   b. Exchange transaction is to facilitate sales to customers
   c. Exchange transaction lacks commercial substance

3. A nonmonetary transaction has commercial substance if the entity's future cash flows are expected to significantly change as a result of the exchange. Tax cash flows that arise solely because the tax business purpose is based on achieving a specified financial reporting result are not considered in cash flows.

E. If a nonmonetary exchange, which is recorded at book value, contains boot received, the portion of the gain recognized should be limited to the ratio [Boot ÷ (Boot received + FMV of asset received)] times the gain.

1. Firm paying boot should not recognize gain.

F. Liquidation distributions to owners should not be accounted for at fair value if a gain results (loss may be recognized).

1. Use historical cost
2. Other nonreciprocal distributions to owners should be accounted for at fair value if fair value

   a. Is objectively measurable
   b. Would be clearly realizable if sold

G. Fair value should be determined in accordance with SFAS 157, *Fair Value Measurements*

1. If one party could elect to receive cash instead of monetary asset, the amount of cash is evidence of fair value

H. Nonmonetary transaction disclosures should include

1. Nature of the transactions
2. Basis of accounting
3. Gains and losses recognized

FASB INTERPRETATION NO. 30 ACCOUNTING FOR INVOLUNTARY CONVERSIONS OF NONMONETARY ASSETS TO MONETARY ASSETS

When involuntary conversions of nonmonetary assets (e.g., fixed assets) to monetary assets (e.g., insurance proceeds) occur, the difference between the assets' cost and the monetary assets received should be reported as a gain or loss. If an unknown amount of monetary assets are to be received in a later period, gain (loss) is estimated per SFAS 5. Could be extraordinary per APB 30.

SFAS 153 Exchanges of Nonmonetary Assets—An Amendment of APB Opinion No. 29 (ASC Topic 845—Nonmonetary Transactions)

A. Requires that nonmonetary exchanges should be measured based on fair values unless certain conditions are met. It removes the distinction of "similar" and "dissimilar" assets found in APB 29 and outlines exceptions to fair value treatment. The statement also clarifies when APB 29 does not apply. The provisions of the statement are to be applied prospectively.

B. A nonmonetary exchange is a reciprocal transfer only if the transferor has no substantial continuing involvement in the asset, and the risks and rewards of ownership are transferred.

C. APB 29, *Accounting for Nonmonetary Exchanges,* does not apply to

1. Business combination accounted for under SFAS 141
2. Transfer of nonmonetary assets between companies under common control
3. Acquisition of nonmonetary assets or services on the issuance of capital stock
4. Stock issued or received in stock dividends and stock splits
5. A transfer of assets in exchange for an equity interest in entity
6. A pooling of assets in a joint undertaking to find, develop, or produce gas or oil
7. Exchange of a part of an operating interest owned for a part of another operating interest owned by another party
8. Transfers of financial assets within the scope of SFAS 140

D. Measure exchange based on fair value unless

1. Fair value is not determinable
2. It is an exchange transaction to facilitate sales to customers
3. The transaction lacks commercial substance

E. Commercial Substance

1. A nonmonetary change has commercial substance if the entity's future cash flows are expected to be significantly changed as a result of the exchange of assets.

   a. Configuration (risk, timing, and amount) of future cash flows differs significantly from that of the asset transferred.
   b. Entity-specific value of the asset differs from the entity-specific value of asset transferred, and that difference is significant in relation to fair values exchanged. Entity specific value can be computed per SFAC 7 by using expectations about use

2. If transaction has commercial substance, the exchange is measured at fair value.
3. If transaction lacks commercial substance, measure based on recorded amount of nonmonetary asset relinquished.
4. Cash flows from tax effect are not considered in determining if the transaction has commercial substance.

ARB 43—Chapter 1A Rules[5] Adopted by Membership (ASC Topics 310, 505, 605, and 850)

Four rules recommended by the Committee on Cooperation with Stock Exchanges in 1934. The last rule is from another 1934 Institute committee.

1. Profit is realized at the point of sale unless collection is not reasonably assured.
2. Capital (paid-in) surplus should not be charged with losses or expenses, except in quasi reorganizations.
3. Receivables from officers, employees, and affiliates must be separately disclosed.
4. Par value of stock issued for assets cannot be used to value the assets if some of the stock is subsequently donated back to the corporation.

APB 18 The Equity Method for Investments (ASC Topics 323, 325, 850)

A. The equity method should be used for corporate joint ventures.
B. The equity method should be applied to investments where less than 50% ownership is held but the investor **can exercise significant influence over operating and financing policies of the investee.**

1. Twenty percent (20%) or more ownership should lead to presumption of substantial influence, unless there is evidence to the contrary.
2. Conversely, less than 20% ownership leads to the presumption of no substantial influence unless there is evidence to the contrary.
3. The 20% test should be based on voting stock outstanding and disregard common stock equivalents.
4. The following procedures should be used in applying the equity method:

   a. Intercompany profits should be eliminated.
   b. Difference between cost and book value of net assets acquired should be accounted for per SFAS 141 and 142.
   c. The investment account and investor's share of investee income should be presented as single amounts in investor statements with the exception of d. below.
   d. Investor's share of discontinued operations, extraordinary items, cumulative effects of accounting changes, and prior period adjustments of investee should be so presented in statements of investor.

---

[5] The references in parentheses are from the FASB Accounting Standards—Current Texts: Volumes 1 and 2, John Wiley & Sons, Inc. These are included only for facilitating the use of the Current Texts for candidates who have access to them.

 e. Investee capital transactions should be accounted for as are subsidiary capital transactions in consolidated statements.

 f. Gains on sale of investment are the difference between selling price and carrying value of investment.

 g. When investee and investor fiscal periods do not coincide, use most recent investee statement and have consistent time lag.

 h. Losses, not temporary in nature, of investment value should be recognized by investor.

 i. Investor's share of investee loss should not be recorded once investment account is written to zero. Subsequent income should be recognized after losses not recognized are made up.

 j. Investor's share of investee's earnings should be computed after deducting investee's cumulative preferred dividends whether declared or not.

 k. If an investor's holding falls below 20%, discontinue applying the equity method but make no retroactive adjustment.

 l. When an investor's holding increases from a level less than 20% to a level equal to or greater than 20%, the investment account and retained earnings of the investor should be adjusted retroactively to reflect balances as if the equity account had been used. This is accounted for like a prior period adjustment.

5. Statements of investors applying the equity method should disclose

 a. Investees and percentages held

  (1) Accounting policies followed
  (2) Treatment of goodwill, if any

 b. Aggregate market value of investment (not for subsidiaries)

 c. When investments are material to investor, summarized information of assets, liabilities, and results of operations of investee may be necessary

 d. Conversion of securities, exercise of warrants, or issuances of investee's common stock which significantly affects investor's share of investee's income

---

FASB INTERPRETATION NO. 35 CRITERIA FOR APPLYING THE EQUITY METHOD OF ACCOUNTING FOR INVESTMENTS IN COMMON STOCK. Interprets APB 18.

 Investors owning between 20 and 50% of an investee may **not** be able to exercise significant influence over the investee's operating and financial policies. The presumption of significant influence stands until overcome by evidence to the contrary, such as: (1) opposition by the investee, (2) agreements under which the investor surrenders shareholder rights, (3) majority ownership by a small group of shareholders, (4) inability to obtain desired information from the investee, (5) inability to obtain representation on investee board of directors, etc. Whether contrary evidence is sufficient to negate the presumption of significant influence is a matter of judgment requiring a careful evaluation of all pertinent facts and circumstances, in some cases over an extended period of time. Application of this interpretation resulting in changes to or from the equity method shall be treated per APB 18, paras 19l and 19m.

FASB INTERPRETATION NO. 1 ACCOUNTING CHANGES RELATED TO THE COST OF INVENTORY

 Changes in the cost composition of inventory is an accounting change and must conform to APB 20, including justification for the change. Preferably should be based on financial reporting objectives rather than tax-related benefits.

SFAS 57 Related-Party Disclosures (ASC Topic 850—Related-Party Disclosures)

A. Definitions

1. **Affiliate**—Party is controlled by another enterprise that controls, or is under common control with another enterprise, directly or indirectly

2. **Control**—Power to direct or cause direction of management through ownerships contract, or other means

3. **Immediate family**—Family members whom principal owners or management might control/influence or be controlled/influenced by

4. **Management**—Persons responsible for enterprise objectives who have policy-making and decision-making authority

 a. For example, board of directors, chief executive and operating officers, and vice-presidents
 b. Includes persons without formal titles

5. **Principal owners**—Owners of more than 10% of a firm's voting interests

 a. Includes known beneficial owners

6. **Related parties**—Affiliates, equity method investees, employee benefit trusts, principal owners, management or any party that can significantly influence a transaction

B. FS shall include disclosures of material transactions between related parties except

1. Compensation agreements, expense allowances, and other similar items in the ordinary course of business
2. Transactions which are eliminated in the preparation of consolidated/combined FS

C. Disclosures of material transactions shall include

1. Nature of relationship(s)
2. Description of transaction(s), including those assigned zero or nominal amounts
3. Dollar amounts of transactions for each income statement period and effect of any change in method of establishing terms
4. Amounts due to/from related parties, including terms and manner of settlement

D. Representations concerning related-party transactions shall not imply that terms were equivalent to those resulting in arm's-length bargaining unless such statement can be substantiated.
E. When a **control** relationship exists, disclose such relationship even though no transactions have occurred.

ARB 43— Chapter 7A Quasi Reorganization (ASC Topic 852)

Describes what is permitted before and after quasi reorganization.

A. Procedure in readjustment

1. A clear report should be made to shareholders to obtain consent for the proposed restatements of assets and shareholders' equity.
2. Write-down of assets should not go below fair value.
3. If potential losses exist, provide for maximum probable loss.
4. When determined, amounts should be written off first to retained earnings and then to capital surplus.

B. Procedure after readjustment

1. After readjustment, accounting should be similar to that appropriate for a new company
2. A new, dated retained earnings account should be created

   a. Dated for ten years to indicate when the reorganization occurred.

SFAS 165—Subsequent Events (ASC Topic 855)

A. Scope—applies to accounting and disclosure for subsequent events not addressed in other GAAP
B. Defines subsequent events as transactions that occur after the balance sheet date but before financial statements are issued or available to be issued

1. Two types of subsequent events

   a. Recognized subsequent events are conditions that existed as of the balance sheet date
   b. Unrecognized subsequent events are conditions that did not exist as of the balance sheet date

C. Effects of recognized subsequent events should be recognized at the balance sheet date (warranty estimates, litigation settlement, and bankruptcy of client with receivables)
D. Effects of nonrecognized subsequent events should be disclosed in a footnote if the financial statements would be misleading if not disclosed
E. Entity must disclose the date through which the subsequent events have been evaluated and the date the financial statements were issued or available to be issued

SFAS 166—Accounting for Transfers of Financial Assets—An Amendment of FASB Statement No. 140 (ASC Topic 860)

A. Modifies SFAS 140 and eliminates the concept of a qualifying special-purpose entity
B. Limits the portions of financial assets that are eligible for derecognition

SFAS 140 Accounting for Transfers and Servicing of Financial Assets and Extinguishment of Liabilities (ASC Topic 860—Transfers and Servicing)

A. Provides accounting and reporting standards for transfers and servicing of financial assets and extinguishment of liabilities

B. Transfer of Assets

1. Necessary conditions to qualify as a sale

   a. Transferred assets have been isolated from the transferor or its creditors,
   b. Transferee has the unconstrained right to pledge or exchange the transferred assets, and
   c. Transferor does not maintain effective control over the transferred assets through

      (1) An agreement that obligates the transferor to repurchase or redeem them before their maturity, or
      (2) The ability to unilaterally cause the holder to return specific assets
      (3) An agreement that requires the transferor to repurchase the assets at a favorable price

2. Upon any transfer of assets, the transferor shall

   a. Initially recognize and measure at fair value the servicing assets and servicing liabilities that require recognition
   b. Allocate the previous carrying amount between the assets sold and the interests that continue to be held by the transferor based on relative fair values at the date of transfer
   c. Continue to carry in its balance sheet any interest it continues to hold in the transferred assets

3. Upon any completion of a transfer of assets which satisfies the conditions of a sale, the transferor shall

   a. Derecognize all assets sold
   b. Recognize all assets obtained and liabilities incurred in consideration as sale proceeds
   c. Initially measure at fair value assets obtained and liabilities incurred in a sale
   d. Recognize in earnings any gain (loss) on sale

4. Upon any completion of a transfer of assets which satisfies the conditions of a sale, the transferee shall

   a. Recognize all assets obtained and liabilities incurred at fair value

5. If transfer of assets does not meet the criteria for a sale, the transfer shall be accounted for as a secured borrowing with pledge of collateral

C. Servicing Assets and Liabilities

1. Recognize and initially measure at fair value a servicing asset or servicing liability if enter into a servicing contract in any of the following situations:

   a. Transfer of the servicer's financial assets that meets the requirements for sale accounting
   b. Transfer of the servicer's financial assets to a qualifying SPE in a guaranteed mortgage securitization in which transferor retains the securities and classifies them as available-for-sale or trading securities
   c. An acquisition or assumption of an obligation that does not relate to the financial assets of the servicer or its consolidated affiliates

2. If entity transfers financial assets to a qualified SPE in a guaranteed mortgage securitization and transferor retains all securities and classifies them as held-to-maturity securities, may either recognizing the servicing assets or servicing liabilities separately or report them with the asset being serviced

3. Measure servicing assets and servicing liabilities with one of two methods

   a. Amortization method

      (1) Initially record at fair value
      (2) Amortize in proportion to and over the period of estimated net servicing income or net servicing loss
      (3) Assess for impairment or increased obligation based on fair value.

   b. Fair value method

      (1) Initially record at fair value
      (2) Measure at fair value at each reporting date
      (3) Report changes in fair value in earnings in the period in which the change occurs

4. Election must be made for each class of servicing assets and servicing liabilities
5. Once an election is made to use the fair value method, election cannot be reversed
6. Report servicing assets and servicing liabilities measured at fair value separately on the balance sheet from amortized assets in one of two ways

   a. Display separate line items for amounts valued at fair value and amounts measured by amortization method, **or**
   b. Present aggregate amounts for all servicing assets and liabilities, and disclose parenthetically the amount that is measured in fair value that is included in the aggregate amount

D. Financial Assets Subject to Prepayment

1. Shall be measured like investments in debt securities classified as available-for-sale or trading

E. Secured Borrowing and Collateral

1. Pledge

    a. Debtor grants a security interest in certain assets
    b. Collateral is transferred to the secured party

2. Accounting for noncash collateral

    a. Debtor to separate asset on balance sheet into an encumbered asset section if secured party has right to sell or repledge collateral
    b. Secured party recognizes the proceeds from sale and obligation to return collateral if it sells collateral pledged to it
    c. Debtor defaults under terms of agreement and is no longer entitled to redeem the pledged asset

        (1) Derecognize the pledged asset
        (2) Secured party recognizes collateral as an asset at fair value
        (3) If collateral already sold, secured party derecognizes its obligation to return collateral.

F. Extinguishment of Liabilities

1. Debtor shall derecognize a liability when it has been extinguished

    a. Debtor pays the creditor and is relieved of its obligation for the liability
    b. Debtor is legally released from being obligor under the liability, either judicially or by the creditor.

G. Required Disclosures

1. Collateral

    a. Policy for requiring collateral or other security due to repurchase agreements or securities lending transactions
    b. Carrying amount and classification of pledged assets as collateral that are not reclassified and separately reported in the balance sheet
    c. The fair value of collateral that can be sold or repledged and information about the sources and uses of that collateral

2. Extinguished debt

    a. General description of transaction
    b. Amount of debt that was considered extinguished at end of period

3. Description of assets set aside for satisfying scheduled payments of a specific obligation
4. Nonestimable fair value of assets

    a. Description of the assets or liabilities
    b. The reasons why it is not practicable to estimate the assets or liabilities

5. For all servicing assets and servicing liabilities

    a. Management's basis for determining its classes
    b. Description of risks, the instruments used to mitigate income statement effect of changes in fair value (Quantitative information, including fair value at beginning and end of period is encouraged but not required)
    c. Amount of contractually specified servicing fees, late fees, and ancillary fees for each period on income statement, with description of where each amount is reported in income statement

6. For servicing assets and servicing liabilities measured at fair value

    a. For each class, the activity including

        (1) Beginning and ending balances
        (2) Additions
        (3) Disposals
        (4) Changes in fair value from changes in valuation inputs or assumptions used, other changes in fair value
        (5) Other changes that affect balance and description of changes

    b. Description of the valuation techniques used to estimate fair value, with qualitative and quantitative information about assumptions used in the model

7. For servicing assets and servicing liabilities amortized

   a. For each class, the activity including

     (1) Beginning and ending balances
     (2) Additions
     (3) Disposals
     (4) Amortization
     (5) Application of valuation allowance to adjust carrying value
     (6) Other than temporary impairments
     (7) Other changes that affect balance and description of changes

   b. For each class, the fair value at the beginning and end of period if practicable to estimate the value
   c. Description of the valuation techniques used to estimate fair value, with qualitative and quantitative information about assumptions used in the model
   d. The risk characteristics of the underlying financial assets used to stratify servicing assets for measuring impairment
   e. The activity by class in any valuation allowance for impairment of servicing assets, including beginning and ending balances, additions charged, recoveries made, and write-downs charged against the allowance for each period

8. Transfer of securitized financial assets accounted for as a sale

   a. Accounting policies for measuring the retained interest
   b. Characteristics of securitizations and the gain (loss) from sale
   c. Key assumptions used in measuring the fair value of retained interests at time of securitization
   d. Cash flows between the securitization SPE and the transferor

9. Retained interests in secured financial assets

   a. Accounting policies for subsequently measuring retained interests
   b. Key assumptions used in subsequently measuring fair value of retained interests
   c. Sensitivity analysis or stress test showing hypothetical effect of unfavorable variations on the retained interest's fair value, including limitations of analysis
   d. Securitized assets

     (1) Total principal outstanding, portion derecognized, and portion that continues to be recognized
     (2) Delinquencies at end of period
     (3) Credit losses, net of recoveries

SFAS 156 Accounting for Servicing of Financial Assets (ASC Topic 860—Transfers and Servicing)

SFAS 156, issued in March 2006, amends SFAS 140. It provides that an election may be made to use the fair value method to value servicing assets and servicing liabilities. Election must be made for each class of servicing assets and servicing liabilities. Once the election is made, it cannot be reversed. SFAS 156 allows balance sheet disclosure to be presented in one of two ways: either displayed as separate line items for amounts valued at fair value and amounts measured by the amortization method, **or** by presenting aggregate amounts for all servicing assets and liabilities with a parenthetical disclosure for the amount that is measured using fair value. Additional footnote disclosures are required for all servicing assets, with separate disclosures for servicing assets measured at fair value and servicing assets measured by the amortization method.

See the outline of SFAS 140, paragraphs B, C, and G.

INDUSTRY (ASC TOPIC 900)

SFAS 7 Accounting and Reporting by Development Stage Companies (ASC Topic 915—Development Stage Entities)

A. A company, division, component, etc., is in the development stage if

  1. Substantially all efforts are devoted toward establishing the business, or
  2. Principal operations are underway but have not produced significant revenues

B. Example activities of development stage companies

  1. Financial planning
  2. Raising capital
  3. Exploring or developing natural resources

    4. R&D
    5. Establishing sources of supply
    6. Acquiring property, plant, equipment, etc.
    7. Personnel recruitment and training
    8. Developing markets
    9. Production start-up

C. No special accounting standards apply to development stage companies.

    1. Report revenue in the income statement as in normal operations
    2. Expense costs as one would for a company in normal operations
    3. Capitalize costs as one would for a company in normal operations

        a. Determine cost recoverability within entity for which statements are being prepared

D. Development stage company statements include

    1. A balance sheet with cumulative net losses termed "deficit accumulated during development stage"
    2. An income statement with revenues and expenses for both current period and cumulative expenses and revenues from the inception of the development stage
    3. A statement of cash flows for both current period and cumulative amounts from inception
    4. Statement of owner's investment including

        a. Dates of issuance and number of shares, warrants, etc.
        b. Dollar amounts must be assigned to each issuance

            (1) Dollar amounts must be assigned for noncash consideration

        c. Dollar amounts received for each issuance or basis for valuing noncash consideration

    5. Identification of statements as those of a development stage company
    6. During the first period of normal operations, notes to statements should disclose that company was, but is no longer, in the development stage

SFAS 45 Accounting for Franchise Fee Revenue (ASC Topic 952—Franchisors)

A. Definitions

    1. **Franchisee**—Party who has been granted business rights
    2. **Franchisor**—Party who grants business rights
    3. **Area franchise**—Agreement transferring franchise rights within a geographical area permitting the opening of a number of franchise outlets
    4. **Continuing franchise fee**—Consideration for continuing rights granted by the agreement (general or specific) during its life
    5. **Franchise agreement**—Essential criteria

        a. Contractual relation between franchisee and franchisor
        b. Purpose is distribution of a product, service, or entire business concept
        c. Resources contributed by both franchisor and franchisee in establishing and maintaining the franchise
        d. Outline of specific marketing practices to be followed
        e. Creation of an establishment that will require and support the full-time business activity of the franchisee
        f. Both franchisee and franchisor have a common public identity

    6. **Initial franchise fee**—Consideration for establishing the relationship and providing some initial services
    7. **Initial services**—Variety of services and advice (e.g., site selection, financing and engineering services, advertising assistance, training of personnel, manuals for operations, administration and recordkeeping, bookkeeping and advisory services, quality control programs)

B. Franchise fee revenue from individual sales shall be recognized when all material services or conditions relating to the sale have been substantially performed or satisfied by the franchisor.

    1. Substantial performance means

        a. Franchisor has no remaining obligation or intent to refund money or forgive unpaid debt
        b. Substantially all initial services have been performed
        c. No other material conditions or obligations exist

    2. If large initial franchise fee is required and continuing franchise fees are small in relation to future services, then portion of initial franchise fee shall be deferred and amortized over life of franchise.

C. Continuing franchise fees shall be reported as revenue as fees are earned and become receivable from the franchise. Related costs shall be expensed as incurred.

D. Direct franchise costs shall be deferred until related revenue is recognized.

1. These costs should not exceed anticipated revenue less estimated additional related costs.

E. Disclosure of all significant commitments and obligations that have not yet been substantially performed are required

1. Notes to the FS should disclose whether the installment or cost recovery method is used.
2. Initial franchise fees shall be segregated from other franchise fee revenue if significant.

SFAS 116 Accounting for Contributions Received and Contributions Made (ASC Topic 958—Not-for-Profit Entities)

Establishes accounting standards for contributions received or made for all types of entities, not-for-profit, and business enterprises.

A. Contributions—defined
Contributions can be defined as an unconditional promise to give cash or other assets to an entity. A cancellation of a liability is also considered a contribution.

B. Contributions received (donee accounting)

1. Shall be capitalized by the donee at FMV of the item and recognized as revenue in period received.
2. Contributions with donor imposed restrictions shall be reported as restricted revenues or gains unless the restrictions are met in the same reporting period.
3. Receipts of unconditional promises to give the payments due in the future shall be reported as restricted support unless the donor intends the funds to be used for current operations.
4. Not-for-profit organizations shall recognize the expiration of donor-imposed restrictions as they expire.

C. Contributions made (donor accounting) shall be recognized at FMV as expense in period the item is donated

1. Donation expense should be classified under other expense on the income statement.
2. If difference exists between the FMV and book value of the item, then gain or loss on disposal will be recognized.

SFAS 117 Financial Statements of Not-for-Profit Organizations (ASC Topic 958—Not-for-Profit Entities)

Establishes the reporting standards for the general-purpose external financial statements of not-for-profit organizations.

A. A complete set of financial statement for a not-for-profit organization shall include

1. A statement of financial position
2. A statement of activities
3. A statement of cash flows
4. Accompanying notes

B. Voluntary health and welfare organizations shall also include a statement of functional expenses

C. The statement of financial position provides relevant information bout liquidity, financial flexibility, and the interrelationship of the organization's assets and liabilities

1. Assets and liabilities should be aggregated in reasonably homogenous groups
2. Cash or other assets received with a donor-imposed restriction that limits their use to long-term purposes should not be classified with cash or other assets that are available for current use
3. Information about liquidity may be provided by one or more of the following

   a. Sequencing assets according to their nearness of conversion to cash and liabilities according to maturity
   b. Classifying assets and liabilities as current and noncurrent
   c. Note disclosure about liquidity and maturity

4. A statement of position shall present

   a. Permanently restricted net assets
   b. Temporarily restricted net assets
   c. Unrestricted net assets

D. The statement of activities is designed to provide information about

1. The effects of transactions and other events that change the amount and nature of net assets
2. The relationships of those transactions and other events and circumstances to each other
3. How the organization's resources are used

E. The statement of activities should show the change in permanently restricted net assets, temporarily restricted net assets, and unrestricted net assets for the period

1. Generally, revenues and expenses shall be reported at gross amounts
2. However, gains and losses may be shown at net amounts if they result from peripheral or incidental or from events and circumstances that are beyond the control of management
3. Expenses should be presented according to their functional classification

F. The statement of cash flows is designed to provide information about cash receipts and payments of the organization during the period

SFAS 124 Accounting for Certain Investments Held by Not-for-Profit Organizations (ASC Topic 958—Not-for-Profit Entities)

A. Requires all equity investments and debt instruments to be valued at their fair values, with the exception of

1. Equity investments accounted for on the equity method.
2. Equity investments without readily determinable fair values.

B. Gains and losses on investments shall be reported in the statement of activities as increases or decreases in unrestricted net assets unless their use is temporarily or permanently restricted.

C. Dividend, interest, and other investment income shall be reported in the period earned as increases in unrestricted net assets unless the use of the assets received is limited by donor-imposed restrictions.

D. Donor-restricted investment income is reported as an increase in temporarily restricted net assets or permanently restricted net assets, depending on the type of restriction.

E. Disclosures

1. The composition of investment return
2. A reconciliation of investment return to amounts reported in the statement of activities
3. The aggregate carry amount of investments by major types
4. The basis for determining the carrying values
5. The methods and assumptions used to determine fair values
6. The aggregate amount of deficiencies for donor-restricted endowment funds
7. Significant concentrations of market risk

SFAS 158 Employers' Accounting for Defined Benefit Pension and Other Postretirement Plans (An Amendment of FASB Statements 87, 88, 106, and 132[R]) (ASC Topic 715—Compensation—Retirement Benefits and ASC Topic 958—Not-for-Profit Entities)

A. Recognize funded status of benefit plans

1. Aggregate status of all overfunded plans and show as noncurrent asset on balance sheet
2. Aggregate status of all underfunded plans, and show as current liability, noncurrent liability, or both on balance sheet.
3. Recognize as other comprehensive income the gain and loss and the prior service costs or credits that arise during the period but are not a part of pension expense.

B. Effective for fiscal years ending after December 15, 2008, the measurement date is the employer's fiscal year-end balance sheet date.

C. Disclosures

1. Funded status of the plans, and the amounts recognized in the balance sheet, showing separately the noncurrent assets, current liabilities, and noncurrent liabilities recognized.
2. Disclose the net gain or loss, net prior service cost or credit recognized in OCI for the period, and any reclassification adjustments of OCI that are recognized in pension cost.
3. The amounts in accumulated OCI that have not yet been recognized as pension costs. Show separately the following items:

    a. Net gain or loss
    b. Net prior service cost or credit
    c. Net transition asset or obligation

4. The amount and timing of any plan assets expected to be returned to the employer during the next 12-month period after the most recent balance sheet date.

SFAS 164 Not-for-Profit Entities: Mergers and Acquisitions—Including an Amendment of FASB Statement No. 142 (ASC Topic 958)

The authors believe that this topic is too specialized for the CPA exam.

SFAS 66 Accounting for Sales of Real Estate (ASC Topics 360, 605, and 976)

A. Other than retail land sales

1. Use the full accrual method if the following criteria are satisfied:

   a. Sale is consummated
   b. Buyer's initial and continuing investments demonstrate a commitment to pay for the property
   c. Seller's receivable is not subject to future subordination
   d. Risks and rewards of ownership have been transferred

2. When the criteria are not met and dependent upon the particular circumstance, use one of the following methods:

   a. Installment method
   b. Cost recovery method
   c. Deposit method
   d. Reduced profit method
   e. Percentage-of-completion

B. Retail land sales (not outlined due to specialized nature)

SFAS 86 Accounting for the Costs of Computer Software to Be Sold, Leased, or Otherwise Marketed (ASC Topic 985—Software)

A. Establishes standards of financial accounting and reporting for the costs of computer software to be sold, leased, or otherwise marketed as a separate product or as part of a product or process, whether internally developed and produced or purchased.

B. Research and development costs consist of all costs to establish technological feasibility.

1. Evidence of technological feasibility

   a. Process of creating the computer software product includes a detailed program design **or**
   b. Process of creating the computer software product includes a product design and a completed working model.

C. Capitalization costs include costs incurred subsequent to establishing technological feasibility.

1. Capitalization shall cease when product is available for general release to customers.

D. Amortization of capitalized software costs is performed on a product-by-product basis.

1. Annual amortization is the greater of

   a. The amount computed using the ratio current gross product revenues to total current and anticipated future gross product revenues **or**
   b. S-L method using the estimated economic life of the software product

2. Amortization begins when product is available for general release to customers.
3. Unamortized capitalized costs cannot exceed the net realizable value (NRV) of that software product. Any excess shall be written off at the end of the year.

E. Inventory costs include costs incurred for duplicating software materials and for physically packaging the product.

1. Costs of maintenance and customer support are charged to expense.

F. FS disclosures shall include

1. Unamortized computer software costs
2. Total amount charged to amortization expense and amounts written down to NRV

MISCELLANEOUS

SFAS 145 Rescission of FASB Statements No. 4, 44, and 64, Amendment of FASB Statement No. 13, and Technical Corrections (Rescinds SFAS 4, 44, and 64 and amends SFAS 13)

A. Rescinds SFAS 4, 44, and 64 to no longer allow treatment of extinguishment of debt as an extraordinary item in the statement of income

B. Amends SFAS 13 to require that when a modification of a capital lease terms gives rise to a new agreement classified as an operating lease, the lessee should account for the new agreement under the sale-leaseback requirements of SFAS 98 (see outline)

SFAS 147 Acquisitions of Certain Financial Institutions, An Amendment of FASB Statements No. 72 and 144 and FASB Interpretation No. 9

The authors believe that this topic is too specialized for the CPA exam.

SFAS 152 Accounting for Real Estate Time Sharing Transactions—An Amendment of FASB Statements No. 66 and 67
(Amends SFAS 66 and SFAS 67)

Requires real estate time-sharing transactions to be accounted for as nonretail land sales. AICPA SOP 04-2 provides guidance on accounting for real estate time-sharing transactions. This statement also amends SFAS 67 (*Accounting for Costs and Initial Rental Operations of Real Estate Projects*), so that SFAS 67 does not apply to real estate time-sharing transactions. Restatement of previously issued financial statements is not permitted.

SFAS 162 The Hierarchy of Generally Accepted Accounting Principles

A. Identifies the sources of accounting principles for US GAAP
B. Descending order of authority for accounting principles is as follows:

1. FASB Statements of Accounting Standards and Interpretations, FASB Staff Positions, AICPA Accounting Research Bulletins, and Accounting Principles Board Opinions not superseded by the FASB.
2. FASB Technical Bulletins, and if cleared by the FASB, the AICPA Industry Audit and Accounting Guides and Statements of Position.
3. AICPA Accounting Standards Executive Committee Practice Bulletins that have been cleared by the FASB, consensus positions of the FASB Emerging Issues Task Force (EITF), and the topics discussed in Appendix D of the EITF Abstracts.
4. Implementation guides (Q&As) published by the FASB staff; AICPA Accounting Interpretations; AICPA Industry Audit and Accounting Guides and Statements of Position not cleared by the FASB; and practices that are widely recognized and prevalent generally or in industry.

C. If accounting treatment is not specified by a pronouncement in the highest category, then use the next highest level of authority. If accounting treatment is not specified in any other category, then consider the accounting principles for similar transactions or events within the given categories, and use other accounting literature.
D. Other accounting literature includes FASB Concept Statements, AICPA Issues Papers, International Financial Reporting Standards, pronouncements of other professional associations or regulatory agencies, Technical Information Service Inquiries and Replies included in AICPA Technical Practice Aids, and accounting textbooks, handbooks, and articles.

SFAS 163 Accounting for Financial Guarantee Insurance Contracts—An Interpretation of FASB Statement No. 60

The authors believe that this topic is too specialized for the CPA exam.

STATEMENTS OF FINANCIAL ACCOUNTING CONCEPTS (SFAC)

Statements of Financial Accounting Concepts (SFAC) set forth financial accounting and reporting objectives and fundamentals that will be used by the FASB in developing standards. While practitioners may also use SFAC in areas where promulgated GAAP does not exist, it is important to note that the SFAC do not constitute authoritative GAAP. Accordingly, SFAC do not come under Ethics Rule 203.

SFAC 1 Objectives of Financial Reporting by Business Enterprises—Superseded by SFAC 8

SFAC 2 Qualitative Characteristics of Accounting Information—Superseded by SFAC 8

SFAC 3 Elements of Financial Statements—Superseded by SFAC 6

SFAC 4 Objectives of Financial Reporting of Nonbusiness Organizations

The authors believe that this concept is not on the CPA Exam.

SFAC 5 Recognition and Measurement in Financial Statements of Business Enterprises

A. Statement addresses principal items that a full set of FS should show and provides fundamental recognition criteria to use in deciding which items to include in FS.

1. Recognition criteria presented are not radical change from current practice
2. Only applies to business enterprises

B. FS

1. A principal means of communicating financial information to those outside an entity
2. Some useful information is better provided by other means of financial reporting, such as notes to the statements or supplementary information (SFAC 1).
3. Objectives of financial reporting (which encompasses FS) are detailed in SFAC 1.
4. Full set of FS should show

   a. Financial position at end of period
   b. Earnings for period
   c. Comprehensive income for period
   d. Cash flows for period
   e. Investments by and distributions to owners during period

5. Are intended as "general-purpose" statements and, therefore, do not necessarily satisfy all users equally well
6. Simplifications, condensations, and aggregations are necessary and useful, but focusing on one figure (i.e., "the bottom line") exclusively should be avoided.
7. FS interrelate and complement each other.
8. Information detailed in 4. above is provided by the following individual financial statements:

   a. **Statement of Financial Position**

      (1) Provides information about entity's assets, liabilities, and equity and their relationships to each other at a particular point in time
      (2) Does not purport to show the value of an entity

   b. **Statement of Earnings and Comprehensive Income**

      (1) Shows how the equity of an entity increased or decreased from all sources (other than from transactions with owners) during period
      (2) Item "earnings" is similar to present net income term but does not include certain accounting adjustments recognized in current period (i.e., change in accounting principle).
      (3) Earnings is a performance measure concerned primarily with cash-to-cash cycles.
      (4) Comprehensive income includes all recognized changes in equity except those from transactions with owners (SFAC 6).
      (5) The terms "gains" and "losses" are used for those items included in earnings.
      (6) The terms "cumulative accounting adjustments" and "other nonowner changes in equity" are used for those items excluded from earnings but included in comprehensive income.

   c. **Statement of Cash Flows**

      (1) Shows entity's cash flows from operating, investing, and financing activities during a period

   d. **Statement of Investments by and Distributions to Owners**

      (1) Shows capital transactions of entity which are increases and decreases in equity from transactions with owners during period

9. FS help users assess entity's liquidity, financial flexibility, profitability, and risk.
10. Full set of FS based on concept of financial capital maintenance—a return is achieved only after capital has been maintained or recovered.

C. Recognition criteria

1. Recognition is presentation of item in both words and numbers that is included in the totals of the financial statements (SFAC 6).
2. Item should meet four fundamental recognition criteria to be recognized

   a. **Definitions**—item is element of FS as defined by SFAC 6
   b. **Measurability**—item has a relevant attribute that is measurable with sufficient reliability

      (1) Five measurement attributes are used in current practice

         (a) Historical cost (historical proceeds)
         (b) Current (replacement) cost
         (c) Current market value
         (d) Net realizable (settlement) value
         (e) Present (discounted) value of future cash flows

(2) Statement suggests that use of different attributes will continue

(3) The monetary unit of measurement of nominal units of money is expected to continue to be used

   c. **Relevance**—item has capacity to make a difference in users' decisions (SFAC 2)

   d. **Reliability**—item is representationally faithful, verifiable, and neutral (SFAC 2)

     (1) Reliability may affect timing of recognition due to excessive uncertainties

     (2) A trade-off may sometimes be needed between relevance and reliability because waiting for complete reliability may make information untimely

D. Guidance in applying recognition criteria

  1. Need to identify which cash-to-cash cycles are substantially complete

  2. Degree of skepticism is needed (SFAC 2)

  3. **Revenues** and **gains**

    a. Generally not recognized until realizable (SFAC 6)

      (1) Realizable means assets received or held are readily convertible to known amounts of cash or claims to cash

    b. Not recognized until earned (APB 4, SFAC 6)

  4. **Expenses** and **losses**

    a. Generally recognized when economic benefits are consumed or assets lose future benefits

    b. Some expenses are recognized when associated revenues are recognized (e.g., cost of goods sold).

    c. Some expenses are recognized when cash is spent or liability incurred (e.g., selling and administrative salaries).

    d. Some expenses are allocated by systematic and rational procedures to periods benefited (e.g., depreciation and insurance).

E. Recognition of changes in assets and liabilities

  1. Initial recognition generally based on current exchange prices at date of recognition

  2. Changes can result from two types of events

    a. Inflows and outflows

    b. Changes in amounts which can be a change in utility or substance (e.g., depreciation) or changes in price

  3. Current price information may only be used if it is reliable, cost justified, and more relevant than alternative information.

SFAC 6 Elements of Financial Statements
(Replaces SFAC 3)

A. Statement contains definitions of FS elements

  1. Definitions provide a significant first screen in determining content of FS.

    a. Possessing characteristics of a definition of an element is necessary but not sufficient condition for including an item in FS

    b. To qualify for inclusion in FS an item must

      (1) Meet recognition criteria (e.g., revenue recognition tests)

      (2) Possess a relevant attribute which can be measured reliably (e.g., historical cost/historical proceeds)

B. Elements of FS of both business enterprises and not-for-profit organizations

  1. **Assets** are probable future economic benefits controlled by a particular entity as a result of past transactions or events.

    a. Characteristics of assets

      (1) Probable future benefit by contribution to future net cash inflows

      (2) Entity can obtain and control access to benefit

      (3) Transaction or event leading to control has already occurred

    b. Asset continues as an asset until collected, transferred, used, or destroyed.

    c. Valuation accounts are part of related asset.

  2. **Liabilities** are probable future sacrifices of economic benefits, arising from present obligations of a particular entity that result from past transactions or events.

a. Characteristics of liabilities

   (1) Legal, equitable, or constructive duty to transfer assets in future
   (2) Little or no discretion to avoid future sacrifice
   (3) Transaction or event obligating enterprise has already occurred

b. Liability remains a liability until settled or discharged.
c. Valuation accounts are part of related liability.

3. **Equity** (net assets) is the owner's residual interest in the assets of an entity that remains after deducting liabilities.

  a. Business enterprises

    (1) Characteristics of equity

      (a) The source of distributions by enterprise to its owners
      (b) No unconditional right to receive future transfer of assets; depends on future profitability
      (c) Inevitably affected by enterprise's operations and circumstances affecting enterprise

    (2) Transactions or events that change owners' equity include revenues and expenses; gains and losses; investments by owners; distributions to owners; and changes within owners' equity (does not change total amount)

  b. Not-for-profit organizations

    (1) Characteristics of net assets (equity)

      (a) Absence of ownership interest
      (b) Operating purposes not centered on profit
      (c) Significant receipt of contributions, many involving donor-imposed restrictions

    (2) Classes of net assets

      (a) **Permanently restricted net assets** is the part of net assets of a not-for-profit organization resulting from

        1] Contributions and other inflows of assets whose use by the organization is limited by donor-imposed stipulations that neither expire by passage of time nor can be fulfilled or otherwise removed by actions of the organization
        2] Other asset enhancements and diminishments subject to same kinds of stipulations
        3] Reclassifications from (or to) other classes of net assets as a consequence of donor-imposed stipulations

      (b) **Temporarily restricted net assets** is the part of net assets of a not-for-profit organization resulting from

        1] Contribution and other inflows of assets whose use by the organization is limited by donor-imposed stipulations that either expire by passage of time or can be fulfilled and removed by actions of the organization pursuant to those stipulations
        2] Other asset enhancements and diminishments subject to same kinds of stipulations
        3] Reclassifications to (or from) other classes of net assets as a consequence of donor-imposed stipulations, their expiration by passage of time, or their fulfillment and removal by actions of the organization pursuant to those stipulations

      (c) **Unrestricted net assets** is the part of net assets of a not-for-profit organization that is neither permanently restricted nor temporarily restricted by donor-imposed stipulations. They result from

        1] All revenues, expenses, gains, and losses that are not changes in permanently or temporarily restricted net assets and
        2] Reclassifications from (or to) other classes of net assets as a consequence of donor-imposed stipulations, their expiration by passage of time, or their fulfillment and removal by actions of the organization pursuant to those stipulations

    (3) Transactions and events that change net assets include revenues and expenses, gains and losses, and changes within net assets that do not affect assets or liabilities (including reclassifications between classes of net assets).
    (4) Changes in classes of net assets of not-for-profit organizations may be significant because donor-imposed restrictions may affect the types and levels of services that a not-for-profit organization can provide.

      (a) Characteristics of change in permanently restricted net assets

           1] Most increases in permanently restricted net assets are from accepting contributions of assets that donors stipulate must be maintained in perpetuity. Only assets that are not by their nature used up in carrying out the organization's activities are capable of providing economic benefits indefinitely. Gifts of cash, securities, and nonexhaustible property are examples.

       (b) Characteristics of change in temporarily restricted net assets

           1] Most increases in temporarily restricted net assets are from accepting contributions of assets that donors limit to use after specified future time or for specified purpose. Temporary restrictions pertain to contributions with donor stipulations that expire or can be fulfilled and removed by using assets as specified.

       (c) Characteristics of change in unrestricted net assets

           1] Change in unrestricted net assets for a period indicates whether organization has maintained the part of its net assets that is fully available (free of donor-imposed restrictions) to support the organization's services to beneficiaries in the next period.

4. **Revenues** are increases in assets or decreases in liabilities during a period from delivering goods, rendering services, or other activities constituting the entity's major or central operations.

   a. Characteristics of revenues

     (1) Accomplishments of the earning process
     (2) Actual or expected cash inflows resulting from central operations
     (3) Inflows reported gross

5. **Expenses** are decreases in assets or increases in liabilities during a period from delivery of goods, rendering of services, or other activities constituting the entity's major or central operations.

   a. Characteristics of expenses

     (1) Sacrifices involved in carrying out earnings process
     (2) Actual or expected cash outflows resulting from central operations
     (3) Outflows reported gross

6. **Gains (losses)** are increases (decreases) in equity from peripheral transactions of entity excluding revenues (expenses) and investment by owners (distribution to owners).

   a. Characteristics of gains and losses

     (1) Result from peripheral transactions and circumstances that may be beyond control
     (2) May be classified according to sources or as operating and nonoperating
     (3) Change in equity reported net

7. **Accrual accounting** and **related concepts** include

   a. **Transaction**—external event involving transfer of something of value between two or more entities
   b. **Event**—a happening of consequence to an entity (internal or external)
   c. **Circumstances**—a set of conditions developed from events which may occur imperceptibly and create possibly unanticipated situations
   d. **Accrual accounting**—recording "cash consequence" transactions as they occur rather than with movement of cash; deals with process of cash movement instead of beginning or end of process (per SFAC 1)

     (1) Based on cash and credit transactions, exchanges, price changes, changes in form of assets and liabilities

   e. **Accrual**—recognizing revenues and related asset increases and expenses and related liability increases as they occur; expected future cash receipt or payment follows recognition of revenue (expense)
   f. **Deferral**—recognizing liability for cash receipt with expected future revenue or recognizing asset for cash payment with expected future expense; cash receipt (payment) precedes recognition of revenues (expenses)
   g. **Allocation**—process of assigning or distributing an amount according to a plan or formula

     (1) Includes amortization

   h. **Amortization**—process of systematically reducing an amount by periodic payments or write-downs
   i. **Realization**—process of converting noncash resources and rights into money; refers to sales of assets for cash or claims to cash

     (1) Realized—identifies revenues or gains or losses on assets sold
     (2) Unrealized—identifies revenues or gains or losses on assets unsold

    j. **Recognition**—process of formally recording an item in financial statements

       (1) Major differences between accrual and cash basis accounting is timing of recognition of income items

    k. **Matching**—simultaneous recognition of revenues with expenses which are related directly or jointly to the same transaction or events

C. Elements of FS exclusive to business enterprises

  1. **Investments by owners** are increases in net assets resulting from transfers by other entities of something of value to obtain ownership.

  2. **Distributions to owners** are decreases in net assets resulting from transferring assets, rendering services, or incurring liabilities by the enterprise to owners.

  3. **Comprehensive income** is the change in equity of an entity during a period from transactions and other events of nonowner sources (i.e., all equity amount changes except investment and distributions).

    a. Term "comprehensive" income is used instead of net earnings (net income) because the board is reserving "earnings" for a component part of comprehensive income yet to be determined.[6]

    b. Concept of capital maintenance or recovery of cost is needed in order to separate return **on** capital from return **of** capital.

    c. Financial capital maintenance concept vs. physical capital maintenance concept

       (1) Financial capital maintenance—objective is to maintain purchasing power
       (2) Physical capital maintenance—objective is to maintain operating capacity

    d. Comprehensive income is return on financial capital.

    e. Characteristics, sources, and components of comprehensive income include

       (1) Cash receipts (excluding owner investments) less cash outlays (excluding distributions to owners) over life of enterprise

          (a) Recognition criteria and choice of attributes to be measured affect timing, not amount.

       (2) Specific sources of income are

          (a) Transactions between enterprise and nonowners
          (b) Enterprise's productive efforts
          (c) Price changes, casualties, and other interactions with environment

       (3) **Earnings process** is the production and distribution of goods or services so firm can pay for goods and services it uses and provide return to owners.
       (4) Peripheral activities may also provide income.
       (5) Components of comprehensive income

          (a) Basic components—revenues, expenses, gains and losses
          (b) Intermediate components result from combining basic components

       (6) Display considerations (e.g., items included in operating income) are the subject of another SFAC.

SFAC 7 Using Cash Flow Information and Present Value in Accounting Measurements

A. Statement provides

  1. A framework for using future cash flows as the basis for accounting measurements

    a. At initial recognition
    b. In **fresh-start measurements**—measurements in period following initial recognition that establish a new carrying amount unrelated to previous amounts and accounting conventions.
    c. For the **interest method of allocation**—reporting conventions that use present value techniques in the absence of a fresh-start measurement to compute changes in the carrying amount of an asset or liability from one period to the next. Like depreciation and amortization conventions, interest methods are grounded in notion of historical cost.

  2. General principles that govern the use of present value

    a. Especially when uncertainties exist in

---

[6] Although SFAS 130 has defined comprehensive income as including net income plus other comprehensive income, it has not yet changed the components that comprise net income. Additionally, prior period adjustments are still reported in the retained earnings statement, not as comprehensive income.

(1) The amount of future cash flows
(2) The timing of future cash flows, or
(3) Both (1) and (2)

    3. Common understanding of objective of present value in accounting measurements
    4. **Guidance on measurement** issues **only—recognition issues are not addressed by SFAS 7.**

B. Statement does not specify when fresh-start measurements are appropriate

    1. FASB expects to decide whether a particular situation requires a fresh-start measurement (or some other accounting response) on a project-by-project basis.

C. Objective of present value in an accounting measurement is to capture, to the extent possible, the economic difference between sets of estimated cash flows

    1. Without present value, a $3,000 cash flow due tomorrow and a $3,000 cash flow due in fifteen years appear the same.
    2. Because present value distinguishes between cash flows that might otherwise appear similar, a measurement based on the present value of estimated future cash flows provides more relevant information than a measurement based on the undiscounted sum of those cash flows.
    3. A present value measurement that fully captures the economic differences between various sets of future cash flows would necessarily include the following elements:

        a. An estimate of the future cash flow (or in more complex cases, series of future cash flows at different times)
        b. Expectations about possible variations in the amount or timing of those cash flows
        c. The time value of money, represented by the risk-free rate of interest
        d. The price for bearing the uncertainty inherent in the asset or liability
        e. Other sometimes unidentifiable factors, including liquidity and market imperfections

D. To provide relevant information in financial reporting, present value must represent some observable measurement attribute of assets or liabilities.

    1. In the absence of observed transaction prices, accounting measurements at initial recognition and fresh-start measurements should attempt to capture the elements that taken together would comprise a market price if one existed, that is, fair value.

        a. The **fair value** of an asset (or liability) is the amount at which that asset or liability could be bought (or incurred) or sold (or settled) in a current transaction between willing parties.

    2. While the expectations of an entity's management are often useful and informative, the marketplace is the final arbiter of asset and liability values.
    3. The entity must pay the market's price when it acquires an asset or settles a liability in a current transaction, regardless of its intentions or expectations.
    4. For some assets and liabilities, management's estimates may be the only available information.

        a. In this case, the objective is to estimate the price likely to exist in the marketplace, if there were a marketplace.

E. The techniques used to estimate future cash flows and interest rates will vary from one situation to another depending on the circumstances surrounding the asset or liability in question. Certain general principles govern any application of present value techniques in measuring assets or liabilities.

    1. To the extent possible, estimated cash flows and interest rates should reflect assumptions about the future events and uncertainties that would be considered in deciding whether to acquire an asset or group of assets in an arm's-length transaction for cash.
    2. Interest rates used to discount cash flows should reflect assumptions that are consistent with those inherent in the estimated cash flows. Otherwise, the effect of some assumptions will be double-counted or ignored. For example, an interest rate of 12% might be applied to contractual cash flows of a loan. That rate reflects expectations about future defaults from loans with particular characteristics. That same 12% rate should not be used to discount expected cash flows because those cash flows already reflect assumptions about future defaults.
    3. Estimated cash flows and interest rates should be free from both bias and factors unrelated to the asset, liability, or group of assets or liabilities in question. For example, deliberately understating estimated net cash flows to enhance the apparent future profitability of an asset introduces bias into the measurement.
    4. Estimated cash flows or interest rates should reflect the range of possible outcomes rather than a single most-likely, minimum, or maximum possible amount.

F. An accounting measurement that uses present value should reflect the uncertainties inherent in the estimated cash flows. Otherwise items with different risks may appear similar.

G. Accounting applications of present value have typically used a single set of estimated cash flows and a single interest rate. SFAC 7 introduces the expected cash flow approach.

1. The expected cash flow approach focuses on explicit assumptions about the range of possible estimated cash flows and their respective possibilities.
2. The traditional approach treats those uncertainties implicitly in the selection of an interest rate.
3. By incorporating a range of possible outcomes, the expected cash flow approach accommodates the use of present value techniques when the timing of cash flows is uncertain.

H. The measurement of liabilities involves different problems from the measurement of assets.

1. The most relevant measurement of an entity's liabilities at initial recognition and fresh-start measurements should always reflect the credit standing of the entity.

I. Interest method of allocation

1. Present value techniques are also used in periodic reporting conventions known collectively as **interest methods of allocation**.
2. Financial statements usually attempt to represent the changes in assets and liabilities from one period to the next. By using current information and assumptions, fresh-start measurements capture all the factors that create change, including

   a. Physical consumption of assets (or reduction of liabilities)
   b. Changes in estimates, and
   c. Holding gains and losses that result from price changes

3. Accounting allocations are planned approaches designed to represent only consumption or reduction.
4. Changes in estimates may receive some recognition, but the effects of a change often have been spread over future periods.
5. Holding gains and losses are generally excluded from allocation systems.
6. In principle, the purpose of all accounting allocations is to report changes in the value, utility, or substance of assets and liabilities over time.
7. Accounting allocations attempt to relate the change in an asset or liability to some observable real-world phenomenon.

   a. An interest method of allocation relates changes in the reported amount with changes in present value of a set of future cash flows.

8. Allocation methods are only representations (not measurements) of an asset or liability.
9. While an interest method could be applied to any asset or liability, it is generally considered more relevant than other methods when applied to assets and liabilities that exhibit one or more of the following characteristics:

   a. The transaction giving rise to the asset or liability is commonly viewed as a borrowing or lending
   b. Period-to-period allocation of similar assets or liabilities employs an interest method
   c. A particular set of estimated future cash flows is closely associated with the asset or liability
   d. The measurement at initial recognition was based on present value

10. Like all allocation systems, the manner in which an interest method of allocation is applied can greatly affect the pattern of income or expense. In particular, the interest method requires a careful description of the following:

    a. The cash flows to be used (promised cash flows, expected cash flows, or some other estimate)
    b. The convention that governs the choice of an interest rate (effective rate or some other rate)
    c. How the rate is applied (constant effective rate or a series of annual rates)
    d. How changes in the amount or timing of estimated cash flows are reported

11. In most situations, the interest is based on contractual cash flows and assumes a constant effective interest rate over the life of those cash flows.

    a. That is, the method uses promised cash flows (rather than expected cash flows) and bases the interest rate on the single rate that equates the present value of the promised cash flows with the initial price of the asset or liability.

12. In reality, actual cash flows often occur sooner or later in greater or lesser amounts than expected. Changes from the original estimate of cash flows, in either timing or amount, can be accommodated in the interest amortization scheme or included in a fresh-start measurement of the asset or liability.

    a. Presently, the FASB doesn't address the conditions that might govern the choice between those two approaches.

13. If a change occurs in the amount or timing of estimated cash flows and the item is not remeasured, the interest amortization scheme must be altered to incorporate the new estimate of cash flows.

    a. The following techniques have been used to address the changes in estimated cash flows:

        (1) A prospective approach computes a new effective interest rate based on the carrying amount and remaining cash flows.
        (2) A catch-up approach adjusts the carrying amount to the present value of the revised estimated cash flows, discounted at the original effective interest rate.
        (3) A retrospective approach computes a new effective interest rate based on the original carrying amount, actual cash flows to date, and remaining estimated cash flows. The new effective interest rate is then used to adjust the carrying amount to the present value of the revised estimated cash flows, discounted at the new effective interest rate.

    b. The FASB considers the catch-up approach to be preferable to other techniques for reporting changes in estimated cash flows because

        (1) It is consistent with the present value relationships portrayed by the interest method, and
        (2) It can be implemented at a reasonable cost

        Under the catch-up approach, the recorded amount of an asset or liability (assuming estimated cash flows do not change) is the present value of the estimated future cash flows discounted at the original effective interest rate. If a change in estimate is effected through the catch-up approach, the measurement basis after the change will be the same as the measurement basis for the same asset or liability before the change in estimate (estimated cash flows discounted at the original effective rate).

    c. The prospective approach obscures the impact of changes in estimated cash flows and, as a result, produces information that is both less useful and less relevant. The interest rate that is derived under the prospective approach is unrelated to the rate at initial recognition or to current market rates for similar assets and liabilities. The amount that remains on the balance sheet can be described as "the unamortized amount," but no more.

    d. In some pronouncements, the retrospective approach has been used. Some consider it the most precise and complete of the three techniques listed above. However, the retrospective approach requires that entities retain a detailed record of all past cash flows. The costs of maintaining these detailed records usually outweigh any advantage provided by this approach.

SFAC 8 Conceptual Framework for Financial Reporting

Overview: Statements of Financial Accounting Concepts

A. Joint project between FASB and IASB

   Divided into chapters. New chapters added as project is completed
   Not part of the Accounting Standards Codification

B. Financial accounting concepts are fundamentals on which standards of financial accounting and reporting are based. Defines financial accounting concepts broader than financial statements and other data.

Chapter 1—The Objective of General-Purpose Financial Reporting

A. Objective of general-purpose financial reporting is to provide information useful to existing and potential investors, lenders, and other creditors.

   1. Primary users are investors, lenders, and other creditors.
   2. Primary users rely on financial reports.
   3. Provides information for primary users to assess prospects for future net cash flows.
   4. Managements, regulators, and other members of the public may use financial information, but are not considered primary users.

B. Information needed about

   1. Resources of the entity.
   2. Claims against the entity.
   3. Changes in economic resources and claims.
   4. How efficiently and effectively the entity's management and governing board have discharged their responsibilities to use those resources.
   5. Information is not designed to show value of an entity, but provide information for users to estimate the value of the reporting entity.

C. Financial reporting based on estimates, judgments, and models.

D. Financial reporting includes

1. Resources and claims against resources.
2. Changes in economic resources and claims.
3. Changes in resources and claims not resulting from financial performance.
4. Financial performance reflected by accrual accounting.
5. Financial performance reflected by past cash flows.

Chapter 3—Qualitative Characteristics of Useful Financial Information

A. The Hierarchy of Accounting Qualities

1. Decision usefulness.
2. Cost-benefit constraint.
3. Materiality threshold (relates to relevance).

B. Fundamental Qualitative Characteristics

1. Relevance

   a. Capable of making a difference in user's decision.
   b. Must have predictive value, confirmatory value or both.
   c. Has predictive value if it can be used as an input to predict future outcomes.
   d. Has confirmative value if it provides feedback about previous evaluations.

2. Faithful Representation

   a. Must faithfully represent phenomena that it purports to represent
   b. Must be complete, neutral, and free from error
   c. Complete all information necessary for a user to understand the phenomena depicted
   d. Neutral without bias toward a particular user
   e. Not accurate in all respects, but free from material error

C. Enhancing Qualitative Characteristics

1. Comparability enables user to identify and understand similarities and differences.
2. Verifiability occurs when different sources reach consensus or agreement on an amount of representation of an item.
3. Timeliness requires that information is available to a decision maker when it is useful to make the decision.
4. Understandability involves classifying, characterizing, and presenting information clearly and concisely.

REGULATION

The Regulation section of the CPA exam covers a combination of Professional Responsibilities, Business Law, and Federal Taxation.

These topics are covered in a total of 17 modules.

Exam Content Overview

Preparing for the Regulation Exam

Regulation is a section of the exam that includes both business law and taxation topics. **In preparing for the Regulation exam, you should take a systematic approach such as the one detailed in Chapter 1.**

First, in approaching your study, you should become acquainted with the nature of the Regulation exam itself. The content specification outlines are printed below.

Relatedly, you should evaluate your competence by working 10 to 20 multiple-choice questions from each of the modules (23–39) in Volume 2. This diagnostic routine will acquaint you with the specific nature of the questions tested on each topic as well as indicate the amount of study required per topic. You should work toward an 80% correct response rate as a minimum on each topic.

Second, study the content of modules 23–39 emphasizing the concepts of each topic such as legal liability of accountants, elements of a contract, and taxable income. You may have to refer to your textbooks, etc., for topics to which you have had no previous exposure.

Third, work the multiple-choice and task-based simulations under examination conditions.

AICPA CONTENT AND SKILLS SPECIFICATIONS

The AICPA Content and Skills Specifications for the Uniform CPA Exam sets forth the coverage of topics on the Regulation exam. This outline was issued by the AICPA and is effective beginning in 2011. The first part of the outline describes the topical coverage of the Regulation exam, and the second part provides some insights into the skills tested on all sections of the Uniform CPA exam.

Content Specification Outlines (CSOs)

The Regulation section tests knowledge and understanding of ethics, professional and legal responsibilities, business law, and federal taxation.

Ethics, Professional and Legal Responsibilities, and Business Law

These topics test knowledge and understanding of professional and legal responsibilities of certified public accountants. Professional ethics questions relate to tax practice issues and are based on the AICPA Code of Professional Conduct, Treasury Department Circular 230, and rules and regulations for tax return preparers. Business law topics test knowledge and understanding of the legal implications of business transactions, particularly as they relate to accounting, auditing, and financial reporting. This section deals with federal and widely adopted uniform state laws or references identified in this CSO. In addition to demonstrating knowledge and understanding of these topics, candidates are required to demonstrate the skills required to apply that knowledge in performing their responsibilities as certified public accountants. To demonstrate such knowledge and skills, candidates will be expected to perform the following tasks:

- Identify situations that might be unethical or a violation of professional standards, perform research and consultations as appropriate, and determine the appropriate action.
- Recognize potentially unethical behavior of clients and determine the impact on the tax services being performed.
- Demonstrate the importance of identifying and adhering to requirements, rules, and standards that are established by licensing boards within their state, and which may place additional professional requirements specific to their state of practice.
- Apply business law concepts in evaluating the economic substance of client transactions, including purchase agreements, loans and promissory notes, sales contracts, leases, side agreements, commitments, contingencies, and assumption of liabilities.
- Evaluate the legal structure of an entity to determine the implications of applicable laws and regulations on how a business is organized, governed, and operates.

Federal Taxation

These topics test knowledge and understanding of concepts and laws relating to federal taxation (income, gift, and estate). The areas of testing include federal tax process, procedures, accounting, and planning, as well as federal taxation of property transactions, individuals, and entities (which include sole proprietorships, partnerships, limited liability entities, C corporations, S corporations, joint ventures, trusts, estates, and tax-exempt organizations). In addition to demonstrating knowledge and understanding of these topics, candidates are required to demonstrate the skills required to apply that knowledge in providing tax preparation and advisory services and performing other responsibilities as certified public accountants. To demonstrate such knowledge and skills, candidates will be expected to perform the following tasks:

- Evaluate the tax implications of different legal structures for business entities.
- Apply analytical reasoning tools to assess how taxes affect economic decisions related to the timing of income/expense recognition and property transactions.
- Consider the impact of multijurisdictional tax issues on federal taxes.
- Identify the differences between tax and financial accounting.
- Analyze information and identify data relevant for tax purposes.
- Identify issues, elections, and alternative tax treatments.
- Research issues and alternative tax treatments.
- Formulate conclusions.
- Prepare documentation to support conclusions and tax positions.
- Research relevant professional literature.

The outline below specifies the knowledge in which candidates are required to demonstrate proficiency.

I. Ethics, Professional, and Legal Responsibilities (15%–19%)

A. Ethics and Responsibilities in Tax Practice

1. Treasury Department Circular 230
2. AICPA Statements on Standards for Tax Services
3. Internal Revenue Code of 1986, as amended, and Regulations related to tax return preparers

B. Licensing and Disciplinary Systems

1. Role of state boards of accountancy
2. Requirements of regulatory agencies

C. Legal Duties and Responsibilities

1. Common law duties and liability to clients and third parties
2. Federal statutory liability
3. Privileged communications, confidentiality, and privacy acts

II. Business Law (17%–21%)

A. Agency

1. Formation and termination
2. Authority of agents and principals
3. Duties and liabilities of agents and principals

B. Contracts

1. Formation
2. Performance
3. Third-party assignments
4. Discharge, breach, and remedies

C. Uniform Commercial Code

1. Sales contracts
2. Negotiable instruments
3. Secured transactions
4. Documents of title and title transfer

D. Debtor-Creditor Relationships

1. Rights, duties, and liabilities of debtors, creditors, and guarantors
2. Bankruptcy and insolvency

E. Government Regulation of Business

1. Federal securities regulation

2. Other federal laws and regulations (antitrust, copyright, patents, money-laundering, labor, employment, and ERISA)

F. Business Structure (Selection of a Business Entity)

1. Advantages, disadvantages, implications, and constraints
2. Formation, operation, and termination
3. Financial structure, capitalization, profit and loss allocation, and distributions
4. Rights, duties, legal obligations, and authority of owners and management

III. Federal Tax Process, Procedures, Accounting, and Planning (11%–15%)

A. Federal Tax Legislative Process

B. Federal Tax Procedures

1. Due dates and related extensions of time
2. Internal Revenue Service (IRS) audit and appeals process
3. Judicial process
4. Required disclosure of tax return positions
5. Substantiation requirements
6. Penalties
7. Statute of limitations

C. Accounting Periods

D. Accounting Methods

1. Recognition of revenues and expenses under cash, accrual, or other permitted methods
2. Inventory valuation methods, including uniform capitalization rules
3. Accounting for long-term contracts
4. Installment sales

E. Tax Return Elections, Including Federal Status Elections, Alternative Treatment Elections, or Other Types of Elections Applicable to an Individual or Entity's Tax Return

F. Tax Planning

1. Alternative treatments
2. Projections of tax consequences
3. Implications of different business entities
4. Impact of proposed tax audit adjustments
5. Impact of estimated tax payment rules on planning
6. Role of taxes in decision making

G. Impact of Multijurisdictional Tax Issues on Federal Taxation (Including Consideration of Local, State, and Multinational Tax Issues)

H. Tax Research and Communication

  1. Authoritative hierarchy
  2. Communications with or on behalf of clients

IV. Federal Taxation of Property Transactions (12%–16%)

A. Types of Assets

B. Basis and Holding Periods of Assets

C. Cost Recovery (Depreciation, Depletion, and Amortization)

D. Taxable and Nontaxable Sales and Exchanges

E. Amount and Character of Gains and Losses, and Netting Process

F. Related-Party Transactions

G. Estate and Gift Taxation

  1. Transfers subject to the gift tax
  2. Annual exclusion and gift tax deductions
  3. Determination of taxable estate
  4. Marital deduction
  5. Unified credit

V. Federal Taxation of Individuals (13%–19%)

A. Gross Income

  1. Inclusions and exclusions
  2. Characterization of income

B. Reporting of Items from Pass-Through Entities

C. Adjustments and Deductions to Arrive at Taxable Income

D. Passive Activity Losses

E. Loss Limitations

F. Taxation of Retirement Plan Benefits

G. Filing Status and Exemptions

H. Tax Computations and Credits

I. Alternative Minimum Tax

VI. Federal Taxation of Entities (18%–24%)

A. Similarities and Distinctions in Tax Treatment among Business Entities

  1. Formation
  2. Operation
  3. Distributions
  4. Liquidation

B. Differences between Tax and Financial Accounting

  1. Reconciliation of book income to taxable income
  2. Disclosures under Schedule M-3

C. C Corporations

  1. Determination of taxable income/loss
  2. Tax computations and credits, including alternative minimum tax
  3. Net operating losses
  4. Entity/owner transactions, including contributions and distributions
  5. Earnings and profits
  6. Consolidated returns

D. S Corporations

  1. Eligibility and election
  2. Determination of ordinary income/loss and separately stated items
  3. Basis of shareholder's interest
  4. Entity/owner transactions, including contributions and distributions
  5. Built-in gains tax

E. Partnerships

  1. Determination of ordinary income/loss and separately stated items
  2. Basis of partner's/member's interest and basis of assets contributed to the partnership
  3. Partnership and partner elections
  4. Transactions between a partner and the partnership
  5. Treatment of partnership liabilities
  6. Distribution of partnership assets
  7. Ownership changes and liquidation and termination of partnership

F. Trusts and Estates

  1. Types of trusts
  2. Income and deductions
  3. Determination of beneficiary's share of taxable income

G. Tax-Exempt Organizations

  1. Types of organizations
  2. Obtaining and maintaining tax-exempt status
  3. Unrelated business income

References—Regulation Ethics, Professional and Legal Responsibilities, and Business Law

- AICPA Code of Professional Conduct
- AICPA Statements on Standards for Tax Services
- Revised Model Business Corporation Act
- Revised Uniform Limited Partnership Act
- Revised Uniform Partnership Act
- Securities Act of 1933
- Securities Exchange Act of 1934
- Sarbanes-Oxley Act of 2002
- Uniform Commercial Code
- Current textbooks covering business law, auditing, accounting, and ethics

Federal Taxation

- Internal Revenue Code of 1986, as amended, and Regulations
- Treasury Department Circular 230
- Other administrative pronouncements
- Case law
- AICPA Model Tax Curriculum
- Current Federal tax textbooks

Skill Specification Outlines

The Skill Specification Outlines (SSOs) identify the skills to be tested on the Uniform CPA Examination. There are three categories of skills, and the weightings will be implemented through the use of different question formats in the exam. For each of the question formats, a different set of tools will be available as resources to the candidates, who will need to use those tools to demonstrate proficiency in the applicable skills categories.

Weights

The percentage range assigned to each skill category will be used to determine the quantity of each type of question, as described below. The percentage range assigned to each skill category represents the approximate percentage to which that category of skills will be used in the different sections of the CPA Examination to assess proficiency. The ranges are designed to provide flexibility in building the examination, and the midpoints of the ranges for each section total 100%. No percentages are given for the bulleted descriptions included in these definitions. The presence of several groups within an area or several topics within a group does not imply equal importance or weight will be given to these bullets on an examination.

Skills Category	Weights (FAR, REG, AUD)	Weights (BEC)
Knowledge and Understanding	50%–60%	80%–90%
Application of the Body of Knowledge	40%–50%	–
Written Communication	–	10%–20%

Knowledge and Understanding. Multiple-choice questions will be used as the proxy for assessing knowledge and understanding, and will be based upon the content topics as outlined in the CSOs. Candidates will not have access to the authoritative literature, spreadsheets, or database tools while answering these questions. A calculator will be accessible for the candidates to use in performing calculations to demonstrate their understanding of the principles or subject matter.

Application of the Body of Knowledge. Task-based simulations will be used as the proxy for assessing application of the body of knowledge and will be based upon the content topics as outlined in the CSOs. Candidates will have access to the authoritative literature, a calculator, spreadsheets, and other resources and tools which they will use to demonstrate proficiency in applying the body of knowledge.

Written Communication will be assessed through the use of responses to essay questions, which will be based upon the content topics as outlined in the CSOs. Candidates will have access to a word processor, which includes a spell-check feature.

Outlines

The outlines below provide additional descriptions of the skills that are represented in each category.

Knowledge and Understanding. Expertise and skills developed through learning processes, recall, and reading comprehension. Knowledge is acquired through experience or education and is the theoretical or practical understanding of a subject; knowledge is also represented through awareness or familiarity with information gained by experience of a fact or situation. Understanding represents a higher level than simple knowledge and is the process of using concepts to deal adequately with given situations, facts, or circumstances. Understanding is the ability to recognize and comprehend the meaning of a particular concept.

Application of the Body of Knowledge, including Analysis, Judgment, Synthesis, Evaluation, and Research. Higher-level cognitive skills that require individuals to act or transform knowledge in some fashion. These skills are inextricably intertwined and thus are grouped into this single skill area.

- Assess the Business Environment

  - Business Process Evaluation: Assess and integrate information regarding a business's operational structure, functions, processes, and procedures to develop a broad operational perspective; identify the need for new systems or changes to existing systems and/or processes.
  - Contextual Evaluation: Assess and integrate information regarding client's type of business or industry.
  - Strategic Analysis—Understand the Business: Obtain, assess, and integrate information on the entity's strategic objectives, strategic management process, business environment, the nature of and value to customers, its products and services, extent of competition within its market space, etc.).

- Business Risk Assessment: Obtain, assess, and integrate information on conditions and events that could impede the entity's ability to achieve strategic objectives.
- Visualize Abstract Descriptions: Organize and process symbols, pictures, graphs, objects, and other information.

- Research

  - Identify the appropriate research question.
  - Identify key search terms for use in performing electronic searches through large volumes of data.
  - Search through large volumes of electronic data to find required information.
  - Organize information or data from multiple sources.
  - Integrate diverse sources of information to reach conclusions or make decisions.
  - Identify the appropriate authoritative guidance in applicable financial reporting frameworks and auditing standards for the accounting issue being evaluated.

- Application of Technology

  - Use electronic spreadsheets to perform calculations, financial analysis, or other functions to analyze data.
  - Integrate technological applications and resources into work processes.
  - Use a variety of computer software and hardware systems to structure, utilize, and manage data.

- Analysis

  - Review information to determine compliance with specified standards or criteria.
  - Use expectations, empirical data, and analytical methods to determine trends and variances.
  - Perform appropriate calculations on financial and nonfinancial data.
  - Recognize patterns of activity when reviewing large amounts of data or recognize breaks in patterns.
  - Interpret financial statement data for a given evaluation purpose.
  - Forecast future financial statement data from historical financial statement data and other information.
  - Integrate primary financial statements: using data from all primary financial statements to uncover financial transactions, inconsistencies, or other information.

- Complex Problem Solving and Judgment

  - Develop and understand goals, objectives, and strategies for dealing with potential issues, obstacles, or opportunities.
  - Analyze patterns of information and contextual factors to identify potential problems and their implications.
  - Devise and implement a plan of action appropriate for a given problem.
  - Apply professional skepticism, which is an attitude that includes a questioning mind and a critical assessment of information or evidence obtained.
  - Adapt strategies or planned actions in response to changing circumstances.
  - Identify and solve unstructured problems.
  - Develop reasonable hypotheses to answer a question or resolve a problem.
  - Formulate and examine alternative solutions in terms of their relative strengths and weaknesses, level of risk, and appropriateness for a given situation.
  - Develop creative ways of thinking about situations, problems, and opportunities to create insightful and sound solutions.
  - Develop logical conclusions through the use of inductive and deductive reasoning.
  - Apply knowledge of professional standards and laws, as well as legal, ethical, and regulatory issues.
  - Assess the need for consultations with other professionals when gray areas, or areas requiring specialized knowledge, are encountered.

- Decision Making

  - Specify goals and constraints.
  - Generate alternatives.
  - Consider risks.
  - Evaluate and select the best alternative.

- Organization, Efficiency, and Effectiveness

  - Use time effectively and efficiently.
  - Develop detailed work plans, schedule tasks and meetings, and delegate assignments and tasks.
  - Set priorities by determining the relevant urgency or importance of tasks and deciding the order in which they should be performed.
  - File and store information so that it can be found easily and used effectively.

Written Communication. The various skills involved in preparing written communication, including

- Basic writing mechanics, such as grammar, spelling, word usage, punctuation, and sentence structure.
- Effective business writing principles, including organization, clarity, and conciseness.
- Exchange technical information and ideas with coworkers and other professionals to meet goals of job assignment.
- Documentation

    - Prepare documents and presentations that are concise, accurate, and supportive of the subject matter.
    - Document and cross-reference work performed and conclusions reached in a complete and accurate manner.

- Assist client to recognize and understand implications of critical business issues by providing recommendations and informed opinions.
- Persuade others to take recommended courses of action.
- Follow directions.

RESEARCHING INCOME TAX ISSUES[1]

Research components of Regulation section will involve a research database that includes the Internal Revenue Code (IRC) or the Statements of Standards for Tax Services (TS).

The Internal Revenue Code of 1986, as Amended (commonly called IRC, or simple the Code) is the most important source of federal income tax law. The IRC is actually Title 26 of the United States Code. The US Code is the complete set of laws passed by Congress. All laws dealing with one topic are consolidated under one title of the US Code. For example, Title 10 of the US Code contains all of the military laws of the United States.

Any changes when Congress passes a new tax law are integrated in the Code. The Code has been amended almost every year since it was reformed in 1986. Prior to that, the Code was reorganized in 1954, and from then until 1986, it was known as the Internal Revenue Code of 1954, as Amended. Before the IRC of 1954, the tax law was contained in the Internal Revenue Code of 1939, the first IRC. Before 1939, the tax law was an unorganized series of tax acts.

Code Organization

There are many different subdivision to the Code, each with a different purpose and name. The Code is divided into subtitles, chapters, parts, subparts, and sections. Some common subtitles of the Code are

Subtitle A	Income Taxes
Subtitle B	Estate and Gift Taxes
Subtitle C	Employment Taxes
Subtitle D	Miscellaneous Excise Taxes
Subtitle E	Alcohol, Tobacco, and Certain Excise Taxes
Subtitle F	Procedures and Administration

Each Subtitle is divided into chapters. The chapters contained in Subtitle A are

Chapter 1	Normal and Surtaxes
Chapter 2	Tax on Self-Employment Income
Chapter 3	Withholding Tax and Nonresident Aliens and Foreign Corporations
Chapter 4	[Repealed]
Chapter 5	Tax on Transfers to Avoid Income Tax
Chapter 6	Consolidated Returns

The chapters are again subdivided into numerous subchapters. Some of the notable subchapters of Chapter 1 are

Subchapter A	Determination of Tax Liability
Subchapter B	Computation of Taxable Income
Subchapter C	Corporate Distributions and Adjustments
Subchapter E	Accounting Periods and Methods
Subchapter I	Natural Resources
Subchapter K	Partners and Partnerships
Subchapter N	International Taxation
Subchapter S	Tax Treatment of S Corporations

Each subchapter may be further divided into parts and subparts, as needed.

The smallest unique part of the Code is the section. The section is normally the basic reference when citing a provision of the Internal Revenue Code. In day-to-day tax practice, reference to larger divisions of the Code such as subtitles and chapters is generally disregarded. Currently, the sections in the Code are numbered from 1 to over 9,000, albeit many

---

[1] This section was prepared by Gerald E. Whittenburg, Ph.D., CPA. For more information about tax research refer to West's *Federal Tax Research*, 6th Edition (Thomas South-Western)

numbers are skipped to allow for future expansion of the tax law. Each Code section may be further subdivided into subsections, paragraphs, subparagraphs, and clauses. As an example, the following Code section reference is to the definition of the term medical for purposes of the medical care deduction:

Citation: Section 213(d)(1)(A), where

213 is the Section Number
(d) is the Subdivision
(1) is the Paragraph
(A) is the Subparagraph

The tax practitioner can be assured that there is only one Section 213 in the Code and that this is a specific tax reference that cannot be confused with any other provision of the Code.

Database Searching

Searching a database consists of the following five steps:

1. Define the issue. What is the research question to be answered?
2. Select the database to search (e.g., the IRC).
3. Choose a keyword or table of contents search.
4. Execute the search. Enter the keyword(s) or click on the appropriate table of contents item and complete the search.
5. Evaluate the results. Evaluate the research to see if an answer has been found. If not, try a new search.

EXAMPLE

Bill and Betty support their 18-year old daughter and her husband who live with and are supported by them. Both the daughter and her husband are full-time students at a local community college and have no income. Bill and Betty would like to know if their daughter's husband qualifies as a dependent on their tax return. The research database search would be as follows:

1. Define the issue. Does a daughter's husband qualify as a relative for dependant purposes?
2. Select the database to search. Internal Revenue Code.
3. Choose appropriate keywords. "Son-in-law," or "dependent."
4. Execute the search. A search should find Section 152(a)(8).
5. Evaluate the results. A son-in-law is a qualified relative.

Advanced Searches

On the Regulation exam you can also perform advanced searches, including

1. Searching for citations that contain two or more keywords.
2. Searching for citations that contain either or both keywords.
3. Searching for citations that contain the first set of keyword(s) but not the second.
4. Searching for citations that contain an exact phrase.
5. Searching for citations that contain words near each other.

The advanced search also allows you to select options for the search. One alternative allows you to retrieve alternative word terms. For example, using this approach with a search on the word "cost" would also retrieve sections containing the word "costing." A synonyms option allows you to retrieve sections that contain words that mean the same as the specified word. You also have the option to search only on the selected sections of the literature.

PROFESSIONAL RESPONSIBILITIES AND BUSINESS LAW

As indicated previously, this section consists of 11 modules designed to facilitate your study for the Professional Responsibilities and Business Law portion of the Regulation section of the Uniform CPA Examination. The table of contents at the right describes the content of each module.

The professional responsibilities and business law portion of the Regulation exam tests the candidate's

1. Ability to recognize legal problems
2. Knowledge of legal principles with respect to the topics listed above
3. Ability to apply the legal principles to the problem situation in order to derive the textbook solution

According to the content specification outline for the Regulation exam, professional responsibilities and business law will constitute about 36% of the exam. Of the 36% about 17% will cover ethics and professional and legal responsibilities, and about 19% will cover business law topics. Refer to "Self-Study Program" in Chapter 1 for detailed suggestions on how to study these topics, outlines, and questions. The basic procedure for each of the twelve professional responsibilities and business law modules is

1. Work 1/4 of the multiple-choice questions to indicate your proficiency and familiarity with the type and difficulty of questions.
2. Study the outlines in this volume.
3. Work the remaining multiple-choice questions. Study the answer explanations of those you missed or had trouble with.
4. Work the simulation problems.

It is important to note that it is very unlikely that the Regulation exam will have simulations on the topics of professional responsibilities and business law. The AICPA has indicated that all simulations will include a research component and the research database on the Regulation exam is a income tax database. Therefore, you should assume that the simulations will relate to taxation topics.

Sources of the Law

Law comes from both statutes and common law. Common law has evolved through court decisions. Decisions of higher courts are binding on lower courts in the same jurisdiction. Statutory law has priority over common law; therefore, common law applies when no statute covers the issue in question. Court cases can also be used to interpret the meaning of statutes.

Some of the law tested on the CPA exam comes from federal statutory law. Examples of this are the Security Act of 1933, the Securities Exchange Act of 1934, and the Sarbanes-Oxley Act of 2002. Other law affected heavily by federal statutes includes bankruptcy law, a good portion of employment law, and parts of accountants' legal liability as provided in the securities laws. The AICPA uses the guideline that federal laws are tested six months following their effective date.

Most of business law is regulated by the individual states and therefore may differ from state to state. However, several uniform laws have been adopted by many states. One example is the Uniform Commercial Code (UCC) which has been adopted by all states (sometimes with changes) except Louisiana, and also is the law in the District of Columbia. This uniform law and others are not federal laws but are laws that each jurisdiction may choose to adopt by statute. Often these uniform laws are amended. For example, the UCC has been amended a few times. The AICPA has published the guideline that the "uniform acts [are tested] one year after their adoption by a simple majority of jurisdictions." This is also interpreted to mean that as these uniform laws are amended, the amended version is tested one year after a simple majority of jurisdictions have adopted it.

When the states have not adopted uniform laws, general rules of law can still be stated by examining how the majority of states settle an area of law either with their own common law or their own statutes. These are called the majority rule when it can be shown that a majority of jurisdictions have settled the legal issue the same way. The CPA exam generally tests the majority rules; however, it tests some minority rules that are considered very significant. For example, the CPA exam has tested in the accountants' legal liability area, both the majority rule and a minority rule known as the Ultramares decision, as discussed in Module 23. The AICPA has generally not published guidelines on when such minority rules are tested or when new majority rules would be tested.

Module 23: Professional and Legal Responsibilities

Overview

This module covers the general standards of care and ethics that must be followed by CPAs. CPAs are authorized to practice by the various state boards of accountancy. They must follow the rules of these bodies which generally follow the AICPA *Code of Professional Conduct*. The AICPA and the state societies cooperate on enforcing the ethics of the profession.

Accountants' civil liability arises primarily from contract law, the law of negligence, fraud, the Securities Act of 1933, and the Securities Exchange Act of 1934. The first three are common law and largely judge-made law, whereas the latter two are federal statutory law.

The agreement between an accountant and his/her client is generally set out in a carefully drafted engagement letter. Additionally, the accountant has a duty to conduct his/her work with the same reasonable care as an average accountant. This duty defines the standard used in a negligence case. It is important to understand

1. When an accountant can be liable to his/her client.
2. When an accountant can be liable to third parties.
3. That an accountant is liable to the client and to all third parties that relied on the financial statements when the accountant committed fraud, constructive fraud, or was grossly negligent; furthermore in these cases, the accountant can be assessed punitive damages.
4. The extent of liability under the Securities Act of 1933 and the Securities Exchange Act of 1934 as well as how they differ from each other and from common law.

The CPA examination also tests the dual nature of the ownership of the accountant's working papers. Although the accountant owns the working papers and retains them as evidence of his/her work, confidentiality must be maintained. Therefore, the CPA cannot allow this information to reach another without the client's consent. In general, privileged communications between a CPA and the client are not sanctioned under federal statutory law or common law, but the privilege is in existence in states that have passed statutes granting such a right.

CPAs also have specific rules and regulations that affect their practice as tax preparers which are covered in this module. Before beginning the reading you should review the key terms at the end of the module.

A. Regulation of the Profession

Permits to practice as a CPA are granted by the boards of accountancy in the various states and other jurisdictions. These boards also regulate the profession and may suspend or revoke a CPA's certificate. While all boards require successful completion of the CPA examination, the requirements for education and experience vary.

1. To audit issuers (public companies) the CPA in charge of the engagement must have a permit to practice issued by a state board of accountancy. In addition, that individual's firm must be registered with the appropriate state board of accountancy, and the Public Company Accounting Oversight Board (PCAOB).

2. State boards have their own codes of professional ethics. However, they generally follow the AICPA *Code of Professional Conduct*. Therefore, violation of an AICPA rule also generally involves violation of a state board rule.
3. AICPA *Code of Professional Conduct* is applicable to all AICPA members, not merely those in public practice.
4. The Code provides minimum levels of acceptable conduct relating to all services performed by CPAs, unless wording of a standard specifically excludes some members.

B. Disciplinary Systems of the Profession and Regulatory Bodies

1. The AICPA *Code of Professional Conduct* is interpreted and enforced by the Professional Ethics Executive Committee (PEEC), a senior technical committee of the AICPA.
2. State accountancy boards ethics rules are enforced by the various state boards of accountancy.
3. If CPAs are members they must also adhere to the ethics requirements of their state societies of CPAs. The codes of ethics of these bodies are also very similar to the AICPA Code of Professional Conduct. Virtually all state societies have agreements with AICPA to allow joint enforcement of ethics complaints through the Joint Ethics Enforcement Program (JEEP). This means there is a single investigation and, if warranted, a single settlement agreement or joint trial board hearing.

   a. Enforcement of rules regarding competitive bidding is excluded from the JEEP process.

4. Joint trial board may discipline CPAs—possible results include

   a. No violation/dismissal
   b. Admonishment (publication of the admonishment is mandatory)
   c. Corrective action required (e.g., additional continuing professional education)
   d. Suspension for up to two years
   e. Expulsion from AICPA

      (1) The CPA may still practice public accounting using valid license issued by a state

         (a) Violation of state board code, however, can result in revocation of CPA certificate and loss of ability to practice public accounting. State board codes generally mirror the AICPA *Code of Professional Conduct*.

      (2) Any member who departs from rulings or interpretations has burden justifying it in any disciplinary proceedings.
      (3) A member of the AICPA may be expelled or suspended without hearing for any of the following:

         (a) The member's CPA certificate or license or permit to practice is revoked by state as a disciplinary measure.
         (b) The member is convicted of a crime punishable by imprisonment for more than one year.
         (c) The member files or aids in filing a fraudulent tax return for client or self.
         (d) The member intentionally fails to file his or her required tax return.

      (4) AICPA Professional Ethics Division may investigate ethics violations and may sanction those that are less serious using less severe remedies.
      (5) In addition, court decisions have consistently held that even if an individual is not a member of AICPA, that individual is still expected to follow profession's *Code of Professional Conduct*.

5. Securities Exchange Commission actions against accountants.

   a. After a hearing, the SEC can revoke or suspend an accountant from practicing before the SEC if the accountant willfully violated federal securities laws or regulations, or has acted unethically or unprofessionally. If a CPA is suspended from practicing before the SEC, he or she cannot serve as auditor for issuer (public company).
   b. The SEC can revoke or suspend an accountant from practicing before the SEC upon conviction of felony or misdemeanor in which moral turpitude was involved.
   c. The SEC can penalize accountants with civil fines and mandates to pay profits gained from violations of securities laws and regulations.

6. Disciplinary actions against CPA firms.

   a. A state board of accountancy has the power to bar a CPA firm from practicing in the state.
   b. The SEC can prohibit an accountant or an accounting firm from doing work for an issuer (public company).
   c. The PCAOB investigates and sanctions registered firms for violations of standards of performance. Firms must be registered with the PCAOB to perform audits or reviews of the financial statements of issuer (public company) clients.

(1) Registered CPA firms must have inspections by the PCAOB staff.

   (a) Firms with more than 100 publicly traded clients (issuers) must be inspected each year.
   (b) Firms with 100 or less publicly traded clients must be inspected every three years.

(2) When investigations lead to alleged violations a hearing will be held by the PCAOB.
(3) The PCAOB hearing may result in sanctions being imposed on the firm or the individuals involved, including suspension or revocation of a firm's registration, suspension or bar of an individual from associating with a registered public accounting firm, or civil monetary penalties.
(4) The PCAOB may also impose other remedial measures, such as

   (a) Improvements in the firm's quality control or training.
   (b) Independent monitoring of the audit work of a firm or individual within a firm.

> **NOW REVIEW MULTIPLE-CHOICE QUESTIONS 1 THROUGH 4 IN VOLUME 2**

C. Accountant's Legal Liabilities

1. Common Law Liability to Clients

Common law is law that has historically been derived from court interpretations of what is fair and equitable. Most of common law has now been codified in state statutes. CPAs have responsibilities to their clients that are codified in common law.

  a. Liability to clients for breach of contract

    (1) The relationship between the client and the CPA is that of an employer and an independent contractor. A CPA may be held liable to a client if the accountant fails to perform substantially as agreed under contract (the engagement letter).

      (a) Duties under contract may be

        1] Implied—The accountant owes duty in contract to perform in nonnegligent manner.
        2] Express—The accountant owes duty to perform under terms of the contract.

          a] This duty can extend liability beyond that which is standard under a normal audit.
          b] Typically, the terms are expressed in engagement letter that should specify clearly and in writing the following:

            i] The nature and scope of engagement to avoid misunderstandings between the CPA and client.
            ii] The procedures and tests to be used.
            iii] That the engagement will not necessarily uncover fraud, defalcations, errors, or illegal actions, unless the CPA agrees to greater responsibility.
            iv] Engagement letter should be signed by at least the client (accountant will typically sign also) but oral contract for audit still enforceable without engagement letter.

      (b) An accountant (CPA) is said to be in privity of contract with client when contract exists between them.

        1] The reverse is also true (i.e., client is in privity of contract with CPA).

      (c) An accountant is not an insurer of financial statements and thus does not guarantee against losses from error or fraud.

        1] A "normal" financial statement audit is not intended to uncover fraud, shortages, or defalcations, in general but is meant to provide audit evidence needed to express opinion on fairness of financial statements. The audit is designed to provide reasonable assurance of detecting material errors and fraud.

      (d) An accountant is not normally liable for failure to detect fraud, etc. **unless**

        1] "Normal" audit or review would have detected it
        2] The accountant by agreement has undertaken greater responsibility such as a fraud audit
        3] The wording of audit report indicates greater responsibility

> **EXAMPLE**
>
> A CPA has been hired by a client to perform an audit. A standard engagement letter is used. During the course of the audit, the CPA fails to uncover a clever embezzlement scheme by one of the client's employees. The CPA is not liable for the losses unless a typical, reasonable audit should have resulted in discovery of the scheme.

    (e) In an audit or review of financial statements, the accountant is under duty to investigate when he or she discovers or becomes aware of suspicious items.

        1] The investigation should extend beyond management's explanations.

  (2) The client should not interfere or prevent accountant from performing.

> **EXAMPLE**
>
> A CPA firm issues its opinion a few days late because of its client's failure to supply needed information. The CPA firm is entitled to the full fee agreed upon under the contract (engagement).

  (3) When a breach of contract occurs

    (a) The accountant is not entitled to compensation if breach is major.

> **EXAMPLE**
>
> Miller failed to complete the audit by the agreed date. If time is of the essence so that the client receives no benefit from the audit, Miller is not entitled to compensation.

    (b) The accountant is entitled to compensation if there are only minor errors but the client may deduct from fees paid any damages caused by breach.

    (c) The client may recover any damages caused by breach even if accountant is not entitled to fee.

    (d) In general, punitive damages are not awarded for breach of contract.

 b. Liability to clients based on negligence

  (1) Elements needed to prove negligence against accountant

    (a) The accountant has a duty to perform with same degree of skill and judgment possessed by average (reasonable) accountant.

        1] This is the standard used in cases involving ordinary negligence (or simply called negligence).

        2] Different phrases are used for this standard, including duty to exercise due care, duty of skill of an average, reasonable accountant (or CPA), duty to act as an average (or reasonable) accountant (or CPA) would under the circumstances, or duty of judgment of an ordinary, prudent accountant (or CPA).

        3] Standard for accountants is guided by

           a] State and federal statutes

           b] Court decisions

           c] Contract with client

           d] GAAS and GAAP (persuasive but not conclusive)

              i] Failure to follow GAAS virtually establishes lack of due care but reverse not true (i.e., following GAAS does not automatically preclude negligence but is strong evidence for presence of due care)

           e] Customs of the profession (persuasive but not conclusive)

> **EXAMPLE**
>
> Will, a CPA, issued an unqualified opinion on the financial statements of X Company. Included in the assets was inventory stated at cost when the market was materially below cost. This violation of GAAP can be used to establish that Will was negligent. Also, the client can sue under contract law because Will has an implied duty in the contract to not be negligent.

> A CPA, while performing the annual audit, detects material errors in the previously issued audit report. The CPA has a duty to correct these material errors.
>
> A CPA failing to warn a client of known internal control deficiency is falling below this standard.

  (b) The accountant breached duty owed of average reasonable accountant.
  (c) Damages or losses resulted from the breach.

    1] Damages are limited to actual losses that use of reasonable care would have avoided.
    2] Punitive damages are not normally allowed for ordinary negligence.
    3] Contributory negligence may be a complete defense by CPA in many states if client's own negligence substantially contributed to the accountant's failure to perform audit adequately.

> **EXAMPLE**
>
> A CPA failed to detect a material fraud in an audit of the client's financial statements. However the CPA had communicated to the client for a number of years a significant deficiency in internal control that allowed the fraud to occur. The client ignored the recommendations and failed to correct the deficiency in internal control. The client's contributory negligence may in some states prevent the client from recovering losses from the CPA for negligence. In other states it will reduce the liability of the CPA.

  (d) A causal relationship must exist between fault of accountant and damages of plaintiff and the cause must be proximate (i.e., foreseeable).

> **EXAMPLE**
>
> A CPA negligently fails to discover during an audit that several expensive watches are missing from the client's inventory. Subsequently, an employee is caught stealing some watches. He confesses to stealing several before the audit and more after the audit when he found out he did not get caught. Only 5 of the watches can be recovered from the employee, who is unable to pay for those stolen. The CPA may be liable for those losses sustained after the audit if discovery could have prevented them. However, the CPA normally would not be liable for the watches taken before the audit when the loss is not the proximate result of the negligent audit. But if there were watches that could have been recovered at the time of the audit but can't be now, the CPA could be liable for those watches even though they were taken before the audit.

  c. The accountant's liability is not based solely on honest errors of judgment; liability requires at least negligence under common law.
  d. Liability to client for fraud, gross negligence, or constructive fraud

    (1) Common law fraud of accountant is established by the following elements:

      (a) Misrepresentation of material fact or accountant's expert opinion
      (b) Scienter, shown by either

        1] Intent to mislead with accountant's knowledge of falsity, or
        2] Reckless disregard of the truth.

      (c) Reasonable or justifiable reliance by injured party
      (d) Actual damages

    (2) Called constructive fraud or gross negligence if when proving above four elements, reckless disregard of the truth is established instead of knowledge of falsity.

> **EXAMPLE**
>
> During the course of an audit, a CPA fails to verify the existence of the company's investments which amounted to a substantial portion of the assets. Many of these, it is subsequently found, were nonexistent. Even in the absence of intent to defraud, the CPA is liable for constructive fraud based on reckless disregard of the truth.
>
> Care and Less Co., CPAs, uncover suspicious items during the course of their audit of Blue Co. Because their audit steps did not require the additional steps needed to check into these suspicious items, the CPAs failed to uncover material errors. Even if a typical audit would not have required these additional audit steps, the CPAs are liable for the damages that result because they have a duty to look into such circumstances when they come to their attention.

(3) Contributory negligence of client is not a defense available for accountant in cases of fraud, constructive fraud, or gross negligence.
(4) Privity of contract is not required for plaintiff to prove fraud, constructive fraud, or gross negligence.
(5) Punitive damages may be added to actual damages for fraud, constructive fraud, or gross negligence.

NOW REVIEW MULTIPLE-CHOICE QUESTIONS 5 THROUGH 15 IN VOLUME 2

2. Common Law Liability to Third Parties (Nonclients)

a. Privity of contract.

(1) In typical accountant-client relationship, there usually is no privity of contract between the accountant and third parties who rely on the financial statements. However, in some cases the client is not the company being audited.

> **EXAMPLE**
>
> Dudley Company is considering acquiring Tyler Company. Dudley engages Wilson, CPA to audit Tyler to obtain assurance that Tyler's financial statements are not materially misstated. Dudley is the client because it engaged Wilson. Accordingly, Dudley would be able to hold Wilson liable for breach of contract or ordinary negligence.

(2) Traditionally, accountants could use the defense of no privity against suing third parties in contract and negligence cases.

(a) Ultramares decision is leading case in which the accountants were held liable for ordinary negligence only to parties who primarily benefit from the audit or the audited financial statement.

> **EXAMPLE**
>
> First Bank requested Goodman Company to obtain an audit to receive a needed loan. Adam, CPA audited the financial statements of Goodman knowing that the Goodman was obtaining the audit to satisfy the request of First Bank. In this case, First Bank would be considered a primary beneficiary of the audit and, therefore, First Bank would have the same rights as the client under common law.

1] This generally means only the client or third-party beneficiaries since these are in privity of contract with accountant.
2] However, a third party who can prove fraud or constructive fraud (gross negligence) may recover from the accountant.

(b) This is a significant **minority** rule today.

b. More recently, many courts have expanded liability to other some third parties. The following distinctions should be understood:

(1) Foreseen party—A third party who the accountant knew would rely on financial statements, or member of limited class that accountant knew would rely on financial statements, for specified transaction.

(a) The **majority rule** is that the accountant is liable to foreseen third parties for ordinary negligence.

1] The rationale for not allowing liability to more third parties is that accountants should not be exposed to liability in indeterminate amount to indeterminate class.

> **EXAMPLE**
>
> A CPA agrees to perform an audit for ABC Client knowing that the financial statements will be used to obtain a loan from XYZ Bank. Relying on the financial statements, XYZ Bank loans ABC $100,000. ABC goes bankrupt. If XYZ can establish that the financial statements were not fairly stated, thus causing the bank to give the loan, and if negligence can be established, most courts will allow XYZ Bank to recover from the CPA.
>
> Assume the same facts as in the example above except that XYZ Bank was not specified. Since the CPA knew that some bank would rely on these financial statements, the actual bank is a foreseen party since it is a member of a limited class and most courts will allow for liability.

(b) The accountant is liable for fraud, constructive fraud, or gross negligence to all parties whether foreseen or not.

(2) Distinguish foreseen party and foreseeable party

(a) Foreseeable party—Any party that accountant could reasonably foresee would receive financial statements and use them.

1] The **majority rule** is that accountant **not** liable to foreseeable parties for negligence.

> **EXAMPLE**
>
> A CPA is informed that financial statements after being audited will be used to obtain a loan from a bank. The audited financial statements are also shown to trade creditors and potential investors. The bank is a foreseen third party but these other third parties are not actually foreseen parties and generally cannot recover from the CPA for ordinary negligence. They may qualify as foreseeable third parties since creditors or investors are the types of parties whom an accountant should reasonably foresee as users of the audited financial statements.

2] Some courts now hold that accountant is liable for negligence to parties that are merely foreseeable.

c. To be awarded damages against the accountant a third party must prove

(1) Losses (damages),
(2) Negligence (either ordinary or gross negligence depending on the type of party and nature of state law) by the CPA,
(3) Proximate cause (i.e., reliance on the work of the CPA caused the losses).

d. Concepts of liability

(1) In many cases in which third-parties sue the accountant, the accountant is not the only party at fault. Typically, management of the company is also responsible for the losses of third parties. It is common that both the accountant and management are named as defendants in these cases. If the defendants lose the case, state courts vary in how the obligation to pay damages is allocated.

(a) **Joint liability.** In a state that applies joint liability, both the accountant and management are liable up to the full amount of the obligation. If management has no funds, the entire amount may be collected from the accountant

(b) **Several liability.** In a state that applies several (proportionate liability), the accountant and management are only obligated to pay their respective share of the damages based on the degree of responsibility for the losses.

> **EXAMPLE**
>
> First bank extended a line of credit in the amount of $1,000,000 to Carey Corporation in reliance on financial statements audited by Gordon, CPA. The financial statements were materially misstated by management, and Gordon did not detect the misstatement. Assume that First Bank prevailed in a lawsuit against management and Gordon. Management was found to be 60% responsible and Gordon was found to be 40% responsible for First Bank's losses of $1,000,000. In a state that applies the concept of several liability, management would be obligated to pay $600,000 (60% x $1,000,000) and Gordon would be obligated to pay $400,000 (40% x $1,000,000). Gordon would not be obligated to pay more even if management had no ability to pay its obligation.

(c) **Joint and several liability.** . In a state that applies joint and several liability, each of the parties are responsible for the full amount of the obligation but may seek to get reimbursement from the other parties. Most state courts apply joint and several liability.

> **EXAMPLE**
>
> If the state in the previous example applies the concept of joint and several liability, First Bank could seek to collect the entire $1,000,000 from Gordon. Gordon would then have to pursue management for its $600,000 share.

| NOW REVIEW MULTIPLE-CHOICE QUESTIONS 16 THROUGH 21 IN VOLUME 2 |

3. Statutory Liability to Third Parties—Securities Act of 1933

    a. General information on the Securities Act of 1933

        (1) Covers regulation of initial sales of securities registered under 1933 Act

            (a) Requires registration of initial issuances of securities with SEC and makes it unlawful for registration statement to contain untrue **material** fact or to omit **material** fact.

                1] Material fact—One about which average prudent investor should be informed.
                2] Most potential accountant liability occurs because registration statement (and prospectus) includes audited financial statements.
                3] Accountant's legal liability arises for untrue material fact or omission of material fact in registration statement (or prospectus).
                4] Securities Act of 1933 does not include periodic reports to SEC or annual reports to stockholders (these are in the 1934 Act below).

    b. Parties that may sue

        (1) Any purchaser of registered securities

            (a) Plaintiff need not be initial purchaser of security.
            (b) Purchaser generally must prove that specific security was offered for sale through registration statement.

                1] Exchange and issuance of stock based on a merger counts as a sale.

        (2) Third parties can sue without having privity of contract with accountant under Federal Securities Acts.

    c. Liability under Section 11 of the 1933 Act.

        (1) This imposes liability on auditors (and other experts) for misstatements or omissions of material fact in certified financial statements or other information provided in registration statements. The registration statement is the document that is used to sell the securities and, in general, includes

            (a) A description of the company's properties and business
            (b) A description of the security to be offered for sale
            (c) Information about the management of the company
            (d) Financial statements certified by independent accountants

        (2) To be awarded damages against the accountant, the plaintiff (purchaser of the securities) must prove

            (a) Damages were incurred.
            (b) There was material misstatement or omission in financial statements or included in registration statement.
            (c) If these two facts are proven, it is sufficient to win against the CPA and shifts burden of proof to the CPA accountant who may escape liability by proving one of the following defenses:

                1] "Due diligence," that is, after reasonable investigation, the accountant had reasonable grounds to believe and did believe that statements were not materially misstated.

                NOTE: Although the basis of liability is not negligence, an accountant who was at least negligent will probably not be able to establish "due diligence."

                2] Plaintiff knew financial statements were incorrect when investment was made.
                3] Lack of causation—loss was due to factors other than the misstatement or omission in the financial statements.
                4] Following generally accepted auditing standards is generally valid as a defense for CPA.

            (d) The plaintiff **need not** prove reliance on financial statements unless security was purchased at least twelve months after effective date of registration statement.
            (e) The plaintiff **need not** prove negligence or fraud.

d. Damages

(1) The difference between amount paid and market value at time of suit.
(2) If sold, difference between amount paid and sale price.
(3) Damages cannot exceed price at which security was offered to public.
(4) The plaintiff cannot recover decrease in value after suit is brought and the accountant is given the benefit of any increase in market value during the suit.

e. Statute of limitations

(1) Action must be brought against accountant within one year from discovery (or when discovery should have been made) of false statement or omission in financial statements.
(2) Or if earlier, action must be brought within three years after security offered to public.

f. This liability can arise from negligence in reviewing events subsequent to date of certified balance sheet. The CPA firm is responsible for reviewing for material events that occur up until the effective date of the registration statement.

(1) This is referred to as S-1 review when made for registration statement under securities regulations.

EXAMPLE

An accountant performed an audit and later performed an S-1 review to review events subsequent to the balance sheet date. The accountant did not detect certain material events during this S-1 review even though there was sufficient evidence to make the accountant suspicious. Further investigation was required to avoid liability.

NOW REVIEW MULTIPLE-CHOICE QUESTIONS 22 THROUGH 29 IN VOLUME 2

4. Statutory Liability to Third Parties—Securities Exchange Act of 1934

a. The Securities Exchange Act of 1934 regulates securities sold on national stock exchanges.

(1) Includes securities traded over-the-counter and other equity securities where the corporation has more than $10 million in total assets and the security is held by 500 or more persons at the end of a fiscal year.
(2) Requires each company to furnish to SEC an annual report (Form 10-K) which includes financial statements (not necessarily the same as an annual report to shareholders) to be audited in accordance with PCAOB standards by a registered firm. It also requires the company to file quarterly reports (Form 10-Qs) which include quarterly financial statements reviewed by a registered firm.
(3) Accountant civil liability comes from two sections—10 and 18.

(a) Section 10 (including Rule 10b-5)—makes it unlawful to

1] Employ any device, scheme, or artifice to defraud.
2] Make untrue statement of material fact or omit material fact.
3] Engage in act, practice, or course of business to commit fraud or deceit in connection with purchase or sale of security.

(b) Section 18—makes it unlawful to make false or misleading statement with respect to a material statement unless done in "good faith."

b. Purchasers **and** sellers of registered securities may sue under these sections. Note that under the 1933 Act only purchasers may sue.

c. Proof requirements—Section 10, including Rule 10b-5

(1) The plaintiff (purchaser or seller) must prove damages resulted in connection with purchase or sale of a registered security in interstate commerce.
(2) The plaintiff must prove there was a material misstatement or omission in information released by the issuer (public company).

(a) Information may, for example, be in the form of audited financial statements in report to stockholders or in Form 10-K.

(3) The plaintiff must prove justifiable reliance on financial information.
(4) The plaintiff must prove existence of **scienter** (the intent to deceive, manipulate, or defraud).

      (a) Includes reckless disregard of truth or knowledge of falsity.

      (b) Negligence alone will not subject accountant to liability under this section but lack of good faith will.

    (5) Note that these proof requirements differ in very significant ways from proof requirements under the 1933 Act.

    (6) The plaintiff cannot recover if he or she is reckless or fraudulent.

  d. Proof requirements—Section 18

    (1) The plaintiff (purchaser or seller) must prove

      (a) That damages were incurred.

      (b) There was a material misstatement or omission on report (usually Form 10-K) filed with SEC.

      (c) The plaintiff read and relied on defective report.

    (2) Then the burden of proof is shifted to the accountant who may escape liability by proving s/he acted in "good faith."

      (a) Although basis of liability here is not negligence, an accountant who has been grossly negligent typically will not be able to establish "good faith."

      (b) An accountant who has been only negligent will probably be able to establish "good faith."

  e. Damages

    (1) Generally, damages are calculated as the difference between amount paid by the plaintiff and market value at time of suit.

    (2) If sold, damages are calculated as the difference between amount paid and sale price.

5. Summary of auditors' defenses under Securities Act of 1933 and Securities Exchange Act of 1934*

- **Defenses** available to auditors:

	1934 Act	1933 Act
1. Audit was performed with **due care**	Yes	Yes
2. Misstatement was immaterial	Yes	Yes
3. Plaintiff had prior knowledge of misstatement	Yes	Yes
4. Plaintiff did not rely on information	Yes	No
5. Misstatement was not cause of loss	Yes	Yes

- Due diligence is a defense for the 1933 Act **only** (Do not use for liability under the 1934 Act)

    * Prepared by Debra R. Hopkins, Northern Illinois University

---

NOW REVIEW MULTIPLE-CHOICE QUESTION 30 THROUGH 33 IN VOLUME 2

D. Legal Considerations Affecting the Accountant's Responsibility

1. Accountant's working papers

  a. Consist of evidence, notes, computations, etc. that accountant accumulates when doing professional work for client.

  b. Working papers are owned by accountant unless there is agreement to the contrary.

  c. Ownership is essentially custodial in nature and it serves two purposes:

    (1) To preserve confidentiality of client information. Without client consent, an accountant cannot allow transmission of information in working papers to another party. However, an accountant must produce working papers upon being given an enforceable subpoena, or if agreeing to provide access to working papers to a government agency is part of the agreement with the client.

      (a) Subpoenas should be limited in scope and for a specific purpose.

      (b) The accountant may challenge a subpoena as being too broad and unreasonably burdensome.

2. Privileged communications between accountant and client generally is not provided by state or federal laws.

  a. Only a few states have enacted laws providing for privileged communications.

  b. Federal law does not recognize privileged communications.

  c. If the accountant is acting as agent for (hired by) an individual who has privileged communication such as an attorney, then accountant's communications are privileged.

  d. To be considered privileged, an accountant-client communication must

(1) Be located in a jurisdiction where privileged communication is recognized.
(2) Have been intended to be confidential at time of communication.
(3) Not have privilege waived by the client.

e. If considered privileged, valid grounds exist for the accountant to refuse to testify in court concerning these matters.

(1) This privilege is, in general, for benefit of client.
(2) Can be waived by client.
(3) If part of the privileged communication is allowed, all of privilege is lost.

f. ACIPA *Code of Professional Conduct* prohibits disclosure of confidential client data unless

(1) The client consents. If the client is a partnership, each partner is actually a client and therefore must give consent.
(2) To comply with GAAS and GAAP.
(3) To comply with enforceable subpoena (e.g., courts where privilege is not recognized).
(4) Disclosure is made in conjunction with a quality (peer) review of the CPA firm's practice.
(5) The AICPA is responding an investigation by the AICPA ethics division or trial board.

g. An interpretation of the *Code of Professional Conduct* allows a CPA to provide confidential client information to a third-party service provider (e.g., a tax return preparation provider) without the client's permission. However, the CPA must enter into a contractual agreement with the service provider to maintain the confidentiality of the information and be reasonably assured that the third-party service provider has appropriate procedures in place to prevent the unauthorized release of confidential information to others.

h. US Supreme Court has held that tax accrual files are not protected by accountant-client privilege.

3. Accountants also should be familiar with privacy laws that may affect their practice. Privacy is defined as "the rights and obligations of individuals and organizations with respect to the collection, use, retention, and disclosure of personal information."

a. Accountants that prepare individual tax returns or provide nonbusiness tax or financial advice must be familiar with the provisions of the Gramm-Leach Blilcy (Financial Modernization) Act of 1999.

(1) Accountants are prohibited from disclosing to a nonaffiliated third party any nonpublic personal information about their clients.
(2) Related FTC regulations require accountants to develop, implement, and maintain a comprehensive information security program that outlines the ways in which they protect client information.
(3) Accountants are responsible for maintaining the confidentiality of information that is outsourced for processing (e.g., outsourced tax return preparation to a firm in a foreign country).

b. The Internal Revenue Code prohibits tax preparers from "knowingly" or "recklessly" disclosing or using tax-related information other than in connection with the preparation of the return. Treasury Department regulations allow information to be used for certain other purposes but only if a consent is obtained from the individual.

4. Illegal acts by clients

a. Situations in which there may be a duty to notify parties outside the client

(1) Form 8-K disclosures. When a change is auditor is reported by a Form 8-K (as required by securities laws), the client must disclose the reason for the change and the auditor must agree with the reason stated by the client or indicate how the auditor disagrees.
(2) Disclosure to successor auditor. Upon a change in auditor, the predecessor auditor must accurately and completely respond to inquiries by the successor auditor after the client has given consent.
(3) Disclosure in response to subpoena.
(4) Disclosure to funding agency for entities receiving governmental financial assistance.

5. CPA certificates are issued under state (not federal) jurisdiction.
6. Acts of employees.

a. Accountant is liable for acts of employees in the course of employment.

> **EXAMPLE**
>
> XYZ, a partnership of CPAs, hires Y to help perform an audit. Y is negligent in the audit, causing the client damage. The partners cannot escape liability by showing they did not perform the negligent act.

     b. Professional liability insurance typically is used to cover such losses.

7. The duty to perform an audit is not delegable because it is a contract for personal services unless client agrees to delegation.
8. Generally, the basis of relationship of accountant to his or her client is that of independent contractor.
9. Insurance

     a. The accountants' professional liability (malpractice) insurance covers their negligence.
     b. A fidelity bond protects client from accountant's fraud.
     c. A client's insurance company is subrogated to client's rights (i.e., has same rights of recovery of loss against accountant that client had).
     d. The portions of debts incurred in violation of securities laws not covered by insurance are not dischargeable in bankruptcy by the accountant.

10. Reliance by an auditor on other auditor's work

     a. The principal auditor is still liable for all work unless the audit report clearly indicates divided responsibility.
     b. The principal auditor cannot rely on unaudited data; must disclaim or qualify opinion.

11. Subsequent events and subsequent discovery

     a. The accountant is generally not liable for the effect of events occurring subsequent to the date of the audit report.

       (1) Liability extends to effective date of registration for reports filed with SEC.

     b. The accountant may be held liable if subsequently discovered facts that existed at report date indicate statements were misleading **unless**

       (1) An immediate investigation is conducted
       (2) Prompt revision of statements is possible
       (3) The SEC and persons known to be relying on statements are notified by the client or the accountant

     c. The accountant is liable if he or she makes assurances that there are no material changes after fieldwork or report date when in fact there are material changes. Therefore, the accountant should perform sufficient audit procedures before giving this assurance.

12. Liability from preparation of unaudited financial statements, including compiled and reviewed financial statements for nonissuers (nonpublic companies)

     a. Financial statements are unaudited if

       (1) No auditing procedures have been applied.
       (2) Insufficient audit procedures have been applied to express an opinion (e.g., inquiries and analytical procedures applied in a review engagement).

     b. The accountant may liable in these types of engagements

       (1) Failure to mark each page, "unaudited," or "See Accountant's Compilation Report," or "See Accountant's Review Report."
       (2) Failure to issue a disclaimer of opinion, or an appropriately worded compilation or review report.
       (3) Failure to follow appropriate AICPA Statements on Standards for Accounting and Review Services.
       (4) Failure to inform client of any discovery of indications of major issues; for example, circumstances indicating presence of fraud.

NOW REVIEW MULTIPLE-CHOICE QUESTIONS 34 THROUGH 41 IN VOLUME 2

E. Criminal Liability

1. Sources of liability

     a. Securities Act of 1933 and Securities Exchange Act of 1934

       (1) An accountant can be held criminally liable for **willful** illegal conduct.

         (a) Intentional misleading omission of material facts
         (b) Putting false information in registration statement

       (2) Subject to fine of up to $10,000 and/or up to five years prison
       (3) Examples of possible criminal actions include

        (a) CPA aids management in a fraudulent scheme.

        (b) CPA covers up prior year financial statement misstatements.

   b. Criminal violations of the Internal Revenue Code

      (1) For willfully preparing false return (perjury)

      (2) For willfully assisting others to evade taxes (tax evasion)

   c. Criminal liability under RICO (Racketeer Influenced and Corrupt Organizations) Act

      (1) Covers individuals affiliated with businesses or associations involved in a pattern of racketeering.

         (a) Racketeering includes organized crime but also includes fraud under the federal securities laws as well as mail fraud.

           1] Accountants are subject to criminal penalty through affiliation with accounting firm or business involved in racketeering.

         (b) A pattern of racketeering means at least two illegal acts of racketeering in previous ten years.

      (2) RICO has also been expanded to allow civil suit by private parties.

         (a) Treble damages allowed (to encourage private enforcement).

         (b) It has been held to apply against accountants even without a criminal indictment or conviction.

EXAMPLE

A CPA firm is convicted of a number of violations of securities laws in a short period of time. The CPA firm could potentially be held liable under RICO for a pattern of violations of laws.

NOW REVIEW MULTIPLE-CHOICE QUESTIONS 42 THROUGH 43 IN VOLUME 2

F. Responsibilities of Auditors under Private Securities Litigation Reform Act

  1. Auditors who audit financial statements under Federal Securities Exchange Act of 1934 are required to establish procedures to

   a. Detect material illegal acts,

   b. Identify material related-party transactions, and

   c. Evaluate ability of firm to continue as going concern.

  2. If auditor detects possible illegal activity, he or she must inform audit committee or board of directors.

   a. If senior management or board fails to take remedial action and if illegal activities are material so that departure from standard audit report or auditor resignation is indicated, the auditor shall report this to board of directors.

      (1) Board has one day to notify SEC of this report.

         (a) If not done, auditor must furnish SEC with copy of auditor's report to board and/or resign from audit.

  3. Civil liability may be imposed by SEC for the auditor's failures under the Act.

   a. Auditors are protected from private civil suits for these reports to SEC under this Act.

  4. Amends Federal Securities Act of 1933 and Federal Securities Exchange Act of 1934.

   a. Law passed to reduce lawsuits against accounting firms and issuers of securities

      (1) SEC's enforcement of securities laws not affected by the Act because the law governs private litigation.

  5. The act creates a "safe harbor" from legal liability for preparation of forward-looking statements.

   a. Including projections of income, revenues, EPS, and company plans for products and services.

   b. To fall within safe harbor, written or oral forward-looking statement should include cautions and identify assumptions and conditions that may cause projections to vary.

   c. Purpose is to encourage company to give investors more meaningful information without fear of lawsuits.

  6. Discourages class action lawsuits for frivolous purposes

   a. Accomplished by

       (1) Providing for stringent pleading requirements for many private actions under Securities Exchange Act of 1934

       (2) Awards costs and attorneys' fees against parties failing to fulfill these pleading requirements

  7. Changes rules on joint and several liability, so that liability of defendants is generally proportionate to their degree of fault

     a. This relieves the accountants (and others) from being "deep pockets" beyond their proportional fault.

     b. Exception—joint and several liability is imposed if defendant **knowingly** caused harm.

EXAMPLE

Plaintiffs suffered $2 million in damages from securities fraud of a company. The auditors of the company are found to be 15% at fault. If the auditors did not act knowingly, they can be held liable for the 15% or $300,000. If they acted knowingly, they can be held liable for up to the full $2 million based on joint and several liability.

---

     c. Accountants may be held liable for the proportionate share of damages they actually (and unknowingly) caused plus an additional 50% where principal defendant is insolvent.

> **NOW REVIEW MULTIPLE-CHOICE QUESTIONS 44 THROUGH 49 IN VOLUME 2**

G. Responsibilities under Sarbanes-Oxley Act

  1. Sarbanes-Oxley Act, also known as Public Company Accounting Reform and Investor Protection Act

  2. New federal crimes involving willful nonretention of audit and review workpapers

     a. Retention required for five years (in some cases seven years).

     b. Makes illegal the destruction or falsifying of records to impede investigations.

     c. Provides for fines or imprisonment up to twenty years or both.

     d. Applies to an accountant who audits an issuer of securities (public company).

       (1) It also applies to others such as attorneys, consultants, and company employees.

     e. Act requires SEC to issue new rules and then periodically update its rules on details of retaining workpapers and other relevant records connected with audits or reviews.

  3. Created the Public Company Accounting Oversight Board (PCAOB).

     a. PCAOB is a nonprofit corporation not federal agency.

       (1) Violation of rules of the PCAOB are treated as violation of Securities Exchange Act of 1934 with its penalties.

     b. The PCAOB consists of five members.

       (1) Two members must be or have been CPAs.

       (2) Three members cannot be or cannot have been CPAs.

       (3) None of Board members may receive pay or profits from CPA firms.

     c. Board regulates firms that audit SEC registrants, not accounting firms of private companies.

     d. Main functions of Board are to

       (1) Register and conduct inspections of public accounting firms

         (a) This replaces peer reviews for the part of a CPA firm's practice that involves audits of issuers (public company clients)

         (b) CPA firms that audit more than 100 issuers (public companies) are inspected annually.

         (c) CPA firms that audit from 1 to 100 issuers (public companies) are inspected every three years.

         (d) Special inspections may be performed in addition to the regular inspections.

       (2) Set standards on auditing, quality control, independence, or preparation of audit reports

         (a) May adopt standards of existing professional groups or new groups.

         (b) Accounting firm must have second partner review and approve each audit report.

         (c) Accounting firm must report on examination of internal control along with description of material weaknesses.

     (3) The PCAOB may regulate the nature and extent of nonaudit services that CPA firms may perform for issuer audit clients

     (4) Enforce compliance with professional standards, securities laws relating to accountants and audits

     (5) Perform investigations and disciplinary proceedings on registered public accounting firms

     (6) May perform any other duties needed to promote high professional standards and to improve auditing quality

     (7) Material services must receive preapproval by audit committee, and fees for those services must be disclosed to investors

4. Additional responsibilities and provisions

  a. A company must disclose whether it has adopted code of ethics for company's principal executive officer, principal accounting officer, principal financial officer or controller.

     (1) A company may have separate codes of ethics for different officers or may have broad code of ethics covering all officers and directors.

     (2) A company is not required to adopt code of ethics but if it has not, it must disclose the reasons why.

  b. Company officials found liable for fraud cannot use bankruptcy law to discharge that liability.

  c. Attorneys practicing before SEC representing issuers must report evidence of material violations by the company or its officers, directors, or agents of securities laws or breach of fiduciary duties

     (1) The report must be made to the chief legal officer or the chief executive officer.

       (a) If management does not respond appropriately, then the attorney must report the evidence "up the ladder" to audit committee of the board of directors, another committee of independent directors, or finally to the entire board of directors.

  d. The SEC adopted new rules requiring more events to be reported on Form 8-K and shortening filing deadlines for most reportable events to four business days after the date the event occurs.

     (1) If the company becomes directly or contingently liable for material obligation arising from an off-balance-sheet arrangement, it must describe this matter including its material terms and nature of arrangement.

  e. The company must disclose several items if a director has resigned or refused to stand for reelection because of disagreement with company's practices, operations or policies, or if the director has been removed for cause.

     (1) The company must disclose such items as circumstances regarding disagreement with company.

  f. If a new executive officer is appointed, the company must disclose information such as his or her name, the position, and description of any material terms of the employment agreement between company and officer.

5. The act lists several specific service categories that the issuer's public accounting firm cannot legally do, even if approved by audit committee, such as

  a. Bookkeeping or other services relating to financial statements or accounting records
  b. Financial information systems design and/or implementation
  c. Appraisal services
  d. Internal audit outsourcing services
  e. Management functions
  f. Actuarial services
  g. Investment or broker-dealer services
  h. Certain tax services, such as tax planning for potentially abusive tax shelters
  i. Board permitted to exempt (on case by case basis) services of audit firm for audit client

Note that the act does **not** restrict the auditor from performing these services for to nonaudit clients or to private companies. Also, the act permits the auditor as a registered public accounting firm to perform nonaudit services not specifically prohibited (e.g., tax services) when approved by issuer's audit committee.

6. The act prohibits the audit partner having primary responsibility for the issuer's audit's and the audit partner who reviews the audits from serving for more than five consecutive years (i.e., the audit partners must be rotated every five years).

  a. If public company has hired an employee of an audit firm to be its CEO, CFO, or CAO within the previous year, the audit firm may not audit that public company.

7. The act requires increased disclosure of off-balance-sheet transactions.
8. The act mandates that pro forma financial disclosures be reconciled with figures done under GAAP.
9. The act creates new federal laws against destruction or tampering with audit workpapers or documents that are to be used in official proceedings.

10. The act increases protection of whistleblowers from retaliation because of participation in proceedings against firms in securities fraud.

   a. Also, provides that employees may report securities fraud directly to the audit committee and may provide the information anonymously and confidentially.

11. Public Companies may not make or modify personal loans to officers or directors with few exceptions.
12. Annual reports filed with SEC that contain financial statements need to incorporate all material corrections noted by CPA firms.
13. Each company must disclose on a current basis information on financial condition that the SEC determines is useful to public.
14. The SEC is authorized to discipline professionals practicing before SEC.

   a. SEC may censure, temporarily bar or permanently bar him or her for

      (1) Lack of qualifications needed
      (2) Improper professional conduct
      (3) Willful violation of helping another violate securities laws or regulations

15. The auditor must report to the issuer's audit committee.
16. The auditors must retain workpapers for five years.

   a. Failure to do so is punishable by prison term of up to ten years.

17. Sarbanes-Oxley Act directed SEC to perform various tasks including several studies to formulate regulations; some of these studies have deadlines in the future and are expected to be used to promulgate new important regulations—others have been completed, resulted in regulations by SEC, and have force of law including the following:

   a. Require disclosure of differences between pro forma financial results and GAAP.
   b. Require that "critical" accounting policies be reported from auditors to audit committee.
   c. Companies are required to disclose if they have adopted a code of ethics.
   d. Disclosure of names of "financial experts" who serve on a company's audit committee.
   e. Actions are prohibited that fraudulently manipulate or mislead auditors.
   f. New conflict of interest rules were established for analysts.
   g. The SEC may petition courts to freeze payments by companies that are extraordinary.

18. CEOs and CFOs of most large companies listed on public stock exchanges are now required to certify financial statements filed with SEC.

   a. This generally means that they certify that information "fairly represents in all material respects the financial conditions and results of operations" of those companies and that

      (1) The signing officer reviewed the report.
      (2) The company's report does not contain any untrue statements of material facts or does not omit any statements of material facts to the best of his or her knowledge.
      (3) The company has an internal control system in place to allow honest certification of financial statements.

         (a) Or if any deficiencies in internal control exist, they must be disclosed to the auditors.

19. Blackout periods were established for issuers of certain security transaction types that limit companies' purchase, sale, or transfer of funds in individual accounts.
20. Stiffer penalties for other white-collar crimes including federal law covering mail fraud and wire fraud

H. Additional Statutory Liability Against Accountants

1. Auditors are required to use adequate procedures to uncover illegal activity of client.
2. Civil liability is proportional to degree of responsibility.

   a. One type of responsibility is through the auditors' own carelessness.
   b. Another type of responsibility is based on auditor's assisting in improper activities that he or she is aware or should be aware of.

NOW REVIEW MULTIPLE-CHOICE QUESTIONS 50 THROUGH 55 IN VOLUME 2

I. Responsibilities of Tax Return Preparers

1. **Preparer**—an individual who prepares for compensation, or who employs one or more persons to prepare for compensation, any federal tax return, or a substantial portion thereof, including income, employment, excise, exempt organization, gift, and estate tax returns.

   a. Compensation must be received and can be implied or explicit (e.g., accountant who prepares individual return of the president of a company, for which he performs the audit, for no additional fee as part of a prior agreement **has** been compensated [implied]).

   b. The performance of the following acts will not classify a person as a preparer:

      (1) Preparation of a return for a friend, relative, or neighbor free of charge even though the person completing the return receives a gift of gratitude from the taxpayer;

      (2) The furnishing of typing, reproducing, or other mechanical assistance in preparing a return; and

      (3) Preparation by an employee of a return for his or her employer, or an officer of the employer, or for another employee if he or she is regularly employed by that employer.

   c. Preparation of a tax return includes giving advice on events that have occurred at the time the advice is given if the advice is directly relevant to determining the existence, character, or amount of a schedule, entry, or other portion of a tax return.

2. **AICPA Statements on Standards for Tax Services**

   a. **Tax Return Positions**

      (1) With respect to tax return positions, a CPA

         (a) Should determine and comply with the standards that are imposed by the applicable taxing authority with respect to recommending a tax return position, or preparing or signing a tax return.

         (b) The CPA should

            1] Satisfy the reporting standard and disclosure requirements of the applicable taxing authority, or

            2] If the taxing authority has no written standard (or it is of lower level), the following should be applied:

               a] For undisclosed positions, realistic possibility of success

               b] For disclosed positions, reasonable basis

         (c) In assisting the taxpayer in tax planning related to a tax shelter, the practitioner should inform the taxpayer of the penalty risks associated with the tax position recommended that does not possess sufficient authority to satisfy the more likely than not standard.

         (d) Should not prepare or sign a tax return if the CPA knows the return takes a position that the CPA could not recommend under (b) above.

         (e) Notwithstanding (b) and (c), a CPA may recommend a position for which there is a reasonable basis so long as the position is adequately disclosed on the return or claim for refund. In determining whether a given standard has been satisfied, a CPA should consider a well-reasoned construction of the applicable stature, well-reasoned articles or treatises, and pronouncements issued by the applicable taxing authority.

         (f) Should advise the client of the potential penalty consequences of any recommended tax position.

      (2) A CPA should not recommend a tax position that exploits the IRS audit process, or serves as a mere arguing position advanced solely to obtain leverage in bargaining with the IRS.

      (3) A CPA has both the right and the responsibility to be an advocate for the client.

   b. **Realistic Possibility and More Likely Than Not Standards**

      (1) The CPA should consider the weight of each authority (e.g., Code, Regs., court decisions, well-reasoned treaties, article in professional tax publications, etc.) in determining whether these standards are met, and may rely on well-reasoned treatises and articles in recognized professional tax publications.

      (2) Realistic possibility of success may require as much as a **one-third likelihood** of success.

      (3) The more likely than not standard requires more than 50% probability of success.

   c. **Answers to Questions on Returns**

      (1) A CPA should make a reasonable effort to obtain from the client and provide appropriate answers to all questions on a tax return before signing as preparer.

      (2) When reasonable grounds for omitting an answer exist, the CPA is not required to provide an explanation on the return of the reason for omission. Reasonable grounds for omitting an answer include

      (a) Information is not readily available and the answer is not significant in terms of taxable income or tax liability.
      (b) Uncertainty as to meaning of question.
      (c) Answer is voluminous and return states that data will be supplied upon examination.

  d. **Procedural Aspects of Preparing Returns**

    (1) A CPA may in good faith rely without verification upon information furnished by the client or by third parties, and is not required to audit, examine, or review books, records, or documents in order to independently verify the taxpayer's information.

      (a) However, the CPA should not ignore implications of information furnished and should make reasonable inquires if information appears incorrect, incomplete, or inconsistent.
      (b) When feasible, the CPA should refer to the client's past returns.

    (2) Where the IRS imposes a condition for deductibility or other treatment of an item (e.g., requires supporting documentation), the CPA should make appropriate inquiries to determine whether the condition for deductibility has been met.
    (3) When preparing a tax return, a CPA should consider information known from the tax return of another client if that information is relevant to the return being prepared, and such consideration does not violate any rule regarding confidentiality.

  e. **Use of Estimates**

    (1) Where data is missing (e.g., result of a fire, computer failure), estimates of the missing data may be made by the client.
    (2) A CPA may prepare a tax return using estimates if it is impracticable to obtain exact data, and the estimated amounts are reasonable.
    (3) An estimate should not imply greater accuracy than actually exists (e.g., estimate $1,000 rather than $999.32).

  f. **Departure from Position Previously Concluded in an IRS Proceeding or Court Decision**

    (1) Unless the taxpayer is bound to a specified treatment in the later year, such as by a formal closing agreement, the treatment of an item as part of concluding an IRS proceeding or as part of a court decision in a prior year, does not restrict the CPA from recommending a different tax treatment in a later year's return.
    (2) Court decisions, rulings, or other authorities more favorable to the taxpayer's current position may have developed since the prior proceeding was concluded or the prior court decision was rendered.

  g. **Knowledge of Error: Return Preparation**

    (1) The term "error" as used here includes any position, omission, or method of accounting that, at the time the return is filed, fails to meet the standards as outlined in a. and b. above. An error does not include an item that has an insignificant effect on the client's tax liability.
    (2) A CPA should inform a client promptly upon becoming aware of a material error in a previously filed return or upon becoming aware of a client's failure to file a required return. A CPA

      (a) Should recommend (either orally or in writing) measures to be taken.
      (b) Is not obligated to inform the IRS of the error, and may not do so without the client's permission, except where required by law.

    (3) If the CPA is requested to prepare the client's current return, and the client has not taken appropriate action to correct an error in a prior year's return, the CPA should consider whether to continue a professional relationship with the client or withdraw.

  h. **Knowledge of Error: Administrative Proceedings**

    (1) When a CPA is representing a client in an IRS proceeding (e.g., examination, appellate conference) with respect to a return that contains an error of which the CPA has become aware, the CPA should promptly inform the client and recommend measures to be taken.
    (2) The CPA should request the client's permission to disclose the error to the IRS, and lacking such permission, should consider whether to withdraw from representing the client.

  i. **Form and Content of Advice to Clients**

    (1) No standard format is required in communicating written or oral advice to a client, but CPA should comply with standards of taxing authority

(2) In deciding on the form of advice provided (e.g., oral or written) the CPA should consider the importance of the transaction and the amounts, the specific or general nature or the inquiry, the technical complexity involved, the existence of authorities and precedents, the sophistication of the taxpayer, the type of transaction and whether it is subject to heightened reporting or disclosure, and the potential penalties involved.

(3) A CPA may choose to communicate with a client when subsequent developments affect previous advice. Such communication is only required when the CPA undertakes this obligation by specific agreement with the client.

3. **Treasury Department Circular 230**

a. **Rules Governing Authority to Practice**

(1) Practice before the IRS comprehends all matters connected with a presentation to the IRS including (but not limited to) preparing and filing documents, corresponding and communicating with the IRS, rendering written advice with respect to any entity, transactions, plan or arrangement, and representing a client at conferences, hearings, and meetings.

(2) Practice before the IRS is limited to CPAs, attorneys, enrolled agents (EAs), and for limited purposes enrolled actuaries, enrolled retirement plan agents, and registered tax return preparers (RTRP). Enrollment as an EA, retirement plan agent, or RTRP is granted if the individual is at least 18 years old and demonstrates competence in tax matters by passing an examination. Additionally, certain former employees of the IRS may be granted the right to practice as an enrolled agent by virtue of service and experience.

(a) Practice as a RTRP is limited to preparing and signing tax returns and claims for refund, and other documents for submission to the IRS. A RTRP may represent taxpayers before revenue agents, customer service representatives, or similar employees of the IRS during an examination if the RTRP signed the tax return or claim for refund for the taxable year or period under examination.

(b) A RTRP's right to practice does not permit such individual to represent the taxpayer before appeals officers, revenue officers, counsel, or similar employees of the IRS. Similarly, a RTRP is not authorized to provide tax advice to a client except as necessary to prepare a tax return, claim for refund, or other documents to be submitted to the IRS.

(3) All paid tax return preparers (including CPAs, attorneys, and EAs) must register with the IRS, pay an annual fee, and obtain a Preparer Tax Identification Number (PTIN) before preparing or signing taxpayers' tax returns or claims for refund. The IRS Office of Professional Responsibility will oversee PTIN registrations, enrollment, and renewal processes, and will oversee future testing and continuing education requirements.

(4) Individuals may appear on their own behalf before the IRS. Also, an individual who is not a practitioner may represent a taxpayer before the IRS in limited situations. This group includes members of the taxpayer's immediate family; full-time employees may represent their employers; an officer or full-time employee may represent a corporation; a general partner or full-time employee of a partnership may represent the partnership; and trusts, receiverships, guardianships, or estates may be represented by their trustees, receivers, guardians, or executors.

b. **Duties and Restrictions Relating to Practice Before the IRS**

(1) A practitioner must promptly submit records or information in any matter before the IRS unless the practitioner believes in good faith and on reasonable grounds that the records or information are privileged.

(2) A practitioner must, at the request of a client, promptly return the client's records. The client's records include all documents and electronic media provided to the practitioner. The existence of a dispute over fees generally does not allow the practitioner to retain records.

(3) A practitioner who becomes aware that a client has not complied with the revenue laws or has made an error in or omission from any return must advise the client promptly of the fact of such noncompliance, error, or omission, and must advise the client of the consequences under the law of such noncompliance, error, or omission.

(4) A practitioner must exercise due diligence in preparing returns and documents relating to IRS matters, as well as in determining the correctness of oral and written representations to clients and the Department of the Treasury. A practitioner may rely on the work product of another person if the practitioner used reasonable care in engaging, supervising, training, and evaluating the person.

(5) A practitioner may not charge an unconscionable fee and generally may not charge a contingent fee for preparing an original return. However, a contingent fee may be charged in connection with the IRS's examination of an original tax return, or an amended return or claim for refund or credit. Also, a contingent fee may be charged for services rendered in connection with any judicial proceeding arising under the Code.

(6) A practitioner may publish the availability of a written fee schedule including fixed fees for specific routine services, hourly rates, ranges of fees for specific services, and the fee charged for an initial consultation.

The practitioner may charge no more than the published fees for at least 30 days after the last date on which the fee schedule was published.

(7) A practitioner may not use any form of public communication or private solicitation containing a false, fraudulent, or coercive statement or claim, nor a misleading or deceptive statement or claim. Enrolled agents may not utilize the word "certified" or imply an employer/employee relationship with the IRS.

(8) Tax advisors should provide clients with the highest quality representation concerning Federal tax issues by adhering to best practices in providing advice and in preparing or assisting in the preparation of a submission to the IRS.

(9) A practitioner who prepares returns may not endorse nor negotiate any federal tax refund check issued to a client by the government.

c. **Standards for Returns and Advising**

(1) A practitioner may not willfully, recklessly, or through gross incompetence sign a tax return or claim for refund that the practitioner reasonably should know contains a position that lacks a **reasonable basis**, is an unreasonable position, or is a willful attempt to understate tax liability or a reckless or intentional disregard of rules and regulations. The prohibition also applies to advising a client to take a position on a tax return or claim for refund that lacks a reasonable basis, or preparing a portion of a tax return or claim for refund containing a position that lacks a reasonable basis. The reasonable basis standard may require at least a 20% probability of a position being sustained on its merits.

(2) A practitioner may not advise a client to take a position on a document, affidavit, or other paper submitted to the IRS that is **frivolous**, nor advise a client to submit documents with the intent of delaying or impeding the administration of federal tax laws. A frivolous position is one without basis in fact or law, or that espouses a position that the courts have held to be frivolous or groundless.

(3) A practitioner must inform a client of any penalties that are likely to apply to a position taken on a return, and must inform the client of any opportunity to avoid penalties by disclosure and the requirements of adequate disclosure.

(4) A practitioner may rely in good faith without verification upon information furnished by the client, but must make reasonable inquiries if the information furnished appears to be incorrect, incomplete, or inconsistent with other facts.

(5) Practitioners providing written advice must adhere to specific standards. Written advice is categorized as either (1) covered opinions, or (2) all other written advice. More stringent standards apply to covered opinions because taxpayers may rely on a practitioner's covered opinion to avoid penalties.

   (a) Written advice is generally considered to be a **covered opinion** if it involves a *listed transaction*, or a place or arrangement the *principal purpose* of which is tax avoidance, or any plan or arrangement in which tax avoidance is a *significant purpose* if the advice is either a *reliance opinion, a marketed opinion*, subject to confidentiality, or subject to contractual protection.

   (b) Advice that does not constitute a covered opinion is subject to more relaxed standards but practitioners must not base their advice on unreasonable assumptions nor rely on unreasonable representations of the taxpayer or others.

   (c) Written advice is a **reliance opinion** if the advice concludes that it is more likely than not (a greater than 50% likelihood) that one or more significant federal tax issues would be resolved in the taxpayer's favor. Written advice (other than advice on listed transactions and advice having the principal purpose of tax avoidance or evasion) *is not treated as a reliance opinion* if the practitioner prominently discloses in the written advice that it was not intended or written by the practitioner to be used, and that it cannot be used by the taxpayer, for the purpose of avoiding penalties that may be imposed on the taxpayer.

   (d) As a result, most practitioners include a standard disclaimer with written correspondence that is intended as informal advice and explicitly not intended to satisfy the reliance opinion requirements. A typical disclaimer may read:

   > Please be advised that any federal tax advice in this communication, including any attachments or enclosures, was not intended or written to be used, and it cannot be used, by any person or entity for the purpose of avoiding penalties imposed under the Internal Revenue Code.

4. **Preparer Penalties**

   a. A preparer is subject to a penalty equal to the greater of $1,000, or 50% of the income derived (or to be derived) by the preparer with respect to the return or refund claim if any part of an understatement of liability with respect to the return or claim is due to an undisclosed position on the return or refund claim for which there is *not* **substantial authority**.

(1) Substantial authority exists if the weight of authorities supporting the position is substantial in relation to the weight of those that take a contrary position. The substantial authority standard may require at least a 40% probability of being sustained on its merits.
(2) The penalty can be avoided by

   (a) An adequate disclosure of the questionable position on the return or refund claim.
   (b) A showing that there was **a reasonable basis** for the position. The reasonable basis standard may require at least a 20% probability of being sustained on its merits.

(3) A higher **more likely than not** standard applies if the position is with respect to a tax shelter as defined in Sec. 6662 (d)(2)(C)(ii) or a reportable transaction to which Sec. 6662A applies. This standard requires a more than 50% probability of being sustained on its merits.
(4) The penalty can also be avoided if the preparer can show there was a reasonable cause for the understatement and that the return preparer acted in good faith.

b. If any part of an understatement of liability with respect to a return or refund claim is due (1) to a willful attempt to understate tax liability by a return preparer with respect to the return or claim, or (2) to any reckless or intentional disregard of rules or regulations, the preparer is subject to a penalty equal to the greater of $5,000, or 50% of the income derived (or to be derived) by the preparer with respect to the return or refund claim.

(1) This penalty is reduced by the penalty paid in a. above.
(2) Rules and regulations include the Internal Revenue Code, Treasury Regulations, and Revenue Rulings.

c. Additional penalties may be imposed on preparers if they fail to fulfill the following requirements (unless failure is due to reasonable cause):

(1) Preparer must sign returns done for compensation.
(2) Preparer must provide a copy of the return or refund claim to the taxpayer no later than when the preparer presents a copy of the return to the taxpayer for signing.
(3) Returns and claims for refund must contain the social security number of preparer and identification number of preparer's employer or partnership (if any).
(4) Preparer must either keep a list of those for whom returns were filed with specified information, or copies of the actual returns, for three years.
(5) Employers of return preparers must retain a listing of return preparers and place of employment for three years.
(6) Preparer must not endorse or negotiate a refund check issued to a taxpayer.
(7) Preparer must not disclose information furnished in connection with the preparation of a tax return, unless for quality or peer review, or under an administrative order by a regulatory agency.

NOW REVIEW MULTIPLE-CHOICE QUESTIONS 56 THROUGH 78 IN VOLUME 2

KEY TERMS

Common Law. Law that has historically been established by judicial precedents. Much common law has now been codified in state statutes. This law is the source of liability to clients and third parties (not covered by securities laws).

Constructive fraud. Failure to even use slight care. Constructive fraud is often referred to as gross negligence.

Contributory negligence. Negligence on the part of the plaintiff that contributed to that party's losses. Contributory negligence will typically mitigate some or all of the defendant's damages.

Due diligence. The standard of care required under filings under the Securities Act of 1933. To establish "due diligence" an accountant must have made a reasonable investigation, and must have had reasonable grounds to believe and did believe that that the registration statement (including the financial statements) were not misleading.

Fraud. A misrepresentation intended to mislead another party or a representation made with a reckless disregard for its truth.

Joint and several liability. A concept of liability that is similar to joint liability except that if all of the judgment is recovered from one defendant that party may attempt to collect from other defendants their proportionate shares of the judgment. As an example, assume a bank files suit against both the CPA firm and management for misleading financial statements, and the CPA firm is found to be 30% liable and management is found to be 70% liable. The bank may recover 100% of the judgment from the CPA firm and it is up to the CPA firm to collect from management its share of the judgment.

Joint Ethics Enforcement Program (JEEP). A joint program of the American Institute of Certified Public Accountants (AICPA) and state CPA societies to jointly investigate ethics violations.

Joint liability. A liability concept in which any joint defendant may be forced to pay the entire amount of a judgment. As an example, if a bank files suit against both the CPA firm and management for misleading financial statements, the bank may recover the entire amount from management or the CPA firm.

Negligence. Failure to perform with the level of skill and judgment possessed by a typical professional. Negligence is often referred to as ordinary negligence.

Primary beneficiary. A party other than the client who primarily benefits from the contracted services provided by the CPA. As an example, if the CPA is aware that an audit is being performed at the request of the client's bank, the bank is a primary beneficiary of the contract between the CPA and the client. Under common law a primary beneficiary has the same rights as the client.

Privileged communication. Communication that is not subject to disclosure in court or administrative proceedings. Privilege must be established by law, and generally the communication between an accountant and a client is not privileged.

Privity. A mutual relationship established between parties typically established by a contract. The client and third-party beneficiaries are in privity with the CPA in a contract to provide services.

Public Company Accounting Oversight Board (PCAOB). A nonprofit organization created by the Sarbanes-Oxley Act to oversee the audits of public companies (issuers).

Public Company Accounting Reform and Investor Protection (Sarbanes-Oxley) Act. An act that set a new set of enhanced standards for public company boards, management, and public accounting firms. The Act established the Public Company Accounting Oversight Board (PCAOB).

Racketeer Influenced and Corrupt Organization (RICO) Act. An act designed to allow prosecution of organized criminals. However, the Act has been used to pursue CPA firms who engage in multiple instances (a pattern) of wrongful acts. Civil actions under the Act can result in recovery of treble damages.

Securities Act of 1933. A federal securities act that covers the initial registration of securities.

Securities Exchange Act of 1934. A federal securities act that covers the secondary purchase and sale of securities.

Several liability. A concept of liability in which joint defendants are responsible for only their proportionate share of the judgment. As an example, assume that a bank files suit against both the CPA firm and management for misleading financial statements, and the CPA firm is found to be 30% liable and management is found to be 70% liable. The bank may recover only 30% of the judgment from the CPA firm. The remaining amount must be recovered by the bank from management.

State boards of accountancy. State boards that regulate the practice of public accountancy in a state or jurisdiction. All individual CPAs and CPA firms must be licensed to practice in the states where they practice.

Statements on Standards for Tax Services. AICPA standards for CPAs that perform tax services for clients.

Treasury Department Circular 230. Regulatory requirements regarding the authority to practice before the Internal Revenue Service.

US Securities Exchange Commission (SEC). A federal agency with primary responsibility for enforcing the federal securities laws and regulating the securities industry.

Module 24: Federal Securities Acts

Overview

The bulk of the material tested on the exam from this area comes from the Securities Act of 1933, as amended, and the Securities Exchange Act of 1934, as amended. Topics included under the scope of the 1933 Act are registration requirements, exempt securities, and exempt transactions. The purposes of the 1933 Act are to provide investors with full and fair disclosure of a security offering and to prevent fraud. The basic prohibition of the 1933 Act is that no sale of a security shall occur in interstate commerce without registration and without furnishing a prospectus to prospective purchasers unless the security or the transaction is exempt from registration.

The purpose of the 1934 Act is the establishment of the Securities Exchange Commission to assure fairness in the trading of securities subsequent to their original issuance. The basic scope of the 1934 Act is to require periodic reports of financial and other information concerning registered securities, and to prohibit manipulative and deceptive devices in both the sale and purchase of securities.

The exam often tests on the Federal Securities Acts; however, this is sometimes combined with accountant's liability or is included within questions concerning corporate or limited partnership law. You should also expect questions on the Sarbanes-Oxley Act of 2002 and the Dodd-Frank Act of 2010. Before beginning the reading you should review the key terms at the end of the module.

A. Securities Act of 1933 (Generally applies to initial issuances [primary offerings] of securities)

1. The purposes of the 1933 Act are to provide potential investors with full and fair disclosure of all material information relating to issuance of securities (such that a prudent decision to invest or refrain from investing can be made) and to prevent fraud or misrepresentation.

   a. This is accomplished by

      (1) Requiring a registration statement to be filed with Securities Exchange Commission (SEC) before either a public sale or an offer to sell securities in interstate commerce

         (a) This is the fundamental thrust of the 1933 Act.
         (b) The SEC is a government agency comprised of commissioners and its staff that was created to administer and enforce the Federal Securities Laws. The Commission interprets the acts, conducts investigations, adjudicates violations, and performs a rule-making function to implement the acts.

            1] Can subpoena witnesses
            2] Can obtain injunction preventing sale of securities
            3] Cannot assess monetary penalties without court proceedings
            4] Cannot prosecute criminal acts

      (2) Requiring prospectuses to be provided to investors with, or before, the sale or delivery of the securities to provide public with information given to the SEC in registration statement.
      (3) Providing civil and criminal liabilities for failure to comply with these requirements and for misrepresentation or fraud in the sale of securities even if not required to be registered.

   b. The SEC does not evaluate the merits or value of securities

      (1) The SEC can only compel full and fair disclosure.
      (2) In theory, the public can evaluate the merits of the security when provided with full and fair disclosure.
      (3) The SEC's function is not to detect fraud or to stop offerings where fraud or unethical conduct is suspected.
      (4) The SEC's functions are also to

         (a) Regulate securities markets
         (b) Maintain fair markets

       (c) Protect investors

       (d) Review corporate financial statements

       (e) Enforce securities laws

       (f) Provide guidance for accounting rules

  c. The major items you need to know include

       (1) That a registration statement and prospectus are usually required

       (2) Which transactions are exempt from registration

       (3) Which securities are exempt from registration

       (4) What the liability is for false or misleading registration statements

2. Definitions

  a. Security—any note, stock, bond, certificate of interest, debenture, investment contract, etc., or any interest or instrument commonly known as a security.

    (1) The general idea is that investor intends to make a profit on the investment through the efforts of others rather than through his/her own efforts.

> **EXAMPLE**
>
> Ward is a general partner of WDC partnership in Washington, D.C. Usually, Ward's interest would not be considered a security because a general partner's interest typically involves participation in the business rather than mere investment.

       (a) Includes limited partnership interests

       (b) Includes rights and warrants to subscribe for the above

       (c) Includes treasury stock

       (d) Investment contract is a security when money is invested in a common enterprise with profits to be derived from the effort of others

> **EXAMPLE**
>
> Blue Corporation in Florida owns several acres of orange trees. Blue is planning on selling a large portion of the land with the orange trees to several individuals in various states on a row-by-row basis. Each purchaser gets a deed and is required to purchase a management contract whereby Blue Corporation maintains all the land and oranges and then remits the net profits to the various purchasers. Even though it may appear that each individual purchased separately the land with the oranges and a management contract, the law looks at the "big picture" here. Since in reality the individuals are investing their money, and the profits are derived from the efforts of others, the law treats the above fact pattern as involving securities. Therefore, the Securities Acts apply.

  b. Person—individual, corporation, partnership, unincorporated association, business trust, government.

  c. Controlling person—has power, direct/indirect, to influence the management and/or policies of an issuer, whether by stock ownership, contract, position, or otherwise.

> **EXAMPLE**
>
> A 51% stockholder is a controlling person by virtue of a majority ownership.

> **EXAMPLE**
>
> A director of a corporation also owns 10% of that same corporation. By virtue of the stock ownership and position on the board of directors, he has a strong voice in the management of the corporation. Therefore, he is a controlling person.

  d. Insiders—(applies to the Securities Exchange Act of 1934) include officers, directors, and owners of more than 10% of any class of an issuer's equity securities.

    (1) Note that debentures are not included because not equity securities.

    (2) For purposes of this law to avoid a "loophole," insiders include "beneficial owners" of more than 10% of the equity stock of issuer.

(a) To determine the amount of "beneficial ownership," add to the individual's equity ownership, equity stock owned by

    1] Owner's spouse
    2] Owner's minor children
    3] Owner's relative in same house
    4] Owner's equity stock held in trust in which owner is beneficiary

---

EXAMPLE

Linda owns 6% of the common stock of ABC Company in Philadelphia. Her spouse owns 3% of ABC Company's common stock. The stock was also placed in the name of their two minor children, each owning 1% of ABC Company's common stock. Linda has beneficial ownership of 11% of the equity securities of ABC Company so she is an insider for the 1934 Act. Note that her husband also qualifies as an insider.

EXAMPLE

Use the same facts as in the previous example except that all four individuals owned debentures of ABC Company. Since these are not equity securities, none qualifies as an insider.

EXAMPLE

Robert is an officer who owns 4% of the common stock of XYZ Company in Washington, DC. Since Robert is an officer, he is an insider even though the ownership level is below 10%.

---

e. Underwriter—any person who has purchased from an issuer with a view to the public distribution of any security or participates in such undertaking.

    (1) Includes any person who offers or sells for issuer in connection with the distribution of any security.
    (2) Does not include person who sells or distributes on commission for underwriter (i.e., dealers).

f. Sales of securities are covered by the Securities Act of 1933

    (1) Issuance of securities as part of business reorganization (e.g., merger or consolidation) constitutes a sale and must be registered with SEC unless the issue otherwise qualifies as an exemption from the registration requirements of 1933 Act.
    (2) Issuance of stock warrants is considered a sale so that requirements of 1933 Act must be met.
    (3) Employee stock purchase plan is a sale and therefore must comply with the provisions of the 1933 Act. The company must supply a prospectus to each employee to whom stock is offered.
    (4) Stock dividends or splits are not sales.

g. Registration statement—the statement required to be filed with SEC before initial sale of securities in interstate commerce.

    (1) Includes financial statements and all other relevant information about the registrant's property, business, directors, principal officers, together with prospectus, and any amendment, report, or document filed as part of the statement or incorporated therein by reference.
    (2) It is against law to sell, offer to sell, or offer to purchase securities before filing a registration statement.
    (3) The registration statement and prospectus becomes public upon filing.

        (a) The effective date of registration statement is 20th day after filing.
        (b) It is against the law to sell securities until the effective date but issuer may **offer** securities upon filing registration statement.
        (c) Such offers may be made

            1] Orally
            2] By tombstone ads that identify security, its price, and who will take orders
            3] By a "red-herring prospectus"

                a] Legend in red ink (thus, red-herring) is printed on this preliminary prospectus indicating that the prospectus is "preliminary" and that a registration statement has been filed but has not become effective.

    h. Prospectus—any notice, circular, advertisement, letter, or communication offering any security for sale (or merger).

        (1) May be a written, radio, or television communication.

            (a) SEC adopted new "plain English" rule for important sections of companies' prospectuses, including risk factor sections.

        (2) After the effective date of the registration statement, communication (written or oral) will not be considered a prospectus if

            (a) Prior to or at same time, a written prospectus was also sent.
            (b) If it only states from whom written prospectus is available, identifies security, states price, and who will execute orders for it (i.e., tombstone ad).

3. Registration requirements

    a. Registration is required under the Act if the securities are to be offered, sold, or delivered in interstate commerce or through the mail.

        (1) Interstate commerce means trade, commerce, transportation, or communication (e.g., telephone call) among more than one state or territory of US. This is interpreted very broadly to include trade, commerce, etc. that is within one state but affects interstate commerce.

> **EXAMPLE**
>
> A corporation issues securities to individuals living only in Philadelphia. It is further shown that this issuance affects trade in Delaware. Interstate commerce is affected because although Philadelphia is of course in one state, the effects on at least one other state allow the Federal Securities Acts to take effect under our Constitution. Therefore, registration of these securities is required under the Federal Law unless exemptions are found as discussed later.

        (2) Unless it is an exempted security or exempted transaction as discussed later.

    b. The issuer has primary duty of registration

        (1) Any person who sells unregistered securities that should have been registered may be liable to a purchaser (unless transaction or security is exempt).
        (2) Liability cannot be disclaimed in writing or orally by the issuer.
        (3) This liability not dischargeable in bankruptcy.

    c. The information required, in general, in registration statements

        (1) Financial statements audited by independent CPA
        (2) Names of the issuer, directors, officers, general partners, underwriters, large stockholders, counsel, etc
        (3) The risks associated with the securities
        (4) A description of property, business, and capitalization of issuer
        (5) Information about management of issuer
        (6) A description of security to be sold and use to be made by issuer of proceeds

    d. The prospectus is also filed as part of registration statement

        (1) It generally must contain same information as registration statement, but it may be condensed or summarized.

    e. The registration statement and prospectus are reviewed by SEC

        (1) Amendments are almost always required by SEC.
        (2) The SEC may issue stop-order suspending effectiveness of registration if statement appears incomplete or misleading.
        (3) Otherwise the registration becomes effective on 20th day after filing (or on 20th day after filing amendment). The twenty-day period is called the waiting period.
        (4) It is unlawful for company to sell the securities prior to approval (effective registration date). However, preliminary prospectuses are permitted once registration statement is filed.

    f. Applies to both corporate and noncorporate issuers.
    g. The registration covers a single distribution, so second distribution must also be registered.
    h. The shelf registration is an exception to requirement that each new distribution of nonexempt securities requires a new filing.

     (1) It allows certain qualified issuers to register securities once and then offer and sell them on a delayed or continuous basis "off the shelf."

     (2) Advantage is that issuer can respond better to changing market conditions affecting stock.

  i. Different registration forms are available

     (1) Form S-1 is basic long-form registration statement.

     (2) Additional forms now required based on Sarbanes-Oxley Act that require non-GAAP financial measures to be presented so that they reconcile to the most directly comparable GAAP financial measure. The goal is to reduce concerns regarding improper use of non-GAAP financial measures.

     (3) Forms S-2 and S-3

        (a) These forms were adopted by SEC to ease much of burden of disclosures required under federal securities regulation.

        (b) They require less detailed disclosures than Form S-1.

        (c) They integrate information required under 1933 and 1934 Acts. Firms already on file with SEC under 1934 Act may incorporate much information by reference to avoid additional disclosure.

     (4) Forms SB-1 and SB-2

        (a) These forms permitted for small businesses under Regulation S-B.

           1] They reduce amount of financial and nonfinancial information required when registering under 1933 Act and when reporting quarterly information under 1934 Act.

           2] A small business issuer is generally one that has revenues less than $25 million.

4. Exempt securities (need not be registered but still subject to antifraud provisions under the Act).

  a. Commercial paper (e.g., note, draft, check, etc.) with a maturity of nine months or less.

     (1) Must be for commercial purpose and not investment.

> **EXAMPLE**
>
> OK Corporation in Washington, DC, wishes to finance a short-term need for more cash for current operations. OK will do this by issuing some short-term notes which all have a maturity of nine months or less. These are exempt from the registration requirements.

  b. Intrastate issues—securities offered and sold only within one state.

     (1) The issuer must be resident of state and doing 80% of business in the state and must use at least 80% of sale proceeds in connection with business operations in the state.

     (2) All offerees and purchasers must be residents of state.

     (3) For nine months after last sale by the issuer, resales can only be made to residents of state.

     (4) All of a particular issue must qualify under this rule or this exemption cannot be used for any sale of the issue.

> **EXAMPLE**
>
> A regional corporation in need of additional capital makes an offer to the residents of the state in which it is incorporated to purchase a new issue of its stock. The offer expressly restricts sales to only residents of the state and all purchasers are residents of the state.

  c. Small issues (Regulation A)—issuances up to $5,000,000 by issuer in 12-month period may be exempt if

     (1) There is a notice filed with SEC.

     (2) An offering circular (containing financial information about the corporation and descriptive information about offered securities) must be provided to offeree. Financial statements in offering circular need not be audited.

     (3) Nonissuers can sell up to $1,500,000 in 12-month period.

> **NOTE:** An offering circular (statement) is required under Regulation A instead of the more costly and time-consuming prospectus.

  d. Securities of governments, banks, quasi governmental authorities (e.g., local hospital authorities), savings and loan associations, farmers, co-ops, and common carriers regulated by ICC. Public utilities are not exempt.

e. Security exchanged by the issuer exclusively with its existing shareholders so long as

   (1) No commission is paid.
   (2) Both sets of securities must have been issued by the same person.

EXAMPLE

A stock split is an exempt transaction under the 1933 Act and thus, the securities need not be registered at time of split.

---

f. Securities of nonprofit religious, educational, or charitable organizations.
g. Certificates issued by receiver or trustee in bankruptcy.
h. Insurance and annuity contracts.

5. Exempt transactions or offerings (still subject, however, to antifraud provisions of the Act; may also be subject to reporting requirements of the 1934 Act).

a. Sale or offer to sell by any person **other than** an issuer, underwriter, or dealer

   (1) Generally covers sales by individual investors on their own account.
   (2) May be a transaction by broker on customer's order. It does not include solicitation of these orders.
   (3) Exemption does not apply to sales by controlling persons because they are considered an underwriter or issuer.

b. **Regulation D** establishes three important exemptions in Rules 504, 505, and 506 under the 1933 Act.

   (1) Rule 504 exempts an issuance of securities up to $1,000,000 sold in 12-month period to any number of investors (this is also known as seed capital exemption).

      (a) General offering and solicitations are permitted under Rule 504 as long as they are restricted to "accredited investors," such as banks, insurance companies, high-worth individuals, etc.
      (b) The issuer need not restrict purchasers' right to resell securities.
      (c) No specific disclosure is required.
      (d) The issuer must send notice of offering to SEC within 15 days of first sale of securities.

   (2) Rule 505 exempts issuance of up to $5,000,000 in 12-month period.

      (a) No general offering or solicitation is permitted within 12-month period.
      (b) Permits sales to 35 unaccredited (nonaccredited term sometimes used) investors and to unlimited number of accredited investors within 12 months.

         1] Accredited investors are, for example, banks, savings and loan associations, credit unions, insurance companies, broker dealers, certain trusts, partnerships, and corporations, also natural persons having joint or individual net worth exceeding $1,000,000 or having joint or individual net income of $200,000 for two most recent years.
         2] SEC must be notified within fifteen days of first sale.

      (c) The issuer must restrict the purchasers' right to resell the securities; in general must be held for two years or else exemption is lost.
      (d) These securities typically state that they have not been registered and that they have resale restrictions.
      (e) Unlike under Rule 504, if nonaccredited investor purchases these securities, audited balance sheet must be supplied (i.e., disclosure is required) as well as other financial statements or information, if readily available.

         1] If purchased only by accredited investors, no disclosure required.

   (3) Rule 506 allows private placement of unlimited amount of securities.

      (a) In general, the same rules apply here as outlined under Rule 505. (Note that under the provisions of the Jumpstart Our Business Startups (JOBS) Act general solicitation and advertising for Rule 506 offerings is allowed. This Act will be eligible for testing beginning in January 2013)
      (b) However, an additional requirement is that the unaccredited investors (up to 35) must be sophisticated investors (individuals with knowledge and experience in financial matters) or be represented by individual with such knowledge and experience.

> **EXAMPLE**
>
> A growing corporation is in need of additional capital and decides to make a new issuance of its stock. The stock is only offered to 10 of the president's friends who regularly make financial investments of this sort. They are interested in purchasing the stock for an investment and each of them is provided with the type of information that is regularly included in a registration statement.

    (4) Disclosures for offerings under $2,000,000 have been simplified to be similar to disclosures under Regulation A.

    (5) A controlling person who sells restricted securities may be held to be an underwriter (and thus subject to the registration provisions) unless requirements of Rule 144 are met when controlling person is selling through a broker.

        (a) If the following are met, the security can be sold without registration:

            1] The broker performs no services beyond those of typical broker who executes orders and receives customary fee.

            2] Ownership (including beneficial ownership) for at least two years.

            3] Only limited amounts of stock may be sold—based on a specified formula.

            4] Public must have available adequate disclosure of the issuer corporation.

            5] Notice of sale must be filed with SEC.

    (6) Small issuers sometimes use offerings over Internet to investors and often use regulation to avoid registration. (Note the JOBS Act of 2012 has provisions that make it easier for firms to make Internet offerings. However, the provision will not be effective or testable on the CPA exam until after the SEC develops the related rules.)

  c. Postregistration transactions by dealer (i.e., dealer is not required to deliver prospectus) if the transaction is made at least 40 days after first date security was offered to public, or after 90 days if it is issuer's first public issue. This exemption does not apply to sales of securities that are leftover part of an allotment from the public issue.

6. Antifraud provisions

  a. Apply even if securities are exempt or the transactions are exempt as long as interstate commerce is used (use of mail or telephone qualifies) to sell or offer to sell securities.

  b. Included are schemes to defraud purchaser or making sale by use of untrue statement of material fact or by omission of material fact.

    (1) Proof of negligence is sometimes sufficient rather than proof of scienter.

    (2) Protects purchaser, not seller.

7. Civil liability (i.e., private actions brought by purchasers of securities).

  a. The purchaser may recover if he or she can establish that

    (1) It was a purchase of a security issued under a registration statement containing a misleading statement or omission of a material fact, and purchaser may also recover if issuer or any person sold unregistered securities for which there is no exemption.

    (2) Suffered economic loss.

    (3) Privity of contract is **not** necessary.

> **EXAMPLE**
>
> Third parties who have never dealt with issuer but bought securities from another party have a right to recover when the above is established despite lack of privity.

    (4) Need **not** prove that the defendant intended to deceive.

    (5) The purchaser need **not** rely on registration statement to recover.

  b. The purchaser of securities may recover from (1) the issuer, (2) any directors, partners or underwriters of the issuer, (3) anyone who signed the registration statement, and (4) experts of authorized statements (e.g., attorneys, accountants, engineers, appraisers). Liability is not discharged in bankruptcy.

  c. The burden of proof is shifted to defendant in most cases; however, except for the issuer, defendant may use "due diligence" defense.

   (1) The due diligence defense can be used successfully by defendant by proving that

      (a) As an expert, s/he had reasonable grounds after reasonable investigation to believe that his/her own statements were true and/or did not contain any omissions of material facts by the time the registration statement became effective.

> **EXAMPLE**
>
> Whitewood, a CPA, performs a reasonable audit and discovers no irregularities.

      (b) S/he relied on an expert for the part of the registration statement in question and did believe (and had reasonable grounds for such belief) that there were no misstatements or material omissions of fact.

> **EXAMPLE**
>
> Greenwood, a CPA, relies on an attorney's work as a foundation for his own work on contingent liabilities.

      (c) S/he did reasonably believe that after a reasonable investigation, statements not in the province of an expert were true or that material omissions did not exist.

> **EXAMPLE**
>
> Lucky, an underwriter, made a reasonable investigation on the registration statement and did reasonably believe no impropriety existed even though misstatements and omissions of material facts existed. Note that the issuer is liable even if s/he exercised the same care and held the same reasonable belief because the issuer is liable without fault and cannot use the due diligence defense.

NOTE: The issuer is liable even if s/he exercised the same care and held the same reasonable belief because the issuer is liable without fault and cannot use the due diligence defense.

  d. The seller of the security is liable to purchaser if interstate commerce or mail is used, and if the registration is not in effect and should be, or if the registration statement contains misstatements or omissions of material facts. The purchaser may recover the amount paid plus interest less any income received by the purchaser. The buyer may ask for rescission of sale instead of damages.

  e. The statute of limitations is the earlier of these dates:

    (1) Two years after discovery is made of fraud, deceit, or manipulation involving contravention of securities laws; or

    (2) Five years after such violation of securities laws involving fraud, deceit, or manipulation

8. Criminal liability

  a. If person intentionally (willfully) makes an untrue statement or intentionally omits a material fact, or willfully violates SEC Act or regulation.

    (1) Reckless disregard of the truth may also qualify.

    (2) Tampering with documents to be used in official proceedings do qualify.

  b. If person uses interstate commerce or mail to fraudulently sell any security.

  c. Person is subject to fine or imprisonment up to twenty years or both.

    (1) Injunctions are also available.

  d. Criminal liability results even if securities are exempt or transactions are exempt.

9. Increased protection for whistle-blowers of public companies

> **NOW REVIEW MULTIPLE-CHOICE QUESTIONS 1 THROUGH 26 IN VOLUME 2**

B. Securities Exchange Act of 1934 (Generally applies to subsequent trading of securities—must comply separately with 1933 Act if applicable, that is, initial issuances rather than subsequent trading).

1. Purposes of the Act

a. To federally regulate securities exchanges and securities traded thereon
b. To require periodic disclosure by issuers of equity securities
c. To require adequate information be provided in various transactions
d. To prevent unfair use of information by insiders
e. To prevent fraud and deceptive practices

2. Following securities must be registered with SEC

a. Over-the-counter and other equity securities traded in interstate commerce where corporation has assets of more than $10 million and 500 or more shareholders. Equity securities include stock, rights to subscribe to stock, or securities convertible into stock. (Note that a provision of the Jumpstart Our Business Startups (JOBS) Act increases this threshold to 500 unaccredited shareholders or 2,000 total shareholders. It also provides that the threshold will not consider shares obtained by a shareholder as a part of a qualified employee compensation plan. This Act will be eligible for testing beginning in January 2013.)
b. Securities that are traded on any national securities exchange must be registered. Securities exempted under 1933 Act may still be regulated under 1934 Act.
c. Securities offered by issuer who was required to register under 1933 Act.

3. Required disclosures in registration include

a. Names of officers and directors
b. Nature of business
c. Financial structure of firm
d. Any bonus and profit-sharing provisions

4. Sanctions available to SEC under the 1934 Act

a. Revocation or suspension of registration
b. Denial of registration
c. Permanent or temporary suspension of trading of securities (injunction)
d. May order accounting and disgorgement of gains made illegally
e. May sanction individuals violating foreign laws
f. May require large traders to identify selves

5. Exempt securities

a. Obligations of US government, guaranteed by, or in which US government has interest.
b. Obligations of state or political subdivision, or guaranteed thereby.
c. Securities of federally chartered bank or savings and loan institution.
d. Securities of common carrier regulated by ICC.
e. Industrial development bonds.

6. Issuers of securities registered under the 1934 Act must file the following reports with SEC.

a. Annual reports (Form 10-K) must be certified by independent public accountant.
b. Quarterly reports (Form 10-Q) must be filed for each of first three fiscal quarters of each fiscal year of issuer.

(1) Must be reviewed by CPA.
(2) Not required to be reported on by CPA.

c. Event reports (Form 8-K) when material events occur such as change in corporate control, significant change or revaluation of assets, or change in amount of issued securities. In most cases the form must be filed within four days after the material event occurs.
d. Similar reports must be provided to shareholders. However, annual report need not be given if issuer had to disclose under 1934 Act only because it made a registered offering under 1933 Act.

7. Whether registered under 1934 Act or not, the securities registered during the previous year under 1933 Act must have periodic reports filed with SEC by issuers.

8. Proxy solicitations

a. Proxy—grant of authority by shareholder to someone else to vote his/her shares at a meeting.
b. A proxy solicitation provisions apply to solicitation (by any means of interstate commerce or the mails) of holders of securities required to be registered under the 1934 Act—must be reported to SEC.
c. A proxy statement must be sent with proxy solicitation.

(1) It must contain disclosure of all material facts concerning matters to be voted upon.

(a) Either misstatements or omissions of material facts are violations of proxy rules.
(b) Material means that it would likely affect vote of average shareholder on proposed action.

(2) The purpose is for fairness in corporate action and election of directors.

d. The requirements of the proxy itself

(1) Indicate on whose behalf solicitation is made
(2) Identify clearly and impartially each matter to be acted on

e. Some of inclusions in the proxy material

(1) Proposals by shareholders that are a proper subject for shareholders to vote on
(2) Financial statements for last two years, certified by independent accountant, if

(a) Solicitation is on behalf of management.
(b) It is for annual meeting at which directors are to be elected.

f. Any person who owns at least 5% or has held stock for six months or more has right of access to lists of share-holders for lawful purpose.
g. The proxy statement, proxy itself, and any other soliciting material must be filed with SEC.
h. Brokers are required to forward proxies for customers' shares held by broker.
i. Incumbent management is required to mail proxy materials of insurgents to shareholders if requested and expenses are paid by the insurgents.
j. Remedies for violation of proxy solicitation rules

(1) Civil action by aggrieved shareholder for damages caused by material misinformation or omissions of material facts
(2) Or injunctions are possible
(3) Or the court may set aside vote taken and require a new proxy solicitation with full and fair disclosure

9. Tender offers

a. A tender offer is invitation by buyer (bidder) to shareholders of targeted company to tender shares they own for sale for price specified over a period of time.
b. Reporting and disclosure requirements apply to tender offers to provide shareholders full disclosure by both the bidder and targeted company.

10. Short-swing profits

a. A corporation is entitled to recover profits from any insider who sells stock of company within six months of its purchase.
b. Profits that can be recovered are calculated by matching highest sale price with lowest purchase price found within six months.
c. Losses cannot be used to offset these profits.

11. Antifraud provisions—very broad scope

a. It is unlawful to manipulate process and create appearance of active trading (not good-faith transactions by brokers).
b. It is unlawful to use any manipulative or deceptive devices in purchase or sale of securities.

(1) Applies to all securities, whether registered or not (as long as either mail, interstate commerce, or a national stock exchange is used)—this is important.
(2) Includes any act, practice, or scheme which is deceptive or manipulative (against SEC rules and/or regulations)—most importantly, it is unlawful to make any false statement of a material fact or any omission of a material fact that is necessary to make statement(s) not misleading (in connection with purchase or sale of security, whether registered or not).

(a) This is Rule 10b-5 promulgated by the SEC under Section 10(b) of the Act.

> **NOTE:** There are no exemptions under Rule 10b-5.

(3) The plaintiff must prove

(a) The defendant made material false statement or omission of material fact in connection with purchase or sale of securities.

1] The basic test of materiality is whether a reasonable person would attach importance to the fact in determining his/her choice of action in the transaction.

> **EXAMPLE**
>
> A broker offers to sell a stock and omits to tell the purchaser that the corporation is about to make an unfavorable merger.

    (b) The defendant acted with scienter which is either knowledge of falsity, or reckless disregard for the truth.

        1] Negligence is not sufficient.
        2] Note that with antifraud provisions under the **1933** Act scienter need not necessarily be proven.

    (c) The defendant must have relied upon false statements or omissions.
    (d) The defendant who suffers damages may sue for monetary damages, or rescind the transaction.

(4) Applies to brokers who intend to never deliver securities or who intend to misappropriate proceeds of sales. The SEC by US Supreme Court ruling has power to sue brokers for fraud.
(5) Applies to any seller, buyer, or person who lends his/her name to statements used in the buying and selling of securities. Cross reference this to the 1933 Act that only applies to sellers or offerors of securities.
(6) Applies to insider who buys or sells on inside information until it is disseminated to public.

    (a) Includes a broad scope of insiders such as officers, directors, accountants, lawyers, employees at the various levels of firm, consultants, agents, representatives of firm, and any other persons owing a fiduciary duty to company.

(7) Even if exempt from registration under 1934 Act, still subject to antifraud provisions.
(8) Extensive potential liability for insiders

    (a) Must forego trading if one has such knowledge until public has information

        1] Includes insiders and anyone with knowledge (e.g., accountant, attorney, engineer)
        2] Illegal for person (tipper) to give inside information to another person (called tippee)
        3] Tippee is liable if acts on inside information until information is known by public

           a] Tipper is liable for illegal profits of tippee.

12. Civil liability

    a. Any person (including an accountant) who intentionally (willfully) manipulates a security may be liable to the buyer or seller of that security if the buyer or seller is damaged.

> **NOTE:** Both buyers and sellers may recover under the 1934 Act.

    b. Any person who makes a misleading (or of course false) statement about any material fact in any application, report, or document is liable to an injured purchaser or seller if s/he relied on the statement, and did not know it was false or misleading.

      (1) Privity of contract is not necessary.
      (2) However, the party sued can avoid liability if s/he can prove s/he acted in good faith, and had no knowledge that the statements were materially misleading or false. The SEC may collect liability funds for victims of securities fraud.

13. Criminal liability

    a. Has been increased due to Sarbanes-Oxley Act

      (1) Individuals in violation of Rule 10b-5 may be put in prison for up to 20 years and/or may be fined for up to five million dollars.

        (a) May be put in prison for up to 25 years and/or fined for willful violation of 1934 Act.

      (2) Corporations or partnerships are subject to fines of up to 25 million dollars.

    b. Criminal liability can also be used for intentional false or misleading statements on material facts provided in applications, reports, or other documents under this Act.

14. The Bankruptcy Abuse Prevention and Consumer Protection Act of 2005 prohibits discharge of any debts incurred in violation of securities laws.
15. Both private parties and SEC now have civil remedies against violators of 1934 Act.

    a. Private parties may recover from those who violate rule 10b-5 as well as from others sharing responsibility such as attorneys, accountants, corporations.

        (1) Private parties may also rescind contracts to purchase contacts when violations hurt them.

    b. SEC authorized to give awards to individuals that provide information leading to prosecution of insider-trading violators.

16. Statute of limitations extended for securities fraud
17. Reporting requirements of insiders under 1934 Act

    a. Must file statement with SEC

        (1) Discloses amount of equity securities
        (2) Time of statement disclosure

           (a) When securities registered
           (b) When registration statement becomes effective
           (c) Within ten days of person attaining insider status

        (3) Insider must report any changes in ownership within 10 days.

18. Foreign Corrupt Practices Act

    a. Unlawful for any domestic company or its officers or employees or agents to offer or give to foreign officials or to political party or political officials something of value to influence decisions.

        (1) Excluded are routine governmental actions that do not involve official's discretion such as processing applications or permits.
        (2) Amendment includes attempt by supplier to obtain any improper advantage is unlawful.

    b. Requires companies having registered securities to maintain system of internal control and to maintain accurate accounting and to protect integrity of independent audits.
    c. Actions of foreign citizens or organizations committed within US also covered.

19. Regulation Fair Disclosure (Reg FD) from SEC requires corporation to disseminate its data equally among investors and analysts to help avoid conflicts of interest by analysts.

    a. If one mistakenly gives out inside information s/he must disclose it publicly as soon as is practicable and always within 24 hours or less.
    b. Applies also to giving nonpublic information to shareholders who are likely to trade based upon it.

NOW REVIEW MULTIPLE-CHOICE QUESTIONS 27 THROUGH 42 IN VOLUME 2

C. The Sarbanes-Oxley Act of 2002

1. The act covers all public companies.
2. Section 906 certification provision of Act requires that each periodic report that contains financial reports of the issuer must be accompanied with written statement of CEO or CFO that certifies that reports comply fully with relevant securities laws and also fairly present the financial condition of company in all material aspects.

    a. Any officer who makes certification while knowing it does not comply with SEC requirements can be fined up to $1,000,000 or imprisoned for up to 10 years, or both.

        (1) Officers can be fined for up to $5,000,000 or imprisoned for up to 20 years, or both, for willful violation of this certification requirement.
        (2) SEC now permitted to freeze payments to officers and directors during investigation of wrongdoings.
        (3) SEC may now prevent unfit individuals from serving as officers or directors of public companies.

    b. CEO and CFO must give up any bonuses, incentive-based pay and profits on sales of stock that they received during 12-month time before financial statements are required to be restated because of omissions or misstatements of material facts.

3. Section 302 certification makes officers responsible for maintaining effective internal controls and requires principal executive and financial officers to disclose all significant internal control deficiencies to issuer's auditors and audit committee.

    a. Management must now evaluate any changes in internal control methods.

    b. Officers and directors of an issuer or their agents are prohibited from fraudulently influencing or coercing auditors to render financial statements materially misleading.

4. Act amends Securities Exchange Act of 1934 to make it illegal for issuer to give various types of personal loans to or for any executive officer or director.
5. CEO and CFO must give up any bonus, any compensation that is equity based or incentive based, or any profit from sale of corporation's securities during period when corporation was required to restate financial statements due to wrongdoings.

    a. CEO and CFO must give up these bonuses and profits even if wrongdoings were not by them but also if they were by any other officer or employee.

    b. Act requires that any wrongdoing officer give up profits from stock sales or bonuses received due to stock being overpriced because of false information.

        (1) Act allows not only that improper gains be recovered but also any remedy needed to protect investors.

6. Attorneys are required to report to chief legal counsel or CEO such things as material violations of securities laws or breach of fiduciary duties. Attorneys must report this to audit committee (or another committee) or board of directors if counsel or CEO does not take action.
7. Companies must disclose material off-balance sheet liabilities and transactions.

    a. Amendments require management disclosure of information needed by users of financial statements to better understand off-balance sheet arrangements involving such things as their business purpose, market risk, credit risk, liquidity, or other material effects.

8. Pro forma information disclosed to public in financial reports, press releases, etc., must not contain any untrue statement of a material fact or omit any material fact.

    a. Pro forma information must also be reconciled with financial statements prepared in accordance with GAAP.

9. SEC now requires that reports by insiders that disclose their securities holdings must be filed electronically with SEC to result in earlier public notification and wider public availability of this information.

    a. Issuers having corporate Web sites must also post such information quickly.

10. New rules require disclosures, both financial and nonfinancial, to aid public in assessing risk better pertaining to companies (e.g., disclosing off-balance sheet financing).

    a. Also, aid in purpose of Act to produce reports under Securities Acts that are timely and reliable.

D. The Wall Street Reform and Consumer Protection (Dodd-Frank) Act of 2010

The Dodd-Frank Act was passed as a reaction to the recent financial crisis. The Act was designed "to promote the financial stability of the United States by improving accountability and transparency in the financial system, to end "too big to fail," to protect the American taxpayer by ending bailouts, to protect consumers from abusive financial services practices, and for other purposes."

1. The Act created the Financial Stability Oversight Council that is charged with identifying threats to the financial stability of the US, promoting market discipline, and responding to emerging risks. The Council will identify significant nonbank financial firms and regulate these institutions, and prescribe risk management standards for payment, clearing, and settlement activities by financial market institutions.
2. The Act increased the types of financial companies that could be seized and liquidated by the FDIC to include insurance companies and nonbank financial companies.
3. The Act requires previously exempt US and non-US advisors of hedge funds, private equity funds, and other private investment vehicles to register with the SEC under the Advisors Act. It also provides for additional reporting requirements for registered and nonregistered advisors.
4. The Act eliminated the Office of Thrift Supervision, distributing its responsibilities to other agencies.
5. The Act created the Federal Insurance Office to regulate insurance companies.
6. The Act created the Bureau of Consumer Financial Protection to regulate the offering of consumer products and services (e.g., credit counseling, check-cashing, etc.) under the federal consumer financial laws.
7. The Act prohibits any "banking entity" from engaging in proprietary trading, or sponsoring or investing in a hedge fund or private equity fund (the Volcher rule).
8. The Act gives authority to the Commodity Futures Trading Commission and the SEC to regulate the derivatives (swaps) markets, including the regulation of swap dealers and major swap participants.
9. The Act has provisions to help prevent conflicts of interests and increase transparency by credit rating agencies.
10. The Act includes broad changes in executive compensation policies for public companies, including

    a. Requiring the national exchanges to issue new listing rules requiring companies to develop and implement compensation-recovery arrangements (clawback policies). The Act states that when noncompliance with a financial-reporting requirement leads to an accounting restatement, the company is required to recover from any current or former executive officer all excessive incentive-based compensation paid over the preceding three-year period.

    b. Requiring that all members of the compensation committee of the board of directors be independent.

    c. Requiring a shareholder nonbinding vote on the prior year's executive compensation at least every three years, and a vote at least every six years as to whether the vote on compensation should be held more often.

    d. Requiring a nonbinding vote by shareholders on "golden parachutes" to be provided to executives as a result of major transactions.

11. The Act provides that the SEC will increase its compliance activities regarding securities trading, and will pay awards to whistle-blowers for providing information about violations of securities laws that result in aggregate monetary sanctions in excess of $1 million.

    a. A whistle-blower is eligible to receive 10 to 30% of the monetary penalty if the information is derived from independent knowledge or analysis of the whistle-blower and not known to the government from any other source.

    b. Tips can be made anonymously (through an attorney) with the whistle-blower only being identified to the SEC after determination that an award will be given.

    c. A broad group of individuals are eligible including employees, customers, and suppliers. Individuals that are generally excluded from eligibility include

        (1) Officers, directors, trustees, or partners of an entity, when those individuals learned of information about the misconduct in question from another person or in connection with the company's processes for identifying potential illegal conduct.

        (2) Employees whose main job functions involve compliance or internal audit, or persons who are employed by a firm hired to perform audit or compliance functions or to investigate possible violations of the law.

        (3) Employees of public accounting firms performing an engagement required by the securities laws.

    However, the above individuals may be still eligible if it appears that the company is attempting to behave in a way that would harm investors or inhibit an investigation, or 120 days have passed since they notified the company of the violation.

    d. Whistle-blowers are encouraged to report the information through the normal internal corporate governance system by an indication that doing so will be considered when determining the amount of the award.

12. The act requires mortgage securitizers or originators to retain an economic interest (at least 5%) in a portion of the credit risk of any securitized asset that they create and sell.

E. Exemptions for Smaller and Emerging Companies

1. Smaller reporting companies have reduced requirements for disclosure of financial and nonfinancial information for initial filings (1933 Act) and periodic reporting (1934 Act). Smaller reporting companies are those that

    a. Have a common equity public float (market capitalization) of less than $75 million, or
    b. Are unable to calculate their public float and have annual revenues of $50 million or less.

2. The Dodd-Frank Act permanently exempted these smaller reporting companies (nonaccelerated filers) from the requirement to have integrated audits of their internal controls.

3. The JOBS Act of 2012 significantly reduced the registration and reporting requirements of "emerging growth companies." Notably, these companies are exempt for at least 5 years from the requirement to have integrated audits of their internal controls, and the Dodd-Frank provisions regarding executive compensation. A company qualifies as an emerging growth company if its initial public offering (IPO) was after December 8, 2011, and it had less than $1 billion of total annual gross revenues during its last completed fiscal year. A company no longer qualifies as an emerging growth company after the earliest of (1) the completion of a fiscal year in which the company has gross revenues of $1 billion or more, (2) the completion of the fiscal year of the 5th anniversary of the company's IPO, (3) the issuance of $1 billion in nonconvertible debt in the prior 3-year period, or (4) the company becoming a larger accelerated filer under SEC guidelines. (Note the JOBS Act will not be eligible for testing until January 2013.)

F. Internet Securities Offering (ISO) (Direct Public Offerings [DPO])

1. ISO used primarily by small businesses to accumulate capital.
2. SEC created electronic database of corporate information.

    a. Allows access to much data formerly available only to big institutions.

        (1) Thus tends to level playing field between small investors and large investors.
        (2) Also, tends to level playing field between small and large businesses.

   b. Allows electronic filing.
   c. Companies may market securities faster and more cheaply by circumventing paperwork of investment bankers.
   d. These securities are typically riskier because often avoid screening processes of various professionals.

3. In general, securities laws and regulations apply to ISO.
4. Prospectuses may be placed online.
5. Secondary market for securities may also be accomplished on websites.

G. Electronic Signatures and Electronic Records

1. Federal law specifies that no agreement, record, or signature required by federal securities laws or state laws can be denied legal effect because it is electronic record or contains electronic signature.

   a. Also applies to electronic signatures between investment advisors, brokers, dealers, and customers.
   b. SEC may specify manner of file retention but may not discriminate against any specific technology in effort to promote advances in technology.

H. State "Blue-Sky" Laws

1. These are state statutes regulating the issuance and sale of securities.

   a. They contain antifraud and registration provisions.

2. Must be complied with **in addition** to federal laws.
3. Exemptions from federal laws are not exemptions from state laws.

NOW REVIEW MULTIPLE-CHOICE QUESTIONS 43 THROUGH 45 IN VOLUME 2

KEY TERMS

Insiders. Includes officers, directors, and owners of more than 10% of any class of an issuer's equity securities.
Prospectus. Any notice, circular, advertisement, letter, or communication offering any security for sale (or merger).
Proxy. Grant of authority by a shareholder to someone else to vote the shareholder's shares at a meeting.
Registration statement. The statement required to be filed with the SEC before the initial sale of securities can occur.
Security. Any debt or equity interest in a company including a note, stock, bond, certificate of interest, debenture, investment contract, etc.
Underwriter. Any person who has purchased from an issuer with a view to the public distribution of any security, or a party who participates in such an undertaking.

Module 25: Business Structure

Overview

A sole proprietorship has only one owner, which creates both advantages and disadvantages. A partnership is an association of two or more persons to carry on a business as co-owners for profit. The major areas tested on partnerships are the characteristics of a partnership, comparisons with other structures, rights and liabilities of the partnership itself, the rights, duties, and liabilities of the partners among themselves and to third parties, the allocation of profits and losses, and the rights of various parties, including creditors, upon dissolution.

The law of joint ventures is similar to that of partnerships with some exceptions. Note that the joint venture is more limited in scope than the partnership form of business. The former is typically organized to carry out one single business undertaking or a series of related undertakings; whereas, the latter is formed to conduct ongoing business.

Subchapter S corporations are those corporations that elect to be taxed similar to partnerships under Subchapter S. Corporations that do not make this election are called Subchapter C corporations. In both cases, a corporation is an artificial person that is created by or under law and which operates under a common name through its elected management. It is a legal entity, separate and distinct from its shareholders. The corporation has the authority vested in it by statute and its corporate charter. The candidate should understand the characteristics and advantages of the corporate form over other forms of business organization.

Basic to preparation for questions on corporation law is an understanding of the following: the liabilities of a promoter who organizes a new corporation; the liability of shareholders; the liability of the corporation with respect to the preincorporation contracts made by the promoter; the fiduciary relationship of the promoter to the stockholders and to the corporation; the various circumstances under which a stockholder may be liable for the debts of the corporation; the rights of shareholders particularly concerning payment of dividends; the rights and duties of officers, directors, and other agents or employees of the corporation to the corporation, to stockholders, and to third persons; subscriptions; and the procedures necessary to merge, consolidate, or otherwise change the corporate structure.

State laws are now widely based on the Revised Business Corporation Act upon which changes to this module are based.

For all the business structures listed in this module you should know the basic characteristics of each. The Examiners expect you to understand the basic strengths and weaknesses of each business structure and to be able to select the appropriate business structure for given situations. Before beginning the reading you should review the key terms at the end of the module.

A. Nature of Sole Proprietorships

1. There is only one owner of business

   a. Business is not a separate legal entity apart from owner
   b. Owner does not share power or decision making with other owners

2. Advantages over other business structures

    a. Sole proprietorship is simplest type of business structure

        (1) Easy to form and to operate

            (a) Federal or state governments do not require formal filing or approval to begin operation

                1] If business is operating under name other than that of sole proprietor, most states require that it file fictitious name statement with government

    b. Business can be sold without need to obtain approval from others such as shareholders or partners
    c. Owner has right to make all business decisions such as direction company should go, who to hire or fire, etc.
    d. If business generates profit, sole owner need not share it with other owners or investors
    e. The profits of the business are taxed on the personal tax return of the owner—profits are taxed only once

3. Disadvantages over other business structures

    a. If company has loss, sole proprietor suffers all of it
    b. Sole proprietorship cannot obtain capital from partners, shareholders, etc.

        (1) Capital is limited by funds the owner has or can borrow

    c. Sole proprietor has unlimited personal liability

NOW REVIEW MULTIPLE-CHOICE QUESTION 1 IN VOLUME 2

B. Nature of Partnerships

1. A partnership is an association of two or more persons to carry on a business as co-owners for profit

    a. The phrase "to carry on a business" includes almost every trade, occupation, or profession

        (1) It does not include passive co-ownership of property (e.g., joint tenants of a piece of land)
        (2) Partnerships do not include nonprofit unincorporated associations (e.g., labor unions, charitable organizations, clubs)

    b. Co-ownership of the "business" (and not merely of assets used in a business) is an important element in determining whether a partnership exists

        (1) The most important and necessary element of co-ownership (and thereby partnership) is profit sharing

            (a) Need not be equal, but is treated equally unless otherwise stated
            (b) Receipt of a share of profits is *prima facie evidence* (raises a presumption) of a partnership

                1] Presumption rebutted by establishing that profit sharing was only for payment of debt, interest on loan, services performed, rent, etc.

        (2) Another important element of co-ownership is joint control

            (a) Each partner has an equal right to participate in management. Right to manage may be contracted away to a managing partner

        (3) Under Revised Uniform Partnership Act, now adopted by majority of states, partner is no longer co-owner of partnership property

2. Partnership relationship creates a fiduciary relationship between partners

    a. Fiduciary relationship arises because each partner is an agent for partnership and for each other in partnership business

3. Partnership relationship is based on contract but arrangements may be quite informal

    a. Agreement can be inferred from conduct (e.g., allowing someone to share in management and profits may result in partnership even though actual intent to become partner is missing)

4. Draws heavily on agency law because each partner is an agent as well as a principal of partnership

    a. Most rules can be changed in individual cases by agreement between parties affected (e.g., rights and duties between partners)

> **EXAMPLE**
>
> A, B, and C form a partnership in which all three partners agree that A is liable for all of the product liability cases against the partnership. This agreement is enforceable between A, B, and C but not against other parties that never agreed to this. Therefore, as long as A is solvent, B and C can collect from A even though a third party recovers from all of them on a product liability problem.

5. Generally, any person (entity) who has the capacity to contract may become a partner

   a. Corporations
   b. Minors—but contract of partnership is voidable
   c. Partnerships can become partners

6. Common characteristics of partnerships

   a. Limited duration
   b. Transfer of ownership requires permission from other partners
   c. May sue and be sued as separate legal entities
   d. Unlimited liability of partners for partnership debts
   e. Ease of formation, can be very informal
   f. Partnership does not pay federal income tax; partners must include their share of partnership operations on their tax returns

NOW REVIEW MULTIPLE-CHOICE QUESTIONS 2 THROUGH 4 IN VOLUME 2

C. Formation of Partnership

1. By agreement, express or implied

   a. Agreement to share profits is *prima facie evidence* that partnership exists

      (1) Need not agree to share losses because agreement to share profits assumes sharing of losses
      (2) Sharing of gross receipts does not establish partnership

   b. Partnership not implied if profits received for some other purpose such as for payment of debt, wages, or lease

2. Creation of a partnership may be very informal, either oral or written

   a. Written partnership agreement not required unless within Statute of Frauds (e.g., partnership that cannot be completed within one year)

> **EXAMPLE**
>
> A, B, and C form a partnership that, although they expect it to last for several years, has no time period specified. This partnership agreement may be oral.

> **EXAMPLE**
>
> X, Y, and Z organize XYZ partnership which by agreement will last at least five years. This partnership agreement must be in writing.

      (1) Usually wise to have in writing even if not required by statute or contract law

   b. Filing not required

3. Articles of copartnership (partnership agreement)—not legally necessary, but a good idea to have
4. Fictitious name statutes require partners to register fictitious or assumed names

   a. Failure to comply does not invalidate partnership but may result in fine
   b. The purpose is to allow third parties to know who is in partnership

D. Partner's Rights and Operation of Partnership

1. Partnership agreement, whether oral or written, is the controlling law for the partnership

2. The Revised Uniform Partnership Act (RUPA) is a law that fills in when relevant provisions are not contained in the partnership agreement

3. Look first to what the partnership agreement says; if the agreement is silent or the Examiners have not given you a relevant provision of the partnership agreement, then apply the RUPA rules that follow below. Remember the partnership agreement supersedes RUPA.

4. Partnership interest

   a. Refers to partner's right to share in profits and return of contribution on dissolution
   b. Is considered personal property
   c. Does not include specific partnership property, merely right to use it for partnership purposes
   d. Freely assignable without other partner's consent

      (1) Assignee is not substituted as a partner without consent of all other partners
      (2) Assignee does **not** receive right to manage partnership, to have an accounting, to inspect books, to possess or own any individual partnership property—merely receives rights in the assigning partner's share of profits and return of partner's capital contribution (unless partners agree otherwise)

         (a) Typically, assignments are made to secure a loan

---

EXAMPLE

C, a CPA, wishes to obtain a large loan. He is a member of a CPA firm and assigns rights in his partnership to the bank to secure the loan.

---

      (3) Assignor remains liable as a partner
      (4) Does not create dissociation unless assignor also withdraws

5. Partnership property

   a. Includes

      (1) Property acquired with partnership funds unless different intent is shown
      (2) Property not acquired in partnership name is partnership property if

         (a) Partner acquires title to it in his/her capacity as a partner, or
         (b) Property acquired with partnership funds

   b. Not assignable or subject to attachment individually, only by a claim on partnership

      (1) Property may be assigned by agreement of all partners
      (2) Any partner can assign or sell property if for the apparent purpose of carrying on the business of the partnership in the usual way

   c. Upon partner's death, his/her estate is entitled to deceased partner's share of profits and capital, but not to any specific partnership property

      (1) Remaining partners have duty to account to the heirs of the deceased for value of interest
      (2) Heirs not automatically partners

6. Participate in management

   a. Right to participate equally in management

      (1) Ordinary business decisions by a majority vote
      (2) Unanimous consent needed to make fundamental changes, which include

         (a) Admitting new partners
         (b) Any action outside the scope of the normal partnership business
         (c) Any action contrary to the partnership agreement, or amending the partnership agreement

   b. Power to act as an agent for partnership in partnership business
   c. Also has right to inspect books and have full knowledge of partnership affairs
   d. Silent partner is one who does not help manage

      (1) Still has personal, unlimited liability

7. Share in profits and losses

   a. Profits and losses are shared equally unless agreement specifies otherwise

(1) Even if contributed capital is not equal
(2) For example, agreement may specify one partner to receive greater share of profits for doing more work, etc., while losses still shared equally

b. If partners agree on unequal profit sharing but are silent on loss sharing, losses are shared per the profit-sharing proportions

(1) May choose to share losses in a different proportion from profits

---

EXAMPLE

A, B, and C form a partnership with capital contributions as follows: A, $100,000; B, $20,000; and C, $20,000. Their agreement is silent on how to split profits or losses. Therefore, profits and losses will be split equally.

EXAMPLE

Same as above except that they agree to give A 50% of the profits and B and C each get 25%. Profits as well as losses will be split based on these stated percentages.

EXAMPLE

Assume that A, B, and C agree to a 50%, 25%, 25% split if there is a profit but to a 20%, 40%, 40% split, respectively, for any annual losses. If there is a $100,000 annual loss, A will suffer $20,000 and B and C each will suffer $40,000 of the loss.

---

8. Other rights

a. Indemnification for expenses incurred on behalf of the partnership
b. General partners may be creditors, secured or unsecured, of the partnership

(1) May receive interest on loans
(2) No interest on capital contributions unless stated in partnership agreement

c. No right to salary for work performed because this is a duty unless they agree otherwise

(1) It is common for partners to agree to pay salaries, especially if only one or two do most of the work, but do not assume this on the CPA exam; the Examiners must tell you that the partners have agreed to pay a partner a salary.

d. May obtain formal accounting of partnership affairs

(1) Each partner has the right if used reasonably

9. Every partner owes a fiduciary duty to every other partner (this is important). These fiduciary duties are essentially the same duties that are discussed in Module 32, section C.2.

a. Each must act in best interest of others

(1) May pursue own self-interest as long as it is not competition and does not interfere with partner's duty to partnership
(2) Any wrongly derived profits must be held by partner for others
(3) Must abide by partnership agreement
(4) Liable to others partners for liability caused by going beyond actual authority

10. Incoming partners new to partnership have same rights as previous partners

a. Requires consent of all partners to admit new partner unless otherwise stated in the partnership agreement
b. Profit sharing, loss sharing, and capital contributions are by agreement between all partners
c. A partnership may also be partner of separate partnership if all partners agree

---

NOW REVIEW MULTIPLE-CHOICE QUESTIONS 5 THROUGH 10 IN VOLUME 2

E. Relationship to Third Parties

1. Partners are agents of the partnership; therefore the liability rules discussed in Module 32, section D. are applicable to partnerships

    a. Can bind partnership to contracts with third parties

       (1) Even where no actual authority, can bind partnership where there is apparent authority
       (2) Third parties are reasonable believing that a partner has authority to enter into contracts on the partnership's behalf
       (3) Contract must be for something related to the normal partnership business for apparent authority to exist

> **EXAMPLE**
>
> A, B, and C form a partnership to sell widgets. Contrary to the wishes of B and C, A decides to buy in the partnership name some "super-widgets" from T. Even though A did not have actual authority to buy these, T can enforce the contract based on apparent authority. A, of course, breached his fiduciary duty to B and C.

> **EXAMPLE**
>
> A and B have a partnership to sell furniture in a retail outlet. A and B agreed that neither would buy more than $10,000 of furniture from suppliers without the consent of the other. A, however, buys $20,000 of furniture from a regular supplier who was unaware of this limitation. When the supplier attempts to deliver, B refuses the furniture. Since A has apparent authority, the supplier can enforce the contract for the full $20,000.

    b. Partnership is not liable for acts of partners outside the scope of the partnership business

> **EXAMPLE**
>
> A partner of a hardware store attempts to buy some real estate in the name of the partnership. Here apparent authority does not exist.

    c. Partnership is liable for partner's torts committed in course and scope of business and for partner's breach of trust (i.e., misapplication of third party's funds)

> **EXAMPLE**
>
> A partner takes a third party's money on behalf of the partnership to invest in government bonds. Instead he uses it himself to build an addition onto his home. Both partner and partnership are liable to the investor.

> **EXAMPLE**
>
> A partner, while driving on partnership business, injures a third party. If the partner is negligent, the partnership is also liable.

2. Unanimous consent of partners is needed unless otherwise stated in the partnership agreement (so no apparent authority) for

    a. Admission of a new partner
    b. Amending the partnership agreement
    c. Assignment of partnership property
    d. Making partnership a surety or guarantor
    e. Admitting to a claim against partnership in court
    f. Submitting partnership claim to arbitrator
    g. Any action outside the scope of the partnership business

3. Partner's liability is personal, that is, extends to all his/her personal assets (not just investment in partnership) to cover all debts and liabilities of partnership

    a. Partners are jointly and severally liable for all debts

(1) The RUPA requires creditors to first attempt collection from partnership before partners unless partnership is bankrupt

b. Partners may split losses or liability between themselves according to any proportion agreed upon; however, third parties can still hold each partner personally liable despite agreement

(1) If any partner pays more than his/her agreed share, s/he can get reimbursed from other partners

> **EXAMPLE**
>
> X, Y, and Z as partners agreed to split losses 10%, 20%, and 70% respectively. A third party recovers $100,000 from X only based on a partnership tort. X can get $20,000 from Y and $70,000 from Z so that she ends up paying only her 10%.

> **EXAMPLE**
>
> Same as before except that Y is insolvent. X can recover the proportionate share from Z or $87,500 ($100,000 × 70%/80%).

> **EXAMPLE**
>
> A, B, and C are partners who agree to split losses 10%, 10%, and 80%, respectively. Y sues the partners for a tort based on the partnership business. C files for bankruptcy. Y can recover from A and B and is not bound by the agreement between A, B, and C.

c. New partners coming into a partnership are liable for existing debts only to the extent of their capital contributions (i.e., the new partners have no personal liability on these preexisting debts)

(1) Unless new partners assume personal liability for old debts

d. Partners withdrawing are liable for existing liabilities

e. Partners withdrawing are liable for subsequent liabilities unless notice of withdrawal or death is given to third parties

(1) Actual notice to creditors who previously dealt with partnership
(2) Constructive (e.g., published) notice is sufficient for others who merely knew of partnership's existence
(3) Notice can also be provided by filing a statement of dissociation with the state's secretary of state

(a) 90 days after statement is filed third parties have notice that partner is no longer affiliated with the partnership, regardless of whether the third party has actually seen the statement
(b) Failure to file a statement, or give other adequate notice, may allow third parties to believe partner is still a partner for up to 2 years after the partner's departure

f. Estates of deceased partners are liable for partners' debts

g. Liability of withdrawing partner may be limited by agreement between partners but agreement is not binding on third parties (unless they join in on agreement)

h. Partners are not criminally liable unless they personally participate in some way or unless statute prescribes liability to all members of management (e.g., environment regulation or sale of alcohol to a minor)

> **NOW REVIEW MULTIPLE-CHOICE QUESTIONS 11 THROUGH 15 IN VOLUME 2**

F. Termination of a Partnership

1. The process of termination begins when a partner dissociates from the partnership

a. Dissociation occurs when a partner ceases to be associated with the partnership
b. Actions that constitute dissociation are

(1) Partner withdraws from the partnership

(a) Partner leaves voluntarily in accordance with the partnership agreement
(b) Partner leaves voluntarily in violation of the partnership agreement

(c) Partner is forced to leave the partnership because of a vote by other partners or partner violated partnership agreement

(2) Partner engages in conduct that interferes with the ability of the partnership to conduct business
(3) Bankruptcy of a partner
(4) Death of a partner
(5) Incapacity of a partner

2. After dissociation occurs the partnership will either

   a. Commence dissolution and liquidation (winding up), or
   b. Continue the partnership business

3. Dissolution can occur by

   a. Prior agreement (e.g., partnership agreement)
   b. Present agreement of partners
   c. By decree of court in such cases as

      (1) Partner continually or seriously breaches partnership agreement
      (2) Partner guilty of conduct that harms business

   d. Assignment, selling, or pledging of partnership interest does **not** cause dissolution even if there is no consent of other partners
   e. Under RUPA, unlike previous law, partner's withdrawal, death, or bankruptcy does **not** automatically cause dissolution of partnership

      (1) Partners that own majority of partnership may choose to continue general partnership within ninety days of partners' withdrawal, death, or bankruptcy
      (2) Any partner has power to dissociate from partnership even if had agreed not to, but is liable for breach of such a contract

4. Winding up

   a. Remaining partners may elect to wind up and terminate partnership or not wind up and continue business

5. Order of distribution upon termination of general partnership

   a. To creditors including partners as creditors
   b. Capital contributions and profits or losses are calculated together

      (1) Partners may receive money or even need to pay money at this stage

6. Partners are personally liable to partnership for any deficits in their capital accounts and to creditors for insufficiency of partnership assets

---

EXAMPLE

A, B, and C formed the ABC partnership. The capital contributions were A $50,000, B $30,000, and C $20,000. After three years, the partners voted to dissolve the partnership. After liquidating its assets and paying off its creditors, ABC had $40,000 in cash. The $40,000 needs to be used to pay back the aforementioned capital contributions, but there is still $60,000 that will go unpaid. The $60,000 is treated as a loss. Each partner will have to pay his/her proportionate share of the $60,000. Since there is no information on how the partners agreed to split profits or losses, the RUPA rule of splitting profits and losses equally must apply. Therefore each partner will need to pay $20,000 to the partnership. Once that is done, the partnership will then pay each partner his/her capital contribution.

---

   a. Priority between partnership creditors and partner's personal creditors

      (1) Partnership creditors have first priority to partnership assets; any excess goes to personal creditors
      (2) Usually, personal creditors have first priority to personal assets; any excess goes to partnership creditors

7. During the winding up process all partners actual authority is terminated, other than those partners who are engaged in the winding up process

   a. No new business is permitted, other than transactions necessary to wind up
   b. Apparent authority can still exist, however

8. Partners can bind other partners and the partnership on contracts until third parties who have known of the partnership are given notice of dissolution

    a. Actual notice must be given to third parties who have dealt with the partnership prior to dissolution

    b. Constructive notice (e.g., notice in newspaper) is adequate for third parties who have only known of the partnership

    c. Partnership may also file a statement of dissolution with the state's secretary of state. All third parties are assumed to have knowledge of the dissolution 90 days after the filing, thus eliminating any apparent authority

9. The partnership may choose to continue instead of dissolving if

    a. A majority of the remaining partners, after dissociation, vote to continue the partnership business

    b. A continuation agreement (clause) is contained in the partnership agreement

10. If the partnership continues, only the dissociated partner's actual authority is terminated

    a. Notice, however, must be provided to remove the apparent authority of the dissociated partner

       (1) Actual notice to creditors who previously dealt with partnership

       (2) Constructive (e.g., published) notice is sufficient for others who merely knew of partnership's existence

       (3) Notice can also be provided by filing a statement of dissociation with the state's secretary of state

          (a) 90 days after statement is filed, third parties have notice that partner is no longer affiliated with the partnership, regardless of whether the third party has actually seen the statement

          (b) Failure to file a statement, or give other adequate notice, may allow third parties to believe partner is still a partner for up to 2 years after the partner's departure

---

NOW REVIEW MULTIPLE-CHOICE QUESTIONS 17 THROUGH 19 IN VOLUME 2

G. Limited Partnerships

1. Revised Uniform Limited Partnership Act (RULPA) is designed to modernize law because today many limited partnerships are very large with many limited partners.

    a. RULPA has been adopted by majority of states

2. Creation of limited partnership

    a. Unlike general partnership that requires no formal procedures to create it, limited partnership requires compliance with state statute to create it

    b. Must file certificate of limited partnership with secretary of state; if the partnership does not, it will be treated as a general partnership

       (1) Must be signed by all general partners and include names of all general partners

          (a) Name and address of the limited partnership

          (b) Name and address of its agent

          (c) Latest date the partnership is to dissolve

          (d) Names of limited partners not required

          (e) Must amend certificate of partnership to show any additions or deletions of general partners

             1] Must also amend certificate if any general partner becomes aware of false information in certificate

    c. Requires at least one general partner and at least one limited partner

       (1) Sole general partner may be a corporation

       (2) Liability of limited partner(s) is limited to amount of capital contributions (with some exceptions below)

    d. General or limited partners' capital contributions may not only be in cash, services performed, or property, but may also now be in promise to perform services, to give cash, or property in future

    e. Name of limited partner may not be used in name of limited partnership unless name is also name of a general partner.

       (1) If a limited partner **knowingly or negligently** allows his/her name to be part of limited partnership name, then the partner is personally liable to creditors who extend credit to business (unless creditors knew that limited partner was not a general partner)

    f. "Limited partnership" words or abbreviation must be in firm's name

    g. Partnership interests may be purchased with cash, property, services rendered, promissory note

    h. Defective formation of limited partnership causes limited partners to be liable as general partners

(1) Under RULPA, partner who believes s/he is limited partner may avoid liability of general partner if upon learning of defective formation either

   (a) Withdraws from partnership and renounces all future profits
   (b) Files amendment or new certificate that cures defect

(2) However, limited partner is liable for past transactions before withdrawal or amendment to any third party transacting business while believing partner was general partner

i. Foreign limited partnership is one doing business in given state but was formed in another state

   (1) Foreign limited partnership must register with secretary of state before doing business in state

3. Rights of partners in limited partnership

   a. General partners manage partnership
   b. Limited partners invest

      (1) Limited partner who substantially manages partnership like general partner obtains liability like general partner to third parties who believed s/he was general partner
      (2) Limited partner allowed to do following without risking loss of limited liability

         (a) Acting as an agent or employee of limited partnership
         (b) Consulting with and advising general partner or limited partnership about partnership business
         (c) Approving or disapproving amendments to limited partnership agreement
         (d) Voting on dissolution or winding up of limited partnership
         (e) Voting on loans of limited partnership
         (f) Voting on change in nature of business
         (g) Voting on removal of a general partner
         (h) Bringing derivative lawsuit on behalf of limited partnership
         (i) Being surety for limited partnership

   c. Profit or loss sharing

      (1) Profits or losses are shared as agreed upon in certificate agreement

         (a) Losses and any liability are limited to capital contributions for limited partners
         (b) If no agreement on profit and losses exists, then shared based on percentages of capital contributions

            1] Note how this differs from a general partnership in which losses and profits are shared equally unless agreed otherwise

   d. Admission of new partner requires written agreement of all partners unless partnership agreement provides otherwise
   e. Limited partnership interests (right to profits) may be assigned in part or in whole

      (1) Similar to general partnerships, assignee is only a creditor of the partner
      (2) Assignee acquires no rights of the limited partner other than the right to the limited partner's right to profits

   f. Limited partners have right to inspect partnership books and tax return information
   g. Can be a limited and general partner at same time

      (1) Has rights, powers, and liability of a general partner
      (2) Has rights against other partners with respect to contribution as a limited partner and also as a general partner

   h. Limited partners may own competing interests
   i. Limited partner may be a secured or unsecured creditor of partnership
   j. Limited partner may not withdraw capital contribution if it impairs creditors

4. Duties of partners

   a. General partners owe fiduciary duties to general and limited partners—limited partners in general do not owe fiduciary duties since they do not engage in the management of the business.

5. Dissolution of limited partnership takes place upon the following events:

   a. Completion of time period specified in certificate
   b. Upon event specified in partnership agreement
   c. Unanimous written consent of all partners
   d. Dissolution of court decree when not practical to continue partnership

e. Event that causes partnership business to be illegal

f. Withdrawal of general partner by retirement, removal, bankruptcy (but not mere insolvency), fraud against other partners, insanity, death

    (1) Unless all partners agree in writing to continue business

    (2) Unless partnership agreement allows partners to continue business

    (3) Withdrawal of limited partner does not cause dissolution

    (4) Death of limited partner does not cause dissolution

6. If partnership not continued, winding up takes place with the following distribution of assets of partnership in order of priority

    a. To creditors including partners who are creditors

    b. To partners and ex-partners to pay off unpaid distributions

    c. To partners to return capital contributions

    d. To partners for partnership interests in proportions they share in distributions

    e. Note that in these priorities general and limited partners share equally

    f. Also, note that partners can vary their rights by agreement of all parties affected

7. Upon dissolution, remaining partners typically complete winding-up process

8. Dissolution of a limited partnership requires the filing of a dissolution document with the state.

> **NOW REVIEW MULTIPLE-CHOICE QUESTION 19 THROUGH 29 IN VOLUME 2**

H. Joint Ventures

1. Joint venture—An association of two or more persons (or entities) organized to carry out a single business undertaking (or series of related undertakings) for profit

    a. Generally, corporations may engage in joint ventures

> **EXAMPLE**
>
> X Corporation, O Corporation, and N Corporation decide to form a joint venture to bring oil from the north to the south of Alaska.

2. Law of joint ventures is similar to that of partnerships with some exceptions

    a. Each joint venturer is not necessarily an agent of other joint venturers—limited power to bind others; there is no apparent authority for joint venturers

    b. Death of joint venturer does not automatically dissolve joint venture

    c. Joint venture is interpreted as special form of partnership

        (1) Fiduciary duties of partners in partnership law apply

        (2) Each member has right to participate in management

        (3) Liability is unlimited and each joint venturer is personally liable for debts of joint venture

3. Generally a joint venture is not required to file a document or certificate with the state

> **NOW REVIEW MULTIPLE-CHOICE QUESTION 30 IN VOLUME 2**

I. Limited Liability Companies (LLC)

1. Laws for this form of business generally follow the Revised Uniform Limited Liability Company Act (RULLCA 2006)

2. LLC is not considered a corporation but a majority of states provide

    a. All owners (often called members) have limited liability and therefore no personal liability

        (1) Liability of owners limited to their capital contributions (including any obligation to make contributions) plus any equity in LLC

            (a) Typically, limited liability is retained even if members fail to follow usual formalities in conducting business

> **EXAMPLE**
>
> Members of LLC fail to keep minutes of the LLC's meetings. This failure does **not** expose them to personal liability for the debts of the LLC.

      1] Note that if a **corporation** does not follow the corporate formalities such as corporate meetings with relevant minutes, the corporate veil can be pierced, thus the corporate entity is disregarded and then shareholders of company obtain personal liability for corporation's debts

        a] This is another important advantage of LLC

  (2) Compare with limited partnership in which only limited partners can have limited liability

  (3) In many states a sole proprietorship may be formed into LLC to obtain its advantages

b. LLC must be formed according to limited liability company statute of the state in which it is formed

  (1) Some general partnerships or limited partnerships convert over to an LLC in which case partners retain liability they had in former partnership; they obtain benefits as new members of LLC only for transactions that take place after conversion date to LLC

  (2) LLC is foreign LLC in other states in which it does business, and laws of state where it was formed typically govern LLC in those other states

c. LLC is separate legal entity so can sue or be sued in own name

  (1) Foreign LLC must register with secretary of state and obtain a certificate of authority to transact business in the state before doing business in another state, or cannot sue in state courts

d. The name of a LLC must include the words "limited liability company" or "limited company" or the abbreviation "L.L.C.," "LLC," "L.C.," or "LC" to give notice to public

e. To form LLC, one or more persons may act as organizers by filing a Certificate of Organization with secretary of state

  (1) May be amended by filing amendment with secretary of state

  (2) The Operating Agreement specifies the manner in which the company will conduct and wind up operations

f. Think of an LLC as a large S corporation

  (1) There is no limit on the number of members (owners/shareholders)

  (2) The LLC itself is not taxed; the tax liability flows through the LLC to the individual members

3. Member (owner) of LLC has no interest in any specific property in LLC but has interest (personal property interest) in LLC in general

a. Member has right to distributions according to profit and loss sharing agreed upon in operating agreement

  (1) Under the majority of state laws, in the absence of an agreement otherwise, members divide profits in proportion to their capital contributions

  (2) Under the RULLCA, in absence of agreement otherwise, members divide profits and losses equally

  (3) If the question does not specify RULLCA assume the majority state rule

  (4) Members may agree to divide profits differently than losses based on different formulas

> **EXAMPLE**
>
> The members agree that the various members each receive profits and losses on bases that are different for each member. Member Q, for example, receives 15% if there is a profit in a given year, but suffers a loss of 20% if the LLC were to suffer a loss. Member R, however, is allocated 12% whether there is a profit or a loss. This is enforceable since the members agree to it.

b. Member has management interest

  (1) Includes rights to manage affairs of firm, vote within firm, and get information about LLC

  (2) Unless agreed otherwise, each member has equal voice in management

c. Member may assign financial interest (right to profits) in LLC unless operating agreement specifies otherwise

  (1) Assignee does not become member, only receives assignor's share of profits assigned unless other members agree otherwise

(2) Member may not assign any other right, including the right to be a member, without the consent of the other members

d. Right to information

(1) Members of member-managed companies (and managers in manager-managed companies) have right to receive (without demand) business information to properly exercise their rights and duties.

(2) Other members, on demand, may inspect information (e.g., books and records) during reasonable times, at the business location and for appropriate purpose

e. Members may be dissociated as members at any time, by notification of desire to dissociate, expulsion, sale of interest, etc.

4. Authority and duties in LLCs

a. When LLC designated as member-managed LLC, all members have authority to bind LLC under agency law to contracts on behalf of LLC

b. When LLC designated as manager-managed LLC, only managers have authority to bind LLC to contracts for LLC

(1) LLC is bound only to contracts that

(a) Either LLC has authorized under agency law, or

(b) Are made in the ordinary course of business

c. In either case

(1) Authority of both members and managers to bind LLC to contracts can be restricted in a statement of authority (filed with the Secretary of State) or in operating agreement

(2) Apparent authority of either members or managers to make contracts with third parties not affected for those who have proper notice of restrictions on contract-making authority

(a) Restrictions in statement of authority are deemed proper notice to third parties if they are filed with Secretary of State

(b) Restrictions in operating agreement are deemed to be proper notice to those third parties who actually receive direct notification of those restrictions

5. Other compensation

a. Member who is not manager has no right to compensation for services performed

(1) Exception is for services performed in winding up LLC

b. Managers of LLCs receive compensation according to agreed contract

c. LLC must reimburse members and managers for payments they made in name of LLC

d. LLC is required to indemnify managers and/or members

6. Fiduciary duties owed by members and managers to LLC; these are essentially the same fiduciary duties discussed in Module 32, section C.2.

a. Managers of manager-managed LLC and members of member-managed LLC owe LLC fiduciary duties

(1) Both owe duty of loyalty and due care to LLC

(a) Duty of loyalty includes

1] To account to the company and hold as trustee for it any property, profit, or benefit derived by the member

2] To refrain from dealing with the company on behalf of a party having an adverse interest in the company

3] To refrain from competing with the company

(b) Duty of due care includes

1] Act with the care that a person in a like position would reasonably exercise and in a manner the member reasonably believes to be in the best interests of the company

(c) The member shall discharge the duties under the operating agreement and exercise any rights consistently with the contractual obligations or good faith and fair dealings

b. A member of a manager-managed company does not have any fiduciary duty to the company or other members solely as a result of being a member

7. Dissolution of LLC

    a. Most state LLC statutes cause LLC to dissolve when

        (1) All members agree in writing to dissolution
        (2) Time period passes or event happens as specified in operating agreement
        (3) Member withdraws, is voted out, dies, goes bankrupt, or becomes incompetent

           (a) Most states allow remainder of members to continue LLC if agreed upon unanimously

        (4) Court order dissolves it

8. Distribution of assets upon dissolution are made in following priorities:

    a. To creditors including managers and members except for their shares in the distribution of profits
    b. To members and past members for unpaid distributions unless agreed otherwise
    c. To members to receive back capital contributions, unless agreed otherwise
    d. To members for their distributions as agreed in operating agreement, or if not agreed upon, in proportion to contributions they had made

9. Dissolution of a LLC may require the filing of a dissolution document with the state.

> **NOW REVIEW MULTIPLE-CHOICE QUESTIONS 31 THROUGH 35 IN VOLUME 2**

J. Limited Liability Partnerships (LLP)

1. Majority of states now allow LLP
2. Formation of LLP

    a. Must file articles of LLP with Secretary of State
    b. Statutes of all jurisdictions require firm's name to include phrase of limited liability partnership or registered limited liability partnership or initials LLP or RLLP to notify public
    c. Majority of states require only majority, not unanimous, approval of partners to become LLP
    d. Generally, laws of state in which the LLP is formed govern affairs of the LLP in all other states
    e. The LLP often works well for professionals who want to do business as professionals in a partnership but still pass through tax benefits while limiting personal liability of the partners
    f. Most states allow an easy transition from conventional partnership into limited liability partnership
    g. Most common law and statutory law from partnership law applies to LLP

3. Liability provisions of partners in LLP

    a. Under traditional general partnerships and limited partnerships, big disadvantage is that general partners in both firms have unlimited personal liability for partnership obligations

        (1) Most states allow LLP to be formed so the general partners have no personal liability for the contractual obligations of the firm

> **EXAMPLE**
>
> The ABC LLP got a loan from 1st Bank. ABC subsequently defaulted on the loan. 1st Bank may only satisfy its claim against ABC; it may not go after the individual partners even if partnership assets are exhausted.

        (2) Partners also have no personal liability for the debts arising from the torts of the LLP. Partners do have personal liability, however

           (a) If the partner actually committed the tort
           (b) In most states for the torts committed by parties under the partners' supervision or control

> **EXAMPLE**
>
> Anson is a partner in the ABC LLP. Dietz is a junior partner at ABC and is under Anson's supervision. Dietz commits malpractice. Dietz has personal liability for the damages arising from the malpractice because Dietz committed the tort. Anson has personal liability because Anson is Dietz's supervisor.

   b. Popular for professionals such as accounting firms and law firms

NOW REVIEW MULTIPLE-CHOICE QUESTION 36 IN VOLUME 2

K. Subchapter C Corporations

  1. Under Federal Subchapter S Revision Act, all corporations are divided into two categories

     a. Subchapter S corporations are discussed later in this module

     b. Subchapter C corporations are all corporations that are not Subchapter S corporations

       (1) Majority of this module covers "regular corporation" also referred to as Subchapter C corporation

          (a) In general, most provisions for Subchapter C corporations and Subchapter S corporations are similar such as limited liability of shareholders and structure of corporate management

              1] Main distinction is tax treatment

NOW REVIEW MULTIPLE-CHOICE QUESTIONS 37 THROUGH 40 IN VOLUME 2

L. Characteristics and Advantages of Corporate Form

  1. Limited liability

     a. Generally a shareholder in a corporation risks only his/her investment

  2. Transferability of ownership interest

     a. Shares in corporations are represented by stocks and can be freely bought, sold, or assigned unless shareholders have agreed to restrictions

  3. Continuous life

     a. Unlike a partnership, a corporation is not terminated by death of a shareholder, or his/her incapacity

       (1) Regarded as perpetual, and continues to exist until dissolved, merged, or otherwise terminated

  4. Separate entity

     a. A corporation is a legal entity in itself and is treated separately from its stockholders

       (1) Can take, hold, and convey property
       (2) Can contract in own name with shareholders or third parties
       (3) Can sue and be sued

  5. Financing

     a. Often easier to raise large amounts of capital than in other business organizations by issuance of stock or other securities (e.g., bonds)
     b. More flexible because can issue different classes of stock and/or bonds to suit its needs and market demands

  6. Corporate management

     a. Persons who manage corporations are not necessarily shareholders and therefore may be more qualified
     b. Management of a corporation is usually vested in board of directors elected by shareholders
     c. Directors could be removed from office before their elected term is finished only for cause under common law

       (1) Increasingly states have been passing laws that allow directors to be removed at any time with shareholders' consent

NOW REVIEW MULTIPLE-CHOICE QUESTIONS 41 THROUGH 45 IN VOLUME 2

M. Disadvantages of Corporate Business Structure

  1. Tax treatment

     a. Tax burdens may be more than on other business structures because of double taxation

     (1) This often happens when income is taxed at corporate level and then dividends paid from after-tax income are taxed again at shareholder level

     (2) Corporation may alleviate double taxation as Subchapter S corporation by being taxed similar to partnership

2. Costs of incorporating, because must meet formal creation requirements
3. Formal operating requirements must be met
4. If the corporation goes public

    a. There substantial costs of compliance with federal securities laws
    b. May be subject to hostile takeover

NOW REVIEW MULTIPLE-CHOICE QUESTION 46 IN VOLUME 2

N. Types of Corporations

1. Domestic corporation is one that operates and does business within the state in which it was incorporated
2. Foreign corporation is one doing business in any state except the state in which it was incorporated

    a. Foreign corporations, if "doing business" in a given state, are not exempt from many requirements and details that domestic corporations must meet

      (1) Doing business in state is typically defined as maintaining an office or selling personal property in state

        (a) These are not considered doing business in state

          1] Defending against a lawsuit
          2] Holding bank account
          3] Using mail to solicit orders
          4] Collecting debts
          5] Using independent contractors to make sales

      (2) Foreign corporations can be required to qualify to do business in state; accomplished by obtaining certificate of authority from state

        (a) Must appoint agent to receive service of process for suits against corporation
        (b) Must pay specified fees
        (c) Must file information with secretary of state

3. Professional corporations are ones under state laws that allow professionals to incorporate (e.g., doctors, accountants, attorneys)

    a. All states allow professional corporations
    b. Typically, shares may be owned only by licensed professionals
    c. Retain personal liability for their professional acts (i.e., personal liability for malpractice)
    d. Obtain other corporation benefits (e.g., limited liability for corporate debts, some tax benefits)

4. Model Statutory Close Corporation Supplement was passed to allow corporations to choose to be close corporations.

    a. Often helps corporations made up of entrepreneurial individuals
    b. Close corporations can also be called closely held corporations or closed corporations
    c. Only corporations having 50 or fewer shareholders may choose status of statutory close corporations

      (1) To choose such status, two-thirds of shares of each class of shares of corporation must approve it
      (2) Articles of corporation must contain a statement it is a statutory close corporation
      (3) All share certificates must clearly state they are issued by statutory close corporation

    d. Close corporations may function without some of formalities of operating corporations

      (1) If all shareholders approve, close corporation may function without board of directors

        (a) It is then managed by shareholders

      (2) Close corporation need not hold shareholders' meetings unless at least one shareholder demands in writing that meetings be held
      (3) Basically, shareholders may treat close corporation as a partnership for purposes of governing

        (a) Very importantly, statutory close corporation status allows shareholders to have limited liability

(4) Usually the transfer of ownership interests (sale of stock) is restricted

5. **De facto** corporation has been formed in fact but has not been formed properly under the law

   a. Usually defective because of some small error
   b. Now, filing by secretary of state of Articles of Incorporation is deemed conclusive proof that incorporators did all that was necessary to incorporate

      (1) Third parties cannot now challenge that corporation exists
      (2) Only state can challenge existence and dissolve or cancel corporation

6. **De jure** corporation has been formed correctly in compliance with the incorporation statute

> **NOW REVIEW MULTIPLE-CHOICE QUESTIONS 47 THROUGH 51 IN VOLUME 2**

O. Formation of Corporation

1. Promoters are persons who form corporations and arrange capitalization to begin corporations

   a. Promoter handles issuing of the prospectus, promoting stock subscriptions, and drawing up charter
   b. Promoter has a fiduciary relationship with corporation, and is not permitted to act against interests of corporation

      (1) Does not prevent personal profit if fully disclosed

   c. Promoter is not an agent of the corporation, because the corporation is still not in existence

      (1) Any agreements (preincorporation contracts) made by promoter are not binding on the future corporation unless adopted by the corporation after it comes into existence

         (a) Requires actual resolution of board of directors
         (b) Normally promoter is personally liable on contract. Adoption by corporation does not relieve promoter; **novation is required to relieve promoter.** The other party must agree to substituting the corporation

            1] Promoter has liability even if promoter's name does not appear on contract
            2] However, promoter is not liable if third party clearly states that s/he would look only to corporation for performance

         (c) Corporation is not liable to promoter for his/her services unless adopted by corporation

2. Formed only under state incorporation statutes ("Creature of statute")
3. Incorporation

   a. Articles of Incorporation (corporate charter) are filed with the state and contain

      (1) Proposed name of corporation and initial address
      (2) Purpose of corporation
      (3) Powers of corporation
      (4) Name of registered agent of corporation
      (5) Name and address of each incorporator

         (a) Incorporators may be promoters

      (6) Number of authorized shares of stock

   b. First shareholders' meeting

      (1) Stock certificates issued to shareholders
      (2) Resignation of temporary directors and election of new

   c. At same meeting or subsequent meeting, directors

      (1) Elect officers
      (2) Adopt or reject preincorporation contracts
      (3) Begin business of corporation
      (4) Adopt initial bylaws

         (a) These need not be filed with any government agency
         (b) Provide specific rules for management

4. Articles of Incorporation may be subsequently amended

    a. Approval of any adversely affected shareholders of amendment needed

        (1) Often majority vote or sometimes two-thirds vote required

            (a) Dissenting minority shareholders may assert right of appraisal and therefore receive fair value for shares

                1] Fair value is value just before vote

NOW REVIEW MULTIPLE-CHOICE QUESTIONS 52 THROUGH 57 IN VOLUME 2

P. Corporate Financial Structure

1. Definitions

    a. Uncertificated securities—securities not represented by written documents
    b. Authorized stock—amount permitted to be issued in Articles of Incorporation (e.g., amount and types)
    c. Issued stock—authorized and delivered to shareholders
    d. Unissued stock—authorized but not yet issued
    e. Outstanding stock—issued and not repurchased by the corporation (i.e., it is still owned by shareholders)
    f. Treasury stock—issued but not outstanding (i.e., corporation repurchased it)

        (1) Are not votable and do not receive dividends
        (2) Corporation does not recognize gain or loss on transactions with its own stock
        (3) Must be purchased out of unreserved or unrestricted earned surplus as defined below and as permitted by state law

            (a) If Articles of Incorporation so permit or if majority of voting shareholders permit, unrestricted capital surplus (see below) may also be used

        (4) May be distributed as part of stock dividend
        (5) May be resold without regard to par value
        (6) Can be resold without regard to preemptive rights
        (7) No purchase of treasury stock may be made if it renders corporation insolvent

    g. Canceled stock—stock purchased or received by corporation that is canceled

        (1) No longer issued or outstanding
        (2) Makes room for more stock to be issued

    h. Par-value stock

        (1) Par value is amount set in Articles of Incorporation
        (2) Stock should be issued for this amount or more
        (3) May subsequently be traded for any amount
        (4) Creditors may hold purchaser liable if stock originally purchased at below par

            (a) Contingently liable for difference between amount paid and par value
            (b) Subsequent purchaser also liable unless purchased in good faith without notice that sale was below par

    i. No-par stock—stock issued without a set par value

        (1) May have a stated value

    j. Stated capital (legal capital)—number of shares issued times par value (or stated value)

        (1) If no par or stated value, then includes total consideration received by corporation

            (a) Under limited circumstances, portion may be allocated by board of directors to capital surplus as permitted by law

        (2) Dividends normally may not be declared or paid out of it
        (3) Following also increase stated capital by number of shares increased times par value (or stated value)

            (a) Exercise of stock option
            (b) Small common stock dividend

        (4) Following do not change stated capital

            (a) Acquisition or reissuance of treasury stock under cost method

    (b) Stock splits

        1] Increase number of shares issued and decrease par or stated value (e.g., 2-for-1 stock split doubles the number of shares issued and cuts in half the par or stated value)

        2] Do not distribute assets or capital

    (c) Payment of organization costs

  k. Earned surplus (retained earnings)—cumulative amount of income (net of dividends) retained by the corporation during its existence or since a deficit was properly eliminated

    (1) Note that under modern terminology, this is correctly referred to as retained earnings as indicated above; since laws written using old terms, CPA candidates should be familiar with old as well as new terms as learned in accounting

  l. Net assets—excess of total assets over total debts

  m. Surplus—excess of net assets over stated capital

  n. Capital surplus—entire surplus of corporation less earned surplus

    (1) Note that paid-in capital is considered capital surplus

  o. Contributed capital—total consideration received by corporation upon issuance of stock

2. Classes of stock

  a. Common stock usually gives each shareholder one vote per share and is entitled to dividends if declared by the directors

    (1) Has no priority over other stock for dividends

    (2) Shareholders entitled to share in final distribution of assets

    (3) Votes may be apportioned to shares in other ways (e.g., one vote per ten shares)

    (4) Corporation may issue more than one class of common stock with varying terms (e.g., class may have no voting rights or different par value, etc.)

    (5) All stock is common stock unless specifically told otherwise

  b. Preferred stock is given preferred status as to some characteristic of the stock, often liquidations and dividends, but the Examiners will state what the preference is

    (1) Usually nonvoting stock; however, assume it is voting stock unless the Examiners specifically state otherwise

    (2) Dividend rate is generally a fixed rate

    (3) Cumulative preferred means that if a periodic dividend is not paid at the scheduled time, it accumulates and must be satisfied before common stock may receive a dividend

      (a) These arrearages are not liabilities of corporation until declared by board of directors

        1] Disclosed in footnotes to financial statements

      (b) Noncumulative preferred means that if the dividend is passed, it will never be paid

    (4) Participating preferred stock participates further in corporate earnings remaining after a fixed amount is paid to preferred shares

      (a) Participation with common shares is generally on a fixed percentage basis

  c. Callable (or redeemable) stock may be redeemed at a fixed price by the corporation

    (1) Call price is fixed in Articles of Incorporation or may be subject to agreement among shareholders themselves

  d. Convertible preferred gives shareholder option to convert preferred stock to common stock at a fixed exchange rate

3. Marketing of stock

  a. Stock subscriptions are contracts to purchase a given number of shares in an existing corporation or one to be organized

    (1) Subscription to stock is a written offer to buy and is not binding until accepted by the corporation

    (2) Under the Model Business Corporation Act, preincorporation stock subscriptions are irrevocable for six months

    (3) Once accepted, the subscriber becomes liable

      (a) For the purchase
      (b) As a corporate shareholder

  b. Watered stock

    (1) Stock is said to be watered when the cash or property exchanged is less than par value or stated value
    (2) Stock must be issued for consideration equal to or greater than the par or stated value under most state laws

      (a) No-par stock may be issued for consideration that the directors determine to be reasonable

    (3) Creditors of the corporation may recover from the stockholders the amount of water in their shares; that is, the amount the stockholders would have paid to the corporation had they paid the full amount required (i.e., par value less amount paid)

      (a) If the corporation becomes insolvent
      (b) Subsequent purchaser of watered stock is not liable unless s/he had knowledge thereof

  c. Valid consideration or value for shares can be any benefit to corporation

    (1) Including cash, property, services performed, intangible property, promissory notes, other securities, or services contracted to be performed in future

      (a) Directors have duty to set value on property received

        1] Directors' value set is conclusive unless fraud shown

4. Debt securities (holders are not owners but creditors)

  a. Debenture is instrument for long-term **unsecured** debt
  b. Bond is instrument for long-term **secured** debt

NOW REVIEW MULTIPLE-CHOICE QUESTIONS 58 THROUGH 69 IN VOLUME 2

Q. Powers and Liabilities of Corporation

1. Corporations generally have following powers

  a. To acquire their own shares (treasury stock) or retire their own shares

    (1) Typically limited to amount of surplus

  b. To make charitable contributions
  c. To guarantee obligations of others only if in reasonable furtherance of corporation's business
  d. Loans to directors require shareholder approval
  e. Loans to employees (even employees who are also directors) do not need shareholder approval and are appropriate if they benefit corporation
  f. Generally, a corporation may also be a partner of a partnership

2. Crimes

  a. Corporations are liable for crimes they are capable of committing
  b. Punishment generally consists of fines or forfeiture, although directors have been faced with prison sentences for crimes of the corporation

3. Contracts

  a. Rules under agency law apply in corporate dealings with third parties; see Module 32, Section D. 1-7
  b. The corporation is the principal
  c. Corporate officers, employees, and the board of directors are the agents
  d. Individual directors are not agents of the corporation; therefore an individual director cannot have apparent authority to enter into a contract on behalf of the corporation

4. Torts

  a. Corporations are liable for the damages resulting from torts committed by their officers, agents, or employees within the course and scope of their corporate duties
  b. Rules of agency law apply; see Module 32, section D. 8-15

5. *Ultra vires* acts

  a. Illegal and *ultra vires* acts are not the same

(1) Illegal acts are acts in violation of statute or public policy

> **EXAMPLE**
>
> False advertising.

(2) Whereas *ultra vires* acts are merely beyond the scope of the corporate powers (i.e., a legal act may be *ultra vires*)

> **EXAMPLE**
>
> Although legal to become a surety, the Articles of Incorporation may not allow it.

    b. The state's attorney general may dissolve corporation for *ultra vires* act

    c. Stockholders have right to object to ultra vires acts

    d. Directors or officers may be sued by shareholders on behalf of the corporation or by the corporation itself if there are damages to the corporation for *ultra vires* acts

> **NOW REVIEW MULTIPLE-CHOICE QUESTIONS 70 THROUGH 72 IN VOLUME 2**

R. Directors and Officers of Corporations

1. Directors are elected by shareholders
2. Directors' duties and powers

    a. A director as an individual has no power to bind the corporation—must act as a board member at a duly constituted meeting of the board

        (1) Majority vote of those present is needed for most business decisions if quorum is present

        (2) Action may be taken by board with no meeting

            (a) Unless prohibited by Articles of Incorporation or by corporate bylaws, and

            (b) There must be unanimous written consent by board members for action to be taken

    b. Powers and duties in general

        (1) Declaration of dividends

        (2) Selection of officers

        (3) Must comply with Articles of Incorporation. The Articles of Incorporation can only be amended by voting shareholders.

        (4) Typically delegate some authority (e.g., day to day or routine matters to officers and agents)

        (5) Directors are not entitled to compensation unless so provided in articles, bylaws, or by a resolution of the board passed before the services are rendered

            (a) May be reimbursed for expenses incurred on behalf of corporation

3. Director's liability

    a. General rule is that directors must exercise ordinary care, due diligence in performing the duties entrusted to them by virtue of their positions as directors, and acts in a manner he or she believes to be in the best interests of the corporation

        (1) Directors are liable for own torts committed even if acting for corporation

            (a) Corporation is **also** liable if committed within the scope of corporate duties

        (2) Business judgment rule—as long as director is acting in good faith s/he will not be liable for errors of judgment unless s/he is negligent

        (3) Directors are chargeable with knowledge of the affairs of the corporation

            (a) If director does not prevent (intentionally or negligently) wrongs of other directors, may be held liable

            (b) Normally may rely on reports of accountants, officers, etc. if reasonable judgment used

        (4) If corporation does not actually exist, then director as well as others in business have personal liability

    b. Directors liable for negligence if their action was the cause of the corporation's loss

(1) Corporation may indemnify directors (also officers, employees, agents) against suits based on their duties for the corporation if acted in good faith and in best interests of corporation

    (a) Also applies to criminal actions if s/he reasonably believed that actions were lawful

(2) Corporation may purchase liability insurance for officers and directors

    (a) Corporation pays premiums
    (b) Policies usually cover litigation costs as well as judgment or settlement costs

c. Directors owe a fiduciary duty to the corporation

(1) Owe fiduciary duties of loyalty, due care, and obedience to the corporation. These are the fiduciary duties of an agent. Even though individual directors are not considered agents of the corporation, directors owe the fiduciary duties of an agent.

(2) Conflicts of interest

    (a) Transactions of a corporation with director(s) or other corporation in which director(s) has interest are valid as long as at least one of the following can be established

        1] Conflict of interest is disclosed or known to board and majority of disinterested members approve of transaction
        2] Conflict of interest is disclosed or known to shareholders and those entitled to vote approve it by a majority
        3] Transaction is fair and reasonable to corporation

> **EXAMPLE**
>
> A plot of land already owned by a director is sold at the fair market value to the corporation. This contract is valid even without approval if the land is needed by the corporation.

d. Directors are personally liable for *ultra vires* acts of the corporation unless they specifically dissented on the record

e. Directors are personally liable to corporation for approving and paying dividends that are illegal

(1) Directors who act in good faith may use defense of business judgment rule

4. Officers

a. Typically operate day-to-day business

(1) Delegated from directors

b. An officer of the corporation is an agent and can bind corporation by his/her individual acts if within the scope of his/her authority as set forth in the bylaws

c. Officers and directors may be the same persons

d. Officers are selected by the directors for a fixed term under the bylaws

(1) If a term is not definite, it is governed by the directors

e. Officers have a fiduciary duty to corporation

f. Courts recognize a fiduciary duty owed by majority shareholders to minority shareholders when the majority shareholders have de facto control over the corporation

5. Officers, like directors, are liable for own torts, even if committed while acting for corporation

a. Corporation is also liable if officer was acting within the scope of his/her authority

6. Requirements of the Sarbanes-Oxley Act of 2002

a. Requires all members of the audit committee of the board of directors to be independent and one must be a financial expert

b. The audit committee must appoint, compensate, and oversee the work of the firm's public accounting firm

c. The CEO and CFO must certify that the financial statements are fairly presented

d. Prohibits officer or director from exerting improper influence on the conduct of the audit

e. CEO and CFO must return compensation that was derived from misstated financial statements resulting from material noncompliance with the reporting requirements

┌───┐
│   **NOW REVIEW MULTIPLE-CHOICE QUESTIONS 73 THROUGH 81 IN VOLUME 2**   │
└───┘

S. Stockholder's Rights

1. Right to transfer stock by endorsement and delivery or by separate assignment

    a. Stock certificates are negotiable instruments
    b. Limitations on transfer may be imposed, but they must be reasonable

        (1) UCC requires that any restrictions must be plainly printed on the certificate to be effective against third party
        (2) These limitations are most often imposed in closely held corporations

    > **EXAMPLE**
    >
    > Existing shareholders of the corporation may have first option to buy.

2. Stockholder has no right to manage corporation unless s/he is also officer or director

    a. If stockholder is also an officer, the stockholder retains limited liability unlike limited partner who participates in management

3. Right to vote for election of directors, decision to dissolve the corporation, and any other fundamental corporate changes

    a. Governed by the charter and class of stock owned
    b. Annual meetings are required as specified in the bylaws
    c. Stockholders may have voting agreements that are enforceable which provide that they will vote a certain way on issues or vote for specified people for the board of directors
    d. Cumulative voting may be required (i.e., a person gets as many votes as s/he has shares times the number of directors being elected)

    > **EXAMPLE**
    >
    > 100 shares × 5 directors is 500 votes.

        (1) Gives minority shareholders an opportunity to get some representation by voting all shares for one or two directors

    e. Can vote by proxy—an assignment of voting rights
    f. Directors have the power to amend or repeal the bylaws unless reserved to the shareholders by the Articles of Incorporation
    g. Amendment of the Articles of Incorporation and approval of fundamental corporate changes such as a merger, consolidation, or sale of all assets generally require majority approval by shareholders

4. Right to dividends

    a. Shareholder generally has no right to dividends unless they are declared by the board of directors

        (1) Power to declare is discretionary based on the board's assessment of business needs

    b. Dividends become a liability of corporation only when declared

        (1) True for all types of stock such as common stock or even cumulative preferred stock

    c. Cash dividends may be paid out of unrestricted and unreserved earned surplus (retained earnings) unless corporation already is or will be insolvent because of dividend

        (1) Some states have other regulations, sometimes allowing reductions in other accounts, too
        (2) Under Model Business Corporation Act, dividends are prohibited that cause total liabilities to exceed total assets after effect of the distribution is considered. Dividends may not be declared if payment of same will cause the corporation to become insolvent.

5. Right of stockholders to inspect books and records exists

    a. These books and records include minute books, stock certificate books, stock ledgers, general account books

   b. Demand must be made in good faith and for a proper purpose

     (1) May get list of shareholders to help wage a proxy fight to attempt to control corporation

     (2) May not get list of shareholders or customers to use for business mailing list

6. Preemptive right

   a. This is the right to subscribe to new issues of stock (at fair market value) so that a stockholder's ownership will not be diluted without the opportunity to maintain it

---

EXAMPLE

A corporation has one class of common stock. Stockholder A owns 15%. A new issue of the same class of stock is to be made. Stockholder A has the right to buy 15% of it.

---

   b. Usually only applies to common stock, not preferred

   c. Not for treasury stock

   d. There is no preemptive right to purchase stock unless Articles of Incorporation so provide; on the CPA exam the Examiners must tell you the shareholder has a preemptive right or it does not exist

7. Stockholder's right to sue

   a. Stockholder can sue in his/her own behalf where his/her interests have been directly injured, for example

     (1) Denial of right to inspect records

     (2) Denial of preemptive right if provided for

   b. Stockholders can sue on behalf of the corporation (i.e., a derivative suit)

     (1) In cases where a duty to the corporation is violated and corporation does not enforce, for example

       (a) Director violates his/her fiduciary duty to corporation

       (b) Illegal declaration of dividends (e.g., rendering corporation insolvent)

       (c) Fraud by officer on corporation

     (2) Unless demand would be futile, must first demand that directors sue in name of corporation and then may proceed if they refuse

       (a) Suit may be barred if directors make good faith business judgment that the suit is not in corporation's best interests

     (3) Damages go to corporation

8. Right to a pro rata share of distribution of assets on dissolution after creditors have been paid

---

NOW REVIEW MULTIPLE-CHOICE QUESTIONS 82 THROUGH 87 IN VOLUME 2

T. Stockholder's Liability

1. Generally stockholder's liability is limited to his/her price paid for stock

2. May be liable to creditors for

   a. Original issue stock sold at below par value

     (1) Contingently liable for the difference between par value and original issuance price

   b. Unpaid balance on no-par stock

   c. Dividends paid which impair capital if the corporation is insolvent

3. Piercing the corporate veil—courts disregard corporate entity and hold stockholders personally liable

   a. Rarely happens but may occur if

     (1) Corporation used to perpetrate fraud (e.g., forming an undercapitalized corporation)

     (2) Owners/officers do not treat corporation as separate entity

     (3) Shareholders commingle assets, bank accounts, financial records with those of corporation

     (4) Corporate formalities not adhered to

4. Majority shareholders owe fiduciary duty to minority shareholders and to corporation

    a. Even shareholder who controls corporation (majority ownership not now needed) has fiduciary duty

---

NOW REVIEW MULTIPLE-CHOICE QUESTIONS 88 THROUGH 90 IN VOLUME 2

U. Substantial Change in Corporate Structure

1. Merger

    a. Union of two corporations where one is absorbed by other

        (1) Surviving corporation issues its own shares (common and/or preferred) to shareholders of original corporations

2. Consolidation

    a. Joining of two (or more) corporations into a single new corporation
    b. All assets and liabilities are acquired by the new company
    c. New corporation is liable for debts of old corporations

3. Requirements to accomplish a merger or consolidation

    a. Boards of both corporations must prepare and submit plan to shareholders of both corporations
    b. Approval of board of directors of both companies
    c. Shareholders of both corporations must be given copy or summary of merger plan
    d. Majority vote of shareholders of each corporation
    e. Surviving corporation gets all assets and liabilities of merging corporations
    f. Dissatisfied shareholders of subsidiary may dissent and assert appraisal rights, thereby receiving the fair market value of their stock

4. Dissolution

    a. Once corporation is dissolved, it may do business only to wind up and liquidate business

        (1) Liquidation is the winding up of affairs and distribution of assets

            (a) Liquidation occurs in the following order

                1] Expenses of liquidation and creditors
                2] Preferred shareholders
                3] Common shareholders

        (2) Termination occurs when winding up and liquidation are completed

    b. May be done by voluntary dissolution or involuntary dissolution by state for cause

        (1) Voluntary dissolution occurs when board of directors passes resolution to dissolve

            (a) Resolution must be ratified by majority of stockholders entitled to vote

    c. Shareholder may petition for judicial dissolution if directors or shareholders are deadlocked

5. Dissolution of a corporation requires the filing of a dissolution document with the state.

NOW REVIEW MULTIPLE-CHOICE QUESTIONS 91 THROUGH 96 IN VOLUME 2

V. Subchapter S Corporation

1. When corporation elects to be Subchapter S corporation it can avoid double taxation by not paying tax at the corporate level

    a. Instead, the corporation income flows through to the income tax returns of the individual shareholders
    b. Shareholders report the income or loss even when income not distributed to them
    c. This flow-through may nevertheless be an advantage under some situations

2. Rules involving the criteria needed to be met to be taxed as a Subchapter S corporation can change to one's detriment, creating another potential disadvantage of needing to stay abreast of rule changes

    a. Some of the rules to watch out for involve

(1) Corporation must be incorporated in the US and have only one class of stock
(2) Number of shareholders Subchapter S corporation can have is limited to no more than 100 shareholders
(3) Shareholders are limited to individuals, estates, qualified trusts, and similar entities
(4) No foreign ownership of shares
(5) The corporation cannot have excessive amounts of passive income

> **NOW REVIEW MULTIPLE-CHOICE QUESTION 97 IN VOLUME 2**

KEY TERMS

Business judgment rule. Officers and/or directors of a corporation will not breach their fiduciary duty of care by simply making a poor business decision. Rather their action must be negligent to breach the duty of care.

C corporation. The assumed corporate form unless party affirmatively selects S corporation status. The typical form for large publically traded companies subject to double taxation. Generally, no personal liability for shareholders.

Dissociation. When a partner is no longer affiliated with the partnership.

Dissolution. The process of ending a partnership.

General partnership. An association of two or more persons to carry on a business as co-owners for profit. Partners have unlimited personal liability.

Joint venture. An association of two or more persons/entities engaged in a business for a specific purpose.

Limited liability company (LLC). A business entity that is run primarily like a general partnership, but affords its members (owners) limited liability.

Limited liability partnership. A general partnership that affords its partners limited liability from the actions of the other partners.

Limited partner. In a limited partnership this partner has no personal liability; however, the limited partner is not allowed to participate in the running of the business.

Limited partnership. A partnership with two types of partners ; general and limited. General partners have unlimited liability; limited partners have no personal liability.

Partnership interest. The partner's right to profits. This is freely transferable. Contrast this with the ownership interest, the right to be a partner, which can only be transferred with the consent of all the other partners.

S-corporation. A type of corporation which must be affirmatively elected by the organizers. Taxed like a partnership, but the shareholders have no personal liability.

Sole proprietorship. One-owner business, owner has unlimited liability.

Ultra vires (Latin). An action that goes beyond the power or the authority of the corporation. Such actions violate the fiduciary duty of obedience.

Winding up. The liquidation of the partnership.

Module 26: Contracts

Overview

Contract rules provide a foundation for many other law topics; consequently, a good understanding of the material in this module will aid you in comprehending the material in other modules.

It is important that you realize that there are two sets of contract rules to learn. The first is the group of common-law contract rules that, in general, apply to contracts that are not a sale of goods. Examples of contracts that are covered by the common law include real estate, insurance, employment, and professional services. The second set is the contract rules contained in Article Two of the Uniform Commercial Code (UCC). The UCC governs transactions involving the sale of goods (i.e., tangible personal property). Hence, if the contract is for the sale or purchase of tangible personal property, the provisions of the UCC will apply, and not the common law. For every contract question, it is important that you determine which set of rules to apply. Fortunately many of the rules under the two sets are the same. The best way for you to master this area is to first study the common-law rules for a topic. Then review the rules that are different under the UCC. Since the common law and the UCC rules have much in common, you will be learning contract law in the most understandable and efficient manner.

Contract law is tested by multiple-choice questions. You need to know the essential elements of a contract because the CPA examination tests heavily on offer and acceptance. Also, understand that an option is an offer supported by consideration. Distinguish between an option and a firm offer and understand how these are affected by revocations and rejections. You need to comprehend what consideration is and that it must be bargained for to be valid. The exam also requires that you understand that "past consideration" and moral obligations are not really consideration at all. You should have a solid understanding of the Statute of Frauds.

Once a contract is formed, third parties can obtain rights in the contract. An assignment is one important way this can happen.

If a contract is not performed, one of the parties may be held in breach of contract. Note that the possible remedies include monetary damages, specific performance, liquidated damages, and anticipatory repudiation. Before beginning the reading you should review the key terms at the end of the module.

A. Essential Elements of a Contract

1. Offer
2. Acceptance

   a. When offer and acceptance have occurred, an agreement is said to have been made

3. Consideration
4. Legal capacity
5. Legality (legal purpose)
6. Reality of consent

   a. Technically not a true element, but important to consider because may be necessary for enforceability of contract

912

7. Statute of Frauds

   a. Not a true element, but each factual situation should be examined to determine whether it applies because certain contracts must be in writing to be enforceable, as explained later

B. Types of Contracts

1. Express contract—terms are specifically stated orally or in writing
2. Implied contract—terms of contract not specifically stated, but some or all of terms are inferred from conduct of parties and/or circumstances

> **EXAMPLE**
>
> Hardy enters a fast food restaurant and orders a combo meal; there is an implied contract that Hardy will pay for the food and the restaurant will provide the food, even though those terms were never specifically stated.

3. Executed contract—terms have been fully performed
4. Executory contract—terms have not been fully performed by both parties
5. Unilateral contract

   a. One party gives promise for completion of requested act
   b. There is no legal obligation, no contract, unless the promise undertakes the action

> **EXAMPLE**
>
> I promise to pay you $10 if you wash my car. If you wash my car, I must pay you $10. If you do not wash my car, I owe you nothing, but you are not under any obligation to wash my car.

6. Bilateral contract

   a. Each party exchanges promises
   b. Creates a legal obligation for both parties

> **EXAMPLE**
>
> You promise to wash my car next Friday and I promise to pay you $10. Each of us has a legal obligation: You must wash my car and I must pay you $10.

7. Voidable contract—one that is enforceable unless party that has right pulls out of contract
8. Void contract—one that is not enforceable by either party

C. Discussion of Essential Elements of a Contract

1. Offer

   a. May be either written or oral (or sometimes by actions)

> **EXAMPLE**
>
> Offeror takes can of soup to check out stand and pays for it without saying anything.

   b. Requirements of a valid offer

      (1) Intent: An indication that the offeror desired to enter into a bargain

         (a) Courts use an objective standard: Would reasonable person think that offer had been intended?
         (b) Subjective intent (what offeror actually intended or meant) is not considered
         (c) Promises made in apparent jest are not offers

> **EXAMPLE**
>
> A licensed real estate agent offers to sell your home for a 4% commission; if a reasonable person thinks that this is a serious offer, then an offer exists, even if the real estate agent was joking.

(d) Statements of intent are not offers

> **EXAMPLE**
>
> "I am going to sell my car for $400." This is a statement of intent, not an offer.

(e) Invitations to negotiate (preliminary negotiations) are not offers (e.g., price tags or lists, auctions, inquiries, general advertisements)

> **EXAMPLE**
>
> Mary offers to pay Lucas, an attorney, $500 to create an estate plan for her. Lucas responds that he would not create an estate plan for anything less than $1000. Mary says she accepts Lucas's offer to do the estate plan for $1000. There is no contract. Lucas did not intend to make an offer; rather, Lucas was letting Mary know that she needed to raise her offer considerably. These are only preliminary negotiations.

(2) Definite and/or certain: Sufficiently specific terms so that the offeror and the offeree know what their obligations are.

(a) Courts allow some reasonable terms to be left open if customary to do so

> **EXAMPLE**
>
> C calls P, a plumber, to come and fix a clogged drain. No price is mentioned. However, upon P's completion of the work, he has the right to collect customary fee from C.

(3) Communicated: must be communicated to offeree by offeror or his/her agent

(a) Offeree may learn of a public offer (e.g., reward) in any way; s/he merely needs knowledge of it
(b) Offeror may limit who may accept the offer

> **EXAMPLE**
>
> This offer is only available to people 18 years of age and older. Even if Carlos, who is 17, heard the offer, he could not accept the offer because he does not satisfy the conditions of the offer.

c. Mistakes in transmission of offer are deemed to be offeror's risk because s/he chose method of communication; therefore, offer is effective as transmitted
d. Termination of offer can occur either by the actions of the parties or by operation of law

(1) Actions of the contracting parties

(a) Offeror's actions

1] Offeror specifically limits length of the offer

> **EXAMPLE**
>
> Offeror states that offer will remain open until June 9th. Offer ends on June 9th.

2] Revocation by the offeror

a] If offeree learns by reliable means that offeror has already sold subject of offer, it is revoked
b] Generally, offeror may revoke offer at any time prior to acceptance by offeree
c] Revocation is effective when received by offeree
d] An **option**, or an option contract, is an offer that is supported by consideration and cannot be revoked before stated time

> **EXAMPLE**
>
> On March 1, Madison offers to Potter a parcel of land for $50,000. Potter responds that he needs to think about it and asks Madison if she will hold the offer open for him. Madison writes on a note that she will hold the offer open for Potter until March 15. On, March 10, Bailey offers Madison $60,000 for the same parcel

of land that she had offered to Potter. Madison agreed to sell the land to Bailey and immediately notified Potter that she revoked her offer to Potter. Madison's offer to Potter terminated as soon as she told Potter of the revocation. This is true despite her written promise to hold the offer open until March 15.

On March 1, if Potter had instead given Madison consideration, for example $50, if Madison would hold the offer open until March 15, then Madison cannot revoke the offer until after March 15, and she could not sell the property to Bailey during that same time period.

    3] Offeree's actions

        a] Rejection of the offer
        b] Counteroffer: A rejection by the offeree couple with a new offer

            Warning: Be careful to distinguish a counteroffer from a mere inquiry. An inquiry does not terminate an offer, while a counteroffer will terminate an offer.

EXAMPLE

Madison offers to sell a parcel of land to Potter for $50,000. Potter asks Madison if she would be willing to take less than $50,000. Potter may still accept Madison's original offer to sell for $50,000. If, however, in response to Madison's original offer, Potter stated I'll give you $45,000 for the land, then that is a counteroffer and Madison's original offer is terminated.

---

        c] Both rejections and counteroffers are effective when received by the offeror

  (2) Some offers terminate automatically by operation of law: If any of the following events occurs the offer is terminated:

    (a) Death of either party
    (b) Incapacity of either party
    (c) The subject matter of the offer is destroyed
    (d) The proposed contract becomes illegal

EXAMPLE

X offers to rent to Y an upstairs floor for a cabaret. Thereafter, the city adopts a fire code making use of the premises illegal without substantial rebuilding.

---

2. Acceptance: When an offeree agrees to the offeror's terms

  a. May be written or oral
  b. Offer may be accepted only by person to whom it was directed

    (1) Use objective test—to whom would a reasonable person believe it to be directed?
    (2) Rewards can usually be accepted by anyone who knows of them, except for those who have a preexisting duty, such as a law enforcement officer.

  c. Offeree must have knowledge of offer in order to accept

EXAMPLE

D advertises a reward of $100 for the return of his pet dog. G, unaware of the offer, returns D's dog. G cannot require that D pay the $100 (if he later hears of the offer) because he was unaware of the offer when he returned the dog. He could not "accept" an offer he did not know existed.

---

  d. Intent to accept is required

    (1) Courts generally find click-on agreements legally enforceable when the offeree completes the contract online by clicking on a button that shows acceptance

      (a) Main issue is that offeree did clearly intend to accept offer by this action

  e. Acceptance must generally be in form specified by offer
  f. Acceptance must be unequivocal and unconditional (mirror image rule) under common law

(1) An acceptance that attempts to change terms of offer is not acceptance, but is both a rejection and a counteroffer

> **EXAMPLE**
>
> O offers to sell some real estate for $100,000 cash. E says "I accept. I'll give you $50,000 now and $50,000 plus 13% interest one year from now."

    (a) Mere inquiry or request is not a counteroffer so offer remains in effect

> **EXAMPLE**
>
> O gives the same offer as above but this time E asks if O would accept $50,000 now and $50,000 plus 13% interest one year from now. The offer is neither accepted nor terminated.

    (b) An attempted counteroffer given to electronic agent such as web page or voice mail is not effective when it does not have ability to evaluate counteroffer

(2) A condition which does not change or add to terms of contract is not a counteroffer (i.e., a condition that is already part of contract because of law, even though not expressed in previous negotiations)

g. Silence is not acceptance unless

(1) Offer indicated silence would constitute acceptance (e.g., offer states "your silence is acceptance," and offeree intended his/her silence as acceptance)
(2) Offeree has taken benefit of services or goods and exercised control over them when s/he had opportunity to reject them
(3) Through prior dealings, by agreement between parties, or when dictated by custom, silence can be acceptance

h. Acceptances are valid when sent (Mailbox Rule)

(1) If acceptance is made by method specified in offer or by same method used by offeror to communicate the offer, acceptance is effective when sent (e.g., when placed in mail or when telegram is dispatched)

> **EXAMPLE**
>
> Offeror mails a written offer without stating the mode of acceptance. Offeree mails acceptance. Offeror, before receipt, calls offeree to revoke the offer. The contract exists because acceptance was effective when mailed and revocation of offer came too late.

    (a) Exception: If offeree sends rejection and then acceptance, first received is effective even though offeree sent acceptance by same method used by offeror

(2) Methods of acceptance, other than those specified in the offer, are considered effective when actually received by offeror
(3) Late acceptance does not create a contract—it is a counteroffer and a valid contract is formed only if original offeror then accepts
(4) If acceptance is valid when sent, a lost or delayed acceptance does not destroy validity

> **EXAMPLE**
>
> R wires an offer to E asking her to accept by mail. The acceptance is correctly mailed but never arrives. There is a valid agreement.

(5) Offeror can change above rules by stating other rule(s) in offer

> **EXAMPLE**
>
> Offeror mails a written offer to offeree stating that acceptance is valid only if **received** by the offeror within ten days. Offeree mails back the acceptance within ten days but it arrives late. Acceptance has not occurred even though the offeree used the same method.

i. Once there is an offer and acceptance, an agreement is formed

  (1) Details can be worked out later
  (2) Formalization often occurs later
  (3) Attempted revocations or rejections after agreement is formed are of no effect

j. Offers, revocations, rejections, and counteroffers are valid when received (under both common law and UCC)

  (1) Compare with rules for acceptances which are sometimes valid when sent and other times are valid when received

> **EXAMPLE**
>
> S offers to sell his land to B for $20,000. The offer is mailed to B. Later that same day, S changes his mind and mails B a revocation of this offer. When B receives the offer, she mails her acceptance. B receives the revocation the day after she mailed the acceptance. S and B have a valid contract because the acceptance was valid when sent but the revocation would have been valid when B received it. Once the offer is accepted, any attempted revocation will not be valid.

> **EXAMPLE**
>
> Use the same facts as above except that the offeree uses a different method than the mailed acceptance. If B receives the revocation before S receives the acceptance, there is no contract.

k. Auctions

  (1) Bid is offer
  (2) Bidder may retract bid until auctioneer announces sale completed
  (3) If auction is "with reserve," auctioneer may withdraw goods before s/he announces completion of sale
  (4) If auction "without reserve," goods may not be withdrawn unless no bid made within reasonable time
  (5) Auctions are "with reserve" unless specified otherwise

l. Online auctions

  (1) Many individuals and businesses are conducting auctions online

    (a) Becoming increasingly popular as buyers and sellers rely on fluidity of contract-making abilities

NOW REVIEW MULTIPLE-CHOICE QUESTIONS 1 THROUGH 9 IN VOLUME 2

3. Formation Defenses: Although offer and acceptance appear to present, if one of the following formation defenses occurs, then there may not be an agreement.

  a. Fraud—includes following elements

    (1) Misrepresentation of a material fact

      (a) Can be falsehood or concealment of defect
      (b) Silence is not misrepresentation unless there is duty to speak, for example,

        1] Fiduciary relationship between parties
        2] Seller of property knows there is a dangerous latent (hidden) defect

      (c) Must be statement of past or present fact

        1] Opinion (e.g., of value) is not fact

          a] Experts' opinion does constitute fraud

> **EXAMPLE**
>
> An expert appraiser of jewelry appraises a diamond to be worth $500 when he knows it is actually worth $1,500. This fulfills the "misrepresentation of a material fact" element and also scienter element. If the remaining elements of fraud are met, then there is fraud.

        2] Opinions about what will happen in future (expert or not) do not satisfy fact requirement

> **EXAMPLE**
>
> A real estate agent tells a prospective buyer that the income property she is considering purchasing will earn at least 50% more next year than last year.

        3] Puffing or sales talk is not fact

> **EXAMPLE**
>
> A seller claims her necklace is worth $1,000. The buyer pays $1,000 and later finds out that he can buy a very similar necklace from another seller for $700. Even if the other elements of fraud are present, this opinion does not constitute fraud.

        4] Presently existing intention in mind of the speaker is fact

  (2) Intent to mislead—"scienter"

    (a) Need knowledge of falsity with intent to mislead, **or**
    (b) Reckless disregard for truth can be substituted

        1] If all elements (1) through (4) are present but reckless disregard is proven instead of actual knowledge of falsity, then it is called constructive fraud

  (3) Reasonable reliance by injured party

    (a) One who knows the truth or might have learned it by a reasonable inquiry may not recover
    (b) One cannot reasonably rely on opinions about future

  (4) Resulting in injury
  (5) Remedies for fraud

    (a) Defrauded party may affirm agreement and sue for damages under tort of deceit, or if party is sued on contract, then s/he may set up fraud in reduction of damages, or
    (b) Defrauded party may rescind contract and sue for damages that result from the fraud

  (6) Fraud may occur

    (a) In the inducement

        1] The misrepresentation occurs during contract negotiations
        2] Creates voidable contract at option of defrauded party

> **EXAMPLE**
>
> A represents to B that A's car has been driven 50,000 miles when in fact it has been driven for 150,000 miles. If B purchases A's car in reliance on this misrepresentation, fraud in the inducement is present, creating a voidable contract at B's option.

    (b) In the execution

        1] Misrepresentation occurs in actual form of agreement
        2] Creates void contract

> **EXAMPLE**
>
> Larry Lawyer represents to Danny that Danny is signing his will, when in fact he is signing a promissory note payable to Larry. This promissory note is void because fraud in the execution is present.

  (7) Fraud is also called intentional misrepresentation

b. Negligent misrepresentation and innocent misrepresentation

  (1) Both involve an innocent misstatement made in good faith (i.e., no scienter)
  (2) All other elements same as fraud

(3) Creates right of rescission (cancellation) in injured party—to return both parties to their precontract positions to extent practicably possible (i.e. the contract is voidable)

    (a) Does not allow aggrieved party to sue for damages

c. Mistake: Where at least one party to the agreement believes that a material fact is true, but the fact is not true.

    (1) Mutual mistake (i.e., by both parties) about material characteristics of subject matter in contract makes contract voidable by either party

> **EXAMPLE**
>
> S and B make a contract in which B agrees to buy a boat from S. Although neither party knew it at the time, this boat had been destroyed before this contract was made. This is a mutual mistake about the existence of the boat; therefore, either party may void this contract by law. Note that legally either party may pull out although usually only one party may wish to do so.

        (a) Also exists when both parties reasonably attach different meanings to word or phrase
        (b) Also called bilateral mistake
        (c) Mistake about value of subject matter is not grounds for voiding contract

    (2) Unilateral mistake generally does not allow party to void contract

        (a) Exception: If non-mistaken part knowingly takes advantage of the mistaken party

> **EXAMPLE**
>
> A subcontractor submits a bid to do the electrical work for a new building. The bid was $10,000; the fair value for such work is approximately $100,000 and the general contractor accepts the bid with knowledge of this error. The subcontractor can successfully use unilateral mistake as a defense and void the agreement.

d. Duress—a contract entered into because of duress can be voided because of invalid consent

    (1) Any acts or threats of violence or extreme pressure against party or member of party's family, which in fact deprives party of free will and causes him/her to agree, is duress

> **EXAMPLE**
>
> X threatens to criminally prosecute Y unless he signs a contract. This contract is made under duress.

        (a) May involve coercion that is social or economic that leaves him/her with no reasonable alternative

    (2) Physical duress in which party agrees to contract under physical force
    (3) Extreme duress causes agreement to be void
    (4) Ordinary duress creates voidable agreement

e. Undue influence—unfair persuasion of one person over another which prevents understanding or voluntary action

    (1) Usually occurs when very dominant person has extreme influence over weaker person

        (a) Weakness can result from physical, mental, or emotional weakness or combinations of these

    (2) Also occurs through abuse of fiduciary relationship (e.g., CPA, attorney, guardian, trustee, etc.)
    (3) Normally causes agreement to be voidable

4. Consideration—an act, promise, or forbearance that is offered by one party and accepted by another as inducement to enter into agreement

a. Consideration requires an exchange of promises (i.e., each party must promise to undertake an obligation that he or she was not previously obligated to perform).

> **EXAMPLE**
>
> B pays S $500 for S's stereo that he hands over to B. B's consideration is the $500. S's consideration is the stereo.

> **EXAMPLE**
>
> S gives B a stereo today. B promises to pay S $500 in one week. The promise to pay $500, rather than the $500 itself, is the consideration. Thus, the element of consideration is met today.

> **EXAMPLE**
>
> A hits and injures P with his car. P agrees not to sue A when A agrees to settle out of court for $10,000. A's promise to pay the money is consideration. P's promise to refrain from bringing a lawsuit is consideration on his/her side.

> **EXAMPLE**
>
> Using the fact pattern above, further assume that it is not clear whether A is at fault. The settlement (contract) is still enforceable if made in good faith because of possible liability.

b. Consideration must be legally sufficient, this includes

   (1) A promise to do something that one was not previously obligated to do
   (2) A promise to refrain from something that one has a legal right to do

> **EXAMPLE**
>
> Thomas promises his uncle that he will not drink alcohol for 10 months in exchange for his uncle's promise to pay him $1,000. If Thomas is a minor and prohibited by state law from drinking alcohol, then Thomas has not provided consideration, since Thomas has no legal right to drink. Conversely, if Thomas is legally allowed to drink, then his promise does constitute consideration.

c. Legal sufficiency does not concern itself with the adequacy of consideration (i.e., the law is not concerned whether the exchanged consideration is a fair deal).

> **EXAMPLE**
>
> In the previous example involving Thomas and his uncle, the court does not care whether Thomas's act of not drinking is worth $1,000. Rather the court is concerned that each party provided some consideration.

d. Consideration must be bargained for (this is essential)

   (1) Agreement to accept from debtor a lesser sum than owed is unenforceable if the debt is a liquidated (undisputed) debt

> **EXAMPLE**
>
> C agrees to accept $700 for a $900 debt that D owes C. The amount is not disputed. D still owes C the additional $200.

     (a) But if debtor incurs a detriment in addition to paying, creditor's promise to accept lesser sum will be binding

> **EXAMPLE**
>
> X owes Y $1,000. Y agrees to accept $500 and X will also install Y's new furnace at no additional cost.

     (b) Note that agreement to accept a lesser sum is enforceable if amount of debt is unliquidated (disputed) because both parties give up right to more favorable sum

> **EXAMPLE**
>
> C claims that D owes him $1,000. D claims that the amount owed is $600. If C and D agree to settle this for $700, the agreement is supported by consideration since C gave up the right to attempt to collect more than $700 and D gave up the right to attempt settlement for a lesser sum.

(2) Preexisting legal duty is not sufficient as consideration because no new legal detriment is suffered by performing prior obligation

> **EXAMPLE**
>
> Agreement to pay police officer $200 to recover stolen goods is unenforceable.

> **EXAMPLE**
>
> X promises to pay Y, a jockey, $50 to ride as hard as he can in the race. Y already owes his employer, Z, that duty so there is no consideration to enforce the agreement.

    (a) Agreement to pay more to finish a job, such as building a house, is unenforceable unless unforeseen difficulties are encountered (e.g., underground stream or marshy land under a house)

(3) Past consideration (consideration for a prior act, forbearance, or agreement) is not sufficient for new contract because it is not bargained for

(4) Moral obligation is not consideration

    (a) In majority of states the following need no consideration

        1] Promise to pay debt barred by statute of limitations.
        2] Promise to pay debt barred by bankruptcy. Promise must adhere to strict rules stated in Bankruptcy Reform Act of 1978 concerning reaffirmations of dischargeable debts.

(5) Modifying existing contracts

    (a) Modification of contract under the common law needs new consideration on both sides to be legally binding

> **EXAMPLE**
>
> S agrees in a written contract to sell a piece of land to P for $40,000. S later changes his mind and demands $50,000 for the same piece of land. The original contract is enforceable (at $40,000) even if P agrees to the increased price because although P has agreed to give more consideration, S has not given any new consideration.

    (b) Under UCC, a contract for sale of goods may be modified orally or in writing without consideration if in good faith

> **EXAMPLE**
>
> S agrees to sell P 300 pairs of socks for $1.00 each. Due to rapid price increases in S's costs, he asks P if he will modify the price to $1.20 each. P agrees. The contract as modified is enforceable because it is covered under the UCC and does not need new consideration on both sides.

    (6) Illusory contracts are not supported by consideration (e.g., party agrees to sell all he/she wishes)

e. In majority of states, seals placed on contracts are not substitutes for consideration
f. Best-efforts contracts are contacts which parties are to use best efforts to complete contract's objectives
g. Promissory estoppel may act as substitute for consideration and renders promise enforceable—promisor is estoppel from asserting lack of consideration

    (1) Elements

        (a) Detrimental reliance on promise
        (b) Reliance is reasonable and foreseeable

        (c) Damage results (injustice) if promise is not enforced

    (2) Usually applied to gratuitous promises but trend is to apply to commercial transactions. At least recovery of expenses is allowed.

> **EXAMPLE**
>
> A wealthy man in the community promises to pay for a new church if it is built. The church committee reasonably (and in good faith) relies on the promise and incurs the expenses.

  h. Mutuality of obligation—means both parties must be bound or neither is bound

    (1) Both parties must give consideration by paying or promising to pay for the act, promise, or forbearance of the other with something of legal value

  i. Promise to donate to charity is enforceable based on public policy reasons

5. Legal Capacity

  a. An agreement between parties in which one or both lack the capacity to contract is void or, in some cases, voidable

  b. Minors: In a majority of states these are people under the age of 18.

    (1) A minor may contract, but agreement is voidable by minor

        (a) Adult is held to contract unless minor disaffirms

    (2) If minor has purchased nonnecessaries, when minor disaffirms, s/he is required to give back any part s/he still has

        (a) Minor may recover all of consideration given
        (b) In most courts, minor need not pay for what s/he cannot return

    (3) Minor is liable for reasonable value of necessaries furnished to him/her

        (a) Minor may disaffirm contract if it is executory (i.e., not completed)
        (b) Necessaries include food, clothing, shelter, education, etc., considering his/her age and position in life
        (c) Many states have passed laws which make certain contracts enforceable against minors such as contracts which involve

            1] Medical care
            2] Life insurance
            3] Psychological care
            4] Loans for education

    (4) Minor may disaffirm contract at any time until a reasonable time after reaching majority age

        (a) Failure to disaffirm within reasonable time after reaching majority acts as ratification (e.g., one year is too long in the absence of very special circumstances such as being out of the country)

    (5) Minor may choose to ratify within a reasonable time after reaching age of majority

        (a) By words, either orally or in writing but must ratify all, or
        (b) By actions that indicate ratification
        (c) Ratification prior to majority is not effective

    (6) If minor misrepresents his/her age when making contract, most states still allow minor to disaffirm

        (a) Some courts allow minor to disaffirm contract, but allow other party to sue for fraud
        (b) Some allow minor to disaffirm if minor returns consideration in similar condition
        (c) Other courts will not allow minor to disaffirm especially if it was a business contract

  c. Incompetent persons

    (1) Contract by person adjudicated insane is void

        (a) Insane person need not return consideration

    (2) Contracts made by those with diminished capacity (e.g., compulsive spending disorder) are voidable

        (a) Where courts hold such agreements voidable, restitution is condition precedent to disaffirmance

d. Legal capacity of one intoxicated is determined by his/her ability to understand and by degree of intoxication

    (1) Contracts are enforceable, in general, unless extent of intoxication at time contract made was so great that intoxicated party did not understand terms or nature of contract—then contract voidable at option of one intoxicated if s/he returns items under contract

6. Legality

  a. Agreement is generally unenforceable if it is illegal or violates public policy

  b. When both parties are guilty, neither will be aided by court (i.e., if one party had already given some consideration, s/he will not get it back)

    (1) But if one party repudiates prior to performance, s/he may recover his/her consideration

> **EXAMPLE**
>
> X contracts to buy stolen goods from Y. If X pays Y but then repents and refuses to accept the stolen goods, X may recover the money he paid Y.

  c. When one party is innocent, s/he will usually be given relief

    (1) A member of a class of people designed to be protected by statute is considered innocent (e.g., purchaser of stock issued in violation of blue-sky laws)

  d. Types of illegal contracts (contracts that may not be enforceable due to public policy concerns)

    (1) Agreement to commit crime or tort

      (a) If agreement calls for intentional wrongful interference with a valid contractual relationship, it is an illegal agreement

    (2) An agreement to not press criminal charges for consideration is illegal

> **EXAMPLE**
>
> A has embezzled money from his employer. The employer agrees to not press charges if A pays back all of the money. Such an agreement is not enforceable, since employer has an obligation to cooperate with criminal investigations.

    (3) Services rendered without a license when statute requires a license

      (a) Two types of licensing statutes

        1] Regulatory licensing statute—one that seeks to protect public from incapable, unskilled, or dishonest persons

          a] Contract is unenforceable by either party
          b] Even if work done, other need not pay because not a contract

> **EXAMPLE**
>
> X, falsely claiming to have a CPA license, performs an audit for ABC Company. Upon learning the true facts, ABC may legally refuse to pay X any fees or expenses.

        2] Revenue-seeking statute—purpose is to raise revenue for government

          a] Contract is enforceable

> **EXAMPLE**
>
> Y, based on a contract, performed extensive yard work for M. M then finds out that Y failed to obtain a license required by the local government to raise revenue. M is obligated to pay Y the agreed-upon amount.

    (4) Usury (contract for greater than legal interest rate)
    (5) Contracts against public policy

      (a) Contracts in restraint of trade such as covenant not to compete after end of an employment contract

      1] Courts must balance need of former employer such as protection of trade secrets or customer base with need of employee to practice his/her line of work

      2] Typically, contract will restrict employee from competing in named areas for stated period of time

      3] Employer must show that covenant not to compete is needed to protect interests of employer and that restraints are reasonable as to geographical area and as to time period

  (b) Upon sale of business, seller agrees to not compete with sold type of business in named areas for stated period of time

      1] Courts will look at reasonableness as to geographical area, reasonableness as to time, and whether covenant is unduly restrictive for public's need

      2] Courts are generally more likely to enforce a covenant not to compete in the sale of a business rather than such a covenant in an employment contract because the parties in the sale of a business are viewed as having equal bargaining power.

  (c) Exculpatory clauses are clauses found in contracts in which one party tries to avoid liability for own negligence

      1] Generally, such clauses are enforceable if it attempts to excuse merely negligent behavior

      2] If the clause tries to excuse intentional or reckless behavior then the clause is unenforceable

---

EXAMPLE

Sally decides to go skiing. When she buys her lift ticket, she signs a clause where she agrees to not hold the owners of the mountain liable for any injuries that Sally suffers while skiing. If Sally is injured while skiing as a result of the conduct of the owners of the ski resort, Sally can still recover against the ski resort if she can show that the injuries were due to reckless or intentional conduct on the part of the owners.

NOW REVIEW MULTIPLE-CHOICE QUESTIONS 10 THROUGH 27 IN VOLUME 2

D. Written Contracts

1. Generally, an oral contract is as enforceable as a written contract
2. The Statute of Frauds, however, requires that certain types of contracts be evidenced by a writing to be enforceable.

  a. Evidenced by a writing means either

    (1) That the contract, itself, be in writing, or

    (2) That there is sufficient written evidence to prove the existence of a contract

3. Contracts that need to be evidenced by a writing

  a. An agreement to sell or transfer any interest in land (real estate)

    (1) Includes buildings, easements, and contracts to sell real estate

    (2) Part performance typically satisfies Statute of Frauds even though real estate contract was oral, but this requires

      (a) Possession of the land

      (b) Either part payment or making of improvements on real estate

      (c) Many courts require all three

  b. An agreement that cannot be performed within one year from the making of agreement

    (1) Contract that can be performed in exactly one year or less may be oral

---

EXAMPLE

W agrees to hire X for ten months starting in four months. This contract must be in writing because it cannot be performed until fourteen months after the agreement is made.

---

    (2) Any contract which can conceivably be completed in one year, irrespective of how long the task actually takes, may be oral

> **EXAMPLE**
>
> A agrees to paint B's portrait for $400. It actually is not completed until over a year later. This contract did not have to be in writing because it was possible to complete it within one year.

(3) If performance is contingent on something which could take place in less than one year, agreement may be oral

> **EXAMPLE**
>
> "I will employ you as long as you live." Party could possibly die in less than one year.

(4) But if its terms call for more than one year, it must be written even if there is possibility of taking place in less than one year

> **EXAMPLE**
>
> "I will employ you for five years." The employee's death could occur before the end of five years, but the terms call for the writing requirement under the Statute of Frauds.

(5) Generally, if one side of performance is complete but other side cannot be performed within year, it is not within Statute (i.e., may be oral). Especially true if performance has been accepted and all that remains is the payment of money.

> **EXAMPLE**
>
> X agrees to pay E $6,000 salary per month and a bonus of $50,000 if he works for at least two years. After two years, X refuses to pay the bonus. The $50,000 is payable and the Statute of Frauds is no defense here.

   (a) An agreement to answer for debt or default of another (contract of guaranty, see suretyship in Module 31)

      1] A secondary promise is within this section of the Statute of Frauds (i.e., must be in writing)

> **EXAMPLE**
>
> "If Jack doesn't pay, I will."

      2] A primary promise is not within this section of the Statute of Frauds because it is in reality the promisor's own contract

> **EXAMPLE**
>
> "Let Jack have it, and I will pay."

      3] Promise for benefit of promisor may be oral ("Main Purpose Doctrine")

> **EXAMPLE**
>
> Promisor agrees to answer for default of X, because X is promisor's supplier and he needs X to stay in business to keep himself in business.

      4] Promise of indemnity (will pay based on another's fault, for example, insurance) is not within Statute

  c. Agreement for sale of goods for $500 or more is required to be in writing under UCC

> **EXAMPLE**
>
> Oral contract for the sale of fifty calculators for $10 each is not enforceable.

> **EXAMPLE**
>
> Oral contract to perform management consulting services over the next six months for $100,000 is enforceable because the $500 rule does not apply to contracts that come under common law.

> **EXAMPLE**
>
> Same as previous example except that the agreed time was for fourteen months. This one is required to be in writing to be enforceable because of the one-year rule.

(1) Exceptions to writing requirement (these are important)

    (a) Oral contract involving specially manufactured goods (i.e., not saleable in ordinary course of business) if seller has made substantial start in their manufacture (or even made a contract for necessary raw materials) is enforceable

    (b) Oral contract is enforceable against party who admits it in court but not beyond quantity of goods admitted

    (c) Goods that have been paid for (if seller accepts payment) or goods which buyer has accepted are part of enforceable contract even if oral

> **EXAMPLE**
>
> B orally agrees to purchase 10,000 parts from S for $1 each. B later gives S $6,000 for a portion of the parts. S accepts the money. In absence of a written agreement, B may enforce a contract for 6,000 parts but not for the full 10,000 parts.

(2) Modifications of written contracts involve two issues under UCC

    (a) New consideration on both sides is not required under UCC although it is required under common law

        1] Under UCC, modification must be done in good faith

    (b) Modified contract must be in writing if contract, as modified, is within Statute of Frauds (i.e., sale of goods for $500 or more)

> **EXAMPLE**
>
> S agrees orally to sell B 100 widgets for $4.80 each. B later agrees, orally, to pay $5.00 for the 100 widgets due to changed business conditions. The modified contract is not enforceable because it must have been in writing. Therefore, the original contract is enforceable.

> **EXAMPLE**
>
> Same as above except that the modification is in writing. Now the modified contract is enforceable despite the fact that S is giving no new consideration.

> **EXAMPLE**
>
> X and Y have a written contract for the sale of goods for $530. They subsequently both agree orally to a price reduction of $40. The modified contract for $490 is enforceable.

(3) Parties may exclude future oral agreements in a signed writing
(4) Agreement for sale of intangibles over $5,000 must be in writing (e.g., patents, copyrights, or contract rights)

    (5) Sale of securities must be in writing

       (a) Must include price and quantity

4. The Statute of Frauds is a rule of evidence; thus, the Statute only applies to executory contracts

    a. The Statute requires a writing to act as proof of the existence of a contract
    b. If the parties have already executed (performed) the contract, there is no need for written evidence because the parties' performance is evidence that a contract existed.

5. The writing requirement

    a. The Statute of Frauds does not require that the actual contract be in writing, rather that there is a writing, or writings, that prove the existence of a contract.
    b. The writing requirement may be satisfied by one writing or by combining multiple writings
    c. A sufficient writing must

       (1) Identify the parties to the contract,
       (2) Identify the subject matter of the contract, and
       (3) Be signed by the party to be charged (the party we are seeking to hold liable for the contract).

EXAMPLE

On May 1, 2011, Patrick provides a written offer to Rod for Rod to work for Patrick from August 1, 2011 until June 30, 2012. Rod accepts the offer orally on May 3, 2011. On July 15, 2011, Rod receives a better job offer from George and informs Patrick that Rod will not work for Patrick. Patrick sues Rod for breach of contract.

Analysis: First this contract is covered by the Statute of Frauds since it cannot be performed within 1 year from the date of formation. (May 3, 2011–June 30, 2012) Patrick's written offer to Rod satisfies two of the conditions for a writing: Identifies the parties and the nature of the contract. Patrick's writing, however, is only signed by Patrick, not Rod. Since Rod is the party to be charged, the writing is not sufficient and the Statute of Frauds will prevent Patrick from enforcing the employment contract against Rod.

NOTE: If Rod had responded to Patrick's offer via e-mail, instead of orally, then the contract is binding upon both parties. Patrick's written offer, as discussed above, satisfies two of the conditions for a writing; Rod's e-mail would provide the signature of the party to be charged. Combining the two writings would satisfy the Statute of Frauds.

---

6. Noncompliance with Statute of Frauds (i.e., failure to make a writing) will make contract unenforceable
7. Parol evidence rule

    a. Applies only if a written contract exists
    b. Provides that any written agreement intended by parties to be final and complete contract (called an integration) may not be contradicted by previous or contemporaneous (written or oral) evidence

       (1) Applies to such written contracts whether Statute of Frauds required writing or not
       (2) Evidence of integration is often shown by a clause such as "This agreement is the complete agreement between the parties; no other representations have been made."

EXAMPLE

A and B enter into a home purchase agreement which is intended as a complete contract. B wishes to introduce oral evidence into court that the price of $150,000 that was in the home purchase agreement was put in to get a larger loan from a bank. B claims that they orally agreed the price would be $130,000. The oral evidence is not allowed to contradict the written contract under the parol evidence rule.

---

       (3) Exceptions (party may present oral proof)

         (a) To prove the existence of a formation (e.g., fraud, forgery, duress, mistake, failure of consideration; see part C.3 of this outline above).
         (b) To show terms not inconsistent with writing that parties would not be expected to have included

> **EXAMPLE**
>
> Builder promises orally to use reasonable care not to damage nearby trees when building a house.

    (c) To explain intended meaning of an ambiguity (proof cannot contradict terms in contract but can explain them)

    (d) To show condition precedent—proof can be presented to show a fact or event must occur before agreement is valid

    (e) Under UCC, written terms may be supplemented or explained by course of dealing, usage of trade, or course of performance

  (4) Does not apply to subsequent transactions (e.g., promises made after original agreement, or separate and distinct agreement made at same time as written contract)

> **EXAMPLE**
>
> M and N have a complete written employment contract. Later, M and N orally modify the contract with M agreeing to pay more and N agreeing to take on more duties. The oral evidence is allowed because it arose subsequent to the written contract.

8. Contracting using faxes

  a. Legal issues arise with use of faxes

    (1) Was an agreement really reached?

      (a) Courts examine faxes to see if "meeting of minds" actually took place under common law principles

    (2) Validity of signatures sent by faxes

      (a) Majority of courts that have examined this issue conclude that signatures sent by fax are valid

9. Contracting online

  a. When individuals make contracts over the Internet, basic rules of contract law still apply; however, this technology has created and will create more additional legal issues—only some of which have been settled

  b. E-SIGN Act—Federal law that makes electronic signatures valid like written ones, also makes electronic documents as valid as ones on paper

    (1) Electronic signatures are also referred to as e-signatures

      (a) Challenge is to verify that one using e-signature is person s/he claims to be

    (2) Electronic document is valid only if it is in form that is retainable and is accurately reproduced

    (3) Some documents are exempt from E-SIGN Act such as wills, court papers, and foreclosures

    (4) Act is considered important to promote use of technology

      (a) Does not provide uniform standard for authenticating e-signatures

        1] However, recommended methods to authenticate e-signatures include

          a] Use devices that recognize iris of user's eye or other portions of eye

          b] Use devices that recognize fingerprints

          c] Use secret passwords

          d] Use cards to identify persons such as "smart cards"

      (b) Various states are adopting statutes that provide for procedures to determine validity of e-signatures

      (c) Many companies enter into written contracts to accept electronic data and e-signatures between them

      (d) Companies and individuals may use exceptions that exist under statute of frauds without need to resort to E-SIGN Act or state statutes

    (5) Federal law has following provisions to protect consumers

      (a) Consumers need to consent to receiving electronic contracts and records

      (b) Businesses required to tell consumers of their right to receive hard-copy documents of electronic transactions

      (c) Consumers must be able to indicate or demonstrate they have access to electronic records for businesses to send them electronic records

10. Computer shrink-wrap licenses and contracts generally enforceable

    a. Sale of shrink-wrap licenses is often conducted over Internet

    b. Individual or company often buys these without seeing or reviewing them first (thus the term shrink-wrap)

       (1) Court cases have held these shrink-wrap licenses or goods purchased online to be enforceable especially if purchaser has time to examine them with right of return

11. Federal antispam law does not prohibit spam but instead allows businesses to spam when they do not lie in spam

12. Internet and online transactions are changing how goods and services are paid for

    a. Some methods have developed for electronic payment

       (1) Person-to-person payment often called PayPal is a system in which buyer authorizes payment of goods or services and seller goes to a site to provide information needed to authorize payment—amount is deducted from buyer's bank account

       (2) Virtual credit card is a system used by ones who doubt security of Internet

          (a) System creates new credit card number for each transaction which cannot be reused

       (3) Digital cash is a method whereby retailers create their own currency on the Internet and customers with the right software can purchase the currency to pay for items with their currency account

          (a) It is good for those who wish not to use credit cards on the web

       (4) Digital Wallets is a one-stop payment location authorized by a buyer so retailers can be paid from the wallet when given access by the buyer

       (5) Virtual points allow web users to accumulate points which can be used to make purchases

          (a) These systems must have a sufficient number of retailers to make them work well

       (6) Virtual escrow is a method in which a third party handles the Internet transaction and makes sure seller has performed according to the contract before releasing payment from buyer

> **NOW REVIEW MULTIPLE-CHOICE QUESTIONS 28 THROUGH 37 IN VOLUME 2**

E. Assignment and Delegation

1. Assignment is the transfer of a right under a contract by one person to another
2. Delegation is the transfer of duties under a contract
3. Generally, a party's rights in a contract are assignable and duties are delegable

    a. No consideration is needed for valid assignment

       (1) Gratuitous assignments are revocable

> **EXAMPLE**
>
> A owes B a debt for services B performed for A, but B has been unable to collect because A has been in financial difficulty. B may gratuitously assign this debt to X if X can collect it. If A's financial position improves, B may revoke the assignment to X and collect the debt himself or assign it to another for consideration.

    b. Rights may be assigned without delegating duties, or duties may be delegated without assigning rights

    c. Partial assignments may be made (e.g., only assign part of one's rights such as right to receive money)

    d. An assignment of a contract is generally taken to mean both assignment of rights and delegation of duties unless language or facts indicate otherwise

    e. Exceptions to ability to make assignments and delegations

       (1) Contract involving personal services, trust, or confidence (e.g., an artist cannot delegate his/her duty to paint a portrait)

          (a) With permission, these can be delegated

          (b) Note that a contractor building a house according to a blueprint can delegate his/her duty to someone qualified

       (2) Provision of contract or statute prohibits assignment or delegation

(a) Trend is to look with disfavor on prohibitions against assignments where only a right to money is concerned

(b) The UCC makes prohibition against assignment of monetary rights ineffective

(3) If assignment would materially change risk or burden of obligor

(a) For example, insurance contracts, requirement and output contracts, and contracts where personal credit is involved

f. A delegation of duties is not an anticipatory breach

> **EXAMPLE**
>
> X Company contracted to deliver certain goods to Y. If X Company is low on these goods, it may delegate this duty to S Company, its subsidiary. It is not an anticipatory breach because X has not indicated that performance will not occur.

4. An assignment generally extinguishes any rights of assignor but a delegation does not relieve delegator of his/her duties

a. The assignee acquires assignor's rights against obligor and has exclusive right to performance
b. If obligor has notice of assignment, s/he must pay assignee, not assignor

(1) If obligor has no notice, s/he may pay assignor and assignee can only recover from assignor

5. Party taking an assignment generally steps into shoes of assignor—s/he gets no better rights than assignor had

a. Assignee is subject to any defenses obligor could assert against assignor
b. If assignee releases obligor, then assignor is also released

> **EXAMPLE**
>
> A and B enter into a contract in which B agrees to pay A $300 for a stereo he received. A assigns his right to the $300 to C. C then releases B from the obligation of paying C the $300. This also releases A.

6. Assignor for value makes implied warranties to assignee that

a. Assignor will do nothing to impair rights of assignee
b. Assignor has no knowledge of any fact that would impair value of assignment

7. If assignor makes more than one assignment of same right, there are two rules to be applied depending upon the state

a. First assignment prevails regardless of notices (majority rule)
b. First assignee to give notice to obligor prevails (minority rule)

NOW REVIEW MULTIPLE-CHOICE QUESTIONS 38 THROUGH 40 IN VOLUME 2

F. Third-Party Beneficiary Contracts

1. Contracting parties enter into agreement intended to benefit third party(ies)

a. Creditor beneficiary—a debtor contracts with a second party to pay the debt owed to creditor (third-party beneficiary)

> **EXAMPLE**
>
> X owes C $100. X contracts with Y to paint Y's house if Y will pay C $100. C is a creditor beneficiary.

> **EXAMPLE**
>
> B buys some real estate from S and agrees to assume S's mortgage that is owed to XYZ bank. XYZ is a creditor beneficiary because B and S made a contract in which B agreed to pay XYZ. If B later defaults,

XYZ may recover from either B or S. XYZ may recover from S based on the original contract. XYZ may recover from B because XYZ is a creditor beneficiary.

EXAMPLE

Buyer purchases some property subject to a mortgage that the seller owes a bank. The bank is not a third-party beneficiary because buyer did not agree to pay the mortgage. The seller is still the only debtor on the mortgage.

---

   b. Donee beneficiary—almost the same as creditor beneficiary except promisee's intent is to confer a gift upon third party through promisor's performance

---

EXAMPLE

X contracts to buy Y's car if Y will deliver it to D, X's son; D is a donee beneficiary.

---

   c. Incidental beneficiary—third party who receives an unintended benefit from a contract. S/he obtains **no** rights under the contract

---

EXAMPLE

X and Y contract to build an apartment building. A, a nearby store owner, would benefit from increased business and is an incidental beneficiary.

---

2. Only intended beneficiary (creditor or donee) can maintain an action against contracting parties for nonperformance

   a. Intent of the promisee controls
   b. Creditor beneficiary can proceed against either contracting party

---

EXAMPLE

X owes C $100. X contracts with M to paint M's house if M will pay C $100. If X does not paint M's house, C may sue X because X still owes C $100. C may also sue M, because M now owes C $100 under the contract. C is a creditor beneficiary and can sue either party.

---

   c. Donee beneficiary can proceed against the promisor only

---

EXAMPLE

X contracts to buy Y's car if Y will deliver it to D. If Y does not deliver the car, D may sue Y. However, D may not sue X because it was a gift from X, not an obligation.

---

3. If the third-party beneficiary contract is executory, the parties may rescind and defeat the third party's rights

---

EXAMPLE

X owes C $100. X contracts with Y to paint Y's house if Y will pay C $100. X and Y may rescind the contract before Y pays C $100. Then there is no contract for C to enforce; however, C may still sue X for the $100 owed. Or in other words, C has no third-party rights on an executory contract.

---

4. The promisor can assert any defenses against third-party beneficiary that s/he has against promisee

---

NOW REVIEW MULTIPLE-CHOICE QUESTIONS 41 THROUGH 45 IN VOLUME 2

G. Performance of Contract

1. Duty to perform may depend upon a condition

    a. Condition precedent is condition that must occur before stated promise or duty in contract becomes due

    > **EXAMPLE**
    >
    > B agrees to plant trees on specified land once C removes an old tennis court from the land. Until C removes the tennis court, B has no obligation to plant the trees.

    b. Condition subsequent is condition that when it occurs it modifies or takes away a duty specified in contract

    > **EXAMPLE**
    >
    > M agrees to rent N a certain home until M finds a buyer.

    c. Satisfaction as a condition—normally when a contract guarantees satisfaction, this means agreement is performed when a reasonable person would be satisfied. However, if agreement is expressly conditioned upon personal satisfaction of one of contracting parties, then performance does not occur until that party is actually satisfied.

2. Tender of performance is an offer to perform (e.g., offer to pay debt)

    > **EXAMPLE**
    >
    > X has contracted to buy goods from Y with delivery and payment to take place concurrently. X must offer the money to Y before Y has breached the contract for failure to deliver.

3. Under the **doctrine of substantial performance** (very important), performance is satisfied if

    a. There has been substantial performance (i.e., **deviations are minor**), and
    b. There has been **good-faith** effort to comply with contract
    c. Then damages for deviations are deducted from price if above are met
    d. This is often used in relation to construction contracts

4. Payment of less than agreed-upon sum does not fulfill obligation unless both parties compromise based on a bona fide dispute as to amount owed
5. Standards of interpretation of contracts

    a. For ordinary words, courts use normal meaning in dictionary
    b. For technical words, courts use technical meaning supplied by expert testimony if necessary
    c. Any ambiguity in contract is construed against party who drafted contract
    d. Typed words prevail over preprinted words—handwritten words prevail over both preprinted and typed words
    e. When both parties are members of same profession or trade, words are given meaning in that profession or trade unless contract states otherwise

NOW REVIEW MULTIPLE-CHOICE QUESTIONS 46 THROUGH 47 IN VOLUME 2

H. Discharge of Contracts

1. By agreement—new consideration is necessary, but often it is supplied by a promise for a promise (e.g., both parties agreeing to release other party of contractual obligation)

    a. Both parties may mutually agree to rescind contract—mutual rescission

        (1) Both parties of a contract may agree to satisfy contract by doing something different called accord and satisfaction

            (a) An accord is an agreement to substitute new performance for the original performance.
            (b) Satisfaction is the performance of the accord.

    b. A novation is an agreement between three parties, the original two parties to the agreement and a new party, where the new party takes the place of one of the original parties to the contract.

(1) Original party, who has been replaced, has no obligation or rights under the original contract.

(2) New party has all rights and liabilities of original party.

> **EXAMPLE**
>
> X has agreed to do some accounting work for Y for $2,000. Since X is very busy, X, Y, and Z all agree to let X out of the contract and insert Z in his place. This is a novation. X and Y no longer have any obligations to each other.

> **EXAMPLE**
>
> A party purchases land and assumes a mortgage. The original mortgagor is still liable unless a novation has occurred.

2. By performance becoming objectively impossible

   a. But mere fact of performance becoming more costly does not excuse performance

> **EXAMPLE**
>
> A agreed to sell a specified quantity of corn to B at specified prices. He had planned to sell his own corn until his crop was destroyed. Even though he may make less profit or even suffer a loss, he can still fulfill the contract by purchasing the corn from others to resell to B under his contract.

3. Breach of contract

   a. If party breaches contract s/he will probably have to pay damages (see I. Remedies immediately below in this outline)

   b. Courts consider most breaches to be nonmaterial and award money damages as the usual remedy.

   c. If breach is material, the nonbreaching party's performance will be excused.

4. Anticipatory breach (repudiation) is renunciation before performance is due

   a. May sue at once, or

   b. Cancel contract, or

   c. Wait until time performance is due or for a reasonable time and then sue, but nonrepudiating party has duty to mitigate damages

   d. If other party has not changed position in reliance upon the repudiation, repudiating party can retract repudiation and perform at appointed time, thereby discharging his/her contractual obligation

> **EXAMPLE**
>
> X agrees to convey and Y agrees to pay for land on April 1. On February 1, Y learns that X has sold the land to Z. Y may sue before April 1, or he may wait and sue on April 1.

> **EXAMPLE**
>
> M agrees to deliver 1,000 widgets to Q by December 1. Three months before that date, M says, he will be unable to deliver on December 1.

5. Bankruptcy discharges a party's contractual obligations

6. Statute of Limitations requires that most lawsuits, including breach of contract lawsuits, be filed in a timely manner

   a. The time begins from the date of the breach of the contract.

   b. If lawsuit is not filed in the time permitted by the law, then the injured party is barred from filing the lawsuit.

   c. Claim (lawsuit) may be revived if breaching party admits to the breach even after Statute of Limitations has expired.

> **EXAMPLE**
>
> Laurie Yur, an attorney, promised to do some legal work for Carrie Client, who paid Yur $500. Yur never performed the work. Several years later, after the Statute of Limitations had expired, Client wrote Yur a letter stating that Yur needed to return the $500 plus interest or Client would sue Yur for breach of contract. If Yur does nothing, Client will be unsuccessful because the Statute of Limitations bars Client's lawsuit. If, however, Yur responds by stating, "Too bad, while I did breach the contract, it is too late for you," then the Statute of Limitations begins to run again. Thus Client could successfully bring the lawsuit, since Yur admitted her breach.

NOW REVIEW MULTIPLE-CHOICE QUESTIONS 48 THROUGH 51 IN VOLUME 2

I. Remedies

1. Monetary damages

   a. Purpose is to place injured party in as good a position as s/he would have occupied if contract had been performed

   b. Actual or compensatory damages are equal to amount caused by breach

      (1) This is the **most common remedy** under contract law

   c. Consequential damages

      (1) These are damages that arise as a consequence of the breach (e.g., lost profits)

      (2) Only awarded by the court if the consequential damages are foreseeable to the breaching party. Courts rarely find these damages to be foreseeable.

   d. Punitive damages are generally not allowed in contract law

   e. Liquidated damage clause is a provision agreed to in a contract to set the amount of damages in advance if a breach occurs

      (1) These are used instead of awarding actual compensatory damages

      (2) Not enforceable if punitive; therefore, amount set in advance must be reasonably based on what actual damages are expected to be

   f. Party injured by breach must use reasonable care to minimize loss because s/he cannot recover costs that could have been avoided—called mitigation of damages

> **EXAMPLE**
>
> One who receives perishables which are not the goods bargained for must take reasonable steps to prevent loss from spoilage.

> **EXAMPLE**
>
> X contracts to fix Y's car. After X begins work, Y breaches and says "Stop." X cannot continue to work and incur more costs (i.e., put in more parts and labor).

2. Rescission—cancellation of contract whereby parties are placed in position they were in before contract was formed

3. Specific performance—compels performance promised

   a. Used when money damages will not suffice (e.g., when subject matter is unique, or rare, as in contract for sale of land)

   b. Injured party may seek compensatory damages if s/he reasonably chooses them

   c. Not available to compel personal services

4. Restitution—return of consideration to injured party

5. Injunction—compels an act or restrains an act

6. Release—one party relieves other party of part of obligations in contract

7. Waiver—one party voluntarily gives up some right in contract either by express agreement or by consistently not enforcing such right in past

8. Arbitration—resolution of dispute, outside of judicial system, agreed to by disputing parties
9. Reformation—if parties have failed to express true intentions in contract, court may reform it to express true intentions of contract

> **NOW REVIEW MULTIPLE-CHOICE QUESTIONS 52 THROUGH 56 IN VOLUME 2**

J. Jurisdiction over Defendant for Online Transactions

1. Courts generally grant plaintiffs personal jurisdiction over defendants in foreign state if plaintiff intentionally engaged in commercial activities for use outside of home state
2. Generally, Web sites or advertising by persons or entities seen by others in other jurisdictions do not create personal jurisdiction to allow lawsuits in those other jurisdictions

   a. Minimum contacts such as actively selling products are needed to require defendant to defend self in other state

3. Parties to contracts made online may agree to use law of given jurisdiction just as in other contracts

   a. Often, Web sites put forum selection clause at end of home page in case lawsuit is brought against online company

      (1) Some courts may not enforce these clauses since they are not negotiable and thus lead to adhesion contracts

         (a) Increasing trend is not to enforce these unless they are fair and reasonable

4. Courts typically invalidate state laws that regulate the Internet when those laws extend to activities outside their state and place a burden on interstate commerce

K. Interference with Contractual Relations

1. Happens when a party to a contract shows that defendant's interference with other party's performance of such contract wrongfully caused plaintiff to lose benefit of performance of that contract

   a. Typically defendant must have **intended** to cause said breach of contract and defendant's conduct must be improper

      (1) For example, when a contract's performance is stopped by bribery, criminal actions, or threats of violence

KEY TERMS

Suffixes "-or" and "-ee." These suffixes are used frequently in the law, but especially in contract law. The "-or" indicates the person performing the action, for example, the promisor is making a promise, the assignor is making an assignment, the offeror makes an offer, etc. The "-ee" is the receiver of the action, for example, the promisee is a person to whom the promise is made, the assignee is someone who receives the assignment, the offeree is a person to whom an offer is made, etc.

Acceptance. An unequivocal expression to enter into a contract based on the terms provided in the offer.

Capacity. The mental ability to understand the nature of the terms of the contract.

Compensatory damages. The most common remedy for breach of contract. Designed to pay the nonbreaching party for the amount of loss that has been suffered.

Consideration. Something that has value in the eyes of the law that induces another to enter into a contract

Contract. Promises that the courts will enforce.

Counteroffer. When an offeree alters the terms of the original offer, which terminates the original offer. The offeree now becomes the offeror.

Formation defenses. These actions invalidate what otherwise would be mutual assent. The actions include duress, fraud, mistake, and undue influence. While offer and acceptance appear to be present on the surface, the presence of a formation defense shows a lack of true mutual assent.

Mirror image rule. An acceptance must precisely reflect (mirror) the offer to be a valid acceptance

Mitigation of damages. The nonbreaching party has an obligation to keep damages as low as is reasonably possible.

Mutual assent. Parties have voluntarily come to a common understanding of the terms of the bargain. Mutual assent is the combination of a valid offer and a valid acceptance.

Offer. An unequivocal expression of party's willingness to enter into a contract.

Parol evidence rule. Prevents the introduction of any documents, testimony, or any evidence that contradicts the language of a **written** contract. This rule only forbids that evidence that arose prior to, or at the same time, that the written contract was created.

    Promissory estoppel. An implied contract at law, where a court rules that a contract exists even though an element of a contract is missing. Court will possibly use this where a promissee has reasonably relied on a promisor's promise and that reliance has injured the promisee.

    Specific performance. A remedy that is available for unique items, where money damages would not be adequate to compensate the nonbreaching party. Effectively, the court orders the breaching party to perform the original promise under the contract.

    Statute of Frauds. A rule of evidence that requires certain contracts be in writing or have written evidence to support the contracts' existence.   These include contracts that transfer interests in real property (real estate); cannot, by the terms of the contract, be possibly performed within 1 year; answer for the debts of another; or involve the sale of **goods** for $500 or more.

Module 27: Sales

Overview

The law of sales governs contracts for the sale of goods. Since a sale of goods is involved, Article 2 of the Uniform Commercial Code (UCC) applies. A sale of goods under the UCC is the sale of tangible, moveable property. Be sure that when you are faced with a contract question to determine whether the contract involved the sale of goods you will apply the UCC rules outlined in this module. If the contract involved something other than goods, then you want to use the common law rules outlined in Module 26.

One of the areas tested in sales is product liability. When studying this area, you should pay particular attention to the different legal theories under which an injured party may recover. Realize that an injured party may recover under the legal theories of breach of warranty, negligence, and strict liability. It is important that you know the circumstances under which these theories may be used. Other areas that are often tested are warranties; disclaimers; risk of loss; and remedies, rights, and duties of the buyer and seller.

You should understand that a binding contract may be present under the UCC if the parties intend to be bound, even though certain elements of a contract may be missing. These open terms will be filled by specific provisions of the UCC. The parties to a sale need not be merchants for the UCC to apply; however, some rules vary if merchants are involved in the sales contract.

As you study this area, note that it builds on much of the material under contracts in the previous module. Therefore, as you study this area you should review the contract law rules, especially those in the previous module that apply to the UCC. Before beginning the reading you should review the key terms at the end of the module.

A. Contracts for Sale of Goods

1. Article 2 of the Uniform Commercial Code, in general, controls contracts for the sale of goods for any dollar amount

   a. "Goods" include tangible personal property (whether specially manufactured or not)

      (1) Does not include sales of investment securities, accounts receivable, contract rights, copyrights, or patents

> **EXAMPLE**
> S sells B a stereo. The UCC applies.

> **EXAMPLE**
> S sells a home to B. The common law rules rather than the UCC rules apply to this contract since it involves the sale of real property.

> **EXAMPLE**
> F sells to M several bushels of wheat. The UCC applies to fungible goods also (i.e., goods in which one unit is considered the equivalent of the other units).

    b. In general, UCC applies to sales and leases of hardware as well as to sales and licensing of software.

        (1) However, if software is heavily customized based on services of consultant, common law applies.

    c. Article 2 of UCC has been passed into law by every state (except Louisiana which has adopted only portions of UCC)

        (1) Federal courts also use principles in Article 2 for sales of goods.

    d. UCC applies whether sale is between merchants or consumers but some rules change if merchant involved

> **EXAMPLE**
>
> S sells his used refrigerator to B, a neighbor. The UCC applies to this transaction.

    e. The UCC, unlike the common law, implies that a contract exists where it is the intent of the parties to create a contract, even though some technical element of contract may be missing

2. General concepts

    a. Merchant—one who deals in the kind of goods being sold, or one who holds self out as having superior knowledge and skills as to the goods involved, or one who employs another who qualifies as a merchant

    b. Good faith

        (1) The UCC assume that parties entering into sales contracts will do so in good faith

        (2) Good faith means that parties will be honest with each other

        (3) Additionally for merchants it also means to observe reasonable commercial standards of fair dealing in the trade

    c. UCC supplies missing terms for contracts

        (1) Under common law if terms are missing there is no contract because the terms are not definite

        (2) UCC fills in missing terms if parties have shown intent to enter into a contract

    d. When terms of a sales contract are unclear the terms can be explained by

        (1) Course of dealing: If parties have had previous dealings, we look to see how the unclear term was interpreted or acted upon by the parties in the past

        (2) Usage of trade: How the term is typically used in the particular trade, business, or industry.

B. Forming the Contract for the Sale of Goods

1. The UCC adopts most of the common law rules for contracts

    a. Assume the common law rule is the same as the UCC rule

    b. What follows are the changes that the UCC makes to the common law rules

2. Offer

    a. Offer under the UCC can be less definite

    b. Generally the UCC permits:

        (1) Open price terms: A reasonable/market price will be supplied if necessary.

        (2) Open quantity terms

            (a) Quantity term does need to be included for contracts over $500, under the Statute of Frauds

            (b) Quantity term does not, however have to be precise

            (c) Output contracts are permissible: Buyer promises to purchase all that a seller can produce

            (d) Requirements contracts are permissible: Seller will provide the quantity of goods that the buyer needs

    c. Firm offer rule

        (1) Promise to hold an offer open, even if not supported by consideration, is irrevocable if the promise is

            (a) In writing, **and,**

            (b) Made by a merchant.

        (2) If firm offer does not state specific time, it will remain open for reasonable time, based on the nature of the subject matter not to exceed three months

> **EXAMPLE**
>
> M, a merchant, agrees in a letter signed by M to sell B 1,000 widgets, with the offer to remain open for five weeks. Even if M tries to revoke this offer before the five-week period, B may still accept.

> **EXAMPLE**
>
> M, a merchant, agrees in signed writing to sell B 1,000 widgets, stating that the offer will remain open for 120 days. B accepts the offer on the 95th day. If nothing has occurred to terminate the offer prior to acceptance, offer and acceptance are present. The irrevocable nature of this offer would end after three months, but the offer would not automatically terminate. The offer would remain in existence for the stated period (120 days) unless terminated by other means.

3. Acceptance

    a. UCC rejects the mirror image rule; instead the UCC focuses on the parties' intent to be bound

    b. The intent to be bound approach creates some problems

> **EXAMPLE**
>
> I offer to sell you 1,000 pens for $100 and ship them via UPS; you accept, but you want them shipped via Federal Express. Under the UCC there is a contract because we both agreed to the sale/purchase of the pens. But how should the goods be shipped: UPS or Federal Express? The answer is contained in the material below entitled Battle of forms.

    c. Battle of forms—between merchants, additional terms included in the acceptance become part of the contract unless

        (1) Original offer precludes such, or

        (2) New terms materially alter the original offer, or

        (3) The original offeror gives notice of his/her objection within a reasonable time

> **EXAMPLE**
>
> In the above example, if we are both merchants, then the additional/changed term you proposed: shipping via Federal Express would become part of the contract unless I make a timely objection.

        (4) If the parties are not merchants, then the offeror needs to expressly accept the additional/changed term.

    d. Accommodation

        (1) When a seller ships substitute goods because the seller does not have the goods ordered by the buyer

        (2) If the buyer accepts substituted goods, a contract exists

        (3) If buyer refuses substituted goods, then there is no contract

        (4) If seller provides notice to buyer that shipment is only an accommodation, seller's actions are not viewed as an acceptance

> **EXAMPLE**
>
> Value Hardware placed an order with Odin Industries for 800 Thor hammers on June for delivery on August 15. On June 3, Odin sent Value a written acceptance. On August 12, Odin shipped 800 Asgard hammers because Odin was out of Thor hammers. Odin also stated on the invoice that the shipment was an accommodation. The hammers arrived at Value on August 15. Odin has breached the contract. Once a seller has accepted an order, the seller cannot simply substitute goods and call it an accommodation.

> **EXAMPLE**
>
> Assume Value placed the same order, on June 1 and stated, "I need the hammers as soon as possible." Odin responded by shipping the 800 Asgard hammers on June 3 with a note stating that the shipment was an

accommodation. If Value accepts, there is a contract. If Value does not accept, then Value can return the hammers and there is no contract.

4. a. Under the UCC, a contract may be modified without new consideration if done in good faith

> **EXAMPLE**
>
> B agrees in a contract to buy 300 electrical parts for $1.00 each from S. B later points out to S that he can get the same parts from D for $.90 each and asks for a price reduction. S reduces the price to $.90 each. This new contract is enforceable even though B gave no new consideration. Note that if S had required B to pay the $1.00 as originally agreed, B would be in breach of contract if he failed to go through with the original contract.

b. Common law requires new consideration on both sides for any modification

> **EXAMPLE**
>
> B agreed, in a written contract, to pay $10,000 to S for certain real estate. Later, B said he was having difficulty getting the $10,000 so S agreed to reduce the price to $9,000. S can still enforce the full $10,000 because B gave no new consideration for the modification.

5. Legality and Capacity are the same under the UCC and the common law
6. Under the UCC version of Statute of Frauds, contracts for sale of goods for $500 or more must be in writing or be evidenced by a writing.

   a. A sufficient writing

      (1) Must contain quantity term
      (2) Signature of party to be charged
      (3) Indicate the existence of a contract

   b. If the contract is between merchants, then a written confirmation is sufficient to serve as a writing unless objection is made within 10 days of receiving the confirmation

> **EXAMPLE**
>
> Pat operates a fish market. Pat phoned Shelley, a fish wholesaler, to see if Shelley could sell Pat 200 pounds of sockeye salmon for $1,000 for delivery in two weeks. Shelley agreed and e-mailed Pat a written confirmation of Pat's order. Pat did not respond to the e-mail. When the fish is delivered two weeks later is Pat obligated to take delivery? Yes, the contract falls under the UCC provision of the Statute of Frauds: Salmon is a good and the contract exceeds $500. Although the signature of the party to be charged, Pat, is not present here; Shelley's written confirmation is sufficient since both parties are merchants.
>
> **NOTE:** If Pat was not a merchant, then the writing is not sufficient to satisfy the Statute of Frauds and Pat could refuse delivery.

   c. If contract is modified, must be in writing if after modification it is for $500 or more

> **EXAMPLE**
>
> B agrees in a contract to buy widgets from S for $500. Later, S agrees to a reduction in price to $490. The first contract must be in writing (absent any exceptions), but the modified contract may be oral.

   d. Exceptions to writing requirement (these are important)

      (1) Oral contract involving specially manufactured goods (i.e., not saleable in ordinary course of business) if seller has made substantial start in their manufacture (or even made a contract for necessary raw materials) is enforceable
      (2) Oral contract is enforceable against party who admits it in court, but not beyond quality of goods admitted
      (3) Goods that have been paid for (if seller accepts payment) or goods which buyer has accepted are part of enforceable contract even if oral

> **EXAMPLE**
>
> B orally agrees to purchase 10,000 parts from S for $1 each. B later gives S $6,000 for a portion of the parts. S accepts the money. In absence of a written agreement, B may enforce a contract for 6,000 parts but not for the full 10,000 parts.

C. Performance of the Sales Contract

1. Seller's performance

    a. Tender: A party is ready, willing, and able to perform the obligations of the contract.
    b. Place of tender (performance) is the seller's place of business, unless contract provides otherwise

        (1) Parties may choose place of tender by contract
        (2) This is one of the UCC's "gap" filling provisions: It only applies if the parties have not accounted for the place of tender in the contract

    c. Perfect tender rule

        (1) Seller's tender of goods must conform exactly, to the terms of the contract
        (2) If Seller's tender is not perfect, buyer may:

            (a) Reject the whole lot of goods
            (b) Accept the whole lot of goods
            (c) Accept some units and reject the remaining units

> **EXAMPLE**
>
> Wonka ordered 5,000 orange gaskets from Acme. The gaskets are used in various machines that Wonka uses to produce candy. Acme timely delivered 5,000 gaskets in five crates of 1,000 gaskets each. When Wonka opened the crates he saw that the gaskets were yellow instead of orange. Even if the color has no affect on how the gaskets work, Wonka may still reject the lot. If Wonka needed 1,500 gaskets immediately, Wonka could accept two crates, or 2,000 gaskets. Wonka cannot, however, split a shipping unit, a crate, so if he needs 1,500 gaskets, he will need to accept two crates.

        (3) Exceptions

            (a) Agreement by parties that seller did not need to perfectly tender
            (b) Seller cures (fixes) the defect
            (c) Installment contracts: Buyer may only reject a defective installment, not entire contract

> **EXAMPLE**
>
> Wonka orders 5,000 orange gaskets from Acme to be delivered in boxes of 500 each month for the next 10 months. Acme perfectly tendered for the first three months, but in the fourth month Acme sent yellow gaskets instead. Wonka may reject only the shipment in the fourth month.

2. Buyer's performance

    a. Payment is due at the time of delivery
    b. Buyer has a right to inspect the goods prior to payment; except for good that were shipped COD (Cash on delivery)
    c. Buyer should inspect goods at time of delivery to preserve buyer's remedies against a seller who has shipped defective or nonconforming goods
    d. Buyer may reject good if goods are defective

        (1) Buyer must disclose nature of the defect to seller. (Gives seller opportunity to cure defect)
        (2) Buyer must either return goods or hold goods with reasonable care

    e. Buyer may accept goods

        (1) Buyer may revoke prior acceptance if

            (a) Seller did not provide promised cure, or
            (b) Goods contained hidden defect: A hidden defect is a defect that the buyer could not perceive with reasonable inspection at the time of delivery

3. Excused performance: Either buyer or seller's obligation to perform may be excused if any of the following occur

   a. Destruction of the goods prior to performance
   b. Commercial impracticality: Performance has become excessively expensive or difficult due to unforeseeable events
   c. Assurance of performance

      (1) If there is a reasonable basis to believe that the other party will not perform as promised, the uncertain party may

         (a) Make a written demand for adequate assurance of performance
         (b) A response assuring performance must be provided within a reasonable time, not exceeding 30 days.
         (c) Failure to respond in a timely fashion is evidence of anticipatory repudiation

   d. Anticipatory repudiation: One party clearly indicates that it is unwilling, or unable, to perform the contract as promised
   e. Cooperation necessary for performance was not provided

> **EXAMPLE**
>
> Wonka ordered 5,000 orange gaskets from Acme. Wonka promised to provide Acme with a specific orange dye. Despite repeated requests from Acme, Wonka never provided the dye. Acme's performance of coloring the gadgets orange is excused.

   f. Performance is not excused when substitute performance is possible

> **EXAMPLE**
>
> Wonka ordered 5,000 orange gaskets from Acme. Acme agreed to ship the gaskets by truck to Wonka's factory. At the time of delivery there was a trucker's strike. The strike does not excuse Acme's performance. Acme could have the gaskets delivered by train or some other method of transportation.

   g. Consignment—Arrangement in which agent (consignee) is appointed by consignor to sell goods if all the following conditions are met:

      (1) Consignor keeps title to goods,
      (2) Consignee is not obligated to buy or pay for goods,
      (3) Consignee receives a commission upon sale, and
      (4) Consignor receives proceeds of sale.

   h. Document of title—Any document that in the regular course of business is accepted as adequate evidence that the person in possession of the document is entitled to receive, hold, and dispose of the document and the goods it covers
   i. Bill of lading—A document of title that is issued by a private or common carrier in exchange for goods delivered to it for shipment. It may be negotiable or nonnegotiable.
   j. Warehouse receipt—A document of title issued by a person engaged in the business of storing goods (i.e., a warehouseman). It acknowledges receipt of the goods, describes the goods stored, and contains the terms of the storage contract. It may be negotiable or nonnegotiable.

D. Transfer of Title (Property Rights)

1. Transfer of title to third parties

   a. These are situations where a person acquires the property and then tries to transfer ownership of the acquired property to another person (a third party)
   b. If party having voidable title transfers goods to a good-faith purchaser for value, the latter obtains good title

      (1) Examples in which there is voidable title

         (a) Goods paid for with a check subsequently dishonored
         (b) Goods obtained by fraud, mistake, duress, or undue influence
         (c) Goods obtained from minor
         (d) Thieves and/or finders of property have **void** title

> **EXAMPLE**
>
> B buys a stereo from S but the check bounces. P, a good-faith purchaser, pays B for the stereo. S cannot get the stereo from P but must recover money from B.

> **EXAMPLE**
>
> Same as above except that B stole the stereo. P does not obtain title of the stereo. S can recover the stereo from P.

    c. If a person entrusts possession of goods to a merchant who deals in those goods, a good-faith purchaser for value obtains title to these goods, unless s/he knew that this merchant did not own the goods.

> **EXAMPLE**
>
> C leaves his watch at a shop for repairs. The shop mistakenly sells the watch to B who is unaware of C's interest. C cannot force B to turn over the watch because B now has title. Of course, C can recover monetary damages from the shop.

2. Transfer of title from a seller to a buyer

    a. Once goods exist and are identified to the contract, the parties may agree as to when title passes

        (1) Sale cannot take place until goods exist and have been identified to the contract

            (a) Identification—occurs when the goods that are going to be used to perform the contract are shipped, marked or otherwise designated as such

            (b) Identification gives buyer

                1] An insurable interest in the goods once they are identified to contract

                2] Right to demand goods upon offering full contract price once other conditions are satisfied

    b. Otherwise, title generally passes when the seller completes his/her performance with respect to physical delivery

        (1) If a destination contract, title passes on tender at destination (i.e., buyer's place of business)

        (2) If a shipping (point) contract, title passes when seller puts goods in the possession of the carrier

    c. If seller has no duty to move the goods

        (1) Title passes upon delivery of documents of title

> **EXAMPLE**
>
> Delivery of negotiable or nonnegotiable warehouse receipt passes title to buyer.

        (2) If no document of title exists, title passes at the time and place of contracting if the goods are identifiable

        (3) If goods not identified, there is only a contract to sell; no title passes

    d. Rejection (justified or not) of goods or a justified revocation of acceptance by buyer reverts title to seller

    e. Taking a security interest is irrelevant to passage of title

E. Risk of Loss

  1. Risk of loss is independent of title under UCC, but rules regarding the transfer of both are similar

  2. General rules when seller ships goods that conform to the contract

    a. Parties may agree as to which party bears risk of loss or has title; otherwise UCC rules below apply

    b. Shipment contract

        (1) Risk of loss transfers to buyer when the goods are delivered to the common carrier

        (2) Generally designated as "FOB seller's warehouse," but any indication of the seller's place of business is sufficient

> **EXAMPLE**
>
> Seller is in San Francisco and buyer is in Chicago: FOB San Francisco.

    (a) Other shipment contract designations

        1] CIF: Cost, insurance, and freight are included in price
        2] C & F: Shipping contract in which cost and freight are included in price

  c. In international sales shipment contracts under United Nations Convention for the International Sale of Goods, risk of loss passes to buyer upon delivery to first carrier for transmission to buyer.

    (1) This can be modified by agreement.

  d. Destination contract

    (1) Risk of loss transfer to buyer when the goods reach their intended destination and are tendered to the buyer
    (2) Usually designated as "FOB buyer's place of business"

  e. If no shipping terms are specified, then the presumption is a shipment contract
  f. Trial sales: Seller is allowing buyer to try the good prior to the actual sale

    (1) Sale on approval: Goods may be returned even if they conform to the contract

      (a) Goods not considered sold until buyer approves or accepts as sale
      (b) Seller retains title and risk of loss until buyer accepts goods
      (c) Creditors of buyer cannot reach goods until buyer accepts

    (2) Sale or return: Goods may be returned even if they conform to the contract

      (a) Goods bought for use or resale
      (b) Sale is final if goods not returned during period specified
      (c) Buyer obtains risk of loss and title until goods are returned
      (d) Creditors of buyer can reach the goods while in buyer's possession, unless notice of seller's interest is posted or filed as required

  g. If risk of loss is not covered by above rules, then

    (1) Merchant sellers transfer the risk of loss when buyer takes physical possession of goods
    (2) Nonmerchant sellers transfer risk of loss to buyer upon tender

> **EXAMPLE**
>
> Max agreed to purchase a used drum set from Buddy. Buddy is not in the business of selling musical instruments. Buddy tendered delivery to Max, after receiving Max's check in the mail. Max told Buddy that he would stop by the following week and pick up the drum set. The next night, after a huge storm, Buddy's basement flooded, and ruined the drum set. Who bears the loss of the drum set? Max will bear the loss because the risk transferred to Max upon tender. Note: If Buddy had been a merchant, Buddy would bear the loss.

  h. If goods are held in warehouse and seller has no right to move them, risk of loss passes to buyer

    (1) Upon proper negotiation of a negotiable document of title
    (2) Within a reasonable time after delivery of a nonnegotiable document of title
    (3) Once warehouseman acknowledges buyer's right to goods if no document of title

3. Sales involving breach of contract

  a. If seller breaches (typically seller has shipped nonconforming goods)

    (1) Risk of loss remains with seller until cure by seller or acceptance by buyer to extent of buyer's deficiency in insurance coverage
    (2) Title passes under original terms despite delivery of nonconforming goods

> **EXAMPLE**
>
> Wonka orders 5,000 orange gaskets from Acme. The contract states that the gaskets will be shipped FOB Acme's warehouse. While the gaskets are in transit to Wonka's warehouse, the gaskets are destroyed when

the common carrier transporting the gaskets is involved in an accident. A review of the common carrier's bill of lading reveals that Acme had shipped 5,000 yellow gaskets, instead of orange gaskets.

Analysis: Title to the gaskets passed to Wonka because this is a shipment contract. Normally, the shipment contract would also place the risk of loss upon Wonka as well. However, since Acme shipped nonconforming gaskets (yellow instead of orange), the risk of loss never transferred to Wonka, so Acme bears the loss here.

b. If buyer breaches, risk of loss passes to buyer to extent of seller's deficiency in insurance for a commercially reasonable time.

4. Risk of loss can be covered by insurance. In general, party has an insurable interest whenever s/he can suffer damage.

   a Buyer usually allowed an insurable interest when goods are identified to the contract
   b Seller usually has an insurable interest so long as s/he has title or a security interest

F. Product Liability—a manufacturer or seller may be responsible when a product is defective and causes injury or damage to a person or property. There are three theories under which manufacturers and sellers may be held liable. (In each fact pattern, consider all three, although proof of any one creates liability.)

1. Warranty Liability—purchaser of a product may sue based on the warranties made

   a. Warranty of title

      (1) Seller warrants good title, rightful transfer, and freedom from any security interest or lien of which the buyer has no knowledge

> **EXAMPLE**
>
> A seller of stolen goods would be liable to a buyer for damages.

      (2) Merchant warrants goods to be free of rightful claim of infringement (e.g., patent or trademark), unless buyer furnished specifications to seller for manufacture of the goods
      (3) Can only be disclaimed by specific language or circumstances that give buyer reason to know s/he is receiving less than full title

         (a) Cannot be disclaimed by language such as "as is"

   b. Express warranties (may be written or oral)

      (1) Any affirmation of fact or promise made by the seller to the buyer that relates to the goods and becomes part of the basis of the bargain creates an express warranty that the goods shall conform to the affirmation or promise

         (a) Sales talk, puffing, or a statement purporting to be merely the seller's opinion does not create a warranty
         (b) Must form part of the basis of bargain

            1] Would include advertisements read by buyer
            2] Normally would not include warranties given after the sale or contract was made

         (c) No intent to create warranty is needed on the part of the seller
         (d) Seller or buyer may be merchant or consumer

      (2) Any description of the goods which is made part of the basis of the bargain creates an express warranty that the goods shall conform to the description
      (3) Any sample or model that is made part of the basis of the bargain creates an express warranty that the goods shall conform to the sample or model
      (4) It is not necessary to the creation of an express warranty that the seller use formal words such as "warranty" or "guarantee"

   c. Implied warranties

      (1) Warranty of merchantability—goods are fit for ordinary purpose

         (a) This warranty also guarantees that goods are properly packaged and labeled
         (b) This warranty applies if

1] Seller must be a merchant with respect to goods of the kind being sold, and

2] Warranty is not modified or excluded

3] Then if goods not fit for ordinary use, breach of this warranty occurs

(2) Warranty of fitness for a particular purpose

(a) Created when the seller knows of the particular use for which the goods are required and further knows that the buyer is relying on skill and judgment of seller to select and furnish suitable goods for this particular use

> **EXAMPLE**
>
> A buyer relies upon a paint salesperson to select a particular exterior house paint that will effectively cover existing siding.

(b) Buyer must actually rely on seller's skill and judgment

(c) Product is then warranted for the particular expressed purpose and seller may be liable if the product fails to so perform

(d) Applicable both to merchants and nonmerchants

d. UCC, being consumer oriented, allows these warranties to extend to parties other than the purchaser even without privity of contract (contractual connection between parties)

(1) Extends to a buyer's family and also to guests who may reasonably be expected to use and/or be affected by the goods and who are injured

> **EXAMPLE**
>
> A dinner guest breaks a tooth on a small piece of metal in the food. Note that in food, the substance causing injury normally must be foreign, not something customarily found in it (bone in fish).

e. Disclaimers—warranty liability may be escaped or modified by disclaimers (also available at common law without rules defining limits of disclaimers)

(1) A disclaimer of merchantability can be written or oral but must use the word "merchantability" unless implied warranties are disclaimed as in (3) below

(2) To disclaim the implied warranty of fitness for a particular purpose, the disclaimer must be in writing and conspicuous

(3) Both the warranty of merchantability and fitness for a particular purpose can be disclaimed by oral or written language such as "as is" or "with all faults"

(4) Written disclaimers must be clear and conspicuous

(5) If the buyer has had ample opportunity to inspect the goods or sample, there is no implied warranty as to any defects which ought reasonably to have been discovered

(6) Implied warranties may be excluded or modified by course of dealings, course of performance, or usage of trade

(7) A disclaimer inconsistent with an express warranty is not effective (i.e., a description of a warranty in a contract cannot be disclaimed)

(8) Limitations on consequential damages for personal injuries are presumed to be unconscionable and thus unenforceable if on consumer goods

2. Negligence

a. Must prove the following elements

(1) Duty of manufacturer to exercise reasonable (due) care to the injured party

(a) Consider likelihood of harm, seriousness of harm

(b) May be based on violation of statute but this is not necessary

(2) Breach of duty of reasonable care

(a) Insufficient instructions may cause breach of duty

(b) Did the manufacturer/seller fail to act as a reasonable manufacturer/seller?

(3) Manufacturer's failure to exercise reasonable care caused the injury/damages.

        (a) Direct cause: In general, if injury would not have happened without defendant's conduct, there is cause in fact

        (b) Proximate cause: Negligence set into motion an unbroken chain of events which led to injury/damages

    (4) Injury/damages: The plaintiff must be able to show that s/he has suffered some recognizable loss

  b. Privity of contract is not needed because suit not based on contract

> **EXAMPLE**
>
> A car manufacturer is negligent in the manufacture and design of brakes and as a result, a driver is severely injured. The driver may sue the manufacturer even if he bought the car from a retailer.

> **EXAMPLE**
>
> In the example above, even a pedestrian injured because of the brake problem may recover from the manufacturer.

  c. Defenses to negligence

    (1) Contributory negligence

        (a) That is, plaintiff helped cause accident
        (b) Complete bar to recovery
        (c) Most states instead use comparative negligence in which damages are allocated between plaintiff and defendant based on relative fault

    (2) Assumption of risk

3. Strict product liability

  a. Manufacturers, sellers, and lessors who normally deal in this type of product are liable to users of products without proof of fault or lack of reasonable care if following other elements are proven

    (1) Product was defective when sold

        (a) Based on poor design, inadequate warnings, improper assembly, or unsafe materials

    (2) Defect is unreasonably dangerous to user

        (a) Based on normal expectations

    (3) Product reaches user without significant changes
    (4) Defect caused the injury

  b. Defense of acting with reasonable care, contributory negligence, comparative negligence, disclaimer or lack of privity is unavailable

    (1) Assumption of risk and misuse are defenses

> **EXAMPLE**
>
> Herb is injured while lifting up his power lawnmower to trim his hedges. Manufacturer would not be liable since product was not being used for intended purpose.

4. American Law Institute has published its Restatement (Third) of Torts: Product Liability

  a. This is significant development and many courts now cite it
  b. However, treat it as a minority rule which has not superceded important long-standing rules of negligence
  c. Restatement (Third)'s product liability rule basically states those in business of selling or distributing defective products are liable for harm to individuals or property resulting from such defect

    (1) Rule covers not only manufacturers but other sellers engaged in business of selling such products that caused harm to plaintiffs
    (2) Note that Restatement (Third) does **not** require products to be unreasonably dangerous

  d. Restatement (Third) adds to general rule above by establishing three types of product defects

(1) Manufacturing defects

    (a) Take place when product does not conform with its intended use when leaves manufacturer

> **EXAMPLE**
>
> Flawed products, damaged products, or products assembled incorrectly.

(2) Inadequate warnings and instructions

    (a) Manufacturers and sellers liable for failing to warn or instruct about reasonably foreseeable harms

        1] Need not warn of generally known or obvious risks

(3) Design defects

    (a) A product has a design defect if its foreseeable risk of harm could have been avoided or reduced by different design

NOW REVIEW MULTIPLE-CHOICE QUESTIONS 1 THROUGH 35 IN VOLUME 2

G. Remedies under Sales Law

1. In general, either party may, upon breach by other, cancel the contract and terminate executory obligations

    a. Unlike common law rescission, however, cancellation does not discharge a claim for damages

2. Seller's remedies

    a. Seller has right to cure nonconformity (i.e., tender conforming goods)

        (1) Within original time of contract, or
        (2) Within reasonable time if seller thought nonconforming tender would be acceptable
        (3) Seller must notify buyer of his intention to cure

    b. Seller may resell goods if buyer breaches before acceptance

        (1) May be public or private sale

            (a) If private, must give notice to buyer who breached; otherwise, losses cannot be recovered
            (b) If seller resells in a commercially reasonable manner, s/he may recover any loss on the sale from the buyer who breached, but s/he is not responsible to buyer who breached for profits made on resale
            (c) In any event, good-faith purchasers take free of original buyer's claims

    c. If seller learns that buyer is insolvent and buyer does not have the document of title, seller may stop delivery of goods in carrier's possession unless buyer pays cash

    d. Seller may recover goods received by an insolvent buyer if demand is made within ten days of receipt

        (1) However, if the buyer has made a written misrepresentation of solvency within three months before delivery, this ten-day limitation does not apply
        (2) If buyer is insolvent, seller may demand cash to make delivery

    e. Seller may recover damages

        (1) If buyer repudiates agreement or refuses goods, seller may recover the difference between market price at time of tender and contract price, plus incidental damages, minus expenses saved due to buyer's breach
        (2) If the measure of damages stated above in (1) is inadequate to place the seller in as good a position as performance would have, then the seller can sue for the lost profits, plus incidental damages, less expenses saved due to the buyer's breach

            (a) Loss profits are consequential damages and as such are recoverable when foreseeable by breaching party

        (3) The seller can recover the full contract price when

            (a) The buyer has already accepted the goods
            (b) Conforming goods have been destroyed after the risk of loss had transferred to buyer
            (c) The seller is unable to resell the identified goods

f. Under Uniform Computer Information Transactions Act (UCITA), licensor of its software has special self-help remedies available to protect its software, the right to be paid for usage, or its trade secrets.

(1) Licensor may use bugs, etc., that disable that software from further misuse if certain requirements are met

(a) Licensee must have specifically agreed to that self-help remedy
(b) Licensor must give licensee at least fifteen days notice before using that remedy as well as who licensee can contact about any questions
(c) Licensor is not permitted to use this remedy if there is a significant risk of personal injury or public safety, or if there is a significant risk to information of other parties

3. Buyer's remedies

a. Buyer may reject nonconforming goods, either in entirety or any commercial unit (e.g., bale, carload, etc.)

(1) Buyer has right to inspect goods before acceptance or payment

(a) Must do so in reasonable time and give notice to seller (failure may operate as acceptance)
(b) Buyer must have reasonable time to inspect

(2) Buyer must care for goods until returned
(3) If buyer is a merchant, s/he must follow reasonable instructions of seller (e.g., ship, sell)

(a) Right to indemnity for costs

(4) If goods are perishable or threatened with decline in value, buyer must make reasonable effort to sell
(5) Buyer has a security interest in any goods in his/her possession to the extent of any payments made to seller and any expenses incurred

(a) S/he may sell the goods to recover payments

b. Under Uniform Computer Information Transactions Act (UCITA), consumers who make electronic errors while ordering have special rights, if consumer, upon learning of error, does following

(1) Immediately notifies seller that s/he made error (as soon as s/he learns of error)
(2) Buyer does not use or benefit from information, software or products ordered
(3) Delivers all copies to seller or destroys them at seller's request
(4) Buyer in error pays all costs of processing and shipping to seller
(5) Note that nonconsumer buyer may not use these more favorable provisions of this Act

> **EXAMPLE**
>
> Buyer intends to purchase one copy of a DVD from ABC Company. The buyer, who is purchasing this DVD for consumer use, mistakenly orders ten copies from ABC's website. The buyer is protected by following the steps given above.

c. Buyer may recover damages measured by the difference between the contract price and the market value of the goods at the time buyer learns of the breach, plus any incidental damages and consequential damages

(1) Consequential damages are damages resulting from buyer's needs that the seller was aware of at the time of contracting
(2) Consequential damages cannot be recovered if buyer could reasonably have prevented these (mitigation of damages)

d. Buyer has the right of cover

(1) Buyer can buy substitute goods from another seller—buyer will still have the right to damages after engaging in "cover"

(a) Damages are difference between cost of cover and contract price, plus incidental and consequential damages
(b) Failure to cover does not bar other remedies

e. Once goods to the contract have been identified, buyer obtains rights in those goods

(1) Identification occurs when goods under contract are

(a) Shipped
(b) Marked as part of the contract, or
(c) In some way designated as part of contract

      (2) Buyer obtains

          (a) Insurable interest in those goods, and

          (b) Right to obtain goods, called replevin, upon offering contract price

              1] Replevin (suing for possession of the goods wrongfully held by the seller) is not allowed if buyer can cover

    f. Buyer may obtain specific performance if goods are unique or in other proper circumstances even if goods are not identified to the contract

      (1) Proper circumstances may exist when other remedies (such as monetary damages or remedy of cover) are inadequate

---

EXAMPLE

S agrees to sell B an antique car of which only one exists. If S later refuses to go through with the contract, B may require S to sell him the unique car under the remedy of specific performance.

---

4. Statute of limitations for sale of goods is four years

    a. An action for breach must be commenced within this period
    b. Parties may agree to reduce to not less than one year but may not extend it
    c. Statute of limitations begins running when the contract is breached

> **NOW REVIEW MULTIPLE-CHOICE QUESTIONS 36 THROUGH 48 IN VOLUME 2**

H. Leases under UCC

1. Law governing leases has been slow to develop and has been "tacked on" for various other areas of law such as property law and secured transactions
2. Now Article 2A of the UCC applies to any transaction creating a lease regardless of form
3. Article 2A is now law in majority of states
4. Article 2A is quite lengthy, but for purpose of CPA exam, note that its provisions are similar to Article 2 except that Article 2A applies to leases and Article 2 applies to sales of goods
5. Under Article 2A

    a. Lessor is person who transfers right to possess named goods and to use them in described ways by lessee

6. Note the following provisions where Article 2A is similar to Article 2:

    a. Statute of frauds except that stated minimum is $1,000 instead of $500 that applies to sales of goods

      (1) There are three exceptions to Statute of Frauds whereby leases need not be in writing even if for $1000 or more (note that these are similar to three exceptions to Statute of Frauds for sales of goods)

          (a) Specially manufactured goods when goods are not suitable for sale or lease in the ordinary course of lessor's business

          (b) Lessor or lessee admits to oral lease in court proceedings

              1] Only enforceable up to quantity admitted

          (c) Part acceptance in which lease is enforceable up to amount accepted by lessee

---

EXAMPLE

E leases under an oral agreement 900 personal computers. A, the lessor, ships 400 of the personal computers to E. After accepting the 400, E decides she does not want to lease the other 500. E is liable for the lease of the 400 personal computers under the part acceptance exception even though the agreement was oral. She would be liable for the lease of the full 900 personal computers if the agreement had been for less than $1,000 which is not the case here.

---

    b. Rules on acceptance, revocation of acceptance, and rejection of goods
    c. Remedies are similar to sellers' and buyers' remedies including the important concept of cure
    d. Principles for performance include anticipatory repudiation or breach, (including use of adequate assurance to avoid a breach), and the concept of impracticability

    e. Leases may be assigned

    f. Use general principles of contract and sales law for these

       (1) Warranties

       (2) Parol evidence

       (3) Firm offers

       (4) Risk of loss rules

       (5) Concept of unconscionable agreements

    g. Provision for sublease by lessee

    h. Leased goods may become fixtures

    i. Lessor has right to take possession of leased property after default without requirement of court adjudication

7. Leases under Article 2A of UCC may be in any manner sufficient to show by words or conduct that lessor and lessee intended to form a lease of identified goods

8. Finance lease is three-party transaction in which lessor acquires title or right to possess goods from supplier

    a. Lessor does not manufacture or supply goods for lessee but third-party supplier does according to lease agreement

I. Contracts for the International Sales of Goods (CISG)

1. Contracts for sales of goods between persons or companies of different countries follow the important rules of CISG

2. Many provisions of CISG are similar to UCC provisions but differences are handled under CISG because USA has this treaty with many countries in South America, Central America, North America, and most countries in Europe

    a. By Constitutional Law, CISG has priority over UCC when it applies and when it conflicts with UCC

    b. The following are important areas where CISG and UCC are different

       (1) Price terms

          (a) May be left open under UCC, in which case UCC provides that price is reasonable price at time of delivery

          (b) CISG requires that price term be included for there to be a contract

             1] CISG allows exception if method to determine price in future is clearly specified in contract

       (2) Time contract formed

          (a) Unlike UCC, CISG specifies that contract is formed only when acceptance is received by offeror

          (b) Also under CISG, acceptance happens at moment requested act is performed, not at the time notice is given of acceptance to offeror

       (3) Acceptances

          (a) CISG provides that there is no contract if terms in acceptance are different from terms in offer

             1] Acceptance is effective if differences are not material

               a] However, almost ever term in contract under CISG is considered material

       (4) Irrevocable offers

          (a) UCC allows offers that are not supported by consideration to be irrevocable if they are written and also meet certain other criteria

          (b) CISG allows offeror to make offer irrevocable by orally stating so

       (5) Written contracts

          (a) UCC has $500 rule for sales of goods

          (b) CISG provides that sales contracts may be oral with no rule regarding amount of money

             1] Also provides that proof of contract can be by any reasonable means

       (6) Parties are encouraged to have choice-of-language and choice-of-law clauses in contracts to help settle any disputes

KEY TERMS

Destination contract. An agreement that generally transfers title and risk of loss of the goods to the buyer when the goods reach their destination, usually the buyer's place of business.

Firm offer. An offer that is irrevocable despite the lack of consideration from the offeree to hold the offer open. Offer must be in writing and made by a merchant to be firm.

Good faith. Parties will operate honestly in the course of the transaction; think of trying to honor the spirit of the agreement more than the literal agreement.

Goods. Moveable personal property

Implied warranty. A guarantee that automatically exists, unless it is disclaimed by the seller. Some examples include the warranty of title, the implied warranty of merchantability, and the implied warranty of fitness for a particular purpose.

Merchant. A person who regularly buys or sells the goods that are involved in the contract.

Perfect tender rule. The goods that the seller delivers must conform exactly to the terms of the contract.

Risk of loss. Parties to the contract allocate which party will bear the loss if the goods are damaged or destroyed.

Shipment contract. An agreement that generally provides that title and risk of loss pass to the buyer when the seller delivers the goods to the common carrier.

Strict product liability. Sellers are held responsible for injuries that their goods cause, even if the seller exercised due care.

Tender. When a party to the contract is ready, willing, and able to perform the promise of the contract.

Transfer of title. Ownership of goods is transferred from the seller to the buyer.

Warranty. A guarantee concerning the quality, performance, or other characteristic of the good.

Module 28: Commercial Paper

Overview

Coverage of commercial paper includes the types of negotiable instruments, the requirements of negotiability, negotiation, the holder in due course concept, defenses to a claim of liability, and the rights of parties to a negotiable instrument. The functions of commercial paper are to provide a medium of exchange that is readily transferable like money and to provide an extension of credit. It is easier to transfer than contract rights and not subject to as many defenses as contracts are. To be negotiable, an instrument must

1. Be written
2. Be signed by the maker or drawer
3. Contain an unconditional promise or order to pay
4. State a fixed amount in money
5. Be payable on demand or at definite time
6. Be payable to order or bearer

These requirements must be present on the **face** of the instrument. Instruments that do not comply with these provisions are nonnegotiable and are transferable only by assignment. The assignee of a nonnegotiable instrument takes it subject to all defenses, whereas a holder of a negotiable instrument may avoid certain defenses.

A central theme of exam questions on negotiable instruments is the liability of the primary parties and of the secondarily liable parties under various fact situations. Similar questions in different form emphasize the rights that a holder of a negotiable instrument has against primary and secondary parties. Your review of this area should emphasize the legal liability arising upon execution of negotiable commercial paper, the legal liability arising upon various types of endorsements, and the warranty liabilities of various parties upon transfer or presentment for payment. A solid understanding of the distinction between real and personal defenses is required. Also tested is the relationship between a bank and its customers. Before beginning the reading you should review the key terms at the end of the module.

A. General Concepts of Commercial Paper

1. Commercial paper has two important functions

    a. Used as a substitute for money

    > **EXAMPLE**
    >
    > One often pays a bill with a check instead of using cash.

    b. Used as extension of credit

    > **EXAMPLE**
    >
    > X gives a promissory note to Y for $100 that is due one year later.

2. To encourage commercial paper to be transferred more easily by making it easier to be collected, **negotiable** commercial paper was established

    a. If an instrument is negotiable, favorable laws of Article 3 of UCC apply as discussed in this module
    b. If an instrument is nonnegotiable, laws of ordinary contract law apply (i.e., assignment of contract rights)

(1) Assignees of contract rights can get only the rights given by the assignor and therefore are burdened by any defenses between prior parties

---

EXAMPLE

C receives a nonnegotiable instrument from B. C now wishes to collect from A, the one who had issued the nonnegotiable note to B when he purchased some goods from B. Assume that A would have owed B only two-thirds of the amount stated on the instrument due to defects in the goods. Since C obtained only the rights that B had under an assignment under contract law, C can only collect two-thirds from A on this nonnegotiable instrument.

---

3. It is helpful to get "the big picture" of negotiable instruments (negotiable commercial paper) before covering details

    a. Whether an instrument is negotiable is determined by only looking at its form and content on the face (front) of the instrument

        (1) This allows individuals seeing an instrument to determine whether it is negotiable

        (2) If a person has a negotiable instrument and also is a holder in due course (discussed later), s/he may collect on instrument despite simple contract defenses

B. Types of Commercial Paper

1. Article 3 of UCC describes two types of negotiable commercial paper

    a. A draft (also called bill of exchange)

        (1) Has three parties in which one person or entity (drawer) **orders** another (drawee) to pay a third party (payee) a sum of money

---

EXAMPLE

June 5, 2011

On June 5, 2012, pay to the order of Bob Smith
$1,000 plus 10% annual interest from June 5, 2011

    To: ABC Corporation

        (Signed) Sue Van Deventer

The above is a draft in which Sue Van Deventer is the drawer, ABC Corporation is the drawee, and Bob Smith is the payee

---

        (a) A check

           1] Is a special type of draft that is payable on demand (unless postdated) and drawee must be a bank; banks include savings and loan associations, credit unions, and trust companies

           2] One writing check is drawer (and customer of drawee bank)

    b. A note (also called a promissory note)

        (1) Unlike a draft or check, is a two-party instrument

           (a) One party is called the maker—this party **promises** to pay a specified sum of money to another party called the payee

---

EXAMPLE

> July 10, 2011
>
> I promise to pay to the order of Becky Hoger $5,000 plus 10% annual interest on July 10, 2012.
>
> (Signed) Bill Jones

The above is a note in which Bill Jones is the maker and Becky Hoger is the payee.

---

(2) May be payable on demand or at a definite time

(a) Certificate of deposit (CD): Is an acknowledgement by a financial institution of receipt of money and a promise to repay it. The financial institution is the maker and the customer is the payee.

(b) Most commonly tested note on the CPA exam is a promissory note; see the example above with Bill Jones as the maker.

NOW REVIEW MULTIPLE-CHOICE QUESTIONS 1 THROUGH 5 IN VOLUME 2

C. Requirements of Negotiability

1. All of the following requirements must be on face of instrument for it to be a negotiable instrument (be sure to know these)

2. To be negotiable, the instrument must

   a. Be written
   b. Be signed by maker or drawer
   c. Contain an unconditional promise or order to pay
   d. State a fixed amount in money
   e. Be payable on demand or at a definite time
   f. Be payable to order or to bearer, unless it is a check

3. Details of requirements of negotiability

   a. Must be in writing

      (1) Satisfied by printing, typing, handwriting or any other reduction to physical form that is relatively permanent and portable
      (2) The UCC has a very liberal definition of a writing under Article 3; it is difficult not to satisfy this requirement

   b. Must be signed by maker (of a note or CD) or drawer (of a draft or check)

      (1) Signature includes any symbol used with intent to authenticate instrument

         (a) Rubber stamp, initials, letterhead satisfy signing requirement
         (b) Assumed name or trade name operates as that party's signature
         (c) Signature may be anywhere on face of instrument

      (2) Again, very liberal interpretation.

   c. Must contain an unconditional promise or order to pay

      (1) This is really two requirements

         (a) That the instrument contains an order or a promise to pay, and
         (b) That the promise or order be unconditional

      (2) If payment depends upon (is subject to) another agreement or event, then it is conditional and therefore destroys negotiability

> **EXAMPLE**
>
> An instrument that is otherwise negotiable states that it is subject to a particular contract. This condition destroys the negotiability of this instrument.

> **EXAMPLE**
>
> An instrument states: "I, Janice Jones, promise to pay to the order of Richard Riley, $1,000 if the stereo delivered to me is not defective." This instrument is not negotiable whether the stereo is defective or not because it contains a conditional promise.

    (a) However, the following are permitted and do not destroy negotiability

        1] Instrument may state its purpose

> **EXAMPLE**
>
> On a check, the drawer writes "for purchase of textbooks."

        2] Instrument may refer to or state that it arises from another agreement; note here that it is not subject to that agreement. Being "subject to" destroys negotiability.
        3] Instrument is permitted to show that it is secured by a mortgage or by collateral
        4] Instrument is permitted to contain promise to provide extra collateral
        5] Instrument is permitted to limit payment out of particular fund

    (b) The key to determining if the promise/order is conditional is, does the language in the instrument make the actual payment subject to some event?

(3) Promises

    (a) Are usually contained in a note
    (b) Must be an affirmative obligation to pay, not a mere acknowledgement of a debt.

> **EXAMPLE**
>
> Deb Tore gives a piece of paper to Lance Lender, which states, "IOU $500," signed Deb Tore. Deb's IOU only acknowledges the debt; she never promised to pay Lance. This instrument is nonnegotiable since it does not contain either a promise or an order to pay money. IOUs are nonnegotiable.

(4) Orders

    (a) Are usually contained in a draft
    (b) The order is a command or a direction to the drawee to pay
    (c) On a check this is the word "Pay"

> **NOTE:** The order **is not** the "order of" language on a check; it is the command, "pay"

d. Must state a fixed amount in money—called sum certain under former law

    (1) Amount of principal, but not interest, must be determinable from instrument without need to refer to other sources

        (a) Stated interest rates are allowed because amount can be calculated

> **EXAMPLE**
>
> A negotiable note states that $1,000 is due one year from October 1, 2001 at 14% interest.

> **EXAMPLE**
>
> A note states that $1,000 is payable on demand and bears interest at 14%. This also is negotiable because once payment is demanded, the amount of interest can be calculated.

(b) Variable interest rates are allowed and do not destroy negotiability even if formula for interest rate or amount requires reference to information outside of negotiable instrument

> **EXAMPLE**
>
> The following does not destroy negotiability in an otherwise negotiable instrument: Interest rates tied to some published key interest rate, consumer index market rate, etc.

(c) If interest rate based on legal rate or judgment rate (fixed by statute), then negotiability not destroyed
(d) Stated different rates of interest before and after default or specified dates are allowed
(e) Stated discounts or additions if instrument paid before or after payment dates do not destroy negotiability
(f) Clauses allowing collection costs and attorney's fees upon default are allowed because they reduce the risk of holding instruments and promote transferability
(g) Must be payable only in money; option to be payable in money or something else destroys negotiability because of possibility that payment will not be in money.

> **EXAMPLE**
>
> A note is payable in $1,000 or its equivalent in gold. This note is not negotiable.

(2) Foreign currency is acceptable even though reference to exchange rates may be needed due to international trade realities

e. Must be payable on demand or at a definite time

(1) On demand includes

(a) Payable on sight
(b) Payable on presentation
(c) No time for payment stated

(2) It is a definite time if payable

(a) On a certain date, or
(b) A fixed period after sight, or
(c) Within a certain time, or
(d) On a certain date subject to acceleration; for example, when a payment is missed, total balance may become due at once
(e) On a certain date subject to an extension of time if

1] At option of holder, or
2] At option of maker or drawer only if extension is limited to a definite amount of time

> **EXAMPLE**
>
> Promissory note which states, I promise to pay to the order of Will Smith $1000 on May 15, 2014, but if I lose my job, payment will be made on August 1, 2014. This instrument is negotiable, since any party taking the instrument knows that the latest they will be paid is August 1, 2014.

(3) It is not definite if payable on an act or event that is not certain as to time of occurrence

> **EXAMPLE**
>
> An instrument contains a clause stating that it is payable ten days after drawer obtains a bank loan. This destroys negotiability because it is unknown when, or even if, the drawer will obtain the loan.

f. Must be payable to order or to bearer **(these are critical words of negotiability and are often a central issue on the CPA exam)**

(1) Instrument is payable to order if made payable to the order of

(a) Any person, including the maker, drawer, drawee, or payee
(b) Two persons together or alternatively
(c) Any entity

(2) Instrument is also payable to order if it is payable "to A or order"
(3) Instrument other than a check is not payable to order if it is only payable to a person (e.g., "Pay John Doe")

EXAMPLE

A draft that is otherwise negotiable states: "Pay to XYZ Corporation." This statement destroys negotiability because the draft is not payable "to the order of" XYZ Corporation.

(a) It is not negotiable
(b) "Pay to the order of John Doe" would be negotiable

(4) If a **check** says "pay to A," it is negotiable order paper—this is not true of other instruments
(5) Instrument is payable to bearer if it is payable to

(a) "Bearer"
(b) "Cash"
(c) "A person or bearer" is bearer paper if "bearer" handwritten; however, "pay to John Doe, the bearer" is not negotiable because it is not payable to order or to bearer but to a person and simply refers to him as the bearer
(d) "Order of bearer" or "order of cash"
(e) Pay to the order of (payee left blank) is bearer paper unless holder inserts payee's name

(6) Instrument cannot be made payable to persons consecutively (i.e., maker cannot specify subsequent holders)

D. Interpretation of Ambiguities in Negotiable Instruments

1. Contradictory terms

a. Words control over figures
b. Handwritten terms control over typewritten and printed (typeset) terms
c. Typewritten terms control over printed (typeset) terms

2. Omissions

a. Omission of date does not destroy negotiability unless date necessary to determine when payable

---

EXAMPLE

A check is not dated. It is still negotiable because a check is payable on demand.

EXAMPLE

A draft states that it is payable thirty days after its date. If the date is left off, it is not payable at a definite time and, therefore, it is not negotiable. However, an authorized party may fill in the appropriate date and make the instrument negotiable.

---

b. Omission of interest rate is allowed because the judgment rate of interest (rate used on a court judgment) is automatically used
c. Statement of consideration or where instrument is drawn or payable not required

3. Other issues

a. Instrument may be postdated or antedated and remain negotiable

(1) Bank is not liable for damages to customer if it pays on postdated check before date on check unless individual notifies bank not to pay check earlier in a separate written document
(2) Once customer does this, bank is liable for any damages caused by early payment

b. Instrument may have a provision that by endorsing or cashing it, the payee acknowledges full satisfaction of debt and remain negotiable

c. If an instrument is payable to order of more than one person

(1) Either payee may negotiate or enforce it if payable to him/her in the alternative

> **EXAMPLE**
>
> "Pay $100 to the order of X or Y." Either X or Y may endorse it.

(2) All payees must negotiate or enforce it if **not** payable to them in the alternative

d. If not clear whether instrument is draft or note, holder may treat it as either

e. UCC requires only that a negotiable instrument need be written, must lend itself to permanence, and must be easily transferable (i.e., movable).

> **NOW REVIEW MULTIPLE-CHOICE QUESTIONS 6 THROUGH 16 IN VOLUME 2**

E. Negotiation

1. There are two methods of transferring commercial paper

  a. By assignment

  (1) Assignment occurs when transfer does not meet all requirements of negotiation

  (2) Assignee can obtain only same rights that assignor had, and is subject to any defenses that can be asserted against assignor

  b. By negotiation

  (1) One receiving negotiable instrument by negotiation is called a holder

  (2) If holder further qualifies as a holder in due course (as discussed later) s/he can obtain **more rights** than what transferor had

  (3) There are two methods of negotiation, which is dependent on whether the transferor is trying to negotiate order paper or bearer paper

   (a) Order paper is a negotiable instrument that is payable to a specific party (e.g., "Pay to the order of Acme Corp.")

    1] Transferred by physical delivery of the instrument **and** endorsement
    2] A holder needs possession of the instrument and any necessary endorsements

   (b) Bearer paper is a negotiable instrument that is payable to any party (e.g., "Pay to cash")

    1] Transferred by delivery alone
    2] Holder only needs possession of the instrument
    3] Subsequent parties may require endorsements (even though UCC does not) for identification
    4] Holder may, in any event, endorse it if s/he chooses to do so

  (4) Endorsement (Indorsement) refers to signature of payee, drawee, accommodation endorser, or holder

2. Types of endorsements

  a. Blank endorsement

  (1) Does not specify any endorsee

> **EXAMPLE**
>
> A check made payable to the order of M on the front can be endorsed in blank by M writing only his signature on the back.

  (2) Converts order paper into bearer paper

  (3) Note that bearer paper may be negotiated by mere delivery; hence a finder, or even a thief, can be a valid holder

> **EXAMPLE**
>
> B endorses a check in blank that had been made payable to his order. He lost it and C found it who delivered it to D. D is a valid holder since C's endorsement was not required.

b. Special endorsement

   (1) Indicates specific person to whom endorsee wishes to negotiate instrument

   > **EXAMPLE**
   >
   > On the back of a check payable to the order of M. Jordan he signs as follows: Pay to L. Smith, (signed) M. Jordan.

   (a) Note that words "pay to the order of" are not required on back as endorsements—the instrument needs to be payable to order or to bearer on front only

   (b) Also, note that if instrument is not payable to order or to bearer on its face, it **cannot** be turned into a negotiable instrument by using these words in an endorsement on the back

   > **EXAMPLE**
   >
   > A particular instrument would have been negotiable except that on the front it was payable to A. On the back, A signed it. "Pay to the order of B, (signed) A." This does not convert it into a negotiable instrument.

   (2) Bearer paper may be converted into order paper by use of special endorsement

   > **EXAMPLE**
   >
   > A check made out to cash is delivered to Carp. Carp writes on the back; Pay to Durn, (signed) Carp. It was bearer paper until this special endorsement.

   > **EXAMPLE**
   >
   > Continuing the previous example, Durn simply endorses it in blank. The check is bearer paper again.

   (3) If last (or only) endorsement on instrument is a blank endorsement, any holder may convert that bearer paper into order paper by writing "Pay to X," etc., above that blank endorsement

c. Restrictive endorsement is an attempt by the endorser to restrict further negotiation; some restrictions are enforceable, others are not.

   (1) Valid restrictive endorsements

      (a) Collection endorsements (e.g. "for deposit only" or "pay any bank")
      (b) Endorsements in trust (e.g. "Pay Smith for Jones")

   (2) Invalid restrictive endorsements

      (a) The following endorsements are viewed by the law as saying "Pay to the order of Smith;" the rest of the language in the endorsement is simply ignored or altered by the law.

         1] Pay to Smith, if Smith washes my car
         2] Pay to Smith only

      (b) Remember the endorsements cannot affect negotiability, thus order language is not required in an endorsement

      (c) Endorsements cannot prohibit further negotiation; to the extent the endorsement attempts to limit further negotiation, the language is ignored.

d. Qualified endorsement

   (1) Normally, endorser, upon signing, promises automatically to pay holder or any subsequent endorser the amount of instrument if it is later dishonored
   (2) Qualified endorsement disclaims this liability

> **EXAMPLE**
>
> Ann Knolls endorses "Without recourse, (signed) Ann Knolls."

    (3) Qualified endorsements, otherwise, have same effects as other endorsements

  e. Combinations of endorsements occur

    (1) Special qualified endorsement

> **EXAMPLE**
>
> "Pay to Pete Bell without recourse, (signed) Tom Lack." Tom Lack has limited his liability and also Pete Bell's endorsement is needed to negotiate this instrument further.

    (2) Blank qualified endorsement

> **EXAMPLE**
>
> "Without recourse, (signed) D. Hamilton."

    (3) Endorsement that is restrictive, qualified, and blank

> **EXAMPLE**
>
> "For deposit only, without recourse, (signed) Bill Coffey."

3. If payee's name misspelled, s/he may endorse in proper spelling or misspelling or both; but endorsee may require both
4. If an order instrument is transferred for value without endorsement, transferee may require endorsement from transferor
5. Federal law standardizes endorsements on checks—endorser should turn check over and sign in designated area

  a. Purpose is to avoid interference with bank's endorsements
  b. Endorsements placed outside this area do not destroy negotiability but may delay clearing process.

6. If check has statement that it is nonnegotiable, check is still negotiable

  a. This is not true of other negotiable instruments whereby such statement destroys negotiability

NOW REVIEW MULTIPLE-CHOICE QUESTIONS 17 THROUGH 21 IN VOLUME 2

F. Holder in Due Course

1. Concept of **holder in due course** (also called **HDC**) is very important for CPA exam purposes. A HDC is entitled to payment on negotiable instrument **despite personal defenses** that maker or drawer of instrument may have

  a. Recall that an assignee of contract rights receives only rights that assignor had (i.e., assignee takes subject to all defenses that could have been asserted against assignor)
  b. Likewise, an ordinary holder of a negotiable instrument has same rights as assignee

2. To be holder in due course, a taker of instrument must

  a. Be a **holder** of a properly negotiated negotiable instrument
  b. Give **value** for instrument

    (1) Holder gives value if s/he

      (a) Pays or performs agreed consideration; be careful, an executory promise (promise to give value in the future is not value. Promise must actually have been performed.

> **EXAMPLE**
>
> DeMaurice gave $3000 to Roger for a $5000 promissory note and promised to pay Roger an additional $1000 in one month. One week after the initial payment, and before making the final payment to Roger, DeMaurice found out that Roger had stolen the note from Jerry. DeMaurice qualifies as a holder in due course for $3,750. Once DeMaurice learns of the theft he cannot further qualify as a holder in due course. When DeMaurice made the initial payment of $3000, he did not know of the theft, so he qualifies as a holder in due course to the extent he has actually provided value. So why does DeMaurice qualify for $3750 and not just $3000? The law recognizes that DeMaurice was never going to pay $5000 for the $5000 instrument. Instead, he purchased the note at a discount. DeMaurice has paid 75% ($3000/$4000) of what he intended to pay, so the law states that he is entitled to 75% of the face value of the instrument: $3750.

   (b) Takes as a satisfaction of a previous existing debt
   (c) Gives another negotiable instrument
   (d) Acquires a security interest in the instrument (e.g., the holder takes possession of the instrument as collateral for another debt)

  (2) A bank takes for value to the extent that credit has been given for a deposit and withdrawn

    (a) FIFO method is used to determine whether it has been withdrawn (money is considered to be withdrawn from an account in the order in which it was deposited)

  (3) Value does not have to be for full amount of instrument

    (a) Purchase at a reasonable discount is value for full face amount of instrument

> **EXAMPLE**
>
> Purchase of a $1,000 instrument in good faith for $950 is considered full value, but purchase of the same instrument for $500 is not considered full value when market conditions show that the discount is excessive.
>
> **NOTE:** Do not just assume that a large discount is excessive; the Examiners need to provide you with facts that indicate the discount is excessive. Do not forget during the recent financial crisis, there were instruments being sold for pennies on the dollar.

 c. Take in **good faith**

  (1) Good faith defined as honesty in fact and observance of reasonable commercial standards of fair dealing

 d. Take **without notice** that the instrument is overdue, has been dishonored, or that any person has a defense or claim of ownership to the instrument

  (1) Holder has notice when s/he knows or has reason to know (measured by objective "reasonable person" standard)
  (2) Overdue

> **EXAMPLE**
>
> I offer to sell you a $10,000 promissory note for $9,000. The note was payable last week. You should be suspicious since I could go to the maker of the note and collect $10,000 immediately; why would I sell it to you for only $9000, unless there was something wrong with the note? Therefore you cannot qualify as a holder in due course.

    (a) Instrument not overdue if default is on payment of interest only
    (b) Domestic check, although payable on demand, is overdue ninety days after its date

  (3) Defense or claim

    (a) Obvious signs of forgery or alteration so as to call into question its authenticity
    (b) Incomplete instrument or irregular instrument
    (c) If purchaser has notice of any party's claim, or that all parties have been discharged

  (4) There is no notice of a defense or claim if

    (a) It is antedated or postdated
    (b) S/he knows that there has been a default in payment of interest
    (c) The note was purchased at a reasonable discount.

(5) But if one acquires notice **after** becoming a holder and giving value, s/he may still be a HDC to the extent of the value given (see the above example under value with DeMaurice and Roger)

3. Payee of a negotiable instrument may qualify as a HDC if meets all requirements

NOW REVIEW MULTIPLE-CHOICE QUESTIONS 22 THROUGH 25 IN VOLUME 2

G. Rights of a Holder in Due Course

1. The general rule is that a transfer of a negotiable instrument to a HDC cuts off all **personal defenses** against a HDC

   a. Personal defenses are assertable against ordinary holders and assignees of contract rights to avoid payment

   > **EXAMPLE**
   >
   > Art Dobbs negotiates a note to Mary Price in payment of a stereo. Mary negotiates this note to D. Finch who qualifies as a HDC. When Finch seeks payment, Dobbs points out that Price breached the contract by never delivering the stereo. Finch, as a HDC, still has the right to collect because breach of contract is a personal defense. Dobbs then has to seek recourse directly against Price.

2. Some defenses are assertable against any party including a HDC—these defenses are called **real (or universal) defenses**

3. Types of **personal defenses**

   a. Breach of contract, including breach of warranty
   b. Lack or failure of consideration
   c. Prior payment

   > **EXAMPLE**
   >
   > Maker of a negotiable note pays on the note but does not keep or cancel the note. A subsequent party who qualifies as a HDC seeks to collect on this same note. Maker, having only a personal defense, must pay the HDC even though it was paid previously.

   d. Unauthorized completion

   > **EXAMPLE**
   >
   > X signs a check leaving the amount blank. He tells Y to fill in the amount necessary to buy a typewriter. Y fills in $22,000 and negotiates the check to a HDC. The HDC may enforce the full amount of the check against X.

   e. Fraud in the inducement

   (1) Occurs when person signs a negotiable instrument and knows what s/he is signing; however, s/he was induced into doing so by intentional misrepresentation

   f. Nondelivery

   (1) Occurs when bearer instrument is lost or stolen

   > **EXAMPLE**
   >
   > M issues a note that is bearer paper. It is stolen by T who sells it to a HDC. The HDC wins against M.

   g. Ordinary duress or undue influence

   (1) Most types of duress are considered a personal defense unless they become very extreme and thus are considered real defenses

> **EXAMPLE**
>
> Jessica threatened to post some unflattering pictures of Anthony on Facebook. Anthony writes Jessica a check so Jessica will not post the pictures. Anthony would only have a personal defense against paying the check.

  h. Mental incapacity

    (1) Personal defense if state law makes transaction voidable
    (2) Real defense if state law makes transaction void

> **EXAMPLE**
>
> Contracts of people who have been adjudicated incompetent are void; those people would have a real defense against enforcement of a negotiable instrument. People who only suffer from some diminished capacity would only have a personal defense.

  i. Illegality

    (1) Personal defense if state law makes transaction voidable
    (2) If state law makes it void, then real defense

  j. Theft by holder or subsequent holder after theft

4. Real Defenses

  a. Forgery

    (1) Forgery of maker's or drawer's signature does not act as his/her signature

      (a) Does allow forger to be held liable

> **EXAMPLE**
>
> X forges M's name on a note and sells it to P. P cannot collect from M whether she is a HDC or not. Her recourse is against X. The UCC recognizes the forged signature as X's signature, not M's. So even though the instrument states "M," in the eyes of the law it states "X."

  b. Bankruptcy
  c. Fraud in the execution

    (1) Occurs when a party is tricked into signing a negotiable instrument believing it to be something else

      (a) This defense will not apply if signer, based on his/her age, experience, etc., should have known what was happening

    (2) Recall that fraud in the inducement is a personal defense

  d. Minority (or infancy)

    (1) When minor may disaffirm contract under state law, then is a real defense for a negotiable instrument

  e. Mental incapacity, illegality, or extreme duress

    (1) Real defenses if transaction is void under state law

  f. Material alteration of instrument

    (1) Is actually only partially a real defense

      (a) If dollar amount was altered, then HDC can collect according to original terms—a non-HDC collects nothing
      (b) If an instrument was incomplete originally and then completed without authorization, HDC can enforce it as completed—a non-HDC collects nothing

    (2) Material alteration exists when terms between any two parties are changed in any way including

      (a) Changes in amount, rate of interest, or days

> **EXAMPLE**
>
> Janice Parks negotiates a $200 negotiable note to Jim Bivins. Bivins deftly changes the amount to $500 and transfers it to E. Melvin for $500 who qualifies as a HDC. The HDC can collect only the original $200 from Janice Parks.

> **EXAMPLE**
>
> Same facts as before except that the material alteration is poorly done by Jim Bivins so that E. Melvin could not qualify as a holder in due course because the change was obvious. E. Melvin cannot collect even the original $200.

    (b) Additions to writing or removal of part of instrument
    (c) Completion of instrument without authorization
    (d) Considered "material" even if small change such as a penny
    (e) But not material alteration if done to correct error on address, math computations, or to place marks on instrument for audit purposes. Alterations that are not material are neither real nor personal defenses so all non-HDCs as well as HDCs can enforce the instrument.
    (f) Not a real defense if maker's or drawer's negligence substantially contributed to the alteration—is a personal defense

5. Holder through a holder in due course ("Shelter Rule")

  a. A party who does not qualify as a HDC but obtains a negotiable instrument from a HDC has the standing of HDC.
  b. Obtains all rights of a HDC

    (1) Based on fact that is an assignee that gets rights of previous party
    (2) Also called shelter provision

  c. A HDC "washes" an instrument so that any holder thereafter can be a holder through a holder in due course

> **EXAMPLE**
>
> A HDC transfers a note to H.V. Shelton who knew that the maker of the note has a personal defense. Shelton does not qualify as a HDC but has the same rights because he is a holder through a holder in due course.

> **EXAMPLE**
>
> Extending the example, H.V. Shelton gives the note to B. Evans. B. Evans does not qualify as a HDC (no value given) but is a holder through a holder in due course.

NOTE: Be careful to remember that in the above examples if the Examiners were to ask you if Shelton or Evans is a HDC, the answer is no. If you are asked do Shelton or Evans have the rights of a HDC, the answer is yes.

  d. Exceptions

    (1) If a party reacquires an instrument, his/her status remains what it originally was

> **EXAMPLE**
>
> P acquires a check from the payee. Neither qualifies in this case as a holder in due course. P delivers the check to Q who qualifies as a HDC. If the check is negotiated back to P, his rights remain those of a non-HDC.

    (2) One who was involved in fraud or illegality affecting the instrument may not subsequently become a holder through a holder in due course

6. Federal Trade Commission Rule significantly limits HDC status in consumer credit transactions

a. This federal law takes precedence over state UCCs
b. Law was passed because it was felt standard HDC rule was causing hardship on consumers who signed notes promising to pay retailers for goods purchased which were defective. Retailer could sell notes to other parties cutting off important remedies against retailer who sold defective goods.
c. FTC rule applies to consumer credit transactions when

   (1) Consumer signs installment sales contract containing waiver of defenses
   (2) Consumer signs sales contract containing promissory note
   (3) Retailer arranges financing with a separate party for consumer financing

d. Lenders and sellers of negotiable instruments must put notice defenses consumers could use against sellers
e. Payments for goods or services using checks are not covered by FTC rule
f. Note that rule does not apply to any nonconsumer transactions and does not apply to any consumer noncredit transactions

---

EXAMPLE

Connie Consumer purchases goods for consumer use and writes out a check. Subsequent holders are governed by ordinary HDC law.

NOW REVIEW MULTIPLE-CHOICE QUESTIONS 26 THROUGH 35 IN VOLUME 2

H. Liability of Parties—There are two general types of warranties on negotiable instruments: contractual liability and warranty liability. This explains who is responsible to pay the holder/holder in due course.

1. Contractual liability

a. This is the liability for payment of the instrument's face value.
b. Applies to any party who signs negotiable instrument. This could include a maker, drawer, acceptor of a draft, or endorser.
c. Primary liability

   (1) The holder/HDC must first seek payment from this party
   (2) The primary party on a note is the maker
   (3) The primary party on a draft is the acceptor of a draft

      (a) This is a drawee who accepts the instrument for payment
      (b) If drawee dishonors (refuses to make payment) the draft, then no party has primary liability on the draft

d. Secondary liability

   (1) If primary party does not pay, then the holder/HDC may either

      (a) Sue the primary party to force the primary party to pay, or
      (b) Seek payment from a secondary party

   (2) Secondary parties are

      (a) Endorsers of any instrument
      (b) Drawers on a draft
      (c) There is no secondary liability on a draft if the draft was accepted by the drawee

   (3) Several conditions must be met to hold a secondary party liable for payment

      (a) Presentment (demand for payment) of the instrument to the primary party by the holder/HDC
      (b) Dishonor (refusal to pay) of the instrument by the primary party
      (c) Timely notice of the dishonor provided to the endorsers (notice is not required for the drawer)

         1] Banks, and similar institutions, must provide notice by midnight of the next banking day
         2] All other parties have 30 days to provide notice of the dishonor

e. Drawers, **except** drawers of a check, and endorsers may avoid secondary liability by signing without recourse
f. Upon certification of check, drawer and all previous endorsers are discharged from liability because bank has accepted check and agreed to pay it
g. A holder/HDC may only seek to collect from prior signatory parties, not subsequent signers

> **EXAMPLE**
>
> Assume that first John and then Paul previously endorsed a note that is in George's possession. Later George transfers the instrument, by endorsement, to Ringo. Ringo presents the note to the primary party Peter for payment; Peter dishonored the note. Ringo then notified all the endorsers of the dishonor and sought payment from Paul, who paid Ringo. Paul could now proceed against John for secondary liability because John signed the note prior to Paul. Paul cannot, however, collect from George because George endorsed after Paul.

2. Warranty liability—two types under which holder can seek payment from secondary parties are transfer warranties and presentment warranties

   a. Transfer warranties—transferor gives following transfer warranties whenever negotiable instrument is transferred for consideration

      (1) Transferor has good title, which means that there are

         (a) No missing endorsements
         (b) No unauthorized endorsements

      (2) All signatures are genuine or authorized
      (3) Instrument has not been materially altered
      (4) No defense of any party is good against transferor
      (5) Transferor has no notice of insolvency of maker, drawer, or acceptor

   b. These warranties generally allocate the loss to parties that dealt face to face with wrongdoer and thus were in best position to prevent or avoid forged, altered, or stolen instruments

      (1) Party bearing loss must then seek payment if possible, from one who forged, altered, or stole instrument

   c. Note that transferor, if s/he did not endorse, makes all five warranties only to immediate transferee but if transferor did endorse, makes them to all subsequent holders taking in good faith

   d. Presentment warranties—holder/HDC presenting negotiable instrument for payment or acceptance and all prior transferors of the instrument provide presentment warranties to the party who pays on the instrument. The presentment warranties for an unaccepted draft are

      (1) The warrantor is entitled to enforce the instrument (i.e. warrantor has good title)
      (2) Warrantor has no knowledge that drawer's signature is forged or unauthorized
      (3) The instrument was not altered

   e. Presentment warranty for all other instruments (other than unaccepted drafts) is only the first warranty listed: Good title.

   f. To recover under warranty liabilities (either transfer or presentment warranties), party does not have to meet conditions of proper presentment, dishonor, or timely notice of dishonor that are required under contractual liability against endorsers

   g. Recovery under a warranty theory only allows the injured party to receive what they paid for the instrument. The injured party is not entitled to recover the face value, as s/he would be able to under contract liability, unless the injured party actually paid the face value of the instrument.

3. Signatures by authorized agents

   a. Drawers or makers at times authorize agents to sign negotiable instruments on behalf of such drawers or makers

      (1) Organizations such as corporations often use corporate officers or employees to be agents to sign their negotiable instruments

         (a) Drawers or makers are liable and agent is not personally liable on negotiable instrument if agent's signature clearly discloses both agency status and identity of drawer or maker

      (2) Individuals may also use agents to sign negotiable instruments and same law applies

> **EXAMPLE**
>
> A negotiable instrument has the following signature, signed entirely by A. Underwood, the authorized agent: Mary Johnson, by A. Underwood, agent.

> **EXAMPLE**
>
> If A. Underwood had simply signed Mary Johnson as she had authorized, this would also bind Mary Johnson.

> **EXAMPLE**
>
> If A. Underwood had signed his name only, he is liable. The principal is not liable even if the agent intended her to be because her name is not on the instrument.

4. Accommodation party is liable on the instrument in the capacity in which s/he has signed even if taker knows of his/her accommodation status

> **EXAMPLE**
>
> Accommodating maker is liable as a maker would be.

> **EXAMPLE**
>
> Accommodating endorser is liable as an endorser would be.

   a. Accommodation party is one who signs to lend his/her name to other party

> **EXAMPLE**
>
> Father-in-law endorses a note for son-in-law so creditor will accept it.

      (1) Notice of default need not be given to accommodation party
      (2) The accommodation party has right of recourse against accommodated party if accommodation party is held liable

5. Discharge of parties

   a. Once primary party pays, all endorsers are discharged from liability
   b. Cancellation of prior party's endorsement discharges that party from liability

      (1) Oral renunciation or oral attempt to discharge a party is not effective

   c. Intentional destruction of instrument by holder discharges prior parties to instrument

6. Liability on instruments with forged signatures

   a. Person whose signature was forged on instrument is not liable on that instrument

      (1) Unless later ratifies it

   b. Forged signature operates as signature of forger
   c. Therefore, if signature of **maker or drawer** is forged, instrument can still be negotiated between parties and thus a holder can acquire good title

      (1) Recall that forgery is a real defense so that innocent maker or drawer cannot be required to pay even a HDC—forger can be required to pay if found

   d. However, a **forged endorsement** does **not** transfer title; thus, persons receiving it after forgery cannot collect on it

      (1) Three important exceptions to rule that forged endorsements cannot transfer title are imposter rule, fictitious payee rule, and negligence of maker or drawer—these cause maker or drawer to be liable

         (a) **Imposter rule** applies when maker or drawer issues a note or draft to an imposter thinking s/he actually is the real payee—when that imposter forges the real payee's name, this effectively negotiates this note or draft so that a subsequent holder (if not part of scheme) can collect from maker or drawer

1] Note that this rule normally places loss on person who was in best position to avoid this scheme (i.e., maker or drawer)

a] Of course, upon payment, maker or drawer may try to collect from imposter

> **EXAMPLE**
>
> J. Loux owes Larsen (whom she has not met) $2,000. Sawyer, claiming to be Larsen, gets Loux to issue him a check for $2,000. Sawyer forges Larsen's endorsement and transfers the check to P. Jenkins. Jenkins can collect from Loux because of the imposter rule exception.

> **EXAMPLE**
>
> If in the example above, J. Loux had given the check to the real Larsen and he lost it, the imposter rule would not apply even if someone found the check and forged Larsen's endorsement. No one after the forgery can collect on the check.

2] This imposter rule exception also applies if an imposter pretends to be **agent** of the named payee

(b) **Fictitious payee rule** applies when maker, drawer, or his/her agent (employee) issues a note or a check to a fictitious payee—then maker, drawer, or employee forges the endorsement—subsequent parties can enforce the note or check against the maker or drawer

1] Actually payee may be a real person as long as maker, drawer, or other person supplying name never intended for that payee to ever get payment

> **EXAMPLE**
>
> R. Stewart submits a time card for a nonexistent employee and the employer issues the payroll check. Stewart forges the endorsement and transfers it to L. Reed. Reed wins against the employer even though the employer was unaware of the scheme at the time.

(c) If person's negligence substantially contributes to the forgery that person is prevented from raising the defense of forgery and thus holder wins

> **EXAMPLE**
>
> D. Wolter has a signature stamp and leaves it lying around. Unauthorized use of the stamp is not a defense against a holder as Wolter's negligence substantially contributed to the forgery. If the forger could be caught, Wolter could sue the forger for losses.

NOW REVIEW MULTIPLE-CHOICE QUESTIONS 36 THROUGH 44 IN VOLUME 2

I. Additional Issues

1. Types of drafts—although they follow general rules of drafts, definitions are helpful

   a. Trade acceptance is a draft in which a seller of goods extends credit to buyer by drawing a draft on that buyer directing him/her to pay seller a sum of money on a specified date

      (1) Trade acceptance also requires signature of buyer on face of instrument—called acceptance—buyer is also called acceptor at this point
      (2) Then seller may negotiate trade acceptance at a discount to another party to receive immediate cash
      (3) Seller is normally both drawer and payee of a trade acceptance

   b. Banker's acceptance is a draft in which drawee and drawer are a bank
   c. Sight draft is one payable upon presentment to drawee
   d. Time draft is one payable at a specified date or payable a certain period of time after a specified date
   e. Money order is a draft purchased by one party to pay payee in which the third party is typically post office, a bank, or a company

2. Definitions for certain types of checks are also helpful

a. Traveler's check is purchased from a bank (or company)—drawer (traveler) must sign twice for purposes of identification (once at the time s/he purchases the check and again at the time s/he uses the check)—drawee is bank or company—payee is one who gets paid

   (1) Technically, drawee must be a bank to be a true "check"—if drawee is not a bank then traveler's check is actually a draft

b. Cashier's check is a check in which drawer and drawee are the same bank with a separate party being the payee

   (1) This is still considered a "three-party" instrument even though drawer and drawee are same bank

c. Certified check is a check that payor bank has agreed in advance to pay so that bank becomes primarily liable

d. Teller's check (bank draft) is draft drawn by one bank on another bank

J. Banks

1. Banks include savings and loan associations, credit unions, and trust companies

2. Relationship between bank and depositor is debtor-creditor

   a. Even though the depositor has funds in the bank, a payee cannot force a drawee to make payment

   b. Only drawer has an action against drawee-bank for wrongfully dishonoring a check—based on contract between customer (drawer) and bank

   c. Bank required to report to IRS any transaction or series of related transactions greater than $10,000

      (1) Ordinary checks are exempted but cash and other types of checks such as cashier's checks come under reporting requirement

   d. Bank must report to IRS suspected crimes involving $1,000 or more in funds

   e. It is a crime to structure or assist in structuring transactions to evade these reporting requirements

      (1) May be punishable by money penalties or under criminal law

3. Checks

   a. Banks are not obligated to pay on a check presented more than six months after date

      (1) But they may pay in good faith and charge customer's account

   b. Even if check creates an overdraft, a bank may charge customer's account

   c. Bank is liable to drawer for damages caused by wrongful dishonor of a check

      (1) Wrongful dishonor may occur if the bank in error believes funds are insufficient when they are sufficient

   d. Payment of bad checks (e.g., forgery of drawer or altered checks)

      (1) Bank is liable to drawer for payment on bad checks unless drawer's negligence contributed because bank presumed to know signatures of its drawers

      (2) If drawer fails to notify bank of forgery or alterations within thirty days of bank statement, the drawer is held liable on subsequent forgeries or alterations done in same way by same person

         (a) In any event, drawer must give notice of forgeries or alterations within one year to keep bank liable or else drawer is liable. This applies to even nonrepeat cases as well as when bank was paying bad faith.

> **EXAMPLE**
>
> G. Wilson forges the name of M. Gibson on a check in an artful way. A subsequent HDC cashes this check at the drawee bank. The bank is liable on this check and cannot recover from either the HDC or M. Gibson as long as Gibson notifies the bank of the forgery within one year. The loss falls on the bank because the bank should know its drawer's signature.

         (b) Forgeries of endorsements are treated differently—depositor has three years to notify bank and also bank may charge check back to party that presented check to bank. Recall that one cashing check gave warranty that all signatures are genuine.

> **EXAMPLE**
>
> D issues a check to P. P loses the check which is found by X. X forges the endorsement and transfers it to H. Finally, H cashes the check at the drawee bank. D soon notifies the bank of the forgery. The bank may charge it back to H (whether or not a HDC) but not to D.

   e. Bank is not liable for early payment of postdated check unless drawer notified bank to not pay check until date on check

   f. Oral **stop payment order** is good for fourteen days; written stop payment order is good for six months and is renewable

     (1) Stop payment order must be given so as to give bank reasonable opportunity to act on it

     (2) Bank is liable to drawer if it pays after effective stop payment order only when drawer can prove that the bank's failure to obey the order caused drawer's loss. If drawer has no valid defense to justify dishonoring instrument, then bank has no liability for failure to obey stop payment order.

> **EXAMPLE**
>
> W. Paisley buys a TV set from the Burke Appliance Store and pays for the set with a check. Later in the day Paisley finds a better model for the same price at another store. Paisley telephones his bank and orders the bank to stop payment on the check. If the bank mistakenly pays Paisley's check two days after receiving the stop payment order, the bank will not be liable if Paisley could not rightfully rescind his agreement with the Burke Appliance Store. With these facts, Paisley suffered no damages from the bank's mistake.

     (3) If drawer stops payment on the check, s/he is still liable to holder of check unless s/he has a valid defense (e.g., if holder qualifies as a holder in due course then drawer must be able to assert a real defense to free him/herself of liability)

   g. Bank is entitled to a depositor's endorsement on checks deposited with the bank

     (1) If missing, bank may supply endorsement to negotiate check

   h. Banks may choose which checks are charged to account first when several checks received in same day

NOW REVIEW MULTIPLE-CHOICE QUESTIONS 45 THROUGH 46 IN VOLUME 2

K. Electronic Fund Transfer Act and Regulation E

1. Applied to consumer electronic fund transfers
2. For lost or stolen debit cards, customer is liable for

   a. Limit of $50 if notifies bank within two days of discovery of loss or theft
   b. Limit of $500 if notifies bank after two days, but before sixty days after unauthorized use appears on customer's bank statement
   c. Limit of $500 does not apply if fails to notify bank before sixty-day period
   d. Note how these rules are very different from those that apply to lost or stolen credit cards

3. Bank is liable for failure to pay electronic fund transfer when customer has sufficient funds in account
4. Unauthorized use of electronic fund transfer is felony under federal law

   a. Banks and their officers must comply with strict rules for prevention or be subject to strict fines and/or imprisonment

L. Fund Transfers under UCC Article 4A

1. Applies to commercial electronic fund transfers

   a. Adopted by majority of states
   b. Does not apply to consumer transfers
   c. Applies to any method of transfer including electronic or mail

2. When party gives payment order to bank and that bank or another bank pays too much money or to wrong party, that bank in error is liable for error

   a. Then bank has burden of recovery for wrongfully paid amount

M. Transfer of Negotiable Documents of Title

1. Transfer of documents of title is very similar to transfer of negotiable instruments under commercial paper
2. A document of title symbolizes ownership of the item it describes.
3. Types of documents of title

  a. Bill of lading is a document issued by a common carrier (a person engaged in the business of transporting or forwarding goods) and given to seller evidencing receipt of the goods for shipment
  b. A warehouse receipt is a document issued by a warehouseman (a person engaged in the business of storing goods for hire) and given to seller evidencing receipt of goods for storage

    (1) Warehouse receipt must contain the following terms:

      (a) Location of the warehouse
      (b) Date the receipt was issued
      (c) Statement to whom the goods will or can be delivered
      (d) Rates (charges) for storing the goods
      (e) Description of the goods.
      (f) Signature of the warehouseman

4. Form

  a. Document of title is negotiable if face of the document contains words of negotiability (order or bearer)

    (1) Document of title containing promise to deliver goods to the order of a named person is an order document

      (a) If person is named on face of document or, if there are endorsements, on back of document and last endorsement is a special endorsement, then document is an order document

        1] Proper negotiation requires delivery of document and endorsement by named individual(s)

    (2) Document of title containing a promise to deliver the goods to bearer is bearer document

      (a) If "bearer" is stated on face of document or, if there are endorsements on back of document and last endorsement is a blank endorsement, it is a bearer document

        1] Proper negotiation merely requires delivery of document

  b. Nonnegotiable (straight) documents of title are assigned, not negotiated

    (1) Assignee will never receive any better rights than assignor had

5. Due negotiation—document of title is "duly negotiated" when negotiated to a holder who takes it in good faith in the ordinary course of business without notice of a defense and pays value

  a. Value does not include payment of a preexisting (antecedent) debt—this is an important difference from value concept required to create a holder in due course for commercial paper

6. Holder by due negotiation acquires rights very similar to those acquired by a holder in due course

  a. These rights include

    (1) Title to document
    (2) Title to goods
    (3) All rights accruing under law of agency or estoppel, including rights to goods delivered after document was issued, and
    (4) The direct obligation of the issuer to hold or deliver the goods according to terms of document

  b. A holder by due negotiation defeats similar defenses to those defeated by a holder in due course for commercial paper (personal but not real defenses)
  c. A document of title procured by a thief upon placing stolen goods in a warehouse confers no rights in the underlying goods

    (1) This defense is valid against subsequent holder to whom document of title has been duly negotiated
    (2) Therefore, original owner of goods can assert better title to goods than a holder who has received document through due negotiation

7. Rights acquired in absence of due negotiation

  a. Transferee of a document, whether negotiable or nonnegotiable, to whom document has been delivered, but not duly negotiated, acquires title and rights which his/her transferor had or had actual authority to convey

8. Transferor for value warrants that

  a. Document is genuine
  b. S/he has no knowledge of any fact that would impair its validity or worth, and
  c. His/her negotiation or transfer is rightful and fully effective with respect to document of title and goods it represents

NOW REVIEW MULTIPLE-CHOICE QUESTIONS 47 THROUGH 50 IN VOLUME 2

N. Agencies Involved in Banking

1. Federal Reserve

   a. Central bank of US which regulates US monetary system and oversees bank holding companies

2. FDIC is US entity which insures customer deposits against bank failure

   a. Also created to help maintain public confidence and encourage stability in our financial system by promoting sound banking practices

3. OCC is arm of Treasury Department established to regulate and supervise national banks and federal branches of foreign banks

   a. Its objective is to promote safety and soundness of banking system
   b. Conducts on-site examination of banks

4. CFTC is US agency established to ensure open and efficient operation of futures markets which have grown from trading agricultural futures to more sophisticated financial products

5. OTS issues and enforces regulation governing nation's savings and loan industry

   a. This bureau is responsible for helping to ensure safety and soundness of deposits in thrift banks

6. Agencies involved in banking could be tested on CPA exam especially because of recent debates among business people and politicians over how to better regulate banks

   a. There is widespread consensus that current regulatory system does not work well enough
   b. Many are recommending merging the SEC and the CFTC, reflecting the blurred lines between securities and commodities

KEY TERMS

Bearer paper. A negotiable instrument that is payable to whomever possesses it.

Contract liability. When a party is responsible to pay the holder/HDC the face value of the instrument.

Draft. A type of negotiable instrument that contains an order to pay money. A draft has three parties: A drawer, a drawee, and the payee.

Drawer. The person who creates the draft and signs the draft on its face.

Drawee. The party that the drawer has instructed to pay the payee; typically this is the drawer's bank.

Endorsement. A signature, usually on the back of a negotiable instrument, by the payee or some other holder. The endorsement is **necessary** to further negotiate the instrument when the instrument is order paper.

Face value. The amount for which the instrument is payable.

Holder. A person who has possession of a negotiable instrument, and the instrument has all necessary endorsements.

Holder in due course (HDC). A holder with enhanced rights in the negotiable instrument. Those rights include the best claim of ownership, and HDC's claims for payment cannot be denied because of a personal defense.

Maker. The person who creates a note and has primary liability for its payment.

Negotiable. A characteristic of an instrument that means the instrument is freely transferable from one party to another.

Negotiation. The actual transfer of ownership of a negotiable instrument from one party to another. Negotiation can be accomplished by delivery alone if the instrument is bearer paper; if the instrument is order paper, then it must be transferred by delivery and the necessary endorsements.

Note. A two-party (the maker and payee) negotiable instrument that contains a promise to pay money.

Order paper. An instrument that is payable to a particular party.

Payee. The party to whom the negotiable instrument was originally payable.

Primary liability. The party from whom the holder/HDC of a negotiable instrument must first seek payment: the maker of a note or the acceptor of a draft.

Secondary liability. Parties who are liable to the holder/HDC if the primary party dishonors the instrument: endorsers and drawers.

Warranty liability. Responsibility to a holder/HDC to return the money actually paid for the negotiable instrument.

Module 29: Secured Transactions

Overview

The concept of secured transactions is important to modern business. A creditor often requires some security from the debtor beyond a mere promise to pay. In general, the creditor may require the debtor to provide some collateral to secure payment on the debt. The creditor then becomes known as a secured party because the debt repayment has additional assurance of collateral rather than just the mere promise to repay. If the debt is not paid, the creditor then can resort to the collateral. Under revised Article 9 of the UCC, the collateral is generally personal property or fixtures. You need to understand the concept of attachment as discussed in this module. You also need to understand the important concept of perfection discussed in this module that allows a secured party to obtain greater rights over many third parties. Be sure to understand the three methods by which perfection can be accomplished. The examination also covers rules of priorities when competing interests exist in the same collateral. Before beginning the reading you should review the key terms at the end of the module.

A. The Elements of Secured Transactions

1. The parties

    a. Secured party is the person/bank that provides credit to the debtor and takes an interest in the debtor's collateral to help assure repayment of the debt.

        (1) Debtor is entity (or person) that owes either payment or some specified performance to the secured party.
        (2) Security interest is legal interest in collateral that secures either payment or debtor's specified performance of some obligation
        (3) Security agreement is transaction that creates security interest

2. Types of collateral

    a. Goods: Moveable, tangible personal property, which is classified by the initial reason the debtor bought the goods (these classifications are very important)

        (1) Consumer goods are goods that were purchased for personal use
        (2) Equipment is goods that were purchased for use in a business
        (3) Inventory is goods that were purchased for sale or lease to a third party

> **EXAMPLE**
>
> Think of a computer. If I purchased a computer for use in my home, it is a consumer good. If I purchased a computer to use for my business, even if it is in my home, then the computer is equipment. If I purchased the computer to resell at my computer store, then it is inventory.

        (4) Fixtures are goods that have been attached permanently or relatively permanently to real property
        (5) Farm products are goods produced on a farm such as livestock or crops.

    b. Indispensible paper: Collateral evidenced by a writing

        (1) Instruments, which include negotiable instruments (see Module 28) as well as stock, bonds, and other investment securities.

    (2) Chattel paper is a writing that provides evidence of the monetary obligation and the security interest in the good. Basically, a piece of paper that recites the indebtedness.

    (3) Documents of title, such as bills of lading and warehouse receipts (This is discussed in more detail in Module 28, subsection M.)

  c. Intangibles include

    (1) Account, or account receivable

    (2) Commercial tort claim

    (3) General intangibles, includes anything else that may be considered collateral, such as intellectual property rights or goodwill.

3. The security agreement

  a. This is an agreement between the debtor and the creditor, which gives the creditor a security interest in the debtor's collateral.

  b. Requirements of a valid security agreement

    (1) The agreement must be in writing, unless the creditor has physical possession of the collateral (a pledge)

    (2) Must be signed by the debtor; creditor's signature is not required

    (3) A reasonable description of the collateral

B. Attachment of Security Interests

1. Attachment is a term used to describe the moment when security interest is enforceable against a debtor by the secured party

2. Security interest is said to attach when all of the following occur in any order (these are important)

  a. Secured party gives value (value is any consideration that supports any contract)

    (1) Preexisting claim (although not consideration) is value

> **EXAMPLE**
>
> D already owes S $5,000 on a previous debt. Subsequently, D signs a security agreement giving S an interest in some furniture owned by D. Value has been given by S based on the previous debt.

> **EXAMPLE**
>
> A bank grants a loan to allow B to purchase a washer and dryer. This extension of credit is a typical type of value.

  b. Debtor has rights in collateral

    (1) Debtor must have rights in collateral

      (a) Ownership interest suffices or having some right to possession of collateral but debtor is not required to have actual legal title

> **EXAMPLE**
>
> M obtains a loan from a bank to purchase a sofa. She signs a security agreement granting the credit union a security interest in any sofa that she will buy with this loan. Attachment cannot occur until she buys a sofa. Note that the other two elements of attachment have occurred.

  c. A valid security agreement (See A.3. above for requirements of security agreement) unless the secured party has a pledge (physical possession of the collateral)

> **NOW REVIEW MULTIPLE-CHOICE QUESTIONS 1 THROUGH 6 IN VOLUME 2**

C. Perfecting a Security Interest

1. Entails steps **in addition to** attachment (with one exception discussed later) to give secured party priority over many other parties that may claim collateral

    a. Attachment focuses primarily on rights between creditor and debtor

    b. Perfection, however, perfection focuses on rights between various **other parties** that may claim an interest in same collateral

        (1) Generally, perfecting a security interest gives (constructive) **notice to other parties** that the perfecting party claims an interest (security interest) in certain collateral

        (2) Only an attached security interest can be perfected

2. There are three primary ways that an attached security interest may be perfected—these are important

    a. Most security interests either can or must be perfected by filing financing statement(s) in the appropriate state office

    b. Secured party takes possession of collateral, or in certain cases takes control

    c. Automatic perfection can occur, but only with consumer goods

3. Depending on the type of collateral there may be only one or several ways to perfect

4. Perfection by filing financing statement(s)

    a. Financing statement requirements

        (1) Names of the debtor and the secured party

        (2) Indication of collateral covered; descriptions such as "all assets" are sufficient

        (3) Signatures are not required on a financing statement; the debtor's signature, however, is required on the security agreement, see A.3. above.

        (4) Minor errors in financing statement do not invalidate it if they are not seriously misleading

        (5) Law now allows that filing may be done either electronically or in writing

    b. Filings last for five years but can be continued with a continuation statement if filed within six months of expiration

    c. Financing statements can be refiled for each new five-year period

5. Perfection by secured party's possession or control of collateral

    a. Possession means actual physical possession of the collateral

---

EXAMPLE

Clint needed some cash so he took his saxophone to a pawnbroker. The pawnbroker loaned Clint $100 and took the saxophone as collateral.

---

    b. Control is similar to possession, but control applies to collateral that cannot be physically possessed (e.g., electronic documents of title, deposit accounts, or investment property)

    c. Secured party must use reasonable care to preserve collateral and may charge reasonable expenses to do so

6. Automatic perfection

    a. Under the following conditions, perfection is accomplished by completing attachment with no further steps

        (1) **Purchase money security interest in consumer goods**

            (a) Purchase money security interest (PMSI) occurs in two important cases

                1] Seller retains security interest in same item sold on credit to secure payment

                2] Another party such as bank provides loan for and retains security interest in same item purchased by debtor

            (b) "In consumer goods" means that goods are bought primarily for personal, family, or household purposes

---

EXAMPLE

B buys a refrigerator for his home from Friendly Appliance Dealer on credit. Friendly has B sign a written security agreement. Because all three elements needed for attachment took place, this is automatic perfection. This is true because the refrigerator is a purchase money security interest in consumer goods.

> **EXAMPLE**
>
> Same as previous example except that Second Intercity Bank provides the loan having B sign a security agreement. This is also a purchase money security interest in consumer goods. Perfection takes place when all three elements of attachment occur.

> **EXAMPLE**
>
> In the two examples above, if B had purchased the refrigerator for use in a restaurant, the collateral would be equipment. Therefore, automatic perfection would not occur. However, the secured party could file a financing statement to perfect the security interest in both cases.

    (2) PMSIs may arise in other goods such as equipment and inventory, but there is no automatic perfection in those goods because they are not consumer goods.

    (3) Perfection by attachment does not occur for motor vehicles, trailers, or both—perfected by a lien on certificate of title filed with state

        (a) Automatic perfection is **not** effective against bona fide purchaser for value who buys goods from consumer for consumer use

            1] **Is effective,** however, if secured party had **filed**

> **EXAMPLE**
>
> B purchases a washer and dryer from Dear Appliances for use in his home giving Dear a security interest, then sells the washer and dryer to C for a fair price for C's household use. C is unaware of the security interest that Dear has in the washer and dryer. Dear's PMSI is not effective against C.

> **EXAMPLE**
>
> Same example as above except that Dear had filed a financing statement. Dear wins because filing is effective even against a subsequent bona fide purchaser such as C even if he buys for consumer use.

> **EXAMPLE**
>
> In the two examples above, if C had purchased the items from B for other than consumer use, C is **not** free of Dear's security interest. This is so because the rule only applies to bona fide purchasers for consumer use. The extra step of filing would not be needed.

            2] **Is effective** if subsequent purchaser knows of security interest before buying

> **EXAMPLE**
>
> An appliance dealer sells a freezer to Jack for family use. Assume attachment has occurred. Jack then sells it to Cindy who is aware of the security interest that the dealer still has in the freezer. Even if Cindy is buying this for household use, she takes it subject to the security interest.

    (4) Sale of promissory notes

    (5) Assignment of health care insurance to health care provider

    (6) Temporary automatic perfection for twenty days for instruments, certificated securities, negotiable documents, and proceeds of sale of perfected security interest

D. Other Issues under Secured Transactions

  1. Security interests in goods acquired in the future

    a. An after-acquired property clause, sometimes referred to as a floating lien, allows the secured party to acquire a security interest in good that the debtor acquires in the future

      (1) Not permitted to be used on consumer goods

      (2) Typically used for inventory and equipment

> **EXAMPLE**
>
> Fred agreed to buy Billy's furniture store. Billy financed the sale himself and took a security interest in all current inventory and equipment and all after-acquired inventory and equipment. Bill filed a financing statement covering this transaction.
>
> Analysis: Billy has a perfected security interest in all current inventory and equipment. If and when Fred purchases additional furniture for resale or goods, such as a computer, for use in the store, then Fred will have a security interest in those goods as well.

2. Computer software embedded in goods is treated as part of those goods and not as software
3. Field warehousing is used to perfect security interest (analogous to possession or control)

   a. Debtor keeps inventory on his/her premises under control of third party such as bonded warehouseman or secured party's employee
   b. Secured party keeps control over inventory such as use of separate room or fenced-off portion with sign showing secured party's control

4. Consignments

   a. Consignment of security interest

      (1) If it is a "true consignment," consignee is simply a sales agent who does not own the goods but sells them for consignor

         (a) "True consignment" exists when

            1] Consignor retains title to goods
            2] Consignee has no obligation to buy goods
            3] Consignor has right to all proceeds (pays consignee commission)

> **EXAMPLE**
>
> Manufacturer (consignor) gives possession of goods to a marketing representative (consignee) to sell those goods on commission.

         (b) To perfect his/her interest, a consignor must

            1] File a financing statement under secured transactions law and give notice to the consignee's creditors who have perfected security interests in the same type of goods. Notice must contain description of the goods to be delivered and be given before the consignee receives possession of goods

> **EXAMPLE**
>
> P delivers goods to A on consignment. The consignment is a "true consignment" in that P has title to the goods and pays A a commission for selling the goods. Any goods that are unsold are returned by A to P. A does not pay for any unsold goods. Creditors of A can assert claims against the goods that A possesses unless P has given notice to the creditors. The general way to accomplish this is by filing a financial statement under the secured transactions law.

      (2) If transaction is not a true consignment because it is actually a **sale** from creditor to debtor in which debtor then owns the goods, look for a security agreement. Attachment and perfection occur as in typical secured transaction

NOW REVIEW MULTIPLE-CHOICE QUESTIONS 7 THROUGH 14 IN VOLUME 2

E. Priorities

1. If more than one party claims a security interest in same collateral, rules of priority should be examined. These rules determine which party has the best rights to the collateral. This is extremely important, both on the exam and in real life, because frequently the value of the collateral is insufficient to pay all creditors and the first creditor gets paid in full before the lower priority creditor receives anything.
2. A secured party will prevail over an unsecured party. Unsecured parties are usually referred to as general creditors.
3. If both parties are secured, then the following rules apply:

a. If neither party is perfected, then the interest that attached first prevails
b. A perfected party will prevail over an unperfected party
c. If both parties are perfected, then generally, the first interest that was perfected prevails.

   (1) A very important exception may arise if one of the party's perfected interests is a PMSI
   (2) A PMSI may take priority over all other security interests, even those security interests perfected prior to the PMSI.
   (3) For the PMSI to gain this "super priority" status certain rules must be followed; the rules vary depending on what type of goods the PMSI has perfected in
   (4) If the goods are equipment or consumer goods, then the PMSI party has 20 days after the debtor receives possession of the collateral to perfect the PMSI

       (a) If the PMSI party follows this rule, then it will prevail over other perfected security interests in the same collateral.

EXAMPLE

Fred agreed to buy Billy's furniture store. Billy financed the sale himself and took a security interest in all current inventory and equipment and all after-acquired inventory and equipment. Billy filed a financing statement covering this transaction on June 1, 2010. On May 29, 2011, Fred purchased and took delivery of a new computer from Mega for use at his store. Fred purchased the computer on credit and entered into a security agreement with Mega giving Mega a security interest in the computer that Fred had purchased. Mega filed a financing statement covering this transaction on June 10, 2011. If Fred defaults on his payments to Mega and Billy, who has priority to the recently purchased computer?

Analysis: Although Billy's security interest in after-acquired equipment arose first, Mega has a PMSI in the computer and perfected within the 20-day window, so Mega will prevail. If Mega had waited until June 25th to perfect its interest in the computer, Mega would have a PMSI, but would not gain the priority over Billy because Mega did not perfect within the 20-day window.

       (b) Technically the 20-day rule does apply to consumer goods, but the creditor with a PMSI in consumer goods does not need to file a financing statement since perfection occurs automatically.

   (5) If the goods are inventory, the PMSI party must perform two tasks to gain priority over earlier perfected interests:

       (a) Perfection must occur prior to or simultaneously to the debtor receiving the inventory

       NOTE: There is no 20-day window for inventory.

       (b) Written notice must be given to all holders of prior perfected security interests in the collateral

---

EXAMPLE

Fred agreed to buy Billy's furniture store. Billy financed the sale himself and took a security interest in all current inventory and equipment and all after-acquired inventory and equipment. Billy filed a financing statement covering this transaction on June 1, 2010. Fred purchased some furniture to resell in his store from Highpoint Furniture Corp. Highpoint sold the furniture to Fred on credit and took a PMSI in the furniture it sold Fred. If Highpoint wants to get priority over Billy's earlier perfected interest on future inventory, Highpoint must provide written notice to Billy of its PMSI and perfect its interest in the furniture. Both tasks must be performed prior to the furniture being delivered to Fred.

---

4. Secured creditors versus subsequent buyers of collateral

   a. Buyers in the ordinary course of business take free of any security interest whether perfected or not (be sure to know this one)

      (1) In general, buying in the ordinary course of business means buying from inventory of a person or company that normally deals in those goods
      (2) Buyer has priority even if s/he knows that security agreement exists but buyer must have possession
      (3) Purpose is to allow purchasers to buy from merchants without fear of security agreements between merchants and other parties

---

EXAMPLE

S, a dealer in stereos, obtained financing from L by securing the loan with her inventory in stereos. B purchases one of the stereos from that inventory. B takes the stereo free of the security interest that L has in the inventory of S whether it is perfected or not.

---

   b. Distinguish between buyers in the ordinary course of business and the subsequent bona fide purchaser from consumers

   (1) The latter defeats only a purchase money security interest in consumer goods (perfection on attachment) unless filing takes place—applies to sale by consumer to consumer

   (2) The former applies whether buyer is consumer or not but seller is dealer in those goods

---

EXAMPLE

See previous example. The result is the same whether or not B was a consumer when he bought the stereo in the ordinary course of business from S.

EXAMPLE

Refer again to the same example using S, L, and B. Now let's add on one more security interest in that B is buying the stereo on credit from S and for his own personal use. Attachment has occurred. There is perfection by attachment because between B and S, it is a purchase money security interest in consumer goods. If B sells the stereo to N, his neighbor, for consumer use, then N takes the stereo free of the perfected security interest (unless S had filed or N had notice of the security interest).

---

5. Secured creditors versus other creditors

   a. Possessor of negotiable document of title has priority over other creditors

   b. Lien creditor (e.g., repairman or contractor)

   (1) Has priority over an unperfected security interest

      (a) Knowledge of security interest is immaterial

   (2) Has priority over a security interest perfected after attachment of the lien unless it is a purchase money security interest perfected within the 20-day grace period

   (3) A security interest perfected before the lien usually has priority

   c. Trustee in bankruptcy as a lien creditor

   (1) Trustee has the rights of a lien creditor from the date of filing of petition in bankruptcy

      (a) So has priority over a security interest perfected after date of filing petition unless it is a purchase money security interest perfected within the 20-day grace period

   (2) Trustee also takes the position of any existing lien creditor

   (3) A security interest perfected before the bankruptcy trustee usually has priority

---

NOW REVIEW MULTIPLE-CHOICE QUESTIONS 15 THROUGH 24 IN VOLUME 2

F. Rights of Parties upon Default

1. If collateral consists of claims (e.g., receivables), the secured party has the right of collection from third parties

   a. Secured party may notify third party to pay secured party directly

   b. Secured party must account for any surplus and debtor is liable for any deficiency

   c. Secured party may deduct his/her reasonable expenses

2. Secured party may retain collateral already in his/her possession or may take possession or control from debtor

   a. May do so him/herself if s/he can without breach of the peace. Breaching the peace means violating the law. Typically the issue is trespass, in other words, secured party may not trespass to repossess the collateral.

   b. Otherwise, s/he must use judicial process to foreclose on collateral

   c. Secured party has duty to take reasonable care of collateral in his/her possession

       (1) Expenses to protect collateral are responsibility of debtor

3. If secured party proposes to satisfy obligation by retaining the collateral, s/he must

    a. Send written notice to debtor

    b. Must notify other secured parties (who have sent written notice of their interest), unless consumer goods

    c. Can only retain consumer goods if debtor has paid less than 60% of the purchase price or obligation

       (1) If 60% or more has been paid for a PMSI in consumer goods, secured party must sell collateral within ninety days after taking possession or be liable to the debtor unless debtor waives this right to sale **after** the default

4. Secured party may sell collateral

    a. May be a public or a private sale

    b. Must use commercially reasonable practices—this right cannot be waived by debtor

    c. Must sell within a reasonable time

    d. Must notify debtor of time and place of public sale or time after which private sale will occur unless collateral is perishable, threatens to decline in value, or is type sold on a recognized market

       (1) Must also notify other secured parties (who have sent written notice of their interest) unless collateral consists of consumer goods

    e. Secured party may buy at any public sale and also at a private sale if rights of debtor protected

    f. Distribution of the sale proceeds. The following are paid in order, with each level paid in full before any money is distributed to the next level.

       (1) Secured party's expenses
       (2) Secured part's debt
       (3) Junior security interests
       (4) Any remainder to the debtor

5. Debtor has right to redeem collateral before secured party disposes of it by paying

    a. Entire debt, and
    b. Secured party's reasonable expenses

6. Most remedies can be varied by agreement if reasonable

    a. Provision that secured party must account for any surplus to debtor cannot be varied by agreement

7. Good-faith purchaser (i.e., for value and with no knowledge of defects in sale) of collateral takes free of debtor's rights and any secured interest or lien subordinate to it

    a. Receives debtor's title
    b. If sale was improper, remedy of debtor is money damages against secured party who sold collateral, not against good-faith purchaser

NOW REVIEW MULTIPLE-CHOICE QUESTIONS 25 THROUGH 30 IN VOLUME 2

G. Other Rights of Parties

1. Debtor has right to request that creditor show proof of unpaid debt or request that creditor correct incorrect filings on collateral

    a. Creditor must either show that debt or filing is correct or make correction

2. When debtor pays debt in full, s/he has right to termination statement of creditor which creditor files or in some cases provides to debtor

    a. This provides notice that earlier filing has been satisfied

3. After expenses are paid for repossessing collateral, storage, and reselling collateral, excess proceeds go to secured party, then to other lien holders

KEY TERMS

   Attachment. When the secured party's security interest becomes enforceable against the debtor.

   Collateral. Property that is subject to a security interest. It is used to help assure a secured party that the debt will be repaid.

   Consumer goods. A type of collateral that was purchased for personal use.

   Debtor. The party in a secured transaction who owes an obligation to the secured party.

   Default. When the debtor fails to make scheduled payment to a secured party. When this occurs it allows the secured party to take action against the collateral.

   Equipment. A type of collateral that was purchased for a business use.

   Financing statement. A document filed with the state government that perfects security interest in collateral

   Floating lien. A security interest in the future inventory or equipment that the debtor acquires.

   Inventory. A type of collateral that was purchased for resale.

   Perfection. When the secured party's security interest is enforceable against third parties. Perfection cannot occur before attachment.

   Pledge. When the secured party perfects by taking possession of the collateral.

   Purchase money security interest (PMSI). Arises when the secured party extends credit to the debtor to purchase a specific good. The secured party takes a security interest in that specific good.

   Secured party. A creditor who receives a promise from a debtor to repay a debt and the debtor also provides collateral to assure repayment of the debt.

   Security agreement. The contact between the debtor and secured party, which creates a security interest in the collateral.

   Security interest. The interest in the collateral that helps to assure repayment of the debt.

Module 30: Bankruptcy

Overview

The overall objective of bankruptcy law is to allow honest insolvent debtors to surrender most of their assets and obtain release from their debts. A secondary purpose is to give creditors fair opportunity to share in the debtor's limited assets in proportion to their claims.

Bankruptcy questions normally emphasize when involuntary and voluntary proceedings can be conducted, the federal exemptions, the role of the trustee in bankruptcy, preferential transfers, priorities of the creditors, and conditions under which debts may be discharged in bankruptcy. Although bankruptcy under Chapter 7 is emphasized on the CPA examination, you should also be familiar with the other portions of this module. Recently, for example, Chapter 11 on Business Reorganizations has received some increased treatment. Before beginning the reading you should review the key terms at the end of the module.

> **NOTE:** Various dollar amounts in this module have been increased so the dollar amounts in various textbooks may be too low under current bankruptcy law.

A. Alternatives to Bankruptcy Proceedings

1. Creditors may choose to do nothing

   a. Expense of collection may exceed what creditors could recover
   b. Creditors may expect debtor to pull through

2. Creditors may rush to satisfy their claims individually through legal proceedings (i.e., legal judgments, garnishing of wages, etc.; these are discussed in more detail in Module 31.)

   a. Bankruptcy proceedings may result anyway, especially if some creditors are dissatisfied

3. Receiverships

   a. This provides for general administration of debtor's assets by a court appointee (a receiver) for benefit of all parties; these are discussed in more detail in Module 31.

4. Agreements can be used to avoid bankruptcy such as composition agreements with creditors whereby creditors agree to accept less; these are discussed in more detail in Module 31.

   a. Creditors who do not agree may force debtor into bankruptcy

B. Bankruptcy in General

1. Bankruptcy is based mostly on federal law
2. Bankruptcy provides a method of protecting creditors' rights and granting the debtor relief from his/her indebtedness

   a. Debtor is permitted to have a fresh start free of previous debt.
   b. Creditors are treated more fairly according to the priorities stated in bankruptcy laws to effect an equitable distribution of debtor's property

C. Types of Bankruptcy

1. Chapter 7

    a. Liquidation: Turning the majority of the debtor's assets into cash to pay debts

    b. Subject to the conditions discussed below; any debtor may file for Chapter 7 **except:**

        (1) Railroads

        (2) Banking institutions

        (3) Insurance companies

  2. Chapter 11

    a. Reorganization of debts

    b. Usually businesses who do not want to liquidate choose Chapter 11, but most debtors who qualify for Chapter 7 bankruptcy qualify for Chapter 11

        (1) Railroads may file under Chapter 11

        (2) Stockbrokers and commodity brokers are not eligible for Chapter 11

  3. Chapter 13

    a. Reorganization of debts primarily for individuals

    b. Similar to Chapter 11, but more streamlined

D. Filing the Bankruptcy Petition

  1. Filing the petition stays most other legal proceedings

    a. This effectively stops creditors, current and future, from pursuing claims against the debtor, except in bankruptcy court.

    b. A stay does not apply to actions concerning paternity, alimony, or child support (i.e., those matters may be pursued outside the bankruptcy court).

  2. Educational requirements

    a. Consumer filers must receive credit counseling from an approved agency within 180 days prior to filing the petition.

        (1) Failure to obtain a certificate of completion from counseling agency will result in a dismissal of the bankruptcy petition

        (2) Does not apply to debtors who are incapacitated, disabled, or on active duty in a military zone

    b. Consumers seeking a discharge of their debts, under either Chapter 7 or 13, must also attend an approval financial management course or their discharge will be denied.

E. Chapter 7 Voluntary Bankruptcy Petitions

  1. Voluntary bankruptcy petition is a formal request by debtor for an order of relief

    a. Petition is filed with court along with list of debtor's assets and liabilities

    b. Debtor is automatically given an order of relief upon filing of petition

    c. The Bankruptcy Abuse and Protection Act of 2005 imposes criteria that a consumer debtor must meet to prove that the debtor is not abusing the Bankruptcy Code. In other words, the law is trying to assure that debtors with the ability to repay their debts are not declaring bankruptcy.

        (1) The law presumes abuse unless the debtor's monthly income exceeds certain dollar limits. The law does permit the deduction of monthly living expenses when calculating monthly income.

        (2) Other special circumstances such as a medical conditions or service in the armed forces will be considered.

        (3) If the debtor's income exceeds the statutory amount and the debtor is unable to remove the presumption of abuse, the debtor may proceed under Chapter 13 instead.

    d. Petition may be filed by husband and wife jointly

  2. There is no minimum number of creditors required to file for bankruptcy

> **NOW REVIEW MULTIPLE-CHOICE QUESTIONS 1 THROUGH 4 IN VOLUME 2**

F. Chapter 7 Involuntary Bankruptcy Petitions

  1. Involuntary bankruptcy petition may be filed with bankruptcy court by creditors requesting an order for relief

  2. Requirements to file petition

a. If there are fewer than twelve creditors, a single creditor may file the petition as long as his/her claim aggregates $14,425 in excess of any security s/he may hold

   (1) Claims must be undisputed
   (2) If necessary, more than one creditor may join together to have combined debts of more than $14,425 of unsecured claims

> **EXAMPLE**
>
> Poor-R-Us Company is not paying its debts as they become due. Its creditors are A (owed $15,000), B (owed $8,000), and C (owed $10,000). A alone may file the involuntary petition to force the company into bankruptcy; however, if A does not wish to do so, neither B nor C **separately** may force the company into bankruptcy because of failure to meet the $14,425 test. B and C may join together to file the petition.

> **EXAMPLE**
>
> XYZ Corporation is unable to pay current obligations. XYZ has three creditors: L (owed $15,000 which is secured by personal property), M (owed $30,000 of which one-half is secured), and N (owed $16,000 of which none is secured). L may not file an involuntary bankruptcy petition but can use the personal property to pay off the debt. Either M or N can file the petition.

> **EXAMPLE**
>
> Trump Inc. is not paying its debts as they become due. Trump has two creditors: Hart and Diamond. Hart claims Trump owes him $18,000, while Diamond claims she is owed $6,000. Trump admits to owing Diamond $6,000, but in good faith claims to owe Hart $12,000. Hart cannot force Trump into bankruptcy by himself. The bankruptcy court will only count the $12,000 toward the $14,425 because that amount is not in dispute. If Hart wants to force Trump into bankruptcy Hart must get Diamond to join the petition.

b. If there are twelve or more creditors, then at least three must sign the petition and they must have claims that aggregate $14,425 in excess of any security held by them

   (1) Claims must be undisputed
   (2) Claims subject to bona fide dispute are not counted in above $14,425 tests

> **EXAMPLE**
>
> Poor, Inc. is unable to meet its current obligations as they are becoming due because of severe business difficulties. It owes over $20,000 to a dozen different creditors. One of the unsecured creditors, Green, is owed $15,000. Green may not force Poor, Inc. into Chapter 7 bankruptcy because even though Green is owed more than $14,425, Green must be joined by two other creditors, even if their claims are very small.

> **EXAMPLE**
>
> Same facts as above except that Poor, Inc. has only eleven creditors. Now Green alone may force Poor, Inc. into bankruptcy under Chapter 7.

c. Creditors who file petition in bankruptcy may need to post a bond that indemnifies debtor for losses caused by contesting petition to avoid frivolous petitions

   (1) Bankruptcy court may award damages including attorneys' fees to debtor who successfully challenges involuntary bankruptcy petition against creditors filing petition
   (2) If petition was made in bad faith, punitive damages may also be awarded

3. Exempt from involuntary bankruptcy are

   a. Persons (individuals, partnerships, or corporations) owing less than $14,425
   b. Farmers
   c. Charitable organizations

4. Bankruptcy not available for deceased person's estate, but once bankruptcy has begun, it is not stopped if bankrupt (debtor) dies
5. An order for relief will be granted if the requirements for filing are met, and

   a. The petition is uncontested; or
   b. The petition is contested; and

      (1) The debtor is generally not paying his/her debts as they become due; or
      (2) During the 120 days preceding the filing of the petition, a custodian was appointed or took possession of substantially all of the property of the debtor

---

EXAMPLE

Debtor assigns his property for the benefit of his creditor.

---

   c. Note that the above rules involve a modified insolvency in the "equity sense" (i.e., debtor not paying debts as they become due). The rest of the Bankruptcy Act uses insolvency in the "bankruptcy sense" (i.e., liabilities exceed fair market value of all nonexempt assets). The use of insolvency in the equity sense for involuntary proceedings is important.

NOW REVIEW MULTIPLE-CHOICE QUESTIONS 5 THROUGH 10 IN VOLUME 2

G. Chapter 7 Bankruptcy Proceedings (also called a liquidation or straight bankruptcy)

1. Take place under federal law

   a. An order of relief is sought
   b. Court appoints interim trustee
   c. Filing petition automatically stays other legal proceedings against debtor's estate until bankruptcy case is over or until court orders otherwise
   d. Debtor may regain property in possession of interim trustee by filing court approved bond

---

EXAMPLE

Mortgage foreclosure by savings and loan will be suspended against debtor.

---

2. First creditors' meeting

   a. Debtor furnishes a schedule of assets, their locations, and a list of creditors
   b. Claims of debtors are deemed allowed unless objected to, in which case the court will determine their validity

      (1) Claims must be filed within six months of first creditors' meeting
      (2) Contingent and unliquidated claims are estimated
      (3) Any attorneys' fees above those ruled reasonable by court are disallowed when objected to by creditors

   c. Trustee may be elected by creditors in Chapter 7 proceeding

      (1) If no election requested by creditors, interim trustee appointed by court continues in office

3. Trustee—the representative of the estate

   a. Trustee has right to receive compensation for services rendered based on value of those services (rather than only on size of estate)
   b. Duties—to collect, liquidate, and distribute the estate, keeping accurate records of all transactions
   c. Trustee represents estate of bankrupt (debtor)

4. Property of the estate

   a. Property presently owned by debtor as of the filing date
   b. Property owed to debtor by third parties that can be recovered by trustee
   c. Property acquired by the estate after the filing date of the petition is generally not part of the estate. The following are exceptions to this rule; thus the following are included in the estate:

> **EXAMPLE**
>
> Mitch filed Chapter 7 bankruptcy on April 1. Mitch received a paycheck on April 15; the paycheck is not part of the estate.

(1) Property received by debtor within 180 days after filing of petition by following methods: inheritance, life insurance, property settlement with spouse

> **EXAMPLE**
>
> Mitch filed Chapter 7 bankruptcy on April 1. Mitch received an inheritance of $5,000 on June 1, when his aunt dies unexpectedly. The $5,000 is part of the estate.

(2) Income from property owned by estate after petition is filed

> **EXAMPLE**
>
> Mitch filed Chapter 7 bankruptcy on April 1. Mitch received a royalty check of $400 from a book he had published the previous January. The $400 is part of the estate.

5. Exempt property: Property that does not go to the estate

   a. Keeps any interests in joint tenancy property if those interests are exempt under other nonbankruptcy law, and
   b. Debtor usually has option of choosing either exemptions under state law or exemptions under the Bankruptcy Code
   c. The Examiners expect you to be familiar with the Bankruptcy Code exemptions; the dollar amounts for this area are generally not tested.

      (1) $21,625 equity in principal residence including co-op or mobile home
      (2) $3,450 equity in one motor vehicle
      (3) $2,175 in books and tools of one's trade
      (4) $550 per item qualifying for personal, family, or home use (has an aggregate ceiling of $11,525)
      (5) $1,450 in jewelry
      (6) Life insurance with accrued dividends and interest to $11,525
      (7) Unmatured life insurance contracts
      (8) Social security benefits
      (9) Unemployment compensation
      (10) Disability, illness, or unemployment benefits
      (11) Alimony and child support
      (12) Veteran's benefits
      (13) Prescribed health aids
      (14) Public assistance
      (15) Pensions and retirement benefits needed for support and ERISA qualified
      (16) Lost earnings payments
      (17) Wrongful death payments that bankrupted party depended on
      (18) Wages up to maximum of specified formula (75% of person's disposable income or 30 times federal minimum wage
      (19) Crime victim's compensation
      (20) Interest in any property not to exceed $1,150 plus $10,825 of any unused portion of the homestead exemption (item [1] above); can be used to protect any type of property including cash
      (21) Specified personal injury awards up to $21,625 (not to include pain and suffering or monetary loss)

   d. Above exemptions doubled for married couples

6. Duties of trustee under Chapter 7 bankruptcy (i.e., a liquidation)

   a. In general, to liquidate and sell assets owned to pay creditors based on priorities discussed later and to examine propriety of claims brought by creditors

      (1) Considers how best to sell, use, or lease property of estate to act in best interest of estate
      (2) Acquires all legal assets owed to estate for equitable distribution to creditors
      (3) Trustee makes interim reports and presents final accounting of the administration of the estate to the court

7. Powers of trustee

   a. Trustee may take any legal action necessary to carry out duties

      (1) Trustee may utilize any defense available to the debtor against third parties
      (2) Trustee may continue or cease any legal action started by the debtor for the benefit of the estate

   b. Trustee, with court approval, may employ professionals (e.g., accountants and lawyers) to assist trustee in carrying out duties that require professional expertise

      (1) Employed professional must not hold any interest adverse to that of debtor (i.e., to avoid conflicts of interest)
      (2) Employed professional has right to receive compensation for reasonable value of services performed

         (a) Reasonable fee is based on amount and complexity of services rendered, not on size of estate

      (3) Trustee, with court approval, may act in professional capacity if capable and be compensated separately for professional services rendered

   c. Trustee must within sixty days of the order for relief assume or reject any executory contract, including leases, made by the debtor

      (1) Any not assumed are deemed rejected
      (2) Trustee must perform all obligations on lease of nonresidential property until lease is either assumed or rejected
      (3) Rejection of a contract is a breach of contract and injured party may become an unsecured creditor
      (4) Trustee may assign or retain leases if good for bankrupt's estate and if allowed under lease and state law
      (5) Rejection or assumption of lease is subject to court approval

   d. Trustee may set aside liens (those which arise automatically under law) if lien

      (1) Becomes effective when bankruptcy petition is filed or when debtor becomes insolvent
      (2) Is not enforceable against a bona fide purchaser when the petition is filed
      (3) In the case of a security interest, is not perfected before filing of bankruptcy petition

   e. Trustee **may set aside transfers made within one year prior** to the filing of the bankruptcy petition if

      (1) The transfer was made with intent to hinder, delay, or defraud any creditor. The debtor need not be insolvent at time of transfer.
      (2) Debtor received less than a reasonably equivalent value in exchange for such transfer or obligation and the debtor was insolvent at the time, or became insolvent as a result of the transfer

   f. Trustee may also set aside preferential transfers of nonexempt property to a creditor made within the **previous ninety days** prior to the filing of the petition

      (1) Preferential transfers are those made for **preexisting debts** that enable the creditor to receive more than s/he would have otherwise under a Chapter 7 liquidation proceeding

         (a) Includes a security interest given by debtor to secure antecedent debt

---

EXAMPLE

Debtor paid off a loan, before the loan was due, to BB Bank sixty days before Debtor filed a bankruptcy petition. This is a preferential transfer.

EXAMPLE

Debtor gave CC Bank a security interest in some office furniture he owns to secure a previous loan CC Bank had granted him. This is a preferential transfer if Debtor gave the security interest within ninety days of the filing of bankruptcy. The reason for this is that it gives the creditor (bank) greater rights than it had before.

EXAMPLE

Debtor prepaid some installments on an installment loan on equipment. This is also a preferential transfer.

---

(2) Preferential transfers **made to insiders** within the **previous twelve months** may be set aside

    (a) Insiders are close blood relatives, officers, directors, controlling stockholders of corporations, or general partners of partnerships

> **EXAMPLE**
>
> S is a secured creditor of XYZ Co. that is in Chapter 7 bankruptcy. S is not an insider.

> **EXAMPLE**
>
> One year ago Herb purchased a car on credit from Ike. Thirty days before filing for bankruptcy, Herb, while insolvent, makes a payment to Ike concerning the auto. This is a preferential transfer. If Ike were Herb's brother, this preference could have been set aside if it had occurred, for example, 120 days before the filing of the petition while Herb was insolvent (insider preference).

(3) Exceptions to trustee's power to avoid preferential transfers

    (a) A contemporaneous exchange between creditor and debtor whereby debtor receives new value

> **EXAMPLE**
>
> Herb, while insolvent, purchases a car for cash from Ike within ninety days of filing a petition in bankruptcy. The trustee could not avoid this transaction because Herb, the debtor, received present (i.e., contemporaneous) value (the car) for the cash transferred to Ike, the creditor. This is not a voidable preference.

    (b) Transfer made in the ordinary course of business is not a voidable preference, nor is the perfected security interest that arises from it (if filed within forty-five days of creation of that debt)

> **EXAMPLE**
>
> Debtor pays the utility bill for the business.

    (c) A security interest given by debtor to acquire property that is perfected within ten days after such security interest attaches

    (d) Consumer debts less than $600

    (e) Business debts less than $5,850

  g. When the bankruptcy trustee sets aside a transaction, the trustee places the parties back in their original positions.

> **EXAMPLE**
>
> Rhonda "sells" her car to her sister for $200. The car had a fair market value of $10,000. Two weeks later Rhonda declares bankruptcy. The trustee will set the aforementioned transaction aside. As a result, the estate will get the car and Rhonda's sister will get back her $200.

8. Trustee may be sued or sue on behalf of estate

NOW REVIEW MULTIPLE-CHOICE QUESTIONS 11 THROUGH 17 IN VOLUME 2

H. Claims

1. Property rights—where claimant has a property right, property is turned over to claimant, because not considered part of debtor's estate

  a. Reclamation is a claim against specific property by a person claiming it to be his/hers

> **EXAMPLE**
>
> A person rented a truck for a week and in the meantime he becomes bankrupt. The lessor will make a reclamation.

    b. Trust claim is made by beneficiary for trust property when the trustee is bankrupt

> **EXAMPLE**
>
> Trustee maintains a trust account for beneficiary under a trust set up in a will. Trustee becomes bankrupt. The trust account is not part of trustee's estate. The beneficiary may claim the trust account as his property.

    c. Secured claim when creditor has a security interest (e.g., mortgage in property or security interest under UCC)

       (1) As long as trustee does not successfully attack the security—basically, security interest must be without defects to prevail against trustee (i.e., perfected security interests)

       (2) Secured status may be achieved by subrogation (e.g., surety is subrogated to creditor's collateral)

    d. Setoffs are allowed to the extent the bankrupt and creditor have mutual debts whether unsecured or not

2. Filing of claims

    a. All claims must be filed within six months after the first creditors' meeting

3. Proof of claims

    a. Timely claims are deemed allowed unless creditor objects

       (1) Contingent and unliquidated claims may be estimated

    b. Claims below are not allowed if an objection is made

       (1) Unenforceable claims (by law or agreement)

       (2) Unmatured interest as of date of filing bankruptcy petition

       (3) Claims that may be offset

       (4) Property tax claim in excess of the property value

       (5) Insider or attorney claims in excess of reasonable value of services as determined by court

       (6) Alimony, maintenance, and support claims for amounts due after bankruptcy petition is filed (they are not dischargeable)

       (7) Landlord's damages for lease termination in excess of specified amounts

       (8) Damages for termination of an employment contract in excess of one year's wages

       (9) Certain employment tax claims

I. Priority of Claims (be sure to know)

1. Secured creditors

    a. Technically, they are not a part of the priorities because they never become part of the bankrupt estate. Valid security interests though, perfected prior to the filing of the bankruptcy petition, supersede the bankruptcy trustee's interest. Therefore, these secured creditors' claims must be satisfied first to see if there are any assets left over for the bankruptcy estate.

       (1) If the value of the collateral is sufficient to pay off the secured party, then any excess will go to junior secured parties. If there is any money left after all secured parties are paid, then the trustee may use that money as part of the estate to pay the general creditors (discussed below).

       (2) If the value of the collateral is insufficient to satisfy the claim of the secured party, the secured party will receive the money from the collateral and the remaining debt that the secured party is owed will be treated as a general obligation.

       (3) The secured party must have a security interest in the specific collateral or the secured party has no priority to the collateral.

> **EXAMPLE**
>
> Sandy Clause Corp., a toy wholesaler, was petitioned involuntarily into bankruptcy under Chapter 7 of the Federal Bankruptcy Code on July 21, 2011. Keebler Inc., has a perfected PMSI in some toys that it has sold to Clause. Clause owes Keebler $30,000 and has not been paying Keebler or its others creditors' debts as

> they have become due. When Clause's assets were liquidated the toys were sold for $40,000. Keebler will be paid in full; the extra $10,000 will go to the bankruptcy trustee and be used to pay the general creditors.

EXAMPLE

Same facts as above except the toys are only sold for $25,000. Keebler will receive the $25,000. Keebler will be treated as a nonpriority general creditor for the remaining $5,000 it is owed.

---

2. Unsecured creditors' (general creditors) claims are paid in full at each level of priority before any lower level is paid. If there are insufficient assets to pay any given level, then assets are prorated at that level and the next levels receive nothing.

    a. Priority general creditors

        (1) Domestic support obligations (e.g., child support, alimony)
        (2) Administration costs

            (a) Includes fees to accountants, attorneys, trustees, and appraisers as well as expenses incurred only in recovering, preserving, selling, or discovering property that should be included in debtor's estate

---

EXAMPLE

Bee, Ware, and Watch, a partnership of CPAs, performed professional services for Dee-Funct Company before it was forced into bankruptcy by its creditors. These fees are not put in the first priority but the last because they do not qualify as administration costs.

            (b) Also includes reasonable fees, salary, or wages needed for services such as operating the business after the bankruptcy action begins

        (3) Claims arising in ordinary course of debtor's business after involuntary bankruptcy petition is filed but before order for relief is entered
        (4) Wages, salaries, and commissions, including vacation, severance, and sick leave owing to bankrupt's employees up to $11,725 per employee earned within 180 days before the petition in bankruptcy was filed (or cessation of business, whichever occurred first)

            (a) Any amount earned in excess of $11,725 is treated as a general claim as explained in (11) below
            (b) This priority does not include officers' salaries

        (5) Contributions to employee benefit plans within the prior 180 days, limited to $11,725 per employee, reduced by amount received as wage preference
        (6) Claims on storage of grain or fish up to $5,775 for each individual
        (7) Consumer deposits for undelivered goods or services limited to $2,600 per individual

---

EXAMPLE

Mary placed a $3,000 deposit for a $10,000 wedding dress at Barb's Bridal Boutique. Before the dress was delivered Barb declared bankruptcy. Mary's claim for $2,600 would fall at this level; the remaining $400 will fall to the nonpriority general creditor group below.

---

        (8) Taxes (federal, state, and local)
        (9) Obligations to an insured bank
      (10) Debts arising from motor vehicle accidents while under the influence of drugs or alcohol
      (11) General (unsecured) creditors that filed timely proofs of claims

            (a) Includes amounts owed to secured creditors in excess of amount for which security sells
            (b) Includes amounts owed to priority general creditors that exceed the priority amount
            (c) Unsecured claims filed late (unless excused) are paid after timely claims

NOW REVIEW MULTIPLE-CHOICE QUESTIONS 18 THROUGH 19 IN VOLUME 2

J. Discharge of the Debtor

1. A discharge is the release of a debtor from all his/her debts not paid in bankruptcy; the debtor has no further obligation even for the debts that were not paid at all or partially paid
2. Creditors not paid are prohibited from any further debt collection on the discharged debts.
3. There are, however, some **nondischargeable debts,** which are discussed in detail below
4. Debtor must be an individual to be discharged

   a. Business organizations do not receive a discharge because they no longer exist; all of their assets have been liquidated.
   b. Conversely, debtors need to be discharged to get a fresh start.

5. Debtor must be adjudged an "honest debtor" to be discharged
6. Discharge will only be granted once every 8 years
7. Acts that bar discharge of **all** debts

   a. Improper actions during bankruptcy proceeding

      (1) Making false claims against the estate
      (2) Concealing property
      (3) Transfer of property after filing with intent to defeat the law (i.e., fraudulent transfer)
      (4) Making any false entry in or on any document of account relating to bankrupt's affairs
      (5) These acts are also punishable by fines and imprisonment

   b. Failing to satisfactorily explain any loss of assets
   c. Refusing to obey court orders
   d. Removing or destroying property within twelve months prior to filing of petition with intent to hinder, delay, or defraud any creditor
   e. Destroying, falsifying, concealing, or failing to keep books of account or records unless such act is justified under the circumstances
   f. "Substantial abuse" of bankruptcy by individual debtor with primarily consumer debts
   g. A preferential transfer does **not** bar discharge (but can be set aside)

K. Debts Not Discharged by Bankruptcy (even though general discharge allowed)

1. Taxes within three years of filing bankruptcy petition
2. Loans for payment of federal taxes
3. Unscheduled debts unless creditor had actual notice of proceedings (i.e., where bankrupt failed to list creditor and debt)

EXAMPLE

In a petition in bankruptcy, a mistake was made so that a debt owed to ABC Company was listed as owed to XYZ Company. The debt to ABC is not discharged unless ABC somehow was aware of the mistake.

---

4. Alimony, separate maintenance, or child support
5. Liability due to theft or embezzlement
6. Debts arising from debtor's fraud about his/her financial condition or fraud in connection with purchase or sale of securities

---

EXAMPLE

Obtaining credit using false information such as materially fraudulent financial statements that the creditor relied on.

---

7. Willful and/or malicious injuries to a person or property of another (intentional torts)

   a. Unintentional torts (i.e., negligence) and breaches of contract are dischargeable

8. Congress amended Bankruptcy Code making it more difficult for student loans to be discharged in bankruptcy

   a. This was prompted because many students have had large student loans to pay for tuition and living expenses

      (1) Upon graduation some students have few assets and may be inclined to file for bankruptcy trying to get student loans discharged

b. Student loans are defined by bankruptcy code to include those loans made or guaranteed by units of government

   (1) Recent additions include loans for students made also by nongovernmental commercial institutions such as banks

      (a) Also includes stipends, scholarships or benefits given by educational institutions

c. Bankruptcy Code now provides that student loans can be discharged in cases of "undue hardship" to debtor and any dependants

   (1) "Undue hardship" is defined very strictly so s/he needs to basically show payment would negate payment of basic necessities of food or shelter

   (2) Cosigners such as parents who guarantee family member's student loan must meet same "undue hardship" test to discharge obligation

9. Governmental fines or penalties imposed within prior three years
10. Those from a prior bankruptcy proceeding in which the debtor waived discharge or was denied discharge
11. Liability incurred by operating any vehicle, vessel or aircraft while legally intoxicated
12. To avoid the practice of "loading up on luxury goods" before bankruptcy, there is a presumption of non-dischargeability for

   a. Consumer debts to a single debtor under specified conditions for luxury goods or services made within 60 days of filing

   b. Certain cash advances based on consumer credit taken within 60 days of filing

13. Any debt from violation of securities laws including those under Sarbanes-Oxley Act
14. Sarbanes-Oxley Act makes it criminal for any person to intentionally falsify, destroy, or cover up records intending to influence proper investigation or administration of matters involving bankruptcy cases
15. Debts owed to pension plans, profit sharing plans or similar employee plans
16. Homeowner association, condo, or cooperative fees

L. Revocation of Discharge

1. Discharge may be revoked if

   a. Bankrupt committed fraud during bankruptcy proceedings unknown to creditors seeking revocation

   > **EXAMPLE**
   >
   > A bankrupt conceals assets in order to defraud creditors.

      (1) Must be applied for within one year of discharge

   b. Bankrupt acquired rights or title to property of estate and fraudulently failed to report this

   c. Bankrupt refused to obey lawful court order or refused to testify when not in violation of his/her constitutional right against self-incrimination

M. Reaffirmation

1. Debtor promises to pay a debt that will be discharged. The Code makes it difficult to reaffirm dischargeable debt.

   a. To be enforceable, reaffirmation of dischargeable debt must satisfy the following conditions:

      (1) Reaffirmation must take place before discharge granted
      (2) Must be approved by bankruptcy court
      (3) Debtor is allowed sixty days to rescind reaffirmation once agreed to

         (a) Debtor must have received appropriate warnings from the court or attorney on effects of reaffirmation, and

         (b) If also involves consumer debt not secured by real property, court must approve new agreement as being in best interests of debtor and not imposing undue hardship on debtor

NOW REVIEW MULTIPLE-CHOICE QUESTIONS 20 THROUGH 26 IN VOLUME 2

N. Business Reorganization—Chapter 11

1. Goal is to keep financially troubled firm in business

    a. It is an alternative to liquidation under Chapter 7 (straight bankruptcy)

    b. In general, allows debtor to keep assets of business

2. Can be initiated by debtor (voluntary) or creditors (involuntary)

    a. Available to individuals, partnerships, or corporations including railroads. Other entities ineligible to be debtors under Chapter 7 are ineligible under Chapter 11.

    b. If involuntary, same requirements must be met as needed to initiate a Chapter 7 involuntary proceeding

3. Creditor's committee is appointed after the order for relief is entered. This committee essentially functions as the bankruptcy trustee.

    a. Investigation of debtor's financial affairs is conducted

    b. Committee is made up of unsecured creditors only

    c. If debtor's management capable of continuing business, no trustee is appointed

    d. If debtor's management is not considered capable of running business, then trustee is appointed to conduct business

    e. Trustee may also be appointed if it is in the best interest of the creditors

    f. Committee will create a reorganization plan; however, the debtor has an exclusive right to file its own plan within 120 days after the order for relief is entered.

4. A reorganization plan

    a. Allows for continued operation of business unless court orders otherwise

    b. Provides for payment of part or all of debts over extended period

        (1) Payment to creditors comes primarily from future income

    c. Must divide claims into classes of similar claims, and claims within a class must be treated equally.

> **EXAMPLE**
>
> A reorganization plan might put employees who are owed back wages in one class, shareholders in another class, and unpaid suppliers in a third class. Assume that the plan calls for the suppliers to be paid 70 cents for each dollar owed. All suppliers must get 70 cents, some cannot get 80 cents, and others only 60 cents on the dollar.

    d. Plan may provide for some creditors to receive stock in place of debt

        (1) Preferred shareholders may be converted to common shareholders

        (2) Common shareholders may forfeit shares of stock

        (3) Typically, claimants receive reduced amounts

    e. Approval of reorganization plan needs

        (1) Over ½ of creditors in each committee owed at least 2/3 of the total debt in that class, and

        (2) Acceptance of stockholders holding at least 2/3 in amount of the stock

        (3) Complete reorganization plan can still be approved by court if court determines plan is fair even if some committees fail to approve it; called "cram down" power

    f. Priority general creditors must be paid in full (e.g., bankruptcy administrative fees, employee wages up to $11,725 per employee; see Section I.2.a. of this outline for further examples).

5. Fast tracking provides for small businesses (having debt less than $2,190,000) which cuts out much of red tape of bankruptcy proceedings

6. After court confirms plan and issues final decree

    a. Debtor is discharged from debts that arose before confirmation of plan, except

        (1) Those agreed to continue under the recognized plan

        (2) Those exempted by law (e.g., taxes; see part K. of this outline for further examples)

7. Court may convert Chapter 11 reorganization into Chapter 7 straight bankruptcy if fairer

8. SEC has limited power to participate in bankruptcy reorganizations

9. When debtor keeps and operates business, debtor has right to retain employees and professionals it used before reorganization

> **EXAMPLE**
>
> Debtor, after a Chapter 11 reorganization, wishes to keep its CPA firm. This is permitted.

O. Debts Adjustment Plans—Chapter 13

1. Most individuals are eligible if

   a. Have regular income, and
   b. Owe unsecured debts of less than $360,475, and
   c. Owe secured debts of less than $1,081,400

2. Initiated when debtor files voluntary petition in bankruptcy court

   a. Creditors may not file involuntary petition under Chapter 13
   b. Filing of petition stays all collection and straight bankruptcy proceedings against debtor
   c. Debtor has exclusive right to propose plan

      (1) If debtor does not file plan, creditors may force debtor into involuntary proceeding under Chapter 7

   d. Plan will be confirmed or denied by court without approval of unsecured creditors

      (1) However, unsecured creditors must receive as much as they would get under Chapter 7, and

         (a) Either be paid in full, or
         (b) Have all debtor's disposable income committed to plan
         (c) Plan may put claims in different classifications but may not discriminate unfairly against any of designated classes and each claimant within same classification must receive same treatment

      (2) If debts to unsecured creditors are not paid in full, plan must commit to payments for three years. If debtor's monthly income exceeds the state's average median annual income, plan must make payment for five years.

   e. Court must appoint trustee in Chapter 13 cases
   f. Debtor engaged in business may continue to operate that business subject to limitations imposed by court
   g. Completion of plan discharges debtor from debts dischargeable by law. Nondischargeable debts are similar to those under Chapter 7 of the Bankruptcy Code (see section K. of this outline)

> **NOW REVIEW MULTIPLE-CHOICE QUESTIONS 27 THROUGH 30 IN VOLUME 2**

P. The Bankruptcy Abuse Prevention and Consumer Protection Act of 2005

1. Amends various parts of US Bankruptcy Code including consumer bankruptcies and business bankruptcies
2. Provisions under new Act allow trade creditors to treat large portions, sometimes most or even all of vendors' claims as being administrative expenses, significantly increasing their priority status.
3. This Act creates a new Bankruptcy Code section that imposes limits on the payment of severance pay or retention bonuses to key employees in a Chapter 11 case

   a. Retention bonuses are permitted only if key employees have good-faith offers from other businesses at the same or greater compensation

4. For consumer cases, the time between discharges has been increased so that Bankruptcy Code will deny discharge to a Chapter 7 debtor if that debtor received either a Chapter 7 or Chapter 11 discharge in a case filed within 8 years of filing of pending case

   a. Prior law said 6 years between such discharges under Chapter 7 or Chapter 11
   b. Under the new act, Chapter 13 debtors have a few different time limitations when combined with the various chapters.

5. This Bankruptcy Abuse Prevention and Consumer Protection Act of 2005 creates a new Chapter 15 of the US Bankruptcy Code on cross-border insolvency cases

   a. Meant to make bankruptcy proceedings across international borders more functional

      (1) Favors and promotes cooperation and communication with both foreign courts and foreign representatives

╔══╗
║   **NOW REVIEW MULTIPLE-CHOICE QUESTION 31 IN VOLUME 2**   ║
╚══╝

Q. Bankruptcy Fees

1. In recent years, bankruptcy specialists have made much larger fees. Rising fees have elicited major objections coming from

   a. Federal watchdogs
   b. Organized labor
   c. Major creditors of bankrupt companies

2. Major complaint is that lawyers and other advisors have been taking too many fees and leaving less money for others in the bankruptcy
3. Thus bankruptcy is more likely testable on CPA Exam because it is now on minds of many

KEY TERMS

Chapter 7 bankruptcy. Debtor liquidates assets, except exempt assets, to pay creditors.

Chapter 11 bankruptcy. Debtor reorganizes debts to pay creditors; primarily used by businesses.

Chapter 13 bankruptcy. Debtor reorganizes debts to pay creditors; primarily used by individuals.

Creditor's committee. A group of unsecured creditors who essentially function as the bankruptcy trustee in Chapter 11 cases.

Discharge. After debtor completes bankruptcy, debtor is relieved of all previous debt except debts that are nondischargeable. This allows debtor to get a financial fresh start.

Estate. The debtor's assets that are used to pay the creditors.

Insider. A party who has a close relationship with the debtor. Relevant in the area of preferential transfers: Transactions with insiders are examined by the trustee for 1 year prior to the filing of the bankruptcy petition.

Involuntary petition. Debtor is sued by creditors and forced into bankruptcy.

Liquidation. The process of turning assets into cash to pay creditors.

Order for relief. Granted, in most cases, to the debtor upon the filing of the bankruptcy petition. Allows debtor to stop paying creditors until the bankruptcy can be finalized.

Preferential transfer. When the debtor provides payment or security to a creditor, which would allow creditor to collect more than the creditor would have under Chapter 7 bankruptcy. If such a transfer took place 90 days prior to the filing of the bankruptcy petition, the trustee may set the transaction aside. This is done to assure all creditors are treated fairly.

Reaffirmation. When a debtor voluntarily chooses to repay a debt that otherwise would be fully discharged under the Bankruptcy Code.

Reorganization (rehabilitation). A debtor retains assets, as opposed to liquidating the assets, and agrees to pay creditors out of future earnings under Chapters 11 or 13 of the Bankruptcy Code.

Stay. A court order that prevents further collection actions by creditors. The stay is issued upon the filing of the bankruptcy petition, but does not apply to family law issues.

Trustee. The bankruptcy trustee presides over the bankruptcy estate and organizes the estate for the court. The trustee determines what the assets and liabilities of the estate are.

Voluntary petition. A debtor chooses to file bankruptcy, as opposed to being forced into bankruptcy by creditors.

Module 31: Debtor-Creditor Relationships

Overview

The first part of this module discusses the rights and duties of debtors and creditors. One of the important areas is the idea of a lien. Note the different types of liens and their effect on debtors and creditors. Also covered are the concepts of composition agreements with creditors and assignments for the benefit of creditors. These can be used as alternatives to bankruptcy.

This module also discusses the concepts of guaranty and suretyship. These two are nearly the same concept. The main difference is that the guarantor is typically secondarily liable to the creditor, whereas the surety is normally primarily liable to the creditor. The rights and duties are otherwise almost the same for both the guarantors and the sureties. Before beginning the reading you should review the key terms at the end of the module.

A. Rights and Duties of Debtors and Creditors

1. Liens are creditors' claims on real or personal property to secure payment of debt or performance of obligations
2. Mechanic's lien or materialman's lien

   a. Statutory lien on real property (real estate) to secure payment of debts for services or materials to improve real property

   > **EXAMPLE**
   >
   > Worker puts a new roof on an owner's building. Since the owner has not paid, the worker puts a lien on the building to secure payment. The worker may, after giving notice to the owner, foreclose on the property.

3. Artisan's lien

   a. Occurs when one repairs or improves personal property for another and retains possession of that personal property

   > **EXAMPLE**
   >
   > A has a mechanic repair his car. Upon completion of the repairs, the mechanic retains possession of the car until A pays for the repairs.

   b. Artisan's lien terminates when creditor receives or is offered payment or when s/he gives up possession of property
   c. Artisan's lien generally has priority over other liens or interests as long as creditor retains possession of the personal property
   d. If debtor does not pay, most statutes allow lienholder to give notice to owner and then to sell property

4. Innkeeper's lien allows hotel to keep possession of guest's baggage until hotel charges are paid
5. Tax lien is imposed by federal, state, or local governments to secure the payment of taxes
6. Attachment is a court-ordered seizure of property due to lack of payment **prior** to court judgment for past-due debt

   a. If creditor wins at trial, property is sold to pay off debt
   b. There are certain constitutional requirements to protect debtors because property is seized based on word of creditors
   c. Writ of attachment allows creditor to take possession of personal property to satisfy debt pursuant to successful legal action

7. Writ of execution is remedy in which court order directs sheriff to seize debtor's property which can then be sold at judicial sale to pay off creditor

   a. Any excess over debt owed is paid to debtor
   b. Some property is exempt from seizure

8. Garnishment allows creditor to seize property, usually money, owed to debtor by third party

   a. Garnishment involves seizing debtor's property possessed by third parties such as banks (debtor's bank account) or employers (debtor's wages)

   > **EXAMPLE**
   >
   > Creditor obtains a writ of garnishment from the court to collect from a bank $5,000 in the debtor's bank account.

   b. State and federal laws limit amount of wages that can be garnished

9. Judgment lien

   a. Occurs when a party is awarded damages by a court and the party files a lien against property to secure payment
   b. Debtor sometimes fraudulently tries to prevent creditor from satisfying a judgment (fraudulent conveyance)

      (1) Evidence of fraud includes one or more of the following:

         (a) Transfer of all assets
         (b) Debtor maintains use or possession of property after the alleged transfer
         (c) Secret transfer
         (d) Transfer made to a family member
         (e) Transfer made for inadequate consideration
         (f) Transfer done in anticipation of litigation

      (2) Conveyance is usually set aside

   > **EXAMPLE**
   >
   > Debtor appears to sell all interest in some property but in fact names herself as the beneficiary as she conveys the legal title to the trustee.

10. Composition agreement with creditors (also called composition of creditors' agreement)

    a. Occurs by two or more creditors' agreement with debtor to accept less than full amount of debt as full satisfaction of debt
    b. Based on contract law so needs new consideration to be enforceable

       (1) New consideration is construed as two or more creditors each agreeing to accept less than full amount

          (a) Note that all creditors need not be part of agreement
          (b) Creditors need not be treated equally but treatment must be disclosed and agreed to by affected parties

       (2) Once debtor pays creditors at agreed rates, those debts are discharged

          (a) If debtor does not perform as agreed in composition agreement, creditors may choose to enforce either original debts or reduced debts under composition agreement.
          (b) Creditors not part of agreement are not bound by agreement and thus may resort to bankruptcy law or settle debt by own method

11. Assignment for the benefit of creditors

    a. Debtor voluntarily transfers all of his/her assets to an assignee (or trustee) to be sold for the benefit of creditors
    b. Assignee takes legal title

       (1) Debtor must cease all control of assets

    c. No agreement between creditors is necessary

       (1) Creditors who accept assignment receive pro rata share of debt they are owed
       (2) Dissatisfied creditors may file a petition in bankruptcy and assignments may be set aside

    d. Debts are not discharged unless they are paid in full by assignee

12. Homestead exemption

    a. In addition to providing exemptions against execution on debtor's assets, also provides exception for debtor's home so that unsecured creditors and trustees in bankruptcy may not satisfy debts from equity in debtor's home

       (1) However, mortgage liens and IRS tax liens take priority over homestead exemption

13. Fair Debt Collection Practices Act restricts how creditors may collect debts

    a. Collection agencies are prevented from contacting debtor-consumer at inconvenient hours, inconvenient places, or at work if employer objects

       (1) Also generally prevented from directly contacting debtor represented by an attorney

    b. Collection agencies may not use methods that are abusive or misleading
    c. Debt collector must provide debtor written notice of amount of debt and to whom the debt is owed within five days of first communication
    d. When debtor contests validity of debt, collection attempts must cease until collector sends debtor verification
    e. Debt collectors must bring suit in court near debtors residence or in jurisdiction where contract signed
    f. If debt collector violates Act, that person is liable for actual damages plus other damages such as court costs and attorneys' fees
    g. Federal Trade Commission enforces this Act

       (1) May use cease and desist orders against debt collector
       (2) Civil lawsuits for damages are also allowed

    h. Act applies to collection agent collecting debt for another—does not apply if creditor collects own debt

14. Truth-in-Lending Act requires lenders and sellers to disclose credit terms on loans to consumer-debtors

    a. Disclosures include finance charges and annual percentage rate of interest charged
    b. Consumer has right to rescind credit within three days
    c. The Bankruptcy Abuse Prevention and Consumer Protection Act of 2005 not only has far-reaching effects on US Bankruptcy Code (see Module 30), but also affects the Truth-in-Lending Act

       (1) The following are important provisions that are testable on the CPA exam:

          (a) Consumer lenders required to make additional disclosures in credit card statements relating to minimum payments, late fees, and introductory rates

             1] Also required to disclose toll-free number that consumer may call for estimate of time required to repay balance by making only minimum payments

          (b) Consumer lenders required to make more disclosures on tax consequences of home equity loans, and Internet-based credit card solicitations
          (c) Preserves defenses and claims of consumers against predatory loans sold by bankruptcy trustees that are covered by Truth-in-Lending Act

15. Equal Credit Opportunity Act prohibits discrimination in consumer credit transactions based on marital status, sex, race, color, religion, national origin, age, or receipt of welfare, or because applicant has exercised legal rights

    a. If creditor denies or revokes credit or worsens credit terms, must provide notice to debtor of specific reasons for adverse action
    b. Provides for civil and criminal penalties

16. Fair Credit Reporting Act prohibits consumer reporting agencies from including in consumer reports any inaccurate or obsolete information

    a. Information includes creditworthiness, mode of living, character, reputation in general
    b. Consumer is allowed access to credit reports
    c. If consumer disagrees with information in report, agency must investigate and correct if appropriate

       (1) If dispute remains, consumer may file statement of his/her version that becomes part of permanent consumer's credit record

17. Fair Credit Billing Act allows consumer to complain of billing errors and requires creditor to either explain or correct them

    a. If dispute remains, debtor may use lawsuit.

18. Fair Credit and Charge Card Disclosure Act requires disclosure of annual percentage rate, membership fee, etc. for credit or charge card solicitations or applications

     a. Credit card holder's liability is limited to $50 per credit card for unauthorized charges due to lost or stolen credit cards

         (1) Additional limitation—not liable for any charges after holder notifies issuer

> **EXAMPLE**
>
> Abel carelessly lost his credit card. He quickly notified the issuer. The person who found the card charged $100 on the card. All of this was after the issuer was notified that the card was lost. Abel is not liable for any of the unauthorized charges.

19. Bank debit cards

     a. Banks are liable for wrongful dishonor for failure to pay electronic fund transfer when customer has sufficient funds in account

---

NOW REVIEW MULTIPLE-CHOICE QUESTIONS 1 THROUGH 6 IN VOLUME 2

B. Nature of Suretyship and Guaranty

1. In both suretyship and guaranty, third party promises to pay debt owed by debtor if debtor does not pay

     a. Third party's credit acts as security for debt to creditor

     b. Purpose of a suretyship agreement is to protect creditor by providing creditor with added security for obligation and to reduce creditor's risk of loss

> **EXAMPLE**
>
> In order for D to obtain a loan from C, S (who has a good credit standing) promises to C that he, S, will pay debt if D does not.

2. Suretyship and guaranty agreements involve three parties

     a. Creditor (C in above example)

         (1) Obligee of principal debtor

     b. Principal debtor (D in above example)

         (1) Has liability for debt owed to creditor

     c. Surety (S in above example) or guarantor

         (1) Promises to perform or pay debt of principal debtor

         (2) Also referred to as accommodation party or consignor

3. Suretyship and guaranty contracts are similar, but many courts distinguish them as such

     a. In strict suretyship, the surety promises to be responsible for the debt and is **primarily** liable for debt

         (1) Creditor can demand payment from surety when debt is due

         (2) Unconditional guaranty is the standard suretyship relationship in which there are no further conditions required for guarantor to be asked to pay if debtor does not

> **EXAMPLE**
>
> G agreed in writing to act as surety when D took out a loan with C, the lender. If D does not pay, C may proceed directly against G. C need not try to collect from D first.

         (a) Creditor need not attempt collection from debtor first

         (b) Creditor need not give notice of debtor's default

b. In contrast to suretyship, in guaranty contract, guarantor is normally **secondarily liable**

   (1) Guarantor can be required to pay debt only after debtor defaults and creditor demands payment from debtor
   (2) Sometimes guaranty contract requires creditor to both seek payment from debtor and bring suit if necessary, but do not assume that the creditor must sue the debtor first unless the Examiners specifically state that a lawsuit is required against the debtor before proceeding against the guarantor.

      (a) Called guarantor of collection

> **NOTE:** With those few exceptions noted in this outline, the rights and duties of both guarantors and sureties are essentially the same and the remainder of this outline will generally use surety and guarantor interchangeably.

4. Examples of typical suretyship and guaranty arrangements

   a. Seller of goods on credit requires buyer to obtain a surety to guarantee payment for goods purchased
   b. Bank requires owners or directors of closely held corporation to act as sureties for loan to corporation
   c. Endorser of negotiable instrument agrees to pay if instrument not paid
   d. In order to transfer a check or note, transferor may be required to obtain a surety (accommodation endorser) to guarantee payment
   e. Purchaser of real property expressly assumes seller's mortgage on property (i.e., promises to pay mortgage debt)

      (1) Seller then has become surety

5. Suretyship and guaranty contracts should satisfy elements of contracts in general

   a. If surety's or guarantor's agreement arises at same time as the contract between creditor and debtor, no separate consideration is needed

      (1) If creditor gave loan or credit before surety's promise, separate consideration is necessary to support surety's new promise

---

EXAMPLE

C loaned $200,000 to D. Terms provided that the loan is callable by C with one month notice to D. C gave the agreed notice and exercised her right to call the loan. D requested a sixty-day extension. C agreed to the extension when S agreed to be a surety on this loan. There is consideration for the new surety agreement since C gave up the right to call the loan sooner.

      (a) Consideration need not be received by surety— often it is principal debtor that benefits

   b. Surety's agreement to answer for debt or default of another must be in writing

      (1) Recall that under the Statute of Frauds under contract law, this is one of the types of contracts that must be in writing
      (2) However, if guarantor's promise is primarily for his/her own benefit, ("Main Purpose Doctrine") it need not be in writing

---

EXAMPLE

S agrees to pay D's debt to D's creditor if he defaults. The main motive of S is to keep D in business to assure a steady supply of an essential component. S's agreement need not be in writing.

EXAMPLE

A del credere agent is one who sells goods on credit to purchasers for the principal and agrees to pay the principal if the customers do not. Since his promise is primarily for his own benefit, it need not be in writing.

---

6. Third-party beneficiary contract is not a suretyship contract

   a. Third-party beneficiary contract is one in which third party receives benefits from agreement made between promisor and promisee, although third person is not party to contract

> **EXAMPLE**
>
> Father says: "Ship goods to my son and I will pay for them." This describes a third-party beneficiary contract, not a suretyship arrangement. Father is not promising to pay the debt of another, but rather engaging in an original promise to pay for goods that creditor delivers to son.

7. Indemnity contract is not a suretyship contract

    a. An indemnity contract is between two parties (rather than three) whereby indemnitor makes a promise to a potential debtor, indemnitee, (not to creditor as in suretyship arrangement), to indemnify and reimburse debtor for payment of debt or for loss that may arise in future. Indemnitor pays because it has assumed risk of loss, not because of any default by principal debtor as in suretyship arrangement.

> **EXAMPLE**
>
> Under terms of standard automobile collision insurance policy, insurance company agrees to indemnify automobile owner against damage to his/her car caused by collision.

8. Warranty (sometimes called guaranty) is not same as the type of guaranty under suretyship law

    a. Warranties arise under, for example, real property law or sales law

        (1) Involve making representations as to facts, title, quality, etc. of property

9. Capacity to act as surety or guarantor

    a. In general, individuals that have capacity to contract
    b. Partnerships may act as sureties unless partnership agreement expressly prohibits it from entering into suretyship contracts
    c. Individual partner normally has no authority to bind partnership as surety
    d. Modern trend is that corporations may act as sureties

> **NOW REVIEW MULTIPLE-CHOICE QUESTIONS 7 THROUGH 8 IN VOLUME 2**

C. Creditor's Rights and Remedies

1. Against principal debtor

    a. Creditor has right to receive payment or performance specified in contract
    b. Creditor may proceed immediately against debtor upon default, unless contract states otherwise
    c. When a debtor has more than one debt outstanding with same creditor and makes a part payment, debtor may give instructions as to which debt the payment is to apply

        (1) If debtor gives no instructions, creditor is free to apply part payment to whichever debt s/he chooses; fact that one debt is guaranteed by surety and other is not makes no difference in absence of instructions by debtor

2. Against surety

    a. Creditor may proceed immediately against surety upon principal debtor's default

        (1) Unless contract requires it, it is not necessary to give surety notice of debtor's default
        (2) Since surety is immediately liable, s/he can be sued without creditor first attempting to collect from debtor

3. Against guarantor of collection

    a. A guarantor of collection's liability is conditioned on creditor notifying guarantor of debtor's default and creditor first attempting to collect from debtor
    b. Creditor must exhaust remedies by going against debtor before guarantor of collection's liability arises, even by lawsuit if necessary
    c. The specific language "guarantor of collection" must be used on the CPA Exam for these rules to apply; normally the Examiners are testing the ordinary surety.
    d. Note that a guarantor of collection is different than a mere guarantor. A creditor only needs to request payment from the debtor before proceeding against a guarantor, whereas the creditor must exhaust all legal remedies against the debtor before proceeding against a guarantor of collection.

4. Against security (collateral) held by surety or creditor

    a. Upon principal debtor's default, creditor may resort to collateral to satisfy debt

        (1) If creditor does resort to collateral, any excess collateral or amount realized by its disposal over debt amount must be returned to principal debtor

        (2) If collateral is insufficient to pay debt, creditor may proceed against surety or debtor for balance due (deficiency)

    b. Creditor is not required to use collateral; creditor may instead proceed immediately against surety or principal debtor

> **NOW REVIEW MULTIPLE-CHOICE QUESTIONS 9 THROUGH 12 IN VOLUME 2**

D. Surety's/Guarantor's Rights and Remedies

1. When the debt or obligation for which surety has given promise is due

    a. Exoneration

        (1) Surety may require (by lawsuit if necessary) debtor to pay obligation if debtor is able before surety has paid

        (2) Exoneration is not available if creditor demands prompt performance from surety

    b. Surety may request creditor to resort first to collateral if surety can show collateral is seriously depreciating in value, or if surety can show undue hardship will otherwise result

2. When surety pays debt or obligation

    a. S/he is entitled to right of reimbursement from debtor

        (1) May recover only actual payments to creditor

        (2) Surety is entitled to resort to collateral as satisfaction of right of reimbursement

        (3) Surety's payment after having received notice of principal debtor's valid defense against creditor causes surety to lose right of reimbursement

    b. S/he has right of subrogation

        (1) Upon payment, surety obtains same rights against principal debtor that creditor had

            (a) That is, surety steps into creditor's shoes

            (b) If debtor is bankrupt, surety is subrogated to rights of creditor's priority in bankruptcy proceeding

> **EXAMPLE**
>
> C, the creditor, required D, the debtor, to put up personal property as collateral on a loan and to also use S as a surety on the same loan. Upon D's default, C chooses to resort to S for payment. Upon payment, S may now sell the collateral under the right of subrogation because the creditor could have used the same right of sale of the collateral.

3. Creditor owes duty to surety to disclose, before surety agrees to contract, any information about material risks that are greater than surety aware of

    a. Creditor must also disclose facts inquired by surety

E. Surety's/Guarantor's Defenses

1. Surety may generally exercise defenses on contract that would be available **to debtor**

    a. Breach or failure of performance by **creditor**

    b. Impossibility or illegality of performance

    c. Creditor obtains debtor's promise by fraud, duress, or misrepresentation

    d. Statute of limitations

    e. Except that surety may **not use** debtor's **personal** defenses as discussed later

2. Surety may take advantage of **own** contractual defenses

    a. Fraud or duress

        (1) If creditor obtains surety's promise by fraud or duress, contract is voidable at surety's option

---

EXAMPLE

Creditor forces X to sign suretyship agreement at threat of great bodily harm.

---

    (2) If creditor gets principal debtor's promise using fraud or duress, then surety not liable

        (a) Exception: surety is liable if was aware of fraud or duress before s/he became surety

    (3) Fraud by principal debtor on surety to induce a suretyship agreement will **not** release surety if creditor has extended credit in good faith

        (a) But if creditor had knowledge of debtor's fraudulent representations, then surety may avoid liability

---

EXAMPLE

Y asked Ace to act as surety on a loan from Bank. In order to induce Ace to act as surety, Y made fraudulent representations concerning its financial position to Ace. This fraud by Y will not release surety, Ace, if the creditor, Bank, had no knowledge of the fraud and extended credit in good faith. But if Bank had knowledge of Y's fraudulent representations, then Ace has a good defense and can avoid liability. Note that if Bank finds out about Y's fraudulent representations after Bank has extended credit, Ace has no defense.

---

  b. Suretyship contract itself is void due to illegality

  c. Incapacity of surety (e.g., surety is a minor)

  d. Failure of consideration for suretyship contract

    (1) However, when surety's and principal debtor's obligations are incurred at same time, there is no need for any separate consideration beyond that supporting principal debtor's contract; if surety's undertaking is entered into subsequent to debtor's contract, it must be supported by separate consideration (see section B.5.a. of this outline)

  e. Suretyship agreement is not in writing as required under Statute of Frauds

  f. Creditor fails to notify surety of any material facts within creditor's knowledge concerning debtor's ability to perform

---

EXAMPLE

Creditor's failure to report to surety that debtor has defaulted on several previous occasions.

EXAMPLE

Creditor's failure to report to surety that debtor submitted fraudulent financial statements to surety to induce suretyship agreement.

---

  g. Surety, in general, may use any obligations owed by creditor to surety as a setoff against any payments owed to creditor

    (1) True even if setoff arises from separate transaction

3. Acts of creditor or debtor materially affecting surety's obligations

  a. Tender of performance by debtor or surety and refusal by creditor will discharge surety

    (1) However, tender of performance for obligation to pay money does not normally release principal debtor but stops accrual of interest on debt

  b. Release of principal debtor from liability by creditor without consent of surety will also discharge surety's liability

    (1) But surety is not released if creditor specifically reserves his/her rights against surety

        (a) However, surety upon paying may then seek recovery from debtor

NOTE: If the Examiners test this issue of the creditor releasing the debtor, they usually have the creditor reserve its rights against the surety; thus the surety is still liable to the creditor. The reason the release of the debtor does not materially affect the surety's obligation is that the surety is primarily liable to the creditor. Thus, the creditor already had the authority to pursue the debt directly from the surety.

c. Release of surety by creditor

   (1) Does **not** release principal debtor because liable whether or not surety is liable

d. Proper performance by debtor or satisfaction of creditor through collateral will discharge surety

e. Variance in terms and conditions of contract subsequent to surety's undertaking

   (1) Accommodation (noncompensated) surety is completely discharged for any change in contract made by creditor on terms required of principal debtor

   (2) Commercial (compensated) surety is completely released if modification in principal debtor's contract materially increases risk to surety

      (a) If risk not increased materially, then surety not released but his/her obligation is reduced by amount of loss due to modification

   (3) Surety may consent to modifications so that they are not defenses

   (4) Surety is not released if creditor modifies principal debtor's duties to be beneficial to surety (i.e., decreases surety's risk)

EXAMPLE

Creditor reduces interest rate on loan to principal debtor from 12% to 10%.

---

   (5) Modifications that affect rights of sureties based on above principles

      (a) Extension of time on principal debtor's obligation, but only to the extent that the extension causes a loss to the surety and only that additional loss will be discharged.

      (b) Change in amount, place, or manner of principal debtor's obligations

      (c) Modification of duties of principal debtor

      (d) Substitution of debtor's or delegation of debtor's obligation to another

         1] Note how this may result in change in risk to the surety

      (e) Release, surrender, destruction, or impairment of collateral by creditor before or after debtor's default releases surety by amount decreased

---

EXAMPLE

S is a surety on a $10,000 loan between Creditor and Debtor. Creditor is also holding $1,000 of Debtor's personal property as collateral on the $10,000 loan. Before the loan is paid, Creditor returns the collateral to Debtor. This action releases S from $1,000 of the $10,000 loan.

EXAMPLE

S is a compensated surety for a loan between Debtor and Creditor. The loan had also been secured by collateral. Upon default, Creditor took possession of the collateral but let it get damaged by rain. The collateral was impaired by $500. Creditor also sought payment from S, the compensated surety. S may reduce his payment to Creditor by $500.

---

   (6) In order to release surety, there must be an actual alteration or variance in terms of contract and not an option or election that principal debtor can exercise under express terms of original agreement which surety has guaranteed

---

EXAMPLE

Tenant and landlord entered into a two-year leasing agreement which expressly contained an option for an additional year which could be exercised by tenant, with X acting as surety on lease contract. If tenant exercises this option, X still remains bound as surety.

---

4. Following are not defenses of surety/guarantor

  a. Personal defenses of principal debtor

        (1) Death of debtor or debtor's lack of capacity (e.g., debtor is a minor or was legally insane when contract was made)

        (2) Insolvency (or discharge in bankruptcy) of debtor

           (a) Possibility of debtor's insolvency is a primary reason for engaging in a surety arrangement

        (3) Personal debtor's setoffs

           (a) Unless debtor assigns them to surety

    b. Creditor did not give notice to surety of debtor's default or creditor did not first proceed against principal debtor

        (1) Unless a conditional guarantor and creditor violated condition

    c. Creditor does not resort to collateral

    d. Creditor delays in proceeding against debtor unless delay exceeds statute of limitations

    e. When creditor is owed multiple debts by same debtor, creditor may choose to apply payment to any of the debts unless debtor directs otherwise—surety cannot direct which debt payment applies to

> **EXAMPLE**
>
> Debtor owes two debts to Creditor. S is acting as a surety on one of these debts. When Debtor makes a payment, Creditor applies it to the debt on which S is not a surety since Debtor did not indicate which one. The surety has no defense from these facts and is not released.

NOW REVIEW MULTIPLE-CHOICE QUESTIONS 13 THROUGH 20 IN VOLUME 2

F. Cosureties

  1. Cosureties exist when there is more than one surety for same obligation of principal debtor to same creditor

    a. Not relevant whether or not cosureties are aware of each other or became cosureties at different times

        (1) Must be sureties for same debtor for same obligation

    b. Cosureties need not be bound for same amount; they can guarantee equal or unequal amounts of debt

        (1) Collateral, if any, need not be held equally

    c. Cosureties need not sign same document

  2. Cosureties are jointly and severally liable to creditor

    a. That is, creditor can proceed against any of the sureties jointly or against each one individually to extent surety has assumed liability

    b. If creditor sues multiple sureties, s/he may recover in any proportion from each, but may not recover more than debtor's total obligation

    c. Proceeding against one or more sureties does not release remaining surety or sureties

  3. Right of contribution exists among cosureties

    a. Right of contribution arises when cosurety, in performance of debtor's obligation, pays more than his/her proportionate share of total liability, and thereby entitles cosurety to compel other cosureties to compensate him/her for excess amount paid (i.e., contribution from other cosureties for their pro rata share of liability)

  4. Cosureties are only liable in contribution for their proportionate share

    a. Cosurety's pro rata share is proportion that each surety's risk (i.e., amount each has personally guaranteed) bears to total amount of risk assumed by all sureties by using the following formula:

$$\frac{\text{Dollar amount individual cosurety personally guaranteed}}{\text{Total dollar amount of risk assumed by all cosureties}}$$

> **EXAMPLE**
>
> X and Y are cosureties for $5,000 and $10,000, respectively, of a $10,000 debt. Each is liable in proportion to amount each has personally guaranteed. Since X guaranteed $5,000 of debt and Y guaranteed $10,000 of debt, then X is individually liable for 1/3 ($5,000/$15,000) of debt and Y is individually liable for 2/3 ($10,000/$15,000) of debt. If debtor defaults on only $3,000 of debt, X is liable for $1,000 (1/3 × $3,000) and Y is liable for $2,000 (2/3 × $3,000). Although creditor may recover $3,000 from either, each cosurety has right of contribution from other cosurety.

> **EXAMPLE**
>
> Refer to the preceding example. If the creditor recovers all of the $3,000 debt from Y, then Y, under the right of contribution, can recover $1,000 from X so that each will end up paying his/her proportionate amount.

5. Each cosurety is entitled to share in any collateral pledged (either held by creditor or other cosurety) in proportion to cosurety's liability for debtor's default

> **EXAMPLE**
>
> If in above illustration, cosurety Y held collateral pledged by debtor worth $900, both cosureties X and Y would be entitled to share in collateral in proportion to their respective liabilities. X would be entitled to 1/3 ($5,000/$15,000) of $900 collateral, or $300; and Y would be entitled to 2/3 ($10,000/$15,000) of $900 collateral, or $600.

6. Discharge or release of one cosurety by creditor results in a reduction of liability of remaining cosurety

   a. Remaining cosurety is released only to extent of released cosurety's pro rata share of debt liability (unless there is a reservation of rights by creditor against remaining cosurety)

> **EXAMPLE**
>
> A and B are cosureties for $4,000 and $12,000, respectively, on a $12,000 debt. If creditor releases cosurety A, cosurety B is released to extent of cosurety A's liability. Each is liable in proportion to amount each has personally guaranteed. Since A guaranteed $4,000 of debt and B guaranteed $12,000 of debt, then A is individually liable for 1/4 ($4,000/$16,000) of debt and B is individually liable for 3/4 ($12,000/$16,000) of debt, that is, $9,000. Therefore, cosurety B is released of A's pro rata liability of $3,000 (1/4 × $12,000), and only remains a surety for $9,000 ($12,000 − $3,000) of debt.

7. A cosurety is not released from obligation to perform merely because another cosurety refuses to perform

   a. However, upon payment of full obligation, cosurety can demand a pro rata contribution from his/her nonperforming cosurety
   b. Cosurety is not released if other cosureties are **unable** to pay (i.e., dead, bankrupt)

      (1) In which case, modify the formula found at Section F.4.a. by taking those cosureties that cannot pay completely out of formula and use it with all remaining cosureties

8. Cosureties have rights of exoneration, reimbursement, and subrogation like any surety

NOW REVIEW MULTIPLE-CHOICE QUESTIONS 21 THROUGH 27 IN VOLUME 2

G. Surety Bonds

1. An acknowledgment of an obligation to make good the performance by another of some act or responsibility

   a. Usually issued by companies which for a stated fee assume risk of performance by bonded party
   b. Performance of act or responsibility by bonded party discharges surety's obligation

2. Performance bonds are used to have surety guarantee completion of terms of contracts

   a. Construction bond guarantees builder's obligation to complete construction

          (1) If builder breaches contract, surety can be held liable for damages but not for specific performance (i.e., cannot be required to complete construction)

            (a) Surety may complete construction if chooses to

3. Fidelity bonds are forms of insurance that protects an employer against losses sustained due to acts of dishonest employees.
4. Official bond is guaranteeing that public officials will faithfully execute their duties.
5. Surety bonding company retains right of subrogation against bonded party

KEY TERMS

Bond. A contract involving a compensated surety.

Contribution. When a cosurety pays more than its proportionate share of the debt it can demand payment from other consureties so that each surety is paying its proportionate share of the debt.

Cosurety. Two or more sureties are guaranteeing the same debt.

Guarantor. Similar to a surety, but a guarantor is secondarily liable to the creditor. Thus, in the event that the debtor defaults the creditor must at least ask the debtor to pay, but it the event the debtor says no, then the creditor may seek payment from the guarantor.

Reimbursement. If the surety pays the debt, the surety is entitled to receive whatever it paid to the creditor from the debtor.

Subrogation. After the surety has paid the debt it acquires the rights of the creditor and may now exercise those rights against the debtor. Thus, if the debtor had given the creditor collateral, the surety would have rights against the collateral.

Surety. A party who promises to pay the debts of another party. Sureties are primarily liable to the creditor.

Module 32: Agency

Overview

Agency is a relationship in which one party (agent) is authorized to act on behalf of another party (principal). The law of agency is concerned with the rights, duties, and liabilities of the parties in an agency relationship. Important to this relationship is the fact that the agent has a fiduciary duty to act in the best interest of the principal. A good understanding of this module is important because business structure applies the concepts of agency frequently.

The CPA exam emphasizes the creation and termination of the agency relationship, the fiduciary duties that the agent owes to the principal, the undisclosed as well as the disclosed principal relationship, unauthorized acts or torts committed by the agent within the course and scope of the agency relationship and principal's liability for agent's unauthorized contracts. Before beginning the reading you should review the key terms at the end of the module.

A. Characteristics

1. Agency is a relationship between two parties, whereby one party (agent) agrees to act on behalf of the other party (principal) with respect to third parties. A contract is not required but is frequently present.

    a. Agent is subject to control of principal
    b. Agent is a fiduciary and must act for the benefit of principal
    c. Agent's specific authority is determined by the principal but generally agent has authority to bind the principal contractually with third parties

B. Examples of Principals and Agents

1. Employer (principal) and Employee (agent)

    a. Employee is a type of agent in which employee's physical conduct is subject to control by employer
    b. Business structures (e.g., corporations, partnerships, limited partnerships) are principals; their various employees are agents.

        (1) Employees include corporate officers, but not directors, general partners, and other employees such as professional support staff.

    c. Some older CPA questions may use the terms master (principal) and servant (agent)
    d. The employer/employee relationship is the most commonly tested principal-agent relationship on the CPA Exam

2. Independent contractor distinguished from employee/agent

    a. Not subject to control of employer as to methods of work
    b. Not subject to regular supervision as an employee
    c. Employer controls results only (independent contractor controls the methods)
    d. Typically an independent contractor is paid by the job, while an employee is paid a salary or an hourly wage on a continuous basis.
    e. Often independent contractors provide their own tools/supplies for a job, while an employee usually has tools/supplies provided by the principal.
    f. The distinction is important because generally employer is not liable for torts committed by independent contractor, but the employer can be held liable for the torts of an agent (see Section B.3. of this outline)

        (1) Unless independent contractor is employed to do something inherently dangerous (e.g., blasting)
        (2) Unless employer was negligent in hiring independent contractor

    g. Independent contractor may also be an agent in certain cases

> **EXAMPLE**
>
> An attorney represents a client in tax court.

3. Special agency situations

    a. Power of attorney: A person authorizes another person to act as his/her representative.

    > **EXAMPLE**
    >
    > Catherine recognizes that she is not as mentally sharp as she once was and is fearful that she may one day lack capacity to manager her own affairs. Catherine executes a power of attorney giving James, her adult son, power of attorney.

    (1) Principal, in writing, grants authority to agent

        (a) Only principal need sign because the principal is the only party relinquishing a legal right, and the law needs evidence of the principal's intent to do so.

        (b) This is similar to the idea of needing the signature of the party to be charged from contract law.

    (2) Agent need not be an attorney but anyone with capacity to be agent

    (3) Power of attorney may grant general authority or restricted authority

    b. Broker—special agent acting for either buyer or seller in business transactions (e.g., real estate broker)

    c. Exclusive—only agent the principal may deal with for a certain purpose during life of the contract (e.g., real estate broker who has sole right to sell property except for personal sale by principal)

    d. Del credere—a sales agent who, prior to the creation and as a condition of the agency, guarantees the accounts of the customers to his/her principal (if the customers fail to pay)

    (1) Guarantee is not within the Statute of Frauds (i.e., it is not required to be in writing)

    e. E-agent is computer program or electronic method to take some action without specific human review

    > **EXAMPLE**
    >
    > P authorizes an online search to find the lowest price of a certain product found through online stores.

    f. A general agent is an agent with a broad range of powers; a special agent is one that engages in only one specific type of transaction for the principal.

    > **EXAMPLE**
    >
    > Cathy hires Nancy, a licensed real estate agent, to sell Cathy's house. Nancy is a special agent.

    g. Subagent: An agent who is hired by another agent.

    (1) Generally, agents have no authority to hire subagents unless principal so authorizes

    h. Relationship resembling agency

    (1) Agency coupled with an interest—agent has an interest in subject matter through a security interest

        (a) For example, mortgagee with right to sell property on default of mortgagor

            1] Agreement stipulating agent is to receive profits or proceeds does not by itself create an agency coupled with an interest

        (b) Principal does not have the power to terminate agency coupled with an interest

        (c) Actually not an agency relationship because one who creates this relationship surrenders power—fact patterns may still use terms of principal and agent

C. Methods of Creation

1. Contract

    a. Generally the agency contract need not be in writing in situations where the agent enters into agreements which themselves fall under the Statute of Frauds

> **EXAMPLE**
>
> A, in his capacity as agent of P, signs a contract for the sale of goods costing $600. Even though the sales contract must normally be in writing under the UCC version of the Statute of Frauds, the agency agreement between A and P need not be expressed in writing.

    (1) But if agency contract cannot be completed within one year, it must be in writing

> **EXAMPLE**
>
> P agrees to pay A as his agent and to keep him as his agent for two years.

    (2) In some states, agency contract needs to be written if agent is to buy or sell a specific piece of real estate named in agency contract

  b. Capacity

    (1) Principal must be able to give legal consent

      (a) Minors (person under age of majority, that is, 18 or 21) can, in most jurisdictions, appoint an agent, but minor may disaffirm agency

      (b) If act requires some legal capacity (e.g., legal age to sell land), then principal must meet this requirement or agent cannot legally perform even if s/he has capacity. Capacity cannot be increased by appointment of an agent.

    (2) An agent must merely have sufficient mental and physical ability to carry out instructions of his/her principal

      (a) Can bind principal even if agent is a minor or legally unable to act for self

      (b) Principal will be responsible for contract that the minor agent entered into on principal's behalf. Principal cannot use minor's lack of capacity as a defense.

  c. Consideration is not required to enter into a valid principal-agency relationship. When consideration is missing, this is known as a gratuitous agency.

2. Agency can also be implied by the conduct or lack of conduct by either the principal or agent that allows third parties to reasonably believe an agency exists; this is agency by estoppel.

> **EXAMPLE**
>
> Marcus put up a sign outside of Paula's restaurant that says, "Valet parking for Paula's $10.00." Paula's never hired Marcus or asked Marcus to do this, but Paula knew that parking was a problem, so she decided not to say anything. Third parties (customers in this case) can reasonably believe that Marcus is Paula's agent, creating agency by estoppel.

3. An agent must merely have sufficient mental and physical ability to carry out instructions of his/her principal

  a. Can bind principal even if agent is a minor or legally unable to act for self

  b. Corporations, unincorporated associations, and partnerships may act as agents

  c. A mental incompetent or an infant of tender years may not be an agent

D. Duties (Obligations) and Rights

1. Principal's duties (obligations) to agent

  a. Most of the principal's duties to the agent are determined by the employment agreement (principal/agent) contract that the principal and agent enter into.

  b. Compensate agent as per agreement, or, in the absence of an agreement, pay a reasonable amount for the agent's service

  c. Reimburse agent for reasonable expenses, unless their agreement states otherwise, and indemnify agent against loss or liability for duties performed at the principal's direction which are not illegal

  d. Duty to cooperate with agent and assist him/her perform duties as agreed to between principal and agent

  e. Inform agent of risks (e.g., physical harm, pecuniary loss)

  f. May have remedies of discharging agent, restitution, damages, and accounting, or an injunction

g. Principal does not owe agent any fiduciary duties; only the agent is a fiduciary in the principal-agent relationship.

2. Agent's duties (obligations) to principal

a. Agent is a fiduciary and must act in the best interest of the principal and with loyalty
b. Carry out instructions of principal exercising reasonable care and skill
c. Account to the principal for profits and property that rightfully belong to the principal and not commingle funds

> **EXAMPLE**
>
> Agent makes authorized purchase order from Mega Corp. As a token of its appreciation, Mega provides two tickets to a sporting event for agent. The gift of tickets needs to be disclosed to the principal, otherwise the agent is breaching a fiduciary duty.

d. Duty not to compete or act adversely to principal

(1) Includes not acting for oneself unless principal knows and agrees

e. Give any information to principal that s/he would want or need to know
f. After termination, must cease acting as agent

E. Liability to Third Parties

1. When a third party (typically a customer, client, or business associate) suffers a loss as a result of the principal's and/or agent's actions, who is responsible for the loss?
2. Before determining liability, ask why the third party is suing. Was the third party's loss due to breach of contract or the commission of a tort?
3. Contract liability is based on two issues:

a. What authority did the agent have to enter into the contract with the third party?
b. Was the principal disclosed to the third party?

4. The authority that the agent has depends on from whom the agent received the authority

a. **Actual authority** comes from the principal

(1) Express actual authority is explicit power that the principal gives to the agent to enter into a contract.
(2) Implied actual authority arises from express authority.

> **EXAMPLE**
>
> King owns several hardware stores and hires Smith to manage one of the stores. King tells Smith that Smith is in charge of the personnel at his store, but that King is the exclusive purchaser of inventory for sale.
>
> Analysis: Smith has express authority to hire/fire employees for the store he manages. Smith has implied authority to enter into contracts that a manager would normally have in this situation, such as selling merchandise. That is an example of implied authority. Smith has no actual authority to buy inventory for the store.

b. **Apparent authority** comes from a third party's **reasonable**, but mistaken, belief that the agent has actual authority to enter into the contract.

(1) Apparent authority occurs where the principal's words, actions, lack of words, or lack of action allows a **reasonable** third party to believe that the agent has actual authority to enter into a contract for the principal.
(2) Focus on whether the third party's belief is reasonable.

> **EXAMPLE**
>
> King owns several hardware stores and hires Smith to manage one of the stores. King gives Smith authority to purchase up to $500 of inventory for the store. King never informed the companies that sold to the store of the dollar limit on Smith's authority. Over several years Smith has made several purchases of Abbot deck stain to resell at the store. While the purchases were always for several hundred dollars, none of the purchases exceeded $500. King always paid Abbot when he was billed. Recently, Smith made a purchase for $600 of Abbot deck stain.

> Analysis: Even though Smith did not have actual authority to purchase more than $500 of deck stain, Smith is cloaked with apparent authority. King's failure to inform Abbot of the limitation and the fact that King has approved of similar past purchases allows Abbot to reasonably believe that Smith has authority.

EXAMPLE

Marcus put up a sign outside of Paula's restaurant that says, "Valet parking for Paula's $10.00." Paula's never hired Marcus or asked Marcus to do this, but Paula knew that parking was a problem, so she decided not to say anything. Third parties (customers in this case) can reasonably believe that Marcus is Paula's agent, creating agency by estoppel.

Analysis: Even though Marcus is not an agent, third parties can reasonably assume that Marcus is an agent and therefore has authority as well.

---

  c. No authority occurs where the agent has neither actual nor apparent authority

5. Disclosure of the principal to the third party

  a. Disclosed principal occurs when the third party knows of the existence of the principal **and** knows the identity of the principal
  b. Partially disclosed principal occurs when the third party knows of the existence of the principal, but does not know the identity of the principal
  c. Undisclosed principal is when the third party does not know of the existence of the principal.

6. Principal's contract liability to third parties

  a. If agent acts with authority, either actual or apparent, the principal is liable, regardless of disclosure status.
  b. If agent acts with no authority, then the principal is not liable, **unless the principal ratifies the contract**

   (1) Ratification occurs when a principal chooses to be bound by the terms of an unauthorized contract. Ratification is valid when all of the following are true:

    (a) Third party knew of the principal's existence at the time the contract was entered into
    (b) The principal has knowledge of all the material facts of the contract
    (c) Third party does not withdraw from contract prior to ratification

   (2) Ratification must be for the entire contract (i.e., the principal cannot choose to be bound by just part of the contract). Therefore ratification cannot occur when the principal is undisclosed since the third party was unaware of the existence of the principal.
   (3) Ratification can be explicit or implied from the principal's actions

7. Agent's contract liability to third parties

  a. If the principal is disclosed and agent has authority, either actual or apparent, agent has no liability.
  b. If the principal is partially disclosed or undisclosed, the principal is personally liable, regardless of authority.
  c. If the agent acts without authority, then the agent is personally liable.

   (1) Exception: If the principal ratifies the contract, the agent is relieved of personal liability

8. Tort liability arises when the conduct of the agent creates a loss for third party.
9. Torts can arise from

  a. Careless conduct or negligence, or
  b. Purposeful conduct: Intentional tort

10. The agent is always personally liable for the tort
11. The principal's liability for the agent's tort depends upon whether the agent's tort was committed in the **scope of employment**.
12. If the agent's tort occurred in the scope of employment, then the principal is liable for the tort under the doctrine of *respondeat superior*
13. Scope of employment means that the agent is engaged in the performance of the agency relationship

  a. Generally, if the tort occurs during working hours, at the workplace, while doing the tasks that the agent is employed to perform, then the tort is in the scope of employment.
  b. Torts that occur slightly outside the work environment are still considered in the scope of employment; these are known as detours.

c. Torts that occur substantially outside the work environment are still considered outside the scope of employment; these are known as frolics.

EXAMPLE

Juan Valdez is having a cup of coffee at work. Juan accidently spills some coffee on a client during a business meeting. Juan's tort is clearly in the scope of employment.

EXAMPLE

Juan Valdez is having a business meeting at his company's office with a client who is from a foreign country. After the meeting concludes, the client expresses concern about being able to tell the cab driver his next destination. Juan grabs a cup of coffee and escorts the client out of the building to hail a cab and assist the client with the cab driver. While hailing the cab, Juan inadvertently spills coffee on the client. This is a mere detour and Juan's tort would be in the scope of employment.

EXAMPLE

After work, Juan Valdez, stops in the Beanery Café to grab a cup of coffee. Juan happens to see a client sitting at another table and goes over to say hello. Juan then accidently spills the coffee on the client. This is a frolic. Juan has left the workplace and he is on personal time. This was not a business meeting, just a casual or social occurrence. Juan is outside the scope of employment.

---

d. The issue is not whether the principal authorized the particular activity that the employee engaged in; rather does the agent's activity fall within the scope of employment.

EXAMPLE

Assume in the previous example, where Juan escorted the client out of the building, that the employer has a policy that employees cannot leave the office building without permission during working hours. Juan will still be considered in the scope of employment because his actions were related to work and Juan is furthering the interests of the principal by assisting a client.

---

14. Intentional torts are normally outside the scope of employment.

EXAMPLE

If, in any of the previous examples, Juan purposefully dumped coffee on the client, then Juan's tort is outside the scope of employment.

---

a. Most intentional torts are also crimes.
b. Intentional torts which are foreseeable and relate to the job are normally in the scope of employment.

EXAMPLE

A bouncer at a bar pushes an unruly patron in an attempt to get the patron off the premises. This intentional tort, battery, is in the scope of employment.

---

c. Intentional torts committed to primarily benefit the principal are usually in the scope of employment.

15. If an agent commits a tort in the scope of employment, then the principal and agent are jointly and severally liable.

a. Joint liability means that the injured third party can sue both the principal and the agent in the same lawsuit
b. Several liability means to separate liability; thus the injured third party could choose just to sue the principal or just to sue the agent.

NOW REVIEW MULTIPLE-CHOICE QUESTIONS 1 THROUGH 24 IN VOLUME 2

F. Termination of Principal-Agent Relationship

1. Termination occurs either by the actions of the parties (principal and/or agent) or by operation of law.
2. Acts of the parties

    a. By agreement

       (1) Time specified in original agreement (e.g., agency for one year)
       (2) Mutual consent to terminate
       (3) Accomplishment of objective (e.g., agency to buy a piece of land) .

    b. Principal or agent may terminate agency

       (1) Party that terminates is liable for breach of contract if termination is before specified period of time

          (a) One still has power to terminate relationship even though s/he has no right to terminate (i.e., results in breach of contract)

EXAMPLE

A and P agree to be agent and principal for six months. P terminates A after two months. P is liable to A for breach of contract for the damages that this wrongful termination causes A. However, P does have the power to remove A's authority to act on behalf of P.

---

       (2) If either party breaches duties owed, other party may terminate agency without liability
       (3) If no time is specified in agency, then either party may terminate without liability

    c. Agency coupled with an interest is irrevocable

       (1) Refers to cases in which agent has actual interest in property involved in this agency, see B.3.h. of this outline.

3. Termination by operation of law: The law automatically ends the principal-agent relationship

    a. If subject of agreement becomes illegal or impossible
    b. Death, insanity, or court determined incompetence of either party

       (1) Exception is an agency coupled with an interest

    c. Bankruptcy of principal terminates the relationship

       (1) Bankruptcy of agent does not affect unless agent's solvency is needed for performance

    d. If subject matter necessary for the performance of the relationship is destroyed

4. Notice of termination to third parties

    a. Termination eliminates any actual authority that the agent had.
    b. Apparent authority could still exist, if third parties are unaware that the principal-agent relationship was terminated.
    c. To eliminate apparent authority, notice of the termination must be provided to third parties.

       (1) Constructive notice (e.g., publishing in a newspaper or a trade journal) is sufficient to third parties who have not previously dealt with agent

---

EXAMPLE

P fired A, who had been P's agent for a few years. P published in the newspaper that A was no longer his agent. A subsequently made a contract with X purporting to bind P to the contract. X had never dealt with P and A before but was aware that A had been P's agent. X was not aware that A had been fired because he had not read the notice. X cannot hold P to the contract because of the constructive notice. X does not have to read it for the constructive notice to be valid.

---

       (2) Actual notice (e.g., orally informing or sending a letter, etc.) must be given to third parties who have previously dealt with agent unless third party learns of termination from another source

> **EXAMPLE**
>
> A, while acting as an agent of P, had previous dealings with T. P fires A but A makes a contract with T purporting to act as P's agent. T can still hold P liable unless he received actual notice of termination.

> **EXAMPLE**
>
> Same as above except that the principal gave constructive notice. T may hold P liable.

> **EXAMPLE**
>
> Same as above except that although P only gave constructive notice through a trade journal, T happened to read it. This qualifies as actual notice. Therefore, unlike above, T may not hold P liable.

    d. Notice is **not required** when termination occurs due to operation of law

> **EXAMPLE**
>
> A, while acting as an agent of P, had previous dealings with T. P is declared incompetent in a judicial proceeding and T is unaware of P's incapacity. No notice was given of P's incapacity. T may not hold P liable on the contract. The moment P was declared incompetent the agency terminated due to operation of law. At that moment, A lost all authority, including apparent authority.

NOW REVIEW MULTIPLE-CHOICE QUESTIONS 25 THROUGH 27 IN VOLUME 2

KEY TERMS

Actual authority. The power given by a principal to an agent that allows the agent to enter into contracts upon the principal's behalf.

Agent. A party who works on behalf of another party known as the principal.

Apparent authority. When a third party reasonably believes that an agent has actual authority even though the agent lacks actual authority.

Disclosed principal. A principal who is known by the third party.

Fiduciary duties. The obligations that an agent owes to a principal that require the agent to act in the best interests of the principal.

Independent contractor. A party who works for another party, but is not subject to the control of the other party; therefore an independent contractor generally does not create liability for the other party.

Joint and several liability. When a principal and agent can both be held liable by the third party or the third party may choose to sever liability and only hold either the principal or the agent liable.

Partially disclosed principal. When the third party knows of the existence of the principal, but does not know the principal's identity.

Principal. The party for whom the agent acts.

Ratification. When a principal approves of a contract that was entered into by an agent lacking authority. Ratification means that the principal is now liable for the contract.

Respondeat superior (Latin). Literally means that the superior should be held responsible. When an agent commits a tort in the scope of employment, then the principal is liable for the agent's tort.

Scope of employment. Agent's actions that occur substantially in the work environment.

Third party. Term in principal/agent law that applies to a party who is interacting with either the principal or the agent. The principal and agent are the first two parties.

Undisclosed principal. When the third party to a contract does not know that a principal exists.

Module 33: Regulation of Business Employment, Environment, and Antitrust

Overview

Issues on this topic are based on the Workers' Compensation Laws and Federal Social Security Rules including the Federal Insurance Contributions Act (FICA) and the Federal Unemployment Tax Act (FUTA). These laws supplement the law of agency. In this area, emphasis is placed on the impact that state and federal laws have on the regulation of employment.

To adequately understand these materials, you should emphasize the theory and purpose underlying the Workers' Compensation Laws. You should also focus on the effect that these laws have on employers and employees. Notice the changes these laws have made on common law.

Upon looking at the Federal Social Security Laws, emphasize the coverage and benefits of the respective programs.

Also, focus on the various discrimination laws.

Be familiar with the various environmental laws; you do not need to know them in great detail, but you must be familiar with the purpose and the basics of each provision.

Candidates should also understand the important parts of the Sherman Act, the Clayton Act, the Robinson-Patman Act, and the Federal Trade Commission Act. These laws as amended form the basis for Antitrust Law which is now testable on the CPA exam. Before beginning the reading you should review the key terms at the end of the module.

A. Federal Social Security Act

1. Main purpose of Act is as name implies (i.e., attainment of the social security of people in our society)

   a. Basic programs include

      (1) Old age insurance
      (2) Survivor's and disability insurance
      (3) Hospital insurance (Medicare)
      (4) Unemployment insurance

   b. Sources of financing for these programs

      (1) Old-age, survivor's, disability, and hospital insurance programs are financed out of taxes paid by employers, employees, and self-employed under provisions of Federal Insurance Contributions Act and Self-Employment Contributions Act
      (2) Unemployment insurance programs are financed out of taxes paid by employers under the Federal Unemployment Tax Act and various state unemployment insurance laws

2. Federal Insurance Contributions Act (FICA)

   a. Imposes social security tax on employees, self-employed, and employers
   b. Social security tax applies to compensation received that is considered to be wages
   c. In general, tax rates are same for both employer and employee
   d. Taxes are paid only up to base amount that is also changed frequently

        (1) If employee pays FICA tax on more than base amount, s/he has right to refund for excess

           (a) May happen when employee works for two or more employers; these two or more employers, however, do not get refunds

    e. FICA is also used to fund Medicare, **not Medicaid**

        (1) There is no earnings cap for the Medicare portion, thus employees pay the Medicare portion of the tax on all earned wages.

    f. It is employer's duty to withhold employee's share of FICA from employee's wages and remit both employee's amount and employer's equal share to government

        (1) Employer subject to fines for failure to make timely FICA deposits

           (a) Also, employer subject to fine for failure to supply taxpayer identification number

        (2) Employer is required to match FICA contributions of employees on dollar-for-dollar basis

        (3) If employer neglects to withhold, employer may be liable for both employee's and employer's share of taxes (i.e., to pay double tax)

           (a) Once employer pays, s/he has right to collect employee's share from employee

           (b) Employer may voluntarily pay not only its share but also employee's share

               1] Employee's share is deductible by employer as additional compensation and is taxable to the employee as compensation

        (4) Employer is required to furnish employee with written statement of wages paid and FICA contributions withheld during calendar year

    g. Taxes paid by employer are deducted on tax return of employer

        (1) But employee may not deduct taxes paid on his/her tax return

    h. Neither pension plans nor any other programs may be substituted for FICA coverage

        (1) Individuals receiving payments from private pension plans may also receive social security payments

3. Self-Employment Contributions Act

    a. Self-employed persons are required to report their own taxable earnings and pay required social security tax
    b. Self-employment income is net earnings from self-employment
    c. Tax rates paid on self-employment income up to base amount

        (1) Since self-employed does not have employer to match the rate, tax rate is that of employer and employee combined
        (2) Base amount and tax rate are subject to amendment
        (3) Base rate is reduced by any wages earned from another employer during year because wages are subject to FICA
        (4) Self-employed can deduct half of FICA tax paid on his/her income tax form

4. Unemployment Insurance (Federal Unemployment Tax Act—FUTA)

    a. Tax is used to provide unemployment compensation benefits to workers who lose jobs and cannot find replacement work
    b. Federal unemployment tax must be paid by employer if employer employs one or more persons covered by Act

        (1) Deductible as business expense on employer's federal income tax return
        (2) Not deductible by employee because not paid by employee

    c. Employer must also pay a state unemployment tax

        (1) An employer is entitled to credit against his/her federal unemployment tax for state unemployment taxes paid
        (2) State unemployment tax may be raised or lowered according to number of claims against employer
        (3) If employer pays a low state unemployment tax because of good employment record, then employer is entitled to additional credit against federal unemployment tax

5. Coverage under Social Security Act is mandatory for qualifying employees

    a. Person may not elect to avoid coverage
    b. Part-time and full-time employees are covered
    c. Compensation received must be "wages"

6. Definitions

a. Wages—all compensation for employment

   (1) Include

      (a) Money wages
      (b) Contingent fees
      (c) Compensation in general even though not in cash
      (d) Base pay of those in the service
      (e) Bonuses and commissions
      (f) Most tips
      (g) Vacation and dismissal allowances

   (2) Exclude

      (a) Wages greater than base amount
      (b) Reimbursed travel expenses
      (c) Employee medical and hospital expenses paid by employer
      (d) Employee insurance premiums paid by employer
      (e) Payment to employee retirement plan by employer

b. Employee—person whose performance is subject to physical control by employer not only as to results but also as to methods of accomplishing those results

   (1) Partners, self-employed persons, directors of corporations, and independent contractors are not covered by unemployment compensation provisions since they are not "employees"

      (a) Are covered as self-employed persons for old-age, survivor's, and disability insurance program purposes

   (2) Independent contractor distinguished from an employee

      (a) Independent contractor not subject to control of employer or regular supervision as employee
      (b) That is, employer seeks results only and contractor controls method

---

EXAMPLE

A builder of homes has only to produce the results.

---

   (3) Officers and directors of corporations are "employees" if they perform services and receive remuneration for these services from corporation

c. Employment—all service performed by employee for person employing him/her

   (1) Must be continuing or recurring work
   (2) Services from following are exempt from coverage

      (a) Student nurses
      (b) Certain public employees
      (c) Nonresident aliens

   (3) Services covered if performed by employee for employer without regard to residence or citizenship

      (a) Unless employer not connected with US

   (4) Domestic workers, agricultural workers, government employees, and casual workers are governed by special rules

d. Self-employment—carrying on trade or business either as individual or in partnership

   (1) Wages greater than base amount are excluded
   (2) Can be both employed (in one job) and self-employed (another business), but must meet requirements of trade or business (i.e., not a hobby, occasional investment, etc.)
   (3) Includes director fees if director is not otherwise employed by the corporation.

e. Employer

   (1) For Federal Unemployment Tax Act (FUTA) need only employ one person or more for some portion of a day for twenty weeks, or pays $1,700 or more in total wages in any calendar quarter
   (2) In general, may be individual, corporation, partnership, trust, or other entity

7. Old-age, survivor's, and disability insurance benefits

   a. Availability of benefits depends upon attainment by individual of "insured status"

      (1) Certain lengths of working time are required to obtain insured status

   b. An individual who is "fully insured" is eligible for following benefits

      (1) Survivor benefits for widow or widower and dependents
      (2) Benefits for disabled worker and his/her dependents
      (3) Old-age retirement benefits payable to retired worker and dependents

         (a) Reduced benefits for retirement at age sixty-two

      (4) Lump-sum death benefits

   c. Individual who is "currently insured" is eligible for following benefits

      (1) Limited survivor benefits

         (a) In general, limited to dependent minors or those caring for dependent minors

      (2) Benefits for disabled worker and his/her dependents
      (3) Lump-sum death benefits
      (4) Survivors or dependents need not have paid in program to receive benefits
      (5) Divorced spouses may receive benefits

   d. Amount of benefits defined by statute which changes from time to time and depends upon

      (1) Average monthly earnings, and
      (2) Relationship of beneficiary to retired, deceased, or disabled worker

         (a) For example, husband, wife, child, grandchild—may be entitled to different benefits

      (3) Benefits increased based on cost of living
      (4) Benefits increased for delayed retirement

8. Reduction of social security benefits

   a. Early retirement results in reduced benefits

      (1) Retirement age is increasing in steps

   b. Returning to work after retirement can affect social security benefits

      (1) Income from private pension plans, savings, investments, or insurance does not affect benefits because not earned income
      (2) Income from limited partnership is considered investment income rather than self-employment income

9. Unemployment benefits

   a. Eligibility for and amount of unemployment benefits governed by state laws
   b. Does not include self-employed
   c. Generally available only to persons unemployed through no fault of their own; however, not available to seasonal workers if paid on yearly basis (e.g., professional sports player in off-season)
   d. One must have worked for specified period of time and/or earned specified amount of wages

> **NOW REVIEW MULTIPLE-CHOICE QUESTIONS 1 THROUGH 9 IN VOLUME 2**

B. Workers' Compensation Act

1. Workers' compensation is a form of strict liability whereby employer is liable to employee for injuries or diseases sustained by employee which arise out of and in course of employment

   a. Also may include those only partially sustained in course of employment
   b. Employee is worker subject to control and supervision of employer
   c. Distinguish from independent contractor (See Module 32, section B.2.)

2. Purpose

   a. To give employees and their dependents benefits for job-related injuries or diseases with little difficulty

       (1) Previously, employee had to sue employer for negligence to receive any benefits in form of damages

       (2) Employee usually cannot waive his/her right to benefits

   b. Cost is passed on as an expense of production

   c. **No fault need be shown;** payment is automatic upon satisfaction of requirements

       (1) Removes employer's common law defenses of

          (a) Assumption of risk

          (b) Negligence of a fellow employee—employer formerly could avoid liability by proving it was another employee's fault

          (c) Contributory negligence—injured employee was also negligent

3. Regulated by states

   a. Except that federal government employees are covered by federal statute

   b. Each state has its own statute

4. Generally, there are two types of statutes

   a. Elective statutes

       (1) If employer rejects, s/he loses the three common law defenses against employee's common law suit for damages so most accept

   b. Compulsory statutes

       (1) Require that all employers within coverage of statute provide benefits

       (2) Majority of states have compulsory coverage

5. Insurance used to provide benefits

   a. In lieu of insurance policy, employer may assume liability for workers' compensation claims but must show proof of financial responsibility to carry own risk

6. Legislative scope

   a. Workers' compensation coverage extends to all employees who are injured on the job or in the course of the employment (i.e., while acting in furtherance of employer's business purpose)

   b. Coverage also extends to occupational diseases and preexisting diseases that are aggravated by employment

   c. Coverage does not extend to employee while traveling to or from work

   d. Out-of-state work may be covered if it meets above mentioned criteria

   e. All states have workers' compensation law; most employees covered

   f. Must be employee; coverage does not extend to independent contractors

   g. Public employees are often covered

7. Legal action for damages

   a. Employers covered by workers' compensation insurance are generally exempt from lawsuits by employees

       (1) If employee does not receive benefits covered under workers' compensation, s/he may sue insurance company that agreed to cover workers

   b. Benefits under workers' compensation laws received by employee are in lieu of action for damages against employer and such a suit is barred

       (1) Employer assumes liability in exchange for employee giving up his/her common law rights to sue employer for damages caused by the job (e.g., suit based on negligence)

       (2) When employee is covered by workers' compensation law, his/her sole remedy against employer is that which is provided for under appropriate workers' compensation act

       (3) However, if employer **intentionally** injures employee, employee may proceed against employer based on intentional tort in addition to recovering under workers' compensation benefits

   c. Employee is entitled to workers' compensation benefits **without regard to fault**

       (1) Negligence or even gross negligence of injured employee is not a bar to recovery

       (2) Employee's negligence plays no role in determination of amount of benefits awarded

       (3) Failure of employee to follow employer's rules is not a bar to recovery

       (4) However, injuries caused by intentional self-infliction, or intoxication of employee, can bar recovery

    d. When employer fails to provide workers' compensation insurance or when employer's coverage is inadequate, injured employee may sue in common law for damages, and employer cannot resort to usual common law defenses

      (1) When employer uninsured, many states have a fund to pay employee for job-related injuries

        (a) State then proceeds against uninsured company
        (b) Penalties imposed

  8. Actions against third parties

    a. Employee's acceptance of workers' compensation benefits does not bar suit against third party whose negligence or unreasonably dangerous product caused injury

      (1) If employee sues and recovers from third party, employer (or its insurance carrier) is entitled to compensation for workers' compensation benefits paid to employee

        (a) Any recovery in excess of workers' compensation benefits received belongs to injured employee
        (b) To the extent that recovery duplicates benefits already obtained from employer (or carrier), that employer (or carrier) is entitled to reimbursement from employee

> **EXAMPLE**
>
> Kraig, an employee of Badger Corporation, was injured in an auto accident while on the job. The accident was due to the negligence of Todd. Kraig can recover under workers' compensation and also fully recover from Todd in a civil court case. However, Kraig must reimburse the workers' compensation carrier to the extent the recovery from Todd duplicates benefits already obtained under workers' compensation laws.

    b. If employee accepts workers' compensation benefits, employer (or its insurance carrier) is subrogated to rights of employee against third party who caused injury

      (1) Therefore, if employee elects not to sue third party, employer (or its insurance carrier) obtains employee's right of action against third person

  9. Claims

    a. Employees are required to file claim forms on timely basis

  10. Benefits

    a. Medical

      (1) Provides for medical care to injured or diseased employee

    b. Disability

      (1) This is partial wage continuation plan

    c. Death

      (1) Various plans and schedules provide payments to widow(er) and minor children

    d. Special provisions

      (1) Normally, statutes call for specific scheduled payments for loss of limb or eye
      (2) Also, if employee's injury is of a nature that prevents his/her returning to his/her occupation, plan may pay cost of retraining

    e. Normally not subject to waiver by employee

NOW REVIEW MULTIPLE-CHOICE QUESTIONS 10 THROUGH 16 IN VOLUME 2

C. Employee Safety

  1. Occupational Safety and Health Act (OSHA)

    a. OSHA applies to almost all employers except federal government, state governments, and certain industries subject to other safety regulations
    b. Purpose of OSHA is to promote safety standards and job safety
    c. Occupational Safety and Health Administration (OSHA) administers this law

(1) OSHA develops and enforces standards in work place on health and safety
(2) OSHA investigates complaints and makes inspections of workplace

    (a) Employers can require OSHA to get search warrant for inspection

        1] Search warrant issued based on probable cause

            a] High employee complaint rate can form basis for probable cause

(3) Employers required to keep records of job-related injuries and report serious accidents to OSHA
(4) Employers required to comply with regulations set by OSHA
(5) Employers are prohibited from discriminating against or discharging employees for exercising his/her rights under OSHA
(6) OSHA may assess civil penalties for violations
(7) Employers may be criminally liable if willful violation results in death of employee

    (a) Possible fine, imprisonment, or both

NOW REVIEW MULTIPLE-CHOICE QUESTION 17 IN VOLUME 2

D. Employment Discrimination

1. Title VII of the 1964 Civil Rights Act forbids discrimination in employment on the basis of race, color, religion, sex, or national origin

    a. Applies to employers and labor unions having fifteen or more employees whose business affects interstate commerce; also applies to government employers and employment agencies
    b. Job discrimination applies to discrimination in hiring, promotion, transfers, firing, compensation, etc.
    c. Enforced by Equal Employment Opportunity Commission (EEOC) which is a federal government administrative agency, or by lawsuits of private individuals
    d. Not necessarily illegal to treat employees differently, but

        (1) Illegal discrimination occurs when employee treated differently because of his/her race, color, religion, sex, or national origin; this is referred to as disparate treatment.
        (2) Illegal discrimination may occur when employer adopts seemingly neutral rules that adversely affect a member of a protected class

> **EXAMPLE**
>
> Rules requiring certain standards on weight and/or height have historically discriminated against women as a class since generally men are taller and weigh more.

        (3) Illegal discrimination may be proven statistically to show pattern of discrimination
        (4) Defendant may have defenses to Title VII violations

            (a) In those certain instances where sex, religion, or national origin is a bona fide (Latin—good faith) occupational qualification (BFOQ) reasonably necessary to the normal operation of that particular enterprise

                1] Courts construe this defense narrowly

            (b) Bona fide seniority or merit system
            (c) Professionally developed employment testing and education requirements

                1] Employers must be able to show that the test/educational requirements are job related and/or related to job performance if the test is adversely affecting a protected class.

            (d) National security reasons
            (e) Employer only needs to make reasonable accommodations for discrimination based on religion
            (f) No BFOQs exist for discrimination on the basis of race or color

    e. Sexual harassment

        (1) Quid pro quo (Latin—this for that) is intentional harassment involving promotions, job offers, job benefits, in exchange for sexual relations. It also includes sex in exchange for not being fired, demoted, etc.
        (2) Hostile work environment involves harassment that creates an offensive or intimidating work environment. This can include jokes, lewd comments, graphic pictures, etc.

    f. Remedies for a successful claimant under Title VII

        (1) Back pay
        (2) Job or promotion
        (3) Retroactive seniority
        (4) Compensatory damages, and in extreme cases punitive damages, for cases involving intentional discrimination

2. Age Discrimination in Employment Act

    a. Discrimination by employers with 20 or more employees, unions, employment agencies, and federal government
    b. Generally applies to individuals at least forty years old
    c. Very similar in application to Title VII except discrimination is based on age.

3. Vocational Rehabilitation Act of 1973 applies to employers with federal contracts over $2,500

    a. Employers required to take affirmative action to employ and advance qualified handicapped individuals

4. Americans with Disabilities Act (ADA)

    a. Forbids companies and most other entities from discriminating against qualified persons with a disability in various employment decisions including hiring, firing, promotion, and pay

        (1) Qualified individual with disability means person who can perform essential functions of job either with or without reasonable accommodation

            (a) Reasonable accommodation may include acquiring new equipment, modifying facilities, restructuring jobs, modifying work schedules, etc. unless employer can show undue hardship based on significant expense or hardship
            (b) ADA does not protect person using illegal drugs unless rehabilitated and no longer using drugs

        (2) Disabilities include physical impairments, mental impairments, medical conditions, and/or perceived impairments

    b. ADA protects disabled persons from discrimination and guarantees them equal access to, among others,

        (1) Public services including public transportation and public accommodations
        (2) Public services operated by private entities

    c. Enforcement may be by attorney general or by private legal action

5. Pregnancy Discrimination Act

    a. Actually a 1978 amendment to Title VII
    b. Employers prohibited from discriminating against employees becoming pregnant or giving birth

        (1) Unmarried and married woman are covered
        (2) Employers' health and disability insurance must cover pregnancy the same as any other medical condition

6. Vietnam Era Veterans Readjustment Assistance Act

    a. Employers with federal contracts of $10,000 or more must take affirmative action in hiring and promoting qualified veterans of the Vietnam War or qualified disabled veterans

7. Equal Pay Act

    a. Requires equal pay for equal work for both sexes
    b. Differences in pay may be based on merit, quality of work, seniority, shift differentials
    c. Enforced by Equal Employment Opportunity Commission (EEOC)
    d. To remedy violations, back pay may be required and wages of wronged employees must be raised to eliminate disparity

        (1) Other employees' wages may not be reduced instead

8. Family and Medical Leave Act

    a. Covers employees employed for at least twelve months for at least 1250 hours by employers having at least fifty employees
    b. Employees have the right to up to twelve workweeks of leave during a twelve-month period for any of following reasons

      (1) Employee's own serious health problem

      (2) To care for serious health problem of parent, spouse, or child

      (3) Birth and care of baby

      (4) Child placed with employee for adoption or foster care

  c. Leave of twelve weeks may be done intermittently for cases of serious health problems of employee or his/her covered relatives

  d. Typically, leave is without pay

  e. When employee returns, s/he must get back same or equivalent position

  f. Returning employee cannot lose benefits due to leave

  g. Employers who deny these rights to employee are civilly liable for damages

9. Health Insurance Portability and Accountability Act

  a. Restricts using exclusions for preexisting conditions in employer sponsored group health insurance policies

10. Whistle-Blower Protection Act

  a. Federal law that protects federal employees from retaliation by employers for reporting employer legal violations

  b. Majority of states also have laws that protect whistle-blowers from employers' retaliation

> **NOW REVIEW MULTIPLE-CHOICE QUESTIONS 18 THROUGH 25 IN VOLUME 2**

E. Federal Fair Labor Standards Act

1. Applies to all businesses that affect interstate commerce
2. All covered employees must be paid at least "the minimum wage"

  a. Employees younger than twenty may be hired for a somewhat lower "opportunity wage" for ninety calendar days

3. Covered workers who work more than forty hours per week must be paid time and a half
4. Some employees are not covered under some or all of the minimum wage and time-and-a-half provisions

  a. For example, professionals, executives, outside salespersons

5. Some employees must get at least minimum wage but are not covered by the overtime rules

  a. For example, taxi drivers, railroad employees

6. Employees may be paid based on various time bases such as hourly, weekly, monthly, etc.
7. Enforced by Department of Labor and may include fines and/or prison

F. National Labor Relations Act (NLRA)

1. Provides that employees have right to join, assist, or form labor organizations
2. Enforced by the National Labor Relations Board (NLRB)
3. NLRB runs and supervises union elections
4. If union is elected, then management and union must collectively bargain

  a. Mandatory bargaining subjects are topics that both sides **must** negotiate about in good faith. These subjects are

      (1) Wages

      (2) Hours, and

      (3) Other conditions of employment (e.g., benefits, safety conditions, seniority rules, etc.)

  b. Illegal bargaining subjects are topics that neither side may bring up (e.g., anything that would violate the NLRA such as an unfair labor practice [UFLP]). Examples include

      (1) Featherbedding, which requires employers to pay employees for work not actually performed

      (2) Involving other parties not directly involved in the labor dispute

  c. Permissive bargaining subjects are topics that either side **may** negotiate about. If a subject is not mandatory or illegal, then it is permissive.

5. Strikes, employees refusing to work, are generally legal, but a strike can only be about a mandatory bargaining subject.

6. Certain employees are **not covered** by the NLRA. This does not mean these employees cannot create unions, but they are not protected by the provisions of the NLRA

   a. Government employees
   b. Agricultural employees
   c. Management level employees
   d. Railroad employees

7. The Landrum-Griffin Act amended the NLRA to regulate union abuses against its own members

   a. Requires extensive financial reporting involving unions
   b. Provides for civil and criminal action against misdeeds of union officers
   c. Provides for bill of rights for union members in conducting meetings and elections

NOW REVIEW MULTIPLE-CHOICE QUESTIONS 26 THROUGH 28 IN VOLUME 2

G. Federal Consolidated Omnibus Budget Reconciliation Act (COBRA)

1. Provides that when employee quits, s/he may keep same group health insurance coverage for eighteen months for that former employee and spouse

   a. Former employee pays for it
   b. Trade Act increases election period to keep same coverage

2. Applies to employers with 20 or more employees

H. Pensions

1. Employee Retirement Income Security Act (ERISA)

   a. Does not require employer to set up pension plan
   b. If employer does set up plan, it must meet certain standards

      (1) Generally, employee contributions to pension plan vest immediately
      (2) In general, employee's rights to employer's contributions to pension plan vest from five to seven years after beginning employment based on formulas in law
      (3) Standards on investment of funds are set up to avoid mismanagement
      (4) Employers cannot delay employee's participation in pension plan
      (5) Covered plans must give annual reports to employees in plan
      (6) Plan must be in writing
      (7) Plan manager must be named. Manager is a fiduciary.

2. In noncontributory pension plan, employee does not pay but employer pays for all
3. Maximum punishments for violations of Act by individuals increased to imprisonment of ten years and fine of $100,000—by entities, maximum fine is increased to $500,000
4. Sarbanes-Oxley Act requires administrators of employee benefit and profit sharing plans to provide participants and beneficiaries thirty-day advance notice of blackout periods when their rights are temporarily suspended to make changes in plan

   a. Criminal penalties increased by significantly greater fines and longer imprisonment terms

      (1) Based on intent of reducing excesses of some corporations and holding officers and directors more accountable

   b. Prohibits officers and directors from acquiring or transferring stock for services to corporation during blackout periods

NOW REVIEW MULTIPLE-CHOICE QUESTIONS 29 THROUGH 31 IN VOLUME 2

I. Worker Adjustment and Retraining Notification Act

1. Provides that employers before they close a plant or have mass layoffs must give sixty days notice to employees as well as to state and local officials
2. Act allows shorter notice period in case of emergencies or failing companies
3. Applies to businesses with 100 or more employees

J. Federal Employee Polygraph Protection Act and Drug Testing

1. Private employers may not require employees or prospective employees to take lie detector test or make adverse employment decisions based on such tests or refusals to take them

    a. Act allows polygraph tests to be used by

        (1) Security services hiring employees to protect public health and safety
        (2) Employers that deal with national defense issues
        (3) Drug manufacturers and distributors

    b. Government employers exempted
    c. Private employer may use lie detector tests as part of investigation of economic loss when employer has reason to suspect individual

        (1) Employer is limited in topics of questions that violate privacy especially in topics not directly related to investigation of economic loss

2. Drug testing by public employers and private employers of prospective employees has increased very significantly in the past few years

    a. Employees and job applicants frequently view this as an invasion of privacy
    b. Employers see drug testing as a way to decrease possible liability and also as a way to increase productivity
    c. Generally courts rule preemployment drug screening is legal because job applicants have a lower expectation of privacy than current employees

        (1) Courts generally hold current employees can be tested if either employer has reasonable suspicion employee is drug-impaired or all employees who have had accidents are tested for drugs

K. Employer Rights to E-mail

1. Courts consistently rule employees have no expectation of privacy using employer's e-mail systems

    a. Most employers warn employees about this limitation on privacy at work

        (1) Lack of this warning does not affect employer's rights to review employees' e-mail

2. Unsolicited bulk e-mail or spam has caused problems for both employers and employees

    a. Lawyers have creatively used the traditional tort of trespass to stop some of these problems in cyberspace

L. Environmental Regulation

1. Under common law

    a. Parties may be liable under doctrine of nuisance

        (1) Based on party using property in manner that unreasonably interferes with another's right to use and enjoy property
        (2) Typically, monetary damages is remedy rather than injunction
        (3) Often, plaintiffs need to show their injury is distinct from harm of public in general

    b. Businesses may be liable for negligence

        (1) Plaintiff shows that his/her harm was caused by business polluter who failed to use reasonable care to prevent foreseeable harm

    c. Businesses may be liable under strict liability if involved in ultra hazardous activities

    > **EXAMPLE**
    >
    > B is in the business of transporting radioactive materials. Strict liability may be used which makes B liable for all damages it causes without the need to prove negligence.

2. Under federal statutory laws

    a. Environmental Protection Agency (EPA)

        (1) Administrative agency set up to ensure compliance with environmental protection laws
        (2) EPA may enforce federal environmental laws by use of administrative orders and/or civil penalties

            (a) May also refer criminal or civil actions to Department of Justice

(3) EPA also adopts regulations and conducts research on environment and effects of pollution

(4) Most environmental statutes provide for criminal liability

    (a) Generally, corporate officers must be "blameworthy," based on ability to prevent or correct, to be criminally liable

(5) EPA generally uses civil suits more than criminal prosecutions because civil suits require preponderance of evidence to win but criminal convictions require proof beyond a reasonable doubt

(6) Private citizens may also sue violators or may sue EPA to enforce compliance with laws

(7) States may also sue violators

b. National Environmental Policy Act

    (1) Requires all federal agencies consider environmental factors in all major decisions

        (a) Requires preparation of environmental impact statement (EIS) when federal action or proposed laws significantly affect environment

            1] Shows expected impact on environment
            2] Describes adverse consequences of action that are unavoidable
            3] Must examine alternatives to achieve goals
            4] For EIS, environment means more than natural environment—can include aesthetic, cultural, and national heritage interests, etc.

        (b) Federal agency must consider environmental impact prior to project

        (c) If federal government needs to grant a permit to a private party, then typically private party will need to submit EIS

        (d) If agency finds no EIS is warranted, it must prepare and make available to public document called "Finding of No Significant Impact" with reasons for no action needed

c. Clean Air Act

    (1) EPA is required to create national ambient air quality standards (NAAQS)

        (a) Primary standards are created to protect the public health
        (b) Secondary standards are created to protect public welfare (e.g., crops, animals, structures)

    (2) States must then submit a state implementation plan (SIP) detailing how the state will achieve the NAAQS

    (3) Provides that EPA set air quality standards for mobile sources, such as autos, and stationary sources, such as factories

        (a) Recent amendments now require more, including some smaller businesses to be regulated by Clean Air Act such as many paint shops, bakeries, and dry cleaners

        (b) Recent amendments have also encouraged cities and counties to impose residential regulations such as no-burn days for fireplaces, regulations on reducing numbers of fireplaces in certain areas, or restrictions on charcoal barbeques

        (c) EPA notes air in some buildings is more polluted than outside air

    (4) New stationary sources constructed after a NAAQS must show that they are using the best technological system of emissions reduction

    (5) Regulates various toxic pollutants, including those that affect acid rain and ozone layer

    (6) Act allows private citizens to sue violators of Act and also state or federal officials who fail to take action under the law

        (a) Those winning successful citizens' lawsuits can get attorneys' fees and court costs and punitive damages

        (b) Court may also order EPA to perform its duties and impose civil penalties

    (7) Encourages and requires use of alternative fuels to help meet pollution goals

    (8) Federal government may force recall of automobiles violating emission regulations

    (9) EPA can assess stated civil penalties per violation

        (a) When company finds it cost effective to violate Clean Air Act, EPA may wage penalty equal to benefit company received by not complying

        (b) Criminal fines and imprisonment for intentional violations have recently been made harsher

            1] Most violations under Act are now felonies rather than misdemeanors
            2] Act allows that any responsible corporate officers can be criminally liable

(10) Amendments to Clean Air Act allow companies to trade some rights to pollute
(11) Recent Supreme Court case says that Clean Air Act does not require EPA to consider cost in making air clean

    (a) EPA required to strictly reduce certain toxic pollutants such as mercury

(12) Areas that have already met or exceeded clean air requirements are prohibited from any significant deterioration of their current air quality

d. Clean Water Act

    (1) EPA sets standards to reduce, eliminate, or prevent pollution of rivers, seas, ponds, wetlands, streams, etc.

        (a) For example, controls dredging or filling of rivers and wetlands
        (b) Also by amendments, requires acid rain control program

    (2) Implemented similar to Clean Air Act: EPA creates framework of clean water standards and states are responsible for making sure that the federal standards are met
    (3) Owners of point sources such as floating vessels, pipes, ditches, and animal feeding operations must obtain permits which control water pollution

        (a) Nonpoint sources such as farms, forest lands, and mining are exempt

    (4) Broad in scope—includes regulation of discharge of heated water (e.g., by nuclear power plant or electric utilities)

        (a) EPA awards grants for programs to notify public of potential exposure to disease-causing organisms in coastal recreation waters

            1] Many states are now directed to increase monitoring programs for recreational water for such things as E. coli
            2] Applies to coastal regions on oceans and Great Lakes

    (5) Provides for fines and prison for neglect or knowing violations or endangerment (i.e., knowingly putting person in imminent danger of death or serious bodily harm)

e. Safe Drinking Water Act

    (1) Regulates safety of water supplied to homes by public water systems

        (a) EPA required to prepare new list every three years that identifies contaminants that EPA is considering for future regulation and for drinking water research, monitoring, and health advisory guidance
        (b) Recently identified threat to water systems is from terrorism

            1] Recent law requires activities at local, state, and national levels to help public health community to respond to threat of terrorism

    (2) Prohibits discharge of waste into wells for drinking water

f. Oil Pollution Act

    (1) Requires establishment of oil pollution cleanup contingency plans by tanker owners and operators to handle worst case spills under adverse weather conditions
    (2) Requires that new tankers have double hulls
    (3) Requires phase-in of double hulls on existing oil tankers and barges

g. Noise Control Act

    (1) Regulates noise pollution and encourages research on its effects
    (2) EPA establishes noise standards for products sold in US
    (3) Violations may result in fines, imprisonment, or injunctions

h. Resource Conservation and Recovery Act

    (1) Creates permit system to regulate businesses that store, use, or transport hazardous waste
    (2) Requires companies to keep strict records of hazardous waste from "cradle to grave" transport
    (3) Producers required to label and package correctly hazardous materials that are to be transported
    (4) Fines and prison for violators

        (a) Can be doubled for certain violations

    (5) Also, household waste regulated

   i. Toxic Substances Control Act

     (1) Mandates testing and regulation of chemicals that pose unreasonable risk to health or environment

        (a) Requires testing before marketing allowed

     (2) Requires special labeling of toxic substances

   j. Federal Insecticide, Fungicide, and Rodenticide Act

     (1) Provides that pesticides and herbicides must be registered with EPA before sale
     (2) EPA can

        (a) Deny registration
        (b) Certify them for general or restricted use
        (c) Suspend registration if emergency or imminent danger
        (d) Grant conditional registration when useful until effects known

     (3) Limits set for amount of pesticide residue permitted on crops for human or animal consumption
     (4) Act has labeling requirements
     (5) Violators subject to fine and imprisonment
     (6) Private party may petition EPA to suspend or cancel registration

   k. Federal Environmental Pesticide Control Act

     (1) All who distribute pesticides must register them with EPA
     (2) EPA uses cost-benefit analysis to decide to register pesticides rather than deciding if they will pose health hazard

   l. Comprehensive Environmental, Compensation, and Liability Act (CERCLA)

     (1) Often known as the Superfund legislation
     (2) Levies taxes on manufacturers of certain dangerous chemicals
     (3) Identifies hazardous waste sites needed to be cleaned up
     (4) Regulates generation and transportation of hazardous substances

        (a) Does not regulate petroleum or natural gas

     (5) Government can impose broad liability for cleanup costs and environmental damages

        (a) Parties have **joint and several liability** and include

           1] **Current owners and operators** of site
           2] **Past owners and operators** of site
           3] Persons who **transported** waste to site
           4] Persons who arranged to have waste transported

        (b) With limited exceptions, the standard is based on **strict liability** for all cleanup costs
        (c) One who is responsible for portion of waste can be liable for all cleanup costs
        (d) Liability is retroactive under this statute
        (e) CERCLA lender liability—one important issue is when a lender has responsibility for cleanup when it takes possession of real property due to a foreclosure sale or a deed in lieu of foreclosure

           1] Recent statute specifically excludes lender from CERCLA liability in most situations when it takes possession of real estate due to foreclosure
           2] Lender is still liable under CERCLA if it participates in management or operational affairs of the facility foreclosed on
           3] Lender can do any of following and NOT be liable under CERCLA

               a] Lease the property
               b] Sell the property
               c] Monitor or enforce terms of security agreement involved
               d] Provide financial advice
               e] Restructure loan terms
               f] Mandate debtor to take action on hazardous materials

        (f) CERCLA does **not** make polluters liable to private parties; they generally use private suits under common law

   m. Emergency Planning and Community Right-to-Know Act

      (1) Companies having specified amounts of extremely hazardous substances must notify state and local agencies and also must issue annual reports of releases of specified toxic chemicals that result from operations

         (a) This information is available to public

   n. International protection of ozone layer

      (1) Many countries, including US, have agreed to reduce or eliminate certain chemicals believed to harm ozone layer

   o. Nuclear Waste Policy Act

      (1) Creates national plan to dispose of highly radioactive nuclear waste
      (2) State may regulate emissions of radioactive particles under Clean Air Act

   p. Energy Independence and Security Act

      (1) Purpose of Act is to move US toward greater energy independence, to increase production of clean renewable fuels, to increase efficiency of products, vehicles, and buildings, among others
      (2) Automakers required to boost fleet-wide gas mileage to specified standards

         (a) Applies to all passenger vehicles including light trucks

      (3) Requires vehicle technology and transportation electrification

         (a) Incentives given for development of plug-in hybrids

      (4) Requires specified standards for greater efficiency for lightbulb or similar energy savings
      (5) New initiatives to improve efficiency of highway, sea, and railroad infrastructure
      (6) Creation of Office of Climate Change and Environment in Department of Transportation
      (7) Modernization of electricity grid to improve efficiency
      (8) Small business loans toward improving energy efficiency
      (9) Creation of training program for green jobs (i.e., energy efficiency and renewable energy workers)
    (10) Taxpayer funding for increased funding of biofuels added to gasoline

   q. Marine Protection, Research, and Sanctuaries Act

      (1) Regulates dumping into oceans
      (2) Establishing marine sanctuaries

   r. Endangered Species Act

      (1) Enforced by both EPA and Department of Commerce
      (2) Protects both endangered as well as threatened species

   s. Pollution Prevention Act

      (1) Provides incentives to industry to prevent some pollution from initially being formed

   t. SEC requires that companies report in financial statements their environmental liabilities

3. Environmental Compliance Audits

   a. These are systematic, objective reviews designed to evaluate compliance with federal and state regulations and laws on environment

      (1) Some states have environmental audit privilege laws. In these states, businesses' environmental audits are exempt from discovery in a lawsuit.

   b. Purposes of audit

      (1) To discover violations or questionable practices to allow company to avoid litigation
      (2) Voluntary discovery allows companies to avoid criminal sanctions
      (3) To meet disclosure requirements under securities laws

NOW REVIEW MULTIPLE-CHOICE QUESTION 32 THROUGH 44 IN VOLUME 2

M. Telephone Consumer Protection Act

1. Restricts use of prerecorded messages
2. Act requires that in order to use prerecorded messages, a live person must introduce prerecorded message and receive from telephoned person permission to play that message

   a. Act exempts calls by nonprofit organizations, calls made for emergencies, and calls to businesses
   b. Act does not cover personal phone calls

N. Federal Telecommunications Act

1. Prevents local or state governments from preventing entry of the growing telecommunications industry

O. Identity Theft

1. Hackers can collect much information on individuals to piece together information on them to, in many cases, obtain credit or make purchases or obtain government benefits
2. Increased penalties for identity theft to help reduce it
3. FTC is appointed to help victims of identity theft to restore credit and minimize impacts of identity theft
4. All banks, savings associations, and credit unions are required to have an identity theft prevention program

P. Antitrust Law

1. The main purpose of federal antitrust laws is to promote the production and distribution of goods and services in the most economical and efficient manner by preserving free, competitive markets

   a. Also promotes fairness and gives consumer a wider choice

2. Regulation (for our concerns) is by federal law, so interstate commerce must be affected before the activity is regulated

   a. If there is a substantial economic effect on interstate commerce, then federal law governs

   (1) Even if a business is only carried on within a state, it may substantially affect interstate commerce if it

       (a) Competes or deals with businesses that do business among several states, or
       (b) Purchases or sells a substantial amount of products that come from or wind up in interstate commerce

> **EXAMPLE**
>
> Wholesale dealers in a state agree to divide the state market among them. This agreement is intrastate but it reduces the chances for out-of-state dealers to enter the local market and therefore the agreement affects interstate commerce.

3. If the contract in restraint of trade is illegal, it is unenforceable by the parties, in addition to possible criminal or civil penalties and injunctions

   a. Vertical restraints are agreements between parties from different levels of the distribution chain (i.e., between manufacturer and retailer)
   b. Horizontal restraints are agreements between parties of the same level of the distribution chain (i.e., between two retailers or two manufacturers)

4. Some contracts in restraint of trade **are** legal and enforceable

   a. Seller of a business agrees not to compete with the buyer

   (1) Only valid if for a reasonable time and a reasonable geographic area and if a proper business interest is sought to be protected

       (a) Reasonable time is what is fair under the circumstances to protect buyer (e.g., one year)
       (b) Reasonable area would be where the business is conducted (e.g., neighborhood). If business is statewide, then restriction can be for whole state

> **EXAMPLE**
>
> Seller of a bakery covenants not to compete in the immediate locality for one year. This is a reasonable area and also a reasonable length of time.

   b. Similarly, partners and employees can covenant not to compete with partnership or employer while relationship lasts and for a reasonable time thereafter and within a reasonable area

c. Buyer or lessee of property may covenant not to use it in competition with, or to the injury of the seller or lessor

(1) Same standards of reasonableness apply

5. Exceptions to the antitrust laws

a. Labor unions unless they join with nonlabor group and act in violation
b. Patents are a twenty-year monopoly; fourteen years for design patents
c. Copyrights are a monopoly for the author's life plus seventy years

(1) For publishers, 95 years after publication or 120 years after creation

d. Trademarks are a monopoly with an indefinite number of renewals if still used
e. Insurance business that is covered by state regulations
f. US exporters may cooperate to compete with foreign entities
g. State allowed to have quotas on oil marketed for interstate commerce
h. Agricultural cooperatives
i. State government actions

(1) These are industries comprehensively regulated by the state
(2) Utilities, insurance are examples of industries where this is true

j. Legislative activities such as lobbying
k. Professional baseball, no other sports, just baseball

6. Enforcement of the Antitrust Laws

a. Justice Department

(1) Enforces Sherman Act and Clayton Act
(2) Only enforcement entity that may seek criminal penalties

b. Federal Trade Commission (FTC)

(1) Enforces Clayton Act and Federal Trade Commission Act
(2) May only pursue civil enforcement

c. Private parties

(1) Entitled to treble (triple) actual damages and reasonable attorney fees if successful.
(2) May only pursue civil enforcement

Q. Sherman Act of 1890

1. Contracts, combinations, conspiracies, or agreements in restraint of trade are illegal under Section 1 of the Sherman Act.

a. The agreement must be between separate economic entities

> **EXAMPLE**
>
> McDonald's can decide that all of its stores will sell Quarter Pounders for $1.99. McDonald's cannot agree with Burger King that if Burger King will charge at least $3.50 for a Whopper, McDonald's will sell Quarter Pounders for $3.50.

b. Only unreasonable restraints are illegal
c. There are two approaches that courts use to determine whether the restraint is unreasonable:

(1) The per se rule
(2) The rule of reason

d. The per se rule means that the restraint is automatically illegal

(1) Certain activities are viewed as so inherently anticompetitive that there can be no valid justification to engage is such activities
(2) Generally, the per se rule applies to horizontal restraints of trade. (See section 2. of this outline below)
(3) Activities that do not fall under the per se rule are analyzed under the rule of reason

e. The rule of reason balances the precompetitive effects of the agreement versus the anticompetitive effects of the agreement

(1) If on balance, the agreement is more procompetitive than anticompetitive, the agreement is legal
(2) Conversely, if the agreement is more anticompetitive, then the agreement is illegal

2. Horizontal restraints of trade involve agreements between competitors

> **EXAMPLE**
>
> An agreement between McDonald's and Burger King.

a. Many horizontal restraints are analyzed under the per se rule because they tend to directly reduce competition
b. Per se horizontal restraints include

(1) Price fixing (agreement)

(a) Whether it actually affects prices or not
(b) Whether the fixed price is fair or not (presumed unfair)
(c) Dollar volume is unimportant; existence of any price fixing agreement is illegal
(d) An actual agreement is not necessary if the parties have a tacit understanding and adhere to it
(e) Includes quantity limitations and minimum, maximum, buying, and selling prices

(2) Joint boycotts (i.e., group agreements not to deal with another) are per se violations
(3) Horizontal territorial limitation is a per se violation

> **EXAMPLE**
>
> Two competitors agree not to sell in each other's section of the city.

c. Not all horizontal agreements are illegal per se

(1) A joint venture is analyzed under the rule of reason because most anticompetitive effects are temporary
(2) Trade and professional organization agreements are examined under the rule of reason

3. Vertical restraints of trade involve agreements between businesses at different levels in the distribution chain

> **EXAMPLE**
>
> McDonald's entering into an agreement with Coke to use only Coca Cola products in McDonald's restaurants

a. All vertical restraints are subject to a rule of reason analysis (i.e. there are no per se violations for vertical restraints)
b. Resale price maintenance (Vertical price fixing)

(1) Manufacturer's may suggest a retail price; this is legal because there is no agreement.
(2) Manufacturer's may refuse to sell to retailers who promise to sell at suggested price. This is a unilateral decision by the manufacturer, so there is no agreement.

> **EXAMPLE**
>
> Colgate toothpaste tells Mega Mart that it must resell Colgate at a price of no less than $2 a tube. Mega Mart refuses and Colgate does not sell toothpaste to Mega Mart. Since there is no agreement between Colgate and Mega, there cannot be a violation of Section 1 of the Sherman Act.

c. Rule of reason analysis for vertical restraints usually focuses on interbrand and intrabrand competition.

(1) Interbrand competition is the competition between different brands of the same product.

> **EXAMPLE**
>
> Campbell's soup and Progresso soup.

(2) Intrabrand competition is between the same brands at different places.

> **EXAMPLE**
>
> The price of Campbell's soup at different competing supermarkets.

(3) Generally interbrand competition is viewed as more beneficial to consumers
(4) Thus, many vertical restraints which injure or limit intrabrand competition, but enhance or promote inter-brand competition, are usually legal under the rule of reason

d. Vertical territorial limitations, often contained in franchising agreements, where franchisee receives an exclusive right to sell in a specific territory but is precluded from selling in any area are only illegal if unreasonable (Rule of Reason)

> **EXAMPLE**
>
> A distributor requires dealer to sell only in X suburban area.

2. Monopolization violates Section 2 of the Sherman Act

a. Section 2 makes it illegal for a firm to obtain or maintain a monopoly; it is not illegal to actually have a monopoly
b. Unlike Section 1 of the Sherman Act, there is no agreement necessary to violate Section 2 of the Sherman Act
c. Monopoly is the power to exclude competition and/or to control prices; a firm does not need 100% of the market to have a monopoly under the antitrust laws

(1) Percentage share of the relevant market is a determining factor

(a) Generally, 70% of the relevant market is a presumption of monopoly power
(b) Less than 50% of the relevant market there is a presumption of no monopoly power
(c) A much lower percentage will suffice if the charge is attempting to monopolize rather than holding monopoly power

(2) The relevant market consists of the product market and the geographic market

(a) Product market consists of commodities reasonably interchangeable by consumers

> **EXAMPLE**
>
> In a case involving a cellophane wrapping manufacturer, the product market was flexible wrapping material.

(b) Geographic market is the area in which the defendant and competitors sell the product

> **EXAMPLE**
>
> A geographic market for a major beer brewer is national while for a taxi company it is very local.

d. Intent is also required to violate Section 2

(1) Therefore, to engage in illegal monopolization there needs to be monopoly power and intent
(2) If no intent, or monopoly is thrust on defendant, then not illegal

(a) Growth resulting from superior product, quality of management, or historical accident is not illegal
(b) There must not be any predatory or coercive conduct

> **EXAMPLE**
>
> There are several hotels in a town. Business drops and all but one close. The remaining hotel has taken no action to get the others to close. Although the remaining hotel has a monopoly, it was thrust upon the hotel and is therefore not illegal.

3. Sanctions (not mutually exclusive, both civil and governmental prosecution available)

a. Injunctions, forced divisions, forced divestiture (by individuals, corporations, or government)

(1) Government may seize property shipped in interstate commerce and violating party forfeits it

b. Criminal penalties (by government)

c. Treble damages (by individuals and corporations)

    (1) That is, actual damages (e.g., loss of profits, multiplied by three)

    (2) Plus attorney fees and court costs

    (3) Instituted to encourage private parties to enforce the antitrust laws

R. Clayton Act of 1914

1. Supplemented the Sherman Act to prohibit a corporation from acquiring the stock of a competing corporation (merger) where the effect **might** substantially lessen competition or tend to create a monopoly

    a. Acquisitions tending to create a monopoly are violations

        (1) No actual monopoly need be created

        (2) To stop monopolistic trends in their incipiency

        (3) Applies where there is a reasonable likelihood the merger or acquisition will substantially lessen competition

        (4) As under the Sherman Act, use the percentage of market (product and geographic) test

    b. Amendment of 1950 added the prohibition of the acquisition of assets of another corporation where the effect might lessen competition

        (1) Thus both asset and stock acquisitions are covered

        (2) Includes vertical mergers (sellers-buyers) and conglomerate mergers (e.g., not in same industry) as well as horizontal mergers (competitors)

> **EXAMPLE**
>
> A shoe manufacturer buys out one of its retailers. This is a vertical merger.

> **EXAMPLE**
>
> A shoe retailer buys out another shoe retailer. This is a horizontal merger.

> **EXAMPLE**
>
> A pen manufacturer buys out a clothing retailer. This is a conglomerate merger.

    c. Suit may be brought either before or after completion of the merger

        (1) For example, preliminary injunction to prevent violation

        (2) For example, forced divestiture anytime after completion of a merger if competitor threatened

    d. Under "failing company doctrine," a merger that is anticompetitive may be allowed if

        (1) The acquired company is failing, and

        (2) There is no other willing purchaser whose acquisition of the company would reduce competition less

    e. Factors to determine whether a merger will result in a substantial lessening of competition include

        (1) Market concentration

            (a) If the market is controlled by just a few firms, then it is more likely that the merger will result in a substantial lessening of competition.

            (b) If the market is controlled by many firms, then it is less likely that the merger will result in a substantial lessening of competition.

        (2) Entry barriers to the market are how difficult or how easy it is for new firms to enter the market. If entry barriers are high, it is more likely a merger will result in a substantial lessening of competition.

        (3) Generally, horizontal mergers are the most likely to result in a substantial lessening of competition, and conglomerate mergers are the least likely to do so.

2. Interlocking directorates are prohibited under the Clayton Act

   a. Applies to a director sitting on boards of two or more competing corporations that are "large"
   b. No proof required that this will lessen competition
   c. Remedy typically is to required offending director to resign one of the director positions

3. Tying arrangements

   a. Occurs where seller forces buyer to take one or more other products as a condition to acquiring the desired product

> **EXAMPLE**
>
> A manufacturer of a very popular line of jeans requires its retailers to also stock the manufacturer's line of shirts in order to obtain the jeans.

   b. Elements of a tying arrangement

     (1) Two separate products

       (a) Tying product is the product that is actually desired. In the example above, the tying products are the jeans.
       (b) Tied product is the product that the buyer is being "forced" to purchase. In the above example, the tied products are the shirts.

     (2) There must be economic power in the tying market. Economic power can be shown by either

       (a) A market share of 30% or more in the tying market, or
       (b) The product is unique. Uniqueness can often be demonstrated by an intellectual property right such as a patent or a copyright.

> **EXAMPLE**
>
> When the movie *Gone with the Wind* was released, movie theaters were told that they would also have to take a movie called *Getting Gertie's Garter*. While *Gone with the Wind* did not have a 30% market share, it was a unique production, and thus qualifies as economic power.

     (3) Substantial commerce in the tied market

   c. Generally, all three elements must be met for the tying arrangement to be considered illegal

S. Robinson-Patman Act of 1936

1. Prohibits price discrimination
2. Price discrimination is when a seller charges different prices to different buyers of the same good.

> **EXAMPLE**
>
> Thor's Hammers Inc. charges Home Depot $3.00 per hammer, but it charges Mom and Pop Hardware $3.50 per hammer.

3. Price differences are permitted if there is a cost justification

> **EXAMPLE**
>
> Home Depot buys an entire truckload of hammers: Mom and Pop Hardware buys 1/20 of a truckload of hammers. The lower transportation costs for Home Depot can be passed on to Home Depot in the form of a lower price without violating the law.

4. Sellers may also temporarily reduce prices in one region to meet the price of a lower-priced competitor

T. Federal Trade Commission Act of 1914

1. Created the Federal Trade Commission (FTC)

   a. FTC has authority to enforce most of the antitrust laws, but not criminal violations
   b. FTC has exclusive authority to enforce this Act's prohibitions (i.e., individuals may not enforce)
   c. FTC has authority to determine what practices are unfair or undesirable

2. Prohibits unfair methods of competition and deceptive practices involving advertising, telemarketing, electronic advertising

   a. FTC has exclusive authority under this Act and can determine what is unfair
   b. FTC may stop unfair and deceptive practices in their incipiency (i.e., before an actual violation occurs) as well as after a violation occurs

---

EXAMPLE

An oil company agreed with a tire company that the oil company would promote the sale of the tire company's accessories to the oil company's independent dealers. There was no tying or overt coercion in these promotions to the independent dealers, but the dominant position of the oil company over its dealers created strong potential for stifling competition. The agreement was therefore an unfair method of competition.

---

   c. Unfairness standards

      (1) Cause of substantial injury to competitors or consumers
      (2) Offends public policy
      (3) Oppressive or unscrupulous practices

3. Sanctions

   a. Cease and desist orders

      (1) Civil penalty for each violation
      (2) Each day of continued violation is separate offense
      (3) FTC may also use cease and desist orders for the Sherman Act and Clayton Act

NOW REVIEW MULTIPLE-CHOICE QUESTION 45 THROUGH 47 IN VOLUME 2

KEY TERMS

Employment Law

   Age Discrimination in Employment Act (ADEA). Law that prohibits discrimination against people who are 40 and older.
   Americans with Disabilities Act (ADA). Prohibits discrimination against differently abled persons. Includes both physical and mental disabilities.
   Bona fide occupational qualification (BFOQ). An employer's defense to a claim of employment discrimination based on Title VII. The employer is claiming to have a legitimate reason, usually related to job qualifications, for what appears to be discrimination.
   Consolidated Omnibus Budget Reconciliation Act (COBRA). Allows former employees, at their own expense, to continue coverage of their group health plan for up to 18 months after losing their job.
   Employee Retirement Income Security Act (ERISA). Regulates pension plans for companies that choose to have pensions.
   Fair Labor Standards Act (FLSA). Federal law that regulates minimum wage, employment hours, and child labor.
   Family and Medical Leave Act. Allows employees to take up to 12 weeks of unpaid leave to deal with family and medical issues.
   Federal Insurance Contributions Act (FICA). Law that requires employers and employees to each pay half of the social security tax. Self-employed individuals must pay the entire tax.
   Federal Unemployment Tax Act (FUTA). Provides temporary payments to workers who have lost their jobs through no fault of their own.
   National Labor Relations Act (NLRA). Legislation that regulates the union/management relationship.
   Occupational Safety and Health Act (OSHA). Creates workplace standards of health and safety.
   Social Security Act. Provides income/benefits to retirees, disabled workers, and dependents of deceased workers.

Title VII of the 1964 Civil Rights Act. Prohibits discrimination on the basis of race, color, religion, national origin, or gender in all aspects of employment.

Worker's compensation. Provides payments to workers for injuries that are sustained at work or that arise out of work. This is a no-fault system.

Environmental Law

Clean Air Act. Establishes air quality standards that states enforce.

Clean Water Act. Establishes water quality standards that states enforce.

Comprehensive Environmental Response, Compensation, and Liability Act (CERCLA). Creates a strict liability system for the cleanup of hazardous waste sites and spills.

Environmental compliance audit. A voluntary review by a company to ensure that it is in compliance with the various environmental laws.

Environmental impact statement. A report required for any federal action that will significantly impact the environment.

Environmental Protection Agency (EPA). Primary enforcer and administrator of environmental laws and regulations.

State implementation plan. Plan submitted by a state to show the EPA how the state will achieve the environmental standards set by the EPA.

Antitrust

Horizontal restraint. An agreement among competing economic entities that limits competition.

Merger. Two separate economic entities that combine into one company. Only mergers that will result in a substantial lessening of competition violate the antitrust laws.

Monopolization. When a firm has monopoly power in the relevant market and keeps others out of the market through methods other than legitimate competition.

Monopoly power. A firm has the ability to exclude competitors and control prices in the relevant market.

Per se rule. Applies to inherently anticompetitive activities that are automatically illegal.

Price discrimination. Sellers charging different buyers different prices for the same product.

Relevant market. Refers to the meaningful areas of competition both geographically and by product.

Restraint of trade. An agreement that limits competition.

Rule of reason. If a restraint of trade does not fall under the per se rule, then it is analyzed under the rule of reason, which balances the procompetitive effects of the agreement versus the anticompetitive effects.

Treble damages. One of the remedies for a private party who successfully proves an antitrust violation; the private party receives three times its actual damages.

Tying arrangement. Seller of a desired product forces a buyer to purchase an additional product if the buyer wants the desired product.

Vertical restraint of trade. An agreement between separate economic entities in the chain of distribution that limits competition.

Module 34: Property

Overview

Property entails items capable of being owned (i.e., the rights related to the ownership of things that society will recognize and enforce). Property is classified as real or personal, and as tangible or intangible. Protection of property and settlement of disputes concerning property is a major function of the legal system.

The candidate should be able to distinguish between personal and real property and between tenancies in common, joint tenancies, and tenancies by the entirety. The candidate also should understand that an instrument given primarily as security for real property is a mortgage and be able to distinguish between the legal results arising from "assumption" of a mortgage and taking "subject to" a mortgage. Other questions concerning mortgages require basic knowledge of the concepts of novation, suretyship, subrogation, and redemption.

Questions on deeds may distinguish between the legal implication of warranty deeds, quitclaim deeds, and special warranty deeds. Both mortgages and deeds should be publicly recorded, and the questions may require the candidate to identify a priority and constructive notice. The most important topics under lessor-lessee law are the Statute of Frauds, the effect of a sale of leased property, assignment, and subleasing. Before beginning the reading you should review the key terms at the end of the module.

A. Distinctions between Real and Personal Property

1. Real property (realty)—includes land and things attached to land in a relatively permanent manner

> **EXAMPLE**
>
> A building is erected on a parcel of land. Both the land and the building are real property.

   a. Crops harvested are not real property because they are separate from land
   b. Growing crops are generally part of land and therefore realty

      (1) Growing crops can be sold separately from land in which case they are considered personal property

         (a) True whether buyer or seller will sever growing crops from land

2. Personal property (personalty)—property not classified as real property or a fixture

   a. May be either

      (1) Tangible—subject to physical possession

> **EXAMPLE**
>
> Automobiles and books are tangible personal property.

(2) Intangible—not subject to physical possession but subject to legal ownership

> **EXAMPLE**
>
> Contractual rights to receive payment for automobiles sold and intellectual property, such as copyrights, are intangible personal property.

3. Fixture—item that was originally personal property but which is affixed to real property in relatively permanent fashion such that it is considered to be part of real property

   a. Several factors are applied in determining whether personal property that has been attached to real property is a fixture

      (1) Affixer's objective intent as to whether property is to be regarded as personalty or realty
      (2) Method and permanence of physical attachment to real property

         (a) If item cannot be removed without material injury to real property, it is generally held that item has become part of realty (i.e., a fixture)

      (3) Adaptability of use of personal property for purpose for which real property is used

         (a) If personal property is necessary or beneficial to use of real property, more likely that item is fixture
         (b) But if use or purpose of item is unusual for type of realty involved, it normally would be personal property

   b. Trade fixture is a fixture installed by tenant in connection with business on leased premises

> **EXAMPLE**
>
> A tenant who is leasing premises for use as grocery store installs refrigeration unit on property. Refrigeration unit is integral to conducting of business for which tenant occupies premises and therefore qualifies as trade fixture.

      (1) Trade fixtures remain personal property, giving tenant right to remove these items upon expiration of lease

         (a) If item is so affixed to real property that removing it would cause substantial damage, then it is considered part of realty

B. Personal Property Can Be Acquired By

1. Gift—a present, voluntary transfer of property without consideration

   a. Necessary elements

      (1) Donative intent by donor
      (2) Delivery
      (3) Acceptance by donee (usually presumed)

   b. Promise to make a gift is unenforceable because it is not a contract due to lack of consideration given by donee
   c. Inter vivos gift is made while donor is living and is irrevocable once completed
   d. Gift causa mortis is a conditional gift in contemplation of death and is automatically revoked if the donor does not die of impending illness or crisis causing gift

2. Will or intestate succession

   a. Property passes under terms of will that is valid at death (i.e., dies testate)
   b. If deceased has no valid will (i.e., dies intestate) then property passes under laws of state

3. Finding personal property

   a. Mislaid property

      (1) Happens when owner **voluntarily** puts the property somewhere but forgets to take it
      (2) Finder does **not** obtain title to mislaid property

         (a) Owner of premises becomes caretaker in case true owner of mislaid property comes back

b. Lost property

   (1) Happens when owner **involuntarily** leaves property somewhere
   (2) Finder has title to lost property which is valid against all parties except the true owner

> **EXAMPLE**
>
> A loses his watch. B finds it but C attempts to take it from B even though both know it is not C's watch. B has the right to keep it from C.

c. Abandoned property

   (1) Generally, finder has title valid against all parties including owner that abandoned property

> **NOW REVIEW MULTIPLE-CHOICE QUESTIONS 1 THROUGH 5 IN VOLUME 2**

C. Bailments

1. Bailment exists when owner of personal property gives possession without giving title to another (bailee)—for example, dry cleaners or valet at restaurant—bailee has duty to either return personal property to bailor or to dispose of it as directed by owner
2. Requirements for creation

   a. Delivery of personal property to bailee
   b. Possession by bailee
   c. Bailee has duty to return property or dispose of property as directed by owner

3. Types of bailments

   a. For benefit of bailor (i.e., bailee takes care of bailor's property)
   b. For mutual benefit (i.e., bailee takes care of bailor's property for a fee)
   c. For benefit of bailee (i.e., bailor gratuitously allows bailee use of his/her property)

4. Bailee's duty of care

   a. Older view depended on the type of bailment (i.e., slight care if for benefit of bailor, ordinary care if for mutual benefit, extreme care if for benefit of bailee)
   b. Now general rule is bailee must take reasonable care in light of the facts and circumstances

     (1) Type of bailment is determined by given facts and the facts are used to determine what is reasonable care

       (a) Bailee is absolutely liable for delivery to improper person

         1] But a receipt or ticket that is for identification of bailor entitles bailee to deliver bailed goods to holder of ticket without liability

   c. Bailee has absolute liability for unauthorized use of property
   d. Bailee usually cannot limit liability with exculpatory clauses

> **EXAMPLE**
>
> A coat check ticket often limits liability on its back side. If the ticket is to be just a means of identification, then the bailee's liability is not limited. If the bailor is aware of the liability limitations statement, liability may be limited if reasonable.

5. Bailee has duty to use property as directed to fulfill purpose of bailment only

   a. Liable to bailor for misuse
   b. In cases of theft, destruction of property, or failing to return property, this constitutes tort of conversion
   c. Bailee may normally limit liability for his/her negligence but not for intentional conduct

6. Bailee is not an agent of bailor, so bailor is not responsible for bailee's actions
7. Bailments normally terminated by

   a. Fulfillment of purpose of bailment
   b. Agreement to terminate by both bailor and bailee
   c. Bailee using property inappropriately

8. Common carriers are licensed to provide transportation for public

   a. Liability is based on strict liability, so common carriers are liable for damage to goods being transported even if loss caused by third parties or by accidents

      (1) Exceptions—common carrier not liable for

         (a) Acts of shipper, such as improperly packing goods to be shipped
         (b) Acts of God, such as earthquakes
         (c) Acts of public enemies
         (d) Loss because of inherent nature of goods

      (2) Common carriers allowed to limit liability to dollar amount specified in contract

D. Intellectual Property and Computer Technology Rights

1. Two general but competing goals

   a. Incentives to create products and services

      (1) By granting property rights so creators have incentive to create and market

   b. Provide public access to intellectual property and computer ideas and uses

      (1) By limiting intellectual and computer technology rights so that public has access to this

2. Copyright law

   a. Protects original works (e.g., literary, musical, or artistic works)

      (1) Expressions of ideas are generally copyrightable—ideas may not by themselves be copyrighted
      (2) Amendments to Copyright Act give added protection to computer hardware and computer software

   b. Copyrights created after January 1, 1978, are valid for life of author plus seventy years

      (1) Are valid for 95 years from publication date when owned by publishing house, or 120 years from creation date, whichever expires first

   c. Registration of copyright not required because copyright begins when author puts expression in tangible form

      (1) Registration, however, gives copyright owner, in case of infringement, rights to statutory damages and attorneys' fees

   d. Works published after March 1, 1989, no longer need copyright notice on them
   e. Fair use doctrine allows use for limited purposes without violating copyright

      (1) Examples include portions for comment, news reporting, research, or teaching

> **EXAMPLE**
>
> Professor hands out copies of a portion of copyrighted work to each member of the class.

      (2) Accessing a digital work is not protected by fair use doctrine

   f. Consumer Software Copyright Act amends copyright law to include computer programs as creative works protected by federal copyright law

      (1) Covers not only portions of computer program readable by humans but also binary language portions normally read by computer
      (2) Covers general items in program such as its basic structure and organizations

   g. Remedies include stated statutory damages or actual damages including profits attributed to infringement of copyright—injunctions also allowed

      (1) Higher damages can be statutorily assessed for willful infringement

   h. Criminal penalties of fines and imprisonment are allowed for willful infringement
   i. No Electronic Theft Act (NET Act)

      (1) Act criminalizes copyright infringement over Internet whether or not for financial gain where retail value of copyrighted works exceeds $1,000
      (2) Provides for imprisonment and fines

3. Patent Law

   a. Covers machines, processes, art, methods, composition of matter, new and useful improvements including genetically engineered plants or animals

   b. Mere ideas are not covered

      (1) But practical applications may be

      (2) Cyber business plans can be patented when they use a practical application of formulas, calculations, or algorithms because they produce results that are useful, tangible, and concrete even though some have argued these cyber plans are intangible.

   c. Invention must be novel, useful, and not obvious

   d. Patents administered by US Patent and Trademark Office

      (1) Inventor may not obtain patent if invention was on sale or in public use in US at least one year before attempt to obtain patent

   e. Generally, patents are valid for twenty years from when patent application was filed

      (1) By treaties, patents generally receive international protection for twenty years

      (2) Design patents are valid for fourteen years from date of issuance of patent

   f. Owner of patent must mark it using word patent to give notice to others

      (1) May also use "Pat" abbreviation

   g. US gives patent protection to first inventor to invent rather than first to file for that patent

      (1) Most countries give protection to the first to file the patent

   h. Earlier views of computer software often categorized it as based on ideas and thus not patentable—more recent authority and court decisions protect software and Internet business methods as patentable

      (1) Financial and business models used over the Internet can also be patented

---

EXAMPLE

Pratt Company patented a computer program that used mathematical formulas to constantly improve a curing process for synthetic rubber upon receiving feedback in the process. This computer program was patentable because Pratt did not attempt to patent the mathematical formula to exclude others from using the formula but patented the process.

EXAMPLE

River.com Inc. receives a patent for the company storing customers' shipping (and billing information) with a one-click ordering system to reduce customers' need to reenter data on future orders.

EXAMPLE

Dual Softie, Inc. receives a patent that allows purchasers of automobiles over Internet to select options they want on the auto.

EXAMPLE

Silvernet, Inc. patents a system that pays individuals who respond to online surveys.

---

   i. Even when patent issued by US Patent Trade Office (PTO), PTO may reexamine and reject patent

      (1) Patent may be overturned or narrowed in case brought to court

      (2) Unlike earlier, computer-related patents focus now on whether they are novel and nonobvious rather than on whether they can be patented at all

   j. Patent law is exclusively federal law

      (1) There is no state patent law

    k. Remedies include injunctions, damages including lost profits traceable to infringement, or assessment of reasonable royalties

        (1) If infringement is willful, inventor may be awarded treble damages and require infringer to also pay attorney's fees

    l. US Supreme Court recently affirmed important part of patent law providing that one cannot escape liability for patent infringement by making only insubstantial changes to a patent and attempting to claim it to be a new patent

    m. Paris convention—allows patent protection in many foreign countries

        (1) Most comprehensive agreement between nations involving intellectual property
        (2) Signed by nearly all industrialized countries and by many developing countries
        (3) Generally, allows a one-year grace period for inventors to file in other countries once inventor files for patent protection in first country

4. Trade Secrets Law

    a. Economic Espionage Act makes it federal crime to use trade secrets

        (1) Trade secrets include such information as financial, engineering, scientific, technical, software programs, or codes

            (a) Also protects processes used by company

        (2) Federal law helps protect against computer hackers who steal trade secrets such as data bases and computer lists.

    b. Alternative to protection by copyright or patent
    c. Protects formulas, patterns, devices, or compilations of information that give business an advantage over competitors

        (1) Must be secret that others have difficulty in acquiring except by improper means
        (2) Owner must take reasonable steps to guard trade secret
        (3) Can cover computer hardware and software

    d. Remedies for violations include breach of contract, breach of fiduciary duties, wrongful appropriation of trade secret, injunction, theft, and espionage

        (1) Civil law as well as criminal law may be used

    e. Trade secret protection by law may be lost if

        (1) Owner of trade secret fails to take steps to keep it secret, or
        (2) Other person independently discovers what was subject of trade secret

    f. Methods to help protect trade secret include

        (1) Licensing of software

            (a) Prohibit copying except for backup copies

        (2) Provide in license that it is terminated for any breach of confidentiality
        (3) Sell software in object code instead of source code
        (4) Have employees and buyers sign confidentiality agreements

5. Semiconductor Chip Protection Act

    a. Amends copyright laws
    b. Prohibits taking apart chips to copy them

        (1) Allows such act if used to create new chip rather than copy
        (2) Not prohibiting copying if design embodies the unoriginal or commonplace

    c. Protection is for ten years from time of registration or first commercial application, whichever is first
    d. Permits civil recovery and penalties up to $250,000 for chip piracy
    e. Reverse engineering of chips allowed if it creates some new innovation

6. Federal Counterfeit Access Device and Computer Fraud and Abuse Act has criminalized many intentional, unauthorized uses of computer to

a. Obtain classified information to hurt US
b. Collect credit or financial information protected by privacy laws

> **EXAMPLE**
>
> Obtaining credit card limits and credit card numbers by accessing credit card accounts.

c. Modify material financial data in computers
d. Destroy or alter computer data to hurt rightful users

> **EXAMPLE**
>
> A person intentionally transfers a computer virus to a company computer.

7. Trademarks under Lanham Act

a. Purposes

(1) To provide identification symbol for company's product
(2) To guarantee consistent quality of all goods from same source
(3) Advertising

b. Protection for trademark for distinctive graphics, words, shapes, packaging, or sounds

> **EXAMPLE**
>
> Coca-Cola has a trademark for its distinctive bottle.

(1) Colors may be trademarked now if they are associated with particular goods such that those colors are identified with that brand

c. Marks normally need to be distinctive to be protected

(1) Secondary meaning of things not inherently distinctive can develop to make them protectable

> **EXAMPLE**
>
> Microsoft registered "Windows" as a trademark when "Windows" acquired its secondary meaning.

> **EXAMPLE**
>
> Windows store cannot be used as a trademark because it sells windows to put on homes and is thus generic rather than distinctive.

d. Generic words like software cannot be protected

(1) Many words that were once trademarks have become generic so are no longer protectable

> **EXAMPLE**
>
> Escalator was originally a brand name but is no longer protectable due to its generic use. Other examples are Yo-Yo and Dry Ice.

> **EXAMPLE**
>
> Xerox takes out advertisements explaining that Xerox is not a verb, but instead say "copy" the document. Xerox is trying to protect its trademark by trying not to let the name grow into common usage.

e. Trademark rights in US are obtained initially by its use in commerce

(1) For distinctive marks, generally first seller to use trademark owns it

(2) Company can register trademark

    (a) Although this is not required, provides constructive notice to others of claim of trademark

(3) Online company may register domain name as trademark with US Patent and Trademark Office

    (a) Various companies may use same trademark for different types of goods or services but only one company may register the domain name

> **EXAMPLE**
>
> Both Star Fences Inc. and Star Insurance Company wish to use Star.com. Only one may do so.

    (b) Cybersquatting is registering sites and domain names that are confusingly or deceptively similar to other existing trademarks

        1] Congress passed the Federal Anticybersquatting Consumer Protection Act to help stop cybersquatting and to provide clearer standards of proof and remedies for this activity such as injunctions to stop the activity as well as money damages

f. Loss of trademark rights

    (1) Actual abandonment when not used in ordinary course of business

        (a) Presumption of abandonment if not used for three years unless owner can prove intent to use trademark

    (2) Constructive abandonment—Company allows trademark to lose its distinctiveness by frequent and common usage

g. Trademark infringement

    (1) Can infringe on trademark whether registered or not
    (2) Proof of infringement

        (a) Establish trademark is valid—federally registered mark is prima facie valid
        (b) Priority of usage
        (c) Violation against trademark if similarities will likely cause confusion in minds of prospective or actual purchasers

    (3) 1995 Trademark Dilution Act expands the Lanham Act to protect a weakening of a famous mark's ability to distinguish goods. Prior law required the infringing trademark to cause confusion as to the source of the product.

h. Remedies for infringement

    (1) Injunction against use
    (2) Lost profits caused by confusion
    (3) Attorneys' fees in some situations

8. Other symbols under Lanham Act

a. Certification mark

    (1) Used to certify characteristics such as origin by geographical location, origin by organization, mode of manufacture.

> **EXAMPLE**
>
> Product XYZ receives the Good Housekeeping Seal of Approval.

b. Collective mark

    (1) Used to identify that product or service is provided by certain collective group, union, or fraternal society.

c. Service mark

    (1) Used to identify that services come from certain company or person

> **EXAMPLE**
>
> All of the shops of a group of shops called The Green Roof Plaza have similar style of roofs painted in the same shade of green.

    d. Similar to trademarks, these additional three types of trade symbols need to be distinctive and not deceptive so that prospective customers do not confuse these products or services with others

        (1) Registration is not required but advisable because it provides federal protection for ten years

            (a) Renewable for as many additional ten-year periods as desired

9. Invasion of Privacy—Increased computer use puts on more pressure

    a. Computer Matching and Privacy Act

        (1) Regulates computer systems used to determine eligibility for various government programs such as student financial aid

    b. Right to Financial Privacy Act

        (1) Restricts government access to financial institution records without customer approval

    c. Family Educational Rights and Privacy Act

        (1) Grants adult students and parents of minors access and right to correct records at institutions of higher learning

10. Palming off results when one company sells its product by confusing buyers and leading them to believe they are purchasing another company's product

    a. Proof of palming off requires that there is likely to be confusion due to the appearance or name of the competing product

11. Counterfeit Access Device and Computer Fraud and Abuse Act

    a. Crime to obtain financial institution's financial records
    b. Crime to use cards, codes, counterfeit devices, etc. to obtain valuable items or to transfer funds without authorization

12. Information Infrastructure Protection Act

    a. Helps protect individuals or companies from another's unauthorized use of or access to computer's data

        (1) Law encompasses computer hackers, transmitting computer viruses or worms, etc.

13. Identity Theft and Assumption Deterrence Act is federal law that makes identity theft and identify fraud felonies

    a. Act also helps victims of identity theft by having Federal Trade Commission aid them to erase effects of identity theft and to aid them to restore their credit

14. Digital Millennium Copyright Act

    a. Federal law based on treaties with other countries to minimize pirating and distribution of copyrighted works
    b. Provides civil and criminal penalties against those that circumvent antipiracy protections or manufacture or sell such equipment to allow circumvention

        (1) Also provides civil and criminal penalties for unauthorized access to copyrighted digital works by circumventing technology that protects such intellectual property

            (a) It is not required that accessed information be misused
            (b) Mere access is sufficient under this Act

        (2) This Act also modifies fair use doctrine of copyright law for digital protected works so that it is now illegal to merely access these works by circumventing the encryption technology that protects these

            (a) Fair use doctrine is unchanged for nondigital works so that misuse, not mere access of copyrighted works is required

    c. Internet Service Provider (ISP) is generally not liable for customers' copyright infringement unless ISP became aware of infringement and failed to correct problem

15. Uniform Computer Information Transactions Act (UCITA) requires that the following be in writing:

     a. Contracts for licensing of information rights for over $5,000

     b. Contracts for licensing of information services that cannot be performed within one year

     c. User agrees to contract by clicking, for example, on "I agree prompt button"

16. Federal Telecommunications Act passed

     a. To increase competition in telecommunications market

     b. Preempts any state or local government laws that have effect of minimizing or eliminating competition in telecommunications market

       (1) Such as county laws that prohibit ability of company to provide telecommunications service

17. Online dispute resolution is becoming increasingly used to resolve disputes

     a. Advantages include low cost, fast communication, and often no need to bring in third parties

     b. Disadvantage includes hard to enforce settlement because no court or sheriff involved

18. Internet Treaties

     a. Grants between many signing nations providing copyright protection for computer programs, producers' rights, performers' rights over the Internet

       (1) Includes rental copies, transmissions over satellite, encrypted signals, and any type of media

---

> **NOW REVIEW MULTIPLE-CHOICE QUESTIONS 6 THROUGH 13 IN VOLUME 2**

E. Interests in Real Property

1. Present interests

     a. Fee simple absolute

       (1) Highest estate in law (has the most ownership rights)

       (2) May be transferred inter vivos (while living), by intestate succession (without will), or by will (testate at death)

       (3) May be subject to mortgages, state laws, etc.

> **EXAMPLE**
>
> Most private residences are fee simple absolute estates although they are commonly subject to mortgage.

     b. Fee simple defeasible

       (1) Fee simple determinable—upon the happening of the stated event the estate automatically reverts to the grantor

> **EXAMPLE**
>
> Conveyance to the holder of an interest was, "to A as long as A uses it for church purposes." The interest will revert back to the grantor or his heirs if the property is not used for church purposes.

       (2) Fee simple subject to condition subsequent—upon the happening of the stated event the grantor must take affirmative action to divest the grantee of the estate

> **EXAMPLE**
>
> Conveyance to the holder of the interest was "to A, but if liquor is ever served on the premises, the grantor has right to enter the premises." The grantor has power of termination so as to repossess the premises.

     c. Life interest (life estate)—an interest whose duration is usually measured by the life of the holder but may be measured by lives of others

> **EXAMPLE**
>
> Conveyance of land, "to A so long as she shall live."

    (1) Upon termination (death), property reverts to grantor or grantor's heirs, or to a named remainderman
    (2) Usual life interest can be transferred by deed only (i.e., not by a will because it ends on death)
    (3) Holder of a life interest (life tenant) is entitled to ordinary use and profits of land but may not commit waste (injure interests of remainderman)

        (a) Must maintain property (in reasonable state of repair)
        (b) May not misuse property

  d. Leaseholds—see Lessor-Lessee at end of this module, section N.

2. Future interest (holder of this interest has right to or possibility of possession in the future)

  a. Reversion—future interest reverts back to transferor (or his/her heirs) at end of transferee's estate

    (1) Usually kept when conveying a life interest or an interest for a definite period of time

> **EXAMPLE**
>
> X conveys, "to Y for life" or "to Y for ten years." X has a reversion.

  b. Remainder—future interest is in a third party at the end of transferee's estate

> **EXAMPLE**
>
> X conveys, "to Y for life, remainder to Z and her heirs."

3. Concurrent interest—two or more persons (cotenants) have undivided interests and concurrent possessory rights in real or personal property—each has a nonexclusive right to possess whole property

  a. Tenancy in common

    (1) A concurrent interest with no right of survivorship (interest passes to heirs, donee, or purchaser)

> **EXAMPLE**
>
> A and B each own 1/2 of Greenacre as tenants in common. If B dies, then A still owns 1/2 and B's heirs own the other half.

    (2) Unless stated otherwise, multiple grantees are presumed to be tenants in common
    (3) Tenant in common may convey individual interest in the whole but cannot convey a specific portion of property

        (a) Unless there is a judicial partition to split up ownership

           1] Creditors may sue to compel a partition to satisfy individual's debts

  b. Joint tenancy

    (1) A concurrent interest with all rights of ownership going to the surviving joint tenants (i.e., have rights of survivorship)

        (a) To create a joint tenancy, all of following unities are required: time, title, interest, and possession
        (b) Cannot be transferred by will because upon death, other cotenants own it
        (c) Corporation may not be joint tenant

> **EXAMPLE**
>
> A and B each own 1/2 of Redacre as joint tenants. If B dies, A owns all of Redacre because of her right of survivorship. B's heirs do not receive any interest.

(2) If rights in property conveyed without consent of others, new owner becomes a tenant in common rather than joint tenant; remaining cotenants are still joint tenants

> **EXAMPLE**
>
> A, B, and C are joint tenants of Greenacre. A sells his interest to D without the consent of B and C. D is a tenant in common with a one-third interest in the whole. B and C are still joint tenants (with the right of survivorship) each having a one-third undivided interest.

c. Tenancy by the entirety

   (1) Joint interest held by husband and wife

   (2) To transfer, both must convey

   (3) Each spouse has a right of survivorship

   (4) Divorce creates a tenancy in common

   (5) Creditors of one spouse cannot place a lien or satisfy a judgment against property held in this manner. The creditor must be a creditor of both spouses.

4. Nonpossessory interests in land

  a. Easement is right to enter another's land and use it in limited way. Very common for utility companies, for example, to have easements on private property for the benefit of all; usually provided for when the property is divided.

> **EXAMPLE**
>
> A is granted an easement to drive over a certain segment of B's land.

   (1) Methods of creation

     (a) Express grant in deed

     (b) Express reservation in deed

> **EXAMPLE**
>
> S sells B some land whereby in the deed S reserves an easement to walk across the land.

     (c) By necessity

> **EXAMPLE**
>
> A owns a piece of land that blocks B's access to any public road. B has the right to use A's land for access to the public road.

  b. Profit is right to enter another's land and remove items such as trees, grass, or gravel

   (1) Profits may be created by grant or by reservation

> **NOW REVIEW MULTIPLE-CHOICE QUESTIONS 14 THROUGH 21 IN VOLUME 2**

F. Contracts for Sale of Land

1. Generally precede transfers of land. Often includes escrows.

> **EXAMPLE**
>
> An earnest money agreement. The purchaser puts the money down to show his seriousness while he investigates the title and arranges for a mortgage.

  a. Generally, agreement must

   (1) Be in writing and signed by party to be bound

(a) To satisfy Statute of Frauds under contract law

(2) Identify land and parties
(3) Identify purpose
(4) Contain terms or promises
(5) Contain purchase price

b. Assignable unless prohibited in contract

2. If not expressed, there is an implied promise that seller will provide a marketable title (implied warranty of marketability)

a. A marketable title is one reasonably free from doubt. Does not contain such defects as breaks in chain of title, outstanding liens, or defective instruments in past (chain of title).

(1) Zoning restrictions do not make a title unmarketable

b. Agreement may provide for marketable or "insurable" title

(1) Insurable title is one that a title insurance company will insure against defects, liens, and invalidity

c. If title is not marketable, purchaser may

(1) Rescind and recover any down payment
(2) Sue for damages
(3) Sue for specific performance with a reduction in price

3. Risk of loss before deed is conveyed (e.g., if house burns who bears the burden?)

a. General rule is purchaser bears the risk of loss, subject to terms of the contract
b. Courts may look to who has the most ownership rights and benefits (normally buyer)
c. Either party can insure against risk of loss

G. Types of Deeds

1. Warranty deeds contain the following covenants (unconditional promises) by grantor

a. Grantor has title and right to convey it
b. Free from encumbrances except as disclosed in the deed

> **EXAMPLE**
>
> O conveys by warranty deed Blackacre to P. There is a mortgage still unpaid on Blackacre. Unless O discloses this mortgage to P, O has violated the covenant that the deed be free from encumbrances.

c. Quiet enjoyment—neither grantor nor third party with rightful claim will disturb grantee's possession

2. Bargain and sale deed (grant deeds)

a. Generally, only covenants that grantor has done nothing to impair title (e.g., s/he has not created any encumbrances)
b. Does not warrant against prior (before grantor's ownership) impairments

3. Quitclaim deed conveys only whatever interest in land the grantor has. No warranty of title is made by grantor.

a. It is insurable, recordable, and mortgagable as with any other deed

H. Executing a Deed

1. Deed must have description of the real estate

a. Purchase price generally not necessary in deed

2. There must be delivery for deed to be effective; there must be an intent on part of grantor to pass title (convey) to grantee

a. Possession of the deed by grantee raises a presumption (rebuttable) of delivery
b. A recorded deed raises a presumption (rebuttable) of delivery
c. A deed given to a third party to give to grantee upon performance of a condition is a delivery in escrow

(1) Escrow agent—intermediary between the two parties who holds deed until grantee pays, then gives deed to grantee and money to grantor

    d. Destruction of deed does not destroy title

  3. Deed must identify the buyer and seller

  4. Must have the seller's signature

I. Recording a Deed

1. Gives constructive notice to the world of grantee's ownership (this is important)

  a. Protects grantee (new owner) against subsequent purchasers

> **EXAMPLE**
>
> X sells land to Y. Y records his deed. Later X sells land to Z. Z loses against Y because Y recorded the deed giving constructive notice of the prior sale.

    (1) However, deed is valid between immediate parties without recording

  b. Most recording statutes provide that subsequent purchaser (bona fide) who takes without notice of the first sale has priority

    (1) Under a notice-type statute, a subsequent bona fide (good-faith) purchaser, whether s/he records or not, wins over previous purchaser who did not record before that subsequent purchase

> **EXAMPLE**
>
> A sells the same piece of property in a state having a notice-type statute to B and C in that order. B did not record the purchase. C is unaware of the sale to B and is thus a bona fide purchaser. C defeats B. Note that C should record the purchase or run the risk of another bona fide purchaser (i.e., D defeating C's claim).

    (2) Under a race-notice type (notice-race) statute, the subsequent bona fide purchaser wins over a previous purchaser only if s/he also records first (i.e., a "race" to file first) (Historically the Examiners have tested the notice-race statute most frequently)

> **EXAMPLE**
>
> X sells some property to Y and then to Z, a good-faith purchaser. After the sale to Z, Y records the purchase and then Z records the purchase. Although Y wins in a state having a race-notice statute, Z wins in a state having a notice-type statute.

> **EXAMPLE**
>
> Same as above except that Z does not record, both results above are not affected.

    (3) Under a race statute, the first to record deed wins

  c. Notice refers to actual knowledge of prior sale or constructive knowledge (i.e., one is deemed to be aware of what is filed in records)

  d. To be a purchaser, one must give value that does not include antecedent debts

J. Title Insurance

1. Generally used to insure that title is good and to cover the warranties by seller

  a. Not required if contract does not require it

2. Without title insurance, purchaser's only recourse is against grantor and s/he may not be able to satisfy the damages

  a. Standard insurance policies generally insure against all defects of record and defects grantee may be aware of, but not defects disclosed by survey and physical inspection of premises

  b. Title insurance company is liable for any damages or expenses if there is a title defect or encumbrance that is insured against

    (1) Certain defects are not insured by the title policy

(a) These exceptions must be shown on face of policy

c. Title insurance does not pass to subsequent purchasers

K. Adverse Possession

1. Possessor of land who was not owner may acquire title if s/he holds it for the statutory period

   a. The statutory period is the running of the statute of limitations. Varies by state from five to twenty years.
   b. The statute begins to run upon the taking of possession
   c. True owner must commence legal action before statute runs or adverse possessor obtains title
   d. Successive possessors may tack (cumulate required time together)

      (1) Each possessor must transfer to the other. One cannot abandon or statute begins over again for the next possessor.

   e. True owner of a future interest (e.g., a remainder, is not affected by adverse possession)

   > **EXAMPLE**
   >
   > X dies and leaves his property to A for life, remainder to B. A pays little attention to the property and a third party acquires it by adverse possession. When A dies, B is entitled to the property regardless of the adverse possession but the statute starts running against B.

2. Necessary elements

   a. Open and notorious possession

      (1) Means type of possession that would give reasonable notice to owner

   b. Hostile possession

      (1) Must indicate intentions of ownership

         (a) Does not occur when possession started permissively or as cotenants
         (b) Not satisfied if possessor acknowledges other's ownership

      (2) Color of title satisfies this requirement. When possession is taken under good-faith belief in a defective instrument or deed purporting to convey the land.

   c. Actual possession

      (1) Possession of land consistent with its normal use (e.g., farm land is being farmed)

   d. Continuous possession

      (1) Need not be constant, but possession as normally used

   e. Exclusive possession

      (1) Possession to exclusion of all others

NOW REVIEW MULTIPLE-CHOICE QUESTIONS 22 AND 31 IN VOLUME 2

L. Easement by Prescription

1. Person obtains right to use another's land (i.e., easement) in way similar to adverse possession
2. Same elements are used as for adverse possession except for exclusive possession—state laws require several years to obtain this

   > **EXAMPLE**
   >
   > X cuts across Y's land for several years in such a way that she meets all of the same requirements as those needed for adverse possession except for exclusive possession. X obtains an easement to use the path even if Y later tries to stop X.

M. Mortgages

1. Lien on real property to secure payment of loan

a. Mortgage is an interest in real property and thus must satisfy Statute of Frauds

   (1) Must be in writing and signed by party to be charged

      (a) Party to be charged in this case is mortgagor (i.e., party taking out mortgage, the borrower)

   (2) Must include description of property and debt to be incurred

b. Debt is usually evidenced by a promissory note
c. Mortgage must be delivered to mortgagee (i.e., lender)
d. Mortgage may be given to secure future advances
e. Purchase-money mortgage is created when seller takes a mortgage from buyer at time of sale

   (1) Or lender furnishes money with which property is purchased

2. Mortgage may be recorded and receives the same benefits as recording a deed or recording an assignment of contract

   a. Gives constructive notice of the mortgage

      (1) But mortgage **is effective** between mortgagor and mortgagee and third parties, who have actual notice, even without recording

   b. Protects mortgagee against subsequent mortgagees, purchasers, or other takers
   c. Recording statutes for mortgages are like those used for recording deeds

      (1) Under a notice-type statute, a subsequent good-faith mortgagee has priority over previous mortgagee who did not file

         (a) This is true whether subsequent mortgagee files or not; but of course if s/he does not file, a subsequent good-faith mortgagee will have priority.

> **EXAMPLE**
>
> Banks A, B, and C, in that order, grant a mortgage to a property owner. None of these record the mortgage and none knows of the others. Between A and B, B has priority. However, C has priority over B.

> **EXAMPLE**
>
> Same facts as before, however, B does record before C grants the mortgage. B has priority over A again. B also has priority over C because now C has constructive notice of B and thus has lower priority.

         (b) Notice is either actual notice or constructive notice based on recording

      (2) Under a race-notice type (notice-race) statute, the subsequent good-faith mortgagee wins over a previous mortgagee only if s/he also records first
      (3) Under a race statute, the first mortgagee to record mortgage wins
      (4) First mortgage to have priority is satisfied in full (upon default) before next mortgage to have priority is satisfied

         (a) Second mortgagee can require first mortgagee to resort to other property for payment if first mortgagee has other property available as security

3. When mortgaged property is sold the buyer may

   a. Assume the mortgage (if the mortgagee allows)

      (1) If "assumed," the buyer becomes personally liable (mortgage holder is third-party beneficiary)
      (2) Seller remains liable (unless released by mortgagee by a novation)

         (a) Mortgagee may hold either seller or buyer liable on mortgage

      (3) Normally the mortgagee's consent is needed due to "due on sale clauses"

         (a) Terms of mortgage may permit acceleration of principal or renegotiation of interest rate upon transfer of the property

   b. Take subject to the mortgage

(1) If buyer takes "subject to" then buyer accepts **no** liability for mortgage and seller is still primarily liable

(2) Mortgagee may still foreclose on the property even in the hands of buyer

    (a) Buyer may pay mortgage if s/he chooses to avoid foreclosure

(3) Mortgagee's consent to allow buyer to take subject to the mortgage is not needed unless stipulated in mortgage

  c. Novation—occurs when purchaser assumes mortgage and mortgagee (lender) releases in writing the seller from the mortgage

> **EXAMPLE**
>
> O has mortgaged Redacre. He sells Redacre to T. T agrees to assume mortgage and mortgagee bank agrees in writing to substitute T as the only liable party in place of O. Because of this novation, O is no longer liable on the mortgage.

4. Rights of parties

  a. Mortgagor (owner, debtor) retains possession and right to use land

    (1) May transfer land encumbered by mortgage

  b. Mortgagee (creditor) has a lien on the land

    (1) Even if mortgagor transfers land, it is still subject to the mortgage if it has been properly recorded

  c. Mortgagee has right to assign mortgage to third party without mortgagors' consent

  d. Upon mortgagor's default, mortgagee may assign mortgage to third parties or mortgagee may foreclose on the land

    (1) Foreclosure requires judicial action that directs foreclosure sale

      (a) Court will refuse to confirm sale if price is so low as to raise a presumption of unfairness

      (b) However, court will not refuse to confirm sale merely because higher price might have been received at a later time

    (2) Mortgagor usually can save real estate (redeem the property) by use of equity of redemption

      (a) Pays interest, debt, and expenses

      (b) Exists until foreclosure sale

      (c) Cannot be curtailed by prior agreement

    (3) After foreclosure sale debtor has right of redemption if state law grants statutory right of redemption

      (a) Affords mortgagor one last chance to redeem property

      (b) Pays off loan within statutory period

    (4) If mortgagee forecloses and sells property and mortgagor does not use equity of redemption or right of redemption

      (a) Mortgagee must return any excess proceeds from sale to mortgagor

        1] Equity above balance due does not give right to mortgagor to retain possession of property

      (b) If proceeds from sale are insufficient to pay note, mortgagor is still indebted to the mortgagee for deficiency

        1] Grantee of the mortgagor who **assumed** mortgage would also be liable for deficiency, but one who took **subject to** the mortgage would not be personally liable

5. Mortgage lenders are regulated by Real Estate Settlement Procedures Act (RESPA)

  a. Provides home buyers with extensive information about settlement process and helps protect them from high settlement fees

6. Deed of trust—also a nonpossessory lien on real property to secure a debt

  a. Like a mortgage, debtor retains possession of land and creditor has a lien on it

  b. Legal title is given to a trustee to hold

    (1) Upon default, trustee may sell the land for the benefit of creditor

7. Sale on contract

    a. Unlike a mortgage or a deed of trust, the seller retains title to property

    b. Purchaser takes possession and makes payments on the contract

    c. Purchaser gets title when debt fully paid

8. When mortgaged property is sold or destroyed, the proceeds from sale or insurance go to mortgagee with highest priority until it is completely paid, then the proceeds, if any, go to any mortgagees or other interest holders, with the next highest priority, etc.

> **NOW REVIEW MULTIPLE-CHOICE QUESTIONS 32 THROUGH 39 IN VOLUME 2**

N. Lessor-Lessee

1. A lease is a contract and a conveyance

    a. Contract is the primary source of rights and duties

    b. Contract must contain essential terms including description of leased premises

    c. May be oral if less than one year

2. Types of leaseholds

    a. Periodic tenancy

        (1) Lease is for a fixed time such as a month or year but it continues from period to period until proper notice of termination

        (2) Notice of termination normally must be given in the same amount of time as rent or tenancy period (i.e., if tenancy is from month to month then the landlord or tenant usually must give at least one month's notice)

    b. Tenancy for a term (also called tenancy for years)

        (1) Lease is for a fixed amount of time (e.g., lease of two years or six months)

        (2) Ends automatically at date of termination

    c. Tenancy at sufferance

        (1) Created when tenant remains in property after lease expires

        (2) Landlord has option of treating tenant as trespasser and ejecting him/her or treating him/her as tenant and collecting rent

    d. Tenancy at will

        (1) Property is leased for indefinite period of time

        (2) Either party may terminate lease at will

3. Lessor covenants (promises) and tenant's rights

    a. Generally, lessor's covenants are independent of lessee's rights; therefore, lessor's breach does not give lessee right to breach

    b. Right to possession—lessor makes premises available to lessee

        (1) Residential lease for real estate entitles tenant to exclusive possession of property during period of lease unless otherwise agreed in lease

    c. Quiet enjoyment—neither lessor nor a third party with a valid claim will evict lessee unless tenant has breached lease contract

    d. Fitness for use—premises are fit for human occupation (i.e., warranty of habitability)

    e. In general, if premises are destroyed through no fault of either party, then contract is terminated

> **EXAMPLE**
>
> Landlord's building is destroyed by a sudden flood. Tenant cannot hold landlord liable for loss of use of building.

    f. Lessee may assign or sublease unless prohibited or restricted in lease

        (1) Assignment is transfer by lessee of his/her entire interest reserving no rights

      (a) Assignee is in privity of contract with lessor and lessor may proceed against him/her for rent and breaches under lease agreement

      (b) Assignor (lessee) is still liable to lessor unless there is a novation or release

      (c) Lease may have clause that requires consent of lessor for subleases

           1] In which case, consent to each individual sublease is required

           2] Lack of consent makes sublease voidable

      (d) Clause prohibiting sublease does not prohibit assignment

    (2) A sublease is the transfer by lessee of less than his/her entire interest (e.g., for three months during summer, then lessee returns to it in the fall)

      (a) Lessee (sublessor) is still liable on lease

      (b) Lessor has no privity with sublessee and can take no action against him/her for rent, but certain restrictions of original lease run with the land and are enforceable against sublessee

      (c) Sublessee can assume obligations in sublease and be liable to pay landlord

      (d) Clause prohibiting assignment does not prohibit sublease

  g. Subject to lease terms, trade fixtures attached by lessee may be removed if can be removed without substantial damage to premises

  h. Tenant can use premises for any legal purpose unless lease restricts

4. Lessee's duties and lessor's rights

  a. Rent—due at end of term or period of tenancy unless otherwise agreed in lease

    (1) No right to withhold rent even if lessor is in breach (unless so provided by lease or by statute)

    (2) Nonpayment gives lessor right to sue for it or to bring an eviction suit or both

  b. Lessee has obligation to make ordinary repairs. Lease or statute may make lessor liable.

    (1) Structural repairs are lessor's duty

  c. If tenant wrongfully retains possession after termination, lessor may

    (1) Evict lessee, or

    (2) Treat as holdover tenant and charge with fair rental value, or

    (3) Tenancy becomes one of period-to-period, and lessee is liable for rent the same as in expired lease

5. Termination

  a. Expiration of lease

  b. Proper notice in a tenancy from period-to-period

  c. Surrender by lessee and acceptance by lessor

  d. Death of lessee terminates lease except for a lease for a period of years

    (1) Death of lessor generally does not terminate lease

  e. Eviction

    (1) Actual eviction—ousting directly

    (2) Constructive eviction—allowing conditions which make property unusable if lessor is liable for condition of premises

  f. Transfer of property does not affect tenancy

    (1) New owner cannot rightfully terminate lease unless old owner could have (e.g., breach by tenant)

      (a) However, if tenant purchases property then lease terminates

NOW REVIEW MULTIPLE-CHOICE QUESTIONS 40 THROUGH 43 IN VOLUME 2

KEY TERMS

Bailee. A party who is entrusted to hold the goods of another person.

Bailment. When a party entrusts goods to another party.

Bailor. The party who gives his/her own goods to another to hold.

Common carrier. A party who transports goods for hire and is strictly liable for any damage to those goods. Damages are generally limited by statute though.

Copyright. Intellectual property right that provides protection for the original expression of an idea.

Deed. A written instrument that transfers ownership of real property.

Easement. A legal right to use another's property in a specific manner.

Fair use doctrine. Allows copyrighted material to be used without paying royalties. Use is generally limited to educational, news and other not-for-profit purposes.

Joint tenancy. A type of co-ownership of real property with the right of survivorship.

Landlord. The owner of the leased premises.

Lease. A contract used to rent real property for a period of time.

Mortgage. A security interest in real property.

Mortgagee. The party with the security interest in the real property (the lender).

Mortgagor. The party who uses his/her real property as collateral to secure a loan (the borrower).

Notice statute. A law that applies to the recording of interests in real property. Notice states allow parties who take an interest in real property without notice to have a superior interest than a party who had an earlier interest.

Notice-race statute. A law that applies to the recording of interests in real property. Notice-race states allow parties who take an interest in real property without notice to have a superior interest than a party who had an earlier interest if the subsequent party records before the party with the earlier interest.

Patent. An intellectual property right that gives an inventor the exclusive right to use the invention.

Race statute. A law that applies to the recording of interests in real property. Race statutes give the superior interest to whichever party records its interest first.

Real estate contract. A written instrument that contains the terms of the bargain to transfer real property.

Real property. Land, the interests in land, and the permanent structures attached to the land.

Recording. The filing of property interests with the appropriate local government that allows the party who records to protect its interest against subsequent parties.

Tenancy by the entirety. A type of co-ownership of real property that is only available to married couples. Helps to protect the property from claims of individual creditors.

Tenant. The party who rents the rental property and acquires a right to use the premises.

Tenants in common. A type of co-ownership of real property that does not include the right of survivorship.

Title insurance. Insures against defects of title of the real property.

Trademark. A distinctive mark, word, symbol, design, etc. that a manufacturer/seller uses to identify its goods.

Trade secrets. Information that a business does not want disclosed to the public. Business must take extraordinary measures to keep the information private.

FEDERAL TAXATION

As indicated previously, this section consists of five modules designed to facilitate your study for the Federal Taxation portion of the Regulation section of the Uniform CPA Examination. The table of contents at the right describes the content of each module.

Federal taxation is tested in the Regulation section of the exam. According to the AICPA's Content Specification Outline, federal taxation should account for about 64% of the Regulation section. Of this 64%, about 16% will test the federal income taxation of individuals, about 21% will test the federal income taxation of entities, about 13% will test income tax procedures and accounting issues, and about 14% will test the taxation of property transactions.

You will want to note that the Regulation exam contains both multiple-choice questions and task-based simulations. Since the database for the Regulation exam is the income tax code and regulations (IRC) and Statements on Standards for Tax Services (TS), all simulations will involve taxation topics. You can expect three multiple-choice testlets consisting of 72 questions, and one testlet containing 6 short task-based simulations.

The multiple-choice questions test detailed application of the Internal Revenue Code and tax regulations. The instructions indicate that "answers should be based on the Internal Revenue Code and Tax Regulations in effect for the tax period specified in the item. If no tax period is specified, use the current Internal Revenue Code and Tax Regulations." On recent examinations, approximately 60% of the multiple-choice questions have specified the preceding taxable year, while the remaining 40% have no year specified.

As a practical matter, the examiners generally avoid testing on recent tax law changes, and have indicated that the **exam will generally cover federal tax regulations in effect 6 months before the beginning of the examination window**. Also note that you are not expected to know amounts that change between years because of being indexed for inflation (e.g., the dollar amount of personal exemption, standard deduction, etc.).

The summary tax outlines presented in this chapter begin by emphasizing individual taxation. Because of numerous common concepts, partnership and corporate taxation are later presented in terms of their differences from individual taxation (i.e., learn individual taxes thoroughly and then learn the special rules of partnership and corporate taxation). Interperiod and intraperiod tax allocation questions are presented in Module 14, Deferred Taxes, of the Financial Accounting and Reporting Volume.

The property transactions outline has been inserted between individual taxation and the partnership and corporate tax outlines because property transactions are common to all types of taxpayers, and generally are tested within every tax problem, both PTAX and CTAX, as well as ITAX.

The next section presents a detailed outline of the individual tax formula, and outlines of two basic federal income tax returns: Form 1065—Partnership; and Form 1120—Corporation. These outlines are an intermediary step between the simple formula outline (below) and the outlines of the detailed rules.

Formula Outline for Individuals

Gross income
–"Above the line" deductions
Adjusted gross income
– Total itemized deductions (or standard deduction)
– Exemptions
Taxable income
× Tax rates
– Tax credits
Tax liability

OVERVIEW OF FEDERAL TAX RETURNS

Problems requiring computation of taxable income require that you be familiar with the outlines below. The tax return outlines help you "pull together" all of the detailed tax rules. The schedule and form identification numbers are provided for reference only; they are not tested on the examination.

Review the outlines presented below. The outlines will introduce you to the topics tested on the exam and their relationship to final "tax liability."

Form 1040—Individuals

A. Income

1. Wages, salaries, tips, etc.
2. Interest (Sch. B)
3. Dividend income (Sch. B)
4. Income other than wages, dividends, and interest (The gross income reported on the schedules below is already reduced by corresponding deductible expenses. Only the net income [or loss] is reported on Form 1040.)

   a. State and local income tax refunds
   b. Alimony received
   c. Business income or loss (Sch. C)
   d. Capital gain or loss (Sch. D)

   e. Other gains or losses (Form 4797)
   f. Taxable IRA distributions, pensions, and annuities
   g. Rents, royalties, partnerships, S corporations, estates, trusts, etc. (Sch. E)
   h. Unemployment compensation, social security
   i. Other

B. Less "Above the Line" Deductions (also known as "Deductions **for** AGI")

1. One-half of self-employment tax
2. Moving expenses
3. Self-employed health insurance deduction
4. IRA deduction

5. Payments to a Keogh retirement plan
6. Penalty on early withdrawal of savings
7. Student loan interest deduction
8. Alimony paid
9. Tuition and fees deduction
10. Health savings account deduction

C. Adjusted Gross Income
D. Less Itemized Deductions (Sch. A), (or standard deduction), including

1. Medical and dental expenses
2. Taxes
3. Interest expense
4. Contributions
5. Casualty and theft losses
6. Miscellaneous

    a. Subject to 2% of AGI limitation
    b. Not subject to 2% of AGI limitation

E. Less Exemptions
F. Taxable Income

1. Find your tax in the tables, or
2. Use tax rate schedules

G. Additional Taxes

1. Alternative minimum tax (Form 6251)
2. Parents' election to report child's interest and dividends (Form 8814)
3. Lump-sum distribution from qualified retirement plans (Form 4972)

H. Less Tax Credits

1. General business credit

    a. Investment credit (Form 3468)

    b. Alcohol fuels credit
    c. Low-income housing credit
    d. Disabled access credit
    e. Employer social security credit

2. Credit for the elderly or the disabled (Sch. R)
3. Credit for child and dependent care expenses (Form 2441)
4. Child tax credit
5. Education credits (Form 8863)
6. Adoption credit (Form 8839)
7. Foreign tax credit (Form 1116)
8. Credit for prior year minimum tax

I. Tax Liability
J. Other Taxes

1. Self-employment tax (Sch. SE)
2. Advance earned income credit payments
3. Social security tax on unreported tip income (Form 4137)
4. Tax on IRAs and other retirement plans (Form 5329)
5. Household employment taxes (Sch. H)

K. Less Payments

1. Tax withheld on wages
2. Estimated tax payments
3. Earned income credit
4. Amount paid with an extension
5. Excess FICA paid
6. Credit for federal tax on special fuels (Form 4136)
7. Credit from a regulated investment company (Form 2439)

L. Amount Overpaid or Balance Due

Form 1065—Partnerships

A. Income

1. Gross sales less returns and allowances
2. Less cost of goods sold
3. Gross profit
4. Ordinary income from other partnerships and fiduciaries
5. Net farm profit
6. Ordinary gain or loss (including depreciation recapture)
7. Other

B. Less Deductions

1. Salaries and wages (other than to partners)
2. Guaranteed payments to partners
3. Rents
4. Interest expense
5. Taxes
6. Bad debts
7. Repairs
8. Depreciation
9. Depletion
10. Retirement plans
11. Employee benefit program contributions
12. Other

C. Ordinary Income (Loss) from trade or business activity
D. Schedule K (on partnership return) and Schedule K-1 to be prepared for each partner

1. Ordinary income (loss) from trade or business activity
2. Income (loss) from rental real estate activity
3. Income (loss) from other rental activity
4. Portfolio income (loss)

    a. Interest
    b. Dividends
    c. Royalties
    d. Net short-term capital gain (loss)
    e. Net long-term capital gain (loss)
    f. Other portfolio income (loss)

5. Guaranteed payments
6. Net gain (loss) under Sec. 1231 (other than casualty or theft)
7. Other
8. Charitable contributions

9. Sec. 179 expense deduction
10. Deductions related to portfolio income
11. Other
12. Credits

    a. Credit for income tax withheld
    b. Low-income housing credit
    c. Qualified rehabilitation expenditures related to rental real estate
    d. Credits related to rental real estate activities

13. Other

14. a. Net earnings (loss) from self-employment
    b. Gross farming or fishing income
    c. Gross nonfarm income

15. Tax preference items

    a. Depreciation adjustment on property placed in service after 12/31/86
    b. Tax-exempt private activity bond interest

16. Investment interest expense
17. Foreign income taxes

Form 1120—Corporations

A. Gross Income

1. Gross sales less returns and allowances
2. Less cost of goods sold
3. Gross profit
4. Dividends
5. Interest
6. Gross rents
7. Gross royalties
8. Net capital gains
9. Ordinary gain or loss
10. Other income

B. Less Deductions

1. Compensation of officers
2. Salaries and wages (net of jobs credit)
3. Repairs
4. Bad debts
5. Rents
6. Taxes
7. Interest
8. Charitable contributions
9. Depreciation
10. Depletion
11. Advertising
12. Pension, profit-sharing plan contributions
13. Employee benefit programs
14. Other
15. Net operating loss deduction
16. Dividends received deduction

C. TAXABLE INCOME times tax rates
D. Less tax credits equals **TAX LIABILITY**

Module 35: Individual Taxation

Overview

This module covers the area of individual taxation in the same order in which topics appear in the individual tax formula. The module begins with exclusions and progresses to items to be included in gross income, tax accounting periods and methods, business income and deductions including depreciation, and deductions subtracted from gross income to arrive at adjusted gross income. Next reviewed is the standard deduction as well as the various categories of itemized deductions, together with personal and dependency exemptions, all of which are subtracted from adjusted gross income to arrive at taxable income. This is followed by a review of filing status, alternative minimum tax, and the various tax credits for which an individual might be eligible. The module concludes with an overview of farming income and expenses, tax procedures including assessments and claims for refund, choice of courts, and taxpayer penalties.

This section outlines (1) gross income in general, (2) exclusions from gross income, (3) items to be included in gross income, (4) tax accounting methods, and (5) items to be included in gross income net of deductions (e.g., business income, sales, and exchanges).

I. GROSS INCOME ON INDIVIDUAL RETURNS

A. In General

1. **Gross income** includes all income from whatever source derived, unless specifically excluded

   a. Does not include a return of capital (e.g., if a taxpayer loans $6,000 to another and is repaid $6,500 at a later date, only the $500 difference is included in gross income)

   b. The income must be **realized** (i.e., there must be a transaction which gives rise to the income)

   (1) A mere appreciation in the value of property is not income (e.g., value of one's home increases $2,000 during year. Only if the house is sold will the increase in value be realized)

   (2) A transaction may be in the form of actual receipt of cash or property, accrual of a receivable, or sale or exchange

   c. The income must also be **recognized** (i.e., the transaction must be a taxable event, and not a transaction for which nonrecognition is provided in the Internal Revenue Code)

   d. An **assignment of income** will not be recognized for tax purposes

   (1) If income from property is assigned, it is still taxable to the owner of the property.

   > **EXAMPLE**
   >
   > X owns a building and assigns the rents to Y. The rents remain taxable to X, even though the rents are received by Y.

   (2) If income from services is assigned, it is still taxable to the person who earns it.

   > **EXAMPLE**
   >
   > X earns $200 per week. To pay off a debt owed to Y, he assigns half of it to Y. $200 per week remains taxable to X.

2. Distinction between exclusions, deductions, and credits

   a. **Exclusions**—income items which are not included in gross income

   (1) Exclusions must be specified by law. Remember, gross income includes all income except that specifically excluded.

   (2) Although exclusions are exempt from income tax, they may still be taxed under other tax rules (e.g., gifts may be subject to the gift tax).

   b. **Deductions**—amounts that are subtracted from income to arrive at adjusted gross income or taxable income

   (1) Deductions for adjusted gross income (above the line deductions)—amounts deducted from gross income to arrive at adjusted gross income

   (2) Itemized deductions (below the line deductions)—amounts deducted from adjusted gross income to arrive at taxable income

   c. **Credits**—amounts subtracted from the computed tax to arrive at taxes payable

B. Exclusions from Gross Income (not reported)

1. Payments received for **support** of minor children

   a. Must be children of the parent making the payments

   b. Decree of divorce or separate maintenance generally must specify the amount to be treated as child support, otherwise payments may be treated as alimony

2. **Property settlement** (division of capital) received in a divorce

3. **Annuities** and pensions are excluded to the extent they represent a return of capital

   a. Excluded portion of each payment is

   $$\frac{\text{Net cost of annuity}}{\text{Expected total annuity payments}} = \text{Payment received}$$

   b. "Expected total annuity payments" is calculated by multiplying the annual return by

    (1) The number of years receivable if it is an annuity for a definite period

    (2) A life expectancy multiple (from IRS tables) if it is an annuity for life

  c. Once this exclusion ratio is determined, it remains constant until the cost of the annuity is completely recovered. Any additional payments will be fully taxable.

> **EXAMPLE**
>
> Mr. Jones purchased an annuity contract for $3,600 that will pay him $1,500 per year beginning in 2012. His expected return under the contract is $10,800. Mr. Jones' exclusion ratio is $3,600 ÷ $10,800 = 1/3. For 2012, Mr. Jones will exclude $1,500 × 1/3 = $500; and will include the remaining $1,000 in gross income.

  d. If the taxpayer dies before total cost is recovered, unrecovered cost is allowed as a miscellaneous itemized deduction on the taxpayer's final tax return.

4. **Life insurance proceeds** (face amount of policy) are generally excluded if paid by reason of death

  a. If proceeds are received in **installments,** amounts received in excess of pro rata part of face amount are taxable as interest.

  b. **Dividends** on unmatured insurance policies are excluded to the extent not in excess of cumulative premiums paid.

  c. **Accelerated death benefits** received under a life insurance policy by a *terminally or chronically ill* individual are generally excluded from gross income

    (1) Similarly, if a portion of a life insurance contract on the life of a terminally or chronically ill individual is assigned or sold to a viatical settlement provider, proceeds received from the provider are excluded.

    (2) For a chronically ill individual, the exclusion is limited to the amount paid by the individual for unreimbursed long-term care costs. Payments made on a per diem basis, up to $300 per day for 2011, are excludable regardless of actual long-term care costs incurred.

  d. All interest is taxable if proceeds are left with insurance company under agreement to pay only interest.

  e. If insurance proceeds are paid for reasons other than death or under c. above, or if the policy was obtained by the beneficiary in exchange for valuable consideration from a person other than the insurance company, all proceeds in excess of cost are taxable. Annuity rules apply to installment payments.

> **EXAMPLE**
>
> Able was the owner and beneficiary of a $30,000 life insurance policy on Baker. Able sold the policy for $10,000 to Carr who subsequently paid $6,000 of premiums. If Baker dies, Carr's gross income from the proceeds of the life insurance policy would total $30,000 – ($10,000 + $6,000) = $14,000.

  f. **Company-owned life insurance.** In the case of an *employer-owned* life insurance contract, the amount of insurance proceeds that can be excluded from gross income by the employer (or related person) is generally *limited* to the sum of the premiums and other amounts paid by the policyholder for the contract. However, the full amount of proceeds paid at death can be excluded if specified notice and consent requirements as well as additional requirements are met.

    (1) The notice and consent requirements specify that the employee must (a) be notified in writing of the intent to insure the employee's life and the maximum amount for which the employee could be insured, (b) provide written consent to being insured and acknowledge that coverage may continue after the employee terminates employment, and (c) be informed in writing that the employer (or related person) will be the beneficiary of proceeds payable upon the death of the employee.

    (2) Additionally, the insured must have been an employee at any time during the 12-month period before the insured's death, or at the time the contract was issued was a director or highly compensated employee. Alternatively, the proceeds must be paid to a member of the insured's family or designated beneficiary of the insured, or the proceeds are used to buy an equity (or capital or profits) interest in the employer from insured's heir.

5. Certain **employee benefits** are excluded

  a. **Group-term life insurance** premiums paid by employer (the **cost of up to $50,000** of insurance coverage is excluded). Exclusion not limited if beneficiary is the employer or a qualified charity.

  b. Insurance premiums employer pays to fund an accident or health plan for employees are excluded.

  c. **Accident and health benefits** provided by employer are excluded if benefits are for

(1) Permanent injury or loss of bodily function
(2) Reimbursement for medical care of employee, spouse, or dependents

    (a) Employee cannot take itemized deduction for reimbursed medical expenses
    (b) Exclusion may not apply to highly compensated individuals if reimbursed under a discriminatory self-insured medical plan

d. Employees of small businesses (50 or fewer employees) and self-employed individuals may qualify for a **medical savings account** (MSA) if covered under a high-deductible health insurance plan. An MSA is similar to an IRA, except used for health care.

    (1) Employer contributions to an employee's MSA are excluded from gross income (except if made through a cafeteria plan), and employee contributions are deductible for AGI.
    (2) Contributions are limited to 65% (75% for family coverage) of the annual health insurance deductible amount.
    (3) Earnings of an MSA are not subject to tax; distributions from an MSA used to pay qualified medical expenses are excluded from gross income.

e. **Meals or lodging** furnished for the convenience of the employer on the employer's premises are excluded.

    (1) For the convenience of the employer means there must be a noncompensatory reason such as the employee is required to be on duty during this period.
    (2) In the case of lodging, it also must be a condition of employment.

f. Employer-provided educational assistance (e.g., payment of tuition, books, fees) derived from an employer's qualified **educational assistance program** is excluded up to maximum of **$5,250** per year through 2012. The exclusion applies to both undergraduate as well as graduate-level courses, but does not apply to assistance payments for courses involving sports, games, or hobbies, unless they involve the employer's business or are required as part of a degree program. Excludable assistance does not include tools or supplies that the employee retains after completion of the course, nor the cost of meals, lodging, or transportation.

g. Employer payments to an employee for **dependent care assistance** are excluded from an employee's income if made under a written, nondiscriminatory plan. Maximum exclusion is **$5,000** per year ($2,500 for a married person filing a separate return).

h. **Qualified adoption expenses** paid or incurred by an employer in connection with an employee's adoption of a child are excluded from the employee's gross income. For 2012, the maximum exclusion is **$12,650** per eligible child (including special needs children) and the exclusion is ratably phased out for modified AGI between $189,710 and $229,710.

i. **Employee fringe benefits** are generally excluded if

    (1) **No additional-cost services**—for example, airline pass
    (2) **Employee discount** that is nondiscriminatory
    (3) **Working condition fringes**—excluded to the extent that if the amount had been paid by the employee, the amount would be deductible as an employee business expense
    (4) **De minimis fringes**—small value, impracticable to account for (e.g., coffee, personal use of copying machine)
    (5) **Qualified transportation fringes**

        (a) Up to $125 per month for 2012 can be excluded for employer-provided transit passes and transportation in a commuter highway vehicle if the transportation is between the employee's home and work place.
        (b) Up to $240 per month for 2012 can be excluded for employer-provided parking on or near the employer's place of business.

    (6) **Qualified moving expense reimbursement**—an individual can exclude any amount received from an employer as payment for (or reimbursement of) expenses which would be deductible as moving expenses if directly paid or incurred by the individual. The exclusion does not apply to any payment (or reimbursement of) an expense actually deducted by the individual in a prior taxable year.

j. **Workers' compensation** is fully excluded if received for an occupational sickness or injury and is paid under a workers' compensation act or statute.

6. Accident and health insurance benefits derived from policies **purchased by the taxpayer** are excluded, but not if the medical expenses were deducted in a prior year and the tax benefit rule applies.
7. **Damages for physical injury or physical sickness** are excluded.

   a. If an action has its origin in a physical injury or physical sickness, then all damages therefrom (other than puni-tive damages) are excluded (e.g., damages received by an individual on account of a claim for loss due to a physical injury to such individual's spouse are excludible from gross income).

   b. Damages (other than punitive damages) received on account of a claim of wrongful death, and damages that are compensation for amounts paid for medical care (including medical care for emotional distress) are excluded.

   c. Emotional distress is not considered a physical injury or physical sickness. No exclusion applies to damages received from a claim of employment discrimination, age discrimination, or injury to reputation (even if ac-companied by a claim of emotional distress).

   d. Punitive damages generally must be included in gross income, even if related to a physical injury or physical sickness.

8. **Gifts, bequests, devises, or inheritances** are excluded.

   a. Income subsequently derived from property so acquired is not excluded (e.g., interest or rent).

   b. "Gifts" from employer except for noncash holiday presents are generally not excluded.

9. The receipt of **stock dividends** (or stock rights) is generally excluded from income, but the FMV of the stock received will be included in income if the distribution

   a. Is on preferred stock

   b. Is payable, at the election of any shareholder, in stock or property

   c. Results in the receipt of preferred stock by some common shareholders, and the receipt of common stock by other common shareholders

   d. Results in the receipt of property by some shareholders, and an increase in the proportionate interests of other shareholders in earnings or assets of the corporation

> **NOW REVIEW MULTIPLE-CHOICE QUESTIONS 1 THROUGH 14 IN VOLUME 2**

10. Certain **interest income** is excluded.

   a. Interest on obligations of a **state** or one of its political subdivisions (e.g., **municipal** bonds), the District of Columbia, and US possessions is generally **excluded** from income if the bond proceeds are used to finance tra-ditional governmental operations.

   b. Other state and local government-issued obligations (private activity bonds) are generally fully taxable. An ob-ligation is a private activity bond if (1) more than 10% of the bond proceeds are used (directly or indirectly) in a private trade or business and more than 10% of the principal or interest on the bonds is derived from, or secured by, money or property used in the trade or business, or (2) the lesser of 5% or $5 million of the bond proceeds is used (directly or indirectly) to make or finance loans to private persons or entities.

   c. The following bonds are **excluded from the private activity bond category** even though their proceeds are not used in traditional government operations. The interest from these bonds is excluded from income.

     (1) Qualified bonds issued for the benefit of schools, hospitals, and other charitable organizations

     (2) Bonds used to finance certain exempt facilities, such as airports, docks, wharves, mass commuting facili-ties, etc.

     (3) Qualified redevelopment bonds, small-issue bonds (i.e., bonds not exceeding $1 million), and student loan bonds

     (4) Qualified mortgage and veterans' mortgage bonds

   d. Interest on **US obligations** is **included** in income.

11. **Savings bonds for higher education**

   a. The accrued interest on Series EE US savings bonds that are redeemed by the taxpayer is excluded from gross income to the extent that the aggregate redemption proceeds (principal plus interest) are used to finance the higher education of the taxpayer, taxpayer's spouse, or dependents.

     (1) The bonds must be issued after December 31, 1989, to an individual age twenty-four or older at the bond's issue date.

     (2) The purchaser of the bonds must be the sole owner of the bonds (or joint owner with his or her spouse). Married taxpayers must file a joint return to qualify for the exclusion.

     (3) The redemption proceeds must be used to pay qualified higher education expenses (i.e., tuition and required fees less scholarships, fellowships, and employer-provided educational assistance) at an accredited univer-sity, college, junior college, or other institution providing postsecondary education, or at an area vocational education school.

(4) If the redemption proceeds exceed the qualified higher education expenses, only a pro rata amount of interest can be excluded.

EXAMPLE

During 2012, a married taxpayer redeems Series EE bonds receiving $6,000 of principal and $4,000 of accrued interest. Assuming qualified higher education expenses total $9,000, accrued interest of $3,600 ($9,000/$10,000 × $4,000) can be excluded from gross income.

---

b. If the taxpayer's modified AGI exceeds a specified level, the exclusion is subject to phaseout as follows:

Filing status	2012 AGI phaseout range
Married filing jointly	$109,250 – $139,250
Single (including head of household)	$72,850 – $87,850

(1) The reduction of the exclusion is computed as

$$\left(\frac{\text{Excess AGI}}{\substack{\$15,000 \\ (\$30,000 \text{ for joint returns})}} \right) \times \left(\substack{\text{Otherwise} \\ \text{excludable} \\ \text{interest}} \right) = \text{Reduction}$$

(2) If the taxpayer's modified AGI exceeds the applicable phaseout range, no exclusion is available.

EXAMPLE

Assume the joint return of the married taxpayer in the above example has modified AGI of $129,250 for 2012. The reduction would be ($20,000/$30,000) × $3,600 = $2,400. Thus, of the $4,000 of interest received, a total of $1,200 could be excluded from gross income.

NOW REVIEW MULTIPLE-CHOICE QUESTIONS 15 THROUGH 22 IN VOLUME 2

12. **Scholarships and fellowships**

   a. A **degree candidate** can exclude the amount of a scholarship or fellowship that is used for tuition and course-related fees, books, supplies, and equipment. Amounts used for other purposes including room and board are included in income.
   b. Amounts received as a grant or a tuition reduction that represent payment for teaching, research, or other services are generally not excludable.
   c. Nondegree students may not exclude any part of a scholarship or fellowship grant.
   d. The exclusion from gross income also applies to scholarships with obligatory service requirements received by degree candidates at qualified educational organizations from the national Health Service Corps Scholarship Program and the F. Edward Hebert Armed Forces Health Professions Scholarship Program through 2012.

13. Political contributions received by candidates' campaign funds are excluded from income, but included if put to personal use.
14. Rental value of parsonage or cash rental allowance for a parsonage is excluded by a minister.
15. **Discharge of indebtedness** normally results in income to debtor, but may be **excluded** if

   a. A discharge of certain student loans pursuant to a loan provision providing for discharge if the individual works in a certain profession for a specified period of time
   b. A discharge of a corporation's debt by a shareholder (treated as a contribution to capital)
   c. The discharge is a gift
   d. The discharge is a purchase money debt reduction (treat as a reduction of purchase price)
   e. Debt is discharged in a bankruptcy proceeding, or debtor is insolvent both before and after discharge

   (1) If debtor is insolvent before but solvent after discharge of debt, income is recognized to the extent that the FMV of assets exceeds liabilities after discharge
   (2) The amount excluded from income in e. above must be applied to reduce tax attributes in the following order

      (a) Net Operating Loss (NOL) for taxable year and loss carryovers to taxable year
      (b) General business credit

  (c) Minimum tax credit
  (d) Capital loss of taxable year and carryovers to taxable year
  (e) Reduction of the basis of property
  (f) Passive activity loss and credit carryovers
  (g) Foreign tax credit carryovers to or from taxable year

  (3) Instead of reducing tax attributes in the above order, taxpayer may elect to first reduce the basis of depreciable property

16. **Lease improvements.** Increase in value of property due to improvements made by lessee are excluded from lessor's income unless improvements are made in lieu of fair value rent.

17. **Foreign earned income exclusion.** An individual meeting either a bona fide residence test or a physical presence test may elect to exclude up to $95,100 of income earned in a foreign country for 2012. Qualifying taxpayers also may elect to exclude additional amounts based on foreign housing costs.

  a. To qualify, an individual must be a (1) US citizen who is a foreign resident for an uninterrupted period that includes an entire taxable year (bona fide residence test), or (2) US citizen or resident present in a foreign country for at least 330 full days in any twelve-month period (physical presence test).
  b. An individual who elects to exclude the housing cost amount can exclude only the lesser of (1) the housing cost amount attributable to employer-provided amounts, or (2) the individual's foreign earned income for the year.
  c. Housing cost amounts not provided by an employer can be deducted for AGI, but deduction is limited to the excess of the taxpayer's foreign earned income over the applicable foreign earned income exclusion.

> **NOW REVIEW MULTIPLE-CHOICE QUESTIONS 23 THROUGH 25 IN VOLUME 2**

C. Items to Be Included in Gross Income

  Gross income includes all income from any source except those specifically excluded. The more common items of gross income are listed below. Those items requiring a detailed explanation are discussed on the following pages.

1. Compensation for services, including wages, salaries, bonuses, commissions, fees, and tips

  a. Property received as compensation is included in income at FMV on date of receipt.
  b. Bargain purchases by an employee from an employer are included in income at FMV less price paid.
  c. Life insurance premiums paid by employer must be included in an employee's gross income except for group-term life insurance coverage of $50,000 or less.
  d. Employee expenses paid or reimbursed by the employer unless the employee has to account to the employer for these expenses and they would qualify as deductible business expenses for employee.
  e. **Tips** must be included in gross income

  (1) If an individual receives less than $20 in tips while working for one employer during one month, the tips do not have to be reported to the employer, but the tips must be included in the individual's gross income when received.
  (2) If an individual receives $20 or more in tips while working for one employer during one month, the individual must report the total amount of tips to the employer by the tenth day of the following month for purposes of withholding of income tax and social security tax. Then the total amount of tips must be included in the individual's gross income for the month in which reported to the employer.

2. Gross income derived from business or profession
3. Distributive share of partnership or S corporation income
4. Gain from the sale or exchange of real estate, securities, or other property
5. Rents and royalties
6. Dividends
7. **Interest** including

  a. Earnings from savings and loan associations, mutual savings banks, credit unions, etc.
  b. Interest on bank deposits, corporate or US government bonds, and Treasury bills

  (1) Interest from US obligations is included, while interest on state and local obligations is generally excluded.
  (2) If a taxpayer elects to amortize the bond premium on taxable bonds acquired after 1987, any bond premium amortization is treated as an offset against the interest earned on the bond. The amortization of bond premium reduces taxable income (by offsetting interest income) as well as the bond's basis.

  c. **Interest on tax refunds**
  d. Imputed interest from interest-free and low-interest loans

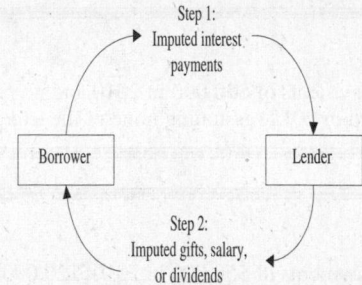

(1) Borrower is treated as making imputed interest payments (subject to the same deduction restrictions as actual interest payments) which the lender reports as interest income.

(2) Lender is treated as making gifts (for personal loans) or paying salary or dividends (for business-related loans or corporation-shareholder loans) to the borrower.

(3) Rate used to impute interest is tied to average yield on certain federal securities and is compounded semi-annually; if the federal rate is greater than the interest rate charged on a loan (e.g., a low-interest loan), impute interest only for the excess.

    (a) For demand loans, the deemed transfers are generally treated as occurring at the end of each year, and will fluctuate with interest rates.

    (b) For term loans, the interest payments are determined at the date of the loan and then allocated over the term of the loan; lender's payments are treated as made on date of loan.

(4) No interest is imputed to either the borrower or the lender for any day on which the aggregate amount of loans between such individuals (and their spouses) does not exceed $10,000.

(5) For any day that the aggregate amount of loans between borrower and lender (and their spouses) does not exceed $100,000, imputed interest is limited to borrower's "net investment income;" no interest is imputed if borrower's net investment income does not exceed $1,000.

EXAMPLE

Parents make a $200,000 interest-free demand loan to their unmarried daughter on January 1, 2011. Assume the average federal short-term rate is 3% for 2011. If the loan is outstanding for the entire year, under Step 1, the daughter is treated as making a ($200,000 × 3% × 1/2) + ($203,000 × 3% × 1/2) = $6,045 interest payment on 12/31/11, which is included as interest income on the parents' 2011 tax return. Under Step 2, the parents are treated as making a $6,045 gift to their daughter on 12/31/11. (Note that the gift will be offset by annual exclusions totaling $26,000 (for 2011) for gift tax purposes as discussed in Module 39.)

---

8. **Alimony** and separate maintenance payments

  a. Alimony is included in the recipient's gross income and is deductible toward AGI by the payor. In order for a payment to be considered as alimony, the payment must

    (1) Be made **pursuant to a decree** of divorce or written separation instrument
    (2) Be made in **cash** and received **by or on behalf** of the payee's spouse
    (3) **Terminate upon death** of the recipient
    (4) Not be made to a member of the same household at the time the payments are made
    (5) Not be made to a person with whom the taxpayer is filing a joint return
    (6) Not be characterized in the decree or written instrument as other than alimony

  b. **Alimony recapture** may occur if payments sharply decline in the second or third years. This is accomplished by making the payor report the recaptured alimony from the first and second years as income (and allowing the payee to deduct the same amount) in the third year.

    (1) Recapture for the second year occurs to the extent that the alimony paid in the second year exceeds the third-year alimony by more than $15,000.

    (2) Recapture for the first year occurs to the extent that the alimony paid in the first year exceeds the average alimony paid in the second year (reduced by the recapture for that year) and third year by more than $15,000.

    (3) Recapture will not apply to any year in which payments terminate as a result of the death of either spouse or the remarriage of the payee.

    (4) Recapture does not apply to payments that may fluctuate over three years or more and are not within the control of the payor spouse (e.g., 20% of the net income from a business).

> **EXAMPLE**
>
> If a payor makes alimony payments of $50,000 in 2010 and no payments in 2011 or 2012, $50,000 – $15,000 = $35,000 will be recaptured in 2012 (assuming none of the exceptions apply).

> **EXAMPLE**
>
> If a payor makes alimony payments of $50,000 in 2010, $20,000 in 2011, and nothing in 2012, the recapture amount for 2011 is $20,000 – $15,000 = $5,000. The recapture amount for 2010 is $50,000 – ($15,000 + $7,500) = $27,500. The $7,500 is the average payments for 2011 and 2010 after reducing the $20,000 year 2011 payment by the $5,000 of recapture for 2011. The recapture amounts for 2010 and 2011 total $32,500 and are reported in 2012.

   c. Any amounts specified as **child support** are not treated as alimony.

      (1) Child support is not gross income to the payee and is not deductible by the payor.

      (2) If the decree or instrument specifies both alimony and child support, but **less is paid than required,** then amounts are first allocated to child support, with any remainder allocated to alimony.

      (3) If a specified amount of alimony is to be reduced upon the happening of some **contingency relating to a child,** then an amount equal to the specified reduction will be treated as child support rather than alimony.

> **EXAMPLE**
>
> A divorce decree provides that payments of $1,000 per month will be reduced by $400 per month when a child reaches age twenty-one. Here, $400 of each $1,000 monthly payment will be treated as child support.

9. **Social security,** pensions, annuities (other than excluded recovery of capital)

   a. Up to 50% of social security retirement benefits may be included in gross income if the taxpayer's provisional income (AGI + tax-exempt income + 50% of the social security benefits) exceeds a threshold that is $32,000 for a joint return, $0 for married taxpayers filing separately, and $25,000 for all other taxpayers. The amount to be included in gross income is the lesser of

      (1) 50% of the social security benefits, or

      (2) 50% of the excess of the taxpayer's provisional income over the base amount.

> **EXAMPLE**
>
> A single taxpayer with AGI of $20,000 received tax-exempt interest of $2,000 and social security benefits of $7,000. The social security to be included in gross income is the lesser of
>
> $$1/2 \ (\$7,000) = \$3,500; \text{ or}$$
>
> $$1/2 \ (\$25,500 - \$25,000) = \$250.$$

   b. **Up to 85%** of social security retirement benefits may be included in gross income for taxpayers with provisional income above a higher second threshold that is $44,000 for a joint return, $0 for married taxpayers filing separately, and $34,000 for all other taxpayers. The amount to be included in gross income is the lesser of

      (1) 85% of the taxpayer's social security benefits, or

      (2) The sum of (a) 85% of the excess of the taxpayer's provisional income above the applicable higher threshold amount plus (b) the smaller of (i) the amount of benefits included under a. above, or (ii) $4,500 for single taxpayers or $6,000 for married taxpayers filing jointly.

   c. **Rule of thumb:** Social security retirement benefits are fully excluded by low-income taxpayers (i.e., provisional income less than $25,000); 85% of benefits must be included in gross income by high-income taxpayers (i.e., provisional income greater than $60,000).

   d. **Lump-sum distributions** from qualified pension, profit-sharing, stock bonus, and Keogh plans (but not IRAs) may be eligible for special tax treatment.

      (1) The portion of the distribution allocable to pre-1974 years is eligible for long-term capital gain treatment.

      (2) If the employee was born before 1936, the employee may elect ten-year averaging.

(3) Alternatively, the distribution may be rolled over tax-free (within sixty days) to a traditional IRA, but subsequent distributions from the IRA will be treated as ordinary income.

10. **Income in respect of a decedent** is income that would have been income of the decedent before death but was not includible in income under the decedent's method of accounting (e.g., installment payments that are paid to a decedent's estate after his/her death). Such income has the same character as it would have had if the decedent had lived and must be included in gross income by the person who receives it.

11. Employer supplemental unemployment benefits or strike benefits from union funds

12. Fees, including those received by an executor, administrator, director, or for jury duty, or precinct election board duty

13. Income from discharge of indebtedness unless specifically excluded

14. **Stock options**

   a. An **incentive stock option** receives favorable tax treatment.

   (1) The option must meet certain technical requirements to qualify.
   (2) No income is recognized by employee when option is granted or exercised.
   (3) If employee holds the stock acquired through exercise of the option at least two years from the date the option was granted, and holds the stock itself at least one year, the

   (a) Employee's realized gain will be long-term capital gain
   (b) Employer receives no deduction

   (4) If the holding period requirements above are not met, the employee has ordinary income to the extent that the FMV at date of exercise exceeds the option price.

   (a) Remainder of gain is short-term or long-term capital gain.
   (b) Employer receives a deduction equal to the amount employee reports as ordinary income.

   (5) An incentive stock option may be treated as a nonqualified stock option if a corporation so elects at the time the option is issued.

   b. A **nonqualified stock option** is included in income when received if option has a determinable FMV.

   (1) If option has no ascertainable FV when received, then income arises when option is exercised; to the extent of the difference between the FV when exercised and the option price.
   (2) Amount recognized (at receipt or when exercised) is treated as ordinary income to employee; employer is allowed a deduction equal to amount included in employee's income.

   c. An **employee stock purchase plan** that does not discriminate against rank and file employees

   (1) No income when employee receives or exercises option
   (2) If the employee holds the stock at least two years after the option is granted and at least one year after exercise, then

   (a) Employee has ordinary income to the extent of the lesser of

   1] FMV at time option granted over option price, or
   2] FMV at disposition over option price

   (b) Capital gain to the extent realized gain exceeds ordinary income

   (3) If the stock is not held for the required time, then

   (a) Employee has ordinary income at the time of sale for the difference between FV when exercised and the option price. This amount also increases basis.
   (b) Capital gain or loss for the difference between selling price and increased basis

15. **Prizes and awards** are generally taxable.

   a. Prizes and awards received for religious, charitable, scientific, educational, artistic, literary, or civic achievement can be excluded only if the recipient

   (1) Was selected without any action on his/her part,
   (2) Is not required to render substantial future services, and
   (3) Designates that the prize or award is to be transferred by the payor to a governmental unit or a tax-exempt charitable, educational, or religious organization
   (4) The prize or award is excluded from the recipient's income, but no charitable deduction is allowed for the transferred amount.

    b. **Employee achievement awards** are excluded from an employee's income if the cost to the employer of the award does not exceed the amount allowable as a deduction (generally from $400 to $1,600).

      (1) The award must be for length of service or safety achievement and must be in the form of tangible personal property (cash does not qualify).

      (2) If the cost of the award exceeds the amount allowable as a deduction to the employer, the employee must include in gross income the greater of

        (a) The portion of cost not allowable as a deduction to the employer, or

        (b) The excess of the award's FMV over the amount allowable as a deduction.

16. **Tax benefit rule.** A recovery of an item deducted in an earlier year must be included in gross income to the extent that a tax benefit was derived from the prior deduction of the recovered item.

    a. A tax benefit was derived if the previous deduction reduced the taxpayer's income tax.

    b. A recovery is excluded from gross income to the extent that the previous deduction did not reduce the taxpayer's income tax.

      (1) A deduction would not reduce a taxpayer's income tax if the taxpayer was subject to the alternative minimum tax in the earlier year and the deduction was not allowed in computing AMTI (e.g., state income taxes).

      (2) A recovery of state income taxes, medical expenses, or other items deductible on Schedule A (Form 1040) will be excluded from gross income if an individual did not itemize deductions for the year the item was paid.

EXAMPLE

Individual X, a single taxpayer, did not itemize deductions but instead used the standard deduction of $5,800 for 2011. In 2012, a refund of $300 of 2011 state income taxes is received. X would exclude the $300 refund from income in 2012.

EXAMPLE

Individual Y, a single taxpayer, had total itemized deductions of $5,900 for 2011, including $800 of state income taxes. In 2012, a refund of $400 of 2011 state income taxes is received. Y must include $100 ($5,900 – $5,800) of the refund in income for 2012.

---

17. Embezzled or other illegal income
18. **Gambling winnings**
19. **Unemployment compensation** must generally be included in gross income. However, for 2009 only, up to $2,400 of unemployment compensation could be excluded from gross income.

NOW REVIEW MULTIPLE-CHOICE QUESTIONS 26 THROUGH 43 IN VOLUME 2

D. Accounting Periods

1. The term **taxable year** refers to a taxpayer's annual accounting period. Annual accounting period means the annual period that the taxpayer uses to compute income in keeping his books.

    a. **Calendar year** is a period of 12 months ending on December 31.

    b. **Fiscal year** is a period of 12 months ending on the last day of a month other than December.

    c. **52-53 week year** is an annual period always ending on the same day of the week (e.g., last Sunday of a month, or the Sunday closest to the end of a month).

2. Taxpayer establishes an accounting period by filing first tax return. A taxpayer who does not keep books (e.g., an employee with wage income) must use a calendar year.

3. Rules for adoption of taxable year.

    a. **Corporation** that is a "C" corporation (other than a personal service corporation) may adopt any taxable year that it chooses. A **personal service corporation** generally must adopt a calendar year.

    b. **Sole proprietor** must use same taxable year for business as is used for personal return.

    c. **Partnership** is a pass-through entity and generally must use the same tax year as that used by its partners owning more than 50% of partnership income and capital. A different taxable year may be permitted if there is a substantial business purpose.

    d. **S corporation** is a pass-through entity and generally must adopt a calendar year. A different taxable year may be permitted if there is a substantial business purpose.

    e. **Estate** may adopt any taxable year for its income tax return that it chooses.

    f. **Trust** (other than charitable and tax-exempt trusts) must adopt a calendar year.

4. Substantial business purpose and IRS approval are generally required to **change a taxable year**. Taxpayers can request permission to change a year by filing Form 1128, Application for Change in Accounting Period, by the 15th day of the second month after the close of a short period.

    a. The business purpose requirement may be satisfied if the taxpayer is requesting a change to a natural business year. The business purpose test will be met if the taxpayer receives at least 25% of its gross receipts in the last two months of the selected year, and this 25% test has been satisfied for three consecutive years.

    b. The IRS may require that certain conditions be met before it approves a request for change (e.g., the IRS may require partners to switch to the same year as is being requested by the partnership).

5. Some changes in tax years require *no* approval.

    a. Newly married individuals may adopt the taxable year of the other spouse without prior approval.

    b. A corporation (other than an S Corporation) may change its year if its taxable year has not changed within the past 10 years ending with the calendar year of change; the resulting short period does not have a NOL; the corporation's annualized taxable income for the short period is at least 90% of its taxable income for the preceding year; and the corporation's status (e.g., personal holding company) for the short period is the same as the preceding year.

    c. A newly acquired subsidiary that will be included in a consolidated return must change its taxable year to the same year as used by its parent.

6. Taxable periods of less than 12 months

    a. If due to beginning or ending of taxpayer's existence, tax is computed in normal way (e.g., corporation is formed, or individual dies). The taxpayer's exemptions and credits are not prorated. In the case of a decedent, the income tax return can be filed as if the decedent lived throughout the entire tax year.

    b. If the short period is due to a *change in taxable year*, taxable income generally must be **annualized**. However, a new subsidiary that has a short year because of being included in a consolidated return is not required to annualize.

        (1) When annualizing, an individual cannot use the tax tables and must itemize deductions. Personal exemptions must be prorated.

        (2) Taxable income is multiplied by 12 and divided by the number of months in short period.

        (3) The tax is computed and multiplied by the number of months in the short period, then divided by 12.

EXAMPLE

Pearl Corp. is a C Corporation that has been using a fiscal year ending June 30. It changes to a fiscal year ending September 30 for 2011. Pearl must file a tax return for its fiscal year ending June 30, 2011, as well as a tax return for its short period beginning July 1, 2011, and ending September 30, 2011. Pearl determines that its taxable income for the short period ending September 30 is $30,000. Because Pearl's short period is the result of a change in taxable year, Pearl must annualize its taxable income for the short period and determine its tax as follows:

Taxable income $30,000 × 12/3	=	$120,000
Tax on $120,000	=	$ 30,050
Tax for short period $30,050 × 3/12	=	$ 7,513

E. Tax Accounting Methods

    Tax accounting methods often affect the period in which an item of income or deduction is recognized. Note that the classification of an item is not changed, only the time for its inclusion in the tax computation.

1. Cash method or accrual method is commonly used.

    a. **Cash method** recognizes income when first received or constructively received; expenses are deductible when paid.

(1) **Constructive receipt** means that an item is unqualifiedly available without restriction (e.g., interest on bank deposit is income when credited to account).

(2) Not all receipts are income (e.g., loan proceeds, return of investment); not all payments are deductible (e.g., loan repayment, expenditures benefiting future years generally must be capitalized and deducted over cost recovery period).

b. Under the cash method, expenses are generally deductible when paid. Payment by check is considered payment so long as the check is honored by the bank. A payment by credit card is considered a payment at the time of the charge.

(1) Generally, a capital expenditure or prepayment that results in a benefit that extends substantially beyond the end of the tax year does not result in an immediate deduction. However, a cash method taxpayer is not required to capitalize a payment so long as (1) the benefit does not extend beyond 12 months after the first date that the benefit is received, and (2) the benefit does not extend beyond the end of the taxable year following the taxable year in which payment is made.

> **EXAMPLE**
>
> On December 1, 2011, a calendar-year taxpayer pays a $10,000 property insurance premium with a 1-year term that begins on February 1, 2012. The amount paid must be capitalized and is not deductible for 2011 because the benefit attributable to the $10,000 payment extends beyond the end of the taxable year following the taxable year in which the payment is made. The premium will be deductible over the period to which it relates.

> **EXAMPLE**
>
> Assume the same facts as in the example above, except that the policy has a term beginning on December 15, 2011. The 12-month rule applies to the $10,000 payment because the benefit attributable to the payment extends neither more than 12 months beyond December 15, 2011, nor beyond the end of the taxable year following the taxable year in which the payment is made. Thus, the taxpayer is not required to capitalize the payment, and may deduct the $10,000 payment in 2011.

(2) The 12-month rule in (1) above does not apply to prepaid interest, which generally must be deducted over the loan period to which it is allocated.

c. The cash method cannot generally be used if inventories are necessary to clearly reflect income, and cannot generally be used by C corporations, partnerships that have a C corporation as a partner, tax shelters, and certain tax-exempt trusts. However, the following may use the cash method:

(1) A qualified personal service corporation (e.g., corporation performing services in health, law, engineering, accounting, actuarial science, performing arts, or consulting) if at least 95% of stock is owned by specified shareholders including employees.

(2) An entity (other than a tax shelter) if for every year it has average annual gross receipts of **$5 million or less** for any prior three-year period and provided it does not have inventories for sale to customers.

(3) A **small business taxpayer** with average annual gross receipts of **$1 million or less** for any prior three-year period can use the cash method and is excepted from the requirements to account for inventories and use the accrual method for purchases and sales of merchandise.

(4) A **small business taxpayer** is eligible to use the cash method of accounting if, in addition to having average gross receipts of more than $1 million and less than $10 million, the business meets any one of three requirements.

    (a) The principal business activity is **not** retailing, wholesaling, manufacturing, mining, publishing, or sound recording;

    (b) The principal business activity is the provision of services, or custom manufacturing; or

    (c) Regardless of the principal business activity, a taxpayer may use the cash method with respect to any separate business that satisfies (a) or (b) above.

(5) A taxpayer using the accrual method who meets the requirements in (3) or (4) can change to the cash method but must treat merchandise inventory as a material or supply that is not incidental (i.e., only deductible in the year actually consumed or used in the taxpayer's business).

d. **Accrual method** must be used by taxpayers (other than small business taxpayers) for purchases and sales when inventories are required to clearly reflect income.

(1) **Income** is recognized when "all events" have occurred that fix the taxpayer's right to receive the item of income and the amount can be determined with reasonable accuracy.

(2) An **expense** is deductible when "all events" have occurred that establish the fact of the liability and the amount can be determined with reasonable accuracy. The all-events test is not satisfied until **economic performance** has taken place.

    (a) For property or services to be provided **to the taxpayer,** economic performance occurs when the property or services are actually provided by the other party.

    (b) For property or services to be provided **by the taxpayer,** economic performance occurs when the property or services are physically provided by the taxpayer.

(3) An exception to the economic performance rule treats certain **recurring items of expense** as incurred in advance of economic performance provided

    (a) The all-events test, without regard to economic performance, is satisfied during the tax year;

    (b) Economic performance occurs within a reasonable period (but in no event more than 8.5 months after the close of the tax year);

    (c) The item is recurring in nature and the taxpayer consistently treats items of the same type as incurred in the tax year in which the all-events test is met; and

    (d) Either the amount is not material or the accrual of the item in the year the all-events test is met results in a better matching against the income to which it relates.

2. **Special rules** regarding methods of accounting

  a. **Rents and royalties received in advance** are included in gross income in the year received under both the cash and accrual methods.

    (1) A **security deposit** is included in income when not returned to tenant.

    (2) An amount called a "security deposit" that may be used as final payment of rent is considered to be advance rent and included in income when received.

> **EXAMPLE**
>
> In 2011, a landlord signed a five-year lease. During 2011, the landlord received $5,000 for that year's rent, and $5,000 as advance rent for the last year (2015) of the lease. All $10,000 will be included in income for 2011.

  b. Dividends are included in gross income in the year received under both the cash and accrual methods.

  c. No advance deduction is generally allowed for accrual method taxpayers for estimated or contingent expenses; the obligation must be "fixed and determinable."

3. The **installment method** applies to gains (not losses) from the disposition of property where at least one payment is to be received after the year of sale. The installment method does not change the character of the gain to be reported (e.g., ordinary, capital, etc.), and is required unless the taxpayer makes a negative election to report the full amount of gain in year of sale.

  a. The installment method **cannot be used** for property held for sale in the ordinary course of business (except time-share units, residential lots, and property used or produced in farming), and cannot be used for sales of stock or securities traded on an established securities market.

  b. The amount to be reported in each year is determined by the formula

$$\frac{\text{Gross profit}}{\text{Total contract price}} \times \text{Amount received in year}$$

    (1) **Contract price** is the selling price reduced by the seller's liabilities that are assumed by the buyer, to the extent not in excess of the seller's basis in the property.

> **EXAMPLE**
>
> Taxpayer sells property with a basis of $80,000 to buyer for a selling price of $150,000. As part of the purchase price, buyer agrees to assume a $50,000 mortgage on the property and pay the remaining $100,000 in 10 equal annual installments together with adequate interest.
>
> The contract price is $100,000 ($150,000 − $50,000); the gross profit is $70,000 ($150,000 − $80,000); and the gross profit ratio is 70% ($70,000 ÷ $100,000). Thus, $7,000 of each $10,000 payment is reported as gain from the sale.

> **EXAMPLE**
>
> Assume the same facts as above except that the seller's basis is $30,000. The contract price is $120,000 ($150,000 – mortgage assumed but only to extent of seller's basis of $30,000); the gross profit is $120,000 ($150,000 – $30,000); and the gross profit ratio is 100% ($120,000 ÷ $120,000). Thus, 100% of each $10,000 payment is reported as gain from the sale. In addition, the amount by which the assumed mortgage exceeds the seller's basis ($20,000) is deemed to be a payment in year of sale. Since the gross profit ratio is 100%, all $20,000 is reported as gain in the year the mortgage is assumed.

(2) Any depreciation recapture under Secs. 1245, 1250, and 291 must be included in income in the year of sale. Amount of recapture included in income is treated as an increase in the basis of the property for purposes of determining the gross profit ratio. Remainder of gain is spread over installment payments.

> **EXAMPLE**
>
> Baxter sells equipment with an adjusted basis of $50,000 to a buyer for $50,000 cash plus a $50,000 interest-bearing note to be paid next year. The equipment had originally cost $90,000, and Baxter had deducted depreciation of $40,000 on the equipment. Baxter realizes a gain of $100,000 – $50,000 = $50,000 on the installment sale, and must immediately recognize gain to the extent of Sec. 1245 depreciation recapture of $40,000, which is not eligible for installment reporting. The gross profit ratio is determined after adding the $40,000 of recapture to the $50,000 of adjusted basis, resulting in a gross profit ratio of 10% [$100,000 – $90,000)/$100,000]. As a result, the $40,000 of depreciation recapture plus 10% × $50,000 cash payment = $5,000 must be recognized this year, while the remaining 10% × $50,000 = $5,000 of gain will be recognized next year when payment on the note is received.

(3) The receipt of readily tradable debt or debt that is payable on demand is considered the receipt of a payment for purposes of the installment method. Additionally, if installment obligations are pledged as security for a loan, the net proceeds of the loan are treated as payments received on the installment obligations.

(4) Installment obligations arising from nondealer sales of property used in the taxpayer's trade or business or held for the production of rental income (e.g., factory building, warehouse, office building, apartment building) are subject to an interest charge on the tax that is deferred on such sales to the extent that the amount of deferred payments arising from all dispositions of such property during a taxable year and outstanding as of the close of the taxable year exceeds $5,000,000. This provision does not apply to installment sales of property if the sales price does not exceed $150,000, to sales of personal use property, and to sales of farm property.

4. **Percentage-of-completion** method can be used for contracts that are not completed within the year they are started.

   a. Percentage-of-completion method recognizes income each year based on the percentage of the contract completed that year.
   b. Taxpayer may elect not to recognize income or account for costs from a contract for a tax year if less than 10% of the estimated total contract costs have been incurred as of the end of the year.

NOW REVIEW MULTIPLE-CHOICE QUESTIONS 44 THROUGH 59 IN VOLUME 2

F. Business Income and Deductions

1. **Gross income** for a business includes sales less cost of goods sold plus other income. In computing cost of goods sold

   a. Inventory is generally valued at (1) cost, or (2) market, whichever is lower
   b. Specific identification, FIFO, and LIFO are allowed
   c. If LIFO is used for taxes, it must also be used on books
   d. Lower of cost or market cannot be used with LIFO

2. All **ordinary** (customary and not a capital expenditure) and **necessary** (appropriate and helpful) **expenses** incurred in a trade or business are deductible.

   a. Business expenses that violate public policy (fines or illegal kickbacks) are not deductible.
   b. No deduction or credit is allowed for any amount paid or incurred in carrying on a trade or business that consists of trafficking in controlled substances. However, this limitation does not alter the definition of gross income (i.e., sales less cost of goods sold).

c. Business expenses must be reasonable.

    (1) If salaries are excessive (unreasonable compensation), they may be disallowed as a deduction to the extent unreasonable.

    (2) Reasonableness of compensation issue generally arises only when the relationship between the employer and employee exceeds that of the normal employer-employee relationship (e.g., employee is also a shareholder).

    (3) Use test of what another enterprise would pay under similar circumstances to an unrelated employee.

d. In the case of an individual, any charge (including taxes) for basic local telephone service with respect to the **first telephone line** provided to any residence of the taxpayer shall be treated as a nondeductible personal expense. Disallowance does not apply to charges for long-distance calls, charges for equipment rental, and optional services provided by a telephone company, or charges attributable to additional telephone lines to a taxpayer's residence other than the first telephone line.

e. **Uniform capitalization rules** (UNICAP) generally require that all costs incurred (both direct and indirect) in manufacturing or constructing real or personal property, or in purchasing or holding property for sale, must be capitalized as part of the cost of the property.

    (1) These costs become part of the basis of the property and are recovered through depreciation or amortization, or are included in inventory and recovered through cost of goods sold as an offset to selling price.

    (2) The rules apply to inventory, noninventory property produced or held for sale to customers, and to assets or improvements to assets constructed by a taxpayer for the taxpayer's own use in a trade or business or in an activity engaged in for profit.

    (3) Taxpayers subject to the rules are required to capitalize not only direct costs, but also most indirect costs that benefit the assets produced or acquired for resale, including general, administrative, and overhead costs.

    (4) Retailers and wholesalers must include in inventory all costs incident to purchasing and storing inventory such as wages of employees responsible for purchasing inventory, handling, processing, repackaging and assembly of goods, and off-site storage costs. These rules do not apply to "small retailers and wholesalers" (i.e., a taxpayer who acquires personal property for resale if the taxpayer's average annual gross receipts for the three preceding taxable years do not exceed $10,000,000).

    (5) Interest must be capitalized if the debt is incurred or continued to finance the construction or production of real property, property with a recovery period of twenty years, property that takes more than two years to produce, or property with a production period exceeding one year and a cost exceeding $1 million.

    (6) The UNICAP rules do not apply to advertising, selling, and research and experimentation expenditures, mine development and exploration costs, property held for personal use, and to freelance authors, photographers, and artists whose personal efforts create the product.

f. **Business meals, entertainment, and travel**

    (1) Receipts must be maintained for all lodging expenditures and for other expenditures of **$75** or more except transportation expenditures where receipts are not readily available.

    (2) Adequate contemporaneous records must be maintained for business meals and entertainment to substantiate the amount of expense, for example, who, when, where, and why (the 4 W's).

    (3) Business meals and entertainment must be directly related or associated with the active conduct of a trade or business to be deductible. The taxpayer or a representative must be present to satisfy this requirement.

    (4) The amount of the otherwise allowable deduction for business meals or entertainment must be reduced by 50%. This **50% reduction rule** applies to all food, beverage, and entertainment costs (even though incurred in the course of travel away from home) after determining the amount otherwise deductible. The 50% reduction rule will not apply if

        (a) The full value of the meal or entertainment is included in the recipient's income or excluded as a fringe benefit.

        (b) An employee is reimbursed for the cost of a meal or entertainment (the 50% reduction rule applies to the party making the reimbursement).

        (c) The cost is for a traditional employer-paid employee recreation expense (e.g., a company Christmas party).

        (d) The cost is for samples and other promotional activities made available to the public.

        (e) The expense is for a sports event that qualifies as a charitable fund-raising event.

        (f) The cost is for meals or entertainment sold for full consideration.

    (5) The cost of a ticket to any entertainment activity is limited (prior to the 50% reduction rule) to its face value.

(6) No deduction is generally allowed for expenses with respect to an entertainment, recreational, or amusement facility.

 (a) Entertainment facilities include yachts, hunting lodges, fishing camps, swimming pools, etc.
 (b) If the facility or club is used for a business purpose, the related out-of-pocket expenditures are deductible even though depreciation, etc. of the facility is not deductible.

(7) No deduction is allowed for dues paid to country clubs, golf and athletic clubs, airline clubs, hotel clubs, and luncheon clubs. Dues are generally deductible if paid to professional organizations (accounting, medical, and legal associations), business leagues, trade associations, chambers of commerce, boards of trade, and civic and public service organizations (Kiwanis, Lions, Elks).

(8) **Transportation and travel expenses** are deductible if incurred in the active conduct of a trade or business.

 (a) Deductible transportation expenses include local transportation between two job locations, but excludes commuting expenses between residence and job.
 (b) Deductible travel expenses are those incurred while temporarily "away from tax home" overnight including meals, lodging, transportation, and expenses incident to travel (clothing care, etc.).

  1] Travel expenses to and from domestic destination are fully deductible if business is the primary purpose of trip.
  2] Actual automobile expenses can be deducted, or taxpayers can use standard mileage rate of 55.5¢ per mile beginning July 1, 2011, for all business miles (plus parking and tolls).
  3] No deduction is allowed for travel as a form of education. This rule applies when a travel expense would otherwise be deductible only on the ground that the travel itself serves educational purposes.
  4] No deduction is allowed for expenses incurred in attending a convention, seminar, or similar meeting for investment purposes.

g. Deductions for **business gifts** are limited to **$25** per recipient each year.

 (1) Advertising and promotional gifts costing $4 or less are not limited.
 (2) Gifts of tangible personal property costing $400 or less are deductible if awarded as an employee achievement award for length of service or safety achievement.
 (3) Gifts of tangible personal property costing $1,600 or less are deductible if awarded as an employee achievement award under a qualified plan for length of service or safety achievement.

  (a) Plan must be written and nondiscriminatory.
  (b) Average cost of all items awarded under the plan during the tax year must not exceed $400.

h. **Bad debts** are generally deducted in the year they become worthless.

 (1) There must have been a valid "debtor-creditor" relationship.
 (2) A **business bad debt** is one that is incurred in the trade or business of the lender.

  (a) Deductible against ordinary income (toward AGI)
  (b) Deduction allowed for partial worthlessness

 (3) Business bad debts must be deducted under the specific charge-off method (the reserve method generally cannot be used).

  (a) A deduction is allowed when a specific debt becomes partially or totally worthless.
  (b) A bad debt deduction is available for accounts or notes receivable only if the amount owed has already been included in gross income for the current or a prior taxable year. Since receivables for services rendered of a **cash method** taxpayer have not yet been included in gross income, the receivables cannot be deducted when they become uncollectible.

 (4) A **nonbusiness bad debt** (not incurred in trade or business) can only be deducted

  (a) If totally worthless
  (b) As a short-term capital loss

 (5) Guarantor of debt who has to pay takes same deduction as if the loss were from a direct loan

  (a) Business bad debt if guarantee related to trade, business, or employment
  (b) Nonbusiness bad debt if guarantee entered into for profit but not related to trade or business

i. A **hobby** is an activity not engaged in for profit (e.g., stamp or card collecting engaged in for recreation and personal pleasure).

(1) Special rules generally limit the deduction of hobby expenses to the amount of hobby gross income. No net loss can generally be deducted for hobby activities.

(2) Hobby expenses are deductible as itemized deductions in the following order:

   (a) First deduct taxes, interest, and casualty losses pertaining to the hobby.

   (b) Then other hobby operating expenses are deductible to the extent they do not exceed hobby gross income reduced by the amounts deducted in (a). Out-of-pocket expenses are deducted before depreciation. These hobby expenses are aggregated with other miscellaneous itemized deductions that are subject to the 2% of AGI floor.

EXAMPLE

Glenn is an engineer who races a Formula Three car as a hobby. This year Glenn received a salary of $97,000 from his employer and won $3,000 in various car races, while incurring $9,000 of out-of-pocket expenses in his racing hobby. Glenn must include the $3,000 of prizes in his gross income, raising his AGI to $100,000. His $9,000 of hobby expenses are only deductible to the extent of $3,000. Assuming that Glenn itemizes his deductions but has no other miscellaneous itemized deductions, his hobby expenses would result in a deduction of $3,000 − (2% × $100,000) = $1,000.

---

(3) An activity is presumed to be for profit (not a hobby) if it produces a net profit in at least three out of five consecutive years (two out of seven years for horses).

NOW REVIEW MULTIPLE-CHOICE QUESTIONS 60 THROUGH 69 IN VOLUME 2

---

3. **Net operating loss**

   a. A NOL is generally a business loss but may occur even if an individual is not engaged in a separate trade or business (e.g., a NOL created by a personal casualty loss).

   b. A NOL may be carried **back two years** and carried **forward twenty years** to offset taxable income in those years.

   (1) Carryback is first made to the second preceding year.

   (2) Taxpayer may elect not to carryback and only carryforward twenty years.

   (3) A three-year carryback period is permitted for the portion of the NOL that relates to casualty and theft losses of individual taxpayers, and to NOLs that are attributable to presidentially declared disasters and are incurred by taxpayers engaged in farming or by a small business.

   (4) A *small business* is any trade or business (including one conducted by a corporation, partnership, or sole proprietorship) with average annual gross receipts of $5 million or less for the three-year tax period preceding the loss year.

   c. The following cannot be included in the computation of a NOL:

   (1) Any NOL carryforward or carryback from another year

   (2) Excess of capital losses over capital gains. Excess of nonbusiness capital losses over nonbusiness capital gains even if overall gains exceed losses

   (3) Personal and dependency exemptions

   (4) Excess of nonbusiness deductions (usually itemized deductions) over nonbusiness income

      (a) The standard deduction is treated as a nonbusiness deduction.

      (b) Contributions to a self-employed retirement plan are considered nonbusiness deductions.

      (c) Casualty losses (even if personal) are considered business deductions.

      (d) Dividends and interest are nonbusiness income; salary and rent are business income.

   (5) The domestic production activities deduction (DPAD).

   (6) Any remaining loss is a NOL and must be carried back first, unless election is made to carryforward only.

EXAMPLE

George, single with no dependents, started his own delivery business and incurred a loss from the business for 2011. In addition, he earned interest on personal bank deposits of $1,800. After deducting his itemized deductions for interest and taxes of $9,000, and his personal exemption of $3,700, the loss shown on George's Form 1040 was $20,700. George's net operating loss would be computed as follows:

Taxable income		$(20,700)
Nonbusiness deductions	$9,000	
Nonbusiness income	−1,800	7,200
Personal exemption		3,700
Net operating loss		$(9,800)

NOW REVIEW MULTIPLE-CHOICE QUESTIONS 70 THROUGH 72 IN VOLUME 2

---

4. Limitation on deductions for **business use of home**. To be deductible

   a. A portion of the home must be used exclusively and regularly as the *principal place of business,* or as a meeting place for patients, clients, or customers.

      (1) Exclusive use rule does not apply to the portion of the home used as a day care center and to a place of regular storage of business inventory or product samples if the home is the sole fixed location of a trade or business selling products at retail or wholesale.
      (2) If an employee, the exclusive use must be for the convenience of the employer.
      (3) A home office qualifies as a taxpayer's *principal place of business* if

         (a) It is the place where the primary income-generating functions of the trade or business are performed; or
         (b) The office is used to conduct administrative or management activities of the taxpayer's business, and there is no other fixed location of the business where substantial administrative or management activities are performed. Activities that are administrative or managerial in nature include billing customers, clients, or patients; keeping books and records; ordering supplies; setting up appointments; and forwarding orders or writing reports.

   b. Deduction is limited to the excess of gross income derived from the business use of the home over deductions otherwise allowable for taxes, interest, and casualty losses.
   c. Any business expenses not allocable to the use of the home (e.g., wages, transportation, supplies) must be deducted before home use expenses.
   d. Any business use of home expenses that are disallowed due to the gross income limitation can be carried forward and deducted in future years subject to the same restrictions.

EXAMPLE

Taxpayer uses 10% of his home exclusively for business purposes. Gross income from his business totaled $750, and he incurred the following expenses:

	Total	10% Business
Interest	4,000	$400
Taxes	2,500	250
Utilities, insurance	1,500	150
Depreciation	2,000	200

Since total deductions for business use of the home are limited to business gross income, the taxpayer can deduct the following for business use of his home: $400 interest; $250 taxes; $100 utilities and insurance; and $0 depreciation (operating expenses such as utilities and insurance must be deducted before depreciation). The remaining $50 of utilities and insurance, and $200 of depreciation can be carried forward and deducted in future years subject to the same restrictions.

---

5. Loss deductions incurred in a trade or business, or in the production of income, are limited to the amount a taxpayer has "**at risk**."

   a. Applies to all activities except the leasing of personal property by a closely held corporation (5 or fewer individuals own more than 50% of stock)
   b. Applies to individuals and closely held regular corporations
   c. Amount "at risk" includes

      (1) The cash and adjusted basis of property contributed by the taxpayer, and
      (2) Liabilities for which the taxpayer is personally liable; excludes nonrecourse debt.

   d. For real estate activities, a taxpayer's amount at risk includes "qualified" nonrecourse financing secured by the real property used in the activity.

(1) Nonrecourse financing is qualified if it is borrowed from a lender engaged in the business of making loans (e.g., bank, savings and loan) provided that the lender is not the promoter or seller of the property or a party related to either; or is borrowed from or guaranteed by any federal, state, or local government or instrumentality thereof.

(2) Nonrecourse financing obtained from a qualified lender who has an equity interest in the venture is treated as an amount at risk, as long as the terms of the financing are commercially reasonable.

(3) The nonrecourse financing must not be convertible, and no person can be personally liable for repayment.

e. Excess losses can be carried over to subsequent years (no time limit) and deducted when the "at risk" amount has been increased.

f. Previously allowed losses will be recaptured as income if the amount at risk is reduced below zero.

6. **Losses and credits from passive activities** may generally only be used to offset income from (or tax allocable to) passive activities. Passive losses may not be used to offset active income (e.g., wages, salaries, professional fees, etc.) or portfolio income (e.g., interest, dividends, annuities, royalties, etc.).

> **EXAMPLE**
>
> Ken has salary income, a loss from a partnership in whose business Ken does not materially participate, and income from a limited partnership. Ken may offset the partnership loss against the income from the limited partnership, but not against his salary income.

> **EXAMPLE**
>
> Robin has dividend and interest income of $40,000 and a passive activity loss of $30,000. The passive activity loss cannot be offset against the dividend and interest income.

a. Applies to individuals, estates, trusts, closely held C corporations, and personal service corporations

(1) A closely held C corporation is one with five or fewer shareholders owning more than 50% of stock.

(2) Personal service corporation is an incorporated service business with more than 10% of its stock owned by shareholder-employees.

b. **Passive activity** is any activity that involves the conduct of a trade or business in which the taxpayer does "not materially participate," any rental activity, and any limited partnership interest.

(1) Material participation is the taxpayer's involvement in an activity on a regular, continuous, and substantial basis considering such factors as time devoted, physical duties performed, and knowledge of or experience in the business.

(2) Passive activity does not include (1) a working interest in any oil or gas property that a taxpayer owns directly or through an entity that does not limit the taxpayer's liability, (2) operating a hotel or transient lodging if significant services are provided, or (3) operating a short-term equipment rental business.

c. **Losses** from passive activities may be deducted only against income from passive activities.

(1) If there is insufficient passive activity income to absorb passive activity losses, the excess losses are carried forward indefinitely to future years.

(2) If there is insufficient passive activity income in subsequent years to fully absorb the loss carryforwards, the unused losses from a passive activity may be deducted when the taxpayer's entire interest in the activity that gave rise to the unused losses is finally disposed of in a fully taxable transaction.

(3) Other dispositions

(a) A transfer of a taxpayer's interest in a passive activity by reason of the taxpayer's death results in suspended losses being allowed (to the decedent) to the extent they exceed the amount of the step-up in basis allowed.

(b) If the disposition is by gift, the suspended losses are added to the basis of the gift property. If less than 100% of an interest is transferred by gift, an allocable portion of the suspended losses is added to the basis of the gift.

(c) An installment sale of a passive interest triggers the recognition of suspended losses in the ratio that the gain recognized in each year bears to the total gain on sale.

(d) If a formerly passive activity becomes an active one, suspended losses are allowed against income from the now active business (if the activity remains the same).

d. **Credits** from passive activities can only be used to offset the tax liability attributable to passive activity income.

    (1) Excess credits are carried forward indefinitely (subject to limited carryback during the phase-in period).
    (2) Excess credits (unlike losses) cannot be used in full in the year in which the taxpayer's entire passive activity interest is disposed of. Instead, excess credits continue to be carried forward.
    (3) Credits allowable under the passive activity limitation rules are also subject to the general business credit limitation.

e. Although a **rental activity** is defined as a passive activity regardless of the property owner's participation in the operation of the rental property, a special rule permits an individual to offset up to $25,000 of income that is **not** from passive activities by losses or credits from rental real estate if the individual **actively participates** in the rental real estate activity.

    (1) "Active participation" is less stringent than "material participation" and is met if the taxpayer personally operates the rental property; or, if a rental agent operates the property, the taxpayer participates in management decisions or arranges for others to provide services.
    (2) An individual is not considered to actively participate in a rental real estate activity unless the individual's interest in the activity (including any interest owned by the individual's spouse) was at least 10% of the value of all interests in the activity throughout the year.
    (3) The active participation requirement must be met in both the year that the loss arises and the year in which the loss is allowed.
    (4) For losses, the $25,000 amount is reduced by 50% of AGI in excess of $100,000 and fully phased out when AGI exceeds $150,000. For this purpose, AGI is computed before including taxable social security, before deducting IRA contributions, and before the exclusion of interest from Series EE bonds used for higher education.
    (5) For low-income housing and rehabilitation credits, the $25,000 amount is reduced by 50% of AGI in excess of $200,000 and fully phased out when AGI exceeds $250,000.

f. If a taxpayer meets certain eligibility requirements, losses and credits from rental real estate activities in which the taxpayer materially participates are not subject to the passive loss limitations. This provision applies to individuals and closely held C corporations.

    (1) Individuals are eligible if (a) more than half of all the personal services they perform during the year are for real property trades or businesses in which they materially participate, and (b) they perform more than 750 hours of service per year in those real estate activities. On a joint return, this relief is available if either spouse separately satisfies the requirements.
    (2) Closely held C corporations are eligible if more than 50% of their gross receipts for the taxable year are derived from real property trades or businesses in which the corporation materially participated.
    (3) Suspended losses from any rental real property that is not treated as passive by the above provision are treated as losses from a former passive activity. The deductibility of these suspended losses is limited to income from the activity; they are not allowed to offset other income.

g. The passive activity limitation rules do not apply to losses disallowed under the at risk rules.

NOW REVIEW MULTIPLE-CHOICE QUESTIONS 73 THROUGH 77 IN VOLUME 2

G. Depreciation, Depletion, and Amortization

Depreciation is an allowance for the exhaustion, wear and tear of property used in a trade or business, or of property held for the production of income. The depreciation class of property is generally determined by reference to its Asset Depreciation Range (ADR) guideline class. Taxpayers must determine annual deductions based on the applicable property class, depreciation method, and averaging convention.

1. For property placed in service prior to 1981, the basis of property reduced by salvage value was recovered over its useful life using the straight-line, declining balance, or sum-of-the-years' digits method. Whether an accelerated method of depreciation could be used depended on the classification and useful life of the property, and whether it was new or used when acquired. The Accelerated Cost Recovery System (ACRS) was used to recover the basis of depreciable property placed in service after 1980 and before 1987.

2. **Modified Accelerated Cost Recovery System (MACRS)**

    a. MACRS is **mandatory** for most depreciable property placed in service **after 1986**.
    b. Salvage value is completely ignored under MACRS; the method of cost recovery and the recovery period are the same for both new and used property.

c. **Recovery property** includes all property other than land, intangible assets, and property the taxpayer elects to depreciate under a method not expressed in terms of years (e.g., units of production or income forecast methods). Recovery property placed in service after 1986 is divided into six classes of personal property based on ADR midpoint life and into two classes of real property. Each class is assigned a recovery period and a depreciation method. Recovery deductions for the first six classes are based on the declining balance method, switching to the straight-line method to maximize deductions.

   (1) **3-year, 200% class.** Includes property with an ADR midpoint of four years or less (except for autos and light trucks) and certain horses
   (2) **5-year, 200% class.** Includes property with an ADR midpoint of more than four and less than ten years. Also included are autos and light trucks, computers and peripheral equipment, office machinery (typewriters, calculators, copiers, etc.)
   (3) **7-year, 200% class.** Includes property with an ADR midpoint of at least ten and less than sixteen years. Also included are property having no ADR midpoint and not classified elsewhere, and office furniture and fixtures (desks, files, etc.)
   (4) **10-year, 200% class.** Includes property with an ADR midpoint of at least sixteen and less than twenty years
   (5) **15-year, 150% class.** Includes property with an ADR midpoint of at least twenty years and less than twenty-five years
   (6) **20-year, 150% class.** Includes property with an ADR midpoint of twenty-five years or more, other than real property with an ADR midpoint of 27.5 years or more
   (7) **27 1/2-year, straight-line class.** Includes residential rental property (i.e., a building or structure with 80% or more of its rental income from dwelling units)
   (8) **39-year, straight-line class.** Includes any property that is neither residential real property nor property with a class life of less than 27.5 years

d. Instead of using the declining balance method for three-year through twenty-year property, taxpayers can elect to use the straight-line method over the MACRS class life. This is an annual class-by-class election.
e. Instead of using the 200% declining balance method for three-year through ten-year property, taxpayers can elect to use the 150% declining balance method. This is an annual class-by-class election.
f. An **alternative depreciation system** (ADS) provides for straight-line depreciation over the property's ADS class life (twelve years for personal property with no ADS class life, and forty years for real property).

   (1) A taxpayer may elect to use the alternative system for any class of property placed in service during a taxable year. For real property, the election is made on a property-by-property basis.
   (2) Once made, the election is irrevocable and continues to apply to that property for succeeding years, but does not apply to similar property placed in service in a subsequent year, unless a new election is made.
   (3) The alternative system must be used for foreign use property, property used 50% or more for personal use, and for purposes of computing earnings and profits.

g. An **averaging convention** is used to compute depreciation for the taxable year in which property is placed in service or disposed of under both the regular MACRS and alternative depreciation system.

   (1) **Personal property** is treated as placed in service or disposed of at the midpoint of the taxable year, resulting in a **half-year** of depreciation for the year in which the property is placed in service or disposed of. However, no depreciation is allowed for personal property disposed of in the same taxable year in which it was placed in service.

> **EXAMPLE**
>
> A calendar-year taxpayer purchased machinery (5-year, 200% class) for $10,000 in January 2011 and elected not to take bonus depreciation. Because of the averaging convention, the MACRS depreciation for 2011 will be ($10,000 × 40% × 1/2) = $2,000.

   (2) A **midquarter** convention must be used if more than 40% of all personal property is placed in service during the last quarter of the taxpayer's taxable year. Under this convention, property is treated as placed in service (or disposed of) in the middle of the quarter in which placed in service (or disposed of).

> **EXAMPLE**
>
> In January 2011 a calendar-year taxpayer purchased used machinery for $10,000. In December 2011 the taxpayer purchased additional used machinery for $30,000. All machinery was assigned to the 5-year, 200% class. No other depreciable assets were purchased during the year.

> Since the machinery placed in service during the last three months of the year exceeded 40% of the depreciable basis of all personal property placed in service during the taxable year, all machinery must be depreciated using the midquarter convention. The taxpayer may claim 3.5 quarters depreciation on the machinery acquired in January ($10,000 × 40% × 3.5/4 = $3,500), and only 1/2 quarter of depreciation for the machinery acquired in December ($30,000 × 40% × .5/4 = $1,500).

(3) **Real property** is treated as placed in service or disposed of in the middle of a month, resulting in a **half-month** of depreciation for the month disposed of or placed in service.

> **EXAMPLE**
>
> A calendar-year taxpayer purchased a warehouse (39-year property) for $150,000 and placed it in service on March 26, 2012. Because of the mid-month convention, the depreciation for 2012 will be ($150,000 × 9.5/468 months) = $3,045.

h. **Bonus (additional first-year) depreciation** equal to **50%** of the adjusted basis of qualified property is available for qualifying property acquired after December 31, 2007, and placed in service before January, 1, 2013 (or before January 1, 2014, in the case of property with a long production period and certain noncommercial aircraft). The 2010 Tax Relief Act increased the bonus depreciation percentage to **100% for qualified property acquired after September 8, 2010, and before January 1, 2012**, and placed in service before January 1, 2012 (or before January 1, 2013, in the case of property with a long production period and certain noncommercial aircraft).

(1) *Qualified property* includes new MACRS property with a recovery period of 20 years or less (most tangible personal property), off-the-shelf computer software, and qualified leasehold property. Original use of the property must begin with the taxpayer, and the property's business use must exceed 50%. Property with a long production period is property that has a production period exceeding one year and a cost exceeding $1 million.

(2) Bonus depreciation is computed before regular MACRS depreciation, but after any amount expensed under Sec. 179.

(3) There is no annual dollar limit on the amount of bonus depreciation that can be taken, nor is it affected by a short tax year, or the date during the year that the property was placed in service.

(4) The bonus depreciation deduction and regular MACRS depreciation on bonus depreciation property are allowed in full for AMT purposes (i.e., there is no AMT depreciation adjustment).

(5) A taxpayer may elect not to take bonus depreciation for any class of property (e.g., 5-year, 7-year) for a tax year.

> **EXAMPLE**
>
> During August 2010, a taxpayer purchases new 5-year MACRS property for $2,000. The additional first-year depreciation would be $2,000 × 50% = $1,000. Regular MACRS deprecation for 2010 using the 200% declining balance and the half-year convention would be ($2,000 – $1,000) × 2/5 × 1/2 = $200. As a result, the total deduction for this property for 2010 would be $1,000 + $200 = $1,200.

> **EXAMPLE**
>
> A taxpayer purchases $600,000 of new 5-year MACRS property during March 2010 and elects to expense $500,000 of its cost under Sec. 179. Bonus depreciation would be ($600,000 – $500,000) × 50%= $50,000. MACRS depreciation using the 200% declining balance method and the half-year convention would be [$600,000 – ($500,000 – $50,000)] × 2/5 ×1/2= $10,000. Thus, the total deduction for this property for 2010 would be $500,000 +$50,000 + $10,000 = $560,000.

> **EXAMPLE**
>
> A calendar-year taxpayer purchases $600,000 of new 5-year MACRS property during May 2011 and places it is service during 2011. The entire cost of $600,000 can be deducted for 2011 using 100% bonus depreciation.

i. The cost of **leasehold improvements** made by a lessee generally must be recovered over the MACRS recovery period of the underlying property without regard to the lease term. For *qualified leasehold improvement property* (i.e., an improvement to the interior portion of nonresidential real property), *qualified restaurant property, and qualified retail improvement property* generally placed in service after October 22, 2004, and before January 1, 2012, cost is recovered over a 15-year recovery period using the straight-line method and half-year convention (unless the midquarter convention applies). Upon the expiration of the lease, any unrecovered adjusted basis in abandoned leasehold improvements is treated as a loss.

j. **Sec. 179 expense election.** A taxpayer (other than a trust or estate) may annually elect to treat the cost of qualifying depreciable property as an expense rather than a capital expenditure.

    (1) Qualifying property is generally recovery property that is new or used tangible personal property acquired by purchase from an unrelated party for use in the active conduct of a trade or business. Off-the-shelf computer software with a useful life of more than one year is treated as qualifying property that may be expensed.

    (2) For tax years beginning in 2010 and 2011, a taxpayer may elect to treat qualified real property as Sec. 179 property. Qualified real property generally consists of qualified leasehold improvements, qualified restaurant property, and qualified retail improvement property.

    (3) The maximum cost that can be annually expensed is **$500,000** for tax years beginning in 2010 and 2011, but is reduced dollar-for-dollar by the cost of qualifying property that is placed in service during the taxable year that exceeds $2 million. For 2012, the maximum expense deduction is $139,000, with the phaseout beginning when the cost of qualified property exceeds $560,000.

    (4) The amount of expense deduction is further limited to the taxable income derived from the active conduct by the taxpayer of any trade or business. Any expense deduction disallowed by this limitation is carried forward to the succeeding taxable year.

    (5) If property is converted to nonbusiness use at any time, the excess of the amount expensed over the MACRS deductions that would have been allowed must be recaptured as ordinary income in the year of conversion.

    (6) The amount of cost that can be expensed under Sec. 179 for a sport utility vehicle (SUV) placed in service after October 22, 2004, is limited to $25,000. This limitation applies to an SUV that is exempt from the limitations in k., below, because its gross vehicle weight exceeds 6,000 pounds.

k. Special restriction apply to the depreciation and expensing of passenger automobiles with a gross vehicle weight (GVW) of 6,000 pounds or less. For a passenger automobile first placed in service during 2012, the amount of MACRS (including expensing) deductions is limited to $3,160 in the year placed in service, $5,100 for the second year, $3,050 for the third year, and $1,875 for each year thereafter. These amounts are indexed for inflation.

    (1) These limits are reduced to reflect personal use (e.g., if auto is used 30% for personal use and 70% for business use, limits are [70% × $3,160] = $2,212 for the year of acquisition, [70% × $5,100] = $3,570 for the second year, etc.).

    (2) If automobile is not used more than 50% for business use, MACRS is limited to straight-line depreciation over five years.

        (a) Use of the automobile for income-producing purposes is not counted in determining whether the more than 50% test is met, but is considered in determining the amount of allowable depreciation.

        > **EXAMPLE**
        >
        > An automobile is used 40% in a business, 35% for production of income, and 25% for personal use. The 200% declining balance method cannot be used because business use is not more than 50%. However, depreciation limited to the straight-line method is allowed based on 75% of use.

        (b) If the more than 50% test is met in year of acquisition, but business use subsequently falls to 50% or less, MACRS deductions in excess of five-year straight-line method are recaptured.

    (3) Bonus depreciation for passenger automobiles with a GVW of 6,000 pounds or less is capped at $8,000. To qualify, the auto must be new and its original use must begin with the taxpayer after December 31, 2007, and before January 1, 2013, and the auto must be predominantly used for business. The $8,000 increase applies for qualifying automobiles unless the taxpayer elects not to use bonus depreciation.

> **EXAMPLE**
>
> An individual purchased a new automobile and places it in service during 2012. If the first year depreciation limit otherwise would be $3,160, it is increased by $8,000 so that the maximum depreciation for 2012 would be $11,160.

> **EXAMPLE**
>
> Assume the same facts as in the preceding example except that the individual uses the auto 70% for business and 30% for personal use. The maximum depreciation for 2012 would be $11,160 × 70% = $7,812.

> **EXAMPLE**
>
> A calendar-year taxpayer purchases a new SUV (with a gross vehicle weight greater than 6,000 pounds) for $80,000 during 2011. Assuming the new SUV will be 100 percent used for business the entire $80,000 cost of the new SUV can be deducted for 2011 using 100% bonus depreciation.

l. Transportation property other than automobiles (e.g., airplanes, trucks, boats, etc.), entertainment property (including real property), and any computer or peripheral equipment not used exclusively at a regular business establishment are subject to the same more than 50% business use requirement and consequent restrictions on depreciation as are applicable to automobiles.

   (1) Failure to use these assets more than 50% for business purposes will limit the deductions to the straight-line method.
   (2) If the more than 50% test is met in year of acquisition, but business use subsequently falls to 50% or less, MACRS deductions in excess of the applicable straight-line method are recaptured.

> **NOW REVIEW MULTIPLE-CHOICE QUESTIONS 78 THROUGH 85 IN VOLUME 2**

3. **Depletion**

   a. Depletion is allowed on timber, minerals, oil, and gas, and other exhaustible natural resources or wasting assets.
   b. There are two basic methods to compute depletion for the year.

   (1) **Cost** method divides the adjusted basis by the total number of recoverable units and multiplies by the number of units sold (or payment received for, if cash basis) during the year.

      (a) Adjusted basis is cost less accumulated depletion (not below zero).

> **EXAMPLE**
>
> Land cost $10,050,000 of which $50,000 is the residual value of the land. There are 1,000,000 barrels of oil recoverable. If 10,000 barrels were sold, cost depletion would be ($10,000,000 ÷ 1,000,000 barrels) × 10,000 = $100,000.

   (2) **Percentage** method uses a specified percentage of gross income from the property during the year.

      (a) Deduction may not exceed 50% of the taxable income (before depletion) from the property.
      (b) May be taken even after costs have been recovered and there is no basis
      (c) May be used for domestic oil and gas wells by "independent producer" or royalty owner; cannot be used for timber
      (d) The percentage is a statutory amount and generally ranges from 5% to 20% depending on the mineral.

4. **Amortization** is allowed for several special types of capital expenditures

   a. **Business start-up costs** (e.g., survey of potential markets, expenses of securing prospective distributors or suppliers, advertising, employee training) are deductible in the year paid or incurred if the taxpayer is currently in a similar line of business as the start-up business. If not in a similar line of business and the new business is

   (1) Not acquired by the taxpayer, then start-up costs are not deductible.

(2) Acquired by the taxpayer, start-up costs must be capitalized. However, a taxpayer may elect to deduct up to $5,000 of start-up costs for the tax year in which business begins. The $5,000 amount must be reduced (but not below zero) by the amount by which start-up costs exceed $50,000. Remaining expenditures are deducted ratably over the 180-month period beginning with the month in which business begins. Note that for a taxable year beginning in 2010 only, up to $10,000 of start-up costs could be expensed, with the $10,000 amount reduced dollar-for-dollar by start-up costs in excess of $60,000.

b. Pollution control facilities can be amortized over sixty months if installed on property that was placed in operation prior to 1976. The pollution control investment must not increase output, capacity, or the useful life of the asset.

c. Patents and copyrights may be amortized over their useful life.

(1) Seventeen years for patents; life of author plus fifty years for copyrights
(2) If become obsolete early, deduct in that year

d. Research and experimental expenses may be amortized over sixty months or more. Alternatively, may be expensed at election of taxpayer if done so for year in which such expenses are first incurred or paid.

e. Intangible assets for which the Code does not specifically provide for amortization are amortizable over their useful lives.

5. **Sec. 197 intangibles**

a. Most **acquired intangible assets** are to be amortized over a fifteen-year period, beginning with the month in which the intangible is acquired (the treatment of self-created intangible assets is not affected). Sec. 197 applies to most intangibles acquired either in stand-alone transactions or as part of the acquisition of a trade or business.

b. An amortizable Sec. 197 intangible is any qualifying intangible asset which is acquired by the taxpayer, and which is held in connection with the conduct of a trade or business. Qualifying intangibles include goodwill, going concern value, workforce, information base, know-how, customer-based intangibles, government licenses and permits, franchises, trademarks, and trade names.

c. Certain assets qualify as Sec. 197 intangibles only if acquired in connection with the acquisition of a trade or business or substantial portion thereof. These include covenants not to compete, computer software, film, sound recordings, videotape, patents, and copyrights.

d. Certain intangible assets are expressly excluded from the definition of Sec. 197 intangibles including many types of financial interests, instruments, and contracts; interests in a corporation, partnership, trust, or estate; interests in land; professional sports franchises; and leases of tangible personal property.

e. No loss can be recognized on the disposition of a Sec. 197 intangible if the taxpayer retains other Sec. 197 intangibles acquired in the same transaction or a series of transactions. Any disallowed loss is added to the basis of remaining Sec. 197 intangibles and recovered through amortization.

H. Domestic Production Activities Deduction (DPAD)

1. The deduction is available to all taxpayers including C corporations, farming cooperatives, estates, trusts, and their beneficiaries, and partners and shareholders of S corporations (not to partnerships or S corporations themselves).

2. The DPAD equals 9% of the *lesser of* the taxpayer's (1) qualified production activities income (QPAI), or (2) taxable income (or in the case of an individual, trust, or estate, adjusted gross income) computed before this deduction. The amount of the allowable deduction for any taxable year is limited to 50% of the W-2 wages paid by the taxpayer for the taxable year allocable to the taxpayer's domestic production gross receipts (DPGR). W-2 wages include wages, tips and other compensation as well as elective deferrals to 401(k) and certain other plans.

EXAMPLE

Assume unrelated manufacturing corporations A, B, and C incurred the following amounts for the current taxable year. Their Sec. 199 DPAD would be computed as follows:

	A	B	C
Qualified production activities income	$200,000	$200,000	$200,000
Taxable income	$100,000	$300,000	$300,000
Lesser of above	$100,000	$200,000	$200,000
Tentative deduction (9% × lesser amount)	$ 9,000	$ 18,000	$ 18,000
W-2 wages paid	$ 30,000	$ 40,000	$ 30,000
Wage limitation (50% × wages)	$ 15,000	$ 20,000	$ 15,000
Sec. 199 DPAD deduction	$ 9,000	$ 18,000	$ 15,000

> Corporation A's deduction equals 9% of its taxable income of $100,000 or $9,000. Corporation B's deduction equals 9% of its QPAI of $200,000, or $18,000. Corporation C's tentative deduction of 9% of its QPAI of $200,000, or $18,000, is limited to 50% of the $30,000 of W-2 wages that it paid, or $15,000.

    a. QPAI is equal to the excess of DPGR over the sum of the cost of goods sold allocable to such receipts, and other expenses and deductions allocable to such receipts.

    b. If a manufacturer produces some of its finished products at an overseas facility and some of its products at a US plant, only income from the products produced in the US will qualify for the deduction. As a result, the taxpayer must segregate qualifying gross receipts from nonqualifying gross receipts, and must apportion the cost of goods sold and other expenses and deductions accordingly. A taxpayer can treat all gross receipts as DPGR if less than 5% of the taxpayer's gross receipts are non-DPRG.

3. Qualified production activities eligible for the deduction *include* (1) the manufacture, production, growth or extraction of tangible personal property such as goods, clothing, or food, as well as computer software and music recordings within the US; (2) film production if at least 50% of the total compensation relating to the production is for services performed within the US; and (3) construction or substantial renovation of residential and nonresidential buildings, and infrastructure such as roads, power lines, water systems, and communication facilities, as well as engineering and architectural services performed in the US relating to such property. Qualified production activities *do not include* the sale of food and beverages prepared by the taxpayer at a retail establishment, and the transmission or distribution of electricity, natural gas, or potable water.

II. "ABOVE THE LINE" DEDUCTIONS

"Above the line" deductions are taken from gross income to determine adjusted gross income. Adjusted gross income is important, because it may affect the amount of allowable charitable contributions, medical expenses, casualty losses, and miscellaneous itemized deductions. The deductions that reduce gross income to arrive at adjusted gross income are

1. Business deductions of a self-employed person (see Business Income and Deductions)
2. Losses from sale or exchange of property (discussed in Module 36: Transactions in Property)
3. Deductions attributable to rents and royalties
4. One-half of self-employment tax
5. Moving expenses
6. Contributions to self-employed retirement plans and IRAs
7. Deduction for interest on education loans
8. Penalties for premature withdrawals from time deposits
9. Alimony payments
10. Jury duty pay remitted to employer
11. Costs involving discrimination suits
12. Expenses of elementary and secondary teachers

A. The treatment of **reimbursed employee business expenses** depends on whether the employee makes an adequate accounting to the employer and returns amounts in excess of substantiated expenses.

    1. Per diem reimbursements at a rate not in excess of the federal per diem rate and 55.5¢ per mile are deemed to satisfy the substantiation requirement if employee provides time, place, and business purpose of expenses.

    2. If the employee **makes an adequate accounting** to employer and reimbursements equal expenses, or if the employee substantiates expenses and returns any excess reimbursement, the reimbursements are excluded from gross income and the expenses are not deductible.

    3. If the employee **does not make an adequate accounting** to the employer or does not return excess reimbursements, the total amount of reimbursement is included in the employee's gross income and the related employee expenses are deductible as miscellaneous itemized deductions subject to the 50% limitation for business meals and entertainment and the 2% of AGI floor (same as for unreimbursed employee business expenses).

B. Expenses attributable to **property held for the production of rents or royalties** are deductible "above the line."

    1. **Rental of vacation home**

        a. If there is any personal use, the **amount deductible** is

$$(1) \quad \frac{\text{No. of days rented}}{\text{Total days used}} \times \text{Total expenses} = \text{Amount deductible}$$

        (2) Personal use is by taxpayer or any other person to whom a fair rent is not charged.

        b. **If used as a residence,** amount deductible is further limited to rental income less deductions otherwise allowable for interest, taxes, and casualty losses.

(1) Used as a residence if personal use exceeds greater of fourteen days or 10% of number of days rented
(2) These limitations do not apply if rented or held for rental for a continuous twelve-month period with no personal use.

EXAMPLE

Use house as a principal residence and then begin to rent in June. As long as rental continues for twelve consecutive months, limitations do not apply in year converted to rental.

---

   c. If used as a residence (above) and **rented for less than fifteen days** per year, then income therefrom is not reported and rental expense deductions are not allowed.

EXAMPLE

Taxpayer rents his condominium for 120 days for $2,000 and uses it himself for 60 days. The rest of the year it is vacant. His expenses are

Mortgage interest	$1,800
Real estate taxes	600
Utilities	300
Maintenance	300
Depreciation	2,000
	$5,000

Taxpayer may deduct the following expenses:

	Rental expense	Itemized deduction
Mortgage interest	$1,200	$600
Real estate taxes	400	200
Utilities	200	--
Maintenance	200	--
Depreciation	--	--
	$2,000	$800

Taxpayer may not deduct any depreciation because his rental expense deductions are limited to rental income when he has made personal use of the condominium in excess of the fourteen-day or 10% rule.

C. For 2011 and 2012, a **self-employed** individual can deduct (6.2%/10.4%) = 59.6% of applicable OASDI taxes and 50% of applicable Medicare (HI) taxes [e.g., if the amount of self-employment tax that an individual must pay for 2011 consists of OASDI taxes of $5,200 and HI taxes of $1,450, the self-employed individual can deduct ($5,200 × 59.6%) + ($1,450 × 50%) − $3,824 in arriving at AGI].

D. A **self-employed** individual can **deduct 100%** of the **premiums for medical insurance** for the individual, spouse, and dependents in arriving at AGI.

   1. This deduction cannot exceed the individual's net earnings from the trade or business with respect to which the plan providing for health insurance was established. For purposes of this limitation, an S corporation more-than-two-percent shareholder's earned income is determined exclusively by reference to the shareholder's wages received from the S corporation.

   2. No deduction is allowed if the self-employed individual or spouse is eligible to participate in an employer's subsidized health plan. The determination of whether self-employed individuals or their spouses are eligible for employer-paid health benefits is to be made on a calendar month basis.

   3. Any medical insurance premiums not deductible under the above rules are deductible as an itemized medical expense deduction from AGI.

   4. The deduction for medical insurance premiums can also be subtracted in computing an individual's self-employment tax.

E. Moving Expenses

   1. The distance between the former residence and new job (d_2) must be **at least fifty miles** farther than from the former residence to the former job (d_1) (i.e., $d_2 - d_1 \geq 50$ miles). If no former job, new job must be at least fifty miles from former residence.

   2. Employee must be **employed** at least thirty-nine weeks out of the twelve months following the move. Self-employed individual must be employed seventy-eight weeks out of the twenty-four months following the move (in addition to thirty-nine weeks out of first twelve months). Time test does not have to be met in case of death, taxpayer's job at new location ends because of disability, or taxpayer is laid off for other than willful misconduct.

3. **Deductible** moving expenses include the costs of moving household goods and personal effects from the old to the new residence, and the costs of traveling (including lodging) from the old residence to the new residence. Actual auto expenses can be deducted, or taxpayer can use standard rate of 23.5¢ per mile beginning July 1, 2011.

4. **Nondeductible** moving expenses include the costs of meals, househunting trips, temporary lodging in the general location of the new work site, expenses incurred in selling an old house or buying a new house, and expenses in settling a lease on an old residence or acquiring a lease on a new residence.

NOW REVIEW MULTIPLE-CHOICE QUESTIONS 86 THROUGH 91 IN VOLUME 2

F. Contributions to Certain Retirement Plans

1. Contributions to an **Individual Retirement Account** (IRA)

   a. If neither the taxpayer nor the taxpayer's spouse is an active participant in an employer-sponsored retirement plan or a Keogh plan, there is no phaseout of IRA deductions.

      (1) The maximum deduction for an individual's contributions to an IRA is generally the lesser of

         (a) **$5,000,** or
         (b) 100% of compensation (including alimony)

      (2) For married taxpayers filing a joint return, up to $5,000 can be deducted for contributions to the IRA of each spouse (even if one spouse is not working), provided that the combined earned income of both spouses is at least equal to the amounts contributed to the IRAs.

   b. For 2012, the IRA deduction for individuals who are active participants in an employer retirement plan or a Keogh plan is proportionately phased out for married individuals filing jointly with AGI between $92,000 and $112,000, and for single individuals with AGI between $58,000 and $68,000.

      (1) An individual will not be considered an active participant in an employer plan merely because the individual's spouse is an active participant for any part of the plan year.

      (2) The maximum deductible IRA contribution for an individual who is not an active participant, but whose spouse is, will be proportionately phased out at a combined AGI between $173,000 and $183,000.

   c. Under the **phaseout rule,** the $5,000 maximum deduction is reduced by a percentage equal to adjusted gross income in excess of the lower AGI amount (above) divided by $10,000 ($20,000 for married filing jointly). The deduction limit is rounded to the next lowest multiple of $10.

      (1) A taxpayer whose AGI is not above the applicable phaseout range can make a $200 deductible contribution regardless of the proportional phaseout rule. This $200 minimum applies separately to taxpayer and taxpayer's spouse.

      (2) A taxpayer who is partially or totally prevented from making deductible IRA contributions can make **nondeductible IRA contributions**.

      (3) Total IRA contributions (whether deductible or not) are subject to the $5,000 or 100% of compensation limit.

EXAMPLE

For 2012, a single individual who has compensation income (and AGI) of $64,000 and who is an active participant in an employer-sponsored retirement plan would be subject to a limit reduction of $3,000 computed as follows: $5,000 × [($64,000 − $58,000) ÷ $10,000)] = $3,000. Thus, the individual's deductible IRA contribution would be limited to $5,000 − $3,000 = $2,000. However, the individual could make nondeductible IRA contributions of up to $3,000 more.

EXAMPLE

For 2012, a single individual who has compensation income (and AGI) of $65,800 and who is an active participant in an employer-sponsored retirement plan would normally be limited to an IRA deduction of $5,000 − [($67,800 − $58,000) ÷ $10,000] × $5,000 = $100. However, because of the special rule in (2) above, a $200 IRA contribution deduction is allowable.

---

d. An individual at least age 50 before the close of the taxable year can make an additional "catch-up" contribution of $1,000 to an IRA. Thus, for 2012, the maximum IRA contribution and deduction for an individual at least age 50 is $5,000 + $1,000 = $6,000.

e. The 10% penalty tax on early withdrawals (pre-age 59 1/2) does not apply to amounts withdrawn for "qualified higher education expenses" and "first-time homebuyer expenses" ($10,000 lifetime cap), nor to distributions made to unemployed individuals for health insurance premiums, and distributions to the extent that deductible medical expenses exceed 7.5% of AGI.

   (1) Qualified higher education expenses include tuition, fees, books, supplies, and equipment for postsecondary education for the taxpayer, taxpayer's spouse, or any child or grandchild of the taxpayer or the taxpayer's spouse.

   (2) Qualified first-time homebuyer distributions must be used in 120 days to buy, build, or rebuild a first home that is a principal residence for the taxpayer or taxpayer's spouse. Acquisition costs include reasonable financing or other closing costs.

2. Contributions to a **Roth IRA** are not deductible, but qualified distributions of earnings are tax-free. Individuals making contributions to a Roth IRA can still make contributions to a deductible or nondeductible IRA, but maximum contributions to all IRAs is limited to $5,000 for 2012. ($6,000 if the individual is at least age 50).

   a. For 2012, eligibility for a Roth IRA is phased out for single taxpayers with AGI between $110,000 and $125,000, and for joint filers with AGI between $173,000 and $183,000.

   b. Unlike traditional IRAs contributions may be made to Roth IRAs even after the individual reaches age 70 1/2.

   c. Qualified distributions from a Roth IRA are not included in gross income and are not subject to the 10% early withdrawal penalty. A qualified distribution is a distribution that is made after the five-year period beginning with the first tax year for which a contribution was made and the distribution is made (1) after the individual reaches age 59 1/2, (2) to a beneficiary (or the individual's estate) after the individual's death, (3) after the individual becomes disabled, or (4) for the first-time homebuyer expenses of the individual, individual's spouse, children, grandchildren, or ancestors ($10,000 lifetime cap).

   d. Nonqualified distributions are includible in income to the extent attributable to earnings and generally subject to the 10% early withdrawal penalty. Distributions are deemed to be made from contributed amounts first.

   e. For tax years beginning before 2010, taxpayers (other than individuals filing separately) with AGI of less than $100,000 could convert assets in traditional IRAs to a Roth IRA at any time without paying the 10% tax on early withdrawals, although the deemed distributions of IRA assets is included in income. For tax years beginning after December 31, 2009, the AGI and filing status limitations are eliminated, allowing higher-income taxpayers to convert traditional IRAs to Roth accounts.

3. Contributions can be made to an **education IRA** (Coverdell Education Savings Account) of up to $2,000 per beneficiary (until the beneficiary reaches age eighteen), to pay the costs of a beneficiary's higher education for tax years beginning before 2013.

   a. Contributions are not deductible, but withdrawals to pay the cost of a beneficiary's education expenses are tax-free.

   b. Any earnings of an education IRA that are distributed but are not used to pay a beneficiary's education expenses must be included in the distributee's gross income and are subject to a 10% penalty tax.

   c. Under a special rollover provision, the amount left in an education IRA before the beneficiary reaches age 30 can be rolled over to another family member's education IRA without triggering income taxes or penalties.

   d. Eligibility is phased out for single taxpayers with modified AGI between $95,000 and $110,000, and for married taxpayers with modified AGI between $190,000 and $220,000.

   e. Expenses that may be paid tax-free from an education IRA include expenses for enrollment (including room and board, uniforms, transportation, computers, and Internet access services) in elementary or secondary schools, whether public, private, or religious. Furthermore, taxpayers may take advantage of the exclusion for distributions from education IRAs, the Hope and lifetime learning credits, and the qualified tuition program in the same year.

4. **Self-employed** individuals (sole proprietors and partners) may contribute to a qualified retirement plan (called H.R.-10 or Keogh Plan).

   a. The maximum contribution and deduction to a defined-contribution self-employed retirement plan is the lesser of

   (1) $50,000, or 100% of earned income for 2012.

   (2) The definition of "earned income" includes the retirement plan and self-employment tax deductions (i.e., earnings from self-employment must be reduced by the retirement plan contribution and the self-employment tax deduction for purposes of determining the maximum deduction).

b. A taxpayer may elect to treat contributions made up until the due date of the tax return (including extensions) as made for the taxable year for which the tax return is being filed, if the retirement plan was established by the end of that year.

5. An employer's contributions to an employee's **simplified employee pension (SEP) plan** are deductible by the employer, limited to the lesser of 25% of compensation (up to a compensation ceiling of $250,000 for 2012) or $50,000.

a. The employer's SEP contributions are excluded from the employee's gross income.
b. In addition, the employee may make deductible IRA contributions subject to the IRA phaseout rules (discussed in 2.c. above).

6. A **savings incentive match plan for employees (SIMPLE)** is not subject to the nondiscrimination rules (including top-heavy provisions) and certain other complex requirements generally applicable to qualified plans, and may be structured as an IRA or as a 401(k) plan.

a. Limited to employers with 100 or fewer employees who received at least $5,000 in compensation from the employer in the preceding year.

(1) Plan allows employees to make elective contributions of up to $11,500 of their pretax salaries for 2010 and 2011 (expressed as a percentage of compensation, not a fixed dollar amount) and requires employers to match a portion of the contributions.
(2) Eligible employees are those who earned at least $5,000 in any two prior years and who may be expected to earn at least $5,000 in the current year.

b. Employers must satisfy one of two contribution formulas.

(1) Matching contribution formula generally requires an employer to match the employee contribution dollar-for-dollar up to 3% of the employee's compensation for the year.
(2) Alternatively, an employer can make a nonelective contribution of 2% of compensation for each eligible employee who has at least $5,000 of compensation from the employer during the year.

c. Contributions to the plan are immediately vested, but a 25% penalty applies to employee withdrawals made within two years of the date the employee began participating in the plan.

G. Deduction for Interest on Education Loans

1. An individual is allowed to deduct **up to $2,500** for interest on qualified education loans. However, the deduction is not available if the individual is claimed as a dependent on another taxpayer's return.
2. A *qualified education loan* is any debt incurred to pay the qualified higher education expenses of the taxpayer, taxpayer's spouse, or dependents (as of the time the debt was incurred), and the education expenses must relate to a period when the student was enrolled on at least a half-time basis. However, any debt owed to a related party is not a qualified educational loan (e.g., education debt owed to family member).
3. Qualified education expenses include such costs as tuition, fees, room, board, and related expenses.
4. For 2010 through 2012, the deduction is phased out for single taxpayers with modified AGI between $60,000 and $75,000, and for married taxpayers with modified AGI between $120,000 and $150,000.

H. Deduction for Qualified Tuition and Related Expenses

1. For 2007 through 2011, individuals are allowed to deduct qualified higher education expenses in arriving at AGI. The deduction is limited to $4,000 for individuals with AGI at or below $65,000 ($130,000 for joint filers). The deduction is limited to $2,000 for individuals with AGI above $65,000, but equal to or less than $80,000 ($130,000 and $160,000 respectively for joint filers).
2. Taxpayers with AGI above these levels, married individuals filing separately, and an individual who can be claimed as a dependent are not entitled to any deduction.
3. *Qualified tuition and related expenses* means tuition and fees required for enrollment of the taxpayer, taxpayer's spouse, or dependent at a postsecondary educational institution. Such term does not include expenses with respect to any course involving sports, games, or hobbies, or any noncredit course, unless such course is part of the individual's degree program. Also excluded are nonacademic fees such as student activity fees, athletic fees, and insurance expenses.
4. The deduction is allowed for expenses paid during the tax year, in connection with enrollment during the year or in connection with an academic term beginning during the year or the first three months of the following year.
5. If a taxpayer takes a Hope credit or lifetime learning credit with respect to a student, the qualified higher education expenses of that student for the year are not deductible under this provision.

I. Penalties for Premature Withdrawals from Time Deposits

1. Full amount of interest is included in gross income.
2. Forfeited interest is then subtracted "above the line."

J. Alimony or Separate Maintenance Payments Are Deducted "Above the Line."
K. Jury Duty Pay Remitted to Employer

1. An employee is allowed to deduct the amount of jury duty pay that was surrendered to an employer in return for the employer's payment of compensation during the employee's jury service period.
2. Both regular compensation and jury duty pay must be included in gross income.

L. Costs Involving Discrimination Suits

1. Attorneys' fees and court costs incurred by, or on behalf of, an individual in connection with any action involving a claim for unlawful discrimination (e.g., age, sex, or race discrimination) are allowable as a deduction from gross income in arriving at AGI.
2. The amount of deduction is limited to the amount of judgment or settlement included in the individual's gross income for the tax year.

M. Expenses of Elementary and Secondary Teachers

1. For tax years beginning before 2012, eligible educators are allowed an above-the-line deduction for up to $250 for unreimbursed expenses for books, supplies, computer equipment (including related software and services) and supplementary materials used in the classroom.
2. An eligible educator is a kindergarten through grade 12 teacher, instructor, counselor, principal, or aide working in a school for at least 900 hours during the school year.
3. For joint filers, if both spouses are eligible, the maximum deduction is $500, but neither spouse can deduct more than $250 of expenses.

> **NOW REVIEW MULTIPLE-CHOICE QUESTIONS 92 THROUGH 102 IN VOLUME 2**

III. ITEMIZED DEDUCTIONS FROM ADJUSTED GROSS INCOME

Itemized deductions reduce adjusted gross income, and are sometimes referred to as "below the line" deductions because they are deducted from adjusted gross income. Itemized deductions (or a standard deduction) along with personal exemptions are subtracted from adjusted gross income to arrive at taxable income.

A taxpayer will itemize deductions only if the taxpayer's total itemized deductions exceed the applicable standard deduction that is available to nonitemizers. The amount of the standard deduction is based on the filing status of the taxpayer, whether the taxpayer is a dependent, and is indexed for inflation. For 2012, additional standard deductions are allowed for age and blindness.

Filing status	Basic standard deduction 2012
a) Married, filing jointly; or surviving spouse	$11,900
b) Married, filing separately	5,950
c) Head of household	8,700
d) Single	5,950

A dependent's basic standard deduction is limited to the lesser of (1) the basic standard deduction for single taxpayers of $5,950 or (2) the greater of (a) $950, or (b) the dependent's earned income plus $300. For example, a dependent who receives wages (earned income) of $1,200 would have a basic standard deduction of $1,200 + $300 = $1,500.

An unmarried individual who is not a surviving spouse, and is either age sixty-five or older or blind, receives an additional standard deduction of $1,450 for 2012. The standard deduction is increased by $2,900 if the individual is both elderly and blind. The increase is $1,150 for 2012 for each married individual who is age sixty-five or older or blind. The increase for a married individual who is both elderly and blind is $2,300. An elderly or blind individual who may be claimed as a dependent on another taxpayer's return may claim the basic standard deduction plus the additional standard deduction(s). For example, an unmarried dependent, age sixty-five, with only unearned income would have a standard deduction of $950 + $1,450 = $2,400.

The major itemized deductions are outlined below. It should be remembered that some may be deducted in arriving at AGI if they are incurred by a self-employed taxpayer in a trade or business, or for the production of rents or royalties.

A. Medical and Dental Expenses

1. Medical and dental expenses paid by taxpayer for himself, spouse, or dependent (relationship, support, and citizenship tests are met) are deductible in year of payment, if not reimbursed by insurance, employer, etc. A child of divorced or separated parents is treated as a dependent of both parents for this purpose.

2. Computation—unreimbursed medical expenses (including *prescribed* medicine and insulin, and medical insurance premiums) are deducted to the extent **in excess of 7.5%** of adjusted gross income.

EXAMPLE

Ralph and Alice Jones, who have adjusted gross income of $20,000, paid the following medical expenses: $900 for hospital and doctor bills (above reimbursement), $250 for prescription medicine, and $600 for medical insurance. The Joneses would compute their medical expense deduction as follows:

Prescribed medicine	$ 250
Hospital, doctors	900
Medical insurance	600
	$1,750
Less 7.5% of AGI	−1,500
Medical expense deduction	$ 250

---

3. Deductible medical care does not include **cosmetic surgery** or other procedures, unless the surgery or procedure is necessary to ameliorate a deformity arising from, or directly related to, a congenital abnormality, a personal injury resulting from an accident or trauma, or a disfiguring disease. In addition, to be deductible, the procedure must promote proper body function or prevent or treat illness or disease (e.g., LASIK and radial keratotomy are deductible; teeth whitening is not deductible).

   a. Cosmetic surgery is defined as any procedure directed at improving the patient's appearance and does not meaningfully promote the proper function of the body or prevent or treat illness or disease.

   b. If expenses for cosmetic surgery are not deductible under this provision, then amounts paid for insurance coverage for such expenses are not deductible, and an employer's reimbursement of such expenses under a health plan is not excludable from the employee's gross income.

4. Expenses incurred by physically handicapped individuals for **removal of structural barriers** in their residences to accommodate their handicapped condition are fully deductible as medical expenses. Qualifying expenses include constructing entrance or exit ramps, widening doorways and hallways, the installation of railings and support bars, and other modifications.

5. **Capital expenditures** for special equipment (other than in 4. above) installed for medical reasons in a home or automobile are deductible as medical expenses to the extent the expenditures exceed the increase in value of the property.

6. **Deductible** medical expenses include

   a. Fees for doctors, surgeons, dentists, osteopaths, ophthalmologists, optometrists, chiropractors, chiropodists, podiatrists, psychiatrists, psychologists, and Christian Science practitioners

   b. Fees for hospital services, therapy, nursing services (including nurses' meals you pay for), ambulance hire, and laboratory, surgical, obstetrical, diagnostic, dental, and X-ray services

   c. Meals and lodging provided by a hospital during medical treatment, and meals and lodging provided by a center during treatment for alcoholism or drug addiction

   d. Amounts paid for lodging (but not meals) while away from home primarily for medical care provided by a physician in a licensed hospital or equivalent medical care facility. Limit is $50 per night for each individual.

   e. Medical and hospital insurance premiums

   f. *Prescribed* medicines and insulin

   g. Transportation for needed medical care. Actual auto expenses can be deducted, or taxpayer can use standard rate of 23.5¢ per mile beginning July 1, 2011 (plus parking and tolls).

   h. Special items and equipment, including false teeth, artificial limbs, eyeglasses, hearing aids, crutches, guide dogs, motorized wheelchairs, hand controls on a car, and special telephones for deaf

   i. The cost of stop-smoking programs and the cost of participation in a weight-loss program as a treatment for the disease of obesity qualify. However, the costs of reduced-calorie diet foods are not deductible if these foods merely substitute for food the individual would normally consume.

7. Items **not deductible** as medical expenses include

   a. Bottled water, maternity clothes, and diaper service

   b. Household help, and care of a normal and healthy baby by a nurse (but a portion may qualify for child or dependent care tax credit)

   c. Toothpaste, toiletries, cosmetics, etc.
   d. Weight-loss expenses that are not for the treatment of obesity or other disease
   e. Trip, social activities, or health club dues for general improvement of health
   f. Nonprescribed medicines and drugs (e.g., over-the-counter medicines)
   g. Illegal operation or treatment
   h. Funeral and burial expenses

8. Reimbursement of expenses deducted in an earlier year may have to be included in gross income in the period received under the tax benefit rule.

9. Reimbursement in excess of expenses is includible in income to the extent the excess reimbursement was paid by policies provided by employer.

> **NOW REVIEW MULTIPLE-CHOICE QUESTIONS 104 THROUGH 115 IN VOLUME 2**

B. Taxes

1. The following taxes are **deductible as a tax** in year paid if they are imposed on the taxpayer:

   a. **Income tax** (state, local, or foreign)

     (1) The deduction for state and local taxes includes amounts withheld from salary, estimated payments made during the year, and payments made during the year on a tax for a prior year.
     (2) A refund of a prior year's taxes is not offset against the current year's deduction, but is generally included in income under the tax benefit rule.

   b. For tax years beginning before January 1, 2012, an individual may elect to deduct state and local general sales taxes in lieu of state and local income taxes. The amount that can be deducted is either the total of actual general sales taxes paid as substantiated by receipts, or an amount from IRS-provided tables, plus the amount of general sales taxes paid with regard to the purchase of a motor vehicle, boat, or other items prescribed in Pub. 600.

     (1) The sales taxes imposed on food, clothing, medical supplies, and motor vehicles may be deducted even if imposed at a rate lower than the general rate.
     (2) In the case of sales taxes on motor vehicles that are higher than the general rate, only an amount up to the general rate is allowed. The sales tax on boats is deductible only if imposed at the general sales tax rate.

   c. **Real property taxes** (state, local, or foreign) are deductible by the person on whom the taxes are imposed.

     (1) When real property is sold, the deduction is apportioned between buyer and seller on a daily basis within the real property tax year, even if parties do not apportion the taxes at the closing. Real property taxes are allocated to the buyer beginning with the date of sale.
     (2) **Assessments** for improvements (e.g., special assessments for streets, sewers, sidewalks, curbing) are generally not deductible, but instead must be added to the basis of the property. However, the portion of an assessment that is attributable to repairs or maintenance, or to meeting interest charges on the improvements, is deductible as taxes.

   d. **Personal property taxes** (state or local, not foreign) are deductible if ad valorem (i.e., assessed in relation to the value of property). A motor vehicle tax based on horsepower, weight, or model year is not deductible.

2. The following taxes are **deductible only as an expense** incurred in a trade or business or in the production of income (above the line):

   a. Social security and other employment taxes paid by employer
   b. Federal excise taxes on automobiles, tires, telephone service, and air transportation
   c. Customs duties and gasoline taxes
   d. State and local taxes not deductible as such (stamp or cigarette taxes) or charges of a primarily regulatory nature (licenses, etc.)

3. The following taxes are **not deductible**:

   a. Federal income taxes
   b. Federal, state, or local estate or gift taxes
   c. Social security and other federal employment taxes paid by employee (including self-employment taxes)
   d. Social security and other employment taxes paid by an employer on the wages of an employee who only performed domestic services (i.e., maid, etc.)

NOW REVIEW MULTIPLE-CHOICE QUESTIONS 116 THROUGH 124 IN VOLUME 2

C. Interest Expense

1. The classification of interest expense is generally determined by tracing the use of the borrowed funds. Interest expense is not deductible if loan proceeds were used to produce tax-exempt income (e.g., purchase municipal bonds).

2. No deduction is allowed for prepaid interest; it must be capitalized and deducted in the future period(s) to which it relates. However, an individual may elect to deduct *mortgage points* when paid if the points represent interest and mortgage proceeds were used to buy, build, or substantially improve a principal residence. Otherwise points must be capitalized and deducted over the term of the mortgage.

3. **Personal interest.** No deduction is allowed for personal interest.

   a. Personal interest **includes** interest paid or incurred to purchase an asset for personal use, credit card interest for personal purchases, interest incurred as an employee, and interest on income tax underpayments.

   b. Personal interest **excludes** qualified residence interest, investment interest, interest allocable to a trade or business (other than as an employee), interest incurred in a passive activity, and interest on deferred estate taxes.

> **EXAMPLE**
>
> X, a **self-employed** consultant, finances a new automobile used 80% for business and 20% for personal use. X would treat 80% of the interest as deductible business interest expense (toward AGI), and 20% as nondeductible personal interest.

> **EXAMPLE**
>
> Y, an **employee**, finances a new automobile used 80% in her employer's business and 20% for personal use. All of the interest expense on the auto loan would be considered nondeductible personal interest.

4. **Qualified residence interest.** The disallowance of personal interest above does not apply to interest paid or accrued on acquisition indebtedness or home equity indebtedness secured by a security interest perfected under local law on the taxpayer's principal residence or a second residence owned by the taxpayer.

   a. **Acquisition indebtedness.** Interest is deductible on up to $1,000,000 ($500,000 if married filing separately) of loans secured by the residence if such loans were used to acquire, construct, or substantially improve the home.

      (1) Acquisition indebtedness is reduced as principal payments are made and cannot be restored or increased by refinancing the home.
      (2) If the home is refinanced, the amount qualifying as acquisition indebtedness is limited to the amount of acquisition debt existing at the time of refinancing plus any amount of the new loan that is used to substantially improve the home.

   b. **Home equity indebtedness.** Interest is deductible on up to $100,000 ($50,000 if married filing separately) of loans secured by the residence (other than acquisition indebtedness) regardless of how the loan proceeds are used (e.g., automobile, education expenses, medical expenses, etc.). The amount of home equity indebtedness cannot exceed the FV of the home as reduced by any acquisition indebtedness.

> **EXAMPLE**
>
> Allan purchased a home for $380,000, borrowing $250,000 of the purchase price that was secured by a fifteen-year mortgage. In 2011, when the home was worth $400,000 and the balance of the first mortgage was $230,000, Allan obtained a second mortgage on the home in the amount of $120,000, using the proceeds to purchase a car and to pay off personal loans. Allan may deduct the interest on the balance of the first mortgage acquisition indebtedness of $230,000. However, Allan can deduct interest on only $100,000 of the second mortgage as qualified residence interest because it is considered home equity indebtedness (i.e., the loan proceeds were not used to acquire, construct, or substantially improve a home). The interest on the remaining $20,000 of the second mortgage is nondeductible personal interest.

   c. The term "residence" includes houses, condominiums, cooperative housing units, and any other property that the taxpayer uses as a dwelling unit (e.g., mobile home, motor home, boat, etc.).

d. In the case of a residence used partly for rental purposes, the interest can only be qualified residence interest if the taxpayer's personal use during the year exceeds the greater of fourteen days or 10% of the number of days of rental use (unless the residence was not rented at any time during the year).

e. Qualified residence interest does not include interest on unsecured home improvement loans, but does include mortgage prepayment penalties.

f. Qualified *mortgage insurance premiums* paid or accrued before January 1, 2012, in connection with acquisition indebtedness are deductible as qualified residence interest. However, for every $1,000 ($500 if married filing separately) by which the taxpayer's AGI exceeds $100,000 the amount of premiums treated as interest is reduced by 10%. The deduction does not apply to mortgage insurance contracts issued before January 1, 2007, nor to premiums allocable to any period after December 31, 2011.

5. **Investment interest.** The deduction for investment interest expense for noncorporate taxpayers is limited to the amount of net investment income. Interest disallowed is carried forward indefinitely and is allowed only to the extent of net investment income in a subsequent year.

> **EXAMPLE**
>
> For 2011, a single taxpayer has investment interest expense of $40,000 and net investment income of $24,000. The deductible investment interest expense for 2011 is limited to $24,000, with the remaining $16,000 carried forward and allowed as a deduction to the extent of net investment income in subsequent years.

a. Investment interest expense is interest paid or accrued on indebtedness properly allocable to property held for investment, including

   (1) Interest expense allocable to portfolio income, and
   (2) Interest expense allocable to a trade or business in which the taxpayer does not materially participate, if that activity is not treated as a passive activity

b. Investment interest expense excludes interest expense taken into account in determining income or loss from a passive activity, interest allocable to rental real estate in which the taxpayer actively participates, qualified residence interest, and personal interest.

c. Net investment income includes

   (1) Interest, rents, dividends (other than qualified dividends), and royalties in excess of any related expenses, and
   (2) The net gain (all gains minus all losses) on the sale of investment property, but only to the extent that the net gain exceeds the net capital gain (i.e., net LTCG in excess of net STCL).

d. A taxpayer may elect to treat **qualified dividends** and **net capital gain** (i.e., an excess of net LTCG over net STCL) as investment income. However, if this election is made, a taxpayer must reduce the amount of qualified dividends income and net capital gain otherwise eligible for reduced maximum tax rates by the amount included as investment income.

> **EXAMPLE**
>
> Assume a taxpayer has the following items of income and expense for 2011:
>
> | | |
> |---|---|
> | Interest income | $ 15,000 |
> | Net long-term capital gain | 18,000 |
> | Investment interest expense | 25,000 |
>
> The taxpayer's deduction for investment interest expense is generally limited to $15,000 for 2011 unless the taxpayer elects to include a portion of the net LTCG in the determination of the investment interest expense limitation. If the taxpayer elects to treat $10,000 of the net LTCG as investment income, all of the taxpayer's investment interest expense will be deductible. But by doing this, $10,000 of the net LTCG will be taxed at ordinary tax rates, leaving only the remaining $8,000 of net LTCG to be taxed at preferential rates.

e. Only investment expenses (e.g., rental fees for safety-deposit box rental, investment counseling fees, subscriptions to investment periodicals) remaining after the 2% of AGI limitation are used in computing net investment income.

f. Income and expenses taken into account in computing the income or loss from a passive activity are excluded from net investment income.

NOW REVIEW MULTIPLE-CHOICE QUESTIONS 125 THROUGH 131 IN VOLUME 2

D. Charitable Contributions

Contributions to qualified domestic charitable organizations are deductible in the year actually paid or donated (for both accrual- and cash-basis taxpayers) with some carryover allowed. A "pledge" is *not* a payment. Charging the contribution on your credit card *does constitute payment.*

1. **Qualified organizations** include

    a. A state, a US possession or political subdivision, or the District of Columbia if made exclusively for public purposes
    b. A community chest, corporation, foundation, etc., operated exclusively for charitable, religious, educational, scientific, or literary purposes, or for the prevention of cruelty to children or animals, or for fostering national or international amateur sports competition (unless they provide facilities or equipment)

       (1) No part of the earnings may inure to any individual's benefit
       (2) May not attempt to influence legislation or intervene in any political campaign

    c. Church, synagogue, or other religious organizations
    d. War veterans' organizations
    e. Domestic fraternal societies operating under the lodge system (only if contribution used exclusively for the charitable purposes listed in b. above)
    f. Nonprofit cemetery companies if the funds are irrevocably dedicated to the perpetual care of the cemetery as a whole, and not a particular lot or mausoleum crypt

2. Dues, fees, or assessments paid to qualified organizations are deductible to the extent that payments exceed benefits received. Dues, fees, or assessments are not deductible if paid to veterans' organizations, lodges, fraternal organizations, and country clubs

3. Out-of-pocket expenses to maintain a **student** (domestic or foreign) in a taxpayer's home are deductible (limited to $50/month for each month the individual is a full-time student) if

    a. Student is in 12th or lower grade and not a dependent or relative
    b. Based on written agreement between taxpayer and qualified organization
    c. Taxpayer receives no reimbursement

4. Payments to qualified organizations for goods or services are deductible to the extent the amount paid exceeds the fair market value of benefits received.

5. A taxpayer who makes a payment to or for the benefit of a college or university and is thereby entitled to purchase tickets to athletic events is allowed to deduct 80% of the payment as a charitable contribution. Any payment that is attributable to the actual cost of tickets is not deductible as a charitable contribution.

6. Unreimbursed out-of-pocket expenses incurred while rendering services to a charitable organization without compensation are deductible, including actual auto expenses or a standard rate of 14¢ per mile.

7. For tax years beginning after August 17, 2006, no deduction will be allowed for **contributions of cash**, checks, or other monetary gifts unless the donor maintains either a canceled check, a receipt, letter or other written communication from the donee, indicating the donee's name, contribution date, and the amount.

8. No charitable deduction is allowed for any **contribution of $250 or more** unless the donor obtains written acknowledgment of the contribution from the donee organization including a good-faith estimate of the value of any goods or services provided to the donor in exchange for the contribution. The acknowledgement must be received by the earlier of the date the taxpayer's return is filed, or the due date (including extensions) for filing the taxpayer's return. A canceled check is not sufficient substantiation for a contribution of $250 or more.

9. For any noncash property donation **exceeding $500 in value,** the taxpayer must maintain a written record containing (1) the approximate date and manner of acquisition of the property, and (2) the cost or other basis of the property if it was held less than twelve months. Additionally, a description of the donated property must be included with the return for the tax year in which the contribution was made. If the donated item exceeds **$5,000** in value, the taxpayer is required to obtain a qualified appraisal and attach a summary of the appraisal to the return. If the donated item exceeds **$500,000** in value, a qualified appraisal must be attached to the return. Similar noncash items, whether donated to a single donee or multiple donees, must be aggregated for purposes of determining whether the above dollar thresholds are exceeded.

10. **Nondeductible** contributions include contributions to/for/of

    a. Civic leagues, social clubs, and foreign organizations
    b. Communist organizations, chambers of commerce, labor unions
    c. The value of the taxpayer's time or services

d. The use of property, or less than an entire interest in property
e. Blood donated
f. Tuition or amounts in place of tuition
g. Payments to a hospital for care of particular patients
h. "Sustainer's gift" to retirement home
i. Raffles, bingo, etc. (but may qualify as gambling loss)
j. Fraternal societies if the contributions are used to defray sickness or burial expenses of members
k. Political organizations
l. Travel, including meals and lodging (e.g., trip to serve at charity's national meeting), if there is any significant element of personal pleasure, recreation, or vacation involved

11. Contributions of property to qualified organizations are **deductible**

   a. At fair market value when FMV is below basis
   b. At basis when fair market value exceeds basis and property would result in short-term capital gain or ordinary income if sold (e.g., gain would be ordinary because of depreciation recapture or if property is inventory)
   c. If contributed property is *capital gain property* that would result in LTCG if sold (i.e., generally investment property and personal-use property held more than one year), the amount of contribution is the property's FMV. However, if the contributed property is *tangible personal capital gain property* and its use is unrelated to the charity's activity, the amount of contribution is restricted to the property's basis.
   d. Appraisal fees on donated property are a miscellaneous itemized deduction.

12. For contributions of **vehicles** (automobiles, boats, and airplanes) with a claimed value exceeding $500 after December 31, 2004, the charitable deduction is limited to the gross proceeds received by the charitable organization upon subsequent sale of the vehicle. Additionally, the donee organization must provide the donor with a written acknowledgement within 30 days of (1) the contribution of the qualified vehicle, or (2) the date of sale of the qualified vehicle. If the vehicle is not sold, the donee must provide certification of the intended use of the vehicle and the intended duration of use.

13. For contributions of **patents** and other **intellectual property** made after June 3, 2004, the amount of deduction is limited to the lesser of (1) the taxpayer's basis for the property, or (2) the property's FMV. A donor is also allowed an additional charitable deduction for certain amounts in the year of contribution and in later years based on a specified percentage of qualified donee income received or accrued by the charity from the donated property.

14. The overall limitation for contribution deductions is **50%** of adjusted gross income (before any net operating loss carryback). A second limitation is that contributions of long-term capital gain property to charities in Section 14.a. below (where gain is not reduced) are limited to **30%** of AGI. A third limitation is that some contributions to certain charities are limited to **20%** of AGI or a lesser amount.

   a. Contributions to the following are taken first and may be taken up to **50%** of AGI limitation

      (1) Public charities

         (a) Churches
         (b) Educational organizations
         (c) Tax-exempt hospitals
         (d) Medical research
         (e) States or political subdivisions
         (f) US or District of Columbia

      (2) All private operating foundations, that is, foundations that spend their income directly for the active conduct of their exempt activities (e.g., public museums)
      (3) Certain private nonoperating foundations that distribute proceeds to public and private operating charities

   b. Deductions for contributions of **long-term capital gain property** (when the gain is not to be reduced) to organizations in Section 14.a. above are limited to **30%** of adjusted gross income; but, taxpayer may elect to reduce all appreciated long-term capital gain property by the potential gain and not be subject to this 30% limitation.
   c. Deductions for contributions to charities that do not qualify in Section 14.a. above (generally private nonoperating foundations) are subject to special limitations.

      (1) The deduction limitation for gifts of

         (a) Ordinary income property is the lesser of (1) 30% of AGI, or (2) (50% × AGI) – gifts to charities in Section 14.a. above
         (b) Capital gain property is lesser of (1) 20% of AGI, or (2) (30% × AGI) – gifts of long-term capital gain property to charities in Section 14.a. above where no reduction is made for appreciation

A CHARITABLE CONTRIBUTION FLOWCHART FOR INDIVIDUALS

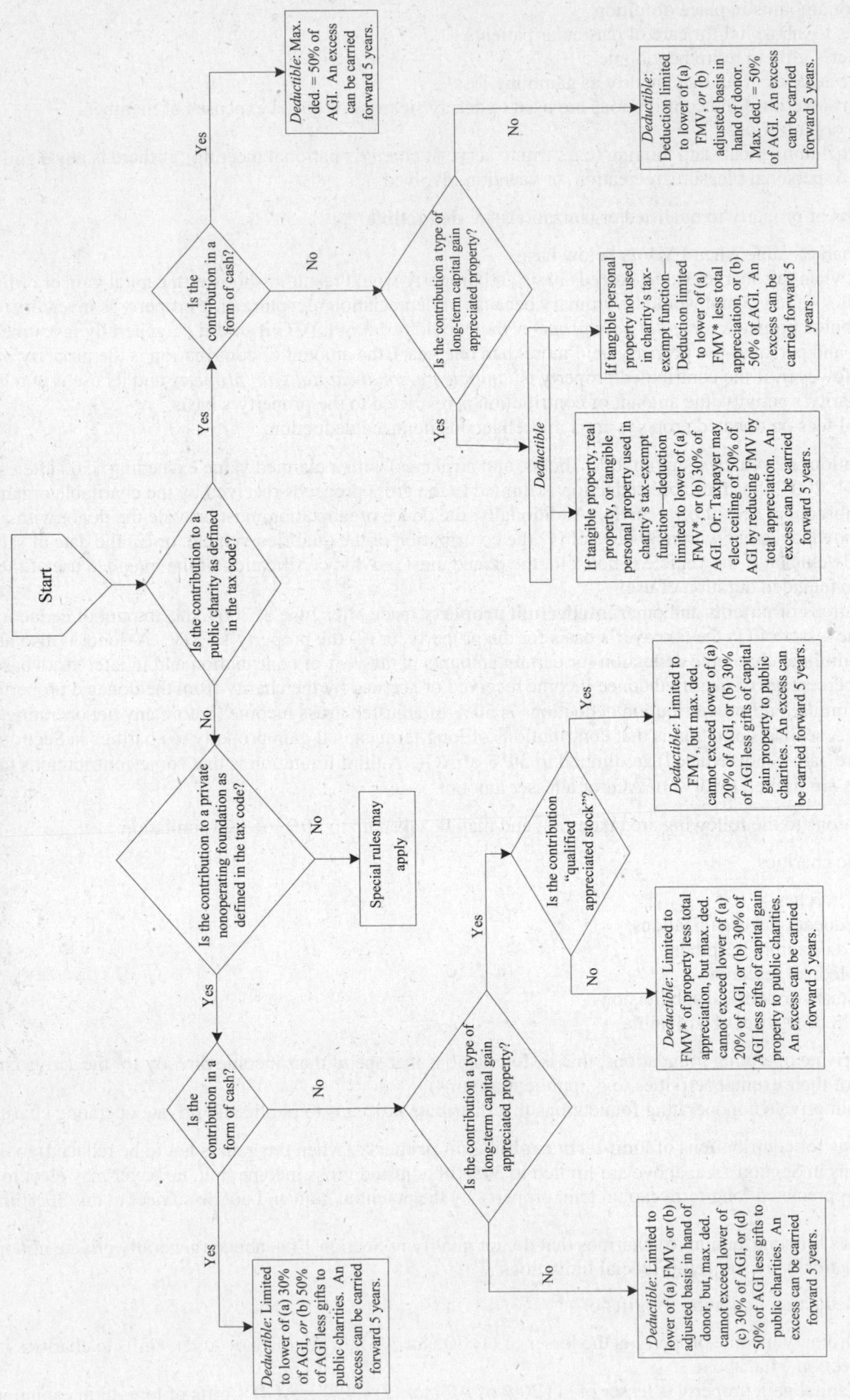

Start

Is the contribution to a public charity as defined in the tax code?

Yes → **Is the contribution in a form of cash?**

Yes → *Deductible:* Max. ded. = 50% of AGI. An excess can be carried forward 5 years.

No → **Is the contribution a type of long-term capital gain appreciated property?**

No → *Deductible:* Deduction limited to lower of (a) FMV, or (b) adjusted basis in hand of donor. Max. ded. = 50% of AGI. An excess can be carried forward 5 years.

Yes → **Deductible**

If tangible personal property not used in charity's tax-exempt function— Deduction limited to lower of (a) FMV* less total appreciation, or (b) 50% of AGI. An excess can be carried forward 5 years.

If tangible property, real property, or tangible personal property used in charity's tax-exempt function—deduction limited to lower of (a) FMV*, or (b) 30% of AGI. Or: Taxpayer may elect ceiling of 50% of FMV by reducing FMV by total appreciation. An excess can be carried forward 5 years.

No → **Is the contribution to a private nonoperating foundation as defined in the tax code?**

No → Special rules may apply

Yes → **Is the contribution in a form of cash?**

Yes → *Deductible:* Limited to lower of (a) 30% of AGI, or (b) 50% of AGI less gifts to public charities. An excess can be carried forward 5 years.

No → **Is the contribution a type of long-term capital gain appreciated property?**

Yes → **Is the contribution "qualified appreciated stock"?**

Yes → *Deductible:* Limited to FMV, but max. ded. cannot exceed lower of (a) 20% of AGI, or (b) 30% of AGI less gifts of capital gain property to public charities. An excess can be carried forward 5 years.

No → *Deductible:* Limited to FMV* of property less total appreciation, but max. ded. cannot exceed lower of (a) 20% of AGI, or (b) 30% of AGI less gifts of capital gain property to public charities. An excess can be carried forward 5 years.

No → *Deductible:* Limited to lower of (a) FMV, or (b) adjusted basis in hand of donor, but, max. ded. cannot exceed lower of (c) 30% of AGI, or (d) 50% of AGI less gifts to public charities. An excess can be carried forward 5 years.

AGI = adjusted gross income.
FMV = fair market value
* The FMV of depreciable property given to a charitable organization must be reduced by the potential ordinary gain generated by depreciation recapture.

(2) These deductions are taken after deductions to organizations in Section 14.a. above without the 30% limitation on capital gain property in Section 14.b. above.

> **EXAMPLE**
>
> An individual with AGI of $9,000 made a contribution of capital gain appreciated property with a FMV of $5,000 to a church, and gave $2,000 cash to a private nonoperating foundation. Since the contribution to the church (before the 30% limit) exceeds 50% of AGI, no part of the contribution to the foundation is deductible this year. Assuming no election is made to reduce the contribution of the capital gain property by the amount of its appreciation, the current deduction for the contribution to the church is limited to 30% × $9,000 = $2,700.

15. Contributions in excess of the 50%, 30%, or 20% limitation can be carried forward for **five years** and remain subject to the 50%, 30%, or 20% limitation in the carryforward years.

> **EXAMPLE**
>
> Ben's adjusted gross income is $50,000. During the year he gave his church $2,000 cash and land (held for investment more than one year) having a fair market value of $30,000 and a basis of $22,000. Ben also gave $5,000 cash to a private foundation to which a 30% limitation applies.
>
> Since Ben's contributions to an organization to which the 50% limitation applies (disregarding the 30% limitation for capital gain property) exceed $25,000 (50% of $50,000), his contribution to the private foundation is not deductible this year. The $2,000 cash donated to the church is deducted first. The donation for the gift of land is not required to be reduced by the appreciation in value, but is limited to $15,000 (30% × $50,000). Thus, Ben may deduct only $17,000 ($2,000 + $15,000). The unused portion of the land contribution ($15,000) and the gift to the private foundation ($5,000) are carried over to the next year, still subject to their respective 30% limitations.
>
> Alternatively, Ben may elect to reduce the value of the land by its appreciation of $8,000 and not be subject to the 30% limitation for capital gain property. In such case, his current deduction would be $25,000 ($2,000 cash + $22,000 land + $1,000 cash to private foundation), but only the remaining $4,000 cash to the private foundation would be carried over to the next year.

NOW REVIEW MULTIPLE-CHOICE QUESTIONS 132 THROUGH 141 IN VOLUME 2

E. Personal Casualty and Theft Gains and Losses

Gains and losses from casualties and thefts of **property held for personal use** are not subject to the Sec. 1231 netting process. Instead, personal casualty and theft gains and losses are **separately netted,** without regard to the holding period of the converted property.

1. A **casualty loss** must be identifiable, damaging to property, and sudden, unexpected, or unusual. Casualty losses **include**

    a. Damage from a fire, storm, accident, mine cave-in, sonic boom, or loss from vandalism
    b. Damage to trees and shrubs if there is a decrease in the total value of the real estate
    c. A loss on personal residence that has been rendered unsafe by reason of a disaster declared by the President and has been ordered demolished or relocated by a state or local government

2. Losses **not deductible** as casualties include

    a. Losses from the breakage of china or glassware through handling or by a family pet
    b. Disease, termite, or moth damage
    c. Expenses incident to casualty (temporary quarters, etc.)
    d. Progressive deterioration through a steadily operating cause and damage from normal process. Thus, the steady weakening of a building caused by normal or usual wind and weather conditions is not a casualty loss.
    e. Losses from nearby disaster (property value reduced due to location near a disaster area)
    f. Loss of future profits from, for example, ice storm damage to standing timber that reduces the rate of growth or the quality of future timber. To qualify as a casualty, the damage must actually result in existing timber being rendered unfit for use.

3. Casualty loss is deductible in the year the loss occurs.

a. Theft loss is deductible in the year the loss is discovered.
b. Loss in a federally declared disaster area is deductible either in the year loss occurs or the preceding year (by filing an amended return).

4. The **amount of loss** is the lesser of (1) the decrease in the FMV of the property resulting from the casualty, or (2) the adjusted basis of the property. The amount of loss must be reduced by

a. Any insurance or reimbursement, and
b. $100 floor for each separate nonbusiness casualty

5. An individual is not permitted to deduct a casualty loss for damage to **insured property** not used in a trade or business or in a transaction entered into for profit unless the individual files a timely insurance claim with respect to the loss. Casualty insurance premiums are considered a personal expense and are not deductible.

6. If personal casualty and theft **gains exceed losses** (after the $100 floor for each loss), then all gains and losses are treated as capital gains and losses.

> **EXAMPLE**
>
> An individual incurred a $5,000 personal casualty gain, and a $1,000 personal casualty loss (after the $100 floor) during the current taxable year. Since there was a net gain, the individual will report the gain and loss as a $5,000 capital gain and a $1,000 capital loss.

7. If losses **(after the $100 floor for each loss) exceed gains,** the losses (1) offset gains, and (2) are an ordinary deduction from AGI to the extent **in excess of 10% of AGI**.

> **EXAMPLE**
>
> An individual had AGI of $40,000 (before casualty gains and losses), and also had a personal casualty loss of $12,000 (after the $100 floor) and a personal casualty gain of $3,000. Since there was a personal casualty net loss, the net loss will be deductible as an itemized deduction of [$12,000 – $3,000 – (10% × $40,000)] = $5,000.

> **EXAMPLE**
>
> Frank Jones' lakeside cottage, which cost him $13,600 (including $1,600 for the land) on April 30, 1991, was partially destroyed by fire on July 12, 2011. The value of the property immediately before the fire was $46,000 ($24,000 for the building and $22,000 for the land), and the value immediately after the fire was $36,000. He collected $7,000 from the insurance company. It was Jones' only casualty for 2011 and his AGI was $20,000. Jones' casualty loss deduction from the fire would be $900, computed as follows:
>
> | | |
> |---|---:|
> | Value of entire property before fire | $46,000 |
> | Value of entire property after fire | −36,000 |
> | Decrease in fair market value of entire property | $10,000 |
> | Adjusted basis (cost in this case) | $13,600 |
> | Loss sustained (lesser of decrease in FMV or adjusted basis) | $10,000 |
> | Less insurance recovery | −7,000 |
> | Casualty loss | $ 3,000 |
> | Less $100 floor | – 100 |
> | Loss after $100 floor | $ 2,900 |
> | Less 10% of AGI | −2,000 |
> | Casualty loss deduction | $ 900 |

NOW REVIEW MULTIPLE-CHOICE QUESTIONS 142 THROUGH 146 IN VOLUME 2

F. Miscellaneous Deductions

1. The following miscellaneous expenses are only deductible to the extent they (in the aggregate) **exceed 2% of AGI**.

a. **Outside salesman expenses** include all business expenses of an employee who principally solicits business for his/her employer while away from the employer's place of business.
b. All **unreimbursed employee expenses** including

(1) Employee **education** expenses if

    (a) Incurred to maintain or improve skills required in employee's present job, or to meet requirements to keep job

    (b) Deductible expenses include unreimbursed transportation, travel, tuition, books, supplies, etc.

    (c) Education expenses are not deductible if required to meet minimum educational requirements in employee's job, or the education qualifies the employee for a new job (e.g., CPA review course) even if a new job is not sought

    (d) Travel as a form of education is not deductible

  (2) **Other deductible unreimbursed employee expenses** include

    (a) Transportation and travel (including 50% of meals and entertainment)

    (b) Uniforms not adaptable to general use

    (c) Employment agency fees to secure employment in same occupation

    (d) Subscription to professional journals

    (e) Dues to professional societies, union dues, and initiation fees

    (f) Physical examinations required by employer

    (g) A college professor's research, lecturing, and writing expenses

    (h) Amounts teacher pays to a substitute

    (i) Surety bond premiums

    (j) Malpractice insurance premiums

    (k) A research chemist's laboratory breakage fees

    (l) Small tools and supplies

  c. Tax counsel, assistance, and tax return preparation fees

  d. Expenses for the production of income other than those incurred in a trade or business or for production of rents and royalties (e.g., investment counsel fees, clerical help, safe-deposit box rent, legal fees to collect alimony, etc.)

2. The following miscellaneous expenses are **not subject to the 2% floor,** but instead are **deductible in full**.

  a. Gambling losses to the extent of gambling winnings

  b. Impairment-related work expenses for handicapped employees

  c. Estate tax related to income in respect of a decedent

  d. Deduction for repayment of amounts under a claim of rights if over $3,000.

  e. Amortizable bond premium on bonds acquired before October 23, 1986

  f. Casualty and theft losses of income-producing property

  g. The balance of an employee's investment in an annuity contract where the employee dies before recovering the entire investment

3. Examples of **nondeductible expenses** include

  a. Fees and licenses, such as auto licenses, marriage licenses, and dog tags

  b. Home repairs, insurance, rent

  c. Personal legal expenses

  d. Life insurance

  e. Burial expenses

  f. Capital expenditures

  g. Illegal bribes and kickbacks

  h. Fines and tax penalties

  i. Collateral

  j. Commuting to and from work

  k. Professional accreditation fees

  l. Bar examination fees and incidental expenses in securing admission to the bar

  m. Medical and dental license fees paid to obtain initial licensing

  n. Campaign expenses of a candidate for any office are not deductible, nor are registration fees for primary elections, even if taxpayer is the incumbent of the office to be contested.

  o. Cost of midday meals while working late (except while traveling away from home)

  p. Political contributions

NOW REVIEW MULTIPLE-CHOICE QUESTIONS 147 THROUGH 152 IN VOLUME 2

IV. EXEMPTIONS

Personal exemptions are similar to itemized deductions in that they are deducted from adjusted gross income. Personal exemptions are allowed for the taxpayer, spouse, and dependent if the dependent is a US citizen or resident.

1. The personal exemption amount is $3,700 for 2011, $3,800 for 2012.
2. Personal exemption for **taxpayer**

    a. Full exemption even if birth or death occurred during the year
    b. No personal exemption for taxpayer if eligible to be claimed as a dependent on another taxpayer's return

3. Exemption for **spouse**

    a. Exemption on joint return
    b. Not allowed if divorced or legally separated at end of year
    c. If a separate return is filed, taxpayer may claim spouse exemption only if the spouse had no gross income and was not the dependent of another taxpayer.

4. Exemption for a **dependent** who is either a *qualifying child* or a *qualifying relative*. A full exemption is allowed even if birth or death occurred during the year. To be a dependent, an individual must be a citizen, national, or resident of the US, or a resident of Canada or Mexico.

    a. An individual must satisfy additional tests relating to relationship, age, abode, and support to be classified as a qualifying child. A **qualifying child**

        (1) Must be the taxpayer's child or a descendant of the taxpayer's child, or the taxpayer's sibling (including half and step siblings) or a descendant of the taxpayer's sibling. *Taxpayer's child* includes son, daughter, stepson, or stepdaughter, or eligible foster child. A legally adopted child or an individual placed with the taxpayer for legal adoption is treated as a child of the taxpayer by blood.
        (2) Must be younger than the taxpayer and must be under age nineteen, or must be a full-time student for at least five months during year and under age twenty-four as of the close of the year. The age test does not apply to a child who is permanently and totally disabled.
        (3) Must have the same principal place of abode as the taxpayer for more than half of the taxpayer's tax year.
        (4) Must not have provided more than one-half of his or her own support during the calendar year in which the taxpayer's tax year begins. If the child is the taxpayer's child and is a full-time student, amounts received as scholarships are not considered support.
        (5) Must not file a joint return with his or her spouse, unless filed solely for refund of tax withheld.
        (6) Cannot be claimed as a dependent on more than one return, even though the child satisfies the qualifying child tests for two or more taxpayers. If none of the taxpayers is the child's parent, the child is a qualifying child for the taxpayer with the highest AGI. If only one of the taxpayers is the child's parent, the child is a qualifying child for that parent. If two of the taxpayers are the child's parents and they do not file a joint return together, the child is a dependent of the parent with whom the child resided for the longest period during the year. If equal time spent with each parent, the parent with the highest AGI is entitled to the exemption.

    b. An individual must satisfy five additional tests to be classified as a qualifying relative. A **qualifying relative**

        (1) Must *not* be a qualifying child (as defined above).
        (2) **Joint return.** Dependent cannot file a joint return, unless filed solely for refund of tax withheld.
        (3) **Member of household or related.** Dependent must either live with the taxpayer for the entire year or be a relative (closer than cousin).

            (a) *Relatives* includes ancestors, descendants, brothers and sisters, uncles and aunts, nephews and nieces, half and step relationships, and in-laws.
            (b) Relationships established by marriage are not ended by death or divorce.
            (c) A person temporarily absent for vacation, school, or sickness, or indefinitely confined in a nursing home meets the member of household test.
            (d) A person who died during the year but was a member of household until death, and a child who is born during the year and is a member of household for the rest of year, meet the member of household requirement.

        (4) **Gross income.** Dependent had gross income less than $3,700 ($3,800 for 2012). Gross income does not include tax-exempt income (e.g., nontaxable social security).
        (5) **Support.** Taxpayer must furnish over one-half of support.

            (a) Includes food, clothing, FV of lodging, medical, education, recreation, and certain capital expenses.

    (b) Excludes life insurance premiums, funeral expenses, nontaxable scholarships, income and social security taxes paid from a dependent's own income.

  c. A **multiple support agreement** may be used if no one person furnishes more than 50% of the support of a dependent. Then a person can be treated as having provided more than half of a dependent's support if (1) over half of the support was received from persons who each would have been entitled to claim the exemption had they contributed more than half of the support, (2) **more than 10%** of the support was provided by the person claiming the exemption, and (3) each other person who contributed more than 10% of the support signs a written declaration stating that he or she will not claim the exemption.

  d. A special rule applies to a child who receives over one-half of the child's support from the **child's parents who are divorced** or legally separated, or who lived apart at all times during the last six months of the year, if the child was in the custody of one or both parents for more than one-half of the year.

    (1) The child will be treated as the qualifying child or qualifying relative of the noncustodial parent if any of the following requirements are satisfied:

      (a) The parents' divorce or separation instrument provides that the noncustodial parent is entitled to the dependency exemption.

      (b) The custodial parent provides the IRS with a signed, written declaration waiving the child's dependency exemption.

      (c) A pre-1985 divorce decree or written separation agreement entitles the noncustodial parent to the exemption and that parent provides at least $600 for the child's support.

    (2) These special rules do not apply if over one-half of the support of the child is treated as having been received from a taxpayer under a multiple support agreement.

  e. If an individual is a dependent of another taxpayer for any taxable year, the individual will be treated as having no dependents for such taxable year.

> **NOW REVIEW MULTIPLE-CHOICE QUESTIONS 153 THROUGH 165 IN VOLUME 2**

V. TAX COMPUTATION

A. Tax Tables

1. Tax tables contain precomputed tax liability based on taxable income.

  a. AGI less itemized deductions and exemptions
  b. Filing status

    (1) Single
    (2) Head of household
    (3) Married filing separately
    (4) Married filing joint return (even if only one had income)
    (5) Surviving spouse (qualifying widow[er] with dependent child)

2. Tax tables must be used by taxpayers unless taxable income is $100,000 or more.

B. Tax Rate Schedules

1. For 2011 the tax rates for individuals are as follows:

Tax rate	Joint return surviving spouse		Married filing separately	
10%	$ 0	– $ 17,000	$ 0	– $ 8,500
15%	$ 17,001	– $ 69,000	$ 8,501	– $ 34,500
25%	$ 69,001	– $139,350	$ 34,501	– $ 69,675
28%	$139,351	– $212,300	$ 69,676	– $106,150
33%	$212,301	– $379,150	$106,151	– $189,575
35%	$379,151 and over		$189,576 and over	

Tax rate	Head of household		Single	
10%	$ 0	– $ 12,150	$ 0	– $ 8,500
15%	$ 12,151	– $ 46,250	$ 8,501	– $ 34,500
25%	$ 46,251	– $119,400	$ 34,501	– $ 83,600
28%	$119,401	– $193,350	$ 83,601	– $174,400
33%	$193,351	– $379,150	$174,401	– $379,150
35%	$379,151 and over		$379,151 and over	

2. **Kiddie tax on unearned income.** The earned income of a child of any age and the unearned income of a child 24 years or older as of the end of the taxable year is taxed at the child's own marginal rate. However, the **unearned income in excess of $1,900** (for 2011 and 2012) of a child under age eighteen is generally taxed at the rates of the child's parents.

   a. This rule also applies to 18-year-old children, as well as 19-to 23-year-old children who are full-time students, if they do not provide at least half of their support with earned income.
   b. Unearned income will be taxed at the parents' rates regardless of the source of the assets creating the child's unearned income so long as the child has at least one living parent as of the close of the tax year and does not file a joint return.
   c. The amount taxed at the parents' rates equals the child's unearned income less the sum of (1) any penalty for early withdrawal of savings, (2) $950, and (3) the greater of $950 or the child's itemized deductions directly connected with the production of unearned income.

      (1) Directly connected itemized deductions are those expenses incurred to produce or collect income, or maintain property that produces unearned income, including custodian fees, service fees to collect interest and dividends, and investment advisory fees. These are deductible as miscellaneous itemized deductions subject to a 2% of AGI limitation.
      (2) The amount taxed at the parents' rates cannot exceed the child's taxable income.

> **EXAMPLE**
>
> Janie (age 11) is claimed as a dependent on her parents' return and in 2011 receives dividend income of $10,000, and has no itemized deductions. Janie's taxable income would be $9,050 ($10,000 – $950 basic standard deduction). The amount of Janie's income taxed at her parents' tax rates would be $8,100 [$10,000 – ($950 + $950)], with the remaining $950 of taxable income taxed at Janie's tax rate.

> **EXAMPLE**
>
> Brian (age 12) is claimed as a dependent on his parents' return and in 2011 receives interest income of $15,000 and has itemized deductions of $1,200 that are directly connected to the production of the interest income. The amount of Brian's income taxed at his parents' tax rates is $12,850 [$15,000 – ($950 + $1,200)].

> **EXAMPLE**
>
> Kerry (age 10) is claimed as a dependent on her parents' return and in 2011 receives interest income of $12,000, has an early withdrawal penalty of $350, and itemized deductions of $400 that are directly connected to the production of the interest income. The amount of Kerry's income taxed at her parents' tax rates is $9,750 [$12,000 – ($350 + $950 + $950)].

   d. A child's tax liability on unearned income taxed at the parents' rates is the child's share of the increase in tax (including alternative minimum tax) that would result from adding to the parents' taxable income the unearned income of their children subject to this rule.
   e. If the child's parents are divorced, the custodial parent's taxable income will be used in determining the child's tax liability.
   f. If child's parents are divorced and both parents have custody, the taxable income of the parent having custody for the greater portion of the calendar year will be used in determining the child's tax liability.

3. **Reporting unearned income of a child on parent's return.** For 2011 and 2012, parents may elect to include on their return the unearned income of their child under age eighteen whose income consists solely of interest and dividends and is between $950 and $9,500.

   a. The child is treated as having no gross income and does not have to file a tax return for the year the election is made.
   b. The electing parents must include the child's gross income in excess of $1,900 on their return for the tax year, resulting in the taxation of that income at the parents' highest marginal rate. Also, the parents must report additional tax liability equal to 10% of the child's income between $950 and $1,900.
   c. The election cannot be made if estimated tax payments were made for the tax year in the child's name and social security number, or if the child is subject to backup withholding.

C. Filing Status

1. Married persons (married at year-end or at time of death of spouse) can file joint return or separate returns.
2. **Qualifying widow(er) with dependent child** (i.e., surviving spouse) may use joint tax rates for the two years following the year in which the spouse died.

   a. Surviving spouse must have been eligible to file a joint return in the year of the spouse's death.
   b. Dependent son, stepson, daughter, or stepdaughter must live in household with surviving spouse.
   c. Surviving spouse must provide more than 50% of costs of maintaining a household that was the main home of the child for the entire year.

3. **Head of household** status applies to an unmarried person (other than a qualifying widow(er) with dependent child) who provides more than 50% of costs of maintaining a household which, for more than one-half of the year, is the principal place of abode for

   a. A *qualifying child* of the taxpayer (e.g., taxpayer's children, siblings, step-siblings, and their descendants under age nineteen, or under age twenty-four and a student), but not if such qualifying child is married at the end of the taxable year and is not a dependent of the taxpayer because of filing a joint return, or was not a citizen, resident, or national of the US, nor a resident of Canada or Mexico.
   b. Relative (closer than cousin) for whom the taxpayer is entitled to a dependency exemption for the taxable year.
   c. Parents need not live with head of household, but parents' household must be maintained by taxpayer (e.g., nursing home) and parents must qualify as taxpayer's dependents.
   d. Cannot qualify for head of household status through use of multiple support agreement, or if taxpayer was a nonresident alien at any time during taxable year.
   e. Unmarried requirement is satisfied if legally separated from spouse under a decree of separate maintenance, or if spouse was a nonresident alien at any time during taxable year.

4. **Cost of maintaining household**

   a. *Includes* rent, mortgage interest, taxes, insurance on home, repairs, utilities, and food eaten in the home.
   b. *Excludes* the cost of clothing, education, medical expenses, vacations, life insurance, transportation, rental value of home, value of taxpayer's services.

> **NOW REVIEW MULTIPLE-CHOICE QUESTIONS 166 THROUGH 172 IN VOLUME 2**

D. Alternative Minimum Tax (AMT)

1. The alternative minimum tax for noncorporate taxpayers is computed by applying a two-tiered rate schedule to a taxpayer's alternative minimum tax base. A 26% rate applies to the first $175,000 of a taxpayer's alternative minimum taxable income (AMTI) in excess of the exemption amount. A 28% rate applies to AMTI greater than $175,000 ($87,500 for married taxpayers filing separately) above the exemption amount. This tax applies to the extent that a taxpayer's AMT exceeds the amount of regular tax.
2. A taxpayer's AMT is generally the amount by which the applicable percentage (26% or 28%) of AMTI as reduced by an exemption amount and reduced by the AMT foreign tax credit exceeds the amount of a taxpayer's regular tax as reduced by the regular tax foreign tax credit.
3. AMT computation formula

```
        Regular taxable income
  +  (–)  Adjustments
  +       Tax preferences
  =  Alternative minimum taxable income
  –       Exemption amount
  =  Alternative minimum tax base
  ×       26% or 28%
  =  Tentative before foreign tax credit
  –       AMT foreign tax credit
  =  Tentative minimum tax
  –       Regular tax liability (reduced by regular tax foreign tax credit)
  =  AMT (if positive)
```

4. **Exemption.** AMTI is offset by an exemption. However, the AMT exemption amount is phased out at the rate of 25% of AMTI between certain specified levels. For 2011, the exemption and phaseout ranges are

Filing status	AMT exemption	Phaseout range
Married filing jointly;		
Surviving Spouse	$74,450	$150,000 – $447,800
Single; Head of Household	$48,450	$112,500 – $306,300
Married filing separately	$37,225	$ 75,000 – $223,900

In the case of a child under the age of eighteen, the AMT exemption (normally $48,450) is limited to the child's earned income plus $6,800 (for 2011).

5. **Adjustments.** In determining AMTI, taxable income must be computed with various adjustments. Example of adjustments include

   a. For real property placed in service after 1986 and before 1999, the difference between regular tax depreciation and straight-line depreciation over forty years.

   b. For personal property placed in service after 1986, the difference between regular tax depreciation using the 200% declining balance method and depreciation using the 150% declining balance method (switching to straight-line when necessary to maximize the deduction).

   c. Excess of stock's FMV over amount paid upon exercise of incentive stock options.

   d. The medical expense deduction is computed using a 10% floor (instead of the 7.5% floor used for regular tax).

   e. No deduction is allowed for home mortgage interest if the loan proceeds were not used to buy, build, or improve the home.

   f. No deduction is allowed for personal, state, and local taxes, and for miscellaneous itemized deductions subject to the 2% floor for regular tax purposes.

   g. No deduction is allowed for personal exemptions and the standard deduction.

   h. For long-term contracts, the excess of income under the percentage-of-completion method over the amount reported using the completed-contract method.

   i. The installment method cannot be used for sales of dealer property.

6. **Preference items.** The following are examples of preference items added to taxable income (as adjusted above) in computing AMTI:

   a. Tax-exempt interest on certain private activity bonds reduced by related interest expense that is disallowed for regular tax purposes. Tax-exempt interest on private activity bonds issued in 2009 and 2010 is not an item of tax preference.

   b. Accelerated depreciation on real property and leased personal property placed in service before 1987—excess of accelerated depreciation over straight-line

   c. The excess of percentage depletion over the property's adjusted basis

   d. 7% of the amount of excluded gain from the sale of Sec. 1202 qualified small business stock (QSBS). However, there is no tax preference for QSBS gains qualifying for the 100% exclusion.

7. **Tax credits.** Generally, an individual's tax credits are allowed to reduce regular tax liability, but only to the extent that regular income tax liability exceeds tentative minimum tax liability.

   a. For 2010 and 2011, all nonrefundable personal credits are allowed to offset both regular tax liability and the alternative minimum tax.

   b. An individual's AMT is also reduced by the alternative minimum tax foreign tax credit, the alcohol fuels credit, the renewable electricity production credit, and several other specified credits.

8. **Minimum tax credit.** The amount of AMT paid (net of exclusion preferences) is allowed as a credit against regular tax liability in future years.

   a. The amount of the AMT credit to be carried forward is the excess of the AMT paid over the AMT that would be paid if AMTI included only exclusion preferences (e.g., disallowed itemized deductions and the preferences for excess percentage depletion, and tax-exempt interest).

   b. The credit can be carried forward indefinitely, but not carried back.

   c. The AMT credit can only be used to reduce regular tax liability, **not** future AMT liability.

NOW REVIEW MULTIPLE-CHOICE QUESTIONS 173 THROUGH 179 IN VOLUME 2

E. Other Taxes

1. **Social security** (FICA) tax is imposed on both employers and employees (withheld from wages). The FICA tax has two components: old age, survivor, and disability insurance (OASDI) and medicare hospital insurance (HI). The OASDI rate is 6.2% and the HI rate is 1.45%, resulting in a combined rate of 7.65% that normally applies to both employees and employers. For 2011 and 2012, the employee OASDI rate is reduced to 4.2%, resulting in a

combined employee rate of 5.65%. However, the employer portion is not reduced, so that rate remains at 7.65% for employers for 2011 and 2012. For 2011 and 2012, the OASDI portion is capped at $106,800, while the HI portion (1.45%) applies to all wages. For 2012, the OASDI portion is capped at $110,100.

2. **Federal unemployment** (FUTA) tax is imposed only on employers at a rate of 6.2% of the first $7,000 of wages paid to each employee. A credit of up to 5.4% is available for unemployment taxes paid to a state, leaving a net federal tax of 0.8%.

3. **Self-employment** tax is imposed on individuals who work for themselves (e.g., sole proprietor, independent contractor, partner). The combined self-employment tax rate is 15.3% for 2010 (13.3% for 2011 and 2012), of which the medicare portion is 2.9%.

   a. The full self-employment tax is capped at $106,800 for 2011 ($110,100 for 2012), while the medicare portion (2.9%) applies to all self-employment earnings.

   b. Income from self-employment generally includes all items of business income less business deductions. Does not include personal interest, dividends, rents, capital gains and losses, and gains and losses on the disposition of business property.

   c. Wages subject to FICA tax are deducted from $106,800 for 2011($110,100 for 2012) in determining the amount of income subject to self-employment tax.

   d. No tax if net earnings from self-employment are less than $400.

   e. A deduction equal to one-half of the self-employment tax rate (7.65%) multiplied by the taxpayer's self-employment income (without regard to this deduction) is allowed in computing the taxpayer's net earnings from self-employment. The purpose of this deduction is to allow the amount on which the self-employment tax is based to be adjusted downward to reflect the fact that employees do not pay FICA tax on the amount of the FICA tax that is paid by their employers.

   f. For years other than 2011 and 2012, individuals deduct one-half of their total self-employment tax for AGI. For 2011 and 2012, the deduction for AGI equals 59.6% of their 10.4% OASDI tax, plus one-half of their 2.9% Medicare tax.

EXAMPLE

A taxpayer has self-employment income of $50,000 before the deemed deduction for 2011. The deemed deduction is $50,000 × 7.65% = $3,825, resulting in net earnings from self-employment of $50,000 – $3,825 = $46,175 and a self-employment tax of $46,175 × 13.3% = $6,141. In computing AGI, the taxpayer is allowed to deduct 59.6% of the $4,802 of OASDI tax, plus 50% of the $1,339 of Medicare tax for a total deduction of $3,531.

EXAMPLE

A taxpayer has self-employment income of $120,000 before the deemed deduction for 2011. The deemed deduction is $120,000 × 7.65% = $9,180, resulting in net earnings from self-employment of $120,000 – $9,180 = $110,820. The taxpayer's self-employment tax will be ($106,800 × 13.3%) + [($110,820 – $106,800) × 2.9%] = $14,321. In computing AGI, the taxpayer is allowed to deduct 59.6% of the $11,107 of OASDI tax, plus 50% of the $3,214 of Medicare tax for a total deduction of $8,227.

NOW REVIEW MULTIPLE-CHOICE QUESTIONS 180 THROUGH 186 IN VOLUME 2

VI. TAX CREDITS/ESTIMATED TAX PAYMENTS

Tax credits directly reduce tax liability. The tax liability less tax credits equals taxes payable. Taxes that have already been withheld on wages and estimated tax payments are credited against tax liability without limitation, even if the result is a refund due to the taxpayer.

A. General Business Credit

1. It is comprised of numerous credits including the (1) investment credit (energy and rehabilitation), (2) work opportunity credit, (3) welfare-to-work credit, (4) alcohol fuels credit, (5) research credit, (6) low-income housing credit, (7) enhanced oil recovery credit, (8) disabled access credit, (9) renewable resources electricity production credit, (10) empowerment zone employment credit, (11) Indian employment credit, (12) employer social security credit, (13) orphan drug credit, (14) new markets tax credit, (15) small-employer pension plan startup cost credit, and (16) the employer-provided child care credit.

2. The general business credit is allowed to the extent of "net income tax" less the greater of (1) the tentative minimum tax or (2) 25% of "net regular tax liability" above $25,000.

    a. "Net income tax" means the amount of the regular income tax plus the alternative minimum tax, and minus nonrefundable tax credits (except the alternative minimum tax credit).
    b. "Net regular tax liability" is the taxpayer's regular tax liability reduced by nonrefundable tax credits (except the alternative minimum tax credit).

> **EXAMPLE**
>
> An individual (not subject to the alternative minimum tax) has a net income tax of $65,000. The individual's general business credit cannot exceed $65,000 – [25% × ($65,000 – $25,000)] = $55,000.

3. A general business credit in excess of the limitation amount is carried back one year and forward twenty years.

B. Business Energy Credit

1. The business energy credit is 10% to 30% for qualified investment in property that uses solar, geothermal, or ocean thermal energy. The property must be constructed by the taxpayer, or if acquired, the taxpayer must be the first person to use the property.
2. The recoverable basis of energy property must be reduced by 50% of the amount of business energy credit.

C. Credit for Rehabilitation Expenditures

1. Special investment credit (in lieu of regular income tax credits and energy credits) for qualified expenditures incurred to substantially rehabilitate old buildings. Credit percentages are (1) 10% for nonresidential buildings placed in service before 1936 (other than certified historic structures), and (2) 20% for residential and nonresidential certified historic structures.
2. **To qualify** for credit on other than certified historic structures

    a. 75% of external walls must remain in place as external or internal walls
    b. 50% or more of existing external walls must be retained in place as external walls
    c. 75% or more of existing internal structural framework must be retained in place

3. A building's recoverable basis must be reduced by 100% of the amount of rehabilitation credit.

D. Work Opportunity Credit

1. Credit is generally 40% of the first $6,000 of qualified first year wages paid to each qualified new employee who begins work before January 1, 2012. For qualified summer youth employees, the credit is 40% of the first $3,000 of wages for services performed during any ninety-day period between May 1 and September 15.
2. Qualified new employees include a (1) qualified IV-A recipient, (2) qualified veteran, (3) qualified ex-felon, (4) designated community resident, (5) vocational rehabilitation referral, (6) qualified summer youth employee, (7) qualified food stamp recipient, (8) qualified SSI recipient, (9) long-term family assistance recipients, (10) unemployed veterans, and (11) disconnected youth.
3. Employer's deduction for wages is reduced by the amount of credit.
4. Taxpayer may elect not to claim credit (to avoid reducing wage deduction).

E. Alcohol Fuels Credit

1. A ten cents per gallon tax credit is allowed for the production of up to fifteen million gallons per year of ethanol by an eligible small ethanol producer (i.e., one having a production capacity of up to sixty million gallons of alcohol per year).
2. The tax credit for ethanol blenders is sixty cents per gallon for 190 or greater proof ethanol and forty-five cents per gallon for 150 to 190 proof ethanol.

F. Low-Income Housing Credit

1. The amount of credit for owners of low-income housing projects depends upon (1) whether the taxpayer acquires existing housing or whether the housing is newly constructed or rehabilitated, and (2) whether or not the housing project is financed by tax-exempt bonds or other federally subsidized financing. The applicable credit rates are the appropriate percentages issued by the IRS for the month in which the building is placed in service.
2. The amount on which the credit is computed is the portion of the total depreciable basis of a qualified housing project that reflects the portion of the housing units within the project that are occupied by qualified low-income individuals.
3. The credit is claimed each year (for a ten-year period) beginning with the year that the property is placed in service. The first-year credit is prorated to reflect the date placed in service.

G. Disabled Access Credit

1. A tax credit is available to an eligible small business for expenditures incurred to make the business accessible to disabled individuals. The amount of this credit is equal to 50% of the amount of the eligible access expenditures for a year that exceed $250 but do not exceed $10,250.
2. An eligible small business is one that either (1) had gross receipts for the preceding tax year that did not exceed $1 million, or (2) had no more than 30 full-time employees during the preceding tax year, and (3) elects to have this credit apply.
3. Eligible access expenditures are amounts incurred to comply with the requirements of the Americans with Disabilities Act of 1990 and include amounts incurred for the purpose of removing architectural, communication, physical, or transportation barriers that prevent a business from being accessible to, or usable by, disabled individuals; amounts incurred to provide qualified readers to visually impaired individuals, and amounts incurred to acquire or modify equipment or devices for disabled individuals. Expenses incurred in connection with new construction are not eligible for the credit.
4. This credit is included as part of the general business credit; no deduction or credit is allowed under any other Code provision for any amount for which a disabled access credit is allowed.

H. Empowerment Zone Employment Credit

1. The credit is generally equal to 20% of the first $15,000 of wages paid to each employee who is a resident of a designated empowerment zone and performs substantially all services within the zone in an employer's trade or business.
2. The deduction for wages must be reduced by the amount of credit.

I. Employer Social Security Credit

1. Credit allowed to food and beverage establishments for the employer's portion of FICA tax (7.65%) attributable to reported tips in excess of those tips treated as wages for purposes of satisfying the minimum wage provisions of the Fair Labor Standards Act.
2. No deduction is allowed for any amount taken into account in determining the credit.

J. Employer-Provided Child Care Credit

1. Employers who provide child care facilities to their employees during normal working hours are eligible for a credit equal to 25% of qualified child care expenditures, and 10% of qualified child care resource and referral expenditures. The maximum credit is $150,000 per year, and is subject to a ten-year recapture rule.
2. *Qualified child care expenditures* include amounts paid to acquire, construct, and rehabilitate property which is to be used as a qualified child care facility (e.g., training costs of employees, scholarship programs, compensation for employees with high levels of child care training).
3. To prevent a double benefit, the basis of qualifying property is reduced by the amount of credit, and the amount of qualifying expenditures that would otherwise be deductible must be reduced by the amount of credit.

K. Credit for the Elderly and the Disabled

1. Eligible taxpayers are those who are either (1) 65 or older or (2) permanently and totally disabled.

   a. Permanent and total disability is the inability to engage in substantial gainful activity for a period that is expected to last for a continuous twelve-month period.
   b. Married individuals must file a joint return to claim the credit unless they have not lived together at all during the year.
   c. Credit cannot be claimed if Form 1040A or 1040EZ is filed.

2. Credit is **15%** of an initial amount reduced by certain amounts excluded from gross income and AGI in excess of certain levels. The amount of credit is limited to the amount of tax liability.

   a. Initial amount varies with filing status.

      (1) $5,000 for single or joint return where only one spouse is 65 or older
      (2) $7,500 for joint return where both spouses are 65 or older
      (3) $3,750 for married filing a separate return
      (4) Limited to disability income for taxpayers under age 65

   b. Reduced by annuities, pensions, social security, or disability income that is excluded from gross income
   c. Also reduced by 50% of the excess of AGI over

      (1) $7,500 if single
      (2) $10,000 if joint return
      (3) $5,000 for married individual filing separate return

> **EXAMPLE**
>
> H, age 67, and his wife, W, age 65, file a joint return and have adjusted gross income of $12,000. H received social security benefits of $2,000 during the year. The computation of their credit would be as follows:
>
> | | | |
> |---|---:|---:|
> | Initial amount | | $7,500 |
> | Less: social security | $2,000 | |
> | 50% of AGI over $10,000 | 1,000 | 3,000 |
> | Balance | | 4,500 |
> | | | × 15% |
> | Amount of credit (limited to tax liability) | | $ 675 |

L. Child and Dependent Care Credit

1. The credit may vary from **20% to 35%** of the amount paid for qualifying household and dependent care expenses incurred to enable taxpayer to be gainfully employed or look for work. Credit is 35% if AGI is $15,000 or less, but is reduced by 1 percentage point for each $2,000 (or portion thereof) of AGI in excess of $15,000 (but not reduced below 20%).

> **EXAMPLE**
>
> Able, Baker, and Charlie have AGIs of $10,000, $20,000, and $50,000 respectively, and each incurs child care expenses of $2,000. Able's child care credit is $700 (35% × $2,000); Baker's credit is $640 (32% × $2,000); and Charlie's credit is $400 (20% × $2,000).

2. **Eligibility** requirements include

   a. Expenses must be incurred on behalf of a qualifying individual and must enable taxpayer to be gainfully employed or look for work
   b. Married taxpayer must file joint return. If divorced or separated, credit available to parent having custody longer time during year
   c. A **qualifying individual** must have the same principal place of abode as the taxpayer for more than one-half of the tax year. A qualifying individual includes

      (1) The taxpayer's qualifying child (e.g., taxpayer's child, stepchild, sibling, stepsibling, or descendant of any of these) under age thirteen, or
      (2) Dependent or spouse who is physically or mentally incapable of self-care

   d. **Qualifying expenses** are those incurred for care of qualifying individual and for household services that were partly for care of qualifying individual to enable taxpayer to work or look for work

      (1) Expenses incurred outside taxpayer's household qualify only if incurred for a qualifying individual who regularly spends at least eight hours each day in taxpayer's household
      (2) Payments to taxpayer's child under age nineteen do not qualify
      (3) Payments to a relative do not qualify if taxpayer is entitled to a dependency exemption for that relative

3. **Maximum amount of expenses** that qualify for credit is the least of

   a. Actual expenses incurred, or
   b. **$3,000** for one, **$6,000** for two or more qualifying individuals, or
   c. Taxpayer's earned income (or spouse's earned income if smaller)
   d. If spouse is a student or incapable of self-care and thus has little or no earned income, spouse is treated as being gainfully employed and having earnings of not less than $250 per month for one, $500 per month for two or more qualifying individuals

> **EXAMPLE**
>
> Husband and wife have earned income of $15,000 each, resulting in AGI of $30,000. They have one child, age 3. They incurred qualifying household service expenses of $1,500 and child care expenses at a nursery school of $2,200.

Household expenses	$1,500
Add child care outside home	2,200
Total employment-related expenses	$3,700
Maximum allowable expenses	$3,000
Credit = 27% × $3,000	$ 810

M. Foreign Tax Credit

1. Foreign income taxes on US taxpayers can either be deducted or used as a credit at the option of the taxpayer each year.
2. The credit is limited to the overall limitation of

$$\frac{\text{TI from all foreign countries}}{\text{Taxable income + Exemptions}} \times \quad (\text{US tax} - \text{Credit for elderly})$$

3. The limitation must be computed separately for passive income (i.e., dividends, interest, royalties, rents, and annuities).
4. Foreign tax credit in excess of the overall limitation is subject to a one-year carryback and a ten-year carryforward.
5. There is no limitation if foreign taxes are used as a deduction.

NOW REVIEW MULTIPLE-CHOICE QUESTIONS 187 THROUGH 195 IN VOLUME 2

N. Earned Income Credit

1. The earned income credit is a **refundable** tax credit for eligible low-income workers. Earned income includes wages, salaries, and other employee compensation (including union strike benefits), plus earnings from self-employment (after the deduction for one-half self-employment taxes). Earned income excludes income from pensions and annuities, and investment income such as interest and dividends.
2. For 2012, the earned income credit is allowed at a rate of 34% of the first $9,320 of earned income for taxpayers with one qualifying child, is allowed at a rate of 40% on the first $13,090 of earned income for taxpayers with two qualifying children, and is allowed at a rate of 45% of the first $13,090 of earned income for an individual with three or more qualifying children. The maximum credit is reduced by 15.98% (21.06% for two or more qualifying children) of the amount by which earned income (or AGI if greater) exceeds $17,090 ($22,300 for married taxpayers filing jointly).
3. To be eligible for the credit an individual must

   a. Have earned income and a return that covers a twelve-month period
   b. Maintain a household for more than half the year for a qualifying child in the US
   c. Have a filing status other than married filing a separate return
   d. Not be a qualifying child of another person
   e. Not claim the exclusion for foreign earned income
   f. Not have disqualified income in excess of $3,200

4. **A qualifying child** must be

   a. The taxpayer's child, adopted child, eligible foster child, stepchild, sibling, stepsibling, or descendant of any of these who has the same principal place of abode as the taxpayer for more than one-half of the tax year, and is
   b. Under age nineteen, or a full-time student under age twenty-four, or permanently and totally disabled.
   c. If a custodial parent would be entitled to a child's dependency exemption but for having released it to the noncustodial parent for purposes of the earned income credit.

5. **Disqualified income** includes both taxable and tax-exempt interest, dividends, net rental and royalty income, net capital gain income, and net passive income.
6. **A reduced earned income credit** is available to an individual who does not have qualifying children if (1) the individual's principal place of abode for more than half the tax year is in the US, (2) the individual (or spouse) is at least age twenty-five (but under sixty-five) at the end of the tax year, and (3) the individual does not qualify as a dependency exemption on another taxpayer's return. For 2012, the maximum credit is 7.65% of the first $6,210 of earned income, and is reduced by 7.65% of earned income (or AGI if greater) in excess of $7,770 ($12,980 for married taxpayers filing jointly).
7. The earned income credit is refundable if the amount of credit exceeds the taxpayer's tax liability. Individuals with qualifying children who expect a refund because of the earned income credit may arrange to have up to 60% of the credit added to paychecks. The ability to receive advance payment of the earned income credit was repealed for tax years beginning after 2010.

O. Credit for Adoption Expenses

1. A nonrefundable credit of up to $12,650 (for 2012) for qualified adoption expenses incurred for each eligible child (including a child with special needs). The adoption credit was refundable for 2010 and 2011.

    a. An *eligible child* is an individual who has not attained the age of 18 as of the time of the adoption, or who is physically or mentally incapable of self-care.
    b. Married taxpayers generally must file a joint return to claim the credit.
    c. The credit is phased out ratably for modified AGI between $189,710 and $229,710.

2. *Qualified adoption expenses* incurred or paid during a tax year prior to the year in which the adoption is finalized may be claimed as a credit in the tax year following the year the expense was incurred. Adoption expenses incurred during the year the adoption becomes final or in the year following the finalization of the adoption are claimed in the year they were incurred. Qualified adoption expenses are taken into account in the year the adoption becomes final and include all reasonable and necessary adoption fees, court costs, attorney fees, and other expenses that are directly related to the legal adoption by the taxpayer of an eligible child. However, expenses incurred in carrying out a surrogate parenting arrangement or in adopting a spouse's child do not qualify for the credit.

P. Child Tax Credit (CTC)

1. The amount of the credit is $1,000 per qualifying child through 2012.
2. A *qualifying child* is a US citizen or resident who is the taxpayer's child, adopted child, eligible foster child, step-child, step-sibling, or descendant of any of these who is less than seventeen years old as of the close of the calendar year in which the tax year of the taxpayer begins.
3. The child tax credit begins to phase out when modified adjusted gross income reaches $110,000 for joint filers, $55,000 for married taxpayers filing separately, and $75,000 for single taxpayers and heads of households. The credit is reduced by $50 for each $1,000, or fraction thereof, of modified AGI above the thresholds.
4. The CTC is refundable to the extent of 15% of the taxpayer's earned income in excess of $3,000 (for 2010 through 2012), up to the per child credit amount of $1,000 per child. Taxpayers with more than two children may calculate the refundable portion of the credit using the excess of their social security taxes (i.e., taxpayer's share of FICA taxes and one-half of self-employment taxes) over their earned income credit, if it results in a larger amount. The amount of refundable CTC reduces the amount of nonrefundable CTC.

Q. American Opportunity Credit (AOC)

1. For the *first four years* of a postsecondary school program, qualifying taxpayers may elect to take a tax credit of 100% for the first $2,000 of qualified tuition, fees, and course materials (not room and board), and a 25% credit for the next $2,000 of such expenses, for a total credit of up to $2,500 a year per student.
2. The credit is available on a *per student basis* and covers tuition payments for the taxpayer as well as the taxpayer's spouse and dependents.

    a. To be eligible for the credit, the student must be enrolled on at least a half-time basis for one academic period during the year.
    b. If a student is claimed as a dependent of another taxpayer, only that taxpayer may claim the education credit for the student's qualified tuition and related expenses. However, if the taxpayer is eligible to, but does **not** claim the student as a dependent, only the student may claim the education credit for the student's qualified tuition and related expenses.

3. The credit is phased out ratably for single taxpayers with modified AGI between $80,000 and $90,000, and for joint filers with a modified AGI between $160,000 and $180,000.
4. 40% of the credit is refundable.
5. The nonrefundable portion of the credit can be claimed against a taxpayer's AMT as well as regular tax liability.
6. For a tax year, a taxpayer may elect only one of the following with respect to one student: (1) the AOC credit, or (2) the lifetime learning credit.

R. Lifetime Learning Credit

1. A nonrefundable 20% tax credit is available for up to $10,000 of qualified tuition and related expenses per year for graduate and undergraduate courses at an eligible educational institution.
2. The credit may be claimed for an unlimited number of years, is available on a *per taxpayer basis*, covers tuition payments for the taxpayer, spouse, and dependents.
3. Similar to the AOC credit, if a student is claimed as a dependent of another taxpayer, only that taxpayer may claim the education credit for the student's qualified tuition and related expenses. However, if the taxpayer is eligible to, but does **not** claim the student as a dependent, only the student may claim the education credit for the student's qualified tuition and related expenses.

4. The credit is phased out for single taxpayers with a modified AGI between $51,000 and $61,000, and for joint filers with modified AGI between $102,000 and $122,000.
5. For a tax year, a taxpayer may elect only one of the following with respect to one student: (1) the AOC credit, or (2) the lifetime learning credit.

> **EXAMPLE**
>
> Alan paid qualified tuition and related expenses for his dependent, Betty, to attend college. Assuming all other relevant requirements are met, Alan may claim either a Hope Scholarship credit or lifetime learning credit with respect to his dependent, Betty, but not both.

> **EXAMPLE**
>
> Cathy paid $2,000 in qualified tuition and related expenses for her dependent, Doug, to attend college. Also during the year, Cathy paid $600 in qualified tuition to attend a continuing education course to improve her job skills. Assuming all relevant requirements are met, Cathy may claim the Hope Scholarship credit for the $2,000 paid for her dependent, Doug, and a lifetime learning credit for the $600 of qualified tuition that she paid for the continuing education course to improve her job skills.

> **EXAMPLE**
>
> The facts are the same as in the preceding example, except that Cathy paid $4,500 in qualified tuition and related expenses for her dependent, Doug, to attend college. Although a Hope Scholarship credit is available only with respect to the first $4,000 of qualified tuition and related expenses paid with respect to Doug, Cathy **cannot** add the $500 of excess expenses to her $600 of qualified tuition in computing the amount of her lifetime learning credit.

> **EXAMPLE**
>
> Ernie has one dependent, Frank. During the current year, Ernie paid qualified tuition and related expenses for Frank to attend college. Although Ernie is eligible to claim Frank as a dependent on Ernie's federal income tax return, Ernie does **not** do so. Therefore, assuming all other relevant requirements are met, Frank is allowed an education credit on Frank's federal income tax return for his qualified tuition and related expenses paid by Ernie, and Ernie is not allowed an education credit with respect to Frank's education expenses. The result would be the same if Frank had paid his qualified tuition expenses himself.

S. Credit for Qualified Retirement Savings

1. The amount of nonrefundable credit is from 10% to 50% of up to $2,000 of elective contributions to IRAs and most retirement plans. The credit rate (10% to 50%) is based on AGI, and the credit is in addition to any deduction or exclusion that would otherwise apply to the contributions.
2. Only individuals filing joint returns with AGI of $56,500 or less, filing as a head of household with AGI of $42,375 or less, and filing other returns with AGI of $28,250 or less qualify for the credit.
3. The credit is available to an individual taxpayer at least eighteen years old at the close of the tax year who is not a full-time student nor claimed as a dependent on another taxpayer's return.

T. First-time Homebuyer Credit

1. An individual who is a first-time homebuyer of a principal residence in the US after December 31, 2008, and before May 1, 2010, is allowed a refundable tax credit for 10% of the purchase price, up to a maximum of $8,000 ($4,000 for a married individual filing separately).
2. A first-time homebuyer is an individual (and, if married, their spouse) who had no present ownership interest in a principal residence in the prior 3-year period ending on the date of home purchase.
3. This credit has no repayment requirement but must be recaptured if the home is sold or ceases to be a principal residence of the taxpayer or taxpayer's spouse within 36 months of the date of purchase. The repayment will be due on the tax return for the year in which the home is sold or ceases to be a principal residence.
4. 2009 legislation extended and expanded the credit for purchases made after Nov. 6, 2009, and before May 1, 2010. The maximum credit remains at $8,000 for a first-time homebuyer, but a reduced refundable credit of up to $6,500 is available for taxpayers who have owned and used a residence as a principal residence for any 5-consecutive-year period during the 8-year period ending on the date of purchase of a new principal residence.

5. For purchases after Nov. 6, 2009, the credit is phased out for modified AGI between $125,000 and $145,000 ($225,000 and $245,000 on a joint return). However, the credit is not available to an individual under age 18 on date of purchase, to dependents, nor on the purchase of a home costing more than $800,000. An election can be made to treat any qualifying 2010 purchase as made on December 31, 2009, for purposes of claiming the credit on a 2009 return.

> **NOW REVIEW MULTIPLE-CHOICE QUESTIONS 196 THROUGH 203 IN VOLUME 2**

U. Estimated Tax Payments

1. An individual whose regular and alternative minimum tax liability is not sufficiently covered by withholding on wages must pay estimated tax in quarterly installments or be subject to penalty.
2. Quarterly payments of estimated tax are due by the 15th day of the 4th, 6th, and 9th month of the taxable year, and by the 15th day of the 1st month of the following year.
3. For 2012, individuals (other than high-income individuals) will incur no penalty if the amount of tax withheld plus estimated payments are at least equal to the lesser of

   a. 90% of the current year's tax,
   b. 90% of the tax determined by annualizing current-year taxable income through each quarter, or
   c. 100% of the prior year's tax.

4. For 2012, high-income individuals must use 110% (instead of 100%) if they base their estimates on their prior year's tax. A person is a high-income individual if the AGI shown on the individual's return for the preceding tax year exceeds $150,000 ($75,000 for a married individual filing separately).
5. The penalty is based on the difference between the required annual payment (i.e., lesser of a., b., or c. above) and the amount paid.
6. Generally no penalty if

   a. Total tax due was less than $1,000;
   b. Taxpayer had no tax liability for prior year (i.e., total tax was zero), prior year was a twelve-month period, and taxpayer was a US citizen or resident for entire year; or
   c. IRS waives penalty because failure to pay was the result of casualty, disaster, or other unusual circumstances.

VII. FILING REQUIREMENTS

A. Form 1040 must generally be filed if gross income at least equals the sum of the taxpayer's standard deduction plus personal exemptions allowable (e.g., generally $5,950 + $3,800 = $9,750 for single taxpayer for 2012).

1. The additional standard deduction for age ($1,450) is included in determining an individual's filing requirement; the additional standard deduction for blindness and dependency exemptions are not included.

> **EXAMPLE**
>
> A single individual age 65 and blind who **cannot** be claimed as a dependency exemption by another taxpayer must file a return for 2012 if the individual's gross income is at least $5,950 + $3,800 + $1,450 = $11,200

2. An individual who can be claimed as a dependency exemption by another taxpayer must file a return if the individual either has (1) unearned income in excess of the sum of $950 plus any additional standard deductions allowed for age and blindness, or (2) total gross income in excess of the individual's standard deduction (i.e., earned income plus $300 up to the normal amount of the basic standard deduction—$5,950 for single taxpayer—plus additional standard deductions for age and blindness).

> **EXAMPLE**
>
> A single individual age 65 who can be claimed as a dependency exemption by another taxpayer must file a return for 2012 if the individual has unearned income (e.g., interest and dividends) in excess of $950 + $1,450 = $2,400.

3. Self-employed individual must file if net earnings from self-employment are **$400** or more.
4. A married individual filing separately must file if gross income is $3,800 or more for 2012.

B. Return must be filed by 15th day of 4th calendar month following close of taxable year.

C. An automatic six-month extension of time for filing the return can be obtained by filing Form 4868 by the due date of the return, and paying any estimated tax due.

NOW REVIEW MULTIPLE-CHOICE QUESTIONS 204 THROUGH 207 IN VOLUME 2

VIII. FARMING INCOME AND EXPENSES

A. A farming business involves the cultivating of land or raising or harvesting of any agricultural or horticultural commodity. It does not include contract harvesting, or the buying or reselling of plants or animals grown or raised by another person.

B. An individual engaged in farming must file Schedule F (Form 1040), Farm Income and Expenses. Additionally, a farmer must also file Schedule SE in order to compute self-employment tax on farm earnings. Completing Schedule F for farming is similar to completing a Schedule C which is used by sole proprietors. Partnerships engaged in farming must file Form 1065, while corporations engaged in farming must file the appropriate Form 1120.

C. The income and expenses from farming are generally treated in the same manner as the income and expenses from any other business. Similarly, the general rules that apply to all cash and accrual taxpayers also apply to farming businesses.

1. A cash-basis farmer who receives insurance proceeds as a result of the destruction or damage to crops may elect to include the proceeds in income for the year after the year of damage if the farmer can show that the income from the crops would normally have been reported in the following year.

2. Income from the sale of a crop is normally reported in the year of sale. However, if the farmer has pledged all of part of the crop production to secure a Commodity Credit Corporation loan, the farmer may elect to report the loan proceeds as income in the year received rather than reporting income in the year the crop is sold. The amount reported as income becomes the farmer's basis for the crop and is used to determine gain or loss upon the sale of the crop.

3. A farmer may generally deduct soil and water conservation expenditures that are consistent with a conservation plan approved by a federal or state agency. However, the deduction is annually limited to 25% of the farmer's gross income from farming. Excess expenses can be carried over for an unlimited number of years subject to the 25 % limitation in each carryover year.

   a. Expenses related to the draining of wetlands or to land preparation for the installation of center pivot irrigation systems may not be deducted under this provision.

   b. Land clearing expenses must be capitalized and added to the farmer's basis in the land.

EXAMPLE

A farmer had gross income from Farm A of $25,000 and gross income from Farm B of $19,000 for the current year. During the year the farmer spent $16,000 on Farm B for soil and water conservation expenditures under a plan approved by a state agency. For the current year, the farmer's deduction of the $16,000 of soil and water conservation expenditures would be limited to ($25,000 + $19,000) × 25% =$11,000.

---

4. Cash-basis farmers can generally deduct prepaid feed costs in the year of payment if the deduction does not materially distort income. However, no deduction is allowed for advance payments for feed, seed, fertilizer, or other supplies to the extent such prepayments exceed 50% of total deductible farming expenses (excluding the prepaid items).

EXAMPLE

During December 2011, a calendar-year farmer purchased a 6-month supply of feed for $6,000 and also purchased $2,000 of seed to be used in the subsequent spring planting season. The farmer's other farm expenses totaled $9,000. In this case the farmer's 2011 deduction for prepaid feed and seed would be limited to 50% × $9,000 = $4,500.

---

5. The cost of most tangible personal property used in a farming business cannot be depreciated under the 200% declining balance method, but instead is generally recovered using the MACRS 150% declining balance method over a 5-year recovery period.

6. An individual engaged in farming can elect to determine current year tax liability by averaging, over the previous three years, all or part of his/her current year income from farming.

IX. TAX PROCEDURES

A. Audit and Appeal Procedures

1. Taxpayer makes determination of tax when return is filed.
2. Examination of questionable returns may be conducted by correspondence, in an IRS office (i.e., office audit), or at taxpayer's place of business (i.e., field audit).
3. If taxpayer does not agree with the changes proposed by the examiner and the examination was made in an IRS office or by correspondence, the taxpayer may request a meeting with the examiner's supervisor.
4. If no agreement is reached, or if the examination was conducted in the field, the IRS will send the taxpayer a copy of the examination report and a letter stating the proposed changes (**thirty-day letter**).
5. A taxpayer has thirty days to (1) accept deficiency, (2) appeal the examiner's findings, or (3) may disregard the thirty-day letter and wait for a statutory notice of deficiency (**ninety-day letter**).
6. If taxpayer has appealed and agreement is not reached at appellate level of IRS, a ninety-day letter is sent.
7. Taxpayer has ninety days to file a petition in the Tax Court.

   a. Assessment and collection are prohibited so long as the taxpayer can petition the Tax Court. Payment of deficiency is not required before going to Tax Court.
   b. If a petition is not filed within ninety days, the tax deficiency is assessed and the amount is subject to collection if not paid within ten days.

B. Choice of Courts

1. A taxpayer may begin tax litigation in any of three courts: the US Tax Court; US district courts; or US Court of Federal Claims.
2. **Tax Court** is a court of national jurisdiction that hears only tax cases. It is composed of 19 judges who are specialists in the tax area that travel to approximately 100 cities throughout the US to hear tax cases. Although a jury trial is not available, a major advantage of the Tax Court is that the tax does not have to be paid before the taxpayer goes to Court. The Tax Court issues regular and memorandum decisions, both of which can be used as precedent.

   a. The IRS has adopted an *acquiescence policy* for regular Tax Court decision that it loses. *Acquiescence* indicates that the IRS will follow the decision in future situation, involving similar facts and issues. *Nonacquiescence* indicates that the IRS will not follow the decision and can be expected to litigate in situations involving similar facts and issues.
   b. Decisions of the Tax Court are appealed to US Court of Appeals. As a matter of policy known as the *Golsen Rule*, the Tax Court will follow the law of the circuit to which a case is appealable.
   c. A taxpayer may take a case to the Small Tax Case Division if the disputed amount does not exceed $50,000. Procedures are simplified and taxpayers can represent themselves without an attorney. Cases are heard by special commissioners instead of a Tax Court judge, and a possible disadvantage is that a decision is binding and cannot be appealed.

3. Each state has at least one **US district court** which is independent of other district courts. District courts adjudicate all types of cases, not just tax cases.

   a. A district court is the only court in which a jury trial is available, which may be advantageous to the taxpayer if the case involves a sympathetic issue.
   b. Unlike a proceeding in the Tax Court, taxpayers must first pay the tax and then file suit in district court for refund.
   c. Decisions of a district court are appealed to the US Court of Appeals.

4. **US Court of Federal Claims** is a court of national jurisdiction. A jury trial is not available and taxpayers must first pay tax and then file suit for refund. Decisions are appealed to US Court of Appeals for the Federal Circuit.
5. There are 11 geographical **Circuit Courts of Appeals** plus one for the District of Columbia and one for the Federal Circuit. Lower court decisions are generally appealable to the court of appeals for an individual's place of residence, or in the case of a corporation, its principal place of business. Decisions of the Appellate Courts have more authority than lower court decisions. The losing party may appeal to the US Supreme Court.
6. **US Supreme Court** normally hears tax cases only if they involve a conflict regarding the treatment of an item between circuits of the Appeals courts. Decisions of the Supreme court are the law of the land and take precedence over all other court decisions.

C. Assessments

1. The normal period for assessment of a tax deficiency is **three years** after the due date of the return or three years after the return is filed, whichever is later.
2. The assessment period is extended to **six years** if gross income omissions exceed 25% of the gross income stated on the return.

3. There is no time limit for assessment if no return is filed, if the return is fraudulent, or if there is a willful attempt to evade taxes.

4. If a taxpayer fails to include any required information on a tax return or statement relating to a listed transaction, the statute of limitations with respect to that listed transaction will not expire until one year after the date the information is provided to the IRS.

5. Assessment period (normally three years) is suspended for 150 days after timely mailing of deficiency notice (90-day letter) to taxpayer.

6. Within sixty days after making the assessment, the IRS is required to provide a notice and demand for payment. If tax is not paid, the tax may be collected by levy or by court proceedings started within ten years of assessment.

D. Collection from Transferees and Fiduciaries

1. Transferee provisions are a method of collecting a predetermined tax that the transferor taxpayer cannot pay.
2. Generally transferor must be insolvent, or no longer in existence (e.g., corporation was dissolved).
3. Generally transferees are liable only to the extent of property received from the transferor taxpayer.

E. Closing Agreement and Compromise

1. A closing agreement is a final determination of tax liability that is binding on both the IRS and taxpayer.
2. A compromise is a writing-down of the tax liability. The IRS has broad authority to compromise in the event that doubt exists as to the existence of actual tax liability or because of the taxpayer's inability to pay.

F. Claims for Refund

1. An income tax refund claim is made on Form 1040X. Form 843 should be used to file a refund claim for taxes other than income taxes. Form 1045 may be used to file for a tentative adjustment or refund of taxes when an overpayment of taxes for a prior year results from the carryback of a current year's net operating loss.

2. Period for filing refund claims

    a. Refund claim must be filed within **three years** from date return was filed, or **two years** from payment of tax, whichever is later. If return filed before due date, the return is treated as filed on due date.
    b. Three-year period is extended to seven years for claims resulting from bad debts or worthless securities.
    c. If refund claim results from a carryback (e.g., NOL), the three-year period begins with the return for the year in which the carryback arose.

3. Suit for refund

    a. Only recourse from IRS's disallowance of refund claim is to begin suit in court within two years of notice of disallowance.
    b. If IRS fails to act on refund claim within six months, the taxpayer may treat it as disallowed.

G. Interest

1. Interest is allowed on overpayments from date of overpayment to thirty days before date of refund check.

    a. If an overpayment, amounts of tax withheld and estimated payments are deemed paid on due date of return.
    b. No interest is allowed if refund is made within forty-five days of later of (1) return due date or (2) actual filing of return.

2. For underpayments of tax, the interest rate is equal to the three-month Treasury bill rate plus three percentage points. For overpayments, the interest rate is equal to the federal short-term rate plus two percentage points.

H. Taxpayer Penalties

1. Penalties may be imposed for late filing or failure to file, and late payment of tax.

    a. **Late filing** or failure to file penalty is 5% of the net tax due per month (up to 25%).
    b. **Late payment** of tax penalty is 0.5% of the net tax due per month (up to 25%).

    (1) For any month to which both of the above apply, the late filing penalty is reduced by the late payment penalty so that the maximum is 5% per month (up to 25%).
    (2) For returns not filed within sixty days of due date (including extensions), the IRS may assess a minimum late filing penalty which is the lesser of $100 or the amount of net tax due.

2. An **accuracy-related penalty of 20%** of the underpayment applies if the underpayment of tax is attributable to one or more of the following: (1) negligence or disregard of rules and regulations, (2) any substantial understatement of income tax, (3) any substantial valuation overstatement, (4) any substantial overstatement of pension liabilities, or (5) any substantial gift or estate tax valuation understatement.

a. Accuracy-related penalty does not apply if the underpayment is due to reasonable cause, or there is adequate disclosure and the position has a reasonable basis for being sustained.

b. **Negligence penalty** applies to any careless, reckless, or intentional disregard of rules or regulations, and any failure to make a reasonable attempt to comply with the provisions of the tax law. Penalty is imposed only on the portion of tax liability due to negligence, and can be avoided by adequate disclosure of a position that has a reasonable basis.

c. **Substantial understatement of income tax penalty** applies if the understatement exceeds the greater of (1) 10% of the tax due, or (2) $5,000 ($10,000 for most corporations). Penalty can be avoided by adequate disclosure of a position that has a reasonable basis, or if there is substantial authority for the position taken.

d. **Substantial valuation misstatement penalty** may be imposed if the value (or adjusted basis) of property stated on the return is 150% or more of the amount determined to be correct.

   (1) Penalty applies to the extent resulting income tax underpayment exceeds $5,000 ($10,000 for most corporations).

   (2) Penalty is applied at a 40% rate if gross overvaluation is 200% or more of the amount determined to be correct.

e. **Substantial overstatement of pension liabilities penalty** applies if the amount of stated pension liabilities is 200% or more of the amount determined to be correct. Penalty is 40% if misstatement is 400% or more, but penalty is not applicable if resulting underpayment is $1,000 or less.

f. **Gift or estate tax valuation misstatement penalty** applies if the value of property on a gift or estate return is 50% or less of the amount determined to be correct.

   (1) Penalty is 40% if valuation used is 25% or less of amount determined to be correct.

   (2) No penalty if resulting understatement of tax is $5,000 or less.

3. A separate accuracy-related penalty applies to **tax shelter transactions**. The penalty is 30% of the tax understatement if the taxpayer fails to disclose a listed transaction or other reportable transaction with a significant tax-avoidance purpose. A lower penalty of 20% of the tax understatement applies if there is disclosure.

   a. The penalty may be waived for reasonable cause if the taxpayer made adequate disclosure, the position is (or was) supported by substantial authority, and the taxpayer reasonably believed the position was more-likely-than-not correct.

   b. Even if a taxpayer reasonably believed that its position was correct, the penalty cannot be waived if there was no disclosure.

4. **Civil fraud penalty** is 75% of the portion of underpayment attributable to fraud. The accuracy-related penalty does not apply to the portion of underpayment subject to the fraud penalty.

NOW REVIEW MULTIPLE-CHOICE QUESTIONS 208 THROUGH 217 IN VOLUME 2

KEY TERMS

Accounting method. The rules used to determine the tax year in which income and expenses are reported for tax purposes. Two major overall methods of accounting are the cash method and the accrual method.

Accounting period. The period of time, usually 12 months, used by a taxpayer for the determination of taxable income. Taxpayers who do not keep records must use a calendar year, while taxpayers who do keep books and records generally may choose between a calendar year and a fiscal year. A fiscal year is a tax year that ends on the last day of a month other than December.

Adjusted gross income (AGI). Unique to individual taxpayers, it generally represents an individual's gross income less business expenses, expenses attributable to the production of rents and royalty income, the capital loss deduction, and certain personal expenses (deductions *for* AGI).

Amount realized. The amount received by a taxpayer from the sale or other disposition of property. The amount realized includes the sum of cash and the fair market value of any other property or services received, plus any debt of the taxpayer assumed by the buyer. Determining the amount realized is the starting point for arriving at the taxpayer's realized gain or loss.

At-risk limitation. Under the at-risk rules, a taxpayer's deductible loss from an activity is limited to the amount the taxpayer has at risk in the activity at the end of the taxable year. The initial amount at risk is generally the sum of the amount of cash and the adjusted basis of property contributed to the activity, plus amounts borrowed for use in the activity for which the taxpayer is personally liable.

Cash method. A method of accounting under which the taxpayer generally reports income for the taxable year in which payments are actually or constructively received. Expenses are deductible when paid.

Gross income. All income from whatever source derived including (but not limited to) compensation for services, gains from property, interest, rents, royalties, dividends, alimony, and income from discharge of indebtedness.

Material participation. The level of participation by a taxpayer in an activity that determines whether the activity is a passive activity or an active trade or business. Material participation can be achieved by meeting any one of the seven tests provided in Regulations.

Passive loss. A loss generated from a passive activity. Generally, passive losses are not allowed to offset trade or business income or portfolio (investment) income.

Realized gain or loss. The gain or loss determined by taking the amount realized from the sale or exchange of property and subtracting the property's adjusted basis.

Statute of limitations. The period of time after which a taxpayer's return is no longer subject to assessment, and the taxpayer can no longer file a claim for refund. The normal stature of limitations is generally three years from the alter of the date the tax return is filed, or its due date.

Stock redemption. The acquisition by a corporation of its own stock from a shareholder in exchange for property. A shareholder's redemption of stock may be treated as an exchange if it meets specified requirements, or otherwise will be treated as a dividend.

Tax benefit rule. The recovery of an item that was deducted in a prior year (e.g., state income tax refund) must be included in gross income for the year of recovery to the extent that the deduction of the item in the prior year produced a tax benefit by reducing the taxpayer's tax.

Module 36: Transactions in Property

Overview

This module presents the income tax consequences of property transactions including the sale, exchange, or other disposition of property. Basis is covered first with a review of the basis of property acquired by purchase, gift, and from a decedent. Tax-deferred transactions are covered next with a review of like-kind exchanges, involuntary conversions, and the sale of a principal residence. Next, sales and exchanges of securities are reviewed as well as the treatment of losses and expenses incurred in transactions with related taxpayers. Finally, capital gains and losses, as well as gains and losses from business property including Sec. 1231 and depreciation recapture are reviewed. Not only is it important to determine the extent of gain or loss recognition, but it is also important to be able to determine whether the character of the recognized gain or loss is capital, Sec. 1231, or ordinary.

A. Sales and Other Dispositions

A sale or other disposition is a transaction that generally gives rise to the recognition of gain or loss. Gains or losses may be categorized as ordinary or capital. If an exchange is nontaxable, the recognition of gain or loss is generally deferred until a later sale of the newly acquired property. This is accomplished by giving the property received the basis of the old property exchanged.

1. The **basis of property** to determine gain or loss is generally its cost or purchase price.

   a. The **cost** of property is the amount paid for it in cash or the FMV of other property, plus expenses connected with the purchase such as abstract of title fees, installation of utility services, legal fees (including title search, contract, and deed fees), recording fees, surveys, transfer taxes, owner's title insurance, and any amounts the seller owes that the buyer agrees to pay (e.g., back taxes and interest, recording or mortgage fees, charges for improvements or repairs, sales commissions).

   b. If property is acquired subject to a debt, or the purchaser assumes a debt, this debt is also included in cost.

   > **EXAMPLE**
   >
   > Susan purchased a parcel of land by paying cash of $30,000 and assuming a mortgage of $60,000. She also paid $400 for a title insurance policy on the land. Susan's basis for the land is $90,400.

   c. If **acquired by gift,** the basis for gain is the basis of the donor (transferred basis) increased by any gift tax paid attributable to the net appreciation in the value of the gift.

      (1) Basis for loss is lesser of gain basis (above), or FMV on date of gift.
      (2) Because of this rule, no gain or loss is recognized when use of the basis for computing loss results in a gain, and use of the basis for computing gain results in a loss.

   > **EXAMPLE**
   >
   > Jill received a boat from her father as a gift. Father's adjusted basis was $10,000 and FMV was $8,000 at date of gift. Jill's basis for gain is $10,000, while her basis for loss is $8,000. If Jill later sells the boat for $9,200, no gain or loss will be recognized.

      (3) The increase in basis for gift tax paid is limited to the amount (not to exceed the gift tax paid) that bears the same ratio to the amount of gift tax paid as the net appreciation in value of the gift bears to the amount of the gift.

(a) The amount of gift is reduced by any portion of the $13,000 annual exclusion allowable with respect to the gift.

(b) Where more than one gift of a present interest is made to the same donee during a calendar year, the $13,000 exclusion is applied to gifts in chronological order.

EXAMPLE

Tom received a gift of property with a FMV of $103,000 and an adjusted basis of $73,000. The donor paid a gift tax of $18,000 on the transfer. Tom's basis for the property would be $79,000 determined as follows:

$$\$73{,}000 \text{ basis } + \left[\$18{,}000 \text{ gift tax } \times \frac{(\$103{,}000 \text{ FMV} - \$73{,}000 \text{ basis})}{(\$103{,}000 \text{ FMV} - \$13{,}000 \text{ exclusion})} \right] = \$79{,}000$$

---

d. If **acquired from decedent,** basis is property's FMV on date of decedent's death, or alternate valuation date (generally six months after death).

(1) Use FMV on date of disposition if alternate valuation is elected and property is distributed, sold, or otherwise disposed of during six-month period following death.

EXAMPLE

Ann received 100 shares of stock as an inheritance from her uncle Henry, who died January 20, 2012. The stock had a FMV of $40,000 on January 20, and a FMV of $30,000 on July 20, 2012. The stock's FMV was $34,000 on June 15, 2012, the date the stock was distributed to Ann.

If the alternate valuation is not elected, or no estate tax return is filed, Ann's basis for the stock is its FMV of $40,000 on the date of Henry's death. If the alternate valuation is elected, Ann's basis will be the stock's $34,000 FMV on June 15 (the date of distribution) since the stock was distributed to Ann within six months after the decedent's death.

---

(2) FMV rule not applicable to appreciated property acquired by the decedent by gift within one year before death if such property then passes from the donee-decedent to the original donor or donor's spouse. The basis of such property to the original donor (or spouse) will be the adjusted basis of the property to the decedent immediately before death.

(3) The portion of jointly held property that is included in a decedent's estate is considered to be acquired from the decedent (i.e., its basis is FMV on date of death, or the alternate valuation). The basis for the portion of jointly held property not included in a decedent's estate is its cost or other basis.

NOW REVIEW MULTIPLE-CHOICE QUESTIONS 1 THROUGH 13 IN VOLUME 2

---

e. The executor of the estate of a decedent who died during 2010 may elect to apply the IRC as if the reinstatement of the federal estate tax by the Tax Relief Act of 2010 had not occurred. If this election is made, the federal estate tax would not apply to the decedent's estate, but a **modified carryover basis** will result. Then the basis of assets transferred by the estate will generally be the lesser of (1) the decedent's adjusted basis, or (2) the fair market value of the property at the date of the decedent's death. (Assume the election to have the federal estate tax not apply has been made in the examples in this section).

EXAMPLE

Alan dies during 2010, owning X Corp. stock with a basis of $20,000 and a FMV of $30,000. The estate's basis for the stock will be $20,000.

EXAMPLE

Baker dies during 2010, owning Y Corp. stock with a basis of $15,000 and a FMV of $10,000 on the date of Baker's death. The estate's basis for the stock will be $10,000.

---

(1) Under the modified carryover basis rules, the basis of property owned by the decedent at date of death can be increased (but not above FMV at date of death) by (1) an aggregate basis increase of $1,300,000, plus (2) built-in losses and loss carryovers (e.g., the amount of any capital loss carryover and Net Operating

Loss (NOL) carryover from the decedent's last tax year, plus the sum of the amount of any losses that would have been allowable to the decedent if the property acquired from the decedent had been sold at FMV immediately before the decedent's death). The basis increase for a specific item of property is the portion of the aggregate basis increase that is allocated to the property.

> **EXAMPLE**
>
> Carter dies during 2010 (without unused carryover and losses) owning stock that cost $700,000 and having a FMV of $6,000,000 at the date of Carter's death. The basis of the stock can potentially be increased by an aggregate basis of adjustment of $1,300,000 to $2,000,000.

(2) An additional basis increase of up to $3,000,000 is available for qualified spousal property passing to the decedent's spouse. Qualified spousal property means property owned by the decedent at date of death that is transferred outright to the surviving spouse as well as qualified terminable interest property. Qualified terminable interest property means property which passes from the decedent and in which the surviving spouse has a qualifying income interest fro life. The basis increase for a specific item of property is the portion of the aggregate spousal basis increase that is allocated to the property. The basis increase adjustment is not allowed to increase the property's basis above FMV at date of the decedent's death.

> **EXAMPLE**
>
> In the above example, if Carter died during 2010 and left the stock to his surviving spouse, the stock's basis of $700,000 could potentially be increased by $1,300,000 plus $3,000,000, to $5,000,000.

(3) The increase adjustments under (1) and (2) above generally do not apply to property acquired by the decedent by gift or inter vivos transfer for less than adequate and full consideration during the 3-year period ending on the date of the decedent's death.

f. The basis of **stock received as a dividend** depends upon whether it was included in income when received.

(1) If included in income, basis is its FMV at date of distribution.
(2) If nontaxable when received, the basis of shareholder's original stock is allocated between the dividend stock and the original stock in proportion to their relative FMVs. The holding period of the dividend stock includes the holding period of the original stock.

> **EXAMPLE**
>
> T owns 100 shares of XYZ Corp. common stock that was acquired in 2008 for $12,000. In 2012, T received a nontaxable distribution of 10 XYZ Corp. preferred shares. At date of distribution the FMV of the 100 common shares was $15,000, and the FMV of the 10 preferred shares was $5,000. The portion of the $12,000 basis allocated to the preferred and common shares would be
>
> $$\text{Preferred} = \frac{\$5,000}{\$20,000}\ (\$12,000) = \$3,000$$
>
> $$\text{Common} = \frac{\$15,000}{\$20,000}\ (\$12,000) = \$9,000$$

g. The basis of **stock rights** depends upon whether they were included in income when received.

(1) If rights were nontaxable and allowed to expire, they are deemed to have no basis and no loss can be deducted.
(2) If rights were nontaxable and exercised or sold

   (a) Basis is zero if FMV of rights is less than 15% of FMV of stock, unless taxpayer elects to allocate basis
   (b) If FMV of rights at date of receipt is at least 15% of FMV of stock, or if taxpayer elects, basis is

$$\frac{\text{FMV of rights}}{\text{FMV of rights} + \text{FMV stock}} \times (\text{Basis in stock})$$

(3) If rights were taxable and included in income, basis is their FMV at date of distribution.

NOW REVIEW MULTIPLE-CHOICE QUESTIONS 14 THROUGH 16 IN VOLUME 2

h. Detailed rules for basis are included in following discussions of exchanges and involuntary conversions.

2. In a sale, the gain or loss is generally the difference between

    a. The cash or fair market value received, and the adjusted basis of the property sold
    b. If the property sold is mortgaged (or encumbered by any other debt) and the buyer assumes or takes the property subject to the debt

        (1) Include the amount of the debt in the amount realized because the seller is relieved of the obligation

> **EXAMPLE**
>
> Property with a $10,000 mortgage, and a basis of $15,000, is sold for $10,000 cash and buyer assumes the mortgage. The amount realized is $20,000, and the gain is $5,000.

        (2) If the amount of the mortgage exceeds basis, use the same rules.

> **EXAMPLE**
>
> Property with a $15,000 mortgage, and a basis of $10,000, is given away subject to the mortgage. The amount realized is $15,000, and the gain is $5,000.

    c. Casual sellers of property (as opposed to dealers) reduce selling price by any selling expenses.

3. In a **taxable exchange,** the gain or loss is the difference between the adjusted basis of the property exchanged and the FMV of the property received. The basis of property received in a taxable exchange is its FMV.

4. **Nontaxable exchanges** generally are not taxed in the current period. Questions concerning nontaxable exchanges often require a determination of the basis of property received, and the effect of boot on the recognition of gain.

    a. **Like-kind exchange**—an exchange of business or investment property for property of a like-kind

        (1) Does not apply to property held for personal use, inventory, stocks, bonds, notes, intangible evidences of ownership, and interests in a partnership
        (2) Property held for business use may be exchanged for investment property or vice versa.
        (3) Like-kind means "same class of property."

            (a) Real property must be exchanged for real property; personal property must be exchanged for personal property within the same General Asset Class or within the same Product Class. For example

                1] Land held for investment exchanged for apartment building
                2] Real estate exchanged for a lease on real estate to run thirty years or more
                3] Truck exchanged for a truck

            (b) Exchange of personal property for real property does not qualify.
            (c) Exchange of US real property for foreign real property does not qualify.

        (4) To qualify as a like-kind exchange (1) the property to be received must be identified within 45 days after the date on which the old property is relinquished, and (2) the exchange must be completed within 180 days after the date on which the old property is relinquished, but not later than the due date of the tax return (including extensions) for the year that the old property is relinquished.
        (5) The **basis of like-kind property received** is the basis of like-kind property given.

            (a) + Gain recognized
            (b) + Basis of boot given (money or property not of a like-kind)
            (c) − Loss recognized
            (d) − FMV of boot received

        (6) If unlike property (i.e., boot) is received, its basis will be its FMV on the date of the exchange.
        (7) If property is exchanged solely for other like-kind property, no gain or loss is recognized. The basis of the property received is the same as the basis of the property transferred.
        (8) If boot (money or property not of a like-kind) is given, no gain or loss is generally recognized. However, gain or loss is recognized if the boot given consists of property with a FMV different from its basis.

> **EXAMPLE**
>
> Land held for investment plus shares of stock are exchanged for investment real estate with a FMV of $13,000. The land transferred had an adjusted basis of $10,000 and FMV of $11,000; the stock had an adjusted basis of $5,000 and FMV of $2,000. A $3,000 loss is recognized on the transfer of stock. The basis of the acquired real estate is $12,000 ($10,000 + $5,000 basis of boot given – $3,000 loss recognized).

(9) **If boot is received**

    (a) Any realized gain is recognized to the extent of the lesser of (1) the realized gain, or (2) the FMV of the boot received

    (b) No loss is recognized due to the receipt of boot

> **EXAMPLE**
>
> Land held for investment with a basis of $10,000 was exchanged for other investment real estate with a FMV of $9,000, an automobile with a FMV of $2,000, and $1,500 in cash. The realized gain is $2,500. Even though $3,500 of "boot" was received, the recognized gain is only $2,500 (limited to the realized gain). The basis of the automobile (unlike property) is its FMV $2,000; while the basis of the real estate acquired is $9,000 ($10,000 + $2,500 gain recognized – $3,500 boot received).

(10) **Liabilities** assumed (or liabilities to which property exchanged is subject) on either or both sides of the exchange are treated as boot.

    (a) Boot received—if the liability was assumed by the other party

    (b) Boot given—if the taxpayer assumed a liability on the property acquired

    (c) If liabilities are assumed on both sides of the exchange, they are offset to determine the net amount of boot given or received.

> **EXAMPLE**
>
> A owns investment land with an adjusted basis of $50,000, FMV of $70,000, but which is subject to a mortgage of $15,000. B owns investment land with an adjusted basis of $60,000, FMV of $65,000, but which is subject to a mortgage of $10,000. A and B exchange real estate investments with A assuming B's $10,000 mortgage, and B assuming A's $15,000 mortgage. The computation of realized gain, recognized gain, and basis for the acquired real estate for both A and B is as follows:
>
> | | A | | B |
> |---|---|---|---|
> | FMV of real estate received | $65,000 | | $70,000 |
> | + Liability on old real estate assumed by other party (boot received) | 15,000 | (1) | 10,000 |
> | Amount realized on the exchange | $80,000 | | $80,000 |
> | – Adjusted basis of old real estate transferred | –50,000 | | – 60,000 |
> | – Liability assumed by taxpayer on new real estate (boot given) | –10,000 | (2) | – 15,000 |
> | Gain realized | $20,000 | | $ 5,000 |
> | Gain recognized (1) minus (2) | $ 5,000 | | $ -- |
> | | | | |
> | Basis of old real estate transferred | $50,000 | | $60,000 |
> | + Liability assumed by taxpayer on new real estate (boot given) | 10,000 | | 15,000 |
> | + Gain recognized | 5,000 | | -- |
> | – Liability on old real estate assumed by other party (boot received) | –15,000 | | – 10,000 |
> | Basis of new real estate acquired | $50,000 | | $65,000 |

    (d) Boot given in the form of an assumption of a liability does **not** offset boot received in the form of cash or unlike property; however, boot given in the form of cash or unlike property does offset boot received in the form of a liability assumed by the other party.

> **EXAMPLE**
>
> Assume the same facts as above except that the mortgage on B's old real estate was $6,000, and that A paid B cash of $4,000 to make up the difference. The tax effects to A remain unchanged. However, since the $4,000 cash cannot be offset by the liability assumed by B, B must recognize a gain of $4,000, and will have a basis of $69,000 for the new real estate.

(11) If within two years after a like-kind exchange between related persons [as defined in Sec. 267(b)] either person disposes of the property received in the exchange, any gain or loss that was not recognized on the exchange must be recognized (subject to the loss limitation rules for related persons) as of the date that the property was disposed of. This gain recognition rule does not apply if the subsequent disposition was the result of the death of one of the persons, an involuntary conversion, or where neither the exchange nor the disposition had tax avoidance as one of its principal purposes.

> **NOW REVIEW MULTIPLE-CHOICE QUESTIONS 17 THROUGH 22 IN VOLUME 2**

b. **Involuntary conversions**

(1) Occur when money or other property is received for property that has been destroyed, damaged, stolen, or condemned (even if property is transferred only under threat or imminence of condemnation).

(2) If payment is received and gain is realized, taxpayer may **elect not to recognize gain** if converted property is replaced with property of similar or related use.

    (a) Gain is recognized only to the extent that the amount realized exceeds the cost of the replacement.

    (b) The **replacement** must be purchased within a **period** beginning with the earlier of the date of disposition or the date of threat of condemnation, and ending two years after the close of the taxable year in which gain is first **realized** (three years for condemned business or investment real property, other than inventory or property held primarily for resale).

    (c) **Basis of replacement property** is the cost of the replacement decreased by any gain not recognized.

> **EXAMPLE**
>
> Taxpayer had unimproved real estate (with an adjusted basis of $20,000) which was condemned by the county. The county paid him $24,000 and he reinvested $21,000 in unimproved real estate. $1,000 of the $4,000 realized gain would not be recognized. His tax basis in the new real estate would be $20,000 ($21,000 cost – $1,000 deferred gain).

> **EXAMPLE**
>
> Assume the same facts as above except the taxpayer reinvested $25,000 in unimproved real estate. None of the $4,000 realized gain would be recognized. His basis in the new real estate would be $21,000 ($25,000 cost – $4,000 deferred gain).

(3) If property is converted directly into property similar or related in service or use, complete nonrecognition of gain is mandatory. The basis of replacement property is the same as the property converted.

(4) The meaning of **property similar or related in service or use** is more restrictive than "like-kind."

    (a) For an owner-user—property must be functionally the same and have same end use (business vehicle must be replaced by business vehicle that performs same function).

    (b) For a lessor—property must perform same services for **lessor** (lessor could replace a rental manufacturing plant with a rental-wholesale grocery warehouse even though tenant's functional use differs).

    (c) A purchase of at least 80% of the stock of a corporation whose property is similar or related in service or use also qualifies.

    (d) More liberal "like-kind" test applies to real property held for business or investment (other than inventory or property held primarily for sale) that is converted by seizure, condemnation, or threat of condemnation (e.g., improved real estate could be replaced with unimproved real estate).

(5) If property is not replaced within the time limit, an amended return is filed to recognize gain in the year realized.

    (6) Losses on involuntary conversions are recognized whether the property is replaced or not. However, a loss on condemnation of property held for personal use (e.g., personal residence) is not deductible.

c. **Sale or exchange of principal residence**

    (1) An individual may **exclude** from income up to **$250,000** of gain that is realized on the sale or exchange of a residence, if the individual owned and occupied the residence as a principal residence for an aggregate of *at least two of the five years* preceding the sale or exchange. The amount of excludable gain is increased to **$500,000** for married individuals filing jointly if either spouse meets the ownership requirement, and both spouses meet the use requirement.

        (a) The sale of a residence that had been jointly owned and occupied by the surviving and deceased spouse is entitled to the $500,000 gain exclusion provided the sale occurs no later than 2 years after the date of death of the individual's spouse.

        (b) The exclusion does not apply to property acquired in a like-kind exchange after October 22, 2004, if the sale or exchange of the property occurs during the five-year period beginning with the date of acquisition of the property.

        (c) Gain in excess of the $250,000 (or $500,000) exclusion must be included in income even though the sale proceeds are reinvested in another principal residence.

    (2) The exclusion is determined on an individual basis.

        (a) A single individual who otherwise qualifies for the exclusion is entitled to exclude up to $250,000 of gain even though the individual marries someone who has used the exclusion within two years before the marriage.

        (b) In the case of married taxpayers who do not share a principal residence but file joint returns, a $250,000 exclusion is available for a qualifying sale or exchange of each spouse's principal residence.

    (3) Special rules apply to divorced taxpayers.

        (a) If a residence is transferred to a taxpayer incident to a divorce, the time during which the taxpayer's spouse or former spouse owned the residence is added to the taxpayer's period of ownership.

        (b) A taxpayer who owns a residence is deemed to use it as a principal residence while the taxpayer's spouse or former spouse is given use of the residence under the terms of a divorce or separation.

    (4) A taxpayer's period of ownership of a residence includes the period during which the taxpayer's deceased spouse owned the residence so long as the taxpayer does not remarry before date of sale.

    (5) Tenant-stockholders in a cooperative housing corporation can qualify to exclude gain from the sale of the stock.

    (6) If the taxpayer does not meet the two-year ownership or use requirements, a pro rata amount of the $250,000 or $500,000 exclusion applies if the sale or exchange is due to a change in place of employment, health, or unforeseen circumstances. A taxpayer is deemed to satisfy the change in employment condition if the taxpayer moves at least fifty miles from his former place of employment, or if previously unemployed at least fifty miles from his former residence. To satisfy the change of health condition, the taxpayer must be instructed to relocate by a physician for health reasons (e.g., advanced age-related infirmities, severe allergies, emotional problems). Unforeseen circumstances include natural or man-made disasters such as war or acts of terrorism, cessation of employment, death, divorce or legal separation, and multiple births from the same pregnancy.

> **EXAMPLE**
>
> Harold, an unmarried taxpayer, purchased a home in a suburb of Chicago on October 1, 2010. Eighteen months later his employer transferred him to St. Louis and Harold sold his home for a gain of $200,000. Since Harold sold his home because of a change in place of employment and had owned and used the home as a principal residence for eighteen months, the exclusion of his gain is limited to $250,000 × 18/24 = $187,500.

    (7) If a taxpayer was entitled to take depreciation deductions because the residence was used for business purposes or as rental property, the taxpayer cannot exclude gain to the extent of any depreciation allowed or allowable as a deduction after May 6, 1997.

> **EXAMPLE**
>
> Ron sold his principal residence during 2012 for a gain of $20,000. He used one room of the residence for business and deducted $1,000 of depreciation in 2011. Although Ron meets the ownership and use tests to exclude residence sale gain from income, he can exclude only $20,000 – $1,000 = $19,000 from income. The remaining $1,000 of gain is taxable and must be included in gross income.

(8) For sales and exchanges of a principal residence after 2008, the exclusion does not apply to the amount of gain allocated to periods of nonqualified use after December 31, 2008. *Nonqualified use* is generally any use other than as a principal residence.

   (a) Nonqualified use does not include (1) any portion of the 5-year period ending on the date of sale or exchange after the last use of the property as a principal residence; (2) any period of 10 years or less when the taxpayer or spouse is serving on extended duty in the military; and, (3) any period of two years or less for temporary absence due to a change of employment, health, or unforeseen circumstances.

   (b) To determine the amount of gain allocated to nonqualified use, multiply the gain by the following fraction:

$$\frac{\text{Total nonqualified use during period of ownership after 2008}}{\text{Total period of ownership}}$$

   (c) Any gain recognized because of post-May 6, 1997 depreciation [see (7) above] is not taken into account in determining the amount of gain allocated to nonqualified use.

> **EXAMPLE**
>
> On January 2, 2009, Diane buys a residence for $400,000 and uses it as rental property for two years, claiming $30,000 of depreciation deductions. On January 2, 2011, Diane converts the property to her principal residence. She moves out on January 11, 2013, and sells the property for $700,000 on January 2, 2014, resulting in a gain of $700,000 – $370,000 = $330,000.
>
> The $30,000 of gain that is attributable to depreciation deductions must be included in income. Of the remaining $300,000 of gain, 2 years/5 years × $300,000 = $120,000 of gain is allocated to nonqualified use and is not eligible for exclusion. Since the remaining gain of $300,000 – $120,000 = $180,000 does not exceed the maximum exclusion ($250,000), Diane can exclude a total of $180,000 of gain from gross income. As a result, Diane must include $330,000 – $180,000 = $150,000 in gross income. Finally, note that the period from January 11, 2013, to January 2, 2014, is after she last used the home as her principal residence so it is not a period of nonqualified use.

(9) Gain from the sale of a principal residence generally cannot be excluded from gross income if, during the two-year period ending on the date of the sale, the taxpayer sold another residence at a gain and excluded all or part of that gain from income. However, part of the gain may be excluded if the sale is due to a change in employment, health, or unforeseen circumstances. If the taxpayer cannot exclude the gain, it must be included in gross income.

> **EXAMPLE**
>
> In September 2009, Anna purchased a new principal residence. In November 2009, Anna sold her old residence for a gain of $50,000. Since she met the ownership and use tests, Anna excluded the $50,000 gain from gross income for 2009. On October 10, 2011, Anna sold the residence she had purchased in September 2009 for a gain of $30,000. The sale was not due to a change in place of employment, health, or unforeseen circumstances. Because Anna had excluded gain from the sale of another residence within the two-year period ending on October 10, 2011, she cannot exclude the gain on this sale.

(10) A loss from the sale of personal residence is not deductible.

NOW REVIEW MULTIPLE-CHOICE QUESTIONS 23 THROUGH 26 IN VOLUME 2

d. **Exchange of insurance policies.** No gain or loss is recognized on an exchange of certain life, endowment, and annuity contracts to allow taxpayers to obtain better insurance.

5. **Sales and exchanges of securities**

   a. Stocks and bonds are not included under like-kind exchanges
   b. Exchange of stock of same corporation

      (1) Common for common, or preferred for preferred is nontaxable
      (2) Common for preferred, or preferred for common is taxable, unless exchange qualifies as a recapitalization

   c. Exercise of conversion privilege in convertible stock or bond is generally nontaxable.
   d. The first-in, first-out (FIFO) method is used to determine the basis of securities sold unless the taxpayer can specifically identify the securities sold and uses specific identification.
   e. **Capital gains exclusion for small business stock**

      (1) A noncorporate taxpayer can exclude 50% of capital gains resulting from the sale of qualified small business stock (QSBS) held for more than five years. The exclusion is increased to 75% if the QSBS was acquired after February 17, 2009, and before September 28, 2010, and 100% for QSBS acquired after September 27, 2010, and before January 1, 2012.
      (2) To qualify, the stock must be acquired directly (or indirectly through a pass-through entity) at its original issuance.
      (3) A qualified small business is a C corporation with $50 million or less of capitalization. Generally, personal service, banking, leasing, investing, real estate, farming, mineral extraction, and hospitality businesses do not qualify as eligible small businesses.
      (4) Gains eligible for exclusion are limited to the greater of $10 million, or 10 times the investor's stock basis.

         (a) 7% of the excluded gain is generally treated as a tax preference for AMT purposes. However, there is no tax preference for gains qualifying for the 100% exclusion.
         (b) Only gains net of exclusion are included in determining the investment interest expense and capital loss limitations.

   f. **Rollover of capital gain from publicly traded securities**

      (1) An individual or C corporation may elect to roll over an otherwise currently taxable capital gain from the sale of publicly traded securities if the sale proceeds are used to purchase common stock or a partnership interest in a specialized small business investment company (SSBIC) within sixty days of the sale of the securities.
      (2) An SSBIC is a partnership or corporation licensed by the Small Business Administration under the Small Business Investment Act of 1958 as in effect on May 13, 1993.
      (3) The amount of gain eligible for rollover is limited to $50,000 per year for individuals (lifetime cap of $500,000) and $250,000 per year for corporations (lifetime cap of $1 million).
      (4) The taxpayer's basis in the SSBIC stock or partnership interest must be reduced by the gain that is rolled over.

   g. **Market discount bonds**

      (1) Gain on the disposition of a bond (including a tax-exempt bond) that was acquired for a price that was less than the principal amount of the bond is treated as taxable interest income to the extent of the accrued market discount for bonds purchased after April 30, 1993.
      (2) Accrued market discount is the difference between the bond's cost basis and its redemption value at maturity amortized over the remaining life of the bond.

   h. **Wash sales**

      (1) Wash sale occurs when stock or securities (or options to acquire stock or securities) are sold at a loss and within **thirty days before or after the sale,** substantially identical stock or securities (or options to acquire them) in the same corporation are purchased.
      (2) Wash sale loss is not deductible, but is added to the basis of the new stock.
      (3) Wash sale rules do not apply to gains.

EXAMPLE

C purchased 100 shares of XYZ Corporation stock for $1,000. C later sold the stock for $700, and within thirty days acquired 100 shares of XYZ Corporation stock for $800. The loss of $300 on the sale of stock is not recognized. However, the unrecognized loss of $300 is added to the $800 cost of the new stock to arrive at the basis for the new stock of $1,100. The holding period of the new stock includes the period of time the old stock was held.

---

(4) Does not apply to dealers in stock and securities where loss is sustained in ordinary course of business.

   i. **Worthless stock and securities**

     (1) Treated as a capital loss as if sold on the last day of the taxable year they become worthless.

     (2) Treated as an ordinary loss if stock and securities are those of an **80% or more owned corporate subsidiary** that derived more than 90% of its gross receipts from active-type sources.

6. **Losses on deposits in insolvent financial institutions**

   a. Loss resulting from a nonbusiness deposit in an insolvent financial institution is generally treated as a nonbusiness bad debt deductible as a short-term capital loss (STCL) in the year in which a final determination of the amount of loss can be made.

   b. As an alternative, if a reasonable estimate of the amount of loss can be made, an individual may elect to

     (1) Treat the loss as a personal casualty loss subject to the $100 floor and 10% of AGI limitation. Then no bad debt deduction can be claimed.

     (2) In lieu of (1) above, treat up to $20,000 as a miscellaneous itemized deduction subject to the 2% of AGI floor if the deposit was not federally insured. Then remainder of loss is treated as a STCL.

EXAMPLE

An individual with no capital gains and an AGI of $70,000, incurred a loss on a federally insured deposit in a financial institution of $30,000. The individual may treat the loss as a $30,000 STCL subject to the $3,000 net capital loss deduction limitation, with the remaining $27,000 carried forward as a STCL; or, may treat the loss as a personal casualty loss and an itemized deduction of [($30,000 – $100) – (10% × $70,000)] = $22,900. If the deposit had **not** been federally insured, the individual could also have taken a miscellaneous itemized deduction of [$20,000 – (2% × $70,000)] = $18,600, with the remaining $10,000 treated as a STCL (i.e., $3,000 net capital loss deduction and a $7,000 STCL carryover).

> **NOW REVIEW MULTIPLE-CHOICE QUESTIONS 27 THROUGH 31 IN VOLUME 2**

7. **Losses, expenses, and interest between related taxpayers**

   a. **Loss is disallowed** on the sale or exchange of property to a related taxpayer.

     (1) Transferee's basis is cost; holding period begins when transferee acquires property.

     (2) On a later resale, any gain recognized by the transferee is reduced by the disallowed loss (unless the transferor's loss was from a wash sale, in which case no reduction is allowed).

     (3) **Related taxpayers** include

       (a) Members of a family, including spouse, brothers, sisters, ancestors, and lineal descendants

       (b) A corporation and a more than 50% shareholder

       (c) Two corporations which are members of the same controlled group

       (d) A person and an exempt organization controlled by that person

       (e) Certain related individuals in a trust, including the grantor or beneficiary and the fiduciary

       (f) A C corporation and a partnership if the same persons own more than 50% of the corporation, and more than 50% of the capital and profits interest in the partnership

       (g) Two S corporations if the same persons own more than 50% of each

       (h) An S corporation and a C corporation if the same persons own more than 50% of each

---

EXAMPLE

During August 2011, Bob sold stock with a basis of $4,000 to his brother Ray for $3,000, its FMV. During June 2012, Ray sold the stock to an unrelated taxpayer for $4,500. Bob's loss of $1,000 is disallowed; Ray recognizes a STCG of ($4,500 – $3,000) – $1,000 disallowed loss = $500.

---

     (4) **Constructive stock ownership rules** apply in determining if taxpayers are related. For purposes of determining stock ownership

       (a) Stock owned, directly or indirectly, by a corporation, partnership, estate, or trust is considered as being owned proportionately by its shareholders, partners, or beneficiaries.

    (b) An individual is considered as owning the stock owned, directly or indirectly, by his brothers and sisters (whole or half blood), spouse, ancestors, and lineal descendants.

    (c) An individual owning stock in a corporation [other than by (b) above] is considered as owning the stock owned, directly or indirectly, by his partner.

  b. The disallowed loss rule in a. above does not apply to transfers between spouses, or former spouses incident to divorce, as discussed below.

  c. Any loss from the sale or exchange of property between corporations that are members of the same **controlled group** is deferred (instead of disallowed) until the property is sold outside the group. Use controlled group definition found in Module 37, D.2., but substitute "more than 50%" for "at least 80%."

> **EXAMPLE**
>
> Mr. Gudjob is the sole shareholder of X Corp. and Y Corp. During 2011, X Corp. sold nondepreciable property with a basis of $8,000 to Y Corp. for $6,000, its FMV. During 2012, Y Corp. sold the property to an unrelated taxpayer for $6,500. X Corp.'s loss in 2011 is deferred. In 2012, X Corp. recognizes the $2,000 of deferred loss, and Y Corp. recognizes a gain of $500.

  d. An accrual-basis payor is effectively placed on the cash method of accounting for purposes of deducting accrued interest and other expenses owed to a related cash-basis payee.

    (1) No deduction is allowable until the year the amount is actually paid.

    (2) This rule applies to pass-through entities (e.g., a partnership and **any** partner; two partnerships if the same persons own more than 50% of each; an S corporation and **any** shareholder) in addition to the related taxpayers described in a.(3) above, but does not apply to guaranteed payments to partners. This rule also applies to a personal service corporation and **any** employee-owner.

> **EXAMPLE**
>
> A calendar-year S corporation accrued a $500 bonus owed to an employee-shareholder in 2011 but did not pay the bonus until February 2012. The $500 bonus will be deductible by the S corporation in 2012, when the employee-shareholder reports the $500 as income.

8. **Transfers in part a sale and in part a gift**

  a. If a transfer of property is in part a sale and in part a gift, the transferor recognizes gain to the extent that the amount realized exceeds the transferor's adjusted basis for the property transferred. However, no loss can be recognized by the transferor.

  b. The basis of the property to the transferee is generally the greater of (1) the amount paid by the transferee for the property, or (2) the transferor's basis for the property at the time of the transfer. However, for purposes of determining a loss, the basis of the property in the hands of the transferee shall not be greater than the fair market value of the property at the time of the transfer.

> **EXAMPLE**
>
> Alan transfers property to his sister, Brianna, for $60,000. The property has a basis of $40,000 and a FMV of $90,000 at date of transfer. Alan must recognize a gain of $60,000 – $40,000 = $20,000, and has made a gift to Brianna of $90,000 – $60,000 = $30,000. Brianna's basis for the property is $60,000.

> **EXAMPLE**
>
> Brenda transfers property to her brother, Carl, for $30,000. The transferred property has a basis of $40,000 and a FMV of $90,000 at date of transfer. Brenda's realized loss of $40,000 – $30,000 = $10,000 cannot be recognized, and she has made a gift to Carl of $90,000 – $30,000 = $60,000. Carl's basis for the property is $40,000.

> **EXAMPLE**
>
> David transfers property to his son, Evan, for $30,000. The property has a basis of $90,000 and a FMV of $60,000 at date of transfer. David's realized loss of $90,000 – $30,000 = $60,000 cannot be recognized, and

> he has made a gift to Evan of $60,000 – $30,000 = $30,000. Evan's basis for the property is $90,000. However, for purposes of determining a loss on a later sale or other disposition of the property by Evan, the property's basis is limited to its FMV at date of transfer of $60,000.

9. **Transfer between spouses**

   a. No gain or loss is generally recognized on the transfer of property from an individual to (or in trust for the benefit of)

      (1) A spouse (other than a nonresident alien spouse), or
      (2) A former spouse (other than a nonresident alien former spouse), if the transfer is related to the cessation of marriage, or occurs within one year after marriage ceases

   b. Transfer is treated as if it were a gift from one spouse to the other.
   c. Transferee's basis in the property received will be the transferor's basis (even if FMV is less than the property's basis).

EXAMPLE

H sells property with a basis of $6,000 to his spouse, W, for $8,000. No gain is recognized to H, and W's basis for the property is $6,000. W's holding period includes the period that H held the property.

---

   d. If property is transferred to a **trust** for the benefit of a spouse or former spouse (incident to divorce)

      (1) Gain is recognized to the extent that the amount of liabilities assumed exceeds the total adjusted basis of property transferred.
      (2) Gain or loss is recognized on the transfer of installment obligations.

10. Gain from the sale or exchange of property will be entirely ordinary gain (no capital gain) if the property is depreciable in hands of transferee and the sale or exchange is between

   a. A person and a more than 50% owned corporation or partnership
   b. A taxpayer and any trust in which such taxpayer or spouse is a beneficiary, unless such beneficiary's interest is a remote contingent interest
   c. Constructive ownership rules apply; use rules in Section 7.a.(4)(a) and (b) above

---

NOW REVIEW MULTIPLE-CHOICE QUESTIONS 32 THROUGH 37 IN VOLUME 2

B. Capital Gains and Losses

1. Capital gains and losses result from the "sale or exchange of capital assets." The term **capital assets** includes investment property and property held for personal use. The term specifically **excludes**

   a. Stock in trade, inventory, or goods held primarily for sale to customers in the normal course of business
   b. Depreciable or real property used in a trade or business
   c. Copyrights or artistic, literary, etc., compositions created by the taxpayer

      (1) They are capital assets only if purchased by the taxpayer.
      (2) Patents are generally capital assets in the hands of the inventor.

   d. Accounts or notes receivable arising from normal business activities
   e. US government publications acquired other than by purchase at regular price
   f. Supplies of a type regularly used or consumed by a taxpayer in the ordinary course of the taxpayer's trade or business

2. Whether short-term or long-term depends upon the **holding period**

   a. Long-term if held more than one year
   b. The day property was acquired is excluded and the day it is disposed of is included.
   c. Use calendar months (e.g., if held from January 4 to January 4 it is held exactly one year)
   d. If stock or securities which are traded on an established securities market (or other property regularly traded on an established market) are sold, any resulting gain or loss is recognized on the date the trade is executed (transaction date) by both cash and accrual taxpayers.

e. The holding period of property received in a nontaxable exchange (e.g., like-kind exchange, involuntary conversion) includes the holding period of the property exchanged, if the property that was exchanged was a capital asset or Sec. 1231 asset.

f. If the basis of property to a prior owner carries over to the present owner (e.g., gift), the holding period of the prior owner "tacks on" to the present owner's holding period.

g. If using the lower FMV on date of gift to determine loss, then holding period begins when the gift is received.

> **EXAMPLE**
>
> X purchased property on July 14, 2011, for $10,000. X made a gift of the property to Z on June 10, 2012, when its FMV was $8,000. Since Z's basis for gain is $10,000, Z's holding period for a disposition at a gain extends back to July 14, 2011. Since Z's $8,000 basis for loss is determined by reference to FMV at June 10, 2012, Z's holding period for a disposition at a loss begins on June 11.

h. Property acquired from a decedent is generally given long-term treatment, regardless of how long the property was held by the decedent or beneficiary, and is treated as property held more than twelve months.

3. Computation of capital gains and losses for **all taxpayers**

   a. First net STCG with STCL and net LTCG with LTCL to determine

      (1) Net short-term capital gain or loss (NSTCG or NSTCL)
      (2) Net long-term capital gain or loss (NLTCG or NLTCL)

   b. Then net these two together to determine whether there is a net capital gain or loss (NCG or NCL)

4. The following rules apply to individuals:

   a. Capital gains offset capital losses, with any remaining net capital gains included in gross income.
   b. Net capital gains are subject to tax at various rates, depending on the type of assets sold or exchanged and length of time the assets were held.

      (1) Capital gain from assets held one year or less is taxed at the taxpayer's regular tax rates (up to 35%).
      (2) Capital gain from the sale of collectibles held more than twelve months (e.g., antiques, art, metals, gems, rugs, stamps, coins, alcoholic beverages) is taxed at a maximum rate of 28%.
      (3) Capital gain attributable to unrecaptured depreciation on Sec. 1250 property held more than twelve months is taxed at a maximum rate of 25%.
      (4) Capital gain from assets held more than twelve months (other than from collectibles and unrecaptured depreciation on Sec. 1250 property) is taxed at a rate of 15% (or for tax years beginning before January 1, 2013, 0% for individuals in the 10% or 15% tax bracket).
      (5) For installment sales of assets held more than twelve months, the date an installment payment is received (not the date the asset was sold) determines the capital gains rate that should be applied

   c. Gains and losses (including carryovers) within each of the rate groups are netted to arrive at a net gain or loss. A net loss in any rate group is applied to reduce the net gain in the highest rate group first (e.g., a net short-term capital loss is applied to reduce any net gain from the 28% group, then the 25% group, and finally to reduce gain from the 15% group).

> **EXAMPLE**
>
> Kim, who is in the 35% tax bracket, had the following capital gains and losses for calendar-year 2011:
>
> | | |
> |---|---:|
> | Net short-term capital loss | $(1,500) |
> | 28% group—collectibles net gain | 900 |
> | 25% group—unrecaptured Sec. 1250 net gain | 2,000 |
> | 15% group—net gain | 5,000 |
> | Net capital gain | $ 6,400 |
>
> In this case, the NSTCL of $1,500 first offsets the $900 of collectibles gain, and then offsets $600 of the unrecaptured Sec. 1250 gain. As a result of this netting procedure, Kim has $1,400 of unrecaptured Sec. 1250 gain that will be taxed at a rate of 25%, and $5,000 of capital gain that will be taxed at a rate of 15%.

   d. If there is a **net capital loss** the following rules apply:

      (1) A net capital loss is a deduction in arriving at AGI, but limited to the lesser of

         (a) $3,000 ($1,500 if married filing separately), or

      (b) The excess of capital losses over capital gains

  (2) Both a NSTCL and a NLTCL are used dollar-for-dollar in computing the capital loss deduction.

> **EXAMPLE**
>
> An individual had $2,000 of NLTCL and $500 of NSTCL for 2011. The capital losses are combined and the entire net capital loss of $2,500 is deductible in computing the individual's AGI.

  (3) Short-term losses are used before long-term losses. The amount of net capital loss that exceeds the allowable deduction may be carried over for an unlimited period of time. Capital loss carryovers retain their identity; short-term losses carry over as short-term losses, and long-term losses carry over as long-term losses in the 28% group. Losses remaining unused on a decedent's final return are extinguished and provide no tax benefit.

> **EXAMPLE**
>
> An individual has a $4,000 STCL and a $5,000 LTCL for 2011. The $9,000 net capital loss results in a capital loss deduction of $3,000 for 2011, while the remainder is a carryover to 2012. Since $3,000 of the STCL would be used to create the capital loss deduction, there is a $1,000 STCL carryover and a $5,000 LTCL carryover to 2012. The $5,000 LTCL carryover would first offset gains in the 28% group.

  (4) For purposes of determining the amount of excess net capital loss that can be carried over to future years, the taxpayer's net capital loss for the year is reduced by the lesser of (1) $3,000 ($1,500 if married filing separately), or (2) adjusted taxable income.

      (a) Adjusted taxable income is taxable income increased by $3,000 ($1,500 if married filing separately) and the amount allowed for personal exemptions.

      (b) An excess of deductions allowed over gross income is taken into account as negative taxable income.

> **EXAMPLE**
>
> For 2011, a single individual with no dependents had a net capital loss of $8,000, and had allowable deductions that exceeded gross income by $4,000. For 2011, the individual is entitled to a net capital loss deduction of $3,000, and will carry over a net capital loss of $5,300 to 2012. This amount represents the 2011 net capital loss of $8,000 reduced by the lesser of (1) $3,000, or (2) – $4,000 + $3,000 + $3,700 personal exemption = $2,700.

  5. **Corporations** have special capital gain and loss rules.

    a. Capital losses are only allowed to offset capital gains, not ordinary income.

    b. A **net capital loss** is carried back three years, and forward five years to offset capital gains in those years. All capital loss carrybacks and carryovers are treated as **short-term** capital losses.

> **EXAMPLE**
>
> A corporation has a NLTCL of $8,000 and a NSTCG of $2,000, resulting in a net capital loss of $6,000 for 2011. The $6,000 NLTCL is not deductible for 2011, but is first carried back as a STCL to 2008 to offset capital gains. If not used up in 2008, the STCL is carried to 2009 and 2010, and then forward to 2012, 2013, 2014, 2015, and 2016 to offset capital gains in those years.

    c. Although an alternative tax computation still exists for a corporation with a net capital gain, the alternative tax computation applies the highest corporate rate (35%) to a net capital gain and thus provides no benefit.

> **NOW REVIEW MULTIPLE-CHOICE QUESTIONS 38 THROUGH 53 IN VOLUME 2**

C. Personal Casualty and Theft Gains and Losses

    Gains and losses from casualties and thefts of property held for personal use are separately netted, without regard to the holding period of the converted property.

  1. If gains exceed losses (after the $100 floor [$500 floor for 2009] for each loss), then all gains and losses are treated as capital gains and losses, short-term or long-term depending upon holding period.

> **EXAMPLE**
>
> An individual incurred a $25,000 personal casualty gain, and a $15,000 personal casualty loss (after the $100 floor) during the current taxable year. Since there was a net gain, the individual will report the gain and loss as a $25,000 capital gain and a $15,000 capital loss.

2. If losses (after the $100 floor [$500 floor for 2009] for each loss) exceed gains, the losses (1) offset gains, and (2) are an ordinary deduction from AGI to the extent in excess of 10% of AGI.

> **EXAMPLE**
>
> An individual had AGI of $40,000 (before casualty gains or losses), and also had a personal casualty loss of $25,000 (after the $100 floor) and a personal casualty gain of $15,000. Since there was a net personal casualty loss, the net loss will be deductible as an itemized deduction of [$25,000 – $15,000 – (10% × $40,000)] = $6,000.

D. Gains and Losses on Business Property

Although property used in a business is excluded from the definition of "capital assets," Sec. 1231 extends capital gain and loss treatment to business assets if the gains from these assets exceed losses. However, before Sec. 1231 becomes operative, Sections 1245, 1250, and 291 provide for recapture of depreciation (i.e., gain is taxed as ordinary income to the extent of certain depreciation previously deducted).

1. All gains and losses are **ordinary** on business property **held one year or less**.
2. **Section 1231**

   a. All property included must have been held for **more than one year**.

      (1) Section 1231 gains and losses include those from

         (a) Sale or exchange of property used in trade or business (or held for production of rents or royalties) and which is not

            1] Inventory
            2] A copyright or artistic composition

         (b) Casualty, theft, or condemnation of

            1] Property used in trade or business
            2] Capital assets held in connection with a trade or business, or a transaction entered into for profit

         (c) Infrequently encountered items such as cut timber, coal and domestic iron ore, livestock, and unharvested crop

   b. The combining of Sec. 1231 gains and losses is accomplished in **two steps**. **First,** net all casualty and theft gains and losses on property held for more than one year.

      (1) If the losses exceed gains, treat them all as ordinary losses and gains and do not net them with other Sec. 1231 gains and losses.
      (2) If the gains exceed losses, the net gain is combined with other Sec. 1231 gains and losses.

   c. **Second,** net all other Sec. 1231 gains and losses (except casualty and theft net loss per above).

      (1) Include casualty and theft net gain
      (2) Include gains and losses from condemnations (other than condemnations on nonbusiness, non-income-producing property)
      (3) Include gains and losses from the sale or exchange of property used in trade or business

   d. If losses exceed gains, treat all gains and losses as ordinary.
   e. If gains exceed losses, treat the Sec. 1231 net gain as a long-term capital gain.

> **EXAMPLE**
>
> Taxpayer has a gain of $10,000 from the sale of land used in his business, a loss of $4,000 on the sale of depreciable property used in his business, and a $2,000 (noninsured) loss when a car used in his business was involved in a collision.

The net gain or loss from casualty or theft is the $2,000 loss. The net casualty loss of $2,000 is treated as an ordinary loss and not netted with other Sec. 1231 gains and losses.

The $10,000 gain is netted with the $4,000 loss resulting in a net Sec. 1231 gain of $6,000, which is then treated as a long-term capital gain.

f. Net Sec. 1231 gain will be treated as ordinary income (instead of LTCG) to the extent of nonrecaptured net Sec. 1231 losses for the five most recent taxable years.

(1) Losses are deemed recaptured in the chronological order in which they arose
(2) Any Sec. 1231 gain recharacterized as ordinary income consists first of gain in the 28% group, then gain in the 25% group, and finally gain in the 15% group

---

EXAMPLE

Corp. X, on a calendar year, has a net Sec. 1231 gain of $10,000 for 2011. For the years 2006 through 2010, Corp. X had net Sec. 1231 losses totaling $8,000. Of the $10,000 net Sec. 1231 gain for 2011, the first $8,000 will be treated as ordinary income, with only the remaining $2,000 treated as long-term capital gain.

---

3. **Section 1245 Recapture**

a. Requires the recapture as **ordinary income** of all gain attributable to

(1) **Post-1961 depreciation** on the disposition of Sec. 1245 property
(2) **Post-1980 recovery deductions** on the disposition of Sec. 1245 recovery property (including amount expensed under Sec. 179 expense election)

b. Sec. 1245 property generally includes depreciable tangible and intangible personal property, for example

(1) Desks, machines, equipment, cars, and trucks
(2) Special-purpose structures, storage facilities, and other property (but not buildings and structural components); for example, oil and gas storage tanks, grain storage bins and silos, and escalators and elevators

c. Sec. 1245 recovery property means all ACRS recovery property placed in service after 1980 and before 1987 other than nineteen-year real property that is classified as real residential rental property, real property used outside the US, subsidized low-income housing, and real property for which a straight-line election was made.

> NOTE: If the cost of nineteen-year nonresidential real property placed in service before 1987 was recovered using the prescribed percentages of ACRS, the gain on disposition is ordinary income to extent of all ACRS deductions. Such recapture is not limited to the excess of accelerated depreciation over straight-line. However, if the straight-line method was elected for nineteen-year real property, there is no recapture and all gain is Sec. 1231 gain.

d. Sec. 1245 does not apply to real residential rental property and nonresidential real property placed in service after 1986 because only straight-line depreciation is allowable.

e. Upon the disposition of property subject to Sec. 1245, any recognized gain will be ordinary income to the extent of all depreciation or post-1980 cost recovery deductions.

(1) Any remaining gain after recapture will be Sec. 1231 gain if property held more than one year.

EXAMPLE

Megan sold equipment used in her business for $11,000. The equipment had cost $10,000 and $6,000 of depreciation had been taken, resulting in an adjusted basis of $4,000. Megan's recognized gain is $11,000 − $4,000 = $7,000. Since the equipment was Sec. 1245 property, the gain must be recognized as Sec. 1245 ordinary income to the extent of the $6,000 of depreciation deducted. The remaining $1,000 gain ($7,000 gain − $6,000 ordinary income) is recognized as Sec. 1231 gain.

EXAMPLE

Assume the same facts as in the preceding example, except the equipment was sold for $9,000. Megan's recognized gain would be $9,000 − $4,000 = $5,000. Now, since the $6,000 of depreciation deducted exceeds the recognized gain of $5,000, the amount of Sec. 1245 ordinary income would be limited to the recognized gain of $5,000. There would be no Sec. 1231 gain.

> **EXAMPLE**
>
> Assume the same facts as in the first example, except the equipment was sold for only $3,500. Megan's sale of the equipment now results in a recognized loss of $3,500 – $4,000 = ($500). Since there is a loss, there would be no Sec. 1245 depreciation recapture and the $500 loss would be classified as a Sec. 1231 loss.

(2) If the disposition is not by sale, use FMV of property (instead of selling price) to determine gain.

    (a) When boot is received in a like-kind exchange, Sec. 1245 will apply to the recognized gain.

> **EXAMPLE**
>
> Taxpayer exchanged his old machine (adjusted basis of $2,500) for a smaller new machine worth $5,000 and received $1,000 cash. Depreciation of $7,500 had been taken on the old machine. The realized gain of $3,500 ($6,000 – $2,500) will be recognized to the extent of the $1,000 boot, and will be treated as ordinary income as the result of Sec. 1245.

    (b) Sec. 1245 recapture does not apply to transfers by gift (including charitable contributions) or transfers at death.

4. **Section 1250 Recapture**

    a. Applies to all real property (e.g., buildings and structural components) that is not Sec. 1245 recovery property.

      (1) If Sec. 1250 property was held twelve months or less, gain on disposition is recaptured as ordinary income to extent of all depreciation (including straight-line).

> **EXAMPLE**
>
> Alan, who is in the 35% tax bracket, owned an office building purchased for $900,000 during March, 2011. The building was sold for $890,000 during February, 2012, when its adjusted basis was $880,000. Since the building was not held for more than one year, the $10,000 gain is treated as ordinary income and is subject to tax at Alan's 35% rate.

      (2) If Sec. 1250 property was held more than twelve months, gain is recaptured as ordinary income to the extent of post-1969 **additional depreciation** (generally depreciation in excess of straight-line).

> **EXAMPLE**
>
> Baker, who is in the 35% tax bracket, owned an office building purchased for $900,000 during March 2011. Baker deducted $30,000 of straight-line depreciation, and sold the building for $890,000 during May 2012. Since the building was held for more than one year and only straight-line depreciation was deducted, there is no Sec. 1250 recapture. However, the $890,000 – $870,000 = $20,000 of Sec. 1231 gain represents unrecaptured Sec. 1250 depreciation and will be subject to tax at a maximum rate of 25% if treated as LTCG.

> **EXAMPLE**
>
> Curt, who is in the 35% tax bracket, sold an office building with an adjusted basis of $40,000 for $350,000. The building had been purchased for $400,000 in 1980 and $360,000 of accelerated depreciation had been deducted. Straight-line depreciation would have totaled $330,000.
>
> | | |
> |---|---:|
> | Total gain ($350,000 – $40,000) | $310,000 |
> | Sec. 1250 ordinary income ($360,000 – $330,000) | (30,000) |
> | Sec. 1231 gain | $280,000 |
>
> The $30,000 of ordinary income will be taxed at 35%, while the $280,000 of Sec. 1231 gain represents unrecaptured Sec. 1250 depreciation and is subject to tax at a maximum rate of 25% if treated as LTCG.

5. **Section 291 Recapture**

    a. The ordinary income element on the disposition of Sec. 1250 property by **corporations** is increased by 20% of the additional amount that would have been ordinary income if the property had instead been Sec. 1245 property or Sec. 1245 recovery property.

EXAMPLE

Assuming the same facts as in the above example except that the building was owned and sold by Ajax Corporation, the computation of gain would be

Total gain ($350,000 – $40,000)	$310,000
Sec. 1250 ordinary income ($360,000 – $330,000)	(30,000)*
Additional ordinary income—20% of $280,000 (the additional amount that would have been ordinary income if the property were Sec. 1245 property)	(56,000)*
Sec. 1231 gain	$224,000

* All $86,000 ($30,000 + $56,000) of recapture is referred to as Sec. 1250 ordinary income.

---

6. **Summary of Gains and Losses on Business Property.** The treatment of gains and losses (other than personal casualty and theft) on property held for **more than one year** is summarized in the following **four steps** (also enumerated on flowchart at end of this section):

   a. Separate all recognized gains and losses into four categories

   (1) Ordinary gain and loss
   (2) Sec. 1231 casualty and theft gains and losses
   (3) Sec. 1231 gains and losses other than by casualty or theft
   (4) Gains and losses on capital assets (other than by casualty or theft)

   > **NOTE:** (2) and (3) are only temporary classifications and all gains and losses will ultimately receive ordinary or capital treatment.

   b. Any gain (casualty or other) on Sec. 1231 property is treated as ordinary income to extent of Sec. 1245, 1250, and 291 depreciation recapture.
   c. After depreciation recapture, any remaining Sec. 1231 casualty and theft gains and losses on business property are netted.

   (1) If losses exceed gains—the losses and gains receive ordinary treatment
   (2) If gains exceed losses—the net gain is combined with other Sec. 1231 gains and losses in d. below

   d. After recapture, any remaining Sec. 1231 gains and losses (other than by casualty or theft), are combined with any net casualty or theft gain from c. above.

   (1) If losses exceed gains—the losses and gains receive ordinary treatment
   (2) If gains exceed losses—the net gain receives LTCG treatment (except ordinary income treatment to extent of nonrecaptured net Sec. 1231 losses for the five most recent tax years)

EXAMPLE

Taxpayer incurred the following transactions during the current taxable year:

Loss on condemnation of land used in business held fifteen months	$ (500)
Loss on sale of machinery used in business held two months	(1,000)
Bad debt loss on loan made three years ago to friend	(2,000)
Gain from insurance reimbursement for tornado damage to business property held ten years	3,000
Loss on sale of business equipment held three years	(4,000)
Gain on sale of land held four years and used in business	5,000

The gains and losses would be treated as follows: Note that the loss on machinery is ordinary because it was not held more than one year.

Ordinary	Sec. 1231 Casualty	Other Sec. 1231	Capital L-T	S-T
$(1,000)	$3,000	$ (500)		$(2,000)*
		(4,000)		
		5,000		
	$3,000 →	3,000		
		$3,500 →	$3,500	
$(1,000)			$3,500	$(2,000)

* A nonbusiness bad debt is always treated as a STCL.

TAX TREATMENT OF GAINS AND LOSSES (OTHER THAN PERSONAL CASUALTY AND THEFT) ON PROPERTY HELD MORE THAN ONE YEAR

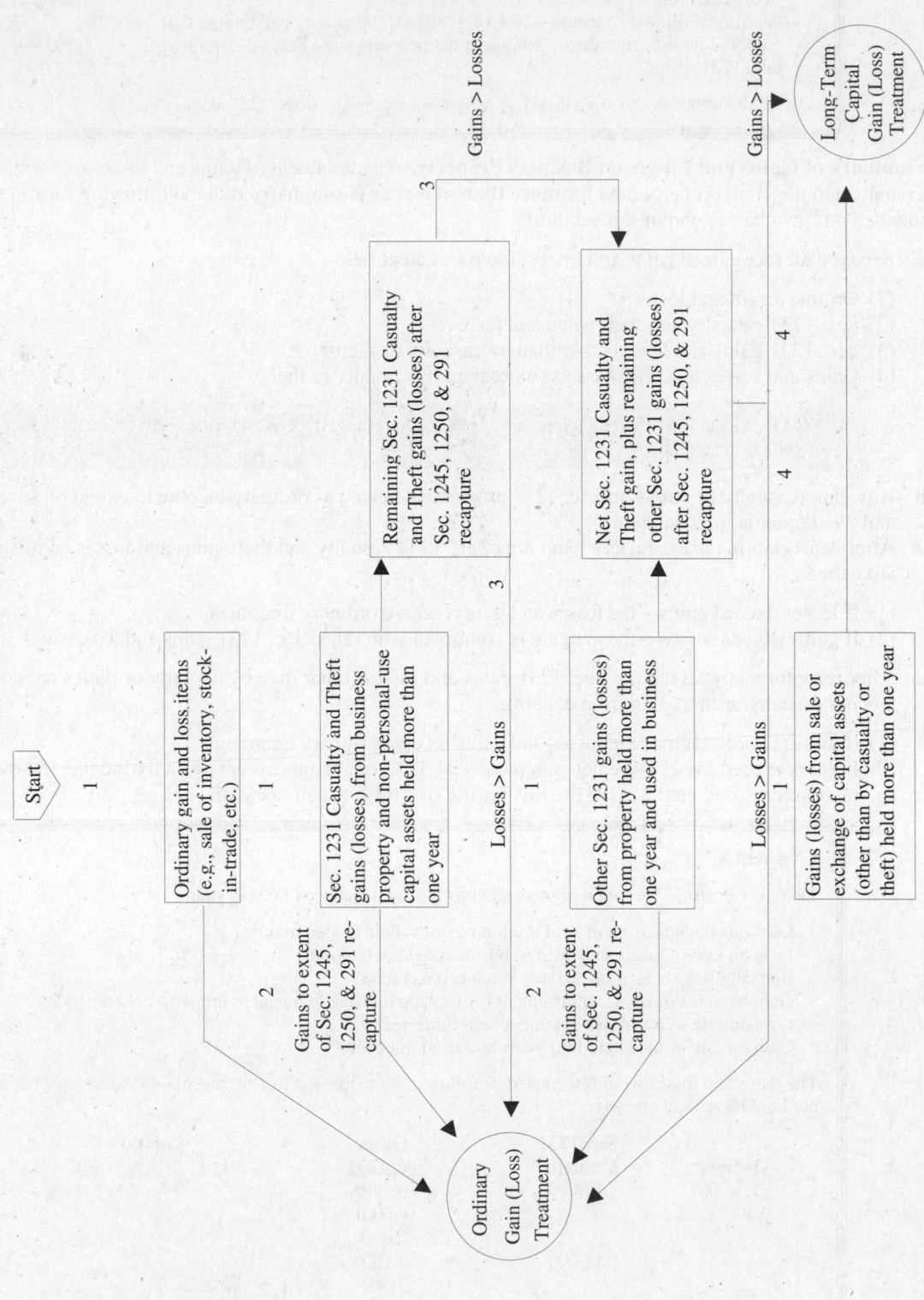

┌───┐
│   NOW REVIEW MULTIPLE-CHOICE QUESTIONS 54 THROUGH 56 IN VOLUME 2   │
└───┘

KEY TERMS

Adjusted basis. The original cost or other basis of property increased by capital improvements and reduced by depreciation and losses.

Boot. Cash or other property not permitted to be received tax-free in certain nontaxable transactions. The receipt of boot will generally cause a realized gain to be recognized to the extent of the lesser of the fair market value of such boot received or the amount of realized gain.

Capital asset. Generally all assets except inventory, notes and accounts receivable, and depreciable and nondepreciable property used in a trade or business. Capital assets generally consist of property held for investment and property held for personal use.

Involuntary conversion. Occurs when money or other property is received for property that has been destroyed, damaged, stolen, or condemned. Generally the recognition of any realized gain resulting from an involuntary conversion can, at the taxpayer's election, be deferred if the taxpayer reinvests the proceeds of conversion within a specified period of time in property that is similar or related in service or use.

Like-kind exchange. An exchange of property held for productive use in a trade or business or for investment (excluding inventory, stocks and bonds, and partnership interests) for property of a like kind. Real property must be exchanged for real property, personal property must be exchanged for personal property within the same general asset class. Generally no gain is recognized unless unlike property (boot) is received.

Long-term capital gain or loss. Gain or loss realized from the sale or exchange of a capital asset held for more than one year.

Related-taxpayer transactions. Generally no loss can be recognized from the sale or exchange of property between related taxpayers. Related taxpayers included members of a family (spouse, brothers, sisters, ancestors, and lineal descendants), and an individual and a more than 50% owned entity. Additionally, gains resulting from transactions between related taxpayers that might otherwise be classified as capital or Sec. 1231 gains may instead be taxed as ordinary income.

Section 1231 property. Depreciable and nondepreciable property used in a trade or business and held for more than one year. Inventory, accounts and notes receivable, US government publications, copyrights, literary, musical, or artistic compositions in the hands of their creator are excluded from the definition.

Section 1245 property. Generally depreciable personal property used in a trade or business or held for the production of income (e.g., machinery, equipment, trucks, autos).

Section 1245 recapture. The gain from the sale or exchange of Sec. 1245 property must be reported as ordinary income to the extent of the lesser of (1) all depreciation (including straight-line), or (2) the recognized gain.

Section 1250 property. Any real property (e.g., building) that (1) is not Sec. 1245 property and (2) is subject to the allowance of depreciation.

Section 1250 recapture. The gain from the sale or exchange of Sec. 1250 property must be reported as ordinary income to the extent that actual depreciation deductions exceeded what straight-line would have been. If Sec. 1250 property was held twelve months or less, gain on disposition is recaptured as ordinary income to the extent of all depreciation (including straight-line).

Wash sale. A loss from the sale of stock or securities is disallowed because the taxpayer, within 30 days before or after the sale, has acquired stock or securities that are substantially identical to those sold.

Module 37: Partnership Taxation

Overview

This module presents the federal tax treatment of partnerships and partners. The tax consequences of partnership formation are covered first, followed by a review of the pass-through of partnership income and loss to partners. A partner's basis for a partnership interest is covered next, with emphasis on the effect of partnership liabilities on a partner's basis. Next reviewed are the special rules that apply to transactions with controlled partnerships, as well as the limitations that apply to a partnership's adoption of a tax year. The module continues with a review of the tax effects of a partner's sale of a partnership interest, and concludes with a review of the rules that apply to a partnership's distribution of property to partners in both current and liquidating distributions. It is important to be able to determine a partner's basis for distributed property, as well as the effect of the distribution on the partner's basis for the partnership interest.

Partnerships are organizations of two or more persons to carry on business activities for profit. For tax purposes, partnerships also include a syndicate, joint venture, or other unincorporated business through which any business or financial operation is conducted. Partnerships do not pay any income tax, but instead act as a conduit to pass through tax items to the partners. Partnerships file an informational return (Form 1065), and partners report their share of partnership ordinary income or loss and other items on their individual returns. The nature or character (e.g., capital, ordinary, Sec. 1231) of income or deductions is not changed by the pass-through nature of the partnership.

A. Entity Classification

1. Eligible business entities (a business entity other than an entity automatically classified as a corporation) may choose how they will be classified for federal tax purposes by filing Form 8832. A business entity with at least two members can choose to be classified as either an association taxable as a corporation or as a partnership. A business entity with a single member can choose to be classified as either an association taxable as a corporation or disregarded as an entity separate from its owner.

    a. An eligible business entity that does not file Form 8832 will be classified under default rules. Under default rules, an eligible business entity will be classified as a partnership if it has two or more members, or disregarded as an entity separate from its owner if it has a single owner.

    b. Once an entity makes an election, a different election cannot be made for sixty months unless there is more than a 50% ownership change and the IRS consents.

2. **General partnerships** exist when two or more partners join together and do not specifically provide that one or more partners is a limited partner. Since each general partner has unlimited liability, creditors can reach the personal assets of a general partner to satisfy partnership debts, including a malpractice judgment against the partnership even though the partner was not personally involved in the malpractice.

3. **Limited partnerships** have two classes of partners, with at least one general partner (who has the same rights and responsibilities as a partner in a general partnership) and at least one limited partner. A limited partner generally cannot participate in the active management of the partnership, and in the event of losses, generally can lose no

more than his or her own capital contribution. A limited partnership is often the preferred entity of choice for real estate ventures requiring significant capital contributions.

4. **Limited liability partnerships** differ from general partnerships in that with an LLP, a partner is not liable for damages resulting from the negligence, malpractice, or fraud committed by other partners. However, each partner is personally liable for his or her own negligence, malpractice, or fraud. LLPs are often used by service providers such as architects, accountants, attorneys, and physicians.

5. **Limited liability companies** that do not elect to be treated as an association taxable as a corporation are subject to the rules applicable to partnerships (a single-member LLC would be disregarded as an entity separate from its owner). An LLC combines the nontax advantage of limited liability for each and every owner of the entity, with the tax advantage of pass-through treatment, and the flexibility of partnership taxation. The LLC structure is generally available to both nonprofessional service providers as well as capital-intensive companies.

6. **Electing large partnerships** are partnerships that have elected to be taxed under a simplified reporting system that does not require as much separate reporting to partners as does a regular partnership. For example, charitable contributions are deductible by the partnership (subject to a 10% of taxable income limitation), and the Sec. 179 expense election is deducted in computing partnership ordinary income and not separately passed through to partners. To qualify, the partnership must not be a service partnership nor engaged in commodity trading, must have at least 100 partners, and must file an election to be taxed as an electing large partnership. A partnership will cease to be an electing large partnership if it has fewer than 100 partners for a taxable year.

7. **Publicly traded partnerships** are partnerships whose interests are traded on an established securities exchange or in a secondary market and are generally taxed as C corporations.

B. Partnership Formation

1. As a general rule, **no gain or loss** is recognized by a partner when there is a contribution of property to the partnership in exchange for an interest in the partnership. There are three situations where gain must be recognized.

   a. A partner must recognize gain when property is contributed which is subject to a liability, and the resulting decrease in the partner's individual liability exceeds the partner's partnership basis.

      (1) The excess of liability over adjusted basis is generally treated as a capital gain from the sale or exchange of a partnership interest.
      (2) The gain will be treated as ordinary income to the extent the property transferred was subject to depreciation recapture under Sec. 1245 or 1250.

EXAMPLE

A partner acquires a 20% interest in a partnership by contributing property worth $10,000 but with an adjusted basis of $4,000. There is a mortgage of $6,000 that is assumed by the partnership. The partner must recognize a gain of $800, and has a zero basis for the partnership interest, calculated as follows:

Adjusted basis of contributed property	$ 4,000
Less: portion of mortgage allocated to other partners (80% × $6,000)	(4,800)
Partner's basis (not reduced below 0)	$ 0

---

   b. Gain will be recognized on a contribution of property to a partnership in exchange for an interest therein if the partnership would be an investment company if incorporated.

   c. Partner must recognize compensation income when an interest in partnership capital is received in exchange for **services rendered**.

EXAMPLE

X received a 10% capital interest in the ABC Partnership in exchange for services rendered. On the date X was admitted to the partnership, ABC's net assets had a basis of $30,000 and a FMV of $50,000. X must recognize compensation income of $5,000, and would have a basis of $5,000 for the partnership interest.

---

2. Property contributed to the partnership has the same **basis** as it had in the contributing partner's hands (a transferred basis).

   a. The basis for the partner's partnership interest is increased by the adjusted basis of property contributed.
   b. No gain or loss is generally recognized by the partnership upon the contribution.

3. The **partnership's holding period** for contributed property includes the period of time the property was held by the partner.

4. A **partner's holding period** for a partnership interest includes the holding period of property contributed, if the contributed property was a capital asset or Sec. 1231 asset in the contributing partner's hands.

5. Although not a separate taxpaying entity, the partnership must make most elections as to the tax treatment of partnership items. For example, the partnership must select a taxable year and various accounting methods which can differ from the methods used by its partners. Partnership elections include an overall method of accounting, inventory method, the method used to compute depreciation, and the election to expense depreciable assets under Sec. 179.

6. A partnership may elect to deduct up to $5,000 of organizational expenditures for the tax year in which the partnership begins business. The $5,000 amount must be reduced (but not below zero) by the amount by which **organizational expenditures** exceed $50,000. Remaining expenditures can be deducted ratably over the 180-month period beginning with the month in which the partnership begins business.

   a. For amounts paid or incurred after September 8, 2008, the partnership is deemed to have made the election to amortize costs and does not have to attach a statement to its return. Alternatively, the partnership may elect to capitalize its costs on a timely filed return (including extensions) for the taxable year in which the partnership begins business.

   b. Similar rules apply to partnership start-up expenditures.

   c. Partnership syndication fees (expenses of selling partnership interests) are neither deductible nor amortizable.

NOW REVIEW MULTIPLE-CHOICE QUESTIONS 1 THROUGH 9 IN VOLUME 2

C. Partnership Income and Loss

1. Since a partnership is not a separate taxpaying entity, but instead acts as a conduit to pass-through items of income and deduction to individual partners, the partnership's reporting of income and deductions requires a two-step approach.

   a. **First,** all items having special tax characteristics (i.e., subject to partial or full exclusion, % or dollar limitation, etc.) must be segregated and taken into account separately by each partner so that any special tax characteristics are preserved.

      (1) These special items are listed separately on Schedule K of the partnership return and include

         (a) Capital gains and losses
         (b) Sec. 1231 gains and losses
         (c) Charitable contributions
         (d) Foreign income taxes
         (e) Sec. 179 expense deduction
         (f) Interest, dividend, and royalty income
         (g) Interest expense on investment indebtedness
         (h) Net income (loss) from rental real estate activity
         (i) Net income (loss) from other rental activity

   b. **Second,** all remaining items (since they have no special tax characteristics) are ordinary in nature and are netted in the computation of partnership ordinary income or loss from trade or business activities

      (1) Frequently encountered ordinary income and deductions include

         (a) Sales less cost of goods sold
         (b) Business expenses such as wages, rents, bad debts, and repairs
         (c) Guaranteed payments to partners
         (d) Depreciation
         (e) Amortization (over 180 months or more) of partnership organization and start-up expenditures
         (f) Sec. 1245, 1250, etc., recapture
         (g) See Form 1065 outline at beginning of chapter for more detail

2. The **character** of any gain or loss recognized on the disposition of property is generally determined by the nature of the property in the hands of the partnership. However, for contributed property, the character may be based on the nature of the property to the contributing partner before contribution.

   a. If a partner contributes **unrealized receivables,** the partnership will recognize ordinary income or loss on the subsequent disposition of the unrealized receivables.

   b. If the property contributed was **inventory** property to the contributing partner, any gain or loss recognized by the partnership on the disposition of the property within five years will be treated as ordinary income or loss.

c. If the contributed property was a **capital asset,** any loss later recognized by the partnership on the disposition of the property within five years will be treated as a capital loss to the extent of the contributing partner's unrecognized capital loss at the time of contribution. This rule applies to losses only, not to gains.

3. A person sitting for the examination should be able to calculate a partnership's ordinary income by adjusting partnership book income (or partnership book income by adjusting ordinary income).

EXAMPLE

A partnership's accounting income statement discloses net income of $75,000 (i.e., book income). The three partners share profit and losses equally. Supplemental data indicate the following information has been included in the computation of net income:

	DR.	CR.
Net sales		$160,000
Cost of goods sold	$ 88,000	
Tax-exempt income		1,500
Sec. 1231 casualty gain		9,000
Section 1231 gain (other than casualty)		6,000
Section 1250 gain		20,000
Long-term capital gain		7,500
Short-term capital loss	6,000	
Guaranteed payments ($8,000 per partner)	24,000	
Charitable contributions	9,000	
Advertising expense	2,000	
	$129,000	$204,000

Partnership ordinary income is $66,000, computed as follows:

Book income		$ 75,000
Add:		
Charitable contributions	$ 9,000	
Short-term capital loss	6,000	15,000
		$ 90,000
Deduct:		
Tax-exempt income	$ 1,500	
Sec. 1231 casualty gain	9,000	
Section 1231 gain (other than casualty)	6,000	
Long-term capital gain	7,500	24,000
Partnership ordinary income		$ 66,000

Each partner's share of partnership ordinary income is $22,000.

---

4. Three sets of rules may limit the amount of partnership loss that a partner can deduct.

a. A partner's distributive share of partnership ordinary loss and special loss items is deductible by the partner only to the extent of the **partner's basis** for the partnership interest at the end of the taxable year [Sec. 704(d)].

(1) The pass-through of loss is considered to be the last event during the partnership's taxable year; all positive basis adjustments are made prior to determining the amount of deductible loss.

(2) Unused losses are carried forward and can be deducted when the partner obtains additional basis for the partnership interest.

EXAMPLE

A partner who materially participates in the partnership's business has a distributive share of partnership capital gain of $200 and partnership ordinary loss of $3,000, but the partner's basis in the partnership is only $2,400 before consideration of these items. The partner can deduct $2,600 of the ordinary loss ($2,400 of beginning basis + $200 net capital gain). The remaining $400 of ordinary loss must be carried forward.

---

b. The deductibility of partnership losses is also limited to the amount of the partner's **at-risk basis** [Sec. 465].

(1) A partner's at-risk basis is generally the same as the partner's regular partnership basis with the exception that liabilities are included in at-risk basis only if the partner is personally liable for such amounts.

(2) Nonrecourse liabilities are generally excluded from at-risk basis.

(3) Qualified nonrecourse real estate financing is included in at-risk basis.

c. The deductibility of partnership losses may also be subject to the **passive activity loss limitations** [Sec. 469]. Passive activity losses are deductible only to the extent of the partner's income from other passive activities (see Module 36).

    (1) Passive activities include (a) any partnership trade or business in which the partner does not materially participate, and (b) any rental activity.

    (2) A limited partnership interest generally fails the material participation test.

    (3) To qualify for the $25,000 exception for active participation in a rental real estate activity, a partner (together with spouse) must own at least 10% of the value of the partnership interests.

NOW REVIEW MULTIPLE-CHOICE QUESTIONS 10 THROUGH 15 IN VOLUME 2

D. Partnership Agreements

1. A partner's distributive share of income or loss is generally determined by the partnership agreement. Such agreement can have different ratios for income or loss, and may agree to allocate other items (e.g., credits and deductions) in varying ratios.

    a. Special allocations must have **substantial economic effect**.

        (1) Economic effect is measured by an analysis of the allocation on the partners' capital accounts. The special allocation (a) must be reflected in the partners' capital accounts, (b) liquidation distributions must be based upon the positive capital account balances of partners, and (c) there must be a deficit payback agreement wherein partners agree to restore any deficit capital account balances.

        (2) An allocation's economic effect will **not** be substantial if the net change recorded in the partners' capital accounts does not differ substantially from what would have been recorded without the special allocation, and the total tax liability of all partners is less.

    b. If no allocation is provided, or if the allocation of an item does not have substantial economic effect, the partners' distributive shares of that item shall be determined by the ratio in which the partners generally divide the income or loss of the partnership.

    c. **If property is contributed** by a partner to a partnership, related items of income, deduction, gain, or loss must be allocated among partners in a manner that reflects the difference between the property's tax basis and its fair market value at the time of contribution.

EXAMPLE

Partner X contributes property with a tax basis of $1,000 and a fair market value of $10,000 to the XYZ Partnership. If the partnership subsequently sells the property for $12,000, the first $9,000 of gain must be allocated to X, with the remaining $2,000 of gain allocated among partners according to their ratio for sharing gains.

        (1) If contributed property has a built-in loss, the built-in loss is taken into account only for determining the amount of partnership items allocated to the contributing partner. For purposes of determining the amount of partnership items allocated to other partners, the basis of contributed property is treated as being equal to FMV at date of contribution. If the contributing partner's interest is transferred or liquidated, the partnership's basis in the property for all future allocations will be based on its FMV at date of contribution, and the built-in loss will be eliminated.

        (2) If property contributed to a partnership is distributed within seven years to a partner other than the partner who contributed such property, the contributing partner must recognize the precontribution gain or loss to the extent that the precontribution gain or loss would be recognized if the partnership had sold the property for its fair market value at the time of distribution.

        (3) The above recognition rule will not generally apply if other property of a like-kind to the contributed property is distributed to the contributing partner no later than the earlier of (1) the 180th day after the date on which the originally contributed property was distributed to another partner, or (2) the due date (without extension) for the contributing partner's return for the tax year in which the original distribution of property occurred.

    d. If there was any change in the ownership of partnership interests during the year, distributive shares of partnership interest, taxes, and payments for services or for the use of property must be allocated among partners by assigning an appropriate share of each item to each day of the partnership's taxable year.

> **EXAMPLE**
>
> Z becomes a 40% partner in calendar-year Partnership XY on December 1. Previously, X and Y each had a 50% interest. Partnership XY uses the cash method of accounting and on December 31 pays $10,000 of interest expense that relates to its entire calendar year. Z's distributive share of the interest expense will be ($10,000 ÷ 365 days) × 31 days × 40% = $340.

2. **Distributable shares** of income and guaranteed payments are reported by partners for their taxable year during which the end of the partnership fiscal year occurs. All items, including guaranteed payments, are deemed to pass through on the last day of the partnership's tax year.

   a. **Guaranteed payments** are payments to a partner determined without regard to income of the partnership. Guaranteed payments are deductible by the partnership and reported as income by the partners.

> **EXAMPLE**
>
> Z (on a calendar-year) has a 20% interest in a partnership that has a fiscal year ending May 31. Z received a guaranteed payment for services rendered of $1,000 a month from 6/1/11 to 12/31/11 and $1,500 a month from 1/1/12 to 5/31/12. After deducting the guaranteed payment, the partnership had ordinary income of $50,000 for its fiscal year ended 5/31/12. Z must include $24,500 in income on Z's calendar-year 2012 return ($50,000 × 20%) + ($1,000 × 7) + ($1,500 × 5).

   b. Partners are generally not considered to be employees for purposes of employee fringe benefits (e.g., cost of $50,000 of group-term life insurance, exclusion of premiums or benefits under an employer accident or health plan, etc.). A partner's fringe benefits are deductible by the partnership as guaranteed payments and must be included in a partner's gross income.

3. **Family partnerships** are subject to special rules because of their potential use for tax avoidance.

   a. If the business is primarily service oriented (capital is not a material income-producing factor), a family member will be considered a partner only if the family member shares in the management or performs needed services.
   b. Capital is not a material income-producing factor if substantially all of the gross income of the business consists of fees, commissions, or other compensation for personal services (e.g., accountants, architects, lawyers).
   c. A family member is generally considered a partner if the family member actually owns a capital interest in a business in which capital is a material income-producing factor.
   d. Where a capital interest in a partnership in which capital is a material income-producing factor is treated as created by gift, the distributive shares of partnership income of the donor and donee are determined by first making a reasonable allowance for services rendered to the partnership, and then allocating the remainder according to the relative capital interests of the donor and donee.

> **NOW REVIEW MULTIPLE-CHOICE QUESTIONS 16 THROUGH 30 IN VOLUME 2**

E. Partner's Basis in Partnership

1. A partner's **original basis** is generally determined by the manner in which the partnership interest was acquired (e.g., contribution of property, compensation for services, purchase, gift, received from decedent).
2. As the partnership operates, the partner's basis for the partnership interest increases or decreases.

   a. A partner's basis is increased by the adjusted basis of any subsequent capital contributions.
   b. Also, a partner's basis is **increased** by any distributive share of

      (1) Partnership ordinary income
      (2) Capital gains and other special income items
      (3) Tax-exempt income of the partnership
      (4) The excess of the deduction for depletion over the partnership's basis of the property subject to depletion

   c. A partner's basis is **decreased** (but not below zero) by

      (1) The amount of money and the adjusted basis of other property distributed to the partner
      (2) The partner's distributive share of partnership ordinary loss and special expense items, as well as nondeductible items not properly chargeable to capital
      (3) The amount of the partner's deduction for depletion on oil and gas wells

> **EXAMPLE**
>
> In the example in Section C. 3, one partner's tax basis (who had a $15,000 tax basis at the beginning of the year) would be $40,000 at the end of the year, calculated as shown below.
>
> | | | |
> |---|---|---|
> | Beginning partnership basis | | $15,000 |
> | Add: | | |
> | Distributive share of partnership ordinary income | 22,000 | |
> | Tax-exempt income | 500 | |
> | Sec. 1231 casualty gain | 3,000 | |
> | Section 1231 gain (other than casualty) | 2,000 | |
> | Long-term capital gain | 2,500 | 30,000 |
> | | | $45,000 |
> | Less: | | |
> | Short-term capital loss | $ 2,000 | |
> | Charitable contributions | 3,000 | 5,000 |
> | Ending partnership basis | | $40,000 |

d. **Changes in liabilities** affect a partner's basis.

   (1) An **increase** in the **partnership's liabilities** (e.g., loan from a bank, increase in accounts payable) increases each partner's basis in the partnership by each partner's share of the increase.

   (2) Any **decrease** in the **partnership's liabilities** is considered to be a distribution of money to each partner and reduces each partner's basis in the partnership by each partner's share of the decrease.

   (3) Any **decrease** in a partner's **individual liability** by reason of the assumption by the partnership of such individual liabilities is considered to be a distribution of money to the partner by the partnership (i.e., partner's basis is reduced).

   (4) Any **increase** in a partner's **individual liability** by reason of the assumption by the partner of partnership liabilities is considered to be a contribution of money to the partnership by the partner. Thus, the partner's basis is increased.

> **EXAMPLE**
>
> The XYZ partnership owns a warehouse with an adjusted basis of $120,000 subject to a mortgage of $90,000. Partner X (one of three equal partners) has a basis for his partnership interest of $75,000. If the partnership transfers the warehouse and mortgage to Partner X as a current distribution, X's basis for his partnership interest immediately following the distribution would be $15,000, calculated as follows:
>
> | | |
> |---|---|
> | Beginning basis | $ 75,000 |
> | Individual assumption of mortgage | + 90,000 |
> | | $165,000 |
> | Distribution of warehouse | −120,000 |
> | Partner's share of decrease in partnership's liabilities | − 30,000 |
> | Basis after distribution | $ 15,000 |

> **EXAMPLE**
>
> Assume in the example above that one of the other one-third partners had a basis of $75,000 immediately before the distribution. What would the partner's basis be immediately after the distribution to Partner X? $45,000 (i.e., $75,000 less 1/3 of the $90,000 decrease in partnership liabilities).

e. A partner's basis for the partnership is adjusted in the following order: (1) increased for all income items (including tax-exempt income); (2) decreased for distributions; and (3) decreased by deductions and losses (including nondeductible items not charged to capital).

> **EXAMPLE**
>
> A partner with a basis of $50 for his partnership interest at the beginning of the partnership year receives a $30 cash distribution during the year and is allocated a $60 distributive share of partnership ordinary loss, and an $8 distributive share of capital gain. In determining the extent to which the ordinary loss is deductible by the partner, the partner's partnership basis of $50 is first increased by the $8 of capital gain and reduced by the $30 cash distribution to $28, so that his deductible ordinary loss is limited to his remaining basis of $28.

NOW REVIEW MULTIPLE-CHOICE QUESTIONS 31 THROUGH 37 IN VOLUME 2

F. Transactions with Controlled Partnerships

1. If a person engages in a transaction with a partnership other than as a member of such partnership, any resulting gain or loss is generally recognized. However, if the transaction involves a **more than 50% owned partnership,** one of three special rules may apply. Constructive ownership rules apply in determining whether a transaction involves a more than 50% owned partnership.

   a. **No losses** are deductible from sales or exchanges of property between a partnership and a person owning (directly or indirectly) more than 50% of the capital or profits interests in such partnership, or between two partnerships in which the same persons own (directly or indirectly) more than 50% of the capital or profits interests. A gain later realized on a subsequent sale by the transferee will not be recognized to the extent of the disallowed loss.

   > **EXAMPLE**
   >
   > Partnership X is owned by three **equal** partners, A, B, and C, who are brothers. Partnership X sells property at a loss of $5,000 to C. Since C owns a more than 50% interest in the partnership (i.e., C constructively owns his brothers' partnership interests), the $5,000 loss is disallowed to Partnership X.

   > **EXAMPLE**
   >
   > Assume the same facts as in the above example. C later resells the property to Z, an unrelated taxpayer, at a gain of $6,000. C's realized gain of $6,000 will not be recognized to the extent of the $5,000 disallowed loss to the Partnership X.

   b. If a person related to a partner does not indirectly own a more than 50% partnership interest, a transaction between the related person and the partnership is treated as occurring between the related person and the partners individually.

   > **EXAMPLE**
   >
   > X owns 100% of X Corp. and also owns a 25% interest in WXYZ Partnership. X Corp. sells property at a $1,200 loss to the WXYZ Partnership. Since X Corp. is related to partner X (i.e., X owns more than 50% of X Corp.), the transaction is treated as if it occurred between X Corp. and partners W, X, Y, and Z individually. Therefore, the loss disallowed to X Corp. is $1,200 × 25% = $300.

   c. A **gain** recognized on a sale or exchange of property between a partnership and a person owning (directly or indirectly) more than 50% of the capital or profits interests in such partnership, or between two partnerships in which the same persons own (directly or indirectly) more than 50% of the capital or profits interests, will be treated as **ordinary income** if the property is **not a capital asset** in the hands of the transferee.

   > **EXAMPLE**
   >
   > Assume the same facts as in the preceding example. Further assume that F is the father of W, Y, and Z. F sells investment property to Partnership WXYZ at a gain of $10,000. If the property will not be a capital asset to Partnership WXYZ, F must report the $10,000 gain as ordinary income because F constructively owns a more than 50% partnership interest (i.e., F constructively owns his children's partnership interests).

   d. A **gain** recognized on a sale or exchange of property between a partnership and a person owning (directly or indirectly) more than 50% of the capital or profits interests in such partnership will be treated as **ordinary income** if the property is **depreciable property** in the hands of the transferee.

NOW REVIEW MULTIPLE-CHOICE QUESTIONS 38 THROUGH 41 IN VOLUME 2

G. Taxable Year of Partnership

1. When a partnership adopts (or attempts to change) its taxable year, it is subject to the following restrictions:

    a. A partnership must adopt the taxable year used by one or more of its partners owning an aggregate interest of more than 50% in profits and capital (but only if the taxable year used by such partners has been the same for the lesser of three taxable years or the period the partnership has existed).

    > **EXAMPLE**
    >
    > A partnership is formed by a corporation (which receives a 55% partnership interest) and five individuals (who each receive a 9% partnership interest). The corporation has a fiscal year ending June 30, while the individuals have a calendar year. The partnership must adopt a fiscal year ending June 30.

    b. If partners owning a more than 50% interest in partnership profits and capital do not have the same year-end, the partnership must adopt the same taxable year as used by all of its principal partners (i.e., a partner with a 5% or more interest in capital or profits).

    c. If its principal partners have different taxable years, the partnership must adopt the taxable year that results in the least aggregate deferral of income to partners.

2. A different taxable year than the year determined above can be used by a partnership if a **valid business purpose** can be established and IRS permission is received. The business purpose test will be met if a partnership receives at least 25% of its gross receipts in the last two months of a twelve-month period, and this "25% test" has been satisfied for three consecutive years.

    > **EXAMPLE**
    >
    > Partnership X is owned by three equal partners—A, B, and C, who use a calendar year. Partnership X has received at least 25% of its gross receipts during the months of June and July for each of the last three years. Partnership X may be allowed to change to a fiscal year ending July 31.

3. A partnership that otherwise would be required to adopt or change its tax year (normally to the calendar year) may **elect to use a fiscal year if the election does not result in a deferral period longer than three months,** or, if less, the deferral period of the year currently in use.

    a. The "deferral period" is the number of months between the close of the fiscal year elected and the close of the required year (e.g., if a partnership elects a tax year ending September 30 and a tax year ending December 31 is required, the deferral period of the year ending September 30 is three months).

    b. A partnership that elects a tax year other than a required year must make a "required payment" which is in the nature of a refundable, noninterest-bearing deposit that is intended to compensate the government for the revenue lost as a result of tax deferral. The required payment is due on May 15 each year and is recomputed for each subsequent year.

4. The **taxable year** of a partnership ordinarily **will not close** as a result of the death or entry of a partner, or the liquidation or sale of a partner's interest. But the partnership's taxable year closes as to **the partner** whose **entire interest** is sold or liquidated. Additionally, the partnership tax year closes with respect to a deceased partner as of date of death.

    > **EXAMPLE**
    >
    > A partner sells his entire interest in a calendar-year partnership on March 31. His pro rata share of partnership income up to March 31 is $15,000. Since the partnership year closes with respect to him at the time of sale, the $15,000 is includible in his income and increases the basis of his partnership interest for purposes of computing gain or loss on the sale. However, the partnership's taxable year does not close as to its remaining partners.

    > **EXAMPLE**
    >
    > X (on a calendar year) is a partner in the XYZ Partnership that uses a June 30 fiscal year. X died on April 30, 2012. Since the partnership year closes with respect to X at his death, X's final return for the period January 1 through April 30 will include his share of partnership income for the period beginning July 1, 2011, and

ending April 30, 2012. His share of partnership income for May and June 2012 will be reported by his estate or other successor in interest.

> **NOW REVIEW MULTIPLE-CHOICE QUESTIONS 42 THROUGH 45 IN VOLUME 2**

H. Partnership's Use of Cash Method

1. The cash method cannot generally be used if inventories are necessary to clearly reflect income and cannot generally be used by tax shelters and partnerships that have a C corporation as a partner.
2. Any partnership (other than a tax shelter) can use the cash method if for every year it has average gross receipts of **$5 million or less** for any prior three-year period and does not have inventories for sale to customers.
3. A small partnership with average annual gross receipts of **$1 million or less** for any prior three-year period can use the cash method and is excepted from the requirements to account for inventories and use the accrual method for purchases and sales of merchandise.

I. Termination or Continuation of Partnership

1. A partnership will terminate when it no longer has at least two partners.
2. A partnership and its taxable year will terminate for all partners if there is a sale or exchange of 50% or more of the **total interests** in partnership capital and profits within a twelve-month period.

   a. Sales or exchanges of at least 50% during any twelve-month period cause a termination.

   > **EXAMPLE**
   >
   > The calendar-year ABC Partnership has three equal partners, A, B, and C. B sold his interest to D on November 1, 2011, and C sold his interest to E on April 1, 2012. The ABC Partnership is considered terminated on April 1 because at least 50% of the total interests have been sold within a twelve-month period.

   b. If the same partnership interest is sold more than once during a twelve-month period, the sale is counted only once.

   > **EXAMPLE**
   >
   > The calendar-year RST Partnership has three equal partners, R, S, and T. T sold his interest to X on December 1, 2011, and X sold his interest to Y on May 1, 2012. The RST Partnership is not terminated because multiple sales of the same partnership interest are counted only once.

3. In a **merger** of partnerships, the resulting partnership is a continuation of the merging partnership whose partners have a more than 50% interest in the resulting partnership.

   > **EXAMPLE**
   >
   > Partnerships AB and CD merge on April 1, forming the ABCD Partnership in which the partners' interests are as follows: Partner A, 30%; B, 30%; C, 20%; and D, 20%. Partnership ABCD is a continuation of the AB Partnership. The CD Partnership is considered terminated and its taxable year closed on April 1.

4. In a **division** of a partnership, a resulting partnership is a continuation of the prior partnership if the resulting partnership's partners had a more than 50% interest in the prior partnership.

   > **EXAMPLE**
   >
   > Partnership ABCD is owned as follows: A, 40%; and B, C, and D each own a 20% interest. The partners agree to separate and form two partnerships—AC and BD. Partnership AC is a continuation of ABCD. BD is considered a new partnership and must adopt a taxable year, as well as make any other necessary tax accounting elections.

NOW REVIEW MULTIPLE-CHOICE QUESTIONS 46 THROUGH 51 IN VOLUME 2

J. Sale of a Partnership Interest

1. Since a partnership interest is usually a capital asset, the sale of a partnership interest generally results in **capital gain or loss**.

    a. Gain is excess of amount realized over the adjusted basis for the partnership interest.

    b. Include the selling partner's share of partnership liabilities in the amount realized because the selling partner is relieved of them.

> **EXAMPLE**
>
> Miller sold her partnership interest to Carter for $150,000 cash, plus Carter's assumption of Miller's $60,000 share of partnership liabilities. The amount realized by Miller on the sale of her partnership interest is $150,000 + $60,000 = $210,000.

2. **Gain is ordinary** (instead of capital) to extent attributable to unrealized receivables or appreciated inventory (Sec. 751 items).

    a. The term **unrealized receivables** generally refers to the accounts receivable of a cash method taxpayer, but for this purpose also includes any potential recapture under Secs. 1245, 1250, and 1252.

    b. The term **inventory** includes all assets except capital assets and Section 1231 assets.

> **EXAMPLE**
>
> X has a 40% interest in the XY Partnership. Partner X sells his 40% interest to Z for $50,000. X's basis in his partnership is $22,000 and the cash-method partnership had the following receivables and inventory:
>
> | | Adjusted basis | Fair market value |
> | --- | --- | --- |
> | Accounts receivable | 0 | $10,000 |
> | Inventory | 4,000 | 10,000 |
> | Potential Sec. 1250 recapture | 0 | 10,000 |
> | | $4,000 | $30,000 |
>
> X's total gain is $28,000 (i.e., $50,000 – $22,000). Since the Sec. 1250 recapture is treated as "unrealized receivables" and the inventory is appreciated, X will recognize ordinary income to the extent that his selling price attributable to Sec. 751 items ($30,000 × 40% = $12,000) exceeds his basis in those items ($4,000 × 40% = $1,600), that is, $10,400. The remainder of X's gain ($28,000 – $10,400 = $17,600) will be treated as capital gain.

NOW REVIEW MULTIPLE-CHOICE QUESTIONS 52 THROUGH 56 IN VOLUME 2

K. Pro Rata Distributions from Partnership

1. Partnership recognizes no gain or loss on a distribution.
2. If a single distribution consists of **multiple items of property,** the distributed property reduces the partner's basis for the partnership interest in the **following order:**

    a. Money,

    b. Adjusted basis of unrealized receivables and inventory, and

    c. Adjusted basis of other property.

3. Partner recognizes **gain** only to the extent **money received exceeds the partner's partnership basis.**

    a. Relief from liabilities is deemed a distribution of money.

    b. Gain is capital except for gain attributable to unrealized receivables and substantially appreciated inventory.

    c. The receipt of property (other than money) will not cause the recognition of gain.

> **EXAMPLE**
>
> Casey had a basis of $9,000 for his partnership interest at the time that he received a nonliquidating partnership distribution consisting of $5,000 cash and other property with a basis of $3,000 and a FMV of $8,000. No gain is recognized by Casey since the cash received did not exceed his partnership basis. Casey's $9,000 basis for his partnership interest is first reduced by the $5,000 cash, and then reduced by the $3,000 basis of other property, to $1,000. Casey will have a basis for the other property received of $3,000.

4. Partner recognizes **loss** only upon **complete liquidation** of a partnership interest through receipt of only money, unrealized receivables, or inventory.

   a. The amount of loss is the basis for the partner's partnership interest less the money and the partnership's basis in the unrealized receivables and inventory received by the partner.
   b. The loss is generally treated as a capital loss.
   c. If property other than money, unrealized receivables, or inventory is distributed in complete liquidation of a partner's interest, no loss can be recognized.

> **EXAMPLE**
>
> Day had a basis of $20,000 for his partnership interest before receiving a distribution in complete liquidation of his interest. The liquidating distribution consisted of $6,000 cash and inventory with a basis of $11,000. Since Day's liquidating distribution consisted of only money and inventory, Day will recognize a loss on the liquidation of his partnership interest. The amount of loss is the $3,000 difference between the $20,000 basis for his partnership interest, and the $6,000 cash and the $11,000 basis for the inventory received. Day will have an $11,000 basis for the inventory.

> **EXAMPLE**
>
> Assume the same facts as in the preceding example except that Day's liquidating distribution consists of $6,000 cash and a parcel of land with a basis of $11,000. Since the liquidating distribution now includes property other than money, receivables, and inventory, no loss can be recognized on the liquidation of Day's partnership interest. The basis for Day's partnership interest is first reduced by the $6,000 cash to $14,000. Since no loss can be recognized, the parcel of land must absorb all of Day's unrecovered partnership basis. As a result, the land will have a basis of $14,000.

5. In **nonliquidating (current) distributions,** a partner's basis in distributed property is generally the same as the partnership's former basis in the property; but is **limited** to the basis for the partner's partnership interest less any money received.

> **EXAMPLE**
>
> Sara receives a current distribution from her partnership at a time when the basis for her partnership interest is $10,000. The distribution consists of $7,000 cash and Sec. 1231 property with an adjusted basis of $5,000 and a FMV of $9,000. No gain is recognized by Sara since the cash received did not exceed her basis. After being reduced by the cash, her partnership basis of $3,000 is reduced by the basis of the property (but not below zero). Her basis for the property is limited to $3,000.

6. **If multiple properties are distributed** in a liquidating distribution, or if the partnership's basis for distributed properties exceed the partner's basis for the partnership interest, the partner's basis for the partnership interest is allocated in the following order:

   a. Basis is first allocated to unrealized receivables and inventory items in an amount equal to their adjusted basis to the partnership. If the basis for the partner's interest to be allocated to the assets is less than the total basis of these properties to the partnership, a **basis decrease** is required and is determined under (1) below.
   b. To the extent a partner's basis is not allocated to assets under a. above, basis is allocated to other distributed properties by assigning to each property its adjusted basis in the hands of the partnership, and then increasing or decreasing the basis to the extent required in order for the adjusted basis of the distributed properties to equal the remaining basis for the partner's partnership interest.

(1) A **basis decrease** is allocated

    (a) First to properties with unrealized depreciation in proportion to their respective amounts of unrealized depreciation (but only to the extent of each property's unrealized depreciation), and

    (b) Then in proportion to the respective adjusted basis of the distributed properties.

EXAMPLE

A partnership distributes two items of property (A and B) that are neither unrealized receivables nor inventory to Baker in liquidation of his partnership interest that has a basis of $20.

	Partnership basis	FMV
Property A	$15	$15
Property B	15	5
Total	$30	$20

Basis is first allocated $15 to A and $15 to B (their adjusted bases to the partnership). A $10 basis decrease is required because the assets' bases of $30 exceeds Baker's basis for his partnership interest of $20. The $10 decrease is allocated to B to the extent of its unrealized depreciation. Thus, Baker has a basis of $15 for property A and a basis of $5 for property B.

---

(2) A **basis increase** is allocated

    (a) First to properties with unrealized appreciation in proportion to their respective amounts of unrealized appreciation (but only to the extent of each property's unrealized appreciation), and

    (b) Then in proportion to the relative FMVs of the distributed properties.

EXAMPLE

A partnership distributes two items of property (C and D) that are neither unrealized receivables nor inventory to Alan in liquidation of his partnership interest that has a basis of $55.

	Partnership basis	FMV
Property C	$ 5	$40
Property D	10	10
Total	$15	$50

Basis is first allocated $5 to C and $10 to D (their adjusted bases to the partnership). The $40 basis increase (Alan's $55 basis less the partnership's basis for the assets $15) is then allocated to C to the extent of its unrealized appreciation of $35, with the remaining $5 of basis adjustment allocated according to the relative FMV of C and D [i.e., $4 to C (for a total basis of $44) and $1 to D (for a total basis of $11)]

---

7. Payments made in liquidation of the interest of a retiring or deceased partner are generally treated as partnership distributions made in exchange for the partner's interest in partnership property. Such payments generally result in capital gain or loss to the retiring or deceased partner.

    a. However, payments made to a retiring or deceased general partner in a partnership in which capital is **not** a material income-producing factor must be reported as ordinary income by the partner to the extent such payments are for the partner's share of unrealized receivables or goodwill (unless the partnership agreement provides for a payment with respect to goodwill).

    b. Amounts treated as ordinary income by the retiring or deceased partner are either deductible by the partnership (treated as guaranteed payments), or reduce the income allocated to remaining partners (treated as a distributive share of partnership income).

    c. Capital is **not** a material income-producing factor if substantially all of the gross income of the business consists of fees, commissions, or other compensation for personal services (e.g., accountants, doctors, dentists, lawyers).

NOW REVIEW MULTIPLE-CHOICE QUESTIONS 57 THROUGH 69 IN VOLUME 2

L. Non-Pro Rata Distributions from Partnership

1. A non-pro rata (disproportionate) distribution occurs when

    a. A distribution is disproportionate as to a partner's share of unrealized receivables or substantially appreciated inventory. Inventory is **substantially appreciated** if its FMV exceeds 120% of its basis.

(1) Partner may receive more than the partner's share of these assets, or

(2) Partner may receive more than the partner's share of other assets, in effect giving up a share of unrealized receivables or substantially appreciated inventory

b. The partner may recognize gain or loss.

(1) The gain or loss is the difference between the FMV of what is received and the basis of what is given up.

(2) The gain or loss is limited to the disproportionate amount of unrealized receivables or substantially appreciated inventory that is received or given up.

(3) The character of the gain or loss depends upon the character of the property given up.

c. The partnership may similarly recognize gain or loss when there is a disproportionate distribution with respect to substantially appreciated inventory or unrealized receivables.

EXAMPLE

A, B, and C each own a one-third interest in a partnership. The partnership has the following assets:

	Adjusted basis	FMV
Cash	$ 6,000	$ 6,000
Inventory	6,000	12,000
Land	9,000	18,000
	$21,000	$36,000

Assume that A has a $7,000 basis for his partnership interest and that all inventory is distributed to A in liquidation of his partnership interest. He is treated as having exchanged his 1/3 interest in the cash and the land for a 2/3 increased interest in the substantially appreciated inventory. He has a gain of $3,000. He received $8,000 (2/3 × $12,000) of inventory for his basis of $2,000 (1/3 × $6,000) in cash and $3,000 (1/3 × $9,000) of land. The gain is capital if the land was a capital asset. The partnership is treated as having received $8,000 (FMV of A's 1/3 share of cash and land) in exchange for inventory with a basis of $4,000 (basis of inventory distributed in excess of A's 1/3 share). Thus, the partnership will recognize ordinary income of $4,000.

M. Optional Sec. 754 Adjustment to Basis of Partnership Property

1. On a distribution of property to a partner, or on a sale by a partner of a partnership interest, the partnership may elect to adjust the basis of its assets to **prevent any inequities** that otherwise might occur. Once an election is made, it applies to all similar transactions unless IRS approves revocation of the election.

2. Upon the **distribution of partnership property,** the basis of remaining partnership property will be adjusted for **all** partners.

   a. Increased by

   (1) The amount of gain recognized to a distributee partner, and

   (2) The excess of the partnership's basis in the property distributed over the basis of that property in the hands of distributee partner

---

EXAMPLE

If the election were made under the facts used in K.5, the $2,000 of basis that otherwise would be lost will be allocated to remaining partnership Sec. 1231 property.

---

   b. Decreased by

   (1) The amount of loss recognized to a distributee partner, and

   (2) The excess of basis of property in hands of distributee over the prior basis of that property in the partnership

3. Upon the **sale or exchange of a partnership interest,** the basis of partnership property to the **transferee** (not other partners) will be

   a. Increased by the excess of the basis of the transferee's partnership interest over the transferee's share of the adjusted basis of partnership property

   b. Decreased by the excess of transferee's share of adjusted basis of partnership property over the basis for the transferee's partnership interest

---

EXAMPLE

Assume X sells his 40% interest to Z for $80,000 when the partnership balance sheet reflects the following:

XY Partnership

	Basis	FMV
Assets		
Accounts Receivable	$ 0	$100,000
Real Property	30,000	100,000
Capital		
X (40%)		$ 80,000
Y (60%)		120,000

Z will have a basis for his partnership interest of $80,000, while his share of the adjusted basis of partnership property will only be $12,000. If the partnership elects to adjust the basis of partnership property, it will increase the basis of its assets by $68,000 ($80,000 – $12,000) solely for the benefit of Z. The basis of the receivables will increase from 0 to $40,000 with the full adjustment allocated to Z. When the receivables are collected, Y will have $60,000 of income and Z will have none. The basis of the real property will increase by $28,000 to $58,000, so that Z's share of the basis will be $40,000 (i.e., $12,000 + $28,000).

N. Mandatory Adjustments to Basis of Partnership Property

1. A partnership is required to make a Sec. 743 adjustment to the basis of partnership property upon a transfer of a partnership interest by sale or exchange or on the death of a partner if the partnership has a substantial built-in loss immediately after such transfer. For this purpose, a partnership has a substantial built-in loss if the partnership's adjusted basis for partnership property exceeds the FMV of such property by more than $250,000.

2. A partnership is required to make a Sec. 734 downward basis adjustment to partnership property in the event of a partnership distribution with respect to which there is a substantial basis reduction. For this purpose, a substantial basis reduction means a downward adjustment of more than $250,000 that would be made to the basis of partnership property if a Sec. 754 election were in effect with respect to the distribution.

KEY TERMS

Current distribution. A nonliquidating partnership distribution made to a partner (i.e., the distribution does not terminate the partner's partnership interest.

Limited liability partnership. Differs from general partnerships in that with an LLP, a partner is not liable for damages resulting from the negligence, malpractice, or fraud committed by other partners. However, each partner is personally liable for his or her own negligence, malpractice, or fraud.

Limited partnership. A partnership with two classes of partners, with at least one general partner and at least one limited partner. A limited partner generally cannot participate in the active management of the partnership, and in the event of losses, generally can lose no more than his or her capital contribution.

Liquidating distribution. A single distribution, or one of a planned series of distributions, that completely terminates a partner's interest in the partnership.

Partnership ordinary income or loss. All partnership items that do not have to be separately stated (because they have no special tax characteristics) and can be combined and just the net amount is passed through to partners.

Sec. 751 property. A partnership's unrealized receivables (including the recapture potential in depreciable assets) and appreciated inventory. The gain on sale of a partnership interest generally must be recognized as ordinary income to the extent of the selling partner's share of unrealized receivables and appreciated inventory. These assets are sometimes referred to as *hot assets*.

Sec. 754 election. An optional election that can be made by a partnership to adjust the basis of its assets to prevent any inequities that might occur as a result of the partnership's distribution of property or the sale by a partner of a partnership interest.

Overview

This module covers corporate taxation and reviews the rules that apply throughout the life cycle of a corporation. The tax consequences of corporate formation are covered first, followed by a review of some of the special rules that apply to the income and deductions of a corporation, including the charitable contributions deduction and the dividends received deduction. The Schedule M-1 reconciliation of book income to taxable income, and the tax concepts of affiliated and controlled groups are next reviewed. This is followed by a review of the tax treatment of corporate distributions to shareholders and their taxability as dividends. Next reviewed are the tax consequences of a complete liquidation, as well as the accumulated earnings and personal holding company penalty taxes. The module then continues with a review of the special rules that apply to S corporations and their shareholders, and the tax effects of corporate reorganizations. The module concludes with a comparison of C corporations, S corporations, and partnerships.

I. CORPORATIONS

Corporations are separate taxable entities, organized under state law. Although corporations may have many of the same income and deduction items as individuals, corporations are taxed at different rates and some tax rules are applied differently. There also are special provisions applicable to transfers of property to a corporation, and issuance of stock.

A. Transfers to a Controlled Corporation (Sec. 351)

1. **No gain or loss** is recognized if property is transferred to a corporation solely in exchange for stock and immediately after the exchange those persons transferring property control the corporation.

   a. **Property** includes everything but services.
   b. **Control** means ownership of at least 80% of the total combined voting power and 80% of each class of nonvoting stock.
   c. **Receipt of boot** (e.g., cash, short-term notes, securities, etc.) will cause recognition of gain (but not loss).

      (1) Corporation's assumption of liabilities is treated as boot only if there is a tax avoidance purpose, or no business purpose.
      (2) Shareholder recognizes gain if liabilities assumed by corporation exceed the total basis of property transferred by the shareholder.

2. **Shareholder's basis for stock** = Adjusted basis of property transferred

   a. + Gain recognized
   b. − Boot received (assumption of liability always treated as boot for purposes of determining stock basis)

3. **Corporation's basis for property** = Transferor's adjusted basis + Gain recognized to transferor.

EXAMPLE

Individuals A, B, & C form ABC Corp. and make the following transfer to their corporation:

Item transferred	A	B	C
Property – FMV	$10,000	$8,000	$ --
– Adjusted basis	1,500	3,000	--
Liability assumed by ABC Corp.	2,000	--	--
Services	--	--	1,000
Consideration received			
Stock (FMV)	$ 8,000	$7,600	$1,000
Two-year note (FMV)	--	400	--
Gain recognized to shareholder	$ 500[a]	$ 400[b]	$1,000[c]
Basis of stock received	--	3,000	1,000
Basis of property to corp.	2,000	3,400	1,000[d]

[a] Liability in excess of basis: $2,000 – $1,500 = $500
[b] Assumes B elects out of the installment method
[c] Ordinary compensation income
[d] Expense or asset depending on nature of services rendered

---

a. For Sec. 351 transactions after October 22, 2004, if the aggregate adjusted basis of transferred property exceeds its aggregate FMV, the corporate transferee's aggregate basis for the property is generally limited to its aggregate FMV immediately after the transaction. Any required basis reduction is allocated among the transferred properties in proportion to their built-in loss immediately before the transaction.

b. Alternatively, the transferor and the corporate transferee are allowed to make an irrevocable election to limit the basis in the stock received by the transferor to the aggregate FMV of the transferred property.

EXAMPLE

Amy transferred Lossacre with a basis of $6,000 (FMV of $2,000) and Gainacre with a basis of $4,000 (FMV of $5,000) to ABE Corp. in exchange for stock in a Sec. 351 transaction. Since the aggregate adjusted basis of the transferred property ($10,000) exceeds its aggregate FMV ($7,000), ABE's aggregate basis for the property is limited to $7,000. The required basis reduction of $3,000 would reduce ABE's basis for Lossacre to $3,000 ($6,000 – $3,000). Amy's basis for her stock would equal the total basis of the transferred property, $10,000.

Alternatively, if Amy and ABE elect, ABE's basis for the transferred property will be $6,000 for Lossacre and $4,000 for Gainacre, and Amy's basis for her stock will be limited to its FMV of $7,000.

NOW REVIEW MULTIPLE-CHOICE QUESTIONS 1 THROUGH 7 IN VOLUME 2

B. Section 1244—Small Business Corporation (SBC) Stock

1. Sec. 1244 stock permits shareholders to deduct an **ordinary loss** on sale or worthlessness of stock.

    a. Shareholder must be the original holder of stock, and an individual or partnership.
    b. Stock can be common or preferred, voting or nonvoting, and must have been issued for money or property (other than stock or securities)
    c. Ordinary loss limited to **$50,000 ($100,000** on joint return); any excess is treated as a capital loss.
    d. The corporation during the five-year period before the year of loss, received less than 50% of its total gross receipts from royalties, rents, dividends, interest, annuities, and gains from sales or exchanges of stock or securities.

EXAMPLE

Jim (married and filing a joint return) incurred a loss of $120,000 from the sale of Sec. 1244 stock during 2011. $100,000 of Jim's loss is deductible as an ordinary loss, with the remaining $20,000 treated as a capital loss.

---

2. If Sec. 1244 stock is received in exchange for property whose FMV is less than its adjusted basis, the stock's basis is reduced to the FMV of the property to determine the amount of ordinary loss.

> **EXAMPLE**
>
> Joe made a Sec. 351 transfer of property with an adjusted basis of $20,000 and a FMV of $16,000 in exchange for Sec. 1244 stock. The basis of Joe's stock is $20,000, but solely for purposes of Sec. 1244 the stock's basis is reduced to $16,000. If Joe subsequently sold his stock for $15,000, $1,000 of his loss would be treated as an ordinary loss under Sec. 1244, with the remaining $4,000 treated as a capital loss.

3. For purposes of determining the amount of ordinary loss, increases in basis through capital contributions or otherwise are treated as allocable to stock which is not Sec. 1244 stock.

> **EXAMPLE**
>
> Jill acquired 100 shares of Sec. 1244 stock for $10,000. Jill later made a $2,000 contribution to the capital of the corporation, increasing her stock basis to $12,000. Jill subsequently sold the 100 shares for $9,000. Of Jill's $3,000 loss, ($10,000 ÷ $12,000) × $3,000 = $2,500 qualifies as an ordinary loss under Sec. 1244, with the remaining ($2,000 ÷ $12,000) × $3,000 = $500 treated as a capital loss.

4. SBC is any domestic corporation whose aggregate amount of money and adjusted basis of other property received for stock, as a contribution to capital, and as paid-in surplus, does not exceed $1,000,000. If more than $1 million of stock is issued, up to $1 million of qualifying stock can be designated as Sec. 1244 stock.

> **NOW REVIEW MULTIPLE-CHOICE QUESTIONS 8 THROUGH 11 IN VOLUME 2**

C. Variations from Individual Taxation

1. Filing and payment of tax

    a. A corporation generally must file a Form 1120 every year even though it has no taxable income. A short-form Form 1120-A may be filed if gross receipts, total income, and total assets are each less than $500,000.

    b. The return must be filed by the fifteenth day of the third month following the close of its taxable year (e.g., March 15 for calendar-year corporation).

    (1) An automatic six-month extension may be obtained by filing Form 7004.
    (2) Any balance due on the corporation's tax liability must be paid with the request for extension.

    c. Estimated tax payments must be made by every corporation whose estimated tax is expected to be $500 or more. A corporation's estimated tax is its expected tax liability (including alternative minimum tax) less its allowable tax credits.

    (1) Quarterly payments are due on the fifteenth day of the fourth, sixth, ninth, and twelfth months of its taxable year (April 15, June 15, September 15, and December 15 for a calendar-year corporation). Any balance due must be paid by the due date of the return.
    (2) No penalty for underpayment of estimated tax will be imposed if payments at least equal the lesser of

        (a) 100% of the current year's tax (determined on the basis of actual income or annualized income), or
        (b) 100% of the preceding year's tax (if the preceding year was a full twelve months and showed a tax liability).

    (3) A corporation with $1 million or more of taxable income in any of its three preceding tax years (i.e., **large corporation**) can use its preceding year's tax only for its first installment and must base its estimated payments on 100% of its current year's tax to avoid penalty.
    (4) If any amount of tax is not paid by the original due date, interest must be paid from the due date until the tax is paid.
    (5) A failure-to-pay tax delinquency penalty will be owed if the amount of tax paid by the original due date of the return is less than 90% of the tax shown on the return. The failure-to-pay penalty is imposed at a rate of 0.5% per month (or fraction thereof), with a maximum penalty of 25%.

2. Corporations are subject to

    a. **Regular tax rates**

	Taxable income	Rate
(1)	$0-$50,000	15%
(2)	$50,001-$75,000	25

Taxable income	Rate
(3) $75,001-$10 million	34
(4) Over $10 million	35

(5) The less-than-34% brackets are phased out by adding an additional tax of 5% of the excess of taxable income over $100,000, up to a maximum additional tax of $11,750.

(6) The 34% bracket is phased out for corporations with taxable income in excess of $15 million by adding an additional 3% of the excess of taxable income over $15 million, up to a maximum additional tax of $100,000.

b. Certain personal service corporations are not eligible to use the less-than-35% brackets and their taxable income is taxed at a flat 35% rate.

> **NOW REVIEW MULTIPLE-CHOICE QUESTIONS 12 THROUGH 20 IN VOLUME 2**

c. **Alternative minimum tax (AMT)**

(1) **Computation.** The AMT is generally the amount by which 20% of alternative minimum taxable income (AMTI) as reduced by an exemption and the alternative minimum tax foreign tax credit, exceeds the regular tax (i.e., regular tax liability reduced by the regular tax foreign tax credit). AMTI is equal to taxable income computed with specified adjustments and increased by tax preferences.

(2) **Exemption.** AMTI is offset by a $40,000 exemption. However, the exemption is reduced by 25% of AMTI over $150,000, and completely phased out once AMTI reaches $310,000.

(3) **AMT formula**

	Regular taxable income before Net Operation Loss (NOL) deduction
+	Tax preference items
+(–)	Adjustments other than Adjusted Current Earnings (ACE) and NOL deduction
	Pre-ACE AMTI
+(–)	ACE adjustment (75% of difference between pre-ACE AMTI and ACE)
–	AMT NOL deduction (limited to 90% of pre-NOL AMTI)
	AMTI
–	Exemption ($40,000 less 25% of AMTI over $150,000)
	Alternative minimum tax base
×	20% rate
	Tentative AMT before foreign tax credit
–	AMT foreign tax credit
	Tentative minimum tax (TMT)
–	Regular income tax (less regular tax foreign tax credit)
	Alternative minimum tax (if positive)

(4) **Preference items.** The following are examples of items added to regular taxable income in computing pre-ACE AMTI:

(a) Tax-exempt interest on private activity bonds (net of related expenses). However, tax-exempt interest on private activity bonds issued in 2009 and 2010 is not an item of tax preference.

(b) Excess of accelerated over straight-line depreciation on real property and leased personal property placed in service before 1987

(c) The excess of percentage depletion deduction over the property's adjusted basis

(d) The excess of intangible drilling costs using a ten-year amortization over 65% of net oil and gas income

(5) **Adjustments.** The following are examples of adjustments to regular taxable income in computing pre-ACE AMTI:

(a) For real property placed in service after 1986 and before 1999, the difference between regular tax depreciation and straight-line depreciation over forty years

(b) For personal property placed in service after 1986, the difference between regular tax depreciation using the 200% declining balance method and depreciation using the 150% declining balance method

(c) The installment method cannot be used for sales of inventory-type items

(d) Income from long-term contracts must be determined using the percentage of completion method

(6) **ACE.** ACE is a concept based on a corporation's earnings and profits, and is calculated by making adjustments to pre-ACE AMTI.

AMTI before ACE adjustment and NOL deduction

Add:	Tax-exempt interest on municipal bonds (less expenses); except not interest on tax-exempt bonds issued in 2009 or 2010.
	Tax-exempt life insurance death benefits (less expenses)
	70% dividends-received deduction
Deduct:	Depletion using cost depletion method
	Depreciation using ADS straight-line for all property (this adjustment eliminated for property placed in service after 1993)
Other:	Capitalize organizational expenditures and circulation expenses
	Add increase (subtract decrease) in LIFO recapture amount (i.e., excess of FIFO value over LIFO basis)
	Installment method cannot be used for nondealer sales of property
	Amortize intangible drilling costs over five years

ACE
– Pre-ACE AMTI
_____
Balance (positive or negative)
× 75%
_____
ACE adjustment (positive or negative)

EXAMPLE

Acme, Inc. has adjusted current earnings of $100,000 and alternative minimum taxable income (before this adjustment) of $60,000. Since adjusted current earnings exceeds pre-ACE AMTI by $40,000, 75% of this amount must be added to Acme's AMTI. Thus, Acme's AMTI before exemption for the year is [$60,000 + ($40,000 × 75%)] = $90,000.

(a) The ACE adjustment can be positive or negative, but a negative ACE adjustment is limited in amount to prior years' net positive ACE adjustments.

(b) The computation of ACE is *not* the same as the computation of a corporation's E&P. For example, federal income taxes, penalties and fines, and the disallowed portion of business meals and entertainment would be deductible in computing E&P, but are not deductible in computing ACE.

(7) **Minimum tax credit.** The amount of AMT paid is allowed as a credit against regular tax liability in future years.

  (a) The credit can be carried forward indefinitely, but not carried back.
  (b) The AMT credit can only be used to reduce regular tax liability, not future AMT liability.

(8) **Small corporation exemption.** A corporation is exempt from the corporate AMT for its first tax year (regardless of income levels). After the first year, it is exempt from AMT if it passes a gross receipts test. It is exempt for its second year if its first year's gross receipts do not exceed $5 million. To be exempt for its third year, the corporation's average gross receipts for the first two years must not exceed $7.5 million. To be exempt for the fourth year (and subsequent years), the corporation's average gross receipts for all prior three-year periods must not exceed $7.5 million.

EXAMPLE

Zero Corp., a calendar-year corporation, was formed on January 2, 2006, and had gross receipts for its first four taxable years as follows:

Year	Gross receipts
2007	$ 4,500,000
2008	9,000,000
2009	8,000,000
2010	6,500,000

Zero is automatically exempt from AMT for 2007. It is exempt for 2008 because its gross receipts for 2007 do not exceed $5 million. Zero also is exempt for 2009 because its average gross receipts for 2007-2008 do not exceed $7.5 million. Similarly, it is exempt for 2010 because its average gross receipts for 2007-2009 do not exceed $7.5 million. However, Zero will lose its exemption from AMT for 2011 and all subsequent years because its average gross receipts for 2008-2010 exceed $7.5 million.

NOW REVIEW MULTIPLE-CHOICE QUESTIONS 21 THROUGH 28 IN VOLUME 2

3. Gross income for a corporation is computed much the same as for individual taxpayers. However, there are a few differences.

    a. A corporation does not recognize gain or loss on the **issuance of its own stock** (including treasury stock), or on the lapse or acquisition of an option to buy or sell its stock (including treasury stock).

        (1) It generally recognizes gain (but not loss) if it distributes appreciated property to its shareholders.

        (2) **Contributions to capital** are excluded from a corporation's gross income, whether received from shareholders or nonshareholders.

            (a) If property is received from a shareholder, the shareholder recognizes no gain or loss, the shareholder's basis for the contributed property transfers to the corporation, and the shareholder's stock basis is increased by the basis of the contributed property.

            (b) If property is received as a capital contribution from a nonshareholder, the corporation's basis for the contributed property is zero.

                1] If money is received, the basis of property purchased within one year afterwards is reduced by the money contributed.

                2] Any money not used reduces the basis of the corporation's existing property beginning with depreciable property.

    b. No gain or loss is recognized on the **issuance of debt**.

        (1) Premium or discount on bonds payable is amortized as income or expense over the life of bonds.

        (2) Ordinary income/loss is recognized by a corporation on the repurchase of its bonds, determined by the relationship of the repurchase price to the net carrying value of the bonds (issue price plus or minus the discount or premium amortized).

        (3) Interest earned and gains recognized in a bond sinking fund are income to the corporation.

    c. Gains are treated as ordinary income on sales to or from a more than 50% shareholder, or between corporations which are more than 50% owned by the same individual, if the property is subject to depreciation in the hands of the buyer.

NOW REVIEW MULTIPLE-CHOICE QUESTIONS 29 THROUGH 33 IN VOLUME 2

---

4. Deductions for a corporation are much the same as for individuals. However, there are some major differences.

    a. Adjusted gross income is not applicable to corporations.

    b. A corporation may elect to deduct up to $5,000 of **organizational expenditures** for the tax year in which the corporation begins business. The $5,000 amount must be reduced (but not below zero) by the amount by which organizational expenditures exceed $50,000. Remaining expenditures can be deducted ratably over the 180-month period beginning with the month in which the corporation begins business.

> **EXAMPLE**
>
> A calendar-year corporation was organized and began business during 2011 incurring $4,800 or organizational expenditures. The corporation may deduct the $4,800 of organizational expenditures for 2011.

> **EXAMPLE**
>
> A calendar-year corporation was organized during February, 2011 incurring organizational expenditures of $6,000. Assuming the corporation begins business during April, 2011, its maximum deduction for organizational expenditures for 2011 would be $5,000 + [($6,000 - $5,000) × 9/180] = $5,050.

> **EXAMPLE**
>
> A calendar-year corporation was organized during February, 2011 incurring organizational expenditures of $60,000. Assuming the corporation begins business during April, 2011, its maximum deduction for organizational expenditures for 2011 would be $60,000 × 9/180 = $3,000.

(1) For amounts paid or incurred after September 8, 2008, the corporation is deemed to have made the election, but instead may choose to forgo the deemed election by clearly electing to capitalize its costs on a timely filed return (including extensions) for the taxable year in which the corporation begins business.

(2) For amounts paid on or before October 22, 2004, a corporation could have elected to amortize organizational expenditures over not less than 60 months, beginning with the month that business begins.

(3) For amounts paid or incurred before September 9, 2008, the election must be made by the due date for filing the tax return (including extensions) for the tax year in which the corporation begins business, and applies to expenditures incurred before the end of the tax year in which the corporation begins business (even if the amounts have not yet been paid by a cash-method corporation).

(4) Organizational expenditures include expenses of temporary directors and organizational meetings, state fees for incorporation, accounting and legal service costs incident to incorporation (e.g., drafting bylaws, minutes of organizational meetings, and terms of original stock certificates).

(5) Expenditures connected with issuing or selling shares of stock, or listing stock on an exchange are neither deductible nor amortizable. Expenditures connected with the transfer of an asset to the corporation must be capitalized as part of the cost of the asset.

> **NOW REVIEW MULTIPLE-CHOICE QUESTIONS 34 THROUGH 37 IN VOLUME 2**

c. The deduction for **charitable contributions** is **limited to 10% of taxable income** before the contributions deduction, the dividends received deduction, a NOL carryback (but after carryover), a capital loss carryback (but after carryover), and the domestic production activities deductions (DPAD).

(1) Generally the same rules apply for valuation of contributed property as for individuals except

    (a) Deduction for donations of inventory and other appreciated ordinary income-producing property is the donor's basis plus one-half of the unrealized appreciation but limited to twice the basis, provided

        1] Donor is a corporation (but not an S corporation)
        2] Donee must use property for care of ill, needy, or infants
        3] Donor must obtain a written statement from the donee that the use requirement has been met
        4] No deduction allowed for unrealized appreciation that would be ordinary income under recapture rules

    (b) Deduction for donation of appreciated scientific personal property to a college or university is the donor's basis plus one-half the unrealized appreciation but limited to twice the basis, provided

        1] Donor is a corporation (but not an S corporation, personal holding company, or service organization)
        2] Property was constructed by donor and contributed within two years of substantial completion, and donee is original user of property
        3] Donee must use property for research or experimentation
        4] Donor must obtain a written statement from the donee that the use requirement has been met
        5] No deduction allowed for unrealized appreciation that would be ordinary income under recapture rules

(2) Contributions are deductible in period paid (subject to 10% limitation) unless corporation is an accrual method taxpayer and then deductible (subject to 10% limitation) when authorized by board of directors if payment is made within 2 1/2 months after tax year end, and corporation elects to deduct contributions when authorized.

(3) Excess contributions over the 10% limitation may be carried forward for up to five years.

EXAMPLE

The books of a calendar-year, accrual method corporation for 2010 disclose net income of $350,000 after deducting a charitable contribution of $50,000. The contribution was authorized by the Board of Directors on December 24, 2010, and was actually paid on January 31, 2011. The allowable charitable contribution deduction for 2010 (if the corporation elects to deduct it when accrued) is $40,000, calculated as follows: ($350,000 + $50,000) × .10 = $40,000. The remaining $10,000 is carried forward for up to five years.

> **NOW REVIEW MULTIPLE-CHOICE QUESTIONS 38 THROUGH 44 IN VOLUME 2**

d. A **100% Dividends Received Deduction (DRD)** for dividends received from affiliated (i.e., at least 80% owned) corporations if a consolidated tax return is not filed.

  (1) If a consolidated tax return is filed, intercompany dividends are eliminated and not included in consolidated gross income.
  (2) See Section D. for discussion of affiliated corporations

e. An **80% DRD** is allowed for qualified dividends from taxable domestic unaffiliated corporations that are **at least 20% owned**.

  (1) DRD may be **limited to 80% of taxable income** before the 80% dividends received deduction, the net operating loss deduction, and a capital loss carryback.

> **EXAMPLE**
>
> A corporation has income from sales of $20,000 and dividend income of $10,000, along with business expenses of $22,000. Since taxable income before the DRD would be $8,000 (less than the dividend income), the DRD is limited to $6,400 (80% × $8,000). Thus, taxable income would be $1,600 ($8,000 – $6,400).

  (2) Exception: The 80% of **taxable income limitation does not apply** if the full 80% DRD creates or increases a net operating loss.

> **EXAMPLE**
>
> In the example above, assume that all facts are the same except that business expenses are $22,001. Since the full DRD ($8,000) would create a $1 net operating loss ($7,999 – $8,000), the taxable income limitation would not apply and the full DRD ($8,000) would be allowed.

f. Only a **70% dividends received deduction** (instead of 80%) is allowed for qualified dividends from taxable domestic unaffiliated corporations that are **less than 20% owned**.

  (1) A 70% of taxable income limitation (instead of 80%) and a limitation exception for a net operating loss apply as in e.(1) and (2) above.
  (2) If dividends are received from both 20% owned corporations and corporations that are less than 20% owned, the 80% DRD and 80% DRD limitation for dividends received from 20% owned corporations is computed first. Then the 70% DRD and 70% DRD limitation is computed for dividends received from less than 20% owned corporations. For purposes of computing the 70% DRD limitation, taxable income is reduced by the total amount of dividends received from 20% owned corporations.

> **EXAMPLE**
>
> A corporation has taxable income before the dividends received deduction of $100,000. Included in taxable income are $65,000 of dividends from a 20% owned corporation and $40,000 of dividends from a less than 20% owned corporation. First, the 80% DRD for dividends received from the 20% owned corporation is computed. That deduction equals $52,000 [i.e., the lesser of 80% of the dividends received (80% × $65,000), or 80% of taxable income (80% × $100,000)].
>
> Second, the 70% DRD for the dividends received from the less than 20% owned corporation is computed. That deduction is $24,500 [i.e., the lesser of 70% of the dividends received (70% × $40,000), or 70% of taxable income after deducting the amount of dividends from the 20% owned corporation (70% × [$100,000 – $65,000])].
>
> Thus, the total dividends received deduction is $52,000 + $24,500 = $76,500.

g. A portion of a corporation's 80% (or 70%) DRD will be disallowed if the dividends are directly attributable to **debt-financed portfolio stock**.

  (1) "Portfolio stock" is any stock (except stock of a corporation if the taxpayer owns at least 50% of the voting power and at least 50% of the total value of such corporation).
  (2) The DRD percentage for debt-financed portfolio stock = [80% (or 70%) × (100% – average % of indebtedness on the stock)].

> **EXAMPLE**
>
> P, Inc. purchased 25% of T, Inc. for $100,000, paying with $50,000 of its own funds and $50,000 borrowed from its bank. During the year P received $9,000 in dividends from T, and paid $5,000 in interest expense on the bank loan. No principal payments were made on the loan during the year. If the stock were not debt financed, P's DRD would be $9,000 × 80% = $7,200. However, because half of the stock investment was debt financed, P's DRD is $9,000 × [80% × (100% − 50%)] = $3,600.

(3) The reduction in the DRD cannot exceed the interest deduction allocable to the portfolio stock indebtedness.

> **EXAMPLE**
>
> Assume the same facts as above except that the interest expense on the bank loan was only $3,000. The reduction in the DRD would be limited to the $3,000 interest deduction on the loan. The DRD would be ($9,000 × 80%) − $3,000 = $4,200.

h. **No DRD** is allowed if the dividend paying stock is held **less than 46 days** during the 91-day period that begins 45 days before the stock becomes ex-dividend. In the case of preferred stock, no DRD is allowed if the dividends received are for a period or periods in excess of 366 days and the stock has been held for less than 91 days during the 181-day period that begins 90 days before the stock becomes ex-dividend.

i. The **basis of stock** held by a corporation must be reduced by the nontaxed portion of a nonliquidating **extraordinary dividend** received with respect to the stock, unless the corporation has held the stock for more than two years before the dividend is announced. To the extent the nontaxed portion of an extraordinary dividend exceeds the adjusted basis of the stock, the excess is recognized as gain for the taxable year in which the extraordinary dividend is received.

(1) The nontaxed portion of a dividend is generally the amount that is offset by the DRD.

(2) A dividend is considered "extraordinary" when it equals or exceeds 10% (5% for preferred stock) of the stock's adjusted basis (or FMV if greater on the day preceding the ex-dividend date).

(3) Aggregation of dividends

    (a) All dividends received that have ex-dividend dates that occur within a period of 85 consecutive days are treated as one dividend.

    (b) All dividends received within 365 consecutive days are treated as extraordinary dividends if they in total exceed 20% of the stock's adjusted basis.

(4) This provision is not applicable to dividends received from an affiliated corporation, and does not apply if the stock was held during the entire period the paying corporation (and any predecessor) was in existence.

> **EXAMPLE**
>
> Corporation X purchased 30% of the stock of Corporation Y for $10,000 during June 2010. During December 2010 X received a $20,000 dividend from Y. X sold its Y stock for $5,000 in March 2011.
>
> Because the dividend from Y is an extraordinary dividend, the nontaxed portion (equal to the DRD allowed to X) $20,000 × 80% = $16,000 has the effect of reducing the Y stock basis from $10,000 to $0, with the remaining $6,000 recognized as gain for 2010. At time of sale, the excess of sale proceeds over the reduced stock basis $5,000 − $0 = $5,000 is also recognized as gain.

NOW REVIEW MULTIPLE-CHOICE QUESTIONS 45 THROUGH 50 IN VOLUME 2

---

j. **Losses** in the ordinary course of business are deductible.

(1) Loss is **disallowed** if the sale or exchange of property is between

    (a) A corporation and a more than 50% shareholder,

    (b) A C corporation and an S corporation if the same persons own more than 50% of each, or

    (c) A corporation and a partnership if the same persons own more than 50% of the corporation, and more than 50% of the capital and profits interest in the partnership.

    (d) In the event of a disallowed loss, the transferee on subsequent disposition only recognizes gain to the extent it exceeds the disallowed loss.

(2) Any loss from the sale or exchange of property between corporations that are members of the same **controlled group** is **deferred** (instead of disallowed) until the property is sold outside the group. See controlled group definition in Section D.2., except substitute "more than 50%" for "at least 80%."

(3) An accrual method C corporation is effectively placed on the cash method of accounting for purposes of deducting accrued interest and other expenses owed to a related cash method payee. No deduction is allowable until the year the amount is actually paid.

EXAMPLE

A calendar-year corporation accrues $10,000 of salary to an employee (a 60% shareholder) during 2010 but does not make payment until February 2011. The $10,000 will be deductible by the corporation and reported as income by the employee-shareholder in 2011.

---

(4) **Capital losses** are deductible only to the extent of capital gains (i.e., may not offset ordinary income).

    (a) Unused capital losses are carried back three years and then carried forward five years to offset capital gains.

    (b) All corporate capital loss carrybacks and carryforwards are treated as **short-term**.

(5) Bad debt losses are treated as ordinary deductions.

(6) Casualty losses are treated the same as for an individual except

    (a) There is no $100 floor

    (b) If property is completely destroyed, the amount of loss is the property's adjusted basis

    (c) A partial loss is measured the same as for an individual's nonbusiness loss (i.e., the lesser of the decrease in FMV, or the property's adjusted basis)

(7) A corporation's **NOL** is computed the same way as its taxable income.

    (a) The dividends received deduction is allowed without limitation, and no deduction is allowed for the domestic production activities deduction (DPAD).

    (b) No deduction is allowed for a NOL carryback or carryover from other years, and no deduction is allowed for the domestic production activities deduction (DPAD).

    (c) A NOL is generally carried back two years and forward twenty years to offset taxable income in those years. However, a three-year carryback is permitted for the portion of a NOL that is attributable to a presidentially declared disaster and is incurred by a small business corporation (i.e., a corporation whose average annual gross receipts are $5 million or less for the three-tax-year period preceding the loss year). A corporation may elect to forego carryback and only carry forward twenty years.

  k. Depreciation and depletion computations are same as for individuals.

  l. Research and development expenditures of a corporation (or individual) may be treated under one of three alternatives

    (1) Currently expensed in year paid or incurred

    (2) Amortized over a period of sixty months or more if life not determinable

    (3) Capitalized and depreciated over determinable life

  m. Contributions to a pension or profit-sharing plan

    (1) Defined benefit plans

      (a) Maximum deductible contribution is actuarially determined.

      (b) There also are minimum funding standards.

    (2) Defined contribution plans

      (a) **Maximum deduction** for contributions to qualified profit-sharing or stock bonus plans is generally limited to 25% of the compensation paid or accrued during the year to covered employees.

      (b) If more than 25% is paid, the excess can be carried forward as part of the contributions of succeeding years to the extent needed to bring the deduction up to 25%.

NOW REVIEW MULTIPLE-CHOICE QUESTIONS 51 THROUGH 58 IN VOLUME 2

---

5. In working a corporate problem, certain calculations must be made in a specific order [e.g., charitable contributions (CC) must be computed before the DRD]. The following memory device is quite helpful:

	Gross income	
–	Deductions (except CC and DRD)	
	Taxable income before CC and DRD	
–	CC (limited to 10% of TI before CC, DRD, capital loss carryback, and NOL carryback)	
	Taxable income before DRD	
–	DRD (may be limited* to 80% or 70%) of TI before DRD, capital loss carryback, and NOL carryover or carryback)	
	Taxable income	
×	Applicable rates	
	Tax liability before tax credits	
–	Tax credits	
	Tax liability	

* Limitation not applicable if full 80% (or 70%) of dividends received creates or increases an NOL.

6. A person sitting for the CPA examination should be able to **reconcile book and taxable income**.

   a. If you begin with book income to calculate taxable income, make the following adjustments:

      (1) **Increase book income** by

         (a) Federal income tax expense
         (b) Excess of capital losses over capital gains because a net capital loss is not deductible
         (c) Income items in the tax return not included in book income (e.g., prepaid rents, royalties, interest)
         (d) Charitable contributions in excess of the 10% limitation
         (e) Expenses deducted on the books but not on the tax return (e.g., amount of business gifts in excess of $25, nondeductible life insurance premiums paid, 50% of business meals and entertainment)

      (2) **Deduct from book income**

         (a) Income reported on the books but not on the tax return (e.g., tax-exempt interest, life insurance proceeds)
         (b) Expenses deducted on the tax return but not on the books (e.g., MACRS depreciation above straight-line, charitable contribution carryover)
         (c) The dividends received deduction

   b. When going from taxable income to book income, the above adjustments would be reversed.

   c. **Schedule M-1** of Form 1120 provides a reconciliation of income per books with taxable income before the NOL deduction and DRD, and must be completed by corporations with less than *$10 million* of total assets. Schedule M-1 items are either *permanent* book-to-tax differences (e.g., tax-exempt interest) or *temporary* differences (e.g., accelerated depreciation used on tax return while straight-line used per books). The starting point on Schedule M-1 is net income (or loss) per books. Additions and subtractions are then made to reflect the differences between financial and tax accounting. The end result is the amount of taxable income before the NOL deduction and DRD that is reported on the current year return.

      (1) Items added to book income include

         (a) Federal income tax expense that was deducted per books
         (b) Excess of capital losses over capital gains deducted per books but not deductible for tax purposes
         (c) Income subject to tax in the current year but not included in current year book income (e.g., receipt of prepaid rent)
         (d) Expenses deducted per books but not allowed in computing taxable income (e.g., 50% of business meals and entertainment, expenses incurred in the production of tax-exempt income, charitable contributions in excess of the 10% of taxable income limitation).

      (2) Items subtracted from book income include

         (a) Income reported on books this year not included in the tax return (e.g., tax-exempt interest, nontaxable life insurance proceeds)
         (b) Deductions on the return not charged against book income this year (e.g., tax depreciation in excess of book depreciation, domestic production activities deduction)

EXAMPLE

A corporation discloses that it had net income after taxes of $36,000 per books. Included in the computation were deductions for charitable contributions of $10,000, a net capital loss of $5,000, and federal income taxes paid of $9,000. What is the corporation's TI?

Net income per books after tax	$36,000
Nondeductible net capital loss	+ 5,000
Federal income tax expense	+ 9,000
Charitable contributions	+10,000
Taxable income before CC	$60,000
CC (limited to 10% × 60,000)	– 6,000
Taxable income	$54,000

d. **Schedule M-2** of Form 1120 analyzes changes in a corporation's Unappropriated Retained Earnings per books between the beginning and end of the year.

Balance at beginning of year
  Add: Net income per books
          Other increases
  Less: Dividends to shareholders
  Other decreases (e.g., addition to reserve for contingencies)
  Balance at end of year

> **NOW REVIEW MULTIPLE-CHOICE QUESTIONS 59 THROUGH 72 IN VOLUME 2**

e. **Schedule M-3** Net Income (Loss) Reconciliation must be completed and attached to a corporation's Form 1120 if the corporation's total assets at the end of the tax year equal or exceed **$10 million**. A corporation filing Schedule M-3 must not complete Schedule M-1. A corporation with total assets less than $10 million can elect to complete Schedule M-3 instead of completing Schedule M-1.

(1) Total assets at the end of the year must be determined using the same method as used for financial statement purposes. If a corporation uses the accrual method for financial statement purposes and the cash method for tax purposes, the corporation's total assets must be determined using the accrual method.

   (a) In the case of a US consolidated tax group, total assets at the end of the tax year must be determined based on the total year-end assets of all includible corporations, net of eliminations for intercompany transactions and balances between the includible corporations.

   (b) A corporation is not required to file Schedule M-3 if total assets at the end of the current year are less than $10 million, even though the corporation was required to file Schedule M-3 for the preceding tax year.

   (c) No schedule M-3 is required for taxpayers filing Form 1120-REIT (Real Estate Investment Trusts); Form 1120-RIC (Regulated Investment Companies); Form 1120-H (Homeowners Associations); and Form 1120-SF (Settlement Funds).

(2) Schedule M-3 consists of three parts: Part I adjusts worldwide income per books to worldwide book income for only those corporations includible on the tax return; Part II reconciles income and loss items for includible corporations; and Part III reconciles expense and deduction items. The total of items for Part III carry over to Part II for the overall reconciliation.

   (a) Schedule M-3 requires much greater detail (Parts II and III contain a total of 66 line items) than Schedule M-1 (10 line items) because it requires taxpayers to separately list each type of transaction that gives rise to a book-tax difference and to identify whether each difference is permanent or temporary.

   (b) Parts II and III each contain four columns: (a) income statement items; (b) temporary differences; (c) permanent differences; and, (d) tax return items. Part III requires a corporation to separate its book federal income tax expense between its current income tax expense and its deferred income tax expense. If its financial statements do not separately report current and deferred income tax expense, all income tax expense should be reported as current income tax expense in Part III.

   (c) A US consolidated tax group required to file Schedule M-3 must file multiple Schedules M-3. It must file one Schedule M-3, Parts I, II, and III to reflect the activity of the entire US consolidated tax group. Additionally, a separate Schedule M-3 Parts II and III must be completed for the parent corporation and each subsidiary to reflect each corporation's separate activity. Lastly, it generally is necessary to complete Parts II and III of a separate Schedule M-3 to eliminate differences related to intercompany transactions, and to include limitations on deductions (e.g., charitable contributions and capital loss limitations) and carryover amounts. As a result, a US consolidated group consisting of a parent corporation and three subsidiary corporations would have to complete a total of six Schedules M-3.

   (d) A corporation or group of corporations that files a Form 1120 and is required to file Schedule M-3, must also file Schedule B (Form 1120), Additional Information for Schedule M-3 Filers. In the case of a consolidated group, a parent corporation files only one Schedule B (Form 1120) for the entire consolidated group.

(e) **Schedule UTP** (Uncertain Tax Positions) must be completed and attached to Form 1120 if the corporation (1) has total assets of at least $100 million, and (2) the corporation has taken a tax position on its return and the corporation or a related party has either recorded a reserve with respect to that position in audited financial statements, or did not record a reserve because the corporation expects to litigate the position.

1] A tax position taken on a tax return is a tax position that would result in an adjustment to a line item on that return if the position is not sustained.

2] Schedule UTP requires a concise description of each uncertain tax position. Additionally, the corporation must rank each listed tax position by size, must indicate whether each position is temporary or permanent, and must disclose whether a tax position is greater than 10% of the aggregate amount of reserves for all tax positions.

3] If the corporation or a related party determined that, under applicable accounting standards, either no reserve was required for a tax position taken on a return because the amount was immaterial for audited financial statement purposes, or that a tax position was sufficiently certain so that no reserve was required, then the tax position is not required to be reported on Schedule UTP.

D. Affiliated and Controlled Corporations

1. An **affiliated group** is a parent-subsidiary chain of corporations in which **at least 80%** of the combined voting power and total value of all stock (except nonvoting preferred) are owned by includible corporations.

   a. They may elect to file a consolidated return. Election is binding on all future returns.
   b. If affiliated corporations file a consolidated return, intercompany dividends are eliminated in the consolidation process. If separate tax returns are filed, dividends from affiliated corporations are eligible for a 100% dividends received deduction.
   c. Possible advantages of a consolidated return include the deferral of gain on intercompany transactions and offsetting operating/capital losses of one corporation against the profits/capital gains of another.

EXAMPLE

P Corp. owns 80% of the stock of A Corp., 40% of the stock of B Corp., and 45% of the stock of C Corp. A Corp. owns 40% of the stock of B Corp. A consolidated tax return could be filed by P, A, and B.

EXAMPLE

Parent and Subsidiary file consolidated tax returns using a calendar year. During 2010, Subsidiary paid a $10,000 dividend to Parent. Also during 2010, Subsidiary sold land with a basis of $20,000 to Parent for its FMV of $50,000. During 2011, Parent sold the land to an unrelated taxpayer for $55,000.

The intercompany dividend is eliminated in the consolidation process and is excluded from consolidated taxable income. Additionally, Subsidiary's $30,000 of gain from the sale of land to Parent is deferred for 2010. The $30,000 will be included in consolidated taxable income for 2011 when Parent reports $5,000 of income from the sale of that land to the unrelated taxpayer.

---

2. A **controlled group** of corporations is limited to an aggregate of $75,000 of taxable income taxed at less than 35%, one $250,000 accumulated earnings credit, one Sec. 179 expense election, and one $40,000 AMT exemption. There are three basic types of controlled groups.

   a. **Parent-subsidiary**—Basically same as P-S group eligible to file consolidated return, except ownership requirement is 80% of combined voting power **or** total value of stock. Affiliated corporations are subject to the controlled group limitations if the corporations file separate tax returns.
   b. **Brother-sister**—Two or more corporations if 5 or fewer persons who are individuals, estates, or trusts own stock possessing more than 50% of the total combined voting power, or more than 50% of the total combined voting power, or more than 50% of the total value of all shares of stock of each corporation, taking into account the stock ownership of each person only to the extent such stock ownership is identical with respect to each corporation.

EXAMPLE

Individual shareholder	Corporations		Stock considered
	W	X	for 50% test
A	30%	20%	20%
B	5	40	5%
C	30	35	30%
D	15	5.	5%
E	20	--	--
	100%	100%	60%

Corporations W and X are a controlled group since five or fewer individuals own more than 50% of each corporation when counting only identical ownership.

EXAMPLE

Individual shareholder	Corporations		Stock considered
	Y	Z	for 50% test
F	80%	5%	5%
G	10	90	10
H	10	5	5
	100%	100%	20%

Y and Z are not a controlled group since shareholders F, G, and H do not own more than 50% of Y and Z when counting only identical stock ownership.

c. **Combined**—The parent in a P-S group is also a member of a brother-sister group of corporations.

EXAMPLE

Individual H owns 100% of the stock of Corporations P and Q. Corporation P owns 100% of the stock of Corporation S. P, S, and Q are members of one controlled group.

NOW REVIEW MULTIPLE-CHOICE QUESTIONS 73 THROUGH 79 IN VOLUME 2

E. Dividends and Distributions

1. Ordinary corporate distributions

a. Corporate distributions of property to shareholders on their stock are subject to a **three-step** treatment.

   (1) Dividend—to be included in gross income
   (2) Return of stock basis—nontaxable and reduces shareholder's basis for stock
   (3) Gain—to extent distribution exceeds shareholder's stock basis

b. The **amount** of distribution to a shareholder is the cash plus the FMV of other property received, reduced by liabilities assumed.

c. A shareholder's tax **basis** for distributed property is the property's FMV at date of distribution (not reduced by liabilities).

d. A **dividend** is a distribution of property by a corporation to its shareholders out of

   (1) Earnings and profits of the current taxable year (CEP), computed at the end of the year, without regard to the amount of earnings and profits at the date of distribution; or,
   (2) Earnings and profits accumulated after February 28, 1913 (AEP).

EXAMPLE

Corporation X has earnings and profits of $6,000 and makes a $10,000 distribution to its sole shareholder, A, who has a stock basis of $3,000. The $10,000 distribution to A will be treated as a dividend of $6,000, a nontaxable return of stock basis of $3,000, and a capital gain of $1,000.

(a) CEP are first allocated to distributions on preferred stock, then to common stock.

(b) CEP are allocated pro rata to multiple distributions on the same class of stock if distributions exceed CEP.

(c) AEP are allocated to distributions in the order in which the distributions are made.

EXAMPLE

A corporation has both preferred and common stock outstanding and no accumulated earnings and profits. For the current year, it has current earnings and profits of $15,000, and during the year distributes cash of $10,000 to its preferred shareholders, and $10,000 to its common shareholders. The $15,000 of CEP are first allocated to the distribution to the preferred shareholders, making all $10,000 taxable as a dividend. The remaining $5,000 of CEP is then allocated to the $10,000 distribution to common shareholders, making only $5,000 taxable as a dividend.

EXAMPLE

A corporation has accumulated earnings and profits of $4,000 and current earnings and profits of $20,000. During the current year its distributes $15,000 to its common shareholders in March, and another $15,000 to its common shareholders in October. The $20,000 of CEP are allocated pro rata to the two distributions, making $10,000 of the March distribution and $10,000 of the October distribution taxable as a dividend. The AEP of $4,000 are then allocated to the March distribution. As a result, $14,000 of the March distribution and $10,000 of the October distribution are taxable as a dividend.

---

e. The **distributing corporation recognizes gain** on the distribution of appreciated property as if such property were sold for its FMV. However, no loss can be recognized on the nonliquidating distribution of property to shareholders.

EXAMPLE

A corporation distributes property with a FMV of $10,000 and a basis of $3,000 to a shareholder. The corporation recognizes a gain of $10,000 – $3,000 = $7,000.

---

(1) If the distributed property is subject to a liability (or if the distributee assumes a liability) and the FMV of the distributed property is less than the amount of liability, then the gain is the difference between the amount of liability and the property's basis.

EXAMPLE

A corporation distributes property with a FMV of $10,000 and a basis of $3,000 to a shareholder, who assumes a liability of $12,000 on the property. The corporation recognizes a gain of $12,000 – $3,000 = $9,000.

---

(2) The type of gain recognized (e.g., ordinary, Sec. 1231, capital) depends on the nature of the property distributed (e.g., recapture rules may apply).

2. **Earnings and profits**

   a. **Current earnings and profits** (CEP) are **similar to book income,** but are computed by making adjustments to taxable income.

      (1) Add—tax-exempt income, dividends received deduction, excess of MACRS depreciation over depreciation computed under ADS, etc.

      (2) Deduct—federal income taxes, net capital loss, excess charitable contributions, expenses relating to tax-exempt income, penalties, etc.

   b. **Accumulated earnings and profits** (AEP) represent the sum of prior years' CEP, reduced by distributions and net operating loss of prior years.

   c. CEP are increased by the gain recognized on a distribution of appreciated property (excess of FMV over basis).

   d. Distributions reduce earnings and profits (but not below zero) by

      (1) The amount of money

      (2) The face amount (or issue price if less) of obligations of the distributing corporation, and

      (3) The adjusted basis (or FMV if greater) of other property distributed

(4) Above reductions must be adjusted for any liability assumed by the shareholder, or the amount of liability to which the property distributed is subject.

EXAMPLE

Z Corp. has two 50% shareholders, Alan and Baker. Z Corp. distributes a parcel of land (held for investment) to each shareholder. Gainacre with a FMV of $12,000 and an adjusted basis of $8,000 is distributed to Alan, while Lossacre with a FMV of $12,000 and an adjusted basis of $15,000 is distributed to Baker. Each shareholder assumes a liability of $3,000 on the property received. Z Corp. must recognize a gain of $4,000 on the distribution of property to Alan, but cannot recognize the loss on the distribution to Baker.

	Alan	Baker
Dividend ($12,000 – $3,000)	$ 9,000	$ 9,000
Tax basis for property received	12,000	12,000
Effect (before tax) on Z's earnings & profits:		
	Alan	**Baker**
Increased by gain (FMV-basis)	4,000	0
Increased by liabilities distributed	3,000	3,000
Decreased by greater of FMV or adjusted basis of property distributed	(12,000)	(15,000)

NOW REVIEW MULTIPLE-CHOICE QUESTIONS 80 THROUGH 91 IN VOLUME 2

3. **Stock redemptions**

   a. A stock redemption is **treated as an exchange,** generally resulting in capital gain or loss treatment to the shareholder if at least one of the following five tests is met. The constructive stock ownership rules of Sec. 318 generally apply in determining whether the following tests are met:

      (1) The redemption is not essentially equivalent to a dividend (this has been interpreted by Revenue Rulings to mean that a redemption must reduce a shareholder's right to vote, share in earnings, and share in assets upon liquidation; and after the redemption the shareholder's stock ownership [both direct and constructive] must not exceed 50%), or

      (2) The redemption is substantially disproportionate (i.e., after redemption, shareholder's percentage ownership is less than 80% of shareholder's percentage ownership prior to redemption, and less than 50% of shares outstanding), or

      (3) All of the shareholder's stock is redeemed, or

      (4) The redemption is from a noncorporate shareholder in a partial liquidation, or

      (5) The distribution is a redemption of stock to pay death taxes under Sec. 303.

   b. If none of the above tests are met, the redemption proceeds are treated as an ordinary Sec. 301 distribution, **taxable as a dividend** to the extent of the distributing corporation's earnings and profits.

   c. A corporation cannot deduct amounts paid or incurred in connection with a redemption of its stock (except for interest expense on loans used to purchase stock).

NOW REVIEW MULTIPLE-CHOICE QUESTIONS 92 THROUGH 94 IN VOLUME 2

4. **Complete liquidations**

   a. Amounts received by **shareholders** in liquidation of a corporation are treated as received in exchange for stock, generally resulting in capital gain or loss. Property received will have a basis equal to FMV.

   b. A **liquidating corporation** generally recognizes gain or loss on the sale or distribution of its assets in complete liquidation.

      (1) If a distribution, gain or loss is computed as if the distributed property were sold to the distributee for FMV.

      (2) If distributed property is subject to a liability (or a shareholder assumes a liability) in excess of the basis of the distributed property, FMV is deemed to be not less than the amount of liability.

   c. **Distributions to related persons**

      (1) No loss is generally recognized to a liquidating corporation on the distribution of property to a related person if

(a) The distribution is not pro rata, or

(b) The property was acquired by the liquidating corporation during the five-year period ending on the date of distribution in a Sec. 351 transaction or as a contribution to capital. This includes any property whose basis is determined by reference to the adjusted basis of property described in the preceding sentence.

(2) Related person is a shareholder who owns (directly or constructively) more than 50% of the corporation's stock. The constructive ownership rules of Sec. 267 apply for purposes of determining whether a person owns more than 50%.

d. **Carryover basis property**

(1) If a corporation acquires property in a Sec. 351 transaction or as a contribution to capital at any time after the date that is two years before the date of the adoption of the plan of complete liquidation, any loss resulting from the property's sale, exchange, or distribution can be recognized only to the extent of the decline in value that occurred subsequent to the date that the corporation acquired the property.

(2) The above rule applies only where the loss is not already completely disallowed by c.(1) above, and is intended to apply where there is no clear and substantial relationship between the contributed property and the conduct of the corporation's business. If the contributed property is actually used in the corporation's business, the above rule should not apply if there is a business purpose for placing the property in the corporation.

EXAMPLE

During September 2010, a shareholder makes a capital contribution which includes property unrelated to the corporation's business with a basis of $15,000 and a FMV of $10,000 on the contribution date. Within two years the corporation adopts a plan of liquidation and sells the property for $8,000. The liquidating corporation's recognized loss will be limited to $10,000 – $8,000 = $2,000.

---

e. **Liquidation of subsidiary**

(1) **No gain or loss** is recognized to a **parent corporation** under Sec. 332 on the receipt of property in complete liquidation of an **80% or more owned subsidiary**. The subsidiary's basis for its assets along with all tax accounting attributes (e.g., earnings and profits, NOL, and charitable contribution carryforwards) will transfer to the parent corporation.

(2) **No gain or loss** is recognized to a **subsidiary corporation** on the distribution of property to its parent if Sec. 332 applies to the parent corporation.

(a) If the subsidiary has debt outstanding to the parent, nonrecognition also applies to property distributed in satisfaction of the debt.

(b) Gain (but not loss) is recognized on the distribution of property to minority (20% or less) shareholders.

(3) Nonrecognition does not extend to minority shareholders. A minority shareholder's gain or loss will be recognized under the general rule at 4.a. above.

EXAMPLE

Parent Corp. owns 80% of Subsidiary Corp., with the remaining 20% of Subsidiary stock owned by Alex. Parent's basis in its Subsidiary stock is $100,000, while Alex has a basis for her Subsidiary stock of $15,000. Subsidiary Corp. is to be liquidated and will distribute to Parent Corp. assets with a FMV of $200,000 and a basis of $150,000, and will distribute to Alex assets with a FMV of $50,000 and a basis of $30,000. Subsidiary has an unused capital loss carryover of $10,000. The tax effects of the liquidation will be as follows:

Parent Corp. will not recognize gain on the receipt of Subsidiary's assets in complete liquidation, since Subsidiary is an at least 80%-owned corporation. The basis of Subsidiary's assets to Parent will be their transferred basis of $150,000, and Parent will inherit Subsidiary's unused capital loss carryover of $10,000.

Alex will recognize a gain of $35,000 ($50,000 FMV – $15,000 stock basis) from the liquidation. Alex's tax basis for Subsidiary's assets received in the liquidation will be their FMV of $50,000.

Subsidiary Corp. will not recognize gain on the distribution of its assets to Parent Corp., but will recognize a gain of $20,000 ($50,000 FMV – $30,000 basis) on the distribution of its assets to Alex.

┌───┐
│   **NOW REVIEW MULTIPLE-CHOICE QUESTIONS 95 THROUGH 103 IN VOLUME 2**   │
└───┘

5. **Stock purchases treated as asset acquisitions**

   a.   An acquiring corporation that has purchased at least 80% of a target corporation's stock within a 12-month period may elect under Sec. 338 to have the purchase of stock treated as an acquisition of assets.
   b.   Old target corporation is deemed to have sold all its assets on the acquisition date, and is treated as a new corporation that has purchased those assets on the day after the acquisition date.

      (1) Acquisition date is the date on which at least 80% of the target's stock has been acquired by purchase within a 12-month period.
      (2) Gain or loss is generally recognized to old target corporation on deemed sale of assets.
      (3) The deemed sales price for the target corporation's assets is generally the FMV of the target's assets as of the close of the acquisition date.

F. **Personal Holding Company and Accumulated Earnings Taxes**

   1.   Personal holding companies (PHC) are subject to a penalty tax on undistributed PHC income to discourage taxpayers from accumulating their investment income in a corporation taxed at lower than individual rates.

      a.   A **PHC** is any corporation (except certain banks, financial institutions, and similar corporations) that meets two requirements.

         (1) During anytime in the last half of the tax year, five or fewer individuals own more than 50% of the value of the outstanding **stock** directly or indirectly, **and**
         (2) The corporation receives at least 60% of its adjusted ordinary gross **income** as "PHC income" (e.g., dividends, interest, rents, royalties, and other passive income)

      b.   Taxed at ordinary corporate rates on taxable income, plus 15% tax rate on undistributed PHC income
      c.   The PHC tax

         (1) Is **self-assessing** (i.e., computed on Sch. PH and attached to Form 1120); a six-year statute of limitations applies if no Sch. PH is filed
         (2) May be avoided by dividend payments sufficient in amount to reduce undistributed PHC income to zero

      d.   The PHC tax is computed as follows:

   Taxable Income
   +   Dividends-received deduction
   +   Net operating loss deduction (except NOL of immediately preceding
         year allowed without a dividends-received deduction)
   −   Federal and foreign income taxes
   −   Charitable contributions in excess of 10% limit
   −   Net capital loss
   −   Net LTCG over NSTCL (net of tax)
         Adjusted Taxable Income
   −   Dividends paid during taxable year
   −   Dividends paid within 2 1/2 months after close of year (limited to 20%
         of dividends actually paid during year)
   −   Dividend carryover
   −   Consent dividends
         Undistributed PHC Income
   ×   15%
         Personal Holding Company Tax

      e.   **Consent dividends** are hypothetical dividends that are treated as if they were paid on the last day of the corporation's taxable year. Since they are not actually distributed, shareholders increase their stock basis by the amount of consent dividends included in their gross income.
      f.   PHC tax liability for a previous year (but not interest and penalties) may be avoided by payment of a deficiency dividend within ninety days of a "determination" by the IRS that the corporation was a PHC for a previous year.

   2.   Corporations may be subject to an **accumulated earnings tax** (AET), in addition to regular income tax, if they accumulate earnings beyond reasonable business needs in order to avoid a shareholder tax on dividend distributions.

a. The tax is not self-assessing, but is based on the IRS' determination of the existence of tax avoidance intent.
b. AET may be imposed without regard to the number of shareholders of the corporation, but does not apply to personal holding companies.
c. **Accumulated earnings credit** is allowed for greater of

   (1) $250,000 ($150,000 for personal service corporations) minus the accumulated earnings and profits at end of prior year, or
   (2) Reasonable needs of the business (e.g., expansion, working capital, to retire debt, etc.).

d. Balance of accumulated taxable income is taxed at 15% tax rate
e. The AET may be avoided by dividend payments sufficient in amount to reduce accumulated taxable income to zero.
f. The accumulated earnings tax is computed as follows:

    Taxable Income
   +   Dividends-received deduction
   +   NOL deduction
   –   Federal and foreign income taxes
   –   Excess charitable contributions (over 10% limit)
   –   Net capital loss
   –   Net LTCG over net STCL (net of tax)
      Adjusted Taxable Income
   –   Dividends paid last 9 1/2 months of tax year and 2 1/2 months after close
   –   Consent dividends
   –   Accumulated earnings credit
      Accumulated Taxable Income
   ×   15%
      Accumulated Earnings Tax

NOW REVIEW MULTIPLE-CHOICE QUESTIONS 104 THROUGH 122 IN VOLUME 2

G. S Corporations

An S corporation generally pays no corporate income taxes. Instead, it functions as a pass-through entity (much like a partnership) with its items of income, gain, loss, deduction, and credit passed through and directly included in the tax computations of its shareholders. Electing small business corporations are designated as S corporations; all other corporations are referred to as C corporations.

1. **Eligibility** requirements for S corporation status

   a. Domestic corporation
   b. An S corporation may own any percent of the stock of a C corporation, and 100% of the stock of a qualified subchapter S subsidiary.

      (1) An S corporation cannot file a consolidated return with an affiliated C corporation.
      (2) A *qualified subchapter S subsidiary* (QSSS) is any domestic corporation that qualifies as an S corporation and is 100% owned by an S corporation parent, which elects to treat it as a QSSS. A QSSS is not treated as a separate corporation and all of its assets, liabilities, and items of income, deduction, and credit are treated as belonging to the parent S corporation.

   c. Only **one class of stock** issued and outstanding. A corporation will not be treated as having more than one class of stock solely because of differences in voting rights among the shares of common stock (i.e., both voting and nonvoting common stock may be outstanding).
   d. **Shareholders** must be individuals, estates, or trusts created by will (only for a two-year period), voting trusts, an Electing Small Business Trust (ESBT), a Qualified Subchapter S Trust (QSST), or a trust all of which is treated as owned by an individual who is a citizen or resident of the US (i.e., Subpart E trust).

      (1) A QSST and a Subpart E trust may continue to be a shareholder for two years beginning with the date of death of the deemed owner.
      (2) Code Sec. 401(a) qualified retirement plan trusts and Code Sec. 501(c) charitable organizations that are exempt from tax under Code Sec. 501(a) are eligible to be shareholders of an S corporation. The S corporation's items of income and deduction will flow through to the tax-exempt shareholder as unrelated business taxable income (UBIT).

   e. No nonresident alien shareholders
   f. The number of shareholders is limited to 100.

(1) Husband and wife (and their estates) are counted as one shareholder.
(2) Each beneficiary of a voting trust is considered a shareholder.
(3) If a trust is treated as owned by an individual, that individual (not the trust) is treated as the shareholder.
(4) All members of a family can elect to be treated as one shareholder. The election may be made by any family member and will remain in effect until terminated. Members of a family include the common ancestor, the lineal descendants of the common ancestor, and the spouses (or former spouses) of the common ancestor and lineal descendants. The common ancestor cannot be more than six generations removed from the youngest generation of shareholders at the time the S election is made.

2. An **election must be filed** anytime in the preceding taxable year or on or before the fifteenth day of the third month of the year for which effective.

   a. All shareholders on date of election, plus any shareholders who held stock during the taxable year but before the date of election, must consent to the election.

      (1) If an election is made on or before the fifteenth day of the third month of taxable year, but either (1) a shareholder who held stock during the taxable year and before the date of election does not consent to the election, or (2) the corporation did not meet the eligibility requirements during the part of the year before the date of election, then the election is treated as made for the following taxable year.
      (2) An election made after the fifteenth day of the third month of the taxable year is treated as made for the following year.

   b. A newly formed corporation's election will be timely if made within two and one-half months of the first day of its taxable year (e.g., a calendar-year corporation formed on April 6, 2011, could make an S corporation election that would be effective for its 2011 calendar year if the election is filed on or before June 20, 2011).
   c. A valid election is effective for all succeeding years until terminated.
   d. The IRS has the authority to waive the effect of an invalid election caused by a corporation's inadvertent failure to qualify as a small business corporation or to obtain required shareholder consents (including elections regarding qualified subchapter S trusts), or both. Additionally, the IRS may treat late-filed subchapter S elections as timely filed if there is reasonable cause justifying the late filing.

3. **LIFO recapture.** A C corporation using LIFO that converts to S status must recapture the excess of the inventory's value using a FIFO cost flow assumption over its LIFO tax basis as of the close of its last tax year as a C corporation.

   a. The LIFO recapture is included in the C corporation's gross income and the tax attributable to its inclusion is payable in four equal installments.
   b. The first installment must be paid by the due date of the tax return for the last C corporation year, with the three remaining installments due by the due dates of the tax returns for the three succeeding taxable years.

4. A corporation making an S election is generally required to **adopt or change to (1) a year ending December 31,** or (2) a fiscal year that is the same as the fiscal year used by shareholders owning more than 50% of the corporation's stock.

   a. An S corporation may use a different fiscal year if a valid business purpose can be established (i.e., natural business year) and IRS permission is received. The business purpose test will be met if an S corporation receives at least 25% of its gross receipts in the last two months of the selected fiscal year, and this 25% test has been satisfied for three consecutive years.

   > **EXAMPLE**
   >
   > An S corporation, on a calendar year, has received at least 25% of its gross receipts during the months of May and June for each of the last three years. The S corporation may be allowed to change to a fiscal year ending June 30.

   b. An S corporation that otherwise would be required to adopt or change its tax year (normally to the calendar year) may elect to use a fiscal year if the election does not result in a deferral period longer than three months, or, if less, the deferral period of the year currently in use.

      (1) The "deferral period" is the number of months between the close of the fiscal year elected and the close of the required year (e.g., if an S corporation elects a tax year ending September 30 and a tax year ending December 31 is required, the deferral period of the year ending September 30 is three months).
      (2) An S corporation that elects a tax year other than a required year must make a "required payment" which is in the nature of a refundable, noninterest-bearing deposit that is intended to compensate the government for

the revenue lost as a result of tax deferral. The required payment is due on May 15 each year and is recomputed for each subsequent year.

5. An S corporation must **file Form 1120S** by the fifteenth day of the third month following the close of its taxable year (e.g., March 15 for a calendar-year S corporation).

   a. An automatic six-month extension may be obtained by filing Form 7004.
   b. Estimated tax payments must be made if estimated tax liability (e.g., built-in gains tax, excess net passive income tax) is expected to be $500 or more.

6. **Termination** of S corporation status may be caused by

   a. Shareholders owning **more than 50%** of the shares of stock of the corporation consent to **revocation** of the election.

      (1) A revocation made on or before the fifteenth day of the third month of the taxable year is generally effective on the first day of such taxable year.
      (2) A revocation made after the fifteenth day of the third month of the taxable year is generally effective as of the first day of the following taxable year.
      (3) Instead of the dates mentioned above, a revocation may specify an effective date on or after the date on which the revocation is filed.

> **EXAMPLE**
>
> For a calendar-year S corporation, a revocation not specifying a revocation date that is made on or before 3/15/11 is effective as of 1/1/11. A revocation not specifying a revocation date that is made after 3/15/11 is effective as of 1/1/12. If a revocation is filed 3/11/11 and specifies a revocation date of 7/1/11, the corporation ceases to be an S corporation on 7/1/11.

   b. The corporation's **failing to satisfy any of the eligibility requirements** listed in 1. Termination is effective on the date an eligibility requirement is failed.

> **EXAMPLE**
>
> A calendar-year S corporation with common stock outstanding issues preferred stock on April 1, 2011. Since its S corporation status terminates on April 1, it must file an S corporation tax return (Form 1120S) for the period January 1 through March 31, and a C corporation tax return (Form 1120) for the period April 1 through December 31, 2011. Both tax returns would be due by March 15, 2012.

   c. Passive investment income exceeding 25% of gross receipts for three consecutive taxable years if the corporation has subchapter C earnings and profits at the end of each of those years.

      (1) Subchapter C earnings and profits are earnings and profits accumulated during a taxable year for which the corporation was a C corporation.
      (2) Termination is effective as of the first day of the taxable year beginning after the third consecutive year of passive investment income in excess of 25% of gross receipts.

> **EXAMPLE**
>
> An S corporation with subchapter C earnings and profits had passive investment income in excess of 25% of its gross receipts for its calendar years 2008, 2009, and 2010. Its S corporation status would terminate 1/1/11.

   d. Generally once terminated, S corporation status can be reelected only after five non–S corporation years.

      (1) The corporation can request IRS for an earlier reelection.
      (2) IRS may treat an inadvertent termination as if it never occurred.

7. An **S corporation** generally pays no federal income taxes, but may have to pay a tax on its built-in gain, or on its excess passive investment income if certain conditions are met.

   a. The S corporation is treated as a **pass-through entity;** the character of any item of income, expense, gain, loss, or credit is determined at the corporate level, and passes through to shareholders, retaining its identity.
   b. An S corporation must recognize gain on the distribution of appreciated property (other than its own obligations) to its shareholders. Gain is recognized in the same manner as if the property had been sold to the distributee at its FMV.

> **EXAMPLE**
>
> An S corporation distributes property with a FMV of $900 and an adjusted basis of $100 to its sole share-holder. Gain of $800 will be recognized by the corporation. The character of the gain will be determined at the corporate level, and passed through and reported by its shareholder. The shareholder is treated as receiving a $900 distribution, subject to the distribution rules discussed in Section G.11.

   c. Expenses and interest owed to any cash-method shareholder are deductible by an accrual-method S corporation only when paid.

> **EXAMPLE**
>
> An accrual-method calendar-year S corporation accrues $2,000 of salary to a cash-method employee (a 1% shareholder) during 2010, but does not make payment until February 2011. The $2,000 will be deductible by the corporation in 2011, and reported by the shareholder-employee as income in 2011.

   d. An S corporation will not generate any earnings and profits. All items are reflected in adjustments to the basis of shareholders' stock and/or debt.

   e. S corporations must make estimated tax payments for the tax liability attributable to the built-in gains tax, excess passive investment income tax, and the tax due to investment credit recapture.

   f. The provisions of subchapter C apply to an S corporation, except where inconsistent with subchapter S. For example, an S corporation can use Secs. 332 and 337 to liquidate an acquired subsidiary, and can make a Sec. 338 election if otherwise qualified.

8. A **shareholder** of an S corporation must separately take into account (for the shareholder's taxable year in which the taxable year of the S corporation ends) (1) the shareholder's pro rata share of the corporation's items of income (including tax-exempt income), loss, deduction, or credit the separate treatment of which could affect the tax liability of **any** shareholder, plus (2) the shareholder's pro rata share of all remaining items which are netted together into "ordinary income (loss) from trade or business activity."

   a. Some of the **items which must be separately passed through** to retain their identity include

     (1) Net long-term capital gain (loss)
     (2) Net short-term capital gain (loss)
     (3) Net gain (loss) from Sec. 1231 casualty or theft
     (4) Net gain (loss) from other Sec. 1231 transactions
     (5) Tax-exempt interest
     (6) Charitable contributions
     (7) Foreign income taxes
     (8) Depletion
     (9) Investment interest expense
    (10) Dividend, interest, and royalty income
    (11) Net income (loss) from real estate activity
    (12) Net income (loss) from other rental activity
    (13) Sec. 179 expense deduction (limited to $500,000 for 2011)

   b. All separately stated items plus the ordinary income or loss are allocated on a **per share, per day basis** to anyone who was a shareholder during the year. Items are allocated to shareholders' stock (both voting and nonvoting) but not to debt.

     (1) A shareholder who disposes of stock in an S corporation is treated as the shareholder for the day of disposition. A shareholder who dies is treated as the shareholder for the day of the shareholder's death.

> **EXAMPLE**
>
> Alan owned 100% of a calendar-year S corporation's stock on January 1, 2010. Alan sold all his stock to Betty on January 31. Assuming the S corporation had $365,000 of ordinary income for the entire 2010 calendar year, the amount allocated to Alan would be $31,000 (31 days × $1,000 per day), and the amount allocated to Betty would be $334,000 (334 days × $1,000 per day).

     (2) The per share, per day rule will not apply if

(a) A shareholder's interest is completely terminated and all affected shareholders consent to allocate items as if the corporation's taxable year consisted of two years, the first of which ends on the date the shareholder's interest was terminated. The closing of the books method applies only to the affected shareholders. *Affected shareholders* include the shareholder whose interest was terminated and shareholders to whom the terminating shareholder transferred shares during the year.

EXAMPLE

Assume in the above example that the S corporation had net income of $40,000 for the month of January. If both Alan and Betty consent, $40,000 would be allocated to Alan, and $325,000 would be allocated to Betty.

(b) An S corporation's election is terminated on other than the first day of the taxable year, and all shareholders during the S short year and all persons who were shareholders on the first day of the C short year consent to allocate items using the corporation's financial accounting records.

EXAMPLE

Bartec Corporation, with ordinary income of $365,000 for calendar year 2010, had its S status terminated on February 1, 2010, when the Post Partnership became a shareholder. Assuming Bartec's shareholders do **not** elect to allocate items using Bartec's financial accounting records, the ordinary income for calendar year 2010 of $365,000 would be allocated on a daily basis between Bartec's S short year and its C short year. Thus, the amount of income to be reported on Bartec's S return would be $365,000/365 days (31 days) = $31,000. The remaining $365,000 – $31,000 = $334,000 of ordinary income would be reported on Bartec's C return for 2010.

---

(3) The per share, per day rule **cannot** be used if

(a) There is a sale or exchange of 50% or more of the stock of the corporation during an S termination year. Financial accounting records must be used to allocate items.

(b) A Sec. 338 election is made. Then the gains and losses resulting from the Sec. 338 election must be reported on a C corporation return.

9. Three sets of rules may limit the amount of S corporation loss that a shareholder can deduct.

   a. A shareholder's allocation of the aggregate **losses and deductions** of an S corporation can be deducted by the shareholder to the extent of the **shareholder's basis for stock plus basis of any debt** owed the shareholder by the corporation [Sec. 1366 (d)].

   (1) An excess of loss over combined basis for stock and debt can be carried forward indefinitely and deducted when there is basis to absorb it.

EXAMPLE

An S corporation incurred losses totaling $50,000. Its sole shareholder (who materially participates in the business and is at-risk) had a stock basis of $30,000 and debt with a basis of $15,000. The shareholder's loss deduction is limited to $45,000. The losses first reduce stock basis to zero, then debt basis is reduced to zero. The excess loss of $5,000 can be carried forward and deducted when there is basis to absorb it.

---

   (2) Once reduced, the basis of debt is later increased (but not above its original basis) by *net undistributed income*.

EXAMPLE

An S corporation incurred a loss of $20,000 for 2010. Its sole shareholder (who materially participates in the business and is at-risk) had a stock basis of $10,000 and debt with a basis of $15,000. The pass-through of the $20,000 loss would first reduce stock basis to zero, and then reduce debt basis to $5,000.

Assume that for 2011, the same S corporation had ordinary income of $10,000, and made a $4,000 cash distribution to its shareholder during the year. The first $4,000 of basis increase resulting from the pass-through of income would be allocated to stock in order to permit the $4,000 distribution to be nontaxable. The remaining basis increase (net **un**distributed income of $6,000) would restore debt basis to $11,000 (from $5,000).

---

b. The deductibility of S corporation losses is also limited to the amount of the shareholder's **at-risk basis** at the end of the taxable year [Sec. 465].

(1) A shareholder's amount at-risk includes amounts borrowed and reloaned to the S corporation if the shareholder is personally liable for repayment of the borrowed amount, or has pledged property not used in the activity as security for the borrowed amount.

(2) A shareholder's amount at-risk does not include any debt of the S corporation to any person other than the shareholder, even if the shareholder guarantees the debt.

c. The deductibility of S corporation losses may also be subject to the **passive activity loss limitations** [Sec. 469]. Passive activity losses are deductible only to the extent of the shareholder's income from other passive activities (See Module 36).

(1) Passive activities include (a) any S corporation trade or business in which the shareholder does not materially participate, and (b) any rental activity.

(2) If a shareholder "actively participates" in a rental activity and owns (together with spouse) at least 10% of the value of an S corporation's stock, up to $25,000 of rental losses may be deductible against earned income and portfolio income.

10. A shareholder's S corporation **stock basis** is **increased** by all income items (including tax-exempt income), plus depletion in excess of the basis of the property subject to depletion; **decreased** by all loss and deduction items, nondeductible expenses not charged to capital, and the shareholder's deduction for depletion on oil and gas wells; and **decreased** by distributions that are excluded from gross income. Stock basis is **adjusted in the following order:**

a. Increased for all income items
b. Decreased for distributions that are excluded from gross income
c. Decreased for nondeductible, noncapital items
d. Decreased for deductible expenses and losses

> **EXAMPLE**
>
> An S corporation has tax-exempt income of $5,000, and an ordinary loss from business activity of $6,000 for calendar year 2010. Its sole shareholder had a stock basis of $2,000 on January 1, 2010. The $5,000 of tax-exempt income would pass through to the shareholder, increasing the shareholder's stock basis to $7,000, and would permit the pass-through and deduction of the $6,000 of ordinary loss, reducing the shareholder's stock basis to $1,000.

> **EXAMPLE**
>
> An S corporation had an ordinary loss from business activity of $6,000 and made a $7,000 cash distribution to its sole shareholder during calendar year 2010. The sole shareholder had a stock basis of $8,000 on January 1, 2010. The $7,000 cash distribution would be nontaxable and would reduce stock basis to $1,000. As a result, only $1,000 of the $6,000 ordinary loss would be allowable as a deduction to the shareholder for 2010. The remaining $5,000 of ordinary loss would be carried forward and deducted by the shareholder when there is stock or debt basis to absorb it.

11. The **treatment of distributions** (Cash + FMV of other property) to shareholders is determined as follows:

a. Distributions are **nontaxable** to the extent of the Accumulated Adjustments Account (AAA) and are applied to **reduce the AAA and the shareholder's stock basis.**

(1) The AAA represents the cumulative total of undistributed net income items for S corporation taxable years beginning after 1982.

(2) If there is more than one distribution during the year, a pro rata portion of each distribution is treated as made from the AAA.

(3) The AAA can have a negative balance if expenses and losses exceed income.

(4) No adjustment is made to the AAA for tax-exempt income and related expenses, and Federal taxes attributable to a year in which the corporation was a C corporation. Tax-exempt income and related expenses are reflected in the corporation's Other Adjustments Account (OAA).

(5) For purposes of determining the treatment of a distribution, the amount in the AAA at the close of any taxable year is determined without regard to any **net negative adjustment** (i.e., the excess of reductions over increases to the AAA for the taxable year) for such taxable year.

b. Distributions in excess of the AAA are treated as **ordinary dividends** to the extent of the corporation's **accumulated earnings and profits (AEP).** These amounts represent earnings and profits that were accumulated (and never taxed to shareholders) during C corporation taxable years.
c. Distributions are next **nontaxable** to the extent of **remaining stock basis** and are applied to reduce the OAA and paid-in capital.
d. Distributions **in excess of stock basis** are treated as **gain** from the sale of stock.

EXAMPLE

A calendar year S corporation had subchapter C accumulated earnings and profits of $10,000 at December 31, 2009. During calendar year 2010, the corporation had net income of $20,000, and distributed $38,000 to its sole shareholder on June 20, 2010. Its shareholder had a stock basis of $15,000 at January 1, 2010.

The $20,000 of net income passes through and is includible in gross income by the shareholder for 2010. The shareholder's stock basis is increased by the $20,000 of income (to $35,000), as is the AAA which is increased to $20,000. Of the $38,000 distribution, the first $20,000 is nontaxable and (1) reduces stock basis to $15,000, and (2) the AAA to zero; the next $10,000 of distribution is reported as dividend income (no effect on stock basis); while the remaining $8,000 of distribution is nontaxable and reduces stock basis to $7,000.

---

12. Health and accident insurance premiums and other **fringe benefits** paid by an S corporation on behalf of a more than 2% sharcholder-employee are deductible by the S corporation as compensation and includible in the shareholder-employee's gross income on Form W-2.
13. An S corporation (that previously was a C corporation) is taxed on its **net recognized built-in gain** if the gain is (1) attributable to an excess of the FMV of its assets over their aggregate adjusted basis as of the beginning of its first taxable year as an S corporation, and (2) is recognized within **ten years** after the effective date of its S corporation election.

a. This provision generally applies to C corporations that make an S corporation election after December 31, 1986.
b. For an S corporation's 2011 tax year, the recognition period is reduced to five years (e.g., the recognition period will end at the beginning of 2011 if the S election was made for the 2006 tax year). For S corporation tax years beginning in 2009 and 2010, the recognition period is reduced to seven years (e.g., the recognition period will end at the beginning of 2009 if the S election was made for the 2002 tax year).
c. To determine the tax, (1) take the lesser of (a) the net recognized built-in gain for the taxable year, or (b) taxable income determined as if the corporation were a C corporation (except the NOL and dividends-received deductions are not allowed); (2) subtract any NOL and capital loss carryforwards from C corporation years; (3) multiply the resulting amount by the highest corporate tax rate (currently 35%); and (4) subtract any general business credit carryovers from C corporation years and the special fuels tax credit.
d. Any net recognized built-in gain that escapes the built-in gains tax because of the taxable income limitation is carried forward and is subject to the built-in gains tax to the extent the corporation subsequently has other taxable income (that is not already subject to the built-in gains tax) for any taxable year within the ten-year recognition period.
e. Recognized built-in gain **does not include** gain from the disposition of an asset if

(1) The asset was not held by the corporation when its S election became effective (e.g., an asset was purchased after the first day of its S election), or
(2) The gain is attributable to appreciation that occurred after the S election became effective (e.g., an asset is sold for a gain of $1,000, but $600 of its appreciation occurred after the first day of its S election; the corporation would be taxed on only $400 of gain).

f. The total amount of net recognized built-in gain that will be taxed to an S corporation is limited to the aggregate net unrealized built-in gain when the S election became effective.
g. The **built-in gains tax** that is paid by an S corporation is **treated as a loss** sustained by the S corporation during the taxable year. The character of the loss is determined by allocating the loss proportionately among the recognized built-in gains giving rise to such tax.

EXAMPLE

For 2010, an S corporation has taxable income of $100,000, which includes a $40,000 long-term capital gain that is also a recognized built-in gain. Since its recognized built-in gain of $40,000 is less than its taxable income, its built-in gains tax for 2010 is $40,000 × 35% = $14,000. Since the built-in gain was a long-term capital gain, the built-in gains tax paid of $14,000 is treated as a long-term capital loss. As a result, a net long-term capital gain of $26,000 ($40,000 LTCG – $14,000 LTCL) passes through to shareholders for 2010.

> **EXAMPLE**
>
> For 2010, an S corporation has taxable income of $10,000, which includes a $40,000 long-term capital gain that is also a recognized built-in gain. Since its taxable income of $10,000 is less than its recognized built-in gain of $40,000, its built-in gains tax for 2010 is limited to $10,000 × 35% = $3,500. As a result, a net long-term capital gain of $40,000 – $3,500 = $36,500 passes through to shareholders for 2010.
>
> The remaining $30,000 of untaxed recognized built-in gain would be suspended and carried forward to 2011, where it would again be treated as a recognized built-in gain. If the S corporation has at least $30,000 of taxable income in 2011 that is not already subject to the built-in gains tax, the suspended gain from 2010 will be taxed. As a result, the amount of built-in gains tax paid by the S corporation for 2011 will be $30,000 × 35% = $10,500, and will pass through to shareholders as a long-term capital loss, since the original gain in 2010 was a long-term capital gain.

14. If an S corporation has subchapter C accumulated earnings and profits, and its **passive investment income exceeds 25% of gross receipts,** a tax is imposed at the highest corporate rate on the lesser of (1) excess net passive income (ENPI), or (2) taxable income.

   a. $$ENPI = \left(\begin{array}{c} \text{Net passive} \\ \text{income} \end{array} \right) \times \left(\frac{\text{Passive investment income } - (25\% \text{ of Gross receipts})}{\text{Passive investment income}} \right)$$

   b.   **Passive investment income** means gross receipts derived from dividends, interest, royalties, rents, annuities, and gains from the sale or exchange of stock or securities. However, dividends from an affiliated C corporation subsidiary are not treated as passive investment income to the extent the dividends are attributable to the earnings and profits derived from the active conduct of a trade or business by the C corporation.

   c.   The tax paid reduces the amount of passive investment income passed through to shareholders

> **EXAMPLE**
>
> An S corporation has gross receipts of $80,000, of which $50,000 is interest income. Expenses incurred in the production of this passive income total $10,000. The ENPI is $24,000.
>
> $$ENPI = \left(\$50,000 - \$10,000 \right) \times \left(\frac{\$50,000 - (25\% \times \$80,000)}{\$50,000} \right) = \$24,000$$

NOW REVIEW MULTIPLE-CHOICE QUESTIONS 123 THROUGH 152 IN VOLUME 2

H. Corporate Reorganizations

   Certain exchanges, usually involving the exchange of one corporation's stock for the stock or property of another, result in deferral of gain or loss.

1. There are seven different **types** of reorganizations which generally result in nonrecognition treatment.

   a.   Type A—statutory mergers or consolidations

      (1) Merger is one corporation absorbing another by operation of law
      (2) Consolidation is two corporations combining in a new corporation, the former ones dissolving

   b.   Type B—the use of solely voting stock of the acquiring corporation (or its parent) to acquire at least 80% of the voting power and 80% of each class of nonvoting stock of the target corporation

      (1) No boot can be used by the acquiring corporation to acquire the target's stock
      (2) Results in the acquisition of a controlled subsidiary

   c.   Type C—the use of solely voting stock of the acquiring corporation (or its parent) to acquire substantially all of the target's properties

      (1) In determining whether the acquisition is made for solely voting stock, the assumption by the acquiring corporation of a liability of the target corporation, or the fact that the property acquired is subject to a liability is disregarded.
      (2) "Substantially all" means at least 90% of the FMV of the target's net assets, and at least 70% of its gross assets.

(3) The target (acquired) corporation must distribute the consideration it receives, as well as all of its other properties, in pursuance of the plan of reorganization.

d. Type D—a transfer by a corporation of part or all of its assets to another if immediately after the transfer the transferor corporation, or its shareholders, control the transferee corporation (i.e., own at least 80% of the voting power and at least 80% of each class of nonvoting stock)

    (1) Although it may be acquisitive, this type of reorganization is generally used to divide a corporation.
    (2) Generally results in a spin-off, split-off, or split-up

e. Type E—a recapitalization to change the capital structure of a single corporation (e.g., bondholders exchange old bonds for new bonds or stock)

f. Type F—a mere change in identity, form, or place of organization (e.g., name change, change of state of incorporation)

g. Type G—a transfer of assets by an insolvent corporation or pursuant to bankruptcy proceedings, with the result that former creditors often become the owners of the corporation

2. For the reorganization to be tax-free, it must meet one of the above definitions and the exchange must be made under a plan of reorganization involving the affected corporations as parties to the reorganization. It generally must satisfy the judicial doctrines of continuity of shareholder interest, business purpose, and continuity of business enterprise.

a. **Continuity of shareholder interest**—The shareholders of the transferor (acquired) corporation must receive stock in the transferee (acquiring) corporation at least equal in value to 50% of the value of all of the transferor's formerly outstanding stock. This requirement does not apply to Type E and Type F reorganizations.

b. **Continuity of business enterprise**—The transferor's historic business must be continued, or a significant portion (e.g., 1/3) of the transferor's historic assets must be used in a business. This requirement does not apply to Type E and Type F reorganizations.

3. **No gain or loss** is generally recognized to a **transferor corporation** on the transfer of its property pursuant to a plan of reorganization.

a. The **transferee corporation's basis for property** received equals the transferor's basis plus gain recognized (if any) to the transferor.

b. Gain is recognized on the distribution to shareholders of any property other than stock or securities of a party to the reorganization (e.g., property the transferor retained and did not transfer to the acquiring corporation), as if such property were sold for its FMV.

4. No gain or loss is recognized by a corporation on the disposition of stock or securities in another corporation that is a party to the reorganization.

a. No gain or loss is generally recognized on the distribution of stock or securities of a controlled subsidiary in a qualifying spin-off, split-off, or split up. However, the distributing corporation must recognize gain on the distribution of its subsidiary's stock if immediately after the distribution, any person holds a 50% or greater interest in the distributing corporation or a distributed subsidiary that is attributable to stock acquired by purchase during the five-year period ending on date of distribution.

b. Gain is recognized on the distribution of appreciated boot property.

5. If a **shareholder receives boot** in a reorganization, gain is recognized (but not loss).

a. Boot includes the FMV of an excess of principal (i.e., face) amount of securities received over the principal amount of securities surrendered.

> **EXAMPLE**
>
> In a recapitalization, a bondholder exchanges a bond with a face amount and basis of $1,000, for a new bond with a face amount of $1,500 and a fair market value of $1,575. Since an excess face amount of security ($500) has been received, the bondholder's realized gain of $575 will be recognized to the extent of the fair market value of the excess [($500/$1,500) × $1,575] = $525.

b. Recognized gain will be treated as a dividend to the extent of the shareholder's ratable share of earnings and profits of the acquired corporation if the receipt of boot has the effect of the distribution of a dividend.

    (1) Whether the receipt of boot has the effect of a dividend is determined by applying the Sec. 302(b) redemption tests based on the shareholder's stock interest in the acquiring corporation (i.e., as if only stock had been received, and then the boot was used to redeem the stock that was not received).
    (2) The receipt of boot will generally not have the effect of a dividend, and will thus result in capital gain.

6. A shareholder's **basis for stock and securities received** equals the basis of stock and securities surrendered, plus gain recognized, and minus boot received.

> **EXAMPLE**
>
> Pursuant to a merger of Corporation T into Corporation P, Smith exchanged 100 shares of T that he had purchased for $1,000, for 80 shares of P having a FMV of $1,500 and also received $200 cash. Smith's realized gain of $700 is recognized to the extent of the cash received of $200, and is treated as a capital gain. Smith's basis for his P stock is $1,000 ($1,000 + $200 recognized gain – $200 cash received).

7. **Carryover of tax attributes**

    a. The tax attributes of the acquired corporation (e.g., NOL carryovers, earnings and profits, accounting methods, etc.) generally carry over to the acquiring corporation in an acquisitive reorganization.

    b. The amount of an **acquired corporation's NOL** carryovers that can be utilized by the acquiring corporation for its first taxable year ending after the date of acquisition is **limited by Sec. 381** to

$$\frac{\text{Acquiring corporation's TI before}}{\text{NOL deduction}} \quad \times \quad \frac{\text{Days after acquisition date}}{\text{Total days in taxable year}}$$

> **EXAMPLE**
>
> Corporation P (on a calendar year) acquired Corporation T in a statutory merger on October 19, 2010, with the former T shareholders receiving 60% of P's stock. If T had an NOL carryover of $70,000, and P has taxable income (before an NOL deduction) of $91,500, the amount of T's $70,000 NOL carryover that can be deducted by P for 2010 would be limited to
>
> $$\$91,500 \quad \times \quad \frac{73}{365} = \$18,300$$

    c. If there is a **more than 50% change in ownership** of a loss corporation, the taxable income for any year of the new loss (or surviving) corporation may be reduced by an NOL carryover from the old loss corporation only to the extent of the value of the old loss corporation's stock on the date of the ownership change multiplied by the "long-term tax-exempt rate" **(Sec. 382 limitation)**.

        (1) An ownership change has occurred when the percentage of stock owned by an entity's 5% or more shareholders has increased by more than 50 percentage points relative to the lowest percentage owned by such shareholders at any time during the preceding 3-year testing period.

        (2) For the year of acquisition, the Sec. 382 limitation amount is available only to the extent allocable to days after the acquisition date.

$$\text{Section 382 limitation} \quad \times \quad \frac{\text{Days after acquisition date}}{\text{Total days in taxable year}}$$

> **EXAMPLE**
>
> If T's former shareholders received only 30% of P's stock in the preceding example, there would be a more than 50 percentage point change in ownership of T Corporation, and T's NOL carryover would be subject to a Sec. 382 limitation. If the FMV of T's stock on October 19, 2010, was $500,000 and the long-term tax-exempt rate were 3%, the Sec. 382 limitation for 2010 would be ($500,000 × 3%) × (73/365 days) = $3,000.
>
> Thus, only $3,000 of T's NOL carryover could be deducted by P for 2010. The remaining $70,000 – $3,000 = $67,000 of T's NOL would be carried forward by P and can be used to offset P's taxable income for 2011 to the extent of the Sec. 382 limitation (i.e., $500,000 × 3% = $15,000).

> **NOW REVIEW MULTIPLE-CHOICE QUESTIONS 153 THROUGH 162 IN VOLUME 2**

II. COMPARISON OF C CORPORATIONS, S CORPORATIONS, AND PARTNERSHIPS

	C Corporations	**S Corporations**	**Partnerships**
Formation	Generally can be formed tax free. No gain or loss for transferors if requirements of Sec. 351 are satisfied (i.e., transferors of property must own at least 80% of stock immediately after transfer). No gain or loss to corporation when issuing stock. Corporation will have a transferred basis for property received; shareholders will have basis for stock equal to basis of property transferred.	Same as for C corporation.	Generally can be formed tax free. Unlike corporations, there is no 80% control test. Property will have a transferred basis to partnership; partners will have a basis for partnership interest equal to basis of property transferred.
Operation	Separate taxpaying entity. Corporate taxable income taxed at corporate rates. Corporate earnings taxed to shareholders as dividends if distributed.	Pass-through entity. Generally pays no corporate income tax. Income, deduction, loss, and credit items retain their characteristics when passed through to be reported on shareholder returns.	Pass-through entity. Pays no entity level income taxes. Income, deduction, loss, and credit items retain their characteristics when passed through to be reported on partner returns.
Nonliquidating Distributions			
Effect on owner	Taxable as dividends to shareholders to extent made out current or accumulated E&P. Distributions in excess of E&P treated as a nontaxable reduction of stock basis, and will result in capital gain to the extent in excess of stock basis.	Generally treated as nontaxable return of stock basis, and will result in capital gain to the extent in excess of stock basis. Taxable as dividend income to the extent made out of accumulated E&P from C years.	Generally nontaxable to partners, but gain recognized if money or FMV of securities received by partner exceed the partner's basis for partnership interest.
	Noncash property distributions measured by FMV; property received will have FMV basis to distributee.	Same as for C corporation shareholders.	Noncash property distributions generally measured by partnership's basis for the distributed property; property will generally have a transferred basis to the distributee partner.
Effect on entity	Gain (but not loss) recognized on distributions to shareholders as if corporation had sold property for FMV.	Same as for C corporation.	Generally no gain or loss recognized by partnership unless distribution is disproportionate and Sec. 751 applies.
Liquidating Distributions			
Effect on owner	Shareholder treats distributions as received in exchange for stock, generally resulting in capital gain or loss. Noncash property received will have a FMV basis to distribute.	Same as for C corporation shareholders.	Partner generally recognizes *no* gain or loss on receipt of liquidating distributions unless distribution is disproportionate and Sec. 751 applies. Partner can recognize loss if liquidating distribution consists solely of money, unrealized receivables, or inventory. Noncash property received will generally have a transferred basis, but limited to the partner's basis for the partnership interest.
Effect on entity	Generally gain as well as loss recognized on liquidating distributions of property to shareholders.	Same as for C corporations	Generally no gain or loss is recognized by partnership unless liquidating distribution is disproportionate and Sec. 751 applies.

KEY TERMS

Accumulated adjustments account. An S corporation account that reflects the cumulative total of undistributed net income previously taxed to shareholders. Distributions from the AAA are generally treated as nontaxable and are a return of a shareholder's stock basis.

Accumulated earnings tax. A penalty tax imposed on a corporation (in addition to regular income tax) if it accumulates earnings in excess of reasonable business needs in order to avoid a shareholder tax on dividend distributions. The tax is not self-assessing, and does not apply to personal holding companies.

Affiliated corporations. A parent-subsidiary chain of corporations in which at least 80% of the voting power (and total value) of stock is owned by includable corporations. An affiliated group may elect to file a consolidated tax return.

Controlled group. Two or more corporations owned by the same individuals or entities. Controlled groups include parent-subsidiary corporations, brother-sister corporations, and combined groups. The two or more corporations that make up a controlled group are in the aggregate limited to the tax benefits available to a single corporation.

Dividend. A corporate distribution of property to shareholders on their stock that is made from the corporation's current or accumulated earnings and profits.

Dividends received deduction (DRD). A deduction allowed a corporation for dividends received from other taxable domestic corporations. The percentage used varies according to the percentage of stock owned in the dividend paying corporation. If the stock ownership percentage is less than 20%, the DRD is 70% of the dividends received. If the stock ownership percentage is at least 20% but less than 80%, the DRD is 80% of the dividends received. If the stock ownership percentage is at least 80%, the DRD percentage is 100% (if a consolidated return is not filed).

Organizational expenditures. Include expenses of temporary directors and organizational meetings, state fees for incorporation, and accounting and legal service costs incident to incorporation. A corporation may immediately expense the first $5,000 (subject to phaseout) of organizational expenditures and generally amortize the remainder over a period of 180 months beginning with the month that business begins.

Personal holding company tax. A penalty tax imposed on a personal holding company (in addition to regular income tax) to discourage individuals from placing investment property in a corporation in order to have investment income taxed at lower corporate rates. The tax is self-assessing.

S corporation. A qualifying small business corporation for which an election has been made to be taxed under the provisions of Subchapter S of the IRC. An S corporation generally pays no corporate income tax and is treated as a pass-through entity. An S corporation's items of income, gain, loss, deduction, and credit pass through to shareholders and are reported on the tax returns of its shareholders.

Sec. 1244 stock. Stock issued by a qualifying small business corporation that entitles the original holder to deduct an ordinary loss (rather than a capital loss) if the stock is disposed of at a loss or becomes worthless. The annual ceiling on ordinary loss treatment is $50,000 ($100,000 for married individuals filing jointly).

Module 39: Other Taxation Topics

Overview

This module presents a review of several independent taxation topics. Coverage is first presented regarding the federal gift, estate, and generation-skipping transfer taxes. Next reviewed is the income taxation of estates and trusts. That is followed by coverage of exempt organizations. Multijurisdictional taxation is then reviewed, including state and local taxation (SALT) and international taxation. Next, the module provides a review of the sources of federal tax authority including the federal tax legislative process, as well as the Internal Revenue Code, regulations, and rulings. The module concludes with an overview of some tax planning possibilities.

I. GIFT AND ESTATE TAXATION

The estate, gift, and generation-skipping transfer (GST) taxes form a unified transfer tax system. The estate tax is based on property transferred at an individual's death, while the gift tax is based on property transferred during an individual's lifetime. The generation-skipping transfer tax ensures that property does not skip a generation without a transfer tax being assessed. The estate tax, gift tax, and GST share a single progressive tax rate schedule.

The Tax Relief Act of 2010 reinstated the federal estate tax and generation-skipping transfer (GST) taxes to the estates of decedents dying and GSTs made after December 31, 2009, and before January 1, 2013. Reinstatement of these taxes was accompanied by a higher applicable exclusion amount of $5 million, and a lower maximum tax rate of 35%. The higher applicable exclusion amount of $5 million and maximum tax rate of 35% also apply to the federal gift tax for gifts made after December 31, 2010. Additionally, beginning in 2011, the estate of a surviving spouse will be entitled to the

1192 Module 39: Other Taxation Topics

unused portion of his or her predeceased spouse's applicable exclusion amount if the appropriate election is made by the predeceased spouse's estate.

The executor of the estate of a decedent who died during calendar-year 2010 may elect to apply the IRC as if the reinstatement of the federal estate tax by the Tax Relief Act of 2010 had not occurred. If this election is made, the federal estate tax will not apply to the decedent's estate, and the estate's assets will have a modified carryover basis instead of a stepped-up fair market value basis.

A. The Gift Tax

1. Gift Tax Formula

Gross gifts (cash plus FMV of property at date of gift)		$xxx
Plus: One-half of spouse's gifts to third parties if gift splitting elected		x
Less:		
One-half of gifts to third parties treated as given by spouse if gift splitting elected	$ x	
Annual exclusion (up to $13,000 per donee)	x	
Unlimited exclusion for tuition or medical expenses paid on behalf of donee	x	
Unlimited exclusion for gifts to political organizations	x	
Charitable gifts (remainder of charitable gifts after annual exclusion)	x	
Marital deduction (remainder of gifts to spouse after annual exclusion)	x	xx
Taxable gifts for current year		$ xx
Add: Taxable gifts for prior years		x
Total taxable gifts		$ xx
Transfer tax on total taxable gifts		$ xx
Less: Transfer tax on taxable gifts made prior to current year		x
Transfer tax for current year		$ xx
Transfer tax credit	$ xx	
Less: Transfer tax credit used in prior years	x	x
Net gift tax liability		$ xx

2. A **gift** is a transfer for less than adequate consideration in money or money's worth. A gift *occurs* when a transfer becomes complete and is measured by its fair market value on that date. A gift becomes **complete** when the donor has relinquished dominion and control and no longer has the power to change its disposition, whether for the donor's benefit or for the benefit of another.

   a. The creation of joint ownership in property is treated as a gift to the extent the donor's contribution exceeds the donor's retained interest.

   b. The creation of a joint bank account is not a gift; but a gift results when the noncontributing tenant withdraws funds.

   c. The transfer of property to a revocable trust is not a completed gift because the transferor may demand the return of the property or change the beneficiaries of the trust.

3. Gross gifts less the following deductions equal taxable gifts:

   a. **Annual exclusion**—of up to $13,000 per donee is allowed for gifts of present interests (not future interests). A **present interest** is an unrestricted right to the immediate use, possession, or enjoyment of property or the income from property. A **future interest** includes reversions, remainders, and other interests that are limited to commence in use, possession, or enjoyment at some future date or time.

     (1) Trusts for minors (Sec. 2503(c) trusts) allow parents and other donors to obtain an annual exclusion for gifts to trusts for children under age twenty-one even though the trust does not distribute its income annually. To qualify, the trust must provide

        (a) Until the beneficiary reaches age twenty-one, the trustee **may** pay the income and/or the underlying assets to the beneficiary, and,

        (b) Any income and assets not distributed must pass to the beneficiary when the beneficiary reaches age twenty-one. If the beneficiary dies before age twenty-one, the income and underlying assets are either payable to the beneficiary's estate, or are payable to any person the minor may appoint if the minor possesses a general power of appointment over the trust property.

     (2) **Crummey** trusts allow a donor to obtain an annual exclusion upon funding a discretionary trust. This type of trust is more flexible than a Sec. 2503(c) trust because the beneficiary can be of any age and the trust can terminate at any age. To qualify, a beneficiary must have the power to demand a distribution equal to the lesser of the donor's annual exclusion ($13,000), or the beneficiary's pro rata share of the amount transferred to the trust each year

b. **Gift-splitting**—a gift by either spouse to a third party may be treated as made one-half by each, if both spouses consent to election. Gift-splitting has the advantage of using the other spouse's annual exclusion and unified transfer tax credit.

> **EXAMPLE**
>
> H is married and has three sons. H could give $26,000 per year to each of his sons without making a taxable gift if H's spouse (W) consents to gift-splitting.
>
> | | H | W |
> |---|---|---|
> | Gifts | $78,000 | |
> | Gift-splitting | (39,000) | $39,000 |
> | Annual exclusion (3 × $13,000) | (39,000) | (39,000) |
> | Taxable gifts | $ 0 | $ 0 |

c. **Educational and medical exclusion**—an unlimited exclusion is available for amounts **paid on behalf of a donee** (1) as tuition to an educational organization, or (2) to a health care provider for medical care of donee.

d. **Political gifts**—an unlimited exclusion is available for the transfer of money or other property to a political organization.

e. **Charitable gifts**—(net of annual exclusion) are deductible without limitation.

f. **Marital deduction**—is allowed without limitation for gifts to a donor's spouse.

(1) The gift must not be a terminable interest (i.e., donee spouse's interest ends at death with no control over who receives remainder).

(2) If donor elects, a gift of **qualified terminable interest** property (i.e., property placed in trust with income to donee spouse for life and remainder to someone else at donee spouse's death) will qualify for the marital deduction if the income is paid at least annually to spouse and the property is not subject to transfer during the donee spouse's lifetime.

(3) In lieu of a marital deduction, gifts to an alien spouse are eligible for an annual exclusion of up to $139,000 for 2012 ($136,000 for 2011).

4. The **tax computation** reflects the **cumulative nature** of the gift tax. A tax is first computed on lifetime taxable gifts, then is reduced by the tax on taxable gifts made in prior years in order to tax the current year's gifts at applicable marginal rates. Any available transfer tax credit is then subtracted to arrive at the gift tax liability.

a. For 2011, the transfer tax credit is $1,730,800, which is equivalent to an exemption of the first $5 million of taxable gifts from the gift tax.

b. For 2012, the transfer tax credit is $1,772,800, which is equivalent to an exemption of the first $5,120,000 of taxable gifts from the gift tax.

5. A **gift tax return** (Form 709 United States Gift [and Generation-Skipping Transfer] Tax Return) must be filed on a calendar-year basis, with the return due and tax paid on or before April 15th of the following year.

a. A donor who makes a gift to charity is not required to file a gift tax return if the entire value of the donated property qualifies for a gift tax charitable deduction.

b. If the donor dies, the gift tax return for the year of death is due not later than the due date for filing the decedent's federal estate tax return (generally nine months after date of death).

6. The **basis of property acquired by gift**

a. Basis for gain—basis of donor plus gift tax attributable to appreciation

b. Basis for loss—lesser of gain basis or FMV at date of gift

c. The increase in basis for gift tax paid is limited to the amount (not to exceed the gift tax paid) that bears the same ratio to the amount of gift tax paid as the net appreciation in value of the gift bears to the amount of the gift.

(1) The amount of gift is reduced by any portion of the $13,000 annual exclusion allowable with respect to the gift.

(2) Where more than one gift of a present interest is made to the same donee during a calendar year, the $13,000 exclusion is applied to gifts in chronological order.

> **EXAMPLE**
>
> Joan received property with a FMV of $60,000 and an adjusted basis of $80,000 as a gift. The donor paid a gift tax of $12,000 on the transfer. Since the property was not appreciated in value, no gift tax can be added in the basis computation. Joan's basis for computing a gain is $80,000, while her basis for computing a loss is $60,000.

> **NOW REVIEW MULTIPLE-CHOICE QUESTIONS 1 THROUGH 9 IN VOLUME 2**

B. The Estate Tax

1. Estate Tax Formula

Gross estate (cash plus FMV of property at date of death, or alternate valuation date)		$xxx
Less:		
Funeral expenses	$x	
Administrative expenses	x	
Debts and mortgages	x	
Casualty losses	x	
State death taxes	x	
Charitable bequests (unlimited)	x	
Marital deduction (unlimited)	x	xx
Taxable estate		$xxx
Add: Post-76 adjusted taxable gifts		xx
Total taxable life and death transfers		$xxx
Transfer tax on total transfers		$ xx
Less:		
Post-76 gift taxes (specially computed at estate tax rates in effect at time of death)	$x	
Transfer tax credit ($1,730,800 for 2011)	x	
Foreign death and prior transfer tax credits	x	x
Net estate tax liability		$ xx

2. **Gross estate** includes the FMV of all property in which the decedent had an interest at time of death.

   a. **Concurrently held property**

   (1) If property was held by tenancy in common, only the FMV of the decedent's share is included.
   (2) Include one-half the FMV of community property, and one-half the FMV of property held **by spouses** in joint tenancy or tenancy by the entirety.
   (3) Include one-half of FMV if the property held by two persons in joint tenancy was acquired by gift, bequest, or inheritance (1/3 if held by three persons, etc.).
   (4) If property held in joint tenancy was acquired by purchase by **other than spouses,** include the FMV of the property multiplied by the percentage of total cost furnished by the decedent.

   b. The FMV of transfers with retained life estates and revocable transfers are included in the gross estate.
   c. Include the FMV of transfers intended to take effect at death (i.e., the donee can obtain enjoyment only by surviving the decedent, and the decedent prior to death had a reversionary interest of more than 5% of the value of the property).
   d. Include any property over which the decedent had a **general power of appointment** (i.e., decedent could appoint property in favor of decedent, decedent's estate, or creditors of decedent or decedent's estate).
   e. Include the value of life insurance proceeds from policies payable to the estate, and policies over which the decedent possessed an "incident of ownership" (e.g., right to change beneficiary).
   f. Include income in respect of a decedent.
   g. Include gifts of life insurance within three years of the decedent's date of death.
   h. Include gift tax paid on all transfers made within three years of death.

3. Property is included at **FMV at date of decedent's death**; or executor may elect to use FMV at **alternate valuation date** (generally a date six months subsequent to death), if such election will reduce both the gross estate and the federal estate tax liability.

   a. If alternate valuation is elected, but property is distributed, sold, exchanged, or otherwise disposed of within six months of death, then use FMV on date of distribution, sale, exchange or other disposition.
   b. Election is irrevocable and applies to all property in estate; cannot be made on an individual property basis.

4. **Estate tax deductions** include funeral expenses, administrative expenses, debts and mortgages, casualty losses during the estate administration, state death taxes, charitable bequests (no limit), and an unlimited marital deduction for the FMV of property passing to a surviving spouse.

   a. A terminable interest granted to surviving spouse will not generally qualify for marital deduction.

   b. If executor elects, the FMV of "qualified terminable interest property" is eligible for the marital deduction if the income from the property is paid at least annually to spouse and the property is not subject to transfer during the surviving spouse's lifetime.

   c. Property passing to a surviving spouse who is not a US citizen is not eligible for the estate tax marital deduction, except for property passing to an alien spouse through a qualified domestic trust (QDT).

   d. Property passing from a nonresident alien to a surviving spouse who is a US citizen is eligible for the estate tax marital deduction.

   e. An unlimited charitable deduction is available for amounts transferred by bequest, devise, or legacy to qualified charitable organizations, including foreign charities. However, the amount of charitable deduction must be reduced by any estate, legacy, or inheritance taxes that are payable in whole or in part from the bequest, devise, or legacy.

   f. The decedent's medical and funeral expenses are allowed as deductions on the estate tax return Form 706. However, if the decedent's medical expenses are paid within twelve months of death, they instead can be deducted on the decedent's final income tax return Form 1040 if the estate's executor makes the appropriate election to waive the deduction on the decedent's estate tax return. The decedent's medical and funeral expenses are never allowed as deductions on the estate's income tax return Form 1041.

5. Post-76 taxable gifts are added back to the taxable estate at date of gift FMV. Any gift tax paid is *not* added back.

6. A transfer tax is computed on total life and death transfers, then is reduced by the tax already paid on post-76 gifts, the unified tax credit, foreign death tax credit, and prior transfer tax credit (i.e., percentage of estate tax paid on the transfer to the present decedent from a transferor who died within past ten years).

7. Effective for deaths occurring after 2010, the estate of a surviving spouse may qualify to utilize the unused portion of the estate tax applicable exclusion amount ($5 million for 2011) of his or her last predeceased spouse. To take advantage of this provision, a special election must have been made by the predeceased spouse's estate. The applicable exclusion amount for a surviving spouse will be the sum of a basic exclusion amount ($5 million for 2011), plus the aggregate deceased spousal unused exclusion amount. The provision applies to only unused exclusion of the last deceased spouse. It is not possible for individuals who have been married multiple times to tack on multiple applicable exclusion amounts of their predeceased spouses.

EXAMPLE

Henry died in 2011 with a taxable estate of $2 million. An election is made on Henry's estate tax return to permit his wife, Wilma, to use his unused exclusion of $3 million. Wilma, who had not made any lifetime taxable gifts, dies in 2012 with a taxable estate of $9 million. The total applicable exclusion amount available to Wilma's estate will consist of her basic exclusion amount of $5,120,000 plus the $3 million of Henry's unused exclusion amount, for a total exclusion of $8,120,000.

---

8. **Form 706** United States Estate (and Generation Skipping Transfer) Tax Return must be filed if the decedent's **gross estate exceeds $5,000,000 for 2011 ($5,120,000 for 2012)**. The return must be filed within **nine months** of decedent's death, unless an extension of time has been granted.

9. The **basis of property acquired from a decedent** is generally the FMV at date of decedent's death, or the alternate valuation date if elected for estate tax purposes.

   a. Use FMV on date of disposition if alternate valuation is elected and property is distributed, sold, or otherwise disposed of during the six-month period following death.

   b. FMV rule does not apply to appreciated property acquired by the decedent by gift within one year before death if such property then passes from the donee-decedent to the original donor or donor's spouse. The basis of such property to the original donor (or spouse) will be the adjusted basis of the property to the decedent immediately before death.

EXAMPLE

Son gives property with FMV of $40,000 (basis of $5,000) to terminally ill father within one year before father's death. The property is included in father's estate at FMV of $40,000. If property passes to son or son's spouse, basis will remain at $5,000. If passed to someone else, the property's basis will be $40,000.

II. GENERATION-SKIPPING TAX

This tax is imposed on transfers in addition to the federal gift and estate taxes and is designed to prevent individuals from escaping an entire generation of gift and estate taxes by transferring property to, or in trust for the benefit of, a person that is two or more generations younger than the donor or transferor.

A. The tax approximates the transfer tax that would be imposed if property were actually transferred to each successive generation, and is imposed on taxable distributions, taxable terminations, and direct skips to someone at least two generations below that of the donor or transferor.

1. A taxable distribution is a distribution out of a trust's income or corpus to a beneficiary at least two generations below that of the grantor (unless the grandchild's parent is deceased and was a lineal descendant of the grantor) while an older generation beneficiary has an interest in the trust.
2. A taxable termination means that by reason of death, expiration of time, or otherwise, the interest of a nonskip person terminates (i.e., someone less than two generations below the donor or transferor) and a skip person (i.e., someone at least two generations below the donor or transferor) becomes the recipient of the trust property or the only beneficiary.
3. A direct skip occurs when one or more generations are bypassed altogether and property is transferred directly to, or in trust for, a skip person.

B. The generation-skipping transfer tax is imposed at a flat rate that equals the maximum unified transfer tax rate of 35%.
C. Exemptions available

1. A $5,000,000 exemption per transferor for 2011 ($5,120,000 for 2012)
2. An unlimited exemption is available for a direct skip to a grandchild if the grandchild's parent is deceased and was a lineal descendant of the transferor

> **NOW REVIEW MULTIPLE-CHOICE QUESTIONS 10 THROUGH 26 IN VOLUME 2**

III. INCOME TAXATION OF ESTATES AND TRUSTS

Although estates and trusts are separate taxable entities, they will not pay an income tax if they distribute all of their income to beneficiaries. In this respect they act as a conduit, since the income taxed to beneficiaries will have the same character as it had for the estate or trust.

A. **US Income Tax Return for Estate or Trust (Form 1041)** must be filed by an estate if it has gross income of **$600** or more, or has a beneficiary who is a nonresident alien. Form 1041 must be filed by a trust if it has gross income of **$600** or more, any *taxable income*, or a beneficiary who is a nonresident alien.

1. Return is due by the 15th day of the fourth month following the close of the estate or trust's taxable year.
2. A **trust must adopt a calendar year** as its taxable year. An estate may adopt a calendar year or any fiscal year.
3. For 2012, estate and trusts are taxed as follows:

   a. First $2,400 of taxable income is taxed at 15%
   b. Over $2,400 but not over $5,600 is taxed at 25%
   c. Over $5,600 but not over $8,500 is taxed at 28%
   d. Over $8,500 but not over $11,650 is taxed at 33%
   e. Over $11,650 is taxed at 35%

4. The alternative minimum tax applies to estates and trusts and is computed in the same manner as for individuals. The AMT exemption for an estate or trust is $22,500.
5. Estates and trusts are generally required to make estimated tax payments using the rules applicable to individuals. However, estates do not have to make estimated payments for taxable years ending within two years of the decedent's death. .

B. **Classification of Trusts**

1. **Simple trust** is one that (1) is required to distribute all of its income to beneficiaries each year, (2) cannot make charitable contributions, and (3) makes no distribution of trust corpus (i.e., principal) during the year.
2. **Complex trust** is any trust other than a simple trust.

C. **Computation of Estate or Trust Taxable Income**

1. **Gross income** for an estate or trust is generally the same as for individual taxpayers.

   a. Generally no gain or loss is recognized on the transfer of property to beneficiaries to satisfy specific bequests.

b. Gain or loss is recognized on the transfer of property to beneficiaries in lieu of cash to satisfy specific cash bequests.

2. **Allowable deductions** for an estate or trust are generally the same as for an individual taxpayer.

 a. A personal **exemption** is allowed.

  (1) $600 for estate
  (2) $300 for trusts required to distribute all income currently
  (3) $100 for all other trusts

 b. Charitable contributions can be made by estates and trusts (other than simple trusts).

  (1) Contributions can be deducted without limitation if paid out of income.
  (2) Contributions are not deductible to the extent paid out of tax-exempt income.

 c. Expenses incurred in the production of tax exempt income are not deductible.
 d. Capital losses offset capital gains and a net capital loss of up to $3,000 can be deducted with the remainder carried forward.
 e. Any unused capital loss and net operating loss (NOL) carryovers from the decedent's final Form 1040 are not allowed as deductions.

3. An **income distribution deduction** is allowed for distributions of income to beneficiaries.

 a. **Distributable net income (DNI)** is the maximum amount of deduction for distributions to beneficiaries in any taxable year and also determines the amounts and character of the income reported by the beneficiaries.
 b. Generally, DNI is the same as the estate's or trust's taxable income computed before the income distribution deduction with the following modifications:

  (1) Add

   (a) Personal exemption
   (b) Any net capital loss deduction (limited to $3,000)
   (c) Tax exempt interest (reduced by related nondeductible expenses)

  (2) Subtract

   (a) Net capital gains allocable to corpus
   (b) Extraordinary dividends and taxable stock dividends allocated to corpus of simple trust

 c. Deduction will be the lesser of DNI or the amount distributed to beneficiaries (i.e., taxable income required to be distributed, plus other amount of taxable income distributed).

D. Treatment of Simple Trust and Beneficiaries

1. Income is taxed to beneficiaries, not to trust.
2. Beneficiaries are taxed on the income required to be distributed (up to DNI), even though not actually distributed during the year.
3. Income passes through to beneficiaries retaining its characteristics (e.g., tax-exempt income passes through retaining its exempt status).
4. If multiple beneficiaries, DNI is prorated in proportion to the amount of required distribution to each beneficiary.

E. Treatment of Complex Trust and Beneficiaries

1. A two-tier income distribution system is used.

 a. First tier: Distributions of the first tier are income amounts that are required to be distributed and include distributions that can be paid out of income or corpus, to the extent paid out of income.
 b. Second tier: Distributions of the second tier are all other amounts that are actually paid during the year or are required to be paid.

2. DNI is first allocated to distributions in the first tier. Any remaining DNI is prorated to distributions in the second tier.

EXAMPLE

A trust has DNI of $9,000. The trust instrument requires that $6,000 of income be distributed annually to Alan. Further, it permits distributions to Baker and Carr of income or corpus in the trustee's discretion. For the current year, the trustee distributes $6,000 to Alan, $4,000 to Baker, and $2,000 to Carr.

> Since Alan's distribution is a first tier distribution, all $6,000 distributed is taxable to Alan. This leaves only $3,000 of DNI to be allocated to the second tier distributions to Baker and Carr. Since DNI would be allocated in proportion to the amounts distributed, $2,000 of Baker's distribution and $1,000 of Carr's distribution would be taxable.

F. Grantor Trusts are trusts over which the grantor (or grantor's spouse) retain substantial control. The income from a grantor trust is generally taxed to the grantor, not to the trust or beneficiaries. A grantor trust generally exists if any of the following conditions are present:

1. Trust income will, or in the grantor's or nonadverse party's discretion may be, distributed to the grantor or grantor's spouse (or used to pay life insurance premiums of either).
2. The grantor (or nonadverse party) has the power to revoke the trust.
3. The grantor (or grantor's spouse) holds a reversionary interest worth more than 5% of trust corpus.
4. The grantor (or nonadverse party) can deal with trust property in a nonfiduciary capacity (e.g., purchase trust assets for less than adequate consideration or borrow trust property at below market rate).
5. The grantor (or grantor's spouse) or nonadverse party controls the beneficial enjoyment of the trust (e.g., ability to change beneficiaries).

G. Termination of Estate or Trust

1. An estate or trust is not entitled to a personal exemption on its final return.
2. Any unused carryovers (e.g., NOL or capital loss) are passed through to beneficiaries for use on their individual tax returns.
3. Any excess deductions for its final year are passed through to beneficiaries and can be deducted as miscellaneous itemized deductions.

NOW REVIEW MULTIPLE-CHOICE QUESTIONS 27 THROUGH 41 IN VOLUME 2

IV. EXEMPT ORGANIZATIONS

A. Types of Organizations

1. Tax-exempt organizations are listed by class of organization in the Internal Revenue Code. Generally, an exempt organization serves some common good, is operated as a not-for-profit entity, its net earnings do not inure for the benefit of specified individuals, and the organization does not exert undue political influence. To obtain exempt status, the organization must be one of those specifically identified in the Code, and generally must apply for and receive an exemption.

IRC 501	Type of Organization	Description
(c) (1)	Federal and Regulated Agencies	Federal Credit Unions, FDIC, Federal Land Bank
(c) (2)	Title Holding Corporation for Exempt Organization	Corporation holding title to fraternity or sorority house
(c) (3)	Religious, Educational, Charitable, Scientific, Literary, Testing for Public Safety, Foster National or International Amateur Sports Competition, Prevention of Cruelty to Children or Animals Organizations	Activities of a nature implied by description of class of organization (e.g., church, school, museum, zoo, planetarium, Red Cross, Boy Scouts of America)
(c) (4)	Civic Leagues, Social Welfare Organizations, and Local Associations of Employees	Promotion of community welfare (e.g., community association, volunteer fire companies, garden club, League of Women Voters)
(c) (5)	Labor, Agricultural, and Horticultural Organizations	Educational or instructive, to improve conditions of work, and to improve products and efficiency (e.g., teacher's association)
(c) (6)	Business Leagues, Chamber of Commerce, Real Estate Boards, etc.	Improvement of business conditions of one or more lines of business (e.g., trade of professional associations, Chambers of Commerce)
(c) (7)	Social and Recreation Clubs	Recreation and social activities (e.g., Country Club, Sailing Club, Tennis Club)

IRC 501	Type of Organization	Description
(c) (8)	Fraternal Beneficiary Societies and Associations	Lodge providing for payment of life, sickness, accident, or other benefits to members
(c) (9)	Voluntary Employees' Beneficiary Associations	Providing for payment of life, sickness, accident, or other benefits to members
(c)(10)	Domestic Fraternal Societies and Associations	Lodge devoting its net earnings to charitable, fraternal, and other specified purposes, but no life, sickness, or accident benefits to members
(c)(11)	Teachers' Retirement Fund Associations	Payment of retirement benefits to teachers
(c)(12)	Benevolent Life Insurance Associations, Mutual or Cooperative Telephone Companies, etc.	Activities of a mutually beneficial nature
(c)(13)	Cemetery Companies	Operated for benefit of lot owners who purchase lots for burial
(c)(14)	State Chartered Credit Unions	Loans to members
(c)(15)	Mutual Insurance Companies or Associations	Providing insurance to members substantially at cost
(c)(16)	Farmers Cooperative Organizations to Finance Crop Operations	Financing of crop operations in conjunction with activities of marketing or purchasing association
(c)(17)	Supplemental Unemployment Benefit Trusts	Payment of supplemental unemployment compensation benefits
(c)(19)	Member of Armed Forces Post or Organization	Veterans of Foreign Wars (VFW)
(d)	Religious and Apostolic Associations	Communal religious community that conducts business activities. Members must include pro rata share of organization's income in their gross income
(e)	Cooperative Hospital Service Organizations	Performs cooperative service for hospitals (e.g., centralized purchasing organization)
(k)	Child Care Organizations	Provides care for children

2. **Sec. 501(c)(3) organizations** (religious, educational, charitable, etc.) generally must apply for exemption by filing Form 1023 within fifteen months from the end of the month in which they were organized. To qualify, (1) the organization must meet an organizational and operational test, (2) no part of the organization's net earnings can inure to the benefit of private shareholders or individuals, and (3) the organization cannot, as a substantial part of its activities, attempt to influence legislation (unless it elects an exception permitting certain lobby expenditures) or directly participate to any extent in a political campaign for or against any candidate for public office.

   a. Some organizations do not have to file for exemption (e.g., churches or an organization [other than a private foundation] normally having annual gross receipts of not more than $5,000). They automatically are exempt if they meet the requirements of Sec. 501(c)(3).

   b. The **organizational test** requires the articles of organization limit the organization's purposes to one or more exempt purposes described in Sec. 501(c)(3), and must not expressly empower the organization to engage in activities that are not in furtherance of its one or more exempt purposes, except as an insubstantial part of its activities.

   c. The **operational test** requires that an exempt organization be operated exclusively for an exempt purpose. An organization will be considered to be operated exclusively for an exempt purpose only if it engages primarily in activities that accomplish its exempt purpose. An organization will not be so regarded if more than an insubstantial part of its activities is not in furtherance of an exempt purpose.

   d. **Inurement** is private benefit provided to insiders who have the institutional opportunity to direct the organization's resources to themselves, to entities in which they have an interest, or to family members. Inurement issues may arise because of excessive compensation, payment of excessive rent, receipt of less than fair value from sales of property, and inadequately secured loans.

   e. An organization (other than churches and private foundations) can elect to replace the substantial part of activities test with a limit defined in terms of expenditures for influencing legislation. **Attempting to influence legislation** includes (1) any attempt to influence any legislation through an effort to affect the opinions of the general public (i.e., grassroots lobbying), and (2) any attempt to influence any legislation through communication with any member or employee of a legislative body, or with any government official or employee who may participate in the formulation of legislation (i.e., direct lobbying).

    (1) Attempting to influence legislation does **not** include appearing before or communicating with any legislative body with respect to a possible decision of that body that might affect the powers, duties, exempt status, or the deduction of contributions to the organization.

    (2) If the election to be subject to the lobbying expenditures limits (instead of the substantial part of activities test) is made, an organization will not lose its exempt status unless it normally makes lobbying expenditures in excess of 150% of lobbying nontaxable amount or normally makes grassroots expenditures in excess of 150% of grassroots nontaxable amount.

    (3) If the election is made, an organization will be subject to a 25% excise tax on the excess of its lobbying and grassroots expenditures over the lobbying and grassroots nontaxable amounts.

3. **Private foundations** are Sec. 501(c)(3) organizations other than churches, educational organizations, hospitals or medical research organizations operated in conjunction with hospitals, endowment funds operated for the benefit of certain state and municipal colleges and universities, governmental units, and publicly supported organizations.

    a. An organization is **publicly supported** if it normally receives at least one-third of its total support from governmental units and the general public (e.g., support received in the form of gifts, grants, contributions, membership fees, gross receipts from admissions, sales of merchandise, etc.)

    b. Private foundations may be subject to taxes based on investment income, self-dealing, failure to distribute income, excess business holdings, investments that jeopardize charitable purposes, and taxable expenditures. The initial taxes (with the exception of the tax on investment income) are imposed because the organization engages in prohibited transactions. Additional taxes are imposed if the prohibited transactions are not corrected with a specified period.

4. **Feeder organizations** do not qualify for tax-exempt status. A feeder organization carries on a trade or business for the benefit of an exempt organization and remits its profits to the exempt organization.

B. Filing Requirements

1. Most exempt organizations must file an **annual information return** Form 990 (Return of Organization Exempt from Income Tax). Organizations **not** required to file Form 990 include churches, federal agencies, organizations whose annual gross receipts do not exceed $50,000, and private foundations.

2. Exempt organizations with **unrelated business income** must file Form 990-T (Exempt Organization Business Income Tax Return) if the organization has gross income of at least $1,000 from an unrelated trade or business. The obligation to file Form 990-T is in addition to the obligation to file Form 990. Additionally, Form 990-T may be required even though Form 990 is not required to be filed.

3. **Private foundations** must annually file Form 990-PF (Return of Private Foundation). If an organization is subject to any of the excise taxes imposed on private foundations, Form 4720 (Return of Certain Excise Taxes on Charities and Other Persons) must be filed with Form 990-PF.

4. Small exempt organizations whose gross receipts are $50,000 or less are required to annually file an electronic Form 990-N (e-Postcard). Organizations eligible to file the 990-N can instead elect to file Form 990.

5. Exempt organizations who are *not* eligible to file the 990-N but have gross receipts less than $200,000 and total assets less than $500,000 are required to file Form 990-EZ or Form 990.

6. Forms 990, 990-EZ, 990-T, 990-PF, and 990-N are generally due by the 15th day of the 5th month after the end of the tax year (e.g., May 15th for a calendar-year organization).

7. An exempt organization that fails to file its required return for three consecutive years will lose its tax-exempt status. The revocation of the organization's tax-exempt status will not take place until the filing due date for the third year.

NOW REVIEW MULTIPLE-CHOICE QUESTIONS 42 THROUGH 56 IN VOLUME 2

C. Unrelated Business Income (UBI)

1. **UBI** is income from a business that is (1) **regularly carried on**, and (2) is **unrelated** to the organization's exempt purpose. A business is substantially related only if the activity (not its proceeds) contributes importantly to the accomplishment of the exempt purposes of the organization.

2. Income derived from debt-financed property unrelated to the exempt function of the organization is included in UBI. The amount of such income to be included in UBI is based on the proportion of average acquisition indebtedness to the property's average adjusted basis.

3. Income from commercial product advertising in journals and other publications is generally UBI.

4. Activities specifically treated as resulting in **related income** (not UBI) include

    a. An activity where substantially all work is performed without compensation (e.g., a church runs a second-hand clothing store with all work performed by volunteers).

   b. A trade or business carried on for the convenience of students or members of a charitable, religious, or scientific organization (e.g., university bookstore).

   c. The sale of merchandise received as gifts or contributions.

   d. Income from dividends, interest, annuities, and royalties. However, such income will be included in UBI if it results from debt-financed investments.

   e. Income derived from renting real property. However, income derived from renting personal property is considered UBI unless the personal property is leased with the real property and personal property rents do not exceed 10% of total rents.

   f. Conducting bingo games if the games are not in violation of any state or local law, and are conducted in a jurisdiction that ordinarily confines bingo games to exempt organizations.

5. UBI is **taxed to the extent in excess of $1,000**. UBI is taxed at regular corporate rates if the organization is a corporation, taxed at rates applicable to trusts if the organization is a trust.

6. An organization must make estimated tax payments if it expects its tax for the year to be more than $500.

NOW REVIEW MULTIPLE-CHOICE QUESTIONS 57 THROUGH 64 IN VOLUME 2

V. MULTIJURISDICTIONAL TAXATION

A. State and Local Taxation (SALT)

1. There are various types of state and local taxes such as income, sales, use, property, franchise, employment, excise, severance, and estate and inheritance taxes. Each state controls the taxation of persons within its jurisdiction and may apply tax rules that differ from the rules that are applied in other states.

2. The US Constitution prohibits a state from taxing a nonresident unless the nonresident has sufficient connection to the state. The presence or activity required within a state before the state may tax a nonresident is referred to as **nexus**. There are different nexus standards for different types of taxes. Simply engaging in an activity or a business transaction within a state may be sufficient to result in nexus for income tax purposes in many states. Property ownership, derivation of income from sources within a state, or the presence of an office within a state also may produce nexus. On the other hand, nexus is generally *not* established merely because of the solicitation of sales of tangible personal property within a state.

3. For *state income tax*, many states conform to the federal income tax model, with a state relying on information from a federal return for its own tax base. As a result, a state income tax base might begin with federal taxable income which is then modified by adjustments required by state law (e.g., no deduction allowed for state income taxes).

4. When a business can be taxed by more than one state, it becomes necessary to develop rules that **allocate** particular types of income to specific states, and to **apportion** other types of income among the several states that can tax it.

   a. **The Uniform Division of Income for Tax Purposes Act (UDITPA)** provides rules for allocating and apportioning a multistate or multinational enterprise's nonbusiness and business income among states and foreign countries. The Multistate Tax Commission adopted model regulations that interpret the UDITPA provisions.

   b. Under UDITPA, **nonbusiness income** is allocated as follows:

     (1) Interest and dividends are allocated to the state of the taxpayer's commercial domicile.

     (2) Net rents and royalties from real property are allocated to the state in which the property is located.

     (3) Capital gains and losses from sales of real property are allocated to the state where the property is located.

     (4) Capital gains and losses from the sale of intangible personal property are allocated to the state of the taxpayer's commercial domicile.

     (5) Net rents and royalties from tangible personal property are allocated to a state to the extent that the property is utilized within that state. Alternatively, all rents and royalties from tangible personal property will be allocated to the state of the taxpayer's commercial domicile if the taxpayer is not organized in or taxable in the state in which the property is utilized.

     (6) Capital gains and losses from sales of tangible personal property are allocated to a state if the property was situated in that state at the time of sale. Alternatively, the gains and losses will be allocated to the state of the taxpayer's commercial domicile if the taxpayer is not taxable in the state in which the property was situated.

     (7) Patent and copyright royalties are allocated to a state to the extent that the patent or copyright is utilized by the payer in the state. Alternatively, the royalties will be allocated to the state of the taxpayer's commercial domicile if the taxpayer is not taxable in the state in which the patent or copyright was utilized.

c. States use various formulas to apportion a taxpayer's **business income** derived from multistate operations. Although the formulas used may differ, the objective is to derive an apportionment percentage to determine the amount of income subject to tax in each state. UDITPA recommends a formula using three equally weighted factors: sales, payroll, and property. Business income is then apportioned to a state by multiplying the taxpayer's business income by a fraction; the numerator of which is the total of the sales factor plus the payroll factor plus the property factor, and the denominator is three (3), to average the factors. Many states that levy an income tax use a modified three-factor formula in which sales are double-weighted (i.e., the sales factor is counted twice and the factor total is divided by four). Some states use just one or two of the factors.

   (1) The **sales factor** is the ratio of total sales to in-state customers divided by total sales from all sales made by the taxpayer. *Total sales* means total net sales after discounts and returns.
   (2) The **payroll factor** is the ratio of compensation paid to employees working in a state divided by the total compensation paid by the taxpayer.
   (3) The **property factor** is the ratio of the average cost of real and tangible personal property owned or rented and located in a state divided by the total average cost of all such property owned or rented by the taxpayer.

EXAMPLE

Assume Multistate Corp. conducts business in several states and provided relevant information as follows:

	Total	State A
Sales	$4,000,000	$1,000,000
Average property	5,000,000	2,000,000
Compensation	1,000,000	200,000
Business taxable income before apportionment	500,000	

State A uses the UDITPA apportionment formula to compute state taxable income for Multistate Corp.'s business income. The sales factor for State A would be $1,000,000 / $4,000,000 = 25%. The property factor would be $2,000,000 / $5,000,000 = 40%. The compensation factor would be $200,000 / $1,000,000 = 20%. The apportionment factor would be (25% + 40% + 20%) / 3 = 28.33%. As a result, $500,000 × 28.33% = $141,667 of Multistate Corp.'s business income would be taxed by State A.

EXAMPLE

Assume State A in the above example gives double weight to the sales factor. The apportionment factor would be (25% + 25% + 40% + 20%) / 4 = 27.5%.

---

5. Under the **unitary** concept, if one company in a group of entities has nexus with a state, the state's apportionment factor is applied to the unitary income of the entire group. A **unitary business** is a single economic enterprise that is made up either of separate parts of a single business entity, or of a commonly controlled group of business entities that are sufficiently interdependent, integrated, and interrelated through their activities. Whether business activities constitute a unitary business is subjective and the courts generally give states great latitude in deciding whether a particular set of activities constitute a unitary business. Under the factors-of-profitability test, business activities will be treated as a unitary business if they are functionally integrated, have centralized management, and show economies of scale.

6. Many states have enacted provisions that require **combined reporting** in applying the unitary business concept to related entities. In a combined return a taxpayer must apply the unitary concept to the combined income of the entities making up the unitary business. Most states have established a 50% ownership rule as the threshold for combined reporting purposes though some states have chosen to use a different percentage.

NOW REVIEW MULTIPLE-CHOICE QUESTIONS 65 AND 66 IN VOLUME 2

B. International Taxation

1. **US Taxation of Foreign Persons.** Nonresident foreign persons generally are subject to US tax on two categories of income: (1) *income that is effectively connected with a US trade or business (ECI)*, and (2) certain passive types of US source income commonly referred to as *fixed or determinable annual or periodical income (FDAP)*.

   a. A foreign person's **income that is effectively connected with a US trade or business (ECI)** is subject to tax at regular graduated income tax rates and deductions are allowed in computing the amount subject to tax. A trade or business generally is defined by case law as profit-oriented activities that are regular, substantial, and continuous. Effectively connected with a US trade or business means that (1) the income is derived from assets held for use in the conduct of a US business, and (2) the activity of the US business was a material factor in the realization of the income. Under an income tax treaty, the US may instead agree to tax business profits of a treaty resident only if the profits are attributable to a **permanent establishment** (PE) in the US. A PE is a fixed place of business through which business is wholly or partially carried on. Simply maintaining storage facilities within the US generally does not by itself amount to a PE.

b. Generally, a nonresident alien who performs personal services within the US is considered to be engaged in a US trade or business. However, the performance of personal services will not constitute a US trade or business if (1) the nonresident alien is present in the US for 90 days or less during the tax year, (2) the amount of compensation received for US services is $3,000 or less, and (3) the nonresident alien works for either a foreign person who is not engaged in a US trade or business, or the foreign office of a US person.

c. **Fixed and determinable annual or periodical income (FDAP)** is generally subject to a 30% withholding tax that is applied to the gross amount of income with no deductions allowed. Withholding of tax occurs at the source of payment (i.e., the person paying the income is required to withhold the tax and remit it to the IRS). FDAP primarily is from passive, nonbusiness activities *including* such items as interest, dividends, rents, royalties, and annuities. FDAP generally *excludes* gain from the sale or exchange of real or personal property, and income that is excluded from gross income by US persons. The 30% withholding tax rate may be reduced or even eliminated by an applicable income tax treaty.

d. **Sourcing rules** are used to determine whether items of income will be deemed to be US source and consequently subject a nonresident foreign person to US taxation. Although the sourcing rules may be modified by tax treaty, the sourcing rules for specific types of income include

    (1) Interest—the domicile of the payor
    (2) Dividends —whether the payor is a US or foreign corporation
    (3) Rents—the location of the property
    (4) Royalties—the location where the property is used
    (5) Gain on sale of real property—the location of the property
    (6) Gain on sale of inventory—the location where title to the inventory passes
    (7) Services—the location where the services are performed

2. **US Taxation of US Persons on Foreign Activities.** US persons are subject to US tax on their worldwide income. A US person includes a citizen or resident of the US, a domestic partnership or corporation, and any estate or trust other than a foreign estate or trust

a. A US corporation is subject to tax on its worldwide income, including the income of a *foreign branch*. In contrast, a US corporation is generally not taxed on the net income of a *foreign subsidiary* corporation until the income is repatriated in the form of dividends to the parent corporation.

> **EXAMPLE**
>
> A US corporation's foreign subsidiary has $1,000 of earnings but makes no distributions to its US parent during the year. The US corporation is not taxed on the $1,000 of earnings of its foreign subsidiary.

b. Certain types of income, referred to as **subpart F income**, of a *controlled foreign corporation* are subject to current US taxation even though the earnings are not distributed to the US parent corporation. **A controlled foreign corporation (CFC)** is a foreign corporation whose stock is more than 50% owned (by vote or value) by US shareholders that own at least 10% of the combined voting power of the foreign corporation's stock. The US shareholders get a corresponding basis increase for their CFC stock for the amount of subpart F income taxed to them but not received in the form of dividends. A later distribution of those earnings will be nontaxable and will reduce their basis for the CFC stock.

> **EXAMPLE**
>
> US corporation M owns all the stock of foreign subsidiary N which has $1,000 of earnings from subpart F income but makes no distributions to M during the year. M is currently taxed on the $1,000 of subpart F income of N, and increases its basis for its N stock by $1,000.

c. **Subpart F income** generally includes foreign passive income as well as certain types of foreign business income that can be readily shifted between taxing jurisdictions to take advantage of a lower foreign tax rate. Included in Subpart F income is income from a CFC's insurance of risks outside its country of creation or organization, foreign base company income, amounts attributable to international boycott participation, and amounts attributable to illegal bribes and kickbacks. Two examples of **foreign base company income** are *foreign personal holding company income,* and *foreign base company sales income.*

(1) **Foreign personal holding company** income generally includes such items as dividends, interest, royalties, rents, annuities, and income from personal service contracts.

(2) **Foreign base company sales income** generally consists of income attributable to sales of personal property if three requirements are met: (1) the subject purchase or sale must be to, from, or on behalf of, a related party (a related party includes all individuals and entities owning, directly or indirectly, more than 50% of the CFC's stock), (2) the purchase or sale must be for use, consumption, or disposition outside of the CFC's country of incorporation, and (3) the personal property must be manufactured, grown, produced, or extracted outside of the CFC's country of incorporation.

As a result of the above requirements, certain sales of personal property will be excluded from foreign base company sales income. For example, Subpart F income does not include income from the sale of personal property that was manufactured, produced, or constructed by the CFC. Also, it does not include income from the purchase and sale of property if the property is used in the jurisdiction wherein the CFC is incorporated.

d. **A foreign tax credit** against US income tax, for income taxes paid to a foreign country, mitigates the double taxation of foreign-source income. However, the amount of allowable foreign tax credit is limited to the US income tax imposed on the foreign source income.

$$\text{Overall limitation is } \frac{\text{Foreign source taxable income}}{\text{Worldwide taxable income}} \times \text{(US income tax)}$$

(1) The overall limit on the foreign tax credit must be computed on a separate basis for several income categories including passive category income such as interest and dividends, and general category income, which includes most income other than passive category income. As a result, the foreign tax credit cannot exceed the lesser of the amount of foreign income taxes paid or accrued, or the limitation amount, for each category.

(2) Foreign income taxes paid in excess of the overall limitation can be carried back 1 year and forward 10 years and used to the extent that the taxpayer is below the limitation in those years.

(3) An individual with $300 or less ($600 for married filing jointly) of creditable foreign income taxes is exempt from the overall limitation if all foreign-source income is passive investment income.

(4) Taxpayers have the option of deducting foreign income taxes in lieu of taking a credit.

e. In addition to the foreign taxes actually paid, a US corporation that receives dividends from a *10% or more owned foreign corporation* (based on voting stock) is entitled to a deemed paid foreign tax credit for the foreign income taxes paid by that foreign corporation with respect to such dividends. A corporation taking the **deemed paid credit** must *gross-up* (increase) the amount of dividend income that it received by the foreign income tax paid on those dividends. The deemed paid credit is subject to the FTC limitation.

EXAMPLE

A US corporation receives a dividend of $75 from a wholly owned foreign subsidiary that has paid $25 of foreign income taxes on the earnings to which the dividend relates. The US corporation's dividend income of $75 is grossed-up by the $25 of foreign income taxes paid by its subsidiary, to $100. The US corporation is then eligible for a foreign tax credit for the $25 of foreign income taxes that it is deemed to have paid.

---

3. **Transfers of Property to Foreign Corporations**

a. Gain (but not loss) is generally recognized on the transfer of property by a US person to a foreign corporation notwithstanding the deferral provision of Subchapter C that otherwise would apply. This prevents gains from escaping US taxation and is accomplished by providing that a "foreign corporation" shall not be considered a corporation for purposes of the Subchapter C provisions (e.g., Sec. 351 transfer to a controlled corporation, Sec. 332 liquidation of a subsidiary, Sec. 361 transfer of property pursuant to a corporate reorganization).

EXAMPLE

US Corporation P owns property with a value of $1 million that has a zero tax basis. Corporation P transfers title to the property to its foreign subsidiary, Corporation S, in exchange for all of the stock of Corporation S. If Sec. 351(a) applied, no gain would be recognized on the transfer of the appreciated property to S. Thereafter, S could sell the property and recognize the gain. Assuming that S does not distribute its earnings to P and that Subpart F does not apply, the gain would escape US taxation. However, since foreign Corporation S is not considered a corporation for purposes of applying Sec. 351, P's realized gain of $1 million on the transfer of property to S is recognized and subject to US taxation.

---

b. The above recognition rule does *not* apply to any property transferred to a foreign corporation for use by such foreign corporation in the active conduct of a trade or business outside of the US. Exceptions requiring gain recognition apply to transfers of certain types of property that are likely to be promptly resold or are highly fungible such as receivables, copyrights, inventory, installment obligations, foreign currency or foreign-currency-denominated investments, and interests in leased property.

4. **Transfer Pricing**

a. When businesses in different countries that are owned or controlled by the same interests sell products or services or make loans between themselves, they have the opportunity to affect each other's taxable income and thereby reduce the overall tax liability of the group. This can be accomplished by shifting taxable income from a high-tax country to a lower-tax country.

b. To restrict this artificial shifting of income, Code Sec. 482 gives the IRS the authority to apportion and allocate income, deductions, and credits as is necessary in order to prevent the evasion of taxes or to clearly reflect income.

c. Generally, Sec. 482 requires that organizations under common control conduct business between themselves as if they were unrelated. That is, in determining the taxable income of a taxpayer from transactions with related organizations, the standard to be applied is that of a taxpayer *dealing at arm's length with an unrelated taxpayer*.

EXAMPLE

A US Corporation causes income which it has earned by means of its property or activity to be received by its foreign subsidiary, and thus shields such income from US taxation. Sec. 482 empowers the IRS to allocate the income to the US corporation.

EXAMPLE

A US Corporation sells its product to an independent third party as well as to its foreign subsidiary, each of whom operate as distributors of its product in a foreign market. The unit price charged the independent distributor is $200, while the unit price charged its foreign subsidiary is $125. If the US corporation dealt with its subsidiary at "arm's length," then the unit price charged the foreign subsidiary would have been $200. The IRS may utilize Sec. 482 to allocate $75 of profit from the subsidiary to the US corporation.

d. Because it may be difficult for a taxpayer to determine what price might be used by unrelated taxpayers dealing at arm's length, the IRS permits taxpayers to enter into an Advance Pricing Agreement (APA)) with the IRS on the best method for determining arm's length prices for transfers between taxpayers owned or controlled by the same interests. Pursuant to an APA, a taxpayer and the IRS agree as to the transfer pricing method to be used to determine the transfer prices for specified transactions.

NOW REVIEW MULTIPLE-CHOICE QUESTIONS 67 THROUGH 70 IN VOLUME 2

VI. SOURCES OF FEDERAL TAX AUTHORITY

A. Federal Tax Legislative Process

1. Tax legislation usually begins in the House of Representatives. Hearings are held before the Ways and Means Committee. Members of the Committee draft a bill, and after having been approved by the Committee, it is sent to the House for debate and vote by the full House membership. A tax bill passed by the House is sent to the Senate Finance Committee.

2. The Senate Finance Committee may amend bill or draft its own bill, and when approved by the finance Committee, the bill is sent to the Senate floor for debate before the Senate and possible additional amendments.

3. If the House- and Senate-passed versions of the tax bill differ, the tax bill is sent to the House-Senate Conference Committee for resolution of any differences. The modified bill, when approved by the Conference Committee, is sent back to the House and Senate for approval in its final form.

4. The uniform bill, after passage by the House and Senate, goes to the president for signing. If the president signs the bill it becomes law. If the president vetoes the bill, at least a two-thirds vote of the House and at least a two-thirds vote of the Senate are needed to override the presidential veto for the tax bill to become law.

5. Most tax legislation simply amends the current Internal Revenue Code of 1986. Note that the IRS does *not* write the tax law, and the Internal Revenue Code was not written by the IRS. Tax legislation is passed by Congress and signed by the president to become law.

B. The **Internal Revenue Code (IRC)** is the basic foundation of federal tax law, and represents a codification of the federal tax laws of the United States.

1. A series of self-contained revenue acts were first codified into an organized framework with the Internal Revenue Code of 1939. Subsequently, the 1939 IRC was reorganized and replaced with the 1954 IRC. In 1986, the Code's name was changed to the IRC of 1986, and has been frequently amended since then (e.g., Jobs and Growth Tax Relief Reconciliation Act of 2004).

2. The Internal Revenue Code of 1986 is actually Title 26 of the United States Code, and is generally divided into an orderly framework as follows: Subtitles; Chapters; Subchapters; Parts; Subparts; Sections; and Subsections.

3. **Subtitles** are denoted with a capital letter, with most pertaining to a general area of tax law as follows:

Subtitle	Topic
A	Income Taxes
B	Estate and Gift Taxes
C	Employment Taxes
D	Miscellaneous Excise Taxes
E	Alcohol, Tobacco, and Certain Other Excise Taxes
F	Procedure and Administration
G	The Joint Committee on Taxation
H	Financing of Presidential Election Campaigns
I	Trust Fund Code
J	Coal Industry Health Benefits
K	Group Health Plan Requirements

4. Each subtitle generally contains a number of **chapters** that are numbered in ascending order throughout the Code. Each chapter generally contains the tax rules that relate to a more narrowly defined area of law than is addressed by a subtitle. For example, Subtitle A—Income Taxes is divided as follows:

Chapter	Topic
1	Normal Taxes and Surtaxes
2	Tax on Self-Employment Income
3	Withholding of Tax on Nonresident Aliens and Foreign Corporations
4	[Repealed]
5	[Repealed]
6	Consolidated Returns

5. Chapters of the IRC are further divided into **subchapters** with each subchapter pertaining to a more narrowly defined area of tax law than is addressed by a chapter. For example, Chapter 1, Normal Taxes and Surtaxes includes Subchapter C—corporate distributions and adjustments, Subchapter K—partners and partnerships, and Subchapter S—tax treatment of S corporations and shareholders.

6. Subchapters are generally divided into **parts,** which are then frequently divided into subparts. Additionally, subparts are divided into **sections** that represent the organizational division of the Internal Revenue Code to which persons dealing with tax matters most often refer (e.g., Sec. 351 transfers to a controlled corporation, Sec. 1231 gains and losses, Sec. 1245 recapture).

7. Code sections are often divided into smaller divisions that may include subsections, paragraphs, subparagraphs, and clauses. Sections are denoted by numbers (1, 2, 3, etc.), subsections by lowercase letters (a, b, c, etc.), paragraphs by numbers (1, 2, 3, etc.), subparagraphs by capital letters (A, B, C, etc.), and clauses by lowercase roman numerals (i, ii, iii, etc.). This organizational scheme is important because the IRC contains many cross references which indicate the scope or limit the application of a provision.

EXAMPLE

Sec. 7701 is a definitional section that begins. "When used in this title…" and then goes on to provide a series of definitions. As a result, a definition found in Sec. 7701 applies to all of the Internal Revenue of Code of 1986.

EXAMPLE

Code Sec. 311(b) provides a gain recognition rule that applies to a corporation when it distributes appreciated property to a shareholder. However, its application is limited in that it only applies to distributions described in Subpart A (i.e., Code Secs. 301 through 307). Code Sec. 311(b)'s position within the overall Code framework is as follows:

Title: Internal Revenue Code of 1986

Subtitle A: Income Taxes

Chapter 1: Normal taxes and surtaxes

Subchapter C: Corporate distributions and adjustments

Part I: Distributions by corporations

Subpart B: Effects on corporation

Section 311: Tax liability of corporation on distributions

Subsection (b): Distributions of appreciated property

Paragraph (1): In general. If—

Subparagraph (A): "a corporation distributes property…in a distribution to which Subpart A applies…"

C. The IRC gives the Treasury Department or its delegate (the Commissioner of Internal Revenue) the authority to issue Regulations to provide administrative interpretation of the tax law. These regulations may be separated into two broad categories: legislative and interpretive. **Legislative regulations** are those issued by the IRS under a specific grant of authority to prescribe the operating rules for a statute (e.g., "the Secretary shall prescribe such regulations as he may deem necessary," or "under regulations prescribed by the Secretary") and have the force and effect of law. The consolidated tax return regulations are an example of legislative regulations. In contrast, **interpretive regulations** are issued pursuant to the general rule-making authority granted to the IRS under Sec. 7805(a) and provide guidance regarding the IRS's interpretation of a statute. Although interpretive regulations do not have the force and effect of law, they are generally accorded substantial weight by the courts.

1. Regulations may also be categorized as proposed, temporary, or final regulations. Regulations are generally issued as **Proposed regulations** allowing interested parties a period of time of at least thirty days to comment and suggest changes. As a result of the comments received, the IRS may make changes to a proposed regulation before being published as a final regulation. Proposed regulations do not carry the same authority as temporary or final regulations. **Temporary regulations** are generally issued following recent tax legislation to provide interim guidance until final regulations are adopted. Temporary regulations (issued after 11/20/88) must be concurrently issued as proposed regulations, and these temporary regulations expire no later than three years from date of issue. Prior to its expiration, a temporary regulation is given the same weight as a final regulation. **Final regulations** are issued after public comments on proposed regulations are evaluated. Final regulations supersede any existing temporary regulations.

2. Regulations are organized in a sequential system with numbers preceding and following a decimal point. The numbers preceding the decimal point indicate the type of regulation or applicable area of tax law to which they pertain, while the numbers immediately following a decimal point indicate the IRC section being interpreted. Some of the more common prefixes include

Number	Type
1	Income Tax
20	Estate Tax
25	Gift Tax
301	Administrative and Procedural Matters
601	Procedural Rules

The numbers and letters to the right of the section number indicate the regulation number and smaller divisions of the regulation (e.g., paragraph, subparagraph). These regulation numbers and paragraphs do not necessarily correspond to the subsection of the Code being interpreted. For example, Reg. 1.267(d)-1(a)(4) provides four examples of the application of Code Sec. 267(d) concerning the determination of recognized gain where a loss was previously disallowed. The citation represents subparagraph (4) of paragraph (a) of the first regulation interpreting Code Sec. 267(d). The citation of a temporary regulation includes a "T" which indicates the nature of the regulation as temporary. For example, 1.45D-1T is a temporary regulation that explains the rules and conditions for claiming the new markets tax credit of Code Sec. 45.

D. Revenue rulings have less force and effect than regulations, but are second to regulations as important administrative sources of federal tax law. A revenue ruling gives the IRS's interpretation of how the Code and regulations apply to a specific fact situation, and therefore indicates how the IRS will treat similar transactions. Revenue rulings can be relied upon as authority by all taxpayers, and are published in the Internal Revenue Bulletin and later in the Cumulative Bulletin. The current status of a revenue ruling can be checked in the most current index to the Cumulative Bulletin. **Revenue procedures** announce administrative practices followed by the IRS, and are published in the Internal Revenue Bulletin and later in the Cumulative Bulletin. Revenue procedures provide guidelines that taxpayers must meet in order to obtain a revenue ruling, and also indicate areas in which the IRS will not issue revenue rulings. A **private letter ruling** is a written statement issued to the taxpayer who requested advice concerning a specific transaction. Although issued only to a specific taxpayer, private letter rulings are useful because they indicate how the IRS may treat a similar transaction, and are included in the list of substantial authority upon which a taxpayer may rely to avoid certain statutory penalties.

VII. TAX PLANNING

Tax planning should not be done in isolation, but instead should be a part of a taxpayer's overall financial goals, and integrated with nontax considerations. Three general tax planning strategies involve (1) the timing of income and deductions, (2) the shifting of income and deductions between taxpayers, and (3) the conversion of the character of income and deductions.

A. Timing

The tax accounting period in which an expense is deducted or in which income is recognized effects the real tax savings or cost because of the time value of money. A simple tax planning strategy would be to accelerate a tax deduction to an earlier period, while deferring the recognition of income to a later period.

1. **Installment sale.** A taxpayer may want to structure the casual sale of an asset so that at least one payment is received in the year(s) following the year of sale. By using the installment method and spreading the gain over multiple years, the taxpayer's gain will be deferred and may be taxed in lower brackets.

2. **Net operating loss.** A taxpayer should carefully consider whether to carry back an NOL or elect to forgo the carryback period. A taxpayer may want to only carry the loss forward if the taxpayer anticipates being in a higher marginal tax bracket in carryforward years.

3. **Casualty loss.** If a casualty loss is sustained in a presidentially declared disaster area, the taxpayer may make an election to deduct the loss in the year preceding the year in which the loss was incurred in order to obtain a more immediate tax benefit for the loss deduction.

4. **Medical expenses.** Because of the 7.5% of AGI threshold for deducting medical expenses, taxpayers often are unable to take a deduction for unreimbursed medical expenses. However, it may be possible to take a medical expense deduction if the expenses are bunched into one year. Medical expenses are generally deductible when paid, but can be deducted in the year charged to a credit card.

5. **Itemized deductions.** If a taxpayer's total itemized deductions are approximately the same as the standard deduction, a taxpayer may benefit from bunching itemized deductions into a year in which the taxpayer intends to itemize, with the intention of taking the standard deduction in the following year. By alternating standard deduction and itemized deductions years, the taxpayer may be able to maximize deductions over a multiyear time frame.

6. **Alternative minimum tax.** If a taxpayer is not subject to AMT in 2011 but expects to be in 2012, accelerate expenses that are not deductible for AMT into 2011. For example, consider paying off home equity debt since the interest expense is usually not deductible for AMT purposes. Alternatively, if the taxpayer expects to pay an AMT in 2011 but not in 2012, consider accelerating ordinary and short-term capital gain income into 2011 while deferring expenses not deductible for AMT into 2012 (e.g., state and local income taxes, real estate taxes, miscellaneous deductions in the 2% category).

7. **Short-term capital gain.** If a taxpayer has short-term capital gains (which are taxed at ordinary income tax rates), consider selling capital assets that will generate capital losses in order to offset the short-term capital gain. Taxpayers are allowed to deduct up to $3,000 of net capital loss against ordinary income each year, with any net capital loss in excess of $3,000 carried forward to future years.

8. **Estimated tax.** An exception that can be used to avoid an underpayment penalty for the current year is for a taxpayer to make estimated payments and withholdings which in total are at least equal to 100% (110% if prior year AGI was greater than $150,000) of the tax liability for the prior year. Income tax withholdings are considered paid equally throughout the year, even if the taxes are withheld near the end of the year. If a taxpayer anticipates that taxes for the current year are underpaid, consider adjusting withholdings for the remainder of the year to avoid the underpayment penalty.

B. Income and Deduction Shifting

This planning strategy seeks to take advantage of the differences in tax rates between taxpayers, or between taxing jurisdictions. The goal is to shift income from high-tax rate to low-tax rate taxpayers or jurisdictions, and to shift deductions from low-tax rate to high-tax rate taxpayers or jurisdictions.

1. **Children.** Parents can reduce their family's income tax by shifting income that would otherwise be taxed at higher rates to their children whose income is taxed at lower rates. Even if the kiddie tax applies, the first $1,900 of unearned (e.g., interest) income will be taxed at the child's rates. Additionally, if the child has no earned income (e.g., wage), the child's unearned income will be partially offset by a limited basic standard deduction of $950.

2. **Gift tax exclusion.** A taxpayer interested in family wealth planning may want to consider the annual gift tax exclusion when gifting appreciated assets to family members. There is an annual $13,000 exclusion (for 2011) per donee for gifts of a present interest. This means that up to $13,000 of gifts can be given to a donee without making a taxable gift. Additionally, if the appreciated assets are given to family members not subject to the kiddie tax who

are in the lowest two brackets, the capital gain on sale of the assets will be taxed at a 0% rate as opposed to the 15% rate if sold by the parents.

3. **Sec. 529 plan.** A Sec. 529 educational savings plan could be established for a child or grandchild. Using a special election, a taxpayer could currently fund up to five years of annual exclusions into the plan without making a taxable gift. This would permit up to $65,000 to be deposited into a child's Section 529 plan where the principal would grow tax-deferred, and later distributions used for the child's college costs would be exempt from tax.

4. **Owners and their businesses.** Incorporating a business and thus shifting income from an individual to a C corporation may result in lower current taxation of the business income (e.g., first $50,000 of corporate taxable income taxed at 15% rate). Alternatively, business income could be shifted from a corporation to an owner through tax-deductible expenses paid to the owner (e.g., compensation, rent, interest) allowing the owner to avoid the double taxation of corporate profits. Additionally, corporate level taxes could generally be completely avoided by making an S corporation election which would shift all income and deductions to the S corporation's shareholders.

C. Conversion

This planning strategy involves converting ordinary income that would be taxed at regular rates into income that will be taxed at a preferential rate. Additionally, this strategy might be applied to convert deductions that would be subject to limitations into ordinary deductions that are deductible without limitation.

1. **Sale of a company.** If considering the sale of a business, a taxpayer may attempt to structure the transaction as a sale of the company's stock rather than a sale of the company's assets. A sale of the company's stock generally results in gain eligible for reduced capital-gains rates, as opposed to a sale of assets which may be taxed as ordinary income.

2. **Qualified dividends.** A taxpayer may want to consider replacing investments generating interest income taxed at regular rates, with stocks paying qualified dividends that are taxed at a reduced rate of 15%, or 0% if the taxpayer is in the 10% or 15% bracket. In order to qualify for the reduced rate, the underlying stock upon which a dividend is paid must be held for at least 61 days during the 121-day period beginning 60 days before the ex-dividend date (91 days of the 181-day period for preferred stock).

3. **Passive activities.** A taxpayer may be able to increase participation in what would otherwise be a "passive activity" in order to classify the activity as an active business activity whose losses are currently deductible. Alternatively, a taxpayer might be able to decrease participation in a profitable business activity in order to classify the income as passive activity income that could then be sheltered by losses generated from other passive activities.

KEY TERMS

Estate tax. A tax imposed on the transfer of property at death. The tax is part of the unified transfer tax system and takes into account transfers an individual made during lifetime and at death.

Generation-skipping tax. A tax on the transfer of property to, or in trust for the benefit of, a person that is two or more generations younger than the donor or transferor and is designed to prevent individuals from escaping an entire generation of gift and estate taxes. It is imposed in addition to federal gift and estate taxes.

Gift tax. A tax imposed on the transfer of property during an individual's lifetime. The tax is imposed upon the donor of the gift and is based upon the fair market value of the property on the date of gift.

Grantor trust. A trust over which the grantor (or grantor's spouse) retains substantial control. The income of a grantor trust is taxed to the grantor, not to the trust or beneficiaries.

Revenue ruling. Gives the IRS's interpretation of how the IRC and regulations apply to a specific fact situation, and therefore indicates how the IRS will treat similar transactions.

Simple trust. A trust that is required to distribute all of its income to beneficiaries each year, cannot make charitable contributions, and makes no distributions of trust corpus (i.e., principal) during the year.

UDITPA. The Uniform Division of Income for Tax Purposes Act which provides rules for allocating and apportioning a multistate or multinational enterprise's nonbusiness and business income among states and foreign counties.

Unrelated business income. Income of an exempt organization from a business that is regularly carried on, and is unrelated to the organization's exempt purpose. UBI is subject to tax to the extent in excess of $1,000. .

BUSINESS ENVIRONMENT AND CONCEPTS

As indicated previously, this section consists of 8 modules designed to facilitate your study for the Business Environment and Concepts section of the Uniform CPA Examination. The table of contents at the right describes the content of each module.

The content of the Business Environment and Concepts (BEC) examination includes a number of general business and accounting topics. The areas are covered as shown below.

Topic	Percentage
Corporate Governance	16-20
Economic Concepts and Analysis	16-20
Financial Management	19-23
Information Systems and Communication	15-19
Strategic Planning	10-14
Operations Management	12-16

The BEC section of the exam tests knowledge and skills using multiple-choice questions and written communication skills using task-based simulations.

The basic concepts for preparation are the same as for other sections of the exam. You need to have the skills and knowledge necessary to solve both **how** (number crunching) and **why** (conceptual) type questions. In addition, you must be prepared for the simulations that require written communication.

First, become acquainted with the nature of the BEC exam itself. With the computerization of the exam, the AICPA has issued a set of content specifications. These content specifications are printed below.

Relatedly, you should evaluate your competence by working 10 to 20 multiple-choice questions from each of the modules (40-47). This diagnostic routine will acquaint you with the specific nature of the questions tested on each topic as well as indicate the amount of study required per topic. However, do not get discouraged. Remember, more difficult questions are more heavily weighted in determining your score. See discussion of self-study programs (Chapter 2) and examination grading (Chapter 3).

Second, study the content of modules 40-47, emphasizing the mechanics of each topic such as economic concepts, strategic performance measurement, working capital management, etc. Use simple examples, journal entries, and diagrams to get a handle on the basic concepts underlying each topic. You may have to refer to your textbooks, etc., for topics to which you have had no previous exposure.

Third, work as many multiple-choice questions as time allows and take the sample examination at the end of this manual.

Fourth, prepare for the simulations by studying the methods to improve your writing skills presented in Chapter 3 of this manual, and **practice**, **practice**, **practice** writing short memos.

AICPA CONTENT AND SKILLS SPECIFICATIONS

The AICPA Content and Skills Specifications for the Uniform CPA Exam set forth the coverage of topics on the Business Environment and Concepts exam. This outline was issued by the AICPA and is effective beginning in 2011. The first part of the outline describes the topical coverage of the Business Environment and Concepts exam, and the second part provides some insights into the skills tested on all sections of the Uniform CPA exam.

Content Specification Outlines (CSOs)

The Business Environment and Concepts section tests knowledge and skills necessary to demonstrate an understanding of the general business environment and business concepts. The topics in this section include knowledge of corporate governance; economic concepts essential to understanding the global business environment and its impact on an entity's business strategy and financial risk management; financial management processes; information systems and communications; strategic planning, and operations management. In addition to demonstrating knowledge and understanding of these topics, candidates are required to apply that knowledge in performing audit, attest, financial reporting, tax preparation, and other professional responsibilities as certified public accountants. To demonstrate such knowledge and skills, candidates will be expected to perform the following tasks:

- Demonstrate an understanding of globalization on the business environment.
- Distinguish between appropriate and inappropriate governance structures within an organization (e.g., tone at the top, policies, steering committees, strategies, oversight, etc.)
- Assess the impact of business cycles on an entity's industry or business operations.
- Apply knowledge of changes in the global economic markets in identifying the impact on an entity in determining its business strategy and financial management policies, including managing the risks of inflation, deflation, commodity costs, credit defaults, interest rate variations, currency fluctuation, and regulation.
- Assess the factors influencing a company's capital structure, including risk, leverage, cost of capital, growth rate, profitability, asset structure, and loan covenants.

- Evaluate assumptions used in financial valuations to determine their reasonableness (e.g., investment return assumptions, discount rates, etc.)
- Determine the business reasons for and explain the underlying economic substance of transactions and their accounting implications.
- Identify the information systems within a business that are used to process and accumulate transactional data, as well as provide monitoring and financial reporting information.
- Distinguish between appropriate and inappropriate internal control systems, including system design, controls over data, transaction flow, wireless technology, and internet transmissions.
- Evaluate whether there is appropriate segregation of duties, levels of authorization, and data security in an organization to maintain an appropriate internal control structure.
- Obtain and document information about an organization's strategic planning processes to identify key components of the business strategy and market risks.
- Develop a time-phased project plan showing required activities, task dependencies, and required resources to achieve a specific deliverable.
- Identify the business and operational risks inherent in an entity's disaster recovery/business continuity plan.
- Evaluate business operations and quality control initiatives to understand its use of best practices and the ways to measure and manage performance and costs.

The outline below specifies the knowledge in which candidates are required to demonstrate proficiency:

I. Corporate Governance (16%–20%)

A. Rights, Duties, Responsibilities, and Authority of the Board of Directors, Officers, and Other Employees

1. Financial reporting
2. Internal control (including COSO or similar framework)
3. Enterprise risk management (including COSO or similar framework)

B. Control Environment

1. Tone at the top—establishing control environment
2. Monitoring control effectiveness
3. Change control process

II. Economic Concepts and Analysis (16%–20%)

A. Changes in Economic and Business Cycle— Economic Measures/Indicators

B. Globalization and Local Economies

1. Impacts of globalization on companies
2. Shifts in economic balance of power (e.g., capital) to/from developed from/to emerging markets

C. Market Influences on Business Strategies

D. Financial Risk Management

1. Market, interest rate, currency, liquidity, credit, price, and other risks
2. Means for mitigating/controlling financial risks

III. Financial Management (19%–23%)

A. Financial Modeling, Projections, and Analysis

1. Forecasting and trends
2. Financial and risk analysis
3. Impact of inflation/deflation

B. Financial Decisions

1. Debt, equity, leasing

2. Asset and investment management

C. Capital Management, Including Working Capital

1. Capital structure
2. Short-term and long-term financing
3. Asset effectiveness and/or efficiency

D. Financial Valuations (e.g., Fair Value)

1. Methods for calculating valuations
2. Evaluating assumptions used in valuations

E. Financial Transaction Processes and Controls

IV. Information Systems and Communications (15%–19%)

A. Organizational Needs Assessment

1. Data capture
2. Processing
3. Reporting
4. Role of information technology in business strategy

B. Systems Design and Other Elements

1. Business process design (integrated systems, automated, and manual interfaces)
2. Information Technology (IT) control objectives
3. Role of technology systems in control monitoring
4. Operational effectiveness
5. Segregation of duties
6. Policies

C. Security

1. Technologies and security management features
2. Policies

D. Internet—Implications for Business

1. Electronic commerce
2. Opportunities for business process reengineering

3. Roles of internet evolution on business operations and organization cultures

E. Types of Information System and Technology Risks

F. Disaster Recovery and Business Continuity

V. Strategic Planning (10%–14%)

A. Market and Risk Analysis

B. Strategy Development, Implementation, and Monitoring

C. Planning Techniques

1. Budget and analysis
2. Forecasting and projection
3. Coordinating information from various sources for integrated planning

VI. Operations Management (12%–16%)

A. Performance Management and Impact of Measures on Behavior

1. Financial and nonfinancial measures
2. Impact of marketing practices on performance
3. Incentive compensation

B. Cost Measurement Methods and Techniques

C. Process Management

1. Approaches, techniques, measures, and benefits to process-management-driven businesses
2. Roles of shared services, outsourcing, and offshore operations, and their implications on business risks and controls
3. Selecting and implementing improvement initiatives
4. Business process reengineering
5. Management philosophies and techniques for performance improvement such as Just in Time (JIT), Quality, Lean, Demand Flow, Theory of Constraints, and Six Sigma

D. Project Management

1. Project planning, implementation, and monitoring
2. Roles of project managers, project members, and oversight or steering groups
3. Project risks, including resource, scope, cost, and deliverables

References—Business Environment and Concepts

- The Committee of Sponsoring Organizations of the Treadway Commission (COSO)

  - Internal Control—Integrated Framework
  - Enterprise Risk Management

- Sarbanes-Oxley Act of 2002

  - Title III, Corporate Responsibility
  - Title IV, Enhanced Financial Disclosures
  - Title VIII, Corporate and Criminal Fraud Accountability

- Current Business Periodicals
- Current Textbooks on

  - Accounting Information Systems
  - Budgeting and Measurement
  - Corporate Governance
  - Economics
  - Enterprise Risk Management
  - Finance
  - Management
  - Management Information Systems
  - Managerial Accounting
  - Production Operations
  - Project Management

Skill Specification Outlines (SSOs)

The Skill Specification Outlines (SSOs) identify the skills to be tested on the Uniform CPA Examination. There are three categories of skills, and the weightings will be implemented through the use of different question formats in the exam. For each of the question formats, a different set of tools will be available as resources to the candidates, who will need to use those tools to demonstrate proficiency in the applicable skills categories.

Weights

The percentage range assigned to each skill category will be used to determine the quantity of each type of question, as described below. The percentage range assigned to each skill category represents the approximate percentage to which that category of skills will be used in the different sections of the CPA Examination to assess proficiency. The ranges are designed to provide flexibility in building the examination, and the midpoints of the ranges for each section total 100%.

No percentages are given for the bulleted descriptions included in these definitions. The presence of several groups within an area or several topics within a group does not imply equal importance or weight will be given to these bullets on an examination.

Skills category	Weights (FAR, REG, AUD)	Weights (BEC)
Knowledge and Understanding	50%–60%	80%–90%
Application of the Body of Knowledge	40%–50%	–
Written Communication	–	10%–20%

Knowledge and Understanding. Multiple-choice questions will be used as the proxy for assessing knowledge and understanding, and will be based upon the content topics as outlined in the CSOs. Candidates will not have access to the authoritative literature, spreadsheets, or database tools while answering these questions. A calculator will be accessible for the candidates to use in performing calculations to demonstrate their understanding of the principles or subject matter.

Application of the Body of Knowledge. Task-based simulations will be used as the proxy for assessing application of the body of knowledge and will be based upon the content topics as outlined in the CSOs. Candidates will have access to the authoritative literature, a calculator, spreadsheets, and other resources and tools which they will use to demonstrate proficiency in applying the body of knowledge.

Written Communication will be assessed through the use of responses to essay questions, which will be based upon the content topics as outlined in the CSOs. Candidates will have access to a word processor, which includes a spell-check feature.

Outlines

The outlines below provide additional descriptions of the skills that are represented in each category.

Knowledge and Understanding. Expertise and skills developed through learning processes, recall, and reading comprehension. Knowledge is acquired through experience or education and is the theoretical or practical understanding of a subject; knowledge is also represented through awareness or familiarity with information gained by experience of a fact or situation. Understanding represents a higher level than simple knowledge and is the process of using concepts to deal adequately with given situations, facts, or circumstances. Understanding is the ability to recognize and comprehend the meaning of a particular concept.

Application of the Body of Knowledge, Including Analysis, Judgment, Synthesis, Evaluation, and Research. Higher-level cognitive skills that require individuals to act or transform knowledge in some fashion. These skills are inextricably intertwined and thus are grouped into this single skill area.

- Assess the Business Environment

  - Business Process Evaluation: Assessing and integrating information regarding a business's operational structure, functions, processes, and procedures to develop a broad operational perspective; identify the need for new systems or changes to existing systems and/or processes.
  - Contextual Evaluation: Assessing and integrating information regarding client's type of business or industry.
  - Strategic Analysis—Understanding the Business: Obtaining, assessing and integrating information on the entity's strategic objectives, strategic management process, business environment, the nature of and value to customers, its products and services, extent of competition within its market space, etc.).
  - Business Risk Assessment: Obtaining, assessing and integrating information on conditions and events that could impede the entity's ability to achieve strategic objectives.
  - Visualize Abstract Descriptions: Organize and process symbols, pictures, graphs, objects, and other information.

- Research

  - Identify the appropriate research question.
  - Identify key search terms for use in performing electronic searches through large volumes of data.
  - Search through large volumes of electronic data to find required information.
  - Organize information or data from multiple sources.
  - Integrate diverse sources of information to reach conclusions or make decisions.
  - Identify the appropriate authoritative guidance in applicable financial reporting frameworks and auditing standards for the accounting issue being evaluated.

- Application of Technology

  - Using electronic spreadsheets to perform calculations, financial analysis, or other functions to analyze data.
  - Integration of technological applications and resources into work processes.
  - Using a variety of computer software and hardware systems to structure, utilize, and manage data.

- Analysis

  - Review information to determine compliance with specified standards or criteria.
  - Use expectations, empirical data, and analytical methods to determine trends and variances.
  - Perform appropriate calculations on financial and nonfinancial data.
  - Recognize patterns of activity when reviewing large amounts of data or recognize breaks in patterns.
  - Interpretation of financial statement data for a given evaluation purpose.
  - Forecasting future financial statement data from historical financial statement data and other information.
  - Integrating primary financial statements: using data from all primary financial statements to uncover financial transactions, inconsistencies, or other information.

- Complex Problem Solving and Judgment

  - Develop and understand goals, objectives, and strategies for dealing with potential issues, obstacles, or opportunities.
  - Analyze patterns of information and contextual factors to identify potential problems and their implications.
  - Devise and implement a plan of action appropriate for a given problem.
  - Apply professional skepticism, which is an attitude that includes a questioning mind and a critical assessment of information or evidence obtained.
  - Adapt strategies or planned actions in response to changing circumstances.
  - Identify and solve unstructured problems.
  - Develop reasonable hypotheses to answer a question or resolve a problem.
  - Formulate and examine alternative solutions in terms of their relative strengths and weaknesses, level of risk, and appropriateness for a given situation.
  - Develop creative ways of thinking about situations, problems, and opportunities to create insightful and sound solutions.
  - Develop logical conclusions through the use of inductive and deductive reasoning.
  - Apply knowledge of professional standards and laws, as well as legal, ethical, and regulatory issues.
  - Assess the need for consultations with other professionals when gray areas, or areas requiring specialized knowledge, are encountered.

- Decision Making

  - Specify goals and constraints.
  - Generate alternatives.
  - Consider risks.
  - Evaluate and select the best alternative.

- Organization, Efficiency, and Effectiveness

  - Use time effectively and efficiently.
  - Develop detailed work plans, schedule tasks and meetings, and delegate assignments and tasks.
  - Set priorities by determining the relevant urgency or importance of tasks and deciding the order in which they should be performed.
  - File and store information so that it can be found easily and used effectively.

Written Communication. The various skills involved in preparing written communication, including

- Basic writing mechanics, such as grammar, spelling, word usage, punctuation, and sentence structure.
- Effective business writing principles, including organization, clarity, and conciseness.
- Exchange technical information and ideas with coworkers and other professionals to meet goals of job assignment.
- Documentation

  - Prepare documents and presentations that are concise, accurate, and supportive of the subject matter.
  - Document and cross-reference work performed and conclusions reached in a complete and accurate manner.

- Assist client to recognize and understand implications of critical business issues by providing recommendations and informed opinions.
- Persuade others to take recommended courses of action.
- Follow directions.

Overview

This module focuses on the related topics of corporate governance, internal control, and enterprise risk management. Corporate governance is designed to compensate for the agency problem resulting from the fact that corporations are managed by professional management that may not operate them in the best interest of the shareholders. Corporate governance includes the policies, procedures and mechanism that are established to control management. The major controls over management include compensation systems, boards of directors (including major committees), external auditors, internal auditors, attorneys, regulators, creditors, securities analysts, and internal control systems.

Internal control is defined by COSO as a process, effected by the entity's board of directors, managements, and other personnel designed to provide reasonable assurance regarding the achievement of objectives in the categories of (1) reliability of financial reporting, (2) effectiveness and efficiency of operations, and (3) compliance with applicable laws and regulations. It can be viewed as including five components: (1) the control environment, (2) the risk assessment process, (3) control activities, (4) information and communication, and (5) monitoring. It is important to realize that internal control is not perfect. It has a number of limitations, including management can override internal control, controls that rely on segregation of duties can be circumvented with collusion, internal control can break down due to bad judgment or misunderstanding of duties, and internal control cannot be perfect because its cost cannot exceed its benefits.

COSO has also developed a framework for enterprise risk management. Enterprise risk management is a process designed to identify potential events that may affect the entity, and manage risk to be within its risk appetite, to provide reasonable assurance regarding the achievement of entity objectives. It consists of eight interrelated components, including (1) internal environment, (2) objective setting, (3) event identification, (4) risk assessment, (5) risk response, (6) control activities, (7) information and communication, and (8) monitoring. All of these components work together to allow an organization to identify risks to achieving the organization's objectives and appropriately manage those risks. Before beginning the reading you should review the key terms at the end of the module.

A. Corporate Governance

In the corporate form of organization, owners (shareholders) are separated from operations (management) of the firm. This creates an agency problem in that management (the agents) may not act in the best interest of the shareholders (the principals). Managers may be tempted to engage in self-serving activities, such as shirking, taking too little or too much risk, or consuming excessive perks. Effective corporate governance involves developing an appropriate legal structure, and establishing appropriate incentives (i.e., forms of compensation) and monitoring devices to prevent this inappropriate activity.

Shareholders are a major stakeholder of the corporation, but there are others, including employees, customers, suppliers, government regulators, and society.

1. **Legal Structure of Corporations**

    a. **Articles of incorporation.** Corporations are almost universally incorporated under the laws and regulations of one of the states. A corporation is formed with the filing of **articles of incorporation** with the secretary of state who issues a certificate of incorporation. The articles of incorporation include

    (1) Proposed name of the corporation and initial address
    (2) Purpose of the corporation
    (3) The powers of the corporation
    (4) The name of the registered agent of the corporation
    (5) Name and address of each incorporator
    (6) Number of authorized shares of stock and types of stock

The articles of incorporation may be subsequently amended by approval of shareholders (often a majority vote but sometimes two-thirds vote required). Shareholders dissenting from the amendments may assert their right to sell their shares to the corporation for fair value before the vote. The **bylaws** of the corporation set forth how the directors and/or officers are elected/selected, how meetings are conducted, the types and duties of officers, and the required meetings. In addition, the bylaws should prescribe the process for bylaw amendment. For good governance all officers and directors should be provided with a copy of the corporation's bylaws.

b. **Shareholders.** Common shareholders provide the basic capital of the corporation and elect the board of directors. Annual meetings of shareholders are required as set forth in the bylaws. Certain matters require vote of the shareholders, such as amendment of the articles of incorporation and fundamental changes affecting the corporation, such as mergers and liquidations. Sarbanes-Oxley, which is discussed later in this module, also prescribes certain matters that must be voted on by shareholders. The common shareholders are the last to receive their capital in the event of liquidation of the corporation. Other rights of the common shareholders include

   (1) Right to receive dividends if declared by the board of directors
   (2) Right to subscribe to stock issues so that their ownership is not diluted as set forth in the Articles of Incorporation (preemptive right)
   (3) Right to inspect books and records in good faith and for a proper purpose
   (4) Right to sue on behalf of the corporation if officers and directors do not for reasons such as director violation of fiduciary duty, illegal declaration of dividends, or fraud by an officer (referred to as a derivative suit)

Shareholders have no right to manage the corporation unless they are also officers or directors. Preferred shareholders generally have no voting rights but they have preference as to dividends and receipt of capital upon liquidation of the company.

In many cases common shareholders have **cumulative voting rights** in the election of directors allowing them to cast 1 vote for each director of the corporation for each share of stock they own. This allows minority shareholders to have an opportunity to elect directors by voting all their votes for one or two directors.

c. **Boards of directors.** The board of directors is charged with running the corporation on behalf of the shareholders and other stakeholders. It is responsible for providing strategic direction and guidance about the establishment of the key business objectives of the corporation. Examples of duties of the board include

   (1) Determining the mission of the corporation
   (2) Selection and removal of the chief executive officer
   (3) Amending the bylaws, unless this is a responsibility of the shareholders
   (4) Determining management compensation
   (5) Decisions regarding declaration and payment of dividends
   (6) Decisions regarding major acquisitions and capital structure
   (7) Advising management
   (8) Providing governance oversight, with the assistance of internal and external auditors
   (9) Ensuring accurate financial reporting by the corporation
   (10) Risk management

Directors are elected by the common shareholders and have no individual power to bind the corporation. The power resides in the board collectively. A majority vote of directors present is needed for most business decisions providing a quorum is present. Actions may be taken with no meeting if allowed by the corporation's articles of incorporation or bylaws. However, there must be unanimous written consent by board members for action to be taken without a meeting.

Directors must exercise ordinary care and due diligence in performing their duties, and act in a manner that they believe is in the best interest of the corporation. In addition, they must disclose any conflicts of interest. The **business judgment rule** is a case law-derived concept that provides that a corporate director may not be held liable for errors in judgment providing the director acted with good faith, loyalty, and due care. Directors, however, maybe held personally liable for approving and paying dividends that are illegal. Directors are also responsible for their own torts (wrongful acts) even if they are acting on behalf of the corporation.

The directors' **duty of loyalty** means that they must put the interest of the corporation before their personal interest.

EXAMPLE

Assume a director is approached with a business opportunity that would be of interest to and benefit the corporation. However, the director is also interested in the opportunity. The director must first offer the opportunity to the corporation before pursuing it on his or her own behalf.

d. **Officers.** Officers operate the company based on the authority delegated to them by the board of directors. An officer of the corporation is an agent that can bind the corporation within the scope of his or her authority. A corporation is not bound by acts of an officer acting beyond the scope of his or her authority. The officers of the corporation are responsible for the fair presentation of the corporation's financial reports, including the financial statements. Sarbanes-Oxley requires the chief financial officer and chief executive officer to certify to financial statements. Officers have a fiduciary duty to the corporation and are liable for their own torts. Finally, the Sarbanes-Oxley Act generally prohibits personal loans to officers or directors of a public company.

2. **Forms of Executive Compensation**

   Various types of compensation are used to attempt to align management behavior with the objectives of the shareholders. A key objective in setting executive compensation is to align management's decisions and actions with the long-term interests of shareholders (e.g., long-term stock price). If managers are given too much fixed compensation, they may become too complacent and not take appropriate risks to increase share price. If managers are given too much incentive compensation based on operating profit or short-term stock price, they have incentives to manage profit or take excessive risks to maximize their compensation. Common types of management compensation are described below.

   a. **Base salary and bonuses**—Using this system, managers are compensated based on performance which is typically measured by accounting profit. Compensation systems based on accounting measures of profit are problematic because accounting profit can be manipulated or managed. For example, the timing of research and development and maintenance expenditures may be altered to manage profit and maximize bonuses. Managers may put too much focus on short-term profits instead of focusing on maximizing the long-term wealth of shareholders.

   b. **Stock options**—The use of stock options as a form of compensation provides managers with an incentive to manage the corporation to increase the stock price, which is consistent with the goal of shareholders. A disadvantage of stock options is that managers may have an incentive to increase the stock price in the short-term at the expense of long-term stock value, even by manipulating accounting income to increase stock price. In addition, stock options may encourage management to take on risks that are that are in excess of shareholders' risk appetite. Finally, if the stock price falls substantially, the stock options may be so underwater that they no longer provide an incentive to management.

   c. **Stock grants**—Stock grants involve issuing shares of stock as part of management's compensation. Two common types of stock grants are

   (1) Restricted stock—The issuance of stock that cannot be sold by the manager for a specific period of time, usually about 10 years. This form of compensation is effective because it encourages managers to undertake operations that increase the long-term value of the corporation's stock price.

   (2) Performance shares—The issuance of stock to management if certain levels of performance are met. If the price of the corporation's stock increases, the value of the manager's compensation increases.

   d. **Executive perquisites (perks)**—Management also may get various perquisites such as retirement benefits, use of corporate assets, golden parachutes, and corporate loans.

   e. **The best forms of executive compensation**—It is generally believed that the best compensation systems include a combination of fixed compensation and incentive compensation that is related to long-term stock price.

EXAMPLE

A company may establish incentive compensation in the form of stock options or stock that can be exercised or sold only after being held for a long period of time (e.g., 5 to 10 years).

Bonuses are effective if they are based on a composite of performance measures in addition to net profit, such as the amount of research and development expenditures, the corporation's market share, the number of new products developed, and/or the percentage of stock held by institutional investors (who tend to hold the stock for the long term). Such performance systems are often referred to as a balanced scorecard.

3. **Monitoring Devices**

   Various devices exist in the United States to monitor management behavior. Some of the devices are internal (e.g., the board of directors and internal auditors), while others are external (e.g., external auditors, analysts, credit agencies, attorneys, the SEC, and the IRS).

   a. **Board oversight.** To be effective at providing governance oversight, board members must be competent and a majority of the board members should be independent. Independence means the board member is not part of management of the corporation and does not receive significant benefit from the corporation other than compensation as a board member. Directors also must be adequately trained and be provided with complete and accurate information to carry out the board's functions. Officers, employees or major stockholders who are on the board of directors are referred to as **inside directors**. The **Wall Street Reform and Consumer Protection (Dodd-Frank) Act of 2010** requires public corporations to disclose why or why not the chairman of the board is also the chief executive officer.

Boards of directors should have a set of governance guidelines that are reviewed and revised annually. These guidelines will set forth the board organization, which will include its various committees and subcommittees. Committees that are particularly important to effective corporate governance include (1) the nominating/corporate governance committee, (2) the compensation committee, and (3) the audit committee.

(1) The nominating/corporate governance committee (1) oversees board organization, including committee assignments, (2) determines director qualifications and training, (3) develops corporate governance principles, and (4) oversees CEO succession.

(2) The audit committee plays a critical role in corporate governance. The Sarbanes-Oxley Act defines the audit committee as a "committee established by and amongst the board of directors of an issuer for the purpose of overseeing the accounting and financial reporting processes of the issuer; and audits of the financial statements of the issuer." A major responsibility of the audit committee is the appointment, compensation and oversight of the corporation's external auditor, including the resolution of any disagreements between management and the external auditor. An independent audit committee is mandated by the Sarbanes-Oxley Act and regulations of the NYSE and NASDAQ. Other important characteristics of an audit committee include

    (a) The Sarbanes-Oxley Act provides that at least one member should be a "financial expert." The names of the financial experts must be disclosed. If the firm does not have a financial expert, it must provide an explanation. A financial expert is one that possesses all of the following attributes:

        1] An understanding of generally accepted accounting principles and financial statements;
        2] Experience in preparing, auditing, analyzing, or evaluating financial statements of the breadth and complexity expected to be encountered with the company;
        3] An understanding of internal controls and procedures for financial reporting; and
        4] An understanding of audit committee functions.

    These attributes may be acquired through (1) education and experience as a principal financial officer, controller, public accountant, or equivalent, (2) experience supervising an individual in one of the positions in (1), (3) experience overseeing or assessing the performance of companies or public accountants with respect to preparing, auditing or evaluating financial statements, or (4) other relevant experience.

    (b) The audit committee should appoint, determine compensation of, and oversee the work of the corporation's external auditor.
    (c) External auditors must report directly to the audit committee.
    (d) Internal auditors should have direct access to the audit committee.
    (e) The audit committee should establish procedures for the receipt and treatment of complaints regarding accounting or auditing matters, including submission of concerns by employees (whistle-blowers).
    (f) Section 302 of the Sarbanes-Oxley Act makes officers responsible for maintaining effective internal control and requires the principal executive and financial officers to disclose all significant internal control deficiencies to the company's auditors and audit committee.

(3) The compensation committee (1) reviews and approves CEO compensation based on meeting performance goals, (2) makes recommendations to the board with respect to incentive and equity-based compensation plans, and (3) attempts to align incentives with shareholder objectives and risk appetite. The **Dodd-Frank Act** established a requirement that all members of the compensation committee of public companies must be independent. In addition, shareholders must be allowed a nonbinding vote on executive compensation at least every three years, and a vote at least every six years as to whether the vote on compensation should be held more often. Finally, the act also requires a nonbinding vote by shareholders on "golden parachutes" to be provided to executives as a result of major transactions.

b. **New York Stock Exchange (NYSE) & NASDAQ Rules Related to Corporate Governance and Director Independence.** Among other items, the NYSE and NASDAQ require listed corporations to

(1) Have a majority of independent directors on their boards.
(2) Make determination of independence of members and provide information to investors about the determination. Specific NYSE and NASDAQ rules that make a director not independent include

    (a) A director is not independent if s/he has been an employee of the corporation or an affiliate in the last 5 years (3 years for NASDAQ).

(b) A director is not independent if a family member has been an officer of the corporation or affiliate in the last 5 years (3 years for NASDAQ).

(c) A director is not independent if s/he was a former partner or employee of the corporation's external auditor in the last 5 years (3 years for NASDAQ).

(d) A director is not independent if s/he or a family member in the last 3 years received more than $120,000 (for a twelve-month period) in payments from the corporation other than for director compensation.

(e) A director is not independent if s/he is an executive of another entity that receives significant amounts of revenue from the corporation.

(3) Identify certain relationships that automatically preclude a board member from being independent.

(4) Have nonmanagement directors meet at regularly scheduled executive sessions.

(5) Adopt and make publically available a code of conduct applicable to all directors, officers and employees, and disclose any waivers of the code for directors or executive officers.

(6) Have an independent audit committee. In addition, nominating/corporate governance and compensation decisions must be made by independent committees (or a majority of independent directors for NASDAQ).

> **NOTE:** It is important to remember that judgment must be used to determine whether a director is independent. For example, based on the facts and circumstances it may be concluded that a director is not independent even though s/he receives less than $120,000 in payments (other than director compensation).

c. **Internal auditors.** Internal auditors perform audits of the risk management activities, internal control, and other governance processes for the corporation. Such audits are often referred to as assurance services. The results of these audits should be communicated directly to the audit committee of the board of directors. The NYSE requires its listed companies to maintain an internal audit function to provide management and the audit committee with ongoing assessments of the company's risk management processes and system of internal control.

The Institute of Internal Auditors (IIA) is a professional organization of internal auditors. Among other activities, the IIA has issued International Standards for the Professional Practice of Internal Auditing and a Code of Ethics for internal auditors. This organization also administers the Certified Internal Auditor (CIA) program. To become a CIA an individual must pass a multipart exam and have a minimum of two years of internal audit experience (or its equivalent). The CIA designation helps to demonstrate that the individual is competent to perform internal audits.

The International Standards for the Professional Practice of Internal Auditing, much like generally accepted auditing standards, include rules and interpretations. They cover the two types of services that internal auditors perform, assurance services and consulting services. Assurance services involve providing an independent assessment of governance, risk management or control processes of an organization. Examples include assurance about financial presentation, compliance, performance, and system security. Consulting services involve advisory related services to improve an organization's governance, risk management or control processes. Examples of consulting services include training, advising, and facilitating. The internal auditing standards are broken down into attribute standards (related to the characteristics of the internal audit activity) and performance standards (related to the quality of internal audit activities). The International Standards also include implementation standards that expand upon the attribute and performance standards. Aspects of the International Standards for the Professional Practice of Internal Auditing that relate particularly to corporate governance include

(1) The purpose, authority, and responsibility of the internal audit activity should be formally defined in the internal audit charter. The internal audit charter should recognize the need to adhere to the Code of Ethics and International a Standards for the Professional Practice of Internal Auditing.

(2) The internal audit activity must be independent and internal auditors must be objective in performing their work. Independence for the internal auditor activity is achieved by organizational independence, which means auditors cannot be influenced by the management of the functional areas that they audit. Accordingly, the chief audit executive should report to a level within the organization that allows the internal audit activity to fulfill its responsibilities. For effective organizational independence, the chief audit executive ideally should report functionally to the audit committee and administratively to the chief executive officer of the corporation. This helps to prevent their work from being influenced by management of the corporation. In addition, individual internal auditors must have an impartial, unbiased attitude and avoid conflicts of interest. If independence is impaired, the details of the impairment should be disclosed to appropriate parties.

EXAMPLE

Assume that an internal auditor managed the shipping department of the business before transferring to the internal audit department. That auditor should not be charged with auditing activities in the shipping department for the period he served as manager because independence could be impaired.

---

(3) Internal audit engagements must be performed with proficiency and due professional care. Proficiency means that the internal auditors must possess the knowledge, skills, and competencies needed to perform their individual responsibilities. This includes a sufficient knowledge of key IT risks and controls, and IT audit techniques, and a sufficient knowledge to evaluate fraud risk.

(4) Internal auditors must enhance their skills with continuing professional development and the chief audit executive must develop and maintain a quality assurance and improvement program.

(5) The internal audit activity must evaluate the effectiveness and contribute to the improvement of the corporation's risk management processes, and assist the management in maintaining effective controls by evaluating their effectiveness and efficiency and promoting continuous improvement.

(6) The chief audit executive must establish risk-based plans to determine audit priorities.

(7) The chief audit executive must establish and maintain a system to monitor the disposition of audit results communicated to management.

d. **External auditors.** The external auditor is responsible for performing an audit of the corporation's financial statements and internal control in accordance with standards of the Public Company Accounting Oversight Board (PCAOB). The external auditor is a major external corporate governance monitoring device for a corporation. The external audit helps assure that corporation financial reports are accurate and management is not engaging in fraudulent financial reporting.

Section 404 of the Sarbanes-Oxley Act requires that management acknowledge its responsibility for establishing adequate internal control over financial reporting and provide an assessment in the annual report of the effectiveness of internal control. For large public corporations (accelerated filers), it also requires that external auditors attest to management's report on internal control as part of the audit of the financial statements.

External auditors are required to communicate to the audit committee information that will help the committee perform its oversight function, including the following matters:

(1) Auditor responsibility to form and express an opinion.

(2) An audit does not relieve management or the audit committee with their responsibilities for governance.

(3) Planned scope and timing of the audit.

(4) Significant audit findings, including:

   (a) Auditor views of qualitative aspects of significant accounting practices.
   (b) Significant difficulties encountered during the audit.
   (c) Disagreements with management.
   (d) Other findings or issues which the auditor believes are significant and relevant.
   (e) Uncorrected misstatements other than those that are trivial.

(5) Material corrected misstatements.

(6) Significant issues discussed with management.

(7) Auditor's views about significant matters on which management consulted with other accountants.

(8) Written representations the auditor is requesting.

(9) Significant deficiencies and material weaknesses in internal control.

Section 802 prohibits a person from knowingly destroying, mutilating, or concealing records or documents to impede or influence the investigation of any department or agency of the United States. The penalty is a fine or imprisonment for not more than 20 years, or both.

e. **Investment banks and securities analysts.** Investment bankers help corporations issue equity and debt offerings. Therefore, they represent an external monitoring device because they must evaluate the company prior to becoming involved in selling the securities.

Securities analysts analyze companies to attempt to develop recommendations to "buy," "hold," or "sell" a particular corporation's stock. Therefore, securities analysts act as an external monitoring device because they use financial and nonfinancial information, including information about corporate management to make their recommendations. An issue with considering the recommendations of analysts is potential conflicts of interest. For example, analysts may be employed by firms that also perform investment banking activities, and the analyst's recommendations may be influenced by the fees received from the corporation for investment banking services. Regulations adopted by the SEC attempt to control these conflicts of interest by, among other requirements, requiring analysts to certify that their compensation will not be impacted by their recommendations.

f. **Creditors.** Creditors also act as an external monitoring device. Debt agreements contain covenants (requirements) that must be complied with to prevent the creditor from taking actions such as accelerating payment terms. Creditors monitor compliance by the corporation with the covenants of these agreements. One limitation of creditors as a monitoring device is that they monitor largely based on information provided by management. However, they do often engage external auditors to perform procedures to provide assurance about the corporation's compliance with certain covenants of the loan agreements.

g. **Credit rating agencies.** Credit rating agencies rate the creditworthiness of corporate bonds. Credit rating agencies are an external corporate monitoring device much like securities analysts. The biggest criticism of credit rating agencies is that they may improperly set the initial rating and are slow to downgrade the rating once the corporation gets in financial difficulty.

> **NOTE:** The Dodd-Frank Act has provisions that help prevent conflicts of interests and increase transparency by credit rating agencies.

h. **Attorneys.** Corporate legal counsel provide another external monitoring device in that they review securities filings and provide management advice on legal matters.

i. **The Securities and Exchange Commission (SEC).** The SEC is responsible for protecting investors; maintaining fair, orderly, and efficient markets; and facilitating capital formation. In achieving these responsibilities, the SEC enforces the US securities laws. The SEC consists of five presidentially appointed Commissioners. The SEC's activities act as an important external monitoring device for corporate government. The divisions and offices of the SEC that are particularly relevant to corporate governance include

(1) Division of Corporate Finance—This division reviews documents of publicly held companies that are filed with the SEC. Through the review process, the Division checks to see if companies are meeting disclosure requirements and seeks to improve the quality of the disclosures by companies.

(2) Division of Enforcement—This division assists the SEC in executing its law enforcement function by recommending the commencement of investigations of securities law violations, recommending which cases to take to court, and prosecuting these cases on behalf of the Commission.

(3) The Office of the Chief Accountant—The Chief Accountant advises the Commission on accounting and auditing, oversees the development of accounting principles, and approves the auditing rules put forward by the Public Company Accounting Oversight Board (PCAOB).

Several provisions of the Sarbanes-Oxley Act improved the SEC's power as an external monitoring device, including:

(1) Section 906 of the Sarbanes-Oxley Act requires the chief executive officer (CEO) and the chief financial officer (CFO) to certify the accuracy and truthfulness of periodic financial reports filed with the SEC. If the certification of the reports is later found to be inaccurate, the CEO and CFO can be found criminally liable and face imprisonment of 10 to 20 years. Also, civil penalties can involve fines of up to $5 million.

(2) Under Sarbanes-Oxley, any person who knowingly perpetrates or attempts a scheme to defraud any other person by misrepresenting or making false claims in connection with the purchase or sale of securities can be fined or imprisoned for up to 25 years, or both. While securities fraud has long been an offense under the other securities acts, Sarbanes-Oxley made prosecution much easier.

(3) The destruction, mutilation, alteration, concealment, or falsification of documentation with the intent to obstruct or influence an investigation that is ongoing or being considered can result in fines or imprisonment of up to 20 years.

(4) Sarbanes-Oxley prohibits any acts of retaliation against employees who alert the government to possible violations of securities laws (whistle-blowers). The punishment for a violation of this provision can include fines or imprisonment of up to 10 years or both.

The Dodd-Frank act provides that the SEC will pay awards to whistle-blowers for providing information about violations of securities laws that result in aggregate monetary sanctions in excess of $1 million. The Act and related rules provide that

(1) A whistle-blower is eligible to receive 10 to 30% of the monetary sanction if the information is derived from independent knowledge or analysis of the whistle-blower and not known to the government from any other source.

(2) Tips can be made anonymously (through an attorney) with the whistle-blower only being identified to the SEC after determination that an award will be given.

(3) A broad group of individuals are eligible including employees, customers, and suppliers. Individuals that are generally excluded from eligibility include

(a) Officers, directors, trustees, or partners of an entity, when those individuals learned of information about the misconduct from another person or in connection with the company's processes for identifying potential illegal conduct.

(b) Employees whose main job functions involve compliance or internal audit, or persons who are employed by a firm hired to perform audit or compliance functions or to investigate possible violations of the law.

(c) Employees of public accounting firms performing an engagement required by the securities laws.

However, the above individuals may be still eligible if it appears that the company is attempting to behave in a way that would harm investors or inhibit an investigation, or 120 days have passed since they notified the company of the violation.

(4) Whistle-blowers are encouraged to report the information through the normal internal corporate governance system of the company by an indication that doing so may increase the amount of the award.

The Jumpstart Our Business Startups (JOBS) Act exempted "emerging growth companies" for a maximum of 5 years from the date of their initial public offering from certain requirements that apply to larger public companies, including

(1) Certain disclosure requirements.
(2) The requirement for an integrated audit of internal control.
(3) The requirements regarding shareholder votes on executive compensation.

j. **The Internal Revenue Service (IRS).** The IRS acts as an external governance device by requiring certain accounting information on the corporation's income tax return. The IRS also audits corporations' tax returns, and enforces penalties for filing false tax returns.

k. **Corporate takeovers.** Takeovers also act as a corporate governance device. If management is performing poorly, the corporation may be subject to takeover by a firm that believes it can more efficiently utilize the corporation's resources. This provides an incentive for management to operate the corporation consistent with the interests of the shareholders. Corporations sometime engage in strategies to prevent a takeover, such as **a poison pill** defense. A poison pill defense triggers an option for the shareholders to purchase additional shares at a discount if someone attempts to acquire a controlling interest in the corporation. Such defenses are controversial because they inhibit an active market for corporate control.

NOW REVIEW MULTIPLE-CHOICE QUESTIONS 1 THROUGH 28 IN VOLUME 2

B. Internal Controls

There are a number of internal control frameworks used as benchmarks. The most commonly used framework in the US is *Internal Control—Integrated Framework* developed by COSO. According to COSO internal control is

A process, effected by the entity's board of directors, management, and other personnel designed to provide reasonable assurance regarding the achievement of objectives in the categories of (1) reliability of financial reporting, (2) effectiveness and efficiency of operations, and (3) compliance with applicable laws and regulations.

As can be seen from the definition, internal control has three objectives: (1) reliability of financial reporting, (2) efficiency and effectiveness of operations, and (3) compliance with applicable laws and regulations.

NOTE: Internal control that provides absolute assurance of achieving these objectives is not possible in terms of reasonable cost. Well-designed internal control can only provide reasonable assurance of achieving the objectives.

Under COSO internal control can be viewed as including five components: (1) the control environment, (2) the risk assessment process, (3) control activities, (4) information and communication, and (5) monitoring.

1. The Control Environment

The control environment sets the tone of an organization by influencing the control consciousness of people. It may be viewed as the foundation for the other components of internal control. Control environment factors include integrity and ethical values; commitment to competence; board of directors or audit committee; management's philosophy and operating style; organizational structure; assignment of authority and responsibility; and human resource policies and practices.

a. Integrity and ethical values. The effectiveness of internal control depends on the communication and enforcement of integrity and ethical values. Management should establish a tone at the top of the organization that encourages appropriate behavior. Top management should communicate these values through a code of conduct, official policies, and by example.

b. Commitment to competence. Effective internal control depends on having employees that possess the skills and knowledge essential to performing their jobs, especially when they are responsible for performing important control functions.

c. Board of directors or audit committee. The control environment is significantly influenced by the effectiveness of the board of directors and its audit committee. The characteristics and requirements for an effective board and audit committee were discussed above in the section on corporate governance.

d. Management's philosophy and operating style. The manner in which management runs the organization can have a significant effect on the control environment. Management that takes undue risks or stresses making profit goals by any means can create an environment where employees are motivated to engage in unethical or illegal activities.

e. Organizational structure. An effective organizational structure provides a basis for planning, directing and controlling operations.

f. Assignment of authority and responsibility. Personnel need a clear understanding of their responsibilities and the rules and regulations that govern their actions. Authority and responsibility is communicated through documents such as job descriptions and organizational charts.

g. Human resource policies and procedures. The control environment is enhanced by effective policies and practices for hiring, training, evaluating, counseling, promoting, and compensating employees.

2. **Risk Assessment**

Effective internal control requires that management have a system of risk assessment. Risk assessment is management's process for identifying, analyzing, and responding to risks. Risks in a company can arise from two sources:

a. Internal risk factors, such as changes in personnel, new information systems, new products, etc.

b. External risk factors, such as economic conditions, competition, etc.

The risk assessment process is described more fully in the section on enterprise risk management.

3. **Control Activities**

Control activities are policies and procedures that help ensure that management directives are carried out. These policies and procedures promote actions that address the risks that face the organization. Typical controls include

a. **Performance reviews**—Reviews of actual current performance versus budgets, forecasts, and prior period performance. Performance reviews involve the use of both operating and financial data.

b. **Information processing controls**—Controls to check the accuracy and completeness of data, and the authorization of transactions. The two broad groupings of information system controls include

   (1) General controls—Control activities over data center operations, system software acquisition and maintenance, access security, and application system development and maintenance.

   (2) Application controls—Control activities designed to ensure that particular applications (e.g., payroll) are accurately and completely processing data, and that transactions are properly authorized. Application controls are further segregated into

      (a) Input controls—Controls to ensure that data are input accurately and completely, and transactions are authorized.

      (b) Processing controls—Controls to ensure that data is processed accurately.

      (c) Output controls—Controls over the distribution of and accuracy of output.

   (3) Physical controls—Control activities that encompass the physical control over assets and records, such as secured facilities and authorization procedures for access to computer programs and files.

   (4) Segregation of duties—Control activities that involve assigning different people the responsibilities of authorizing transactions, recording transactions, and maintaining custody of assets. Segregation of duties helps assure that an individual cannot both perpetrate an error or fraud and also conceal it. Segregation of duties can be circumvented by collusion among employees.

4. **Information and Communication**

To make effective decisions, managers must have access to timely, reliable, and relevant information. Information systems should be implemented to capture information and process, summarize and report the information on an accurate and timely basis. To be effective, the information and communication system must accomplish the following goals for transactions

a. Identify and record all valid transactions.

b. Describe the transactions on a timely basis.

c. Measure the value of the transactions properly.

d. Record transactions in the proper time period.

e. Properly present and disclose transactions.

f. Communicate responsibilities to employees.

5. **Monitoring**

Monitoring of controls is a process used to assess the quality of internal control performance over time. Monitoring may be achieved by performing ongoing activities or by separate evaluations. Ongoing monitoring activities include regularly performed supervisory and management activities, such as continuous monitoring of customer complaints, or reviewing the reasonableness of management reports. Separate evaluations are monitoring activities that are performed on a nonroutine basis, such as periodic audits by the internal auditors.

In 2009 COSO issued Guidance on monitoring Internal Control Systems that elaborates on the monitoring component of internal control. Individuals that monitor controls within an organization are referred to as evaluators.

a. Characteristics of **Evaluators**—evaluators should be competent and objective in the particular circumstances. Competence refers to the evaluator's knowledge of internal control and related processes, including how controls should operate and what constitutes a deficiency. The evaluator's objectivity refers to whether that person can evaluate the controls without concern about possible consequences of discovering deficiencies.

b. Internal control systems fail because

(1) They are not designed or implemented properly;

(2) They are properly designed and implemented but environment changes have occurred making the controls ineffective; or

(3) They are properly designed and implemented but the way they operate has changed making the controls ineffective.

c. In all situations, a baseline understanding of internal control system's effectiveness in an area serves as the starting point for monitoring. This baseline understanding allows organizations to design ongoing and separate monitoring procedures. Monitoring may be considered as consisting of the following sequence of activities (monitoring-for-change control continuum):

(1) Control baseline—Establishing a starting point that includes a supported understanding of the existing internal control system.

(2) Change identification—Identifying through monitoring changes in internal control that are necessary because changes in the operating environment have taken place, such as changes in regulations or changes in the economic environment.

(3) Change management—Evaluating the design and implementation of the changes, and establishing a new baseline. An effective change management process enables management to control (1) change requests, (2) change analyses, (3) change decisions, and (4) change planning, implementation, and tracking. When a change occurs in an organization, it often has an effect on other areas of the organization. It is important that the change management process considers these effects and incorporates them into the analysis, planning, and implementation phases of the change. Also, a system of documentation should be established to ensure that changes are authorized, communicated, and documented. Finally, changes should be thoroughly tested before being implemented. If employees are not adequately trained on new processes, control may break down.

(4) Control revalidation/update—Periodically revalidating control operation when no known changes have occurred.

d. It is important to understand that this entire sequence does not reside solely in the monitoring component of internal control. For example, changes in the operating environment might be identified through risk assessment.

e. The effectiveness and efficiency of monitoring can be enhanced by linking it to the results of the risk assessment component of internal control. This allows evaluators to focus monitoring attention on controls that address meaningful risks (referred to as key controls). Key controls often have the following characteristics:

(1) Their failure could materially affect the area's objectives, and other controls would not be expected to detect the failure on a timely basis; and

(2) Their operation might prevent or detect other control failures before they had an opportunity to become material to the organization's objectives.

f. For key controls the evaluator should determine what constitutes sufficient suitable evidence that the control is operating as designed. This evidence is of two types:

(1) Direct evidence—Evidence obtained from observing the control and reperforming it.
(2) Indirect evidence—Evidence that identifies anomalies that may signal control change or failure (e.g., evidence derived from operating statistics, key risk indicators, key performance indicators, and comparative industry data).

g. Ongoing monitoring is generally better than separate monitoring because ongoing monitoring operates continuously and can offer the first opportunity to identify and correct control deficiencies.
h. Technology has enhanced an organization's ability to monitor internal controls and risk. Internal control systems can have embedded modules that look for unusual or suspicious transactions or relationships. This makes it more efficient and effective for management to perform ongoing monitoring.
i. Monitoring includes reporting results to appropriate personnel both within and outside of the organization.

6. **Limitations of Internal Control**

As we indicated previously, internal control provides reasonable, but not absolute, assurance that specific entity objectives will be achieved. Even the best internal control may break down because

a. Human judgment in decision making can be faulty.
b. Breakdowns can occur because of human failures such as simple errors or mistakes.
c. Controls, whether manual or automated, can be circumvented by collusion.
d. Management has the ability to override internal control.
e. Cost constraints (the cost of internal control should not exceed the benefits expected to be derived).
f. Custom, culture, and the corporate governance system may inhibit fraud, but they are not absolute deterrents.

7. **Controls over Business Processes**

Organizations use various approaches to executing and controlling financial transactions. Some are still very manual in nature. However, more and more transactions are being processed completely by the technology through private links within and between companies, or over the Internet. All transactions have risks that must be controlled.

A fundamental control over transactions is segregation of duties. For each transaction cycle, the functions of authorization, approval (for certain types of transactions), execution (custody of assets), and recordkeeping should be segregated. In a manual accounting system, segregation of duties is achieved by having different individuals physically performing the functions. In a technology-based system, the computer performs many of these processes and segregation of duties is achieved by controlling access to terminals and through the use of passwords. Of course in a technology-based system control is achieved over processing and data by appropriate information technology controls as discussed in Module 41.

The tables below presents two major processes (transaction cycles) including the risks and examples of controls that might be used to mitigate those risks.

Sales & Collections Business Process

Risk	Nature of the Process	Example Controls
Inaccurate or incomplete sales data and lack of security over sales order information	Sales orders inputted manually	Password control over terminals to assure that sales are authorized by sales department; accuracy and completeness controls over inputs*; physical controls over terminals and files
	Sales over the Internet	Encryption of transmitted data; accuracy and completeness controls over inputs; password control over access to information to maintain a segregation of duties; data controls to ensure that sales prices are accurately inputted and updated
Sales to customers that are not creditworthy	Outsource credit to credit card company	Protect credit card information with password control and physical security over terminals and files
	Organization has credit department that extends credit	Credit department should be independent of sales function and approve credit limits; effective practices for collecting credit information to make evaluations to grant credit
Maintaining too much or too little inventory	Inventory control and management	Use of a perpetual inventory system; use of techniques such as just-in-time, economic order quantity, and reorder points as methods of managing inventory: heavy reliance on technology to determine when and how much to order
Inaccurate filling of orders	Manual filling of orders	Have an individual not involved in filling the order check it for accuracy
	Technology used to fill orders	Input controls to assure information is correct in computer fulfillment process; use technology such as bar code scanners to pack goods

Risk	Nature of the Process	Example Controls
Inaccurate billing of customers	Manual billing process	Individual doing billing match sales order to shipping document to assure the accuracy of billing invoice; use of prenumbered documents and accounting for all documents; invoice checked for clerical accuracy by an individual not involved in preparation; billing department is independent of individuals maintaining receivables records; account for numerical sequence of documents
	Technology used for billing	Accuracy and completeness input controls to assure billing information is accurate and based on accurate shipping information input by shipping personnel; accuracy and completeness controls to assure that pricing information is accurate and based on authorization from the sales department; password control over terminals to insure segregation of duties
Failure to bill for shipment	Manual billing process	Accounting for all prenumbered shipping documents
	Technology used for billing	Accuracy and completeness input controls to assure that all shipping information is entered to the system for billing
Errors or fraud in processing and depositing cash receipts	Cash receipts received through the mail	Segregation of cash handling from accounts receivable records or use of a lockbox at a financial institution
	Electronic funds transfer system	Control over access to the system through the use of a password system; use of accuracy and completeness controls over input of cash receipt information
Accounts may be written off without authorization	Manual	Individual independent of sales and cash receipts should be authorized to write off accounts; use of prenumbered authorization forms; accounting for all forms
	Technology-based system	Access to terminal for authorization by independent individual should be restricted by password system

* Accuracy and completeness controls include controls such as validity checks, missing data checks, logic checks, limit tests, etc.

Acquisitions & Payments Process

Risk	Nature of the Process	Example Controls
Ordering unneeded goods	Manual or technology-based system	Use of a perpetual inventory system; ordering based on inventory management techniques, such as just-in-time, economic order quantity, and reorder points
Purchasing goods from unauthorized vendors	Manual or technology-based system	Establish preferred vendor relationships; establish criteria for authorized vendors
		Creation of purchase orders; accuracy and completeness controls over inputting purchasing information into the computer; password control over terminals
Receiving goods that were not ordered	Manual system	Matching of purchase order to goods received
	Technology-based system	Computer comparison of purchase information input by the purchasing department with information on goods received inputted by the receiving department
Receiving goods that are damaged or inferior	Manual or technology-based system	Inspect goods received
Payment for goods not received	Manual system	Matching of purchase orders with receiving reports; accounting for all prenumbered documents; individual authorized to sign checks is independent of those maintaining records and receiving goods; check signer cancels supporting documentation
	Computer generation of payments based on purchase and receiving information	Accuracy and completeness input controls for purchase and receiving information; segregation of those maintaining records and processing payments from those authorized to make payments; password control to ensure segregation of duties

Risk	Nature of the Process	Example Controls
Payment for purchase twice	Manual system	Cancel supporting documents for all payments
	Technology-based system	Control access to receiving and purchasing information by use of passwords and appropriate segregation of duties
Unauthorized cash payments	Manual system	Segregation of duties of accounting and authorized check signers; reconciliation of bank account by individual independent of individuals preparing and signing checks
	Technology-based system	Passwords and controls over terminals prevent issuance of unauthorized payments; reconciliation of bank account by computer or independent individual
Loss or theft of assets	Manual or technology-based system	Periodic reconciliations of physical assets to accounting records by individuals independent of individuals having custody of the assets and individuals maintaining the accounting records for the assets; examples include reconciliations of bank accounts, taking physical inventories, and inventories of supplies and equipment

    a. **Additional controls over inventories**

        (1) Perpetual inventory records for large dollar items
        (2) Prenumbered receiving reports prepared when inventory received; receiving reports accounted for
        (3) Adequate standard cost system to cost inventory items
        (4) Physical controls against theft
        (5) Written inventory requisitions used
        (6) Proper authorization of purchases and use of prenumbered purchase orders

    b. **Controls over payrolls**

        (1) Segregate: Timekeeping
                     Payroll preparation
                     Personnel
                     Paycheck distribution

        (2) Time clocks used where possible
        (3) Job time tickets reconciled to time clock cards
        (4) Time clock cards approved by supervisors (overtime and regular hours)
        (5) Treasurer signs paychecks
        (6) Unclaimed paychecks controlled by someone otherwise independent of the payroll function (locked up and eventually destroyed if not claimed). In cases in which employees are paid cash (as opposed to checks) unclaimed pay should be deposited into a special bank account.
        (7) Personnel department promptly sends termination notices to the payroll department.

    c. **Controls over fixed assets**

        (1) Major asset acquisitions are properly approved by the firm's board of directors and properly controlled through capital budgeting techniques.
        (2) Detailed records are available for property assets and accumulated depreciation.
        (3) Written policies exist for capitalization vs. expensing decisions.
        (4) Depreciation properly calculated.
        (5) Retirements approved by an appropriate level of management.
        (6) Physical control over assets to prevent theft.
        (7) Periodic physical inspection of plant and equipment by individuals who are otherwise independent of property, plant, and equipment (e.g., internal auditors).

8. **Reporting on Internal Control**

    Section 404 of the Sarbanes-Oxley Act requires management to establish and maintain effective internal control over financial reporting and document the system. In addition, it requires management to provide a report on the effectiveness of the system. Management's report should include the following

    a. A statement of management's responsibility for establishing and maintaining adequate internal control over financial reporting for the corporation.
    b. A statement identifying the framework used by management to conduct the required assessment of the effectiveness of the corporation's internal control over financial reporting (e.g., COSO).

c. An assessment of the effectiveness of the corporation's internal control over financial reporting as of the end of the company's most recent fiscal year, including an explicit statement as to whether the internal control over financial reporting is effective. If there are any material weaknesses, they should be disclosed.

d. If applicable, a statement that the corporation's registered public accounting firm that audited the financial statements included in the annual report has issued an attestation report on management's assessment of the company's internal control over financial reporting. Larger public corporations (accelerated filers) are required to have their external auditors attest to, and report on, the effectiveness of internal control over financial reporting. The Dodd-Frank Act permanently exempted small corporations from this requirement.

NOW REVIEW MULTIPLE-CHOICE QUESTIONS 29 THROUGH 42 IN VOLUME 2

C. Enterprise Risk Management

In addition to an internal control framework, COSO has also developed a framework for enterprise risk management (ERM). The framework defines ERM as follows:

Enterprise risk management is a process, effected by an entity's board of directors, management and other personnel, applied in a strategy setting and across the enterprise, designed to identify potential events that may affect the entity, and manage risk to be within its risk appetite, to provide reasonable assurance regarding the achievement of entity objectives.

ERM helps align the risk appetite of the organization with its strategy, enhances risk response decisions, reduces operational surprises and losses, identifies and manages cross-enterprise risks, provides integrated responses to multiple risks, helps the organization seize opportunities, and improves the deployment of capital.

A key aspect of ERM is the identification and management of events that have a negative impact, positive impact, or both. Events with negative impact represent risks. Events with positive impact may offset negative impacts or represent opportunities. The risk management process involves (1) identifying risks, assessing risks, prioritizing risks, determining risk responses, and monitoring risk responses.

Everyone in the organization has some responsibility for ERM. The best run organizations have a culture of risk management that is understood by every employee. Many organizations assign a risk officer, financial officer, and/or internal auditor with key support responsibilities. The internal control of the organization is an integral part of the organization's ERM system.

1. **Components of ERM**

   According to COSO, ERM consists of eight interrelated components, including (1) internal environment, (2) objective setting, (3) event identification, (4) risk assessment, (5) risk response, (6) control activities, (7) information and communication, and (8) monitoring.

   a. **Internal environment**

      The internal environment is the basis for all other components of ERM, providing discipline and structure. It encompasses the tone of the organization, and sets the basis for how risk is viewed and addressed by an organization's people, including risk management philosophy and risk appetite, and integrity and ethical values.

      The board of directors is a critical part of the internal environment. The board provides oversight over management's implementation of ERM, helping to make sure that it is effective.

      Integrity and ethical values help insure that management and other individuals within the organization are not inclined to engage in unethical or illegal activities. Management sets an ethical tone by action and example, and communicates the tone through codes of conduct and established policies. Management also should avoid the use of incentives and temptations to engage in unethical behavior, unless effective controls are established to prevent such behavior.

      Other factors that contribute to an effective internal environment include competent, well-trained employees, an appropriate organizational structure, properly assigned authority and responsibility, and effective human resource policies and procedures.

      An important aspect of the organization's internal environment is its risk appetite. **Risk appetite** is the amount of risk an organization is willing to accept to achieve its goals. It reflects the organization's culture and operating style and is directly related to the organization's strategy. Some organizations consider risk appetite qualitatively (e.g., low, moderate, high) while others consider risk quantitatively (e.g. in percentages). **Risk tolerance** relates to the organization's objectives. It is the acceptable variation with respect to a particular objective.

> **EXAMPLE**
>
> Assume a company has an objective of 97% customer satisfaction rating. However, the company may tolerate as low as a 94% customer satisfaction rating. The difference between 97% and 94% represents the company's risk tolerance with respect to the customer satisfaction rating.

b. **Objective setting**

Objectives must exist before management can identify potential events affecting their achievement. Enterprise risk management ensures that management has in place a process to set objectives and that the chosen objectives support and align with the organization's mission and are consistent with its risk appetite. The organization's mission sets forth in broad terms what the organization aspires to achieve. Strategic objectives are high-level goals aligned with the organization's mission. These high-level objectives are linked and integrated with the specific objectives established for various activities. By setting objectives the organization can identify critical risk factors, which are the key things that must go right for the objectives to be met.

Objectives may be divided into three categories: (a) operations objectives, which relate to the effectiveness and efficiency of operations, (b) reporting objectives, which relate to reliable reporting of internal and external, financial and nonfinancial information, and (c) compliance objectives which relate to adherence to laws and regulations.

c. **Event identification**

Potential internal and external events affecting achievement of an organization's objectives must be identified, distinguishing between risks and opportunities. An event is an incident that occurs or might occur that affects implementation of strategy or achievement of objectives. Events may be negative (risks), positive (opportunities) or both. Risks require a response while opportunities should be channeled back to management's strategy or objective-setting processes. Some events may be external in nature, such as those resulting from economic, natural environment, political, social, or technological factors. Other events result from internal factors such as the organization's infrastructure, personnel, processes, or technology.

Event identification techniques include

(1) Event inventories. Developing a detailed listing of potential events.
(2) Internal analysis. This may be done at regular staff meetings. It may involve using information from other stakeholders, such as customers, suppliers, etc.
(3) Escalation or threshold triggers. Management predetermines limits that cause an event to be further assessed.

> **EXAMPLE**
>
> A company may identify a potential pricing issue when competitor sales prices change by a predetermined percentage.

(4) Facilitated workshops or interviews. This technique involves soliciting information about events from management and staff. For example, a facilitator may lead a discussion of events that might affect achieving an organization's objectives.
(5) Process flow analysis. Involves breaking processes down into inputs, tasks, responsibilities, and outputs to identify events that might adversely affect the process.
(6) Leading event indicators. This technique involves monitoring data correlated to events, to identify when the event is likely to occur.
(7) Loss event data methodologies. By developing repositories of data on past loss events, management can identify event trends and the root causes of events. Management can also perform **black swan analysis** which involves evaluating the occurrence of events that had negative effects and were unanticipated or viewed as highly unlikely.

d. **Risk assessment**

Risks are analyzed, considering likelihood and impact, as a basis for determining how they should be managed. Management should assess both inherent risk and residual risk for an event. Inherent risk is the risk to the organization if management does nothing to alter its likelihood or impact. Residual risk is the risk of the event after considering management's response. Risks are assessed in terms of their likelihood of occurring and their impact (e.g., financial effect). Management often uses qualitative techniques to assess risk when risks do not lend themselves to quantification or when sufficient reliable data is not available to use a quantitative model. Probabilistic or nonprobabilistic models may be used to quantify risk. Probabilistic models associate a range of events and the resulting impact with the likelihood of those events based on certain assumptions. Examples of probabilistic models include value at risk, cash flow at risk, earnings at risk, and development of credit and operational loss distributions. Nonprobabilistic models use subjective assumptions in estimating the impact of events without quantifying an associated likelihood. Examples of nonprobabilistic models include sensitivity measures, stress tests, and scenario analysis.

e. **Risk response**

In this aspect of ERM, management selects risk responses that are consistent with the risk appetite of the organization including

(1) Avoidance. This response involves exiting the activity that gives rise to the risk.
(2) Reduction. This response involves taking action to reduce risk likelihood or impact, or both. For example, this might involve managing the risk or adding additional controls to processes.
(3) Sharing. This response involves reducing risk likelihood or impact by transferring or sharing a portion of the risk. Techniques for sharing include insurance, hedging, and outsourcing.
(4) Acceptance (retention). No action is taken because the risk is consistent with the risk appetite of the organization.

All risk responses must be assessed in terms of their costs and benefits to select the responses that should be implemented.

f. **Control activities**

Policies and procedures should be established and implemented to help ensure the risk responses are effectively carried out.

g. **Information and communication**

Relevant information is identified, captured, and communicated to enable people to carry out their responsibilities. Information is needed at all levels of the organization to identify, assess and respond to risks. Communication should effectively convey the importance and relevance of effective ERM, the organization's objectives, the organization's risk appetite and risk tolerances, a common risk language, and the roles and responsibilities of personnel in effecting and supporting the components of ERM.

h. **Monitoring**

The entire ERM process should be monitored to make needed modifications. Monitoring is accomplished by ongoing management activities, and separate evaluations, such as those performed by internal auditors.

2. **Limitations of ERM**

In considering limitations of ERM, three distinct concepts must be recognized:

a. Risk relates to the future which is uncertain,
b. ERM provides information about risks of achieving objectives but it cannot provide even reasonable assurance that objectives will be achieved, and
c. ERM cannot provide absolute assurance with respect to any of the objective categories. Specific limitations include the following:

(1) The effectiveness of ERM is subject to the limitations of the ability of humans to make judgments about risk and impact.
(2) Well-designed ERM can break down.
(3) Collusion among two or more individuals can result in ERM failures.
(4) ERM systems can never be perfect due to cost-benefit constraints.
(5) ERM is subject to management override.

> **NOW REVIEW MULTIPLE-CHOICE QUESTIONS 43 THROUGH 50 IN VOLUME 2**

KEY TERMS

Articles of incorporation. The document filed with the secretary of the state to obtain a certificate of incorporation.

Audit committee. The committee of the board of directors that oversees the accounting and financial reporting processes of the company and oversees the audits of the financial statements of the company. The Sarbanes-Oxley Act requires all members to be independent.

Black swan analysis. Evaluating the occurrence of events that had negative effects and were unanticipated or viewed is highly unlikely.

Board of directors. The body charged with running the corporation on behalf of the shareholders.

Business judgment rule. A case law-derived concept that provides that a corporate director may not be held liable for errors in judgment providing the director acted with good faith, loyalty, and due care.

Compensation committee. The committee of the board of directors that reviews and approves executive compensation, makes recommendations to the board regarding incentive-based compensation, and attempts to align incentives with shareholder objectives and risk appetite. The Dodd-Frank Act requires all members to be independent.

Corporate bylaws. Set forth how the directors and/or officers are selected, how meetings are conducted, the types and duties of officers, and the required meetings.

Duty of loyalty. A concept that provides that directors and officers must put the interest of the corporation before their personal interest. Accordingly, if a director is approached with a business opportunity that would be of interest to and benefit the corporation, he or she must first offer the opportunity to the corporation before pursuing it on his or her own behalf.

Enterprise risk management. A process designed to identify potential events that may affect the organization, and manage risk to be within its risk appetite, to provide reasonable assurance regarding the achievement of organizational objectives.

Evaluator. An individual that monitors internal control within an organization.

Executive perquisites. Executive benefits other than compensation, such as retirement, use of corporate assets, golden parachutes, and corporate loans.

Inherent risk. The risk to the organization if management does nothing to alter its likelihood or impact.

Residual risk. The risk of the event after considering management's response.

Risk appetite. The amount of risk an organization is will to accept to achieve its objectives.

Risk assessment. Analyzing the potential (likelihood and impact) effects of a risk.

Risk tolerance. The acceptable variation with respect to achieving a particular objective.

Module 41: Information Technology

Overview

Computers have become the primary means used to process financial accounting information and have resulted in a situation in which auditors must be able to use and understand current information technology. Accordingly, knowledge of information technology implications is included in the Business Environment & Concepts section of the CPA exam. In addition, auditing procedures relating to information technology (IT) are included in the Auditing & Attestation portion of the CPA exam.

This module describes various types of information technology and describes the major types of controls that are used to assure the accuracy, completeness, and integrity of technology processed information.

Ideally, to effectively reply to technology-related questions, you should have previously studied or worked in computerized business environments. However, if you do not have this background, we believe that the information in this module should prepare you to perform reasonably well on a typical exam. Keep in mind that the review of these materials cannot make you an expert, and a module such as this cannot cover all possible topics related to information technology. However, this material should help you to understand the complexities introduced by computers in sufficient detail to answer most questions. Before beginning the reading you should review the key terms at the end of the module.

A. Information Systems Within a Business

1. **Definition**—An information system processes data and transactions to provide users with the information they need to plan, control and operate an organization, including

   a. Collecting transaction and other data
   b. Entering it into the information system
   c. Processing the data
   d. Providing users with the information needed
   e. Controlling the process

2. **Manual vs. Computer Systems**

   a. On an overall basis, manual accounting systems have in most circumstances been replaced by computerized accounting information systems of various types, although portions of many systems remain manual.
   b. Computer processing tends to reduce or eliminate processing time, and prevent computational errors and errors in processing routine transactions (when fraud is not involved).

3. **General Types of IT Systems**

   a. **Office automation systems**—Designed to improve productivity by supporting daily work of employees (e.g., word processing, spreadsheets, presentation tools, e-mail, electronic calendars, contact management software)
   b. **Transaction processing systems**—Involve the daily processing of transactions (e.g., airplane reservation systems, payroll recording, cash receipts, cash disbursements)
   c. **Management reporting systems**—Designed to help with the decision making process by providing access to computer data

      (1) **Management information systems**—Systems designed to provide past, present and future information for planning, organizing and controlling the operations of the organization
      (2) **Decision support systems**—Computer-based information systems that combine models and data to resolve nonstructured problems with extensive user involvement
      (3) **Expert systems**—Computer systems that apply reasoning methods to data in a specific relatively structured area to render advice or recommendations, much like a human expert

1235

(4) **Executive information systems**—Computerized systems that are specifically designed to support executive work

> **NOTE:** It is helpful to consider these two distinct roles for systems—that is, (a) recording transactions of various types versus (b) providing support for decision making. These topics are discussed in detail under topic B.2. (Methods of Processing).

4. Systems Design and Process Improvement

Designing and implementing a new information and control system provides an opportunity to reexamine business processes, especially if the new system is an enterprise resource planning (ERP) system. Management can take advantage of the capabilities of the technology to redesign business processes making them more efficient and effective. The traditional methodology for developing information systems is the systems development lifecycle (SDLC). This methodology is characterized by its phases, each representing a specific set of development activities. Typically, the SDLC phases include: planning, analysis, design, development, testing, implementation and maintenance.

a. The Planning Phase
Major activities in the planning phase include

(1) Identify the problem(s) that proposed system will solve.
(2) Define the system to be developed. This involves identifying and selecting the system to be developed based on the strategic goals of the organization.
(3) Determine the project scope. This activity sets the project's boundaries by providing a clear understanding of what the new system will do and how it will be evaluated. A project scope document is used to describe the project scope. During the process of systems design, the scope of the project may be revisited and revised.
(4) Develop a project plan. The project plan defines the activities that will be performed, and the individuals and resources that will be used. A project manager is individual that develops the plan and tracks its progress. The plan establishes project milestones which set forth dates by which certain activities need to be performed.
(5) Evaluate the initial feasibility of the project. Feasibility analysis may involve multiple measures including determining the project's technical, organizational, and economic feasibility.

b. The Analysis Phase
This phase involves teams including end users, information technology specialists, systems analysts, and process design specialists to understand the requirements for the proposed system. Typically, processing, data, and logic models are produced during this phase to help determine the system requirements. A needs assessment may also be performed. A needs assessment involves determining the requirements for the system in terms of processes, data capture, information and reporting. Next, an analysis is performed on the existing system along the same dimensions. Then, a gap analysis is performed to examine the differences (gaps) between the required system and the existing system. Finally priorities will be established for the gaps (requirements) which will be documented in a requirements definition document, which will receive sign-off from the end users. It is during this phase that a company can take advantage of the processes inherent in the new system to improve existing processes. System specification documents contain information on basic requirements which include

(1) Performance levels
(2) Reliability
(3) Quality
(4) Interfaces
(5) Security and privacy
(6) Constraints and limitations
(7) Functional capabilities
(8) Data structures and elements

c. The Design Phase
The primary goal of the design phase is to build a technical blueprint of how the proposed system will work. The components that are typically designed during this phase include

(1) Databases
(2) User interfaces for input and output
(3) Required reports
(4) Programs
(5) Infrastructure and controls

d. **The Development Phase**

During the development phase the documents from the design phase are transformed into the actual system. In the design phase the platform on which the system is to operate is built or purchased off-the-shelf and customized and databases are developed.

e. **The Testing Phase**

The testing phase involves verifying that the system works and meets the business requirements as set forth in the analysis phase. The testing phase is obviously critical. The following types of test should be performed:

(1) *Unit testing.* Unit testing involves testing the units or pieces of code.

(2) *System testing.* System testing involves testing of the integration of the units or pieces of code into a system.

(3) *Integration testing.* Integration testing involves testing whether the separate systems can work together.

(4) *User acceptance testing.* User acceptance testing determines whether the system meets the business requirements and enables users to perform their jobs efficiently and effectively.

f. **The Implementation Phase**

The implementation phase involves putting the system in operation by the users. In order to effectively implement the system detailed user documentation must be provided to the users, and the users must be adequately trained. An organization may choose from a number of implementation methods including:

(1) *Parallel implementation.* This method uses both systems until it is determined that the new system is operating properly. This has the advantages of a full operational test of the new system with less risk of a system disaster. The disadvantage of this method is the additional work and cost during the period in which both systems are operating.

(2) *Plunge implementation.* Using this method the organization ceases using the old system and begins using the new system immediately. This method is less costly than the parallel method but it has higher risk of a system breakdown.

(3) *Pilot implementation.* This method involves having a small group of individuals using the new system until it is seen to be working properly. This has the advantage of providing a partial operational test of the new system at a lower cost than parallel implementation.

(4) *Phased implementation.* This method involves installing the system in a series of phases.

g. **The Maintenance Phase**

This phase involves monitoring and supporting the new system. In this phase the organization provides ongoing training, help desk resources, and a system for making authorized and tested changes to the system.

> **NOW REVIEW MULTIPLE-CHOICE QUESTIONS 1 THROUGH 14 IN VOLUME 2**

B. Characteristics of IT Systems—General

1. **Types of Computers, Hardware, and Software**

   a. **Types of computers (in order of size and power)**

      (1) **Supercomputers**—Extremely powerful, high-speed computers used for extremely high-volume and/or complex processing needs.

      (2) **Mainframe computers**—Large, powerful, high-speed computers. While less powerful than supercomputers, they have traditionally been used for high-volume transaction processing. Clusters of lower cost, less powerful "servers" are increasingly taking over the processing chores of mainframe computers.

      (3) **Servers**—High-powered microcomputers that "serve" applications and data to clients that are connected via a network (e.g., web servers, database servers). Servers typically have greater capacity (faster processors, more RAM, more storage capacity) than their clients (microcomputers) and often act as a central repository for organizational data. Servers today are often configured as a "virtual machine," meaning multiple operating systems can coexist and operate simultaneously on the same machine. Virtual machines are appealing because they lower hardware costs and they create energy savings.

      (4) **Microcomputers (e.g., desktop computers, laptop computers)**—Designed to be used by one person at a time, they are often called personal computers. Typically used for word processing, e-mail, spreadsheets, surfing the web, creating and editing graphics, playing music, and gaming.

      (5) **Tablets/Smart Phones/Personal Digital Assistants** (e.g., iPad, iPhone, Android, Blackberry). These are typically smaller, handheld wireless devices that depend on WiFi and/or cellular technology for communication. Many of these devices support touch screen input.

b. **Hardware—Physical equipment**

(1) **Central processing unit (CPU)**—The principal hardware components of a computer. It contains an arithmetic/logic unit, primary memory, and a control unit. The major function of the CPU is to fetch stored instructions and data, decode the instructions, and carry out the instructions.

    (a) **Arithmetic/logic unit**—Performs mathematical operations and logical comparisons.

    (b) **Primary memory (storage)**—Active data and program steps that are being processed by the CPU. It may be divided into RAM (random-access memory) and ROM (read-only memory). Application programs and data are stored in the RAM at execution time.

    (c) **Control unit**—Interprets program instructions and coordinates input, output, and storage devices.

(2) **Secondary storage**

    (a) **Storage devices**

        1] **Magnetic tape**—Slowest type of storage available because data is stored sequentially. Primarily used for archiving purposes today.

        2] **Magnetic disks**—The most common storage medium in use on computers today. Magnetic disks are also called "hard disks" or "hard disk drives" (HDD). Data can be accessed directly.

        3] **RAID (Redundant array of independent [previously, inexpensive] disks)**—A way of storing the same data redundantly on multiple magnetic disks

            a] When originally recorded, data is written to multiple disks to decrease the likelihood of loss of data.

            b] If a disk fails, at least one of the other disks has the information and continues operation.

        4] **Compact Discs**—Discs (CDs) and Digital Video Discs (DVDs)—Both are the same physical size and both use optical technology to read and write data to the disc.

        5] **Solid State Drives (SSDs)**—Use microchips to store data and require no moving parts for read/write operations. SSDs are faster and more expensive per gigabyte than CDs, DVDs, and HDDs. SSDs are increasingly being used in place of HDDs in microcomputers but cost and limited capacity have constrained their adoption as a primary storage device. SSDs are more commonly used for auxiliary storage. SSDs that are "pluggable" are often called "thumb drives," "flash drives," or "USB drives" (because they use a USB interface to "plug" into other devices).

        6] **Cloud-Based Storage**—Also called "Storage as a Service" (SaaS). This type of storage is hosted offsite, typically by third parties, and is accessed via the Internet.

    (b) **Manner in which information is represented in a computer**

        1] **Digital**—A series of binary digits (0s and 1s). One binary digit is called a "bit." A series of 8 bits is referred to as a "byte." One byte can form a letter, a number, or a special character (e.g., 00000111 is the binary equivalent of the decimal number 7).

        2] **Analog**—The representation that is produced by the fluctuations of a continuous signal (e.g., speech, temperature, weight, speed, etc.). Rather than using 0s and 1s to represent information, analog signals use electrical, mechanical, hydraulic or pneumatic devices to transmit the fluctuations in the signal itself to represent information.

    (c) **Related computer terms**

        1] **Online**—Equipment in direct communication with, and under the control of, the CPU. Online also refers to having a connection to the Internet.

        2] **Off-line**—Equipment not in direct communication with the CPU; the operator generally must intervene to connect off-line equipment or data to the CPU (e.g., mount a magnetic tape of archival data). Off-line also refers to the absence of an Internet connection.

        3] **Console**—A terminal used for communication between the operator and the computer (e.g., the operator of a mainframe computer)

        4] **Peripheral equipment**—All non-CPU hardware that may be placed under the control of the central processor. Classified as online or off-line, this equipment consists of input, storage, output, and communication.

        5] **Controllers**—Hardware units designed to operate specific input-output units

        6] **Buffer**—A temporary storage unit used to hold data during computer operations

        7] **MIPS**—Millions of instructions per second; a unit for measuring the execution speed of computers

(3) **Input devices**

    (a) **Keying data—Data entry devices**

        1] **Key-to-tape** and **key-to-disk** in which data is entered on magnetic tape and/or disk respectively, and then read into a computer

    (b) **Online entry**

        1] **Visual display terminal/monitors**—Uses keyboard to directly enter data into computer

            a] **Input interface**—A program that controls the display for the user (usually on a computer monitor) and that allows the user to interact with the system

            b] **Graphical user interface (GUI)** uses icons, pictures, and menus instead of text for inputs (e.g., Windows).

            c] **Command line interface**—Uses text-type commands

        2] **Mouse, joystick, light pens**—Familiar devices that allow data entry

        3] **Touch-sensitive screen**—Allows users to enter data from a menu of items by touching the surface of the monitor

    (c) **Turnaround documents**—Documents that are sent to the customer and returned as inputs (e.g., utility bills)

    (d) **Automated source data input devices**

        1] **Magnetic tape reader**—A device capable of sensing information recorded as magnetic spots on magnetic tape

        2] **Magnetic ink character reader (MICR)**—Device that reads characters that have been encoded with a magnetic ink (e.g., bank check readers)

        3] **Scanner**—A device that reads characters on printed pages

        4] **Automatic teller machine (ATM)**—A machine used to execute and record transactions with financial institutions

        5] **Radio Frequency Identification (RFID)**—Uses radio waves to track and input data. Increasingly used for inventory and contactless payment systems. RFID tags can be read wirelessly by RFID readers; does not require line-of-sight access like bar code technology (e.g., Mobil's Speedpass® payment systems, FasTrak® toll collection system).

        6] **Point-of-sale (POS) recorders**—Devices that read price and product code data (e.g., recall purchasing groceries—items are frequently passed over a POS recorder). POS recorders ordinarily function as both a terminal and a cash register.

            a] POS processing allows one to record and track customer orders, process credit and debit cards, connect to other systems in a network, and manage inventory. Generally, a POS terminal has as its core a personal computer, which is provided with application-specific programs and input/output devices for the particular environment in which it will serve.

            b] POS terminals are used in most industries that have a point of sale such as a service desk, including restaurants, lodging, entertainment, and museums. For example, a POS system for a restaurant is likely to have all menu items stored in a database that can be queried for information in a number of ways.

            c] Increasingly, POS terminals are also Web-enabled, which makes remote training and operation possible, as well as inventory tracking across geographically dispersed locations.

        7] **Voice recognition**—A system that understands spoken words and transmits them into a computer.

    (e) **Electronic commerce** and **electronic data interchange**—Involves one company's computer communicating with another's computer. For example, a buyer electronically sending a purchase order to a supplier. Discussed in further detail in section C.5. of this module.

(4) **Output devices**

    (a) Many automated source data input devices and electronic commerce/electronic data interchange devices [(3)(d) and (e) above] are capable of outputting data ("writing" in addition to "reading") and therefore become output devices as well as input devices.

    (b) **Monitors**—Visually display output

    (c) **Printers**—Produce paper output

    (d) **Plotters**—Produce paper output of graphs

    (e) **Computer output to microfilm or microfiche (COM)**—Makes use of photographic process to store output

 c. **Software—Computer programs that control hardware**

   (1) **Systems software**

     (a) **Operating system**—Manages the input, output, processing and storage devices and operations of a computer (e.g., Windows, Linux, Unix)

       1] Performs scheduling, resource allocation, and data retrieval based on instructions provided in job control language

     (b) **Utility programs**—Handle common file, data manipulation and "housekeeping" tasks

     (c) **Communications software**—Controls and supports transmission between computers, computers and monitors, and accesses various databases

   (2) **Applications software**—Programs designed for specific uses, or "applications," such as

     (a) Word processing, graphics, spreadsheets, email, and database systems

     (b) Accounting software

       1] **Low-end**—All in one package, designed for small organizations

       2] **High-end**—Ordinarily in modules (e.g., general ledger, receivables)

       3] **Enterprise Resource Planning (ERP)**—Designed as relatively complete information system "suites" for large and medium size organizations (e.g., human resources, financial applications, manufacturing, distribution). Major vendors are well known—SAP, PeopleSoft, Oracle, and J.D. Edwards.

         a] Advantages of ERP systems—Integration of various portions of the information system, direct electronic communication with suppliers and customers, increased responsiveness to information requests for decision-making

         b] Disadvantages of ERP systems—Complexity, costs, integration with supplier and customer systems may be more difficult than anticipated

   (3) **Software terms**

     (a) **Compiler**—Produces a machine language object program from a source program language

     (b) **Multiprocessing**—Simultaneous execution of two or more tasks, usually by two or more CPUs that are part of the same system

     (c) **Multitasking**—The simultaneous processing of several jobs on a computer

     (d) **Object program**—The converted source program that was changed using a compiler to create a set of machine readable instructions that the CPU understands

     (e) **Source program**—A program written in a language from which statements are translated into machine language; computer programming has developed in "generations"

       1] Machine language (composed of combinations of 1's and 0's that are meaningful to the computer).

       2] Assembly language—A low-level programming language that uses words (mnemonics) instead of numbers to perform an operation. Assembly language must be translated to machine language by a utility program called an *assembler*. Generally, an assembly language is specific to a computer architecture and is therefore not portable like most high-level languages.

       3] "High-level" programming languages such as COBOL, Basic, Fortran, C++, and Java.

         a] C++ and Java are considered object-oriented programs (OOP) in that they are based on the concept of an "object" which is a data structure that uses a set of routines, called "methods," which operate on the data. The "objects" are efficient in that they often are reusable in other programs.

         b] Object-oriented programs keep together data structures and procedures (methods) through a procedure referred to as encapsulation. Basic to object-oriented programs are the concepts of a class (a set of objects with similar structures) and inheritance (the ability to create new classes from existing classes).

       4] An "application-specific" language usually built around database systems. These programs are ordinarily closer to human languages than the first three generations (e.g., SQL, Structured Query Language: an instruction to create a report might be *Extract all Customers where "Name" is Jones*).

       5] A relatively new and developing form that includes visual or graphical interfaces used to create source language that is usually compiled with a 3rd or 4th generation language compiler.

(f) **Virtual memory (storage)**—Online secondary memory that is used as an extension of primary memory, thus giving the appearance of larger, virtually unlimited internal memory

(g) **Protocol**—Rules determining the required format and methods for transmission of data

(4) **Programming terms**

(a) **Desk checking**—Review of a program by the programmer for errors before the program is run and debugged on the computer

(b) **Debug**—To find and eliminate errors in a computer program. Many compilers assist debugging by listing errors in the program such as invalid commands

(c) **Edit**—To correct input data prior to processing

(d) **Loop**—A set of program instructions performed repetitively a predetermined number of times, or until all of a particular type of data has been processed

(e) **Memory dump**—A listing of the contents of storage

(f) **Patch**—A section of coding inserted into a program to correct a mistake or to alter a routine

(g) **Run**—A complete cycle of a program including input, processing and output

2. **Methods of Processing**

a. **Batch or online real-time**

(1) **Batch**

(a) Transactions flow through the system in groups of like transactions (batches). For example, all cash receipts on accounts receivable for a day may be aggregated and run as a batch.

(b) Ordinarily leaves a relatively easy-to-follow audit trail.

(2) **Online real-time** (also referred to as **direct access processing**)

General: Transactions are processed in the order in which they occur, regardless of type. Data files and programs are stored online so that updating can take place as the edited data flows to the application. System security must be in place to restrict access to programs and data to authorized persons. Online systems are often categorized as being either online transaction processing systems or online analytical processing systems.

(a) **Online transaction processing (OLTP)**

1] Databases that support day-to-day operations

2] Examples: airline reservations systems, bank automatic teller systems, and Internet Web site sales systems

(b) **Online analytical processing (OLAP)**

1] A category of software technology that enables the user to query the system (retrieve data), and conduct an analysis, etc., ordinarily while the user is at a PC. The result is generated in seconds. OLAP systems are primarily used for analytical analysis.

> **EXAMPLE**
>
> An airline's management downloads its OLTP reservation information into another database to allow analysis of that reservation information. At a minimum, this will allow analysis without tying up the OLTP system that is used on a continuous basis; the restructuring of the data into another database is also likely to make a more detailed analysis possible.

2] Uses statistical and graphical tools that provide users with various (often multidimensional) views of their data, and allows them to analyze the data in detail.

3] These techniques are used as **decision support systems** (computer-based information systems that combine models and data in an attempt to solve relatively unstructured problems with extensive user involvement).

4] One approach to OLAP is to periodically download and combine operational databases into a **data warehouse** (a subject-oriented, integrated collection of data used to support management decision-making processes) or a **data mart** (a data warehouse that is limited in scope).

a] **Data mining**—Using sophisticated techniques from statistics, artificial intelligence and computer graphics to explain, confirm and explore relationships among data (which is often stored in a data warehouse or data mart)

b] Business intelligence (BI)—A combination of systems that help aggregate, access, and analyze business data and assist in the business decision-making process.

5] **Artificial intelligence (AI)**—Computer software designed to help humans make decisions. AI may be viewed as an attempt to model aspects of human thought on computers. AI ordinarily deals with decisions that may be made using a relatively structured approach. It frequently involves using a computer to quickly solve a problem that a human could ultimately solve through extremely detailed analysis.

6] **Expert system**—One form of AI. A computerized information system that guides decision processes within a well-defined area and allows decisions comparable to those of an expert. Expert knowledge is modeled into a mathematical system.

EXAMPLE

An expert system may be used by a credit card department to authorize credit card purchases so as to minimize fraud and credit losses.

---

b. **Centralized, Decentralized, or Distributed**

(1) **Centralized**

(a) Processing occurs at one location.

(b) Historically, this is the model used in which a mainframe computer processes data submitted to it through terminals.

(c) Today, centralized vs. decentralized processing is often a matter of degree—how much is processed by a centralized computer vs. how much by decentralized computers.

(2) **Decentralized**

(a) Processing (and data) are stored on computers at multiple locations.

(b) Ordinarily the computers involved are not interconnected by a network, so users at various sites cannot share data.

(c) May be viewed as a collection of independent databases, rather than a single database.

(d) End-user computing (topic C.4. below) is relatively decentralized.

(3) **Distributed**

(a) Transactions for a single database are processed at various sites.

EXAMPLE

Payroll is processed for Minneapolis employees in Minneapolis, and for Santa Fe employees in Santa Fe. Yet the overall payroll information is in one database.

(b) Processing may be on either a batch or online real-time basis.

(c) An overall single data base is ordinarily updated for these transactions and available at the various sites.

3. **Methods of Data Structure**

a. **Data organization for computer operations**

(1) **Bit**—A binary digit (0 or 1) which is the smallest storage unit in a computer.

(2) **Byte**—A group of adjacent bits (usually 8) that is treated as a single unit, or character, by the computer. Printable alphanumeric characters (e.g., A-Z, a-z, 0-9); special characters (e.g., $, %, !, @, etc.) and unprintable control codes (e.g., those that control peripheral devices such as printers) can be represented by an 8-bit Byte. Character-encoding schemes for computers, such as ASCII and UTF-8, ensure universal interpretation of the 8-bit codes.

(3) **Field**—A group of related characters (e.g., a social security number).

(4) **Record**—An ordered set of logically related fields. For example, all payroll data (including the social security number field and others) relating to a single employee.

(5) **File**—a group of related records (e.g., all the weekly pay records year-to-date), which is usually arranged in sequence.

(6) **Table**—A group of related records in a relational database with a unique identifier (primary key field) in each record.

(7) **Database**—A group of related files or a group of related tables (if a relational database).

(8) **Array**—In a programming language, an aggregate that consists of data objects with attributes, each of which may be uniquely referenced by an index (address). For example, an array may be used to request input of various payroll information for a new employee in one step. Thus an array could include employee name, social security number, withholdings, pay rate, etc.—for example (John Jones, 470-44-5044, 2, $18.32, ...). Name would be indexed as 1 (or zero), with each succeeding attribute receiving the next higher number as an address. Also arrays may be multidimensional. They are often used with object-oriented programming such as C++ and Java.

(9) **Master file**—A file containing relatively permanent information used as a source of reference and periodically updated with a detail (transaction) file (e.g., permanent payroll records).

(10) **Detail or transaction file**—A file containing current transaction information used to update the master file (e.g., hours worked by each employee during the current period used to update the payroll master file).

b. **Data file structure**

(1) **Traditional file processing systems**—These systems focus upon data processing needs of individual departments. Each application program or system is developed to meet the needs of the particular requesting department or user group. For accounting purposes these systems are often similar to traditional accounting systems, with files set up for operations such as purchasing, sales, cash receipts, cash disbursements, etc.

(a) **Advantages of traditional processing systems**

1] Currently operational for many existing (legacy) systems
2] Often cost effective for simple applications

(b) **Disadvantages of traditional processing systems**

1] Data files are dependent upon a particular application program.
2] In complex business situation there is much duplication of data between data files.
3] Each application must be developed individually.
4] Program maintenance is expensive.
5] Data may be isolated and difficult to share between functional areas.

(2) **Database systems**

(a) **Definitions**

1] **Database**—A collection of interrelated files, ordinarily most of which are stored online.

a] **Normalization**—The process of separating the database into logical tables to avoid certain kinds of updating difficulties (referred to as "anomalies").

2] **Database system**—Computer hardware and software that enables the database(s) to be implemented.

3] **Database management system**—Software that provides a facility for communications between various applications programs (e.g., a payroll preparation program) and the database (e.g., a payroll master file containing the earnings records of the employees).

4] **Data independence**—Basic to database systems is this concept which separates the data from the related application programs.

5] **Data modeling**—Identifying and organizing a database's data, both logically and physically. A data model determines what information is to be contained in a database, how the information will be used, and how the items in the database will be related to each other.

a] **Entity-relationship modeling**—An approach to data modeling. The model (called the Entity-Relationship diagram, or ERD) divides the database in two logical parts—entities (e.g. "customer," "product") and relations ("buys," "pays for").

b] **Primary key**—The field(s) that make a record in a relational database table unique.

c] **Foreign key**—The field(s) that are common to two (or more) related tables in a relational database.

d] **REA data model**—A data model designed for use in designing accounting information databases. REA is an acronym for the model's basic types of objects: **R**esources—Identifiable objects that have economic value, **E**vents—An organization's business activities, **A**gents—People or organizations about which data is collected.

6] **Data Dictionary** (also referred to as a **data repository** or **data directory** system)—A data structure that stores meta-data.

a] **Meta-data**—Definitional data that provides information about or documentation of other data managed within an application or environment. For example, data about data elements, records and data structures (length, fields, columns, etc.).

7] **Structured query language (SQL)**—The most common language used for creating and querying relational databases (see (b)3] below), its commands may be classified into three types.

a] **Data definition language (DDL)**—Used to define a database, including creating, altering, and deleting tables and establishing various constraints.

b] **Data manipulation language (DML)**—Commands used to maintain and query a database, including updating, inserting in, modifying, and querying (asking for data). For example, a frequent query involves the joining of information from more than one table.

c] **Data control language (DCL)**—Commands used to control a database, including controlling which users have various privileges (e.g., who is able to read from and write to various portions of the database).

(b) **Database structures**

1] **Hierarchical**—The data elements at one level "own" the data elements at the next lower level (think of an organization chart in which one manager supervises several assistants, who in turn each supervise several lower level employees).

2] **Networked**—Each data element can have several owners and can own several other elements (think of a matrix-type structure in which various relationships can be supported).

3] **Relational**—A database with the logical structure of a group of related spreadsheets. Each row represents a record, which is an accumulation of all the fields related to the same identifier or key; each column represents a field common to all of the records. Relational databases have in many situations largely replaced the earlier developed hierarchical and networked databases.

4] **Object-oriented**—Information (attributes and methods) are included in structures called object classes. This is the newest database management system technology

5] **Object-relational**—Includes both relational and object-oriented features.

6] **Distributed**—A single database that is spread physically across computers in multiple locations that are connected by a data communications link. (The structure of the database is most frequently relational, object-oriented, or object-relational.)

(c) **Database controls**

1] **User department**—Because users directly input data, strict controls over who is authorized to read and/or change the database are necessary.

2] **Access controls**—In addition to the usual controls over terminals and access to the system, database processing also maintains controls within the database itself. These controls limit the user to reading and/or changing (updating) only authorized portions of the database.

a] **Restricting privileges**—This limits the access of users to the database, as well as operations a particular user may be able to perform. For example, certain employees and customers may have only read, and not write, privileges.

b] **Logical views**—Users may be provided with authorized *views* of only the portions of the database for which they have a valid need.

3] **Backup and recovery**—A database is updated on a continuous basis during the day. Three methods of backup and recovery include

a] **Backup of database and logs of transactions** (sometimes referred to as "systems logs"). The approach is to backup the entire database several times per week, generally to magnetic tape. A log of all transactions is also maintained. If there is extensive damage to a major portion of the database due to catastrophic failure, such as disk crash, the recovery method is to restore the most recent past copy of the database and to reconstruct it to a more current state by reapplying or redoing transactions from the log up to the point of failure.

b] **Database replication.** To avoid catastrophic failure, another approach is to replicate the database at one or more locations. Thus, all data may be recorded to both sets of the database.

c] **Backup facility.** Another approach is to maintain a backup facility with a vendor who will process data in case of an emergency.

   Further information on backup and recovery is included under Disaster Recovery—D.11 of this module.

4] **Database administrator (DBA)**—Individual responsible for maintaining the database and restricting access to the database to authorized personnel.

5] **Audit software**—Usually used by auditors to test the database; see Auditing with Technology Module.

(d) **Advantages of database systems**

1] **Data independence**—Data can be used relatively easily by differing applications.

2] **Minimal data redundancy**—The manner in which data is structured results in information being recorded in only one place, thus making updating much easier than is the case with traditional file systems.

3] **Data sharing**—The sharing of data between individuals and applications is relatively easy.

4] Reduced program maintenance.

5] Commercial applications are available for modification to a company's needs.

(e) **Disadvantages of database systems**

1] Need for specialized personnel with database expertise

2] Installation of database costly

3] Conversion of traditional file systems (legacy systems) costly

4] Comprehensive backup and recovery procedures are necessary.

> **NOW REVIEW MULTIPLE-CHOICE QUESTIONS 15 THROUGH 52 IN VOLUME 2**

C. Characteristics of IT Systems—Specific

1. Types of Networks

a. Background

(1) A network is a group of interconnected computers and terminals.

(2) The development of **telecommunications**—The electronic transmission of information by radio, fiber optics, wire, microwave, laser, and other electromagnetic systems—has made possible the electronic transfer of information between networks of computers. This topic is discussed in detail later in this module.

b. Classified by geographical scope

(1) **Personal area network** (PAN)—A computer network that is centered around an individual and the personal communication devices he/she uses. PANs can be associated with both wireless and wired communication devices (e.g., the Bluetooth devices we use with our mobile phones for driving; the USB devices that we connect to our computers).

(2) **Local area networks** (LAN)—Privately owned networks within a single building or campus of up to a few miles in size. Because this topic has been emphasized in AICPA materials, it is discussed further later in this module.

(3) **Metropolitan area network** (MAN)—A larger version of a LAN. For example, it might include a group of nearby offices within a city.

(4) **Wide area networks** (WAN)—Networks that span a large geographical area, often a country or continent. It is composed of a collection of computers and other hardware and software for running user programs.

c. Classified by ownership

(1) **Private**—One in which network resources are usually dedicated to a small number of applications or a restricted set of users, as in a corporation's network.

(a) A typical approach is to lease telephone lines that are dedicated to the network's use.

(b) Also, traditional EDI systems (discussed below) use a private network.

(c) Advantages: Secure, flexible, performance often exceeds that of public.

(d) Disadvantage: Costly

(2) **Public**—Resources are owned by third-party companies and leased to users on a usage basis (also referred to as public-switched networks [PSN]).

(a) Access is typically through dial-up circuits.

(b) Example: Applications using the Internet.

(c) Advantages and disadvantage: In general, the opposite of those for private networks, but certainly a significant disadvantage is that they are less secure.

1] Improvements in Internet communications will decrease the disadvantages and will lead to a dramatic increase in the use of public networks (e.g., rapid increases in the use of Internet-based electronic commerce).

(3) **Cloud computing/cloud services**—The use and access of multiple server-based computational resources via a digital network (WAN, Internet connection using the World Wide Web, etc.). A user accesses the server resources using a computer, netbook, tablet computer, smart phone, or other device. With cloud computing, applications are provided and managed by the cloud server and data is stored remotely in the cloud configuration. Users do not download and install applications on their own device or computer; all processing and storage is maintained by the cloud server. Cloud services may be offered by a cloud provider or by a private organization.

(a) Risks of cloud computing

1] Information security and privacy—users must rely on the cloud providers' data access controls.
2] Continuity of services—user problems may occur if the cloud provider has disruptions in service.
3] Migration—users may have difficulty in changing cloud providers because there are no data standards.

d. **Classified by use of Internet**

General: The following all use the Internet. They have in common that data communications are ordinarily through **Hypertext Markup Language (HTML)** and/or **Extensible Markup Language (XML)**—languages used to create and format documents, link documents to other Web pages, and communicate between Web browsers. XML is increasingly replacing HTML in Internet applications due to its superior ability to tag (i.e., label) and format documents that are communicated among trading partners.

Extensible Business Reporting Language (XBRL) is an XML-based language being developed specifically for the automation of business information requirements, such as the preparation, sharing, and analysis of financial reports, statements, and audit schedules. XBRL is used in filings with the SEC that are made available on EDGAR, the SEC's Electronic Data Gathering and Retrieval database.

(1) **Internet**—An international collection of networks made up of independently owned computers that operate as a large computing network. Internetwork communication requires the use of a common set of rules, or protocols (TCP), and a shared routing system (IP).

(a) Primary applications of the Internet include

1] E-mail
2] News dissemination
3] Remote log-in of computers
4] File transfer among computers
5] Electronic commerce

(b) Terminology

1] **Hypertext Transfer Protocol (HTTP)**—The primary Internet protocol for data communication on the World Wide Web.
2] **Uniform Resource Locator (URL)**—A standard for finding a document by typing in an address (e.g., www.azdiamondbacks.com). URLs work in much the same way as addresses on mail processed by the postal department.
3] **World Wide Web (the web or WWW)**—A framework for accessing linked resources (e.g., documents, pictures, music files, videos, etc.) spread out over the millions of machines all over the Internet.
4] **Web browser**—Client software (e.g., Internet explorer, Firefox, Chrome, Mosaic, etc.) that provides the user with the ability to locate and display web resources.
5] **Web servers**—The software that "serves," (i.e., makes available) web resources to software clients. web servers (e.g., Apache and Internet Information Server [IIS]) typically run on "server" hardware. However, many computing devices today support their own web server software.
6] **Firewall**—A method for protecting an organization's computers and computer information from outsiders. A firewall consists of security algorithms and router communications protocols that prevent outsiders from tapping into corporate database and e-mail systems.
7] **Router**—A communications interface device that connects two networks and determines the best way for data packets to move forward to their destinations.
8] **Bridge**—A device that divides a LAN into two segments, selectively forwarding traffic across the network boundary it defines; similar to a switch.

9] **Switch**—A device that channels incoming data from any of multiple input ports to the specific output port that will take the data toward its intended destination.

10] **Gateway**—A combination of hardware and software that links to different types of networks. For examples, gateways between e-mail systems allow users of differing e-mail systems to exchange messages.

11] **Proxy server**—A server that saves and serves copies of web pages to those who request them (e.g., potential customers). When a web page is requested, the proxy server is able to access that page either through its cache (reserve of web pages already sent or loaded) or by obtaining it through the original server. A proxy server can both increase efficiency of Internet operations and help assure data security.

12] **Web 2.0**—2nd generation of the web. Refers to era of web-based collaboration and community-generated content via web-based software tools such as

   a] **Blog**—An asynchronous discussion, or web log, led by a moderator that typically focuses on a single topic. Similar to an electronic bulletin board. Blogs are an efficient way to share information, views, and opinions.

   b] **Wiki**—An information-gathering and knowledge-sharing website that is developed collaboratively by a community or group, all of whom can freely add, modify, or delete content.

   c] **Twitter**—A micro-variation of a blog. Restricts input (tweets) to 140 characters. Commonly used to "follow" friends and celebrities. Increasingly companies are using Twitter to inform followers.

   d] **RSS/ATOM Feeds—Really Simple Syndication**—An XML application that facilitates the sharing and syndication of website content by subscription. RSS feeds are automatically checked by RSS-enabled client software (including most browsers and RSS readers) for new website content on a regular basis.

13] **TCP/IP (Transmission Control Protocol/Internet Protocol)**—The basic communication language or protocol of the Internet. It has two layers. The higher layer assembles messages or files into smaller packets that are transmitted over the Internet. The lower layer assigns IP addresses and insures that messages are delivered to the appropriate computer.

14] **IP address**—The number that identifies a machine as unique on the Internet.

15] **ISP (Internet Service Provider)**—An entity that provides access to the Internet.

(c) The nature of the Internet has resulted in the spread of a series of malicious programs (often through email) that may adversely affect computer operations, including

   1] **Virus**—A program (or piece of code) that requests the computer operating system to perform certain activities not authorized by the computer user. Viruses can be easily transmitted through use of files that contain macros that are sent as attachment to e-mail messages.

      a] **Macro**—A stored set of instructions and functions that are organized to perform a repetitive task and can be easily activated, often by a simple keystroke combination. Most macros serve valid purposes, but those associated with viruses cause problems.

      b] Unexpected changes in, or losses of, data may be an indication of the existence of a virus on one's computer.

      c] E-mail attachments and *public domain software* (generally downloadable from the Internet at no cost to users) are notorious sources of viruses.

   2] **Trojan horse**—A malicious, security-breaking program that is disguised as something benign, such as a game, but actually is intended to cause IT damage.

   3] **Worm**—A program that propagates itself over a network, reproducing itself as it goes.

   4] **Antivirus software**—Is used to attempt to avoid the above types of problems. But the rapid development of new forms of viruses, Trojan horses, and worms results in a situation in which antivirus software developers are always behind the developers.

   5] **Botnet**—A network of computers that are controlled by computer code, called a "bot," that is designed to perform a repetitive task such as sending spam, spreading a virus, or creating a distributed denial of service attack.

(2) **Intranet**—A local network, usually limited to an organization, that uses internet-based technology to communicate within the organization.

(3) **Extranet**—Similar to an intranet, but includes an organization's external customers and/or suppliers in the network.

e. **Database client-server architecture**

General: When considering networks, it is helpful to consider their architecture (design). Bear in mind that the architecture must divide the following responsibilities (1) input, (2) processing, and (3) storage. In general, the client-server model may be viewed as one in which communications ordinarily take the form of a request message from the client to the server asking for some service to be performed. A "client" may be viewed as the computer or **workstation** of an individual user. The server is a high-capacity computer that contains the network software and may provide a variety of services ranging from simply "serving" files to a client to performing analyses.

(1) **Overall client-server systems**—A networked computing model (usually a LAN) in which database software on a server performs database commands sent to it from client computers

Illustration of Client/Server Architecture

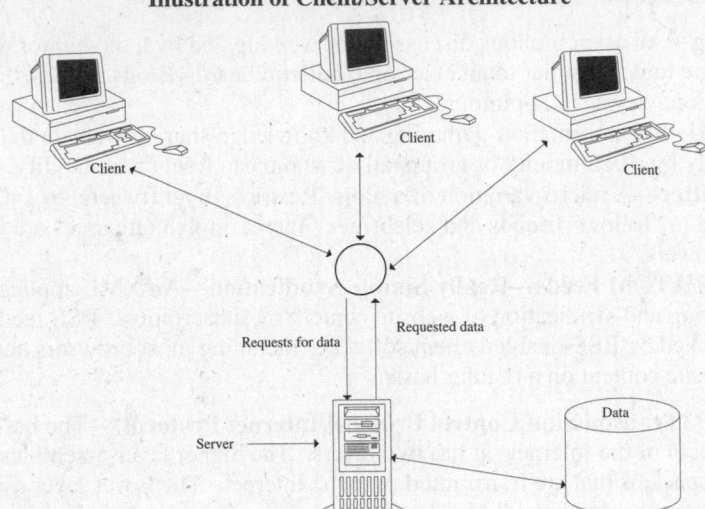

(2) **Subtypes of client/server architectures**

(a) **File servers**—The file server manages file operations and is shared by each of the client PCs (ordinarily attached to a LAN). The three responsibilities (input/output, processing, and storage) are divided in a manner in which most input/output, and processing occurs on client computers rather than on the server. The file server acts simply as a shared data storage device, with all data manipulations performed by client PCs.

(b) **Database servers**—Similar to file servers, but the server here contains the database management system and thus performs more of the processing.

> **NOTE:** The above two architectures are referred to as "two-tier" architecture—client tier and server database tier.

(c) **Three-tier architectures**—A client/server configuration that includes three tiers. The change from the above systems is that this architecture includes another server layer in addition to the two tiers discussed above. For example, application programs (e.g., a transaction processing monitor that controls the input of transactions to the database) may reside on the additional server rather than on the individual clients. This system of adding additional servers may generalize to additional tiers and thus become **n-tier** architecture. Examples of other servers that may be added are as follows:

1] **Print server**—Make shared printers available to various clients.

2] **Communications server**—May serve a variety of tasks, such as acting as a gateway (i.e., means of entrance) to the internet or to the corporate intranet.

3] **Fax server**—Allow clients on the network to share the hardware for incoming and outgoing fax transmissions.

4] **Web server**—Stores and serves web pages on request.

(3) **Distributed systems**—These systems connect all company locations to form a distributed network in which each location has its own input/output, processing, and storage capabilities. These local computers also pass data among themselves and possibly to a server (often referred to as a "host" in this context) for further processing. An illustration of this type of system is presented in the database section of this outline.

2. **Local Area Networks (LANs)**—Privately owned networks within a single building or campus of up to a few miles in size.

   a. **Software**

      (1) Software allows devices to function cooperatively and share network resources such as printers and disk storage space.

      (2) Common services

         (a) Network server
         (b) File server
         (c) Print server
         (d) Communications server

   b. **Hardware components**

      (1) **Workstations**—Ordinarily microcomputers.
      (2) **Peripherals**—For example, printers, network attached storage (NAS) devices, optical scanners, fax board.
      (3) **Transmission media**—Physical path that connect components of LAN, ordinarily twisted-pair wire, co-axial cable, or optical fiber. LANs that are connected wirelessly are called WLANs or WiFi networks.
      (4) **Network interface cards**—Connect workstation and transmission media.

   c. **Control implications**

      (1) General controls are often weak (e.g., controls over development and modification of programs, access and computer operations).
      (2) Controls often rely upon end users, who may not be control conscious.
      (3) Often users may not be provided adequate resources for problem resolution, troubleshooting and recovery support.
      (4) Controlling access and gaining accountability through logging of transactions enforces a segregation of duties.
      (5) Good management controls are essential—for example, access codes, passwords.
      (6) LAN software ordinarily does not provide security features available in larger scale environments.

> **NOTE:** Tests of controls may address whether controls related to the above are effective.

   d. LANs generally make possible the computer audit techniques that may be performed either by internal auditors or external auditors.

3. **Microcomputers**

   a. The proliferation of microcomputers (e.g., personal computers [PC], laptop computers) has had a profound effect on information systems. A small-business client will probably use a PC to run a commercially purchased general ledger package (off-the-shelf software). Segregation of duties becomes especially difficult in such an environment because one individual may perform all recordkeeping (processing) as well as maintain other nonrecordkeeping responsibilities.

   b. A larger client may use a network of PCs that may or may not be linked to a large corporate mainframe computer. In all systems, management policies should be in place regarding the development and modification of programs and data files.

   c. Regardless of the system, the control objectives remain the same. When small computers are involved, the following points need to be considered:

      (1) **Security**—Security over small computers, while still important, may not be as critical as security over the data and any in-house developed software. Most companies can easily replace the hardware, but may suffer a severe setback if the data and/or in-house developed software is lost. Access to the software installation files should be controlled and backup copies should be made. Access to the hard drive must be restricted since anyone turning on the power switch can read the data stored on those files. Also, a control problem may exist because the computer operator often understands the system and also has access to the input data. The management of the company may need to become more directly involved in supervision when a lack of segregation of duties exists in data processing.

      (2) **Verification of processing**—Periodically, an independent verification of the applications being processed on the small computer system should be made to prevent the system from being used for personal projects. Also, verification helps prevent errors in internally developed software from going undetected. Controls should be in operation to assure the accuracy of in-house created spreadsheets and databases.

      (3) **Personnel**—Centralized authorization to purchase hardware and software should be required to ensure that appropriate purchasing decisions are made, including decisions that minimize software and hardware com-

patibility difficulties. Software piracy and viruses may be controlled by prohibiting the loading of unauthorized software and data on company-owned computers.

    (a) Software is copyrighted, and violation of copyright laws may result in litigation against the company.

    (b) A company may control possible software piracy (the use of unlicensed software) by employees by procedures such as:

        1] Establishing a corporate software policy

        2] Maintaining a log of all software purchase

        3] Auditing individual computers to identify installed software

4. **End-User Computing (EUC)**—The end user is responsible for the development and execution of the computer application that generates the information used by that same end user.

    a. User substantially eliminates many of the services offered by an MIS department.

    b. Risks include

      (1) End-user applications are not always adequately tested before implemented.

      (2) More client personnel need to understand control concepts.

      (3) Management often does not review the results of applications appropriately.

      (4) Old or existing applications may not be updated for current applicability and accuracy.

    c. Overall physical access controls become more difficult when companies leave a controlled MIS environment and become more dependent upon individual users for controls.

    d. Control implications

      (1) Require applications to be adequately tested before they are implemented

      (2) Require adequate documentation

      (3) Physical access controls, including

        (a) Clamps or chains to prevent removal of hard disks or internal boards

        (b) Diskless workstations that require download of files

        (c) Regular backup

        (d) Security software to limit access to those who know user ID and password

        (e) Control over access from outside

        (f) Commitment to security matters written into job descriptions, employee contracts, and personnel evaluation procedures

      (4) Control access to appropriate users

        (a) Passwords and user IDs

        (b) Menus for EUC access to database

        (c) Protect system by restricting user ability to load data

        (d) When end user uploads data, require appropriate validation, authorization, and reporting control

        (e) Independent review of transactions

        (f) Record access to company databases by EUC applications.

      (5) Control use of incorrect versions of data files.

        (a) Use control totals for batch processing of uploaded data.

      (6) Require backup of files.

      (7) Provide applications controls (e.g., edit checks, range tests, reasonableness checks).

      (8) Support programmed or user reconciliations to provide assurance that processing is correct.

> **NOTE:** Since end-user computing relies upon microcomputers, the controls here required for microcomputers and EUC are similar. Also, tests of controls may address whether controls related to the above are effective.

5. **Electronic Commerce**

    a. **General:** Electronic commerce involves individuals and organizations engaging in a variety of electronic transactions with computers and telecommunication networks. The networks involved may be publicly available (e.g., the Internet) or private to the individuals and organizations involved (e.g., through telephone lines privately leased by the parties involved). Wide acceptance of the Internet (more specifically, that portion of the Internet referred to as the World Wide Web, or the web) is currently leading to a great expansion in electronic commerce.

b. Five areas of risk associated with electronic commerce IT systems (as well as to varying degrees with other IT systems) are (1) security, (2) availability, (3) processing integrity, (4) online privacy, and (5) confidentiality. See section E.1 of this module for a discussion.

c. Use of the web is growing rapidly as both the number and types of electronic transactions increase. However, many believe that risks such as those listed above are currently impairing its growth.

(1) As discussed further in the Reporting Module, the AICPA and the Canadian Institute of Chartered Accountants have developed a form of assurance referred to as the "WebTrust Seal of Assurance" that tells potential customers that the firm has evaluated a Web site's business practices and controls to determine whether they are in conformity with WebTrust principles.

(2) Digital certificates, also referred to as digital IDs, are a means of assuring data integrity.

(a) A digital certificate (signature) allows an individual to digitally sign a message so the recipient knows that it actually came from that individual and was not modified in any manner.

(b) Ordinarily the message is encrypted and the recipient decrypts it and is able to read the contents.

(3) **Encryption**—The conversion of data into a form called a cipher text, that cannot be easily understood by unauthorized people. **Decryption** is the process of converting encrypted data back into its original form so it can be understood. The conversion is performed using an algorithm and key which only the users control.

(a) **Algorithm**—A detailed sequence of actions to perform to accomplish some task (in this case to encrypt and/or decode data).

(b) **Key**—In the content of encryption, a value that must be fed into the algorithm used to decode an encrypted message in order to reproduce the original plain text.

(c) **Private key system**—An encryption system in which both the sender and receiver have access to the electronic key, but do not allow others access. The primary disadvantage is that both parties must have the key.

(d) Encryption is important in a variety of contexts, including any time two or more computers are used to communicate with one another, and even to keep private information on one computer.

(e) The machine instructions necessary to encrypt and decrypt data constitute **system overhead;** that is, they slow down the rate of processing.

(4) To assure continuity in the event of a natural disaster, firms should establish off-site mirrored Web servers.

d. **Electronic funds transfer (EFT)**—Making cash payments between two or more organizations or individuals electronically rather than by using checks (or cash).

(1) Banks first became heavily involved with EFT; it is now a major part of most types of electronic commerce.

(2) EFT systems are vulnerable to the risk of unauthorized access to proprietary data and to the risk of fraudulent fund transfers; controls include

(a) Control of physical access to network facilities.

(b) Electronic identification should be required for all network terminals authorized to use EFT.

(c) Access should be controlled through passwords.

(d) Encryption should be used to secure stored data and data being transmitted. See section C.5.c.(3) for more information on encryption.

e. **Electronic data interchange (EDI)**—The electronic exchange of business transactions, in a standard format, from one entity's computer to another entity's computer through an electronic communications network.

(1) Traditionally, the definition of electronic commerce has focused on EDI. Currently, Web-based commerce is replacing a portion of these EDI systems.

(2) Risks related to EDI

(a) EDI is commonly used for sales and purchasing, and related accounts. The speed at which transactions occur often reduces amounts receivable (payables) due to electronic processing of receipts (payments). Another effect is to make preventive controls particularly desirable, since detective controls may be too late.

(b) In these systems, documents such as purchase orders, invoices, shipping forms, bills of lading, and checks are replaced by electronic transactions.

1] For example, in electronic funds transfer systems, a form of EDI, electronic transactions replace checks as a means of payment. As discussed below, EDI is often conducted on private networks.

        2] To determine that transactions are properly processed, effective audit trails for both internal auditors and external auditors include activity logs, including processed and failed transactions, network and sender/recipient acknowledgment of receipt of transactions, and proper time sequence of processing.

        3] In some EDI applications, portions of the documentation of transactions are retained for only short period of time; this may require auditors to pay particular attention to controls over the transactions and to test controls on a timely basis when records remain available.

(3) Methods of communication between trading partners

  (a) **Point-to-point**—A direct computer-to-computer private network link

    1] Automakers and governments have traditionally used this method.

    2] Advantages

      a] No reliance on third parties for computer processing.

      b] Organization controls who has access to the network.

      c] Organization can enforce proprietary (its own) software standard in dealings with all trading partners.

      d] Timeliness of delivery may be improved since no third party is involved.

    3] Disadvantages

      a] Must establish connection with each trading partner

      b] High initial cost

      c] Computer scheduling issues

      d] Need for common protocols between partners

      e] Need for hardware and software compatibility

  (b) **Value-added network (VAN)**

    1] A VAN is a privately owned network that routes the EDI transactions between trading partners and in many cases provides translation, storage, and other processing. It is designed and maintained by an independent company that offers specialized support to improve the transmission effectiveness of a network. It alleviates problems related to interorganizational communication that results from the use of differing hardware and software.

    2] A VAN receives data from sender, determines intended recipient, and places data in the recipient's electronic mailbox.

    3] Advantages

      a] Reduces communication and data protocol problems since VANs can deal with differing protocols (eliminating need for trading partners to agree on them).

      b] Partners do not have to establish the numerous point-to-point connections.

      c] Reduces scheduling problems since receiver can request delivery of transactions when it wishes.

      d] In some cases, VAN translates application to a standard format the partner does not have to reformat.

      e] VAN can provide increased security.

    4] Disadvantages

      a] Cost of VAN

      b] Dependence upon VAN's systems and controls

      c] Possible loss of data confidentiality

  (c) **Public networks**—For example, the Internet-based commerce solutions described earlier

    1] Advantages

      a] Avoids cost of proprietary lines

      b] Avoids cost of VAN

      c] Directly communicates transactions to trading partners

      d] Software is being developed which allows communication between differing systems.

    2] Disadvantages

      a] Possible loss of data confidentiality on the Internet

      b] Computer or transmission disruption

      c] Hackers and viruses

      d] Attempted electronic frauds

(d) **Proprietary networks**—In some circumstances (e.g., health care, banking) organizations have developed their own network for their own transactions. These systems are costly to develop and operate (because of proprietary lines), although they are often extremely reliable.

(4) Controls required for other network systems are required for EDI systems. In addition, disappearance of "paper transactions" and the direct interrelationship with another organization's computer makes various authentication and encryption controls particularly important for these transactions.

(a) **Authentication**—Controls must exist over the origin, proper submission, and proper delivery of EDI communications. Receiver of the message must have proof of the origin of the message, as well as its proper submission and delivery.

(b) **Packets**—A block of data that is transmitted from one computer to another. It contains data and authentication information.

(c) **Encryption**—The conversion of plain text data into cipher text data used by an algorithm and key which only the users control. See section C.5.c.(3) for more information on encryption.

(5) The AICPA Auditing Procedures Study, *Audit Implications of EDI,* lists the following benefits and exposures of EDI:

(a) Benefits

1] Quick response and access to information
2] Cost efficiency
3] Reduced paperwork
4] Accuracy and reduced errors and error-correction costs
5] Better communications and customer service
6] Necessary to remain competitive

(b) Exposures

1] Total dependence upon computer system for operation
2] Possible loss of confidentiality of sensitive information
3] Increased opportunity for unauthorized transactions and fraud
4] Concentration of control among a few people involved in EDI
5] Reliance on third parties (trading partners, VAN)
6] Data processing, application and communications errors
7] Potential legal liability due to errors
8] Potential loss of audit trails and information needed by management due to limited retention policies
9] Reliance on trading partner's system

6 **Telecommunications**—The electronic transmission of information by radio, wire, fiber optic, coaxial cable, microwave, laser, or other electromagnetic system

a. Transmitted information—Voice, data, video, fax, other
b. Hardware involved:

(1) Computers for communications control and switching
(2) Transmission facilities such as copper wire, fiber optic cables, microwave stations and communications satellites
(3) Modems may be used to provide compatibility of format, speed, etc.

c. Software controls and monitors the hardware, formats information, adds appropriate control information, performs switching operations, provides security, and supports the management of communications.
d. While telecommunications is **not** an end of itself, it enables technologies such as the following:

(1) Electronic data interchange
(2) Electronic funds transfer
(3) Point of sale systems
(4) Commercial databases
(5) Airline reservation systems

e. Controls needed

(1) System integrity at remote sites
(2) Data entry
(3) Central computer security
(4) Dial-in security

(5) Transmission accuracy and completeness

(6) Physical security over telecommunications facilities

> **NOTE:** Tests of controls may address whether controls related to the above are effective.

7. **Computer Service Organizations (Bureaus, Centers)**—Computer service organizations record and process data for companies. These organizations allow companies (users) to do away with part of the data processing function. While many computer service organizations simply record and process relatively routine transactions for a client (e.g., prepare payroll journals and payroll checks), a VAN is a service organization that takes a broader role of providing network, storing, and forwarding (mailbox) services for the companies involved in an EDI system.

> **NOW REVIEW MULTIPLE-CHOICE QUESTIONS 53 THROUGH 96 IN VOLUME 2**

D. Control Objectives for Information and Related Technology (COBIT)

1. The Information Systems Audit and Control Association (ISACA) has developed a framework, referred to as COBIT, for information technology (IT) and IT governance. The COBIT framework is business-oriented in that it provides a systematic way of integrating IT with business strategy and business risk. To satisfy business objectives, information needs to conform to the following criteria:

   a. Effectiveness—information should be relevant to the business process and delivered in a timely, accurate, consistent, and useable manner.

   b. Efficiency—information should be developed through the optimal use of resources (i.e., in the most economic or productive manner).

   c. Confidentiality—sensitive information should be protected from unauthorized disclosure.

   d. Integrity—information should be accurate and complete and consistent with business values and expectations.

   e. Availability—information should be available when it is required by business processes.

   f. Compliance—business processes should comply with applicable laws, regulations, and contractual arrangements.

   g. Reliability—appropriate information should be available for management to operate the entity and exercise its fiduciary and governance responsibilities.

2. In implementing the COBIT framework, the company's enterprise strategy is translated into a set of business objectives, which include IT business objectives. The IT group achieves these business objectives by establishing processes and employing the following resources:

   a. Applications—automated systems and manual procedures that process the information.

   b. Information—the data, in all their forms, input, processed and output by the information systems.

   c. Infrastructure—the technology and facilities (i.e., hardware, operating systems, networking, and the environment that houses and supports them) that enable the processing of information.

   d. People—the personnel required to plan, organize, acquire, implement, deliver, support, monitor and evaluate information systems and services. The people could be internal, outsourced, or contracted.

3. COBIT defines IT activities in a process model within four domains (Plan, Build, Run and Monitor):

   a. Plan and organize—encompasses the strategy and tactics to identify the manner in which IT can best contribute to the achievement of business objectives.

   b. Acquire and implement—encompasses the identification, acquisition or development, and implementation of IT solutions.

   c. Deliver and support—encompasses the delivery of the required IT solutions and services.

   d. Monitor and evaluate—encompasses the assessment of IT's quality and compliance with control requirements.

4. To assist in implementation of the framework, COBIT identifies 34 processes generally used by companies, and for each of the processes it has defined control objectives and process and application controls.

5. IT systems should also be measurement driven. COBIT deals with measurement issues by providing

   a. Maturity models—models used to evaluate the sophistication of IT processes rated from a maturity level of nonexistent (0) to optimized (5).

   b. Performance goals and metrics—used to demonstrate how processes meet business and IT goals by using outcome measures (key goal indicators) and key performance indicators (KPIs).

   c. Activity goals—used to establish what needs to happen inside a process to achieve the required performance and how to measure it.

E. Effect of IT on Internal Control

> **NOTE:** We have already discussed the effect of a computer on internal control of several systems under C. (microcomputers, end-user computing, and electronic commerce). In this section we discuss the effect in general terms as presented in the AICPA Audit Guide, **Consideration of Internal Control in a Financial Statement Audit**. This section presents information on controls a company may have. We begin by discussing overall principles of a reliable system and overall risks. We then consider the effect of a computer on internal control using the five components of internal control—control environment, risk assessment, information and communication, monitoring, and control activities.

1. **Principles of a Reliable System and Examples of Overall Risks**

   a. A reliable system is one that is capable of operating without material error, fault, or failure during a specified period in a specified environment.

   b. One framework for analyzing a reliable system is presented by the AICPA's Trust Services. Trust Services, which provide assurance on information systems, use a framework with five principles of a reliable system— (1) security, (2) availability, (3) processing integrity, (4) online privacy, and (5) confidentiality. Accordingly, when a principle is not met a risk exists.

Principle	Examples of Risks
1. *Security.* The system is protected against unauthorized access (both physical and logical)	Physical access—A lack of physical security allows damage or other loss (e.g., theft) to the system • Weather • Acts of war • Disgruntled employees or others Logical access—A lack of security over access to the system allows • Malicious (or accidental) alteration of, or damage to, files and/or the system • Computer based fraud • Unauthorized access to confidential data
2. *Availability.* The system is available for operation and use as committed or agreed. The system is available for operation and use in conformity with the entity's availability policies.	System failure results in • Interruption of business operations • Loss of data
3. *Processing Integrity.* System processing is complete, accurate, timely, and authorized.	Invalid, incomplete, or inaccurate • Input data • Data processing • Updating of master files • Creation of output
4. *Online Privacy.* Personal information obtained as a result of e-commerce is collected, used, disclosed, and retained as committed or agreed.	Disclosure of customer information (or that of others) such as • Social security numbers • Credit card numbers • Credit rating • Medical conditions
5. *Confidentiality.* Information designated as confidential is protected as committed or agreed.	Examples of confidential data that might be disclosed • Transaction details • Engineering details of products • Business plans • Banking information • Legal documents • Inventory or other account information • Customer lists • Confidential details of operations

> **NOTE:** Make certain that you are familiar not only with the above principles, but are familiar with the nature of the various risks relating to computer processing.

2. **Control Environment**

   a. Recall the seven factors of the control environment:

I - Integrity and ethical values
C - Commitment to competence
H - Human resource policies and practices
A - Assignment of authority and responsibility
M - Management's philosophy and operating style
B - Board of directors or audit committee participation
O - Organizational structure

b. Although all seven factors may be affected by computer processing, the organizational structure is modified to include an information systems department (EDP department). It is helpful to keep in mind that the information systems department is involved with two distinct functions—systems development and data processing.

c. Steps in the *system development lifecycle:*

(1) Software concept—identify the need for the new system.
(2) Requirements analysis—determine the needs of the users.
(3) Architectural design—determining the hardware, software, people, etc. needed.
(4) Coding and debugging—acquiring and testing the software.
(5) System testing—testing and evaluating the functionality of the system.

d. Organizational structure

(1) **Segregation controls**

(a) Segregate functions between information systems department and user departments.

1] User departments are the other departments of the company that utilize the data prepared by the information systems department.

(b) Do not allow the information systems department to initiate or authorize transactions.

(c) At a minimum, segregate programming, data entry, operations, and the library function within the information systems department.

(d) A more complete segregation of key functions within the information systems department may be possible; one way to separate key functions is as follows:

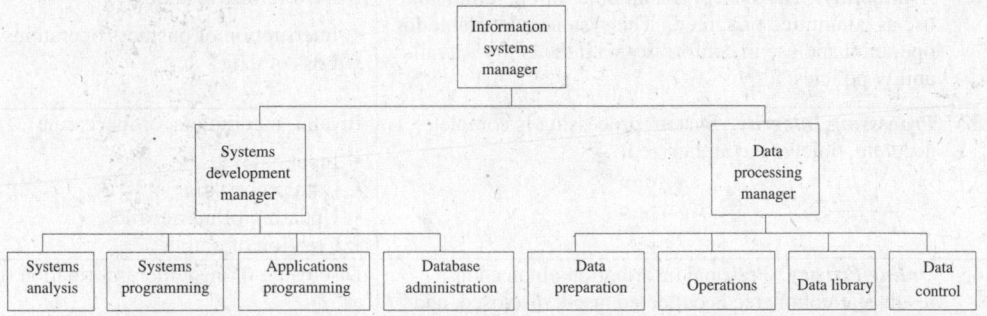

1] **Systems analysis**—The systems analyst analyzes the present user environment and requirements and may (1) recommend specific changes, (2) recommend the purchase of a new system, or (3) design a new information system. The analyst is in constant contact with user departments and programming staff to ensure the users' actual and ongoing needs are being met. A system flowchart is a tool used by the analyst to define the systems requirements.

2] **Systems programming**—The systems programmer is responsible for implementing, modifying, and debugging the software necessary for making the hardware work (such as the operating system, telecommunications monitor, and the database management system). For some companies the term "software engineer" is viewed as similar or identical to that of systems programmer. For others, the software engineer is involved with the creation of designs used by programmers.

3] **Applications programming**—The applications programmer is responsible for writing, testing, and debugging the application programs from the specifications (whether general or specific) provided by the systems analyst. A program flowchart is one tool used by the applications programmer to define the program logic.

4] **Database administration**—In a database environment, a database administrator (DBA) is responsible for maintaining the database and restricting access to the database to authorized personnel.

5] **Data preparation**—Data may be prepared by user departments and input by key to storage devices.

6] **Operations**—The operator is responsible for the daily computer operations of both the hardware and the software. The operator supervises operations on the operator's console, accepts any required input, and distributes any generated output. The operator should have adequate documentation available to run the program (a run manual), but should not have detailed program information.

      a] Help desks are usually a responsibility of operations because of the operational nature of their functions (for example, assisting users with systems problems and obtaining technical support/vendor assistance).

    7] **Data library**—The librarian is responsible for custody of the removable media (i.e., magnetic tapes or disks) and for the maintenance of program and system documentation. In many systems, much of the library function is maintained and performed electronically by the computer.

    8] **Data control**—The control group acts as liaison between users and the processing center. This group records input data in a control log, follows the progress of processing, distributes output, and ensures compliance with control totals.

Ideally, in a large system, all of the above key functions should be segregated; in a small computer environment, many of the key functions are concentrated in a small number of employees. For purposes of the CPA exam remember that, at a minimum, an attempt should be made to segregate *programming, operations,* and the *library* functions. Large organizations typically have a chief information officer (CIO) that oversees all information technology and activities.

(e) Electronic commerce has resulted in a number of new web-related positions, including

    1] **Web administrator (web manager)**—Responsible for overseeing the development, planning, and the implementation of a website. Ordinarily a managerial position.

    2] **Web master**—Responsible for providing expertise and leadership in the development of a website, including the design, analysis, security, maintenance, content development, and updates.

    3] **Web designer**—Responsible for creating the visual content of the website.

    4] **Web coordinator**—Responsible for the daily operations of the website.

    5] **Internet developer**—Responsible for writing programs for commercial use. Similar to a software engineer or systems programmer.

    6] **Intranet/Extranet developer**—Responsible for writing programs based on the needs of the company.

3. **Risk Assessment**

a. Changes in computerized information systems and in operations may increase the risk of improper financial reporting.

4. **Information and Communication**

a. The computerized accounting system is affected by whether the company uses small computers and/or a complex mainframe system.

    (1) For small computer systems, purchased commercial "off-the-shelf" software may be used.

        (a) Controls within the software may be well known.

        (b) Analysis of "exception reports" generated during processing is important to determine that exceptions are properly handled.

    (2) For complex mainframe systems a significant portion of the software is ordinarily developed within the company by information systems personnel.

        (a) Controls within the software are unknown to the auditor prior to testing.

        (b) As with small computer systems, analysis of exception reports is important, but controls over the generation of such reports must ordinarily be tested to a greater extent.

5. **Monitoring**

a. Proper monitoring of a computerized system will require adequate computer skills to evaluate the propriety of processing of computerized applications.

b. A common method of monitoring for inappropriate access is review of system-access log.

c. IT can also facilitate monitoring.

    (1) IT can constantly evaluate data and transactions based on established criteria and highlight items that appear to be inconsistent or unusual.

    (2) IT can capture samples of items for audit by internal auditors.

6. **Control Activities—Overall**

a. Control activities in which a computer is involved may be divided into the following categories:

   (1) Computer **general** control activities.
   (2) Computer **application** control activities.

   Programmed application control activities.
   Manual follow-up of computer exception reports.

   (3) **User** control activities to test the completeness and accuracy of computer processed controls.

   The following illustration, adapted from the AICPA Audit Guide, *Consideration of Internal Control in a Financial Statement Audit*, summarizes the relationships among the controls.

COMPUTER CONTROL ACTIVITIES

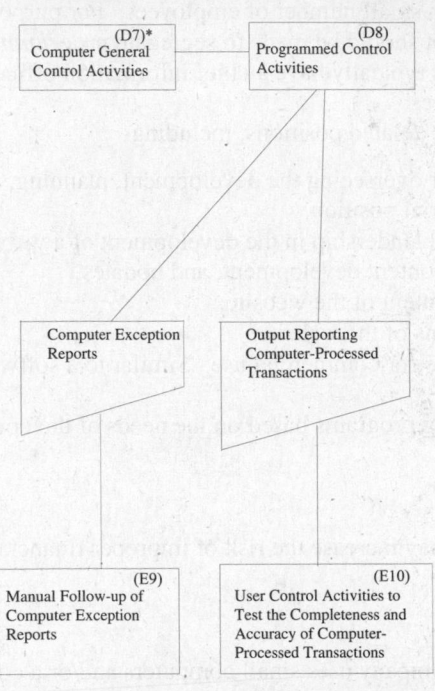

* Section below in which control discussion is presented.

EXPLANATION OF COMPUTER CONTROL ACTIVITIES

Computer General Control Activities control program development, program changes, computer operations, and access to programs and data. These control activities increase the assurance that programmed control activities operate effectively during the period.

Computer Application Control Activities

Programmed Control Activities relate to specific computer applications and are embedded in the computer program used in the financial reporting system. The concepts presented here related to programmed control activities may also apply to other activities within the computer accounting system.

Manual Follow-Up of Computer Exception Reports involves employee follow-up of items listed on computer exception reports. The effectiveness of application control activities that involve manual follow-up of computer reports depends on the effectiveness of both the programmed control activities that produce the exception report and the manual follow-up activities.

User Control Activities to Test the Completeness and Accuracy of Computer Processed Transactions represent manual checks of computer output against source document or other input, and thus provide assurance that programmed aspects of the accounting system and control activities have operated effectively.

7. **Computer General Control Activities**

> **NOTE:** General control activities affect all computer applications. There are four types of general controls—(a) developing new programs and systems, (b) changing existing programs and systems, (c) controlling access to programs and data, and (d) controlling computer operations.

a. **Developing new programs and systems**

   (1) **Segregation controls**

      (a) User departments participate in systems design.
      (b) Both users and information systems personnel test new systems.
      (c) Management, users, and information systems personnel approve new systems before they are placed into operation.
      (d) All master and transaction file conversions should be controlled to prevent unauthorized changes and to verify the accuracy of the results.
      (e) Programs and systems should be properly documented (see Section F. of outline).

   (2) **Computer hardware is extremely reliable.** This is primarily due to the chip technology. However, it is also due to the controls built into the hardware and systems software to provide for a self-diagnostic mechanism to detect and prevent equipment failures. The following are examples of such controls:

      (a) **Parity check**—A special bit is added to each character that can detect if the hardware loses a bit during the internal movement of a character.

(b) **Echo check**—Primarily used in telecommunications transmissions. During the sending and receiving of characters, the receiving hardware repeats back to the sending hardware what it received and the sending hardware automatically resends any characters that were received incorrectly.

(c) **Diagnostic routines**—Hardware or software supplied by the manufacturer to check the internal operations and devices within the computer system. These routines are often activated when the system is booted up.

(d) **Boundary protection**—Most CPUs have multiple jobs running simultaneously (multiprogramming environment). To ensure that these simultaneous jobs cannot destroy or change the allocated memory of another job, the systems software contains boundary protection controls.

(e) **Periodic maintenance**—The system should be examined periodically (often weekly) by a qualified service technician.

(3) **Documentation.** Systems and programs should be adequately documented. System specification documents should detail such matters as performance levels, reliability, security and privacy, constraints and limitations, functional capabilities, and data structure and elements.

b. **Changing existing programs and systems**

(1) Suggestions for changes (from users and information system personnel) should be documented in a change request log.

(2) Proper *change control* procedures (also referred to as *modification controls*) should be in place.

(a) The information systems manager should review all changes.
(b) The modified program should be appropriately tested (often using test data).
(c) Details of all changes should be documented.
(d) A *code comparison program* may be used to compare source and/or object codes of a controlled copy of a program with the program currently being used to process data.

1] This will identify any unauthorized changes (this approach may also be used by CPAs).

c. **Controlling access to programs and data**

(1) **Segregation controls**

(a) Access to program documentation should be limited to those persons who require it in the performance of their duties.
(b) Access to data files and programs should be limited to those individuals authorized to process data.
(c) Access to computer hardware should be limited to authorized individuals such as computer operators and their supervisors.

(2) **Physical access to computer facility**

(a) **Limited physical access**—The physical facility that houses the computer equipment, files, and documentation should have controls to limit access only to authorized individuals. Possible controls include using a guard, automated key cards, and manual key locks, as well as the new access devices that permit access through fingerprints or palm prints.
(b) **Visitor entry logs**—Used to document those who have had access to the area.

(3) **Hardware and software access controls**

(a) **Access control software** (user identification)—The most used control is a combination of a unique *identification code* and a confidential *password*.

1] Passwords should be made up of a combination of alphabetic, numeric, and symbol elements.
2] Passwords should be changed periodically.
3] Passwords should be disabled promptly when an employee leaves the company.

(b) **Call back**—Call back is a specialized form of user identification in which the user dials the system, identifies him/herself, and is disconnected from the system. Then either (1) an individual manually finds the authorized telephone number or (2) the system automatically finds the authorized telephone number of the individual and calls back.

(c) **Encryption**—Data is encoded when stored in computer files and/or before transmission to or from remote locations (e.g., through use of modems and telephone lines). This coding protects data, since to use the data unauthorized users must not only obtain access, but must also translate the coded form of the data. Encryption performed by physically secure hardware (often special-purpose computers) is ordinarily more secure, but more costly than that performed by software. See section C.5.c.(3) for more information on encryption.

  d. **Controlling computer operations**

   (1) **Segregation controls**

    (a) Operators should have access to an ***operations manual*** that contains the instructions for processing programs and solving routine operational program issues, but not with detailed program documentation.

    (b) The control group should monitor the operator's activities and jobs should be scheduled.

   (2) **Other controls**

    (a) **Backup and recovery**—Discussed in Section D.11. in this module

    (b) **Contingency processing**—Detailed contingency processing plans should be developed to prepare for system failures. The plans should detail the responsibilities of individuals, as well as the alternate processing sites that should be utilized. Backup facilities with a vendor may be used to provide contingent sites in case of an emergency. This topic is discussed further in Section D.11. of this module.

    (c) **Internal and external labels**—External labels are gummed-paper labels attached to storage media which identify the file. Internal labels perform the same function through the use of machine readable identification in the first record of a file. The use of labels allows the computer operator to determine whether the correct file has been selected for processing.

8. **Computer Application Control Activities—Programmed Control Activities**

> **NOTE:** Programmed application controls apply to a specific application rather than multiple applications. These controls operate to assure the proper input and processing of data. The input step converts human-readable data into computer-readable data. Ensuring the integrity of the data in the computer is critical during processing. The candidate should be prepared to identify the following common controls in a multiple-choice question.

  a. **Input controls**

   (1) **Overall controls**

    (a) Inputs should be properly authorized and approved.

    (b) The system should verify all significant data fields used to record information (editing the data).

    (c) Conversion of data into machine-readable form should be controlled and verified for accuracy.

   (2) **Input validation (edit) controls**

    (a) **Preprinted form**—Information is preassigned a place and a format on the input form.

    (b) **Check digit**—An extra digit added to an identification number to detect certain types of data transmission errors. For example, a bank may add a check digit to individuals' 7-digit account numbers. The computer will calculate the correct check digit based on performing predetermined mathematical operations on the 7-digit account number and will then compare it to the check digit.

    (c) **Control, batch, or proof total**—A total of one numerical field for all the records of a batch that normally would be added, (e.g., total sales dollars).

    (d) **Hash total**—A control total where the total is meaningless for financial purposes (e.g., a mathematical sum of employee social security numbers).

    (e) **Record count**—A control total of the total records processed.

    (f) **Limit (reasonableness) test**—A test of the reasonableness of a field of data, given a predetermined upper and/or lower limit (e.g., for a field that indicates auditing exam scores, a limit check would test for scores over 100).

    (g) **Menu driven input**—As input is entered, the operator responds to a menu prompting the proper response (e.g., What score did you get on the Auditing part of the CPA Exam [75-100]?).

    (h) **Field check**—A control that limits the types of characters accepted into a specific data field (e.g., a pay rate should include only numerical data).

    (i) **Validity check**—A control that allows only "valid" transactions or data to be entered into the system (e.g., a field indicating sex of an individual where 1=female and 2=male—if the field is coded in any other manner it would not be accepted).

    (j) **Missing data check**—A control that searches for blanks inappropriately existing in input data (e.g., if an employee's division number were left blank an error message would result).

    (k) **Field size check**—A control of an exact number of characters to be input (e.g., if part numbers all have 6 digits, an error message would result if more or less than 6 characters were input).

    (l) **Logic check**—Ensures that illogical combinations of input are not accepted (e.g., if the Tuba City branch has no company officers, an error message would result if two fields for a specified employee indicated that the employee worked as an officer in Tuba City).

(m) **Redundant data check**—Uses two identifiers in each transaction record (e.g., customer account number and the first five letters of customer's name) to confirm that the correct master file record is being updated.

(n) **Closed-loop verification**—A control that allows data entry personnel to check the accuracy of input data. For example, the system might retrieve an account name of a record that is being updated, and display it on the operator's terminal. This control may be used instead of a redundant data check.

(3) **Processing controls**

Overall: When the input has been accepted by the computer, it usually is processed through multiple steps. Processing controls are essential to ensure the integrity of data. Essentially all of the controls listed for input may also be incorporated during processing. For example, processed information should include limit tests, record counts, and control totals. In addition, external labels should be used on removable media, with internal header and trailer labels used to determine that all information on a file has been read.

> **NOTE:** Previously, the professional standards divided application controls into three categories—input, processing, and output. The current categories of application controls (programmed and manual) and user controls have replaced that breakdown. As an aid to discussing controls we distinguish between input and processing above. User control activities include the essentials of the previous "output" controls.

9. **Application Controls—Manual Follow-Up of Computer Exception Reports**

   a. These controls involve employee (operator and/or control group) follow-up of items listed on computer exception reports. Their effectiveness depends on the effectiveness of both the programmed control activities that produce the reports and the manual follow-up activities.

10. **User Control Activities to Test the Completeness and Accuracy of Computer-Processed Controls**

    a. These manual controls, previously referred to as *output controls,* include

       (1) Checks of computer output against source documents, control totals, or other input to provide assurance that programmed aspects of the financial reporting system and control activities have operated effectively.
       (2) Reviewing computer processing logs to determine that all of the correct computer jobs executed properly.
       (3) Maintaining proper procedures and communications specifying authorized recipients of output.

    b. These procedures are often performed by both the control group and users.
    c. In some systems, user departments evaluate the reliability of output from the computer by extensive review and testing; in others, users merely test the overall reasonableness of the output.

11. **Disaster Recovery and Business Continuity**

    a. A plan should allow the firm to

       (1) Minimize the extent of disruption, damage, and loss.
       (2) Establish an alternate (temporary) method for processing information.
       (3) Resume normal operations as quickly as possible.
       (4) Train and familiarize personnel to perform emergency operations.

    b. A plan should include priorities, insurance, backup approaches, specific assignments, period testing and updating, and documentation, as described below.

       (1) **Priorities**—Which applications are most critical?
       (2) **Insurance to defer costs**
       (3) **Backup approaches**

          (a) Batch systems—The most common approach is the *Grandfather-Father-Son* method. A master file (e.g., accounts receivable) is updated with the day's transaction files (e.g., files of cash receipts and credit sales). After the update, the new file master file is the son. The file from which the father was developed with the transaction files of the appropriate day is the grandfather. The grandfather and son files are stored in different locations. If the son were destroyed, for example, it could be reconstructed by rerunning the father file and the related transaction files.
          (b) Online databases and master files systems

             1] **Checkpoint**—Similar to grandfather-father-son, but at certain points, "checkpoints," the system makes a copy of the database and this "checkpoint" file is stored on a separate disk or tape. If a problem occurs the system is restarted at the last checkpoint and updated with subsequent transactions.

2] **Rollback**—As a part of recovery, to undo changes made to a database to a point at which it was functioning properly

3] **Backup facilities**

a] **Reciprocal agreement**—An agreement between two or more organizations (with compatible computer facilities) to aid each other with their data processing needs in the event of a disaster. This is sometimes referred to as a mutual aid pact.

b] **Hot site**—A commercial disaster recovery service that allows a business to continue computer operations in the event of computer disaster. For example, if a company's data processing center becomes inoperable, that enterprise can move all processing to a hot site that has all the equipment needed to continue operation. This is also referred to as a recovery operations center (ROC) approach.

c] **Cold site**—Similar to a hot site, but the customer provides and installs the equipment needed to continue operations. A cold site is less expensive, but takes longer to get in full operation after a disaster. This is sometimes referred to as an "empty shell" in that the "shell" is available and ready to receive whatever hardware the temporary user needs.

d] **Internal site**—Large organizations with multiple data processing centers sometimes rely upon their own sites for backup in the event of a disaster.

NOTE: Be aware that most approaches to control for catastrophic failures rely upon backup of the entire system in one form or another. Also, various combinations of the above approaches may be used.

e] **Mirrored web server**—An exact copy of a website which is the best way to back up the website.

(4) **Specific assignments, including having individuals involved with**

(a) Arranging for new facilities.
(b) Computer operations.
(c) Installing software.
(d) Establishing data communications facilities.
(e) Recovering vital records.
(f) Arranging for forms and supplies.

(5) **Periodic testing and updating of plan**
(6) **Documentation of plan**

NOW REVIEW MULTIPLE-CHOICE QUESTIONS 97 THROUGH 141 IN VOLUME 2

F. Flowcharting

General: Flowcharts analytically describe some aspect of an information system. Flowcharting is a procedure to graphically show the sequential flow of data and/or operations. The data and operations portrayed include document preparation, authorization, storage, and decision making. The more common flowcharting symbols are illustrated below. Knowledge of them would help with occasional multiple-choice questions and with problems that present a detailed flowchart that must be analyzed.

1. Common Flowcharting Symbols

	Document	This can be a manual form or a computer printout
	Computer Operation	Computer process which transforms input data into useful information
	Manual Operation	Manual (human) process to prepare documents, make entries, check output, etc.
	Decision	Determines which alternative path is followed (IF/THEN/ELSE Conditions)

Input/Output	General input or output to a process. Often used to represent accounting journals and ledgers on document flowcharts
Online Storage	Refers to direct access computer storage connected directly to the CPU. Data is available on a random access basis
Disc Storage	Refers to data stored on a magnetic disk
Off-Line Storage	Refers to a file or indicates the mailing of a document (i.e., invoices or statements to customers). A letter in the symbol below the line indicates the order in which the file is stored. (N-Numerical, C-Chronological, A-Alphabetical)
Display	Visual display of data and/or output on a terminal screen
Batch Total Tape	Manually computed total before processing (such as the number of records to be processed). This total is recomputed by the computer and compared after processing is completed.
Magnetic Tape	Used for reading, writing, or storage on sequential storage media
Manual Data Entry	Refers to data entered through a terminal keyboard or key-to-tape or key-to-disk device
Annotation	Provides additional description or information connected to symbol to which it annotates by a dotted line (not a flowline)
Flowline	Shows direction of data flow, operations, and documents
Communication Link	Telecommunication line linking computer system to remote locations
Start/Termination	Used to begin or end a flowchart. (Not always used or shown in flowcharts on the CPA exam.) May be used to show connections to other procedures or receipt/ sending of documents to/from outsiders
On Page Connector	Connects parts of flowchart on the same page
Off Page Connector	Connects parts of flowchart on separate pages

2. **Types and Definitions**

   a. **System flowchart**—A graphic representation of a data processing application that depicts the interaction of all the computer programs for a given system, rather than the logic for an individual computer program.
   b. **Program flowchart**—A graphic representation of the logic (processing steps) of a computer program.
   c. **Internal control (audit) flowchart** or **document flowchart**—A graphic representation of the flow of documents from one department to another, showing the source flow and final disposition of the various copies of all documents. Most flowcharts on the CPA exam have been of this type.

3. **Other Documentation Charting Techniques**

   a. **Decision table**—Decision tables use a matrix format that lists sets of conditions, and the actions that result from various combinations of these conditions. See Module 3 on internal control for an example of a decision table.

   b. **Data flow diagram (DFD)**—Presents logical flows of data and functions in a system. For example, a data flow diagram for the delivery of goods to a customer would include a symbol for the warehouse from which the goods are shipped and a symbol representing the customer. It would not emphasize details such as computer processing and paper outputs.

NOW REVIEW MULTIPLE-CHOICE QUESTIONS 142 THROUGH 149 IN VOLUME 2

KEY TERMS

Because the content of this module is largely terminology, a set of key terms is not provided.

Module 42: Economics, Strategy, and Globalization

Overview

This module covers three interrelated topics: economics, business strategy, and globalization. The module begins with a discussion of microeconomic and macroeconomic concepts. These concepts are important in determining effective strategies for a business. It is important to understand the effects of the macroeconomic factors on the business, including actions by governments that impact global markets. Business managers must also understand the nature of the markets that the company purchases and sells in. These factors provide inputs into strategy formulation for the firm. Because business is truly global, managers must understand the global economy and how global factors provide opportunities and risks for their companies. Before you begin the reading, you should review the key terms at the end of the module.

MICROECONOMICS

A. Microeconomics focuses on the behavior and purchasing decisions of individuals and firms. In a market economy goods and services are distributed through a system of prices. Goods and services are sold to those willing and able to pay the market price. The market price is determined based on demand and supply.

B. Demand

Demand is the quantity of a good or service that consumers are willing and able to purchase at a range of prices at a particular time. Therefore, market demand for a product is actually a schedule of the amount that would be purchased at various prices, with all other variables that affect demand being held constant. Graphically a demand curve shows an inverse relationship between the price and quantity demanded. That is, less products are demanded at higher prices. Illustrated below is the demand schedule and demand curve for Product X.

Market Demand for Product X

Price per unit	Quantity Demanded
$70	2,000
60	2,500
50	3,000
40	4,000
30	6,000
20	10,000

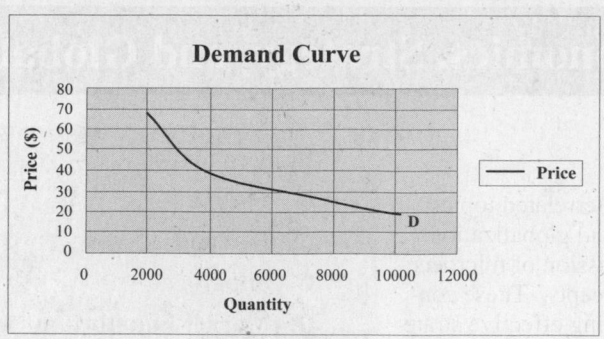

As illustrated, at a price of $50, 3,000 units of Product X will be bought. If the price of Product X changes, more or less will be bought.

1. **Demand curve shift.** A demand curve shifts when demand variables other than price change. For example, if the price of substitute products for Product X increase in price, the demand for Product X would shift upward and to the right. A demand curve shift is illustrated in the graph below.

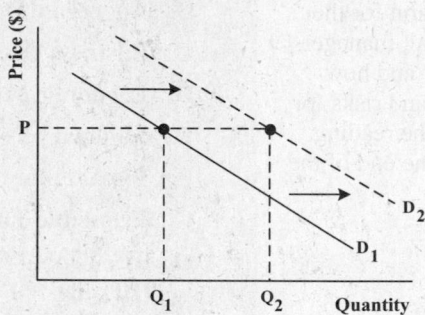

2. Variables that may cause a demand curve shift include changes in the price of other goods and services, consumer tastes, spendable income, wealth, and the size of the market. The table below summarizes the effects of these factors on the demand for a particular product.

Factors Affecting the Demand for a Product other than Its Price

Factor	Effect
Price of other goods and services (e.g. substitute goods)	**Direct relationship.** As goods that may be purchased instead go up in price the demand for the product goes up. As an example, if the price of pork increases the demand for beef may increase.
Price of complement products (i.e., products that must be used with the product or enhance its usefulness)	**Inverse relationship.** As the prices of complement goods go up, the demand for the product goes down. As an example, if the price of hamburger increases the demand for hamburger buns decreases.
Expectations of price increase	**Direct relationship.** If the price of the good is expected to increase in the future, there will be an increase in demand.
Consumer income and wealth	**Generally a direct relationship.** As consumer income (wealth) goes up the demand for many products (normal goods) goes up. However, there are certain **goods that are inferior** (e.g., bread, potatoes, etc.) and the demand for such goods actually goes up as consumer income (wealth) goes down. This is because consumers buy more inferior goods when they are short of money.
Consumer tastes	**Indeterminate relationship.** The effect depends on whether the shift is towards or away from the product.
Size of the market	**Direct relationship.** As the size of the market increases, the demand for the product will increase.
Group boycott	**Inverse relationship.** If a group of consumers boycott a product, demand will be decreased.

3. **Price elasticity of demand.** The elasticity of demand measures the sensitivity of demand to a change in price. It is calculated as follows:

$$E_D = \frac{\text{Percentage change in quantity demanded}}{\text{Percentage change in price}}$$

To make results the same regardless of whether there is an increase or decrease in price, the amount is usually calculated using the *arc method* as shown below.

$$E_D = \frac{\text{Change in quantity demanded}}{\text{Average quantity}} \div \frac{\text{Change in price}}{\text{Average price}}$$

EXAMPLE

Assume that you are operating a hot dog stand and sell hot dogs for $2.50. Your usual demand for hot dogs is 200 per day. To increase sales, you decide to run a $1.50 hot dog special and you sell 400 hot dogs for the day. The price elasticity of hot dogs is calculated as follows:

The change in quantity demanded = 200 (400 − 200)

The change in price = $1.00 ($2.50 − $1.50)

The average quantity = 300 [(200 + 400) ÷ 2]

The average price = $2.00 [($2.50 + $1.50) ÷ 2]

$$E_D = \frac{\text{Change in quantity demanded}}{\text{Average quantity}} \div \frac{\text{Change in price}}{\text{Average price}}$$

$$= \frac{200}{300} \div \frac{\$1.00}{\$2.00}$$

$$= .667 \div .5$$

$$= 1.334$$

Interpretation of the demand elasticity coefficient. If E_D is greater than 1, demand is said to be elastic (sensitive to price changes). If E_D is equal to 1, demand is said to be unitary (not sensitive or insensitive to price changes). If E_D is less than 1, demand is said to be inelastic (not sensitive to price changes).

The price elasticity of demand coefficient allows management to calculate the effect of a price change on demand for the product. In the example above, a 10% decrease in the price of a hot dog results in a 13.34% (10% × 1.334) increase in demand. The elasticity of demand is greater for a product when there are more substitutes for the good, a larger proportion of income is spent on the good, or a longer period of time is considered.

NOTE: The demand for luxury goods tends to be more elastic than for necessities.

4. **Relationship between price elasticity and total revenue.** Total revenue from the sale of a good is equal to the price times the quantity. Price elasticity is an important concept because if demand is elastic an increase in sales price results in a decrease in total revenue for all producers. If demand is unitary total revenue remains the same if price changes, and total revenue increases if price is increased when demand is inelastic. These relationships are shown in the following table:

Effect of Price Changes on Various Types of Goods

Price Change	Elastic Demand E > 1	Inelastic Demand E < 1	Unitary Demand E = 1
Price increase	Total revenue decreases	Total revenue increases	Total revenue does not change
Price decrease	Total revenue increases	Total revenue decreases	Total revenue does not change

In the example of the hot dog stand above, we calculated price elasticity to be 1.334. Therefore, demand is elastic and, as expected, we find that the price decline resulted in an increase in total revenue, $600 ($1.50 × 400) versus $500 ($2.50 × 200).

Price elasticity is an important concept because it reveals whether the firm is likely to be able to pass on cost increases to its customers. Obviously, when demand is inelastic the firm can increase its price with less of a negative impact.

5. **Income elasticity of demand.** Income elasticity of demand measures the change in the quantity demanded of a product given a change in income. Income elasticity is calculated as follows:

$$E_I = \frac{\text{Percentage change in quantity demanded}}{\text{Percentage change in income}}$$

The income elasticity of demand can be used to describe the nature of the product. The demand for normal products increases as consumer income increases. For example, the demand for **normal goods,** such as beefsteaks increases as consumer income increases. Therefore, E_I for beefsteaks is positive. The demand for **inferior goods,** such as beans, decreases as income increases; E_I is negative. The demand for inferior goods increases as income declines, because when individuals have less money they substitute these less expensive goods for normal goods.

6. **Cross-elasticity of demand.** Cross-elasticity of demand measures the change in demand for a good when the price of a related or competing product is changed. For example, Coca Cola Company would be interested in knowing how an increase in the price of Pepsi would affect the sales of Coca Cola. The coefficient of cross-elasticity is calculated as follows:

$$E_{XY} = \frac{\text{Percentage change in the quantity demanded of Product X}}{\text{Percentage change in the price of Product Y}}$$

In our case Pepsi would be Product Y, the competing product with the price change, and Coca Cola would be Product X. The coefficient describes the relationship between the two products. If the coefficient is positive, the products are substitutes (like Pepsi and Coca Cola). If the coefficient is negative, the products are complements (like hamburger and hamburger buns) and if the coefficient is zero, the products are unrelated. The table below illustrates these relationships.

Cross-Elasticity of Demand

Coefficient	Relationship between goods
Coefficient of cross-elasticity positive ($E_{xy} > 0$)	Substitutes
Coefficient of cross-elasticity negative ($E_{xy} < 0$)	Complements
Coefficient of cross-elasticity zero ($E_{xy} = 0$)	Unrelated

---

EXAMPLE

Assume that the cross-elasticity of demand for Product X in relation to Product Y is calculated to be 2.00. If the price of Product Y increases by 5%, then the demand for Product X would increase by 10% (5% × 2.00).

---

7. **Consumer demand and utility.**

a. As illustrated previously, the demand curve for a particular good is downward sloping. As the price of the good declines, consumers will purchase more because of substitution and income effects. The **substitution effect** refers to the fact that as the price of a good falls, consumers will use it to replace similar goods. As an example, as the price of pork falls, consumers will purchase more pork than other types of meat. The **income effect** refers to the fact that as the price of a good falls, consumers can purchase more with a given level of income.

b. An individual demands a particular good because of the utility (satisfaction) he or she receives from consuming it. The more goods an individual consumes the more total utility the individual receives. However, the marginal (additional) utility from consuming each additional unit decreases. This is referred to as the **law of diminishing marginal utility**.

c. A consumer maximizes utility from spending his or her income when the marginal utility of the last dollar spent on each commodity is the same. Utility maximization may be presented mathematically as shown below.

$$\frac{\text{Marginal Utility of A}}{\text{Price of A}} = \frac{\text{Marginal Utility of B}}{\text{Price of B}} = \frac{\text{Marginal Utility of Z}}{\text{Price of Z}}$$

d. To simplify this concept most economics books illustrate marginal utility with only two types of goods (e.g., chocolate bars and cans of soda). They construct a series of **indifference curves** which illustrate the combinations of chocolate bars and soda that provide equal utility. The optimal level of consumption of the two goods is then found where the individual's **budget constraint** line intersects the highest possible utility curve. At this point the individual receives the greatest amount of utility for the amount of money available. This relationship is illustrated below.

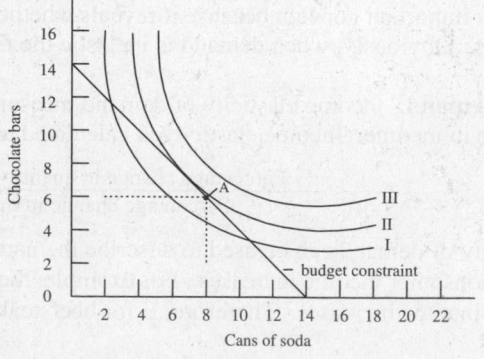

As illustrated, the individual gets the greatest satisfaction for the funds available at point A.

e. Consumption decisions depend on many factors but the main one is **personal disposable income**. This is the amount of income consumers have after receiving transfer payments from the government (e.g., welfare payments) and paying their taxes. When their personal disposable income goes up, consumers buy more. They buy less when it goes down.

f. The relationship between changes in personal disposable income and consumption is described by a **consumption function**. The function is typically described as follows:

$$C = c_0 + c_1 Y_D$$

Where

C = Consumption for a period

Y_D = Disposable income for the period

c_0 = The constant

c_1 = The slope of the consumption function

The important factor from the above function is the slope, c_1. It measures the consumer's **marginal propensity to consume (MPC)** describing how much of each additional dollar in personal disposable income that the consumer will spend. A consumption function is shown graphically below.

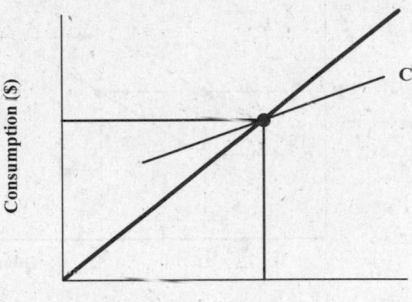

Disposable income ($)

g. The **marginal propensity to save (MPS)** is the percentage of additional income that is saved. Since a consumer can either spend or save money, the marginal propensity to consume plus the marginal propensity to save is equal to one as shown below.

$$MPC + MPS = 1$$

h. Certain nonincome factors may also affect consumption, including

(1) Expectations about future prices of goods
(2) Quantity of consumer liquid assets
(3) Amount of consumer debt
(4) Stock of consumer durable goods
(5) Attitudes about saving money
(6) Interest rates

C. Supply

A supply curve shows the amount of a product that would be supplied at various prices. Graphically a supply curve shows a direct relationship between price and quantity sold. The higher the price the more products that would be supplied. A supply schedule and supply curve for Product X are presented below.

Market Supply for Product X

Price per unit	Quantity supplied
$70	10,000
60	6,000
50	4,000
40	1,800
30	1,000
20	500

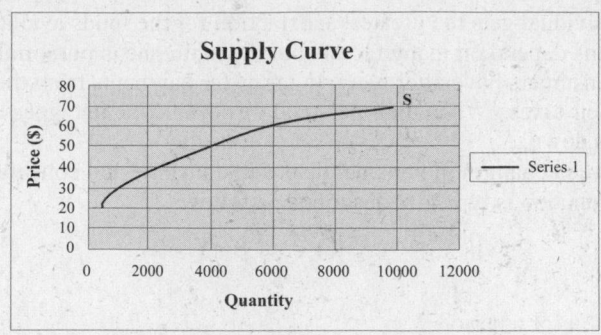

A change in the market price of the product results in a shift along the existing supply curve. For example, at $50, the market would supply 4,000 units but if the price changes to $60, the amount supplied will increase to 6,000.

1. **Supply curve shift.** A supply curve shift occurs when supply variables other than price change. As an example, if the costs to produce the product increase, the supply curve would shift upward and to the left. A shift in the supply curve is illustrated below.

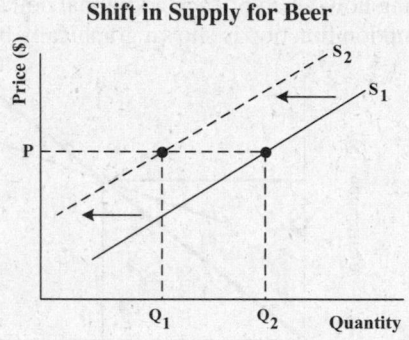

2. Variables that cause a supply curve shift include changes in the number or size of producers, changes in various production costs (wages, rents, raw materials), technological advances, and government actions. The effects of these variables are shown in the table below.

Factors Affecting the Supply of a Product other than Its Price

Factor	Effect
Number of producers	**Direct relationship.** Generally an increase in the number of producers will cause an increase in the amount of goods supplied at a given price.
Change in production costs or technological advances	**Inverse relationship.** As production costs go up fewer products will be supplied at a given price. If costs go down, more products will be produced.
Government subsidies	**Direct relationship.** Subsidies in effect reduce the production cost of goods and, therefore, increase the goods supplied at a given price.
Government price controls	Price controls would tend to limit the amount of goods supplied by holding the price artificially low.
Prices of other goods	**Inverse relationship.** If other products can be produced with greater returns, producers will produce those goods.
Price expectations	**Direct relationship.** If it is expected that prices will be higher for the good in the future, production of the good will increase.

3. **Elasticity of supply.** The elasticity of supply measures the percentage change in the quantity supplied of a product resulting from a change in the product price. The elasticity of supply is calculated as follows:

$$E_s = \frac{\text{Percentage change in quantity supplied}}{\text{Percentage change in price}}$$

- Supply is said to be elastic if $E_s > 1$, unitary elastic if $E_s = 1$, and inelastic if $E_s < 1$.
- Elastic supply means that a percentage increase in price will create a larger percentage increase in supply.

D. Market Equilibrium

A product's equilibrium price is determined by demand and supply; it is the price at which all the goods offered for sale will be sold (i.e., quantity demanded = quantity supplied). The equilibrium price is the price at which the demand and supply curve intersect as shown below.

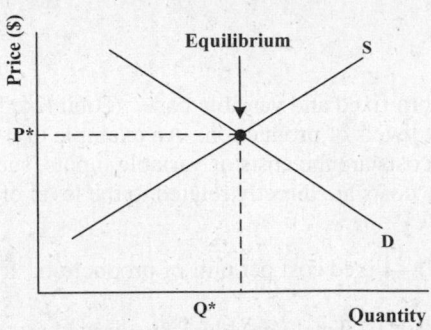

1. **Government intervention.** Government actions may change market equilibrium through taxes, subsidies, and rationing. For example, a subsidy paid to farmers will reduce the cost of producing a particular farm product and, therefore, cause the equilibrium price to be lower than it would be without the subsidy. Import taxes, on the other hand, would increase the cost of an imported product causing the equilibrium price to be higher.

   a. **Price ceiling.** A price ceiling is a specified maximum price that may be charged for a good. If the price ceiling is set for a good below the equilibrium price, it will cause good shortages because suppliers will devote their production facilities to producing other goods.

   b. **Price floor.** A price floor is a minimum specified price that may be charged for a good. If the price floor is set for a good above the equilibrium price, it will cause overproduction and surpluses will develop.

   Therefore, we see that government intervention in terms of taxes, subsidies, or price controls interfere with the free market and can result in an inefficient allocation of resources. Too many resources are devoted to certain sectors of the economy at the expense of other sectors.

2. **Externalities.** Another factor that causes inefficiencies in the pricing of goods in the market is the existence of externalities. **Externalities** is the term used to describe damage to common areas that is caused by the production of certain goods. A prominent example of an externality is pollution. Because these externalities are not included in the production costs of the goods, the supply is higher and the price is lower than is appropriate. Government laws and regulations (e.g., Environmental Protection Agency regulations) attempt to force firms to change their production methods to make externalities part of the cost of production. This causes the market price of these products to be a more accurate reflection of the cost of the goods to society.

3. **The effects of shifts in demand and supply.** The effects on equilibrium of shifts in demand and supply are shown in the following graphs.

Increase in Demand and New Equilibrium   **Increase in Supply and New Equilibrium**

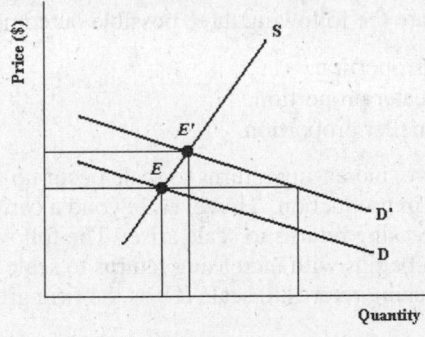   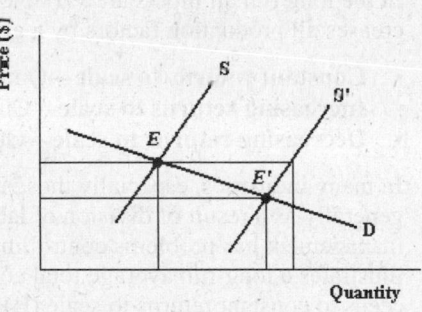

The effects of shifts in demand and supply can be complex especially when both shift simultaneously. The following table describes the effects of these changes:

Change in demand or supply	Effect
1. Increase (decrease) in demand, no change in supply	Equilibrium price will increase (decrease) and quantity purchased will increase (decrease)
2. Increase (decrease) in supply, no change in demand	Equilibrium price will decrease (increase) and quantity purchased will increase (decrease)
3. Both demand and supply increase (decrease)	Quantity purchased will increase (decrease) and the new equilibrium price is indeterminate
4. Demand increases and supply decreases	Equilibrium price will increase and quantity purchased is indeterminate.
5. Demand decreases and supply increases	Equilibrium price will decrease and quantity purchased is indeterminate

E. Costs of Production

1. **Short-run total costs.**

    a. In the short run, firms have both fixed and variable costs. Total fixed costs are those that are committed and will not change with different levels of production. An example of a fixed cost is the rent paid on a long-term lease for a factory. Variable costs are the costs of variable inputs, such as raw materials, variable labor costs, and variable overhead. These costs are directly related to the level of production for the period. In the short run, costs behave as follows:

    • **Average fixed cost (AFC)**—Fixed cost per unit of production. It goes down consistently as more units are produced.
    • **Average variable cost (AVC)**—Total variable costs divided by the number of units produced. It initially stays constant until the inefficiencies of producing in a fixed-size facility cause variable costs to begin to rise.
    • **Marginal cost (MC)**—The added cost of producing one extra unit. It initially decreases but then begins to increase due to inefficiencies.
    • **Average total cost (ATC)**—Total costs divided by the number of units produced. Its behavior depends on the makeup of fixed and variable costs.

    b. The cause of the inefficiencies described above is referred to as the **law of diminishing returns**. This law states that as we try to produce more and more output with a fixed productive capacity, marginal productivity will decline. The graph below illustrates the relationships between various short-run costs.

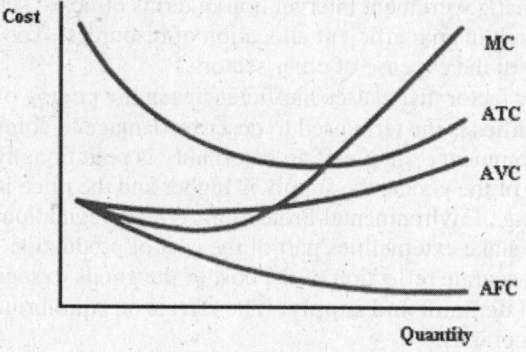

2. **Long-run total costs.**

    a. In the long run all inputs are variable because additional plant capacity can be built. If in the long run a firm increases all production factors by a given proportion, there are the following three possible outcomes:

    • **Constant returns to scale**—Output increases in same proportion.
    • **Increasing returns to scale**—Output increases by a greater proportion.
    • **Decreasing returns to scale**—Output increases by a smaller proportion.

    b. In many industries, especially those that are capital intensive, increasing returns to scale occur up to a point, generally as a result of division of labor and specialization in production. However, beyond a certain size, management has problems controlling production and decreasing returns to scale arise. The following graph illustrates a long-run average total cost (ATC) curve which begins with increasing returns to scale (A), and proceeds to constant returns to scale (B), and eventually decreasing returns to scale (C) as the firm grows.

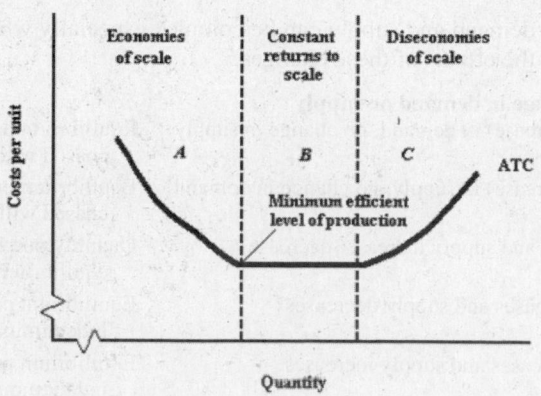

3. **Profits.** Economists refer to two different types of profit.

   a. **Normal profit**—The amount of profit necessary to compensate the owners for their capital and/or managerial skills. It is just enough profit to keep the firm in business in the long run.

   b. **Economic profit**—The amount of profit in excess of normal profit. In a perfectly competitive market, economic profit cannot be experienced in the long run.

F. Production

1. Management makes production decisions based on the relationship between marginal revenue and marginal cost. **Marginal revenue** is the additional revenue received from the sale of one additional unit of product. A good should be produced and sold as long as the marginal cost (MC) of producing the good is less than or equal to the marginal revenue (MR) from sale of that good. This relationship is shown in the following graph.

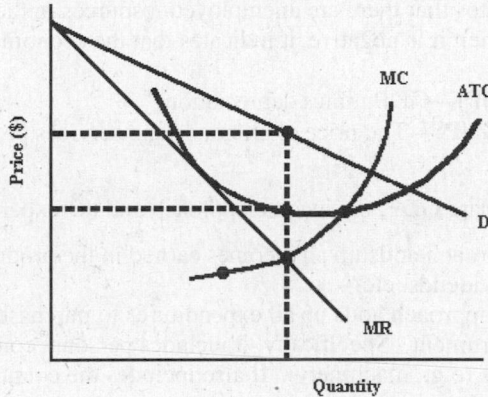

2. The price of input resources (e.g., labor, raw materials, etc.) is determined by demand and supply. If the price of an input increases, demand will decline. On the other hand, demand will increase if the price declines. In making decisions about the employment of resources, management considers the marginal product for each input resource. The **marginal product** is the additional output obtained from employing one additional unit of a resource. The change in total revenue from employing one additional unit of a resource is referred to as the **marginal revenue product**.

EXAMPLE

Thorp Corporation produces Product G and has developed the following chart illustrating relationships between number of workers producing the product, the number of units produced, and the revenue generated.

Number of workers	Products produced	Revenue generated
4	100	$200,000
5	120	$240,000
6	139	$275,000
7	157	$300,000

The marginal product of employing the 6th worker is equal to 19 (139 – 120), and the marginal revenue product is equal to $35,000 ($275,000 – $240,000).

---

3. The **marginal revenue per-unit** is calculated by dividing the marginal revenue product by the increase in products produced by employing one additional unit of resource. Using the above example of employing a 6th worker, the marginal revenue per-unit is equal to $1,842.11 [$35,000 (marginal revenue product) ÷ 19 (139 – 120) increase in products produced].

4. To be competitive management must produce the optimal output in the most efficient manner. The cost of production in the long run is minimized when the marginal product (MP) per dollar of every input (resource) is the same. Similar to utility maximization for a consumer, the least cost formula is

$$\frac{\text{MP of input A}}{\text{Price of input A}} = \frac{\text{MP of input B}}{\text{Price of input B}} = \frac{\text{MP of input C}}{\text{Price of input C}} = \frac{\text{MP of input Z}}{\text{Price of input Z}}$$

NOW REVIEW MULTIPLE-CHOICE QUESTIONS 1 THROUGH 48 IN VOLUME 2

MACROECONOMICS

A. Macroeconomics looks at the economy as a whole. It focuses on measures of economic output, employment, inflation, and trade surpluses or deficits. It also examines the spending of the three major segments of the economy, consumers, business, and government. The levels of economic activity is measured using a number of benchmarks, including

- **Nominal Gross Domestic Product (GDP)**—The price of all goods and services produced by a domestic economy for a year at current market prices.
- **Real GDP**—The price of **all** goods and services produced by the economy at price level adjusted (constant) prices. Price level adjustment eliminates the effect of inflation on the measure.
- **Potential GDP**—The maximum amount of production that could take place in an economy without putting pressure on the general level of prices. The difference between **potential GDP** and **real GDP** is called the GDP gap. When it is positive, it indicates that there are unemployed resources in the economy and we would expect unemployment. Alternatively, when it is negative, it indicates that the economy is running above normal capacity and prices should begin to rise.
- **Net Domestic Product (NDP)**—GDP minus depreciation.
- **Gross National Product (GNP)**—The price of all goods and services produced by labor and property supplied by the nation's residents.

1. There are two ways to calculate GDP, the income approach and the expenditure approach.

   a. The income (output) approach adds up all incomes earned in the production of final goods and services, such as wages, interest, rents, dividends, etc.
   b. The expenditure (input) approach adds up all expenditures to purchase final goods and services by households, businesses, and the government. Specifically, it includes personal consumption expenditures, gross private investment in capital goods (e.g., machinery). It also includes the country's net exports. The tables below illustrate these computations.

The Income Side of GDP

Compensation to employees	6,010
Corporate profits	767
Net interest	554
Proprietor's income	743
Rental income of persons	143
National income	8,217
Plus: indirect taxes	794
Minus: other, including statutory discrepancy	(160)
Net national product	8,851
Plus: consumption of fixed capital	1,351
Gross national product	10,202
Plus: payments of factor income to other countries	341
Minus: receipts of labor income from other countries	(335)
Gross domestic product	10,208

The Product Side of GDP

Personal consumption expenditures	7,065
Gross private domestic fixed investment	
Business	1,246
Residential	446
Government purchases	
Federal	616
State and local	1,223
Net exports	(330)
Changes in business inventories	(58)
Gross domestic product	10,208

B. Aggregate Demand and Supply

1. An aggregate demand curve depicts the demand of consumers, businesses, and government as well as foreign purchasers for the goods and services of the economy at different price levels. The aggregate demand curve looks like the demand curve for a single product (presented above); it is inversely related to price level. The price level affects aggregate demand for several reasons.

a. **Interest rate effect**—As price levels increase (inflation increases) nominal interest rates increase causing a decrease in interest sensitive spending. Interest sensitive spending includes spending for items such as houses, automobiles, and appliances.

b. **Wealth effect**—When price levels increase, the market value of certain financial assets decreases (e.g., fixed rate bonds) causing individuals to have less wealth and therefore they reduce their consumption.

c. **International purchasing power effect**—When domestic price levels increase relative to foreign currencies, foreign products become less expensive causing an increase in imported goods and a decrease in exported goods. This decreases the aggregate demand for domestic products.

2. An aggregate demand curve shifts when consumers, businesses, or governments are willing to spend more or less, or when there is an increase or decrease in the demand for domestic products abroad (i.e., an increase or decrease in net exports). Government can affect aggregate demand through its own spending levels, taxes, and monetary policy. For example, a reduction in individual or corporate taxes increases the spendable income of consumers or businesses. This would be expected to increase spending.

3. An aggregate supply (output) schedule presents the relationship between goods and services supplied and the price level, assuming that all other variables that affect supply are held constant. While there is not complete agreement on the shape of the aggregate supply curve, it is generally depicted as shown below.

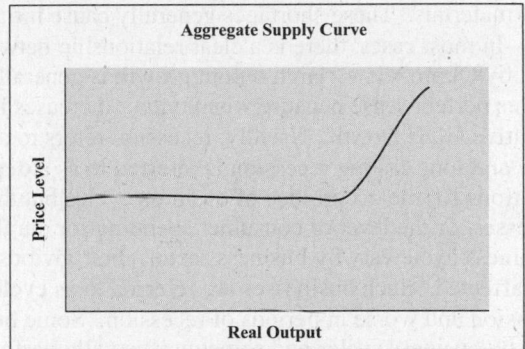

As shown, prices remain relatively constant until the economy reaches near capacity, at which time prices begin to increase at a significant rate. Shifts in the aggregate supply curve may be caused by technology improvements, changes in resource availability, or changes in resource costs.

4. Equilibrium GDP occurs when the output level of the economy creates just enough spending to purchase the entire output.

5. **The multiplier.** The multiplier refers to the fact than an increase in spending by consumers, businesses, or the government has a multiplied effect on equilibrium GDP. The reason for this is that increased spending generates increases in income to businesses and consumers which in turn increases their spending, which again increases the income of other consumers and businesses, etc. Therefore, the increased spending ripples through the economy increasing GDP by much more than the original increase in spending. The effect of the multiplier can be estimated by examining an economy's **marginal propensity to consume (MPC)** and **marginal propensity to save (MPS)**. From our previous discussion we know that additional income is either spent or saved as shown below.

$$MPS + MPC = 1$$

The multiplier may be calculated from the following formula:

$$\frac{1}{MPS} \times \quad \text{Change in spending}$$

EXAMPLE

If MPS is .25 (MPC = .75) and spending increases by $1,000,000, the increase in equilibrium GDP is calculated below.

$$\frac{1}{.25} \times \$1,000,000 = \$4,000,000$$

C. Business Cycles

1. A business cycle is a fluctuation in aggregate economic output that lasts for several years. Business cycles are recurring but vary in terms of both length and intensity. They are depicted as a series of peaks and troughs. A peak marks the end of a period of economic expansion and the beginning of a recession (contraction) while a

trough marks the end of a recession and the beginning of an economic recovery (expansion). The chart below illustrates the nature of the business cycle.

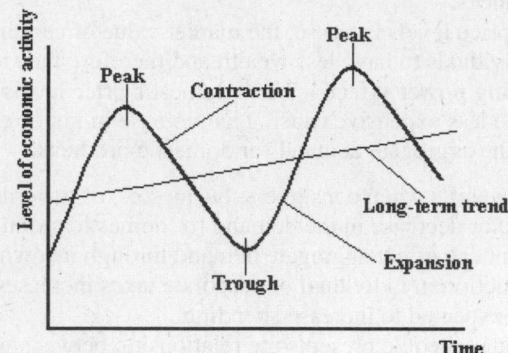

2. Economic contractions are characterized by a decrease in real gross domestic product (GDP) due to reduced spending. In a period of expansion, real GDP is increasing. At the peak real GDP generally surpasses potential GDP causing a scarcity of labor and materials. These shortages generally cause inflation.

3. **Unemployment and Output**—In most cases, there is a clear relationship between the change in unemployment and GDP growth, as explained by Okum's law. High output growth is generally associated with a decrease in the unemployment rate. This makes perfect sense because when output increases less.

4. A **recession** is a period of negative GDP growth. Usually, recession refers to at least two consecutive quarters of negative GDP growth. A deep and long-lasting recession is referred to as a **depression**.

5. There are a number of explanations for the occurrence of business cycles but they generally relate to the level of investment spending by businesses, or the level of consumer spending for durable goods (e.g., automobiles and appliances). The effects of a business cycle vary by business sector. For obvious reasons, heavy manufacturing is one of the sectors that is most affected. Such businesses are referred to as **cyclical** businesses because they perform better in periods of expansion and worse in periods of recession. Some business sectors are called **defensive** because they are affected little by business cycles and some may actually perform better in periods of recession.

6. Economists attempt to predict business cycles using economic indicators. Some indicators lead future economic trends, others coincide with economic trends, and still others lag economic trends. The Conference Board, a private research group, has developed the following list of indicators:

   a. Leading indicators

   - Average weekly hours, manufacturing
   - Average weekly initial claims for unemployment insurance
   - Manufacturer's new orders, consumer goods and materials
   - Vendor performance, slower deliveries diffusion index
   - Manufacturer's new orders, nondefense capital goods
   - Building permits, new private housing units
   - Stock prices, 500 common stocks
   - Money supply, M2
   - Interest rate spread, 10-year Treasury bonds less federal funds
   - Index of consumer expectations

   b. Coincident indicators

   - Employees on nonagricultural payrolls
   - Personal income less transfer payments
   - Industrial production
   - Manufacturing and trade sales

   c. Lagging indicators

   - Average duration of unemployment
   - Inventories to sales ratio, manufacturing and trade
   - Labor cost per unit of output, manufacturing
   - Average prime rate
   - Commercial and industrial loans
   - Consumer installment credit to personal income ratio
   - Consumer price index for services

7. **Investment.** Investment includes expenditures for residential construction, inventories, and plant and equipment. The most important determinant of business investment is expectations about profitability. Accordingly, the following factors affect investment spending:

   a. **The rate of technology growth.** In periods of high technology growth, firms tend to invest more because new products and innovations tend to be more profitable.

   b. **The real interest rate (nominal rate minus the inflation premium).** Lower real interest rates reduce the cost of investment.

   c. **The stock of capital goods.** If there are already enough capital goods in the economy to meet aggregate demand there is little incentive to invest.

   d. **Actions by the government.** Government fiscal policy can be used to stimulate investment spending (e.g., reductions in taxes, tax incentives, or increased government spending).

   e. **The acquisition and operating cost of capital goods.** As the purchase price or operating cost of plant and equipment decreases, firms will invest more.

   Investment spending is the most volatile portion of GDP. **Autonomous investment** includes expenditures made by businesses based on expected profitability that are independent of the level of national income. That is, they are constant regardless of whether the economy is expanding or contracting. **Induced investment** is incremental spending based on an increased level of economic activity.

8. **Accelerator theory.** Accelerator theory states that as economic activity increases, capital investment must be made to meet the level of increased demand. The increased capital investment in turn creates additional economic demand which further feeds the economic expansion.

D. Economic Measures

Previously we described several important measures of economic activity: GDP, GNP, etc. In this section we will describe other economic measures, such as rates of unemployment, inflation, and personal disposable income.

1. **Unemployment**

   The unemployment rate is the percent of the total labor force that is unemployed at a given time. Individuals may be unemployed because of frictional, structural, or cyclical causes.

   a. **Frictional unemployment** occurs because individuals are forced or voluntarily change jobs. At any point in time some individuals will be temporarily unemployed while they look for a job. New entrants into the workforce also fall into this category.

   b. **Structural unemployment** occurs due to changes in demand for products or services, or technological advances causing not as many individuals with a particular skill to be needed. Structural unemployment is reduced by retraining programs.

   c. **Cyclical unemployment** is caused by the condition in which real GDP is less than potential GDP. Therefore, such unemployment increases during recessions and decreases during expansions.

2. **Inflation**

   a. **Inflation** is the rate of increase in the price level of goods and services, usually measured on an annual basis.

   b. **Deflation** is a term used to describe a decrease in the price levels. While Japan has experienced deflation in prices recently, the US has not experienced an annual rate of decrease in price level since the 1930s. Deflation is very damaging because businesses do not want to borrow money and pay it back with money that has more purchasing power, and they do not want to invest in plant and equipment given that the cost of plant and equipment is declining.

   c. High rates of inflation are not good for the economy either. It generally causes economic activity to contract and redistributes income and wealth.

   d. A price index measures the prices of a basket of goods and/or services at a point in time in relation to the prices in a base period.

      (1) **The consumer price index** (CPI) measures the price that urban consumers paid for a fixed basket of goods and services in relation to the price of the same goods and services purchased in some base period.

      (2) **The producer price index** (PPI) measures the prices of finished goods and materials at the wholesale level.

      (3) **The GDP deflator** measures the prices for net exports, investment, government expenditures, and consumer spending. It is the most comprehensive measure of price level.

3. **Causes of inflation.** There are generally two causes for inflation that are commonly referred to as demand-pull and cost-push.

   a. **Demand-pull** inflation occurs when aggregate spending exceeds the economy's normal full-employment output capacity. It generally occurs at the peak of a business cycle and is characterized by real GDP exceeding potential GDP. Because labor is short companies bid up the price and inflation occurs.

b. **Cost-push** inflation occurs from an increase in the cost of producing goods and services. It is usually characterized by decreases in aggregate output and unemployment because consumers are not willing to pay the inflated prices.

There is an inverse relationship between inflation and unemployment. When the unemployment rate is low, inflation tends to increase. Inflation tends to decrease when the unemployment rate is high. This relationship is depicted by the **Phillips curve**.

4. **Personal disposable income** is the amount of income that individuals receive and have available to purchase goods and services. Personal disposable income has a significant effect on the economy because it is a large determinant of consumer demand. Personal disposable income is equal to **personal income** minus personal taxes.

5. **Interest rates.** Interest is the price paid for the use of money. Economists typically focus on the risk-free or pure rate of interest. In practice, interest rates are also affected by credit risk, maturity, and administrative costs. As with other commodities, interest rates are determined by demand and supply. The intersection of the demand and supply curves for money determines the equilibrium price or interest rate. On the demand side, firms borrow money to make investments in assets and will continue to borrow as long as investment return exceeds the interest rate at which the funds are borrowed. The supply of funds is affected by the past and current savings of individuals and firms, but it is also affected by the monetary policy of the government. Interest rates are often quoted as

a. **Real interest rate**—Interest rate in terms of goods. These rates are adjusted for inflation.

b. **Nominal interest rate**—Interest rate in terms of the nation's currency. These are the rates that are quoted by financial institutions and in the financial pages of newspapers. The difference between the real rate and the nominal rate is the inflation premium, which represents the expected inflation rate. The higher the expected inflation rate the larger the inflation premium. The interest rate charged to a particular business or individual will be higher than the nominal rate due to **credit risk,** which is the risk that the firm will not pay the interest or principal of the loan.

6. **Government budget surplus (deficit)**—The excess (deficit) of government taxes in relation to government transfer payments and purchases. To finance a deficit the government issues debt (e.g., Treasury bonds).

7. **Money.** Money in an economy serves three major purposes—a medium of exchange; a common denominator to measure prices, revenue, expenses, and income; and a store of value allowing individuals and firms to save. Economists use three basic measures of money, M_1, M_2, and M_3. M_1 includes only currency and demand deposits, M_2 is equal to M_1 plus savings accounts and small-time deposits (less \$100,000), and M_3 is equal to M_2 plus other (larger) time deposits. In regulating the economy the Federal Reserve focuses on M_2.

E. Monetary Policy

Depository institutions (banks, savings and loans, and credit unions, etc.) borrow savers' money and lend the money to consumers, businesses, and governments. The Federal Reserve (the US central bank), through its open market controls the actions of depository institutions and can affect the supply of money in the following ways:

1. **Reserve requirements.** When a bank lends money, it gives the borrower a check drawn on the bank itself. The Federal Reserve controls a bank's ability to issue check-writing deposits by imposing a reserve requirement on checking deposits. The institution must hold in reserve (much of which is on deposit at a Federal Reserve Bank) a certain percentage of their total checking deposits. The Federal Reserve can influence interest rates by changing the reserve requirements and therefore increasing or decreasing the supply of money. However, making changes in reserve requirements is rarely done.

2. **Open-market operations.** A more common instrument of monetary policy is open-market operations (by the **Federal Open-Market Committee**), which involves the purchase or sale of government securities using the Federal Reserve Bank deposits. If the Federal Reserve purchases government securities, they are able to increase the monetary supply and, therefore, put downward pressure on interest rates. When a central bank is purchasing government securities and expanding the money supply, it is called an **expansionary open-market operation**. If a central bank is selling government securities it is said to be pursuing a **contractionary open-market operation,** because this reduces the money supply.

3. **The discount rate.** When a bank has a reserve deficiency it may borrow funds from a Federal Reserve Bank. By setting the discount rate for such borrowing, the Federal Reserve can influence interest rates in the economy.

4. **Economic analysis.** In making its monetary decisions, the Federal Open-Market Committee does extensive economic analysis. In speeches by the members and when providing the basis for its decisions insights are provided into the state of the economy. This information also may have an effect on economic factors such as interest rates, business spending, and the stock prices.

5. The Federal Reserve uses monetary policy to attempt to sustain economic growth while keeping inflation under control. Monetary policy works on the principle that a decrease in interest rates will stimulate the economy, and an increase in interest rates will slow the economy. Lower interest rates tend to encourage consumer and business spending because finance charges are lower. Higher interest rates tend to discourage spending because finance charges are higher. It also encourages saving because the return on savings is higher.

6. The effects of monetary policy depend on their effects on the expectations of investors, businesses, and consumers. If monetary expansion leads the financial markets to revise their expectations about inflation, interest rates and output, the effect on output will be dramatic. On the other hand, if expectations remain unchanged, the effects will be minimal.

7. **Rational expectations** assume that investors, firms, and consumers develop expectations about inflation, interest rates, and output based on a consideration of all available information. This is contrasted to adaptive expectations in which investors, firms and consumers adjust their expectations based on new information. As an example, if they find that inflation is higher than expected, they adjust their expectation upward.

F. Fiscal Policy

Fiscal policy is government actions, such as taxes, subsidies, and government spending, designed to achieve economic goals. As an example, a reduction of taxes increases personal disposable income, which will serve to stimulate economic activity. The economy may also be stimulated through increased government spending. An increase in deficit, either due to an increase in government spending or to a decrease in taxes, is called a fiscal expansion. On the other hand, increases in taxes to reduce a deficit is called fiscal contraction.

1. **Taxes.** Taxes are levied by a government based on two general principles: (1) the ability to pay (e.g., progressive income taxes), and (2) derived benefit (e.g., gasoline taxes used to pay for roads). The following are the major types of taxes:

   a. **Income tax.** Income taxes are levied on taxable income. In the US the rate structure is generally progressive. However, there are a number of social and economic incentives built into the system that dilute its progressive structure.
   b. **Property tax.** Property taxes are levied based on wealth. They generally are progressive based on the value of the property.
   c. **Sales tax.** Sales taxes are levied based on the amount of income spent. Sales taxes are viewed as regressive because low-income individuals pay the same percentage rate as high-income individuals.
   d. **Wage taxes.** The most significant wage tax in the US is the social security tax. This tax is borne both directly (the employee's share) and indirectly (the employer's share) by employees because without the tax, wages would be higher.
   e. **Value-added tax.** A tax commonly used in other industrial nations is the value-added tax (VAT). Value-added taxes are levied on the increase in value of each product as it proceeds through production and distribution processes. Ultimately, the tax is paid by the final consumer. The VAT is thought to encourage savings because it taxes consumption instead of earnings.

2. Both monetary and fiscal policy take time to have the desired effects for a number of reasons, including

   a. Consumers take time to adjust their consumption based on changes in personal disposal income
   b. Firms take time to adjust investment based on changes in sales
   c. Firms take time to adjust spending based on changes in interest rates
   d. Firms take time to adjust production based on changes in sales

3. Fiscal policies can have a large effect on the size of budget deficits. In the long and medium run, a budget deficit reduction is likely to be beneficial to the economy. Lower budget deficits usually mean more savings and investment, and therefore, more output. In the short run, a reduction in budget deficit leads to reductions in spending and therefore less output.

G. Economic Theories

1. **Classical economic theory**—This theory holds that market equilibrium will eventually result in full employment over the long run without government intervention. This theory does not support the use of fiscal policy to stimulate the economy.
2. **Keynesian theory**—This theory holds that the economy does not necessarily move towards full employment on its own. It focuses on the use of fiscal policy (e.g., reductions in taxes and government spending) to stimulate the economy.
3. **Monetarist theory**—This theory holds that fiscal policy is too crude a tool for control of the economy. It focuses on the use of monetary policy to control economic growth.
4. **Supply-side theory**—This theory holds that bolstering an economy's ability to supply more goods is the most effective way to stimulate growth. A decrease in taxes (especially for businesses and individuals with high income) increases employment, savings, and investments and is an effective way to stimulate the economy. The tax revenue lost from the reduction in taxes is more than offset by the increase in taxes from increased economic activity. However, this predicted effect only occurs when rates are too high. The **Laffer Curve** attempts to explain how consumers react to changes in rates of income tax. The curve illustrates that if taxes are already too low decreasing them will result in less tax revenue.

5. **Neo-Keynesian theory**—This theory combines Keynesian and monetarist theories. It focuses on using a combination of fiscal and monetary policy to stimulate the economy and control inflation.

> **NOW REVIEW MULTIPLE-CHOICE QUESTIONS 49 THROUGH 80 IN VOLUME 2**

H. The Global Economy and International Trade

Economic globalization refers to the increasing economic interdependence of national economies across the world through a rapid increase in cross-border movement of goods, service, technology and capital. It has led to a single world market in which developed economies have integrated with less developed countries by means of foreign direct investment, the reduction of trade barriers, and the modernization of the developing countries. The comparative advantages of natural resources or low-cost labor attract businesses and capital to developing (emerging) economies.

International trade is very important to almost every business. If a country has an **absolute advantage** (e.g., low-cost labor, technology) in the production of a particular good, there is an incentive for that country to produce more than its citizens need to export the good to countries with higher production costs. This is especially true if it also has a comparative advantage to producing the good. A **comparative advantage** means that country has no alternate uses of its resources that would involve a higher return (i.e., the **opportunity costs** are less). In the long term, production of specific goods and services will migrate to countries that have a **comparative advantage**. By exploiting its comparative advantages and exporting goods and services, a nation can import the goods for which it has a comparative disadvantage. In this manner all nations will be better off.

Michael Porter developed a "diamond of national advantage" to explain how a country can create new advanced factor endowments that contribute to the country's comparative advantage. The four points of the diamond can be described as

- **Factor Conditions**—A country can create its own important factors such as skilled resources and technology infrastructure. The stock of factors at a given time is less important than the country's potential. A country can overcome shortages of factors through innovation.
- **Demand Conditions**—A country has a comparative advantage for a particular product when it has a strong domestic market because the firms in the country devote more attention to the product than in other countries.
- **Related and Supporting Industries**—A country has a comparative advantage for a product when the supporting industries are strong because of the cost effective and innovative inputs that result.
- **Firm Strategy, Structure, and Rivalry**—Different types of comparative advantages accrue from different business organizational structures (e.g., hierarchal, matrix, extended family structures). Also, intense rivalry of an industry in a country tends to lead to a competitive advantage for that country's industry globally.

1. **Obstacles to free trade.** Even though trade can be a source of major gains, many nations restrict free trade by various means, for example by imposing tariffs and quotas. That is, they engage in protectionism. An import **tariff** is a tax on an imported product. Tariffs are designed to discourage the consumption of goods from foreign companies or to raise revenue, or both. A trigger price mechanism automatically imposes a tariff barrier against cheap imports by imposing a duty on all imports below a trigger price. An import **quota** is a restriction on the amount of a good that may be imported during a period. Finally, an **embargo** is a total ban on the importation of specific goods.

An exporting country may elect to establish a **voluntary export restraint** to limit the quality of goods that can be exported to appease importing countries and keep them from imposing stiffer import restrictions.

Another barrier to trade that a country may impose is a **foreign-exchange control**. A foreign exchange control is a control imposed by a government on the purchase or sale of foreign currencies by residents, or on the purchase or sale of local currency by nonresidents. Examples of such controls include

   a. Banning the use of foreign currency in the country.
   b. Banning possession of foreign currency by citizens.
   c. Restricting currency exchange to government-approved exchangers.
   d. Fixed exchange rates.

Trade restrictions are advocated by labor unions and firms making products that are more inexpensively produced in other nations. Thus, trade restrictions generally impose a burden on society as a whole because they reduce the availability of goods and increase their prices. Arguments in favor of trade restrictions include

   a. To protect domestic labor against inexpensive foreign labor
   b. To reduce domestic unemployment
   c. To protect young or infant industries
   d. To protect industries important to the nation's defense

Other arguments against unrestricted trade include the fact that the businesses of developed nations are disadvantaged by social laws in their countries that do not exist in developing countries (e.g., laws restricting pollution, child labor, minimum wage, etc.), and by disproportionate taxing of domestic manufacturing.

Trade restrictions in the US are advocated by labor and firms in the US in industries that have lost their competitive advantage, such as producers of shoes, textiles, and steel. Some firms and industries in the US have been able to regain their competitive advantage through the introduction of new technology.

Most of the arguments for trade restrictions are not valid. Trade restrictions generally have negative effects in that economic activity is inappropriately shifted to less-productive protected industries, resulting in a decline in total world output.

2. **Dumping.** A **dumping** pricing policy is a form of predatory pricing in which a manufacturer in one country exports a product at a price that is lower than the price charged in its home market or below the company's cost of production. Under the World Trade Organization (WTO) Agreement, dumping is condemned (not prohibited) if it causes material injury to a domestic industry in the importing country. US firms can file an antidumping petition with the International Trade Organization when products are being sold at less than "fair value," as defined by Department of Commerce regulations. If the firm's case is proved, antidumping duties may be imposed on goods imported from the dumper's country.

3. **Export subsidies** are payments made by a government to encourage the production and export of specific products. Such payments may be made in various ways, including special tax benefits. **Countervailing duties** are duties imposed by an importing country to neutralize the negative effects of export subsidies.

4. The **World Trade Organization (WTO)** is an organization of countries designed to supervise and liberalize trade among participating countries. It facilitates trade agreements among participants and provides a resolution process to enforce the agreements. Under the WTO provisions, members afford all other members favored nation status, which means a member country will not establish trade barriers that discriminate against other members.

5. **North American Free Trade Agreement (NAFTA)**

   a. NAFTA is a free trade agreement between the countries of Canada, Mexico, and the US. It was adopted by the US Congress in 1993. NAFTA offers a number of advantages for US businesses including

      (1) The ability to take advantage of the lower labor costs in Mexico for such functions as manufacturing and assembly.
      (2) The opening of new markets for goods of US industries that have a comparative advantage, such as technology.

   b. Disadvantages to US businesses and labor markets include

      (1) Some US industries, such as producers of shoes and apparel, are concerned that the firms will be hurt by the availability of less expensive products from Mexico.
      (2) Certain jobs in the US will be lost because of the availability of lower-cost labor in Mexico combined with more lax environmental laws and regulations.

6. **Balance of payments.** The balance of payments is an account summary of a nation's transactions with other nations. It has three major sections: the current account, the capital account, and the official reserve account.

   a. **Current account**—Shows the flow of goods and services and government grants for a period of time.

      (1) The **balance of trade** for a period is the difference between the total goods exported and the total goods imported.
      (2) The **balance on goods and services** is the difference between the total value of goods and services exported and the total value of goods and services imported.
      (3) When a nation exports more than it imports a **trade surplus** occurs.
      (4) When a nation imports more than it exports a **trade deficit** occurs.

   b. **Capital account**—Shows the flow of investments in fixed and financial assets for a period of time.
   c. The **balance of payments** surplus or deficit is the amount that nets the current and capital accounts. In other words, when the sum of the outflows exceeds the inflows a deficit in balance of payment occurs. The deficit is settled in currency of other nations, or by an increase in the holdings of the nation's currency by other nations. A deficit is an unfavorable balance of payments while a surplus is a favorable balance of payments.
   d. **Official reserve account**—Shows the changes in the nation's reserves (e.g., gold and foreign currency).

7. **The International Monetary Fund (IMF)** has a pool of currencies from which member countries can borrow to meet short-term deficits in balance of payments.

8. The **G-20** is a group of finance ministers and central bank governors from 20 economies (the European Union and 19 countries). It studies, reviews, and promotes discussion of policy issues affecting global financial stability, and seeks to address issues that go beyond the responsibilities of its individual members.

9. The **European Union (EU)** is an economic and political union of 27 countries primarily in Europe. The EU has developed a single market through a standardized system of laws that apply to all member countries. An economic and monetary union known as the **eurozone** (officially the euro area) is composed of 17 member countries that use the euro currency. The European Central Bank establishes monetary policy for the members of the eurozone.

I. Foreign Exchange Rates

Firms that do business internationally must be concerned with exchange rates, which are the relationships among the values of currencies. For example, a US firm selling products in Europe is very interested in the relationship of the euro to the US dollar.

1. **Factors influencing exchange rates.** As with any other market, the exchange rate between two currencies is determined by the supply of, and the demand for, those currencies. However, these rates are also subject to intervention by the central banks of countries. Therefore, exchange rates are often said to be determined by **managed float**. In general, the following factors will affect the exchange rate of a particular currency:

    a. **Inflation.** Inflation tends to deflate the value of a currency because holding the currency results in reduced purchasing power.

    b. **Interest rates.** If interest returns in a particular country are higher relative to other countries, individuals and companies will be enticed to invest in that country. As a result there will be increased demand for the country's currency.

    c. **Balance of payments.** Balance of payments is used to refer to a system of accounts that catalogs the flow of goods between the residents of two countries. If country X is a net exporter of goods and therefore has a surplus balance of trade, countries purchasing the goods must use country X's currency. This increases the demand for the currency and therefore its relative value.

    d. **Government intervention.** Through intervention (e.g., buying or selling the currency in the foreign exchange markets), the central bank of a country may support or depress the value of its currency.

    e. **Other factors.** Other factors that may affect exchange rates are political and economic stability, extended stock market rallies, or significant declines in the demand for major exports.

2. The **exchange rate regime** is the way a country manages its currency in respect to currencies of other countries. The basic types of exchange rate regimes include

    a. **Floating exchange rate**—One in which the exchange rate is dictated by market factors as described previously.

    b. **Pegged exchange rate**—One in which the country's central bank keeps the rate from deviating too far from a target band or value.

    c. **Fixed exchange rate**—One in which the rate is tied to the value of another currency, such as the US dollar or the euro.

    d. **Managed exchange rate**—One in which the country's central bank attempts to control the movement in currency value.

3. **Spot rates and forward rates.** The spot rate for a currency is the exchange rate of the currency for immediate delivery. On the other hand, the forward rate is the exchange rate for a currency for future delivery. For example, a forward contract might obligate a company to purchase or sell euros at a specific exchange rate three months hence. The difference between the spot rate and the forward rate is referred to as the discount or premium. If the forward rate is less (greater) than the spot rate, the market believes that the value of the currency is going to decline (increase).

EXAMPLE

Assume that a multinational company sells products to a French company for a receivable payable in 60 days in the amount of 10,000 euros. If at the time of the sale the exchange rate is 1.25 US dollars to the euro, the sale is equal to $12,500 (1.25 × 10,000). If the euro depreciates by 2% against the US dollar in the 60-day period between the sale and collection, the firm has experienced a loss. The 2% depreciation would mean that the new exchange rate is 1.225 (1.25 × 98%) euros to the US dollar. Therefore, the firm has lost $12,500 − $12,250 (1.225 × 10,000) = $250.

---

4. The forward premium or discount of one currency with respect to another is calculated using the following formula:

$$\frac{\text{Forward rate} - \text{Spot rate}}{\text{Spot rate}} \times \frac{\text{Month (or days) in year}}{\text{Months (or days) in forward period}}$$

> **EXAMPLE**
>
> Assume the 180-day forward rate for the British Pound is $1.612 and the spot rate is $1.610. The forward premium is calculated to be 0.5% {[($1.612 – $1.610) / $1.60] × (360 days/180 days)}. Note that the result is a premium because the forward rate is higher than the spot rate.

5. The foreign exchange risk for a multinational company is divided into two types: **translation (accounting) risk** and **transaction risk**. Translation risk is the exposure that a multinational company has because its financial statements must be converted to its functional currency.

6. Transaction risk relates to the possibility of gains and losses resulting from income transactions occurring during the year. The example above involving the sale of goods for a receivable in euros illustrates transaction risk. Transaction risk can cause volatility in reported earnings that motivates management to use strategies to minimize the company's exposure. Companies can use various forms of contracts to hedge foreign currency risk, including

   a. **Options**—Allow, but do not require, the holder to buy (call) or sell (put) a specific or standard commodity or financial instrument, at a specified price during a specified period of time (American option) or at a specified date (European option).

   b. **Forwards**—Negotiated contracts to purchase and sell a specific quantity of a financial instrument, foreign currency, or commodity at a price specified at origination of the contract, with delivery and payment at a specified future date.

> **EXAMPLE**
>
> Assume that Company X has agreed to deliver 20,000 units of product in six months to a Japanese company who will pay for the product in yen. To mitigate the risk of losses from devaluation of the yen, Company X could enter into a forward contract to sell the yen for delivery in six months. This contract in effect locks in the price for the sale in terms of US dollars. Alternatively, Company X could purchase a put option allowing them to put the yen up for sale at a specific price in six months.

   c. **Futures**—Forward-based standardized contracts to take delivery of a specified financial instrument, foreign currency, or commodity at a specified future date or during a specified period generally at the then-market price.

   d. **Currency swaps**—Forward-based contracts in which two parties agree to exchange an obligation to pay cash flows in one currency for an obligation to pay in another currency.

   e. **Money market hedge**—A second way to eliminate the transaction risk described in b. is to borrow money in yen when the agreement is executed. This strategy immediately converts the yen to US dollars. Then, when the yen are collected from the sale, the loan can be repaid, resulting in no foreign exchange loss or gain over the six-month period.

J. Foreign Investment

1. Foreign direct investments are usually quite large and many are exposed to **political risk**. Repatriation (transfer) of a foreign subsidiary's profits may be blocked. In the extreme case a foreign government may even expropriate (take) the firm's assets. Strategies to reduce risk include the use of joint ventures, financing with local-country capital, and the purchase of insurance.

2. **Transfer pricing.** Transfer pricing is the price at which services or products are bought and sold across international borders between related parties. As an example, if a US parent company purchases products from its French subsidiary, a transfer price must be established for the products. Because the transfer price affects the parent and subsidiary's net income, it affects the taxes that the firm pays in the US and France. Multinational companies can minimize their overall tax burden by using transfer prices to minimize net income in jurisdictions with higher income tax rates, and maximizing net income in jurisdictions with lower income tax rates. However, many governments have established tax regulations that are designed to help ensure that transfer prices estimate market prices.

NOW REVIEW MULTIPLE-CHOICE QUESTIONS 81 THROUGH 99 IN VOLUME 2

THE EFFECTS OF THE GLOBAL ECONOMIC ENVIRONMENT ON STRATEGY

A firm's objectives are the overall plans for the firm as defined by management. Management attempts to achieve these objectives by developing strategies (operational actions). However, achieving management's objectives is always subject to business risks faced by the firm. **Business risks** are conditions that threaten management's ability to execute strategies and achieve the firm's objectives. A comprehensive understanding of the firm's internal and external environments is necessary for management to understand the firm's present condition and its business risks. This understanding includes comprehension of both the general and industry environments.

A. The **general environment** includes the following factors:

- Economic—Inflation rates, interest rates, budget deficits, personal saving rate, gross domestic product, etc.
- Demographic—Population size, workforce, ethnic mix, income distribution, geographic distribution, etc.
- Political and legal—Antitrust laws, tax laws, deregulation philosophies, etc.
- Sociocultural—Workforce diversity, environmental concerns, shifts in consumer preferences, etc.
- Technological segment—Societal innovations in technology and products, focus of the economy on research and development, etc.
- Global—Important global political events, developments in global markets, etc.

The general aspects of the environment are out of the control of management of the firm. Management must adapt to its general environment.

B. The **industry environment** is the set of factors that influence the firm's competitive actions. Michael Porter developed a model for industry analyses that focuses on five forces: (1) competitors, (2) potential entrants into the market, (3) equivalent products, (4) bargaining power of customers, and (5) bargaining power of input suppliers.[1]

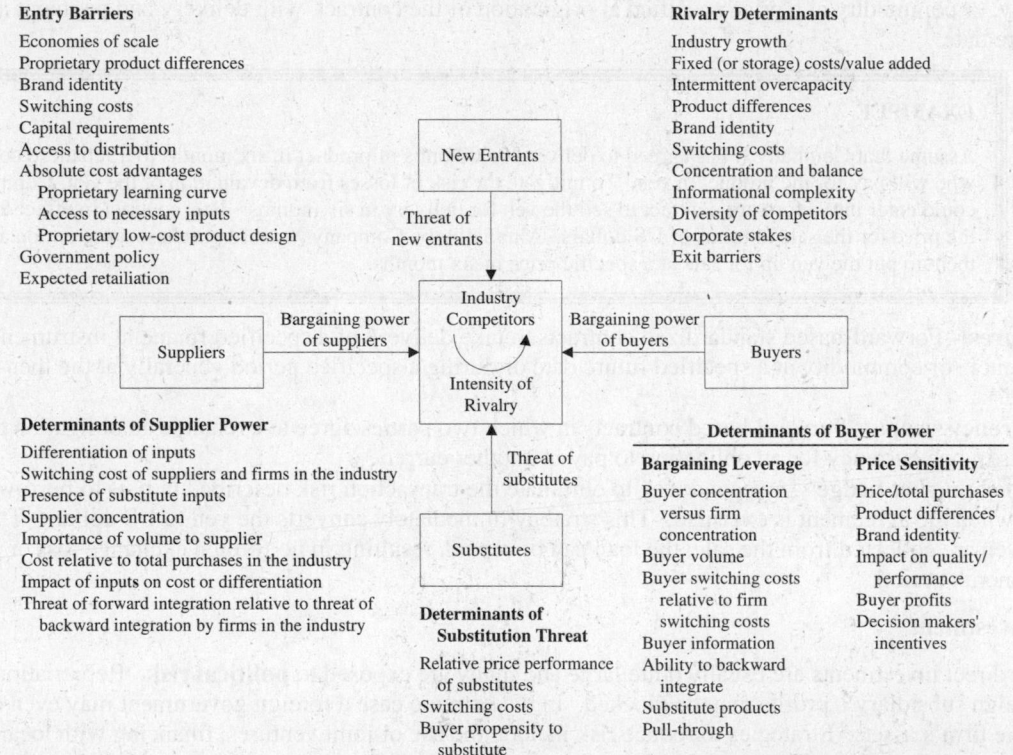

1. The industry environment directly affects the firm and the types of strategies it must develop to compete. It is most relevant to the firm's profit potential. Management attempts to position the firm where it can influence the industry factors and successfully defend against their influence. **Remember, management has little or no control over the general environment factors but through its actions may have significant influence over industry factors.** Generally, the larger the firm's market share the more influence it can have on its industry environment.

2. Since firms must make strategic decisions that involve long-term commitments (e.g., investments in technology, plant, etc.), management must not only deal with the current environment, it must forecast the future. Effective management must analyze and forecast the general environment to identify opportunities and threats to the firm. In doing so, the following techniques are used:

   a. **Scanning**—A study of all segments in the general environment. The objective is to predict the effects of the general environment on the firm's industry. Management can use this information to modify its strategies and operating plans. Scanning of the general environment is critical to firms in volatile industries. Sources of in-

---

[1] M. Porter, *Competitive Strategy*, New York Free Press (1980).

formation for scanning include trade publications, newspapers, business publications, public polls, government publications, etc.

b. **Monitoring**—A study of environmental changes identified by scanning to spot important trends. As an example, the trend in aging of the population in this country would definitely be important to firms that provide services to retired individuals. Effective monitoring involves identifying the firm's major stakeholders (e.g., customers, investors, employees, etc.).

c. **Forecasting**—Developing probable projections of what might happen and its timing. As an example, management might attempt to forecast changes in personal disposable income or the timing of introduction of a major technological development.

d. **Assessing**—Determining changes in the firm's strategy that are necessary as a result of the information obtained from scanning, monitoring, and forecasting. It is the process of evaluating the implications of changes in the general environment on the firm.

C. Industry Analysis

1. An industry is a group of firms that produce products that are substitutes or close substitutes. Industries are often classified by their fundamental economics as perfect competition, pure monopoly, monopolistic competition, and oligopoly.

   a. **Perfect (Pure) competition**

      (1) An industry is perfectly competitive if

         (a) It is composed of a large number of sellers, each of which are too small to affect the price of the product or service
         (b) The firms sell a virtually identical product
         (c) Firms can enter or leave the market easily (i.e., no barriers to entry)

      There are few perfectly competitive markets; common examples include the commodity markets, such as markets for wheat, soybeans, and corn.

      (2) In this market, the **firm's demand curve** is perfectly elastic (horizontal). The firm can sell as many goods as it can produce at the equilibrium price but no goods at a higher price. The firm is a price taker. The **market demand curve** is downwards sloping. Therefore, demand will increase if all suppliers lower prices and will decrease if all suppliers raise their prices.

      (3) In a perfectly competitive market a firm will continue to produce and sell products until the margin cost is greater than marginal revenue.

      (4) Theoretically, no economic profits can be generated in the long run. The price will reflect the costs plus the normal profit of the most efficient producers.

      (5) In a perfectly competitive market there is no product differentiation and the key to being successful is being the lowest cost producer in the marketplace. Innovation is restricted to attempting to make production, distribution, and sales processes more efficient.

   b. **Pure monopoly**

      (1) A pure monopoly is a market in which there is a single seller of a product or service for which there are no close substitutes. A monopoly may exist for one or more of the following reasons:

         (a) Increasing returns to scale
         (b) Control over the supply of raw materials
         (c) Patents (e.g., a drug manufacturer)
         (d) Government franchise (e.g., a public utility)

      (2) Monopolies that exist when economic or technical conditions permit only one efficient supplier are called **natural monopolies.**

      (3) The monopolist sets the price for the product (unless it is set by regulation). The demand curve for the firm is negatively sloping; the company must reduce price to sell more output. The firm will continue to produce and sell products as long as the marginal revenue is greater than average variable cost.

      (4) Entry barriers make it possible for the firm to make economic profit in the long run.

      (5) In pure monopoly, the company has little market incentive to innovate or control costs. The company has no market control on the price it charges. As a result pure monopolies are generally subject to government regulation. Price boards generally review the company's prices and costs. From a strategic standpoint monopolistic firms want to create a positive image with the public to forestall additional regulation. Therefore any advertising expenditures they incur tend to be for public relations. These firms also spend a lot of effort attempting to influence laws and regulations. They can increase total revenue if they can engage in price discrimination by market segment (e.g., charging business customers more than individual customers).

(6) The US government has passed legislation to discourage the development of monopolies because prices are higher and output less in such markets as compared to competitive markets. These laws include the Sherman Act of 1890, the Clayton Act of 1914, the Robinson-Patman Act of 1936, and the Celler-Kefauver Anti-Merger Act of 1950.

c. **Monopolistic competition**

(1) Monopolistic competition is characterized by many firms selling a differentiated product or service. The differentiation may be real or only created by advertising, and there is relatively easy entry to the market but not as easy as in a perfectly competitive market. This type of market is prevalent in retailing, including the markets for groceries, detergents, and breakfast cereals.

(2) The demand curve in a monopolistic competitive market is negatively sloped and firms tend to produce and sell products until the marginal revenue is less than average variable cost. Therefore, goods tend to be priced somewhat higher than in a perfectly competitive market but less than in a monopoly. Also, there tends to be underproduction as compared to a perfectly competitive market.

(3) The strategies of firms in monopolistic competitive markets tend to focus on product or service innovation. Companies may spend heavily on product development. Customer relations and advertising necessarily are important to firm strategies.

d. **Oligopoly**

(1) Oligopoly is a form of market characterized by significant barriers to entry. As a result there are few (generally large) sellers of a product. Because there are few sellers the actions of one affect the others. An example of an oligopoly is the automobile industry. Other examples are found in the production of steel, aluminum, cigarettes, personal computers, and many electrical appliances.

(2) Oligopolists often attempt to engage in nonprice competition (e.g., by product differentiation or providing high levels of service). However, during economic downturns and periods of overcapacity, price competition in an oligopolistic market can turn fierce.

(3) The kinked-demand-curve model seeks to explain the price rigidity in oligopolistic markets. This model holds that the demand curve is kinked down at the market price because other oligopolists will not match price increases but will match price decreases. Generally, in the oligopolistic market there is a price leader that determines the pricing policy for the other producers.

(4) If left unregulated, ologopolists tend to establish **cartels** that engage in price fixing. Regulations in the US prohibit collusion by firms to set prices.

2. The competitive market of the firm determines the intensity of competition and threats to new entrants to the industry. However, the firm must also consider the threat of substitute products, bargaining power of suppliers, and bargaining power of its customers.

3. **Threat of substitute products.** Substitute products are goods or services from outside a given industry that perform similar functions. As an example, plastic containers constrain the price of glass containers.

4. **Bargaining power of suppliers.**

a. The power of suppliers affects a firm's ability to negotiate price or quality concessions. When suppliers have a good deal of power, they will be able to increase prices, and the firm purchasing those supplies may or may not be able to pass the cost on to its customers. Suppliers have power, for example, when the market is dominated by a few large companies, the industry firms are not significant customers for suppliers, or there are large costs to switching to another supplier.

b. The supplier market also includes the firm's labor market. The firm's ability to influence wage rate will depend on the other firms that are competing for the labor, and actions of the government and labor unions.

c. A **monopsony** is a market where only one buyer exists for all sellers. A monopsonist has monopoly power in the purchase of a resource. The marginal cost curve for a monopsonist is different from other firms' in that each time it purchases an additional unit of product or labor it increases the cost of all of the resource.

5. **Bargaining power of customers.** The power of customers determines the firm's ability to increase prices or lower quality of their products. When customers are powerful, the firm has difficulty passing cost increase on to them. Therefore the firm must concentrate on controlling costs. Customers are powerful, for example, when they purchase a large percentage of the industry output, they could switch to another product with little cost, the industry's products are standardized and the customers pose a threat to integrate backward into the firm's market.

6. **Techniques for industry analysis.** Firms use a variety of techniques to analyze their industries. In this section we will describe three of those techniques, competitor analysis, price elasticity analysis, and target market analysis.

a. **Competitor analysis.** In formulating strategy, management must consider the strategies of the firm's competitors. Competitor analysis is of vital importance to devising strategies in concentrated industries. Competitor analysis involves two major activities: (1) gathering information about competitors' capabilities, objectives, strategies, and assumptions (competitor intelligence), and (2) using the information to understand the competitors' behavior. Management uses a number of sources of information for competitor analysis including the competitor's

- Annual reports and SEC filings
- Interviews with analysts
- Press releases

However, management must also consider information derived from the actions of the competitor such as the following:

- Research and development projects
- Capital investments
- Promotional campaigns
- Strategic partnerships
- Mergers and acquisitions
- Hiring practices

In a competitor analysis, management seeks to understand

- What are the competitor's objectives?
- What can and is the competitor doing based on its current strategy?
- What does the competitor assume about the industry?
- What are the competitor's strengths and weaknesses?

Information from the analysis of the competitor's objectives, assumptions, strategy and capabilities can be developed into a **response profile** of possible actions that may be taken by the competitor under varying circumstances. This will allow management to anticipate or influence the competitor's actions to the firm's advantage.

b. **Price elasticity analysis.** Recall that the price elasticity of demand measures the effect of a change in price on the demand for the product. It is calculated with the following equation:

$$E_D = \frac{\text{Change in quantity demanded}}{\text{Average quantity}} \div \frac{\text{Change in price}}{\text{Average price}}$$

In order to develop a pricing strategy, management may perform price elasticity analysis of product or service. By observing the effects of price changes management can obtain a better understanding of the relationship. Regression analysis may be used to perform a more sophisticated analysis.

EXAMPLE

Assume that Carlton Corp. manufactures Product X, a commodity-type product. Management is attempting to understand the price elasticity of the product to assist in planning production levels. Management has collected the following historical data regarding the price and aggregate demand for Product X. The prices have been price-level adjusted to take out the effects of inflation.

Date	Price	Quantity Sold	Date	Price	Quantity Sold
1/1/X1	$5.00	10,000	3/31/X2	$4.00	14,500
3/31/X1	4.50	13,000	6/30/X2	4.25	13,000
6/30/X1	4.00	15,000	9/30/X2	5.00	10,500
9/30/X1	5.50	9,000	1/1/X3	5.50	9,000
1/1/X2	5.25	10,000	3/31/X3	6.00	7,500

Management decides to use regression analysis on a spreadsheet program to assist with estimating the relationship between price and quantity demanded. The results of the analysis are illustrated below.

	A	B	C	D	E	F	G
1	**SUMMARY OUTPUT**						
2							
3							
4	**Regression Statistics**						
5	Multiple R	0.986247					
6	R Square	0.972684					
7	Adjusted R						
8	Square	0.969269					
9	Standard Error	447.0297					
10	Observations	10					
11							
12	**ANOVA**						
13		df	SS	MS	F	Significance F	
14	Regression	1	56926316	56926316	284.8658	1.54E-07	
15	Residual	8	1598684	199835.5			
16	Total	9	58525000				
17							
18		Coefficients	Standard error	t Stat	P-value	Lower 95%	Upper 95%
19	Intercept	29030.7	1068.801	27.16194	3.64E-09	26566.04	31495.36
20	X variable 1	-3649.12	216.2063	-16.878	1.54E-07	-4147.7	-3150.55

As expected, the results indicate that there is a very significant relationship between price and aggregate demand for the product. The adjusted R Squared indicates that about 97% of the variance in quantity demanded is explained by price. The equation for simple regression is as follows:

$$y = a + bx$$

Where

      y = the dependent variable—in this case demand volume
      a = the y-axis intercept
      b = the slope of the line
      x = the independent variable—in this case price

Assuming that management wants to predict aggregate demand if the price was set at $5.75, we can use the equation that was developed from the analysis. Under the column Coefficients we see Intercept of 29030.7 and X variable 1 (price) of 3649.12. The equation to predict aggregate demand would be

Demand	=	a + (b)Price
	=	29030.7 + (-3649.12 × Price)
	=	29030.7 + (-3649.12 × 5.75)
	=	8,048

At a price of $5.75, the firm should expect aggregate demand to be about 8,048. Notice that the slope of the line (b) is negative indicating a negative relationship between demand and price, which is what we would expect. Regression analysis is explained in detail in Module 47.

D. Strategic Planning

      Strategic planning involves identifying an organization's long-term goals and determining the best approaches to achieving those goals. To facilitate strategic planning an organization may establish a planning department, committee, or planning officer. Strategic planning should include involvement from decision makers at all company levels—the corporate, business, and functional levels. It is important to get as many stakeholders as possible involved in the process. Because strategic decisions have a huge impact on the company and require large commitments of financial resources, top management must approve and embrace the strategic plan.

      Strategic planning begins with the development or review of the organization's mission. The **mission** sets forth the purpose of the organization, including its distinguishing characteristics. The organization may also develop a **vision** which sets forth where the organization would like to be in the future.

      Next, a situational analysis will be performed which involves collection and evaluation of past and present economical, political, social, and technology data (an **environmental scan**) to (1) identify internal and external forces that may affect the organization's performance and choice of strategies, and (2) to assess the organization's strengths, weaknesses, opportunities, and threats (a **SWOT analysis**).

The SWOT analysis is then used to develop strategies to minimize risks and take advantage of major opportunities. This analysis is usually displayed in a SWOT matrix.

SWOT Matrix

	Strengths	**Weaknesses**
Opportunities For example, unfilled customer need, new technologies, etc.	*Strength-opportunity strategies* Strategies to pursue opportunities that are a good fit for the firm's strengths.	*Weakness-opportunity strategies* Strategies to overcome weaknesses to pursue opportunities.
Threats For example, shifts in consumer tastes away from the firm's product, new regulations, etc.	*Strength-threat strategies* Strategies to use strengths to overcome threats.	*Weakness-threat strategies* Defensive strategies to prevent the firm's weaknesses from making it highly vulnerable to threats.

After performing the situational analysis, specific strategies will be developed consistent with the mission and vision of the organization. Then, the strategies will be implemented within the organization. Effective implementation requires communication of the strategies throughout the organization and establishment of incentives and performance expectations that are consistent with the strategies. Finally, controls and outcome measures should be developed and monitored to provide feedback on whether the strategies are effectively implemented and achieving the desired results.

1. **Generic Business Strategies.** Generic business strategies are generally classified as being product differentiation or cost leadership. These two strategies have been broken down by Michael Porter into industry wide or market segment strategy as illustrated below.

Target Scope	**Advantage**	
	Low Cost	Product Uniqueness
Broad (Industry-Wide)	Cost Leadership Strategy	Differentiation Strategy
Narrow (Market Segment)	Focus Strategy (low cost)	Focus Strategy (differentiation)

a. **Product differentiation.** Product differentiation involves development of a unique product to make it more attractive to the target market or to differentiate it from competitors' products. Products may be differentiated in the following ways:

(1) Physical characteristics (e.g., aesthetics, durability, reliability, performance, serviceability, features, etc.)
(2) Perceived differences (e.g., advertising, brand name, etc.)
(3) Support service differences (e.g., exchange policies, assistance, after-sale support, etc.)

By differentiating its products, the firm may be able to charge higher prices than its competitors or higher prices for the same products sold in different market segments.

b. **Cost leadership.** Striving for cost leadership fundamentally involves focusing on reducing the costs and time to produce, sell, and distribute a product or service. A number of techniques are used to attempt to reduce costs and time, including process reengineering, lean manufacturing (production), supply chain management, strategic alliances, and outsourcing.

(1) **Process reengineering** involves a critical evaluation and major redesign of existing processes to achieve breakthrough improvements in performance. Process reengineering differs from total quality management (TQM) in that TQM involves gradual improvement of processes, while reengineering often involves radical redesign and drastic improvement in processes. Many of the significant improvements in processes over the last few years have been facilitated with innovations in information technology.

(2) **Lean manufacturing** is a management technique that involves the identification and elimination of all types of waste in the production function. Operations are reviewed for those components, processes, or products that add cost rather than value. A basic premise underlying lean manufacturing is by focusing on improving design, increasing flexibility, and reducing time, defects, and inventory, costs can be minimized.

(3) **Supply chain management.**

(a) The term supply chain describes the flow of goods, services, and information from basic raw materials through the manufacturing and distribution process to delivery of the product to the consumer, regardless of whether those activities occur in one or many firms.

NOTE: A supply chain is illustrated below.

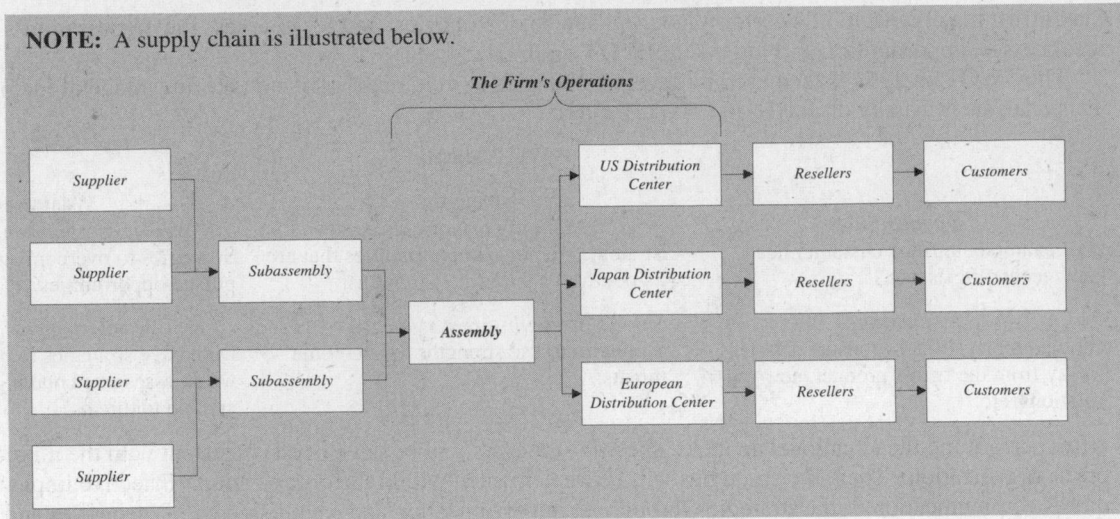

As shown, the firm's operations include only the assembly and distribution processes. Other firms supply raw materials, perform subassembly, and are the resellers of the final product. In viewing the supply chain, it is critical to go beyond the firm's immediate suppliers and customers to encompass the entire chain.

(b) To improve operations and manage the relationships with their suppliers many firms use a process known as **supply chain management**. A key aspect of supply chain management is the sharing of key information from the point of sale to the final consumer back to the manufacturer, the manufacturer's suppliers, and the suppliers' suppliers. As an example, if a manufacturer/distributor shares its sales forecasts with its suppliers and they in turn share their sales forecasts with their suppliers, the need for inventories for all firms is significantly decreased. The manufacturer/distributor, for example, needs far less raw materials inventory than normally would be the case because its suppliers are aware of the manufacture's projected needs and is prepared to have the materials available when needed. Specialized software facilitates this process of information sharing along the supply chain network.

(c) Supply chain management also focuses on improving processes to reduce time, defects, and costs all along the supply chain. By focusing on the entire supply chain, management may evaluate the full cost of inefficient processes, defective materials, and inaccurate forecasts of sales.

(d) However, supply chain management presents the company with a number of problems and risks including those arising from

1] Incompatible information systems
2] Refusal of some companies to share information
3] Failure of suppliers or customers to meet their obligations

2. **Target market analysis.**

a. In implementing a generic strategy a firm will often use target market analysis. A firm's target market is a market in which the firm actually sells or plans to sell its product or services. A thorough understanding of the market is key to accurate sales forecasts. Just defining the market in geographic terms is not enough. Management should perform target market analysis to understand exactly who the firm's customers are. Management needs to understand why customers purchase the firm's product or service. For an individual customer the purpose might be to satisfy a basic need, to make things easier, or for entertainment. Target market analysis generally involves market segmentation, which involves breaking the market into groups that have different levels of demand for the firm's product or service. For example, a clothing store like the GAP, that sells clothing primarily for teens, is interested in the size of the segment of the market—the number of teens in the geographical area that the store serves. Segmentation may be performed along any dimension that defines the firm's market, including

(1) Demographics (e.g., sex, education, income, etc.)
(2) Psychographics (e.g., lifestyle, social class, opinions, activities, attitudes, etc.)

b. If the firm's customers are businesses, segmentation might be performed in terms of other relevant dimensions including

(1) Industry
(2) Size (in terms of sales, total employees, etc.)

(3) Location

(4) How they purchase (e.g., seasonality, volume, who makes the purchasing decision)

Unlike individuals, businesses purchase products to increase revenue, decrease costs, or maintain status quo.

c. Target market analysis may be essential to the firm's success. The greater the understanding management has of the firm's market, the more effective it can be at making marketing decisions. Advertising, for example, can be tailored to particular market segments. The firm may even be able to use differential pricing in which they charge different prices to different market segments. As an example, airlines have long attempted to develop fare schedules and restrictions that segment the business traveler from the vacation traveler because the business traveler will generally pay more for a ticket.

3. **Strategic alliances** involve collaborative agreements between two or more firms. They may be organized as joint ventures, equity ventures, equity investments, or simple agreements (such as comarketing or codevelopment agreements). Firms enter into strategic alliances for a number of reasons, including to

a. Refocus the firm's efforts on its core competencies and value creation activities
b. Speed innovation
c. Compensate for limited resources
d. Reduce risk

4. **Globalization involves developing strategies to deal with, and capitalize on, markets in other countries.** Companies in developed countries are able to compete with companies in developing countries in a number of ways, including

- Use of sophisticated technology to reduce costs
- Effective process management
- Innovation in products or services
- Product quality
- Customer service
- Adopting a global strategy

In operating in a global economy, it is important that executives understand the cultural differences among countries. Differences in customs, values, and behavior result in problems that can only be managed by cross-cultural communication and interaction. These cultural differences affect negotiations, personnel management, and commerce.

Multinational companies generally pursue a global strategy in which they locate and consolidate operations in countries with the greatest strategic advantages. Organizations that pursue a global strategy can benefit in a number of ways, including

- Pooling international production to one or a few locations can achieve increased economies of scale
- Manufacturing costs can be cut by moving production to low-cost countries
- A firm that can switch production among different countries has increased bargaining power over labor, suppliers, and host governments
- Worldwide access to resources, labor, suppliers and customers

5. **Outsourcing** involves contracting for the performance of processes by other firms. Outsourcing provides a way for firms to focus on their core competencies and value creation activities. Any processes, such as information technology, human resources, product service, etc., for which the firm does not have a competitive advantage may be outsourced to other firms that can perform the process more effectively or efficiently. In doing so, the firm may be able to decrease its costs.

Outsourcing can present a firm with new risks. For example, agreements must be appropriately structured to allow the firm to control performance, quality and ethical employment practices of the other firm. Also, the firm may face risks to its reputation due to low quality or for outsourcing jobs, especially if the work is outsourced to another country.

E. Estimating the Effects of Economic Changes

1. Successful management involves being able to anticipate changes in economic conditions and competitor actions and devising strategies and plans to react to those changes. To begin with, management must thoroughly understand the effects of economic changes on the firm. "How will demand for the firm's products or services be affected?" and "How will the change affect the firm's costs?" are key questions. In order to estimate the effects, management will collect and analyze historical data. Quantitative techniques such as regression analysis may be used. Management will also examine the effects of any competitor analysis that has been performed. The following table illustrates the process.

Economic change	Estimated effects	Response
1. Management of an airline predicts an economic downturn that will cause a significant decline in business travel.	• Revenue from business travel will decline. • The firm is in an oligopolistic market, and competitors will react to the economic downturn by reducing fares.	• Execute a preemptive price decrease in the vacation travel segment of the business. • Disguise the price decrease by selling the fares with travel packages and through Priceline.
2. A financial institution predicts a significant increase in interest rates.	• The increase will increase the institution's cost of capital and therefore increase its interest expense. Based on historical data, the estimated effect is an increase in interest expense of 15%. • Because the institution has a significant amount of long-term loans at fixed rates, the increase cannot be passed on to a significant segment of its customers.	• Management decides to use interest rate swaps to minimize the effects of the projected interest rate increase.
3. Management of an appliance manufacturer expects an upturn in economic activity resulting in an increase in demand for the firm's products. The upturn is expected to increase the cost of raw materials.	• Revenue will increase due to increased sales and costs will increase.	• The increase in demand is built into the firm's forecasts to assure that products will be available. • Management decides to purchase futures contracts to hedge the cost of raw materials.

2. On the CPA exam you can expect questions that will require you to determine the effects of economic changes and competitor actions on the firm's financial results. If no data to predict the effect of the change are provided, the solution to the question will merely require you to predict the direction of the change. For example, if personal disposable income increases, how are sales for a chain of jewelry stores affected? Obviously, the effect will be an increase in sales. However, without historical data on the effect of changes in personal disposable income on jewelry sales there would be no way to determine the extent of the effect. Other questions may provide you with indications of the effects of economic changes allowing the determination of a more precise answer. For example, if you were provided with the price elasticity of demand for a product, say 1.5, and told that the price was to be increased by 10% you could estimate the effects of the price increase on demand using the formula for price elasticity as shown below.

$$E_D = \frac{\text{Percentage change in quantity demanded}}{\text{Percentage change in price}}$$

We know that the percentage change in quantity demanded can be calculated as follows:

$$
\begin{aligned}
\text{Percentage change in quantity demanded} \quad &= \quad E_D \times \text{Percentage change in price}\\
&= \quad 1.5 \times 10\%\\
&= \quad 15\%
\end{aligned}
$$

Still other questions might provide you with historical data on the effect of changes in economic variables on the firm's results, and ask you to estimate the impact of some anticipated change in economic conditions on the firm's future financial results.

NOW REVIEW MULTIPLE-CHOICE QUESTIONS 100 THROUGH 126 IN VOLUME 2

KEY TERMS

Absolute advantage. An advantage a country has over other countries in the production of a good or service.

Business cycle. A fluctuation in aggregate economic output that lasts for several years.

Comparative advantage. An advantage a country has in producing a good or service because it has no alternative users of its resources that would involve a higher return.

Consumption function. Depicts the relationship between changes in personal disposable income and consumption.

Cost leadership. A strategy that involves focusing on reducing the costs and time to produce, sell, and distribute a product or service.

Demand. The quantity of a good or service that a consumer is willing and able to purchase at a given price.

Deflation. The rate of decline in the price level of goods and services.

Depression. A deep and long-lasting recession.

Dumping. A form of predatory pricing in which a manufacturer in one country exports a product at a price that is lower than the priced charged in its home country.

Economic profit. The amount of profit in excess of normal profit.

Export subsidies. Payments made by a government to encourage the production and export of specific products.

Government budget surplus (deficit). The excess (deficit) of government taxes in relation to government transfer payments and purchases.

Inflation. The rate of increase in the price level of goods and services.

Marginal product. The additional output obtained from employing one additional unit of resource (e.g., one additional worker).

Marginal revenue. The additional revenue received from the sale of one additional unit of a product.

Marginal revenue product. The change in total revenue from employing one additional unit of a resource.

Market equilibrium. The price at which all the goods offered for sale will be sold.

Monopolistic competition. A market characterized by many firms selling a differentiated product or service.

Nominal gross domestic product. The price of all goods and services produced by a domestic economy for a year at current market prices.

Nominal interest rate. The interest rate in terms of the nation's currency.

Normal profit. The amount of profit necessary to compensate the owners for their capital and/or managerial skills.

Oligopoly. A market characterized by significant barriers to entry. As a result there are few sellers of the product.

Personal disposable income. The amount of income that individuals receive and have available to purchase goods and services.

Potential gross domestic product. The maximum amount of production that could take place in an economy without putting pressure on the general level of prices.

Price ceiling. A specified maximum price that may be charged for a good, usually established by a government. A price ceiling will cause good shortages.

Price floor. A specified minimum price that may be charged for a good, usually established by a government. A price floor will cause overproduction of the good.

Product differentiation. A strategy that involves modification of a product to make it more attractive to the target market or to differentiate it from competitors' products.

Pure competition. An industry in which there are a large number of sellers of virtually identical products or services. No individual seller is able to affect the market price.

Pure monopoly. A market in which there is a single seller of a product or service for which there are no close substitutes.

Real gross domestic product. The price of all goods and services produced by a domestic economy at price level adjusted (constant) prices.

Real interest rate. The interest rate adjusted for inflation.

Recession. A period of negative gross domestic product growth.

Substitution effect. The fact that as the price of a good or service falls, consumers will use it to replace similar goods or services.

Supply. The quantity of a good or service that will be supplied by producers at a given price.

Unemployment rate. The percentage of the total labor force that is unemployed at a given time.

Module 43: Financial Risk Management and Capital Budgeting

Overview

This module describes the relationship between risk and return and the use of various techniques to manage financial risk. There is an inverse relationship between risk and return. Companies attempt to maximize return within the risk tolerance level of its owners. There are a number of ways in which management attempts to mitigate risk including diversification and hedging.

This module also covers the concepts of the time value of money. Understanding the topic of the time value of money is essential for successful completion of the BEC exam. You must understand the mechanics as well as the concepts. Specifically, you should understand how present value techniques are used to value financial assets and liabilities.

The concepts of present value provide the basis for the last topic in this module–capital budgeting. Capital budgeting is the term used to describe the process of evaluating and controlling capital investments. The most effective capital budgeting techniques rely on present value techniques. Before beginning the reading you should review the key terms at the end of the module.

A. Risk and Return

There is a trade-off between risk and returns when considering investments—to achieve higher returns an investor must assume greater risk. This relationship is illustrated by the following chart that presents the means and standard deviations of real returns from stocks, bonds, and Treasury bills over a ten-year period. The results are as would be expected: stocks earned significantly higher returns but also with significantly higher risk (variance). The chart can be used to compute the **equity risk premium**. The equity risk premium is equal to the 8.7% real return on stocks minus the risk-free real return as measured by the return on Treasury bills, 1%, or 7.7% (8.7% – 1.0%). The average risk premium on common stock versus bonds over the ten-year period is about 6.6% (8.7% – 2.1%).

Real Returns of US Investments 1900 – 2000

Assets	Mean return (%)	Standard deviation (%)	Highest year (%)	Lowest Year (%)
Stocks	8.7	20.2	56.8	−38.0
Bonds	2.1	10.0	35.1	−19.3
Bills	1.0	4.7	20.0	−15.1
Inflation	3.3	5.0	20.4	−10.8

SOURCE: Dimson and Marsh, **Triumph of the Optimists,** (Princeton, NJ: Princeton University Press: 2002)

To understand why riskier investments offer a premium, it is necessary to make some assumptions about preferences of investors. Most financial models assume that investors are **risk averse**. Risk aversion does not mean investors will not take risks; it means that they must be compensated for taking risk. Most investors, and the market as a whole, are considered by most analysts to be risk averse. However, certain investors may exhibit different behavior.

1. **Risk-neutral investors**—Investors that prefer investments with higher returns whether or not they have risk. These investors disregard risk.
2. **Risk-seeking investors**—Investors that prefer to take risks and would invest in a higher-risk investment despite the fact that a lower-risk investment might have the same return.

B. Return on a Single Asset

1. Investment return is the total gain or loss on an investment for a period of time. It consists of the change in the asset's value (either gain or loss) plus any cash distributions (e.g., cash flow, interest, or dividends). The return is illustrated by the following equation:

$$R_{t+1} = \frac{P_{t+1} - P_t + CF_{t+1}}{P_t}$$

Where

R_{t+1}	=	The investment return from time t to $t+1$
P_{t+1}	=	The asset's price (market value) at $t+1$
P_t	=	The asset's price (market value) at t
CF_{t+1}	=	Cash flow received from the asset from t to $t+1$

This formula measures return on an *ex post* basis (after the fact) and, therefore, does not consider risk. Managers have to evaluate investments on an *ex ante* basis and, therefore, must use **expected returns** and **estimates of risk**.

2. **Estimating Expected Returns**

A common way to estimate expected returns is based on prior history. One could simply calculate the average historical returns on a similar investment to get the expected return. When making this computation two approaches are often used.

a. **Arithmetic average return**—Computed by simply adding the historical returns for a number of periods and dividing by the number of periods.
b. **Geometric average return**—This computation depicts the compound annual return earned by an investor who bought the asset and held it for the number of historical periods examined. If returns vary through time, the geometric average will always fall below the arithmetic average.
c. It is generally recommended that the arithmetic average return be used for assets with short holding periods and the geometric average return be used for assets with longer holding periods.

3. **Estimating Risk**

a. Measures of risk also are often developed from historical returns. Many financial analysts assume that the pattern of historical returns of large numbers of similar investments approximates a **normal distribution** (bell shaped curve) with the mean being the expected return and the variance, or standard deviation, measuring the dispersion around the expected return. Therefore, the most common estimates of risk come from the variance or standard deviation of historical returns. Remember, if you assume that the distribution is normal, about 95% of the returns will fall within the range created by expected return ± two standard deviations.
b. For many investments, management does not have significant historical data on returns to calculate the mean and variance. In these cases management must resort to **subjective** estimates of risk.

EXAMPLE

Assume that a defense contractor has the possibility of getting a lucrative government contract. The government intends to announce the winner of the contract today. An investor estimates that the probability of the firm getting the contract is 60%, in which case the stock price will increase 20%. If the contractor does not get the contract, the stock price is estimated to decline by 10%. Today's expected return on the stock investment would be computed as follows:

$$\text{Expected return} = 0.60(20\%) + 0.40(-10\%) = 8.0\%$$

The variance of the return is measured by the following formula:

$$\text{Variance} = E\{[R - E(R)]^2\}$$

Where

R = A random possible return

E(R) = The expected value of the return

Therefore to get the variance, we simply sum the squared deviations of the possible returns from the expected return weighted by their probability, as shown below.

Variance $= 0.60(20\% - 8\%)^2 + 0.40(-10\% - 8\%)^2$

Variance $= 216\%$

The standard deviation, which is equal to the square root of the variance, is calculated below.

$$\text{Standard deviation} = \sqrt{216\%} = 14.70\%$$

Therefore, the investor can make a decision about whether to invest in the stock knowing that the expected return is 8.0% with a standard deviation of 14.70%.

C. Portfolio Returns and Risk

1. **Expected Returns of a Portfolio**

   When an investor invests in a portfolio of assets, the expected returns are simply the weighted-average of the expected returns of the assets making up the portfolio. The expected return may be calculated with the following formula:

   $$E(R_p) = w_1 E(R_1) + w_2 E(R_2) + w_3 E(R_3)\ldots$$

   Where

$E(R_p)$	=	The expected return on the portfolio
$w_{1,2,3}$	=	The weight of each of the assets (1,2,3, etc.) in the portfolio
$E(R_{1,2,3})$	=	The expected return of each of the assets (1, 2,3, etc.) in the portfolio

   ### EXAMPLE

   Assume that an investor has two assets (or types of assets) in his or her portfolio. Asset 1 is 60% of the portfolio, and it has an expected return of 10%. Asset 2 is 40% of the portfolio, and it has an expected return of 5%. The expected return of the portfolio is calculated below.

   $$E(R_p) = 0.60(10\%) + 0.40(5\%) = 8\%$$

2. **The Variance of Portfolio Returns**

   a. The variance of portfolio returns depends on three factors

      (1) The percentage of the portfolio invested in each asset (the weight)
      (2) The variance of the returns of each individual asset
      (3) The covariance among the returns of assets in the portfolio. The covariance captures the degree to which the asset returns move together over time. If returns on the individual assets move together, there is little benefit to holding the portfolio. On the other hand, if returns on some assets in the portfolio go up when returns on other assets in the portfolio go down, holding the portfolio reduces overall risk.

   b. Portfolios allow investors to diversify away unsystematic risk. **Unsystematic risk** is the risk that exists for one particular investment or a group of like investments (e.g., technology stock). By having a balanced portfolio, investors can theoretically eliminate this risk. **Systematic risk** relates to market factors that cannot be diversified away. All investments are to some degree affected by them. Examples of systematic risk factors include fluctuations in GDP, inflation, interest rates, etc.

3. **Measuring the Systematic Risk of an Individual Investment**

   The variance of an individual investment captures the total risk of the investment, both systematic an unsystematic. However, since unsystematic risk can be eliminated by diversification, the variance of a specific investment is not a particularly useful measure when considering a portfolio of investments. A standardized measure that has been developed to estimate an investment's systematic risk is beta.

   $$\text{Beta} = b_i = \frac{\sigma_{im}}{\sigma_m^2}$$

   The beta of a particular investment equals the covariance of the investment's returns with the returns of the overall portfolio divided by the portfolio's variance. It measures how the value of the investment moves with changes in the value of the total portfolio. Therefore, it can be used to evaluate the effect of an individual investment's risk on the risk of the entire portfolio.

4. An individual investor has a **risk preference function** which describes the investor's trade-off between risk and return. A portfolio that falls on the line described by this function is an **efficient portfolio**.

D. Interest Rates

Interest represents the cost of borrowing funds. Therefore, consideration of interest rates is a critical aspect of financing decisions. In this section, we will review aspects of interest rates that are significant to financing decisions.

1. Interest Rates and Risk

As discussed above, risk and return are directly related. Investors and creditors must be paid a premium for assuming higher degrees of risk. In determining the appropriate interest rate to accept, investors and creditors consider the business risks of the loan or investment. The following business risks are relevant:

- **Credit or default risk**—The risk that the firm will default on payment of interest or principal of the loan or bond. This may be divided into two parts: the individual firm's creditworthiness (or risk of default) and **sector risk** (the risk related to economic conditions in the firm's economic sector).
- **Interest rate risk**—The risk that the value of the loan or bond will decline due to an increase in interest rates.
- **Market risk**—The risk that the value of the loan or bond will decline due to a decline in the aggregate value of all the assets in the economy.

Credit risk is an example of an unsystematic (unique) risk. It is unique to the particular loan or investment. Credit risk can be eliminated by diversification (e.g., by investing in a portfolio of loans or bonds). Market and interest rate risks are part of systematic risk that must be accepted by the investor.

2. Stated Versus Effective Annual Interest Rates

Management must make objective comparisons of loan costs or investment returns over different compounding periods. In order to put interest rates on a common basis for comparison, management must distinguish between the **stated interest rate** and the **effective annual interest rate**. While the stated rate is the contractual rate charged by the lender, the effective annual rate is the true annual return to the lender. The simple annual rate may vary from the effective annual rate because interest is often compounded more often than annually. The formula for calculating the effective annual rate from the stated rate is presented below.

$$EAR = \left(1 + \frac{r}{m}\right)^m - 1$$

Where

r = The stated interest rate
m = Compounding frequency

EXAMPLE

Assume that management is evaluating a loan that has a stated interest rate of 8% with compounding of interest quarterly. Since compounding is quarterly, m is equal to 4 because interest is compounded 4 times each year. Using the following equation, the effective annual rate may be computed as follows:

$$EAR = \left(1 + \frac{.08}{4}\right)^4 - 1$$

$$EAR = .0824 = 8.24\%$$

Management may now compare this 8.24% rate to other options on an effective interest basis.

---

3. The Term Structure of Interest Rates

The term structure of interest rates describes the relationship between long- and short-term rates. These relationships are important in determining whether to use long-term fixed or variable rate financing. A yield curve is used to illustrate the relative level of short-term and long-term interest rates at a point in time. At any point in time a yield curve may take any one of the following three forms:

a. **Normal yield curve**—An upward sloping curve in which short-term rates are less than intermediate-term rates which are less than long-term rates.
b. **Inverted (abnormal) yield curve**—A downward-sloping curve in which short-term rates are greater than intermediate-term rates which are greater than long-term rates.
c. **Flat yield curve**—A curve in which short-term, intermediate-term and long-term rates are all about the same.
d. **Humped yield curve**—A curve in which intermediate-term rates are higher than both short-term and long-term rates.

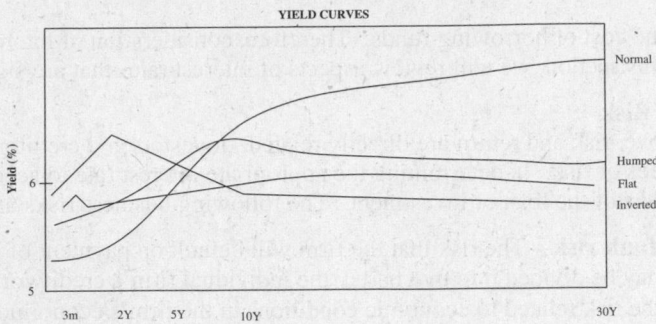

Long-term rates are usually higher (as described by the normal yield curve) because they involve more interest rate risk. Therefore, lenders require higher **maturity risk premiums** for long-term lending. However, market rates are also affected by expectations about the future levels of inflation, defaults, and liquidity, which can vary with the maturity date. These factors cause the relationships depicted by the inverted or humped yield curves.

There are a few theories that attempt to explain the shape of the yield curve, including

(1) **Liquidity preference (premium) theory.** This theory states that long-term rates should be higher than short-term rates, because investors have to be offered a premium to entice them to hold less liquid and more price-sensitive securities. Remember if interest rates increase and an investor holds a fixed-rate long-term security, the value of the security will decline.

(2) **Market segmentation theory.** This theory states that treasury securities are divided into market segments by the various financial institutions investing in the market. Commercial banks prefer short-term securities to match their short-term lending strategies. Savings and loans prefer intermediate-term securities. Finally, life insurance companies prefer long-term securities because of the nature of their commitments to policy-holders. The demand for various term securities is therefore dependent on the demands of these segmented groups of investors.

(3) **Expectations theory.** This theory explains yields on long-term securities as a function of short-term rates. Specifically, it states that long-term rates reflect the average of short-term expected rates over the time period that the long-term security will be outstanding. Under this theory long-term rates tell us about market expectations of short-term rates. When long-term rates are lower than short-term rates, the market is expecting short-term rates to fall. Since interest rates are directly tied to inflation rates, long-term rates also tell us about the market's expectations about inflation. If long-term rates are lower than short-term rates, the market is indicating a belief that inflation will decline.

All of the theories and factors described above make it very difficult to predict interest rates, in general, and much less for varying maturities. Therefore, sound financial policy calls for using a combination of long- and short-term debt, and equity, to enable the firm to survive in any interest rate environment.

The mix of long- and short-term debt also affects the firm's financial statements. A heavy reliance on short-term or variable-rate debt means that interest expense and, therefore, net income will be more variable. This increases the financial risk of the firm and will cause creditors and investors to demand higher rates to compensate for the increased risk.

> **NOW REVIEW MULTIPLE-CHOICE QUESTIONS 1 THROUGH 18 IN VOLUME 2**

DERIVATIVES AND HEDGING

A. The Nature of Derivatives

1. A derivative is a financial instrument or contract whose value is derived from some other financial measure (underlyings, such as commodity prices, stock prices, interest rates, etc.) and includes payment provisions.

2. Common examples of derivatives include the following:

    a. **Options**—Allow, but do not require, the holder to buy (call) or sell (put) a specific or standard commodity or financial instrument, at a specified price during a specified period of time (American option) or at a specified date (European option).

    b. **Forwards**—Negotiated contracts to purchase and sell a specific quantity of a financial instrument, foreign currency, or commodity at a price specified at origination of the contract, with delivery and payment at a specified future date.

    c. **Futures**—Forward-based standardized contracts to take delivery of a specified financial instrument, foreign currency, or commodity at a specified future date or during a specified period generally at the then market price.

    d. **Currency swaps**—Forward-based contracts in which two parties agree to exchange an obligation to pay cash flows in one currency for an obligation to pay in another currency.

    e. **Interest rate swaps**—Forward-based contracts in which two parties agree to swap streams of payments over a specified period of time. An example would be an interest-rate swap in which one party agrees to make payments based on a fixed rate of interest and the other party agrees to make payments based on a variable rate of interest.

    f. **Swaption**—An option of a swap that provides the holder with the right to enter into a swap at a specified future date with specified terms, or to extend or terminate the life of an existing swap. These derivatives have characteristics of an option and an interest rate swap.

3. Forward contracts and swaps are often created and exchanged by **financial intermediaries,** such as

    a. Commercial banks
    b. Insurance companies
    c. Pension funds
    d. Savings and loan associations
    e. Mutual funds
    f. Finance companies
    g. Investment bankers
    h. Money market funds
    i. Credit unions

The other party to the contract or agreement is referred to as the **counterparty**.

B. Risks in Using Derivatives

1. **Credit risk**—The risk of loss as a result of the counterparty to a derivative agreement failing to meet its obligation.
2. **Market risk**—The risk of loss from adverse changes in market factors that affect the fair value of a derivative, such as interest rates, foreign exchange rates, and market indexes for equity securities.
3. **Basis risk**—The risk of loss from ineffective hedging activities. Basis risk is the difference between the fair value (or cash flows) of the hedged item and the fair value (or cash flows) of the hedging derivative. The entity is subject to the risk that fair values (or cash flows) will change so that the hedge will no longer be effective.
4. **Legal risk**—The risk of loss from a legal or regulatory action that invalidates or otherwise precludes performance by one or both parties to the derivative agreement.

C. Uses of Derivatives

1. **Speculation**—As an investment to speculate on price changes in various markets.
2. **Hedging**—To mitigate a business risk that is faced by the firm. Hedging is an activity that protects the entity against the risk of adverse changes in the fair values or cash flows of assets, liabilities, or future transactions. A hedge is a defensive strategy.

D. Financial Statement Effects of Derivative Transactions

The financial statement effects of derivative transactions is governed primarily by Statement of Financial Accounting Standards 133 (SFAS 133), *Accounting for Derivative Instruments and Hedging Activities.* In this section we will briefly review the requirements of that standard.

1. SFAS 133 provides guidance on three types of hedging activities.

    a. **Fair value hedge**—A hedge of the changes in the fair value of a recognized asset or liability, or of an unrecognized firm commitment, that are attributable to a particular risk.

    b. **Cash flow hedge**—A hedge of the variability in the cash flows of a recognized asset or liability, or of a forecasted transaction, that is attributable to a particular risk.

    c. **Foreign currency hedges**

        (1) A fair value hedge of an unrecognized firm commitment or a recognized asset or liability valued in a foreign currency (a foreign currency fair value hedge).

        (2) A cash flow hedge of a forecasted transaction, an unrecognized firm commitment, the forecasted functional-currency-equivalent cash flows associated with a recognized asset or liability, or a forecasted intercompany transaction (a foreign currency cash flow hedge).

        (3) A hedge of a net investment in a foreign operation.

2. In general, SFAS 133 requires an entity to report all derivatives as assets and liabilities in the statement of financial position, measured at fair value. Unrealized gains and losses attributed to changes in a derivative's fair value are accounted for differently, depending on whether the derivative is designated and qualifies as a hedge.

    a. **Accounting for a fair value hedge**—The change in the fair value of a derivative designated and qualifying as a fair value hedge is recognized in earnings and is offset by the portion of the change in the fair value of the hedged asset or liability that is attributable to the risk being hedged. Accordingly, the carrying amount of the hedged asset or liability is adjusted for changes in fair value. If the hedge is completely effective, the change in the derivative's fair value will equal the change in the hedged item's fair value. Therefore, there will be no effect on earnings. However, if the hedge is not completely effective, earnings will be increased or decreased for the difference between the changes in the fair values of the derivative and the hedged item.

    b. **Accounting for a cash flow hedge**—The effective portion of the change in the fair value of a derivative designated and qualifying as a cash flow hedge is reported in other comprehensive income, and the ineffective portion is reported in earnings.

    c. **Accounting for foreign hedges**—The accounting for foreign exchange hedges is very similar to the accounting for fair value and cash flow hedges as describe above.

3. **Valuing Derivatives**

    As indicated above, derivatives are valued on financial statements at fair values, which is the current market price of the derivative. Quoted market prices in active markets are the best source of fair value and may be used for many derivatives. If a quoted market price is not available, valuation techniques are used to estimate the fair value, such as option-pricing models, matrix pricing, option-adjusted spread models, and fundamental analysis. We will briefly describe two commonly used methods.

    a. The **Black-Scholes option-pricing model** is a mathematical model for estimating the price of stock options, using the following five variables:

    - Time to expiration of the option
    - Exercise or strike price
    - Risk-free interest rate
    - Price of the underlying stock
    - Volatility of the price of the underlying stock

    Other methods that are used to value options include Monte-Carlo simulation and binomial trees.

    b. The **zero-coupon method** is used to determine the fair value of interest rate swaps. The zero-coupon method is a present value model in which the net settlements from the swap are estimated and discounted back to their current value. The key variables in the model include

    - Estimated net settlement cash flows (explained in the example below)
    - Timing of the cash flows as specified by the contract
    - Discount rate

    > **EXAMPLE**
    >
    > Assume that management enters into an agreement to swap payments on a fixed-rate liability for a variable rate. If interest rates decline, the firm will receive a net positive cash flow from the swap because the amount received on the fixed rate will be greater than the amount due on the variable rate. The opposite is true if rates increase. The zero-coupon method estimates future cash flows by calculating the net settlement that would be required if future interest rates are equal to the rates implied by the current yield curve. That amount is discounted to determine the current fair value of the swap for financial reporting purposes.

E. Hedging Examples

> **EXAMPLE**
>
> On January 1, 20X1, a firm forecasts that it will need $10,000,000 in financing December 31, 20X1. Management decides that the appropriate form of financing is a bond issue of 10 years with a fixed interest rate. The market rate at which the firm can issue the debt is based on the Treasury rate, which is the yield on US Treasury bonds. On January 1, 20X1, the Treasury rate is 4%. Since the Treasury rate is the risk-free rate, the firm's actual rate would be higher to compensate the investor for risk of default on the bonds. Assume that based on the firm's credit rating and economic conditions, the credit spread is two basis points. Therefore, the firm's interest rate at January 1, 20X1, is equal to 6% (4% risk free rate + 2% credit spread). Management would like to lock in the risk-free component of interest today to hedge against an increase in rates. The firm hedges the transaction by entering into futures contracts to sell $10,000,000 in 5-year Treasury

bonds at the forward rate of 4%. A position such as this, in which the firm is committed to sell something it does not own, is referred to as a **short position**. Around December 31, 20X1, management intends to purchase the contracts to close out its short position. Assume that the interest rate for Treasury bonds increases by one basis point from January 1, 20X1, to December 31, 20X1. If the interest rate on Treasury bonds increases by 1% from the 4% rate at the beginning of the year, the price of the bonds will decrease to allow an investor to earn 5% on the Treasury bonds. Therefore, management can buy futures contracts at much less than the price they were sold at and realize a gain. If the futures contracts for the Treasury bonds can be purchased at $9,400,000 the gain would be $600,000 ($10,000,000 – $9,400,000). Since this is a hedge, the gain would be reported in other comprehensive income rather than ordinary income. Assume that the bond financing that was issued by the firm on December 31, 20X1, was at 7 ½ %, the 5% risk-free rate plus a 2 ½ % credit spread. Hedge accounting would in effect reduce the interest rate on the debt by the 1% increase in the risk-free rate. From an accounting standpoint the gain on the Treasury bond futures contracts would be amortized to reduce interest expense by 1% over the life of the bond. Notice that the credit spread increased from January 1, 20X1, to December 31, 20X1, by ½%. Credit risk cannot be hedged, and therefore, the effective rate (after amortization of the hedging gain) on the bond issue actually increased from the forecasted 6% (4% + 2%) at the beginning of the year to 6 ½% (4% + 2 ½%).

EXAMPLE

Several years ago a firm entered into a $20,000,000, ten-year noncallable debt agreement. The agreement calls for variable interest payments tied to the London Interbank Offered Rate (LIBOR). LIBOR is currently 4.5% but management is concerned about the volatility of current rates and wants to lock in a fixed rate for this debt. The firm enters into an interest rate swap to pay 7% fixed interest for the remaining term of the loan instead of the variable rate. In this way it is able to hedge its interest rate risk. Instead of having a variable interest expense over the life of the loan, the firm will have a fixed rate of 7%. The financial statement effects of this transaction would be recognition of a 7% fixed rate of interest over the life of the loan as opposed to the variable rate.

EXAMPLE

Assume that a firm carries approximately $200,000 in short-term financing at variable interest rates and management is concerned about the current instability of short-term interest rates. To lock in the current rate for a year, management decides to sell on the futures market $200,000 in Treasury notes to be delivered one year from today. Again, this sale gives the firm a **short position.** The futures contracts will sell at approximately the current yield on the short-term Treasury securities. If interest rates rise, the firm will pay more interest on its short-term debt but it will also experience a gain on the futures contract because the price of Treasury notes will decline. Near the end of the year, the firm will purchase Treasury note contracts to close its short position. If the Treasury note contracts can be purchased for $180,000 at the end of the year, the firm's gain on the contract would be calculated as shown below.

Sales price Treasury note contracts (beginning of year)	$200,000
Purchase price of Treasury note contracts (end of year)	180,000
Gain on the contracts	$ 20,000

If the hedge was completely effective, the $20,000 gain on the futures contracts will offset the increase in interest expense experienced by the firm due to the increase in short-term interest rates. From an accounting standpoint, the gain on the contracts would be used to reduce interest expense in operating income.

NOW REVIEW MULTIPLE-CHOICE QUESTIONS 19 THROUGH 27 IN VOLUME 2

PRESENT VALUE

This section reviews the basic concepts related to time value of money.

A. The Time Value of Money

On the CPA exam, you do not have to know the complex formulas that are used to compute time value of money factors (TVMF). The factors will be given to you or enough information will be given to you so that you can easily compute them or use a spreadsheet tool to compute them. Your main focus of attention should be centered on understanding which TVMF should be used in a given situation.

> **NOTE:** The following abbreviations are used in the material that follows:
>
>   i = interest rate
>   n = number of periods or rents

1. **Future Value (FV) of an Amount** (future value of $1)

    The future value of an amount is the amount that will be available at some point in the future if an amount is deposited today and earns compound interest for "n" periods. The most common application is savings deposits. For example, if you deposited $100 today at 10%, you would have $110 [$100 + ($100 × 10%)] at the end of the first year, $121[$100 + ($110 × 10%)] at the end of the second year, etc. The compounding feature allows you to earn interest on interest. In the second year of the example you earn $11 interest: $10 on the original $100 and $1 on the first year's interest of $10.

2. **Present Value (PV) of a Future Amount** (present value of $1)

    The present value of a future amount is the amount you would pay now for an amount to be received "n" periods in the future given an interest rate of "i." A common application would be the money you would lend today for a noninterest-bearing note receivable in the future. For example, if you were lending money at 10%, you would lend $100 for a $110 note due in one year or for a $121 note due in two years.

    The present value of $1 is the inverse of the future value of $1. Thus, given a future value of $1 table, you have a present value of $1 by dividing each value into 1.00. Look at the present value of $1 and future value of $1 tables on the next page. The future value of $1 at 10% in five years is 1.611. Thus, the present value of $1 in five years would be 1.00 ÷ 1.611 which is .621 (check the table). Conversely, the future value of $1 is found by dividing the present value of $1 into 1.00, that is, 1.00 ÷ .621 = 1.611.

3. **Compounding**

    When interest is compounded more than once a year, two extra steps are needed. First, **multiply** "n" by the number of times interest is compounded annually. This will give you the total number of interest periods. Second, **divide** "i" by the number of times interest is compounded annually. This will give you the appropriate interest rate for each interest period. For example, if the 10% was compounded semiannually, the amount of $100 at the end of one year would be $110.25 [(1.05)^2] instead of $110.00. The extra $.25 is 5% of the $5.00 interest earned in the first half of the year.

4. **Future Value of an Ordinary Annuity**

    The future value of an ordinary annuity is the amount available "n" periods in the future as a result of the deposit of an amount (A) at the end of every period 1 through "n." Compound interest is earned at the rate of "i" on the deposits. A common application is a bond sinking fund. A deposit is made at the end of the first period and earns compound interest for n-1 periods (not during the first period, because the deposit is made at the end of the first period). The next to the last payment earns one period's interest, that is, $n - (n-1) = 1$. The last payment earns no interest, because it is deposited at the end of the last (nth) period. Remember that in the FUTURE AMOUNT OF AN ORDINARY ANNUITY TABLE, all of the factors for any "n" row are based on one less interest period than the number of payments.

TIME VALUE OF MONEY FACTOR (TVMF) TABLES

Future Value (Amount) of $1

n	6%	8%	10%	12%	15%
1	1.060	1.080	1.100	1.120	1.150
2	1.124	1.166	1.210	1.254	1.323
3	1.191	1.260	1.331	1.405	1.521
4	1.262	1.360	1.464	1.574	1.749
5	1.338	1.469	1.611	1.762	2.011

Present Value of $1

n	6%	8%	10%	12%	15%
1	.943	.926	.909	.893	.870
2	.890	.857	.826	.797	.756
3	.840	.794	.751	.712	.658
4	.792	.735	.683	.636	.572
5	.747	.681	.621	.567	.497

Future Value (Amount) of an Ordinary Annuity of $1

n	6%	8%	10%	12%	15%
1	1.000	1.000	1.000	1.000	1.000
2	2.060	2.080	2.100	2.120	2.150
3	3.184	3.246	3.310	3.374	3.473
4	4.375	4.506	4.506	4.641	4.993
5	5.637	5.867	6.105	6.353	6.742

Present Value of an Ordinary Annuity of $1

n	6%	8%	10%	12%	15%
1	.943	.926	.909	.893	.870
2	1.833	1.783	1.736	1.690	1.626
3	2.673	2.577	2.487	2.402	2.283
4	3.465	3.312	3.170	3.037	2.855
5	4.212	3.993	3.791	3.605	3.352

5. Present Value of an Ordinary Annuity

The present value of an ordinary annuity is the value today, given a discount rate, of a series of future payments. A common application is the capitalization of lease payments by either lessors or lessees. Payments "1" through "n" are assumed to be made at the end of years "1" through "n," and are discounted back to the present.

EXAMPLE

Assume a five-year lease of equipment requiring payments of $1,000 at the end of each of the five years, which is to be capitalized. If the discount rate is 10%, the present value is $3,791 ($1,000 × 3.791). The behavior of the present value of the lease payment stream over the five-year period is shown below. Note that the liability (principal amount) grows by interest in the amount of 10% during each period and decreases by $1,000 at the end of each period.

```
   0                1                2                3                4                5

$3,791 + 380 Int. =   $4,171
                    − 1,000 Pay
                      $3,171 + 320 Int. =   $3,491
                                          − 1,000 Pay
                                            $2,491 + 250 Int. =   $2,741
                                                                − 1,000
                                                                  $1,741 + 170 Int. =   $1,911
                                                                                      − 1,000
                                                                                        $ 911 + 91 Int. =   $1,002
                                                                                                          − 1,000
                                                                                                            2*
```

* Due to rounding

---

6. Distinguishing a Future Value of an Annuity from a Present Value of an Annuity

Sometimes confusion arises in distinguishing between the future value (amount) of an annuity and the present value of an annuity. These two may be distinguished by determining whether the total dollar amount in the problem comes at the beginning (e.g., cost of equipment acquired for leasing) or at the end (e.g., the amount needed to retire bonds) of the series of payments as illustrated below.

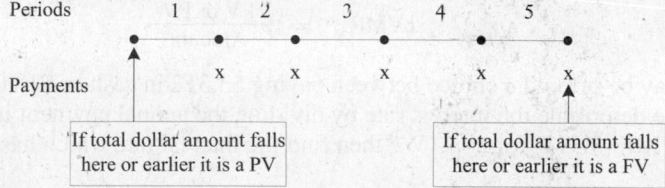

Remember: if the total amount comes at the end of the series of payments, it is a **future value** of annuity situation. If the total amount comes at the beginning of the series of payments, it is a **present value** of annuity situation. The total dollar amount may be given in the problem or you may have to compute it; either way, it makes no difference in determining whether a problem involves a present value or future value situation.

Some students feel the need to "convert" all time value of money problems into either present value or future value problems, depending on which they're most comfortable with. This process involves more work and more chance for errors, because an additional TVMF equation must be solved in the conversion. This is inefficient, and unnecessary, if you are able to correctly identify between the two initially. Become proficient at determining present value and future value situations, so that you may efficiently select the correct TVMF from the corresponding table.

7. Annuities Due

In some cases, the payments or annuities may not conform to the assumptions inherent in the annuity tables. For example, the payments might be made at the beginning of each of the five years instead of at the end of each year. This is an annuity due (annuity in advance) in contrast to an ordinary annuity (annuity in arrears). Both annuity due and ordinary annuity payments are represented by the "x's" in the illustration below.

Periods		1	2	3	4	5
Annuity		x	x	x	x	x
Annuity Due	x	x	x	x	x	

If the payments in the 5-period lease example above were made at the beginning of the period, the present value of the first payment which is made today is $1,000 (i.e., the TVMF is 1.00). The remaining 4 payments comprise an ordinary annuity for 4 periods as you can see on the above diagram. Always use time diagrams to analyze application of annuities.

To convert either a future value of an ordinary annuity or the present value of an ordinary annuity factor to an annuity due factor, multiply the ordinary annuity factor times $(1 + i)$. For the above lease example, you would find the present value of an ordinary annuity factor for $n = 5$ which is 3.993. Then multiply 3.993 by 1.08 to arrive at the annuity due factor, 4.312. The present value of the payments would be $4,312 ($4.312 × $1,000). Notice that the present value of the annuity due in the above example is $319 greater than the present value of the ordinary annuity because the payments are moved closer to the present.

8. Interest Rates

Usually, you will be given the interest rate for a time value problem but it is important to remember that the interest rate is generally made up of two components—the expected inflation/deflation rate (which affects the relative value of the currency), and the inflation adjusted return for the particular investment (which is determined by the risk of the investment).

9. TVMF Applications

The basic formula to use is

$$FV \text{ or } PV = TVMF \times Amount$$

If an annuity is involved, the amount is the periodic payment or deposit; if not, it is a single sum. Note that FV or PV is determined by three variables: time, interest rate, and payment. TVMF represents two variables: time and interest rate. The tables usually have the interest rate on the horizontal axis and time on the vertical axis. The above formula may also be stated as

$$Amount = \frac{FV \text{ or } PV}{TVMF}$$

For example, if we need to accumulate $12,210 in five years to repay a loan, we could determine the required annual deposit with the above formula. If the savings rate were 10%, we would divide the FV ($12,210) by the TVMF of the future value of annuity, n=5, i=.10 (6.105) and get $2,000. Thus, $2,000 deposited at the end of each of five years earning 10% will result in $12,210. This formula may also be used to find future values of an amount, present values of amounts, and annuities in the same manner.

Another variation of the formula is

$$TVMF = \frac{FV \text{ or } PV}{Amount}$$

For example, we may be offered a choice between paying $3,312 in cash or $1,000 a year at the end of each of the next four years. We determine the interest rate by dividing the annual payment into the present value of the annuity to obtain the TVMF (3.312) for n=4. We then find the interest rate which has the same or similar TVMF (in this case 8%).

Alternatively, using the above formula, we may know the interest rate but not know the number of payments. Given the TVMF, we can determine "n" by looking in the TVMF table under the known interest rate. Remember the TVMF reflects two variables: time and interest rate.

B. Valuation of Bonds

Bonds generally provide for periodic fixed interest payments at a coupon (contract) rate of interest. At issuance, or thereafter, the market rate of interest for the particular type of bond may be above, the same, or below the coupon rate. If the market rate exceeds the coupon rate, the book value will be less than the maturity value. The difference (discount) will make up for the coupon rate being below the market rate.

Conversely, when the coupon rate exceeds the market rate, the bond will sell for more than maturity value to bring the effective rate to the market rate. This difference (premium) will make up for the coupon rate being above the market rate. When the coupon rate equals the market rate, the bond will sell for the maturity value.

The market value of a bond is equal to the maturity value and interest payments discounted to the present. You may have to refer to the discussion of time value of money concepts in the previous section before working with the subsequent material. Finally, when solving bond problems, candidates must be careful when determining the number of months to use in the calculation of interest and discount/premium amortization. For example, candidates frequently look at a bond issue with an interest date of September 1 and count three months to December 31. This error is easy to make because candidates focus only on the fact that September is the ninth month instead of also noting whether the date is at the beginning or end of the month.

1. **Bond Valuation Example**

   $10,000 in bonds, semiannual interest at 6% coupon rate, maturing in six years, and market rate of 5%.

   a. Find present value of maturity value. Use present value of $1 factor. Discount $10,000 back 12 periods at 2 1/2% interest (Factor = .7436). (Semiannual compounding is going to be required to discount the semiannual payments so it is also assumed here.)

   $$\$10,000 \quad \times \quad .7436 \quad = \quad \$7,436$$

   b. Find the present value of the annuity of twelve $300 interest payments. Use present value of an ordinary annuity of $1 factor for twelve periods at 2 1/2% interest (Factor = 10.26).

   $$\$300 \quad \times \quad 10.26 \quad = \quad \$3,078$$

   c. Today's value is $10,514 (7,436 + 3,078)

CAPITAL BUDGETING

A. Capital budgeting is a technique to evaluate and control long-term investments. There are six stages to capital budgeting.

1. **Identification stage.** Management determines the type of capital projects that are necessary to achieve management's objectives and strategies.
2. **Search stage.** Management attempts to identify alternative capital investments that will achieve management's objectives.
3. **Information-acquisition stage.** Management attempts to revaluate the various investments in terms of their costs and benefits.
4. **Selection stage.** Management chooses the projects that best meet the criteria established.
5. **Financing stage.** Management decides on the best source of funding for the project. This process is described in Module 45.
6. **Implementation and control stage.** Management undertakes the project and monitors the performance of the investment.

This section will focus primarily on the techniques management uses to evaluate various projects. However, these techniques may also be used to monitor their performance. Capital budgeting alternatives are typically evaluated using discounted cash flow techniques. Such techniques involve evaluation of an investment today in terms of the present value of future cash returns from the investment. The objective is to identify the most profitable or best investment alternative. The cash returns can take two forms depending on the nature of the project. If the project will produce revenue, the return is the difference between the cash revenues (inflows) and cash expenses (outflows). Other projects generate cost savings (e.g., cash outflows for labor that are not made because a new machine is more efficient). The latter are, in effect, reductions in outflows, which for simplicity, can be treated as cash inflows. Conceptually, the results of both types of projects are the same. The entity ends up with more cash by making the initial capital investment.

The following terminology is useful to the understanding of capital budgeting analysis:

a. **Sunk, past, or unavoidable costs** are committed costs that are not avoidable and are therefore irrelevant to the decision process.
b. **Avoidable costs** are costs that will **not** continue to be incurred if a department or product is terminated.
c. **Committed costs** arise from a company's basic commitment to open its doors and engage in business (depreciation, property taxes, management salaries).
d. **Discretionary costs** are fixed costs whose level is set by current management decisions (e.g., advertising, research and development).
e. **Relevant costs** are future costs that will change as a result of a specific decision.
f. **Differential (incremental) cost** is the difference in cost between two alternatives.
g. **Opportunity cost** is the maximum income or savings (benefit) foregone by rejecting an alternative.
h. **Outlay (out-of-pocket) cost** is the cash disbursement associated with a specific project.

The choice among alternative investing decisions can be made on the basis of several capital budgeting models:
(1) Payback or discounted payback; (2) Accounting rate of return; (3) Net present value, (4) Excess present value index, and (5) Internal (time-adjusted) rate of return.

B. Payback and Discounted Payback

The **payback** method evaluates investments on the length of time until recapture (return) of the investment. For example, if a $10,000 investment were to return a cash flow of $2,500 a year for eight years, the payback period would be four years. If the payback period is to be computed after income taxes, it is necessary to calculate cash flow as shown below, remembering that depreciation itself does not consume cash. Assuming an eight-year life with no salvage value and a 40% income tax rate, the after-tax payback period would be computed as follows:

Cash flow: $2,500 × (1 − 40%) = $1,500
Tax savings from depreciation: $1,250 × 40% = $500
Cash flow after tax: $1,500 + $500 = $2,000
$10,000 ÷ $2,000 = 5 years

The payback method has a number of limitations. First, it ignores total project profitability and therefore has little or no connection to maximization of shareholder value. Second, the method is not really effective in taking into account the time value of money.

The **discounted payback** method is essentially the same as the payback method except that in calculating the payback period, cash flows are first discounted to their present value. This is only a minor improvement over the conventional payback method. It still ignores any cash flows after the cutoff period and therefore does not consider total project profitability.

Using the above example, assume that the cost of capital for the firm is 8%. The discounted payback would be calculated as shown below.

Discounted payback

Cash flow after taxes = $2,000

Year	Cash flow	Present value factor	Present value of cash flow	Cumulative present value
1	$2,000	.926	$1,852	$1,852
2	2,000	.857	1,714	3,566
3	2,000	.794	1,588	5,154
4	2,000	.735	1,470	6,624
5	2,000	.681	1,362	7,986
6	2,000	.630	1,260	9,246
7	2,000	.583	1,166	10,412
8	2,000	.540	1,080	11,492

From the table we see that the discounted payback occurs in year 7. Specifically, it occurs when $754 ($10,000 − $9,246) of cash flow is received in that year. By dividing the $754 needed cash flow by the total $1,166 cash flows in year 7, that we need .65 of year 7 cash flows. Therefore, the discounted payback period is 6.65 years.

C. Accounting Rate of Return

The **accounting rate of return** (ARR) method computes an approximate rate of return which ignores the time value of money. It is computed as follows:

ARR = Annual net income ÷ Average (or initial) investment

Using the same example and assuming the annual cash flows approximate annual net income before depreciation and taxes for the project, the ARR before taxes is

($2,500 − $1,250) ÷ ($10,000 ÷ 2) = 25%

The ARR after taxes is

[($2,500 − $1,250) × 60%] ÷ ($10,000 ÷ 2) = 15%

Note that the numerator is the increase in **net income**, not **cash flows**, so depreciation is subtracted. The average investment is one-half the initial investment because the initial investment is depreciated down to 0 by the end of the project. If a problem asked for ARR based on **initial** investment, you would not divide the investment by 2.

The advantage of the accounting rate of return method is that it is simple and intuitive. It also is often the measure that is used to evaluate management. However, it has a number of limitations including

- The results are affected by the depreciation method used
- ARR makes no adjustment for project risk
- ARR makes no adjustment for the time value of money

D. Net Present Value

The **net present value** (NPV) method is a discounted cash flow method which calculates the present value of the future cash flows of a project and compares this with the investment outlay required to implement the project. The net present value of a project is defined as

$$\text{NPV} \quad = \quad \text{(Present value of future cash flows)} \quad - \quad \text{(Required investment)}$$

The calculation of the present value of the future cash flows requires the selection of a discount rate (also referred to as the target or hurdle rate). The rate used should be the minimum rate of return that management is willing to accept on capital investment projects. The rate used should be no less than the cost of capital—the rate management currently must pay to obtain funds. A project which earns exactly the desired rate of return will have a net present value of 0. A positive net present value identifies projects which will earn in excess of the minimum rate. For example, if a company desires a minimum return of 6% on an investment of $10,000 that has an expected return of $2,500 for five years, the present value of the cash flows is $10,530 ($2,500 × 4.212: 4.212 is the TVMF for the present value of an annuity, n = 5, i = 6%; see the previous section on Present Value Concepts). The net present value of $530 ($10,530 – $10,000) indicates that the project will earn a return in excess of the 6% minimum desired. If the requirement were for a net-of-tax return of 6%, and the net-of-tax cash flow were $23,000, that amount would be multiplied by 4.212. This would result in a present value of $96,876 for the cash inflows, which is less than the $100,000 initial outlay. Therefore, this investment should not be made.

The NPV method is based on cash flows and would ignore depreciation if taxes were not considered. As shown earlier, however, depreciation results in a tax savings (tax shield) that must be factored into the evaluation. For example, assume that a company is considering the purchase of equipment costing $20,000 for use in a new project. MACRS is used to depreciate equipment for tax purposes, under which the machine has a useful life of seven years. The required rate of return of the company is 8%. The present value of the tax savings from depreciation would be as follows:

Year	Income tax deduction for depreciation	Income tax savings at 30% tax rate	8% Discount factor	Present value at 8%*
1	$2,858	$ 857	.926	$ 794
2	4,898	1,469	.857	1,259
3	3,498	1,049	.794	833
4	2,498	749	.735	551
5	1,786	536	.681	365
6	1,784	535	.630	337
7	1,786	536	.583	312
8	892	268	.540	145
				$4,596

* Tax savings × Discount factor

Therefore, $4,596 would be included in the NPV computation as a cash inflow from the equipment.

The **excess present value (profitability) index** computes the ratio of the present value of the cash inflows to the initial cost of a project. It is used to implement the net present value method when there is a limit on funds available for capital investments. Assuming other factors are equal, this is accomplished by allocating funds to those projects with the highest excess present value indexes.

First, the net present value of each alternative is calculated using the minimum required rate of return. Then the excess present value index is computed

$$\frac{\text{Present value of future net cash inflows}}{\text{Initial investment}} \quad \times \quad 100 \quad = \quad \text{Excess present value index}$$

If the index is equal to or greater than 100%, the project will generate a return equal to or greater than the required rate of return.

Net present value methods are the most widely accepted methods of evaluating a capital expenditure. Their advantages include

- Presents results in dollars which are easily understood
- Adjusts for the time value of money
- Considers the total profitability of the project
- Provides a straightforward method of controlling for the risk of competing projects—higher-risk cash flows can be discounted at a higher interest rate
- Provides a direct estimate of the change in shareholder wealth resulting from undertaking a project

The limitations of net present value methods include

- May not be considered as simple or intuitive as some other methods
- Does not take into account the management flexibility with respect to a project—management may be able to adjust the amount invested after the first year or two depending on the actual returns

E. Internal Rate of Return

The **internal (time-adjusted) rate of return** (IRR) method is another discounted cash flow method. It determines the rate of discount at which the present value of the future cash flows will exactly equal the investment outlay (i.e., the rate that results in a NPV of zero). This rate is compared with the minimum desired rate of return to determine if the investment should be made. The internal rate of return is determined by setting the investment today equal to the discounted value of future cash flows. The discounting factor (rate of return) is the unknown. The TVMF for the previous example is

$$
\begin{aligned}
\text{PV (investment today)} &= \text{TVMF} \times \text{Cash flows} \\
\$100,000 &= \text{TVMF} \times \$25,000 \\
\text{TVMF} &= 4.00
\end{aligned}
$$

The interest rate of a TVMF of 4.00 where n = 5 is approximately 8%. The after-tax rate of return is determined using the $23,000 after-tax cash inflow amount as follows:

$$
\begin{aligned}
\$100,000 &= \text{TVMF} \times \$23,000 \\
\text{TVMF} &= 4.35
\end{aligned}
$$

The interest rate of a TVMF of 4.35 where n = 5 is approximately 5%. The answers are worded "less than 5%, but greater than 0%," "less than 7%, but greater than 5%," etc.

The relationship between the NPV method and the IRR method can be summarized as follows:

NPV	IRR
NPV > 0	IRR > Discount rate
NPV = 0	IRR = Discount rate
NPV < 0	IRR < Discount rate

If the firm has sufficient funds to undertake all projects, the calculated internal rate of return on a project is compared to a prespecified **hurdle rate** which is the firm's minimum acceptable rate of return for the project. The hurdle rate is determined based on the market rate of return for projects with similar levels of risk.

1. The advantages of the internal rate of return method include

    a. Adjusts for the time value of money
    b. The hurdle rate is based on market interest rates for similar investments
    c. The results tend to be a little more intuitive than the results of the net present value method

2. Limitations of the internal rate of return method include

    a. Depending on the cash flow pattern there may be no unique internal rate of return for a particular project—there may be multiple returns depending on the assumptions used
    b. Occasionally, there may be no real discount rate that equates the project's NPV to zero
    c. The technique also has limitations when evaluating mutually exclusive investments as described in the next section

F. Mutually Exclusive Projects

1. Until now, we have assumed that management can invest in any project that meets the particular criteria being used. However, at times management must decide on one of several projects that are all acceptable. In other words, management must decide on the best project. This situation is often described as **capital rationing**.
2. To decide on the best investment, management must examine the characteristics of each. One way of summarizing the characteristics of an investment is through the use of the **net present value profile**. The profile allows us to portray the net present value of projects at different discounts rates.

EXAMPLE

Management is considering investment in one of two projects, both of which involve an initial investment of $20,000. Future cash flows from the two projects are shown below.

Year	Investment A	Investment B
1	$3,000	$18,000
2	4,000	6,000
3	5,000	2,400
4	10,000	
5	10,000	

The following graph shows the net present value for the two investments.

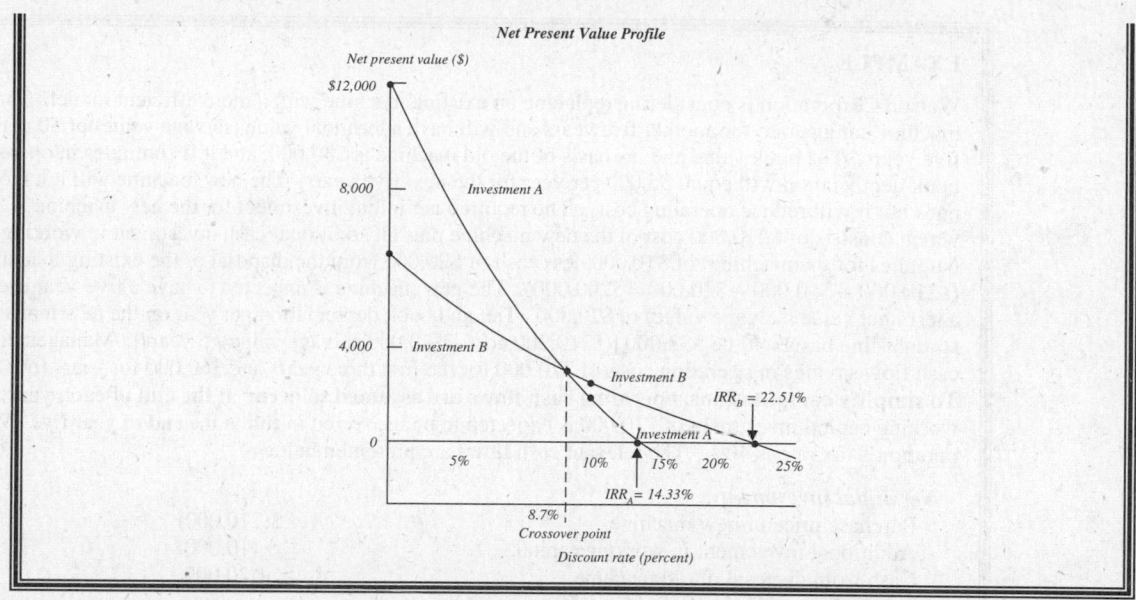

3. Comparing the two investments, we see that at low discount rates Investment A has a higher net present value. Investment B has a higher net present value at higher discount rates. This is because most of the return from Investment B is loaded toward the early years of the investment. The crossover point is at 8.7%, at lower discount rates Investment A should be selected, and at higher rates Investment B should be accepted.

4. Net present value works better than the internal rate of return in a situation in which a choice must be made among a group of investments. The internal rate of return method is based upon an important assumption when comparing investments of different lives and different cash flow patterns. The method implicitly assumes that the cash inflows from an investment can be reinvested at the same internal rate of return. For example, assume a company must choose between two projects, C and D. The IRR on project C is 15% with a life of five years, while the IRR of project D is 13% with a life of ten years. Project C would be the one selected under the IRR criteria. However, the internal rate of return method assumes that the cash inflows from the project can be reinvested at 15%. If the cash inflows can only be reinvested at 9%, then project B may be the better alternative. **Therefore, we see that traditional IRR criteria may not arrive at the best solution in all cases.** As a result, many firms rely on net present value criteria when evaluating competing proposals.

G. Determining Future Cash Flows

1. In evaluating investment alternatives, one of the first challenges is determining the future cash flows that are relevant to the decision. Simply stated, relevant cash flows are those that are expected to differ among the alternatives. Examples of relevant cash flows include

   a. The initial investment in long-term tangible or intangible assets for each investment alternative
   b. Any initial investment in working capital for each investment alternative (e.g., inventories, accounts receivable, etc.)
   c. Cash flow from the sale of any assets being replaced
   d. Differences in cash flows from operations under the alternatives (e.g., cash inflows from sales and/or cash outflows for operating costs)

      - Remember to focus on cash flows not accounting income
      - Payments for incremental income taxes should be included
      - Depreciation expense does not affect cash flows but the firm receives a tax savings (shield) from depreciation expense. It reduces taxable income and therefore reduces tax payments. Remember it is tax depreciation that generates the tax shield, and book depreciation may differ from tax depreciation.

   e. Cash flows at the end of the expected life of the project.

      - Terminal disposal price of any long-term tangible or intangible assets. If the tax basis (Initial cost – Tax depreciation taken) is expected to be different from the disposal price, the tax gain or loss will generate a tax inflow or outflow.
      - Recovery of any working capital investment—This investment will be recovered at the end of the project by liquidation of inventories, accounts receivable, etc. There are generally no tax implications of this recovery because it is assumed that the cash received will be equal to the book value (tax basis) of the working capital items.

EXAMPLE

Watson Corporation is considering replacing an existing machine with a more efficient model. The existing machine can operate for another five years and will have a terminal value (salvage value) of $0 at the end of five years. The book value and tax basis of the old machine is $30,000, and if it continues in operation, tax and book depreciation will equal $6,000 per year for the next five years. The new machine will not increase revenues but it will reduce operating costs. The required net initial investment for the new machine is $200,000, which consists of $210,000 cost of the new machine plus an additional cash investment in working capital (supplies for the machine) of $10,000, less cash of $20,000 from the disposal of the existing machine ($210,000 + $10,000 – $20,000 = $200,000). The new machine is expected to have a five-year useful life and a terminal value (salvage value) of $20,000. Tax and book depreciation per year on the new machine on a straight-line basis will be $38,000 [($210,000 cost – $20,000 salvage value)/ 5 years]. Management expects a cash flow savings in operating costs of $70,000 for the first three years and $60,000 for years four and five. **To simplify computations, operating cash flows are assumed to occur at the end of each year.** The working capital investment of $10,000 is expected to be recovered in full at the end of year five. Watson Corporation's tax rate is 40%. The relevant cash flows are presented below.

Net initial investment

Purchase price of new machine		$(210,000)
Additional investment in working capital		(10,000)
Cash from disposal of old machine		20,000
Total effect of disposal of old machine:		
Cash from disposal	$20,000	
Less: Tax basis	(30,000)	
Loss on sale of old machine	(10,000)	
Tax rate	40%	
Tax benefit from sale of old machine		4,000
Net initial investment		$(196,000)

Operating cash flow for years 1 through 3

Cost savings before income taxes		$ 70,000
Less income taxes (40% × $70,000)		(28,000)
Cost savings after taxes		42,000
Tax savings from depreciation:		
Depreciation on new machine	$38,000	
Less depreciation on old machine	6,000	
Depreciation differential	$32,000	
Tax rate	40%	
Tax savings from incremental depreciation		12,800
Cash flow after taxes for years 1 through 3		$ 54,800

Operating cash flow for years 4 and 5

Cost savings before income taxes		$ 60,000
Less income taxes (40% × $60,000)		(24,000)
Cost savings after taxes		36,000
Total savings from depreciation:		
Depreciation on new machine	$38,000	
Less depreciation on old machine	6,000	
Depreciation differential	$32,000	
Tax rate	40%	
Tax savings from incremental depreciation		12,800
Cash flow after taxes for years 4 and 5		$ 48,800

Cash flow at end of year 5

Terminal price of new machine	$ 20,000
Recovery of working capital investment	10,000
Cash flow at end of year 5	$ 30,000

The pattern of relevant cash flows from investment in the new machine is summarized below.

		Relevant Cash Flows				
	0	**1**	**2**	**3**	**4**	**5**
Initial investment	$(196,000)					
Operating cash flow (after tax)		$54,800	$54,800	$54,800	$48,800	$48,800
Terminal price of new machine						20,000
Recovery of working capital						10,000
Total relevant cash flows	$(196,000)	$54,800	$54,800	$54,800	$48,800	$78,800

Assuming that Watson Corporation's cost of capital is 10%, the net present value of purchasing the new machine is calculated below.

Year	Cash flow	Present value factor (10%)	Present value
0	$(196,000)	1.000	$(196,000)
1	54,800	.909	49,813
2	54,800	.826	45,265
3	54,800	.751	41,155
4	48,800	.683	33,330
5	78,800	.621	48,935
Net present value			$22,498

The results indicate that when using the net present value criteria, management should purchase the new machine.

EXAMPLE

Taylor Corporation is considering investing in one of the following two projects. Taylor's marginal tax rate is 25% and its cost of capital is 10%

Investment A

Initial investment	$150,000
Operating effects for 5-year useful life:	
Cash basis revenues	$200,000
Cash basis expenses	(160,000)
Net cash flow from operations (before taxes)	$ 40,000
Tax depreciation on the investment each year	$ 25,000
Terminal value of investment at end of 5 years	$ 25,000

Investment B

Initial investment	$210,000
Operating effects for 6-year useful life:	
Cash basis revenues	$250,000
Cash basis expenses	(200,000)
Net cash flow from operations (before taxes)	$ 50,000
Tax depreciation on the investment each year	$ 35,000
Terminal value of investment at end of 6 years	$ 0

The cash flows from the two projects may be scheduled out as follows:

Investment A

	0	1	2	3	4	5
			Relevant Cash Flows			
Initial investment	$(150,000)					
Operating cash flow (before taxes)		$40,000	$40,000	$40,000	$40,000	$40,000
Taxes on operating cash flows (25%)		(10,000)	(10,000)	(10,000)	(10,000)	(10,000)
Tax savings from added depreciation (25% × $25,000)		6,250	6,250	6,250	6,250	6,250
Terminal price of investment						25,000
Total relevant cash flows	$(150,000)	$36,250	$36,250	$36,250	$36,250	$61,250

Investment B

	0	1	2	3	4	5	6
				Relevant Cash Flows			
Initial investment	$(210,000)						
Operating cash flow (before taxes)		$50,000	$50,000	$50,000	50,000	$50,000	$50,000
Taxes on operating cash flows (25%)		(12,500)	(12,500)	(12,500)	(12,500)	(12,500)	(12,500)
Tax savings from added depreciation (25% × $35,000)		8,750	8,750	8,750	8,750	8,750	8,750

| | | Terminal value of investment | | | | | | 0 |
| | | Total relevant cash flows | $(210,000) | $46,250 | $46,250 | $46,250 | $46,250 | $46,250 | $46,250 |

		Investment A		Investment B	
Year	Present value factor (10%)	Cash flow	Present value	Cash flow	Present value
0	1.000	$(150,000)	$(150,000)	$(210,000)	$(210,000)
1	.909	36,250	32,951	46,250	42,041
2	.826	36,250	29,943	46,250	38,203
3	.751	36,250	27,224	46,250	34,734
4	.683	36,250	24,759	46,250	31,589
5	.621	61,250	38,036	46,250	28,721
6	.564			46,250	26,085
			$2,913		$(8,627)

The results indicate that when using the net present value criteria, Investment A should be accepted and Investment B rejected.

H. Considering Risk in Capital Budgeting

Risk as applied to capital budgeting is defined in terms of variability of the possible outcomes from a given investment. **Projected cash flows are not known with certainty.** Like individual investors, it is assumed that management is **risk averse**—that is, given the same rate of return they would prefer an investment with less uncertainty. A number of statistical techniques have been developed to measure the extent of risk inherent in a particular situation.

1. **Probability Analysis**

   One way to include risk in the capital budgeting analysis is to assign probabilities to possible outcomes. The probabilities provide a mathematical way of expressing uncertainty about the outcomes. They may be based on past experience, industry ratios and trends, economic forecasts, interviews with executives, or sophisticated simulation techniques.

   a. The set of all possible outcomes from an investment with a probability assigned to each outcome is referred to as a **probability distribution**. Probability distributions may be discrete or continuous. A **discrete distribution** identifies a **limited number of potential outcomes** and assigns probabilities to each of the outcomes. A **continuous distribution** theoretically defines an infinite number of possible outcomes. A commonly used continuous distribution is the **normal distribution** (bell-shaped curve). The normal distribution is useful because it approximates many real-world situations and it can be completely described with only two statistics, its mean and its standard deviation. Normal distributions have the following fixed relationships between distance from the mean and area under the curve:

Distance in standard deviations from the mean	Area under the curve
1.00	68.3%
1.64	90.0%
1.96	95.0%
2.00	95.4%
2.57	99.0%

   Therefore, by knowing the mean (expected value) and the standard deviation, management can construct a confidence interval for a particular outcome. As an example, 95% of the outcomes will fall within the mean (expected value) plus or minus 1.96 standard deviations. The following chart illustrates this point in graphic form:

   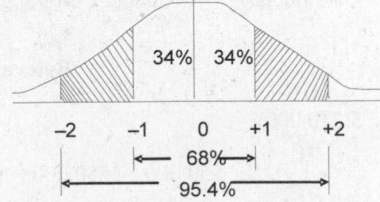

   b. Once outcomes are determined and probabilities assigned, management can compute two important statistical measures—the expected value and the standard deviation. The following formula can be used to calculate the expected return:

$$\hat{k} = \sum_{i=1}^{n} k_i p_i$$

Where

$\hat{k}$ = the expected value of the returns

k = the returns from the various possible outcomes

p = the probabilities assigned to the possible outcomes

The standard deviation can be calculated using the following formula:

$$\sigma = \sum_{i}^{n} (k_i - \hat{k})^2 p_i$$

EXAMPLE

Assume a firm is considering investing in a project with the following possible outcomes and related probabilities.

Outcome (present value of future cash flows)	Probability of outcome	Assumption
$100,000	.2	Pessimistic
$150,000	.6	Most likely
$200,000	.2	Optimistic

The expected return would be $150,000 as calculated below.

k		p		
$100,000	×	.2	=	$20,000
$150,000	×	.6	=	90,000
$200,000	×	.2	=	40,000
$\hat{k}$			=	$150,000

The standard deviation of the expected return would be $31,623 as calculated below.

$$\sigma = \sum_{i}^{n} (k_i - \hat{k})^2 p_i$$

$k_i - \hat{k} = (k_i - \hat{k})$	$(k_i - \hat{k})^2$	$p_i \times (k_i - \hat{k})^2$	$\sqrt{\text{Square root}}$
$100,000 - 150,000 = -50,000$	2,500,000,000	500,000,000	$\sqrt{1,000,000,000}$
$150,000 - 150,000 = 0$	0	0	
$200,000 - 150,000 = 50,000$	2,500,000,000	$\dfrac{500,000,000}{1,000,000,000}$	$= \$31,623$

---

c. The standard deviation provides a rough estimate of how far each outcome falls away from the mean. Generally, the larger the standard deviation, the greater the risk. However, the standard deviation as a measure of risk has a significant limitation. Its size depends on the size of the investment. The $31,623 may seem reasonable in relation to these possible outcomes, but what if the expected value of the investment was only $60,000. The standard deviation would be quite large. Therefore, it is difficult to use the standard deviation in comparing risk for investments of different sizes.

d. To eliminate the size difficulty analysts have developed a preferred measure, the **coefficient of variation**, which is simply the standard deviation divided by the expected value of the investment, as shown below.

$$\text{Coefficient of variation} = \frac{\sigma}{\hat{k}}$$

For the investment described above, the coefficient of variation would equal .2108 as calculated below.

$$\text{Coefficient of variation} = \frac{\$31,623}{\$150,000} = .2108$$

The coefficient of variation provides a measure of risk that is normalized for the size of the investment. Therefore, it allows comparisons across investments of varying size.

2. **Risk-Adjusted Discounted Rate**

a. A popular approach to adjust for risk involves using different discount rates for proposals with different levels of risk. Using this technique, management is applying **risk-adjusted discount rates**. A project with a normal level of risk is discounted at the firm's cost of capital and projects with greater levels of risk are discounted at higher rates.

b. Using the coefficient of variation as a risk measure, management could set different categories of risk with different risk premiums as shown in the following table:

(Risk coefficient of variation)	Discount rate
0.40 or less	10.0%
0.41 to 0.70	13.0%
0.71 to 1.00	16.0%
1.01 to 1.30	20.0%

Alternatively, management might simply establish qualitative measures of risk as shown below.

Risk (example)	Discount rate
Low risk (replace old equipment)	7.0%
Normal risk (add plant capacity	10.0%
Moderately above normal risk (new market)	15.0%
High risk (new product in foreign market)	20.0%

EXAMPLE

Assume that management is evaluating two alternative projects, Investment A and Investment B. Investment A has a normal level of risk and should be discounted at the firm's cost of capital, 10%. Investment B, on the other hand, has a significantly higher level of risk and management believes that 15% is the appropriate discount rate. Assume that Investment A would require an investment of $30,000, and Investment B would require an investment of $28,000. The table below presents the discounted cash flow for the two projects.

Investment A (10% discount rate)			**Investment B (15% discount rate)**		
Year			Year		
1	$10,000 × 0.909 =	$ 9,090	1	$5,000 × 0.870 =	$4,350
2	20,000 × 0.826 =	16,520	2	7,000 × 0.756 =	5,292
3	10,000 × 0.751 =	7,510	3	10,000 × 0.658 =	6,580
		$33,120	4	10,000 × 0.572 =	5,720
	Investment	30,000	5	10,000 × 0.497 =	4,970
	Net present value	$ 3,120			$26,912
				Investment	28,000
				Net present value	$(1,088)

As can be seen from the table, Investment A would be acceptable because it has a positive net present value. Project B would be rejected because its net present value is negative.

---

3. **Time-Adjusted Discount Rates**

Management's ability to accurately forecast cash flows diminishes as they are forecast further out in time. Therefore, cash flows projected in later years of a project's life are much more uncertain than those forecasted in the early years. Economic conditions, interest rates, inflation rates, etc., may fluctuate very significantly over a number of years in the future. This would imply that the cash flows later in a project's life should be discounted at higher rates than those in the first years. The table below illustrates how this might be done.

Time period	Discount rate
Years 1 through 4	10.0%
Years 5 through 8	13.0%
Years 9 through 12	16.0%

4. **Sensitivity Analysis**

Most capital budgeting problems require management to make many assumptions before arriving at the investment's net present value. For example, forecasting projected cash flows may require assumptions about demand, costs of production, selling price, etc. When using sensitivity analysis, managers explore the importance of these assumptions. First, managers compute the expected (most likely) results. Then, management allows one variable to change while holding the others constant, and the net present value is recomputed. By repeating the process with all the important variables, management can determine how sensitive the net present value is to changes in each major assumption. Therefore, sensitivity analysis involves exploring "what if" situations to determine the variables to which the outcomes are particularly sensitive. Management can then challenge its assumptions about these sensitive variables.

5. **Scenario Analysis**

Scenario analysis is a more complex variation of sensitivity analysis. Instead of exploring the effects of a change in one variable, management develops a scenario that might happen if a number of related variables change. As an example, if demand is lower than expected, sales price might have to be reduced, and unit production costs might be higher. Normally, management develops a most likely scenario and one or more pessimistic and optimistic ones. This is useful in illustrating the range of the possible net present values, and therefore the risk of the investment.

6. **Simulation Models**

Computer simulation software makes it possible to model the effects of even more economic conditions on the results of an investment project. Monte Carlo simulation uses random variables for inputs distributed around the expected means of the economic variables. As an example, management may expect short-term interest rates to be about 4% over the life of the project with a standard deviation of 1.5%. This data would be input and the program would generate simulated results using random interest rates from a probability distribution with a mean of 4% and a standard deviation of 1.5%. Therefore, instead of just developing several possible outcomes for a project, management can generate a range of outcomes with a standard deviation. Some simulation models generate probability acceptance curves for capital budgeting decisions. These curves inform management of the probabilities of having a positive net present value for the project.

7. **Decision Trees**

Most investment decisions are more complex than simply determining the net present value of future cash flows for a period of time and deciding to invest if the project has a positive net present value. Management often faces a series of decisions that may affect the value of the investment. Let's assume that management is deciding whether to introduce a new product. Management is evaluating whether to make an investment in the new product and test market it in a small geographical area. If the product sells well, management will expand the test market to a larger area. Finally, if the product does well in the larger area, management will introduce the product nationally, and there are several possible net present values from the product depending on how well it sells on a national basis. The project may be abandoned based on the results of either marketing test. A decision tree provides a visual representation of these decision points and potential decisions. The value of a decision tree is that it forces management to think through a series of "if then" scenarios that describe how the firm might react based on future events.

EXAMPLE

Assume that a firm is considering a $1,250,000 investment in a new product. Management intends to test-market the product in a small market and if the product hits at least a moderate level of demand, management will expand the test market area. Otherwise, management will abandon the project with no value. Management believes that the probability of meeting a moderate level of sales in the initial test market is 50%. If the product sells at least a moderate level in the expanded test area, management will launch the product nationally. Otherwise, management will abandon the project with no value. Management believes that the probability of the product performing well in the expanded market area is 75%. If the product is launched nationally, management believes the following three outcomes are possible:

Possible outcome	Probability	Net present value of future cash flows
Pessimistic sales	25%	$2,000,000
Most likely sales	50%	$4,000,000
Optimistic sales	25%	$6,000,000

The decision tree below depicts this investment opportunity.

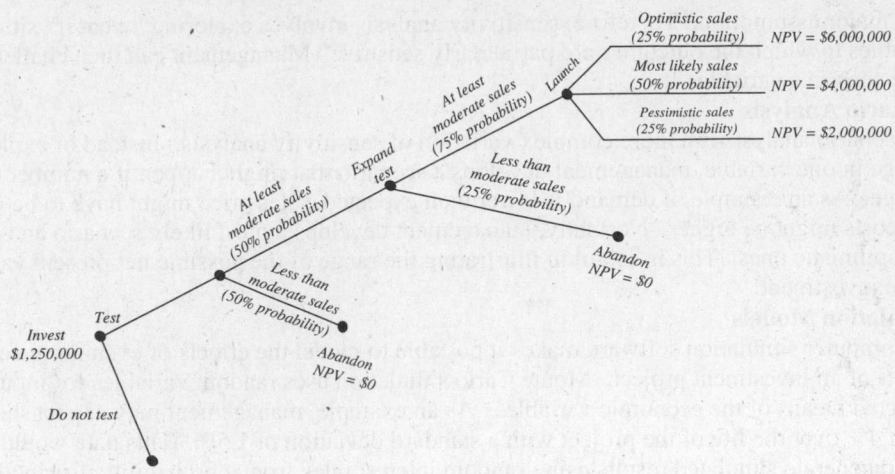

The appropriate way to calculate the expected net present value for the investment using a decision tree is to begin at the end and work backward to the initial decision from one decision point to another.

Expected net present value of future cash flows if the product is launched

Net present value of outcomes	Probability	Expected net present value
$2,000,000	25%	$ 500,000
$4,000,000	50%	2,000,000
$6,000,000	25%	1,500,000
		$4,000,000

The $4,000,000 in expected net present value in the previous step is used to calculate the expected net present value of future cash flows at the point of deciding whether to expand the market test.

Outcome	Net present value of outcomes	Probability	Expected net present value
Moderate sales (launch)	$4,000,000	75%	$3,000,000
Less than moderate sales (abandon)	0	25%	0
			$3,000,000

The $3,000,000 in expected net present value from the previous step is used to calculate the expected net present value of future cash flows at inception.

Outcome	Net present value of outcomes	Probability	Expected net present value
Moderate sales (expand test)	$3,000,000	50%	$1,500,000
Less than moderate sales (abandon)	0	50%	0
			$1,500,000

The final expected net present value after considering the initial investment is calculated below.

Expected net present value of cash flows	$1,500,000
Initial investment	1,250,000
Expected net present value of the investment	$ 250,000

Since the expected net present value is positive, the results indicate that the project should be accepted.

8. Real Options

Another technique that takes into account the dynamic nature of an investment decision is one that views an investment as a real option. This technique assumes that once management makes an initial investment, it has an option to take a number of future actions that will change the value of the investment. Therefore, the initial decision can be viewed as purchasing an option. Since net present value ignores the option value of an investment it sometimes does not provide the correct answer.

EXAMPLE

Assume that management is considering bidding on the rights to extract oil from a proven site over the next five years. The extraction costs are expected to be $22 per barrel. Oil is currently selling for $21 per barrel and management does not know whether the price will go up or down over the next five years. Using net present value with an expected price for the oil of $21, management would clearly decide not to make the investment. The expected value of the production costs, $22 per barrel, is greater than the expected sales price of the oil, $21 per barrel.

We get a different answer using the real option approach. Remember, the firm is not obligated to extract the oil, it only has an option to do so. Management knows that oil prices are very volatile and at least some time over the five-year period oil will sell for more than $22 per barrel. Therefore, the investment has value and management may reasonably bid on the rights. The net present value method understates or overstates a project's value depending on whether the investment creates or eliminates options for the firm. To correct this deficiency, the real options approach adds or subtracts an option value for the investment to get a more realistic value for the project.

$$\text{Project value} = \text{NPV} \pm \text{Option value}$$

The option value is estimated much like the option value of a financial instrument is estimated. For a particular investment, the option may be a number of types, including

a. **Expansion options**—Management may receive an option to expand the investment. An example of this option is a new product investment in which management has an option to expand production after the initial investment.

b. **Abandonment options**—Management almost always has an option to abandon a project.

c. **Follow-up investment options**—Management may receive other investment opportunities when investing in the project. The expansion option is really a subset of this type of option, but follow-up investment options are more complex. As an example, investing in a particular research and development project might offer management options for other related projects.

d. **Flexibility options**—Management may be provided with the ability to take advantages of changes in economic circumstances. As an example, an investment in machinery that can be used to produce a number of different products provides management with operating flexibility.

9. **Lease Versus Buy**

In capital budgeting, it is also important to evaluate whether it may be more advantageous to lease the asset rather than purchase it. In making a lease-versus-buy decision, management will often compare the two alternatives using discounted cash flow. Depending on the circumstances, leasing may provide an attractive alternative for a number of reasons, including

- There may be tax advantages to structuring the acquisition as a lease.
- Leasing may require less initial investment.
- Leasing will require less formal borrowing which may be restricted by loan coverants tied to the company's other debt.
- Certain leases do have to be capitalized and therefore will not require recognition of debt on the company's balance sheet.

10. **Portfolio Risk**

a. Theoretically, management should evaluate all possible combinations of investment projects to determine which set will provide the best trade-off between risk and return. This process is very similar to an investor's process of putting together a portfolio of financial investments. Conceptually, the sets of portfolios that meet management's trade-off between risk and return can be visualized as falling on an indifference curve or **risk preference function**. A risk preference function, as presented in the graph below, illustrates the **efficient frontier** for portfolio investments. Any portfolio of investments that falls on the line is an efficient portfolio (e.g., A, B, and C); it meets management's objectives with respect to the trade-off between risk and return. Any portfolio that falls to the right is not efficient.

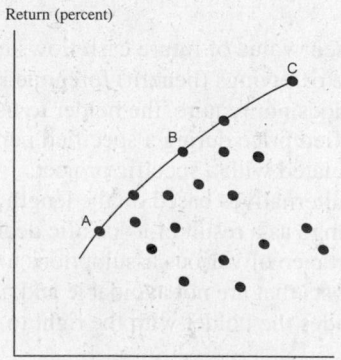

Return (percent)

Risk level (beta coefficient of variation

b. When considering a new investment to be added to an existing portfolio, management must consider the effect of the investment on the overall risk of the portfolio. Whether or not an individual investment will change the overall risk of the firm depends on its relationship to other investments in the portfolio. If a casualty insurance company purchases the casualty insurance division of another firm, there is little risk reduction. Highly correlated investments do nothing to diversify away risk. Investments that are negatively correlated do reduce overall risk. Investments that are negatively correlated are those with performance that moves in opposite directions with changing economic conditions. Simply illustrated, if you match an investment that performs poorly during recessions with one that performs well during recessions, the risk of the two investments combined is much less than the risk of them individually.

c. A measure that is used to express the extent of the correlation between a set of investments is the **coefficient of correlation** from multiple regression analysis. (Multiple regression is illustrated in Module 47.) This measure takes a value of from +1 to –1. The table below illustrates the relationship between the coefficient of correlation and the extent of risk reduction for the portfolio.

Significant risk reduction		Some risk reduction		Little risk reduction	
-1	-.5	0	+.5		+1

NOW REVIEW MULTIPLE-CHOICE QUESTIONS 28 THROUGH 85 IN VOLUME 2

KEY TERMS

Avoidable costs. Costs that will not continue to be incurred if a particular course of action is taken.

Cash flow hedge. A hedge of the variability in the cash flows of a recognized asset or liability or of a forecasted transaction that is attributable to a particular risk.

Committed costs. Costs related to the company's basic commitment to open its doors (e.g., depreciation, property taxes, management salaries, etc.).

Credit (default) risk. The risk that a firm will default on payment of interest or principal of a debt.

Currency swaps. Forward-based contracts in which two parties agree to exchange an obligation to pay cash flows in one currency for an obligation to pay in another currency.

Differential (incremental) cost. The difference in cost between two alternative courses of action.

Discretionary costs. Fixed costs whose level is set by current management decisions (e.g., advertising, research and development, etc.).

Fair value hedge. A hedge of the changes in fair value of a recognized asset or liability, or of an unrecognized firm commitment.

Forwards. Negotiated contracts to purchase and sell a specific quantity of a financial instrument, foreign currency, or commodity at a price specified at the origination of the contract, with delivery and payment at a specified future date.

Futures. Forward-based standardized contracts to take delivery of a specified financial instrument, foreign currency, or commodity at a specified future date or during a specified period generally at the then market price.

Interest rate risk. The risk that the value of a debt instrument will decline due to an increase in prevailing interest rates.

Interest rate swaps. Forward-based contracts in which two parties agree to swap streams of payments over a specified period of time. These contracts are often used to trade variable-rate instruments for fixed-rate instruments.

Internal rate of return method. Uses the rate of return that equates investment with future cash flows to evaluate investment alternatives.

Market risk. The risk that the value of a debt instrument will decline due to a decline in the aggregate value of all assets in the economy.

Net present value method. Uses the present value of future cash flows to evaluate investment alternatives.

Opportunity cost. The maximum income or savings (benefit) foregone by rejecting an alternative.

Options. An instrument that allows, but does not require, the holder to buy (call) or sell (put) a specific or standard commodity or financial instrument, at a specified price during a specified period of time or at a specified date.

Outlay cost. The case disbursement associated with a specific project.

Payback method. Evaluates investment alternatives based on the length of time until the investment is recaptured.

Relevant costs. Future costs that will change as a result of a specific decision.

Sensitivity analysis. Exploring the importance of various assumptions to forecasted results.

Sunk (unavoidable) costs. Committed costs that are not avoidable and are therefore irrelevant to future decisions.

Swaption. An option of a swap that provides the holder with the right to enter into a swap at a specified future date with specified terms.

Systematic risk. The risk related to market factors which cannot be diversified away.

Unsystematic risk. The risk that exists for one particular investment or a group of like investments. This risk can be diversified away.

Module 44: Financial Management

Overview

This module describes major aspects of financial management. Financial management deals with the various types of monetary decisions that must be made by managers in a company, along with the tools and analyses used to make those decisions.

Financial management includes the following five functions:

1. **Financing function**—Raising capital to support the firm's operations and investment programs.
2. **Capital budgeting function**—Selecting the best projects in which to invest firm resources, based on a consideration of risks and return.
3. **Financial management function**—Managing the firm's internal cash flows and its capital structure (mix of debt and equity financing) to minimize the financing costs and ensure that the firm can pay its obligations when due.
4. **Corporate governance function**—Developing an ownership and corporate governance system for the firm that will ensure that managers act ethically and in the best interest of stakeholders.
5. **Risk-management function**—Managing the firm's exposure to all types of risk.

This module focuses primarily on the financing, financial management and financial risk management functions. It is divided into four sections. The first section reviews the concepts of working capital management, the second section deals with the topic of a firm's capital structure, asset and liability valuation is described in the third section, and the final section focuses on business mergers. Before beginning the reading you should review the key terms at the end of the module.

WORKING CAPITAL MANAGEMENT

A. Working capital management involves managing and financing the current assets and current liabilities of the firm. The primary focus of working capital management is managing inventories and receivables.

1. **Managing the Firm's Cash Conversion Cycle**

   The cash conversion cycle of a firm is the length of time between when the firm makes payments and when it receives cash inflows. This cycle is illustrated below.

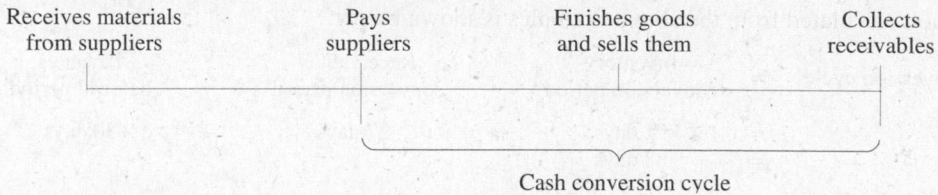

Receives materials from suppliers — Pays suppliers — Finishes goods and sells them — Collects receivables

Cash conversion cycle

To enable more detailed analysis, the cash conversion cycle may be analyzed using the following three periods:

- Inventory conversion period
- Receivables collection period
- Payables deferral period

a. **Inventory conversion period**—The average time required to convert materials into finished goods and sell those goods.

$$\text{Inventory conversion period} = \frac{\text{Average inventory}}{\text{Cost of goods sold per day*}}$$

* In some references this ratio is calculated using sales per day instead of cost of goods sold per day

---

EXAMPLE

Assume that average inventory is $10,000,000 and annual cost of goods sold are $40,000,000; the inventory conversion period is equal to 91 days, as calculated below.

$$\text{Inventory conversion period} = \frac{\$10,000,000}{\$40,000,000/365 \text{ days}}$$

$$= 91 \text{ days}$$

---

b. **Receivables collection period (days sales outstanding)**—The average time required to collect accounts receivable.

$$\text{Receivables collection period} = \frac{\text{Average receivables}}{\text{Credit sales per day}}$$

EXAMPLE

Assume that the average receivables balance is $3,000,000 and credit sales are $40,000,000; the receivables collection period is equal to 27 days as calculated below.

$$\text{Receivables collection period} = \frac{\$3,000,000}{\$40,000,000/365 \text{ days}}$$

$$= 27 \text{ days}$$

---

c. **Payables deferral period**—The average length of time between the purchase of materials and labor and the payment of cash for them.

$$\text{Payables deferral period} = \frac{\text{Average payables}}{\text{Purchases per day}}$$

$$= \frac{\text{Average payables}}{\text{Cost of goods sold}/365}$$

EXAMPLE

Assume that the average payables balance for labor and materials is $2,500,000 and cost of goods sold is $30,000,000; the payables deferral period is 30 days as calculated below.

$$\text{Payables deferral period} = \frac{\$2,500,000}{\$30,000,000/365 \text{ days}}$$

$$= 30 \text{ days}$$

---

d. The cash conversion cycle nets the three periods described above and, therefore, measures the time period from the time the firm pays for its materials and labor to the time it collects its cash from sales of goods. The conversion period calculated from the above examples is shown below.

$$\text{Cash conversion cycle} = \frac{\text{Inventory}}{\text{conversion period}} + \frac{\text{Receivables}}{\text{conversion period}} - \frac{\text{Payables}}{\text{deferral period}}$$

$$= 91 \text{ days} + 27 \text{ days} - 30 \text{ days}$$
$$= 88 \text{ days}$$

e. Effective working capital management involves shortening the cash conversion cycle as much as possible without harming operations. This strategy improves profitability because the longer the cash conversion cycle, the greater the need for financing. We will now turn our attention to the management of each type of current asset.

2. **Cash Management**

A firm should attempt to minimize the amount of cash on hand while maintaining a sufficient amount to (1) take advantage of trade discounts, (2) maintain its credit rating, and (3) meet unexpected needs.

a. Firms hold cash for two basic purposes

- *Transactions.* Cash must be held to conduct business operations.
- *Compensation to financial institution.* Financial institutions require minimum balances (1) for certain levels of service or (2) as a requirement of loan agreements. Such minimums are referred to as **compensating balances**.

b. Firms prepare cash budgets to make sure that they have adequate cash balances to:

- Take advantage of **cash discounts**. Suppliers often offer lucrative discounts for early payment of invoices.
- Assure that the firm maintains its credit rating.
- Take advantage of favorable business opportunities, such as opportunities for business acquisitions. These amounts are sometimes called **speculative balances**.
- Meet emergencies, such as funds for strikes, natural disasters, and cyclical downturns. These amounts are sometimes called **precautionary balances**.

c. A key technique for cash management is managing float. **Float** is the time that elapses relating to mailing, processing, and clearing checks. A float exists for both the firm's payments to suppliers and the firm's receipts from customers. **Effective cash management involves extending the float for disbursements and shortening the float for cash receipts.**

d. **Zero-balance accounts.** This cash management technique involves maintaining a regional bank account to which just enough funds are transferred daily to pay the checks presented. Regional banks typically receive the checks drawn on their customers' accounts in the morning from the Federal Reserve. The customer can then be notified as to the amount of cash needed to cover the checks and arrange to have that amount of cash transferred to the account. This arrangement has two advantages:

- Checks take longer to clear at a regional bank, providing more float for cash disbursements.
- Extra cash does not have to be deposited in the account for contingencies.

A zero-balance account is cost-effective if the amount the firm saves on interest costs from the longer float is adequate to cover any additional fees for account maintenance and cash transfers.

EXAMPLE

A firm has an opportunity to establish a zero-balance account system using three different regional banks. The total amount of the maintenance and transfer fees is estimated to be $5,000 per year. The firm believes that it will increase the float on its operating disbursements by an average of three days, and its cost of short-term funds is 4%. Assuming that the firm estimates its average daily operating disbursements to be $50,000, should the firm establish the accounts?

The solution to this problem is found by comparing the $5,000 cost in fees to the benefit in terms of reduced interest costs. If the float on the average is lengthened by three days, the firm gets the use of $150,000 of additional funds ($50,000 per day × 3 days). The annual value of the use of an extra $150,000 in funds is measured by the interest savings, or $6,000 ($150,000 × 4%). Therefore, the firm would save an estimated $1,000 ($6,000 − $5,000) by establishing the zero-balance accounts.

---

e. **Lockbox system.** In a lockbox system, customer payments are sent to a post office box that is maintained by a bank. Bank personnel retrieve the payments and deposit them into the firm's bank account. This technique has the following advantages:

- Increases the internal control over cash because firm personnel do not have access to cash receipts.
- Provides for more timely deposit of receipts which reduces the need for cash for contingencies.

If management is evaluating the feasibility of establishing a lockbox system solely based on the cash flow benefit, the system is cost effective if the interest costs saved due to obtaining more timely deposits is sufficient to cover the net increase in costs of cash receipt processing (bank fees less internal costs saved from having the bank process receipts). The computation would be similar to the one illustrated above for a zero-balance account.

> **EXAMPLE**
>
> Assume that a firm is evaluating whether to establish a lockbox system. The following information is available to make the decision:
>
> - The bank will charge $25,000 per year for the process and the firm will save approximately $8,000 in internal processing costs. Therefore, the estimated net additional cost of processing the receipts is $17,000 ($25,000 – $8,000).
> - The float for cash receipts will be reduced by an estimated two days. Therefore, the firm will receive use of the cash receipts on the average two days earlier.
> - Average daily cash receipts are equal to $300,000 and short-term interest costs are 4%.
>
> Should the firm establish the lockbox system?
>
> Based solely on cash flow considerations, the firm should establish the system if the interest savings is greater than the increased costs. In this case, the amount of interest savings is measured by multiplying the increase in average funds, $600,000 ($300,000 per day × 2 days), by the interest cost, 4%. The firm will save an estimated $24,000 ($600,000 × 4%) in annual interest costs. Therefore, the cost savings for the lockbox system is estimated to be $7,000, the savings in interest cost less the net increase in processing costs ($24,000 – $17,000). The real benefit may be even greater, because of the intangible value of the increase in internal control from having the bank process cash receipts. This reduces the firm's business risk.

f. **Concentration banking.** Another way to speed up collection of payments on accounts is concentration banking. Using this technique, customers in an area make payments to a local branch office rather than firm headquarters. The local branch makes deposits in an account at a local bank. Then, surplus funds are periodically transferred to the firm's primary bank. Since these offices and banks are closer to customers, the firm gets the use of the funds more quickly. The float related to cash receipts is shortened. However, transferring funds between accounts can be costly. Wire transfers generally involve a significant fee. A slower but less expensive way of transferring funds is through the use of **official bank checks** (depository transfer checks) which are preprinted checks used to make transfers.

> **EXAMPLE**
>
> Assume that a firm is considering establishing a concentration banking system and has the following information to make the decision:
>
> - The concentration banking arrangement will allow access to the firm's average $100,000 daily cash receipts from customers two days faster.
> - Bank maintenance and transfer fees are estimated at $4,000 per year.
> - The firm's short-term borrowing cost is 3.5%.
>
> Should the firm establish the concentration banking system?
>
> Again, in evaluating the decision, management must compare the interest savings, $7,000 [($100,000 per day × 2 days) × 3.5%] to the additional costs, $4,000. Thus, management would save $3,000 ($7,000 – $4,000) by establishing the concentration banking system.

g. **Electronic funds transfer.** Electronic funds transfer is a system in which funds are moved electronically between accounts without the use of a check. As an example, through a terminal at a supermarket a customer's payment is automatically charged with a "debit card" against the customer's bank account before he or she leaves the store. Electronic funds transfer systems actually take the float out of both the receipts and disbursements processes.

h. **International cash management.** Multinational firms can use various systems, including electronic systems, to manage the cash accounts they hold in various countries. Carefully managing international accounts may provide management with opportunities to increase earnings. As an example, management may be able to transfer funds to a country in which interest rates are higher, allowing increased returns on investments.

3. **Marketable Securities Management**

   In most instances firms hold marketable securities for the same reasons they hold cash. Such assets can generally be converted to cash very quickly, and marketable securities have an advantage over cash in that they provide an investment return. There are many securities to choose from for short-term investment. The factors that are considered in making the choice include:

- **Minimum investment required**—Some investments, such as high-yield certificates of deposit, require larger investments.
- **Safety**—The risk to principal.

- **Marketability (liquidity)**—Relates to the speed with which the investment can be liquidated.
- **Maturity**—The length of time the funds are committed.
- **Yield**—Generally, the higher the yield the better. However, additional yield comes with higher risk or longer maturity.

Because short-term investments must be available to meet the current cash needs of the firm, the most important considerations with respect to these investments are liquidity and safety. Major types of short-term investments include

a. **Treasury bills (T-bills)**—Short-term obligations of the federal government. Although treasury bills are initially offered with maturities of from 91 to 182 days, existing T-bills may be purchased on the market with virtually any maturity date up to 182 days. T-bills are popular short-term investments because the active market ensures liquidity.

b. **Treasury notes**—Government obligations with maturities from one to ten years. These securities are appropriate for the investment of short- to intermediate-term funds.

c. **Treasury Inflation Protected Securities (TIPS)**—Government obligations that pay interest that equates to a real rate of return specified by the US Treasury, plus principal at maturity that is adjusted for inflation. These are useful to a firm that wants to minimize interest rate risk.

d. **Federal agency securities**—Offerings of government agencies, such as the Federal Home Loan Bank. These securities offer security, liquidity (active market), and pay slightly higher yields than treasury issues.

e. **Certificates of deposit (CD)**—Savings deposits at financial institutions. There is actually a two-tier market for CDs—small CDs ($500 – $10,000) with lower interest rates and large ($100,000 or more) with higher interest rates. There is a secondary market for large CDs, providing some liquidity. Interest yields are higher on CDs than for government securities but CDs are not as liquid or as safe. CDs are normally insured up to $100,000 by the federal government.

f. **Commercial paper**—Large unsecured short-term promissory notes issued to the public by large creditworthy corporations. Commercial paper has a two- to nine-month maturity period and is usually held to maturity by the investor because there is no active secondary market.

g. **Banker's acceptance**—A draft drawn on a bank for payment when presented to the bank. Banker's acceptances generally arise from payments for goods by corporations in foreign countries. The corporation receiving the banker's acceptance may have to wait 30-90 days to present the acceptance for payment. As a result, a secondary market has developed for the sale of these instruments at a discount. Therefore, management may purchase banker's acceptances as short-term investments. Banker's acceptances involve slightly more risk than government securities but also offer slightly higher yields.

h. **Eurodollar certificate of deposit**—Eurodollars are US dollars held on deposit by foreign banks and in turn lent by the banks to anyone seeking dollars. To obtain dollars, foreign banks offer Eurodollar certificates of deposit. As an investment, Eurodollar certificates of deposit pay higher yields than treasury bills or certificates of deposit at large US banks.

i. **Money market funds**—Shares in a fund that purchases higher-yielding bank CDs, commercial paper, and other large-denomination, higher-yielding securities. Money market funds allow smaller investors to participate in these markets.

j. **Money market accounts**—Similar to savings accounts, individual or business investors deposit idle funds in the accounts and the funds are used to invest in higher-yielding bank CDs, commercial paper, etc.

k. **Equity and debt securities**—Management may also decide to invest in the publicly traded stocks and bonds of other corporations. Such investments have greater risk than other short-term investments, but they also offer higher average long-term returns. If management invests in such securities it should purchase a balanced portfolio to diversify away the **unsystematic risk** (e.g., default risk) of the individual investments.

4. **Inventory Management**

Effective inventory management starts with effective forecasting of sales and coordination of purchasing and production. The two goals of inventory management are

- To ensure adequate inventories to sustain operations, and
- To minimize inventory costs, including carrying costs, ordering and receiving costs, and cost of running out of stock.

a. **Production pattern.** If the firm has seasonal demand for its products, management must decide whether to plan for level or seasonal production. Level production involves working at a consistent level of effort to manufacture the annual forecasted amount of inventory. Level production results in the most efficient use of labor and facilities throughout the year. However, it also results in inventory buildups during slow sales periods. This results in additional inventory holding costs. Seasonal production involves increasing production during periods of peak demand and reducing production during slow sales periods. Seasonal production often has additional operating costs for such things as overtime wages and maintenance.

EXAMPLE

A firm has projected the following data for the two alternatives of level production and seasonal production. The firm's short-term interest cost is 7%.

	Level production	Seasonal production
Average inventory	$200,000	$150,000
Production costs	$1,000,000	$1,010,000

Which alternative is preferable?

Under the level production alternative, the firm would incur an additional $3,500 (($200,000 – $150,000) × 7%) in inventory holding costs, but it would also save $10,000 ($1,010,000 – $1,000,000) in production costs. Therefore, level production would be the best production alternative. It would save the firm $6,500 ($10,000 – $3,500).

---

b. **Inventory and Inflation.** A firm's inventory policy also might be affected by inflation (deflation). As an example, if a firm uses silver as a raw material, the firm could experience significant gains or losses simply because of price fluctuations that occur in the silver market. Price instability occurs in a number of markets, such as copper, wheat, sugar, etc. The problem may be partially controlled by holding low levels of inventory. Another way would be to hedge the price movement with a futures contract to sell silver at a specified price in the future. In this manner, if the price of the silver falls, reducing the value of the inventory, the value of the future contract would rise to completely or partially offset the inventory loss.

c. **Supply chain.** The term **supply chain** describes a good's production and distribution. It illustrates the flow of goods, services, and information from acquisition of basic raw materials through the manufacturing and distribution process to delivery of the product to the consumer, regardless of whether those activities occur in one or many firms. To manage inventories and their relationships with their suppliers many firms use a process known as **supply chain management.** A key aspect of supply chain management is the sharing of key information from the point of sale to the final consumer back to the manufacturer, to the manufacturer's suppliers, and to the suppliers' suppliers. As an example, if a manufacturer/distributor shares its sales forecasts with its suppliers and they in turn share their sales forecasts with their suppliers, the need for inventories for all firms is significantly decreased. The manufacturer/distributor, for example, needs far less raw materials inventory than normally would be the case because its suppliers are aware of the manufacturer's projected needs and are prepared to have the materials available when needed. Specialized software facilitates the process of information sharing along the supply chain network.

d. **Economic order quantity**

How much to order? The amount to be ordered is known as the **economic order quantity** (EOQ). The EOQ minimizes the sum of the ordering and carrying costs. The total inventory cost function includes **carrying costs** (which increase with order size) and **ordering costs** (which decrease with order size). The EOQ formula is derived by setting the annual carrying costs equal to annual ordering cost or by differentiating the cost function with respect to order size.

$$EOQ = \sqrt{\frac{2aD}{k}}$$

Where

a = cost of placing one order
D = annual demand in units
k = cost of carrying one unit of inventory for one year.

When to reorder? The objective is to order at a point in time so as to avoid **stockouts** but not so early that an excessive **safety stock** is maintained. Safety stocks may be used to guard against stockouts; they are maintained by increasing the lead time (the time that elapses from order placement until order arrival). Thus, safety stocks decrease stockout costs but increase carrying costs. Examples of these costs include

Carrying costs of safety stock (and inventory in general)	Stockout costs
1. Storage	1. Profit on lost sales
2. Interest	2. Customer ill will
3. Spoilage	3. Idle equipment
4. Insurance	4. Work stoppages
5. Property taxes	

The amount of safety stock held should minimize total stockout and carrying costs, as shown below.

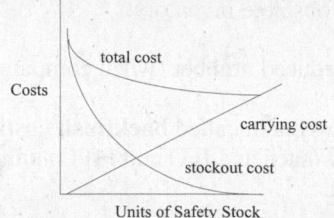

The most common approach to setting the optimum safety-stock level is to examine previous lead-time periods to determine the probabilities of running out of stock (a stockout) for different assessed levels of safety stock.

e. **Inventory Management and MRP.** Materials requirements planning (MRP) is a computerized system that manufactures finished goods based on demand forecasts. Demand forecasts are used to develop bills of materials that outline the materials, components, and subassemblies that go into the final products. Finally, a master production schedule is developed that specifies the quantity and timing of production of goods, taking into account the lead time required to purchase materials and to manufacture the various components of finished products. A key weakness of MRP is that it is a "push through" system. Once the master schedule is developed goods are pushed through the production process whether they are needed or not. Therefore, inventories may accumulate at various stages, especially if there are production slowdowns or unreliable demand forecasts. **MRP II** was developed as an extension of MRP and it features an automated closed loop system. That is, production planning drives the master schedule which drives the materials plans which is input to the capacity plan. It uses technology to integrate the functional areas of a manufacturing company.

f. **Just-in-Time (JIT) Purchasing.** JIT is a demand-pull inventory system which may be applied to purchasing so that raw material arrives just as it is needed for production. The primary benefit of JIT is **reduction of inventories, ideally to zero**. Because of its non-value-added nature, inventory is regarded as undesirable. In a JIT system, suppliers inspect their own goods and make frequent deliveries of materials, which are placed into production immediately upon receipt. This process eliminates the need for incoming inspection and the storeroom. Suppliers all along the supply chain are informed through specialized software (e.g., enterprise resource systems) about the forecasted demand for their products allowing them to plan to supply the items when needed.

Obviously, the most important aspect of a JIT purchasing system is selection of, and relationships with, suppliers. If suppliers do not make timely delivery of defect-free materials, stockouts and customer returns will occur and they will be more pronounced. In addition, if sales forecasts are not reliable, goods ordered will vary from what is expected, causing inventories to build up somewhere along the supply chain.

g. **JIT Production.** JIT methodology can also be applied to production. JIT production is a "demand pull" system in which each component of a finished good is produced when needed by the next production stage. The production process is driven by the demand. It begins with an order by the customer triggering the need for a finished good and works its way back through each stage of production to the beginning of the process. A JIT system strives to produce high-quality products that meet the customer's needs on a timely basis and at the lowest possible cost. Obviously, JIT production reduces inventories to a minimal level. To accomplish JIT production, management must

- **Emphasize reducing production cycle time (manufacturing lead time) and setup time.** Cycle time is the time required to complete a product from the start of its production until it is finished. Setup time is the time required to get equipment and materials ready to start working on the product. The time for both is cut to a minimum in a JIT system.
- **Emphasize production flexibility.** Plant layout is organized around **manufacturing cells** that produce a product or type of product with the workers being able to operate a number of the different machines. Machinery is purchased that can be used for multiple functions.
- **Emphasize solving production problems immediately.** If it is discovered that parts are absent or defective, production is corrected on the spot. This practice contrasts with traditional systems, in which the production of defective products often continues because defective goods are sitting in inventory—awaiting sale and thus ultimate feedback from the customer. In a JIT system, each worker is responsible for the quality of his or her own work. Thus, JIT results in reductions in scrap and rework.
- **Focus on simplifying production activities.** The goal of JIT is to identify and eliminate non-value-added activities. Less factory space is used for inventory storage and production activities, and materials handling between workstations is streamlined.

JIT purchasing and production systems offer many advantages over traditional systems, including the following:

- Lower investments in inventories and in space to store inventory.
- Lower inventory carrying and handling costs.

- Reduced risk of defective and obsolete inventory.
- Reduced manufacturing costs.
- The luxury of dealing with a reduced number (when compared with traditional systems) of reliable, quality-oriented suppliers.
- JIT allows a simplified costing system called **backflush costing**. The lack of inventories in a JIT system makes choices about cost-flow (such as LIFO and FIFO) unimportant—all manufacturing costs are simply run through cost of goods sold.

On the other hand, JIT systems can break down with disastrous results if (1) suppliers do not provide timely delivery of quality materials, (2) employers are not well trained or supervised, or (3) technology and equipment are not reliable.

h. **Enterprise Resource Planning (ERP) Systems.** ERP systems are enterprise-wide computerized information systems that connect all functional areas within an organization. By sharing information from a common database, marketing, purchasing, production, distribution, and customer relations management can be effectively coordinated. ERP systems also facilitate supply chain management by connecting the firm electronically to its suppliers and customers.

5. Receivables Management

Effective receivables management involves systems for deciding whether or not to grant credit and for monitoring the receivables. Obviously, management should establish consistent credit evaluation procedures that balance the costs of lost sales with the costs of credit losses (uncollectible accounts). The firm's credit policy consists of the following four variables:

- Credit period—The length of time buyers are given to pay for their purchases.
- Discounts—Percentage provided and period allowed for discount for early payment.
- Credit criteria—Required financial strength of acceptable credit customers. Firms often use a statistical technique called **credit scoring** to evaluate a potential customer.
- Collection policy—Diligence used to collect slow-paying accounts.

a. The credit period and discount policies will be the major determinant of the eventual size of the receivables balance. If a firm has $10,000 in credit sales per day and allows 30 days for payment, the firm will carry an approximate balance of $300,000 ($10,000 × 30). If the firm extends the terms to 45 days, the receivables balance will swell to approximately $450,000 ($10,000 × 45).

b. In making an individual credit decision, management must determine the level of credit risk of the customer based on prior records of payment, financial stability, current financial position, and other factors. Credit information is available from sources such as **Dun & Bradstreet Information Services** to make such decisions. Dun & Bradstreet makes available its Business Information Report (BIR) and a number of credit scoring reports.

c. To provide overall monitoring of receivables, management will often use measures such as the days sales outstanding and aging schedules. The days sales outstanding provides an overall measure of the accumulation of receivables and is calculated as follows:

$$\text{Days sales outstanding} = \frac{\text{Receivables}}{\text{Sales per day}}$$

EXAMPLE

Assume that a firm's outstanding receivables balance is $2,000,000 and annual sales is $52,000,000; the days sales outstanding is calculated below.

$$\text{Days sales outstanding} = \frac{\$2,000,000}{\$52,000,000/365 \text{ days}} = 14 \text{ days}$$

An aging schedule breaks down receivables by age, as shown below.

Age of Account (Days)	Amount	Percentage
0-10	$1,355,000	67.7
11-30	505,000	25.3
31-45	90,000	4.5
46-60	43,000	2.2
Over 60	7,000	0.3
Total	$2,000,000	100.0

By monitoring days sales outstanding and the aging schedule, management can detect adverse trends and evaluate the performance of the credit department.

---

d. Management of accounts receivable also involves determining the appropriate credit terms and criteria to maximize profit from sales after considering the cost of holding accounts receivable and losses from uncollectible accounts.

EXAMPLE

Assume that management believes that if they relax the firm's credit standards, sales will increase by $240,000. The firm's average collection period for these new customers will be 60 days and the payment period for existing customers is not expected to change. Management expects 5% losses from uncollectible accounts for these new customers. If variable costs are 75% of sales, and the cost of financing accounts receivable is 10%, should management decide to relax credit standards? The answer to this question involves comparing incremental revenues to incremental costs as shown below.

Incremental revenue	$240,000
Variable costs ($240,000 × 75%)	(180,000)
Uncollectible account expense ($240,000 × 5%)	(12,000)
Interest cost on additional average receivables ($40,000 × 10%)	(4,000)
Incremental revenue	$44,000

The interest cost is calculated by recognizing that if collection takes approximately 60 days, there will be approximately 60 days sales outstanding during the year. Average outstanding receivables is calculated as

$$\text{Average outstanding receivables} = (\text{Sales}/360 \text{ days}) \times 60 \text{ days}$$
$$= (\$240,000/360) \times 60$$
$$= \$40,000$$

---

6. **Financing Current Assets**

a. Because many firms have seasonal fluctuations in the demand for their products or services, current assets tend to vary in amount from month to month. Conventional wisdom would say that such assets should be financed with current liabilities—accounts payable, commercial bank loans, commercial paper, etc. However, a certain amount of current assets are required to operate the business in even the slowest periods of the year. This amount of current assets is called the amount of **permanent current assets**. Permanent current assets are more appropriately financed with long-term financing, such as stock or bonds. Additional current assets (inventory, accounts receivable, etc.) are accumulated during periods of higher production and sales. These current assets are called **temporary current assets,** and they may be appropriately financed with short-term financing.

b. Various strategies are used to finance current assets. Since short-term debt is less expensive than long-term, firms generally attempt to finance current assets with short-term debt. However, use of extensive amounts of short-term debt is **aggressive** in that firms must pay off the debt or replace it as it comes due. A business recession may render the firm unable to meet these obligations. In addition, the amount of interest expense over time will be more volatile because the firm has not locked in an interest rate on a long-term basis. More **conservative** strategies involve financing some current assets with long-term debt which involves a more stable interest rate. However, as indicated above long-term debt tends to be more expensive, and the provisions or **covenants** of long-term debt agreements generally constrain the firm's future actions. Finally, prepayment penalties may make early repayment of long-term debt an expensive proposition.

c. Illustrated in the graph below is a conservative short-term investment strategy in which permanent current assets are financed with long-term debt.

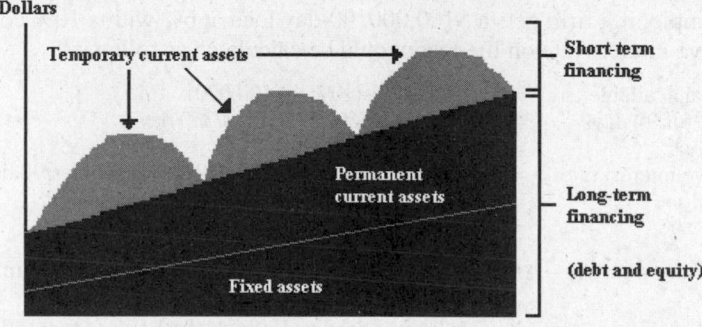

d. The **maturity matching** or **self-liquidating approach** to financing assets involves matching asset and liability maturities. This strategy minimizes the risk that the firm will be unable to pay its maturing obligations. This method is often referred to as a hedging approach.

e. Generalizations about the cost, riskiness, and flexibility of short-term versus long-term debt depend on the type of short-term debt being used. We will now turn our attention to the different sources of short-term funds.

7. **Sources of Short-Term Funds**

a. **Accounts payable (trade credit).** Firms generally purchase goods and services from other firms on credit. Trade credit, especially for small firms, is a very significant source of short-term funds. A major advantage of trade credit is that it arises in the normal course of conducting business and bears no interest cost, providing it is paid on time.

   Many firms have credit terms that allow a cash discount for early payment of the invoice. For example, a firm might sell on terms of 2/10, net 30, which means that payment is due in thirty days and a 2% discount is allowed for payment within 10 days. Generally, it is a good financial decision to take advantage of such discounts because the rate of interest realized for early payment is significant. The approximated cost of not taking the discount is calculated with the following formula:

$$\frac{\text{Discount percent}}{100\% - \text{Discount percent}} \times \frac{365 \text{ days}}{\text{Total pay period} - \text{Discount period}}$$

With our example of 2/10, net/30, the discount percentage is 2%, the total pay period is 30 days, and the discount period is 10 days. Therefore, the nominal annual cost is equal to 37.2% as calculated below.

$$\text{Nominal annual cost} = \frac{2\%}{100\% - 2\%} \times \frac{365 \text{ days}}{30 \text{ days} - 10 \text{ days}}$$
$$= 37.2\%$$

The nominal rate does not consider the effects of compounding. Therefore, the effective annual rate is significantly higher than the 37.2%.

b. **Short-term bank loans.** Notes payable to commercial banks represents the second most important source of short-term funds. We will now turn our attention to key features of bank loans.

   Maturity—While banks do make long-term loans, the majority of their lending has a maturity date of one year or less. Business loans typically mature every 90 days requiring the firm to pay or renew the loan on a regular basis.

   Promissory note—Notes are executed using a signed promissory note. The note specifies the terms of the agreement.

   Interest—The rate for short-term bank loans fluctuates with changes in short-term interest rates as measured by such indexes as

   - *Prime rate*—The rate a bank charges its most creditworthy customers. The rate increases for customers with more credit risk. As an example, a customer might have a rate of prime plus 100 basis points, which would be equal to the prime rate plus one percent. One basis point is equal to one hundredth of one percent (0.01%).
   - *London Interbank Offered Rate (LIBOR)*—This rate is important because of the availability of dollars for loan on the international market. US companies can decide to borrow money in the US financial markets, London, or any other major money market center. LIBOR reflects price of funds in the international market.

   Compensating balances—Loan agreements may require the borrower to maintain an average demand deposit balance equal to some percentage of the face amount of the loan. Such requirements increase the effective interest rate of the loan, because the firm does not get use of the full amount of the loan principal. As an example, if a firm gets a $100,000, 90-day loan at 6% with a 10% compensating balance arrangement, the effective interest rate on the loan would be calculated as follows:

Principal available	=	$100,000 − (10% × $100,000)
Interest for 90 days	=	$100,000 × 6% × (90 days/360 days)
	=	$1,500
Effective interest rate	=	Interest paid/Principal available × (360 days/90 days
	=	$1,500/$90,000 × (360 days/90 days)
	=	6.67%

   Informal line of credit—An informal specification of the maximum amount that the bank will lend the borrower.

   Revolving credit agreements—A line of credit in which the bank is formally committed to lend the firm a specified maximum amount. The bank typically receives a commitment fee as a part of the agreement. Revolving credit arrangements are often used for intermediate-term financing.

Letter of credit—An instrument that facilitates international trade. A letter of credit, issued by the importer's bank, promises that the bank will pay for the imported merchandise when it is delivered. It is designed to reduce the risk of nonpayment by the importer.

c. **Commercial paper.** Commercial paper is a form of unsecured promissory note issued by large, creditworthy firms. It is sold primarily to other firms, insurance companies, pension funds, banks, and mutual funds. Commercial paper typically has maturity dates that vary from one day to nine months. This form of financing is very favorable for corporations with the financial strength to issue it. The rate is often 2 to 3% less than the prime rate and there are no compensating balance requirements. However, the market is less predictable than bank financing.

d. **Accounts receivable financing.**

   (1) **Pledging of receivables.** Pledging accounts receivable involves committing the receivables as collateral for a loan from a financial institution. The financial institution will evaluate the receivables to see if they are of sufficient quality to serve as collateral. The interest rate will depend on the financial strength of the firm and the quality of the receivables. Typically, the financial institution will lend 60 to 80% of the value of the receivables and the outstanding balance of the loan will fluctuate with the amount of the receivables outstanding. Interest is computed based on the outstanding loan balance and tends to be quite high. However, for small or troubled companies the interest rate will be less than for unsecured loans.

   (2) **Factoring.** When accounts receivable are factored, they are sold outright to a finance company. In such situations, the finance company is often directly involved in the credit decisions, and will submit the funds to the firm upon acceptance of the account. For taking the risk, the finance company is generally paid a fee of from 1 to 3% of the invoices accepted. In addition, the finance company receives the interest rate for advancing the funds.

EXAMPLE

Assume that a finance company charges a 2% fee and a 12% annual interest rate for factoring the firm's receivables which are payable in 30 days. The effective annual rate of interest on this arrangement would be calculated as follows:

   2% Fee
   1% Interest for 1 month (12% annual/12)
   3% Monthly × 12 = 36% annual rate

Obviously, with the high rates associated with factoring, it is only considered by firms that have few other options.

---

   (3) **Asset-backed public offerings.** Large firms recently have begun floating public offerings of debt (e.g. bonds) collateralized by the firm's accounts receivable. Because they are collateralized, such securities generally carry a high credit rating, even though the issuing firm may have a lower credit rating. Therefore, this form of accounts receivable financing can be advantageous. The creation of asset-backed securities is also called **securitization of assets**.

e. **Inventory financing.** A firm may also borrow funds using its inventory as collateral. The extent of the feasibility of this strategy depends on the marketability of the inventory. Obviously, widely traded raw materials such as lumber, metals, and grains are easily used as collateral. The methods used by lenders to control the pledged inventories include

   • **Blanket Inventory Lien**—This is simply a legal document that establishes the inventory as collateral for the loan. No physical control over inventory is involved.
   • **Trust Receipt**—An instrument that acknowledges that the borrower holds the inventory and that proceeds from sale will be put in trust for the lender. Each item is tagged and controlled by serial number. When the inventory is sold, the funds are transferred to the lender and the trust receipt is cancelled. This form of financing is also referred to as *floor planning* and is widely used for automobile and industrial equipment dealers.
   • **Warehousing**—This is the most secure form of inventory financing. The inventory is stored in a **public warehouse** or under the control of public warehouse personnel. The goods can only be removed with the lender's permission.

f. **Hedging to reduce interest rate risk.** Firms that must borrow significant amounts of short-term variable rate funds are exposed to high levels of interest rate risk. If interest rates go up suddenly, the firm could experience a significant increase in interest costs. To mitigate this interest rate risk, management may decide to hedge the risk with derivatives purchased or sold in the **financial futures market**. Derivatives and hedging strategies are described in Module 44.

> **NOW REVIEW MULTIPLE-CHOICE QUESTIONS 1 THROUGH 80 IN VOLUME 2**

CAPITAL STRUCTURE

This section focuses on determining the appropriate **capital structure** of the firm which involves a combination of debt and equity.

A. Long-Term Debt

The characteristics of the various forms of financing available to the firm help determine the funding sources that are most appropriate.

1. **Public and Private Debt**

    Debt is increasingly a source of funds for US corporations. In issuing debt, management must first decide whether to issue the debt privately or publicly.

    a. **Private debt** is of two principal types. The first type is loans from financial institutions (either an individual institution or a syndicated loan from multiple institutions). Such loans almost universally have a floating interest rate that is tied to a base rate, usually **LIBOR** (the London Interbank Offered Rate) or the US bank prime interest rate. The second type of private debt involves the **private placement** of unregistered bonds sold directly to accredited investors (often pension funds or insurance companies). Such debt is typically less expensive to issue than public debt.

    b. In the United States, **public long-term debt** offerings involve selling SEC registered bonds directly to investors. The bond agreement specifies the par value, the coupon rate, and the maturity date of the debt. The par value is the face amount of the bond and most corporate bonds have a $1,000 face amount. The coupon rate is the interest rate paid on the face amount of the bond. Since most bonds pay a fixed rate of interest, the market value of the bond fluctuates with changes in the market interest rate. The maturity date is the final date on which repayment of the bond principal is due.

EXAMPLE

Baker Corporation issued $500,000 in 6% bonds, maturing in 20 years. Assuming that the bonds were issued at face value and interest is paid semiannually, the coupon rate of 6% is paid in installments of $30 (3% × $1,000) every six month for each $1,000 bond. Total annual interest for the firm every year is $30,000 ($500,000 × 6%). If the market rate of interest increases to 7% after the bonds are issued, the market value of the bonds will decline to an amount that will allow a new purchaser to realize a 7% yield to maturity. On the other hand, if the market rate of interest decreases to 5%, the market price of the bond will increase to an amount that will allow the new purchaser to earn only a 5% yield to maturity. This example illustrates the **interest rate risk** that investors assume when they purchase long-term fixed-rate bonds.

---

    c. A debt market with increasing importance is the market for **Eurobonds**. A Eurobond is a bond payable in the borrower's currency but sold outside the borrower's country. As an example, the bond of a US firm, payable in US dollars, might be sold in Germany, London, and Japan through an international syndicate of investment bankers. The registration and disclosure requirements for Eurobonds are less stringent than those of the SEC for US issued bonds. Therefore, the cost of issuance is less.

2. **Debt Covenants and Provisions**

    a. **Debt covenants.** Both private and public debt agreements contain restrictions, known as **debt covenants**. Such covenants allow investors (lenders) to monitor and control the activities of the firm. Otherwise, management could make decisions that would be detrimental to the interests of the debt holders. Negative covenants specify actions the borrower cannot take, such as restrictions on

        (1) The sale of certain assets.
        (2) The incurrence of additional debt.
        (3) The payment of dividends.
        (4) The compensation of top management.

    Positive covenants specify what the borrower must do and include such requirements as:

        (1) Provide audited financial statements each year.
        (2) Maintain certain minimum financial ratios.
        (3) Maintain life insurance on key employees.

These covenants restrict the action of management and are an important consideration in determining the type of financing to obtain. In addition, major covenants must be disclosed in the footnotes to the firm's financial statements. Now, let's turn our attention to some typical provisions of debt agreements.

b. **Security provisions.** Debt may be secured or unsecured. Secured debt is one in which specific assets of the firm are pledged to the bondholders in the event of default. Based on their security provisions debt may be classified as follows:

(1) **Mortgage bond**—A bond secured with the pledge of specific property. The securing property is typically property or plant assets.

(2) **Collateral trust bond**—A bond secured by financial assets of the firm.

(3) **Debenture**—A bond that is not secured by the pledge of specific property. It is a general obligation of the firm. Because of the **default risk,** such bonds can only be issued by firms with the highest credit rating. Debentures typically have a higher yield than mortgage bonds and other secured debt.

(4) **Subordinated debenture**—A bond with claims subordinated to other general creditors in the event of bankruptcy of the firm. That is, the bondholders receive distributions only after general creditors and **senior** debt holders have been paid. As you would expect, subordinated debentures have higher yields than senior unsecured debt.

(5) **Income bond**—A bond with interest payments that are contingent on the firm's earnings. Obviously, these bonds also have a high degree of risk and carry even higher yields. These types of bonds are often associated with firms undergoing restructuring.

c. **Methods of payment.** Bonds may be paid as a single sum at maturity, or through:

(1) **Serial payments—Serial bonds** are paid off in installments over the life of the issue. Serial bonds may be desirable to bondholders because they can choose their maturity date.

(2) **Sinking fund provisions**—The firm makes payments into a sinking fund which is used to retire bonds by purchase.

(3) **Conversion**—The bonds may be convertible into common stock and this may provide the method of payment.

(4) **Redeemable**—A bondholder may have the right to redeem the bonds for cash under certain circumstances (e.g., if the firm is acquired by another firm).

(5) **A call feature**—The bonds may have a call provision allowing the firm to force the bondholders to redeem the bonds before maturity. Call provisions typically call for payment of a 5 to 10% premium over par value to redeem the bonds. Investors generally do not like call features because they may be used to force them to liquidate their investment.

3. **Bond Yields**

a. There are three different yields that are relevant to bonds: the **coupon rate,** the **current yield,** and **yield to maturity**.

EXAMPLE

Assume that a bond has a par value of $1,000 and pays 12% interest, $120 ($1,000 × 12%) per year for the remaining term of 10 years. The bond is currently selling for $900.

- The coupon rate (nominal yield) is equal to the 12% stated rate.
- The current yield is the stated interest payment divided by the current price of the bond.

$$\frac{\$120}{\$900} = 13.33\%$$

- The yield to maturity is the interest rate that will equate future interest payments and the maturity payment to the current market price. The future interest payments are $120 per year and the principal payment is $1,000 received at the end of 10 years. The current price of the bond is $900, and the yield to maturity can be estimated with the following formula:

$$YM = \frac{\text{Annual interest payment} + \dfrac{\text{Principal payment} - \text{Bond price}}{\text{Number of years to maturity}}}{0.6 \,(\text{Price of bond}) + 0.4 \,(\text{Principal payment})}$$

$$= \frac{\$120 + \dfrac{\$1,000 - \$900}{10}}{0.6\,(\$900) + 0.4\,(\$1,000)}$$

$$= 13.83\%$$

b. The price of a bond is dependent on the current **risk-free interest rate** and the **credit risk** of the particular bond. Bond rating agencies have rating systems for bonds to capture credit risk. For example, Moody's Investor Service provides the following nine categories of ranking:

Aaa	Aa	A	Baa	Ba	B	Caa	Ca	C

Lowest risk   Highest risk

    Companies that invest in a significant amount of bonds may decide to share the credit risk by purchasing credit default insurance.

    For additional discussion of the valuation of bonds, review the section on present value in Module 44.

4. **Other Types of Bonds**

    a. **Zero-coupon rate bonds**—These types of bonds do not pay interest. Instead they sell at a deep discount from the face or maturity value. The return to the investor is the difference between the cost and the bond's maturity value. The advantage of these bonds is that there are no interest payment requirements until the bonds mature. In addition, the amortization of interest is tax-deductible even though the firm is not making any interest payments.

    b. **Floating rate bonds**—The rate of interest paid on this type of bond floats with changes in the market rate (usually monthly or quarterly). Therefore the market price of the bond does not fluctuate as widely. **Reverse floaters** are floating rate bonds that pay a higher rate of interest when other interest rates fall and a lower rate when other rates rise. Reverse floaters are riskier than normal bonds.

    c. **Registered bonds**—These bonds are registered in the name of the bondholder. Interest payments are sent directly to the registered owners.

    d. **Junk bonds**—These bonds carry very high-risk premiums. Junk bonds often have resulted from **leveraged buyouts** or are issued by large firms that are in troubled circumstances. They may appeal to investors who feel they can diversify the risk by purchasing a portfolio of the bonds in different industries.

    e. **Foreign bonds**—These bonds are international bonds that are denominated in the currency of the nation in which they are sold. Foreign bonds might serve as an effective hedge for a firm that is heavily invested in assets in the foreign country.

    f. **Eurobonds**—As described above, these bonds are international bonds that are denominated in US dollars.

5. **Advantages and Disadvantages of Debt Financing**

    In deciding whether debt should be used as a form of financing, management must keep in mind the following advantages and disadvantages. The advantages of debt financing include

- Interest is tax-deductible.
- The obligation is generally fixed in terms of interest and principal payments.
- In periods of inflation, debt is paid back with dollars that are worth less than the ones borrowed.
- The owners (common stockholders) do not give up control of the firm.
- Debtors do not participate in excess earnings of the firm.
- Debt is less costly than equity. Therefore, the use of debt, up to some limit, will lower the firm's cost of capital. Cost of capital is discussed later in this module.

Disadvantages of debt financing include

- Interest and principal obligations must be paid regardless of the economic position of the firm.
- Interest payments are fixed in amount regardless of how poorly the firm performs.
- Debt agreements contain covenants that place restrictions of the flexibility of the firm.
- Excessive debt increases the risk of equity holders and therefore depresses share prices.

6. **Leasing as a Form of Financing**

    a. Another potential source of intermediate or long-term financing involves leasing assets. From a financial statement standpoint, leases may be capital leases or operating leases. **Capital leases** are those that meet any one of the following four conditions as set forth in SFAS 13:

        (1) The arrangement transfers ownership of the property to the lessee by the end of the lease.
        (2) The lease contains a bargain purchase option at the end of the lease. The option price must be sufficiently low so exercise of the option appears reasonably certain.
        (3) The lease term is equal to 75% or more of the estimated life of the leased property.
        (4) The present value of the minimum lease payments equals 90% or more of the fair value of the leased property at the inception of the lease.

    If a lease meets one of these conditions, the firm must record the leased asset and related liability on its balance sheet, and account for the asset much like it would a purchased asset. The asset is recorded at the present value of the future lease payments and amortized (depreciated). A liability is recorded at the same amount and each lease payment involves payment of interest and principal on the obligation.

b. An **operating lease** is one that does not meet the criteria to be treated as a capital lease. Operating leases are treated as rental agreements; the asset and obligation are not recorded on the firm's balance sheet. The lease payments are expensed as rent as they are incurred.

c. A **sale-leaseback** is a transaction in which the owner of the property sells the property to another and simultaneously leases it back. Such arrangements often provide financing and tax advantages.

d. Leases have a number of advantages over purchasing the asset and financing through other means, including

- A firm may be able to lease an asset when it does not have the funds or credit capacity to purchase the asset.
- The provisions of a lease agreement may be less stringent than a bond indenture.
- There may be no down payment requirement.
- Creditor claims on certain types of leases, such as real estate, are restricted in bankruptcy.
- The cost of a lease to the lessee may be reduced because the lease may be structured such that the lessor retains the tax benefits.
- Operating leases do not require recognition of a liability on the financial statement of the lessor.

e. On the other hand, the dollar cost of leasing an asset is often higher than the cost of purchasing the asset.

B. Equity

This section describes the use of various forms of equity used for long-term financing.

1. **Common Stock**

   The ultimate owners of the firm are the common shareholders. They generally have control of the business and are entitled to a residual claim to income of the firm after the creditors and preferred shareholders are paid. Common stock ownership involves a high degree of risk. The investor is the last in line to receive earnings and distributions upon liquidation of the firm. On the other hand, common stockholders have the potential opportunity to receive very high returns. The return of the common stockholder includes dividends and appreciation in the value of the stock.

   a. **Classes of common stock.** Most firms issue only one class of common stock. However, a firm may issue a second class of stock that differs with respect to the stockholders' right to vote or receive dividends. As an example, if the current stockholders do not wish to give up control of the firm, a class B stock might be issued that has limited voting rights. Obviously, the class B stock would sell for less than the class A stock as a result of the restriction.

   b. **Stock warrants.** Stock warrants are sometimes issued with bonds to increase their marketability. A stock warrant is an option to buy common stock at a fixed price for some period of time. Once the bond is sold, the stock warrants often may be sold separately and are traded on the market.

   c. **Advantages of issuing common stock**

   - The firm has no firm obligation, which increases financial flexibility.
   - Increased equity reduces the risk to borrowers and, therefore, will reduce the firm's cost of borrowing.
   - Common stock is more attractive to many investors because of the future profit potential.

   d. **Disadvantages of common stock**

   - Issuance costs are greater than for debt.
   - Ownership and control is given up with respect to the issuance of common stock.
   - Dividends are not tax-deductible by the corporation whereas interest is tax-deductible.
   - Shareholders demand a higher rate of return than lenders.
   - Issuance of too much common stock may increase the firm's cost of capital.

2. **Preferred stock** is a hybrid security. Preferred shareholders are entitled to receive a stipulated dividend and, generally, must receive the stipulated amount before the payment of dividends to common shareholders. In addition preferred stockholders have a priority over common stockholders in the event of liquidation of the firm. Common features of preferred stock include

   - **Cumulative dividends**—Most issues are cumulative preferred stock and have a cumulative claim to dividends. That is, if dividends are not declared in a particular year, the amount becomes in arrears and the amount must be paid in addition to current dividends before common shareholders can receive a dividend.
   - **Redeemability**—Some preferred stock is redeemable at a specified date. This makes the stock very similar to debt. On the firm's balance sheet such stock is often presented between debt and equity (the so-called mezzanine).
   - **Conversion**—Preferred stock may be convertible into common stock.
   - **Call feature**—Preferred stock, like debt, may have a call feature.

- **Participation**—A small percentage of preferred shares are participating, which means they may share with common shareholders in dividends above the stated amount.
- **Floating rate**—A small percentage of preferred shares have a floating rather than fixed dividend rate.

a. Advantages of issuing preferred stock

- The firm still has no obligation to pay dividends until they are declared, which increases financial flexibility.
- Increased equity reduces the risk to borrowers and, therefore, will reduce the firm's cost of borrowing.
- Common stockholders do not give up control of the firm.
- Preferred stockholders do not generally participate in superior earnings of the firm.

b. Disadvantages of preferred stock

- Issuance costs are greater than for debt.
- Dividends are not tax-deductible by the corporation whereas interest is tax-deductible.
- Dividends in arrears accumulated over a number of years may create financial problems for the firm.

3. Convertible Securities

A convertible security is a bond or share of preferred stock that can be converted, at the option of the holder, into common stock. When the security is initially issued it has a **conversion ratio** that indicates the number of shares that the security may be converted into.

The advantage of convertible securities is the fact that investors require a lower yield because of the prospects that conversion may result in a significant gain.

The major disadvantage is that conversion dilutes the ownership of other common stockholders.

4. Spin-Offs

A spin-off occurs when a public diversified firm separates one of its subsidiaries, distributing the shares on a pro rata basis to the existing stockholders. Spin-offs are often part of management's strategy to turn its focus to its core businesses.

5. Tracking Stocks

A tracking stock is a specialized equity offering that is based on the operations and cash flows of a wholly owned subsidiary of a diversified firm. They are hybrid securities, because the subsidiary is not separated from the parent, legally or operationally. The stock simply is entitled to the cash flows of the subsidiary and, therefore, the trading stock trades at a valuation based on the subsidiary's expected future cash flows. Managers that issue trading stock believe that stockholder wealth will be maximized by separate valuation of two or more parts of the consolidated group.

6. Venture Capital

Venture capital is a pool of funds that is used to make actively managed direct equity investments in rapidly growing private companies. Such funds may be institutionally managed or involve ad hoc investments by wealthy individuals. In addition to capital, professional venture capitalists provide managerial oversight and business advice to the companies. Venture capitalists generally plan to exit the investment within three to seven years by selling the stock to another firm or by initiating a public offering of the stock. Venture capital provides a good source of capital for promising private companies, but it is expensive and management gives up significant control.

7. Going Public

As a private firm grows, one decision that must be made is whether and when to go public. Going public involves registering the firm's shares with the SEC. From that point on, the firm must comply with the reporting and other requirements of the SEC and the exchange on which the stock trades.

a. Advantages of going public

- An initial public offering provides the firm with access to a larger pool of equity capital.
- Publicly traded stock may be used for acquisitions of other firms. If a private company decides to acquire another company it generally must do so with cash.
- The firm can offer stock options and other stock-based compensation to attract and retain qualified managers.
- Going public provides the owners of the private company liquidity for their investments. These individuals can more easily sell portions of their stock in the firm and diversify their portfolio with other investments.

b. Disadvantages of going public

- Significant costs and management effort must be put into an initial public offering.
- There are significant costs of being public related to compliance with the securities laws and SEC and stock exchange regulations. These costs have been significantly increased by the provisions of the Sarbanes-Oxley Act of 2002.

- Being public necessarily causes management to be focused on maximizing stock price. This may or may not be in the best long-term interest of the firm.
- Management must provide a great deal of information about the firm to investors.

8. **Employee Stock Ownership Plans (ESOPs)**

Firms often reward management and key employees with stock or stock options as part of their compensation. These plans are designed to motivate management to focus on shareholder value. ESOPs are sometimes used as a vehicle for a **leveraged buyout**. ESOPs have certain tax advantages to the employees, and compensation expense may or may not have to be recognized by the firm.

9. **Going Private**

Some public corporations have decided (often to concentrate control) to go private. These transformations are sometimes executed through a **leveraged buyout** (LBO). In an LBO large amounts of debt are used to buy all or a voting majority of the shares of stock outstanding. Obviously, the firm, after the LBO, is heavily leveraged with much greater risk.

C. Evaluating the Best Source of Financing

To understand completely the considerations involved in making financing decisions, one must understand the concepts of leverage and cost of capital.

1. **Leverage**

The finance literature generally discusses two types of leverage: operating leverage and financial leverage.

a. **Operating leverage.** Operating leverage measures the degree to which a firm builds fixed costs into its operations. If fixed costs are high a significant decrease in sales can be devastating. Therefore, all other things being equal, the greater a firm's fixed costs the greater its **business risk**. On the other hand, if sales increase for a firm with a high degree of operating leverage, there will be a larger increase in return on equity. The degree of operating leverage (DOL) may be computed using the following formula:

$$DOL = \frac{\text{Percent change in operating income}}{\text{Percent change in unit volume}}$$

Highly leveraged firms, such as Ford Motor Company, enjoy substantial increases in income when sales volume increases. Less leveraged firms enjoy only modest increases in income as sales volume increases.

b. **Financial leverage.** Financial leverage measures the extent to which the firm uses debt financing. While the use of debt can produce high returns to stockholders, it also increases their risk. Since debt generally is a less costly form of financing, a firm will generally attempt to use as much debt for financing as possible. However, as more and more debt is issued, the firm becomes more leveraged and the risk of its debt increases, causing the interest rate on additional debt to rise. Therefore, the optimal capital structure for a firm involves a mixture of debt and equity. The degree of financial leverage (DFL) for a firm may be computed using the following formula:

$$DFL = \frac{\text{Percent change in EPS}}{\text{Percent change in EBIT}}$$

Where

EPS = Earnings per share
EBIT = Earnings before interest and taxes

EXAMPLE

Let's examine two different leverage strategies. Under Plan 1 (the leveraged plan) management borrows $400,000 and sells 20,000 shares of common stock at $10 per share. Under Plan 2 (the conservative plan) the firm borrows $100,000 and issues 50,000 shares of stock at $10 per share. The debt bears interest at 10% and the firm has a 40% tax rate. These alternatives are illustrated below.

	Plan 1	Plan 2
Debt (10 % interest)	$400,000	$100,000
Common stock	200,000	500,000
Total financing	$600,000	$600,000
Common stock	20,000 shares	50,000 shares

Now let's examine two sets of financial results. First, assume that the firm loses $200,000 before interest and taxes (EBIT). The financial results under the two different financing scenarios is shown below.

	Plan 1	**Plan 2**
EBIT	$(200,000)	$(200,000)
Interest (10% × principal)	(40,000)	(10,000)
Earnings before taxes	$(240,000)	$(210,000)
Tax benefit (40% × EBT)	96,000	84,000
Net loss	$(144,000)	$(126,000)
Loss per share	($7.20)	($2.52)

Next, assume that the firm earns $200,000 before interest and taxes. Again, the financial results under the two different financing scenarios is shown below.

	Plan 1	**Plan 2**
EBIT	$200,000	$200,000
Interest (10% × principal)	(40,000)	(10,000)
Earnings before taxes	$160,000	$190,000
Tax expense (40% × EBT)	(64,000)	(76,000)
Net earnings	$96,000	$114,000
Earnings per share	$4.80	$2.28

As you can see from the tables, the more leveraged strategy results in much higher earnings for common stockholders when the firm performs well. However, it results in much larger loss per share when the firm performs poorly. These examples clearly illustrate the major advantages and disadvantages of financial leverage.

2. Cost of Capital

A firm's cost of capital is an important concept in discussing financing decisions, especially those involving financing capital projects (long-term financing). If a firm can earn a return on an investment that is greater than its cost of capital, it will increase the value of the firm. The cost of capital for a firm is the weighted-average cost of its debt and equity financing components. The cost of the various components are determined as described below.

a. The **cost of debt** is equal to the interest rate of the loan adjusted for the fact that interest is deductible. Specifically, the cost is calculated as the interest rate times one minus the marginal tax rate. As an example, if a firm's interest rate on a long-term debt is 6% and its marginal tax rate is 30%, the cost of the debt is 4.2% (0.06 × (1.00 - .30)). Remember in considering the cost of new debt, costs of issuing the debt (floatation costs) must be considered. For example, assume the firm issues at face value $20,000,000 of 6% coupon bonds and floatation costs are equal to $1,000,000. The maturity date of the bonds is in 10 years and interest is payable semiannually. To compute the cost of the debt, management should determine the interest rate (internal rate of return) that equates the future interest and principal payments with the present value of the debt. This is equivalent to the bond issue's yield to maturity. To get an accurate yield one would need to use a computer or programmable calculator. However, the following formula may be used to approximate the yield on bonds.

$$YM = \frac{\text{Annual interest payment} + \dfrac{\text{Principal payment} - \text{Bond price}}{\text{Number of years to maturity}}}{0.6 \,(\text{Price of bond}) + 0.4 \,(\text{Principal payment})}$$

$$= \frac{\$1,200,000 + \dfrac{\$20,000,000 - \$19,000,000}{10}}{0.6 \,(\$19,000,000) + 0.4 \,(\$20,000,000)}$$

$$= 6.70\%$$

b. The **cost of preferred equity** is determined by dividing the preferred dividend amount by the issue price of the stock. For example, if 1,000 shares of $8.00 preferred stock is issued for $102,500, the cost of preferred stock is equal to 7.8% ($8,000/$102,500).

c. The **cost of common equity** is greater than that of debt or preferred equity because common shareholders assume more risk. Thus, they demand a higher return for their investment. Common equity is raised in two ways: (1) by retaining earnings, and (2) by issuing new common stock. Equity raised by issuing stock has a somewhat higher cost due to the flotation costs involved with new stock issues.

3. The Cost of Existing Common Equity

Firms use a number of techniques to estimate the cost of existing common equity including the Capital Asset Pricing Model, the Arbitrage Pricing Model, the Bond-Yield-Plus approach, and the Dividend-Yield-Plus-Growth-Rate approach.

a. **The Capital Asset Pricing Model (CAPM) Method.** One method of estimating the cost of common equity is by using the CAPM. The steps involved in estimating CAPM are

(1) Estimate the risk-free rate of interest, k_{RF}. Generally, firms use the either the US Treasury bond rate or the short-term Treasury bill rate.

(2) Estimate the stock's beta coefficient, b_i for use as an index of the stock's risk. The beta coefficient measures the correlation between the price volatility of the stock market and the price volatility of an individual firm's stock. If the stock price consistently rises and falls to the same extent as the overall market, the stock's beta would be equal to 1.00. Higher betas indicate more volatility and more risk. Betas are computed and reported by financial reporting services.

(3) Estimate the expected rate of return on the market, k_M. This is the expected rate of return on stock investments with similar risk. This factor is designed to capture systematic risk of the stock investment.

(4) Use the following equation to calculate the CAPM which can be used as an estimate of the cost of equity capital.

$$k_s \text{ (CAPM)} = k_{RF} + (k_M - k_{RF})b_i$$

EXAMPLE

Assume the risk-free interest rate (k_{RF}) is equal to 5%, the expected market rate of interest (k_M) is equal to 10%, and the stock's beta coefficient (b_i) is equal to 0.9 for a given stock; CAPM is calculated as follows:

$$
\begin{aligned}
k_s &= 5\% + (10\% - 5\%)(0.9) \\
&= 5\% + (5\%)(0.9) \\
&= 5\% + 4.5\% \\
&= 9.5\%
\end{aligned}
$$

Thus, an estimate of the cost of existing common equity is 9.5%

---

b. **Arbitrage pricing model.** As indicated previously, investors face two different types of risk for an investment.

- Systematic risk—Market risk that cannot be diversified away.
- Unsystematic risk—The risk of the specific investment that can be eliminated through diversification.

CAPM uses only one variable to capture systematic risk, the market rate of return or k_m. The arbitrage pricing model uses a series of systematic risk factors to develop a value that reflects the multiple dimensions of systematic risk. For example, systematic risk may be affected by future oil prices, exchange rates, interest rates, economic growth, etc. The formulation of the arbitrage pricing model is as follows:

$$r_p = b_1(k_1 - k_{RF}) + b_2(k_2 - k_{RF}) + b_3(k_3 - k_{RF}) \ldots$$

Where

r_p = The risk premium on the particular investment. This is the amount that should be added to the risk-free rate to get an estimate of the cost of capital.

k_{rf} = The risk-free interest rate.

$b_{1,2,3}$ = The betas for the individual risk factors (e.g., exchange rate risk, oil price risk, interest rate risk, etc.).

$k_{1,2,3}$ = The market interest rate associated with each of the risk factors.

As you can see, the amounts in the parentheses are equal to the risk premium associated with each of the factors, (i.e., the market rate for each factor minus the risk-free rate).

c. **Bond-yield-plus approach.** The bond-yield-plus approach simply involves adding a risk premium of 3 to 5% to the interest rate on the firm's long-term debt.

d. **Dividend-yield-plus-growth-rate approach.** The dividend-yield-plus-growth-rate (dividend valuation) approach estimates the cost of common equity by considering the investors' expected yield on their investment. Specifically, the following formula is used:

$$k_s = \frac{D_1}{P_0} + \text{Expected g}$$

Where

D_1 = Next expected dividend

P_0 = Current stock price

g = Growth rate in earnings

EXAMPLE

Assume that a firm's stock sells for $25, its next annual dividend is estimated to be $1 and its expected growth rate is 6%. The cost of existing common equity would be calculated as follows:

$$k_s = \frac{D_1}{P_0} + \text{Expected } g$$

$$k_s = \frac{\$1}{\$25} + 6\%$$
$$= 4\% + 6\%$$
$$= 10\%$$

4. **The Cost of New Common Stock**

If a firm is issuing new common stock, a slightly higher return must be earned. This higher return is necessary to cover the cost of distribution of the new securities (floatation or selling costs). As an example, assume that the cost of capital for existing stockholders is 10% and the current share price of the stock is $25. Also, assume that the cost of floating the new stock issue is $2 per share, the next expected dividend is $1, and the expected growth rate in earnings for the firm is 6%. Using the dividend-yield-plus-growth-rate approach the cost of issuing new stock would be calculated using the following formula:

$$k_s = \frac{D_1}{P_0 - F} + \text{Expected } G$$

Where

D_1 = Next expected dividend
P_0 = Current stock price
G = Growth rate in earnings
F = Flotation cost per share

$$k_s = \frac{D_1}{P_0 - F} + \text{Expected } G$$

$$k_s = \frac{\$1}{\$25 - \$2} + 6\%$$

$$= 10.35\%$$

5. **Evaluating the Cost of Capital—An Example**

Assume that Café Roma operates a chain of coffee shops located in the Northwest. Management has decided to undertake an aggressive expansion program into California and is considering the following three financing options to obtain the $38,000,000 needed.

a. Issuance of $40,000,000 bonds with an 8% coupon rate. After floatation costs the firm would receive approximately $39,000,000, and the effective yield would equal 8.5%.

b. Issuance of $40,000,000 in 6% preferred stock that would yield approximately $38,000,000 after floatation costs.

c. Issuance of 2,000,000 shares of common stock at $20 per share that would yield approximately $38,000,000 after floatation costs.

The current market value of Café Roma's common stock is $20 per share, and the common stock dividend for the year is expected to be $1 per share. Investors are expecting a growth rate in earnings and dividends for the firm of 5%. The firm is subject to an effective tax rate of 40%.

To determine which of the alternatives is least expensive in terms of cost of capital, the cost of each alternative would be calculated as shown below.

Cost of bond issue	=	Interest rate × (1.00 – The effective rate)
	=	8.5% (1.00 – .40)
	=	5.1%

Cost of preferred stock	=	Total dividend amount/Total issuance price
	=	The annual dividend amount/Issue price
	=	(6% × $40,000,000)/$38,000,000
	=	$2,400,000/$38,000,000
	=	6.3%

$$\text{Cost of common stock} \quad = \quad \frac{D_1}{P_0 - F} + \text{Expected G}$$

$$= \quad \frac{\$1}{\$20 - \$1} + 5\%$$

$$= \quad 10.3\%$$

Because total floatation costs are $2,000,000 [(2,000,000 × $20) – $38,000,000], floatation costs per share are $1 ($2,000,000/2,000,000).

6. **Optimal Capital Structure**

a. The optimal capital structure defines the mix of debt, preferred, and common equity that causes the firm's stock price to be maximized. The optimal or target capital structure involves a trade-off between risk and return. Incurring more debt generally leads to higher returns on equity but it also increases the risk borne by the stockholders of the firm. From a theoretical standpoint a firm's optimal capital structure is the one that minimizes the weighted-average cost of capital as shown in the graph below.

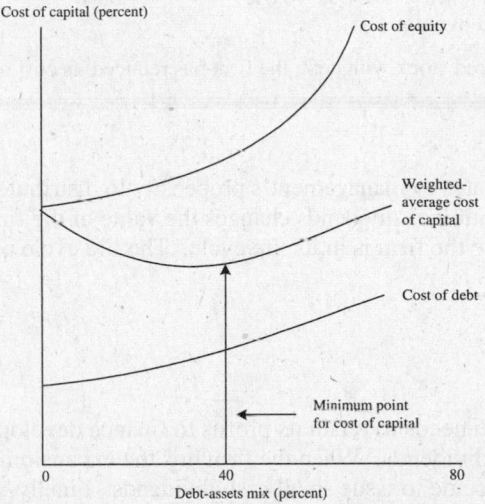

In practice, the following factors generally affect a firm's capital structure strategies:

(1) *Business risk.* The greater the inherent risk of the business the lower the optimal debt to equity ratio.
(2) *Tax position.* A major advantage of debt is the tax deductibility of interest payments. If the firm has a low marginal tax rate, debt becomes less advantageous as a form of financing.
(3) *Financial flexibility.* Financial flexibility is the ability of the firm to raise capital on reasonable terms under adverse conditions. Less debt should be assumed by firms with less financial flexibility.
(4) *Management conservatism or aggressiveness.* A firm's target capital structure will be affected by the risk tolerance of management. More aggressive management may take on more debt.

b. **Weighted-average cost of capital (WACC).** In determining the optimum capital structure, management often calculates the firm's weighted-average cost of capital. This process involves taking the cost of the various types of financing (debt, preferred equity, common equity, etc.) and weighting each by the actual or proposed percentage of total capital. A computation of weighted-average cost of capital is presented below.

Weighted-Average Cost of Capital

	Cost (after tax)	Weight	Weighted Cost
Debt	4.2%	40%	1.68%
Preferred stock	7.8%	10%	0.78%
Common stock	10.0%	50%	5.00%
Weighted-average			7.46%

As illustrated, the weighted-average cost of capital for the firm is 7.46%. Management can now use this model to evaluate various forms of proposed financing options in terms of their effects on the firm's average cost of capital.

EXAMPLE

Assume that management, with the capital structure described in the table above, is considering calling the preferred stock and issuing 7% debentures. Assume that the costs to call the preferred shares are negligible and the firm's effective tax rate is 30%. What would be the effect on the firm's weighted-average cost of capital?

The cost of the new debentures is calculated below.

$$\text{Cost of new debt} = 7\% \, (1.00 - \text{The effective tax rate})$$
$$= 4.9\%$$

The following table recalculates the weighted-average cost of capital for the firm.

Weighted-Average Cost of Capital

	Cost (after tax)	Weight	Weighted Cost
Existing debt	4.2%	40%	1.68%
New debt	4.9%	10%	0.49%
Common stock	10.0%	50%	5.00%
Weighted-average			7.17%

By replacing the preferred stock with debt, the firm has reduced its cost of capital to 7.17%

D. Dividend Policy

1. The dividend policy of a firm relates to management's propensity to distribute earnings to stockholders. While it is unclear as to whether the distribution of dividends changes the value of the firm's stock, one of the major influences on dividend policy is where the firm is in its life cycle. The life cycle of a firm has the following four stages:

     a. Development stage
     b. Growth stage
     c. Expansion stage
     d. Maturity stage

     In its first two stages the firm needs to retain its profits to finance development and growth. If any dividends are issued, they tend to be stock dividends. When the firm hits the expansion stage, its need for investment declines and management may decide to issue small cash dividends. Finally, if the firm is successful in its maturity stage, it will tend to begin issuing regular and growing cash dividends.

2. Most people argue that the relevance of dividends is in their *information content.* Dividends **signal** to investors that management believes that the firm had a good year. Increases in dividends tend to increase share prices, while reductions tend to depress share prices. As a result, management is hesitant to decrease dividends.

3. Other factors that affect management's dividend policy include

- *Legal requirements*—Most states forbid firms to pay dividends that would impair the initial capital contributions to the firm.
- *Cash position*—Cash must be available to pay the dividends.
- *Access to capital markets*—If the firm has limited access to capital markets, management is more likely to retain the earnings of the firm.
- *Desire for control*—Retaining earnings results in less need for management to seek other forms of financing which might come with restrictions on management's actions.
- *Tax position of shareholders*—Stockholders must pay taxes on dividends and wealthier individuals pay higher taxes.
- *Clientele effect*—Some firms may have a strategy of attracting investors that require a dividend, such as retired individuals.
- *Investment opportunities*—Retained earnings should be reinvested in the firm if the firm can earn a return that exceeds what the investor can earn on another investment with similar risk.

4. **Other Types of Dividends**

     a. **Stock dividends** are payments to existing stockholders of a dividend in the form of the firm's own stock. As an example, a 10% stock dividend would involve the issuance of 10% more shares to each stockholder. Such dividends are designed to signal to investors that the firm is performing well, but it does not require the firm to distribute cash.

     b. **Stock splits** are similar to stock dividends but they are generally designed to reduce the stock's price to a target level that will attract more investors. As an example, a 2-for-1 stock split doubles the number of shares outstanding and it would be expected that the price of the stock would drop approximately in half.

E. Share Repurchases

Firms will often repurchase some of their shares to have them available for executive stock options or acquisitions of other firms. However, management of some firms have undertaken other repurchase programs based on the following rationales:

- It sends a positive signal to investors that management believes the stock is undervalued.
- It reduces the number of shares outstanding and thereby increasing earnings per share.
- It provides a temporary floor for the stock.

Many analysts question the validity of these rationales. As an example, the impact on earnings per share is uncertain because investing the cash in operations instead of spending it to repurchase stock might actually increase earnings per share to a greater extent.

F. Financial Markets

Financial markets are markets in which financial assets are traded. Such markets facilitate borrowing and lending, sale of previously issued securities, and sale of newly issued securities. **Primary markets** are markets in which newly issued securities are sold, and **secondary markets** are markets in which previously issued securities are sold. Examples of markets for stocks and debt include the New York Stock Exchange, the US government bond market, and NASDAQ. Futures and option contracts are traded on exchanges such as the Chicago Board of Trade and the Chicago Mercantile Exchange. A rising market is referred to as a **bull market**, and a declining or lethargic market is referred to as a **bear market**. The major players in markets include

1. **Brokers**—Commissioned agents of buyers or sellers.
2. **Dealers**—Similar to brokers in that they match buyers and sellers. However, dealers can and do take positions in the assets and buy and sell their own inventory.
3. **Investment banks**—Assist in the initial sale of newly issued securities by providing advice, underwriting, and sales assistance.
4. **Financial intermediaries**—Financial institutions that borrow one form of financial asset (e.g., a savings deposit) and distribute the asset in another form (e.g., a commercial loan).

NOW REVIEW MULTIPLE-CHOICE QUESTIONS 81 THROUGH 132 IN VOLUME 2

ASSET AND LIABILITY VALUATION

An important aspect of financial management is the valuation of assets and liabilities. Valuations are needed for a number of purposes including investment evaluation, capital budgeting, mergers and acquisitions, financial reporting, tax reporting, and litigation. The major types of valuation models include

1. Market values obtained from active markets for identical assets
2. Market values derived from active markets for similar but not identical assets
3. Valuation models

A. Using Active Markets for Identical Assets

The most straightforward method of valuing a financial instrument is using prices for identical instruments in an active market. The use of such markets is appropriate if they have sufficient volume of transactions to insure that the market price is reliable.

B. Using Active Markets for Similar Assets

Another method for valuing instruments involves deriving values from the market prices of similar but not identical instruments. The key to this method of valuation is accurate adjustment for differences that exist between the instrument being valued and the instrument that is traded in the market. For example, the price might need to be adjusted for such factors as restrictions on sales, or differences in maturity dates, exercise dates, block sizes, credit risk, etc. Financial models are often used to adjust the value of the instrument for these differences.

C. Valuation Models

A method that can be used in the absence of an active market is determining estimated fair value based on a valuation model, such as discounted cash flows. Such valuations generally rely on assumptions about future events and conditions that affect income and cash flows. These assumptions could materially affect the fair value estimate. Accordingly, they must be examined to determine whether they are reasonable and consistent with existing market information, the economic environment and past experience. For example, in determining the fair value of a rare asset for which market information is not available, consideration should be given to sales of similar assets, the general economic environment in which the asset is used, and past experiences with similar assets. As another example, discount rates for calculating discounted cash flows must reflect market expectations of future rates and be consistent with the level of risk inherent in the future cash flows.

In determining estimates of fair values it is also important that the model being used is appropriate based on the nature of the asset and current economic conditions.

MERGERS

A. Business mergers involve many of the considerations involved in the acquisition of any asset or group of assets. However, there are additional considerations.

    1. Firms often acquire other firms due to **synergies**; the two firms can perform more effectively together than separately. Synergies arise from operating or financial economies, as well as managerial efficiency.

    2. Management may also acquire a firm for diversification or tax considerations, or to take advantage of a bargain purchase.

B. Types of Mergers

    1. **Horizontal merger**—When a firm combines with another in the same line of business.

    2. **Vertical merger**—When a firm combines with another firm in the same supply chain (e.g., a combination of a manufacturer with one of its suppliers).

    3. **Congeneric merger**—When the merging firms are somewhat related but not enough to make it a vertical or horizontal merger.

    4. **Conglomerate merger**—When the firms are completely unrelated. These types of mergers provide the greatest degree of diversification.

C. Several methodologies are used to value **target firms,** including

    1. **Discounted cash flow analysis**—Application of capital budgeting techniques to an entire firm rather than a single investment.

        a. Two key items are needed for this valuation method

            (1) A set of pro forma financial statements are developed that project the incremental cash flows that are expected to result from the merger.

            (2) A discount rate, or cost of capital, to apply to the projected cash flows. The appropriate discount rate is the cost of equity rather than an overall cost of capital. The discount rate used must reflect the underlying riskiness of the target firm's operations (future cash flows).

        b. A risk analysis should be performed with the cash flows (e.g., sensitivity analysis, scenario analysis, etc.).

    2. **Market multiple method**—Applies a market-determined multiple to some measure of earnings such as net income or earnings per share.

D. An acquisition may be accomplished through a purchase of the assets of the firm or a purchase of a controlling interest in the firm's stock. The acquisition may be for cash or the acquiring firms stock.

E. Goodwill is recognized as the difference between the fair market value of the identifiable assets and the total purchase price of the firm. Goodwill remains on the financial statements of the combined firms unless it becomes impaired.

> **NOW REVIEW MULTIPLE-CHOICE QUESTIONS 133 THROUGH 138 IN VOLUME 2**

KEY TERMS

Arbitrage pricing model. Uses a series of systematic risk factors to develop a value that reflects the multiple dimensions of systematic risk.

Cash discounts. Discounts for early payment of accounts.

Compensating balance. Required minimum level of deposit based on loan agreement.

Concentration banking. Payments from customers are routed to local branch offices rather than firm headquarters. This reduces collection time.

Cost of capital. The weighted-average cost of a firm's debt and equity financing components.

Debenture. A bond that is not secured by the pledge of specific property.

Economic order quantity. An inventory technique that minimizes the sum of inventory ordering and carrying costs.

Electronic funds transfer. The movement of funds electronically without the use of a check.

Factoring. The sale of receivables to a finance company.

Financial leverage. Measures the extent to which the firm uses debt financing.

Float. The time that elapses relating to mailing, processing, and clearing checks.

Inventory conversion period. The average length of time required to convert materials into finished goods and sell the goods.

Just-in-time production. A demand-pull system in which each component of a finished good is produced when needed by the next stage of production.

Just-in-time purchasing. A demand-pull inventory system in which raw materials arrive just as they are needed for production. It minimizes inventory holding costs.

Lockbox system. A system in which customer payments are sent to a post office box that is maintained by the company's bank. This reduces collection time and improves controls.

Mortgage bond. A bond secured with the pledge of specific property.

Operating leverage. Measures the degree to which a firm builds fixed costs into its operations.

Payables deferral period. The average length of time between the purchase of materials and labor and the payment of cash for them.

Precautionary balances. Cash available for emergencies.

Receivables collection period. The average length of time required to collect accounts receivable.

Speculative balances. Cash available to take advantage of favorable business opportunities.

Subordinated debenture. A bond with claims subordinated to other general creditors.

Supply chain. Describes the processes involved in a good's production and distribution.

Warehousing. Inventory financing in which the inventory is held in a public warehouse under the lender's control.

Module 45: Performance Measures

Overview

Organizational performance measures (including financial and nonfinancial measures) are used for a variety of purposes including: resource allocation, incentive compensation, divisional and business unit evaluation, budgeting and planning, and setting targets. Performance measures are used to manage and monitor performance in many areas of the organization including: financial, customer, internal processes, employees, and suppliers.

Organizational performance measures should be aligned to the strategy of the organization and useful in executing that strategy.

Strategy describes how an organization uses its activities and resources to achieve its objectives. For a business, the objective is to ethically maximize financial value. **Execution** includes the performance measures used (1) to ensure the strategy of the organization is being executed and (2) to monitor performance. To be successful, an organization must have an effective strategy and an effective execution system in place, including performance measures that closely link to the strategy. Before beginning the reading you should review the key terms at the end of the module.

A. Financial and Nonfinancial Performance Measures

Both financial and nonfinancial performance measures are needed to manage an organization. Financial measures gauge performance, profitability, or costs and are expressed as dollar amounts, ratios, or other forms. Nonfinancial performance measures are expressed in nonmonetary terms and include measures of customer satisfaction, customer retention, on-time delivery, quality, employee satisfaction, etc.

B. Balanced Scorecard and Performance Measures

The balanced scorecard, a performance measurement system that includes financial and nonfinancial performance measures, was developed by Kaplan and Norton.

1. **What Is the Balanced Scorecard?**

    The **balanced scorecard** is a strategic performance measurement and management framework for implementing strategy by translating an organization's mission and strategy into a set of performance measures. These performance measures are generally in four primary perspectives: **financial, customer, internal business processes, and learning and growth.**

2. **Four Perspectives of the Balanced Scorecard**

    a. **Financial perspective.** This perspective focuses on return on investment and other supporting financial performance measures. Example performance measures include profitability, return on invested capital, and revenue growth.

    b. **Customer perspective.** This perspective focuses on performance in areas that are most critical to the customer. Example performance measures include customer satisfaction and customer retention.

    c. **Internal business processes perspective.** This perspective focuses on operating effectively and efficiently and includes performance measures on cost, quality and time for processes that are critical to the customers. It focuses on business processes, which are the structured activities of an organization that produce a product or service. Example performance measures include number of defects and cycle time.

    d. **Learning and growth perspective.** This perspective focuses on performance measures relating to employees, infrastructure, teaming and capabilities necessary for the internal processes to achieve customer and financial objectives. Example performance measures include employee satisfaction, hours of training per employee, and information technology expenditures per employee.

3. **Components of the Balanced Scorecard**

    a. **Strategic objectives.** A statement of what the strategy must achieve and what is critical to its success.
    b. **Performance measures.** Describe how success in achieving the strategy will be measured and tracked.
    c. **Baseline performance.** The current level of performance for the performance measure.
    d. **Targets.** The level of performance or rate of improvement needed in the performance measure.
    e. **Strategic initiatives.** Key action programs required to achieve strategic objectives.

    Strategic objectives focus on **what** is to be achieved. Strategic initiatives focus on **how** it will be achieved and performance measures, baseline performance and targets relate to how it will be **measured**.

    The **value chain** in the balanced scorecard framework is the sequence of business processes in which usefulness is added to the products or services of a company and includes the **innovation process**, **operations process**, and **post-sales process**. The value chain is one way to describe the internal process perspective in the balanced scorecard and its performance measures.

4. **Characteristics of the Balanced Scorecard**

    Characteristic of the balanced scorecard include the following:

    - **Strategy-focused.** Performance measures are driven by mission, vision and strategy. The balanced scorecard communicates the strategy to all members of the organization.
    - **Balanced.** Performance measures are "balanced" in terms of financial and nonfinancial measures, leading and lagging measures and internal (internal processes) and external (customer) measures. Accordingly, the scorecard highlights suboptimal tradeoffs that managers may make when they fail to consider operational and financial measures together.
    - **Includes both financial and nonfinancial measures.** Performance measures include traditional financial measures, as well as nonfinancial measures.
    - **Cause-and-effect linkages.** Performance measures are connected using cause-and-effect linkages. Performance measures include **performance drivers** (leading indicators) and **outcome performance measures** (lagging indicators). The focus on cause and effect linkages limits the number of measures used by identifying the most critical ones.
    - **Unique to the strategy.** Performance measures are unique and customized to an organization's strategy.

5. **Strategy Maps and Cause-and-Effect Linkages**

    Strategy maps are diagrams of the cause-and-effect relationships between strategic objectives. When looking at cause and effect linkages in the balanced scorecard framework, it is important to remember that the classification of performance measures as leading or lagging is not a dichotomy, but rather must be considered as a continuum. For example, customer satisfaction may be a leading indicator (performance driver) to return on investment (the lagging indicator or outcome measure). However, customer satisfaction may be a lagging indicator to on-time delivery (the leading indicator).

EXAMPLE

Balanced scorecard

The following is a simple example of a balanced scorecard. Within each of the four perspectives are key strategic objectives and related performance measures.

Financial Perspective

Strategic objective	Performance measure
Increase return on investment (ROI)	ROI
Revenue growth	Percent growth in revenue
Increase profitability	Net income as a percentage of sales

Customer Perspective

Strategic objective	Performance measure
Increase customer satisfaction	Customer satisfaction ratings
Increase customer share	Revenue per customer
Attract new customers	Number of new customers
	Revenue from new customers

Internal Business Processes Perspective

Strategic objective	Performance measure
Improve on-time delivery	Percentage of on-time deliveries
Improve quality performance	Number of rejects

Learning and Growth Perspective

Strategic objective	Performance measure
Train employees on quality tools	Hours of training on quality tools
Use information systems to manage on-time delivery status	Percent of employees using information system

In this example, we see possible cause and effect relationships. Increasing the training in the use of quality tools may improve on-time delivery performance which may improve customer satisfaction and therefore increase return on investment. The connection between customer satisfaction and return on investment at some companies is based on the following observation: more satisfied customers pay invoices faster, therefore accounts receivable turnover (a component of return on assets) increases and return on investment increases.

6. **Performance Measures in the Balanced Scorecard**

Here are examples of performance measures that are classified within the four perspectives of the balanced scorecard.

Financial perspective
Return on investment
Economic profit
Economic value added
Cash flow ROI
Free cash flow
Net income/sales ratio
Sales/asset ratio
Revenue growth
Revenue from new products (existing customers)
Revenue from new products (new customers)
Cost of sales %

Customer perspective
Customer satisfaction
Customer retention
Customer acquisition
Percentage of highly satisfied customers
Depth of relationship
Percentage of business from customer referrals
Customer satisfaction with new product/service offerings

Internal process perspective
On-time delivery
Cost per unit
Percentage of late orders
Total cost of quality
Cycle time
Process efficiency
Capacity utilization
Inventory turnover
Lead times (order to delivery)

Internal process perspective
Percentage of on-time deliveries
Time to resolve customer complaints
Inventory obsolescence
Order backlog
Number of leads/conversion rate
Hours with customers
Time spent with target accounts
Number of new projects based on client input
Number of joint projects
Number of technology and product partners
Number of patents
Total time from concept to market
Time from pilot to full production
Manufacturing-process yield
Number of failures, defects and customer returns
Warranty costs
Number of safety incidents

Learning and growth perspective
Employee satisfaction and engagement
Employee turnover
Employee objectives linked to the balanced scorecard
Employee awareness of the strategy
Percentage of employees trained in total quality management
Number of six-sigma black belts
Performance improvement from employees' suggestions
Percentage of ideas and best practices shared across organization
Percentage of R&D employees to total employees
R&D expenditure as a percent to sales revenue

NOW REVIEW MULTIPLE-CHOICE QUESTIONS 1 THROUGH 13 IN VOLUME 2

C. Value-Based Management (VBM) and Financial Performance Measures

VBM involves the use of value-based metrics (performance measures) in a strategic management system and as such may be viewed as a financial scorecard. The spectrum of value-based metrics include performance measures such as: return on investment (ROI), economic profit, economic value added (EVA), cash flow ROI, and residual income.

When is it appropriate to use economic value added measures (EVA) (or other value-based metrics) as a performance measure? EVA is particularly useful for incentive compensation, resource allocation and investor relations. Executive compensation and incentive compensation firmwide have been the most popular target of EVA. The premise is "pay for performance" where performance is defined as creating financial value (earning a return above the cost of capital). Using EVA alone can have certain disadvantages by failing to reflect all the pathways to value creation. This limitation can be minimized by integrating EVA with a balanced scorecard framework which would avoid the temptation to focus only on low-hanging fruit (cost reduction and increased asset intensity) but miss the opportunity to create additional value through growth strategies.

1. Return on Investment (ROI)

Return on investment is the ratio of a measure of "return" divided by a measure of "investment." There are various ways to measure ROI including: return on assets (ROA), return on net assets (RONA) and return on equity (ROE). ROI is most often computed using net income (income after interest and taxes) but it also may be computed using operating income or operating income after taxes.

2. DuPont ROI Analysis

DuPont ROI analysis looks at ROI as driven by two factors: return on sales (net income/sales) and asset turnover (sales/total assets). The calculation of DuPont ROI is as follows:

$$\text{ROI} = \text{Net income/total assets}$$
$$= \text{Net income/sales} \times \text{Sales/average investment}$$
$$= \text{Return on sales} \times \text{Asset turnover ratio}$$

The DuPont method highlights the two basic ways to improve profits: (1) increasing income per dollar of sales, and (2) using assets to generate more sales.

EXAMPLE

The following selected data pertain to the Amy Division of Cara Products, Inc. for 2012:

Sales	$20,000,000
Average invested capital (total assets)	5,000,000
Net income	1,250,000
Cost of capital	10%

ROI (based on total assets) and DuPont ROI would be calculated as follows:

$$
\begin{aligned}
\text{DuPont ROI} \quad &= \quad 1,250,000/5,000,000 = 25\% \\
&= \quad 1,250,000/20,000,000 \times \\
&\qquad 20,000,000/5,000,000 \\
&= \quad 6.25\% \times 4.0 \\
&= \quad 25\%
\end{aligned}
$$

The return on sales of 6.25% times the asset turnover ratio of 4.0 equals the ROI of 25%.

3. **Residual Income**

Residual income is net income (or operating income after taxes) minus a cost of capital based on capital invested in a division or project.

$$
\begin{aligned}
\text{Residual income} \quad &= \quad \text{Net income} - \text{Interest on investment} \\
&= \quad \text{Net income} - (\text{Required rate of return} \times \text{Invested capital})
\end{aligned}
$$

EXAMPLE

Using the data from the previous example for Amy Division

Sales	$20,000,000
Average invested capital	5,000,000
Net income	1,250,000
Required rate of return	10%

$$
\begin{aligned}
\text{Residual income} \quad &= \quad \$1,250,000 - (10\% \times \$5,000,000) \\
&= \quad \$1,250,000 - 500,000 \\
&= \quad \$750,000
\end{aligned}
$$

Remember that the ROI was 25% for this company and the required interest rate is 10%. The difference between the ROI and the required interest rate (cost of capital) is sometimes called the **spread**. In this case the spread can be computed as follows:

$$
\begin{aligned}
\text{Spread} \quad &= \quad \text{ROI} - \text{Cost of capital} \\
&= \quad 25\% - 10\% \\
&= \quad 15\%
\end{aligned}
$$

Notice that the residual income of $750,000 divided by the invested capital of $5,000,000 equals the spread of 15%.

---

4. **Residual Income Profile**

The **residual income profile** is a graphical way to look at the relationship between residual income and ROI.
The residual income profile shows the interrelationship between residual income and ROI. The vertical axis shows residual income in dollars. The horizontal axis shows the implicit cost of capital and ROI.
The formula for the residual income profile is

$$\text{Residual income} = \text{Net income} - i\,(\text{invested capital})$$

Where: i = cost of capital or required rate of return for computing residual income

The formula for the residual income profile is the same as the formula for residual income with the required rate of return as the coefficient. As the required rate of return increases, residual income decreases. Where residual income is zero, the required rate of return equals the ROI.

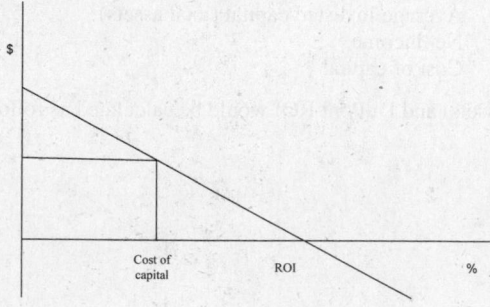

EXAMPLE

The following information is available for Iceman, Inc. for 2012:

Net income	$ 300,000
Average invested capital	$2,000,000
Cost of capital	12%

The ROI and residual income are computed below.

$$\text{ROI} = \frac{\$300,000}{\$2,000,000} = 15\%$$

$$\begin{aligned} \text{Residual income} &= \$300,000 - (12\% \times 2,000,000) \\ &= \$300,000 - 240,000 \\ &= \$60,000 \end{aligned}$$

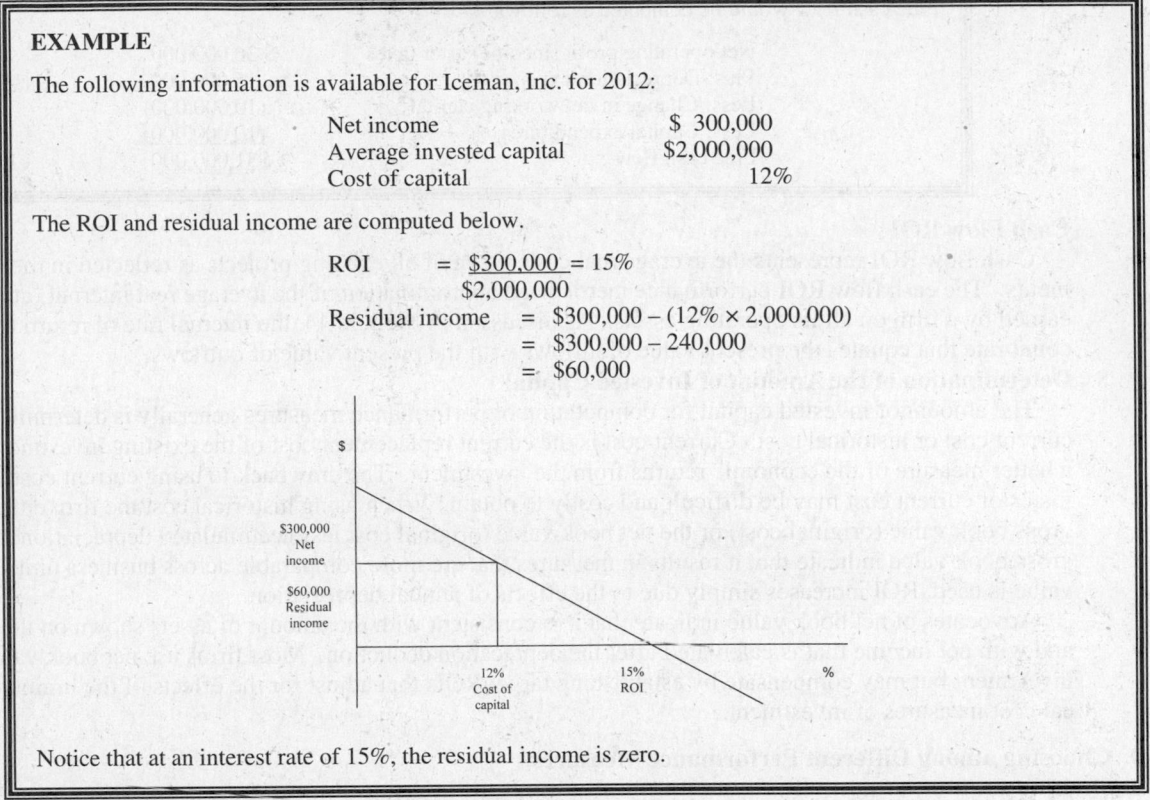

Notice that at an interest rate of 15%, the residual income is zero.

5. Economic Profit and EVA

Economic profit and economic value added measures stress the importance of making investments only when the return exceeds cost and, in the process, value to the stockholder is maximized. Economic profit is accounting profit minus the cost of capital. EVA is a variation of economic profit. Economic Value Added (EVA) is net operating profit (income) after taxes (NOPAT) minus the after-tax weighted-average cost of capital (WACC) multiplied by total assets (TA) minus current liabilities (CL) (net assets).

$$\text{EVA} = \text{Net operating profit after taxes (NOPAT)} - [(\text{TA} - \text{CL}) \times \text{WACC}]$$

Market value added is the difference between the market value of a company (both equity and debt) and the capital that lenders and shareholders have entrusted to it over the years in the form of loans, retained earnings and paid-in capital. Market value added is a measure of the difference between "cash in" (what investors have contributed) and "cash out" (what they could get by selling at today's prices).

6. Free Cash Flow

Free cash flow can be computed as follows:

Free cash flow = Net operating profit after taxes (NOPAT) + Depreciation and amortization – Capital expenditures – The change in working capital requirements

EXAMPLE

The following information is available for Armstrong Enterprises:

Net operating profit (income) after taxes	$36,000,000
Depreciation expense	15,000,000
Change in net working capital	10,000,000
Capital expenditures	10,000,000
Invested capital (TA – CL)	90,000,000
Weighted-average cost of capital	10%

EVA would be computed as follows:

Net operating profit (income) after taxes	$36,000,000
Less: capital charge on invested capital	
(90,000,000 × 10%)	(9,000,000)
Economic value added	$27,000,000

Free cash flow would be computed as follows:

Net operating profit (income) after taxes	$ 36,000,000
Plus: Depreciation expense	+ 15,000,000
Less: Change in net working capital	(10,000,000)
Less: Capital expenditures	(10,000,000)
Free cash flow	$31,000,000

7. **Cash Flow ROI**

   Cash flow ROI represents the average real cash return of all existing projects as reflected in the financial statements. The cash flow ROI performance metric is an approximation of the average real internal rate of return earned by a firm on all its operating assets. As discussed in Module 44, the internal rate of return (IRR) is the discount rate that equates the present value of inflows with the present value of outflows.

8. **Determination of the Amount of Invested Capital**

   The amount of invested capital for computation of performance measures generally is determined in two ways: current cost or historical cost. Current cost is the current replacement cost of the existing investment and provides a better measure of the economic returns from the investment. The drawback to using current cost is that the estimates of current cost may be difficult and costly to obtain. When using historical cost the firm either uses the gross book value (original cost) or the net book value (original cost less accumulated depreciation). Advocates of gross book value indicate that it results in measures that are more comparable across business units. If net book value is used, ROI increases simply due to the effects of annual depreciation.

   Advocates of net book value indicate that it is consistent with the amount of assets shown on the balance sheet and with net income that is calculated after the deprecation deduction. Most firms use net book value to measure investment but may compensate by establishing target ROIs that adjust for the effects of the limitations of historical cost measures of investment.

D. Choosing among Different Performance Measures

1. Choosing among different performance measures involves understanding how the performance measure will be used. Is it being used for executive compensation, resource allocation or business unit performance evaluation? It also involves understanding how well the performance measure enables management to execute business strategy and monitor how well it is being executed. Here are some guidelines for choosing among different performance measures.

   a. **Strategy-focused.** How well does the performance measure reflect the strategy of the organization? This is where the balanced scorecard framework and the performance measures within the balanced scorecard framework can be useful. A well-designed balanced scorecard will include the right mix of performance measures to communicate and operationalize the strategy.

   b. **Economic reality and cash flow.** How well does the performance measure reflect the economic reality that a firm must earn a return on capital invested in excess of its cost of capital in order to create financial value? Here is where Value Based Management and its metrics (ROI, economic profit, free cash flow, and cash flow ROI) can be useful.

   c. **Quality of the performance measure.** The relevance and reliability of the performance measures also should be considered. For example, relevant and reliable manager performance measures are ones that are sensitive to factors within the control of the manager and not sensitive to factors beyond the manager's control.

2. The most common financial measures used for performance measurement include return on investment (ROI), residual income (RI), economic value added (EVA), and return on sales (ROS). It is important to distinguish between those measures that are used to evaluate the business unit and those that are used to evaluate a manager's performance.

3. Performance measures should not encourage decisions that maximize the measure in the short run but are in conflict with the long-term goals of the firm. For example, a manager could decide to postpone machine maintenance to make ROI for a particular year look better, but the decision may cause long-run profits to suffer. The focus on short-run performance may be mitigated by using measures with multiple-year time horizons or by using a combination of financial and nonfinancial measures. Compensation tied to changes in the value of the firm's stock also encourages managers to take a long-run perspective, because stock prices reflect the future value of current management decisions.

4. A focus on ROI as a performance measure may cause a lack of goal congruence. As an example, managers of very profitable business units may reject projects that from a firm-wide perspective should be accepted. In such situations, RI rather than ROI provides a performance measure that better aligns the goals of business unit managers with the goals of the overall organization.

> ### EXAMPLE
>
> Borke Company's cost of capital is 10%. One of Borke Company's division managers has the opportunity to invest in a project that will generate $45,000 of net income per year for eight years on an initial investment of $300,000. The division's current income is $250,000 from a total divisional asset base of $1,000,000. The manager should accept the project since it offers a 15% return and the company's cost of capital is 10%. Chances are the manager will reject the project since it will lower the division current ROI from
>
> $$\frac{\$250,000}{\$1,000,000} \ = \ 25\% \quad \text{to} \quad \frac{\$250,000+45,000}{\$1,000,000+300,000} \ = \ 22.7\%$$
>
> In this case the use of ROI has led to an incorrect decision.

NOW REVIEW MULTIPLE-CHOICE QUESTIONS 14 THROUGH 37

E. Traditional Financial Statement Analysis

One type of commonly used set of financial measures is derived from traditional financial statement analysis. Financial statement analysis involves the calculation and comparison of financial statement ratios. Financial ratios used to evaluate the financial position and operations of firms typically are classified into the following five categories:

1. **Profitability ratios**
   - Gross margin
   - Operating profit margin
   - Return on assets
   - Return on equity
   - Dividend payout ratio

2. **Asset utilization ratios**
   - Receivable turnover
   - Average collection period
   - Inventory turnover
   - Fixed asset turnover
   - Total asset turnover

3. **Liquidity ratios**
   - Current ratio
   - Quick or acid ratio

4. **Debt utilization ratios**
   - Debt to total assets
   - Debt to equity
   - Times interest earned

5. **Market ratios**
   - Price/earnings ratio
   - Market/book ratio

The calculation of these ratios will be illustrated using the following financial statements from Home Depot.

The Home Depot, Inc. and Subsidiaries
CONSOLIDATED BALANCE SHEETS

Amounts in millions, except per share data	February 2, 2003	February 3, 2002
Assets		
Current assets:		
Cash and cash equivalents	$ 2,188	$ 2,477
Short-term investments, including current maturities of long-term investments	65	69
Receivables, net	1,072	920
Merchandise inventories	8,338	6,725
Other current assets	254	170
Total current assets	11,917	10,361

Amounts in millions, except per share data	*February 2, 2003*	*February 3, 2002*
Property and equipment, at cost:		
Land	5,560	4,972
Buildings	9,197	7,698
Furniture, fixtures and equipment	4,074	3,403
Leasehold improvements	872	750
Construction in progress	724	1,049
Capital leases	306	257
	20,733	18,129
Less accumulated depreciation and amortization	3,565	2,754
Net property and equipment	17,168	15,375
Notes receivable	107	83
Cost in excess of the fair value of net assets acquired, net of accumulated amortization of $50 at February 2, 2003, and $49 at February 3, 2002	575	419
Other assets	244	156
Total assets	$30,011	$26,394

Liabilities and Stockholders' Equity		
Current liabilities:		
Accounts payable	$ 4,560	$3,436
Accrued salaries and related expenses	809	717
Sales taxes payable	307	348
Deferred revenue	998	851
Income taxes payable	227	211
Other accrued expenses	1,134	938
Total current liabilities	8,035	6,501
Long-term debt, excluding current installments	1,321	1,250
Other long-term liabilities	491	372
Deferred income taxes	362	189
Total liabilities	$10,209	8,312

Stockholders' Equity		
Common stock, par value $0.05; authorized: 10,000 shares, issued and outstanding 2,362 shares at February 2, 2003, and 2,346 shares at February 3, 2002	118	117
Paid-in capital	5,858	5,412
Retained earnings	15,971	12,799
Accumulated other comprehensive loss	(82)	(220)
Unearned compensation	(63)	(26)
Treasury stock, at cost, 69 shares at February 2, 2003	(2,000)	--
Total stockholders' equity	19,802	18,082
Total liabilities and stockholders' equity	$30,011	$26,394

The Home Depot, Inc. and Subsidiaries
CONSOLIDATED STATEMENTS OF EARNINGS

Fiscal Year Ended

Amounts in millions, except per share data	February 2, 2003	February 3, 2002	January 28, 2001
Net Sales	$58,247	$53,553	$45,738
Cost of merchandise sold	40,139	37,406	32,057
Gross profit	18,108	16,147	13,681
Operating expenses:			
Selling and store operating	11,180	10,163	8,513
Preopening	96	117	142
General and administrative	1,002	935	835
Total operating expenses	12,278	11,215	9,490
Operating income	5,830	4,932	4,191
Interest income (expense):			
Interest and investment income	79	53	47
Interest expense	(37)	(28)	(21)
Interest, net	42	25	26
Earnings before provision for income taxes	5,872	4,957	4,217
Provision for income taxes	2,208	1,913	1,636
Net earnings	$3,664	$3,044	$2,581

Weighted-average common shares	2,336	2,335	2,315
Basic earnings per share	$1.57	$1.30	$1.11
Diluted weighted-average common shares	2,344	2,353	2,352
Diluted earnings per share	$1.56	$1.29	$1.10

1. **Profitability Ratios**

    Profitability ratios measure how effective a firm is at generating profit from operations. They are some of the most closely watched and widely quoted financial ratios. Management attempts to maximize these ratios to maximize firm value.

    a. **Gross margin** measures the percentage of each sales dollar remaining after payment for the goods sold.

    $$\text{Gross margin} = \frac{\text{Gross profit}}{\text{Net sales}} = \frac{\$18,108}{\$58,247} = 31.09\%$$

    Remember that gross profit is equal to net sales minus cost of goods sold.

    b. To find the proportion of revenue that finds its way into profits, analysts look at profit margin. Profit margin is calculated as net income divided by net sales, as shown below.

    $$\text{Profit margin} = \frac{\text{Net income after interest and taxes}}{\text{Net sales}} = \frac{\$3,664}{\$58,247} = 6.29\%$$

    c. **Operating profit margin** measures the percentage of each sales dollar that remains after the payment of all costs and expenses except for interest and taxes. This ratio is followed closely by analysts because it focuses on operating results. Operating profit is often referred to as earnings before interest and taxes or EBIT.

    $$\text{Operating profit margin} = \frac{\text{Operating profit}}{\text{Net sales}} = \frac{\$5,830}{\$58,247} = 10.01\%$$

    d. **Return on assets (return on investment)** measures the percentage return generated on the assets available (investment). This ratio may be calculated as

    $$\text{Return on assets} = \frac{\text{Net income after interest and taxes}}{\text{Average total sales}} = \frac{\$3,664}{\$28,203} = 12.99\%$$

    $$\begin{aligned} \text{Average total assets} &= (\text{Ending total assets} + \text{Beginning total assets})/2 \\ &= (\$30,011 + \$26,394)/2 \\ &= \$28,203 \end{aligned}$$

    As discussed previously, return on investment is calculated and dissected in a number of ways and is very important to value-based management.

    e. **Return on equity** measures the percentage return generated to common stockholders.

    $$\text{Return on equity} = \frac{\text{Net income after interest and taxes}}{\text{Average common stockholders' equity}} = \frac{\$3,664}{\$18,942} = 19.34\%$$

    $$\begin{aligned} \text{Average stockholders' equity (SE)} &= (\text{Ending SE} + \text{Beginning SE})/2 \\ &= (\$19,802 + \$18,082)/2 \\ &= \$18,942 \end{aligned}$$

    f. **The dividend payout ratio** measures the dividend paid in relation to net earnings. If Home Depot's dividend for the year was $0.22, the dividend payout is calculated as

    $$\begin{aligned} \text{Dividend payout ratio} &= \frac{\text{Cash dividend per common share}}{\text{Earnings per common share}} \\ &= \frac{\$0.22}{\$1.57} \\ &= .14 \text{ or } 14\% \end{aligned}$$

2. **Asset Utilization (Activity) Ratios**

    Asset utilization ratios measure the time it takes to convert various assets to sales or cash. Asset utilization ratios are used to measure the efficiency with which assets are managed. For this reason, they are often called **asset management ratios**.

    a. **Receivables turnover** measures the number of times per year the balance of receivables is collected. This is a very important measure of the efficiency with which management is managing accounts receivable.

    $$\text{Receivables turnover} = \frac{\text{Net credit Sales}}{\text{Average accounts receivable}}$$

This ratio cannot be computed for Home Depot since the company does not break out the amount of credit sales.

b. The **average collection period** measures the average number of days it takes to collect an account receivable. This ratio is also referred to as **the number of days of receivable** and **the number of days' sales in receivables**.

$$\text{Average collection period} = \frac{\text{Average accounts receivable}}{\text{Average sales per day}}$$

Again, this ratio cannot be calculated for Home Depot because the company does not break out the amount of credit sales.

c. **Inventory turnover** measures the efficiency with which a firm utilizes (manages) its inventory.

$$\text{Inventory turnover} = \frac{\text{Cost of goods sold}}{\text{Average inventory}} = \frac{\$40,139}{\$7,532} = 5.33 \text{ times}$$

$$
\begin{aligned}
\text{Average inventory} &= (\text{Ending inventory} + \text{Beginning inventory})/2 \\
&= (\$8,338 + \$6,725)/2 \\
&= \$7,532
\end{aligned}
$$

d. A related measure is the number of days' sales in inventory.

$$
\begin{aligned}
\text{Number of days' sales in inventory} &= \frac{\text{Average inventory}}{\text{Cost of goods sold} / 365} \\
&= \frac{\$7,532}{\$40,139 / 365} \\
&= 68.49 \text{ days}
\end{aligned}
$$

e. **Fixed asset turnover** measures the efficiency with which the firm uses its fixed assets.

$$\text{Fixed asset turnover} = \frac{\text{Sales}}{\text{Average net fixed assets}} = \frac{\$58,247}{\$16,272} = 3.58 \text{ times}$$

$$
\begin{aligned}
\text{Average fixed assets} &= (\text{Ending fixed assets} + \text{Beginning fixed assets})/2 \\
&= (\$17,168 + \$15,375)/2 \\
&= \$16,272
\end{aligned}
$$

f. **Total asset turnover** measures the efficiency with which the firm uses its total assets.

$$\text{Total asset turnover} = \frac{\text{Sales}}{\text{Average total assets}} = \frac{\$58,247}{\$28,203} = 2.07 \text{ times}$$

3. **Liquidity Ratios**

Liquidity ratios measure the firm's ability to meet its short-term obligations as they come due.

a. The **current ratio** is the most common measure of short-term liquidity. It is sometimes referred to as the **working capital ratio** because net working capital is the difference between current assets and current liabilities.

$$\text{Current ratio} = \frac{\text{Current assets}}{\text{Current liabilities}} = \frac{\$11,917}{\$8,035} = 1.48 \text{ times}$$

- **Current assets** include cash and cash equivalents, net accounts receivable, marketable securities classified as current, inventories and prepaid expenses.
- **Current liabilities** include accounts payable, short-term notes payable, current maturities of long-term debt, unearned revenue, and other accrued liabilities.

Changes in the current ratio can be misleading. As an example, if management simply borrows money from a bank and invests the funds in marketable securities, both current assets and current liabilities go up by an identical amount. Net working capital is unaffected but the current ratio changes. Thus the current ratio is subject to "window dressing" by management.

b. The **quick (acid) ratio** provides a more conservative measure of short-term liquidity. It takes out inventory because in times of financial difficulty inventory may be saleable only at liquidation value.

$$\text{Quick ratio} = \frac{\text{Current assets} - \text{Inventory}}{\text{Current liabilities}} = \frac{\$11,917 - 8,338}{\$8,035} = .45$$

4. **Debt Utilization Ratios**

Debt utilization ratios measure the effectiveness with which management finances the assets of the firm. They are used to evaluate the financial leverage of the firm.

a. The **debt to total assets** measures the proportion of total assets financed with debt and, therefore, the extent of financial leverage.

$$\text{Debt to total assets} = \frac{\text{Total liabilities}}{\text{Total assets}} = \frac{\$10,209}{\$30,011} = 34.02\%$$

b. The **debt to equity ratio** also measures the extent of the firm's financial leverage.

$$\text{Debt to equity ratio} = \frac{\text{Total liabilities}}{\text{Total equity}} = \frac{\$10,209}{\$19,802} = 51.56\%$$

c. The **times interest earned** measures the firm's ability to make contractual interest payments.

$$\text{Times interest earned} = \frac{\text{Earnings before interest and taxes}}{\text{Interest expense}} = \frac{\$5,830}{\$37} = 157.57\%$$

5. **Market Ratios**

Market ratios involve measures that consider the market value of the firm's common stock.

a. The **price/earnings (PE) ratio** is the most commonly quoted market measure. Assuming that Home Depot's stock price is $34.00, the price/earnings ratio would be computed as follows:

$$\text{Price/earning} = \frac{\text{Stock price per share}}{\text{Earnings per share}} = \frac{\$34}{\$1.57} = 21.66$$

b. The **market/book ratio** provides another evaluation of how investors view the firm's past and future performance. To calculate the ratio, the book value per share of the firm's stock must first be calculated.

$$\text{Book value per share} = \frac{\text{Common stock equity}}{\text{Number of shares of common stock outstanding}}$$

$$= \frac{\$19,802}{\$2,362} = \$8.38 \text{ per share}$$

Again, assuming a $34 market price per share of common stock, the market/book ratio is calculated as follows:

$$\text{Market/book ratio} = \frac{\text{Market value per share of common stock}}{\text{Book value per share of common stock}}$$

$$= \frac{\$34.00}{\$8.38} = 4.06$$

6. **Interpreting Financial Ratios**

How does one decide whether a particular ratio is good or bad? To get value from ratio analysis, the measures must be compared to benchmarks. There are two basic approaches to this analysis, horizontal analysis and cross-sectional analysis. While **horizontal analysis** involves an evaluation of the firm's ratios and trends over time, **cross-sectional analysis** involves benchmarking the ratios against ratios of similar firms at a point in time. Industry averages are often used for cross-sectional analysis. Averages for industries are published by the US Department of Commerce, Dun & Bradstreet, Robert Morris Associates, and others. Researching data on firms in the same industry is facilitated through the Standard Industrial Classification (SIC) system.

The figure below illustrates horizontal (trend) and cross-sectional analysis of a firm's income statement. The figure also illustrates a **common-size** income statement, in which all revenues and expenses are presented as a percentage of net sales. A common-size balance sheet presents all assets, liabilities and stockholders' equity as a percentage of total assets. The development of common-size financial statements is also known as **vertical analysis**.

Carson Corporation

	Dollars (000s omitted)			Common-size statements		
			Percent			**Industry averages**
	20X6	**20X7**	**change**	**20X6**	**20X7**	**20X7**
Gross sales	78,428	82,212	4.8	103%	105%	104%
Less: Returns and Allowances	2,284	4,235	85.4	3%	5%	4%
Net sales	76,144	77,977	2.4	100%	100%	100%
Cost of goods sold	46,213	46,478	0.6	61%	60%	58%
Gross profit	29,931	31,499	5.2	39%	40%	42%
Selling & administrative expenses	20,105	22,487	11.8	26%	29%	28%
Income from operations	9,826	9,012	−8.3	13%	12%	14%
Interest expense	1,930	1,584	−17.9	3%	2%	3%
Net income before taxes	7,896	7,428	−5.9	10%	10%	11%
Income taxes	3,807	2,971	−22.0	5%	4%	4%
Net income	4,089	4,457	9.0	5%	6%	7%
EPS	0.78	0.84	10.5			
Ratios						
Current	1.7	1.9				2.1
Quick	1.0	1.1				1.3
Receivables turnover	5.3	5.6				5.1
Days' sales in ending receivables	68.1	64.3				65.6
Inventory turnover	4.7	3.2				3.5
Days' sales in ending inventory	76.0	75.0				74.4
Interest expense/outstanding debt	0.11	0.08				0.09

Horizontal (Trend) analysis	Vertical analysis	Cross-sectional analysis

To use ratio analysis effectively, analysts must be aware of the relationship between the items used in calculating the ratio. For example, in comparing the gross margin of a company over time, it should be remembered that this ratio may be affected by the fact that cost of goods sold is made up of fixed and variable costs or the fact that the sales mix has changed.

7. **Limitations of Financial Ratios**

While comparing the firm's ratios with those of similar firms in the same industry provides information about the performance of the firm, it does have limitations.

a. Other firms in the industry may not be comparable due to differences in size, diversification of operations, accounting principles used, different year-ends, etc.
b. Industry averages may not be reliable (e.g., based on too small a sample of firms).
c. There are variations in the way ratios are calculated.
d. Financial statements contain estimates that might distort results.
e. Ratios are only financial measures and do not provide a balanced view of performance.

F. **Benchmarking and Best Practices**

Benchmarking is the continuous process of comparing the levels of performance in producing products and services and executing activities against the best levels of performance. It is the search for and implementation of "best practices." There are different types of benchmarking including:

• *Internal benchmarking* compares similar operations within different units of the same organization.
• *Competitive benchmarking* targets processes and methods used by an organization's direct competitors.
• *Functional or industry benchmarking* compares similar functions within the same broad industry.
• *Generic benchmarking* compares processes that are independent of industry.

Best practices are the best ways to perform a process. Best practices represent the means by which world-class organizations have achieved superior performance. However, no practice can be considered a "best practice" for all organizations or in all situations. The advice of Dr. W. Edwards Deming applies to benchmarking: "Adapt, don't adopt."

Benchmarks are the performance metrics used in benchmarking.

NOW REVIEW MULTIPLE-CHOICE QUESTIONS 38 THROUGH 55 IN VOLUME 2

G. Quality Control Principles and Tools

1. **Total Quality Management (TQM)** focuses on managing the organization to excel in quality in all dimensions of products and services for customers.

2. **Six-Sigma Quality**

    What is six-sigma? A statistical measure expressing how close a product comes to its quality goal. One-sigma means 68% of products are acceptable; three-sigma means 99.7%. Six-sigma is 99.999997% perfect: 3.4 defects per million parts.

    Six-sigma black belts must attend a minimum of four months of training in statistical and other quality improvement methods. Six-sigma black belts are experts in the six-sigma methodology. They learn and demonstrate proficiency in the DMAIC methodology and statistical process control (SPC) techniques within that methodology. DMAIC is the structured methodology for process improvement within the six-sigma framework. It stands for define, measure, analyze, improve, and control.

3. **Quality Award Programs**

    There are a number of quality award programs. Here is a summary of some of the major programs.

    - **Malcolm Baldrige National Quality Award** is an award that was established in 1987 to recognize total quality management in American industry. The Baldrige award is given to businesses—manufacturing and service, small and large—and to education and health care organizations that apply and are judged to be outstanding in seven areas: leadership, strategic planning, customer and market focus, information and analysis, human resource focus, process management, and business results. Congress established the award program in 1987 to recognize US organizations for their achievements in quality and performance and to raise awareness about the importance of quality and performance excellence as a competitive edge. The award is not given for specific products or services. Three awards may be given annually in each of these categories: manufacturing, service, small business, education, and health care.
    - **The Deming Prize** is named after American statistician Dr. W. Edwards Deming, who developed the quality concepts for Japanese industry after World War II.
    - **European Quality Award.** The European Quality Award is Europe's most prestigious award for organizational excellence. It is open to every high-performing organization in Europe and focuses on recognizing excellence and providing detailed, independent feedback to all applicants to help them on their continuing journey to excellence.

4. **ISO Quality Standards**

    ISO 9000 Series is a series of standards agreed upon by the International Organization for Standardization (ISO) and adopted in 1987. ISO 9000 evolved in Europe. The ISO Series consists of five parts numbered 9000 through 9004.

    ISO 14000 series was developed to control the impact of an organization's activities on the environment and focuses on reducing the cost of waste management, conserving energy and materials, and lowering distribution costs.

5. **Quality Tools and Methods**

    a. **Total quality control (TQC).** The application of quality principles to all company activities. Also known as total quality management (TQM).

    b. **Continuous improvement and Kaizen**

    Continuous improvement (CI) seeks continual improvement of machinery, materials, labor, and production methods, through various means including suggestions and ideas from employees and customers.

    Kaizen is the Japanese art of continuous improvement. A philosophy of continuous improvement of working practices that underlies total quality management and just-in-time business techniques.

    PDCA (Plan-Do-Check-Act) Also called the Deming Wheel, focuses on the sequential and continual nature of the CI process.

    c. **Cause-and-effect analysis**

    Cause-and-effect (fishbone or Ishikawa) diagrams identify the potential causes of defects. Four categories of potential causes of failure are: human factors, methods and design factors, machine-related factors, and materials and components factors. Cause-and-effect diagrams are used to systematically list the different causes that can be attributed to a problem (or an effect). A cause-and-effect diagram can aid in identifying the reasons why a process goes out of control.

    A **Pareto chart** is a bar graph that ranks causes of process variations by the degree of impact on quality. The Pareto chart is a specialized version of a histogram that ranks the categories in the chart from most frequent to least frequent. A related concept, the "Pareto Principle" states that 80% of the problems come from 20% of the causes. The Pareto Principle states that: "Not all of the causes of a particular phenomenon occur with the same frequency or with the same impact."

d. **Control charts and robust design**

> **Control charts** are statistical plots derived from measuring factory processes; they help detect "process drift," or deviation, before it generates defects. Control charts also help spot inherent variations in manufacturing processes that designers must account for to achieve "robust design."

> **Robust design** is a discipline for making designs "production-proof" by building in tolerances for manufacturing variables that are known to be unavoidable.

e. **Poka-yoke (mistake-proofing).** Poka-yoke involves making the workplace mistake-proof. For example, a machine fitted with guide rails permits a part to be worked on in just one way.

H. Cost of Quality

Cost of quality is based on the philosophy that failures have an underlying cause, prevention is cheaper than failures, and cost of quality performance can be measured. Cost of quality consists of four components.

- Prevention cost
- Appraisal cost
- Internal failure cost
- External failure cost

1. **Prevention cost.** The cost of prevention is the cost of any quality activity designed to help do the job right the first time. Examples of prevention cost include:

   - Quality engineering
   - Quality training
   - Quality circles
   - Statistical process control activities
   - Supervision of prevention activities
   - Quality data gathering, analysis, and reporting
   - Quality improvement projects
   - Technical support provided to suppliers
   - Audits of the effectiveness of the quality system

2. **Appraisal cost.** The cost of quality control including testing and inspection. It involves any activity designed to appraise, test, or check for defective products. Examples of appraisal costs include:

   - Test and inspection of incoming materials
   - Test and inspection of in-process goods
   - Final product testing and inspection
   - Supplies used in testing and inspection
   - Supervision of testing and inspection activities
   - Depreciation of test equipment
   - Maintenance of test equipment
   - Plant utilities in the inspection area
   - Field testing and appraisal at customer site

3. **Internal failure cost.** The costs incurred when substandard products are produced but discovered before shipment to the customer. Examples of internal failure costs include:

   - Scrap
   - Spoilage
   - Rework
   - Rework labor and overhead
   - Reinspection of reworked products
   - Retesting of reworked products
   - Downtime caused by quality problems
   - Disposal of defective products
   - Analysis of the cause of defects in production
   - Reentering data because of keying errors
   - Debugging software errors

4. **External failure cost.** The cost incurred for products that do not meet requirements of the customer and have reached the customer. Examples of external failure costs include

   - Cost of field servicing and handling complaints
   - Warranty repairs and replacements

- Product recalls
- Liability arising from defective products
- Returns and allowances arising from quality problems
- Lost sales arising from reputation for poor quality

I. Business Process Management

Business process management focuses on continuously improving processes to align all activities with the desires and needs of the customer. As a managerial approach, business process management views processes as strategic assets that must be understood, managed, and improved. To improve processes, management focuses on both the human and technological aspect of processes, and the interaction of the two. Many organizations are finding it productive to improve processes by focusing on this human—technology interaction, as they try to develop technology that is designed for a task and the way the particular individual works.

The life cycle of business process management includes design, modeling, execution, monitoring, and optimization.

1. **Design**

   The design phase involves identification of existing processes and design of process improvements. Good process design is critical to preventing problems over the life of the process.

2. **Modeling**

   In the modeling phase management simulates the process in a test environment and performs "what if" analysis to try to determine how it will work under varying conditions.

3. **Execution**

   Execution involves installing software, training personnel, and implementing the new processes. It also involves testing the new processes.

4. **Monitoring**

   The monitoring phase is continuous after the execution phase. It involves tracking the processes with performance statistics.

5. **Optimization**

   This phase of the life cycle involves retrieving performance statistics from modeling or monitoring and identifying potential bottlenecks or other problems for additional improvement of the process.

   As processes are analyzed for improvement, it is sometime discovered that processes that were once performed by several departments should be centralized in one department. For example, employee training might become a centralized process to improve efficiency and effectiveness. Alternatively, management may decide to outsource a process to an external organization, or even outsource a process to an organization in another country (often referred to as off-shoring). There are a number of reasons that an organization may decide to outsource or off-shore, including costs saving, quality improvement, tax benefit, scalability, or to focus on core competencies. However, such strategy may present additional risks, including

   - *Quality risk.* The company may have less control over the quality of outsourced or off-shored activities.
   - *Language risk.* Control over activities and customer service may be affected by language issues.
   - *Information security risk.* Control over confidential company or customer information may be put at risk.
   - *Intellectual property risk.* Information about the company's products and processes may be put at risk.
   - *Public opinion risk.* The company's reputation may be put at risk because it is off-shoring jobs.
   - *Social responsibility risk.* The company's reputation may be put at risk based on the practices of the organizations used in other countries.

   Obviously, the company can implement policies and controls, including requiring effective operating agreements, to mitigate these risks.

6. **Other techniques that focus on improving processes include**

   a. **Reengineering (business process reengineering)** is the fundamental rethinking and redesign of business processes to achieve improvements in critical measures of performance such as cost, quality, service speed and customer satisfaction. The scope of reengineering can affect operations and manufacturing processes, as well as financial and administrative processes such as accounts payable and procurement and can impact internal controls.

   b. **Lean manufacturing philosophy.** Lean manufacturing is an operational strategy focused on achieving the shortest possible cycle time by eliminating waste. It is based on increasing the value-added work by eliminating waste and reducing incidental work. The technique often decreases the time between a customer order and shipment, and it is designed to improve profitability, customer satisfaction, throughput time, and employee morale.

   c. **Theory of constraints (TOC)** refers to methods to maximize operating income when faced with some bottleneck operations. **Bottleneck resources** are any resource or operation where the capacity is less than the demand placed upon it. **Nonbottleneck resources** have capacity greater than demand. The objective of TOC is to increase *throughput contribution* while decreasing *investment* and *operating costs*. **Throughput contribution** is revenues minus the direct materials cost of goods sold. **Investment** is the sum of materials, cost in direct materials, work in process and finished goods inventories; research and development costs; and the costs of equipment and buildings. **Operating costs** include the salaries and wages, rental expense, utilities, and depreciation.

d. **Workflow Analysis** examines the overall flow of work to find ways to improve the flow. It focuses on identifying non-value-added activities and interdependence among various departments. By eliminating non-value-added activities and improving the coordination among departments, efficiencies may be achieved.

NOW REVIEW MULTIPLE-CHOICE QUESTIONS 56 THROUGH 71 IN VOLUME 2

KEY TERMS

Balanced scorecard. A strategic performance measurement system that includes financial and nonfinancial performance measures. The measures are in the four perspectives of financial, customer, internal business processes, and learning and growth.

Cash flow ROI. The average real cash return on all existing projects as reflected in the financial statements.

Continuous improvement. Seeks continual improvement of machinery, materials, labor, and production methods by soliciting suggestions and ideas from employees and customers.

Cost of quality. A technique that is based on the philosophy that failures have an underlying cause, prevention is cheaper than failures, and cost of quality performance can be measured.

Cross-sectional analysis. Involves benchmarking the firm's ratios against ratios of similar firms at a point in time.

Economic profit. Accounting profit minus the cost of capital.

Economic value added. Net operating profit after taxes minus the after-tax weighted-average cost of capital multiplied by total assets minus current liabilities.

Free cash flow. Net operating profit after taxes plus depreciation and amortization minus capital expenditures minus the change in working capital requirements.

Horizontal analysis. Involves an evaluation of the firm's ratios and trends over time.

Kaizen. The Japanese art of continuous improvement.

Pareto chart. A bar graph that ranks causes of process variations by the degree of impact on quality.

Strategy maps. Diagrams of the cause and effect relationships between strategic objectives.

Residual income. Net income minus a cost of capital based on capital invested in the project or division.

Residual income profile. A graphical way to look at the relationship between residual income and return on investment.

Total quality management. Focuses on managing the firm to excel in quality in all dimensions of products and services for customers.

Value-based management. Involves the use of value-based metrics in a strategic management system.

Module 46: Cost Measurement

Overview

A primary purpose of cost measurement is to allocate the costs of production (direct materials, direct manufacturing labor, and manufacturing overhead) to the units produced. It also provides important information for management decisions, such as product pricing decisions. Cost measurement is achieved through a costing system (job-order, process, activity-based) as described in this module. Before you begin the reading, you should review the key terms at the end of the module.

A. Cost of Goods Manufactured

Regardless of which costing system is used, a cost of goods manufactured (CGM) statement is prepared to summarize the manufacturing activity of the period. CGM for a manufacturing firm is equivalent to purchases for a merchandising firm. Although it may take different forms, essentially the CGM statement is a summary of the direct materials and work in process (WIP) accounts.

$$BWIP + DM + DML + MOH - EWIP = CGM$$

A typical CGM statement is presented below.

Uddin Company
COST OF GOODS MANUFACTURED
Year Ended December 31, 2007

Direct materials

Inventory, Jan. 1	$ 23,000	
Purchases	98,000	
Materials available for use	121,000	
Inventory, Dec. 31	16,000	
Direct materials used		$105,000
Direct manufacturing labor		72,000

Factory overhead

Indirect labor	$ 14,000	
Supplies	4,000	
Utilities	8,000	
Depreciation	13,000	
Other	3,000	42,000
Manufacturing costs incurred, 2007		219,000
Add work in process inventory, Jan. 1		25,000
Manufacturing costs to account for		244,000
Deduct work in process inventory, Dec. 31		30,000
Cost of goods manufactured (completed)		$214,000

The result of the CGM statement is used in the cost of goods sold (CGS) statement or cost of goods sold section of the income statement, as indicated below.

Uddin Company
COST OF GOODS SOLD
Year Ended December 31, 2007

Finished goods, Jan. 1	$ 40,000
Add cost of goods manufactured (completed) per statement above	214,000
Cost of goods available for sale	254,000
Deduct finished goods, Dec. 31	53,000
Cost of goods sold	$201,000

B. Cost Flows

Before discussing any particular costing system, it is important to understand the flow of costs through the accounts, as summarized in the diagram below.

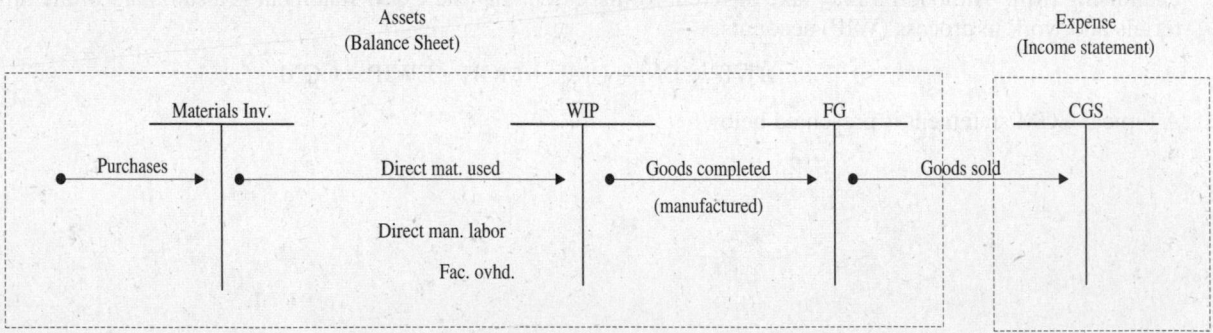

Analyze the diagram carefully before proceeding. The details will be explained further in the next few pages.

C. Job-Order Costing

Job-order costing is a system for allocating costs to groups of unique products. It is applicable to the production of customer-specified products such as the manufacture of special machines and even to cost a particular service (e.g., providing legal services for the client of a law firm). Each job becomes a cost center for which costs are accumulated. A subsidiary record (job-order cost sheet) is needed to keep track of all unfinished jobs (work in process) and finished jobs (finished goods). Note that the total of unfinished job cost sheets will equal the work in process balance.

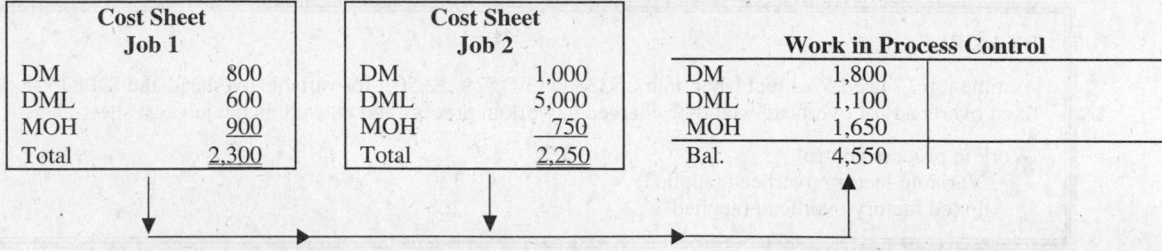

The balances on the job-order cost sheets are also the basis for the entries transferring completed goods to finished goods inventory and transferring the cost of goods shipped to customers to cost of goods sold. The work in process account is analyzed below.

Work in Process Control	
1. Beginning balance	
2. Direct materials used	
3. Direct labor used	
4. Overhead applied	5. Cost of goods manufactured (CGM)
6. Ending balance	

A similar analysis can be performed on the finished goods account.

Finished Goods Control	
1. Beginning balance	
2. Cost of goods manufactured	3. Cost of goods sold (CGS)
4. Ending balance	

D. Accounting for Overhead

Accounting for manufacturing overhead is an important part of job-order costing and any other costing system. Overhead consists of all manufacturing costs other than direct materials and direct manufacturing labor. The distinguishing feature of manufacturing overhead is that while it must be incurred in order to produce goods, **it cannot be directly traced to the final product** as can direct materials and direct manufacturing labor. Therefore, overhead must be **applied,** rather than directly charged, to goods produced. The overhead application process is described below.

1. Overhead items are grouped by cost behavior (e.g., fixed and variable).
2. The fixed and variable overhead costs are estimated for the forthcoming period (e.g., $200,000 for variable overhead and $400,000 for fixed overhead).
3. A denominator (activity) base is chosen (see discussion below). A common choice is direct labor hours or machine hours.
4. The actual activity level is estimated for the forthcoming year (e.g., 80,000 hours).
5. Determine the normal capacity of the facility (e.g., 100,000 hours).
6. Determine the predetermined overhead rates:

   a. For variable overhead use actual activity level

   $$\frac{\text{Estimated variable overhead costs}}{\text{Estimated actual activity level}} = \frac{\$200,000}{80,000 \text{ hours}} = \$2.50/\text{hour}$$

   b. For fixed overhead use normal capacity

   $$\frac{\text{Estimated fixed overhead costs}}{\text{Normal capacity}} = \frac{\$400,000}{100,000 \text{ hours}} = \$4.00/\text{hour}$$

7. As actual overhead costs are incurred, they are debited to the factory overhead accounts.

Variable factory overhead (actual)	900	
Various accounts		900
Fixed factory overhead (actual)	1,000	
Various accounts		1,000

8. As jobs are completed, the predetermined overhead rate(s) is used to apply overhead to these jobs.

```
EXAMPLE

Assume job 17 used 52 direct labor hours, $338 [$130 (52 x $2.50)] for variable overhead and $208 (52 x $4) for
fixed overhead] of overhead would be charged to work in process and entered on the job cost sheet.

   Work in process control                        338
       Variable factory overhead (applied)              130
       Fixed factory overhead (applied)                 208
```

US financial reporting standards require the allocation of fixed production overhead to inventory based on the normal capacity of the production facilities. Normal capacity is the production expected to be achieved over a number of periods or seasons under normal circumstances. The actual level of production may be used if it approximates normal capacity. Therefore, for financial reporting purposes companies must use normal capacity to allocate fixed overhead but the actual activity level is used to allocate variable overhead.

To allocate the costs of overhead to units produced, an **activity base** must be chosen for use in the computation of a predetermined overhead rate. This activity base should bear a causal relationship to the incurrence of overhead costs. Examples of activity bases are

1. Direct manufacturing labor hours
2. Direct manufacturing labor cost
3. Machine hours

For example, overhead may result from (be a function of) hours worked regardless of who works, which would mean that direct manufacturing labor hours should be the activity base. If, on the other hand, more overhead costs were incurred because of heavily automated operations, machine hours might be a more appropriate activity base.

However, for internal purposes, management may use a number of approaches to determine the activity level, as shown below.

Approach	Definition
Theoretical capacity	Output is produced efficiently 100% of the time.
	↓
Practical capacity	ADJUSTED FOR: factors such as days off, downtime, etc. Output is produced maximum percentage of time practical (75-85%).
	↓
Normal capacity	ADJUSTED FOR: long-run product demand. Average annual output necessary to meet sales and inventory fluctuations over 4-5-year period.
	↓
Expected annual capacity	ADJUSTED FOR: current year fluctuations. Expected output for current year.

Note that theoretical capacity is larger than practical capacity, which is larger than normal volume. Expected annual capacity fluctuates above and below normal volume.

At year-end fixed overhead may be

1. **Overapplied**—More is applied than incurred because

    a. Overhead costs were overestimated,
    b. Actual activity was greater than normal capacity, and/or
    c. Actual overhead costs were less than expected.

2. **Underapplied**—Less overhead is applied than incurred because

    a. Overhead costs were underestimated,
    b. Actual activity was less than normal capacity, and/or
    c. Actual overhead costs were more than expected.

E. Disposition of Under- and Overapplied Overhead

1. If the under- or overapplied overhead is immaterial, it is frequently written off to cost of goods sold on grounds of expediency.

```
        Cost of goods sold (debit or credit)              xx
            Factory overhead (debit or credit)                 xx
```

2. If the amount of under- or overapplied variable overhead is significant, then an adjustment must be made to all goods which were costed at the erroneous application rate during the current period. The goods with the incorrect costs will be in three accounts: Work in Process Control, Finished Goods Control, and Cost of Goods Sold.

   Proration may be made based upon total ending balance (before proration) of the three accounts or on some other equitable basis. The exam will normally give specific directions on what allocation base should be used.

   The amount of under- or overapplied fixed overhead should always be charged to cost of goods sold.

F. Service Department Cost Allocation

A large firm will have several production departments, each of which may compute a separate predetermined overhead rate. A problem arises when a **service** (support) department (maintenance, receiving, etc.) incurs costs and benefits multiple production departments.

Costs of these service departments must be allocated to production departments because all manufacturing costs must ultimately be traced to products. For example, the costs of the materials-handling cost center may need to be allocated to the production departments (and possibly other service departments). Apportionment of service department costs should be based on meaningful criteria such as

1. Services provided
2. Services available
3. Benefits received
4. Equity

Examples of apportionment bases are

1. Square feet for building costs
2. Usage for electricity
3. Employees for cafeteria, personnel, and first aid
4. Usage for materials handling, maintenance, etc.

Service department costs can be allocated by

1. Direct method
2. Step method
3. Reciprocal method

1. Direct Method

The direct method simply allocates the costs of each service department to each of the producing departments based on a relative level of the apportionment base. For example, if a service department had costs of $140,000, and producing departments X and Y used 80% and 20% of the apportionment base, X and Y would be assigned $112,000 and $28,000 respectively. Note that the direct method ignores use of services by other service departments. For example, the direct method would ignore the fact that service department A uses the services of service department B. The essence of the direct method is shown in the following diagram.

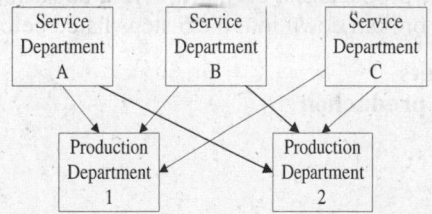

2. Step Method

The step method allocates service department costs to other service departments as well as production departments. The allocation process is

a. Select the service department serving the most other service departments

   (1) When more than one service department services an equal number of service departments, select the department with the highest costs

b. Allocate the costs of the service department selected in step a. to the production departments and other service departments based on a relative level of the apportionment base as in the direct method.

c. Allocate the costs of each remaining service department selected in the same manner as described in step a.

d. Costs of service departments are never allocated back to departments whose costs have already been allocated.

NOTE: The step method ignores the fact that reciprocal services are used between some service departments.

EXAMPLE

DEPARTMENTS

	Service		Production		
	A	**B**	**1**	**2**	**Totals**
Costs	$4,000	$6,000	$38,000	$42,000	$90,000
Use of A		10%	40%	50%	100%
Use of B	30%		40%	30%	100%

Direct Method—Allocate A's and B's costs directly to production departments 1 and 2.

	A	B	1	2
Costs prior to allocation	4,000	6,000	38,000	42,000
Allocation of A's costs*	(4,000)		1,778	2,222
Allocation of B's costs**		(6,000)	3,429	2,571
	0	0	43,207	46,793

* 4/9 and 5/9
** 4/7 and 3/7 $90,000

Step Method—Allocate B's costs (B has more costs than A) to departments A, 1, and 2. Next allocate A's costs to departments 1 and 2; you cannot allocate A's costs back to B, as B's costs have already been allocated.

	A	B	1	2
Costs prior to allocation	4,000	6,000	38,000	42,000
Allocation of B's costs*	1,800	(6,000)	2,400	1,800
Allocation of A's costs ($4,000 + $1,800)**	(5,800)		2,578	3,222
	0	0	42,978	47,022

* 3/10, 4/10, and 3/10
** 4/9 and 5/9 $90,000

3. Reciprocal Method

The reciprocal method provides a way to adjust for the reciprocal services provided among the service departments. Using this method, service department costs and service department reciprocal service relationships are described by a linear equation. Then, the equations are solved simultaneously providing a more precise allocation of costs to production departments because it considers the mutual services provided among the service departments.

G. Process Costing

Process costing, in contrast to job-order costing, is applicable to a continuous process of production of the same or similar goods, for example, oil refining and chemical production. Since the product is uniform, there is no need to determine the costs of different groups of products and each processing department becomes a cost center.

Process costing computations can be broken down into the 5 steps listed below.

1. Visualize the **physical flow of units**
2. Compute the **equivalent units of production**
3. Determine **costs to allocate**
4. Compute **unit costs**
5. **Allocate total costs** to

   a. Goods completed
   b. Ending work in process

Note that the five steps above can be memorized using the acronym: PECUA (**P**hysical Flow, **E**quivalent Units of Production, **C**osts to Allocate, **U**nit Costs, **A**llocate Costs).

1. Flow of Units

The cost flow diagram shown under Section B in this module is the same for process costing except there will typically be several WIP accounts (i.e., one for every department). When solving a process costing problem, it is helpful to visualize the physical flow of units, as illustrated in the diagram below.

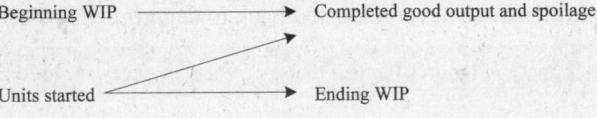

The units in BWIP are either completed or become spoiled. Units started during the period but not completed become EWIP.

2. **Equivalent Units of Production (EUP)**

An EUP is the amount of work equivalent to completing one unit from start to finish. In a process costing system, products are assigned costs periodically (usually monthly). At any one moment some units are incomplete which makes the EUP calculations necessary to allocate manufacturing costs between

1. Goods finished during the period (cost of goods manufactured)
2. Ending work in process

The two primary EUP methods used for process costing are first-in, first-out (FIFO) and weighted-average (WA). Past questions on the exam have emphasized the weighted-average method. Under the weighted-average approach, current costs are combined with prior period costs, and all units are carried at an average cost of production. Importantly, the method assumes that all units completed during a period are started and completed during that period. As a result, the **percentage** of work done last period on the beginning work in process inventory is ignored.

3. **Simple Process Costing Example**

The BW Toy Company uses a weighted-average process cost system to collect costs. Data relevant to 2007 production is given below. Assume we begin with 800 units 25% complete for labor and overhead (conversion costs), and 100% complete for materials because they are introduced at the start of the process. We start 4,200 units. 4,000 units are completed, while 1,000 remain in EWIP (20% complete for labor and overhead and 100% complete for materials). No spoilage exists. The costs are summarized in the following T-account:

Work in Process Control

BWIP				
materials	900			
labor + OH	532	1,432	???	Goods finished
Current				
materials	4,200			
labor + OH	14,000	18,200		
EWIP		???		

Step 1: The physical flow of units is accounted for.

BWIP	800
Started	4,200
To account for	5,000
Units completed	4,000
EWIP	1,000
Accounted for	5,000

Step 2: The units completed and ending work in process are converted to equivalent units.

		Equivalent units	
Description	Total	Direct mtls.	Conv.
Physical units to account for			
Beginning inventory	800		
Units started	4,200		
Units to be accounted for	5,000		
Equivalent units of production			
Good units completed and transferred out	4,000	4,000*	4,000**
Ending WIP	1,000	1,000*	200
Units accounted for	5,000	5,000	4,200

* These units are 100% complete with respect to materials because materials are introduced at the start of the process.

** These units are 100% complete with respect to conversion because all units completed are **assumed** to be started and completed during the period.

Steps 3 and 4: Determine costs to allocate and equivalent unit costs.

Manufacturing costs			
Beginning inventory	$ 1,432	$ 900	$ 532
Current costs	18,200	4,200	14,000
Total costs to account for	$19,632	$ 5,100	$14,532
Cost per equivalent unit		$ 1.02*	$ 3.46**

* Notice the resulting costs are averages: $5,100 ÷ 5,000 equivalent units = $1.02.

** $14,532 ÷ 4,200 equivalent units = $3.46.

Step 5: Allocate total costs to goods completed and ending work in process.

Units completed [4,000 x ($1.02 + $3.46)]		$17,920
Ending WIP:		
Mat. (1,000 x $1.02)	$1,020	
Conv. (200 x $3.46)	692	1,712
Total costs accounted for		$19,632

The allocation is accomplished by multiplying the individual equivalent unit figures by the unit costs.

4. **EUP for Material**

   In the above example, material was assumed to be added at the beginning of the production process. Material can also be added at different points in the process (e.g., 10%, 70%) or gradually during the process.

5. **FIFO Work in Process Assumption**

   The FIFO approach is not as popular as the weighted-average approach on the exam. Thus, we will focus solely on the calculation of equivalent units. With FIFO, the first batch into production (i.e., the beginning work in process inventory) is assumed to be the first batch completed. This batch is treated as a separate, distinct layer— separate from goods that are started and completed during the period.

   The weighted-average assumption (all goods are assumed to be started and completed during the period) no longer holds for FIFO. Thus, any work done last period on the beginning work in process inventory must be taken into consideration. After all is said and done, the equivalent unit figures reflect the work done during the current accounting period. Also, the only difference between the two methods is the treatment of the beginning work in process inventory.

   The equivalent-unit calculations for BW Toy follow.

Description	Total	Direct mtls.	Conv.
Physical units to account for			
Beginning inventory	800		
Units started	4,200		
Units to be accounted for	5,000		
Equivalent units of production			
Good units completed and transferred out:			
From beg. WIP	800	0*	600**
Started and completed	3,200	3,200***	3,200***
Ending WIP	1,000	1,000	200
Units accounted for	5,000	4,200	4,000

   * All material was introduced last period.
   ** 75% of the work was necessary this period to complete the units.
   *** 100% of the materials and conversions were introduced this period.

6. **Spoilage (Scrap) in Process Costing**

   The following terms are commonly used:

   • **Spoilage (scrap)**—Inferior goods either discarded or sold for disposal value
   • **Defective units**—Inferior goods reworked and sold as normal product

   A major distinction is made between normal and abnormal spoilage.

   a. Normal spoilage is the cost of spoiled units caused by the nature of the manufacturing process (i.e., which occur under efficient operating conditions).

      (1) Normal spoilage is a necessary cost in the production process and is, therefore, a **product cost**.

   b. Abnormal spoilage is the cost of spoiled units which were spoiled through some unnecessary act, event, or condition.

      (1) Abnormal spoilage is a **period cost** (e.g., "loss on abnormal spoilage").
      (2) Abnormal spoilage costs should not be included in cost of goods sold.

      Spoilage must be considered in EUP calculations. For example, if spoilage is discovered at the 60% point in processing and 100 units of abnormal spoilage are discovered, 60 EUP have occurred. The amount of abnormal loss would be the cost of 60 EUP (processing) plus the materials added to 100 units of production up to the 60% point. In contrast, if the spoilage was considered normal in nature, the spoilage cost would be treated as a product cost and simply added to the cost of the good units completed.

7. **Spoilage in Job Costing**

   In a job-order costing system, the costs of normal spoilage and defective units can be handled in two different ways. When spoilage is attributable to general factory conditions, net spoilage costs are allocated to all jobs through overhead application (i.e., estimated spoilage costs are included with other overhead in the computation of the overhead application rate). Alternatively, when spoilage is attributable to exacting job specifications, net spoilage costs are charged to specific jobs. With this approach, spoilage is **not** reflected in the predetermined overhead rate. Under both methods, the proceeds from the sale of spoiled goods should be offset against the cost of spoiled goods produced. Net spoilage cost would be charged to factory overhead in the first case and left in work in process in the second case.

Costs of abnormal spoilage should **not** be charged to jobs but should be written off as a loss of the period.

H. Hybrid-Costing System

Because of the nature of their operations certain manufacturers use costing systems that blend characteristics of both the job-order and process costing systems. Such so-called hybrid-costing systems are often used by firms that manufacture a relatively large number of closely related standardized parts (e.g., automobile manufacturers and clothing manufacturers). An example of a hybrid-costing system is the **operation-costing system** that applies costs to batches of similar, but not identical, products. Direct materials are traced directly to each batch, similar to job costing. Conversion costs are traced to each operation and allocated to products that pass through the operation.

I. Backflush Costing

When a firm uses a **just-in-time (JIT)** production system, as described in Module 45, management may decide to use backflush costing for their products. Instead of using accounting records to track costs of goods as they are purchased and go through the production process, backflush costing uses normal or standard costs to work backward to "flush out" the costs of the goods finished or sold. Backflush costing does not strictly adhere to generally accepted accounting principles. However, because of the negligible amount of inventories that is characteristic of JIT production systems, the difference is often not material.

NOW REVIEW MULTIPLE-CHOICE QUESTIONS 1 THROUGH 37 IN VOLUME 2

J. Activity-Based Costing

Activity-based costing (ABC) is based upon two principles. First, activities consume resources. Second, these resources are consumed by products, services, or other cost objectives (output). ABC allocates overhead costs to products on the basis of the resources consumed by each activity involved in the design, production, and distribution of a particular good. This is accomplished through the assignment of costs to homogeneous cost pools that represent specific activities and then the allocation of these costs, using appropriate cost drivers, to the product. ABC may be used in conjunction with either job order or process costing systems.

Central to ABC are the activities performed to fulfill organizational objectives (producing products or services for customers). Activities may be value-added or non-value-added. **Value-added activities** are those which customers perceive as increasing the worth of a product or service and for which customers are willing to pay. They include only production activities. **Nonvalue-added activities** increase the cost of a product but do not increase its value to customers. Examples include materials handling and rework. Packaging is required for some products such as milk or potting soil, but it may be non-value-added for other products such as books (it is also costly and takes up huge amounts of landfill space). Thus, these activities may be eliminated and/or restructured without customers perceiving a decline in the value of the product/service. An activity (process) map is a flowchart which indicates all activities involved in the production process and identifies both value-added and non-value-added activities.

Cost drivers are those activities which have a direct cause and effect relationship to the incurrence of a particular cost. Traditional costing uses only variable and fixed or total overhead cost pools and views cost drivers at the output unit level, wherein costs are allocated based on labor hours, machine hours, etc. Some costs though, such as setup costs, vary at the batch level (batch-level costs) and should be spread over the units in the batch to which they relate (**not** machine hours). Product-sustaining (process-level) costs such as engineering change orders should be assigned to the products for which the orders were issued. Facility-sustaining costs incurred at the organizational level support operations and can only be arbitrarily assigned to products. As shown by the following table, ABC uses both transaction-related (e.g., purchase orders) and volume-related (e.g., machine hours) cost drivers. Traditional product costing tends to use only volume-related cost drivers.

Activity	Cost driver
Purchase of materials	Number of purchase transactions
Receiving	Number of shipments received
Disbursing	Number of checks issued
Setup costs	Number of setups or setup hours
Machining	Number of machine hours
Repair costs	Number of machine hours
Engineering changes to products	Number of engineering change notices

The activities listed above are all examples of direct activities which can be traced to an output or service. In contrast, indirect activities such as human resources are not directly attributable to output. The cost of indirect activities may be allocated or simply labeled as nontraceable.

To illustrate, ABC traces the costs of setup activities to the production batch that caused the setup costs to be incurred. The cost of each setup is then spread over the units in that batch. On the other hand, a traditional costing system would typically allocate setup costs as overhead on the basis of a volume-related cost driver such as direct manufacturing labor hours. Assume that product A and product B incur setup costs as follows:

	A	B	Total
Production volume	7,500	10,000	
Batch size	250	1,000	
Number of setups	30	10	
Total setup costs incurred	$60,000	$20,000	$80,000
Total cost per setup	$2,000	$2,000	
Direct manuf. labor hours/unit	3	3	
Total direct manuf. labor hours	22,500	30,000	52,500
Setup cost per DMLH ($80,000 ÷ 52,500)			$1.52
Traditional setup cost/unit			
A ($1.52 x 3 DMLH required)	$ 4.56		
B ($1.52 x 3 DMLH required)		$ 4.56	
ABC setup cost/unit			
A ($2,000/setup ÷ 250 units/batch)	$ 8.00		
B ($2,000/setup ÷ 1,000 units/batch)		$ 2.00	

In this case, products A and B are assigned different total setup costs. However, because they require the same number of direct manufacturing labor hours per unit, traditional costing allocates equal setup costs per unit to both products. In effect, one product picks up cost that was caused by another product (cross-subsidization), which distorts product costing information. ABC assigns different setup costs per unit to each product because **each unit** of product A demands more resources for setup activity than does **each unit** of product B. Note that the **total** setup cost remains the same under either method.

Activity-based management (ABM) integrates ABC with other concepts such as Total Quality Management (TQM) and target costing to produce a management system that strives for excellence through cost reduction, continuous process improvement, and productivity gains.

K. Joint Products

Joint products are two or more products produced together up to a split-off point where they become separately identifiable. They cannot be produced by themselves. For example, a steak cannot be produced without also producing roasts, ribs, liver, hamburger, etc. Other industries which produce joint products include

1. Chemicals   3. Mining
2. Lumber   4. Petroleum

Joint products incur common, or joint costs, before the split-off point. The split-off point is the point of production at which the joint products can be individually identified and removed from the joint, or common, process. The joint products can then be sold or processed further. Costs incurred after the split-off point for any one of the joint products are called separable costs.

Common costs are allocated to the joint products at the split-off point, usually on the basis of sales value at the split-off point, estimated net realizable value (NRV) at split-off point, or some physical measure. The estimated net realizable value method allocates joint costs using the estimated sales values of the joint products after further processing less the separable processing costs. Of the first two methods listed, the sales value at split-off method **must** be used if a sales value at split-off point exists. The following example illustrates the sales value at split-off and estimated net realizable value methods.

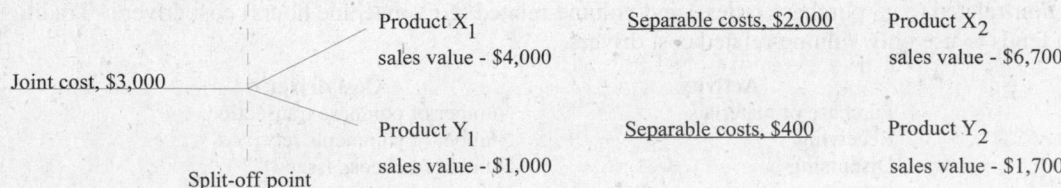

SALES VALUE AT SPLIT-OFF

Product	Sales value @ split-off	Ratio	x	Joint costs	=	Allocated joint costs
X_1	$4,000	$\dfrac{\$4,000}{\$5,000}$	x	$3,000	=	$2,400
Y_1	$1,000	$\dfrac{\$1,000}{\$5,000}$	x	$3,000	=	$ 600
Total	$5,000					$3,000

If the sales value at split-off is not available or one did not exist, we would use the estimated net realizable value method (NRV).

ESTIMATED NET REALIZABLE VALUE METHOD (NRV)

Product	Final sales value	–	Separable costs	=	Estimated net realizable value	Ratio	x	Joint costs	=	Allocated joint costs
X_2	$6,700	–	$2,000	=	$4,700	$\dfrac{\$4,700}{\$6,000}$	x	$3,000	=	$2,350
Y_2	$1,700	–	$ 400	=	$1,300	$\dfrac{\$1,300}{\$6,000}$	x	$3,000	=	$ 650
Total					$6,000					$3,000

Physical measures (units, pounds, etc.) generally are not used because of the misleading income statement effect. With an allocation based on pounds, steak would show a big profit while ground beef would be a consistent loser; each pound would carry the same cost although steak sells for much more per pound.

Joint cost allocation is performed for the purpose of inventory valuation and income determination. However, joint costs should be **ignored** for any internal decisions including the decision on whether to process a joint product beyond the split-off point. Such costs are not relevant to the sell or process further decision. The **sell or process further** decision should be based on incremental revenues and costs beyond the split-off point. If incremental revenue from further processing exceeds incremental costs, then process further. If incremental costs exceed incremental revenues, then sell at the split-off point. In the previous example in which we assumed a sales value at the split-off point, both X_1 and Y_1 should be further processed.

	Incremental revenue		Incremental cost		Advantage of further processing
X_1:	$6,700 – $4,000 = $2,700	–	$2,000	=	$700
Y_1:	$1,700 – $1,000 = $ 700	–	$ 400	=	$300

If X_1 could have sold for only $5,500 after further processing, the incremental revenue ($1,500) would not cover the incremental cost ($2,000), and X_1 should not be further processed.

L. By-Products

By-products, in contrast to joint products, have little market value relative to the overall value of the product(s) being produced. Joint (common) costs are usually not allocated to a by-product. Instead, by-products are frequently valued at market or net realizable value (NRV) and accounted for as a contra production cost, that is, a reduction in the joint costs that will be allocated to the joint products.

Rather than recognizing by-product market value as a reduction of production cost, it is sometimes recognized when sold and disclosed as

1. Ordinary sales
2. Other income
3. Contra to cost of sales

Given the variety of approaches, the exam will normally specify the method that is to be followed.

> **NOW REVIEW MULTIPLE-CHOICE QUESTIONS 38 THROUGH 53 IN VOLUME 2**

M. Estimating Cost Functions

A **cost function** is a mathematical expression of how a cost changes with changes in the level of activity. Cost functions may be illustrated on a graph with the x-axis measuring the level of activity and the y-axis measuring the corresponding total cost. Underlying cost functions is the belief that the level of activity explains the total costs, and that the relationship is linear (expressed as a straight line) within the relevant range. The relevant range is the range of costs for which the relationships are predictable. The following three types of cost functions may be observed:

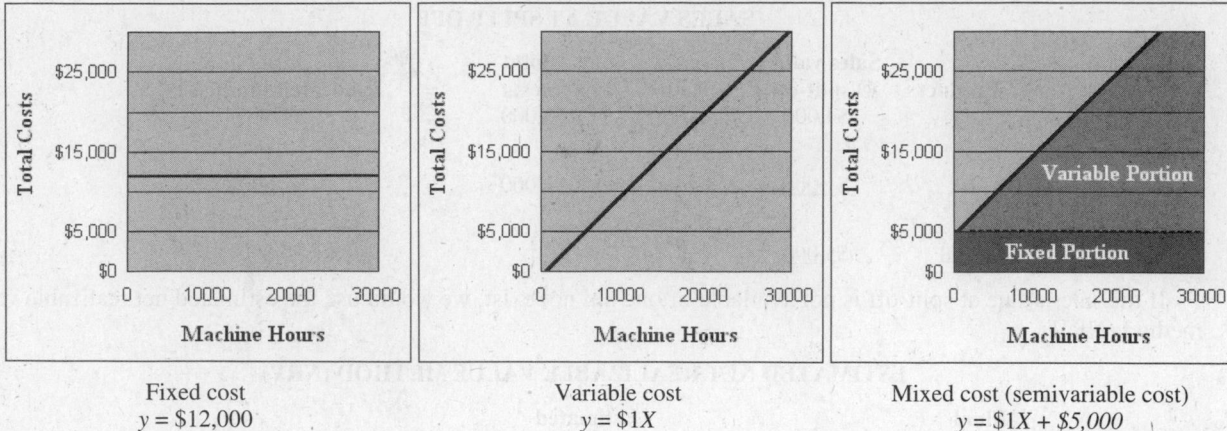

Fixed cost
y = $12,000

Variable cost
y = $1X

Mixed cost (semivariable cost)
y = $1X + $5,000

As illustrated, the fixed cost is a constant amount of $12,000 over the relevant range, and the variable cost is equal to $1 per machine hour over the relevant range. The mixed cost is made up of $5,000 in fixed cost and $1 per unit of variable cost.

As indicated previously, one of the most important aspects of estimating a cost function is determining whether there is a causal relationship between the level of activity (the cost driver) and the cost. A causal relationship is necessary to developing reliable cost predictions.

There are four different basic approaches to cost estimation.

1. **Industrial engineering (work-measurement) method**—Estimates of cost functions are derived from analyzing the physical relationships between inputs (e.g., direct labor hours) and outputs. As an example, a time and motion study might be used to determine how many hours it takes to assemble a table. This method of developing cost functions is time-consuming and costly.

2. **Conference method**—Estimates of cost functions are derived from analysis and opinions about cost relationships by individuals from various departments. This method can be done quickly but may not be as reliable as those that are based on quantitative methods.

3. **Account analysis method**—Estimates of cost functions are derived by analyzing ledger accounts and designating them as containing fixed costs, variable costs, or mixed costs. This is a widely used method but to be reliable it must be performed by individuals who understand operations.

4. **Quantitative methods**—Estimates of cost functions are derived using formal mathematical models. Using quantitative methods, management identifies a cost and one or more cost drivers to be used to predict the cost. Then they collect historical data to estimate the cost function. A number of quantitative methods are used, including

   a. **Scattergraph method.** The scattergraph method is a graphical approach to computing the relationship between two variables. The dependent variable is plotted on the vertical axis and the independent variable on the horizontal axis. A straight line is then drawn through the observation points which best describes the relationship between the two variables. In the graph below, the broken line illustrates the relationship. This method lacks precision, because by freely drawing the line through the points, it is possible to obtain a line that does not minimize the deviations of the points from the line.

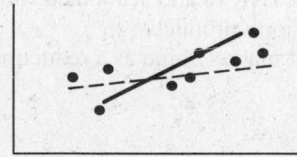

   b. **High-Low method.** The high-low method computes the slope for the variable rate based on the highest and lowest observations.

$$\text{Slope} = \frac{\text{Change in cost between high and low points}}{\text{Change in activity between high and low points}}$$

This method is illustrated using the following observations for factory maintenance costs (DMLH = Direct manufacturing labor hours).

Month	DMLH	Factory maintenance cost
1	45,000 (low)	$110,000
2	50,000	115,000
3	70,000	158,000
4	60,000	135,000
5	75,000 (high)	170,000
6	65,000	145,000

The difference in cost is divided by the difference in activity to obtain the variable cost. The fixed cost can then be computed by using either the high observation or the low observation. The same result will be obtained with either one. The computation for separating factory maintenance cost is detailed below.

Variable rate computation

$$\frac{\$170,000 - \$110,000}{75,000 - 45,000} = \$2/\text{DMLH}$$

Fixed rate computation

$$\$170,000 - (75,000 \times \$2) = \$20,000$$

or

$$\$110,000 - (45,000 \times \$2) = \$20,000$$

The high-low method is a rather crude technique compared to regression analysis. For example, this method may be inaccurate if the high and low points are not representative (i.e., are outliers) as illustrated by the solid line in the chart included with the discussion of the scattergraph method.

c. **Regression analysis.** Regression (least squares) analysis determines the functional relationship between variables with a measure of probable error. For example, you may wish to determine the relationship of electricity cost to level of activity. Based on activity levels and electricity charges of past months, the following chart (scattergraph) might be prepared.

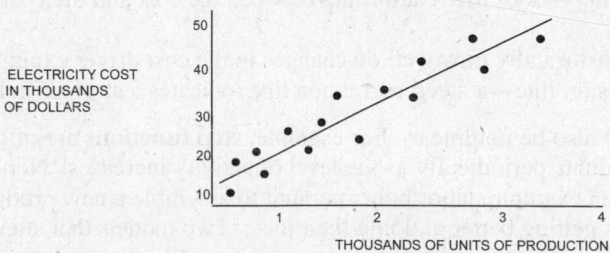

As production increases, electric costs increase. The relationship appears linear. Linearity is an assumption underlying regression. If the power costs begin to fall after 3,000 units of production, the relationship between electricity and production would not be linear, and linear regression would not be appropriate.

The method of least squares fits a regression line between the observation points such that the sum of the squared vertical differences between the regression line and the individual observations is minimized. The simple regression equation for a linear cost function is

$$y = a + bx$$

Where

y = estimated total cost
a = constant, the portion of the cost that is fixed over the relevant range
b = the slope, the amount by which the cost changes based on changes in the level of activity over the relevant range
x = the level of activity as measured by the cost driver

The goodness of the least squares fit (i.e., how well the regression line fits the observed data) is measured by the coefficient of determination (R^2). The better the line fits the observed data points (i.e., the closer the observed data points are to the line), the closer R^2 will be to 1.00 — R^2s of 90–99% are considered very good. However, you must remember that a high R^2 does not prove that there is a cause and effect relationship between the two variables.

If only one independent variable exists, the analysis is known as simple regression (as in the above example). **Multiple regression** consists of a functional relationship with multiple independent variables (e.g., cost may be a function of several cost drivers). Multiple regression is described in detail in the next module.

d. **Correlation analysis.** Correlation is the relationship between variables. If the variables move with each other, they have a direct relationship (positive correlation) as in A. If the variables move in opposite directions, they have an inverse relationship (negative correlation) as in B.

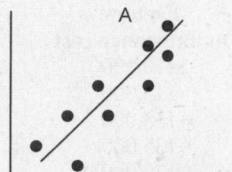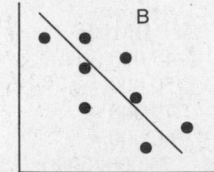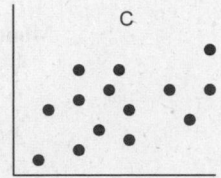

The degree and direction of correlation is measured from –1 to 1. The sign (negative or positive) describes whether the relationship is inverse or direct. The coefficient of correlation is measured by

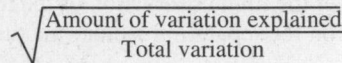

$$\sqrt{\frac{\text{Amount of variation explained}}{\text{Total variation}}}$$

If all of the observations were in a straight line, all of the variation would be explained and the coefficient of correlation would be 1 or –1 depending upon whether the relationship is positive or negative. If there is no correlation, as in C above, the coefficient of correlation is 0.

> **NOTE:** The coefficient of correlation is similar in concept to the coefficient of determination discussed above in "method of least squares." The coefficient of determination cannot have a negative value, as can the coefficient of correlation, because the coefficient of determination is based on squared deviations (i.e., if you square a negative number, the result is positive).

Management often has a choice of cost drivers to use in estimating a particular cost. In evaluating the best driver to use, management should consider

- Economic plausibility—does the relationship between the cost and the cost driver make intuitive economic sense?
- Goodness of fit—historically how well do changes in the cost driver explain total costs?
- Slope of the regression line—a steep regression line indicates a stronger relationship than a flatter line.

Cost functions may also be nonlinear. For example, **step functions** are often encountered in which the cost increases in discrete amounts periodically as the level of activity increases. Nonlinear functions also occur due to **learning curves**. As an example, labor hours per unit to assemble a new product may decline as production increases due to workers getting better at doing their jobs. Two models that attempt to capture the effect of learning are

- **Cumulative average-time model**—The cumulative average time per unit declines by a constant percentage each time the quantity of units produced doubles.
- **Incremental unit-time learning model**—The incremental unit time needed to produce the last unit declines by a constant percentage each time the cumulative quantity of units produced doubles.

NOW REVIEW MULTIPLE-CHOICE QUESTIONS 54 THROUGH 57 IN VOLUME 2

KEY TERMS

Job order costing is a system for allocating costs to groups of unique products made to customer specifications.

Process costing is a system for allocating costs to homogeneous units of a mass-produced product.

Hybrid-costing is a system that blends the characteristics of both the job order and process costing systems. Firms using this system typically produce large numbers of closely related products.

Activity-based costing (ABC) is a cost system that focuses on activities, determines their costs, and then uses appropriate cost drivers to trace costs to the products based on the activities. The following terminology is encountered in ABC:

A **cost driver** is a factor that causes a cost to be incurred. Cost drivers may be volume-related (e.g., repair costs may depend on the volume of machine hours) and transaction-related (purchasing costs may depend on the number of purchase transactions).

Cost pools are groupings of related costs accumulated together to be allocated to a product or some other cost object.

Non-value-added costs are the cost of activities that can be eliminated without the customer perceiving a decline in product quality or performance.

Value-added cost is the cost of activities that **cannot** be eliminated without the customer perceiving a decline in product quality or performance.

A **value chain** is the sequence of business functions in which value is added to a firm's products or services. This sequence includes research and development, product design, manufacturing, marketing, distribution, and customer service.

Engineered costs are determined from industrial engineering studies that examine how activities are performed and if/how performance can be improved.

Activity-based management (ABM) integrates ABC with other concepts such as Total Quality Management (TQM) and target costing to produce a management system that strives for excellence through cost reduction, continuous process improvement, and productivity gains.

Backflush costing is a costing system that omits recording some or all of the journal entries to track the purchase and production of goods. Goods are costed after they have been completed.

A **cost management system (CMS)** is a planning and control system that measures the cost of significant activities, identifies non-value-added costs, and identifies activities that will improve organizational performance.

Product costs are costs that can be associated with the production of specific goods. Product costs attach to a physical unit and become an expense in the period in which the unit to which they attach is sold. Product costs normally include direct manufacturing labor, direct materials, and factory overhead. **Period costs** cannot be associated (or matched) with manufactured goods (e.g., advertising expenditures). Period costs become expenses when incurred.

Prime costs are easily traceable to specific units of production and include direct manufacturing labor and direct materials. **Direct costs** are those easily traced to a specific business segment (e.g., product, division, department). **Indirect costs** are not easily traceable to specific segments and include factory overhead.

Direct materials is the cost of materials directly and conveniently traceable to a product. Minor material items (nails, glue) are not deemed conveniently traceable. These items are treated as **indirect materials** along with production supplies.

Direct manufacturing labor is the cost of labor directly transforming a product. This theoretically should include fringe benefits, but frequently does not. This is contrasted with **indirect manufacturing labor,** which is the cost of supporting labor (e.g., material-handling labor, factory supervisors).

Factory (manufacturing) overhead normally includes indirect manufacturing labor costs, supplies cost, and other production facility costs such as plant depreciation, taxes, etc. It is comprised of all manufacturing costs that are not direct materials or direct manufacturing labor.

Conversion costs include direct manufacturing labor and manufacturing overhead. They are the costs of converting direct materials into finished products.

Cost assignment encompasses both **cost tracing** (assignment of direct costs to a cost object) and **cost allocation** (assignment of indirect costs to the cost object). A **cost object** is the item (product, department, process, etc.) for which cost is being determined.

Direct materials inventory includes the cost of materials awaiting entry into the production system. **Work in process inventory** includes the cost of units being produced but not yet completed. **Finished goods inventory** includes the cost of units completed but unsold.

Actual activity level is the level of production actually occurring for the period.

Normal activity level is the production level expected to be achieved over a number of periods or seasons under normal circumstances.

Cycle time (or **throughput time**) is the time required to complete a good from the start of the production process until the product is finished.

Product life-cycle costing tracks the accumulation of costs that occur starting with the research and development for a product and ending with the time at which sales and customer support are withdrawn.

Computer-integrated manufacturing (CIM) is a highly automated and integrated production process that is controlled by computers.

A **flexible manufacturing system (FMS)** is a series of computer-controlled manufacturing processes that can be **easily** changed to make a variety of products.

Joint costs are costs common to multiple products that emerge at a split-off point. **Joint costing** is a system of assigning joint costs to **joint products** whose overall sales values are relatively significant. When a product has insignificant sales value relative to the other products, it is called a **by-product**.

Cost estimation is the examination of past relationships of costs and level of activity to develop predictions of future costs.

Fixed costs do not vary with the level of activity within the relevant range for a given period of time (usually one year), for example, plant depreciation.

Variable costs vary proportionately **in total** with the activity level throughout the relevant range (e.g., direct materials).

Stepped costs (or semifixed costs) are fixed over relatively short ranges of production levels (e.g., supervisors' salaries). Fixed, variable, and semifixed costs are diagrammed below.

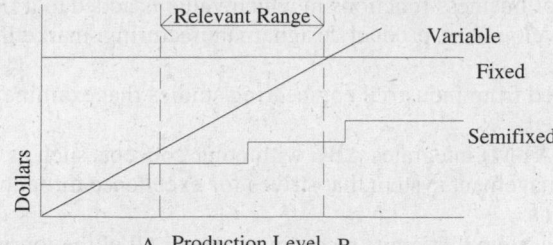

Mixed costs (semivariable) are costs that have a fixed component and a variable component. These components are separated by using the scattergraph, high-low, or linear regression methods.

Relevant range is the operating range of activity in which cost behavior patterns are valid (A to B in the preceding illustration). Thus, it is the production range for which fixed costs remain constant (e.g., if production doubles, an additional shift of salaried foremen would be added and fixed costs would increase).

Nonlinear cost function is a cost function that is not described by a straight line over the relevant range.

Learning curve is a function that demonstrates how productivity improves as workers become more proficient at producing the product.

Overview

This module discusses a number of tools used internally for financial planning, control, and analysis. In the area of financial planning, the module focuses on cost-volume-profit analysis. An understanding of the behavior of costs is essential to effective management of an organization. The module also examines the tools managers use to make effective financial decisions, including forecasting, budgeting, and regression analysis.

In the area of control, the module focuses on the establishment of standards and variance analysis. Finally, the module reviews the techniques used to perform specific tasks or make particular types of decisions, including project management, product and service pricing, transfer pricing, and short-term differential cost analysis. Before beginning the reading you should review the key terms at the end of the module.

A. Cost-Volume-Profit (CVP) Analysis

1. Overview

Cost-volume-profit (CVP) analysis provides management with profitability estimates at all levels of production in the relevant range (the normal operating range). CVP (or breakeven) analysis is based on the firm's profit function. Profit is a function of sales, variable costs, and fixed costs.

$$\text{Profit (NI)} = \text{Sales (S)} - \text{Fixed Costs (FC)} - \text{Variable Costs (VC)}$$

When profit is zero
$$0 = S - FC - VC$$
$$S = FC + VC$$

Fixed costs are constant in the relevant range, but both sales and variable costs are a function of the level of activity, and vary with respect to a single, output-related driver (e.g., units manufactured or sold). For example, if widgets are sold at $2.00/unit, variable costs are $.40/unit, and fixed costs are $20,000, breakeven is 12,500 units.

$$X = \text{Units of production and sales to breakeven}$$
$$\$2.00X = \$.40X + \$20,000$$
$$\$1.60X = \$20,000$$
$$X = 12,500 \text{ units (breakeven point)}$$

The cost-volume-profit relationship is diagrammed below.

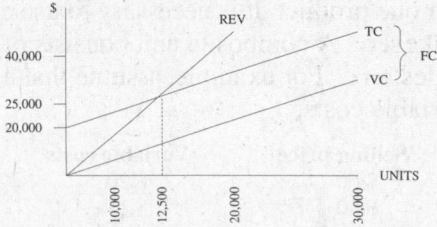

The breakeven point can be thought of as the amount of contribution margin (sales minus variable costs) required to cover the fixed costs, or the point of zero profit. In the previous example, the unit contribution margin (CM) is $1.60 ($2.00 – $.40). Thus, sales of 12,500 units are required to cover the $20,000 of fixed costs. This illustrates the possibility of two shortcut approaches.

Shortcut 1

$$\text{Units to break even} = \frac{\text{Fixed costs}}{\text{Unit CM}} = \frac{\$20,000}{\$1.60} = 12,500 \text{ units}$$

Shortcut 2

$$\begin{array}{ll} \text{Dollars to} \\ \text{break even} \end{array} = \frac{\text{Fixed costs}}{\text{CM percentage (ratio)}} = \frac{\text{Fixed costs}}{\dfrac{\text{CM per unit}}{\text{Selling price}}} = \frac{\$20,000}{\dfrac{\$1.60}{\$2.00}} = \frac{\$20,000}{80\%} = \$25,000 \text{ sales dollars}$$

A number of variations on the basic CVP calculation are found on the CPA exam. These are illustrated in the following paragraphs:

a. **Target net income.** Selling price is $2, variable cost per unit is $.40, fixed costs are $20,000, and desired net income is $5,000. What is the level of sales in units?

Equation ⟶ Sales = VC + FC + NI
$$\$2X = \$.4X + \$20,000 + \$5,000$$

Shortcut ⟶ $$\frac{FC + NI}{CM} = \frac{\$20,000 + \$5,000}{\$1.60}$$

Solution ⟶ 15,625 units

b. **Target net income-percentage of sales.** Same facts, except desired net income is 30% of sales. What is the level of sales in units?

Equation ⟶ Sales = VC + FC + NI
$$\$2X = \$.4X + \$20,000 + .30(\$2X)$$

Solution ⟶ 20,000 units

c. **No per-unit information given.** Fixed costs are $20,000, and variable expenses are 20% of sales. What is the breakeven level of sales in dollars?

Equation ⟶ Sales = VC + FC
$$S = .2(S) + \$20,000$$

Shortcut ⟶ $$\frac{FC}{CM\%} = \frac{20,000}{80\%}$$

Solution ⟶ $25,000 sales dollars

d. **Decision making.** Selling price is $2, variable cost per unit is $.40, and fixed costs are $20,000. Purchasing a new machine will increase fixed costs by $5,000, but variable costs will be cut by 20%. If the selling price is cut by 10%, what is the breakeven point in units?

Equation ⟶ Sales = VC + FC
$$\$1.8X = \$.32X + \$25,000$$

Shortcut ⟶ $$\frac{FC}{CM} = \frac{\$25,000}{\$1.48}$$

Solution ⟶ 16,892 units

2. **Breakeven: Multiproduct Firm**

If a firm makes more than one product, it is necessary to use composite units to find the number of units of each product to breakeven. A composite unit consists of the proportionate number of units which make up the firm's sales mix. For example, assume that a firm has two products with the following selling prices and variable costs.

Product	Selling price	Variable costs	Contribution margin
A	$.60	$.20	$.40
B	$.40	$.15	$.25

Also assume that the sales mix consists of 3 units of A for every 2 units of B (3:2) and fixed costs are $34,000.

The **first** step is to find the composite contribution margin.

$$\text{Composite contribution margin} = 3(\$.40) + 2(\$.25) = \$1.70$$

Next compute the number of composite units to breakeven.

$$\frac{\$34,000 \text{ fixed costs}}{\$1.70 \text{ composite contribution margin}} = 20,000 \text{ composite units}$$

Finally, determine the number of units of A and B at the breakeven point by multiplying the composite units by the number of units of A (i.e., 3) and the number of units of B (i.e., 2) in the mix.

$$A: 20,000 \times 3 = \underline{60,000} \text{ units}$$
$$B: 20,000 \times 2 = \underline{40,000} \text{ units}$$

3. **Assumptions of CVP Analysis**

When applying CVP to a specific case and in interpreting the results therefrom, it is important to keep in mind the assumptions underlying CVP which are listed below.

a. Selling price does not change with the activity level
b. The sales mix remains constant
c. Costs can be separated into fixed and variable elements
d. Variable costs per unit are constant
e. Total fixed costs are constant over the relevant range
f. Productivity and efficiency are constant
g. Units produced = Units sold

B. **Variable (Direct) and Absorption (Full) Costing**

Variable (direct) costing is a form of inventory costing. Variable costing considers fixed manufacturing costs as period rather than product costs. It is advocated because, for internal reporting, it presents a clear picture of performance when there is a significant change in inventory. However, remember that variable costing is not acceptable as GAAP for external reporting.

Variable and absorption costing methods of accounting for fixed manufacturing overhead differ: under variable costing, fixed manufacturing overhead is expensed whereas under absorption costing, such amounts are treated as a product cost and inventoried. The treatment of fixed manufacturing overhead often results in different levels of net income between the absorption and variable costing methods. The differences are timing differences, which result from recognizing the fixed manufacturing overhead as an expense.

1. In the period incurred—variable costing
2. In the period in which the units to which fixed overhead has been applied are sold—absorption costing

The relationship between variable costing (VC) income and absorption costing (AC) income follows:

Sales = Production (no change in inventory) — No difference in income
Sales > Production (inventory decreases) — VC income greater than AC income
Sales < Production (inventory increases) — VC income less than AC income

EXAMPLE

Production begins in period A with 5,000 units. Fixed manufacturing costs equal $5,000 and variable manufacturing costs are $1/unit. Sales were 4,000 units at $3/unit. In period B, units produced and production costs were the same as in period A. Sales were 6,000 units at $3/unit.

	Variable costing Period A	Period B	Absorption costing Period A	Period B
Sales	$12,000	$18,000	$12,000	$18,000
Less costs	9,000	11,000	8,000	12,000
Profit	$3,000	$7,000	$4,000	$6,000

With absorption costing, $1 of fixed manufacturing overhead is attached to each unit produced ($5,000 ÷ 5,000 units). Notice that both variable and absorption costing recognized $10,000 profit in periods A + B. Variable costing income in period A was less than absorption income, because production exceeded sales which resulted in $1,000 of fixed costs being **inventoried** under AC that were **expensed** under VC.

	Fixed costs expensed Period A	Period B	Variable costs expensed Period A	Period B	Total costs expensed Period A	Period B
Variable	$5,000*	$5,000*	$4,000	$6,000	$9,000	$11,000
Absorption	4,000**	6,000**	4,000	6,000	8,000	12,000

* The same every period.
** $1 per unit x number of units sold.

The yearly income difference between the two methods can normally be reconciled as follows:

Change in inventory units × Fixed overhead per unit (e.g., 1,000 units × $1)

If the example above included either variable or fixed selling costs, they would be handled the same under either method—deducted in total on the income statement in the period in which they were incurred.

Note that the format of the income statement changes under variable costing to reflect the alternate treatment given to the fixed manufacturing costs and to emphasize the contribution margin. The recommended format under variable costing follows:

Sales
– <u>Variable manufacturing costs</u>
= Manufacturing contribution margin
– <u>Variable selling and administrative expenses</u>
= Contribution margin
– <u>Fixed manufacturing, selling, and administrative expenses</u>
= <u>Net income</u>

> **NOW REVIEW MULTIPLE-CHOICE QUESTIONS 1 THROUGH 20 IN VOLUME 2**

C. Financial Planning

1. Financial planning is the process of:

   a. Analyzing the investment and financing alternatives available to a firm
   b. Forecasting the future consequences of the alternatives
   c. Deciding which alternatives to undertake
   d. Measuring subsequent performance against established goals

2. Financial planning must be tied to the strategic plans of top management. Good financial planning can help managers ensure that their financing strategies are consistent with their capital budgets. It also highlights the investing and financing decisions necessary to support management's strategic plans.

3. Management often uses a **financial planning model** to help assess the consequences of alternative operating and financial strategies. Such models range from those that are fairly simple to those that incorporate hundreds of variables and equations, using specialized software. The input to the models generally consists of current financial statements and expectations about future conditions.

4. In developing the financial plan, management generally will prepare a series of pro forma financial statements, one of which will represent the forecast. The forecast depicts the firm's most-likely future financial results. However, effective financial planning generally requires the development of a series of possible scenarios to allow management to plan for various contingencies. Sensitivity analysis may be used with the model to explore the effects of changes in significant variables on the firm's performance. In addition, financial planning can be used to explore the implications of the various decision alternatives.

Financial Planning Model

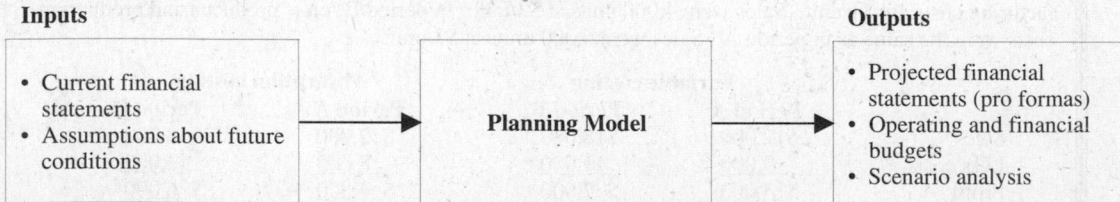

As shown in the exhibit above, the outputs of the financial planning process are pro forma financial statements, operating and financial budgets for the firm, and scenario analysis that explores other possible outcomes.

D. Budgeting

1. To be most effective, the firm's budget should be an integral part of the strategic plan. It must reflect management's objectives and plans. A **master budget** summarizes the results of all of the firm's individual budgets into a set of projected financial statements and schedules. Specifically the master budget summarizes the results of the following two major budgets:

   a. **The operating budget**—The budgeted income statement and supporting schedules.
   b. **The financial budget**—The capital budget, cash budget, and the budgeted balance sheet and statement of cash flows.

2. Budgets are prepared for some set period of time, usually one year. However, some budgets must be broken down into shorter time frames. For example, a cash budget is usually prepared monthly to allow management to plan for

the firm's cash needs. Many firms use **rolling budgets** which are continually updated as time passes. As an example, a 12-month rolling budget adds a future month and drops the current month as it ends.

3. Budgets may be constructed in a number of ways.

   a. Top-down mandated approach—Upper-level management establishes the budget parameters and it is passed down through the organization to each operating unit.

      (1) Advantages include quick preparation time and clear communication of management's objectives.
      (2) Disadvantage is that lower-level management and employees may view it to be dictatorial and not fully embrace and accept the budget.

   b. Participative (bottom-up) is driven by involving lower-level management and employees.

      (1) Advantages are that employees may more readily accept the budget, morale may be improved, and budget input is provided by a larger number of individuals.
      (2) Disadvantages are that the process is time-consuming, and managers may try to pad their budgets.

   c. Many budgets are prepared using a blended approach that combines aspects of the top-down and bottom-up methods.

4. A budget displays a plan of action for future operations. The most important functions of a budget are to coordinate the various functional activities of the firm and to provide a basis for control of the activities. Budgets may be prepared for all elements of the value chain, which includes R&D, design, production, marketing, distribution, customer service, and administration. The budgets process begins with an estimate of sales and then proceeds systematically as outlined below.

   a. Develop a sales forecast
   b. Develop a production schedule to calculate production costs and costs of goods sold
   c. Estimate other expenses and revenues
   d. Complete the pro forma financial statements and budgets

Pictorially, this process is shown below.

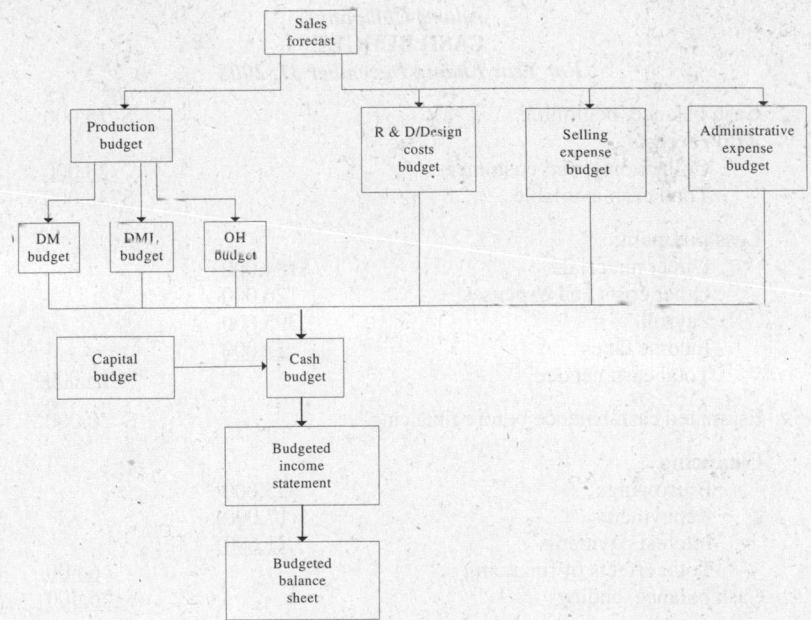

5. The basic formats of some of the key budgets are presented below.

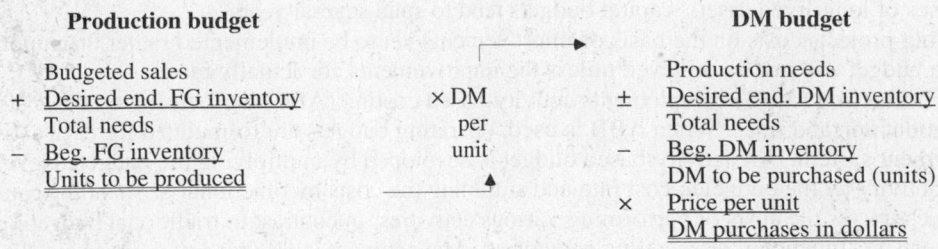

Production budget

    Budgeted sales
+   Desired end. FG inventory
    Total needs
−   Beg. FG inventory
    Units to be produced

× DM
per
unit

DM budget

    Production needs
±   Desired end. DM inventory
    Total needs
−   Beg. DM inventory
    DM to be purchased (units)
×   Price per unit
    DM purchases in dollars

Note that before proceeding to the cash budget, DM purchases would have to be converted to **payments** for DM purchases, based on some payment schedule (e.g., 70% in month of purchase, 30% in month following). On the CPA exam you may be given questions that require you to calculate cash inflows from sales or cash outflows for expenses.

EXAMPLE

Assume that a firm sells all of its products on credit and collects 40% of the receivables in the month of sale, 50% in the following month, and 9% in the month after that. If the firm had the following monthly sales, how much is the estimated collections in June?

January	February	March	April	May	June
$20,000	$25,000	$30,000	$10,000	$20,000	$30,000

June's collections would consist of 40% of June's sales, 50% of May's sales, and 9% of April's sales. Therefore, June's collections would be estimated to be $22,900 [($30,000 × 40%) + ($20,000 × 50%) + ($10,000 × 9%)].

---

6. Remember it is cash collections and cash payments that go into the cash budget, as shown below. Also remember that depreciation is not a cash expense.

        Cash budget
        Beginning cash balance
   + Receipts (collections from customers, etc.)
        Cash available
   − Payments (materials, expenses, payroll, etc.)
        Estimated cash balance before financing
 +/− Financing (planned borrowing or short-term investing to bring cash to desired balance)
  = Ending cash balance

To illustrate, Adams Company prepared the following cash budget for 2008.

Adams Company
CASH BUDGET
For Year Ending December 31, 2008

Cash balance, beginning		$ 15,000
Add receipts		
Collections from customers		723,000
Total cash available		$738,000
Less payments		
Direct materials	$184,000	
Other costs and expenses	126,000	
Payroll	395,000	
Income taxes	13,000	
Total cash needed		718,000
Estimated cash balance before financing		$ 20,000
Financing		
Borrowings	$25,000	
Repayments	(17,000)	
Interest payments	(1,600)	
Total effects of financing		6,400
Cash balance, ending		$ 26,400

7. The **capital (capital expenditures) budget** displays the financial effects of purchases and retirements of long-lived assets. This information is needed to budget the cash and financing needs of the firm. Because of the need to plan for purchases of long-lived assets, capital budgets tend to span several years.

8. **Kaizen budgeting** projects costs on the basis of improvements yet to be implemented rather than upon current conditions. The budget will not be achieved unless the improvements are actually made.

9. **Activity-based budgeting (ABB)** complements activity-based costing (ABC) by focusing on the costs of activities necessary for production and sales. When ABB is used, operating budgets are formulated for each activity in the activity management system. An activity-based budget is developed by multiplying the budgeted level of the cost driver for each activity by the budgeted cost rate and summing the costs by functional or spending categories. ABB budgeting estimates the costs of performing various activities, in contrast to traditional budgeting which directly budgets costs for functional or spending categories. Management is provided with more insight into what causes costs and is in a much better position to control them.

10. **Developing an Operating Budget—An Example**

This example is designed to provide an overview of the process of developing an operating budget. On the CPA exam, you can expect multiple-choice questions that will deal with particular aspects of the process. As an example, you might be given manufacturing costs and inventory levels and be asked to compute cost of goods manufactured.

In our example, Snyder Corporation is developing a financial plan for the year ending December 31, 2008. The company has two primary products, Product A and Product B. Based on an assessment of the projected economic conditions, management has developed forecasted sales of Product A of 25,000 units at a sales price of $100, and forecasted sales of Product B of 30,000 units at a sales price of $120. Therefore, total forecasted sales is $6,100,000.

Assume that management wants an inventory of 1,200 units of Product A and 1,000 units of Product B at year-end. The beginning inventory is shown in the following schedule.

Schedule 1—Beginning Finished Goods Inventory

	Product A	Product B	Total
Units	1,200	1,200	
Cost per unit	$ 70	$ 80	
Total cost	$84,000	$96,000	$180,000

There was no work-in-process beginning inventory and none is anticipated at the end of the year. This information can then be used to prepare the production schedule shown below.

Schedule 2—Production Schedule

	Product A	Product B
Projected unit sales	25,000	30,000
Desired ending inventory	1,200	1,000
Beginning inventory	(1,200)	(1,200)
Units to be produced	25,000	29,800

Once the production schedule is developed, management can develop the raw materials usage budget and budgets for labor and overhead. Information to develop these schedules can be obtained from the following product specifications schedule.

Schedule 3—Product Specifications

	Product A	Product B	Estimated Cost
Materials			
Silver	7 oz.	6 oz.	$5.15 per oz.
Red Oak	1 b.f.		$3.95 per b.f.
Teak		1 b.f.	$6.10 per b.f.
Direct Labor	½ hour	¾ hour	$ 40 per hour

Schedule 4—Direct Materials Usage Budget

Physical Units	Silver oz.	Red Oak b.f.	Teak b.f.	Total
Product A				
Silver	175,000			
Red Oak		25,000		
Product B				
Silver	178,800			
Teak			29,800	
To be used in production	353,800	25,000	29,800	
Cost Budget				
Available from beginning inventory				
Silver 4,000 oz. @ $5.00 per oz.	$ 20,000			
Red Oak 1,000 b.f. @ $4.00 per b.f.		$ 4,000		
Teak 1,000 b.f. @ $6.00 per b.f.			$ 6,000	
From purchases				
Silver $5.15 × (353,800 – 4,000)	1,801,470			
Red Oak $3.95 × (25,000 – 1,000)		94,800		
Teak $6.10 × (29,800 – 1,000)			175,680	
Cost of direct materials to be used	$1,821,470	$98,800	$181,680	$2,101,950

Schedule 5—Direct Manufacturing Labor Budget

Product A
(25,000 × ½ hour × $40 per hour) $ 500,000
Product B
(29,800 × ¾ hour × $40 per hour)   894,000
                                                          $1,394,000

Schedule 6—Manufacturing Overhead Budget (at 34,850 budgeted direct labor hours)

Variable overhead costs:
Supplies	$ 60,000
Indirect labor	135,000
Maintenance	50,000
Electricity	100,000
Miscellaneous	30,000

Fixed overhead costs:
Depreciation	$306,400	
Insurance	40,000	
Plant supervision	90,000	
Miscellaneous	25,000	
Total manufacturing overhead		$836,400

Overhead application rate:
Direct labor hours
Product A (25,000 × ½ hour)	12,500	
Product B (29,800 × ¾ hour)	22,350	
Total direct labor hours		34,850
Application rate ($836,400 / 34,850)		$ 24 per hour

Based on the budgeted amounts of materials, labor, and overhead, management can now determine the unit production cots, and the ending inventories and costs of goods sold budgets as shown below.

Schedule 7—Unit Production Costs

	Product A	Product B
Materials	$40	$37
Direct labor	20	30
Manufacturing overhead ($24 per DLH)	12	18
	$72	$85

Schedule 8—Cost of Goods Sold Budget

	Schedule		
Beginning finished goods inventory	1		$ 180,000
Direct materials used	4	$2,101,950	
Direct labor	5	1,394,000	
Manufacturing overhead	6	836,400	
Cost of goods manufactured			4,332,350
Cost of goods available for sale			4,512,350
Deduct ending finished goods inventory			171,400
Cost of goods sold			$4,340,950

With estimates of sales and general and administrative expenses and the tax rate, management can now prepare the pro forma income statement for next period as shown below.

Snyder Corporation
PRO FORMA INCOME STATEMENT
For the Year Ending December 31, 2008

Sales	$6,100,000
Cost of goods sold	4,340,950
Gross profit	1,759,050
General & administrative expenses	1,020,000
Operating income (EBIT)	739,050
Interest expense	260,000
Earnings before taxes	479,050
Taxes (30%)	143,715
Net income	$ 335,335

E. Forecasting Methods

1. Management may choose from a number of methods for forecasting the firm's sales. Such methods are generally classified as qualitative or quantitative techniques. Qualitative approaches base the forecast on management judgment. Examples of qualitative techniques include:

   a. Executive opinions
   b. Sales-force polling
   c. Customer surveys

2. Structured approaches, such as the **Delphi technique,** may be used to assist in developing qualitative forecasts. This technique develops consensus among a group about the future through a series of structured questionnaires and an iterative process. The results of prior questionnaires are used to develop subsequent questionnaires until consensus is achieved.

3. Quantitative approaches to the development of forecasts may be broken down into three major types: (1) approaches based on historical data, (2) approaches based on observed associations, (3) approaches based on forecasts of consumer behavior. Examples include the following:

   a. Approaches based on historical data:

      (1) **Naive models**—These models are based exclusively on historical observation of sales or other variables. As an example, management might examine historical data on sales by product line and make a subjective estimate of the next period's sales.
      (2) **Moving average**—This technique simply uses the average of sales for the most recent periods to predict the next period's sales.
      (3) **Exponential smoothing**—This technique is similar to moving average but the more recent sales data are weighted more heavily than older data in computing the forecast. Underlying the technique is the belief that more recent data are more relevant to predictions of future sales.
      (4) **Decomposition of time series**—This technique is especially appropriate when sales are seasonal or cyclical in nature. The technique examines prior sales data and estimates seasonal and cyclical effects. When these effects are extracted from the prior data, historical trends may be observed and projected into the future. Once the trends are used to develop initial forecasts, seasonal and cyclical effects are reintroduced to develop the final forecast.

   b. Approaches based on observed associations:

      (1) **Regression analysis**—This technique estimates sales based on an observed relationship between sales (the dependent variable) and one or more predictors of sales (independent variables).
      (2) **Econometric models**—Involve the use of regression analysis to model the firm's sales based on economic data. For example, forecasts of personal disposable income, interest rates, etc. might be used to develop an estimate of future sales.

   c. Approaches based on forecasts of consumer behavior:

      (1) **Markov techniques**—These techniques attempt to forecast consumer purchasing by considering factors such as brand loyalty and brand switching behavior. These data are used to predict changes in the firm's market share, which is then used to develop the sales forecast.

4. **Regression Analysis**

   As described in Module 46, regression is a technique for estimating mathematically the average relationship between a dependent variable (y) and one or more independent variables (x). Simple regression involves only one independent variable and the estimation equation is shown below.

   $$y = a + bx + e$$

   Where

   y = the dependent variable
   x = the independent variable
   a = the y-intercept or constant value
   b = the slope of the regression line
   e = an error term that is assumed to be normally distributed with a mean of 0

   Since the random error term (e) is assumed to have a zero mean, it is ignored and the equation becomes simply

   $$y = a + bx$$

   a. Major assumptions underlying regression analysis include

(1) The relationship is linear within the relevant range.
(2) The variance of the error (residual) term is constant. A violation of this assumption is referred to as **heteroscedasticity**. While it does not affect the accuracy of the regression estimates (a and b), heteroscedasticity does reduce the reliability of the estimates of standard errors and therefore affects the precision of any estimates developed from the equation.
(3) The error (residual) values are independent.
(4) The error values are normally distributed around the regression line.

b. **Trend Analysis**

Regression might be used as a tool in performing trend analysis. In this case regression analysis is used to fit a trend line to a time series of data. As an example, assume that management believes that sales for the next period might be estimated based on the trend of prior sales. The following data have been collected:

Period	Sales	Period	Sales
1	$60,000	6	$67,500
2	$62,000	7	$69,000
3	$62,500	8	$71,000
4	$65,000	9	$71,500
5	$66,500	10	$72,500

The output of regression analysis of this data using a spreadsheet program is illustrated below.

Summary Output

Regression Statistics

Multiple R	0.994088
R Square	0.988211
Adjusted R Square	0.986738
Standard Error	498.4825
Observations	10

	Df	SS	MS	F	Significance F
Regression	1	1.67E+08	1.67E+08	670.6128	5.31E–09
Residual	8	1987879	248484.8		
Total	9	1.69E+08			

	Coefficients	Standard error	t-Stat	P-value	Lower 95%	Upper 95%
Intercept	58933.33	340.5284	173.0644	1.39E–15	58148.07	59718.59
Period	1421.212	54.88112	25.89619	5.31E–09	1294.656	1547.768

c. **Goodness of fit** measures how well the predicted values of the dependent variable match the actual amounts. Regression analysis computes a measure of goodness of fit, the **coefficient of determination**. The coefficient of determination (adjusted R Squared) in this case indicates that 98.6738% of the variance in sales is explained by the time series (period).

d. The significance of the relationship is measured by the t-Statistic. In this case, the t-Statistic for Period is 25.89619 which is very significant. The P-value of 5.31E–09 (0.00000000531) indicates that there is an extremely low probability (0.000000531%) that this relationship occurred by chance.

e. From the coefficients section we see that the equation to predict sales is as follows:

$$\text{Sales} = 58933.33 + (1421.212 \times \text{Period})$$

If we wanted to predict sales for period 11, we would simply substitute 11 for the period and calculate the estimate as shown below.

$$\begin{aligned} \text{Sales} &= 58933.33 + (1421.212 \times 11) \\ &= \$74{,}566.66 \end{aligned}$$

5. **Multiple Regression**

Multiple regression is used when management wishes to forecast sales using two or more associated variables. As an example, assume that management of a growing toy manufacturer believes that an accurate estimate of sales can be obtained with two variables—expenditures for advertising and the number of newly introduced toys. Management has collected the following data:

Period	Sales	Advertising expenditures	Number of new toys	Period	Sales	Advertising expenditures	Number of new toys
1	$40,000,000	$1,000,000	5	6	$49,000,000	$1,000,000	12
2	$45,000,000	$1,250,000	7	7	$54,000,000	$1,600,000	12
3	$44,000,000	$ 900,000	9	8	$52,000,000	$1,500,000	4
4	$48,000,000	$1,500,000	9	9	$55,000,000	$1,500,000	13
5	$50,000,000	$1,200,000	14	10	$57,000,000	$1,500,000	15

a. The output of regression analysis of this data using a spreadsheet program is illustrated below.

Summary Output

Regression Statistics

Multiple R	0.910234
R Square	0.828526
Adjusted R Square	0.779534
Standard Error	2506160
Observations	10

	Df	SS	MS	F	Significance F
Regression	2	2.12E+14	1.06E+14	16.91129	0.002088
Residual	7	4.4E+13	6.28E+12		
Total	9	2.56E+14			

	Coefficients	Standard error	t-Stat	P-value	Lower 95%	Upper 95%
Intercept	24678459	4466529	5.525199	0.000883	14116805	35240114
Advertising	13.63897	3.302376	4.130049	0.004404	5.830102	21.44785
New Toys	705906.9	224772.5	3.140539	0.016367	174404.7	1237409

b. The **coefficient of determination** (Adjusted R Squared) is .779534. As discussed above, this is a measure of goodness of fit. In this case 77.9534% of the variation in sales is explained by advertising expenditures and the number of new toys introduced.

c. The equation for predicting sales is shown below.

$$\text{Estimated sales} = \$24{,}678{,}459 + (13.63897 \times \text{Ad. Exp.}) + (705{,}906.9 \times \text{No. New Toys})$$

d. For the next period, assume that management estimates that $1,600,000 will be spent on advertising and 10 new toys will be introduced. The estimated sales for the period would be calculated as follows:

$$\text{Estimated sales} = \$24{,}678{,}459 + (13.63897 \times \$1{,}600{,}000) + (705{,}906.9 \times 10)$$
$$\text{Estimated sales} = \$53{,}559{,}880$$

e. Other important regression statistics to consider include

   (1) **The Standard Error of the Estimate and Confidence Level**—The standard error of the estimate, in this case 2,506,160, is the standard deviation of the regression. This number can be used to establish confidence intervals around the estimate of sales. If the manager wants a prediction to be 95% confident, the confidence interval would be the estimated value from the equation ± $2,506,160 × 2.3436. The 2.3436 is derived from a normal curve area table that shows the relative area under a normal curve from one standard deviation to another. For a normal distribution, 95% of the values fall within 2.3436 standard deviations from the mean. Using the estimated sales number calculated above, $53,559,880, management can be 95% confident that sales for the next period will fall within the range calculated below.

$$95\% \text{ Confidence Interval} = \$53{,}559{,}880 \pm \$2{,}506{,}160 \times 2.3436$$
$$= \$47{,}686{,}443 \text{ to } \$59{,}433{,}317$$

   (2) **The F-Statistic**—This statistic provides an overall measure of the significance of the regression equation. In the above case the F-Statistic is 16.91129 and is significant at the .002088 level. This means that there is only about a two-tenths of one percent chance (0.2088%) that the relationship occurred by chance.

   (3) **The t-Statistics**—Each independent variable will have a t-Statistic which indicates its significance. In the above case, the t-Statistics are 4.130049 and 3.140539 with P-values of .004404 and .016367, respectively. The P-values measure the level of significance of each variable to the equation. In this case both are significant at less than the .05 (5%) level, which means that there is less than a 5% probability that the relationship occurred by chance.

f. Previously, we described the assumptions underlying regression. In evaluating the results, consideration should be given to two related issues.

(1) **Multicollinearity**—When using more than one independent variable there may be a high correlation between the independent variables. This will cause the equation to be in error and may produce spurious forecasts. Indicators of multicollinearity include low *t*-Statistics for variables that should be important, or variables with coefficients with illogical signs (e.g., a negative relationship between advertising and sales).

(2) **Autocorrelation**—Remember from the discussion above regression analysis assumes that the error term is randomly distributed and independent. If the errors are serially correlated this can again distort the results. Autocorrelation may indicate that a major independent variable is not included in the model. The Durbin-Watson statistic provides a test for autocorrelation.

F. Flexible Budgets

A flexible budget is a budget adjusted for changes in volume. In the planning phase, a flexible budget is used to compare the effects of various activity levels on costs and revenues. In the controlling phase, the flexible budget is used to help analyze actual results by comparing actual results with a flexible budget for the level of activity achieved in the period. Standard costing naturally complements flexible budgeting. However, even without standard costing, flexible budgeting can be used based upon actual costs and quantities of outputs (although lack of input data precludes computation of price and efficiency variances).

Presented below is a sample flexible budget for overhead costs.

FACTORY OVERHEAD
FLEXIBLE BUDGET

	18,000	20,000	22,000
Direct manufacturing labor hours			
Variable factory overhead			
Supplies	$ 18,000	$ 20,000	$ 22,000
Power	99,000	110,000	121,000
Idle time	3,600	4,000	4,400
Overtime premium	1,800	2,000	2,200
Total ($6.80 per DMLH)	$122,400	$136,000	$149,600
Fixed factory overhead			
Supervision	$ 15,000	$ 15,000	$ 15,000
Depreciation	32,000	32,000	32,000
Power	8,000	8,000	8,000
Property taxes	5,000	5,000	5,000
Insurance	1,500	1,500	1,500
Total	$ 61,500	$ 61,500	$ 61,500
Total overhead	$183,900	$197,500	$211,100

> **NOW REVIEW MULTIPLE-CHOICE QUESTIONS 21 THROUGH 49 IN VOLUME 2**

G. Responsibility Accounting

Responsibility accounting allocates those revenues and/or assets which a manager can control to that manager's responsibility center and holds the manager accountable for operating results. If a manager is only responsible for costs, his/her area of responsibility is called a **cost center**. Cost centers represent the most basic activities or responsibilities. Nonrevenue generating departments (purchasing and billing, for example) are usually organized as cost centers.

If the manager is responsible for both revenues and costs, his/her area of responsibility is called a **profit center**. A contribution income statement similar to the one shown below would be prepared for each profit center. Finally, if the manager is responsible for revenues, costs, and asset investment, his/her area of responsibility is called an **investment center**.

H. Segmented Reporting and Controllability

Variable (Direct) and Absorption (Full) Costing reports (as described in Section B) can be broken into further detail to emphasize controllability.

1. Variable manufacturing costs are deducted from sales to obtain **manufacturing contribution margin**.
2. Variable selling and administrative expenses are deducted from manufacturing contribution margin to obtain **contribution margin**.
3. Fixed costs controllable by segment managers at various levels (e.g., division, department) are deducted from contribution margin to obtain the **controllable contribution** at that level.
4. Fixed costs controllable by others at various levels are deducted from controllable contribution to obtain the **segment contribution** at that level.
5. Costs common to all operations are finally deducted to obtain **income before taxes**.

EXAMPLE CONTRIBUTION APPROACH INCOME STATEMENT

	Total	Segment 1	Segment 2
Sales	$600	$350	$250
–Variable manufacturing costs	220	115	105
Manufacturing contribution margin	380	235	145
–Variable selling and admin. exp.	100	70	30
Contribution margin	280	165	115
–Controllable, traceable fixed costs	80	35	45
Controllable contribution	200	130	70
–Uncontrollable, traceable fixed costs	90	60	30
Segment contribution	$110	$ 70	$ 40
–Unallocable common costs	60*		
Income before taxes	$ 50		

* Not allocated to any segment of the firm. Examples include corporate office salaries and advertising for firm name.

Costs not controllable by a subdivision (cost or profit center) of a firm should not be allocated to the subdivision for evaluation or decision making purposes (see Section G. Responsibility Accounting).

Contribution margin data can be used in a variety of situations, including planning (CVP analysis) and decision making (which products to emphasize, which products should be retained and which should be eliminated, and so forth).

I. Standards and Variances

Standard costs are predetermined target costs which should be attainable under efficient conditions. The tightness, or attainment difficulty, of standard costs should be determined by the principles of motivation (e.g., excessively tight standards may result in employees feeling that the standards are impossible to achieve; consequently, they may ignore them). Standard costs are used to aid in the budget process, pinpoint trouble areas, and evaluate performance.

The tightness of standards is generally described by one of two terms. **Ideal** standards reflect the absolute minimum costs which could be achieved under perfect operating conditions. **Currently attainable** standards should be achieved under efficient operating conditions. Generally, currently attainable standards are set so they will be difficult, but not impossible, to achieve. Currently attainable standards are most often used since they are more realistic for budgeting purposes and are a better motivational tool than ideal standards.

Variances are differences between actual and standard costs. The total variance is generally broken down into subvariances to further pinpoint the causes of the variance.

1. Variance Analysis

In calculating the variances for direct material and direct manufacturing labor the following symbols will be employed as defined:

AP: Actual price paid per unit of input (e.g., price per foot of lumber, per hour of labor, per ton of steel, etc.)
SP: Standard price per unit of input
AQ: The actual quantity of input (feet, hours, tons, etc.) used in production
SQ: The standard quantity of input that should have been used for the good units produced

Variances can be computed using the diagram approach that follows.

2. Material Variances

The diagram for computing material variances is

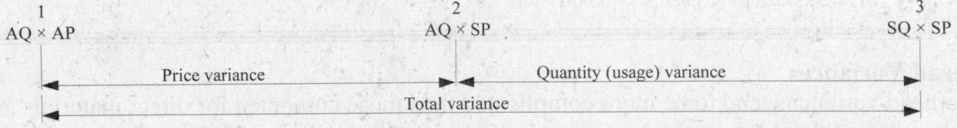

The price variance is unfavorable if AP > SP; the quantity variance is unfavorable if AQ > SQ. Favorable variances arise when actual amounts are less than standard amounts.

The only alternative allowed on the variances above concerns the material price variance. The price variance can be recognized when material is placed in production (as assumed in the previous discussion) or when material is purchased (which is desirable for early identification and control). If the price variance is to be recognized at the time of purchase, AQ (for the price variance **only**) becomes quantity **purchased** rather than quantity **used**.

The materials price variance is generally considered to be the responsibility of the purchasing department, while the materials quantity variance is the responsibility of the production department or production design engineers.

EXAMPLE

The following data relate to DFW Manufacturing, which produced 5,000 units of product during the period:

Direct materials standard per finished unit: 2 lbs. @ $1.60 per lb.

Actual: 10,100 lbs purchased @ $1.65 per lb., 9,500 lbs. used in production

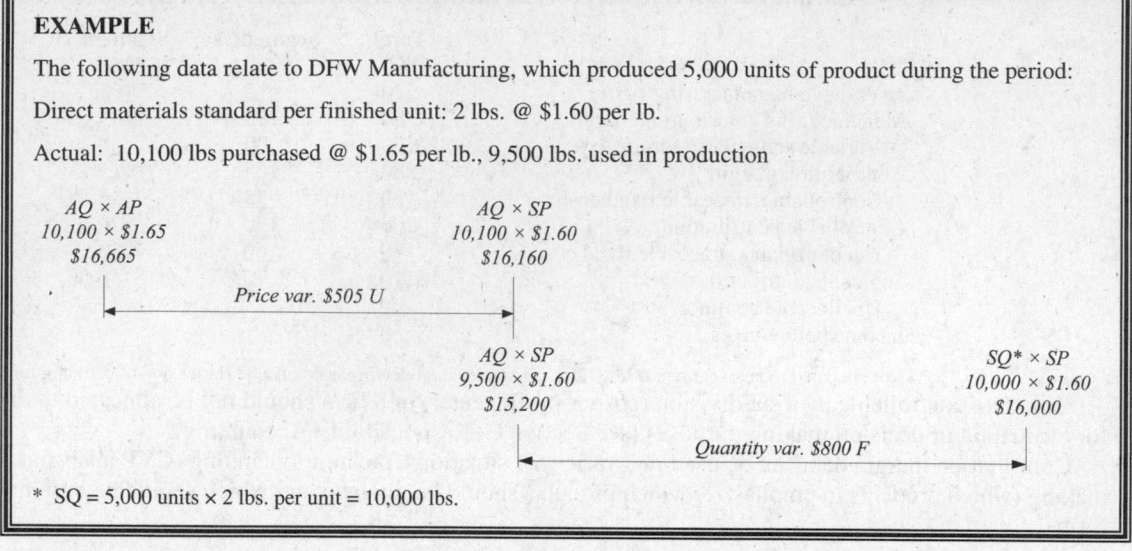

$AQ \times AP$
$10,100 \times \$1.65$
$\$16,665$

$AQ \times SP$
$10,100 \times \$1.60$
$\$16,160$

Price var. $505 U

$AQ \times SP$
$9,500 \times \$1.60$
$\$15,200$

$SQ^* \times SP$
$10,000 \times \$1.60$
$\$16,000$

Quantity var. $800 F

* SQ = 5,000 units × 2 lbs. per unit = 10,000 lbs.

---

3. Labor Variances

The computational form of the labor variances is similar to the calculation of material variances—except that the price being used changes from price per pound of material to price (rate) per hour of labor, and the quantity changes from pounds, yards, etc., to hours. Therefore, the diagrams are the same, although the terminology differs.

Material variance		**Labor variance**
Price	→	Rate
Quantity	→	Efficiency

Both labor variances are usually considered to be the responsibility of the production department or production design engineers.

EXAMPLE

The following data relate to DFW Manufacturing. Recall that the company produced 5,000 units of product during the period:

Direct labor standard per finished unit: 3 hours @ $2.50 per hour

Actual: 15,400 hours worked @ $2.60 per hour

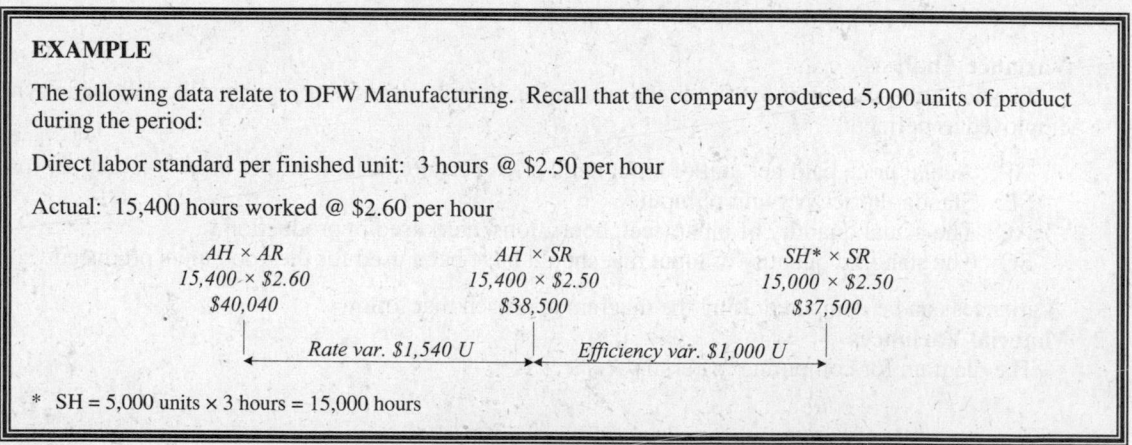

$AH \times AR$
$15,400 \times \$2.60$
$\$40,040$

$AH \times SR$
$15,400 \times \$2.50$
$\$38,500$

$SH^* \times SR$
$15,000 \times \$2.50$
$\$37,500$

Rate var. $1,540 U   Efficiency var. $1,000 U

* SH = 5,000 units × 3 hours = 15,000 hours

---

4. Overhead Variances

Overhead variances tend to be more complicated than those computed for direct materials and direct labor, primarily because of the different computation methods that are available. The easier approach to master is a parallel of the variance grids shown earlier, with overhead being subdivided into fixed and variable elements. Variable overhead parallels the calculation of direct labor variances; fixed overhead, in contrast, requires a minor modification. The general setup approach follows:

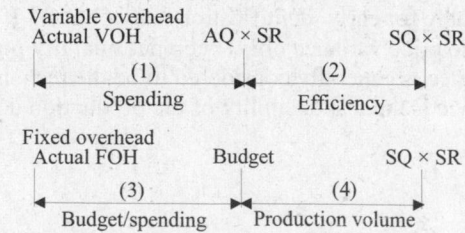

Variable overhead
Actual VOH $AQ \times SR$ $SQ \times SR$
     (1)   (2)
     Spending   Efficiency

Fixed overhead
Actual FOH   Budget $SQ \times SR$
     (3)   (4)
     Budget/spending   Production volume

Notice the use of AQ and SQ. On virtually all CPA exams, direct labor hours is the base used to apply overhead to production.

EXAMPLE

To illustrate the proper approach, we will continue to focus on DFW Manufacturing, which applies overhead to production on the basis of hours. Recall from the earlier calculations that 5,000 units were manufactured. 15,400 hours were worked, and each unit is supposed to take 3 hours of labor time. Additional data follow.

Estimated (standard) factory overhead based on a "normal capacity" of 16,000 labor hours:

Variable	3 hours @ $1.50
Fixed	3 hours @ $0.50*

Actual overhead cost for the period

Variable	$22,800
Fixed	$ 8,100

* $8,000 budgeted fixed overhead costs ÷ 16,000 direct labor hours

Variable Overhead

	$AQ \times SR$	$SQ \times SR$
Actual	15,400 × $1.50	15,000 × $1.50
$22,800	$23,100	$22,500

|⎣___ *Spending var. $300 F* ___⎦___ *Efficiency var. $600 U* ___⎦|

Fixed Overhead

		$SQ \times SR$
Actual	*Budget*	15,000 × $0.50
$8,100	$8,000	$7,500

|⎣__ *Spending/budget var. $100 U* __⎦ *Production volume var. $500 U* ⎦|

This example illustrates several key points.

According to the information presented, DFW has a capacity to work 16,000 hours, which is the equivalent of 5,334 units (16,000 ÷ 3 hours per unit). Since the firm produced only 5,000 units, the production volume variance is unfavorable.

Overhead in the SQ × SR column ($22,500 + $7,500 = $30,000) is the amount applied to production. Since actual overhead was $30,900 ($22,800 + $8,100), overhead is $900 underapplied. This latter amount will always coincide with the combination of all four variances ($300F – $600U – $100U – $500U = $900U).

The 3-variance approach. The 3-variance method results in the calculation of three variances rather than the four just illustrated. The **only** difference between these two approaches is in the calculation of the spending variance, which is a combination of (1) and (3) to create a total spending variance as shown below.

|⎣___ (1) + (3) ___⎦___ (2) ___⎦___ (4) ___⎦|
| Total spending | Efficiency | Production volume |

For DFW, the total spending variance is $200F ($300F – $100U).

The 2-variance approach. The 2-variance approach results in the calculation of only two variances: the production volume variance shown earlier and a combined spending/efficiency variance (see the following diagram).

|⎣___ (1) + (2) + (3) ___⎦___ (4) ___⎦|
| Budget | Production volume |
| (Controllable) | |

This latter variance for DFW is $400U ($300F – $100U – $600U).

Some computational hints. These variance approaches are fairly straightforward if you start with the 4-variance method and then work backwards to arrive at the 3-variance approach and then work that backwards to arrive at the last method. Occasionally, the exam may not give you enough data to perform all calculations to do this. The following hints have proven to be extremely helpful:

- The production volume variance is the same no matter what approach is used.
- The efficiency variance is the same for the 3- and 4-variance approach.

- When in doubt, you can calculate the total variance (the difference between actual total overhead and applied overhead [SQ × SR]), subtract the variances that you can compute, and the result, a forced figure, will often be the variance that is requested by the examiners.

Miscellaneous. The budget variance (also called the controllable variance) arises when the amount spent on both fixed and variable overhead differs from the amount budgeted for the actual hours worked.

The production volume variance is solely a **fixed** overhead variance. It is caused by under- or overutilization of capacity. If actual output is less than (more than) capacity activity, an unfavorable (favorable) output level variance results. The capacity volume is the activity level used to set the predetermined fixed overhead rate for product costing purposes (see Module 47).

5. **Disposition of Variances**

If insignificant, variances are frequently written off to cost of goods sold on the grounds of expediency. (ARB 43 states that you may report inventories using standard costs if they are based on currently attainable standards.) If significant, the variances must be allocated among the inventories and cost of goods sold, usually in proportion to the ending balances. Remember, SFAS 151 requires that fixed overhead costs be allocated based on normal capacity and variances related to fixed overhead volume should be allocated only to cost of goods sold (treated as a period cost).

> **NOW REVIEW MULTIPLE-CHOICE QUESTIONS 50 THROUGH 70 IN VOLUME 2**

J. Project Management

A project is a series of activities and tasks that

- Have specific definable objectives,
- Have defined start and end dates,
- Are subject to funding constraints,
- Consume resources, people, equipment, etc., and
- Cut across various functional areas of the organization.

Projects are usually planned and executed by multidisciplinary teams, consisting of individuals from different functional areas and led by a project manager. Team members must be knowledgeable and able to work together to plan and execute work in a team setting. Some projects are assigned a project oversight or steering group which takes responsibility for the business issues related to the project. These committees are responsible for approving budgetary strategy, defining and realizing benefits, and monitoring risks, quality and timeliness.

Effective project management involves efficiently achieving the project objectives within time and cost constraints. To achieve effective project management, the project leader must manage the four basic elements of a project, including

1. Resources—people, equipment, materials, etc.
2. Time—task durations, task interdependencies, the critical path, etc.
3. Money—costs, contingencies, profit, etc.
4. Scope—project size, goals, requirements, etc.

The processes involved in project management include project initiation, project planning, project execution, project monitoring and control, and project closure.

1. Project initiation includes

   a. Selection of the best project given resource constraints.
   b. Recognizing the benefits of the project.
   c. Authorizing the project. The project must have full support of management of the organization. Since projects often cross functional lines, a commitment by top management of the organization is critical to the success of any project.
   d. Assigning the project manager (leader). The project manager should be competent and have sufficient authority to get access to needed resources and people the project manager should have planning skills, organizational skills, negotiating skills, administration skills, resource allocation skills, and entrepreneurial skills. A **project charter** authorizes the project, and sets forth the project manager's authority and responsibility.

2. Project planning involves determining the activities that need to be performed, who should perform them, and when the activities need to be completed. Planning includes

   a. Defining the work requirements.
   b. Defining the quality and quantity of the work.
   c. Indentifying the needed resources.

   d. Scheduling the activities and tasks.

   e. Indentifying and assessing risks.

     The planning process results in a number of documents. The scope of the work is often set forth in a **statement of work (SOW),** which is a narrative description of the work to be performed to complete the project, including the deliverables. One of the most common reasons for a scope change in a project is a poorly defined statement of work.

     The statement of work often includes the **project specifications,** which is a detailed listing of the man-hour, equipment, and materials requirements. The **milestone schedule** sets forth the start date, the end date and other major milestones involved in completing the project. Finally, the **work breakdown structure (WBS)** breaks the project into manageable, independent, and measureable elements that can be budgeted and for which responsibility can be assigned. The WBS provides a basis for costing, risk analysis, control, and scheduling the project.

     Many companies use a **life-cycle approach** in planning, in which project planning is divided into defined phases, such as conceptualization, feasibility study, etc. At the end of each phase an assessment is done to evaluate the success of the phase and determine whether the next phase should be undertaken.

3. Many different techniques are used to schedule and control a project, including

   a. Gantt chart—a type of bar chart that illustrates the scheduled start and finish of elements of a project over time.

   b. Milestone chart—a type of chart that illustrates the milestones for a project over time.

   c. Line of balance—a type of chart that illustrates the series of activities that are related. It is appropriate where a project has a series of repetitive activities.

   d. Network diagram—illustrates the logical representation of activities that defines the sequence of the work of a project. It illustrates the path of a project. A network diagram has advantages over other forms of techniques because it (1) illustrates the interdependencies between activities, (2) identifies critical paths in a project, (3) facilitates risk analysis for the activities in the project, and (4) enables management to evaluate the effect of an activity delay on the project completion date.

   e. Program Evaluation and Review Technique (PERT)—PERT is a network technique that formally focuses on the interdependency of activities and the time required to complete an activity to schedule and control the project. This technique focuses on the **critical path**, which is the shortest amount of time necessary to accomplish the project. Any slippage in the time of performing the activities along the critical path will result in a delay in completion of the project. Therefore, management knows which activities and events are most critical to timely completion of the project. PERT uses three time estimates (optimistic, most likely, and pessimistic) to derive expected time to complete a particular task. In PERT analysis **slack time** is the difference between the expected time and the latest time the activity can be completed without delaying the project. PERT is probabilistic in nature which allows the calculation of the risk in completing the project. PERT is typically used where there is a high variability of completion times, such as research and development projects.

   f. PERT cost—allows the addition of resource cost considerations to the schedule produced by the PERT technique. This allows the inclusion of cost uncertainty into the analysis.

   g. Critical Path Method (CPM)—CPM is similar to PERT but it only uses one time estimate that represents the normal time to complete an activity. CPM is used for projects where there is less variability in time estimates. CPM includes a procedure for time/cost tradeoff to minimize the sum of direct and indirect project costs.

   h. Graphical Evaluation and Review Technique (GERT)—GERT is similar to PERT but it has the advantage of allowing looping and branching based on the results of a particular activity. It is appropriate for projects that may be completed in a number of ways.

   i. **Project crashing** is a term used to describe the practice of adding resources to shorten selected activity time on the critical path of a project. In effect, the manager is trading off money for time. Therefore, each activity may be viewed as having two types—a normal (planned) time and the crash time (the shortest possible time).

   j. Another technique that is often used in conjunction with any of these scheduling techniques is **ABC analysis**. ABC analysis involves the categorization of tasks into groups. These groups are often marked A, B, and C—hence the name. Activities are ranked upon the following general criteria:

     A–Tasks that are perceived as being urgent and important.
     B–Tasks that are important but not urgent.
     C–Tasks that are neither urgent nor important.

     Then, each group is rank-ordered in priority. This technique is particularly applicable to project management because it focuses attention on the critical activities or tasks.

     Risk management is also applicable to project management. Project risks include those related to costs overruns, time slippage, inappropriately defined scope, and dissatisfaction with the deliverables. The steps in the risk management of a project include (1) identification of risks, (2) quantifying the risks, (3) prioritizing risks, and (4) developing a risk response. Like any type of risk management the response may involve such activates as developing controls or shifting the risk to another party.

4. Project execution includes

    a. Negotiating for the team members.
    b. Directing the work.
    c. Managing team members to improve performance.

Management of a project requires much the same skills as managing any function. However, if the project crosses functional lines, the management process becomes complicated. Problems in project management typically arise from one of the following:

- Organizational uncertainty. The working relationship between the project manager and the functional managers has not been adequately defined by senior management.
- Unusual decision pressures. Project managers must make quick decisions in uncertain situations and with incomplete information. Senior management must recognize these difficulties and support the project manager's decisions.
- Inadequate senior management support. Delays in approval, inability to resolve reporting conflicts, and delays in providing resources can significantly delay or derail projects.

5. Project monitoring and control includes

    a. Tracking progress of the project.
    b. Comparing actual outcomes to predicted outcomes.
    c. Analyzing variances and their effects.
    d. Making adjustments.

Many of the typical management techniques are used to control projects, including budgets, variance analysis, and status analysis. The scheduling techniques discussed above also facilitate control of the project by allowing management to focus its attention on critical activities.

6. Project closure includes

    a. Determining that all work has been completed.
    b. Closure of the contract, financial charges, and paperwork.

K. Product and Service Pricing

Product pricing requires the use of judgment by the cost accountant and management to maximize the entity's profits and to increase shareholder wealth. To find the combination of sales price and volume yielding the greatest profits, management must make many assumptions regarding customer preferences, competitors' reactions, economic conditions, cost structures, etc. In maximizing shareholders' wealth, management must consider not only product costs but must also react to external changes, for example, a competitor's price on a relatively undifferentiated product. Additionally, management must consider the company's cost of capital in determining a desired **rate of return**. This rate of return represents the desired minimum markup on the cost of goods.

Costs are usually the starting point in determining prices. In the long run, all costs, including fixed costs, must be considered. However, decisions involving short-range pricing, such as a special order, may be evaluated on the basis of contribution margin. The **contribution margin approach** considers all relevant variable costs plus any additional fixed costs needed to sustain the new production level. Which costs are relevant is determined by analyzing how total costs of each component of the value chain will change if the order is accepted.

Cost-plus pricing is one model for the pricing decision; prices are set at variable costs plus a percentage markup, at full manufacturing or service cost plus a percentage markup, or at target ROI per unit. The percentage markup must cover fixed costs and profit (variable approach), operating expenses and a profit (full cost approach), or invested capital (target ROI approach). Consider the following example:

Annual sales—10,000 units		Invested capital—$100,000		Target ROI—15%
Manufacturing costs:		Operating costs:		
Fixed	$20,000	Fixed	$10,000	
Variable	$3/unit	Variable	$2.50/unit	

If price is set at total variable cost plus 60% ($5.50 × 160%), or full manufacturing cost plus 76% ($5.00 × 176%), the selling price would be $8.80. The selling price under the target ROI approach is calculated as follows:

Invested capital	$100,000
× Target ROI	× 15%
Total target ROI	15,000
÷ Annual sales	÷ 10,000
Target oper. inc. per unit	1.50
+ Cost base (total cost)	+ 8.50
Selling price	$ 10.00

Note that the rate of markup ($1.50/$8.50 = 17.65%) has nothing to do with target ROI (15%), which expresses operating income as a percentage of **investment**.

Another alternative is **target pricing**, which sets prices at the amount that consumers are willing to pay based on their perceived value of the product or service. Based on targeted prices and income, a target cost is determined; the targeted cost is the estimated cost of the product or service that yields the targeted income at the target price. To meet target costs, a company must often improve its products or increase efficiency. **Value engineering** examines all components of the value chain to find opportunities for improvements and cost reduction. Activity-based costing helps to identify opportunities for cost reduction by improving specific activities.

Finally, the use of **standard costs** that are attainable eliminates the effect of unusual efficiency/ inefficiency on price.

L. Transfer Pricing

Decentralization of profit or investment centers requires pricing policies for optional internal transfers of intermediate goods or services between those centers. The transfer price represents revenue to the selling subunit and cost to the purchasing subunit, which are included in the operating income of the divisions. The goal of transfer pricing is to provide autonomous segment managers with incentive to maximize profits of the company as a whole, not just the performance of their own divisions.

In theory, outlay cost plus opportunity cost should determine the transfer price. However, opportunity cost may be difficult or impossible to measure. Therefore, three transfer pricing alternatives exist: cost-based price, market price, and negotiated price. Transfer prices based on cost may consider variable manufacturing costs, total manufacturing (absorption) costs, or full product costs. Actual costs are unstable (vary seasonally, etc.) and allow the producing division to pass its inefficiencies to the buyer; thus, standard costs should be used. Any variances from standard affect the operating income of the selling division (cannot be passed on).

A transfer price based on **full cost** includes the transferring division's fixed costs (absorption costing). A problem with full cost transfer pricing is that special orders at below full cost but above variable cost may be rejected because they result in losses for the selling division even though the contribution to fixed costs benefits the company as a whole (suboptimization). Thus, the use of full cost for transfer pricing could lead to poor motivation and dysfunctional decision making.

A **full product cost** transfer price includes absorption manufacturing cost plus a share of other costs of the value chain, such as R&D or other administrative, selling, or general expenses.

A transfer price based on the **market price** of similar products or services is justified if a competitive market exists for the product/service. A market transfer price may also be based on the transferring division's price to outside customers. However, if any costs can be avoided by selling internally rather than externally (e.g., commissions, advertising) then the market price should be reduced by these cost savings. Market transfer prices are useful because they are objective, they avoid the need to define cost, and because they show each division's contribution to company profit.

Alternatively, two divisions may establish a **negotiated transfer price**. Cost and market price information may be useful in the bargaining process, but it is not required that the transfer price be specifically related to either. However the resulting transfer price should fall within a range limited by a ceiling and a floor. The ceiling, which is the lowest external market price, helps the purchasing subunit keep costs down. The floor equals the transferring division's outlay plus opportunity costs, so the seller can cover costs. The transfer price serves to divide this amount between the divisions involved, which affects divisional operating income and thus performance measurement and responsibility accounting.

To enhance cooperation between divisions, prevent suboptimization by managers, encourage the transferring division to maximize income, and provide the purchasing division with cost information relevant for short-term decision making, a **dual transfer pricing** system may be established. Here, transfers are recorded by the selling subunit at one price while the purchaser records the transfer at a different transfer price.

M. Short-Term Differential Cost Analysis

Differential cost decisions include:

1. Sell or process further (see also Section K., Module 47)
2. Special order
3. Outsourcing (make or buy)
4. Closing a department or segment
5. Sale of obsolete inventory
6. Scarce resources

These decisions would better be described as differential cost and **revenue** decisions, since basically the decision maker must consider differences in costs and revenues over various alternatives. All other things being equal, the alternative providing the greatest profit (or cost savings) should be chosen.

Three concepts relate to most differential cost decisions.

1. **The only relevant costs or revenues are those expected future costs and revenues that differ across alternatives.** If an alternative leads to increased revenues (costs) as compared to the present method used or other alternative considered, then these revenues (costs) are **relevant** (i.e., a differential cash flow).

2. **All costs incurred in the past (sunk costs) are irrelevant, unless they have future tax ramifications.** Past costs include joint costs, the cost of obsolete inventory, and fixed costs (in the short run).

3. **Opportunity cost, the income obtainable from an alternative use of a resource, must be considered.** If an alternative is profitable and that alternative is rejected in favor of others, the benefits foregone become a "cost" to be evaluated in the decision-making process.

To work a relevant cost problem, you must first identify the type of decision that is involved. Once you have identified the decision, you can determine which costs and revenues are relevant for accepting or rejecting an alternative and in reaching a decision. For example, in a decision to sell at split-off or process further, joint costs are irrelevant and a decision to process further is made if incremental revenue exceeds incremental cost. Finally, a decision is made based on the benefit or loss that would be derived from each alternative.

The table presented below summarizes various differential cost decisions and includes only **quantitative** factors.

Decision	Description	Decision guideline
1. Sell or process further	Should joint products be sold at split-off or processed further?	Ignore joint costs. Process further if incremental revenue exceeds incremental cost.
2. Special order	Should a discount-priced order be accepted when there is idle capacity?	If regular sales are not affected, accept order when the revenue from the order exceeds the incremental cost. Fixed production costs are usually irrelevant—they remain the same no matter what the company does.
3. Outsourcing (make or buy)	Should a part be manufactured or bought from a supplier?	Choose lower cost option. Fixed costs usually are irrelevant. Often opportunity costs are present.
4. Closing a department or segment	Should a segment of the company, such as a product line, be terminated?	Compare existing contribution margin with alternative. Consider any changes in future fixed costs.
5. Sale of obsolete inventory	Should obsolete inventory be reworked or junked?	Cost of inventory is sunk and ignored. Choose alternative with greatest excess of future revenue over future cost.
6. Scarce resources	Which products should be emphasized when capacity is limited?	Determine scarce resource (e.g., machine hours). Emphasize products with greatest contribution margin per unit of scarce resource.

Qualitative factors may be equally important in nonroutine decisions. For example, in the outsourcing decision, qualitative factors include

1. Quality of purchased part compared to manufactured part
2. Relationships with suppliers
3. Quickness in obtaining needed parts

Uncertainty also affects decision making. See the probability section at the end of this module for further discussion.

An example of a differential cost decision (special order) is presented below, comparing the simpler, more efficient **incremental** approach with the equally effective but more cumbersome **total** approach. Unless a problem requires the total approach, use of the incremental approach will save valuable exam time.

EXAMPLE

Potts Co. manufactures cookware. Expected annual volume of 100,000 sets per year is well below full capacity of 150,000. Normal selling price is $40/set. Manufacturing cost is $30/set ($20 variable and $10 fixed). Total fixed manufacturing cost is $1,000,000. Selling and administrative expenses are expected to be $500,000 ($300,000 fixed and $200,000 variable). A catalog company offers to buy 25,000 sets for $27/set. No extra selling and administrative costs would be caused by the order, and acceptance will not affect regular sales. Should the offer be accepted?

INCREMENTAL APPROACH

Incremental revenue (25,000 × $27)	$ 675,000
Incremental cost (25,000 × $20)	(500,000)
Benefit of accepting order (contribution margin)	$ 175,000

TOTAL APPROACH

		Without order		With order
Sales (100,000 × $40) less Variable costs:		$4,000,000	[+(25,000 × $27)]	$4,675,000
Manufacturing	(100,000 × $20)	(2,000,000)	[+(25,000 × $20)]	(2,500,000)
Sell. and admin.	(100,000 × $2)	(200,000)		(200,000)
		1,800,000		1,975,000
Contribution margin less Fixed costs:				
Manufacturing		(1,000,000)		(1,000,000)
Sell. and admin.		(300,000)		(300,000)
Operating income		$ 500,000		$ 675,000

At first glance, it may appear that the order should not be accepted because the selling price of $27 is less than the $30 manufacturing cost per set. However, fixed costs do not increase if the order is accepted and are therefore irrelevant to this decision. The result is that, with either the incremental or the total approach, operating income is increased by $175,000. Therefore, Potts Company should accept the order.

NOW REVIEW MULTIPLE-CHOICE QUESTIONS 71 THROUGH 88 IN VOLUME 2

KEY TERMS

Activity-based budgeting. A budgeting approach that focuses on the cost of activities required to produce and sell products. It is an extension of activity-based costing.

Avoidable costs. Costs that will **not** continue to be incurred if a department or product is terminated.

Benchmarking. Requires that products, services, and activities be continually measured against the best levels of performance either inside or outside the organization.

Budget. A quantification of the plan for operations. A **flexible budget** is a budget that is adjusted for changes in volume. **Performance reports** compare budgeted and actual performance.

Budgetary slack. The practice of underestimating revenues and overestimating expenses to make budgeted targets more easily achievable.

Committed costs. Arise from a company's basic commitment to open its doors and engage in business (e.g., depreciation, property taxes, management salaries, etc.).

Contribution margin. Equals revenue less **all** variable costs.

Controllable costs. Can be affected by a manager during the current period (e.g., amount of direct manufacturing labor per unit of production is usually under the control of a production supervisor). Uncontrollable costs are those that cannot be affected by the individual in question (e.g., depreciation is not usually controllable by the production supervisor).

Cost management. Refers to the approaches and activities used by management to make planning and control decisions for the firm.

Cost-volume-profit (CVP) analysis. A planning tool used to analyze the effects of changes in volume, sales mix, selling price, variable expense, fixed expense, and profit.

Differential (incremental) cost. The difference in cost between two alternatives.

Discretionary costs. Fixed costs whose level is set by current management decisions (e.g., advertising, research and development, etc.).

Financial planning models. Support the financial planning process by making it easier to construct projected financial scenarios. These models incorporate the interrelationships among operating activities, financial activities, and other factors that affect the business, and range from simple models to those that incorporate hundreds of equations.

Financial budget. The cash budget, the capital budget, the budgeted balance sheet, and the budgeted statement of cash flows.

Fixed costs. Costs that do not vary with the level of activity within the relevant range for a given period of time (usually one year), for example, plant depreciation.

Incremental budgeting. Involves developing budgets that require only justification for increases in the funding over the prior period.

Life-cycle budgeting. Involves estimating the revenues and costs attributable to each product from initial research and development to its final customer and support.

Management by exception. Focuses attention on material deviations from plans (e.g., variances in a performance report) while allowing areas operating as expected to continue to operate without interference.

Master budget. A comprehensive expression of management's operating and financial plans for a future period that is summarized as budgeted financial statements. It consists of the operating and financial budgets.

Mixed costs (semivariable). Costs that have a fixed component and a variable component. These components are separated by using the scattergraph, high-low, or linear regression methods.

Multiple regression. A model that estimates the relationship between a dependent variable and two or more independent variables. It may be used to develop sales forecasts.

Operating budget. The budgeted income statement and related schedules.

Opportunity cost. The maximum income or savings (benefit) foregone by rejecting an alternative.

Outlay (out-of-pocket) costs. The cash disbursement associated with a specific project.

Planning. Involves selecting goals and choosing methods to attain those goals. **Control** is the implementation of the plans and evaluation of their effectiveness in attaining goals.

Relevant costs. Future costs that will change as a result of a specific decision.

Relevant range. The operating range of activity in which cost behavior patterns are valid. Thus, it is the production range for which fixed costs remain constant (e.g., if production doubles, an additional shift of salaried foremen would be added and fixed costs would increase).

Responsibility accounting. Measures subunit performance based on the costs and/or revenues assigned to responsibility centers.

Standard costs. Predetermined target costs.

Sunk, past, or unavoidable costs. Committed costs which are not avoidable and are therefore irrelevant to the decision process.

Tactical profit plan. A defined short-term financial plan that includes assigned responsibilities at all levels.

Target costing. Identifies the estimated cost of a new product that must be achieved for that product to be priced competitively and still produce an acceptable profit. Often the product is redesigned and the production process simplified several times before the target cost can be met.

Transfer pricing. The determination of the price at which goods and services will be "sold" to profit or investment centers via internal company transfers.

Variable (direct) costing. Costing that considers all fixed manufacturing overhead as a period cost rather than as a product cost. Conversely, **absorption (full) costing** considers fixed manufacturing overhead to be a product cost. The treatment of fixed manufacturing cost as a period cost rather than as a product cost is the only difference between variable costing and absorption costing. All other costs (i.e., variable manufacturing, fixed selling, and variable selling) are treated the same under both systems. Variable costing is not acceptable for external reporting per GAAP.

Variable costs. Costs that vary proportionately **in total** with the activity level throughout the relevant range (e.g., direct materials).

Variances. Differences between standards and actual results.

Zero-based budgeting. Involves developing budgets from the ground up by requiring each program or department to justify its level of funding.

Index

1417

limitations of financial ratios, 1356
liquidity ratios, 1354
profitability ratios, 1351, 1353
unusual or infrequent items, 405
financial structure (corporations), 903
financing
current assets, 1327
debt, 1332
evaluating best source of, 1335
cost of capital, 1336
cost of existing common equity, 1336
cost of new common stock, 1338
for optimal capital structure, 1339
leverage, 1335
leasing as form of, 1332
sources of short-term funds, 1328
financing (accounting cycle), 125
financing activities
defined, 599
on statements of cash flows, 599, 600
transactions included in, 600
financing function, 1319
financing stage (capital budgeting), 1305
financing statement, 982
fine payments, 546
firewalls, 1246
firm commitment
defined, 650
FC denominated, 646
unrecognized, 645
firm offer, 952
first-in, first-out (FIFO), 431, 441
first-time homebuyer tax credit, 1119
fiscal policy, 1278
fiscal year, 1076, 1154
fishbone diagrams, 1357
fitness for a particular purpose, warranty of, 946
fixed and determinable annual or periodical income (FDAP), 1203
fixed asset turnover, 1354
fixed assets, 442
Accounting Standards Codification, 460
acquisition cost, 442
biological, 463
capital vs. revenue expenditures, 450
capitalization of interest, 442
computer software costs, 459
controls over, 1230
defined, 442, 464
depletion, 456
depreciation, 451, 453
development stage enterprises, 460
disposal of, 454
gain on sale of, 606
goodwill, 456
IFRS rules for, 461
impairment of, 455, 463
insurance, 456
intangible, 456, 462
intercompany transactions, 623
investment property, 461
key terms, 463

nonmonetary exchanges, 445
plant, property, and equipment, 461
purchase groups of (basket purchase), 450
research and development costs, 459
start-up costs, 458
US GAAP vs. IFRS rules for, 387
fixed costs, 1397
fixed exchange rate, 1281
fixed overhead variance, 1392
fixed sample size approach, 224
fixtures, 1041
flat yield curve, 1297
flexibility options, 1317
flexible budgets, 1388, 1397
float
defined, 1321, 1342
in cash management, 1321
managed, 1281
floating exchange rates, 1281
floating lien, 982
floating rate
bonds, 1332
preferred stock, 1334
floor
defined, 429, 441
flow of units, 1366
flowcharting, 1262
flowcharting software, 237
FLSA (Fair Labor Standards Act), 1025, 1038
FOB destination, 441
FOB shipping point, 441
follow-up investment options, 1317
forecasted transactions
defined, 650
foreign currency denominated, 646
forecasting (industry environment), 1284
forecasting methods, 1385
foreign activities, US taxation of US persons on, 1203
foreign base company income, 1203
foreign base company sales income, 1204
foreign bonds, 1332
foreign corporations, 901
transfer of property to, 1204
Foreign Corrupt Practices Act of 1977, 98, 131, 882
foreign currency hedges, 640, 645
accounting for, 1300
defined, 1299
foreign currency statements
defined, 677
translation of. *See* foreign currency translation
foreign currency transactions, 637, *See also* derivative instruments
defined, 650, 807
SFAS 48, 807
foreign currency translation, 671
Accounting Standards Codification, 676
defined, 677
FASB Interpretation No. 37, 817
financial statement translations, 671

IFRS rules for, 677
in highly inflationary economies, 676
key terms, 677
objective of, 671
SFAS 48, 807
SFAS 52, 768
foreign earned income exclusion, 1072
foreign exchange rates, 1281
foreign investment, 1283
foreign operations (segment reporting), 659
foreign personal holding company, 1204
foreign persons, US taxation of, 1202
foreign tax credit, 1117, 1204
foreign-exchange control, 1280
foreseeable party, 855
foreseen party, 854
forged endorsements, 968
Form 8-K, 419
Form 8-K/6-K, 419, 425
Form 10-K, 420
Form 10-K/20-F, 419, 425
Form 10-Q, 419, 420, 425
Form 1120 schedules, 1171
Form 1120S filing, 1181
Form 706, 1196
form of practice, AICPA rule for, 68
Form S-1/F-1, 419, 425
formation defenses
contracts, 917
defined, 935
forward contract
defined, 651
discount or premium on, 650
forward exchange contracts, 646, 651, 817
forward rates, 1281
forwards, 1283, 1298, 1318
foundations, 1200
four-column cash reconciliation, 466
fractional year depreciation, 454
franchise agreements, 382, 822
franchise fee revenue (SFAS 45), 822
franchisee, 822
franchisor, 822
fraud
AU 312, 266
AU 316, 280
contracts, 917
defined, 79, 93, 161, 193, 869
engagement planning, 83
liability to clients for, 853
fraud risk factors
AU 316, 282, 286
defined, 93, 162
fraudulent financial reporting, 83
AU 316, 281, 282
defined, 93, 162
materiality
engagement planning, 83
free cash flow, 1349, 1360
free rent (leases), 525
free trade, obstacles to, 1280
fresh-start measurements, 831
frictional unemployment, 1277
fringe benefits